HANDBOOK OF RESEARCH ON TEACHING

Fourth Edition

HANDBOOK OF RESEARCH ON TEACHING
Fourth Edition

Edited by

Virginia Richardson

AMERICAN EDUCATIONAL RESEARCH ASSOCIATION
WASHINGTON, D.C.

47182224

Copyright © 2001 by the American Educational Research Association

Published by
American Educational Research Association
1230 17th Street, NW
Washington, DC 20036-3078

Printed in the United States of America

First Impression 2002

Library of Congress Cataloging-in-Publication Data

Handbook of research on teaching / edited by Virginia Richardson.—4th ed.
   p. cm.
  Includes bibliographical references and index.
  ISBN 0-935302-26-3
  1. Education—Research—United States. I. Richardson, Virginia, 1940–
II. American Educational Research Association.

LB1028 .H315 2001
370'.7'2—dc21   2001045075

Contents

Special Topics in Qualitative Methodology

PART 3: SUBJECT MATTER

PART 4: THE LEARNER

PART 5: POLICY

PART 6: TEACHERS AND TEACHING

Preface

The editing of a handbook that is devoted to describing research in a well-established, yet still evolving, field is a formidable task. It involves developing a framework for describing the field, inventing an approach for dividing the field into sections and chapters, identifying particular authors, persuading them to write chapters, following the progress of the chapters, sending the chapters out for review, making suggestions for changes—and finally, writing a Preface. This Preface describes the decisions that were made by the Editorial Advisory Board and me in relation to the content and organization of this handbook, as well as in relation to the nature of the sections and chapters as they eventually came together in this volume.

The project began a number of years ago when the publications committee of the American Educational Research Association (AERA) informed me that I was nominated to become the editor of the fourth edition of the *Handbook of Research on Teaching*. If interested, I was to write a letter to the committee suggesting how I would approach the task were I chosen as editor. In that letter, I stressed the need for three emphases that would guide the development of the framework for the *Handbook*. The first emphasis was to attempt to place the field of research on teaching within a larger foundational context, that is, to place research on teaching within the many descriptive and normative ideas about thinking, learning, and action that were and still are swirling around us. The purpose of this emphasis was to provide students and scholars of research on teaching with an understanding of the field as it operates within the larger frame of social scholarship. The second emphasis was on including research on teaching and pedagogy that is not always described within research on teaching chapters but that might instead be considered multicultural, ethnic, and gender studies. And the third was to ensure inclusion of research on teaching that has been conducted outside the boundaries of the United States.

An Editorial Advisory Board was selected that provided advice on both the standard conceptions of research on teaching and the emphases described above. We met in Tucson, Arizona, over a 3-day period and again at a 1-day meeting during an AERA conference. The purposes of the first session were to determine the overall frame and approach of the *Handbook,* to map the sections and chapters, and to begin to suggest possible authors for the chapters. The following sections explain some of the issues with which we had to deal to determine chapter titles, content, and potential authors.

The Purpose of a Handbook

It was agreed that the *Handbook of Research on Teaching* has been and should continue to be written for students of and scholars in research on teaching. The *Handbook* is also meant for scholars in other fields who want to look in depth at an area within research on teaching. The emphasis in the chapters is placed on representing and organizing research that has been conducted, with some attention to suggesting lines of future research. The Board agreed that the *Handbook* is not meant to be interpretations of research for the sole purpose of the improvement of practice. Obviously, much of the research is useful in practice, and, in fact, some chapters deal specifically with the use of research in practice. However, this *Handbook* is not one that translates research into practice suggestions. Further, it is meant to describe research that has already been conducted rather than to explain underdeveloped areas that require more research attention.

The State of the Field

Very few areas of conflict in the field of research on teaching were represented in the publication of the *Handbook of Research on Teaching, Third Edition.* Perhaps the strongest disagreements revolved around the various methods of conducting research on teaching. However, détente between qualitative and quantitative (Rist, 1977) had pretty well arrived by 1986. Since the third *Handbook* was conceived, much has happened that has, in the words of some, created chaos in the field. Many research threads do not necessarily overlap, and the work conducted within one approach may not be understood or even be understandable to those in another. Between the time of the last *Handbook* (Wittrock, 1986) and this one, there has been turbulence in research on teaching similar to that in other fields. Postmodernism raises questions that jar the very foundations of our understanding of research. Those questions concern the nature of knowledge, who owns it, who produces it, and how it may be used. This commotion goes beyond the old qualitative–quantitative controversy as elucidated in the 1986 *Handbook,* particularly with Erickson's (1986) chapter. It now focuses on the very nature of research and knowledge, its representation, and the uses of research in the improvement of practice.

As members of the Editorial Advisory Board struggled with developing an approach to the *Handbook* that related to the state of the field, they discussed two suggestions. The first approach was to unscramble the field, that is, to place some order over it. The sense here was that, by tidying up the field, we had an opportunity to affect future research, making it, perhaps, more coherent. The second approach was to try to represent the nature of the field, that is, to represent the alternative if not competing approaches to the study of teaching. Of course, we understood that the act of writing chapters and placing them between the covers of one volume is an interpretive process. Any attempt to summarize a field places a stamp on it. But the consensus of the Board was to represent the field of research on teaching—excellence, chaos, warts, and all.

What to Include, What to Exclude, and How to Organize

Although we reached an agreement quite rapidly on the overall approach to representing the field, our concerns then focused on how we would fit all that we wanted in one volume and how it would be organized. We quickly agreed that this *Handbook* would not just include the same chapter titles as the 1986 *Handbook* with updated content. The field had simply changed too much to consider this option, although—particularly in the subject-matter section—some of the same titles appear. A second consideration in this set of decisions focused on the proliferation of research handbooks now available to scholars. This proliferation is particularly the case for handbooks that describe research on a particular content or subject-matter area. Handbooks now exist in many subject-matter areas (e.g., reading, mathematics, science, music, art, etc.). In each of those handbooks, one can find chapters that touch on the content that would be of interest in the *Research on Teaching* handbook. What, then, would a chapter titled "Research on Teaching Mathematics" include? It could not really summarize a complete subject-matter handbook or several editions thereof. Did we really need the subject-matter chapters now that almost all topics had their own handbooks?

In addition to considering the availability of handbooks in many subject-matter areas, we also assessed the expectation of scholars and students concerning the inclusion of chapters. We agreed, for example, that scholars and students would expect subject-matter chapters; therefore, they are included in this *Handbook.* We also decided that the chapters would focus on work that had been conducted since the 1986 *Handbook.* This decision helped us to determine the nature and content of the chapters. For example, considerably more work since 1986 has addressed issues of qualitative than quantitative methodology, suggesting that this *Handbook* should emphasize qualitative methodology. We also decided that, in addition to chapters of the standard length, we would include a set of shorter chapters. These shorter chapters would allow us to include a number of topics that, although they do not necessarily warrant a large handbook chapter themselves, could stand on their own, rather than be buried within a subsection of a larger chapter.

The titles of the sections are quite standard with few surprises: Foundations; Methodology; Subject Matter; The Learner; Policy; Teachers and Teaching; Social and Cultural Contexts and the Role of the Teacher; and Instruction. Three of these sections, however, will be discussed below because of the somewhat unusual ways in which they were organized and configured.

Foundations

We usually think of educational foundations as education ideas that are considered and scholarship that is conducted within social disciplines such as philosophy, history, economics, anthropology, and sociology. Interestingly, educational psychology is not considered as foundational scholarship and usually warrants its own department within schools of education.

With respect to the study of teaching, a considerable amount of the research has been conducted within the frame of educational psychology. Thus, in previous handbooks of research on teaching, educational psychology was ever-present in most chapters that summarized the research. Several chapters in each *Handbook* have represented foundations, such as chapters on philosophy and history of teaching as well as a "frameworks"-type chapter.

In this *Handbook,* we attempt to locate research on teaching within broader and more inclusive frameworks of current social and philosophical thinking. Of the two long "frameworks" chapters, one represents a traditional approach to research on teaching (Floden), and one operates at the edges (Hamilton & McWilliam). In addition, a series of short chapters examine research on teaching as it relates to important ideas and seminal thinkers. Those thinkers, although not necessarily in the field of research on teaching, have certainly affected it. This selection is not meant to represent an inclusive list of social theorists who have affected our ways of thinking in the field. The works are, however, meant as examples that suggest the importance of considering the field of research on teaching as affecting and being affected by broad intellectual trends in social thinking.

Methodology

Historically, the various editions of the *Handbook on Teaching* have had considerable effects on research methodology in research on teaching and in general educational research. For example, Campbell and Stanley's (1967) seminal chapter on experimental and quasi-experimental designs appeared in the first *Handbook* (Gage, 1967), Rosenshine and Furst's (1973) chapter on classroom observation was published in the second *Handbook* (Travers, 1973), and Erickson's (1986) influential chapter on interpretive research is found in the third *Handbook* (Wittrock, 1986). We spent considerable time analyzing trends in research methodology since the 1986 *Handbook,* intending to continue this tradition.

Our first concern focused on the recent effect that qualitative methodology has had on the field. While qualitative methodology began to enter the field during the late 1970s, interest in and use of these methodologies have expanded considerably since the conception of the 1986 *Handbook.* Several handbooks are now devoted to qualitative methodology (Denzin & Lincoln, 1994; Lecompte, Milroy, & Preissle, 1992). In addition, journals such as the *American Educational Research Journal,* although not always dominated by articles using qualitative methodology, are certainly publishing a sizable number.

In the meantime, several important quantitative breakthroughs have significantly affected our understandings of the teaching–learning process in large-scale data analysis. Thus, it was important to represent both fields. The quantitative chapter (Crawford & Impara) addresses the importance of quantitative approaches for the use of research on teaching in policy development and in the improvement of education. Several chapters were planned for the qualitative subsection. We also sensed that qualitative methodology is not a unified or singular field; to portray all ways of thinking within one chapter by one or even several authors would be difficult. Thus, we planned a large chapter (Donmoyer) and a number of small ones. The large chapter would describe the proliferation of qualitative methodologies, and the small ones would address specific issues and aspects in this approach to research.

Subject Matter

The subject-matter chapters raised some interesting issues about what we could expect within such chapters given that other handbooks devoted to research on subject matter had been published, each with a considerable number of chapters that focused on teaching and instruction. Our solution was that the *Handbook*'s chapters should be relatively short, analytical–conceptual summaries of research summaries that included considerations of research methodology and next steps. In addition, we determined that a large chapter focusing on curriculum and teaching (Leinhardt) would be extremely helpful at this time.

Topics Not Included

If, from the reader's standpoint, chapters are missing from this *Handbook,* several explanations may be provided. The first is that the particular topic, though important and interesting, has not received enough research attention since 1986 to warrant a full chapter. The second reason that a chapter may not be found in the *Handbook* is a chapter may have been planned but never completed. In several instances, chapters were not completed and, therefore, could not be included in this edition of the *Handbook.* The third reason is that a conscious decision was made to not devote a full chapter to a particular topic, for example, the topic of educational technology. We concluded that educational technology would be scattered throughout the chapters, and, given the state of the educational technology field—particularly its relationship to research on teaching—it did not justify its own chapter. Yet it is quite clear at this point that this topic should have received the attention that a chapter devoted to the topic can provide. Although many chapters discuss work on educational technology, those instances are scattered and are not organized around the specific topic of educational technology. In hindsight, then, a chapter devoted to educational technology should have been included in this *Handbook.* Undoubtedly, readers will identify other topics that should have received their own chapters.

The Finished Product

I expect that many different judgments will be made about the nature and worth of this edition of the *Handbook.* From my standpoint, we accomplished what we set out to do. More foundational chapters appear in this volume, a number of specific chapters are devoted to equity and multicultural topics (those issues are also addressed in other chapters), and the research extends beyond the United States.

As it is, the *Handbook* presents a quite complete picture of research on teaching that really cannot be described as "chaotic." It certainly does reflect, however, the current and sometimes competing schools of thought about the nature of possibilities for the research and writing about social action that is devoted to teaching. Although the chapters reflect the field, many chapters in this volume are destined to affect the field of research on teaching as well as other areas of educational research and social action. Again, some chapters and topics in the methodology section speak to fields beyond research on teaching as do some chapters within foundations and subject-matter sections. Within the chapters that are devoted specifically to research on teaching, the quite different lenses that are used to approach the topic, for example, teaching as dialogue (Burbules & Bruce), may help us continue the exploration of teaching action in all its interesting formations and complexities.

In all, the chapters are deep and suggest a robust field of research that is characterized by evolving research methodologies and strong, diverse conceptual frameworks. Importantly, such chapters also suggest that this field of research maintains a strong interest and involvement in and concern for educational practice, which is an important consideration as we contemplate the purposes of educational research. Ultimately, educational research should inform practice—policy, school administration, teaching, instruction, and parenting. And above all, it should speak to student learning and to student development in the important aspects of human life, including the cognitive, moral, physical, emotional, artistic, and social. The ideas, information, and questions in this volume will guide our educational practice and continuing research for the years to come.

ACKNOWLEDGMENTS

I wish to thank the many people who have helped with this massive task. Deborah Anders, University of Arizona; Cathie Fallona, University of Southern Maine; the Editorial Advisory Board members; the chapter reviewers; the publication staff at AERA; and my friends and family who have tolerated my various mental states while traversing the ups and downs of this long and difficult process. I also thank Chris Clark and his graduate students at Michigan State University who provided critical feedback on the organization of the *Handbook*.

REFERENCES

Campbell, D. T., & Stanley, C. (1967). Experimental and quasi-experimental designs for research on teaching. In N. Gage (Ed.), *Handbook of research on teaching* (pp. 171–246). Chicago: Rand McNally.

Denzin, K., & Lincoln, S. (Eds.). (1994). *Handbook of qualitative research*. Thousand Oaks, CA: Sage.

Erickson, F. (1986). In M. Wittrock (Ed.), *Handbook of research on teaching* (3rd ed., pp. 119–161). New York: Macmillan.

Gage, N. (Ed.). (1967). *Handbook of research on teaching*. Chicago: Rand McNally.

Lecompte, M., Milroy, W. L., & Preissle, J. (Eds.). (1992). *The handbook of qualitative research in education*. San Diego: Academic Press.

Rist, R. (1977). On the relations among educational research paradigms: From disdain to détente. *Anthropology and Education Quarterly, VIII*(2), 42–49.

Rosenshine, B., & Furst, N. (1973). The use of direct observation to study teaching. In R. M. W. Travers (Ed.), *Second handbook of research on teaching* (pp. 122–183). Chicago: Rand McNally.

Travers, R. M. W. (Ed.). (1973). *Second handbook of research on teaching*. Chicago: Rand McNally.

Wittrock, M. (Ed.). (1986). *Handbook of research on teaching* (3rd ed.). New York: Macmillan.

Virginia Richardson
University of Michigan

HANDBOOK OF RESEARCH ON TEACHING

Fourth Edition

Part I
Foundations

1.
Research on Effects of Teaching: A Continuing Model for Research on Teaching

Robert E. Floden
Michigan State University

A simple story is often told about changes in research on teaching over the past two decades. According to this story, early research on teaching was a behaviorist-influenced search, first for correlates of student achievement and, ultimately, for the causal links that could be used to enhance achievement. This model, the story continues, ultimately failed because it neglected the meanings teachers and students make in their classrooms and because scholars have shown that a search for causal networks in human affairs is bound to be fruitless. The model has been replaced by research activities that seek to uncover shared and individual meanings or even to "problematize" teaching as a social endeavor.

In their chapter in this volume, for example, Hamilton and McWilliam (chapter 2) recount the history of research on teaching, beginning (as I will begin presently) with Gage's chapter in the initial *Handbook of Research on Teaching* (Gage, 1963b). They chronicle the doubts about social science that came from social scientists and other scholars. These authors convey the impression that the vision in Gage's *Handbook* chapter was abandoned, to be replaced by "the splintering and unruly terrain of ideas which inform a contemporary educational understanding of difference and marginality" (Hamilton & McWilliam, this volume). Of the general approach Gage advocated, they say: "The old methods survived; but they did not flourish" (Hamilton & McWilliam, this volume). Considering Gage's recent writings, they see inconsistencies: "That is, his contradictory comments in 1996 merely affirm the depth of the intellectual crisis that surfaced in the 1960s and 1970s. To use a label that Joseph Schwab used in 1970, research on teaching had become 'moribund'" (Hamilton & McWilliam, this volume). Readers of this analysis might get the impression that "the old methods" have been abandoned, smashed by hammers of complex systems, multiple interpretive frames, and postmodern doubt.

This chapter acknowledges the growth in scholarly interest in interpretation and deconstruction but argues that the academic progeny of Gage's early description of research on teaching are many and healthy. Current research on teaching includes many research areas that can be seen as building on Gage's search for characteristics of teaching likely to lead to changes in student learning. Although the simple story is reasonably accurate in its portrayal of early research, it underestimates the contributions and continuing use of research models that search for causally relevant connections between teaching and student achievement. Other models of research (e.g., ethnographic approaches) have been added to the mix of research under way, but studies that search for ways to make teaching more effective in raising student achievement remain vital lines of work, of great interest to practitioners and policymakers, as well as to other researchers.

The chapter by Hamilton and McWilliam offers detailed discussions of research that has eschewed a search for teaching's effects on learning. This chapter will refer to such work only in passing, focusing attention instead on areas of research that continue the quest for causally relevant links to student achievement. Some such work focuses on the connection between teaching and learning; other work looks backward to examine the factors that influence teaching; still other studies examine the intermediate processes that connect teaching and learning.

In some discussions of research, varying uses of key terms lead researchers to talk past each other, or simply to feel confused. One can be accused of being a "positivist," for example, even though none of the characteristics of positivism apply (Phillips, 1983). Similarly, many varieties of thought have been characterized as "postmodern," making it difficult to frame an assessment of the broad category (Howe, 1998).

To lend some consistency to this chapter, I introduce a new phrase to identify research done in keeping with the model articulated by Gage. I will use "effects of teaching" to describe the line of research that moves from Gage through contemporary work. The defining characteristic of such work is its goal of identifying associations between characteristics of teaching and student learning. Interest is primarily in causal connections, though many investigators are cautious about making causal claims. Other terms have been used to describe such work, notably "process–product" research and "criteria of effectiveness" (Gage's own early term). These alternative labels, however, have negative connotations or direct attention away from the central task of finding connections between teaching and learning.

Past *Handbook*s, especially the first and third, have included chapters that painted the field in broad strokes, offering a simple way of looking at much of the recent work, recognizing that close examination of any area would show departures from the sweeping vision. Those chapters provide a glimpse of the gradual changes in research on teaching, starting from Gage's description and moving forward, with the mainstream of work based on the model of research on the effects of teaching.

In the first *Handbook* (Gage, 1963a), Gage argued that research aimed at linking variations in teaching and teachers to variations in desired student outcomes had become the central model. In Shulman's article in the third *Handbook,* he described Gage's model, commented on work that extended it by including variations in student activity, broadened it through greater attention to meaning and thought, and then proposed a further modification to include greater attention to teachers' subject-matter knowledge.

Although Shulman and Gage argued for or described changes in research models, Shulman's description also noted that most work continued to fit what I am calling the research on effects of teaching model. My chapter again gives most emphasis to continuity. Hamilton and McWilliam describe the growth of alternative approaches; here I argue that many vigorous streams of current research can be seen as part of a stable tradition, seeking warranted, fairly general claims about the effects of teaching on student learning. Hamilton and McWilliam note that Gage recently defended the value of social science, saying that it "should return to the task of eliciting 'long-lasting generalizations . . . essential to long-lasting theory'" (Hamilton & McWilliam).

My overall argument begins with a review of how talk about the search for knowledge about the effects of teaching has evolved since Gage's seminal piece, sets these changes in the broad currents of change in social science, then gives examples of research that represent either the contemporary search for connections between teaching and learning or extensions of the model that consider influences on teaching (e.g., education policies) and factors that mediate between teaching and learning (e.g., student activity).

Descriptions of Mainstream Research Traditions

Both the first and third editions of the *Handbook of Research on Teaching* (Gage, 1963a; Wittrock, 1986) included chapters that discuss dominant "paradigms" for research on teaching. Gage (Gage, 1963b) used his chapter in the first *Handbook* to argue that a discussion of frameworks would be helpful, to propose an overarching framework for research on teaching, and to describe more specific frameworks that fit under that general framework. Gage used the term "paradigms" to refer to models of research. Gage made no reference to the seminal work by Kuhn (Kuhn, 1962) on paradigms in science, but Gage's usage is compatible with at least some of the meanings Kuhn assigned to the term. For Gage,

> paradigms are models, patterns, or schemata. Paradigms are not theories; they are rather ways of thinking or patterns for research. . . . When one has chosen a paradigm for his research, he has made crucial decisions concerning the kinds of variables and relationships between variables that he will investigate. Paradigms for research imply a kind of commitment, however preliminary or tentative, to a research program. (1963b, p. 95)

The examples Gage gave of paradigms in social science illustrated the generality of the concept. The examples included a taxonomy of statistical techniques as well as an approach to analyzing case histories of psychopathology. All the paradigms exemplified categorization of variables. For the statistical methods, the variables described the procedures (e.g., the number of dependent variables included), rather than characteristics of a social phenomena. For the psychopathology, the paradigm specified categories of influence (e.g., events in early life, traumatic events) and distinguished them from current symptoms.

The paradigm can serve as a unifying format for organizing research, setting all the statistical methods that involve a single dependent variable, for example, apart from those that involve either none or more than one. Sometimes, as with the case from psychopathology, the paradigm also suggests a approach to be taken in the study itself, that is, that the researcher should identify the variables present in a case history, representing them in a diagram that includes the sets of variables in the paradigm.

The paradigm to which Gage devoted the most attention is what he called the "criterion of effectiveness" paradigm for research on teaching. At its core, the paradigm specified two types of variables: a criterion variable and its predictors. The paradigm also indicated the general approach to be taken in each study:

> . . . identify or select a criterion (or set of criteria) of teacher effectiveness. This criterion then becomes the dependent variable. The research task is then (1) to measure this criterion, (2) to measure the potential correlates of this criterion, and (3) to determine the actual correlations between the criterion and its potential correlates. (1963b, p. 114)

The discussion of this paradigm makes evident that Gage was interested in correlates that were not simply accidentally related to changes in the criterion. His interest was in correlates that would warrant claims that changes in the correlate would result in changes in the criterion, that teaching would have a (somewhat) predictable effect. The word "effectiveness" itself connotes attention to "effects," not simply "associations." A concern for the adage that "correlation does not imply causation" may have led Gage to avoid causal language, but the language of effectiveness leaves little doubt that the goal was to identify causal links.

As an early chapter in the first *Handbook*, Gage's model of research might correspond to the research approaches reviewed in later chapters. Although some chapters reported on such research, other chapters in Gage's *Handbook* were based on apparently different models of research. The chapter by Getzels and Jackson (1963) on teacher personality, for example, concentrated on the search for teacher personality types, particularly on existing approaches to personality measurement. Yet even this chapter used the effects of teaching model as an orienting goal. Their focus on measurement resulted from a need to develop valid measures before pursuing effects rather than from a deliberate move away from trying to identify effects. "Ultimately, the results of teacher personality research are presumed to be relevant to the problem of selection and prediction" (Getzels & Jackson, 1963, p. 575).

By calling his model "criteria of effectiveness," Gage emphasized the centrality of identifying just what forms of student learning are of interest. Raising that question opens the possibility that the effects of teaching to be considered will not be student learning at all but might be classroom climate or student attitudes. Connections to current educational context can be seen more clearly, however, if Gage's phrase is replaced by "effects of teaching."

The first *Handbook* showed that the effects of teaching model was used in most research on teaching. The use of this model continued through the second *Handbook*. So, up through the mid-1970s, most of research on teaching was based on the model of looking for associations between some measure of student learning (most often achievement tests) and variables describing classrooms, including both teacher actions and those of the students.

By the third *Handbook,* research based on other models had become more prevalent. In his chapter on research paradigms, Shulman (1986) described how the research on classroom ecology and research on teacher cognition have joined effects of teaching (both process–product models and models that introduce student activities as part of the process of producing effects) as major lines of work. Shulman advocated use of all approaches, seeing strengths and limitations in each. He portrayed the several newcomer paradigms as choosing different methods or points of focus rather than developing an approach that unequivocally represented "progress." He recommended "disciplined eclecticism" in which careful thought about purposes and assumptions linked to different methods was used to guide creation of a mixed strategy. Proper consideration of what each element in the mix contributed required researchers to understand a range of methods. Shulman was optimistic that researchers who understood various methods would be able to make sense of varied bodies of work.

> [W]hen investigators have learned to speak each other's languages, to comprehend the terms in which other programs' research questions are couched, then processes of deliberation over findings can yield the hybrid understandings not possible when members of individual research programs dwell in intellectual ghettos of their own construction. (1986, p. 33)

Both Gage and Shulman portrayed an orderly evolution of research approaches, drawn from work in related social sciences and disciplined by the methodological strictures of those fields. Gage suggested that the search for correlations with student outcomes unifies and should continue to unify research on teaching. Shulman reported that such research (he referred specifically to process–product research) was still active, indeed that it was the "most vigorous and productive of the programs of research on teaching during the past decade" (Shulman, 1986, p. 9). He described the emergence of other research paradigms as an increase in the tools available, advocating the disciplined use of tools appropriate to each investigation. Adding research methods from other disciplines yields additional insights, which complement those from process–product research. In Shulman's view, the field as a whole was progressing. "Both our scientific knowledge of rules and principles . . . and our knowledge of richly described and critically analyzed cases combine to define the knowledge base of teaching" (p. 32). Implicit in Shulman's presentation was the assumption that all the paradigms of research could be used to improve student performance. Those constructing such studies may base part of their arguments on common sense or collateral studies by other investigators (e.g., using international studies of second language learning to support the assumption that teacher choices about instructional mathematics content will influence student achievement), but the undergirding premise was that creating additional disciplined knowledge about teaching and teachers would improve student learning.

Changing Tides in the Humanities

In various university humanities departments, discussions of several varieties of postmodernism were well under way as the authors of the third *Handbook* prepared their chapters. The movement had not, at that point, gotten much attention from researchers on teaching. In the index of the third *Handbook,* there is one reference to Derrida (in a passage on aesthetic theories in the chapter on art teaching), none to Lyotard, none to Rorty, all authors among the most prominent exponents of the mix of assertions loosely labeled as "postmodern." The general tenor of these assertions is that any search for firmly supported knowledge is bound to be fruitless, because all human observation and understanding are mediated by language and context, with no possibility of establishing processes for adjudicating among competing views of the world. Working from a variety of examples (some from psychological experiments) showing the context dependence of human perception and reasoning, the postmodernists describe their unwillingness to accept, for example, the belief that disciplined modes of inquiry yield conclusions that are in any sense more trustworthy than or preferable to conclusions built on causal observation or ideology.

Such postmodern doubt [what Lyotard (1987, p. 74) called "incredulity to metanarratives"] has shaken some convictions about the possibility of progress in social science. Philosophy of science, especially references to Kuhn (1962), Feyerabend (1975), and Lakatos (1971), has been used to refute the idea that growth of understanding can be a goal. Such studies have also been used as the basis for claiming that distinctions cannot be made among different methods of investigating human behavior, including methods for the study of teaching (e.g., Eisner, 1992). These sea changes in the academy have been used to critique research models (e.g., research on the effects of teaching) that presume an ability to discover "real" causally relevant associations between teaching and student learning. They have complicated discussions of criteria to be used in evaluating the credibility and generalizability of claims from case studies aimed at understanding meaning making. Some teacher narratives, or researcher narratives about teachers they know well, occupy a blurred boundary area between research and memoir (Casey, 1995).

This intellectual current thus attempts to wash away the progressive trail that Gage and Shulman built in their descriptions of research on teaching's history. If no method of obtaining evidence is better than any other, then research activities merely develop a series of interpretations, with no reason for believing later ones to be more trustworthy than the earlier.

In the past 20 years, discussions in philosophy of science have built a counter case to the apparent relativism of Kuhn and others. A central tenet to the argument for the superiority of disciplined inquiry is that it is reasonable to follow the methods of a discipline, even though those methods can sometimes lead to erroneous conclusions. Laudan (1996), for example, noted that, although it might be *possible* to defend any claim in the face of contradictory evidence, it is not *reasonable* to do so. So the argument that disciplined inquiry should not be privileged because the investigators *might* have ignored contradictory evidence loses force; such bull-headed adherence to an initial claim would not have been reasonable. At its broadest, the argument is that the possibility of error should make one cautious, but does not provide grounds for giving equal credence to all knowledge claims.

In the context of educational research, claims about the relativity of knowledge have led both to a spirited defense of disciplined inquiry and to a growth in research areas in which specific differences in interpretive standpoint have seemed worth pursuing. Educational theorists such as Margaret Eisenhart, Kenneth Howe, and D.C. Phillips have argued that more trustworthy bases for knowledge can and should be identified (Eisenhart & Howe, 1992; Howe, 1992; Phillips, 1990). Although their arguments have not convinced those taking the most relativistic stance, they do offer others a reasoned basis for continuing to pursue systematic inquiry.

The attention to the role of perspective and interpretation has also prompted inquiry that embodies a purposeful shift in perspective, from the vantage point of socially privileged groups (especially socially advantaged White males) to the vantage points of groups less privileged, such as women, teachers, and the poor. Feminist studies of teaching have challenged interpretive frameworks that seemed based on a traditional "male" view. Studies by Gilligan (1982) of moral development laid the groundwork for arguments by Noddings that contemporary schooling has treated "feminine" traits as inferior to "masculine" characteristics. Noddings (1984), for example, sees *caring* as a central virtue. Caring, according to Noddings, has been neglected because it was associated with women, whereas reason and achievement were associated with men. Applying the feminist perspective to teaching, Noddings (1992) pressed for a more prominent role for care in schools, and McAninch (1993) suggested that teacher education be reconsidered in light of the feminine virtues. Other scholars (Weiler, 1995) have insisted that efforts to professionalize teaching are built on a flawed model of "professional," stressing autonomy and specialized knowledge (seen as masculine) over connection and community (seen as feminine).

Just as the lower power and status of women has led research to neglect their perspectives, the low position of teachers in school systems and in society generally has led to research with little attention to the view from the teacher's seat. Research by, for, and among teachers has been seen as an antidote to research that seemed to discount teachers' perspectives (Cochran-Smith & Lytle, 1992). Studies that start from the point of view of historically disadvantaged groups may give reason to question an assumed consensus about the purposes and role of schooling (Delpit, 1995; Lareau, 1989).

As this *Handbook* reveals, research on teaching has incorporated these varying viewpoints, including arguments for the impossibility of well-supported knowledge about teaching. The addition of different viewpoints is described in the chapter in this *Handbook* by Hamilton and McWilliam. Such studies from other viewpoints have not, however, meant the abandonment of work more closely tied to Gage's research on teaching effects. Such studies of effects have, however, shifted to follow changing societal views about curriculum, teaching, and the appropriate relationships among teachers, administrators, and the public.

Shifts in Content Standards and Shifts in Teaching

In the wake of "A Nation at Risk" (National Commission on Excellence in Education, 1983), U.S. educators began another round of curriculum revisions for K–12 schools. Graduation standards were raised. Organization of subject matter began to develop more challenging standards for student performance (e.g., National Council of Teachers of Mathematics, 1989). This shift led to questions about the standard achievement tests in use, pointing to differences between their content and the newly adopted goals for student learning (Frederiksen, 1984).

Because many studies of teaching effects had used these tests as criterion measures, the applicability of such research was called into question, as was the usefulness of research supporting skills-oriented approaches to professional development (Little, 1993). When policymakers turned the results of research on the effects of teaching into prescriptions for classroom performance, many researchers and teachers attacked the way such transformation of research into practice ignored the variability of effects across classroom contexts (Fenstermacher, 1979; Kepler, 1980). Although the policy use and abuse was not necessarily connected to the model of research used (Floden, 1981), many researchers, dismayed by the ways their findings were used, expressed doubts about the search for generalizable connections between teaching and learning.

When the work on teaching effects was under fire, research-supported recommendations for teaching were replaced by a variety of approaches, described variously (and loosely) as Socratic, progressive, constructivist, pragmatist, and Deweyian. These approaches all claim to be taking account of recent research on learning, which stresses the importance of students' active engagement. Different lines of work—cognitive and situative—are associated with contemporary constructivist approaches (see, e.g., Greeno, Collins, & Resnick, 1996), approaches to teaching differ in what they mean by "active engagement" and in what role they believe the teacher should play in the classroom. From a cognitive perspective, "active engagement" means that the student uses his or her existing cognitive structures to make sense of the welter of signals coming through the senses. From the situative perspective, in contrast, the student's active engagement is a connection to an ongoing social process, such as serving as an apprentice to a more knowledgeable member of the community (Collins, Brown, & Newman, 1989; Lave & Wenger, 1991). Correspondingly, teaching becomes creating learning environments for individual students to explore or fostering communities of learning, respectively. A modern behaviorist might even agree that students should be actively engaged, meaning that instruction must give students opportunities to receive feedback on their responses to the teacher.

Teaching, as well as learning, has come to be seen as being more dependent on social and historical context. For some scholars, this expanded focus implies a redirection of research on teaching toward studies of individual teachers in their particular settings (Connelly & Clandinin, 1996). Such a position resembles the postmodern tenet that general knowledge is a vain quest and has provoked a parallel rebuttal, namely that the lack of infallible knowledge about each particular situation does not preclude the productive use of information about teaching across a wide variety of contexts (Floden & Klinzing, 1990).

These changes in student goals and recommendations for teaching might be seen as reducing the utility of studies that focused on basic skills or on methods of direct instruction. The changes might, alternatively, be seen as raising questions about how research could be conducted to understand the significance of the changes for knowledge about teaching. Do the principles of effective classroom management become invalid when instruction seeks more student engagement (of some particular sort)? Or does the openness associated with student activity make it even more important to follow those general principles? Prior research should not be abandoned but should be reevaluated, searching to determine how conclusions might change in new contexts.

As shown through examples in the remainder of this chapter, many researchers have continued to pursue research within the effects of teaching paradigm. They see the contemporary views of learning as adding complexity to the analyses of how teaching and learning are related, but they have not given up the goal of uncovering connections between teaching and learning that can support the improvement of education. They seek instrumental theory and research that might guide, in part, the design of teaching practices that will increase student learning on more challenging subject matter. The concerns about policy misuse continue, but as attention has shifted away from direct instruction, research findings seem to have less frequently been translated into prescriptions for what *all* teachers must do.

Research in the "Modern" Tradition

Research in various postmodern modes is more common than at the time of the third *Handbook*. Its radical departure from prior work—in method, epistemology, and subject matter—has given it high visibility. But most current research can be seen as an extension of the effects of the teaching paradigm Gage described in the first *Handbook*. Researchers have broadened Gage's model but have done so in the interest of answering his basic question and discovering how to put the answers to use in improving education.

Gage's question can be paraphrased as "What characteristics of teachers and teaching are linked, in some causally relevant way, to desired student outcomes?" At that time, teacher and teaching characteristics were primarily thought of as teacher behaviors and personality traits and links to student outcomes were thought about as correlation coefficients.

Early process–product studies form part of a larger model of influences on student learning. The effects of teaching paradigm posits some association between teaching and student learning, but the larger picture steps back as it looks for influences on teaching (e.g., education policies or learning experiences for learners), looks more carefully at the array of characteristics teachers possess, and looks forward to the mediating role classroom characteristics and student activities play in connecting what teachers do to what students learn.

Researchers in subsequent years worked with the same broad question about links between teaching and student outcomes, but they introduced other ideas about what characteristics of teachers and teaching were likely to be linked with which student outcomes. Thus, for example, investigators looked for connections between teachers' formal qualifications and student achievement or used assessments of student performance to describe student outcomes.

One current "hot" topic is whether insisting that teachers meet standards for licensure has any effect on student achievement. The claim is central to the reform agenda of the National Commission on Teaching and America's Future (NCTAF), which is working with policymakers in many states to make policy changes that should increase student learning (National Commission on Teaching and America's Future, 1996; National Commission on Teaching and America's Future, 1997).

Most of the research work on effects of teacher qualifications has used a "production function" model from economics in which large-scale databases are used to estimate coefficients in multiple regression equations. In a recent study, Goldhaber and Brewer (2000) used data from the National Educational Longitudinal Study of 1988 to analyze the contribution teacher qualifications make to student achievement. To separate effects of teacher qualifications from other causes of student achievement, the authors used as covariates indicators for other likely influences. These covariates included prior achievement and indicators of the socioeconomic status of the school (percentage of minority and percentage of free or reduced lunch). The authors conclude that, in mathematics, teachers with training in mathematics (a mathematics degree or certification as a mathematics teacher) "outperform" those teachers lacking preparation in mathematics but that teachers on emergency license perform about as well as those teachers with a standard credential.

This example is one of a set of studies that prominently figure in ongoing policy debates. As the word "outperform" suggests, these studies are seen as uncovering the instrumental links between characteristics of teachers and the academic achievement of their students. Some previous studies have supported the finding that teachers' subject-matter training affects student achievement but have concluded, contrary to Goldhaber and Brewer, that teachers with a regular, rather than emergency, license have a greater effect on student achievement (Darling-Hammond, 1998; Ferguson, 1991). Other studies have drawn conflicting conclusions about the overall contributions teacher characteristics make to student achievement (Hanushek, 1986; Hedges, Laine, & Greenwald, 1994).

The interest in these studies is evidence of the policy interest in continuing work on the effects of teaching. With the political momentum driven by work of NCTAF, policymakers are considering whether specific policy recommendations are worth pursuing (Darling-Hammond, 1998). They are asking for studies that will indicate which policy changes will affect student achievement. Studies of the effects of teaching deliver some answers to these questions. The sometimes disparate answers show that further work is needed to refine definitions (e.g., of a qualified teacher) and methodology. Neither policymakers nor researchers see the disagreements as indications of the postmodern demise of research on teaching. Indeed, the vigor of the debates suggests that studies of the effects of teaching are taken as an important source of information.

In response, the U.S. Department of Education has initiated two major, 5-year research initiatives to learn more about the connections among teaching policy, teacher education, teacher characteristics, teaching practice, and student achievement. The Center for the Study of Teaching and Policy, with headquarters at the University of Washington, is carrying out a range of studies aimed at describing the effects of policies on teaching and, ultimately, on student learning (Center for the Study of Teaching and Policy, 1998). The National Partnership on Excellence and Accountability in Teaching, with headquarters in Washington, D.C., combined studies of the effects of teaching, teacher education, and teaching policy with partnership initiatives aimed at enacting changes in the education system (National Partnership on Excellence and Accountability in Teaching, 1999).

Policy studies have expanded the effects of teaching paradigm beyond simple connections between teaching and learning, but sometimes (as in the production function studies) leave classroom processes out of the picture. An updated model might start with the one Dunkin and Biddle (1974) include in their early, seminal book on research on teaching, then add policy variables. Dunkin and Biddle divided variables measured in research on teaching into presage (how teachers got to be the way they are), context (what students, schools, and communities are like), process (what teachers and students do in the classroom), and product (what students learn). The term "process–product research" refers to studies that focus on the last two areas, treating presage and context as background sources of variation. The effects of teaching paradigm, as originally defined, also looks only at process and product.

That limitation, however, can be seen as a strategic choice in how to move forward within a more fundamental paradigm, a search for ways to trace student learning back, through teaching processes, to other factors (e.g., teacher education and education policy) that may have an ultimate effect on students.

These are extensions of the paradigm, not a rejection of the idea that research can discover connections between teaching and practice. As such, they operate in the face of postmodern attacks on the possibility for justified knowledge about human endeavors. They proceed on the assumption that research, if done well, can lead to an increase in understanding about the causal links between teaching and learning as well as about the factors that influence teaching. The following sections will sketch the range of ways that the effects of teaching paradigm has been expanded as more has been learned. These expansions elaborate the effects of teaching paradigm; they do not abandon it.

Studies in the Process–Product Tradition

Process–product research may have been roundly criticized (e.g., Fenstermacher, 1979), but it has continued as a major stream of work. The amount of work within this model declined in the late 1970s as the large research grants needed for large correlational studies evaporated. Some large-scale studies are still being conducted, joined by smaller studies that are guided by particular models of what classrooms should look like. In some cases, information about mediations between teaching and learning is collected, but the goal of central importance is finding causal connections between teaching and learning.

The largest, most visible, study examining the connection is the Third International Mathematics and Science Study (TIMSS) (Schmidt, McKnight, & Raizen, 1997). Public attention to this massive, multicountry study has emphasized the student achievement data. The study was designed, however, to explain differences in achievement, not just to document them. To that end, two forms of teacher process data were collected. A survey of teacher practice was developed and pilot tested in several countries. The survey was then given to the teachers whose students participated in the TIMSS student testing, yielding the data needed to search for associations between process and product in a variety of countries.

In three countries (United States, Japan, and Germany), TIMSS also gathered process data by making videotapes of a nationally representative sample of teachers. The rationale for this costly research investment was that it would provide data on teaching process necessary for explaining differences in student achievement, by searching for associations between what teaching is like and what students learn. Publications reporting these associations have not yet appeared as of this writing, but, when they do, they are likely to gain wide attention. Questions about the basic links between teaching and learning remain of substantial public interest.

A second large study in the process–product tradition is the Project STAR (Student-Teacher Achievement Ratio) study of the effects of class size (Mosteller, Light, & Sachs, 1996). With the support of the Tennessee government, researchers randomly selected teachers to have smaller class sizes than those of their colleagues. The study's central question was "Does small class size lead to higher student achievement?" Class size is a crude teaching variable, because teachers may vary greatly in the use to which they put the resources released, but its very simplicity has made it appealing to the public and to policymakers. Because teachers in the STAR study were randomly selected to receive fewer students, this process–product study has a better than usual basis for determining which associations between teaching and learning are causally relevant.

Partly on the basis of this study, President Clinton has been pushing for a large federal investment in class size reduction, and several states have also invested in this reform. Changes to smaller class size have created further opportunities to study the effects of small class size on teaching and the effects of those changes in teaching to improvements in student learning. A consortium of research institutions, for example, is looking at the effects of class size reduction in California (Stecher, Stasz, & Ormseth, 1998). The longitudinal study will use multiple methodologies (e.g., observation, case studies, and survey) to describe the effects of class size reduction on teaching and to identify the effects those changes in teaching have on student learning. The financial support from the California Department of Education is evidence that policymakers take a strong interest in the effects of policies on teaching and learning.

On a smaller scale, studies of the effects of particular curricula can be seen as effects of teaching studies. In this case, the variation in teaching practice is created by trying to get a group of teachers to adopt a new instructional model. The search for connections to student learning is then made by comparing the results of those taught to use the new model with the results of some control group. Often these studies collect information on what teachers do in their classrooms, partly as a check to see whether the curriculum was implemented as intended, partly as a way to understand which parts of the model are most associated with student learning. In either case, these studies give prominence to effects of the teaching component.

Slavin and his colleagues, for example, have been examining the data on the most popular comprehensive school reform programs (Slavin & Fashola, 1998; Wasik & Slavin, 1993). Slavin's own "Success for All" has received the most intensive examination. The program has been operating in some districts for more than a decade, so longitudinal data are available on 55 schools, each of which is compared with a control school matched to the experimental school on poverty level, prior achievement level, and ethnicity. This ongoing longitudinal investigation shows an average effect size of about half a standard deviation on scores from three national reading tests: the Woodcock Reading Mastery Test, the Durrell Analysis of Reading Difficulty, and the Gray Oral Reading Test (Slavin & Madden, 1999). Data on teaching practice in some of these classrooms allow the investigators to look for associations between teaching process and student learning. They have found that, in general, schools that closely followed the program model had higher achievement scores (Nunnery et al., in press).

Recently, a review of research on school-wide reform models found that only 3 of 24 models studied have strong evidence of effects on student achievement (Herman, 1999). Another four models have "promising" research evidence. The policy interest in such studies of the effects of teaching is indicated by recent legislation, which has begun to specify that programs receiving funding must be based on reliable research. In keeping with that focus on reliable research, the ratings of the strength of supporting evidence was based on the number of studies "using rigorous methodologies," which was judged "according to methodological criteria such as sample size, duration of the study, appropriateness of comparison groups, and relevance of measurement instruments." The review was commissioned by the major national associations of teachers and administrators, major groups of educational practitioners, which are among those seeking research on the effects of teaching.

Unpacking Classroom Practices

As mentioned earlier, Doyle's classroom mediation paradigm (Doyle, 1978) elaborated the process–product paradigm by adding attention to student classroom activity, both as associated with teacher actions and as associated with student learning. This addition can be thought of either as a way of making the effects of teaching more transparent (because it revealed more about *how* teaching had its effects) or as a guide for selecting what aspects of teaching to measure (because teaching that has no effect on student activity seems unlikely to affect student learning).

The importance of student mediating processes has been underscored by lines of research on student understanding of subject matter and on the social construction of classroom knowledge. To date, these research programs have mostly been working back from student learning to the activities students engage in, stopping short of empirical examination of what teaching yields the student activities associated with learning. There are exceptions, however, that will be discussed below.

Research on Student Understanding

Since Piaget, researchers have been investigating the interpretations students make of their educational experiences. Initially, studies served mainly as dramatic demonstrations that students had robust conceptions of subject matter, different from those the teacher hoped them to develop (e.g., Erlwanger, 1973). Investigators would, for example, follow up apparently accurate student responses (e.g., about properties of light), asking students to give more detailed explanations. When pressed, students often revealed reasoning and beliefs contrary to what was currently accepted in their discipline.

With that point clearly established, researchers began to map conceptions of students in different contexts, so that teaching might be informed by a prediction of what conceptions might provide obstacles for teaching. Roth (1991), for example, has developed several units designed to surface students' conceptions of photosynthesis, then offer the teacher ways to assist students in moving toward a conception consistent with scientific thought. To complete the picture for the effects of teaching paradigm, studies like this are being expanded to examine whether the changes in teaching associated with these materials lead to improvements in student learning.

Social Construction of Classroom Knowledge

Work on classrooms in which students are more actively engaged has grown in popularity. Terms such as "community of learners," "social cognition," and "construction of knowledge" signal an interest in teaching models designed to move the teacher off center stage, giving a bigger role to the students. The idea has precursors and roots in American progressive education but in this cycle cites social learning theories for theoretical support.

Researchers and practitioners use the terms in such a wide

variety of ways that any research study can examine only one particular version of an associated teaching approach. Like research on student understanding, these studies often start by trying to understand how classroom social processes are related to student learning. With that information in hand, investigators can begin to examine what characteristics of teaching will foster the social processes that lead ultimately to student learning.

Building from the work of Vygotsky and his followers (van der Veer & Valsiner, 1991; Vygotsky, 1962; Wertsch, 1985), Cobb and his collaborators have undertaken a program of work examining how elementary school student interactions around mathematics are related to student learning and how particular approaches to teaching support or impede those student interactions. With the focus on clearly defined areas of mathematics content (e.g., moving from counting by ones to counting by 10s and ones), these investigators describe what goes on in classrooms and what students learn from their classroom experiences. In some studies, the descriptions of students' progress are presented as case studies of learning (e.g., Cobb, 1995), with no mention of the teachers' role in promoting understanding. But in other work, teachers participated in a 1-week summer institute and were given activities to use in their classrooms. By working from a social constructivist theory of learning, the researchers hoped that the teachers would promote discussion of mathematical ideas,

> highlighting conflicts between alternative interpretations or solutions, helping students develop productive small-group collaborative relationships (Wood & Yackel, 1990), facilitating mathematical dialogue between students (Wood, Cobb, & Yackel, 1989), implicitly legitimizing selected aspects of contributions to a discussion in light of their potential fruitfulness for further mathematical constructions (Wood & Yackel, 1990), redescribing students' explanations in more sophisticated terms that are none the less comprehensible to students, and guiding the development of taken-to-be-shared interpretations when particular representational systems are established (Cobb, Yackel, & Wood, 1989). (Cobb et al., 1991, p. 7)

The inservice was intended to build teachers' understanding of mathematics and mathematics learning, not to "program the teachers to act in a predetermined way" (Cobb et al., 1991, p. 14). Teachers were expected to use these general understandings to adapt their instruction to the specific students in their classes, with support across the school year from the research staff.

The study showed how research on the effects of teaching can be carried out in line with a social constructivist approach, which changes the role of teacher from a font of information to a class discussion leader and builder of classroom community. The effects of the changes in teacher role were examined by comparing students' scores on several tests with the scores of students in comparison classes in the same three schools. Students in the "constructivist" classrooms scored higher than the control students on tests (one nationally standardized test and one developed by the project) emphasizing conceptual understanding; they scored the same as the control students for tests emphasizing computation. The latter result is notable because critics of mathematics reforms have claimed that gains in understanding are made at the expense of computational skill—

not the case here. It is studies like this that can guide teachers and curriculum developers as they design instruction in light of the social constructivist theories of Vygotsky and others.

Brown and her colleagues have also built on Vygotsky, focusing on how development can be fostered by working in the "zone of proximal development" between tasks students can do independently and tasks they can do with assistance (from the teacher, from peers, from technology, etc.). Early work (e.g., Brown & Palinscar, 1982) promoted students' ability to read with understanding by training them to lead discussions, following a pattern that begins with asking a question, includes trying to clarify and predict, and ends with giving a summary. Students who cannot initially use these comprehension strategies independently get experience with the strategies with the support of the teacher and other students in the group. That participation, with supports, pushes the child's development, so that the child can later use the strategies when reading independently. The approach builds on Vygotsky's insights that learning and development are social processes. The effects of reciprocal teaching come not just from learning comprehension strategies but from building an interpretive community "whose interaction with texts was as much a matter of community understanding and shared experience as it was strictly textual interpretation" (Brown, 1994, pp. 6–7).

Building on this work on reading, the Community of Learners project (Brown & Campione, 1994) has expanded teaching aimed at developing interpretive communities to include other subject areas (e.g., science) and to include experts from outside the school (e.g., by e-mail). Refinement of this model has been accompanied by ongoing studies of the effects of such communities on student learning, building support for theoretical developments and for practical implementation. The "design experiments" Brown is conducting work from practical implementation to theoretical refinement and back, in the spirit of the effects of teaching approach. These experiments show the important role teachers play, even in instruction based on the theory that students construct knowledge. "An essential role for teachers is to guide the discovery process toward forms of disciplined inquiry that would not be reached without expert guidance" (Brown, 1994, p. 9).

Looking Out to the Influences on Teaching

Attention to students helps to understand how changes in teaching might lead to stronger connections with student learning. Attention to how and why teaching changes can fill out another section of the research on teaching map. Rather than assuming that teaching is a static enterprise, this work focuses on how teaching can be changed. Because formal methods for changing teaching (e.g., teacher education, professional development) are only part of the picture, studies can be broadly construed as investigating teachers' learning, which may be shaped by early experience and peer identification as much as by programs designed to affect what teachers know and do.

Investigators studying opportunities for teacher learning often see their work as ultimately, though perhaps distantly, connected to student learning. Thus, the significance of teacher policy studies is justified by a presumed connection (possibly supported by research) between how teachers change as a result of the policy and what students of such teachers are likely to learn. That connection suggests that this work should be seen in the context of the effects of teaching paradigm.

Early research on teaching lumped influences on what teachers knew and did into the category of "presage variables" (Dunkin & Biddle, 1974). Through the period of the second *Handbook,* investigations of connections between these variables and teaching received limited attention. The third *Handbook* contains no chapter looking at the connections between education policies and teaching. A separate handbook on teaching and policy (Shulman & Sykes, 1983) was published 3 years before the third *Handbook,* but its content apparently had not made its way into the research on teaching community.

The *Handbook* chapter on teacher education (Lanier & Little, 1986) also gave surprisingly little attention to the effects—on teachers or on students—of teacher education and professional development. As with studies of policy-teaching connections, research was being conducted beyond what was reported in this *Handbook,* including projects led by Feiman-Nemser and Buchmann (1986) and by Zeichner and Tabachnick (1985). The number of studies on teacher learning has grown substantially since 1986.

Many of these studies, perhaps most of them, use the language of opportunities for teacher learning; others use the language of influence on teachers. The difference in language colors interpretations. Saying that a teacher has an opportunity to learn gives the impression of autonomy and choice, whereas saying that a teacher has been influenced suggests the possibility of coercion. Arguments for use of one set of terms over another appear periodically, but both forms remain in use. A hybrid language of "influence on teacher learning" will be used for the remainder of this chapter.

Influences on teacher learning include teacher education and professional development, education policies, teachers' life histories and career stages, and the social contexts of teaching. A brief look at the work in each of these categories will aid in understanding how they fit with studies of the effects of teaching, especially what assumptions must usually be made to tie the work empirically to student learning.

Influence of Teacher Education and Professional Development

Research on methods used in teacher education and professional development goes back 30 years to studies of microteaching as a method for teachers to learn instructional skills (Allen & Ryan, 1969). Microteaching was subsequently studied extensively, supporting an approach to skills learning that remains in wide use, both in the United States and in other countries. Research on skill training for experienced teachers has also been extensively studied, to the point in which a model combining modeling, practice with feedback, and coaching is generally accepted (Joyce & Showers, 1988; Little, 1993). Such research makes the connection to student learning by selecting skills found to be associated with some student outcomes.

Research has also addressed the effects of field experience (e.g., Zeichner & Tabachnick, 1981). Because these studies often look at effects on teachers' general orientations to teaching rather than at effects on particular instructional practices, the

connection to student learning is a loose one, which is based on intuitions about teaching, in contrast to the tighter link for studies of skill training.

Little research has addressed how entire programs of teacher education affect teachers' learning. One exception is the Teacher Education and Learning to Teach (TELT) study conducted by Kennedy and her colleagues (National Center for Research on Teacher Education, 1988). The study focused on a dozen teacher education programs, both preservice and inservice, looking at how teachers learned to teach mathematics and writing to diverse learners. One recent analysis (Kennedy, 1998) examined the effects these teacher education programs had on teachers' "espoused ideals and their immediate concerns in particular classroom situations" (p. 166). Earlier research on the effects of teacher education had focused on features of program structure, such as the length of field experience or the arrangements for connecting methods classes to work in schools. Kennedy looked instead at the *substantive* orientation of programs, contrasting programs focusing on "the traditional themes of classroom management and associated topics" with those that "directly addressed the teaching of school subjects such as writing" (p. 21). She found that

> These substantive orientations made a difference. Teachers who participated in traditional management-oriented programs became even more concerned about prescriptions by the end of their programs than they had been in the beginning, while teachers in reform-oriented programs reduced their concerns about prescriptions and increased their concerns about students' strategies and purposes. . . . Virtually all of the changes in teachers' interpretations of these particular situations [posed by the researchers] were consistent with the programs' substantive orientation. (Kennedy, 1998, p. 21)

Kennedy's work is an example of the effects of teaching paradigm, looking at effects of teacher education on teachers in the context of reform.

Influence of Policy

Policy studies have gained increased attention in education, as indicated by the creation of a separate division within the American Educational Research Association. Researchers typically see their work as relevant to improvements in student learning, but investigations that go all the way from policy to student learning remain rare. Some studies analyze policies, leaving the connections to teaching practice as untested assumptions. When studies do collect information on teaching practice, they often use a blend of observation and self-report.

The Content Determinants project conducted a series of studies examining various influences on teachers' choices about what to teach in fourth-grade mathematics (Porter, Floden, Freeman, Schmidt, & Schwille, 1988). The project argued that such content decisions were important because other research had demonstrated that student learning of particular content was affected by the amount of time students spent engaged in studying that content (Carroll, 1963). Thus, this research team made a link from policy to teaching to student learning, with their research focus on the first link and prior research supporting the second link. To explore the influences on teaching, the investigators analyzed the content of a range of policy instruments—textbooks, tests, objectives, and others—and compared it with the content of teachers' instruction. The content of instruction was recording, using combinations of observations, interviews, and teacher logs. Results from the research, such as that teachers were (in the 1970s) receiving contradictory messages about what to teach, have been incorporated into contemporary discussions of alignment and standards based reform.

The Educational Policy and Practice Study (EPPS) (Cohen & Ball, 1990) used a similar methodology in its studies of the effects of state mathematics and reading policies. In work in California, these investigators made repeated visits to elementary school teachers in three school districts. The work used vivid examples to argue that changes in official goals for mathematics were not enough to change classroom practice, because teachers needed to learn more (about mathematics and about some approaches to teaching) before they could move beyond endorsing a new rhetoric.

By adding a statistically representative state survey, linked to student achievement data, the EPPS work added a stronger basis for conclusions about the effects of policies on teaching practices and the effects of those practices on student learning. The survey asked teachers questions about their instructional practices, their knowledge of the state mathematics reform, and the opportunities teachers had to learn how to teach in ways suggested by the new state mathematics framework. The survey was sent to a sample of 1,000 teachers, representative of the second- to fifth-grade teachers in the state. Student results on state tests were obtained for those teachers so that teaching could be linked to learning. The authors conclude that:

> Teaching practice and student performance are likely to improve when educational improvement is focused on learning and teaching academic content, and when curriculum for improving teaching overlaps with curriculum and assessment for students. (Cohen & Hill, 1998, p. 11)

Note that these studies of policy and teaching practice do not claim the ability to predict what individual teachers or students will do. The conclusions are rather about "likely" effects. That way of phrasing results acknowledges the claims that research on teaching cannot produce "certain" (i.e., infallible) knowledge, particularly about individual cases. The investigators have not, however, followed some postmodern authors who jump from lack of certainty to nihilism. Rather, the authors make important claims about general tendencies, claims that have been picked up in the discussions of education reform.

Influence of Colleagues

Teachers can learn from each other, outside the confines of a program of inservice education. Much past research focused on the conservative effects new teachers experience when they join a school. Studies in the past decade, however, have shifted to studies of the positive effects of connections with colleagues. After Little (1982) described schools where teachers talked to each other about ways to improve instruction, other investiga-

tors began to examine what teachers learned from interactions with their building colleagues and with broader teacher networks. Much of this research focuses on teachers' satisfaction with what they get from network participation (Lieberman & McLaughlin, 1994), leaving connections to student learning as an assumption supported by teachers' sense of what is helpful.

The departmental organization of secondary schools affects collegial influence, because association is within content area rather than with teachers in the school as a whole. Research from the Center on Teaching Context (McLaughlin & Talbert, in press) has examined the effects on teachers of the contexts—students in the classroom, subject-matter department, school, district, state—in which teaching is embedded. In 16 schools, spread across seven school districts in California and Michigan, the investigators combined intensive, repeated interviews and observations with a survey, which included items that permitted comparison with national samples. Although the study did not include achievement measures for all the students in these schools, the investigators used classroom observations to get a sense of what students were doing and seemed to be learning. They saw some settings where students seemed bored and disengaged; others where students eagerly pursued challenging academic projects.

> We visited schools in which the kinds of students who would have been turned-off and tuned-out in most urban high schools instead talked to us with animation about learning and about their schoolwork. In an alternative high school for youth who were not succeeding in a "regular" high school, for example, we listened to students critiquing Hemingway, and then reading their own writing and commenting to peers on ways to strengthen theirs. In an urban school dedicated to the performing arts, we found students intent on their writing, music, and staging the school's dramatic production. (McLaughlin & Talbert, 2001)

By working up from these differences among students, the investigators found that the teachers getting their students engaged in challenging work were supported by communities in their schools in which teachers shared "a commitment to examining and improving their practice." These communities, in turn, were fostered by subject-matter departments and by principals who shared this commitment. The subject matter of the departments also mattered, with teachers in sequential subjects like mathematics reporting more coordination with colleagues and more pressure for content coverage than other teachers (Stodolsky & Grossman, 1995). These results shed light on the sources of difference in teachers' practices and beliefs, using examples of particular pupils to complete the link to student learning.

Teachers' Life and Career Stages

Early research on teacher personality types found little to report, concluding that measures of personality were too problematic to support connections to student learning (Getzels & Jackson, 1963). Perhaps because of such early failure, research on teachers' personal circumstances has received little attention from others doing research on teaching in the United States. In other countries, in contrast, researchers have been studying teachers' life histories, looking for patterns of change (Floden & Huberman, 1989). Because life history is not a variable that can be manipulated, it is difficult to make empirical connections between life history and student learning. Some results, however, suggest plausible linkages. For example, teachers typically engage vigorously in reform activities early in their careers but, disappointed by the payoff for such investments, are less willing to invest in change later in their careers. They are, however, still willing to invest in their students (Huberman, 1989). This developmental trajectory suggests that younger teachers are more likely to shift their instruction as goals for student learning change.

Research on Teachers' Mental Lives

Objections to the behaviorist aspects of process–product research led many researchers to shift their attention to descriptions of teacher knowledge and teacher thinking. By using studies in cognitive psychology as a model, researchers investigated how teachers thought about their teaching, how they made decisions about instruction, what they believed about how students learn, and so on. Shulman (1986) included these cognitive studies in his review of the field but argued that the studies were not paying enough attention to the subject matter about which teachers were thinking and teaching.

In the ensuing years, many researchers have followed Shulman's advice, looking carefully at what teachers know of and about the subjects they teach, at what teachers think about how that subject matter can be learned and should be taught, and at how teachers learn to think differently about subject matter. Most such research has described teachers' understandings (Leinhardt, 1990) and how those understandings are formed by teacher education and other experiences (e.g., Ball, 1989).

Links between teacher cognition and student learning are often based on the commonsense argument that teachers who know more about their subject will produce better results with students. More recent studies, however, have empirically connected teacher knowledge to student learning. The study described earlier by Cobb and his colleagues (Cobb et al., 1991) makes the link to student achievement as do the studies by the Cognitively Guided Instruction (CGI) group at the University of Wisconsin–Madison (Carpenter, Fennema, Peterson, Chiang, & Loef, 1989). Both studies used comparison groups to support inferences about the effects of differences in teaching. The CGI group makes their interest in the effects of teaching explicit: "The purpose of this study was to investigate whether providing teachers access to explicit knowledge derived from research on children's thinking in a specific content domain would influence the teachers' instruction and their students' achievement" (Carpenter et al., 1989, p. 500). As in Cobb's work, the investigators found connections between teaching and learning, but they were left with puzzles about their operation and their variability. But, as with the other studies of the effects of teaching, the incompleteness and uncertainty about the research results does not leave the researchers with a postmodern sense that no conclusions are possible. Instead, they conclude by indicating that their work supports a path for improving student achievement by enhancing teachers' knowledge.

Although many unanswered questions remain, our results suggest that giving teachers access to research-based knowledge about students' thinking and problem solving can affect teachers' beliefs about learning and instruction, their classroom practices, their knowledge about their students, and most important, their students' achievement and beliefs. (Carpenter et al., 1989, p. 530)

Conclusion

As noted at the beginning of this chapter, recent publications often begin with a claim that educational research has changed in light of the rise of postmodernism. Constas, for example, in a critique of some postmodernists, says:

Over the past several years, it appears that the writing of the educational research community has undergone a consistent series of changes. . . . I would argue that the most radical change found in the current discourse of educational inquiry stems from the intellectual movement variously referred to as 'the postmodern condition' (Lyotard, 1984), "the condition of postmodernity" (Harvey, 1989), and "unmarked modernity" (Spivak, 1990). . . .

As a distinctive intellectual approach to comprehending and solving problems, postmodernism abandons the enlightenment ambitions of unity, certainty, and predictability. . . . Using the notion of chaos as an explanatory metaphor, postmodernism doggedly questions the view of a world founded on the aspiration of progressive betterment. (Constas, 1998, p. 26)

Looking specifically at recent research on teaching, Hamilton and McWilliam (this volume) portray the line of research on the effects of teaching as "moribund." These accounts leave readers thinking that researchers, practitioners, and policymakers should abandon hopes for research on teaching that can lead to improvements in education.

The research programs illustrated in this chapter are visible evidence that research on teaching effects is vital and highly regarded. The education community's appetite for evidence on the connections between teaching and learning seems larger than ever. The complexity of teaching and learning make absolute certainty and predictability unreasonable expectations, but research evidence on the average effect of policies, programs, and practices figures prominently in public debates about the future direction of education. Moreover, work on these studies is not fraught with doubts prompted by the recognition that every study is open to some questions about its focus, objectivity, and validity. Instead, discussions seek to explain differences in conclusions by arguing the specifics of methods used, interpretations made, and implications drawn. In examining the overall import of production function studies, for example, Hedges and his colleagues (Hedges et al., 1994) began a debate with Hanushek (1989, 1994). The debate assumes the possibility of using research to understand the impact of changing educational inputs, such as more qualified teachers or additional professional development; it does not degenerate into general angst about the very possibility of worthwhile research. Debates about methods and interpretations are compatible with belief in the value of research on teaching effects. The scientific "metanarrative" lives on.

Many policymakers and funding agencies are now asking researchers for more evidence regarding effects on student learning. Although the complexity of the education system often makes such effects difficult to identify, the demands for evidence will encourage investigators to contrive research designs that will deliver. The sought for connection has been achieved in a variety of studies, spread across the areas sketched here. Successful attempts to find causal connections refute the radical critics who deny the possibility of causal understandings in the human sciences. Instructional programs, such as described above, led by Slavin, Brown, Cobb, and Carpenter, draw on research in their initial design and then demonstrate the effects of those designs on what students learn. Such studies will raise expectations for research, inspiring other scholars to elaborate knowledge of causal links.

The connections between teaching and learning would be easier to demonstrate if an empirically supported theory of teaching, connected to learning, were in hand. With confidence in claims about links between teaching and learning, researchers could concentrate their efforts on links between teaching and the several factors that influence it. A theory of teaching is a worthy goal; it is unlikely to be attained in the near future. The effects of direct instruction on skill learning have been established, but claims about connections have yet to be demonstrated between teaching for active engagement in learning and new content standards. For such teaching, experts disagree enough about what teaching should be like that it makes little sense to ask about the effects of the general approach.

As the chapters in this *Handbook* illustrate, work in a postmodern vein has gained a place in research on teaching, but it has not displaced the line of work that Gage (Gage, 1963b) promoted in the first of these handbooks. Indeed, that work has expanded, encompassing realms that explain how teaching affects learning and how the overall environment affects teaching and learning. My prognosis is that research on the effects of teaching, built on strong research designs from multiple methodologies, will make increasing contributions to educators' understandings of how to improve education for all.

REFERENCES

Allen, D., & Ryan, K. (1969). *Microteaching.* Reading, MA: Addison-Wesley.
Ball, D. L. (1989). *Breaking with experience: The role of a preservice methods course* (IP 89–10). E. Lansing, MI: National Center for Research on Teacher Learning, College of Education, Michigan State University.
Brown, A. L. (1994). The advancement of learning. *Educational Researcher, 23*(8), 4–12.
Brown, A. L., & Campione, J. C. (1994). Guided discovery in a community of learners. In K. McGilly (Ed.), *Classroom lessons: Integrating cognitive theory and classroom practice* (pp. 229–270). Cambridge, MA: MIT Press/Bradford Books.
Brown, A. L., & Palinscar, A. S. (1982). Inducing strategic learning from texts by means of informed, self-control training. *Topics in Learning and Learning Disabilities, 2*(1), 1–18.
Carpenter, T. P., Fennema, E., Peterson, P. L., Chiang, C.-P., & Loef, M. (1989). Using knowledge of children's mathematics thinking in classroom teaching: An experimental study. *American Educational Research Journal, 26*(4), 499–531.
Carroll, J. (1963). A model for school learning. *Teachers College Record, 64,* 723–733.
Casey, K. (1995). The new narrative research in education. In M. W. Apple (Ed.), *Review of research in education. 1995–1996* (Vol. 21,

pp. 211–253). Washington, DC: American Educational Research Association.
Center for the Study of Teaching and Policy. (1998). *Policy and excellent teaching: Focus for a national research center. Center description and synopsis of research program.* Seattle, WA: University of Washington.
Cobb, P. (1995). Cultural tools and mathematical learning. *Journal for Research in Mathematics Education, 26*(4), 362–385.
Cobb, P., Wood, T., Yackel, E., Nicholls, J., Wheatley, G., Trigatti, B., & Perlwitz, M. (1991). Assessment of a problem-centered second-grade mathematics project. *Journal for Research in Mathematics Education, 22*(1), 3–29.
Cobb, P., Yackel, E., & Wood, T. (1989). Young children's emotional acts while doing mathematical problem solving. In D. B. McLeod & V. M. Adams (Eds.), *Affect and mathematical problem solving: A new perspective* (pp. 117–148). New York: Springer-Verlag.
Cochran-Smith, M., & Lytle, S. (1992). Communities for teacher research: Fringe or forefront? *American Journal of Education, 100,* 298–323.
Cohen, D. K., & Ball, D. L. (1990). Policy and practice: An overview. *Educational Evaluation and Policy Analysis, 12,* 233–239.
Cohen, D. K., & Hill, H. C. (1998). *State policy and classroom performance: Mathematics reform in California* (Policy Brief RB-23-January 1998). Philadelphia: Consortium for Policy Research in Education, Graduate School of Education, University of Pennsylvania.
Collins, A., Brown, J. S., & Newman, S. E. (1989). Cognitive apprenticeship: Teaching the craft of reading, writing, and mathematics. In L. B. Resnick (Ed.), *Knowing, learning, and instruction: Essays in honor of Robert Glaser.* Hillsdale, NJ: Lawrence Erlbaum Associates.
Connelly, M., & Clandinin, D. J. (1996). Teachers' professional knowledge landscapes. *Educational Researcher, 21*(1), 145–158.
Constas, M. A. (1998). The changing nature of educational research and a critique of postmodernism. *Educational Researcher, 27*(2), 26–33.
Darling-Hammond, L. (1998). Teachers and teaching: Testing policy hypotheses from a national commission report. *Educational Researcher, 27*(1), 5–15.
Delpit, L. (1995). *Other people's children: Cultural conflict in the classroom.* New York: The New Press.
Doyle, W. (1978). Paradigms for research on teacher effectiveness. In L. S. Shulman (Ed.), *Review of research in education* (Vol. 5). Itasca, IL: Peacock.
Dunkin, M. J., & Biddle, B. J. (1974). *The study of teaching.* New York: Holt, Rinehart and Winston.
Eisenhart, M. A., & Howe, K. R. (1992). Validity in educational research. In M. D. LeCompte, W. Millroy, & J. Preissle (Eds.), *The handbook of qualitative research in education* (pp. 643–680). San Diego, CA: Academic Press.
Eisner, E. (1992). Objectivity in educational research. *Curriculum Inquiry, 22*(1), 9–15.
Erlwanger, S. H. (1973). Benny's conception of rules and answers in IPI mathematics. *Journal of Children's Mathematical Behavior, 1*(2), 7–26.
Feiman-Nemser, S., & Buchmann, M. (1986). The first year of teacher preparation: Transition to pedagogical thinking. *Journal of Curriculum Studies, 18*(3), 239–256.
Fenstermacher, G. (1979). A philosophical consideration of recent research on teacher effectiveness. *Review of Research in Education, 6,* 157–185.
Ferguson, R. (1991). Paying for public education: New evidence on how and why money matters. *Harvard Journal on Legislation, 28,* 465–498.
Feyerabend, P. (1975). *Against method.* Medawah, NJ: Humanities Press.
Floden, R. E. (1981). Does the triple play retire the side? Research methods and methods of teacher education. In C. J. B. Macmillan (Ed.), *Philosophy of education 1980. Proceedings of the thirty-sixth annual meeting of the Philosophy of Education Society* (pp. 163–173). Normal, IL: Philosophy of Education Society.
Floden, R. E., & Huberman, M. (1989). Teachers' professional lives:

The state of the art. *International Journal of Educational Research, 13,* 455–466.

Floden, R. E., & Klinzing, H. G. (1990). What can research on teacher thinking contribute to teacher preparation? *Educational Researcher, 19*(5), 15–20.

Frederiksen, N. (1984). The real test bias: Influences of testing on teaching and learning. *American Psychologist, 39*(3), 193–202.

Gage, N. L. (Ed.). (1963a). *Handbook of research on teaching.* Chicago: Rand McNally.

Gage, N. L. (1963b). Paradigms for research on teaching. In N. L. Gage (Ed.), *Handbook of research on teaching* (pp. 94–141). Chicago: Rand McNally.

Getzels, J. W., & Jackson, P. W. (1963). The teacher's personality and characteristics. In N. L. Gage (Ed.), *Handbook of research on teaching* (pp. 506–582). Chicago: Rand McNally.

Gilligan, C. (1982). *In a different voice: Psychological theory and women's development.* Cambridge, MA: Harvard University Press.

Goldhaber, D. D., & Brewer, D. J. (2000). Does teacher certification matter?: High school teacher certification status and student achievement. *Educational Evaluation and Policy Analysis, 22,* 129–145.

Greeno, J. G., Collins, A. M., & Resnick, L. (1996). Cognition and learning. In D.C. Berliner & R. C. Calfee (Eds.), *Handbook of educational psychology* (pp. 15–46). New York: Simon & Schuster Macmillan.

Hanushek, E. (1986). The economics of schooling: Production and efficiency in public schools. *Journal of Economic Literature, 24,* 1141–1178.

Hanushek, E. A. (1989). The impact of differential expenditures on school performance. *Educational Researcher, 18*(4), 45–51.

Hanushek, E. A. (1994). Money might matter somewhere: A response to Hedges, Laine, and Greenwald. *Educational Researcher, 23*(4), 5–8.

Harvey, D. (1989). *The condition of postmodernity.* Minneapolis, MN: University of Minnesota Press.

Hedges, L., Laine, R., & Greenwald, R. (1994). A meta-analysis of the effects of differential school inputs on student outcomes. *Educational Researcher, 23*(3), 5–14.

Herman, R. (1999). *An educator's guide to schoolwide reform* [On-line]. American Institutes for Research. Available: http://www.aasa.org/Reform/index.htm [cited 1999, June 7].

Howe, K. R. (1992). Getting over the quantitative-qualitative debate. *American Journal of Education, 100*(2), 236–256.

Howe, K. R. (1998). The interpretive turn and the new debate in education. *Educational Researcher, 27*(8), 13–20.

Huberman, M. (1989). The professional life cycle of teachers. *Teachers College Record, 91,* 31–58.

Joyce, B., & Showers, B. (1988). *Student achievement through staff development.* New York: Longman.

Kennedy, M. M. (1998). *Learning to teach writing: Does teacher education make a difference?* New York: Teachers College Press.

Kepler, K. (1980). BTES: Implications for preservice education of teachers. In C. Denham & A. Lieberman (Eds.), *Time to learn* (pp. 139–157). Washington, DC: National Institute of Education, U.S. Department of Health, Education, and Welfare.

Kuhn, T. S. (1962). *The structure of scientific revolutions.* Chicago: University of Chicago Press.

Lakatos, I. (1971). *Philosophical papers.* Cambridge, UK: Cambridge University Press.

Lanier, J. E., & Little, J. W. (1986). Research on teacher education. In M. C. Wittrock (Ed.), *Handbook of research on teaching* (3rd ed., pp. 527–569). New York: Macmillan.

Lareau, A. (1989). *Home advantage: Social class and parental intervention in elementary education.* New York: Falmer Press.

Laudan, L. (1996). *Beyond positivism and relativism.* Boulder, CO: Westview Press.

Lave, J., & Wenger, E. (1991). *Situated learning: Legitimate peripheral participation.* Cambridge, UK: Cambridge University Press.

Leinhardt, G. (1990). Capturing craft knowledge in teaching. *Educational Researcher, 19*(2), 18–25.

Lieberman, A., & McLaughlin, M. W. (1994). Networks for educational change: Powerful and problematic. *Phi Delta Kappan, 63,* 673–677.

Little, J. W. (1982). Norms of collegiality and experimentation: Workplace conditions of school success. *American Educational Research Journal, 19,* 325–340.

Little, J. W. (1993). Professional development in a climate of educational reform. *Educational Evaluation and Policy Analysis, 15,* 129–152.

Lyotard, J. (1987). The postmodern condition. In K. Baynes, J. Bohman, & T. McCarthy (Eds.), *After philosophy: End or transformation?* (pp. 67–94). Cambridge, MA: MIT Press.

Lyotard, J. F. (1984). *The postmodern condition: A report on knowledge* (G. Bennington & B. Massumi, Trans.). Minneapolis, MN: University of Minnesota Press.

McAninch, A. R. (1993). *Teacher thinking and the case method: Theory and future directions.* New York: Teachers College Press.

McLaughlin, M., & Talbert, J. (2001). *Professional communities and the work of high school teaching.* Chicago: University of Chicago Press.

Mosteller, F., Light, R. J., & Sachs, J. A. (1996). Sustained inquiry in education: Lessons from skill grouping and class size. *Harvard Educational Review, 66,* 797–842.

National Center for Research on Teacher Education. (1988). Teacher education and learning to teach: A research agenda. *Journal of Teacher Education, 39*(6), 27–32.

National Commission on Excellence in Education. (1983). *A nation at risk.* Washington, DC: U.S. Government Printing Office.

National Commission on Teaching and America's Future. (1996). *What matters most: Teaching for America's future.* New York: Author.

National Commission on Teaching and America's Future. (1997). *Doing what matters most: Investing in quality teaching.* New York: Author.

National Council of Teachers of Mathematics. (1989). *Curriculum and evaluation standards for school mathematics.* Reston, VA: Author.

National Partnership on Excellence and Accountability in Teaching. (1999). Untitled web page [On-line]. Available: http://www.npeat.org/about.htm [cited 1999, June 7].

Noddings, N. (1984). *Caring: A feminine approach to ethics and moral education.* Berkeley, CA: University of California Press.

Noddings, N. (1992). *Challenge to care in schools: An alternative approach to education.* New York: Teachers College Press.

Nunnery, J., Slavin, R. E., Ross, S. M., Smith, L. J., Hunter, P., & Stubbs, J. (in press). An assessment of Success for All program component configuration effects on the reading achievement of at-risk first grade students. *American Educational Research Journal.*

Phillips, D.C. (1983). After the wake: Postpositivist educational thought. *Educational Researcher, 12*(5), 4–12, 16.

Phillips, D.C. (1990). Subjectivity and objectivity: An objective inquiry. In E. Eisner & A. Peshkin (Eds.), *Qualitative inquiry in education: The continuing debate* (pp. 19–37). New York: Teachers College Press.

Porter, A., Floden, R., Freeman, D., Schmidt, W., & Schwille, J. (1988). Content determinants in elementary school mathematics. In D. A. Grouws, T. J. Cooney, & D. Jones (Eds.), *Effective mathematics teaching* (pp. 96–113). Reston, VA: National Council of Teachers of Mathematics.

Roth, K. (1991). Learning to be comfortable in the neighborhood of science: An analysis of three approaches to elementary school teaching. In W. Saul & S. A. Jagusch (Eds.), *Vital connections: Children, science, and books.* Portsmouth, NH: Heinemann.

Schmidt, W. H., McKnight, C. C., & Raizen, S. A. (1997). *A splintered vision: An investigation of U.S. science and mathematics education.* Boston: Kluwer Academic Press.

Shulman, L. S. (1986). Paradigms and research programs in the study of teaching: A contemporary perspective. In M. C. Wittrock (Ed.), *Handbook of research on teaching* (3rd ed., pp. 3–36). New York: Macmillan.

Shulman, L. S., & Sykes, G. (Eds.). (1983). *Handbook on teaching and policy.* New York: Longman.

Slavin, R. E., & Fashola, O. S. (1998). *Show me the evidence! Proven and promising programs for America's schools.* Thousand Oaks, CA: Corwin Press.

Slavin, R. E., & Madden, N. A. (1999). *Success for all, roots and wings: 1999 summary of research on achievement outcomes* [On-line]. Available: http://www.successforall.net/sumresch99.html [cited 1999, June 6].

Spivak, G. (1990). The postmodern condition: The end of politics? In S. Harasym (Ed.), *The post-colonial critic.* New York: Routledge.

Stecher, B., Stasz, C., & Ormseth, T. (1998, September). *Class size reduction: What have we learned?* Paper presented at the 1998 national Comprehensive Systems for Educational Accountability and Improvement (CRESST) conference: R&D Results, Los Angeles, CA.

Stodolsky, S. S., & Grossman, P. L. (1995). The impact of subject matter on curricular activity: An analysis of five academic subjects. *American Educational Research Journal, 32,* 227–249.

van der Veer, R., & Valsiner, J. (1991). *Understanding Vygotsky: A quest for synthesis.* Cambridge, MA: Blackwell.

Vygotsky, L. (1962). *Thought and language.* Cambridge, MA: MIT Press.

Wasik, B. A., & Slavin, R. E. (1993). Preventing early reading failure with one-to-one tutoring: A review of five programs. *Reading Research Quarterly, 28,* 178–200.

Weiler, K. A. (1995). Women and the professionalization of teaching. In L. W. Anderson (Ed.), *International encyclopedia of teaching and teacher education* (2nd ed., pp. 76–80). New York: Elsevier Science.

Wertsch, J. V. (1985). *Vygotsky and the social formation of mind.* Cambridge, MA: Harvard University Press.

Wittrock, M. C. (Ed.). (1986). *Handbook of research on teaching* (3rd ed.). New York: Macmillan.

Wood, T., Cobb, P., & Yackel, E. (1989, March). *Change in teaching mathematics: A case study.* Paper presented at the annual meeting of the American Educational Research Association, San Francisco.

Wood, T., & Yackel, E. (1990). The development of collaborative dialogue within small group interactions. In L. P. Steffe & T. Wood (Eds.), *Transforming children's mathematics education. International perspectives* (pp. 244–252). Hillsdale, NJ: Lawrence Erlbaum Associates.

Zeichner, K., & Tabachnick, B. R. (1981). Are the effects of university teacher education washed out by school experience? *Journal of Teacher Education, 32*(3), 7–11.

Zeichner, K., & Tabachnick, B. R. (1985). The development of teacher perspectives: Social strategies and institutional control in the socialization of beginning teachers. *Journal of Education for Teaching, 11,* 1–25.

2.

Ex-Centric Voices That Frame
Research on Teaching

David Hamilton
Umeå University, Sweden

Erica McWilliam
Queensland University of Technology, Australia

The first *Handbook of Research on Teaching* was published in 1963, the same year that Betty Friedan published *The Feminine Mystique,* and the same year that buses and trains brought over a quarter of a million people to Washington for the largest human rights demonstration in the history of the American republic. These events are markers for this chapter. The handbook represented an attempt to cumulate the social science wisdom of the first half of the 20th century, while the anger and hopes expressed by Betty Friedan and the main speaker in Washington, Martin Luther King Jr., represented a different reading of the same epoch.

The first handbook sought to synthesize a new science of teaching. Future improvements in classroom teaching were to be based on "creative examination of the past" and "imaginative appropriation" of other work in the behavioral sciences. Educational practice, that is, was to be harmonized with the law-derived, instrumental implications of 20th century science, themselves clearly expressed in the theme of the 1933 Chicago World's Fair: Science Explores: Technology Executes: Mankind Conforms.

Friedan and King, conversely, expressed a different social agenda: fair worlds rather than world fairs. The fabric of schooling, teaching, and learning was politically dysfunctional. It needed an overhaul. Pursuit of greater mechanical efficiency was not the solution. Schooling, teaching, and learning deserved to be reorganized and reconstituted within a different framework.

Didactics and Pedagogy

The differentiation of pedagogy from didactics can be identified with this new framework. Originally, didactics composed the art of teaching. It embraced procedures for the efficient transmission—or inculcation—of received knowledge. In the words of one of its pioneers, Wolfgang Ratke (1571–1635), didactics prescribed that "all work fell to the teacher" and that, as a consequence, "young learners should sit still, listen, and be silent" (quoted in Michel, 1978, p. 65; see also McLintock, 1972).

Modern pedagogy, however, broke away from didactics. Its emergence stems from 19th century, German-led reactions to the rise of the natural and physical sciences. How, for instance, were the earlier scientific assumptions of Descartes and Newton to be applied to social behavior? Should the nascent educational sciences be located within the physical sciences? Or were they to find a home in the emergent human sciences? Should the knowledge base of educational practice to be derived from processes of explanation (Erklärung) or from activities of interpretation and understanding (Verstehen)?

Didactics and pedagogics separated along these lines. Interpretative pedagogic questions entered English-language scientific communities through the mediation of German-influenced scholars, like John Dewey and George Herbert Mead, and, much later, alongside the exploration—similarly provoked by German thinking—of "qualitative" research in the 1960s (see, for example, Schwandt, 1994; Biesta, 1997).

The authors wish to thank Ervin V. Johanningmeier (University of South Florida) and Ruth Vinz (Teachers College, Columbia University) for their reviews of the outline and draft chapter.

Against this background, pedagogic perspectives regard teaching as a process, not a technique. It is more a variety of two-way communication than a mode of one-way transmission or delivery. In turn, teaching is held to be more about transformative relationships of production and exchange than about distributive mechanisms for the dissemination and consumption of knowledge. Pedagogic thinking, therefore, prioritizes the constitution of learning over the execution of teaching. Paulo Freire, for instance, suggests that teachers and learners are both "in" and "with" the world. They have the capacity to reflect upon its circumstances and transform these circumstances through collective and conscious action (Freire, 1970, p. 452).

Thus, pedagogic action seeks to replace the educational commonplace "What should they know?" with the more profound question "What should they become?" It accepts the interpretative maxim that "once you know what you are doing, you are no longer doing it." And, not least, pedagogic thinking recognizes that all forms of teaching and learning coexist in a web of economic, social, and cultural differences that links, yet also separates, teachers and learners.

During the 1960s such forms of understanding were ill-articulated and insecure (see Lusted, 1986). The term "pedagogy," for instance, is absent from the 2,000 earliest entries in the ERIC (Educational Resources Information Center) database (1962–63). At that time, there was no obvious English-language pedagogic mainstream, like the behavioral sciences, with which educationists could identify. By default, then, pedagogic thinking emerged as a heterodox diaspora, ideas and practices of which still coexist and intermingle with the didactic, behavioral science, paradigm of the first *Handbook of Research on Teaching*. It is no accident, therefore, that this chapter can be read as a commentary on the seven-fold increase in the appearance of "pedagogy" in ERIC between 1981 and 1993 (i.e., from 0.0011 to 0.0081%).

Contents

The purpose of this chapter is to revisit the pedagogic diaspora, to review its conceptual commonalities and differences, and to record its ever-changing horizons. But our task cannot be honored by means of a simple cause-and-effect narrative. We cannot assume that change has motivations that are rational, developments that are linear and effects that are cumulative. The challenge for us here is to embrace a terrain of ideas constituted as much by surprises and disruptions, leaps and discontinuities, deviations and regressions, as by any systematic and ordered processes of evolution.

To map what we have termed "ex-centric" events, we work across the grain of history, blurring the boundaries of chronology and, to some extent, the borderlands between education and elsewhere. Nevertheless, we acknowledge the importance of structure to any form of storytelling, including this narrative about a pedagogic diaspora. Our story, then, is structured around four themes that overlap, bleeding into—or transfusing—one another.

In the first section we explore teaching as didactics, indicating what discontinuities, confusions, and debates were at work within and beyond the explanation of "best practice" offered in the first *Handbook of Research on Teaching*. The second section maps a corpus of work that became linked to notions about participant observation, anthropology, and ethnography in the 1960s and that further proliferated in the 1970s. It recounts work that, wittingly or unwittingly, stood outside the boundaries of psychostatistical or didactic research. Such work sought—through its interpretative stance—to "tell it like it is."

This flowering of narratives around teaching was both abetted and disrupted by the politicized social world of the 1960s. Critical, oppositional, and contestational pedagogies began to be differentiated from liberal humanistic diagnoses of classroom life.

In the third section we go on to map the new sociology of knowledge as an avant-garde tradition of the 1980s and 1990s, one that pitted itself against instrumentalism so it could set priorities for the problematic identity politics of different groups (e.g., African Americans) that are engaged in their own reconceptualizations of teaching and learning.

The fourth section is our attempt to show how poststructural theoretical developments (particularly emanating from new French theory) have been controversial and disturbing across the entire spectrum of research on teaching. Such theory rejects not only positivism but also the antipositivist, antiempirical reaction that, in the 1990s, continued to claim authenticity—and superiority—as a defensible modernist, critical, and feminist alternative.

The First Handbook of Research on Teaching

The title page and preface of the first *Handbook of Research on Teaching* (Gage, 1963a) indicate that it arose from a "project of the American Educational Research Association." Its 1,218 pages were planned as "an aid in the training of workers in research on teaching." Its overall intention was to "improve the conceptual and methodological equipment used in teaching." And it was to accomplish these goals by bringing teaching "into more fruitful contact with the behavioral sciences." Nevertheless, the confident tone of this preface masks a silence. By the early 1960s, the behavioral sciences already faced epistemological disruptions, some of which can be discerned in the first handbook.

The handbook's fundamental allegiance to the behavioral sciences was reflected in its "conceptual orientation." Each chapter was to "flow" from consideration of three major classes of variables: "central variables, relevant variables, and site variables." Central variables stood surrogate for "a behavior or characteristic of teachers"; relevant variables denoted "antecedents, consequents, or concurrents" of the central variables; and site variables referred to a cluster of ancillary measures that "did not need to vary," were "held constant," or merely characterized the "situation in which the [other] variables are studied."

The "problems and findings," which occupied 14 chapters in the first handbook, were "embedded" within a variety of "other chapters." These carried, respectively, "something" of the "historical, philosophical, and theoretical background" of research on teaching (three chapters) and "even more" about the "methodology of research on teaching" (six chapters).

Chains of Reasoning

Gage's solo chapter, "Paradigms for Research on Teaching" (Gage, 1963b) presented the keynote argument. It made the presumption that, "in the long run, the researchers" task is to "seek out the relationships between variables" (p. 96). Further, Gage accepted that such modes of logic and rationality—which Descartes (1596–1650) had identified as "long chains of reasonings" (Descartes, 1968, p. 41)—would underwrite a social technology. Scientists cease to be mere spectators in the world. They acquire the capacity to become, in Descartes's terms, actors "in all the dramas which [are] being played there" (p. 50) or, in Gage's terms, scientists whose knowledge increases "our power to understand, predict, and control events of a given kind" (p. 96).

Chains of reasonings were, Descartes believed, "quite simple and easy" and could be imagined as "linked in the same way" (1968, p. 41). Providing no false terms are included and that the selected terms are kept in the "right order," nothing is "so distance that one does not reach it eventually, or so hidden that one cannot discover it" (p. 41). Gage presumed, likewise, that the relationship between variables is straightforward. To this extent, Gage discounted the warning about "particularly" acute "problems of measurement and the nature and use of models, mathematical and nonmathematical" (p. 44) issued by May Brodbeck in the previous chapter of the first handbook, "Logic and Scientific Method in Research on Teaching" (Brodbeck, 1963). Without apparent reference to these difficulties, Gage reduced the logic of the behavioral sciences to a commonsensical, linear chain of articulations, inferences, and conclusions:

> We understand an event by relating it logically to others. We predict an event by relating it empirically to antecedents in time. [And] We control an event by manipulating the independent variables to which it is functionally related. (Gage, 1963b, p. 96)

Gage also attempts to apply this reductionist model to teaching. It, too, is represented as a linear, connected production process. Teaching is "any interpersonal influence" aimed at changing the ways in which other persons "can or will behave." Further, Gage argues, this influence has to "impinge" upon potential learners through their "perceptual and cognitive processes." That is, teaching is an activity whereby potential learners extract "meaning" from the "objects and events that teachers bring to their sense" (pp. 96–97).

Gage's language at this point is revealing. His association of "can or will behave" and "getting meaning" in the same paragraph is notable. It seems to have been prompted by a view that gained prominence in the late 1950s (e.g., Bruner, 1960)—that teaching is a cognitive rather than a behavioral technology. Gage appeared comfortable with this viewpoint:

> The acquisition of the kinds of cognitive knowledge and understanding at which schooling is aimed cannot be reduced, in this conception of the learner and of what is to be learned, to any mere set of stimulus-response connections, no matter how thoroughly elaborated. (p. 138)

Yet, in the section on "Teaching and Cognitive Processes," Gage appears to discount this cognitive premise. He wavers,

reinvoking Cartesian notions of right order and consequent success:

> Maximum advantage should be taken of the cognitive properties of learners and subjects. Properly organized subject matter presented to learners whose cognitive development and processes are correctly understood will produce learning. (p. 138)

Ultimately, Gage's hesitation or uncertainty remained unresolved in the first handbook. The final sentence of "Paradigms for Research on Teaching" can be read as a call for further research; but it is also a call for continued adherence to a Cartesian view of the behavioral sciences:

> The logical organization of content in instructional media, the similarity and also "colinearity" . . . between teachers' cognitive structures and those of their pupils, and other logical dimensions of teaching behavior should be operationally defined and investigated as to their significance for attaining educational objectives. (p. 139)

In the process, it seems, Gage reduced meaning and understanding to the differentiation of a linear sequence of events and a corresponding concatenation of variables. Brodbeck's hesitation over measurement problems was disregarded. The connection between cognition, meaning, and behavior was simplified, not clarified.

Continuity and Discontinuity

Brodbeck's cautionary voice was not alone in the first handbook. Comparable caveats are voiced elsewhere—notably in Harry Broudy's "Historic Exemplars of Teaching Method" and Donald Campbell and Julian Stanley's "Experimental and Quasi-Experimental Designs for Research on Teaching."

Broudy's is the first chapter in the 1963 handbook. Its location, however, can be interpreted at two levels. It can be read as a prologue, a respectful homage to canonical ideas inherited from previous centuries, or it can be read as an account of prescientific practices that, by design or default, serves to privilege the superiority of the scientific perspective promulgated in the succeeding chapters. Indeed, this ambiguity about continuity and discontinuity seems to have entered Broudy's own argument. At one level it is unreservedly contextual: "What sort of teaching theory will command interest during a given period of history depends on what sort of learnings carry a premium in that period" (Broudy, 1963, p. 1). Broudy continues with the same line of argument. "If these 'conjectures' about educational theorists are not 'wholly awry,'" he suggests, the "lifestyle of an age may be discerned in the great teachers of that age" (p. 1). Yet, Broudy also turns this functionalist argument on its head. He claims that great teachers (e.g., Socrates and Abelard) acquire their greatness because they not only represent but also "protest against" the values of an age (p. 1).

Broudy's reflexivity recognizes that all teaching is located in time and space; yet it also suggests that, simultaneously, some forms of teaching are universally transgressive and transcendental. While his contextual premise detracts from the air of universalism in the rest of the handbook, his simultaneous appeal to the essentialism or the classical status of Socrates and others can, just as easily, be read as further justification for the behavioral science paradigm and its transcendental capacity to provide "organizational anticipations" of the "perennial" problems that will arise "in the days to come" (p. 42).

Campbell and Stanley's chapter is also a comment upon the Cartesian method. Their chapter is sometimes regarded as an extension of Ronald Fisher's earlier work on the design of field experiments. Certainly, it harks back to the 1920s, when Ronald Fisher was employed at Rothamsted agricultural research station (35 km northwest of London) to examine whether the station's long-term records were, in its director's words, "suitable for proper statistical examination" (quoted in Box, 1978, p. 96). Fisher's efforts at Rothamsted generated a series of seminal papers concerned, among other things, with the design and interpretation of field experiments. Fisher brought these ideas together in a single volume, *The Design of Experiments,* first published in 1935. By dint of randomization and the internal replication of experimental treatments, Fisher believed that investigators could control uncertainty, could achieve "rigorous and unequivocal inference" and, in turn, could make "decisive conclusions" about crop yield (Fisher, 1949, pp. 4, 2).

Like many classic papers, however, "Experimental and Quasi-Experimental Designs for Research on Teaching" is probably more frequently cited than consulted. To claim it falls within the Fisherian paradigm is, however, a serious misreading. It is only necessary to reach the third sentence to find that it is "*not* a chapter on experimental design in the Fisher . . . tradition" (Campbell & Stanley, 1963, p. 171). On the following page, too, Campbell and Stanley write of their "disillusionment" with "experimentation in education."

Accordingly, Campbell and Stanley's chapter should be read in a different light. It is about the validity of inferences made under conditions of uncertainty. The key term in their title is "quasi-experimental," not "experimental." The fundamental question that they raise is: What kind of inferences can be drawn from quasi-experiments conducted under conditions of quasi-control? What, in short, are the rationality costs associated with such "ambiguity of inference" (Campbell et al., 1974; reprinted in Campbell, 1988, p. 191).

Nevertheless, there is a deeper sense in which the works of Fisher and of Campbell and Stanley converged. They shared a concern for investigational rigor. They focused on the management of uncertainty rather than the establishment of truth. Put another way, they grappled with the distinction between closed and open systems. Fisher regarded natural systems "as if" (Latin: quasi) they could be closed, whereas Campbell and Stanley adopted a more restrained view of the possibilities of closure, echoing a later denotation of quasi—"almost."

Determinism

The historical significance of such systems' thinking is conventionally linked with an 18th century conjecture of the Frenchman, Pierre Simon Laplace (1749–1827). Laplace's *Physical Essays on Probabilities* (1795), published in the same decade as the appearance of the term "social science" (Baker, 1975, appendix B), posited the possibility of a fully rational and determinist world:

Given for one instance an intelligence which could comprehend all the forces by which nature is animated and the respective situation of the beings who compose it . . . nothing would be uncertain and the future, as the past, would be present to its eyes. (quoted in Hacking, 1990, pp. 11–12)

Laplace's translated words merit careful scrutiny. They are couched as a conditional, if-then, proposition. But Laplace's conjecture became a utopian dream for the social sciences, a dream that succeeding generations believed could be brought to life. Gage's contribution to the first handbook, for instance, included a typical post-Fisherian formulation of this dream:

Farmers need to know something about how plants grow, and how they depend on soil, water, and sunlight. So teachers need to know how children learn, and how they depend on motivation, readiness, and reinforcement. But farmers also need to know how to farm—how to till the soil, put in the seed, get rid of weeds and insects, harvest the crop, and get it to market. If our analogy applies even loosely, teachers similarly need to know how to teach—how to motivate pupils, assess their readiness, act on the assessment, present the subject, maintain discipline, and shape a cognitive structure. Too much of educational psychology makes the teacher infer what he needs to do from what he is told about learners and learning. Theories of teaching would make explicit how teachers behave, why they behave as they do, and with what effects. (p. 133)

But this "agricultural botany" paradigm (Parlett, 1972) for research on teaching probably reached its apogee in the following decade—in the form of Michael Dunkin and Bruce Biddle's exhaustive review of *The Study of Teaching* (1974) and Neville Bennett's intensive study of *Teaching Styles and Pupil Progress* (1976). Dunkin and Biddle noted the existence of a "never-ending supply" of models for teaching (p. 31). Yet most of these models, they felt, had only a weak connection with educational practice. They were little more than remote idealizations. Dunkin and Biddle's response was more grounded. *The Study of Teaching* considered "not what teaching is about theoretically, nor what it should be like, but rather what has been found out about it in empirical research" (p. 31). "To paraphrase a famous American [Martin Luther King Jr.]," they wrote in their preface, "Our dream is of an educational system whose procedures are governed by research and by theories that are empirically based." Nevertheless, Dunkin and Biddle also chose to impose "boundaries" on their task, limiting their review to situations where, for instance, a teacher is closeted with "a group of 30 or more pupils of approximately equal age"; where the teacher "is more likely to be a woman"; where pupils and teachers "only enter the school for a period of from four to seven hours"; and where classrooms "tend to have a flag, patriotic pictures, a waste basket, a pencil sharpener, supply cupboards, and exhibits of work by pupils or of materials pertinent to the subjects taught" (pp. 32–34).

Given their selective sampling, it is perhaps not surprising that Dunkin and Biddle conclude that the "process of teaching is surprisingly invariant across the United States and throughout the Western world" (p. 32) and, likewise, that the practice of teaching has "changed so little during a century that has seen such sharp changes in other social forms" (p. 36).

Nevertheless, Dunkin and Biddle's initial chapter—"Outlook and Orientation"—concludes with a cautionary note. Their work, they suggest, is not "everything you've always wanted to know about teaching." Rather, much of what they present "concerns not what we know but what we genuinely *don't* know about teaching." Indeed, their conclusion is almost a lament: "Perhaps the beginning of wisdom is to discover how very little we know as yet and what to do to rectify that lack" (p. 7).

Neville Bennett was more upbeat in *Teaching Styles and Pupil Progress*. He claimed to have identified causal connections between teaching (compare: teaching styles) and learning (compare: pupil progress). Duly armed with "research evidence," Bennett offered results that, according to his codirector's foreword, had "unequivocal" implications. "Formal methods of teaching" are, by contrast with "informal" pedagogic procedures, associated with "greater progress in the basic skills" (pp. ix, viii–ix).

Eventually, however, Bennett abandoned his original claims. A research team, including himself, suggested in a reanalysis of the original data that Bennett's findings were more equivocal than originally imagined. They found "convincing evidence" that Bennett's sample of teachers should be divided not into two distinct groups (formal and informal) but, rather, into three "overlapping" clusters (formal, informal, and mixed). Further, the response patterns of the various groups of teachers did not consistently—nor statistically—favor formal teaching over informal methods (Aitken, Bennett. & Hesketh, 1981, pp. 170–173)

Retractions and Recantations

More substantial cautionary comments, including retractions and recantations, also began to emerge in the 1970s, in the work, for instance, of Donald Campbell, Lee J. Cronbach, and Samuel Messick. Donald Campbell's intervention came, according to the editor of his "selected papers," in the form of a "classic recanting" (in Campbell, 1988, p. 336). Campbell wrote:

> In past writings . . . I have spoken harshly of the single-occasion, single-setting (one shot) case study . . . because it combined such a fewness of points of observation, and such a plethora of available causal concepts. . . . Recently, in a quixotic and ambivalent article, "Degrees of Freedom" (1975), I have recanted, reminding myself that such studies regularly contradict the prior expectations of authors, and are convincing and informative to sceptics like me. (Campbell, 1988, p. 373)

Elsewhere in his reflections Campbell looked back, among other things, to the first handbook's "Experimental and Quasi-Experimental Designs for Research on Teaching," where his original judgment had been that "such [one-shot case] studies have such a total absence of control as to be of almost no scientific value" (Campbell & Stanley, 1963, p. 178). By the 1970s, however, Campbell accepted that much social research necessarily relied on "extensive study," by an "outsider," of a "single foreign setting" (1988, p. 377). "This is not to say," he added, that "such commonsense naturalistic observation is objective, dependable, or unbiased. But it is all we have. It is the only

route to knowledge—noisy, fallible, and biased though it be" (p. 377).

Campbell's revision of his earlier argument arose because he had come to recognize the legitimacy of a "major source of discipline" in case study settings. Insofar as case study inquiry entails "thorough local acquaintance," the theory used to account for phenomena also generates predictions or expectations of "dozens of other aspects of the culture" (p. 388). The theory, that is, has multiple implications that, in turn, can be internally checked against other data collected in the case study. And Campbell concluded his retraction by recognizing that "intensive cross-cultural case study has a discipline and a capacity to reject theories" that had been "neglected" in earlier reviews of research design (p. 380).

Moreover, Campbell's writings have repeatedly returned to the distinction between quantitative and qualitative (or interpretative) research. He argues, according to his editor, that all science depends on "qualitative knowing," that postpositivist social science recognizes that "all knowing is presumptive," and that, in turn, "all observations and facts are theory-laden" (p. 335). This viewpoint, which is often traced back to Thomas Kuhn's *The Structure of Scientific Revolutions* (1962) in Anglo-American thought, and to Immanuel Kant's *The Critique of Pure Reason* (1781) in German thought, is most easily demonstrated in optical illusions—as Campbell does in 1978 in "Qualitative Knowing in Action Research" (also reprinted in his selected papers, 1988). Campbell, like other postpositivists, assumes not only that all facts are theory-laden but, as in the archetypical instance of optical illusions, there is more to seeing than meets the eye. Campbell accepts this canon of postpositivist thought. Every act of seeing is also necessarily an act of interpretation. Moreover, Campbell accepts the consequential unity of quantitative and qualitative analysis. The proposition—"there are 10 children," for example—is both a quantitative and a qualitative statement. It is quantitative because it responds to the question "How many?" And it is qualitative because it is equally a response to the question "What kind of?" (*qualis* is the Latin word for "What kind of"). In an important sense, then, Campbell's papers in the 1970s not only linked qualitative and quantitative research but also, in the process, invested qualitative inquiry with a degree of legitimacy previously unknown in the realms of mainstream research on teaching.

Cronbach's comments were also a retraction. His presidential address to the American Psychological Association in 1957 had advanced a version of Laplace's rationale:

> Our job is to invent constructs and to form a network of laws which permits prediction. From observations we must infer a psychological description of the situation and of the present state of the organism. Our laws should permit us to predict, from the situation, the behavior of [the] organism-in-context. (Cronbach, 1957, pp. 681–682)

By 1974, however, Cronbach took a different view—when he addressed the American Psychological Association in response to an award for his "distinguished scientific contribution" to psychology. In the intervening decades, Cronbach reported, he had encountered "inconsistencies" that led him to confess that the "line of investigation I advocated in 1957 no longer seems sufficient" (1975, p. 119).

Cronbach's unease arose from the same kind of interpretative problems encountered by Campbell and Stanley; namely, difficulties that trouble open systems subject only to quasi-control. In the event, Cronbach abandoned the confident stance he had taken in the 1950s. Investigators, he suggested, should eschew the erection of "theoretical palaces."

> The goal of our work [he continued] . . . is not to amass generalization atop which a theoretical tower can someday be erected. The special task of the social scientist in each generation is to pin down the contemporary facts. Beyond that, he shares with the humanistic scholar and the artist in the effort to gain insight into contemporary relationships, and to realign the culture's view of man with present realities. (p. 126)

Samuel Messick expressed comparable uncertainties about prediction and control. In an invited address to the American Psychological Association divisions of Educational Psychology and Evaluation and Measurement in 1979, Messick revisited a "deceptively simple" distinction that he had made in the 1960s; namely, that psychometric tests should be evaluated against two sets of criteria: their "measurement properties" and their "potential social consequences." In turn, Messick suggested that these criteria were fundamentally different. The appraisal of measurement properties is a "scientific and technical" issue that can be resolved by reference to the psychometric properties of tests; whereas the "potential social consequences" of a test pose a different set of ethical questions. Test use, therefore, requires not only an initial set of technical warrants but also consequential "justification" by reference to "social values" (Messick, 1980, p. 1012).

This difference between the "evidential" and "consequential" grounds for test use is equivalent to the distinction between experimental and quasi-experimental research design. The validity of test use must be inferred rather than measured. It is a postpositivist activity. It requires judgment rather than calculation; and, accordingly, it admits the vulnerability of test use, including the possibility of ill-judged decisions about the utility of such devices.

The net result of Messick's review was his revised position that validity is a "general imperative" in measurement and that it can be conceived as the "overall degree of justification for test interpretation and use" (p. 1014). In terms of this chapter, the inclusion of judgment means that decision making with regard to testing is a practical rather than a technical (or measurement) matter. It echoes Campbell's concerns about "ambiguities of inference" and Cronbach's doubts about "theoretical palaces."

Overall, then, Campbell, Cronbach, and Messick's work in the 1970s undermined a Laplacian and technical view of the social sciences and scientific inference. The social world may not be a closed system the subsequent states of which can be predicted from earlier configurations. Human beings are not billiard balls confined within the carpentered regularities of the billiard table. And individual actions cannot be reduced to the algorithms of a social technology. Nevertheless, resolute and repeated attempts have been made to collapse the world and its workings into this social engineering framework. For nearly 200 years, Laplace's tentative efforts to square the circle of determinism held the fate of the social sciences in the English-speaking world.

In Search of Science

Yet, in the 1970s, Campbell, Cronbach, and Messick turned Laplace's conjecture upside down. Their arguments—boosted by their own professional authority—were released into the social science community through the medium of prestigious settings and journals. Their reluctant, revisionist ideas had an impact not only upon researchers fumbling with their own inchoate postpositivist concerns, but also upon mainstream enthusiasts for variables-based research on teaching—like Nathaniel Gage.

Gage articulated his own posthandbook uncertainties in *The Scientific Basis of the Art of Teaching* (1978), arising from lectures given at Teachers College, Columbia University. Gage's thinking in the 1970s differed substantially from the conspectus of the first handbook. Three of his revisions are relevant to this chapter. First, he offered a less didactic view of teaching, making no reference to behavior or objectives:

> By *teaching* I mean any activity on the part of one person intended to facilitate learning on the part of another. Although the activity often involves language, it need not do so, nor need teaching rely solely on rational and intellectual processes. We can teach by providing silent demonstrations for our students or models for them to imitate. And we often teach by fostering attitudes and appreciations the rational components of which are suffused with affect. (Gage, 1978, p. 14)

Second, Gage put distance between himself and the idea that teaching is a rule- or law-following activity. Instead, he suggested that teaching is an artistic endeavor. It occupies the "room" created whenever there are "departures" from "what is implied by rules, formulas, and algorithms" (p. 15). And, third, Gage believed that the art of "classroom teaching" has only a contingent—or quasi—relationship with its "scientific basis" (p. 16).

Such artistry assumes that teachers know "when to follow the implications of the laws, generalizations, and trends and, especially, when not to" (p. 18). Reaffirming Cronbach's (1975) worries about interference from extraneous or unrecognized variables, he cautions that, "when any additional variable interacts to influence the relationship between two variables, we are unwise to follow the implications of a simple two-variable relationship" (p. 18). Gage, therefore, eschewed his earlier confidence in prediction and control. Instead, his Teachers' College lectures were premised on the contrary view that

> A science of teaching . . . is erroneous. It implies that good teaching will some day be attainable by closely following rigorous laws that yield high predictability and control. (p. 17)

Gage's revised position was that teachers, as educational scientists, use "judgment, intuition, and insight" in "handling the unpredicted" phenomena that arise from the unanticipated "contingencies" of classroom life (p. 17).

The historical significance of these 1970s discontinuities, inversions, and confusions in research on teaching is that the foundationalism offered by Descartes and Laplace began to show signs of structural weakness. The value-laden ranking of methods from "hard" to "soft" began to buckle under the pressure of so-called "rigor" versus "relevance" considerations. The insulation between words like "evidence," "knowledge," "information," "meaning," and "understanding" began to be broached, facilitating multiple interpretations of sense data. Finally, the substitution of open for closed systems of theory building allowed distinctions to be more readily drawn between goal-driven technique (for closed systems) and value-contingent practice (for open systems).

In the period after 1963, the social science view of research on teaching did not live up to the expectations of the Editorial Advisory Board of the first handbook (viz. W. J. McKeakie, Harold E. Mitzel, H. H. Remmers, David V. Tiedeman, R. M. W. Travers, Ralph W. Tyler, and John Withall). It began to be bowed down by ideological baggage that it had accumulated over more than 3 centuries (i.e., since Descartes's *Discourse on Method,* 1639). The advancement of the behavioral sciences became vulnerable to the same kind of criticisms about reliability and validity (or scientificity) that had devalued and marginalized other forms of social science. Moreover, no simple replacements were forthcoming. Although qualitative methods were sometimes advanced as an alternative paradigm—a position skeptically reviewed in the editors' contributions to the *Handbook of Qualitative Research* (Denzin & Lincoln, 1994)—research on teaching became—and has remained—a diaspora. It is not a field of divergent models or paradigms that can be taxonomically juxtaposed to one another. Rather, as the remainder of this chapter will show, research on teaching is a blurred genre, a kaleidoscope of unstable patterns, a palimpsest of multiple reinscriptions.

Reinscriptions

Even Gage's work can be analyzed in such terms. Despite his contribution to the first handbook, despite what he called the "counsels of despair" of Cronbach and others, and despite the cautionary tone of his Teachers' College lectures, Gage "continued" the search for "long-lasting generalizations" (e.g., Gage, 1996, p. 5; see also Gage, 1989). But, more than 30 years after the first handbook, he still found it difficult to square the Cartesian circle. He conceded that associations, derived from meta-analysis, remained "imperfect" and only "fairly" generalizable (Gage, 1996, p. 14). Nevertheless, Gage found such imperfections to be a source of platonic inspiration, of ideals. The search for perfection—however remote—is held to be paramount:

Behavioral sciences should indeed reject trying to be positive in the sense of seeking a certainty that tolerates no exceptions to generalizations. . . . But behavioral scientists should not reject trying to be positive . . . an attitude that affirms the value of the generalizations and theory thus far achieved. (pp. 14–15)

Telling It Like It Is

Yet, by the 1970s such macho views of research had already been characterized as "moribund" (Schwab, 1978, p. 287). The field of research on teaching—as exemplified in the first hand-book—had become unable to "continue its work and to contribute significantly to the advancement of education." It required "new principles which will generate a new view of the character and variety of its problems." To conclude, Schwab suggested that a "renascence" of practical inquiry required "energies" to be diverted

from theoretic pursuits (such as the pursuit of global principles and comprehensive patterns, the search for stable sequences and invariant elements, the construction of taxonomies of supposedly fixed or recurrent kinds) to . . . other modes of operation. (1978, pp. 287–288)

Schwab's criticism was a significant intervention. Although directed toward the curriculum field, it was equally applicable to research on teaching. *Understanding Curriculum: An Introduction to the Study of Historical and Contemporary Curriculum Discourses* (Pinar, Reynolds, Slattery, & Taubman, 1995), which can read alongside this chapter, reports the consequences of Schwab's criticisms within the curriculum field. A comparable response, however, occurred within research on teaching. It, too, gave its attention to understanding and, in the process, began to embrace varieties of pedagogic thinking that reached back, through Dewey, to 19th century German notions of Lebenswelt (life world) and Erlebnis (lived experience; see Ermath, 1978, and Schwandt, 1994). Research on teaching, that is, began to pay renewed attention to the understandings—or interpretations—of practitioners.

The Life World of Teaching

One classic exemplar of such inquiry already existed: Willard Waller's *The Sociology of Teaching,* originally published in 1932, and reprinted for the third time in 1967. Waller's work was prepared at the State College, Pennsylvania. Its perspectives on practice can be characterized in several ways. *The Sociology of Teaching* was social psychological, because it examined the life worlds of an important occupational grouping in American society. It was psychological because it explored the groups' attitudes; it was anthropological because it studied their cultural practices; and it was ethnographic because it treated them as "others," that is as an occupational group whose location behind the schoolhouse door screened them from public scrutiny.

The scene is set by the opening words of Waller's original preface:

What this book tells is what every teacher knows, that the world of school is a social world. Those human beings who live together in the school, though deeply severed in one sense, nevertheless spin a tangled web of interrelationships; that the web and the people in it make up the social world of the school. It is not a wide world, but, for those who know it, it is a world compact with meaning. It is a unique world. It is the purpose of this book to explore it. I believe that all teachers, great and small, have need of insight into the social realities of school life, that they perish, as teachers, for lack of it.

Later in the same preface, Waller accepted that his task was not to "attack the school, nor talk overmuch about what ought to be, but only about what is." Accordingly, he accepted that he should not "gloss over weak spots or . . . apologize for existing things." But, to achieve these levels of veracity, Waller also recognized that "to show the school as it really is," it is necessary to report "concrete situations typical of the typical school." Finally, Waller used "a certain amount of fictional material," which was based on "good insight," for its "illustrative" value.

Written as a textbook, The *Sociology of Teaching* included chapters on such topics as the school as a social organism, school and community, some interpretations of life in the school, the teacher-pupil relationship, and what teaching does to teachers. And its last two chapters are "A Principal Reason Why Institutions Do Not Function" and a series of "Recommendations." Waller's theoretical framework is captured in these titles. He believed that teachers gain "social insight" from "experience." But he accepted that such insight is only "rough" and "fragmentary." It needed to "be fitted into a larger picture and to be pieced out with completer [sic] knowledge" (p. 1). Using the "folk talk" of teachers, Waller's aspiration was to "isolate causal mechanisms involved in . . . the interactions of human beings . . . in the institution of the school" (p. 2).

The Sociology of Teaching was intended to be "essentially constructive." It was an attempt to "found a new understanding of the schools" and to find "such remedies for existing ills as that new understanding dictates" (p. 4). Waller's reference, however, to the "ills" of schooling suggests that *The Sociology of Teaching* also stemmed from a social-Darwinist or pathological view of schooling. Out-of-date schools, classrooms, and teachers need to be protected against becoming eugenic casualties in the survival of the fittest. In short, they needed to be reintegrated into progressive revisions of the body politic.

Psychoanalysis

Psychoanalytic thought also supported a restorative model of teaching. Freud's attention to mental life—the term "psychoanalysis" was first used in 1896—was shaped by two observations pertinent to the study of teaching. First, Freud claimed that human suffering arises from the repression of early sexual experiences. Second, he proposed that such suffering can only be relieved if it is also relived (i.e., through analysis). Thus, intellectual growth was, Freud felt, ineluctably tied to the reliving and relieving of early psychic experience.

Shell-shocked casualties of World War 1 also focused attention on the relief of psychic disturbance. Treatment centers were established behind the lines of the western front and, even before the ceasefire, analysts generalized their experience to other constituencies of sufferers. Adolescent disturbances were treated in the same way—in the creation, for instance, of a self-governing psychoanalytic republic in rural southern England managed by a young American, Homer Lane (1875–1935).

Lane had been superintendent of playgrounds in Detroit, Michigan. Later, on a farm outside Detroit he ran the Ford Republic, which gave delinquent boys opportunities to govern their own lives. Lane became well known—even notorious—among penal reformers. He moved to the United Kingdom in 1909 and was invited to take over the Little Commonwealth in 1913, recruiting many of its members from London Magistrates Courts. To break down social hostility, Lane eschewed the conventional attitudes of adults. It is reported, for instance, that Lane "believed in ordinary goodness and not original sin" (Croall, 1983, p. 82). The Little Commonwealth closed down in 1918.

Lane's thinking was influenced by Oscar Pfister of Zurich (see Armytage, 1975; p. 331), who wrote *Love in Children and Its Aberrations* (English edition, 1914) and *Psychoanalysis in the Service of Education* (1922). But, ultimately, the place of Lane in the history of research on teaching is indirect. One of the visitors to the Little Commonwealth in its final months was a trainee soldier, A. S. Neill, who subsequently described Lane as the "most influential factor in my life" (Quoted in Armytage, 1975, p. 318). Lane introduced Neill to the ideas of Sigmund Freud and, through the agency of writing about his own school (Summerhill), Neill devoted the rest of his life to the psychoanalytic emancipation of learners and learning.

In 1960 a selection of Neill's writings—from *The Problem Child* (1926), *The Problem Parent* (1932), *That Dreadful School* (1937), and *The Free Child* (1953)—was published in the United States under the title *Summerhill: A Radical Approach to Child-Rearing.* It sold 24,000 copies in its first year and 100,000 in 1968. According to Neill's biographer, it had sold 2 million copies by 1970 and "was required reading in at least 600 American university courses" (Croall, 1983, p. 353). By comparison, the first U.S. edition of *The Problem Child* (1928) had sold only 140 copies in the first 9 months after publication, (Croall, 1983, p. 346).

The conduct of analyses, the relief of inhibitions, and the resultant release of energy remained central to psychoanalysis. Yet, the practical implications of Freud's original insights were open to debate. Different interpretations yielded a wide range of psychoanalytically based child-rearing practices. If Neill served on the libertarian wing of the movement, others, like Susan Isaacs, espoused a more "disciplinarian" viewpoint (Armytage, 1975, p. 323). Isaacs's Malting House School, near Cambridge (England), became a crucible for the testing of these ideas, using the children of university teachers as its raw materials. According to Isaacs's writings about Malting House School, children were given the maximum opportunity to explore, through play, the world around them. Visited by Melanie Klein and Jean Piaget, Malting House School became a lighthouse institution. Subsequently appointed to a new department of child development at the University of London Institute of Education, Isaacs, through her teaching and writings, also helped to release nursery and infant teachers from their own inhibitions about employing play in a secure environment.

Education and Culture

The association of psychoanalysis with human behavior also attracted the attention of anthropologists. Was human development, they inquired, the result of nature or culture? Margaret Mead (1901–1978), for instance, was one of four research students sent overseas by Franz Boas, her professor at Columbia University. Her task, in Samoa, was to examine the question:

> How much of [a child's] development follows regular laws? How much or how little and in what ways is it dependent upon early training, upon the personality of its parents, its teachers, its playmates, the age into which it is born? (Mead, 1963, p. 10)

In the event, Mead reported that adolescent life in Samoa was easy and casual, not a life of stress and conflict. Moreover, her analysis supported Boas' cultural thesis—that adolescence in the United States and elsewhere had cultural rather than biological causes.

At the same time, her comparative analysis fed into wider debates about the mental as well as the physical well-being of children. Benjamin Spock's *Common Sense Book of Baby and Child Care* (1946) had been preceded, for instance, by *The Psychological Aspects of Pediatric Practice* (Spock & Huschka, 1938), published by the Committee on Mental Hygiene of the New York State Charities Aid Association. And a further integration of psychoanalysis and anthropology arose in the shape of Erik Erikson's *Childhood and Society* (first published in 1950). Erikson's general approach was to "reconcile historical and psychological methodologies" and, in the process, to come to terms with the "function of childhood in the fabric of society" (1963, pp. 403–404). He believed, for instance, that child care should not only take account of the intellectual progress of children but also critical periods in their moral and sexual development.

In effect, anthropologists and psychoanalysts underwrote a clinical view of child rearing and school teaching. And the popularity of works like Spock's *Baby and Child Care* and A. S. Neill's *Summerhill* allowed unconventional ideas about child raising—however controversial—to gain attention within a community that was much larger than the public and private school system. These clinical ideas were underwritten by parents interested in the fortunes of their own children. In the process, such ideas were deemed applicable to the healthy development of all children.

Sensitivity to different cultures of education also seems to have had an impact on mainstream anthropology. George Spindler's *Education and Anthropology* (1955) emerged, for instance, from a working seminar of 12 educationists and 12 anthropologists (including Margaret Mead), held the previous year at Carmel Valley, California. This conference also seems to have been a methodological bridgehead. Previous anthropologists, like Spindler, had accepted that they were outside the educational mainstream. It was "methodological heresy" at that time, George Spindler later reported with his coworker Louise Spindler, to recommend anything but "correlational and neoexperimental research methods to serious educational researchers," even though anthropologists had been doing "natural history in their fieldwork for about half a century" (Spindler & Spindler, 1987, p. 9).

Other Worlds

Close-up, interpretative, or clinical study of teachers and teaching extended to other domains during the 1950s. The rural and overseas settings investigated by Waller and Mead were complemented by the investigation of more metropolitan communities. Early natural histories surfaced as nonfiction novels, with Edward Blishen's *Roaring Boys: A Schoolmaster's Agony* (1955) and Evan Hunter's *Blackboard Jungle* (1954) becoming notable examples. *Blackboard Jungle* also became a film in 1955, backed by Bill Haley's classic orchestration of "Rock Around the Clock," and it also reappeared in 1984 in the Arbor House Library of Contemporary Americana.

Other literary works that also made the transition from novel to film include *To Sir With Love (Reminiscences of a Negro Teacher in London)* (Braithwaite, 1959, film: 1967, also a Read-

er's Digest condensed book, vol. 35), and *Up the Down Staircase* (Kaufman, 1966, film: 1967). Indeed, *Blackboard Jungle, To Sir with Love,* and *Up the Down Staircase* are recorded in the ninth edition of Halliwell's Film Guide (1993) as, respectively, a "seminal fifties melodrama," "sentimental nonrealism" and an "earnest, well-acted, not very likeable melodrama" (see also Dalton, 1995).

The melodramatic features of these works—as mediated by Hollywood—was a function of their literary realism and dramatic potential. They could be packaged as victory narratives—portrayals of alien life worlds that, almost unwittingly, had been stumbled upon by literate, white-collar professionals.

These cinematic narratives, however, also provided creative space for a complementary articulations—autobiographies, muckraking journalism, self-help manuals. One such example was *36 Children* (1967), which was based on Herbert Kohl's experiences in the New York City school system from 1962 to 1965. The "sketches" collated in *36 Children* had already appeared in *Urban Review* and the *New York Review of Books.* They recounted the author's experience of confronting 36 "black faces" at an elementary school in Harlem, where he was equipped with a "barren classroom, no books, a battered piano, broken windows and desks, falling plaster, and an oppressive darkness" (p. 1). Kohl's writings were realist but, like other influential writings in the genre, they were also transcendental. The author's voice spoke about an alien world in such a manner as to draw the attention and empathy of a much wider audience. A British contributor to the genre (Edward Blishen), for instance, was able to comment on the back cover of the English edition that "What Mr. Kohl discovered during that year . . . is relevant to teaching anywhere: marvellously exciting."

The 232-page narrative of *36 Children* is divided into two parts. Under the heading "Teaching," 186 pages are taken up with episodes in the lives of Kohl and the 36 class members. On these occasions, Kohl wrote as both a participant and an observer: "I am convinced that the teacher must be an observer of his class as well as a member of it" (p. 21), an interpretative standpoint that had been absent from his teacher training sojourn at Teachers College, Columbia University.

The story in *36 Children* is is about how one teacher came to terms with the loneliness, hopelessness, and alienation of school teaching. But, as noted, it was also a narrative of collaboration and hope. Indeed, Kohl's hopes were expressed through the imagery of dreaming. The latter section of *36 Children* is titled "A Dream Deferred," a phrase taken from a poem by Langston Hughes. By this stage in his narrative, Kohl had begun to taste the bittersweet of teaching. Having challenged, coached, and cajoled them and having sought to sow and nurture the seed of their educational self-transformation, Kohl's students left him. They moved across the street to junior high school, to a "new, more chaotic and difficult world" (p. 186). But Kohl knew, when he chose the Langston Hughes poem, that the seed he had planted might, like a "raisin in the sun," dry up, "fester," "stink," and "sugar over." But, following the poet's prompting, Kohl was also sensitive to another possibility. A seed also poses the transformative question: "Does it explode?"

Kohl's text focused on educational ideas and educational practices. He reported his own curriculum and pedagogic efforts, his own storytelling, his own anecdotes. These stories have pedagogic merit. They constitute an analysis of a year-long action-research project. They are a representation of schooling. They are an analysis of the complexities that teachers can encounter in the maelstrom of classroom life. Above all, they are presented in the form of an open, unfinished text, one that invites the annexation of different scenarios, contrasting accounts, alternative explanations. To this degree, *36 Children* was a hermeneutic (i.e., interpretative) contribution to the literature on teaching. It promoted a sophisticated reading of classroom life. It did not endorse a univocal or universal solution. Instead, every reader was invited to generalize the book's analysis to their own political and practical contexts.

Yet, *36 Children* was also a child of its time. It is a passionate story. It does not conform to the stoic quasi-disinterest of 20th century behavioral research. The reliability of Kohl's observations and the validity of his interpretations can be challenged and reinscribed in many different ways. But Kohl's personal testament was released into a public forum that was much wider, and no less critical, than the readership of the first *Handbook of Research on Teaching*. As a cumulation of experience, it was well positioned to inform the practice of other educators.

That Line

While Herbert Kohl was teaching in New York City, another former student of Oxford University, Jonathan Kozol, was teaching in a segregated classroom of the Boston public schools and, simultaneously, writing for journals like the *Atlantic Review,* the *New Republic,* and the *New York Review of Books.* "Disheartened by conditions in my school building and being an habitual note taker," Kozol soon began to "amass a large number of envelopes of handwritten notes." Fueled by subsequent events, these field notes grew into a manuscript and, eventually, into *Death at an Early Age: The Destruction of the Hearts and Minds of Negro Children in the Boston Public Schools* (Kozol, 1967).

Kozol, like Kohl, became an activist in his schoolroom experiences. *Death at an Early Age* recounts a political story. In the preface to the English edition, Kozol suggested that it

documents . . . one of the climactic and historic moments in this national tragedy [of race division]. It is a story of national failure, of the cowardice and cruelty of a particular city, of the hesitation and consequent self-compromise of any number of well-intending individuals. I have spoken, in these pages, of a death of the heart in Negro children. But there is another death, too: it is the death of an entire people. (p. 15)

Three quarters of *Death at an Early Age* is taken up, like Kohl's book, with stories about Kozol's interactions with the personalities of Boston classroom life: the art teacher, the math teacher, the reading teacher, special students. Its opening lines are indicative:

Stephen is eight years old. A picture of him standing in front of the bulletin board on Arab Bedouins shows a little light-brown person staring with unusual concentration at a chosen spot upon the floor. Stephen is tiny, desperate, unwell. (p. 17)

Many of these classroom events took place alongside national, local, and personal reactions to the struggle for civil rights. Within the school there was "that line" (p. 36); within Massachu-

setts there was to be a report on "racial imbalance" in the state schools (p. 132); and, nationally, reaction had been focused by the death, in 1965, of Reverend Reeb of Selma, Alabama.

Further, much of Kozol's text focuses upon the assimilationist and compensatory substance of the school curriculum and related textbooks. Indeed, Kozol reports the dismissal he faced as a result of teaching Langston Hughes's "Ballad of the Landlord," a poem not on the official course of study (p. 184ff). When interviewed at the school department, Kozol was told: "You're out. You cannot teach in the Boston schools again."

He continued: "I left her office, but, before I left the building, I stopped at a table and I took out a pad of paper and wrote down what she had said" (p. 188).

Within the context of this chapter, the writings of Kohl and Kozol are not unique. Muckraking journalism about classroom practices has a history that goes back at least as far as Rice's late-19th-century studies of the teaching of reading (see Tyack, 1974, p. 55ff). But Kozol and Kohl are historically significant for two different reasons. They not only recount a struggle over civil rights, their analyses also portray a struggle between didactic and pedagogic practices. They offer a different view of schooling, albeit one that has existed on the margins for many years. But they move it center stage. They present it to a wider audience, itself infected with thinking about civil rights and public schooling. Both write of their dreams, of new horizons, of rekindled powers, of human dignity.

Complexity

There is a further reason for featuring Kohl and Kozol in this chapter. The year 1965 saw the publication of another volume the substance of which appears far from the daily travails of Public School 79, New York (to whose pupils it is dedicated). The title of the work is *The Age of Complexity,* its author was Herbert Kohl, and it included an extract from *The Red Raincoat* (1965), a novel by Jonathan Kozol.

The *Age of Complexity* is a comment on the fact that "European and Anglo-American philosophies seem to be worlds apart" (p. 11). Kohl's premise was that

At the outset of this century many people felt that this world was exceedingly simple and that its structure could be reflected through language. Either language could be reduced to an all-inclusive "logical" system, or essences and principles that would reveal reality in all its naked elegance and simplicity could be uncovered. At the turn of the century, and even after the Great War that no one quite believed in, the quest for simplicity was rife. . . . By the end of the Second World War simplicity was irretrievably dead in Western Europe, along with uncounted millions. (p. 15)

This premise prefigured Kohl's writing task: to reconcile modernity with complexity. "To be 'modern' in Europe and America," he wrote, "is to give up simple explanations of man and the world, to embrace complexity once and for all, and to try, somehow, to manage it" (p. 15). *The Age of Complexity* focused on the prophets of modernity, "small voices," non-Americans like Lawrence, Nietzsche, Wittgenstein, Heidegger, Sartre, and Camus. It sought to go beyond the "simplifications of the past," which were "inadequate when faced with the world of the last 20 years" (pp. 16–17). Modern philosophy, therefore, is not only a philosophy of "complexity and of disillusionment," it is also a philosophy of "rediscovery" (p. 15). It allows the reorientation of human beings whenever they recognize that there could "never again be a simple system of thought" (p. 16). Kohl's acknowledgment of complexity also entailed a view that "contemporary philosophy" should not only have a concern for the "*ordinary, day-to-day life* man must live in this trying world" but also "man's capacity to rise, occasionally, to this life and experience" (p. 14).

In turn, Kohl believed that such complexity could be identified, named, and transcended through poetry, the plastic arts, film, and fiction. The extract from Kozol's *The Red Raincoat* is a short story about a disturbed boy who "could easily be put into some classical psychiatric category." Kohl selected it because "the reader might be interested in trying to understand the boy's world on its own terms," that is, as "an exercise in existential psychiatry" (p. 173). It is an account of a young boy who projects himself through a personal temporal world. His life exists in the here and now; yet it is also a transcendental life—in that it is moving into the future. In addition, Adam— the subject of Kozol's story—exists in a contingent culture, a world that is already there.

Adam is out with his father and two sisters to buy new raincoats. Seemingly silenced by his talkative sisters, he eventually voices the statement that "I'm getting a raincoat, too." He waits his turn. His sisters are fitted with red waterproofs when, suddenly, Adam's father chooses him a blue one. Adam protests that he wanted to have the same as his sisters. The purchase proceeds, with Adam standing "immobile, entombed (as he felt) within the unwanted coat" (p. 178). Later, Adam hears his parents go out. He takes the blue coat from the closet and, using dressmaking scissors, cuts it to pieces. He then goes to the empty bedroom of one of his sisters. With "enormous excitement," he dons a red raincoat, puts out his arms and spins around. The final words of Kozol's extract are: "What he wished, more than anything else, was that his mother and father would come in on him now" (pp. 180–181).

The works of Kohl and Kozol are journalistic and immediate; but they are also contingent and transcendental. They told it like it is; but they could also be read as offering a way forward. They were sources of both political and pedagogic inspiration and practice. They detailed the predicament of teachers, denials of social justice; and, not least, possibilities for classroom transformations.

Social Justice

But, given their historical and geographical settings, *36 Children* and *Death at an Early Age* might also be read as a problem of "black skin, white masks," the title of another influential text of the 1960s, written by a psychiatrist from Martinique, Frantz Fanon, who took part in the Algerian Revolution against the French in the 1950s (Fanon, 1967). Fanon's work was an analysis of "Black consciousness" (p. 134) and its organic links with the overcoming of "negritude" (132):

> It is not out of my bad nigger's misery, my bad nigger's teeth, my bad nigger's hunger that I will shape a torch with which to burn down the world, but it is the torch that was already there, waiting for that turn of history. (p. 134)

But that turn of history had already arrived in the 1960s. Malcolm X was assassinated in Harlem in 1965; Black rebellions— or "20th century slave revolts" (Marable, 1984, p. 103)—occurred in major cities across the United States in the spring and summer months of 1964–1968, leading to 250 deaths, 10,000 serious injuries, and 60,000 arrests; and Martin Luther King Jr. was assassinated in Memphis on April 4, 1968.

These events brought the claims of Black Power—modulated as much through poetry and song as through protest and proclamation—to wider attention. And the parallel conflict in Vietnam—where U.S. ground forces had grown from 14,000 in 1963 to 267,000 in 1966 (Williams, McCormick, Gardner, & Lafeber, 1975, p. 220)—broadened the boundaries of political awareness.

The problems of freedom and identity noted by Erikson and Neill were recast by many groups to embrace a rejection of domination and to embrace a reconstruction of alternative forms of life in general, and classroom life in particular. Rejection and reconstruction were analyzed, shared, and expressed in many ways. Thus, the self-confessed social scientist and journalist, Charles Silberman, was responsible for *Crisis in Black and White* (1964) as well as *Crisis in the Classroom: The Remaking of American Education* (1971). A welter of sources indicated to Silberman that, in effect, the crisis in Black and White— itself "part of the larger crisis of American society"—could not be resolved unless

> all who have a stake in the remaking of American education— teachers and students, school board members and taxpayers, public officials and civic leaders, newspaper and magazine editors and readers, television directors and viewers, parents and children—are alerted to what is wrong and what needs to be done. (1971, p. vii)

Silberman's works capture the sense of unease that pervaded the 1960s. The cultural and political problem had become raising society, not children. *Crisis in Black and White* recognized that the "problem of Negro education" had been strongly influence by the appearance of James Bryant Conant's *Slums and Suburbs* (1961). But it also commented that Conant had "recommended" the worst kind of society- and child-rearing solution—namely, an "increase in vocational education" (p. 253). Similarly, *Crisis in the Classroom* suggested that "our most pressing educational problem . . . is not how to increase the efficiency of the schools; it is how to create and maintain a humane society" (p. 203).

Rejection and reconstruction also figured in reappraisals made by writers oppressed by the status quo. These discussions touched all sections of American society—if only because everyone had been touched by the events of the 1960s. But, more important, these discussions were shared across social divides, drawing new groups into such thinking and practices, and causing irruptions within existing groups—as when bell hooks chose the title *Ain't I a Woman: Black Women and Feminism* (1982) from a similar speech by Sojourner Truth delivered at an antislavery rally in 1852 (hooks, 1982, p. 160).

New Voices, Silent Languages

Thus, thinking about teaching, learning, and classroom life was refreshed from a source that entered and intermingled with the groundwater of educational thought. Again, forms of pedagogic thinking achieved a presence in the academy. Important sources of such sweet water include Philip Jackson's *Life in Classrooms* (1968) and Louis Smith and William Geoffrey's *The Complexities of an Urban Classroom: An Analysis Toward a General Theory of Teaching* (1968). Neither Jackson nor Smith were strangers to the world of thinking about teaching. Both had already established places in the academy as psychologists. Jackson had coauthored, with Jacob Getzels, a chapter in the first *Handbook of Research on Teaching,* and Louis Smith had coauthored, with B. B. Hudgins, a college textbook, *Educational Psychology* (1964).

Jackson had begun gathering classroom material in 1962, from a small number of elementary school classrooms in Palo Alto, California (where he was a fellow at the Center for Advanced Study in the Behavioral Sciences). These data inspired Jackson to "take off in new directions." His observations, which continued after Jackson's return to Chicago, were written up "most especially" for teachers, administrators, and others whose daily work brings them into "direct contact with classroom life." Jackson's goal was to "arouse the reader's interest" and possibly to "awaken his concern over aspects of school life that seem to be receiving less attention than they deserve" (preface).

Smith also began to rethink his academic work "several years" before the publication of *Complexities.* That publication arose partly as a result of comments by William Geoffrey, then a "student in a graduate class" (p. 1n), and partly from Smith and Geoffrey's joint recognition that " the social problem of urban education is a major issue in contemporary American society" (p. 2). To "understand" the full impact of urban teaching and to guide "practical innovation," Smith felt that there was a "need to understand the full impact of urban teaching through the eyes of the regular practicing teacher in his day-to-day work in the "real world" of his classroom" (p. 2).

In both cases, too, Jackson and Smith distanced themselves from the behavioral science perspectives of the first *Handbook of Research on Teaching.* Jackson, for instance, argued that the understanding and tactics of the learning theorist and the human engineer are of "less potential value to the practicing educator than is commonly assumed" (p. 159). Likewise, he contrasted the "complexity of the teacher's work and the simplicity of the conditions under which much of our formal learning theory has been generated" (p. 160).

Like Schwab, Jackson disavowed the conceptual orientation of the first handbook. The "complexity" of the teacher's work arises from the fact that teaching focuses itself on a "complex organism, working toward complex goals, in a complex setting" (p. 161). Accordingly, "experienced teachers . . . know or come to know that the path of educational progress more closely resembles the flight of a butterfly than the flight of a bullet" (pp. 166–167). Moreover, Jackson was even led to "wonder" whether the teacher's "primary concern is learning, after all" (p. 161). Indeed, Jackson further highlighted the complexity of teaching when he suggested that, in terms of the meanings that learners extract from teaching (compare: Gage), the "hidden curriculum" may be at least as potent as the visible curriculum (p. 33).

Like Jackson, Smith and Geoffrey's audience included "the layman," who, they felt, "should profit from the extended detail reported in the field note excerpts" (p. v). Their book, that is,

"centers on complexity" (p. vii) addressed through the compilation and interpretation of a "microethnography of the classroom" (p. 3). Yet, Smith and Geoffrey hardly knew what they might find—"our nets were spread to catch some elusive quarry" (p. 6). Just as Jackson had been drawn to unveil the hidden curriculum of classroom life, Smith and Geoffrey were no less curious to decode the "silent language" of schooling.

As these illustrations suggest, the refreshed intellectual circumstances of the late 1960s were postpositivist in at least two respects. It was accepted that school classrooms are differentially structured in the eyes of their beholders. And it was increasingly recognized that, in their turn, these structures are also expressions of differences in power and control.

Such perspectives on teaching and learning found further expression in two books published in English at the turn of the 1970s: *Pedagogy of the Oppressed* (Freire, 1971) and *Knowledge and Control* (Young, 1971). Both books associated the word "pedagogy" with the silent languages and hidden curricula of schooling. Freire, for instance, relabeled earlier didactic ideas (compare: Ratke's) as the "banking" or "narrative" concept of education (chapter 2):

> Narration (with the teacher as narrator) leads the students to memorize mechanically the narrated content. Worse still, it turns them into "containers," into receptacles to be filled by the teacher. The more completely he fills the receptacles, the better a teacher he is. The more meekly the receptacles permit themselves to be filled , the better students they are. (p. 45)

Further, Freire identified 10 features of the banking concept, ranging from "the teacher teaches and the students are taught" through "the teacher is the subject of the learning process, while the pupils are mere objects" to "the teacher talks and the student listens—meekly" (pp. 46–47).

Freire then offered the "problem-solving method" as a replacement for the banking conception. From such a perspective, students become "critical coinvestigators" with their teachers. Collectively, they engage in a "constant unveiling of reality." Whenever faced with problems relating to themselves "in the world and with the world," students and teachers "feel increasingly challenged and obliged to respond to that challenge" (p. 54). Problem-posing education "roots itself in the dynamic present." Human beings are "in the process of *becoming*" within an "unfinished reality" (pp. 56–57).

Comparable statements linking pedagogy to power and the politics of teaching and learning are voiced by Basil Bernstein in a key contribution to *Knowledge and Control:*

> How a society selects, classifies, distributes, and evaluates the educational knowledge that it considers to be public, reflects both the distribution of power and the principles of social control. . . . Formal educational knowledge can be considered to be realized through three message systems: curriculum, pedagogy, and evaluation. Curriculum defines what counts as valid knowledge, pedagogy defines what counts as the valid transmission of knowledge, and evaluation defines what counts as a valid realization of this knowledge on the part of the taught. (Bernstein, 1971, p. 47; see also Bourdieu, Passeron, & Martin, 1994)

From such reappraisals of teaching and learning, pedagogics became identified with a parallel set of questions about the reproduction and distribution of political power. Pedagogy was seen to be about forms of classroom life, about social values as well as social relations. Ever since the 1970s, research on teaching has had to confront—or abjure—such opportunities to reformulate "telling it like it is."

Saying It Otherwise

"Tell it like it is" was an imperative to do more than raise awareness of social injustice. It also meant articulating a problem-posing agenda from which a better social order could emerge. Contestation over what ought to be, whether as debates over valid research methods, as social psychological angst in literature and film, or as civil disobedience and public protest, was serving to heighten awareness of the active political character not simply of schooling, but of language itself. A new educational order would entail, at one and the same time, a new linguistic order. Questions of identity and marginality had not lost their political character or their significance for teachers as social reconstructionists. However, being a teacher and a social advocate would increasingly involve contesting the natural or normal language being used to frame good teaching.

In the service of this new linguistic order, an embryonic but vociferous band of educators located themselves squarely in the liberatory social movements of the 1960s and 1970s and their related politics of difference. Teaching and learning as a critical politics of education were to be redefined in the 1970s by notions of reproduction and resistance that were rooted in the historical materialism of Karl Marx and Antonio Gramsci and that were elaborated in the writings of Jurgen Habermas, Pierre Bourdieu, and Paulo Freire. Later, many of the educators who drew on and informed this new sociology of knowledge would increasingly find themselves resisting, rejecting, or accommodating the discursive turn of Michel Foucault, Jacques Derrida, Jean-Francois Lyotard, and other new French theorists. In turn, this very dichotomy—materiality or discourse—would itself be made problematic in queer and posthumanist social analysis. It is only at the end of the 1990s that such theorizing is being applied to research on teaching and learning.

For many of those disaffected by the social institutions of late capitalism, social activism as political protest provided a politicized and politicizing vocabulary of liberation. Yet the promise of liberation for all marginalized social groups would not be squarely on the political agenda until the injustices experienced by Black Americans were acknowledged at the broadest political level as both pervasive and deeply offensive. The fact of Blackness, as Fanon (1967) has described it, was the difference that made a difference in the radical politics of the anti-Vietnam and Civil Rights era. The 1960s and 1970s had heard a clear clarion call to freedom in streets of Washington, D.C., and Mississippi, in the utterances of Martin Luther King Jr. and Malcolm X. It was also heard in the foundational feminist writings of Betty Friedan and Germaine Greer. However, in the decade after 1963 the embryonic feminist project of liberation would play second fiddle to the peace and Civil Rights movements, as they fixed the global gaze on racial injustice and the obscenity of war. The peace and Civil Rights movements also overshadowed the Hispanic-American liberation movement, the Native American liberation movement, and the gay rights movement, all of which existed in embryonic form at that time.

Thus, many of the contradictions and paradoxes around the identity politics of those involved in the civil rights march would not be on the agenda until much later. Categories of difference were fixed by the need for unity against an oppressive social system. Thus, speaking on behalf of African Americans or on behalf of women would not invite the criticisms from within that were forthcoming in later years, as single-issue or one (essential) identity politics fragmented into multiple and diverse positionings of the self. The sorts of contradictions that were present at the time—for example, the number of Anglo men and women who attended the march, leaving women of color behind to do the invisible work of cleaning their houses (Greene, 1996)—would not be scrutinized until much later. Partly because other injustices against minorities had not yet seen the political light of day, the civil rights march appeared to unite all minorities as a spectacle of social democracy at work. It stood as an optimistic symbolic enactment of the real possibility of liberation for both oppressed and oppressor. "We shall overcome" had a simple message of collective concerted action that was an impossible achievement for the Million Man March more than 30 years later, where the unresolved and unstable nature of minority politics was so starkly visible.

Direct social action, in particular the peace movement and the Civil Rights movement, made available to the culturally silent a vocabulary of liberation (Goulet, in Freire, 1987, xii) to be used in the service of social justice and civil rights. Emancipation, transformation, conscientization, revolution, these terms rather than empowerment (which would appear in a later generation of educational literature), were part of a new language that would be generated to speak the condition of oppression and its elimination. For many educators, this new language flagged the hope that schools and universities might be transformed to deliver truly democratic education. Instead of subjugating the powerless, it might allow both manipulator and manipulated to take a hard look at power and its abuse. This hope reiterated a long-standing, perennial theme across the social spectrum regardless of ideological orientation—that reformed schooling (as a key culprit in any current malaise), will provide the means to social salvation.

During the late 1960s, much progressive experimentation with schooling was tied specifically to liberationist politics. The emphasis was on schools as mutually supportive communities oriented less to transmission of subject content than to learner needs in the context of the realities of a capitalist political economy. Similarities have recently been drawn between this period of school reform and two earlier periods—the turn of the century and the 1930s, when, according to Linda Darling-Hammond (1996), there was a proliferation of highly successful schools that failed to replicate their successes and thus vanished in the succeeding decades (p. 9). For Darling-Hammond, the limited shelf life of such experimentation had as much to do with their marginal status in the politics of educational policy development as it had to do with the nature of the pedagogical demands being made on teachers within these schools (p. 9).

Not all alternative educationists of the time worked from the assumption that schooling should or could be liberating. Ivan Illich, for example, refused to see schooling, whether reformed or not, as anything other than an enduring social problem. In *Deschooling Society* (1971), Illich elaborated his project of demythologizing schooling, a project that has continued to unsettle formulae for alternative schooling ever since. He argued:

> We cannot begin a reform of education unless we first understand that neither individual learning nor social equality can be enhanced by the ritual of schooling. We cannot go beyond the consumer society unless we first understand that obligatory public schools inevitably reproduce such a society, no matter what is taught in them. (pp. 43–44)

Conceptual Tools for Pedagogical Deconstruction

Educational liberationists—whether identifying with the specific agendas of reformist social movements (e.g., African American liberation, women's liberation) or with differing versions of social reconstruction that had been based on the work of Marx, Dewey, or Freire—were certainly aware that schools and university classrooms would not serve a social reconstructionist agenda without changed curricula and teaching methods. Socially reconstructive pedagogical processes would be required of new a generation of radical teachers to draw attention to the ways in which certain knowledge—and thus certain groups of people—had been subjugated. A plethora of literature was generated in the 1970s by curriculum theorists (e.g., Apple, 1979; Bourdieu & Passeron, 1977; Young, 1971), educational sociologists (e.g., Jencks, 1979; Bernstein, 1975), and political economists (e.g., Bowles & Gintis, 1976; Karier, Violas, & Spring, 1973) that focused attention on the role of schools in perpetuating existing inequalities in society by legitimating cultural practices and institutional arrangements.

A key imperative of this sort of literature as a form of inquiry into teaching and learning practices was its framing of pedagogy as an explicitly interpretive, deconstructive, and reconstructive task (Apple, 1979; Ramsay 1975; Willis, 1977). Deconstruction would expose the injustices of current institutional arrangements. It involved unpacking the structure of educational texts (writing, speech, technology) in order to unmask the real beneficiaries of this version of educational truth and thereby to allow a newly constructed social order that would be based on the fundamental principles of social justice. The question "Whose interests are served by any particular version of good educational order?" was and still is the driving logic of such critiques. The idea is that education as a competing system of beliefs can be demonstrated to be linked to broader social and political ideologies of class, race, and gender inequality. Ecology, disability, sexuality, and age would later make this an increasingly complex landscape of critique. For example, two studies of the cultures boys that continue to be important for educators—Paul Willis's *Learning to Labour: How Working Class Kids Get Working Class Jobs* (1977) and Bob Connell's *Masculinities* (1995)—work out of different conceptualizations of identity, the latter proceeding from a more elaborated reading of class, sexuality, and gender dynamics than the former.

Understanding individuals as social subjects has become increasingly important to this literature of deconstructive pedagogy. The French structuralist Louis Althusser contributed significantly to the deconstructive educational project through his elaboration of relationship of subjectivity and power—that is, his notion of the way ideology functions to produce social subjects. In "Ideology and State Apparatuses" (1971), Althusser explains that ideology is the system of representation by means of which we live in cultures as their products and agents. Ideology transforms human beings (biological materials) into social subjects but also obscures the processes by which the subject is constituted, thereby enabling the subject to consider this production natural. In that consciousness is considered self-evident, inevitable, and natural, what consciousness contains is therefore ideological. Yet, it is also material, in that it is produced by Ideological State Apparatuses (ISAs)—those institutions, rituals, and practices that compose sociocultural life. Through these ISAs, the subject is hailed to both recognize and fail to recognize itself in the institutions and practices that constitute it (p. 163). Ideology, then, in Althusser's view, transforms individuals into subjects by presenting them with particular positions or signs of a possible future that serve the dominant interests in a society.

It was the importance Althusser placed on the linguistic production of identity that was to be so useful to education-as-deconstruction in the 1980s. For example, Jean Anyon (1983), Michael Apple (1982a, 1982b), and Henri Giroux (1983) use this idea to move educational deconstruction away from Bowles and Gintis's (1976) notion of the direct correspondence between schools and capitalism. While still insisting on the marginalizing effects of schooling for minorities, these writers analyzed schools and classroom as sites of cultural reproduction, where contestation and resistance are also possible. If identity is provided out of available language, and if such languages are shifty, contradictory, and always in competition, then the structural political economy of schooling cannot rule out resistance, because it cannot fix the process of identity production for teachers or students.

The shiftiness of language was not only a theme of critical pedagogy—the deconstructive and politicizing educational literature of the 1980s and early 1990s—but it is also apparent in the shifting tenor of the literature of educational critique itself, as it moved from the influence of German political philosophers increasingly to take up French poststructuralist accounts of power and subjectivity. Typified by the work of Michael Apple, Stanley Aronowitz, Henri Giroux, and Peter McLaren, critical pedagogy sought, with varying degrees of success, to draw attention to the insufficiency of discursively constructed categories in taken-for-granted language use in education. As a structuralist enterprise in the mid-1980s (e.g., Apple, 1986; Aronowitz & Giroux, 1985; Giroux & McLaren, 1986), critical pedagogy opposed both an old order based on behaviorist models of teaching and a new order that further refined such scientific models in terms of industrial effectiveness or fast capitalist logic.

What it meant to be critical was aligned with conceptions of critical thinking derived from Germany's Frankfurt school of political thought, (e.g., Habermas, 1971; Horkheimer & Adorno, 1972) rather than with John Dewey's understanding of the term. That is, critical pedagogy looked to new social movements and collective action to overturn and transform the mass deception produced by commodity fetishism. While Dewey's call had certainly been for a transformative pedagogy, it did not draw on a revolutionary discourse of liberation as radical political action.

The work of Jurgen Habermas (1971) certainly had appeal for a new generation of educational writers seeking to put social justice in the forefront of the schooling agenda. The Habermasian notion of technocratic consciousness (1971, pp. 107–122) was put to work by the new sociologists, who were trying to see beyond Marxist notions of reproduction and resistance (Wexler, 1987, p. 44). These new sociologists (e.g., Bates, 1983; Henry, Knight, Lingard, & Taylor, 1988) applied Habermasian understandings of technocratic rationality to their structuralist accounts of the role of schools and governments to show how what counts as legitimate knowledge has come to be constructed and in whose interests this knowledge operates.

French sociologist Pierre Bourdieu was also influential in moving ideological studies of education away from correspondence theories of education, and in shaping conceptualizations of schooling as cultural reproduction. In Bourdieu and Passeron's *Reproduction: In Education, Society and Culture* (1977), Bourdieu's interest in the interplay between everyday social interaction and the realm of esoteric or abstract ideas provides important insights into the relationship between educational institutions, questions of power, and cultural modes of domination. A central problem for educational analysis, as he saw it, was that the whole educational enterprise tends to prevent one from thinking about Kant in relation to pajamas or about pajamas while reading Marx (Bourdieu, 1980, p. 40). The call to noble social and political ideals must be accompanied by engagement with the concrete and the mundane.

Deconstructive Research on Teaching

As an imperative to educational reform in the 1980s, the social reconstructionist or reconceptualist agenda was pitted against any technicalization of the process of production and exchange that takes place in the interaction of teacher and learner and from the knowledge jointly produced (Lusted, 1986). Advocates drew attention to the conditions necessary to maximize opportunities for effecting social reform. In particular, they focused on the power relations within which knowledge is produced. Reconceptualizing work like that of William Pinar (1981) and Joe Kincheloe (1989) blamed positivistic, ahistorical, and depoliticized analyses of liberal and conservative educational critics for the failure of education to engage or transform teachers and students. They took up the newly forged tools of structuralist sociological critique to oppose mainstream discourse communities in education, in particular those versions of cognitive science and humanistic psychology that were held to abet and underwrite the values of competitive individualism in educational work.

Thus, deconstructive educational researchers in the 1980s set about confronting mainstream mythologies (e.g., the ideology of individual differences) and attempting to generate possibilities for denormalizing social processes in their pedagogical work. Claims to value-free knowledge or neutral methodology were made decidedly problematic. Critical educational research began to interrogate Eurocentric and androcentric knowledges and cultural practices in terms of their capacity to delegitimate the claims of those disadvantaged by their identity position in terms of race, class, culture, gender, and ecology.

Armed with structuralist accounts of institutional and social power, new sociologists used critical pedagogy to unpack, locate, or interpret teaching and learning practices, rather than merely opposing or criticizing mainstream models schooling or education per se. Overall, actual technique in pedagogical instruction merited much less attention in applications of the new sociology of knowledge than the development of a radical political language. Nevertheless, while continuing to frame teachers' work as ideological, new sociologists did begin to look more closely at the mundane practices of teachers' work. For example, the teacher survival strategies (e.g., joke telling, flirting, drilling) that were documented by Woods (1979, pp. 149–167) were understood to be, in some senses, a response to inequitable relations of power (e.g., Hargreaves, 1978; Henry et al., 1988). Concern was also expressed that the curriculum, despite being mediated and modified by teachers and students in a range of ways, "continued to operate as an expression of [inequitable] power" (Stone, 1981, p. 55). As a result, minorities would experience curricula as repressive, despite policy directions that had the appearance of enlightened thinking in relation to minorities (see Troyna & Hatcher, 1992, pp. 200–204).

The idea of a hidden curriculum of learnings that mirrored dominant patterns of social class had been available in educational research since the Lippett and White (1958) study. This study recorded the behavior of four groups of 10-year-old boys in response to what Lippett and White describe as authoritarian, democratic, and laissez-faire models of teacher leadership. The study pointed to the range of learning outcomes that appeared to be in no way related to the official curriculum or subject content. Deconstructive work done to map the hidden curriculum as a troublesome educational politics (Connell, Ashenden, Kessler, & Dowsett, 1982; Dale, 1977; Dreeben, 1968; Hargreaves, 1978; Illich, 1971; Whitty & Young, 1976) questioned the legitimacy of all those who spoke with authority and certainty about educational practice.

This challenge was to manifest itself in more persistent calls for teachers to intervene in their own practices as part of an emancipatory school politics. For 4 decades, scholars had been noting both the unique opportunities that existed for teachers to be their own researchers and the potential of participatory research to inform the theory-practice nexus in education (e.g., Buckingham, 1926; Corey, 1953; Lewin, 1946). As emancipatory or socially critical models of research, later participatory or action research models, for example the Deakin model of Stephen Kemmis, Wilfred Carr, and Robin McTaggart (Carr & Kemmis, 1986; Kemmis & McTaggart, 1988; McTaggart, 1991), were pitted against scientism and, in turn, found themselves constantly having to respond to criticisms about their own subjectivism and relativism (Adelman, 1989; Wallace, 1987).

Despite such critiques, the broader imperative to inquire into the mundane daily practices of teachers had an important impact on educational research in that teachers themselves were best placed to do this sort of research. In teacher education, important developments included the use of biography as a research tool in socialization inquiry (Barone, 1987; Zeichner & Grant, 1981), a greater interest in the means by which reflective inquiry could take place (Ross & Hannay, 1986; Zeichner, 1987; Zeichner & Liston, 1987), and the acknowledgment of revitalized action research as an important component of teacher education reform (Brent & Hodges, 1988; Elliot, 1988). Studies such as those focusing on teacher dialogue (e.g., Raphael, 1985; Strieb, 1985) indicated a move among teachers to gain power over their teaching as a result of being in charge of the creation of teacher knowledge rather than being subjugated by the ideas of others. Importantly, Duckworth's (1986) research stressed the need to elevate the criterion of sense making in order to better understand practice and the need to elevate the subject of the study as a meaning maker, to avoid researching down on teachers or students.

Alongside such factory floor initiatives, a few larger academic studies explored school processes in terms of social and cultural production and reproduction. Peter McLaren's *Schooling as a Ritual Performance* (1986), an ethnographic study of secondary schooling, was a deliberate attempt to challenge the limits of present methods of interpreting school life. Likewise, Nancy Lesko (1988) in her book titled *Symbolizing Society: Stories, Rites, and Structure in a Catholic High School* continued to move away from overly rational and arid school descriptions toward an understanding of a school as possessing a symbolic order whose multileveled and metaphorical nature, when deconstructed, revealed important insights into what school means and what its effects are. This sort of phenomenological and ethnographic work drew attention to the language through which human beings give meaning to their educational experiences, the linguistic context in which this occurs, and the social relations of the research act itself.

Other work of an ethnographic type focusing on the sociolinguistics of cultural reproduction studied how classroom talk functions to inform student interpretations of their educational world (Bartlett, 1987; Green, 1983; Green & Harker, 1982; Morine-Dershimer, 1985). Bartlett's work on text, context, and pupil attention (1987) is noteworthy in its conception of teacher action as text that is mediated through contemporary networks of social relationships. He demonstrated the possibility of building upon elements of empirical and interpretive research paradigms to reconstruct social theory relevant to the study of social action. This helped educators to address not simply the problem of sociolinguistic estrangement, but the impoverished theory and method through which such estrangement is generated and maintained.

Feminism and Deconstructive Work and as Deconstructive Work on Teaching

Feminist educational researchers applauded both the move to consider the social character of language and the move to new methods for interrogating language at the site of practice (Greene, 1986; Grundy, 1989). Nevertheless, they also warned against a fascination with innovative methods for their own sake, arguing that the applications of findings out of context could lead to the sort of misrepresentation that creates new rules to govern and constrain teacher behavior rather than to promote professional autonomy (Evertson, 1987).

As it had done a decade earlier, the work of Paulo Freire continued to make an important contribution to feminist research on teaching. In *Pedagogy of the Oppressed* (1971), Freire had attended to the processes by which it becomes possible to reflect on educational tasks in an empowering way by bringing forth the contradictions or limit situations that characterize the reality of the participants. In seeking to end education's complicity in reproducing gendered inequality, feminists like Francis Maher (1985) and Ira Shor (1987) drew on Freire's emancipatory agenda to resist and replace the banking model of classroom teaching practice. However, such feminists also warned against Freirean idolatry taking the place of the development of critical consciousness in the project of a liberating education.

For neo-Marxist feminists, empowerment must transcend individual workplace competency or even broader notions of personal fulfillment. They therefore distanced themselves from their more moderate or liberal sisters (Acker, 1987). In the new generation of radical scholarship emerging out of the heightened politicized and politicizing social and cultural agendas of the 1960s and early 1970s, empowerment would mean liberation or emancipation in the sense of freedom from discrimination, poverty, and social injustice. The focus was still on power as a repressive effect of structural inequality, a possession of the few at the expense of the many. Thus, the matter of who gets to speak as an "authority" in the government of the day, the church, the family, the classroom, the academic tome, would remain a focus of critique. Feminists were therefore particularly interested in analyzing pedagogical processes as the lived experiences of girls and women. They called for a more rigorous scrutiny of the daily pedagogical practices used in tertiary institutions by those who train future teachers (Culley & Portuges, 1985; Gore, 1987; Lewis, 1990).

It was feminist writers in particular (e.g., Culley & Portuges, 1985; Culley, Diamond, Edwards, Lennox, & Portuges, 1985; Friedman, 1985; Schniedewind, 1985) who took up the challenge to provide a more thorough exploration of how politicizing educators might exercise authority with rather than authority over their students and themselves (Gore, 1993, p. 68). This involved promoting collaborative and cooperative models over dialectic one-way instructional techniques (see Weiler, 1991). The personal and pedagogical empowerment that resulted would be pitted against patriarchy, given that patriarchal structures denied all women, including teachers, the authority of their own, differently lived experience of the world. In *Bitter Milk: Women and Teaching* (1988), Madeleine Grumet argued that issues particular to women's lived experience inevitably slide down under the discourse, weighted down by centuries of talk about education dominated by the history and preoccupation of male experience (p. xix). Grumet sought to differentiate a middle way of seeking empowerment for teachers and students from a previous generation of liberationists who, she claimed, collapsed schooling system into an economic system and thus ignored "experiences of family life, of bearing, delivering and nurturing children . . . [and] . . . the language of the body, the world we carry on weight-bearing joints, the world we hear in sudden hums and giggles" (p. xv). This middle way would bring new phenomenological, psychoanalytic, and feminist perspectives to bear on neo-Marxist analyses of educational practice. It would challenge those versions of difference that were based on simple dichotomies and special psychological categorizations.

Later deconstructions of educational practice—for example, the work of feminists like Elizabeth Ellsworth (1989), Carmen Luke and Jennifer Gore (1992), and Deborah Britzman (1995)—would move analyses on to consider how the very language of critique itself might have repressive effects, despite the good intentions of the teacher to work on behalf of the vulnerable. Their work would reconfigure the politics of vulnerability in educational writing, because it would challenge the essentialist assumptions about class, race, and gender that had become so important to deconstructive research in education as a structuralist project.

The Otherness of the Other

For almost 2 decades after the civil rights march on Washington, Black-White politics had been a catalyst for, and at times had overshadowed, other diverse experiences of difference. In many respects the politics of difference had been enacted as a pecking order of difference, in which race and class—and later gender—had been privileged, and this had important consequences for other agendas of minorities. Increasingly, the question "Who gets to speak for whom about what and why?" worked to fracture allegiances and cut across alignments forged in the heady days of the early 1970s. By the mid-1980s it became increasingly evident that social justice was too often being translated into entrenched them-and-us oppositions. The capacity of social movements to mobilize people around a coherent set of essential principles for action based on categories such as gender, class, or race could be seen as both a strength and a weakness.

In 1981 Betty Friedan wrote of a necessary second stage of feminist politics, one that was emerging in the light of the conflicts and contradictions felt by those "trying to live in terms of first-stage feminism and the emergence of full-scale backlash with and after the [1980] Reagan election" (Friedan, 1981, p. 4). This second stage, she argued, should take up some of the thornier problems of the enactment of feminism as a reactive politics in order to push beyond critique and refusal of the "feminine mystique"—the title of her foundational feminist work published in 1963. She was not signaling an end to reaction as an on-going political necessity, but the importance of understanding feminism's reactions as "half-truths" (p. 31), with their own limited view of personhood and, thus, of possibility. This more reflective and reflexive tone in the politics of resistance was, among other more noble things, a product of fatigue—the fatigue of the women campaigners themselves and the fatigue of first-stage politics of liberation as a system of language use. In the case of the women's movement, the truncating of women's liberation to women's lib, and the designation of women as libbers signaled not simply the trivializing of feminist agendas in the commercial media, but also the exhaustion of a vocabulary of resistance that had served well the reactive politics of the 1960s and 1970s.

By the mid-1980s, there was an increasing discomfort with the self-congratulatory and somewhat evangelical tone that characterized politicizing pedagogical work as a system of rhetoric. In 1989, Elizabeth Ellsworth's paper "Why Doesn't This Feel Empowering: Working Through the Repressive Myths of Critical Pedagogy" captured a new mood of dis-ease about the social reconstructionist agenda. In it Ellsworth expressed not simply a concern to address the politics of identity in her own radical classroom, but her disquiet about what were apparently the repressive effects of so-called emancipatory discourses in general. Her analysis of the defiant speech of her own students

was important to the reconfiguration of the work of deconstructing teaching and learning as a political and moral project. What had become troubling to a new generation of political writers, including black feminist educators like bell hooks (1984), was the way structuralist positionings threatened to fix difference and thus absorb it into the orthodox and the familiar.

Denaturalizing Difference

This reflexive turn in deconstructive pedagogy provided a new set of challenges to modes of social scientific inquiry. It was not simply a turn away from positivism, but also from the antipositivist, antiempiricist impetus that animated educational politics as a modernist enterprise, particularly the neo-Marxist foundations of the new sociology of knowledge. As the dominant epistemic faiths of the modern period, both positivism and its doppelganger Marxism had, according to Dick Hebdige (1988), dissolved as oppositions (p. 192). Postpositivisms as postmodernist phenomena came quickly to represent a challenge to any epistemological vantage point claiming totalistic knowledge (Jay, 1988, p. 5). The modernist metaphor of knowledge as a tree with fixed center and branching limbs would be increasingly irrelevant to any research based on this new set of assumptions.

French poststructuralism provided much of the theoretical framework for the new analyses of social and cultural practices spawned by this epistemological break. Jacques Derrida was a key figure in mobilizing the linguistic turn across the humanities and social sciences. In *Structure, Sign, and Play in the Discourses of the Human Sciences* (1970), Jacques Derrida had not been content merely to disrupt purely material understandings of ideology, but he had refused a center or a point of presence which would disallow anything but the free-play of structure (Derrida, 1970, pp. 247–248). As Philip Wexler (1987, p. 134) puts it, Derrida's aim, in common with other poststructuralists, was to assert terms for describing the decomposition of fixed centers of metaphysics, choosing to focus on the means of producing the meanings of various discourses, rather than their origins or social foundations. In using Derrida, marginal writers must therefore refuse the very idea of a center or margin that can be located. Difference should not to be read as a terrain of fixed political positions but an ex-centric, contingent, and shifty diaspora.

Derrida's deconstruction of texts within the history of philosophy forced the acknowledgment of the oppositions, exclusions, dichotomies, and distinctions that characterize the texts of Western metaphysics. His complex concept of différance—the condition of difference and of the binary oppositional structure of difference-sameness within which it exists—allows for the use of a text's own system of logic against itself. This moved deconstructive inquiry to challenge all sorts of them-and-us assumptions, whether it was feminists challenging the binary logic of phallocentrism, queer theorists challenging the binary logic of hetero-homo sexuality, or any other cultural critic. Language makes difference an endless problematic.

For educational researchers, the actual project of extracting a deconstructive method from Derrida's work has been very difficult. The intertextual nature of Derridean readings and his destabilization of the binary logic of Western texts has unsettled conventional deconstructive thinking, yet to date applications are being made to educational theory and methodology rather than to specific research on teaching and learning. Feminist theorists, for example, while continuing to be skeptical of Derrida's apoliticism, have found his intertextual deconstruction useful as a conceptual framework for the reading of culture (Cornell & Thurschwell, 1987; Suleiman, 1986).

As a new decade dawned, feminist researchers began to acknowledge, by means of a doubled movement of inscription and subversion, the ways that feminism is both outside and yet inscribed within Western language systems, patriarchal rationality, and imperialistic practices (Lather, 1991a). By 1990 feminist pedagogy had become identified with challenging any form of minority oppression—racism, classism, homophobia, and heterosexism—as well as gender inequality. Collections of feminist works such as *Feminism and Education* (Bourne, Masters, Amin, Gonick, & Gribowski, 1994) and *The Feminist Classroom* (Maher & Tetreault, 1994) reflect this broader politics in their advocacy on behalf of the educationally vulnerable. Yet, importantly, these feminist writings also reflect a reluctance to see feminism as occupying the highest moral ground of practice. This new spirit of reflexivity is evidenced in Maher and Tetreault's introduction to *The Feminist Classroom:*

> When we began our study, we had a somewhat simplistic and dichotomized view of the authoritarian, male-dominated, traditional classroom versus the idealized feminist teacher, a notion taken from many early descriptions of feminist teaching practices, including Maher's own. Like the construct of woman's nature in some feminist theories, such as Carol Gilligan's, of the early 1980s, this feminist teacher was democratic rather than authoritarian, cooperative rather than competitive, and concerned with connected and relational rather than separate and irrational approaches to learning. . . . Meanwhile we had been hiding ourselves—as knowers, as researchers, as engaged feminists. . . . Still thinking that we could describe what was really going on. (p. 12)

In following the profound linguistic turn in social theory that Derrida's work exemplifies, critical feminist educators began to focus less on truth and more on the production of truth effects. Patti Lather's (1991b) conception of a postpositivist research methodology as one that works both within and against the complexity, contingency, and fragility of its own discursive practices is an example of this sort of application to educational research as a feminist poststructuralist project. Erica McWilliam's *In Broken Images: Feminist Tales for a Different Teacher Education* (1994) provides an exemplar of such within and against logic applied to a research project on teaching. The book documents McWilliam's doctoral research with preservice teachers, in which she used Lather's theorizing of method to trouble her own clear images about the value of deconstructive pedagogy and the presumed conservatism of her students.

Denaturalizing difference has been made possible not simply through new theorizing of textuality but also of power. Since the late 1980s, French poststructuralist writer Michel Foucault has been most influential in moving contemporary understandings of power away from structuralist attempts to define what power is and from concomitant analyses of the origins of power. In *Power/Knowledge: Selected Interviews and Other Writings 1972–1977* (1980) Foucault explains that knowledge and power are inseparable and interrelated, in that there is no power relation without the correlative constitution of a field of knowledge, nor knowledge that does not presuppose and constitute at the same time, power relations (p. 59). Thus, to examine issues of the exercise of power in classrooms or anywhere else is to examine the processes and struggles of power-knowledge that determine the forms and possible domains of knowledge. Power, then, is not owned by institutions or social groups but exists in relationships that are discursively constructed. All knowledge, indeed, is constructed through discourses.

Discourses, for Foucault, are practices, not simply a group of signs, inasmuch as they systematically form the objects of which they speak (1972, p. 49). Because they embody meaning and social relationships, discourses constitute both our selves as subjects and the power relations within which we live and work. The power of discourses to constrain the possibilities of thought derives from their capacity to order and combine words in particular ways, changing their meaning and their effects through deploying them in ways that exclude or displace other possible combinations. Thus, the exercise of power through the effects of discourse is "always a way of acting upon . . . acting subjects by virtue of their acting or being capable of action" (Foucault, 1982, p. 220). For Foucault, this exercise of power incites, induces, seduces, and makes easier or more difficult (p. 220). In this sense, discourse as both an instrument and an effect of power can be both the means to prevent an opposing strategy and the means by which an oppositional strategy can begin.

While Foucault does allow the potentiality for collective transformation through emancipatory power-knowledge, there is no doubt that he was generally negative about the possibility of individual subjects being able to take this sort of control over their own lives. Thus, to take up this sort of conceptualizing of power relations is to disallow notions of endless progress or the possibility of utopian social transformation. For Foucault (1978), a plurality of resistances replaces the pure law of the revolutionary (p. 95), and these resistances are often transitory and mobile rather than fixed and class based.

While Foucault, like Derrida, presented educational researchers with no ready-made framework for analyzing power in educational discourse, his work did signal the importance of maintaining an awareness of the potentially oppressive role of ostensibly liberating forms of discourse and the possibility of resistance. Given women's own histories of marginalization and subjugation, many feminists found that Foucauldian notions of power and resistance confirmed their own practices, including their refusal of hierarchical organization or representation. Further, Foucault's work abetted strategically located strikes at power's most vulnerable places (Grosz, 1990, p. 92). Valerie Walkerdine's *Counting Girls Out* (1989) and *School Girl Fiction* (1990) are examples of such feminist applications to educational research, in that they draw attention to the positive as well as the repressive effects of schooling and popular culture in terms of the multiple ways girls engage with these social phenomena.

Because Foucault understood signifying processes as formative of the subject, Foucauldian analyses are likely to proceed from a commitment to historical analysis of the social world. Two examples of such an imperative being applied to analyses of teaching are available in Ian Hunter's *Rethinking the School: Subjectivity, Bureaucracy, Criticism* (1994) and David Kirk's *Schooling Bodies: School Practice and Public Discourse 1880–1940* (1998). Both authors refuse traditional accounts of the historical development of schooling, taking up instead Foucauldian imperatives to inquire into schooling as an assemblage of contingent improvisations (Hunter, 1994, p. 438) and as a set of techniques for producing and regulating disciplinary society (Kirk, 1998, p. 3).

Ian Hunter's *Rethinking the School* is significant as a departure from the orthodox treatments of both the school and the state that are available in liberal and Marxist accounts. Hunter rejects the tidying logic of a dialectic reconciliation of two sets of principles—the objectives of government and the spiritual milieu of the subject (Hunter, 1995, pp. 439–440)—arguing that it produces a misreading of the institution and of its relations with the state as all of a piece. He insists that schooling as a set of systemic practices has been produced out of a fusion of two autonomous technologies of human existence, which he calls techniques for the moral training and governance of modern citizens and techniques of pastoral Christianity (Hunter, 1994, p. 31).

Unlike Hunter's book, David Kirk's *Schooling Bodies* (1998) does not demand of the reader a strong grasp of poststructuralist theoretical shifts and modes of educational analysis. It is a "history of physical training, medical inspection and sport in Australian schools 1880–1940" (Preface) in which Kirk shows how layer upon layer of public and disciplinary discourse came to be laid down, reinscribed, and placed under erasure in a formative period in Australian physical education history. In keeping with other Foucauldian scholars, Kirk insists that public discourses are never fixed, nor does history always unfold in predicable, even rational, ways. Thus, he notes that the time periods prewar, interwar, and World War 2, pre and post, are problematic in many respects, and, like other Foucauldian scholars, he refuses to read history as a story about progress toward the present.

Foucault's analysis of the nature of discursive practices enables researchers to approach text as both an object in its own right and also as an interactive event, an instance of the process and product of social meaning in a particular context of power-knowledge discourse that is encapsulated within it. The challenge of letting all voices speak can therefore be understood as the challenge of creating (or denying) a linguistic space for others as producers of different knowledge(s). This denies a singular cause-and-effect logic at work in the construction of a fixed or essential social identity, or in descriptions of pedagogical work.

Thus, the imperative coming from new French theory to education has been to focus increasingly on the accidents—the discontinuities, surprises, leaps, regressions—that produce the fragmented and unstable social world of education, rather than on maintaining a united call to social justice as a macropolitical struggle. This imperative is evident in the changing tenor of critical pedagogical writing in the late 1980s and early 1990s, as critical educational writers attempted to come to terms with this postmodern challenge to epistemic faiths, neo-Marxist or otherwise. Instead of generating a big picture or grand narrative about why large-scale systems or structures have risen or declined, poststructuralist educational analysts have begun to examine the mundane daily practices of education in an attempt to explain how certain versions of good teaching and learning have come to be intelligible as effective practice (e.g., Hunter, 1988; Meadmore & Symes, 1996; Meredith & Tyler, 1993). This sort of patient documentation of daily practice is not used to extrapolate either to the macropolitical or to the personal.

Few examples of such patient documentation exist in relation to teaching. One book that is a pioneer in the field is *Child and Citizen: Genealogies of Schooling and Subjectivity* (Meredyth & Tyler, 1993), an edited collection of articles linked by a common interest in the relation between schooling and government, between the child and the citizen, and between the adherence to educational principles and the administration of educational programs (p. 4). Importantly, the various chapters serve to question some central assumptions about liberal education, including the idea that child-centered pedagogy is pitted against normative and corrective functions of education (e.g., Patterson, 1993; Tyler, 1993).

A second example is provided by Jennifer Gore's research into how power operates in classrooms. In "On the Use of Empirical Research for the Development of a Theory of Pedagogy" (in press), Gore explains her attempt to redress the philosophical nature of pedagogical deconstruction by engaging in systematic collection and analysis of data in order to inquire into power's inescapability and pedagogy's operation on the body (p. 1). Her research involved intensive documentation of four pedagogical sites (a high school physical education class, a 1st-year teacher education cohort, a women's discussion group, and a feminist reading group) over a period of 6 months. In describing her work as "taming Foucault" (p. 5), Gore indicates her own understanding of the risks involved in bringing Foucauldian scholarship and traditional empirical methods of data collection together. Interestingly, she argues that a major finding of the study was how much similarity was documented between radical or deconstructive pedagogy and mainstream pedagogy (p. 6).

The Individual as (Multiple) Subject

In their interrogation of schooling as a set of technologies for producing a new type of citizen, Foucauldian educational writers brought a new language system into play. It is a language that refuses and unsettles old orthodoxies, including both a dominant order of scientific or instrumentalist practice, and a reconceptualist order informed by neo-Marxist and other politically and economically oriented scholarship (including feminism, psychoanalysis, phenomenology, hermeneutics, and historical discussions of the field of curriculum). The new language seemed to serve the documentation of minutiae of practice better than the master narratives of the Freirean or Deweyan sort. As a set of vocabularies for articulating practice, the new language attempted to avoid common binary formulations that characterize both mainstream and radical texts as humanist projects—individual-society, cognitive-affective, agency-structure, center-margin, public-private and so on. The point of such avoidance, as feminists like Patti Lather saw it, was to unfix those categories of difference that define women and others by their difference from the Anglo, masculine, heterosexist norm:

> Philosophically speaking, the essence of the postmodern argument is that dualisms which continue to dominate Western thought are inadequate for understanding a world of multiple causes and effects interacting in complex and nonlinear ways, all of which are rooted in a limitless array of historical and cultural specificities. (Lather, 1991c, p. 21)

Rather than totalize difference as a special social or educational category, the imperative here was to invite the proliferation of difference, insisting that historically produced human complexity would always defy neat categorization. Simply put, difference will always leak.

To contend with this leakage of modernist categories of difference, poststructuralist researchers preferred to speak of human beings as subjects rather than individuals. Henriques, Holloway, Urwin, Venn, and Walkerdine's *Changing the Subject: Psychology, Social Regulation, and Subjectivity* (1984) was one of the first feminist collections to flag the significance of these shifts for social scientific research. In this collection, a number of feminist social analysts challenged the individual-society binary generated out of psychology-sociology debates in the 1960s and 1970s for its failure to address the socially produced individual (pp. 4–5). They asserted that, despite radical critiques, notions of the human constructed in empirical-behaviorist psychology have congealed into liberal intransigence, with the value of individualism becoming the norm.

> The force of humanist psychology (and social science) is increasingly tied to an insecure claim about who can best defend the interests of the individual . . . individualism is both the theoretical Achilles heel of humanist psychology and the crucial condition for the insertion of its discourse in the practices which produce the existing state of affairs. (p. 12)

When the individual is privileged as the focus of various organizational activities, they argue, the social and power relations of institutions within which people function are ignored. In this way the individual of psychology and the individualization of industry establish and maintain a system of mutual support (p. 56).

In education, this system could be seen to be maintained in part through the dominance of behaviorism in the process-product curriculum research of the 1970s. As such, behaviorism was the bête noire of liberationists who reject its simplistic understandings of the nature of teacher work and, hence, its appropriateness for programs of teacher preparation. Yet, the argument was not simply with behaviorism. It was also with an educational system that was maintained, according to Grumet (1989), through the successful pairing of behaviorism with the romanticism of a humanistic psychological tradition in which a collective political will is marginalized. For Grumet, accountability, the ideology of collective responsibility implicit in the behavioral objectives of competency-based teacher education programs, was complemented by humanistic psychology's romantic conception of individual expression and creativity, the ideology of individual responsibility. These discursive elements,

in combination, she argued, denied teachers an understanding of the political nature of their work and, in turn, contributed to the professional disempowerment of teachers (Grumet, 1989, p. 13). The 1980s box office success of two classroom-focused American films, *Stand and Deliver* in 1988 (Musca & Menendez, 1988) and *Dead Poets' Society* in 1989 (Haft & Weir, 1989), in which a male teacher is triumphant, transformative, and heroic despite the obstacles of poverty or tradition, is testimony to the power of this individualizing and romantic imperative to account for pedagogical success in the popular imagination at that time.

While poststructuralists have embraced the structuralist concern to avoid romanticizing or pathologizing accounts of the individual, they have refused the reconstructionist formulae for correcting the individualizing imperative, rejecting the idea that society can be transformed without a recognition of the place and importance of changing subjects in relation to that social transformation (Henriques, Holloway, Urwin, Venn, & Walkerdine, 1984, p. 91). The starting point for poststructuralists has been at understanding and transforming subjectivity, giving privilege to neither society nor individual as a starting point. What matters is how a human being turns him or herself into a subject (Foucault, 1988). By focusing on the discursive technologies at work to produce the self as a social subject, poststructuralist educators sought to highlight the invented nature of the conventions for articulating difference, and so refused the idea of difference as natural or given.

Not all feminist educators have been comfortable with this linguistic turn. The very strangeness of the new dialects continued to be a stumbling block, especially for those for whom cognitive science or humanistic psychology had been the conceptual frameworks for interrogating educational practice. Some, however, like Patti Lather (1995) and Deborah Britzman (1995), insisted on the importance of "troubling [the] clarity" (Lather, 1995) of the natural order. However, for most educators, such new vocabularies have been less welcome, producing a proliferation of research dialects from which many have felt estranged. In 1993 Maxine Greene commented on the relatively small and precious world (p. 208) of poststructuralist educational writers. As the decade ends, this continues to be the scenario.

Language Games in Pedagogical Research

Clearly the proliferation of difference in educational research as a landscape of language has been both necessary and problematic. Where mainstream educational psychology has a preference for speaking of teaching and learning, both neo-Marxist and poststructuralist writers have been more likely to use the term pedagogy to describe the totality of classroom events and relationships. Yet, while poststructuralist writers also make use of the term pedagogy in the sense that David Lusted understood it in the mid-1980s, there is a marked difference in the treatment of power relations. For poststructuralists, power is always productive, and this productivity has positive as well as negative effects on persons who are the subjects of and subject to it.

Thus, in place of theories of schooling as social reproduction (e.g., Bowles & Gintis, 1976), poststructuralist analyses of pedagogy have examined classroom events as a set of technologies for the moral training of a new public. Ian Hunter (1988), for example, documents developments in the teaching and learning of English as a form of moral governance, intended to fix a particular difference from both academic and home values in a newly trained rather than traditionally educated citizenship. Such an analysis provides some explanation for the prevalence of and insistence upon the need for a teacher to be personal friend and confidant of students. In keeping with Foucauldian notions of power as productive in both positive and negative ways, Hunter is not explicitly arguing for or against such practices, but merely argues how they do a particular sort of work in the moral training of citizens.

Other very significant movements in educational language occur around the notion of difference. Where mainstream educational psychology continues to speak of the special needs of individuals or even special needs groups, because of sociocultural background or disability, critical pedagogy has spoken of marginal voices that need to be moved to the center (Herrington & Curtis, 1990). Peter McLaren's *Schooling as Ritual Performance* (1989), for example, argues that the concept of voice in critical pedagogy is an important means of contextualizing pedagogy within historical and cultural variables as they interact to make certain conversations possible between teachers and students. Yet, both of the above notions are troubled by recent poststructuralist writing, given the poststructuralist refusal of the idea of a center of practice or power, and the refusal of a stable, rational, unitary self that produces a singular voice or maintains a singular sociocultural position (e.g., Poynton, 1996).

However, poststructuralist literature does share with earlier deconstructive pedagogy the idea that knowledge is produced rather than given as content (Wexler, 1987, pp. 98–120). Consequently, issues of context can no longer be regarded as peripheral to educational research. Instead, they become integral to an emergent focus on multiple realities. As Landon Beyer (1988) describes it, truth becomes supplanted by warranted assertability, knowledge by judgment, and ahistoricism by social and cultural context-valuation (p. 80). This means that both critical pedagogues and poststructuralists frame research as more tentative and more provocative, with the focus shifting from prediction and prescription to disclosure and deconstruction.

Poststructuralist educational research does not proceed from traditional scientific assumptions about the nature of knowledge, including the logic that sets quantitative against qualitative as the either/or of legitimate inquiry. However, the break is not with rationalism, but with the association of what is rational with a configuration of the subject as autonomous, implicitly male, neutral, contextless, and transcendental (Poster, 1989, p. 5). The poststructuralist call for a different relationship of educational research to teaching does not reiterate the progressive call for more qualitative studies, greater eclecticism, or simply for allowing more voices to speak through action research and political advocacy. Instead, the poststructuralist imperative claims to draw attention to how teachers become reinscribed through their practices in the very politics of truth that they might claim to oppose (Gore, 1991, p. 48). It asks about the otherness of the other—how different from any prevailing or

hegemonic notion of difference a human being might understand themselves and others to be.

Carmen Luke's *White Women in Interracial Families: Reflections on Hybridization, Feminine Identities and Racialized Othering* (1995) is an example of such work. Here Luke writes to challenge race-based theories of identity that tend to totalize identity and race as fixed in embodied difference, regardless of whether those differences are theorized on constructivist or essentialist grounds (p. 51).

Postcolonialism and Marginality

The fact that structuralist and poststructuralist critiques of education are not always easily differentiated is evident in the related field of postcolonial educational writing. Here alternative language systems continue to bleed into one another, at the same time producing new critiques of the center, and of each other. The very term postcolonial is suggestive of the way such cross-fertilization produces hybrid bodies of research. This work exists somewhere within and outside of a Marxist concern to question certain processes of history and a poststructuralist agenda that pits itself against all totalizing systems. For postcolonial writers, it is the totalizing system of the massive imperial center (Slemon, 1988, p. 10) that is the object of critique. The way that global, for example, might come to stand for American, or vice versa, is one post-cold war concern that might be labeled postcolonial.

Cameron McCarthy's (1995) reading of postcolonial schooling is a recent exemplar of the hybridization of postcolonial research. In his analysis of the production of adolescent identity in Barbadian public schools, McCarthy notes the ironies, paradoxes, and recuperations that abound as colonizer practices get appropriated and reworked over time in local communities. McCarthy notes that such schooling techniques are paradoxical as cultural markers in the postcolony (p. 344). He argues that specific techniques (such as singing the school song) work as imperfect apparatuses of social normalization (p. 333) rather than as means for directly controlling school populations. While he focuses on techniques such as singing and reciting set pieces of poetry, prose, and drama as effective modes of moral, political, and spiritual inculcation, he also demonstrates that their work is not limited to inculcation.

Given the importance of the mother tongue in colonial cultures, many other postcolonial writers have closely interrogated pedagogical techniques as particular systems of language use in colonial and neocolonial systems of education in recent decades. By the time of the 1963 civil rights march in Washington, some belated attempts had been made in Africa and parts of the British Commonwealth to expand the curriculum of schools and universities to allow local or indigenous content. However, in the growing mood of resistance to the dominant culture as a colonial hangover, critics condemned these moves as token gestures at best. For example, developments relating to the English Department in the Arts Faculty, University of Nairobi were seen as a rather apologetic attempt to smuggle African writing into an English syllabus (Ngugi, 1972). In the same decade, other postcolonial writers like Arun Mukherjee (Canada) (1978) were noting the pervasiveness of Anglocentric assumptions about literary excellence and standards as well as the effects of these in giving privilege to certain systems of language use, and therefore certain social and cultural identities.

In those countries marginalized by 19th-century European imperialism and 20th-century American imperialism, education and the techniques of its enactment in state or missionary, primary, or secondary schools continued to be the massive cannon in the artillery of the empire (Ashcroft, Griffith & Tiffin, 1995, p. 425). Its power is its ability to achieve for the colonizer what Antonio Gramsci (1971) called "domination by consent," the cheap form of social control made available when the newly educated subject is positioned as a part of the continuing imperial apparatus. That is, it is a technique for inviting the colonized to see themselves in a picture of colonization as culturally progressive (e.g., Viswanathan, 1987).

The tenor of such critiques has been taken up again more recently in Peter McLaren's *Postmodernism, Postcolonialism and Pedagogy* (1995), an edited collection that is an illustration of how new and old, modernist and postmodernist educational critiques continue to be reworked, with all of the accommodations and dangerous liaisons that this must involve. Such stitching together of critique as patchwork and pastiche has been in keeping with the agendas of marginal educational scholarship at the end of the millennium.

Impersonalizing Pedagogy

In the 1990s, ex-centric education might have moved away from the evangelistic tone that characterized much of the reconceptualist work of the 1980s, but the move was neither backward nor forward to other certainties. With poststructuralism's insistence that all utopias come wrapped in barbed wire (Hebdige, 1988, p. 196), calls to liberation or transformation in and through the classroom have been met with skepticism from many quarters. There has been a preference for climbing down from the quasi-religious visions of an earlier generation of critique to more moderate estimates of pedagogical possibility, for example, that a teacher might enable rather than transform.

An aspect of this work that is noteworthy is the fact that it often draws for inspiration on work that is outside the disciplines of education altogether. The analyses of teaching that are presented in collections such as *Jane Gallop Seminar Papers* (Matthews, 1994) and *Pedagogy, Technology and the Body* (McWilliam & Taylor, 1996) offer an eclectic range of interpretations of pedagogical work that move in and out of disciplinary boundaries. Where the *Jane Gallop Seminar Papers* draw on literary criticism, psychoanalysis, and philosophy for the conceptual frameworks, evading traditional educational discourses almost entirely, *Pedagogy, Technology and the Body* looks inside and outside the classroom and the discipline of education, turning also to popular media and culture as important sites of pedagogical work. Both collections are interested in pedagogy in terms of the relational but shift the analysis of teacher-student relations by foregrounding the importance of desire and bodies in the classroom.

As part of this posthumanist reconfiguring of the relational in teaching, the place of the personal in pedagogical work has been revisited. *Pedagogy: The Question of Impersonation* (Gallop, 1995) and *Making a Place for Pleasure in Early Childhood*

Education (Tobin, 1997) are two collections in which new interrogations of the personal—whether as politics or as individual growth and development—unsettle the comfort zones of humanistic pedagogy. In the former collection, the Freirean model as the epitome of student-centered teaching is criticized as a fantasy of good teaching (Amirault, 1995, p. 67), particularly when applied to higher education contexts. In the latter, Leavitt and Power (1997) speak of the isolating effects of individualizing pedagogy as a disembodied activity in early childhood education.

So too does the heterosexuality of pedagogical orthodoxy come under scrutiny in both collections. Lesbian and gay analyses have been important in denaturalizing many master (heterosexist) narratives about teaching and learning. Joseph Litvak (1995), for example, argues that the discipline of heterosexuality frames much of what teachers and students perform in classrooms, policing the erotics of the classroom in ways that disallow exploration of alternatives to sexual harassment and melancholic heterosexuality (p. 26). Gail Boldt (1997) and Jonathan Silin (1997) both point to silences about the place of sexuality in the early childhood classroom, including the way idealized gender norms work to frame the natural identity of young children.

Importantly, this new wave of pedagogical analyses struggles with the issue of difference as *alterity,* which means "a confrontation with the incommensurability of that which cannot be reduced to a version of oneself" (Simon, 1995, p. 90). Roger Simon speaks of the classroom as a place of meeting and pedagogy as an act of provocation, in which the teacher must come face to face with difference. His concern is to challenge the human tendency to reduce the other to the same by insisting that teachers face an other, to "refract categories of difference, rather than confirm them" (p. 92). This sort of politicizing of the pedagogical relationship lurks around the relational, the intimate, the sexual—the erotics of education—and, as such, it is another departure from rational, disembodied readings of pedagogical work.

In recent pedagogical rethinking, the personal is interrogated as both a troubling aspect of pedagogy and as a relation suppressed in the interests of preserving notions of pedagogical objectivity (Frank, 1995; hooks, 1993; Simon 1995). Ambivalence about the personal or autobiographical has become a meeting point of psychoanalytic feminism and radical feminist analyses of curriculum and pedagogy. Madeleine Grumet (1995), whose credentials as a curriculum theorist are well established, argues: "[t]he personal is a performance, an appearance contrived for the public, . . . these masks enable us to perform the play of pedagogy" (p. 37).

Far from denigrating the pedagogical masks of teacher and learner as superficial and unauthentic, Grumet and others are now questioning the value of this very reality-contrivance distinction in teaching. In fragmenting such distinctions she and other such writers (e.g., Gunew & Yeatman, 1993) fragment the very politics of difference itself. It is no longer necessary or desirable to project the burden of authenticity onto the minority (Gunew & Yeatman, 1993, p. xvii), nor the burden of more authentic practice onto the feminist or the progressive teacher. There is more telling work to do.

Conclusion

In speaking of pedagogical work as a contrivance, Grumet fingers the lack of innocence of pedagogical work. We too would want to signal that this piece of writing, as pedagogical work, is not innocent. It is, as all other stories told in this fourth handbook, a contrivance and an exercise in seduction.

We have invented categories for elaborating education as a field of pedagogical possibility in the last few decades of the millennium—"The First Handbook of Research on Teaching," "Telling it like it is," "Saying it Otherwise," "The Otherness of the Other." These inventions are both useful and problematic as textual technologies; they permit some forms of knowledge and leave out others.

They have permitted an interrogation of some core assumptions in the first handbook about the nature of teaching and the sort of scientific inquiry that ought to be pursued to augment, enhance, and even overturn such knowledge. They have allowed documentation of the impetus to realism that characterized some of the bottom-up pedagogical writing of the 1960s and early 1970s. They have worked to illustrate the links forged from the 1960s onward between institutionalized education on the one hand and a macropolitical climate of resistance and civil disobedience in the name of social justice on the other. They have struggled to articulate the splintering and unruly terrain of ideas that inform a contemporary educational understandings of difference and marginality.

However, in doing this work they have also disallowed much in the way of relevant discussions of education in the margins. They have abetted us in producing a text that perhaps accords more educational significance to events in the year 1963 than may be wise or prudent. Moreover, our fictive categories are by now well on the way to becoming fixed categories in a process that we no longer control. Perhaps in getting such a chapter written we cannot hope to get it right. Condemned as we authors are to the constraints of time and space, our text is merely one reading, not the ultimate reading, of marginal educational research as a diaspora of the last 3 decades.

REFERENCES

Acker, S. (1987). Feminist theory and the study of gender and education. *International Review of Education, 33*(4), 419–435.

Adelman, C. (1989). The practicality ethic takes priority over methodology. In W. Carr (Ed.), *Quality in teaching: Arguments for a reflective profession* (pp. 173–182). London: Falmer Press.

Aitken, M., Bennett, S. N., & Hesketh, J. (1981). Teaching styles and pupil progress: A re-analysis. *British Journal of Educational Psychology, 51,* 170–186.

Althusser, L. (1971). Ideology and state apparatuses. In *Lenin and philosophy and other essays* (B. Brewster, Trans.) (pp. 121–173). London: New Left Books.

American Psychological Association, American Educational Research Association, and National Council on Measurement in Education. (1974). *Standards for educational and psychological tests.* Washington, DC: American Psychological Association.

Amirault, C. (1995). The good teacher, the good student: Identifications of a student teacher. In J. Gallop (Ed.), *Pedagogy: The question of impersonation* (pp. 64–78). Bloomington and Indianapolis, IN: Indiana University Press.

Anyon, J. (1983). Intersections of gender and class: Accommodation and resistance by working-class and affluent females to contradictory sex ideologies. In S. Walker & L. Barton (Eds.), *Gender, class, and education* (pp. 132–148). Sussex, England: Falmer Press.

Apple, M. (1979). *Ideology and curriculum.* New York: Routledge and Kegan Paul.

Apple, M. (1982a). *Cultural and economic reproduction in education.* Boston and London: Routledge and Kegan Paul.

Apple, M. (1982b). *Education and power.* Boston and London: Routledge and Kegan Paul.

Apple, M. (1986). *Teachers and texts: A political economy of class and gender relations in education.* New York: Routledge and Kegan Paul.

Armytage, W. H. G. (1975). Psychoanalysis and teacher education II. *British Journal of Teacher Education, 1,* 317–334.

Aronowitz, S., & Giroux, H. (1985). *Education under siege.* South Hadley, MA: Bergin and Garvey.

Ashcroft, B., Griffith, G., & Tiffin, H. (Eds.), (1995). *The post-colonial studies reader.* London: Routledge.

Baker, K. M. (1975). *Condorcet: From natural philosophy to social mathematics.* Chicago: University of Chicago Press.

Barone, T. (1987). Educational platforms, teacher selection, and school reform: Issues emanating from a biographical case study. *Journal of Teacher Education, 38*(2), 12–17.

Bartlett, L. (1987). *In the beginning: Text, context, and pupil attention.* Unpublished doctoral dissertation, University of Queensland, Brisbane, Australia.

Bates, R. (1983). Educational administration and cultural transmission. In R. Browne & L. Foster (Eds.), *Sociology of education* (pp. 73–82). Melbourne, Australia: Macmillan.

Bennett, S. N. (1976). *Teaching styles and pupil progress.* London: Open Books.

Bernstein, B. (1971). On the classification and framing of educational knowledge. In M.F.D. Young (Ed.), *Knowledge and control: New directions for the sociology of knowledge* (pp. 47–69). London: Collier-Macmillan.

Bernstein, B. (1975). *Class, codes, and control: Towards a theory of educational transmission.* London: Routledge and Kegan Paul.

Beyer, L. (1988). *Knowing and acting: Inquiry, ideology, and educational studies.* London: Falmer Press.

Biesta, G. J. J. (1997, March). *George Herbert Mead's lectures on philosophy of education in the University of Chicago (1910–1911).* Presented at the annual meeting of the American Educational Research Association, Chicago, IL.

Blishen, E. (1955). *Roaring boys: A schoolmaster's agony.* London: Thames & Hudson.

Boldt, G. (1997). Sexist and heterosexist responses to gender bending. In J. Tobin (Ed.), *Making a place for pleasure in early childhood education* (pp. 188–213). New Haven, CT, and London: Yale University Press.

Bourdieu, P. (1980). *Questions de sociologie.* Paris: Minuit.

Bourdieu, P., & Passeron, J. (1977). *Reproduction in education, society, and culture.* London and Beverly Hills, CA: Sage.

Bourdieu, P., Passeron, J.-C., & Martin, M. de St. (1994). *Academic discourse: Linguistic misunderstanding and professorial power* (R. Teese, Trans.). Cambridge, UK: Polity Press.

Bourne, P., Masters, P., Amin, N., Gonick, M., & Gribowski, L. (Eds.). (1994). *Feminism in education.* Toronto, Canada: Centre for Women's Studies in Education.

Bowles, S., & Gintis, H. (1976). *Schooling in capitalist America.* New York: Basic Books.

Box, J. F. (1978). *R. A. Fisher: The life of a scientist.* New York: Wiley.

Braithwaite, E .R. (1959). *To sir, with love: Reminiscences of a Negro teacher in London.* London: Bodley Head.

Brent, L., & Hodges, R. (1988, February). *Pre-service teacher education: Research on the application of the scientist-practitioner model in an undergraduate program.* Presented at the annual meeting of the American Association of Colleges for Teacher Education, New Orleans, LA.

Britzman, D. (1991). *Practice makes practice.* Albany, NY: State University of New York Press.

Britzman, D. (1995). Is there a queer pedagogy? Or stop reading straight. *Educational Theory, 45*(2), 151–165.

Brodbeck, M. (1963). Logic and scientific method in research on teaching. In N. L. Gage (Ed.), *Handbook of research on teaching* (pp. 44–93). Chicago: Rand McNally.

Broudy, H. (1963). Historic exemplars of teaching method. In N. L. Gage (Ed.), *Handbook of research on teaching* (pp. 1–43). Chicago: Rand McNally.

Bruner, J. S. (1960). *The process of education.* Cambridge, MA: Harvard University Press.

Buckingham, B. (1926). *Research for teachers.* New York: Silver, Burdett.

Butler, J. (1990). *Gender trouble: Feminism and subversion.* New York and London: Routledge.

Campbell, D. T. (1978). Qualitative knowing in action research. In M. Brenner, P. Marsh, & M. Brenner (Eds.), *The social contexts of research* (pp. 184–209). London: Croom Helm.

Campbell, D. T. (1988). *Methodology and epistemology for social science: Selected papers* (E.S. Overman, Ed.). Chicago: University of Chicago Press.

Campbell, D. T., Riecken, H. W., Boruch, R. F., Caplan, N., Glennan, T. K., Pratt, J., Rees, A., & Williams, W. (1974). Quasi-experimental designs. In H. W. Riecken & R. F. Boruch (Eds.), *Social experimentation: A method for planning and evaluating social intervention* (pp. 87–116). New York: Academic Press.

Campbell, D. T., & Stanley, J. C. (1963). Experimental and quasi-experimental designs for research on teaching. In N. L. Gage (Ed.), *Handbook of research on teaching* (pp. 171–246). Chicago: Rand McNally.

Carr, W., & Kemmis, S. (1986). *Becoming critical: Education, knowledge, and action research.* London: Falmer Press.

Conant, J. B. (1961). *Slums and suburbs.* New York: McGraw-Hill.

Connell, R. W. (1995). *Masculinities.* Sydney, Australia: Allen & Unwin.

Connell, R. W., Ashenden, D. J., Kessler, S., & Dowsett, G. W. (1982). *Making the difference: Schools, families, and social division.* Sydney, Australia: Allen & Unwin.

Corey, S. (1953). *Action research to improve school practices.* New York: Teachers College Press.

Cornell, D., & Thurschwell, A. (1987). Feminism, negativity, intersubjectivity. In S. Benhabib & D. Cornell (Eds.), *Feminism as critique* (pp. 143–162). Minneapolis, MN: University of Minnesota Press.

Croall, J. (1983). *Neill of Summerhill: Permanent rebel.* London: Routledge.

Cronbach, L. (1957). The two disciplines of scientific psychology. *American Psychologist, 12,* 671–684.

Cronbach, L. J. (1975). Beyond the two disciplines of scientific psychology. *American Psychologist, 30,* 116–127.

Culley, M., Diamond, A., Edwards, L., Lennox, S., & Portuges, C. (1985). The politics of nurturance. In M. Culley & C. Portuges (Eds.), *Gendered subjects: The dynamics of feminist teaching* (pp. 11–20). New York: Routledge.

Culley, M., & Portuges, C. (Eds.). (1985). *Gendered subjects: The dynamics of feminist teaching.* New York: Routledge.

Dale, R. (1977). *The structural context of teaching.* Milton Keynes, UK: Open University Press.

Dale, R. (1981). Education and the capitalist: Contributions and contradictions. In M. Apple (Ed.), *Cultural and economic reproduction in education* (pp. 24–41). London: Routledge and Kegan Paul.

Dalton, M. M. (1995). The Hollywood curriculum: Who is the "good" teacher? *Curriculum Studies, 3*(1), 23–44.

Darling-Hammond, L. (1996). The right to learn and the advancement of teaching: Research, policy, and practice for democratic education. *Educational Researcher, 25*(6), 5–17.

Denzin, N. K., & Guba, Y. S. (1994). *Handbook of qualitative research.* Thousand Oaks, CA: Sage.

Derrida, J. (1970). Structure, sign, and play in the discourse of the human sciences. In R. Macksey & E. Donato (Eds.), *The language of criticism and the sciences of man: The structuralist controversy.* Baltimore: Johns Hopkins University Press.

Descartes, R. (1968). *Discourse on method and the meditations.* Harmondsworth, UK: Penguin.

Dreeben, R. (1968). *On what is learned in school.* London: Addison Wesley.

Duckworth, E. (1986). Teaching as research. *Harvard Educational Review, 56,* 481–495.

Dunkin, M., & Biddle, B. (1974). *The study of teaching.* New York: Holt, Rinehart and Winston.

Elliot, J. (1988). Educational research and outsider-insider relations. *International Journal of Qualitative Studies in Education, 1*(2), 54–62.

Ellsworth, E. (1989).Why doesn't this feel empowering: Working through the repressive myths of critical pedagogy. *Harvard Educational Review, 59*(3), 297–324. Erikson, E. H. (1963). *Childhood and society* (2nd. ed.). New York: Norton.

Ermath, M. (1978). *Wilhelm Dilthey: The critique of historical reason.* Chicago: University of Chicago Press.

Evertson, C. (1987). Creating conditions for learning: From research to practice. *Theory into Practice, 26*(1), 44–50.

Fanon, F. (1967, originally published in 1952). *Black skin, white masks* (C. L. Markmann, Trans.). New York: Grove Press.

Fisher, R. A. (1949). *The design of experiments* (5th ed.). Edinburgh, Scotland: Oliver & Boyd.

Foucault, M. (1972). *The archeology of knowledge.* London: Tavistock.

Foucault, M. (1978). *The history of sexuality, vol. 1.* New York: Pantheon.

Foucault, M. (1980). *Power/knowledge: Selected interviews and other writings 1972–1977.* New York: Pantheon.

Foucault, M. (1982). Afterword: The subject and power. In H. Dreyfus & P. Rabinow (Eds.), *Michel Foucault: Beyond structuralism and hermeneutics* (pp. 208–228). Brighton, England: Harvester Press.

Foucault, M. (1988). Technologies of the self. In L. Martin, H. Gutman, & P. Hutton (Eds.), *Technologies of the self: A seminar with Michel Foucault* (pp. 1–49). Amherst, MA: University of Massachusetts Press.

Frank, A. W. (1995). Lecturing and transference: The undercover work of pedagogy. In J. Gallop (Ed.), *Pedagogy: The question of impersonation* (pp. 28–35). Bloomington and Indianapolis, IN: Indiana University Press.

Freire, P. (1970). Cultural action and conscientization. *Harvard Educational Review, 40,* 452–477.

Freire, P. (1971). *Pedagogy of the oppressed* (M. B. Ramos, Trans.). Harmondsworth, UK: Penguin.

Freire, P. (1987). *The politics of education: Culture, power and liberation.* South Hadley, MA: Bergin and Garvey.

Friedan, B. (1965). *The feminine mystique.* Harmondsworth, UK: Penguin. (Original work published 1963).

Friedan, B. (1981). *The second stage.* New York: Summit Books.

Friedman, S. S. (1985). Authority in the feminist classroom: A contradiction in terms? In M. Culley & C. Portuges. (Eds.), *Gendered subjects: The dynamics of feminist teaching* (pp. 203–208). New York: Routledge.

Gage, N. L. (Ed.). (1963a). *Handbook of research on teaching.* Chicago: Rand McNally.

Gage, N. L. (1963b). Paradigms for research on teaching. In N. L. Gage (Ed.), *Handbook of research on teaching* (pp. 94–140). Chicago: Rand McNally.

Gage, N. L. (1978). *The scientific basis of the art of teaching.* New York: Teachers College Press.

Gage. N. L. (1989). The paradigm wars and the aftermath. *Teachers College Record, 91,* 135–50.

Gage, N. L. (1996). Confronting counsels of despair for the behavioral sciences. *Educational Researcher, 25*(3), 5–15.

Gallop, J. (Ed.). (1995). *Pedagogy: The question of impersonation.* Bloomington and Indianapolis, IN: Indiana University Press.

Giroux, H. (1983). *Theory and resistance in education.* South Hadley, MA: Bergin and Garvey.

Giroux, H. & McLaren, P. (1986). Teacher education and the politics of engagement: The case for democratic schooling. *Harvard Educational Review, 56,* 213–238.

Gore, J. (1987). Reflecting on reflective teaching. *Journal of Teacher Education, 38*(2), 33–39.

Gore, J. (1991). On silent regulation: Emancipatory action research in preservice teacher education. *Curriculum Perspectives, 11*(4), 47–51.

Gore, J. (1993). *The struggle for pedagogies: Critical and feminist discourses as regimes of truth.* New York: Routledge.

Gore, J. (1997). On the use of empirical research for the development of a theory of pedagogy. *Cambridge Journal of Education, 27*(2), 211–221.

Gramsci, A. (1971). *Selections from the prison notebooks of Antonio Gramsci* (Q. Hoare & G. Nowell Smith, Eds.). London: Lawrence and Wishart.

Green, J. (1983). Research on teaching as a linguistic process: A state of the art. In E. Gordon (Ed.), *Review of Research in Education, 10* (pp. 151–252). Washington, DC: American Educational Research Association.

Green, J., & Harker, J. (1982). Gaining access to learning: Conversational, social and cognitive demands of group participation. In L. Wilkinson (Ed.), *Communicating in the classroom* (pp. 183–221). New York: Academic Press.

Greene, M. (1986). Reflection and passion in teaching. *Journal of Curriculum and Supervision, 2,* Fall, 68–81.

Greene, M. (1993). Reflections on postmodernism and education. *Educational Policy, 7*(2), 206–211.

Greene, M. (1996, April). *The shudders of identity.* Willystine Goodsell Address to Research on Women in Education, annual meeting of American Educational Research Association, New York, NY.

Grosz, E. (1990). Contemporary theories of power and subjectivity. In S. Gunew (Ed.), *Feminist knowledge: Critique and construct* (pp. 59–120). London: Routledge.

Grumet, M. (1988). *Bitter milk: Women and teaching.* Amherst, MA: University of Massachusetts.

Grumet, M. (1989). Generations: Reconceptualist curriculum theory and teacher education. *Journal of Teacher Education, 40*(1), 13–17.

Grumet, M. (1995). Scholae personae: Masks for meaning. In J. Gallop (Ed.), *Pedagogy: The question of impersonation* (pp. 36–45). Bloomington and Indianapolis, IN: Indiana University Press.

Grundy, S. (1989). Beyond professionalism. In W. Carr (Ed.), *Quality in teaching: Arguments for a reflective profession* (pp. 79–100). London: Falmer Press.

Gunew, S., & Yeatman, A. (Eds.). (1993). *Feminism and the politics of difference.* Sydney, Australia: Allen & Unwin.

Guy-Sheftall, B. (Ed.). (1995). *Words of fire: An anthology of African-American feminist thought.* New York: New Press.

Habermas, J. (1971). *Toward a rational society.* London: Heinemann.

Hacking, I. (1990). *The taming of chance.* Cambridge, UK: Cambridge University Press.

Haft, S. (Producer), & Weir, P. (Director). (1989). *Dead poets' society* [Feature film]. Warner/Touchstone/Silver Screen.

Halliwell, L. (1993). *Halliwell's film guide* (9th ed.). London: Harper Collins.

Hargreaves, A. (1978). The significance of classroom coping strategies. In L. Barton and R. Meighan (Eds.), *Sociological interpretations of schooling and classrooms: A reappraisal* (pp. 73–100). Driffield, UK: Nafferton.

Hebdige, D. (1988). *Hiding in the light: On images and things.* New York: Routledge and Kegan Paul.

Henderson, J. (1988). A Curriculum response to the knowledge base reform movement. *Journal of Teacher Education, 39*(5), 13–17.

Henriques, J., Holloway, W., Urwin, C., Venn, C., & Walkerdine, V. (Eds.). (1984). *Changing the subject: Psychology, social regulation, and subjectivity.* London and New York: Methuen.

Henry, M., Knight, J., Lingard, R., & Taylor, S. (Eds.). (1988). *Understanding schooling: An introduction to the sociology of Australian education.* Sydney, Australia, and London: Routledge.

Herndon, J. (1969). *The way it spozed to be: A report on the classroom war behind the crisis in our schools.* New York: Bantam Books. (Original work published 1968)

Herrington, A., & Curtis, M. (1990). Teachers and teaching: Basic writing: Moving the voices on the margin to the center. *Harvard Educational Review, 60*(4), 489–496.

Higgins, K. (1982). Making it in your own world: Women's studies in Freire. *Women's Studies International Forum, 5*(1), 87–98.

Holt, J. (1964). *How children fail.* New York: Pitman.

hooks, b. (1982). *Ain't I a woman: Black women and feminism.* Boston: South End Press (citations taken from the parallel edition published by Pluto Press, London).

hooks, b. (1984). *Feminist theory: From margin to center.* Boston: South End Press.

hooks, b. (1993). Eros, eroticism, and the pedagogical process. *Journal of Cultural Studies, 7*(1), 58–63.

Horkheimer, M., & Adomo, T. W. (1972). *Dialectic of enlightenment.* New York: Herder and Herder.

Hunter, E. (1954). *The blackboard jungle.* New York: Simon & Schuster.

Hunter, I. (1988). *Culture and government: The emergence of literary education.* London: Macmillan.

Hunter, I. (1994). *Rethinking the school: Subjectivity, bureaucracy, criticism.* St. Leonards, New South Wales, Australia: Allen & Unwin.

Hunter, I. (1995). Armed pluralism (response to critics). *Discourse: Studies in the Cultural Politics of Education, 16,* 437–441.

Illich, I. (1971). *Deschooling society.* New York: Harper & Row.

Jackson, P. W. (1968). *Life in classrooms.* New York: Holt, Rinehart and Winston.

Jay, M. (1988). *Fin-de-siecle socialism and other essays.* New York: Routledge and Kegan Paul.

Jencks, C. (1979). *Who gets ahead?* New York: Basic Books.

Kant, I. (1793). *The critique of pure reason.* London: Dent. (Original work published 1781).

Karier, C. J., Violas, P., & Spring, J. (Eds.). (1973). *Roots of crisis: American education in the twentieth century.* Chicago: Rand McNally.

Kaufman, B. (1964). *Up the down staircase.* Englewood Cliffs, NJ: Prentice-Hall.

Kemmis, S., & McTaggart, R. (1988). *The action research planner* (3rd ed.). Geelong, Victoria, Australia: Deakin University Press.

Kincheloe, J. (1989). *Getting beyond the facts: Teaching social studies in the late twentieth century.* New York: Lang.

Kirk, D. (1998). *Schooling bodies: School practice and public discourse, 1880–1940.* Leicester, UK: University of Leicester.

Kohl, H. (1965). *The age of complexity.* New York: Mentor Books.

Kohl, H. (1976). *36 children.* Harmondsworth, UK: Penguin.

Kozol, J. (1967). *Death at an early age: The destruction of the hearts and minds of Negro children in the Boston public schools.* New York: Houghton Mifflin (quotations taken from the English published by Penguin, 1968).

Kuhn, T. S. (1962). *The structure of scientific revolutions.* Chicago: University of Chicago Press.

Lather, P. (1991a). *Getting smart: Feminist research and pedagogy with/in the postmodern.* New York: Routledge.

Lather, P. (1991b). Deconstructing/deconstructive inquiry: The politics of knowing and being known. *Educational Theory, 41*(2), 153–173.

Lather, P. (1991c). *Feminist research in education: Within/against.* Geelong, Victoria, Australia: Deakin University Press.

Lather, P. (1995, April). *Troubling clarity: The politics of accessible language.* Paper presented at the annual meeting of the American Educational Research Association, San Francisco, CA.

Leavitt, R. L., & Power, M. B. (1997). Civilizing bodies: Children in day care. In J. Tobin (Ed.), *Making a place for pleasure in early childhood education* (pp. 39–75). New Haven, CT, and London: Yale University Press.

Lesko, N. (1988). *Symbolizing society: Stories, rites, and structure in a Catholic high school.* New York: Falmer Press.

Lewin, K. (1946). Action research and minority problems. *Journal of Social Issues, 2,* 34–46.

Lewis, M. (1990). Interrupting patriarchy: Politics, resistance, and transformation in the feminist classroom. *Harvard Educational Review, 60*(4), 467–489.

Lippett, R., & White, R. K. (1958). An experimental study of leadership and group life. In E. E. Maccoby, T. M. Newcomb, & E. L. Hartley (Eds.), *Readings in Social Psychology.* Eastbourne, UK: Holt, Rinehart and Winston.

Litvak, J. (1995). Discipline, spectacle, and melancholia in and around the gay studies classroom. In J. Gallop (Ed.), *Pedagogy: The question of impersonation* (pp. 19–27). Bloomington and Indianapolis, IN: Indiana University Press.

Luke, C. (1995). White women in interracial families: Reflections on hybridization, feminine identities, and racialized othering. *Feminist Issues, 14*(2), 49–72.

Luke, C., & Gore, J. (Eds.). (1992). *Feminisms and critical pedagogy.* New York: Routledge.

Lusted, D. (1986). Why pedagogy? *Screen, 27*(5), 2–14.

Maher, F. A. (1985). Toward a richer theory of feminist pedagogy: A comparison of "liberation" and "gender" models for teaching and learning. *Journal of Education, 169*(3), 91–100.

Maher, F. A., & Tetreault, M. K. T. (Eds.) (1994). *The feminist classroom.* New York: Basic Books.

Marable, M. (1984). *Race, reform and rebellion: The second reconstruction in black America.* Jackson, MS: University Press of Mississippi.

Matthews, J. (Ed.). (1994). *Jane Gallop seminar papers, proceedings of the Jane Gallop seminar and public lecture "the teachers breasts," June 1993.* Canberra, Australia: The Humanities Research Centre.

McCarthy, C. (1995). School music and the production of adolescent identity in the postcolony. *Discourse: Studies in the Cultural Politics of Education, 16*(3), 331–346.

McLaren, P. (1986). *Schooling as a ritual performance.* London: Routledge and Kegan Paul.

McLaren, P. (1988). Language, structure, and the language of subjectivity. *Critical Pedagogy Networker 1*(2, 3), 1–10.

McLaren, P. (1989). *Life in schools.* New York: Longman.

McLaren, P. (Ed.) (1995). *Postmodernism, postcolonialism, and pedagogy.* Albert Park, Australia: James Nicholas.

McLintock, R. (1972). Towards a place for study in a world of instruction. *Teachers College Record, 73,* 161–205.

McTaggart, R. (1991). *Action research: A short modern history.* Geelong, Victoria, Australia: Deakin University Press.

McWilliam, E. (1994). *In broken images: Feminist tales for a different teacher education.* New York: Teachers College Press.

McWilliam, E., & Taylor, P. G. (Eds.). (1996). *Pedagogy, technology, and the body.* New York: Peter Lang.

Mead, M. (1963). *Growing up in New Guinea: A study of adolescence and sex in primitive societies.* Harmondsworth, UK: Penguin. (Original work published 1930).

Meadmore, D., & Symes, C. (1996). Of uniform appearance: A symbol of school discipline and governmentality. *Discourse: Studies in the Cultural Politics of Education, 17*(2), 209–225.

Meredyth, D., & Tyler, D. (Eds.). (1993). *Child and citizen: Genealogies of schooling and subjectivity.* Brisbane, Australia: ICPS.

Messick, S. (1980). Test validity and the ethics of assessment. *American Psychologist, 35,* 1012–1027.

Michel, G. (1978). *Die Welt als Schule: Comenius und die Didaktische Bewegung.* Hannover, Germany: Schroedel.

Miller, S. (1990). Foucault on discourse and power. *Theoria, 76,* 115–125.

Morine-Dershimer, G. (1985). *Talking, listening, and learning in elementary classrooms.* White Plains, NY: Longman.

Mukherjee, A. P. (1978). *The twice-born fiction: Themes and techniques of the Indian novel in English.* Delhi, India, and London: Heinemann.

Musca, T. (Producer), & Menendez, R. (Director). (1988). *Stand and Deliver* [Feature film]. Warner/American Playhouse.

Neill, A. S. (1962). *Summerhill: A radical approach to education.* New York: Hart.

Ngugi, W. T. (1972). *Homecoming: Essays.* London: Heinemann.

Parlett, M. R. (1972). Evaluating innovations in teaching. In H. J. Butcher & E. Rudd (Eds.), *Contemporary problems in research in higher education* (pp. 144–154). London: McGraw-Hill.

Patterson, A. (1993). Personal response and English teaching. In D. Meredith & D. Tyler (Eds.), *Child and citizen: Genealogies of schooling and subjectivity* (61–86). Brisbane, Australia: ICPS.

Pinar, W. F. (Ed.). (1981). *Curriculum theorizing: The reconceptualists.* Berkeley, CA: McCutchan.

Pinar, W. F., Reynolds, W. M., Slattery, P., & Taubman, P. M. (1995). *Understanding curriculum: An introduction to the study of historical and contemporary curriculum discourses.* New York: Lang.

Poster, N. (1989). *Critical theory and poststructuralism: In search of a context.* London: Cornell.

Poynton, C. (1996). Giving voice. In E. McWilliam & P. G. Taylor (Eds.), *Pedagogy, technology, and the body* (pp. 103–112). New York: Peter Lang.

Pusey, M. (1983). The control and rationalisation of schooling. In R. Browne & L. Foster (Eds.), *Sociology of education* (3rd ed.) (pp. 401–409). Melbourne, Australia: Macmillan.

Ramsay, P. D. K. (1975). *The family and the school in New Zealand society.* Melbourne, Australia: Pitman.

Raphael, R. (1985). *The teacher's voice.* Portsmouth, NH: Heinemann.

Ravetz, J. (1971). *Science and its social problems.* New York: Oxford University Press.

Rist, R. C. (1980). Blitzkrieg ethnography: On the transformation of a method into a movement. *Educational Researcher, 9*(2), 8–10.

Rorty, R. (1980). Pragmatism, relativism, and irrationalism. *Proceedings and Addresses of the American Philosophical Association, 53,* 719–738.

Rorty, R. (1982). *The consequences of pragmatism.* Sussex, UK: Harvester Press.

Ross, E., & Hannay, L. (1986). Towards a critical theory of reflective inquiry. *Journal of Teacher Education, 37*(4), 9–15.

Schniedewind, N. (1985). Cooperatively structured learning: Implications for feminist pedagogy. *Journal of Thought: Special Issue: Feminist Education, 20*(3), 65–73.

Schubert, W. (1989). Reconceptualizing and the matter of paradigms. *Journal of Teacher Education, 40*(1), 27–32.

Schwab, J. J. (1978). *Science, curriculum, and liberal education: Selected essays* (I. Westbury & N. Wilkof, Eds.). Chicago: University of Chicago Press.

Schwandt, T. A. (1994). Constructivist, interpretivist approaches to human inquiry. In N. K. Denzin & Y. K. Guba (Eds.), *Handbook of qualitative research* (pp. 118–137). Thousand Oaks, CA: Sage.

Shaker, P., & Kridel, C. (1989). The return to experience: A reconceptualist call. *Journal of Teacher Education, 1*(1), 2–8.

Shor, I. (1987). *Freire for the classroom.* Portsmouth, NH: Boynton and Cook.

Silberman, C. E. (1964). *Crisis in black and white.* New York: Vintage Books.

Silberman, C. E. (1971). *Crisis in the classroom: The remaking of American education.* New York: Vintage Books.

Silin, J. (1997). The pervert in the classroom. In J. Tobin (Ed.), *Making a place for pleasure in early childhood education* (pp. 214–134). New Haven, CT, and London: Yale University Press.

Simon, R. (1995). Face to face with alterity: Postmodern Jewish identity and the Eros of pedagogy. In J. Gallop (Ed.), *Pedagogy: The question of impersonation* (pp. 90–105). Bloomington and Indianapolis, IN: University of Indiana Press.

Slemon, S. (1988). Magic realism as postcolonial discourse. *Canadian Literature, 116,* 9–23.

Smith, L. M., & Geoffrey, W. (1968). *The complexities of an urban classroom: An analysis toward a general theory of teaching.* New York: Holt, Rinehart and Winston.

Smith, L. M., & Hudgins, B. B. (1964). *Educational psychology.* New York: Knopf.

Spindler, G. D. (Ed.). (1955). *Education and anthropology.* Stanford, CA: Stanford University Press.

Spindler, G. D. (1984). Roots revisited: Three decades of perspective. *Anthropology and Education Quarterly, 15,* 3–10.

Spindler, G. D., & Spindler, L. (Eds.). (1987). *Interpretative ethnography: At home and abroad.* Hillsdale, NJ: Lawrence Erlbaum Associates.

Spock, B. M. (1946). *The common sense book of baby and child care.* New York: Duell, Sloan & Pearce.

Spock, B. M., & Huschka, M. (1938). *The psychological aspects of pediatric practice.* New York: State Committee on Mental Hygiene of the State Charities Aid Association.

Stone, M. (1981). The education of the black child. In A. James & R. Jeffcoate (Eds.), *The school in the multicultural society* (pp. 45–57). London: Harper & Row.

Strieb, L. (1985). *A (Philadelphia) teacher's journal.* Grand Forks, ND: North Dakota Study Group on Evaluation.

Suleiman, S. (1986). (Re)writing the Body: The politics and poetics of female eroticism. In S. Suleiman (Ed.), *The female body in western culture* (pp. 7–29). Cambridge, MA: Harvard University Press.

Tobin, J. (Ed.). (1997). *Making a place for pleasure in early childhood.* New Haven, CT, and London: Yale University Press.

Troyna, B., & R. Hatcher (1992). *Racism in children's lives: A study of mainly white primary schools.* London: Routledge.

Tyack, D. (1974). *The one best system: A history of American urban education.* Cambridge, MA: Harvard University Press.

Tyler, D. (1993). Making better children. In D. Meredith & D. Tyler (Eds.), *Child and citizen: Genealogies of schooling and subjectivity* (pp. 35–60). Brisbane, Australia: ICPS.

Viswanathan, G. (1987). The beginnings of English literary study in British India. *Oxford Literary Review, 9*(1–2), 2–26.

Walkerdine, V. (1989). *Counting girls out.* London: Virago.

Walkerdine, V. (1990). *School girl fictions.* London: Verso.

Wallace, M. (1987). A historical review of action research: Some implications for the education of teachers in their managerial role. *Journal of Education for Teaching, 13*(2), 97–115.

Waller, W. (1967). *The sociology of teaching.* New York: Wiley.

Weiler, K. (1991). Freire and a feminist pedagogy of difference. *Harvard Educational Review, 61,* 449–474.

Wexler, P. (1987). *Social analysis of education: After the new sociology.* New York: Routledge.

Whitty, G., & Young, M. F. D. (1976). *Explorations in the politics of school knowledge.* Driffield, UK: Nafferton.

Williams, W. A., McCormick, T., Gardner, L., & Lafeber, W. (1975). *America in Vietnam: A documentary history.* New York: Norton.

Willis, P. (1977). *Learning to labour: How working class kids get working class jobs.* Farnborough, UK: Saxon.

Wills, W. D. (1964). *Homer Lane: A biography.* London: Allen & Unwin.

Woods, P. (1979). *The divided school.* London: Routledge and Kegan Paul.

Young, M. F. D. (Ed.). (1971). *Knowledge and control: New directions for the sociology of knowledge.* London: Collier-Macmillan.

Zeichner, K. (1987). Preparing reflective teachers: An overview of instructional strategies which have been employed in pre-service teacher education. *International Journal of Educational Research, 11*(5), 565–575.

Zeichner, K., & Grant, C. (1981). Biography and social structure in the socialization of student teachers: A re-examination of the pupil control ideologies of student teachers. *Journal of Education for Teaching, 7*(3), 298–314.

Zeichner, K., & Liston, D. (1987). Teaching student teachers to reflect. *Harvard Educational Review, 57,* 23–48.

Foundational Issues and Thinkers in Research on Teaching

3.

"Family Connections" as a Factor in the Development of Research on Teaching

Greta Morine-Dershimer
University of Virginia

Family Connections Analogy

The development of any field of research is heavily influenced by prior research. Publications play an important role, for the methodological design and questions addressed in productive new studies build on earlier studies and reviews of related research. These links are generally made explicit in the articles that report on research. The face-to-face interactions of researchers as they discuss the problems and issues with which they are wrestling also have an important impact on the development of any field of research. These links and relationships are less well known, and are rarely made explicit in publications. This chapter explores some of the ways in which such relationships have influenced the development of the field of research on teaching.

The chapter is based on an analogy which suggests that relationships between and among researchers are like relationships within families. Conventionally, the doctoral advisor is like a parent to graduate students, passing on a particular research tradition, much like family customs or family heirlooms might be passed on to the next generation within a family. Students (children) graduate (reach adulthood) and leave the university (home) to begin their own careers (families), carrying on the handed-down customs, and polishing the heirlooms associated with the research traditions in which they were raised.

New forms of family have sprung up in our society in recent years, and these forms have parallels in new types of relationships between and among researchers. These new types of relationships have contributed to the reshaping of some research traditions and the initiation of some new approaches to research on teaching. An examination of the "family connections" reflected in traditional and newer forms of research relationships can provide an interesting perspective on the role of social interaction in methodological and topical shifts in the recent history of the field of research on teaching. This perspective is developed in a series of cases that exemplify each of several forms of familial-research relationships. The cases were developed through written communications, telephone interviews, and e-mail interchanges with the researchers involved.

It is important to note that it was impossible to include all the people who have contributed important work to the field of research on teaching within the cases investigated for this chapter. The focus here is on the impact that collaborative relationships have had upon recognized developments within the field. Most of the particular developments identified in these cases have been featured in one or more of several relatively recent historical reviews of the field (Brophy, 1989; Gage, 1989; Shulman, 1987, 1992); thus, they have been acknowledged as influential in establishing some critical change in the direction of the research agenda. Critical developments in the field that are generally attributed to an individual or to short-term collaborative efforts rather than to an extended collaborative relationship are not highlighted in the cases presented here. This in no way reflects on the importance of these contributions to the field. Most of the collaborators identified in the cases presented here have worked together over an extended period on a series of studies or publications. They have been associated with one or more of the influential developments in the field, and, in many instances, their work has received some form of recognition or award from AERA. They also illustrate specific types of family connections. In addition to these criteria, cases were selected to provide some geographic and institutional variety. Because of limited time and space, only a few cases could be included in each category of relationship. Failure to include any well-known pair of collabo-

---

The author wishes to thank Carolyn Evertson of Vanderbilt University and Michael Dunkin of University of New South Wales (now retired) for their helpful comments on drafts of the chapter.

rators in no way reflects on the value of their contributions to the field.

The cases included here highlight developments in the field of research on teaching during the quarter century spanning the period from the 1970s to the 1990s. Space limitations precluded full reporting of the individual cases. Instead, the vital statistics for individual cases are presented in a series of tables, organized by category of family relationship, and discussion focuses on patterns and themes derived from cross-case analysis.

Traditional Parent-to-Child Inheritance

The relationship of doctoral advisor to doctoral student in the research universities of the United States is analogous to the relationship of parent to child in most American families. The doctoral advisor structures much of the early learning of the entering graduate student and begins the process of socializing the student into the community of scholars. One critical difference between the two types of relationship should be noted, however. While the infant child has no opportunity to select his or her parent, many doctoral students do consciously select the professors who will serve as their academic mentors. Thus, they can exert some control over the direction of their professional development.

Five cases (see Table 3.1) exemplify the impact of this traditional type of professional relationship on the field of research on teaching. They are organized primarily in chronological sequence, and focus on three different periods of development in the field. Barak Rosenshine was a student of N. L. Gage at Stanford in the 1960s, and Susan Florio-Ruane studied with Courtney Cazden at Harvard in the 1970s, while Sigrun Gudmundsdóttir worked with Lee Shulman at Stanford, and David Hansen worked with Philip Jackson at Chicago in the 1980s. The fifth case illustrates an interesting variation on the traditional pattern. In Adrienne Alton-Lee's work with Graham Nuthall at the University of Canterbury in New Zealand, the mentoring relationship grew into a true collaborative effort extending well beyond the period of graduate study.

Relatives and Family Friends

Several other types of common family relationships are analogous to less common collaborative research relationships which have influenced development of the field of research on teaching. Three of these types of relationships are exemplified here, each illustrated by a single case (see Table 3.2).

THE "DUTCH UNCLE" ROLE

A "Dutch uncle" is typically a family friend, who visits occasionally and displays a particular interest in the children in the household, frequently bringing toys and candy for the youngest and offering friendly advice to adolescents about any problems they may be experiencing. In academic circles, a role similar to that of a Dutch uncle may be played by researchers who generously respond to queries from graduate students who are neither their advisees nor students in their courses. They may provide advice about specific studies to be reviewed or particular methodologies to be investigated. Typically, these interactions

are brief, but, occasionally, the relationship persists over a longer period of time. In the past, as in the family setting, proximity was an important contributor to the establishment of a Dutch uncle relationship between an experienced and a novice researcher, but today such relationships may be readily facilitated by communication on the Internet. The case illustrating this type of relationship involved extensive advice from Ned Flanders on development of the interactive observation system that was used by Jane Stallings in her landmark study of teaching and learning in early childhood programs.

SIBLINGS MODERNIZING THE FAMILY BUSINESS

Recent doctoral graduates who have been prepared in the same institution and whose preparation has placed an emphasis on the same research tradition rarely begin their professorial careers teaching together at a single institution. When such a circumstance occurs, the ensuing professional relationship can be seen as analogous to siblings entering a successful family business. The pair may choose to continue the research tradition (family business) with little change, or they may engage in sibling rivalry and compete with each other to achieve honors and rewards. Successful programs of research probably best maintain their influence and productivity if such heirs to a research tradition support each other professionally in the new setting as they seek to focus their research more sharply on newly emergent issues. When this happens, the professional relationship is analogous to siblings modernizing the family business. The case illustrating this type of relationship involved the work of Ronald Marx and Philip Winne in adding the mediating variable of pupil cognitions to the process-product paradigm.

DISTANT COUSINS

Some interesting cross-national collaborative relationships have occurred in the field of research on teaching, and these are analogous to interactions between distant cousins. Researchers in such relationships might visit each other on occasion, but much of their communication is by mail (now e-mail). These circumstances limit the extent of their collaborative efforts to some degree, but some very productive contributions to the field have resulted from these types of relationships, nonetheless. Australian Michael Dunkin is notable for these types of collaborations, having worked with Bruce Biddle on an early, influential review of research on teaching (Dunkin & Biddle, 1974) and with N. L. Gage on development of an influential international research journal, *Teaching and Teacher Education.* The collaboration of distant cousins illustrated here focuses on Gage's and Dunkin's simultaneous realization that the international scope of the field of research on teaching could be enhanced by creation of such an international journal.

Traditional Marriages

Collaborative research relationships in which the partners have been prepared in different institutions (families) but under similar research traditions (cultures) are analogous to traditional marriages in which the two partners come from similar cultural, socioeconomic, and religious backgrounds and share many

Table 3.1. "Parent-Child" Inheritance

MENTORING PAIRS	PROFESSIONAL PREPARATION	ELEMENTS OF MENTORSHIP	RELATED PUBLICATIONS
N.L. GAGE Purdue University, 1947–48 University of Illinois, 1948–62 Stanford University, 1962–87	Ph.D., Purdue, 1947 MENTORS: Hermann H. Remmers, B.F. Skinner (undergraduate years)	Rosenshine became a research assistant for Gage when the Stanford R&D Center on Teaching was funded. His dissertation was part of the first study for the Center. Gage was on his dissertation committee. Rosenshine's literature review particularly impressed Gage by its thoroughness.	Gage, N.L. (Ed.). (1963) Handbook of research on teaching. Rosenshine, B. (1971) Teaching behaviours and student achievement.
BARAK ROSENSHINE Temple University, 1966–70 University of Illinois at Champaign-Urbana, 1970–94	History teacher, 6 years Ph.D., Stanford, 1967 MENTORS: Robert Bush, Dwight Allen, Fred McDonald, N.L. Gage DISSERTATION: correlational process-product study of teacher effectiveness in explaining during lectures FELLOW PH.D. CANDIDATES: David Berliner, James Cooper, Kevin Ryan	After Rosenshine's graduation, Gage obtained funds through the International Association for the Evaluation of Educational Achievement (IEA) for Rosenshine to review the process-product studies available at the time. Rosenshine became noted for his influential research reviews.	Rosenshine, B., & Furst, N. (1973) The use of direct observation to study teaching. Rosenshine, B., & Stevens, R. (1986) Teaching functions. Gage, N.L. (1989) The paradigm wars and their aftermath: A "historical" sketch of research on teaching since 1989. Rosenshine, B., Meister, C., & Chapman, S. (1996) Teaching students to generate questions: A review of the intervention studies.
COURTNEY CAZDEN Harvard University, 1965–1995	Primary teacher, 9 years Ed.D., Harvard, 1965 MENTOR: Roger Brown	Cazden was Florio-Ruane's advisor for her master's degree, and served on her dissertation committee, chaired by Erickson. A series of informal meetings of key sociolinguistic researchers from Harvard, Rockefeller University, and UC San Diego included Florio-Ruane and other doctoral students. Cazden provided a model of linking research to practice by her year of teaching (1974–75) in San Diego schools with Mehan as observer and research collaborator (Mehan, 1979).	Cazden, C., Johns, V. & Hymes, D. (Eds.). (1972) Functions of language in the classroom. Cazden, C. (1986) Classroom discourse. Florio-Ruane, S. (1987) Sociolinguistics for educational researchers. Florio-Ruane, S. (1990) The written literacy forum: An analysis of teacher–researcher collaboration.
SUSAN FLORIO-RUANE Michigan State University, 1978–present	Middle school teacher, 3 years Ed.D., Harvard, 1978 MENTORS: Frederick Erickson, Courtney Cazden DISSERTATION: ethnographic study on socialization of K-1 students to classroom communication norms FELLOW Ed.D. CANDIDATES: Jeffrey Shultz, Don Dorr-Bremme	Florio-Ruane went on to conduct productive research on writing as a communicative process.	Florio-Ruane, S. (1997) To tell a new story: Reinventing narratives of culture, identity, and education.
LEE SHULMAN Michigan State University, 1963–82 Stanford University, 1982–present	Ph.D., Chicago, 1963 MENTORS: Joseph Schwab, Benjamin Bloom, Frederick Lighthall	Gudmundsdottir was a research assistant in Shulman's Knowledge Growth in Teaching project. Her dissertation was a part of that project; Shulman was dissertation advisor. His view of advising emphasized the value of a community of researchers thinking together, with resulting reciprocal influence. He modeled a process of thinking about research through "thinking aloud" dialogues with the group of research assistants.	Shulman, L.S. (1986) Paradigms and research programs in the study of teaching: A contemporary perspective. Shulman, L.S. (1987) Knowledge and teaching: Foundations of the new reform. Gudmundsdottir, S., & Shulman, L. (1987) Pedagogical content knowledge in social studies.
SIGRUN GUDMUNDSDOTTIR University of Iceland, 1986–89 Norwegian University of Science and Technology, 1989–present	Elementary teacher (Scotland and Iceland), 6 years Ph.D., Stanford, 1988 MENTORS: Lee Shulman, Milbrey McLaughlin, Nel Noddings, Denis Phillips DISSERTATION: ethnographic study on pedagogical content knowledge of experienced secondary teachers FELLOW PH.D. CANDIDATES: Pamela Grossman, Anna Richert, Suzanne Wilson, Samuel Wineburg	Gudmundsdottir extended the concept of pedagogical content knowledge to emphasize its narrative quality. In Norway she found a common interest with the classical German "didaktikk" specialists.	Gudmundsdottir, S. (1991) Ways of seeing are ways of knowing: The pedagogical content knowledge of an expert teacher. Gudmundsdottir, S. (1995) The narrative nature of pedagogical content knowledge.

Table 3.1. (continued)

MENTORING PAIRS	PROFESSIONAL PREPARATION	ELEMENTS OF MENTORSHIP	RELATED PUBLICATIONS
PHILIP JACKSON Wayne State University, 1954–55 University of Chicago, 1955–1998 DAVID HANSEN University of Illinois at Chicago, 1990–present	Ph.D., Columbia University, 1954 MENTORS: Arthur T. Jersild, Irving Lorge, Millie Almy, Arthur I. Gates Secondary history teacher, 1 yr; Peace corps teacher, 2 yrs.; Great Books Foundation staff development, 4 yrs. Ph.D., University of Chicago, 1990 MENTORS: Philip Jackson, Sophie Haroutunian-Gordon, Robin Lovin, Rick Shweder DISSERTATION: "philosophical ethnography" of the moral significance of everyday classroom practice FELLOW PH.D. CANDIDATES: Rene Arcilla, Karen Alston, Robert Boostrom, Steven Jones, Jerry Pillsbury	Hansen was a research assistant on Jackson's Moral Life of Schools project, a 3–4 year collaborative effort of researchers and teachers. His dissertation grew out of the project and Jackson was his dissertation advisor. Their work together focused on "finding a language" to talk about the moral dimensions of teaching. Jackson's early work was in educational psychology, and Hansen's in social science, but both came to use ethnographic approaches for observation in classrooms, and philosophical approaches for analysis of classroom data. They share a love of poetry, and a conception of writing as a craft. These interests serve to make finding a language "a permanent challenge." Hansen continues to write about teaching as a moral practice, and has extended the work to include teaching as a calling.	Jackson, P.W. (1968) Life in classrooms. Jackson, P.W. (1992) Untaught lessons. Boostrom, R.E., Hansen, D.T., & Jackson, P.W. (1993) Coming together and staying apart: How a group of teachers and researchers sought to bridge the "research/practice" gap. Jackson, P.W., Boostrom, R., & Hansen, D.T. (1993) The moral life of schools. Hansen, D.T. (1993) From role to person: The moral layeredness of classroom teaching. Hansen, D.T. (1995) The call to teach. Hansen, D.T. (1996) In class with Philip W. Jackson.
GRAHAM NUTHALL University of Canterbury, Christchurch, NZ, 1966–2001 ADRIENNE ALTON-LEE University of Canterbury, 1984–93 Victoria University at Wellington, 1993–1999 New Zealand Ministry of Education, 2000–present	Ph.D., Illinois, 1966 MENTOR: B. Othanel Smith Primary teacher, 3 years Ph.D., University of Canterbury, 1984 MENTOR: Graham Nuthall DISSERTATION: case studies of pupils' experiences with content in relation to short- and long-term learning	Nuthall was the dissertation advisor for Alton-Lee. He initiated her into a research tradition of classroom observation. She introduced him to an approach that was unusual at the time (small sample of participants, in-depth data collection, consideration of cognitive learning in a social and cultural context). Following the dissertation study, Nuthall advised that replication was needed before serious publication. The two then collaborated as equals on a series of follow-up studies, alternating leadership according to tasks and interests: Alton-Lee, emphasis on case studies and gender analysis; Nuthall, amalgamating and predicting from case data, relating the work to learning theory and prior research on teaching.	Nuthall, G., & Church, J. (1973) Experimental studies of teaching behaviour. Alton-Lee, A.G., Densem, P.A., & Nuthall, G.A. (1991) Imperatives of classroom research: Understanding what children learn about gender and race. Alton-Lee, A.G., & Nuthall, G.A. (1992) A generative methodology for classroom research. Nuthall, G.A., & Alton-Lee, A.G. (1992) Understanding how students learn in classrooms.

Table 3.2. "Relatives and Family Friends"

COLLABORATORS	PROFESSIONAL PREPARATION	COLLABORATIVE WORK	RELATED PUBLICATIONS
NED FLANDERS University of Minnesota, 1949–61 University of Michigan, 61–69 Far West Laboratory for Educational Research and Development, 1970–75	Ph.D., Chicago, 1949 MENTOR: Herbert Thelen DISSERTATION: laboratory study of anxiety during learning in two "social climates," (responsive vs. dominant teacher) FELLOW PH.D. CANDIDATES: John Goodlad, David Krathwohl	Stallings at SRI was assigned to develop an observation system for the Follow Through evaluation study. She needed an "opinion-free" system to accurately depict and compare the various program models.	Flanders, N.A. (1970) Analyzing teaching behavior. Stallings, J. (1975) Implementation and child effects of teaching practices in Follow Through classrooms.
JANE STALLINGS Stanford Research Institute, 1969–80 Vanderbilt University, 1983–86 University of Houston, 1986–90 Texas A&M, 1990–1999	Ph.D., Stanford, 1970 MENTORS: Richard E. Snow, Fannie Shaftel, Eleanor Maccoby, N.L. Gage DISSERTATION: ATI study of children's sequencing ability in relationship to reading methods (phonics/whole-word) FELLOW PH.D. CANDIDATES: Richard Shavelson	Flanders, on leave at the Center for Advanced Study in the Behavioral Sciences, served as a friendly consultant, advising Stallings on development of systematic observation categories. They visited classrooms together to test tentative categories and developed a matrix for efficient recording of data.	Stallings, J. (1977) Learning to look: A handbook on classroom observation and teaching models. Stallings, J., Needels, M., & Sparks, G.M. (1987) Observation for the improvement of classroom learning.
RONALD MARX Simon Fraser University, 1978–90 University of Michigan, 1990–present	Ph.D., Stanford, 1978 MENTORS: Pauline Sears, N.L. Gage, Richard E. Snow DISSERTATION: Lens model study of teachers' judgments of students' cognitive and affective states in lessons	Marx and Winne collaborated with fellow doctoral students at Stanford on a well-known factorial study of teacher structuring, soliciting, responding, and reacting.	Winne, P.H., & Marx, R.W. (1982) Students' and teachers' views of thinking processes involved in classroom learning. Marx, R.W. (1983) Student perceptions in classrooms.
PHILIP WINNE Simon Fraser University, 1978–present	Ph.D., Stanford, 1978 MENTORS: N.L. Gage, Lee Cronbach, Richard Snow DISSERTATION: ATI experimental study on teacher effectiveness FELLOW PH.D. CANDIDATES: (for both): Christopher Clark, Penelope Peterson	They began college teaching together at Simon Fraser. Their collaboration there began with a conference paper that became a published article, introducing the "cognitive mediation" variable into the process-product paradigm. Two collaborative studies based on their model followed.	Winne, P.H. (1985) Steps toward promoting cognitive achievements. Winne, P.H., & Marx, R.W. (1987) The best tools teachers have—their students' thinking.
MICHAEL DUNKIN Macquarie University, 1968–80 University of Sydney, 1981–91 University of New South Wales, 1991–96	Junior high teacher, 5 years Ph.D., University of Queensland, 1967 MENTORS: William J. Campbell, G. W. Bassett, Bruce Biddle DISSERTATION: survey of primary teachers with observational case studies on warmth and directiveness.	In 1983 Dunkin and Gage each independently discussed an idea for an international journal on research on teaching with officials of Pergamon Press. Maxwell, head of Pergamon, proposed Dunkin as Editor of the journal, and Gage as chair of the Editorial Board. Further discussion led to Gage's appointment as Editor, with Dunkin and Sara Delamont as Associate Editors. Teaching and Teacher Education began publication in 1985, and has become a well-respected international journal, with Dunkin, Neville Bennett and Greta Morine-Dershimer as subsequent Editors.	Dunkin, M. J., & Biddle, B. (1974) The study of teaching. Dunkin, M.J., & Barnes, J. (1986) Research on teaching in higher education. Dunkin, M.J. (1987) The international encyclopedia of teaching and teacher education. Gage, N.L. (1988) The founding of Teaching and Teacher Education: An international journal of research and studies.
N.L. GAGE Purdue University, 1947–48 University of Illinois, 1948–62 Stanford University, 1962–87	Ph.D., Purdue, 1947 MENTORS: Hermann H. Remmers, B.F. Skinner (undergraduate years) DISSERTATION: correlational study of high school students' attitudes toward minorities, using Guttman scaling and factorial design		

common interests. The collaborative researchers are apt to have similar views about appropriate issues to be investigated and acceptable methodology to be pursued. While they may bring somewhat different specific skills and knowledge to a cooperative task as a result of differences in prior professional experiences, the perspectives that they have in common can facilitate communication and ease the collaborative process.

The two cases (see Table 3.3) that illustrate this type of research relationship are organized in chronological sequence and highlight developments related to the impact of teacher perceptions of pupils on learning outcomes. Jere Brophy and Thomas Good investigated the effects of teacher expectations on pupil learning. Penelope Peterson and Elizabeth Fennema together with Thomas Carpenter examined the impact of changes in teachers' thinking about pupils' mathematical problem-solving abilities on classroom teaching and learning.

Mixed Marriages

Collaborative research relationships in which the partners have been prepared at different institutions (families) and in very different research traditions (cultures) are analogous to mixed marriages, which are unions between couples who come from families that differ sharply in cultural, socioeconomic, or religious backgrounds. Like mixed marriages, such research relationships have become increasingly prevalent and increasingly well accepted in recent years, but some early collaborative efforts were frowned on by members of the research traditions (cultures) in which the collaborative partners had been reared. The different professional backgrounds of researchers in these types of collaborative relationships require that they make a concerted effort to understand each other's perspectives. But the adaptations in research methods (rituals) that result can provide new conceptions which enrich the field of research on teaching.

The four cases (see Table 3.4) that illustrate this type of research relationship are sequenced chronologically and illustrate some of the changes that have occurred over time in attempts to relate research on teaching to classroom practice. Carolyn Evertson and Judith Green provided a comprehensive analysis of classroom observation, bridging the chasm that separated categorical systems from ethnographic approaches. Hilda Borko and Margaret Eisenhart united alternative perspectives on knowledge, derived from cognitive psychology and anthropology, to examine experienced teachers' ideas and practices in reading instruction and the process of novice teachers' learning to teach mathematics. David Berliner and Ursula Casanova joined forces to provide classroom teachers with research-based knowledge about teaching as viewed by a researcher and by a practitioner. Linda Darling-Hammond and Ann Lieberman linked the world of policy analysis to the world of classroom practice in their work on the restructuring of schools.

Communes, or Intentional Communities

Modern-day communes are seen by their inhabitants as intentional communities in which people unrelated by blood join together in some form of cooperative living. The sharing of responsibilities and resources creates a positive energy, enabling

members to lead more productive and satisfying lives. In much the same way, groups of classroom teachers, teacher educators, or researchers, who form collaborative communities with the intention of improving their work, share resources (knowledge and experiences) and responsibilities (provide feedback and support for each other) as they work (study) together to create more productive lives (learning environments) for students and teachers.

This type of professional relationship is illustrated by two cases (see Table 3.5). One describes the collaboration of Marilyn Cochran-Smith and Susan Lytle, who pioneered in creating and conceptualizing intentional communities of teachers engaged in investigating their own practice. The other focuses on a network of African-American researchers, spread out around the United States, but which maintained close communication via telephone and e-mail. Members of this network were initially identified for this set of cases by Gloria Ladson-Billings, and the network is represented here by three active participants: Ladson-Billings, Michele Foster, and Jacqueline Jordan Irvine.

Cross-Case Patterns and Themes

In addition to the interesting vital statistics from the individual professional histories of some prominent and influential researchers provided in the tables presented here, the full cases on which the tables are based provide insights into the process of collaboration and depict the impact that collaborative research relationships have had, and may continue to have, on the development of the field of research on teaching. This section identifies patterns that are evident across the set of cases. Three main arenas for collaboration are discussed: professional preparation, research, and dissemination.

Patterns of Professional Preparation

Several features of their professional preparation were reportedly important for the researchers in these cases. The features included the "recycling" of exciting experiences by major professors, the provision of formative concepts and models, the sense of reciprocal learning, the introduction to significant others, and the opportunity for collaborative practice.

RECYCLING EXCITING EXPERIENCES

One interesting feature of the cases in the "parent-child" category is the apparent tendency for professors to provide doctoral students with experiences similar to those they deemed critical to their own early professional development. For example, Gage recounted the early opportunity provided by his doctoral advisor, Hermann Remmers, to serve on an AERA Committee on Criteria of Teaching Effectiveness and help prepare the committee report (Barr et al., 1953). This experience led to Gage's later appointment in 1955 as chair of an AERA Committee on Teacher Effectiveness. The first edition of the *Handbook of Research on Teaching* (Gage, 1963) was initiated by Gage as a task for this subsequent committee. Thus, the opportunity for committee work provided to Gage by Remmers was the initial link in a chain of experiences that culminated in the publication of

Table 3.3. "Traditional Marriages"

COLLABORATORS	PROFESSIONAL PREPARATION	COLLABORATIVE WORK	RELATED PUBLICATIONS
JERE BROPHY University of Texas at Austin, 1968–76 Michigan State University, 1976–present	Ph.D., Chicago, 1967 MENTORS: Robert D. Hess, Virginia Shipman DISSERTATION: observation study of mother–child interaction in urban black families FELLOW PH.D. CANDIDATES: (clinical psychologists, none in research on teaching)	Brophy and Good both began college teaching at UT, Austin. They had a common interest in seeing how teacher expectations were communicated to pupils. Both had looked at dyadic interactions in their dissertation studies. They developed a dyadic coding system together to test their model of teacher expectation effects. Their collaborative work continued in further studies of the dynamics of teacher-student relationships and process-outcome studies of teacher effects (affective and achievement outcomes), as well as publication of a textbook and research reviews.	Brophy, J.E., & Good, T.L. (1970) Teachers' communication of differential expectations for children's classroom performance: Some behavioral data. Good, T.L. (1981) Teacher expectations and student perceptions: A decade of research. Brophy, J.E. (1983) Research on the self-fulfilling prophecy and teacher expectations. Brophy, J.E., & Good, T.L. (1986) Teacher behavior and student achievement. Good, T.L., & Brophy, J.E. (1997) Looking in classrooms. (7th edition).
THOMAS GOOD University of Texas at Austin, 1968–71 University of Missouri, 1971–91 University of Arizona, 1991–present	Ph.D., Indiana, 1967 MENTORS: Joanne Prentice, Richard Turner DISSERTATION: field study of teacher expectation effects on pupil response opportunities FELLOW PH.D. CANDIDATES: Myron Dembo, Richard Coop		
PENELOPE PETERSON University of Wisconsin, Madison, 1976–87 Michigan State University, 1987–97 Northwestern University, 1997–present	Ph.D., Stanford, 1976 MENTORS: N.L. Gage, Richard Snow, Bruce Joyce, Lee Shulman DISSERTATION: ATI study on effects of student anxiety, achievement orientation, and teacher behavior on student achievement and attitude FELLOW PH.D. CANDIDATES: Christopher Clark, Ronald Marx, Philip Winne	Peterson collaborated with fellow doctoral students at Stanford. She and Fennema met at Wisconsin, Madison and admired each other's work. After receiving tenure, Peterson joined Fennema in studies of gender differences in the learning of mathematics. In an effort to combine research on learning with research on teaching, Peterson and Fennema worked with Thomas Carpenter in a study on Cognitively Guided Instruction (CGI). Participant teachers, who were given information on children's "invented" ways of solving story problems, changed instructional procedures and students' math achievement improved.	Fennema, E. (1974) Mathematics learning and the sexes: A review. Peterson, P.L., Marx, R.W., & Clark, C.M. (1978) Teacher planning, teacher behavior, and student achievement. Fennema, E., & Peterson, P.L. (1986) Teacher-student interactions and sex-related differences in mathematics. Peterson, P.L., Carpenter, T.P., & Fennema, E. (1989) Teachers' knowledge of students' knowledge and cognition in mathematics problem solving. Peterson, P.L., Fennema, E., & Carpenter, T.P. (1991) Using children's mathematical knowledge.
ELIZABETH FENNEMA University of Wisconsin, Madison, 1969–96	Elementary Teacher, 3 years Ph.D., Wisconsin, Madison, 1969 MENTORS: Vere DeVault, Thomas Romberg, Herbert Klausmeier DISSERTATION: experimental study comparing children's learning with concrete vs symbolic math tools FELLOW PH.D. CANDIDATES: Thomas Carpenter, Douglas Grouws, Douglas McLeod, Mary Montgomery Lindquist		

Table 3.4. "Mixed Marriages"

COLLABORATORS	PROFESSIONAL PREPARATION	COLLABORATIVE WORK	RELATED PUBLICATIONS
CAROLYN EVERTSON University of Texas at Austin, 1970–81 Educational Consultant, 1981–83 Vanderbilt University, 1983–present	Elementary Teacher, 1 year Ph.D., University of Texas at Austin, 1972 MENTORS: Frank Wicker, Jere Brophy, Frances Fuller DISSERTATION: experimental study of children's paired–associate learning with 4 types of instructional materials FELLOW PH.D. CANDIDATES: Anita Woolfolk Hoy, Claire Ellen Weinstein	Green invited Evertson to present a colloquium at Delaware. They began to converse about research, and wrote an NIE proposal for a collaborative study linking instruction and management to student learning. This led to a series of studies in several states.	Evertson, C., Anderson, C., Anderson, L., & Brophy, J. (1980) Relationships between classroom behaviors and student outcomes in junior high mathematics and English classes. Green, J.L. (1983) Research on teaching as a linguistic process: A state of the art.
JUDITH GREEN Kent State University, 1977–80 University of Delaware, 1980–84 Ohio State University, 1984–90 University of California at Santa Barbara, 1990–present	Elementary Teacher, 10 years Ph.D., University of California at Berkeley, 1977 MENTORS: Robert Ruddell, John Gumperz, Millie Almy, Paul Amon DISSERTATION: descriptive/statistical study comparing 2 classroom observation systems across 11 teachers, teaching the same lesson FELLOW PH.D. CANDIDATES: Celia Genishi, Judith Harker	Evertson was invited to coauthor a chapter on observation in the 3rd Handbook of Research on Teaching, representing systematic observation. She invited Green as a coauthor representing ethnographic/sociolinguistic approaches. They rejected the editorial board's request for a "nuts and bolts" chapter, and wrote on the relationship between theory and method.	Evertson, C., Weade, R., Green, J., & Crawford, J. (1985) Effective management and instruction: An exploration of models. Evertson, C.M., & Green, J.L. (1986) Observation as inquiry and method.
HILDA BORKO System Development Corporation, 1978–80 Virginia Polytechnic Institute and State University, 1980–85 University of Maryland, 1985–91 University of Colorado, 1991–present	Secondary Math Teacher, 4 years Ph.D., University of California at Los Angeles, 1978 MENTORS: Richard Shavelson, Eva Baker, Leigh Burstein DISSERTATION: experimental policy-capturing study modeling teacher judgments about student aptitudes in relation to their organizational/management decisions FELLOW PH.D. CANDIDATES: Nancy Russo Atwood, Joel Cadwell	Borko and Eisenhart both began college teaching at Virginia Tech in 1980. Gary Fenstermacher saw them as a "natural pair," as both came from research traditions, and educational research was being promoted at Virginia Tech at that time. They applied for an NIE grant on learning to read, and were approved for funding, then the money was withdrawn. Virginia Tech provided graduate assistants to support the study anyway.	Borko, H., & Eisenhart, M. (1986) Students' conceptions of reading and their reading experiences in school. Borko, H., & Shavelson, R.J. (1990) Teachers' decision making. Eisenhart, M., & Cutts-Dougherty, K. (1991) Social and cultural constraints on students' access to school knowledge.
MARGARET EISENHART Virginia Polytechnic Institute and State University, 1980–87 University of Colorado, 1987–present	Ph.D., University of North Carolina, Chapel Hill, 1980 MENTOR: Dorothy Holland DISSERTATION: ethnographic study comparing gender-related interaction patterns with race-related interaction patterns in intermediate classrooms FELLOW PH.D. CANDIDATES: (anthropologists, none involved in research on teaching)	Their work linked a teacher decision-making focus (Borko) with a student social interaction focus (Eisenhart). Later work involved a study of learning to teach mathematics, combining cognitive and sociocultural perspectives on learning.	Eisenhart, M., Borko, H., Underhill, R.G., Brown, C.A., Jones, D., & Agard, P.C. (1993) Conceptual knowledge falls through the cracks: Complexities of learning to teach mathematics for understanding. Eisenhart, M., & Borko, H. (1993) Designing classroom research: Themes, issues, and struggles.

Table 3.4. (continued)

COLLABORATORS	PROFESSIONAL PREPARATION	COLLABORATIVE WORK	RELATED PUBLICATIONS
DAVID BERLINER University of Massachusetts, 1968–70 Far West Laboratory for Educational Research and Development, 1970–77 University of Arizona, 1977–87 Arizona State University, 1987–present	Ph.D., Stanford, 1968 MENTORS: Fred McDonald, Lee Cronbach DISSERTATION: experimental study of the effects of test-like events and note-taking on learning from lectures FELLOW PH.D. CANDIDATES: James Cooper, Barak Rosenshine, Kevin Ryan, Gavriel Salomon, Leonard Cahen	Berliner and Casanova met when she was a research associate at NIE and he was a visiting scholar there. They often discussed problems associated with encouraging teachers to read and use educational research. Opportunities to collaborate in addressing this issue were enhanced by their marriage in 1986. Berliner and Casanova instituted a regular column in the Instructor Magazine, in which Berliner would summarize a study, and Casanova would comment on how teachers could relate the research to classroom practice. Articles from the 6-year series were later published in a book. The pair also piloted and oversaw development of an NEA series of 9 volumes of Readings in Educational Research.	Berliner, D.C., & Rosenshine, B.V. (Eds.). (1987) Talks to teachers: A festschrift for N.L. Gage. Casanova, U. (1987) Ethnic and cultural differences. Berliner, D.C., & Casanova, U. (1993, 1996) Putting research to work in your school. Berliner, D.C., Casanova, U., & Powell, J.H. (Eds.). (1994) Readings in educational research: Intelligence. Casanova, U., Berliner, D.C., & Powell, J. H. (Eds.). (1994) Readings in educational research: Cognition.
URSULA CASANOVA University of Arizona, 1985–87 Stanford University, 1987–88 Arizona State University, 1988–present	Elementary/Junior High Spanish Teacher, 7 years Elementary Principal, 5 years Ph.D., University of Arizona, 1985 MENTORS: Suzanne Shafer, Nicholas Appleton, Elizabeth Brandt DISSERTATION: descriptive study of elementary school secretaries FELLOW PH.D. CANDIDATES: (none involved in research on teaching)		
LINDA DARLING-HAMMOND Rand Corporation, 1979–89 Teachers College, Columbia, 1989–1998 Stanford University, 1998–present	Secondary/college Teacher, 5 years Ed.D., Temple University, 1978 MENTORS: Bernard Watson, Arthur Wise (RAND) DISSERTATION: policy study on school finance reform in Pennsylvania.	This pair connected when Lieberman asked Darling-Hammond to write a report for the Task Force on Professionalism in NYC. The report noted the need for a center for school reform. When Darling–Hammond was hired at Teachers College, she raised seed money to start such a center, and Lieberman returned to TC to organize it. When NCREST was established, they became co-directors. The National Center on Restructuring Education, Schools, and Teaching (NCREST) promoted school reform by addressing both policy and practice through research and the formation of networks. Darling-Hammond provided expertise on policy studies and Lieberman on networking.	Darling-Hammond, L. (1994) Professional development schools: Schools for developing a profession. Darling-Hammond, L., Ancess, J., & Falk, B. (1995) Authentic assessment in action: Studies of schools and students at work. Lieberman, A. (1995) The work of restructuring schools: Building from the ground up. Darling-Hammond, L. (1996) What matters most. Lieberman, A. (1996) Networks and reform in American education. Darling-Hammond, L. (1997) The right to learn: A blueprint for schools that work.
ANN LIEBERMAN University of California at Los Angeles, 1969–71 University of Massachusetts, 1971–73 Teachers College, Columbia, 1973–86 University of Washington, 1986–89 Teachers College, Columbia, 1989–1998 Stanford University, 1998–present	Elementary Teacher, 4 years Ed.D., University of California at Los Angeles, 1969 MENTORS: C. Wayne Gordon, John Goodlad DISSERTATION: large-scale survey on effects of principal leadership on teachers' morale, professionalism, and style in classroom.		

Table 3.5. "Communes" or Intentional Communities

COLLABORATORS	PROFESSIONAL PREPARATION	COLLABORATIVE WORK	RELATED PUBLICATIONS
MARILYN COCHRAN-SMITH University of Pennsylvania, 1982–96 Boston College, 1996–present SUSAN LYTLE University of Pennsylvania, 1982–present	Elementary Teacher, 6 years Ph.D., University of Pennsylvania, 1982 DISSERTATION: ethnographic study of literacy learning in young children FELLOW PH.D. CANDIDATES: Susan Lytle Secondary English Teacher, 6 years Peace Corps, 2 years Ph.D., University of Pennsylvania, 1982 DISSERTATION: qualitative-quantitative study of comprehension processes of adolescents FELLOW PH.D. CANDIDATES: Marilyn Cochran-Smith	Cochran-Smith and Lytle were in the University of Pennsylvania Language and Literacy degree program together. Their intensive collaboration began in 1986 when they began to connect their work in two separate projects involving teachers as researchers. As they worked individually with teacher groups on collaborative investigations of teaching and learning, they worked together to conceptualize, develop, and refine the collaborative process, concluding that what counts as "knowledge" in research on teaching needed to be rethought. Together they received a major Spencer Foundation grant for their work on "Teacher Inquiry and the Epistemology of Teaching." The teachers' sharing of research, begun in small collaborative groups, expanded to sharing across groups, and then to presentations at local and national conferences.	Cochran-Smith, M. & Lytle, S. (1990) Research on teaching and teacher research: The issues that divide. Lytle, S., & Cochran-Smith, M. (1990) Learning from teacher research: A working typology. Cochran-Smith, M., & Lytle, S. (1992) Interrogating cultural diversity: Inquiry and action. Cochran-Smith, M. & Lytle, S. (Eds.). (1993) Inside/outside: Teacher research and knowledge. Lytle, S., & Cochran-Smith, M. (1994) Inquiry, knowledge, and practice. Lytle, S., & Cochran-Smith, M. (1996) Disrupting university culture: The case of teacher research.
MICHELE FOSTER University of Pennsylvania, 1987–91 University of North Carolina, Chapel Hill (post-doctoral fellow) and Spencer Foundation Fellowship, 1989–91 UC Davis, 1991–94 Claremont Graduate School, 1994–present JACQUELINE JORDAN IRVINE Emory University, 1979–present GLORIA LADSON-BILLINGS Santa Clara University, 1989–91 University of Wisconsin, Madison, 1991–present	Elementary teacher, 3 years Ed.D., Harvard, 1987 DISSERTATION ADVISOR: Courtney Cazden DISSERTATION: ethnography of communication study of Black female community college teacher with predominantly Black students FELLOW Ed.D. CANDIDATES: Lisa Delpit Ph.D., Georgia State University, 1979 POST-DOCTORAL MENTORS: Faustine Jones-Wilson (Howard, ret.), Anne Pruitt (Ohio State, ret.) DISSERTATION: quantitative experimental study on gender roles K–12 teacher, 12 years Ph.D., Stanford, 1984 MENTORS: Sylvia Wynter, James Gibbs, Larry Cuban DISSERTATION: ethnographic study of citizenship and values among 8th graders in a predominantly Black school FELLOW PH.D. CANDIDATES: Anna Richert, Renee Clift	Ladson-Billings, Irvine, and Foster are representative members of a larger group of African-American researchers involved in research on teaching, who have an active informal support network operating on several levels. Experienced researchers provide feedback to each other, and publish together; more experienced researchers serve as national mentors for younger researchers. Many members of this network had difficulty finding mentors during their doctoral work, and feel fairly isolated even in the institutions where they work at present. Thus the network provides a critical support system. The work of this group is "mission-driven," focused on issues of helping children of color to succeed in school, and energized by the commitment to give back to the African-American community, following the custom of "each one teach one."	Irvine, J.J. (1990) Black students and school failure: Policies, practices, and prescriptions. Irvine, J.J. (1991) Beyond role models: An examination of cultural influences on the pedagogical perspectives of black teachers. Ladson-Billings, G. (1994) The dreamkeepers: Successful teachers of African American children. Ladson-Billings, G. (1995) Toward a theory of culturally relevant pedagogy. Foster, M. (1995) Talking that talk: The language of control, curriculum, and critique. Irvine, J.J. & Foster. M. (Eds.). (1996) Growing up African American in Catholic schools. Foster, M. (1997) Black teachers on teaching.

the *Handbook,* an event that was influential in Gage's subsequent career. In a similar way, Gage promoted an important career opportunity for Rosenshine. Impressed by Rosenshine's dissertation literature review, which was "exactly what I wanted for the first *Handbook,* but didn't always get" (Gage, personal communication, September 17, 1996), Gage was granted funds by the International Association for the Evaluation of Educational Achievement (IEA) for Rosenshine to review the correlational and experimental studies relating teacher behavior to student achievement. The resultant publication (Rosenshine, 1971) launched Rosenshine as a prominent reviewer of process-product research. Rosenshine reports that Gage, as an advisor on that publication, insisted that he prepare a separate table for each of the instructional behaviors he was studying, with each table containing all the research results for that behavior. "This 'suggestion,' which I strongly opposed, resulted in the tables that gave the research results for instructional behaviors such as 'clarity,' 'enthusiasm,' and 'indirectness' . . . and made a tremendous difference in how we could look at the results of the studies" (Rosenshine, personal communication, October 1, 1996). Rosenshine dedicated the book to Gage in appreciation for the intellectual and emotional help he had provided.

As another example of this tendency for professors to provide opportunities for doctoral students similar to those they had benefited from themselves, Cazden commented on her attendance at a small conference in 1965, sponsored by the U.S. Office of Education, where she met several leaders in what was then the new field of sociolinguistics, including Dell Hymes, John Gumperz, and Joshua Fishman. It was a meeting which served to induct her into "a small and exciting community of inquiry" (Cazden, personal communication, August 29, 1996). In 1979, Florio-Ruane participated in a similar induction experience, when Cazden and a small group of people who were engaged in related research began a series of informal meetings that included doctoral students. Florio-Ruane notes that through her mentors, Cazden and Erickson, she met and learned from "faculty members at other institutions pioneering in sociolinguistics and the ethnography of communication and their application to studies of teaching, as well as their graduate students, who became valued peers and later colleagues" (Florio-Ruane, personal communication, July 1996).

Not all of these formative learning experiences felt positive initially. Jackson notes that Irving Lorge "offered me some of the sharpest and harshest judgments and advice of all my professors, much of which lives on, and I find myself acting his part in my relationships with students, sometimes by being too harsh, I fear" (Jackson, personal communication, November 11, 1997). In one striking episode, Jackson asked Lorge how long it might take him to write his dissertation, and Lorge responded, "I can't be sure, but my guess is that you write slowly and badly." Jackson recalls, "That was like throwing a bucket of cold water on me. . . . but I thought, I might never change the 'slowly' part, but I could change the 'badly' part, so I worked on it. And I stress writing with my students" (Jackson, personal communication, November 6, 1997). Hansen (1996) has written about an episode in his own doctoral studies when Jackson commented on his writing. "He was incredibly attentive to language, and I appreciate now, in a way I never did then, how much time that took. He really does take writing seriously, and

really sought to help students with their writing" (Hansen, personal communication, November 7, 1997). Hansen indicates that while Jackson could be very critical, his comments were never personal. "He didn't beat around the bush, and it was not always comfortable, but strangely enough, never dispiriting. . . . I learned the importance of spending that kind of time [on my own writing]" (Hansen, personal communication, November 7, 1997).

FORMATIVE CONCEPTS AND MODELS

Faculty mentors provided doctoral students in many of these cases with critical concepts and professional models that they still perceive as fundamental to their work as educators and researchers. Florio-Ruane credited Cazden as the source for her views on patterns of early acquisition of language, multidisciplinary perspectives on classroom discourse, and the connections between research and practice. Winne noted that Gage "taught me the meaning of scholarship—read everything, write more, then edit for accuracy, clarity, and logic" (personal communication, August 7, 1996). Peterson's ability to analyze the quantitative data and then use qualitative data to "make it speak to people" (Fennema, personal communication, September 13, 1996) was a trait much admired by Fennema. Peterson explained that "I got that idea from Dick Snow. He always used to say you've got to psychologize it. I guess what people today would say is, tell a story about the data" (Peterson, personal communication, September 13, 1996).

Faculty mentors also served as models for professional roles. Florio-Ruane noted that her sense of the importance of serving actively in professional organizations resulted from such modeling, and led to her service as President of the Council on Anthropology and Education, following in the footsteps of both Cazden and Erickson. Gudmundsdóttir commented on Shulman's impact as teacher of a qualitative research methods course. The course Shulman helped launch at Stanford was the starting point for her in designing her own course, and she believes that it was the same for her classmates. "I have this Bakhtinian vision of that course popping up all over the world in one form or another, with Lee's 'voice' [ventriloquizing] through us, who were in that class and are now teaching it in our new contexts" (Gudmundsdóttir, personal communication, September 19, 1996). Alton-Lee described the model of researcher provided by Nuthall. "As a scholar of depth of thought, integrity, incredibly high standards (although he used to counsel me not to always seek perfection), Graham created a standard which I still use" (Alton-Lee, personal communication, January 14, 1997). Commenting on Jackson as a mentor, Hansen reported that "being in Phil's presence was a significant thing for me in my education as a scholar and as a person. What I learned from him is what it looks like when you love something . . . and really want to understand it" (Hansen, personal communication, November 7, 1997).

Not all researchers in these cases found the types of models that they craved during their doctoral work. Cochran-Smith and Lytle named no professors who served as mentors during their doctoral studies and noted that they served as mentors for each other when they began working together after graduation. Ladson-Billings commented on the difficulty that some

African-American doctoral candidates at Stanford had finding advisors who were able to assist with the kinds of issues the candidates wished to address. Foster said simply, "I had no mentors as a graduate student" (Foster, personal communication, November 3, 1997). She currently serves as a mentor to Black graduate students and junior faculty at a number of institutions around the United States, reading and reacting to over 150 manuscripts a year. She firmly believes what she was told as a graduate student: As an African American she would have to do more work and better work to get the same amount of recognition as white researchers. "That's what I want for Black graduate students. I don't want them to be average. I want them to be superior" (Foster, personal communication, November 13, 1997).

RECIPROCAL LEARNING

Despite the rather widespread belief that graduate students are there to learn from their professors, the cases investigated here suggest that the learning flows in more than one direction. As Shulman opined in an interview with Gudmundsdóttir published in *Norsk Pedagogisk Tidsskrift* (Gudmundsdóttir, 1992):

> The best kind of doctoral training occurs when you make possible a small community of doctoral students who become mentors and support and educators of one another. . . . [W]hen there is a community, a group of four or five, seven or nine students, who read each other's work, who criticize each other's work, who stimulate one another, it only means that every student now has ten teachers instead of just one. I also get stimulated. I learn so much from the students and they know it. (Shulman, as quoted by Gudmundsdóttir, 1992)

The sense of reciprocal learning between professor and student, or mentor and "mentee," was reiterated by several others. Gage reportedly got the idea of process-product research from Stanley Rudin, one of his research associates at Illinois; Rudin, in turn, had gotten the idea from Ross Stagner, his mentor in the Psychology Department at Illinois. "That (idea) was like a bright light going on over my head" (Gage, personal communication, September 17, 1996). Jackson noted that Hansen "is an extremely patient and careful listener to what people say. . . . That sensitivity was invaluable in our project, where we spent a lot of time listening to teachers' talk . . . and David brought to that a very, very sensitive ear" (Jackson, personal communication, November 6, 1997). The sense of being able to contribute something back was also important for doctoral students. Alton-Lee explained that "In my research as the first teacher affiliate [at the University of Canterbury], I challenged the focus on group results, and showed them how essential it was to trace the way an individual student understood and constructed new concepts" (Alton-Lee, personal communication, January 14, 1997).

This aspect of professional development does not end when doctoral studies are completed. Irvine, discussing her interactions with Vanessa Siddle Walker, a younger colleague at Emory, indicated that "being women, we help each other, and sometimes we are our harshest critics. We feel like we can get honest feedback from [each other]. We help each other in conceptualizing and thinking about our work, so it's an invaluable resource" (Irvine, personal communication, August 2, 1996).

SIGNIFICANT OTHERS

While major advisors served a clear mentoring role for the researchers in these cases, they were not the only influential individuals in their early professional development. The cross-fertilization of ideas provided by contact with a variety of experienced researchers was probably most evident in the experiences of Peterson, Marx, and Winne during their doctoral studies at Stanford. In addition to working with Gage, who provided experience in process-product research on teaching, they worked extensively with Richard Snow, who was engaged in aptitude-treatment-interaction (ATI) studies of learning. Winne also participated with Berliner and Gall in a Far West Laboratory experimental study of higher-order questioning (Gall et al., 1978) while Peterson and Marx worked with Bruce Joyce in an experimental study of teacher thinking (Peterson, Marx, & Clark, 1978) and discussed research on teacher thinking at length with Shulman, who was spending a sabbatical year at the Center for Advanced Study in the Behavioral Sciences. Peterson has described the interaction with Joyce and Shulman as "transformative," (Peterson, 1994, p. 99), and it seems highly probable that the mix of perspectives that these three were exposed to during this period contributed substantially to their subsequent interest in research that examined relationships between teacher and pupil cognitions and behavior. Gudmundsdóttir commented on Shulman's generosity in "sharing his contacts and friendships with his graduate students, expecting us to love and respect them as he did" (Gudmundsdóttir, personal communication, July 22, 1997). As a result, she developed close relationships with Pinchas Tamir and Miriam Ben-Peretz from Israel, who introduced her to members of the International Study Association on Teacher Thinking (ISATT).

Members of Ladson-Billings' network frequently mentioned significant others as contributors to their professional development. Ladson-Billings herself actively sought out faculty members outside the School of Education at Stanford to obtain advice and received helpful support from James Gibbs and George Spindler of the anthropology department and Sylvia Wynter, chair of African-American Studies. Irvine cited African-American women at different institutions, Faustine Jones-Wilson (Howard) and Anne Pruitt (Ohio State), as her primary role models.

Significant others were not limited to experienced researchers. Many of the researchers in these cases commented on how much they learned from fellow doctoral students. For Florio-Ruane, the fellow students contributing to her learning "then as now" came not just from Harvard (see Table 1) but also from the University of Pennsylvania (Evelyn Jacob), Stanford (Katie Anderson-Levitt, Doug Campbell), Berkeley (Sarah Michaels), and the Kamehameha Early Education Project (Kathryn Au). Gudmundsdóttir noted the contributions of the more "advanced" doctoral students at Stanford (Max Angus, Renee Clift, Anna Richert, and Gary Sykes).

OPPORTUNITIES FOR COLLABORATIVE PRACTICE

Many of the researchers in these cases had some experience with collaborative research during their doctoral programs, which may have made them more amenable to such activity in their later work. Peterson, Marx, and Winne collaborated with fellow doctoral students Clark and Stayrook on a factorial study of teacher structuring, soliciting, and reacting (Clark et al., 1979) under the guidance of Gage. Borko and Eisenhart both had experience with collaborative research in their respective disciplines (Borko at UCLA in educational psychology and Eisenhart at UNC in anthropology); then at about the time of completing their studies, each worked in a cross-disciplinary project outside her university setting. Good had two different experiences in collaborative research with fellow students at Indiana during his doctoral studies. Both were student-initiated activities that occurred outside the established doctoral curriculum. He found these to be instructive experiences, and indicated that "collaboration is useful in trying to develop a sense of what you know, what you don't know, why you think something works, and what would help to move you forward in your understanding" (Good, personal communication, April 25, 1997). As part of her dissertation study, Florio-Ruane pioneered collaboration between a university-based researcher and a teacher and published what has been acknowledged as the first such collaborative study in the educational anthropology literature (Florio & Walsh, 1981). Hansen had collaborative experiences with other doctoral students in analyzing classroom talk for a project of Harootunian-Gordon's, and an extended 3-year collaboration with Jackson, fellow research assistant Boostrom, and 18 teachers in the Moral Life of Schools project from which his dissertation was drawn. In the meetings of the latter group, he noted, "What stands out vividly as an endlessly exciting, challenging, at times frustrating part of that project . . . was finding a language in which we could talk together about the moral life of schools and classrooms" (Hansen, personal communication, November 7, 1997).

EXPOSURE TO NEW AND VARIED PERSPECTIVES

What all these types of developmental professional experiences had in common was the opportunity to work with and learn from a variety of people with a variety of perspectives. This sort of opportunity would appear to be an important factor contributing to the ability and interest these researchers displayed in their later professional work. Many of the types of experiences reported here were not planned elements of the doctoral programs involved, but perhaps more programs should provide such experiences on a systematic basis. In addition, more professors could possibly acknowledge more openly and regularly the ways in which they have learned and are learning from their students. This reciprocal learning would seem to be an important contributor to the continued development of the field of research on teaching. Finally, graduate schools of education need to acknowledge and systematically reward the inter-institutional mentoring role played by faculty members in networks like the one represented here by Foster, Irvine, and Ladson-Billings. Many institutions may be unaware of the degree to which their minority-group students receive such outside support, but the extensive mentoring provided to those students clearly exploits the sense of mission which drives the work of such network members.

Patterns of Productive Research Collaboration

Several factors were important contributors to the establishment of productive research collaborations for the participants in the cases reported here. These included proximity, stage of professional development, available resources, and expanded thinking. A problem encountered was the professional risk seemingly involved in collaboration.

PROXIMITY

It is clear that serendipity was an important factor in the establishment of most of the collaborative relationships examined here. In most instances, two people who happened to be working at the same institution found that they had similar interests and began to explore these together. But factors beyond mere proximity operated to promote or inhibit collaborative efforts. Marx and Winne had worked together as graduate students at Stanford, but their initial collaborative effort at Simon Fraser was fueled by three additional factors: they shared a physically isolated trailer office, they felt a bit of intellectual isolation from Canadian colleagues by virtue of their U.S. roots, and they needed to have a paper to present in order to get conference travel funds. These combined factors led to their joint conference paper, later published in the *Journal of Educational Psychology* (Winne & Marx, 1977), in which they introduced their cognitive mediational model. In contrast, Peterson and Fennema first met in a women's lunch group organized by Fennema at the University of Wisconsin at Madison, then began to read and admire each other's work. Although Peterson was intrigued by Fennema's studies of gender differences in mathematics learning, she was concerned about the possible negative impact of collaborative research in general, and gender-based research in particular, on tenure and promotion decisions in the male-dominated educational psychology department. In 1980, after holding her interest in abeyance for four years, she informed Fennema that, having received tenure, she finally felt free to pursue collaborative research on gender issues.

The collaborations of Flanders with Stallings and Borko with Eisenhart provide another type of variation in the general pattern of mutually initiating collaborative efforts because of common interests. Their initial contacts were prompted by the advice of other researchers whom they respected. Stallings was at the Stanford Research Institute (SRI), assigned to develop an interactive observational system for the Follow Through study. Program sponsors had rejected a "check-off" observation system, and Stallings quickly discovered that the field notes she was accustomed to taking would not provide the cross-site comparison essential for the research. Colleagues suggested that she meet with Flanders, then a fellow at the Center for Advanced Study in the Behavioral Sciences. He showed her how to develop systematic observation categories. "Never a paid consultant . . . he was generous, kind, and helpful, and really listened" (Stallings, personal communication, August 8, 1996). Borko and Eisenhart were new faculty members at the Virginia Polytechnic Institute and State University in the fall of 1980. Though they were trained in different research traditions (cognitive psychology and anthropology), Gary Fenstermacher, then chair of the program area in Social Foundations, saw them as a natural pair. He suggested to each separately that they should get to know each other. Because Virginia Tech was trying to induce the education faculty to engage in more research, the collaborative research activities of Borko and Eisenhart received institutional encouragement and support.

The collaborations of Evertson with Green and Darling-Hammond with Lieberman are in sharp contrast to the general pattern, for Green and Lieberman were each proactive in initiating contacts with researchers at distant institutions whose work they admired. Green had read Evertson's work but had never met her when she invited Evertson to present a faculty colloquium at the University of Delaware. The dialogue begun on that occasion led initially to a collaborative research proposal, funded under the National Institute of Education Field-Initiated Grants program, and eventually to their collaboration as coauthors of the chapter, "Observation as Inquiry and Method," for the third *Handbook of Research on Teaching* (Wittrock, 1986). Evertson and Green never had the advantage of working in the same institution to support continued interaction, but they managed to meet together frequently, using research-project travel funds, as they wrote their chapter. Proximity was essential for the collaborative efforts of Darling-Hammond and Lieberman, but it took some effort to arrange that opportunity. While working with Goodlad's Puget Sound Educational Consortium, Lieberman initiated contact with Darling-Hammond at Rand Corporation, inviting her to prepare a report for a task force on teacher professionalism in New York City. As a result of that report, Lieberman argued that New York needed a center for school reform. When Darling-Hammond was hired at Teachers College, she obtained seed money for such a center. Lieberman moved back to Teachers College specifically to work with Darling-Hammond, and the two became codirectors of NCREST, the National Center for Restructuring Education, Schools, and Teaching.

Another variation in the formation of collaborative activities is evident in the Ladson-Billings network. Ladson-Billings and Foster met when both had Spencer Foundation Fellowships in the same 2-year period. Ladson-Billings met Irvine at a Project 30 conference in Monterey, California, where Irvine was a plenary speaker. Foster and Irvine met when they were both serving on an advisory panel for Educational Testing Service (ETS). Members of this network meet face-to-face mainly at conferences. Most of their interaction occurs by telephone or e-mail. Some members do have colleagues nearby with whom they collaborate. Ladson-Billings has coedited a book with Carl Grant (Grant & Ladson-Billings, 1997), a colleague at Wisconsin, Madison. Irvine mentors Vanessa Siddle Walker, a junior colleague at Emory, and works in Atlanta public schools with Lisa Delpit. The network is essential, however, because, as Ladson-Billings notes, "Most of us are fairly isolated. There's one or two of us at an institution. The more prestige associated with the institution, the fewer of us there are" (Ladson-Billings, personal communication, October 28, 1997).

Despite the variety in methods of initiating interaction in the cases considered here, proximity was clearly a contributing factor in most of the collaborative efforts. Given the serendipitous nature of the majority of these meetings and pairings, it is worth questioning whether the field of research on teaching might have taken some rather different directions if these particular relationships had never developed.

STAGE OF PROFESSIONAL DEVELOPMENT

A second factor of apparent influence in the establishment of most of these collaborative research relationships was the stage of professional development. In many instances, one or both partners in the collaborative pairs were novice professors, researchers, or both when they began to interact. Brophy and Good each had newly minted Ph.D.s when they were hired at the University of Texas at Austin in 1967, and each held a joint appointment in the Department of Educational Psychology and the Research and Development Center for Teacher Education. Their collaborative research began almost immediately, fueled by their common interest in teacher expectations, a hot topic because of the Pygmalion in the Classroom study (Rosenthal & Jacobson, 1968). Similarly, Marx and Winne, Borko and Eisenhart, and Cochran-Smith and Lytle all began their collaborative work during the first four years after completing their degrees. Stallings, Peterson, and Green, who were not more than four years beyond their degree work when their collaborations began, each collaborated with a researcher—Flanders, Fennema, and Evertson, respectively—who was older and more experienced.

The exception to this general pattern was Darling-Hammond's partnership with Lieberman, for these two were both professionally experienced when their collaboration at NCREST began. Given the general pattern, however, one must wonder whether the adaptation and accommodation required of individuals engaged in productive and innovative collaboration becomes prohibitively difficult as researchers develop more experience and expertise. It is worth noting that although these collaborations were all very productive, and positive personal relationships were maintained long after the active research collaboration ended, the close collaborations for many of these pairs came to a close as they became more seasoned researchers.

AVAILABLE RESOURCES

Two factors related to available resources also contributed to the productivity of most of these collaborative research relationships. First, there was funding support provided from federal sources or private foundations for most of the studies conducted by these collaborators. In fact, during the period when much of this work was done, funding agencies were actively encouraging collaborative and interdisciplinary research. Second, the opportunity for extended interaction in a relaxing setting contributed to the development of new ideas and shared perceptions, according to the reports of these researchers. In some instances, such opportunities were readily available. Winne and Marx, for example, shared office space in a trailer that was out in the woods and physically isolated from other faculty. A refrigerator stocked with liquid refreshments contributed to the relaxed atmosphere that supported their productive afternoon bull sessions. In other instances such as the planned meetings of Evertson and Green, the opportunities for relaxed discussion were deemed essential, and were deliberately created by the collaborators. Their working procedures provided food for body and mind. "We had smoked white fish . . . and played computer games. . . . We spent extended periods of time together talking about the social history and looking at the roots of the work . . . [to] understand what was the intellectual base of the field" (Green, personal communication, July 30, 1996).

A remarkable exception to academic tradition was the decision of Dean Marvin Lazerson at the University of Pennsylvania to award a 5-year endowed chair jointly to Cochran-Smith and Lytle. This award came before either had received tenure, and provided them with some extra resources for their work on teacher research. These two had opportunity for extended interaction, but not in a relaxed setting. They were running separate inquiry projects with groups of teachers, each with different funding sources, yet their common interests made them natural allies. Working together across projects and with the doubly intense pressures provided by the multiple contexts involved was particularly time-consuming, but they perceived this environment as particularly generative.

Time and money are essential resources for most productive research, but based on the experience of the researchers interviewed for this chapter, additional time for exploration and melding of alternative viewpoints appears to be a critical factor for innovative collaborative research.

EXPANDED THINKING

The participants in these cases all commented on the ways in which the collaborative work had stretched their thinking and had enriched both their conceptions of research and their perceptions of teaching and learning. Even in the "traditional marriage" category of collaboration, the differences in background and experience were such that mutual learning occurred. The data from these cases suggest that this sense of expanded consciousness was valued as much as the more public rewards accorded to the work of these collaborators. The following testimonials include many illustrative comments.

1. Marx and Winne. "Phil has a tenacious mind and he wants to analyze EVERYTHING down to its elemental components. . . . I brought the more molar and human interaction perspective to our work. In terms of basic premises about our understanding of the world, I have more of a moral philosophy point of view whereas Phil has a more epistemological point of view" (Marx, personal communication, August 3, 1996). "This tension was invigorating and we had some real knock-down arguments. But we were always simpatico in some very special way. . . . Our friendship prevented any enmity from discoloring what we did" (Winne, personal communication, August 7, 1996).
2. Nuthall and Alton-Lee. "[Adrienne] convinced me that case studies were necessary. I found ways of amalgamating case study data and predicting from one case to another. She convinced me that social processes (including gender) were deeply imbedded in the process and did much of the gender analysis. I provided some of the background in learning theory and in previous research on teaching" (Nuthall, personal communication, August 12, 1996). "It was a case of walking in and out of each other's minds" (Alton-Lee, personal communication, January 14, 1997).
3. Borko and Eisenhart. "We tried to join Hilda's interest in psychology with my interest in anthropology, both in terms of the theoretical perspectives that we brought to [the research] and also the methodological techniques that we had been working with separately" (Eisenhart, personal communication, August 13, 1996). "We must have talked for hours about knowledge, and tried to figure out what the idea of knowledge meant to us—to a psychologist who saw knowledge as residing within an individual and to an anthropologist who saw knowledge as residing within a culture. . . . We've talked over the years about this, but in that initial conversation I thought we were talking in two foreign languages" (Borko, personal communication, August 13, 1996).

One must ask what factors led these researchers to be open to an expansion of their conceptions of research and their ideas about teaching and learning. Many of the collaborators commented on their general dissatisfaction with their own dissertation topics or methodology. For example, Evertson commented on her dissertation study, which examined children's paired-associate learning using pictures, words, photographs, and real objects. Once the dissertation was completed, she noted, "It was clear to me . . . that there wasn't anywhere to go with it. . . . I could never figure out a way that it would be very relevant to what a teacher needs to deal with in the classroom" (Evertson, personal communication, July 30, 1996). Like Evertson, several of these researchers felt that what they learned from their dissertation studies was not particularly useful for improvement of practice. Thus they were probably more open to considering alternative methodologies and research questions.

Many of these collaborative researchers were women, and several of the women saw their gender as an important contributor to their thoughtful explorations of alternative perspectives. However, several pairs of males and also male-female combinations collaborated. While gender did not seem to be a critical factor for success, there were some interesting gender-related differences in the language used to describe collaborative interaction. The women tended to describe their conceptual interactions as discussions or conversations, while the men tended to describe them as productive arguments. For example, Lytle noted that her image of collaboration was "Marilyn and I sitting at a computer, talking about nitty-gritty methods that we were involved in and the teacher struggles, and we would talk them through, . . . work it out, and think about the implications of that for conceptualizing the work" (Lytle, personal communication, August 19, 1996). In contrast, Good commented:

Jere's and my original research resulted from an argument in terms of whether we would find [certain] things in classroom settings. I think that kind of healthy exchange—what type of evidence would you want? what would convince you? how would you know?—these are pretty exciting questions when you're beginning to see the world from someone else's point of view but, at the same time, you're as-serting your point of view, and you're finding fair, interesting ways to explore the phenomena together. (Good, personal communication, April 25, 1997)

While questions to be addressed and methodological ap-proaches to be pursued have been the main topics of conversa-tion or argumentation for most of these collaborative pairs, Ladson-Billings' network has a different focus. The network bridges a variety of research disciplines (e.g., Irvine in educa-tional psychology, Foster in sociolinguistics, Ladson-Billings in anthropology), but this presents no barrier according to Lad-son-Billings.

We all have a sense of urgency, and see this as a moral and almost cultural obligation. . . . We understand that people might frame the questions differently, . . . [but] rarely have I had to question my col-laborators' motivation or ethics, because we [all] have a sense of how high the stakes are. . . . The sense of relief that comes from working with people in my network is that the ethical stuff gets put on the table first, and we will ask the question of what benefit is this going to be for the community in which we are working. (Ladson-Billings, personal communication, October 28, 1997)

PROFESSIONAL RISK

It is important to acknowledge that the research and publica-tions of these collaborative researchers were not universally ac-claimed. In many instances, their work met with mixed reac-tions. This type of response is probably typical for research that pushes the boundaries of any field. Indeed, it is important that such research, like all research, be subjected to careful analysis and objective critique. In some instances, however, the criti-cisms faced by these researchers have focused on their attempts to forge links between opposing research paradigms or pro-grams. Some process-product researchers, for example, sug-gested that Evertson was disloyal for allowing the *Handbook* chapter on observation (Evertson & Green, 1986) to be tainted by the ethnographic perspective, while a review of qualitative research (Jacobs, 1987) criticized the chapter as "atheoretical." Similar pressures to conform were described by Lytle and Cochran-Smith, who noted that occasionally when teachers in their groups were invited to publish their research, the people who wanted them to publish also wanted them to alter the re-search to make it more like academic research in form and voice. This research team has been struggling to support teach-ers who are trying to invent various new forms of writing for presenting their work. "These ways don't necessarily match per-fectly with what has been done in the academy" (Cochran-Smith, personal communication, August 19, 1996).

While the research itself was eventually generally accepted in all these cases, these types of criticisms had an impact on some researchers' identification with professional reference groups. For example, Borko and Eisenhart never published jointly in either educational psychology or anthropology journals. When Borko was asked to chair the educational psychology program area at Colorado, she was told by some that she was not an educational psychologist. Eisenhart felt that she had to keep up a separate track of research in anthropology and confessed that "I did feel quite schizophrenic for a good ten years there" (Eisen-

hart, personal communication, August 13, 1996). As the pe-riod of their cooperative research was concluded (an amicable separation in all cases), some of these collaborative partners re-turned to comfortable homes in their original research tradi-tions (cultures or families), but others felt relegated to a kind of limbo, unable to fit in easily with their original membership group, and unwilling to be completely adopted into the research group of their collaborative partner. Thus the formation of a productive and innovative collaborative research relationship is not without some professional risk.

For the Ladson-Billings network, the mentoring and support that members provide each other serves to minimize the profes-sional risk associated with conducting research outside the mainstream. Their sense of professional risk is compounded by feelings of risk associated with position in the overall popu-lation.

When you feel as if you are not always valued by the general popula-tion, as African Americans and as women, you don't want to send your work out to be critiqued by just anybody; you have to be care-ful who you send your work out to, because in its early drafts it might be harshly and unfairly criticized. (Irvine, personal communi-cation, August 2, 1996)

ENCOURAGING COLLABORATIVE EFFORTS

The patterns of productive research collaboration revealed in these cases have in common the element of encouragement. Proximity, available resources, and a sense of expanded think-ing all encourage continued interaction. Researchers in early ca-reer stages can find encouragement for their ideas by sharing them with a collaborative partner. Even professional risk can be encouraging in a counterintuitive way, for there is a certain excitement and stimulation in stepping beyond tradition to tread uncharted paths. The continued growth and development of research on teaching will depend to a large extent on main-taining such sources of encouragement and on locating or in-venting new sources of support for collaborative efforts.

Patterns in the Development of Research Dissemination

Collaborators in these cases have contributed to changes in the dissemination of research, as well as the conduct of research. Shifts have occurred in the audiences addressed, the ways in which research is shared, and the role of teachers in the re-search and dissemination process.

DISSEMINATION TO RESEARCHERS

Several of the collaborative pairs included here have contrib-uted to the dissemination of research on teaching. Changes have occurred in this area also. Early dissemination efforts were aimed almost exclusively at the educational research commu-nity, often with the goal of convincing others that research on teaching could produce results befitting an emergent scientific basis for the art of teaching. The early work of Gage (1963) exemplifies this type of effort. The subsequent reviews by Ro-senshine (1971), Dunkin and Biddle (1974), and Brophy and Good's next-generation review (1986) were also directed toward researchers, but had the somewhat different goal of pointing out directions for the improvement of research. Like the collaborative research reports, these dissemination efforts were not always well received. Rosenshine notes that "the height of my popularity was when I was most vague, . . . reporting on studies of teacher clarity and enthusiasm, . . . concepts which were sufficiently ambiguous" (Rosenshine, personal communication, October 4, 1996). When he wrote articles praising the methodology of Stallings' Follow Through study, "it was a bombshell . . . and people were very upset" (Rosenshine, personal communication, October 4, 1996) because the results supported direct instruction, contrary to current views of good teaching at that time. Rosenshine was undeterred by these reactions, however. Stallings recalls that Rosenshine studied her data, and began trumpeting the results. She viewed him as a kind of "town crier" (Stallings, personal communication, August 8, 1996) in his zeal to inform others about the results of well-designed studies of teaching and saw this role as providing an important service to the profession.

The journal, *Teaching and Teacher Education,* initiated as a result of efforts by Gage and Dunkin, expanded dissemination geographically, providing researchers with a greater awareness of international developments in research on teaching. Gage was a member of the advisory board for the first edition of the *International Encyclopedia of Education* (Husen & Postlethwaite, 1985), published by Pergamon Press. The idea for an international journal grew out of discussions of this advisory board. Robert Maxwell, the head of Pergamon Press, endorsed the idea. Maxwell initially invited Dunkin to serve as editor of *Teaching and Teacher Education* (*TATE*). Dunkin had coedited with distinction the section on "Teaching and Teacher Education" in the *International Encyclopedia of Education* and had been chosen to edit the single-volume encyclopedia on teaching and teacher education (Dunkin, 1987). He knew the international experts and recommended people to serve as the first members of the journal's editorial board. Maxwell invited Gage to chair the editorial board, but Gage declined, believing that the arrangement of two leadership positions would be unwieldy. Subsequently, Maxwell named Gage as editor, possibly in the belief that sales in the United States would be greater with a well-known American editor. Gage selected Dunkin and Sara Delamont (University College, Cardiff, UK) as the two associate editors. Gage wrote the statement of the scope and purpose of the journal and served as editor for the first six issues. When eye problems made editing duties difficult, Gage resigned as editor, and Dunkin was appointed editor, serving in that capacity for 6 years.

A major benefit of *TATE* has been to introduce American researchers to the work of their counterparts in other countries. As Sara Delamont puts it, American researchers "need to know that the network is international and that this is a good thing" (Delamont, personal communication, July 31, 1996). Neville Bennett, *TATE* editor from 1992 to 1998, has expressed similar views, noting that "U.S. researchers in general (there are some remarkable exceptions) are a pretty ethnocentric lot, and we Europeans have the feeling that our research does not travel west half as well as theirs travels east" (Bennett, personal communication, August 1, 1996). From Australia, Dunkin has observed that "Americans were not the only ones who did not know the international literature. The Brits were just as ethnocentric" (Dunkin, personal communication, September 9, 1997).

DISSEMINATION TO TEACHERS

David Berliner was also an early associate editor of *TATE,* thereby acknowledging the importance of dissemination of research on teaching to an international audience of researchers. In his work with Casanova, however, the audience for dissemination of research shifted sharply. Berliner and Casanova were concerned with making research on teaching more accessible to practitioners, and chose the *Instructor* magazine as an appropriate vehicle for reaching that audience, partly as a result of Berliner's role as a member of the *Instructor* Advisory Board. From 1983 to 1989 they wrote a joint column, "Putting Research to Work," highlighting studies which dealt with issues relevant to teachers, which could be readily synthesized in the space allotted, and which reflected their philosophy of worthwhile educational practice. The column was well received by practitioners, and Berliner was often introduced to practitioner audiences as coauthor of the column, rather than as a prominent educational psychologist. The columns were subsequently published in book form (Berliner & Casanova, 1993/1996). This pair also worked with colleagues at the National Education Association (NEA) and graduate students to develop and publish an eight-volume series, *Readings in Educational Research,* presenting primary research articles on teacher-chosen topics (e.g., Casanova, Berliner, & Powell, 1994). A general introduction to the topic, annotations of the articles, and discussion questions are included in each volume.

FACE-TO-FACE DISSEMINATION

Not all dissemination of research on teaching occurred through publications, even in the early stages of development of the field. Both Flanders and Stallings, independently and at different points in time, worked with classroom teachers to provide them with feedback on their interactive behavior, using the category systems they had developed. Both used research results to suggest desirable models of productive interaction patterns, but each encouraged teachers to choose the types of changes they wished to make to improve their own teaching. Evertson has indicated that her work with Green changed the way she thought about the relationship of classroom observation to teacher development. She went from a training model ("just tell them what to do and make them practice, practice, practice") to an inquiry-based model. She now believes that "teachers must begin to find their own voice and come forward with their own explanatory models for what occurs. . . . This is a much more powerful way of helping people move through the change process in their own development" (Evertson, personal communication, August 8, 1996).

Darling-Hammond and Lieberman, in their work as codirectors of the National Center for Restructuring Education, Schools, and Teaching (NCREST), also worked directly with teachers in an alternative format for disseminating research on teaching. They engaged groups of teachers in affiliated schools in dialogue and discourse about research. Lieberman's interests have long focused on how the individual fits within the organization and how networks of teachers can create the conditions for school change. Forming teacher networks to promote school restructuring fit well with her commitments. NCREST also targeted policy makers in their dissemination efforts, aiming to document (and eventually improve) school practice from both the "inside-out" and the "outside-in."

> [We've] struggled with how you bring the tools of social science to bear in a way that also understands the work from the perspective of those who do it, and therefore communicates to other practitioners in ways that are not romanticized or ungrounded, but are rigorous and also responsive to [their] concerns. (Darling-Hammond, personal communication, August 7, 1996)

DISSEMINATION BY TEACHER-RESEARCHERS

The approach of Cochran-Smith and Lytle (1993) introduced another important shift in thinking about dissemination of research on teaching. Experienced and prospective teachers in their teacher-researcher communities engaged in studies of teaching and learning in their own classrooms, shared their research with each other, and eventually moved to disseminate their work more broadly to teachers, teacher educators, and researchers through conference presentations and publications. Cochran-Smith notes that teachers' interests in these research communities "were really about understanding and ultimately altering and improving their work with kids and adolescents, and when teacher research and inquiry helped them do that better, there was an enormous commitment" (Cochran-Smith, personal communication, August 19, 1996). Lytle explains that improvement of their teaching "is the primary investment that many teachers make. . . . But some of them make dual investments, [becoming] also invested in being part of the national conversation" (Lytle, personal communication, August 19, 1996). Thus, teachers in these groups see themselves as the creators of knowledge to be disseminated rather than the targets of information created by researchers from academia.

Clearly, over time the audiences for research on teaching have expanded dramatically, and the venues for sharing information derived from research have evolved to include face-to-face interaction in school settings. The changes in patterns of dissemination have been consistent with the changes in topical interests addressed by research, and these two aspects of the field may have had an interactive influence on each other. As research has focused more on teacher cognitions and explored more links between teaching and learning, the results may have become more interesting, useful, and meaningful to practitioners, making dissemination to teachers more feasible. At the same time, as researchers and teacher educators have become more committed to dissemination of research to an audience of teachers through direct dialogue and discussion, the inherent interest of teachers in the thinking of their students may have encouraged researchers to focus more on the pupil cognition aspect of classroom interaction. Certainly the advent of teacher research has increased the influence teachers have on the directions of research on teaching.

More and more researchers have become actively engaged in teacher education in recent years, and future dissemination efforts will predictably focus more sharply on prospective teachers. One important question to be addressed is the degree to which teacher research, work on the moral dimensions of teaching, and studies of culturally relevant pedagogy will enter into the teacher education curriculum. A more important issue, perhaps, is the process by which such research will be shared with prospective teachers. Lessons learned about the effectiveness of dialogue and discussion with experienced teachers should be a sound basis for designing such future dissemination efforts.

Teaching Experience as a Possible Factor in Development of the Field

An interesting characteristic of many of the collaborative researchers identified here was their prior experience as teachers before beginning their doctoral work. As noted in Tables 3.1–3.5, 18 of the 32 researchers in these cases had experience teaching in K–12 public school settings: Rosenshine, Cazden, Florio-Ruane, Gudmundsdóttir, Hansen, Alton-Lee, Dunkin, Fennema, Evertson, Green, Borko, Casanova, Darling-Hammond, Lieberman, Cochran-Smith, Lytle, Foster, and Ladson-Billings. In several instances, they have commented on the ways in which their teaching experience influenced their approaches to the conduct of research and the implementation of research results.

Doctoral students in education who have had teaching experience are certainly not rare, but apparently prior to the 1970s, such students rarely became committed researchers. Gage recalled his delight when Winne and Peterson entered the doctoral program at Stanford:

> They were bright young people, and they were exactly what I'd been yearning for for years, namely, people who came into graduate work in education directly out of their undergraduate programs, because at Illinois and at Stanford until then, they typically were people who had gotten teaching experience and, sometimes, administrative experience, and then they would show up as graduate students in education. They showed up at the age of 28, typically with a spouse, some children, and a mortgage, and they were in a hurry to get out and go to work and make a living. So that research for those graduate students was a kind of strange interlude, something they had never done before and would never do again. . . . Winne and Peterson and others were members of a bright new generation of graduate students . . . and they were wonderful. They were eager, they had a research orientation and research values, and they were very smart. (Gage, personal communication, September 17, 1996)

While Gage viewed Winne's and Peterson's dearth of teaching experience as an asset, Winne was in fact drawn to graduate study in part by the difficulties he faced during his brief period of student teaching, and Peterson regarded her lack of classroom experience as a handicap to be overcome, for it affected the way she was perceived by faculty colleagues at Wisconsin and by the teachers whose classrooms she wished to study. The prevalence of former teachers among the productive researchers in these cases suggests that the bright new generation of graduate students that Gage and other professors encountered in the early 1970s were not merely imbued with a "research orientation." They were lured not only by a commitment to the improvement of teaching and learning but also by a belief that

Figure 3.1. Early topics in research on teaching.

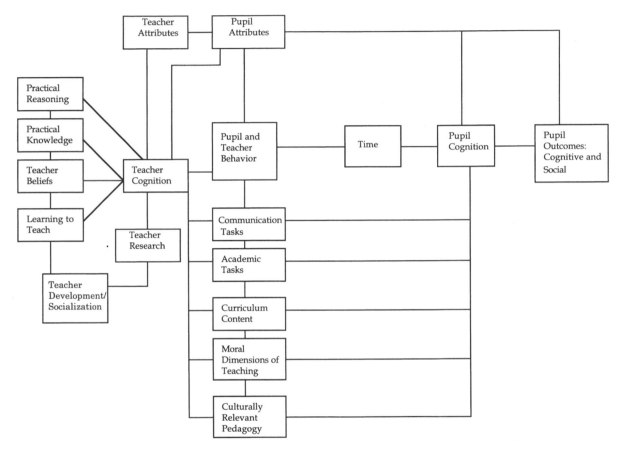

Figure 3.2. Expanded field of research on teaching.

research on teaching could contribute substantially to such an improvement. These were qualities that Peterson and Winne shared with doctoral students who were more experienced in classroom practice.

Figures 3.1 and 3.2 present a graphic representation of the principal topics addressed by research on teaching in the early 1970s (Figure 3.1), compared with those included in more recent reviews (Figure 3.2). Almost all of the researchers identified in the cases described here have contributed research linked in some way to the topic of teacher cognitions, shown in its present expanded form in Figure 3.2. The transformation from experienced teacher to committed researcher was an important chapter in the professional lives of many of the collaborative researchers in the cases chronicled here. It is certainly reasonable to conjecture that the subsequent transformation of research on teaching, which since 1970 has greatly increased in complexity and has become heavily invested in examining the

myriad forms of teacher cognitions, is due at least in part to the presence of former teachers in the corps of active researchers investigating classroom processes.

Two other types of changes that have occurred over time may also be related to the presence of former teachers in the ranks of active researchers. There has been increased attention to pupil cognitions as a critical aspect of research on teaching, and there has been a persistent drive toward linking research on teaching to research on learning. This was evident in Winne and Marx's introduction of the mediating variable of pupil cognitions and in Peterson and Fennema's research incorporating Carpenter's studies of children's mathematical thinking. Evertson and Green saw their ability to consider in depth the relationship of teaching to learning as an essential feature of their collaboration. Borko and Eisenhart reportedly held long conversations about whether knowledge resided in the individual or in the culture, and they considered their ability to link the individual and the sociocultural environment in their conceptual model of the learning of teachers as evidence of their development as collaborators. Members of Ladson-Billings' network saw the study of teaching as an essential part of their mission to improve the learning of African-American students. Perhaps the most comprehensive work illuminating the connection between studies of teaching and studies of learning was that of Alton-Lee and Nuthall in the six studies of their Understanding Teaching and Learning Project (Alton-Lee & Nuthall, 1992).

These developments could well stem from the perspectives of experienced teachers turned researchers. Teachers must pay attention to the thinking and learning of their students if they are to make informed judgments about the efficacy of their teaching. As researchers, former teachers might naturally focus on pupil cognitions as a critical ingredient in any investigation of effective teaching. The teacher-researchers who have worked with Cochran-Smith and Lytle have had this type of focus in many of their investigations (Cochran-Smith & Lytle, 1993).

Possible Impact of Collaboration on Future Directions of Research on Teaching

As research on teaching has focused more on teacher and pupil cognitions and on the links between teaching and learning, some of the research collaborators depicted in these cases have begun to reflect on the changes that have occurred both in their own thinking about research and dissemination and in their conceptions of teaching and learning. The process of collaboration has prodded these researchers toward an increased awareness of the intellectual families in which they were raised, and has allowed them to acknowledge the potential value of relationships that enable them to build on the strengths of more than one tradition. Having become more cognizant of influences on their own thinking, some have become interested in exploring such influences in others or in sharing awareness of influences upon their thinking with other researchers. Evertson and Green, for example, examined the roots of several illustrative studies in their chapter, "Observation as Inquiry" (Evertson & Green, 1986), by interviewing the researchers about their intellectual histories. Borko and Eisenhart have written a book on research design for novice researchers that uses personal stories about their own research experiences to dispel some of the mystique surrounding research (Eisenhart & Borko, 1993). Peterson has written about the evolution of her beliefs about research, and she concludes by noting that because "we are asking teachers to be more reflective about and critical of their own beliefs and practices . . . we need to think about these questions and work to become more reflective and critical of our own beliefs and practices as researchers" (Peterson, 1994).

Peterson has taken her own advice and has actively promoted such exploration by others, in addition to her self-explorations. She has coedited a book in which a series of women educators explore the relationships between their life experiences and the issues they have addressed in their research (Neumann & Peterson, 1997). The approach is reminiscent of the work of Clandinin and Connelly (1995), who investigated the ways in which teachers' personal histories influence their practical knowledge about teaching.

This type of inquiry may well prompt a new phase of research on teaching in which a kind of personal epistemology is entered into the record together with other methodological features of a study. In some ways this would seem to be a next logical step in the direction of strengthening the links between studies of teaching and studies of learning and expanding the investigations of teacher and pupil cognitions. Inquiry into the cognitions of researchers and identification of the ways in which researchers' prior experiences and learning influence not only the questions that they raise but also the methods that they use to investigate classroom teaching and learning could make public what is now tacit knowledge in much of research on teaching. Researchers, teachers, and policymakers might better understand why they know what they currently know about teaching, and catch a glimpse of the unexplored issues that have yet to be investigated.

It is clear from these cases that the process of research collaboration has had an impact not only on the thinking of the individuals involved but also on the movement of the field of research on teaching as a whole. Just as individual researchers may gain valuable insights into their beliefs and practices through reflection on their personal and intellectual histories, so current and future generations of researchers may learn valuable lessons from periodic examinations of the professional relationships influencing the historical development of the field.

REFERENCES

Alton-Lee, A. G., Densem, P. A., & Nuthall, G. A. (1991). Imperatives of classroom research: Understanding what children learn about gender and race. In J. Morss & T. Linzey (Eds.), *Growing up: Lifespan development and the politics of human learning* (pp. 93–117). Auckland: Longman Paul.

Alton-Lee, A. G., & Nuthall, G. A. (1992). A generative methodology for classroom research. *Educational Philosophy and Theory: Special Issue on Educational Research Methodology, 24*(2), 29–55.

Barr, A. S., Bechdolt, B. V., Gage, N. L., Orleans, J. S., Pace, C. R., Remmers, H. H., & Ryans, D. G. (1953). Second report of the committee on criteria of teacher effectiveness. *Journal of Educational Research, 46*(9), 641–658.

Berliner, D.C., & Casanova, U. (1996). *Putting research to work in your school.* Arlington Heights, IL: IRI/Skylight Training and Publishing. (Original work published 1993).

Berliner, D.C., Casanova, U., & Powell, J. H. (Eds.). (1994). *Readings in educational research: Intelligence.* Washington, DC: National Education Association.

Berliner, D.C., & Rosenshine, B. V. (1987). *Talks to teachers: A festschrift for N. L. Gage.* New York: Random House.

Boostrom, R. E., Hansen, D. T., & Jackson, P. W. (1993). Coming together and staying apart: How a group of teachers and researchers sought to bridge the "research/practice" gap. *Teachers College Record, 95*(1), 35–44.

Borko, H., & Eisenhart, M. (1986). Students' conceptions of reading and their reading experiences in school. *Elementary School Journal, 86*(5), 589–611.

Borko, H., & Shavelson, R. J. (1990). Teachers' decision making. In B. Jones & L. Idol (Eds.), *Dimensions of thinking and cognitive instruction* (pp. 311–346). Hillsdale, NJ: Lawrence Erlbaum Associates.

Brophy, J. E. (1983). Research on the self-fulfilling prophecy and teacher expectations. *Journal of Educational Psychology, 75*(5), 631–661.

Brophy, J. E. (1989). Introduction to volume 1. In J. E. Brophy (Ed.), *Advances in research on teaching* (Vol. 1, pp. xi-xix). London: JAI Press, Inc.

Brophy, J. E., & Good, T. L. (1970). Teachers' communication of differential expectations for children's classroom performance: Some behavioral data. *Journal of Educational Psychology, 61*(5), 365–374.

Brophy, J. E., & Good, T. L. (1986). Teacher behavior and student achievement. In M. C. Wittrock (Ed.), *Handbook of research on teaching* (3rd ed., pp. 328–375). New York: Macmillan.

Casanova, U. (1987). Ethnic and cultural differences. In V. Richardson-Koehler (Ed.), *Educators' handbook: A research perspective* (pp. 370–393). New York: Longman.

Casanova, U., Berliner, D.C., & Powell, J. H. (Eds.). (1994). *Readings in educational research: Cognition.* Washington, DC: National Education Association.

Cazden, C. B. (1986). Classroom discourse. In M. C. Wittrock (Ed.), *Handbook of research on teaching* (3rd ed., pp. 432–463). New York: Macmillan.

Cazden, C. B., John, V., & Hymes, D. (Eds.). (1972). *Functions of language in the classroom.* New York: Teachers College Press.

Clandinin, D. J., & Connelly, F. M. (1995). *Teachers' professional knowledge landscapes.* New York: Teachers College Press.

Clark, C. M., Gage, N. L., Marx, R. W., Peterson, P. L., Stayrook, N. G., & Winne, P. H. (1979). A factorial experiment on teacher structuring, soliciting, and reacting. *Journal of Educational Psychology, 71*(4), 534–552.

Cochran-Smith, M., & Lytle, S. (1990). Research on teaching and teacher research: The issues that divide. *Educational Researcher, 19*(2), 2–11.

Cochran-Smith, M., & Lytle, S. (1992). Interrogating cultural diversity: Inquiry and action. *Journal of Teacher Education, 43*(2), 104–115.

Cochran-Smith, M., & Lytle, S. (1993). *Inside/outside: Teacher research and knowledge.* New York: Teachers College Press.

Darling-Hammond, L. (1994). *Professional development schools: Schools for developing a profession.* New York: Teachers College Press.

Darling-Hammond, L. (1996). *What matters most: Teaching for America's future.* New York: National Commission on Teaching and America's Future.

Darling-Hammond, L. (1997). *The right to learn: A blueprint for schools that work.* San Francisco: Jossey-Bass.

Darling-Hammond, L., Ancess, J., & Falk, B. (1995). *Authentic assessment in action: Studies of schools and students at work.* New York: Teachers College Press.

Dunkin, M. J. (Ed.). (1987). *The international encyclopedia of teaching and teacher education.* Oxford: Pergamon Press.

Dunkin, M. J., & Barnes, J. (1986). Research on teaching in higher education. In M. C. Wittrock (Ed.), *Handbook of research on teaching* (3rd ed., pp. 754–757). New York: Macmillan.

Dunkin, M. J., & Biddle, B. (1974). *The study of teaching.* New York: Holt, Rinehart, & Winston.

Eisenhart, M., & Borko, H. (1993). *Designing classroom research: Themes, issues, and struggles.* Needham Heights, MA: Allyn & Bacon.

Eisenhart. M., Borko, H., Underhill, R. G., Brown, C. A., Jones, D., & Agard, P. C. (1993). Conceptual knowledge falls through the cracks: Complexities of learning to teach mathematics for understanding. *Journal for Research in Mathematics Education, 24*(1), 8–40.

Eisenhart, M., & Cutts-Dougherty, K. (1991). Social and cultural constraints on students' access to school knowledge. In E. Hiebert (Ed.), *Literacy for a diverse society: Perspectives, programs, and policies* (pp. 28–43). New York: Teachers College Press.

Evertson, C., Anderson, C., Anderson, L., & Brophy, J. (1980). Relationships between classroom behaviors and student outcomes in junior high mathematics and English classes. *American Educational Research Journal, 17*(1), 43–60.

Evertson, C. M., & Green, J. L. (1986). Observation as inquiry and method. In M. C. Wittrock (Ed.), *Handbook of research on teaching* (3rd ed., pp. 162–213). New York: Macmillan.

Evertson, C., Weade, R., Green, J., & Crawford, J. (1985). *Effective classroom management and instruction: An exploration of models.* Final Report (NIE-G-83-0063). Washington, DC: National Institute of Education.

Fennema, E. (1974). Mathematics learning and the sexes: A review. *Journal for Research in Mathematics Education, 5*(3), 129–164.

Fennema, E., & Peterson, P. L. (1986). Teacher-student interactions and sex-related differences in mathematics. *Teaching and Teacher Education, 2*(1), 19–42.

Flanders, N. (1970). *Analyzing teaching behavior.* New York: Addison-Wesley.

Florio-Ruane, S. (1987). Sociolinguistics for educational researchers. *American Educational Research Journal, 24*(2), 185–198.

Florio-Ruane, S. (1990). The written literacy forum: An analysis of teacher-researcher collaboration. *Journal of Curriculum Studies, 22*(4), 313–328.

Florio-Ruane, S. (1997). To tell a new story: Reinventing narratives of culture, identity, and education. *Anthropology and Education Quarterly, 28*(2), 152–162.

Florio, S., & Walsh, M. (1981). The teacher as colleague in classroom research. In H. T. Trueba, G. P. Guthrie, & K. H. Au (Eds.), *Culture and the bilingual classroom* (pp. 87–101). Rowley, MA: Newbury House.

Foster, M. (1995). Talking that talk: The language of control, curriculum, and critique. *Linguistics and Education, 7*(2), 129–150.

Foster, M. (1997). *Black teachers on teaching.* New York: New Press.

Gage, N. L. (Ed.). (1963). *Handbook of research on teaching.* Chicago: Rand McNally.

Gage, N. L. (1988). The founding of *Teaching and Teacher Education: An international journal of research and studies. Teaching and Teacher Education, 4*(2), i–ii.

Gage, N. L. (1989). The paradigm wars and their aftermath: A "historical" sketch of research on teaching since 1989. *Educational Researcher, 18*(7), 4–10.

Gall, M. D., Ward, B. A., Berliner, D.C., Cahen, L. S., Winne, P. H., Elashoff, J. D., & Stanton, G. C. (1978). Effects of questioning techniques and recitation on student learning. *American Educational Research Journal, 15*(2), 175–199.

Good, T. L. (1981). Teacher expectation and student perceptions: A decade of research. *Educational Leadership, 38*(5), 415–422.

Good, T. L., & Brophy, J. E. (1997). *Looking in classrooms* (7th ed.). New York: Harper & Row.

Grant, C., & Ladson-Billings, G. (Eds.). (1997). *A dictionary of multicultural education.* Phoenix: Oryx Press.

Green, J. L. (1983). Research on teaching as a linguistic process: A state of the art. In E. W. Gordon (Ed.), *Review of research in education: Vol. 10* (pp. 151–252). Washington, DC: American Educational Research Association.

Gudmundsdóttir, S. (1991). Ways of seeing are ways of knowing: The pedagogical content knowledge of an expert teacher. *Journal of Curriculum Studies, 23*(5), 409–421.

Gudmundsdóttir, S. (1992). Interview with Lee Shulman. *Norsk Pedagogisk Tidsskrift, 76*(2), 111.

Gudmundsdóttir, S. (1995). The narrative nature of pedagogical content knowledge. In H. McEwan & K. Egan (Eds.), *Narrative in teaching, learning, and research* (pp. 24–38). New York: Teachers College Press.

Gudmundsdóttir, S., & Shulman, L. (1987). Pedagogical content knowledge in social studies. *Scandinavian Journal of Educational Research, 31*(2), 59–70.

Hansen, D. T. (1993). From role to person: The moral layeredness of classroom teaching. *American Educational Research Journal, 30*(4), 651–674.

Hansen, D. T. (1995). *The call to teach.* New York: Teachers College Press.

Hansen, D. T. (1996). In class with Philip W. Jackson. In C. Kridel, R. V. Bullough, Jr. & P. Shaker (Eds.), *Teachers and mentors: Profiles of distinguished twentieth-century professors of education* (pp. 127–138). New York: Garland Publishing.

Husen, T., & Postlethwaite, N. (Eds.). (1985). *International encyclopedia of education.* Oxford: Pergamon Press.

Irvine, J. J. (1990). *Black students and school failure: Policies, practices, and prescriptions.* New York: Greenwood Press.

Irvine, J. J. (1991). Beyond role models: An examination of cultural influences on the pedagogical perspectives of black teachers. *Peabody Journal of Education, 66*(4), 51–63.

Irvine, J. J., & Foster, M. (Eds.). (1996). *Growing up African-American in Catholic schools.* New York: Teachers College Press.

Jackson, P. W. (1968). *Life in classrooms.* New York: Holt, Rinehart and Winston.

Jackson, P. W. (1992). *Untaught lessons.* New York: Teachers College Press.

Jackson, P. W., Boostrom, R., & Hansen, D. T. (1993). *The moral life of schools.* San Francisco: Jossey-Bass.

Jacobs, E. (1987). Qualitative research traditions: A review. *Review of Educational Research, 57*(1), 1–50.

Ladson-Billings, G. (1994). *The dreamkeepers: Successful teachers of African American children.* San Francisco: Jossey-Bass.

Ladson-Billings, G. (1995). Toward a theory of culturally relevant pedagogy. *American Educational Research Journal, 32*(3), 465–491.

Lieberman, A. (1995). *The work of restructuring schools: Building from the ground up.* New York: Teachers College Press.

Lieberman, A. (1996). Networks and reform in American education. *Teachers College Record, 98*(1), 7–45.

Lytle, S., & Cochran-Smith, M. (1990). Learning from teacher research: A working typology. *Teachers College Record, 92*(1), 83–103.

Lytle, S., & Cochran-Smith, M. (1994). Inquiry, knowledge, and practice. In S. Hollingsworth & H. Sockett (Eds.), *Teacher research and educational reform* (pp. 22–51). 93rd Yearbook of the National Society for the Study of Education. Chicago, IL: University of Chicago Press.

Lytle, S., & Cochran-Smith, M. (1996, April). Disrupting university culture: The case of teacher research. Paper presented at the American Educational Research Association conference, New York.

Marx, R. W. (1983). Student perceptions in classrooms. *Educational Psychologist, 18*(3), 145–164.

Mehan, H. (1979). *Learning lessons: Social organization in a classroom.* Cambridge, MA: Harvard University Press.

Neumann, A., & Peterson, P. L. (Eds.). (1997). *Learning from our lives: Women, research and autobiography in education.* New York: Teachers College Press.

Nuthall, G. A., & Alton-Lee, A. G. (1992). Understanding how students learn in classrooms. In M. Pressley, K. Harris, & J. Guthrie (Eds.), *Promoting academic competence and literacy in school* (pp. 57–87). San Diego: Academic Press.

Nuthall, G. A., & Church, J. (1973). Experimental studies of teaching behaviour. In G. Chanan (Ed.), *Towards a science of teaching* (pp. 9–25). Windsor, Berkshire, UK: National Foundation for Educational Research.

Peterson, P. L. (1994). Research studies as texts: sites for exploring the beliefs and learning of researchers and teachers. In R. Garner & P. Alexander (Eds.), *Beliefs about text and instruction with text* (pp. 93–120). Hillsdale, NJ: Lawrence Erlbaum Associates.

Peterson, P. L., Carpenter, T. P., & Fennema, E. (1989). Teachers' knowledge of students' knowledge and cognition in mathematics problem solving. *Journal of Educational Psychology, 81*(4), 558–569.

Peterson, P. L., Fennema, E., & Carpenter, T. P. (1991). Using children's mathematical knowledge. In B. Means, C. Chelemer, & M. S. Knapp (Eds.), *Teaching advanced skills to at-risk children* (pp. 68–101). San Francisco: Jossey-Bass.

Peterson, P. L., Marx, R. W., & Clark, C. M. (1978). Teacher planning, teacher behavior, and student achievement. *American Educational Research Journal, 15*(3), 417–432.

Rosenshine, B. (1971). *Teaching behaviours and student achievement.* Windsor, Berkshire, UK: National Foundation for Educational Research.

Rosenshine, B., & Furst, N. (1973). The use of direct observation to study teaching. In R. M. W. Travers (Ed.), *Second handbook of research on teaching* (pp.122–183). Chicago: Rand McNally.

Rosenshine, B., Meister, C., & Chapman, S. (1996). Teaching students to generate questions: A review of the intervention studies. *Review of Educational Research, 66,* 181–221.

Rosenshine, B., & Stevens, R. (1986). Teaching functions. In M. C. Wittrock (Ed.), *Handbook of research on teaching* (3rd ed., pp. 376–391). New York: Macmillan.

Rosenthal, R., & Jacobson, L. (1968). *Pygmalion in the classroom: Teacher expectation and pupils' intellectual development.* New York: Holt, Rinehart and Winston.

Shulman, L. S. (1986). Paradigms and research programs in the study of teaching: A contemporary perspective. In M. C. Wittrock (Ed.), *Handbook of research on teaching* (3rd ed., pp. 3–36). New York: Macmillan.

Shulman, L. S. (1987). Knowledge and teaching: Foundations of the new reform. *Harvard Educational Review, 57*(1), 1–22.

Shulman, L. S. (1992). Research on teaching: A historical and personal perspective. In F. K. Oser, A. Dick, & J. L. Patry (Eds.), *Effective and responsible teaching* (pp. 14–29). San Francisco: Jossey-Bass.

Stallings, J. (1975). Implementation and child effects of teaching practices in Follow Through classrooms. *Monographs of the Society for Research in Child Development, 40*(7–8), 1–133.

Stallings, J. (1977). *Learning to look: A handbook on classroom observation and teaching models.* Belmont, CA: Wadsworth.

Stallings, J., Needels, M., & Sparks, G. M. (1987). Observation for the improvement of classroom learning. In D.C. Berliner & B. V. Rosenshine (Eds.), *Talks to teachers: A festschrift for N. L. Gage* (pp.129–158). New York: Random House.

Winne, P. H. (1985). Steps toward promoting cognitive achievements. *Elementary School Journal, 85*(5), 673–693.

Winne, P. H., & Marx, R. W. (1977). Reconceptualizing research on teaching. *Journal of Educational Psychology, 69*(6), 668–678.

Winne, P. H., & Marx, R. W. (1982). Students' and teachers' views of thinking processes involved in classroom learning. *Elementary School Journal, 82*(5), 493–518.

Winne, P. H., & Marx, R. W. (1987). The best tools teachers have—their students' thinking. In D.C. Berliner & B. V. Rosenshine (Eds.), *Talks to teachers: A festschrift for N. L. Gage* (pp. 267–304). New York: Random House.

Wittrock, M. C. (Ed.). (1986). *Handbook of research on teaching* (3rd ed.). New York: Macmillan.

4.
Dewey After Derrida

Jim Garrison
Virginia Polytechnic Institute and State University

Mary Leach
The Ohio State University

The texts of Derrida seem inextricably connected to the word deconstruction. Yet, Derrida insists, "The word 'deconstruction,' like all other words, acquires its value only from its inscription in a chain of possible substitutions. . . . The word has interest only . . . where it replaces and lets itself be determined by such other words as . . . 'trace,' 'différance,' 'supplement'" (see Kamuf, 1991, p. 275). The reader immediately senses the elusiveness of Derrida's thought. His writings do not limit themselves to merely making a point; they perform and enact it. His texts, by virtue of both their singularity and their intrinsic relation to generality, perform the action of opening themselves up to the incalculable, the unpredictable, the nonprogrammatic. They exhibit his effort to call out a response by the other for whose arrival they have opened the way. Always on the move, Derrida allows no word, no concept, no nonconcept to master him or inhibit the play of language. Derrida himself does not think deconstruction a "good word" and concludes, "It deconstructs itself" (Kamuf, pp. 274 and 275). Derrida lives in a world without a stable center or circumference. Everyone does; that is one lesson his philosophy teaches.

Explicating the texts of Derrida is exhausting enough; doing the same for the often misunderstood texts of Dewey multiplies the difficulty. Combining them so that each is reflected critically in the mirror of the other seems almost foolhardy; like fools, we rush in. We will explicate Derrida, using what Rodolphe Gasché refers to as the "infrastructure" of "différance" (just as we will explicate Dewey using the structure of his "generic traits"). Gasché (1994) asserts, "The traits that make up an infrastructure are without exception traits of pointing away from (themselves), being marked in advance by an Other, referring to an Other, and so on" (p. 7). However complete one thinks his or her system is, however fixed or finished, there are always other possibilities, other interpretations.

Substituting "trace" for "différance" the following passage provides some excuse for our folly: "We must begin wherever we are and the thought of the trace . . . has already taught us that it was impossible to justify a point of departure absolutely. *Wherever we are:* in a text where we already believe ourselves to be" (Derrida, 1976, p. 162). It is possible to trace a series of substitutions forever. It resembles looking up words in a dictionary, where the definition of one word requires looking up the definition of others. For Derrida, there is no master word, no ultimate foundation of meaning that must end the series. We begin within texts signed "Jacques Derrida," where we believe it fruitful for researchers on teaching to begin. We also begin with a discussion of "différance" and of the ethical, political, and institutional nature of Derrida's thought. Gross oversimplifications are unavoidable in the cramped space where we believe ourselves to be in the larger work of this handbook, as well as in the work of Derrida and Dewey.

Différance and the Place of the Ethical, Political, and Institutional in Derrida

Derrida (1982) starts his explication of différance with a description of the function of the sign:

> The sign is usually said to be put in the place of the thing itself, the present thing, "thing" here standing equally for meaning or referent. The sign represents the present in its absence. . . . The sign, in this sense, is deferred presence. (p. 9)

The metaphysics of presence, along with the related idea of logocentrism, dominates Western thought. Seeing is believing, so, presumably, whatever is (metaphysically) present and apparent to the attentive mind is (epistemologically) indubitably true.

The authors wish to thank reviewers Larry Hickman (Southern Illinois University) and Patti Lather (The Ohio State University).

Logical inference may be understood as a chain (or trace) of connecting propositions (or symbols). Logical inference assumes identity (e.g., $x = x$, or, if $x = a$ and $x = b$, then $a = b$). Identity is the center of logocentric thought. Yet the "x" on the left in $x = x$ is different (in space) from the one on the right, and (temporally) it was written first. They are functionally equivalent for many purposes, but these "x's" are not identical. Correct inference should, supposedly, terminate in the presence of the ultimate reference of the symbols. For example, logical deductions from hypothesized laws of theoretical physics should, if experiments are performed correctly, eventuate in experiences that present evidence for the laws. Something like the same pattern supposedly holds for research on teaching, whether qualitative or quantitative. Derrida denies this possibility.

Différance indicates a double meaning in all language. First, there is "difference"; the sign is different from the signified. Second, there is "deferred presence." For most structuralist thinkers, any system of signs (e.g., a theory, a text, a narrative) eventually terminates either in some master word in the system or in some "transcendental signified," that is, something outside the symbolic system to which all the symbols individually or in grammatical combination refer. (See Derrida, 1976, p. 158.) These symbolic systems are usually considered either naturalistic elements in experience like "raw data" or some ideal meaning like "rationality." The transcendental signified terminates the play of signs because it is, supposedly, the presence of the indubitable self-identical thing, the referent. Derrida denies the existence of the transcendental signified and thereby challenges most of Western epistemology and metaphysics. Derrida (1978), though, does understand the desire to escape the anxiety of uncertainty:

> The concept of centered structure is in fact the concept of a play based on a fundamental ground, a play constituted on the basis of a fundamental immobility and a reassuring certitude, which itself is beyond the reach of play. And on the basis of the certitude anxiety can be mastered . . . a history—whose origin may always be reawakened or whose end may always be anticipated in the form of presence. (p. 279)

The promise is false, but the human need is real.

There is no ultimate beginning or ending in Derrida's world, nor is there a bottom (or top) to being for us to ever know. Derrida (1978) rejects the metaphysics of invariable presence and its retinue:

> The entire history of the concept of structure . . . must be thought of as a series of substitutions of center for center, as a linked chain of determinations of the center. . . . It could be shown that all names related to fundamentals, to principles, or to the center have always designated an invariable presence—*eidos, arche, telos, energeia, ousia* (essence, existence, substance, subject). . . . (pp. 279–280)

Eidos refers to something's characteristic property, or essence. *Arche* refers to ultimate origin, foundation, or first principle. *Energeia* is the functioning of a capacity or potential to achieve its fulfillment and actualization. It conjoins with *entelecheia* (that is, the capacity or force) to achieve its perfect self-actualization. For instance, a properly functioning acorn will become a giant oak. *Telos* refers to completion, end, or purpose; it also connects with *entelecheia*. *Ousia* refers to ultimate substance or subject.

Statements such as those above lead many to accuse Derrida of nihilism. Derrida is a nihilist in the sense of alleging that beliefs and values have no eternal, immutable, or indubitable foundations. He deprives us of metaphysical, or theological, comfort. Yet Derrida is not a nihilist because he is not asserting that existence is senseless and useless. Nihilists whimper because they do not think existence has any meaning; for Derrida, meaning is endlessly created. Perhaps we need a new word for those who drown in the ocean of infinite meaning within which humankind swims. Derrida is not a nihilist, nor is he afraid of our experience of swimming.

Against those who see him as destructive, Derrida argues, "Deconstruction certainly entails a moment of affirmation. Indeed, I cannot conceive of a radical critique which would not be ultimately motivated by some sort of affirmation, acknowledged or not. Deconstruction always presupposes affirmation" (see Kearney, 1984, p. 118). Derrida is quite clear about what he wants to affirm; deconstruction, for him is "an openness towards the other" (see Kearney, 1984, p. 124). Deconstruction problematizes because it constantly points away from itself toward absence and otherness. It welcomes in advance the excluded other. Derrida states deconstruction's affirmation thus:

> I mean that deconstruction is, in itself, a positive response to an alterity, or openness that necessarily calls, summons, or motivates it. Deconstruction is therefore vocation—a response to a call. The other, as the other than self, the other that opposes self-identity. . . . The other precedes philosophy and necessarily invokes and provokes the subject before any genuine questioning can begin. It is in this rapport with the other that affirmation expresses itself. (See Kearney, 1995, p. 168.)

Deconstruction urges recognition and respect for what is different, left out, or queer. It is this positive response to the other, to those persons and situations different from the "norm," that, in writing our paper, we want most to urge the community of researchers on teaching to consider. What is called for is not the arrogance of institutionalized knowledge, with its rigid concepts, categories, and identities, but acknowledgment, respect, and recognition.

In an essay on "Metaphysics and Essence," Derrida (1978) urges,

> *Respect* for the other *as what it is:* other. Without this acknowledgment, which is not a knowledge, or let us say without this "letting-be" of an existent (Other) as something existing outside me in the essence of what it is (first in its alterity), no ethics would be possible. . . . The "letting-be" concerns all possible forms of the existent and even those which, by essence, cannot be transformed into "objects of comprehension." (p. 138)

This is ontological respect; it is an openness that recognizes and respects what is not understood. It is a kind of piety before the mysteries of nature, including human nature. Metaphysically, researchers should let being be in its otherness, even when they cannot comprehend it. Otherwise, ethics is impossible because ethical relations begin in respect for the particular, even if unknowable, being of other beings, especially other human beings. Logocentrism drives out difference; it reduces everything to the essences, categories, and norms of the knower. This is the violence concealed in modernity's appeal to "rationality." Deconstruction exposes an ethics of acknowledgment. It opens a site for the consideration of the implications of scientific knowledge as a primary practice for ethical knowing. In writing our paper, we want to affirm the inescapable ethics of all "knowledge" in research on teaching.

Modernity assumes that progress automatically occurs if we can master nature. In the social sciences modernity means mastering human nature. The tool of mastery is reason. As an abstract noun, reason tends to be totalizing, that is, it tends to deny, repress, and violate otherness, difference, and uniqueness as deviations from the norm. Derrida challenges all norms by raising critical concerns about what it is that structures these. What is it that structures meanings, practices, or "laws" that promise mastery? His work opens questions about why certain practices become intelligible, valued, or deemed as traditions, while other practices become impossible, denigrated, or unimaginable as normal.

Carol Gilligan (1982) dared to question the consequences of Lawrence Kohlberg applying the norms of Kantian rule governed morality to the study of all moral development. She claimed to hear "a different voice" of morality associated most frequently with women who thought in terms of webs of connection and who refused to think strictly in terms of a hierarchy of rules. One may read Gilligan as deconstructing Kohlberg's text of the normative moral self. Similarly, we might also wonder why White males score so much better on the norm-referenced Scholastic Aptitude Test. Deconstructing theories of research in moral development, or the research that goes into constructing academic achievement tests, may disclose a logic of identity that serves as a tool of domination.

Unlike claims to detached, dispassionate, and neutral rationality that rests on indubitable metaphysical or epistemological foundations, Derrida (1981) declares, "Deconstruction . . . is not *neutral*. It *intervenes*" (p. 93). It intervenes, for instance, to deconstruct the master words used by masters of political domination to exclude participation in the political process by others different from them. This domination is all too easily translated into research on teaching when embedded in the norms and presuppositions of research questions. Deconstruction challenges the logocentric construction of (for example, White male) identity as exclusively "normal." For his part, Dewey (1930/1984a) decried, "The efforts of those engaged in what is euphemistically called a science of education aim at setting so-called norms" (p. 132).

Deconstruction shakes the foundations of oppression, and it is this shaking that shapes our nonneutral investment in it and brings us to our task in this paper of playing the texts associated with the names "Dewey" and "Derrida" off each other creatively. Nor are we neutral in choosing to emphasize the ethical, political, and institutional in Derrida's work. In a decentered world, not only may people begin wherever they think they are, but also they may move toward whatever they think is most desirable.

Deconstruction can be read as a philosophy of connection-disconnection and inclusion-exclusion. It mitigates against fixed borders and hierarchies, and it can be used to deconstruct oppressive social, political, and institutional constructions. That is the way we approach the deconstructive texts written under the name "Derrida." Derrida (1982) states that "we will designate as *différance* the movement according to which language, or any code . . . is constituted 'historically' as a weave of differences" (p. 12). We will look long and hard at Derrida's "The Laws of Reflection: Nelson Mandela," in *Admiration, or Nelson Mandela* (1987), as a testimonial to Derrida's (and Mandela's) deconstruction of an oppressive system of laws, an illegal legal code. We believe Derrida's efforts in this essay both reflect his political response to apartheid and reveal the political responsibility of his deconstructive practices. After looking at Derrida's mode of approach in deconstructing metaphysical assumptions, we will address Dewey's very different way of "doing" deconstruction on the metaphysics of presence, one of the primary concerns in Derrida's writing and one reason that he writes in the style he does.

Mandela and the Deconstructive Laws of Reflection

Derrida has recognized that the currently available codes for taking any political stance are not at all adequate to radical deconstruction. The impression that deconstruction is apolitical prevails only, he claims, "because all our political codes and terminologies still remain fundamentally metaphysical, regardless of whether they originate from the right or the left" (see Kearney, 1984, pp. 107–126). Thus he is obliged to address any political theory or discussion of politics obliquely through the posing of questions of singularity, universality, alterity, and difference. He must also address such related topics as the ethics of relating and responding. This is his strategy in his essay "The Laws of Reflection: Nelson Mandela." In the essay, Derrida produces a reading of the "law" that he argues is reflected in a singular person and in the proper name Nelson Mandela. It is a structure of "law" that Mandela, in all his particularity, opens up and calls forth to transgress the determined historicity of the law as Western law. Mandela, in his specificity, constitutes for Derrida a gathering in action of singular traits, an apparatus of reflection that gives birth to "the law itself, the law above other laws" . . . "a law beyond legality" (Derrida, 1987, pp. 11, 42). It is instantiated in his name, in his reflection upon the law, and in his reflection of it (pp. 15, 34). This is no routine exercise, for Derrida is not proclaiming or acclaiming Mandela a great man. Derrida is paying homage, admiring Mandela for his interrogation of the meaning of the law and his interrogation of its origin, its aims, and its limits. Derrida shows Mandela as a figure inquiring after the grounding of the ground itself.

As a proper name, which, like a date, "comes to mark itself as the one and only time," the name "Mandela" is a singularity that relates to the other. He (his name) is inscribed within a common geopolitical history, tradition, and set of problematics. As a human being, his vocation is that of a "man of the law," and as such, he both reflects it and reflects upon it in the living of his life (Derrida, 1987, p. 26). Mandela reflects the law, but not in a simple speculative reversal because the law in South Africa in 1987 had been usurped, represented by an oppressive White minority. His becomes the name of the "law" by the laws

of reflection. They work this way. In struggling against apartheid, Mandela inspires admiration by the admiration he feels
for the logic of the law. This admiration that demonstrates for
something that, by its very nature, tends toward universality
and generality, makes him, a singular person, admirable to his
friends and to his enemies alike. Without reducing différance
(in this case, his own particularity), Mandela forces "difference," a multiple mirroring involving the "law," of which he is
clearly within, and the law, of which he is clearly outside.

Derrida's text, as well as its subject, produces a gathering of
a multitude of nonsymmetrical and nonspeculative reflections
that cannot refer to or represent any totality nor create any
unity or synthesis. Derrida's analysis is one reflecting on "what
makes *this* individual the individual that he is" (Gasché, 1994,
p. 17). The hypothesis in the words of Derrida (1987) is that
Mandela "becomes admirable for having, with all his force, admired, and for having made a force of his admiration, a combat-
ive, untreatable, and irreducible power" (p. 15). Derrida per-
forms this movement of reflections outside a logic of exclusive
either/ors, thereby freeing the idea of difference from normative
connotations. In thinking difference differently, he demonstrates a distinction between the conceptualizable difference of
common sense (different from the norm) and a difference that
is not brought back into the order of the same (Mandela, both
a man of the law and a man outside it). Difference here is neither an identity nor a difference between identities. The figure
of Mandela deconstructs Western moral law and its basis in
the logical law of identity. Mandela's law makes its production
possible by transversal of responsibility to a questioning, to the
interrogative demand for a just structure of law. He, his name,
and his life irrevocably move the discourse of politics to its ethical relation among human beings.

In this essay and others, Derrida refuses Habermas's claim,
for example that there exists a necessary link between universalism, rationalism, and modern democracy. Yet, he is strongly
committed to the democratic project. He shows Mandela as a
figure reflecting the lack of availability of an Archimedean
point—such as reason—that could guarantee the possibility of
a mode of argumentation that would have transcended its particular conditions of enunciation. The institution of apartheid
could not be made secure by any rational grounding. He shows
that the distinction between the public man and the private
man, important as it is for democratic politics, is not one of
essence. Mandela's life problematizes that differentiation; it reflects that differentiation as an unstable frontier constantly tres-
passed, with personal autonomy investing public aims and the
private becoming politicized.

The "Laws of Reflection" elaborates a nonfoundationalist
thinking about democracy that we believe presents a convincing
case for the importance of deconstruction for politics and ethics. The radical democratic principles Mandela forces by the
mobilization of passions and sentiments can be defended only
in a situated, contextualist manner, as being constitutive of his
form of life. Derrida argues that he expresses democratic values,
not by appealing to some neutral ground for some transcendental rationalist argument that is based on politically neutral
premises, nor by seeing the individual as prior to society, as
abstracted from social and power relations, language, and
culture. His name consists in the legitimization of conflict,

keeping democratic hope alive by the refusal to eliminate it
through the imposition of an authoritarian South African
structure of law.

Derrida attends to the excess within the closure of the law by
his homage to Mandela. He complicates the play of reflexivity
of the code of politics in which the two concepts of "original"
and "image" mirror each other, intensifying the gap and slip-
page between "original" and "copy," between the thing and its
disguise. His writing reminds us of the chain of significations
in which the word "law" is caught. He writes of Mandela,

> As a lawyer worthy of that name, he sets himself *against the code in
> the code,* reflects the code, but making visible thereby just what the
> code in action rendered unreadable. . . . His reflection . . . does not
> reproduce; it produces the visible. This production of light is jus-
> tice—moral or political. (p. 34)

We believe that good research on teacher education must involve careful reflection on the moral, political, and scientific
codes that control its construction. This approach means that
the stories that research on teacher education tells itself will
become interested in the archaeology of its own construction,
the sedimentary grounds of its own authority. Researchers encountering the "texts" of schooling and culture will move to
acknowledge both the structure of the narration of the stories
and what it is that structures its modes of intelligibility. As contextualized knowledge tales, "research" then foregrounds the
contingent nature of our understanding of school, with its social
situations that have complexities that are subject to a variety
of knowings.

The categories that we use to describe ourselves and others,
the meaning of our methods and aims, and the maze of dualisms in which we have explained our intentions and our tools
to ourselves have become sites of contention.

Derrida, Dewey, and the Double Bind of Postmodern Criticism

The prominent neopragmatist, Richard Bernstein (1992), admires Derrida's philosophy of deconstruction. He particularly
admires its openness to differences and attention to the violence
wrought by exclusionary laws, norms, and codes (see chapters
6 and 7). Although he sees deconstruction as a powerful tool
for critiquing exclusive social and political (and, we add, educational) practices, Bernstein thinks that such radical openness
finds it difficult to take a strong position in ethical, political, or
institutional struggles. He believes, correctly in our opinion,
that there no ethics or politics are possible without taking some,
at least temporary, position. Derrida's dilemma (what Bernstein
calls "the double bind") is that he wants to ameliorate the violence of Western thought by challenging logocentrism and the
metaphysics of presence without falling into nihilistic relativism. Derrida recognizes the problem:

> But the difficulty is to gesture in opposite directions at the same
> time: on the one hand, to preserve a distance and suspicion with
> regard to the official political codes governing reality; on the other,
> to intervene here and now in a practical and engaged manner when-
> ever the necessity arises. . . . I try where I can to act politically while
> recognizing that such action remains incommensurate with my in-
> tellectual project of deconstruction. (Kearney, 1984, p. 120)

Small wonder that Derrida often expresses worry about problems regarding responsibility even as he writes situated, contextualized texts such as "The Laws of Reflection."

"Metaphysically," writes Derrida (1978), "the best liberation from violence is a certain putting into question, which makes the search for an *archia* tremble" (p. 141). Dewey's philosophy of reconstruction liberates us from ethical violence by including the other in the same way as Derrida's deconstruction; that is, by making logocentrism and *arche* (the entire metaphysics of presence) tremble. He does so in ways that do not lead into Derrida's "double bind" and to his difficulties with responsibility. Dewey provides a solution to the postmodern problem with responsible criticism.

Dewey's Deconstruction of the Metaphysics of Presence (*Eidos, Energeia,* and *Entelecheia*) and His Reconstruction

Charles Sanders Peirce, the author of American pragmatism, was a "convergent realist" who thought science could, if carried on long enough, eventually discover all the eternal essences and necessary laws of existence. Peirce (1878/1965) proclaims, "The progress of investigation carries them [scientists] by a force outside of themselves to one and the same conclusion . . . embodied in the conception of truth and reality" (p. 268). The notion of scientists carried by forces beyond their control to some preordained conclusion is an obvious expression of the metaphysic of presence. Here inquiry is driven to its perfect *telos* by the force of a concealed *energeia*. The perfect *telos* is knowledge of eternal, necessary, and indubitable ultimate foundations or first principles (the *arche*) and essences (*eidos*). Many educational researchers share this vision.

Derrida argues that the metaphysics of presence, along with logocentrism, suppresses difference and excludes otherness by reducing everything to the same identity or norm in a timeless present, often at the origin. Peirce identifies forces pushing existence toward complete perfection (*entelecheia*) at the end of inquiry, but the result is the same. Peirce (1878/1965) concludes,

> But the identity of a man consists in the consistency of what he does and thinks. . . . The individual man, since his separate existence is manifested only by ignorance and error, so far as he is anything apart from his fellows, and from what he and they are to be, is only a negation.

> This is man, . . . proud man, Most ignorant of what he's most assured, His glassy essence. (p. 189)

"Man's" glassy essence is to mirror the eternal and immutable *eidos* that will be revealed at the end of history. Insofar as any individual is unique, or different, she or he is only a negation of essential truth. We will now see how William James and John Dewey reconstruct Peirce's pragmatism.

James rejects any notion of a permanent antecedent-fixed essence or identity for researchers to discover. For him there is no perfect end of inquiry; there are only practical purposes. James (1890/1950) insisted that

> The only meaning of essence is teleological, and that classification and conception are purely teleological weapons of the mind. The

essence of a thing is that one of its properties which is so important for my interests that in comparison with it I may neglect the rest. (p. 335)

As with Derrida, James rejects any logocentric notion of essence. Any scheme of theoretical or methodological essences, classifications, or conceptions can be deconstructed by questioning the practical purposes (including social, political, and economic interests) for which they were initially constructed. Logical rules of inference, statistical techniques, or methods of data collection and interpretation are all teleological weapons of the researcher's mind, constructed for her practical purposes. They help secure what is desired (e.g., higher test scores); they are tools for solving problems (e.g., high dropout rates) and achieving valued ends (e.g., multicultural understanding). Reinterpret the purpose, redefine the problem, question the value, and one may deconstruct an essence quickly. Many errors occur because researchers fail to recognize that they create the fundamental categories, concepts, and essences of inquiry as much as they discover them.

Dewey (1925/1981) makes a careful distinction between existence and essence:

> Essence . . . is but a pronounced instance of meaning; to be partial, and to assign a meaning to a thing as *the* meaning is but to evince human subjection to bias. . . . Essence is never existence, and yet it is the essence, the distilled import of existence: the significant thing about it, its intellectual voucher. (p. 144; also see Sleeper pp. 114–116)

Bias in inquiry is inevitable because human beings inquire for their purposes. It does no harm as long as everyone acknowledges the theory-laden character of inquiry and admits that, as Dewey put it, "The same existential events are capable of an infinite number of meanings" (p. 241). Derrida too recognizes the infinite semantic density of existence. Inquiry is the process of distilling logical essences from metaphysical existence. A fallacy, indeed, "the philosophic fallacy," occurs when, in traditional metaphysics, "Essences were hypostatized into original and constitutive forms of all existence" (pp. 51, 145). Metaphysics is about existence, while logic is about essences. Dewey is an epistemological constructivist (see Garrison, 1995). Essences for him are consequences of inquiry that are made, not discovered. Yet they are made out of events found in antecedent existence. Operational definitions supply rigorous essences (and identities), but we must never forget that they are contingent constructs that are developed for our research purposes.

Strangely, James continued to comprehend necessity and causation as metaphysical. Dewey does for a logocentric understanding of necessity and causation what James did for essences. In practical reasoning, researchers inquire to secure what they need or desire. For Dewey, all reasoning was practical reasoning and necessity was practical necessity based on human interest and purpose. Ralph Sleeper (1986) observes "the [scientific] explanation has not so much been 'discovered' as 'produced' by the process of inquiry. The character of 'necessity,' therefore, is 'purely teleological' and contingent" (p. 37). Both contingency and necessity are grasped only as moments in the constant movement of practical inquiry:

Contingent and necessary are thus the correlative aspects of one and the same fact. . . . Contingency referring to the separation of means from end . . . necessity being the reference of means to an end which has still to be got. Necessary means needed; contingency means no longer required—because already enjoyed. (Dewey 1893/1971, p. 29)

Necessity is to be understood logically "only with reference to the development of [practical] judgment, not with reference to objective things or events" (p. 19). Following James's treatment of essences, Dewey comprehends necessity as a logical and not as an ontological concept. As with logical essences, necessary laws depend on the inquirer's practical purposes and, therefore, are endlessly subject to deconstruction.

Dewey includes the idea of causation in his analysis of necessity: "We call it 'means and ends' when we set up a result to be reached in the future . . . we call it 'cause and effect' when the 'result' is given and the search for means is a regressive one" (p. 36). Here again he affirms "the supreme importance of our practical interests" (p. 36). As with essences (*eidos*) and necessity (part of the *arche*), Dewey assimilates the idea of causation (*energeia* or *telos*) to logic instead of metaphysics, but in a way that destroys logocentrism.

Dewey (1938/1986) eventually extended his deconstruction of the metaphysics of presence and logocentrism to include the forms of logic themselves. Sleeper (1986) observes that for Dewey "the normative rules [of logic] must be discovered in and through the successes and failures of inquiry" (p. 83). Dewey (1938/1986) himself alleges, "All logical forms . . . arise within the operation of inquiry and are concerned with the control of inquiry so that it may yield warranted assertions. . . . The forms *originate* in operations of inquiry" (p. 11). There are no metaphysical origins in Dewey's philosophy, which does not mean that things do not emerge in the process of inquiry. For Dewey, those "things" include not only essences, necessity, and causation, but also the very forms of inquiry themselves, such as methodology and logical structures (for instance, the principle of noncontradiction).

Dewey's Deconstruction of the Metaphysics of Presence (*Ousia*)

In Dewey's (1925/1981) philosophy, "nature is viewed as consisting of events rather than substances; it is characterized by histories, that is, by continuity of change proceeding from beginnings to endings. Consequently, it is natural for genuine initiations and consummations to occur in experience" (pp. 5–6). For Dewey, existence, the subject matter of metaphysics, is about events; it is about processes, not ultimate substances (*ousia*). Dewey's fundamental Darwinian intuition is that everything is in flux; everything changes; whatever is constructed will someday be either intellectually deconstructed or physically destroyed.

In his essay, "The Influence of Darwinism on Philosophy," Dewey (1909/1977) discusses the source of his organic and evolutionary theory of nature:

In laying hands upon the sacred ark of absolute permanency, in treating forms that have been regarded as types of fixity and perfection as originating and passing away, the *Origin of Species* intro-duced a mode of thinking that in the end was bound to transform the logic of knowledge, and hence the treatment of morals, politics and religion. (p. 3)

Later Dewey (1920/1982) would argue that "change rather than fixity is now a measure of 'reality' . . . change is omnipresent," or again, "natural science is forced by its own development to abandon the assumption of fixity and to recognize that what for it is actually 'universal' is process." (pp. 114, 260). Surprisingly, research on teaching seems not to have learned this lesson.

For Dewey, the events of natural existence are a mixture of both the precarious and the stable; he insisted on an "ineradicable union in nature of the relatively stable and the relatively contingent" (Dewey, 1925/1981, p. 56). For him, "the things of ordinary experience contain within themselves a mixture of the perilous and uncertain with the settled and uniform" (p. 5). It has been estimated that 99% of all species that have ever lived are not extinct (Parker, 1992, p. 570). A species is an essence, an *eidos*. Dewey's neo-Darwinian insight is to realize that what holds for biological forms or essences also holds for ontological and logical forms as well. The essence of things, including the objects postulated by theories and methods of science, are relatively stable, yet their existence is precarious. Dewey declares, "A thing may endure . . . and yet not be everlasting; it will crumble before the gnawing tooth of time, as it exceeds a certain measure" (p. 63). That things endure, that they are relatively stable, is all that researchers on teaching need to engage in rational research and responsible criticism.

As a pragmatist, Dewey emphasizes the importance of the relatively stable and fixed more than Derrida does. This view permits him to take critical positions more readily. Still, every contingent construction for Dewey is subject to deconstruction and reconstruction. In this process, Dewey seems to put the accent on the constructive and reconstructive phase more than on the deconstructive. Dewey's neo-Darwinism imparts an urgency to his philosophy of reconstruction that is missing from Derrida's deconstruction. This may be the way out of Derrida's "double bind" and a more responsible attitude to take.

Dewey's Deconstruction of the Metaphysics of Presence (*Arche*)

Dewey's metaphysics is consistent with his logic and philosophy of nature. The role of metaphysics in Dewey's philosophy is ill understood. Early in his career, Dewey (1930/1984b) adhered to neo-Hegelianism. Hegel argued, as did Peirce later, that the course of events was moving toward the concrete realization of the good, the beautiful, and the true at the end of history. Dewey slowly "drifted away from Hegelianism" (p. 154). As he did, Dewey ceased to write about metaphysics at all. Once Dewey entirely abandoned neo-Hegelianism, he also abandoned the idea of cosmic purposes (*telos*) fulfilling themselves in history, any eternal eschatology, and any ultimate beginning (*arche*) as controlling the course of events.

When, after years of silence on the subject, Dewey formulated a new metaphysics, he started by rejecting the idea of ultimate metaphysical origin, foundation, or *arche*. There is no ultimate cosmic beginning (*arche*), center, or ending (*telos*) in

Dewey's world any more than there is in Derrida's. Dewey (1915/1979) stated,

> Hence it may be said that a question about ultimate origin or ultimate causation is either a meaningless question, or else the words are used in a relative sense to designate the point in the past at which a particular inquiry breaks off. . . . The term "ultimate" has meaning only in relation to the particular existence in question. (p. 5)

The inquiry begins wherever the inquirers are, in some situation they find themselves, and it concludes whenever the needs and purposes that initiated the inquiry are satisfied.

Dewey believed that there was a distinctive role for a metaphysics of existence apart from logic and scientific inquiry:

> I wish to suggest that while one may accept as a preliminary demarcation of metaphysics from science the more "ultimate traits" with which the former deals, it is not necessary to identify these ultimate traits with temporally original traits. (p. 4)

Dewey strove to provide a role for metaphysics in practical inquiry, but it is so different from the metaphysics of presence that it is hard to recognize. What, though, did Dewey mean by "irreducible traits," or what he later called "generic traits"? The answer, we think, is something very much like what Derrida called infrastructures.

Derrida's "Infrastructures" and Dewey's "Generic Traits": The Metaphysics of Absence and the Other

For Derrida, operative terms like "deconstruction," "différance," and "trace" are infrastructures; they are "nonconcepts," or "undecidables." What does he mean by infrastructures? Gasché (1994) identifies Derrida's ideas of "substitution," "trace," "supplementarity," or "différance" as infrastructures that attempt to "articulate the laws and limits of intelligibility. . . . The traits that make up an infrastructure are without exception traits of pointing away from (themselves), being marked in advance by an Other, referring to an Other and so on. . . . They can thus never give rise to a unity" (p. 6). The law of différance is a reminder that there are always other possibilities beyond any actual system, however perfectly unified. Infrastructures are not transcendental conditions for the possibility of something. Instead, their irreducible tensions are openings to other and indeterminate possibilities. Dewey's generic traits resemble Derrida's infrastructures.

Derrida declares différance "a nonconcept in that it cannot be defined in terms of oppositional predicates; it is neither *this* nor *that;* but rather this *and* that (e.g., the act of differing and of deferring) without being reducible to a dialectical logic of either" (Kearney, 1984, p. 110). Derrida (1973) insists, "For us, difference remains a metaphysical name. . . . 'Older' than Being itself, our language has no name for such a difference (1973, pp. 158–159). Rorty (1991) wonders, "How can différance . . . be *more* than the vacuous nonexplanations characteristic of a negative theology? (p. 113). Rorty (1982) passes a similar judgment on Dewey's metaphysics of generic traits; he is mistaken about both.

We have seen that Richard Bernstein particularly admires deconstruction's openness to the other. Bernstein (1992) believes there is "a deep tendency in Western philosophy to reduce (violently) 'the Other' to 'the Same'" (pp. 73–74). Bernstein concludes: "We must resist the dual temptation of *either* facilely assimilating the alterity of 'the Other' to what is 'the Same' . . . *or* simply dismissing (or repressing) the alterity of 'the Other' as being of no significance" (p. 74). Bernstein believes Derrida succeeds in overcoming metaphysical violence by working beyond the exclusive either/ors of Western thought. As Bernstein indicates, "His 'logic' here is a 'both/and' rather than 'either/ or' . . . it is not the 'logic' . . . in which all difference and oppositions are ultimately reconciled" (p. 72). The logic of Derrida's infrastructures is neither this nor that; but rather this and that. This tension is the "logic" of poetry; it is the opening through which the possible may become actual and novel meaning can be made. The same logic holds for Dewey's generic traits.

Rarely does anyone call attention to the structure of Dewey's generic traits (Garrison, 1985, is an exception). Dewey's generic traits display a pluralistic both/and structure that complements the nonuniversalizable both/and "logic" that Bernstein so admires in the work of Derrida. Recall that for Dewey events are both precarious and stable. A nonuniversalizable both/and "logic" structures the generic traits of Dewey's metaphysics:

> We live in a world which is an impressive and irresistible mixture of sufficiencies, tight completenesses, order, recurrences which make possible predication and control, and singularities, ambiguities, uncertain possibilities, processes going on to consequences as yet indeterminate. They are mixed not mechanically [or dialectically] but vitally like the wheat and tares of the parable. We may recognize them separately but we cannot divide them, for unlike wheat and tares they grow from the same root . . . change gives meaning to permanence and recurrence makes novelty possible. A world that was wholly risky would be a world in which adventure is impossible, and only a living world can include death. Such facts have been celebrated by thinkers like Heracleitus and Lao-tzu; they have rarely been frankly recognized as fundamentally significant for the formation of a naturalistic metaphysics. (p. 47)

This is a remarkable passage, one that lies at the core of Dewey's entire philosophy, including his philosophy of education. The field of education ignores it entirely. Dewey's generic traits do not provide "a permanent neutral matrix for future inquiry," as Rorty (1982, p. 80) claims; instead, it describes a creative, poetic space where new meaning is made. Dewey's generic traits and Derrida's infrastructures are compatible with poetry, but they do not describe the ground of transcendental rationality.

Dewey is a naturalist. Most people assume that commits him to a simpleminded faith in mechanical natural science; that is false. Dewey viewed nature organically, as a fertile, poetic place where new meanings may be born. In Latin, nature (*natura*), is derived from *nasci* ("to be born"); it translated the Greek *physis* that derived from *phyo,* meaning "bring forth" or "make to grow."

The reference to Heracleitus and Lao-tzu above suggests a unity of opposites, but this metaphysics goes far beyond that. It is ever open, inclusive, and moving. The world we live in is a mixture of both rest and flux. Existence is a mixture of both particularity and universality, both life and death. The differences between each conjoint pair implicate and call out for the other in its definition. This is a both/and structure without final reconciliation or universalizability. The generic traits of existence are always open to other poetic possibilities, other values, other essences to consider and criticize. Dewey's is a pluralistic universe.

A Pluralistic Universe

The universe, for Dewey, is infinitely pluralistic. Derrida derived many of his ideas by reflecting on Heidegger. Dewey developed his ideas by reconstructing the infinite pluralism of William James. In his essay "Realism Without Monism Or Dualism" Dewey (1922/1983a) declares, "Neither is the disjunction between monistic and dualistic realism exhaustive. There remains pluralistic realism, which is precisely the theory I have advanced" (p. 54). Dewey commits himself to infinite pluralism, although James articulates the stance better. James asserts, "The uneasiness which keeps the never-resting clock of metaphysics in motion, is the consciousness that the nonexistence of this world is just as possible as its existence" (James, 1896/1979, p. 63). We must defer all meanings forever in a never-resting world. James feels that "when all things have been unified to the supreme degree, the notion of a possible other than the actual may still haunt our imagination and prey upon our system" (p. 64). James concludes, "The difference between monism and pluralism is perhaps the most pregnant of all the differences in philosophy" (p. 5). Let us explore this pragmatic difference.

James (1909/1971) states the pluralistic thesis this way:

> Pragmatically interpreted, pluralism or the doctrine that it [the universe] is many means only that the sundry parts of reality may be externally related. Everything you can think of, however vast or inclusive, has on the pluralistic view a genuinely "external" environment of some sort or amount. Things are "with" one another in many ways, but nothing includes everything, or dominates over everything. The word "and" trails along after every sentence. (pp. 273–274)

Regardless how perfect and internally complete (*entelecheia*) something seems, there is always something other, something external, something absent that trails along to alter its meaning. That is how Dewey and James would have understood "différance," as difference and deferral. Existence in the metaphysics of infinite pluralism discloses itself to be permanently both internally unified and externally incomplete; it evolves because it involves an openness toward the other. A pluralistic universe is never complete; its ultimate meaning is deferred forever. The "and" that always "trails along" implies an indeterminate, although not capricious, continuation. We think, and feel, that something comes after the "and." We expect something different, something other, must happen, but what, we cannot exactly say. Infinite pluralism is incompatible with the monistic universe of Hegel and Peirce. There is no end of history for the infinite pluralist. There is always room to make more meaning and to reach out to the other (person, interpretation, and essence).

So far as we are aware, no one has ever called attention to the open pluralistic both/and structure of Dewey's generic traits of existence. Infinite pluralism ensures that there will always be differences and that final meaning (aesthetic, ethical, and cognitive) will be deferred forever. This pluralism leads to "the generic insight into existence that alone can define metaphysics in any empirical [naturalistic] sense," because metaphysical knowledge is itself "an added fact of existence, and a curious doubling" (p. 310). The universe changes as things are called into and out of existence, which means the generic traits, or infrastructures, may require revision. It is not a permanent neutral matrix for future inquiry. It is just part of the pragmatic ethos that assures us there will never be any permanent neutral matrix of cosmic rationality to which researchers can make their appeal.

Metaphysics, Criticism, and Context: Finding a Temporary Position for Creative Criticism

Bernstein (1992) complains that criticism of all kinds has been "drawn into a grand Either/Or: either there is a rational grounding of the norms of critique or the conviction that there is such a rational grounding is itself a self-deceptive illusion" (p. 8). Most criticism of research on teaching falls into such grand either/ors. Instead of assuming either one or the other opinion must be the right one, he suggests an alternative. Bernstein believes that we must acknowledge that critique goes on forever, the final meaning not only of what is critiqued, but of critique itself, is forever deferred. Bernstein (1992) concludes, "I do not think we can any longer responsibly claim that there is or can be a final reconciliation in which all difference, otherness, opposition and contradiction are reconciled" (p. 8). Bernstein suggests that we think of criticism (including the critique of research on teaching) as constituted by a "logic" that avoids conceptual universals or the logic of either/or. He is advocating a both/and "logic" rather than the logocentrism of perfect identity. This conviction is why Bernstein (1992) admires the way "Derrida deconstructs the Either/Or itself" (p. 184). Bernstein should admire Dewey's generic traits as tools of criticism as much as he does Derrida's infrastructures.

Nonetheless, Bernstein remains concerned with the question: "*How can we 'warrant'* . . . *the ethical-political 'positions' we do take?* This is *the* question that Derrida never satisfactorily answers. . . . What are we to do after we realize that all *archai* tremble?" (p. 191). Dewey responds to these questions better than Derrida does, although the difference is more one of emphasis and attitude than fundamental philosophical disagreement. Both emphasize the cyclic relation between criticism and creativity. In the critical-creative cycle of construction-deconstruction-reconstruction, Derrida tends to emphasize deconstruction, whereas Dewey accents reconstruction.

For Dewey (1925/1981) "philosophy is inherently criticism" (p. 298). Criticism of what one wonders. Dewey answers, "Criticism is discriminating judgment, careful appraisal, and judgment is appropriately termed criticism wherever the subject-matter of discrimination concerns goods or values" (p. 298). Our fate is bound up with the goods and values we desire and strive to secure. Criticism of research on teaching must, therefore, go far beyond determining whether it is technically competent, valid, and sound. Research on teaching is undertaken to aid us in securing our ideal values; those values must also be continually criticized. Ideals are often possibilities other than the real. Truly effective research must recognize this, which is why we must have constant critique.

Dewey wonders, "If philosophy be criticism, what is to be said of the relation of philosophy to metaphysics?" (p. 308). Dewey answers his question thus:

> [Both] qualitative individuality and constant relations, contingency and need, movement and arrest are common traits of all existence. This fact is source both of values and of their precariousness. . . . Any theory that detects and defines these traits is therefore but a ground-map of the province of criticism, establishing base lines to be employed in more intricate triangulations. (pp. 308–309)

The first sentence restates the both/and structure of the generic traits; the second reaffirms their connection to value discrimination. To live well, or at all, one must secure those things that they need and desire. The generic traits of existence mutually define, condition, and constrain one another within a single unified event much as concave and convex may spatially unify and define each other within a single curve. For example, "Permanence and flux . . . are names given to various phases of their conjunction," Dewey declared, "and the issue of living depends upon the art with which these things [traits] are adjusted to each other" (p. 67). The both/and structure of Dewey's naturalistic metaphysics makes inquiry both necessary and possible. Knowing the proportion of the generic traits mixed in a particular existential context (for example, the mixture of necessity and contingency) provides clues to what we may intelligently hope to creatively actualize.

For Dewey (1931/1985a), "the most pervasive fallacy of philosophic thinking goes back to neglect of context" (p. 5). The concerns that motivate criticism arise out of a concrete practical context; it is context that fixes the proper position for responsible criticism. Dewey did not think one could be in doubt at will. One finds one's self thrown into doubt when her or his usual ways of responding to a situation fail. The state of doubt is not merely cognitive; it is affective as well. The task of inquiry is to effectively transform some situation thereby relieving doubt and discomfort by restoring effective action in one's specific ethical, political, and institutional position. After one makes the *arche* tremble and collapses logocentrism, there are still present problems to which only inquiry allows agents to respond intelligently. Derrida pays homage to Mandela for being an (individual) man both of and outside the (universal) law in the specific context of South African politics.

Dewey describes three deepening spheres of context. The first and "most limited consideration, is the range and vitality of the experience of the thinker himself" (p. 20). Everyone has a unique genetic inheritance (consider fingerprints) and personal history. The inquirer is an indispensable part of any context:

> There is present . . . the background of the experimenter. This includes the antecedent state of theory which has given rise to his problem. It takes in his purpose in arranging the apparatus, including the technical knowledge which makes a controlled experiment possible. . . . There are the habits and present disposition of the subject, his capacity to give attention and to make verbal responses, etc. (p. 7)

Present in any context of inquiry is the experimenter's embodied habits of conduct (including emotions), ways of knowing, purposes, interests, and bias:

> Another aspect of context is that which I have called "selective interest." Every particular case of thinking is what it is because of some attitude, some [theoretical] bias. . . . There is selectivity (and rejection) found in every operation of thought. There is care, concern, implicated in every act of thought. . . . Bias for impartiality is as much a bias as is partisan prejudice. . . . One can only see from a certain standpoint. (p. 14)

Dewey held a pluralistic, standpoint theory of epistemology. Research on teaching is deceptive (and possibly self-deceptive) if it thinks it can be theory and value neutral. It is also deceptive if it thinks it can be socioculturally unbiased.

The "next wide circle or deepened stratum of context resides in what I have referred to as culture" (p. 21):

> In the first instance there is a background of culture; in the second, of theory. There is no thinking which does not present itself on a background of tradition, and tradition has an intellectual quality that differentiates it from blind custom. Traditions are ways of interpretation and of observation, of valuation, of everything explicitly thought of. (p. 12)

The religious, political, and scientific beliefs and values that determine the culture of a people and age are always part of any inquiry, including inquiry into teaching. Cultural tradition partially determines the context of every inquiry and locates the position and point of criticism.

The last level is a cloaked reference to the generic traits:

> Finally, there is the context of the make-up of [all] experience itself. It is dangerous to begin at this point. . . . But the boundless multiplicity of the concrete experience of humanity when they are dealt with gently and humanely, will naturally terminate in some sense of the structure of any and all experience. . . . Those who try to interpret these indications may run the risk of being regarded by some other philosophers as not philosophers at all. They may, however, console themselves with the reflection that they are concerning themselves with that inclusive and pervasive context of experience in which philosophical thinking must, for good or ill, take place. (p. 21)

As experienced, the generic traits of existence are the ultimate context for all criticism. The generic traits of our experience of existence, along with their both/and structure, provide the largest context for inquiry or critique; one ignores them at his or her risk.

Poetry: The Power of Creative Criticism

Criticism examines the purposes, goods, interests, and values that guide educational research. That is why Dewey concludes that "the most far-reaching question of all criticism [is]: the relationship between existence and value, or as the problem is often put, between the real and ideal" (p. 310). Infinite pluralism provides an intuitive understanding of the often misunderstood notion of the union of both the actual and the possible, existence and value, the real and the ideal. Unity is a temporary achievement of inquiry, an ever moving trace of différance.

For Dewey, the task of inquiry in a pluralistic universe is to transform some disruptive situation into a unified whole (see 1938/1986, p. 108). For Dewey, as for Derrida, one must begin wherever they are, or in whatever context they believe themselves to be. For Dewey, though, the concrete, embodied lived situation provides severe constraint on real possibility. The task of inquiry, including research on teaching, is to connect the ideal with the actual to transform the present situation. Ideas, hypotheses, etc., mediate between the undesirable actuality and the ideal possibility.

Inquiry, mediation, making connection, actualizing possibilities—this process is creation. Dewey (1917/1980) asserts,

> [T]he doctrine that intelligence develops within the sphere of action for the sake of possibilities not yet given is the opposite of a doctrine of mechanical efficiency. Intelligence as intelligence is inherently forward-looking. . . . A pragmatic intelligence is a creative intelligence, not a routine mechanic. (p. 45)

Inquiry, including scientific inquiry into teaching, is an art that mediates and, thereby, creates connection and continuity. Creation continues forever in a pluralistic universe. The actual at any given time is only a small part of the real.

Matthew Arnold's dictum that "poetry is criticism of life" impressed Dewey (1934/1987) although he wondered "how it was criticism?" (p. 349). Dewey's answer is that the imaginative experience of possibilities can contrast disturbingly with actual conditions. He calls this "the most penetrating 'criticism'" (p. 349). It is important to inquire into and judge the truth function of propositions stating duties, virtues, and values, but the most powerful form of criticism goes beyond knowledge of actual conditions to explore pluralistic possibilities. Dewey (1932/1985b) remarks, "Reflection cannot be limited to the selection of one end out of a number which are suggested by conditions. Thinking has to operate creatively to form new ends [or values]" (p. 185). In a pluralistic, ever-open universe, the most powerful form of criticism is the one open to other and widely diverse possibilities. If Derrida and Dewey are right, there is a playful aesthetic component involved in any critical, reflective approach to research on teaching.

Those, unlike Dewey, who do not grasp the critical importance of creative play, often deride Derrida for his lack of seriousness. Dewey, nonetheless, does appear to constrain the field of play in ways Derrida does not. Dewey (1930/1984c) declares,

> Ideals express possibilities; but they are genuine ideals only in so far as they are possibilities of what is now moving. Imagination can set them free from their encumbrances and project them as a guide in attention to what now exists. But, save as they are related to actualities, they are pictures in a dream. (p. 112)

Actual circumstance constrains Derrida's poetic imagination much less than it does Dewey's. One may enjoy completely free imaginative play when she is at leisure and is safe and secure. Often our most desperate needs are first glimpsed only as a dream or fantasy. Dreams and fantasies, though, can be dangerous, even deadly, in a world where 99% of species that have ever existed are now extinct. Derrida is right to emphasize play;

it is a delight and a necessity for survival. Still, excessive deconstruction can lead to destruction in a Darwinian world. Dewey seems to understand this threat better than Derrida does. That is why he places greater emphasis on reconstruction than he does on deconstruction. For Dewey, freedom is always firmly situated. That is why he chooses to emphasize real possibility grounded in the current actual state of concrete affairs, rather than abstract logical possibility. The horizon separating real possibilities from those too distant to actualize is difficult to discriminate for even the most experienced captain of the ship of responsible critique. Sailing the ship of continuous critique means constantly searching the open horizon for material to reconstruct the vessel while remaining afloat.

For Dewey (1930/1984a), "Creation and criticism are companions." This statement clearly puts the accent on construction and reconstruction rather than deconstruction in Dewey's theory of criticism. For him construction-deconstruction-reconstruction was a living rhythmic cycle:

> Creation and criticism cannot be separated because they are the rhythm of output and intake, of expiration and inspiration, in our mental breath and spirit. . . . Production [construction] that is not followed by criticism [including deconstruction] becomes a mere gush of impulse; criticism that is not a step further than creation deadens impulse and ends in sterility. (pp. 140–141)

Derrida also recognizes this rhythm, but his philosophical attitude puts the emphasis in a different place, thereby making it needlessly difficult to take a critical position in the context of concrete practices like teaching and research on teaching. Dewey concludes, "Creative activity is our great need; but criticism, self-criticism, is the road to its release" (p. 143). Deconstructive criticism is the best road to release, but creative reconstruction provides a position for tending to our greatest need. We believe Derrida and Dewey in conjunction can provide a critically creative philosophy for improving research on teaching.

Dewey concludes: "To work exclusively within the context provided by the sciences themselves is to ignore their vital context, the place of science in life" (p. 19). Research on teaching is a policy science carried out by biased human beings intended to improve a preeminent cultural practice.

Implications for Research on Teaching

A conversation on Deweyan reconstruction and Derridean deconstruction yields many important implications for research on teaching. To begin, many familiar pragmatic admonitions to researchers receive novel reformulation. First, we can abandon foundationalism. There simply are no eternal metaphysical, logical, or epistemological foundations for research on teaching to make an appeal. Second, researchers are encouraged to comprehend the contingency of their research constructions. All theoretical and methodological concepts, categories, structures, standards, norms, essences, and identities are forever deconstructable. Contingent constructions can always be decentered and critically deconstructed and, if desired, reconstructed; they can also simply be destroyed when the purposes that motivated the research are abandoned.

Another implication is that responsible research on teaching requires locating, or perhaps creating, a position that may serve as a fulcrum of effective critique. This requires attending carefully to the context of research.

A third implication that is reinforced by appreciating the cycle of construction-deconstruction-reconstruction is pluralism. Methodological and theoretical pluralism in research is reaffirmed. Derrida (1978) remarks that "to renounce the other is to enclose oneself within solitude (the bad solitude of solidity and self-identity)" (p. 91). There are always other perspectives, other possibilities; research must strive to include them even as it acknowledges it will fail. Construction-deconstruction-reconstruction should put researchers on teaching doubly on guard. First, they should be constantly alert to possible falsification of their constructs. Second, they should be constantly alert for other perspectives on the problems they are trying to solve and the tools they use to solve them. Pluralistic openness to others partially constitutes openness to falsification.

The most important implication of construction-deconstruction-reconstruction for research on teaching is the elevation of ethics and aesthetics as constitutive of good research. The ideas of moral law and natural law cannot be pulled entirely apart from this perspective. Enlightenment modernity privileges knowledge and cognition above ethical recognition, or artistic creation.

Logocentrism obeys the exclusive logic of either/or; it violently reduces everything to the same, the identical, the normal. Other possibilities, other interpretations, other perspectives are rejected as simply mistaken, or deviant. This logic is finite, monistic, and precludes creativity once the correct construction (category or identity) has been built. Any difference from the norm, the standard, the correct is labeled and remediated, incarcerated, or driven away. This is the violence of hegemony of "reason." It excludes anyone or anything that does not fit its categories, concepts, essences, or identities. This is the core of intellectual colonialism; it is the fate of Nelson Mandela. Who he is before the law resembles the fate of millions of students and teachers before the politically and institutionally normalizing results of research on teaching.

For Derrida, the reduction of every difference of the other to the same, the identical, is ethical as well as intellectual violence; or rather ethical violence is committed with intellectual weapons of domination and control (see Derrida, 1978, chapter 4). Research on teaching must be on guard against the scientistic violence of closure and exclusion. What is called research on teaching often becomes research done on teachers. Teachers are often strangely prominent among those others whose voices are most brutally silenced; their opinions, their perspectives, their interpretations are ignored; they are thoroughly colonized. To the threat of colonialism, many researchers, especially qualitative "participant researchers" rely on something like methodological sympathy. They try to walk a mile in the teachers' shoes, but they rarely get very far. Too often sympathy, that is, a caring understanding of the others, is just another weapon of colonialism. The problem is that such sympathetic "understanding" is usually constructed using the researchers' canons of reasonable action. Such sympathy can be the cruelest weapon of all. Remember, missionaries usually accompanied soldiers in wars of colonial conquest.

Construction-deconstruction-reconstruction requires a more aesthetic approach to the critique of research on teaching. The playful inventions of différance decenter the conventions of research and critique. They allow us to see that poetry, or perhaps something beyond poetry, is the most penetrating criticism because it operates to create other possibilities. It is impossible for researchers, or those they do research with (or "on"), to be free without alternative possibilities. Freedom is one of the most important reasons to remain open to the perspective of others and to engage in poetic criticism. The logic of both/and allows criticism to continue forever along dispersed lines of différance between the actual and the possible. Good research on teaching creates other possibilities.

Finally, construction-deconstruction-reconstruction requires researchers to alter their attitudes toward what they may hope to accomplish. Progress is one of the unquestioned dogmas of modernity. In research on teaching, progress means arriving at something regarding teaching that at least resembles Thorndike's laws of learning. The progressive passion is to determine at least a few eternal laws, norms, concepts, categories, essences, and identities. Researchers want to store up a progressively larger storehouse of knowledge. Deconstruction devastates Enlightenment ideals of rational progress, but surely Dewey's philosophy of reconstruction must be a bulwark of progressivism. It is not. Dewey explicitly rejects modern ideals of progress. If humankind is a creative participant in an unfinished and unfinishable universe, there is no ultimate destination for inquiry into teaching to carry us.

As Dewey sees it, progress was not, as with Hegel and Peirce, a movement toward some eternal fixed Ideal, Good, or Value. Instead, progress means local reconstruction, that is, transforming a situation from worse to better. Dewey (1922/1983b) writes:

> Progress is present reconstruction adding fullness and distinctness of meaning. . . . Unless progress is a present reconstructing, it is nothing. . . . Progress means increase of present meaning, which involves multiplication of sensed distinctions as well as harmony, unification. (pp. 195–196)

For Dewey, and Derrida, there are no cosmic purposes guaranteeing progress in advance; there were only people like teachers and researchers of teaching trying to make things better. Dewey (1922/1983b) reflects:

> There is something pitifully juvenile in the idea that "evolution," progress, means a definite sum of accomplishment which will forever stay done, and which by an exact amount lessens the amount still to be done, disposing once and for all of just so many perplexities and advancing us just so far on our road to a final stable and unperplexed goal. (p. 197)

The road of inquiry, including research on teaching, never ends. We do not need to think that things are getting better, or that there is some cosmic backup story that guarantees success, to do our best. That is part of maturity; it is the attitude of the meliorist in contrast to the optimist:

> Meliorism is the belief that the specific conditions which exist at one moment, be they comparatively bad or comparatively good, in any event may be bettered. It encourages intelligence to study the positive means of good . . . and to put forth endeavor for improvement of conditions. It arouses confidence and a reasonable hope-

fulness as optimism does not. Too readily optimism makes the men who hold it callous and blind to the sufferings of the less fortunate, or ready to find the cause of troubles of others in their personal viciousness. (Dewey, 1920/1982, pp. 181–182)

We may be meliorists even at moments when our world is in ruins. We can seek to ameliorate a situation even in a disintegrating world. Such situations often confront caregivers, such as teachers. Instead of an attitude of technical progress, it might be better if researchers of teaching took a more modest melioristic attitude toward their work.

The chief defects of bad research on teaching are not flawed theory, method, or technique; they are ignoring context, ethics, and aesthetics.

Caveats

We exposited the texts titled "Derrida" and "Dewey" where we thought it best for researchers on teaching to begin. It was necessary to oversimplify to the extreme. We have emphasized points of agreement between Dewey and Derrida, while ignoring their differences. Here, at the end, we must issue a caveat that, although the similarities between these two thinkers are striking and surprising, they are different from each other. For one thing, Dewey's naturalism is much more comfortable talking about science and the philosophy of nature. Dewey also has a much more Darwinian, biological approach to philosophy. Derrida is much more at home deconstructing language, writing and discourse, and expositing texts. Finally, both of these thinkers are in need of further inquiry into the cultural play of power and its multiple effects.

An Author's "After Words"

It may be clear to the attentive reader that Jim's voice and my own do not come together in a cohesive or seamless whole. This writing cannot provide the reader an easy, unproblematic conclusion to any of the difficult issues raised by joint inquiry. My own effort in this was offered in the hope of finding a way to hold open the question of the relation between Dewey and Derrida so as to explore both the possibility of their coincidence and the necessity of their distinction. As I envisioned this "conversation," Derrida would introduce his own work to Dewey by acknowledging that his writing, indeed all writing, including Dewey's own, is "double-bound." Any radical criticism necessarily produces words at war with themselves. They must struggle to exempt themselves from the very grammar in which they are caught up and by which they mean. Inevitably they are qualified, "written under erasure," hedged as Derrida does, with inevitable quotation marks. If writings (of radical ideas) emerge always within a history, they would subvert and take their sense from that history even as they would undo that history's claim to mastery over their sense making. These writings must necessarily employ tools, devices that Derrida refers to as "ploys of designification." Derrida works not only to exemplify the both/and, but also the neither/nor that is demanded in any exterior form of a critical rupture and a redoubling (see Derrida, 1978, p. 247). The moment we approach any philosophical notion no longer by thinking to refute it but by asking how it

can be said, the ground shifts beneath the traditional arguments.

For a number of good reasons, not the least being time constraints, the outcome of this paper is not compatible with mine. Perhaps this anomaly is unavoidable if our earlier claims that "inquiry begins wherever the inquirer is" are warranted. Two inquirers would seem bound to produce varied readings of the limits and possibilities of both Derrida's and Dewey's projects.

That Jim and I hold different views is no cause for alarm. Our controversies over interpretation are what "inquiry" is all about, and in my view, are symptomatic of the unstable and shifting moment in the current time of philosophical scholarship. That Jim and I do not agree but have written together anyway may serve to raise interesting questions for educational research on the authority of language, the "truth" of any text, the effects of writing, and the excess produced that is not recouperable to one single judgment of meaning. We present an instance of contradictory interpretations that can perhaps agitate traditional notions of a writer, a reader, or a researcher isolated from subject positions, the histories, discourses, and practices that constitute both philosophical thought and current educational imperatives (see Spivak, 1985; Rutsby & Wiltgen, 1991; Greene, 1994).

An Other Author's "After Words"

I realized the offer to coauthor a paper titled "Dewey After Derrida" would pose a challenge. Initially, I assumed a simple division of labor. Mary would explicate and advocate Derrida, while I would do the same for Dewey. I thought it would be easy to show that Dewey's pragmatism is superior to Derrida's relativism. It did not work out that way. Derrida is not a relativist. Other surprises awaited, as Mary directed me to many passages in Derrida stunningly similar to statements by Dewey. I was overwhelmed, and my understanding was altered.

The proof that Dewey rejects the metaphysics of presence as stridently as Derrida does is impressive (see also Garrison, 1999). So is the evidence that Dewey's generic traits resemble Derrida's infrastructures. Most Deweyans will be shocked; I was. It will be difficult to explain away the many passages cited in support of these surprising claims. Eventually, I argue that the only real difference between Dewey's philosophy of reconstruction and Derrida's philosophy of deconstruction is where they put the emphasis in the construction-deconstruction-reconstruction cycle. Mary knows this cannot be right. So do I now, but there is no more time for us to continue the conversation.

I have assimilated Derrida to Dewey in a way that deemphasizes their differences and subtly gives Dewey the victory. Mary wants to preserve and accentuate the differences (différances?) in hopes of having a more creative dialogue. She is confident that Dewey, the philosopher of reconstruction, who reconstructed himself many times, would have done so again in a critical encounter with Derrida. The reader has read only a frozen moment in a mobile conversation. Here is the most important thing I have learned thus far: It is not enough to tolerate the tensions of difference and alterity; one must learn to delight in the dance of difference and make meaning in the opening provided when we are open to the movements of the other.

REFERENCES

Bernstein, R. (1992). *The new constellation.* Cambridge, MA: The MIT Press.

Derrida J. (1973). In *Speech and phenomena* (David B. Allison, Trans.). Evanston, IL: Northwestern University Press.

Derrida, J. (1976). *Of grammatology* (G. C. Spivak, Trans.). Baltimore: Johns Hopkins Press.

Derrida, J. (1978). *Writing and difference* (A. Bass, Trans.). Chicago: University of Chicago Press.

Derrida, J. (1981). *Positions* (A. Bass, Trans.). Chicago: University of Chicago Press.

Derrida, J. (1982). *Margins of philosophy* (A. Bass, Trans.). Chicago: University of Chicago Press.

Derrida, J. (1987). The laws of reflection: Nelson Mandela. In J. Derrida & M. Tlili (Eds.), *Admiration, or Nelson Mandela.* New York: Seaver Books, Henry Holt and Company.

Dewey, J. (1971). The superstition of necessity. In J. A. Boydston (Ed.), *John Dewey: The early works* (Vol. 4, pp. 19–36). Carbondale, IL: Southern Illinois University Press. (Original work published 1893)

Dewey, J. (1977). The influence of Darwinism on philosophy. In J. A. Boydston (Ed.), *John Dewey: The middle works* (Vol. 4, pp. 3–14). Carbondale, IL: Southern Illinois University Press. (Original work published 1909)

Dewey, J. (1979). The subject-matter of metaphysical inquiry. In J. A. Boydston (Ed.), *John Dewey: The middle works* (Vol. 8, pp. 3–13). Carbondale, IL: Southern Illinois University Press. (Original work published 1915)

Dewey J. (1980). The need for a recovery of philosophy. In J. A. Boydston (Ed.), *John Dewey: The middle works* (Vol. 10, pp. 3–48). Carbondale, IL: Southern Illinois University Press. (Original work published 1917)

Dewey, J. (1981). Experience and nature. In J. A. Boydston (Ed.), *John Dewey: The later works* (Vol. 1). Carbondale, IL: Southern Illinois University Press. (Original work published 1925)

Dewey, J. (1982). Reconstruction in philosophy. In J. A. Boydston (Ed.), *John Dewey: The middle works* (Vol. 12, pp. 77–250). Carbondale, IL: Southern Illinois University Press. (Original work published 1920)

Dewey, J. (1983a). Realism without monism or dualism. In J. A. Boydston (Ed.), *John Dewey: The middle works* (Vol. 13, pp. 40–60). Carbondale, IL: Southern Illinois University Press. (Original work published 1922)

Dewey, J. (1983b). Human nature and conduct. In J. A. Boydston (Ed.), *John Dewey: The middle works* (Vol. 14). Carbondale, IL: Southern Illinois University Press. (Original work published 1922)

Dewey, J. (1984a). Construction and criticism. In J. A. Boydston (Ed.), *John Dewey: The later works* (Vol. 5, pp. 128–143). Carbondale, IL: Southern Illinois University Press. (Original work published 1930)

Dewey, J. (1984b). From absolutism to experimentalism. In J. A. Boydston (Ed.), *John Dewey: The later works* (Vol. 5, pp. 147–160). Carbondale, IL: Southern Illinois University Press. (Original work published 1930)

Dewey, J. (1984c). Individuality in our day. In. J. A. Boydston (Ed.), *John Dewey: The later works* (Vol. 5, pp. 111–123). Carbondale, IL: Southern Illinois University Press. (Original work published 1930)

Dewey, J. (1985a). Context and thought. In J. A. Boydston (Ed.), *John Dewey: The later works* (Vol. 6). Carbondale, IL: Southern Illinois University Press. (Original work published 1931)

Dewey, J. (1985b). Ethics. In J. A. Boydston (Ed.), *John Dewey: The later works* (Vol. 7). Carbondale, IL: Southern Illinois University Press. (Original work published 1932)

Dewey, J. (1986). Logic: The theory of inquiry. In J. A. Boydston (Ed.), *John Dewey: The later works* (Vol. 12). Carbondale, IL: Southern Illinois University Press. (Original work published 1938)

Dewey, J. (1987). Art as experience. In J. A. Boydston (Ed.), *John Dewey: The later works* (Vol. 10). Carbondale, IL: Southern Illinois University Press. (Original work published 1934)

Garrison, J. (1985). Dewey and the empirical unity of opposites. *Transactions of the Charles S. Peirce Society,* Vol. XXI, No. 4, 549–561.

Garrison, J. (1994a). Realism, Deweyan pragmatism, and educational research. *Educational Researcher, 23*(1), 5–14.

Garrison, J. (1995). Deweyan pragmatism and the epistemology of contemporary social constructivism. *American Educational Research Journal, 32*(4), 710–740.

Garrison, J. (1999). John Dewey, Jacques Derrida, and the metaphysics of presence. *Transactions of the Charles S. Peirce Society,* Vol. XXXV, No. 2, pp. 346–347.

Gasché, R. (1994). *Inventions of difference.* Cambridge, MA: Harvard University Press.

Gilligan, C. (1982). *In a different voice: Psychological theory and women's development.* Cambridge, MA: Harvard University Press.

Greene, M. (1994). Epistemology and educational research: The influence of recent approaches to knowledge. *Review of Research in Education, 20,* 423–464.

James, W. (1950). *The principles of psychology.* New York: Dover Publications, Inc. (Original work published 1890)

James, W. (1979). *The will to believe.* Cambridge, MA: Harvard University Press. (Original work published 1896)

James, W. (1971). A pluralistic universe. In R. B. Perry (Ed.), *Essays in radical empiricism and a pluralistic universe* (pp. 1–352). New York: E. P. Dutton & Co. (Original work published 1909)

Kamuf, P. (Ed.). (1991). Letter to a Japanese friend. In *A Derrida reader* (pp. 269–276). New York: Columbia University Press.

Kearney, R. (Ed.). (1984). Deconstruction and the other. In *Dialogues with contemporary continental thinkers* (pp. 105–133). Manchester, UK: Manchester University Press.

Kearney, R. (Ed.). (1995). Jacques Derrida: Deconstruction and the other. In *States of mind: Dialogues with contemporary thinkers* (pp. 156–176). New York: New York University Press.

Parker, S. P. (Ed.). (1992). *McGraw-Hill encyclopedia of science & technology* (7th ed., Vol. 6, pp. 570–572). New York: McGraw-Hill.

Peirce, C. S. (1965). Some consequences of four incapacities. In C. Hartshorne & P. Weiss (Eds.), *Collected papers of Charles Sanders Peirce* (Vol. V, pp. 156–189). Cambridge, MA: The Belknap Press of Harvard University. (Original work published 1878)

Rorty, R. (1982). In *Consequences of pragmatism* (pp. 72–89). Minneapolis: University of Minnesota Press.

Rorty, R. (1991). Two meanings of "logocentrism": A reply to Norris. In *Essays on Heidegger and others: Philosophical paper* (Vol. 2, pp. 107–118). Cambridge: Cambridge University Press.

Rutsby, R. L., & Wiltgen, J. (1991). Marx after Elvis. *Strategies, 6,* 3–17.

Sleeper, R. (1986). *The necessity of pragmatism.* New Haven, CT: Yale University Press.

Spivak, G. (1985). Scattered speculations on the question of value. *Diacritics, 15*(4), 73–93.

5.
Reflections on Teaching

Maxine Greene
Teachers College, Columbia University

My reflections on the project and process of teaching arise from my pondering (and wondering about) my own classroom experiences, the choices I have made, and the conversations with those who shared and those who differed sharply with my views. The fact that my concerns have centered in the domains of the arts and humanities and that I have been much preoccupied with social imagination—the capacity to look at social arrangements as if they could be otherwise—is not of incidental relevance. Conceiving of myself mainly as an educational philosopher, I have taken seriously the charge on the part of the analytic philosopher to counter confusions in the use of language that interfere with understanding just as I have tried to remain aware of vagueness, fixity of belief, and one-dimensional thinking. I have never, however, believed it sufficient to take the analyst's or the linguistic philosopher's approach to teaching and the situations in which teaching takes place.

Affected as I have been by John Dewey's explorations of experience and by the existential phenomenologist's view of consciousness and being in the world, my notions of teaching are much involved with notions of human relationship, intersubjectivity, the pursuit of various kinds of meaning, and the sense of untapped possibility—of what might be, what ought to be, what is not yet. My interest in the arts and the aesthetic has made me insist on the centrality of the arts in the modes of human sense making that teachers are asked to keep alive. This interest has, moreover, moved me to point to the paradigmatic nature of the artistic encounter regarding the construction of meaning and being actively present to what surrounds.

As time has gone on, feminist ideas have intensified what began as a discomfort with hollow abstraction, with distancing and disengagement, with a very gradual recognition of the worth of tasks and obligations associated with family and domestic life. Connectedness, responsibility, attentiveness: These concepts began to seem more and more significant when considering teaching. Likewise, the kind of caring that sustained others' desires to become what they chose to be seemed increasingly important. Since the 1960s, particularly, the sufferings linked to feelings described as invisibility, nobodiness, and voicelessness have infused my approach to the teaching act as have the conceptions of human rights and civil rights, including the right to full membership in a community.

The fact and possibility of acknowledged diversity have had an influence along with conceptions of multiculturalism or the recognition that diversity and difference are more than individual. Diversity and difference are consequences of cultural, ethnic, and class differences and are to be taken into account in the quest for social justice and, at once, for a common ground. I often try to keep in mind the startling realization that those I hope to move to learn are not—and do not have to be—versions of my White, studious, middle-class, urban, literary self. Meanwhile, I strain—and try to convince others to strain—to pay heed to long-stifled voices, not all with sympathetic things to say. Attending to these voices is a matter, as Cynthia Ozick writes, of trying (as teacher and as human being) to imagine "the familiar hearts of strangers" (1989, p. 283). We need to recognize ourselves as being, in some degree, strangers. That recognition means refusing to be caught in the familiar or in that which is taken for granted. For the social phenomenologist Alfred Schutz, "Strangeness and familiarity are not limited to the social field but are general categories of our interpretation of the world." Once we encounter in experience something we did not know before, he continues, we begin a process of inquiry; we attempt to catch the meaning of what stands out from the ordinary. Trying to integrate our inquiry with the meanings we have funded over time, we transform our experience into an additional element of what we believe we know. Doing so, "we have enlarged and adjusted our stock of experience" (1964, p. 105).

That mode of transforming seems to have marked, over time, my approach to teaching. The questions still multiply today as the humbling phenomena of difference and what might be

The author wishes to acknowledge the support of Professor Donna Kerr, University of Washington, and Professor William Pinar, Louisiana State University. She is grateful to both and privileged by their approval.

called the extraordinary confront me day by day. At one time, I thought of teaching as mainly a matter, as Stanley Cavell says of "conveying the 'hang' of something . . . familiar, for example, in conservatories of music, but also, I should guess, in learning a new game or entering any new territory or technique or apprenticing for a trade" (1976, pp. 103–104). I also approached teaching as a matter of teaching the rudiments, the low-level things, or as teaching the habits of mind that would free learners to go beyond and begin teaching themselves. My focus was on communicating certain procedures, methods, and processes that would enable people to teach themselves, because I certainly understood that, on some level, learners had to choose to learn. I probably was beginning to see what Martin Heidegger meant when he asked why teaching is more difficult than learning.

> Not because the teacher must have a larger store of information, and have it always ready. Teaching is more difficult than learning because what teaching calls for is this: to let learn. The real teacher, in fact, lets nothing else be learning than—learning. His conduct, therefore, often produces the impression that we properly learn nothing from him, if by "learning" we now suddenly understand the procurement of useful information. (1972, p. 15)

For Heidegger (and for me, after a while), the teacher has to learn what it is to learn to let others learn.

There is considerable agreement that people are moved to learn when they ask themselves questions—questions that demand answers if restlessness or hunger or unhappiness is to be allayed. This provoking of learning suggests the necessity for the teacher somehow to create classroom situations that provoke or at least to allow for the asking of such questions. In recent years, we have become familiar with journal keeping, storytelling, and poetry writing, commonly used on all levels of education. We also have discovered that, when people—whether young children or teachers-to-be or practicing teachers—are given opportunities to articulate, or to give some kind of shape to their lived experience, all kinds of questions may arise. Gaps appear in the narratives; awarenesses of lacks and deficiencies become visible; bright moments and epiphanies highlight the dark times, the fears, the felt failures.

Suggestions for what this awareness of what is lacking may imply can be found in Virginia Woolf's memories of her own youth, in her remembered feelings of the ground giving way and old assurances being destroyed. Ordinary life, she wrote, contained a large amount of what she described as "cotton wool," meaning nonbeing, life not lived consciously (1976, pp. 71–72). Very few teachers are insensitive to the number of their pupils who experience life that way. Then Woolf talked about examples of "shocks" that aroused her: one, when her brother continued to beat her after she dropped her fists in a fight with him, and she felt the foolishness of trying to hurt another person; another, when she heard her parents say that a family friend had killed himself; a third, when she began wondering about what was earth and what was flower as she stared at a plant with a spread of leaves. These were instances, she said, of "exceptional moments"—one ending in satisfaction when she realized the wholeness of the plant, half flower, half earth, the others ending in despair, because she did not understand.

For the teacher willing to pay heed, what is significant is the sense of powerlessness Woolf associated with not understanding. Of the exceptional moments she remembered, therefore, certain ones brought a kind of horror with them: "They seemed dominant, myself passive" (p. 72). Then she wrote,

> This suggests that as one gets older one has a greater power through reason to provide an explanation; and that this explanation blunts the sledgehammer force of the blow. I think this is true, because though I still have the peculiarity that when I receive these sudden shocks, they are now always welcome; after the first surprise, I always feel instantly that they are particularly valuable. And so I go on to suppose that the shock-receiving capacity is what makes me a writer. I hazard the explanation that a shock is at once in my case followed by the desire to explain it. (p. 72)

By finding words, Woolf put "severed parts together" in an intuition of the wholeness of things. For a while, the lived world made a new kind of sense.

These reminiscences contrast the story that Claudia tells in Toni Morrison's *The Bluest Eye,* but both Woolf and Morrison may make the same demand on a teacher who is eager to enable students to overcome the powerlessness they feel. The story has to do with Pecola Breedlove, who is unloved, convinced of her own ugliness, and yearning to look like the White Shirley Temple and to have blue eyes. Pecola is humiliated, perplexed, used, and raped by her own father. Then she loses the baby he gave her. Claudia, who tries to befriend and understand, talks (in the beginning and at the end) about marigolds not growing in their neighborhood and wonders whether that was because Pecola lost her baby. Claudia then wonders whether she and her sister are responsible because they did not say the right words when they planted the marigold seeds. As Claudia said:

> For years I thought my sister was right: it was my fault. I had planted them too far down in the earth. It never occurred to either of us that the earth itself was unyielding. We had dropped our seeds in our own little plot of black dirt. Our innocence and faith were no more productive than his lust and despair. What is clear now is that of all that hope, fear, lust, love, and grief, nothing remains but Pecola and the unyielding earth. Cholly Breedlove is dead; our innocence too. The seeds shriveled and died; her baby too. There is really nothing more to say—except why. But since why is difficult to handle, one must take refuge in how. (1970, pp. 5–6)

If Claudia confronted her teacher with that revelation—finding the why so difficult to handle—the teacher would be fairly convinced of her feeling of passivity or powerlessness. Here, too, we can see a need to devise the kind of classroom situation in which a learner can pose such a question, can speak to others about it once she puts it into words, and somehow can be helped to discover how to go about responding and resolving, if only for the time being.

In this case, the need to contextualize the events and the questions is clearer. Actually, in both cases, the teacher should make some effort to move from the incidents themselves to what impinges on them, to what surrounds. In the case of Virginia Woolf's brother Thody, the issues of British family life at the time, the role of the boy in the British family, and the connection between thoughtless violence and upper-class schoolboys may all be part of the context, and those concepts may suggest a problem that goes beyond the simple account of the boy and girl using their fists in the garden. In the fictional world of Claudia and Pecola, they contend with the fearsome roles of poverty, of discrimination, of the plight of southern migrants in the north, of homelessness, and of the need not to be "outside." They also experience the effect of popular White culture on African-American children: the demeaning influence of Shirley Temple as rendered on the screen, on china cups, and in the faces of ubiquitous dolls. Clearly, in the case of public school teaching, much depends on the students' level of development, as well as on whether or not students are ready for initiation into subject matters that might open the way to new perspectives on these problems. In my own teaching and in the communities of teacher education, I have tried to pay attention to lived lives; to life stories; and to the cultural, historical, economic, and sociological frameworks in which they take place. At once, I have stressed the fruitfulness of using novels, films, drama, and even painting in effecting connections and in shedding light or going beyond.

The ways in which a teacher responds to the development of a classroom situation depends a great deal, as I have tried to tell my own students, upon that teacher's sense of teaching as both project and process. Thinking of teaching as a project, I have tapped existential views of the ways in which human beings create identities by means of the projects they choose and of their ways of gearing into the world. For Jean-Paul Sartre (1963), a project implies going beyond a situation and what the human being "succeeds in making of what he has been made. . . . The most rudimentary behavior must be determined both in relation to the real and present factors which condition it and in relation to a certain object, still to come, which it is trying to bring into being. This is what we call *the project*" (1963, p. 91). A project involves actions we choose to perform; it involves the ways in which we address issues such as the question of our students and ourselves becoming different—something they and we are not yet.

For Alfred Schultz (1964), the "texture of meaning" that distinguishes a culture originates in such actions and such choices. The objective relations of the surrounding world (or the school, or the neighborhood) are experienced as "contexts of interests, as a hierarchy of problems to be solved, as systems of projects" (p. 288). The connections between project and existing meaning system, as well as between activity and culture, may offer to the teacher or the teacher-to-be an alternative to the condition of a clerk or functionary, who may be someone defined by her or his place in the bureaucracy. To speak of choosing the self or of creating an identity by means of a project suggests to the professional something more than determination by outside forces. To be acquainted on any level, for instance, with the plight of Pecola Breedlove or with the difficulty that Claudia faces in finding out why is to be called to take a position of some kind, to involve students in a particular kind of way.

If teaching has been defined as a project having to do with protectiveness, or with shielding the young from failures and disappointments from what Hamlet called "the slings and arrows of outrageous fortune," then the implication may well be that certain young people are simply incapable of understanding or resistance. However, in trying to protect a child who is at risk in these times, we face a degree of absurdity. In fact, we may well find something unethical in refusing (or not noticing) students' need to be part of a sustaining, if not a critical, community. The choice is not between leaving a child or young person on a front line without help and protecting that person by ignoring her or his lived reality. Much has to do with the way the teacher has chosen to define the project of teaching. Much has to do with the way the teacher responds to what Schutz calls the "contexts of interests" in the impinging world or the "hierarchy of problems to be solved" (p. 288): the poverty tearing at the lives of so many, the lack of what teachers recognize as role models, random humiliations, violence, drug dealing, and addictions. Obviously, these words apply primarily to urban ghettos and to members of those minority groups who seem appointed for suffering. Urban teachers are all too familiar with the hopelessness, the dead eyes, of far too many youth. Most often, those teachers see themselves as liberal and progressive. They relish questions; they reject imposition; they are committed to individual freedom. In some fashion, they become paradigm cases for what happens in many teachers' lives as they (in Sartre's sense) work to combat their own conditioning, to move beyond.

Lisa Delpit, concentrating on "other people's children" (1995) writes about the paternalism she finds in the attitudes of White liberal colleagues when they talk of the need of Black children to be "given voice" (pp. 18–19).

> Progressive white teachers seem to say to their black students: "Let me help you find your voice. I promise not to criticize one note as you search for your own song." But the black teachers say, "I've heard your song loud and clear. Now, I want to teach you to harmonize with the rest of the world." (p. 11)

Delpit finds suspect the underemphasis on skill training in these days. Skills, she says, represent "useful and usable knowledge which contributes to a student's ability to communicate effectively in standard, generally acceptable literary forms" (p. 19). She acknowledges, as I certainly do, the importance of teaching skills through meaningful communication in meaningful contexts. The Black student has to be helped, at the same time, to engage in critical and creative thinking on the basis of the habits of mind or the skills that are necessary for that student to open the doors in the wider world. Obviously, this is one of the key issues in anyone's conception of teaching.

The British philosopher John Passmore (1980) deals with this issue by talking about "closed" and "open" capacities. Closed capacities include the ability to count, to find one's way home, to dress oneself. The competencies to which closed capacities give rise include telling time, mastering a vocabulary in another language, playing tic-tac-toe, and later on—for some at least—solving equations. Such capacities (or habits or skills) can be taught through training, student practice, repetition, and concentration. Open capacities, in contrast, are never finally taught, and students cannot be trained to master them.

> For what is the test that a pupil has acquired an open capacity? The test is this: that the pupil can take steps which he has not been taught to take, which in some measure surprise the instructor . . . in the sense that the teacher has not taught his pupil to take pre-

cisely that step and his taking it does not necessarily follow as an application of a principle which the teacher has instructed in. The pupil in other words has come to be, in respect to some exercise of some capacity, inventive. (Passmore, 1980, p. 42)

Passmore, in his analytical language, is also talking about students teaching themselves, understanding something they have not been taught to understand, becoming unpredictably different, and going beyond. Like Delpit, Freire, and Dewey, however, Passmore knows that open capacities have to be taught on the ground of closed capacities and that critical and creative consciousness cannot be nurtured without certain habits of mind.

The same is clearly the case with privileged students, although the presumption that basic skills or critical thinking have to be taught seldom makes itself felt. Skills are often taken for granted, in part because the teacher's past experience overlaps that of the students. The point does not have to be made, as it does with "other people's children," that the mainstream language or the language of power is a necessity if people are to succeed in the world. However, even in middle-class, White schools, what must be taught may be reduced to discrete competencies; education may be thought of as a mode of technical training. Whatever decision is made goes back, it would appear, to the nature of the teachers' projects, especially in these days when teacher choice and collaboration have become significant.

When I think of project, I think (again) of the way in which teachers choose their identities or negotiate them by the ways they take action in the world. Choosing to be a teacher (or agreeing to be one), a person singles out a particular mode of engaging the world. To say that choice is impossible, given the press of things, is in some fashion to say that teaching and learning are impossible, because both depend on a considerable degree of voluntariness. Nevertheless, to view the selves and identities being chosen or created as fixed or isolated quantities is a mistake. The self, John Dewey wrote, is not something "fixed antecedent to action; it is not something ready-made, but something in continuous formation through choice of action. . . ." (1916, p. 408). No separation exists, he said, between interest and self: "Self and interest are two names for the same fact; the kind and amount of interest actively taken in a thing reveals and measures the quality of selfhood which exists" (p. 408).

What must be added to Dewey is the fact that the self is not to be regarded in total autonomy, as in the old individual tradition. People's selves, we tend to realize, emerge from intersections of many factors: gender, ethnic, class. Teachers, arriving at specific schools and taking up the work assigned, arrive as men and women and are sometimes homosexual; they cannot leave their Whiteness or their Blackness, let us say, behind; they cannot wholly deny their original class membership, no matter what the degree of their mobility. Teacher educators need to recognize this and to encourage the self-reflectiveness that might enable teachers-to-be to understand the contingency of many of their tastes and opinions—even their conceptions of what teaching is and ought to be.

Seyla Benhabib, referring to the work of Alasdair MacIntyre, Charles Taylor, and Michael Sandel (1992, pp. 90ff), reviews the critique of the so-called "unencumbered self" and reminds her readers of the many views that focus on the priority of association over individuation. Too frequently, teachers are thought of as autonomous and, therefore, personally accountable for what happens in their classrooms. In fact, they emerge from some sort of community as they enter the associated life of the school. This does not mean that they automatically transport into the classrooms (or ought to) what they have come to value in the course of their experiences. It does mean, however, that they should be asked not only to take a critical look at what they have internalized from significant others' points of view but also to be conscious of the need to look through others' perspectives in order to attain what Hannah Arendt called "an enlarged way of thinking" (1961, p. 220).

An approach to teaching, perhaps, essentially in these times, ought to take into account the tensions and ambivalences that different people bring to the teaching process because of their own histories and the choices they have made. The White liberal colleague that Lisa Delpit describes or the transformative thinker that we find in so much radical literature today must take into account a larger and more multi-faceted community that is composed of distinctly diverse individuals, many of whose fundamental commitments differ from those professed by teachers and by the schools. The protective, charitable, seriously liberating self may not arouse or empower certain students to learn how to learn. The teacher who comes in contact with students through and by means of technical expertise may reach certain ones and leave others by the wayside. The restless, skeptical self or the teacher willing to make audible her or his own doubts and ideals may be at odds with the dominant order in the school. The parents, wary of such innovations as sex and AIDS education, may not appreciate being told that looking through other people's eyes is important.

Teachers (like me) who look back, say, on works such as *Romeo and Juliet, Moby Dick, To the Lighthouse, Invisible Man,* or *The Plague* as an always overflowing reservoir of resonant experiences and insights may take umbrage at suggestions for a popular culture component or a "hip-hop" curriculum that obviously engages youngsters in the school. If, indeed, "self and interest are two names for the same fact," as Dewey said (1916, p. 408), the teacher may feel a loss of authenticity and integrity when repressing a passionately felt interest. For me, provocative teaching cannot take place unless the teacher's interests are engaged, unless a self in the making is fully present to others—present not only in body but also in mind, not only emotionally but also cognitively, not only imaginatively but also analytically. For me, the teacher must communicate a kind of passion—a consciousness of risk and possibility—no matter how much blankness, disinterest, or difference of opinion is expressed by others.

Aware of the variety of perspectives in each classroom, as well as aware of student experiences that the teacher could not conceivably share, the teacher can still pose the questions that continue to arouse each student. Such questions should set forth the accommodations made and the reasons for them, and should point to the perspectives opened for individuals to look through—even in the face of all the refusals that students articulate—all their unwillingness to "see." If the familiar and the strange do mark different moments of interpretation for teachers and their students, if, indeed, only the shock of the unfamiliar moves people to pose questions, then deliberate efforts ought to be made to challenge any immersion in that which is taken for granted.

I have before turned to Walker Percy's *The Moviegoer* to suggest what such a challenge may (at least metaphorically) entail. The narrator is Binx Bolling, who is so immersed in the normal and the everyday that he has long since stopped noticing anything about it. But, then, his peaceful existence becomes complicated, and the idea of a search occurs to him.

> What is the nature of the search? you ask. Really it is very simple, at least for a fellow like me; so simple that it is easily overlooked. The search is what anyone would undertake if he were not sunk in the everydayness of his own life. This morning, for example, I felt as if I had come to myself on a strange island. And what does such a castaway do? Why he pokes around the neighborhood and he doesn't miss a trick. To become aware of the possibility of the search is to be on to something. Not to be on to something is to be in despair. (1979, p. 13)

Of considerable interest, Percy uses as the epigraph for his book a phrase from Soren Kierkegaard's *The Sickness Unto Death:* ". . . the specific character of despair is precisely this: it is unaware of being despair." "To be on to something" may be a matter of taking a look at one's own situation as if it were someone else's, at least so it begins to look unfamiliar—perhaps like a "strange island." To poke around in the way described is actually to begin an inquiry and to begin it precisely and carefully, because the person is abruptly "on to something" as never before.

Existentialists might call Binx's encounter an encounter with nothingness: a gap or a space between what has been expected and has not yet taken place, between what has been hoped for and what may fulfill that hope, between an answer sought and an answer found. The encounter may manifest itself as a sense of lack, of deficiency, or of something suddenly seen as in need of repair. This moment of slow, almost grudging awakening has been and is still being dramatized in literature, particularly, in novels. *Moby Dick* begins with such a moment, when Ishmael finds himself looking into coffin warehouses and thinks it is time to go to sea. *The Plague* (Camus, 1948) begins in such a moment, with the citizens of Oran submerged in habit; everyone is bored, and few have any intimations of the coming unusual, unfamiliar events. When the pestilence arrives, they deny it or resign themselves; only when Tarrou comes and organizes sanitary squads does some kind of action seem possible, and the plague becomes the concern of all.

> Hitherto, surprised as he may have been by the strange things happening around him, each individual citizen had gone about his business as usual. . . . And no doubt he would have continued doing so. But once the town gates were shut, every one of us realized that all, the narrator included, were, so to speak, in the same boat, and each would have to adapt himself to the new conditions of life. Thus, for example, a feeling normally as individual as the ache of separation from those one loves suddenly became a feeling in which all shared alike—and together with fear—the greatest affliction of the long period of exile that lay ahead. (Camus, 1948, p. 61)

The power of this figure for me is in the way it makes me think of the connection between shared experience or intersubjectiv-

ity and learning to adapt. And to adapt must demand some ability to understand.

In *The Myth of Sisyphus,* Camus (1955) offers a metaphor for those of us reflecting on the act of teaching. He is writing about the routines of ordinary life, the unthinking fashion in which people accept the mechanical aspect of existence. He describes the deadly rhythm of daily labor and daily movement back and forth.

> But one day the "why" arises and everything begins in that weariness tinged with amazement. "Begins"—this is important. Weariness comes at the end of the acts of a mechanical life, but at the same time it inaugurates the impulse of consciousness. It awakens consciousness and provokes what follows. What follows is the gradual return into the chain or it is the definitive awakening. . . . For everything begins with consciousness and nothing is worth anything except through it. (1955, p. 13)

This quotation from Camus evokes Virginia Woolf's distinction between being and nonbeing (Woolf, 1976), as it does John Dewey's opposing of the routine, the mechanical, the anaesthetic to the aesthetic experience, and the experience of full consciousness (Dewey, 1931).

To speak of consciousness, of course, is to speak of thrusting into the world around us and actively grasping the appearances of things. It is to speak of acts of perceiving, believing, imagining, and conceptualizing and to speak of the ways they effect relationships between the living, situated being and what surrounds. To speak of consciousness, too, is to hold in mind the likelihood that the conscious being (unlike the finished objects of the physical world) is always becoming, projecting, or striving toward what is not yet. Even as many of our students cling to the familiar or to forms that seem to confirm what they already know, even as they reach back to the chain of unreflective habit, they are, on some level, rejecting objectness. They would not be in a classroom otherwise; they hope for something, something they do not understand, something they expect. And part of teaching is to come in contact with that sense of incompleteness. Indeed, the craft of teaching involves that capacity to make contact; it is another way of addressing our students' freedom.

To heighten consciousness, then, means to provoke diverse people to pay heed to the particularities of the worlds they inhabit—the "stuff" or the facticity that makes it so hard to open spaces for choosing. It means encouraging people to use their imaginations, but (as Dewey said) not so that imagination can simply run loose and go in search primarily of emotional satisfaction. "When we find the successful display of our energies checked by uncongenial surroundings, natural and social," Dewey wrote, "the easiest way out is to build castles in the air and let them be a substitute for an actual achievement which involves the pains of thought. So in overt action we acquiesce and build up an imaginary world in mind" (1916, p. 405). What he was warning against was the use of imagination as a means of withdrawal from "uncongenial surroundings" instead of as a means of stimulating transformative thinking.

The point of imagining a better community or a better school is to begin to seek out ways of changing the uncongenial community or school that actually exists. Teachers realize on some level that most young people, when faced with an unfamiliar problem, reach out tentatively and diffusely. Lacking experience or understanding, young people have no means at hand for altering aspects of their community. They may know nothing about building playgrounds, laying out a flower garden in an empty lot, or rehabilitating an apartment for a homeless family. Concerned enough and finding themselves engaged with other students who have begun to care about what is lacking, they may seek out someone who can convey "the hang" of laying floorboards, for instance, of mounting shelves, or of measuring for the needed window glass. Once they have mastered the fundamental skills demanded by rehabilitation, they can begin to understand what is involved in the entire project, what part they are playing in the repair, and what it all has to do with their classmates or with poor people passing in the street.

Obviously, not all teaching deals with practical acts like these. Relatively few teachers can look at concrete results and tell themselves that something must have happened in the workroom or the classroom, because the students have started going beyond what was taught by rote. Those students are now talking about how curtains should be hung, how a double bed might be maneuvered through the door, or how the bathtub might be kept clean enough to serve more than one family. More than a degree of craft and a special kind of care on the part of teachers are required if students' interests are to be directed to an activity that takes on meaning for them. For Dewey, what was important was engagement in a

progressively cumulative undertaking under conditions that engage interest and require reflection. Given a consecutive activity embodying the student's own interest, where a definite result is to be obtained, and where neither routine habit nor the following of dictated directions nor capricious improvising will suffice, the rise of conscious purpose, conscious desire, and deliberate reflection are inevitable. They are inevitable as the spirit and quality of an activity having specific consequences, not as forming an isolated realm of inner consciousness. (1916, pp. 406–407)

For Dewey too, this engagement is a matter of active learning: of being actively in the world, of being moved by desire, and of discovering what it can signify to be in a search.

Of course, when conscious purpose and desire arise, imagination can draw people on to act on what is possible. Reflectiveness may be grasped anew by those attuned to association and by those who recognize the connection between multiple perspectives and a richness of thought. We must recognize a range of vantage points, must seriously consider the reasons for decisions and conclusions, and must realize that, likely, full consensus may never be possible. The real challenge of teaching is to be found in the connection between the words uttered by the teacher (or the gestures, the admonitions, the modeling activities, the questions posed, the thought processes made visible) and the choice of the students to go beyond what they have been taught. To me, this challenge to go beyond seems to be true even where the disciplines are concerned.

The disciplines, as I see them, are deliberate selections of materials that are ordered and systematized for the sake of providing particular kinds of perspectives on what human beings know. Such perspectives ought always to be conceived to be provisional and open to revision, as in the case of physics, mathematics, economics, and even literary criticism. If we know that these perspectives are human fabrications that were invented in response to human interests of various kinds, then students may be helped to see that encounters with them are aspects of their quests for meaning; such perspectives are modes of imparting some coherence to the world.

This understanding that the disciplines provide provisional perspectives may be the case even when the best-known disciplines that are taught in schools are identified with what Michael Apple calls "official knowledge" (1993). This phrase means that the texts and curricular materials used to transmit knowledge about the past and present are full of ideological content, which may include temptations to false consciousness, as well as deliberate distortions that support and justify existing power arrangements. We need only to recall some of the presentations of American history: (a) the obliteration of lived Black experiences, (b) the mystifications with regard to slavery, (c) the falsifying of Native American cultural and political life, (d) the caricaturing and demeaning of minorities, and (e) the exclusion of women except in subordinate roles. Perhaps most potent of all have been the renderings of the United States as the world's savior, the appointed champion of the developed world regarding peasant stirrings in the so-called undeveloped world. If the distinctive subject matter disciplines are taken to structure experience in such a fashion as properly to represent "reality," the so-called official conversation into which teachers are to initiate the young becomes, in many ways, indefensible. Yet these objectifying approaches are, for many, the only lenses available through which to order what otherwise appears to be a confusion of facts and events.

Teachers realize today, as I have come to realize, the arbitrariness of specialized perspectives. We know about the "blurring" of the disciplines; we know that each discipline is inevitably stamped with points of view, usually those of the powerful, the dominant academic (White, male, upper-class) group. At once, we know how much many of them have revealed to us and how many roads they have opened. All we can do is multiply the disciplinary approaches we use as sources of perspective as we incorporate diverse authors, more and more diverse witnesses, and more and more diverse forms of narrative. Just as important is an insistence on the interpretive approach on the part of the teacher and learner: a recognition that location, situation, and life history play legitimate parts in shaping the interpretation.

A northern shopkeeper's son, protected by his and his family's Whiteness, can never read or interpret the story of a lynching in a nearby town as the family of the victim does, no matter how much guilt the White neighbors experienced, no matter how intent they are on reform. Men are seldom able to study the 19th century infantilization of women with anything like the sense of what it signifies, which women immediately feel. Homosexuals respond to accounts of AIDS tragedies with a consciousness of mortality different from that of their most committed supporters. Newcomers in a community look at the codes and practices observed by its inhabitants with a curiosity, wonder, or surprise never felt by those who "belong." Not one of the above examples means that the teacher or the learner cannot understand what she or he has never lived through, what

Schutz called "strange." This approach only suggests that multiple sources need to be consulted, that things must be viewed from several directions, and that the conversation must widen and must become more and more inclusive.

If, indeed, the case is that "reality" must be understood as interpreted experience, then teaching demands intensified attention to the processes of interpretation, decoding, and sense making. Inside and outside the study of literature exist what Stanley Fish describes as "interpretive communities" (1980) that share certain strategies of reading. The fact that many communities exist, however, does not mean a total relativism of interpretation, which is something teachers must take seriously. Shared experiences, shared social practices, and shared ways of speaking connect various interpretations and provide a promise of something common, even while allowing for differing vantage points. Edward Said, concerned about specialization and exclusion, reaches for an "interpretive community." He goes on to say:

> If a community is based principally on keeping people out and on defending a tiny fiefdom . . . on the basis of a mysteriously pure subject's inviolable integrity, then it is a religious community. The secular realm I have presupposed requires a more open sense of community as something to be won and as audiences as human beings to be addressed. (1983, p. 152)

It is a matter, as it is in education generally, of reconciling diversity and distinctiveness with something held in common, something nourishing and shared.

Maurice Merleau-Ponty, troubled more than 30 years ago by an "absolute artificialism, such as we see in the ideology of cybernetics, where human creations are derived from a natural information process, itself conceived on the model of human machines," warned against what might happen if we ignore what we know of our lived situations and translate our experience into "abstract indices" (1964, p. 160). He went on:

> Scientific thinking, a thinking which looks on from above, and thinks of the object-in-general, must return to the "there is" which underlies it: to the site, the soil of the sensible and opened world such as it is in our life and for our body—not that possible body which we may legitimately think of as an information machine but that actual body I call mine, this sentinel standing quietly at the command of my words and acts. (p. 160)

He pictured associated bodies coming forward—others who shared being and the perceived world with him—and he called for science's "agile and improvisatory thought to ground itself upon things themselves. . . ." These lines are taken from "Eye and Mind" (Merleau-Ponty, 1964), an essay largely about painting and about being open to the world by means of vision, movement, and the engagement of the body. In teaching, I will often refer to or use the arts (dance, perhaps, and painting and poetry) to try to restore in a moment of cybernetics and abstract indices that idea of the "there is" that underlies, which is the idea of returning to the "sensible and opened world such as it is in our life and for our body." On the ground of that world, I believe with Merleau-Ponty and Dewey, is where meanings are sedimented, layered, and funded.

Of course I believe that students have to be taught what being

open to the world signifies and to move from the "natural attitude" where everything, including the objective world around, is taken as given, normal, and the same for everyone (Schutz, 1967). Holding on to the natural attitude, people do not question, do not see voids and deficiencies, and do not reach beyond themselves in a quest for meaning. Hoping for the "why" and the new beginning, as well as hoping for a felt discomfort within what Camus called the "chain of habitual life," I try to provoke students to enter new realities. They need to enter what Schutz called "provinces of meaning," each with its own cognitive style, its own way of experiencing the self in relation to the world, and its own "accent of reality" that makes it distinguishable from other provinces (1967, pp. 229–234). Indeed, Schutz talks of "shock experiences" when we find ourselves moving, say, from the province of disinterested science to the province of religion, or from the realm of dreams to the realms of commonsense life on the street.

Schutz describes, for instance, what happens when a person leaps into the province of theoretical thought and, for a while, suspends her or his subjective point of view. This suspension shows that "Not the undivided self, but only a partial self, a taker of a role, a 'Me', namely, the theoretician, 'acts' within the province of scientific thought" (p. 239). This partial self lacks the actuality of involvement that is regained in the province of the arts and some of the social sciences, as subjectivity may be regained and experiences connected with the body and its movements. These different provinces of meaning are names, Schutz said, for different tensions of consciousness "now living in working acts, now passing through a daydream, now plunging into the pictorial world of a painting, now indulging in theoretical contemplation. All these different experiences are experiences within my inner time; they belong to my stream of consciousness; they can be remembered and reproduced" (p. 258). The possibility of their being remembered means they can be communicated and can become part of the conversation I have been trying to keep alive—the conversation that ought to illuminate the world of everyday life as it enriches meaning and relationship and as it expands what is to be understood.

I know one can never fully know. I suspect we will never reach a full consensus on what is taken to be true and right, and I rather hope people will see the value in tension, in the wide-awakeness that comes with a consciousness of difference and incompleteness. I think I teach for wide-awakeness and for a more reflective, more physical, and less ossified living in the world. I recall Mikhail Bakhtin writing about ambivalence and laughter entering the life of literature and philosophy—of laughter even in the Platonic dialogues "immersing thought itself in the joyful relativity of evolving existence and not permitting it to congeal in abstractly dogmatic (monologic) ossification" (1984, p. 164). Should we use critical consciousness? Yes, I try to provoke it through my teaching. Imaginative encounters? Yes, I try to offer occasions, ordinarily in the domains of art. Dialogue? Yes. And a physical, passionate presentness to things, and laughter here and there, and song? I try to offer opportunities for all these in my teaching.

I will conclude with some lines from the poet Wistawa Szymborska's (1996) recent Nobel lecture. She is talking about inspiration, which she says she does not really understand. But she says it is not the exclusive privilege of poets or artists.

There is, there has been, there will always be, a certain group of people whom inspiration visits. It's made up of all those who've consciously chosen their calling and do their job with love and imagination. It may include doctors, teachers, gardeners—I could list a hundred more professions. Their work becomes one continuous adventure as long as they manage to keep discovering new challenges in it. Difficulties and setbacks never quell their curiosity. A swarm of new questions emerges from every problem they solve. Whatever inspiration is, it's born from a continuous "I don't know." (1996, pp. 27–28)

I hope that quotation tells you what I try to do when I teach. But I don't know. I reach, but I wonder; I pose more questions. But I don't know.

REFERENCES

Apple, M. (1993). *Official knowledge.* New York: Routledge.

Arendt, H. (1961). *Between past and future.* New York: Viking.

Bakhtin, M. (1984). *Problems of Dostoyevsky's poetics.* Minneapolis: University of Minnesota.

Benhabib, S. (1992). *Situating the self: Gender, community, and postmodernism in contemporary ethics.* New York: Routledge.

Camus, A. (1948). *The plague.* New York: Knopf.

Camus, A. (1955). *The myth of Sisyphus.* New York: Knopf.

Cavell, S. (1976). *Must we mean what we say?* New York: Cambridge University Press.

Delpit, L. (1995). *Other people's children.* New York: The New Press.

Dewey, J. (1916). *Democracy and education.* New York: Macmillan.

Dewey, J. (1931). *Art as experience.* New York: Minton, Balch.

Fish, S. (1980). *Is there a text in this class?: The authority of interpretive communities.* Cambridge, MA: Harvard University Press.

Heidegger, M. (1972). *What is called thinking.* New York: Harper & Row.

Merleau-Ponty, M. (1964). Eye and mind. In *The primacy of perception* (pp. 159–190). Evanston, IL: Northwestern University Press.

Morrison, T. (1970). *The bluest eye.* New York: Washington Square Press.

Ozick, C. (1989). *Metaphor and memory.* New York: Knopf.

Passmore, J. (1980). *The philosophy of teaching.* Cambridge, MA: Harvard University Press.

Percy, W. (1979). *The moviegoer.* New York: Knopf.

Said, E. W. (1983). Opponents, audiences, constituencies, and community. In H. Foster (Ed.), *The anti-aesthetic: Essays on postmodern culture* (pp. 135–159). Port Townsend, WA: Bay Press.

Sartre, J.-P. (1963). *Search for a method* (H. Barnes, Trans.). New York: Knopf.

Schutz, A. (1964). *Studies in social theory: Collected papers Vol. 2.* The Hague: Martinus Nijhoff.

Schutz, A. (1967). On multiple realities. In *The problem of social reality: Collected papers Vol. 1.* The Hague: Martinus Nijhoff.

Szymborska, W. (1996, December 30). The Nobel lecture. *The New Republic,* pp. 27–28.

Woolf, V. (1976). A sketch of the past. In *Moments of being.* New York: Harcourt Brace Jovanovich.

6.

Teaching as Communicative Action: Habermas and Education

David Coulter
The University of British Columbia

The Handbook of Research on Teaching comprises answers to three questions: What is teaching? What is good teaching? How can people become better teachers? Most of the chapters are concerned with answering the first question and some with the second and third. But, by implication at least, all three questions necessarily involve conceptions of goodness, which is a risky subject in a "postmodern" world. Determining value in societies without consensus about ethical and moral foundations is precarious. Teachers often talk of good teaching, good teachers, and good schools unproblematically. Educational researchers generally avoid directly tackling questions of goodness in teaching. Goodness is either implied or defined operationally by using, for example, the success of students on achievement tests or by reputation. "Effective schools" and "effective teachers" attain ends that are presumed good.

Some scholars continue to pursue these questions, however, as they try to work through ways to think directly about values, goodness, justice, and reason—all the concepts that have become so contentious in contemporary scholarship. Arguably one of the most influential and controversial figures, although working outside the study of education, is Jürgen Habermas, the German philosopher–sociologist who has redefined critical theory over the past 30 years. Habermas has become a cult figure for many other scholars and has spawned a small cultural industry of people interpreting his work. Putting aside prejudices about trendiness, I think that if we are serious in generating research on teaching that is committed to advancing education in and for a more democratic society, then we need to grapple with the particular resources that Habermas indirectly offers for thinking about teaching and education. I hope to show how his work addresses the three central questions of the Handbook.

Habermas has been remarkably consistent in pursuing the same issues for almost 40 years. At a time when scholars commonly limit their scope to a narrow range of problems, Habermas has attempted a broad, comprehensive analysis of modern society, its history, its present situation, and its prospects. This attempt has meant grappling with both European and Anglo–American streams of philosophy, including pragmatism, hermeneutics, and phenomenology, plus different areas of sociology and social science such as structural-functionalism, systems theory, linguistics, and ethnomethodology.

Habermas weaves his understanding of many diverse thinkers into a remarkably coherent corpus. His work is especially challenging for readers: The scope of his scholarship is such that few readers can follow and critically evaluate all the diverse sources that are part of his argument (certainly I do not include myself in this group). Further, while his destination may be consistent, the roads taken have been varied, having had occasional false starts and dead ends. This variation, in turn, is further exacerbated by some readers who choose to appropriate and develop lines of Habermas's thinking that he himself has abandoned.

Multiple and competing versions of Habermas's thinking add to the difficulty of understanding his work. While all of these barriers make reading Habermas daunting, I believe the effort is worthwhile: He provides rich and powerful conceptual resources for thinking about the moral conditions necessary for a just sense of that most critical educational act: communication. He does not avoid questions of meaning and value, nor does he confine himself to deconstructing other attempts. Instead, he embraces the challenge and tackles the issues involved in replying to Aristotle's question of how best to live.

Early Directions

Habermas's work can be divided into two phases: that of the 1960s and 1970s, a period grounded in notions of fundamental human interests, and that of the past two decades, a period based on language. In *Knowledge and Human Interests* (Habermas, 1968/1971), he began an effort to explain human action and reason by using a theory of three quasi-transcendental cognitive interests: the technical, the practical, and the emancipatory. Those three serve as the basis for three different forms of knowledge and three different types of sciences.

Technical interests are concerned with humans' need to control the physical environment, and they lead to natural sciences and the research programs that are based on those assumptions. Practical interests involve a furthering of understanding between people and of coordinating human action; such interests lead to hermeneutic–interpretive sciences. Emancipatory interests are concerned with the freedom from distorted, ideological communication; they engender critique, a type of self-reflection that allows humans to "grasp invariant regularities of social action as such and when they express ideologically frozen relations of dependence" (Habermas, 1968/1971, p. 310). Some programs concerning educational action research are intended to embody emancipatory interests by encouraging participants to uncover their ideological assumptions (e.g., Carr & Kemmis, 1986).

This theory attracted much attention and much criticism of the ambiguity with which self-reflection is defined, of the kind of status of the three quasi-transcendental interests, and of the continuing emphasis on epistemological concerns (R. Bernstein, 1985). Convinced of the legitimacy of those criticisms and of how they point to the vestiges of the philosophy of consciousness and the philosophy of the subject in his own work, Habermas began a somewhat different course, one that emphasizes the intersubjective and dialogical character of human action. Since 1981—beginning with *The Theory of Communicative Action* (Habermas, 1981/1984, 1987)—he no longer speaks of fundamental human interests, instead grounding his work on the presuppositions of language. This linguistic turn is both a dramatic shift and a continuation and refinement of his previous work: "[T]he insights contained in the original trichotomy of human interests are conceptually transformed in a new register within the context of his theory of communicative action" (R. Bernstein, 1985, p. 17).

Habermas's change in course has not been followed by all of his readers, a separation that results in curious phenomena such as (a) teacher action research approaches based on ideas that Habermas no longer pursues (e.g., Carr & Kemmis, 1986) or (b) reviews of his work that unproblematically combine his theory of communicative action with knowledge and human interests (e.g., Ewert, 1991). This difficulty in following his changes is a recurring problem for readers of Habermas. Richard Bernstein (1985, p. 15) describes Habermas as "a genuine dialectical thinker" who carefully listens to his critics and then changes course when convinced.

Other examples of such shifts involve concepts such as the ideal speech situation and discourse, plus distinctions such as moral–ethical and public–private, all of which are mentioned later in text. While this continuous development may complicate the appropriation of Habermas's ideas in fields like education, it can also add to the richness of the resources available. It has the added benefit of actually exemplifying some of what he tries to write about.

The Theory of Communicative Action

Communicative Action and Reason in the Lifeworld

In the switch from grounding his work in knowledge and human interests to grounding it in language and dialogue, Haber-

mas both refines and transforms concepts. The distinction between technical interests on the one hand and practical and emancipatory interests on the other is carried forward into two categories of action: strategic and communicative. The tripartite division of *Knowledge and Human Interests* (Habermas, 1968/1971) is also echoed in three "worlds": the objective, the social, and the subjective. Humans act in relation to at least one of those worlds, and their actions can be grouped into two general orientations to act: strategic or communicative. In strategic action, people attempt to influence the objective world (or the social world conceived objectively). In communicative action, humans attempt to come to an understanding with others about something in the objective world, social world, or subjective world that will allow them to coordinate action with others. The medium for this coordination is language.

Habermas constructs his ideas about language using resources from G. H. Mead's symbolic interactionalism, Austin's theory of speech acts, Wittgenstein's language games, and Gadamer's hermeneutics. Habermas argues (a) that to pursue ends or to coordinate actions with others, humans require language, and (b) that speech is a form of action, social action. Language permits the creation of a common lifeworld, that is, the shared resources for interpreting objective, social, and subjective worlds:

> Subjects acting communicatively always come to an understanding in the horizon of a lifeworld. Their lifeworld is formed from more or less diffuse, always unproblematic, background convictions. This lifeworld background serves as a source of situation definitions that are presupposed by participants as unproblematic . . . [and] also stores the interpretive work of preceding generations. (Habermas, 1981/1984, p. 70)

Language allows people to acquire and sustain their identities by being initiated into particular traditions, which, in turn, allows them to coordinate social actions, either by pursuing their chosen ends (strategic orientation) or by common agreement (communicative orientation). Language allows people to define themselves and their relationship to the objective world or social world. And it is through language that people attempt to come to an understanding with one another by making unavoidable validity claims to truth, rightness, and truthfulness

> according to whether the speaker refers to something in the objective world (as the totality of existing states of affairs), to something in the shared social world (as the totality of the legitimately regulated interpersonal relationships of a social group), or to something in his own subjective world (as the totality of experiences to which one has privileged access). (Habermas, 1983/1990, p. 58)

It is the understood acceptance to redeem validity claims—if necessary—that permits communication between partners in dialogue and forms the basis for Habermas's conception of reason. Habermas claims that "[r]eaching understanding is the inherent telos of human speech" (1981/1984, p. 287) upon which other uses of language are parasitic. Reason and language are inextricably entwined. Habermas's seemingly strong claim for the status of language and reason is tempered somewhat because what counts as reason in a particular society varies. Habermas's communicative rationality is, therefore, grounded universally but is determined in particular historical and social contexts. People work out what counts as reason by agreeing to redeem the validity claims they must make to truth, rightness, and truthfulness, all of which are embedded in language. Language thus becomes Habermas's new foundation for a theory of moral human action.

While Habermas's theory applies to all forms of communication, it is not hard to see the theory's particular relevance to the classroom as a carefully structured sphere of communicative action. Classrooms are places, for example, where many claims to truth, rightness, and truthfulness are reviewed and rehearsed, tested and tried on, as students learn what counts as reason through the achievement of new levels of language proficiency in dialogue with teachers and classmates.

Strategic Action, Instrumental Reason, and System

Habermas is not, however, claiming that modern human action is only about achieving understanding. Complex societies are not simply amalgams of lifeworlds but are systems as well. Any society sustains itself in relationship to both the natural and social worlds, and modern societies involve systems and organizations that coordinate action. The complement of communicative action is strategic action. In communicative action, actors attempt to understand one another; in strategic action they attempt to influence their environment (which includes other people) to achieve defined ends:

> Success in [strategic] action is . . . dependent on other actors, each of whom is oriented to his own success and behaves cooperatively only to the degree that fits with his egocentric calculus of utility. Thus strategically acting subjects must be cognitively so equipped that for them not only physical objects but decision-making systems can appear in the world. (Habermas, 1981/1984, p. 87–88)

The controlling medium of the economic and administrative systems of modern societies is not language but the generalized media of exchange: money and administrative power. Actors, when acting strategically, do not treat one another as individual dialogical partners but as assets or barriers to achieving their ends. Teachers act strategically in planning and managing their classes; students act strategically when pursuing better grades. The school is both a system and a lifeworld.

If communicative action involves using language and communicative reason to warrant validity claims and if it can be judged by the capacity to redeem those claims, then strategic action and instrumental reasoning involves using the media of money and administrative power to achieve purposes and can be judged by the efficiency of the match of means to ends. Those resources are used by Habermas in his analysis of modernity. For Habermas, the lifeworld and social systems are interdependent, each with its own forms of action and reason, but systems are intended to support the lifeworld. Instead, the opposite often occurs: Social systems "colonize" the lifeworld and allow "cognitive-instrumental rationality to achieve a one-sided dominance not only in our dealings with external nature, but also in our understanding of the world and in the communicative practice of everyday life" (Habermas, 1981/1984, p. 66).

Habermas (1981/1984, p. 342) argues that many of the problems of modernity are not simply the result of contradictions between social systems and the lifeworld. Instead, they are caused by the effects of the steering media—money and administrative power—that "replace language as the mechanism for coordinating action. They set social action loose from integration through value consensus and switch it over to purposive rationality steered by media." This change is often done "behind the backs" of those affected; that is, actors are unaware of the effects of the steering media. Habermas advocates a decolonization of the lifeworld by the development of that form of reason proper to the lifeworld: communicative rationality. A linguistically rationalized lifeworld would counteract media-steered systems.

Classrooms are venues for both communicative and strategic action. While Habermas seldom writes about teaching directly, when he does, he underlines the dangers of systems overwhelming the lifeworld of students and teachers. He describes the fundamental problem facing schools as

> a fight for or against the colonization of the lifeworld. . . . The protection of pupils' and parents' rights against educational measures (such as promotion or nonpromotion, examinations and tests, and so forth), or from acts of the school or the department of education that restrict basic rights (disciplinary penalties), is gained at the cost of a judicialization and bureaucratization that penetrates deep into the teaching and learning process. (Habermas, 1981/1987, p. 371)

All of which leads to such familiar phenomena in schools as "depersonalization, inhibition of innovation, breakdown of responsibility, immobility, and so forth" (Habermas, 1981/1987, pp. 371–372). Habermas is concerned with providing resources to better understand and combat this colonization; his most important conceptual tool is discourse ethics.

Discourse Ethics

The previous description of the lifeworld and its unproblematic background assumes agreement about people's understandings of their objective and social worlds and about how they understand themselves. But this consensus, if present, is fragile. Challenges to any one of an actor's validity claims about truth, rightness, or truthfulness can disrupt that consensus. The repair of this disruption requires actors to try to reforge their lifeworld consensus in forms of discourse or, minimally, to clarify the differences that separate them:

> Thus the rationality proper to the communicative practice of everyday life points to the practice of [discourse] as a court of appeal that makes it possible to continue communicative action with other means when disagreements can no longer be repaired with everyday routines and yet are not to be settled by the direct or strategic use of force [in strategic action]. (Habermas, 1981/1984, pp. 17–18)

Communicative rationality requires a theory of argumentation, or discourse. In contesting lifeworld assumptions, Habermas claims that "the unforced force of the better argument" should prevail and that such dialogues should be free of coercion, manipulation, distortion, or other barriers to rational discussion. Discourse presumes ideal speech situations in which conditions of symmetry and reciprocity predominate, including that all people who wish to may initiate and continue dialogue; that they may raise, question, and pursue any assertion; and that they will not repress others.

Two important cautions seem warranted. First, the conditions of discourse apply only to situations where fundamental validity claims in the lifeworld have been challenged and argumentation is warranted, which is not a common occurrence. For example, normal classroom communication does not usually include challenges to the fundamental beliefs of the students or teacher. Second, Habermas's use of the term "ideal speech situation" is unfortunate and is one that he now regrets. It has sometimes been taken as a possibility that might be achieved in some form (e.g., Carr & Kemmis, 1986), instead of a regulative ideal presupposed by argumentation: "If we want to enter into argumentation, we must take these presuppositions of argumentation as a matter of fact, despite the fact that they have an ideal content to which we can only approximate in reality" (Habermas, 1991/1993, p. 164).

As any teacher can attest, but as some research on classroom discourse fails to acknowledge, the conditions of ideal discourse can never be met in practice: Not everyone affected can always be involved, we can never purge language of all hidden distortions, and discourse has no mechanism to bring about closure. The best, most exciting classroom discussions in which teachers and students are challenging fundamental assumptions about important issues are truncated by school bells, for instance. So while the ideal of discourse is consensus, Habermas is not arguing that all discourses fail if consensus is not reached. His point is more modest: One of the conditions for entering a discourse is the possibility of its success. That is, we can then achieve understanding. Otherwise, the attempt at dialogue would seem futile. In practice, discourse may succeed only in clarifying the perspectives that continue to separate participants.

Habermas distinguishes between types of discourses, depending on the action orientation and validity claims being challenged. Typologies have changed as he has developed his theory partly in response to critics, changes that can lead to confusion for readers. For example, in *The Theory of Communicative Action* (Habermas, 1981/1984, 1987), he lists theoretical, explicative, and practical discourses, as well as aesthetic criticism and therapeutic critique. Later, he talks of moral and evaluative discourses (Habermas, 1983/1990). In more recent work (Habermas, 1991/1993), he lists pragmatic, ethical, and moral discourses. He then adds procedurally regulated bargaining (Habermas, 1992/1996); this version is the one I outline here with an eye to its applicability as a framework analyzing both classroom discourse and teaching as a form of communicative action.

Pragmatic discourses concern expediency in strategic action and entail argumentation about means–ends matches in the objective world; language is used to transmit empirical knowledge to assist in choosing appropriate means or in selecting between valued goals. Pragmatic discourses assume an unproblematic background of shared values. Much of the research discussion about teaching is pragmatic discourse. From this standpoint, the ends of what constitutes good teaching are presumed and the empirical research attempts to help in matching possible means to those ends. When ends become problematic, how-

ever, participants may choose to engage in ethical or moral discourse.

Ethical discourse is concerned with issues of self-understanding and identity and how best to live a particular society, which is paradoxically a subject for dialogue because such self-understanding can come only in dialogue with others: "[Ethical questions] pose themselves from the perspective of members who, in the face of important life issues, want to gain clarity about their shared form of life and about the ideals they feel should shape their common life" (Habermas, 1992/1996). Success in ethical discourse results in increased understanding of a historically transmitted form of life. School communities can sometimes be involved in ethical discourse when attempting to clarify their values, their identity.

In contrast, moral discourses require breaking with the specific historical contexts and identities of participants so that the participants may justify universal norms: "[Moral] discourse represents the ideal extension of each individual communication community from within. In this forum, only those norms that express a common interest of all affected can win justified assent" (Habermas, 1991/1993, p. 13). Success in moral discourse involves having the participants transcend the ethnocentric perspective of a particular form of life, and it results in universal norms that would meet with the considered agreement of all those affected. Discussions of what is worthwhile—and educational—in any human society will involve moral discourses.

Habermas recognizes that in complex modern societies neither ethical nor moral discourse may be a viable alternative; thus, he has recently added another option. The issue at stake may affect diverse groups in different ways without any clear generalizable interest or priority emerging. Consensus cannot be reached; common understanding is not possible. Rather than ignore the issue or resort to strategic action, parties may resort to bargaining, a form of strategic action with at least some of the features of discourse including, for example, procedural fairness. "Fair bargaining, then, does not destroy the discourse principle but rather indirectly presupposes it" (Habermas, 1992/1996, p. 167).

The bulk of political decision making involves bargaining and compromise and is very familiar to those working in schools. Habermas worries that—as part of the colonization of the lifeworld—ethical and moral questions about the good and the right are either ignored in pragmatic discourses or redefined into strategic issues to be regulated either by strategic action or bargaining. Conceptions of goodness in teaching, for example, are often not confronted in public dialogue, but are unproblematically assumed in discussions about effective teaching or are settled by bureaucratic fiat or by politically bargained job descriptions. The relationship between ethical and moral discourses, however, requires elaboration, especially the connection to other Habermasian distinctions such as justification and application or public and private.

Ethical and Moral Discourses

In his conceptions of the ethical and moral, Habermas aims to fuse two streams of moral theory: (a) abstract, universalistic Kantian theory and (b) communitarian, contextual Aristotelian theory. He tries to reconcile those very different conceptions of morality by working out the relationships between the ethical and the moral, by connecting these discourses with separate discourses of justification and application, and by providing a venue or public sphere for such discourses.

The most important division is between the ethical and moral, that is, the good and the just. Ethical argumentation is contained within particular contexts or communities; moral argumentation transcends individual social–historical contexts. This distinction applies especially to discussions of education, which is concerned with living both in particular societies and, generally, in human society. Schools, whether in Canada, the United States, France, or Japan, prepare the young for living in particular communities and for living with other humans globally. Habermas's response to the plurality of modern societies is to work out a relationship between a concrete notion of the ethical and an abstract conception of the moral. He maintains that the moral can be determined free of any particular context because moral discourse is based on the validity claims that are fundamental to any language:

> Concepts such as truth, rationality, and justification play the *same* role in *every* language community, even if they are interpreted differently and applied in accordance with different criteria. And this fact is sufficient to anchor the same universalistic concepts of morality and justice in different, even competing, forms of life and show that they are compatible with different conceptions of the good—on the assumption that the "comprehensive doctrines" and "strong traditions" enter into unrestricted dialogue with one another instead of persisting in their claims to an exclusivity in a fundamentalistic manner. (Habermas, 1991/1993, p. 105; italics in original)

He argues for a conception of morality in which what is moral is not determined by the introspective self, but in dialogue with others. What educational aims are and what counts as good teaching, for example, are not decided by educational philosophers or administrators or teachers but by actual dialogues of those involved (which, of course, include educational philosophers, administrators, and teachers).

Habermas, Richard Bernstein (1983, p. 184) argues, ". . . speaks with two voices, which can be called the 'transcendental' and the 'pragmatic.'" To connect those two voices—the universal moral and the local ethical—Habermas develops a two-stage process for the extrication of moral questions from concrete ethical life and then for the reinsertion of agreed-upon norms back into that life: justification and application. In modern societies with many conflicting moral–ethical frameworks, problematic social issues cannot be easily resolved by referring to a background of shared values. Instead, those issues have to be abstracted from their everyday contexts to be treated rationally in dialogue, resulting in the possibility of universally valid norms. But the cognitive advantage gained by abstraction must be undone. Norms have to be applied appropriately to concrete life situations. This insertion is again accomplished through a dialogue, but one in which the guiding principle is not universalization, but appropriateness: "What must be determined here is which of the norms already accepted as valid is appropriate in a given case in the light of all of the relevant features of the situation conceived as exhaustively as possible" (Habermas, 1991/1993, p. 14). Moral discourse thus requires dialogues

of both justification and application. In developing this conception, Habermas attempts to link the Kantian generalizable other with the concrete other of neo-Aristotelians.

Discourses of justification and application require venues, or private and public spaces—an issue that has concerned Habermas for his entire career. In such early work as *The Structural Transformation of the Public Sphere* (1962/1989), Habermas traces European bourgeois political life from the 17th to the mid-20th centuries; he describes the blurring of the public and the private, the assumption of public power by private organizations, and the penetration of the private by the state. These transformations result in the replacing of any genuine public dialogue with the reification of public opinion, a commodity that can be manufactured and manipulated. Much of Habermas's project since 1962 can be read as an attempt to create a framework for dialogue that is in the public sphere and in which moral and ethical action can be dialogically grounded.

In developing such a model of public space, Habermas tries to create a thicker, less-procedural model than the usual individualistic, neutral, liberal conception. At the same time, he tries to avoid the elitism of a republican, Arendtian conception (Benhabib, 1992). He proposes a discursive model of public space in which the conditions of the ideal speech situation—including, for example, nonrepression—act as constraints. Habermas (1992/1996) proposes multiple, overlapping publics in which people construct individual and collective identities, as well as the norms that bind them together in democratic dialogue.

Discussions of "public" also require defining "private," that is, deciding the boundaries between the two. Habermas's initial attempt to separate the public from the private attracted criticism, particularly from feminists, because of the rigidity of his separation of the public from the private (e.g., Benhabib, 1992; Fraser, 1992). Yet at the same time, other critics (e.g., Moon, 1991) expressed concern that if public and private become enmeshed in one another; nothing is left that is genuinely private. Habermas's newest response is to again rely on a conception of dialogue and to distinguish between discussing topics and regulating them: "Making something that has so far been considered a private matter a topic for public discussion does not yet imply any *infringement* of individual rights. . . . To talk about something is not necessarily the same as meddling in another's affairs" (Habermas, 1992/1996, p. 313; italics in original).

It is possible to discuss child abuse, poverty, and racism, for example, while protecting the privacy of individuals. However, making a decision about when something previously private needs to become public is itself a judgment subject to public scrutiny. Teachers can raise issues of child poverty without necessarily making public the private lives of poor children, but teachers must publicly act when encountering a starving or abused child. Researchers such as Jonathan Kozol (1991, 1995) and Shirley Brice Heath (1983) struggle with the ethical and moral issues involved with researching the lives of children in schools. As researchers, they make public the previously hidden (and private) lives of the children and adults they study, while at the same time they must struggle to protect the privacy of those same people. Habermas argues that deciding the boundaries between public and private cannot be left to legislators, judges, administrators, or researchers, that is, those working within social systems. Debates about public–private require the kind of discourse in a democratic public sphere in which all are involved: Such debates inevitably make claims to truth, truthfulness, and rightness. Discourse ethics is, therefore, both a moral theory and a democratic theory.

Communicative Action and Democracy

Habermas's work on democracy follows that of two other important 20th-century democratic thinkers: John Dewey and Hannah Arendt. Like them, he is concerned with developing a theory of democratic legitimacy that, in turn, is tied to dialogue. One way to understand Habermas's work is an attempt to construct a democratic dam against the dehumanizing forces of modernity by encouraging public dialogue. Indeed, he directly quotes Dewey in explaining that "the essential need, in other words, is the improvement of methods and conditions of debate, discussion, and persuasion" (Dewey quoted by Habermas, 1992/1996, p. 304). Habermas argues for a conception of democracy with multiple publics in which pragmatic, ethical, and moral discourses allow the justification and application of general social norms. Benhabib describes the challenge well:

> Democratic debate is like a ball game where there is no umpire to definitively interpret the rules of the game and their application. Rather in the game of democracy the rules of the game no less than their interpretation and even the position of the umpire are essentially contestable. (1992, pp. 106–107)

I want to pursue Benhabib's analogy to illustrate aspects of Habermas's project. To the players, their ball game is the lifeworld, one they collectively construct in public dialogue. Problems occur periodically in deciding what is appropriate equipment, what rules apply, or whether people are faithful to the game. When such issues occur, all those involved are involved in establishing a new consensus. As the game becomes more popular, more and more players become involved, leading to the establishment of administrative systems, that is, leagues, rules, coaches and umpires who may serve the game, or deform it. Eventually, the game becomes professionalized. Now, owners, coaches, players, unions, and agents determine what the game is and how it should be played. Rather than serve the players, these people control the players; the system colonizes the lifeworld of the participants. The only recourse, according to Habermas, is to reestablish institutions and systems that serve the players and in which the purposes, rules, and structures are again open to debate.

Certainly, my use of this analogy dangerously simplifies Habermas, ignoring, for example, his concern for why the players choose to become involved in the ball game and how they should treat one another. Nonetheless, I hope the analogy does bring his issues and concerns into some form of relief. For Habermas, for example, norms and values—the game and its rules—are not given to the players but are determined by these players and are always subject to debate. In the normal course of a game, these aspects are all taken for granted, but when problematic, they become the subject of discourse. We can walk away from the game, but not the lifeworld.

Discussions of democracy lead to the most common criticism of Habermas: his supposed idealism. Is it realistic to expect the players to stop the game and to rationally debate both the purpose of the game and its rules? This course would be clearly utopian. But this approach is not what Habermas is advocating. He is not arguing for democratic dialogue as a decision-making strategy. Instead, he maintains that the systems and the ways of acting and reasoning are essential to coordinating human action and understanding in complex, large, modern societies. We cannot play the game without organization and rules. The challenge is to prevent the systems we have established to support our actions from deforming those actions. The check on those systems is language and its presuppositions.

If we return to the ball game analogy, the only recourse we have to control of the game by owners, coaches, unions, and agents is ongoing dialogue among the players about what the game is really about. In this effort, Habermas provides resources both for understanding what is happening and for improving the methods and conditions of debate.

If those same resources were to be used in grappling with the three critical questions that I claim for this Handbook, the normative subtext of the three questions would involve democracy. Indeed, the three questions might be subsumed in one: How can teachers help to create and foster democratic dialogues in which they and their students, together with others, decide how best to live? In fostering such discussions, teachers would still be strategic actors working within schooling systems. They would be communicative actors supporting the lifeworld of their various communities, but they world also be partners and initiators of pragmatic, ethical, and moral discourses in which the match of means to ends would be examined, the ends and means of schooling would be questioned, and the assumptions of the participants would be periodically challenged. Classrooms and schools would become public spaces in which teachers, students, and community members together decide goodness.

These resources, of course, add to the complexity of teaching. Deciding when to act strategically or communicatively, when to resort to discourse, what kind of discourse, with whom, and how—all of these are decisions that teachers must make. For Habermas, those decisions are, in turn, subjects for public dialogue. Habermas contributes criteria for judging the quality of the dialogues and of the decisions, that is, the criteria for deciding goodness.

According to Habermas, goodness involves claims to truth, rightness, and truthfulness that are debated publicly by all who are affected under conditions that come as close as possible to approximating the ideal speech conditions of symmetry and reciprocity. Goodness, determined in democratic dialogue, provides criteria for judging dialogues and decisions, including, for example, whether strategic action supports or colonizes the lifeworlds of participants. Those efforts occur in multiple and overlapping public and private spaces, in classrooms and staff rooms, on soccer fields, in supermarkets. Democratic public spheres "come into existence whenever and wherever all affected by general and social political norms of action engage in a practical discourse, evaluating their validity" (Benhabib, 1992, p. 105). Such a conception of teaching has implications for the roles of all who are involved with schools and, indeed, with the conception of schooling in democratic societies, hence my claims for Habermas's importance for readers of the Handbook.

Criticisms and Appropriations

All of the earlier discussion is contentious. Habermas's work creates problems for those who seek to understand his ideas and to appropriate them for education. While I cannot deal with such issues in any detail here, I can provide a sense of some of the difficulties by examining a couple of topics and how those topics have been treated by Habermas and by his critics.

Criticisms

There is scarcely an aspect of Habermas's project that has not attracted substantial and sustained criticism, both dismissive and appreciative. Much is inaccurate; Habermas's work seems to contribute to misreading and confusion. While some of the difficulty of reading Habermas is due to (a) the scope and developmental character of his work, (b) the difficulties of translation, and (c) the requirements for broad background knowledge, some of the problem is the result of how he frames and pursues his argument. As the dialectical thinker that Richard Bernstein describes, Habermas often seems to create sharp dichotomies and then to work toward synthesis. That is, he frames his argument in polarities and then tries to work out the relationships between poles, sometimes with more success than others. Communicative–strategic action, lifeworld–system, moral–ethical, justification–application, and public–private are some of his key dichotomies.

While some of the oppositions are not as stark as I have outlined in my necessarily brief sketch of his project, I believe that they fairly characterize Habermas's thinking and that interpreting Habermas inevitably involves a critique of his categories and of how he defines the relationships between contrasting concepts. Some interpreters accept his stark oppositions without reference to how he subsequently tries to soften them and to define the relationship between the polarities. I want to use communicative–strategic and the moral–ethical as examples of these dichotomies and of how Habermas and his critics treat them. Such distinctions are also key to developing Habermasian conceptions of teaching and education.

Communicative and strategic action are oriented to understanding and to success, respectively, and this opposition is sometimes characterized by critics as a consensus theory of truth versus distortion and oppression (e.g., Lakomski, 1994). Participants can choose either to construct the truth together or to attempt to impose their version of the truth. Habermas softens this dichotomy in three ways. First, he does not argue that the truth can ever be definitely discovered or created; the ideal speech situation is just that, ideal. It is meant as a "counterfactual construct" that is presumed by discourse, but it can never be achieved in practice. While the ultimate goal may be an unattainable universal consensus, this consensus may, in practice, be a provisional agreement or just an improved understanding of the issues that divide. Teachers and parents may, for example, never arrive at a common notion of education, but they can develop greater understanding of other perspectives.

Second, Habermas distinguishes between communicative action and discourse. The former comprises the taken-for-granted constructs of the social world; the latter involves argumentation that results when those agreed assumptions have become problematic. A world in which all social agreements were contested would be chaotic, and for teachers to attempt to problematize all aspects of their students lifeworlds would be both irresponsible and futile (Williams, 1985).

Finally, Habermas more recently (1992/1996) argues that strategic and communicative action are actually enmeshed in contexts and cannot be so neatly separated. Interaction runs through different phases in which participants negotiate the coordination of their actions. The entire exchange is subsequently judged for its orientation to achieving control or understanding: "[S]trategic *elements* within a use of language oriented to reaching understanding can be distinguished from strategic *actions* through the fact that the entire sequence of a stretch of talk stands . . . under the presuppositions of communicative action" (Habermas, 1981/1984, p. 331; italics in original). Teachers need some measure of control of their classrooms; the degree and purpose of that control requires judgment that should be subject to review.

Another often criticized dichotomy is Habermas's separation of the ethical from the moral. That is, he divides issues that are located within a particular historical–ethical form of life from issues that are of a universal concern involving justice. This approach has an obvious connection to education and involves both the values of the local community and the norms of human society in general. I believe the development of this distinction can be traced to Habermas's various conceptions of discourse.

In *The Theory of Communicative Action* (Habermas, 1981/ 1984, 1987), discourses involving norms (practical) were distinguished from those concerning values (aesthetic criticism). Criticism concerning this separation (e.g., Benhabib, 1986) motivated Habermas to revise and clarify this aspect of his work. In *Moral Consciousness and Communicative Action* (Habermas, 1983/1990), he separates moral and evaluative questions. In *Justification and Application* (Habermas, 1991/1993), he describes pragmatic, ethical, and moral discourses. Later, in *Between Facts and Norms* (Habermas, 1992/1996), he adds bargaining. The sharp separations that characterized earlier work become blurred. While norms still have to be extracted from everyday practice and justified in argumentation, they must also be reinserted into particular lifeworlds through discourses of application. The focus of his work has shifted from the justification of universal norms to their selection and application:

> Postconventional morality provides no more than a procedure for impartially judging disputed questions. It cannot pick out a catalog of duties or even designate a list of hierarchically ordered norms, but it expects subjects to form their own judgments. . . . Normally the basic [norms] themselves—entailing such duties as equal respect of each person, distributive justice, benevolence toward the needy, loyalty, and sincerity—are not disputed. Rather, the abstractness of these highly generalized norms leads to problems of application as soon as a conflict goes beyond the routine interactions in familiar contexts. (Habermas, 1992/1996, p. 115)

Questions of which norm applies to what features of which context create a far more complex picture of moral discourse than the original rigid dichotomy. While the early version of discourse ethics was accused of maintaining rigid boundaries between the moral and the ethical (e.g., Benhabib, 1986, 1992), his current version can be seen as almost neo-Aristotelian in its embrace of context (J. M. Bernstein, 1995). Habermas has gone so far in complicating the relationship between the universal and the particular that he runs the risk of blurring one into the other, a very ironic situation for someone who is usually accused of being neo-Kantian.

What is apparent is that issues of ethical and moral import require dialogues, and some exchanges need to be broader than others. Education and teaching involve both ethical and moral questions and, therefore, call for both local and broad discussion in multiple publics. What is ethical, what is moral, or what is educational cannot be defined by any one of these forums. Those definitions must be determined in actual dialogues that, in turn, have led to having some of those appropriating his work see it as being more suitable as a political theory than as a moral theory (Cohen & Arato, 1992).

Appropriation

The difficulties in interpretation have contributed to problems in the appropriation of Habermas's ideas for education. Habermas has generally not been well served by those who appropriate his work. Many of the same problems I have just outlined are common: Dependence on rigid dichotomizes or confusion about how the dialectical synthesis is attempted. Even the most sophisticated of interpretations—for example, that of Robert Young (1990, 1992)—has some of those characteristics. I want to use Young as an example of how Habermas has been interpreted for education and teaching because I believe Young's work is perhaps the best version to date and yet it still has some of those problems. Young quite properly scolds others for their uncritical use of emancipation and for the problematization of students' lifeworlds, that is, the privileging of discourse:

> It is not the main function of critical educators to attack the lifeworld of students—to "make trouble." Rather, it should be to assist students to make an effective job of reconstructing the already problematic parts of their life-world through communicative, problem-solving learning. (Young, 1990, p. 71)

Young also adroitly deals with a number of other issues that have been consistently mishandled by those interpreting Habermas for teaching, including, for example, the role of the ideal speech situation and the asymmetrical relationship between students and teachers. But Young too seems to use stark dichotomies, notably the division of classroom types into methods and discourse catergories. Methods teachers objectify students and knowledge as they cover the curriculum; discourse teachers invite students to construct knowledge with them. Young does try to soften the contrast:

> The issue is not one of black hats and white hats, but of definitions of the educational task and the teaching role. The discourse classroom is characterized by what Dewey called "normal communication," which he distinguished from mechanical communication in a manner very like Habermas's distinction between communicative and strategic action. (Young, 1992, p. 87)

But Habermas no longer makes the distinction between strategic and communicative action so stark; they are enmeshed in

one another as I described earlier. Teachers, therefore, must be involved with both methods and discourse aspects of teaching.

Further, even if Young's divisions were accepted as useful initial categories, he then begs the question of who is involved both in determining occasions for educative classroom discourse and in judging the quality of that discourse. In *Critical Theory and Classroom Talk* (1992), Young rightly focuses on the capacities of young children to be involved in examining their own actions with the assistance of their teacher. But the education of children is a shared ethical and moral responsibility, and many are left out of this dialogue: parents, other teachers, and the immediate and larger community. Again, using Habermas's theory, Young concentrates on one public space with limited involvement, and many public spaces with broad involvement need to be created. The challenge that Habermas poses is the creation of multiple public spaces in which moral and ethical action can be democratically grounded; classroom and schools provide few public (or genuinely private) spaces in which education can be created.

Resources for Teaching and the Study of Teaching

Habermas provides important resources for thinking about teaching in and for a democracy. For Habermas, teaching is both strategic action and communicative action, and it requires teachers to use both instrumental and communicative reason to create and sustain their lifeworlds and those of their students. In such efforts, teachers and students inevitably confront issues of goodness and justice that can ultimately be decided only in dialogue with one another and with other affected parties in which all involved presume that the unforced force of the better argument and not administrative power or position will prevail. In trying to resolve various claims to truth, rightness, and truthfulness, parties inevitably attempt to create certain conditions that support and sustain democratic dialogue. Teachers can become better teachers by helping themselves and their students forge better understandings of themselves, their social world, and their objective world. This understanding involves developing the lifeworld and resisting its colonization by economic and administrative systems.

Habermas's work has equally important implications for those who seek to research and to promote educational and democratic teaching. Researchers of teaching would continue to contribute empirical research to pragmatic discourses, thereby allowing teachers to match effective means to particular ends. That is, they would contribute to strategic action.

But following Habermas, more educational researchers would not avoid, but would directly tackle, questions of goodness in teaching; they would contribute to communicative action. They would examine whether or not the ends being pursued strategically are worthwhile, or if schooling systems are colonizing the lifeworlds of students, teachers, administrators, and parents. They would respectfully seek to challenge some of the unproblematic background convictions that make up the lifeworlds of those in schools and that raise issues for ethical and moral discourses. They would initiate, encourage, and join democratic dialogues about good teaching as equal partners with valuable, but not decisive, contributions to make. They would seek to involve and support the silent and marginalized in such discussions. They would also critique those dialogues, uncovering the inevitable less-than-ideal aspects of speech. They would support others in initiating and sustaining public dialogues.

Researchers of teaching would also be involved in dialogues about their own research and their own educational teaching. None of this effort is absent from research on teaching now, but I would also argue that it is not common enough. I believe that attention to Habermas's work would help make this kind of teaching and this kind of research more widespread. To borrow Maxine Greene's wonderful phrase: more teachers and researchers would be wide awake. They would strive

> to bring the school community into an open discussion, to consider the moral issues in the light of over-arching commitments, to talk about what is actually known and what is merely hypothesized. At the very least, there would be wide-awakeness. (Greene, 1978, p. 45)

REFERENCES

Benhabib, S. (1986). *Critique, norm, and utopia.* New York: Columbia University Press.

Benhabib, S. (1992). *Situating the self: Gender, community, and postmodernism in contemporary ethics.* New York: Routledge.

Bernstein, J. M. (1995). *Recovering ethical life: Jürgen Habermas and the future of critical theory.* New York: Routledge.

Bernstein, R. J. (1983). *Beyond objectivism and relativism: Science, hermeneutics, and praxis.* Philadelphia: University of Pennsylvania Press.

Bernstein, R. J. (1985). Introduction. In R. J. Bernstein (Ed.), *Habermas and modernity* (pp. 1–32). Cambridge, MA: MIT Press.

Carr, W., & Kemmis, S. (1986). *Becoming critical: Education, knowledge, and action research.* Philadelphia: Falmer Press.

Cohen, J. L., & Arato, A. (1992). *Civil society and political theory.* Cambridge, MA: MIT Press.

Ewert, G. D. (1991). Habermas and education: A comprehensive overview of Habermas in educational literature. *Review of Educational Research, 61*(3), 345–378.

Fraser, N. (1992). Rethinking the public sphere: A contribution to the critique of actually existing democracy. In C. Calhoun (Ed.), *Habermas and the public sphere* (pp. 109–142). Cambridge, MA: MIT Press.

Greene, M. (1978). *Landscapes of learning.* New York: Teachers College Press.

Habermas, J. (1971). *Knowledge and human interests* (J. Shapiro, Trans.). Boston: Beacon. (Original work published 1968)

Habermas, J. (1984). *The theory of communicative action: Vol. I, Reason and the rationalization of society* (T. McCarthy, Trans.). Boston: Beacon. (Original work published 1981)

Habermas, J. (1987). *The Theory of communicative action: Vol. II, Lifeworld and system: A critique of functionalist reason* (T. McCarthy, Trans.). Boston: Beacon. (Original work published 1981)

Habermas, J. (1989). *The structural transformation of the public sphere: An inquiry into a category of bourgeois society* (T. Burger, Trans., with the assistance of F. Lawrence). Cambridge, MA: MIT Press. (Original work published 1962)

Habermas, J. (1990). *Moral consciousness and communicative action* (C. Lenhardt & S. Weber Nicholson, Trans.). Cambridge, MA: MIT Press. (Original work published 1983)

Habermas, J. (1993). *Justification and application: Remarks on discourse ethics* (C. P. Cronin, Trans.). Cambridge, MA: MIT Press. (Original work published 1991)

Habermas, J. (1996). *Between facts and norms: Contributions to a discourse theory of law and democracy* (W. Rehg, Trans.). Cambridge, MA: MIT Press. (Original work published 1992)

Heath, S. B. (1983). *Ways with words: Language, life, and work in communities and classrooms.* New York: Cambridge University Press.

Kozol, J. (1991). *Savage inequalities.* New York: HarperCollins.

Kozol, J. (1995). *Amazing grace.* New York: HarperCollins.

Lakomski, G. (1994). Critical theory and education. In T. Husen & T. N. Postlethwaite (Eds.), *The International Encyclopedia of Education.* White Plains, NY: Permagon.

Moon, J. D. (1991). Constrained discourse and public life. *Political Theory, 19,* 202–229.

Williams, B. (1985). *Ethics and the limits of philosophy.* Cambridge, MA: Harvard University Press.

Young, R. E. (1990). *A critical theory of education: Habermas and our children's future.* New York: Teachers College Press.

Young, R. E. (1992). *Critical theory and classroom talk.* Philadelphia: Multilingual Matters Ltd.

7.
The Caring Teacher

Nel Noddings
Stanford University and Teachers College, Columbia University

What does it mean to be a caring teacher? In educational research, there are many ways to approach this question. We might ask teachers what they mean by caring, or we might ask students to describe caring teachers. We might identify outstanding teachers—teachers described by their students as caring—and do a form of educational hagiography. We might even try to operationalize caring by reducing it to a set of traits or behaviors and then devise an instrument to measure it. The task for philosophers of education is to analyze the concept thoroughly so that connections to other concepts are revealed, the consequences of adopting one definition or another are explored, and important related issues are identified. This chapter is designed to demonstrate how a philosopher approaches the task of describing the caring teacher.

What Does It Mean to Care?

One of the first things we notice when we set out to analyze what it means to care is that caring manifests itself in a wide variety of ways. Not only does caring differ across cultures and occupational settings but also it even differs in the same individual as he or she meets different persons in different situations. In education, a teacher might be tough with one student and gentle, almost permissive, with another in roughly similar situations and, in both cases, rightly be called caring. Each of us has an idea of caring, and that idea clearly affects the way we talk about caring and what we expect to see when someone claims to care. My own idea, or ideal, of caring has surely entered my analysis (Noddings, 1984, 1992a), but I tried at the outset to find a description that would fit all the cases we want to include.

A second objective for those of us influenced by Deweyan pragmatism is to develop a concept that will be useful in our daily lives and work. Dewey urged philosophers to abandon concepts that have outgrown their usefulness for social life. In that tradition, Richard Rorty (1989) has encouraged philoso-

phers and other thoughtful people to introduce new vocabularies as our problems change. What we seek, then, is a view of caring that is phenomenologically accurate and highly useful for our work in education. We must be concerned not only with the clarity of our description but also with the consequences of employing it in both research and practice.

Third, if we are committed to the vocabulary of care, we have to address the issues that have arisen in its use. A prominent issue today is the persistent identification of caring with an attitude or feeling. As a mere feeling, caring seems to conflict with the hard intellectual and managerial work of teaching; at least, it seems relatively unimportant (a nice, added touch) in contrast to the central tasks of education. I will show that this is what philosophers call a *pseudoproblem*. The word *caring* can, of course, be used to refer to an attitude, but it can also be used to describe a relation or to point to something far deeper and more important—a way of being in the world.

Fourth, we have to be aware of the special setting in which the concept will be applied. For example, the demands of caring may come into conflict with the current interest in professionalization, and the historical association of caregiving with women may aggravate that conflict.

Because our first goal is to produce a description or definition of caring that will fit all cases, let's start with a *caring encounter,* a meeting between two people—a carer and a cared-for—and ask what characterizes these two people as they meet.

If we examine how we are when we care, we see, first, that we are attentive; we try to receive what the other is telling or showing us. In such an encounter, we are not laying our own conceptual structures on the situation (although we will inevitably do this as we eventually decide what to do); for some moments at least, we are receptive. Simone Weil (1977) emphasized the receptive nature of this attention when she wrote:

In the first legend of the Grail, it is said that the Grail . . . belongs to the first comer who asks the guardian of the vessel, a king three-

The author wishes to thank reviewer George Noblit (University of North Carolina), graduate students in philosophy of education at Stanford University, and James Paul (University of South Florida) for helpful suggestions.

quarters paralyzed by the most painful wound, "What are you going through?" (p. 51)

Weil continued:

> The love of our neighbor in all its fullness simply means being able to say to him: What are you going through? It is a recognition that the sufferer exists, not only as a unit in a collection, or a specimen from the social category labeled "unfortunate," but as a man, exactly like us. (1977, p. 51)

This receptivity is, of course, a prelude to response. When I attend (and it may be to one bubbling over with enthusiasm or joy as well as to a sufferer), I allow myself to be moved by the other's needs and feelings. I experience what I have called, in a fuller analysis (Noddings, 1984, 1992a), *motivational displacement*. My motive energies flow toward the projects of the other. Often I want to remove the pain, share the joy, solve the problem, or promote the project of the other. But this flow of energy can be blocked by fatigue or reluctance; it can also be appropriately blocked if I evaluate the other's desire and disapprove of it. But caring does not necessarily end in the latter case. Now I may need to find a form of response that will persuade the other that he or she is mistaken (or even morally wrong) in his or her project. If, as often happens in teaching, the teacher regards a student's complaint as unjustified, he or she cannot simply dismiss it. In caring, one must try to find what lies behind the complaint and help the student to understand better both his own attitude and that of the carer's. In another passage, Weil lays a heavy burden on carers who find themselves in this position:

> Every time that there arises from the depths of a human heart the childish cry . . . "why am I being hurt?", then there is certainly an injustice. For if, as often happens, it is only the result of a misunderstanding, then the injustice consists in the inadequacy of the explanation. (1977, p. 315)

I would not use the language of justice in most situations (for usually it is not a matter of justice, and surely some people, in some situations, are hurt justly), but her basic point underscores the responsibility of the carer. Even when we have to say no, we have the responsibility to convey our continued concern to the cared-for. Conscientious parents and teachers know that it often takes prolonged conversation to convey care convincingly when the proposed projects of young people must be reevaluated or rejected. When the cared-for recognizes our care, the caring relation is complete. The carer is characterized by receptive attention and motivational displacement; the cared-for contributes by acknowledging the care, sometimes directly, sometimes in seemingly spontaneous growth that can be easily traced (whether voiced or not) to the efforts of the carer.

Anyone who has taught feels the importance of this cycle: the receptivity and motivational displacement, the outflow of motive energy (sometimes repeated to the point of fatigue), the responsive grin, a spark in the student's eye, a spurt of growth, or a courteous gesture toward a fellow student—some sign that the caring has been completed. Without such signs, teachers become exhausted or, in today's language, "burned out."

This is a good point at which to pause in my analysis and consider the problems that emerge for some critics of caring as a moral orientation. One obvious point is that the maintenance of caring relations puts a tremendous burden on carers. Because caring has for so long been regarded as women's work, there is a danger that endorsing it will support the continued exploitation of women. (See Diller, 1996, for a substantial list of feminist philosophers who have voiced this objection.) The situation is further aggravated in occupations such as teaching and nursing whose members are mostly women. (For an account of the difficulties in nursing, see Reverby, 1987.) I think the critics are right to worry about caring as solely a women's ethic but wrong to deny its heritage in women's experience. Just as right-thinking men are now sharing opportunities long withheld from women, women should be generous in extending opportunities to men to care in the direct way long expected of women. The caring orientation (or ethic of care) cannot be responsibly confined to women (Held, 1993; Tronto, 1993), but neither can it be discarded.

A second concern raised occasionally by educational researchers is that to insist on the contribution from the cared-for to the caring relation makes research very difficult. Wouldn't it be easier just to decide what behaviors constitute caring and then go out and look for them? This concern for the smooth execution of research is reminiscent of an earlier move to separate teaching and learning (Komisar & Macmillan, 1967; Macmillan & Nelson, 1968). Of course, it would be far easier to decide exactly what behaviors constitute teaching and then observe people performing (or failing to perform) them than to study the highly complex interactions of teachers and students through which learning is accomplished. But we have learned that the connection cannot be dissolved so easily. Teaching is a relational concept. The label *caring* is, in this interactional view, also relational; it applies to the relation, not simply to the carer. If we accept a relational definition of caring, then we must consider the response of the cared-for.

The exigencies of research are not the only factors that drive some critics to separate carer and cared-for. A long tradition in philosophy called *virtue ethics* also plays a role. Dating at least to Aristotle, it is a form of ethics that puts great emphasis on the character of moral agents; the good and the right are displayed and achieved through the exemplary conduct of a society's most virtuous citizens. If the ethic of care were a form of virtue ethics, we would certainly want to discuss caring as a virtue, and this interpretation would facilitate the research program mentioned above. But, although we certainly use *caring* to reflect a sense of virtue—we say, for example, "He is a caring person"—the sense I find most useful is one applied to the relation, not just to the carer.

When we use *caring* to refer to a relation, our attention is drawn to both parties and also to the situation in which they find themselves. A failure of caring may, then, be traced to the carer, the cared-for, or the situation. The approach is thoroughly relational and encourages us to look beyond the virtue of the carer. The caring teacher alluded to in the chapter title is not best construed as one who possesses certain stable, desirable traits that might be identified before she steps into a classroom. Rather, a caring teacher is someone who has demonstrated that she can establish, more or less regularly, relations of care in a wide variety of situations. This approach reminds us, too, that a teacher who fails in one situation may succeed in another and vice versa.

I started this analysis by looking at caring encounters and seeking those features that all such encounters have in common. How much of myself is in the features that I see everywhere? It is interesting to me that Simone Weil used a story to introduce her claims about attention and receptivity. I, too, have used stories extensively, but it could well be that the stories I have examined and what I have extracted from them are products of my predispositions. I think it is fair to say, however, that stories of care appear again and again in accounts of women's lives (Addams, 1985; Auchincloss, 1985; Berson, 1994; Blount, 1996; Boucher, 1982; Day, 1952; Reverby, 1987), and one would be hard put to provide a comprehensive list of references documenting the centrality of care in women's lives. In addition to historical and biographical material, I have used the novels of Jane Austen, Pearl Buck, Mary Gordon, Doris Lessing, Anne Perry, and Virginia Woolf. Thus, although I cannot deny that my own predisposition set me on a search for stories of women's caring, those stories were not hard to find, and a mere list of them would fill volumes.

The present analysis started not only from my own experience (as all such analyses must) but also with a conceptual simplification. The encounter was used as the site of analysis. Clearly, a thorough analysis would have to include an examination of caring over time, caring for more than one person simultaneously, and caring that is in conflict with other legitimate demands and expectations. As educators, we have to be concerned with all three of these aspects of care. In particular, what enhances or impedes caring in teaching?

Before we tackle that important question, however, we should note what has been accomplished in this first section: We sought a definition or description of caring that would accommodate a wide range of manifestations, but we also wanted it to exclude some claims to care. Saying "because I care" has too often been used to justify cruelty and self-righteousness. Therefore, I have insisted that the reaction of the cared-for is essential in establishing a relation as one of caring. The cared-for's rejection of a claim does not by itself invalidate a claim to care; time may change rejection to acceptance. But rejection of a claim raises a question, and that is the important point here. Any relation in which one person claims to care and the recipient of that care denies the claim is one that demands close scrutiny. One does not care simply because one claims to do so. Now we can turn to questions about caring in professional life, especially in teaching.

Caring and Professional Life

A major impediment to caring in teaching is the confusion we have already discussed about the nature of caring. If one supposes that caring is merely a nice attitude, an attitude that ignores poor behavior and low achievement in favor of helping students to feel good, then, of course, caring will be seen as antithetical to professional conduct. But this is just wrong. A carer, faithfully receiving the cared-for over time, will necessarily want the best for that person; that is part of what it means to care. Assessment of wanting the best involves considering both the felt needs of the other and the values of the carer. We cannot in good conscience put our motive energy at the disposal of another's purposes if we evaluate those purposes as somehow bad. Neither can we entirely resist imposing some of our values on those for whom we bear some responsibility. However, it is clear that caring implies a continuous drive for competence. In the virtue sense, it refers to a person who continually strives for the competence required to respond adequately to the recipients of care; in the relational sense, it refers to situations regularly displaying the kinds of interaction in which both parties are growing. For teaching, both senses are captured by Milton Mayeroff when he writes, "To care for another person, in the most significant sense, is to help him grow and actualize himself" (1971, p.1).

Although the conceptual misunderstanding about caring as a soft, fuzzy notion is easily dispelled (at least theoretically), there are genuine conflicts between caring and professionalization, and they are not unique to teaching. These conflicts are also recognized in nursing (Reverby, 1987; Watson, 1985), medicine (Candib, 1995), and law (Lesnick, Dvorkin, & Himmelstein, 1981). Caring requires relations intimate enough for personal understanding; professionalization presses for distance and a certain aloofness. Caring invites communication in whatever language both parties can use effectively; professionalization encourages the growth of a jargon only insiders can use. Caring demands that competent carers remain close to the recipients of care; professionalization entices the professional to move beyond direct care into supervision of some form. (For a fuller discussion of the issues raised by professionalization, see Metzger, 1987; Noddings, 1992b.)

Conflicts between caring and professionalization have occurred at every level in education. In school administration, for example, the conflict dates to the early part of this century. Sometimes the conflict took the form of an attack on democratic procedures; arguments were launched against the participation of laypersons in school affairs, and it was suggested that all decisions be made at appropriate professional levels. The stories of Ella Flagg Young, Susan Dorsey, and Julia Richman (Blount, 1996) show graphically how several women in powerful positions (superintendents in Chicago, Los Angeles, and New York respectively) consistently used methods congruent with a caring orientation even though equally powerful men were speaking publicly against their mode of administration. The debate continues today (Beck, 1994).

For caring teachers today, the demand to teach everyone the same material may pose a great dilemma. Teachers agree that all children must acquire certain skills, but many fine teachers believe not only that children gain skills at very different rates, but also that children should be allowed to pursue different interests beyond these skills. Both Dewey and Rousseau support teachers in this belief. Dewey (1916) wrote:

> The general aim translates into the aim of regard for individual differences among children. Nobody can take the principle of consideration of native powers into account without being struck by the fact that these powers differ in different individuals. The difference applies not merely to their intensity, but even more to their quality

and arrangement. As Rousseau said: "Each individual is born with a *distinctive* temperament. . . . We indiscriminately employ children of different bents on the same exercises; their education destroys the special bent and leaves a dull uniformity. Therefore after we have wasted our efforts in stunting the true gifts of nature we see the short-lived and illusory brilliance we have substituted die away, while the natural abilities we have crushed do not revive." (p. 116)

Professionalism and caring are not inherently in conflict. Indeed, it is useful to make a distinction between professionalism and professionalization (or professionism) (Metzger, 1987). *Professionalism* refers to the internal workings of a profession and the concern of a profession's members to do the best possible job for their clients; *professionalization* refers to external criteria such as status, salary, specialization, and control. The latter criteria are not unimportant, but when they dominate the concerns of professionalism and produce a single vision—a single definition of what it means, for example, to be a good teacher—conflicts arise. In an edition of another *Handbook* on teaching, a group of elementary school teachers expressed their great disappointment in a system that disregarded their professional (and deeply caring) judgment and pressed them constantly to produce higher test scores (Boston Women's Teachers' Group, 1983). These teachers believed, with Dewey and Rousseau, that children should be treated as individuals. They valued caring relationships but found themselves unable to establish such relations—even criticized for spending time to do so. Today, a narrow definition of professional teaching as teaching that produces specific academic achievements still pervades the field and produces a conflict that could be avoided by more careful consideration of what it means to teach and what it means to be a caring teacher.

Although the conflict discussed above is avoidable, there are tensions between professionalism and caring that have to be faced regularly. As professionals, we all hold some vision of what it means to be educated. Further, as specialists, we often accord our own specialty an elevated place in the list of things students should learn. But as carers, many of us are reluctant to coerce our students into standard courses of study. For example, over many years of mathematics teaching, I came to believe that, although I loved math, it was neither right nor educationally necessary to force all students (or even the majority) into academic mathematics. However, although I still believe this, an uneasy tension attends this conclusion. I want to be sure that students make well-informed decisions, that they know what they are risking when they accept or reject a particular educational opportunity. To me, this is vitally important. Caring teachers not only listen to students and respect their legitimate interests, but they also share their wisdom with students. In Martin Buber's (1965) words, they present a "selection of the effective world" to their students. The tension cannot be resolved by either authoritarian coercion or permissiveness masquerading as respect. One always worries: Should we talk further? Are students excused from algebra by negligence rather than informed choice? Does the student really know what he's doing? Would it hurt if I pushed a bit harder?

The tension exists not only between professionalism and caring but within caring itself. Children have been known to accept dreadful forms of coercion as caring (Miller, 1983; Orwell,

1956). What are we to say of such relationships? The carer insists that he or she cares, listens, and acts in the best interests of the child. The child—although unhappy, sometimes desperately so—agrees. Literature is replete with examples. Samuel Butler's (1944) *The Way of All Flesh* describes caring gone awry over several generations. Cases range from the extremes described by Miller, Orwell, and Butler to everyday comments of students about their teachers: "Ms. A really cares—she makes us work hard and gives out a lot of bad grades and detentions. She's tough!"

Sometimes such relationships meet more than the technical phenomenological criteria of care; over time, some do produce both growth and the competence to care. These relationships make our task even more difficult. A person may claim to care and justify his or her acts on the grounds of caring, and we, as caring observers, may be appalled at the behaviors so justified. Yet, there are times when the claim is, in time, justified in the cared-for. The important thing to remember is that every claim to care must eventually be grounded in the response of the cared-for and that every instance in which the cared-for rejects the claim of caring must be examined in careful detail.

It is vitally important today to recognize that caring is manifested in different ways across cultures (Webb-Dempsey, Wilson, Corbett, & Mordecai-Phillips, 1996). Strictness and toughness do not in themselves signal either caring or not caring. Some modes of care are scorned because of misunderstanding, but surely others are genuinely pathological. As third-person carers, we are quite sure that healthy children would not assess the treatment they are undergoing as caring. Alice Miller (1983) has documented the cases of several members of the Nazi high command; all were rigidly raised in highly moralistic homes, and all were forbidden to express their unhappiness. They were also prepared to pass along to the next generation a mode of destructive child rearing. All of these parents told their children that the cruelty they endured was "for your own good." Similarly, George Orwell, in describing the cruelty he endured as a child at his elementary school, Crossgates, notes that children believe adults. Even when he was whipped for stumbling in his Latin translations, Orwell did not think to question the headmaster's tactics. After all, under these methods, small boys did in fact learn Latin, English grammar, and the dates of historical events. Probably Orwell (1956) would not have said that he was "cared for," but he writes: "I hated Bingo and Sim [wife and headmaster], with a sort of shamefaced, remorseful hatred, but it did not occur to me to doubt their judgment" (p. 431).

Thus the tension runs deep in caring. We can deny the status of caring to the cases described by Miller and Orwell on the grounds of the children's unhappiness, but there are many cases in which unhappiness and fear are so well buried that we cannot detect them easily. We learn to walk a fine line—we share and persuade but try to stop short of coercion, and sometimes we must allow ourselves to be persuaded.

The problem under discussion is particularly important in today's liberal societies. Traditional liberals have never quite known what to do with children. Valuing freedom and noninterference, we have still had to raise acceptable children. How long and to what degree should we tell our children what they must do? Do we best prepare them for life in a free society by forcing them to acquire the skills and information characteristic of people who succeed in such societies? Or must they be given opportunities to practice freedom, as Dewey (1916) suggested? It would be foolish and dishonest to say that we have no vision at all of what it means to be educated, but if that vision begins to define liberty itself—one is only free if one becomes what he or she should be—then, as Isaiah Berlin (1984) warned, it "renders it easy for me to conceive of myself as coercing others for their own sake, in their, not my, interest" (p. 24).

It is clear from the discussion so far that I do not think the tension between shaping students toward some preestablished ideal and encouraging them to grow in directions they themselves choose can be resolved. It is a tension that has to be lived. The question now arises how best to establish a climate in which caring and professionalism are compatible. Under what conditions do caring and caring professionals flourish?

Encouraging Care in Teaching

The relational nature of caring as I have been describing it requires attention not only to the responses and reactions of students to their teachers' attempts to care but also to the settings in which teachers work. Relations between administrators and teachers can help to provide a setting in which caring can flourish. Recall that we defined a caring teacher as one who regularly establishes caring relations—not merely as one who possesses certain virtues. The setting in which teachers work can make it more or less likely that they will succeed in establishing such relations or even that they will try to do so.

As empirical studies accumulate (Beck, 1994; Deiro, 1996; Eaker-Rich & Van Galen, 1996; Rose, 1995), we see again and again that administrators can encourage caring both by respecting their teachers' efforts to care and by modeling care. (See also an extensive bibliography available through the Lilly Endowment.) Taking time to talk openly and in nonspecialized language with parents can help to forge relations of care (Beck & Newman, 1996; Mercado et al., 1996). Current studies underscore the wisdom of earlier administrators such as Young, Dorsey, and Richman. The case of Ella Flagg Young (Blount, 1996) is especially instructive on the power of conversation. She spent much time talking and listening to her teachers and even held regular conversation sessions in her own home.

The conversations between Young and her teachers and between principal Mary Story and students, teachers, and parents (Beck & Newman, 1996) seem to have been genuine dialogues. They were characterized by open-ended exploration, mutual listening, and a commitment to respond helpfully if a need arose. A student at Story's school remarked that he liked the school because "they paid attention and were organized" (Beck & Newman, 1996, p. 195). Attention, of course, is a basic criterion of care, and being organized is reasonable preparation for the competent response that should follow motivational displacement. One wants to help and so organizes her resources so that appropriate responses can be made expeditiously.

Administrators can help also by recognizing the wide variety of ways in which teachers show their care. Studies that reveal these different ways (Deiro, 1996; Dempsey & Noblit, 1996; Rose, 1995) should help administrators to appreciate and encourage the healthy ways in which caring and professional judgment are combined by good teachers. To use one's authority

and mandate as a change agent to press the entire faculty into one mold is counterproductive. Of course, to work with very different ways of caring is more complicated, and sometimes teachers need to be protected from their own fine impulses—for example, when a teacher spends a great deal of time outside school hours with a student (Deiro, 1996) and risks accusations of sexual involvement.

Teachers may need protection for other reasons as well. Gay men and lesbians may need support and encouragement to use appropriate touch in the their classrooms; they should not be forbidden to care (King, 1996; Kissen, 1996). Teachers with AIDS need to feel both cared for and that their own efforts to care are still appreciated (Zappulla, 1997). Teachers of color need to be heard when they describe modes of caring that seem right for their own people (Walker, 1993; Webb-Dempsey, Wilson, Corbett, and Mordecai-Phillips, 1996). Indeed, conversations across cultural lines can contribute to growth on all sides. Such conversation may also reveal irreconcilable differences and teach us all to define successful conversation less in terms of consensus and more in terms of being together and living sensitively with difference.

At the policy level, attention to care can raise cautions in campaigns for both justice and increased academic achievement. For example, educators are beginning to realize that the well-intentioned drive for desegregation in schools concealed an unintended arrogance. Are all-Black schools inherently unequal? Do Black children need the presence of white children to learn well? Or is the inequality contingent and remediable? Strong political or national arguments for eliminating single-race (and single-gender) schools may be offered, of course, but the educational arguments are less persuasive. Several writers have documented the caring that characterizes single-race schools and what is lost when these schools are closed in the name of a great social good, desegregation (Dempsey & Noblit, 1996; Walker, 1993). When caring is a major concern, policymakers might move more cautiously in trying to accomplish single, great goals.

Similarly, educators have learned the hard way that considerations of curriculum should not dominate policy decisions. In the 1960s, guided by James Conant (1959, 1967) and others, American policymakers opted for larger schools and more highly specialized curricula. The idea was to compete more successfully with Russian technology. With hindsight, educators now realize that we should have asked what would happen to the sense of community as school populations were moved into larger and more impersonal situations. What happens to the spirit of care and community when people become strangers to one another? Today, there are many cries for smaller schools and for building community.

If we are to establish relations of care and trust, certain continuities are required (Noddings, 1992a). Teachers and students need to stay together long enough to know one another. Students learn over time what to expect of a teacher; the teacher learns to know students as individuals and to respond to their legitimate differences. There is no good reason why students and teachers who want to do so should not be encouraged to stay together for several years. The clause *who want to do so* is important because care cannot be coerced. Care must be modeled, invited, encouraged, and nurtured; it cannot be mandated.

Continuity of place also matters. Students—perhaps all people—take better care of a facility if they feel a personal attachment to it. We give far too little attention today to encouraging (or even recognizing) a sense of place and the role it plays in learning and awareness. Often the sense of place is deliberately wiped out in well-intentioned efforts to present a uniform curriculum good for all contemporary places. Some schools have even been built without windows so that students will not be distracted from their place-free studies. But place is regarded by many aestheticians and philosophers as an extension of self (Casey, 1993). Literature, too, attests to the centrality of place (Proust, 1981). Further, educators outside the system of formal education have shown us vividly how the evocation of place can restore communication, induce awareness, and prepare the way for learning (Reynolds, 1995).

The school is, for both teachers and students, a dwelling place (Martin, 1992). It is not just a place to conduct the business of learning. As a dwelling place, it needs to be so constructed that it encourages two major ways to dwell: dwelling-as-residing and dwelling-as-wandering (Casey, 1993). To feel safe, secure, and cared for—characteristic of dwelling-as-residing—gives children the courage to wander forth both physically and intellectually into new territory. As care guides policymaking, we are led to think less about efficiency and even justice writ large and more about the immediate and long-term effects of our policies on individual children and the communities that support each child's growing individuality.

Thus, in establishing and maintaining climates of care, we should return to the emphasis on conversation with which we started this section. Educators need to talk about care and its connection to rules, pedagogy, and purposes. Many rules that are instituted to keep things running smoothly may be antithetical to caring. In my own high school teaching, for example, I regularly disregarded a rule to report tardies. First, I did not want to waste time on this clerical duty, but more importantly, I wanted to treat students with respect and to encourage them to take responsibility for their own behavior. Therefore, we arranged the room so that latecomers could take seats near the door, and it was agreed that they would wait quietly to consult their peers about whatever they missed. Of course, if chronic tardiness occurred, I talked with the offenders. The point is that, if we approach teaching from the moral orientation of caring, everything we do is examined in its light. Such conversations among teachers are good in themselves, but they should also help to support teachers in their commitment to care.

Summary

I have tried to show how philosophical research lays a foundation for both empirical research and reflection on practice. A relational definition of caring encourages exploration of the contributions made by both carer and cared-for. It also prompts us to examine the situations in which caring is supposed to take place.

In some professional settings, conflicts arise between caring and professionalization. These conflicts are particularly keen when an occupation (such as nursing or teaching) is striving for professional recognition. Then the temptation is to copy recognized professions and forget the central mission, which is to do what is in the best interests of the recipients of care. At its worst, professionalization may oppress educators with a single view of what it means to be a good teacher, and the rich variety of ways to care may be lost.

Finally, a relational definition led us to consider ways in which educators might establish climates of care. Administrators can contribute by caring directly for the teachers under their supervision and also by modeling care in all their interactions. Policymakers can use care as a basic moral orientation and examine propositions for reform reflectively. What will be the effects on care if we adopt a particular reform? Are there ways to address issues of justice without abandoning care? The conversation induced and maintained by care should enhance caring throughout the system.

REFERENCES

Addams, J. (1985). *Jane Addams on education* (E. C. Lagemann, Ed.). New York: Teachers College Press.

Auchincloss, L. (1985). *Pioneers and caretakers.* Boston: G. K. Hall.

Beck, L. (1994). *Reclaiming educational administration as a caring profession.* New York: Teachers College Press.

Beck, L., & Newman, R. L. (1996). Caring in one urban high school. In D. Eaker-Rich & J. A. Van Galen (Eds.), *Caring in an unjust world* (pp. 171–198). Albany: State University of New York Press.

Berlin, I. (1984). Two concepts of liberty. In M. Sandel (Ed.), *Liberalism and its critics* (pp. 15–36). New York: New York University Press.

Berson, R. (1994). *Marching to a different drummer: Unrecognized heroes of American history.* Westport, CT: Greenwood Press.

Blount, J. M. (1996). Caring and the open moment in educational leadership. In D. Eaker-Rich & J. A. Van Galen (Eds.), *Caring in an unjust world* (pp. 13–30). Albany: State University of New York Press.

Boston Women's Teachers' Group (1983). Teaching: An imperilled "profession." In L. S. Shulman & G. Sykes (Eds.), *Handbook of teaching and policy* (pp. 261–299). New York: Longman.

Boucher, S. (1982). *Heartwomen.* San Francisco: Harper & Row.

Buber, M. (1965). *Between man and man.* New York: Macmillan.

Butler, S. (1944). *The way of all flesh.* Garden City, NY: Doubleday.

Candib, L. (1995). *Medicine and the family: A feminist perspective.* New York: Basic Books.

Casey, E. S. (1993). *Getting back into place.* Bloomington: Indiana University Press.

Conant, J. B. (1959). *The American high school today: A first report to interested citizens.* New York: McGraw-Hill.

Conant, J. B. (1967). *The comprehensive high school: A second report to interested citizens.* New York: McGraw-Hill.

Day, D. (1952). *The long loneliness.* San Francisco: Harper & Row.

Deiro, J. A. (1996). *Teaching with heart.* Thousand Oaks, CA: Corwin Press.

Dempsey, V., & Noblit, G. (1996). Caring and continuity. In D. Eaker-Rich & J. A. Van Galen (Eds.), *Caring in an unjust world* (pp. 113–128). Albany: State University of New York Press.

Dewey, J. (1916). *Democracy and education.* New York: Macmillan.

Diller, A. (1996). The ethics of care and education: A new paradigm, its critics, and its educational significance. In A. Diller, B. Houston, D. P. Morgan, & M. Ayim (Eds.), *The gender question in education* (pp. 89–104). Boulder, CO: Westview Press.

Diller, A., Houston, B., Morgan, K. P., & Ayim, M. (1996). *The gender question in education.* Boulder, CO: Westview Press.

Eaker-Rich, D., & Van Galen, J. A. (Eds.). (1996). *Caring in an unjust world.* Albany: State University of New York Press.

Held, V. (1993). *Feminist morality.* Chicago: University of Chicago Press.

King, J. R. (1996). Uncommon caring. In D. Eaker-Rich & J. A. Van Galen (Eds.), *Caring in an unjust world* (pp. 47–60). Albany: State University of New York Press.

Kissen, R. M. (1996). Forbidden to care. In D. Eaker-Rich & J. A. Van

Galen (Eds.), *Caring in an unjust world* (pp. 61–84). Albany: State University of New York Press.

Komisar, B. P. & Macmillan, C. J. B. (Eds.). (1967). *Analytical concepts in education.* Chicago: Rand McNally.

Lesnick, H., Dvorkin, E. & Himmelstein, J. (Eds.). (1981). *Becoming a lawyer: A humanistic perspective on legal education and professionalism.* St. Paul, MN: West.

Macmillan, C. J. B. & Nelson, T. (Eds.). (1968). *Concepts of teaching.* Chicago: Rand McNally.

Martin, J. R. (1992). *The school home: Rethinking schools for changing families.* Cambridge, MA: Harvard University Press.

Mayeroff, M. (1971). *On caring.* New York: Harper & Row.

Mercado, C. I., and Members of the Bronx Middle School Collaborative. (1996). Caring as empowerment. In D. Eaker-Rich & J. A. Van Galen (Eds.), *Caring in an unjust world* (pp. 171–198). Albany: State University of New York Press.

Metzger, W. P. (1987). A spectre is haunting American scholars: The spectre of "professionism." *Educational Researcher, 16*(6), 10–21.

Miller, A. (1983). *For your own good* (H. Hannun & H. Hannun, Trans.). New York: Farrar, Strauss, Giroux.

Noddings, N. (1984). *Caring: A feminine approach to ethics and moral education.* Berkeley: University of California Press.

Noddings, N. (1992a). *The challenge to care in schools.* New York: Teachers College Press.

Noddings, N. (1992b). The professional life of mathematics teachers. In D. A. Grouws (Ed.), *Handbook of research on mathematics teaching and learning* (pp. 197–208). New York: Macmillan.

Orwell, G. (1956). *The Orwell reader.* New York: Harcourt, Brace.

Proust, M. (1981). *Remembrance of things past.* Vol. 1, *Swann's way.* (C. K. S. Moncrieff & T. Kilmartin, Trans.). New York: Random House.

Reverby, S. (1987). *Ordered to care.* Cambridge: Cambridge University Press.

Reynolds, R. A. (1995). *Bring me the ocean.* Acton, MN: Vander-Wyk & Burnham.

Rorty, R. (1989). *Contingency, irony, and solidarity.* Cambridge: Cambridge University Press.

Rose, M. (1995*). Possible lives: The promise of public education in America.* New York: Houghton Mifflin.

Tronto, J. (1993). *Moral boundaries: A political argument for an ethic of care.* New York: Routledge.

Walker, E. V. S. (1993). Caswell County Training School, 1933–1969: Relationships between community and school. *Harvard Educational Review, 63*(2), 161–182.

Watson, J. (1985). *Nursing: Human science and human care.* Norwalk: CT: Appleton-Century-Crofts.

Webb-Dempsey, J., Wilson, B., Corbett, D., & Mordecai-Phillips, R. (1996). Understanding caring in context. In D. Eaker-Rich & J. A. Van Galen (Eds.), *Caring in an unjust world* (pp. 85–109). Albany: State University of New York Press.

Weil, S. (1977). *Simone Weil reader* (G. A. Panichas, Ed.). Mt. Kisco, NY: Moyer Bell Ltd.

Zappulla, C. (1997). *Suffering in silence.* New York: Peter Lang.

8.
(Mis)Understanding Paulo Freire

Donaldo Macedo
University of Massachusetts, Boston

Ana Maria Araújo Freire
Pontifícia Universidade Católica, São Paulo, Brazil

According to Herbert Kohl, the renowned educator and social critic Paulo Freire is perhaps "the most significant educator in the world in this last half of the century" (Kohl, 1997). His insightful theories represent an important answer to the capitalist "banking model" of education that has generated and continues to generate greater and greater failure. As a result, many North American liberal and neoliberal educators are looking to Paulo Freire's pedagogy as an alternative. No longer can it be argued that Freire's pedagogy is appropriate only in Third World contexts. For one thing, we are experiencing a rapid "Third Worldization" of North America, where inner cities come to resemble, more and more, the shantytowns of the Third World, with high levels of poverty, violence, illiteracy, human exploitation, homelessness, and human misery. The abandonment of our inner cities and the insidious decay of their infrastructures, including their schools, makes it very difficult to maintain the artificial division between the First World and the Third World. One can just as easily find Third World misery in the First World inner cities as one can discover First World opulence in the oligarchies in El Salvador, Guatemala, and many other Third World nations. The Third-Worldization of North American inner cities has also produced large-scale educational failures that have created minority student dropout rates that range from 50% in the Boston public school system to more than 70% in the school systems of larger metropolitan areas like New York City.

Conservative educators have recoiled, by and large, from this landscape of educational failure in an attempt to salvage the status quo and to contain the "browning," or changing skin pigmentation, of the United States. These conservative educators have attempted to reappropriate the educational debate and to structure the educational discourse in terms of competition and the privatization of schools. The hidden curriculum of the proposed school privatization movement consists of taking resources from poor schools that are on the verge of bankruptcy to support private or well-to-do schools. "Private school choice" is only private to the degree that it generates private profit while being supported by public funds. What is rarely discussed in the North American school debate is the fact that public schools are part and parcel of the fabric of any democratic society. In fact, conservative educators fail to recognize that a democratic society that shirks its public responsibility is a democracy in crisis. A society that equates for-profit privatization with democracy is a society with confused priorities. A democratic society that believes (falsely—one need only consider the savings and loan debacle and the Wall Street scandals, for example) that quality, productivity, honesty, and efficiency can be achieved only through for-profit privatization is a society that displays both an intellectual and ethical bankruptcy of ideas. If we accept the argument that private is best, we should once again consider Jack Beaty's question: "Would we set up a private Pentagon to improve our public defense establishment?" (Beaty, 1992). Would the private-is-best logic eradicate the ongoing problems in the military that range from rampant sexual harassment to expenditures that are both outrageous (more than $600 for a toilet seat) and wasteful (billions of dollars for airplanes that don't fly)? Most Americans would find the privatization of the Pentagon utterly absurd, claiming that a strong defense is a national priority. Similarly, we contend that instead of dismantling public education further, we should make it a national public priority. We also contend that U.S. public education should be a top priority; the safeguarding of U.S. democracy rests much more on the creation of an educated, smart citizenry than on the creation of smart bombs.

In the face of the market notion of school reform in the United States, many liberal and neoliberal educators have rediscovered Freire's ideas as an alternative to the conservative domestication of education that equates free-market ideology with democracy. However, part of the problem with some of these pseudocritical educators is that, in the name of liberation pedagogy, they reduce Freire's leading ideas to a method. According to Stanley Aronowitz, the North American fetish for method has allowed Freire's philosophical ideas to be "assimilated to the prevailing obsession of North American education, following a tendency in all human and social sciences, with methods of verifying knowledge and, in schools, of teaching that is, transmitting knowledge to otherwise unprepared students" (Aronowitz, 1993, p. 8).

This fetish for method works insidiously against the ability to adhere to Freire's own pronouncement against importing and exporting methodology. In a long conversation Paulo had with Donaldo Macedo about this issue, Freire said: "Donaldo, I don't want to be imported or exported. It is impossible to export pedagogical practices without reinventing them. Please tell your fellow American educators not to import me. Ask them to recreate and rewrite my ideas."

Before problematizing the reduction of Freire's leading philosophical ideas to a mechanistic method, first we must comment on the "Paulo Freire Method," because it is still widely used today, with some adaptations, all over the world. Second, when one speaks of Freire and literacy, one often reduces Freire's thoughts on literacy to a mere set of techniques associated with the learning of reading and writing. We must clarify, especially for the sake of those who are new to Freire's thinking.

Freire's "invitation" to adult literacy learners is, initially, that they look at themselves as persons living and producing in a given society. He invites learners to come out of the apathy and the conformism—akin to being "dismissed from life"—in which they often find themselves. Freire challenges them to understand that they are themselves the makers of culture and guides them to learn the anthropological meaning of culture. They are shown that the popular classes' lower status is the result, not of divine determination or fate but, rather, of the economic, political, and ideological contexts of the society in which they live.

When men and women realize that they themselves are the makers of culture, they have accomplished, or nearly accomplished, the first step toward feeling the importance, the necessity, and the possibility of owning reading and writing. They become literate, politically speaking. Then, as they discuss the object to be known and the representation of reality to be decoded, the members of a "culture circle" respond to questions generated by the group coordinator, thereby gradually deepening their readings of the world. The ensuing debate makes possible a rereading of reality from which may well result the literacy learner's engaging in political practices aimed at social transformation.

What? Why? How? To what end? For whom? Against whom? By whom? In favor of whom? In favor of what? These are questions that provoke literacy learners to focus on the substantiveness of things, that is, their reasons for being, their purposes, the ways they do things, and so on.

Literacy activities require research into what Freire calls the "minimum vocabulary universe" among literacy learners. Through work on this universe, words that are used to integrate the literacy program become chosen. These words, about seventeen of them, called "generative words," should be phonemically rich words and necessarily ordered in increasing phonetic difficulty. They should be read within the widest possible context of the literacy learners' life and of the local language, thus, also becoming national. Decoding the written word, which follows the decoding of a coded existential situation, implies certain steps that must be strictly followed.

Let us examine the word *tijolo* (brick), which Freire used as the first generative word in his work in Brasilia in the 1960s. This word was chosen to facilitate the reader's understanding because Brasilia was a city under construction at the time.

1. The generative word tijolo is presented, inserted in the representation of a concrete situation: men at work at a construction site.
2. The word is simply written: tijolo.
3. The same word is written with its syllables separated: ti-jo-lo.
4. The "phonemic family" of the first syllable is presented: ta-te-ti-to-tu.
5. The phonemic family of the second syllable is presented: ja-je-ji-jo-ju.
6. The phonemic family of the third syllable is presented: la-le-li-lo-lu.
7. The phonemic families of the word being decoded are presented: ta-te-ti-to-tu ja-je-ji-jo-ju la-le-li-lo-lu.

    This set of "phonemic families" of the generative word has been termed the "discovery form," for it allows the literacy learner to put together "pieces," that is, to come up with new phonemic combinations that will necessarily result in words of the Portuguese language.
8. Vowels are presented: *a-e-i-o-u.*

In sum, the moment the literacy learner is able to articulate syllables to form words, he or she is literate. The process, obviously, requires deepening, that is, a postliteracy component. The effectiveness and validity of Freire's method lie in using the learners' reality as the starting point, in beginning with what they already know, ranging from the pragmatic value of the things and the facts of their daily lives to their existential situations. By respecting and starting from common sense, Freire proposes overcoming it.

Freire's method follows methodological and linguistic rules but also goes beyond them, for it challenges men and women who are becoming literate to take ownership of the written code and to politicize themselves, to acquire a view of language and the world as a totality. Freire's method also rejects mere narrow-minded and mind narrowing repetition of phrases, words, and syllables as it proposes that the learners "read the world" and "read the word," which, as Paulo Freire emphasizes, are inseparable actions. Thus, he is against *"cartilhas,"* or literacy workbooks. In short, Paulo Freire's work is more than a method for literacy education; it is a broad and deep understanding of education that has its political nature at the core of its concerns.

We would conclude these comments on the "Paulo Freire Method" by saying that the literacy education of the Brazilian people (for when Freire created the Method he never expected it to spread around the world) was, in the good sense of the phrase, an educational tactic designed to achieve a necessary result: the politicizing of the Brazilian people. In this sense, the Method is revolutionary, for it can lift those who do not yet know the written word out of their conditions of submission, immersion, and passivity. The revolution as Freire envisioned it does not presuppose an inversion of the oppressed-oppressor poles; rather, it intends to reinvent, in communion, a society where exploitation and the verticalization of power do not exist, where the disenfranchised segments of society are not excluded or interdicted from reading the world.

Paulo Freire was in exile for almost 16 years precisely because he understood education this way and because he fought to give a large number of Brazilians access to an asset traditionally denied them: the act of reading the world by reading the word.

As becomes abundantly clear, Freire's method of teaching peasants how to read was designed to be a method, not as an end in itself, but as part of a larger goal of politicizing the Brazilian peasants so they could also read the world and connect the world with the word. For this reason, Freire's main ideas about the act of knowing transcend the methods for which he is known. In fact, according to Linda Bimbi, "The originality of Freire's work does not reside in the efficacy of his literacy methods, but, above all, in the originality of its content designed to develop our consciousness" as part of a humanizing pedagogy (Bimbi as cited in Gadotti, 1989, p. 32). According to Freire, "A humanizing education is the path through which men and women can become conscious about their presence in the world. The way they act and think when they develop all of their capacities, taking into consideration their needs, but also the needs and aspirations of others" (Freire & Betto, 1985, p. 15).

Freire developed students' abilities to be aware of their presence in the world through the dialogic model for which he is also known. Unfortunately, many educators who embrace his notion of dialogue mechanistically reduce the epistemological relationship of dialogue to a vacuous, comfortable, feel-good zone. Reduced in this way, the dialogic model loses its clear view of the object of knowledge under study and reduces dialogue to a mere conversation about individuals' lived experiences.

With that said, we can begin to understand why some educators, in their attempt to cut the chains of oppressive educational practices, blindly advocate the dialogic model. In turn, they create a new form of methodological rigidity that is laced with benevolent oppression, done under the guise of democracy, and justified by saying that it is for the students' own good. Many of us have witnessed pedagogical contexts in which we have been implicitly or explicitly required to speak, to talk about our experience as an act of liberation. We all have been at conferences where the speaker was chastised because he or she failed to locate himself or herself in history; in other words, he or she failed to give primacy to his or her experiences while addressing issues of critical democracy, regardless of whether or not the speaker had important and insightful things to say. This approach to an overstretched identity politics is tantamount to dismissing Marx because he did not entrance us with his personal life experiences.

The dialogic method as a process of sharing experiences is often reduced to a form of group therapy that focuses on the psychology of the individual. Although some educators may claim that this process creates a pedagogical comfort zone, in my view, it does little beyond making the oppressed feel good about his or her own sense of victimization. In other words, the sharing of experiences should not be understood in psychological terms only. It invariably requires a political and ideological analysis as well. That is, the sharing of experiences must always be understood within a social praxis that entails both reflection and political action. In short, it must always involve a political project with the objective of dismantling oppressive structures and mechanisms.

The overdose of experiential celebration that characterizes some strands of critical pedagogy offers a reductionist view of identity and experience within rather than outside the problematics of power, agency, and history. Educators who overindulge in the legacy and importance of their respective voices and experiences often fail to move beyond a notion of difference structured in polarizing binarisms and uncritical appeal to the discourse of experience (Giroux, in press). They thus invoke a romantic pedagogical model that isolates lived experiences as a process of coming to voice. By refusing to link experiences to the politics of culture and critical democracy, these educators reduce their pedagogy to a form of middle-class narcissism. On the one hand, the dialogic method provides the participants with a group therapy space for stating their grievances, and on the other hand, it offers the educator or facilitator a safe pedagogical zone to deal with his or her class guilt.

By refusing to deal with the issue of class privilege, the pseudocritical educator dogmatically pronounces the need to empower students, to give them voices. These educators are even betrayed by their own language. Instead of creating pedagogical structures that would enable oppressed students to empower themselves, they paternalistically proclaim: "We need to empower students." This position often leads to the creation of what we could call literacy and poverty pimps: While they are proclaiming the need to empower students, they are, in fact, strengthening their own privileged position.

The following example involving a progressive teacher who had been working within a community-based literacy project and who betrayed her liberal discourse—her claim to want to empower the community—will clarify my point. One of the agencies we work with solicited a colleague's help in writing a math literacy proposal for them. The colleague welcomed the opportunity and agreed. One of her ongoing goals is to develop structures that will enable community members and agencies to take the initiative and chart their own course, thus, eliminating the need for our continued presence and expertise. In other words, our success in creating structures that enable community members to empower themselves rests on the degree to which our presence and expertise in the community are no longer necessary because community members have acquired their own expertise, thus, preventing a type of neocolonialism.

When the progressive teacher heard about the math literacy proposal, she was reticent but did not show any outward opposition. However, weeks later, when she learned that the community-based math literacy proposal, written by community members, competed with her own university-based proposal, which was also designed to provide math literacy training to community members, she reacted almost irrationally. She argued that the community agency that had written the math literacy proposal did not follow a democratic process because it had not involved her in the development of the proposal. A democratic and participatory process, in her view, was one that necessarily included her, despite the fact that she is not a member of the particular community that the math literacy grant was designed to serve. Apparently, in her mind, one can be empowered so long as the empowerment does not encroach on the "expert," privileged, powerful position. This position of power is designed to empower others paternalistically.

When the obvious ideological contradictions in her behavior were pointed out, her response was quick, aggressive, and almost automatic: "I'll be very mad if they get their grant and we don't get ours." It became very clear to me that the progressive teacher's real political commitment to the community hinged on the extent to which her "expert" position remained unthreatened. That is, the literacy "expert," do-gooder, antiestablishment persona makes sure that his or her privileged position within the establishment as an antiestablishment "expert" is never replaced by empowered community members.

This colonizing, paternalistic attitude led this same progressive teacher to pronounce publicly, at a major conference, that community people don't need to go to college; because they know so much more than do members of the university community, there is little that the university can teach them. While making such public statements, she was busily moving from the inner city to an affluent suburb, making sure that her children attend better schools.

A similar attitude emerged in a recent meeting to develop a community-university relationship grant proposal. During the meeting, a liberal white professor correctly protested the absence of community members from the committee. However, in attempting to valorize the community knowledge base, she rapidly fell into a romantic paternalism by stating that the community people knew much more than the university professors and should be invited to come to teach the professors rather than having the professors teach the community members. This position not only discourages community members from taking advantage of the cultural capital from which these professors have benefited greatly, but it also disfigures the reality context that makes the university's cultural capital indispensable for any type of real empowerment. It also smacks of a false generosity of paternalism that Freire aggressively opposes:

> The pedagogy of the oppressed animated by authentic humanism (and not humanitarianism) generously presents itself as a pedagogy of man. Pedagogy that begins with the egoistic interests of the oppressors (an egoism cloaked in the false generosity of paternalism) and makes of the oppressed the objects of its humanitarianism, itself maintains and embodies oppression. It is an instrument of dehumanization. (Freire, 1990, p. 39)

The paternalistic pedagogical attitude represents a middle-class narcissism that gives rise to pseudocritical educators who are part of the same instrumentalist approach to literacy that they apply to readers who meet the basic requirements of our contemporary society as proposed by conservative educators. Instrumentalist literacy also includes the highest level of literacy through disciplinary hyperspecialization. Pseudocritical educa-

tors are part of this latter instantiation of instrumentalist literacy to the extent that they reduce Freire's dialogic method to a form of specialization. In other words, the instrumentalist literacy for the poor (in the form of a competency-based, skill-banking approach) and the instrumentalist literacy for the rich (the highest form, which is acquired through the university in the form of professional specialization) share one common feature: They both prevent the development of critical thinking that enables one to read the world critically and to understand the reasons and linkages behind the facts.

The instrumentalist approach to literacy, even at the highest level of specialization (including method as a form of specialization), functions to domesticate the consciousness through a constant disarticulation between the reductionistic and narrow reading of one's field of specialization and the reading of the universe within which one's specialization is situated. If not combated, this inability to link the reading of the word with the world will further debilitate the already feeble democratic institutions and the unjust, asymmetrical power relations that characterize the hypocritical nature of contemporary democracies. At the lowest level of instrumentalist hierarchy, a semiliterate person reads the word but is unable to read the world. At the highest level of instrumental literacy achieved via specialization, the semiliterate person is able to read the text of his or her specialty but is ignorant of all other bodies of knowledge that constitute the world of knowledge. This semiliterate specialist was characterized by José Ortega y Gasset as a "learned ignoramus." That is to say, "he is not learned, for he is formally ignorant of all that does not enter into his specialty; but neither is he ignorant, because he is a 'scientist' and 'knows' very well his own tiny portion of the universe" (Ortega y Gasset, 1932, p. 112).

Because the "learned ignoramus" is mainly concerned with his or her own tiny portion of the world, disconnected from other bodies of knowledge, he or she is never able to relate the flux of information to gain a critical reading of the world. A critical reading of the world implies, according to Freire, "a dynamic comprehension between the least coherent sensibility of the world and a more coherent understanding of the world" (Freire & Macedo, 1987, p. 131). This statement explains, for example, how medical specialists in the United States, who have contributed to a great technological advancement in medicine, cannot understand and appreciate why more than 30 million Americans do not have access to this medical technology and why we still have the highest infant mortality rate among the developed nations.

Finally, we would propose an antimethod pedagogy that refuses the rigidity of models and methodological paradigms. The antimethod pedagogy forces us to view dialogue as a form of social praxis, so that the sharing of experiences is informed by reflection and political action. Dialogue as social praxis "entails that recovering the voice of the oppressed is the fundamental condition for human emancipation" (Aronowitz, 1993, p. 10). The antimethod pedagogy also frees us from the beaten path of certainties and specialties. It rejects the mechanization of intellectualism. In short, it calls for the illumination of Freire's leading ideas, ideas that will guide us toward the critical road of truth, toward the reappropriation of our endangered dignity, and toward the reclaiming of our humanity. No one could argue more pointedly against reducing dialogue and problem posing to a mere method than Freire himself:

Problem posing education is revolutionary futurity. Hence, it is prophetic. Hence it corresponds to the historical nature of man. Hence it affirms men as beings who transcend themselves. Hence it identifies with the movement that engages men as being aware of their incompletion—an historical movement that has its point of departure, its subjects and its objective. (Freire, 1990, p. 30)

Not only does the antimethod pedagogy adhere to Freire's view of education as revolutionary futurity, but also it celebrates the eloquence of António Machado's poem: "Caminante no hay camino, se hace el camino al andar" (Machado, 1962, p. 826). [Traveler, there is no road. The road is made as one walks. (My translation)] However, Freire's view of education as revolutionary futurity also requires other fundamental skills, skills that he discussed eloquently in his last books, *Pedagogy of Freedom* (1999) and *Teachers as Cultural Workers* (1997), but that are seldom taught to us in our preparation as teachers:

We must dare, in the full sense of the word, to speak of love without the fear of being called ridiculous, mawkish, or unscientific, if not antiscientific. We must dare in order to say scientifically, and not as mere blah-blah-blah, that we study, we learn, we teach, we know with our entire body. We do all of these things with feeling, with emotion, with wishes, with fear, with doubts, with passion, and also with critical reasoning. However, we never study, learn, teach, or know with the last only. We must dare so as never to dichotomize cognition and emotion. We must dare so that we can continue to teach for a long time under conditions that we know well: low salaries, lack of respect, and the ever-present risk of becoming prey to cynicism. We must dare to learn how to dare in order to say no to the bureaucratization of the mind to which we are exposed every day. We must dare so that we can continue to do so even when it is so much more materially advantageous to stop daring. (Freire, 1997, p. 3)

REFERENCES

Aronowitz, S. (1993). Paulo Freire's radical democratic humanism. In P. McLaren & P. Leonard (Eds.), *Paulo Freire: A critical encounter.* London: Routledge.

Beaty, J. (1992, August). *The Boston Globe.*

Freire, P. (1990). *Pedagogy of the oppressed.* New York: Continuum Publication.

Freire, P. (1997). *Teachers as cultural workers: Letters to those who dare teach.* Boulder, CO: Westview Press.

Freire, P. (1999). *Pedagogy of freedom: Ethics, democracy, and civic courage.* Boulder, CO: Rowman & Littlefield Publishers.

Freire, P., & Betto, F. (1985). *Essa escola chamada vida.* São Paulo: Atica.

Freire, P., & Macedo, D. (1987). *Literacy: Reading the word and the world.* South Hadley, MA: Bergin and Garvey.

Gadotti, M. (1989). *Convite a leitura de Paulo Freire.* São Paulo: Editora Scipione.

Giroux, H. (in press). The politics of difference and multiculturalism in the era of the Los Angeles uprising. *Journal of the Midwest Modern Language Association.*

Kohl, H. (1997, May 26). Paulo Freire: Liberation pedagogy. *The Nation,* p. 7.

Machado, A. (1962). *Manuel y António Machado: Obras completas.* Madrid: Editorial Plenitud.

Ortega y Gasset, J. (1932). *The revolt of the masses.* New York: Norton.

9.

Through the Mediation of Others:
Vygotskian Research on Teaching

Luis C. Moll
University of Arizona

> *Theories, including sociohistorical and activity theory which seek to understand social practice, do not contain within themselves "prescriptions" for changing these practices. What a theory "means" for practice cannot be read off from texts of the theory. Notions such as "translating theory into practice" or "applying theory to practice" are based on the contrary assumption. They imply, erroneously in my opinion, that grand theoretical propositions can be directly converted into methods for transforming established practices in the contingent here-and-now.*
>
> (Sylvia Scribner, 1990b)

This chapter serves two purposes. It summarizes the basic tenets of a Vygotskian cultural–historical psychology, highlighting the essential role of cultural mediation in Vygotsky's formulation, and it reviews the use of these ideas in education, with special emphasis on research on teaching. In so doing, I have kept in mind Scribner's admonition, not to think of theories, including Vygotsky's ideas, as providing straightforward prescriptions to be directly applied in practice or, for that matter, as providing ready-made research techniques and procedures. Instead, Vygotskian theory offers a general approach, including "conceptual tools and methodological principles, which have to be concretized according to the specific nature of the object un-

der scrutiny" (Engeström, 1993, p. 97). Accordingly, I highlight studies that have developed concepts and models that mediate between Vygotskian theory and research on the practices of teaching.

The current interest in the ideas of Vygotsky dates to the publication 20 years ago of *Mind in Society* (Vygotsky, 1978), an edited compilation of selected articles by the Russian psychologist.[1] This little book, although now disparaged by some critics,[2] had an enormous and unexpected effect (see Cole, 1996, p. 106). It was instrumental in introducing Vygotsky's work to a new generation of readers, with special resonance, as I shall explain, in the field of education. It also served as a catalyst for the ex-

The author wants to thank Esteban Díaz for his helpful comments on a draft of this chapter. This chapter is dedicated to the memory of Angel Rivière: brilliant psychologist, good colleague, and friend.

[1] Vygotsky's work has been available in English since the period from the late 1920s to the early 1930s (see Cole, 1996; Van der Veer & Valsiner, 1991). Prior to the publication of *Mind in Society* (1978), the book *Thought and Language* (1962) was the most prominent and widely read translation of his work, enjoying several printings. This book was an abridged version of the Russian original published in 1934, a few months after Vygotsky's passing. The 1962 English version of *Thought and Language* also included an extended commentary by Jean Piaget that was excluded from subsequent printings. After the initial publication of *Mind in Society* in 1978, and in response to the great interest in Vygotsky's work generated by this book, a revised edition of *Thought and Language* was published in 1986 [see References], and an unabridged version titled *Thinking and Speech* was published as part of the first volume of Vygotsky's collected works in English (see Vygotsky, 1987). *Thought and Language* has also appeared in several languages, and like the English version, these translations have had several versions and reprintings. For biographical information about Vygotsky and discussions of his historical context, see, for example, Blanck (1990), Rosa and Montero (1990), Van der Veer and Valsiner (1991), and Yaroshevsky (1989).

[2] For example, Van der Veer & Valsiner (1994) refer to the book as "the cocktail-type mixing of various of [Vygotsky's] ideas to fit the American audience" (p. 4).

amination of his ideas and for the publication of related books and articles not only in the United States but also in several other countries. Vygotsky's contributions are now widely recognized internationally (Lima, 1995, 1997) including, quite belatedly (for many complicated reasons not of immediate relevance), in his home country (see Van der Veer & Valsiner, 1991).

The last edition of this *Handbook,* published in 1986 (Wittrock, 1986), contained only four articles that referenced Vygotsky. Most prominent was the article by Cazden (1986) on classroom discourse.[3] Since then, citations to the ideas of Vygotsky and to related work have increased dramatically (Doise, Staerkle, & Clémence, 1996), and several important new books and articles have been published (for an extensive bibliography, see Elhammoumi, 1997).[4] For present purposes, it may suffice to mention that a more complete corpus of Vygotsky's work now exists in English as well as in other languages. The six volumes of Vygotsky's collected works are now available in English (Vygotsky, 1987, 1993, 1997b, 1997c, 1998, 1999), and his 1926 book, *Pedagogical Psychology,* was also published recently in English as *Educational Psychology* (Vygotsky, 1997a).[5]

In addition, several related volumes have appeared since the last *Handbook,* including, to mention just a few, those by Castorina, Ferreiro, Kohl de Oliveira, and Lerner (1998); Cole (1996); Cole, Engeström and Vásquez (1997); Daniels (1996); John-Steiner, Panofsky, and Smith (1994); Kozulin (1990); Lantolf and Appel (1994); Ratner (1991); Rogoff (1990); Saxe (1991); Tryphon and Vonèche (1996); Van der Veer and Valsiner (1991, 1994); Wertsch (1985, 1991); and Wood (1998).

A four-volume bilingual series (English and Spanish) that is edited by del Río, Álvarez, and Wertsch has also been published: Rosa and Valsiner (1994); Wertsch and Ramírez (1994); Merced and Coll (1994); and Álvarez and del Río (1994). In addition, several books addressing the educational implications of Vygotsky's ideas are now also available: Álvarez (1997); Baquero (1996); Berk and Winsler (1995); Bodrova and Leong (1996); Daniels (1993); Dixon-Krauss (1996); Forman, Minick, and Stone (1993); Hicks (1996); Kozulin (1998); Lee and Smagorinsky (2000); Moll (1990b); Terré and Bell (1995); Tharp and Gallimore (1988); and Wells (1999).

To prepare this chapter, in addition to identifying the volumes mentioned above, I searched for articles with citations to Vygotsky. Although I limited the search to those published since 1990,[6] I identified more than 300 articles, and this search did not include chapters in books, which have proliferated. I found articles that were either based on Vygotsky or that cited his ideas prominently. These articles were written on diverse topics including the following:

- psychotherapy (Portes, 1999; Wilson & Weinstein, 1992a, 1992b)
- clinical applications (Díaz & Berk, 1995; Schneider & Watkins, 1996)
- children's play (Berk, 1994; Nicolopoulou, 1993)
- moral development (Buzzeli, 1993; Glassman & Zan, 1995)
- motivation and self-esteem (Aidman & Leontiev, 1991; Montero & Huertas, 1997; Rueda & Moll, 1994)
- metacognition and self-regulation (Manning, White, & Daugherty, 1994; McCaslin Rohrkemper, 1989)
- private speech (Díaz & Berk, 1992)
- peer interactions (Tudge, 1992); and community psychology (Odonnel, Tharp, & Wilson, 1993)

More directly connected to the task at hand, I also found articles on the following:

- science and math education (Brissiaud, 1994; Candela, 1995; Nuñes, 1992, 1999; Sierpinska, 1993)
- special education (Cousins, Díaz, Flores, & Hernández, 1995; Englert, Rozendal, & Mariage, 1994; Gindis, 1995; Rosa, 1997; Rueda, 1996; Trent, Artiles, & Englert, 1998; see also, Terré & Bell, 1995)
- bilingualism and second language development (Lantolf, 1994; Donato & McCormick, 1994; Hernández, 1993; see also, Bain, 1996)
- teacher cognition (Manning & Payne, 1993)
- assessment (Day & Cordon, 1993; Meltzer & Reid, 1994)
- reading and writing (Cazden, 1995; Gutiérrez, Baquedano-López, & Turner, 1997; Smagorinsky & Coppock, 1995)
- classroom practices (Holzman, 1995; Pontecorvo & Girardet, 1993; Wells, 1995)

In addition, I found several articles that presented alternative interpretations or elaborations of the zone of proximal development, Vygotsky's well-known concept. These articles were not limited to the field of education (see, e.g., Díaz, Neal, & Vachio, 1991; Englert, Rozendal, & Mariage, 1994; Lacasa, Cosano, & Reina, 1997; Smagorinsky, 1995; Wilson & Weinstein, 1996). Later in this chapter, I will summarize a representative selection of those articles most related to research on teaching, the main focus of this *Handbook.*

But why Vygotsky now? Why have the ideas of a long-deceased (1896–1934) and relatively obscure Russian psychologist from the 1930s become so visible, even vital, near the end of this century? Why is he prominent in the field of education,

---

[3] The 1976 edition of the *Handbook* lists no references to his work.

[4] A serious omission in this otherwise fine bibliography is the work developed in Cuba. Consider that, as Calviño and de la Torre (1996) have pointed out, between 1977 and 1982, coinciding with the resurgence of Vygotsky's ideas in the United States, more than 30 professors (about 75% of the total faculty) from the School of Psychology of the University of Havana had had direct contact with Russian psychologists, some Cuban professors obtaining their advanced degrees in Russia, and others worked in Russia during prolonged visits. See also González Rey (1996).

[5] For additional information about *Educational Psychology* (Vygotsky, 1997a), which was intended as a summary for student teachers but written before his formulation of a cultural–historical theory, see Van der Veer and Valsiner (1991, chap. 4) and Davydov (1995).

[6] I picked 1990 as the starting date for the search because it was the year of publication of my edited volume on Vygotsky and education, which, I believe, contains articles representative of the field since 1986, the publication date of the previous *Handbook.* Among the most important publications related to Vygotsky that appeared before 1990 are the following: Bakhurst (1986), Valsiner (1988), Wertsch (1985), Wood (1998). Also, consult Cole, Engeström, and Vásquez (1997).

which has changed so much since Vygotsky's time? Among other interpretations (see, e.g., Cole et al., 1997, pp. 1–25; Van der Veer & Valsiner, 1994, pp. 1–9), Baquero (1996) has proposed, following Bernstein (1993), that the rise of cultural diversity in schools, specifically, a more ethnically and racially heterogeneous student population, produced a crisis in educational practice that created a receptive context for Vygotsky's cultural–historical perspective. In particular, his ideas about the learning potential of students and the formative role of others, as embodied in the concept of the zone of proximal development, were very well received.

The period that coincides roughly with the publication of *Mind in Society* (Vygotsky, 1978) was also characterized, at least in the United States, (a) by intense interest on issues related to cultural differences in learning and thinking (e.g., Cole & Scribner, 1974; Scribner & Cole, 1981; Wagner & Stevenson, 1982) and (b) by the advent of anthropological, especially ethnographic approaches to education (e.g., Cazden, John, & Hymes, 1972; Spindler, 1974, 1982), including those with an emphasis on understanding the social organization of classroom interactions (e.g., McDermott, 1976; Mehan, 1979; Philips, 1983). This combination of factors—the urgency of addressing issues of language and cultural diversity in practice, a growing preoccupation with the role of culture and context in psychology, and the ascendancy of qualitative approaches in educational research (all of which are still viable)—created fortuitous circumstances for the reintroduction of Vygotsky's ideas (see also, Sinha, 1989, pp. 317–319).

Education was of primary interest to Vygotsky, which is exemplified by his lifelong commitment to practical work (see Blanck, 1990). As Sinha (1989) has suggested, agency, more than anything else, provides the Vygotskian approach with its unifying thread, and agency is central to the substance of both his theory and method (p. 314). So pedagogy in all its cultural forms was intrinsic to his theorizing, and he assigned schooling a major formative role in the mental development of children (Baquero, 1996; Moll, 1990a; Vygotsky, 1934/1963). Therefore, his psychology may not serve as a foundation for education, but education in all its forms serves as a foundation for his psychology.

The Basics of Vygotsky's Psychology

I will not attempt to provide a thorough review of Vygotsky's psychology because extended treatments and varied interpretations are now readily available (e.g., Kozulin, 1990; Rivière, 1984; Van der Veer & Valsiner, 1991; Wertsch, 1985).[7] Instead,

the purpose of this section is to provide an overview of key concepts that may help the readers frame the following sections, which examine the uses of Vygotskian ideas in research on teaching.

With these caveats in mind, let me start, then, by summarizing what I believe is the essence of Vygotsky's psychology: Human thinking develops through the mediation of others.[8] Scribner (1990b) has expressed eloquently a similar idea:

> Vygotsky's special genius was in grasping the significance of the social in things as well as people. The world in which we live in is humanized, full of material and symbolic objects (signs, knowledge systems) that are culturally constructed, historical in origin and social in content. Since all human actions, including acts of thought, involve the *mediation* of such objects ("tools and signs") they are, on this score alone, social in essence. This is the case, whether acts are initiated by single agents or a collective and whether they are performed individually or with others. (p. 92, emphasis added)

As Scribner underscores, the concept of the mediation of human actions (including "acts of thought") is central to Vygotsky's theorizing and is, perhaps, its defining characteristic. Put succinctly, people interact with their worlds, which are "humanized, full of material and symbolic objects," through these mediational means. This mediation of actions through cultural artifacts, especially language in both its oral and written forms, plays a crucial role in the forming and developing human intellectual capacities. Notice that the central point is not simply about the importance of tool and symbol use by human beings; the point has a stronger claim than that. It refers to the essential role of cultural mediation in the constitution of human psychological processes (Bakhurst, 1995).

Kozulin (1995) has pointed out that Vygotsky's notion of mediation includes three large classes of mediators: signs and symbols, interpersonal relations, and individual activities (p. 119).[9] Vygotsky (1978, 1987) concentrated primarily on what he called "psychological tools," which are the semiotic potential of systems of signs and symbols (most significantly, language) in mediating thinking (see also Wertsch, 1985, 1991). Pontecorvo (1993) summarizes well this Vygotskian idea of tool mediation: "Mediation tools include the semiotic systems pertaining to different languages and to various scientific fields; these are procedures, thought methodologies, and cultural objects that have to be appropriated, practices of discourse and reasoning that have to be developed, and play or study practices that have to be exercised" (p. 191).

Without entering into details, Vygotsky (1987) emphasized a double function of language: (a) how it serves communication,

---

[7] See also chapters about Vygotsky in the following books: Bakhurst (1991), Baquero (1996), Luria (1979), and Valsiner (1988). See also Davydov (1995) and Scribner (1990b).

[8] "[W]e might say that through others we become ourselves, and this rule refers not only to the individual as a whole, but also to the history of each separate [psychological] function. This also comprises the essence of the process of cultural development expressed in a purely logical form. The individual becomes for himself what he is in himself through what he manifests for others. This is also the process of forming the individual" (Vygotsky, 1997c, p. 105).

[9] In contrast, Morenza (1997, p. 6) proposes four major types of mediations: (a) social mediation—interactions with other human beings and, especially, the role of social groups in integrating the subject into social practices; (b) instrumental-tool mediation—the use of the instruments created culturally; (c) instrumental-signs mediation—the use of systems of signs or semiotics; and (d) anatomical mediation—the use of physiological systems that permit interaction with the stimuli and information found in the social medium.

enabling human beings to socially coordinate (or discoordinate) their actions with others through meaning; and (b) how, through the internalization of this communication, it comes to mediate intellectual activity through the discourse of inner speech. The development of this capacity for self-regulation through inner speech is what helps to bring actions under the control of thought, a development to which he assigned great importance (see also, e.g., Bakhurst, 1986; Berk & Winsler, 1995; Martí, 1996; Shotter, 1993a, 1993b; Wells, 1994).

Nevertheless, as Foley (1991) has indicated, however crucial language may be to the mediation and development of thinking, the construction of meaning is regulated (or mediated) by social relationships (Wells, 1994). This observation points to the second large class of mediators in Vygotsky's theory, which he referred to as the "social situation of development" (see Minick, 1989). Cole (1996) has suggested that "in order to give an account of culturally mediated thinking it is necessary to specify not only the artifacts through which behavior is mediated but also the circumstances in which the thinking occurs" (p 131). In relation to this contextual emphasis, Vygotsky proposed the concept of the zone of proximal development, the contrast between what a child can do independently, his or her actual level of development, and what a child can do with the assistance of others, the proximal level of development (see Vygotsky, 1978). Contrasting what children can do independently with what they can accomplish with assistance not only provides a more dynamic perspective on their capabilities but also can serve to guide teaching. Instruction, he suggested, should be aimed not at what the child can already do without help but, proximally, at those abilities that are developing and that can only be manifested with the assistance of others.

Much has been written about this concept of the zone of proximal development in recent years (see, e.g., Henderson & Cunningham, 1994; Minick, 1989; Moll, 1990a; Tharp & Gallimore, 1988). For now, let me propose that Vygotsky may have intended the concept not only to be an instructional heuristic or to highlight the importance of social dynamics in assessment but also to emphasize the significance of meaning in the cultural mediation of thinking. The concept of mediation, especially in relation to the role of semiotic systems, most notably speech, privileges the importance of meaning not only as the medium of the social but also as the medium of the mental (see Bakhurst, 1986, 1995). As Vygotsky (1987) put it, "Thought is not only mediated externally by signs. It is mediated internally by meanings" (p. 282). The development or genesis of this meaning, as part of the continuous and reciprocal relations between human beings and their social worlds, is also a central Vygotskian concern (John-Steiner & Mahn, 1996).

In this sense, the concept of the zone of proximal development was used by Vygotsky to capture the relationship in schooling between what he called "everyday" and "scientific" concepts (Vygotsky, 1987, 1934/1994a). The key difference is that scientific, or schooled, concepts such as mammals and reptiles (as compared to everyday concepts such as boats and cars) are systematic (i.e., they form part of and are acquired though a system of formal instruction). The observation that scientific concepts tend to be acquired in school and everyday concepts tend to be acquired out of school is not as important as the characteristic of systematicity (how scientific concepts form part of an organized system of knowledge) and, thus, can be more easily reflected upon and manipulated deliberately.

Consequently, through schooling, these concepts (both scientific and everyday) become objects of study. Furthermore, Vygotsky (1987) also pointed out the reciprocal relationship between everyday and scientific concepts and how they mediate each other. Everyday concepts provide the "conceptual fabric" for developing schooled concepts but the everyday concepts are transformed through their connection to the more systematic concepts. Scientific concepts grow into the everyday, into the domain of personal experience, thus acquiring meaning and significance. However, scientific concepts bring with them conscious awareness and control, which he believed to be two essential characteristics of schooling.

The primacy assigned to cultural mediation and to the social situation of development in Vygotsky's theory does not exclude considering the active, dynamic individual who is also central to his formulation. This emphasis is most evident in Vygotsky's writings about the role of play, especially imaginative or make-believe play, in development (Vygotsky, 1978, 1982). As he wrote:

> Play creates a zone of proximal development in the child. In play, the child always behaves beyond his average age, above his daily behavior; in play it is as though he were a head taller than himself. As in the focus of the magnifying glass, play contains all the developmental tendencies in a condensed form and is itself a major source of development. (Vygotsky, 1978, p. 102)

He proposed that play serves as a unique zone of proximal development: the creation of imaginary situations with their own particular social rules through which the children advance themselves to higher levels of psychological functioning. Notice as well that the focus on the individual does not negate the social dynamics of development.

This preoccupation with the active individual led Vygotsky to propose a developmental or genetic method that involves studying psychological processes in transition. As Sinha (1989) has suggested, "Vygotsky's method was not one of *positing* psychological entities, but of analysing the functional *transformations* wrought by socio-individual developmental processes upon *complexes of activity* manifested in the dynamic organization of behaviour" (pp. 314–315, emphases in original). One example of a developmental method is the "method of double stimulation" in which the experimenter devises a situation or task and provides the subject with some means (or other forms of assistance) that can lead to a solution of the task (Vygotsky, 1978). The focus is on the subject's constructive role, on how he or she uses the available resources or creates new mediational means to solve the task or problem. "Whatever concrete form Vygotsky's method might take in the hands of different empirical investigators," Valsiner (1988) has written, "its emphasis on the *subject's active nature* in his/her relations with other people within the given (structured) environments remains the heart of the matter" (p. 139, emphasis in original).

In a recent summary of the cultural–historical approach, Cole (1996, pp. 104–115) has discussed another issue that is quite relevant to the present discussion: how humans organize life for new generations to rediscover and appropriate mediating artifacts. This intergenerational dynamic is central to the survival of the species. For example, Stetsenko (1993) has pointed out that what was important for Vygotsky was not only culture in its broadest forms—as that variable differs across nations and populations—but also culture as the social "milieu in which the life of the people is embedded." That is, culture is understood as an "accumulation of the social experiences of humanity in the concrete form of means and modes, schemes and patterns of human behaviour, cognition, and communication" (p. 40). Through the process of enculturation, then, older human beings arrange for younger ones to acquire the accumulated cultural artifacts and practices of its group or culture. Here the notion of the zone of proximal development again comes to mind, understood not only in terms of "more capable" others assisting "less capable" ones, but also in terms of how human beings "use social processes and cultural resources of all kinds" to help children construct their futures (Scribner, 1990b, p. 92).

John-Steiner (1995) has called attention to how individuals appropriate "a multiplicity of semiotic means and practices" (which she refers to as "cognitive pluralism") by being part of a sociohistorical milieu in which these tools and practices are used and culturally transmitted. In this sense, schools represent a primary "sociohistorical milieu" at a society's disposal for making many of these critical means and practices widely available. Considering John-Steiner's points in terms of the means and practices—the special forms of social relationships, discourse, technologies, and thinking that can characterize going to school—is a way to understand Vygotsky's claim about the formative capacities of schooling. Research into those means and practices is the topic of the next section.

Bringing the Theory to Observation

In this section, I will cite work, without attempting to be exhaustive, that represents four major trends or characteristics of how Vygotskian ideas are being used in research on teaching (see also, John-Steiner & Mahn, 1996). I will not cover certain topics that some might consider essential, such as concept development, internalization, and private speech, although I will refer to such topics as relevant to the review of the works included. I will also concentrate on research on teaching as it relates to schooling while recognizing, however, that I am not addressing an important literature on teaching and learning in nonschool settings (see, e.g., Lave & Wenger, 1991; Pelissier, 1991; see also, Lave, 1996).

As several authors have observed (e.g., Kozulin, 1995), the general pattern of use of Vygotsky's ideas, especially in education, could be characterized as selective borrowing and interpretation. This pattern results, in part, because a complete corpus of Vygotsky's works has been generally unavailable. In addition, by focusing attention on the social basis of learning and development and by providing general concepts to guide such an approach, the theory lends itself well, as Vygotsky intended, for interdisciplinary combinations and extensions. Put another way, it is relatively easy to find common ground between Vygotsky's ideas and contemporary interdisciplinary currents or trends in various disciplines including psychology (Cole, 1996; Rodríguez Arocho, 1996), anthropology (Holland & Cole, 1995), and linguistics (Nelson, 1996) as well as other areas of inquiry (e.g., Lock, 1999).

This selective borrowing, as Van der Veer and Valsiner (1994) have commented, has produced a number of "blind spots" (pp. 5–6). One blind spot that is most relevant here is that in educational applications the role of the social other (e.g., as found in accounts of the zone of the proximal development) is generally presented as favorable or helpful. That presentation ignores the contradictions or negative educational circumstances that often constitute schooling (see also, Moll, 1990a). I shall return to this topic at the conclusion of this chapter.

Van der Veer and Valsiner (1991) also point out what they consider to be a misleading use of Vygotsky's ideas:

> [N]owadays countless investigators of mother–child dialogues and joint problem solving (with their emphasis on the steering role of the more experienced other in an intimate setting) feel obliged to refer to Vygotsky, although in fact Vygotsky never discussed these situations and instead focused more upon culture as providing tools for thinking. (p. 6)

Be that as it may, if one is borrowing from a theory that provides a social and cultural account of thinking, it seems relevant that one should investigate the social contexts in which learners participate. Thus one could make clear how the interpersonal dynamics within or among those contexts work as constitutive, mediating processes rather than simply to assume (theoretically) their general relevance for thinking. Indeed, all of the studies presented below share, in ways I shall explain, this orientation "toward analyzing and understanding how interactional settings and pragmatic patterns of speech affect forms of arguing, thinking, and learning, through the mediation of a variety of cultural tools" (Pontecorvo, 1993, p. 189). Clearly, within a Vygotskian perspective, social relations provide a major resource for the development of thinking. How this development may be accomplished is a legitimate area of investigation, whether or not Vygotsky discussed these situations.

Moreover, Vygotsky most certainly emphasized (a) the social nature of schooling as he wrote about the "unique forms of co-operation between the child and the adult that is the central element of the educational process" and (b) how, through this interactional process, "knowledge is transferred to the child in a definite system" (Vygotsky, 1987, p. 169; Vygotsky, 1934/1994a). He also wrote about the necessity to conceptualize the educational process as "active on three levels: the student is active, the teacher is active, and the environment created between them is an active one" (Vygotsky, 1926/1997a, as cited by Davydov, 1990/1997, p. xxiv). The act of teaching, therefore, plays a central role in Vygotsky's theorizing because he believed that the capacity to teach and to benefit from instruction is a fundamental attribute of human beings. This belief is at the heart of his proposal about the social genesis of thinking, his oft-cited "general genetic law of cultural development," which notes the transformation from "interpsychological" to "intrapsychological" functioning (Vygotsky, 1981, p. 163).

Let me turn now to the four trends that I have identified in the literature, which I have labeled as follows: theorizing from practice, changing how teachers teach, conducting teaching experiments, and creating activity systems. These four trends, clearly, are not mutually exclusive; the labels are simply meant to capture the main focus of the work. I will present a primary example of each trend, citing additional literature as I proceed.[10] Within each example, Vygotskian ideas are not only supportive of the research but central to its formulation. I conclude the chapter by summarizing the review and by presenting some additional, potentially fruitful areas of future research.

Theorizing from Practice

The group of studies that depict the trend to theorize from practice is characterized by classroom observations of novel teaching practices. The goal in these studies has been to use examples of teaching to clarify or extend Vygotskian theoretical concepts. The general idea is that practice can not only inform and elaborate but also exceed our theoretical notions.

In most cases, the teaching practices featured in these studies were not developed or implemented with Vygotskian principles in mind (e.g., Chang-Wells & Wells, 1993; Clay & Cazden, 1990; Englert, Rozendal, & Mariage, 1994; Lacasa, Cosano, & Reina, 1997; Moll & Whitmore, 1993; Tharp & Gallimore, 1988; Wells, 1995). Nevertheless, the authors considered that certain aspects of these practices, such as the organization of instruction or the teacher's ways of interacting with students, were particularly useful in illuminating theoretical concepts (e.g., the zone of proximal development) or the relationships among concepts.[11]

The primary example I have selected for commentary, however, is from the research of Raphael and colleagues on the Book Clubs program, a literacy instruction approach featuring the study of trade books (Gavelek & Raphael, 1996; Raphael, 1996; Raphael & Goatley, 1994). The research has a strong developmental emphasis; the actions of teachers and students were carefully documented for evidence of student transformations over a period of two years (Gavelek & Raphael, 1996, p. 188). These transformations consisted of students appropriating or taking over the reading strategies that were practiced or instantiated in the program to use them for their own purposes as part of their evolving self-regulation.

The Book Clubs program consists of four interrelated and well-coordinated components. Its central component is the student-led discussion groups called book clubs, and these are supported or enhanced by three other components: reading, writing, and community share. The last component, community share, refers to whole-class instruction about strategies (e.g., ways of discussing a story) or attempts to summarize and discuss what is being read in one of the clubs. The bulk of the reading takes place within each book club where all students in a particular club read the same book. The various clubs may read the same book or thematically related titles depending on the students' interests and the teacher's agenda. The writing component consists of short-term writing, such as log entries in which students respond to what they are reading, and also of long-term writing that may involve reports or essays. Key to the

program is the coordination among these components and how the teacher facilitates different forms of public discussion of books that can serve as a resource for the students' learning and development.

The central thrust of this work, then, a seven-year collaborative effort with teachers, is how language, especially teachers' ways of interacting with students, mediates the relationship between students and their understandings of texts. As Gavelek & Raphael (1996) explain it, the focus of the work is on the ways in which language "plays a central role in the development of literate minds" by "mediating students' abilities to think, feel, and act" (p. 183). The talking about text that teacher and students engage in represents attempts to facilitate not only reading comprehension but also "the very *means* by which students come to acquire and construct new knowledge, new meanings, and new interpretations of text through interactive use of language" (p. 184, emphasis in original). The idea is that students—through their participation in varied and rich discussions about texts that they are reading either collectively or individually—will internalize and personalize (and, thus, transform) these discussions, as well as key concepts about texts, and will use them to guide subsequent ways of understanding what they read. The public language about text—the different ways of talking about books that are coordinated by the teacher and instantiated in a book club curriculum (see Raphael, 1996) comes to eventually form part of the students' private language for thinking about what they read, illustrating the shift from "interpsychological" to "intrapsychological" functioning, as proposed by Vygotsky.

This analysis of the Book Clubs program builds on a conceptual model proposed by Harré (1984) called "The Vygotsky Space" (see Figure 9.1). Briefly put, the model highlights the relationships both between social and individual actions and between public and private domains of action. These relationships are represented by the crossing vertical and horizontal lines in the figure. The Vygotsky Space, then, consists of four parts: (a) public-social, (b) private-social, (c) private-individual, and (d) public-individual. The learners may be characterized as functioning at any given time within any of these four quadrants. The idea, as depicted in Figure 9.1, is that, during their development, learners move recursively through these four different quadrants (see Gavelek & Raphael, 1996, p. 187).

For example, the shift from learning how to talk about a book during community share (public action and social domain, quadrant 1 in the figure) to using or modeling the same strategy or concepts as part of a response log (private action and individual domain) is a way to conceptualize the students' initial transitions or appropriations. A more sophisticated developmental transition may occur when a student then applies these strategies in novel ways as part of subsequent individual work (e.g., as a written essay).

The researchers used this conceptual model to trace the connection between the teachers' instructional strategies (the

---

[10] Although I selected the examples for their illustrative capacities, they also, in part, reflect my biases and research interests. For example, I highlighted two studies that address the teaching of literacy (a central research interest of mine) instead of studies that deal with, say, the teaching of mathematics or art.

[11] The edited volumes by Alvarez and del Río (1994), Dixon-Krauss (1996), Merced and Coll (1994), and Moll (1990b) all contain studies of teaching that are interpreted along Vygotskian lines.

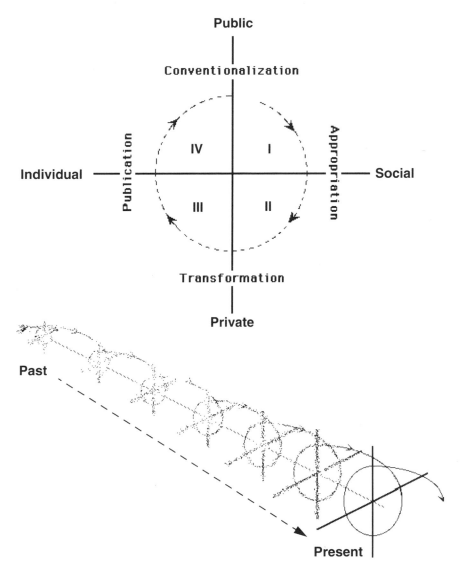

Figure 9.1. The Vygotsky Space (adapted from R. Harré [1984]). (From Gavelek & Raphael, 1996, p. 186.)

teachers' roles) and the students' developmental transformations over 2 years of participation in the Book Club. As they have written (Gavelek & Raphael, 1996), the model "is rich in its capacity to help us conceptualize the relationship between the discourse that students are guided to participate in through social venues and the text-related thinking that they independently demonstrate over time. . . . The model provides a framework for teachers to help students develop facility with and ownership of a range of cognitive and metacognitive strategies" (Gavelek & Raphael, 1996, p. 183, 184).

Thus, a teaching innovation, the Book Clubs, is analyzed using Vygotskian concepts to understand the changes, or the developmental shifts, in the students' ability to take over and independently use strategies for reading that have been presented to them publicly and socially within each of the program's components. Notice that Raphael and colleagues examine both the social interactions and the students' productions for evidence

of qualitative changes in the students' internalization of the reading strategies that underlie this literacy program. This analysis can provide formative feedback to teachers that could shape how they go about instructing students.

Changing How Teachers Teach

The second group of studies attempts, as a central characteristic, to change or modify how teachers teach; that is, the focus is explicitly on changing teachers and their methodology, especially their speech genres and registers within lessons. Building on the Vygotskian emphasis on social interactions as a major factor in cognitive development, teacher-student interactions usually comprise the primary unit of study as well as the leading indicator of positive change. The principal approach has often consisted of concentrated coaching of teachers in controlled, laboratory-like settings or courses and has sometimes involved the videotaping of lessons that are used to conduct interactional analysis and to provide practical feedback (see, e.g., Au, 1990; Jones, Rua, & Carter, 1997; Palincsar, 1986).

The primary example of teacher change comes from the work of Goldenberg and colleagues and the development of the concept of Instructional Conversations (IC) (Gallimore & Goldenberg, 1992; Goldenberg, 1991, 1992/1993; Rueda, Goldenberg, & Gallimore, 1991; Saunders & Goldenberg, 1996, 1999; Saunders, Goldenberg, & Hamann, 1992). This work of Goldenberg and colleagues builds on research conducted as part of the Kamehameha Early Education Program (KEEP) in Hawaii, a well-known, long-term, and successful educational research study with Native Hawaiian students and teachers (e.g., Au, 1979; Tharp & Gallimore, 1988). At the heart of KEEP was the social organization of reading lessons to facilitate the students' motivation, engagement, and comprehension

In brief, building on classroom experimentation with lessons as well as on ethnographic observations of interactional patterns in Native Hawaiian homes, reading lessons were structured to elicit an interaction between teachers and students that is often labeled a "talk-story." These talk-story interactions were designed to increase the students' involvement and comprehension during story reading (Au, 1979). The central characteristic of these interactions was that the teacher was both flexible and responsive to the students' verbal contributions, shaping the interchange of ideas about what they were reading through instructional conversations with the students (for a detailed summary and Vygotskian interpretation of KEEP, see Gallimore & Tharp, 1990; Tharp & Gallimore, 1988; for earlier Vygotskian interpretations of the KEEP research, see Au & Kawakami, 1984; Tharp et al., 1984).

Goldenberg and colleagues have adapted and elaborated the concept of instructional conversations as part of their research with Latino and other students in Los Angeles, California. In particular, building on the notion of assisted performance as related to Vygotsky's concept of the zone of proximal development, they have identified 10 elements (see Table 9.1) that are essential for the creation of instructional conversation lessons

and have produced a rating scale and manual for the training of teachers (Goldenberg, 1991, 1992/1993; Rueda, Goldenberg, & Gallimore, 1991; Saunders & Goldenberg, 1996). The goal has been to develop an applied model that could be used to teach and evaluate how teachers are using the different elements of instructional conversations in their work. For example, these IC elements include whether the teacher is responsive to the students' responses and whether the teacher is asking students to support their arguments or claims. The intent of the rating scale is also to develop an instrument that teachers can use to evaluate (self-regulate) their own teaching.

The work on this applied model has consisted primarily of collaborating with small groups of teachers to develop alternative teaching (and bilingual) practices that are based on the Instructional Conversations model. Teachers are typically videotaped in action in their classrooms for later analysis with researchers (usually once a week) to discuss their teaching and to assess successful approximations in relation to the IC model over time. The researchers report that it takes at least a year of such training for teachers to implement IC effectively in their classrooms. In addition, outcome measures are usually collected from the students, especially comprehension test results and other pre- and posttest measures including sociolinguistic analyses of lessons conducted by IC and non-IC teachers, that help substantiate the effectiveness of the IC intervention (see Saunders & Goldenberg, 1999). Furthermore, the researchers have collected evidence that the IC treatment persists; teachers continue to use IC several years after the training and assistance ends (Saunders & Goldenberg, 1996).

Notice that the emphasis of this research has been on how teachers come to use IC as a mediating artifact in their teaching. The goal of the intervention, generated developmentally, is to facilitate the teachers' self-regulation: their conscious use, clear differentiation, and adaptations of the various IC strategies in their teaching. The explicitness of the IC elements and the deliberateness of the training are intended to produce multiple learning opportunities for teachers that will lead to observable and documentable changes in their teaching. As Saun-

---

Table 9.1   Ten Elements of an Instructional Conversation Adapted from Gallimore & Goldenberg, 1992

INSTRUCTIONAL ELEMENTS

1. *Thematic focus:* The teacher selects a theme or idea to serve as a starting point for focusing the discussion and has a general plan for how the theme will unfold, including how to "chunk" the text to permit optimal exploration of the theme.

2. *Activation and use of background knowledge:* The teacher provides students with pertinent background knowledge for understanding a text and this knowledge is woven into the discussions that follow.

3. *Direct teaching:* When necessary, the teacher provides direct teaching of a skill or concept.

4. *Promotion of more complex language and expression:* The teacher elicits more extended student contributions by using a variety of elicitation techniques (e.g., invitations to expand, questions, restatements).

5. *Elicitation of bases for statements or positions:* The teacher promotes students' use of text, pictures, and reasoning to support an argument or position. The teacher probes for the bases of the students' statements (e.g., "How do you know?").

CONVERSATIONAL ELEMENTS

6. *Fewer "known-answer" questions:* Much of the discussion centers on questions and answers for which there might be more than one correct answer.

7. *Responsivity to student contributions:* While having an initial plan and maintaining the focus and coherence of the discussion, the teacher is also responsive to students' statements and the opportunities they provide.

8. *Connected discourse:* The discussion is characterized by multiple, interactive, connected turns, so that succeeding utterances build upon and extend previous ones.

9. *A challenging, but non-threatening atmosphere:* The teacher creates a "zone of proximal development" where a challenging atmosphere is balanced by a positive affective climate, and the teacher allows students to negotiate and construct meaning of the text.

10. *General participation:* The teacher encourages general participation among students, and they are encouraged to influence the selection of speaking turns.

ders and Goldenberg (1996) put it, "Since the goals and ends of teaching are many and complex, so too must be the means. Exclusive reliance on one or another model or theory is unwise" (p. 158).[12]

Conducting Teaching Experiments

The third group of studies consists of those that involve experimentation with teaching classroom wide. The goal of these studies is generally to introduce theoretically specific changes into the teaching and then to analyze the changes in the process of instruction. Thus, in contrast to the theoretically motivated observations of practice that are discussed above or to the more focused efforts to modify teachers' discourse patterns, teaching experiments attempt to modify, explicitly using alternative theoretical constructs, the classroom teaching system or key aspects of that system (see Brown & Campione, 1994; Brown, Metz, & Campione, 1996; Holzman, 1995; Newman, Griffin, & Cole, 1989; Wells, 1996).

The primary example for this section is from the work of Hedegaard (1990) that was conducted in Danish elementary schools (see also, Hedegaard, 1996, 1998, 1999). I have selected her work because it builds not only on the ideas of Vygotsky but also on the related work of Davydov (1988a, 1988b, 1988c), Elkonin (1971), and Aidarova (1982), all prominent Russian psychologists in the Vygotskian tradition. The key formulation in Hedegaard's work is that of theoretical learning (see also, Engeström, 1987; Karpov & Bransford, 1995; Kozulin, 1995). She builds on the contrast between empirical knowledge and theoretical knowledge, a distinction borrowed primarily from Davydov (1988b, 1988c). As Kozulin (1990, pp. 254–262) explains this contrast, traditional methods of schooling are based primarily on empirical knowledge, with the starting point being what one can immediately observe about the properties of an object. Abstracting from some common features that are observed in a number of objects, one then arrives at a generalization that can be labeled, classified, or turned into a concept (not necessarily a correct one) and that can be taught directly to the students, usually in the form of some verbal definition. With such an emphasis, students fail to understand the critical distinction between everyday and scientific concepts (see Vygotsky, 1987, chap. 6) or to appreciate the logic of both scientific inquiry and the process underlying the development of concepts.

In contrast, theoretical knowledge deals with a connected system of phenomena, not the separate individual phenomenon. The goal of theoretical learning, then, is to develop an understanding of these interconnections prior to or while understanding the concrete phenomena or manifestations (Hedegaard, 1990, p. 352). As Karpov and Bransford (1995) explain:

Theoretical learning is based on supplying students with psychological tools: general and optimal methods for dealing with certain classes of problems that direct the students toward the essential (not simply the common) characteristic of the problems of each class. This psychological tool is then used for solving concrete problems.

In the course of its use, the processes underlying the tool are mastered and internalized by the student. (p. 63)

From the theoretical learning perspective, the starting point for the students is the learning of conceptual (theoretical) models that can serve as a "generalizing," abstract framework for their studies of empirical knowledge. The purpose of teaching, then, is to elaborate those activities that generate theoretical, conceptual reasoning, usually in the form of general models, and to facilitate student inquiries to clarify and extend the models. The goal, in other words, is to foster theoretical learning by starting with the more abstract model and then moving students to the study of the concrete, the empirical subject. That is, the goal is to move students "from the most general relationship characteristic of a given educational subject to its concrete, empirical manifestations" (Kozulin, 1990, p. 259).

To accomplish this theoretical learning, Hedegaard (1990) has proposed what she calls the "double move" in instruction: "The teacher must guide instruction on the basis of general laws, whereas the children must occupy themselves with these general laws in the clearest possible form through their investigation of their manifestations" (p. 357). What Hedegaard proposes is a form of guided investigation or research by the students in which they conduct concrete or practical investigations of a subject while being oriented by a general, theoretical model of the phenomenon they are studying, a model that they formalize or expand through their analysis of the concrete examples. Thus, in this double move, there is always a relationship between theoretical knowledge (the abstract conceptual model) and empirical knowledge (the concrete explorations of the phenomenon).

For example, Hedegaard's (1990) teaching experiment, conducted in an elementary-level classroom over a nine-month period, consisted of a teacher-guided student inquiry into the evolution of species, especially the adaptation (or misadaptation) of animals (e.g., bears) to their environments. As illustrated in Figure 9.2, while the children engage in concrete explorations (Stage 1: the study of animals and nature), they start formulating, with the teacher's help, a "germ-cell" (initial-general) model of what they are studying (Stage 2: the adaptation of different animal species). As they elaborate this general model, they reconceptualize the findings from the concrete explorations (Stage 3: a model of the development of species). In this way, the theoretical model becomes not only an instrument or tool for teaching and learning but also an outcome of the study. "Whereas the teacher's planning must advance from the general to the concrete," she writes, "the children's learning must develop from preconceived actions to symbolization of the knowledge they obtain through their research, finally resulting in a linguistic formulation of relations" (p. 357).

Although Hedegaard reports some problems with the teaching activity, including repetitiousness and the difficulties children encounter as they try to understand the concepts that have been introduced into the teaching process, the children had no

---

[12] Building on the strategy of creating special settings for teachers to examine their work in relation to an explicit model, Goldenberg and colleagues have recently developed a successful schoolwide model of change that incorporates IC as one of several innovations (see Goldenberg, 1996; Goldenberg & Sullivan, 1994).

Stage I: The relation between nature and animal life, and animals' adaptation to a given/specific/particular nature

Stage II: The adaptation of different animal species to the specific nature which is characteristic of a particular biotope (the relation between genetic and functional inheritance)

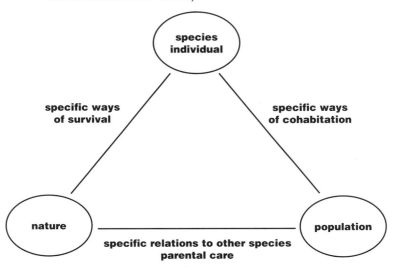

Stage III: The development of a species is determined by changes in the nature and changes in the state of the offspring

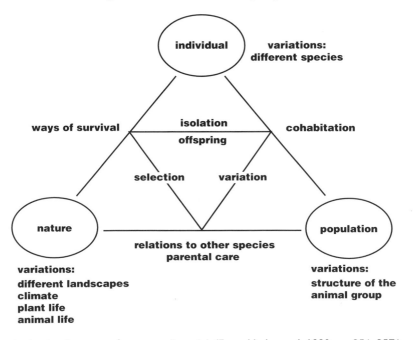

Figure 9.2. Three stages in the development of a germ-cell model. (From Hedegaard, 1990, pp. 356–357.)

problems modeling their subject knowledge, which is central to acquiring theoretical knowledge of the subject (pp. 363–365). Hedegaard (1990) concludes:

> Teaching that promotes children's theoretical concept learning must occur on a basis of profound teacher knowledge of the central concepts of the subject area. . . . The teacher must guide the learning from student involvement with general laws in the clearest possible form. Clearly, practical activities are an important part of teaching; however, these activities must, as mentioned, contain the general laws in their most transparent form. (p. 367)

Creating Activity Systems

The final group of studies characterize the trend to create settings or environments for teaching and learning that deliberately combine cultural resources in fundamentally new ways. These settings and the activity systems that form part of them are built on the basis of Vygotskian principles (see, e.g., Brown & Campione, 1994; Brown, Metz, & Campione, 1996; Cole, 1995, 1996; Gutiérrez, Baquedano-López, & Álvarez, 2001; Holzman, 1995; Moll, 1997; Moll & Greenberg, 1990; Schustack, King, Gallego, & Vásquez, 1994). Creating these settings or environments is the least common innovation because it is the most complicated to create, sustain, and research for a prolonged amount of time.

The emphasis of the projects in this category is unmistakably on theoretically inspired activity systems, systems that also become the medium of research. That is, the primary task is to create or reconstruct social and cultural practices in classrooms and other settings to formulate model systems that resemble, as Scribner (1990b) has suggested, an analytic-investigative device and also that prompt visions of a desired state of affairs to put "in between" an interpretation of theory and the development of practice. Although the focus of studies may differ depending on the investigators or the inquiry at hand, the goal is to produce change, to transform teaching and learning. So, for example, the focus in Brown and Campione's (1994) work has shifted from the teaching of reading comprehension to the design of dynamic learning communities, but the emphasis on agency and change remains at the heart of their system of inquiry and practice (see Brown, 1992). Similarly, the focus of the work of Moll and colleagues (e.g., Moll, Amanti, Neff, & González, 1992; Moll & Díaz, 1987; Moll & González, 1997) has shifted from the researchers identifying and documenting cultural resources in classroom practices to the teachers becoming participant researchers of their students' households as part of an explicit culturally mediated pedagogy. However, throughout the work, the emphasis on agency and change in connecting theory and practice has remained a constant.

I have selected as the primary example of creating activity systems, however, the work of Vásquez and colleagues and, in particular, the activity setting they refer to as "La Clase Mágica" [The Magic Classroom] (Vásquez, 1993, 1994). This activity setting originated as part of a group of related projects called "The 5th Dimension," all of which were community-based,

after-school programs (see, e.g., Cole, 1995, 1996, 1997; Gutiérrez et al., 2001; Nicolopoulou & Cole, 1993; Schustack et al., 1994).

In brief, all of the 5th Dimension projects share a particular social structure that combines play with educational activities and that contains a special set of rules, activities, artifacts, and relationships among participants including, as I shall explain, connections with local universities. As Cole (1995) describes the system, children play games within a loosely structured adventure-world framework that appropriates the games for the goals of promoting reading, writing, problem solving, and knowledge of computer-based communication (p. 171). The latest evaluation, which uses a wide array of instruments (see Cole, 1997), indicates that 5th Dimension participants demonstrate greater cognitive and academic growth than did matched nonparticipants.

The programs are all conducted after school and meet in the afternoons (usually 3 days a week for 2 hours) at a community site such as a youth club, library, or other community setting. The children who participate in the project, mostly elementary-level students, attend schools in the local community. Communities range from impoverished inner-city neighborhoods to affluent suburban sites that are located in different parts of the United States and in other countries.[13] All of the participants are volunteers, including the school children. The adults typically represent an intergenerational mix of (a) undergraduate students who are enrolled in child development or education courses at local universities (acting as on-site tutors and research assistants), (b) graduate students who are majoring in the social sciences, (c) parents and other relatives of the children in the program, (d) local community members, and (e) university faculty who supervise the implementation of activities and conduct research at each site. Data are collected daily on the functioning of each site, especially of the children's activities and progress, and they include fieldnotes, field-developed measures, and audio and video recordings.

The most prominent characteristic of each site is the presence of various computers that are used by the children to play games or to fulfill other educational or communicative activities (see Figure 9.3). The computers serve as an important lure and motivate the children to attend the site regularly. The children's use of the computers is partially regulated, or mediated, by the activities specified in "task cards" found within a 20-room maze that is set up as a visual display on a table or bulletin board. The maze is used symbolically to represent the movement of children through several project activities. Their movement through the maze is recorded in "journey logs," which assess their progress. The newcomers usually start with the first room in the maze, although the selection of a room or an activity may vary depending on the age and expertise of the students. As they master the computer games or activities found in that room, they move progressively to the other rooms represented in the maze. Once they gain expertise, the students assume the expert role and assist novice members with their activities. Throughout, the adults encourage the children to solve problems, formulate goals, and make decisions that will move them

---

[13] As of this writing, the sites were located at various cities in the United States (in California, North Carolina, and Illinois), Mexico, Sweden, Denmark, Russia, Israel, and Australia.

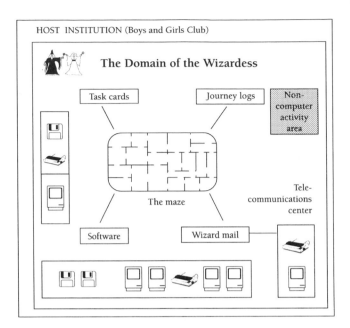

HOST INSTITUTION (Boys and Girls Club)

The Domain of the Wizardess

Task cards   Journey logs   Non-computer activity area

The maze

Tele-communications center

Software   Wizard mail

Figure 9.3. A schematic overview of the 5th Dimension maze and artifacts. (From Cole, 1996, p. 291.)

toward self-regulation, in the Vygotskian sense, within this 5th Dimension setting.

Multiple forms of mediation are found within each site, including personalized support and assistance with the daily tasks. The undergraduates play a key role, teaming with the youngsters to assist them with the activities and submitting field notes to document the children's progress. The site coordinators also play a key role in facilitating the site's functioning by solving problems that may occur during each session. But perhaps the most novel form of mediation is that which is provided by an imaginary "wizard," who can be contacted only though electronic mail and who helps monitor the functioning of the site by providing answers, making suggestions, and even settling disputes (see Figure 9.3). The true identity (and gender) of the wizard at each site is a closely guarded secret, but the students usually suspect that the site coordinator or one of the university students is playing the role of the invisible, all-knowing wizard behind the scenes.

As Cole (1995) describes it, the wizard is an important artifact for mediating power relations between adults and children at the sites. When conflicts or problems arise at the site, "adults as well as children write to the wizard to decide how matters should proceed. It is also important that by pretending to believe in the wizard the adults can collude with the children in the pretension of the wizard's existence and thereby enter into playful relations with them" (p. 177). This imaginary relationship with the wizard and those social relations formed by the other project participants (notably, those between undergraduate students and their younger peers) create multiple social situations for learning that are unlike those found in a typical classroom setting.

La Clase Mágica, although modeled after the 5th Dimension, represents a distinct innovation in its own right. A most

important change is that the site is bilingual in English and Spanish, so that children or any other person can participate in all activities in either language or in both. Another is that the wizard's identity has been adjusted accordingly, becoming El Maga (a neologism combining male and female morphemes), a bilingual and multicultural entity. As Vásquez (1993) explains:

> Transforming the Fifth Dimension was not a simple act of translation from English to Spanish but a fundamental change in the approach to the organization of the pedagogical activity. Although informed throughout by traditional Mexican cultural knowledge, the Fifth Dimension's evolution into La Clase Mágica was not based solely on the children's home culture, rather, it tapped the multiple knowledge sources available in the children's everyday life. Whenever possible, content knowledge and skills from such learning domains as the family, church, sports, and dance groups were written into tasks accompanying the games. The goal was to build upon the background knowledge of the children at the same time that a new set of experiences and a second language were introduced. (p. 208)

La Clase Mágica represents, therefore, a fundamentally new cultural setting, one that borrows strategically but differs significantly from the children's home culture and from the institutional culture of the 5th Dimension. Just as clearly, however, this setting is not meant to replace or replicate classrooms, especially the classrooms' structures. La Clase Mágica is a deliberate attempt to create an alternative and heterogeneous social situation for learning that mediates the children's access to learning tasks in dynamic ways. The children's experiences and background knowledge form part of the foundation of the site, something that is recognizable by all participants and that is validated daily through the routines and practices that constitute the setting.

Along similar lines, three other aspects of this activity system merit mentioning: the internal distribution of languages, the ties with the local community, and the more general "mediating structure." These aspects all have to do with the creation of "additive" conditions for teaching and learning. I refer here to the term *additive* in two ways. In a linguistic sense, the term denotes creating positive conditions to help children add a second language to their repertoire while developing their first language, a challenging task especially when a minority or socially marked language is involved—even under favorable conditions, such as La Clase Mágica (see Vásquez, 1993). I also refer to *additive* in a broader emotional sense that reflects creating conditions that are caring and nurturing and that fully accept the children and their identities. These additive emotional conditions not only accept the children's language and culture as a resource for learning but also allow children an "unmarked identity" while in the program, without any of the school designations and labels that mark someone as "minority," "different," or "deficient."

Most notable of these aspects, especially when considering the additive conditions, is the internal distribution of languages at the site. An important consequence of the particular cultural arrangement of La Clase Mágica is that, to a remarkable extent, language designations and fluency levels, which are so powerful in sorting children in schools, become irrelevant within the site's sociolinguistic context. That is to say, whether the child is monolingual in either Spanish or English or whether the child is bilingual, the tasks and routines that constitute La Clase Mágica accommodate the child. The specific language characteristics of the child never become a barrier to full participation within site. Language does not control or limit involvement because both languages are found everywhere, are fostered, and are used routinely in the performance of all tasks.

The links or ties that are fostered with the local community are also important. La Clase Mágica is an open cultural system where the participation of local residents is feasible and vital to the success of the site. The local residents, especially the children's families, not only represent an additional resource for teaching, contributing their knowledge and experiences, but also help establish on a daily basis the cultural identity of the site, how La Clase Mágica defines itself culturally through the nature and content of its routines. Furthermore, local community participants are also key allies in sustaining the site, helping to define it widely as a worthwhile educational experience for children. The long-term existence of such a nonschool setting depends crucially on the network of support it can generate and on how it can mediate existing constraints, especially given fluctuations in funding. The involvement of parents becomes an essential strategy to help perpetuate the site within its host setting, be it a local club, library, or church.

Finally, the site also functions as a broader "mediating structure" that helps participants establish contacts and linkages with other important educational settings, especially local colleges and universities. In particular, the students get to know personally the university students and faculty as they interact about social and academic matters for a prolonged amount of time (Vásquez, 1996). Building on the ideas of Vygotsky, Wells (1995) has suggested, and it applies well to La Clase Mágica, that "what we learn depends crucially on the company we keep, on what activities we engage in together, and how we do and talk about these activities" (p. 238).

Concluding Remarks

The ideas of Vygotsky have become central to any researcher interested in the cultural constitution of thinking, and his concept of mediation, especially through the actions and discourses of others, has become a key unit of analysis in the study of teaching. As Engeström (1993) has emphasized, however, and as the works cited in this article confirm, the cultural–historical tradition associated with Vygotsky "is not a fixed and finished body of strictly defined statements—it is itself an internationally evolving, multivoiced activity system" (p. 64).

I have summarized four major trends in research on teaching from a Vygotskian perspective and have described four distinct research programs to illustrate these trends. Combined, these programs represent innovative attempts to exploit the rich potential of a Vygotskian conception of thinking for the study of teaching. The first two types of studies (Raphael and colleagues; Goldenberg and colleagues) credit instructional discourse with great powers in the formation of the students' intellectual abilities. Both studies, each in its own way, emphasize that by changing the classroom's oral discourse—the register and genre that prevail within instructional situations—the lessons' potential meaning changes accordingly, creating more ad-

vanced learning opportunities for students. The claim is that the teacher's discourse, or the discourse that the teacher helps organize into lessons, is internalized by students and becomes the basis for subsequent independent actions or self-regulations. Both studies also emphasize, however, the development of carefully structured teaching activities—the medium for the discourse—within which the students actively engage in meaningful interactions with text and can also be provided with explicit information about dealings with texts.

In contrast, the third study (Hedegaard) emphasizes concepts as mediating tools, the children's deliberate elaboration of theoretical models to guide their actions and thinking, and the teacher's role in mediating these practices. The study builds around a double move in teaching, that of facilitating interactions between a developing theoretical model and the students' active research of empirical knowledge. As in the previous studies, Hedegaard's work also emphasizes the joint actions of teachers and students. In this instance, the joint action occurs in formulating and developing the activities that count as theoretical learning within the classroom, the primary objective of instruction.

The final study (Vásquez and colleagues) features a more distributed model of mediation, a cultural system that incorporates a multiplicity of semiotic means including an imaginary character, cross-age tutoring, and several informal routines that constitute the setting. Teaching within this setting is not the responsibility of a single adult. The teaching is distributed, becoming the obligation of all participants, including the children, and teaching is also assumed to occur in the interactions with computers.

Methodologically, all four studies relied primarily on extended observations in situ, with the investigators playing a formative role in the development of the activities under inquiry, well in line with Vygotsky's genetic or developmental approach. The primary concern was to document the nature of the activities, their constitutive practices and discourses, and the dynamics of change or development—of individuals and of the system of activities—over time. Clearly, to "situate" individual development in the sociocultural contexts or systems under study, as a Vygotskian approach requires, remains a considerable challenge.

Significantly, the last example (Vásquez) is the only one where culture explicitly plays a fundamental role in the conception of teaching. It is also, arguably, the only example where the children's personal characteristics are taken into account in the development of the instructional experiences. The three previous examples present more generic models of teaching where the cultural characteristics of the participants, the setting, the content, or the materials are not a central preoccupation. Certainly, however, part of the rationale for the development of Instructional Conversations as a teaching method is that such modes of interactions, with the emphasis on extended discourse and responsivity to student contributions, help the teacher to understand the knowledge, experiences, and values of the students. This understanding enables teachers to contextualize teaching in the cultural experiences of the learner (see also, Goldenberg, 1996). Nevertheless, considerations about culture seem to disappear when the focus is on the techniques of teaching or the general characteristics of discourse; the considerations seem to reappear when the emphasis is on multiple mediations as a characteristic of a social system or on institutional contexts within which we are asking children to learn.

However, the centrality of culture to Vygotskian-based research approaches to teaching may also be a function of the investigators and their particular interests. All four trends contain examples of research that foreground either the cultural experiences of teachers and students or teaching as a cultural practice (see, e.g., Alvarez & del Río, 1994; Moll & Greenberg, 1990; Moll, Tapia, & Whitmore, 1993; Rockwell, 1997). In general, however, it seems ironic that studies based on a cultural–historical theory of thinking may ignore the significance of culture within their specific contexts of study. A similar point has been made about the historical aspects of a cultural–historical approach (see Cole, 1995, 1996; Scribner, 1985). Both points represent important issues for clarification and elaboration in future studies of teaching.

Likewise, Gee (1996), has raised the issue of the lack of a critical perspective (in the political sense) within a Vygotskian approach, a perspective that is also central to the study of teaching. After all, institutions such as schools are not only pedagogical but also political sites with well-known structural constraints and biases, especially in relation to the social class configuration of the students. The point is that these institutional conditions also serve as distal but powerful mediating factors in determining why, how, and what children get to learn, and they represent the broader activity and ideological system within which teaching takes place. As Woolard and Schieffelin (1994) have argued, "The term ideology reminds us that the cultural conceptions we study are partial, contestable and contested, and interest-laden" (p. 58). They continue:

> A naturalizing move that drains the conceptual of its historical content, making it seem universally and /or timelessly true, is often seen as key to ideological processes. The emphasis of ideological analysis on the social and experiential origins of systems of signification counters this naturalization of the cultural. . . . (p. 58)

For similar reasons, Engeström (1993) has been particularly emphatic in proposing a collective but heterogeneous and variable activity system, a unified whole, as the primary unit of analysis without losing sight of active individuals, a prime concern of teaching. "If we take a closer and prolonged look at any institution," he writes, "we get a picture of a continuously constructed collective activity system that is not reducible to series or sums of individual discrete actions, although the human agency is necessarily realized in the forms of actions" (p. 66). His analysis, then, would integrate individuals, mediating tools and actions, institutional contexts, and the history of the systems of activity under inquiry. The theoretical danger of isolating mediated actions as the unit of study, as many Vygotskian studies might be tempted to do, is that "individual experience is described and analyzed as if consisting of relatively discrete and situated actions" while the system of which those actions are a part is either treated as an immutable given or barely described at all (Engeström 1993, p. 66; as cited by Cole, 1996, p. 333).

These more encompassing perspectives that include both (a) the dynamics of institutional contexts as organized systems of social practices and (b) the possibilities of meta-awareness and critique of these contexts and their practices are of particular relevance to studies that address the teaching or schooling of minority children, especially those that live in poverty. These children face special institutional practices such as the devaluation of their home language and culture or outright hostility and denigration by school personnel (see, e.g., Anyon, 1997), which must be addressed, or structurally mediated, to create favorable or additive instructional circumstances. Vásquez's emphasis on embedding the routines and practices of La Clase Mágica within those of the supportive local community and providing the children with a sense of cultural ownership of the resources facilitated by the program stems from concerns about the negative influences of these special institutional practices. As Serpell (1993) has pointed out, the "authority of the claim 'this is my language, my culture, my community' is simultaneously based in a sense of belonging (of being owned and accepted by the group) and in a sense of control (of owning the medium and hence having the power to use it skillfully and innovatively)" (p. 362).

A related issue is how differentially acquired mediational means may influence thinking (see Bain, 1996). Consider that not only is the Vygotskian claim about the social- or tool-mediated nature of learning, broadly speaking, but that his claim is much more context-specific. Vygotsky maintained that the intellectual tools children acquire are directly related to how they interact with others in specific sociocultural environments. He proposed that children internalize and transform the kind of help they receive from others and eventually use the same means of guidance to direct their own actions. Considering this claim, one realizes that the teaching of literacy or mathematics, the development of oral language within schools, or the development of bilingualism at home or school may differ radically depending on the social practices or relationships found within particular institutional contexts. I refer here to more than the general circumstances for learning. I refer to how the specific ideas, attitudes, emotions, and activities that constitute those circumstances control or mediate what literacy or mathematics, for example, may come to mean for children and how it may form part of their lives. In particular, considering that teaching is always affect laden, I am surprised that the study of emotions in relation to the internalization of mediational means such as literacy or mathematics has not been addressed very well in the Vygotskian literature, but it certainly may represent a crucial factor with powerful consequences for children's thinking (see Vygotsky, 1935/1994b).

The four research trends reviewed above suggest that research on teaching, at least as far as the Vygotskian-inspired analyses are concerned, is moving toward a more holistic, integrated understanding of teaching. This movement is manifested not only in the units of study connecting individuals and social context but also in the understanding of how specific social practices, discourse patterns, and uses of artifacts mediate the children's learning and development. An integrated understanding of teaching may fulfill the potential of Vygotsky's idea to provide a unifying framework for the study of human actions, including understanding how teaching, learning, and thinking relate to broader social, cultural, and historical circumstances.

REFERENCES

Aidarova, L. (1982). *Child development and education.* Moscow: Progress.

Aidman, E., & Leontiev, D. (1991). From being motivated to motivating oneself: A Vygotskian perspective. *Studies in Soviet Thought, 42*(2), 137–151.

Álvarez, A. (1997). *Hacia un currículum cultural: La vigencia de Vygotski en la educación* [Toward a cultural curriculum: The relevance of Vygotsky in education]. Madrid: Fundación Infancia y Aprendizaje.

Álvarez, A., & del Río, P. (Eds.). (1994). Education as cultural construction. In P. del Río, A. Álvarez, & J. V. Wertsch (General Editors), *Explorations in sociocultural studies* (Vol. 4). Madrid: Fundación Infancia y Aprendizaje.

Anyon, J. (1997). *Ghetto schooling: A political economy of urban educational reform.* New York: Teachers College Press.

Au, K. (1979). Using the experience-text-relationship method with minority children. *Reading Teacher, 32*(6), 677–679.

Au, K. (1990). Changes in a teacher's views of interactive comprehension instruction. In L. C. Moll (Ed.), *Vygotsky and education* (pp. 271–286). Cambridge, UK: Cambridge University Press.

Au, K., & Kawakami, A. J. (1984). Vygotskian perspectives on discussion processes in small group reading lessons. In P. L. Peterson, L. C. Wilkinson, & M. Hallinan (Eds.), *The social context of instruction: Group organization and group processes* (pp. 209–225). New York: Academic Press.

Bain, B. (1996). *Pathways to the peak of Mount Piaget and Vygotsky: Speaking and cognizing monolingually and bilingually.* Rome: Bulzoni Editore.

Bakhurst, D. (1986). Thought, speech and the genesis of meaning: On the 50th anniversary of Vygotsky's *Myslenie i Rec. Studies in Soviet Thought, 31,* 103–129.

Bakhurst, D. (1991). *Consciousness and revolution in Soviet philosophy.* Cambridge, UK: Cambridge University Press.

Bakhurst, D. (1995). On the social constitution of mind: Bruner, Ilyenkov, and the defence of cultural psychology. *Mind, Culture, and Activity, 2*(3), 158–171.

Baquero, R. (1996). *Vigotsky y el aprendizaje escolar [Vygotsky and school learning].* Buenos Aires: Aique.

Berk, L. (1994). Vygotsky's theory: The importance of make-believe play. *Young Children, 50*(1), 30–39.

Berk, L., & Winsler, A. (1995). *Scaffolding children's learning: Vygotsky and early childhood education.* Washington, DC: National Association for the Education of Young Children.

Bernstein, B. (1993). Foreword. In H. Daniels (Ed.), *Charting the agenda: Educational activity after Vygotsky* (pp. xiii–xxiii). London: Routledge.

Blanck, G. (1990). Vygotsky: The man and his cause. In L. C. Moll (Ed.), *Vygotsky and education* (pp. 31–58). Cambridge, UK: Cambridge University Press.

Bodrova, E., & Leong, D. (1996). *Tools of the mind: The Vygotskian approach to early childhood education.* Englewood Cliffs, NJ: Prentice Hall.

Brissiaud, R. (1994). Teaching and development: Solving missing addend problems using subtraction. *European Journal of Psychology of Education, 9*(4), 343–365.

Brown, A. (1992). Design experiments: Theoretical and methodological challenges in creating complex interventions in classroom settings. *The Journal of the Learning Sciences, 2*(2), 141–178.

Brown, A., & Campione, J. (1994). Guided discovery in a community of learners. In K. McGilly (Ed.), *Classroom lessons: Integrating cognitive theory and classroom practice* (pp. 229–270). Cambridge, MA: MIT Press and Bradford Books.

Brown, A., Metz, K., & Campione, J. (1996). Social interaction and individual understanding in a community of learners: The influence of Piaget and Vygotsky. In A. Tryphon & J. Vonèche (Eds.), *Piaget-Vygotsky: The social genesis of thought* (pp. 145–169). East Sussex, UK: Psychology Press.

Buzzeli, C. (1993). Morality in context: A sociocultural approach to enhancing young children's moral development. *Child and Youth Care Forum, 22*(5), 375–386.

Calviño, M., & de la Torre, C. (1996, January). *La historia despues de Vygotski: Una mirada desde lo vivencial* [The history after Vygotsky: A glance based on lived experiences]. Paper presented at the Conference in Honor of the Centenary of the Birth of L. S. Vygotsky, Havana, Cuba.

Candela, A. (1995). Consensus construction as a collective task in Mexican science classes. *Anthropology and Education Quarterly, 26*(4), 458–474.

Castorina, J. A., Ferreiro, E., Kohl de Oliveira, M., & Lerner, D. (1998). *Piaget-Vygotski: Contribuciones para replantear el debate [Piaget-Vygotski: Contributions to reopen the debate].* México, DF: Paidós.

Cazden, C. (1986). Classroom discourse. In M. C. Wittrock (Ed.), *Handbook of research on teaching* (pp. 432–463). New York: Macmillan.

Cazden, C. (1995). Selective traditions: Readings of Vygotsky in writing pedagogy. In D. Hicks (Ed.), *Discourse, learning, and schooling* (pp. 165–185). Cambridge, UK: Cambridge University Press.

Cazden, C., John, V., & Hymes, D. (Eds.). (1972). *Functions of language in the classroom.* New York: Teachers College Press.

Chang-Wells, G. L. M., & Wells, G. (1993). Dynamics of discourse: Literacy and the construction of knowledge. In E. Forman, N. Minick, & C. A. Stone (Eds.), *Contexts for learning* (pp. 58–90). Oxford, UK: Oxford University Press.

Clay, M., & Cazden, M. (1990). A Vygotskian interpretation of Reading Recovery. In L. C. Moll (Ed.), *Vygotsky and education* (pp. 206–222). Cambridge, UK: Cambridge University Press.

Cole, M. (1995). Cultural–historical psychology: A meso-genetic approach. In L. M. W. Martin, K. Nelson, & E. Tobach (Eds.), *Sociocultural psychology: Theory and practice of doing and knowing* (pp. 168–204). Cambridge, UK: Cambridge University Press.

Cole, M. (1996). *Cultural psychology.* Cambridge, MA: Harvard University Press.

Cole, M. (1997). *Using new information technologies in the creation of sustainable after-school literacy activities: From invention to maximizing the potential.* Third year report, July 1996–June 1997, submitted to the Andrew W. Mellon Foundation. University of California, San Diego: Laboratory of Comparative Human Cognition.

Cole, M., Engeström, Y., & Vásquez, O. (Eds.). (1997). *Mind, culture, and activity.* Cambridge, UK: Cambridge University Press.

Cole, M., & Scribner, S. (1974). *Culture and thought.* New York: Wiley.

Cousins, P. T., Díaz, E., Flores, B., & Hernández, J. (1995). Looking forward: Using a sociocultural perspective to reframe the study of learning disabilities. *Journal of Learning Disabilities, 28*(10), 656–663.

Daniels, H. (Ed.). (1993). *Charting the agenda: Educational activity after Vygotsky.* London: Routledge.

Daniels, H. (Ed.). (1996). *An introduction to Vygotsky.* London: Routledge.

Davydov, V. V. (1988a). Problem of child's mental development: Part 1. *Soviet Education, 30*(8), 44–97.

Davydov, V. V. (1988b). Problem of developmental teaching: Part 2. *Soviet Education, 30*(9), 1–81.

Davydov, V. V. (1988c). Problem of developmental teaching: Part 3. *Soviet Education, 30*(10).

Davydov, V. V. (1995). The influence of L. S. Vygotsky on education theory, research, and practice. *Educational Researcher, 24*(3), 12–21.

Davydov, V. V. (1997). Introduction: Lev Vygotsky and educational psychology. In L. S. Vygotsky, *Educational Psychology* (pp. xxi–xxxix). Boca Raton, FL: St. Lucie Press. (Original work published 1990)

Day, J., & Cordon, L. (1993). Static and dynamic measures of ability: An experimental comparison. *Journal of Educational Psychology, 85*(1), 75–82.

Díaz, R., & Berk, L. (Eds.). (1992). *Private speech: From social interaction to self-regulation.* Hillsdale, NJ: Lawrence Erlbaum Associates.

Díaz, R., & Berk, L. (1995). A Vygotskian critique of self-instructional training. *Development and Psychopathology, 7*(2), 369–392.

Díaz, R., Neal, C., & Vachio, A. (1991). Maternal teaching in the zone of proximal development: A comparison of low-risk and high-risk dyads. *Merrill-Palmer Quarterly Journal of Developmental Psychology, 37*(1), 83–108.

Dixon-Krauss, L. (Ed.). (1996). *Vygotsky in the classroom.* White Plains, NY: Longman.

Doise, W., Staerkle, C., & Clémence, A. (1996). Vygotsky in the East and the West. *Journal of Russian and East European Psychology, 34*(2), 67–96.

Donato, R., & McCormick, D. (1994). A sociocultural perspective on language learning strategies: The role of mediation. *The Modern Language Journal, 78*(4), 453–464.

Elhammoumi, M. (1997). *Socio-Historicocultural psychology: Lev Semenovich Vygotsky (1896–1934): Bibliographical notes.* Lanham, MD: University Press of America.

Elkonin, D. (1971). Toward the problem of stages in the mental development of the child. *Soviet Psychology, 10,* 538–653.

Engeström, Y. (1987). *Learning by expanding: An activity-theoretical approach to developmental research.* Helsinki, Finland: Orienta-Konsultit Oy.

Engeström, Y. (1993). Developmental studies of work as a testbench of activity theory: The case of primary care medical practice. In S. Chaiklin & J. Lave (Eds.), *Understanding practice: Perspective on activity and context* (pp. 64–103). Cambridge, UK: Cambridge University Press.

Englert, C., Rozendal, M., & Mariage, M. (1994). Fostering the search for understanding: A teacher's strategies for leading cognitive development in zones of proximal development. *Learning Disability Quarterly, 17*(3), 187–204.

Foley, J. (1991). Vygotsky, Bernstein, and Halliday: Towards a unified theory of L1 and L2 learning. *Language, Culture, and Curriculum, 4*(1), 17–42.

Forman, E. A., Minick, N., & Stone, C. A. (Eds.). (1993). *Contexts for learning: Sociocultural dynamics in children's development.* Oxford, UK: Oxford University Press.

Gallimore, R., & Goldenberg, C. (1992). Mapping teachers' zone of proximal development: a Vygotskian perspective on teaching and teacher training. In F. Oser, A. Dick, & J.-L. Patry (Eds.), *Effective and responsible teaching: The new synthesis* (pp. 203–221). San Francisco, CA: Jossey-Bass.

Gallimore, R., & Tharp, R. (1990). Teaching mind in society: Teaching, schooling, and literate discourse. In L. C. Moll (Ed.), *Vygotsky and education* (pp. 175–205). Cambridge, UK: Cambridge University Press.

Gavelek, J. R., & Raphael, T. E. (1996). Changing talk about text: New roles for teachers and students. *Language Arts, 73,* 182–192.

Gee, J. P. (1996). Vygotsky and current debates in education: Some dilemmas as afterthoughts to *Discourse, Learning, and Schooling.* In D. Hicks (Ed.), *Discourse, Learning, and Schooling* (pp. 269–282). Cambridge, UK: Cambridge University Press.

Gindis, B. (1995). The sociocultural implication of disability: Vygotsky's paradigm for special education. *Educational Psychologist, 30*(2), 77–81.

Glassman, M., & Zan, B. (1995). Moral activity and domain theory: An alternative interpretation of research with young children. *Developmental Review, 15*(4), 434–457.

Goldenberg, C. (1991). *Instructional conversations and their classroom application.* Washington, DC: Center for Applied Linguistics and the National Center for Research on Cultural Diversity and Second Language Learning.

Goldenberg, C. (1993). Instructional conversations: Promoting comprehension through discussion. *The Reading Teacher, 46,* 316–326. (Original work published 1992)

Goldenberg, C. (1996). Latin American immigration and U.S. schools. *Social Policy Report: Society for Research in Child Development, 10*(1), 1–30.

Goldenberg, C., & Sullivan, J. (1994). *Making change happen in a language-minority school: A search for coherence* (Educational Practice Report #13). Washington, DC: Center for Applied Linguistics.

González Rey, F. (1996, January). *L. S. Vygotski: Presencia y continuidad en el centenario de su nacimiento* [*L. S. Vygotsky: Presence and continuity in the centenary of his birth*]. Paper presented at the Conference in Honor of the Centenary of the Birth of L. S. Vygotsky, Havana, Cuba.

Gutierrez, K. D., Baquedano-López, P., & Álvarez, H. (2001). Literacy as hybridity: Moving beyond bilingualism in urban classrooms. In M. Reyes & H. Halcón (Eds.), *The best for our children: Critical perspectives of literacy for Latino students* (pp. 122–141). New York: Teachers College Press.

Gutiérrez, K., Baquedano-López, P., & Turner, M. G. (1997). Putting language back into language arts: When the radical middle meets the third space. *Language Arts, 74*(5), 368–378.

Harré, R. (1984). *Personal being: A theory for individual psychology.* Cambridge, MA: Harvard University Press.

Hedegaard, M. (1990). The zone of proximal development as the basis for instruction. In L. C. Moll (Ed.), *Vygotsky and education* (pp. 349–371). Cambridge, UK: Cambridge University Press.

Hedegaard, M. (1996). How instruction influences children's concepts of evolution. *Mind, Culture, and Activity, 3*(1), 11–24.

Hedegaard, M. (1998). Situated learning and cognition: Theoretical learning and cognition. *Mind, Culture, and Activity, 5*(2), 114–126.

Hedegaard, M. (1999). Activity theory and history teaching. Y. Engeström, R. Miettinen, & R-L. Punamäki (Eds.), *Perspectives on activity theory* (pp. 282–297). Cambridge, UK: Cambridge University Press.

Henderson, R., & Cunningham, L. (1994). Creating interactive sociocultural environments for self-regulated learning. In D. H. Schunk & B. J. Zimmerman (Eds.), *Self-regulation of learning and performance: Issues and educational applications* (pp. 255–281). Hillsdale, NJ: Lawrence Erlbaum Associates.

Hernández, J. (1993). Bilingual metacognitive development. *The Educational Forum, 57,* 350–358.

Hicks, D. (Ed.). (1996). *Discourse, Learning, and Schooling.* Cambridge, UK: Cambridge University Press.

Holland, D., & Cole, M. (1995). Between discourse and schema: Reformulating a cultural–historical approach to culture and mind. *Anthropology and Education Quarterly, 26*(4), 475–489.

Holzman, L. (1995). Creating developmental learning environments: A Vygotskian practice. *School Psychology International, 16*(2), 199–212.

John-Steiner, V. (1995). Cognitive pluralism: A sociocultural approach. *Mind, Culture, and Activity, 2*(1), 2–11.

John-Steiner, V., & Mahn, H. (1996). Sociocultural approaches to learning and development: A Vygotskian framework. *Educational Psychologist, 31*(3/4), 191–206.

John-Steiner, V., Panofsky, C., & Smith, L. (Eds.). (1994). *Sociocultural approaches to language and literacy.* Cambridge, UK: Cambridge University Press.

Jones, M. G., Rua, M., & Carter, G. (1997, March). *Science teachers' conceptual growth within Vygotsky's zone of proximal development.* Paper presented at the annual meeting of the American Educational Research Association, Chicago, IL.

Karpov, Y., & Bransford, J. (1995). L. S. Vygotsky and the doctrine of empirical and theoretical learning. *Educational Psychologist, 30*(2), 61–66.

Kozulin, A. (1990). *Vygotsky's psychology: A biography of ideas.* Cambridge, MA: Harvard University Press.

Kozulin, A. (1995). The learning process: Vygotsky's theory in the mirror of its interpretations. *School Psychology International, 16*(2), 117–129.

Kozulin, A. (1998). *Psychological tools: A sociocultural approach to education.* Cambridge, MA: Harvard University Press.

Lacasa, P., Cosano, C., & Reina, A. (1997). Aprendices en la zona de desarrollo próximo: ¿Quién y cómo? [Learners in the zone of proximal development: Who and how]. *Cultura y Educación, 6/7,* 9–29.

Lantolf, J. (1994). Sociocultural theory and second language learning: Introduction to the special issue. *Modern Language Journal, 8*(4), 418–420.

Lantolf, J., & Appel, G. (1994). (Eds.). *Vygotskian approaches to second language research.* Norwood, NJ: Ablex.

Lave, J. (1996). Teaching, as learning, in practice. *Mind, Culture, and Activity, 3*(3), 149–164.

Lave, J., & Wenger, E. (1991). *Situated learning: Legitimate peripheral participation.* Cambridge, UK: Cambridge University Press.

Lee, C. D., & Smagorinsky, P. (2000). *Vygotskian perspectives on literacy research: Constructing meaning through collaborative inquiry.* Cambridge, UK: Cambridge University Press.

Lima, E. S. (1995). Vygotsky in the international scene: A brief overview. *Anthropology and Education Quarterly, 26*(4), 490–499.

Lima, E. S. (1997). Replantear la cultura: Las ideas de Vygotski [Reconsidering culture: Vygotsky's ideas]. *Cultura y Educación, 5,* 5–19.

Lock, A. (1999). On the recent origin of symbolically-mediated language and its implications for psychological science. In M. C. Corballis & S. E. G. Lea (Eds.), *The descent of mind: Psychological perspectives on hominid evolution* (pp. 324–355). Oxford, UK: Oxford University Press.

Luria, A. (1978). *The making of mind.* Cambridge, MA: Harvard University Press.

Manning, B., & Payne, B. (1993). A Vygotskian-based theory of teacher cognition: Toward the acquisition of mental reflection and self-regulation. *Teaching and Teacher Education, 9*(4), 361–371.

Manning, B., White, C., Daugherty, M. (1994). Young children's private speech as a precursor to metacognitive strategy use during task engagement. *Discourse Processes, 17*(2), 191–211.

Martí, E. (1996). Mechanisms of internalisation and externalisation of knowledge in Piaget's and Vygotsky's theories. In A. Tryphon & J. Vonèche (Eds.), *Piaget-Vygotsky: The social genesis of thought* (pp. 57–83). East Sussex, UK: Psychology Press.

McCaslin Rohrkemper, M. (1989). Self-regulated learning and academic achievement: A Vygotskian view. In B. Zimmerman & D. Schunk (Eds.), *Self-regulated learning and academic achievement: Theory, research, and practice* (pp. 143–168). New York: Springer.

McDermott, R. P. (1976). *Kids make sense: An ethnographic account of the interactional management of success and failure in one first-grade classroom.* Unpublished doctoral dissertation, Stanford University, Stanford, CA.

Mehan, H. (1979). *Learning lessons.* Cambridge, MA: Harvard University Press.

Meltzer, L, & Reid, D. (1994). New directions in the assessment of students with special needs: The shift toward a constructivist perspective. *Journal of Special Education, 28*(3), 338–355.

Merced, N., & Coll, C. (Eds.). (1994). Teaching, learning and interaction. In P. del Río, A. Alvarez, & J. V. Wertsch (General Editors), *Explorations in sociocultural studies* (Vol. 3). Madrid: Fundación Infancia y Aprendizaje.

Minick, N. (1989). Mind and activity in Vygotsky's work: An expanded frame of reference. *Cultural Dynamics, 2*(2), 162–187.

Moll, L. C. (1990a). Introduction. In L. C. Moll (Ed.), *Vygotsky and education* (pp. 1–27). Cambridge, UK: Cambridge University Press.

Moll, L. C. (1990b). (Ed.). *Vygotsky and education.* Cambridge, UK: Cambridge University Press.

Moll, L. C. (1997). Vygotski, la educación, y la cultura en acción [Vygotsky, education, and culture in action]. In A. Álvarez (Ed.), *Hacia un currículum cultural: La vigencia de Vygotski en la educación* [Toward a cultural curriculum: The relevance of Vygotsky in education] (pp. 39–54). Madrid: Fundación Infancia y Aprendizaje.

Moll, L. C., Amanti, C., Neff, D., & González, N. (1992). Funds of knowledge for teaching: Using a qualitative approach to connect homes and classrooms. *Theory into Practice, 31*(2), 132–141.

Moll, L. C., & Díaz, S. (1987). Change as the goal of educational research. *Anthropology and Education Quarterly, 18*(4), 300–311.

Moll, L. C., & González, N. (1997). Teachers as social scientists: Learning about culture from household research. In P. M. Hall (Ed.), *Race, ethnicity and multiculturalism* (pp. 89–114). New York: Garland.

Moll, L. C., & Greenberg, J. (1990). Creating zones of possibilities: Combining social contexts for instruction. In L. C. Moll (Ed.), *Vygotsky and education* (pp. 319–348). Cambridge, UK: Cambridge University Press.

Moll, L. C., Tapia, J., & Whitmore, K. (1993). Living knowledge: The social distribution of cultural resources for thinking. In G. Salomon (Ed.), *Distributed cognitions: Psychological and educational considerations* (pp. 139–163). Cambridge, UK: Cambridge University Press.

Moll, L. C., & Whitmore, K. (1993). Vygotsky in classroom practice. In E. Forman, N. Minick, & C. A. Stone (Eds.), *Contexts for learning* (pp. 19–42). Oxford, UK: Oxford University Press.

Montero, I., & Huertas, J. A. (1997). Motivación en el aula [Motivation in the classroom]. In J. A. Huertas (Ed.), *Motivación: Querer aprender* [Motivation: Wanting to learn] (pp. 291–324). Buenos Aires: Aique.

Morenza, L. (1997). *Bases teóricas del aprendizaje: La escuela histórico-cultural, la escuela psicogenética, y el enfoque del procesamiento de la información* [Theoretical bases of learning: The cultural–historical school, the psychogenetic school, and the information processing focus]. Unpublished manuscript, University of Havana, Cuba.

Nelson, K. (1996). *Language in cognitive development.* Cambridge, UK: Cambridge University Press.

Newman, D., Griffin, P., & Cole, M. (1989). *The construction zone: Working for cognitive change in schools.* Cambridge, UK: Cambridge University Press.

Nicolopoulou, A. (1993). Play, cognitive development, and the social world: Piaget, Vygotsky, and beyond. *Human Development, 36*(1), 1–23.

Nicolopoulou, A., & Cole, M. (1993). Generation and transmission of shared knowledge in the culture of collaborative learning: The Fifth Dimension, its playworld, and its institutional contexts. In E. A. Forman, N. Minick, & C. A. Stone (Eds.), *Contexts for learning: Sociocultural dynamics in children's development* (pp. 283–314). New York: Oxford University Press.

Nuñes, T. (1992). Cognitive invariants and cultural variation in mathematical concepts. *International Journal of Behavioral Development, 15*(4), 433–453.

Nuñes, T. (1999). Mathematics learning as the socialization of mind. *Mind, Culture, and Activity, 6*(1), 33–52.

Odonnel, C., Tharp, R., & Wilson, K. (1993). Activity settings as the unit of analysis: A theoretical basis for community intervention and development. *American Journal of Community Psychology, 21*(4), 501–520.

Palincsar, A. M. (1986). The role of dialogue in providing scaffolded instruction. *Educational Psychologist, 21*(1 & 2), 73–98.

Pelissier, C. (1991). The anthropology of teaching and learning. *Annual Review of Anthropology, 20,* 75–95.

Philips, S. (1983). *The invisible culture: Communication in classroom and community on the Warm Springs Indian Reservation.* New York: Longman.

Pontecorvo, C. (1993). Forms of discourse and shared thinking. *Cognition and Instruction, 11*(3 & 4), 189–196.

Pontecorvo, C., & Girardet, H. (1993). Arguing and reasoning in understanding historical topics. *Cognition and Instruction, 11*(3 & 4), 365–395.

Portes, P. (1999). *Cultural historical theory and the practice of counseling and psychotherapy.* Paper presented at the annual meeting of the American Educational Research Association, Montreal, Canada.

Raphael, T. E. (1996, October). *Balanced instruction and the role of classroom discourse.* Paper presented at the Wingspread Conference on Balanced Instruction, Racine, WI.

Raphael, T. E., & Goatley, V. M. (1994). The teacher as "more knowledgeable other": Changing roles for teaching in alternative reading instruction programs. In C. Kinzer & D. Leu (Eds.), *Multidimensional aspects of literacy research, theory and practice* (pp. 527–536). Chicago: National Reading Conference.

Ratner, D. (1991). *Vygotsky's sociohistorical psychology and its contemporary applications.* New York: Plenum.

Rivière, A. (1984). La psicología de Vygotski: Sobre la larga proyección de una corta biografía [The psychology of Vygotsky: Regarding the long projection of a short biography]. *Infancia y Aprendizaje, 27–28*(3 & 4), 7–86.

Rockwell, E. (1997). La dinámica cultural en la escuela [The dynamics of culture in school]. In A. Álvarez (Ed.), *Hacia un currículum cultural: La vigencia de Vygotski en la educación* [Toward a cultural curriculum: The relevance of Vygotsky in education] (pp. 21–38). Madrid: Fundación Infancia y Aprendizaje.

Rodríguez Arocho, W. (1996). Vygotski, el enfoque sociocultural y el estado actual de la investigación cognoscitiva [Vygotsky, the sociocultural focus, and the actual state of cognitive research]. *Revista Latinoamericana de Psicología, 28*(3), 455–472.

Rogoff, B. (1990). *Apprenticeship in thinking: Cognitive development in social context.* Oxford, UK: Oxford University Press.

Rosa, A. (1997). De la defectología de Vygotski a la educación personalizada y especial [From Vygotsky's defectology to a personalized and special education]. In A. Álvarez (Ed.), *Hacia un currículum cultural: La vigencia de Vygotski en la educación* [Toward a cultural curriculum: The relevance of Vygotsky in education] (pp. 147–158). Madrid: Fundación Infancia y Aprendizaje.

Rosa, A., & Montero, I. (1990). The historical context of Vygotsky's work: A sociohistorical approach. In L. C. Moll (Ed.), *Vygotsky and education* (pp. 59–88). Cambridge, UK: Cambridge University Press.

Rosa, A., & Valsiner, J. (Eds.). (1994). Historical and theoretical discourse. In P. del Río, A. Álvarez, & J. V. Wertsch (General Editors), *Explorations in sociocultural studies* (Vol. 1). Madrid: Fundación Infancia y Aprendizaje.

Rueda, R. (1996). Language and culture in special education: The changing context. In L. Denti & J. Novak (Eds.), *Multicultures: A monograph on diversity in the field of education* (pp. 1–14). San Jose, CA: San Jose State University.

Rueda, R., Goldenberg, C., & Gallimore, R. (1991). *A manual for the use of the Instructional Conversation Rating Scale.* Unpublished manuscript.

Rueda, R., & Moll, L. C. (1994). A sociocultural perspective on motivation. In H. O'Neil & M. Drillings (Eds.), *Motivation: Theory and research* (pp. 117–137). Hillsdale, NJ: Lawrence Erlbaum Associates.

Saunders, W., & Goldenberg, C. (1996). Four primary teachers work to define constructivism and teacher-directed learning: Implications for teachers assessment. *The Elementary School Journal, 97*(2), 139–161.

Saunders, W., & Goldenberg, C. (1999). The effects of instructional conversations and literature logs on limited- and fluent-English-proficient students' story comprehension and thematic understanding. *The Elementary School Journal, 99*(4), 277–301.

Saunders, W., Goldenberg, C., & Hamann, J. (1992). Instructional conversations beget instructional conversations. *Teaching and Teacher Education, 8,* 199–218.

Saxe, G. (1991). *Culture and cognitive development: Studies in mathematical understanding.* Hillsdale, NJ: Lawrence Erlbaum Associates.

Schneider, P., & Watkins, R. (1996). Applying Vygotskian developmental theory to language intervention. *Language Speech and Hearing Services in Schools, 27*(2), 157–170.

Schustack, M., King, C., Gallego, M., & Vásquez, O. (1994). A computer-oriented after-school activity: Children's learning in the Fifth Dimension and La Clase Mágica. *New Directions for Child Development, 63,* Spring.

Scribner, S. (1985). Vygotsky's uses of history. In J. Wertsch (Ed.), *Communication, culture and cognition* (pp. 119–145). Cambridge, UK: Cambridge University Press.

Scribner, S. (1990a). A sociocultural approach to the study of mind. In C. Greenberg & E. Tobach (Eds.), *Theories of the evolution of knowing* (pp. 107–120). Hillsdale, NJ: Lawrence Erlbaum Associates.

Scribner, S. (1990b). Reflections on a model. *The Quarterly Newsletter of the Laboratory of Comparative Human Cognition, 12*(3), 90–94.

Scribner, S., & Cole, M. (1981). *The psychology of literacy.* Cambridge, MA: Harvard University Press.

Serpell, R. (1993). Interface between sociocultural and psychological aspects of cognition. In E. A. Forman, N. Minick, & C. A. Stone (Eds.), *Contexts for learning: Sociocultural dynamics in children's development* (pp. 357–381). Oxford, UK: Oxford University Press.

Shotter, J. (1993a). Bakhtin and Vygotsky: Internalization as a boundary phenomenon. *New Ideas in Psychology, 11*(3), 379–390.

Shotter, J. (1993b). Vygotsky: The social negotiation of semiotic mediation. *New Ideas in Psychology, 11*(1), 61–75.

Sierpinska, A. (1993). The development of concepts according to Vygotsky. *Focus on Learning Problems in Mathematics, 15*(2 & 3), 87–107.

Sinha, C. (1989). Reading Vygotsky. *History of the Human Sciences, 2*(3), 309–331.

Smagorinsky, P. (1995). The social construction of data: Methodological problems investigating learning in the zone of proximal development. *Review of Educational Research, 65*(3), 191–212.

Smagorinsky, P., & Coppock, J. (1995). The reader, the text, the context: An exploration of a choreographed response to literature. *Journal of Reading Behavior, 27*(3), 271–298.

Spindler, G. (Ed.). (1974). *Education and cultural process.* New York: Holt, Rinehart & Winston.

Spindler, G. (Ed.). (1982). *Doing the ethnography of schooling: Educational anthropology in action.* New York: Holt, Rinehart & Winston.

Stetsenko, A. (1993). Vygotsky: Reflections on the reception and further development of his thought. *Multidisciplinary Newsletter for Activity Theory, 13/14,* 38–45.

Terré, O., & Bell, R. (1995). *La psicología cognitiva contemporanea y sus implicancias en el aprendizaje [Contemporary cognitive psychology and its implications for learning].* Lima, Perú: Ediciones Libro Amigo.

Tharp, R., & Gallimore, R. (1988). *Rousing minds to life.* Cambridge, UK: Cambridge University Press.

Tharp, R., Jordan, C., Speidel, G., Au, K., Klein, T., Calkins, R., Sloat, K, & Gallimore, R. (1984). Product and process in applied developmental research: Education and the children of minority. In M. E. Lamb, A. L. Brown, & B. Rogoff (Eds.), *Advances in developmental psychology* (Vol. III, pp. 91–144). Hillsdale, NJ: Lawrence Erlbaum Associates.

Trent, S. C., Artiles, A. J., & Englert, C. S. (1998). From deficit thinking to social constructivism: A review of theory, research and practice in special education. *Review of Research in Education, 23,* 277–307.

Tryphon, A., & Vonèche, J. (Eds.). (1996). *Piaget-Vygotsky: The social genesis of thought.* East Sussex, UK: Psychology Press.

Tudge, J. (1992). Processes and consequences of peer collaboration: A Vygotskian analysis. *Child Development, 63*(6), 1364–1379.

Valsiner, J. (1988). *Developmental psychology in the Soviet Union.* Sussex, UK: The Harvester Press.

Van der Veer, R., & Valsiner, J. (1991). *Understanding Vygotsky.* London: Blackwell.

Van der Veer, R., & Valsiner, J. (1994). *The Vygotsky reader.* London: Blackwell.

Vásquez, O. (1993). A look at language as a resource: Lessons from La Clase Mágica. In M. B. Arias & U. Casanova (Eds.), *Bilingual education: Politics, practice, and research* (Ninety-second Yearbook of the National Society for the Study of Education, Part 2, pp. 199–224). Chicago: University of Chicago Press.

Vásquez, O. (1994). The magic of La Clase Mágica: Enhancing the learning potential of bilingual children. *Australian Journal of Language and Literacy, 17*(2), 120–128.

Vásquez, O. (1996). A model system of institutional linkages: Transforming the educational pipeline. In A. Hurtado, R. Figueroa, & E. Garcia (Eds.), *Strategic interventions in education: Expanding the Latina/Latino perspective* (pp. 137–166). Santa Cruz: Regents of the University of California, University of California, Santa Cruz.

Vygotsky, L. S. (1962). *Thought and language.* Cambridge, MA: MIT Press.

Vygotsky, L. S. (1963). Learning and mental development at school age. In B. Simon & J. Simon (Eds.), *Educational psychology in the USSR* (pp. 21–34). Stanford, CA: Stanford University Press. (Original work published 1934)

Vygotsky, L. S. (1978). *Mind in society.* Cambridge, MA: Harvard University Press.

Vygotsky, L. .S. (1981). The genesis of higher mental functions. In J. V. Wertsch (Ed.), *The concept of activity in Soviet psychology* (pp. 144–188). Armonk, NY: Sharpe.

Vygotsky, L. S. (1982). *La imaginación y el arte en la infancia [Imagination and art in infancy].* Madrid: Akal.

Vygotsky, L. S. (1986). *Thought and language* (Revised edition). Cambridge, MA: MIT Press.

Vygotsky, L. S. (1987). *The Collected Works of L. S. Vygotsky: Vol. 1. Problems of general psychology* (R. Rieber & A. Carton, Eds.; N. Minick, trans.). New York: Plenum.

Vygotsky, L. S. (1993). *The Collected Works of L. S. Vygotsky: Vol. 2. The fundamentals of defectology* (R. Rieber & C. Stevens, Eds.; J. Knox & C. Stevens, trans.). New York: Plenum.

Vygotsky, L. S. (1994a). The development of academic concepts in school aged children. In R. Van der Veer & J. Valsiner (Eds.), *The Vygotsky reader* (pp. 355–370). Oxford, UK: Blackwell. (Original work published 1934)

Vygotsky, L. S. (1994b). The problem of the environment. In R. Van der Veer & J. Valsiner (Eds.), *The Vygotsky reader* (pp. 339–354). Oxford, UK: Blackwell. (Original work published 1935)

Vygotsky, L. S. (1997a). *Educational Psychology.* Boca Raton, FL: St. Lucie Press. (Original work published 1926)

Vygotsky, L. S. (1997b). *The Collected Works of L. S. Vygotsky: Vol. 3. Problems of the theory and history of psychology* (R. Rieber & J. Wollock, Eds.; R. van der Veer, trans.). New York: Plenum.

Vygotsky, L. S. (1997c). *The Collected Works of L. S. Vygotsky: Vol. 4. The history of the development of higher mental functions* (R. Rieber, Ed.; M. J. Hall, trans.). New York: Plenum.

Vygotsky, L. S. (1998). *The Collected Works of L. S. Vygotsky: Vol. 5. Child psychology* (R. Rieber, Ed.; M. J. Hall, trans.). New York: Plenum.

Vygotsky, L. S. (1999). *The Collected Works of L. S. Vygotsky: Vol. 6. Scientific legacy* (R. Rieber, Ed.; M. J. Hall, trans.). Dordrecht, The Netherlands: Kluwer Academic/Plenum Publishers.

Wagner, D. A., & Stevenson, H. W. (Eds.). (1982). *Cultural perspectives on child development.* San Francisco: Freeman.

Wells, G. (1994). The complementary contributions of Halliday and Vygotsky to a "language-based theory of learning." *Linguistics and Education, 6,* 41–90.

Wells, G. (1995). Language and the inquiry-oriented curriculum. *Curriculum Inquiry, 25*(3), 233–269.

Wells, G. (1996). Using the tool-kit of discourse in the activity of learning and teaching. *Mind, Culture, and Activity, 3*(2), 74–101.

Wells, G. (1999). *Dialogic inquiry: Toward a sociocultural practice and theory of education.* Cambridge, UK: Cambridge University Press.

Wertsch, J. (1985). *Vygotsky and the social formation of mind.* Cambridge, MA: Harvard University Press.

Wertsch, J. (1991). *Voices of the mind.* Cambridge, MA: Harvard University Press.

Wertsch, J. V., & Ramírez, J. D. (Eds.). (1994). Literacy and other forms of mediation action. In P. del Río, A. Álvarez, & J. V. Wertsch (General Editors), *Explorations in sociocultural studies* (Vol. 2). Madrid: Fundación Infancia y Aprendizaje.

Wittrock, M. (Ed.). (1986). *Handbook of research on teaching.* New York: Macmillan.

Wilson, A., & Weinstein, L. (1992a). An investigation into some implications of a Vygotskian perspective on the origins of mind: Psychoanalysis and Vygotskian psychology, 1. *Journal of the American Psychoanalytic Association, 40*(2), 349–379

Wilson, A., & Weinstein, L. (1992b). Language and the psychoanalytic process: Psychoanalysis and Vygotskian psychology, 2. *Journal of the American Psychoanalytic Association, 40*(3), 725–759

Wilson, A., & Weinstein, L. (1996). The transference and the zone of proximal development. *Journal of the American Psychoanalytic Association, 44*(1), 167–200.

Wood, D. (1998). *How children think and learn* (2nd ed). Oxford, UK: Blackwell.

Woolard, K., & Schieffelin, B. (1994). Language ideology. *Annual Review of Anthropology, 23,* 55–83.

Yaroshevsky, M. (1989). *Lev Vygotsky.* Moscow: Progress Publishers.

Part 2
Methodology

10.

Critical Issues, Current Trends, and Possible Futures in Quantitative Methods

John Crawford
Millard Public Schools, Omaha, Nebraska

James C. Impara
University of Nebraska at Lincoln

Our charge for this chapter is to review recent developments in quantitative methods in research on teaching. We have taken an approach that focuses on several critical issues and examines the recent work. We also put forth suggested methods and questions for the future of the research endeavor.

One cannot deal with quantitative methods (or qualitative methods, for that matter) without also dealing with the nature of the questions to be addressed by the research. The diversity within the community of research on teaching is reflected in the editorial by Donmoyer (1996) in which he discusses the proliferation of paradigms, ranging from the traditional to proposals "for counting fictional narratives as educational research" (a reference to Eisner, 1993). Although our intent is not to critique qualitative methods in this chapter, we will contend that those who are, or should be, the consumers of research on teaching have many needs and concerns that are most appropriately addressed through what are usually termed quantitative methods.

Who are the stakeholders in research on teaching? Who is the intended audience, either immediate or more removed? Our contention is that if research on teaching is to inform and improve both teaching and student performance, then it needs a better connection to the concerns of the 15,000-plus public school districts and school boards in our nation. Fictional narrative presented as educational research at a school board meeting would be interesting to see.

If, however, the ultimate audience for the output of research on teaching is the research community itself (about four-fifths of whom are affiliated with higher education, according to AERA membership), then attending to concerns of school boards, teachers, administrators, and superintendents would become less important.

What are the concerns of school boards, teachers, administrators, and superintendents? Pick up almost any issue of *Education Week,* and you will find school districts dealing with decisions about (a) curricula and programs that affect (or purport to affect) student achievement (often as measured with traditional, standardized achievement tests); (b) cost issues—in particular, the degree to which taxpayers and board members in a district or a state believe that they are getting a fair return on each tax dollar; (c) standards, typically content standards; and (d) performance assessments, often driven by the relatively new notion of measuring the attainment of content standards.

Although we do not claim to know the critical issues in all school districts, we can say that from many years of experience in urban, suburban, small town, and rural districts, we would have difficulty arguing against the perception that the above four broad areas are prominent. In addition, the most recent Phi Delta Kappa (PDK)/Gallup poll (Rose, Gallup, & Elam, 1997) provides empirical backup for our assertion that considerable societal value is placed on the above-named issues.

Accordingly, we have organized this chapter to consider what we believe to be critical issues and topics that can be addressed by quantitative research. The major sections include discussion of the following:

The authors appreciate the comments and suggestions by N. L. Gage, Professor Emeritus, Stanford University, on an early draft; still, any shortcomings should be attributed solely to the authors.

- The importance of having between-group comparisons when estimating program effects on outcomes
- The contribution of meta-analysis to discovering consistent, replicable trends and understanding educational effects and relationships
- An assessment of the findings of a large-scale, statewide experiment (the Tennessee study of class size)
- The dependability of performance assessments and whether those assessments are up to the task of determining student competencies in a high-stakes context
- The relationship of measurement to research design and statistical analysis issues
- The considerations in using psychometric decision-rules in placing students into groups (such as mastery versus non-mastery)
- A survey of presenters who were on the Division K (Teaching and Teacher Education) program of AERA, Spring 1997—conducted primarily to gain an understanding of the methods used by current practitioners of research on teaching
- An in-depth analysis of a study on teacher attitudes toward different kinds of research

The final section brings together the earlier sections and suggests directions for future research.

Inferring Program Effects: The Need for Between-Group Studies

Public schools have limited budgets. When trying out new instructional programs or curricula, decision makers want to know whether identified outcomes have been improved as a consequence of implementing the new intervention. Although the debate on qualitative versus quantitative methods may be active in the AERA community, that debate may not be central to the largest problem in public school evaluations. Of major concern is the typical lack of comparison groups (of any kind) in program evaluations.

One doctrine that has not changed in the years since Campbell and Stanley (1963) and Cook and Campbell (1979) is that we are on shaky ground when we try to infer causality from evaluations of single-groups only using pretest and posttest. Unfortunately, this design is the most common one in public school evaluations. In such evaluations, a new program or curriculum is put in place in a pilot setting, with assessments administered at the beginning and end of the pilot (and teachers are obviously aware that they are part of the pilot). Then, (typically positive) gains on the preassessment and postassessment are attributed to the pilot program.

Process data, when present, may consist of interviews of a small number of implementers or surveys of larger numbers of participants. This is the typical evaluation. The absence of a control or comparison group and the use of the same instrument for both pretest and posttest usually guarantees an apparent positive effect on student learning. The decision on whether to continue or expand the program may then rest on costs and opinion about implementation (because positive gains, most likely, will have been achieved). Certainly, cost and implementation are important issues, but most decision makers would also

say that they wanted (and thought they were getting) a good assessment of gain in student achievement as part of the evaluation of the program.

Certainly, exceptions vary from the typical example described above, but this scenario prevails in the vast majority of cases—at least when some type of systematic evaluation is done. The single-group evaluations, with pretests and posttests of Title I programs, are a major case in point (deriving from Tallmadge & Wood, 1978). Unfortunately, positive pre-to-post gains of the students in those programs may be due as much to student maturation, increased familiarity with the test items, or factors unrelated to the program as they are attributable to the program itself.

The difficulty in inferring cause and effect has been the basis for the gold standard of true experiments (involving random assignment to treatment and control groups) in medical research. In recent years, a whole field of medical research has evolved to estimate the size of the placebo effect. The single-group design based on pre-to-post gains in education is essentially indistinguishable from the placebo effect of medical research. Students grow and learn and mature, just as patients sometimes recover in the absence of any real medical treatment. The magnitude of the placebo effect (both in medicine and in education) illustrates the importance of having comparison-group performance to estimate the effect of any treatment.

Moertel, Taylor, Roth, and Tyce (1976) found that 39% of 288 cancer patients reported 50% or more pain relief from placebos. Patients who had a higher level of education, or were farmers, or had a professional occupation, or were women working outside the home and patients who were widowed, separated, or divorced tended to have a higher-than-average placebo response. In a study of antidepressant medications, Wilcox et al. (1992) found that placebo responses varied from an approximate 20% rate up to a rate of 40.8%, depending on patient characteristics and the severity of the illness (patients with milder symptoms had higher placebo response rates).

Turner, Deyo, Loeser, Von Korff, and Fordyce (1994), examined several studies on pain treatment and concluded that placebo effects could be higher than the often-cited one-third of patients demonstrating the response. They found three studies showing positive response to the placebo in the 50–70% improvement range and four studies reporting that from 85% to 100% improved in the placebo condition. Some literature has begun to address the potential of using the placebo effect to improve patients' prognoses outside of the research setting (see e.g., Blair, 1996). Without this research on the magnitude of the placebo effects, determining the true magnitude of the treatment effects under study would be impossible.

One example from educational evaluation may serve to illustrate the importance of having between-group (comparative) data on the effect of educational programs. As standards come to be articulated as specific cut scores on assessments, schools will be identifying students who score below the standard and, therefore, need remediation. Only if the standards remain as content or skill statements *without* accompanying assessment, will this reliance on measurement of standards not arise as an issue. Districts will be very interested in effective programs for getting students up to standards.

Crawford and Brady (1998) evaluated a grant-funded summer school program that was designed to remediate elementary, middle, and high school students' weaknesses in language arts and math. Students were identified as needing remediation during the 1995–96 and 1996–97 school years through assessments with cut scores set by the Angoff method (Angoff, 1971). The Angoff procedures involve judges (teachers) who examine items and estimate the performance of a "just competent" student on each item. Then those item estimations are aggregated to yield a total cut score on the test.

Because not all lower-achieving students were served through the grant-funded summer school, some students, similar to those who were in summer school, did not receive the additional instruction. However, all lower-achieving students did receive some special attention during the school year prior to summer, usually through within-class activities. The reading and math assessments were given in the fall semester, and the writing assessment was given in the spring of each year. Students attending summer school had been identified by test scores, nominated by staff members, and had parents who agreed to the intervention.

Following the 4-week summer school, students were assessed again during the regular school year to see how many scored above the cut scores after the summer school intervention. Consider the following data in Tables 10.1 and 10.2 on the performance of students who participated in the summer school program.

From these data, which are based on just those students in the summer school program, it would be difficult to answer this question: How effective was the summer school intervention? Certainly, the two analyses (seventh- and tenth-grade math), which show 100% of the students above the cut score (following the summer school intervention), make the program appear to be effective, at least at those grade levels, in math. Yet, other students, similarly low achieving, received regular classroom instruction in language arts and math during the school year, which also could have effectively remediated their weaknesses.

Therefore, it was possible to create matched groups of students, for each analysis, in the same grade levels, who had precisely the same pre-achievement scores (before summer) as the intervention students. The comparison students were also matched on free-lunch status. Although it is always possible to envision other potentially important variables as confounding factors, at least we can be assured that the groups being compared were similar on pre-achievement and on a measure representing socioeconomic status. In one set of post hoc analyses, the investigators tested the additional hypothesis that the two groups might differ on the percentage of students in special education. Those post hoc analyses did not show differences in that special education percentage.

Now, reconsider the data in Tables 10.1 and 10.2 by examining the performance of the matched comparison groups alongside the groups of students receiving the summer school treatment, in Tables 10.3 and 10.4.

The data that include the matched comparison-groups create a different picture from that presented by the treatment group alone. Although the seventh- and tenth-grade math analyses did show statistically significant differences, a descriptive view of the findings in a cost-benefit frame may be more enlightening than the probability that group differences could have occurred

Table 10.1. Elementary School Results for Students in Summer School Program

Subject	Percent Above Cut Score
1996–97	
4th Grade Reading Comprehension	51.3%
4th Grade Analytical Writing	78.9%
1997–98	
4th Grade Reading Comprehension	61.1%
5th Grade Mathematics	70.2%

Table 10.2. Middle and High School Results for Students in Summer School Program (1997–98)

Subject	Percent Above Cut Score
7th Grade Mathematics	100%
7th Grade Reading Comprehension	82.1%
10th Grade Mathematics	100%

Table 10.3. Elementary School Results

	Percent Above Cut Score	
Subject	Students in Summer School Program	Students Not in Summer School Program
1996–97		
4th Grade Reading Comprehension	51.3%	47.2%
4th Grade Analytical Writing	78.9%	66.7%
1997–98		
4th Grade Reading Comprehension	61.1%	50.0%
5th Grade Mathematics	70.2%	62.2%

Table 10.4. Middle and High School Results (1997–98)

	Percent Above Cut Score	
Subject	Students in Summer School Program	Students Not in Summer School Program
7th Grade Mathematics	100%	82.4%
7th Grade Reading Comprehension	82.1%	82.9%
10th Grade Mathematics	100%	75.0%

by chance. If we average the posttreatment, above-standard percentage by organizational level, then we would see results as shown in Table 10.5.

The grant provided $799,220 for services for 3,290 students (across 3 years). This grant represents an expenditure of about $243 dollars per pupil. Although this amount may not seem to be a large sum, it does equal 5% of the current total per-pupil expenditure in this school district. Accordingly, a worthwhile and interesting question is "How much improvement resulted

Table 10.5. Elementary and Middle/High School Results for Students in Summer School Program

Organizational Level	Percent Above Cut Score
Elementary	65.4%
Middle/High	94.0%

Table 10.6. Actual Improvement Over Status Quo for Students in Summer School Program

Organizational Level	Treatment	Control	Difference
Elementary	65.4%	56.5%	8.9%
Middle/High	94.0%	80.1%	13.9%

as a consequence of the program?" In the absence of any comparison group, we might be tempted to cite the 65% and 94% figures, representing the proportion of students who were above standards after the summer treatment. However, the actual improvement over the status quo is illustrated in Table 10.6.

In this context, we see that the additional 5% expenditure was associated with an additional 9–14% of students achieving standards. Whether this is a good expenditure of funds may now become a considered value judgement in relation to other alternatives. If we had similar data on other remediation programs (such as special in-class programs, before- or after-school programs, or intensive small-group pullout programs), the board could make an informed decision on the likely greatest benefit per dollar spent. This approach to informed decision making could even result in the conclusion that different remediation programs work best in different grade levels and subject matter areas. (We should note here that regression-to-the-mean effects could have contributed to making both the treatment and control group students score higher after being preselected as relatively low achieving. This possibility is discussed in greater detail later in this chapter.) The main point is that, without a status quo comparison group, estimating the magnitude of treatment effects is impossible. Although an assessment of the percentage above standards of a status quo, no-special-treatment group is not precisely the same as the placebo effect in medicine, it is closely analogous. Patients improve, sometimes without efficacious treatment, and students grow and learn even in the absence of special interventions.

In programmatic work spanning many years, Robert Slavin has carried out a particular version of meta-analysis, "best-evidence synthesis," that gives explicit attention to the importance of between-group comparisons. Slavin's (1986) adaptation of meta-analysis codifies inclusion-criteria for the studies assessed through meta-analytic methods. It facilitates the researcher's ability to formulate a decision-rule that takes methodological adequacy into account. Not only does the method allow rational exclusion of studies based on scope of time (for example, as in brief, lab-type settings) and external validity of the original studies, but also it allows one to elevate the critical importance of between-group evaluation to the highest level of concern in the literature synthesis.

Many factors conspire to make difficult the random assignment of subjects to treatment conditions in educational research. For example, in the previously discussed summer school evaluation, parental agreement (choice) precluded a truly random assignment of students to the summer school program. However, it would not be unreasonable to base a meta-analytic review on just those studies that use true random assignment and also include quasi-experimental work that uses the thoughtful matching of subjects on what are believed to be critical variables related to the outcome of interest. Such "best-evidence" analysis should yield results in which we can have greater confidence than those analyses giving equal weight to studies that use no matching or those that are poorly matched, between-group comparisons (or, worse yet, those that use no comparison groups at all).

Using best-evidence methods, Slavin and others have tackled some of the more significant issues under debate in the educational community. For example, Slavin (1990) addressed the use of ability grouping in secondary schools, finding no evidence that favored the use of ability grouping, despite common practice. Whether students were high or low in prior ability and no matter what the subject area was, Slavin found no evidence favoring ability grouping. In one subject (social studies), Slavin did identify a trend in which heterogeneous placement was more effective. This analysis examined 6 random-assignment experiments, 9 quasi-experiments using matching, and 14 correlational studies using statistical controls.

However, Slavin (1987a) did examine ability grouping in elementary grades and did find some evidence of effects, depending on context. Cross-grade ability grouping in reading and within-class ability grouping in math were associated with positive effects on student achievement.

Using best-evidence methods, Slavin's (1987b) analysis of the mastery-learning literature supported the conclusion that group-based mastery learning methods had no effect on standardized achievement test performance. Evidence of effects on experimenter-made assessments (those made by proponents of mastery learning) was positive, but not enduring. This meta-analysis sparked debate with Guskey (1987) and Anderson and Burns (1987)—a debate that may not be resolved, depending on one's philosophical stance on the appropriateness of standardized achievement tests in this context. At a minimum, though, Slavin's work threw a cautionary note over some of the claims being made for the effectiveness of mastery learning.

Another much-debated area (still, in the 1990s, as it was in the 1970s and 1980s) concerns mainstreaming of special education students. Madden and Slavin (1983) helped inform policymakers by their assessment of methodologically adequate studies of special education students' programming. Their findings favored regular-class placement of special education students for all achievement, behavioral, and social or emotional outcomes. Taken together, findings from the best-evidence adaptation of meta-analysis has made important contributions to research on teaching and to the broader concerns of educational and policy research.

Meta-Analyses and Large-Scale Studies on Resource Effects and Class Size

According to Elmore and Woehlke (1996), meta-analytic methods became the method of choice for *Review of Educational Research* articles for the period from 1978 to 1995. These powerful methods, now used ubiquitously in the social and health sciences, afford the opportunity to delve into a large literature and extract underlying, consistent findings. One of the original propositions of this chapter was that such methods should continue to be used in research on teaching to address social and educational questions of importance. The large number of published meta-analyses on significant topics range broadly from specific instructional-program effects to basic research questions.

For example, the expenditure of funds to incorporate computers into classrooms for student use has been questioned by some. Recently, Khalili and Shashaani (1994) carried out a meta-analysis that followed up earlier work to demonstrate, again, that computer-assisted instruction does meaningfully improve student achievement. Additionally, the ongoing debate regarding the apportionment of nature and nurture effects on IQ is addressed by Devlin, Daniels, and Roeder (1997) in *Nature*. They used results from 212 studies in a sophisticated test of functionally distinct covariance models and concluded that previous heritability estimates have been too high. Their results show heritability at less than 50% and an increased estimate of in utero environmental effects, thereby presenting evidence against much of the basis of *The Bell Curve* (Herrnstein & Murray, 1994), which depends on heritability in the 60–80% range.

The list of examples goes on, but to chronicle the educational questions considered through meta-analysis would take a book-length treatise (or, more likely, several book-length volumes). Our focus here is much more limited. We will spend some time examining the debates on educational–production–functions and class size. The questions concerning input–output production functions deal with whether resources (inputs) are demonstrably associated with student (or school, or district) performance (outputs), as measured typically with standardized achievement tests. This debate ranges from academic journals to state legislatures to front-page news headlines to school tax referendum elections.

We also link the work on the question "Does money matter?" to the class-size research. That linkage exists because 80–85% of school district budgets are typically devoted to salary and benefits, and most of that portion (usually 60–70% and more) consists of teacher salaries. So to ask about the relationship of per-pupil expenditures and student performance is to ask a question with some dependence on class size. (Certainly, the differences in pay scales among geographical regions contribute to variation in per-pupil expenses, but within a state or within a district, much of the variability in costs is affiliated with average class sizes. Most would agree that raising or lowering class size has an effect on budgets.)

One of the more recent public debates in the research community on the magnitude of the education productivity function pits Hedges and colleagues against Hanushek in *Educational Researcher* during 1994 (Hedges, Laine, & Greenwald, 1994a, 1994b; Hanushek, 1994) and in *Review of Educational Research* during 1996 (Greenwald, Hedges, & Laine, 1996a, 1996b; Hanushek, 1996). Reading the point–counterpoint and some near (or actual) ad hominem attacks, one is tempted to applaud Tanner (1998), who poked fun at the debaters. But the seriousness of the contention that resources do not matter and the far-ranging character of that controversy outside the research community pushes us to consider the issue. One is also tempted to suggest that educational research should have been the centerpiece of a recent article (Begley, 1997) pointing out that researcher attitudes, opinions, philosophies, and colleague alignments have a substantive effect on research findings. However, educational research was not mentioned; that article focused on "hard science" disciplines.

We come down on the side of Hedges and colleagues that resources *do* matter in education, because of certain methodological and statistical considerations, class-size research (to be discussed shortly), and common sense. In the 1994 and 1996 publications, Hedges and his colleagues addressed the major criticisms that Hanusek made of their work. In the 1994 *Educational Researcher* article (Hedges, Laine, & Greenwald, 1994a), Hedges made the following points:

- Hanushek's vote-counting methods were imprecise and, in this instance, incorrect in estimating aggregate effects, whereas the combined-significance tests and effect-size tests of Hedges' meta-analyses yielded less-biased assessments of effects.
- Hedges appropriately did not make use of poorly reported studies (the authors of this chapter agree with this approach attending to studies that meet certain methodological criteria). This is similar to Slavin's rational rule-governed culling of studies.
- Hanushek's complaint about the lack of independence in the body of findings was addressed by Hedges et al. (1994a) in their reanalysis (by creating independent subsets of data).
- Hedges acknowledged the heterogeneity of *p*-values in their data and presented evidence that the positive effects still overwhelm the negative effects. (The authors of this chapter note that it is not uncommon in medicine and other fields to have conflicting individual studies, hence, the need for sensitive synthesis methods.)
- Hanushek's contention that Hedges et al. came to the debate with personal biases was unsupported (and, in our view, should be irrelevant).

Similarly Greenwald, Hedges, and Laine (1996b) respond with the following points:

- Hanushek was out of step with the meta-analytic research community in asserting that the studies combined through meta-analysis must be identical (or even highly homogeneous).
- Hanushek's use of multiple results from the same study (e.g., 10 different coefficients from one set of subjects counting as 10 "studies") created problematic interpretations by violating assumptions of independence. Further, in this case, Hanushek systematically overcounted negative results.

- The issue of publication bias was addressed by Greenwald et al. (1996b) in redoing the analysis and putting twice the weight on nonsignificant results; even in this simulation, their conclusions did not change.
- Hanushek complained that Hedges et al. (1994a; Greenwald et al., 1996a) did not provide a "complete description" of their studies, even though they provided more information than Hanushek did.

Greenwald, Hedges and Laine (1996b) conclude

No one is this country is arguing that all of our public schools are doing well enough to meet today's standards. . . .

We recognize that we must look for greater returns on the public's investment in our children. . . .

Our findings, which demonstrate that money, and the resources those dollars buy, do matter to the quality of a child's education. Thus policies must change to ensure that all children have sufficient resources *and* that incentives to spend those resources wisely are in place. (p. 415)

The point of analyzing this issue in some detail in this chapter on quantitative methods is that, without the meta-analytic procedures, this substantive debate would not take place. These methods afford the vehicle for addressing important questions.

The Tennessee Study (Project STAR)

Despite the apparent power and utility of meta-analysis in educational and social science research, some medical researchers have questioned the validity of meta-analyses if the meta-analytic results disagree with those of large-scale randomized experiments. In medicine, LeLorier, Gregoire, Benhaddad, Lapierre, and Derderian (1997) compared 12 large, randomized controlled trials with 19 published meta-analyses dealing with the same substantive questions. Their definition of a large trial was one in which 1,000 patients or more were studied. They make the point that "if there had been no subsequent randomized controlled trial, the meta-analysis would have led to the adoption of an ineffective treatment in 32% of cases . . . and to the rejection of a useful treatment in 33% of cases" (p. 539).

The authors and the editor of the *New England Journal of Medicine* assume that the large-scale true experiments provide the standard; they argue that meta-analyses should be used more as confirmatory evidence and not for decision making. (This contention is not unquestioned, however; for example, see the related correspondence in the January 1, 1998, *New England Journal of Medicine* where discussion continues regarding the utility and importance of meta-analysis findings.)

Typically, education lacks large-scale true experiments to use as the "gold standard." One exceptional study that does qualify as long-term, large-scale, and methodologically sophisticated (using random assignment) is the Project STAR (Student Teacher Achievement Ratio) effort in Tennessee. We agree with the call by Mosteller, Light, and Sachs (1996) for more such studies. The main study making up Project STAR ran from 1985 to 1989; the subsequent Lasting Benefit Study (LBS) tracked students from STAR into 1990–91. Although most of the discussion in the technical reports is restrained and

well-connected to the data, the articles in more practitioner-oriented journals like the *Kappan* (Pate-Bain, Achilles, Boyd-Zaharias, & McKenna, 1992) and the *American School Board Journal* (Nye, Boyd-Zaharias, Fulton, & Wallenhorst, 1992) describe the results with less restraint and fewer qualifications. The study is not without critics and those who question the utility of the findings (Holliday, 1992; Tomlinson, 1990). Still, this study may indeed be the nearest thing that education has to medicine's Framingham Heart Study (e.g., see the discussion in Achilles, Nye, Zaharias, Fulton, & Cain, 1996 and in Achilles, Nye, Zaharias, & Fulton, 1993) and, as such, merits attention here.

In 1985, nearly 7,000 kindergarten students were randomly assigned to classes, and those classes were randomly assigned to one of three treatment conditions:

- Small classes (S) of 13 to 17 students
- Regular-size classes (R) of 22 to 26 students
- Regular-size classes with a full-time aide assigned (RA)

A total of 79 schools were involved from 42 of Tennessee's 138 school districts (i.e., more than 30% of the districts in the state participated). The experimental conditions held while the students were in grades K–3. Following K–3, students returned to status quo classroom instruction. The analyses that were done after third grade make up the Lasting Benefit Study (LBS). The classroom was the unit of analysis; more than 100 classes were in each condition, each year. Teacher and aide turnover was handled by random assignment of new staff members each year. Student outcomes were measured with norm- and criterion-referenced tests, and with other methods such as questionnaires, student self-concept inventories, and measurement of demographic variables. In addition to the LBS, other related studies were the Project Challenge assessment of the lowest socioeconomic status districts in the state, the selection of 21 comparison schools from STAR districts, and a number of dissertation studies.

The report by Achilles, Nye, Zaharias, Fulton, and Cain (1996) summarized the findings by noting that (a) the S-condition classrooms outperformed R and RA classes on student achievement, (b) the S classrooms had fewer discipline problems and spent more time on task, (c) students in S classrooms had fewer in-grade retentions, (d) the White versus non-White test score gap was not as great in S as in R and RA classrooms, and (e) the RA condition produced lower scores than the R group of classes. More important than tests of statistical significance are the between-treatment effect sizes. Achilles et al. (1993) discussed effect sizes (S versus R) for STAR in the .20 to .27 range. Effect was greater in the lower grades.

Project Challenge, although not experimental, applied STAR-based policy to districts in poor, rural counties. Those districts made advances in their rank-order standing of 12 ranks in reading and 25.7 ranks in math (in relation to 138 school districts). Nye, Achilles, Boyd-Zaharias, Fulton, and Wallenhorst (1992) presented effect sizes for the LBS for fourth grade, after all students were back in regular classrooms. Their Table 10.7 (Nye et al., p. 11) has the following data, shown in Table 10.7 here.

Table 10.7. Effect Sizes for Lasting Benefit Study

Subject	Percent Above Cut Score	
	S vs. R Effect Size	RA vs. R Effect Size
Norm-Referenced Tests		
Total Reading	.13	−.05
Total Language	.13	−.02
Total Math	.12	−.06
Science	.12	−.03
Social Science	.11	−.04
Study Skills	.14	−.03
Criterion-Referenced Tests		
Language Arts	.11	−.09
Mathematics	.16	−.04

The average effect size for S versus R is about .13 in the above table; the average RA versus R effect size is −.045. In both cases, the sign is consistent across all eight measures.

Therefore, the K–3 effects may be about one-fourth of a standard deviation (S versus R) and the lasting effect, one year posttreatment, may be about one-eighth of a standard deviation. NCE (Normal Curve Equivalent) scores from nationally normed tests have a population standard deviation of about 21; NCE scores are equal-interval scores suitable for comparisons and inferences. An advantage of .25 *SD* equates to approximately 5 NCE points. The LBS effect similarly translates to a 2.7 NCE point advantage for S classrooms.

To convert the NCE gains to a more common metric, consider what these effects would look like in terms of improvement in national percentile ranks. For example, a 5-point NCE difference would translate to improvement from the 8th to the 12th percentile rank; 5 NCE points would also equate to a student or a group of students improving from the 20th to the 27th percentile rank or from the 60th to the 69th percentile. (NCEs are nonlinearly related to percentiles, although both metrics center on 50 and range from 1 to 99.) Similarly, the 2.7-point NCE advantage of small classes in the LBS could translate to, as examples, improvement from the 30th to the 35th percentile, from the 50th to the 55th percentile, or from the 83rd to the 86th percentile.

Now we return to the cost-benefit question. Results from a large, well-done, and generalizable study demonstrate relatively small but consistent effects of a treatment that consists of merely the modification of class size (although we should note that at least a portion of the apparent consistency of findings is surely due to nonindependence of the measures of achievement). Questions about why the findings do not yield cumulative effects within K–3 and why classrooms with an aide perform (slightly) less well than those without an aide persist. Certainly, the latter finding needs as much discussion as the positive small class-size finding, because a common practice in school districts is to put a paraprofessional aide into classrooms to assist the teacher. Most decision makers would probably not expect such additional resources to be associated with lower student achievement.

Mitchell, Beach, and Badarak (1989) used the STAR data-

base to assess competing models that were intended to help explain the nature of the effects in the data. Their secondary analyses constitute one effort to go beyond mere between-group ANOVAs (analyses of variance) or ANCOVAs (analyses of covariance) and to assess explanatory models. They analyzed three direct-effect models and three indirect-effect models. The direct-effect models included (a) what the authors called "Instructional Overhead," where achievement declines as a simple linear function of increasing class size; (b) a "Classroom Interaction Costs" model, where achievement declines exponentially as class size grows; and (c) a "Distribution of Fixed Resources" model, which uses a logarithmic function in which the achievement curve declines as a function of spreading resources across more and more students (the curve declines sharply when the number of students is relatively small and then gradually flattens out at a lower level as the number becomes larger).

The three indirect effect models deal with certain distributional properties of within-class scores. Model 4 assesses simple "Heterogeneity in Student Capabilities" as defined by the within-class range and standard deviation in achievement (the assumption being that teacher behavior is a linear function of class range or variability in achievement, as measured by the standard deviation). Model 5 proposed that "Instructional Pacing" for the lowest achieving students affected classroom achievement; this proposition regarding the impact of the lowest achieving students was assessed by predictors using (a) the least able student's score, (b) the lowest score's deviation from the class average, and (c) the skewedness of the within-class distributions. Model 6, the "Ability-based Grouping or Achievement Modeling" explanation, takes into account the lowest and highest scoring students and the kurtosis of the class scores (the more closely packed the scores are—in comparison to a normal distribution—the higher the kurtosis score).

Generally, after the data were fit to the different models, results showed that the three direct-effect models were weaker explanatory models. The most potent model (Model 6) was the Ability-Based Grouping or Achievement Modeling theory. One surprise was that Model 4, representing Heterogeneity in Student Capabilities, showed effects in the opposite direction from what the researchers expected. That is, higher classroom ability-score ranges and standard deviations were associated with higher class achievement scores and gains. The authors conclude that "Rather, it appears that teachers—especially during the first three years of school—are able to improve average class performance by allowing the more able students to move out ahead of their slower learning peers" (p. 57). Their interpretation is that this model can also help explain the lack of cumulative effects as students continue in small classes for several years. Namely, "The lack of cumulative gains for students in small classes arose because average class achievement is very heavily influenced by the achievement of the most and least able students in the class" (p. 67). Mitchell et al. (1989) demonstrated the complexity of the data and the types of analyses that can potentially help explain why class size matters. We need more of these kinds of studies on the Tennessee data.

Another study may help us understand why the apparent effects of class size were not greater than they were found to be. Evertson and Randolph (1989) reported observational data from STAR classes and also assessed in-service training given to a subsample of STAR teachers. They did a straightforward and very powerful thing: They went out and looked at STAR classes. What they found was that, for a significant percentage of the time, the "Regular" classes, those with a purported class size of 22 to 26, actually overlapped with class sizes in many of the "Small" classes. This result is akin to finding out that a large number of the control subjects in a randomized trial of a 1-aspirin-per-day regimen have suddenly, on their own, started taking an aspirin each day, even though they were not part of the treatment group for whom that intervention was prescribed. No wonder the effect sizes were not greater, either for the K–3 program (approximately .25 SD) or the LBS (approximately .13 SD).

Evertson and Randolph found that some classes in the "Regular" group, when observed, had 12 to 18 students present, and many in that group (in several analyses, the modal number) were in the range of 18 to 22 students. Some of the smaller numbers observed may have had to do with pullout programs like Title I (whereby students are pulled from their regular classroom for limited supplemental instruction). The "Small" (treatment) classes did appear to be capped at 18. (S-group classes were intended to range from 13 to 17.) Although the groups would still differ significantly in average number of pupils present for instruction, clearly, some contamination of treatment has occurred. This finding by Evertson and Randolph also has the potential to explain why class-size effects do not seem to accumulate across years (along with, perhaps, the statistical modeling-based explanation of Mitchell et al., 1989).

Evertson and Randolph also found extensive use of aides in classes other than those designated as "Regular with Aides." This finding regarding the presence of aides may at least partly account for the small achievement decrement that seems to be associated with the "Regular" versus "Regular-with-Aides" comparisons, although the Evertson and Randolph data do not show consistent differences in the use of aides across grouping conditions. Again, in a large field-based experiment of this type, we should not be surprised to find treatment contamination. Evertson and Randolph did not find differences in their measures of classroom process associated with class type (S versus R versus RA) or with training condition (trained versus not trained). Although their finding of "no difference" in process data makes the explanation of the documented achievement effects no easier, the particular dimensions of classroom life that do *not* covary with class size and (attempted) teacher training are still important to understand.

Although one can find no lack of policy pronouncement that is based on Project STAR data (see, for example, Folger, 1989), the following are the safest statements to make:

- We need more field-based true experiments like Project Star; other states (like California and Oklahoma) that are mandating class sizes should take their lead from Tennessee. Even though the research may appear expensive, it is cheap in relation to the cost of implementation of class size initiatives.
- In addition to the large-scale, between-group studies, we need more work like the Mitchell et al. (1989) modeling

studies and the Evertson and Randolph (1989) classroom process studies that will help to explain the between-group results.
- We need detailed studies of why lowering class size sometimes does not produce higher achievement. For example, comparisons of small-sized classes with higher and lower achievement should be carried out. What are the contextual factors that mitigate treatment effects?
- We need careful cost-comparative analyses of class-size intervention as compared to other ways of improving student achievement. These analyses should be done as parts of the same research project. For example, compare Slavin's Success for All program with across-the-board reductions in class size for cost effectiveness.
- We need to disseminate "negative" results just as widely and in just as many nonresearch publications as we do positive findings. (For example, the results showing use of aides associated with slightly lower achievement should be discussed and should lead to additional studies on why this result regarding aides in classrooms was found.)

Dependability of Performance Assessments

One contention of this chapter is that student learning and the measurement of student achievement need to relocate to a place more central to research on teaching. Having said that, one moves quickly into the issue of the heightened use of so-called performance assessments. Elsewhere in this *Handbook,* integrated assessments in classroom instruction are the focus of discussion. Accordingly, we deal here with some concerns related to the large-scale use of performance assessments as a basis for effective decision making. Whenever assessments affect the lives of students, we may consider those to be high-stakes assessments. This is a broader interpretation of high stakes than one restricting it to mean diploma granting or promotion from one grade to the next. In our view, high stakes could refer to the assignment of a student to supplemental instruction (before or after school, Saturday school, or summer-school programs). Otherwise, at the secondary level, high stakes could refer to the intrusion of the administration or instructional staff into what would usually be the students' choices of elective courses. All these actions affect students' lives.

Generalizability theory provides a powerful tool for estimating the dependability of performance assessments and for obtaining data that may specify the conditions under which assessment of students' capabilities can be considered reliable. Although generalizability theory has been available for more than 25 years (Cronbach, Gleser, Nanda, & Rajaratnam, 1972) and attempts have been made to put the methods in front of a broader research community (e.g., Shavelson & Webb, 1991; Shavelson, Webb, & Rowley, 1989), it is still almost surely underused in educational research and especially in research on teaching. Generalizability is, however, often meaningfully applied in the community of researchers who have expertise in measurement and psychometric issues. The problem is that, in many school districts, performance assessments are being put in place, often for high-stakes purposes, by curriculum and instruction staff members who may not attend adequately, if at all, to the issues of dependability of assessment. In this section, we intend to raise some concerns about using performance assessments and not, by any means, to survey the extant literature. An entirely separate area, also beyond our scope here, is the question of whether the use of performance assessments may actually lead to outcomes indicative of higher-order thinking skills, as is often claimed.

Cronbach, Linn, Brennan, and Haertel (1995) lay out a number of critical issues. Their overriding concern is that policymakers and those who make decisions that are based on assessment results need to consider explicitly the standard error inherent in any measurement of human cognitive abilities. And that view of the standard error (SE) of an assessment is necessarily a complex one, needing to be framed by generalizability theory rather than by classical test theory.

Cronbach et al. (1995) discuss designs that isolate variance components for pupils, tasks, and judges (and interactions among those facets). Their simulation stipulates that each pupil is given eight tasks and the students' products are rated by three judges. The pupil (p) component represents the measurement of the students and is the desired information; the task-related (t) variance reflects the variability in task difficulty; and the variance related to judges (j) reflects the leniency or severity of each judge's ratings. Once the variance components have been estimated, it becomes possible to examine different scenarios (combinations of tasks and judges, in this case) that allow a cost-benefit perspective on gaining the greatest reduction in error per dollar spent. The SE contribution of pt, then, reflects differential performance of students across tasks, and, similarly, the pj term indicates the tendency of a judge (j) to give higher or lower scores than others do to a given pupil (across all tasks). The tj error represents the tendency of a judge to give higher or lower scores on a given task, considering all students.

Cronbach and his colleagues also deal with the need to assess aggregates of students—as nested in classrooms and in schools. A great deal of activity at the state and national levels is pointed toward accountability in the form of rewarding schools with high levels of student performance and bringing negative consequences to bear on schools where students do not perform up to standards. Their primary recommendation is that policymakers and psychometricians should be concerned about multiple sources of error in performance assessments. If inferences are to be made regarding individual students, the simulations of Cronbach et al. (1995) give direction for assessing the accuracy of rating one task with either one, two, or three judges, allowing the decision makers to examine the resulting improvement in reliability. Matrix-design sampling, where eight tasks are scored singly across distributed judges, was shown to result in an increase in the SE from .32 to only .34, which "seems to be an acceptable price to pay for the economy of single scoring" (p. 16). If one is interested in estimating the error in school-level scores, the same issues and overall procedures apply, although the models get more complex—because the pupil-score variance gets decomposed into a pupil-within-class-within-school component, a class-within-school component, and a school component. Although the SE will be higher when the intent is to infer beyond a particular year's measurement of students, for purposes of school accountability, Cronbach and his coauthors make the case for such "infinite" inference, noting that

> Restricting inference to the historical statement would defeat the purpose of many school-accountability uses of assessment results, where inferences reach beyond students recently taught. Note, for example, that analysis of one year's data, developing the SE for the finite student body, cannot support such actions as rewarding a school for satisfactory performance, or imposing sanctions on a school that did poorly; the finite-population analysis provides no basis for assessing the uncertainty in the school mean that arises from random variation in student intake. Nor would the analysis support the inference that the program in school A is better than that in school B, even if they draw on equivalent populations. Nor, thirdly, does the finite-population SE provide a basis for arguing that a school mean higher in Year 2 than in Year 1 implies improved instruction, rather than a fortuitously superior intake of pupils. (p. 21)

In short, those embarking on (or contemplating) effective, so-called high-stakes performance assessment would do well to consider the applications of generalizability theory in the Cronbach et al. (1995) monograph.

Next, we briefly discuss some of the empirical work in this area. Swanson, Norman, and Linn (1995) describe lessons learned from the health sciences regarding the use of performance assessments. They discuss research on (written) patient-management problems, computer-based clinical simulations, oral examinations, and "standardized" patients (live simulations). One set of findings accrues from the difficulty in sampling from the universe of desired behaviors. The context and the construct (underlying knowledge) interact at times in the assessment to yield low generalizability. For example, one study on physical examination skills found relatively low generalizability across skills (compared to, say, the interrater reliability) applied to one anatomic site and across anatomic sites for the same skill. They also describe difficulties in the accuracy of scoring oral exams. Oral exams were eliminated from U.S. medical licensing exams when rater agreement failed to get much higher than a near-chance level. Because the tasks in a performance exam are few in number, we run into problems if we wish to generalize to performance in other, unmeasured contexts. That is, within reasonable time limits allocated to exams, results may not be reproducible across contexts.

Problems also arise with the interpretability of what would usually be called validation correlations. Equating and security concerns also abound with high-stakes performance assessments. Although we find much opinion regarding the effect that alternative forms of assessment have on instruction and learning, this issue is typically not well studied. For example, given that available time is finite, one might wonder what might be eliminated from a curriculum if new, more hands-on instruction is incorporated after, perhaps, the format of assessment has changed? All of these issues are as important for education as they are for medicine.

Shavelson, Baxter, and Pine (1992) present findings on performance assessments in the context of the call for nationwide exams in the public schools. Recognizing the prohibitive cost of actual observations (and judging) of students' science work, they investigated "surrogates" of observations—ranging from notebook reporting to computer simulations to pencil-and-paper tests (short-answer and multiple-choice). Although they found that high interrater reliability was not difficult to obtain, they found much lower intertask reliability—students performed well on one task but not on another. The good news was that performance assessments were able to distinguish among groups of students with different instructional backgrounds (more versus less hands-on instruction before the assessment). However, the performance assessments, like more traditional assessments, were also capable of being well predicted from pencil-and-paper measures of science aptitude. In discussing results from the same data sets in the context of convergent validity, Shavelson, Baxter, and Gao (1993) did not find consistent evidence that different measurement methods converged on comparable findings across students. For example, although observations and notebook reporting correlated .84 in the electricity task, those two methods correlated only .34 in the bugs exercise. The computer-simulation assessment method correlated from .30 to .55 with other methods and tasks. And the short-answer method of measurement had 3 of 13 validity correlations less than .30 and 7 of 13 between .30 and .40.

Linn and Burton (1994) discuss the issue of school-level inferences regarding the percentage of students above or below a cut score. Their analysis of the Shavelson et al. (1993) data showed the relative effect of the task and the school-by-task interaction components to be as great or greater than the percentage of variability attributable to the school. Linn and Burton also simulated the effects of varying the numbers of students sampled within the school and varying the number of tasks in the assessment. Using plus or minus one standard error, one finds that annual school means that are more than 1 SE above or below the mean would be expected in about one-third of the years. If the school's true (universe) score corresponds to a pass rate of 20%, and if the school were measured with only 10 students completing two tasks, the observed pass rate might be expected to be as low as 14% or as high as 48% one-third of the time. Even increasing the number of students to 100 and the number of tasks to five narrowed the boundaries to only 13% to 40%.

Brennan and Johnson (1995) looked at California Assessment Program data and found that, whereas little variance was associated with raters, the task-related variance was relatively large, and the person-by-task interaction was the largest variance component. The importance of this interaction term indicates the difficulty of generalizing inferences regarding students across different tasks. Because of the small variance associated with raters, their results suggest that only one rater would be cost beneficial, but that it would require nine different tasks to reach a generalizability coefficient of .80.

Other studies echo these trends. Wolfe (1996) looked at a large-scale (nationwide) implementation of portfolio-based assessments and found quite variable results. Interrater reliabilities were low enough (especially in science) to call into question the use of scores for making decisions on individual students. Generalizability coefficients (across five portfolio entries) were reasonably high in language arts (.73) but were very low in math and science (.33 and .31, respectively). Barrett (1994) examined writing-task data in the fourth grade. The results again showed

that the number of tasks is very important. With the (perhaps) typical one-task sample, the generalizability coefficient was .50, whereas five tasks would be required to get the dependability measure up to .83.

In addition to the generalizability literature, some cautionary notes have recently begun to appear in more practitioner-oriented publications. In an interview with Brandt (1992), even Grant Wiggins, a strong advocate of the use of performance assessments, acknowledges problems with reliability of performance assessments. Bracey (1993), writing in *School Administrator,* refers to the work on the adequacy of performance assessments at the Center for Research in Evaluation, Standards, and Student Testing. And Roeber (1997), writing for the Council of Chief State School Officers, discusses state-level reform efforts in the context of new assessments. Roeber cites technical challenges such as generalizability and sampling issues, practical concerns such as time required for testing, along with the lag time between the assessment and the feedback to the test takers. Some researchers (e.g., Marcoulides & Goldstein, 1992) have begun to grapple with the resource-allocation questions, namely, what models can be examined to help planners with a cost-benefit decision-rule that can be used when resources are limited (as they always will be) and when new, costly assessments are put forth for implementation.

Performance assessments have taken education by storm in recent years. The idea of a measurement that may somehow be more proximal to subsequent real-life action is one that resonates with teachers, curriculum experts, and others in education. Only recently have some countervailing arguments come forth that essentially question the dependability of the scores and the breadth of the domain being sampled. In view of the current popularity of performance assessments, even in large-scale (accountability-based) programs, one may be a little surprised to find that some (e.g., Terwilliger, 1997) would stridently question the movement. Terwilliger addresses some of the language and intent of Grant Wiggins and other "assessment reformers." He questions the simple view of "face" validity and the lack of empirical evidence found in the rhetoric of Wiggins and others who speak both of "authentic" assessments and the great need for such assessments in education. Terwilliger highly criticizes the use of the term *authentic* and the pejorative adjectives that are attached to measurement resulting from some of the more traditional, standardized tests.

Educational assessment is a complex process that is built on a variety of assumptions about the purposes of education and on a set of data-gathering procedures that need to be judged against a series of both practical and technical standards. The use of labels that impute special status to a specific set of data collection procedures only serves to obscure fundamental assessment questions that must be addressed. For example, questions concerning the validity of assessment techniques help to focus discussion on relevant data instead of arguments about "authenticity." Therefore, terms like "authentic," "genuine," and "real-life" should be reserved for advertising copy and avoided in scholarly discussions of educational assessment. (Terwilliger, 1997, p. 25)

Messick (1995) puts forth a broad view of standards of validity that should be the focus of concern of proponents of performance assessments (and, really, of proponents of any kind of assessments). He takes the traditional validity conceptualization, extends it, and recasts it in the context of the current push toward more performance-like assessments. Messick states that "Validity is an overall evaluative judgment of the degree to which empirical evidence and theoretical rationales support the *adequacy* and *appropriateness of interpretations* and *actions* based on test scores or other modes of assessment." He adds, "Validity is not a property of the test or assessment as such, but rather of the meaning of the test scores" (p. 5, italics in original).

Messick discusses six aspects of construct validity that are worthy of analysis. We briefly recount his discussion here. One issue is the content relevance and representativeness of the assessment. One should ask, "Where is the evidence demonstrating that the content sampled through assessment is truly representative of the domain of interest?" Messick also uses this component to distinguish content standards (being developed by state boards of education all across the country) from performance standards. Some states are putting out content standards at the state level and then turning over the development of performance assessments and standards to local school districts even though they still intend to report out "percent above the standard" statistics in a single array, as if all the districts had used a common assessment and performance standard.

Messick is also concerned with substantive theories and process models of how students engage the content of assessments. That is, in addition to the validity of the content sampled, we need to address the degree to which the assessment actually taps the cognitive process purported to be engaged by the exam task. Where is the "empirical evidence that the ostensibly sampled processes are actually engaged by respondents in task performance" (Messick, 1995, p. 6)?

Messick also includes scoring models and their relation to domain structure as a part of the content-validity concerns. That is, the scoring criteria and rubrics should not be constructed capriciously, just because others have used similar schemes. One should have a defensible rationale for whatever scoring process is used. Because of social pressures in education, score comparability will always be an issue. Either individuals or groups will be compared against each other, or scores will be compared against some external standard. Messick brings generalizability and the meaning of scores together as an aspect of validity. He correctly notes that the greater interest usually lies in the unmeasured: What can we infer from an assessment about students' knowledge or skill base beyond the actual assessment itself?

This issue of generalizability of score inferences across tasks and contexts goes to the very heart of score meaning. Indeed, setting the boundaries of score meaning is precisely what generalizability evidence is meant to address.

However, because of the extensive time required for the typical performance task, there is a conflict in performance assessment between time-intensive depth of examination and the breadth of domain coverage needed for generalizability of construct interpretation. This conflict between depth and breadth of coverage is often viewed as entailing a trade-off between validity and reliability (or generalizability). It might better be depicted as a trade-off between the valid description of the specifics of a complex task performance and the power of construct interpretation. (1995, p. 7)

The question of relationships with external criteria is also included as an aspect of construct validity. That is, "the constructs represented in the assessment should rationally account for the external pattern of correlations" (p. 7). Related to this issue is the desirability of more positive, confirmatory evidence that is presented as part of the technical data with performance assessments. Too often, low or moderate correlations between performance assessments and multiple-choice tests are presented as evidence that the performance assessments "must" be measuring some different construct (usually claimed to be "higher-order thinking skills"). But where is the strong positive correlation between the performance assessment and some external, accepted measure of higher-order thinking skills? Otherwise, the low correlation with so-called traditional tests is impossible to interpret (perhaps, the performance assessment merely has poor reliability and does not correlate higher than .2 or .4 with anything).

Lastly, Messick reminds us not to forget the importance of consequences of the assessment. If claims are put forth for positive benefits of new kinds of assessment, then evidence supporting those claims needs to be presented. Likewise, we need to make sure that any undesired bias in the assessment is kept to a minimum.

That is, low scores should not occur because the assessment is missing something relevant to the focal construct that, if present, would have permitted the affected students to display their competence. Moreover, low scores should not occur because the measurement contains something irrelevant that interferes with the affected students' demonstration of competence. (Messick, 1995, p. 7)

In summary, we agree with Terwilliger (1997) that the rhetoric regarding performance assessments has gotten ahead of the underlying understanding of the psychometric properties of the new assessments. Messick's (1995) thoughtful discussion provides one potential pathway out of the jungle.

The Relation of Measurement to Research Design and Use of Psychometric Decision-Rules

Assessment strategies (broadly defined) are used in many critical ways in research. The most obvious, perhaps, is that dependent variables are typically defined by assessment techniques, and, thus, the psychometric quality of those assessments is critical to making inferences about the variables we are interested in researching. In addition to concerning ourselves about the quality of the measurement of dependent variables, we must recognize that the definition of many independent variables also relies on some form of assessment. This reliance is especially the case for variables used as covariates or variables that are used for classifying research subjects into groups. The criteria used for making classification decisions rely on some form of decision-rule or cut score (or more than one cut score when multiple classification are used). Researchers often develop the measures used in their research, but, at other times, existing measures are used. The quality of the measures must be demonstrated independently of the research question. (An inappropriate approach would be to conduct a study to answer substantive research questions and to use the same study to generate the initial data used as evidence for the psychometric quality of the measure.) Thus, an often-suggested strategy is that extant measures be used whenever possible. How does one find such measures, and, once found, how is their psychometric quality determined for the particular study to be conducted?

The following section of this chapter attempts to accomplish three ends. The first is to raise the issue of the relationship of measurement to the other major components of research methodology: the research design and the statistical analysis. Although this topic could be the focus of an entire chapter, it will be considered briefly as a reminder to attend carefully to the psychometric qualities of any measures used and to recognize the importance of using sound measures in research on teaching. The second question is the issue of setting cut scores (sometimes referred to as performance standards or minimum-passing scores). This discussion relates to the use of psychometric strategies for classifying individuals into two categories (e.g., passing or failing, mastery or nonmastery, having or not having a trait) or into several categories, as is done by the National Assessment of Educational Progress (NAEP) or when students are assigned grades. The third goal is for this section to consider how to locate an extant measure that might be used in a research study.

The Importance of Measurement Quality in Quantitative Research

Discussions (especially in textbooks) of research methods in the social sciences, whether focused on teaching or other areas, typically deal with the topics of research design, statistics, and measurement independently. This way of treating these topics is convenient, but it may contribute to researchers' not attending carefully enough to how these components interact when conducting research. In discussions found in previous editions of this *Handbook,* some methodologists have not ignored the interrelationships among research design, statistics, and measurement. For example, in the first *Handbook of Research on Teaching,* Campbell and Stanley (1963) indicate how some measurement problems are associated with threats to the validity of research designs.

More recently, in the third edition, Linn (1986) discusses these issues from a statistical perspective (extending Cochran's 1968 review of the effect of measurement error on statistics). Included in Linn's discussion are measures of change, and explanations and illustrations in the context of structural equation modeling (e.g., Jöreskog, 1973). Cook and Campbell (1979) expand and extend the discussion on threats to validity presented by Campbell and Stanley. These examples are merely a few of the many research methodologists and statisticians who have addressed the importance of taking the quality of one's measures into account when conducting research. We include this discussion because we believe occasional reminders to the research community are important and worthwhile.

The Relation of Psychometric Quality to Research Design Considerations

A research study that contains no threats to validity is one in which the results are explained by the independent variable(s) under investigation. That is, changes in the dependent variable are due solely to changes in the independent variable. To conduct a study that is completely free of threats to validity is virtually impossible. A threat to the validity of a research study is any alternative explanation (alternative to the independent variable of interest) about why the results came out the way they did. Cook and Campbell (1979) elaborate many threats to the validity of a research study; their discussion includes the threats described by Campbell and Stanley and many more. Among these threats are several that are related explicitly to the psychometric quality of the measures used in the study. (Threats that may have only subtle implications from the psychometric perspective are not discussed here.) Each of these threats is briefly restated here.

THREATS TO INTERNAL VALIDITY

Testing. The effects of taking the same test more than once may increase the participants' familiarity with the test content and result in scores on the dependent variable that reflect something other than the effect of the independent variable(s).

Instrumentation. Changes may occur in the way the dependent variable is measured over the course of the treatment. Such changes could result when (a) an alternate form is used that is not as parallel as desired from the point of view of treatment content; (b) the metric of the measure is not the same throughout the full range of scores—caused by a floor or ceiling effect that compresses the scale at the extremes as compared to the center of the score distribution; and (c) human observers (scorers) become more (or less) competent over the course of the treatment, for example, when the same observers gain confidence (or redefine the criteria) as they become more experienced or when different observers are used at different times, and the observers differ in their perspective on how to score the observations.

Statistical Regression. When tests that are less than perfectly reliable (i.e., all measures of human cognitive abilities) are used to select participants into a treatment because of their extreme scores, the scores on subsequent testing will regress to the mean of the population to which the group belongs. If the selection measure is more than modestly correlated with the dependent variable (and why would a selection measure that is unrelated to the dependent variable be used for selection?), and participants are selected for their extremely high or low scores, then subsequent scores on the dependent variable will tend to regress to the mean of the population to which the participants belong, regardless of any treatment effect.

The reason for this phenomenon is that errors of measurement are greater at the extremes of the distribution than they are at the center of the distribution. An imperfect correlation (any $r < 1.00$) means that standard scores on one variable must be closer to the mean of the standard scores on the other variable (i.e., to a standard score of zero), because

$$\frac{y - \bar{y}}{\text{sd}_y} = r\left(\frac{x - \bar{x}}{\text{sd}_x}\right).$$

In essence, a group that has a very high mean standard score on a test is likely to have a lower standard score on any other variable that is imperfectly correlated with the first test. The regression effect will occur whether the same test is given on both occasions (because even the same test administered on two testing occasions will have less than perfect test–retest reliability) or whether an alternate test is used on one of the occasions. The reverse would be likely to happen for examinees who scored extremely low on the first administration. Therefore, individuals may score higher or lower on a posttest, depending on how they were selected, without regard to any actual effect of independent variables.

Selection Interactions. Selection interactions can occur between (a) selection (the threat to validity associated with having different types of individuals systematically belonging to different treatment groups [e.g., volunteers in the experimental group and the general population in the control group]) and (b) instrumentation (the threat to validity associated with changes in the metric of the dependent variable over the course of the treatment). In the interaction, the major problem occurs when ceiling or floor effects occur and different individuals are more (or less) likely to score at the extreme (Cook & Campbell, 1979).

STATISTICAL CONCLUSION VALIDITY

The Reliability of Measures. To the degree that measures produce unstable scores, they are unlikely to provide estimates of true changes over time. Any of the typical reasons for low estimates of score reliability are sufficient to make this threat a reality. The reason that this threat is related to statistical conclusion validity is that the effect of less than perfectly reliable scores is to increase the error terms of the statistics used to assess treatment effect.

This threat is particularly salient in current research because of the renewed emphasis on performance testing. As discussed previously, such tests may result in scores that have low reliability estimates because they lack content representativeness (thus resulting in low external validity also) or there is low interscorer agreement (a reflection of the internal threat of instrumentation). This threat can be weakened somewhat by three practices. The first practice involves using longer, more comprehensive tests—a practice not always possible because the time needed for extended testing may be prohibitive. The second practice involves using more aggregated units of analysis (e.g., schools rather than classes, classes rather than individuals). Aggregation is often undesirable because aggregated units may not be of particular interest in research on teaching and because the loss of degrees of freedom in the analysis may result in loss of statistical power. The third practice involves correcting for unreliability (attenuation)—a technique applicable only under special conditions that are rarely appropriate in most research settings (because we cannot reasonably project that, in the real world, our measures of outcomes will be without error). Thus, unreliability in the variables used in research may lead to incorrect statistical conclusions. Moreover, to the degree that variables are unreliable, invalid, or both, the substantive conclusions will also be at risk.

The unreliability of measures may be taken into account depending, to some degree, on the statistical model used. For example, in using a structural equations model to conduct the analysis, we can take unreliability of both the independent and dependent variables into account in estimating the effects of the independent variable on the dependent variable (for a clear discussion of this approach, see Linn, 1986, pp. 102–103).

CONSTRUCT VALIDITY THREATS

Construct validity is the degree to which measures (independent and dependent variables) do, in fact, represent the intended underlying constructs. In their discussion of this category of threats to the validity of research designs, Cook and Campbell (1979) examine the importance of collecting certain evidence prior to undertaking a research study. We concur strongly with their approach and mention it here in advance of a more lengthy subsequent discussion of the selection among existing measures versus the development of new measures to be used in conducting research.

Cook and Campbell advocate, as a first step, advanced testing to ensure that the independent variables "alter what they are meant to alter" (p. 60). Their second precursor to conducting a study calls for assessing the divergence of the independent variable, that is, testing the extent to which "an independent variable does not vary with measures of related but different constructs" (p. 60). The third a priori activity is to gain assurance that "the proposed dependent variables should tap into the factors they are intended to measure" (pp. 60–61). In more contemporary measurement terms, this third activity might be restated: The scores from the measure of the dependent variable can be interpreted in terms of the desired variable of interest under the conditions in which the measure will be taken. (Messick, 1989, characterizes these concerns as construct underrepresentation and construct–irrelevant variance.)

Finally, Cook and Campbell (1979) advocate collecting evidence showing that irrelevant factors associated with the measurement of the dependent variable should not be dominant and result in scores that reflect "more or less than was intended" (p. 61). In essence, they advocate that the researcher obtain evidence of the validity of the measures to be used for both the independent and dependent variables before conducting the study. The specific threats to construct validity that have direct implications for the psychometric quality of the measures used to conduct research are described briefly below.

Inadequate Preoperational Explication of Constructs. To avoid this threat, Cook and Campbell (1979) would require researchers to fully and precisely articulate the definition of the constructs in a study before undertaking the study. They say, "The choice of operations should depend on the result of conceptual analysis of the essential features of a construct" (p. 64). Although this description is not explicit with regard to measurement of the variables of interest, it certainly implies that if the choice of operations (measurement of the variables being one of the operations) is not congruent with the measures to be used, then a clear potential threat exists to the interpretation of the results of the study. For example, if a variable of interest is anxiety, then that construct should be explicitly defined, and the measure of the construct should produce scores that can be interpreted in terms of that definition.

Mono-operation Bias. The threat this poses is that conclusions from research studies are weakened when only one form of the variable(s) is measured and are strengthened when multiple forms of both the cause (treatment) and effect (outcome) are permitted. Multiple forms of a treatment introduce different irrelevancies that might help to explain possible effects—effects that would not be studied without such variation in treatments. Cook and Campbell (1979) also elaborate on the importance of having multiple measures of the dependent variable. They admonish the reader that "single operations both underrepresent constructs and contain irrelevancies, [thus] construct validity will be lower in single-exemplar research than in research where each construct is multiply operationalized in order to triangulate on the referent" (p. 65). They contend, perhaps optimistically, that because the cost of multiple measures of outcomes is low, one rarely has an excuse for not obtaining them.

We agree with their advice, but not necessarily that the cost of obtaining multiple measures of the outcome variables is low. Recent advances in latent variable modeling (such as Linear Structural Relations [LISREL] modeling) allow explicit attention to multiple indicators and the underlying construct represented by the indicators.

Mono-method Bias. This threat exists if only one strategy is used to present the treatment or to measure the outcome variable (e.g., use of only paper-and-pencil measures or use of only performance measures). This threat extends the previous one: It suggests that having multiple presentations of treatment (e.g., both live and media presentations of a lesson) and outcome measurement (such as both paper-and-pencil and observational measures) are not enough. Thus, to assess an outcome by using different types of multiple-choice tests would be limiting the generalizability of the construct that represents the outcome.

Evaluation Apprehension. This threat may occur if respondents behave differently when being evaluated by experts, particularly experts in personality adjustment or experts in the assessment of human skills. We believe this threat may be extended to the general condition of test anxiety, such that individuals who feel threatened by the evaluative condition (whether direct assessment by experts or self-report assessment through paper-and-pencil testing) do not produce scores that are valid indications of the treatment effect. This apprehension, which could result in lower scores from some (but not all) respondents, results in confounding the results of a treatment effect with a personality trait or an emotional reaction to measurement.

Experimenter Expectancies. This threat comes about when, during the delivery of treatments, experimenters reveal (wittingly or unwittingly) their expectations to the participants. This threat does not, at first glance, seem to represent a problem of psychometric quality, but we think a clear assessment component is involved. Specifically, if experimenters reveal their expectations to participants, it is very much like teaching the test instead of teaching to the test, which is why medical research is so often conducted with blind or double-blind methods.

Confounding Constructs and Levels of Constructs. This threat, too, does not seem to be directly related to measurement. In this threat, Cook and Campbell indicate that when several discrete levels of a continuous independent variable are manipulated, the absence of an effect at one level does not preclude the potential for an effect at another level. For example, experiments regarding the effect of the quantity of homework might yield different findings, according to the definition of the independent variable. Perhaps no differences are associated with one versus two homework assignments per week, whereas a study of no assignments versus one to two assignments versus three to four assignments versus five assignments might demonstrate effects of the amount of homework. When the independent variable is not linearly related to the dependent variable, or when only a limited range of the independent variable is included in the study, then the outcome may not reflect accurately the effect of the treatment across all levels of the independent variable. The measurement problem arises when separating the independent variable into discrete categories. At issue is the validity of the cut score used to separate participants into groups. Often, little attention is paid to how these cut scores are set; we assume that the classification of the participants is done in a valid way. But unless the cut scores are validated, the potential for this threat exists, even when, otherwise, it might not be a problem.

Interaction of Testing and Treatment. When a pretest tends to have a specific effect on the treatment that would not have occurred without the use of a pretest, then the results of the study will not generalize to treatments that do not involve a pretest. For example, a pretest may sensitize the treatment group to look for certain things to occur in the treatment condition and, thus, result in posttest scores that might not have been so high without the use of the pretest.

Restricted Generalizability Across Constructs. This threat is characterized as one of breadth of inquiry. Often, a particular treatment may affect more than the one or two dependent variables that are the principal focus of the study. To the extent possible, additional variables should also be measured. The psychometric implications of this threat are twofold. First, in the threat's simplest form, the measures may not adequately represent all the outcomes on which to base valid inferences about all the outcomes of the treatment. Narrowly considered, if the treatment is intended to result in both knowledge and skills, and the measures focus only on knowledge, then a validity problem exists. More broadly considered (as we think was intended by Cook & Campbell), for example, if the treatment will result in improved writing because of substantial practicing and feedback from an automated computer program, then improved keyboarding skills may be a secondary outcome that should also be assessed (even though it was not an intended outcome). The second set of psychometric concerns is also related to focusing narrowly on the intended outcomes. As described earlier, scores on performance measures tend not to generalize to other performance measures, even when they seem as though they should be related. This fact reinforces the need to undertake multiple measures of the all the outcomes—those planned and those unplanned.

Order-of-Administration Effect. One additional threat is discussed in neither Campbell and Stanley (1963) nor Cook and Campbell (1979). That threat happens when multiple measures may be used at the pretest, and an order-of-administration effect occurs. This effect is a special case of a reactive effect that may obscure the cause of an outcome. It is likely to occur when both a measure of knowledge and a measure of attitude are administered at both the pretest and posttest stages of a study, and, at the pretest stage, participants are not expected to achieve high scores on the knowledge measure. If participants attempt the knowledge measure first on the pretest, their attitude scores may be lower than if they attempt the attitude measure first. This effect is illustrated in Armstrong and Impara (1990) where two classes of fifth-grade students were administered a test of science content knowledge first, followed by a measure of attitude toward the environment. A second set of two classes was administered the same measures in reverse order. The knowledge scores were essentially equal for both groups, but students who took the knowledge test first had significantly lower scores on the attitude measure (more negative attitudes) than did those who took the attitude measure first. If the differences in the attitude measure were due to the order of testing, then simply reversing the order of testing on the posttest would result in significant differences in attitude. The apparent effect of the treatment would, in reality, be due to the order of testing at the pretest stage.

Setting Cut Scores

In quantitative research, subjects are often assigned to groups (e.g., experimental and control group, masters and nonmasters) that may be formed randomly or may be based on some attribute variable. When the intent is to infer causality, random assignment into groups, whenever possible, is the strategy most often recommended. However, more than two groups often are formed—groups that are based on subjects' classification on some attribute variable in addition to groups formed because of treatments (e.g., males and females in experimental and control groups). Sometimes the attribute variable is directly observable, as is the case with sex. At other times, however, when the attribute variable is a measured variable, the researcher must make decisions about how to determine which subjects should be assigned to the various classifications of the attribute variable. Such a decision requires the researcher to set one or more cut scores. These cut scores may be set to form groups of equal size, or groups may be formed on the basis of some defined amount of the attribute variable that the subjects may have (e.g., course grades or achievement test scores that represent different levels of knowledge).

USING MEASURES TO DEFINE GROUPS OF EQUAL SIZE

When subjects are divided into equal-sized groups according to an attribute variable, the researcher is most concerned with two issues: the range of scores obtained by the subjects on the measure of the attribute variable and the validity of the scores from the measure.

When equal-sized groups are desired, methods such as a median split; taking the top, middle, and bottom one-third of the subjects; or other similar methods that divide the score distribution into equal parts produces the desired groups of equal size (at the outset, at least). Having equal-sized groups is desirable because it may make the statistical analysis more resistant to other potential violations of assumptions. Thus, in these cases, the cut score is set to make it convenient for the researcher. Such classification schemes produce groups that are rank-ordered on the attribute (i.e., subjects in the group with the highest scores have the most of the attribute, those with the lowest scores have the least of the attribute). These methods lead to the most interpretable results when the group of subjects to be used in the study obtain the full range of scores on the measure used to assess the attribute. When the range of scores on the attribute measure is somehow restricted, the conclusions of the study may need to be restricted in a similar way. For example, if an ability measure with a population mean of 100 was used to divide students into high- and low-ability groups, but the range of scores in the study was from 95 to 130 with a median value of 114, drawing conclusions about the differential effectiveness of a teaching module on high- and low-ability students may have questionable validity because the low-ability students may not be very representative of what is usually thought of as low ability. One caution, then, that researchers must take into account, even when using straightforward statistical definitions to assign subjects to attribute groups, is to ensure that the full range of scores is represented. Moreover, when the distribution of scores is very oddly shaped (e.g., multimodal or highly skewed) and results in very different interval widths associated with assignment to groups (e.g., on a measure with a score range of 20 to 100, the low group represents scores of 20 to 25, the middle group has scores from 26 to 37, and the high group, from 38 to 100), the assignment measure may have serious problems, and the results of the study may be affected negatively.

A second caution and, perhaps, the more obvious one is that the measure being used should provide scores that reflect the desired attribute. This need to reflect the desired attribute seems trivial, but we can cite articles in which the measure used to assign subjects to groups (e.g., learning styles) may not have been appropriate for use with the particular subjects in question (e.g., see Coop & Brown, 1970). If the measure used to make attributions is not a good measure of the attribute variable of interest, either because it has not been adequately validated or because it is designed for a different population from that being studied, then the results of the study may be seriously challenged. This problem is discussed above in several of the threats to validity identified by Cook and Campbell (1979).

Thus, we find two risks in assigning subjects to groups on the basis of some measured attribute variable when the objective of the measure is to define groups of equal size. The first risk occurs when the full range of scores is not obtained by the subjects to be divided into groups. This restricted range of scores may result in problems with generalizability. The second risk occurs when the measure may not produce scores that adequately represent the variable of interest, either in general or for the specific population being used in the study. With the second risk, a researcher may not find any differences when differences would otherwise have been found, or the researcher may misinterpret the differences that are found because the measure did not produce scores that could be interpreted in the desired way.

USING MEASURES TO DEFINE GROUPS WITH SPECIFIC ATTRIBUTES

When group formation is based on some cut-score strategy other than those described above, subjects may be misclassified. For example, when classifying students on the basis of their knowledge of subject matter is desirable, and a variable such as grades is used to measure subject-matter knowledge, many students may be misclassified because grades may not reflect subject-matter knowledge. Even if the classification is a gross one (e.g., C+ or higher represents "more knowledgeable" students and C or lower represents "less knowledgeable" students), the students in the respective groups may not accurately represent the desired variable, because many factors other than subject-matter knowledge (e.g., deportment, class participation, and attendance) may be represented by grades (Brookhart, 1994; Frary, Cross, & Weber, 1993). Grades, of course, are problematic for reasons of reliability in addition to the problems with their validity.

In this discussion, the invalidity of the measure is a secondary consideration, however. Of primary interest is the validity of the interpretation of the cut score. That is, if a method is used to classify subjects into groups such as masters and nonmasters or into groups such as below-basic, basic, proficient, and advanced, then few subjects should be misclassified in any group. This is, in part, a reliability problem, but misclassifications that result from a flawed method of setting the cut score represent problems of validity that have clear implications for the interpretation of the outcomes of research.

Setting cut scores to assign individuals to groups can be done five basic ways: normative methods, criterion-referenced methods, empirical methods, examinee-centered methods, and test-centered methods. Each of these methods is discussed briefly, and the strengths and weaknesses of each method in terms of its use in a research context are mentioned.

Normative Methods. In setting the cut score, normative methods use a score-point in the distribution to separate subjects into groups of equal size. The investigator would be using a normative method to use the cut score of one standard deviation above or below, or both above and below the mean. Essentially, normative methods are intended to fill quotas. The cut score is set such that it divides the sample into ordinal classifications without much regard for how much or how little, in an absolute sense, the subjects may have of the attribute. These methods provide an ordering (ranking) of the subjects into groups that have more or less of the attribute (assuming the measure to provide scores that reflect the attribute is adequate). As already noted, when the distributions are oddly shaped (e.g., highly skewed, multimodal) or when scores from the measure are substantially lacking in validity, the method seriously lowers the validity of the research conclusions.

Criterion-Referenced Methods. Criterion-referenced methods typically use some capricious standard for dividing subjects into groups that are thought to represent greater or lesser amounts of some explicitly defined attribute variable. One example is a cut score of 70% to divide those who are masters of some subject content from those who are not masters. We refer to this score as "capricious" because it is usually set without regard for the way the measure is constructed. Measures may be designed to be hard or easy for a given group, but the cut score is fixed regardless of the nature of the posttest score distribution. Many schools use a fixed set of cut points that represent different grade categories (e.g., A = 93–100%; B = 85–92.9%; C = 77–84.9%; D = 70–76.9%; and F = below 70%).

These classifications, and others like them, are completely capricious and, although they will rank order subjects on a variable, the substantive interpretation is essentially without merit because no definition of what constitutes the criterion has been articulated: the content and subranges of the measures used to assign the scores. The substantive interpretation of such classifications may not even be consistent for a single rater (teacher) because the standard may be applied differently for different students on measures used to make a final determination of the grade (an example of the validity threat associated with instrumentation described above). If the interpretations are not useful (valid) for any one teacher, then they are certainly not valid when used across teachers. Thus, one teacher's grade of B may be equivalent, in terms of knowledge of subject matter, to another teacher's grade of A or C, depending on, among other things, the method and content of the measures used to assign the grades. Clearly, criterion-referenced methods for setting the cut scores are inappropriate if the desire is to represent other than the grossest of ordinal scales and if misclassification of subjects into groups is not a serious problem in interpreting the outcomes of some treatment.

Empirical Methods. Empirical methods are those based on statistical methods that rely on some prediction strategy. The most common statistical strategies use some type of linear modeling, either ordinary least squares, logistic regression, or discriminant analysis. In these methods, examinees who score above the cut score have a higher probability of being successful on some criterion and those who score below the cut score have a lower probability of being successful on the criterion. These methods are used occasionally in research studies. They have value when the criterion measure is both reliable and valid (i.e., the score on the criterion is the main focus and not a distant proxy for some unmeasured variable) and when the predictor variable is sufficiently correlated (statistically) with the criterion so that adequate accurate prediction, or classification, is possible.

Empirical methods have serious limitations in many research contexts because the samples often are preselected on some unrelated variable or the range of the variables is seriously restricted, and these factors can reduce considerably the magnitude of the correlation between the predictor and the criterion. When the correlation is low, the number of classification errors increases. Thus, empirical methods are acceptable when the statistical correlations between the predictor(s) and criterion are at least moderately high (say, at least .30 to .50) and when both measures produce reliable and valid scores. To the degree that these conditions do not hold, the methods will result in misclassifications.

With most empirical methods, misclassifications are most likely to occur near the cut score. The more distant subjects are from the cut score, the less likely they will be misclassified (especially if only two classification categories are used). Empirical methods may be of value when two groups are desired and the two most extreme groups can be selected. However, such strategies may also result in a regression-to-the-mean effect when subsequent measures are used. When the cut score is set using empirical methods, the use of the cut score to define groups for research is applicable only insofar as the sample at hand has characteristics like those in the population used to set the original cut score.

In many settings, empirical methods do not work because researchers cannot obtain the full range of performance on the criterion variable. Specifically, in many credentialing settings, individuals who are classified as ineligible for the credential (degree, license, diploma, or certificate) are never measured on the criterion variable. Thus, the range of scores on the criterion variable is restricted to those who pass the credentialing measure. For example, when trying to set a cut score for physicians, empirical methods will not work because we assume that no "incompetent" group is included in the sample that takes the criterion measure. Thus, the restricted range of possible scores on the criterion essentially precludes the use of these methods.

Examinee-Centered Methods. Examinee-centered methods are those that require persons who are knowledgeable about the examinees' competencies to classify them into groups of subjects like the groups will be classified later, using only the measure of interest. The most common methods are the contrasting-groups method and the borderline-groups method (Livingston & Zieky, 1982). The contrasting-groups method requires someone who knows the subjects to assign them to groups such that one group has a high amount of the attribute and the other group has a low amount of the attribute. Often, the classifier is shown the criterion measure and asked to make group assignments on the basis of the subjects' expected performance on the criterion. (The classifier is not permitted to know, in advance, the subjects' scores on the criterion measure.) For example, a teacher may be asked to assign her students to the groups of masters and nonmasters of some specified content to be measured by the criterion test. The test (criterion measure) is given to subjects in both groups, and a cut score somewhere between the average scores of the two groups is set. The cut score depends on the nature of the score distribution and the costs associated with making incorrect classification decisions. The contrasting-groups method often is problematic when the overlap between the scores of the two contrasting groups is high. This overlap happens when the individuals who make the original classification decisions are not accurate in their decisions about group assignment. Such classification errors can occur when the criterion is not clear or when the classifier is basing the decision on something other than knowledge of the subject's competence on the criterion.

As is the case when using empirical methods, the contrasting-groups method is used to set a cut score that is applied to future groups. To the extent that the current sample is similar to the sample used to determine the cut score and all other things are equal, then subjects assigned to groups on the basis of their performance on the criterion measure should be classified reasonably correctly.

The borderline-groups method also requires someone who is knowledgeable about a group of subjects to classify them as

having high, low, and borderline amounts of the attribute (criterion) of interest. Subjects who are classified as borderline are tested, and some central score (often the median) in the distribution is used as the cut score. This method has been criticized as being subject to regression to the mean (Livingston, 1995). It is also subject to the same shortcomings of the contrasting-groups method. That is, it depends on the extent to which the classifications, especially of the borderline group, are correct and on the extent to which the sample being used in the research has characteristics similar to those of the sample used in setting the cut score. Clearly, if regression to the mean is a problem, then misclassification is a potential problem depending on the extent to which the basis for making the group assignment is correlated with the criterion measure. Of course, that correlation may not be available or computable; thus, if the borderline group has been used to set a cut score that serves as the basis for grouping subjects in a research study, some misclassification should be expected.

Test-Centered Methods. Test-centered methods, such as those proposed by Nedelsky (1954), Angoff (1971), and Ebel (1979), and their modifications also have problems. The common element of these three researchers' methods is that each requires a panel of judges to examine each item independently and make a judgment about the performance of target examinees on that item. Of these three methods, the method proposed by Ebel is rarely used and is not discussed.

The Nedelsky method is restricted to use with multiple-choice items. As it is now used in most applications, Nedelsky's method entails having judges examine each item and its response choices and indicate the number of response choices that the target examinee would be able to eliminate as being obviously wrong. The cut score is based on the assumption that the target examinee would select randomly from the response choices that remained after the obvious incorrect choice(s) had been eliminated. Thus, for a test consisting of four-option multiple-choice items, if the target examinee was expected to be able to eliminate one choice for a particular item, the cut score for that item would be 3/4 (.75). The cut score for the test is the sum of the item cut scores.

This method tends to produce systematically lower cut scores than does the Angoff method (Livingston & Zieky, 1989). The major drawback of the Nedelsky method is that it is not considered valid by many potential users because the results of the method do not agree with the judges' perception of the number of examinees who should pass or fail. That is, when judges have a sense of the number of examinees in the pool who would be expected to fail (or pass), the Nedelsky method tends to produce a cut score that fails too few (or passes too many). If a cut score is being used to classify research subjects and that cut score has been set using the Nedelsky method, one may anticipate systematic misclassification of subjects. Moreover, the Nedelsky method is not well suited for dividing subjects into more than two groups. As in the cases discussed above, such a systematic misclassification can lead to conclusions of questionable validity.

The final method we discuss in detail is the method proposed by Angoff (1971), which has been modified considerably over the years in many studies. This method is the most often-used method of setting cut scores on credentialing examinations

(Sireci & Biskin, 1992). It is most often used with multiple-choice items, but it can be used also with performance items (see Hambleton & Plake, 1995). The method typically requires three steps: training judges in the use of the method, estimating examinee performance on each item without knowledge of actual performance, and estimating examinee performance with knowledge of performance of the total group of examinees. Essentially, the Angoff method requires judges to look at an item and estimate, for that item, the proportion of examinees in the target group who will answer the item correctly. After making initial item-performance estimates, judges often are provided actual performance levels for examinees and then another round of estimates is carried out.

Numerous variations are used with this method. Some studies provide actual data immediately following training and have only one round of performance estimates. Other studies provide data to judges more sparingly and use up to three rounds of performance estimates. Shepard (1995) described some serious problems in using the Angoff method when it was applied to setting multiple cut scores with items released by the National Assessment of Educational Progress (NAEP). The Angoff method has also been challenged with claims that invalid cut scores have resulted when the method was used in the way it has been typically been used (Impara, 1997; Impara & Plake, 1997; 1998; Linn & Shepard, 1997). The major problem is that judges are not competent to perform the task they are asked to do. Moreover, the tendency of the items to have modest to low intercorrelations results in judges' cut scores that are inconsistent with judges' perceptions of the number of examinees who should pass. Specifically, if the cut score is at the high end of the distribution (as in the NAEP classification of "Advanced"), the cut score is set too high, and too few examinees are classified in the highest group. The reverse is true for cut scores intended to identify the lowest-performing group—the cut score is set too low, and too few individuals are classified as being in the lowest group. Impara (1997) has suggested some alternative methods that may help resolve the problems under certain conditions when the Angoff method is used.

The final result is that the Angoff method, except under very special conditions in educational settings, may produce cut scores that result in erroneous classifications. Moreover, the nature of the error depends on which tail of the distribution is of interest. The Angoff method, although used with some types of performance items, is not universally the recommended approach. When the test consists of performance items, no methods of setting standards, at present, are highly recommended by psychometric experts.

SUMMARY REGARDING CUT SCORES

In general, investigators will be setting cut scores for conducting research and not setting cut scores to make selection or classification decisions that will have an irreversible effect on the subjects of the research. If that is the case, then probably, a better approach would be to try to maximize the power of the statistical analyses and the robustness of the statistical methods. To get the most power and robustness, researchers should strive for equal group sizes. Thus, the normative methods described above (e.g., median split) will provide for equal-sized groups of research subjects. However, if researchers are conducting a study designed to set a cut score and the individuals classified on the basis of these cut scores will, subsequently, be used as research subjects, then the researchers should read the literature carefully and use either an Angoff procedure as described by Impara (1997) or a mixed method as described by Giraud, Impara, Plake, Hertzog, and Spies (1997).

Sometimes, when using measures developed by others, the author of the measure will recommend cut scores for the purpose of classifying examinees. The new user must verify that these cut scores have been derived appropriately. To do this, one may have to go back to the original source—the test manual, an article in the literature, or some other reference—that provides information on the psychometric quality of the measure. Some of these other sources of information are described below.

Locating Existing Measures

The body of measures that may be used in research on teaching falls into two categories: commercially available and noncommercially available. Commercially available measures are those that must be purchased from a publisher. Noncommercial measures may be found in the literature or obtained from a researcher who developed or modified the measure. We discuss in turn how to learn about the two kinds of measures.

Even after reading our discussion about locating tests, one should first define the constructs to be measured, then contact a research librarian in a research university for help in finding the most appropriate measure. Most research librarians are aware of many resources that provide descriptions and reviews of commercially available tests and research versions of tests. Jordan (1996) provides an excellent strategy for finding suitable tests.

The Internet (World Wide Web) can now be a valuable source of information also. A recent Internet search on "tests and measures" yielded several thousand sites, many of them very useful. Many of the internet sites are linked, so finding one site may lead to helpful others. The two major sources of information about commercially available tests (the Mental Measurements Yearbook series and the Test Critiques series) provide test reviews, but such reviews are not likely to be available at no cost on the Internet. The above-mentioned references that do contain reviews are available in most research libraries. Descriptive information is available for some noncommercial tests on the Internet through the test locator service of the ERIC Assessment and Evaluation division.

The effort required to locate a measure to be used in research is usually justified. The total research effort may require hundreds of hours to design the study, collect and analyze the data, and write the report. The time spent to locate the most appropriate measure(s), thus maximizing the likelihood of actually measuring the construct(s) of interest, is a relatively small part of the total investment. If the researcher develops an original measure, validating it may require an effort at least equivalent to the research that is being planned. This validation process would be a considerable expenditure just to determine if the measure is adequate for the research.

COMMERCIALLY AVAILABLE MEASURES

A commercially available measure does not always meet any particular standards of psychometric or content quality. Many publishers make only inadequate attempts to provide data about the way a measure was developed, about the underlying basis for its development, or about the psychometric quality of the measure. Some of this information may be available, but the technical manuals may not have been produced, because waiting for technical manuals cuts into profit. In other cases, no manual or other information is even scheduled for publication. Thus, the user is responsible to ascertain whether an available measure meets even minimum standards of quality before deciding to use the measure in research.

Information about the test is likely to be available from the publisher. Publishers can be contacted and asked for specimen (or examination) copies of the measure and the associated technical information. (Sometimes a fee will be charged for the specimen set.) However, to decide whether a particular measure might be applicable in the planned research, the researcher should first find out about the available measures and learn the relevant information about them before contacting the publishers.

There are two major publishers that provide general information about commercially available tests. These two publishers produce similar publications, but at different times with different formats. The two publishers are (a) the Buros Institute of Mental Measurements and (b) Pro-Ed. The Buros Institute of Mental Measurements publishes the Mental Measurements Yearbook Series (14 yearbooks have been published between 1938 and 2001—the most recent yearbook is listed in the reference list as Plake and Impara, 2001), and the Tests in Print Series (six have been published, the most recent is Murphy, Impara, and Plake, 2000). Pro-Ed publishes Test Critiques and Tests: A Comprehensive Reference for Assessments in Psychology, Education, and Business (hereafter referred to as TACRA). The most recent editions of the Pro-Ed books are also listed in the reference list (for example, Maddox, 1997).

The TIP and TACRA volumes describe the tests in print as of the date of publication. The descriptions include basic information about the tests: title, purpose, population for whom the test is designated, costs, date of publication, and publisher. Both series have indexes for locating tests on particular topics, and both have indexes of publishers. The TACRA also includes an index not available in TIP—of tests that have gone out of print since the last publication. TIP includes a score index and a broad subject index (neither is available in TACRA). Because some test publishers (mostly the smaller ones) deal with only one of these reference sources, some tests will be located in one source but not the other. For the most part, both sources contain comprehensive information. The Buros series has been in existence longer (since 1938), and, thus, libraries are more likely to carry the Buros books if they do not have both.

The volumes that describe the tests currently in print do not contain reviews of those tests, mainly because, with several thousand tests in print at any one time, to include the reviews along with the descriptions would make the volumes too cumbersome and costly. But these works do indicate where a review can be found, if a test has been reviewed. Of course, TIP indicates the location of reviews only in the MMY, and TACRA directs the reader only to reviews in Test Critiques.

The reviews in the MMY and in Test Critiques contain basic information about the test, its intended uses, and commentary on its psychometric quality. These reviews are a valuable resource for making decisions about using a measure. Because the reviews may not always contain sufficient information for a decision, obtaining a specimen set from the publisher (or finding a library that has a copy of the test) may still be necessary. The MMY is also available in many libraries in electronic form from SilverPlatter™. This service provides the most up-to-date information on tests currently in print.

In summary, two major sources of publications provide descriptions and reviews of tests in the English language. These publications are provided by the Buros Institute of Mental Measurements and Pro-Ed. The Buros Institute has a Web page (http://unl.edu/buros/) that is linked to other sources, some of which are described below.

NONCOMMERCIALLY AVAILABLE TESTS

If a particular test, a test on a particular topic (less likely), or an affordable test cannot be located, the possibility of using a noncommercially available test should be explored. The risk of using such a test is that, in line with what was said above about not assuming commercially available tests are psychometrically sound, the psychometric information available on noncommercial tests may be quite limited, and many of these tests are not well constructed.

A source of information on noncommercially available tests is the ETS Test Collection Catalog (1989–1995). This source also contains information on commercially available tests, but no reviews are referenced; thus, the Buros and Pro-Ed sources should be examined first. Much of the information available in the ETS (Educational Testing Service) catalog is also on-line in the test-locator file of the ERIC/Assessment and Evaluation. The ETS catalog includes references for tests that can be found in the literature. The collection may be the most easily accessible resource for unpublished tests (Jordan, 1996).

When a test is available only in a journal article, tracking it down often becomes very difficult. Even when the citation is given in the ETS Test Collection Catalog, the source may be other than the one given. Jordan (1996) illustrates this problem in a discussion of a search for the Impression Formation Test. The ETS Test Collection Catalog sends the reader to an issue of the journal Educational and Psychological Measurement. The article referenced, however, does not contain a copy of the measure. The measure is described, and the reader will either have to attempt to reconstruct the measure from the description or go to an earlier reference in which the measure is reproduced.

Another source of information about unpublished tests is the Directory of Unpublished Experimental Mental Measures (Goldman, Saunders, Busch, Osborne, & Mitchell, 1974–1995). This series of books has had several publishers; the most recent is the American Psychological Association (APA). These books contain citations of measures found only in the literature. Some 30–40 journals in the behavioral and social sciences are regularly scrutinized to identify measures under development or developed specifically for a particular research question. However, this resource is not always accurate; in one instance, a researcher provided a citation for a commercially available test in the reference list (and the test name was capitalized in the text of the article), but the Directory indicated that the test had been developed by the researcher for use in her research. Thus, a search in a different source for the test under the researcher's name would have been unsuccessful.

In addition to the general resources we have suggested for locating information about commercially and noncommercially available tests, numerous other sources can help locate measures in specialty areas (e.g., substance abuse, gender role). These sources typically concentrate on noncommercially available measures. A search of the Internet by the researcher—after checking with a research librarian (to find out if the librarian has already undertaken such a search)—can be invaluable in locating sources of available tests.

Survey of AERA Presenters of Research on Teaching

Although collecting data to assess where the field is currently positioned and where research on teaching might be headed may be somewhat unusual for a Handbook chapter, it seemed valuable to do, in the opinion of one group of active researchers. The practitioners of research on teaching who were chosen for our study were the presenters in the AERA's Division K program (Teaching and Teacher Education) at the 1997 AERA convention. Certainly, other divisions within AERA have a connection with research on teaching—Division C on Learning and Instruction and Division H on Program Evaluation, for example. However, Division K was most closely allied with the field that is represented in this Handbook. We went through a database provided by AERA headquarters and cross-referenced it against the 1997 program to identify the first author of all presentations in the Division K program.

This identification yielded 347 potential respondents, the population of 1997 Division K first authors on the program. All received a mailed survey with a return envelope in early November, 1997. Responses were requested by November 15, 1997 (allowing nearly 2 weeks for response). Seven returned surveys were unusable (i.e., the potential respondents replied that they did not present at Division K, the surveys had incorrect addresses, or the surveys came back completely blank). A total of 56 returns were usable. (As a point of reference, when the first author of this chapter sends out an annual spring parent survey to about 2,000 parents in a school district—across 28 school buildings—asking for ratings of their schools, the return rate is consistently around 50%.) Although the return rate for the AERA survey was relatively low and somewhat disappointing (16% returned), it does not, in itself, disqualify the results from consideration. (One would have hoped that more researchers would respond to a request for information and opinion about their research for this Handbook chapter.) The Appendix presents a copy of the instrument, the cover letter, a summary of the responses, and transcribed comments.

We have a few indicators available to use in examining the degree to which the 347 Division K presenters might resemble the larger AERA population. Similarly, we can see how the 56 who responded resemble the total group of Division K presenters on these few indicators.

Information from the AERA office showed (as of August, 1997) the total membership of AERA to be 45% males and 55% females. The percentage of the AERA membership reporting their primary employment as being in higher education was 79%.

Using an analysis of names, we estimated the gender breakdown of the 347 Division K presenters to be 106 (30%) males, 224 (65%) females, and 17 (5%) gender unknown. These results suggest that the population of (1997) Division K presenters had proportionately more females than the AERA membership.

Of the 56 presenters who did respond to the survey, 45 (80.4%) were females, 10 (17.9%) were males, and 1 (1.8%) did not respond to the question.

On the questions regarding primary employment, 53 (94.6%) responded "Higher Education," and 3 (5.4%) responded either "Research and Development Center" or "Other."

These data suggest that the responding sample is disproportionately female (in comparison to the presenters in Division K and in relation to AERA in general) and also has a somewhat higher-than-expected percentage who are working in higher education.

Results of the AERA Survey

One of the items asked Division K presenters how long they have been engaged in research on teaching. Figure 10.1 shows the distribution of responses.

The data show nearly one-fourth reporting 5 or fewer years, with the largest group (37%) in the 6- to 10-year response category.

The Appendix contains category summaries of the open-ended responses to Question 1 ("Briefly describe the research . . ."). Of the 52 respondents who gave an answer to Question 1, the category with the most presentations ($N = 22$) addressed postsecondary education. The teaching category (performance pay, teaching methods, reform issues, etc.) included the next highest number of returned surveys ($N = 19$). Five presentations addressed student issues (gender, culture or race, mentoring, etc.). The others ($N = 6$) dealt with research on school (cohort) research or other issues.

Figure 10.2 shows the percentage distribution of responses to Question 2 regarding researchers' characterizations of the primary methodology they used in the 1997 AERA presenta-

Table 10.8. Number of Respondents Comparing "Primary Methodology" 10 Years Ago with Current Methodology

Current	10 Years Ago		
	Largely Quantitative	Combination	Largely Qualitative
Largely Quantitative	2	1	1
Combination	4	7	2
Largely Qualitative	2	8	10

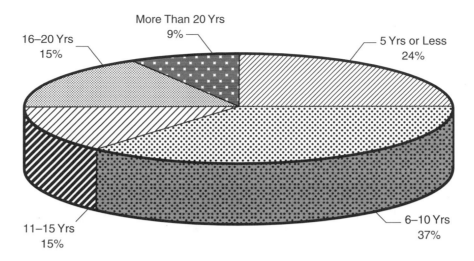

Figure 10.1. How long engaged in research on teaching?

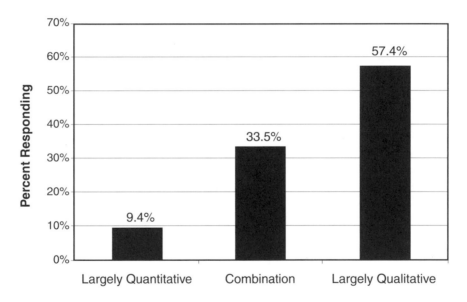

Figure 10.2. Primary methodology in 1997 AERA presentation.

tion (on a 10-point, quantitative-to-qualitative scale). We collapsed the data by combining the bottom three responses (quantitative) and the top three responses (qualitative). The middle four points were collapsed to indicate a combination of qualitative and quantitative methods. The data showed a majority (57.4%) of responses at the qualitative end of the scale.

Question 3 was essentially the same as Question 2, except that it asked hypothetically, "If you were engaged in research on teaching 10 years ago, how would you characterize your primary methodology then?" Of the 56 researchers, 37 responded to this question.

The largest percentage responded in the middle part of the scale—43.2% reporting methods 10 years ago as a "combination" of qualitative and quantitative methods. The percentage responding on the quantitative end of this scale was more than

twice the percentage on the previous item. Table 10.8 summarizes the shifts from 10 years ago to the present.

Of the eight researchers who were "largely quantitative" 10 years ago, only two reported being "largely quantitative" in their methods in 1997. However, of the 13 who reported their methods as "largely qualitative" 10 years ago, only one switched to "largely quantitative" (and 10 remained "largely qualitative"). Of the 16 researchers who reported using a "combination" of methods 10 years ago, 7 remained in the "combination" response category, and 8 switched to the "largely qualitative" category.

The next group of five items used a response scale asking for ratings of the perceived importance of several aspects of current research on teaching. Questions asked about perceived importance of (a) quantitative observational data; (b) qualitative in-

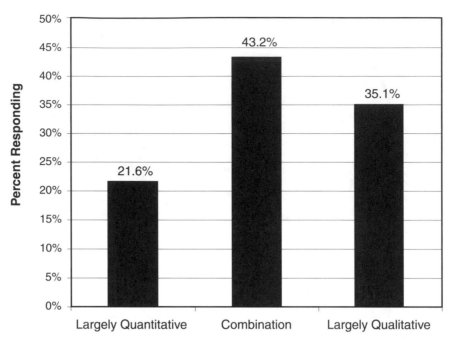

Figure 10.3. Methodology used in research 10 years ago.

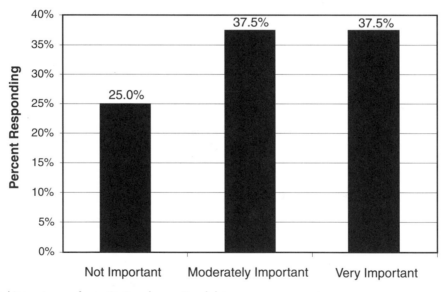

Figure 10.4. Perceived importance of quantitative observational data.

formation on teachers and classrooms; (c) traditional student achievement measures (e.g., multiple-choice, norm-referenced tests); (d) performance assessments of students' abilities and skills; and (e) research suitable for causal inferences. These items all used a five-point scale (from "Not Important at All" to "Very Important"). For the purpose of producing Figures 10.4 through 10.8 to illustrate these data, we collapsed the percentages responding in the bottom two points (labeled "Not Important" in the figure) and in the top two points ("Very Important"). Those responses at the midpoint (3) of the scale were called "Moderately Important."

Of those who responded to the survey, nearly all (94.7%) rated qualitative observational methods as very important. Quantitative observational measurement ratings were more evenly divided—25% "not important," 37.5% "moderately important," and 37.5% "very important." Regarding student assessment, the highest percentage (39.3%) rated traditional, norm-referenced achievement tests as "not important," whereas 89.3% rated performance assessment of students as "very important" in the current direction of research on teaching. Perhaps surprisingly, more responses were in the "very important" category on the item asking about the perceived importance

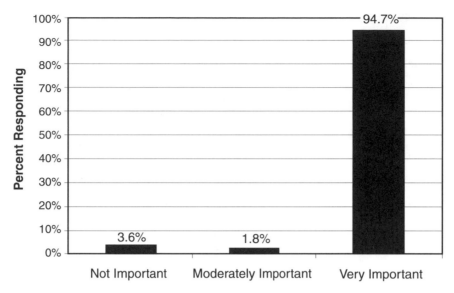

Figure 10.5. Perceived importance of qualitative observational information.

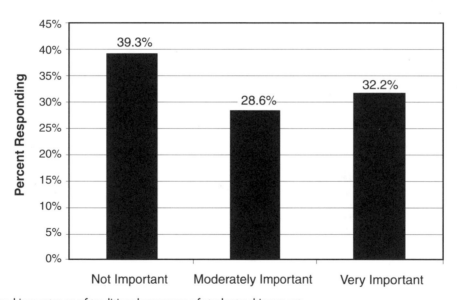

Figure 10.6. Perceived importance of traditional measures of student achievement.

of cause-and-effect research, although more than one-fourth (26.8%) of those responding placed the causal inference type of research on the "not important" end of the scale.

Analyses also examined gender differences on the survey items. Two items showed significant differences between male and female researchers. The item on years in research on teaching showed mean differences favoring the males (F = 8.88, df = 1,52, p = .004)—with an average of 16.80 years versus 9.93 years for females. The variability within males was also significantly higher than for females (SD = 9.30 for males versus 5.85 for females). The one other item showing a statistically significant gender difference was the question asking for a rating on the perceived importance of qualitative information on classrooms (ethnographies, interviews, teacher action research, etc.). Females gave a higher average rating (F = 24.50, df = 1,53,

p < .001) on the perceived importance of this kind of qualitative data (4.73 on a five-point scale versus 3.70 for males). And the within-group variance again differed significantly between male and female researchers (male SD = 1.06; female SD = 0.45).

Analyses also examined relationships between the measure of years in research and responses to the rating items. Most were not significantly correlated. However, a significant curvilinear relation (the quadratic term p-value was .023) did occur between years in research and responses to the question asking for a rating on the "quantitative to qualitative" continuum—as of 10 years ago. The function was an inverted-U, with those respondents who reported 15 to 20 years experience tending to have the highest ratings, thereby reflecting more reliance on qualitative methods (as of 10 years ago). The researchers with fewer or with more years of experience (compared to the 15–20

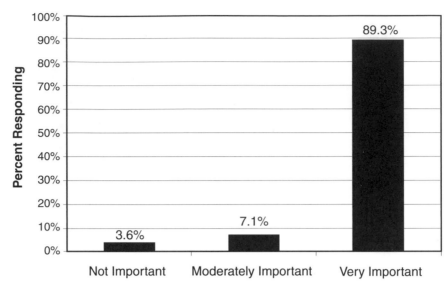

Figure 10.7. Perceived importance of performance assessments of students.

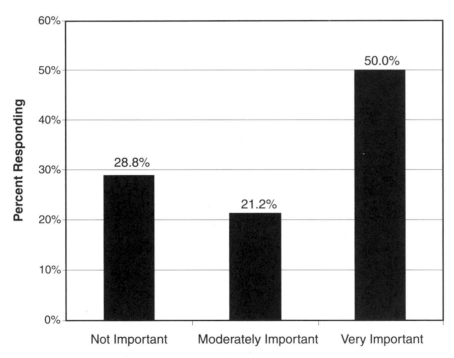

Figure 10.8. Perceived importance of research suitable to causal inference.

year group) tended to give ratings more toward the quantitative end of the scale.

One may reasonably question the representativeness of this study because of the low return rate, however, in the absence of other data, we put these results forth as worthy of consideration. They can be considered as a snapshot of the prevailing attitudes of professional researchers in the area of research on teaching and teacher education. The Appendix shows the transcribed comments of the respondents on the open-ended comments questions. We return to these findings in the summary discussion.

Study of Teacher Attitudes Regarding Research

Kennedy (1996a, 1996b) has carried out thought-provoking work on teacher responses to educational research of several different genres. She presented 100 teachers with research articles of the following types:

- Two comparisons of teaching methods, statistically based and intended to produce generalizations (one in math and one in writing)
- Two autobiographies of teachers (one dealing with the

teaching of science and the other with the teaching of writing)

- One essay analyzing the concept of equality of educational opportunity
- Two reports on writing and mathematics (one a survey of students' writing achievement at several grade levels and the other a case study of one student's understanding of mathematics)
- Two discipline-based studies that examined the "knowledge production processes" in disciplinary fields (one in English and one in science)

The nine research reports were grouped into two packages of five each. One package contained mainly studies dealing with language arts, whereas the other package included studies that spanned a variety of subject areas. Any one teacher, then, received one package of five studies. Even though the studies varied in methods, Kennedy (1996a, p. 11) states that "The studies also shared an important feature. Despite their methodological diversity, they all argued for the kind of conceptually based teaching that contemporary education reformers are asking for. In that sense, they were mutually reinforcing and could have been perceived as an integrated body of work, rather than as five discrete, unrelated studies."

After teachers read their packet of studies, the researchers held discussions with the teachers on each individual study. Then they asked teachers to nominate which of the five studies was most persuasive, which was most relevant, and which influenced their thinking the most. Again, quoting from Kennedy (1996a)

- The question about persuasiveness allows us to see which studies are most likely to pass the truth tests that teachers apply when they review research. If it is the case that they depend for justification on narrative structures or situated events, they should find the case studies and teacher autobiographies to be more persuasive.
- The question about relevance enables us to see the extent to which studies need to be conducted in situations very like their own in order to be relevant, and
- The third question offers them an opportunity to indicate whether the study had some influence on their thinking even if it was not perceived as persuasive or relevant. (pp. 12–13)

Table 10.9, taken from Table 10.2 in Kennedy's study (1996a), shows the percentages of teachers who nominated each of the nine studies as "Most Persuasive," "Most Relevant," and "Influenced Thought Most." The grouping of the nine studies into five categories is Kennedy's grouping. (Percentages do not sum to 100 because studies could have been nominated more than once.)

Following Kennedy, one can look at these data in at least two ways. Table 10.9 essentially presents the studies in rank order of nomination, from top to bottom. The two "traditional" studies (between-group comparisons of different teaching approaches) ranked 1st and 2nd, 3rd and 1st, and 1st and 3rd, respectively, on the "Most Persuasive," "Most Relevant," and "Influenced Thought Most" dimensions. The only other studies with a ranking in the top three were the autobiography of teaching science

Table 10.9. Nominations Across All Studies (*N* = 100 Teachers)

Study	Most Persuasive	Most Relevant	Influenced Thought Most
Comparison Approaches to Teaching Math (*N* = 36)	56%	47%	47%
Comparison Approaches to Teaching Writing (*N* = 100)	48%	56%	40%
Autobiography, Teaching Science (*N* = 36)	39%	50%	39%
Autobiography, Teaching Writing (*N* = 64)	33%	30%	41%
Essay, Analysis of a Concept (*N* = 64)	20%	13%	23%
Survey, Student Achievement in Writing (*N* = 64)	17%	16%	3%
Case Study, Student Understanding of Mathematics (*N* = 36)	8%	14%	14%
Disciplinary, Language (*N* = 36)	11%	6%	3%
Disciplinary, Biology (*N* = 36)	0%	0%	0%

Note: Table reprinted with author's permission, from Kennedy, 1996a.

(2nd on "Most Relevant") and autobiography of teaching writing (2nd on "Influenced Thought Most").

Kennedy's second way of looking at the findings is to compare the studies on the "percent-nominating" metric against the "standard" of 20%—because if each study had been nominated an equal number of times, across all teachers, they would all have had one-fifth of the nominations (i.e., each teacher had five studies). Examined in this way, the four studies in the top part of the table all got more than their share of nominations for all three response dimensions. The traditional between-group comparisons and the autobiographies received from 1.5 times up to nearly three times the expected standard of 20%. The survey of writing, the case study of mathematics, and the two discipline-based reports all received fewer than 20% of the nominations, across the board. The conceptual essay, in the middle of the table, received 20% and 23% of the nominations for "Most Persuasive" and "Influenced Thought Most"; however, for the "Most Relevant" category, it was nominated by only 13% of the teachers.

Kennedy admits to being surprised by these findings. In the earlier-cited quotation, at least for the persuasiveness dimension, she states a hypothesis (although she doesn't term it a hypothesis): "If it is the case that [teachers] depend for justification on narrative structures or situated events, they should find the case studies and teacher autobiographies to be more persuasive" (p. 12). Yet the data demonstrate that the traditional between-group studies were nominated by 56% (math) and 48% (writing) of the teachers as most persuasive. The nearest-ranking studies were the autobiographies, each nominated by less than 40% of the teachers.

Kennedy also takes note of teachers' valuing of sample size. In particular, the fact that the case study of one student was nominated so much less frequently than the survey of student achievement in writing was mentioned. She comments that

These two studies appear in rows six and seven of [Kennedy's] Table 10.2. Let's start with persuasiveness. You can see that 17% of the teachers who read the survey nominated it as most persuasive, whereas only 8% of those who read the case study nominated it as most persuasive. So the teachers have surprised us. And I know, from reading their detailed discussions of these two studies, that the sample sizes did make a difference. Teachers felt the large number of students assessed in the survey increased the study's persuasiveness, and, on the other side, felt that the case study was limited because it included only one student. (p. 14)

That is, with little or no formal training in research methods (external validity or generalizability), the teachers have intuitively incorporated a value system taking sample size into account. At least in this analysis, single-case studies don't persuade very many teachers.

In another paper, Kennedy (1996b) described other, related findings from the same study. The researchers asked teachers what they expected or wanted from research, and they responded:

- 39% wanted research to provide specific prescriptions
- 29% wanted research to provide intellectual stimulation
- 31% wanted both or were ambivalent
  (Kennedy, 1996b, p. 6)

Again, this is a finding with which Kennedy does not seem entirely comfortable. Following presentation of these percentages, she states that

In the research literature these two main ways of using research are called "instrumental uses" and "conceptual uses." From teachers' discussions of what they expected from research, it seems that they were pretty evenly divided between instrumental and conceptual uses of research, though a slightly greater fraction preferred instrumental uses for research. (Kennedy, 1996b, p. 6)

However, someone else might look at 39 versus 29 in the above percentage table and say that 39 is one-third higher than 29, and, when coupled with the data on nominations as "Most Persuasive" and so forth, the results do mean that teachers most highly value traditional, between-group studies that lead to (prescriptive) conclusions (such as "Method A" produced more student learning than "Method B").

Kennedy's explanation of the high value teachers placed on the traditional comparative studies rests on the notion that these two studies dealt with both teaching (methods) and (student) learning. That these two concepts are central to teachers' lives seems unarguable. Her interpretation, however, is that the method used does not cause research to be valued by teachers but rather the inclusion of both teaching and learning as objects of investigation. The interpretation is partly based on the finding that the two qualitative autobiographies (also dealing with both teaching and learning) ranked just behind the traditional studies. This interpretation would be easier to accept as an explanation if the traditional studies had just barely nudged out the autobiographies for the top ranking. However, on two of the three dimensions, the results actually were not close. If we aggregate the response percentages for the two kinds of studies within the top two categories (by using the midpoint between

Table 10.10. Aggregated Response Percentages, Nominations as Most Persuasive, Most Revelant, and Most Influential

Study Type	Most Persuasive	Most Relevant	Influenced Thought Most
Traditional, Comparative Studies	52.0%	51.5%	43.5%
Autobiographies	36.0%	40.0%	40.0%
Difference, Favoring Traditional	16.0%	11.5%	3.5%

the two percentages), we obtain the following results shown in Table 10.10.

Examined in this way, only the "Influenced Thought Most" dimension shows a small advantage for the traditional studies. The percentage for "Most Persuasive" for the traditional studies is nearly half-again higher than the figure for autobiographies, and the percentage for "Most Relevant" is over one-fourth higher for the traditional method studies. These findings, coupled with the earlier-described result showing that more teachers wanted "specific prescriptions" (Kennedy's words), argue that teachers value traditional between-group methods that lead to (or, at least, potentially lead to) statements about "what works" for enhancing student learning. Kennedy reminds us that her sample of 100 teachers might not represent teachers in general—the teachers in her sample were all involved in professional growth activities of one kind or another (either advanced degree work or district-sponsored staff development). So, we might say that the findings of Kennedy's study hold true for teachers who are willing to work beyond the regular teaching day for their professional development.

We should be listening to these teachers. In whatever way they came to the value system that they hold (and our survey of Division K presenters would not suggest that it came from teacher education classes, assuming that most of those responding to the survey teach in colleges of teacher education), they appear to have high regard for just the kind of study that is out of favor these days in research on teaching. Kennedy summed it up best, when she said, "Conversations with these 100 teachers suggest that many of our assumptions about the role of research in teaching are not grounded in reality" (Kennedy, 1996b, p. 9).

Summary Discussion

This chapter aimed at providing an update regarding quantitative methods for the field of research on teaching. Basically, many of the major issues have not changed in the 16 years since Linn (1986) wrote his chapter in the previous Handbook. The need for between-group, randomized designs has not diminished; the reliability of measured outcomes remains important; and structural equation models and the analysis of aggregated units still hold promise and create complexity (and do yield valuable explanations). Instead of focusing solely on research methods, our attempt has been to identify critical issues and to present exemplars from current research that demonstrate findings of substance that would not be obtainable if the associated methodologies were not in place.

Whither Now?

One could argue that the survey of researchers in teaching and teacher education produced findings concerning their values that places the researchers somewhat out-of-step with the concerns of school boards and even with concerns of the teachers in Kennedy's study. However, the promising news may be found in the researchers' open-ended responses to the question "Where do you view the field of research on teaching 10 years in the future?" (See Appendix.) Although we would (admittedly, grossly) characterize the respondents in our survey sample as largely qualitative researchers (according to their pattern of responses in the survey), they said overwhelmingly that the future should hold a thoughtful combination of qualitative and quantitative methods and results.

Although it may be expected for us to speak of a pendulum swinging one way or the other, it may also be an accurate characterization. Elmore and Woehlke (1996) systematically analyzed methods in AERA publications and documented a substantial increase in the use of qualitative methods in the 8 years prior to their publication. Instead of a pendulum metaphor, perhaps a more useful image would be that of two powerful trains moving side-by-side, on parallel tracks, headed in the same direction. Medical research makes great use of case studies (especially to illustrate exceptions to the expected norm; see, for example, Coulter, Kaneshige, & Wyatt, 1997) without giving up randomized experiments. Those who engage in polemical discussion, such as Chambers (1992) (and for a counterargument to Chambers, see Gage, 1994a, 1994b), and hypercritical remarks that reflect their perception of the "atheoretical" nature of process–product research should acquaint themselves with similarly "atheoretical" work in medical science, such as the (process–product) Framingham Heart Study. Medical practitioners have never waited for full-blown theoretical understanding of treatment effects before implementing an effective treatment. Similarly, thanks to the Tennessee study (e.g., Achilles et al., 1993), we now know that smaller class sizes do work, even though we do not understand precisely why. The survey of AERA presenters should be replicated 10 or 15 years from now to see the extent to which the 1997 responses in our survey reflected only a temporary excursion away from essential functions of research on teaching.

We, fortuitously, can look to a recent article in Educational Researcher for opinions from three distinguished past presidents of AERA (Cooley, Gage, & Scriven, 1997) on their visions of educational research in the 21st century. Cooley's great hope is to possibly eliminate the isolation that has kept "folks who are responsible for the educational policies of state and local educational systems" (p. 18) from taking advantage of research done for AERA audiences. His unpublished policy-related data analyses provide a case in point. Gage cites his review (Gage, 1996) of meta-analytic work to demonstrate that "many generalizations in education do hold up across many replications with high consistency" (Cooley, Gage, & Scriven, 1997, p. 19). He goes on to call for future theory development: "The meta-analyses also show that those generalizations now cry out for theories that will tie them together in rational, logical, systematic models and explanatory frameworks" (p. 19). Scriven (writing in Cooley, Gage, & Scriven, 1997) is also critical of the current state of affairs, noting that "the association [AERA] as a group has almost entirely failed to discharge its principal duty to the society that supports it. That duty, it seems, is to identify educational best practice and improve it" (pp. 19–20). He proposes solutions: more (and better) data collection; more sophisticated analyses of expert–practitioner exemplars; more between-group studies that compare (e.g., old with new) programs; and "more sophisticated use of educational product and educational procedure evaluation" (p. 21) in school districts. Like others (e.g., Bradley, 1998, writing in Education Week), he is critical of colleges of education.

Writing in Berliner, Resnick, Cuban, Cole, Popham, and Goodlad (1997), Resnick claims that, because AERA researchers cannot agree on policy and practice (much less on findings of research), an inherent inability to advise decision makers exists. "If you are a decision maker—from politicians to school superintendents or school board members—you have to decide. You have to come down on one hand or the other. When we as researchers say we do not yet know enough, that we need more time to collect and weigh all possible evidence, we are saying, 'We can't help. You'll have to make your decisions without us.' And that is exactly what happens" (p. 15). Her proposed ways to move forward are to develop a short list of priorities for research and stick with it for at least a decade; figure out how to disseminate findings in a way that maximizes clarity and utility; create larger (not smaller) communities within AERA (e.g., have ties across divisions); and get AERA moved out of Washington, D.C.

Conclusions

With all the above in mind, consider the points that this chapter has attempted to make:

1. Continued (and even increased frequency of) studies are needed that use between-group comparisons to strive for (generalizable) causal inferences. True experiments with random assignment to groups are best; quasi-experiments with thoughtful matching are better than description-only or correlation-only analyses. The goal is to generate results that demonstrate method and program effects on student achievement, attitude, or behavior.

2. Meta-analytic methods are important. We are especially drawn to adaptations such as those by Slavin and others. When aggregating findings, the combining of a rational, rule-based selection of studies with meta-analytic procedures allows researchers to focus on methodologically well-done studies. Sometimes using this approach gives answers that are different from analyzing all available studies. One can compensate for the possible introduction of subjectivity in selecting methodologically excellent studies by grouping all studies into the excellent and less-than-excellent categories and determining whether this division yields different results.

3. We must pay attention to the education–production–function debate. This discussion most recently is captured in the point–counterpoint between Hedges (and colleagues) and Hanushek. Although we think the evidence favors the Hedges position (resources do relate to student

outcomes), the debate has been useful, regardless of choices as to the most compelling evidence. The debate deals with the important issues that public schools grapple with every day. Without the methods used by Hedges and his colleagues, the debate would not occur.

4. The Tennessee class-size project should be placed front and center. This important effort demonstrates why we need large-scale, long-term, true experiments. The study both raises questions and answers them, which is a good thing. It also has a direct bearing on the Hedges-Hanushek debate. One of the most common places where schools put additional resources is class-size reduction. The Tennessee project cries out for additional, more detailed studies. For example, what distinguishes small classes that are high achieving from small classes that are not high achieving? Why is there (perhaps counterintuitively) a small, but consistent, decrement associated with putting a teacher's aide in a classroom?

5. The issue regarding the dependability of performance assessments should be put in the spotlight. Although those in the measurement world are fully aware of concerns about phenomena like task-related error, the larger communities of faculty and researchers in colleges of education and leaders of public school curriculum and instruction seem to be less aware. If performance assessments were being used only in classroom settings and being combined with other information that teachers typically have on students, this lack of awareness would not be so great a problem. These assessments, however, are being deployed for high-stakes purposes without sufficient attention to breadth of coverage, generalizability of scores, and validity.

6. The design and statistical analysis issues (first raised by Cook and Campbell) need to be brought squarely into the arena of psychometrics. In this chapter, we examined, in particular, the interplay of the psychometric properties of dependent variables with the researchers' abilities to draw proper inferences from the data. We also examined the methods of placing students or other respondents into groups (such as those who have mastered a particular content area versus those who have not mastered that content). We have also contended that, most of the time, the most cost-effective use of researchers' time is spent in locating adequate measures rather than in constructing them from scratch. And we have provided advice on how to search for sound measurement tools.

7. We need to consider the attitudes and methods of current practitioners of research and their effect on teaching. Although the ongoing work in the field of research on teaching surely has worth, much of it does not directly address the most pressing issues in public schools. This opinion arises from our survey results—low ratings given by the Division K respondents—which indicate that they regard traditional measures of student achievement and quantitative methods as unimportant. The opinion is also based on the fact that fewer than half the respondents did not think between-group studies (that justify causal inference) were important. Nonetheless, even though most of those surveyed fall into the class of researchers not currently engaged in quantitative work, they projected a vision for the future showing a return to a better balance between quantitative and qualitative research. This survey should be repeated from 10 to 15 years in the future.

8. We need to analyze in depth the findings of research on what kinds of studies teachers value and also what teachers expect from research studies. Kennedy's findings (Kennedy 1996a, 1996b) from a good-sized sample of 100 teachers showed that teachers were most persuaded by traditional, between-group comparative studies. The teachers also said that these studies were most relevant and influenced their thought the most (compared to other, more qualitative work). And the percentage of teachers who said they wanted research to yield specific prescriptions was higher than the percentage of teachers who said they wanted intellectual stimulation. These teachers are worth listening to.

APPENDIX: Survey of AERA Researchers

10/30/97

M E M O R A N D U M

TO: Presenters in the AERA, 1997, Division K Program

FROM: John Crawford, Ph.D.   James Impara, Ph.D.
             Millard Public Schools   Buros Institute, Univ. of Nebraska, Lincoln
             Omaha, NE

RE: Attached survey of current methods in research on teaching

As part of the upcoming *Handbook of Research on Teaching,* we have been charged with the study of current methods in use in the research on teaching community. That is why we are now contacting you.

Based on information from the AERA office, you were a first author/presenter at the conference last spring, on the part of the program dedicated to Division K.

We are asking you to take a few minutes to complete the attached survey and return it in the enclosed envelope (a stamp is needed). There are items addressing your own current research programs and your perceptions of the current utility of both quantitative and qualitative methods. We need your responses by November 15, 1997. We have attempted to keep the survey short to increase the likelihood of getting a good return. We need your responses. All the surveys will be handled and encoded confidentially (no identity information will be maintained). *If* you would like a report on the results, please include a business card or a mailing label, and we will send you a report.

Thank you for your cooperation.

If you have questions, call John Crawford, (402) 895-8214.

Attachment

Research on Teaching Survey

Please take a few minutes to respond to the following items. Your responses are important. If the space is insufficient on open-ended items, attach additional pages.

Questions Regarding Your Research and the Field of Research on Teaching

1. Briefly describe the research that was the basis for your AERA Division K presentation in Spring 1997 (the title and a 1- or 2-sentence description):

_____
_____
_____
_____
_____
_____

2. How would you characterize the primary methodology that you used in the research that was presented this past spring at AERA? (Circle one response.)

1	2	3	4	5	6	7	8	9	10
Quantitative				Combination of Quantitative and Qualitative					Qualitative

Comments, if any:

_____
_____
_____

3. *If* you were engaged in research on teaching 10 years ago, how would you characterize the primary methodology that you were using then? (If you were not substantially engaged in research on teaching 10 years ago, please leave this item blank.)

1	2	3	4	5	6	7	8	9	10
Quantitative				Combination of Quantitative and Qualitative					Qualitative

Comments, if any:

_____
_____
_____

4. Now, thinking of the *current* direction in the field of research on teaching, estimate your perception of the *i*mportance of (Circle one response.)

    a. Quantitative observational data (e.g., frequency counts of teacher or student behavior, time allocation indicators, etc.)

1	2	3	4	5
Not Important At All		Moderately Important		Very Important

    b. Qualitative information on teachers, student behavior, classroom climate (information from ethnographic observations/interviews, action research, etc.)

1	2	3	4	5
Not Important At All		Moderately Important		Very Important

c. Traditional measures of student achievement—for example, primarily multiple choice, norm-referenced achievement tests

1	2	3	4	5
Not Important At All		Moderately Important		Very Important

d. Performance or authentic assessments of students' abilities or skills

1	2	3	4	5
Not Important At All		Moderately Important		Very Important

e. Research suitable for cause and effect inferences that can be generalized to a larger, unmeasured population

1	2	3	4	5
Not Important At All		Moderately Important		Very Important

5. Discuss where you view the field of research on teaching 10 years in the future. Focus on 3 or 4 key concepts—for example, what do you see as the prevailing methodology? What may be the substantive questions of interest?

_____

_____

_____

_____

_____

_____

_____

6. In the future, for studies that *do* incorporate *quantitative* methods, what do you view as the major outcome measures (for the field of research on teaching, as now represented by Division K)? What would you estimate to be the process measures of most interest (teacher, school, student variables)?

_____

_____

_____

_____

_____

_____

_____

Background Information

1. How long have you been engaged in research on teaching?

    _____ years

2. Your gender: _____ female   _____ male

3. Which is your primary employment?

    _____ college/university

    _____ private or federally funded R & D lab or center

    _____ public school

    _____ consultant/self-employed

    _____ other: (please specify) _____

Research on Teaching Survey
(Responses from Survey)

1. Briefly describe the research that was the basis for your AERA Division K presentation in Spring 1997 (the title and a 1- or 2-sentence description):

_____

_____

_____

_____

_____

_____

TOPIC AREAS	NUMBER OF RESPONSES FROM SURVEYS
POSTSECONDARY EDUCATION	
Reform Issues	2
Professional Development	11
Pre-Service Issues	4
Recruitment	1
Assessment	2
Mentoring	1
Multicultural Education	1
TOTAL	*22*
TEACHING	
Performance Pay	1
Teaching Methods	9
Multicultural Education	2
Reform Issues	4
Assessment	3
Professionalism	0
TOTAL	*19*
STUDENTS	
Gender Issues	2
Cultural/Racial Issues	1
Mentoring	1
Learning	1
Professionalism	0
TOTAL	*19*
STUDENTS	
Gender Issues	2
Cultural/Racial Issues	1
Mentoring	1
Learning	1
TOTAL	*5*
SCHOOL (COHORT) RESEARCH	3
OTHER	3
OVERALL TOTAL	*52*

2. How would you characterize the primary methodology that you used in the research that was presented this past spring at AERA? (Circle one response.)

1	2	3	4	5	6	7	8	9	10
Quantitative				Combination of					Qualitative
				Quantitative and Qualitative					

Comments, if any:

_____

_____

_____

Survey #	Response
3	Only numbers were some demographic data for descriptive purposes only.
6	These descriptors are woefully inadequate.
8	At this point, more of literary analysis than educational research, I suppose. A precursor to my dissertation study on teacher preparation.
11	Data sources: interviews, observations, interactions, logs, case studies, and quantitative analysis of interactions.
14	Highly post-positivistic—collaborative.
15	Descriptive research was the initial focus, but project is emerging to include a balance of qualitative and quantitative methodology.
18	Survey of CA math teachers (N>700). Interviews and observations with 99 teachers.
28	My paper for the '97 presentation was primarily qualitative (on the subset of the data); currently I'm doing quantitative analysis on the larger data set. My dissertation will center on qualitative analysis of the same data in relation to other measures used in classroom.
31	(a) Use of questionnaires, which were built based on observational data. (b) Use of videotaping, audio-taping of mentoring sessions. (c) Documentation of reflection session by mentors on their practice and thinking/perception. (d) Including the teachers in the research team (participatory role).
32	This was a study that was both ethnographic and narrative.
33	A two-pronged approach: Semistructured interviews with all research directors in all the French training institutions and historical analysis of official texts, reports, daily, administrative, and specialized press; and depth case studies, plus cross-case analysis.
34	Qualitative methods were used to gather data, which were quantified and analyzed using traditional statistical methods.
35	Questionnaires to 1,300 teachers, questionnaires to 200 administrators, interviews in representatives of 10 schools, plus district office.
37	Essays, stories.
42	The papers were based on a series of case studies.
43	Descriptive of our reform process.
45	I provided conceptual frame and discussion of 7 papers.
46	Mine was a philosophical study.
47	Some basic quantitative measures are taken, but most of the work requires qualitative analysis.
49	Correlations, multiple regressions.
50	My research involves reading and analyzing text[book]s.
51	Questionnaires analyzed (reliability correlation) and interviews coded, ranked, and correlated.
53	I have done both—in fact I like "mixed" studies, but reviewers usually prefer one or the other. Questions usually suggest the type of study.

3. *If* you were engaged in research on teaching 10 years ago, how would you characterize the primary methodology that you were using then? (If you were not substantially engaged in research on teaching 10 years ago, please leave this item blank.)

1	2	3	4	5	6	7	8	9	10
Quantitative				Combination of					Qualitative
				Quantitative and Qualitative					

Comments, if any:

_____

_____

_____

Survey #	Response
10	A lot of work with archival/demographic data—unsophisticated statistical analysis—mostly descriptive.
24	If prior to 10 years ago, I would have said more quantitative.
31	Interviews, questionnaires.
43	Single subject research (15 years ago). Just starting qualitative (10 years ago).
45	10 years ago: in findings from a quantitative study, provided a sampling frame for addressing questions about processes (academic and social) at play that differentiated effective classroom managers from less effective managers.
47	As quantitative measures are put in perspective and do not dominate any more, it is highly relevant to use data whenever appropriate.
51	Pretest/posttest and control.
55	Descriptive.

****

5. Discuss where you view the field of research on teaching 10 years in the future. Focus on 3 or 4 key concepts—for example, what do you see as the prevailing methodology? What may be the substantive questions of interest?

_____

_____

_____

Survey #	Response
1	A combination of both quantitative and qualitative.
2	Qualitative—action research. Researchers will try to identify those elements that encourage or discourage student learning. So the emphasis will be on ways students learn, not on ways teachers teach. Schools will be reorganized to accommodate technological influences. Questions of interest may address how students are self-taught and on learning experiences translate information into knowledge.
3	(a) Individual differences, ATIs. (b) Importance of local, contextual variables. (c) Longitudinal studies and life histories of exemplary teachers. (d) Evaluating teaching and teacher education based on student outcomes of the children in school.
4	I think a combination of rich qualitative studies and well-designed quantitative studies of reformed classrooms will prove truthful to research on teaching. Qs of interest (a) diversity—analyzing teaching (+ learning) that reaches out to all students—complexities, challenges, successes. (b) Alternative assessment—exploring teaching (+ learning) through "new" measures—also how teaching is changed (or not) as alternative assessment practices are implemented. (c) Action research, teacher research, collaborative teacher research, and how they contribute to research on teaching.
6	Of interest: having the complex interactions between context (culture, if you will), individuals and the subject matters being addressed. The aim should be to develop rich and theoretically connected portrayals of good teaching/learning and if poor conditions in order to redirect approaches to improvement that could be enacted in particular settings. This research requires many ranges of approaches embedded qualitative, but also needs careful measurement of those things that can be quantified.

Survey #	Response
8	I imagine issues of language and cultural diversity will remain dominant, as well as investigations that explore alternative and performance assessments. I see qualitative methods, particularly discourse analysis and ethnography growing in importance.
10	There will be more blending/mixing of methods. Researchers will be coming to terms with the strengths and weaknesses of many approaches and designing from an eclectic methodological perspective. Topics of interest will include comparisons of traditional vs. charter schools—more emphasis on personal narratives as a preservice tool (continue focus on factors affecting student performance including technology, continue changes in family and socioeconomic structures).
11	I see more effort to connect teacher learning and student learning to deal with subject matter and issues of diversity. I see more comparative, interdisciplinary research.
12	A merger of qual. and quant. to include the personal nature of one with the generalizability of the other.
13	I think it would be unfortunate if either qualitative or quantitative research dominated. Different kinds of questions/subjects require different approaches. For decisions about pedagogies, learning environment, professional development, etc. I think we have a lot more qualitative work to do. But I want to know about macro issues regarding equity, curricular trends, attitudes, etc., which require large statistical studies. I'd like to see a lot more research into norm-referenced testing—only if to improve the tests and our use of them.
14	Collaboration—research ethics—ownership/power—methodologies will continue to emerge—all varieties. Questions: What are important questions? What makes a difference? What involves the researched? Is anything lagging or improving?
15	Teacher as researcher and other forms of participatory research methods should be playing a more important role. Hopefully, we will be closer linked to practice. Multiple data collection techniques—using a type of triangulation. Questions should focus on continuing professional development, lifelong learning and response to change and innovations.
16	Methodologies will be based on the questions of interest and importance of the era. It is hard to tell what those questions might be. My guess, though, is that qualitative methodologies will continue to be used to explore social phenomena that are measurable in terms of quantitative data.
17	While in research circles (some) generalizability might be outmoded, policy people are still hungry for it. In 10 years, hopefully, case study work will be better interpreted by the quantitative united stuff to provide research that is useful to practice and to policy. Over time, perhaps this way the idea that policy serves practice (not the other way around) will gain a strong foothold.
18	The methodologies would continue to respond to the significant research questions. Commonalties of large scale and in-depth studies can generate the most helpful information. My hope is that we have higher standards for the more qualitative research that gets published. Same stuff is horrible and gives narrative a bad name. Research by practitioners needs to be better understood, as does teacher-researcher work.
19	We need better deep descriptions of the complex dynamics of innovative, reflective classroom practice and of how teachers think about that practice and its inherent dilemmas. We need to understand how students construct content understandings and how teachers construct understandings of that construction roles. Finally, research on teaching should explore a variety of issues on teachers cognitive and professional development.
21	I believe there should be a combination of qualitative and quantitative methodologies in the field. Unexplored issues should be investigated qualitatively and the findings of such research should be tested quantitatively. Then a combination of both will enable to fully understand the issues.
22	Cognitive process involved in the teaching-learning interaction should be studies with some robust methods other than merely surface observations.
23	I would imagine the debate about qualitative vs. quantitative to still be in the discussion. I think there will be more quantitative master degrees and dissertations flowing through the system, but I'm not sure they will even be seen as true knowledge. I also see more classroom teachers going to universities that offer qualitative modes of degrees.
24	(a) Prevailing methodologies: greater continuation of qualitative and quantitative. (b) Questions of teacher/school culture, individual student learning in a social context.
25	The effect of culture on teaching and learning. Ethnographic research methodologies. Case methodologies, multicultural education on a global scale.

Survey #	Response
27	I hope the discussions of methodologies turn away from dichotomies and ideologically based struggles and toward examinations of issues and processes associated with more appropriate forms of representation. If our purpose as researchers is to apprehend, understand, and represent/communicate about elements of human experiences, then we need to find more outlandish and generalizable ways of researching human experiences.
28	[Because I'm new to the field], it seems to me that research methodologies and research on teaching move in and out of cycles influenced by larger cultural-political-economic forces. Right now, qualitative approaches are gaining momentum (much to the dismay of the older faculty . . .). In 10 years, I suspect things may swing to the quantitative end of the continuum. What I would like to see is a larger body of research using mixed methods— teams of researchers with qualitative and quantitative expertise, exploring relationships in classrooms and effects of classroom management on social-emotional learning of students. I suspect, however, that in 10 years, a more conservative wave may focus research on teacher accountability for students' academic performance. The 3 Rs and Back to Basics arguments are recycled over and over again.
29	I see the methodologies as a mixture of qualitative and quantitative, of ethnographic surveys and quasi-experiments. I hope that emphasis on the appropriate way to collect data to address a particular research question (including honoring the epistemological assumptions implicit in the question) increases, so that the question is the important focus, not the methodology per se. I hope the methodological focus shifts to trying to ensure the quality of and care with which the methods are applied.
30	Qualitative methodology valuing social contexts of excellence and teachers multiple factions (using qualitative methods to examine them).
31	(a) A combination of qualitative and quantitative. (b) More focus on validity issues—what can we really learn from quantitative studies. (c) Meta-research trends (analysis of numerous qualitative studies on specific issues).
32	(a) I see research as becoming increasingly theoretical. (b) I see an increase in research presentations as performance (aesthetic). (c) I see an increase in participatory research. (d) The opinion poll is going to play a larger and larger role in policy development. (e) Institutions are going to lose any control they currently have over "research." The media will replace research in this role.
33	Substantive questions of interest: school-university partnerships to improve both teacher education and schools. Prevailing methodology: collaborative inquiry.
34	Methodology will be primarily quantitative because of disappointment from qualitative.
35	I hope there is a return to rigor in both qualitative and quantitative methods. There has been a steady decline in the past 10 years. Sooner or later there will have to be acknowledgment of SES as a critical factor. Also, the systematic interaction of family and classroom with student learning.
36	Prevailing methodology will probably swing back to a quantitative focus—or a mixture of qualitative and quantitative. Technology will be researched—its effect on teaching and learning. Issues of diversity will also be studied—although with a different focus.
37	From quant. to qual.
38	Prevailing methodology will move more toward the "radical middle" or the "third space." Questions: How have pupils and systems (education) evolved into what they are? How has culture and the information age affected the thinking and action of pupils and educators? How can learning be made more meaningful for all learners?
40	With luck, we will be using large-scale statistical studies to relate teacher quality with desired student outcomes (more than traditional standardized tests) and also context specific detailed studies of how has "correlated" factors (e.g., teacher education experiences and student opportunities for learning and desired student outcomes) play out.
41	Combination of better technology and shifts in ideas about teaching will lead more and more to classroom and practitioner documentation—collections of student works; accounts of teaching by teachers—word processed-data bases; digitized photos, etc. Increasing role of collaborative studies of teaching and learning—among teachers and between teachers and university folk. What does it take to make schools productive contexts for learning for both students and teachers? How to balance issues of community and diversity within classrooms, schools, and districts.
43	I would like to see more stories of teachers engaged in inquiry and reflection (like Dudley-Marling's book *Messy Reality of Classroom Practice;* Ruth Parker's work with a 5th grade math teacher). Rich descriptions of the challenges of working with diverse learners.

Survey #	Response
45	(a) Access to opportunity to learn as civil rights. (b) Cultural identity development—in classrooms. (c) Multiple sites of learning (home, school, baseball diamond) cross-site comparisons.
47	On-line data (out of professional development community of teachers) will require to be for ethnographic site-based and field ethnography. Reflective literature will benefit desktop publishing. Collaborative teaching will lead to coproduction of materials. Teaching and research will merge in new ways and global virtual learners are likely to become a new standard. New ability to research a single learning activity and keep it productive—global learning projects.
48	We will probably still be struggling with mechanisms understanding achievement, success, and motivation. Quantitative and qualitative methods will come into balance. Teacher qualities, beliefs, and effects.
49	I think a combination of qualitative and quantitative should be the goal. I have found that the qualitative research helps to classify and explain the quantitative.
50	I think research on teaching—and everything else—is influenced by the world historic context. No one can any more predict the direction of research than she can [predict] what will occur in international markets or politics.
51	I'm convinced that ethnographic studies alone will do little more than tell nice stories. Variables that emerge need to be established as constructs and, where possible, measured. Questions include the management issues—at school boards and within school level: how do you change hierarchy of the administration so that innovative and constructive practice is encouraged, rather than suppressed? But then in 10 years, I'll be well out to grass!
52	Methodologies will continue to be mixed. Probably the pendulum will have swung back toward the quantitative side a bit by then. People will want fewer stories and more "hard" generalizable principles by which to guide classrooms and programs. But these will be more intelligent generalizations, tempered by understanding of context.
53	I hope that research will focus on what is appropriate to the question. I believe that quantitative and qualitative research are different ways of knowing—we need multiple perspectives. Quantitative research is as politically motivated as any other—or me, in the human sciences, very little is absolutely true. I hope that we will come to value different methodologies.
54	More focus on learning—more focus on t and ss cognition.
55	More quantitative—large-scale studies to study experts on school reform—qualitative studies focusing on specific smaller populations.

6. In the future, for studies that *do* incorporate *quantitative* methods, what do you view as the major outcome measures (for the field of research on teaching, as now represented by Division K)? What would you estimate to be the process measures of most interest (teacher, school, student variables)?

_____

_____

_____

Survey #	Response
2	Field-based teacher ed. programs (# of teachers hrs prior to ST). How students organize learning tasks? Ways students determine successful completion of tasks? How often teachers introduce new web sites? School design as it encourages multi-age interaction. Quantities of resources—ways used (hour per day), etc.
3	Student variables—yes, not correlations. Maybe regression or multi-variable analysis if the N is big enough to warrant these. Aptitude X treatment interactions.
4	Difficult to understand the question. Having written this, I think outcome measures for quantitative studies: changes in teaching and learning as process measures change. When it comes to process measures, I believe that we should think about all possible variables (teacher, school, student) rather than having different studies focusing on different sets of variables.
6	I have no objection to quant. measures if they are valid. But one should take complex actions as outcomes, not scores on standardized tests, student learning. Broadly defined and development of efficacy are most inept outcomes. I don't believe process can be represented as a variable; I think you need rich descriptions of the work of teachers and students in particular settings.

Survey #	Response
9	Student variables indirect consequence of planned T. intervention with data collected primarily qualitatively.
11	Outcomes: student understanding, student promotion/retention, at-risk student achievement, teacher learning. Process: student understanding, teacher learning.
14	Achievement, whatever that may mean. The difference between quality experience and putting in time. Differences in pedagogical content knowledge.
15	We must deal with student variables. Its difficult to deal with the ethics, power issues, etc., but it is crucial to understand student outcomes. Hopefully, we will focus on multiple outcomes—not just test results.
17	School variables (site, organizational features). "Value added" is a concept that should /could be developed with quantitative methods. Outcome measures: some standardized test scores and some as yet to be developed school-based (developed and done) outcome measures.
19	If we can imagine deeper, more-robust measures of students' understanding—not just answers but processes and pushing the edges of their thinking; and also measures of statistics, confidence, collaborative abilities, maybe of cognitive capacity that might serve as outcomes. My guess is that predictors may need to be multilevel. I really think teaching is inherently cultivated, very specialized, and complex.
22	Outcome measures: problem solving ability in domains, creativity in domains (e.g., math creativity, science creativity . . .). Process Measures: student motivation, effective teacher's knowledge structure, cognitive strategy, and automatic routines.
24	(a) Student learning [outcomes]. (b) All 3 major domains (i.e., teacher, school, and student, plus the important system-level variable [measures]).
28	What's likely: Outcome measures = student academic performance as measured on the most widespread and standardized tests. What I'd like to see: process measures that interest me most are the role of teacher beliefs, school climate, and parent involvement and affiliation with the school in student engagement and learning.
29	Student outcomes: achievement (of all sorts!), effort, academic self-concept, academic future choice, career, interests, etc. Teacher outcomes: career trajectories, beliefs about education (also a process variable), satisfaction, etc. Teacher process: beliefs, values, instructional and assessment strategies, planning and thought. Student processes: effort (also an outcome variable) interest, study and work habits, involvement in the learning community, peer interaction, etc. School and classroom variables: climate, curriculum, instructional policy, etc.
30	Quantitative data support; qualitative analysis.
31	Process measures: student learning, teacher thinking and professional growth. Outcome measures: going beyond the "contextual," identification of mega-trends.
33	It seems to me that quantitative methods are useful for giving general, micro-social information and appreciating the importance of such case study in regard to the whole national and international data.
34	Teacher thinking and behavior, including out of class behavior. Student achievement and thinking—academic, social, and moral.
35	Performance assessment will be with us. As we are learning in Kentucky developing reliable and valid multiple measures is so expensive that it is not going to be worth doing unless we change our paradigms. However, the testing—policy-maker complex is not going to support a meaningful change.
36	Tests will prevail. Student variables.
41	Stability of enrollment in schools—stability of staffing—class size—per pupil spending—staff/pupil ratio, school size, professional development opportunities.
45	I'm not sure I understand the question. The process measures you itemize won't be taken seriously if anyone is depicted in isolation from others.
47	To document the information. Members of the teaching profession are engaged with the integration of the classroom instruction with their homes; schools are large educational systems. Add networks as a new object of knowledge and process measure.

Survey #	Response
49	We must focus on factors that make a difference in student learning. We must continue to search for valid and reliable ways of determining what works—variables having an impact on student learning and ways of quantifying learning that is substantive, invoking higher level thinking, analysis, and synthesis.
51	Teacher behaviors—pupil academic achievement—management ethos, beliefs, and style.
52	(a) Student learning measured in a variety of ways student strategy use. (b) We'll be looking at things like reflection and beliefs, but less globally; we'll have refined those into more precise variables.
53	I think student variables are most valued at a time of educational accountability. As a result of that, teacher variables are also of interest.

REFERENCES

Achilles, C. M., Nye, B. A., Zaharias, J. B., & Fulton, B. D. (1993). Creating successful schools for all children: A proven step. *Journal of School Leadership, 3*(6), 606–621.

Achilles, C. M., Nye, B. A., Zaharias, J. B., Fulton, B. D., & Cain V. (1996). *Education's equivalent of medicine's Framingham heart study.* Paper presented at the Fifth Annual National Conference on Creating the Quality School, March, 1996, Oklahoma City, OK.

Anderson, L. W., & Burns, R. B. (1987). Values, evidence, and mastery learning. *Review of Educational Research, 57,* 215–223.

Angoff, W. H. (1971). Scales, norms, and equivalent scores. In R. L. Thorndike (Ed.), *Educational Measurement* (2nd ed., pp. 508–600). Washington, DC: American Council on Education.

Armstrong, J., & Impara, J. C. (1990). The effects of order of test administration on environmental attitudes. *Journal of Environmental Education, 21*(3), 37–39.

Barrett, T. J. (1994). *Generalizability of writing tasks at fourth grade in the Riverside Unified School District.* Paper presented at the Annual Meeting of the California Educational Research Association Meeting, San Diego, CA.

Begley, S. (1997, April 21). The science wars. *Newsweek,* 54–57.

Berliner, D.C., Resnick, L. B., Cuban, L., Cole, N., Popham, W. J., & Goodlad, J. I. (1997). "The Vision Thing": Educational research and AERA in the 21st century, Part 2. Competing visions for enhancing the impact of educational research. *Educational Researcher, 26*(5), 12–18, 27.

Blair, D. T. (1996). The placebogenic phenomenon: Art in psychiatric nursing. *Journal of Psychosocial Nursing, 34*(8), 11–15.

Bracey, G. W. (1993). Testing the tests. *The School Administrator, 50*(11), 8–11.

Bradley, A. (1998, February 18). Education schools getting heat on reading. *Education Week, 2,* 16–17.

Brandt, R. (1992). On performance assessment: A conversation with Grant Wiggins. *Educational Leadership, 49*(8), 35–37.

Brennan, R. L., & Johnson, E. G. (1995, Winter). Generalizability of performance assessments. *Educational Measurement: Issues and Practice,* 9–12, 27.

Brookhart, S. M. (1994). Teachers' grading practices: Practice and theory. *Applied Measurement in Education, 7,* 279–301.

Campbell, D. T., & Stanley, J. C. (1963). Experimental and quasi-experimental designs for research on teaching. In N. L. Gage (Ed.) *Handbook of research on teaching.* Chicago: Rand McNally.

Chambers, J. H. (1992). *Empiricist research on teaching: A philosophical and practical analysis of its scientific pretensions.* Boston: Kluwer Academic Publishers.

Cochran, W. G. (1968). Errors of measurement in statistics. *Technometrics, 10,* 637–666.

Cook, T. D., & Campbell, D. T. (1979). *Quasi-experimentation: Design and analysis issues for field studies.* Boston: Houghton Mifflin.

Cooley, W. W., Gage, N. L., & Scriven, M. (1997). "The Vision Thing": Educational research in the 21st century, Part 1. Competing visions of what educational researchers should do. *Educational Researcher, 26*(4), 18–21.

Coop, R. H., & Brown, L. D. (1970) Effects of cognitive style and teaching method on categories of achievement. *Journal of Educational Psychology, 61*(5), 400–405.

Coulter, C. L., Kaneshige, A. M., & Wyatt, W. M. (1997). Unusual cause of dysarthria in a patient with cerebrovascular disease. *Archives of Neurology 54,* 515–516.

Crawford, J., & Brady, R. (1998, March). *Evaluation of the Millard Public Schools Excellence in Education summer school program.* Omaha, NE: Millard Public Schools.

Cronbach, L. J., Gleser, G. C., Nanda, H., & Rajaratnam, N. (1972). *The dependability of behavioral measurements.* New York: Wiley.

Cronbach, L. J., Linn, R. L., Brennan, R. L., & Haertel, E. (1995, Summer). *Generalizability analysis for educational assessments* (Monograph). Los Angeles: National Center for Research on Evaluation, Standards, and Student Testing, UCLA.

Devlin, B., Daniels, M., & Roeder, K. (1997). The heritability of IQ. *Nature, 388,* 468–471.

Donmoyer, R. (1996). Educational research in an era of paradigm proliferation: What's a journal editor to do? *Educational Researcher, 25*(2), 19–25.

Ebel, R. E. (1979). *Essentials of educational measurement* (3rd ed.). Englewood Cliffs, NJ: Prentice-Hall.

Education Testing Service, Test Collection. (1989–1995). *The ETS Test Collection Catalog* (Vols. 1–2, 2nd ed.; Vols. 3–6). Phoenix, AZ: Oryz Press.

Eisner, E. (1993). Forms of understanding and the future of educational research. *Educational Researcher, 22*(7), 38–39.

Elmore, P. B., & Woehlke, P. L. (1996). *Research methods employed in* American Educational Research Journal, Educational Researcher, *and* Review of Educational Research from 1978 to 1995. Paper presented at the annual meeting of the American Educational Research Association, New York.

Evertson, C. M., & Randolph, C. H. (1989). Teaching practices and class size: A new look at an old issue. *Peabody Journal of Education, 67*(1), 85–105.

Folger, J. (1989). Lessons for class size policy and research. *Peabody Journal of Education, 67*(1), 123–132.

Frary, R. B., Cross, L. H., & Weber, L. J. (1993). Testing and grading practices and opinions of secondary teachers of academic subjects: Implications for instruction in measurement. *Educational Measurement: Issues and Practices, 12*(3), 23–30.

Gage, N. L. (1994a). The scientific status of research on teaching. *Educational Theory, 44*(4), 371–383.

Gage, N. L. (1994b). The scientific status of the behavioral sciences: The case of research on teaching. An essay review of *Empiricist research on teaching: A philosophical and practical critique of its scientific pretensions. Teaching and Teacher Education, 10*(5), 565–577.

Gage, N. L. (1996). Confronting counsels of despair for the behavioral sciences. *Educational Researcher, 25*(3), 5–15, 22.

Giraud, G., Impara, J. C., Plake, B. S., Hertzog, M., & Spies, R. (1997, October). *Cut score validity in a public school setting.* Paper presented at the annual meeting of the Midwestern Educational Research Association, Chicago.

Goldman, B. A., Saunders, J. L., Busch, J. C., Osborne, W. L., & Mitchell, D. F. (Eds.). (1974–1995). *Directory of unpublished experimental mental measures* (Vols. 1–6). Washington, DC: American Psychological Association.

Greenwald, R., Hedges, L. V., & Laine, R. D. (1996a). The effect of school resources on student achievement. *Review of Educational Research, 66*(3), 361–396.

Greenwald, R., Hedges, L. V., & Laine, R. D. (1996b). Interpreting research on school resources and student achievement: A rejoinder to Hanushek. *Review of Educational Research, 66*(3), 411–416.

Guskey, T. R. (1987). Rethinking mastery learning reconsidered. *Review of Educational Research, 57*, 225–229.

Hambleton, R., & Plake, B. (1995). Using an extended Angoff procedure to set standards on complex performance assessments. *Applied Measurement in Education, 8*, 41–57.

Hanushek, E. A. (1994). Money might matter somewhere: A response to Hedges, Laine, and Greenwald. *Educational Researcher, 23*, 5–8.

Hanushek, E. A. (1996). A more complete picture of school resource policies. *Review of Educational Research, 66*(3), 397–409.

Hedges, L. V., Laine, R. D., & Greenwald, R. (1994a). Does money matter? A meta-analysis of studies of the effects of differential school inputs on student outcomes. *Educational Researcher, 23*(3), 5–14.

Hedges, L. V., Laine, R. D., & Greenwald, R. (1994b) Money does matter somewhere: A reply to Hanushek. *Educational Researcher, 2*(4), 9–10.

Herrnstein, R. J., & Murray, C. (1994). *The bell curve: Intelligence and class structure in American life.* New York: Free Press.

Holliday, W. G. (1992). Should we reduce class size? What the research really says. *The Science Teacher, 59*(1), 14–17.

Impara, J. C. (1997, October). *Setting standards using Angoff's method: Does the method meet the standard?* Invited paper presented to Division D of the Midwestern Educational Research Association, Chicago.

Impara, J. C., & Plake, B. S. (1997). Standard setting: An alternative approach. *Journal of Educational Measurement, 34*, 355–368.

Impara, J. C., & Plake, B. S. (1998). Teachers' ability to estimate item difficulty: A test of the assumptions in the Angoff standard setting method. *Journal of Educational Measurement, 35*, 69–81.

Jordan, R. P. (1996, March). *Searching for information on tests: Reference sources and a search strategy* (Iowa Testing Programs Occasional Papers, #38). Iowa City: University of Iowa Testing Programs.

Jöreskog, K. G. (1973). A general model for estimating a linear structural equation system. In A. S. Goldberger & O. D. Duncan (Eds.), *Structural equation models in the social sciences: Specification, estimation and testing.* New York: Seminal Press.

Kennedy, M. (1996a). *Some common contentions about educational research.* Paper presented at the annual meeting of the American Educational Research Association, Chicago, IL.

Kennedy, M. (1996b, April). *Teacher's responses to educational research.* East Lansing: National Center for Research on Teacher Learning, Michigan State University.

Keyser, D. J., & Sweetland, R. C. (Eds.). (1984–1994). *Test critiques* (Vols. 1–10). Austin, TX: Pro-Ed.

Khalili, A., & Shashaani, L. (1994). The effectiveness of computer applications: A meta-analysis. *Journal of Research on Computing in Education, 2*(1), 48–61.

LeLorier, J., Gregoire, G., Benhaddad, A., Lapierre, J., & Derderian, F. (1997). Discrepancies between meta-analyses and subsequent large randomized, controlled trials. *The New England Journal of Medicine, 337*, 536–542.

Linn, R. L. (1986). Quantitative methods in research on teaching. In M. C. Wittrock, (Ed.), *Handbook of research on teaching* (3rd ed.). New York: Macmillan.

Linn, R. L., & Burton, E. (1994). Performance-based assessment: Implications of task specificity. *Educational Measurement: Issues and Practice, 13*, 5–8, 15.

Linn, R. L., & Shepard. L. (1997, July). *Item-by-item standard setting: Misinterpretations of judge's intentions due to less than perfect item inter-correlations.* Presentation at the Large-scale Assessment Conference, Colorado Springs, CO.

Livingston, S. A. (1995). Standards for reporting the educational achievement of groups. In *Joint Conference on Standard Setting for Large Scale Assessments, Proceedings Volume II* (pp. 39–51). Washington, DC: National Assessment Governing Board, National Center for Educational Statistics.

Livingston, S. A., & Zieky, M. J. (1982). *Passing scores: A manual for setting standards of performance on educational and occupational tests.* Princeton, NJ: Educational Testing Service.

Livingston, S. A., & Zieky, M. J. (1989) A comparative study of standard setting methods. *Applied Measurement in Education, 2*, 121–141.

Madden, N. A., & Slavin, R. E. (1983). Mainstreaming students with mild handicaps: Academic and social outcomes. *Review of Educational Research, 53*(4), 519–569.

Maddox, T. (Ed.). (1997). *Tests: A comprehensive reference for assessments in psychology, education, and business* (4th ed.). Austin, TX: Pro-Ed.

Marcoulides, G. A., & Goldstein, Z. (1992). The optimization of multivariate generalizability studies with budget constraints. *Educational and Psychological Measurement, 52*(2), 301–308.

Messick, S. (1989). Validity. In *Educational Measurement* (3rd ed.). Phoenix, AZ: Oryz Press.

Messick, S. (1995). Standards of validity and the validity of standards in performance assessments. *Educational Measurement: Issues and Practice, 14*(4), 5–8.

Mitchell, J. V., Jr. (Ed.) (1985). *Ninth mental measurements yearbook.* Lincoln, NE: Buros Institute of Mental Measurements, University of Nebraska–Lincoln.

Mitchell, P. E., Beach, S. A., & Badarak, G. (1989). Modeling the relationship between achievement and class size: A re-analysis of the Tennessee project STAR data. *Peabody Journal of Education, 67*(1), 34–74.

Moertel, C. G., Taylor, W. F., Roth, A., & Tyce, F. A. (1976). Who responds to sugar pills? *Mayo Clinic Proceedings, 51*, 96–100.

Mosteller, F., Light, R. J., & Sachs, J. A. (1996). Sustained inquiry in education: Lessons from skill grouping and class size. *Harvard Educational Review, 66*(4), 797–828.

Murphy, L. L., Impara, J. C., & Plake, B. S. (Eds.). (2000). *Tests in print V: An index to tests, test reviews, and the literature on specific tests* (Vols. 1–2). Lincoln, NE: Buros Institute of Mental Measurements, University of Nebraska–Lincoln.

Nedelsky, L. (1954). Absolute grading standards for objective tests. *Educational and Psychological Measurement, 14*, 3–19.

Nye, B. A., Achilles, C. M., Boyd-Zaharias, J., Fulton, B. D., & Wallenhorst, M. P. (1992). *Five years of small-class research: Student benefits derived from reduced student/teacher ratios.* Paper presented at the annual meeting of the American Educational Research Association, San Francisco, CA.

Nye, B. A., Boyd-Zaharias, J., Fulton, B. D., & Wallenhorst, M. P. (1992). Smaller classes really are better. *American School Board Journal, 179*(5), 31–33.

Pate-Bain, H., Achilles, C. M., Boyd-Zaharias, J., & McKenna. B. (1992). Class size does make a difference. *Phi Delta Kappan, 74*, 253–256.

Plake, B. S., & Impara, J. C. (Eds.). (2001). *The fourteenth mental measurements yearbook.* Lincoln, NE: Buros Institute of Mental Measurements, University of Nebraska–Lincoln.

Roeber, E. D. (1997). *The technical and practical challenges in developing innovative assessment approaches for use in statewide assessment programs.* Paper presented at the annual meeting of the American Educational Research Association, Chicago, IL.

Rose, L. C., Gallup, A. M., & Elam, S. M. (1997, September). The 29th annual PDK/Gallup Poll of the public's attitudes toward the public schools. *Phi Delta Kappan, 79*(1), 41–56.

Shavelson, R. J., Baxter, G. P., & Gao, X. (1993). Sampling variability of performance assessments. *Journal of Educational Measurement, 30*, 215–232.

Shavelson, R. J., Baxter, G. P., & Pine, J. (1992). Performance assessments: Political rhetoric and measurement reality. *Educational Researcher, 21*(4), 22–27.

Shavelson, R. J. & Webb, N. M. (1991). *Generalizability theory: A primer.* Newbury Park, CA: Sage.

Shavelson, R. J. Webb, N. M., & Rowley, G. (1989, June). Generalizability theory. *American Psychologist, 44*(6), 922–932.

Shepard, L. A. (1995). Implications for standard setting of the NAE evaluation of NAEP achievement levels. *Joint Conference on Standard Setting for Large Scale Assessments, Proceedings, Volume II* (pp. 143–160). Washington, DC: National Assessment Governing Board, National Center for Educational Statistics.

Sireci, S. A., & Biskin, B. H. (1992). Measurement practices in national licensing examination programs: A survey. *CLEAR Exam Review, 3*(1), 21–25.

Slavin, R. E. (1986). Best-evidence synthesis: An alternative to meta-analysis and traditional reviews. *Educational Researcher, 15*(9), 5–11.

Slavin, R. E. (1987a). Ability grouping and student achievement in elementary schools: A best-evidence synthesis. *Review of Educational Research, 57*(3), 293–336.

Slavin, R. E. (1987b). Mastery learning reconsidered. *Review of Educational Research, 5*(2), 175–213.

Slavin, R. E. (1990). Achievement effects of ability grouping in secondary schools: A best-evidence synthesis. *Review of Educational Research, 60*(3), 471–499.

Swanson, D. B., Norman, G. R., & Linn, R. L. (1995). Performance-based assessment: Lessons from the health professions. *Educational Researcher, 24*(5), 5–11, 35.

Sweetland, R. C., & Keyser, D. J. (Eds.). (1991). *Tests: A comprehensive reference for assessments in psychology, education, and business* (3rd ed.). Austin, TX: Pro-Ed.

Tallmadge, G. K., & Wood, C. T. (1978). *User's Guide: ESEA Title I Evaluation and Reporting System.* Mountain View, CA: RMC Research Corporation.

Tanner, D. (1998). The social consequences of bad research. *Phi Delta Kappan, 79*(5), 344–349.

Terwilliger, J. (1997). Semantics, psychometrics, and assessment reform: A close look at "authentic" assessments. *Educational Researcher, 26*(8), 24–27.

Tomlinson, T. M. (1990). Class size and public policy: The plot thickens. *Contemporary Education, 62*(1), 17–23.

Turner, J. A., Deyo, R. A., Loeser, J. D., Von Korff, M., & Fordyce, W. E. (1994). The importance of placebo effects in pain treatment and research. *Journal of the American Medical Association, 271*(20), 1609–1614.

Wilcox, C. S., Cohn, J. B., Linden, R. D., Heiser, J. F., Lucas, P. B., Morgan, D. L., & DeFrancisco, D. (1992). Predictors of placebo response: A retrospective analysis. *Psychopharmacology Bulletin, 28*(2), 157–162.

Wolfe, E. W. (1996). *A report on the reliability of a large-scale portfolio assessment for language arts, mathematics, and science.* Paper presented at the annual meeting of the National Council for Measurement in Education, New York, NY.

11.
Paradigm Talk Reconsidered

Robert Donmoyer
University of San Diego

The world was once a simpler place. During that time, a phrase like "research on teaching," at least within the United States,[1] conjured up relatively clear and consistent images. Research on teaching was something done by professors (or similar sorts of social scientists) who worked in universities (or similar sorts of knowledge-generating organizations). Such research might employ a range of procedures—everything from surveys to correlational analysis (maybe even case studies done for the purpose of hypothesis generation)—but the ultimate goal was to validate causal relationships between what teachers do and what students learn. Hence, the quasi-experimental study with a representative sample large enough to produce statistically significant findings was considered the ultimate form of research on teaching. Quasi-experimental studies were needed to make survey findings useful, to ensure that inferences about causality drawn from correlational findings were valid, and to certify that the hypotheses generated from case studies were not only internally valid but also generalizable (Good, Biddle, & Brophy, 1975).

The emergence of qualitative research procedures as method-ological options in the 1970s began to complicate things a bit. Initially, for some at least, the complications were not too dramatic. Matthew Miles (1979), for example, dubbed qualitative methods an "attractive nuisance." According to Miles and like-minded scholars, there were some problems associated with using qualitative research procedures (most notably, problems related to internal validity and generalizability); however, qualitative procedures did expand the methodological options available to educational researchers, and, consequently, they did make it easier for researchers to investigate certain kinds of phenomena. In research on teaching, for example, qualitative methods made it possible to investigate teacher thinking (Clark & Peterson, 1986; Clark & Yinger, 1977), a phenomenon that could not be studied easily by methods that focused exclusively on directly observable behavior and that, consequently, provided at best only high inference access to the black box of the human mind.

While some saw the introduction of qualitative methods into the study of teaching and other educational phenomena as an attractive, albeit somewhat problematic, way to expand educa-

The bulk of this paper was written while I was a faculty member and administrator at the Ohio State University. I want to acknowledge that institution's generous support. I also want to express my appreciation to the two reviewers of this chapter, John K. Smith and Jean Clandinin, for their thoughtful critiques and the helpful way the critiques were made. I also wish to acknowledge my Ohio State colleagues, Patti Lather and Nancy Chisin, for their always helpful comments, and the many current and former Ohio State doctoral students with whom I have had the good fortune to interact and who have, in the course of these interactions, sharpened my thinking on the issues discussed in this chapter. This group includes but, of course, is not limited to Gary Anderson, Shawn Batterberry, William Billinghurst, Joanne Burrows, Jeasik Cho, Brian Edmiston, Su Ching Lin, Diana Moyer, Mongaring Musa, Bachrudin Mustafa, Tonette Rocco, Marilyn Scherwindt, James Scheurich, Linda Tillman, Juanita Wagstaff, and Connie Wu.

[1] The focus of this chapter is primarily on research on teaching in the United States or at least on work that has greatly influenced discussions about research on teaching within this country. I readily acknowledge the limits of such ethnocentrism. I also acknowledge the benefits of viewing a phenomenon such as educational research from a more comparative perspective. Mexican scholars with whom I have worked, for instance, indicate that the move to qualitative research in their country represents a move toward empirical research and away from the Marxist-inspired critiques that tended to dominate Mexican scholarship in the past. Not surprisingly, my Mexican friends have a different view of critical ethnography than many scholars in the United States who came to qualitative research from a decidedly different direction. Similarly, if we were to focus on work by our neighbors to the north, we would find a greater emphasis on ontology than one finds in this chapter, in part, because of the influence of Max van Manen's (1990) focus on the importance of attending to the "lived experience" of teachers and students. When space is limited, however, hard choices about focus have to be made, and it is sensible, I believe, for an author of a chapter such as this one to focus on the cultural contexts he or she knows best. Furthermore, a critique of conceptions of research that are operative in the United States can be justified on the grounds that, for better and, all too often, for worse, United States' views of research have had a profound impact on the thinking of scholars throughout the world. I have sat in a seminar room in Indonesia and have been told that quantitative and qualitative research strategies simply cannot be combined. Proponents of this position supported their argument by citing United States scholars, Lincoln and Guba.

tional researchers' methodological options, others almost immediately saw the introduction of such methods into the field as being about much more than methodology. Their position was similar to Talcott Parsons' view of methodological disputes that arose during the advent of the social sciences in the 1800s. In his classic text, *The Structure of Social Action,* Parsons wrote:

> The issues between German idealism and Western European positivism have been more than merely methodological. . . . They have concerned differences over the substantive factors invoked in explanation of human action. (Parsons, 1937, p. 481)

The view that growing interest in the use of qualitative research procedures in educational research signaled much more than an expansion of educational researchers' methodological strategies was clearly articulated in a chapter written by Fred Erickson (1986) in the previous edition of this *Handbook.* In his chapter titled "Qualitative Methods in Research on Teaching," in fact, Erickson, took issue with what Carolyn Evertson and Judith Green (1986) had written in another chapter of the *Handbook*—a chapter that focused on both qualitative and quantitative observation techniques—precisely because Evertson and Green treated qualitative methods merely as techniques. Erickson (1986) wrote that Evertson and Green's

> comprehensive review of a wide range of methods of classroom observation does not emphasize the discontinuities in theoretical presupposition that obtain across the two major types of approaches to classroom research, positivist/behaviorist and interpretive. . . . Green and Evertson are relatively optimistic about the possibility of combining disparate methods and orientations in classroom observation. I am more pessimistic about the possibility, and have become increasingly so in the last few years. (p. 120)

Educational researchers who, like Erickson, viewed the introduction of qualitative procedures as being about something more than research methodology frequently appropriated a concept from Thomas Kuhn's (1962/1970) historically based analysis of the physical sciences to indicate what that "something more" was. Kuhn argued that scientific understanding in the physical sciences is not the result of the progressive accumulation of bits and pieces of information. Rather, according to Kuhn, scientific knowledge and the process of creating such knowledge, in reasonably mature scientific disciplines at least, are grounded in something that Kuhn called "paradigms." Kuhn did not provide a precise definition of the term *paradigm.* (One critic (Masterman, 1970), in fact, counted twenty-two somewhat different ways in which Kuhn used the term in his book, *The Structure of Scientific Revolutions.*) In his book, however, Kuhn did indicate that

> the transition from a paradigm in crisis to a new one from which a new tradition of normal science can emerge . . . is a reconstruction of the field from new fundamentals, a reconstruction that changes some of the field's most elementary theoretical generalizations as well as many of its paradigm methods and applications. . . . When the transition is complete, the profession will have changed its view of the field, its methods, and its goals. (pp. 84–85)

Kuhn also relied on a metaphor from gestalt psychology—along with some important caveats—to clarify what a paradigm

is: "The marks on paper that were first seen as a bird are now seen as an antelope, or vice versa." Kuhn quickly added that the visual gestalt metaphor

> can be misleading. Scientists do not see something *as* something else; instead, they simply see it. . . . In addition, the scientist does not preserve the gestalt subject's freedom to switch back and forth between ways of seeing. Nevertheless, the switch of gestalt, particularly because it is today so familiar, is a useful elementary prototype for what occurs in full-scale paradigm shift. (p. 85)

Thus, for many educational researchers in the 1970s, the emergence and growing acceptance of qualitative research methods was seen as evidence that the field of educational research was undergoing the same sort of "paradigm revolution" that Kuhn's historical analysis suggested occurred intermittently within physical science disciplines.

Interestingly, Erickson, himself, stopped short of characterizing the different "theoretical presuppositions" he associated with the use of qualitative and quantitative methods as Kuhnian paradigms, quite possibly because he was influenced by the thinking on display in another third edition *Handbook* chapter, one written by Lee Shulman (1986) and titled "Paradigms and Research Programs in the Study of Teaching: A Contemporary Perspective." In that chapter Shulman took issue with key components of Kuhn's thinking—especially Kuhn's thinking about the social sciences. Consequently, although Shulman used Kuhn's term, he radically redefined it: "There is a second, weaker sense of paradigm I prefer to use in this chapter," Shulman wrote (1986, p. 5).

Here, I want to critically examine both Kuhnian-inspired paradigm talk and Shulman's "weaker" form of paradigm talk. My argument is a simple one: Both forms of paradigm talk have outlived their usefulness, albeit for quite different reasons. One form of paradigm talk, I will argue, exaggerates differences among research orientations, while the other form underestimates very real and significant—and, in the contemporary context, at least, quite obvious—differences among researchers. In the final portion of the paper, I will present and briefly make the case for using another strategy for simplifying the Pandora's box of complexity that has been unlocked by the qualitative research revolution.

Kuhnian-Inspired Paradigm Talk Reconsidered

Characteristics of Kuhnian-Inspired Paradigm Talk

Patton (1980/1990) encapsulates, in a relatively brief definition, what the term paradigm has come to mean to educational researchers who have been influenced by Kuhn's description of the role of paradigms in the physical sciences. "A paradigm," Patton writes,

> is a world view, a general perspective, a way of breaking down the complexity of the real world. As such, paradigms are deeply embedded in the socialization of adherents and practitioners: paradigms tell them what is important, legitimate, and reasonable. Paradigms are also normative, telling the practitioner what to do without the necessity of long existential or epistemological consideration. (p. 37)

While the paradigms we have been socialized to accept make unnecessary any long discussions about the nature of reality (i.e., ontology) and the nature of knowledge and knowing (i.e., epistemology), Kuhnian-inspired paradigm talk makes unconscious assumptions about such matters conscious and susceptible to critique and reformulation.

Arguably the most influential proponents and practitioners of Kuhnian-inspired paradigm talk within the education field—and in several other fields as well—are Lincoln and Guba. In their widely cited book, *Naturalistic Inquiry,* for example, Lincoln and Guba (1985) embed their discussion of qualitative research methods into a much larger discussion of two different and, according to them, incommensurable paradigms.

LINCOLN AND GUBA'S COMPETING PARADIGMS

The Positivist Paradigm. One paradigm Lincoln and Guba label "positivism." The positivist paradigm, according to Lincoln and Guba (1985), includes a realist ontology: "There is a single tangible reality 'out there' fragmentable into independent variables and processes, any of which can be studied independently of the others; inquiry can converge on that reality until, finally, it can be predicted and controlled" (p. 37). The positivist paradigm also has embedded within it a number of assumptions about knowledge and knowing. For example, according to Lincoln and Guba, a positivist epistomology is rooted in the assumption that "the inquirer and the object [of inquiry] are independent" (p. 37). The positivist paradigm also incorporates the notions that (a) "the aim of inquiry is to develop a nomothetic body of knowledge in the form of generalizations that are truth statements free of time and context (they hold anywhere and at anytime)" (p. 38); (b) "every action [in fact] can be explained as the result (effect) of a real cause that precedes the effect temporally" (p. 38); and (c) inquiry can be value-free if appropriate methods—that is, methods designed to ensure objectivity—are employed.

In their 1985 book, Lincoln and Guba claimed that virtually all educational researchers up to that point had been socialized to accept the positivist paradigm. Consequently, virtually all researchers at the time accepted—without much thought or discussion—the logic undergirding experimental and quasi-experimental research design, and they embraced experimental and quasi-experimental design as the paragon of methodological virtue within the field.

One certainly could find evidence to support this claim within the field of research on teaching. In the preface to the American Educational Research Association's first *Handbook of Research on Teaching,* for example, the first *Handbook*'s editor, N. L. Gage (1963a), discusses the *Handbook*'s organization. Rather than organize the text as a kind of intellectual vaudeville as the editors of this fourth edition of the *Handbook* have (of necessity) done, Gage indicates that, in the first *Handbook,* a single "conceptual framework was to provide an orientation for the entire volume, and each chapter was to flow from this framework" (p. vi). The framework employed includes the following definition:

> Research on teaching is aimed at the identification and measurement of variables in the behavior and characteristics of teachers, at

discovering the antecedents or determiners of these central variables, and at revealing the consequents or effects of these variables. (p. vi)

Further evidence of what Lincoln and Guba call positivist thinking can be found by examining the research methods discussed in the first *Handbook* and by focusing on methodologies that received no attention. The section titled "Methodologies in Research on Teaching," for example, opens with Tatsuoka and Tiedman's (1963) chapter "Statistics as an Aspect of Scientific Method in Research on Teaching" and Campbell and Stanley's (1963a) exceedingly influential "Experimental and Quasi-Experimental Designs for Teaching." Other chapters on research methodology focus on measuring classroom behavior by systematic observation (Medley & Mitzel, 1963), rating methods in research on teaching (Remmers, 1963), testing cognitive ability and achievement (Bloom, 1963), and measuring noncognitive variables in research on teaching (Stern, 1963).

At least as significant as what was included in the first *Handbook* is what was not there: The first handbook contained no discussion of qualitative research procedures. Qualitative methods also were not mentioned in the *Handbook*'s second edition (Travers, 1973). (The second edition of the *Handbook* does contain a chapter titled "Issues in the Analysis of Qualitative Data" (Light, 1973), but this chapter focuses on the statistical analysis of nominal data.) Not until 1986 and the publication of the third *Handbook* (Wittrock, 1986) did chapters on qualitative methods begin to appear. Erickson (1986), in his chapter that was discussed above, explained the delay: "The previous editions of the *Handbook of Research on Teaching* do not contain a chapter devoted to participant observational research," he noted, "because interest in these approaches is so recent" (p. 119).

Interest in qualitative research, according to Lincoln and Guba, was not only recent; it was also a bit heretical. They preface their 1985 book, for example, with the following statement:

> We are all so imbued with the tenets of science that we take its assumptions utterly for granted, so much so that we almost cannot comprehend the possibility that there might be other ways of thinking. And when other ways are suggested, we are inclined to shut our ears, feeling that merely to listen to them is, quite literally, a heresy. (pp. 8–9)

Lincoln and Guba add that their book "proposes such a heresy" (p. 9).

The Naturalist Paradigm. Lincoln and Guba's heresy takes the form of what they called, initially, at least, the "naturalist paradigm," an alternative world-view that incorporates ontological and epistemological assumptions that, Lincoln and Guba argue, are diametrically opposed to and, hence, incommensurate with the realist ontology and objectivist epistemology of positivism. Within the naturalist paradigm, for example, reality is no longer a singular physical entity waiting to be discovered piece by piece. Rather, "there are multiple constructed realities that can be studied only holistically" (Lincoln & Guba, 1985, p. 37). Furthermore, rather than positing a separation between the knower and the known, a naturalist epistemology presumes that "the inquirer and the 'object' of inquiry interact to influence one another" (p. 37). Rather than positing that the aim of inquiry is to produce universal, context-free generalizations or laws, naturalist epistemology suggests that "the aim of inquiry is to develop an ideographic body of knowledge in the form of 'working hypotheses' that describe the individual case" (p. 38). Rather than positing that the world can be explained in terms of cause-effect relationships, the naturalist paradigm posits that "all entities are in a state of mutually simultaneous shaping so that it is impossible to distinguish causes and effects" (p. 38). Finally, rather than articulating a belief in objectivity and value-free inquiry, the naturalist paradigm presumes that "inquiry is [inevitably] value-bound" (p. 38) and, consequently, that it can never be objective.

Lincoln and Guba's alternative paradigm called into question both the feasibility and the desirability of quasi-experimental research. If the world is, indeed, a world of multiple realities, for example, researchers will never be able to uncover the sort of universal, context-free generalizations that Lincoln and Guba claimed positivists sought. Similarly, if "all entities are in a state of mutually simultaneous shaping," quasi-experimental studies, by definition, will grossly oversimplify social actions (not to mention, underestimate their role in shaping the phenomena they supposedly explain).

Simultaneously, Lincoln and Guba's naturalistic paradigm transformed the supposed limitations of qualitative research—for example, its lack of instrumentation and inability to test the generalizability of findings—into virtues. The fact that the human being is the primary instrument in qualitative studies is viewed positively now

because it would be virtually impossible to devise a priori a non-human instrument with sufficient adaptability to encompass and adjust to the variety of realities that will be encountered; because of the understanding that all instruments interact with respondents and objects but that only the human instrument is capable of grasping and evaluating the meaning of that differential interaction; because the intrusion of instruments intervenes in the mutual shaping of other elements and that shaping can be appreciated and evaluated only by a human; and because all instruments are value-based and interact with local values but only the human is in a position to identify and take into account (to some extent) those resulting biases. (Lincoln & Guba, 1985, pp. 39–40)

Similarly, when the emphasis is on context and ideographic knowledge, generalizability (at least as that term was traditionally defined) is no longer an issue. The case study is no longer seen merely as a hypothesis-generating preliminary to the sort of research that will tell us whether the hypotheses that are generated are valid. Indeed, when research is viewed from Lincoln and Guba's naturalistic perspective, the best we can hope for from research is working hypotheses, and the best working hypotheses are those encased in enough information about the cases in which they were generated to make it possible for practitioners to make a reasonable judgment about whether findings are likely to generalize or "transfer" (to use Lincoln and Guba's language) to the situation in which practitioners work.

Thus, according to Lincoln and Guba, the growing interest in qualitative research within the field of educational research

and the social sciences generally signaled much more than an expansion of research methods. To be sure, Lincoln and Guba always acknowledged that the relationship between the naturalist paradigm they espoused and the qualitative methods that seemed so compatible with that paradigm was a loosely coupled one. They recognized early on, for example, that self-described "soft-nosed positivists" like Miles and Huberman (1984a, 1984b/1994) could use qualitative methods without accepting naturalist epistemology or ontology; similarly, Lincoln and Guba kept open the possibility that naturalists might, on occasion, use certain quantitative research procedures such as surveys, particularly for triangulation purposes. For Lincoln and Guba, in short, neither quantification nor the absence of quantification, per se, was significant; rather, what was significant was the deeper logic that tended to (but did not always) undergird the research methodologies that the field has labeled, somewhat inappropriately, qualitative and quantitative. Lincoln and Guba emphasized that although qualitative and quantitative methods could, on occasion, be mixed, these logics were incommensurable.

One had to choose up sides, in other words. One could side with the guardians of traditional views of knowledge, knowing, and reality, or one could join the self-described heretics in what amounted to a holy war to reorient fundamental thinking in the field. One could not simultaneously embrace both the positivist and the naturalist paradigms; commitment to eclecticism was tantamount to intellectual schizophrenia in the thinking of Lincoln and Guba, and the many devotees to qualitative research who were influenced by their thinking.

Paradigm Proliferation and Other Contemporary Modifications

MODIFICATIONS IN LINCOLN AND GUBA'S THINKING

Lincoln and Guba's thinking has evolved in significant ways during the years since *Naturalistic Inquiry* was published. Guba and Lincoln (1989), for instance, have expressed concern that their initial attempt to define the naturalistic paradigm—and, in the process, to articulate criteria that could be used to determine what was credible work within this paradigm—relied too much on concepts and criteria that were parallel to concepts used in the positivist paradigm. "The credibility criterion [which was operationalized by such methodological techniques as peer debriefing, persistent observation, prolonged engagement, and member checks]," they noted, "is parallel to internal validity in that the idea of isomorphism between findings and an objective reality is replaced by isomorphism between constructed realities of respondents and the reconstructions attributed to them" (1989, pp. 236–237).

Guba and Lincoln, in their later writings, did not so much reject the credibility criterion, however; nor did they reject strategies like member checking, peer debriefing, persistent observation, and prolonged engagement—strategies, which, if used, could help determine whether the credibility criterion had been met. Similarly, they did not disavow their notion of transferability, a concept that is clearly an analog for the positivist notion of external validity or generalizability. Rather than dismiss the concepts and methods they advocated in their earlier work, Lincoln and Guba, in their later work, simply lessened their importance by de-emphasizing the significance of research methods in general and by adding additional criteria that were ethical and even political in character. "In the positivist paradigm," Guba and Lincoln (1989) write,

> method has primacy. Method is critical for ensuring the results are trustworthy. But method is only *one consideration* in constructivist inquiry. . . . Relying solely on criteria that speak to methods, as do the parallel criteria, leaves an inquiry vulnerable to questions regarding whether stakeholder rights were in fact honored. (p. 245, emphasis added)

In short, in their later work—most notably in their book, *Fourth Generation Evaluation*—Guba and Lincoln (1989) attempt to redefine their naturalist paradigm (now renamed "the constructivist paradigm") so that it "could have been invented by someone who had never heard of positivism" (p. 245). They made a conscious attempt, in other words, to heighten incommensurability.

Guba and Lincoln's paradigm talk changed in other ways also during the years after they first wrote about the allegedly incommensurable positivist and naturalist paradigms. In a 1990 book edited by Guba, which contained papers presented at a conference to commemorate his retirement from Indiana University, for example, the positivist paradigm was updated and renamed. It became "the postpositivist paradigm" (Phillips, 1990). The new constructivist label was retained for Guba and Lincoln's preferred perspective, but the 1990 book also introduced a third paradigm that was grounded in critical theory (Popkewitz, 1990).

By 1994, in their chapter for the *Handbook of Qualitative Research* (Denzin & Lincoln, 1994), positivism reappears alongside postpositivism (in what is now a four-paradigm typology), though the term seems to reference thinking that is more historical than current. "The term positivism" Guba and Lincoln (1994) write,

> denotes the "received view" that has dominated the formal discourse in the physical and social sciences for 400 years, whereas postpositivism represents efforts of the past few decades to respond in a limited way . . . to the problematic criticisms of positivism. (pp. 108–109)

Also, although constructivism and critical theory remain paradigmatic options in the 1994 article, the term *critical theory* now is followed by the designation, "*et al.*" Guba and Lincoln explain:

> The term *critical theory* is (for us) a blanket term denoting a set of several alternative paradigms, including additionally (but not limited to) neo-Marxism, feminism, materialism, and participatory inquiry. Indeed, critical theory may itself usefully be divided into three substrands: poststructuralism, postmodernism, and a blending of these two. (p. 109)

PARADIGM PROLIFERATION

Guba and Lincoln's transformation of critical theory into a sort of metaparadigm is an attempt to respond to a contemporary phenomenon that could appropriately be labeled "paradigm proliferation." Others also have begun to construct metaparadigms in an attempt to make sense of the increasing number of paradigms that some members see when they view the educational research field. Lather (1992), for example, differentiates deconstruction-oriented paradigms such as poststructuralism and postmodernism from emancipation-oriented paradigms such as critical theory and neo-Marxism in an attempt to bring some conceptual order to the current proliferation of paradigms.

The need for such order is increasingly apparent, for paradigm proliferation will almost certainly continue and even likely accelerate in the future, in part because of a growing tendency in some circles to associate the concept of paradigm with the concept of life experience. For example, certain scholars of color (Dillard, 1997; Stanfield, 1993, 1994) along with some White scholars who are sympathetic with their views (e.g., Scheurich & Young, 1997) have begun to link the paradigm notion with ethnicity, and, in the process, suggest that there are paradigms (or at least that paradigms might be articulated) that are nowhere in evidence in Guba and Lincoln's typology.

In his chapter in the 1994 *Handbook of Qualitative Research,* for example, John Stanfield II chides self-proclaimed Afrocentric scholars for "claiming to be producing knowledge sensitive to the experiences of African-descent peoples as a unique cultural population even as they insist on using Eurocentric logics of inquiry" (p. 182). Stanfield calls, instead, for the development of "indigenous ethnic models of qualitative research" that reflect "novel indigenous paradigms grounded distinctly in the experiences of people of color" (p. 183).

Cynthia Dillard (1997) makes a similar sort of argument. The difference is that her "endarkened epistemology" is as much a product of gender as it is of race and ethnicity. According to Dillard, Black women—by virtue of being Black women and experiencing what Black women experience—operate with an epistemology that is different from both White feminists and Black male scholars such as Stanfield. Other aspects of lived experience—for example, sexual preference (Pinar, 1998)—also have been portrayed as being inextricably intertwined with the process of knowing.

As paradigms have proliferated and Kuhnian-inspired paradigm talk, consequently, has become much more layered and complex, Lincoln and Guba's original dualistic conception of paradigm differences—and even Erickson's (1986) musings about "the discontinuities . . . across the two major types of approaches to classroom research" (p. 120) in the third edition of the *Handbook of Research on* Teaching—seem like quaint antiques. They become artifacts of an earlier era in which the battle lines between competing perspectives in research were clearly drawn and "the paradigm wars" (Gage, 1989) were at least occurring on the same battlefield. Now if we use Gage's "paradigm wars" metaphor, we must imagine the battleground as a sort of intellectual Croatia. In short, Kuhnian-inspired paradigm talk today is radically different from Kuhnian-inspired paradigm talk in the past because of the phenomenon of paradigm proliferation. Furthermore, the contemporary penchant for linking the concept of paradigm with the concept of life experiences virtually guarantees that paradigm proliferation will continue and even accelerate.

In at least one important respect, however, Kuhnian-inspired paradigm talk in an era of paradigm proliferation resembles Kuhnian-inspired paradigm talk in the past: Implicit in both earlier and contemporary forms of Kuhnian-inspired paradigm talk is the notion of radically different epistemologies. That notion, in turn, implies at least some sense of incommensurability, some sense that we must still, of necessity, choose up sides. If anything, the linking of the notion of paradigms with the concept of cultural experience and ethnicity has only reinforced the incommensurability argument because none of us can ever totally walk in another's shoes.

CAN'T WE ALL GET ALONG?

Before concluding the discussion of contemporary variations in Kuhnian-inspired paradigm talk, I want to focus on one more difference between paradigm talk today and paradigm talk in the past: On the surface, at least, Kuhnian-inspired paradigm talk today is considerably less intense and far more conciliatory than it was even a decade or so ago. Even Guba and Lincoln seem to have softened their rhetoric considerably. In the conclusion of their 1994 chapter in the *Handbook of Qualitative Research,* for example, they write:

> The metaphor of the "paradigm wars" described by Gage (1989) is undoubtedly overdrawn. Describing the discussions and altercations of the past decade or two as wars paints the matter as more confrontational than necessary. A resolution of paradigm differences can occur only when a new paradigm emerges that is more informed and sophisticated than any existing one. That is most likely to occur if and when proponents of these several points of view come together to discuss their difference, not to argue the sanctity of their views. Continuing dialogue among paradigm proponents of all stripes will afford the best avenue for moving toward a response and congenial relationship. (p. 116)

This plea for congenial dialogue is put into perspective in Guba and Lincoln's concluding paragraph, however, because, in this paragraph, they reaffirm their belief in the importance of the sort of paradigm talk they have used in the past: "We hope that in this chapter," they write, "we have illustrated the need for such a discussion by clearly delineating the differences that currently exist, and by showing that those differences have significant implications at the practical level. Paradigm issues are crucial; no inquirer, we maintain, ought to go about the business of inquiry without being clear about just what paradigm informs and guides his or her approach." (p. 116)

In short, the title of Guba and Lincoln's handbook article, "*Competing* Paradigms of Qualitative Research," [emphasis added] is not a mistake. In fact, during a session at the 1997 meeting of the American Educational Research Association, Lincoln restated her belief that the competition is still about

incommensurable points of view. One wonders how the discussion of differences and the "continuing dialogue among paradigm proponents of all stripes" that Guba and Lincoln call for can occur if the discussants' views are, indeed, incommensurable. Furthermore, if we, in fact, do hold incommensurable worldviews, how will we all recognize the "new paradigm . . . that is more informed and sophisticated than any existing one" when it miraculously appears?[2]

Kuhnian-Inspired Paradigm Talk and Research on Teaching

Just as Kuhnian-inspired paradigm talk has had a prominent place in the field of educational research in general, it also has been very much a part of important discussions within the subfield of research on teaching. A prominent example is Tom and Valli's chapter titled "Professional Knowledge for Teachers," published in the 1990 *Handbook of Research on Teacher Education* edited by Houston. At the outset of their chapter, Tom and Valli declare that "what counts as knowledge is vigorously contested" (p. 373). They then go on "to explore the contrasting epistemologies of professional knowledge" and to argue that "these formal epistemologies—positivistic, interpretive, and critical—direct our attention to differing professional knowledge" (p. 373). This trinity of epistemologies is nearly identical to the three paradigms Guba (1990) was talking about at the time Tom and Valli's chapter was published. More important, Tom and Valli seem to endorse Guba and Lincoln's incommensurability thesis. They note, for example, that positivism, interpretivism, and critically oriented paradigms

> differ radically in the form and purpose of professional knowledge: generalizations, lawlike if possible, designed to improve teaching effectiveness (positivism); cases, designed to reveal meaning in context (interpretivism); and varied forms of knowledge, designed to expose ways in which favored values are prevented from being realized (critically oriented). The three orientations to knowledge also contrast in their approaches to values: value neutral (positivism), value relative (interpretivism), value centered (critically oriented). (Tom & Valli, 1990, p. 378)

The position taken by Tom and Valli, however, does differ from Lincoln and Guba's paradigm talk in two respects, and it is worth pausing at this point to take note of these two important differences. First, although Tom and Valli endorse Lincoln and Guba's idea about the existence of fundamentally different epistemologies, they say nothing about ontology. This silence about ontological questions makes sense: Lincoln and Guba's claim that naturalistic researchers believe in a world of multiple realities—a claim they label as ontological in character—ultimately seems more an epistemological claim than an ontological one.

---

[2] Considerable time elapsed between the submission of this manuscript in 1999 and receipt of page proofs in 2001. During that time, a second edition of *The Handbook of Qualitative Research* was published in 2000. In their chapter for the new edition of the *Handbook* (which was once again edited by Denzin and Lincoln and published by Sage), Lincoln and Guba retreat from their view that a new, more encompassing paradigm acceptable to positivists and nonpositivists alike would someday emerge. In their chapter for the second edition, they write: "In retrospect, such a resolution [of paradigmatic differences] appears highly unlikely and would probably even be less than useful" (p. 185). They also blur the lines separating nonpositivist paradigms, however, arguing that "there is a great potential for interweaving viewpoints . . ." (p. 167). They make it clear, however, that this interweaving should not occur across the divide that, in their view, continues to separate positivist and nonpositivist world views.

One is reminded of Kant's (1781/1996) argument about cause and effect. Kant noted that the world may, indeed, be a world of causes and effects, but once we make the epistemological assumption that our knowledge of reality is always mediated by the categories in our heads, we must acknowledge that we cannot know whether this is the case. Once we posit that sensory data are filtered through intellectual categories such as the categories of cause and effect, in other words, we are no longer in a position to make claims about what the world is really like. We already have acknowledged that we do not have direct access to reality, and, by implication, we have acknowledged that we cannot answer ontological questions. Similarly, if we accept Lincoln and Guba's epistemological assumption about the inseparability of the knower and the known, we can hardly make claims about what the world really is like. Lincoln and Guba's naturalistic epistemology, in other words, makes ontological questions moot.

Thus, Tom and Valli's decision to jettison the ontological component of Lincoln and Guba's paradigm talk seems prudent. Other scholars have taken a similar tack. Consequently, in recent years, except in the writing of Lincoln and Guba, discussions of paradigm disputes in the United States, both within and outside of the research on teaching field, normally have been framed in epistemological rather than ontological terms.

Tom and Valli's paradigm talk differs from the paradigm talk of Lincoln and Guba in one other important respect: In addition to talking about positivist, interpretivist, and critical epistemologies, Tom and Valli discuss the concept of craft knowledge, a concept they associate with Donald Schön (1983, 1987, 1989, 1991), a scholar who claims both that craft knowledge is rooted in its own epistemology—an epistemology of practice and action—and that the epistemology of practice is largely incommensurable with the theory-oriented ways of knowing that are so prized in universities and similar sorts of settings.

In their chapter, Tom and Valli do not really develop the craft knowledge concept so that it can be seen as functioning on a par with the three more fully developed epistemological stances they discuss. Others, however, have taken up this challenge. Anderson and Herr (1999), for instance, characterize attempts to legitimate teacher action research and the Schön-like epistemology of practice that they claim undergirds such research as "the new paradigm wars," while Cochran-Smith and Lytle (1998) agree that the teacher research movement is rooted in a distinctively different epistemology, although their thinking differs from the thinking of Anderson and Herr in several important respects. Arguably, the most systematic attempt in the research on teaching field to elevate Tom and Valli's craft knowledge to something akin to paradigm status, however, can be found in Gary Fenstermacher's (1994) lead chapter in the 1994 edition of the American Educational Research Association's *Review of Research in Education,* edited by Linda Darling-Hammond (1994).

In his chapter, Fenstermacher (1994) distinguishes between two types of knowledge about teaching, which, according to Fenstermacher, are rooted in fundamentally different epistemologies. One he labels "teacher knowledge: formal." Fenstermacher writes, "The process-product studies of teaching are perhaps the most well-known instance of this form of knowledge" (p. 6). The other he calls "teacher knowledge: practical," a category that includes knowledge characterized by a number of labels in the literature "including practical, personal practical, situated, local relational, and tacit" (p. 6).

Clearly, the two epistemologies that Fenstermacher describes differ markedly from Lincoln and Guba's positivistic and naturalistic epistemologies and even more markedly from Lincoln and Guba's later, more complex category schemes. Indeed, it is virtually impossible to map Fenstermacher's two epistemologies onto the epistemologies discussed by Lincoln and Guba. One wonders, for example, where does knowledge that is produced by the sort of case study research Lincoln and Guba champion—for example, thick description-type knowledge of particular contexts—belong in the dualistic category scheme that Fenstermacher advances, especially if process-product studies of teaching serve as the prototype for knowledge that is classified under the "teacher knowledge: formal" rubric. My purpose, here, however, is not to critique the comprehensiveness or adequacy of Fenstermacher's paradigm framework. Nor am I particularly interested in highlighting differences between the paradigm talk of Lincoln and Guba, on the one hand, and Fenstermacher, on the other. What is significant for this discussion is one important similarity: Fenstermacher endorses Lincoln and Guba's notion that methodological differences are rooted in fundamentally different epistemologies. This endorsement, in turn, links Fenstermacher's thinking with the paradigm talk of Lincoln and Guba. This linkage is even stronger in the writing of some other scholars who discuss Schön's theoretical-practical distinction in epistemological terms.[3]

Problems with Kuhnian-Inspired Paradigm Talk

For the past quarter century, paradigm talk, inspired by Kuhn's description of conceptual change in the physical sciences, has been commonplace within the field of educational research in general and within the field of research on teaching in particular. Problems with Kuhnian-inspired paradigm talk have also arisen, however. In this section of the chapter, I will review both long-standing and more emergent criticisms. The discussion will be organized around four general problems associated with

---

[3] In fairness, it should be noted that Fenstermacher, himself, despite his talk of epistemological differences, stops short of endorsing the Lincoln and Guba incommensurability thesis. Indeed, he seems to want to hold open the possibility that "teacher knowledge: practical" and "teacher knowledge: formal" might have something to offer each other. Others who have talked of an epistemology of practice and who have elevated action research to paradigmatic status, however, have been less reticent to embrace the fundamentals of Kuhnian-inspired paradigm talk. The incommensurability thesis, for example, is very much in evidence in the seminal work of Donald Schön on this topic as well as in the Anderson and Herr (1999) discussion of "the new paradigm wars." In addition, Cochran-Smith and Lytle (1998) have chided Fenstermacher not only for blurring the distinction between "teacher knowledge: practical" and "teacher knowledge: formal" but also for critiquing the teacher research movement with a "teacher knowledge: formal" epistemology. For many, talk of teacher craft knowledge and action research represents an alternative, apparently incommensurable paradigm talk within the research on teaching field.

Kuhnian-inspired paradigm talk which I have labeled (1) the verisimilitude problem; (2) the changing times problem; (3) the need-for-theoretical-pluralism problem; and (4) the balkanization problem.

THE VERISIMILITUDE PROBLEM

One problem is the lack of correspondence between (a) Kuhnian-inspired paradigm talk about incommensurability and the eventual triumph of one paradigm over another, and (b) what many of us see and experience when we examine and do research. One need not be a naive realist—or even a critical realist (House, 1991) for that matter—to expect to find a referent in experience for our linguistic constructions about experience. Even those who argue that language shapes our perceptions of reality—and I would count myself among this group—expect to find some degree of verisimilitude between our linguistic accounts of the world and our experiences in it. If this were not the case, self-described constructivists like Lincoln and Guba long ago would have abandoned totally such methodological strategies as prolonged engagement and member-checking.

There are a number of variations of the verisimilitude problem. Three will be discussed here.

Variation #1: Methodological/Epistemological Impurity. One manifestation of the verisimilitude problem was discussed by qualitative methodologists Miles and Huberman (1984, 1984/ 1994) years ago. They noted that those who do qualitative research—as opposed to those individuals who primarily talk about it—are normally much more eclectic and much less paradigmatically pure than Kuhnian-inspired paradigm talk suggests. "Epistemological purity doesn't get research done," Miles and Huberman concluded (1984, p. 21).

Educational philosopher D.C. Phillips (1983) made a similar sort of argument at the epistemological level. Phillips demonstrated not only that the term *positivism* has had a host of meanings associated with it throughout history (some of which conflict with the definitions found in Kuhnian-inspired paradigm talk) but also that "some of the most boisterous celebrants at positivism's wake are actually more positivistic than they recognize, or have more in common with the positivists than they would care to admit" (p. 7).

While Phillips has pointed out the influence of positivism on the thinking of positivism's critics, a 1987 review of Lincoln and Guba's (1985) *Naturalistic Inquiry* suggested that the authors tend

> to caricature the views of traditional ["positivist"] researchers. . . . For example, Lincoln and Guba declare the following axiom part of the positivist paradigm: "The aim of inquiry is to develop a nomothetic body of knowledge in the form of generalizations that are truth statements free from both time and contexts (they will hold anywhere and at any time)" ([Lincoln & Guba, 1985], p. 38). The history of aptitude X treatment interaction research, however, suggests that large numbers of traditional researchers gave up the search for context-free nomothetic laws a long time ago. Furthermore, even a die-hard process-product researcher such as Gage has acknowledged that artistry will always be required when we apply

> scientific generalizations about teaching to particular teaching contexts. (Donmoyer, 1987b, p. 471)

Variation #2: The Incommensurable-Logical Incompatibility Distinction. More recently, philosopher Richard Bernstein (1991) has argued that incommensurability does not necessarily imply logical incompatibility. (He also indicates that Kuhn, himself, never meant to imply that it did, though this point was certainly missed by many scholars who have appropriated Kuhn's concept.) According to Bernstein, different paradigms often simply focus our attention on different phenomena and ask different sorts of questions. One paradigm may be judged by members of a field to be more appropriate to achieve a field's purposes than another (Toulmin, 1972), but that does not necessarily mean that the two paradigms logically conflict. My physicist friends, for example, assure me that they still think in Newtonian terms when working on certain applied problems, even though, at the cutting edge of the field, the Einsteinian paradigm supplanted Newton's worldview years ago.

Furthermore, even on those occasions when paradigms are basically incompatible, we can still attempt to understand different paradigmatic perspectives and we can use utilitarian criteria to choose which paradigm is most appropriate to accomplish particular purposes and to maximize particular values. Philosopher Peter Cohen (1968), for example, used a utilitarian sort of argument in critiquing philosopher Peter Winch's (1958/1990) classic text, *The Idea of a Social Science and Its Relationship to Philosophy.* The ideas in Winch's book are quite reminiscent of the ideas found in Lincoln and Guba's paradigm talk and include the idea that action in the social world is constructed through social interaction rather than caused by independent variables of one sort or another. In his critique of this particular idea, Cohen acknowledges that "one would agree that the use of the term 'causation' does not have as precise a reference in the social world as it does in the natural world." Then he adds, "But if one is to use such criteria, one wonders what is to be offered in place of 'causation'. . . . In fact, one begins to wonder how social policy would be possible without some idea of causation" (Cohen, 1968, p. 416).

In short, one could agree with Winch and with Lincoln and Guba, for that matter, about the constructed nature of social action, yet still talk in cause-and-effect terms if one accepted Cohen's argument that such talk is useful. In fact, once we assert that we do not have direct access to reality but, rather, that we live, ultimately, in a world of multiple realities of our own construction, one wonders how else we could ground our arguments, resolve conflicts intellectually, and make decisions without resorting to the use of brute force except by appealing to the notion of utility.

Variation #3: Paradigm Proliferation. In recent years, the phenomenon of paradigm proliferation has compounded the verisimilitude problem. Although, in their 1994 *Handbook of Qualitative Research* chapter, Guba and Lincoln still seem to hold open the possibility of "a new paradigm [emerging] . . . that is more informed and sophisticated than any existing one" (p. 116), few others now believe that the field will eventually converge around a single paradigm as the Kuhnian-inspired storyline suggests.

Indeed, some scholars have even argued that Kuhn's convergence storyline does not match up very well with phenomena in the physical sciences (see, e.g., Erickson, 1986; Lakatos, 1970). Whether or not this criticism is fair is a question which is beyond the scope of this discussion. Here, it will be sufficient to state a virtual truism: Talk of convergence around a single paradigm seems inappropriate in a field in which paradigms continue to proliferate and in which the very notion of a paradigm has begun to be associated with ethnic, gender, and other differences.

Summary. The three variations discussed above are all manifestations of the same general problem: the absence of verisimilitude between experience and paradigm talk's characterization of experience. Those who raise this problem suggest that Kuhnian-inspired paradigm talk tells a story that does not match up very well with what educational researchers actually do and how different research perspectives currently function in our field and how they are likely to function in the future.

THE CHANGING TIMES PROBLEM

The changing times problem portrays Kuhnian-inspired paradigm talk in a somewhat more charitable light than does the verisimilitude problem. Those who raise this problem—and I include myself in this group (Donmoyer, 1997)—concede that, at the outset of the qualitative revolution, proponents of Kuhnian-inspired paradigm talk did not get everything right; they also did not get everything wrong, however. For example, a distinction exists between believing that knowledge is essentially discovered and believing that knowledge is, at least in part, constructed. Furthermore, this distinction is not without practical significance. The latter position, for instance, suggests that a researcher bears much more ethical responsibility for the research he or she does than the view that researchers primarily discover empirical truth. Kuhnian-inspired paradigm talk helped clarify distinctions such as this one despite its lack of subtlety (or, one could argue, because of it). In the process, such talk promoted new ways of thinking about and doing research.[4] Indeed, it is hard to fathom how qualitative research—especially some of the avant-garde versions of qualitative research discussed in this edition of the *Handbook*—could have gained acceptance in a field almost exclusively defined by process-product studies of teaching (Gage, 1963a) without the flawed but highly functional Kuhnian-inspired paradigm talk described above.

The problem, from the changing times perspective, is that proponents of Kuhnian-inspired paradigm talk have pretty much won the paradigm wars. Qualitative methods, for instance, have achieved widespread acceptance within our field. This fourth edition of the *Handbook of Research on Teaching*—

which devotes an entire section to a range of qualitative methodology—is evidence of this acceptance.

More important, many of the epistemological tenets of Kuhnian-inspired paradigm talk have gained widespread acceptance. In some sense, at least, we are all constructivists now. Today, for example, most researchers acknowledge that the language used to frame research questions affects research findings; most researchers would agree that the methods used to study a phenomenon shape and constrain what can be discovered; and most researchers now believe the knower cannot be separated from what is known.

Furthermore, most researchers gave up the search for universal laws long ago, along with the expectation that research could provide formulas or recipes for practice. Even traditional quantitative researchers (see, e.g., Hoy & Miskel, 1978/1996) now acknowledge that research serves merely a heuristic function: Research can help practitioners frame questions and possibly provide some probabilistic sense of which answers are likely to be most appropriate to enact in particular settings to achieve certain purposes and maximize particular values. Research findings, however, can never substitute for thinking; they are merely heuristics for thoughtful practitioners to use.

To state this last point another way, virtually all researchers—quantitative and qualitative alike—have embraced Lincoln and Guba's notion of transferability (even though they may not use the term or give appropriate credit to the developers of the concept), along with many of the other ideas Lincoln and Guba associated with their naturalistic paradigm. Even if this epistemological consensus at times exists more at the level of rhetoric than action,[5] the change in rhetoric opens the door for rethinking the utility of Kuhnian-inspired paradigm talk and for seeking an alternative—and potentially more helpful—way of characterizing the diversity within our field. The next two problems that will be discussed below provide an impetus to actively seek such an alternative, since they highlight unfortunate consequences associated with Kuhnian-inspired paradigm talk.

THE NEED-FOR-THEORETICAL-PLURALISM PROBLEM

While the first two problems discussed above focus on discrepancies between Kuhnian-inspired paradigm talk and "what is," the focus of the third problem, which will be discussed in this section, and the fourth problem, to be discussed below, assess the appropriateness of Kuhnian-inspired paradigm talk from the perspective of "what ought to be." A partial articulation of this third problem was offered by Lee Shulman as he discussed his self-described "weaker" form of paradigm talk, which was alluded to above and which will be discussed in detail in the second part of this chapter. In the third edition of this *Handbook,* Shulman (1986) argued that Kuhn erred when he charac-

---

[4] I do not mean to suggest that the early advocates of qualitative research who engaged in Kuhnian-inspired paradigm talk were disingenuous, that they intentionally exaggerated the differences between themselves and more traditional researchers in the field, or that they consciously vilified adherents to traditional ways of doing and thinking about research. To the contrary, Kuhnian-inspired paradigm talk was convincing and functional, in large part, because those who engaged in it were very much true believers in what they had to say.

[5] Not only do actions speak louder than words; they also are harder to change. Furthermore, people take a long time to recognize all the implications of the new ideas they espouse and to reorient totally their thinking, much less their actions.

terized the "very absence of a single dominant paradigm" in the social sciences

> as a development disability, a state of preparadigmatic retardation. Indeed, it is far more likely that for the social sciences and education, the coexistence of competing schools of thought is a natural and quite mature state. . . . Merton argues for the superiority of a set of competing paradigms over the hegemony of a single school of thought. He asserts that theoretical pluralism encourages development of a variety of research strategies, rather than premature closure of investigation consistent with the problematics of a single paradigm. Different paradigms alert research workers to different phenomena of interest, different conceptions of the problem, and different aspects of events likely to be ignored within a single perspective. (p. 5)

Shulman's argument for theoretical pluralism makes even more sense if we extend his thinking by acknowledging that education is not simply an applied social science, as Shulman assumes, but is also a public policy field. Such a claim can easily be defended. After all, even teachers—who in our loosely coupled (Weick, 1976) educational systems, make decisions and establish rules and standard operating procedures, for example, about the grouping of students in their classes, that can profoundly affect students' lives—can be considered policymakers rather than simply implementers of policies developed by others (Schwille, Porter, & Gant, 1980). Furthermore, in an era of site-based and shared decision making, teachers' policymaking authority has begun to extend beyond their own particular classrooms (Donmoyer, 1996b, 1999).

The work of philosopher Stephen Toulmin (1972, 1983) suggests the significance of viewing teaching and education in general as a public policy field. Toulmin notes that policymakers—unlike most applied social scientists—do not simply confront technical problems. To demonstrate this point, he notes that civil engineers probably could reach an agreement about the best place to build a dam. However, the policy group charged with actually making the decision would not necessarily decide to implement the engineers' recommendation because, in public policy fields, multiple criteria—not simply the technical criteria considered by the civil engineers—must be taken into account and somehow balanced. Policymakers, for instance, must consider the economic impact of building a dam in one location rather than another, not to mention the likely political impact of angry voters in the next election. They certainly cannot totally ignore the civil engineers' advice and build the dam in a place where it will collapse. But they will not necessarily choose a location that is rated as "best," using the engineers' technical criteria, because other criteria—other definitions of "best"—need to be taken into account.

Teachers too must confront problems that are not merely technical and, in the process of doing this, must consider—and eventually choose among or find a way to balance—different, even contradictory, criteria. We expect teachers, for example, both to transmit culture (Spindler, 1987) and to encourage their students to critique the cultural ideas being transmitted. Teach-ers must somehow impose order in the classroom (Evertson, 1989) while simultaneously making their students independent and self-directed learners (Florio-Ruane, 1989). Their students must become technically proficient readers, but most of us also want teachers to instill a love of reading in students. In short, teachers must engage in the same sort of balancing act that a policymaking body must engage in when deciding where to build a dam.[6] To make appropriate decisions, in other words, teachers—even more than the researchers Shulman talks about—must be alerted "to different phenomena of interest, different conceptions of the problem, and different aspects of events likely to be ignored within a single perspective" (Shulman, 1986, p. 5). Consequently, when we think of teaching and education more generally as public policy fields, Shulman's critique of Kuhn's thinking—and his defense of theoretical pluralism in a field like education—becomes even more compelling.

THE BALKANIZATION PROBLEM

Theoretical pluralism, of course, is useful only in a public policy field like education only if members of the field are open to looking at phenomena and considering questions from a variety of perspectives. Kuhnian-inspired paradigm talk, however, discourages such activity. When we assume that paradigms are inevitably competitive and that we must, in essence, choose up sides, there is little incentive to view phenomena or consider policy questions from a diverse array of perspectives. Indeed, there is little incentive even to try to learn from those who disagree with us when we assume our opponents operate out of a paradigm that is incommensurable (and, presumably, inferior) to the paradigm we use.

This whole matter of balkanization is, for me at least, the most serious of all the problems associated with Kuhnian-inspired paradigm talk, in part, I suspect, because I have directly experienced the consequences of the sort of balkanization that Kuhnian-inspired paradigm talk engenders. I have grown weary of doctoral students who attempt to immunize their work from criticism by claiming they were working in a different paradigm from that of their critics. I experienced similar frustration while serving as features editor for the American Educational Research Journal, *Educational Researcher*. I remember one letter from the author of a rejected manuscript who complained that the review process was unfair because one of the reviewers had identified himself in his narrative comments as an Australian poststructuralist. The author noted that she was a postmodernist and went on to assert that a poststructuralist should never be called on to review a postmodernist's work because poststructuralists operate out of a different (and, of course, inferior) paradigm. The author also noted two other reasons why the self-described Australian poststructuralist should not have been asked to review her work: (a) the author was Canadian; (b) the author was female and she suspected the reviewer was male.

---

[6] For a more detailed discussion of this argument, see Donmoyer, 1991, 1996b.

This argument can be carried to its logical conclusion: Canada, after all, is a large and culturally diverse place. Often, as much variation exists within cultural groups as between them. Consequently, we could reasonably assume that, in time, we should all have our very own research paradigms, along with the fifteen minutes of fame Andy Warhol promised. (Those of us with less-than-unified selves may actually be able to have more than one paradigm.) When this situation occurs, of course, the only person qualified to critique a paper will be the person who wrote it. Why, we may all even be able to have our very own journals if the American Educational Research Association can figure out how to pay for the printing costs for journals with few subscribers.

Lest my argument here seems a bit too glib, I should clarify that I certainly agree with the proposition that culture affects how and what we know, whether we define culture literally—in terms of ethnicity—or more metaphorically—as either the cultures of practice and the academy, on the one hand, or the "cultures" associated with different academic disciplines and fields of study within the academy, on the other. The problem, I believe, is with making the notion of cultural/"cultural" differences synonymous with the notion of incommensurable epistemologies.

I certainly understand, for example, that my former doctoral student, Linda Tillman (1995), learned different things in her dissertation study about the mentoring of Black faculty members in research universities than I would have learned had I done a comparable study, in part, because she is a Black female and I am a White male. Consequently, the experiences each of us would bring to such a study would be somewhat different, and those differences would result in our doing different things and seeing things differently. Linda, for example, at times asked different questions from those I would have asked. I am certain she was told different things by the Black faculty members whom she interviewed than I would have been told, even if our questions had been the same. Linda might also have been more sensitive to the need to alter traditional data collection procedures to make them more consistent with indigenous communication patterns among members of the culture she was studying (Ladson-Billings, 1995) than I would have been. Furthermore, when Linda's data were collected and she started the analysis process in earnest, she undoubtedly saw things in the data that I probably would have ignored. Perhaps, our different life experiences might even lead us to weigh different sorts of evidence differently. The poll figures about the impact of race on perceptions of the O. J. Simpson trial suggest that it would be wise to at least consider this possibility.

I also would expect practitioners and academicians to ask different sorts of questions and, at times, to value different sorts of information. Practitioners may even prefer that information be encoded in different ways, as the work on narrative research often suggests (Richardson, 1994).

Similarly, within the academy, I fully expect to see significant differences across different disciplines and even across different research orientations within a particular discipline. I would expect, for instance, a researcher socialized into the "culture" of Skinnerian behaviorism and one schooled in and partial to Piagetian views of learning and development to come to a very different understanding about the same kindergarten program that each was asked to assess. Those different understandings, of course, would lead to different assessments of the program and different recommendations for improvement.[7]

Having acknowledged all of the above, however, I also want to argue that it would be unwise to characterize the differences alluded to above as epistemological differences, especially if different epistemologies are assumed to be, by definition, incommensurable. My argument here is a utilitarian one: African-American scholars correctly emphasize that they cannot speak for all scholars of color. The African-American cultural experience, they argue, is in some respects similar to, but is also quite different from, the cultural experiences of, say, Hispanics. The term Hispanic, of course, encompasses many different ethnic groups, but even if we disaggregate the concept and acknowledge that, say, Cuban-Americans and Mexican-Americans will each have their own "indigenous epistemologies," we must still confront the anthropologist's dictum that as much variation exists within cultural groups as between them. We must be open to the possibility, in other words, that individuals within each culture might have their own "indigenous epistemologies." Once we do this, we must also confront the fact that some scholars have begun to challenge the whole notion of the unity of the self. That challenge, in turn, seems to set us up for a sort of infinite regression of proliferating paradigms once we conflate the notions of epistemology and lived experience and assume that variation in the latter implies epistemological variation as well.

My argument here is not simply an arcane and academic argumentum ad absurdum. To the contrary, balkanization has some very real consequences. I have already alluded to the problems that paradigm proliferation poses for journal editors when paradigms are seen as emanating from different epistemologies (Donmoyer, 1996a). Problems also occur for students taking qualitative research courses and for professors who wish to help students make sense of the proliferation of research approaches in our field. Lincoln and Guba's earlier versions of paradigm talk at least simplified things for students. In an era of paradigm proliferation, however, Kuhnian-inspired paradigm talk no longer offers even this pedagogical virtue.

Furthermore, once we use Kuhnian-inspired paradigm talk to characterize cultural, gender, or similar sorts of differences, we have little incentive to try to communicate with those who have had different experiences and, consequently, think and see the world differently from the way we do. Thus, when research perspectives conflict—and even when no logical conflict occurs among perspectives, but when we must still make choices because of things such as limited research funding, limited journal space, and a finite number of faculty lines to be filled in the institutions in which we work—we have little incentive to even try to resolve conflicts intellectually before resorting to the use of brute power to resolve our differences. What is the incentive

---

[7] For a more detailed discussion of this point, see Donmoyer, 1991, 1996b.

to even engage in discussion with—much less to try understand and accommodate—someone whose views we assume a priori are incommensurable with our own?

In short, I certainly accept the proposition that different cultural experiences (whether we define "cultural" literally or more metaphorically) influence the process of knowing in different ways. That statement, in fact, represents, for me, a legitimate and exceedingly defensible and useful epistemological stance. But acceptance of this epistemological position in no way requires us to use Kuhnian-inspired paradigm talk to characterize the differences that different life experiences generate and, in the process, to code our differences as being rooted in incommensurable epistemologies. The negative consequences of such balkanization are exceedingly problematic for the field.

CONCLUSION

At the very least, the four problems associated with Kuhnian-inspired paradigm talk outlined above should encourage us to consider other ways to make sense of the complexity that is characteristic of research on teaching in particular and education research more generally. Of course, an alternative to Kuhnian-inspired paradigm talk already exists within the research on teaching field. As noted at the outset of this chapter, Lee Shulman, in the lead chapter of the third edition of the *Handbook,* explicitly rejected Kuhn's definition and substituted "a second, weaker sense of paradigm." My discussion now turns to a consideration of the sort of paradigm talk that has emerged from Shulman's alternative sense of paradigm.

Revisiting a "Weaker" Form of Paradigm Talk

In his *Handbook* chapter, Shulman writes:

> Social scientists pursue their research activities within the framework of a school of thought that defines proper goals, starting points, methods, and interpretive conceptions for investigations. . . . These schools of thought operate much like Kuhnian paradigms or Lakatosian research programs insofar as they are relatively insular and predictably uniform. However, in no sense are social science fields necessarily dominated by a single school of thought. (Shulman, 1986, p. 5)

Differences between Shulman's and Kuhnian-Inspired Paradigm Talk

Shulman's "second, weaker" form of paradigm talk differs from the Kuhnian-inspired paradigm talk of Lincoln and Guba (and, to some extent, from the paradigm talk of Tom, Valli, and some who speak about a unique epistemology of practice) in at least three important respects. First, Shulman's "weaker" notion of paradigm no longer presumes that different paradigms represent incommensurable epistemologies. Rather, in the chapter Shulman wrote for the third edition of the *Handbook,* paradigms are simply different "research programs." Second, unlike Lincoln and Guba—and also Kuhn, for that matter—Shulman does not expect "a new paradigm . . . [to emerge] that is more informed and sophisticated than existing ones" (Guba & Lin-

coln, 1994, p. 116). Shulman, in fact, argues that "the social sciences and education can be seen as quite different from Kuhn's conception of a mature paradigmatic discipline in the natural sciences" and warns that "the danger for any field of social science or educational research lies in its potential corruption (or worse, trivialization) by a single paradigmatic view" (Shulman, 1986, p. 4). Third, while scholars such as Lincoln and Guba and those who characterize the rise of practitioner research as "the new paradigm wars" emphasize the competitive nature of paradigms, Shulman emphasizes complementarity.

The imagery Shulman uses in developing his self-described, "weaker" view of paradigm talk, in fact, highlights the complementarity notion. Shulman, at one point, compares the results of particular research programs to puzzle pieces that presumably can be arranged to form a coherent (if not totally complete) picture of the phenomenon of teaching. He also compares adherents to particular research programs to the blind men (and presumably women) trying to make sense of an elephant. Needless to say, only when the blind men and women pool their information will they begin to construct a reasonably complete—or at least a more adequate—understanding of the elephant they each have been studying. Similarly, Shulman suggests that we can make sense of the gargantuan phenomenon of teaching only when we piece together the different, but largely complimentary, findings emerging from different research programs.

Gage's Influence

Although he uses Kuhn's concept, Shulman's version of paradigm talk owes more to N. L. Gage than to Thomas Kuhn. In fact, in the American Educational Research Association's very first *Handbook of Research on Teaching,* Gage also appropriated Kuhn's language while altering Kuhn's meaning. The term *paradigm* in Gage's *Handbook* essay became a synonym for "models, patterns or schemata" (Gage, 1963b, p. 95). That weaker meaning of paradigm, in turn, permitted Gage to treat emerging paradigms as components of, rather than challenges to, the process-product conceptualization of research on teaching that he favored.

To be sure, by 1989, Gage was talking of paradigms in a more Kuhnian way. The title of his often cited article—"Paradigm Wars and Their Aftermath"—in fact, was a clear indication of his recognition that the term paradigm could have a stronger meaning than the one he used in 1963 and the one Shulman used in 1986. In his 1989 article, however, Gage makes it clear that the phrase *paradigm wars* is, for him, a description of what was happening at the time rather than a prescription for what ought to be. Gage, in fact, used the rhetorical device of claiming to be writing in the year 2009 and, from that vantage point, wrote quite different "histories" of research on teaching during the period 1989 to 2009. In one scenario, for example, the paradigm wars continued, and researchers who viewed the world differently "huddled together in embattled camps and fought off the aggressions of their opponents" (Gage, 1989, p. 147). The future of educational research and the social sciences in general seemed to be in jeopardy if this scenario got played out.

In Gage's preferred scenario, however, those who huddled in embattled camps finally got the message that Gage had preached back in 1963. Gage, in his role as 2009 historian, acknowledges that members of the research community in general had missed his point initially. (He cites Erickson and, in particular, Erickson's 1986 chapter in the third edition of this *Handbook* as examples of misguided thinking.) But then, from his vantage point "in the future," he goes on to note that eventually

all researchers realized that what might be called the oppositional component of the paradigm was invalid. This component had stated that any paradigm inherently implied an opposition to alternative paradigms. Given their new understanding of the falsity of the oppositional component, researchers realized that there was no necessary antagonism between the objectivists, the interpretivists, and the critical theorists. . . . [It] became apparent that programs of research that had often been regarded as mutually antagonistic were simply concerned with different, but important, topics and problems. There was no essential incompatibility between, for example, process-product research on teaching (the search for relationships between classroom processes and students' subsequent achievements and attitudes) and research that focused on teachers' and students' thought processes and meaning-perspectives. The two kinds of researchers were simply studying different topics. . . . Process-product research was . . . recognized to be compatible with interpretive, ethnographic studies of classroom phenomena. Thus, what Erickson had endorsed as good examples of interpretive research came to be recognized also as examples of process-product research, because they related ways of teaching to what students learned. . . . Classroom processes need not be described solely in terms of behaviors or actions; they could also be described in terms of meaning-perspectives. No calamity whatever befell those who studied teaching in the same investigation with both objective-quantitative and interpretive-qualitative methods. (Gage, 1989, pp. 141–142)

In his role as a 2009 historian, Gage (1989) asks in his preferred history, "So, what happened in research on teaching in the decades after 1989?" Anyone who has read his 1963 *Handbook* chapter will not be surprised by his answer:

As the years went by, the ineluctability of process-product research became ever more apparent. Educators simply wanted to know as much as possible about how different ways of teaching were related to different levels and kinds of student achievement and attitude. . . . The long and important agenda of process-product research continued to be acted on. Processes in teaching were investigated in interpretive and cognitive terms as well as in terms of teachers' and students' actions. Through the use of multiple perspectives, the teachers' pedagogical content knowledge was described in ever more valid ways. (Gage, 1989, p. 144)

Problems with Shulman and Gage's "Weaker" Form of Paradigm Talk

As has already been noted, Gage and Shulman's alternative form of paradigm talk has some obvious advantages over the Kuhnian-inspired paradigm talk critiqued in the first part of this chapter. The most important advantages are (1) that this "weaker" version of paradigm talk acknowledges that multiple perspectives are required in a public policy field like education, and (2) that the jettisoning of the notion of incommensurability lessens, at least somewhat, the push toward balkanization. The alternative forms also have some significant problems, however.

Next I will discuss three general categories of problems. I have labeled them the verisimilitude-changing times problem, the political incommensurability problem, and the inappropriate appropriation problem.

THE VERISIMILITUDE-CHANGING TIMES PROBLEM

Shulman and Gage have their own version of the verisimilitude problem. The contents of this *Handbook of Research on Teaching,* for example, suggest that the history of research on teaching has not unfolded as Gage would have liked. In addition, as is the case with Kuhnian-inspired paradigm talk, recent changes in the intellectual landscape actually heighten the verisimilitude problem. Back in 1986, Shulman may have been able to survey the field and cull from it research programs that could legitimately be characterized as complimentary rather than competitive. Today, however, even researchers' most fundamental notions are being redefined. New views of validity, reliability, theory, and theorizing have arisen, and these new views conflict with, rather than compliment, traditional ways of thinking.

Competing Conceptions of Validity. Patti Lather (1994), for instance, has articulated four poststructuralist-inspired conceptions of validity, which bear absolutely no resemblance to the four types of validity that Campbell and Stanley (1963b/1966) outlined in *Experimental and Quasi-Experimental Designs for Research* or even to the conception of validity advanced by qualitative researchers such as Miles and Huberman (1984b/1994). One of Lather's four types of validity, a type she calls "ironic validity," in fact turns traditional conceptions of validity upside down. From the perspective of ironic validity, a study is valid only if it clearly signals that it is invalid and that the concept of validity, as it has been traditionally defined, is not a viable notion. Lather writes:

Contrary to dominant validity practices where the rhetorical nature of scientific claims is masked with methodological assurances, a strategy of ironic validity proliferates forms, recognizing that they are rhetorical and without foundation, postepistemic, lacking in epistemological support. The text is resituated as a representation of its "failure to represent what it points toward but can never reach." (Lather, 1994, p. 41)

In her chapter in this edition of the *Handbook,* Lather has modified her thinking about validity somewhat, but her modified thinking still represents more of a challenge to rather than an endorsement of traditional thinking.

Rival Views of Reliability. While Lather has redefined traditional conceptions of validity, Gitlin and his colleagues have refashioned the traditional notion of reliability. Gitlin and Russell (1994) in discussing their critical theory-inspired educative research methodology—a methodology that has a "dialogical approach" at its center and has "developing voice among those who have been silenced historically" (p. 186) as its primary purpose—indicate that

within traditional methods, reliability is understood in terms of the ability of independent researchers to come to the same conclusions when the same procedures are used. In contrast, when the aim is the development of voice, it is not expected and is indeed undesirable that independent researcher-subject teams come to the same conclusions. It is also undesirable for the procedures to remain unchanged from context to context. Procedures should be allowed not only to evolve within a specific research study but also to change given the needs and priorities of a particular population. Reliability, therefore, cannot be based on duplicating procedures, but rather must center on attempts to satisfy the underlying principle of voice and its relation to a desired type of school change. (pp. 187–188)

Alternative Approaches to Theory and Theorizing. While scholars such as Gitlin and Lather have challenged traditional conceptions of reliability and validity, some scholars of color have challenged traditional thinking about the nature of theory and theorizing. Christian (1987) expresses this emerging position succinctly and even elegantly when she notes that

> people of color have always theorized quite different from the Western form of logic. And I am inclined to say that our theorizing (and I intentionally use the verb rather than the noun) is often in narrative forms, in the stories we create, in riddles and proverbs, in the play with language, since dynamic rather than fixed ideas seem more to our liking. . . . My folk, in other words, have always been a race of theory—though more in the form of the hieroglyph, a written figure that is both sensual and abstract, both beautiful and communicative. (p. 52)

The notion that storytelling can be a form of theorizing is not associated only with scholars of color, of course. In the early 1980s, Simon and Dippo (1980) characterized storytelling as "theorizing in the concrete." Today we find a burgeoning literature on narrative ways of knowing both inside and outside the research on teaching field (see, e.g., J. Smith, 1997 and the chapter by Gudmundsdóttir in this volume). Why, even a president of the American Educational Research Association—in his presidential address—called for novels to be counted as dissertations in schools and colleges of education (Eisner, 1993), and a prestigious research journal, the *International Journal of Qualitative Studies in Education,* has actually published a paper that the paper's author characterizes as ethnographic fiction. The article includes the traditional disclaimer contained in fictional works: characters and situations in no way represent real people, situations, or events (Tierney, 1993). For many within the field (see Gardner's comments in Donmoyer et al., 1996), however, a paradigm that sanctions fictional writing as a legitimate form of research reporting is not a "complimentary" approach to research. Rather, it represents a perspective that is antithetical to and logically incompatible with traditional thinking.

THE POLITICAL INCOMMENSURABILITY PROBLEM

Even when research orientations are not inherently contradictory or logically incompatible—that is, even when, to use Gage's characterization, "two kinds of researchers were simply studying different topics" (1989, p. 141)—a kind of *political* incommensurability still likely will arise whenever resources (e.g., research funding, journal space, teacher time) are limited. This concept of political incommensurability can be demonstrated by focusing on two chapters—one by Carolyn Evertson and the other by Susan Florio-Ruane—which appeared in the Ameri-

can Association of Colleges of Teacher Education's comprehensive volume, *Knowledge Base for Beginning Teachers* (Reynolds, 1989). Both chapters focus on classroom organization, but each chapter is written from a different disciplinary perspective. Hence, each chapter characterizes the issue of classroom organization and management in quite different ways. In some sense, at least, the two authors are indeed discussing different topics, as Gage's analysis suggests.

Evertson's chapter, for example, is informed by the discipline of educational psychology in general and educational psychologists' process-product studies of teaching in particular. Constructs from process-product research are very much in evidence in the management framework that Evertson lays out in her chapter. For instance, like process-product studies, Evertson's framework conceptualizes teaching in cause-effect terms. Consequently, the teacher is encouraged to be an authoritative figure who consciously, through her or his actions, attempts to maximize the likelihood that certain effects will occur while minimizing the likelihood of other, less-desirable outcomes.

By contrast, the Florio-Ruane (1989) chapter draws on a sociolinguistic knowledge base that, like Lincoln and Guba's naturalistic and Erickson's interpretivist paradigms, tends to see human understanding as constructed through social interaction more than caused by a teacher or some other external force. Thus, Florio-Ruane recommends a very different course of action:

> Significant here for beginning teachers is the realization that a social context awaits in the classrooms where they will comfortably (or uncomfortably) assume social and intellectual authority over children. But, as Waller's work asserts, there is an essential mismatch between such a social arrangement and teachers' work: the education of children. Learners who are subordinates cannot participate in many of the activities and forms of discourse that would lead to genuine education. Thus, beginning teachers need to learn to mitigate aspects of their authority not only because they like children and want to be liked in return, but because they want to teach well. (Florio-Ruane, 1989, p. 166)

Now, it is certainly possible to view Evertson's and Florio-Ruane's work as complimentary. After all, Evertson and Florio-Ruane think of teaching and learning in fundamentally different ways. Therefore, they are trying to maximize quite different values. They are, at the operational level, at least, "simply studying different topics" (Gage, 1989, p. 14). The topics, however, are not so incommensurable that teachers cannot understand each author's position. Indeed, I suspect most of us would want teachers to consider both Evertson's and Florio-Ruane's research-based advice before deciding how to organize their classrooms. One could even imagine a teacher deciding to do some sort of balancing act with the very different management approaches advocated by Evertson and Florio-Ruane: A teacher with responsibility to teach both a skills-oriented course like typing, on the one hand, and a course like English in which students are expected to generate novel interpretations of literature and develop their own voices in their work, on the other hand, might use Evertson's framework to manage the former course but might follow Florio-Ruane's lead in managing the latter. Similarly, a beginning teacher might conclude that the view of learning that undergirds Florio-Ruane's thinking will generate more and better understanding than Evertson's view but might still opt to use Evertson's management framework during his or her first year of teaching. The beginning teacher might use such a combination because he or she concludes that the Evertson approach is more likely to ensure survival for an inexperienced teacher, and he or she values survival more than other things.

Thus, in one sense, Evertson and Florio-Ruane's quite different views of classroom organization could be said to be complementary. Yet one cannot implement Evertson's and Florio-Ruane's advice simultaneously. At any given point in time, hard choices will have to be made. This requirement to choose is what I mean by political incommensurability. Whenever resources are limited (in the Evertson and Florio-Ruane example, the limited resource is time, but in other situations, it could be (a) limited dollars to support research, (b) a limited number of faculty positions to fill, or (c) a scarce amount of space in an academic journal), we have to choose between different values and perspectives. Shulman and Gage's weaker form of paradigm talk—with its emphasis on complementarity—obscures the need to make such choices.

THE INAPPROPRIATE APPROPRIATION PROBLEM

Gage's critique of Erickson, which was alluded to above, demonstrates rather dramatically the potential danger with the "weaker" form of paradigm talk's overemphasis on complementarity. By subsuming all research perspectives under the process-product paradigm, Gage, in effect, obscures Erickson's notion about the interactive, constructed nature of learning. In the process-product paradigm, teaching and learning become sequential processes rather than symbiotic ones, and a student becomes something to be manipulated rather than someone with whom the teacher must interact to jointly construct meaning. Indeed, when reframed in process-product terms, the meanings that so interested Erickson become no more than intervening variables that teachers or others (e.g., administrators, policymakers, curriculum developers) can manipulate to produce the outcomes they want.

Furthermore, Gage's subsuming of Erickson's approach to research under the process-product paradigm obscures the fact that Erickson's chapter in the previous edition of this *Handbook* was not simply about research methodology. It was also, at least in part, about where educational decisions should be made and who should make them. "If classroom teaching in elementary and secondary schools is to come of age as a profession—if the role of the teacher is not to continue to be institutionally infantilized," Erickson writes,

> then teachers need to take the adult responsibility of investigating their own practice systematically and critically, by methods that are appropriate to their practice. . . . Interpretive research on teaching, conducted by teachers with outside-classroom colleagues to provide both support and challenge, could contribute in no small way to the

American schoolteacher's transition to adulthood as a professional. (1986, p. 157)

And why is Erickson's interpretive methodology the appropriate research strategy for helping to upgrade the status and influence of teachers? Because, according to Erickson, teachers "share similar concerns with the interpretive researcher. Teachers too are concerned with specifics of local meaning and local action; that is the stuff of life in daily classroom practice" (1986, p. 156).

Erickson's emphasis on the importance of the local and of teachers at the local level who engage in face-to-face interactions with students (as opposed to researchers and policymakers who try to choreograph teaching practice from afar) is consistent with the symbolic interactionist research tradition that Erickson refers to in order to situate his particular version of qualitative research.[8] Herbert Blumer (1969), the father of symbolic interactionism, argued that human beings act toward things on the basis of the meanings things have for them and that meanings are generated by social interaction. He also argued that meanings are not static but must constantly be constructed and reconstructed by actors during social interaction. Thus, even if meanings and reasons are allowed to substitute for causes in a cause-and-effect explanatory framework—if we treat them, in other words, as independent or possibly as intervening variables—Blumer would not be satisfied. According to Blumer, the cause-and-effect explanatory framework (and, by implication, a process-product explanatory framework) sends an inaccurate message about the nature of human action.

As noted above, this indictment of cause-effect thinking is lost in Gage's attempt to sweep Erickson's methodology under the process-product research rug. In the process, Erickson's symbolic interactionist logic for placing authority for educational decision making in the hands of teachers is also lost. One can still advocate for the importance of teacher professionalism on other grounds. Shulman, in particular, affirms his belief in the importance of teachers. He also asserts—correctly, I believe—"that the search for lawful relationships between teaching and learning . . . does not inexorably lead to the teacher as robot" (Shulman, 1986, p. 29). What is lost when Gage subsumes Erickson's thinking under talk of processes and products, however, is the virtual imperative for making decisions at the classroom level that is implicit in Erickson's symbolic interactionist view of teaching and learning: When one views learning as a process requiring social interaction rather than as a product of certain processes, it simply makes no sense for administrators or state legislatures to attempt to choreograph the teaching-learning process from afar.

SUMMARY

Gage's appropriation of Erickson's thinking into the process-product paradigm Gage champions demonstrates the potential harm associated with the weaker form of paradigm talk's emphasis on complementarity.[9] To be fair, I should note that this

---

[8] It is also, of course, consistent with Lincoln and Guba's paradigm talk and Florio-Ruane's sociolinguistic perspective.

[9] Lest anyone assume that Gage's appropriation of Erickson's thinking under the process-product paradigm is an argument for continuing to engage in the "stronger" Kuhnian-inspired paradigm talk, it should be noted that similar claims about appropriation have been leveled against Fenstermacher's version of Kuhnian-inspired paradigm talk by Cochran-Smith and Lytle (1998).

problem is less evident in the writing of Lee Shulman. However, even in Shulman's work, we find little sense of the hard choices that often will have to be made among different research orientations and the fundamentally different sorts of findings that different research orientations can generate. We find no indication, to use Shulman's own metaphor, that the puzzle pieces might not fit together or that we may need to choose among different puzzle pieces to fill a space. Thus, even at its best, the weaker version of paradigm talk presents an incomplete and less-than-adequate picture of the complex phenomena of teaching, research, and educational decision making.

The problems here are the reverse of the problems associated with Kuhnian-inspired paradigm talk. Whereas Kuhnian-inspired paradigm talk exaggerates the significance of differences in research orientations, the self-described "weaker" form of paradigm talk, with its emphasis on complementarity, inappropriately minimizes the significance of these differences and obscures the hard choices that often will have to be made. Clearly, what is needed is an alternative way of characterizing the very real but nevertheless manageable differences among researchers within our field.

In Search of Another Way of Talking

In this final section, I want to discuss an alternative approach to making sense of the proliferation of perspectives in our field and then to sketch a brief comparative advantage case for its use. To ground that case in as much specificity as possible, I also will describe in some detail a particular conceptual framework that illustrates the general alternative approach I am proposing for making sense of our differences. My main concern here, however, is less with the specifics of that framework and more with the general strategy for making sense of the proliferation of research orientations that framework exemplifies. Indeed, the specific framework I will outline has all of the limitations that conceptual frameworks inevitably have. It is a human construction rather than a mirror image of reality, and, consequently, it is not the only—or even necessarily the best—way to make sense of the educational research field. Furthermore, the framework intentionally oversimplifies reality, for any conceptual framework—if it is to be useful—can never be too baroque. Finally, the framework was constructed and reconstructed at particular points in time to respond to particular problems and accomplish particular purposes.

One set of problems and purposes related to my work as the features editor for the *Educational Researcher.* I used the category scheme I am about to present to select appropriate reviewers for submitted manuscripts and to help me establish appropriate criteria to evaluate reviewers' often conflicting advice and make publication decisions (Donmoyer, 1996a). The framework was initially developed, however, for pedagogical purposes: I wanted to help the students in the courses on qualitative methods that I teach make some sense of the paradigm proliferation in our field, without either exaggerating or obscuring differences among different groups of researchers.

I have little doubt that I, and hopefully my students, will have altered the framework by the time this chapter gets published. Alterations are always required to reflect changes in the field, new understandings of phenomena, or even one's own changing circumstances and needs. In short, what our field does not need is another reified set of categories that cement rather than facilitate thought. So I ask readers not to perseverate too much on the particulars of the conceptual framework outlined below, but to attempt instead to look beyond the particulars to the general strategy for making sense of the differences in our field that the particulars exemplify. It is this general strategy—rather than the illustrative exemplar of the strategy presented here—that I will attempt eventually to defend.

The General Strategy

The general strategy assumes (a) that different research orientations reflect different purposes, (b) that researchers' purposes can be inferred by readers of studies, and (c) that studies can consequently be categorized by referencing the different purposes that can be inferred rather than by positing the existence of radically different epistemologies. I should quickly add a caveat: Unlike certain methodologists who have invoked the notion of purpose to cavalierly dismiss paradigm talk's claims about the ideological aspects of research and to suggest, instead, that decisions about research methods are merely technical and procedural, my assumption is that different purposes reflect different and potentially conflicting values.[10] In other words, I am using the notion of purpose much as philosopher of science Stephen Toulmin (1972, 1983) does. The general strategy is also consistent with Habermas' (1978) notion that different human interests direct and shape different kinds of knowledge and different approaches to knowledge generation.

I must admit, however, that I did not consciously think of either Toulmin or Habermas—or any other theorist, for that matter—when I embraced the general strategy and developed the framework that I present here. In my own mind, at least, the general strategy and the framework I will use to exemplify the general strategy "emerged from the data" as I went about solving a very practical problem. The data in this case were the many different sorts of qualitative studies my students and I were reading in the courses on qualitative research methods that I taught. The problem was that Lincoln and Guba's paradigm-based category scheme did not easily map onto the phenomena my students and I were studying. An article that some students would classify as emerging from a critical paradigm was seen by other students as an example of the constructivist or interpretivist paradigm. I, however, almost inevitably would see elements of each paradigm represented in the article, despite Kuhnian-inspired paradigm talk's claims about incommensurability. Gary Anderson's (1989) critical ethnography is an example of a qualitative approach that quite consciously—and I believe quite successfully—combines supposedly incommensurable paradigms.

Even more problematic was the fact that I saw substantial

---

[10] Sometimes scholars make a distinction between methods and methodology. When this distinction is made, the former term normally refers to techniques and procedures, and the latter term refers to a rationale that links techniques and procedures with more fundamental, nontechnical issues. Clearly, I am concerned with methodology here. My assumption, however, is that methodological discussions need not be grounded in epistemological positions, ontological positions, or both but can, instead, focus on values and purposes.

vestiges of the positivist paradigm—which Lincoln and Guba had supposedly discredited—in virtually every piece of qualitative research I read. It always struck me as odd, for example, when doctoral students in the methodology chapters of their dissertations would reiterate Lincoln and Guba's catechism about multiple realities and would then proceed to lay out detailed procedures for member checking (as Lincoln and Guba, of course, recommend). The researcher was a member of the same species as the people being researched, I thought; if the people being studied lived in realities totally of their own construction, why should we expect the researcher's constructions of these constructions to have any grounding? Why bother to member check if we reject the tenets of positivism so completely? Similarly, I noted that Lincoln and Guba—in the very book in which they associated cause-and-effect thinking with the outdated positivist paradigm they rejected—frequently employed cause-and-effect analysis in making the case for the alternative paradigm that supposedly rejected cause-and-effect thinking (Donmoyer, 1987b).

By the same token, the research strategies that were described and reported in at least some of the articles my students and I were reading did indeed seem different from each other. At times, the differences between research orientations seemed substantial; research orientations even could appear contradictory. (Consider the different views of validity, reliability, and theory discussed above.) Eventually, I was motivated to make some sense of the complexity my students and I encountered so that I, as an instructor in a qualitative methodology class, no longer had to choose between (a) leaving my students dazed and confused by the complexity they encountered when reading qualitative research and methodological discussions, on the one hand, or (b) teaching them what seemed to me to be the increasingly unhelpful fictions embedded in the Lincoln and Guba and the Shulman and Gage versions of paradigm talk, on the other.

In time, I settled on the notion of purpose as the basis for making sense of the differences in our field, in part, I suspect, because of the unconscious influence of theorists like Toulmin and Habermas. Then I set out to see if I could construct a typology of overarching purposes to layer onto the literature that my students and I were studying. My goal was to construct a framework that was both simple enough to be useful and sufficiently complex and encompassing so as not to obscure significant differences on display in the field. Later, as indicated above, I put this framework to use—and, in the process, modified it somewhat—while playing the role of features editor for *Educational Researcher.*

The Exemplary Framework

When I am playing the role of teacher in qualitative methods courses, I have settled—at least for the moment—on a framework built around five relatively discrete purposes: (a) the "truth" seeking purpose, (b) the thick description or local knowledge purpose, (c) the developmental and quasi-historical purpose, (d) the personal essay purpose, and (e) the praxis and social change purpose. The framework is summarized in Table 11.1 and is discussed in more detail below. In the discussion below, I also attempt to (a) clearly differentiate among the various purposes and (b) demonstrate that acceptance of a particular purpose does not require that one posit the existence of a unique epistemology, at least not in an era when most scholars concede that knowledge is a human construction and that answers to empirical questions are relative to the particular linguistic and theoretical frames used to pose particular questions.

THE "TRUTH" SEEKING PURPOSE

Most quantitative research—but also a fair amount of research that could be labeled qualitative—reflects the sort of purposes that traditionally have motivated researchers: (a) to find out the "truth" about something; (b) to determine which answer is more "correct;" and (c) to assess which strategy or program is more "effective." The difference between researchers in the past and most researchers today (whether contemporary researchers use quantitative, qualitative, or some combination of methods) is that most researchers today realize that terms such as *truth, correct,* and *effective* need to be surrounded by quotation marks because such terms refer to characteristics that are not absolute but, rather, are relative to particular ways of conceptualizing the question. Whether the proposition "Students learn more when teachers engage in direct instruction" is true or false depends not simply on the empirical data gathered but also on how the term *learn* is defined and operationalized. Similarly, most people now acknowledge that assessments about effectiveness hinge as much on the definition of effectiveness used (effective for whom? effective for what purpose?) as on the empirical reality being studied. To state this another way: the realization is growing that context—in this case, the political as well as the measurement context—has a potent impact on perceptions of reality and, consequently, on research.

Despite the growing if not yet universal recognition of the need to qualify such concepts as *truth, correctness,* and *effectiveness,* qualitative researchers continue trying to build grounded theory (Glaser & Strauss, 1967; Strauss & Corbin, 1997). Quantitative researchers and even some qualitative researchers continue to explicate and even test a priori theory (Miles & Huberman, 1984b/1994); and evaluation researchers continue to determine the relative effectiveness of the programs, practices, or people they are evaluating. Such activity—although admittedly potentially dangerous if theories and evaluation findings are accepted uncritically and the theorists and researchers' a priori assumptions and frames of reference go unacknowledged and unrecognized—serves a potentially useful function. If the term *truth*—even in quotation marks—is no longer a viable concept, one wonders what our world would be like and on what basis we would make decisions about what to believe and how to act. Undoubtedly, the brutest of politics would have to be used to answer our questions and resolve our policy disputes. Some, of course, would argue that this situation would be preferable to the current situation in which the subtle and potentially insidious politics of knowledge get played out. This argument, however, seems to be primarily instrumental rather than epistemological.

THE THICK DESCRIPTION PURPOSE

Work that fits into this second category attempts to explicate the unique, idiosyncratic meanings and perspectives con-

Table 11.1. Five Overarching Purposes Undergirding Contemporary Qualitative Research

Purpose	Fundamental Questions	Exemplars
The "truth" seeking purpose	What is the correct answer (given a particular way of framing the question)? What is the relative effectiveness of a program, person strategy, or method (given a particular definition of effectiveness)?	Grounded theory-oriented researchers and theory testers, and evaluators who attempt to determine program effectiveness
The thick description purpose	How do the people studied interpret phenomena? What meaning do they attach to events? What category schemes do they employ to make sense of reality?	Emic-oriented anthropologists (e.g., Geertz, 1973, 1983)
The developmental purpose	How does an organization, individual, or group of individuals change over time?	Quasi-historical researchers such as Smith (1982) and stage theory-oriented researchers such as Huberman (1989)
The personal essay purpose	What is the researcher's personal, idiosyncratic interpretation of a situation; what unique and useful meaning can the researcher construct from a situation he or she has studied?	Eisner's (1998) educational connoisseurs, practitioners of Lawrence Lightfoot's (1983) portraiture method, practitioners of Pinar (1994) and Grumet's (1980) autobiographical method, and certain teacher researchers
The praxis and social change purpose	How can we simultaneously learn about and change educators, educational organizations, or both? How can we make advocacy for change part of our research design rather than merely something that occurs after a study is completed?	Collaboratively oriented researchers influenced by critical, feminist, race-oriented and postmodern thought such as Lather (1986, 1994), Gitlin (1994), and Dillard (1997); practitioners of Wasley's (1993) negotiated research and certain forms of action research

structed by individuals, groups of individuals, or both who inhabit a particular context or case being studied. The primary concern here is not with assessing program effectiveness, (although certain evaluation approaches such as Stake's [1975] responsive approach and Parlett and Hamilton's [1977] illuminative model have always presumed that thick description can serve an evaluative function). Nor is the purpose theory development (although theory can certainly be constructed from descriptions of local meaning systems, as ethnologists who build anthropological theory from ethnographies of individual cultures demonstrate). Rather, researchers whose work exhibits this second purpose are concerned with what Geertz (1983) calls local knowledge; they want to understand and communicate how an individual or a particular group of individuals interpret phenomena.

It should be noted that theory and theoretical constructs are not absent from work that is guided by an interest in the thick description of local knowledge. Theory in this orientation, however, plays a quite different role from its role in traditional quantitative research or even in qualitative studies geared toward the development of grounded theory. As Clifford Geertz (1973), the anthropologist who coined the term *thick description,* notes, in this form of research, theory functions as a means, not an end. Theoretical constructs serve primarily a rhetorical function. They are used much as philosopher of history William Dray indicates historians use a theoretical construct such as *revolution.* When an historian sets out to account for the French Revolution, Dray (1957) writes, the historian

is just *not interested* in explaining it as a revolution—as an astronomer might be interested in explaining a certain eclipse as an instance of eclipses; he [sic] is almost invariably concerned with it as different from other members of its class. Indeed, he might even say that his

main concern will be to explain the French Revolution's taking a course unlike any other; that is to say, he will explain it as unique in the sense distinguished above. (p. 47)

Clearly, this second category—with its emphasis on idiosyncrasy and meaning—represents a reasonable facsimile of Lincoln and Guba's naturalistic-constructivist paradigm minus Lincoln and Guba's postulates about an incommensurable epistemology and ontology. The stripping away of Lincoln and Guba's epistemological and ontological talk—and the redefining of the perspective in terms of its overarching purpose—can be justified by the fact that the case for thick description-oriented work can be—and, in fact, often has been—made on utilitarian grounds. Consider, Lincoln and Guba's (1985) transferability argument. Lincoln and Guba, in essence, argue that their concept of transferability is preferable to the traditional notion of generalizability because social phenomena are complex and idiosyncratic. Consequently, the more useful course of action is to support research that lets the research consumer decide whether the findings of a particular study will apply to his or her particular situation (by providing a detailed description of the "sending" setting, which can be compared to the consumers' "receiving" setting) rather than to provide the research consumer with a statistical measure of generalizability, a measure that can be gotten only by using large samples and, in the process, obscuring contextual variables.

THE DEVELOPMENTAL PURPOSE

The third category encompasses a diverse array of work, everything from Louis Smith's (1982) *Kensington Revisited,* a quasi-historical study of an innovative school and the teachers who work there, to Michael Huberman's (1989) study of the career development of teachers, which netted a kind of stage theory. Each of these studies—and most other work that fits under this category—could also be fit under one of the other two categories of studies discussed above. For example, historians are very much concerned with the perceptions of the people they study (Collingwood, 1946). Hence, a quasi-historical study like *Kensington Revisited* could have been classified as a kind of thick description. Huberman's work, conversely, was designed to generate a grounded theory, albeit a special kind of grounded theory. Thus, it could have been grouped under the "truth" seeking category described above.

What differentiates each of these studies from other work in the categories to which they could have been assigned—and what makes it possible to put quasi-historical and stage theory-oriented work in the same category—is a shared interest in development over time. A concern for temporality, in short, is the defining property of this third category, a category with two distinct subcategories: one for work that provides thick descriptions, albeit in a quasi-historical format, and the other for work that abstracts from thick description data a more generalizable stage theory.

The fact that work in this third category could be classified in other ways demonstrates the constructed nature of this particular framework (and, for that matter, all frameworks and category schemes). I decided to create a separate category for developmentally oriented work because it helped me, in my role as teacher of qualitative methods courses, to make distinctions that seemed important to make for my students (to differentiate, for example, between studies in which standard interview techniques could be used and studies that required the elicitation of life history data). Others with different purposes may not find this distinction particularly helpful and may need to modify the scheme I am presenting here or maybe even start from scratch and develop their own frameworks for making sense of the field. Indeed, when I played the role of features editor for the *Educational Researcher,* I did not find this third category particularly helpful. Therefore, in this context, I used a four-part rather than a five-part category framework to do my work. The fact that I altered my framework to reflect the somewhat different needs of different situations reinforces the heuristic nature of this framework. It also reinforces a point made earlier: The field does not need another reified set of categories that cement rather than facilitate members' thinking and acting.

THE PERSONAL ESSAY PURPOSE

When I survey the field, I see a fourth overarching purpose. Work that reflects this fourth purpose, like work that exhibits the thick description and developmental purposes discussed above, is oriented toward the explication of meaning. The difference is that here the meanings being explicated are as much the researcher's as they are those the researcher has stud-

ied. The researcher, in other words, is concerned with sharing a personal interpretation of the phenomena he or she has studied, at least as much as—and possibly more than—with sharing the interpretations of her or his subjects or respondents. The researcher's subjectivity, in short, is intentionally front and center in research reports.

Until recently, this more subjective and personal form of work had not been found within the field of educational research nor in the social sciences more generally. It has always been commonplace in the humanities, however. In this context, it represents a genre referred to as the personal essay. Phillip Lopate (1994), the editor of the anthology titled *The Art of the Personal Essay,* writes in the preface to that book:

> At the core of the personal essay is the supposition that there is a certain unity to human experience. . . . This meant that when . . . [an essayist] was telling about himself, he [sic] was talking, to some degree, about the entire human condition. (p. xxiii)

Those who have begun to advocate the use of or actually use the personal essay genre within education—and I would include in this group Elliot Eisner's (1979, 1993, 1998) educational connoisseurs and critics (see, e.g., Barone, 1983), practitioners of Sarah Lawrence Lightfoot's (1983) portraiture approach to doing research, those who employ the autobiographical method developed by Pinar (1994) and Grumet (1980), and certain teacher researchers who attempt to communicate their "personal practical knowledge" (Connelly & Clandinin, 1990) in the form of narrative essays with the hope of informing and enlightening others[11]—seem to share the assumption about a unity of human experience that transcends the idiosyncrasy of our personal experiences. The rationale for this sort of work also includes the assumption that educational issues are as much conceptual as empirical, that how we frame educational questions is as important as—and to a large extent determines—how we answer them (Donmoyer, 1987a, 1991, 1996b).

As was the case above, we can see similarities with the other purpose-based categories described in this chapter, but once again we also can see significant differences in emphasis. Researchers whose work fits under this category may use theory, but theory development or explication is not their primary purpose. Similarly, research that fits into this fourth category may get reported in narrative form. The narratives, however, will read more like personal essays than like the objective-sounding, quasi-historical accounts discussed above.

Researchers whose work fits into this category also may—and undoubtedly will—report on the meanings and perspectives of those they have studied, but here researchers' interpretation of others' interpretations is foregrounded. To be sure, the difference between work that fits into this personal essay category and thick description-oriented studies is one of degree rather than one of kind. Even in the most systematically exe-

---

[11] Of course, the teacher researcher movement is complex and multifaceted (see, e.g., Cochran-Smith & Lytle, 1993, 1998; Richardson, 1994). It cannot be adequately described by a single category, or possibly even a single category scheme. I personally have been involved in collaborative action research projects with a classroom teacher that exemplified both the "truth" seeking (Yennie-Donmoyer & Donmoyer, 1993) and the thick description (Donmoyer & Yennie-Donmoyer, 1995) purposes discussed above. Furthermore, Cochran-Smith and Lytle (1998) indicate that the teacher researcher movement is about more than the generation of knowledge. (See also the chapter on teacher research by Zeichner & Noffke in this *Handbook.*)

cuted thick description–oriented scholarship, one ultimately gets only the researcher's interpretation of the interpretations of those he or she has studied. In such studies, however, the researcher has attempted—through the use of procedures such as member checking and using "native language" in the reporting of findings—to minimize his or her influence.

Those same procedures, of course, might be used by researchers whose work fits into this fourth category, because all researchers have an ethical obligation to not misrepresent the perspectives of the people they write about. Nevertheless, the central focus in such work is clearly on the researcher's own interpretations. The researcher's interpretations are those that are foregrounded; the meanings and perspectives of those studied intentionally play a more supporting role. Consequently, the primary question we should ask when assessing work that reflects a personal essay purpose is not, "Did the researcher get it right?" Although this question remains important—in large part because of an ethical responsibility to not misrepresent the thoughts and actions of others (Donmoyer, 1987a, 1987c)—the primary concern is, "Does the researcher's work lead me to see educational phenomena differently and to think of educational questions in different ways?"

Needless to say, work generated by this fourth purpose represents a rather radical departure from more traditional views of the role of research in an applied field such as education and requires significantly different assessment criteria than are normally used when the purpose is (a) to find the "true" answer to a question, (b) to discover the most effective strategy, (c) to report as accurately as possible the interpretations of others, or (d) to relate as accurately as possible a chronology of events and the meanings participants associate with these events. An appreciation of work reflecting this fourth purpose, however, does not require acceptance of a different epistemology, at least, once the proposition that all empirical understanding requires some sort of a priori framing has been accepted. This approach simply brings the framing to the foreground rather than keeping it in the background. Whether the benefits of this approach outweigh the costs and whether it is wise to use limited research dollars to support work oriented toward the fourth purpose rather than use limited dollars to support work guided by more traditionally accepted purposes are questions that will undoubtedly continue to be debated. Such debates, however, are basically utilitarian and not epistemological in character.

THE PRAXIS AND SOCIAL CHANGE PURPOSE

The final purpose-based category I will discuss represents an attempt to accommodate some recent work that makes change and reform activity an integral part of the research process. The goal in this work is not simply to bring about change and reform through the publication of research findings (a goal of most researchers in an applied field like education). Rather, in work that fits into this fifth purpose-based category, change and reform become integral parts of the research design by changing the relationship between researchers and subjects/respondents into a less hierarchical, more collaborative one. The specifics of that relationship vary somewhat from study to study, but the general tendency is toward making those being studied into co-researchers who help define the questions to be asked and whose involvement in data collection and analysis goes well beyond the interviewee role and the member-checking process described by Lincoln and Guba. The emphasis, in short, is on eliminating or at least minimizing hierarchical relationships and on promoting learning among all participants in the research process.

Some researchers whose work fits into this category (e.g., Gitlin, 1994; Lather, 1986, 1994) have been influenced by critical, feminist, and, more recently, postmodern theory[12] and the emancipatory agendas that are central to these perspectives and embedded in the notion of praxis. Other change-oriented approaches—e.g., Wasley's (1993) negotiated research and various forms of collaborative action research (see, e.g., Yennie-Donmoyer & Donmoyer, 1993)—share both critical scholars' commitment to making practitioners central players in the research process and their commitment to integrating a change orientation into research activity. Those approaches, however, are not undergirded by critical, feminist, or postmodern theory. They do not, in other words, have an a priori commitment to making the theoretical constructs of race, class, gender, and power central components of the research study.[13]

Before proceeding, I should acknowledge that work in this category might legitimately be seen as emanating from a different epistemology if, as in some Marxist discussions of praxis, we assume that one cannot really know independent of action. This idea, however, does not seem to be central to the case made by contemporary advocates of the praxis and social change perspective. Rather, the case for this sort of work nor-

---

[12] The methodological implications of postmodern thought are not, at this point in time, altogether clear. Hence, where or even whether postmodern-inspired research approaches fit in the framework being presented here is not obvious. In Lather's (1994) work, the impact of postmodern thinking can be seen most readily during the representation phase of the research process, because Lather recommends that the researcher use various rhetorical techniques to undermine his or her authority. Lather's postmodern-inspired strategies seem best classified as a special form of emancipation-oriented work and, consequently, appear to fit into the fifth category in the typology of purposes presented here. Others, however, have begun to draw other sorts of methodological implications from postmodern scholarship (see, e.g., Scheurich, 1997), and it is not so clear that some of these strategies fit so comfortably under the praxis and social change umbrella. We may discover a need, in short, to alter the framework being presented here when the methodological implications of postmodern thought become clearer. Similarly, the methodological implications of race-based critiques of knowledge are less than clear at this point in time. To date, a limited number of attempts have been made to move the discussion to the methodological level. Furthermore, although many of the attempts that have been made (see, e.g., Dillard, 1997; Ladson-Billings, 1995) could be fit into the fifth category outlined above, they might also be fit into several other categories in the purpose-based typology. Once again, careful monitoring is needed, and depending on what this monitoring reveals, significant adjustments in the framework may be required.

[13] I do not mean to suggest that social change-oriented research that is not influenced by critical, feminist, or postmodern theory is atheoretical. Wasley's social change-oriented work, for instance, is clearly influenced by the theoretical work of Seymour Sarason (1996). I am simply trying to distinguish between two kinds of social change-oriented work: one has an a priori commitment to the centrality of the variables of race, class, gender, and power; the other does not exhibit such a priori commitments.

mally emanates from an ethical concern about not exploiting research subjects (Lather, 1986), a utilitarian concern about making it more likely that research will be used by practitioners (Gitlin, Siegel, & Boru, 1989), or both.

Whether involving practitioners in collaborative research does, indeed, make research more usable is a question that undoubtedly will continue to be debated. Similarly, we will almost certainly continue to debate whether the ethical benefits of collaborative research cost too much in terms of rigor and the regulative ideal of objectivity. Once again, however, these debates are largely utilitarian rather than epistemological in character, at least for those who realize that objectivity can be no more than a regulative ideal.

SUMMARY

The above five categories help us make sense of the methodological balkanization within the field of educational research without resorting to either the Kuhnian-inspired or the weaker form of paradigm talk critiqued in the first two sections of this chapter. Why is it more advantageous to characterize methodological difference in terms of purpose rather than epistemology? What do we gain by focusing attention on differing purposes rather than emphasizing the complementarity of research orientations? These are the questions I will address—albeit quite briefly—in the final part of this chapter.

A Comparative Advantage Case

COMPARATIVE ADVANTAGES VIS-À-VIS KUHNIAN-INSPIRED PARADIGM TALK

A category scheme like the one just presented—that is, a category scheme built around researcher purpose—has a number of advantages over ones that assume that the different approaches to research reflect incommensurable epistemologies. Here I will focus on two particularly significant advantages.

First, a category scheme built around the notion of purpose can better accommodate the real world complexity of research practice because it does not preclude classifying a study into two or more categories or seeing both primary and secondary purposes in a study. One cannot embrace incommensurable epistemologies easily (Lincoln & Guba, 1985). Frequently, however, one can pursue multiple purposes simultaneously.

Second, category schemes built around differing purposes still alert us to the need to use different criteria when evaluating qualitative work, but purpose-based categories do not stop cross-perspective discourse before it starts. When people assume they hold incommensurable world views, they find little reason to talk with and listen to each other. Indeed, when incommensurability is assumed, one can easily write off criticism from proponents of another paradigm, because the person being critiqued can legitimately assume that his or her critic really cannot understand. When people see differences as relating to conflicting purposes rather than to incommensurable epistemologies, however, they have more incentive to talk with their critics and less reason to dismiss cavalierly those with whom they disagree. Consequently, at the individual level, we discover a greater opportunity for learning and, at the collective level, a greater likelihood that,

when educational decisions must be made, a range of perspectives will be considered and an appropriate balance between these perspectives will be found.

COMPARATIVE ADVANTAGES VIS-À-VIS THE WEAKER FORM OF PARADIGM TALK

Of course, the importance of considering and accommodating a range of perspectives in the study of teaching was also emphasized by Shulman in making the case for his self-described "weaker" form of paradigm talk. The weaker form of paradigm talk advocated by Shulman and also by Gage, however, tends to overemphasize the complementarity of differing research perspectives and underestimate the hard choices and trade-offs that frequently have to be made in a public policy field like education. By contrast, when the focus is on researchers' differing and sometimes even conflicting purposes, potential value conflicts—and the hard choices required to resolve them—are highlighted.

SUMMARY

Thus, the purpose-based approach to making sense of the diversity within our field seems preferable to both Kuhnian-inspired paradigm talk and the "weaker" form of paradigm talk used by Shulman and Gage. Whether it is wise to characterize this purpose-oriented way of talking as a third type of paradigm talk or whether it is best to now jettison Kuhn's term is, for me, at this point, an open question. The term's acceptance by academic and even popular culture argues for the former strategy; fear of confusion and a concern for clarity are the best reasons to adopt the latter course of action.

Conclusion

Research on teaching and the field of educational research in general has changed dramatically during the years since the American Educational Research Association published its first *Handbook of Research on Teaching.* That first edition of the *Handbook,* after all, was organized around a single conceptual framework, and qualitative research methods were not even mentioned. By contrast, this edition of the *Handbook* views teaching and learning from a number of different perspectives, and the topic of qualitative research has been given a prominent place in the *Handbook's* contents.

One can even see dramatic changes between the third edition of the *Handbook*—published in 1986—and this fourth edition. In the third edition, only two articles discussed qualitative methods. More important, Erickson suggested that only two major conceptions of research were operative in the field. By contrast, today we have a proliferation of research orientations, and this proliferation is clearly displayed, especially in the section of this *Handbook* that is devoted to qualitative research.

In this chapter, I have attempted to map out a new way to make sense of this proliferation of approaches to research on teaching and, more generally, to the field of educational research. My goal has been to find a middle ground between those who portray differing methodologies as invariably complimentary and those who suggest that different methodologies inevitably reflect incommensurable epistemologies. I articulated a classification scheme that was based on researchers' differing purposes, and I sketched out a comparative advantage case for using this sort of scheme rather than either the Kuhnian-inspired or Gage and Shulman's "weaker" version of paradigm talk. My hope is that the purpose-based strategy I have proposed will help us talk with and learn from each other about the complex processes of teaching and learning and that such talk will result in more thoughtful teaching and more balanced educational policymaking.

REFERENCES

Anderson, G. (1989). Critical ethnography in education: Origins, current status and new directions. *Review of Educational Research, 59*(3), 249–270.

Anderson, G., & Herr, K. (1999). The new paradigm wars: Is there room for rigorous practitioner knowledge in schools and universities? *Educational Researcher, 28*(5), 12–21.

Barone, T. (1983). Things of use and things of beauty: The Swain County High School arts program. *Daedalus, 112,* 1–28.

Bernstein, R. J. (1991). *The new constellation: The ethical-political horizons of modernity/postmodernity.* Cambridge, England: Polity Press.

Bloom, B. (1963). Testing cognitive ability and achievement. In N. L. Gage (Ed.), *Handbook of research on teaching* (pp. 379–397). Chicago: Rand McNally.

Blumer, H. (1969). *Symbolic interactionism: Perspective and method.* Englewood Cliffs, NJ: Prentice-Hall.

Campbell, D., & Stanley, J. (1963). Experimental and quasi-experimental designs for research on teaching. In N. L. Gage (Ed.), *Handbook of research on teaching* (pp. 171–246). Chicago: Rand McNally.

Campbell, D., & Stanley, J. (1966). *Experimental and quasi-experimental designs for research.* Chicago: Rand McNally. (Original work published in 1963)

Christian, B. (1987). The race for theory. *Cultural Critiques, 6,* 51–63.

Clark, C., & Peterson, P. (1986). Teachers' thought processes. In M. Wittrock (Ed.), *Handbook of research on teaching* (3rd ed., pp. 255–296). New York: Macmillan.

Clark, C., & Yinger, R. (1977). Research on teacher thinking. *Curriculum Inquiry, 7*(4), 279–304.

Cochran-Smith, M., & Lytle, S. (1993). *Inside outside: Teacher research and knowledge.* New York: Teachers College Press.

Cochran-Smith, M., & Lytle S. (1998). Teacher research: The question that persists. *International Journal of Leadership in Education, 1*(1), 19–36.

Cohen, P. (1968). The very idea of a social science. In I. Lakatos & A. Musgrace (Eds.), *Philosophy of Science* (pp. 407–432). Amsterdam: North-Holland.

Collingwood, R. (1946). *The idea of history.* New York: Oxford University Press.

Connelly, F. M., & Clandinin, D. J. (1990). Stories of experience and narrative inquiry. *Educational Researcher, 19*(5), 2–14.

Darling-Hammond, L. (Ed.). (1994). *Review of research in education* (Vol. 20). Washington, DC: American Educational Research Association.

Denzin, N. K., & Lincoln, Y. S. (1994). Introduction: Entering the field of qualitative research. In N. K. Denzin & Y. S. Lincoln (Eds.), *Handbook of qualitative research* (pp. 1–17). Thousand Oaks, CA: Sage.

Dillard, C. (1997, April). *The substance of things hoped for, the evidence of things not seen: Toward an (en)darkened feminist epistemology.* Paper presented at the annual meeting of the American Educational Research Association, Chicago.

Donmoyer, R. (1987a). Beyond Thorndike/Beyond melodrama. *Curriculum Inquiry 17*(4), 353–363.

Donmoyer, R. (1987b). [Review of the book *Naturalistic inquiry*]. *Teachers College Record, 88,* 470–474.

Donmoyer, R. (1987c). Why case studies? Reflections on Hord and Hall's three images. *Curriculum Inquiry, 17,* 91–102.

Donmoyer, R. (1990). Generalizability and the single case study. In E. Eisner & A. Peshkin (Eds.), *Qualitative research in education: The debate continues* (pp. 175–199). New York: Teachers College Press.

Donmoyer, R. (1991). Postpositivist evaluation: Give me a for instance. *Educational Administration Quarterly, 27,* 265–296.

Donmoyer, R. (1996a). Educational research in an era of paradigm proliferation: What's a journal editor to do? *Educational Researcher, 25*(2), 19–25.

Donmoyer, R. (1996b). The concept of a knowledge base. In F. Murray (Ed.), *The teacher educator's handbook: Building a knowledge base for the preparation of teachers* (pp. 92–119). San Francisco: Jossey-Bass.

Donmoyer, R. (1997, April). *The qualitative/quantitative distinction: Is it really a matter of conflicting epistemologies?* Paper presented at the annual meeting of the American Educational Research Association, Chicago.

Donmoyer, R. (1999). The continuing quest for a knowledge base 1976–1998. In J. Murphy & K. Seashore-Lewis (Eds.), *Handbook of research on educational administration* (pp. 25–43). San Francisco: Jossey-Bass.

Donmoyer, R., Eisner, E., Gardner, H., Stotsky, S., Wasley, P., Tillman, L., Cizek, G., & Gough, N. (1996). Should novels count as dissertations in education? *Research in the Teaching of English, 30*(4), 403–427.

Donmoyer, R., & Yennie-Donmoyer, J. (1995). Data as drama: Reflections on the use of readers theater as a mode of qualitative data display. *Qualitative Inquiry, 1*(4), 402–428.

Dray, W. (1979). *Laws and explanations in history.* Westport, CT: Greenwood Press. (Original work published in 1957).

Eisner, E. (1979). *The educational imagination: On the design and evaluation of school programs.* New York: Macmillan.

Eisner, E. (1993). Forms of understanding and the future of educational research. *Educational Researcher, 22*(7), 5–11.

Eisner, E. (1998). *The enlightened eye: Qualitative inquiry and the enhancement of educational practice.* Upper Saddle River, NJ: Merrill (Prentice Hall).

Erickson, F. (1986). Qualitative methods in research on teaching. In M. Wittrock (Ed.), *Handbook of research on teaching* (3rd ed., pp. 119–161). New York: Macmillan.

Evertson, C., & Green, J. (1986). Observation as inquiry and method. In M. Wittrock (Ed.), *Handbook of research on teaching* (3rd ed., pp. 162–213). New York: Macmillan.

Evertson, D. (1989). Classroom organization and management. In M. C. Reynolds (Ed.), *Knowledge base for the beginning teacher* (pp. 59–70). Elmsford, NY: Pergamon Press.

Fenstermacher, G. D. (1994). The knower and the known: The nature of knowledge in research on teaching. In L. Darling-Hammond (Ed.), *Review of research in education* (Vol. 20, pp. 3–56). Washington, DC: American Educational Research Association.

Florio-Ruane, S. (1989). Social organization of classes and school. In M. C. Reynolds (Ed.), *Knowledge base for the beginning teacher* (pp. 163–172). Elmsford, NY: Pergamon Press.

Gage, N. L. (Ed.). (1963a). *Handbook of research on teaching.* Chicago: Rand McNally.

Gage, N. L. (1963b). Paradigms for research on teaching. In N. L. Gage (Ed.), *Handbook of research on teaching* (pp. 94–141). Chicago: Rand McNally.

Gage, N. L. (1989). The paradigm wars and their aftermath: A "historical" sketch of research on teaching since 1989. *Teachers College Record, 91*(2), 135–150.

Geertz, C. (1973). *The interpretation of cultures: Selected essays.* New York: Basic Books.

Geertz, C. (1983). *Local knowledge: Further essays in interpretive anthropology.* New York: Basic Books.

Gitlin, A. (1994). *Power and method: Political activism and educational research.* London: Routledge.

Gitlin, A., & Russell, R. (1994). Alternative methodologies and the research context. In A. Gitlin (Ed.), *Power and method: Political activism and educational research* (pp. 181–202). London: Routledge.

Gitlin, A., Siegel, M., & Boru, K. (1989). The politics of method: From leftist ethnography to evaluative research. *International Journal of Qualitative Studies in Education, 2*(3), 235–253.

Glaser, B., & Strauss, A. (1967). *The discovery of grounded theory: Strategies for qualitative research.* Chicago: Aldine.

Good, T., Biddle, B., & Brophy, J. (1975). *Teachers make a difference.* New York: Holt, Rinehart and Winston.

Grumet, M. (1980). Autobiography and reconceptualization. *Journal of Curriculum Theorizing, 2,* 155–158.

Guba, E. (Ed.). (1990). *The paradigm dialog.* Newbury Park, CA: Sage.

Guba, E., & Lincoln, Y. (1989). *Fourth generation evaluation.* Newbury Park, CA: Sage.

Guba, E., & Lincoln, Y. (1994). Competing paradigms in qualitative research. In N. K. Denzin & Y. S. Lincoln (Eds.), *Handbook of qualitative research* (pp. 105–117). Thousand Oaks, CA: Sage.

Habermas, J. (1978). *Knowledge and human interests.* London: Heinemann.

House, E. (1991). Realism in research. *Educational Researcher, 20*(6), 2–10.

Houston, W. (Ed.). (1990). *Handbook of research on teacher education.* New York: Macmillan.

Hoy, W., & Miskel, C. (1996). *Educational administration: Theory, research and practice* (5th ed.). New York: Random House. (Original work published in 1978).

Huberman, M. (1989). The professional lifecycle of teachers. *Teachers College Record, 91*(1), 31–57.

Kant, I. (1996). Critique of pure reason. (W. Pluhar, Trans.). Indianapolis, IN: Hackett. (Original work published in 1781)

Kuhn, T. (1970). *The structure of scientific revolutions.* Chicago: University of Chicago Press. (Original work published in 1962)

Ladson-Billings, G. (1995). Toward a theory of culturally relevant pedagogy. *American Educational Research Journal, 32*(3), 465–491.

Lakatos, I. (1970). Falsification and the methodology of scientific research programs. In I. Lakatos & A. Musgrave (Eds.), *Criticism and the growth of knowledge.* Cambridge, UK: Cambridge University Press.

Lather, P. (1986). Research as praxis. *Harvard Educational Review, 56*(3), 257–277.

Lather, P. (1992). Critical frames in educational research: Feminist and poststructural perspectives. *Theory into Practice, 31*(2), 1–13.

Lather, P. (1994). Fertile obsession: Validity after post structuralism. In A. Gitlin (Ed.), *Power and method: Political activism and educational research* (pp. 36–60). London: Routledge.

Lawrence-Lightfoot, S. (1983). *The good high school.* New York: Basic Books.

Light, R. (1973). Issues in the analysis of qualitative data. In R. Travers (Ed.), *Handbook of research on teaching* (2nd ed., pp. 318–381). Chicago: Rand McNally.

Lincoln, Y. (1997, April). *Response made during the paradigm wars revisited.* Session at the annual meeting of the American Educational Research Association, Chicago.

Lincoln, Y. S., & Guba, E. G. (1985). *Naturalistic inquiry.* Newbury Park, CA: Sage.

Lincoln, Y., & Guba, E. (2000). Paradigmatic controversies, contradictions, and emerging confluences. In N. Denzin & Y. Lincoln (Eds.), *Handbook of qualitative research* (2nd ed., pp. 163–188). Thousand Oaks, CA: Sage.

Lopate, P. (1994). Introduction. In P. Lopate (Ed.), *The art of the personal essay* (pp. xxiii–liv). New York: Doubleday.

Masterman, M. (1970). The nature of a paradigm. In I. Lakatos & A. Musgrave (Eds.), *Criticism and the growth of knowledge* (pp. 59–89). Cambridge, UK: Cambridge University Press.

Medley, D., & Mitzel, H. (1963). Measuring classroom behavior by systematic observation. In N. L. Gage (Ed.), *Handbook of research on teaching* (pp. 247–328). Chicago: Rand McNally.

Miles, M. (1979). Qualitative data as an attractive nuisance: The problem of analysis. *Administrative Science Quarterly, 24,* 590–601.

Miles, M., & Huberman, M. (1984). Drawing valid meaning from qualitative data: Toward a shared craft. *Educational Researcher, 13,* 20–30.

Miles, M., & Huberman, M. (1994). *Qualitative data analysis: A sourcebook of new methods.* Beverly Hills, CA: Sage. (Original work published in 1984)

Parlett, M, & Hamilton, D. (1977). Evaluation as illumination: A new approach to the study of innovatory programs. In D. Hamilton, B. MacDonald, C. King, D. Jenkins, & M. Parlett (Eds.), *Beyond the numbers game* (pp. 6–22). Berkeley, CA: McCutchan.

Parsons, T. (1937). *The structure of social action: A study in social theory with special reference to a group of recent European writers.* New York: McGraw-Hill.

Patton, M. Q. (1990). *Qualitative evaluation and research methods.* Newbury Park, CA: Sage. (Original work published in 1980)

Phillips, D. C. (1983). After the wake: Postpositivistic educational thought. *Educational Researcher, 12*(5), 4–12.

Phillips, D. C. (1990). Postpositivistic science: Myths and realities. In E. Guba (Ed.), *The paradigm dialog* (pp. 31–45). Newbury Park, CA: Sage.

Pinar, W. (1994). *Autobiography, politics and sexuality: Essays in curriculum theory, 1972–1992.* New York: Peter Lang.

Pinar, W. (1998). *Queer theory in education.* Mahwah, NJ: Lawrence Erlbaum Associates.

Popkewitz, T. (1990). Whose future? Whose past? Notes on critical theory and methodology. In E. Guba (Ed.), *The paradigm dialog* (pp. 46–66). Newbury Park, CA: Sage.

Remmers, H. H. (1963). Rating methods in research on teaching. In N. L. Gage (Ed.), *Handbook of research on teaching* (pp. 329–378). Chicago: Rand McNally.

Reynolds, M. C. (Ed.). (1989). *Knowledge base for the beginning teacher.* Elmsford, NY: Pergamon Press.

Richardson, V. (1994). Conducting research on practice. *Educational Researcher, 23*(5), 5–10.

Sarason, S. (1996). *Revisiting "The culture of school and the problem of change."* New York: Teachers College Press.

Scheurich, J. (1997). *Research method in the postmodern.* Washington, DC: Falmer Press.

Scheurich, J., & Young, M. (1997). Coloring epistemologies: Are our research epistemologies racially biased? *Educational Researcher, 26*(4), 4–16.

Schön, D. A. (1983). *The reflective practitioner.* New York: Basic Books.

Schön, D. A. (1987). *Educating the reflective practitioner.* San Francisco: Jossey-Bass.

Schön, D. A. (1989). Professional knowledge and reflective practice. In T. J. Sergiovanni & J. H. Moore (Eds.), *Schooling for tomorrow: Directing reforms to issues that count* (pp. 188–206). Boston: Allyn & Bacon.

Schön, D. A. (Ed.). (1991). *The reflective turn.* New York: Teachers College Press.

Schwille, J., Porter, A., & Gant, M. (1980). Content decision making and the politics of education. *Educational Administration Quarterly, 16*(2), 21–40.

Shulman, L. (1986). Paradigms and research programs in the study of teaching: A contemporary perspective. In M. Wittrock (Ed.), *Handbook of research on teaching* (3rd ed., pp. 3–36). New York: Macmillan.

Simon, R., & Dippo, D. (1980). Dramatic analysis: Interpretive inquiry for the transformation of social settings. *Journal of Curriculum Theory, 2,* 109–134.

Smith, J. (1997). The stories educational researchers tell about themselves. *Educational Researcher, 26*(5), 4–11.

Smith, L. (1982). *Kensington revisited: Two years of context from the Milford Chronicles.* (ERIC Document Reproduction Service No. ED 225 231)

Spindler, G. (1987). *Education and the cultural process.* Prospect Heights, IL: Waveland Press.

Stake, R. (1975). *Evaluating the arts in education: A responsive approach.* Columbus, OH: Charles Merrill.

Stanfield, J. H., II. (1993). Epistemological considerations. In J. H. Stanfield II & R. M. Dennis (Eds.), *Race and ethnicity in research methods* (pp. 16–36). Newark Park, CA: Sage.

Stanfield, J. H., II. (1994). Ethnic modeling in qualitative research. In N. K. Denzin & Y. S. Lincoln (Eds.), *Handbook of qualitative research* (pp. 175–188). Thousand Oaks, CA: Sage.

Stern, G. (1963). Measuring noncognitive variables in research on teaching. In N. L. Gage (Ed.), *Handbook of research on teaching* (pp. 398–447). Chicago: Rand McNally.

Strauss, A., & Corbin, J. (1997). *Grounded theory in practice.* Thousand Oaks, CA: Sage.

Tatsuoka, M., & Tiedman, D. (1963). Statistics as an aspect of scientific method in research on teaching. In N. L. Gage (Ed.), *Handbook of research on teaching* (pp. 142–170). Chicago: Rand McNally.

Tierney, W. (1993). The cedar closet. *Qualitative Studies in Education, 6,* 303–314.

Tillman, L. (1995). *Mentoring African American faculty in predominantly White institutions: An investigation of assigned and informal mentoring relationships.* Unpublished doctoral dissertation, The Ohio State University, Columbus, OH.

Tom, A., & Valli, L. (1990). Professional knowledge for teachers. In W. Houston (Ed.), *Handbook of research on teacher education* (pp. 373–392). New York: Macmillan.

Toulmin, S. (1972). *Human understanding.* Princeton, NJ: Princeton University Press.

Toulmin, S. (1983). The construal of reality: Criticism in modern and postmodern science. In W. J. T. Mitchell (Ed.), *The politics of interpretation* (pp. 99–117). Chicago: University of Chicago Press.

Travers, R. (Ed.). (1973). *Handbook of research on teaching* (2nd ed.). Chicago: Rand McNally.

van Manen, M. (1990). *Researching lived experience: Human science for an action sensitive pedagogy.* Albany, NY: State University of New York Press.

Wasley, P. (1993). *Rattling cages: Negotiated research for improved reflective practice.* Paper presented at the annual meeting of the American Educational Research Association, Atlanta.

Weick, K. (1976). Educational organizations as loosely coupled systems. *Administration Science Quarterly, 21,* 1–19.

Winch, P. (1990). *The idea of a social science and its relationship to philosophy.* New York: Humanities Press. (Original work published in 1958)

Wittrock, M. (Ed.). (1986). *Handbook of research on teaching* (3rd ed.). New York: Macmillan.

Yennie-Donmoyer, J., & Donmoyer, R. (1993). Creating a culture of writers with at-risk students. In R. Donmoyer & R. Kos (Eds.), *At-risk students: Portraits, policies, programs, and practices* (pp. 343–369). Albany, NY: State University of New York Press.

Special Topics in Qualitative Methodology

12.

Qualitative Educational Research: The Philosophical Issues

Kenneth R. Howe
University of Colorado at Boulder

This chapter examines qualitative educational research through the lens of philosophy. I sort out the issues in terms of four of philosophy's traditional subareas: epistemology, ontology, political theory, and ethics. As we shall see, the issues overlap and crisscross in many ways.

My task is complicated by the fact that the term "qualitative" as deployed in educational research is markedly vague and ambiguous. This is due in no small way to the ongoing quantitative-qualitative debate within the educational research community, in which the descriptors "quantitative" and "qualitative" have been attached willy-nilly to data, to research methods, and to broader epistemological "paradigms." In light of the foggy climate for discussion this creates, a clearer understanding of the philosophical controversies within qualitative educational research may be obtained by first pausing to briefly describe some of what preceded them.

The most rudimentary meaning of the quantitative-qualitative distinction—as well as the clearest—is associated with data. Categorical data count as qualitative, and ordinal, interval, and ratio data count as quantitative. From here, the distinction has been used less literally, to include research design (i.e., experimental versus nonexperimental) as well as data analysis (i.e., statistical versus interpretive). Data, design, and analysis go together to make up the distinction between quantitative and qualitative "methods" (e.g., Guba, 1987), or "techniques and procedures" (e.g., Smith & Heshusius, 1986). Finally, the quantitative-qualitative distinction has been used in a way far removed from its more straightforward meaning; it also applies to epistemological "paradigms."

Ultimately, participants in the quantitative-qualitative debate conceded the worth and feasibility of combining quantitative and qualitative techniques and procedures, and the debate devolved into what Gage (1989) calls the "paradigm wars." That

is, the worth and feasibility of combining more expansive epistemological paradigms, particularly "positivism" versus various versions of the "new paradigm" (e.g., Guba, 1987) became the locus of contention.

Arguably, the quantitative-qualitative debate should have been a nonstarter, both because it proceeded by stretching the meanings of the terms involved beyond all recognition and because positivism, with which quantitative research is so often identified, is philosophically moribund. But this is not a thesis I need establish here. (See, e.g., Howe, 1985, 1988, 1992.) It is sufficient for my purposes in this chapter to observe that qualitative educational research has secured its place as legitimate and that there are significant philosophical controversies among the views it encompasses. These controversies are the focus of this chapter.

One more preliminary comment. "Interpretivism" is one meaning for "qualitative" that emerged from the quantitative-qualitative debate, and this is how I shall use it throughout this chapter, unless I indicate otherwise. In light of the vagueness and ambiguity described previously, such a stipulation is required for this chapter to unfold in a coherent fashion. More than this, it should also lend greater focus to a conversation that has too often been at cross-purposes.

Epistemology

Rabinow and Sullivan (1987) coined the phrase the "interpretive turn" to describe the epistemological shift under way in the social sciences in the mid- to late-20th century, away from positivism and toward hermeneutics. That Rabinow is an anthropologist and Sullivan is a philosopher symbolizes the merging of the social sciences and the humanities associated with interpretivism. This point is addressed explicitly by Charles

The author wishes to thank James Garrison, Virginia Polytechnic and State University, and Denis Phillips, Stanford University, for their valuable comments on drafts of this chapter.

Taylor in his seminal "Interpretation and the Sciences of Man" (1987). He rejects the view that there can be any scientifically neutral, impersonal language (a central tenet of positivism) with which to describe and interpret human activities. Rather, "we have to think of man [sic] as a *self-interpreting* animal. . . . [T]here is no such thing as the structure of meanings for him independently of his interpretation of them. . . ." (p. 46, emphasis added). (See also Taylor, 1991, 1995.) This general perspective provides the epistemological underpinning for the emphasis on including marginalized and excluded "voices," so prominent today in feminist and postmodernist educational research.

Interpretivists share a constructivist epistemology, generally construed. That is, against classical empiricists and their offspring, the positivists, interpretivists uniformly reject what Dewey called the "spectator view" of knowledge—the view that knowledge is built up piece by piece, by accumulation of an evergrowing and increasingly complex arrangement of passively received observations. Instead, knowledge, particularly in social research, must be seen as actively constructed—as culturally and historically grounded, as laden with moral and political values, and as serving certain interests and purposes.

But this creates a formidable problem for interpretivists: Is knowledge (or what passes for it) merely a cultural-historical artifact? Is it merely a collection of moral and political values? Does it merely serve certain interests and purposes? There are two basic responses to these questions from within the interpretivist (qualitative) camp: postmodernist and transformationist.[1]

Postmodernists seem to answer "yes" to these questions—or at least seem to have no grounds for answering "no." Consider Lyotard's definition of postmodernism: "I define *postmodern* as incredulity toward metanarratives" (1987, p. 74). Briefly, a metanarrative is a grand legitimating story, one important feature of which is its abstraction from time, place, and culture. Metanarratives include grand epistemological stories, such as the inevitable progress science, and grand political stories, such as Marxism and liberalism.

The Marxist and liberal traditions each embrace the goal of the emancipation of humankind, and postmodernists are highly suspicious of them for precisely this reason. Because the goal of emancipation incorporates a peculiarly Western epistemology, pursuing it serves, as Lyotard says, to "terrorize" peoples who had no part in writing it. It is, after all, a time-, place-, and culture-bound story of human knowledge and, accordingly, is a very bad fit for many sociocultural groups. Worse, by presupposing certain conceptions of knowledge and rationality, it masks the manner in which modern Western societies oppress the many others that exist within them and is thus a bad story for Western societies themselves. In the end, it blunts rather than fosters emancipation (e.g., Ellsworth, 1992).

Michel Foucault (1987) shares Lyotard's attitude toward metanarratives and would supplant them with what he calls "genealogy."[2] Foucault's method is to unearth (he has also used the metaphor of archeology) the historical antecedents that have given rise to the rationalization of modern institutions. For Foucault, rationality is irremediably historical and contingent, and there can be no extrahistorical touchstones—metanarratives—of the kind philosophers have sought since Plato. Related to this interpretation of rationality, knowledge and power are inextricably wedded in "regimes of truth" that function to "normalize" persons, that is, to render them acquiescent and "useful" vis-à-vis the institutions of modern society.

This description of the postmodernist incredulity toward metanarratives should be sufficient to elucidate the basis for the general criticism that so routinely leaps to the minds of critics: that postmodernism is hopelessly relativistic and self-defeating; that it cannot, if consistently held, justify any knowledge claims whatsoever. For, if all knowledge claims are thoroughly context-bound and are merely masks for interests and power, then any claims the postmodernists advance themselves are also possessed of these features.

Transformationists, as I call them, join postmodernists in rejecting the traditional philosophical quest for ultimate epistemological touchstones that transcend contingent human experience. But "overcoming epistemology," to use Charles Taylor's phrase (1995, chapter 1), does not entail abandoning knowledge and rationality as illusory. Transformationists see their task as working out defensible conceptions of knowledge and rationality that have contingent human experience as their basis. In this way, the transformationist project is continuous with the emancipatory project of modernity. The postmodernist project, by contrast, is discontinuous. It seeks a fundamental break—or "rupture."

Among transformationists may be counted pragmatists, critical theorists, and (certain) feminists.[3] How such thinkers have worked (and are working) out their conceptions of rationality and knowledge, much less whether they are successful, is not something I can describe in any detail here. Thomas Kuhn (1970) perhaps provides the best general description of the transformationist view when he likens it to Darwinian evolution. In short, there exists no acontextualized criterion of knowledge toward which science must move. Instead, scientific theories are supported to the extent that they handle the problematic better than their competitors do. Criteria for making these judgments exist, but they may not be mechanically applied and are not settled once and for all.

Transformationists take very seriously the avoidance of the inference that embracing the interpretive turn requires effectively abandoning reason. Transformationists prefer their tentative and falliblistic project to postmodernism's all-out attack on reason—an attack they believe winds up nullifying all knowledge claims, including any advanced by postmodernists themselves. As Benjamin Barber (1992) puts this challenge to postmodernism:

---

[1] Dividing views into these two obviously glosses much complexity, both regarding the difficulties in drawing such a line at all and regarding the vast differences among views on either side of the issue. Given the level of generality at which this chapter is written, I think the distinction between postmodernists and transformationists is workable.

[2] Arguably, Foucault is not a postmodernist, but a poststructuralist—and even that is debatable. I will ignore these niceties.

[3] Some feminists are postmodernists, but many belong in the transformationist camp, a few of which include Alison Jaggar, Seyla Benabib, Iris Marion Young, Catharine MacKinnon, Lorraine Code, and Sandra Harding.

Reason can be a smoke screen for interest, but the argument that it is a smoke screen itself depends on reason—or we are caught up in an endless regression in which each argument exposing the dependency of someone else's argument on arbitrariness and self-interest is in turn shown to be self-interested and arbitrary. (p. 109)

The Ontology of the Self

Ontology is that part of philosophy that concerns itself with the kinds of entities that exist and the features they possess. For example, do numbers exist? in what sense? where can we find them? How about social structures? Do selves exist? What features, if any, do different selves share? How are selves formed? Are selves relatively stable or always in flux?

In the previous section, I described interpretivists as embracing a constructivist conception of knowledge. This feature of interpretivism renders the philosophical distinction between epistemology and ontology considerably more artificial than my way of dividing up this chapter may suggest. (See also Taylor, 1987.) For how human beings know and are known, as well as what knowledge consists in, is inextricably bound up with the kinds of things human beings are. And there is a further complication. Because human beings actively construct their social reality, the kinds of things human beings *are* is not necessarily the kinds of things they *must* or *ought to be*. Thus, distinguishing the moral-political from the ontological (and, by extension, from the epistemological) is also artificial—so much so that altogether forestalling the introduction of political-moral ideals until the next section would be counterproductive as well as misleading.

Be they postmodernists or transformationists, interpretivists are like-minded in their rejection of the positivistic conception of human nature, in which human beings are portrayed as passive recipients of stimuli, explicable solely in terms of the operation of exogenous causes. Rather than (or in addition to) this characterization of human nature, interpretivists hold that human beings are self-creating, or, as Brian Fay (1987) puts it, "activist" in their behavior. That is to say, it is not as if human beings are mere molecules in motion, simply pushed to and fro by existing social arrangements and cultural norms. Instead, they actively shape and reshape these constraints on behavior. But there is a problem, and it parallels the one discussed earlier in connection with the nature of knowledge. Are human beings completely active? Is the molecules-in-motion characterization of them totally erroneous?

Insofar as postmodernists seek to "penetrate" and "deconstruct" the workings of social structures, and as transformationists seek to "undistort" communication so as to equalize power and "emancipate" human beings, each presupposes that human beings are not altogether active and that they can indeed be unwittingly pushed to and fro by unseen and unknown causes. Furthermore, because human nature is so malleable, the passive, positivistic conception of human nature can function as a self-fulfilling prophecy. As Dewey (1938) observes in this connection, after years of receiving and then regurgitating information presented by their teachers, school children will develop the habit of expecting (and demanding) that they play this passive role in learning. That is, they will be conditioned to fit the positivist-behaviorist conception of human nature.

So, what is wrong with this conception? Nothing. Nothing, that is, unless we are prepared to commit to the view that this conception ought not guide social and educational research, that some version of the activist conception should. But let me set this observation aside for now in order to look into the controversy between postmodernists and transformationists about the ontology of the self.

Postmodernists attribute to the traditional liberal and Marxist "metanarratives" a commitment to an essential human self, a fixed model of human nature, to which all humankind should aspire and in terms of which all should be measured—things like "rational autonomy" and "species being," respectively. Postmodernists emphasize that, contrary to these "essentialist" conceptions, identities come in many forms, associated with race, class, and gender, among others. Identities must be seen as neither unified nor fixed, but as various and continually "displaced-replaced" (e.g., Lather, 1991a). "Decentering" is the watchword: Placing the universal Everyman allegedly presupposed by Marxist and liberal metanarratives at the center can only function to "normalize" and "terrorize" the many Others on the margins.

On the transformationist view (and here I use John Searle, 1995, as my example), maintaining that something is real does not entail maintaining that it cannot be "constructed," much less that it must be essential and unchangeable. Automobiles, for example, would not be real if this were generally true. But consider money, the existence and nature of which is much less a "brute fact" than automobiles. Money is what Searle calls an "institutional fact"—a kind of fact that grows out of and would not exist but for human social arrangements and "collective intentionality." Nonetheless, money does not come into or go out of existence on the basis of what individual people believe or "construct." For example, suppose someone owes me $1,000. I cannot reject cash payment and demand gold because I happen to believe that currency is worth no more than the paper it is printed on. Whether I like it or not, currency is legal tender for the payment of debts.

The situation is parallel in the case of Searle's less formal, "social facts." Take gender. To be sure, there have been and continue to be institutional facts associated with gender (e.g., exclusion from voting in the past and exclusion from certain forms of military duty today). But more far-reaching are shared beliefs, expectations, know-hows, and practices that make up the social facts of gender. In general, the feminine gender is identified with nurturance and preserving relationship on the one hand, and with a lack of worldliness and the capacity for abstract reasoning on the other hand. Women thus have been historically directed into activities such as homemaking, nursing, and elementary school teaching and away from engineering, politics, and science. Independent of what individual girls and women believe—and like it or not—there is a "gender regimen" (Connell 1987) associated with a particular kind of feminine identity that is, in turn, associated with a large complex of social facts that shape it.

These social facts must be reckoned with in thinking about identity. And a little introspection reveals we cannot construct new identities for ourselves with the ease with which we can don a new set of clothes. Changing our being requires a good deal of time and effort, and there is no guarantee of success.

Partly because of this people often do not want to change, and they believe it is oppressive to expect them to. Instead, people want "recognition" of who they are (Taylor, 1994). And if this general observation about the phenomenology of the self were not true, it would be very difficult to make any sense whatsoever out of the demands to recognize diversity that are so prominent on the current political and educational scenes. Why not just avoid all the fuss by "deconstructing" old identities and putting new ones in their place?

As the preceding paragraph suggests, there is no way to completely separate moral-political commitments from a conception of human nature. This point echoes for a second time my remarks at the beginning of this section, and I will develop the implications in greater detail later. Here, I bracket, as far as possible, the moral-political in order to further look into the controversy between postmodernists and transformationists about the ontology of the self.

Searle (1995) employs the concept of "background of intentionality" to describe the peculiar context of human behavior and development. Against both mentalism (all human behavior is explicable in terms of conscious or unconscious understanding and intent) and behaviorism (all human behavior is explicable in terms of physical movements), Searle maintains that human beings simply have the capacity to gain the know-how required to respond to shared social and institutional facts in accordance with normative expectations, largely by virtue of their linguistic capacity to manage symbols.

Within this general framework, Searle develops the following general schema to explicate the ontological status of social facts: "x counts as y in z." To again take Searle's favorite example, money, the U.S. dollar bill (x) counts as legal tender (y) in the United States (z). One of Searle's fundamental points is that, unlike gold, for example, there is nothing about the physical features of a dollar bill that gives rise to its value and to the normatively sanctioned behaviors that surround it. Rather, its value, its counting as legal tender, is a result of "collective intentionality."

Gender, race, and a whole host of other social categories can be viewed on a similar model, though it might be more suggestively formulated as x marks y in z. Race and gender (x's) each serve to mark a constellation of normatively sanctioned behaviors (y's) associated with various contexts (z's), including the context of schools. (Here I remind the reader that I am bracketing the issue of whether the norms in question are good. Norms need not be morally sanctioned to regulate human behavior.) In this way, although social categories (x's) have no essence independent of what humans have constructed, they, like money, are no less real for that.

Gaining the know-how associated with collective intentionality and learning how to negotiate the social terrain are long and complex tasks. And because identity formation is "dialogical," as Charles Taylor says (1994), individuals unavoidably incorporate into their identities the normative structure associated with social categories and practices. Through many different dialogues in many different contexts people learn what it is to be a man or a women, to be gay or lesbian, or to be an African-American high school student.

It should be observed that the general characterization of the ontology of the self that is provided by thinkers like Searle and Taylor is not one with which all postmodernists must disagree. For instance, Foucault (1979) says: "It would be wrong to say the soul is an illusion, or an ideological effect. On the contrary, it exists, it has reality, it is produced permanently, around, on, within the body . . ." (p. 29).

Postmodernists who suggest that identities may be easily and matter-of-factly "displaced-replaced" must concede that selves have to remain in place at least long enough to be the object of deconstruction. In the case of women, for instance, they may sometimes celebrate the traditional feminine identity they have formed, as in "gynocentric" feminism (Young, 1990), and may sometimes lament it, as in feeling like "a fraud" (Ornstein, 1995). Some similar form of ambivalence—coming out versus remaining closeted, being oppositional versus "acting White," for example—is characteristic of all marginalized groups. And this phenomenon, like the demand for recognition, makes sense only if human identities are relatively stable.

This leaves the controversy about the self between postmodernists and transformationists quite up in the air. All interpretivists ("qualitative" researchers) are constructivists with respect to the ontology of the self: They agree that it is contingently formed and that it has no transcendent "essence." Then how do postmodernists and transformationists differ with respect to the self? The problem here is that the question of the ontology of the self cannot be viewed in the abstract. As I observed several times before, it is thoroughly entangled with epistemology. It is also thoroughly entangled with what (if anything) is adopted as the moral-political mission of social research. And it is here where the differences between postmodernists and transformationists are perhaps most perspicuous.

Political Theory

Neither transformationists nor postmodernists believe present social arrangements are just and democratic, and both seek to identify social structures and norms that serve to oppress people. Each, then, embraces "deconstruction" in this sense. What divides them is the reason for engaging in deconstruction and what comes after it.

In the extreme, deconstruction is done for its own sake, merely to challenge and disrupt the status quo. The question of how social arrangements ought to be transformed so as to better approximate social justice is dismissed, if not greeted with outright hostility. For this is the modernist project, which presupposes norms of rationality and morality around which to forge consensus. But such norms are totally ungrounded and, worse, when promoted by the powers that be, are also inherently oppressive (Ellsworth, 1992; Lyotard, 1987).

Catharine MacKinnon (1989) criticizes this brand of deconstruction on the grounds that it is nothing but playing at a "neo-Cartesian mind game" (p. 137). It goes nowhere politically, if not backwards, for it "raises acontextualized interpretive possibilities that have no real social meaning or real possibility of any, thus dissolving the ability to criticize the oppressiveness of actual meanings without making space for new ones" (1989, p. 137). Like Descartes, radical deconstructionists embrace "hyperskepticism" (Barber, 1992) as their starting point, but, unlike him, they find no "clear and distinct" moorings for knowledge. Indeed, they find no moorings at all.

Transformationists (among whom I include MacKinnon and Barber) charge that, insofar as the aim of radical deconstruction embraces the political goal of eradicating oppression, it undermines its own political project. (See also Bernstein, 1996; Gutmann, 1994; Lyon, 1994; Taylor, 1994; and Barber, 1992.) Radical deconstruction renders unanswerable the question of who the terrorized Others on the margins might be (if not unaskable), for the reality of these Others as Others evaporates under the hot lights of deconstruction. Alternatively, insofar as everyone is to be seen as marginalized, the question of who is oppressed is rendered trivial.

Transformationists concede that identities are not rigidly fixed and that prescribing a particular voice for members of marginalized groups can be condescending, stereotyping, and oppressive. As Henry Louis Gates remarks regarding the feeling he gets from his white colleagues in the academy: It is as if they were to provide him with a script and say, "Be oppositional—please. You look so cute when you're angry" (1992, p. 185). But Gates also warns against taking this observation too far. He writes:

> Foucault says, and let's take him at his word, that the "homosexual" as life form was invented sometime in the 19th century. Now, if there's no such thing as a homosexual, then homophobia, at least as directed toward people rather than acts, loses its rationale. But you can't respond to the discrimination against gay people by saying, "I'm sorry, I don't exist; you've got the wrong guy." (1992, pp. 37–38)

Gates uses this example to identify a tension between what he calls "the imperatives of agency" and "the rhetoric of dismantlement." Homosexuality (or race, or gender) can be conceived of as "only a sociopolitical category," as Gates puts it. But, consistent with my observations in the previous section, that does not mean that such social categories ("constructions") do not exist or are not real in their effects. Acknowledging that members of social groups do not necessarily speak with one voice, acknowledging that identity is, as Cameron McCarthy (1993) puts it, "nonsynchronous," transformationists are on their guard to avoid sliding into the sort of radical dismantlement of group identity Gates warns against, in which all that remains are decentered, radically unstable individuals.

The flip side of the transformationists' worry about the alleged inability of radical deconstruction to make sense out of oppression is its inability to provide any guidance regarding how to educate persons so that they will be moral agents who can, among other things, recognize oppression and work against it. Daniel Dennett (1991), who rejects the Cartesian—or modernist—conception of the self in favor of a postmodernist conception, acknowledges the moral-political dangers in doing so. He thus embraces the idea of getting beyond a merely deconstructive activity to the constructive one of shaping selves of the right kind. Responding to an imagined interlocutor, Dennett writes:

> I think I know what you're getting at. If a self isn't a real thing, what happens to moral responsibility? One of the most important roles of self in our traditional conceptual schemes is as the place where the buck stops, as Harry Truman's sign announced. If selves aren't real—aren't *really* real—won't the buck just get passed on and on,

round and round, forever? . . . The task of constructing a self that can take responsibility is a major social and educational project. . . . (pp. 429–430)

Nick Burbules (1996) makes a point similar to Dennett's when he observes that education is inherently about growth and development and is therefore inherently goal-directed. If Dennett and Burbules are right, it follows that however cautious educators can and ought to be about the norms, dispositions, attitudes, and knowledge they foster, foster some they must. In short, educators and educational researchers alike are required to engage in a constructive political activity.

Perhaps acknowledgment of this point explains why postmodernists in education are, by comparison to postmodernists more generally, relatively unabashed about embracing the project of ending oppression and why they are less likely to limit themselves only to deconstruction (but see Usher & Edwards, 1994). In any case, postmodern educationists appear unable to consistently confine themselves to deconstruction, and, whatever their avowals, to opt for transformation in the end.

Consider the following remark by Elisabeth Ellsworth:

> [I]n a classroom in which "empowerment" is made dependent on rationalism, those perspectives that would question the political interests (sexism, racism, colonialism, for example) expressed and guaranteed by rationalism would be rejected as "irrational" (biased, partial). (1992, p. 98)

But what is the alternative to "rationalism?" As Benjamin Barber asks:

> How can . . . reformers think they will empower the voiceless by proving that voice is always a function of power? . . . How do they think the struggle for equality and justice can be waged with an epistemology that denies standing to reasons and normative rational terms . . . ? (1992, p. 123)

Barber adds: "The powerful toy with reason, the powerless need it, for by definition it is their only weapon" (p. 124).

It would seem there is no way for those who would reject rationalism carte blanche to adequately respond to Barber's challenge. In the end, some overarching (and presumably "modernist") principle or principles must be embraced (Burbules & Rice, 1991). And Ellsworth does exactly this when she proffers the following question as the "final arbiter" for determining the "acceptability" of antiracist actions:

> To what extent do our political strategies and alternative narratives about social difference succeed in alleviating campus racism, while at the same time managing *not to undercut* the efforts of other social groups to win self-definition? (1992, p. 110)

Isn't this a principle guiding political action? Doesn't it have a specific goal? Isn't it (shouldn't it be) rationally agreed to?

Consider Patti Lather's book *Getting Smart* (1991a). The subtitle, *Feminist Research and Pedagogy Withlin Postmodernism,* as well as much of her exposition and vocabulary, suggests she is advancing a straightforward postmodernist approach to educational research, to be distinguished from a modernist (or Enlightenment) one. But Lather explicitly denies that she em-

braces the nihilism associated with thoroughgoing deconstruc-
tionism, and she limits deconstruction to opening up space for
the expression of hitherto silenced voices. In this connection,
she repeatedly and approvingly cites the work of Brian Fay
(1976, 1987), whose project is clearly a transformational one
(however guarded and qualified).

Some self-described postmodernist educationists explicitly
embrace general political principles. For example, Stanley Aronowitz and Henry Giroux (1991) acknowledge the force of the
general sort of criticism advanced by Barber. In response, they
call for a "critical" (versus "apolitical") postmodernism in
which the "postmodern politics of difference" is combined
with the "modernist struggle for justice, equality, and freedom"
(p. 194).

Here we see the line (or "border") between postmodernists
and transformationists explicitly crossed. For "critical postmodernism" cannot be systematically distinguished from the
so-called metanarratives of Marxism and liberalism that it pu-
tatively rejects. The "modernist struggle" continues for Marxism and liberalism, and neither tradition has remained static.
On the contrary, both have evolved so as to better cope with
the "politics of difference," so emphasized in postmodernist
analyses.[4]

As I acknowledged in an earlier note, there are dangers in
trying to divide philosophical stances taken toward the interpretive (qualitative) turn into postmodernist and transformationist. Such danger should be even more evident in light of
the preceding several paragraphs. In educational theory at least,
various views seem to fall on a continuum regarding the degree
to which they embrace transformation. Very few shun transformation altogether.

Those I have been calling postmodernists tread very lightly.
They are highly tentative about what to do in the wake of deconstruction and highly suspicious of those who claim to know
what is best. They also emphasize paying very close attention
to the researcher's own social position and "subjectivities."
Those I have been calling transformationists do not ignore these
concerns, but they are less guarded. They proceed by articulating and employing broad political principles—justice, equality,
and the like—to criticize existing conditions and to suggest the
direction that transformations should take.

Research Ethics

The interpretive (qualitative) turn has significant implications
for the ethics of social research in general and educational research in particular. For convenience, I divide the terrain into
broad versus narrow ethical obligations.

Broad (or external) ethical obligations are anchored in the
broad political goals of social research, and the interpretive
(qualitative) turn jettisons the positivist goal of "technical control" (Fay, 1976). Various ends (academic achievement and increased economic competitiveness, for instance) cannot be
bracketed and set to one side while educational researchers go

about the task of investigating the best means, with an eye toward exerting more effective control. Ends must be left on the
table, themselves remaining part of what needs to be investigated and negotiated. Postmodernists and transformationists
are in substantial agreement to this point. They diverge from
here, however, and their respective responses to the demise
of the positivist "fact-value distinction" may be used to illustrate how.

The fact-value distinction is shorthand for a broad set of distinctions. On the fact side, it also puts rationality, science,
means, cognition, objectivity, and truth. On the value side, it
also puts irrationality, politics, ends, interests, subjectivity, and
power. Postmodernists focus on the value side and collapse the
fact side into it. Thus, we get the picture (in Foucault, for instance) that science, truth, and the like are simply masks for
power. Alternatively, transformationists intermingle the fact
and value sides. Thus, we get the picture (in Habermas, for instance) that, although science and truth can be corrupted—
"distorted"—by power, they are nonetheless redeemable if
checked by the kind of rationality associated with an emancipatory interest.

But here again the difference between postmodernists and
transformationists (at least in education) may be placed on a
continuum. Assume that postmodern educationists do, indeed,
embrace the goal of ending oppression. This puts them in some
general agreement with transformationists. Nonetheless, they
may still complain that transformationists are far too confident
both in how they understand this goal and the means by which
it can be best achieved. It is they—the transformationists—
who have a self-defeating, because overconfident, paternalistic,
and oppressive, project.[5]

In my view, this sort of disagreement can but does not have
to turn on fundamental philosophical questions. It may turn on
strategic questions such as these: When should I bite my
tongue? What's the best way to move things along? What would
be the long-term consequences of intervening now? How can I
get these people to see what's really going on here? Or other
questions may be these: What's my stake in this? Have I failed
to appreciate what's being said? Who am I to interpret this situation by my lights? And so on.

Consider these questions in light of the practice of "female
circumcision." Now, consider them in light of what we know
about the treatment of girls; people of color; and gay, lesbian,
and bisexual youths by public schools. I am suggesting that,
whether they have done so or not, postmodernists and transformationists could end up answering these questions in much the
same way. They could end up agreeing that taking action in a
certain set of circumstances would be ill-advised; they could
end up agreeing that action should be taken but in the form
of some tentative first steps; and so forth. Should postmodern
educationists embrace the view that it is not just bad strategy
to act on certain value judgments—about what is good, bad,
oppressive, and should be changed—in certain circumstances
but that such judgments can (ought to?) never be rendered, then

---

[4] Numerous examples exist in political theory, but, for specific applications of critical theory to education, see Robert Young, 1990, and Nicholas Burbules, 1993. For an application of liberalism, see Kenneth Strike, 1991, and Kenneth Howe, 1997.

[5] See the exchange among Giroux 1988; McLaren, 1988; and Lather, 1991b.

their view is morally and politically untenable from the transformationist's point of view. Worse, it is dangerous.

Narrow (or internal) ethical obligations are closely associated with what is typically thought of as "research ethics," for example, informed consent and confidentiality. The focus here is much more on how research subjects (participants) are to be treated within the conduct of research than on broader political goals.

Of course, the distinction between research ethics in this sense and the broader sense described above is not hard and fast. How participants are to be treated within the conduct of social research cannot be divorced from the overarching aims that that research seeks to achieve, particularly where the positivist fact-value distinction is not available to insulate the two from one another (Howe, 1992). Bearing in mind that broader ethical obligations associated with broader political-epistemological "paradigms" are always lurking in the background, there nonetheless remain ethical implications of the interpretive (qualitative) turn in educational research that may be best understood in terms of the methodological nitty-gritty of "techniques and procedures."

The techniques and procedures of interpretivist research possess two features that experimental and quasi-experimental research lack (at least lack to a relatively significant degree): intimacy and open-endedness (Howe & Dougherty, 1993). Interpretive (qualitative) research is intimate insofar as it reduces the distance between researchers and participants in the conduct of social research. Indeed, the growing preference for the term "participants" (who take an active role in "constructing social meanings") over "subjects" (who passively receive "treatments") testifies to the changed conception of relationships among human beings engaged in social research that has attended the interpretive (qualitative) turn. The face-to-face interactions associated with the pervasive techniques of interviewing and participant observation are in stark contrast to the kind of interactions required to prepare subjects for a treatment. Interpretive research is open-ended insofar as the questions and persons to which interviewing and participant observation may lead can be roughly determined only at the outset. This, too, is in stark contrast to the relatively circumscribed arena of questions and participants that characterizes experimental and quasi-experimental research.

What this means is that researchers employing qualitative techniques and procedures are (whether they want or intend to or not) likely to discover secrets and lies as well as oppressive relationships. These discoveries may put research participants at risk in ways that they had not bargained for and that the researcher had not anticipated. They may also put researchers in the position of having to decide whether they have an ethical responsibility to intervene in some way. (See, e.g., Roman, 1993.) It is for this reason that the barrier between narrow and broad ethical obligations cannot be steadfastly maintained.

Where experimental and quasi-experimental research is not identified with positivism (and I think it shouldn't be, necessarily at least, Howe, 1985, 1988, 1992), researchers in this tradition can face the same problems. For instance, things can simply fall into their laps in the process of explaining a protocol and recruiting subjects; a treatment may prove so obviously effective (or harmful) that the trial should be stopped; and so

forth. Still, the odds of facing unforeseen ethical problems are surely much higher for qualitative researchers. Generally speaking, then, qualitative research is more ethically hazardous than experimental and quasi-experimental research, and requires more careful monitoring for that reason.

Some qualitative researchers have recoiled at this suggestion, on the grounds that the current ways of thinking about and monitoring the ethics of social research are rooted in the experimentalist tradition (Murphy & Johannsen, 1990). They call for loosening or abandoning the human subjects procedures that are in place when it comes to qualitative research. Yvonna Lincoln (1990) takes this one step further by suggesting that qualitative researchers are somehow ethically in the clear because they have repudiated positivism.

Whatever benefits the interpretive (qualitative) turn has brought, I think most qualitative researchers would agree an ethically simpler life is not among them. On the contrary, qualitative researchers themselves have proposed measures that significantly complicate conducting research, such as periodic reaffirmations of consent (Cornett & Chase, 1989) and construing consent on the model of an ongoing "dialogue" (Smith, 1990). In this way, they have acknowledged the increased ethical hazards inherent in the research methods they employ. And this self-consciousness on the part of qualitative researchers is for the good, for these hazards are not going to go away.

Conclusion

Not to beat a dead horse, let me say again that the traditional philosophical debate between positivism and interpretivism—between the quantitative and qualitative "paradigms"—is over. In the wake of the interpretive turn, the philosophical debate is now between those who seek some new understandings of knowledge, rationality, truth, and objectivity (i.e., transformationists) and those who are ready to abandon these concepts as hopelessly wedded to the bankrupt modernist project (i.e., postmodernists).

Interpretivist (qualitative) educational researchers once seemed to have been much more united than they now seem to be. Perhaps their differences were simply submerged for a time, as they sought to gain legitimacy in the face of the then dominant psychological-experimental—"quantitative"—tradition. And perhaps this in turn helps explain the vague, umbrella-like nature of the term "qualitative." But to the extent this impression is accurate, it can still be only part of the story. For it is difficult to see the fracturing that has developed recently within qualitative educational research as somehow really there all along, lurking below the surface. Rather, new positions have been staked out, and feminism and postmodernism have loomed large in this development.

Disagreements among interpretivist (qualitative) educational researchers—on epistemology, ontology, politics, and ethics—are all well and good, for they spur intellectual progress. But the existence of disagreement should not obscure the three important points of agreement. First, "subjectivities" count. This is a general implication of the interpretive turn and the constructivist epistemology that goes with it. Second, social arrangements are irremediably interest-, power-, and value-laden. Accordingly, they need to be carefully examined—"deconstructed"—in this light. And third, the result of educational research should be a more just and democratic system of schooling and, ultimately, a more just and democratic society. That is, the goal of transformation drives educational research.

To be sure, serious disagreements exist between postmodernists and transformationists. But if I am right to place these on a continuum, qualitative educational researchers of all stripes embrace both deconstruction and transformation. They would do well to avoid overblowing their differences on how to understand and balance these in a way that engenders new "paradigm cliques"—a description I once used to diagnose the quantitative-qualitative debate (Howe, 1988)—and that confuses questions about effective strategy with something more philosophically fundamental.

REFERENCES

Aronowitz, S., & Giroux, H. (1991). *Postmodern education.* Minneapolis, MN: University of Minnesota Press.

Barber, B. (1992). *An aristocracy of everyone.* New York: Ballantine Books.

Bernstein, R. (1996, April). *Pragmatism and postmodernism: The relevance of John Dewey.* Paper presented at the annual meeting of the American Educational Research Association, New York, NY.

Burbules, N. (1993). *Dialogue in teaching.* New York: Teachers College Press.

Burbules, N. (1996). Postmodern doubt and philosophy of education. In A. Neiman (Ed.), *Philosophy of education 1995* (pp. 39–48). Urbana, IL: The Philosophy of Education Society.

Burbules, N., & Rice, S. (1991). Dialogue across difference: Continuing the conversation. *Harvard Educational Review, 61*(4), 393–416.

Connell, R. W. (1987). *Gender and power.* Stanford, CA: Stanford University Press.

Cornett, J., & Chase, S. (1989, March). The analysis of teacher thinking and the problem of ethics: Reflections of a case study participant and a naturalistic researcher. Paper presented at the annual meeting of the American Educational Research Association, San Francisco, CA.

Dennett, D. (1991). *Consciousness explained.* New York: Little, Brown and Company.

Dewey, J. (1938). *Experience and education.* New York: Macmillan.

Ellsworth, E. (1992). Why doesn't this feel empowering. In C. Luke & J. Gore (Eds.), *Feminisms and critical pedagogy* (pp. 90–119). New York: Routledge.

Fay, B. (1976). *Social theory and political practice.* London: Unwin Hyman.

Fay, B. (1987). *Critical social science.* Ithaca, NY: Cornell University Press.

Foucault, M. (1979). *Discipline and punish: The birth of the prison.* New York: Vintage Books.

Foucault, M. (1987). Questions of method: An interview with Michel Foucault. In K. Baynes, J. Bohman, & T. McCarthy (Eds.), *After philosophy: End or transformation?* (pp. 100–117). Cambridge, MA: MIT Press.

Gage, N. L. (1989). The paradigm wars and their aftermath: A "historical" sketch of research in teaching since 1989. *Teachers College Record, 91*(2), 135–150.

Gates, H. L. (1992). *Loose canons.* New York: Oxford University Press.

Giroux, H. (1988). Border pedagogy in the age of postmodernism. *Journal of Education, 170*(3), 162–181.

Guba, E. (1987). What have we learned about naturalistic evaluation? *Evaluation Practice, 8*(1), 23–43.

Gutmann, A. (1994). Introduction. In A. Gutmann (Ed.), *Multiculturalism: Examining the politics of recognition* (pp. 3–24). Princeton, NJ: Princeton University Press.

Howe, K. R. (1985). Two dogmas of educational research. *Educational Researcher, 14*(8), 10–18.

Howe, K. R. (1988). Against the quantitative-qualitative incompatibility thesis (or dogmas die hard). *Educational Researcher, 17*(8), 10–16.

Howe, K. R. (1992). Getting over the quantitative-qualitative debate. *American Journal of Education, 100*(2), 236–256.

Howe, K. R. (1997). *Understanding equal educational opportunity: Social justice, democracy, and schooling.* New York: Teachers College Press.

Howe, K. R., & Dougherty, K. (1993). Ethics, IRBs, and the changing face of educational research. *Educational Researcher, 22*(9), 16–21.

Kuhn, T. (1970). *The structure of scientific revolutions.* Chicago: The University of Chicago Press.

Lather, P. (1991a). *Getting smart: Feminist research and pedagogy with/in postmodernism.* New York: Routledge.

Lather, P. (1991b). Post-critical pedagogies: A feminist reading. *Education and Society, 9*(2), 100–111.

Lincoln, Y. (1990). Toward a categorical imperative for qualitative research. In E. W. Eisner & A. Peshkin (Eds.), *Qualitative inquiry in education: The continuing debate* (pp. 277–295). New York: Teachers College Press.

Lyon, D. (1994). *Postmodernity.* Minneapolis, MN: University of Minnesota Press.

Lyotard, J. (1987). The postmodern condition. In K. Baynes, J. Bohman, & T. McCarthy (Eds.), *After philosophy: End or transformation?* (pp. 67–94). Cambridge, MA: MIT Press.

MacKinnon, C. (1989). *Toward a feminist theory of the state.* Cambridge, MA: Harvard University Press.

McCarthy, C. (1993). Beyond the poverty in race relations: Nonsynchrony and social difference in education. In L. Weis & M. Fine (Eds.), *Beyond silenced voices* (pp. 325–346). New York: State University of New York Press.

McLaren, P. (1988). Schooling the postmodern body: Critical pedagogy and the politics of enfleshment. *Journal of Education, 170*(3), 53–83.

Murphy, M., & Johannsen, A. (1990). Ethical obligations and federal regulations in ethnographic research and anthropological education. *Human Organization, 49*(2), 127–134.

Ornstein, P. (1995). *Schoolgirls.* New York: Anchor Books.

Rabinow, P., & Sullivan, W. (1987). The interpretive turn: Emergence of an approach. In P. Rabinow & W. Sullivan (Eds.), *Interpretive social science* (pp. 1–21). Los Angeles: University of California Press.

Roman, L. (1993). Double exposure: The politics of feminist materialist ethnography. *Educational Theory, 43*(3), 279–308.

Searle, J. (1995). *The construction of social reality.* New York: The Free Press.

Smith, J. K., & Heshusius, L. (1986). Closing down the conversation: The end of the quantitative-qualitative debate among educational researchers. *Educational Researcher, 15*(1), 4–12.

Smith, L. M. (1990). Ethics of qualitative field research: An individual perspective. In E. W. Eisner & A. Peshkin (Eds.), *Qualitative inquiry in education: The continuing debate* (pp. 258–276). New York: Teachers College Press.

Strike, K. (1991). The moral role of schooling in a liberal democratic society. In D. H. Monk & J. Underwood (Eds.), *Microlevel school finance: Issues and implications for policy* (pp. 143–180). Cambridge, MA: Ballinger.

Taylor, C. (1987). Interpretation and the sciences of man. In P. Rabinow & W. Sullivan (Eds.), *Interpretive social science: A second look* (pp. 33–81). Los Angeles: University of California Press.

Taylor, C. (1991). *The ethics of authenticity.* Cambridge, MA: Harvard University Press.

Taylor, C. (1994). The politics of recognition. In A. Gutmann (Ed.), *Multiculturalism: Examining the politics of recognition* (pp. 25–74). Princeton, NJ: Princeton University Press.

Taylor, C. (1995). *Philosophical arguments.* Cambridge, MA: Harvard University Press.

Usher, R., & Edwards, R. (1994). *Postmodernism and education.* New York: Routledge.

Young, I. M. (1990). Humanism, gynocentrism, and feminist politics. In *Throwing like a girl and other essays in philosophy and social theory* (pp. 73–91). Bloomington, IN: Indiana University Press.

Young, R. (1990). *A critical theory of education.* New York: Teachers College Press.

13.

Changing Conceptions of Culture and Ethnographic Methodology: Recent Thematic Shifts and Their Implications for Research on Teaching

Margaret Eisenhart
University of Colorado, Boulder

When anthropologist Frederick Erickson wrote the first-ever chapter about qualitative methods for the third edition of *The Handbook of Research on Teaching* (Erickson, 1986), he officially introduced teacher researchers to interpretive scholarship, ethnographic methodology, and their potential for educational research. Relying on interpretive theory from the social sciences and philosophy, Erickson built the case for a new approach to classroom research—an approach that would begin by investigating what actually happens between teachers and students in classrooms, would proceed by developing an interpretation of what actions in the classroom mean for participants, and would end with an argument suggesting how these actions and meanings relate to large-scale patterns of social action and structure, an approach that would be a worthy alternative to the positivistic approach and experimental and survey designs so prevalent in classroom research at the time. Now, little more than 10 years later, research on teaching is replete with studies informed in some way by interpretive scholarship and ethnographic methodology. Erickson's article was part of a sea change in educational research, a change so pervasive that today we can scarcely imagine research on teaching without the interpretive perspective or ethnographic procedures of data collection and analysis.

What has often been missed is that Erickson was also writing about a new emphasis in studies of "culture." A decade before Erickson's article, interpretive scholarship had washed like a wave over cultural anthropology, reorganizing the way many prominent anthropologists thought about culture. Older views of culture as a group's distinct pattern of behaviors, or coherent "way-of-life," lost ground to an interpretive view of culture as "webs of significance," or meanings partially shared and manipulated by those who knew them. About this, Clifford Geertz (after Max Weber) wrote: "I take culture to be those webs, and the analysis of it to be therefore not an experimental science in search of law [to explain behavior] but an interpretive one in search of meaning" (Geertz, 1973b, p. 5).

More recently, new perspectives developed by feminist, ethnic, postmodern, and cultural studies scholars have produced other thematic shifts or "turns" in the definition of culture. In fact, during the past 10 years, several conceptions of culture have been in simultaneous use among anthropologists and others who study and write about education. Yet, many educational researchers seem unaware of these variations and shifts or their implications for research.

Research on teaching, for example, has been unevenly influenced by changing conceptions of culture. In teacher education and literacy education research, newer feminist and postmodern ideas about culture seem to have affected some (but certainly not all) research (e.g., Cochran-Smith, 1991; Florio-Ruane, 1991a, 1991b); in teacher research on bilingual and multicultural education, older ideas about culture (exemplified in part by language) continue to be used as do newer, updated ideas (e.g., González, 1995; González, Moll, Floyd-Tenery, Rivera, Rendón, Gonzales, & Amanti, 1995); in other areas, such as mathematics and science education research, culture is rarely conceptualized, and ideas about it—old or new—do not seem

---

The author would like to thank Hilda Borko, Bradley Levinson, and Patrick McQuillan for their helpful comments on an earlier version of this chapter. She would like to especially thank reviewers Evelyn Jacob (George Mason University) and Margaret LeCompte (University of Colorado) for their ideas and suggestions.

to have affected the direction of reform. The recent history of changing conceptions of culture and the implications for ethnography and educational research are the subjects of this chapter.

In the first section of the chapter, I take up thematic shifts in the conceptions of culture that have been salient in the work of educational anthropologists and sociologists during the past 3 decades. This section culminates with some new directions for the next decade of research on teaching. In the course of the discussion, I mean to stress that each conception has important uses. Newer conceptions focus on features of contemporary life not captured in older versions, but for some research and political purposes older versions remain appropriate and valuable. My purpose is not to build an argument for one fixed or definitive conception of culture, nor is it to imply a linear evolutionary process in which older forms die out when new ones appear. Rather, I hope to reveal the versatility of "culture," the ways it has been reformulated over time, and the potential in pursuing new formulations.

In the second section, I argue that ethnographers (be they educational researchers or not) have been slow to take up some important challenges posed by changing conceptions of culture. Ethnographic methods, such as face-to-face participant observation and ethnographic interviewing, were originally developed as the means to study "culture," defined as the lifestyle of a social group with clear boundaries and distinctive behaviors and beliefs. Today, many ethnographers reject this definition as too simple to capture "culture" in contemporary life, yet they continue to use research methods that presuppose the old definition. Newer conceptions of culture have roused interest in a few new methodological concerns—namely the relationship between researcher and researched and the conventions for writing up research findings—but little has been done to reconceptualize strategies for data collection or analysis. I will suggest some ways this work might proceed.

Changing Conceptions of Culture

Culture as a Way-of-Life that Is an Adaptation to External Conditions

Throughout most of the history of anthropology as well as in public discourse, "culture" has been generally defined as patterns in a way of life characteristic of a bounded social group and passed down from one generation to the next.[1] Whether one's interests were in language use, family life, beliefs and values, cognitive models, school achievement, or classroom climate, anthropologists have searched for and written about culture as evidenced by patterns in the collective behaviors and central orientations of socially distinguishable groups. Social groups identified from the outset by country, region, ethnicity, religion, skin color, social position, first language, or gender

have been and continue to be the most likely subjects of culturally oriented studies in education and beyond. When I reviewed 2 years (1994–1996) of the *Anthropology and Education Quarterly, Educational Researcher,* and the *American Educational Research Journal,* I found that roughly 90% of the articles about "culture" focused on these groups. In these studies, one or more socially salient group is assumed to have a distinct culture, and the research is designed to identify its characteristic features. Questions about intragroup cultural variation or cultural similarities across groups are rarely addressed.

Among anthropologists, this conception of "culture" had clear advantages over its conceptual predecessor, "race," because culture removed difference from the realm of the natural or innate. Rather than something that springs from physical differences among groups, culture (way-of-life) was understood to be a successful adaptation to relatively stable environmental (economic, social, and political) conditions, "a ready-made set of solutions for human problems so that individuals don't have to begin all over again each generation" (Lewis, 1973, p. 239). As such, culture provides a group with a way to live in and make sense of their world, although the culture may arise in conditions of deprivation or oppression. Unless environmental conditions change, culture will remain stable over time. It will be transmitted as a coherent whole to the next generation through the organization of child rearing. From the 1920s through the 1970s, this general conception of culture was used to attack arguments of racial or genetic inferiority applied to many groups, including Native Americans, Irish Americans, Jewish Americans, African Americans, and Mexican Americans (Hicks & Handler, 1978; Stocking, 1979).

Cultural Difference Theory: A Corollary

In this view of culture, cultural similarities are expected when social, economic, and historical conditions are similar; cultural differences are expected when these conditions differ. When members of groups with legacies of adaptation to different external conditions come into contact with each other, their cultural differences are likely to be a cause of miscommunication and misunderstanding, unless sensitive cultural brokers are available to anticipate, explain, and overcome the effects of difference.[2]

This theory of cultural difference has profoundly affected thinking about education in the United States and elsewhere since the 1950s. It is the basis for the now-large body of research that has examined mismatches between the "culture of the school" and the "culture of the home." Using this theory, mismatches are understood in the following way: To the extent that the culture of the school reflects only one home culture—the adaptation of White, privileged-class Americans, then the behaviors and attitudes expected in school are likely to be unfamiliar to students raised in other environments. Without special efforts to teach "culturally different" students the unfa-

---

[1] Although debate about the proper definition of culture has been ongoing in anthropology since the discipline developed, this general definition has been recognized by both those who accept it (e.g., Kroeber & Kluckhohn, 1952) and those who do not (e.g., Keesing, 1974) as the most salient and widely held view. See Brightman (1995) for a recent discussion of various definitions and critiques of them.

[2] It is important to recognize that this conception of culture makes it considerably more consequential for individuals and more resistant to change than many educational researchers have accepted. In educational research, it has been common to conceive of culture as one of several variables the consequences of which can be identified quickly, and, if necessary, overcome by minor changes or short-term interventions.

miliar school culture, these students will, from the first day and through no fault of their own, have difficulty understanding what is expected of them in school. Study after study have demonstrated that, although all children approach school culture as a kind of "second culture" (after the home and neighborhood), White, class-privileged children and their parents find school culture considerably more familiar than do others.

Shirley Brice Heath's book, *Ways with Words* (1983), makes this point compellingly. Heath presents detailed accounts of how children's lives are organized, talked about, and nurtured in three distinct but geographically proximate communities— one Black working class; one White working class; and one Black and White middle class. She illustrates how the children's experiences of using language, time, and space differed in each community and how, in the two working-class communities (but not in the middle-class one), children's use of language, time, and space differed substantially from the uses expected at school. When children from the working-class communities went to school, they behaved in ways consistent with their background experiences at home. These behaviors were misunderstood or unappreciated by middle class-oriented teachers, who characterized the children as "behavior problems" or "slow." Neither teachers nor students knew how to make actions and expectations that were familiar to one group familiar to the other.

The general ideas about culture and cultural difference that are illustrated in Heath's work have inspired 3 decades of research and classroom interventions by all of the leading figures in educational anthropology (for collections of this work, see Jacob & Jordan, 1993; Spindler, 1982; Spindler & Spindler, 1994; Trueba, Rodriguez, Zou, & Cintron, 1993) and by many in other branches of education (see Bruner, 1996 and Cole, 1996 for traces of these ideas in their current work, and the collection by Noblit & Pink, 1987). The authors represented in these works do not all concentrate on the same features of culture— some, like Heath, focus on sociolinguistic patterns; others focus on conceptual categories, "cultural models" of success, valued identities, or "household funds of knowledge." But they share a commitment to the idea that group differences in culture— defined as patterned ways of behaving, thinking, or feeling, formed over time as an adaptation to specific environmental conditions, and learned through socialization in the home community—set the stage for later success and difficulties in school.

This approach to culture and cultural difference has been and continues to be theoretically, practically, and politically powerful. It has successfully accounted for the difficulties of many non-White, non-class-privileged children in mainstream U.S. schools (Miller, 1995), and it has provided direction for the development of instructional and curricular changes that, at least in the short-run, improved these children's success in schools (Gartrell, 1991; Heath, 1983; Mehan, Villanueva, Hubbard, & Lintz, 1996; Vogt, Jordan, & Tharp, 1993). For many years, this view of cultural difference has been a compelling argument in the struggle to gain more equal educational opportunities for nonmainstream students. In various contexts, liberals, progressives, and civil rights advocates have argued successfully that cultural difference is not a legitimate reason to limit or deny educational opportunities (for recent examples focused on immigration issues in California, see the Theme issue of the *Anthropology and Education Quarterly,* 1996, edited by Jose Ma-

cías,) and that the persistence of school outcome differences by cultural group is an important reason for recommitting to affirmative action (Howe, 1997).

Challenges to the Widespread View of Culture and Cultural Difference

For years, there have been challengers to this dominant approach, and the chorus is getting louder. John Ogbu (1978) was one of the first to point out that not all culturally different children do poorly in mainstream schools. Recently immigrated groups, for example, often do well in U.S. schools, while minority groups often do not. The success of some culturally different students is not accounted for by cultural difference theory. Ogbu's insight has led him to develop and test increasingly complex models of the relationship between external conditions, a "cultural frame of reference" (a group's accepted set of ideas about how to behave), and student achievement. In recent formulations (1995a, 1995b), Ogbu has argued that a group's history (e.g., recent immigration versus long-time subordination) will cause them to respond differently, that is, to develop different cultural frames of reference, to similar (immediate) external conditions. When a cultural frame of reference includes a positive assessment of schooling (the case for many immigrant minorities), cultural differences between home and school will be rather easily overcome; when the cultural frame of reference about schooling is negative (as for many subordinate minorities), cultural differences will be hard to overcome. Many others have used, expanded, or modified Ogbu's theory as a means of understanding the school performance of various minority groups (Deyhle, 1992; Deyhle & Margonis, 1995; Fordham & Ogbu, 1986; Gibson, 1993; Matute-Bianchi, 1986; Suárez-Orozco, 1993).

Other critics of cultural difference theory have demonstrated that group differences in orientations toward school are not always or only linked to differences in home communities. Taken-for-granted views of such things as readiness for school, performance in reading, and participation in extracurricular activities, as well as ideas about popularity, romance, or plans for the future, are sometimes shared by groups composed of individuals who do not share a social history or home community (Eckert, 1989; Eisenhart & Graue, 1993; Foley, 1990; Holland & Eisenhart, 1990; Willis, 1977). These various orientations seem to develop as small groups or individuals work out their relationships and identities in relation to the school. Meanings brought to school can be reconfigured, as students and parents respond to what they find there. Drawing on meanings available in various settings but actively appropriated and modified to fit an unfolding context at school, groups of parents, students, and teachers from diverse backgrounds may come to share an orientation to school.

This view of culture, in which the focus shifts toward meanings actively appropriated, constructed, and manipulated in specific contexts and away from ideas about culture as a given "way of life," gained momentum as part of cultural anthropology's shift toward interpretivism. The substance of this shift is described in detail in Erickson's chapter for the third edition of *The Handbook of Research on Teaching* (1986).

In educational anthropology and sociology, the "interpretive turn" did not, however, lead researchers completely away from the effects of external conditions or social structure. Rather, they worked to find new ways of conceptualizing the relationship between actively constructed meaning systems (cultures) and externally imposed conditions (structures). One group particularly active in this work during the late 1970s and early 1980s was the Centre for Contemporary Cultural Studies (CCCS) at the University of Birmingham in Birmingham, England. In his book, *Learning to Labor* (1977), the British sociologist and ethnographer Paul Willis, a member of CCCS working in the tradition of social reproduction theory, exemplifies this work and its contribution to another conception of culture.

Social Reproduction Theory

Following a Marxist interpretation of society, social reproductionists argue that communities and families in capitalist societies are defined and organized primarily by social class position, that is, by their relation to the means of production.[3] A relation to the means of production is lived out in the daily activities (especially the productive activities of making a living) of families and is interpreted through the history and experience of the family and groups of similarly situated families. The interpretation of this "living out" of a class relation is a collective class ideology or "culture," that is, a set of symbolic and conceptual forms by which a group's social class circumstances are made to seem reasonable and "natural." As the basic pattern of daily (labor) activities is repeated from one generation to the next, class-based "culture" is reproduced in successive generations, and the class-based, economic status quo is maintained. Thus, in this view, culture takes on an ambivalence that is not part of the cultural difference tradition or the early interpretive turn. Culture becomes a set of ideas and beliefs for living (a positive, enabling dimension) that camouflages or "mystifies" the social inequities of class-based societies (a negative, disabling dimension) (e.g., Willis, 1977).

In early social reproductionist work in education, the school was seen as a key site for learning one's place in a class society and thus one's class culture (Anyon, 1981; Apple, 1979; Bowles & Gintis, 1976). Numerous studies documented that schools put students to work (i.e., grouped, treated, and taught them) according to the social class position they came from and that they were expected to assume as adults (e.g., Anyon, 1981; Oakes, 1985). Students from working class backgrounds were more likely than their middle-class peers to spend their school days learning procedures, following rules, modifying their behavior, and covering simplified academic material. Middle- and upper-class kids were given greater freedom of movement and expression, as well as more exciting and demanding curricula.

Early social reproductionists argued that schools are engaged in an elaborate process to "mystify" students about the true (i.e., economic) basis for their different activities. This mystification is achieved through the culture of the school, which mediates the relationship between school activities and student success. Specifically, schools define the meaning of "good"

work and behavior in ways that suggest that success in life depends on individual academic success. In the school culture, academic success and thus success in life are defined as a reflection of individual intelligence and personal effort (which they are not, after Bourdieu & Passeron, 1977) rather than a set of tasks that privilege the labor of one social class group, the middle class (which they are). For schools to succeed at this mystification, they must convince students and others that academic achievement is independent of social class background (or race, gender, nationality, etc.). Schools work at this mystification by promoting a particular idea of exchange: Teachers give out knowledge in exchange for students' compliant behavior. Teachers then calculate (grade) student achievement based on how well students meet the terms of this exchange, thereby creating student "academic" groupings and rankings. Students who accept and conform to the exchange are rewarded with good grades, receive the "symbolic capital" of being a good student, and are promised a school credential and a good job later. Students who do not or cannot conform are punished with low grades, receive little or none of the school's symbolic capital, and are threatened with no credential and no good job later. The argument will then be made that these students are not prepared for, nor do they deserve, "good," that is, middle-class, jobs because they did not achieve academically. In this way, the school contributes to reproducing occupational dispositions (beliefs that certain kinds of people are suited for certain kinds of jobs) on which a capitalist society depends.

Willis, sensitive to the research of symbolic interactionists on classroom microdynamics, thought the school's role had to be more complicated than that. In the opening to his ethnography, *Learning to Labor* (1977), Willis wondered: Why would working-class kids (for example), no doubt aware that their status in a capitalist society is low and many of the tasks required of them in school trivial, allow themselves to be treated so poorly by the school? Why didn't these students demand or get better treatment so they would be prepared to move into the middle class?

Willis's answer derived from an argument about culture. Culture in school, he wrote, was not only a symbolic working-out of a given social class position conveyed through the organization of school and the actions of teachers, but it could also be actively and creatively constructed or "produced" by students as they resisted the imposition of the school's organization and ideology.

> Structural determinations act, not by direct mechanical effect, but by mediation through the cultural level where their own relationships become subject to forms of exposure and explanation. . . . Social agents are not passive bearers of ideology, but active appropriators who reproduce existing structures only through struggle, contestation, and a partial penetration of those structures. (Willis, 1977, pp. 173–175)

Willis's book describes how a small group of White working-class high school boys in England, the "lads," produced a

---

[3] For a more detailed treatment of the history and development of the ideas discussed in this section, see Levinson & Holland (1996). Although their review does not focus so directly on "culture," it is an excellent review of similar currents in U.S. educational anthropology and British ethnography of education.

counterculture to a school ideology they did not accept. The lads, who did not do well in school, renounced the school's system of rewards, status, and prestige. They looked elsewhere to find ways of acting that would bring them some rewards and status and help them to make positive sense of their lives. In looking around, they found the elements of more rewarding situations among their friends, in popular culture, and, most importantly, in the shop floor culture of their working-class parents. Under these conditions, groups of students who were not rewarded by the school developed their own group logic or "cultural productions," that is, ways of thinking about themselves, others, and the world, fashioned from the cultural (meaning-laden) resources they found outside of school. Later, Willis defined cultural productions as "discourses, meanings, materials, practices, and group processes [used by groups] to explore, understand, and creatively occupy particular positions in sets of general material possibilities" (1981, p. 59).

Sometimes these cultural productions cast the school as irrelevant, sometimes as a target. Sometimes these cultural productions led students to legitimate activities, sometimes to illegitimate or illegal ones.[4] In the lads' case, their cultural production of status and prestige had ironic consequences: It led them to resist the school, which denigrated them. Yet, in resisting what the school had to offer, the lads cut themselves off from access to the knowledge and the credentials they would need to move up in society. The lads ended up reproducing their lower status in society, despite their production of a culture that opposed (in some flamboyant and immediate ways) that status as it was constructed in school.

But Willis did not believe such an outcome was inevitable. Because the cultural level is actively constructed and sometimes opposes the status quo, the outcome is continually in doubt. It could happen that culture disrupts (rather than transmits) the status quo.

Thus, culture, in this view, becomes a set of symbolic and material forms, affected but not determined by history and structure, actively appropriated or "produced" in groups to bring order and satisfaction to experiences. In consequence, culture includes both enabling and disabling dimensions, both reproductive and transformative possibilities, for those who produce and live by it. This perspective and the studies it has inspired constituted another major shift in the conception of culture and might be referred to as a "productions turn" in studies of culture and education. I will come back to the shift toward "cultural productions" after a discussion of some more recent challenges.

More Recent Challenges to Conceptions of Culture: Ethnic, Feminist, and Postmodern Views

As the shift toward cultural productions was taking place in some circles, new ideas also were coming from other sources. From within anthropology as well as from literary criticism, feminist studies, ethnic studies, and postmodern studies, increasing numbers of scholars were pointing to contemporary phenomena that seemed to defy explanation in conventional cultural terms. From the gathering momentum of their challenges, together with (and not unrelated to) those of interpretivists and social reproductionists, the poststructural critique of culture in the 1990s has taken shape. The meaning of this critique for culture has been to emphasize further the need to decouple "culture" from "social group," and to turn toward "identity."

Recent challenges to old ideas about culture have their origins in empirical evidence from contemporary global events, new social movements, and changing demographics. New modes of transportation, communication, and migration have created mixed or mixed-up social relationships by traditional anthropological standards. The spaces, times, relationships, tasks, and tools that seemed to constitute collectively organized society in the past, took their meanings from culture, and served as the focal points of anthropological research have been transformed with the changing conditions of contemporary life. Today, for example, it is not surprising to hear of a researcher traveling half way around the world to visit a key informant—say, a Hindu priest in India—only to find that he has moved to serve parishioners in Houston (Appadurai, 1991). Similarly, we hear about "a medicine man who at one time feels a deep respect for Mother Earth and at another plans a radical real estate subdivision" (Clifford, 1988, p. 338). It is not uncommon to listen to political or educational debates in which members of the same ethnic or racial group take different sides. It is not unexpected to find homes, neighborhoods, or schools where people speak more than one language in the same conversation. It is not unusual to find children and adults spending hours each day communicating via computer technologies, video games, or popular music that connect them to people, values, and economic networks far removed from home or school. Paul Willis, discussing the increasing allure of popular culture among young people, writes:

> Many of the traditional resources of, and inherited bases for, social meaning, membership, security, and psychic certainty have lost their legitimacy for a large proportion of young people. There is no longer a sense of a "whole culture" with allocated places and a shared, universal value system. . . . [There is no longer a supply of] ready values and models of duty and meaning to help structure the passage into settled adulthood. (Willis, 1990, p. 13)

Today, varied social settings—for child care, education, leisure, and work—take the place of, or function together with, homes and communities to socialize large numbers of children and young people. Widespread access to transportation, the mass media, and computer technology opens avenues of communication far wider and more diverse than in previous generations (Nespor, 1994).

For reasons like these, it is no longer straightforward for anthropologists to plan to study "cultural groups," that is, designated groups of people with coherent, shared value systems,

---

[4] See Jay MacLeod's (1987) *Ain't No Makin' It: Leveled Aspirations in a Low-Income Neighborhood* for a similar account of cultural productions in two American high school-aged peer groups—one Black and one White. MacLeod found that the culture produced in the Black group was considerably more proschool than that of the White group.

households or communities with clearly defined boundaries, or shared funds of knowledge transmitted primarily from adults to their children. Conventional assumptions of culture as coherent and coterminous with social background, language use, region, religion, or ethnicity have become impossible to sustain. Certainly, such changes have been occurring for much longer than the past 10 years, but in anthropology critics from feminist studies, ethnic studies, and postmodern studies have been the ones to drive the point home.[5]

Ethnic, Feminist, and Postmodern Challenges

Ethnic scholars have challenged conventional ideas about culture on the grounds that old ideas freeze group characteristics and ignore issues of power. Ethnic scholars, not recognizing themselves or people like them in older anthropological accounts of their group, have complained about the essentializing and stereotyping of cultural categorization. They object to the way conventional ideas about culture solidify group characteristics, ignore within-group variations, and leave little room for individual creativity, agency, or change (Abu-Lughod, 1991; Hemmings, 1996; Rodriguez, 1982).

Radical ethnic and feminist scholars also have charged that conventional ideas about culture are too indebted to cultural relativism and liberal politics. They argue that the conventional discourse of culture and cultural differences, though intended to correct racist beliefs and serve a progressive politics, has nonetheless contributed to (or been co-opted to) perpetuating racism and sexism. In the United States, for example, African Americans, Mexican Americans, or women are not just another colorful, exotic, or different group; they live within and must somehow deal with structures of racial or gender inequality and cultural dominance. Critics complain that cultural difference theory—with its commitment to consider all cultural adaptations as equally reasonable or successful for those who live within them—tends to divert attention from enduring inequities of power (e.g., James, 1997). Although relations of power continue to block opportunities for some groups regardless of qualification and deny legitimate roles in society for those who differ from or criticize the dominant group, power remains hidden or in the background of most conventional accounts of culture or cultural difference.

Feminists have further protested that the tendency to celebrate culture-as-reasonable-adaptation obscures the ways traditional cultural groups oppress women (Friedman, 1987; Kondo, 1990; McRobbie, 1980), as well as the variation among women. Ethnic, feminist, and gay and lesbian scholarship has made clear that not all people of color, all women, all men, or all people socially identified as members of any group have the same histories, experience the world in the same way, face the same problems, or construct the same meanings.

Particularly during the past decade, increasing numbers of scholars have challenged the idea that individual behaviors, attitudes, or self-identities derive from a coherent and given cultural tradition acquired in the family during childhood. Postmodern scholarship is developing the idea that knowledge (including categories, beliefs, and values that filter or screen ways of seeing the world, i.e., culture) emanates from ongoing shifting and emerging relationships among people in different social positions and with different experiences of the world who come into contact—literally or figuratively—with each other. In this view, culture is not one primordial or coherent thing, fixed in time and space—as many older discussions and much popular theorizing imply—but rather a dynamic, continually emerging set of struggles among people trying to identify themselves in relation to others (Clifford, 1986). In this view, contemporary U.S. culture can be seen as composed of, for example, all of the competing ways in which Black people are constructed as "other" to White people, women are constructed as "other" to men, illegal aliens as "other" to real Americans, and so forth. Culture becomes the set of conflicting, continually changing, often incoherent understandings of self and others that take form among people who regularly communicate with or about each other (Clifford, 1986; Mascia-Lees, Sharpe & Cohen, 1989).

In this context, individuals who live *between* social groups—those of mixed ancestry whom Abu-Lughod (1991) calls "halfies"; those such as South Texans or homosexuals of color who live in the "borderlands" of historically separate groups (Anzaldúa, 1987; Rosaldo, 1989)—have become a central focus of attention. Living at the junctures of different traditions, these individuals must make sense of their lives by crossing, blending, negotiating, or transcending the boundaries of tradition. They are portrayed as the "usual" person-type in contemporary heterogeneous societies (Anzaldúa, 1987; Cohen, 1993; Davidson, 1996; Haig-Brown, 1995; Hemmings, 1996). Research among such individuals suggests that they develop behaviors and attitudes in practice that deal directly with the challenges of being "mixed," "different," or simply, oneself. These individuals are not choosing between one home and one school culture, or between assimilation to the mainstream or maintenance of a coherent ethnic identity; nor is it the case that they necessarily form oppositional cultures (although this is common) or that oppositional cultures are always associated with academic difficulties or restricted future opportunities. About this, Gloria Anzaldúa writes:

> Cradled in one culture, sandwiched between two cultures, straddling all three cultures and their value systems, *la mestiza* undergoes a struggle of flesh, a struggle of borders. . . . Like all people, we perceive the version of reality that our culture communicates. Like others having or living in more than one culture, we get multiple, often opposing messages. The coming together of two self-consistent, but habitually incompatible frames of reference causes *un choque,* a cultural collision. (1987, p. 78)

---

[5] Often dated in the United States from the appearance of James Clifford and George Marcus's (1986) edited volume, *Writing Culture;* Marcus and Michael Fischer's (1986) *Anthropology as Cultural Critique;* and Clifford's (1988)*The Predicament of Culture* postmodern criticism in anthropology has deeper and broader roots. They can be found in earlier works by feminist anthropologists (e.g., diLeonardo, 1984; Rosaldo & Lamphere, 1974), interpretive theorists (e.g., Geertz, 1973b), social reproduction and cultural theorists (e.g., Willis, 1977, and others at the Centre for Contemporary Cultural Studies in Birmingham, England), practice theorists (e.g., Bourdieu, 1977), and philosophers of science (e.g., Foucault, 1980).

In response, individuals fashion meaningful ways of being in the world (identities) from the various material and symbolic resources that are available to them in different settings, with diverse people, and for different purposes. About this, Dorinne Kondo writes: "[People] forge their lives in the midst of ambivalences and contradictions, using the idioms at their disposal" (1990, p. 302); Ann Davidson describes it as a situation in which "identity is constantly recreated, coming forward or retreating to the background in response to the politics and relations that characterize changing social situations" (1996, p. 4).

This body of scholarship suggests that cultures (ways of acting or understanding) are less stable (more situational and ephemeral), more actively constructed (less dependent on transmission), more creative (less given), and more contested (less coherent) than the conventional definition of culture-as-given-adaptation can accommodate. In this view, culture recedes into the conceptual background, while identity moves center stage. The struggle to define and heal a self fractured by competing cultural traditions becomes the focus of attention (Anzaldúa, 1987; Kondo, 1990):

> Culture, from this standpoint, is no reified thing or system, but a meaningful way of being in the world, inseparable from the "deepest" aspects of one's "self." . . . Selves, in this view, can be seen as rhetorical figures and performative assertions enacted in specific situations within fields of power, history, and culture. (Kondo, 1990, pp. 300, 304)

> The struggle is inner . . . played out in the outer terrains. (Anzaldúa, 1987, p. 87)

This approach points toward investigations of identity that trace the ways individuals construct and use meanings of self within historically specific contexts. Thus, interest shifts to identity struggles and the construction of self against the backdrop of cultural tradition. Culture remains important for the traditional orientations and resources it offers, but not as the form in which new possibilities arise. For writers such as Anzaldúa, the possibilities for transcending cultural differences and cultural violence lie, literally and metaphorically, in the mestiza's experience of trying to heal the disjunctures of her life at the intersection of numerous cultural traditions.

In this context, some have suggested abandoning the concept of culture altogether. Lila Abu-Lughod writes that "culture" is the linchpin of an anthropological discourse that "enforce[s] separations that inevitably carry a sense of hierarchy" (1991, p. 138). She continues:

> Anthropology's avowed goal may be "the study of man" . . . [but it] has been and continues to be primarily the study of the non-Western [culturally different] other by the Western [culturally mainstream] self, even if in its new guise it seeks explicitly to give voice to the Other, either textually or through an explication of the fieldwork encounter (1991, p. 139). . . . Culture is the essential tool for making other. As a professional discourse that elaborates on the meaning of culture in order to account for, explain, and understand cultural difference, anthropology also helps construct, produce, and maintain it. Anthropological discourse gives cultural difference . . . the air of the self-evident. (p. 143)

In fact, Abu-Lughod argues, the relationship between the culturally different and the mainstream has been constituted by mainstream domination and projects of assimilation, supported by conventional conceptions of culture and cultural difference.

Abu-Lughod's remedy is to write "*against* culture" by focusing on particular individuals. In her view, this remedy would

> necessarily subvert the most problematic connotations of culture: homogeneity, coherence, and timelessness. Individuals are confronted with choices, struggle with others, make conflicting statements, argue about points of view on the same events, undergo ups and downs in various relationships and changes in their circumstances and desires, face new pressures, and fail to predict what will happen to them in the future. So . . . it becomes difficult to think that the term "Bedouin culture" makes sense when one tries to piece together and convey what life is like for one old Bedouin matriarch. (1991, p. 154)

Abu-Lughod argues that a focus on individual particulars will reveal how similar people are across social groups and thus serve to diminish the worst features of cultural categorization.

Is It Time to Abandon Culture?

In contrast to Abu-Lughod, I am not so sanguine about the value of abandoning culture. I see no good reason to assume that focusing on similarities across individuals will necessarily reduce the tendency to create social hierarchies. On the one hand, there are real social, economic, and power differences that separate people and their experiences; ignoring these differences (as has often been the case in psychology, for example) will not make the hierarchies disappear. On the other hand, as Abu-Lughod makes clear, an exclusive focus on differences leaves out too much of the variety in human life.

I for one am not ready to give up on culture. To do so is to deny that patterned behaviors or intersubjective meanings are significant features of our ability to understand human experience. It is careless to suggest that such things as patterns in conversational turn-taking, rationales for school success and failure, or constructions of student or teacher identity categories are comprehensible in individual terms. The patterns and meanings that people take up and manipulate in particular places and with particular other people are consequential for them. They affect the way people interpret (or "filter") their experiences, the concerns people feel, the preferences they have, the choices they make, and the identities they seek (Kimball, 1976; D'Andrade & Strauss, 1992; Holland & Quinn, 1987; Levinson, Foley, & Holland, 1996). Individuals are not free to choose for themselves any view of the world, any way of acting in class, any definition of success, or any identity. In practice, such choices are constrained by intersubjective understandings of what is possible, appropriate, legitimate, properly radical, and so forth. That is, they are constrained by culture and the enduring social structures that culture mediates. I agree with Sherry Ortner who writes:

> However much we now recognize that cultures are riddled with inequality, differential understanding, and differential advantage, . . . nonetheless they remain for the people who live within them sources of value, meaning, and ways of understanding—and resisting—the world. . . . [Thus the] ethnography of meaningful cultural worlds is [still] a significant enterprise. (Ortner, 1991, p. 187)

These meaningful worlds are not things that educational researchers or policymakers can afford to abandon or neglect.

The way forward, in Ortner's view, is to tread the line between attending to the significance of culture as resource—in the sense of what it provides in the way of order, salience, and value, while at the same time attending to how it is both constituted by and contributes to the reproduction of enduring structures (Ortner, 1991, p. 167; see also diLeonardo, 1984). Ortner cites as good examples of this approach Willis's *Learning to Labor* (1977) and Penny Eckert's *Jocks and Burnouts* (1989), an ethnographic account of how two cultural categories—being a "jock" and being a "burnout"—define a meaningful world for the high school students she studied and simultaneously construct their relationship to larger structures of corporate America.[6] This direction is, I think, especially fruitful for anthropologists and other ethnographers of education. It is a direction currently being developed by scholars who are extending Willis's concept of cultural production with reference to developments in the emerging field of "cultural studies."

Cultural Studies

The field of cultural studies is generally concerned with the subcultures (such as the lads' counterculture) created or used by groups on the margins of society in contemporary U.S. and British society (Hall, 1980; Johnson, 1986–87).[7] In cultural studies,

> Culture is not *a* practice; nor is it simply the descriptive sum of the "mores and folkways" of societies—as it tended to become in certain kinds of anthropology. . . . The "culture" is those patterns of organization, those characteristic forms of human energy which can be discovered as revealing themselves . . . within or underlying *all* social practices. . . . The purpose of the analysis [of culture] is to grasp how the interactions between all these practices and patterns are lived and experienced as a whole, in any particular [historical] period. (Hall, 1980, p. 60)

The "characteristic forms of human energy" that interest cultural studies researchers are "popular" forms of expression, especially the artistic, literary, and musical products of members of subordinate social groups. These researchers rely primarily on tools of literary criticism to analyze these forms of expression and to relate them in patterns. Their goal is to understand how various media forms or "texts"—especially those that members of subordinate groups produce in the concrete situations of their everyday lives—mediate (i.e., organize and make meaningful) a relationship with a dominant group.

Reminiscent of social reproductionist as well as ethnic and feminist scholarship, there is also a critical dimension to cultural studies. In cultural studies, researchers try to understand the way representations both enable creative expression and conceal oppressive social and power relations.

In writing about the contribution of cultural studies to edu-cational research, Levinson and Holland (1996) suggest that by joining ideas from cultural studies with those of cultural production, "culture" becomes the set of meaningful forms that grow out of actual social relations between groups that become dominant or subordinate in a particular context, such as between students who become "jocks" and "burnouts" or "lads" and conformists in a school; forms that are expressed in the texts, discourses (including those of identity), technologies, artifacts, and actions the various groups take up in relation to each other. From the idea of "cultural productions," their view recognizes the significance of collective pattern and meaning, acknowledges the association of culture and social relations (social structure), and allows the possibility of change or transformation arising from the active, creative expressions of groups in communication with each other. From the idea of culture in cultural studies, their view stretches out to accommodate the cultural possibilities in such phenomena as mass communication, global consumerism, economic restructuring, and computer technologies that are the media of so much contemporary life and that have so mixed up older ideas about culture. Better understandings of such phenomena, hold, for me, special promise for culture-oriented studies of education in the near future.

Cultural Productions and the Study of Education

Discussing this promise with respect to studies of education, Levinson and Holland say:

> [T]he larger question is now one of how historical persons are formed in practice, within and against larger societal forces and structures which instantiate themselves in schools and other institutions. Cultural production [informed by cultural studies] is one vision of this process. . . . Through the production of cultural forms, created within the structural constraints of sites such as schools, subjectivities [identities] form and agency develops. . . . [Focusing on cultural production] is a way to show how people creatively occupy the space of education and schooling. This creative practice generates understandings and strategies which may in fact move well beyond the school, transforming aspirations, household relations, local knowledges, and structures of power. (Levinson & Holland, 1996, p. 14)

This expanded view of cultural productions directs anthropologists of education and other educational researchers to investigations of how groups in school organize subjectivities (identities) and the possibilities for individual agency in the expressive forms the groups take up and develop in the activities in which they regularly engage. This approach contrasts with much previous educational research that has focused on "cultural" topics such as preexisting beliefs, attitudes, and values. In previous research, for example, students' (or parents') beliefs about appropriate teacher behavior (e.g., the meaning of direct eye contact, the meaning of being an authority) have been viewed as preexisting cultural features that can either facilitate or block learn-

---

[6] See also Holland & Eisenhart (1990) for an illustration of how the "culture of romance" defines and constructs the lives of some college women; and Fordham (1996) for how the meanings of "being Black" and "acting White" construct the lives of some African-American high school students.

[7] Although it is possible to distinguish people and places primarily associated with "cultural studies" from those primarily associated with ethnic, feminist studies, and postmodern studies, these different arenas of scholarship have heavily influenced each other. See also Levinson & Holland (1996) and Turner (1993) for discussions of the contribution of cultural studies to anthropological perspectives on education.

ing in school. Similarly, teachers' preexisting beliefs about such things as "teacher-as-researcher," "mathematics," or "whole language," are thought to seriously affect teachers' responses to new programs. Beliefs before, during, and after the introduction of an educational reform are often investigated, as an indicator of whether changes associated with new educational practices have taken hold with students or teachers.

A focus on cultural productions suggests looking at student or teacher "beliefs" in a different way. The ongoing expressions of identity and purpose that particular groups of students or teachers produce as "group logics" in their everyday interactions would be the central concern and would be viewed as the means of staying in, growing, or changing in school. These expressions would not be considered reflections of a fixed state-of-mind or enduring beliefs, but a response to past experiences that is simultaneously a commitment to future experiences. They would be investigated not only for how they continue some legacy from the past, but also how they launch individuals into the future. They would be identified, not by individual statements of belief, but by patterns in the ways participants act in classrooms, label their own efforts, and describe themselves to others with whom they normally and regularly interact over time. Additionally, these expressions would not be associated primarily with background factors (e.g., home environment, previous socialization) but with individuals' positions in the ongoing social relations in which they participate, both inside and outside of school.

The cultural production approach provides a more complicated picture of how "beliefs" come to be formed in educational practice, how they give meaning to actions and organize identity, and how and why they contribute to maintaining, and possibly changing, the educational status quo. This is no small project, but the work already accomplished by researchers like Bradley Levinson, Aurolyn Luykx, and Jan Nespor provides fascinating illustrations of how we might begin (see also other articles in Levinson, Foley, & Holland, 1996; Davidson, 1996).

Levinson (1996), for example, traced the discourses (language and interactional forms) used by students in a Mexican secondary school to construct identities for themselves and others. He found the students forming their understanding of selves and others in a field of highly contradictory cultural discourses. Some were dominant or official discourses, for example, the school's discourse of equality; some were not. Students came to think of themselves and others "within and against" these discourses. Levinson's method was to follow the messages about the meaning of school, social success, and individual identity into and through the spaces where members of small groups of students spent their time. After identifying various messages, he then traced their associations or connections to wider scale national discursive forms (see also Weis, 1990; Wexler, 1992). He found, for example, that as students appropriated the school's discourse of equality, they learned to see (or deal with a view of) themselves and others within their particular school as equals, but this sense of equality was achieved, in part, by defining themselves against others—specifically, those who no longer attended secondary school—who were identified as lower status, "unequal." Thus, by appropriating the school's discourse of equality to build relationships within the school, the students were simultaneously constructing a discourse that di-

vided them from many of their friends, relatives, and peers who would not have the advantage of secondary school. They came to differentiate peers and family members in ways they had not previously differentiated them.

> The "fact" of a general secundaria education . . . gets elaborated into a series of cultural distinctions which signify the value of being properly schooled. This process magnifies the *difference* between schooled and unschooled. . . . [It] is the sense of self as educated person [i.e., someone who has completed secondary school] which most powerfully articulates social difference into new configurations. . . . Schooled identity and the category of educated person create new configurations of difference by bringing together and identifying previously opposed or antagonistic identities rooted in distinct [home] cultures. (Levinson, 1996, p. 231)

This difference that the school and students constructed held implications for whom the students interacted with, whom they wanted to know and emulate, how they thought about their past and future, and what they worried about and wished for.

Using a similar approach, Aurolyn Luykx (1996) studied a Bolivian (Aymaran) normal school. As the teacher candidates from various rural areas came together for instruction in preparing to become teachers, they appropriated the national discourse of professional teacher development. In so doing, they began to differentiate themselves from their rural relatives and friends. Yet the teacher education students also maintained discourses from their rural homes, to which they would eventually return as teachers. By careful investigation of these competing discourses, how the teacher education students used and manipulated them, and their connections to larger structural forms, for example, the rural poverty of Bolivia's indigenous population and the economic allure of professional teaching, Luykx was able to reveal the contested terrain of culture and its mixed messages for these students becoming teachers. Her analysis of the Bolivian teacher education students' experiences also suggests a way of seeing the dilemmas of minority teacher candidates in the United States.

> Part of their socialization involved coming to grips with the fact that the achievement of professional status would distance them from their ethnic and class origins, while simultaneously requiring them to live and work among those from whom they had differentiated themselves. Furthermore, their transformation from captive subjects of the educational system into its active agents meant incorporating themselves within an institution which has traditionally threatened the integrity of indigenous culture. As future teachers, they would be called upon to disseminate a worldview opposed to the one they were encouraged to identify with as Aymaras. The only choice [they found] legitimate was to maintain these two ideological loyalties simultaneously, despite their cultural and historical incompatibilities. It may not be an exaggeration to suggest that this dilemma constitutes a collective cultural-psychological crisis which [minority] teachers . . . must traverse on their journey toward personal and professional identity. (Luykx, 1996, p. 246; see also Fordham, 1996, for similar experiences of Black teachers at Capitol High in Washington, D.C.)

Using a different approach, Jan Nespor (1994) traced the networks of affiliation that undergraduate college students in physics and management are joined to as they move through the organizational arrangements, textbook materials, content requirements, and social demands of their college degree programs. The students' movement through the curriculum is conceptualized as a process of consuming and producing the material and symbolic representations made available in the social organization of coursework, and thereby becoming attached to and embodied by wider networks of social relations and meaning that extended far beyond the program, college, and immediate scenes of action. In Nespor's account, the lives of students in physics and management—though they may have entered college with similar backgrounds—are differently arranged by their respective curricula, which lead them to very different productions of college life, professional and social networks, and plans for the future.

One other issue bears mentioning here. Most studies of cultural productions suggest that subordinate groups or their members can, potentially, contribute something new or different that will alter the status quo. However, very few studies have provided examples in which this potential has been realized. One that does is Dorothy Holland and Debra Skinner's (1995) account of songs produced by Nepali women for the annual Tij festival. The women's songs were structured and performed in conventional ways, yet some had novel elements that, once they were performed, added to the personal and collective ways Nepali women could think about their (oppressed) circumstances and act on them. Sara Harkness and her colleagues (Harkness, Super, & Keefer, 1992) described something similar among first-time parents, who formulated new models of "being a parent" from the received wisdom and mistakes they gleaned from other parents, self-help manuals, and their own babies' responses. And, Margaret Eisenhart (1995b) illustrated how talk about "being a mother" and "being a scientist" led women in one workplace to create new ways of thinking about their jobs—ways that put pressure on the work place to accommodate the needs of mothers.

These recent studies of cultural productions illustrate how local practices of cultural production become meaningful and consequential to participants; differentiate otherwise similar individuals; make similar otherwise different people; are connected to wider processes of nationalism, stratification, globalization, and professionalism; and sometimes motivate change. The processes by which teachers, students, and other school participants take on and make meaningful the contemporary cultural possibilities associated with schooling, adult identities, peer groups, leisure activities, work, and citizenship would seem crucial to understanding the conditions and needs of contemporary education. Yet, these processes seem nearly invisible to most educational researchers. Those who abhor insensitivity to (conventional) cultural differences should be chastened to realize that ignoring the contemporary interests of young people and teachers, and the forces which affect their lives, is tantamount to the same thing. Researchers must take more seriously the possibility that, through regular exposure to numerous contemporary cultural possibilities, many of today's young people, including new teachers, are developing interests and identities that are unfamiliar to older generations and unlikely to be piqued by traditional discipline-oriented curricula and instruction.

The focus on cultural productions also suggests that we need some new methods of ethnographic research. In particular, the turn toward cultural productions requires approaches to collecting and analyzing data that can explore structures and meanings—physical and symbolic representations—that stretch across time and space. Put another way, ethnographers' traditional dependence on direct participation and observation—what can be participated in and observed firsthand—must be expanded. Ethnographers must find ways to learn about cultural forms and structural constraints that materially and symbolically organize people in and across times and spaces, as well as what can be "seen" and experienced by a positioned researcher-actor. However, such methodological issues are not the ones that have drawn the interest of most people who are presently engaged in discussions about improving ethnographic techniques, especially in educational research.

Conceptions of Ethnographic Methodology

Changes in ethnographic methodology have not necessarily kept pace with changing ideas about culture. Although feminist, ethnic, and postmodern critics have influenced the way ethnographers think about their relationships with study participants and the styles ethnographers use to write their accounts, methods of site selection, data collection and analysis remain virtually unchanged. In this section, I first review the conventional approach to ethnographic methodology; then I take up some of the challenges and proposed alternatives to it.

The Conventional View of Ethnographic Methodology

The conventional view of ethnographic methodology makes understanding culture dependent on an attentive researcher who comes to understand the lives of others primarily by watching them, listening to them, and participating with them. This firsthand acquaintance with the lives of others produces categories, concepts, pictures, and images that are close to the empirical domain, as others experience or "imagine" it (Blumer, 1969; Geertz, 1973b), and "that can successfully handle and accommodate the resistance offered by the empirical world under study" (Blumer, 1969, p. 23).

To the extent that older conceptions of culture have guided ethnographers' goals, studies have focused on different things and involved the researcher in different ways. For example, ethnographers with a conception of culture as way-of-life have pursued observations, interviews, and participation for the purpose of identifying the categories of activity (e.g., the uses of time, space, and language) that order and give direction to people's lives. The accounts these ethnographers produce describe the categories and suggest their implications for filtering people's experiences and attitudes (e.g., Heath's 1983 account of everyday life in Trackton and Roadville). For the most part, ethnographers working in this tradition have seen themselves as unobtrusive recorders of the flow of activity and faithful reporters of its characteristic patterns.

In contrast, ethnographers with an interpretive conception of culture as an "imaginative universe within which . . . acts are signs" (Geertz, 1973b, p. 13) pursue observations, interviews, and participation in order to grasp the significance others give to acts. As Erickson (1986) put it, interpretive ethnographers aim to be "empirical without being positivistic" (p. 120), to provide an "'objective' analysis . . . of 'subjective' meaning" (p. 127). The accounts these ethnographers produce attempt to represent the meanings (symbolism) of acts, as they are understood by participants (e.g., Geertz's 1973a account of a Balinese cockfight or his 1973b account of a Moroccan sheep raid). These researchers consider themselves active, reflective subjects, who produce the images, concepts, and understanding represented in ethnographic accounts, based on firsthand knowledge of others and deliberate scrutiny of one's own viewpoint in light of others'. However, regardless of the differences between these two groups of ethnographers, both consider the "reality" of others' worlds to be the constraint which checks bias and assures social science.

Challenges to Conventional Ethnography

The challenges to ethnographic research that have come from feminists, ethnic scholars, and postmodernists derive from concerns about perspective and power. In particular, these scholars have decried the one-sidedness of ethnographic procedures and accounts, which give the researcher exclusive control of the research design, the final account, and any subsequent uses of the material. For the most part, ethnographers have decided on the research questions to be asked and the kinds of information to be collected from others. In addition, they have been the ones to make interpretations of the information they collect and to author accounts of "what it's like to be a _____." Informants or study participants have had little say in what was done to them or written about them. Thus, critics have asked: Whose lives or views are really being represented in ethnographic research? If ethnographers purport to represent the lives of others, why don't "others" have greater voice in what is studied and how the results are presented, interpreted, or used? These concerns have led in two directions: to more collaborative models of the relationship between researcher and researched and to experiments in writing (so-called "textualist strategies") that allow more different perspectives or "voices" to be revealed in final accounts. Within anthropology and beyond, these issues have arguably been the most hotly debated topics in ethnographic methodology of the past decade.[8]

The Relationship of Researcher to Researched

Most contemporary critics of the conventional relationship of ethnographer to the people studied have called for more collaborative or "dialogic" relationships in which participants help to set the research agenda and contribute to the data collection, analysis, and writing. This alternative follows from the views of some feminist, ethnic, and postmodern scholars who argue that understanding is personally derived; that is, it is derived from one's negotiated position (identity) in a social context. These authors complain, in consequence, that a single-authored account of culture is no more than the subjective and partial view of one precisely situated person (Clough, 1992; Krieger, 1983,

1996; Richardson, 1990; Tyler, 1986). As such, it has no more claim to accuracy, authenticity, or comprehensiveness than anyone else's view. Further, because individuals' views are affected by the actual circumstances of their lives, views are likely to differ by race, class, gender, and other enduring inequities (such as who is likely to be the researcher and who the researched) that differentially constrain circumstances. One way to overcome these limitations is to involve more different kinds of people in designing the research process and creating the final product. Another is for the researcher to disclose more about his or her own views, commitments, and social position, that is, to become a subject of the research in the way other participants are.

Researchers working in the tradition of critical theory have also complained about conventional ethnography. The processes and products of ethnography, they claim, should do more than account for the actions of others; they should empower participants to take greater charge of their own lives (e.g., Anderson, 1989; Carspecken, 1996; Roman, 1992; Roman & Apple, 1990). Researchers can contribute to empowerment in several ways: by exposing the power inequities that shape a situation, including the research itself; by actively participating in consciousness-raising about power inequities in one's own and others' lives; and by actively taking steps to change unequal power relations.

These debates have made clearer how the ethnographer's social position, cultural perspective, and political stance affect the research relationships he or she forms and, in turn, how the research is done, what is learned, what is written, and what subsequent actions are taken. They also make clear that salient features of the ethnographer will necessarily vary in relation to the group she or he is studying, and that a careful ethnographer must be conscious of both the opportunities and constraints of his or her social relationships in the field and the choices of research relationships that are possible to make.

Writing Ethnography

Ethnography is inevitably a means of representation; accounts of what ethnographers learn from studying others are, as Geertz put it, "our own constructions of other people's constructions of what they and their compatriots are up to" (1973b, p. 9). Conventionally, ethnographers have written these accounts for people like themselves (not the "natives") to read. Recently, postmodern researchers have drawn a great deal of attention to "textualist" issues, that is, questions about how ethnographers write about other people (e.g., Clifford & Marcus, 1986; Van Maanen, 1988). Committed to a view of the researcher as active yet partial and positioned, postmodern scholars stress that ethnographers struggle with their own images or interpretations of an unfamiliar group and the need for written accounts to appeal to a familiar audience. As such, ethnographers inevitably tell about another group by drawing on literary conventions of persuasion that are familiar to them. Thus, it is not others' "reality" that constrains what is written, but the literary conventions

---

[8] Because these feminist, ethnic, and postmodern challenges to ethnography have been extensively discussed elsewhere—see Atkinson & Hammersley (1994); Clifford & Marcus (1986); Van Maanen (1988)—I review them only briefly here.

of inscribing (writing), narrative (storytelling), searching for understanding (formulaic ways of demonstrating that one has gained insight), and "sentimenting" (adding emotion and drama) with which the author is familiar (e.g., Atkinson, 1990; Clifford & Marcus, 1986; Clough, 1992).

Accepting that there is no neutral way of representing the world, postmodern ethnographers have dealt with the resulting anxiety by proposing to change writing, that is, to produce experimental ethnographic texts that present any one "reality" as contested, open-ended, and contingent (Clough, 1992; Marcus & Fischer, 1986, Van Maanen, 1988). Thus, we have impressionist accounts (Van Maanen, 1988), travelogues (Pratt, 1986), theoretical fiction (Cohen, 1993), ethnographic fiction (Tierney, 1993), ethnographic drama (Tanaka, 1997), multi-voiced accounts (Krieger, 1983; Lewis & Simon, 1986; Richardson, 1990; Shostak, 1981; Wolf, 1992), and autoethnography (Ellis, 1995)—all of which have been proposed as more honest as well as more circumspect ways of depicting ethnographic findings and the researcher's role in constructing them. In one way or another, all of these experimental writing strategies acknowledge the central interpretive role of the researcher, allow more voices to be represented in the final account, and leave final conclusions open or ambiguous. As such, they make readers skeptical of conventional, "realist" ethnographies, such as Heath's *Ways With Words* (1983), Willis's *Learning to Labor* (1977), Holland and Eisenhart's *Educated in Romance* (1990), and many others, which present one relatively uncontested, coherent view of culture.[9]

Interestingly, the textualist criticisms of ethnography assume, as Patricia Clough (1992) points out, a dubious distinction between field methods and writing, where the methods remain virtually the same, while the style of written presentation is changed. Field methods of firsthand participation, observation, and open-ended interviewing, as well as some systematic procedures of content analysis, are presupposed; then, the various writing experiments are suggested as better ways of reporting the researcher's findings and experiences. In Clough's (postmodern) view, these approaches ignore what, for her, is the key issue: That questions of ethnographic method have always been "about writing and reading practices and the technologies of their mass (re)production" (Clough, 1992, p. 136). In consequence, her suggestion is to do away with ethnography and replace it with "a social criticism that gives up on data collection and instead offers rereadings of representations in every form of information processing, empirical science, literature, film, television, and computer simulation" (1992, p. 137). This move away from empirical data collection and analysis in favor of textual deconstructions is common among postmodern critics of ethnography.

While the postmodernists are surely correct that ethnographies would be improved by including the interpretations of more and different voices and exercising more caution in forming relationships and making generalizations, they go too far when they suggest that there are no good reasons for ethnographers (or anyone else) to collect or analyze any more data about "other people." For educational researchers in particular, it is one thing to be careful about interpretations and generalizations, quite another to disengage from collecting data that might contribute to improving education. Policymakers and other decision makers will not stop trying to frame the experience of "others" in discourse or making plans that affect "others," while postmodernists deconstruct old accounts.

What is needed are powerful modes of representing what ethnographers know about the world, which, once "made transparent, public and capable of evaluation" (Agar, 1996, p. 13), can instruct but do not invalidate the informed views of others. (See Eisenhart & Howe, 1992, Maxwell, 1996, and Sanjek, 1990, for more detailed discussions of improving ethnographic validity without eliminating ethnography.) Historically, ethnographies of education that revealed experiences of nondominant groups have been used, with some success, to "move the world" (Agar, 1996, p. 13) toward more concern about and sensitivity to these groups and to their educational opportunities. These successes were not accomplished without some cost to participants' desires and voices. Yet, the dangers in this work do not cancel out the value of a research method that, unlike any other, tries to understand how people act in and make sense of their worlds and is committed to doing so before taking or supporting actions that affect those people (Harding & Livesay, 1984; Mc-Call, Ngeva, & Mbebe, 1997).

However, the debates about research relationships and writing styles do not address all of the methodological issues that new conceptions of culture pose. What about methods for investigating contemporary cultural phenomena, such as the mixed-up group affiliations and new technologies referred to in the first section of this chapter? What about methods for exploring the present circumstances, for example, of the families who participated in Heath's 1983 study of Trackton and Roadville? Writing about these families in 1996, Heath says:

> Fieldwork such as that behind *Ways with Words* [1983] has [become] impossible. Present day households and communities of children and youths lack the easily described boundaries of their parents. . . . In many of these households [in 1996], weeks go by when no two members of a household eat at the same time, share any chore, or plan work together. Hours go by when no one is anywhere near home. Over a decade ago, I could generally find the children of Roadville and Trackton at home or at school. Today, with no one at home to organize chores or to watch over play in the community, children and young people scatter and disappear. Youngest children are in daycare centers. School-age children go inside friends' houses to watch television or play video games; they crowd into the vans of community youth athletic leagues and move from sport to sport by season. . . . Older youths either race to their cars when the school bell rings and head for fast-food restaurants or malls, or ride the bus to one another's houses and then scatter to favorite gathering places with their friends. On the go, they listen to car radios or wear headphones and throb to the muffled beat of their compact discs or cassettes. Older and younger children segregate themselves by gender, activity, space, and sounds. . . . If the movement of adults and children in and out of households and their uses of space, time,

---

[9] But see Levinson (in press) for a discussion of the limitations encountered when trying to put ideas about collaboration and multiple voices into research practice.

work and leisure [have changed] so much, then ethnographers must develop new methods of seeing and understanding. . . . Now ethnographers must learn patterns of affiliation in numerous networks of different spaces and times, follow modes of physical transport and learn where [people] meet, and delineate technological means and sources of communication. (Heath, 1996, pp. 370–372)

Changes such as these seem to demand that educational ethnographers who want to understand contemporary culture must develop some additional (and nontextualist) methodological strategies. We need strategies, for example, to explore friendships and other relationships that stretch out across time and space, to identify brief encounters that have special significance, and to analyze activities and entertainment taken up locally but formed and controlled elsewhere. Especially if educational ethnographers intend to be helpful to teachers, students, and parents in the near future, we need ways to explore the new influences and developments which Heath's description so aptly captures.

Nontextualist Methods

In contrast to strategies that focus on collaborative research relationships or reflexive presentations as the means of correcting conventional ethnography, George Marcus (1995) has proposed what he calls "multisite ethnography" (see also Marcus & Fischer, 1986). Multisite ethnographies are

designed around chains, paths, threads, conjunctions, or juxtapositions of locations in which the ethnographer establishes some form of literal, physical presence, with an explicit, posited logic of association or connection among sites that in fact defines the argument of the ethnography (Marcus, 1995, p. 105). Strategies of quite literally following connections, associations, or putative relationships are thus at the very heart of designing multisited ethnographies. (Marcus, 1995, p. 97)

Put another way, multisited ethnographies would investigate the connections among sites that together make up arena of social practice, such as the complex arena of contemporary childhood socialization described by Heath (above).

Multisited ethnography seems an especially appropriate methodology for studying contemporary cultural productions. Using a multisited design, cultural forms taken up or produced in one locale would be followed and explored in other places, allowing a sense of connection to emerge by following paths of circulation. Marcus (1995) suggests several strategies for making this connection. First, ethnographers might follow the cultural productions of the same people when they move from one site to another, as in, for example, studies of young children talking about learning at home, in school, and after school; studies of students' discourse about "growing up" or otherwise socially differentiating themselves as they move from home to school, elementary school to middle school, high school to col-

lege, or school to work; or studies of teachers' discourse about "professionalization" as they move through different stages of their career or between their lives as teachers and parents. Second, ethnographers might examine one form of cultural production, for example, the discourse of computer technologies, or the meaning of "being somebody," as it appears in distinct but related groups, for example, among teachers and students, or among young people at school, at leisure, and at work. Third, ethnographers might follow a narrative or life history, where the salient "sites" are defined by a storyteller and then further explored by the researcher.[10] Finally, ethnographers might follow the discourse about an innovation or reform as it takes shape in various locales and later affects others, for example, the discourse about science education reform when formulated by policymakers and the discourse about the same thing among those who have to implement it. In Mike Rose's book, *Possible Lives* (1995), he tries to imagine what the effects of new educational reforms might be on the lively, impressive classrooms he studied:

We might ask ourselves how a particular proposal would advance or constrain the work we saw in a classroom that had special meaning for us, that caught us up in its intelligence and decency. Would that proposal create or restrict the conditions for other such classrooms to flourish? (Rose, 1995, p. 431)

Rose notes that some of the teachers he observed were discouraged by previous reforms, while others were inspired and motivated by them. Yet, he cannot say what makes the difference. Studies that develop research strategies for following educational reforms or innovations as cultural productions—as they form, are taken up, and compete with others in the lives of teachers, students, and others involved in education—might be able to identify the difference. Identifying the difference might be possible because studies of educational reforms-as-cultural-productions would focus broadly on the meanings and struggles that create the specific, local context for those involved with a reform to act and identify themselves in relation to others and wider scale projects (e.g., a national or state-level reform). A multisited study of cultural productions—such as the discourses of teachers involved in reform, the expressions of young people experiencing the reform, and the struggles of parents to prepare their children for an unknown future—would further offer a broad means of understanding how educational activities, concerns, and needs depend on and are constrained by each other.

Note, however, that multisited design puts conventional ethnographic method at stake in ways that "textualist" approaches to method do not (Marcus, 1995, p. 100). In a multisited design, the "specialness" of one site is lost; what is gained is the ability to make connections among distinctive discourses and practices from site to site. Similarly, in multisite design, the specialness of one "people" or group also is lost; attention is redirected to

---

[10] Studies of "narrative" have become a methodological type in educational research in recent years. See, for example, Riessman (1993) and the 1997 Theme Issue of *Teaching and Teacher Education,* "Narrative Perspectives on Research on Teacher Education." Although I think narrative research, inquiry, and analysis are important methodological approaches for educational research, I approach narratives as a form of cultural production, that is, as a meaningful, situated, and consequential construction of one's life in the world (Eisenhart, 1995a), similar to the way older anthropologists considered life histories to be one manifestation of culture, and not, as some have suggested, a distinct way of knowing.

the cultural forms that connect and construct various people in context, regardless of their previous social affiliations or cultural traditions.

This multisite approach also challenges the privileged position of the strange, the unfamiliar, the different, the subordinated—those groups for whom ethnographers' romantic and progressive impulses have historically been engaged. "[Questions] of resistance, although not forgotten, are often subordinated to different sorts of questions about the shape of systemic processes themselves [e.g., cultural productions] and complicities with these processes among variously positioned subjects" (Marcus, 1995, p. 101), including teachers, students, parents, researchers and their communities.

Marcus is vague about specific methods for collecting and analyzing multisite data. However, others grappling with similar issues have pointed out that, compared to previous ethnographers, ethnographers attempting to follow contemporary people, artifacts, or ideas from place to place are likely to face: more long-distance travel; greater dependence on interviews; greater reliance on what can be learned in short, intensive visits; increased use of electronic forms of communication, and greater attention to the analysis of significant events (in contrast to ongoing interactions) and of the material and symbolic interconnections among contexts, tools, and ideas (e.g., Moore, 1994; Nespor, 1994; Ortner, 1997; Rose, 1995). For ethnographers of education and researchers of teaching, the most profound implications would seem to be, first, the need to develop methods for obtaining information about cultural processes outside of school that bear on the people and outcomes of classrooms and schools; and, second, the need to develop ways of understanding how cultural processes inside and outside of school are interconnected, sustained, or changed. (See Heath & McLaughlin, 1993, for a multisite approach focused on differences between young people in youth organizations versus schools; Ogbu, 1981, for an approach that he calls "multilevel" ethnography; and Eisenhart and Finkel, 1998, for a multisite approach that explores science learning inside and outside of schools.) These considerations suggest the outline of a direction for new methodological strategies that can follow cultural forms, rather than specific groups, in contemporary society.

Conclusion

In comparison to the model of interpretive research outlined by Erickson (1986), cultural and ethnographic researchers today face greater demands to investigate contemporary cultural issues, more options for conducting their research, more issues regarding one's positioning as researcher and writer, and more questions about the validity of their findings and conclusions. These challenges are difficult ones, worthy of ethnographers' serious attention in the near future. In this chapter, I have argued that the revision and expansion of issues, choices, and questions is not a reason to give up on either culture or ethnography. It is, rather, a reason to pay careful attention to new cultural phenomena, new perspectives on culture, and strategic decisions about research design, methods, and reporting. It is also a reason to scale back hopes for universal appeal and to rededicate ourselves to making solid arguments for what ethnographers know and how we know it. As Signithia Fordham (1996) has

recently written, those empowered to write about culture are thus empowered to deeply affect the policies and practices perpetrated on those identified with culture. By the stroke of a pen, we may extend, reshape, transform thinking and perceptions of a group: "Our perceptions of an entire generation could be permanently altered as a result of these ethnographic images" (Fordham, 1996, p. 341). This is no small curse, privilege, or opportunity. The promise in this power is good enough reason not to abandon culture or ethnography, but to rearticulate their versatility and value, try to detach them from their oppressive complicities, and to apply them creatively to contemporary phenomena that affect teachers, students, policymakers, and educational researchers. We must follow cultural forms where we now find them and where they take us, be cognizant of our power and limitations, and figure out the methods we need to do so.

REFERENCES

Abu-Lughod, L. (1991). Writing against culture. In R. Fox (Ed.), *Recapturing anthropology: Working in the present* (pp. 137–162). Santa Fe, NM: School of American Research Press.

Agar, M. (1996). Schon wieder [already again]? Science in linguistic anthropology. *Anthropology Newsletter, 37*(1), 13.

Anderson, G. (1989). Critical ethnography in education: Origins, current status, and new directions. *Review of Educational Research, 59*(3), 249–270.

Anyon, J. (1981). Social class and school knowledge. *Curriculum Inquiry, 11*(1), 3–41.

Anzaldúa, G. (1987). *Borderlands/La frontera: The new mestiza.* San Francisco: Spinsters/Aunt Lute Book Company.

Appadurai, A. (1991). Global ethnoscapes: Notes and queries for a transnational anthropology. In R. Fox (Ed.), *Recapturing anthropology: Working in the present* (pp. 191–210). Santa Fe, NM: School of American Research Press.

Apple, M. (1979). *Ideology and curriculum.* London: Routledge and Kegan Paul.

Atkinson, P. (1990). *The ethnographic imagination: Textual constructions of reality.* New York: Routledge.

Atkinson, P., & Hammersley, M. (1994). Ethnography and participant observation. In N. Denzin & Y. Lincoln (Eds.), *Handbook of qualitative research* (pp. 248–261). Thousand Oaks, CA: Sage.

Blumer, H. (1969). *Symbolic interactionism.* Englewood Cliffs, NJ: Prentice-Hall.

Bourdieu, P. (1977). *Outline of a theory of practice.* Cambridge, England: Cambridge University Press.

Bourdieu, P. & Passeron, J.-C. (1977). *Reproduction in education, society, and culture.* London: Sage.

Bowles, S., & Gintis, H. (1976). *Schooling in capitalist American: Educational reform and the contradictions of economic life.* New York: Basic Books.

Brightman, R. (1995). Forget culture: Replacement, transcendence, reflexification. *Cultural Anthropology, 10*(4), 509–546.

Bruner, J. (1996). *The culture of education.* Cambridge, MA: Harvard University Press.

Carspecken, P. (1996). *Critical ethnography in educational research: A theoretical and practical guide.* New York: Routledge.

Clifford, J. (1986). Introduction: Partial truths. In J. Clifford & G. Marcus (Eds.), *Writing culture: The poetics and politics of ethnography* (pp. 1–26). Berkeley, CA: University of California Press.

Clifford, J. (1988). *The predicament of culture: Twentieth-century ethnography, literature, and art.* Cambridge, MA: Harvard University Press.

Clifford, J., & Marcus, G. (Eds.). (1986). *Writing culture: The poetics and politics of ethnography.* Berkeley, CA: University of California Press.

Clough, P. (1992). *The end(s) of ethnography.* Newbury Park, CA: Sage.

Cochran-Smith, M. (1991). Learning to teach against the grain. *Harvard Educational Review, 61*(3), 279–310.

Cohen, J. (1993). Constructing race at an urban high school: In their minds, their mouths, their hearts. In L. Weis & M. Fine (Eds.), *Beyond silenced voices: Class, race, and gender in United States schools* (pp. 289–308). Albany, NY: State University of New York Press.

Cole, M. (1996). *Cultural psychology: A once and future discipline.* Cambridge, MA: Harvard University Press.

D'Andrade, R., & Strauss, C. (Eds.). (1992). *Human motives and cultural models.* Cambridge, England: Cambridge University Press.

Davidson, A. (1996). *Making and molding identity in schools: Student narratives on race, gender, and academic engagement.* Albany, NY: State University of New York Press.

Deyhle, D. (1992, May). Constructing failure and maintaining cultural identity: Navajo and Ute school leavers. *Journal of American Indian Education, 31,* 21–36.

Deyhle, D., & Margonis, F. (1995). Navajo mothers and daughters: Schools, jobs, and the family. *Anthropology and Education Quarterly, 26*(2), 135–167.

diLeonardo, M. (1984). *The varieties of ethnic experience: Kinship, class, gender among California Italian-Americans.* Ithaca, NY: Cornell University Press.

Eckert, P. (1989). *Jocks and burnouts: Social categories and identity in the high school.* New York: Teachers College Press.

Eisenhart, M. (1995a). The fax, the jazz player, and the self-story teller: How *do* people organize culture? *Anthropology and Education Quarterly, 26*(1), 3–26.

Eisenhart, M. (1995b). Women scientists and the norm of gender neutrality at work. *Journal of Women and Minorities in Science and Engineering, 1*(3), 193–207.

Eisenhart, M., & Finkel, E. (1998). *Women's science: Learning and succeeding from the margins.* Chicago: University of Chicago Press.

Eisenhart, M., & Graue, M. E. (1993). Constructing cultural differences and educational achievement. In E. Jacob & C. Jordan (Eds.), *Minority education: Anthropological perspectives* (pp. 165–179). Norwood, NJ: Ablex.

Eisenhart, M., & Howe, K. (1992). Validity in educational research. In M. LeCompte, W. Millroy, & J. Preissle (Eds.), *The handbook of qualitative research in education* (pp. 643–680). San Diego, CA: Academic Press.

Ellis, C. (1995). *Final negotiations: A story of love, loss, and chronic illness.* Philadelphia: Temple University Press.

Erickson, F. (1986). Qualitative methods in research on teaching. In M. Wittrock (Ed.), *Handbook of research on teaching* (3rd ed., pp. 119–161). New York: Macmillan.

Florio-Ruane, S. (1991a, April). *A conversational interpretation of teacher/researcher collaboration.* Paper presented at the Center for Applied Research and Development, Manassas, VA.

Florio-Ruane, S. (1991b). Conversation and narrative in collaborative research: An ethnography of the written literacy forum. In C. Witherell & N. Noddings (Eds.), *Stories lives tell: Narrative and dialogue in education* (pp. 234–256). New York: Teachers College Press.

Foley, D. (1990). *Learning capitalist culture: Deep in the heart of Tejas.* Philadelphia: University of Pennsylvania Press.

Fordham, S. (1996). *Blacked out: Dilemmas of race, identity, and success in Capital High.* Chicago: University of Chicago Press.

Fordham, S., & Ogbu, J. (1986). Black students' school success: Coping with the burden of "acting white." *The Urban Review, 18*(3), 176–206.

Foucault, M. (1980). Two lectures. In *Power/knowledge: Selected interviews and other writings 1972–1977* (C. Gordon, Ed.) (pp. 78–108). New York: Pantheon Books.

Friedman, M. (1987). Feminism and modern friendship: Dislocating the community. In J. Arthur & W. Shaw (Eds.), *Justice and economic distribution* (pp. 304–319). Englewood Cliffs, NJ: Prentice-Hall.

Gartrell, N. (1991). Coming together: An interactive model of schooling. In M. Burawoy, J. Gamson, & A. Burton (Eds.), *Ethnography unbound: Power and resistance in the modern metropolis* (pp. 203–220). Berkeley, CA: University of California Press.

Geertz, C. (1973a). Deep play: Notes on the Balinese cockfight. In *The interpretation of cultures: Selected essays by Clifford Geertz* (pp. 412–453). New York: Basic Books.

Geertz, C. (1973b). Thick description: Toward an interpretive theory of culture. In *The interpretation of cultures. Selected essays by Clifford Geertz* (pp. 3–30). New York: Basic Books.

Gibson, M. (1993). The school performance of immigrant minorities: A comparative view. In E. Jacob & C. Jordan (Eds.), *Minority education: Anthropological perspectives* (pp. 113–128). Norwood, NJ: Ablex.

Goetz, J., & LeCompte, M. (1984). *Ethnography and qualitative design in educational research.* New York: Academic Press.

González, N. (1995). Processual approaches to multicultural education. *Journal of Applied Behavioral Science, 31*(2), 234–244.

González, N., Moll, L., Floyd-Tenery, M., Rivera, A., Rendón, P., Gonzales, R., & Amanti, C. (1995). Funds of knowledge for teaching in Latino households. *Urban Education, 29*(4), 443–470.

Haig-Brown, C. (1995). Two worlds together: Contradictions and curriculum in first nations adult science education. *Anthropology and Education Quarterly, 26*(2), 193–212.

Hall, S. (1980). Cultural studies: Two paradigms. *Media, Culture and Society, 2,* 57–72.

Harding, J., & Livesay, M. (1984). Anthropology and public policy. In G. McCall & G. Weber (Eds.), *Social science and public policy: The roles of academic disciplines in policy analysis* (pp. 51–90). Port Washington, NY: Associated Faculty Press.

Harkness, S., Super, C., & Keefer, C. (1992). Learning to be an American parent: How cultural models gain directive force. In R. D'Andrade & E. Strauss (Eds.), *Human motives and cultural models* (pp. 163–178). Cambridge, England: Cambridge University Press.

Heath, S. (1983). *Ways with words: Language, life and work in communications and classrooms.* Cambridge, UK: Cambridge University Press.

Heath, S. (1996). *Ways with words: Language, life, and work in communities and classrooms* (Reprinted with new 1966 Epilogue.). Cambridge, UK: Cambridge University Press.

Heath, S., & McLaughlin, M. (Eds.). (1993). *Identity and inner-city youth: Beyond ethnicity and gender.* New York: Teachers College Press.

Hemmings, A. (1996). Conflicting images? Being black and a model high school student. *Anthropology and Education Quarterly, 27*(1), 20–50.

Hicks, G., & Handler, M. (1978). Ethnicity, public policy and anthropologists. In E. Eddy & W. Partridge (Eds.), *Applied anthropology in America* (pp. 292–235). New York: Columbia University Press.

Holland, D., & Eisenhart, M. (1990). *Educated in romance: Women, achievement, and college culture.* Chicago: University of Chicago Press.

Holland, D., & Quinn, N. (Eds.) (1987). *Cultural models in language and thought.* Cambridge, UK: Cambridge University Press.

Holland, D., & Skinner, D. (1995). Contested ritual, contested femininities: (Re)forming self and society in a Nepali women's festival. *American Ethnologist, 22*(2), 279–305.

Howe, K. (1997). *Understanding equal educational opportunity: Social justice, democracy, and schooling.* New York: Teachers College Press.

Jacob, E., & Jordan, C. (Eds.). (1993). *Minority education: Anthropological perspectives.* Norwood, NJ: Ablex.

James, J. (1997, February). *Feminism and anti-racism in the academy: Then and now.* Talk presented at "Talking Across Disciplines," University of Colorado, Boulder, Colorado.

Johnson, R. (1986–87). What is cultural studies anyway? *Social Text,* 17–52.

Keesing, R. (1974). Theories of culture. *Annual Review of Anthropology, 3,* 73–97.

Kimball, S. (1976). The transmission of culture. In J. Roberts & S. Akinsanya (Eds.), *Schooling in cultural context: Anthropological studies in education* (pp. 257–271). New York: David McKay.

Kondo, D. (1990). *Crafting selves: Power, gender, and discourses of identity in a Japanese workplace.* Chicago: University of Chicago Press.

Krieger, S. (1983). *The mirror dance: Identity in a women's community.* Philadelphia: Temple University Press.

Krieger, S. (1996). Beyond subjectivity. In A. Lareau & J. Shultz (Eds.), *Journeys through ethnography: Realistic accounts of fieldwork* (pp. 177–194). Boulder, CO: Westview Press.

Kroeber, A., & Kluckhohn, C. (1952). Culture: A critical review of concepts and definitions. *Papers of the Peabody Museum of American Archaeology and Ethnology, 47.*

Levinson, B. (1996). Social difference and schooled identity at a Mexican *secundaria*. In B. Levinson, D. Foley, & D. Holland (Eds.), *The cultural production of the educated person: Critical ethnographies of schooling and local practices* (pp. 211–238). New York: State University of New York Press.

Levinson, B. (in press). The social commitment of the educational ethnographer: Notes on fieldwork in Mexico and the field of work in the United States. In J. Smyth (Ed.), *Being reflexive in critical educational and social research.* London: Falmer Press.

Levinson, B., Foley, D., & Holland, D. (Eds.). (1996). *The cultural production of the educated person: Critical ethnographies of schooling and local practices.* New York: State University of New York Press.

Levinson, B., & Holland, D. (1996). The cultural production of the educated person. In B. Levinson, D. Foley, & D. Holland (Eds.), *The cultural production of the educated person: Critical ethnographies of schooling and local practices* (pp. 1–54). New York: State University of New York Press.

Lewis, M., & Simon, R. (1986). A discourse not intended for her: Learning and teaching within patriarchy. *Harvard Educational Review, 56*(4), 457–472.

Lewis, O. (1973). The culture of poverty. In T. Weaver (Ed.), *To see ourselves: Anthropology and modern social issues* (pp. 234–240). Glenview, IL: Scott, Foresman and Company.

Luykx, A. (1996). From Indios to profesionales: Stereotypes and student resistance in Bolivian teacher training. In B. Levinson, D. Foley, & D. Holland (Eds.), *The cultural production of the educated person: Critical ethnographies of schooling and local practices* (pp. 239–272). New York: State University of New York Press.

Macías, J. (Ed.). (1996). Theme issue: Racial and ethnic exclusion in education and society. *Anthropology and Education Quarterly, 27*(2).

MacLeod, J. (1987). *Ain't no makin' it: Leveled aspirations in a low-income neighborhood.* Boulder, CO: Westview Press.

Marcus, G. (1995). Ethnography in/of the world system: The emergence of multi-site ethnography. *Annual Review of Anthropology, 24,* 95–117.

Marcus, G., & Fischer, M. (1986). *Anthropology as cultural critique: An experimental moment in the human sciences.* Chicago: University of Chicago Press.

Mascia-Lees, F., Sharpe, P., & Cohen, C. (1989). The postmodern turn in anthropology: Cautions from a feminist perspective. *Signs: Journal of Women in Culture and Society, 15*(1), 7–33.

Matute-Bianchi, M. (1986, November). Ethnic identity and patterns of school success and failure among Mexican-descent and Japanese American students in a California high school: An ethnographic analysis. *American Journal of Education, 95,* 233–235.

Maxwell, J. (1996). *Qualitative research design: An interpretive approach.* Thousand Oaks, CA: Sage.

McCall, G., Ngeva, J., & Mbebe, M. (1997). Mapping conflict cultures: Interpersonal disputing in a South African township. *Human Organization, 56*(1), 71–78.

McRobbie, A. (1980, Spring). Settling accounts with subcultures: A feminist critique. *Screen Education, 34,* 37–49.

Mehan, H., Villanueva, I., Hubbard, L., & Lintz, A. (1996). *Constructing school success: The consequences of untracking low-achieving students.* Cambridge, MA: Harvard University Press.

Miller, L. (1995). *An American imperative: Accelerating minority educational achievement.* New Haven, CT: Yale University Press.

Moore, S. (1994). The ethnography of the present and the analysis of process. In R. Borofsky (Ed.), *Assessing cultural anthropology* (pp. 362–374). New York: McGraw-Hill.

Narrative perspectives on research on teaching and teacher education (1997, theme issue). *Teaching and Teacher Education, 13*(1).

Nespor, J. (1994). *Knowledge in motion: Space, time and curriculum in undergraduate physics and management.* London: Falmer Press.

Noblit, G., & Pink, W. (Eds.). (1987). *Schooling in social context: Qualitative studies.* Norwood, NJ: Ablex.

Oakes, J. (1985). *Keeping track: How schools structure inequality.* New Haven, CT: Yale University Press.

Ogbu, J. (1978). *Minority education and caste: The American system in cross-cultural perspective.* New York: Academic Press.

Ogbu, J. (1981). School ethnography: A multilevel approach. *Anthropology and Education Quarterly, 12*(1), 3–29.

Ogbu, J. (1995a). Cultural problems in minority education: Their interpretations and consequences—part one: Theoretical background. *The Urban Review, 27*(3), 189–205.

Ogbu, J. (1995b). Cultural problems in minority education: Their interpretations and consequences—part two: Case studies. *The Urban Review, 27*(4), 271–297.

Ortner, S. (1991). Reading America: Preliminary notes on class and culture. In R. Fox (Ed.), *Recapturing anthropology* (pp. 163–189). Santa Fe, NM: School of American Research Press.

Ortner, S. (1997). Fieldwork in the postcommunity. *Anthropology and Humanism, 22*(1), 61–80.

Pratt, M. (1986). Fieldwork in common places. In J. Clifford & G. Marcus (Eds.), *Writing culture: The poetics and politics of ethnography* (pp. 27–50). Berkeley, CA: University of California Press.

Richardson, L. (1990). *Writing strategies: Reaching diverse audiences.* Newbury Park, CA: Sage.

Riessman, C. (1993). *Narrative analysis.* Newbury Park, CA: Sage.

Rodriguez, R. (1982). *Hunger of memory: The education of Richard Rodriguez.* Boston: David R. Godine.

Roman, L. (1992). The political significance of other ways of narrating ethnography: A feminist materialist approach. In M. LeCompte, W. Millroy, & J. Preissle (Eds.), *The handbook of qualitative research in education* (pp. 555–594). San Diego, CA: Academic Press.

Roman, L., & Apple, M. (1990). Is naturalism a move away from positivism? Materialist and feminist approaches to subjectivity in ethnographic research. In E. Eisner & A. Peshkin (Eds.), *Qualitative inquiry in education: The continuing debate* (pp. 38–73). New York: Teachers College Press.

Rosaldo, M., & Lamphere, L. (Eds.). (1974). *Woman, culture, and society.* Stanford, CA: Stanford University Press.

Rosaldo, R. (1989). *Culture and truth: The remaking of social analysis.* Boston: Beacon Press.

Rose, M. (1995). *Possible lives: The promise of public education in America.* New York: Penguin Books.

Sanjek, R. (1990). On ethnographic validity. In R. Sanjek (Ed.), *Fieldnotes: The makings of anthropology* (pp. 385–418). Ithaca, NY: Cornell University Press.

Shostak, M. (1981). *Nisa: The life and words of a !Kung woman.* Cambridge, UK: Cambridge University Press.

Spindler, G. (Ed.). (1982). *Doing the ethnography of schooling: Educational anthropology in action.* New York: Holt, Rinehart and Winston.

Spindler, G., & Spindler, L. (Eds.). (1994). *Pathways to cultural awareness: Cultural therapy with teachers and students.* Thousand Oaks, CA: Corwin.

Stocking, G. (1979). Anthropology as kulturkampf: Science and politics in the career of Franz Boas. In W. Goldschmidt (Ed.), *The uses of anthropology* (pp. 33–50). Washington, DC: American Anthropological Association.

Suárez-Orozco, M. (1993). Becoming somebody: Central American immigrants in U.S. inner-city schools. In E. Jacob & C. Jordan (Eds.), *Minority education: Anthropological perspectives* (pp. 129–143). Norwood, NJ: Ablex.

Tanaka, G. (1997, March). *Where is Mkhan'yasi? A fictional play as ethnography.* Paper presented at the American Educational Research Association, Chicago, IL.

Tierney, W. (1993). The cedar closet. *Qualitative studies in education, 6*(4), 303–314.

Trueba, H., Rodriguez, C., Zou, Y., & Cintron, J. (1993). *Healing multicultural America: Mexican immigrants rise to power in rural California.* London: Falmer Press.

Turner, T. (1993). Anthropology and multiculturalism: What is anthropology that multiculturalists should be mindful of? *Cultural Anthropology, 8*(4), 411–429.

Tyler, S. (1986). Post-modern ethnography: From document of the occult to occult document. In J. Clifford & G. Marcus (Eds.), *Writing culture: The poetics and politics of ethnography* (pp. 122–140). Berkeley, CA: University of California Press.

Van Maanen, J. (1988). *Tales of the field: On writing ethnography.* Chicago: University of Chicago Press.

Vogt, L., Jordan, C., & Tharp, R. (1993). Explaining school failure, producing school success: Two cases. In E. Jacob & C. Jordan (Eds.), *Minority education: Anthropological perspectives* (pp. 53–65). Norwood, NJ: Ablex.

Weis, L. (1990). *Working class without work: High school students in a de-industrializing economy.* New York: Routledge.

Wexler, P. (1992). *Becoming somebody: Toward a social psychology of school.* London: Falmer Press.

Willis, P. (1977). *Learning to labor: How working class kids get working class jobs.* New York: Columbia University Press.

Willis, P. (1981). Cultural production is different from cultural reproduction is different from social reproduction is different from reproduction. *Interchange, 12*(2–3), 48–67.

Willis, P. (1990). *Common culture: Symbolic work at play in the everyday cultures of the young.* Boulder, CO: Westview Press.

Wolf, M. (1992). *A thrice told tale: Feminism, postmodernism, and ethnographic responsibility.* Stanford, CA: Stanford University Press.

14.
Narrative Research on School Practice

Sigrún Gudmundsdóttir
Norwegian University of Science and Technology (NTNU)

In the 1960s and 1970s, the so-called "infant school" (ages 5–8) in England and Scotland was the toast of the education profession throughout Europe and the North American continent. It was called open education outside the United Kingdom—open not just in terms of architecture but also in the organization of learning activities. It was, and still is, considered by many teachers, parents, and teacher educators to be more child centered than traditional approaches, because it provides the right kind of educational environment for children to grow, prosper, and learn. Therefore, the publication in 1976 of a comparative study on informal (open) and formal (traditional) teaching methods caused a minor earthquake in the education community in the United Kingdom. This study showed that pupils being taught using formal methods consistently came out with higher test scores on standardized tests than those pupils being taught using the much praised open education approach (Bennett, 1976). It was a correlational study that correlated just about every measurable unit in sight. The researchers could not find any measure where informal teaching methods produced higher test scores. Bennett and associates realized, however, that numbers fail to capture certain aspects of open education. They felt compelled to present the best teacher in the whole study in a short narrative vignette (pp. 97–98). This teacher was an informal teacher. The lesson of this story is that narrative approaches capture better the complexities of classroom practice than do traditional research methods.

In this chapter, I am defining *teaching* as school practice to separate my unit of analysis from the more general terms *teaching* and *practice* because I am interested in practice that arises as a result of teaching in the context of classrooms and schools and because almost all empirical narrative research in educa-

tion is related to school practice. In this respect, I take my lead from Virginia Richardson (1994), who consistently uses "teaching practice" instead of just *practice* or *teaching*. I am using "school practice" because I am uncomfortable with the word *teaching*. By using "school practice," I am widening the unit of analysis to include not just what the teacher does but also what students learn as a result of experiencing school practice. I am reminded of Dewey's (1938/1963) comments when he equated teaching with "selling" and learning with "buying" in the question, "How can you sell anything if nobody buys?" (p. 19). Teaching, in my mind, focuses too much on what the teacher does. Narrative research as a field of study is developing specializations and subdivisions faster than most of us can keep up with them.[1] Within the research tradition that focuses on school practice, the narrative approach is almost exclusively associated with research on school practice, teacher or student-teacher biographies, and autobiographies.

The purpose of the chapter is to ground the narrative project in the cultural-historical activity theory (CHAT) tradition in psychology from where it receives much of its driving force. Within this tradition, narratives have been crowned as a mode of thinking, an expression of "culture's storehouse of knowledge" (Bruner, 1996), and not least as one of our culture's most important and complex meaning-making tools. This gives teachers' understanding about school practice and empirical inquiry a distinct and unmistakable narrative quality (Egan, 1988, 1989, 1995; Gudmundsdóttir, 1995). An important aim of the narrative project is to capture school practice and tell others about it in such a way that this central feature of practice is preserved and maintained. Narrative understanding is a slippery phenomenon to categorize. It is, in many cases, embedded

The author would like to thank reviewers Dana Fox, University of Arizona at Tucson, and Hunter McEwan, University of Hawaii at Manoa. For their helpful comments on earlier drafts, the author also wishes to thank Dorothy Vasquez-Levy, University of Virginia, and David Hansen, University of Illinois at Chicago, and for their informative comments on literature on cultural-historical activity theory (CHAT), the author thanks Carl Ratner, Humboldt State University, and Torlaug Hoel, Norwegian University of Science and Technology (NTNU).

[1] See, for example, Carter & Doyle (1996) for an excellent review of personal narrative and life history in learning to teach, Huberman (1989/1993, 1995) for teachers' life cycles, Butt & Raymond (1989) on teachers' autobiographies, Bloom (1996) and Middleton (1993, 1994, 1996) for a feminist perspective of life history, and a volume titled *Teachers' Stories* edited by Thomas (1995).

in school practice and can only be appropriately expressed in a narrative, because the central features of classrooms are meanings that are built upon other people's meanings and based on interpretations of other people's interpretations.

Narrative research on school practice offers the opportunity to define a researchable unit of analysis that preserves the notion of context. The unit must be a "living proportion of a unified whole that cannot be broken down further" (Vygotsky, 1934/1963, p. 9) and it must be capable of being maintained and developed, including self-development, although internal contradictions and dilemmas may exist. In this way, the unit of analysis can be properly examined in its ever shifting social context of an individual's life history, the institutional context, and the dynamic nature of practice. In narrative research, the primary unit of analysis is defined in terms of *mediated activity* (i.e., what people do, say, and think) in cultural contexts called "school practice."

School Practice as Mediated Activity

Like all human activity, school practice is culturally mediated. Even walking down a road is mediated by some forces. Walking, in that case, is mediated by the road makers who laid out the road according to some master plan that was conceptualized by the town planners and approved by the politicians elected to the city council. The way classrooms are physically set up with carpets and cushions in one corner and different sized tables mediates people's activities in that space. The way activities in classrooms and schools are organized has to do with historical traditions that stretch far back in time, the educational philosophy of the school, and teachers' interpretations of these. Also, specific cultural expectations with regard to the role of teachers mediate how teachers organize space and activities. Teachers inhabit the preculturally defined role of, for example, the kindergarten teacher, the high school English teacher, or the high school physical education teacher (who also may have another role to inhabit as that of the football coach). These different roles leave, of course, a great deal of freedom for individuals to carve out their own approach to the activities embedded in the professional roles as defined by Hansen (1998).

Yet, it is important to note that every action carried out and every word uttered within these roles belongs as much to the context, the role, and the cultural expectations assigned to the roles as they belong to the individual. Actions and words become part of teachers repertoires once they populate them with their ideas, ways of thinking about practice, children, learning, and goals, giving each teacher a distinct style that is firmly placed within a long and rich tradition. From the kindergarten teacher to the subject specialists in secondary schools, a community of like-minded teachers who share ideas about particular school practice precedes any young teacher entering the profession. Great teachers, real and fictional, past and present, who have written or had movies made about their practice have furnished the different roles with lasting images of what

schoolteachers can be at their best. These images, however, don't always travel well across cultures, and they travel even less well across age groups. In addition, each of us, upon entering the profession, does so with our favorite or most-hated teacher firmly printed in our mind. These images can mediate considerable influence on young teachers, in fact, one could say that the voices they represent ventriloquate through the individual teacher's school practice (Gudmundsdóttir & Hoel, 1997). These individual image-making teachers and a string of educational researchers and scholars are like characters in the sense that McIyntyre (1981/1985) proposes, because they shape the plot of past and present school practice and educational discourse in general. Furthermore, McIyntyre (1981/1985) claims that "the ability to recognize [the public figures] is socially crucial because a knowledge of the character provides an interpretation of the actions of those individuals who have assumed the character" (p. 27). These characters constrain, more than most people, the activities of the individuals who inhabit the preculturally defined roles. They carry, so to speak, the burden of the moral authority and integrity embedded in the various culturally predefined roles.

In short, actions and words carried out within a role are like a language in the sense that they exist out there—in other teachers' practices and serving other goals—and from these contexts, they are appropriated by the individual teacher, often through a long apprenticeship.

> Language [school practice] is not a neutral medium that passes freely into the property of people's [individual teachers'] intentions; it is populated—overpopulated—with the intentions of other people [teachers]. Expropriating it, forcing it to submit to one's own intentions and [style], is a difficult and complicated process. (Bakhtin, 1981)[2]

This means that every action and every word carried out within a role is only half the individual teacher's and half the tradition's. Teachers come to inhabit their roles in various ways: They may have acquired them accidentally, they may have chosen their roles, or they may have been called to them (Hansen, 1995).

The traditions that shape school practice have been handed down to each and every teacher since the Jesuits started teaching children in large groups. These traditions have a cultural aspect as each generation of teachers has interpreted the traditions in terms of their current cultural contexts. Moreover, these traditions have an institutional aspect in that the early descriptions of school practice dating back to 1800 appear remarkably similar on the surface to what we have today (i.e., 20–30 students, one teacher, one blackboard, desks in rows, and, often, the one teacher doing most of the talking, etc.). What has fundamentally changed, however, are the intentions (aims and goals), the roles for teachers to inhabit, the image of learning, the learning activities that teachers organize, and how we as teachers think and talk about children, learning, and teaching.

---

[2] Here I am paraphrasing Bakhtin (p. 294). I am replacing, "language," the word Bakhtin uses, with "school practice". Like language, practice carries meaning. I have put brackets around the words that I have replaced.

On the surface, the activities may well be similar, but the mediational forces assigning meaning to many of the activities have radically changed.

Semiotic mediation occurs when action is mediated by verbal and nonverbal signs and symbols of social origins. Vygotsky shows how, as an example of semiotic mediation, an infant's unsuccessful hand gesture acquires the meaning it has in our culture. It starts as a unsuccessful grasping movement by the infant. The caregiver steps in and assigns meaning to that gesture. The movement itself has not changed. The only thing that has changed in this instance is that now this movement has a meaning imposed upon it from the outside. Soon the infant will be using this pointing gesture because she or he has become conscious of the meaning of the gesture. As those of us who have been caregivers for infants know only too well, he or she will in turn be using this communicative gesture to mediate the activities of his or her caregivers. From the perspective of the young infant, she or he has considerably increased her or his communicative repertoire. Vygotsky observes that "the functions of the movement itself have undergone a change here: from a movement directed toward an object it has become a movement directed towards another human being" (Wertsch, 1981, p. 64). Semiotic mediation is directed from humans to other human beings and seeks to influence how they think and act. Just as God created man in his own image, according to the Old Testament, our culture seeks to shape its members in its own form through various forms of culturally mediated activities (Wertsch, 1981).

School practice is one of our cultures most important and complex mediation systems (Cole, 1997). Classrooms are imbued with meaning related to the special kind of social activity that takes place there. This meaning is primarily assigned to classrooms and schools by our culture but also by the individuals, concerned through their many years of experience, from the education system. Most of the goals for people's activities in classrooms are not their own—they are prescribed and handed to us by our culture through the various social relationships we have experienced in the education system. School practice in all its varied forms throughout the world is a system of social relations that is mediated by the different cultural and historical traditions. The concrete manifestations of practice in classrooms depend on the individuals concerned, their relationships, the social order they belong to, their predicament, and, of course, individual factors such as idiosyncratic interpretations. Just imagine with me, if you will, in a given culture or even in a given school, how many classrooms full of learning activities are physically the same yet feel so very different, sometimes, as if they belonged to a different world. If we remove people and their social relationships from classrooms, classrooms as such (where teachers organize learning activities for children) will not exist. They will be only empty shells with some objects inside.

The interest in narrative research within the community of researchers who are studying school practice enables these researchers to take a fresh look at the context of classroom processes, including the possibilities of having an impact on school practice by making the language of practice the central concern in our research. Feminist issues are present in most narrative research on school practice, practically by default. This is not surprising as the majority of teachers are women and the majority of narrative researchers who conduct research on school practice are former teachers themselves, both women and men, who speak the language of practice. Furthermore, narrative research on school practice is characterized by a careful attention to the researcher's interpretative authority for the narrative, the redefinition of the relevant ethical and moral issues, and the informant's voice.

Historical Background

Narrative descriptions of school practice are, however, not new. They date back to the late-18th and early-19th centuries, to the time of Schleiermacher and Dilthey. In Central and Northern Europe, this was a time when an active narrative discourse about school practice was taking place in newspapers, magazines, and privately funded monographs.[3] The contributors to that public discourse were not only teachers but also priests, farmers, novelists, and poets. Teachers contributed on equal footing with others, writing narrative descriptions of what they had done, because they had an urge to tell others about their experiences. These pieces were almost always normative and often contained an explicit moral message (Edvardsen, 1989; Røger, 1991; Strømnes, 1989). By 1850, several new universities had been founded in central and Northern Europe (and North America), and teacher training colleges had been established. A profession of teacher educators was born, and the consequence was that the teacher's voice in the official discourse fell silent. To legitimize education as a "scholarly discipline," teacher educators had to distance themselves from the narrative discourse practiced by teachers (Hopmann, in preparation). Teachers have, however, published, uninterrupted, in their own professional journals, and exceptional teachers have continued to this day to write narrative descriptions of their practices, often in monographs, that are read and valued by their colleagues and student teachers. Their voices ventriloquate through many teachers' school practice today. Current examples of this type of literature are Ashton-Warner (1963), Marshall (1963), and Paley (1990, 1995).[4]

The teacher's voice in the official discourse had been almost completely silenced around 1850, but the voice is emerging once again today, 140 years later, stronger and more forceful, as teacher educators and the younger profession of educational researchers focusing on school practice are rediscovering that narrative research lends itself to the description and analysis of practice. Narratives reemerge as a legitimate way of conducting research on school practice when teachers' voices are heard as coauthors of studies of their own practice, both in their autobiographies and as tellers of their stories in plain language. The

---

[3] According to Hopmann (in preparation), the professionalization of teacher educators took place at a later date in the United Kingdom.

[4] Vivian Paley's voice is even heard in today's official scientific discourse. Her narrative description of her inspiring practice is published in a volume edited by McEwan & Egan (1995), aptly titled *Narrative in Teaching, Learning, and Research*.

interest in narrative reemerges only when researchers become interested in school practice, and only then do we once more hear the teacher's voice in the scientific discourse about school practice.[5] This has become possible because interpretative research has been accepted as a legitimate way of conducting research in educational settings.

What is new, however, is the marriage of several traditions within research on school practice—narrative descriptions of school practice; research on teacher thinking, practical knowledge, teacher research, action research, and educational connoisseurship and criticism (with its close attention to the descriptive language of school practice)—to make what we now call the narrative research tradition in the study of school practice. Narrative research first reappeared within the teacher-thinking research tradition, especially with the distinct genre that developed in the early 1980s called "personal practical knowledge" (Elbaz, 1983; Clandinin, 1986). This research genre takes, as its primary unit of analysis, teachers' (and student teachers') practice and interpretations of the curriculum, their thoughts, beliefs, images, and their students' learning processes. The interest in the development of practice stems from Stenhouse's research group at the University of East Anglia in the United Kingdom in the 1970s. They named their work "action research" with an emphasis on *action*. The aim was to emancipate teachers through an understanding of the political context of school practice and improvements within their own practices.[6] Like action research, narrative research on school practice does not lack ambitions; indeed, it aims to make an impact on school practice by making the teachers involved as partners in the research, and it also aims to increase understanding of the central issues related to the dilemmas of school practice among the larger community of researchers who are conducting formal research on practice (Elbaz, 1997; V. Richardson, 1994; Richardson & Anders, 1994a, 1994b).

Narrative research on school practice is now, in fact, reemerging in the mainstream of the interpretative research family of traditions in the social sciences. Social science researchers, including educational researchers, are gradually abandoning their search for the one great truth. They are increasingly content with describing local processes, "small-scale theories fitted to specific problems and specific situations" (Lincoln, 1993, quoted in Denzin & Lincoln, 1994, p. 11) and events, involving small groups in social interactions, from the participants' perspectives. This has been facilitated by the emergence of what Denzin and Lincoln (1994) call the "fifth moment." It means that we have reached a new horizon in educational research "where messy, uncertain, multivoiced texts, cultural criticism, and new experimental works will become more common, as will more reflexive forms of fieldwork, analysis, and intertextual representation" (Denzin & Lincoln, 1994, p. 15). They also indicate that more engagement (action research) on the behalf of researchers in their research projects is "on the horizon," which fits neatly with the main thrust of narrative research on school practice. After all, school practice is the reason for the existence of our community. We, the community of researchers on school practice, have a moral obligation to ourselves and the community of practitioners (teachers) that we serve to be better informed about the dilemmas of practice so that we are better prepared to help them and ourselves to develop professionally. The narrative approach to research on school practice is appropriate for this task because the basic premise is that knowledge about classrooms is culturally constructed.

Narratives and Narrative Inquiry

What do we mean by *narrative* anyway? The term is highly ambiguous. In order to dispel some of the confusion of meaning in narrative research, Fenstermacher and Richardson (1994) have suggested the following categories: (a) narrative as "a piece of writing," (b) narrative inquiry, and (c) the use of narratives as pedagogical tools. My unit of analysis is, however, limited to narrative inquiry and empirical narrative studies as they are related to school practice or to what Clandinin and Connelly (1990) call the "phenomenon and the inquiry process."

The narrative approach moves research on school practice as a field of study out of the constraints that educational psychology has placed upon our community and enables us to move where we belong—into the realm of human sciences as conceptualized by Dilthey. Narrative as a research genre is a branch of interpretative research with roots in Schleiermacher's biblical scholarship of "Hermeneutische Wissenschaften" and Dilthey's "Geisteswissenschaften" (Erickson, 1986; Jank & Meyer, 1991).[7] Dilthey argued that the physical and human sciences are fundamentally different. One seeks to explain physical phenomena; the other seeks to promote understanding of human interaction—in this case, an understanding of school practice as it evolves in context-specific situations. The hermeneutic circle, or spiral as I would like to call it, is at the heart of a process of meaning making and meaning generating in interpretative research.[8]

Phillips (1992) argues for two types of hermeneutic interpretation. One involves general understanding through the use of symbolic systems where every act of comprehension is, by nature, hermeneutic. This Phillips calls "the weak hermeneutic program." The other involves the systematic use of hermeneutic interpretation as a research tool to approach participants' meanings in a given social interaction. Phillips calls this type of interpretation "the strong hermeneutic program." It is

---

[5] The genre of joint authorship of teacher-researcher research on practice is one of the fastest growing modes of scholarship on the North American continent. It started, however in the 1970s in the United Kingdom under the leadership of Lawrence Stenhouse. Today, it has been awarded its own "Special Interest Group" by the American Educational Research Association.

[6] Today, John Elliot and associates at the University of East Anglia have continued this important research tradition.

[7] See Palmer (1969/1985) for a general introduction to the field of hermeneutics and Phillips (1992) on the different types of hermeneutic understanding.

[8] I prefer, as does Dorothy Vasquez, the notion of the "hermeneutic spiral" rather than "circle," because a circle suggests closure rather than the promotion of an in-depth understanding.

also a kind of grounded theorizing (see Miles & Huberman, 1994) and is the type of data interpretation that is of primary interest in the narrative project.

The aim of interpretation is understanding, and the activity to achieve that is called "text analysis," or the strong hermeneutic program. Mediated action becomes text (or data, to be interpreted like a text) for the following reasons (Ricoeur, 1981).

1. By writing down a description of a mediated action, the action becomes *fixed*. This means that the action is no longer tied to the moment it occurred.

2. By fixing it, the mediated action has become *autonomized*. The action and the meaning have been detached from the moment, event, and persons and have assumed consequences of their own. They leave traces in the social space and become somewhat like artifacts of human activity through collective memory within institutions. Ricoeur points out that we "read" these traces in the social institutions we belong to. Morgan (1993), for example, describes how she set about changing the institutional narrative about a boy in her class. His unruly older siblings, who had attended the school before him, had contributed to a narrative in circulation among the staff that prejudged the boy as a troublemaker.

3. The mediated action can assume importance that goes beyond the initial situation and becomes relevant in other contexts. The episode has been emancipated from the original discourse and may now enter into new interpretative frames where it might assume meanings not intended by the person involved in the original action.

4. The mediated action (as text) is considered to be an open work where the meaning is addressed to a range of readers. "Like a text, human action is an open work, the meaning of which is 'in suspense'. It is because it 'opens up' new references and receives fresh relevance from them that human deeds are also waiting for fresh interpretations which decide their meaning" (Ricoeur, 1981, p. 208). This notion of mediated action as an open text makes it possible to engage in interpretation.

Furthermore, meaning is not just like some content that is thrust upon a text from the outside. Rather, the interactive process of text interpretation in research shapes meaning that was already there in the original mediated action and places it in a theoretical or narrative frame. The result—a "meaningful" text—functions as a generator of multiple new meanings in new contexts and for multiple readers (see Hoel, 1992, 1994; Fox, 1991). An important point to emphasize is that cultural traditions place considerable restriction on the interpretation of "open texts," making them "open" only to culture-specific interpretations.

Creating a narrative text is basically a hermeneutic interpretation, where the meaning of the parts is a function of the narrative as a whole and the meaning of the narrative as a whole depends on the meaning of the parts. Any narrative, fictional or research based, functions at two levels. The first level comprises the mediated actions that have been carefully selected out of a complex situation and have been fixed for inclusion in a narrative. By picking out one episode from a complex social situation, often involving many people, the event has already been infused with meaning, meaning ascribed to it by the narrative under construction, which is the second level. With the second level, the selected episodes (already infused with meaning) become the artifacts with which the narrator (or researcher) creates a narrative or story that will capture what the narrator experienced in such a way that the reader will gain a new insight and a new understanding of the larger issue behind the particular series of incidents. If no larger issue (societal or theoretical) can be found behind the narrative, it is a story best left untold.

Narratives are always told from a theoretical perspective or from the point of view of a larger issue, otherwise they are meaningless. Two researchers, Grant (1991) and Gudmundsdóttir (1991b), were working with different narratives (or theories) while doing fieldwork with the same teacher (at different times). Grant was telling a narrative about Susan Hall as a teacher of critical thinking. Gudmundsdóttir, through a process of grounded theorizing, was developing a narrative about Susan as an excellent teacher displaying impressive pedagogical content knowledge. In developing their stories, both attended to two levels of story making in research: (a) selection of episodes, and (b) combining the selected episodes into a narrative or a story. Both picked out similar episodes (first level) to place in their respective narratives or stories (second level) about her because they were so obvious and striking and so representative of Susan's practice. Both wrote narratives about the way she organized the learning of literature and asked interpretative questions about the literary work. Both researchers infused the second level episodes with different meaning because they were working from distinct theoretical perspectives. According to Susan Hall, although both narrative descriptions of her are so different that a stranger reading them would think that they are of two different teachers, they are in fact both true (Grant & Hall, 1991; Clark, 1991, 1995).[9] This trafficking between the parts (individual episodes—first level) and the whole (theory or the narrative—second level) and how they give meaning to each other constitutes narrative interpretation. Narrative interpretation refers to both the phenomenon under study (practice) and the inquiry process itself (Clandinin & Connelly, 1990).

Friendly critics of narrative research, such as Phillips (1994, 1997), make the point that narratives have to be "true." He is not referring to the possibility that the events reported did not happen. That is a problem for all research, not just narrative research. Phillips is concerned, and rightly so, with the way in which events are infused with meaning by selection, inclusion, or omission in a narrative. Some narratives are simply more "true" than others because they are better contextualized and have more appropriate interpretative frameworks (i.e., second level). However, one has good reason to be skeptical when narrative descriptions of practice—which are always local, provisional, and essentially personal—are used to generalize to situations and contexts where they are clearly out of place.

---

[9] See a set of papers by Shulman, Grant, Gudmundsdóttir, Grant & Hall, and Clark in a 1991 issue of *Journal of Curriculum Studies* 23(5).

Fenstermacher and Richardson (1993) propose that narratives as research reports are "different from the traditional research report," even different from the traditional qualitative or interpretative research report (p. 52). Narrative research is short on descriptions of data sources and analytic categories. As a piece of writing, narrative is closer to literature than social science because the structure is borrowed from literature, both oral and written. The better craftsmen and craftswomen we are, the more likely we are to tell a really good story. All good interpretative researchers, not just the narrative ones, are not only good at fieldwork and data interpretation, but they are also good storytellers in a very traditional sense. Good narrators in educational research owe their persuasive power as much to their narrative competence as to their research skills.

In the construction of a narrative of practice, researchers are always interpreters, situated as Roland Barthes says, between their experiences from the field and their efforts to make sense and describe these experiences. Narrative descriptions, like all descriptions, are never straight copies of the world in the way that a photocopy is a copy of a text. All descriptions, if they are to be meaningful, are also interpretations of other people's interpretations, and to engage in an interpretation is to step into the shoes of an author (Barthes?). Furthermore, as Barthes reminds us, an author is not the one who invents the most artistic tales but the one who achieves the greatest command over a particular culture's narrative codes.

Narratives as Cultural Scaffolds

The narration of experience comes naturally, like learning a language. From a cultural-historical perspective, the origin of thinking is to be found in language that has been appropriated. At the basic level, narrative is linked to language; "someone(s) or something(s) (a noun) acting on (a verb), and other aspects of language function as conceptual elaborations" or other artistic devices (Fuller, 1982). Language, however, is not the same as thinking but, instead, creates scaffolds, like narratives, for practicing talk and thereby facilitates the further appropriation of language into thought (Feldman, 1989). This means that young children learn to tell all sorts of narratives, short and long, as they are mastering the language. They put, for example, events into a temporal sequence or talk themselves through difficult tasks. This connection between language and thinking makes narratives one of the first cultural meaning-making tools appropriated by human beings in their first attempts at sorting out their social worlds.

As children have experiences, through participation in all sorts of social events in their infinite varieties, they also learn to tell stories about them. In this way, they also gradually learn what kind of meaning culture has imposed upon the different events (Nelson, 1989; Cole, 1997). Gradually, they realize that some events are taboo subjects while others are considered ac-

ceptable conversation topics, although the reasons are revealed to them only later in life. Thus, children and adults alike find themselves situated in a world full of meaning together with other human beings whose activities are based on cultural interpretation rather than on some mysterious "intra-psychic events or brute force" (Feldman, 1992). Through years of participation in a given cultural activity, people in all cultures gradually develop distinct ways of knowing about, understanding, and perceiving their shared physical and social reality. (See, for example, Alton-Lee, 1993; Cochran-Smith & Lytle; Clandinin, 1986; Connelly & Clandinin, 1988; Fox, 1993, 1995; Gudmundsdóttir, 1990, 1991, 1995; Hoel, 1997; Kyratzis & Green, 1997.) This way of knowing has been called the narrative mode of thought (Bruner, 1986) and it gives rise to a narrative tool for people to interpret their social experiences and tell others about it.

Thus, for children and adults alike, storytelling is a natural way to recount experience and a practical solution to a fundamental problem in life—creating a reasonable order out of experience. The history of any nation is a complex set of ideas and events needing someone to apply one of the meaning-making tools that are readily available all around us. When faced with the task of organizing the teaching and learning of U.S. history for teenagers in a Californian high school, Harry and David created several stories to address the chaotic situation they faced: textbooks that were "bad history," disjointed and conflicting curriculum requirements, and unmotivated students. They established several narrative structures in the curriculum in the fall and developed them through various activities throughout the year. Through these narrative structures, they were able to infuse the events selected for inclusion in the stories with their sense of what U.S. history is all about and what can be learned from it. These stories were organized so that they would not just capture all the major events in U.S. history but also would enable the two teachers to connect with current events (Gudmundsdóttir, 1988, 1991a).[10] Over the years, they had come to see this way of narrative curriculum making as a natural way of teaching. They both responded to my questions that asked if they knew other ways of curriculum making with another question: "Is there another way?"

Harry and David were experienced (and excellent) teachers and had strong feelings about U.S. history. The two student teachers, who I also studied, similarly, had strong feelings about their school practice. They were responsible for organizing the learning activities of social studies for first-year students. They faced the same chaotic situation as their more experienced teachers: bad textbooks, disjointed and conflicting curriculum requirements, and unmotivated and unruly students. They too tried to appropriate a narrative structure to create order in their curriculum, but found it problematic. They could figure out a story to encompass only one unit at a time. The next unit had another story that often had very little connection to the previ-

---

[10] The teachers were not aware that they used narrative structures to make meaning for themselves and their students. It took an outsider to put things into context. When I told them about the stories, they more or less agreed with me because it made sense. Where we disagreed, I checked my data and focused subsequent observations on the particular "story,"—the story of "Wars"—to gather evidence, both to confirm my story and also to contradict the idea. I met again with the teacher and laid out my evidence. We discussed it, and I explained how I interpreted specific episodes to come to this conclusion. He agreed and said that his moral views on the nature of wars were probably more integrated into his teaching than he was explicitly aware.

ous one. Interestingly, nobody told them to appropriate a narrative structure to create order in their curriculum and classroom (Gudmundsdóttir, 1990a). They did this intuitively and instinctively, like toddlers use narratives as an instrument to figure out how things work, what they mean, and to predict the future (Nelson, 1989). While Harry and David were able to work with several narrative structures in the curriculum that could be characterized as "extended novels," the novice teachers were able to establish only an anthology of "short stories."

Novices and experienced teachers alike intuitively engage in story making and storytelling because narratives are the ultimate teaching tool (Egan, 1988, 1995; Reinertsen, Nordtømme, Eidsvik, Weideman, & Gudmundsdóttir, 1996). For teachers, both young and veteran, the attraction of the narrative approach is that stories create order out of a chaotic situation. Order is achieved along several cognitive dimensions (Robinson & Hawpe, 1986): economy, selectivity, and familiarity. Economy means that narrative order can be applied to almost all aspects of our lives—past, present, and future—something the social studies curriculum deals with. Selectivity is vital, because we cannot pay equal attention to every detail in the curriculum; that is a sure way to a meaningless practice. Instead, the curriculum stories select events to be narrated (first level), assigns significance to them (second level), and places them in the stories. Familiarity is achieved by repetition and the creation of similar accounts of typical events. This makes stories told within a tradition more familiar than stories told in strange settings. Not surprisingly, many experienced teachers probably appropriate the narrative as a meaning-making tool to organize the curriculum, not only to make sense for themselves as teachers but also to aid student learning and thereby link themselves, the subject they are responsible for, and their students to "culture's storehouse of knowledge and procedures" (Bruner & Lucariello, 1989).

Although the narrative is the ultimate organizing tool, a large measure of agency is always present, because the way narratives are organized always involves interpretations of other people's interpretations, be it a textbook or interactions. Besides, no one could tell all there is to tell. In addition, considerable restrictions are imposed on the narrator by the context, audience, medium, and genre chosen for the telling of the story. All these aspects place restrictions on the story making and the storytelling as meaning-making tools and, at the same time, provide the stage for us to exercise agency in our meaning-making activities in the classroom.

Culture supplies a range of narratives for our individual meaning-making activities and keeps generating new forms of subjectivity for us to adopt as we mediate between narratives furnished by our culture and our efforts at organizing experiences and emotions. In this process, the self is not autonomous but is, instead, contingent upon the intersubjective nature of language and culture. In this way, narratives function like scaffolds or scripts to help us make sense and give us the oppor-

tunity to climb to higher ground mentally and intellectually. We use narratives in research on school practice to organize experience so that we can tell others about it and, therefore, initiate the kind of dialogue that is necessary for the type of reflection that is an essential part of the development of any language of practice. When we narrate our experiences in various types of publications, we are, in fact, putting our experiences and ideas into circulation among our colleagues and contributing to a collective enterprise of meaning making about the complexities of practice. The appeal of narrative research as the privileged approach to research on school practice is closely related to the fact that this research approach appropriates culture's primary meaning-making tool. We use narratives all the time because social reality presents itself to us, to a great extent, as a narrative. As a research approach, it mirrors how we, as social beings, make sense of complex social situations every day of our lives.

Narratives, cultural and individual, are emerging as primary units of analysis in the cultural theory of cognition that is inspired by Vygotsky and his Western interpreters in social psychology, education, and cultural anthropology (Kessen, 1993).[11] Vygotski argued that individual responses emerge from the collective life. Moreover, he suggested that intellectual development takes place on two planes: first, on the intermental plane, that is, between people in social interactions; and second, on the intramental plane, that is, the appropriation of the intermental processes (Vygotsky, 1987). This implies that higher mental functions such as thinking, reflection, reasoning, problem solving, or logical memory are carried out in collaboration with others in social and cultural settings (the intermental plane). Narratives exist on the intermental plane, and through a process of appropriation, they become part of an individual's intramental plane. This does not mean that individual narratives are identical copies of cultural narratives; rather, an intrinsic dependency occurs between social activity (the intermental plane) and internal processes (the intramental plane). External social structures are transformed in each member of a given culture to create internal processes. In Leont'ev's (1981) words, "the process of internalization is not the transferal of an external activity to a preexisting internal plane of 'consciousness': it is the process in which this plane is *formed* [italics in original text]" (p. 57). In this way, individual narratives are only restricted variations of larger narratives supplied by our culture (see also Cole, 1985/1995; Hohr, 1996; Ratner, 1991a, 1991b).

Language, both written and spoken, plays a central role in the appropriation of higher mental processes.[12] The appropriation of mediated action is assisted by repeated participation in social interactions in settings such as the kitchen, classroom, and living room. The furniture and tools in these spaces are intended for certain activities. One cooks in kitchens, teaches or learns in classrooms, and socializes in living rooms. Each social setting provides the goal for the activities and defines the frames for appropriate action and the thinking (and emotions) associ-

---

[11] According to Carl Ratner (personal communication, July 1997), Vygotsky never explicitly mentions the word *narrative* in his writings that have been translated into English. His Western interpreters have called their own ideas "narratives," ideas they have derived from Vygotsky's cultural theory of cognition. Much of the work of the Russian scholars is not available in complete translations. What we have instead are the ideas of Vygotsky and Bakhtin ventriloquating through the writing of Bruner, Ratner, and the various publications by Wertsch.

[12] This, of course, has implications for teacher education (see Phelan et al., 1995; Marble, 1997).

ated with each activity. What is important here is that these goals are not our own. Like narratives, they are supplied by our culture (Nelson, 1981). We never question these goals. No one ever explicitly teaches them to us, and we never explicitly learn them. We unconsciously and effortlessly "take them over" as if they have always been ours. These culturally supplied goals for our actions and thinking give rise to the social origins of narratives (Tulviste, 1991).

The Language of Practice

School practice, like any other human activity, is situated in an institutional, historical, and cultural setting. Such settings are associated with the disciplines that have traditionally supplied the field of educational studies with substantive theories and research methodology, giving rise to "*dimension or ways of looking*" at classrooms (Wertsch, 1991). Narrative research enables researchers to define their unit of analysis in a way that cuts across disciplinary boundaries and, at the same time, preserves, in clearly defined units of analysis, as many aspects of the context as possible for a meaningful, systematic, and disciplined inquiry.

Descriptions of school practice begin with the assumption that, like most socially and culturally situated activities, practice is primarily mediated activity, hence, it cannot be stripped of its context. Therefore, the key to any description of school practice, narrative or otherwise, is the notion of the language of practice (Taylor, 1985). It is this "language," Taylor claimed, that "marks distinctions among different possible social acts, relations, [and] structure" (p. 32). Consider the game of chess, for instance. No such thing as the game of chess would exist without the specified checkered board, the specific pieces (called pawns, queens, kings, rooks, bishops, etc.), and the rules for moving them around the board. The vocabulary of chess, such as the concept of the "Sicilian defense," pertains to specific ways to move specific pieces at particular times in a game. Chess, like any other organized social activity, has its own language and systems. For chess, this language describes the practice of playing chess and systems are in place to record the moves. To learn to play chess, one has to master the moves and the language of the practice of playing chess.

However, this analogy of the game of chess has a limitation. Classrooms are not checkered boards populated by lifeless wooden pieces, and even the average teacher is no grand master with thousands of variations of the "Sicilian defense" stored on a computer and in his or her mind to be activated in a cool and calculated manner. But considerable evidence from cultural-historical research in social psychology has been gathered on the connection between language, thought, and action. This body of research and scholarship offers insight into how adults can use language to analyze (or reflect on) complex social situations, a process that can lead to a better understanding and can often result in an improvement in practice (Gudmundsdóttir & Hoel, 1996, 1997; Moen, Dypvik, & Gudmundsdóttir, 1998; Moen & Gudmundsdóttir, 1997; Nilssen, Wangsmo-Cappelen, & Gudmundsdóttir, 1996; Nilssen, Gudmundsdóttir, & Wangsmo-Cappelen, 1999; Reinertsen et al., 1996).

To have a "school practice" one needs an institution, a teacher and students, a curriculum, and the mandate for the teacher to organize learning activities for these students. These social and cultural divisions make further distinctions possible, both in practice and in language, such as learners, learning, subject matter, group work, assignments, grades, assessment, achievement, class discussions, and so on, creating the foundation for a language of school practice. Taylor's point is that this vocabulary does not exist without being embedded in culturally meaningful activities in the classroom. Although the same vocabulary exists in most schools throughout the Western world, it does not always have the same meaning for every teacher role, in any institution, or in any culture. For example, the ideas of *teaching, learning,* and *achieving* carry different meaning in a small infant school in England than in a big American inner-city school. The words are only applications of social life. Without the activities, the words have no meaning. If talking about what it means to teach, learn, and achieve helps to clarify things, then the talking lends support to the claim that "changes in the language of practice . . . are to be seen as changes in the practice itself" (Phelan, McEwan, & Pateman, 1995; see also Morgan, 1993; Richardson & Anders, 1994a, 1994b; Richardson & Hamilton, 1994; Vasquez-Levy, 1993). This interdependence of language and practice is what the cultural-historical school of activity theory in social psychology means by mediated activity.

Taylor's notion of the language of practice makes mediated action an important unit of analysis in all research on social practice. Taylor's notion of the "language of practice" and Bakhtin's (1986) "speech genre" are basically parallel concepts explicating similar social and cultural phenomena. "A speech genre," according to Bakhtin (p. 87), "is not a form of language but a typical form of utterance; as such the genre also includes a certain typical kind of expression that inheres in it." In America, a common greeting is How are you? When uttered as a greeting, this is not a question about health (which it is when the person asking is a doctor on his or her round of the hospital ward). Bakhtin continues "In the genre, the word acquires a particular typical expression. Genres correspond to typical situations of speech communication, typical themes, and, consequently, also particular contacts between the meaning of words and actual concrete reality under typical circumstances" (p. 87). We have different languages of practice for different social and cultural contexts, like a flexible tool kit for use in different social situations. Different contexts have their own languages that are privileged in that situation. An important social skill is to know when to use a particular language of practice, that is, to know in what contexts each language of practice is privileged. For example, we academics speak one language at conferences when making presentations, another when socializing with our friends and colleagues, and yet another language in classrooms. The notion of genre emphasizes the two primary functions of language at work simultaneously, the generative and the enclosing functions. A language needs to be generative in order to function as a tool for self-development. But to function in such a way, it also needs to be able to enclose or crystallize ideas into actions and concepts to facilitate self-development. The notion of genre is essentially another hermeneutic spiral, as are all interpretative activities in which people engage.

The idea of a language of practice assumes that speakers and

actors do not have the kind of freedom that Saussure's notion of *parole* suggests.[13] Saussure suggested that a speaker has
complete freedom to choose, at will, words to combine into
sentences (Saussure, 1914/1974, p. 14). Bakhtin disagrees and
points out that a speaker speaking a language of practice depends upon historical traditions and institutional contexts to
combine thoughts and express utterances both in words and
through the communicative context (Bakhtin, 1986/1996). Moreover, an utterance is always made in response to something
that was uttered before and is expressed also in anticipation
of an answer. Although each utterance is individual in a grammatical sense, the context or social situation in which it is typically used develops its own relatively stable types of these utterances. In this way, the language of playing chess, obviously,
would be completely out of place in the classroom, just as the
language of the classroom would be out of place in the context
of a chess game. The language of school practice is, therefore,
more than just words, it is a cultural reservoir of beliefs, ideas,
ways of doing and seeing, all embedded in a distinct social activity—rather a kind of heteroglossia, to invoke Bakhtin's
(1994) vocabulary. Heteroglossia is

> a perception of language as ideologically saturated and stratified.
> The many social languages participating in heteroglossia at any spe-
> cific moment of its historical existence are all specific points of view
> on the world, forms of conceptualising the world in words. Any so-
> cial language is a concrete socio-linguistic belief system that is uni-
> tary only in the abstract. (pp. 15–16)

In this way, the language of practice does not reflect the social
reality of practice but, instead, produces meaning and, therefore, creates reality. Through the language of practice, social
organizations and relationships are defined and tried out, and
the language of practice becomes the place where our identity
as teachers and researchers, our subjectivity, is conceived. The
language of practice is associated with a special group of
people, or voices, whose collective belief systems ventriloquate
through the language of practice. This culturally situated
"voice" resonates through the individual teachers' (or student
teachers') voices that speak in the many narrative case studies
that have been written within the narrative tradition in research
on school practice. (See, for example, Clandinin, 1986; Connelly & Clandinin, 1988; Elbaz, 1983; Fox, 1995; Thomas, 1995;
Gudmundsdóttir, 1990a, 1990b; Gudmundsdóttir & Hoel,
1996; Kyratzis & Green, 1997; and Alton-Lee, 1993, 1998.)

The language of school practice is the privileged mode of
talking about practice. One could say that a language of practice is privileged to a particular social situation when the participants have achieved such a high degree of intersubjectivity
that they often speak in incomplete sentences or express incomplete thoughts and that the conversation partners automatically
and unconsciously fill in the right missing words with the right
meaning and infuse them with the appropriate emotional expressions. It is a kind of "active understanding" that has been
described by Bakhtin (1994) as the type of understanding that
integrates ideas and words being discussed into a new concep-

tual framework and, in the process, establishes a new network
of ideas that enrich the idea being discussed. "It is precisely
such understanding that the speaker counts on" (p. 76), and
it is this kind of understanding that makes the community of
practitioners who are speaking the language of school practice
feel that their language is the only possible way to express their
thoughts and ideas, even though other modes are theoretically
possible.

Research within different subject matter areas suggests that
learning each subject also involves learning the language of that
subject, or the subjects' subcultures in the words of Grossman
and Stodolsky (1995). Hoel's (1994, 1997) and Fox's (1991)
work on learning and writing about literature suggests that
learning the language of the subculture of literature involves
learning to recognize and hear voices ventriloquating through
the poem, the novel, or the short story that students are working
with. Moreover, Fox's (1996) and Grant's (1995) work on the
portfolio in teacher education shows that learning the language
of practice can be an instrument for claiming one's own voice,
not just repeating someone else's narrative, and for developing
one's own language of practice. Grossman and Stodolsky (1995)
suggest that other subject areas, or subcultures, have their own
language of practice with roots in teaching the particular subject and the parent discipline. (See also Olson, 1977; Marton,
1981; and Säljø, 1988.)

The conversation between those who speak the same language of practice is both the means and the end in that, by
engaging in a dialogue using the language of practice, the language itself changes. This dynamic quality makes the language
of practice capable of self-development. This happens through
a process of collective reflection with conversation partners.
Through this dialogue, interlocutors have the opportunity to
define the situation anew, often in surprising and creative ways.
Huberman's (1989/1993, 1995) study of the lives and experiences of some 160 Swiss teachers is a good example of how
important it is for researchers to be well versed in the language
of school practice and how that skill enables them to engage
in a collective reflective conversation with a teacher that ensures a rich collection of data. Huberman and his coworkers
asked the teachers if they could divide their careers as teachers into periods. None of the teachers had ever thought about
his or her career in these terms. The planned 1 1/2-hour interviews frequently stretched much longer, sometimes lasting several hours.

The language of practice has all the hallmarks of a practice
discourse (Fenstermacher, 1994a). This type of discourse can
be developed through practical arguments. (See the series of
three papers about the theory of practical arguments by Fenstermacher & Richardson, 1993; Morgan, 1993; and Vasquez-
Levy, 1993 in the *Journal of Curriculum Studies*. See also Pendlebury, 1990, about the role of context in shaping practical
arguments.) Central to the development of practical arguments
is the notion of the "Other" in conversations with the teacher
(Fenstermacher & Richardson, 1993; Fenstermacher, 1994b;
Richardson & Hamilton, 1994). This "Other" can be a researcher, a group engaged in a collective activity to change

---

[13] The way Bakhtin uses "communication" in general may come close to Saussure's *parole.*

practice, or it can be also a slice of the self, constructed for the purpose of engaging in dialogue with the teacher about practice. In short, the Other is someone who speaks the language of practice and is there to ask the teacher questions and to guide the teacher along. When Vasquez-Levy (personal communication, April 1997) met her three informants for the first time, they practically "interviewed" her to find out what her "credibility rating" was. One of them wanted to know if she had taught school, "in a real school and lately, too"; in other words, he wanted to know if Vasquez-Levy spoke the language of practice.

Collective reflection between the teacher and the Other has the power to transform and generate change in practice. This dialogue aims to systematically develop justifications that are appropriate for the nature of practice, using the language of practice. This kind of dialogue "may hold more promise for broadening and deepening our understanding of practical knowledge" (Fenstermacher, 1994b, p. 48). This dialogue is well documented in empirical studies on practical arguments (Morgan, 1993; Vasquez-Levy, 1993) where changes in practice were a result of changing the language of practice. One of Vasquez-Levy's informants said, "My beliefs and my actions have changed. I've noticed my language has changed too" (p. 137). Basically, practical arguments, as proposed by Fenstermacher and Richardson (1993) and Fenstermacher (1994b), are systematic and structured reflection over belief systems and actions (semiotic mediation). Practical arguments involve using the language of practice to bring to the surface people's deepest held moral values and beliefs about practice and to explore their manifestations in practice. The plots in the narratives are the premises formulated for the development of practical arguments. The characters are the teachers, who are trying to understand their practice and perhaps change it, and the children, who do not respond as well as they should (Morgan, 1993). This is the very stuff narratives are made of both in research on school practice and in our culture at large.

The questions the Other asks focus on "non-trivial aspects of practice" (Morgan, 1993) as defined by the teacher and shake the teacher out of fossilized routines to initiate a conscious and voluntary examination. Then, and only then, can the language of practice develop in such a way that it can lead to change in practice. The process is long and painful as studies by Morgan (1993), Vasquez-Levy (1993), and Richardson and Anders (1990) show—a process in which the Other needs considerable expertise in addition to fluency in the language of practice. It is guided first by the external Other through explicit reflective dialogue, and then it becomes internalized and routinized as illustrated by one of Vasquez-Levy's informants.[14]

If the cultural reservoir of practice is ventriloquated through the language of practice, then the language of practice, in turn, speaks through narrative inquiry, because it is the privileged mode of capturing and expressing school practice. This feeling of the narrative being privileged in relation to research on school practice most likely encouraged Kathy Carter (1993, 1995) and Walter Doyle (1997) to say that the story is the best way to describe practice. Other modes are theoretically possible, but because both Carter and Doyle are well versed in the language of practice as well as the language of educational research, they clearly believe that narrative research is the only possible way of expressing the language of school practice.

The notion of a language of practice has implications for voice and ethical issues in all interpretative research on school practice. The implication is that ethical issues need to be redefined, and the notion of voice assumes a wider meaning than is currently in circulation among students of school practice. The wider meaning of voice is related to a community of practitioners whose shared beliefs and practices ventriloquate through any individual speaking about school practice, including both teachers and researchers conducting research on practice.

Voice

Almost all researchers and scholars who study school practice refer to voice as the informant's voice. Some, such as Hardgreaves (1996), treat voice almost as if it is fully formed, laying around in contexts, waiting to be turned on by like a tape recorder. The notion of voice that I am promoting is that voice is intimately interconnected with culture, meaning, and mediated activity as is suggested by the empirical work of Acker (1997), Alton-Lee (1993), Clandinin and Connelly (1990), Elbaz (1983), Feuerverger (1997), Fox (1996), Grant (1995), Hoel (1994, 1997), Hollingsworth (1992), Kyratzis and Green (1997), and Richert (1992). In my view, voice is neither turned on nor created. Voices are claimed in the process of collaborative narrative inquiry. One finds no singular voice, because any claimed voice is a heteroglossia of culturally situated voices that ventriloquate through the singular voice that is claimed by an individual. Moreover, one finds no logical beginning (nor an end, for that matter) in regard to a narrating voice. This is recognized by the aviator Beryl Markham (1942/1988) in the opening words of her autobiography: "I should like to begin at the beginning, patiently like a weaver at his loom. I should like to say, 'This is the place to start; there is no other'" (p. 3). Her starting point was an entry in her pilot's log. She starts at Nungawe, an obscure town somewhere on the vast African continent, randomly chosen, because it is "as good as any other."[15] Bagnold (1988) ends his autobiography after a long and adventurous career as a desert explorer with these words: "The proper point at which to end an autobiography is when it becomes unlikely there will be anything further to narrate." Echoing Markham, he says "The age of ninety-one seems a good time [to end]" (p. 196). For both Markham and Bagnold, they find no logical place to start and conclude a narrative.

---

[14] The process of changing practice through practical arguments as described by Fenstermacher & Richardson (1993), Morgan (1993), Vasquez-Levy (1993) and Richardson & Anders (1990, 1994a, 1994b; Richardson & Hamilton, 1994), shares many important similarities with the model proposed by Tharp & Gallimore (1988/1995) concerning "the four stages of the Zone for Proximal Development and beyond."

[15] Beryl Markham was the contemporary in Kenya of Baroness Karen Blixen. She was the first woman to fly across the Atlantic. Characteristically, she flew the Atlantic, not gliding with the eastward wind like Lindbergh did, but against the wind, that is, against the prevailing west winds that blow across the Atlantic ocean from west to east.

In a profession rich in traditions that stretch as far back in history as school practice does, many voices can be claimed and developed into one's own voice either through a process of collaboration or interaction with an Other or through artifacts of practice—the artifacts being a portfolio, developed practical arguments, and the various forms of research texts that involve the use of the language of practice. The process of claiming voice is basically an interaction between an individual's beliefs and experiences (intramental plane) and external voices of practice as manifested in the Other and in the artifacts of practice (intermental plane). The individual's meaning comes into contact with external voices of practice. Through structured interaction between these two, the teacher's meaning changes—as in Fox's (1996), Grant's (1995), and Richert's (1992) work on portfolio in which the concept of the portfolio becomes a site where a heteroglossia of voices are sounded—and the individuals who are compiling their own portfolios cannot escape hearing these voices and are compelled to claim several of them as their own. The implication is that the individual teacher's meaning and understanding is always multivoiced.

With this multivoicedness comes the invisible baggage of our culture's ideologies and ethical issues revealing unequal power relationships. When we as narrative researchers put our ideas into circulation among our colleagues through our narratives, we may at times be doing the narrative project and school practice more harm than good. Narratives, as McEwan (1997) observes, are not always emancipatory; they can also be coercive. Sometimes we, through our narratives of practice, may end up reproducing the gendered, hierarchical, and patriarchal structure of our culture. Our concern with voice should also be extended to a redefinition of subjectivity, from a unitary subjectivity in which individuals are assumed to be unique, fixed, individual, and coherent to a nonunitary subjectivity, where language, ethical issues, relationships, social interactions, pivotal experiences, and development are central (Bloom, 1996). In practice, nonunitary subjectivity leads to honesty in admitting failures and in criticizing one's own subjectivity. The very act of narrating a nonunitary self permits greater self-knowledge that is not just emancipatory but can also lead to improvements in practice.[16]

Our culture promotes unitary subjectivity, especially through the meaning-making tools it provides us with—the narratives. Unitary subjectivity is a myth, claims Bloom, promoted by the masculine domination in our culture. As a result, women's subjectivity is "continually fragmenting from daily experiences from living with the pervasive hierarchical, patriarchal structuring of sexual differences through which women learn to internalize negative and conflicting ideas about what it means to live as a woman" (Bloom, 1996, p. 178). The challenge for us researchers is to improve at interpreting nonunitary subjectivities in the self-representations we face in our work with our informants and to be alert about how nonunitary subjectivity is produced and reproduced in our own narratives of practice. Our challenge is to turn the nonunitary self-representations of our informants into something that resembles emancipatory narratives of practice (McEwan, 1997). A self-narrative becomes emancipatory when it gives up "the myth of a unified subjectivity" and allows for "the subjectivity and the validation of conflict as a source through which women become strong and learn to speak their own experiences" (Bloom, 1996, p. 192).

The thrust of a nonunitary self-representation is strong in the stories of school practice that our informants tell us and the stories we tell of their practice. It works mainly through the narrative structures furnished by culture and appropriated by our informants in their presentation of self, their practices, and us in our narrative inquiry. The narrative scripts to be appropriated are many: "the conquering hero"—we know them from many novels and from Hollywood B movies; "the happy ever after"—we know them from, among others, many commercials ("eat, buy this, and you will be happy"); and the stoic, never-changing characters who pass across the silver screen seemingly unaffected by any event and without a normal existential crisis. Bloom calls these "master narratives of male success." When we (informants and researchers) appropriate these narrative scripts, we are probably unconsciously responding to generic expectations of literary narratives and thereby further silencing an already silenced group, in addition to reproducing the gendered, hierarchical, and patriarchal structure of our culture. One wants to hear the story of an uncomplicated and good teacher, of a teacher who is able to gain control over all the children in the class, and of a teacher who gets all the children in the class to deliver book reports with everybody living happily ever after.

The stories by Elbaz (1983), Vasquez-Levy (1993), and Morgan (1993), however, break away from the narrative script provided by culture in various ways: Elbaz's informant is frustrated; Vasquez-Levy is faced with the complex issue of what constitutes change and progress in practice; Morgan finds many challenges in getting all the children to deliver book reports, and at the end of her narrative, she has not yet achieved that part of her project. She has, however, gained a valuable understanding of the dilemmas in the children's life situations. These are not the conquering-hero or happy-ever-after narratives or the stoic, never-changing characters. Instead, we see in these narratives complex challenges and dilemmas that require compromises and that have no easy solutions on the horizon. They describe nonunitary subjectivities: the teacher's growth, both professional and personal. We see people with feelings, and they are made of flesh and blood. Moreover, their honesty gives us insight into their reflections over their small victories as well as their defeats—their narratives bring us up close to their thoughts and practice (Carter, 1993, 1995; Zellermayer, 1997).[17]

We may not be able to dismantle our culture's patriarchy, but we have an opportunity to rid interpretative research of its nar-

---

[16] Gilligan (1982), in her much acclaimed study of psychological theory and women's development, found it necessary to claim a voice for women in order to capture the language of women's moral development and explore it in practice.

[17] Typical narrative descriptions of practice often cover a relatively short period in both teachers' lives and the focuses of specific aspects of practice. The biographers and autobiographers are left to develop fully the interesting notion that Bloom raises about spirals in one's development and their relation to practice.

rative coercion.[18] We can only say that our informants have claimed a voice of their own through which the language of practice ventriloquates, a voice that does not reproduce the gendered, hierarchical, and patriarchal structure of our culture. Such an emancipation is made possible when we, as researchers, have accepted nonunitary subjectivity as a strength rather than as a weakness and as an alternative discourse in all branches of interpretative research. Otherwise, teachers (male and female) will never have the opportunity to see themselves "outside of masculinist ideologies" and will never gain strength from exploring their own nonunitary subjectivities (Bloom, 1996, p. 193). For female teachers, the result is further fragmentation, invisibility, and alienation. For male teachers, it represents stunted professional and personal growth.

Ethical Issues

Concerns about ethical issues in interpretative research craftsmanship have been constant companions of researchers for a long time, as long as there have been people who call themselves interpretative researchers or ethnographers. The pioneers in ethnography often worked with isolated, illiterate, non-Western cultures. The texts researchers wrote about their fieldwork had no influence whatsoever on the informants' subsequent careers or their lives. Moreover, the researchers were strangers who always departed as soon as their fieldwork was concluded. The ethical issues inherent in this kind of situation were simple. Disguising the tribe and assigning pseudonyms to key informants were standard procedures. If any unsolved ethical dilemmas remained at the end of the fieldwork, they were solved by default when the researcher left. Other possible ethical dilemmas were controlled rather than solved through journal writing. Like the ethnographers of the past, we who conduct narrative research on school practice knock on the doors of the people we want to study and obtain their permission to be a part of their lives for a limited period of time. But that is where the similarity ends. Our informants can read our studies and they may not like what they read. They have careers they care about and their time is precious. They may experience invisible, unequal power relationships in research involving high-status academics male and female (Carter, 1995).

Awareness of ethical issues is an integral part of all narrative research craftsmanship, especially in those cases where researchers are fluent in the language of practice. In these contexts, teachers (as informants) tend to be more personal than they otherwise would have been. Thus, old concerns about ethical issues are being redefined because narrative research on school practice is essentially a moral enterprise rather than a technical one, where researchers and informants see themselves as moral agents in search of a better practice (Elbaz, 1997). This calls for a redefinition of the ethical and moral dimension of research on practice. The suggestion has been made that moral reasoning is dialogical: a dialogue between justice and care, with each notion representing distinct discourse practices (Day & Trappan, 1996). The "justice" voice speaks the language of fairness and equality. Ventriloquating through this voice are many of the great moral philosophers since ancient times. Then, another voice resonates, the voice speaking the language of "caring." Its vocabulary captures interpersonal relationships, feelings, attitudes and flexibility (Noddings, 1991). Thus, solutions to practical ethical dilemmas are never absolute and cast in stone. Instead, solutions can be claimed through a structured dialogical process between the two distinct voices.

A typical moral dilemma for narrative researchers is one in which our informants do not like our story (Alvermann, 1993). Conflicts between informants and researchers often arise about the interpretation of specific events. Informants may question the interpretative authority of researchers. In such cases, Alvermann advocates including the informants' interpretation of reported events in the research reports. Gudmundsdóttir and Hoel (1996) solved this type of dilemma by making the informants coauthors of their own studies. Their comments appeared in two places: as footnotes, to give them an opportunity to comment on specific events where their interpretations differed from the researchers and in the appendix, where the comments were more general in nature and could not be tied to a specific interpretation. Our role as researchers assigns us considerable interpretative authority because our job is to analyze and interpret what we observe, providing we preserve what we consider to be the appropriate moral aspects of the situation. We, as narrative researchers on school practice, do not intend nor want to be mere messengers, writing down the words and actions of someone else.

Concluding Remarks

Many challenges face narrative research on school practice in the future, as is natural for such a relatively young tradition. First, we need to develop more genres for our inquiries and more formats for our reports (see L. Richardson, 1994). Second, student learning as a unit of analysis disappeared with the fading away of the process-product research tradition. We need to widen the units of analysis to include learners and reclaim them as an important element of narrative research on practice. Third, we need to keep close to practice, to the language of practice, and to the lives of teachers. Otherwise, narrative research on school practice could end up, as Huberman (1996) claims, in oblivion.

REFERENCES

Acker, S. (1997). Becoming a teacher educator: Voices of women academics in Canadian faculties of education. [Special theme issue on narrative perspectives in teaching and teacher education]. *Teaching and Teacher Education, 13*(1), 65–74.

Alton-Lee, A. (1993). Reframing classroom research: A lesson from the private world of children. *Harvard Educational Review, 63*(1), 50–84.

Alton-Lee, A. (1998, January). *Theory in practice: Facilitating effective teaching using cycles of action research and in-depth classroom studies.* Keynote address to the 11th International Congress for School Effectiveness and School Improvement, Manchester, UK.

Alvermann, D. (1993). Researching the literal: Of muted voices, second

---

[18] Bloom makes the important point that "unitary subjectivity fictionalizes and reduces malehood as well as female selfhood" (Bloom, 1996, p. 193).

texts, and cultural representations. In D. Leu & C. Kinzer (Eds.), *Examining central issues in literacy research, theory and practice* (pp. 1–10). Washington, DC: The National Teaching Conference, Inc.

Ashton-Warner, S. (1963). *Teacher.* New York: Touchstone.

Bagnold, R. (1988). *Sand, wind and war: Memoirs of a desert explorer.* Tucson: University of Arizona Press.

Bakhtin, M. (1981). *The dialogic imagination.* Austin: University of Texas Press.

Bakhtin, M. (1986). *Speech genre and other essays.* Austin: University of Texas Press.

Bakhtin, M. (1994). The dialogic imagination. In P. Morris (Ed.), *The Bakhtin reader: Selected writings of Bakhtin, Medvedev, Voloshinov* (pp. 74–84). London: Arnold.

Bennett, N. (1976). *Teaching styles and pupil progress.* London: Open Books.

Bloom, L. (1996). Stories of one's own: Nonunitary subjectivity in narrative representation. *Qualitative Inquiry, 2*(2), 176–197.

Bruner, J. (1986). *Actual mind, possible worlds.* Cambridge, MA: Harvard University Press.

Bruner, J. (1996). *The culture of education.* Cambridge, MA: Harvard University Press.

Bruner, J., & Lucariello, J. (1989). Monologue as narrative recreation of the world. In K. Nelson (Ed.), *Narratives from the crib* (pp. 73–79). Cambridge, MA: Harvard University Press.

Butt, R., & Raymond, D. (1989). Studying the nature and development of teachers' knowledge using collaborative autobiography. *International Journal of Educational Research, 13*(4), 403–419.

Carter, K. (1993). The place of story in research on teaching and teacher education. *Educational Researcher, 22*(1), 5–12.

Carter, K. (1995). Teaching stories and local understandings. *The Journal of Educational Research, 88*(6), 326–330.

Carter, K., & Doyle, W. (1996). Personal narrative and life history in learning to teach. In J. Sikula, T. Buttery, & E. Guyton (Eds.), *Handbook of research on teacher education* (2nd ed., pp. 120–142). New York: Macmillan.

Clandinin, J. (1986). *Classroom practice: Teacher images in action.* London: Falmer Press.

Clandinin, J., & Connelly, M. (1990). Story of experience and narrative inquiry. *Educational Researcher, 19*(5), 2–14.

Clark, C. (1991). Real lessons from imaginary teachers. *Journal of Curriculum Studies, 23*(5), 429–433.

Clark, C. (1995). *Thoughtful teaching.* London: Falmer Press.

Cole, M. (1995). The zone of proximal development: Where culture and cognition create each other. In J. Wertsch (Ed.), *Culture, communication, and cognition: Vygotskian perspectives* (pp. 146–161). Cambridge, UK: Cambridge University Press. (Original work published 1985).

Cole, M. (1997). *Cultural psychology.* Cambridge, MA: Harvard University Press.

Connelly, M., & Clandinin, J. (1988). *Teachers as curriculum planners: Narratives of experience.* New York: Teachers College Press.

Day, J., & Tappan, M. (1996). The narrative approach to moral development: From the epistemic subject to dialogical selves. *Human Development, 39,* 67–82.

Denzin, N., & Lincoln, Y. (1994). The fifth movement. In N. Denzin & Y. Lincoln (Eds.), *Handbook of qualitative research* (pp. 575–586). London: Sage Publications.

Dewey, J. (1963). *Experience and education.* New York: Collier Books. (Original work published 1938).

Doyle, W. (1997). Heard any stories lately? [Special theme issue on narrative perspectives in teaching and teacher education]. *Teaching and Teacher Education, 13*(1), 93–99.

Edvardsen, E. (1989). *Den gjenstridige allmue: Skole og levebrød i et nordnorsk kystsamfunn ca. 1850–1900* [The obstinate commoner: School and livelihood in a North Norwegian coastal community]. Oslo: Solum Forlag.

Egan, K. (1988). *Primary understanding: Education in early childhood.* New York: Routledge.

Egan, K. (1989). *Teaching as storytelling: An alternative approach to teaching and curriculum in the elementary school.* Chicago: University of Chicago Press.

Egan, K. (1995). Narrative and learning: A voyage of implications. In H. McEwan & K. Egan (Eds.), *Narrative in teaching, learning, and research* (pp. 116–126). New York: Teachers College Press.

Elbaz, F. (1983). *Teachers' thinking: A study of practical knowledge.* New York: Croom Helm.

Elbaz, F. (1997). Narrative as personal politics. [Special theme issue on narrative perspectives in teaching and teacher education]. *Teaching and Teacher Education, 13*(1), 75–83.

Erickson, F. (1986). Qualitative methods in research on teaching. In M. Wittrock (Ed.), *Handbook of research on teaching* (3rd ed., pp. 119–161). New York: Macmillan.

Feldman, C. (1989). Monologue as problem solving narrative. In K. Nelson (Ed.), *Narratives from the crib* (pp. 98–119). Cambridge, MA: Harvard University Press.

Feldman, C. (1992). The new theory of the theory of mind. [Essay review]. *Human Development, 35,* 107–117.

Fenstermacher, G. (1994a). The knower and the known: The nature of knowledge in research on teaching. *Review of Research in Education, 20,* 3–56.

Fenstermacher, G. (1994b). The place of practical arguments in the education of teachers. In V. Richardson (Ed.), *Teacher change and the staff development process* (pp. 23–42). New York: Teachers College Press.

Fenstermacher, G., & Richardson, V. (1993). The elicitation and reconstruction of practical arguments in teaching. *Journal of Curriculum Studies, 25*(2), 101–114.

Fenstermacher, G., & Richardson, V. (1994). Promoting confusion in educational psychology: How is it done? *Educational Psychology, 29*(1), 49–55.

Feuerverger, G. (1997). "On the edges of the map": A study of heritage language teachers in Toronto. [Special theme issue on narrative perspectives in teaching and teacher education]. *Teaching and Teacher Education, 13*(1), 39–53.

Fox, D. (1991). Building a reading community: "Intertextuality" and the adult reader. "Article of the Year Award" in 1991 from National Council of Teachers of English. Fox, D. (1993). The influence of context, community and culture: Contrasting cases of teacher knowledge development. In D. Leu & C. Kinzer (Eds.), *The forty-second yearbook of the National Reading Conference* (pp. 345–351). Chicago: National Reading Conference.

Fox, D. (1995). From English major to English teacher: Two case studies. *English Journal, 84*(2), 17–25.

Fox, D. (1996). The struggle for voice in learning to teach: Lessons from one preservice teacher's portfolio. In K. Whitmore & Y. Goodman (Eds.), *Whole language voices in teacher education* (pp. 285–296). New York: Stenhouse Publishers.

Fuller, R. (1982). The story as the engram: Is it fundamental to thinking? *Journal of Mind and Behaviour, 3*(2), 127–142.

Gilligan, C. (1982). *In a different voice: Psychological theory and women's development.* Cambridge, MA: Harvard University Press.

Grant, G. (1991). Ways of constructing classroom meaning: Two stories about knowing and seeing. *Journal of Curriculum Studies, 23*(5), 397–408.

Grant, G. (1995). Interpreting text as pedagogy and pedagogy as text. *Teachers and Teaching: Theory and Practice, 1*(1), 87–100.

Grant, G., & Hall, S. (1991). On what is known and seen. *Journal of Curriculum Studies, 23*(5), 423–428.

Grossman, P., & Stodolsky, S. (1995). Content as context: The role of school subjects in secondary school teaching. *Educational Researcher, 24*(8), 5–11.

Gudmundsdóttir, S. (1988). *Knowledge use among experienced teachers: Four case studies of high school teaching.* Unpublished doctoral dissertation, Stanford University, School of Education, Stanford, CA.

Gudmundsdóttir, S. (1990a). Curriculum stories: Four case studies of social studies teaching. In C. Day, P. Denicolo, & M. Pope (Eds.), *Insights into teachers' thinking and practice* (pp. 107–118). London: Falmer Press.

Gudmundsdóttir, S. (1990b). Values in pedagogical content knowledge. *Journal of Teacher Education, 41*(3), 44–53.

Gudmundsdóttir, S. (1991a). Story-maker, story-teller: Narrative structures in curriculum. *Journal of Curriculum Studies, 23*(3), 207–218.

Gudmundsdóttir, S. (1991b). Ways of seeing are ways of knowing: The pedagogical content knowledge of an expert teacher. *Journal of Curriculum Studies, 23*(5), 409–425.

Gudmundsdóttir, S. (1995). The narrative nature of pedagogical knowledge. In H. McEwan & K. Egan (Eds.), *Narrative in teaching, learning, and research* (pp. 24–38). New York: Teachers College Press.

Gudmundsdóttir, S., & Hoel, T. (1996). *Four case studies of reflection chains.* Unpublished report from the Reflect project at the Department of Education, Norwegian University of Science and Technology, Trondheim, Norway. [On-line]. Available: http://www.sv.ntnu/ped/sigrun

Gudmundsdóttir, S., & Hoel, T. (1997, August). *The reflect project: Interactive pedagogy using information technology.* Paper presented at the Biannual Meeting of the European Association for Research on Learning and Instruction, Athens, Greece. [On-line]. Available: http://www.sv.ntnu/ped/sigrun

Hansen, D. (1995). *The call to teach.* New York: Teachers College Press.

Hansen, D. (1998). The moral is in the practice. *Teaching and Teacher Education, 14*(6), 643–656.

Hardgreaves, A. (1996). Revisiting voice. *Educational Researcher, 25*(1), 12–19.

Hoel, T. (1992). *Tanke blir tekst* [Thought into text]. Oslo: Det Norske Samlaget.

Hoel, T. (1994). *Elevsamtaler om skriving i vidaregåande skole: Responsgrupper i teori og praksis* [High school students' conversations about writing: Theory and practice of response groups]. Unpublished doctoral dissertation, Norwegian University of Science and Technology, Trondheim, Norway.

Hoel, T. (1997). Voices from the classroom. [Special theme issue on narrative perspectives in teaching and teacher education]. *Teaching and Teacher Education, 13*(1), 2–16.

Hohr, H. (1996). Opplevelse som erkjennelsesform [Experience as a form of understanding]. *Norsk pedagogisk tidskrift, 5,* 280–289.

Hollingsworth, S. (1992). Learning to teach through collaborative conversation: A feminist approach. *American Educational Research Journal, 29*(2), 373–404.

Hopmann, S. (in preparation). *Die forschulung der Schule* [The schooling of the school].

Huberman, M. (1993). *The lives of teachers.* New York: Teachers College Press. (Original work published 1989).

Huberman, M. (1995). Working with life-history narratives. In H. McEwan & K. Egan (Eds.), *Narrative in teaching, learning, and research* (pp. 127–165). New York: Teachers College Press.

Huberman, M. (1996). Moving mainstream: Taking a closer look at teacher research. *Language Arts, 73*(2), 124–140.

Jank, W., & Meyer, H. (1991). *Didaktische Modelle.* Frankfurt am Main, Germany: Cornelsen Verlag Scriptor GmbH & Co.

Kessen, W. (1993). Rumble or revolution: A commentary. In R. Wozniak & K. Fischer (Eds.), *Development in context: Acting and thinking in specific environments* (pp. 269–279). Mahwah, NJ: Lawrence Erlbaum Associates.

Kyratzis, A., & Green, J. (1997). Jointly constructed narratives in classrooms: Co-constructions of friendship and community through language. [Special theme issue on narrative perspectives in teaching and teacher education]. *Teaching and Teacher Education, 13*(1), 17–37.

Leont'ev, A. (1981). The problem of activity in psychology. In J. Wertsch (Ed.), *The concept of activity in Soviet psychology* (pp. 37–71). Armonk, NY: M. E. Sharpe.

Lincoln, Y. (1993, January). *Notes toward a fifth generation of evaluation: Lessons from the voiceless, or, toward a postmodern politics of evaluation.* Paper presented at the Fifth Annual Meeting of the Southeast Evaluation Association, Tallahassee, FL.

Marble, S. (1997). Narrative visions of schooling. [Special theme issue on narrative perspectives in teaching and teacher education]. *Teaching and Teacher Education, 13*(1), 55–65.

Markham, B. (1988). *West with the night.* London: Penguin Books. (Original work published 1942).

Marshall, S. (1963). *An experiment in education.* Cambridge, UK: Cambridge University Press.

Marton, F. (1981). Phenomenography—Describing the conceptions of the world around us. *Instructional Science, 10,* 177–200.

McEwan, H. (1997). The function of narrative in research on teaching. [Special theme issue on narrative perspectives in teaching and teacher education]. *Teaching and Teacher Education, 13*(1), 85–92.

McEwan, H., & Egan, K. (1995). *Narrative in teaching, learning, and research.* New York: Teachers College Press.

McIyntyre, A. (1985). *After virtue: A study in moral theory.* London: Duckworth. (Original work published 1981).

Middleton, S. (1993). *Educating feminists: Life histories and pedagogy.* New York: Teachers College Press.

Middleton, S. (1994). Schooling and radicalisation: Life histories of New Zealand feminist teachers. In L. Stone (Ed.), *The education feminist reader* (pp. 279–299). London: Routledge.

Middleton, S. (1996). Towards an oral history of educational ideas in New Zealand as a resource for teacher education. *Teaching and Teacher Education, 12*(5), 543–560.

Miles, M., & Huberman, M. (1994). *Qualitative Data Analysis* (2nd ed.). London: Sage.

Moen, T., Dypvik, W., & Gudmundsdóttir, S. (1998, June). Inclusion in education: A Vygotskyan perspective. Paper presented at the Fourth Congress of the International Society for Cultural Research and Activity Theory, Århus, Denmark.

Moen, T., & Gudmundsdóttir, S. (1997). *"Det å send han Tom ut av klassen, e ikkje nån løysing": En kasusstudie av inkluderende prosesser.* Trondheim, Norway: Tapir Press.

Morgan, B. (1993). Practical rationality: A self-investigation. *Journal of Curriculum Studies, 25*(2), 115–124.

Nelson, K. (1981). Social cognition in a script framework. In J. Flavell & L. Ross (Eds.), *Social cognitive development* (pp. 97–118). Cambridge, UK: Cambridge University Press.

Nelson, K. (1989). Monologue as representation of real-life experience. In K. Nelson (Ed.), *Narratives from the crib* (pp. 1–23). Cambridge, MA: Harvard University Press.

Nilssen, V., Wangsmo-Cappelen, V., & Gudmundsdóttir, S. (1996). *"Dæm tænkt på ein heilt anna måte enn ka æ gjor": En kasusstudie av en lærerstudents matematikkundervisning i 2. Klasse* ["The children think so differently from me": A case study of a student teacher teaching second-grade mathematics]. Trondheim, Norway: Tapir.

Nilssen, V., Gudmundsdóttir, S., & Wangsmo-Cappelen, V. (1999). Mentoring the teaching of multiplication: A case study. *European Journal of Teacher Education, 21*(1), 29–45.

Noddings, N. (1991). Stories in dialogue: Caring and interpersonal reasoning. In C. Witherell & N. Noddings (Eds.), *Stories lives tell: Narrative and dialogue in education* (pp. 157–170). New York: Teachers College Press.

Olson, D. (1977). The languages of instruction: On the literate bias of schooling. In R. Anderson, R. Spiro, & W. Montague (Eds.), *Schooling and the acquisition of knowledge* (pp. 65–89). Hillsdale, NJ: Lawrence Erlbaum Associates.

Paley, V. (1990). *The boy who would be a helicopter.* Cambridge, MA: Harvard University Press.

Paley, V. (1995). Looking for the magpie: Another voice in the classroom. In H. McEwan & K. Egan (Eds.), *Narrative in teaching, learning, and research* (pp. 91–99). New York: Teachers College Press.

Palmer, R. (1985). *Hermeneutics.* Evanston: Northwestern University Press. (Original work published 1969).

Pendlebury, S. (1990). Practical arguments and situational appreciation in teaching. *Educational Theory, 40*(2), 171–179.

Phelan, A., McEwan, H., & Pateman, N. (1995). Collaboration in student teaching: Learning to teach in the context of changing curriculum practice. *Teaching and Teacher Education, 12*(4), 335–334.

Phillips, D. (1992). *The social scientist's bestiary.* Oxford, UK: Pergamon Press.

Phillips, D. (1994). Telling it straight: Issues in assessing narrative research. *Educational Psychologist, 29*(7), 5–12.

Phillips, D. (1997). Telling the truth about stories. [Special theme issue on narrative perspectives in teaching and teacher education]. *Teaching and Teacher Education, 13*(1), 101–109.

Ratner, C. (1991a). Contributions of sociohistorical psychology and phenomenology to research methodology. In H. Stam, L. Mos, W. Thorngate & B. Kaplan (Eds.), *Recent trends in theoretical psychology, Volume III.* Berlin: Springer-Verlag.

Ratner, C. (1991b). *Vygotsky's sociohistorical psychology and its contemporary applications.* New York: Plenum.

Reinertsen, A., Nordtømme, N., Eidsvik, R., Weideman, E., & Gudmundsdóttir, S. (1996). *Fagdidaktisk kunnskap i historie belyst gjennom undervising i hendelsene på Eidsvoll i 1814: Tre kasusstudier av lærere i videregåendeskole* [Pedagogical content knowledge in history illustrated through the teaching of the Norwegian constitution: Three case studies of high school teachers]. Trondheim, Norway: Tapir Press.

Richardson, L. (1994). Writing: A method of inquiry. In N. Denzin & Y. Lincoln (Eds.), *Handbook of qualitative research* (pp. 516–529). London: Sage.

Richardson, V. (1994). Conducting research on practice. *Educational Researcher, 23*(5), 5–10.

Richardson, V., & Anders, P. (1990). Final report of the Reading Instruction Study. [Report submitted to OERI, U.S. Department of Education]. University of Arizona, Tucson: School of Education. (ERIC Document Reproduction Service No. ED 030 047)

Richardson, V., & Anders, P. (1994a). The study of teacher change. In V. Richardson (Ed.), *Teacher change and the staff development process* (pp. 159–198). New York: Teachers College Press.

Richardson, V., & Anders, P. (1994b). A theory of change. In V. Richardson (Ed.), *Teacher change and the staff development process* (pp. 199–216). New York: Teachers College Press.

Richardson, V., & Hamilton, M. (1994). The practical argument staff development process. In V. Richardson (Ed), *Teacher change and the staff development process* (pp. 109–134). New York: Teachers College Press.

Richert, A. (1992). The content of student teachers' reflections within different structures for facilitating the reflective process. In T. Russell & H. Munby (Eds.), *Teachers and teaching: From classroom to reflection* (pp. 171–191). London: Falmer Press.

Ricoeur, P. (1981). *Hermeneutics and the human sciences* (J. B. Thompson, Ed. and Trans.). Cambridge, UK: Cambridge University Press.

Robinson, J., & Hawpe, L. (1986). Narrative thinking as a heuristic process. In T. Sarbin (Ed.), *Narrative psychology: The storied nature of human conduct* (pp. 111–125). New York: Praeger.

Røger, H. (1991). *Oppvekst og opplæring i Gudbrandsdalen* [Growing up and schooling in Gudbrandsdal]. Vistra, Norway: Gudbrandsdal lærerlag [Gudbrandsdal Teachers' Union].

Saussure, F. (1974). *Course in general linguistics.* London: Fontana. (Original work published 1915).

Säljø, R. (1988). A text and its meanings: Observations on how readers construe what is meant from what is written. In R. Säljø (Ed.), *The written word: Studies in literate thought and action.* Berlin: Springer-Verlag.

Shulman, L. (1991). Ways of seeing are ways of knowing: Ways of teaching, ways of learning are both teaching. *Journal of Curriculum Studies, 23*(5), 393–395.

Strømnes, Å. (1989). *Lærerrolla til ulike tider* [The teacher's role throughout history]. Oslo: Selskapet for norsk skolehistorie [Association for the history of Norwegian schools].

Taylor, C. (1985). *Philosophy and the human sciences: Philosophical papers 2.* Cambridge, UK: Cambridge University Press.

Tharp, R., & Gallimore, R. (1995). *Rousing minds to life: Teaching, learning and schooling in a social context.* Cambridge, UK: Cambridge University Press. (Original work published 1988).

Thomas, D. (1995). *Teachers' stories.* Buckingham, UK: Open University Press.

Tulviste, P. (1991). *The cultural historical development of verbal thinking.* Commack, NY: Nove Science Publishers.

Vasquez-Levy, D. (1993). The use of practical arguments in clarifying and changing practical reasoning and classroom practice: Two cases. *Journal of Curriculum Studies, 25*(2), 125–143.

Vygotsky, L. (1963). *Thought and language.* Cambridge, MA: MIT Press. (Original work published 1934).

Vygotsky, L. (1987). *The collected works of L. S. Vygotsky: Volume 1. Problems of general psychology.* London: Plenum Press.

Wertsch, J. (1981). The concept of activity in psychology. In J. Wertsch (Ed.), *The concept of activity in Soviet psychology.* Armonk, New York: M. E. Sharpe.

Wertsch, J. (1985). *Vygotsky and the social formation of mind.* Cambridge, MA: Harvard University Press.

Wertsch, J. (1991). *Voices of the mind: A socio-cultural approach to mediated action.* London: Harvester.

Zellermayer, M. (1997). When we talk about collaborative curriculum-making, what are we talking about? *Curriculum Inquiry, 27*(2), 187–214.

15.

Validity as an Incitement to Discourse: Qualitative Research and the Crisis of Legitimation

Patti Lather
The Ohio State University

Where do you find meaning or rigor? Which "ism" is the name of your system? Or, worse yet, what is your obsession? (Serres & Latour, 1995, p. 101)

How scientific knowledge is made credible is a long-standing issue. When Steven Epstein (1996) wrote *Impure Science,* which is about AIDS, activism, and the politics of knowledge, he documented a contemporary example of how scientific fact-making occurs in politicized environments. Epstein's major point is not just that the "context of discovery" is no longer separable from the "context of justification." His much more dramatic point is that the very "calculus of credibility" of what is deemed "good science," the very determination of warrants of validity, has shifted in the science of clinical trials in medical research.

This chapter focuses on similar shifts within the context of research on teaching. It examines discourse-practices of validity in qualitative research in education in order to trace the conditions of the legitimation of knowledge.[1] Beginning with a survey of the various turns in recent framings of the social sciences, I write against the more typical demarcation discourse that calls on such figures as Popper and Lakatos with their "essential," culture-free standards and Kuhn with his disattention to

power outside the community of scientists in the social construction of knowledge. Positing a proliferation of available framings, I write toward discourses of validity that recognize the power and political dimensions of the issue of demarcation. This proliferation is positioned within the "science wars" as more traditional scientists take on what they see as the dangerous focus on science as social construction versus "truth" about "nature."[2] In short, validity is situated as not just one of many issues in science, but as the crux of the issue: the claims of science to a certain privilege in terms of authoritative knowledge.[3]

"I don't need validity," Denzin stated in his discussant commentary at a 1994 American Educational Research Association (AERA) panel. "These are the things poststructuralism and postmodernism teach me." Contra Denzin, in what follows, I position validity as a space of constructed visibility that gives to be seen the unthought in our practices of epistemology and methodology. Here, validity is positioned as both medium and symptom in the (dis)articulation of positivist hegemony. Such a positioning foregrounds the work validity does, the effects of its postpositivist framings, as an especially concentrated point for tracing the relations of power.[4] The chapter is organized around two thematics: first, the shifts in episteme and the consequent

The author wishes to thank Yvonna Lincoln (Texas A&M University) and Steinar Kvale (Psykologisk Institut, Denmark) for reviewing the outline and the draft chapter.

[1] My rationale for hanging on to the term "validity" is to both circulate and break with the signs that code it. What I mean by the term, then, is both mobilizing all the baggage that it carries and, in a doubled movement, using it to rupture validity as a "regime of truth," to displace its historical inscription toward policing the borders between science and not-science. See note 20 for what this doubled move might mean in the context of a "double science."

[2] *Higher Superstition: The Academic Left and Its Quarrels with Science* by Paul Gross and Norman Levitt (1994) is the most noted articulation of the backlash against the critiques of science across feminism, multiculturalism, postmodernism, and the social studies of science. For responses, see Ross (1996).

[3] Kerlinger states in his 1986 *Foundations of Behavioral Research,* "Validity . . . is much more than technique. It bores into the essence of science itself" (p. 432).

[4] My use of the term postpositivist does not follow the 1994 *Handbook of Qualitative Research* where the editors, Denzin and Lincoln, use the term to refer to a revisionist positivism. The broader usage is more typical across philosophy of science, for example, Fiske and Shweder (1986, p. 16) who refer to "the postpositivist intellectual climate of our times."

weakening of homogeneous standards, and second, the proliferation of counterpractices of authority in qualitative research. While not delineating specific validity practices, the major function of the chapter is to posit both the intelligibility and
availability of alternative discourse-practices of validity. Hence,
what follows is not so much an exhaustive survey or a "how-
to" guide as an argument for thinking differently about how we
think about validity in qualitative research in education.[5]

Shifts in Episteme

> There is no pure place outside of power by which the question of
> validity might be raised, and where validity is raised, it is also al-
> ways an activity of power. (Butler, 1995, p. 139)

Various turns have characterized research in the human sciences over the past few decades, shifts that are not so much
linear as multiple, simultaneous, and interruptive. Rather than
nostalgia for a lost world of certain knowledge, to engage and
transvalue these shifts is to move toward a thought of dissensus
rather than consensus, a dissensus not easily institutionalized
into some new regime of truth.[6] Such turns are about the "ruins" of validity, the end of transcendent claims of validity, the
end of grand narratives of validity: validity under erasure.[7] In
such a place of thought, evaluation is seen as a social question
rather than a device of measurement. What is at stake is no
longer the nature of value but its function. Questions of accountability and responsibility are ethical and social. Hence,
my argument is the need to rethink the terms in which we address the issue in such a way that validity becomes a site of an
attempt to transvalue the end of scientificity.[8]

Surveying the various turns reveals the difficulties of deciding
even on what terms to feature (see Table 15.1).

Table 15.1. "Turns" in the Human Sciences

- Linguistic (Rorty, 1967)
- Structural (Althusser, 1971)
- Practical human action (Schwandt, 1996)
- Critical (Fay, 1987)
- Poststructural (Derrida, 1976)
- Rhetorical (Nelson, Megill, & McCloskey, 1987; Simons, 1989)
- Textual (Clifford & Marcus, 1986)
- Narrative (Casey, 1995)
- Historical (McDonald, 1996)
- Ethnographic (Van Maanen, 1995)
- Ethical/theological (Derrida, 1996)

Complicating matters even further is the recent language of
"return," both a return to the real (Foster, 1996) and a return to
objectivity, whether after deconstruction or after feminist and
postcolonial critiques of objectivism (Stanfield, 1994; Harding,
1987, 1991, 1993). Feminist philosopher of science, Sandra
Harding, for example, argues for "strong objectivity" based on
"systematically examining all of the social values shaping a particular research process" (1993, p. 18). Art historian, Steven
Melville, argues for an "objectivity in deconstruction" that emphasizes how "'deconstruction is not what you think'" in its
moves of reversing, undoing, and complicating the linguistic
turn. To turn everything into discourse is not exhaustive of our
engagement with things and how they happen. There is a being
in excess of our languages of knowing, whether we know it or
not. This "objectivity in deconstruction" refuses "to let its notion of objectivity be constrained by the dominant paradigms of
truth" (Melville, 1996, p. 140). It is as if the critiques of truth in
Nietzsche, self-presence in Freud, referential language in Saussure, and metaphysics in Heidegger were finally coming home
to roost in the social sciences (Roseneau, 1992; Hollinger, 1994;
Dickens & Fontana, 1994; Kreiswirth & Carmichael, 1995).

Across this dizzying array of in-movement shifts, these turns
challenge the "view from nowhere" and the traditional foundations of knowledge that continue to undergird so much of
contemporary research in education (Spanos, 1993). Rather
than focusing on the persistence of this traditional world view
in the face of its loss of plausibility, I outline 20th century turns
toward epistemological indeterminacy in order to underscore
contemporary interest in situatedness, perspective, relationality,
narrative, poesis, and blurred genres (Greene, 1994). I then survey across the field of educational inquiry in terms of the variety of available discourses of validity in order to delineate the
weakening of any "one best way approach" to validity. The particular alignment of my reading is how discourse-practices of
validity enter into the circulation and dialogue that make up
the ongoing interplay of the field.

Epistemic Indeterminacy and the Weakening of
Homogeneous Standards

> Exploring the question of value means recognizing that there exists
> no homogeneous standard of value that might unite all poles. . . .
> The question, then, is how we can raise the question of accountabil-
> ity as something that *exceeds* the logic of accounting (Readings,
> 1996, pp. 164–165).

---

[5] Recent handbooks and research reviews contain more exhaustive surveys of the literature: LeCompte, Millroy and Preissle (1992), Denzin and
Lincoln (1994, 2000), Darling-Hammond (1994), and Apple (1995).

[6] The Nietzschean transvaluation of values involves working the pathos of ruined ideals toward an ethical vitalization. Against those who read
him as a nihilist, this move underwrites the new Nietzsche scholarship which positions him as a "protodeconstructionist," working the ruins of
hierarchical binaries toward a healthier being and doing. The work of Judith Butler (1995, p. 131) exemplifies this move: "For that sphere [of
politics] will be the one in which those very theoretical constructions—those without which we imagine we cannot take a step—are in the very
process of being lived as ungrounded, unmoored, in tatters, but also as recontextualized, reworked, in translation, as the very resources from which
a postfoundational politics is wrought." In this move, the concept of ruins is not about an epistemological skepticism taken to defeatist extremes,
but rather a working of repetition and the play of difference as the only ground we have in moving toward new practices (Butler, 1993). For an
example of this sort of inquiry, see Bill Readings's *The University in Ruins* (1996).

[7] To work "under erasure" involves simultaneously troubling and using the concepts we think we cannot think without. It entails keeping something visible but crossed out to avoid universalizing or monumentalizing it, keeping it as both limit and resource. The classic unpacking of this
deconstructive logic is Spivak's translator's preface to Derrida's *Of Grammatology* (1976).

[8] Aronowitz (1995, p. 12) defines scientificity as not so much the actual practices of science as "the permeation of the standard elements of the
scientific attitude into all corners of the social world: seeing is believing; the appeal to 'hard facts' such as statistical outcomes to settle arguments;
the ineluctable faith in the elements of syllogistic reasoning."

In exploring the work of science in an era of blurred genres (Geertz, 1980), validity is a "limit question" of research, one that repeatedly resurfaces, one that can be neither avoided nor resolved. Within a context of epistemic antifoundationalism (West, 1991), validity is about much more than the limits of objectivity: It is the claims of scientificity itself that are put under theoretic pressure. "Where, after the metanarratives, can legitimacy reside?" Lyotard asks (1984, p. xxv). What follows argues that the answer is a reflexivity about research practices that takes into account both the crisis of representation and the limits of reflexivity.[9] Here validity is situated as practices toward spaces of constructed visibility and incitements to see which constitute power-knowledge (Foucault, 1980). This postepistemic focus decenters validity as about epistemological guarantees and shifts it into practices that are situated, multiple, partial, endlessly deferred, a reflexive validity interested in how discourse does its work.

Exemplifying a postepistemic focus, Scheurich (1996) argues that validity is a boundary line for what is acceptable and what is not acceptable in research. Validity is, in short, power, the power to determine the demarcation between science and not-science. Such a postepistemic focus shifts what Kvale (1989) has termed "the validity of the validity question" in some interesting directions. Like Denzin in his "I don't need validity," Wolcott (1990) argues for dismissing validity altogether as too much about the continuation of positivist ideals. On quite the other hand, Roberts (1996), writing about qualitative research in science education, warns that "a niche won is not necessarily a niche held, or a niche held without vigilance" (p. 244). "Still on the defensive," the qualitative "upstart" that fails to provide systematic depth analysis and analytic rigor "threaten[s] the very fragile niche that sound qualitative research has established." This lack of rigor risks consigning all of qualitative research to the determination of not being research at all (p. 248).[10]

Obviating that methodologically and interpretively weak research occurs across the paradigms, Roberts is much about qualitative research getting a hearing in the halls of normative science.[11] Denzin and Wolcott are speaking against this sort of validity that holds qualitative research to a too scientistic accounting. In contrast, Pam Moss, writing out of psychometrics and assessment, argues that all of us are under theoretic pressure in terms of foundational assumptions. In her 1996 *Educational Researcher* article on validity in educational measurement, Moss argues for a reflexive complementarity between varied approaches to the social sciences in order to think reflexively about our taken-for-granted practices and perspectives. Unlike Roberts, Moss sees a reciprocity of accountability in this purposeful engagement across paradigmatic assumptions.

Particularly interested in how assessment practice might benefit from interpretive theory and research, she posits the fallibility and constitutive workings of knowledge claims, the ethical and political implications of epistemological choices, the historical and culturally situated nature of frameworks, the dialectic between researcher and researched, the constraining as well as useful effects of our categories, and the role of power in constructing coherent interpretations. "Who has the authority to construct and evaluate knowledge claims," she asks in her conclusion (p. 26), as she cautions against "a priori criteria abstracted from existing practices." Moss's urging is toward "critical reflection on the very *criteria* of validity that are brought to bear" on concrete situations of research (p. 26, original emphasis). "Enlarging the concept of validity" to open up the field of assessment, she argues for "'epistemic reflexivity'" (p. 27) and "'learning to live with [among] rival pluralistic incommensurable traditions'" (p. 28).[12]

Moss's expansion of validity echoes the argument of Mishler (1990) that the "problem" of validity is about deep theoretical issues that technical solutions cannot begin to address. Ever since Cronbach and Meehl's 1955 essay on the problems with construct validity in psychological testing, validity has been the problem, not the solution. Various postpositivist efforts have been made to resolve the problem: from the naturalistic and constructivist paradigms of Lincoln and Guba (1985, Guba & Lincoln, 1989) that dominated the early discourse of qualitative research in education; to discourse theory (Mishler, 1990); to ethnographic authority (Clifford, 1983; Gordon, 1990; Britzman, 1995); to critical, feminist, and race-based paradigms (Lather, 1986a, b; Gitlin, 1994; Stanfield, 1994; Tuhiwai Smith, 1999); and to more recent poststructuralisms (Cherryholmes, 1988; Kvale, 1995; Lather, 1991). Some efforts toward validity in qualitative research remain deeply inscribed in a correspondence model of truth and assumptions of transparent narration (LeCompte & Goetz, 1982). Others attempt validity practices that take into account the crisis of representation (Lather, 1993; Lenzo, 1995). And some call for new imaginaries altogether, where validity is as much about the play of difference as the

---

[9] Lenzo (1995, p. 19), for example, uses "Justifying Feminist Science" by Linda Alcoff (1992) to argue that we "fool ourselves" if we believe that we can come clean "under the confessing, redemptive, self-reflexive gaze." This is a different sort of concern about the limits of reflexivity than someone like Patai (1994, pp. 64, 67) who derides "postmodernist methodolatry" for encouraging "wading in the morass of our own positionings" through "endless self-scrutiny and anxious self-identification."

[10] Here Roberts echoes a 1994 AERA session, "But Is It Research," where Deborah Britzman concluded her comments with the hope that educational research would become unintelligible to itself. Britzman's statement situates unintelligibility as an ethical imperative and political intervention in terms of disrupting the ways we make sense. To theorize intelligibility is to ask how certain ways of thinking and acting become available to us, while others remain unthought and unperformed (St. Pierre, 1997). Kate McCoy (1997, pp. 333–334) unpacks the idea of intelligibility further within the context of qualitative research: "The idea of intelligibility is linked to the idea of the natural. The things that are most intelligible are the things that seem natural and, consequently, unquestionable. . . . Thus intelligibility has consequences not only for what is sayable and understandable but also for what is doable."

[11] It is this failure to position his critique of qualitative research in relation to the limits of positivism that I disagree with in Roberts, as I share his concern that qualitative data is often underanalyzed. Focusing on the argumentative structure of the research report, Roberts usefully distinguishes between a case story and a case study, with the former being neither systematic nor providing any depth of analysis, the equivalent of a data table in a quantitative study.

[12] Moss is quoting, respectively, Pierre Bourdieu and Richard Bernstein.

repetition of sameness (Scheurich, 1996). Rather than exhausting the problem, all exemplify how the effort to answer the problem of validity is always partial, situated, temporary.

In what follows, I delineate these provisional "solutions" by using the frame of constitutive versus regulatory discourses of validity in a move to displace normative criteria of quality. By way of introduction to this framework, normative criteria posit themselves as universal and attempt to regulate "best way" procedures, whereas constitutive criteria are situated, relational, temporal-historical. Unlike standardized regulatory criteria, constitutive criteria move away from compelling conviction to some essence and toward contextually relevant practices that both disrupt referential logic and shift orientation from the object to the relations of its perception, to its situation of address and reception.[13]

Counter-Practices of Authority: From Quality Criteria to Social Practices

> So here it is
> for you
> a glossary of
> some of my validities
> none of which
> will fit into a wheelbarrow.
> (O'Connor, 1996, p. 19)

Over the past decade or so, various discourse-practices of validity in qualitative research in education have entered and circulated, with differential intelligibilities and effects. Some practices travel well across paradigms and ontologies; some are less nomadic, less border crossers. Critical tensions shift around, from early worries about researcher effects to more recent concerns about "vanity ethnography" (Van Maanen, 1988). In what follows, my concern is not so much with the genesis or the historical unfolding of the concept of validity as with the move from a central structure to a system of differences. My particular interest is in positioning counterpractices of authority as a kind of "indiscipline," movements of cultural and political indiscipline that blur the borders between science and "not-science."

Just a decade ago, most qualitative dissertations in education used Lincoln and Guba's delineation of validity as a sort of mantra. Such widespread usage evidences the importance of a validity discourse appropriate to qualitative research, but most interesting to me is how Guba and Lincoln's early delineation worked in unanticipated ways to undercut representational logic and spawn increasingly postepistemic practices of validity. To pursue this reading, I trace the movement of their thinking across a decade of validity formulations. As I set the stage, my first layer in the story of validity in qualitative research is from the pages of a textbook on educational research picked rather randomly from my shelves, a textbook standard in its consignment of qualitative research to a single chapter.

The Standard Story from the Side of Positivism

Whereas the criteria for the credibility of quantitative research is based on the validity and reliability of instruments and internal validity, in qualitative research the primary criterion is the credibility of the study (McMillan, 1996). Credibility is defined as the extent to which the data, data analysis, and conclusions are believable and trustworthy as based on a set of standard practices. Markers of credibility include triangulation defined as the use of different methods and sampling of people, times, and places. Reliability "is the fit between what occurs and what is recorded," and it is established by detailed field-notes, a team approach, participant confirmation of accuracy of observations, mechanized recording of data (tape recorders, videotapes, photographs), use of participant quotations, and an active search for discrepant data. Internal validity refers to "the match between researchers' categories and interpretations and what is actually true." It is claimed through prolonged engagement, thick description, thorough delineation of research process, and "unobtrusive entry and participation in the setting" (p. 252). Finally, interestingly, external validity shifts from generalizability based on sampling to reader assessment of transferability.

While this treatment of generalization evidences some attention to postpositivist assumptions, the preceding is grounded in the sort of scientificity that is at issue here. Guba and Lincoln (1989), for example, argue that internal validity, as an assessment of the degree of isomorphism between a study's findings and the real world, cannot have meaning as a criterion in a paradigm that rejects a realist ontology. Additionally, external validity or generalizability has little meaning if realities are multiple and constructed. Erickson's idea of "particularizability" (1986) seems more useful: documenting particular cases with "thick" description, so that the reader can determine the degree of "transferability." Most interesting in this standard treatment of validity in qualitative research in education is the rather unremarked work of the concept of "transferability." Displacing a validity of correspondence with a focus on the terms of address, of reception, orientation shifts to the reader who determines the degree to which a study is "transferable" to their own context of interest. I return to the work of this concept later, but I turn now to my next layer in the story of validity, a standard treatment of validity from someone thinking out of postpositivist paradigmatic assumptions.

The Standard Story from the Side of Postpositivism

Qualitative Evaluation and Research Methods by Michael Patton (1980/1990) was one of the most widely used texts before release of the best-selling *Handbook of Qualitative Research* (1994). Patton elaborates on methodical reporting of systematic procedures of data collection and analysis. Particularly concerned about researcher effects, he cautions against the sort of self-importance that often leads to overrating this problem. The key is that "reducing distortions introduced by evaluator predisposition" (p. 475) is based on "empathic neutrality," a kind of impartiality that works to minimize researcher effect while

---

[13] This last move is taken from Hal Foster's *The Return of the Real* (1996), a look at contemporary art criticism.

recognizing that "the data inevitably represent perspective rather than absolute truth" (p. 475). In delineating legitimating practices, Patton surveys across the most frequently noted figures: Lincoln and Guba (1985, 1989) and Miles and Huberman (1984) on specific validity practices, LeCompte and Goetz (1982) and Kirk and Miller (1986) on reliability and validity, Michael Scriven (1972) on rethinking objectivity, Denzin (1989) on triangulation, Peshkin (1988) on subjectivity as a resource, and Cronbach (1975, 1980) on generalizability. The basic assumptions of this canonical discourse on validity in qualitative research in education can be traced by unpacking the work of, arguably, the central figures in the validity debates in the field, Guba and Lincoln.

(Re)reading Lincoln and Guba

When I teach validity in my qualitative research courses, I begin with the summary chart in their 1985 book, *Naturalistic Inquiry*. Here Lincoln and Guba summarize the techniques for establishing trustworthiness as (a) credibility (prolonged engagement and persistent observation; triangulation of sources, methods, and investigators; peer debriefing; negative case analysis; referential adequacy; and member checks); (b) transferability through thick description; (c) dependability and confirmability through an audit trail; and (d) the reflexive journal (p. 328). Each practice is more or less developed, with the member check positioned as "the most crucial technique" (p. 314). All are offered in the hopes of working against prescription and "neoorthodoxy" (p. 330).

By 1989, Guba and Lincoln had moved to a delineation of three different approaches: parallel or quasi-foundational criteria, now called trustworthy criteria; the nature of the hermeneutic process itself; and a new set of nonfoundational criteria, termed the authenticity criteria, inspired by the "gentle" urging of John K. Smith (Lincoln, 1995, p. 286; Smith, 1993). The parallel criteria map onto the 1985 formulation, but they are more clearly located in a postrealist ontology, for example, triangulation is de-emphasized as "too positivist" in its assumptions of "unchanging phenomena" (p. 240). "The hermeneutic process as its own quality control" argues the difficulty of falsity because of the interactive, dialogic nature of the research process.[14] The most noteworthy feature of the authenticity criteria is the break with more traditional methodological criteria into criteria that blur the line between ethics and validity. Termed "fairness" and "ontological, educative, catalytic, and tactical authenticity," the criteria are about balancing viewpoints, encouraging the learning of both researcher and researched, sharing knowledge democratically, and fostering social action. While these categories might be questioned in terms of analytic

distinctions and an untroubled notion of authenticity, my emphasis here is the move of validity from a set of epistemic concepts to a space of relational practices in situated contexts of inquiry.[15]

By 1995, Lincoln shifted fully into an antifoundational discourse interested in research as relational and in fostering of action and social justice. Quality criteria are posited as fluid and emergent, with a focus on criteria that collapse the distinction between rigor and ethics. Tracing both the history and the rationale for the continued importance of "rigor criteria," Lincoln notes her continued use of the parallel foundationalist criteria with her doctoral students as a place to begin. She then delineates emerging criteria that, while all relational, are differently aware of the exclusionary function of quality criteria and the inevitability of partial and incomplete standpoints. Regarding the latter, "detachment and author objectivity" become "barriers to quality, not insurance of having achieved it," as she urges researchers to "'come clean'" about their own stances (p. 280).[16]

Epistemology is situated as an ethical issue, and objectivism is displaced by linking research to social action. Key practices are delineated: the use of multiple voices, reflexivity regarding the relationships and contradictions of research processes, reciprocity as a kind of "intense sharing that opens all lives party to the inquiry to examination" (pp. 283–284), sacredness, defined as an ecological awareness about "that which nourishes and sustains us" (p. 284), and sharing the perquisites of privilege such as royalties, as a way to address the cultural and economic capital that academics make out of the lives of others.[17] This latter includes movement toward action inquiry where participants become active "in reclaiming their own histories and re-creating their lives" (p. 285). My interest here is the move beyond the search for uniform criteria, what Schwandt calls "a farewell to criteriology," and the suggestion that "we might . . . permit criteria to grow indigenously as a natural consequence of the inquiry effort" (Lincoln, 1995, p. 286). This call is for a profusion of situated validities, immanent validities, within the context of a particular inquiry.

Seeing validity as an apparatus of betterment, as a cure for what ails us, Lincoln's panegyric contrasts starkly with Scheurich (1996) who, rather than pay tribute, deconstructs "the masks of validity." Across both positivism and postpositivism, Scheurich organizes discourses of validity into three categories. The first, "originary validity," translates conventional science concerns into postpositivism, for example Lincoln and Guba's parallel criteria. "Successor validity" recasts the concepts that arose in opposition to conventional notions of science, for example the concept of catalytic validity that grows out of advocacy research or "research as praxis" (Lather, 1986a, b). Fi-

---

[14] This position is much undercut by arguments such as Ellsworth (1989), Leach (1992), and Scheurich (1995) on the weight of power in dialogic contexts.

[15] Authenticity discourses assume some essence, some natural, some real, as contested by Baudrillard's (1983) theory of the simulacrum and Derrida's (1976) deconstruction of the metaphysics of presence.

[16] On the limits of "coming clean" through self-reflexivity, Nietzsche cautioned that "unmasking is not about removing from the text a cloak that veils the truth, but rather showing the clothing which an apparent 'nakedness' conceals" (Kofman, 1993, p. 92). Nietzsche's critical project was to make the perspective appear, denaturalize it, and position it as the expression of a hierarchical relationship between forces.

[17] The noninnocence of the use of multiple voices is effected by the role of the researcher in selecting what is included and excluded. One example of an effort to both use and trouble the strategy of multiple voices is *Troubling the Angels: Women Living With HIV/AIDS* by Lather and Smithies (1997).

nally, "interrogated validity" deconstructs the policing function of validity. For example, Cherryholmes (1988, p. 450) argues that construct validity is "of and about power."

Scheurich (1996, p. 5) argues that to the extent discourse-practices of validity are about policing the borders between "the accepted from the not true or the unaccepted or the not yet accepted," they are "imperial" in allowing the same and disallowing the different. At the heart of the Western knowledge project, Scheurich writes, is this "Same/Other power binary" (p. 6) that is more about "'Eating the Other" (quoting bell hooks), than it is about increasing knowledge. "Validity practices are unconscious instantiations of a Western philosophical . . . dualism" (p. 8) that is not about individual conscious intentions but about the Western "civilizational project, an imperial project" (p. 7). To undermine this dualism, he urges new imaginaries of validity that both unmask dualisms and celebrate polyphony and difference, the shifting complexities of truth as multiply perspectival.

As a possibility, Scheurich unpacks my 1993 delineation of transgressive validities—ironic, paralogical, rhizomatic, and situated-embodied-voluptuous.[18] All unsettle truth regimes, implode controlling codes, and work against the constraints of authority. All bring the insufficiencies of language and the production of meaning-effects into the foreground; foster differences and heterogeneity; put conventional discursive procedures under erasure; and embody a situated, partial, positioned, explicit tentativeness. All anticipate a politics that desires both justice and the unknown, generate new locally determined norms of understanding, and proliferate open-ended and context-sensitive criteria that enact practices of engagement and self-reflexivity. All bring ethics and epistemology together. Intended to "incite" the proliferation of validity discourse-practices, my effort leaves Scheurich (1996, p. 10) unsatisfied, however, still worried about the capacity of "our restless civilizational immodesty" to reappear with new masks in its continuing absorption of the other into the same. Turning to the accelerating proliferation of marginalized voices, he calls for "a Bakhtinian dialogic carnival, a loud clamor of a polyphonic, open, tumultuous, subversive conversation on validity" (p. 10).

Mary Hermes evokes such a space in a 1997 paper titled "Research Methods as a Situated Response: Towards a First Nations' Methodology." Hermes speaks as an "outside Indian," from multiple and fluid identity categories, about a research project designed to foster community building and revitalization through collaborative curriculum development. "Where are the methods?" she asks. Listing the practices she used that arose out of the cultural specificities of location, she wishes to complicate by example how relationship produced method. Method becomes a situated response, "specific to the culture, the problem, and the dynamics of the particular context" (p. 13). Method becomes ethics and responsibility, as she shifts her position as knower from expert to "receiver" and "gatherer" of stories, stories that she absorbs and relays rather than

critiquing and interpreting. Speaking of "channeling back to the community" her learnings, her desire is to foster methods that break the dynamics of the exploitative colonial relations of normative research. Evoking "Native American research ethics," she urges a kind of policing that "holds researchers accountable" to "standards" that arise from the communities being researched: "In this way, much more community involvement and participation would become a necessary part of the process of research" (p. 10).

A second exemplar of situated validity is Clark and Moss (1996), who examine the ethical and epistemological issues of collaborative research with students coresearching their own literacy practices. "Questions of ethics are intrinsically tied to issues of epistemology," they argue (p. 521), as they delineate immanent practices of validity that move away from abstract and a priori criteria. As they try to avoid "yet another list of rules and criteria," (p. 523, quoting Mishler), their goal is to sketch what an "open-ended, context-sensitive approach to validity might look like" (p. 525). Their central argument is that to separate out issues of validity and ethics is to move away from the sort of research "with" research participants that characterizes ethnographic action research where all share in the shaping of research, authority is negotiated, understanding does not entail agreement, and multiple perspectives are valued (pp. 520–522). Researching "with" and "for," a host of ethical and epistemological validity issues are raised by their methodological choices around practices of cocreating data and collaborative analysis. While they argue from within the context of in-the-field versus more regulatory ethics and practices of validation, participant involvement in all aspects of the inquiry process is, "in fact, central to maintaining and describing the 'goodness' of this study" (p. 539).

These two exemplars bring us full circle, back to standards that involve the necessary participation of the researched in the conduct of the study. But this return to a policing validity is, paradoxically, within situated contexts. How did we get to such a place, and what does it mean? As a sort of homage to Guba's early penchant for tables, I summarize these ideas in Table 15.2.

Table 15.2. Constitutive Versus Regulatory Practices of Validity

- **Constitutive** practices of validity that construct a relationality, a sociality in which to assess the legitimacy of knowledge claims

  versus a **regulatory** validity that polices the borders between "science" and "not-science"

- **Transgressive** practices of validity that theorize, historicize, situate, and interrogate inquiry as a cultural practice

  versus **correspondence** validity that seeks some essential and compels conviction through relation to some "real" world

---

[18] Moss (1996) ventures that my work on transgressive validity is designed "to shock us into acknowledging the role of power in constructing coherent interpretations." She translates transgressive validity into the context of assessment through an argument for multiple interpretations and voices to subvert authoritative interpretations. "Now, I am not prepared to abandon coherence as an epistemological criterion, but I find the challenge informative," she writes. "At least, it makes me more aware of the consequences of the choices I make—the voices I may be silencing by striving to account for all evidence in a coherent, but possibly manipulative and arbitrary, interpretation" (p. 24).

Such a framing moves validity from a discourse about quality as normative to a discourse of relational practices that evokes an epistemic disruption, a transgression of set forms. Such a move can be further summarized using Scheurich's (1996) categories of regulatory, successor, and interruptive validity (see Table 15.3).

Table 15.3. Regulatory, Successor, and Interruptive Validities

Regulatory validity: homogeneous criteria, for example, trustworthiness criteria of Lincoln and Guba (1985):
- parallel positivist criteria, translate conventional science concerns into postpositivism
- dominant, formulaic, readily available codes of validity
- realist ontology, correspondence to some empirical "real"
- a priori standards, foundational, policing

Successor validity: proliferation of quality criteria, for example, authenticity criteria of Guba and Lincoln (1989), catalytic validity of Lather (1986), and Lather's (1993) parody of transgressive validity:
- exhibits postrealist ontology, for example, triangulation de-emphasized as "too positivist"
- begins to blur the line between ethics and validity, for example, fairness criterion of Guba and Lincoln (1989)
- moves from uniform epistemic concepts to a space of relational practices in situated contexts of inquiry
- assumes validity as a "cure" versus Scheurich's idea of "interrogated validity" that asks questions about policing functions of validity

Interruptive validity: reflexive, situated criteria, for example, Clark and Moss (1996) and Hermes (1997):
- experimental practices that disrupt referential logic and bring ethics and epistemology together
- a move from focus on "capturing the object" to relations of our seeing
- a move from policing to self reflection, antifoundational, self-interruptive
- a focus on critical potential of context-specific validity practices, ranging from revaluation of validity as a site of (dis)articulation, to use of validity to further change the terms of the legitimation of knowledge beyond discrete methods and toward the social uses of the knowledge we construct, in order to use the legitimation crisis to rehearse other practices toward changing the social imaginary about research

Transgression, art critic Hal Foster, writes, is a within-against move, at a point of internal crisis of the symbolic order, not a rupture produced outside, but a fracture traced within. This transgression is not about breaking absolutely with an order, but is about registering its points of both breakdown and breakthrough, "the new possibilities that such a crisis might open up" (Foster, 1996, p. 157). It is the critical potential of a transgressive validity that is my interest, a validity capable of helping us negotiate the complex heterogeneity that characterizes contemporary social sciences. As long as it is held in tension, validity is a construct we surrender at our own loss, a construct whose tensions we work to sustain. We need these tensions; we need them to incite and soothe us and to help us get lost and found as we try to get to that place Britzman (1998) evokes where we are unintelligible to ourselves as we face the inadequacy of thought to its object.

What I am writing about, it is clear to me now, are the turns and returns of practices across time and place, practices that

succeeded however provisionally in disarticulating positivism. Transferability, for example, shifted focus to reader response, a move from a hierarchical array of quality criteria to a horizontal, social axis, arranged across space. Lincoln and Guba's economy of trustworthiness provoked counterdiscourses, all of which worked to loosen positivism and suggest the critical potential of validity to put under theoretic pressure the claims of scientificity.

The revaluation I have attempted here moves toward practices of validity that approach the complications of the word and the world. In this incitement, I have tried to temper the aggressive historicism that claims the end of the old and the birth of the new by focusing on what was emergent but not dominant. Such a move is about a kind of decentering that has always been, a palimpsest of emergent and residual forms (Williams, 1977) instead of a clean break with a past assumed to be no longer of use. The reflexivity I am endorsing is about neither paralysis nor endless self-probing, but about opening new sites for work, a reflexivity that is about relational engagement rather than hermetic self-absorption. Positioning validity as the work of (dis)articulation, I have situated it as a discursive site that registers a passage to the never arrived place where we are sure of our knowledges and our selves.

Given the range of alternatives to standard articulations, educational researchers do not have to default to dominant foundational, formulaic, and readily available codes of validity. The hope is that such livable alternatives will provide a means for educational researchers to take positions regarding the contested bodies of thought and practice that shape contemporary inquiry problematics. Situated in the crisis of authority that has occurred across knowledge systems, the challenge is to make productive use of the dilemma of being left to work from traditions of research and discourses of validity that appear no longer adequate to the task. Between the no longer and the not yet lies the possibility of what was impossible under traditional regimes of truth in the human sciences: the invention of other practices of generative methodology out of recognition of the unnoticed dangers of the techniques we use to conceive and resolve our problems of establishing legitimate knowledge. My central argument is that counterpractices are perpetually becoming available if we render explicit the spaces opened up by the growing acceptance of epistemic antifoundationalism (West, 1991). Hence, my evocation is toward the "horizons toward which experiments work" (Ormiston 1990, p. 239) as we try to understand what is at play in our practices of constructing a science "after truth" (Tomlinson 1989). Here impossibility serves not as a logical concept but as an historical one.

Conclusion: Do We Have to Read Derrida?

Derrida won't have to be "gone through" because there will be another model to take our attention. (Bygrave, 1996, p. 148)

This chapter has delineated what McWilliam (1993) terms "galloping theory" as we try to stay ahead of perpetually reforming knowledge problematics. About more than critical fashions, the motivation for such an effort is to engage in a transvaluative moment regarding the purposes of the social sciences: to use validity to further change the terms of the legitimation of knowledge beyond discrete methods and toward the social uses of the knowledge we construct. Caught between a rock of responsibility and accountability and a soft place of the continued claims of scientism to one-best-way production and legitimation of knowledge, we live out these tensions.[19] The crisis of legitimation occurring across knowledge systems is registered in a cacophony of postpositivism, nonfoundationalism, realisms and postrealisms, warranted assertability, logic of inquiry, construct validity, carefully controlled inference, objectivism, situational validity, and Cronbachian insights regarding the decay of generalizations (Garrison, 1994).

Suffering from our categories of science and research and of the failure of their promise to deliver, our practices are overcoded by the normative; our procedures and operations are too much configured into repetitions of banality. To ask what makes certain possibilities impossible for us, now, in this space called educational research is to press our uncertainties and to calculate the apparatuses of our capture. What would it mean to create a different space in which to undertake other thinking, an aesthetic space, a political space? What would it mean to create new solidarities—fragments of other possibilities—to experiment differently with meanings, practices, and our own confoundings? What happens when normative evaluation is replaced by attention to social effect and a sociological sense of audience within present institutional frames? What would it effect to speak from shifting subject positions where we both pass and don't pass as "scientists," occupying zones of legitimacy only to dismantle them or exploit them as sites of intervention?

The geography of such questions is very different from opposing a dominant culture considered radically other. Such a move is about working within-against the dominant, contesting its borders, tracing our complicity, moving toward some place that might be termed a double science, both science and not-science.[20] To position our work as both within a disciplinary discourse of the human sciences and as a wanderer outside of the science it purports to be is to capture the vitality of the deviations that elude taxonomies in addressing the question of practices of science within a postfoundational context.

As somewhat of a science outlaw, I use the validity debates to ask what becomes possible when all of educational inquiry, positivist and postpositivist alike, is positioned as a site of crisis. Situating educational inquiry as distressed and exceeded, I raise questions about the difficulties and limitations of the categories we use to do our work. We hardly know how to think in such a place, particularly across our paradigmatic divides. But now, out from under scientism, finally, perhaps we can begin to rehearse other practices in order to change the social imaginary about research. To move beyond the normalized apparatuses of our own training toward a social science more answerable to the complications of our knowing is more about "the changing shape of the thinkable" (Gordon 1991, p. 3) than it is about actually existing practices of validity. Such an effort is about how we might invent ourselves into "the surprise of what is not yet possible in the histories of the spaces in which we find ourselves" (Rajchman 1991, p. 163).[21]

REFERENCES

Althusser, L. (1971). *Lenin and philosophy and other essays* (B. Brewster, Trans.). New York: Monthly Review Press.

Apple, M. (Ed.). (1995). *Review of research in education, 1995–96, 21.* Washington, DC: AERA.

Aronowitz, S. (1995). Bringing science and scientificity down to earth. *Cultural Studies Times, 1*(3), 12,14.

Baudrillard, J. (1983). *Simulations* (P. Foss & P. Patton, Trans.). New York: Semiotext(e).

Britzman, D. (1995). The question of belief: Writing poststructural ethnography. *Qualitative Studies in Education, 8*(5), 233–242.

Britzman, D. (1998). *Lost subjects, contested objects: Toward a psychoanalytic inquiry of learning.* Albany: SUNY Press.

Butler, J. (1993). Poststructuralism and postmarxism. *diacritics, 23*(4), 3–11.

Butler, J. (1995). For a careful reading. In S. Benhabib, J. Butler, D. Cornell, & N. Fraser, *Feminist contentions: A philosophical exchange* (pp. 127–144). New York: Routledge.

Bygrave, S. (1996, Spring). Responsibilities on the far side [Review of Rodolphe Gasche, *Inventions of difference: On Jacques Derrida* (Harvard University Press, 1994)]. *New Formations, 28,* 145–148.

Casey, K. (1995). The new narrative research in education. In M. Apple (Ed.), *Review of research in education, 1995–96, 21* (pp. 211–253). Washington, DC: AERA.

Cherryholmes, C. (1988). *Power and criticism: Poststructural investigations in education.* New York: Teachers College Press.

Clark, C., & Moss, P. (1996). Researching *with:* Ethical and epistemological implications of doing collaborative, change-oriented research with teachers and students. *Teachers College Record, 97,* 518–548.

Clifford, J. (1983). On ethnographic authority. *Representations, 1*(2), 118–146.

Clifford, J., & Marcus, G., (Eds.). (1986). *Writing culture: The poetics and politics of ethnography.* Berkeley: University of California Press.

Cronbach, L. (1975). Beyond the two disciplines of scientific psychology. *American Psychologist, 30,* 116–127.

Cronbach, L. (1980). Validity on parole: Can we go straight? *New Directions for Testing and Measurement, 5,* 99–108.

Cronbach, L., & Meehl, P. (1955). Construct validity in psychological tests. *Psychological Bulletin, 52,* 281–302.

Darling-Hammond, L. (Ed.). (1994). *Review of research in education.* Washington, DC: AERA.

Denzin, N. (1989). *The research act* (3rd ed.). Englewood Cliffs, NJ: Prentice Hall.

Denzin, N. (1994, April). Validity after poststructuralism. Paper presented at the annual meeting of the American Educational Research Association, New Orleans, LA.

---

[19] In "Issues of Validity in Openly Ideological Research: Between a Rock and a Soft Place," I recast the familiar metaphor so that the "rock" was the unquestionable need for trustworthiness in data generated by alternative paradigms and the "soft place" was the positivist claim to neutrality and objectivity (Lather, 1986b, p. 65).

[20] Derrida (1982) speaks of a double science: "Deconstruction cannot limit itself or proceed immediately to a neutralization: it must, by means of a double gesture, a double science, a double writing, practice an *overturning* of the classical opposition *and* a general *displacement* of the system. It is only on this condition that deconstruction will provide itself the means with which to *intervene* in the field of oppositions that it criticizes. . . . Deconstruction does not consist in passing from one concept to another, but in overturning and displacing a conceptual order. . . . To leave to this new concept the old name . . . is to maintain the structure of the graft, the transition and indispensable adherence to an effective *intervention* in the constituted historic field" (pp. 329–330, original emphases).

[21] These passages are grafted from the work of John Struik (1993a, b) on heteronormativity as a ruin.

Denzin, N., & Lincoln, Y. (Eds.). (1994). *Handbook of qualitative research.* Thousand Oaks, CA: Sage.

Denzin, N., & Lincoln, Y. (Eds.). (2000). *Handbook of qualitative research* (2nd ed.). Thousand Oaks, CA: Sage.

Derrida, J. (1976). *Of grammatology* (G. Spivak, Trans.). Baltimore: Johns Hopkins University Press.

Derrida, J. (1982). *Margins of philosophy* (A. Bass, Trans.). Chicago: University of Chicago Press.

Derrida, J. (1994). *Specters of Marx: The state of the debt, the work of mourning, and the new international* (P. Kamuf, Trans.). New York: Routledge.

Derrida, J. (1996) By force of mourning. *Critical Inquiry, 22*(2), 171–192.

Dickens, D., & Fontana, A. (Eds.). (1994). *Postmodernism and social inquiry.* New York: The Guilford Press.

Ellsworth, E. (1989). Why doesn't this feel empowering? Working through the repressive myths of critical pedagogy. *Harvard Educational Review, 59*(3), 297–325.

Epstein, S. (1996). *Impure science: AIDS, activism, and the politics of knowledge.* Berkeley: University of California Press.

Erickson, F. (1986). Qualitative methods in research on teaching. In M. C. Wittrock (Ed.), *Handbook of research on teaching* (pp. 119–161). New York: Macmillan.

Fay, B. (1987). *Critical social science.* Ithaca, NY: Cornell University Press.

Fiske, D., & Shweder, R. (Eds.). (1986). *Metatheory in social science: Pluralisms and subjectivities.* Chicago: University of Chicago Press.

Foster, H. (1996). *The return of the real: The avant-garde at the end of the century.* Cambridge: MIT Press.

Foucault, M. (1980). *Power/knowledge* (C. Gordon, Ed. and Trans.). New York: Pantheon.

Garrison, J. (1994). Realism, Deweyan pragmatism, and educational research. *Educational Researcher, 23*(1), 5–14.

Geertz, C. (1980). Blurred genres. *The American Scholar, 49,* 165–179.

Gitlin, A. (Ed.) (1994). *Power and method.* New York: Routledge.

Gitlin, A., Siegel, M., & Boru, K. (1989). The politics of method: From leftist ethnography to educative research. *Qualitative Studies in Education, 2,* 237–53.

Gordon, C. (1991). Governmental rationality: An introduction. In G. Burchell, C. Gordon, & P. Miller (Eds.), *The Foucault effect: Studies in governmentality* (pp. 1–51). Chicago: University of Chicago Press.

Gordon, D. (1990). The politics of ethnographic authority: Race and writing in the ethnography of Margaret Mead and Zora Neale Hurston. In M. Manganaro (Ed.), *Modernist anthropology: From fieldwork to textwork* (pp. 146–162). Princeton: Princeton University Press.

Greene, M. (1994). Epistemology and educational research: The influence of recent approaches to knowledge. In L. Darling-Hammond (Ed.), *Review of research in education* (pp. 423–464). Washington, DC: AERA.

Gross, P., & Levitt, N. (1994). *Higher superstition: The academic left and its quarrels with science.* Baltimore: Johns Hopkins University Press.

Guba, E., & Lincoln, Y. (1989). *Fourth generation evaluation.* Newbury Park, CA: Sage.

Harding, S. (Ed.). (1987). *Feminist methodology.* Bloomington: Indiana University Press.

Harding, S. (1991). *Whose science? Whose knowledge?* Ithaca NY: Cornell University Press.

Harding, S. (Ed.). (1993). *The "racial" economy of science.* Bloomington: Indiana University Press.

Hermes, M. (1997, March). Research methods as a situated response: Towards a first nations' methodology. Paper presented at annual meeting of the American Educational Research Association, Chicago, IL.

Hollinger, R. (1994). *Postmodernism and the social sciences: A thematic approach.* Thousand Oaks, CA: Sage.

Kerlinger, F. (1986). *Foundations of behavioral research* (3rd ed.). New York: Holt, Rinehart & Winston.

Kirk, J., & Miller, M. (1986). *Reliability and validity in qualitative research.* Newbury Park, CA: Sage.

Kofman, S. (1993). *Nietzsche and metaphor* (D. Large, Trans.). Stanford: Stanford University Press.

Kreiswirth, M., & Carmichael, T. (Eds.). (1995). *Constructive criticism: The human sciences in the age of theory.* Toronto: University of Toronto Press.

Kvale, S. (1989). To validate is to question. In S. Kvale (Ed.), *Issues of validity in qualitative research* (pp. 73–92). Sweden: Studentliterature.

Kvale, S. (1995). The social construction of validity. *Qualitative Inquiry, 1*(1), 19–40.

Lather, P. (1986a). Research as praxis. *Harvard Educational Review, 56*(3), 257–277.

Lather, P. (1986b). Issues of validity in openly ideological research: Between a rock and a soft place. *Interchange, 17*(4), 63–84.

Lather, P. (1991). *Getting smart: Feminist research and pedagogy with/in the postmodern.* New York: Routledge.

Lather, P. (1993). Fertile obsession: Validity after poststructuralism. *The Sociological Quarterly, 34*(4), 673–693.

Lather, P., & Smithies, C. (1997). *Troubling the angels: Women living with HIV/AIDS.* Boulder, CO: Westview Press.

Leach, M. (1992). Can we talk? A response to Burbules and Rice. *Harvard Educational Review, 62*(2), 257–271.

LeCompte, M. D., & Goetz, J. P. (1982). Problems of reliability and validity in ethnographic research. *Review of Educational Research, 52*(1), 31–60.

LeCompte, M. D., Millroy, W. L., & Preissle, J. (Eds.). (1992). *The handbook of qualitative research in education.* New York: Academic Press.

Lenzo, K. (1995). Validity and self-reflexivity meet poststructuralism: Scientific ethos and the transgressive self. *Educational Researcher, 24*(4), 17–23.

Lincoln, Y. (1995). Emerging criteria for quality in qualitative and interpretive research. *Qualitative Inquiry, 1*(3), 275–289.

Lincoln, Y., & Guba, E. (1985). *Naturalistic inquiry.* Newbury Park, CA: Sage.

Lyotard, J. F. (1984). *The Postmodern Condition* (G. Bennington & B. Massumi, Trans.). Minneapolis: University of Minnesota Press.

McCoy, K. (1997). White noise—The sound of epidemic: Reading/writing a climate of intelligibility around the "crisis" of difference. *International Journal of Qualitative Studies in Education, 10*(3), 333–347.

McDonald, T. (Ed.). (1996). *The historic turn in the human sciences.* Ann Arbor, MI: University of Michigan Press.

McMillan, J. (1996). *Educational research: Fundamentals for the consumer* (2nd ed.). New York: HarperCollins.

McWilliam, E. (1993). "Post" haste: Plodding research and galloping theory. *British Journal of Sociology of Education, 14*(2), 199–205.

Melville, S. (1996). *Seams: Art as a philosophical context* (J. Gilbert-Rolfe, Ed.). Amsterdam: G. & B. Arts.

Miles, M., & Huberman, A. (1984). Drawing valid meaning from qualitative data: Toward a shared craft. *Educational Researcher, 13*(5), 20–30.

Mishler, E. (1990). Validation in inquiry-guided research: The role of exemplars in narrative studies. *Harvard Educational Review, 60*(4), 415–442.

Moss, P. (1996). Enlarging the dialogue in educational measurement: Voices from interpretive research traditions. *Educational Researcher, Jan–Feb,* 20–28, 43.

Nelson, J., Megill, A., & McCloskey, D. (Eds.). (1987). *The rhetoric of the human sciences: Language and argument in scholarship and public affairs.* Madison: University of Wisconsin Press.

O'Connor, K. (1996). Glossary of validities. *Journal of Contemporary Ethnography, 25*(1), 16–21.

Ormiston, G. (1990). Postmodern differends. In A. Dallery & C. Scott (Eds.), *Crisis in continental philosophy* (pp. 235–283). Albany: SUNY Press.

Patai, D. (1994). (Response) When method becomes power. In A. Gitlin (Ed.), *Power and method* (pp. 61–73). New York: Routledge.

Patton, M. (1990). *Qualitative evaluation and research methods.* Newbury Park, CA: Sage. (Original work published in 1980).

Peshkin, A. (1988). In search of subjectivity—one's own. *Educational Researcher, 17*(7), 17–22.

Rajchman, J. (1991). *Philosophical events: Essays of the 80's.* New York: Columbia University Press.

Readings, B. (1996). *The university in ruins.* Cambridge, MA: Harvard University Press.

Roberts, D. (1996). What counts as quality in qualitative research? *Science Education, 80*(3), 243–248.

Rorty, R. (Ed.). (1967). *The linguistic turn: Essays in philosophical method.* Chicago: University of Chicago Press.

Rorty, R. (1982). *The consequences of pragmatism.* Minneapolis: University of Minnesota Press.

Roseneau, P. (1992). *Post-modernism and the social sciences: Insights, inroads, and intrusions.* Princeton: Princeton University Press.

Ross, A. (Ed.). (1996). *Science wars.* Durham, NC: Duke University Press.

Scheurich, J. (1995). A postmodernist critique of research interviewing. *Qualitative Studies in Education, 8*(3), 230–252.

Scheurich, J. (1996). The masks of validity: A deconstructive investigation. *Qualitative Studies in Education, 9*(1), 49–60.

Schwandt, T. (1996). Farewell to criteriology. *Qualitative Inquiry, 2*(1), 58–72.

Scriven, M. (1972). Objectivity and subjectivity in educational research. In L. G. Thomas (Ed.), *Philosophical redirection of educational research: The seventy-first yearbook of the National Society for the Study of Education.* Chicago: University of Chicago Press.

Serres, M., & Latour, B. (1995). *Conversations on science, culture, and time* (R. Lapidus, Trans.). Ann Arbor: University of Michigan Press.

Simons, H. (Ed.). (1989). *Rhetoric in the human sciences.* London: Sage.

Smith, J. (1993). *After the demise of empiricism: The problem of judging social and educational inquiry.* Norwood, NJ: Ablex.

Spanos, W. (1993). *The end of education: Toward posthumanism.* Minneapolis: University of Minnesota Press.

Spivak, G. (1976). Translator's preface. In J. Derrida, *Of grammatology* (pp. ix–xc). Baltimore: Johns Hopkins University Press.

St. Pierre, B. (1997). An introduction to figurations: A poststructural practice of inquiry. *Qualitative Studies in Education, 10*(3), 279–284.

Stanfield, J. (1994). Ethnic modeling in qualitative research. In N. Denzin & Y. Lincoln (Eds.), *Handbook of qualitative research* (pp. 175–188). Thousand Oaks, CA: Sage.

Struik, J. (1993a). Bodies in trouble and the problem of sexual practices. Paper presented at the Queer Sites Conference, Toronto, Ontario.

Struik, J. (1993b, October). Queer cures. Paper presented at the Bergamo Curriculum Theorizing Conference, Dayton, OH.

Tomlinson, H. (1989). After truth: Post-modernism and the rhetoric of science. In H. Lawson & L. Appignanesi (Eds.), *Dismantling truth: Reality in a post-modern world* (pp. 43–57). New York: St. Martin's Press.

Tuhiwai Smith, L. (1999). *Decolonizing methodologies: Research and indigenous peoples.* London: Zed Books.

Van Maanen, J. (1988). *Tales of the field: On writing ethnography.* Chicago: University of Chicago Press.

Van Maanen, J. (1995). An end to innocence: The ethnography of ethnography. In J. Van Maanen (Ed.), *Representation in ethnography* (pp. 1–35). Thousand Oaks, CA: Sage.

West, C. (1991). Theory, pragmatisms, and politics. In J. Arac & B. Johnson (Eds.), *Consequences of theory* (pp. 22–38). Baltimore: Johns Hopkins University Press.

Williams, R. (1977). *Marxism and literature.* Oxford: Oxford University Press.

Wolcott, H. (1990). On seeking—and rejecting—validity in qualitative research. In E. Eisner & A. Peshkin (Eds.), *Qualitative inquiry in education: The continuing debate* (pp. 121–152). New York: Teachers College Press.

16.
Mixing Social Inquiry Methodologies

Jennifer C. Greene
University of Illinois at Urbana-Champaign

> *There is no reason to assume that dialogue across differences involves either eliminating those differences or imposing one group's view on others; dialogue that leads to understanding, cooperation, and accommodation can sustain differences within a broader compact of toleration and respect.*
>
> (Burbules & Rice, 1991, p. 402)

Creating meaningful forums for such dialogue is the task of 21st-century democracy and also the challenge of 21st-century applied social science. Both our society and our science today are highly pluralistic. In fact, the paradigmatic and methodological pluralism of contemporary social science mirrors the political and cultural pluralism of the larger society. The proliferation of divergent inquiry frameworks within science reflects the contemporary raced, classed, gendered differentiation of the broader society. Impassioned exchanges within the academy about contending views on what constitutes knowledge and how best to do our work parallel the contentious politics of difference that fracture the larger society. To prevent rifts of irreparable magnitude, both the academy and the larger society need to learn more effective ways to respect and honor the differences among us while also striving to name and strengthen our commonalities and our connections.

Within the domain of applied social science, the challenge of honoring difference while strengthening connection is directly addressed by a mixed-method approach to inquiry. A mixed-method approach intentionally incorporates the lenses of more than one inquiry framework—through the collection of different kinds of information, the combined use of different kinds of methods, the maintenance of different philosophical assumptions about social phenomena and our ability to know them, and the inclusion of diverse values and interests. That is, the differences that are respected and promoted in mixed-method inquiry are themselves diverse. Mixed-method inquiry can take different forms in the field. And it can range from relatively modest departures from standard methodologies—for example, the inclusion of a few open-ended interviews to complement a large-scale survey—to more dramatically inventive combinations—for example, the nesting of an ethnography within the logic of experimentation (Maxwell, Bashook, & Sandlow, 1986).

The primary rationale shaping the mixed-method commitment to honor difference is the desire to understand more fully, to generate insights that are deeper and broader, and to develop important knowledge claims that respect a wider range of interests and perspectives. Mixed-method inquiry, that is, rests on the assumptions that each of our ways of knowing offers a meaningful and legitimate view of what we are striving to know and, therefore, that incorporating multiple ways of knowing will enable us to know better and more fully. Each way of knowing contributes a different thread of understanding to the whole cloth being woven, which is richer, more textured, and more complete because of its diverse and multiple threads.

In any discussion of mixing social inquiry methodologies, it must be fully acknowledged that different ways of knowing can invoke tensions and knots of conflict among the different threads of understanding, which can challenge even the most skillful of weavers. In the present mixed-method discussion, the argument is made that it is precisely in these tensions and points of conflict that mixed-method inquiry offers its greatest potential for better understanding. The better understanding is achieved through the creation of an analytic space that doesn't necessarily resolve the tensions but rather uses them—in re-

The author thanks reviewers Hallie Preskill (University of New Mexico) and William Firestone (Rutgers, The State University of New Jersey) and my continuing mixed-method collaborators, Valerie Caracelli and Mel Mark.

spectful conversation—to probe more deeply and stretch the boundaries of what is known in new directions. So, stronger mixed-method designs will be those that invite more diverse ways of knowing and that create dialectic tensions among conflicting claims to know. Recognizing that not all these conflicts may be resolved, the resultant woven cloth may be more nubby and irregular, but is also likely to be more expressive and resplendent.

In the remainder of this chapter, I will elaborate on this view of mixed-method social inquiry. The discussion concentrates on mixing methods from interpretivist-qualitative and postpositivist-quantitative inquiry traditions, for these have cornered much of the debate. The logic of the discussion, however, is intended to apply more broadly to other inquiry methods and frameworks, for example, those framed by feminist, collaborative, action-oriented, and critical perspectives. The next section will discuss more fully the purposes and rationales for mixing methods in applied social inquiry today. This is followed by a presentation of practical design ideas and strategies for mixed-method inquiry, including comments on when a single methodology will suffice and when not to mix methods. A brief conclusion will highlight conceptual and practical mixed-method avenues that warrant further development.

Why Mix Social Inquiry Methodologies

Purposes and rationales for mixing different methods in applied social inquiry are examined first at the technical level of individual method and then at the philosophical level of inquiry framework or logic of justification.

The Debate at the Technical Level of Method

> Every cobbler thinks that leather is the only thing. Most social scientists . . . have their favorite methods. . . . [But now] let us be done with the arguments of "participant observation" *versus* interviewing . . . and get on with the business of attacking our problems with the widest array of conceptual and methodological tools that we possess and they demand. (Trow, 1957, p. 35)

> It is the current absence of total certainty about what constitutes correct practice that leads to the advocacy of multiplism in perspectives and methods. . . . The fundamental postulate of multiplism is that when it is not clear which of several options for question generation or method choice is "correct," all of them should be selected so as to "triangulate" on the most useful or the most likely to be true. (Cook, 1985, pp. 22, 38)

The sensibility of using multiple methods in applied social research has long been recognized within both interpretivist-qualitative and postpositivist-quantitative traditions (among others), as illustrated respectively by the above excerpts from Martin Trow (see also Denzin, 1978) and Thomas Cook (see also Campbell & Fiske, 1959). This recognition builds on the assumed fallibility, limitations, and biases inherent in any given method and seeks to compensate for such constraints by using multiple methods with counterbalancing limitations and biases. The compelling rationale for "multiplism" at this level of method has been to strengthen construct and conclusion validity through the triangulation of information from multiple sources.

Extending this logic—from using multiple methods within an inquiry framework to using multiple methods drawn from different inquiry frameworks—mixing methods—has invoked several other arguments, which have affirmed and reinforced the nearly universal support for the technical sensibility of mixing methods. Primary among these arguments are the following two. First, because social phenomena are so complex and social problems so intractable, all of our methodological tools are needed for understanding and for action. Any single method by itself can render only partial insight from but one perspective. Gabriel Salomon (1991), for example, argued that educational phenomena like classrooms are so complex they warrant the complementary use of both "analytic" and "systemic" approaches and methods, perhaps most feasibly across studies. In similar fashion, C. C. Ragin (1989) argued that comparative social inquiry can best be advanced via a synthesis of "case- and variable-oriented approaches," or approaches that frame complexity by holistically understanding the interrelationships within individual cases and approaches that order complexity by analyzing relationships across the variables that define the cases.

The second mixed-method argument at the technical level underscores the essential interdependence of different methods in all of our claims to know. Referring especially to social program evaluation contexts, Donald Campbell (1974) maintained that qualitative knowing underlies all quantitative inferencing, that an inquirer cannot discern a plausible from an implausible explanation without first-hand, experiential knowledge of the local context. Kenneth Howe (1988) insisted that qualitative beliefs about the phenomena being studied permeate all substantive conclusions and conceptual inferences. Ernest House (1994a) similarly argued that the findings from different methods "come together in the content," whether that content is knowledge about the effectiveness of a particular social intervention or conceptual claims at the level of theory. Fielding and Fielding (1986) noted that in sociology, qualitative fieldwork focuses on the microlevel of individual action, while quantitative inquiry addresses the macrolevel of collective structure. Arguing that these micro- and macrolevels are integrated in daily life and that each "bears within it indirect reference to the existence of the other" (pp. 20–21), "an intimate 'back-and-forth,' testing, critique, and synthesis [of the two approaches] stands the best chance of specifying powerful solutions" to important inquiry problems (pp. 12–13).

In previous research (Greene, Caracelli, & Graham, 1989), I worked with colleagues to organize these various rationales for mixing methods into a set of five distinct mixed-method purposes, each of which can invoke different design and analysis decisions. The conceptual traditions, references, and details supporting these five purposes can be found in that work (1989). These five mixed-method purposes are listed below.

1. In a classic sense, mixing methods for the purpose of *triangulation* seeks convergence, corroboration, and correspondence of results across the different methods. Different methods are used to increase the validity of constructs and inquiry results by counterbalancing known method biases

and limitations. For example, in studying socially deviant behavior such as excessive drinking, unobtrusive measures like garbage analysis could be used to counterbalance known social desirability biases of self-report measures. By definition, triangulation designs use different methods to measure the same constructs or phenomena. Because the construct definition must remain the same across methods, triangulation designs are characteristically limited to just one inquiry paradigm.

2. In a *complementarity* mixed-method design, different methods are used to measure overlapping, but distinct facets of the phenomena under investigation. Results from one method are intended not necessarily to converge with but rather to elaborate, enhance, illustrate, or clarify results from the other. A common complementarity design uses questionnaires to assess the prevalence of a phenomenon—for example, student perceptions of instructional quality—and interviews to assess its meaningfulness—for example, the connections students make between instructional quality and learning. Complementarity increases the interpretability, meaningfulness, and validity of constructs and inquiry results by both counteracting inherent method biases and capitalizing on inherent method strengths.

3. *Development* designs use different methods sequentially in order to use the results of one method to help develop the other method or inform its implementation— as in sampling. For example, the factor analysis results of a questionnaire assessing student perceptions of instructional quality could form one set of themes to be probed in a follow-up interview.

4. Combining methods for purposes of *expansion* occurs when inquirers use different methods for different inquiry components in order to extend the breadth and range of the inquiry. Using observations to measure behavior and self-reports to assess perceptions is a sensible expansion design.

5. Finally, *initiation* designs intentionally seek the discovery of paradox and contradiction, and new perspectives or frameworks via the recasting of questions or results from one method with questions or results from the other method. For example, in a regression analysis examining the relationship between instructional technology use and student motivation, one could include an inductive typology of instructional media generated from extensive teacher interviews. Initiation designs are intended to provoke fresh insights, new concepts, and imaginative interpretations.

This consensual support for the benefits of mixing methods at the technical level has been harder to achieve at the paradigm level of the debate. As discussed in the next section, reframing this debate offers one avenue for progress.

The Debate at the Philosophical Level of Inquiry Paradigm

The juxtaposition of knowledge constructed from different epistemological paradigms [is] encouraged as a way of promoting fruitful, knowledge-creating dialogue, . . . a way of making new "world visions" out of the raw material of our different frameworks for understanding the world. (Mathie, 1996, pp. 57–58)

[Likening qualitative and quantitative research traditions to cultures], we want to preserve the significant differences between the two cultures. Instead of homogenizing research methods and cultures, we would like to see researchers become bicultural. (Kidder & Fine, 1987, p. 57)

In this arena of competing perspectives, multimethod researchers have a vested interest in bridging differences and bringing about common understanding. They may play an almost ambassadorial role similar to that sometimes played by persons who are subjected to cross-pressures in other politicized situations. (Brewer & Hunter, 1989, p. 178)

Dialogue, biculturalism (and multiculturalism), and ambassadorial diplomacy toward common understandings are apt images for the view of mixed-method social inquiry being advanced in this discussion. These images convey norms of reciprocity, respect, and openness while they simultaneously underscore the existence and the acceptance of difference. Even more, these images convey a commitment to actually using our differences to generate more meaningful claims to know and more visionary understandings of our social worlds than would be possible with just a single methodology. This mixed-method stance has evolved from prior conversations about competing frameworks for social inquiry. The key to this evolution has been a reenvisioning of just what differences really matter between and among alternative inquiry frameworks. (For this discussion, a social inquiry framework—a logic of justification, a paradigm—is construed as a set of interlocking assumptions and stances about knowledge, our social world, our ability to know that world, and our reasons for knowing it that collectively warrant certain methods, certain knowledge claims, and certain actions on those claims.) The route to this reenvisioning is traced in the discussion that follows.

Many prior conversations about alternative inquiry frameworks have been dominated by contrasts and debates over core philosophical tenets of these frameworks (e.g., Guba, 1990). Using quantitative and qualitative inquiry traditions as examples, these include debates over realism versus relativism, objectivity versus subjectivity, and nomothetic versus ideographic knowing. While productive for some purposes—for example, exploring nuanced meanings of *scientific realism* (Garrison, 1994; House, 1994b)—these debates have not usefully advanced the mixed-method conversation. Moreover, these debates reflect fundamental philosophical differences that have long histories and that are not likely to be reconciled in our lifetimes (Krantz, 1995). Reconciliation is not even necessarily the right question, at least in the present context of promoting meaningful mixed-method inquiry.

Indeed, one continuing mixed-method stance dubbed the *pragmatic* position (Greene & Caracelli, 1997) maintains that these philosophical differences do not really matter very much to the practice of social inquiry, and so we need not worry about their reconciliation (Bryman, 1988; Patton, 1988). This is because paradigms are best viewed as descriptive characterizations of research practice, not prescriptive dictates about how to practice research. What is more important are the practical demands of inquiry problems. Inquirers should be able to choose whatever will "work best" for a given inquiry problem "without being limited or inhibited" (Patton, 1988, p. 117) by philosophical assumptions. Given the inherent complexity of social scientific problems, often what will work best is a combination or mixture of different kinds of methods.

I agree that inquiry practice should not be driven by the unilateral dictates of abstract philosophical assumptions (Howe, 1988). But, it also should not be exclusively or even primarily shaped by the demands of the inquiry context. To respond with integrity, coherence, and consistency to these demands requires a paradigmatic anchor. In addition to context, that is, "methodology also depends on ontological and epistemological assumptions about the nature of reality and best ways of gaining access to that reality, so that knowledge about it can be formulated" (House, 1994a, p. 15). So, actual inquiry planning and implementation decisions are importantly shaped by both paradigm assumptions and contextual demands such that the epistemological and the practical have a balanced, reciprocal relationship in guiding inquiry practice.

Granting the importance of the epistemological returns us to the problem of irreconcilable paradigmatic differences. The mixed-method question now becomes the following: How can these paradigmatic differences be respected, and while not reconciled, somehow be joined together in the generation of understandings and insights not likely or even possible within just one inquiry paradigm? This mixed-method question reflects a *dialectic* stance (Greene & Caracelli, 1997), which maintains that differences between and among philosophical inquiry paradigms are meaningful and important. In any mixed-method inquiry, therefore, these differences must be honored in ways that maintain the integrity of the disparate paradigms, even as the differences are used toward a dialectical discovery of enhanced understandings.

If philosophical differences among paradigms are irreconcilable, or even might be, then one key to advancement of the mixed-method cause is to recast what constitutes important differences among social inquiry paradigms. Other than assumptions of ontology and epistemology, what are critical features of different inquiry traditions that, although likely to present tensions when combined, are important to preserve precisely because they integrally define those traditions? Or, what are the paradigmatic differences that matter in mixed-method contexts?

One promising alternative here is attention to critical features of the knowledge claims generated by different paradigmatic traditions. The following examples of such features for interpretivism and postpositivism are, again, from Greene & Caracelli (1997):

- Particularity and generality
- Closeness and distance
- Meaning and causality
- The unusual and the representative
- The diversity within the range and the central tendency of the mean
- Social constructions and physical traces
- Integrative synthesis and componential analysis

- Insider and outsider viewpoints
- The contextualized understanding of local meanings and the distanced analysis of regularities
- Connective, relational reasoning and utilitarian, instrumental reasoning

These represent characteristically but not universally different facets of knowledge claims generated from the different inquiry traditions of interpretivism and postpositivism—different, but not necessarily incompatible. Defensible claims to know in interpretive inquiry are characteristically reconstructions of what members of that particular setting have experienced as meaningful. These reconstructions are usually multifaceted, portraying diversity alongside typicality, and holistic, conveying the complexity and nuance of the whole case or story. Defensible claims to know in postpositivist inquiry are characteristically propositions about causal relationships among social phenomena. These propositions have intended generality across settings and intended applicability to broader explanatory theories about patterned regularities in our social worlds. The point here is not about which characteristics accompany which paradigms—reviewers of these ideas have consistently critiqued my alignments. The point is, rather, that there are different characteristics of our social knowledge claims: These different characteristics accompany different techniques and methods (and often, overall methodologies and paradigms), and most importantly, mixed-method inquiry can productively capitalize on merging, blending, and combining these different facets of our social knowing.

Hence, a mixed-method study that does productively combine different ways of knowing would strive for knowledge claims that are grounded in the lives of the participants studied, that have some generality to other participants and other contexts, that offer both contextual understanding and structural explanation, and that isolate factors of particular significance while also integrating the whole. Compared to knowledge claims generated in a single-method study, this mixed-method set of knowledge claims is likely to be more insightful and generative, even if accompanied by continuing unresolved tensions.

Summary

There are many widely endorsed, practical reasons for using multiple, diverse methods in applied social inquiry. These center around the acknowledged fallibility of all methods in tandem with the desire to understand complex social phenomena more completely. The challenge to mixing methods, therefore, lies at the philosophical level. Accepting irreconcilability among the philosophical logics framing different methodologies leaves no space for a mixed-method approach. Such space can be created, however, by pushing to one side concerns about irreconcilable philosophical tenets and centering attention on (a) the contextual demands on methods decisions, and (b) other characteristics of our inquiry methodologies such as characteristics of our knowledge claims, which may still be different but not logically incompatible. Focusing primarily on responsiveness to contextual demands as important for generating more comprehensive and meaningful inferences represents a *pragmatic* mixed-method stance. Focusing primarily on the creative and initiative tensions created when juxtaposing different methodologies represents a *dialectic* stance.

The next section of this chapter offers some practical guidelines for designing mixed-method studies.

How to Mix Social Inquiry Methodologies

Being thoughtful and purposeful about mixed-method designs requires a set of constructs or ideas with which to work during the design process. The five practical mixed-method purposes presented earlier represents one such set. Another set is represented by the pragmatic and dialectic stances on mixing methods at the philosophical level discussed above. Paralleling this latter set are the design constructs of *coordination or cooperation* and *integration or synthesis* (Caracelli & Greene, 1997). Recalling that all mixed-method designs aim for more comprehensive and insightful understandings, *coordinated designs* do so by "bringing into common action or harmonizing" (from Webster's, 1967) data or learnings from different methods that, even as they are joined in harmony, still retain their individual, separate identities. In an *integrated design,* the data or learnings from different methods are "blended, united, dialectically combined into a coherent or higher whole" (from Webster's, 1967) such that the individual learnings become interlaced and embedded within the whole, not distinguishable as separate entities. Note that these design constructs are offered as conceptual handles for the challenges of mixing methods, not as rigid, impermeable classifications. Elaboration and illustration of these ideas follow.

Coordinated Mixed-Method Designs

In a coordinated or cooperative mixed-method design, the different methods are characteristically planned and implemented as discrete, separable sets of activities. Some interaction should occur between the different methods and their findings, but the methods remain distinguishable throughout the inquiry. This interaction, which constitutes the essential mixing of the different methods, is characteristically done at the level of overall inferences, rather than at prior stages of data compilation or analysis.

To illustrate, envision a study about teacher participation in systemic reform initiatives. The inquirers in this study are wondering about the nature, extent, practical classroom value, and structural correlates of such participation. For the purpose of *complementarity* (using different methods to assess different facets of the focal construct of teacher participation), a coordinated mixed-method design in this context might mix a quasi-experimental, pre-post methodology with a case study, ethnographic methodology. For the quasi-experimental methodology, districts involved in systemic reforms could be matched with districts involved in other kinds of reforms, and samples of teachers in both sets of districts could be assessed on structured, quantitative measures of participation in educational change endeavors. For the ethnographic methodology, a purposeful sample of 5–10 teachers, selected as extreme cases of extensive and beneficial participation, could be studied in more depth with qualitative methods of observation and interviewing. As a coordinated or cooperative design, the two methodologies would interact or be harmonized primarily at the level of findings and for purposes of generating more comprehensive, insightful overall study inferences.

The results of the comparative quantitative component might state, for example: *When compared to teachers in districts with a different educational change effort, teachers in districts with systemic reforms report considerably more challenge in translating the reform to their classrooms.*

That statement would be considered along with the results of the indepth qualitative component, which might state, for example: *Teachers who choose to participate extensively in systemic reform initiatives indicate that their participation most meaningfully contributes to their intellectual and professional development, rather than to their practical teaching repertoires.*

Then inferences would be made, for example: *Taken together, these findings suggest a gap at the practical level in systemic reform efforts.*

In a coordinated mixed-method design, therefore, the different methods are often arrayed side-by-side and remain distinguishable, with interaction or harmonizing planned and implemented at the inference phase of inquiry.

To link these design constructs to the prior discussion on mixed-method rationales and purposes, coordinated designs are most consonant with a pragmatic philosophical stance and with the specific mixed-method purposes of triangulation, complementarity, and expansion. A coordinated design invites harmony, not discord, and thereby supports the pragmatic mixed-method inquirer's emphasis on contextual responsiveness rather than on the nodes of tension in the methodologies being mixed (which is the emphasis of the dialectic stance). For the specific mixed-method purposes of triangulation and expansion and, to a lesser extent, complementarity, the different methods should remain separate and distinguishable throughout the study, as they do in a coordinated design.

I wish to reemphasize that although I am suggesting a consonance between the overall mixed-method design construct of coordination and the philosophical mixed-method rationale of practical responsiveness, and between coordination and certain specific mixed-method purposes, coordination is neither limited to these rationales and purposes nor they to it. Consonance here means fit, not rigid categorization. As is clearly indicated in the following discussions of integrated and then iterative designs, these constructs overlap both conceptually and practically. Even so, they are offered as heuristically valuable in planning and implementing good mixed-method studies.

Integrated Mixed-Method Designs

The key feature of an integrated mixed-method design is the blending, synthesis, or union of the different methodologies into a whole that is other than or more than its constituent parts or methods. In this synthesis, the integrity of the different methodologies is honored, such that qualitative data gathered from life history interviews are analyzed and valued for their emic meaning and such that survey results from carefully stratified random samples are analyzed and valued for their generalizability.

Yet, in an integrated design, it is the synthesis of the different methods that is most important, a synthesis that is planned and implemented during the processes of data gathering and analysis rather than at the stage of inference. So in the creation of this synthesis, markers of the individual methods are blended and their discrete identities left behind.

Let me return to the example of studying the nature, extent, practical classroom value, and structural correlates of teacher participation in systemic reform initiatives. An integrative mixed-method study in this context would explicitly endeavor to juxtapose different ways of knowing so as to generate new insights, challenges to accepted wisdom, and alternative meanings for the phenomena of interest. This is the essential meaning of the specific mixed-method purpose of *initiation*. An integrated mixed-method design for this purpose of initiation might mix a large-scale survey of a representative sample of teachers in districts with systemic reform initiatives and ethnographic case studies of a sample of five teachers who were rated "excellent" and selected from two or three of these districts. The survey would concentrate on teacher understandings of systemic reform and their own participation in it. For the case study sample, which would be identified through a peer and supervisor nomination process, the significance of systemic reform would be studied within and connected to the teachers' frameworks and meanings for excellence.

In an integrated design, the essential mixing of methods happens during the inquiry processes of data gathering and especially analysis. The data from the different methods are used generatively and as challenges, one set to the other, towards blending and synthesis. The survey results in the above study might include the following item frequency, for example: *40% of the teachers surveyed reported that their district's systemic reform was having "little or no impact" on their own teaching, 40% reported a "modest impact", and only 20% reported an "impact that is significantly changing how I teach."*

The case study results might include the following theme: *One characteristic common to excellent teachers is the commitment to continuous professional renewal. Said one, "I am always trying out new ideas in my room. These ideas come from other teachers, from the bit of reading I find time to do, and just from my own head."*

A blending of these two data items and, therefore, of the two constructs of reform impact and teaching excellence might generate the following beginnings of a synthesis: *(a) Only teachers who are already excellent become involved in systemic reform efforts in terms of its implications for their own practice; and (b) other teachers will become engaged with systemic reform at the level of their own practice if the reform actively changes teacher cultures to ones that insist upon continuous professional renewal.*

Other data from both the survey and the case studies would also be jointly analyzed to further the refutation and elaboration of these first steps toward a synthesis that would connect the meanings of excellence in teaching and systemic reform and that would incorporate both contextuality and generality, both emic meaning and patterns of regularity, and both the unusual and the representative.

Clearly, the idea of integrated mixed-method designs is most consonant with but, again, not limited to, a dialectic stance on the philosophical sensibility of mixing methods and the specific mixed-method purposes of initiation and complementarity. Complementarity fits comfortably with both coordination and integration.

Integrated designs emphasize the nodes of tension that exist between different methodologies because the tension is seen as the creative, dialectic source of synthesis. Such synthesis, however, is not always readily attainable. To illustrate, Buchanan (1992) probed the challenges of integration in his study of the relationship between moral reasoning and teenage drug use. A sample of 225 eighth graders were given a questionnaire assessing demographics, drug use, and moral thinking. A selected subsample of 95 were also interviewed to gather more indepth information, especially on moral thinking. One mixed-method integration challenge in the study was to connect singular qualitative findings to the quantitative focus on typicality, frequency, and mean responses. A related challenge was the problem of how to incorporate complex qualitative themes into the quantitative or integrative analysis. The following excerpt illustrates this latter challenge.

> In this study . . . one of the major conclusions was that the ascendancy of an ethical code of utilitarian individualism puts *all* teenagers in our society at risk for drug use. [Examples of two teens with] diametrically opposed views on drug use . . . are more revealing for their similarities than their differences. For both Elisha and Alfred, their goals in life . . . are defined in terms of utilities—money and material rewards. The means to achieve these ends are strictly instrumental. They may go by different routes (education vs. drug dealing), but the activities themselves have no intrinsic merit. Education, like drug dealing, is just a means to an end. This calculative, self-interested, utility-maximizing attitude was . . . by far the most salient ethos of the young people interviewed. . . . But these arguments and the evidence presented here can only be made in a qualitative fashion. . . . If we tried to assimilate this factor into a quantitative analysis, the results would be a wash. (pp. 126–127)

Acknowledging the challenges of integration, I also offer some ideas that may be useful in many situations (see also Greene & Caracelli, 1997). First is the idea of using or generating a substantive framework for data synthesis. This substantive framework may consist of theoretical constructs or a theory itself (grounded in the study at hand, generated from elsewhere, or both), a concept map (Novak & and Gowin, 1981; Trochim, 1989) or other spatial-visual representation of the phenomena being studied, or an emergent set of warranted assertions, following Erickson's (1986) schema for interpretive data analysis (see M. L. Smith, 1997). In any of these forms, the substantive framework offers an initial set of concepts, nodes, and directions for integrative synthesis rather than relying on the analytic process to create these. The substantive framework, that is, provides an organized set of conceptual starting places for the integrative analysis. (To be fully consonant with dialectic mixed-method inquiry, the framework itself should be open to revision and reconstitution as part of the processes of analysis and synthesis.)

Second, following similar logic, an action or value-based framework could provide important starting points for an integrative analysis. The action framework might represent decisions that need to be made or critical points of controversy that need to be resolved. The value-based framework might offer consensual bases for synthesizing disparate sets of data. For example, agreement on the importance of equity and social justice in all educational reforms could suggest, for many studies of teaching and reform, integrative analytic starting points like, "In what ways does this reform help teachers and schools serve students equitably? In what ways does the reform offer equity—of opportunity, of reward, of recognition, and so forth—for teachers?"

Third, from prior work (Caracelli & Greene, 1993) come four specific analytic strategies intended to aid and enable interplay and transformation of meaning as different kinds of data are analyzed together. Most of these strategies are also applicable to coordinated mixed-method designs in many contexts. While not new, these strategies are usefully positioned within an dialectic mixed-method framework:

1. *Data transformation* is the conversion or transformation of one data type into the other so that both can be analyzed together. For example, frequencies for qualitative categories and themes can be tallied and then included in a quantitative analysis.
2. *Typology development* is the process which yields a typology (or set of substantive categories) from the analysis of one data type that is then applied as a framework in analyzing the other data type. For example, factor analytic results can be used to cluster qualitative categories, which are then transformed into higher order themes upon further analysis.
3. *Extreme case analysis* is a tool to reach understanding of extreme cases by analyzing one data type via analysis of the other type of data. For example, intensive case studies can reveal distinguishing characteristics of exemplary practice. These characteristics can then be used to regroup cases within the larger sample for further quantitative examination of what constitutes exemplary practice.
4. *Data consolidation* entails jointly reviewing different data sets to create new or consolidated variables or data sets, which are then used in further analyses. For example, the inquiry team may critically and collectively review all of the data available for each case. These reviews are represented as judgments of progress, which are new variables or constructs that are then pursued in further analyses.

One last mixed-method design, the iterative design, which is briefly presented next, actually bridges the coordinated-integrated design classification featured in this section.

Iterative Mixed-Method Designs

Iterative mixed-method designs, which are among the most common in practice, can be either coordinated or integrated designs, depending on their intent and form. The essential feature of an iterative design is its back-and-forth character in which the different methods take turns, offering opportunities for dynamic interplay. Most commonly, the different methods take turns over time, either to develop one method from another, or, more substantively, to focus in progressively on critical insights and understandings. Eckert (1987) illustrates a spiral type of mixed-method design with multiple cycles of iter-

ation between intensive participant observation and extensive surveying to identify patterns of displacement among elderly hotel dwellers in an urban area undergoing revitalization and development. Because the findings from one method served to challenge and reframe the focus and direction of the next method, this study is best considered an integrated study. A sequential iterative study that is coordinated in intent and form is that by Radimer (1990). In this study, intensive interpretivist interviews with a purposeful sample of 32 limited-income mothers yielded a comprehensive conceptual framework for the meaning of hunger in contemporary U.S. society. This framework was then used to develop and pilot test a set of structured survey items measuring hunger. (These Radimer survey items have since been refined and incorporated into large-scale U.S. surveys conducted by the USDA and other monitors of food and income security.)

Summary

Planning the specific contours of a mixed-method study can be aided by the broad design constructs of coordination and integration. In coordinated mixed-method designs the different methods are brought together at the inference phase of inquiry. So, the fundamental mixed-method rationale of understanding more fully is accomplished by planning, implementing, and analyzing the results of different methods separately and then combining these results into overall study inferences. Harmony is the intended result. In integrated mixed-method designs the different methods are blended during the inquiry phases of data gathering and especially analysis. Points of tension between the different methods—for example, emic and etic meanings—are juxtaposed and analytically blended into a dialectic synthesis. It is this synthesis in integrated designs that fulfills the fundamental mixed-method purpose of understanding more fully.

In coordinated designs, the different methods tend to be side-by-side, assessing different components of the inquiry (expansion) or different facets of an inquiry construct (complementarity). Sometimes the different methods in a coordinated design are more iteratively planned and implemented, constituting different phases in the construction of an instrument (development). In integrated designs, the different methods are juxtaposed, usually simultaneously (initiation) but sometimes iteratively (development) for the express purpose of invoking generative insights through dialectic tensions.

Given this reasonably broad framework for mixing methodologies in applied social inquiry, an important question becomes, When not to mix? In brief, mixed-method studies are not advocated (a) when resources are insufficient or (b) when the desire to understand more fully is not of greatest importance. Insufficient resources characterize most applied social inquiry settings. It is my belief that strong mixed-method studies require some parity among the different methods. A token or exploratory inclusion of a few open-ended questions on a structured survey or a small comparison group in an ethnographic case study is unlikely to fulfill mixed-method aspirations. These resources might better be used to enhance and strengthen the primary study methodology, leaving mixed methods for other contexts or perhaps, most realistically, for linkages across studies. With respect to the second limitation on mixing methods (item *b*), many important inquiry contexts feature phenomena of interest that are quite well known, established methodologies that have worked well in the past, and inquiry questions that are circumscribed in scope. Some cost analyses, teacher action research, and sociometric inquiries of student interactions are examples. In these kinds of instances, a mixed-method approach is unlikely to be the most appropriate.

Conclusion

In many fields of applied social inquiry, alternative ways of knowing still battle for legitimacy and space. Even when the battles are primarily in the past—as is true for much educational research—the former protagonists rarely share coffee much less ideas. To counterpoint, mixed-method inquiry is premised on the acceptance of difference as a starting point for more meaningful social science. This chapter has charted some ideas and directions for mixed-method inquiry. Of greatest need is the serious practical application of these ideas in multiple, diverse contexts toward their refinement, elaboration, and ultimate usefulness.

REFERENCES

Brewer, J., & Hunter, A. (1989). *Multimethod research: A synthesis of styles.* Thousand Oaks, CA: Sage.

Bryman, A. (1988). *Quantity and quality in social research.* London: Unwin Hyman.

Buchanan, D. R. (1992). An uneasy alliance: Combining qualitative and quantitative research methods. *Health Education Quarterly, 19,* 117–135.

Burbules, N. C., & Rice, S. (1991). Dialogue across differences: Continuing the conversation. *Harvard Educational Review, 61,* 393–416.

Campbell, D. T. (1974). *Qualitative knowing in action research.* Kurt Lewin Award address presented at the annual meeting of the American Psychological Association, New Orleans, LA.

Campbell, D. T., & Fiske, D. W. (1959). Convergent and discriminant validation by the multitrait-multimethod matrix. *Psychological Bulletin, 56,* 81–105.

Caracelli, V. J., & Greene, J. C. (1993). Data analysis strategies for mixed-method evaluation designs. *Educational Evaluation and Policy Analysis, 15,* 195–207.

Caracelli, V. J., & Greene, J. C. (1997). Crafting mixed-method evaluation designs. In J. C. Greene & V. J. Caracelli (Eds.), *Advances in mixed-method evaluation: The challenges and benefits of integrating diverse paradigms. New Directions for Evaluation No. 74.* San Francisco: Jossey-Bass.

Cook, T. D. (1985). Postpositivist critical multiplism. In R. L. Shotland & M. M. Mark (Eds.), *Social science and social policy* (pp. 21–62). Beverly Hills: Sage.

Denzin, N. K. (1978). *The research act: An introduction to sociological methods.* New York: McGraw Hill.

Eckert, J. K. (1987). Ethnographic research on aging. In S. Reinharz & G. D. Knowles (Eds.), *Qualitative gerontology* (pp. 241–255). New York: Springer.

Erickson, F. E. (1986). Qualitative methods in research on teaching. In M. Wittrock (Ed.), *Handbook of research on teaching* (3rd ed., pp. 119–161). New York: Macmillan.

Fielding, N. G., & Fielding, J. L. (1986). *Linking data. Qualitative Research Methods Series No. 4.* Thousand Oaks, CA: Sage.

Garrison, J. (1994). Realism, Deweyan pragmatism, and educational research. *Educational Researcher, 21*(1), 5–14.

Greene, J. C., & Caracelli, V. J. (1997). Defining and describing the paradigm issue in mixed-method evaluation. In J. C. Greene & V. J. Caracelli (Eds.), *Advances in mixed-method evaluation: The challenges and benefits of integrating diverse paradigms. New Directions for Evaluation No. 74.* San Francisco: Jossey-Bass.

Greene, J. C., Caracelli, V. J., & Graham, W. (1989). Toward a conceptual framework for mixed-method evaluation designs. *Educational Evaluation and Policy Analysis, 11,* 255–274.

Guba, E. G. (Ed.). (1990). *The paradigm dialog.* Thousand Oaks, CA: Sage.

House, E. R. (1994a). Integrating the quantitative and qualitative. In C. S. Reichardt & S. F. Rallis (Eds.), *The qualitative-quantitative debate: New perspectives. New Directions for Program Evaluation No. 61* (pp. 13–22). San Francisco: Jossey-Bass.

House, E. R. (1994b). Is John Dewey eternal? *Educational Researcher, 21*(1), 14–16.

Howe, K. R. (1988). Against the quantitative-qualitative incompatibility thesis, or dogmas die hard. *Educational Researcher, 17*(8), 10–16.

Kidder, L. H., & Fine, M. (1987). Qualitative and quantitative methods: When stories converge. In M. M. Mark & R. L. Shotland (Eds.), *Multiple methods in program evaluation. New Directions for Evaluation No. 35* (pp. 57–75). San Francisco: Jossey-Bass.

Krantz, D. L. (1995). Sustaining vs. resolving the quantitative-qualitative debate. *Evaluation and Program Planning, 18,* 89–96.

Mathie, A. W. M. (1996). *An evaluation system for CUSO: Promoting dialogue across epistemological divides in a learning organization.* Doctoral dissertation, Department of Human Service Studies, Cornell University, Ithaca, NY.

Maxwell, J. A., Bashook, P. G., & Sandlow, L. J. (1986). Combining ethnographic and experimental methods in educational evaluation: A case study. In D. M. Fetterman & M. A. Pitman (Eds.), *Educational evaluation: Ethnography in theory, practice, and politics* (pp. 121–143). Thousand Oaks, CA: Sage.

Novak, J. D., & Gowin, D. B. (1981). *Concept mapping and other innovative strategies.* Unpublished manuscript, Department of Education, Cornell University, Ithaca, NY.

Patton, M. Q. (1988). Paradigms and pragmatism. In D. M. Fetterman (Ed.), *Qualitative approaches to evaluation in education* (pp. 116–137). New York: Praeger.

Radimer, K. L. (1990). *Understanding hunger and developing indicators to assess it.* Doctoral dissertation, Division of Nutrition, Cornell University, Ithaca, NY.

Ragin, C. C. (1989). *The comparative method: Moving beyond qualitative and quantitative strategies.* Berkeley: University of California Press.

Salomon, G. (1991). Transcending the qualitative-quantitative debate: The analytic and systemic approaches to educational research. *Educational Researcher, 20*(6), 10–18.

Smith, M. L. (1997). Mixing and matching: Methods and models. In J. C. Greene & V. J. Caracelli (Eds.), *Advances in mixed-method evaluation: The challenges and benefits of integrating diverse paradigms. New Directions for Evaluation No. 74.* San Francisco: Jossey-Bass.

Trochim, W. M. T. (1989). An introduction to concept mapping for planning and evaluation. *Evaluation and Program Planning, 12,* 1–16.

Trow, M. (1957). Comment on participant observation and interviewing: A comparison. *Human Organization, 16,* 33–35.

Webster's Seventh New Collegiate Dictionary. (1967). Springfield, MA: G. & C. Merriam Company.

17.

Advances in Teacher Assessments and Their Uses

Andrew C. Porter, Peter Youngs, and Allan Odden
University of Wisconsin-Madison

Over the past decade, several states, districts, and national organizations have developed or implemented new approaches to teacher assessment. Some of these approaches feature innovative assessment strategies, such as teacher-developed portfolios, constructed response questions, and assessment center exercises. Others attempt to use traditional methods, including standardized, multiple-choice tests, classroom observations, and structured interviews, in ways that better measure complex teaching performance. In this chapter, we describe many of these new approaches to teacher assessment, examine whether they promote reflective, learner-centered teaching practices, consider their psychometric properties, and discuss their possible uses.

The first section discusses the purposes of various assessments for teachers and a review of research on past and continuing practices in teacher assessment. The second section addresses new approaches to teacher assessment as being developed by the National Board for Professional Teaching Standards (NBPTS), the Educational Testing Service (ETS), and the Interstate New Teacher Assessment and Support Consortium (INTASC). In particular, this section examines the purposes of the assessments being developed by NBPTS, ETS, and INTASC; the conceptions of teaching that underlie them; the processes by which criteria and standards were developed; and the nature of the assessments themselves. In the third section, we review studies of the psychometric properties of these assessments, particularly studies of validity, reliability, and fairness.

In the fourth section, we describe innovative practices in teacher assessment in two states, Connecticut and California, and two districts, Rochester and Cincinnati. Both states have implemented induction programs for beginning teachers, while the districts have each established peer review programs in which accomplished teachers mentor and evaluate beginning

teachers. The fifth section examines efforts to assess teachers in terms of student outcomes, in contrast to efforts to evaluate them in terms of teaching processes. In the sixth section, we consider the implications of these new approaches to teacher assessment for efforts to implement innovative systems of teacher compensation. Finally, the seventh section summarizes the extensive work that has gone on in the area of teacher assessment in recent years, suggests some additional psychometric studies that should be undertaken of various assessments, and considers some of the tensions and limitations in the development and use of new assessments.

Current and Recent Practices in Teacher Assessment

Several researchers have offered ways to conceptualize the purposes of teacher assessment (e.g., Andrews & Barnes, 1990; Natriello, 1990; Darling-Hammond, Wise, & Klein, 1995; Peterson, 1995; Dwyer & Stufflebeam, 1996). First, assessments can be used, along with other measures, to control the movement of teachers into and out of positions at different stages of their careers (Andrews & Barnes, 1990; Natriello, 1990; Dwyer & Stufflebeam, 1996). In particular, assessments can be used in determining whether to (a) admit individuals into teacher education programs; (b) grant licenses to prospective teachers; (c) retain, promote, or dismiss licensed teachers; and (d) award advanced certification to veteran teachers. A second purpose is to influence the performance and professional growth of teachers in particular positions, such as student teachers, initially licensed teachers, and regularly licensed teachers (Andrews & Barnes, 1990; Natriello, 1990). Third, assessments can be used to represent a professional consensus about the knowledge and skills that teachers must have to engage in responsible practice.

The authors wish to thank the following reviewers for their comments: Sharon Conley, University of California, Santa Barbara; Carol Dwyer, Educational Testing Service; Ann Harman, National Board for Professional Standards; Carolyn Kelley, University of Wisconsin, Madison; and Pamela Moss, University of Michigan.

Table 17.1. Dimensions of Assessments for Teachers

Purpose of Assessment:	Admission to Preservice Teacher Education
	Initial Licensure
	Continuing Licensure
	Promoting Professional Practice Beyond Licensure
	Teacher Salary
	Advanced Certification
Type of Assessment:	Assessments of Basic Literacy and Numeracy Skills
	Assessments of Subject Matter Knowledge
	Assessments of Pedagogical Knowledge—Knowledge of Pedagogy—Knowledge of How Students Learn
	Assessments of Teaching Skills (During Clinical Practice)
	Assessments of Gains in Student Learning
Developer of Assessment:	Colleges and Universities
	States
	Educational Testing Service
	Interstate New Teacher Assessment and Support Consort
	National Board for Professional Teaching Standards
	Local Districts
Nature of Assessment:	Standardized, Multiple-Choice Test
	Constructed Response
	Observation and Interview
	Portfolio
	Assessment Center Exercises
When Assessment Occurs:	Before Admission to Preservice Teacher Education
	During Preservice Teacher Education
	Following Completion of Preservice Teacher Education
	During 1st Years of Teaching
	After Receipt of Continuing License
	After Teacher Has Taught for Several Years

This section provides an overview of the various assessments that, along with other measures, serve to control teachers' movement, influence their performance and development, and represent a professional consensus about a knowledge base for teaching. In particular, we will discuss who develops and administers these assessments, the knowledge and skills they measure, when they typically occur, and the activities of which they consist. Table 17.1 provides an overview of these five dimensions for describing teacher assessments. The reader should note that this chapter does not describe assessments for ensuring program accountability. (For information about such assessments, see Darling-Hammond, this volume.)

One purpose of teacher assessment is to determine whether to admit individuals into teacher education programs. In the 1980s, many states began requiring candidates to attain certain levels of performance on tests of basic intellectual skills. The most widely used test was the Pre-Professional Skills Test (PPST) developed by ETS, a standardized, multiple-choice test that assessed basic skills in reading, writing, and mathematics. Some states developed their own tests, though, and others required institutions to choose tests that met certain guidelines. By 1987, more than 20 states had mandated some form of testing for candidates to be admitted into teacher education programs (Office of Educational Research and Improvement, 1987).

There is some disagreement among researchers over whether tests of basic skills should be used in determining whether to admit individuals into formal preparation. Many contend that these tests are necessary to ensure that prospective teachers have competence in reading, writing, and mathematics. In addition, some argue that the tests should be used to advise such

individuals of the likelihood they will later pass tests that are necessary for initial licensure. Conversely, some researchers maintain that tests of basic intellectual skills are unnecessary, for two reasons. First, many teacher education programs raised their admissions requirements significantly during the 1980s (Darling-Hammond & Berry, 1988). Second, in the view of these researchers, basic skills can be tested in assessments of prospective teachers' professional skills, which would occur after the completion of formal preparation. Unfortunately, little data are available to resolve these opposing points of view.

Some teacher educators and researchers assert that assessment of prospective teachers during formal preparation should be based on a professional consensus regarding the knowledge and skills that are necessary for responsible practice. In recent years, there have been several efforts to codify the knowledge and skills that all teachers should have (e.g., Shulman, 1987; Reynolds, 1989; National Board for Professional Teaching Standards, undated; INTASC, 1992; Dwyer, 1994). At some institutions, for example, faculty members are using the INTASC core standards to delineate what students should know and be able to do at different stages of their preparation and to develop assessments to determine whether they can demonstrate those capacities.

At other institutions, by contrast, the faculty members themselves have defined what they expect graduates to know and be able to do and have developed appropriate assessments for measuring these capacities. The faculty at Alverno College, for example, has been using performance-based assessments in teacher education for more than 20 years to "provide an ever more complex picture of the students' development over time"

(Diez, Rickards, & Lake, 1994, p. 13). The Alverno faculty provides explicit criteria to beginning students that describe the capacities they need in various situations. Advanced students, conversely, "having developed a range of capacities to call on in varied situations," are expected, "given a context, to infer the kind of performance elicited, call upon the required abilities, and infer criteria of performance" (Loacker, Cromwell, & O'Brien, 1986, p. 52).

Another purpose of teacher assessment is for use in making decisions regarding initial licensure. From 1977 to 1987, the number of states requiring candidates to pass tests of basic skills, subject-area knowledge, or professional knowledge dramatically increased from 3 to 44 (Office of Educational Research and Improvement, 1987). States varied considerably, though, in the areas tested, the tests used, and the minimum standards set for passing (Goertz & Pitcher, 1985). To assess basic skills, many states used their own assessments or the PPST. Similarly, most states used National Teacher Examination (NTE) Specialty Area exams or their own tests to assess prospective teachers' content area knowledge. Finally, many states used their own assessments or one or more of the tests that composed the NTE Core Battery to assess pedagogical knowledge. The Core Battery included tests of communication skills, general knowledge, and professional knowledge.

Most tests used by states to assess basic skills, subject-matter knowledge, and pedagogical knowledge, including the PPST, NTE Specialty Area exams, and the NTE Core Battery, were standardized, multiple-choice tests. The widespread implementation in the 1980s of the NTE and other competency tests was viewed positively by many educators, researchers, and policymakers for a variety of reasons. First, given that state-approved teacher education programs varied widely in their course content and overall quality, they believed that competency tests based on research on teaching effectiveness would ensure that beginning teachers entered the profession with basic levels of expertise. Second, many proponents supported the use of basic-skills tests prior to admission to teacher education programs to prevent candidates from being denied licensure as a result of their failing such tests after completing professional preparation. Third, subject-matter tests were widely advocated because many believed they would ensure that candidates had basic levels of knowledge in the subjects they were planning to teach.

Despite the prevalent use in the 1980s of the NTE and other paper-and-pencil tests of basic skills, subject-matter knowledge, and professional knowledge, these tests were criticized by researchers for several reasons. First, tests of professional knowledge were faulted for oversimplifying teaching by applying research on teacher effectiveness (e.g., Brophy & Good, 1986; Good & Brophy, 1986) in ways that fail to account for the "many intervening variables concerning classroom organization, teaching strategies, and instructional goals" that influence teachers' work (Darling-Hammond, Wise, & Klein, 1995, p. 53). Given the ambiguity of many of the questions on the NTE test of teaching knowledge, the argument went, the greater a candidate's knowledge of how these variables affected teaching, the more likely he or she was to have difficulty answering these questions (Darling-Hammond, Wise, & Klein, 1995). We were unable to find convincing data on either side of this issue.

Second, paper-and-pencil tests of content knowledge and professional knowledge were criticized for failing to account for the fact that candidates must integrate multiple areas of knowledge in making curricular and pedagogical decisions. In particular, candidates need to bring together knowledge of subject matter, students, and the local context to make appropriate instructional decisions. While tests of content knowledge assessed whether candidates had genuine knowledge of the subject areas they intended to teach, such tests did not reveal whether they were able to apply pedagogical content knowledge in classroom situations (Shulman, 1987). In other words, such tests did not reveal whether candidates' practices reflected awareness of the most appropriate ways of presenting subject matter to students, their most common misconceptions, or the areas they would find most difficult.

For their part, tests of professional knowledge were faulted because of their reliance on process-product research on teaching and for emphasizing issues related to classroom management over the complexities of instructional decision making. While this research attempted "to identify those teaching behaviors and strategies most likely to lead to achievement gains among students," it focused on generic relationships; that is, "behaviors and strategies associated with student academic gains irrespective of subject matter or grade level" (Shulman, 1987, p. 10). Consequently, the findings from this research and their implications for tests of professional knowledge "have been much more closely connected with the management of classrooms than with the subtleties of content pedagogy" (Shulman, 1987, p. 10). In our view, it is clear that the tests of content knowledge and professional knowledge that became prevalent in the 1980s were incomplete.

Investigations of the predictive validity of paper-and-pencil tests of teachers' basic skills found weak results (Haney, Madaus, & Kreitzer, 1987; Haertel, 1991). In a study summarizing research on the NTE between 1940 and 1972, Quirk, Witten, and Weinberg (1973) found very low correlations between candidates' exam scores and (a) their grades in practice teaching and (b) their ratings by college supervisors or principals during the student teaching period. Similarly, Ayers and Qualls (1979) reported that the correlations between candidates' NTE scores and principals' ratings of their teaching were consistently low and rarely statistically significant. For these studies, of course, the appropriateness and quality of the criterion were as much in question as was the validity of the assessments.

Several researchers (e.g., Goertz & Pitcher, 1985; Graham, 1987; Smith, Miller, & Joy, 1988) have found that tests of basic skills, content knowledge, and professional knowledge have had an adverse impact on racial minorities. The number of minorities entering teacher education programs and the percentage that compose the teaching force have both dropped significantly over the past 2 decades (although it is unlikely that these declines can be attributed solely to the effects of teacher testing). Two hypotheses have been put forth to explain the disparate impact of these tests on minority candidates. According to the first hypothesis, minority candidates' poor performance reflects true differences in knowledge and skill, largely because of poor professional preparation. The second hypothesis attributes their poor performance to bias in the tests themselves.

Most teacher assessments have been carefully studied for evidence of possible bias, using panels of experts to review questions and differential item functioning statistics to detect and eliminate items that show bias. In our view, poor performance of minority candidates is not a function of bias in the tests as bias has been traditionally defined. Nevertheless, it may be that minority candidates have compensating strengths not captured by the teacher assessments used thus far.

In the 1980s, in part because of dissatisfaction with standardized, multiple-choice tests, several states implemented performance assessments of beginning teachers. In those states, most of which were in the South, candidates were granted an initial license after they completed their course requirements and passed one or more competency tests. They did not receive a regular license, though, until they had attained a teaching position and passed an on-the-job performance assessment. Among the more prominent of these assessments were the Florida Performance Measurement System (FPMS), the Georgia Teacher Performance Assessment Instruments (TPAI), and the Texas Appraisal System (TAS).

Such assessments were viewed favorably by many educators, researchers, and policymakers, because they were based on empirical research, particularly process-product research on teaching (Kuligowski, Holdzkom, & French, 1993; Pecheone & Stansbury, 1996). By drawing their assessment criteria from the same research base, Florida, Georgia, Texas, and other southern states were able to promote a common understanding of teaching across the region and to provide educators within and across states with a common language for discussing teaching practice (Kuligowski, Holdzkom, & French, 1993). Process-product research also influenced the data-collection methods used in these assessment systems. In some states, low-inference systems were used. The FPMS, for example, focused on the frequency of different teaching behaviors. Other states used higher-inference or modified scripting procedures, including Georgia and Texas, where assessors used 5-point scales to measure the quality of teaching they observed (Pecheone & Stansbury, 1996).

While the FPMS, TPAI, TAS, and other similar performance assessments were fairly popular, they have been criticized for reinforcing a narrow conception of teaching (Darling-Hammond, Wise, & Klein, 1995). By focusing on a uniform set of teaching behaviors and strategies, regardless of the content area or grade level being taught, assessments based on process-product research may lead teachers to follow a fixed set of prescriptions. In the FPMS, for example, the "observers record the frequencies of specific behaviors in two columns—one for 'effective' behaviors, the other for 'ineffective'" without taking account of contextual factors (Darling-Hammond, Wise, & Klein, 1995, p. 64). Consequently, in this and similar systems, teachers are discouraged "from adapting their instruction to the particular subjects and students they are teaching" (Floden & Klinzing, 1990).

In recent years, ETS and INTASC have developed performance-based assessments for evaluating the teaching skills of beginning practitioners. Some states are using the Praxis assessments—developed by ETS—to influence the professional growth of beginning teachers, while others are using Praxis or the INTASC assessments in making decisions about initial licensure. Further, the use of these assessments is likely to become more widespread as increasing numbers of states require beginning teachers to go through induction programs. In induction programs, beginning teachers receive regular guidance and support from mentor teachers during their 1st year of teaching. Such programs enable beginning teachers to develop those teaching skills and dispositions that can be cultivated only through long-term exposure to actual classroom situations (Darling-Hammond, Wise, & Klein, 1995). (The second section of this chapter examines the Praxis and INTASC assessments in detail, while the fourth section describes how they are being used in Connecticut and California.)

Once teachers have earned a continuing license, they are usually evaluated by their principals or other building administrators. Such evaluations typically involve a classroom observation and a brief meeting afterwards. Research indicates that this approach to evaluation has both positive and negative aspects. One positive aspect is that principals are familiar with the school context. This knowledge makes it more likely that, in conducting evaluations, they will take account of such factors as student characteristics, faculty culture, and the social class of the community served by the school. Second, unlike most district and state officials, principals have ongoing relationships with their teachers. Consequently, when evaluations reveal that teachers lack knowledge or skills in certain areas, principals can ensure that they have opportunities to develop such capacities.

At the same time, though, several studies "depict principals as inaccurate raters both of individual teacher performance behaviors and of overall teacher merit" (Peterson, 1995, p. 15). In a recent review of research on teacher assessment, Dwyer and Stufflebeam (1996) found that the main problem with principal ratings is that they lack variability; in other words, principals usually consider all of their teachers to be performing at acceptable levels. In addition, Kauchak, Peterson, and Driscoll reported that evaluations based on principal visits were "perfunctory with little or no effect on actual teaching practice" (1985, p. 33). Further, in a review of research on measurement of teaching for the previous edition of this handbook, Shavelson, Webb, and Burstein (1986) concluded that most evaluations based on classroom observations are unreliable because they take place during a limited time period.

Other studies indicate widespread dissatisfaction among teachers and principals with prevailing assessment practices. Wise, Darling-Hammond, McLaughlin, and Bernstein (1984) reported that the most serious problem with these practices was the role conflict experienced by principals who were serving both as instructional leaders and as evaluators. They found that many principals, seeking to maintain collegial relations with their staff members, were reluctant to criticize them. This reluctance made "the early identification of problem teachers difficult and mask[ed] important variations in teacher performance" (Wise et al., 1984). In another study, Johnson (1990) found that most teachers were aware of the role conflict for principals. Further, many teachers reported that their primary criticism of administrators as evaluators was their lack of competence in carrying out this role (Johnson, 1990).

In response to some of the shortcomings of principal-conducted evaluations, several school districts have implemented peer assistance and review programs. These districts include Cincinnati, Columbus, Poway, Rochester, Seattle, and Toledo. Established through collective bargaining between districts and teachers' unions, these programs provide release time to highly accomplished teachers, often referred to as consulting teachers, to mentor and evaluate (a) beginning teachers and (b) experienced teachers who are experiencing difficulty. Peer assistance and review programs offer two important advantages over traditional systems of teacher evaluation. First, consulting teachers spend much more time observing and meeting with teachers than most principals do. As a result, consulting teachers acquire a more thorough understanding of the contextual factors that influence their teachers' work and can offer more comprehensive advice to help them improve. Second, these programs make it easier to dismiss poorly performing teachers, because they were created through collective bargaining and include due process protections. (Peer assessment programs in two districts, Cincinnati and Rochester, are described in the fourth section of this chapter.)

In addition to those districts that have implemented peer assistance and review programs, many other districts have recently begun to examine new ways of assessing teachers. This increased attention to assessment beyond initial licensure may have been prompted in part by the work of the NBPTS during the past 10 years. To recognize and reward outstanding teaching, NBPTS is developing assessments in different content areas and at different levels of schooling that delineate the knowledge and skills that teachers must have to engage in accomplished practice. These assessments consist of portfolios, including videotapes and essays, and assessment center exercises. Further, NBPTS is encouraging states and districts to reward teachers who, by earning National Board Certification, demonstrate the capacities associated with accomplished practice. (The National Board's assessments are examined in detail in the second section of the chapter.)

In addition to assessments that are designed for evaluating teachers on teaching processes, assessments can also be used to evaluate teachers on student outcomes. There is some disagreement among researchers, though, over whether student achievement gains can be validly used to assess teacher performance (e.g., Berk, 1988; Schalock & Schalock, 1993). In the fifth section of his chapter, we consider some of the challenges to evaluating teachers on student outcomes and describe one approach to evaluating teachers on the basis of the gains of their students, the Tennessee Value-Added Accountability System (TVAAS).

In examining new ways of evaluating regularly licensed teachers, districts need to consider what approaches to teacher compensation, professional development, and assessment are likely to advance teachers' practices. For example, one way for districts to promote professional growth among experienced teachers would be to align their compensation, staff development, and assessment practices with the National Board's standards and assessments. Under the single-salary schedule currently used by most districts, teachers receive pay increases for years of experience, education units, and university degrees, all of which are, at best, loose proxies for indicators of knowledge and skills.

By implementing knowledge- and skills-based pay systems, districts can replace these indirect indicators with more direct measures of teacher knowledge and skills and compensate teachers for what they know and can do (Odden & Kelley, 1997). This approach to teacher compensation, though, requires local assessment practices that are performance based, reflect the complexities of teaching, and occur on a regular basis. In combination with such approaches to local assessment, skills-based pay could provide incentives for teachers to continue refining the capacities that are associated with highly proficient practice and that are required for National Board Certification. (In the sixth section we examine how districts could use new teacher assessments in implementing knowledge- and skills-based pay systems.)

New Advances in Teacher Assessment

In recent years, ETS, INTASC, and NBPTS have all undertaken efforts to develop new systems of teacher assessment that feature performance-based assessments. This section begins by describing the purpose of each of these assessments. Next, the conceptions of teaching underlying them are compared and contrasted. By conception of teaching, we refer to an assessment's assumptions about educational objectives and teacher knowledge, skills, dispositions, and behavior. The section then examines the processes by which criteria or standards were developed for each of the assessments. Finally, the technical aspects of the assessments are described, including the methods, instruments, and sources of evidence used; the time and frequency at which they occurred; and the knowledge and preparation of the assessors. In the following section, we discuss studies of the validity, reliability, and fairness of the assessments.

Purposes of the Praxis, INTASC, and National Board Assessments

In 1988, ETS announced plans to revise the NTE in part because of criticisms that the NTE failed to measure complex teaching knowledge, had poor predictive validity, and had an adverse impact on racial minorities. The revised versions are known collectively as the Praxis Series: Professional Assessments for Beginning Teachers. The Praxis Series consists of three types of assessments, each of which first became available in 1993. The Praxis I assessment is meant to be used either in determining whether to admit candidates into teacher education programs or in making decisions regarding initial licensure. Praxis I measures basic skills in reading, writing, and mathematics and comes in two versions: a paper-and-pencil test and a computerized version. Both versions include multiple-choice questions and an essay question. Unlike the paper-and-pencil version, though, the computerized version is adaptive, in that questions are selected for candidates on the basis of their responses to earlier questions, and enables candidates to select single or multiple responses and to construct their own answers.

The Praxis II assessments are designed for use in determining whether to award candidates initial licensure. Praxis II includes four types of assessments: core tests of content knowledge, in-depth tests of content knowledge, tests of teaching knowledge, and tests of pedagogical content knowledge. The core tests of content knowledge are 2 hours in length and include only multiple-choice questions. In contrast, the in-depth tests of content knowledge feature constructed response questions. The tests of teaching knowledge, known as Principles of Learning and Teaching, include multiple-choice and constructed response questions and are associated with different levels of schooling (e.g., Grades K-6, Grades 5–9, and Grades 7–12). Finally, the tests of pedagogical content knowledge feature constructed response questions.

The Praxis III assessment, which evaluates candidates' teaching skills during their 1st year of teaching, is meant for use in making decisions regarding ongoing licensure. This assessment is based on 19 criteria that represent areas of practice that are relevant across different elementary and secondary school teaching situations. The criteria are organized into the following four domains: (a) organizing content knowledge for student learning, (b) creating an environment for student learning, (c) teaching for student learning, and (d) teacher professionalism (ETS, 1995). Several sources were used in developing the criteria: the perspectives of practicing teachers (obtained through job analyses and pilot testing), the findings of researchers, state requirements for initial licensure, and feedback from a national advisory committee (Dwyer, 1994).

In Praxis III, teachers complete a class profile and an instruction profile and are observed and interviewed by trained assessors. In contrast to Praxis II, there is only one version of Praxis III, which means that the same process is used with all beginning teachers regardless of the subject area or grade level that they teach. Assessors are trained to evaluate candidates' behaviors and decisions with regard to each criterion by examining the profiles and conducting the observations and interviews. States that use Praxis III in making licensure decisions are required by ETS to administer the assessment at least twice during each candidate's 1st year of teaching.

Because of the high costs involved with implementing Praxis III, ETS developed a modified version of the assessment, known as Pathwise. Drawing on the same research base and criteria as Praxis III, Pathwise is used in providing feedback to student teachers and practicing teachers, but it cannot be used in making licensure decisions. For this assessment, teachers complete a class profile and an instruction profile and are observed and interviewed by an assessor. Unlike Praxis III, though, the preobservation interview is not required and assessors do not have to write about each of the 19 criteria. Further, Pathwise includes a formative observation form, on which assessors can write suggestions, and an instruction and reflection profile, on which teachers can reflect in writing on their practice. Several districts and teacher education programs have implemented Pathwise for use with student teachers and 1st-year teachers. (In the fifth section of this chapter, we discuss the use of this assessment in California in the context of an induction program for beginning teachers.)

ETS describes the different assessments that compose the Praxis Series as a tightly coupled package and strongly recommends that states use each of these assessments in their licensure systems. In particular, for each area of licensure, it is recommended that states use all of the available Praxis II assessments, including tests of content knowledge, teaching knowledge, and pedagogical content knowledge, along with Praxis III. Of course, states can choose to just implement the Praxis II core tests of content knowledge along with Praxis III. Such states, as we discuss later, will acquire limited information about candidates' pedagogical content knowledge.

INTASC was created in 1987 by Connecticut and California to provide a forum for states to collaborate on efforts to improve the preparation and professional development of teachers. In 1992, INTASC "articulated performance-based standards for initial licensing of teachers that are built upon and compatible with those of the National Board" (INTASC, 1995b, p. 3). These standards are intended to facilitate the creation of coherent state systems of performance-based licensing by guiding the development of state policies in the areas of teacher education, program approval, licensure, certification, and professional development. Such systems "would more closely resemble the systems of licensing and certification in established professions where candidates are licensed when they pass a rigorous licensing examination" (INTASC, 1995b, p. 7). Several states have already adopted or adapted the core standards in revising their licensing policies, and the National Council for the Accreditation of Teacher Education (NCATE) has incorporated them into its procedures for accrediting teacher education institutions.

When completed, INTASC will have discipline-specific standards in mathematics, English/language arts (E/LA), science, social studies, and fine arts and standards for elementary education and special education. In 1994, several states began collaborating in the development of portfolio assessments based on the INTASC standards in the areas of math and E/LA. These assessments, which are meant for use in determining whether to award ongoing licensure, require teachers to complete several portfolio exercises, referred to as entries, that are integrated around one or two units of instruction. The entries include a description of their teaching context, lesson plans, videotapes of and commentaries about two lessons, and examples of student work. Connecticut played a leadership role in developing the INTASC math and E/LA portfolios and has implemented modified versions of both assessments.

Eventually, INTASC expects to develop portfolio assessments in all seven of the areas in which it is generating standards. The math and E/LA portfolios are designed for middle school and high school teachers in those content areas, while the elementary portfolio will be available for teachers in Grades Prekindergarten (P) through 6. The fine arts and special education portfolios will be designed for all teachers in those areas. In addition to these assessments, INTASC is also developing several subject-area tests and has contracted with ETS to create a test of teacher foundational knowledge. The latter will assess teachers' knowledge of child development and learning theory and of educational foundations. These tests are being designed for use in decisions regarding initial licensure and will be taken upon completion of formal preparation.

NBPTS was established in 1987 as a result of a report by the Carnegie Forum's Task Force on Teaching as a Profession, which called for the founding of a professional body to establish high standards for what teachers need to know and be able to do and to certify teachers who meet them (NBPTS, 1986). The National Board is currently developing advanced standards and performance-based assessments in about 30 certificate areas. One purpose of these assessments is to recognize excellence among continuing teachers, which, in turn, is expected to lead to larger numbers of good teachers. A second purpose is to make teaching more closely resemble other professions by identifying the knowledge, skills, and dispositions teachers must have to engage in accomplished practice and by making advanced certification the province of a professional body.

Each National Board assessment consists of 10 exercises, including 6 portfolio exercises and 4 assessment center exercises. The portfolio exercises include descriptions of the teaching and learning in the teacher's classroom, videotapes of and commentaries on the teacher's interactions with students, and examples of and commentaries on student work. The assessment center exercises require teachers to devise instructional plans, analyze examples of student work, view and respond to videotapes, and participate in simulations.

Two dimensions define the National Board's certificate framework: The first dimension denotes the developmental level of the students being taught, and the second dimension denotes the subject matter specialization of the teacher. The six overlapping developmental levels are early childhood (ages 3–8), middle childhood (ages 7–12), early and middle childhood (ages 3–12), early adolescence (ages 11–15), adolescence and young adulthood (ages 14–18+), and early adolescence through young adulthood (ages 11–18+). Across these six developmental levels, NBPTS plans to develop between 27 and 33 certificates in 15 subject-matter fields. These subject-matter fields include Generalist, English Language Arts, Mathematics, Science, Social Studies-History, Art, English as a New Language, Exceptional Needs Generalist, Foreign Language, Guidance Counseling, Health, Library/Media, Music, Physical Education, and Vocational Education.

During the 1993–94 school year, the National Board field-tested its first two assessments in the Early Adolescence/Generalist (EA/Gen) and the Early Adolescence/English Language Arts (EA/ELA) certificate fields. Between the 1994–95 and the 1997–98 school years, NBPTS developed and began offering five additional assessments. These assessments cover the following certificate fields: Early Childhood/Generalist (EC/Gen), Middle Childhood/Generalist (MC/Gen), Early Adolescence Through Young Adulthood/Art (EAYA/Art), Adolescence and Young Adulthood/Mathematics (AYA/Math) and Adolescence and Young Adulthood/Science (AYA/Science). NBPTS estimates that the seven assessments offered in 1997–98 made National Board Certification available to approximately 48% of the teachers in the United States. In 1999–2000, a total of 18 assessments were offered, which made National Board Certification available to about 85% of the teachers in the United States.

Conceptions of Teaching Underlying the Assessments

The conceptions of teaching underlying the Praxis III, INTASC, and National Board assessments are embodied in the Praxis III assessment criteria (Dwyer, 1994; Dwyer & Villegas, 1992/1993), the INTASC core standards (INTASC, 1992), and the National Board's core propositions (NBPTS, undated), respectively. Many similarities obtain among the three conceptions, although, unlike the others, NBPTS's conception refers to the practices of accomplished teachers.

SUBJECT-MATTER KNOWLEDGE

All three conceptions emphasize the need for teachers to be very knowledgeable about the subject or subjects they teach.

The Praxis III conception states that competent beginning teachers understand the structure of their subject and how its various elements are related to each other (ETS, 1995). Similarly, according to the conception underlying the INTASC assessments, competent beginning teachers are knowledgeable about the central concepts and methods of inquiry in the subject or subjects they teach (INTASC, 1992). Finally, the National Board's conception asserts that accomplished "teachers in command of their subject understand its substance—factual information as well as its central organizing concepts—and the ways in which new knowledge is created" (NBPTS, undated, p. 17).

KNOWLEDGE OF STUDENTS

All three conceptions stress the need for teachers to be knowledgeable about their students. According to the Praxis III and the INTASC conceptions, competent beginning teachers understand that students differ in their cognitive, emotional, social, and physical development and with regard to their abilities, interests, and rates of learning. In addition, both conceptions assert that teachers need multiple strategies for learning about students' families, communities, and cultures. For its part, the National Board's conception states that accomplished teachers "strive to acquire a deep understanding of their students and the communities from which they come" (NBPTS, undated, p. 15).

ABILITY TO ENGAGE STUDENTS IN ACTIVE LEARNING

According to the three conceptions, competent teachers routinely engage their students in active, in-depth learning. The INTASC conception states that competent beginning teachers are able to use knowledge about human motivation and behavior to create classroom environments that promote active engagement in learning (INTASC, 1992). In a similar vein, the conception underlying Praxis III stresses the need for teachers to engage students as active learners (Dwyer & Villegas, 1992/1993) and help them build bridges between what is familiar and the new content to be learned (ETS, 1995). For its part, the National Board's conception asserts that accomplished teachers understand the ways in which students can be motivated and "engage them actively in learning" (NBPTS, undated, p. 24).

REFLECTIVE PRACTICE

All three conceptions stress the need for teachers to engage in reflective practice. According to the Praxis III conception, competent beginning teachers "reflect on classroom events, both to plan next steps for individuals and groups of students and to improve their teaching skills over time" (ETS, 1995, p. 50). Further, such teachers collaborate with others to address issues related to their teaching and to coordinate instruction for groups of students or individuals (ETS, 1995). Similarly, the INTASC conception stresses the need for beginners to constantly assess the effects of their decisions and actions on students, parents, and other teachers; and to collaborate with other teachers "to make the entire school a productive learning environment" (INTASC, 1992, p. 30). As for the National Board's conception, it asserts that the decisions made by accomplished teachers are always "grounded in established theory and reasoned judgment" (NBPTS, undated, p. 28) and that such teachers reflect on their work to assess the outcomes of their efforts and the reasons for their successes and failures.

PEDAGOGICAL CONTENT KNOWLEDGE

Finally, all three conceptions emphasize the need for teachers to have pedagogical content knowledge. INTASC's first principle asserts that beginning teachers should be able to represent and explain concepts in a variety of ways to link them to students' prior understandings. In addition, they should understand how students' learning can be influenced by their "conceptual frameworks and their misconceptions of an area of knowledge" (INTASC, 1992, p. 10). The Praxis III assessment criteria refer "to a teacher's understanding of the structure or hierarchy of a discipline" and their knowledge of how "one element is prerequisite to or related to learning another" (ETS, 1995, p. 18). Further, beginners should be able to create or select "teaching methods, learning activities, and instructional materials or other resources that are appropriate to the students and that are aligned with the goals of the lesson" (ETS, 1995, p. 20). Similarly, according to NBPTS's second proposition, accomplished teachers have "knowledge of the most appropriate ways to present the subject matter to students" and are aware "of the most common misconceptions held by students; the aspects they will find most difficult; and the kinds of knowledge, experience, and skills that students of different ages typically bring to the learning of particular topics" (NBPTS, undated, p. 19).

Processes of Developing Criteria and Standards

ETS used a somewhat different approach in developing the Praxis III assessment criteria than those used by the National Board and INTASC in creating their standards. Researchers at ETS formulated a guiding conception for teaching (Dwyer & Villegas, 1992/1993) that was used as the starting point for creating a set of draft criteria for Praxis III. The criteria were further developed and modified as a result of job analyses, research reviews, and analyses of state licensing requirements. In contrast, each of the National Board and INTASC standards documents was initially developed by a small group of highly proficient teachers and subject-matter experts and then widely circulated to hundreds of educators for comment.

While, as discussed above, these different approaches resulted in remarkably similar conceptions of teaching, they also led to significantly different approaches to assessment. In particular, the National Board and INTASC have developed standards and assessments that are content specific, while the Praxis III criteria and assessment are for use at all grade levels and in all subject areas (although ETS recommends that Praxis III be used in conjunction with Praxis II assessments, which are content specific). In this section, we examine the processes by which the standards and criteria were developed and consider the role of job analyses in ensuring the legal defensibility of teacher performance assessments. Attention to the development process is necessary, since, to a considerable extent, the claim of validity for resulting assessments rests on the perceived validity of the assessment process. (See the third section for further discussion of validity.)

NATIONAL BOARD STANDARDS DOCUMENTS

For each National Board Certification area, a standards committee is created that consists of 12 to 15 people and includes teachers, school administrators, higher education faculty members, and others who have expertise in the appropriate content area and at the appropriate developmental level. Standards committee members begin their work by reading *What Teachers Should Know and Be Able to Do* (NBPTS, undated), which articulates the National Board's five core propositions[1] and describes the conception of teaching underlying its work. Over the next 18 months, committee members meet three or four times to discuss what constitutes outstanding teaching practice in their particular certification area. During these discussions, staff members from the NBPTS assemble a standards document that is based on the committee's deliberations. During the 18-month period, the draft goes through many iterations as the National Board staff solicits comments about it from committee members by telephone and electronic mail.

Once a draft of the standards document has been developed, it is submitted to the National Board's Certification Standards Working Group (CSWG), which consists of members of NBPTS's board of directors and which is responsible for overseeing the work of each of the standards committees. The CSWG suggests ways to revise the draft standards document. After the standards committee makes these revisions, it acquires permission from the CSWG to distribute the standards document for purpose of comment to hundreds of teachers, school administrators, higher education faculty members, and others throughout the country.

The National Board distributes a guide to help people review the standards document and provides a variety of opportunities for them to provide feedback on it. The standards committee reviews the feedback and uses it in making further refinements in the standards document. The revised version is then sent to the CSWG, which either approves it and sends it on to the board of directors for final approval or returns it to the standards committee for additional revisions. The board of directors is a 63-member board that includes teachers, district and state education officials, higher education faculty members, teachers' union representatives, policymakers, and others. By board pol-

---

[1] The National Board's five core propositions are as follows:
1. Teachers are committed to students and their learning.
2. Teachers know the subjects they teach and how to teach those subjects to students.
3. Teachers are responsible for managing and monitoring student learning.
4. Teachers think systematically about their practice and learn from experience.
5. Teachers are members of learning communities.

icy, a majority of the board's members must be teachers who are actively practicing in the classroom at least half-time.

For its part, INTASC established a Standards Drafting Committee to develop its core standards. The committee included representatives of 17 state education agencies, along with professional association staff members, higher education faculty members, and teachers' union representatives. Members of the committee used the National Board's five core propositions as a starting point for exploring the knowledge, skills, and dispositions that beginning teachers should have to practice responsibly and to begin developing the expertise that will eventually allow them to engage in highly accomplished practice. The committee also drew on Alverno College's performance-based approach to assessing student teachers and on recent work in several states that used similar conceptions of teaching.

Like the National Board, INTASC has created several committees to develop its content-area standards. Each committee consists of 12 to 15 people and includes teachers, school administrators, state education agency officials, and others. The majority of subcommittee members are teachers, many of whom have been involved in developing standards with the National Board or various professional associations. Subcommittee members use the INTASC core standards and resource documents produced by professional associations and the National Board to identify the disciplinary and pedagogical concepts deemed essential to competent teaching by beginning teachers in the content area where they have expertise. Once the INTASC standards documents have been developed, they are circulated to teachers, school administrators, higher education faculty members, policymakers, and others and subsequently are revised on the basis of feedback from these individuals.

PRAXIS III CRITERIA

The guiding conception of teaching formulated by Dwyer and Villegas (1992/1993) was used by ETS to create the initial set of Praxis III assessment criteria. ETS then conducted job analyses, research reviews, and analyses of state licensing requirements to establish and synthesize a knowledge base for teaching and to further develop and refine the assessment criteria. The guiding conception was used throughout as a theoretical framework in (a) creating the knowledge base and (b) using the results of the job analyses, research reviews, and analyses of licensing requirements to modify the assessment criteria (Dwyer, 1998).

The first of the job analyses carried out by ETS (Rosenfeld, Freeberg, & Bukatko, 1992; Rosenfeld, Reynolds, & Bukatko, 1992; Rosenfeld, Wilder, & Bukatko, 1992) were large-scale, national surveys that asked teachers in detail about the importance of specific tasks for their own teaching as well as for that of beginning teachers. These surveys were carried out separately for elementary school, middle school, and secondary school teachers, and the teachers' responses were used to refine the initial set of assessment criteria. ETS found a "high degree of similarity of results across different groups doing the rating, and across grade level and subject-matter taught," a finding that

"was highly influential in the decision to create a single set of criteria to be used in assessing different grade levels and subjects taught" (Dwyer, 1994, p. 13). Of course, their findings must be interpreted in light of the nature of the specific tasks to which the teachers were responding. The tasks were not subject specific. (It should be noted, though, that content-specific job analyses were carried out for all of the Praxis II tests of content knowledge.)

Following completion of these national surveys, ETS continued developing a unified set of criteria designed to "identify important aspects of teaching that have validity in a wide variety of contexts" (Dwyer, 1994, p. 13). This set of criteria was reviewed by a national advisory committee, known as the Teacher Program Council. The council consisted of highly accomplished teachers, district administrators, teachers' union officials, and educational researchers. To obtain further information about changes that were needed in the criteria, ETS piloted them in 1992 with beginning and experienced teachers in Delaware and Minnesota (Dwyer, 1994), carried out a series of research studies (Dwyer, 1994), and conducted additional job analyses (Powers, 1992; Wesley, Rosenfeld, & Sims-Gunzenhauser, 1993)

The results from the pilot testing, research studies, and job analyses contributed to the development of a set of criteria that, as we have seen, emphasize the need for teachers to engage their students in active, in-depth learning and to have pedagogical content knowledge. At the same time, these results also led to ETS's decision to create one set of criteria and one assessment for use at all grade levels and in all subject areas. Consequently, even when used in conjunction with the Praxis II tests of pedagogical content knowledge, Praxis III reveals less about whether beginning teachers apply pedagogical content knowledge then INTASC's subject-specific portfolios. (In the next section, we discuss the nature of the Praxis and INTASC assessments.)

In addition to the job analyses carried out while developing the criteria for Praxis III, ETS conducted and reviewed analyses of state regulations and assessment practices regarding teacher licensure. In one study, Street (1991) found that, while many of the state performance assessment systems implemented in the 1980s were organized in different ways, the teaching skills they measured were similar across states. Two other studies (Tracy & Smeaton, 1993; Kuligowski, Holdzkom, & French, 1993) produced similar results. The use of these analyses as a source of data may have further contributed to ETS's decision to develop one set of criteria and one assessment for use at all grade levels and in all subject areas. The performance-based assessments that were developed by most states in the 1980s focused on generic aspects of teacher behavior and often involved checklists of discrete behaviors. In contrast, a number of states have recently developed content-specific teaching standards.

Finally, researchers from ETS conducted a review of research on culturally responsive pedagogy (Villegas, 1991) and completed a synthesis of reviews of effective teaching and studies of learning to teach (Reynolds, 1992). In her review, Villegas identified several qualities that characterize teachers who are able to work effectively with students from diverse backgrounds, many of which were incorporated into the conception of teaching that underlies Praxis III. In her synthesis, Reynolds examined research on the practices of competent experienced teachers and how their practices differ from those of beginning teachers. Reynolds's findings were "directly incorporated into the knowledge base" for Praxis III (Dwyer, 1994, p. 14).

ROLE OF JOB ANALYSES IN ENSURING
LEGAL DEFENSIBILITY

According to case law, job analyses often contribute to ensuring the legal defensibility of assessments used in making licensure decisions. By carrying out extensive job analyses in developing the Praxis III criteria, ETS helped to ensure that Praxis III would be legally defensible in this respect. Conversely, while INTASC did not conduct traditional job analyses, it did ensure the integrity of the processes by which its standards were developed by assembling subject-matter experts to draft them and by widely distributing the drafts to educators throughout the country. In our view, there is a tension between the ETS approach, which ties assessment to current practice, and the heavy reliance of INTASC and the National Board on experts that may lead to assessments that push the field of practice forward. Ultimately, the legality of the various assessments will be determined as they are implemented and used for important decisions such as licensure or compensation.

Technical Factors

The nature, outcomes, and effects of an assessment are influenced by a variety of technical factors, including the methods, instruments, and sources of evidence used; the time and frequency at which assessment occurs; the ways in which data are combined and aggregated and judgments are communicated; and the knowledge and preparation of the assessors (Darling-Hammond, 1990; Peterson, 1995). In this section, we compare and contrast the technical aspects of the Praxis, INTASC, and National Board assessments. We refer here to Praxis III as well as the Praxis II tests of content knowledge, teaching knowledge, and pedagogical content knowledge; and use the INTASC 1995–96 mathematics assessment and the National Board's 1996–97 EA/ELA assessment as prototypes. Although differences obtain among the various INTASC assessments and among the various NBPTS assessments, there are virtually no differences among these assessments on the dimensions discussed here.

The INTASC and NBPTS assessments require teachers to perform exercises that are significantly different from those that compose Praxis II and III. The various Praxis II assessments feature multiple-choice or constructed response questions. In Praxis III, teachers go through at least two assessment cycles over the course of a year, each of which involves describing their teaching context, preparing a lesson plan, teaching a lesson that they have selected, and going through interviews before and after the lesson. In contrast, the INTASC assessments require teachers to submit several portfolio entries that are integrated around one or two units of instruction. These entries include a description of their teaching context, a set of lesson plans from a 2-week period, videotapes of and commentaries about two of these lessons, and samples of student work during this period. In addition, teachers must focus on three of their students as they go through the assessment.

For the National Board assessments, teachers must develop classroom-based portfolios that include videotapes of lessons, commentaries about the videotapes, and samples of student work. In addition, teachers must complete four exercises that are administered at a local assessment center. These four 90-minute exercises are designed to measure candidates' pedagogical content knowledge and, to some extent, their content knowledge.

NATURE OF THE INTASC ASSESSMENTS

For the INTASC mathematics assessment, teachers are required to complete six portfolio entries that are integrated around a single unit of instruction. For the first entry, they must fill out a teaching-context form that calls for information about the community in which their school is located, the socioeconomic status and racial and gender distribution of the students, whether they teach in a middle school or a high school, whether they teach in a public school or a private school, and their access to various types of technology. For this entry, they must write a commentary describing their school, the class they have selected for use in the assessment, and three students on whom they have chosen to focus throughout the assessment.

The second entry requires teachers to "complete a set of lesson plans that detail the mathematics, tasks, discourse, environment, and analysis of learning that occurs throughout this series of lessons" (INTASC, 1995a, p. 22). In addition, they write a commentary for this entry that articulates their objectives and expectations for student learning during the lessons and that describes the mathematical concepts that unify the lessons. In the commentary, teachers describe the tasks that students will be expected to engage in and how these tasks are related to particular mathematical ideas and processes, and they discuss any modifications they will make to ensure the engagement of the three students they have elected to highlight (INTASC, 1995a).

The third and fourth entries in the assessment require teachers to videotape two lessons and include 20 to 30 minutes of the videotape of each lesson in their portfolios. The videotapes are meant to capture the classroom environment and the nature of discourse between candidates and their students and among students. Videotapes are to include the introduction and development of a mathematical concept, whole group and non-whole-group instruction, and students engaged in problem solving (INTASC, 1995a). In addition to the videotapes, each entry requires teachers to include samples of student work and a commentary that describes the objectives of the lesson, the mathematical tasks that were part of the lesson, the mathematical discourse that occurred during the lesson, and their analysis of student learning and their own teaching during the lesson (INTASC, 1995a).

In the fifth entry, teachers describe the assessment or assessments they used to evaluate student learning over the course of the series of lessons. In particular, they are asked to consider what their students have learned to do as a result of the lessons and what they still need to learn. In addition, the teachers must include samples of work from the three students they have chosen to highlight throughout their portfolios. For the final entry, teachers assess the work in their portfolios and describe how they will use it for professional growth. They examine which tasks and what type or types of discourse were most effective in helping students to further their understanding of mathematics. They are also asked to describe the nature of their collaborative work with colleagues during the past year and to identify one aspect of their teaching that they want to improve (INTASC, 1995a). Overall, it takes most teachers 50 to 75 hours to complete all six portfolio exercises.

INTASC's approach to assessing teachers' portfolios is characterized as "integrative and dialogic" (Moss, 1998a). Each portfolio is evaluated by two readers (the background and training of the readers are described below). At first, the readers independently examine and take notes on each of the portfolio entries, recording evidence that is relevant to the interpretive categories. These categories represent the interaction in actual teaching situations among the standards for a given assessment. In mathematics, for example, the interpretive categories include mathematical tasks, mathematical discourse, learning environment, and analysis of teaching and learning.

After the readers have each taken notes on all of the entries, they use a set of guiding questions as they "work together to prepare interpretive summaries with supporting evidence for each category" (Moss, 1996, p. 25). For example, the four guiding questions for the category of mathematical tasks are as follows:

1. What kinds of mathematical tasks does the teacher select?
2. How appropriate are the tasks and activities for the instructional goals and objectives?
3. How appropriate are the tasks for the learners?
4. What happens when the tasks are implemented? (Thompson, 1997, pp. 15–16).

Developing interpretive summaries "requires readers to compare and integrate evidence from multiple parts of the portfolio," which includes integration across different portfolio entries and types of portfolio data. In particular, readers are encouraged to point to evidence that their coreader has failed to notice or challenge their interpretations with counterinterpretations or disconfirming evidence (Moss, 1998a). Readers then use these summaries as they attempt to reach consensus regarding the teacher's overall level of performance. With regard to the mathematics portfolios, for example, readers assign a rating of 1 to 4. Finally, they "prepare a written justification tying the evidence they have analyzed to their decision" (Moss, 1996, p. 25). States that use the INTASC portfolios in making licensure decisions are responsible for establishing cut scores.

NATURE OF THE PRAXIS II AND PRAXIS III ASSESSMENTS

ETS offers Praxis II core tests of content knowledge in more than 20 content areas. In addition, ETS has developed in-depth tests of content knowledge in 17 areas, tests of pedagogical content knowledge in 9 areas, and three tests of teaching knowledge (for different developmental levels). In some content areas, additional advanced content tests have been created. As mentioned earlier, the core content tests are all 2 hours long and include only multiple-choice questions, while the in-depth tests of content knowledge and the tests of pedagogical content knowledge feature constructed response questions. The three tests of teaching knowledge feature both multiple-choice and constructed response questions.

In mathematics, for example, ETS has developed a core test of content knowledge; an in-depth test of content knowledge; a basic test of proofs, models, and problems; an advanced test of proofs, models, and problems; and a test of pedagogical content knowledge. In Spanish, by contrast, tests of core content knowledge, language skills, and pedagogical content knowledge are available.

For Praxis III, each teacher completes a class profile and an instruction profile and is then observed and interviewed by an individual assessor (the backgrounds and training of the assessors are described below). In the class profile, the teachers must describe the content and grade level of the class being observed; the socioeconomic status, racial-ethnic and gender distribution, and level of English proficiency of the students; and the number of students with various exceptionalities. Further, teachers are asked about the "most important classroom routines, procedures, rules, and expectations for student behavior that will be in operation during the observed lesson" and whether there is "anything about the learning environment that [they] think might affect [the] students or the scheduled observation" (ETS, 1995, p. 68).

In the instruction profile, the teachers must describe their goals for the lesson with regard to student learning and how the content of the lesson is related to what students have learned previously and what they'll be learning in the future. The teachers are asked to discuss how, in planning the lesson, they have accommodated the gender of their students and their racial-ethnic backgrounds, levels of English-language proficiency, socioeconomic status, skill levels, and exceptionalities. Further, they must provide information about the teaching methods, learning activities, and instructional materials they plan to use and how these are related to their goals for the lesson (ETS, 1995).

Before the observation, the assessor reviews the class and instruction profiles. In the preobservation interview, teachers are asked several questions, including why they selected the goals, instructional methods, activities, and materials and how they acquire information about their students' prior knowledge and skills and their cultural resources. This interview is semistructured and serves as an important source of key evidence for several criteria, particularly those in Domain A, Organizing Content for Student Learning (ETS, 1995).

During the observation, the assessor records key aspects of what the teacher and students say and do that are related to the criteria, especially those in Domain B, Creating An Environment for Student Learning, and Domain C, Teaching for Student Learning. The criteria for Domain B, for example, are:

B1. Creating a climate that promotes fairness,
B2. Establishing and maintaining rapport with students,
B3. Communicating challenging learning expectations to each student,
B4. Establishing and maintaining consistent standards of classroom behavior, and
B5. Making the physical environment as safe and conducive to learning as possible (ETS, 1995, p. 25).

These notes, taken by the assessor during the observation, are to be objective and descriptive; at this point, the assessor is not forming judgments.

In the postobservation interview, the teacher is asked to reflect on how the lesson went and, if the class departed from the lesson plan, to explain why. This semistructured interview also serves as a source of evidence for several criteria, particularly those in Domain D, Teacher Professionalism. In this interview, the assessor probes to learn whether teachers would do anything differently if they were to teach the lesson to the same class again. In addition, they are asked to discuss some students who were doing well with the instructional tasks and some who were doing poorly (ETS, 1995).

After the postobservation interview is completed, the assessor reviews all of the notes taken during the observation and interviews along with the information from the class profile and instruction profile. The assessor then determines what evidence, positive or negative, exists for each of the 19 criteria, "selects the most salient evidence of performance for each, and transfers it to the Record-of-Evidence form" (ETS, 1995). Finally, the assessor writes a summary statement for each criterion, which links the evidence to the scoring rules for that criterion, and assigns a score from 1.0 to 3.5 for each criterion.

All of the activities associated with the assessment of a single lesson compose an assessment cycle, and it takes teachers 6 to 8 hours to go through such a cycle. The class profile and the instruction profile, which must be ready prior to the observation, can be completed in a few hours, and the interviews and observation typically last 3 or 4 hours. Although, as mentioned earlier, states that use Praxis III in making licensure decisions are required to administer the assessment at least twice during each candidate's 1st year of teaching, ETS anticipates that beginning teachers in many states will go through several assessment cycles. Further, states that use Praxis III are responsible for establishing cut scores and determining how data will be aggregated across criteria and over observations to create a scoring scale.

DIFFERENCES BETWEEN INTASC AND PRAXIS

There are several important differences between the INTASC and Praxis assessments. First, the INTASC portfolios are content-specific assessments, and the readers who evaluate them must have teaching experience in the same content area and at the same level of schooling as those they are assessing. In contrast, Praxis III is designed for use in all subject areas and at all developmental levels, and assessors are not required to have teaching experience in the same subject areas as those they assess. While ETS strongly recommends that states supplement Praxis III with the Praxis II tests of pedagogical content knowledge, some states may elect not to do so.

The INTASC portfolios more fully reveal whether beginning teachers practice in ways that reflect knowledge of the most appropriate ways of presenting subject matter to students, their most common misconceptions, and areas they find most difficult. In contrast, the Praxis measure of pedagogical content knowledge is based on constructed response questions, not on analyses of actual teaching practices. It may be, though, that the Praxis II assessments of pedagogical content knowledge provide a more complete assessment of teacher knowledge in this important area.

A second noteworthy difference is that the INTASC portfolio entries are integrated around one or two instructional units, while the assessment cycles that beginning teachers in Praxis III go through do not necessarily occur during the same unit. By requiring teachers to complete a series of lesson plans for a unit of instruction and write a commentary about them, INTASC is able, unlike Praxis III, to assess teachers' abilities to plan multiple tasks across several lessons within the same unit and to plan multiple means of assessing students.

Third, while both INTASC and Praxis III require candidates to reflect on their own performance on the assessment, they ask candidates to analyze student performance during the lesson or lessons in different ways. During the postobservation interview in Praxis III, candidates are asked to reflect on the lesson they have just taught. In particular, they are asked about the relative effectiveness of the teaching methods, activities, and materials they used and about students who appeared, to the assessor, to be engaged during the lesson as well as students who seemed to have difficulty. Similarly, INTASC requires candidates to reflect on their teaching throughout the series of lessons, particularly the relative effectiveness of the different tasks, types of discourse, and environmental changes that characterized the lessons. In contrast to Praxis III, though, INTASC requires candidates to include a copy of an assessment they used to analyze student learning across several of the lessons, to provide samples of work from the three selected students, and to discuss what they believe these students learned across the series of lessons.

Another important difference is that Praxis III involves live observations, while the INTASC portfolios require teachers to submit videotapes of their instruction. Because it involves live observation, Praxis III enables assessors to see what the teacher and all of the students are doing and to evaluate the teacher's management skills with regard to the entire class. In contrast, by requiring teachers to include videotapes of two lessons, the INTASC portfolios are less likely to provide information about all that is happening, including perhaps teachers' management skills with regard to an entire class. Further, the quality of the video may vary from teacher to teacher in ways unrelated to teaching quality. Video does, however, allow for the use of multiple assessors who can review a teacher's practices at their own pace.

Conversely, the INTASC portfolios enable candidates to choose examples of their teaching that represent their ability to meet INTASC's content-specific standards. In the INTASC mathematics portfolio, for example, candidates are asked to select videotape that includes "the introduction and development of a mathematical concept, whole group and non-whole-group instruction, students engaged in problem solving" and the candidate's "role in facilitating discourse in the classroom, student to student discourse, and the classroom environment" (INTASC, 1995a, p. 29). While candidates may not be able to include evidence of each of these aspects of instruction in each videotaped lesson, they are expected to include all of them over the course of the two lessons featured on videotape.

In contrast, while candidates in Praxis III choose the lessons during which they will be observed and go through two or more assessment cycles over the course of the school year, their teaching during the observations may not accurately represent their ability to meet the Praxis III criteria. In sum, the videos teachers compile for the INTASC portfolios may represent their best practice, as opposed to their typical practice, while the observations in Praxis III may be of lessons that are more representative of their typical practice, but may not illustrate all important dimensions of good teaching (as represented by the Praxis III criteria).

Another noteworthy difference has to do with costs. Because of the length of our section on costs, we have included it below in a separate section.

Sixth, Praxis III is part of a battery of assessments that, as mentioned earlier, includes Praxis I and Praxis II. By using all three of these assessments, states will be able to measure basic intellectual skills, subject-matter knowledge, and teaching skills. While INTASC has announced plans to develop tests of subject-matter knowledge and teaching knowledge, these tests had not been completed as of spring 1998.

Finally, it is important to note that both Praxis III and the INTASC portfolios suffer from being based on a very small, and possibly unrepresentative, sample of teaching practices (Shavelson, Webb, & Burstein, 1986).

COSTS

Since Praxis III and the INTASC portfolios have not yet been implemented statewide (i.e., with all beginning teachers) in any states, we do not have actual data on the costs of implementing these assessments. Instead, we will draw on some preliminary estimates of the costs of implementing induction programs for beginning teachers that feature Praxis III or the INTASC portfolios. (These estimates were provided by ETS and the Connecticut State Department of Education.)

The main costs of an induction program include developing or purchasing an assessment system, pilot testing and validating the system, training mentor teachers, training assessors, administering proficiency tests for assessor candidates, and administering and scoring the assessment. It would cost states much more to develop content-specific teaching standards and portfolio assessments than to purchase Praxis III. States can purchase Praxis III assessment materials for 2,000 beginning teachers for $40,000. In contrast, the estimated cost of developing teaching standards and a portfolio in a single-content area is considerably higher (Fisk, 1997). To reduce the cost of portfolio development, several states have participated in the INTASC Performance Assessment Development Project. In this project, about 10 states contributed $150,000 each from 1994 to 1997 to support the development of the INTASC mathematics and English/language arts portfolios.

In estimating the costs of training mentors and assessors and administering assessor proficiency tests, it was assumed that 2,000 mentors and 170 assessors would be trained (Fisk, 1997; Tsuji, personal communication, September 25, 1997). Under these assumptions, the estimated cost of implementing an induction program featuring Praxis III is approximately $292,000 ($88,000 for mentor training; $170,000 for assessor training; and $34,000 for administering assessor proficiency tests). In contrast, the estimated cost of implementing an induction program featuring the INTASC portfolios is approximately $308,000 ($73,000 for mentor training and $235,000 for assessor training and administering assessor proficiency tests).

The estimated cost of scoring the INTASC portfolios for 2,000 teachers is $250,000 (Fisk, 1997). We were unable to obtain an estimate of the cost of scoring the performance of 2,000 teachers on Praxis III (with each teacher going through two assessment cycles).

In sum, the costs of training mentors and assessors and administering the assessments in both systems are similar, while the costs of developing the INTASC portfolios are greater than the costs of purchasing Praxis III. At the same time, it is important to note three important distinctions between induction programs featuring the INTASC portfolios and those that make use of Praxis III. First, as mentioned above, the INTASC portfolios more fully reveal whether beginning teachers are able to apply pedagogical teaching knowledge. Second, developing an INTASC portfolio is a more rigorous form of professional development than going through two or more Praxis III assessment cycles. Finally, the INTASC portfolio scoring process serves as an important professional development experience for readers. In particular, this process promotes critical inquiry among teachers by requiring them to work collaboratively to integrate multiple sources of evidence in evaluating the portfolios (Moss, Schutz, & Collins, 1998).

NATURE OF THE NBPTS ASSESSMENTS

The National Board's assessments consist of several portfolio and assessment center exercises, each of which is designed to measure teachers' performances on one or more of the standards for that assessment. Many of the portfolio exercises are similar to the exercises that make up the INTASC assessments. From 1991 to 1995, several contractors were hired to develop assessments in six different areas (which were mentioned earlier). The total number of exercises for each of these assessments ranged from 7 to 13. In 1996, the National Board selected ETS to serve as its sole contractor. Beginning in 1996–97, all of the assessments consisted of 10 exercises. For each assessment, the 10 exercises included 6 portfolio exercises and 4 assessment center exercises.

During the first 5 years of pilot testing and implementation (1993–94 to 1997–98), teachers were given 4 to 6 months to develop their portfolios. In the 1996–97 EA/ELA assessment, for example, candidates for National Board Certification were asked to compile portfolios that included: three students' responses to a work of literature; writing samples from three students; a videotape of the teacher exploring an important topic in language arts with a small group of students; a videotape of the teacher discussing an important language arts topic with the whole class; and documentation of teaching activities that involve the teacher's colleagues, school, students' families, and local communities (NBPTS, 1996). For each portfolio entry, teachers must also submit a written commentary in which they contextualize the entry and analyze their teaching.

For the assessment center exercises, candidates for the 1996–97 EA/ELA assessment were asked to plan some teaching based on three to five works of literature and to construct an argument about a teaching scenario based on three professional articles about writing instruction. In addition, they were asked to use four professional articles on second-language learning and bilingualism to describe how they would plan instruction for a particular second-language learner and to recommend reading selections to parents of students ages 11 to 15 (NBPTS, 1996).

For every candidate who goes through the National Board assessment process, two assessors score each assessment exercise on a scale from 0.75 to 4.25 (the backgrounds and training of the assessors are described below). Working independently, the assessors use prompts to seek evidence and to determine whether candidates satisfy certain criteria. For the first 3 years of pilot testing and implementation, after the assessors had independently arrived at scores, candidates received the average of the two scores if they were in the same score family, e.g., 3- (2.75), 3 (3.0), and 3+ (3.25). If the scores were not in the same score family (e.g., 2+ and 3-), however, an adjudication process was triggered (Gregory, 1995). If the scores were still in different score families after adjudication, then a third assessor was brought in.

In 1996–97, the scoring process was changed. Under the new process, the final score for each exercise is the average of the two scores assigned to it. When the scores are 1.25 or less apart, the two are averaged to reach a final score. If the scores are more than 1.25 apart, than a trainer is brought in. For such cases, the trainer's score counts for half the final score and each of the other scores count for one fourth (Thompson & Pearlman, 1997). In all, a candidate's score record has 10 final scores in it, one for each exercise, so at least 20 scores go into determining whether or not a candidate is certified (Thompson & Pearlman, 1997).

To become a National Board Certified Teacher, candidates must earn a score of 275 or higher on a scale from 75 to 425. While candidates receive scores from 0.75 to 4.25 for each of the 10 exercises, these scores are not all weighted equally. In determining a candidate's overall score, the scores for some exercises are multiplied by 10, while others are multiplied by numbers greater than or less than 10. The four classroom-based portfolio exercises are the most heavily weighted, followed by the four assessment center exercises. The two documented accomplishment exercises are given the least weight in the scoring.

In 1996–97, the National Board initiated a new banking policy. Under this policy, NBPTS automatically banks the individual exercise scores of all candidates for a 3-year period once they are notified of their initial scores. During this period, candidates who are not yet certified may retake any combination of portfolio or assessment center exercises on which they received a score below 2.75. If their overall score after retaking the exercises is greater than 2.75, then they can apply the score toward National Board Certification. This process of banking will allow candidates to capitalize on measurement error.

During the pilot testing and administration of the National Board assessments in 1993–94, the assessment center exercises took place over 2 days. In 1994–95 and 1995–96, the exercises took place over the course of a single, 8-hour day. From the beginning of 1993–94 through 1995–96, there were only six to eight assessment centers available throughout the United States, and candidates were required to travel to the centers on a particular weekend in the spring. As of 1996–97, the National Board arranged to have the assessment center exercises carried out at Sylvan Technology Centers, which are located in all 50 states and several territories, including Puerto Rico, Guam, and the U.S. Virgin Islands. Candidates have the option of traveling to the Sylvan Technology Centers on any day of the week during a 3- to 6-week period. The length of this period depends on the number of candidates planning to come to the center.

DIFFERENCES BETWEEN INTASC AND THE NATIONAL BOARD

While the National Board, like INTASC, has multiple assessors evaluate each candidate's performance, it uses a qualitatively different approach to scoring candidates' performances. Each candidate for National Board Certification is evaluated on each assessment exercise by two assessors. In contrast to INTASC assessors, though, National Board assessors determine a score without communicating with their counterpart (i.e., the other assessor who is evaluating the candidate's performance on the same exercise). Further, each National Board assessor is responsible for evaluating a candidate's performance on only one exercise. Each National Board candidate's overall performance is determined by combining scores assigned by individual assessors algorithmically into a composite score.

From the perspective of psychometric theory, the National Board's scoring practices use more independent pieces of information in forming a score and so may have greater reliability. However, INTASC contends that judging assessors who have become familiar with the candidate's abilities across multiple performances may result in a more valid and fair decision and that allowing readers to engage in dialogue about the actual performances may result in a sounder decision that more comprehensively considers the complex evidence available (Moss, 1996). In INTASC's view, further empirical research is necessary to determine the relative strengths and limitations of INTASC's approach to portfolio evaluation as compared to the more traditional approach used by the National Board. Consequently, INTASC is undertaking an extensive program of validity research (see Moss, Schutz, and Collins, 1998). (Several studies that are part of this program are described below.)

Knowledge and Training of Assessors

For each assessment cycle in Praxis III, the teacher is observed and interviewed by an individual assessor. In conducting the assessment, the assessor reviews the classroom and instruction profiles and conducts the observation and interviews. Then the assessor determines what evidence exists for each of the assessment criteria and writes a summary statement and assigns a score for each criterion. ETS expects all of the assessors for Praxis III to be current or former teachers. Assessors are not required, however, to teach in the same content area, or at the same student developmental level, as the teachers they assess. In contrast, INTASC and the National Board require assessors to be teachers in the same content area as the teachers they assess, and NBPTS also requires that they teach at the same developmental level. It should be noted, though, that none of these assessment systems include content-specific assessments at the elementary school level.

In Praxis III, the length of training for assessors is 6 days. Trainers use worksheets, sample records of evidence, simulations, case studies, and videotapes of benchmark samples to help the assessors learn to recognize evidence of the presence or absence of each of the 19 criteria in a range of educational settings. At this point, ETS plans to train a small number of assessor trainers in each state that chooses to implement Praxis III. These individuals, in turn, will train large numbers of assessors across their states.

Assessor trainees go through several exercises to learn to evaluate written information provided by the teacher, to take accurate notes during classroom observations, and to conduct semistructured interviews. They receive feedback from the trainer and their peers as well as the answers to the exercises themselves, and they explore their personal biases. After 4 days of structured activities, the trainees spend a day conducting an assessment cycle with a beginning teacher. Then they come together on the final day to discuss their experiences and take a practice exam and a proficiency exam.

In the proficiency exam, each trainee views a videotape of a beginning teacher presenting a lesson along with the accompanying preobservation and postobservation interviews and reads copies of the actual class and instruction profiles for the videotaped lesson (ETS, 1994). Trainees receive two scores on the exam: an accuracy score and a documentation score. The accuracy score "measures the degree of agreement between scores that the assessor trainee assigns for the 19 criteria and those on the juried Record of Evidence that serves as the official 'answer key'" (ETS, 1994, p. 1). To determine a trainee's documentation score, a panel of Praxis III assessors rates the trainee's documentation for each criterion with respect to three categories: evidence, summary statement, and objectivity. Evidence and summary statements are each rated on a 4-point scale, while objectivity is rated on a 2-point scale. We were unable to learn the standards to which trainees are held.

The National Board's assessors are trained to evaluate performances on a single exercise. The length of training is determined by the exercises they are being trained to score and usually lasts from 3 to 5 days. During the training, trainees learn about the various parts of the scoring system and go through exercises in which they explore their personal biases. Trainers emphasize the "importance of taking on the National Board's criteria as the only lens with which to evaluate cases" and the need to treat all performances with respect (Thompson & Pearlman, 1997, p. 36).

During the training, assessors are given benchmarks, training samples, and qualifying samples. The benchmarks are actual examples of performances at all four levels. The assessors are told the scores of the benchmarks before they read them and asked to look for evidence that matches a particular level descriptor. The benchmarks "are presented in pairs so that assessors can see that there are many ways to meet the description of a level in the rubric" (Thompson & Pearlman, 1997, p. 38). After a pair of benchmarks is presented, the trainer leads a discussion about the salient evidence of each performance and the ways in which the two performances are similar despite surface differences (Thompson & Pearlman, 1997).

Unlike the benchmarks, the scores of the training samples are not known in advance by the assessors. Assessors work independently to score the training samples. Once they are finished, the trainer announces the true score and leads a discussion about the salient evidence of the performance. After scoring the

training samples and discussing them, assessors move into a qualifying round. In this stage, assessors score preselected cases on their own, without discussion, which more closely matches true scoring conditions.

There is some ambiguity to the standards that individuals must meet to become assessors. The National Board examines the scores each assessor gives and the assessor's records of evidence at each stage of the training process. According to NBPTS, assessors must meet a rigorous standard in assessing the preselected cases during the qualifying round.

In contrast to the National Board's assessors, INTASC's readers are trained to evaluate entire portfolios through the use of interpretive categories (Moss, 1996). During the field testing of the mathematics and E/LA portfolios, the length of training for the readers was 6 days. During the training, trainees learn: (a) to use interpretive categories to examine the different components of the portfolios; (b) to take notes on the different components of the portfolios; (c) to use an evaluation scale, which provides examples of benchmark performances, in evaluating the portfolios; and (d) to work with another reader in evaluating the portfolios.

INTASC has established knowledge and dispositional standards that teachers must meet to be accepted into reader training. For example, mathematics readers must know the content and discourse of mathematics; understand how students learn mathematics; understand how their racial, ethnic, socioeconomic, and linguistic backgrounds affect their learning; and know mathematics pedagogy (Thompson, 1997). With regard to dispositions, readers must be willing, for example, to adopt a common framework for evaluating teaching and to make decisions recommending the denial of licensure. It is unclear to us how readers are judged against these standards.

Once teachers have gone through reader training, they must meet four performance standards before they are allowed to evaluate portfolios for licensure. For example, they must demonstrate the ability to write interpretive summaries and assign accurate performance levels, "individually and in pairs, that accurately reflect the work of a beginning teacher" (Thompson, 1997, p. 59). While readers provide some evidence of their ability to meet the performance standards during training, "a calibration test of at least two portfolios is required of readers at the completion of training" (Thompson, 1997, p. 60). Most readers who do not initially meet performance standards continue to participate in training until they are able to calibrate their scores with those of experienced readers.

Psychometric Studies of the Praxis, INTASC, and NBPTS Assessments

The National Board INTASC, and ETS are carrying out a variety of studies of the psychometric properties of their assessments. In this section, we examine each organization's approach to conducting research on validity, reliability, and fairness. In particular, the following types of validity-related evidence are considered: evidence based on test content, evidence related to the procedures used to specify the content domain, criterion-related evidence, evidence based on response processes, and evidence based on consequences of testing. In terms of reliability, we focus on consistency of scores across raters and rater pairs;

consistency of scores across lessons, exercises, and portfolios; and the precision of classification decisions. Finally, with regard to fairness, we examine whether the various assessments result in bias or adverse impact and whether issues of equity are being addressed through process-oriented studies of candidates' opportunity to learn and access to support.

In the preceding discussion, the reader should be mindful of the fact that the National Board and INTASC assessments are sometimes modified from 1 year to the next. For example, the National Board's 1997–98 MC/Gen assessment is different from previous MC/Gen assessments, while INTASC's 1997–98 mathematics assessment is different from its earlier math assessments.

National Board—Completed Studies

The National Board's approach to conducting research on validity, reliability, and fairness draws on psychometric principles and is primarily guided by the requirements of the 1985 *Standards for Educational and Psychological Testing* (American Educational Research Association, American Psychological Association, & National Council on Measurement and Education, 1985). In particular, NBPTS has carried out a variety of studies to (a) obtain validity-related evidence based on assessment content, the procedures used to specify the content domain, response processes, and the consequences of testing; (b) estimate the overall reliability of the assessments; (c) examine the consistency of scores across exercises; and (d) consider several issues related to fairness and equity.

For each of its assessments, the National Board has conducted multiple studies to obtain evidence of content validity (Jaeger, 1998). Expert panels have been assembled for each assessment to evaluate the content validity of the assessment exercises and scoring rubrics. For the 1995–96 MC/Gen assessment, for example, a panel of 19 expert middle childhood teachers "agreed" or "strongly agreed" that each of the 11 content standards represented a critical aspect of the middle childhood domain (Benson & Impara, in Jaeger, 1996c). At least 15 panelists judged all 11 assessment exercises to be "relevant" to 2 or more of the 11 content standards and "important" to 2 or more of the standards. Further, at least 15 of the 19 panelists rated each of the 11 scoring rubrics to be relevant and important to 2 or more of the MC/Gen standards.

Not only do these results provide evidence that the content of the MC/Gen assessment is closely related to the construct to be measured by the assessment, but they also indicate that individual exercises require candidates to integrate knowledge, skills, and dispositions from two or more standards. Studies of the 1995–96 EC/Gen assessment (Benson & Impara, in Jaeger, 1996b) and the 1995–96 EAYA/Art assessment produced similar findings from content-related evidence (Benson & Impara, in Jaeger, 1996a).

Studies have been conducted of the integrity of the processes by which content standards for various National Board assessments have been developed. For example, Hattie (in Jaeger, 1996c) found that the procedures used to develop the standards for the 1994–95 and 1995–96 MC/Gen assessments were procedurally sound; there was much input, criticism, and reaction from accomplished teachers and other experts in the subject area; and the resulting standards were subjected to appropriate professional review. In studies of the 1995–96 EC/Gen assessment (Jaeger, 1996b) and the 1995–96 EAYA/Art assessment (Jaeger, 1996a), Hattie came up with similar findings.

The processes that assessors go through in scoring candidates' responses to individual exercises have been examined. For each assessment, a small group of accomplished teachers was "asked to evaluate the degree to which assessors' bases for scoring candidates' responses were consistent with" the standards for that certification area (Jaeger, 1996c, p. 23). In addition, the teachers were asked to consider whether assessors' judgments of candidates' responses to individual exercises "appeared to be representative of the entire content domain" as defined by the standards associated with that exercise (Jaeger, 1996c, p. 24). For the MC/Gen assessment, for example, panelists examined 84 ratings. In 75 of the ratings (89%), they concluded that the capacities considered by assessors in making a judgment about the candidate's response to a particular exercise were firmly and exclusively grounded in the content standards assessed by the exercise (Jaeger, 1996c). In 67 of the ratings (80%), they reported that the assessors' judgments were representative of the entire content domain assessed by the exercises.

The studies of the consequences of the National Board's assessments are reported below in the section on fairness.

With regard to reliability, studies have been conducted to estimate the overall reliability of each of the assessments. Jaeger (1996b), using a fairly liberal estimate of the standard error of measurement, estimated that, because of measurement error, 19% of the candidates who took the 1994–95 EC/Gen field test with abilities at least as great as the performance standards were not certified. Of the candidates who should not have been certified, an estimated 10% did nonetheless receive certification, again because of measurement error. Overall, 16% of the 195 classification decisions in the 1994–95 administration of the EC/Gen assessment were probably incorrect. In studies of the 1995–96 MC/Gen and EAYA/Art field tests, Jaeger (1996c; 1996a) found that similar percentages of classification decisions were probably incorrect. In interpreting these misclassification percentages, it is important to keep in mind that most, if not all, candidates were experienced teachers. Therefore, these relatively low false-positive and false-negative rates indicate that the assessments can be legitimately used to distinguish between accomplished teachers and other teachers.

In terms of consistency of scores across exercises, it is inappropriate to assume that each exercise in a National Board assessment represents an equivalent measure of the construct underlying that assessment because each NBPTS assessment is used to evaluate candidates within a broad, multifaceted domain. To determine whether the reliability of an assessment might be more reasonably estimated by examining the consistency of scores across subdomains of exercises, Jaeger (1998) applied the stratified coefficient alpha approach to reliability estimation to a National Board assessment that was composed of 11 exercises. He found that the estimated reliability of the assessment increased from 0.82 (when the reliability was estimated without stratifying exercises) to 0.84.

With regard to fairness, the National Board has found that African-American candidates earn National Board Certification at much lower rates than White candidates. From 1993–94 through 1996–97, 43% of White candidates were certified as compared to 11% of African-American candidates. While the certification rate of African-American candidates in 1996–97 (20%) was much higher than it had been previously, it remained far below that of Whites (49%).

To account for the wide disparity in performance between African Americans and Whites, the National Board has examined several potential sources of adverse impact (Bond, 1998). In terms of external sources, NBPTS considered whether the differences in performance on the 1993–94 and 1994–95 assessments could be attributed to years of teaching experience, number of advanced degrees, or amount of support received during portfolio preparation. Bond (1997) found that 62% of all White candidates and 54% of all African-American candidates had advanced degrees (i.e., beyond a bachelor's degree) and that 58% of all White candidates and 62% of all African-American candidates had 10 or more years of teaching experience. Although he did not have information about the quality of the institutions that candidates had attended, Bond (1997) concluded that advanced degrees and years of experience did not explain the difference in performance between Whites and African Americans.

In terms of amount of support, the National Board conducted a study of candidates who participated in the 1993–94 field tests of the EA/Gen and EA/ELA assessments. In this study, 60 White candidates and 37 African-American candidates were interviewed to determine the level of support they received as they prepared their portfolios. In the interviews, candidates were asked to describe the nature of the support they received, whether any of their colleagues assisted them in videotaping their classroom exercises, and whether anyone helped them edit the various reflective essays required in the portfolio (Bond, 1997). Bond (1997) found that White and African-American candidates received comparable support in virtually all categories of collegial, administrative, and technical support.

The National Board has also examined potential sources of adverse impact internal to the assessment itself, including the possible existence of construct-irrelevant variance and potential race-related interactions between assessors and candidates. To examine whether differential performance by race on the 1993–94 EC/Gen assessment was due to differences in writing ability, Bond (1997) compared differences between the two groups across tasks involving more or less writing. The results indicated that the difference in favor of White candidates was larger on the Interpreting Content (IC) exercise, which demanded the most writing of all the exercises, than on the Analyzing Your Lesson (AYL) exercise, which required a minimal amount of writing, but the difference was not statistically significant. (The difference on the IC exercise was 0.75 on a scale from .75 to 4.25, while the difference on the AYL exercise was 0.50.)

National Board—Studies Planned or in Progress

The National Board is currently conducting several studies to identify potential sources of the difference in performance between Whites and African Americans on the 1993–94 and 1994–95 EA/ELA assessments. In one study, a panel of EA/ ELA teachers and researchers will examine whether the EA/ ELA standards and assessment "privilege and honor constructivist, student-centered, and permissive approaches to instruction over didactic, teacher-centered, and more authoritarian instructional styles" (Bond, 1997, p. 15). To perform the evaluation, the panel will scrutinize the EA/ELA standards, the training that assessors go through, and the ways in which assessors apply the scoring scheme.

This study was undertaken in response to a perception that the National Board's assessments give privilege to and honor constructivist, student-centered, and permissive approaches to instruction and, in so doing, systematically disadvantage African-American teachers, because the contexts in which many of them teach (i.e., urban and inner city) require certain styles of instruction. The implied premise of this study is not shared by the National Board or by the authors of this chapter. Whether the criticism and the premise on which it was based are in fact accurate remains to be seen.

In a second study, the National Board will survey and interview both targeted and random samples of African-American EA/ELA teachers to determine (a) what aspects of teaching African-American teachers consider integral to outstanding teaching and (b) whether these teachers' perceptions are consistent with the National Board's vision of outstanding practice. A third study will examine how assessor characteristics interact with candidate characteristics. In particular, it will consider whether African-American assessors, in assessing African-American candidates, attend to aspects of performance that White assessors overlook or even disparage. Further, this study will explore whether assessors whose teaching contexts are similar to candidates they assess value aspects of their performance that other assessors fail to acknowledge.

In a fourth study, the National Board will seek to identify outstanding African-American EA/ELA teachers and support their participation in the process of seeking National Board Certification. After they go through the process, their performance and rate of certification will be compared with those of other candidates. Finally, a fifth study will examine the performances of African-American teachers and White teachers who receive the same evaluation to see if African-American teachers have different patterns of performance across the exercises and, in particular, on the video exercises.

These studies will help to clarify differences in performance on the National Board assessments between African-American and White teachers. The studies may not, however, definitively answer the question of whether the differences are due to bias or competence.

NBPTS is also planning a study that will examine the relationships between teachers' performances on the National Board assessments and (a) the quality of their ongoing teaching practices; (b) the quality of the work produced by their students on classroom assignments and external assessments; and (c) their postassessment professional activities. The study will consider whether National Board Certified Teachers (NBCTs) practice in ways that are superior to those who are denied certification, whether the students of NBCTs achieve at higher levels than students of teachers who perform less well on the National Board assessments, and whether NBCTs are more involved in learning communities outside their classrooms than noncertified teachers. These criterion-validity studies are potentially quite important, although the key to their utility will be getting good measures of the criteria, especially the quality of teaching practices and the value added of student achievement.

ANALYSIS

The National Board's approach to conducting validity research has many strengths and a few shortcomings. One strong point is that NBPTS has developed several innovative strategies for analyzing validity, reliability, and potential impact that are helping to move the measurement field forward. A second strength is that NBPTS has demonstrated content-related validity evidence for each of its assessments. Third, the National Board has undertaken several studies to account for differences in performance between Whites and African Americans in the EA/ELA assessment. Finally, NBPTS is planning a study that will compare the teaching practices, influence on student performance, and professional activities of NCBTs with those of teachers who perform less well on the assessments.

In terms of shortcomings, it is unclear whether teaching performance in particular school environments, as measured by the NBPTS assessments, generalizes to other environments. Consequently, the "generalizability of test interpretation and use" should be investigated (Messick, 1989, p. 6). In terms of consequential validity, the influence these assessments are having on teacher education programs, professional development, and systems of teacher compensation needs to be studied.

INTASC—Completed Studies

In contrast to the National Board, INTASC's validity research agenda draws on both psychometric and hermeneutic principles. For "most sources of evidence, consistent with psychometric principles of validity," INTASC "develop[s] a contrast that has a certain amount of independence built in" (Moss, Schutz, & Collins, 1998). Then, consistent with hermeneutic principles of validity, INTASC reconciles any observed differences dialectically. (For more information about INTASC's validity-research agenda, see Moss, Schutz, & Collins, 1998.)

INTASC has carefully documented the processes by which its standards and portfolios on content-related evidence are developed. It has recorded the credentials and experience of participating teachers and subject-matter experts, charted the evolution of the various assessment components and practices, and created conceptual maps to illuminate the links among the INTASC general principles, the content-specific principles, the portfolio guidelines, and the evaluation criteria (Moss, 1998b).

A series of studies has been conducted to obtain validity evidence based on the processes beginning teachers go through in developing INTASC portfolios. One of these studies involved sending a questionnaire to candidates who planned to undergo the assessment process. The questionnaire asked questions about their educational backgrounds, their ability to perform the portfolio exercises, and their access to mentoring and other resources. It also asked candidates to describe the benefits and drawbacks of going through the portfolio process.

In a related study, INTASC conducted interviews with 18 candidates who had completed the questionnaires. The interview questions were based on the questionnaires. In the study, all 18 candidates reported that completing the portfolios required extensive use of personal time. The estimated time spent ranged from 30 to 80 hours. Candidates also reported a range in the type and degree of support they received from mentors as they went through the process. Some candidates had little or no contact with their mentors, while others had their lesson plans and the portfolio itself reviewed on a regular basis (Collins, Schutz, & Moss, 1997). Of the 18 candidates, 12 felt that their regular teaching activities were reflected by the portfolio, and 15 felt that "their school/district's vision of mathematics (was) consistent with the vision of mathematics education reflected in the INTASC and NCTM [National Council of Teachers of Mathematics] standards" (Collins, Schutz, & Moss, 1997, p. 14). Only four of the candidates, though, felt that their teacher education program prepared them to complete the portfolio.

INTASC has conducted a thorough and objective case study of one reader pair scoring one portfolio (Moss, Schutz, & Collins, 1998). In this study, readers' dialogues and written documentation were examined to determine (a) the extent to which readers' developing interpretations or preconceptions of a candidate's performance are being regularly challenged or tested by the evidence available in the portfolio and by the other member of the pair, (b) the extent to which readers' interpretations reflect comparison and integration of evidence from multiple sections of the portfolio and multiple types of evidence, and (c) the extent to which the comprehensiveness of evidence considered is enhanced by having two members of a pair work together. The study revealed that readers can integrate evidence from different sources, provide additional evidence for each other, and challenge their own assertions by looking for and examining counterexamples (Moss, Schutz, & Collins, 1998).

INTASC—Studies Planned or in Progress

INTASC conducted two criterion studies to examine the relationship between beginning teachers' performances on the portfolios and variables external to the assessment. INTASC compared candidates' performances as evaluated by trained INTASC readers with their performances as assessed by subject-matter experts not trained to serve as assessors. The subject-matter experts are asked to first evaluate the portfolios on the basis of whatever criteria they feel are relevant to the assessment of beginning teaching in their fields and then to review their evaluations after receiving training in the INTASC evaluation process.

Deborah Ball and Anne Ruggles Gere conducted case studies of candidates in their local contexts. The case studies allow INTASC to determine whether the evidence from the portfolios is consistent with evidence gathered from 5-day observations of candidates in their local contexts. By comparing candidates' performances on the INTASC portfolios with partially independent sources of information, this study was designed to illuminate both the strengths and the potential problems of the portfolios (Moss, 1998b).

INTASC plans to conduct studies of interrater pair reliability once it has established performance levels and implemented portfolios on a widespread basis.

In terms of fairness, INTASC has created two Equity Review Panels: one in mathematics and one in English/language arts. Each panel includes teachers, teacher educators, and subject-matter experts. To date, the panels have examined the assessments themselves, and they are beginning to look at the actual performances of candidates. Eventually, both panels will examine whether the assessments (a) provide an appropriate range of opportunities for candidates to display expertise, (b) clearly explain what is valued, (c) allow for differing resource levels and teaching environments, and (d) recognize differing theories about teaching consistent with professional consensus about sound practice. In carrying out these responsibilities, the panels will make use of the results of the process studies described above. In particular, the panels will consider candidates' opportunity to learn and access to support.

No data are available yet on differential impact for the INTASC portfolios.

ANALYSIS

While INTASC's validity research is still in its early stages, the approach it has taken has many strengths. First, by drawing on psychometric and hermeneutic principles in conducting its validity research, INTASC is making an important contribution to the field of measurement; the outcomes of its research will shed light on the strengths and limitations of using both psychometric and hermeneutic principles in construct validation. Second, the planned criterion studies will reveal whether beginning teachers' performances on the portfolios are correlated with other evaluations of their practices. A third strength is the close attention being paid to equity. In particular, the multiple studies of the processes candidates go through in developing portfolios will provide important information about their opportunity to learn and their access to support.

Along with these strengths, INTASC's approach has some weaknesses. First, INTASC has not examined whether teaching performance in particular school environments, as measured by the INTASC portfolios, generalizes to other environments. Second, studies should be carried out to determine the consequences of the INTASC standards and portfolios on teacher education programs and state licensing requirements.

Praxis III—Completed Studies

In conducting research on the validity, reliability, and fairness of Praxis III, ETS, like the National Board, drew on psychometric principles. With regard to content-related evidence of validity, ETS carried out four main activities in developing the criteria for Praxis III: job analyses, analyses of state regulations, research reviews, and expert panel reviews. These activities, all of which are described above, provide content-related evidence of validity.

ETS has conducted several studies of the processes assessors go through in completing an assessment cycle. In one study, for example, Myford and Lehman (1993b) examined how much difficulty assessors experienced in rating the candidate on each criterion, what problems they encountered, and how much confidence they had in their ratings. A total of 93% had no need to reconcile conflicting evidence among criteria; 92% did not have

to infer evidence for certain criteria; and 83% of the assessors reported that they had evidence for all criteria.

Reynolds (1993) carried out an investigation of how two assessors used the measurement instruments to make their judgments. According to her findings, Reynolds made several recommendations to improve the training of assessors. Her recommendations included:

1. Clarify criteria that overlap,
2. Create more opportunities to gather information for criteria that are presently difficult to document, and
3. Discuss ways to decide how much evidence is enough to include for a particular criterion (1993).

In a third study, Myford and Lehman (1993a) surveyed 36 assessors concerning the documentation process. A total of 58% of the assessors reported that they could return to their notes in a year and reconstruct what happened in the classroom, while 42% indicated that they could possibly reconstruct what happened (Myford & Lehman, 1993a). A total of 31% of the assessors felt that their notes contained statements that could be construed as judgments or inferences (which they were not to include) and another 31% stated that their notes possibly contained such statements. Finally, in a rating on a scale of 1 to 5 of how comprehensive they thought their notes were, assessors reported a mean rating of 3.5 (Myford & Lehman, 1993a).

In a fourth study (Reynolds, 1995), recommendations were solicited from assessors regarding how to improve the assessment process. With regard to training, assessors recommended providing assessors feedback during training on the quality of their notes, their selection of evidence for the Record-of-Evidence form, and their choice of rating for the evidence. Assessors also recommended creating exemplars for the Record-of-Evidence form. In addition, assessors suggested making the scoring rules consistent with the criterion definitions and making the domain descriptors similar in length, depth, and breadth across the criteria (Reynolds, 1995). These recommendations were implemented.

Finally, two researchers from ETS examined 36 Record-of-Evidence forms completed by assessors during pilot testing to determine whether assessors differed in the evidence they cited in these forms and whether the completed forms varied in their effectiveness as assessment documents (Camp & Mandinach, 1993). The researchers used a matrix to code each of the 36 forms and to identify issues affecting the quality of the forms. As a result of their analysis, they made several recommendations, all of which were implemented.

As of the 1997–98 school year, ETS had not conducted any predictive or concurrent studies of Praxis III or any studies of the consequences of the assessment.

In terms of reliability, ETS conducted a study to determine how often two assessors observing a lesson agreed on their ratings on each criterion (Livingston, 1993). The study involved 37 different beginning teachers and 43 different assessors. On the scoring scale of 1.0 to 3.5, the two assessors' ratings were within 0.5 of each other 89% of the time, and they were within 1.0 of each other 100% of the time. The average difference between the assessors' ratings was 0.23.

ETS has not conducted any studies of generalizability across lessons for Praxis III.

The content validity and reliability of Praxis I and II have been investigated and are considered excellent according to industry standards.

ANALYSIS

ETS's approach to examining the validity and reliability of Praxis III has a number of strengths. First, ETS used job analyses in developing the criteria for Praxis III, thereby increasing the likelihood that the assessment would be legally defensible. Second, the studies of the processes that assessors go through in evaluating candidates have led to several improvements in the assessment procedure. Third, close attention has been paid to consistency of scores across raters.

In terms of shortcomings, ETS has not conducted any criterion studies, and it has not examined whether teaching in particular school environments, as measured by Praxis III, generalizes to other environments. Given that Praxis III had not been implemented statewide in any states as of the 1999–2000 school year, it was not possible for ETS to conduct any studies of the precision of classification decisions or of adverse impact. When the assessment is implemented statewide in one or more states, it will be important to examine these issues.

States and Districts

This section examines issues related to the implementation of innovative teacher assessments at the state and local levels. In Connecticut and California, performance assessments for beginning teachers are being used in the context of induction programs that provide such teachers with mentoring and support. In addition, a number of other states are pilot testing the Praxis III or INTASC assessments. Several districts have initiated peer assessment programs or other innovative approaches to assessing beginning and experienced teachers. Two such districts, Rochester and Cincinnati, are profiled here.

Connecticut

PURPOSE

In Connecticut, the Beginning Educator Support and Training (BEST) program was implemented prior to the 1989–90 school year and serves all 1st- and 2nd-year teachers and teachers who are new to the state. The purpose of the program is to provide new teachers with mentoring and other forms of support during the critical period of their induction into the profession, while determining whether they have the general and content-specific pedagogical skills necessary to teach effectively. The state assesses new teachers' general teaching skills in their 1st year with the Connecticut Competency Instrument (CCI) and evaluates their content-specific teaching skills in their 2nd year through the use of portfolios.

MENTORING AND OTHER FORMS OF SUPPORT

Each new teacher works with a mentor or a mentor team on a regular basis during their 1st year. Districts are responsible for choosing mentors and can choose teachers, principals, and district administrators to serve in this role. Mentors are required to have teaching experience in the same content area and at the same developmental level as those with whom they work. In addition, new teachers are assigned to mentors who have successfully taught students from the same racial and socioeconomic backgrounds as those they are teaching. With regard to mentor teams, at least one team member must have teaching experience in the appropriate content area. For example, a new elementary school teacher who has students with learning disabilities might have a mentoring team consisting of an experienced elementary school teacher, a special education teacher, and a principal.

In addition to mentoring, the state offers subject-specific seminars to new teachers. These seminars meet six to eight times over the course of a year, focus on issues related to the state's teaching standards, and are led by master teachers who have served as scorers on the state's portfolio assessments (described below) and who have demonstrated the ability to teach adults. In the science seminars, for example, master teachers conduct demonstration lessons and help new teachers analyze the work of teachers and students in science. In these seminars, new teachers collaboratively explore issues of school science learning, such as teaching for understanding, inquiry-oriented learning, and assessing student performance (Lomask, Seroussi, & Budzinsky, 1997). Further, the seminars are designed to promote reflective practice.

A number of universities in Connecticut will offer courses for new teachers and mentors that address the state's teaching standards in particular content areas, teaching strategies associated with the standards, and research that underpins the standards. The courses will be cotaught by university faculty members and master teachers and will require new teachers to write research papers in which they integrate their work in classrooms with research on which the standards in their discipline are based. These courses, as well as the seminars described above, serve as examples of teacher assessments influencing professional development.

CONCEPTIONS OF TEACHING UNDERLYING
THE ASSESSMENTS

The conception of teaching underlying the CCI is similar in many ways to those underlying the Praxis, INTASC, and National Board assessments. The CCI conception states that effective teachers "have a complete understanding of the structures of (their) subject matter, its basic concepts, principles, and procedures" (Armour-Thomas & Szczesiul, undated, p. 3). Such teachers provide learning experiences for their students and interact with them in ways that reflect understanding of their cognitive, social, emotional, and physical development (Armour-Thomas & Szczesiul, undated). According to the CCI conception, effective teachers have high academic expectations for all of their students and engage all of them in active learning. Further, such teachers reflect on each of their lessons, making decisions before, during, and after the act of teaching (Armour-Thomas & Szczesiul, undated, p. 2).

Because of Connecticut's leadership role in developing the INTASC portfolios, the conception of teaching underlying the state's portfolios is identical to that underlying the INTASC conception. In particular, the conception underlying Connecticut's portfolios emphasizes the need for teachers to have a deep understanding of the discipline they teach, to know their students well, to engage them in active, in-depth learning, and to reflect on their practice on a regular basis. In addition, unlike the CCI conception, this conception stresses the need for teachers to have pedagogical content knowledge.

THE PROCESSES OF DEVELOPING STANDARDS

Connecticut has created several committees to develop teaching standards in particular content areas. Each committee consists of teachers, school administrators, higher education faculty members, and others who have expertise in the appropriate content area and at the appropriate developmental level. In developing teaching standards, each committee uses two state-developed documents as a starting point: *A Common Core of Teaching,* which was patterned after the INTASC core standards, and *A Common Core of Learning.* In addition, the committees use documents produced by professional subject-matter associations. For example, the committee that developed the BEST's Professional Science Teaching Standards used *Science for All Americans* (American Association for the Advancement of Science, 1989) and an early draft of the *National Science Education Standards* (National Research Council [NRC], 1994). Practicing teachers are involved in reviewing drafts of the standards documents, and each document must be formally approved by the state board of education.

Connecticut has aligned its teaching standards and portfolios with the standards and assessments it has developed for students in two ways. First, in many content areas, the same personnel have been involved in developing both the student and teaching standards. In particular, the state has tried to ensure that the lead person on the committee that develops the student standards, usually a state curriculum specialist, also runs the committee that develops the teaching standards. Second, Connecticut has made explicit linkages between its standards and assessments for students and its teaching standards and portfolios. In science, for example, students must design a research study, carry out research, and write up a report. For their part, the science teaching standards state that teachers must increase students' understanding of science through inquiry-oriented learning, and the science portfolios require teachers to demonstrate how they facilitate the inquiry process through student-centered research.

The Connecticut Academic Performance Test (CAPT) is administered to 10th-graders and includes assessments in the areas of English/language arts, mathematics, and science. In English/language arts, for example, the CAPT requires students to write an essay in which they describe their understandings of a piece of literature and connect the literature to other pieces of literature. For their portfolio, teachers must provide examples of interpretive dialogue between themselves and students through both videotapes of their instruction and examples of their responses to student writing. In these instances of interpretive dialogue, teachers are expected to demonstrate their ability to promote students' understanding of literature.

NATURE OF THE ASSESSMENTS

During participants' 1st year in the BEST program, mentors use the CCI to assess generic teaching competencies in the areas of instruction, assessment, and classroom management. In developing the CCI, Connecticut was influenced by the assessment systems used by Florida, Georgia, Texas, and other states in the 1980s (discussed in the third section). The CCI uses fewer indicators of teacher quality than these systems, though, and is scored holistically. Mentors observe a lesson, take notes on teacher and student behavior, sort evidence by indicator, and determine whether evidence represents a satisfactory or unsatisfactory performance (Pecheone & Stansbury, 1996). If new teachers do not demonstrate mastery of the competencies in their 1st year, they continue to teach and are assessed again with the CCI during their 2nd year. If their performance on the CCI remains unsatisfactory, they will not earn their provisional certification or be allowed to continue teaching in Connecticut public schools (Pecheone & Stansbury, 1996).

In their 2nd year in the BEST program, new teachers will be expected to complete a content-specific portfolio designed to assess their pedagogical knowledge and skills. The cohort of new mathematics and science teachers who started teaching in Connecticut in 1996–97 submitted portfolios in those areas in 1997–98. In developing its mathematics portfolio, Connecticut collaborated very closely with INTASC; consequently, this portfolio is very similar to the INTASC mathematics portfolio described earlier.

While the state developed its science portfolio on its own, the portfolio tasks for new science teachers are very similar to those required of new mathematics teachers. In particular, new science teachers are required to keep daily logs during a 2-week inquiry-based instructional unit, videotape two lessons from the unit and write analyses of the lessons, assess the work done by two students during the unit, and assess their own performance during the unit (Lomask, Seroussi, & Budzinsky, 1997). In 1998–99, Connecticut implemented portfolios in English/language arts and special education (for the teachers in those areas who began teaching in 1997–98).

For portfolios that are on line, assessors have to determine whether each new teacher's performance meets or does not meet an established standard. Those teachers whose performance is unsatisfactory have the opportunity to go through the portfolio process again during the 3rd year of teaching. If their performance on the portfolio remains unsatisfactory, they will not be eligible for provisional certification and will not be able to continue teaching in public schools in Connecticut.

KNOWLEDGE AND TRAINING OF ASSESSORS

There are two types of assessors in the BEST program. Those assessors who are trained to use the CCI include full-time teachers, principals, other administrators, higher education faculty members, and retired educators. Those assessors who are trained to evaluate portfolios are active teachers who teach in the same content area and at the same developmental level as those whom they assess. Portfolio assessors, also known as readers, receive approximately 50 hours of training. In the training, they learn documentation techniques, develop an understanding of how standards are embedded in indicators, and learn to link evidence from their observations to specific standards. Like the INTASC readers, Connecticut's readers are trained to work collaboratively to determine candidates' scores. Readers are required to take annual proficiency tests in which they independently evaluate three portfolios. In assessing their performance on these tests, the state examines their scores and the evidence they cite for their scores.

COMPLETED PSYCHOMETRIC STUDIES

Connecticut has conducted studies of the validity, reliability, and fairness of its science portfolios and plans to conduct studies of its other portfolios. In addition, INTASC has carried out several studies of its mathematics assessment (codeveloped by Connecticut) and plans to conduct further studies of this assessment and its English/language arts assessment (also codeveloped by Connecticut).

To evaluate the content validity of the BEST's Professional Science Teaching Standards, this document was sent to random samples of 100 science teachers in Connecticut and 100 science educators teaching at universities throughout the United States. The reviewers were asked to use a 5-point Likert scale to indicate the degree to which they agreed with statements about the qualities of the standards. A total of 85 (42%) of the questionnaires were returned and analyzed. The results found that all of the standards were considered to be important and appropriate for science teachers and were aligned with the vision of effective science teaching described in the 1996 National Science Education Standards document (Lomask, Seroussi, & Budzinsky, 1997, p. 13).

In another study, the state assessed the coherence of the various components of the science portfolio. Fifty experienced science educators were asked to review the complete set of assessment materials, consider the technical quality of the teaching standards and portfolio tasks, and examine the internal relations among the standards, tasks, and scoring framework. Thirty-four teachers (68%) completed the review and answered all of the questions. The results indicated that the teachers perceived the assessment documents to be organized and well written and "were able to see the connections among the professional science teaching standards, the portfolio-based assessment tasks, and the evaluation framework for the science portfolios" (Lomask, Seroussi, & Budzinsky, 1997, p. 14).

Two studies were conducted to assess the internal consistency and reliability of the science portfolio. In the first study, correlations were calculated among the intermediate scores assigned to candidates on each of the three evaluation categories—planning, teaching, and assessment. The scores for the three categories were found to be highly correlated (0.65 to 0.73) and to contribute equally to the final portfolio score (Lomask, Seroussi, & Budzinsky, 1997).

The second study examined the consistency of scores given by different pairs of assessors. In this study, 30 portfolios were each scored on a scale of 1 to 5 by two independent pairs of trained assessors. Across all matched pairs, there was exact agreement on the final score for 19 out of the 30 scored portfolios (63%) and adjacent agreement on the scores for 28 portfolios (93%). These results were not considered sufficient for es-

tablishing licensure decisions. As of 1997–98, assessors did not have to identify five levels of performance (as they did in this study). Instead, they will simply have to judge whether each portfolio performance meets an established performance standard, which should reduce classification errors and increase reliability (Lomask, Seroussi, & Budzinsky, 1997).

In a study carried out by the Professional Examination Service, a committee of 15 expert science educators was assembled to analyze the content of the portfolios, the language used in the assessment materials, and teachers' access to support and other resources. The reviewers were asked to answer 10 yes-or-no questions. Analysis of their responses indicated that they strongly supported the fairness of the science portfolio. In particular, 93% of the reviewers answered yes to 9 of the 10 items (Smith & Greenberg, 1996).

In a second study of fairness, Lomask, Seroussi, and Budzinsky (1997) analyzed the portfolio scores received by 57 new teachers who participated in a pilot study of the assessment. The scores were analyzed by several background factors, including gender (of the portfolio developer), school level, subject matter (i.e., biology, chemistry, physics, Earth science, or general science), and socioeconomic status of the school community. For the most part, the analyses indicated that these factors had little effect on teachers' scores. The only significant difference between the mean scores of candidate subgroups was between teachers in two of the seven subgroups for socioeconomic status of the school community. The reader should note, though, that the effect of the candidate's race on performance was not examined in this study, because Connecticut did not have any beginning minority science teachers in the years in which the study was carried out.

(See above for information about studies conducted by INTASC of the processes beginning teachers go through in developing mathematics portfolios and of a case study of one reader pair scoring one mathematics portfolio.)

STUDIES PLANNED OR IN PROGRESS

Connecticut is currently conducting or plans to conduct several validity studies. In terms of criterion validity, the state has portfolio data on several 1st-year teachers who participated in a pilot study of the science portfolio, and the state intends to examine (a) the progression of teacher ability over a 5-year period and (b) connections between teacher ability and student learning. The state will examine the consequential validity of its portfolios through the use of surveys and focus groups.

Connecticut plans to examine the precision of classification decisions for the 1997–98 math and science portfolios.

As mentioned above, INTASC has created a panel to examine equity issues related to the use of the math and English/language arts portfolios.

ANALYSIS

In our view, the BEST program is a model program worth emulating by other states that are concerned about improving student achievement and increasing the quality of teachers entering the profession. By having new teachers go through the CCI and develop portfolios, Connecticut helps to ensure teachers have basic competencies in instruction, assessment, and classroom management, as well as subject-specific pedagogical knowledge and skills. The mentoring and subject-specific seminars provide new teachers with important sources of support, while promoting reflective, learner-centered practice. The BEST program also promotes such practice among experienced teachers by involving them as mentors and assessors. Further, the university courses aligned to state teaching standards may eventually bring alignment to preservice teacher preparation at those institutions. Finally, the state's pioneering efforts to align its standards and assessments for students with its teaching standards and portfolios are likely to have positive effects on student achievement.

Three important issues need to be addressed by states that are considering the implementation of portfolios and induction programs. First, states must establish that their use of portfolios in assessing beginning teachers is legally defensible by demonstrating that such portfolios are valid, reliable, and fair. Connecticut and INTASC have undertaken an aggressive set of reliability and validity studies, especially for the science and mathematics portfolios. They will need to do the same for other subjects.

Second, given that many teacher assessments have had an adverse impact on racial minorities, it will be important for states to ensure that new minority teachers—many of whom work in urban districts serving low-income, minority students—have equitable access to professional and technical support as they go through the portfolio development process. Like Connecticut, other states should take steps to ensure that new minority teachers are assigned to mentors who themselves have successfully taught minority, low-income students in urban schools. They should also ensure that all new teachers have access to videotaping equipment and to personnel who can train them in how to use it.

Finally, states need to recognize that implementing portfolios and induction programs is an expensive investment. In her analysis of the costs of developing a portfolio-based assessment system, Fisk (1997) found that it cost Connecticut $1,026,000 over 3 years to develop and validate teaching standards, develop and pilot test assessments, and carry out full-scale field testing for validation and standard setting, and more work lies ahead. To reduce costs, the state is currently participating in the INTASC Performance Assessment Development Project with 10 other states. As part of this project, the states are developing portfolios in mathematics and English-language arts. While participating in the project enables states to share the costs involved in developing standards and portfolios, they are still responsible for validating the portfolio system within their own state.

In addition, implementing the BEST program on a yearly basis requires $3,623,000 (Fisk, 1997). This figure includes the costs of providing support for new teachers; training CCI assessors and portfolio assessors; administering the CCI and portfolios; scoring, reporting, and providing feedback to candidates; and administering the overall program. While Connecticut could save money by shifting the costs associated with local mentoring programs to districts and eliminating its support seminars and clinics for new teachers, Fisk offers compelling reasons why the state should preserve these aspects of the BEST program. One reason is that mentoring, seminars, and clinics help ensure that new teachers have equitable opportunities to pass the portfolio assessment. Second, these various forms of support are crucial in gaining the support of teachers' organizations for rigorous licensing standards. Finally, the mentoring, seminars, and clinics provide new teachers with important professional development opportunities while engaging experienced teachers in reflective inquiry (Fisk, 1997).

California

PURPOSE

In 1992, the California Legislature initiated the Beginning Teacher Support and Assessment (BTSA) program in Senate Bill (SB) 1422. Jointly sponsored by the California Department of Education (CDE) and the Commission on Teacher Credentialing (CTC), the BTSA program consists of several local projects designed to provide beginning teachers with guidance and support as they enter the profession. In their work with beginning teachers, mentor teachers (or sometimes others) use performance assessments as formative evaluation tools to help identify teachers' strengths and needs. In the BTSA program, mentor teachers are referred to as support providers. At the outset, the program was designed to serve only a small percentage of the new teachers in the state. At that time, priorities for funding local projects included (a) schools and districts with large increases in student populations, (b) schools and districts with particularly diverse student populations, and (c) schools and districts with evidence of low student achievement (Bartell & Ownby, 1994).

In 1996–97, 33 local BTSA projects were funded, serving 4,100 beginning teachers. Of these teachers, 80% were 1st-year teachers and 20% were in their 2nd year. The approximately 3,300 1st-year teachers served by the program in 1996–97 represented about 10% of the 1st-year teachers in the state. It should be noted that the number of new teachers in California increased dramatically beginning in 1995–96 as a result of the state's class-size reduction program. If this program had not been implemented, the BTSA program would have served about 20% of the 1st-year teachers in the state. In the next few years, the number of new teachers is expected to peak and then settle at 24,000 to 26,000.

For 1997–98, the state legislature increased the budget for the BTSA program from $7.5 million to $17 million. Half of the budget increase was used to expand 30 of the 33 existing local BTSA projects and half was used to start 40 new projects. All of the new projects were in operation by the 1998–99 school year. The 73 projects served approximately 10,000 new teachers, representing about 40% of new teachers in the state.

For 1999–2000, the state legislature increased the budget for the BTSA program to $67.5 million. This increase enabled approximately 110 local projects to serve 22,000 new teachers, virtually all of the newly credentialed teachers in California. For each new teacher, the state provides $3,000 and requires the local projects to provide $2,000 in matching funds. As a result, local projects provided $44 million in matching funds in 1999–2000.

Almost all of the new BTSA projects are using the California

Formative Assessment and Support System for Teachers (CFASST), an assessment system that was collaboratively developed by the state, ETS, and WestEd, a regional educational laboratory. CFASST is designed to measure teachers' knowledge and skills with regard to the *California Standards for the Teaching Profession* (CDE & CTC, 1996), which are described below. Most of the older BTSA projects have used the California Teacher Portfolio, developed by WestEd, and Pathwise, developed by ETS, as formative assessment instruments. Some of the older projects have subcontracted with other organizations or developed their own assessments.

MENTORING AND OTHER FORMS OF SUPPORT

The various local BTSA projects assign either one support provider or a team of support providers to each beginning teacher and offer different types of support and professional development opportunities. In one project, for example, experienced teachers serve as mentors to beginning teachers, meeting with them on a weekly basis. In another project, each beginner works with a triad support team that includes a support provider, an assessor, and the principal. In this program, a new teacher meets with a member of their support team at least twice a month. A third project created intradisciplinary triads consisting of one peer coach and two beginning teachers. Triad members observe each other's practice on eight occasions over the course of the school year (Bartell & Ownby, 1994). In addition to conferences with support providers and classroom observations, other forms of support and professional development offered by various projects include demonstration lessons, peer support seminars, and content-specific workshops.

CONCEPTIONS OF TEACHING UNDERLYING THE ASSESSMENTS

The conception of teaching underlying CFASST and the California Teaching Portfolio is embodied in the *California Standards for the Teaching Profession* (CDE & CTC, 1996). The *California Standards* reflect a developmental conception of teaching, according to which "teachers' knowledge, skills, and abilities develop throughout their professional careers" (CDE & CTC, 1996, p. 6). For these capacities to grow over time, the *California Standards* assert that "teachers must become reflective practitioners who actively work to strengthen and augment their knowledge and skills throughout their careers" (CDE & CTC, 1996, p. 6). Further, this conception posits that individual teachers enter the profession at varied levels of experience and ability and develop at different rates in different areas of teaching (CDE & CTC, 1996).

The *California Standards* are organized around the following six interrelated categories of teaching practice, referred to as domains: instructional strategies, classroom environment, subject-matter knowledge, designing instructional experiences, assessing student learning, and professional development and community outreach (CDE & CTC, 1996). Each domain includes several elements. For the domain of subject-matter knowledge, for example, the elements include: demonstrating knowledge of subject matter, organizing curriculum to support student understanding of subject matter, integrating ideas and information, demonstrating student understanding of subject matter through instructional strategies, and using materials, resources, and technologies to make subject matter accessible to students (CDE & CTC, 1996).

The conception of teaching underlying Pathwise is reflected in the Praxis III criteria and shares many similarities with the conception underlying CFASST and the California Teaching Portfolio. Like *the California Standards,* the Praxis III criteria reflect a developmental conception of teaching and emphasize the need for teachers to engage in reflective practice (ETS, 1995). Further, both conceptions stress the need for teachers to be knowledgeable about their students and the subject or subjects they teach, to establish an environment that promotes student learning, to engage students in active, in-depth learning, to use assessment strategies that are aligned with learning goals, and to apply pedagogical content knowledge (CDE & CTC, 1996; ETS, 1995).

THE PROCESSES OF DEVELOPING STANDARDS

The *California Standards for the Teaching Profession,* previously known as the *Draft Framework of Knowledge, Skills, and Abilities for Beginning Teachers in California,* were developed from 1991 to 1997. As part of a 4-year pilot program, the CDE and the CTC contracted with the Far West Laboratory for Educational Research and Development (FWL) to develop a framework of challenging, realistic expectations of the professional skills, abilities, and knowledge needed by beginning teachers. The framework was revised in 1994 on the basis of the work of a task force established by CTC and feedback from educators across the state.

At that point, the state legislature decided to have several local BTSA projects take over the task of developing the framework. Grants were awarded to local projects to have them (a) conduct a validity study and (b) carry out focus groups. For the validity study, BTSA participants from across the state were surveyed. Participants were asked to rate the standards and elements in terms of their importance for beginning teacher support and development. Most of the respondents rated the different aspects of the *Draft Framework* very highly, but the results were not reliable because of the low response rate.

Staff members from the University of California, Santa Cruz (UCSC) New Teacher Project conducted focus groups in Los Angeles, Sacramento, Santa Cruz, and San Diego. As a result of the focus groups, UCSC New Teacher Project staff members decided to reorganize the standards to present them in a holistic way, explicitly connect each standard with the acts of teaching and learning, and create a visual representation of the standards. In addition, focus group participants emphasized the need for the narratives (describing the standards) to represent best practice, as opposed to the practices of beginning teachers.

Drawing on the data from the focus groups and the survey, the standards were revised and released in August 1996. After members of the CDE and the CTC staffs commented on the *Draft Standards,* the standards were revised and released again in November 1996. The November 1996 version was reviewed by members of an advisory panel created in SB 1422 to review teacher credentialing requirements. The advisory panel consisted of representatives from a number of special interest groups and had the power to veto the *Draft Standards.* Instead of vetoing them, though, the panel merely altered some of the language in the narratives and made a few other minor changes.

The *Draft Standards* were then circulated to educators across California and revised on the basis of their feedback. The final version, known as the *California Standards for the Teaching Profession,* was released in July 1997. The process by which the Praxis III assessment criteria, which underlie Pathwise, were developed is described above.

NATURE OF THE ASSESSMENTS

For the first 6 years of the BTSA program, local projects were "encouraged to 'subcontract' with any appropriate assessment entity or to develop their own assessments" (Bartell & Ownby, 1994, p. 16). Consequently, in 1996–97, 13 of the local projects used Pathwise, 11 used the California Teacher Portfolio, and the rest subcontracted with other organizations or developed their own assessments. The results of the assessments were used by beginning teachers and their support providers to develop individualized program plans (IPP) and thereby to ensure that support was most appropriately designed and delivered to meet the beginning teacher's professional needs (Bartell & Ownby, 1994).

For the California Teacher Portfolio, beginning teachers must each write a description of their teaching context and complete entries in several of the six domains. Each entry involves a four-step process known as plan-teach-reflect-act (WestEd, 1997). In this process, the teacher selects a content area and develops a series of lesson plans, teaches the lessons, and reflects on their teaching. Each entry takes 4 to 6 weeks to compile and must include the lesson plans, three to five pieces of student work from the series of lessons, and the teacher's written reflection on his or her work. When the teachers have completed several entries, they critique their domain evidence (e.g., lesson plans, samples of student work, observation notes, and reflective writing), considering what they have learned about their students' needs and their own professional growth (WestEd, 1997).

The beginning teachers develop a research question that is focused on one domain and is based on their findings from their entries. The plan-teach-reflect-act cycle is then used by the teachers to investigate their research question, and their support provider helps them to "collect evidence, critique it, and make changes in (their) practice to improve student performance" (WestEd, 1997, p. 7). The teachers are expected to seek professional development activities that will be based on their findings. Next, the teachers are expected to make a presentation to school colleagues on the basis of the key findings from the portfolio. Finally, the teachers must reflect on what they have learned about their students, themselves, and the art of teaching, and they must design a plan for future professional development (WestEd, 1997).

Pathwise is a modified version of Praxis III and is based on the same research base and criteria as Praxis III. For Pathwise, teachers complete an instruction profile and are observed and interviewed by an assessor, who, in some cases, is their support provider. With Pathwise, though, the preobservation interview is not required and assessors write about the four domains. But they do not have to write about each criterion. Further, Path-

wise includes a formative observation form, on which assessors can write suggestions, and an instruction and reflection profile, on which teachers can reflect in writing on their practice.

Several local BTSA projects have developed their own assessment systems. Each of these systems includes one or more of the following: classroom observations, videotapes of instructions, lesson plans, samples of student work, conferences, and self-reflections.

CFASST was field-tested in 1998–99 by about 50 local projects. The assessment system included the following components: a class-school-community profile, profiles of practice, inquiries, a summary statement, a colloquium, and an individual induction plan. The profiles of practice are classroom observations and interviews that are based on the California standards. The observations and interviews are intended to occur twice over the course of the school year, in November and March. During the interviews, candidates are asked to share examples of student work with the assessors. With regard to the inquiries, each beginning teacher must complete two or three 6- to 8-week investigations of one element from each of the following standards: classroom environment, designing instructional experiences, and assessing student learning.

Teachers receive scores for their performances on each of the elements. A mediated scoring process will be used in which the candidates suggest particular scores and then the support provider and the candidate come to an agreement about each score. The scores will not be combined into an overall score.

KNOWLEDGE AND TRAINING OF ASSESSORS

In the 33 local BTSA projects that were funded in 1996–97, support providers included mentor teachers, other experienced teachers, school administrators, university professors, and student teaching supervisors. In many of these projects, the support providers also served as assessors. For local projects that use the California Teaching Portfolio, the assessors receive training from WestEd. In collaboration with the teachers, the assessors use rubrics, known as conversation guides, to determine the teachers' levels of performance on their entries. The guides describe what teachers know and are able to do at three levels of accomplishment: developing, maturing, and accomplished. The first level describes knowledge, skills, and abilities for a competent novice teacher, while the next two levels describe more advanced knowledge and skills (WestEd, 1997). At the end of their 1st year, beginning teachers should be able to demonstrate that they have met the criteria in the first level for two or more of the domains.

For local BTSA projects that use Pathwise, the assessors receive 2 days of training from the CDE staff or the local project staff.

For local projects that developed their own assessments or subcontracted with other organizations, the nature and amount of assessor training varies. While assessors in some projects receive 1 day of training, others receive up to 6 days of training.

In most of the 40 new projects that will be implemented by 1998–99, support providers will also serve as assessors. For those projects that use CFASST, the support providers will go through 45 hours of training.

STUDIES OF THE BTSA PROGRAM

As of 1997–98, two major studies of the BTSA program had been conducted. One study was carried out during the 1993–94 school year by the CDE. In the study, CDE staff members conducted open-ended interviews with beginning teachers, support providers, and assessors from several of the local BTSA programs. They found that beginning teachers participated in the programs for one of the following three reasons: (a) the teachers were aware that they needed help in coping with the challenges of teaching, (b) they wanted to make use of the professional development opportunities provided by the programs, or (c) they were strongly encouraged by others (teachers, principals, and district office personnel) to participate (Bartell & Ownby, 1994). For their part, veteran teachers reported that they were participating as support providers and assessors in the programs because (a) they felt the programs were valuable, (b) they wanted to support new teachers, (c) they felt they had sufficient experience, or (d) they were encouraged by someone else (Bartell & Ownby, 1994).

In a small number of the local BTSA programs, the support providers also serve as assessors. A total of 67% of the 467 support providers and assessors who responded to an October 1993 questionnaire indicated they served only as support providers, while 13% reported they served only as assessors, and 20% indicated they served in both roles. In interviews with 25 individuals who served in both roles, 24% stated that they found combining the two roles to be at least somewhat problematic, while 76% did not (Bartell & Ownby, 1994). Those who found it difficult to combine roles expressed concerns "that using a formal assessment can be threatening" and that "the information might be used in formal evaluation procedures" (Bartell & Ownby, 1994, p. 28).

Finally, CDE staff members found that 41% of the beginning teachers from the first 15 local BTSA projects focused on the domain of organizing and managing the classroom, while similar percentages concentrated on the domains of instructional strategies and lesson planning. In contrast, significantly fewer teachers focused on the domains of subject matter knowledge, student assessment, or professional development and community outreach. The study did not indicate whether these results were consistent across different levels of schooling.

A second major study was conducted by the California Educational Research Cooperative (CERC) during the 1995–96 school year. This study examined the impact of the BTSA program on (a) the development of beginning teachers' skills and abilities, (b) their confidence in their teaching roles, and (c) their career satisfaction (Mitchell, Scott, Takahashi, & Hendrick, 1997). In the study, CERC staff members solicited survey responses from all of the teachers, support providers and assessors, site administrators, and local BTSA staff members who participated in local projects in 1995–96. Of the 4,255 program participants, 1,520 returned useable questionnaires, including 593 teachers (31%), 564 support providers (42%), 289 site administrators (33%), and 74 BTSA staff members (57%) (Mitchell et al., 1997).

Of the teachers who returned the questionnaire, 45% reported that their support providers work in the same subject area and at the same grade level that they do, and 27% reported that the feedback they received from their principal was sharply divergent from that provided by their support provider (Mitchell et al., 1997). In terms of the BTSA program's impact on teachers' skills and abilities, teachers felt that the program was most beneficial in helping them plan instruction, while support providers, site administrators, and BTSA staff members felt the program was most valuable in helping teachers to organize and manage their classroom.

With regard to confidence in their teaching roles, the study revealed that teachers feel that participation in the BTSA program has had the strongest effect on their ability to seek useful help and feedback from others. In terms of career satisfaction, on average, teachers indicated that they were very satisfied with their decision to become a teacher (4.54 on a 5-point scale), and that they were confident they would remain in teaching for at least 5 years (4.30).

ANALYSIS

There are several important differences between the BTSA programs and Connecticut's BEST program. First, the most commonly used assessments, Pathwise and the California Teacher Portfolio, are not subject-specific assessments. Consequently, they do not measure beginning teachers' pedagogical content knowledge. Second, support providers and assessors in the BTSA programs are not required to have teaching experience in the same content areas as those they are mentoring or assessing. As a result, support providers and assessors may be limited in their ability to help beginning teachers reflect on their practice, engage their students in genuine dialogue, or integrate knowledge of students with content knowledge in making decisions. In addition, they may not be able to help beginners acquire pedagogical content knowledge.

A third noteworthy difference is that the assessments in the BTSA programs are not used in making licensure decisions. Instead, they are used as formative evaluation tools, designed to help beginning teachers improve their practice. This approach reflects the developmental conception of teaching underlying the *California Standards for the Teaching Profession,* which, as mentioned above, asserts that individuals begin teaching with varying amounts of expertise and experience and progress at different rates in different areas of the profession. In contrast, beginning teachers in Connecticut must earn a passing score on the CCI in their 1st year of teaching and on content-specific portfolios during their 2nd or 3rd year to earn an ongoing license. Otherwise, they are not allowed to continue teaching. Because the assessments in the BTSA programs are used as formative evaluation tools, they do not need to meet the same high psychometric standards as the CCI and content-specific portfolios in Connecticut.

Cincinnati

PURPOSE

In the Cincinnati Public Schools, beginning teachers and experienced teachers who are having serious instructional difficulty receive guidance and support from highly accomplished teachers, known as consulting teachers, through the Peer Assistance and Evaluation program. Established through collective bargaining between the district and the Cincinnati Federation of Teachers (CFT), the program has two main purposes. First, it is designed to help induct new teachers, known as interns, into the profession while determining whether they are prepared to teach successfully. Second, it is intended to help experienced teachers who are having difficulty, known as intervention candidates, improve their practice.

MENTORING AND OTHER FORMS OF SUPPORT

Consulting teachers in Cincinnati have teaching experience in the same content area or areas as the teachers they assess and, in most cases, have reached the highest level on the district's career ladder, that of lead teacher. If an insufficient number of lead teachers apply to become consulting teachers, career-level teachers are considered. Neither of these distinctions are based on formal assessments, but rather on confirmation of experience and an application process. Consulting teachers work with a maximum of 14 beginning teachers, although working with a 2nd-year intern or an intervention candidate is the equivalent of working with 1.5 interns. They must formally observe each intern and intervention candidate at least six times over the course of the school year; teach demonstration lessons; and provide subject-specific training sessions, known as practicums, on a monthly basis. Each consulting teacher who is a lead teacher receives a stipend of $5,500. Those consulting teachers who are career-level teachers receive a stipend of $3,000.

NATURE OF ASSESSMENTS

Consulting teachers assess the content knowledge, pedagogical knowledge, and management skills of interns and intervention candidates through classroom observations, during conferences and informal meetings, and by looking at their lesson plans. Consulting teachers also evaluate interns and intervention candidates in relation to their job targets, which are goals they develop in one or more of six categories. The categories are instructional leadership; classroom management; ability to promote emotional growth; relationships with colleagues, parents, and community members; professional development; and human relations.

Most interns are judged successful by their consulting teachers at the end of their 1st year and are promoted to the second level of the district's career ladder, that of resident. If a beginning teacher is not judged to be successful, that teacher may be recommended by the consulting teacher for a 2nd year in the program. If the beginning teacher is not judged to be successful at the end of the 2nd year, the consulting teacher recommends to the district's Peer Review Panel that the teaching contract not be renewed. This panel, which consists of five teachers selected by the CFT president and five administrators appointed by the superintendent, makes a recommendation to the superintendent regarding whether the teacher should be promoted to the resident level or whether the teacher's contract should be terminated. Six votes are necessary for the panel to make a recommendation.

With regard to experienced teachers who are having serious instructional difficulty, a consulting teacher is assigned to conduct an investigation only after the principal has made two observations and the Peer Review Panel has reviewed the documents that summarize the observations. During the investigation, the consulting teacher may conduct observations or interview the teacher and principal. The consulting teacher then writes a report that recommends to the Peer Review Panel whether the teacher should be placed in intervention.

If a teacher is placed in intervention, the consulting teacher then conducts observations and collects information about the teacher's instructional program and teaching practices. After 20 days, the consulting teacher prepares an Intervention Summary Report and recommends either (a) that the intervention process end because of improved performance, (b) that the teacher be dismissed because of deficient performance, or (c) that the intervention process should continue. Again, the Peer Review Panel makes the final decision regarding the teacher's status.

ANALYSIS

In our view, Cincinnati's Peer Assistance and Evaluation program has many important strengths. First, the program promotes high-quality teaching by providing intensive assistance to beginning teachers and intervention candidates while screening out those individuals who are not teaching effectively. A second strength is that highly accomplished, veteran teachers are rewarded for mentoring other teachers, reducing their incentive to seek administrative positions or leave the profession. Third, the process used in the program for removing incompetent teachers is less adversarial than traditional processes used in most other districts. In particular, because of its role in designing the program, the teachers' union does not oppose the dismissal of intervention candidates who fail to improve over time. Finally, assessment in the program is based on a more representative sample of teaching practices than is the case with Praxis III or the INTASC portfolios.

With regard to psychometric properties, it is important to note that the courts would probably hold the Peer Assistance and Evaluation program to less stringent standards than Praxis III or the INTASC portfolios, because it involves ongoing performance appraisal in which consulting teachers serve as both mentors and evaluators. In contrast, the Praxis III assessment cycles and the INTASC portfolios take place during limited time periods, and the Praxis III assessors and INTASC portfolio readers do not also serve as mentors. The courts have rarely held performance appraisal programs in which mentors serve as assessors to high standards in other professions. Nonetheless, we feel that investigation of the psychometric properties of the assessments in Cincinnati's program is warranted.

In terms of validity, Cincinnati is developing a set of teaching standards for consulting teachers to use in their work with interns and intervention candidates. These new standards will provide evidence of content-related validity for the assessments in the Peer Assistance and Evaluation program. Performance appraisal programs such as this one are stronger if they are based on a set of uniform standards and assessment methods. These methods would ensure that consulting teachers have similar conceptions of the domains of content and pedagogical knowledge and that they rely on the same sources of evidence in making evaluation decisions.

Second, the reliability of the assessments is uncertain, because each intern or intervention candidate is evaluated by just one consulting teacher. An interrater reliability study should be conducted, and the results should be used in determining whether having one assessor is appropriate or whether more are needed. Finally, criterion-related studies should be conducted of programs like the Peer Assistance and Evaluation program. One such study could involve examining the quality of the teaching of several 3rd- or 4th-year teachers and then correlating the results with their performances as 1st-year teachers on the assessments in their performance appraisal programs. Of course, determining how to measure the quality of 3rd- and 4th-year teachers would be a key decision for such a study.

For fairness, it would be useful for Cincinnati to examine the rates at which interns from different ethnic groups are promoted to the resident level. If a significant difference exists in the rates at which teachers from different groups are promoted, this difference would be evidence of adverse impact, and investigations for possible bias would be warranted.

Rochester

PURPOSE

In Rochester, all teachers who are tenured and who have received their ongoing license from New York State must go through a formative evaluation process each year. Teachers can choose between Performance Appraisal Review for Teachers (PART), which involves various types of peer assessment, and a more traditional evaluation with a supervisor. PART requires teachers to write a proposal describing the professional development activities in which they plan to engage during the school year. In their proposals, teachers must indicate how their activities will be related to the district's four expectations for teachers (pedagogy, content, school quality, and home involvement) as well as to the School Improvement Plan at their school. In their proposals, teachers must also explain how they will incorporate the following into their appraisals: indicators of student performance, feedback from peers, input from parents, and input from students.

At the end of the school year, teachers complete a year-end progress report in which they describe how their work met one or more of the district's expectations; how their work affected their students, colleagues, or parents; and how their practice changed as a result of their work. They must provide specific evidence in each of these areas.

Teachers who participate in PART must go through a Summative Appraisal (SA) Process every 3 years. In this process, which is known as PART/SA, a team consisting of the principal and two other teachers uses the teacher's PART work to conduct a rigorous review of their teaching over the previous 3 years. One of the two teachers must have teaching experience in the same certification area as the teacher being assessed. At the conclusion of the review, the team determines whether or not the teacher's practice meets the district's professional expectations and related standards.

CONCEPTION OF TEACHING UNDERLYING THE ASSESSMENT

The conception of teaching that underlies PART is embedded in Rochester's four expectations for teachers. The expectation for pedagogy stresses the need for teachers to be committed to their students and to engage them in student-centered learning. According to the expectation for content, teachers should know the subjects they teach and how to help students develop content-related knowledge and skills. With regard to school quality, the conception emphasizes the need for teachers to work collaboratively with colleagues to improve the climate of their schools and to promote student learning. Finally, teachers are expected to promote family involvement in student learning by forming relationships with their students' families (Gillett et al., 1996).

NATURE OF THE ASSESSMENTS

As of the 1997–98 school year, all teachers must decide at the beginning of the year whether to participate in PART/SA or in a more traditional annual evaluation by a supervisor. Within PART/SA, teachers can choose from the following models: (a) program- or school-linked performance appraisal, (b) goal setting, (c) project-based appraisal, (d) comprehensive peer appraisal, and (e) portfolio appraisal.

Program- or school-linked performance appraisal is designed for groups of teachers or an entire faculty that share a common teaching philosophy, are used to working together, and have established a high level of trust. In this process, teachers engage in individual goal setting and collegial reflection. This model focuses on student engagement and performance and, consequently, the assessment of the teachers is based on the success of the program or school as a whole.

In goal setting, individual teachers or groups of teachers identify goals related to one or more of the four expectations and develop plans for achieving them. Teachers who choose the third model, project-based, must design and carry out a project that addresses the four professional expectations. In their projects, they focus on one or two aspects of their work that they feel are representative of their teaching.

Comprehensive peer appraisal involves a thorough assessment of an individual teacher by other teachers in the same content area who have been trained to carry out such assessments. Teachers who have no peers in their building (e.g., art, gym, and foreign-language teachers) may find this model particularly suitable. The fifth model, portfolio, involves a self-appraisal process in which individual teachers or groups assemble classroom and professional materials. This model provides opportunities for dialogue and reflection and can be used to bring order to a broad range of items in a teacher's professional life.

As mentioned above, teachers who participate in PART go through the Summative Appraisal Process every 3 years. In this process, the principal and two teachers examine the teacher's PART plans and the results of their PART work over the previous 3 years. One of the teachers must be licensed in the same content area as the teacher being evaluated. The team also considers data on student performance, input from other teachers, comments from parents, and (if appropriate) comments from students. Then the team meets with the teacher to discuss that individual's teaching over the past 3 years. If the teacher's practice does not meet the district's expectations and related standards, the teacher's salary is frozen and a recommendation for intervention can result. If the teacher's practice meets the expectations, then a pay increase will result, according to the district's salary schedule.

ANALYSIS

In Rochester, Performance Appraisal Review for Teachers and the Summative Appraisal Process together represent a sound approach to assessment of in-service teachers for several reasons. First, PART provides teachers with an alternative to traditional assessment. In particular, the five PART models require teachers to engage in rigorous, reflective self-assessment, and many provide opportunities to collaborate with colleagues in the assessment process. Second, these programs are based on explicit standards, which, in turn, are similar to the National Board's core propositions. As a result, teachers and team members generally have similar conceptions of content and pedagogical knowledge.

Third, PART/SA separates formative and summative assessment. In PART, teachers establish goals for themselves, identify appropriate professional development activities, and participate in them to increase their knowledge and skills. The team members who evaluate their teaching in the SA Process are not directly involved in their PART work. Finally, it is noteworthy that one of the team members must be a teacher who is licensed in the same content area as the teacher being assessed.

While the courts would probably hold the Summative Approval process to less stringent standards than Praxis III or the INTASC portfolios, we feel that the validity, reliability, and fairness of the assessment should still be considered, because important decisions are being made on the basis of the assessment. In terms of validity, by developing expectations for teachers and related standards, the district has ensured that the SA process has some content-related validity. There is an uncertain relationship, though, between the expectations and the evidence about teaching knowledge and practice that accumulates during the PART process. Consequently, it would be useful for Rochester to conduct a study of this relationship.

With regard to reliability, the SA process counteracts leniency among individual assessors and bias caused by teacher-assessor interaction by having three individuals collectively evaluate each teacher. There is no information, though, about agreement among assessors. To obtain such information, the district would need to conduct a study of interrater reliability. In terms of reliability across the assessment, the district ensures greater consistency by having assessors examine multiple sources of evidence. In particular, team members examine a teacher's PART work over a 3-year period and interview the teacher.

For fairness, it would be useful for Rochester to examine the rates at which teachers from different ethnic groups meet the district's expectations and related standards in the PART/SA

process. If a significant difference exists in the rates at which teachers from different groups meet the expectations, this difference would be evidence of adverse impact, and possibilities of bias would need to be considered.

Assessing Teachers in Terms of Student Outcomes

The INTASC portfolios and the National Board assessments provide some information about student performance, because they require candidates to include samples of work from selected students. These assessments do not, however, measure the overall effect that candidates have on the academic progress of their students. While several states and districts have attempted to evaluate teachers in terms of student performance on standardized tests, they have encountered serious obstacles in their efforts. These obstacles have included the confounding of teacher effects with other factors, particularly student and school characteristics, and the nature of the standardized tests. After examining some of these obstacles, this section describes an innovative approach to evaluating teachers' influences on student outcomes, the Tennessee Value-Added Assessment System (TVAAS), and considers its strengths and limitations.

Several researchers warn against using student outcomes in evaluating teachers, because such outcomes are shaped by numerous other factors (e.g., Berk, 1988). These factors include student characteristics such as intelligence, attitude, race-ethnicity, socioeconomic level, sex, and age and school features such as expenditures, class size, schoolwide learning climate, instructional support, and backgrounds and personal characteristics of the staff (Berk, 1988). Some assessment systems use regression to control for the effects of student and school characteristics in measuring teachers' effects on student achievement. There is a large and sophisticated literature on the pros and cons of using regression procedures to control for confounding variables when attempting to establish causal attributions. In any such effort, strong assumptions are made about the inclusion in the model of the right control variables, that the control variables are well measured, and that the nature of the relationships among control variables and outcome variables are appropriately specified.

In considering the use of standardized tests for evaluating teachers in terms of student outcomes, states and districts also need to examine the characteristics of the tests themselves. In particular, they should examine the extent to which the tests have curricular validity. Curricular validity refers to the extent to which the items on a test correspond to the content of the desired curriculum (McClung, 1979). Berk (1988) has suggested that instructional validity, the extent to which the content tested is also the content taught, should be required. We believe that teaching the desired curriculum is a characteristic of teacher quality and so should not be controlled in teacher assessment.

Tennessee

A group of researchers in Tennessee developed a teacher assessment system in the early 1990s that addresses many of the obstacles just described (Sanders, Saxton, & Horn, 1997). TVAAS measures the effects of schools, school districts, and teachers on the academic progress of students in Grades 3 through 8 in reading, language arts, mathematics, science, and social studies. To calculate these effects, the assessment system uses scaled scores from the norm-referenced portion of the Tennessee Comprehensive Assessment Program (TCAP). Each year, all students in Grades 2 through 8 in the state take the TCAP in all five subjects. The scaled scores from the TCAP "form a single, continuous, equal-interval scale across all grades, allowing for measurement of student academic progress from year to year" (Wright, Horn, & Sanders, 1997, p. 58).

Unlike other assessment systems, TVAAS does not use regression to control for the effects of student characteristics in measuring teachers' influence on students' academic progress. Instead, TVAAS uses a longitudinal approach based on Henderson's mixed-model equations (Henderson, 1984). Under this approach, data on individual students are used to control for the effects of their characteristics on their achievement. By "blocking for each student, many of the exogenous influences most often cited as influencing academic progress—educational attainment of parents, socioeconomic level, race, and so on—(can) be partitioned without having direct measures of each one" (Sanders, Saxton, & Horn, 1997, p. 142).

The use of longitudinal data in the Tennessee Value-Added Assessment System introduces a new challenge, though—that of missing student achievement data. TVAAS overcomes this potential problem through the use of mixed-model equations that permit "the use of all test information for each student regardless of how sparse or complete" the data are (Sanders, Saxton, & Horn, 1997, p. 143). Further, the system uses shrinkage estimates to calculate the effects of individual teachers on the progress of their students. This approach makes it very unlikely for teachers with small amounts of student achievement data to have estimates that are significantly different from the average estimates of their school systems.

In our view, TVAAS has several noteworthy strengths. First, the scaled scores from the TCAP form a common metric across Grades 3 through 8. Second, TVAAS overcomes the problems associated with regression methods and missing data through the use of mixed-model equations. Third, the assessment system can be used as a research instrument. For example, "TVAAS data have shown that when students transfer to the lowest grade in a receiving school, their gains are severely retarded in the 1st year" (Sanders, Saxton, & Horn, 1997, p. 141). This finding and others about using this assessment system can help in planning further research or designing policy interventions. Finally, many school administrators have found the information contained in TVAAS reports invaluable in curriculum planning and program evaluation (Sanders, Saxton, & Horn, 1997).

At the same time, it is important to note that TVAAS has some limitations. For one, as the developers of this assessment system observe, "teachers cannot be assessed solely on the basis of TVAAS" (Sanders, Saxton, & Horn, 1997, p. 139). The TCAP consists of standardized, multiple-choice questions that fail to measure complex performance skills. There is also some disagreement among researchers over whether TVAAS takes sufficient account of the different contexts in which teachers work. In particular, some researchers contend that variability in students' backgrounds and in the ways in which schools are organized makes it very difficult to attribute students' academic progress to the efforts of individual teachers.

Along with efforts to evaluate teachers in terms of student outcomes, several states and districts are exploring ways to reward schools for improvements in student performance. Many of these programs provide teachers with small salary bonuses if schoolwide student achievement meets a target for improvement. Research on such programs in Dallas, in Charlotte-Mecklenburg, in Kentucky, and in North Carolina indicates that they can motivate teachers to (a) focus on improving student achievement in core academic subjects and (b) develop the knowledge and skills to accomplish this goal (Clotfelter & Ladd, 1996; Heneman, 1998; Kelley, 1998; Ladd, 1999).

Use of New Teacher Assessments for Compensation

In addition to informing decisions about initial and professional licensure, retention in position, and promotion into leadership roles, the new assessments can be used in making decisions about teacher compensation (Odden, 1998; Milanowski, Odden, & Youngs, 1998). In emerging high-performance organizations, the primary purpose of the human resources system is to manage the recruitment, development, and retention of knowledge and skills (Lawler & Ledford, 1992). As Kelley (1997) and Odden and Kelley (1997) have argued, the goals of the major education reform strategies over the past 2 decades could have been reinforced by a stronger linkage of knowledge and skills to compensation. Compensation systems could be modified to provide rewards and incentives for teachers to acquire the knowledge and skills needed to teach a more rigorous curriculum (Odden & Conley, 1992) and to develop the expertise needed for standards- and school-based education reform (Mohrman, Mohrman, & Odden, 1996).

New forms of compensation, particularly pay for knowledge and skills, are now viewed as one of a set of elements needed to strengthen teaching as a profession. The recent report of the National Commission on Teaching and America's Future (1996) called for enhancing teacher pay schedules with fiscal incentives for expanding their professional expertise, one specific example being a pay increase or bonus for becoming certified by the National Board for Professional Teaching Standards.

The Single-Salary Structure

In the United States, the single-salary schedule has been prevalent for decades. It was created early in the 20th century to root out practices that paid different salaries to elementary and secondary teachers, male and female teachers, and minority and nonminority teachers (Protsik, 1996). This salary schedule uses (a) education units and degrees and (b) years of experience as the objective bases for providing individual teachers with different base salary levels. The notion is that teachers with more education units and degrees and greater experience have more expertise than other teachers and thus should be compensated at higher levels. As currently designed, however, the most common forms of the single-salary schedule are either neutral to or only mildly supportive of the need for teachers to broaden, enhance, or fundamentally change their professional knowledge and skills. Research shows that, on average, after the first few years of teaching, greater experience is not associated with more expertise and success in the classroom (Murnane, 1983).

	Individual	**Organizational**
National	Core Instructional Expertise: Praxis II, III INTASC NBPTS Other	Instructional Skills Unique to School Strategies, e.g., Success for All Roots and Wings Accelerated Schools Modern Red Schoolhouse Edison Project School
Local	Other Desired Individual Knowledge and Skills: Language Skills License in 2nd Field Other	Leadership and Management Expertise, e.g., Financial Management Team Leadership, Coordination Professional Development Curriculum Development

Figure 17.1. Types of knowledge and skills.

New Form of the Single-Salary Schedule

As organizations outside of education restructure into higher-performing entities, they usually change their pay structures to compensate employees directly for the knowledge and skills needed in the work environment (Lawler, 1990; Schuster & Zingheim, 1992; Ledford, 1995). These systems reward employees for developing demonstrable knowledge, skills, and abilities that enable organizational performance. As Heneman and Ledford (1998) note, these systems promote higher performance among employees by defining the skills needed for such performance and embodying a model of skill development within the salary structure. They complement group-based performance awards by providing employees with the skills needed to achieve the organization's performance goals (Lawler, 1990).

It seems likely that knowledge- and skills-based pay systems in education would similarly complement standards- and school-based education reform. To accomplish current reform goals, teachers need better content knowledge, more curricular and instructional strategies, and new skills to engage productively in broader school-based management decisions (Kelley, 1997; Mohrman, Mohrman, & Odden, 1996). If, as Cohen (1996) has argued, schools are likely to have difficulty meeting student achievement standards because teachers lack the needed skills, a human resources strategy that included a pay system based on the knowledge and skills needed to improve student achievement could have a synergistic effect on performance. Further, although engaging in opportunities to acquire knowledge and skills is intrinsically motivating for teachers—they enjoy doing it and feel they are better professionals when they have expanded their professional repertoire (Odden & Kelley, 1997)—adding salary increments for the acquisition of such knowledge and skills would simply provide an extrinsic reward (more pay) to the intrinsic incentive of expanding one's knowledge and skills.

A knowledge- and skills-based pay system requires two key elements: clear descriptions of and standards for the knowledge and skills desired and valid and reliable assessments that determine whether individual teachers' practice meets those standards (Milanowski, Odden, & Youngs, 1998). In terms of standards, one approach discussed by Heneman and Ledford (1998) would be to modify national competency standards to meet local needs and then supplement national-level assessments with locally developed ones.

Several types of knowledge and skill could be considered in constructing a pay system to augment or replace the single-salary schedule. As shown in Figure 17.1, these knowledge and skills can be categorized as being relevant primarily to individual teaching versus organization-wide practices or reforms, in one dimension, and as being generalizable across schools, districts, and state as opposed to being valuable in specific local contexts, in another dimension. With respect to individual teaching, generalizable knowledge and skills could be specified and assessed by national-level programs. These items would be core instructional skills that could be assessed relative to a set of national teaching standards. The knowledge and skills assessed by the Praxis Series or the INTASC portfolios might be seen as appropriate for beginning teachers, while the NBPTS standards could represent a core of expertise expected of accomplished, experienced teachers. Schools or districts might also desire other knowledge and skills with primarily individual application, such as knowledge of the primary languages of students in the school, or a license in a second area for which there was a teacher shortage in that district.

With respect to schools as organizations, some knowledge and skills might be required because of the choice of a specific educational program or organizational form. Schools that choose to use national school reform designs, such as the Roots and Wings or Modern Red Schoolhouse designs of the New American Schools (Stringfield, Ross, and Smith, 1996), may want teachers to develop skills particular to that curriculum approach. These skills could also be specified and assessed at the national level. In contrast, a school or district might want teachers to engage in broader roles, including leadership, training, participation in financial management, and curriculum development. Because different schools and districts will probably desire different levels and combinations of these activities, it seems appropriate to specify the skills needed at the local level and perhaps develop assessments locally as well.

Each of these four areas represents opportunities for creating a knowledge- and skills-based pay increase in a salary schedule. Douglas County, Colorado, has tried variations of these ideas

Years of Teaching	Knowledge and Skills	External or Internal
First two years	Praxis II, Praxis III	External, national
Second or third year	INTASC	External, state
Early career	Locally identified expertise Lead or master teacher Expertise for specific school designs Unbundled National Board exercises	Internal, local Internal, local External, but school specific External, national
Mid- or advanced career	National Board Certification	External, national

Figure 17.2. Knowledge and skill elements over a teacher's career.

for several years; evaluation reports suggest the effort has met with considerable success (Hall & Caffarella, 1996). In late 1997, Robbinsdale, Minnesota, approved a knowledge- and skills-based pay structure for new teachers, in which teachers can increase their salary by up to $15,000.

There are many other ways salary schedules could include knowledge- and skills-based pay elements. Hammond, Indiana, has negotiated a contract that allows National Board Certification to move a teacher to the PhD salary lane. With regard to compensation in Kentucky, becoming a National Board Certified Teacher (NBCT) is equivalent to completing a master's degree plus 30 additional units. Other states and localities either provide assistance for the costs entailed in taking the National Board assessment or provide a salary bonus or permanent salary increase that can equal up to 15% of salary. All of these are examples of essentially retaining the current single-salary structure and either adding an element for National Board Certification or letting it function as the equivalent of some education degree (see the Consortium for Policy Research in Education's teacher compensation Web site (http://www.wcer.wisc.edu/cpre/tcomp/) for descriptions of these and other teacher compensation innovations).

It can be challenging to combine national standards and assessments with locally developed definitions and assessments of skills to form a coherent knowledge- and skills-based pay system. One way to conceptualize such a system is shown in Figure 17.2, which indicates where some of the assessments described in this section could occur during a teacher's career. In this conception, a teacher's career would start after completing college and possibly after passing Praxis II or other assessments of content knowledge, professional knowledge, or pedagogical content knowledge. At this point, the teacher would have an initial teaching license. During the 1st year, the teacher could be required to go through Praxis III or a similar assessment that focuses on beginning teaching skills. Success on this level would be associated with a pay increase (and failure would trigger remedial assistance).

The INTASC portfolios also assess beginning teacher skills. In contrast to Praxis III, they are subject specific and more fully measure teachers' ability to apply pedagogical content knowledge (see section two for more details). Earning a passing score on an INTASC portfolio could be a basis for moving from an initial to a professional teaching license and for another pay increase. Later in their careers, perhaps 5 or 10 years after earning their initial or professional license, the teachers could go through the National Board assessment process. Earning National Board Certification would be an indication of professional mastery. On their salary schedules, a number of districts and states have made earning National Board Certification the equivalent of completing a PhD or a master's degree plus 30 units.

Thus far, there have been very few efforts by districts or states to create teaching standards for the time period between professional licensure, as represented by passing an INTASC portfolio, and National Board Certification. For many teachers, this period will be at least 5 or 10 years. During this period, peer assistance and review programs could be used by districts to (a) provide support to teachers and (b) assess whether they are continuing to acquire and refine important knowledge and skills. Indeed, in most organizations outside of education, assessment for salary increments is usually accomplished through peer assessment (Heneman & Ledford, 1998). This time period could focus on the knowledge and skills needed for specific school designs, lead teacher programs, or outstanding teacher programs (Kelley, 1996). Demonstrating acquisition of such knowledge and skills could lead to a pay increase between that associated with initial or professional licensure and that associated with professional mastery. Another possibility is to provide a pay increase for passing some, but not all, of the exercises on a given National Board assessment or for achieving a score below the level currently required for National Board Certification but above some minimum.

Another issue is the form of pay tied to demonstration of knowledge and skills. As Heneman and Ledford (1998) report, most private sector systems provide permanent base-pay increases for mastering higher levels of knowledge and skill. Base-pay increases for acquiring additional educational credits are, of course, nearly universal in current teacher pay systems. But some private sector organizations have provided bonuses rather than base-pay increases. Heneman and Ledford suggested that providing bonuses may be appropriate where the nature of the competencies needed change frequently (1998). It may make sense to use bonuses to reward knowledge and skills related to specific local programs or those that are more narrowly applicable, while rewarding more portable or broadly applicable competencies with base-pay increases. The system in Douglas County, Colorado (Kelley, 1996), makes use of bonuses to reward the acquisition of specific, locally defined skills.

Odden and Kelley (1997) provide a detailed overview of how a knowledge- and skills-based pay system could be designed for education, with a series of additional models for augmenting or replacing the current teacher salary schedule. They include models that add elements to the current teacher salary structure, and they also propose models that essentially replace the current salary structure and provide all salary increments on the basis of direct measures of knowledge and skill.

To date, there has not been much research on how knowledge- and skills-based pay elements would work in education. Though a few experiments have been attempted and evaluated (Conley & Odden, 1995; Hall & Caffarella, 1996; Odden & Kelley, 1997), more innovations need to be developed, implemented, and researched now that there are so many important advances in teacher standards and assessments. In organizations outside of education, these types of pay innovations have been found to enhance individual expertise, to raise worker morale, and to improve organizational productivity (Heneman & Ledford, 1998), but further research is needed.

Summary and Conclusions

The 1990s will surely go down in education reform history as a period of intense activity and focus on teacher assessment. INTASC and the National Board were both founded in 1987. Work on the Praxis Series, ETS's effort to revise the NTE, began in 1988. For all three assessments, much attention was given initially to articulating standards or criteria for teachers. It has been against these standards and criteria that the development of the assessments has proceeded. The National Council of Teachers of Mathematics' *Content Standards* (1989) and the American Association for the Advancement of Science's *Science for All Americans* (1989) first appeared at this time. Both standards for teachers and standards for students triggered major efforts to revise and upgrade assessments. Thanks to the leadership in a few key states as well as from ETS, INTASC, and the National Board, much progress has been made on the teacher front. Still, uses of these new instruments are just beginning to catch on, and much variability of teacher assessment practices remains at the state and local levels. Of course, a similar variability in reform of student achievement assessment exists as well. Clearly, good assessment of ambitious and demanding standards is hard work, expensive, and not easily implemented on a wide scale, and the payoff of these efforts to reform assessment is not yet known.

What motivated the intense attention to teacher assessment that was begun at the end of the 1980s? Almost certainly, the general concern about the quality of K-12 education in the United States was an impetus. *A Nation at Risk* (National Commission on Excellence in Education, 1983) was a call to arms for the reform of K-12 education in the United States, and since that time virtually no stone has been left unturned in seeking reform. When it comes to concerns about the quality of education and how it might be improved, invariably teachers take center stage. In the reform efforts that followed *A Nation at Risk,* more money has been spent on professional development for teachers than on any other reform instrument. Thus, it is not surprising that teacher assessment would come under close scrutiny and that efforts to upgrade teacher assessment would be a part of the overall reform.

As has been described, previous teacher assessments had, for some time, been under attack. They were accused of being too narrow, focusing sometimes exclusively on teacher literacy skills and other times including only paper-and-pencil tests of teacher subject-matter knowledge and pedagogical knowledge. But what of actual classroom practice? There were efforts to assess teachers in the classroom, but they were criticized for operating at too micro a level. Typically, they consisted of a few hours of classroom observation, spread across a few days, where observers used a checklist of specific behaviors identified by process-product research. Previous assessments were also criticized as being biased, with low pass rates common for members of minority groups. No one seemed to be in support of principal-peer evaluation, which was judged not only to be of low validity, but also, when used for accountability purposes, to put colleagues in conflicting roles. Increasingly, educators and researchers were calling for new teacher assessments that were comprehensive, efficient, and controlled by the profession.

How is it, then, that teacher assessments are to work to improve the quality of education? They can be used for accountability purposes, by aiding in decisions to: admit teachers into teacher education; license teachers; retain, promote, or dismiss teachers; award advance certificates; and provide pay for performance. Teacher assessments can clarify the goals for preservice and in-service teacher education and, in the process, make them both more effective and more efficient. Of course, assessments themselves should not be the target of teacher education; rather, the standards against which the assessments are written should be the target. Still, assessments give those standards bite. Finally, teacher assessments can become an integral part of a professional development program, providing feedback to teachers on their practice and pointing directions as to how they might improve. There may be some tensions, however, between the formative and accountability uses of teacher assessment. Also, the ways in which teacher assessment may serve these purposes can vary, according to whether the assessment is a minimum competency instrument or one that assesses a range of levels of expertise. If the former, then the assessment will have its strongest impact on the weakest teachers and on the weakest teacher training efforts.

Teacher assessments are dependent upon clear knowledge of what constitutes good teaching. What are teachers who do well on the assessments supposed to be able to accomplish? Are they to have the knowledge and skills to be able to produce important gains in student achievement on accepted measures of student achievement? Are they to create a safe and orderly environment for students? Are they to produce students who become good citizens? Are they to be individuals who contribute to their profession in important ways? These are all outcomes. Is there an important difference between assessing the potential to be a good teacher and assessing the extent to which someone is a good teacher? Such a distinction is akin to the aptitude-achievement distinction that is made in assessing student achievement. On the aptitude side, prior experience, training, knowledge, and beliefs can be assessed. On the achievement side, the effects of students' efforts—student achievement gains, citizenship, and contributions to the profession—can be assessed. Between aptitude and achievement are teachers' actions, the content and pedagogy of the instruction they deliver, or, at least, what they do and say about content and pedagogy in simulated settings. It is exactly this area between aptitude and achievement where much of the focus has been for the new teacher assessments.

But what is the knowledge base on which a picture of good teaching is based? Is it sufficient to support the assessments? Obviously, the answer is yes and no. There is an important and emerging literature on good teaching (summarized in various chapters in this volume), and the assessments reviewed here have drawn heavily on that knowledge. But there are clearly points at which the knowledge base is insufficient and where expert judgment and experience have been drawn upon to fill in the gaps. The Praxis Series does the most by way of assessing teacher knowledge, including literacy. Praxis III, the INTASC portfolios, and the National Board assessments all share a heavy emphasis upon assessment of teaching as it occurs in classrooms, though their methods for doing so differ in important ways. None of the three major national efforts put special attention on assessing teachers' beliefs (e.g., about what is the most appropriate content to teach, what students are capable of learning), though these beliefs may have a major impact on teacher practice over the long haul. Perhaps this omission occurred because beliefs are difficult to measure in a valid and reliable way and because there are disagreements about what beliefs may be best to hold.

In defining good teaching, there is a surprisingly strong commonality among the Praxis III criteria; the INTASC core standards; the National Board's core propositions; and the teaching standards in California, Connecticut, and Rochester. This agreement is in alignment with national standards for teaching, where such standards exist (e.g., NCTM and NRC). While it is not exactly clear the extent to which teacher assessments are aligned to content standards for students, they clearly favor teachers who emphasize advanced content, deep understanding, reasoning, and applications over a strong focus on just basic skills and facts. Similarly, a shared conception leans more toward constructivist teaching than toward direct instruction.

Does good teaching vary by context, and to what extent is such variance reflected in the assessments? NBPTS and INTASC take a very strong position in favor of assessing teachers within the context of specific subjects and, to some extent, specific levels of schooling. Subjects are defined somewhat differently by INTASC and the National Board, and the National Board puts more emphasis on distinctions among levels of schooling. To a lesser extent, the Praxis Series recognizes the importance of subject as a context by assessing subject-matter knowledge, although its assessments of teaching practice are generic across subjects and levels of schooling. But good teaching can vary on other dimensions of context as well. Are some teachers better at teaching slow learners and other teachers better at teaching gifted students? Are some teachers effective with the full range of student aptitude? Are some teachers more effective with African-American students, Hispanic students,

or White students? While all of the assessments of teacher practice are completed in the context in which the teacher is teaching at the particular time, no systematic variation on student type is assessed.

Does good teaching lie on a single quantitative dimension, or is good teaching qualitatively different from one developmental level to the next? At the national level, the INTASC portfolios and the Praxis assessments are focused on assessing beginning teachers, while the National Board is focused on assessing accomplished, experienced teachers. Could one instrument cover this entire range of teacher expertise? If not, is the problem simply one of floor and ceiling effects? Could the INTASC portfolios be used in place of the National Board assessments to identify experienced teachers who are accomplished? If not, is it because such teachers are qualitatively different and require a whole different approach to assessment, or is it because the INTASC portfolios lack sufficient ceiling? The same could, of course, be asked of Praxis III. While the answers to these questions are not clear, the fact that the three assessment procedures share similar conceptions of good teaching suggests the difference is more quantitative than qualitative.

Why do Praxis III and the INTASC portfolios both exist when they are designed to serve the same general purposes? One answer is that they began almost simultaneously and quite independently, and so it is more by accident than by design that both have been developed. But that conclusion would not completely fit the data. For example, INTASC plans to develop tests of teacher subject-matter knowledge, despite the fact that the Praxis Series already includes such assessments, suggesting that each developer sees the need to create an individual alternative. The extent to which each is an alternative to the other, however, plays out more in the methods of assessment than it does in the targets of assessment.

As has been said, the Praxis Series does the most comprehensive and thorough job of assessing teacher subject-matter knowledge, with tests of core content knowledge in more than 20 areas and in-depth tests of content knowledge in 17 areas. The Praxis Series is the only national-level assessment to include a basic skills literacy test. In addition, only the Praxis Series includes paper-and-pencil tests of pedagogical knowledge, one at each of the three levels of K-12 schooling, although INTASC is currently developing a test of teaching knowledge. All three national efforts test pedagogical content knowledge. The Praxis Series includes paper-and-pencil tests of pedagogical content knowledge in nine content areas. Pedagogical content knowledge is an integral part of the INTASC and National Board performance assessments of teacher practice.

At the elementary school level, Praxis III, the INTASC portfolios, and the National Board assessments all take a non-subject-specific approach to performance assessment of teacher practice. Beyond the elementary school level, the INTASC portfolios and the National Board assessments both assess teachers within the context of specific subjects, while Praxis III remains a generic approach. In contrast to the National Board assessments, the INTASC portfolios do not distinguish between middle school and high school levels within a subject. Currently, INTASC has math and English/language arts portfolios with plans for portfolios in science, social studies, and fine arts.

The National Board assesses teacher quality in English/language arts, math, science, and art, and implemented assessments in social studies-history in 1998–99. Only the National Board has an early childhood level assessment and it is generic, not subject specific. Both INTASC and the National Board plan to develop assessments in the area of special education.

There are other ways in which Praxis III, the INTASC portfolios, and the National Board assessments differ in their approaches to teacher assessment. Praxis III features direct observations of classroom practice and interviews, while both the National Board and the INTASC portfolios involve videotapes and written commentaries. Each approach has its strengths and weaknesses, as noted previously. In scoring, each Praxis III assessment cycle involves a single assessor, while the National Board uses two independent scorers for each exercise (for a total of at least 20 assessors), and INTASC uses two readers to collaboratively evaluate an entire portfolio. Definitive studies of the strengths and weaknesses of these differing approaches are not yet available. INTASC argues that using a clinical scoring approach and having scorers look across all of a candidate's performances provides a better overall assessment. ETS argues that Praxis III assessors are better able to capture all that is going on than can videotapes.

Although Praxis III and the INTASC portfolios have been nationally developed, they are being administered and used by individual states or districts, which is not true of the National Board assessments. States that implement Praxis III or the INTASC portfolios are responsible for training their own assessors and readers. No evidence is yet available on whether quality deteriorates through this training-of-trainers approach. Also, states using Praxis III and the INTASC portfolios must set their own pass-fail standards and do their own validity studies. The National Board has set a single passing standard that is consistent across all of their assessments.

States have taken quite different approaches to teacher assessment. In Connecticut, for example, assessments are used for accountability purposes and are required of all beginning teachers. Perhaps not surprisingly, given the high-stakes purposes of teacher assessment in Connecticut, the state has an impressive program of reliability and validity studies. California, in contrast, uses assessments primarily to identify teachers' professional development needs. In California, teacher assessment is not required. There is no single model, and some districts participate, while others do not. Rochester is an especially interesting site, in that teacher assessment is required and used for accountability purposes. Six distinctly different options of assessment are available, and, other than Tennessee, Rochester is the only place considered here that uses student achievement as one piece of datum in the overall evaluation of a teacher. What seems to be prevalent, if not common, across all local teacher assessment programs is a focus on induction and an approach that has teachers involved in the assessment of teachers.

In teacher assessment, most of the validation work has been to establish content validity. All three national efforts have relied heavily on expert judgment. In developing the Praxis III criteria, ETS started with a guiding conception of teaching validated through careful job analyses. In contrast, the National Board and INTASC standards documents were initially developed by small groups of highly accomplished teachers and subject-matter experts. Despite these somewhat different starting points, the conceptions of good teaching underlying each of the three approaches are quite similar.

The National Board has conducted a number of reliability and validity studies, with many more planned. INTASC has conducted some studies, but it plans to continue investigating the reliability and validity of its assessment procedures. Further validity studies on Praxis III will be accomplished state by state, as states adopt the procedure. Beyond that, it appears as though ETS has completed its reliability and validity work. Thus far, reliability and validity studies have been conducted almost exclusively by the developers. This pattern may change, though, as use of the assessments becomes more common.

Beyond efforts to establish content validity and some basic aspects of reliability, not much empirical work has been completed and reported. Thus far, few criterion/predictive-validity studies have been completed. One problem here is obtaining a good criterion measure for teacher quality. Further, very little has been completed by way of studying the consequences of the assessments. The National Board has seen an adverse impact on minority candidates and has conducted several studies to try to establish whether or not this effect is a problem of bias. Adverse impact data are not yet available for either Praxis III or the INTASC portfolios.

Clearly, it will be important to examine the consequences of using the various assessments for different purposes. Does systematic use of the INTASC portfolios or Praxis III lead to an increasingly competent teacher corps? Do the teacher assessments and the standards against which they are written become important targets for the design and evaluation of preservice and in-service teacher education, and, if so, do the effectiveness and efficiency of these teacher education efforts improve? If the assessments are used as a basis for higher pay, does this use lead to a better rate of teacher development over time? Assessing the long-term effects of various uses of teacher assessment is difficult, but it still is of interest. Does teacher assessment lead to better citizens, greater student achievement gain, and a more pleasant and supportive school environment?

There are also issues of how pass-fail standards are set. The National Board has done studies reporting probabilities of false positive and false negative identifications. Comparable studies will be conducted of Praxis III and the INTASC portfolios. These are essential for high-stakes assessments. These studies do not, however, address the question of whether standards for performance are set at an appropriate level, not too high and not too low. The case of Praxis III is a state decision. Since both Praxis III and the INTASC portfolios are used in making licensure decisions, in some sense they will represent minimum levels of competency. It is important to note, however, that huge tensions exist in many states and districts regarding the supply of and demand for teachers. These tensions vary over time for a variety of reasons and may inhibit efforts to implement rigorous assessments of beginning teachers.

Although a substantial amount of reliability and validity work has been completed on the new teacher assessments, a great deal remains to be done. One or more generalizability studies that investigate the sampling dimensions of lessons or days; observers versus videotape; scorers or observers or pairs of observers; exercises; or types of students would be much welcomed. Obviously, this recommendation applies to each assessment.

Another useful study would be to follow a cohort over time from admission into teacher education, through formal preparation and induction into the teaching profession, and on to becoming experienced (and perhaps National Board certified) teachers. Such a study could begin to address whether there is a qualitative as well as a quantitative distinction across years and levels of teacher development. Such a study could also look at correlations between early and subsequent measures of teacher quality. Early literacy measures could be used to predict broader measures at the point of induction, which, in turn, could be used to predict measures of experienced teachers. Ideally, this study could be augmented to see how well the various pieces of information from teacher assessments can predict gains in student achievement and other types of long-term outcome measures. It would also be useful to know the concurrent validity between Praxis III and the INTASC portfolios.

A number of tensions exist in the development and use of teacher assessments that must be negotiated. Tension exists between using assessments for accountability versus using them for teacher support and improvement. As we have seen, some try to do both with a single assessment, but that may not work well. Tension exists between assessments that try to move the field forward, pressing for better teachers and better teacher education, versus those that are consistent with current practice and that are, perhaps, more legally defensible. In terms of trying to lead the field, how far out in front of current practice should an assessment (or series of assessments) be to have maximum effect? Also, to stay ahead of the field, how frequently should it (or they) be revised?

When assessment is used to make licensure decisions, tension exists between the goal of excellence and the fact that minimum competency is what is being established. A related issue is the desire to set high standards versus the need for more teachers, especially in certain fields and to work in certain geographic locations. Yet another related issue is the need for more teachers of color and the fact that small percentages of minority candidates are passing the assessments. Finally, tension exists between wanting assessments that are comprehensive and state-of-the-art versus the need to have assessments that are affordable. In particular, there are trade-offs among testing methods with respect to measurement quality (e.g., validity and reliability) and resource requirements (e.g., testing time and the costs for test development, administration, scoring, and analysis) (Klein, 1998). In our view, only time will tell whether the developers or users of Praxis III, the INTASC portfolios, and the National Board assessments have negotiated an appropriate balance among the various tensions described here.

The new assessments have not adequately addressed one important aspect of good teaching. Arguably, the strongest school-controlled predictor of gains in student achievement is the alignment of the enacted curriculum to the measure of student achievement (Porter, 1998). Praxis selects only a few days of observation. Such a small sample cannot hope to capture whether what is being taught is appropriate. INTASC and the National Board take a larger sample of practice, but nothing like a full school year. Further, judging the quality of the content of instruction does not appear to be a major objective. If the new assessments did decide to assess the content of instruction, it would not be an easy task to complete successfully. The first decision to make is what content is important. National professional standards might be expected to answer this question, although these national standards operate at a level of generality that does not translate in a straightforward fashion to specific instruction. Having solved this problem, a useful way to accurately sample a sufficiently long period of instruction must be developed. Some success has been achieved at using teacher logs and teacher surveys to measure the content of the enacted curriculum over a full school year, but these have never been used in high-stakes situations. Whether logs and surveys would maintain their validity in the context of an assessment that is to be used to make licensure, compensation, or other such high-stakes decisions is questionable.

Recent advances in teacher assessment are impressive and exciting. They hold considerable promise for improving the quality of teaching and learning in U.S. schools while simultaneously increasing the status and respect associated with the teaching profession in this country. Further research is needed, though, to examine how these new assessments are being used and their consequences.

REFERENCES

American Association for the Advancement of Science (Project 2061). (1989). *Science for all Americans.* Washington, DC: Author.

American Educational Research Association, American Psychological Association, & National Council on Measurement and Education. (1985). *Standards for educational and psychological testing.* Washington, DC: Authors.

Andrews, T. E., & Barnes, S. (1990). Assessment of teaching. In W. R. Houston (Ed.), *Handbook of research on teacher education* (pp. 569–598). New York: Macmillan.

Armour-Thomas, E., & Szczesiul, E. (undated). *A review of the knowledge base of the Connecticut Competency Instrument.* Hartford, CT: Connecticut State Department of Education.

Ayers, J. B., & Qualls, G. S. (1979). Concurrent and predictive validity of the National Teacher Examination. *Journal of Educational Research, 73*(2), 893.

Bartell, C. A., & Ownby, L. (1994). *Report on implementation of the beginning teacher support and assessment program (1992–1994).* Sacramento, CA: Commission on Teacher Credentialing and California Department of Education.

Berk, R. (1988). Fifty reasons why student achievement gain does not mean teacher effectiveness. *Journal of Personnel Evaluation in Education, 1*(4), 345–364.

Bond, L. (1997). *Adverse impact and teacher certification.* Paper presented at the annual meeting of the American Educational Research Association, Chicago.

Bond, L. (1998). Disparate impact and teacher certification. *Journal of Personnel Evaluation in Education, 12*(2), 211–220.

Brophy, J. E., & Good, T. S. (1986). Teacher behavior and student achievement. In M. C. Wittrock (Ed.), *Handbook of research on teaching* (3rd ed., pp. 328–375). New York: Macmillan.

California Department of Education & Commission on Teacher Credentialing. (1996). *California standards for the teaching profession.* Sacramento, CA: Authors.

Camp, R., & Mandinach, E. (1993). *Formative studies of Praxis III classroom performance assessments. Issues identified in qualitative analysis of record-of-evidence forms.* Princeton, NJ: Educational Testing Service.

Carnegie Forum on Education and the Economy. (1986). *A nation pre-*

pared: Teachers for the 21st century. Washington, DC: Carnegie Forum on Education and the Economy, Task Force on Teaching as a Profession.

Clotfelter, C. T., & Ladd, H. F. (1996). Recognizing and rewarding successful schools. In H. F. Ladd (Ed.), *Holding schools accountable: Performance-based reform in education* (pp. 23–63). Washington, DC: Brookings Institution.

Cohen, D. (1996). Rewarding teachers for student performance. In S. H. Fuhrman & J. O'Day (Eds.), *Rewards and reform: Creating educational incentives that work* (pp. 60–112). San Francisco: Jossey-Bass.

Collins, K. M., Schutz, A. M., & Moss, P. A. (1997). *INTASC candidate interviews: A summary report—Draft.* Washington, DC: INTASC.

Conley, S. C., & Odden, A. (1995). Linking teacher compensation to teacher career development: A strategic examination. *Educational Evaluation and Policy Analysis, 17,* 253–269.

Darling-Hammond, L. (1990). Teacher evaluation in transition: Emerging roles and evolving methods. In J. Millman & L. Darling-Hammond (Eds.), *The new handbook of teacher evaluation: Assessing elementary and secondary school teachers.* Newbury Park, CA: Sage.

Darling-Hammond, L., & Berry, B. (1988). *The evolution of teacher policy.* Santa Monica, CA: RAND Corporation.

Darling-Hammond, L., Wise, A. E., & Klein, S. P. (1995). *A license to teach: Building a profession for 21st-century schools.* Boulder, CO: Westview Press.

Diez, M. E., Rickards, W. H., & Lake, K. (1994). Performance assessment in teacher education at Alverno College. In T. Warren (Ed.), *Promising practices in liberal arts colleges* (pp. 9–18). Lanham, MD: University Press of America.

Dwyer, C. A. (1994). *Development of the knowledge base for the Praxis III classroom performance assessments assessment criteria.* Princeton, NJ: Educational Testing Service.

Dwyer, C. A. (1998). Psychometrics of Praxis III: Classroom performance assessments. *Journal of Personnel Evaluation in Education, 12*(2).

Dwyer, C. A., & Stufflebeam, D. (1996). Teacher evaluation. In D. Berliner & R. Calfee (Eds.), *Handbook of educational psychology.* New York: Macmillan.

Dwyer, C. A., & Villegas, A. M. (1993). *Guiding conceptions and assessment principles for the Praxis Series: Professional assessments for beginning teachers.* Princeton, NJ: Educational Testing Service. (Original work published 1992)

Educational Testing Service. (1994). *Praxis III: Classroom performance assessments—Rating assessor proficiency.* Princeton, NJ: Author.

Educational Testing Service. (1995). *Praxis III: Classroom performance assessments—Orientation guide.* Princeton, NJ: Author.

Fisk, C. W. (1997). *The costs and benefits of designing and implementing a portfolio-based support and assessment system for beginning teachers.* Paper presented at the annual meeting of the American Educational Research Association, Chicago.

Floden, R. E., & Klinzing, H. G. (1990). What can research on teacher thinking contribute to teacher preparation? A second opinion. *Educational Researcher, 19*(5), 15–20.

Gillett, T., Melendez, A., Golden, C., Jackett, D., O'Connell, C., & Robinson, C. M. (1996). *Career in teaching: PART and summative appraisal guidebook.* Rochester, NY: Rochester City School District.

Goertz, M. E., & Pitcher, B. (1985). *The impact of NTE use by states on teacher selection.* Princeton, NJ: Educational Testing Service.

Good, T. S., & Brophy, J. E. (1986). *Educational psychology* (3rd ed.). White Plains, NY: Longman.

Graham, P. A. (1987). Black teachers: A drastically scarce resource. *Phi Delta Kappan, 68*(8), 598–605.

Gregory, K. (1995). *Emerging solutions: The creation of viable scoring systems to assess teacher performance.* Paper presented at the annual meeting of the American Educational Research Association, San Francisco.

Haertel, E. H. (1991). New forms of teacher assessment. In G. Grant (Ed.), *Review of Research in Education, 17,* 3–29.

Hall, E., & Caffarella, E. (1996). *First-year implementation of the Douglas County, Colorado, School District Performance Pay Plan for*

Teachers (1994–95). Greeley, CO: University of Northern Colorado, School of Education.

Haney, W., Madaus, G., & Kreitzer, A. (1987). Charms talismanic: Testing teachers for the improvement of American education. In E. Z. Rothkopf (Ed.), *Review of Research in Education, 14,* 169–238.

Henderson, C. R. (1984). *Applications of linear models in animal breeding.* Guelph, Ontario, Canada: University of Guelph.

Heneman, H. G. (1998). Assessment of the motivational reactions of teachers to a school-based performance award program. *Journal of Personnel Evaluation in Education, 12*(1), 43–59.

Heneman, R. L., & Ledford, G. E. (1998). Competency pay for professionals and managers in business: A review and implications for teacher certification. *Journal of Personnel Evaluation in Education, 12*(2), 103–121.

Interstate New Teacher Assessment and Support Consortium. (1992). *Model standards for beginning teacher licensing and development: A resource for state dialogue.* Washington, DC: Author and Council of Chief State School Officers.

Interstate New Teacher Assessment and Support Consortium. (1995a). *Mathematics teacher performance assessment handbook.* Washington, DC: Author and Council of Chief State School Officers.

Interstate New Teacher Assessment and Support Consortium. (1995b). *Next steps: Moving toward performance-based licensing in teaching.* Washington, DC: Author and Council of Chief State School Officers.

Jaeger, R. M. (1996a). *Conclusions on the technical measurement quality of the 1995–96 operational version of the National Board for Professional Teaching Standards' early adolescence/young adulthood art assessment.* Unpublished manuscript, National Board for Professional Teaching Standards, Southfield, MI.

Jaeger, R. M. (1996b). *Conclusions on the technical measurement quality of the 1995–96 operational version of the National Board for Professional Teaching Standards' early childhood/generalist assessment.* Unpublished manuscript, National Board for Professional Teaching Standards, Southfield, MI.

Jaeger, R. M. (1996c). *Conclusions on the technical measurement quality of the 1995–96 operational version of the National Board for Professional Teaching Standards' middle childhood/generalist assessment.* Unpublished manuscript, National Board for Professional Teaching Standards, Southfield, MI.

Jaeger, R. M. (1998). Evaluating the psychometric qualities of the National Board for Professional Teaching Standards' assessments: A methodological accounting. *Journal of Personnel Evaluation in Education, 12*(2), 184–210.

Johnson, S. M. (1990). *Teachers at work: Achieving success in our schools.* New York: Basic Books.

Kauchak, D., Peterson, K., & Driscoll, A. (1985). An interview study of teachers' attitudes toward teacher evaluation practices. *Journal of Research and Development in Education, 19*(1), 32–37.

Kelley, C. (1996). Implementing teacher compensation reform in public schools: Lessons from the field. *Journal of School Business Management, 8*(1), 37–54.

Kelley, C. (1997). Teacher compensation and organization. *Educational Evaluation and Policy Analysis, 19*(1), 15–28.

Kelley, C. (1998). The Kentucky School-Based Performance Award Program: School-level effects. *Educational Policy, 12*(3), 305–324.

Klein, S. P. (1998). Standards for teacher tests. *Journal of Personnel Evaluation in Education, 12*(2), 123–138.

Kuligowski, B., Holdzkom, D., & French, R. (1993). Teacher performance evaluation in the southeastern states: Forms and functions. *Journal of Personnel Evaluation in Education, 1,* 335–358.

Ladd, H. F. (1999). The Dallas School Accountability and Incentive Program: An evaluation of its impact on student outcomes. *Economics of Education Review, 18*(1), 1–16.

Lawler, E. E. (1990). *Strategic pay.* San Francisco: Jossey-Bass.

Lawler, E. E., & Ledford, G. E. (1992). A skills-based approach to human resource management. *European Management Journal, 10,* 383–391.

Ledford, G. E. (1995). Paying for the skills, knowledge, and competencies of knowledge workers. *Compensation and Benefits Review, 27*(4), 55–62.

Livingston, S. (1993). *Inter-assessor consistency of the Praxis III class-room performance assessment: Spring 1992 preliminary version.* Unpublished report, Educational Testing Service, Princeton, NJ.

Loacker, G., Cromwell, L., & O'Brien, K. (1986). Assessment in higher education: To serve the learner. In C. Adelman (Ed.), *Assessment in higher education: Issues and contexts* (pp. 47–61). Washington, DC: U.S. Department of Education.

Lomask, M., Seroussi, M., & Budzinsky, F. (1997). *The validity of portfolio-based assessment of science teachers.* Paper presented at the annual meeting of the National Association of Research in Science Teaching, Chicago.

McClung, M. S. (1979). Competency testing programs: Legal and educational issues. *Fordham Law Review, 47,* 651–712.

Messick, S. (1989). Meaning and values in test validation: The science and ethics of assessment. *Educational Researcher, 18*(2), 5–11.

Milanowski, A., Odden, A., & Youngs, P. (1998). Teacher knowledge and skill assessments and teacher compensation: An overview of measurement and linkage issues. *Journal for Personnel Evaluation in Education, 12*(2), 83–101.

Mitchell, D. E., Scott, L. D., Takahashi, S. S., & Hendrick, I. G. (1997). *The California Beginning Teacher Support and Assessment Program: A statewide evaluation study.* Riverside, CA: California Educational Research Cooperative.

Mohrman, A., Mohrman, S. A., & Odden, A. (1996). Aligning teacher compensation with systemic school reform: Skills-based pay and group-based performance awards. *Educational Evaluation and Policy Analysis, 18,* 51–71.

Moss, P. A. (1996). Enlarging the dialogue in educational measurement: Voices from interpretive research traditions. *Educational Researcher, 25*(1), 20–28, 43.

Moss, P. A. (1998a). Rethinking validity in the assessment of teaching. In N. Lyons & G. Grant, (Eds.), *With portfolio in hand: Portfolios in teaching and teacher education* (pp. 202–219). New York: Teachers College Press.

Moss, P. A. (1998b). *Response to Porter, Odden, & Youngs.* Paper presented at the annual meeting of the American Educational Research Association, San Diego, CA.

Moss, P. A., Schutz, A. M., & Collins, K. (1998). An integrative approach to portfolio evaluation for teacher licensure. *Journal for Personnel Evaluation in Education, 12*(2), 139–161.

Murnane, R. (1983). Quantitative studies of effective schools: What have we learned? In A. Odden & L. D. Webb (Eds.), *School finance and school improvement: Linkages for the 1980s* (pp. 193–209). Cambridge, MA: Ballinger.

Myford, C. M., & Lehman, P. (1993a). *Formative studies of Praxis III classroom performance assessments. Assessors' evaluation of their own classroom observation notes, interview notes, and record-of-evidence forms.* Princeton, NJ: Educational Testing Service.

Myford, C. M., & Lehman, P. (1993b). *Formative studies of Praxis III classroom performance assessments. Questionnaire results.* Princeton, NJ: Educational Testing Service.

National Board for Professional Teaching Standards. (undated). *What teachers should know and be able to do.* Detroit, MI: Author.

National Board for Professional Teaching Standards. (1996). *National Board Certification portfolio sampler.* Southfield, MI: Author.

National Commission on Excellence in Education. (1983). *A nation at risk: The imperative for educational reform.* Washington, DC: U.S. Department of Education.

National Commission on Teaching and America's Future. (1996). *What matters most: Teaching for America's future.* New York: Author.

National Council of Teachers of Mathematics. (1989). *Curriculum and evaluation standards for school mathematics.* Reston, VA: Author.

National Research Council. (1994). *National science education standards—Draft.* Washington, DC: Author.

Natriello, G. (1990). Intended and unintended consequences: Purposes and effects of teacher evaluation. In J. Millman & L. Darling-Hammond (Eds.), *The new handbook of teacher evaluation: Assessing elementary and secondary school teachers* (pp. 35–45). Newbury Park, CA: Sage.

Odden, A. (1998). *A policymaker's guide to incentives for students, teachers, and schools.* Denver, CO: Education Commission of the States.

Odden, A., & Conley, S. (1992). Restructuring teacher compensation systems. In A. Odden (Ed.), *Rethinking school finance: An agenda for the 1990s* (pp. 41–96). San Francisco: Jossey-Bass.

Odden, A., & Kelley, C. (1997). *Paying teachers for what they know and do: New and smarter compensation strategies to improve schools.* Thousand Oaks, CA: Corwin Press.

Office of Educational Research and Improvement. (1987). *What's happening in teacher testing: An analysis of state teacher testing practices.* Washington, DC: U.S. Department of Education.

Pecheone, R. L., & Stansbury, K. (1996). Connecting teacher assessment and school reform. *The Elementary School Journal, 97*(2), 163–177.

Peterson, K. D. (1995). *Teacher evaluation: A comprehensive guide to new directions and practices.* Thousand Oaks, CA: Corwin Press.

Porter, A. C. (1998). The effects of upgrading policies on high school mathematics and science. In D. Ravitch (Ed.), *Brookings papers on education policy* (pp. 123–172). Washington, DC: Brookings Institution.

Powers, D. E. (1992). *Assessing the classroom performance of beginning teachers: Educators' appraisal of proposed evaluation criteria.* Princeton, NJ: Educational Testing Service.

Protsik, J. (1996). History of teacher pay and incentive reforms. *Journal of School Leadership, 6*(3), 265–289.

Quirk, T. J., Witten, B., & Weinberg, S. F. (1973). Review of studies of the concurrent and predictive validity of the National Teacher Examinations. *Review of Educational Research, 43*(1), 89–113.

Reynolds, A. (1992). What is competent beginning teaching? A review of the literature. *Review of Educational Research, 62*(1), 1–35.

Reynolds, A. (1993). *Formative studies of Praxis assessments. Not all assessors are alike: A case study of two assessors.* Princeton, NJ: Educational Testing Service.

Reynolds, A. (1995). *Formative studies of Praxis III classroom performance assessments. Small- and large-group discussions among assessors.* Princeton, NJ: Educational Testing Service.

Reynolds, M. C. (1989). *Knowledge base for the beginning teacher.* New York: Pergamon.

Rosenfeld, M., Freeberg, N. E., & Bukatko, P. (1992). *The professional functions of secondary school teachers.* Princeton, NJ: Educational Testing Service.

Rosenfeld, M., Reynolds, A., & Bukatko, P. (1992). *The professional functions of elementary school teachers.* Princeton, NJ: Educational Testing Service.

Rosenfeld, M., Wilder, G., & Bukatko, P. (1992). *The professional functions of middle school teachers.* Princeton, NJ: Educational Testing Service.

Sanders, W. L., Saxton, A. M., & Horn, S. P. (1997). The Tennessee Value-Added Assessment System: A quantitative, outcomes-based approach to educational assessment. In J. Millman (Ed.), *Grading teachers, grading schools: Is student achievement a valid evaluation measure?* (pp. 137–162). Thousand Oaks, CA: Corwin Press.

Schalock, H. A., & Schalock, M. D. (1993). Student learning in teacher evaluation and school improvement: An introduction. *Journal of Personnel Evaluation in Education, 4*(1), 103–104.

Schuster, J. R., & Zingheim, P. (1992). *The new pay: Linking employee and organizational performance.* New York: Lexington Books.

Shavelson, R. I., Webb, N. M., & Burstein, L. (1986). Measurement of teaching. In M. C. Wittrock (Ed.), *Handbook of research on teaching* (3rd ed., pp. 569–598). New York: Macmillan.

Shulman, L. S. (1987). Knowledge and teaching: Foundations of the new reform. *Harvard Educational Review, 57*(1), 1–22.

Smith, G. P., Miller, M. C., & Joy, J. (1988). A case study of the impact of performance-based testing on the supply of minority teachers. *Journal of Teacher Education, 39*(4), 45–53.

Smith, I. L., & Greenberg, S. (1996). *Fairness review of CSDE's mathematics and science portfolios—Final report.* Hartford, CT: Professional Examination Service.

Street, M. S. (1991). *Content synthesis of currently used statewide performance assessment instruments.* Princeton, NJ: Educational Testing Service.

Stringfield, S., Ross, S., & Smith, L. (1996). *Bold plans for school restructuring: The New American Schools design.* Mahwah, NJ: Lawrence Erlbaum Associates.

Thompson, B. (1997). *Preparing readers to evaluate INTASC mathemat-*

ics teacher portfolios. Paper presented at the annual meeting of the American Educational Research Association, Chicago.

Thompson, M., & Pearlman, M. (1997). *Template for benchmarking sessions, including benchmark training.* Princeton, NJ: Educational Testing Service.

Tracy, S. J., & Smeaton, P. (1993). State-mandated assisting and assessing teachers: Levels of state control. *Journal of Personnel Evaluation in Education, 6,* 219–234.

Villegas, A. M. (1991). *Culturally responsive pedagogy for the 1990s and beyond.* Princeton, NJ: Educational Testing Service.

Wesley, S., Rosenfeld, M., & Sims-Gunzenhauser, A. (1993). *Assessing the classroom performance of beginning teachers: Teachers' judgments of evaluation criteria.* Princeton, NJ: Educational Testing Service.

WestEd. (1997). *California teacher portfolio.* San Francisco: Author.

Wise, A. E., Darling-Hammond, L., McLaughlin, M. W., & Bernstein, H. T. (1984). *Teacher evaluation: A study of effective practices.* Santa Monica, CA: Rand Corporation.

Wright, S. P., Horn, S. P., & Sanders, W. L. (1997). Teacher and classroom context effects on student achievement: Implications for teacher evaluation. *Journal of Personnel Evaluation in Education, 11,* 57–67.

18.

Practitioner Research

Kenneth M. Zeichner
University of Wisconsin-Madison

Susan E. Noffke
University of Illinois

There is considerable justification for the belief that research methodology will not begin to have the influence that it might have on American education until thousands of teachers, administrators, and supervisors make more frequent use of the method of science in solving their own practical problems.

(Corey, 1953, p. 18)

This fourth edition of the *Handbook of Research on Teaching* is the first time that a chapter has been included about practitioner research. It has always been assumed, in these handbooks at least, that researchers do research about someone else's practice, despite the long history in which those directly involved in educational work have done research on their own practice. Rather than regard practice itself as a form of systematic knowing, the practitioner's role in this view is merely to consume the research produced by others. This same neglect of the knowledge that educators generate in enacting and studying their own practice has been true for most histories of educational research. According to Lagemann (1996), teachers—if mentioned at all in these histories—are seen as research subjects and consumers of research and not as producers of educational knowledge.[1] Despite the volume and variety of practitioner research that has been conducted by teachers and academics, Dewey's (1929) statement about teachers' contributions to educational research being an "unworked mine" remains true in many ways 70 years later.

The little attention that has been given to practitioner research in the academic educational literature, including the handbooks, has viewed it as a form of professional development for practitioners (e.g., Clifford, 1973; Good, 1963). The expres-

sion of this perspective, which often acknowledges the high value that practitioners place on self-study, does not generally address the research as having implications for our understanding of different ways of knowing, nor does it treat seriously and seek to disseminate to others the knowledge produced through research by practitioners. Yet, as Bridget Somekh notes,

If action research is not recognized as a research methodology, the knowledge generated from action research is neither taken seriously nor disseminated widely and effectively. The knowledge is seen merely as an outcome of a professional development process, devalued into something which concerns only the individual who carried out the action research—local, private, and unimportant. In this way, the operation of power in the social system works to neutralize the voice and influence of practitioners and promote the hegemony of traditional academic researchers. (1993a, p. 28)

This century has seen several major criticisms of the involvement of teachers in researching their own practices. The first criticism is that teachers are not properly trained to conduct research and that the research they have conducted has not been up to an acceptable standard (Campbell & Stanley, 1963; Corman, 1957; Foshay, 1994; Hitchcock & Hughes, 1995). Over

The authors wish to acknowledge the Bureau of Educational Research at the University of Illinois-Champaign/Urbana for the assistance of Rita Davis in preparing the references. They would also like to thank Gary L. Anderson, Robin Marion, Bridget Somekh, and Susan Threatt for their comments about earlier drafts of the manuscript.

[1] The term "teacher" will be used in this chapter as a generic term to refer to P–12 educators. The term "academic" will be used to refer to college and university-based educators.

the years, even among those who have acknowledged practitioner research as a form of educational scholarship, some have viewed it as an inferior form of research with less rigorous standards than those of academic research.

> Although action research uses the same methods as regular educational research, many of the rigorous criteria applied to regular educational research can be relaxed in doing action research. (Borg, 1981, p. 249)

Instead of recognizing practitioner research as an indicator of an emergent form of educational science, Hodgkinson (1957) equated practitioner research with "easy hobby games for little engineers" and believed that "research is no place for an amateur." He argued that teachers are unfamiliar with the basic techniques of research and that the inquiries they engage in should be classified as "quantified common sense" rather than as a form of scientific study. (Also see Travers, 1958.) The second criticism, which is based on a positivist view of external validity, is that practitioner research is of questionable value because many studies do not involve the investigation of groups that are representative of larger populations. Therefore, some have felt that it is not possible to generalize from these smaller examined situations and to apply the research to others.

Third, and apart from concerns about teachers' qualifications to conduct research, were concerns that the demands of teachers' jobs make it difficult for them to find time to do research and that, when they do so, their attention is drawn away from their main task of educating students. It is felt that practitioner research is a form of exploitation of teachers that undermines the quality of education for students.

> If the teacher becomes a researcher, there is no reason why she should not be made to become a guidance counselor, nurse, musician, or psychiatrist, in the name of professional responsibility. (Hodgkinson, 1957, p. 77)

It was also felt by some that practitioner research could lead not to teacher development, but to self-delusion and to the greater stagnation of teachers who would use their research merely to justify their current practices.

> Teachers would have greater cause to become stagnant, if they did incorporate action research findings into their teaching, as they could then defend their techniques on the grounds of scientific objectivity, saying that "this is the best way because four years ago we tested it through action research." (Hodgkinson, 1957, p.77)

Despite the emergence of a context in which the socially constructed nature of all scientific inquiry has been recognized (e.g., Harding, 1986), these and other criticisms of the legitimacy of practitioner research as forms of educational inquiry have continued today while self-study research has gained in popularity and while claims about its status as a unique research paradigm have emerged.

For example, Biddle and Anderson (1986), in their chapter on "Theory, Methods, Knowledge, and Research on Teaching" in the third edition of the *Handbook of Research on Teaching*, describe trends in action research (a particular form of practitioner research) briefly in a section titled "Other Discovery Methods." They link action research to Kurt Lewin and the process of involving social scientists in social policy in "countries whose institutions are controlled by the state, such as the Soviet Union" (p. 239). They also specifically note the use of action research in Scandinavian social policy research and development and comment: "It appears less often in countries where social policy is allowed to drift or is planned largely through political means, as in the United States . . ." (p. 239). Although they comment on the connections between action research and the concept of "praxis" (i.e., action informed by reflection), on the use of observation as an adjunct to teacher education, and note that "talented teachers sometimes claim to have adopted such an orientation in their classroom practice," (p. 239) they appear quite skeptical of the usefulness of its outcomes: "However, few systematic insights and findings seem to have been generated as yet for our understanding of teaching by means of action research" (p. 239).

Huberman (1996), as well, has raised important questions about the adequacy of the evidence for many of the claims made about the value of practitioner research and its effects on teaching practice and classrooms. Echoing the criticisms of Hodgkinson (1957), Huberman has questioned the ability of those who study their own practices to rise above or bracket their preconceptions and avoid distortions and self-delusion.

Despite these continuing criticisms of practitioner inquiry as a legitimate form of educational research, there has been growing support for its knowledge-generating potential. In a widespread shift, the conception of teachers as merely consumers of educational research is changing to one of teachers as producers and mediators of educational knowledge (Richardson, 1994a). There has also been a challenge to the notion of college and university academics as the sole producers of educational knowledge (Carr & Kemmis, 1986). Others have challenged the idea of applying the norms and standards of academic educational research to the assessment of practitioner research and have made proposals for a variety of different indicators of research quality. Continuing the line of argument first made early in this century (Buckingham, 1926), Cochran-Smith & Lytle (1993) have asserted that teachers, because of their position in the classroom, can offer special insights into the knowledge-production process that those studying someone else's practice are unable to provide.

While in this chapter we will not examine the adequacy of specific claims that have been made about the value of conducting practitioner research and its impact on practice, we will discuss the general issue of the criteria that should be used to assess the trustworthiness of claims made in practitioner research. In doing so, we will support the view of practitioner research as a legitimate form of educational inquiry that should be evaluated with criteria that overlap with, but that are somewhat different from, those used to assess the trustworthiness of academic educational research.

In the third edition of the *Handbook of Research on Teaching*, Frederick Erickson came very close to bringing practitioner research into his chapter on qualitative research by discussing research collaborations involving academics and teachers: "A few steps beyond collaborative research involving teachers and academic researchers is for the classroom teacher to become the researcher in his or her own right" (1986, p. 157). Erickson went on to argue that more teachers need to take on the responsibility of conducting educational research and that supports should be built into their jobs to make such research possible:

> If classroom teaching in elementary and secondary schools is to come of age as a profession—if the role of teacher is not to continue to be infantilized—then teachers need to take the adult responsibility of investigating their own practice systematically and critically, by methods that are appropriate to their practice. . . . Time needs to be made available in the school day for teachers to do this. Anything less than that basic kind of institutional change is to perpetuate the passivity that has characterized the teaching profession in its relations with administrative supervisors and the public at large. (p.157)

In this chapter, we take that next step and address several specific aspects of practitioner research as a form of educational inquiry. In so doing, it is important for us to acknowledge that we are ourselves practitioner researchers who have—over a period of time—conducted research into our own work as teachers, teacher educators, and facilitators of the practitioner research of others (e.g., Noffke, 1994b; Tabachnick & Zeichner, 1999; Zeichner, 1995a). In the first section, we discuss the similarities and differences among the various traditions of inquiry that have been associated with this broad movement in educational research. We begin with efforts toward the scientific study of education at the end of the 19th century and continue on to contemporary varieties of practitioner research. Throughout that section and in the rest of the chapter, we limit ourselves largely to the English-language literature on practitioner research from several countries.

In the second section, we discuss the various motivations that have been associated with conducting practitioner research— the motives of people who have conducted this research and those of others who have encouraged them to do so. In the third section, we consider the kinds of issues and questions that have been considered in practitioner research together with the methodologies that have been used in collecting and analyzing data. The reader will note that although some practitioner research looks very much like research conducted by academics in colleges and universities, other self-studies carried out by practitioners are quite different from conventional academic research

In the fourth section, we discuss the issue of trustworthiness in practitioner research, and we will consider practitioner research as a way of knowing the following: What are the grounds for placing confidence in the findings of practitioner research? What criteria should be used in distinguishing good work from work that is of a lower quality? Who should make judgments about the quality of practitioner research? Here we address the question of whether practitioner research is a different research paradigm from academic research requiring different evaluative criteria or whether conventional academic standards should be applied in assessing the quality of practitioner studies. We also briefly consider some of the moral and ethical issues that arise

in practitioner research, such as the relations among the participants in the research. Finally, we highlight the limitations of our analyses and identify areas for further inquiry that we feel will strengthen the contribution of practitioner research to the general field of research on teaching.

Multiple Traditions of Practitioner Research

Many scholars (e.g., Wann, 1953; Adelman, 1993) have attributed the origins of practitioner research in education to the work of social psychologist Kurt Lewin and of John Collier, U.S. Commissioner of Indian Affairs from 1933 to 1945. Both men were involved in work that was outside education and that, among other things, sought to counteract racism and oppression and improve intergroup relations (e.g., Collier, 1945; Lewin, 1946).[2] While theirs was clearly an important influence, we see, along with others (e.g., McKernan, 1996; McTaggart, 1991), several other factors contributing to the adaptation of practitioner research as part of the study of educational problems.

Forms of practitioner research today are the culmination of long processes of evolution and contestation, which included efforts both inside and outside education (Noffke, 1997a, 1997b). One such influence arose from tensions within the movement for the scientific study of education, beginning in the late 19th and early part of the 20th century. Hopkins (1950), for example, identified a number of curriculum study projects in the early 1920s (e.g., in Los Angeles and Denver) as well as others in the 1930s, including the well-known "8-year study" (Aiken, 1942) that evidenced many of the characteristics of practitioner research. Thus, he highlighted the benefits as well as the tensions between the work of practitioners and the growing body of external consultants.

Besides the movement for the scientific study of education, other factors affected the development of practitioner research, such as the progressive educational philosophy of John Dewey (Dewey, 1938; Schubert & Lopez-Schubert, 1997) and the sociopolitical conditions of the time, which stimulated a greater concern for promoting democratic means of decision making in many aspects of life (see Kemmis, 1980/1988). As evidenced by the work of Ida B. Wells, W. E. B. DuBois, and Carter G. Woodson, as well as by that of turn-of-the-century feminists (see Reinharz, 1992), the idea that social research can be directly connected to social reconstruction has long been an important parallel to practitioner research. (See also Altrichter & Gstettner, 1993.)

As Anderson, Herr, and Nihlen (1994) point out, a number of calls emerged during the early part of this century for teachers to actively participate in research carried out in their classrooms in cooperation with academic researchers. This cooperation in educational research was, according to Buckingham (1926, 1939), something that would lead to the greater professionalization of teaching and to raising its status in the society even though, in reality, teachers were to serve merely as data collectors for the research of university academics:

---

[2] It has been argued that the Austrian physician, social philosopher, and poet Jacob Moreno was a pioneer in developing the idea of practitioner research (Gunz, 1996).

The teacher has opportunities for research which, if seized, will not only powerfully and rapidly develop the technique of teaching, but will also react to and vitalize and dignify the work of the individual teacher. (Buckingham, 1926, p. iv)

Cooperative research activity between academic researchers and teachers was seen as a way to improve the quality of educational research and to bring it closer to the needs of the field because of the important contributions that teachers could make from their perspective within the classroom (Cutright & Dahl, 1939). Despite the call for teachers to become researchers, the role of teachers in research was mainly to be limited to data collectors in studies designed and controlled by academic researchers. The ideas (a) that teachers could independently design and carry out inquiries on their own practice and (b) that the results of those efforts could have meaning and value for others beyond the settings in which the research was conducted were not commonplace in the early part of this century (Olson, 1990).

At least five major traditions of practitioner research in education have developed during the 20th century. We will not attempt to present a detailed history of those traditions in this chapter. A literature has emerged in the past decade that does a good job of this (e.g., Adelman, 1993; Elliott, 1991; Foshay, 1994; Kemmis, 1980/1988; McKernan, 1996; McTaggart, 1991; Noffke, 1994a, 1997a, 1997b; Olson, 1990; Park, Brydon-Miller, Hall, & Jackson, 1993; Wallace, 1987). Our purpose here is to briefly identify and define those different traditions of practitioner research.

First is the action research tradition that developed out of the work of Collier and Lewin in the United States and that was brought into schools in the United States by Stephen Corey and others at the Horace Mann-Lincoln Institute at Columbia University in the 1950s. Second is the British teacher-as-researcher movement that evolved in the 1960s and 1970s out of the curriculum reform work of British teachers and the supports provided by several academics, such as Lawrence Stenhouse and John Elliott, who were based at the University of East Anglia, and the participatory action research movement in Australia that has many direct links to the British movement.

Third is the contemporary teacher researcher movement in North America that has been developed primarily by teachers, often with the support of their university colleagues and subject-matter associations. Fourth is the recent growth of self-study research by college and university educators who— as teachers and teacher educators— study their own practice, Finally is the tradition of participatory research that (a) evolved out of work in Asia, Africa, and Latin America with oppressed groups and (b) was then adapted to community-wide research in North America that included, but went beyond, the educational sphere.

The Action Research Tradition

Although the central impulse behind action research can be understood to lie in the efforts of many disenfranchised groups to attain greater social justice through careful study, the first use of the term in the United States can be found in the writings of social psychologist Kurt Lewin and U.S. Commissioner of Indian Affairs John Collier, who used it as a way to counteract racial prejudice, to reform agricultural practices, and to promote more democratic forms of leadership in the workplace. Building on the Deweyan idea of inquiry, but also influenced by the movement for the scientific study of education noted earlier, Stephen Corey, Dean of Teachers College at Columbia University and head of the Horace Mann-Lincoln Institute for School Experimentation, and his colleagues brought the term "action research" into educational work. The institute was formed in 1943 to improve the rate of curriculum change in schools and to reduce the gap between research knowledge and instructional practices in classrooms (Olson, 1990). Corey believed that teachers would make better instructional decisions if they conducted research to determine the basis for those decisions and that teachers would be more likely to pay attention to research that they conducted themselves (Corey, 1953).

Corey and his associates at the institute worked cooperatively with teachers, principals, and supervisors in school districts across the United States in the late 1940s and 1950s on various group research efforts in what was referred to as the cooperative action research movement (e.g., Corey, 1953; Cunningham & Miel, 1947; Foshay, Wann, & Associates, 1954). Teams of educators worked together with the staff of the institute in addressing a numerous problems of curriculum, instruction, and supervision. Like Lewin, Corey (1953) saw action research as a cyclical process with each cycle of research affecting subsequent cycles of planning, acting, observation, and reflection. Corey outlined the significant elements of the action research methodology, as follows:

1. The identification of a problem area about which an individual or group is sufficiently concerned to want to take action.
2. The selection of a specific problem and the formulation of a hypothesis or prediction that implies a goal and a procedure for reaching it. This specific goal must be viewed in relation to the total situation.
3. The careful recording of actions taken and the accumulation of evidence to determine the degree to which the goal has been achieved.
4. The inference from this evidence of generalizations regarding the relation between the actions and the desired goal.
5. The continuous retesting of these generalizations in action situations. (Corey, 1953, pp. 40–41)

This understanding of the action research process was generally similar to Lewin's in terms of (a) the focus on the group and (b) the emphasis on the recursive nature of action research process (i.e., the need to allow the initial understanding of a problem defined by practitioners to shift to remain relevant to changing situations):

In a program of action research, it is impossible to know definitely in advance the exact nature of the inquiry that will develop. If initial designs, important as they are for action research, are treated with too much respect, the investigators may not be sufficiently sensitive to their developing irrelevance to the ongoing action situation. (Corey, 1949, pp. 40–41)

Corey's view of the action-research process differed from Lewin's in its emphasis on hypothesis formulation and testing.

In the eyes of Corey's students and those who followed him at the institute, action research was increasingly viewed as a linear problem-solving process as opposed to the recursive cyclical process that it had been under Lewin and Corey. In the work of Hilda Taba (e.g., Taba & Noel, 1957) and others, action research lost the notion of a spiral and became a series of steps to follow. It also became increasingly associated as a form of in-service teacher education as opposed to a methodology for knowledge production (Noffke, 1997b; Shumsky, 1958; Wiles, 1953).

Corey spent much time defending action research as a legitimate form of educational inquiry in terms of the positivist standards of research that were dominant at the time, but he was largely unsuccessful in doing so. Action research was ridiculed and judged by conventional academic standards as discussed at the beginning of this chapter, and it largely disappeared from mainstream U.S. educational literature until the late 1970s, when a new teacher research movement appeared in North America. A shift in the funding of educational research to the federal level; the establishment of the National Institute of Education; the disassociation of the American Educational Research Association from the National Education Association (in 1967); and an increased reliance on a research, development, and dissemination model of educational research in the establishment of research and development centers at universities across the country—all signaled the decline of the cooperative action research movement in the United States (Noffke, 1997b).

The Teacher-as-Researcher Movement in the United Kingdom and the Participatory Action Research Movement in Australia

Following the decline of action research in the United States by the early 1960s, the idea of action research in the field of education emerged in the United Kingdom in the context of school-based curriculum development in the 1960s. According to John Elliott (1991, 1997), who was one of the central players in this movement both as a secondary teacher and as a university academic, this teacher-led movement arose in response to large-scale student disaffection in British secondary modern schools in the 1960s. In Elliott's view, it was from attempts by teachers in some innovative secondary modern schools to restructure and reconceptualize the humanities curriculum that the ideas of teacher-as-researcher, teaching as a reflexive practice, and teaching as a form of inquiry emerged.

It should also be noted that another influence on the development of action research in the United Kingdom before this was the Tavistock Institute of Human Relations, which was set up in 1947 to further practices that psychologists had used during World War 2 to train officers, resettle prisoners, and so forth. There were strong parallels between the work of this institute, which adapted those methods to deal with problems of human relations and group dynamics in industrial settings, and the Research Center for Group Dynamics that Lewin had set up in the United States (Wallace, 1987). Some evidence shows that Lawrence Stenhouse, one of the major proponents of action re-

search in Britain, had been influenced by the work of the Tavistock Institute (Carr & Kemmis, 1986).

According to Somekh (1998), two other influences on development of the teacher-as-researcher movement in Britain were the Educational Priority Areas Programme, which involved collaborative inquiries among academic researchers and teachers (Halsey, 1972), and the U.S.-developed "Man: A Course of Study" (MACOS.) social studies curriculum, which emphasized the idea of students as researchers (Bruner, 1965). According to Somekh, Lawrence Stenhouse was strongly influenced by MACOS, and for many years his university served as the British distributor of the curriculum.

The "bottom up" curriculum reform work initiated by British teachers and later conceptualized and recorded by academics like John Elliott, Lawrence Stenhouse, Jean Rudduck, and Clem Adelman involved many different initiatives designed to make the curriculum more relevant to the lives of students, such as (a) restructuring the content of curriculum around life themes instead of subjects, (b) transforming the instructional process from a transmission mode to a more interactive and discussion-based mode, (c) using multi–age-grouping patterns, and so forth.

A number of major curriculum reform projects were initiated in the 1960s and 1970s by Stenhouse, Elliott, and others who used and further developed the notion of practitioner inquiry as curriculum development. These projects included the Humanities Curriculum Project, which dealt with teaching controversial issues (Stenhouse, 1968); the Ford Teaching Project, which dealt with implementing an inquiry-discovery approach to teaching (Elliott, 1976–77); and the Teacher-Student Interaction and Quality of Learning project, which focused on the problems of "teaching for understanding" within the context of a system of public examinations (Elliott & Ebutt, 1986). All of these projects involved university academics working with teachers and represented a rejection of a standards- or objectives-based view of curriculum development in favor of one that is based on a pedagogically driven conception of curriculum change that depends on teachers' reflections about their practice. According to this view, the act of curriculum theorizing is not so much the application in the classroom of theory learned in the academy as it is the generation of theory from attempts to change curriculum practice in the school (Elliott, 1991). Stenhouse (1975), one of the early academic supporters of this movement, coined the term "teacher as researcher" to signify the dependence of pedagogical change on teachers' capacities for reflection.

Elliott (1997) argues that action research cannot be distinguished as a unique paradigm of research in terms of data-gathering methods. He argues that what distinguishes action research from other forms of educational research are its transformative intentions (i.e., to change practice) and the methodological principles such intentions imply. He summarizes the methodology of action research, as follows:

> It is directed towards the realization of an educational ideal (e.g., as represented by a pedagogical aim),
>
> It focuses on changing practice to make it more consistent with the ideal,

It gathers evidence of the extent to which the practice is consistent/inconsistent with the ideal and seeks explanations for inconsistencies by gathering evidence about the operation of contextual factors,

It problematizes some of the tacit theories which underpin and shape practice (i.e., taken-for-granted beliefs and norms), [and]

It involves practitioners in generating and testing action-hypotheses about how to effect worthwhile educational change. (p. 25)

The efforts of John Elliott, Peter Holly, Bridget Somekh, and many others at the University of East Anglia led to the establishment and development of the Collaborative Action Research Network. This network has sponsored conferences and published many accounts of action research and many works that have furthered discussions about action research methodology (e.g., Edwards & Rideout, 1991; O'Hanlon, 1991). More recently, the group has played a central role in establishing the journal, *Educational Action Research,* which provides an international forum for reports of action research and for the exchange of ideas about action research.

Stephen Kemmis, who had spent some time with Elliott and his colleagues at the University of East Anglia, took action research with him to Australia, and, together with Wilfred Carr, a British educational philosopher, developed an epistemological basis for action research in the critical theory of Habermas (Carr & Kemmis, 1986). This view of "emancipatory" action research that is based in critical theory effectively challenged other models of action research as conservative and positivistic. As in the United Kingdom, Kemmis, Robin McTaggart, and others at Deakin University were able to build on a strong movement among teachers for school-based curriculum development and a context for grassroots involvement in policymaking (Grundy & Kemmis, 1988). Using ideas later articulated in *Becoming Critical,* teachers and other staff members developed a methodology for use in various action research courses and projects (Kemmis & McTaggart, 1988a, b). This model, which was conceptualized as a series of recursive cycles of plan, act, observe, and reflect, has a clear definition of the aims of the research process, as follows:

Action research is a form of *collective* self-reflective enquiry undertaken by participants in social situations in order to improve the rationality and justice of their own social or educational practices, as well as their understanding of these practices and the situations in which these practices are carried out. (Kemmis & McTaggart, 1988b, p. 5)

Although a number of projects of the critical emancipatory type are described in various publications (e.g., Kemmis & Grundy, 1997; Kemmis & McTaggart, 1988a; Tripp, 1990), there is some question as to the degree to which the teachers throughout Australia who became engaged in action research took on the critical-emancipatory purposes that Kemmis and his colleagues emphasized in their work at Deakin (Grundy, 1982). As was the case in the United Kingdom, academics like Kemmis and Tripp (who had also spent time in Britain) worked hard to legitimate action research as research within Australia. Grundy (1997) argues, though, that various political, social,

and educational circumstances had already established the conditions for the further development of practitioner research in Australia:

It is . . . wrong to see the development of participatory action research as a missionary venture in which the gurus, who had come to see the light in a far country, now brought the news to a waiting population. It is clear . . . that there was, both socially and educationally, a milieu already oriented toward teacher participation in the production of educational knowledge. (p.135)

Grundy (1997) identifies a series of political, social, and educational conditions that had fostered a receptivity to the idea of teachers as producers of educational knowledge. Among those were three projects in the 1970s funded by the Commonwealth Schools' Commission: The Innovative Grants Project, the Language and Learning Project, and the Curriculum Development Center. Those projects, as well as (a) changing conceptions of in-service teacher education at the state level and (b) a growth in practitioner research in tertiary institutions, stimulated a lot of school-based curriculum development and evaluation and teachers studying their own practices in Australian schools. Grundy argues that, although the tradition of Australian participatory action research developed with a direct link to the British teacher-as-researcher movement, it eventually developed its own practices and epistemology that distinguished it from British action research.

The North American Teacher Research Movement

In the 1980s, a new movement for teacher research emerged in North America in response to several factors. Anderson et al. (1994) argue that this movement was not derivative of the British teacher-as-researcher movement or a reemergence of the co-operative action research movement of the 1940s and 1950s. They identify many influences on the development of this movement, including (a) the growing acceptance of qualitative and case-study research in education that more closely resembles the narrative forms of inquiry used by practitioners to communicate their knowledge; (b) the pioneering work of many teachers of writing such as Nancy Atwell (1987), who conducted case studies on the teaching of writing; (c) the increased emphasis on action research in university teacher education programs (e.g., Cochran-Smith & Lytle, 1993; Zeichner & Gore, 1995); and (d) the reflective practitioner movement that was inspired by the work of Schön (1983) and that sought to reclaim teachers' knowledge as valid.

Cochran-Smith and Lytle (1993) also discuss other influences on teacher research in North America, such as the National Writing Project; the Breadloaf School of English (Goswami & Stillman, 1987); the National Council of Teachers of English (supporter of many teacher researchers in English-Language Arts education) (e.g., Mohr & Maclean, 1987); Patricia Carini and the teachers at the Prospect School in Bennington, Vermont, who developed methods for documenting the progress of children's learning (e.g., Carini, 1975); and the North Dakota Study Group on Evaluation guided by Vito Perrone (e.g., Perrone, 1989).

This teacher research movement followed a number of years of "interactive research and development" and other forms of collaborative research among university researchers and teachers (e.g., Jacullo-Noto, 1984; Oja & Smulyan, 1989; Tikunoff & Ward, 1983) that involved teachers in some aspects of the research about their practices but that was not a process fully owned by the teachers. This collaborative research, like the research stimulated by the work of Lewin and Corey, involved collaboration between professional researchers and the teachers whose practice was under study. Practitioner research was not then considered as a process that could be identified primarily as the property of individuals who were not professional researchers by vocation (McTaggart, 1991).

Cochran-Smith and Lytle (1993) describe the different varieties of inquiry that have emerged under the rubric of teacher research in North America. Rather than outlining a series of phases or steps of the research process, a practice that was common in the British and Australian action research movements and in the cooperative action research movement in the United States in the 1950s, Cochran-Smith and Lytle (1993) define teacher research very broadly as "systematic intentional inquiry by teachers about their own school and classroom work" (pp. 23–24). They outline two major categories of teacher research: (a) conceptual research, which is theoretical and philosophical, and (b) empirical research, which involves the collection, analysis, and interpretation of data gathered from teachers, schools, and classrooms.

In the category of empirical teacher research, Cochran-Smith and Lytle include (a) journals that provide accounts of classroom life over time (e.g., Streib, 1985), (b) oral inquiries that consist of teachers' oral examinations of their practice in a group setting (e.g., Kanevsky, 1993), and (c) classroom studies that represent teachers' explorations of their work using data based on observations, interviews, and document collection (e.g., Bissex & Bullock, 1987). Under the category of conceptual research, they include teachers' essays and books that represent extended interpretations and analyses of various aspects of schooling. These essays include the works of teachers like Gallas, (1994, 1995, 1998), Hawkins (1969), Kohl, (1967), Kozol (1967), and Paley (1979).

The category of classroom studies includes work that most closely resembles the earlier cooperative research studies in the United States, British action research studies, and traditional forms of academic educational research. Cochran-Smith and Lytle (1993) argue that it would be a mistake to limit the concept of teacher research to the category of classroom studies, as many have done, because this limitation does not enable us to benefit from much of the empirical and conceptual work conducted by teachers. Cochran-Smith and Lytle, as well as Anderson et al. (1994), essentially argue that practitioner research represents a different paradigm of research from academic research, because it gives us access to insider or local knowledge about educational settings. This point of view has important implications for how we think about the epistemology of practitioner research, which is the subject of a later section in this chapter.

A large part of the research that has been conducted by North American teachers within this teacher research movement has not been included in mainstream academic publishing outlets, although some, such as Grimmett and MacKinnon (1992), have described and analyzed practitioner research within conventional academic publishing outlets. In the academic world, few journals (such as *Language Arts*) and certain publishers (such as Heinemann, Stenhouse, and Teachers College Press) have regularly published practitioner research. Several new journals (e.g., *Teacher Research,* the National Educational Association's *Teaching and Change,* and *Network,* the electronic teacher research journal based in Toronto) focus exclusively on practitioner research.

Much practitioner research, however, still remains as part of a fugitive literature that is accessible only locally (Richardson, 1994b). Even here, norms and circumstances often discourage the sharing of work in local settings (McTaggart, 1989; Zeichner, Marion, & Caro-Bruce, 1998). A number of teacher research networks like those in Fairfax County, Virginia; in Madison, Wisconsin; and at the Cooperative Research and Extension Services (CRESS) center sponsored by the University of California at Davis have developed listings by research topics of the abstracts of studies conducted within their networks. In some cases, like the Madison, Wisconsin, school district, those abstracts have been made available on the Internet. The CRESS Center has also published a language arts journal (*Visions and Revisions: Research for Writing Teachers*) and a math journal (*Translation, Rotation, and Reflection*) that provide a forum for the work of teacher researchers. Much practitioner research that is done by teachers in North America is not published anywhere but is shared orally at several regional and national teacher research conferences that occur on a regular basis.

The Tradition of Self-Study Research

Although many of the reports of practitioner research have involved the work of elementary and secondary school teachers and other staff members who have studied their practice, there has also been a growing tradition of research in which college and university faculty members conduct research on their own practice. This research tradition recognizes the fact that we are all practitioners in some sphere of our work (Somekh, 1995). It rejects the ideas that the only role for academics is to generate theories for others to consume and that academics should have a monopoly on knowledge production in education. There has been growing acceptance of self-study research within colleges and universities, especially within the teacher education community.

Although there have long been calls for this kind of research by teacher educators (e.g., Corey, 1955) and college and university faculty members who have conducted inquiries on their own teaching practice (e.g., Duckworth, 1987; Lampert, 1985), recently there has been a tremendous growth in the publication of self-study research (e.g., Feiman-Nemser & Featherstone, 1992; Loughran & Russell, 1997; Richardson, 1997; Russell & Korthagen, 1995; Tabachnick & Zeichner, 1991). There have also been calls for the academy to recognize the legitimacy of high-quality self-study research in tenure and promotion decisions (e.g., Adler, 1993). In 1992, a special interest group, Self-Study of Teacher Education Practices, was formed in the

American Educational Research Association. Just 7 years later, it has become one of the largest interest groups in the association.

The self-study research conducted by college and university faculty members has used various qualitative methodologies and has focused on a wide range of substantive issues. For example, some studies in this genre use narrative life history methods and describe the connections between teacher educators' life experiences and their current teaching practices (Cole & Knowles, 1995; Zeichner, 1995a). In this form, the self-study research most closely resembles the essays and narratives that are commonly found in the North American teacher research movement, and it parallels developments in life history research generally (e.g., Neumann & Peterson, 1997; Thomas, 1995). Although research in this genre seldom follows the pattern of the action research cycles common in the U.S. cooperative action research movement and in the British and Australian teacher researcher movements, some studies, many emanating from the University of Bath and Kingston University in the UK, have connected action research and self-study (e.g., Lomax, 1997). Some self-study research involves inquiries about (a) the use of particular instructional strategies (e.g., Grimmett, 1997; Moje, Remillard, Southerland, & Wade, 1999; Richert, 1991; Teitelbaum & Britzman, 1991) or (b) the implementation of particular educational philosophies in teacher education programs (e.g., Carson, 1997; Macgillivray, 1997; Maher, 1991; Richardson, 1997). Many recent studies focus on the struggles of teacher educators with issues of race, class, and gender (e.g., Cochran-Smith, 1995; Lima, 1998; Martin, 1995) and with working within institutions that do not place a high value on the activity of teacher education (McCall, 1996).

Self-study research has found its way into the academic journals and into a flurry of recent books. Some journals, like *Teaching Education,* have actively recruited and published self-studies on a regular basis. Two teacher education journals, *Action in Teacher Education* (Manning & McLaughlin, 1996) and *Teacher Education Quarterly* (special issue, 1995), have recently published special issues on self-study research.

The Tradition of Participatory Research

Although much of the research in this tradition has taken place in Third World countries in Latin America, Africa, and Asia (e.g., Fals-Borda, 1988; Fals-Borda & Rahman, 1991; Freire, 1982; Tandon, 1988), similar ideas and practices have developed in North America, Europe, and Australia with groups that share characteristics of oppression and domination experienced by many Third World peoples (e.g., Park et al., 1993; Stringer, 1996). According to Hall (1993), the International Council for Adult Education's Participatory Research Project in 1977, which is based in Toronto, was the means by which an initial sharing of methods and practices of participatory research occurred in North America. Other accounts discuss the role of the Highlander Center in the United States in developing and disseminating information and strategies for conducting participatory research (Horton, 1990; Noffke, 1997a).

This research tradition has been closely associated with adult education and literacy movements, although it has also dealt with other social issues and problems, such as land ownership and use, environmental contamination, unemployment, crime and drugs, and so forth. Torres (1992) argues that the development of the ideas of liberation pedagogy and popular education are responsible for the origins of participatory research in Latin America. According to Reason (1994), participatory research has the following double objective:

> One aim is to produce knowledge and action directly useful to a group of people through research, adult education, and sociopolitical action. The second aim is to empower people through a second and deeper level through the process of constructing their own knowledge. (p. 328)

The explicit aim of participatory research is to bring about a more just and humane society, and the research process provides a framework in which people who seek to overcome oppressive situations can come to understand the social forces operating in a situation and can gain strength to engage in collective action (Park, 1993). This broad scope of participatory research, which leads to an examination of issues within a societal framework, is very different from the individual and group foci in other traditions of practitioner research (Brown & Tandon, 1983).

According to Gaventa (1991), three strategies of participatory research have emerged in the North American context. They are as follows:

1. The reappropriation of knowledge—gaining access to knowledge and skills normally considered to be the monopoly of a knowledge elite. This includes what Gaventa refers to as community power structure research in which communities of people gain access to such things as courthouse records about property transactions, housing codes, land and mineral ownership, government records about company finances, and so forth (e.g., Adams, 1975).
2. The development of the people's knowledge—the production and reclaiming of the common person's knowledge and wisdom. An example of this strategy is the housewife researchers who analyzed and documented the health experiences of people in the community in the vicinity of Love Canal, which resulted in a campaign to clean up toxic waste dumps (Levine, 1982).
3. Popular participation in the social production of knowledge. This strategy involves forms of democratic participation and control in defining problems to be studied, setting research priorities, and in determining how the results are to be used. One example is the case of relatively powerless groups in Appalachia demanding a voice in the allocation of public research funds. (Gaventa & Horton, 1981)

Although a numerous research methods are used in participatory research, a general structure of research in this tradition and a set of assumptions are shared by researchers. A key concept in this research is that the subject–object relationship between researcher and researched typical in conventional academic research is turned into a subject–subject relationship (Fals-Borda, 1991; Freire, 1982). Although often an outside person intervenes to mobilize and organize a community for investigation and action, the people in an area being studied assume active roles in the investigation and do not serve as passive objects of study. Typically, ordinary people engage in activities like making up questionnaires and interview schedules that are commonly reserved for technically trained personnel.

Hall (1993) points out that participatory research is based on the epistemological assumption that knowledge is constructed socially through a process of dialogue and that the issues studied and ways of studying them should flow from those involved and should promote dialogue within the community of researchers. The first step in the process is the definition and exploration of the problem to be investigated. The outside researcher typically acts as a discussion organizer, a facilitator, and as a technical resource person.

The researchers (outside and inside) then decide on how data are to be collected and analyzed. Participatory research draws upon a wide range of research methods used in the social sciences, including field observation, archival and library research, personal histories, interviews, and observations. The specific methods that are selected in particular projects take into account the technical and material resources of the community and traditions within the community of communicating and disseminating knowledge (e.g., Hinsdale, Lewis, & Waller, 1995). Hall (1993) describes the selection of approaches according to their potential for drawing out knowledge and analysis in a social and collective way. He identifies a number of research methods not typically found in conventional academic research, including

> Community meetings, video documentaries, community drama, camps for the landless in India, use of drawing and murals, photo novels, sharing of oral histories, community surveys, storytelling, shared testimonies, and many more. (pp. 4331–4332)

Gaventa (1991) argues that once people begin to view themselves as researchers who are able to investigate and change reality for themselves, they will invent indigenous ways of gathering information from the power structure, what he calls "guerrilla research" methods. One example that he gives of this phenomenon is a situation in Appalachia, where coal miners needing information about their employer gained a great deal of useful data by monitoring garbage cans at company headquarters. The data assembled in the research, by whatever methods, serve as topics for collective reflection through dialogue within the community of researchers and provide researchers with ammunition for improving their material conditions.

Those who are engaged in participatory research are typically very critical of nonparticipatory research and often argue that it serves the dominant groups in a society by monopolizing the development and use of knowledge to the disadvantage of the communities in which research takes place, thereby exploiting those communities (Reason, 1994). Participatory research aims to democratize the political economy of knowledge production and to empower oppressed groups so they take effective actions toward improving the conditions in their lives.

These five traditions of practitioner research—action research, the teacher-as-researcher and participatory action re-

search movements in Britain and Australia, the teacher research movement in North America, self-study research, and participatory research—reflect a variety of personal, professional, and political motivations for conducting research. The next section of this chapter will look across those five traditions and will discuss the various motivations that have stimulated practitioner research in education.

Frameworks of Purpose in Practitioner Research

> But can you expect teachers to revolutionize the social order for the good of the community? Indeed we must expect this very thing. The educational system of a country is worthless unless it accomplishes this task. (Woodson, 1933/1977, p. 145)

This quote represents the thoughts behind but one of the many frameworks of purpose in practitioner research. At its core, practitioner research shares with other forms of educational research an emphasis on developing and deepening the understanding of educational practice. Yet practitioner research is both about changing practice as a result of study and about changing practice to understand it. As noted earlier, to some, especially those writing in the British action research tradition, its claim as a distinct research paradigm is based to a large extent on its potential for changing practice (Elliott, 1997). The nature and extent of the change intended, though, is a contested area that varies not only across but also within traditions of practitioner research. Through changing practice, teachers and other educational practitioners become producers, as well as mediators and consumers, of knowledge. For many advocates of and participants in practitioner research, the concept of practice as knowledge production is essential in that it can both embrace the value of individual development and move beyond the local and private context to contribute more broadly to educational and societal improvement.

Fischer (1996) notes that teacher researchers often pursue their own interests in their classroom. He suggests the following categories for understanding the many kinds of reasons one might engage in practitioner research:

> (a) an interest in knowing more about how students learn; (b) wanting to try something new, to innovate in a curriculum area; (c) a desire for change in one's teaching ; and (d) a search for connections and meanings in one's work. (p. 39)

Such motivations are similar to those outlined by Zeichner (1997), who highlights the various kinds of questions that preservice and in-service teachers in Madison, Wisconsin, have pursued. These include questions that are designed

1. To improve practice (e.g., how can I hold better discussions in my classes and have a more learner-centered classroom?);
2. To better understand a particular aspect of practice (e.g., do I conduct my classes in a manner where students feel free to express different opinions and even to disagree with me?);
3. To better understand one's practice in general (e.g., what is going on in my classroom?) (a specific question emerges later);

4. To promote greater equity (e.g., how can I help the girls in my math class feel more confident about their abilities in math and to participate more in class activities?); and

5. To influence the social conditions of practice (e.g., how can I get the school district to reallocate funding to support teacher-initiated professional development work?) (Zeichner, 1997, pp. 10–11).

In addition to identifying examples of the various starting points for practitioner research in their respective contexts, both Fischer (1996) and Zeichner (1997) depict practitioner research as a recursive process that often shifts in focus and that is connected to the dynamics of the school year. This depiction contrasts with linear models of the action-research process, models that are often described in the literature.

The closeness of the relationship between change and practice implied by the term "practitioner research" serves as a reminder that the work of education takes place in a complex social context. As Kemmis and McTaggart (1988a) emphasize in their definition of action research noted earlier, the focus of this version of practitioner research is not only on advancing understanding and practice, but also on improving the situation in which the practice occurs. Although we will differentiate the motivational structures of practitioner research in terms of the personal, professional, and political, all three dimensions are inherently political because they involve issues of power and control (Noffke, 1997a). In practice, those dimensions are interwoven categories rather than orientations belonging to a particular tradition of practitioner research. The separation into categories is thus a construct for illuminating emphases rather than a typology for identifying the worthiness of purposes or traditions.

In this section and the next, an important caution must be understood. Practitioner researchers, like many traditional researchers, do not always report their reasons for engaging in inquiry. Their purposes often must be inferred from the topics of their research (addressed in the next section) and from the tone of their presentation. As with other analyses of practitioner research, we still rely too heavily on works written by academics, which set out theoretical or conceptual frameworks derived from social science theories or which comment on what has been gleaned from studying practitioners, often using traditional research methods. Although we recognize this weakness, we hope the present work represents a continuing step in recognizing practitioners' voices in research on teaching.

Up Close and Personal: Seeing Children, Seeing Oneself

The personal dimension of practitioner research is evident in several ways. First, much of practitioner research involves the careful study of the participants in educational practice, very often involving the students or children—what and how they learn. The research is personal, because it represents not only the search for general principles or theories of school curriculum or classroom instruction but also the search for understanding and improving one's everyday practice.

From the work in the 1950s at the Horace Mann-Lincoln Institute at Teachers College (Foshay et al., 1954), through the work of the Ford Teaching Project (Elliott & Adelman, 1973),

to much of the work in the current traditions of North American teacher research and self-study, a major purpose for engaging in practitioner research has been to gain a better understanding of individual students' thoughts and actions (Banford, 1996; Gallas, 1998; Osborne, 1997) or teachers' experiences with particular educational innovations (Griffiths & Davies, 1993). This purpose recognizes the inherent process of generating and examining theories that are part of educational practice (Elliott, 1991; Handal & Lauvas, 1987; Posch, 1993). In some ways resembling the early child-study movement or case study approach, practitioner research brings us very close to everyday classroom experiences. As such, the research (e.g., Short, Schroeder, Laird, Kaufmann, Ferguson, & Crawford, 1996; Steffy & Hood, 1994) offers great potential for building a case-study literature in education, as has been done in other professions. Many practitioner researchers have expressed concern about both the current educational context and children's lives. As teacher researcher Barbara Morgan noted in the *1994 Yearbook of the National Society for the Study of Education*:

> I think that those of us who tend toward the silent "making do" often do not effectively resist the stupidities of policy and institution. To act in this way harms children. However safe we keep them for the time they stay with us, we cannot protect against damage done by schooling. We must enter the conversation because we are closest to the children, and we have the possibility of bringing the children's voices into the conversation too. We have not spoken enough. We need to speak not as "raw data" but as analytical women (and men) who have rigorously considered their environment and are ready to add new interpretive frames (Threatt, Buchanan, Morgan, Strieb, Sugarman, Swenson, Teel, & Tomlinson, 1994, p. 230).

Morgan's clear concern with the lives of the children in her classroom is strongly linked to a commitment to the potential within teachers for creating new ways of sharing their experiential knowledge with others. The care and nurture of students is integrally connected to the perception of self as teacher (Nias, 1989). Although Morgan's research experience is personal and valued in its individuality, it is also part of an overall political strategy (Noffke & Brennan, 1997) embedded in her classroom practice. As practitioners change their practices and document what they do, they live out as well as problematize particular orientations to the larger social order, including ethical stances on how one should "be" with children in the classroom, and the uneven distribution of knowledge and privilege in society (Griffiths, 1994; Maher, 1991). Although not all teachers embrace a social transformation orientation, all practice embodies a political stance, whether directly or tacitly (Noffke & Brennan, 1997).

A second aspect of the personal dimension is a heightened self-awareness by the practitioner, including the clarification of assumptions about education and the recognition of contradictions between espoused ideas and actual classroom practices. This pattern, evident in the Ford Teaching Project (Elliott, 1976–77) and in subsequent projects in the United Kingdom, parallels early practitioner research in the United States (Shumsky, 1958). Particularly noteworthy here is that curriculum and pedagogical theorizing are being examined in light of the practitioners' experiences (Fecho, 1996). Along with this examination is a strong emphasis on what one is actually doing, rather than intending to do, in P–12 as well as in university classrooms (Peterman, 1997). The personal, in this sense, encompasses both individual classrooms and the theorizing of individual practitioners.

A third aspect of the personal in the practitioner research literature is the examination of the impact of the research process on the practitioner (e.g., Dadds, 1995; McNiff, 1993; Noffke & Zeichner, 1987). Resonating with the work of Lewin and others, the focus of practitioner research often shifts from classrooms, teachers' theories, and children to changes in teachers' basic orientations to practice. Motivations for engaging teachers in research have ranged from creating a greater receptivity among teachers to traditional academic educational research (Tikunoff & Ward, 1983), to encouraging changes in teachers' belief structures and practices, to having practitioners offer contributions to existing lines of theory production in the field (Johnston & Proudford, 1994). Although some attention has been devoted to this personal and often transformative aspect of practitioner research, the impact of such efforts on practitioners' basic belief structures and concepts of self has been largely unexamined in the literature.

One exception is the growing salience in the self-study tradition of narrative, life history, and autobiographical research (Cole & Knowles, 1995; Elijah, 1996), which illustrates how practitioner research often fosters reexamination of tacit views. Although such explorations offer many insights into the role of the personal in change processes, the role of teachers' cultural identities in the transformation of practice has been largely ignored and is clearly an area in need of study.

Another exception is the recent effort to study the impact of conducting practitioner research on teachers' professional development in North America (e.g., Richert, 1996; Troen, Kamii, & Boles, 1997; Zeichner, 1999; Zeichner, Marion, & Caro-Bruce, 1998) and the United Kingdom (e.g., Dadds, 1995). Richert (1996), for example, concludes that participation in a 6-year teacher research project sponsored by the Bay Region IV Professional Development Consortium in California had many important effects on teacher researchers, including the following:

1. It resulted in a renewed feeling of pride and excitement about teaching and in a revitalized sense of self as teacher.
2. The research experience reminded teachers of their intellectual capability and the importance of that capability to their professional lives.
3. The research experience allowed teachers to see that the work that they do in school matters.
4. The research experience reconnected many of the teachers to their colleagues and to their initial commitments to teach.
5. The research experience encouraged teachers to develop an expanded notion of what teachers can and ought to do.

It is important to note that practitioner research does not always, nor perhaps even often, occur in isolation. Many practitioner researchers work in collaboration with children (e.g., Gallas, 1994; Stumbo, 1992). Much work is also "facilitated" by others, often those in universities (e.g., Dockendorf, 1995;

Hollingsworth, 1994; Miller, 1990), or is supported through group meetings with other practitioner researchers (Caro-Bruce & McReadie, 1995; Cochran-Smith & Lytle, 1993; Evans, Stubbs, Frechette, Neely, & Warner, 1987; Marion, 1998). Some of this collaborative inquiry by teachers takes place in the context of teacher study groups (e.g., Saavedra, 1996) or teacher networks (e.g., Watt & Watt, 1993). Questions about "who owns the process" (Johnston & Proudford, 1994) are vital in evaluating the purpose of the research. An understanding of the legacy of Lewin's work in action research is crucial to evaluating whether the personal dimension—the focus on children and self—is also a means to changing the practitioner through involvement in participatory processes (Noffke, 1997b). Participation, a key aspect to many forms of practitioner research, has a very strong impact on the acceptance of innovation and the improvement of "productivity" (Adelman, 1993). Especially in a context in which practitioner research is seen as a strategy for school improvement (Calhoun, 1994; Sagor, 1992), the potential for administrators to manipulate the goals of practitioner researchers needs to be examined.

Finally, a related purpose for engaging in practitioner research within the personal dimension highlights the fine line between research and learning. Perhaps because of the frequent focus on individual teachers in their classrooms, some practitioner research is dominated by psychological, rather than sociological or anthropological, frameworks. Although this work strongly emphasizes research as "systematic inquiry made public" (Stenhouse, 1983, p. 185), it also focuses clearly on research as an individual learning process for the researcher (e.g., McNiff, 1993; Winter, 1989). The work is particularly interesting in its focus on the value of experiential knowledge. Yet it is also important in highlighting the difficulty of articulating the relationship between the personal and social spheres, which is integral to educational practice, and the absence of discussions of identity (Noffke, 1991).

Considered together, these four aspects of the personal emphasize the ways in which many forms of practitioner research have as their central purpose the improvement of practice (Elliott, 1991) and the ways in which the personal aspects form an integral part of that process. As will be seen in a subsequent section, judgments about the quality of the research have to take into account the practice as well as the study of practice.

Knowledge and the Profession of Education

Closely related to the focus of practitioner research on individual improvement of practice is its connection to the overall education profession. This linkage can be seen along three strands: (a) as a contribution to the profession's "knowledge base," (b) as a means of professional development, and (c) as an enhancement of the profession's status. This professional dimension of practitioner research has a long tradition. Corey (1954) emphasized the potential of practitioner research for helping teachers better understand what they are accomplishing in their classrooms. In the Ford Teaching Project, much attention was paid to creating better congruency between teachers' beliefs and practices as they articulated and problematized previously tacit theories. Teachers generated and tested hypotheses and then sought alternative explanations for what they carefully observed. In those efforts, they also considered how such activities contributed to the overall education profession. Practitioners' descriptions of teaching techniques represented substantial contributions, not only as research findings but also as material for further reflection by other practitioners. Both Stenhouse (1975) and Elliott (1991) have highlighted the vital role for teachers in the articulation of curriculum theory and the continuing efforts for its development in practice.

In Australia as well, considerable attention has been paid, at least at the level of academic writing, to practitioner research as a form of knowledge production. Building on Lewin's emphasis on action research as contributing to both the generation of theory and the improvement of the human condition, Carr & Kemmis (1986), writing from a critical social theory perspective, shaped a claim for action research as a distinct form of educational research. In a framework where all forms of knowledge production are seen as representing particular interests, some teachers, administrators, and researchers have developed projects that embody a transformative and emancipatory theory and practice, rather than ones that appear to seek only the accumulation of knowledge (Kemmis & Grundy, 1997).

Such efforts in the United Kingdom and Australia contrast strongly with the early Interactive Research and Development in Teaching projects that emerged in the United States during the same era. With a purpose of bridging theory and practice by uniting university researchers and practitioners, those projects used empirical analytical methods and focused attention primarily on teaching techniques. Rather than shifting the base of educational knowledge to include moral and social issues, the projects intended to create opportunities for practitioners to add to a narrowly proscribed knowledge base for teaching (Jacullo-Noto, 1984; Tikunoff & Ward, 1983). In some ways, that same accumulative stance toward knowledge is evident in the early work of Cochran-Smith and Lytle (1993), but with significant differences:

> Research by teachers represents a distinctive way of knowing about teaching and learning that will alter—not just add to—what we know in the field. Furthermore, we have argued that, as it accumulates and is more widely disseminated, research by teachers will represent a radical challenge to our current assumptions about the relationship of theory and practice, schools and universities, and inquiry and reform. (p. 85)

Although practitioner research is accepted as an emergent form of creating knowledge, the purpose here is to challenge, rather than reinforce, existing forms of knowledge.

Others emphasize practitioner research less as a contender in the knowledge production arena and more as a potential resource for professional development and educational management (Dadds, 1995; Lomax, 1996; O'Hanlon, 1996; Richardson, 1994b; Zuber-Skerritt, 1996). Although the potential of practitioner research to contribute to educational knowledge is not discounted (see Whitehead, 1993), there is more emphasis on its impact on building collaborative professional communities (e.g., Troen et al., 1997) and on informing educational policy (e.g., Atkin, 1994). Although this focus can be seen as connected to the earlier era in the United States when action research was considered more a means of staff development

than as a means of producing knowledge, a significant difference is that, in the contemporary era, the role of practitioner research in enhancing the status of the profession is emphasized more strongly (Sagor, 1992). Constructed in this way, practitioner research highlights the need to examine the meanings of professionalism in educational organizations in light of the interests they represent (Popkewitz, 1994).

As in the personal dimension, struggles over the meaning and status of the profession and professional knowledge occur in political contexts and are representations of various political, economic, and social agendas. In many ways, the current movement in North American teacher research is a clear example of contestation, through research, over the meanings of schooling in the lives of teachers and their students. For example, Wagler (1996) focused his attention not on the individual classroom level, but on ways in which school districts and teacher education institutions could better support networks of innovative teachers. Along similar lines, Russell (in Gitlin, Bringhurst, Burns, Cooley, Myers, Price, Russell, & Tiess, 1992) not only highlights her own voice in educational discourse, but also documents her efforts to establish "professional dialogue sessions" involving teachers and administrators throughout her school.

The self-study tradition focuses beyond individual classrooms. For example, some self-study research is related to the status of teacher education and teacher educators in university structures, particularly those at research universities (e.g., McCall, 1996). By the same token, the British literature on teacher research has long been concerned with issues of professional accountability and autonomy (Elliott, 1991).

Taken together, all of these efforts are an attempt to extend practitioner research beyond the classroom and point to what Lawn (1989) referred to as the "schoolwork research" potential within practitioner research. Rather than relying on external analyses of their work contexts, practitioner researchers directly study and seek to influence aspects of the social and institutional contexts in which they work.

The Political Dimension of Practitioner Research

Although this section outlines aspects of practitioner research that assert a social justice agenda, we assume that all forms of educational research embody particular stances, either to maintain existing lines of power and privilege or to transform them along more just and caring lines. Works that are silent on issues of racial equality, for example, assume political positions as much as those that explore the meaning of such issues. Works that take unproblematized stances toward the role of teachers, the nature of the curriculum, or the processes of learning are likewise political and representative of particular educational positions. Efforts to make schools fulfill their functions more efficiently in relation to given social and economic structures are no less political than those that challenge the form of these structures and their relationship to educational work.

In the participatory research tradition, an overt agenda of social change is integral to the research process. This agenda is explicit in its commitment to economic and social justice issues in both the larger social context and the research process itself. If the political is conceptualized in terms of power issues, then a major political focus in this tradition involves shared power over knowledge issues. The research, therefore, is "from" and "with," rather than "on," and has full participation by those affected by the research process. Participants' knowledge is valued and developed, it uses skills appropriated from dominant groups, and it is then transformed to serve the interests of the larger community (Gaventa, 1991; Park, 1993).

Such agendas are present in other practitioner research traditions, albeit in different forms. For example, an emancipatory agenda often framed by critical social theory is advocated in Australian participatory-action research (Atweh, Kemmis & Weeks, 1998; Carr, & Kemmis, 1986; McTaggart, 1997). The British teacher research tradition has a strong political agenda to shape and retain control over the profession (e.g., Elliott, 1991). Finally, as noted earlier, some efforts in both the self-study and the research traditions within North American teacher research focus on classroom change and embody a pedagogy explicitly tied to developing more humane and just teaching.

Several practitioner research projects have directly addressed issues of gender and schooling. Some projects have been foundation-funded or university-based efforts (Chisholm & Holland, 1986; Johnston & Proudford, 1994; Kelly, 1984; Lock & Minarik, 1997; Tiess in Gitlin et al., 1992; Whyte, 1986) that link teachers and researchers in efforts to uncover and address gender differences in student success. Others have sought ways to understand and change practices that promote racism in education (Donald, Gosling, Hamilton, Hawkes, McKenzie, & Stronach, 1995; Krater, Zeni, & Cason, 1994; Lyman, 1996) or ways to help their pupils understand and challenge social class inequalities (Sylvester, 1994). Some practitioner researchers have focused on teachers' growing awareness of racial identity and of the important role their understanding of culture plays in learning (Cochran-Smith, 1995; McIntyre, 1997; Miller, 1996; Murphy, 1991). Still others have taken on work aimed at creating more inclusive schools (Taylor & Parmar, 1993). This growing literature is still a small part of practitioner research reports, yet it bears much promise for creating educational practices that will make students' experiences in schools more just and equitable.

Open debate about the political agenda question in practitioner research has been limited, at least in public arenas. Whatever forums for discussion of issues of politics in practitioner research emerge, teachers' personal commitment to the children in their classrooms represents a version of the political located in the private, rather than public, sphere. Although much has been written in the academic literature on the tensions between personal and social aims in practitioner research (e.g., Weiner, 1989; Zeichner, 1993), commentators on practitioner research often have not sought to reconcile the tensions between calls for social action beyond the classroom and what many practitioners see as the site of their struggle in the classroom (Griffiths & Davies, 1993). It may be, for example, that the individual nature of some forms of practitioner research, and the frequent focus on individual children or on children as individuals, may help frame research politically in ways similar to other kinds of political movements in the public sphere beyond the classroom.

Melanie Walker (1995), writing about the potential of action

research efforts for both personal development and collective political struggle in the new South Africa, asks fundamental questions important to the overall issue of purposes in practitioner research:

> Finally, then, under new conditions of possibility we must still contest the purposes of action research: Whose problems do we try to understand? Who speaks to and for whom? Who writes and who is written? Who, in the end, benefits? (p. 25)

Although the individual, classroom-focused nature of much practitioner research is necessary for social transformation, it may not be sufficient. Collaborations may be needed that provide individual teacher researchers with potentially greater leverage to challenge institutional and social structures (e.g., Hursh, 1995, 1997).

Practitioner researchers need to explore any types of resources and supports. For example, much of the recent work on critical race theory (e.g., Ladson-Billings & Tate, 1995) could be very useful to practitioner research groups. Also, the emerging community emphasis in some recent teacher research in North America (Banford et al., 1996; Burch & Palanki, 1993; Shockley, Michalove, & Allen, 1995) and the work in the participatory research tradition of practitioner research may be useful in exploring social justice issues more collectively. New ways to communicate about research are still very much needed—ones that recognize and value multiple ways of knowing and forms of theorizing and that assume all educational work, whether in classrooms or university research centers is a form of practice with political implications.

Vision and Voice: The Nature of Practitioner Research

> Last year, I noticed that the children in my class were creating groups segregated by gender, and I wrote about it in my journal as I wrote about other issues and events. What I did *not* do last year was to start out by saying, "I'm going to study gender issues in my classroom," and to limit my observations and notes to that (Strieb, in Threatt et al., 1994, p. 237).
>
> I am struck by how hard it is to talk about teacher research apart from the students we teach. This is what makes the teacher part of teacher research so important and also what makes it so hard to figure out how to deal with the big questions of time, support, purposes, and audiences for this work. (Buchanan, in Threatt et al., 1994, p. 237)

These comments by teachers about their work as researchers give small insights into what it is like to do practitioner research. Questions about the research areas addressed, the methods used to gather and analyze perspectives on practice, the forms and spheres of communication used to share research, and the kinds of claims made on the basis of research need an exhaustive review far beyond the scope of this chapter, especially given the range of traditions and the varied purposes for engaging in the work. Asking questions about the nature of practitioner research is like asking similar questions about other branches of the methodological families of education research. The topics, the procedures for data collection and analysis, and the forms of communicating the research are wide-ranging.

Beginning with the early work of Corey (1953) in the United

States, the nature of action research has been tied to its search for legitimacy in the academic world. Initially conceived as a cyclical process, the research gradually became seen as a more linear, problem-solving, or learning process. Yet even during that era, there were signs that the methods of data collection and analysis were expanding to meet the demands of the kinds of questions that practitioners were interested in studying (Foshay et al., 1954). The inability of accepted research techniques to address the questions most directly tied to practice may have contributed to the decline in action research in the United States noted earlier. Despite this decline, many reports of collaborative action research presented in the Corey and Foshay volumes use a relatively high degree of narrative and first person voice.

By the time the British teacher research movement emerged, great changes were under way in academic educational research. New forms of inquiry, primarily qualitative, were constructing new boundaries for research acceptability (Carr, 1995). The growing acceptance of a search for meaning and for individual cases, rather than for predictability and control, as well as the growth in classroom-based research by academics, may have created a context more conducive to developing new research techniques and forms of communication. Although not excluding surveys and questionnaires as sources of data, practitioner researchers used examples of children's work, teachers' journals, transcripts of class sessions, and classroom photos. These new sources of information were chosen to respond directly to teachers' concerns. Also evident in the publications of the Collaborative Action Research Network and the more recent volumes of *Educational Action Research* is a mixture of project reports, essays, conference talks, and articles examining aspects of the development of the field itself (e.g., Edwards & Rideout, 1991; O'Hanlon, 1991). In those publications, the growth of new forms of research (e.g., Griffiths, 1994) and an expanding international voice are evident. *Educational Action Research* displays a clear ecumenicism in the inclusion of examples from a broad range of practitioner research traditions. In addition, examples in the literature come from higher education, health-related occupations, and other contexts beyond P–12 education.

In Australia as well, the literature includes compilations of historical documents related to the development of the field in a variety of contexts (Kemmis & McTaggart, 1988b), works documenting specific projects (e.g., Bunbury, Hastings, Henry, & McTaggart, 1991), and works showing a growing connection to international projects (e.g., McTaggart, 1997). In the latter works, there has been a turn to identifying the projects as "participatory action research," thus showing a strong affiliation with the participatory research tradition. As in the United Kingdom, the research techniques suggested in the Australian literature reflect a predominance of qualitative data gathering methods. In contrast to much British and North American work, the Australian literature places a greater emphasis on critical collaborative reflection as the primary means of data analysis, closely following a suggested framework for sociopolitical analysis (Kemmis & McTaggart, 1988a). Taken together, the works originating in the United Kingdom and Australia contribute strongly to a widely based discussion of purposes and processes in practitioner research. However, as clearly as the literature on these forms of practitioner research lays out a cyclical process of problem identification, planning, observation, action, and reflection, it may not adequately describe how practitioner researchers actually engage in the process (Elliott, 1991). For example, research topics often emerge over time and are refined and redirected as the process takes place, often in response to the context of the practice, thereby resulting in a messier process than the various conceptual models suggest (Burnaford, Fischer, & Hobson, 1996).

Although reports by practitioners outside North America were difficult for us to access, we can note that in the United Kingdom and Australia attempts have been made to include both conceptual and empirical studies in the same publications. This trend is also evident in several North American publications (e.g., Anderson et al., 1994; Carson & Sumara, 1997; Cochran-Smith & Lytle, 1993; Goswami & Stillman, 1987; Hollingsworth, 1997; Noffke & Stevenson, 1995; Wells, 1993).

In some parts of the North American tradition of teacher research, considerable efforts have been made to generate research techniques that, although modeled on qualitative methods, attempt to respond more directly to the needs of practitioners in classrooms. Many issues of the journal *Teacher Research,* for example, include discussions of particular techniques, and practitioner research handbooks contain detailed descriptions of research methods adapted for classroom use (e.g., Anderson et al., 1994; Hubbard & Power, 1993).

Although methodological issues are salient in the works, even more prominent is the subject matter of the research. As in the earlier Ford Project in the United Kingdom, pedagogical and curricular innovations best characterize much of the work. North American work often focuses on innovations in literacy education or on inquiry-oriented approaches to teaching in different subject areas. Perhaps because of this focus on specific intended changes in individual classroom practices, academic social theory seems to play a much smaller role in analysis here than in other traditions.

Practitioner research has been related to academic educational research and theory in several ways. For example, Troen et al. (1997) describe three patterns that emerged in their analysis of teacher researchers' work in collaborative inquiry seminars in Brookline and Boston, Massachusetts. Teacher researchers in one group began their work by consulting the academic educational research literature and used concepts and ideas from this work in their research plans.

> Teachers in this group found that the ideas that they encountered in books and journal articles resonated with their intuitions about students' and teachers' intellectual lives. The ideas seemed to explain some of the puzzles the teachers had been wrestling with regarding children's approaches to learning and performance on certain classroom tasks. It gave them a language for talking about something they had seen. The teachers suspected the ideas, now articulated and named, had powerful implications for their design of curriculum and their teaching practices. (Troen et al., p. 22)

A second group of teacher researchers began answering their research questions by working in their classrooms and systematically collecting data and reflecting on it. Those teachers deliberately avoided consulting the academic literature at the onset, because they wanted to listen to and learn from their students and to think about what it meant before connecting their research to the work of academic researchers.

> Their strategy was to collect their data and to do a preliminary analysis of it before consulting the research literature. They approached the research literature with findings in hand, looking for corroborating evidence and language to use in discussing their work. (Troen et al., 1997, p. 22)

A third group of teacher researchers focused their work in the classroom and school almost exclusively and selected their teaching colleagues as the audience for their work. Those teachers deliberately bypassed the academic educational research literature because they felt no need to connect with it.

> More often than not, they found it unhelpful and even demeaning and offensive, as much because of the style in which it is written as because of what it had to say. (Troen et al., 1997, p. 22)

Generally, little interaction has occurred between the teacher and academic research literatures in North America (Zeichner, 1995b), although the three patterns noted in the Massachusetts teacher research groups have been described elsewhere (e.g., Fischer, 1996). It is more likely that one can find teacher researchers citing academic research in their work than that one will find academic researchers citing teacher research. This pattern is beginning to change, however, as more teacher research is finding its way into journals and books.

The self-study research tradition in many cases shares with the North American teacher research tradition an individual focus. There are, however, several differences. Perhaps because of their greater proximity to academic debates about research methodology, some self-study researchers emphasize research techniques less and personal-autobiographical methods more. Because of the position of many self-study researchers as both teachers and teacher educators, the examination of their practice often raises issues related to university structures (Adler, 1993). Frequently, those practitioners problematize their own assumptions, as well as the potential for the imposition of their beliefs on preservice teachers (e.g., Ahlquist, 1991; Gore & Zeichner, 1991; Macgillivray, 1997; Zeichner, 1995a).

As noted earlier, participatory research often involves the development of research strategies by the participants themselves. Those strategies include developing ways to gather specific information and finding means to communicate the research that fit the particular context in which the research has been carried out. In some works, the reporting takes forms such as songs, poetry, festivals, drama, and storytelling to communicate the research to those inside the situation. Although written and published texts are sometimes produced in the participatory research tradition (e.g., Hinsdale et al., 1995), those texts are not always the primary focus. Rather, social transformation is the central concern in much participatory research, and the results are reported in forms other than the typical academic report. In most cases, the focus and processes of the research are developed collaboratively by all participants. In a few cases, the research resembles other forms of academic qualitative research, probably a reflection of the researcher's need to negotiate the study in relation to academic requirements (e.g., McIntyre, 1997).

This brief overview was intended to sketch out some of the ways in which practitioner research varies both within and across traditions. In the next two subsections, we attempt to let practitioners' voices form the basis of the description, along with comments by others who have noted patterns in the literature. Although we touch on several traditions, we focus primarily on the teacher research movement in North America. Here, it is important to remember the earlier characterization of practitioner research as a fugitive literature. This characteristic of the research may benefit practitioner researchers, because the external imposition of forms and standards of quality (addressed in the fourth part of the chapter) may be less likely to occur and the sources for further clarification remain close by. For the purposes of this chapter, however, this characteristic is presented as a point of tension.

Although more places have been created for practitioners to share their work, and both of us have collected practitioner reports not published in academic sources and have sought out those collected by others, practitioners have done much work that is not widely available beyond local sites. In addition, (see Cochran-Smith & Lytle's 1993, typology), some research is produced in forms that cannot be easily circulated. Many practitioner researchers strongly feel that the central focus of their studies lies in the practice within classrooms and communities and in the production of alternative forms of communication rather than in the creation of documents for publication. We hope this more in-depth look at the voices from one tradition will enable subsequent analyses to expand to works from other places and traditions, thus adding new dimensions to our understanding of practitioner research.

Closely Watched Children

From the earliest work on practitioner research, a strong emphasis has been placed on the valuable insights to be gained through the careful observation of classroom practice by those most "inside" it. Much work of the Ford Teaching Project in the United Kingdom in the 1970s, for example, involved teachers analyzing transcripts and photos of their classes to understand how students actually worked through attempted curricular innovations (Elliott & Adelman, 1973). Cochran-Smith and Lytle (1993) highlight the strong classroom focus in much of the teacher research work in North America, including a focus on individual children's learning, single class experiences, children's conceptual development and relationships, and documentation of long-term reflections on teaching and learning. A collection edited by Wells (1993) also focuses on efforts to examine in detail the process of working through an inquiry approach to teaching and learning. The progressive nature of many of the changes in practices being studied is fairly consistent. Many studies address pedagogical innovations connected to a developmental approach to curriculum (Kliebard, 1995) and framed in a version of current constructivist theory (Richardson, 1997).

This link to developmental and constructivist academic theories might lead one to conclude that practitioner research frequently consists of studying the implementation of academic reformers' ideas. Indeed, many reports, although carefully detailing the many pitfalls of a particular approach, seem not to critique fundamental assumptions. However, as Tomlinson (in Threat et al., 1994) notes:

> For many years I studied and thought about how students learn. Over time, I gave very little thought to the perceptions the students had about their own learning. What I have learned from the teacher research I have been a part of has created much pain for me. Through interviews with students eligible for special education services, I have gained new insights into their feelings about themselves and the message the process of special education has sent. (p. 235)

For many researchers, such clear struggle with the contradictions in their practice has its roots not in the academic literature alone, but in the confrontation with the evidence elicited through careful attention to students.

As evident in Brankis's (1996) report of research, important differences exist between practitioner research and traditional research development dissemination models:

> At first I felt compelled to read everything that was even remotely related to the topic of using journals in a classroom. However, after some experience, I became more selfish and discriminating. I was drawn to those pieces of research that were done by teachers. There was such a personal element to their writings. Their investment in searching to make a difference for their students was so inspiring. I found a camaraderie with those authors. Those researchers have a story to tell. Their motivation to change their teaching and involve students intimately in the learning process was evident. (pp. 20–21)

What is evident here is that the sharing of practitioner research serves a function perhaps quite different from that of academic writing. It supports classroom practice directly through the substantive detail of the work and the development of supportive networks. Academic reports can be seen to support practice, but in different ways. First, the practice supported is the process of research and not necessarily teaching. Second, although the intention is often to influence classroom practice, the practitioner is not the primary audience. In contrast, the sense of fellow practitioners as audience is carried through much of the practitioner research literature.

Also common in reports of practitioner research is the use of details of classroom conversations (Maher, 1993; Gallas, 1998) and students' work as sources for analysis (e.g., Brankis, 1996; Gallas, 1994). In many cases, much space is devoted to the presentation of excerpts from classroom life with less, but often still significant, attention to critique or connections to academic theory and research. This practice may be a function of the intended audience—the community of other practitioner researchers, as well as the focus on the rich understanding of the participants in practice.

Many handbooks for practitioner research (e.g., Altrichter, Posch, & Somekh, 1993; Anderson et al., 1994) present fairly standard methods of qualitative data collection, including ways to record and collect classroom events and artifacts. However, they include caveats about the need to adapt the strategies to fit into the routines of everyday practice. Hubbard and Power (1993), for example, present clear methods for data collection and analysis as well as ways to connect with "distant teachers"—the writings of others who have wondered about similar things. Many practitioner-research accounts share details about data (e.g., Hammatt-Kavaloski, 1996; Hindley, 1996), whereas others make connections to the academic literature (e.g., Brankis, 1996).

In a recent volume of *Teaching and Change,* Kochendorfer (1997) analyzed the 73 reports of practitioner research that the journal had published. He classified the studies in terms of "what it was the investigators wanted from their research" (p. 157). In many cases, studies sought a "quantifiable answer," wanted to determine the "effects of change," or formulated yes-no research questions about the use of particular instructional strategies (p. 158). More than half the reports were of that form, which serves as a good reminder that some practitioner research mirrors traditional process-product research and uses quantitative rather than qualitative methods.

The nature of practitioner research varies not only across but also within traditions. The process-product research orientation frequently found in some North American works contrasts directly with the more personal and narrative style found in others. In the United Kingdom, the works presented in the Collaborative Action Research Network publications frequently have a very different tone and focus from those in the Bath area. Articles presented in *Educational Action Research* represent a broad range of practices from different fields and countries and show a mixture of narrative, commentary, and methodological discussions. The influence of a particular university or a particular funded project, such as those of the National Writing Project, may play a major role in the nature of the work that is done (Kennedy, 1996). As much as practitioner research may draw on or resemble academic research in its written form, the relationship between the two groups of researchers is sometimes unclear. As Threatt notes:

> Despite my excitement at having other people to talk with, people with unique perspectives and interesting and sometimes valuable information, in some ways, at this point, those relationships seem to me to have a colonial flavor to them. The more friendly and equanimous the relationship, the harder it is for me to explain that feeling and perspective. . . . But it seems to me that someone else is having the discussion we need to have for ourselves and that someone else benefits in an economy that rewards their making sense of our work. (Threatt, et. al., 1994, pp. 231–232)

Although the focus on practice and improving the lives of those in schools is a very salient aspect of practitioner research, this form of research raises questions of voice much in need of addressing.

Who Gets to Tell the Story?

As with the participatory research tradition, the authorship of the story of practice is a major issue in the teacher research tradition in North America. As noted earlier, much practitioner research appears as individual narratives (Gallas, 1994), collective stories of practice (e.g., Marsella, Hussey, Emoto, Kaupp, Lee, Soares, Takushi, & Ushijima, 1994), essays (e.g., Turchi, 1996), or oral inquiries (Anderson, Butts, Lett, Mansdoerfer, & Raisch, 1995). (See Cochran-Smith & Lytle's 1993 typology.) Such reports have several different functions. For example, they allow various audiences to hear teachers' stories. In this sense, they might be seen as teacher narrative studies (Neumann & Peterson, 1997; Thomas, 1995), which use the forms and stan-

dards of that genre. Yet one could argue that those pieces, written perhaps out of a strong sense of growing identity as a practitioner researcher, are qualitatively different. Vida Schaffel
(1996) describes the way she "rethinks" her practice through
her research, as follows:

> Without learning there can be no growth, and without growth there
> can be no change. This holds true for both the student and the
> teacher. I see myself more now as a facilitator rather than as the
> purveyor of knowledge. I am constantly collecting data in my class-
> room while I analyze my own teaching and learning. I view children
> in a more holistic and developmental way than I did previously. I
> am more conscious of "process" and see "product" as being multi-
> dimensional and multifaceted. I am not the same as I was before.
> (p. 30)

The conscious recounting of change in practice and the self-
reflection on her role as educator can be seen as signs that the
intended audience for such narratives may be a significant factor in why such narratives differ from others in the qualitative
research literature.

A recent issue of *Teacher Research* (Power & Hubbard, 1995)
explores this topic of audiences. Although much practitioner
research focuses on other teachers as the audience, other aspects are identified. First, teaching narratives need to be seen
against the backdrop of years of course work in preparation for
teaching that included "research that didn't speak to real stories
of classroom life" (p. iii). As is still the case in much teacher
education, this audience of teachers has been largely ignored
by academic educational research (Zeichner, 1995b). Second,
and perhaps similar to other narratives, some of the reports
seem to deliberately attempt to give the audience insights into
the more difficult aspects of educational change, thereby almost
conveying a message of shared struggle and risk taking.

> Change is not easy. It is lonely being a majority of one and it is hard
> working against the grain. The need to connect with other educators
> is essential for me. . . . It is difficult not to do what I believe; for to
> do otherwise, I would not be true to myself. (Schaffel, 1996, p. 31)

The personal narrative in this sense may be seen as an attempt
to form a collective identity and a sense of shared struggle. Yet
the telling of the story by the author may have the additional
function of developing a strong sense of identity with that practice. As in participatory research, the description is affirming
and potentially makes the critiquing and building of collectivities more possible.

Practitioner research reports, whether narratives, plays, oral
inquiries, poems, or the many other forms of representation
emerging in the literature, might be compared usefully to testimony. As in the work of Menchu (1983), there can be a direct
connection between the recounting of stories of experience and
the struggle for empowerment. As Benmayor (1991) notes:
"'Testimonial' speech acts help foster strong peer identification,
bonding, and a sense of collective" (pp. 161–162). In the literature on participatory research, as well as in the Lewinian
tradition of action research, this aspect to sharing one's work is
very important. Arguably, the reports of practitioner research
taken together represent the struggle for a "pedagogy of hope"
(Freire, 1992).

The breadth of the social vision that sustains practitioner
research is sometimes unclear. Whereas some works seem to
speak to individual practitioners involved in similar work, others appear to work toward more collaborative actions (e.g., Gitlin et al., 1992; Wagler, 1996). In the later works, the enhancement of professional practice is integrally tied to structural
changes in the work of teaching (Lawn, 1989). Some, but by
no means all, appear to embody social critique. As Gitlin and
Thompson (1995) have noted, though, the meaning of politics
varies considerably, even in those versions of practitioner research that accept it as a major goal.

As with academic research, it remains to be seen whether
the various versions of practitioner research will recognize and
critique the affiliative power that they gain through participation in their research communities. For example, as Labaree
(1992) outlined in his work on the professionalization of teaching, the enhancement of the authority of teachers through
means such as forming practitioner research groups could increase the isolation of teachers from the communities they seek
to serve. (See also Zeichner, 1991.) A major question for all
forms of practitioner research is whether researchers will continue to find ways to address the unexamined assumptions and
tacit beliefs the different research traditions embody. The articulation of such a process of self-critique may begin to form a
core of ideas around which an understanding of trustworthiness
in practitioner research may be developed.

Practitioner Research as a Trustworthy Way of Knowing

> I don't think we've done enough work in explicating or validating
> the ways in which we teachers already inquire and make sense in
> our classrooms or the ways in which we already communicate what
> we know. I do not happen to agree that we are a "less theoretical"
> group. Our "theoretical discussion" is carried out differently, more
> embedded in material from the contexts in which we work, in de-
> scriptions of the classroom dynamic, in what we do and say.
> (Threatt, in Threatt et al., 1994, 232–233)

In the decade since the last *Handbook of Research on* Teaching
was published, the area of what is usually called *validity* has
been greatly contested in educational research. Clearly, much
of this current incarnation of the handbook is devoted to emergent debates in this area. For practitioner research, the current
research context offers much in the way of intellectual resources
for thinking about the issue of quality in practitioner research.
We have chosen the term *trustworthiness* as an alternative to the
term *validity* for its invocation of knowledge in relational terms.
As Lincoln (1995) argues:

> Just as the naturalistic/constructivist paradigm effectively brought
> about the irrelevance of the distinction between ontology and epis-
> temology, so too does this paradigm and interpretive social science
> in general bring about the collapse of the distinction between stan-
> dards, rigor, and quality criteria and the formerly separate consider-
> ation of research ethics. In effect, many of the proposed and emerg-
> ing standards for quality in interpretive social science are also
> standards for ethics. (pp. 286–287)

For us, the idea of trustworthiness better captures the need
for practitioner research to justify its claims to know in terms

of the relationships among knowers and knowledges. We agree with Fenstermacher (1994), who argues that the claim to have generated knowledge through practitioner research does not relieve us of the obligation to show the justification or warrant for our claims. Uncritical acceptance of all knowledge that is generated through practitioner inquiry without any attention to research quality will serve only to undermine the acceptance of practitioner research as a legitimate form of knowledge generation in education. The comments in this section are directed to practitioner inquiry where researchers have chosen to make their research public so that others may benefit from it. When practitioner researchers choose to make their inquiries available to others, their work becomes a potential source of knowledge (a) for other researchers and practitioners, (b) for the curriculum of teacher education and professional development programs, and (c) for educational policymakers. We recognize that some practitioners choose to engage in research primarily as a professional development activity and do not wish to make their work public. The following discussion about research quality is not intended to apply to those cases.

When practitioner inquiry is conducted in a P–12 school context, it seems to us that P–12 educators should be the ones who have the most to say about the criteria and procedures that are used to determine the quality of practitioner research studies. Much practitioner research, however, is conducted within the context of award-bearing courses and degree programs in colleges and universities, a situation that necessarily involves academics in assessing the quality of practitioner research. In this chapter, we generally support a situation in which a democratic negotiation of both the criteria and procedures is used to determine research quality and to broaden the way in which the academy thinks about the issue of research quality, including ways of addressing trustworthiness that originate outside the boundaries of conventional academic educational research.

Practitioner research is always deeply contextual. Its claims on truth are integrally related to its realization in practice. For many practitioner researchers, the justification of their labor is as much in the lives of those who practice as it is in its acceptance by those outside the situation. We have chosen to present this portion of the chapter in sections that reflect the juxtaposition of knowledge communities that have an impact on the understanding of practitioner research as a trustworthy way of knowing. In the first section, we frame important trends in the understanding of issues of validity and trustworthiness in academic research against the backdrop of the historical struggle of practitioner research for acceptance as a legitimate way of knowing. In this way, potential resources from academic educational research for thinking about issues of quality in practitioner research are identified and assessed. The second section traces developments in the exploration of those issues within the practitioner research literature itself.

The question of trustworthiness in practitioner research is not a straightforward one. As will be seen, it matters by whom and if criteria are to be developed or allowed to emerge. As was discussed in the earlier description of the uses of data in participatory research, this process, to many practitioner researchers, is one that is fundamentally grassroots and collective in nature. Academic theory and frames can be useful (see Walker, 1995), but they must also be seen in terms of their potential for colonization (Carr, 1995). The section ends with some tentative conclusions that are about issues of quality in practitioner research and that are based on our analysis of the literature and the tremendous diversity of motivations, along with research forms within the practitioner research umbrella.

Academic Sources for Thinking About Issues of Quality in Practitioner Research

> The quality of fundamental research and the quality of action research are judged by different criteria. The value of the former is determined by the amount of dependable knowledge it adds to that already recorded and available to any people who want to familiarize themselves with it. Conversely, the value of action research is determined primarily by the extent to which findings lead to improvement of the practices of the people engaged in the research. (Corey, 1953, p.13)

Stephen Corey, one of the leaders in the cooperative action research movement in the United States in the 1950s, spent a lot of time trying to legitimate action research within the academic community by developing alternative versions of standards of validity (e.g., vertical instead of horizontal generalization). He argued that those standards were more appropriate to the different purposes of action research. As the paper by Hodgkinson (1957) discussed earlier indicates, Corey and others were not very successful in convincing the educational research community in the United States of their point of view. Researchers continued to judge the quality of action research as inferior research by the prevailing positivistic view "that research should be modeled on the natural sciences, using quantitative methods in controlled experiments whose ultimate aim was to establish broad generalizations" (Wallace, 1987, p. 101). For the most part, there was acceptance of practitioner research as a professional development activity of benefit to its participants, but not as a knowledge production activity that could be of benefit to others. Despite pressures to evaluate the quality of the research by positivist criteria, there was also some ambiguity among mainstream educational researchers about the grounds for placing confidence in an action research study:

> Are we to judge according to how much the teachers change, how much the pupils change, how classroom practice is altered, or how good the statistics are? Ordinarily in true research, validity and reliability can be used, but the reports never seem to mention how valid or reliable an action research study was. What are the grounds for placing confidence in action research? (Hodgkinson, 1957, p.78)

Before the emergence of qualitative forms of research in education on a wide scale, the standards of internal and external validity outlined by Campbell & Stanley (1963) served as nearly universal benchmarks to assess the worth of a piece of educational research. Internal validity refers to the credibility of inferences that experimental treatments cause effects under certain well-defined circumstances. External validity refers to generalizing the effects observed under experimental conditions to other populations and contexts.

When educational research entered the so-called postpositivist era and when alternative forms of qualitative and critical inquiries began to gain acceptance within the educational research community, much attention was focused on reconceptualizing the notion of validity and on finding ways to establish the trustworthiness of inquiries for those alternative research methodologies. Very little of this discussion, however (see Carr & Kemmis, 1986; Watkins, 1991; Whitehead, 1989; Winter, 1987, for exceptions), included practitioner research. There were several responses to the task of developing standards to assess the worth of alternative paradigm research. One response exemplified by the work of Denzin (1989) was to show how different research paradigms (or, as he called them, "methodologies") were able to minimize the threats to internal and external validity that had been outlined by Campbell and Stanley (1963) . He showed that each design (e.g., survey, participant observation) has different strengths and weaknesses with respect to minimizing the threats to validity.

A similar tact was taken by Goetz and LeCompte (1984), who developed analogs for conventional types of internal and external validity and for construct validity, which they argued were more appropriate for ethnographic research. They added a set of global criteria for determining a study's validity, such as clarity—the degree to which it is easy to figure out what the study is about and why it was designed in the way it is—and credibility—the degree to which the results are believable. Denzin as well as Goetz and LeCompte focused on adapting conventional notions of validity to encompass alternative research paradigms but did not break away from them completely.

A somewhat more radical position about establishing the validity of educational research was taken by Erickson (1986) and Lincoln and Guba (1985). As Eisenhart and Howe (1992) point out, the work of Erickson, Lincoln, and Guba reflects a deep skepticism (in the case of Erickson) and an outright rejection (in the case of Lincoln and Guba) that conventional notions of validity can be applied to alternative paradigm research that falls outside the bounds of positivist experimental designs. Erickson's (1986) ideas about validity place a lot of emphasis on the way the story is told and the quality of the evidence that is provided for its authenticity. Erickson adds another dimension of validity that is concerned with meeting criteria of quality (e.g., clear, appropriate, useful) with regard to different audiences, including teachers.

Lincoln and Guba (1985) take a more radical turn than Erickson; they advocate for the development of an entirely different set of standards by which to judge the quality of "naturalistic research." In fact, they propose that, because of the different ontological and epistemological basis of naturalistic research, the term *validity* should be abandoned altogether and the term *trustworthiness* substituted instead. Lincoln and Guba (1985) define trustworthiness as follows:

> The basic issue in relation to trustworthiness is simple: How can an inquirer persuade his or her audiences (including self) that the findings of an inquiry are worth paying attention to, worth taking account of? What arguments can be mounted, what criteria invoked, what questions asked, that would be persuasive on this issue? (p. 290)

Lincoln and Guba (1985) go on to propose various standards of trustworthiness that they feel are appropriate for naturalistic inquiry. For example, in relation to the criterion of truth value,

they argue that the main issue is being able to show that the researchers' interpretations of data are credible to those who provided the data. They provide an alternative to a conventional view of external validity, similar to what Stake (1995) has termed *naturalistic generalization.* They argue that the establishment of external validity in naturalistic inquiry is an empirical matter to be largely determined by those who wish to apply the findings of research to other settings. The potential users of research must determine for themselves whether their own contexts are sufficiently similar to the context of the research to make the transfer of results possible and reasonable. Despite the break from the conventional standards of Campbell and Stanley by Lincoln and Guba (1985), their emphasis on the researcher not influencing or manipulating the conditions in the research to any great extent limits the usefulness of their ideas for establishing the trustworthiness of practitioner inquiry where such interventions are at the very heart of the research process.

Another response to reconceptualizing the idea of validity in the postpositivist era of educational research has been to propose a set of general standards that cut across all forms of educational research. This approach is taken by Eisenhart and Howe (1992) and by Eisenhart and Borko (1993), who define all research studies as arguments open to public scrutiny and debate.

> The validity of educational research, regardless of the specific design used, can be determined by how carefully the study is designed, conducted, and presented; how sensitively it treats human subjects; and how well it contributes to important educational issues, including debates about educational theory and practice. (p. 93)

Eisenhart and her colleagues go on to elaborate a set of five general standards for determining the validity of educational research. They argue that these five standards set broad boundaries within which to determine the validity of research using different methodologies, and the standards do not determine the specific strategies and techniques for researchers to use within the different methodologies. Instead, they recognize the need for developing design-specific standards that are subsumed by the five general standards and that articulate the different kinds of knowledge, technical skills, evidence, and so forth required in the different research forms.

First is the issue of the fit between research questions, data collection procedures, and analysis techniques. Here the concern is that the data collection and analysis techniques be suitable for answering the research questions posed and that the research questions should drive the data collection and not vice versa.

> Research studies qua arguments have questionable validity when methodological preferences or matters of convenience, rather than research questions, drive the study design. Validity requires cogently developed designs. (Eisenhart & Howe, 1992, p. 658)

The second standard states that the data collection and analysis techniques used must be competently applied in "a more-or-less" technical sense. Here there is reference to the various guidelines that have been developed on how research instruments should be designed, how sampling should be done and interviews conducted, and so forth. Eisenhart and Howe (1992) argue that

> It is incumbent on educational researchers who wish to demonstrate that their techniques have been competently applied, to locate their work in the historical, disciplinary, or traditional contexts in which the methods have been developed. (p. 659)

The third proposed standard states that educational research studies must be judged against a background of existing theoretical, substantive, or explicit practical knowledge. According to this standard, for research to be considered valid, it must be built on some theoretical tradition or it must contribute to some substantive or practical area. This standard calls for researchers to make explicit their own personal interpretations, a stance that directly contradicts the call for researcher neutrality in positivist and some new paradigm research such as "naturalistic inquiry."

The fourth standard proposed by Eisenhart and Howe (1992) concerns both external and internal value constraints. Initially, with regard to external value (whether the study is worthwhile), the researcher must show how the research is important for informing and improving educational practice. They argue that, although research may be well designed and conducted in a technical sense, this criterion alone is insufficient. To be considered worthwhile, a study must deal with important issues and problems that arise for practitioners, and it should be accessible to the general education community. This approach means that the research must be communicated in ways that are understandable to and debatable by various audiences. With regard to internal value constraints or research ethics, Eisenhart and Howe state that the ethical dimensions of how the researcher interacts with the other participants are crucial for establishing the credibility of research studies. They refer to such elements of human subjects protection as confidentiality, privacy, and truth telling.

The fifth and final standard, comprehensiveness, brings together the first four standards in a holistic way and refers to three things: (a) having the overall clarity, coherence, and competence of the research; (b) balancing the overall technical quality of the research with the risks to participants, and (c) being alert to and able to use knowledge from outside a particular perspective and tradition in which one is working as well as to consider various explanations for what is discovered in a study.

These five standards for determining the validity of educational research are proposed as a unitary construct that must be considered together. Eisenhart and Howe (1992) state that the standards have been formulated in a way that can encompass—without undue constraint—the specific standards and norms of particular research designs. The implications of this work for determining validity in practitioner research have yet to be explored. To do so would require taking each of the five standards and developing their meaning with reference to the paradigm of practitioner research. That task is complicated by the existence of the five different traditions of practitioner research described earlier, by varying motivations for conducting practitioner research, and by the diverse research forms

within this genre. It seems unlikely to us that one broad set of discipline-specific standards within these five general standards could be developed to encompass all of the different traditions, forms, and motivations. None of what is discussed by Eisenhart and her colleagues addresses the specific situation of researchers studying their own practice or the case of openly ideological research that seeks to promote greater social justice.

VALIDITY AND ADVOCACY

Other radical breaks from conventional notions of research validity can be found in the feminist and critical-emancipatory work of Roman (1989), Roman and Apple (1990), and Lather (1991). Those works come close to addressing the issue of the trustworthiness of some aspects of practitioner research, although the thrust of this work is on altering power relations and encouraging research that promotes greater social justice from the perspective of academic researchers. Their work does not explicitly acknowledge practitioners as producers of their own knowledge on their own. Neither Lather nor Roman link their proposals to the tradition of participatory research, which, among all of the traditions of practitioner research, comes closest to their proposals.

Both Lather and Roman question the ways that conventional academic research perpetuates and reinforces power relations in the wider society. They call for a democratization of the research process, where decisions about (a) what to study, (b) how to study it, and (c) what the relations are between researchers and other participants must be worked out with greater respect for the voices and interests of all participants. Adoption of their proposals would result in an ethical standard for judging the quality of educational research, in part, according to the processes used in doing the research. Lather (1986) calls for an interactive and dialogic research process where meanings are negotiated, a process very similar to what is advocated in the tradition of participatory research.

Both Roman and Lather criticize the call for researcher neutrality that was commonly advocated in the naturalistic research community, and they call for a more explicit political stance by educational researchers and for educational research that is more openly committed to building a more just social order. This view of research as praxis is very similar to the emancipatory intent in participatory research.

Lather (1986, 1991), in particular, gives a lot of attention to addressing issues of what she calls empirical accountability, the need to offer grounds for accepting or establishing the trustworthiness of a researcher's description and analysis. She argues that a lack of concern for data credibility in praxis-oriented research will serve to decrease the legitimacy of the knowledge generated and warns that, if we do not develop agreed-upon procedures for determining the credibility of this research, "our theory building will suffer from a failure to protect our work from our own passions and limitations" (p. 69).

Lather proposes systematic attention to triangulation and reflexivity as well as an emphasis on face validity and catalytic validity. With regard to the process issue of triangulation—a method for bringing different kinds of evidence into relation with one another so that they can be compared and contrasted—Lather proposes an expansion of the psychometric definition of multiple measures to include the criteria of multiple data sources, methods, and theoretical schemes-perspectives. The issue of triangulation is a standard of quality that has been a central part of the teacher-as-researcher work in Britain (e.g., Elliott, 1991) and is usually discussed as an important feature of practitioner research in most practitioner research methodology books (e.g., Altrichter et al., 1993). It has also been a standard of validity that has been frequently identified for qualitative research (Erickson, 1986).

In her discussion of construct validity in educational research as praxis, Lather (1991) emphasizes the importance of a self-critical attitude on the part of researchers about how their own preconceptions are affecting the research. She calls for disclosure and self-scrutiny by the researcher of his or her own preconceptions as well as a respect for the "experiences of people in their daily lives to guard against theoretical imposition" (p. 67). Lather (1991) also discusses the importance of reconsidering the concept of face validity. In research as praxis, face validity is addressed by feeding the descriptions, the emerging interpretations, and the conclusions back to research participants and by refining those findings in light of the researchers' reactions.

Finally, given the emancipatory intent of praxis-oriented research, Lather (1991) proposes that the concept of catalytic validity be addressed. She defines catalytic validity as "the degree to which the research process reorients, focuses and energizes participants toward knowing reality in order to transform it" (p. 68). This aspect of validity proposed by Lather is highly similar to Freire's (1970) notion of conscientization (critical consciousness), and is another link between praxis-oriented research and the tradition of participatory research. Despite similarities between the praxis-oriented and emancipatory approach to educational research advocated by Roman and Lather and practitioner research, there is no discussion in their work of practitioners as producers of their own knowledge independent of professional academic researchers. Although Lather's proposals about establishing the credibility of research address research that is emancipatory in intent, not all practitioner research reflects this motivation. The situation of establishing the credibility of research, where practitioners produce knowledge about their own practices and the situations in which they practice, requires attention to the specific conditions of practitioner research.

Although efforts to establish criteria for the validity of qualitative or for praxis-oriented educational research do not explicitly address the situation of self-study, they do contribute to creating a climate within the educational research community that is more receptive to alternative forms of research that fall outside the dominant research paradigms. Because many of the emerging criteria for determining the quality of new paradigm research address the quality of relations among the participants in the research, this body of work (see also Altheide & Johnson, 1994; Altrichter, 1986; Erickson, 1989; Lather, 1993; Lincoln, 1995; Maxwell, 1992; Mishler, 1990; Reason & Rowan, 1981) has contributed to a situation where the boundaries between epistemological and ethical issues that are commonly experienced in discussions of positivist research are beginning to break down. The ethical dimensions of the research process are now commonly viewed as a central part of the process of determining the quality of a piece of research.

> New paradigm inquiry is not, and never will be, second-rate conventional inquiry. It is scientific inquiry that embraces a set of three new commitments: first to new and emergent relations with respondents; second to a set of stances—professional, personal and political—toward the uses of inquiry and toward its ability to foster action; and, finally, to a vision of research that enables and promotes social justice, community, diversity, civic discourse, and caring. (Lincoln, 1995, p. 277–278)

ISSUES OF QUALITY IN NARRATIVES

Another line of work that addresses issues of quality in educational research concerns narrative inquiry. Because of the prevalence of narrative inquiry in some forms of practitioner research, these discussions are relevant to the task of developing ways to assess the quality of practitioner research. Here, as in discussions of trustworthiness in qualitative research, there has been much debate between advocates and critics of narrative inquiry about what makes a good piece of research. Advocates of narrative inquiry, such as Connelly and Clandinin (1990), argue that we have to move beyond the epistemic warrants of reliability, validity, and generalizibility in the conventional sense to judge the worth of narratives and propose several alternative criteria including verisimilitude, plausibility, transferability, and the invitational quality of a study. (See also Polkinghorne, 1988.) Their work echoes Bruner (1986), who argued that good narrative leads to "good stories, believable though not necessarily true" (p. 13). Barone (1992) proposes accessibility, compellingness, and moral persuasiveness as criteria to determine the worth of educational stories. Finally, Van Manen (1990) focuses on the degree to which narrative descriptions are animating and evocative.

Phillips (1994) questions the sufficiency of using such criteria as these in determining the quality of research, and he argues that narrative researchers need to deal much more thoroughly with the issue of truth. He also argues that, because narratives often have important practical consequences (e.g., using them in the formulation of policy), they must be much more than accessible, compelling, and morally persuasive descriptions. Acknowledging Geertz's (1973) point that even a paranoid's delusion and a swindler's story sometimes have coherence and hang together, Phillips proposes what he sees as a number of epistemically relevant tests that could be applied to narrative inquiry to avoid problems of outright lying and self-delusion. In the end, Phillips is quite skeptical about the epistemical respectability of narrative as a knowledge-bearing or explanation-giving genre of research in education. He feels that pronarrative educational researchers often tend to have sociopolitical rather than epistemic grounds for their enthusiasm.

O'Dea (1994), while agreeing with Phillips that narrative researchers cannot afford to skirt the issue of truth, feels that Phillips's critique "somewhat misses the mark by holding up empirical quantitative truth and its attendant virtues, reliability, validity, and generalizibility as the hallmarks of epistemic respectability" (p. 162). She argues from the perspective of literary criticism that these criteria are simply not relevant to the purposes and nature of narrative research and proposes a notion of artistic truth grounded in the idea of authenticity, in being true to oneself. Here, there is the requirement that the researcher honestly take account of what actually occurs in a situation and that she or he also exercises existential freedom in questioning his or her adherence to norms, roles, and attitudes perpetuated by external society. This self-critical attitude is the same kind as that advocated by Lather (1986, 1991). While O'Dea's arguments are compelling and persuasive, she does not provide much guidance in helping us judge whether a narrative study is, in fact, authentic in the literary sense that she defines it.

Fenstermacher and Richardson (1994), in commenting on Phillips's (1994) position, make an important distinction among (a) the narrative itself (the outcome of the narrative method, written or spoken), (b) narrative inquiry (ways of constructing, remembering, or eliciting a story), and (c) narrative use (as devices to promote change in practice). They argue that such analytic distinctions help us to see the need for different forms of warrant with regard to narrative inquiry and to see that epistemic warrant is not always called for in reading or using stories. With regard to narrative as the product of narrative inquiry, Fenstermacher and Richardson believe that there are ways of judging the quality of narratives independent of epistemic warrant. They discuss several literary criteria such as believability and the power to convince or to evoke support—criteria similar to those proposed by advocates of narrative inquiry and discussed above. In considering the process of narrative inquiry, Fenstermacher and Richardson identify several examples of work on narrative method (e.g., research techniques), examples that they feel enhance the epistemic warrant of certain elements of narratives, while they admit that such research methods cannot guarantee their truth in a way that would satisfy Phillips. Finally, in terms of the use of narratives, Fenstermacher and Richardson point out ways that render truth unimportant or irrelevant in relation to other literary criteria such as believability. They conclude that only certain elements of narrative may be warrantable in the traditional scientific sense. They agree with O'Dea's general thesis that certain elements of quality in narrative are more suited for evaluation by literary criteria.

Sources of a Concept of Trustworthiness from within Practitioner Research

There have been several efforts by academics involved in supporting practitioner research (and sometimes involved in conducting it on their own practices) to propose a set of criteria for determining the trustworthiness of practitioner inquiries. One of the most comprehensive discussions of this issue within the academic literature on practitioner research is by Anderson et al. (1994), who share many of the political motivations of Lather and are advocates of practitioner research with a critical spirit. Anderson et al. (1994) argue that, because of the dual goals of understanding and improving practice, academic conceptions of validity are of limited use to the practitioner researcher. They call for a different conception of validity that responds to the purposes and conditions of practitioner re-

search. Because practitioners conduct self-study research for different reasons, Anderson et al. (1994) suggest that the specific purposes for conducting practitioner research should influence the way in which validity is defined.

> If the purpose of practitioner research is to produce knowledge for dissemination in fairly traditional channels (e.g., dissertations, journals), then the criteria for a "valid" study may be different than the criteria of practitioners who organize their research around specific problems within an action context. (p. 29)

Adopting this notion of different conceptions of validity for different kinds of practitioner research would also mean that different kinds of journals would use different criteria in judging the quality of research. For example, the National Education Association-sponsored teacher research journal in the United States, *Teaching and Change,* would use different standards for assessing the quality of research from those used by the *Harvard Educational Review.* This position does not imply that the standards of quality used within an academic context are somehow superior to those used in the school setting.

Anderson et al. (1994) suggest a set of five criteria for assessing the validity of practitioner research. Much of what they propose is highly similar to Lather's proposals for research-as-praxis and draws on some of the ideas set forth in discussions of the validity of academic qualitative research. They do reflect, however, a distinctive quality that is consistent with the specific situation of insiders generating knowledge about their own practice. The intent is that practitioner researchers will draw on different aspects of those criteria, depending on the motivation for and circumstances of their research. The five criteria proposed by Anderson et al. (1994) are as follows:

1. Democratic validity—the extent to which the research is done in collaboration with all parties who have a stake in the problem under investigation, and multiple perspectives and interests are taken into account.
2. Outcome validity—the extent to which actions occur that lead to a resolution of the problem under study or to the completion of an research cycle that results in action.
3. Process validity—the adequacy of the processes used in the different phases of the research such as data collection, analysis, etc. This validity includes the issue of triangulation as a guard against viewing events in a biased way. It also goes beyond research methods to include several general criteria such as plausibility.
4. Catalytic validity—taken directly from Lather's (1991) work. This validity describes the degree to which the research energizes the participants to know reality so they can transform it.
5. Dialogic validity—the degree to which the research promotes a reflective dialogue among all of participants in the research.

Anderson et al. (1994) discuss the issue of generalizibility. Like many who have written about this issue in relation to qualitative and interpretative research, they essentially adopt the notion of naturalistic generalization or transferability advocated by Stake

(1995), where those who wish to use the research also make judgments about the similarities between their own context and that of the research. Anderson et al. (1994) argue that this conception of the usefulness of research beyond the context in which it was conducted fits well with practitioner cultures, where stories are shared regularly among practitioners as part of an oral craft tradition.

The tentative validity criteria proposed by Anderson et al. (1994) draw heavily on postpositivist discussions of validity in academic research and seem broad enough to encompass all of the different traditions of practitioner research and motivations for conducting practitioner research discussed earlier. However, the criteria are still proposed by university academics for researchers who are largely P–12 teachers, a situation that is inconsistent with the goals of Anderson et al. to further democratize educational research. Anderson et al. (1994) imply that evaluative criteria used in the world of P–12 teachers might be different from those used in the academy. They mention two examples of very broad criteria that teachers regularly apply in their work with their students: (a) rigorous vs. sloppy work and (b) analysis vs. mere opinion. But they provide no discussion of the issue of how P–12 teachers might go about assessing the quality of practitioner research.

Another example of an attempt by a university academic to propose a set of criteria for assessing the validity of practitioner research is found in the work of Stevenson (1996). Drawing on the Deakin University definition of action research cited earlier as encompassing the three-fold purpose of improving (a) one's practice, (b) one's understanding of that practice, and (c) the situations in which those practices are carried out, Stevenson proposes a set of 10 criteria that address both the quality of the process of generating knowledge and the quality of the actual changes or improvements in one's practices and the situations that result. Consistent with much of the work on validity in academic qualitative research, those criteria go beyond the epistemological issues of drawing inferences from data and generalizing research to other settings to include attention to issues of ethics, relationships, and politics.

The first criterion requires that the researcher articulate the rationale for and educational significance of the study in a way that connects it to his or her own value commitments and to experiential or theoretical knowledge. The purpose here is to establish the worthwhileness of engaging in the particular piece of research.

Second, the researcher must be able to articulate and justify his or her own intentions and beliefs, a criterion similar to much of the validity literature in qualitative research that challenges the idea that the researcher must remain neutral. Asking for researchers to remain neutral in a research form that is based on commitment, intervention, and action does not make much sense.

The third criterion proposed by Stevenson is identical to the idea of democratic validity proposed by Anderson et al. (1994). Here, there is a requirement that the research be genuinely collaborative in that all parties who are affected by the research are included in the research and their perspectives are respected.

The fourth criterion addresses a problem discussed in the literature as "arrested action research," where the researcher aborts the project before actually taking any action to change the situation or after a single action research cycle that does not resolve the concern. Here the trustworthiness of an action research study would be assessed according to whether or not the research was prematurely aborted.

The fifth standard concerns the representation of multiple perspectives data sources in the research, the criterion of triangulation discussed earlier in relation to Lather's (1991) work.

The sixth criterion for determining the validity of action research requires that there be a constant dialectical interplay between the researcher's values and actions where the values inform the actions and vice versa. This is yet another point where the neutrality of the researcher and the idea of the detached observer are challenged.

The seventh criterion examines the degree to which the research has been systematically conducted (also see Whitehead, 1989) yet is responsive to evolving understandings and circumstances in the research. This standard would place a positive value on a very common occurrence in action research: the changing of the research question or focus over the course of the research.

The eighth criterion refers to the degree to which the research has been transformative, thus leading to a change in the researcher's understandings, actions, or situation. This standard is identical to the notion of catalytic validity proposed by Lather (1991) and by Anderson et al. (1994).

The ninth criterion requires that the researcher make the results of his or her research public and engage in a dialogue about it.

The tenth and final criterion addresses the issue of the external validity or transferability of the research to other settings. Here, like most scholars who have examined this issue in relation to nonexperimental research methods, Stevenson (1996) adopts the idea of "naturalistic generalization" proposed by Stake (1995) and asks for action researchers to provide sufficiently rich descriptions of their contexts so that others will be able to draw analogies to their own situations.

In proposing these 10 criteria for the assessment of the validity of action research, Stevenson acknowledges the limitation of university researchers formulating criteria for determining the quality of action research when so many of those who conduct action research are Kindergarten through Grade 12 educators. While not providing any specific suggestions for how to deal with this problem, Stevenson (1996) argues that

Practitioners must be a central part of the dialogue on standards for the research they conduct and be allowed to formulate criteria for sound action research that is grounded in their own experiences of action research practice. (pp. 9–10)

Another limitation in Stevenson's proposals is that they are aimed only at the action-research tradition and possibly the British and Australian teacher-as-researcher traditions, and they are less applicable to the other traditions. For example, much teacher research in North America does not follow the improvement-oriented, action-research spiral characteristic of the action-research tradition. The goal is often a deeper understanding and fuller documentation of current practices, and there is not always an immediate motivation to change practice or even answer a specific research question. Despite these limitations, Stevenson's work joins the work of Anderson et al. (1994) as one of the few attempts to develop a comprehensive conceptualization of validity specifically for practitioner research.

Another effort to develop ways to assess the trustworthiness of practitioner research comes from the field of adult education. Jacobson (1998), like Stevenson (1996) and Anderson et al. (1994), argues that criteria for the integrity of practitioner research must rest both on the quality of the actions taken by the researchers on the basis of their data (see also Lomax, 1994; Munby, 1995) and on the quality of the data itself:

> The data itself must faithfully represent actions in their contexts, collected through procedures which make it possible to distinguish what is actually happening from what I see happening. Furthermore, data needs to be thorough, based on a variety of sources and probing for meanings associated with actions. . . . Conclusions which are drawn from the data must be applicable to practice and must lead to actions that are critically responsive; that is, responding to what is happening and at the same time questioning what is happening and my own responses to it. Actions taken must be justifiable, grounded in the research rather than in the comfortable routines of teaching. (Jacobson, 1998, pp. 12–13)

Jacobson (1998) developed these ideas about defining the quality of practitioner research while working as an English-as-a-second-language (ESL) instructor at the university level. After presenting his ideas, he goes on to analyze his own practitioner research in relation to them. One additional issue emphasized in Jacobson's perspective on the quality of practitioner research is that the conclusions reached in a study be consistent with the nature of the data.

Probably the most extensive discussion of the issue of trustworthiness in the practitioner research literature is Dadds's (1995) analysis of the validity of three action-research studies completed by Vicki, 1 of 27 teachers enrolled in Dadds's advanced diploma course leading to a master's degree at Cambridge Institute of Education in the United Kingdom. Dadds frames her analysis of this one teacher's research as part of her study of her own practice as a teacher educator. It is her hope that this self-study will help her better understand the learning of the teachers who take her course and will help her improve the course to support teachers' action research.

In framing the discussion of Vicki's research, Dadds proposes the concept of the democratic validation of teacher action-research studies as an alternative to a situation where the academy is the sole arbiter of worthwhileness. This position stems, in part, from Dadds's discomfort in using only academic criteria to assess the action-research projects of the teachers in her classes.

> Many of the teachers' research studies for academic assessment were generating practical processes and outcomes in school of which I had little previous understanding and which our validation criteria failed to capture. (Dadds, 1995, p. 112)

Dadds's position also is a consequence of her general concern about issues of power in validating action research, one that she shares with several others who have written about determining the quality of action research.

> Power is an issue, too, for there is a shared concern about "outsiders" enforcing unnegotiated and inappropriate criteria on teacher action research (Clarke, Dudley, Edwards, Rowland, Ryan, & Winter, 1993; Lomax, 1994). In an essentially democratic research methodology such as action research, it is incongruous to rely upon one, sole arbiter of worthwhileness, so the monolithic validating voice of the academy does not sit comfortably, even though it is an important voice, and one which may thoughtfully enhance the debate. (Dadds, 1995, p. 112)

Under the concept of democratic or multiple perspective validation, the quality of a practitioner research study is determined through a process of negotiation in which the different purposes and audiences served by a piece of research are taken into account. Members of the various audiences served by a research study would contribute their perspectives about the worthwhileness of the research. (See also Gitlin et al., 1992.) In addition to including the academic examiner, any research completed as part of award-bearing courses at colleges or universities could include the teachers' colleagues, her students, and the researcher's own validation reflections.

Dadds (1995) offers a discussion of her developing ideas related to five broad areas within which discourses about the validity of teacher action research could be conducted within a democratic framework. She prefers the use of the term *valuing* rather than *validation* because of the more visible positive respect and regard for teacher knowledge that she thinks it publicly conveys. In this discussion, Dadds argues that action research needs to be assessed in relation to (a) the knowledge that is generated by the research, (b) the quality of the text that is produced to represent the research, (c) the impact of the research on the researcher's practice or situation or both, (d) the impact of the research on the researcher's professional learning and growth, and (e) the quality of the collaboration in the research.

For each of these five areas, Dadds (1995) offers her thoughts about criteria that could possibly be used. For example, with regard to the quality of the knowledge produced through action research, she considers, among other things, the originality of the knowledge in relation to the context of the study (i.e., the degree to which it provides the researcher and others with new insights about their situation), the degree to which multiple perspectives have been taken into account in constructing the research knowledge, and the contribution of the research to others' thinking outside of the situation.

In her analysis, Dadds (1995) makes an important distinction between the research and its representation in textual form. She argues that much of the complexity and richness of action research is often not articulated in the texts that teachers submit in their college and university courses. She raises a number of important questions about the representation of action research that challenge the academy to rethink its approach to validation, an approach that usually requires a written research report.

> If we confine our view of "text" to the more conventional academic research genre . . . we may ignore the appropriateness of other

forms of communication, written or spoken, that may have greater potential for shaping and communicating meaning, for putting the action in action research, for acting as catalysts for institutional action and change. (Dadds, 1995, p. 132)

Dadds raises the possibility of the production of different texts for different audiences, something that Vicki does do in the case example, but she worries about the demands this activity makes on busy teachers. Dadds is more inclined to have the academy broaden its view of what counts as legitimate ways to represent action research to include ways of communicating research that are more relevant to school contexts.

In her discussion of the practical validity of action research, Dadds suggests that "good arguments which gather dust may be less helpful than shaky arguments which oil the wheels of purposeful action" (1995, p. 135). She argues that the determination of practical validity cannot be divorced from consideration of the ethical or moral validity of the work. It is not so much a question of whether practice was affected by the research as it is of whether these changes are desirable within some ethical or moral framework. She argues that we cannot remain neutral in the validation process. Also, like many of those in the postpositivist literature on research quality, Dadds argues that the quality of relations among all of the participants in the research needs to be considered as part of this moral and ethical analysis of the research.

In summary, Dadds, like most of those within the practitioner research literature who have addressed the issue of determining research quality, believes that criteria, standards, and validation processes need to be developed that are more congruent with the nature and purposes of practitioner research than are traditional practices in the academy. She further argues that, given the diversity of this research genre, attempts to develop a common set of criteria for the entire practitioner research community are probably misguided.

The efforts of Anderson et al. (1994), Dadds (1995), Jacobson (1998), and Stevenson (1996) to discuss the issue of establishing the trustworthiness of practitioner research, as well as Eisenhart and Howe's (1992) attempt to propose a set of general criteria to provide the basis for generating quality criteria in different research genres, all make important contributions to creating a situation where practitioner researchers can talk to each other and to others about the quality of research that they do. However, as we have alluded to several times throughout this chapter, there is a serious ethical issue involved in positioning university academics (however well intentioned) as the sole determiners of standards of quality in a field of research where the majority of the researchers are P–12 educators. The silencing of P–12 educators by academics has been a serious problem in educational research and teacher education for many years (Evans et al., 1987; Zeichner, 1995b). It is inexcusable to perpetuate this situation in practitioner research where the intent is to democratize the research process. P–12 educators need to assume a central role in formulating and applying standards for assessing the quality of their own work. This role is likely to assume a form that is very different from the academic accounts summarized in this chapter. One example of the interactive and relational nature that this discourse could assume is a recent dialogue among eight P–12 teacher researchers about a wide range of issues concerning teacher research in North America. including issues of quality (Threatt et al., 1994).

While it is not possible for us to offer any firm resolutions to many of the debates now in progress concerning the basis for determining quality in practitioner inquiry, we can offer a few conclusions based on our assessment of these debates in relation to the nature and purposes of practitioner research. First, it is clear to us that, whatever criteria eventually emerge to define quality in practitioner research, they will need to reflect the different forms and multiple purposes associated with this research genre. In many cases, this means taking into account that most of those who do practitioner research are also full-time teachers. The idea of applying conventional notions of reliability, validity, and generalization to judge practitioner research does not seem justified given the diverse purposes and forms of this research. (See also Altrichter, 1993; Brennan & Noffke, 1997; Chaudhary, 1997; Feldman, 1994; Noffke, 1991.) While in some circumstances it may be appropriate to apply criteria of validity or trustworthiness or both that are adapted from those used to evaluate conventional academic research, there will be circumstances where the use of aesthetic, literary, educational, or moral criteria will be most appropriate. Furthermore, alternative criteria will need to take into account the very diverse contexts associated with the different traditions of practitioner inquiry. These contexts include such things as teachers participating in teacher-initiated research groups, teachers enrolled in school district professional development programs, teachers enrolled in graduate university courses, and teachers who are writing master's papers and PhD dissertations. Assessing the quality of a practitioner research doctoral dissertation will certainly need to be different from judging the quality of a proposal to present research at a practitioner research conference or from making decisions about whether to archive particular research studies in a local database. The idea proposed by Eisenhart and her colleagues to apply and adapt one universal set of general criteria to assess the merit and worth of diverse forms of research remains to be tested, but we are fairly skeptical about the usefulness of this approach with regard to practitioner inquiry.

While academic researchers need not necessarily be involved in assessing school-based practitioner research that is not directly connected to a college or university setting, much practitioner research is done by P–12 teachers who are enrolled in award-bearing courses and degree programs. It is in those situations where we think the democratic negotiation of quality criteria suggested by Dadds (1995) offers much promise.

Given the development of new forms of representation of practitioner inquiry (i.e., we cannot assume a written report as the product of research), criteria for judging the quality of research will need to take into account different forms of representation in addition to the conventional research report. The different forms might include educational action, oral presentation and structured discussion, drama, still photography, film, short story, and poetry (e.g., Lomax & Parker, 1995; McNiff, Lomax, & Whitehead, 1996). We also need to take into account the particular audience to which the representation of the research is directed. Communicating findings to academic researchers, P–12 teachers, policymakers, and the general public or to some combination of the above suggests the need for different strategies for representing research. It is probably important in all contexts, though, for the researcher to make fully transparent the processes used in conducting the research (Lomax, 1994).

Also, as we have noted repeatedly throughout our analysis, the question of who determines the trustworthiness and quality of research is a matter of great importance in a field like practitioner research, where many researchers are P–12 educators. In our view, those educators must have a say in how the issues get resolved with regard to their own work and in practitioner research generally, even when the assessment is situated within the context of award-bearing courses and degree programs. It is ethically questionable to have academics debate the issues only among themselves and then seek to impose their resolutions on P–12 educators.

Ways must be found to include the voices of P–12 educators in the development of ethical guidelines and standards. This may involve the publication of their opinions about practitioner inquiry (e.g., Threatt et al., 1994). In other cases, the meetings of groups such as the annual International Teacher Research Conference, which is held in conjunction with annual American Educational Research Association (AERA) meetings, can be used for this purpose. In one case several years ago, the U.S. Department of Education organized a meeting of P–12 educators and university academics from across the country to discuss a variety of issues related to teacher research, including issues of determining research quality. More of those kinds of efforts are needed to reach out and bring P–12 educators into the public dialogue about research quality. It is important to see that such educators are well represented among those who review practitioner research for presentation at regional and national conferences, including AERA, and for publication in journals and books.

Finally, it is critical that P–12 educators be well represented on the panels that make decisions about the funding of practitioner research initiatives by private entities such as the Spencer and MacArthur Foundations and by public funders such as the U.S. Department of Education. These organizations have funded and continue to fund practitioner research while involving P–12 educators in funding decisions.

From the discussions reported above about validity and trustworthiness in educational research in general, in qualitative research, in narrative research, and in practitioner research, it is clear that the ways that eventually emerge to determine the quality of practitioner research will have a strong moral and ethical component that includes attention to the quality of relationships among the participants in the research. The relationships include those between researchers and their students as well as those among all people affected by a research project. The criteria that emerge will also need to address both how the research was done and what the quality of its representation is.

Finally, because knowledge generation is only one of several potential purposes of practitioner research, criteria for assessing its quality will need to take into account the transformative impact of the research on the researcher's understandings, actions, and situations. Practitioner research that helps researchers to gain new and deeper insights into their practices, to improve the learning situation for their students, and to change their situations will need to be valued for these transformational qualities (see Lomax, 1994; Northfield, 1996) in addition to the attention that is given to the warrants for claims to know.

Conclusion

In this chapter, we first provided a framework for understanding the various traditions of practitioner research and their varied purposes. We have done so with the recognition that this is a small step in working toward addressing the many issues this form of research represents. One issue that needs to be addressed in the future is the development of a dialogue across the various traditions of practitioner research. Currently, there is very little reference in work within one tradition to work from the other practitioner research traditions. This lack of cross-reference is particularly true in the case of participatory research, which seems to have been ignored by many who have written about practitioner research, even by those who appear to share the emancipatory political perspective that is central to participatory research. In our view, much can be gained by looking at literature across the various traditions when examining general issues related to practitioner research, such as issues of research quality and the legitimacy of claims to know. This cross-fertilization of ideas could be useful as it furthers our understanding about the methodological aspects of conducting and representing practitioner research.

A second focus in this chapter has been a discussion of the different purposes associated with practitioner research grouped under the broad categories of personal, professional, and political. We analyzed the different reasons people engage themselves in or are engaged by others in practitioner research, ranging from an interest in better understanding one's own students and improving one's teaching, to generating knowledge about teaching and schooling that can be shared with others, to improving the various social and institutional contexts in which their educational practice is embedded.

A third emphasis in the chapter has been to discuss the nature of practitioner research by focusing on the teacher research tradition in North America. While we hope this analysis has captured some of the important similarities and differences between teacher research and other forms of research, much work in relation to other practitioner research traditions is clearly needed.

Finally, our discussion of issues of quality in practitioner research in this chapter has drawn on literature from different traditions of practitioner research as well as on literature about the quality of academic educational research. We have supported the idea of democratic negotiation of both the criteria and the procedures used in determining the quality of research. We have made a number of general assertions about the issue of quality in practitioner research on the basis of our analysis of both academic and practitioner research literature. We are aware that this discussion barely begins to scratch the surface of what needs to be done to collaboratively develop ways in which the quality of practitioner research can be determined in different contexts. We hope, though, that we have outlined some of the major issues that will need to be resolved in this work. We also hope that our efforts will encourage similar efforts by those in the various practitioner research communities and will stimulate academic researchers to recognize the great potential of practitioner research to inform the development of academic educational research and theory.

In this chapter, we very briefly raised a variety of specific issues that need further inquiry and discussion. For example, constructions of the political dimensions of practitioner research need to be understood in ways that help in seeing not only the political platforms embedded in programs and policies, but also those platforms embodied in classroom practice. Ways need to be found to bridge the current divide between academic discussions of critical and emancipatory goals for practitioner research and practitioners' discussions of the classroom as a site for political struggle.

Another important issue that merits further study is the effect of external funding on the nature of practitioner research. As private foundations such as Spencer and MacArthur and public agencies such as the U.S. Department of Education become more involved in funding practitioner research, we need to examine how this involvement helps shape both the nature of the studies and the ways in which they are represented to the broader public. In doing so, we need to investigate the extent to which the external funding of practitioner research serves to legitimate or challenge particular educational, social, and economic policies.

Another related issue that needs further analysis is the way in which the linking of practitioner research to school improvement efforts by administrators and government officials influences the nature and impact of practitioner research. What happens to practitioner research when the focus for the research is provided by a larger educational reform effort instead of being generated by practitioners within their own classrooms? It is important to investigate the degree to which the increased use of practitioner research as a reform strategy by administrators and government officials signals a use contrary to the intentions of many practitioner researchers—one of regulation and control rather than of discovery and enhancement (Johnston & Proudford, 1994).

Closely related to the increased availability of external funding for practitioner research and the efforts to tie it to broader institutional reforms by administrators is the increased use of practitioner research in preservice teacher education programs. There has been very little investigation of the purposes toward which this work has been directed and the research foci and methodologies used by prospective teacher practitioner researchers. There has also been little study of the impact on learning to teach of the introduction of practitioner research into teacher education curricula.

New ways of understanding and valuing the knowledge of practitioners are clearly emerging, a situation in a sense signified by the very inclusion of this chapter in the handbook, but as we have stated repeatedly throughout the chapter, much of the research of P–12 educators remains very difficult to access beyond and even at the local level. Much effort needs to be devoted to figuring out ways to make this research available to others within and beyond the local communities in which it has been conducted (see, for example, Somekh, 1993b) and to include the perspectives of P–12 educators about the process of practitioner research in the public dialogue about research quality. The potential influence of electronic media on the availability and discussion of practitioner research is a relevant area for further study.

Yet another issue that merits further attention is the expansion of our analysis that has emphasized practitioner research conducted in the United States, Canada, the United Kingdom, and Australia to include the growing attention to practitioner research in other European countries (e.g., Brezmes, 1997; Brock-Utne, 1980; Gómez 1996; Ruiz de Gauna, Diaz, Gonzalez, & Garaizar, 1995; Mayer, 1997; and Schindler, 1993), in Latin America (e.g., Barabtarlo y Zedansky & Poschner, 1998; Dinan & Garcia, 1997; Fals-Borda, 1997; Fosas, 1997; and Geraldi, 1996), in Africa (e.g., Davidoff, Julie, Meerkotter, & Robinson, 1993; Walker, 1988, 1993; 1995; and Zeichner, Amukushu, Muukenga, & Shilamba, 1998), and in Asia (e.g., Chaudhary, 1997; Chuaprapaisilp, 1997; and Phaik-Lah, 1997). While some of this work has been written in or translated into English, greater effort needs to be devoted to studying works that are not available in English and to analyzing how cultural conditions influence the processes and outcomes of practitioner inquiry.

A final issue that deserves study is the organizational context needed to support practitioner research. We need close investigation of the conditions that facilitate and obstruct the ability of educators to conduct research on their own practice. Questions about the importance of research groups and external facilitators to the research process, and of ways in which to lessen the inevitable tensions between teaching and researching are but a few examples of the kinds of issues in need of further study. We hope that this first chapter on practitioner inquiry in an American Educational Research Association *Handbook of Research on Teaching* will stimulate further work on these and other issues.

REFERENCES

Adams, F. (1975). *Unearthing seeds of fire: The idea of Highlander.* Winston-Salem, NC: John F. Blair.

Adelman, C. (1993). Kurt Lewin and the origins of action research. *Educational Action Research, 1*(1), 7–24.

Adler, S. (1993). Teacher education: Research or reflective practice. *Teaching and Teacher Education, 9*(2), 159–167.

Ahlquist, R. (1991). Position and imposition: Power relations in a multicultural foundations class. *Journal of Negro Education, 60*(2), 158–169.

Aiken, W. M. (1942). *The story of the Eight-Year Study.* New York: Harper & Brothers

Altheide, D., & Johnson, J. (1994). Criteria for assessing interpretative validity in qualitative research. In N. Denzin, & Y. Lincoln (Eds.), *Handbook of qualitative research* (pp. 485–499). Thousand Oaks, CA: Sage.

Altrichter, H. (1986). Visiting two worlds: an excursion into the methodological jungle including an optional evening's entertainment at the Rigour Club. *Cambridge Journal of Education, 16*(2), 131–143.

Altrichter, H. (1993). The concept of quality in action research: Giving practitioners a voice in educational research. In M. Schratz (Ed.), *Qualitative voices in educational research* (pp. 40–55). London: Falmer Press.

Altrichter, H., & Gstettner, P. (1993). Action research: A closed chapter in the history of German social science? *Educational Action Research, 1*(3), 329–360.

Altrichter, H., Posch, P., & Somekh, B. (1993). *Teachers investigate their work: An introduction to the methods of action research.* London: Routledge.

Anderson, C., Butts, J., Lett, P., Mansdoerfer, S., & Raisch, M. (1995). Voices in unison: Teacher research and collaboration. *Teacher Research, 2*(2), 117–135.

Anderson, G. L., Herr, K., & Nihlen, A. S. (1994). *Studying your own school: An educator's guide to qualitative practitioner research.* Thousand Oaks, CA: Corwin Press.

Atkin, M. (1994). Teacher research to change policy. In S. Hollingsworth, & H. Sockett (Eds.), *Teacher research and educational reform* (pp. 186–203). Chicago: University of Chicago Press.

Atweh, B., Kemmis, S., & Weeks, P. (Eds.). (1998). *Action research in practice: Partnerships for social justice in education.* New York: Routledge.

Atwell, N. (1987). *In the middle: Writing, reading, and learning with adolescents.* Portsmouth, NH: Boynton/Cook-Heinemann.

Banford, H. (1996). The blooming of Maricar: Writing workshop and the phantom student. In H. Banford, M. Berkman, C. Chin, C. Cziko, B. Fecho, D. Jumpp, C. Miller, & M. Resnick, *Cityscapes: Eight views from the urban classroom* (pp. 3–24). Berkeley, CA: National Writing Project.

Banford, H., Berkman, M., Chin, C, Cziko, C., Fecho, B., Jumpp, D., Miller, C., & Resnick, M. (1996). *Cityscapes: Eight views from the urban classroom.* Berkeley, CA: National Writing Project.

Barabtarlo y Zedansky, A., & Poschner, T. (1998) Participatory action research in teacher education: a method for studying the everyday reality of teaching in Latin America. In G. L. Anderson, & M. Montero-Sieburth (Eds.), *Educational qualitative research in Latin America: The struggle for a new paradigm.* New York: Garland.

Barone, T. (1992). A narrative of enhanced professionalism: Educational researchers and popular storybooks about schoolpeople. *Educational Researcher, 21*(8), 15–24.

Benmayor, R. (1991). Testimony, action research, and empowerment: Puerto Rican women and popular education. In S. B. Gluck, & D. Patai (Eds.), *Women's words: The feminist practice of oral history* (pp. 159–174). New York: Routledge.

Biddle, B. J., & Anderson, D. S. (1986). Theory, methods, knowledge, and research on teaching. In M. C. Wittrock (Ed.), *Handbook of research on teaching* (3rd ed.) (pp. 230–252). New York: Macmillan.

Bissex, G., & Bullock, R. (1987). *Seeing ourselves: Case study research by teachers of writing.* Portsmouth, NH: Heinemann.

Borg, W. R. (1981). *Applying educational research: A practical guide for teachers.* New York: Longman.

Brankis, N. (1996). Discovering the real learner within: Journalkeeping with children. In G. Burnaford, J. Fischer, & D. Hobson (Eds.), *Teachers doing research: Practical possibilities* (pp. 18–24). Mahwah, NJ: Lawrence Erlbaum Associates.

Brennan, M., & Noffke, S. E. (1997). Uses of data in action research. In T. R. Carson & D. Sumara (Eds.), *Action research as a living practice* (pp. 23–43). New York: Peter Lang.

Brezmes, M. S. (1997) A background to action research in Spain. In R. McTaggart (Ed.), *Participatory action research* (pp. 187–202). Albany, NY: State University of New York Press.

Brock-Utne, B. (1980) What is educational action research. *Classroom Action Research Network Bulletin, 4*(10–15).

Brown, L. D., & Tandon, R. (1983). Ideology and political economy in inquiry: Action research and participatory research. *Journal of Applied Behavioral Science, 19*(3), 277–294.

Bruner, J. (1965). *Man: A course of study. Occasional Paper No. 3, Social Studies Curriculum Program.* Cambridge, MA: Educational Services Inc. (Now Educational Development Center).

Bruner, J. (1986). *Actual minds, possible worlds.* Cambridge, MA: Harvard University Press.

Buckingham, B. R. (1926). *Research for teachers.* New York: Silver Burdett & Co.

Buckingham, B. R. (1939). The value of research to the classroom teacher. In AERA and the Department of Classroom Teachers, National Education Association, *The implications of research for the classroom teacher* (pp. 24–37). Washington, DC: National Education Association.

Bunbury, R., Hastings, W., Henry, J., & McTaggart, R. (1991). *Aboriginal pedagogy: Aboriginal teachers speak out.* Geelong, Victoria, Australia: Deakin University Press.

Burch, P., & Palanki, A. (Eds.). (1993). Circles of change: Parent-teacher action research. Theme issue of *Equity and Choice, 10*(1), 1–64.

Burnaford, G., Fischer, J., & Hobson, D. (Eds.). (1996). *Teachers doing research: Practical possibilities.* Mahway, NJ: Lawrence Erlbaum Associates.

Calhoun, E. (1994). *How to use action research in the self-renewing school.* Alexandria, VA: Association for Supervision and Curriculum Development.

Campbell, D. T., & Stanley, J. C. (1963). *Experimental and quasi-experimental designs for research.* Chicago: Rand McNally.

Carini, P. (1975). *Observation and description: An alternative methodology for the investigation of human phenomena.* Grand Forks, ND: University of North Dakota Press.

Caro-Bruce, C., & McCreadie, J. (1995). What happens when a school district supports action research? In S. Noffke & R. Stevenson (Eds.), *Educational action research* (pp. 154–164). New York: Teachers College Press.

Carr, W. (1995). *For education: Towards critical educational inquiry.* Buckingham, UK: Open University Press.

Carr, W., & Kemmis, S. (1986). *Becoming critical: Education, knowledge and action research.* London: Falmer Press.

Carson, T. R. (1997). Reflection and its resistances: Teacher education as a living practice. In T. R. Carson & D. Sumara (Eds.), *Action research as a living practice* (pp. 77–91). New York: Peter Lang.

Carson, T. R., & Sumara, D. (Eds.). (1997). *Action research as a living practice.* New York: Peter Lang.

Chaudhary, A. (1997). Toward an epistemology of participatory research. In R. McTaggart (Ed.), *Participatory action research* (pp. 113–124). Albany, NY: State University of New York Press.

Chisholm, L., & Holland, J. (1986). Girls and occupational choice: Anti-sexism in action in a curriculum development project. *British Journal of Sociology of Education, 7*(4), 353–365.

Chuaprapaisilp, A. (1997), Thai Buddhist philosophy and the action research process. *Educational Action Research , 5*(2), 331–336.

Clarke, J., Dudley, P., Edwards, A., Rowland, S., Ryan, C., & Winter, R. (1993). Ways of presenting and critiquing action research reports. *Educational Action Research, 1*(3), 490–492.

Clifford, G. (1973). A history of the impact of research on teaching. In R. M. W. Travers (Ed.), *Handbook of research on teaching* (2nd ed.) (pp. 1–46). New York: Rand McNally.

Cochran-Smith, M. (1995). Uncertain allies: Understanding the boundaries of race and teaching. *Harvard Educational Review, 65*(4) 541–570.

Cochran-Smith, M., & Lytle, S. L. (1993). *Inside/outside: Teacher research and knowledge.* New York: Teachers College Press.

Cole, A., & Knowles, G. (1995). Methods and issues in a life history approach to self-study. In T. Russell & F. Korthagen (Eds.), *Teachers who teach teachers* (pp. 130–151). London: Falmer Press.

Collier, J. (1945). United States Indian administration as a laboratory of ethnic relations. *Social Research, 12,* 265–303.

Connelly, F. M., & Clandinin, D. J. (1990). Stories of experience and narrative inquiry. *Educational Researcher, 19*(5), 2–14.

Corey, S. M. (1949). Action research, fundamental research, and educational practices. *Teachers College Record, 50,* 509–514.

Corey, S. M. (1953). *Action research to improve school practices.* New York: Teachers College Press.

Corey, S. M. (1954). Hoping? Or beginning to know! *Childhood Education, 30*(5), 208–211.

Corey, S. M. (1955). Implications of cooperative-action research for teacher education. In American Association of Colleges for Teacher Education, *Eighth yearbook of the American Association of Colleges for Teacher Education* (164–172). Oneata, NY: National Education Association.

Corman, B. (1957). Action research: A teaching or research method. *Review of Educational Research, 27*(5), 544–547.

Cunningham, R., & Miel, A. (1947). Frontiers of educational research in elementary school curriculum development. *Journal of Educational Research, 40*(5), 365–372.

Cutright, P. D., & Dahl, M. H. (1939). The application of the scientific method. In AERA and the Department of Classroom Teachers, National Education Association, *The implications of research for the classroom teacher* (pp. 53–65). Washington DC: National Education Association.

Dadds, M. (1995). *Passionate enquiry and school development.* London: Falmer Press.

Davidoff, S., Julie, D., Meerkotter, D., & Robinson, M. (1993) *Emancipatory education and action research.* Pretoria, South Africa: Human Sciences Research Council.

Denzin, N. (1989). *The research act.* Englewood Cliffs, NJ: Prentice Hall.

Dewey, J. (1929). *The sources of a science of education.* New York: Liverright.

Dewey, J. (1938). *Logic: The theory of inquiry.* New York: Henry Holt.

Dinan, J., & Garcia, Y. (1997) Participatory research in Venezuela: 1973–1991. In R. McTaggart (Ed.), *Participatory action research* (pp. 151–186) Albany, NY: State University of New York Press.

Dockendorf, M. (1995). *Within the labyrinth: Facilitating teacher research groups.* Unpublished master's degree thesis, Simon Fraser University, Burnby, B. C. Canada.

Donald, P., Gosling, S., Hamilton, J., Hawkes, N., McKenzie, D., & Stronach, I. (1995). "No problem here": Action research against racism in a mainly white area. *British Educational Research Journal, 21*(3), 263–275.

Duckworth, E. (1987). *"The having of wonderful ideas" and other essays on teaching and learning.* New York: Teachers College Press.

Edwards, G., & Rideout, P. (Eds.). (1991). *Extending the horizons of action research* (Classroom Action Research Network Publication 10C). Norwich, UK: CARN Publications.

Eisenhart, M., & Borko, H. (1993). *Designing classroom research: Themes, issues and struggles.* Boston: Allyn & Bacon.

Eisenhart, M., & Howe, K. (1992). Validity in qualitative research. In M. LeCompte, W. Milroy, & J. Preissie (Eds.), *The handbook of qualitative research in education* (pp. 643–680). San Diego, CA: Academic Press.

Elijah, R. (1996). Professional lives; institutional contexts: Coherence and contradictions. *Teacher Education Quarterly, 23*(3),69–90.

Elliott, J. (1976–77). Developing hypotheses about classrooms from teachers' practical constructs: An account of the work of the Ford Teaching Project. *Interchange, 7*(2), 2–22.

Elliott, J. (1991). *Action research for educational change.* Philadelphia: Open University Press/Milton Keynes.

Elliott, J. (1997). School-based curriculum development and action research in the United Kingdom. In S. Hollingsworth (Ed.), *International action research: A casebook for educational reform* (pp. 17–28). London: Falmer Press.

Elliott, J., & Adelman, C. (1973). Reflecting where the action is: The design of the Ford Teaching Project. *Education for Teaching, 92,* 8–20.

Elliott, J., & Ebutt, D. (Eds.). (1986). *Case studies in teaching for understanding.* Cambridge, UK: Cambridge Institute of Education.

Erickson, F. (1986). Qualitative methods in research on teaching. In M. Wittrock (Ed.), *Handbook of research on teaching* (3rd ed.) (pp. 119–161). New York: Macmillan.

Erickson, F. (1989, March). *The meaning of validity in qualitative research.* A paper presented at the annual meeting of the American Educational Research Association, San Francisco, California.

Evans, C., Stubbs, M., Frechette, P., Neely, C., & Warner, J. (1987). *Educational practitioners: Absent voices in the building of educational theory* (Working Paper N. 170). Wellesley, MA: Center for Research on Women.

Fals-Borda, O. (1988). *Knowledge and people's power.* New Delhi, India: Indian Social Institute.

Fals-Borda, O. (1991). Some basic ingredients. In O. Fals-Borda & M. A. Rahman (Eds.), *Action and knowledge: Breaking the monopoly with participatory research* (pp. 3–12). New York: Apex Press.

Fals-Borda, O. (1997). Participatory action research in Columbia: Some personal feelings. In R. McTaggart (Ed.), *Participatory action research: International contexts and consequences* (pp. 107–124). Albany, NY: State University of New York Press.

Fals-Borda, O., & Rahman, M. A. (Eds.). (1991). *Action and knowledge: Breaking the monopoly with participatory action-research.* New York: Apex Press.

Fecho, B. (1996). Learning from Laura. In H. Banford, M. Berkman, C. Chin, C. Cziko, B. Fecho, D. Jumpp, C. Miller, & M. Resnick, *Cityscapes: Eight views from the urban classroom* (pp. 57–71). Berkeley, CA: National Writing Project.

Feiman-Nemser, S., & Featherstone, H. (1992). *Exploring teaching: Reconstructing an introductory course.* New York: Teachers College Press.

Feldman, A. (1994). Erzberger's dilemma: Validity in action research and science teachers' need to know. *Science Education, 78*(1), 83–101.

Fenstermacher, G. (1994). The knower and the known: The nature of knowledge in research on teaching. In L. Darling-Hammond (Ed.), *Review of Research in Education, 20,* 3–56.

Fenstermacher, G., & Richardson, V. (1994). Promoting confusion in educational psychology: How is it done? *Educational Psychologist, 29*(1), 49–55.

Fischer, J. (1996). Open to ideas: Developing a framework for your research. In G. Burnaford, J. Fischer, & D. Hobson (Eds.), *Teachers doing research: Practical possibilities* (pp. 33–50). Mahwah, NJ: Lawrence Erlbaum Associates.

Fosas, L. O. (1997). Using participatory action research for the reconceptualization of educational practice. In S. Hollingsworth (Ed.), *International action research: A casebook for educational reform* (pp. 219–224). London: Falmer Press.

Foshay, A. W. (1994). Action research: An early history in the U.S. *Journal of Curriculum and Supervision, 9,* 317–325.

Foshay, A. W., Wann, K. D., & Associates. (1954). *Children's social values: An action research study.* New York: Teachers College Press.

Freire, P. (1970). *A pedagogy of the oppressed.* New York: Seabury Press.

Freire, P. (1982). Creating alternative research methods. In B. Hall, A. Gillette, & R. Tandon (Eds.), *Creating knowledge: A monopoly? Participatory research in development* (pp. 29–37). New Delhi, India: Participatory Research Network.

Freire, P. (1992). *A pedagogy of hope.* New York: Continuum.

Gallas, K. (1994). *The languages of learning.* New York: Teachers College Press.

Gallas, K. (1995). *Talking their way into science: Hearing children's questions and theories and responding with curricula.* New York: Teachers College Press.

Gallas, K. (1998). *Sometimes I can be anything: Power, gender and identity in a primary classroom.* New York: Teachers College Press.

Gaventa, J. (1991). Toward a knowledge democracy: Viewpoints on participatory research in North America. In O. Fals-Borda & M. A. Rahman (Eds.), *Action and knowledge: Breaking the knowledge monopoly through participatory research* (pp. 121–131). New York: Apex Press.

Gaventa, J., & Horton, B. D. (1981). A citizens' research project in Appalachia, USA. *Convergence, 14*(3), 30–42.

Geertz, C. (1973). *The interpretation of cultures.* New York: Basic Books.

Geraldi, C. (1996) *Integration of teaching and research in the university.* Paper presented at the Third European Congress of Educational Research, Seville, Spain.

Gitlin, A, Bringhurst, K., Burns, M., Cooley, V., Myers, B., Price, K., Russell, R., & Tiess, P. (1992). *Teachers' voices for school change: An introduction to educative research.* New York: Teachers College Press.

Gitlin, A., & Thompson, A. (1995). Foregrounding politics in action research. *McGill Journal of Education, 30*(2), 131–147.

Goetz, J., & LeCompte, M. (1984). *Ethnography and qualitative design in educational research.* New York: Academic Press.

Gómez, A. I. P. (1996, Sept.). *Human development through action-research in a trade-school for marginal students in Malaga.* Paper presented at the Management for Organizational & Human Development Project Conference, Frascati, Italy.

Good, C. V. (1963). *Introduction to educational research.* New York: Appleton Century Crofts.

Gore, J. M., & Zeichner, K. M. (1991). Action research and reflective teaching in preservice teacher education: A case study from the United States. *Teaching and Teacher Education, 7*(2), 119–136.

Goswami, D., & Stillman, P. R. (Eds.). (1987). *Reclaiming the classroom: Teacher research as an agency for change.* Portsmouth, NH: Boynton/Cook-Heinemann.

Griffiths, M. (1994). Autobiography, feminism and the practice of action research. *Educational Action Research, 2*(1), 71–82.

Griffiths, M., & Davies, C. (1993). Learning to learn: Action research from an equal opportunities perspective in a junior school. *British Educational Research Journal, 19*(1), 43–58.

Grimmett, P. P. (1997). Breaking the mold: Transforming a didactic professor into a learner-focused teacher educator. In T. R. Carson & D. Sumara (Eds.), *Action research as a living practice* (pp. 121–136). New York: Peter Lang.

Grimmett, P. P., & Mackinnon, A. (1992). Craft knowledge and the education of teachers. In G. Grant (Ed.), *Review of Research in Education, 18*, 385–456.

Grundy, S. (1982). Three modes of action research. *Curriculum Perspectives, 2*(3), 23–34.

Grundy, S. (1997). Participatory educational research in Australia: The first wave—1976 to 1986. In R. McTaggart (Ed.), *Participatory action research: International contexts and consequences* (pp. 125–149). Albany, NY: State University of New York Press.

Grundy, S., & Kemmis, S. (1988). Educational action research in Australia: The state of the art (an overview). In S. Kemmis & R. McTaggart (Eds.), *The action research reader* (3rd ed.) (pp. 321–335). Geelong, Victoria, Australia: Deakin University Press.

Gunz, J. (1996). Jacob L. Moreno and the origins of action research. *Educational Action Research, 4*(1), 145–148.

Hall, B. L. (1993). Participatory research. In T. Husen & T. N. Postlethwaite (Eds.), *The international encyclopedia of education* (pp. 4330–4336). Oxford, UK: Pergamon.

Halsey, A. H. (1972). *Educational priority: EPA Problems and policies.* London: Her Majesty's Stationary Office.

Hammatt-Kavaloski, J. (1996). Fostering resiliency. In Madison Metropolitan School District, *Curriculum Integration: Classroom action research, 1995–96* (pp. 73–107). Madison, WI: Madison Metropolitan School District.

Handal, G., & Lauvas, P. (1987). *Promoting reflective teaching.* Milton Keynes, UK: Open University Press.

Harding, S. (1986). *The science question in feminism.* Ithaca, NY: Cornell University Press.

Hawkins, F. P. (1969). *The logic of action: Young children at work.* New York: Pantheon Books.

Hindley, J. (1996). *In the company of children.* York, ME: Stenhouse.

Hinsdale, M. A., Lewis, H. M., & Waller, S. M. (1995). *It comes from the people: Community development and local theology.* Philadelphia: Temple University Press.

Hitchcock, G., & Hughes, D. (1995). *Research and the classroom teacher.* London: Routledge.

Hodgkinson, H. L. (1957). Action research—a critique. *Journal of Educational Sociology, 31*(4), 137–153.

Hollingsworth, S. (1994) *Teacher research: Urban literacy education.* New York: Teachers College Press.

Hollingsworth, S. (Ed.). (1997). *International action research: A casebook for educational reform.* London: Falmer Press.

Hopkins, L. T. (1950). Dynamics in research. *Teachers College Record, 51*(6) 339–346.

Horton, M. (1990). *The long haul: An autobiography.* New York: Doubleday.

Hubbard, R. S., & Power, B. M. (1993). *The art of classroom inquiry: A handbook for teacher-researchers.* Portsmouth, NH: Heinemann.

Huberman, M. (1996). Moving mainstream: Taking a closer look at teacher research. *Language Arts, 73,* 124–140.

Hursh, D. (1995). Developing discourses and structures to support action research for educational reform: Working both ends. In S. E. Noffke, & R. Stevenson (Eds.), *Educational action research: Becoming practically critical* (pp. 141–153). New York: Teachers College Press.

Hursh, D. (1997). Critical, collaborative action research in politically contested times. In S. Hollingsworth (Ed.), *International action research: A casebook for educational reform* (pp. 124–134). London: Falmer Press.

Jacobson, W. (1998). Defining the quality of practitioner research. *Adult Education Quarterly, 48*(3), 125–139.

Jacullo-Noto, J. (1984). Interactive research and development—partners in craft. *Teachers College Record, 86*(1), 208–222.

Johnston, S., & Proudford, C. (1994). Action research—who owns the process? *Educational Review, 46*(1), 3–14.

Kanevsky, R. D. (1993). Descriptive review of a child: A way of knowing about teaching and learning. In M. Cochran-Smith, & S. Lytle (Eds.), *Inside/outside: Teacher research and knowledge* (pp. 159–169). New York: Teachers College Press.

Kelly, A. (1984). Action research: What is it and what can it do? In R. G. Burgess (Ed.), *Issues in educational research* (pp. 129–151). Philadelphia: Falmer Press.

Kemmis, S. (1980/1988). Action research in retrospect and prospect. In S. Kemmis & R. McTaggart (Eds.), *Action research reader* (3rd ed., pp. 27–39). Geelong, Australia: Deakin University Press.

Kemmis, S., & Grundy, S. (1997). Educational action research in Australia: Organizations and practice. In S. Hollingsworth (Ed.), *International action research: A casebook for educational reform* (pp. 40–48). London: Falmer Press.

Kemmis, S., & McTaggart, R. (1988a). *The action research planner* (3rd ed.). Geelong, Australia: Deakin University Press.

Kemmis, S., & McTaggart, R. (Eds.). (1988b). *The action research reader* (3rd ed.). Geelong, Australia: Deakin University Press.

Kennedy, M. (1996). *Teacher conducting research.* East Lansing, MI: National Center for Research on Teacher Learning.

Kliebard, H. M. (1995). *The struggle for the American curriculum, 1893–1958* (2nd ed.). New York: Routledge.

Kochendorfer, L. (1997). Types of classroom teacher action research. *Teaching and Change, 4*(2), 157–173.

Kohl, H. (1967). *Thirty six children.* New York: Bantam.

Kozol, J. (1967). *Death at an early age.* New York: Signet.

Krater, J., Zeni, J., & Cason, N. D. (1994). *Mirror images: Teaching writing in black and white.* Portsmouth, NH: Heinemann.

Labaree, D. F. (1992). Power, knowledge, and the rationalization of teaching: A genealogy of the movement to professionalize teaching. *Harvard Educational Review, 62*(2), 123–154.

Ladson-Billings, G., & Tate, W. F. (1995). Toward a critical race theory of education. *Teachers College Record, 97*(1), 47–68.

Lagemann, E. (1996). *Contested terrain: A history of educational research in the United States, 1890–1990.* Chicago: The Spencer Foundation.

Lampert, M. (1985). How do teachers manage to teach? Perspectives on problems in practice. *Harvard Educational Review, 55*(2), 178–194.

Lather, P. (1986). Issues of validity in openly ideological research: Between a rock and a soft place. *Interchange, 17*(4), 63–84.

Lather, P. (1991). *Getting smart: Feminist research and pedagogy with/in the postmodern.* New York: Routledge.

Lather, P. (1993). Fertile obsession: Validity after poststructuralism. *Sociological Quarterly, 34*(4), 673–693.

Lawn, M. (1989). Being caught in schoolwork: The possibilities of research in teachers' work. In W. Carr (Ed.), *Quality in teaching: Arguments for a reflective profession* (pp. 147–161). London: Falmer Press.

Levine, A. G. (1982). *Love Canal: Science, Politics, and People.* Lexington, MA: D.C. Heath.

Lewin, K. (1946). Action research and minority problems. *Journal of Social Issues, 2*(4), 34–46.

Lima, E. S. (1998) Teachers as learners: The dialectics of improving pedagogical practice in Brazil. In G. Anderson & M. Montero-Sieburth (Eds.), *Educational qualitative research in Latin America: The struggle for a new paradigm* (pp. 141–160). New York: Garland.

Lincoln, Y. (1995). Emerging criteria for quality in qualitative and interpretative research. *Qualitative Inquiry, 1*(3), 275–289.

Lincoln, Y., & Guba, E. (1985). *Naturalistic inquiry.* Thousand Oaks, CA: Sage.

Lock, R. S., & Minarik, L. T. (1997). Gender equity in an elementary classroom: The power of praxis. In S. Hollingsworth (Ed.), *International action research: A casebook for educational reform* (pp. 179–189). London: Falmer Press.

Lomax, P. (1994). Standards, criteria and the problematic of action research within an award bearing course. *Educational Action Research, 2*(1), 113–126.

Lomax, P. (Ed.). (1996). *Quality management in education.* London: Routledge.

Lomax, P. (Ed.). (1997). *Dimensions of the educative relationship: Case studies from teaching and teacher education* (Kingston Hill Research) Surrey, UK: Kingston University.

Lomax, P., & Parker, Z. (1995). Accounting for ourselves: The problematic of representing action research. *Cambridge Journal of Education, 25*(3), 301–314.

Loughran, J., & Russell, T. (1997). *Teaching about teaching: Purpose, passion and pedagogy in teacher education.* London: Falmer Press.

Lyman, K. (1996). Ribbons, racism, and a placenta: The challenges and surprises of culturally relevant teaching. In Madison Metropolitan School District, *Race, class, gender and learning: Classroom action research, 1995–96* (pp. 59–91). Madison, WI: Madison Metropolitan School District.

Macgillivray, L. (1997). Do what I say, not what I do: An instructor rethinks her own teaching and research. *Curriculum Inquiry, 27*(4), 469–488.

Maher, A. (1993). An inquiry into reader response. In G. Wells (Ed.), *Changing schools from within: Creating communities of inquiry* (pp. 81–97). Portsmouth, NH: Heinemann.

Maher, F. (1991). Gender, reflexivity and teacher education: The Wheaton program. In B. R. Tabachnick, & K. Zeichner (Eds.), *Issues and practices in inquiry-oriented teacher education* (pp. 22–34). London: Falmer Press.

Manning, B. H., & McLaughlin, H. J. (Eds.). (1996). Studying our own practice in teacher education. [Special issue]. *Action in Teaching Education, 18,* 1–86.

Marion, R. (1998). *Practitioner research as a vehicle for teacher learning: A case study of one urban school district.* Unpublished doctoral dissertation. University of Wisconsin-Madison.

Marsella, J., Hussey, E., Emoto, C., Kaupp, J., Lee, G., Soares, C., Takushi, F., & Ushijima, T. (1994). Making waves: Explorations in the consequences of teacher research. *Teacher Research, 1*(2), 33–56.

Martin, R. E. (1995). *Practicing what we preach: Confronting diversity in teacher education.* Albany, NY: State University of New York Press.

Maxwell, J. (1992). Understanding and validity in qualitative research. *Harvard Educational Review, 62*(3), 279–300.

Mayer, M. (1997). Action research and the production of knowledge: The experience of an International project on environmental education. In S. Hollingsworth (Ed.). *International action research: A casebook for educational reform* (pp. 112–123). London: Falmer Press.

McCall, A. (1996). Teaching by the rules: Changing the rules in teacher education. *Teacher Education Quarterly, 23*(3) 143–152.

McIntyre, A. (1997). *Making meaning of whiteness: Exploring racial identity with White teachers.* Albany, NY: State University of New York Press.

McKernan, J. (1996). *Curriculum action research.* London: Kogan Page.

McNiff, J. (1993). *Teaching as learning: An action research approach.* London: Routledge.

McNiff, J., Lomax, P., & Whitehead, J. (1996). *You and your action research project.* London: Routledge.

McTaggart, R. (1989) Bureaucratic rationality and the self-educating profession: The problem of teacher privatism. *Journal of Curriculum Studies, 21*(4), 345–361.

McTaggart, R. (1991). *Action research: A short modern history.* Geelong, Australia: Deakin University Press.

McTaggart, R. (Ed.). (1997). *Participatory action research: International contexts and consequences.* Albany, NY: State University of New York Press.

Menchu, R. (1983). *I, Rigoberta Menchu: An Indian woman in Guatemala.* London: Verso.

Miller, C. (1996). No longer "too white": Using multicultural literature to promote academic achievement and cultural understanding. In H. Banford, M. Berkman, C. Chin, C. Cziko, B. Fecho, D. Jumpp, C. Miller, & M. Resnick, *Cityscapes: Eight views from the urban classroom* (pp. 73–97). Berkeley, CA: National Writing Project.

Miller, J. (1990). *Creating spaces and finding voices: Teachers collaborating for empowerment.* Albany, NY: State University of New York Press.

Mishler, E. G. (1990). Validation in inquiry-guided research: The role of exemplars in narrative studies. *Harvard Educational Review, 60*(4), 415–442.

Mohr, M. M., & Maclean, M. S. (1987). *Working together: A guide for teacher-researchers.* Urbana, IL: National Council of Teachers of English.

Moje, E. B., Remillard, J. T., Southerland, S., & Wade, S. (1999). Researching case pedagogies to inform our teaching. In M. Lundeberg, B. Levin, & H. Harrington (Eds.), *Who learns what from cases and how.* Mahwah, NJ: Lawrence Erlbaum Associates.

Munby H. (1995, April). *Gazing in the mirror: Asking questions about validity in self-study research.* A paper presented at the annual meeting of the American Educational Research Association, San Francisco, CA.

Murphy, C. (1991). How can Alaskan Native students be successful in college composition classes? In Alaska Teacher Researchers, *The Far Vision, The close look* (pp. 125–129). Fairbanks, AK: Alaska Teacher Research Network.

Neumann, A., & Peterson, P. (Eds). (1997). *Learning for our lives: Women, research and autobiography in education.* New York: Teachers College Press.

Nias, J. (1989). *Primary teachers talking: A study of teaching as work.* London: Routledge.

Noffke, S. E. (1991). Hearing the teacher's voice: Now what? *Curriculum Perspectives, 11*(4), 55–59.

Noffke, S. E. (1994a). Action research: Towards the next generation. *Educational Action Research, 2*(1), 9–21.

Noffke, S. E. (1994b, Feb.). *Uncovering the incredible whiteness of being.* Symposium paper presented at the 15th Annual Ethnography in Education Research Forum, Philadelphia.

Noffke, S. E. (1997a). Professional, personal, and political dimensions of action research. In M. Apple (Ed.), *Review of Research in Education, 22,* 305–343.

Noffke, S. E. (1997b). Themes and tensions in U.S. action research: Towards historical analysis. In S. Hollingsworth (Ed.), *International action research: A casebook for educational reform* (pp.–16). London: Falmer Press.

Noffke, S. E., & Brennan, M. (1997). Reconstructing the politics of action in action research. In S. Hollingsworth (Ed.), *International action research: A casebook for educational reform* (63–69). London: Falmer Press.

Noffke, S. E., & Stevenson, R. (Eds.). (1995). *Educational action research.* New York: Teachers College Press.

Noffke, S. E., & Zeichner, K. M. (1987, April). *Action research and teacher thinking: The first phase of the action research on action research project at the University of Wisconsin-Madison.* Paper presented at the annual meeting of the American Educational Research Association, Washington, DC.

Northfield, J. (1996, April). *Quality and the self-study perspective on research.* A paper presented at the annual meeting of the American Educational Research Association, New York City.

O'Dea, J. (1994). Pursuing truth in narrative research. *Journal of Philosophy of Education, 28*(2), 161–171.

O'Hanlon, C. (Ed.). (1991). *Participatory Enquiry in Action* (Classroom Action Research Network Publication 10A). Norwich, UK: CARN Publications.

O'Hanlon, C. (Ed.). (1996). *Professional development through action research in educational settings.* London: Falmer Press.

Oja, S. N., & Smulyan, L. (1989). *Collaborative action research: A developmental approach.* London: Falmer Press.

Olson, M. W. (1990). The teacher as researcher: A historical perspective. In M. W. Olson (Ed.), *Opening the door to classroom research* (pp. 1–20). Newark, DE: International Reading Association.

Osborne, M. D. (1997). Balancing individual and the group: A dilemma for the constructivist teacher. *Journal of Curriculum Studies, 29*(2), 183–196.

Paley, V. (1979). *White teacher.* Cambridge, MA: Harvard University Press.

Park, P. (1993). What is participatory research? A theoretical and methodological perspective. In P. Park, M. Brydon-Miller, B. Hall, & T. Jackson (Eds.), *Voices of change: Participatory research in the*

United States and Canada (pp. 1–19). Westport, CT: Bergin & Garvey.

Park, P., Brydon-Miller, M., Hall, B., & Jackson, T. (Eds.). (1993). *Voices of change: Participatory research in the United States and Canada.* Westport, CT: Bergin & Garvey.

Perrone, V. (1989). *Working papers: Reflections on teachers, schools and communities.* New York: Teachers College Press.

Peterman, F. (1997). The lived curriculum of constructivist teacher education. In V. Richardson (Ed.), *Constructivist teacher education: Building new understandings* (pp. 154–163). London: Falmer Press.

Phaik-Lah, K. (1997). The environments of action research in Malaysia. In S. Hollingsworth (Ed.) *International action research: A casebook for educational reform* (pp. 238–243). London: Falmer Press.

Phillips, D.C. (1994). Telling it straight: Issues in assessing narrative research. *Educational Psychologist, 29*(1), 13–21.

Polkinghorne, D. (1988). *Narrative knowing and the human sciences.* Albany, NY: State University of New York Press.

Popkewitz, T. (1994). Professionalism in teaching and teacher education: Some notes on its history, ideology and potential. *Teaching and Teacher Education, 10*(1), 1–14.

Posch, P. (1993). Action research in Environmental Education. *Educational Action Research, 1*(3), 447–455.

Power, B. M., & Hubbard, R. S. (1995). A note from the editors. *Teacher Research, 2*(2), iii–iv.

Reason, P. (1994). Three approaches to participative inquiry. In N. Denzin & Y. Lincoln (Eds.), *Handbook of qualitative research* (pp. 324–339). Thousand Oaks, CA: Sage.

Reason, P., & Rowan, J. (1981). Issues of validity in new paradigm research. In P. Reason & P. Rowan (Eds.), *Human inquiry* (pp. 239–252). New York: Wiley.

Reinharz, S. (1992). *Feminist methods in social research.* New York: Oxford University Press.

Richardson, V. (1994a). Conducting research on practice. *Educational Researcher, 23*(5), 5–10.

Richardson, V.(1994b). Teacher inquiry as professional staff development. In S. Hollingsworth & H. Sockett (Eds.), *Teacher research and educational reform* (pp. 186–203). Chicago: University of Chicago Press.

Richardson, V. (Ed.). (1997). *Constructivist teacher education: Building a world of new understandings.* London: Falmer Press.

Richert, A. (1991). Case methods in teacher education: Using cases to teach teacher reflection. In B. R. Tabachnick, & K. Zeichner (Eds.), *Issues and practices in inquiry-oriented teacher education* (pp. 130–150). London: Falmer Press.

Richert, A. (1996). Teacher research on school change: What teachers learn and why that matters. In K. Kent (Ed.), *Breaking new ground: Teacher action research, a wealth of learning.* Redwood City, CA: Bay Region IV Professional Development Consortium.

Roman, L. (1989, Jan.). *Double exposure: The politics of feminist research.* Paper presented at the Qualitative Research in Education Conference, Athens, Georgia.

Roman, L., & Apple, M. (1990). Is naturalism a move away from positivism? Materialist and feminist approaches to subjectivity in ethnographic research. In E. Eisner (Ed.), *Qualitative inquiry in education* (pp. 38–73). New York: Teachers College Press.

Ruiz de Gauna, P., Diaz, C., Gonzalez, V., & Garaizar, I. (1995) Teachers' professional development as a process of action research. *Educational Action Research, 3*(2), 183–194.

Russell, T., & Korthagen, F. (Eds.). (1995). *Teachers who teach teachers: Reflections on teacher education.* London: Falmer Press.

Saavedra, E. (1996). Teacher study groups: Contexts for transformative learning and action. *Theory into Practice, 35*(4), 271–277.

Sagor, R. (1992). *How to conduct action research.* Alexandria, VA: Association for Supervision and Curriculum Development.

Schaffel, V. (1996). Shifting gears: An urban teacher rethinks her practice. In G. Burnaford, J. Fischer, & D. Hobson (Eds.), *Teachers doing research: Practical possibilities* (pp. 25–31). Mahwah, NJ: Lawrence Erlbaum Associates.

Schindler, G. (1993). The Environment and Schools Initiatives (ENSI): The conflict. *Educational Action Research, 1*(3), 457–468.

Schön, D. (1983). *The reflective practitioner.* New York: Basic Books.

Schubert, W., & Lopez-Schubert, A. (1997). Sources of a theory for action research in the United States of America. In R. McTaggart (Ed.), *Participatory action research: International contexts and consequences* (pp. 203–222). Albany, NY: State University of New York Press.

Self-study and living educational theory. (1995). [Special issue]. *Teacher Education Quarterly, 22.*

Shockley, B., Michalove, B., & Allen, J. (1995). *Engaging families: Connecting home and school literacy communities.* Portsmouth, NH: Heinemann.

Short, K. G., Schroeder, J., Laird, J., Kaufmann, G., Ferguson, M. J., & Crawford, K. M. (1996). *Learning together through inquiry: From Columbus to integrated curriculum.* York, ME: Stenhouse.

Shumsky, A. (1958). *The action research way of learning: An approach to in-service education.* New York: Teachers College Press.

Somekh, B. (1993a). Quality in educational research: The contribution of classroom teachers. In J. Edge & K. Richards (Eds.), *Teachers develop, teachers research: Papers on classroom research and teacher development* (pp. 26–38). Portsmouth, NH: Heinemann.

Somekh, B. (1993b) Teachers generating knowledge: Constructing practical and theoretical understanding from multi-site case studies. In C. Day, J. Calderhead, & P. Denicolo (Eds.), *Research on teacher thinking: Understanding professional development* (pp. 124–147). London: Falmer Press.

Somekh, B. (1995). The contribution of action research to development in social endeavors: A position paper on action research methodology. *British Educational Research Journal, 21*(3), 339–355.

Stake, R. (1995). *The art of case study research.* Thousand Oaks, CA: Sage.

Steffy, S., & Hood, W. J. (1994). *If this is social studies, why isn't it boring?* York, ME: Stenhouse.

Stenhouse, L. (1968). The Humanities Curriculum Project. *Journal of Curriculum Studies, 23*(1), 26–33.

Stenhouse, L. (1975). *An introduction to curriculum research and development.* London: Heinemann Educational Books.

Stenhouse, L. (1983). *Authority, education and emancipation.* London: Heinemann Educational Books.

Stevenson, R. (1996, March). *What counts as "good" action research?* Paper presented at the Ethnography in Educational Research Forum, Philadelphia.

Streib, L. (1985). *A Philadelphia teacher's journal.* Grand Forks, ND: North Dakota Study Group for Teaching and Learning.

Stringer, E. (1996). *Action research: A handbook for practitioners.* Thousand Oaks, CA: Sage.

Stumbo, C. (1992). Giving their words back to them: Cultural journalism in Eastern Kentucky. In N. A. Branscombe, D. Goswami, & J. Schwartz (Eds.), *Students teaching, teachers learning* (pp. 124–142). Portsmouth, NH: Boynton/Cook, Heinemann.

Sylvester, P. S. (1994). Elementary school curricula and urban transformation. *Harvard Educational Review, 64*(3), 309–331.

Taba, H., & Noel, E. (1957). *Action research: A case study.* Washington, DC: Association for Curriculum & Supervision.

Tabachnick, B. R., & Zeichner, K. (Eds.). (1991). *Issues and practices in inquiry-oriented teacher education.* London: Falmer Press.

Tabachnick, B. R., & Zeichner, K. (1999). Action research and the development of conceptual change teaching in science. *Science Education, 83*(3), 309–322.

Tandon, R. (1988). Social transformation and participatory research. *Convergence, 21*(2–3), 5–18.

Taylor, B., & Parmar, S. (Compilers). (1993). *Partners for inclusion.* Vancouver, Canada: British Columbia Teachers Federation.

Teitelbaum, K., & Britzman, D. (1991). Reading and doing ethnography: Teacher education and reflective practice. In B. R. Tabachnick & K. Zeichner (Eds.), *Issues and practices in inquiry-oriented teacher education* (pp. 166–185). London: Falmer Press.

Thomas, D. (Ed.). (1995). *Teachers' stories.* Philadelphia: Open University Press.

Threatt, S., Buchanan, J., Morgan, B., Strieb, L. Y., Sugarman, J., Swenson, J., Teel, K., & Tomlinson, J. (1994). Teachers' voices in the conversation about teacher research. In S. Hollingsworth, & H. Sockett (Eds.), *Teacher research and educational reform* (pp. 222–233). Chicago: University of Chicago Press.

Tikunoff, W. J., & Ward, B. A. (1983). Collaborative research on teaching. *Elementary School Journal, 83*(4), 453–468.

Torres, C. A. (1992). Participatory action research and popular education in Latin America. *Qualitative Studies in Education, 5*(1), 51–62.

Travers, M. W. (1958). *An introduction to educational research.* New York: Macmillan.

Tripp, D. (1990). Socially critical action research. *Theory into Practice, 29*(3), 158–166.

Troen, V., Kamii, M., & Boles, K. (1997, March). *From carriers of culture to agents of change: Teacher-initiated professional development in the learning/teaching collaborative inquiry seminars.* Paper presented at the annual meeting of the American Educational Research Association, Chicago.

Turchi, L. (1996). The elixir of technology and the teacher researcher. *Teacher Research, 4*(1), 104–111.

Van Manen, M. (1990). *Researching lived experience.* Albany, NY: State University of New York Press.

Wagler, M. (1996). Supporting innovative teaching: A model for restructuring schools via teacher networks. In Madison Metropolitan School District, *Elementary and middle school classroom action research 1995–1996* (pp. 89–118). Madison, WI: Madison Public Schools.

Walker, M. (1988). Thoughts of the potential of action research in South African schools. *Cambridge Journal of Education 18*(2), 147–154.

Walker, M. (1993). Developing the theory and practice of action research: A South African case. *Educational Action Research, 1*(1), 95–109.

Walker, M. (1995). Context, critique, and change: Doing action research in South Africa. *Educational Action Research, 3*(1), 9–27.

Wallace, M. (1987). A historical review of action research: Some implications for the education of teachers in their managerial role. *Journal of Education for Teaching, 13*(2), 97–115.

Wann, K. (1953). Action research in schools. *Review of Educational Research, 23*(4), 337–345.

Watkins, K. (1991, April). *Validity in action research.* Paper presented at the annual meeting of the American Educational Research Association, Chicago.

Watt, M. L., & Watt, D. L. (1993). Teacher research, action research: The Logo Action Research Collaborative. *Educational Action Research, 1*(1), 35–63.

Weiner, G. (1989). Professional self-knowledge versus social justice: A critical analysis of the teacher-researcher movement. *British Educational Research Journal, 15(*1), 41–51.

Wells, G. (Ed.). (1993). *Changing schools from within: Creating communities of inquiry.* Portsmouth, NH: Heinemann.

Whitehead, J. (1989). Creating a living educational theory from questions of the kind, "How do I improve my practice?" *Cambridge Journal of Education, 19*(1), 41–52.

Whitehead, J. (1993). *The growth of educational knowledge: Creating your own living educational theories.* Bournemouth, UK: Hyde Publications.

Whyte, J. (1986). *Girls into science and technology.* London: Routledge & Kegan Paul.

Wiles, K. (1953). Can we sharpen the concept of action research? *Educational Leadership, 9*(7), 408–419, 432.

Winter, R. (1987). *Action research and the nature of social inquiry.* Aldershot, UK: Avebury.

Winter, R. (1989). *Learning from experience: Principle and practice in action-research.* London: Falmer Press.

Woodson, C. G. (1933/1977). *The mis-education of the Negro.* New York: AMS Press.

Zeichner, K. (1991). Contradictions and tensions in the professionalization of teaching and democratization of schools. *Teachers College Record, 92*(3), 363–379.

Zeichner, K. (1993). Action research: Personal renewal and social reconstruction. *Educational Action Research, 1*(2), 199–219.

Zeichner, K. (1995a). Reflections of teacher educator working for social change. In T. Russell, & F. Korthagen (Eds.), *Teachers who teach teachers: Reflections on teacher education* (pp. 11–24). London: Falmer Press.

Zeichner, K. (1995b). Beyond the divide of teacher research and academic research. *Teachers and Teaching: Theory and Practice, 1*(2), 153–172.

Zeichner, K. (1997, Oct.). *Action research as a tool for educational and social reconstruction.* Paper presented at the annual meeting of the Brazilian National Association of Postgraduate Education and Educational Research (ANPED), Caxambu, Brazil.

Zeichner, K. (1999, Oct.). Teacher research as professional development for P–12 educators. Washington, DC: U.S. Office of Education.

Zeichner, K., Amukushu, A. K., Muukenga, K. M., & Shilamba, P. P. (1998). Critical practitioner inquiry and the transformation of teacher education in Namibia. *Educational Action Research, 6*(2), 183–203.

Zeichner, K., & Gore, J. (1995). Using action research as a vehicle for student teacher reflection: A social reconstructionist approach. In S. E. Noffke, & R. Stevenson (Eds.), *Educational action research: Becoming practically critical* (pp. 13–30). New York: Teachers College Press.

Zeichner, K., Marion, R., & Caro-Bruce, C. (1998). *The nature and impact of action research in one urban school district.* Final Report. Chicago: The Spencer Foundation.

Zuber-Skerritt, O. (1996). Emancipatory action research for organisational change and management development. In O. Zuber-Skerritt (Ed.), *New directions in action research* (pp. 83–105). London: Falmer Press.

Part 3
Subject Matter

19.

Instructional Explanations: A Commonplace for Teaching and Location for Contrast

Gaea Leinhardt
University of Pittsburgh

Always and everywhere, whether at one extreme or the other, generalities are achieved only by processes of abstraction or idealization. Species are differentiated and defined on the basis of only some *differences and similarities. Many others are ignored. . . . The very fabric of the practical . . . consists of the richly endowed and variable particulars from which theory abstracts or idealizes its uniformities. The road we drive on has bends and potholes not included on the map. We teach not literature, but this novel and that. The child with whom we work is both more and less than the percentile ranks, social class, and personality type into which she falls. Yet, we will drive our car smoothly, convey* Billy Budd *effectively, and teach 'Tilda well only as we take account of conditions of each which are not included in the theories which describe them as roads, literature, and learning child.*

(Schwab, 1978, p. 324)

We observe few objects really closely. As we walk on the earth, we observe the external events at two or three arms' lengths. If we ride a horse or drive an automobile, we are further separated from the immediate surround. We see and photograph "scenery"; our vast world is inadequately described as "landscape." . . . The small and the commonplace are rarely explored.

(Adams, 1983, pp. 34–35)

We begin this chapter, the quotations above notwithstanding, with a discussion of the chapter's location—both literal and figural. If tradition is any guide, this chapter will find itself located in the latter 20% of an enormous handbook. In each of the previous three editions of the *Handbook,* the discussions of teaching specific subjects and grades has always been a part of the concluding section. The location could be interpreted as though the editors viewed the research on teaching and learning subject matter as an afterthought, but I prefer to assume that teaching and learning in the subject areas is a culmination—a summation of what we need to know about the nature of the learners and their understandings, about the nature of the social systems at work in the school, about the professional preparation of teachers, and about the methodologies available to us as we seek to understand how teaching affects learning.

This chapter is located in a set of discourses and in a particu-

The author gratefully acknowledges the advice of reviewers Pamela Grossman and Alan Schoenfeld, the helpful comments and moral support of Suzanne Wilson, the collegial assistance of Joyce Fienberg, and the teachers—including Magdalene Lampert and others who chose to remain anonymous—for allowing her into their classrooms. A special thanks to Virginia Richardson for her patience and support.

lar part of a volume. It is located, on the one hand, within the heated discussion concerning the subject matter specificity versus the subject matter generality of teaching and, on the other hand, within the discussion of how we should interpret excellent teaching and acts of "teaching" in the context of a constructivist psychology. The quotations that start this chapter are meant to suggest that, through close examination of cases of the specific, especially the specifics of subject matter teaching in classrooms, we can understand not only the more general constructs of teaching but also the ways to support and encourage learning.

The chapter is part of an ongoing discussion and elucidation of subject matter teaching and learning roused by Lee Shulman (1974, 1986, 1987) and chorused by Pamela Grossman and Susan Stodolsky (Grossman & Stodolsky, 1994; Stodolsky, 1988). The intent of this chapter is to advance that particular discussion while being aware of the backdrop of the debates mentioned above. The core argument is that the uniqueness of epistemology, language, task, constraints, and affordances of different subjects transform and mold the commonplaces of the instructional landscapes (Schwab, 1978). The assertion is that teaching is specific with respect to task, time, place, participants, and content, and that different subjects vary in those specifics (Doyle, 1992; Greene, 1994; Schwab, 1978). Thus, learning to write an analytic essay in history is unlike solving algebra word problems, even though both can be considered a form of problem solving. The process of polishing and refining an essay over many class periods is different from coming to understand the multiple perspectives from which an historical event can be considered or the multiple solution paths that are possible for a complex mathematical problem, even though revision and flexibility of thinking is present in all three activities (Kieran, 1992; Sfard, 1991; Young & Leinhardt, 1998b).

Collaboratively conducting a science project in which multiple laboratory tools must be chosen and assembled or jointly solving a mathematics problem in which multiple representations must be coordinated or built and then justified is different from collaborating on a history project in which multiple texts must be interpreted, even though collaboration of activity, division of labor, and development of shared goals are present in all three undertakings. Therefore, teaching students in ways that support their problem solving, their revision and reconsideration, and their long-term planning and collaboration in different subjects is also different. At the same time, we must acknowledge that there are commonplaces of teaching; indeed we will, as the title suggests, take one of the common places—instructional explanation—as our central example. Further, we are assuming that teaching is both a long-term undertaking by "the teacher" and a short-term role shared by many different actors in the classroom—students, teachers, texts, and computers.

Following early critiques by Schwab (1978) and Shulman (1974) as well as the more recent ones by Fenstermacher and Richardson (1994), the discussion here is designed to center around educational (rather than psychological or anthropological) so-called "discipline-based" problems. Therefore, the argument that teaching is bound to the specificity of subjects being taught and also to the social context is framed, to the extent possible, in the pragmatic discourse of practices (Schwab,

1978). The point is that this chapter will not center on the discussion of the structure of discourse analysis or on the semantics of activity structures, because those highly relevant constructs are not the central set of questions for this educational issue. Tools for analyzing the situation, however, are borrowed from many disciplines including linguistics, psychology, and anthropology.

The focus or unit of examination in this chapter is the entire classroom discussion as it unfolds around specific tasks, supporting actions, and materials. The focus of the chapter extends beyond the individual learner or the dyad of a particular discussion. The focus is on explanatory discussions as commonly produced resources for members of the classroom in the context of an ongoing, jointly understood curriculum. In this sense, then, the stance is consistent with Sfard's discussion of the two metaphors for education, acquisitional and participatory (Sfard, 1998). In her trenchant review, Sfard distinguishes between the acquisitional metaphor of knowledge as a thing that one can gain and transmit and the more recent consideration of knowledge as an aspect of participatory practice that does not exist separately from the specific contexts and uses of a community of practitioners. Her main point is that we need both metaphors to proceed. The chapter considers explanations to be a particular kind of practice that occurs in classrooms. The practice is most commonly, but not always, shared by teachers and students.

The chapter considers the purpose of explanatory discussion to be unabashedly and unapologetically learning and teaching. By learning, I mean both the increased level of participation in a community of discourse AND the acquisition of new knowledge and skills; I mean the transformation or conceptual alteration of existing knowledge and skills AND the alteration of dispositions toward knowledge and skills in ways that permit and encourage students to participate comfortably in new and expanding communities of discourse. I consider teaching to be those activities that are deliberately designed to facilitate and support learning. In learning how to teach, teachers must be able to both design and deliver a coherent and meaningful explanation just as they must be able to participate in and facilitate a meaningful explanatory discussion that is being led by students.

The issue of identifying and differentiating instructional explanations and monitoring the transformations of such explanations in different subjects is uniquely a problem within the practice of education. However, a duality, a layering, exists even within the commitment to practice, because it includes, in fact, two practices—the practice of teaching and learning in the classroom and the practice of studying such teaching and learning. In this chapter, I focus on the former; I do so because I believe that careful and continued research is needed on the kinds of practices that occur in classrooms and on how teachers can best learn them. The chapter makes use of a second dualism: On the one hand, the chapter centers on differences in the nature of instructional explanations in different subjects and, on the other hand, it uses a core model of such explanations to organize the chapter's central discussion.

We know intuitively that subject matter content affects the nature and practices of teaching. We can easily distinguish a calculus class from a literature class and a beginning reading class from a beginning music class because the tasks, activities, and discourses are so distinct. Naturally, we might find many moments where both the task and the discourse seem intriguingly close to the subjects in a different area—discussions of the aesthetics of a proof or the precision of musical performance might blur boundaries. Moreover, at some levels of description—seat work, board work, testing, open-ended questioning—subject matter becomes totally invisible. However, the invisibility does not mean the differences are not real or are not there, only that they are not seen or acknowledged.

The chapter starts with a review of the claims that teaching differs substantially depending on the specific school subject. I select a critical, identifiable part of the instructional system—instructional explanation—as a way to study teaching systematically in different domains. I explore instructional explanation in some detail, distinguishing it from other forms of explanation, and discuss its components. Then, I turn to an example to elucidate and illustrate our conceptualization. Finally, I conclude with a brief discussion of what this analysis reveals about teaching in the subject areas and teaching in general and how we might proceed to use these insights to educate teachers and to conduct research into teaching.

What Is the Conversation That Is Being Extended?

This chapter extends a particular intellectual conversation about subject matter teaching and learning. The conversation was started by Lee Shulman (1986) and Susan Stodolsky (1988) and was continued by Stodolsky and Pamela Grossman (Grossman & Stodolsky, 1994). In the context of descriptions of effective and ineffective teaching practices, Shulman observed and Stodolsky showed that the differences between teaching in one subject area and teaching in another had been overlooked.[1]

Twenty-five years ago, Shulman addressed the annual meeting of the National Association for Research in Science Teaching in Chicago with a talk titled, "The Psychology of School Subjects: A Premature Obituary" (Shulman, 1974). The published version of this address presents an elegant argument for pursuing a program of research that is neither enamored with theory nor pragmatically opportunistic but that somehow wends its way toward middle-level theories and meaningful understandings of the practice of teaching in specific domains. The argument suggests that, in 1974, we were in a position to tackle the truly complex issues involved in understanding teaching but only if we abandoned simplistic notions of atomistic variables that were impervious to the effects of contextual issues such as subject matter.

Shulman points out, by quoting Brownell (1948), that subjects themselves are different and, therefore, require different acts of teaching.

> Yet, from subject to subject, and within the same subject, arbitrary associations differ; skills differ; concepts differ; and withal, pupil behavior differs. The differences reside, in part, in the intrinsic relations involved; they reside in the opportunities afforded for the use of previous experience; they reside in varying amounts of complexity, they reside in sheer difficulty with respect to mastery. All these differences need to be explored. (Brownell, 1948, p. 496, cited in Shulman, 1974, p. 328)

But if everything is unique, and nothing generalizes, then what is the benefit of close examination? Shulman handles this issue by considering the role of theory in educational research overall and in instructional research in particular. His suggestion was quite radical then, namely, that theory should be used to build up meanings and interpretations. Transforming the initial discussion somewhat, we can imagine that what can be generalized is our capacity to examine the uniqueness of instructional moments rather than the "findings" of instructional outcomes. Theories, Shulman argues, should serve as guides and heuristics for the examination, inspection, and interpretation of teaching and learning: Theories become cognitive tools. This suggestion was precisely the one made by Joseph Schwab in his article, "The Practical: Arts of Eclectic" (Schwab, 1978).

Shulman went on to make the first of several calls for research that elucidates the practices of excellent practitioners within the framework of their teaching content. Shulman posited that teachers needed knowledge of their subject matter and of pedagogical content. Identifying the construct of pedagogical content knowledge was like letting the proverbial genie out of the bottle. Not only did the study of the "Wisdom of Practice" that Shulman engineered grow directly out of that call and out of the definition of pedagogical content knowledge but also a host of other studies emerged that had been waiting in the wings—studies that showed the ways in which teaching of specific subject topics might be considered. The research of Shulman's students and colleagues (Carlsen, 1991; Grossman, 1991; Gudmundsdottir, 1991; Hashweh, 1985; Putnam, 1985; Tamir, 1988, 1991; Wineburg & Wilson, 1991) covered much of the core K–12 curriculum (biology, history, literature, mathematics, and other sciences). These studies, taken together, clarify the range and depth of distinctions among teachers of different subjects, but they also fly in the face of a conception of instruction and learning that imagines a world without teachers.

---

[1] One possible reason for ignoring the systematic investigation of subject matter and its influence on teaching stems from the history of modern educational research. In the late 1960s and early 1970s, much of educational research was heavily supported by federal grants. These grants tended to support classroom research as a component of program evaluations—indeed, evaluations of federally funded programs. But which programs were being federally funded, teaching Shakespeare at the high school level or teaching calculus? Neither. The federal government, under the banner of the Great Society program, funded early childhood interventions and early schooling. Programs such as Head Start and Follow Through emphasized getting a jump on the academic curriculum to come but worked most heavily at establishing commonly effective educational practices in the normally self-contained elementary classrooms.

Logically, the research into those programs would stress those aspects of teaching that were common across subjects. Furthermore, the prominence of behaviorist programs, Piagetian programs, or both tended to emphasize the importance of reinforcement and sequence. That is, they emphasized generic aspects of teaching. The programs being studied were not designed to teach the more advanced content; they were designed to provide critical tools for future learning. If the programmatic efforts had been at the secondary level and had emphasized the preparation of future professionals or the advancement of national competency in science and mathematics, I believe that the research would have been far more closely tied to the interplay between the epistemology of the subject matter and the particular teaching demands.

Shulman stands firmly for teaching and equally firmly for the careful transformation of our ideas about what it means to be an excellent teacher. Clearly, the classroom is a social system. Clearly, all of the parties in the classroom both learn and teach. However, it is the adults, with their life experiences, who assume formal responsibility for assuring that conditions are arranged to promote learning.

Shulman has also provided us with two extensive reviews of the literature that are key to understanding excellent teaching in subject areas (Shulman, 1986; Shulman & Quinlan, 1996). His popular 1986 *Handbook* chapter centers on the ways in which various communities of researchers who address issues of teaching and learning go about their tasks. Communities tend to share sets of important questions and varieties of methods for approaching problems, and they listen to each others' views in respectful and referential ways. The communities share, in other words, paradigms.

In his chapter, Shulman traces the contributions and limitations of the process-product paradigm and the ascendancy of cognitive psychology as a discipline that was willing to address issues of why. His chapter also predicts the rise of sociocultural views in which "why" is considered answerable only if "under what conditions" and "with whom" is well described. Shulman lent support to those trying to understand not only what teachers were doing but also what they were thinking, and in that context, he pointed to a "missing program." That missing program of research, Shulman asserted, would deal with the knowledge and understandings that teachers have about subject matter content and how this understanding plays out in the thoughts and actions of teachers in the classroom.

By 1996, Shulman and his coauthor Kathleen Quinlan, in reviewing the *Comparative Psychology of School Subjects,* traced back to the Judd (1915, 1936) and Thorndike (1922) rivalry the roots of the debate surrounding the significance of subject matter being embedded in teaching and learning (Shulman & Quinlan, 1996). They set up the discussion as a tension between the psychologizing of school subjects and vice versa. In continuing the search for a middle-level theory that eschews this dichotomy (advocated in both the 1974 and 1986 Shulman pieces), Shulman and Quinlan trace Brownell's program of research on the learning of mathematical ideas, research on teaching within the subjects of mathematics and history, and self-reflective research on teaching primarily in mathematics.

In this series of reviews and especially the final one in 1996, Shulman and Quinlan anchor the discussion to a core learning issue—the idea of transfer. Indeed, the importance of transfer coupled with the debate as to its existence has preoccupied much of educational psychology and its critics. By attending to transfer as an issue, Shulman and Quinlan locate one of several possible places to deeply explore how subject matter is important in teaching and learning. In this chapter, I will not plumb those waters but will go to a more fine-grained aspect of the task of teaching and to an educational activity by using "task" in Doyle's (1983) sense and "activity" in the socioculturalists' sense.

Before turning to explanation as one task of teaching, we need to examine another set of evidence that points to the importance of subject matter in teaching. In the late 1970s, Stodolsky collected the data on fifth-grade social studies and mathe-

matics classes that became the core of her book, *The Subject Matters* (1988). Among many important findings in the research was clear evidence that activity structures were different depending on both where in the lesson one was looking and which subject matter one was examining. Although intuitively obvious at some level, the finding represented solid documentation that a substantial portion of the research literature on teaching and effective teaching practices had been ignoring an important issue.

For example, if something as simple as time on task or as subtle as coherent verbal reasoning in a discussion was dependent on the particular subject and particular segment of a lesson, then findings concerning student achievement that ignored these distinctions might be suspect. What Stodolsky's brief 136-page book showed was that teachers routinely reconfigured activity structures depending on the subject matter even when the same teacher taught both subjects.

Stodolsky and others (Berliner, 1983; Bossert, 1979; Leinhardt & Greeno, 1986) used the concept of activity structures and segments as a way of describing the pattern of arrangements for classroom activity and the tasks of that activity. The paradigmatic example of an activity structure is the reading lesson that has one group reading aloud in a reading circle with a teacher while two or more other groups are reading silently at their desks. Mathematics lessons contain similarly recognizable activity structures such as review, presentation, and guided practice. Cognitive analyses of these activities have stressed the arrangement of conditions, the action schemas, and the cognitive goals (Leinhardt & Greeno, 1986).

Later analyses would use similar concepts but would cluster all the activities and goals that served a particular instructional task (Stein, Grover, & Henningsen, 1996). Collectively, the import of this work was that it allowed us to break out of a conceptualization of the class periods as homogeneous and begin to look at the parts of lessons in ways that could highlight distinctions and uniquenesses (within and between them). Naturally, as soon as we recognize that lessons may consist of multiple activity types and multiple tasks, we recognize that the practices of teaching must accommodate and be able to develop these different sorts of tasks.

Building from the discussions led by Shulman and supported by empirical findings, Grossman and Stodolsky (1994) reviewed the evidence surrounding the significance of different school subject matters from the perspective of content as context for teaching. As they say so eloquently,

> Although policymakers and researchers alike have often portrayed teaching as a generic enterprise, schoolteaching is not schoolteaching is not schoolteaching. The work of teaching depends greatly on the specific grade level; the particular subject matter; the school's organization, mission, culture, and location; and the district, state, and national contexts in which teaching and learning occur. (p. 180)

Their main thesis is that the structural and epistemological organizations of disciplines play themselves out in fundamental ways in the lives of teachers, especially secondary teachers. Because Grossman and Stodolsky have done such a thorough and relatively recent job of analyzing the global features of subject matter and its effect on the organization and experiences of teaching, I feel free in this chapter to excuse myself from the normal reviewing task and focus on a rather small part of the picture, instructional explanations.

In recent years, as serious consideration of the constructivist stance on learning has grown and as work has begun to link the constructivist and sociocultural discussions (Cobb, 1994; Cobb & Yackel, 1996), we can see a tendency, in emphasizing these features of the learning setting, to minimize research on the complexity of teaching.[2] In some versions of this argument, both the teacher and teaching would be viewed as doing best if they "softly and suddenly faded away" (Carroll, 1962, p. 89). As researchers try to emphasize the need for teachers to listen and learn from the mental constructions and social goals of their students, the unfortunate suggestion or assumption has been made that any action on the part of the teacher imposes and is deleterious rather than supportive and facilitative. This assumption leaves us in the untenable position of suggesting that the best teaching is to do nothing and that, therefore, we should not strive to work on and improve the most directly improvable portion of the educational system.

Research that extends back to the 1920s and even earlier bears strong witness to both the inherent complexity of effective teaching and the complexity of thinking about teaching as an activity, skill, and art (Barr, 1929; Fenstermacher & Soltis, 1986). The complexity of teaching stems, in part, from its real-time and nonroutinized feature. Only small portions of teaching can be off-loaded into either relatively habitual social scripts (Leinhardt, Weidman, & Hammond, 1987) or more controllable time frames such as preclass planning or postclass analysis (Jackson, 1968). When the class starts, the teacher is contending not only with his or her own beliefs and intentions but also with the continuous revisions and reworkings of those intentions and with beliefs that are based on what is actually going on. (See van Zee & Minstrell, 1997, for an intensive examination of eight minutes of such activity; in the same tradition of fine-grained study, see Schoenfeld, 1998, for a way of representing these processes.)

Teachers are faced with a flow of information about the mood, understanding, and general state of their students and also with a flow of information about progress or lack of it with respect to an intellectual agenda. (See Duesterberg, 1998; Teel, Debruin-Parecki, & Covington, 1998, for ways in which teachers might be thought of as engaged in on-line reflection.) The information about the general state of affairs in the classroom is filtered, considered, and analyzed in different ways depending on the teacher's own sense of what it means to teach well and the teacher's own sense of moral activity with respect to teaching (Durkheim, 1925/1961; Fenstermacher & Soltis, 1986).

At the same time, the core activities of teaching are also being shaped by the students in the environment. Because of the social nature of teaching and because of its intensely dynamic features, it poses, like other real-world, real-time situations, a far more complex problem for analysis than activities such as chess, the "Tower of Hanoi," or even solving difficult algebra word problems (Anzai & Simon, 1979; Simon & Chase, 1973; Zhu & Simon, 1987). If teaching is so complex, why subject it to a peculiarly fine-grained analysis? Why not stay at the more global level? One reason is that learning to teach is difficult, and learning to teach well seems to be almost a matter of chance. Perhaps by analyzing carefully the tasks of teaching and the ways in which those tasks are handled successfully within subject matters, we might find ways to be more supportive of the beginning teacher. One way to examine teaching at this fine-grained level is to compare the details of excellent teaching with those of less successful or less polished teaching.

Individual teachers differ greatly on many features; therefore, contrasting the behaviors of excellent teachers with those of weaker teachers, although revealing, can only tell us so much (Leinhardt, Young, & Merriman, 1995; Wineburg & Wilson, 1988). We need to make some assumptions both about the components on which to focus (here theory helps considerably) and about how to break apart the teaching activity. In considering what is required to be an excellent teacher, we can easily fall into the trap of debating which component is more necessary than the others or which needs to be acquired first.

This concern with issues of importance and primacy has been most vigorously debated in discussions of teacher education. The arguments play themselves out in the following way. One simply cannot teach a sensible interpretation of the northern migration of southern Blacks in the early 20th century unless the class is reasonably ready to learn and is under some sort of control. Therefore, teachers of history, mathematics, and, in fact, all other subjects need to learn about classroom management strategies first. Then they can turn to the subtleties of the content (Berliner 1986, 1992; Borko & Livingston, 1989; Sabers, Cushing, & Berliner, 1991). Furthermore, most new teachers and student teachers are seriously concerned about and frustrated by issues of management and control (Jones & Vesilind, 1995; Rust, 1994). So, one component of teaching that must be studied is management.

However, the argument goes, if one has something compelling and interesting for students to learn and appreciate, then management will follow naturally, according to students' intrinsic motivation and curiosity. Learning strategies for teaching that do not relate to the meaningful content under consideration are pointless (Kemper, 1992; Shulman, 1992). In this view, the most important aspect of teaching is the transformation of knowledge for teaching (Grossman, 1989). If one does not know what to teach or how to make it interesting, no set of management strategies will work. Therefore, emphasize content-based pedagogy first. The difficulty in formulating the debate in this way is that it presumes a particular view of teacher learning, one that requires following a best singular sequence. If we formulate learning to teach as an intricate series of tasks, tools, and practices all within subject matter knowledge, then these can be more easily shared with a mentor and learned by a novice.

Student teachers probably need to move gradually into their teaching environments, carefully taking on responsibility for

---

[2] A notable exception to this trend is the current work of Lampert and her students (Lampert & Ball, 1998), and Ball (1993), Lampert (1985, 1992), and Ball and Lampert (1999).

important parts of the whole lesson arrangement, using and developing multiple knowledge bases together rather than trying to master just one dimension at a time. Carefully annotating and explaining how lessons are working from a theoretically and pragmatically informed position seems a more promising approach for learning to teach than one in which parts of the teaching task are taught in separate methods and content courses. (See Gregg et al., 1997, for a description of a similar teacher education program and Leinhardt, 1993b, for other suggestions.) The point of this discussion is to suggest that an appropriate approach on several levels is to abandon the distinction between content and methods and to turn instead to critical activities that may well be repetitive at some levels but that are uniquely formed by the intellectual situation in which they evolve.

In this section, we have reviewed the origins of the discussion about the ways subject matter influences teaching. The discussion is located, in Schwab's terms, in the particulars. One does not just teach or talk or converse; one teaches someone and something, and those ones and things are the particulars—specific people and specific subjects. Knowing a lot about the subject, in turn, suggests to the teachers different kinds of activities, different kinds of tasks, and different kinds of talk. In the next section, we look at one location where we might observe these differences more clearly.

A Significant Commonplace in Teaching

Just as teaching in a classroom is a dynamic and complex issue, embedded as it is in values and events, so, too, is doing research and writing about that teaching, because research and writing are embedded in a swirl of values about what teaching is and should be as well as what research about teaching should be (Sfard, 1998). The classroom scene presents the researcher with an overabundance of researchable teaching moments and massively conflicting values. How can one select a focusing topic without doing injury to the interweaving connectedness of the whole? Among the cacophony of speech and activity in a classroom, how can one legitimately and defensibly pick only one kind of speech, one kind of activity, and discuss only that?

If we choose one instructional moment to explore carefully, the criteria necessary for identifying a researchable teaching moment must be clear. The researchable teaching moment should be commonly recognizable as being a legitimate part of the instructional landscape; it should be a generally agreed-upon critical aspect of the teaching repertoire—that is, doing it well should matter; it should involve all the major actors in the drama of the class—teachers, content, and students; and it should have the potential to be reflective of differences among subject matter areas, reflective of responsiveness to the unique features of a given student group, and reflective of differences in teaching approaches. It should be a commonplace of the instructional landscape.

Instructional Explanations

Instructional explanations as a location for examining the uniqueness of teaching in different subject matter areas meets the criteria of a good researchable teaching moment. Instruc-

tional explanations are recognizable as part of the instructional landscape by teachers, students, and observers. We know instructional explanations are important, because ample evidence shows that doing them well facilitates learning while doing them poorly interferes with learning (e.g., Eisenhart et al., 1993). When explanations are done well, they help to convey both the content of the domain and the sense of the domain—how the domain asks and answers questions (Schwab, 1978). Instructional explanations involve the major actors in classrooms because they exist in textbooks (Larreamendy-Joerns, 1996), are given by teachers (Wineburg & Wilson, 1991), are given by groups of students working together (Lampert, 1992), and, furthermore, can be used as a form of assessment (Raghavan, Sartoris, & Glaser, 1998). Instructional explanations demonstrate and justify as well as support problem solving and reasoning in the process of developing understanding—they are both a means and an end.

To understand instructional explanations, we first need to distinguish them from other kinds of explanations. Explanations are often defined as systematic answers to "why" questions within a domain. In this chapter, we consider explanations more broadly than that, and we come to a definition, or an approximate definition, after we distinguish instructional explanations from three other major kinds of explanations.

For our purposes, it is useful to consider four families of explanations: common explanations, disciplinary explanations, self-explanations, and instructional explanations (Leinhardt, 1993a). All four share certain features; for example, they depend on an explicit or implicit query, they conform to specific rules of closure or completeness, and they have certain regularities with respect to evidence and audience. But the four types of explanations also differ in the specifics of these very same features: The specific type of query differs, the specific kind of evidence differs, the specific sense of audience differs, and the specific rules for closure differ.

Common explanations are responses to direct and usually simple (if sometimes profound) questions. Why have they rescheduled the board meeting? When are they closing the elementary school? How will we find out when redistricting will go into effect? Why should I go to school? These families of questions are generally short invitations to a short discussion. They rely heavily on the particular relationship between the speakers; that is, the inquiry is directed to someone who probably can engage in producing an answer (even if the answer is only a speculation). The exchange is either face-to-face or virtually so; that is, the exchanges are not separated by large geographic or temporal distances (current electronic exchanges notwithstanding). The appropriateness of the responses depends on the degree to which they satisfy the inquirer. These explanations are common in that they are a part of everyday life and do not depend on an answer that adheres to a domain's set of rules, such as those of history or mathematics. We seek explanatory answers of those who we think can provide them. Common explanations do not require access to a specialized language or form of reasoning; rather, we rely on a social system of rules to determine appropriateness of the discourse.

Common explanations rest on the social setting and surface features of polite exchanges. Developmental researchers are particularly interested in the existence and evolution of these explanations (Callanan & Oakes, 1992; Callanan, Shrager & Moore, 1995; Crowley & Callanan, 1998). Common explanations are significant for educators, because their forms have the potential to either support or collide with educational forms of explanatory discourse. On the one hand, local and personal differences in the pattern of common explanations that are used by a community or group may cause confusion and even pain among students of that group if and when those patterns collide with the expectations of educators or educational institutions. On the other hand, skillfully used, the availability of common explanations as a resource for learning can support knowledge development and can build connections between in- and out-of-school competencies. When common forms of explanation are ignored by educators, a serious failure to communicate with students or to help them make progress toward understanding and learning in the educational setting often occurs (McDermott, 1977).

In contrast to common explanations, disciplinary explanations, as their name suggests, arise from queries embedded in the discipline itself. Education asks questions of effectiveness and social equality, psychology asks questions about universal mechanisms of the mind, history asks questions of cause and consequence, and mathematics asks questions of provability and aesthetics (Schwab, 1978; Thagard, 1992). Explanations in a discipline respond to explicit and implicit questions that exist free of the boundaries of time and place. We tackle problems in mathematics and in physics that were identified in tongues other than our own hundreds of years ago (e.g., consider the joy in and attention paid to the solution of Fermat's Conjecture).

To accommodate the diversity of participants in disciplinary explanations, the form and language of such explanations are somewhat rigid and even ritualized. The formalization helps support communication in the absence of face, voice, and social setting. Disciplinary explanations adhere to precise conventions of completeness and closure as well as to a more tacit set of conventions that surround what constitutes a legitimate question, what the agenda for the discipline is, what is required for evidence to be accepted, and what the rules for refutation are.

These explanations have rules that help the broad and dispersed community of thinkers in the discipline to focus on the task of constructing new knowledge and reformulating extant knowledge (Dunbar, 1995; Schwab, 1978). Interestingly, these explanations are both highly social and highly unsocial. They are social because they are expected and anticipated and because the group that engages in them knows what it is looking for. They are unsocial because they do not require face-to-face interactions and because their audiences are often anonymous.

Although they share features in common, disciplinary explanations differ from each other because the epistemology and formalisms of each discipline differ (Grossman, 1989; Schwab, 1978; Shulman, 1986). Rules of evidence range from rules of formal logic in mathematics and in much of physics to rules of exhaustivity in history. What is considered theory in one discipline is seen as description or simple notation in another. (Consider, for example, how computer science views the "architecture" of a language.) Rules of refutation range from the provision of a single counterexample (in linguistics and mathematics) to the simple strength of the rhetorical form of argument (in literary criticism). The presence or absence of self-reflection or of layering varies from being a critical component of historical explanation to being irrelevant or even annoying and unaesthetic in mathematics.

Finally, what constitutes a legitimate query in one discipline is unrecognizable in another. How does a prion work and does it exist? What is the relationship between rational elliptical curves and modular forms (the Taniyama-Shimura Conjecture)? What is the role of "aunt" in baboon social structure? What is the emission mechanism of a pulsar? What is the role of landscape in the history of cultural identity? What is the role of modern megachurches in the formation of social identity? The kinds of explanatory answers to these questions are different in form, different in representational and notational usage, different in principles, and different in general applicability, both internally and externally, to their fields.

Disciplinary explanations are significant in education for four reasons. First, as students acquire deeper and more epistemic understandings in a domain, they can begin to appropriate features of disciplinary explanations into their own work. Second, instructional explanations must bridge the gap between common and disciplinary explanations and teachers need to understand how the explanations are different. Third, as students advance, they begin to come into contact with more authentic disciplinary explanations, some features of which tend to remain largely unmarked—the particular use of register, for example (Cazden, 1986)—but teachers should know how to flag them. Fourth, as students appropriate disciplinary explanations and integrate them into solutions and discussions of informal topics or within more informal venues, they can use these fledgling disciplinary reasoning skills to engage in knowledge use in authentic ways outside the classroom.

For example, the common high school knowledge level of comets could permit a rich and useful discussion about the discovery of Hale-Bopp—a discussion that might be used to challenge the tragic argument that the comet hid a chariot from outer space.[3] Disciplinary explanations do not provide practical information in the sense of the everyday but they do provide authentic information in an authentic form, in the sense that they are valued by a particular community, and they demonstrate a mode of thinking that has the potential to extend into other areas.

Self-explanations, unlike disciplinary explanations, are a mechanism of learning (Chi, 2000). If disciplinary explanations rest within the guides of the discipline as an entity, self-explanations rest within the guides of the person. Self-explanations are ways to establish meaning, to extend or revise understanding, or strategically and intentionally to improve

---

[3] In 1997, a bright new comet was discovered by two astronomers, Hale and Bopp. The path of the comet and its eventual view was a widely publicized and awaited event. Sadly, one group that waited was Heaven's Gate, a cult that comprised religious fanatics who believed the comet hid a special chariot designed to take them to a higher plane. To catch the chariot, they needed to cast off their physical selves by committing mass suicide. This belief in the meaning of a comet led to the death of 39 cult members.

memory. As the name suggests, self-explanations are given to the self, not to others. Although they may be presented audibly in front of a listener, the target of the explanation is the explainer. Naturally, because the audience is the self, the language used in a self-explanation tends to be highly colloquial, personally referential, fragmentary, and idiosyncratic. Known and understood fragments are left unsaid while areas of concern or confusion may be restated several times.

The prompt for a self-explanation is sometimes a sense of query because an impasse in problem solving or reasoning has been reached, or it is sometimes a need to extend or connect information (Chi, 2000). At upper grade levels and in college we find evidence—in the sciences, at least—that higher levels of self-explanation, especially to targeted material, are associated with higher levels of accomplishment and learning.[4] Individuals also seem to learn better when they are required to explain to others in a more complete or formal way. This action is not, however, what is usually meant by self-explanation.

In contrast to common, disciplinary, and self-explanations, instructional explanations are designed to explicitly teach—to specifically communicate some portion of the subject matter to others, the learners. Instructional explanations can be given by a textbook, a computer, a teacher, or a student, or they can be jointly built through a coherent discourse surrounding a task or text that involves the entire class and the teacher working together. Instructional explanations are natural and frequent pedagogical actions that occur in response to implicit or explicit questions—whether posed by students or teachers. The questions, like those in self-explanations, can arise from real or perceived confusions, as a way of extending or connecting information or concepts, or as a way of anticipating future uses or significances. Instructional explanations support learning, because they model both the types of questions that can be fruitfully asked in a domain and the ways in which such queries are answered. Instructional explanations can help to demonstrate, convince, structure, and convey, and they suggest the appropriate metacognitive behavior for working in a given discipline.

As a consequence of participating in an instructional explanation, either by producing a part of it or hearing and seeing others do so, a student is helped to learn, understand, and use information, concepts, and procedures in flexible and creative ways. Such an explanation is complete when coherence exists among the critical components. The verbal trace of such explanations, therefore, tends to be more exhaustive than the verbal traces of either self- or disciplinary explanations. The form of instructional explanations is less formal and more redundant than that of disciplinary explanations and tends to obey general rules of social discourse.

How do these four types of explanations relate to one another, and what do they have to do with learning and teaching in the subject matter areas? The core underlying default for classroom discourse in general, and instructional explanations in particular, is common social discourse. Teachers and students enter the classroom with a deep knowledge of the principles of conversation. The demands of the classroom promptly

require them to violate some of these principles, but the default condition is, nonetheless, the common ground of conversation. Grice describes a set of conversational "implicatures" that provide a system of constraints for normal conversation and that cluster around a general principle of cooperation; that is, all the players want the conversation to work (Grice, 1989, p. 26).

The cooperative principle has four categories of constraints: quantity—say enough but not too much; quality—do not lie and do not overextend; relation—be relevant and connect comments to the subject at hand; and manner—be clear, unambiguous, brief, and orderly. These elements of the cooperative principle and the "rules" associated with them are implicit and, decidedly, culturally unique. (In many cultures, for example, polite conversation requires a rather lengthy recitation of what is already quite well known to all of the parties involved.) The implicitness and uniqueness of these conversational implicatures allow considerable room for confusion and conflict to occur in the simplest of exchanges when the speakers do not share the same implicit rules or cultural constraints.

We must realize, of course, that the classroom represents a culture, just as the economic and ethnic backgrounds of the students and teachers tend to be markers for culture. In the classroom culture, there may not always be an agreement that the conversation needs to work. There may be a real need for saying a bit too much; there may be social purposes to being a bit irrelevant and not being particularly brief. So it is possible and definitely researchable that there are profound and important differences between the norms of social conversation and those of classroom conversation, not the least of which is the presence or absence of a presumed "cooperative principle" in classroom discourse (see Gutierrez, 1995). The point here is that when instructional discourse in general and instructional explanations in particular seem to fail, we should consider the collisions that might be occurring between conversational systems and instructional ones.

Common explanations may indeed rest on these conversational implicatures; that is, they may work because the speakers in the explanation have a shared understanding of the conversational system. In the classroom, conversational rules and common explanations are used unless an overriding educational situation suggests otherwise, which occurs frequently. For example, in normal conversation, one never asks a question to which one already knows the answer; we do not test each other (unless we are playing complicated mind games, but that does not apply here). As Mehan (1979) pointed out, we would find the following conversational exchange in a social setting improbable and rude:

"What time is it?"
"Eleven fifteen."
"Right."

But such an exchange is not a violation of classroom discourse. Some have suggested that classrooms might be more effective as places of learning if they pursued a more conversational structure and if they also made greater efforts to link the out-of-school knowledge bases to the in-school knowledge de-

---

[4] The precise mechanism for improved learning through self-explanation has been elusive. Research that contrasts prompts for self-explanation with "ordinary" instructional explanation tends to favor the latter or show no advantage for self-explanation. Therefore, when observed as naturally occurring, self-explanation is possibly an indicator of increased attention to important aspects of the learning.

mands. But clearly, even if we may wish to change the nature of classroom conversations, they are different from everyday conversations. In examining classroom conversations, we must take into account the larger cultural assumptions about the responsibilities and meanings of being in school and having a teacher. Otherwise, we sacrifice the positive meanings that are associated with school for the positive meanings that are associated only with connecting socially and with notions of shared authority and responsibility.

If patterns of common explanations are the default condition for social exchange in classrooms, then disciplinary explanations form an upper bound of instructional explanation patterns. Disciplinary explanations constrain the rules of evidence, the linguistic register, and the legitimate class of queries that may be asked, the latter limited to those elements that are truly (authentically) not yet known in a given disciplinary community. (I am not suggesting here that classrooms using a more disciplinary basis for instructional dialogues—such as those in graduate classes—should consider as real only those topics that have never before been explored. Rather, I suggest that, in such classrooms, the exploration itself is wide open and can include as-yet-unanswered queries, in contrast to the more typical classroom search for a known result or replication.) In Gricean terms, that which is "not yet known" inside a discipline is quite small or focused while that which is already assumed is quite large, and redundancy and repetition are minimal. In some ways, acquiring aspects of the disciplinary explanation pattern is also one goal of instruction; that is, a student learning biological principles of evolution should be able to portray a given instance of evolution in terms of evolutionary theory (Ohlsson, 1992).

Instructional explanations occupy a particular place on a continuum of instructional forms: they are more than simple description and demonstration but somewhat less than a full-scale argument. An instructional explanation usually contains an instance of something to be explained; an example of it; a set of discussions that connect what is being explained to particular rules or principles; and, finally, a set of discussions that bound it or limit its applicability, thus, distinguishing it from other closely allied ideas or practices.

Instructional explanations, when developed through a process of group discourse, can be considered the core of meaningful classroom talk. In his work on the use of assessment conversations, Michael Smith (1995) describes ways in which teachers and students, working together, can press toward the careful expression of ideas that make use of evidence, systematic inquiry, and previous conversational elements. In a similar vein, Lauren Resnick and her colleagues consider "accountable talk" one of the hallmarks of their reform efforts (Resnick, Salmon, Zeitz, Wathen, & Holowchak, 1993). Their idea is that in-class discussions should focus on particular issues, seek to establish common ground, and move toward conclusions while respecting and voicing the tenets of the various disciplines. This view is in contrast to one that portrays any and all talk by students as good and any and all talk by teachers as bad.

Locations for Instructional Explanations

If instructional explanations constitute a legitimate instructional moment, one worthy of more careful examination, then to consider where and when in the life of a classroom such explanations occur seems appropriate. I will proceed to address this issue of location in two ways. First, I consider the idea of location globally across subject matters, asking, In what kinds of activities and practices do we find instructional explanations? Second, I consider location in a more fine-grained way, asking, What are the kinds of occasions within specific subject matter areas that prompt instructional explanations?

Tasks and Talk

The activities and practices that harbor instructional explanations and provide opportunities for them to occur are instructional tasks and classroom talk. Tasks are the activities of the class, whether students are watching a filmstrip or building a diorama of an Iroquois village. These tasks constitute the framework for particular kinds of classroom talk, such as directions, planning, short answers, and explanations. Walter Doyle has conducted a 20-year program of work that is centered on the idea of instructional tasks (Doyle, 1979, 1983, 1992; Doyle & Carter, 1984). Although that work has not made direct connection with the socioculturalists' or sociolinguists' discussions of activity and discourse (Cazden, 1986), it is closely allied to those discussions because it is connected to social group activity and to the sense that tasks are products and processes of school-based culture.

Tasks, their design, use, and place form the core of the learning moments in classrooms. Doyle (1992) argues that through the implicit and explicit messages of tasks, the central culture of the class is conveyed. If students are asked to find all the uses of the article "the" in a passage (to paraphrase Doyle's example), or to fill in the one-word responses to blue-inked outlines (my example), the message about literature as a discipline is very different from what it would be if the students were asked to consider the various ways an author has conveyed a message or to consider what that message (or multiple messages) might be (Beck, McKeown, Hamilton, & Kucan, 1997; Wineburg, 1998). Educational tasks range from large-scale, multiperson projects to small-scale, individual exercises and from responses to a brief Haiku to discussions of essays being produced over many days. In all cases, however, instructional tasks set the tone for the work of a classroom and provide a location for instructional explanations. The explanations may be justifications for actions (often in mathematics or science), they may be arguments in support of a particular interpretation (often in history or English), or they may be presentations of new information and its attachment to known principles or previous information.

Tasks, then, constitute one location in the instructional frame that encourages and promotes explanations. Another location is classroom talk. Although I suggested earlier that instructional explanations could occur in textbooks (Beck, McKeown, & Gromoll, 1989), in computer programs (Moore, 1995), or in the discourse of the classroom (Leinhardt, 1987, 1993a), for the purposes of this chapter, I focus on explanations that are part of the discourse of the class. Classroom discourse and its analysis has been the focus of an enormous and burgeoning program of work (see chapter 15, this volume).

Courtney Cazden's (1986) chapter in the *Handbook of Research on Teaching* covers the significant psycholinguistic framework that describes classroom talk, and although it advances our understanding of how the distinct traditions of analysis of such talk developed, it is less connected to the issues of learning a particular kind of content and how that content evolves through the discussions that occur in a classroom. In a series of short papers in a special issue of *Cognition and Instruction,* Pontecorvo and her colleagues began to broach that subject (Pontecorvo, 1993a, 1993b). Here we consider talk to be the means by which we can see explanations being developed in a classroom setting. We are less concerned with the issue of who talks than we are with what gets talked about, what register is used, and what echoing occurs.

Subject Matter Occasions That Prompt Explanations

Having distinguished among a variety of explanation types and having considered where in the context of tasks and discourse we locate instructional explanations, we now must distinguish among a variety of instructional moments. Classroom instruction does not occur as a single blur of activity and discussion. Rather, there are clearly discernible activity structures that are defined by differences in goals, tasks, talk, and action. In-class test taking, spelling bees, drills, reading circles, and project work each have their clear markers in terms of geography and scene. Instructional explanations, although they can occur during many different activities, are themselves a type of activity structure. Instructional explanations occur most frequently during large- or small-group discussions—before, after, or in the middle of doing a task of some kind. But even more than a temporal moment, instructional explanations occur at an intellectual moment—there are clusters of subject matter-based *occasions,* different for each subject area, that prompt and support instructional explanations.

So far, the description of instructional explanations has floated relatively free from any subject matter anchor; however, what prompts a query for an explanation is something embedded in the subject matter itself. I consider here two very different subjects, history and mathematics, using them to describe the kinds of occasions that prompt an explanation. I leave to the reader and future researchers the task of considering what sorts of moments in other disciplines form the occasions for explanation. In describing these differences in the intellectual moments for instructional explanation, we must think in terms of the kinds of epistemic structures that organize a domain. We must also think of the kinds of social and psychological features that challenge the student while learning a domain. It is at the intersection of these that explanations are likely to occur. In this section, I focus on four elements: the events or small paradigmatic features, the long-term undergirding processes that seem harder to grasp, the core principles of a domain, and the metasystems of inquiry in the domain.

History, when described by psychologists, is often characterized as narrative in form and temporal-causal in argument (Perfetti, Britt, Rouet, Georgi, & Mason, 1994). This characterization is not false, but it is incomplete. Certainly, a major feature of history is its event-like narrative structure. Indeed, one of the major occasions for instructional explanations in history is events—the short, action-packed, narrative episodes that include the stories of war and conquest, of massive migrations of people, of revolutions, and of people's lives. Events have actors, purposes, motives, and consequences, and they form narrative-like chains of cause and consequence. Historical events take place in relatively short time frames that are frequently associated with specific dates. When events are the occasion for an explanation, the query is often about causes or consequences and sometimes about the specifics of the occurrence. It is events that get made into films, and events and their dramas are what students remember (Seixas, 1994). An example of such an event-based query that might prompt an instructional explanation is "What were the consequences of John Brown's raid on Harper's Ferry for the congressional debate over slavery?"

History is not just about events, however. It also involves social and political structures that constitute another occasion for instructional explanation. The discussion of these structures tends to have an expository flavor with an emphasis on conditions and relationships. The temporal quality of these structural phenomena is long (extending over centuries or millennia), evolutionary, and often ill defined. We speak of the development of the judicial and economic systems in the United States, punctuated, perhaps, by laws and cases, but a sense of flow and gradualism with an emphasis on comparison and contrast is evident. While the connections between events are causal, the connections between historical structures are relational. Structures can be, and often are, affected by events—the government of France changed during and after the French Revolution—but the explanations of the structures themselves are expository, not narrative, in nature. A query of social structure might be "What were the differences and similarities between the social organization and consequent experiences of westward-migrating European Americans in the early 1800s and the northern-migrating African Americans in the early 1900s?" Evidence suggests that historical structures are harder to learn and require more teaching support than historical events (Kindervater & von Borries, 1997, p. 78; Young & Leinhardt, 1998a).

Another occasion for instructional explanations in history is the themes that cut through and across different events and different types of social organizations. Themes constitute the interpretive principles for the historian. Examples of themes include power, wealth, freedom, and struggle. Many of the more notable historical themes are associated with a particular school of thought, such as the thematic link between Marxism and power. Students of history have the complex task of learning these thematic principles (as ways to reason in history) and of applying them to unique and varied settings. An example of a recent thematic historical inquiry is one posed by Schama (1995) when he asked about the differing role of landscape in construction of historical cultural memory. Instructional explanations of themes are less common than are those of events or historical structures. Thematic explanations tend to be spread out across the cumulation of lessons rather than to be the explicit target of a single instructional episode.

Finally, an occasion for instructional explanations in history is the metasystems of the discipline. (Thus, the four occasions for instructional explanations in history are events, structures, themes, and metasystems.) Among the metasystems to be explained are (a) analysis of specific historical events or structures; (b) synthesis of many such events or structures, often around a theme; (c) hypothesis posing; (d) perspective taking; and (e) interpretation. History is not only about events and circumstances but also about what we make of them: Is the story of the large migration of Europeans across the North American continent a story of pioneer courage, fortitude, and resourcefulness, or is it a story of genocidal oppression and territorial occupation? The well-prepared history student is taught to muster a variety of arguments in support of either position. Learning how to build historical explanations, cases, and arguments prompts instructional explanations of the metasystems of history (see Seixas, 1993; Walvoord & Breihan, 1990). An example of the language that suggests metasystem explanation can be found in the description of Breihan's class (Walvoord & Breihan, 1990, p. 106).

Naturally, many instructional explanations cover more than one occasion and, in fact, blend them together. However, the activity or task, the language and example, and the form of the explanation tend to vary in consistent ways depending on which of the four occasions outlined above is the target for the explanation.

These occasions for instructional explanations—moments in the teaching and learning of a subject when a particular family of exchanges is likely to take place—are quite different in mathematics instruction from those in history. Mathematical contexts for explanations, for example, may be either direct or embedded. Those that are direct deal specifically with the mathematical topic or construct, whereas others are found embedded inside a more elaborate discussion of a problem. Consider, for example, this initiating situation given by Magdalene Lampert in a lesson with fifth graders: "A humpbacked whale eats 2,000 kilograms of fish every day during the feeding season" (5/15). The lengthy instructional explanation of the meaning of the term *average* that followed was deeply embedded inside the originating problem situation. In contrast, another problem situation initiated by the query, "What does 115% of something mean?" is an example of a more direct mathematical occasion that prompts an instructional explanation.

The occasion for instructional explanations in mathematics that is comparable to explanations of events in history is found in the actions that cluster around operations, functions, procedures, and iterations. These actions are the transformers of mathematics. Performing an operation, for example, changes mathematical elements in particular ways that are consistent with mathematical rules and principles. Instructional explanations of operations can vary from a list of procedural steps and their justifications to complex systems of equivalent and parallel actions. Instructional explanations of operations tend to respond to queries of how something might be done: How can we determine the percentage of a figure that is shaded?

These mathematical operations are not done in a vacuum, however. They operate on something—on entities such as number systems, shapes, graphs. Instructional explanations are prompted by the entities and by the operations. Part of what makes mathematics a complex subject is that entities alter the meanings of operations. Thus, decimal fractions impose constraints on the operations of multiplication, altering the operation from that used with whole numbers. Furthermore, some entities, such as fractions or percents, have both operational and measurement characteristics. Explanations of mathematical entities tend to make use of specific representations or models, such as Diennes blocks or Cuisinaire rods. These representational devices are themselves often the target of an instructional explanation and, often, also constrain the explanations. Thus, using a gridlike structure to support an explanation of percent can lead to an overemphasis on the part/whole meaning of percent, which in turn leads to a sense that there is something wrong with ideas such as 115%. Unlike history, mathematical entities bear a specific and definable relationship to each other. The degree to which a teacher understands and is aware of these subtleties within the domain of mathematics dramatically affects his or her ability to explain or to lead an explanation of a particular mathematical idea (Even, 1993; Pólya, 1968; Zaslavsky & Peled, 1996).

Another occasion for instructional explanations in mathematics is found in the principles that form the constraints and affordances that impinge on entities and operations. The principles of mathematics are the fundamental tenets that constrain and afford actions, making some actions "legal" and others "illegal." Explanations of these principles involve the idea that some actions are consistent with previous assumptions of how things work in mathematics whereas others are not. Mathematical principles include, among others, concepts such as associativity, commutivity, and the concept of proof. Interestingly, although principles are not particularly easy to learn, evidence suggests that many students have a strong intuitive grasp of them long before formal introduction (Resnick, 1986). The explanations of mathematical principles in classrooms tend to be largely by example and logical proof.

Finally, the metasystems of mathematics provide an occasion for instructional explanations. Metasystems are the tools of mathematical reasoning. Students must learn them and the circumstances of their use. The metasystems of mathematics are routinely incorporated into textbooks and have been at the center of major analytic research by authors such as Pólya (1968) and Schoenfeld (1983). Mathematical metasystems include the problem-solving heuristics of simplification, extreme cases, and analogy construction. They also include an appreciation for sense making: Is this action consistent? Is this action of value? In addition to the well-studied area of mathematical problem solving is the less-well-studied area of mathematical notation. The selection of what to notate can be thought of as a metasystem in that notations are tools that help to support mathematical reasoning. These tools can also render mathematical results that are opaque to readers who are unfamiliar with a particularly idiosyncratic version of a notational system (see, for example, the accounts of Ramanujan and Hardy in Kanigel, 1991). In the current climate of educational reform, these ideas about the role of metasystems in mathematics instruction are integrated around a set of important discussions of real and complex problems (Henningsen & Stein, 1997; Lehrer & Romberg, 1996).

The explanations, then, are explanations in the context of subject matters and are prompted as part of the justification or clarification of an approach to a problem or a deep issue. Instructional explanations in both history and mathematics have different aspects to them depending on the focus of the explanation, but they are internally self-referential and integrated. The occasions for instructional explanations in mathematics and in history are the educational circumstances that prompt them. Naturally, many explanations occur as the result of more than one occasion or prompt, and in those cases, the neatly distinguishing lines that separate occasions are blurred.

A Caveat on Occasions

To clarify the kinds of occasions for explanations in mathematics and history, I have focused on the talk and ignored the layer of task. The reader should not infer that explanations "sound" distinct. They do not usually have clear linguistic markers, nor do they always occur at a certain spot in a lesson. Explanations occur while the tasks of the class are being enacted. If history students are engaged in a formal debate, then we will find explanation inside the language of the debate. In Wineburg and Wilson's (1991) account of such a debate, we see an explanation of the two arguments about representation in parliament (a rather complex structural explanation). If students in Lampert's mathematics class are debating the meaning of origin, then they are explaining a part of a mathematical entity, the Cartesian system. If students in Minstrell's physics class are discussing which data to keep track of and how to do so, they are explaining the metasystems of science and mathematics (Schoenfeld, 1998; van Zee & Minstrell, 1997).

Model of Instructional Explanation

I have distinguished among different types of explanations and have showed how instructional explanations both depend on and are different from other types of explanations. I have also discussed the kinds of domain-specific occasions that prompt instructional explanations in classrooms. This next section considers a variety of elements that are common to explanations: a sense of query; the use and generation of examples; the role of intermediate representations such as analogies and models; and the system of devices that limits or bounds explanations (identification of errors, principles, and conditions of use). The section also considers how these elements play out in two disciplines, history and mathematics. While the core model of instructional explanations is generic, the development and instantiations of it are based within subject-matter domains. We present the core model with brief examples from specific domains and then use the model as a heuristic for discussing specific ways in which instruction in subject matter varies.[5] The point here is to highlight the differences between the disciplines with respect to these elements so that we can consider how teaching in the disciplines varies. In this section I will try to dance between the general and the particular as described in Schwab's opening quote.

The core model of an instructional explanation can be thought of as a system of interrelated goals (shown in hexagons on Figure 19.1), their supporting actions (shown in rectangles), and the knowledge required to meet the goal successfully (shown as small network icons). In general, goals are implicit

and not visible to an observer, but they can be inferred either by interpreting explicit actions or through interviews with teachers and students about intentions and justifications with respect to teaching and learning (Leinhardt, 1993b; Schoenfeld, 1998). Actions make up the system of skills and behaviors that are visible in terms of language and physical movements within the classroom setting.

To construct a coherent instructional explanation, a teacher must have available the conceptual knowledge that undergirds both the actions and the establishment of goals (i.e., knowledge of what to teach and how to teach). To coordinate, support, and guide the joint construction of a collaborative explanation among students, the teacher needs not only knowledge of what and how to teach but also knowledge about the specific meanings of students' speech and actions. Although rare, we have seen some cases when students, while developing an explanation together, show an awareness of at least some of these goals through their questions or critiques ("We haven't finished!" "How does that show anything?"). The components of the model have been verified by observations of very effective teachers across grade levels and subject areas as well as by observations of the missteps and failures of less competent teachers or struggling beginning teachers (Leinhardt, 1986; Leinhardt, Putnam, Stein, & Baxter, 1991).

The model is comprised of a system of the goals that, when met, produce an explanation. Those goals include the following: (a) establishing a significant query or problem, (b) having a useful set of examples available, (c) having appropriate representations available, (d) attaching the new information that is generated to prior knowledge of the same sort, (e) completing the explanation by identifying core principles, (f) identifying the conditions of use, and (g) resolving the nature of errors. The goals, in turn, are supported by a system of action schemas.

The teaching actions include selecting or building representations, identifying critical features of a skill or concept, selecting critical examples, and showing interconnections. Specific knowledge systems that allow for building and selecting appropriate actions to meet goals are also necessary. I discuss this model below by considering four goals and their supporting actions. Throughout these discussions, other goals and actions in the model are addressed indirectly but not in any precise order that corresponds to the layout on Figure 19.1. The discussion here is intended not to focus on the way such a model could "run," although a version of it has successfully done so,[6] but to focus on the ways in which the complex system of an instructional explanation differs in different subject matter domains.

Query

A central goal for an explanation is to answer an explicit or implicit query. In history classes, the chain of queries tends to be developed into patterns that produce an informed discussion (Leinhardt, 1993c). In mathematics classes, the query tends to serve as a way of solving complex problems by linking prin-

---

[5] This model has been evolving for some time and has appeared in various forms, both published and unpublished (see Leinhardt, 1987, 1988, 1989, 1990, 1993b).

[6] An expanded version of this model has been run as a computer simulation for explaining the factoring of trinomials (Lane, 1998).

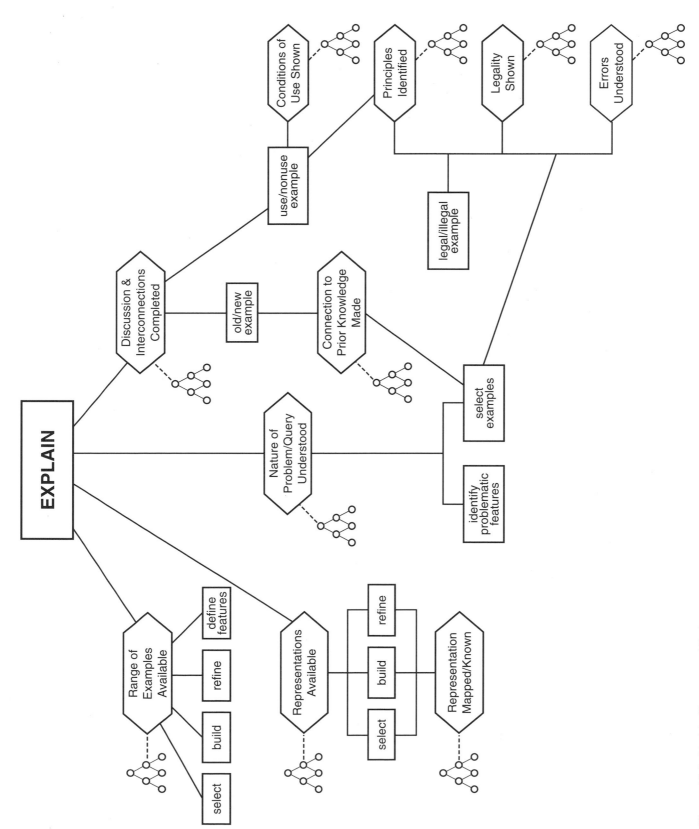

Figure 19.1. Model of Instructional Explanation.

cipled understandings to specific parts of the task (Lampert, 1989). A good explanation problematizes the query in authentic ways—authentic both in terms of the personal experiences of students' lives (see Peterson, Fennema, Carpenter, & Loef, 1989, p. 17) and in terms of the recognizable realism within a domain (see Lampert, 1986, p. 246). Thus, a query that motivates an explanation in mathematics or history can have authenticity because it refers to a real-world problem that is locally or personally important and valid: If you are planning a trip with your family, how can you plan for the cost of gasoline? Which long distance telephone service is most economical given your family's usage patterns? Where is your extended family located and why are they there? A query can also have disciplinary authenticity: How do various groups view themselves with respect to critical elements in the land and landscape? (See Schama, 1995.) What is interesting in a set of ordered pairs when you see them plotted on a graph? (See Lampert reported in Leinhardt, 1993b, p. 19.)

A good query, like a good task, has both an open and a closed quality. It is open in that it suggests many ways of being represented, many approaches to solving it, and multiple possible answers; it is closed in that it can be answered. A good explanation rests on more than giving a title to an issue (as in "Today we will discuss equivalent fractions"); it rests on the foundation of an authentic query. The explicit recognition of the query or problem to be addressed establishes a benchmark against which progress in terms of understanding can be measured in the discussion.

Multiple actions can support the goal of establishing a query, including one or more of the following: the class itself can identify the problems to work on; the teacher can select a problem or issue and post it; and the teacher can describe an open-ended situation from which one of many possible questions can be established for explanation. Additionally, the teacher may detect an important query in the explicit statements of a student: "Well, the numbers that are over 2,000 are . . . are more over 2,000 than the numbers that are under 2,000 are under" (from a lesson by Lampert, 5/15). The translation of this statement might be, "This is how I evaluate a particular estimate of the average without actually calculating the average, and here is my reason." The query might become How can we consider a model for a set of data? In another situation, the teacher may hear an important query in the implicit questions of a student. Good, complex, and meaningful queries can also be found in textbooks; however, the difficulty for teachers is that not all of the start-up problems or core ideas in textbooks make good queries.

To select a query, the teacher needs sophisticated knowledge of the discipline—the way the discipline is put together, what simple things are fundamental. For example, addition with regrouping is neither hard nor fundamental, but the idea that one can rearrange numbers in particular ways sheds significant light on the concepts of place value notation and also foreshadows some strategically important moves in algebra. To recognize and design a significant query requires also that a teacher have deep knowledge of both the particular students in a given class and students in general—their background understandings and potential confusions (Ball & Lampert, 1999). Further, the teacher needs to be able both to design a set of meaningful problems, projects, or exercises and to hear the cues for them in the conversations of her students.

This discernment, construction, and encouragement differentiates an excellent teacher from one who is stumped when the conversation just does not seem to work (Beck et al., 1997). The requisite knowledge develops from an informed understanding of what is important in the domain, what is problematic for students to learn, and how students are likely to be considering the problem initially. When teachers fail to establish a query, the ensuing explanation may be internally coherent, but it remains disconnected from a central issue or problem. In some cases, students may well find questions to which the new ideas relate, but they also may not be able to do so in which case the knowledge becomes classically inert.

EXAMPLE OF QUERIES

The instructional explanations that exist in textbooks of different subjects quite logically have very different implicit or explicit queries around which explanations are built. In *Mathematics in Context* (Wisconsin Center for Education Research & Freudenthal Institute, 1998), the first section of one unit that is devoted to building formulas introduces the idea of representing patterns with formulas. It "explains" the concept through a series of small exercises. The driving query is How many units will be needed? The set of activities accompanying the query leads from a situation in which the student can simply look at a picture and state the answer, to a situation in which the student must use tools of developing a formula to represent the numbers of tiles needed for different explicit patterns and different pattern types. So the fundamental query is How and under what circumstances do we build formulas? The specific setting deals with the designs of walks in gardens. The instruction is supposed to lead the student from being able to construct very simple, one-number formulas to constructing fairly complex formulas that describe large patterns. The explanation is designed to show the student how to do something, how to extend the skill into settings in which other methods that are initially useful gradually lose their utility, and how to justify or prove that their method is accurate.

Consider, in contrast, a common set of historical queries. A common text-based query that leads to an explanation in American history asks some version of the following question: What were the problems facing the United States after the Civil War and how were they to be addressed? The answers to this broad question "explain" the devastating consequences of the war, the social issues facing the South and the newly emancipated African Americans, and the economic tensions that were developing between agrarian and industrial economies. The query is used to open a door into the understanding of which factors need to be considered as one delves into this notable moment in American history. Each layer of the accompanying discussion adds depth to the narrative of events and their causes and consequences.

In-class instructional explanations in mathematics and in history also have fundamentally different core questions. To give the flavor of this difference, consider two questions, one asked by Lampert during the teaching of a section on functions to her fifth-grade class and the other asked by Sterling (pseudonym) during her teaching of a unit in American history to high school students. Lampert says, "Where is the origin on that graph that

I have up there? . . . Now why do you think that T_____ and M_____ have different ideas about where the origin is?" (Lampert, 10/26, lines 489 and on). These questions exemplify what is stated above about important queries coming from an understanding of both the mathematics and the students. Starting with what appeared to be a confusion expressed by one of the students in her class, Lampert launched a series of explanations that lasted two days. A student had expressed the view that the origin was "in the center"; another student had expressed the view that the origin was at zero. The issue is profound both mathematically and psychologically—the idea of an origin and the four quadrants of a Cartesian graph are not obvious and understanding these ideas has definite consequences for students' ability to "see" a function. The query is well worth an explanation and an elaborate one at that.

Consider next this sequence of queries from Sterling's high school American history class:

All right, I may still not be clear about who is actually free? . . . Yes. That's where they are. It's important to note that here we have the Emancipation Proclamation. The law of the land, January 1, 1863. All slaves in the rebellion states will be freed. So who's free? . . . What do you think the purpose of the Emancipation Proclamation really was? (Sterling, 11/29, line 522 and on)

These questions served not only to launch the specific explanation of what the Proclamation was but also to attend to the more nuanced question of why the Emancipation Proclamation was being distributed during the war and what exactly was being accomplished. Who were the readers supposed to be? Using these probes, the teacher and students weave an explanation of events, actors, motivations, and consequences. Agency and intent are significant but so is the continual historical duality. Here is a known event for which we discover both the mythic construction, how Lincoln freed the slaves, and the interpretive construction, which says that after Lincoln announced some slaves were to be freed, he then distributed the information strategically. (See Wineburg, 1998, for an extensive discussion of historical considerations of Lincoln.)

What is getting explained in this lesson is both the specific historical content and a particular stance toward history. At the most general level, these are features shared with mathematics and the explanations that are offered there. In the example above, Lampert is developing both an explanation of origin with her students and a stance toward the careful construction of mathematical entities. But at a more specific level, these explanations are quite different. The search in this history example is for ever deepening layers of meaning and mismeanings; the search in the mathematics example is for clarity and congruence.

Examples in Explanations

A query can be thought of as being at the heart of an explanation, but it should not be assumed to be at the start of an explanation. Explanations can build up around tasks and activities and around a specific series of examples. The generation or selection of examples is a fundamental part of constructing a good explanation. But developing, recognizing, or selecting an appropriate example or counterexample is difficult (Zaslavsky & Peled, 1996). Examples play a critical role in explanations. They connect prior information with new information; they can be used to prompt and resolve errors; they can help to demonstrate the legality of a principle or even to show when a concept does not apply; and they can be used to clarify the core query, that is, to help people see exactly what the question is (Rissland, 1991). But what is an example and how does it work in the construction of an explanation?

An example is an instance. To make use of and learn from an example, several are needed. As Young (1998) has pointed out, the research on examples is vast and covers many domains, but the results from studies on learning are remarkably consistent. For learning to occur, several examples are needed, not just one; the examples need to encapsulate a range of critical features; and the examples need to be unpacked, with the features that make them an example clearly identified. What constitutes an example in mathematics? That depends on what the query is, but here are some examples of examples in different lessons.

In a series of lessons on functions, Lampert helps students to unpack the significance of specific terms through a quick review using several examples. Lampert asks, "What is an ordered pair?" Students respond and then Lampert poses several "for instances," and asks if each is an ordered pair: "a pair of shoes? 2, 10? a, 10? 2, 2?" These one-phrase examples are instances of (a) a colloquial use of the term *pair*—a pair of shoes—but it is not an ordered pair; (b) a real pair of numbers that can be an ordered pair—2, 10; (c) something that looks like an ordered pair but is not because they are not both numbers—a, 10; and (d) something that is an ordered pair but is more restricted than necessary—2, 2. In terms of Figure 19.1, these are examples that have been constructed to serve the goals of having conditions of use understood, having legal and illegal instances clarified, and having discussions of principles. These examples play a critical role in the development of the larger explanation of a function and in the more local explanation of elements of a graph of a function, specifically ordered pairs. The examples are also responses to students' questions that followed Lampert's probes—students were confused about the exact meaning of "the same thing." What was the same, the value of the number or the fact that they were numbers?

Examples in history play a different sort of role, because rarely do we find a situation where a single term is followed by instances that exemplify it. Rather, a large phenomenon can sometimes be labeled as exemplifying an idea or construct. Examples in history, then, are reinspected, unpacked, and annotated to clarify or pull together core ideas or themes. In history, examples play the dual role of instance and problem. Consider the way an example is placed in the larger (written) historical explanation by Sobel (1995). The query is the following: Why was finding a way to measure longitude so critical to navigation, and why was it so difficult?

As the world turns, any line drawn from pole to pole may serve as well as any other for a starting line of reference. The placement of the prime meridian is a purely political decision.

Here lies the real, hard-core difference between latitude and longitude—beyond the superficial difference in line direction that any child can see: The zero-degree parallel of latitude is fixed by the laws of nature, while the zero-degree meridian of longitude shifts like the sands of time. This difference makes fixing latitude child's play, and turns the determination of longitude, especially at sea, into an adult dilemma—one that stumped the wisest minds of the world for the better part of human history.

. . . For lack of a practical method of determining longitude, every great captain in the Age of Exploration became lost at sea despite the best available charts and compasses. From Vasco da Gama to Vasco Núñez de Balboa, from Ferdinand Magellan to Sir Francis Drake—they all got where they were going willy-nilly, by forces attributed to good luck or the Grace of God.

. . . In consequence, untold numbers of sailors died . . . [O]n October 22, 1707, at the Scilly Islands near the southwestern tip of England, four homebound British warships ran aground and nearly two thousand men lost their lives. (Sobel, 1995, pp. 4–7)

The above example contains a definitional section, a litany of famous explorers, and, finally, a poignant pair of sentences that picture homeward-bound sailors running aground and dying, all for the lack of an accurate estimate of longitude—the story of which is the central point of the book. Similarly, teachers use small bits of narrative example to tell a miniature version of the larger story. Students in dynamic classes often offer their own series of examples to bolster their positions as they struggle with learning how to develop an argument.

In developing or selecting an example, teachers are faced with difficult tasks. They must understand the critical features that they need to explicate. These features may be critical because they are important within the subject matter domain or because they are key to the students' understandings. The teacher needs to be aware of the purposes that the example may help to serve: Can the example exemplify the way a principle is to be applied, the way the new ideas connect to the older ones, or the ways in which the question can be problematized? Finally, the teacher needs to have the skills to refine and extend examples posted by students themselves. Examples can fail because they are irrelevant, because they are confusing, or because they themselves are so complex that untangling them leads the instructional explanation astray and the point is lost.

Examples are one kind of tool that serves to support and instantiate aspects of an explanation. In the discussions that produce an explanation, examples can make connections to prior knowledge and conclusions, they can point out under which conditions a particular form of an argument can or should be used, and they can clarify the features of a fundamental query that are themselves problematic. Another tool for the development of an explanation is an effective representation.

Representations

Representations can be "given" in textbooks or can be jointly produced in classrooms. Representations are most frequently discussed by researchers when they are referring to teaching and learning mathematics or the hard sciences. In those domains, the representations can include operational representations, such as Diennes blocks or Cuisinaire rods, or diagrammatic representations, such as drawings of abstract figures or computer simulations (White, 1993). Metaphors or verbal analogies seem to serve a comparable representational function in the humanities or social sciences. However, more concrete representations and more textual analogies both can be used in any of these domains (Joshua & Dupin, 1987). The important feature of representations is that they must connect in relevant and explicit ways to the explanation being developed.

Representations in mathematics can run the risk of having serious negative entailments. For example, a representation such as the pie chart or hundreds square for percent admirably develops the concept of part of a whole. Although a percent can be considered a part of a whole, it is fundamentally a privileged proportion (Parker & Leinhardt, 1995). Percent shows how one ratio relates to a target ratio based on one hundred. Thus, although having 113% makes sense under some circumstances, thinking of 113% as a part of a whole does not make sense. Such a relationship can be shown, but it is not an explanation supported by a representation; rather, it is a confusion in the representation that requires the mathematical knowledge to already be in place for someone to interpret the representation. Beck refers to "asides that overwhelm," and other researchers have described analogies that confuse (Beck, McKeown, & Gromoll, 1989; Gentner, 1989; Holyoak & Thagard, 1995). The examples in the citations above are all instances of representational systems being used to explain in a way that clouds or confuses rather than supports and helps.

Representations, then, are somewhat dangerous tools (Young & Leinhardt, 1998a). To build good representations during an explanation, the teacher needs the knowledge that will allow him or her to (a) select from those representations that are offered in texts, (b) build new representations that truly match the context of the explanation, and (c) refine representations that are offered by students in the course of their own discussions. The knowledge for building good representations, like the knowledge required for identifying important queries or finding good examples, requires a mixture of understanding the subject matter as well as the personal lives and the experiences of the students themselves. The language that accompanies the use of representations and examples requires, in turn, that explicit interconnections be built.

Consider the following representations used in an Addison Wesley mathematics textbook (Eicholz et al., 1991, pp. 165, 168). In two consecutive chapters, students are exposed to the concepts of *greatest common factor* and *least common multiple*. One page shows two separate representations for the greatest common factor. The top half of the page has a picture of a boy with a dialogue balloon over his head that reads,

2 is a factor of both of these numbers
$$2 \times 30 = 60$$
$$2 \times 36 = 72$$

Below that, in a yellow box, is a two-column table with one column labeled "List the Factors" and the other labeled "Prime Factorization." The table shows two methods for finding the greatest common factor. On the page titled "Least Common Multiple," two representations are also shown. One shows two crickets jumping along the ground that has been marked with a ruler-like scale; the second is another two-column table with the columns labeled "List Some Multiples" and "Prime Factorization." All of these representations are themselves quite complex.

The narrative representations—the boy and the crickets—are far less usable and interpretable than the tabular ones. With appropriate supporting discussion, the ideas that the tables are trying to show—that these ideas can be represented in several ways, that the concepts of least common multiple and greatest common factor share an underlying commonality—seem to support an explanation of sorts about the two topics. These representations do not convey their respective messages directly or easily; they require that either the teacher or the students work to build meaning from them and build interconnections between them.

What is often done by even the most artistic of teachers, however, is to pull representations out of the air—and risk that an intriguing representation will not map well to the target concept being explained. An example of the expert use of representations can be seen in the work of George Pólya. In the Mathematical Association of America's (MAA) 1965 film of his teaching, Pólya builds several representations to support an explanation of the five planes problem (Mathematical Association of America, 1965; McQuaide, Fienberg, & Leinhardt, 1991). One of his representations is a tabular chart in which a variety of information is recorded that eventually leads students to recognize a pattern in the data (Leinhardt & Schwarz, 1997). But, of course, the question is as follows: How does one know to construct such a table?

Building the representations themselves is a marvelous pedagogical act that begins with this query: How shall we show this? The result can be an important part of an explanation. But representations in and of themselves do not explain something, which is why "using manipulatives" does not increase understanding by itself. When well-crafted, carefully manipulated, and tightly connected to core problems, manipulatives matter; but standing alone, a pile of counting blocks speaks nothing.

It is instructive to consider what happens when a representation fails. In the following case, reported by Borko and her colleagues, the teacher's lack of pedagogical content knowledge interfered with her ability to help students understand division of fractions (Borko et al., 1992, p. 197). In this lesson, Ms. Daniels reviews the invert-and-multiply procedure, using the problem 3/4 divided by 1/2. A student asks, "I was just wondering why, up there when you go and divide it and down there you multiply it, why do you change over?" In an effort to explain, Ms. Daniels draws a rectangle on the board with three vertical lines dividing it into four congruent parts, one of which she shaded. She says,

> "And say we have a wall, OK, and we divide it into fourths. 1/4 of it is already painted, OK. So we have 3/4 of it left to paint. Right? You agree with me? . . . But we only have enough paint to paint *half of these three fourths* [emphasis added]. So half of 3/4 would be between about right there. Right, do you agree with that?" Ms. Daniels drew a line down the middle of the unshaded portion to divide it in half. ". . . There is 1/4 on each side plus half of a fourth. So now if we look at this, this fourth was divided in half, so we divide this fourth in half and this fourth in half. We are left with 1, 2, 3, 4, 5, 6." [She drew vertical lines to divide each of the remaining unshaded fourths in half.] "And if we had this fourth divided in half it would be what kind of unit?" [She drew a vertical line to divide the shaded fourth in half.] "How many units is my wall divided into now? 1, 2, 3, 4, 5, 6, 7, 8. But 2/8 is already covered. We

see right here that we have enough paint to cover this many more eighths. Right? When we divide it into eighths, leaving us with how many eighths, 1, 2, 3. OK, oh wait. I did something wrong here." (pp. 197–198)

Once Ms. Daniels realizes that she has made an error, she pauses, studying the board, and then she tells the students to "just use our rule for right now" while she thinks of a different way to explain it to them. In this example, two parts of the representation system failed the teacher. First, she was trying to represent the problem 3/4 divided by 1/2, but she said "one half *of* three fourths." This statement refers to the multiplication of fractions. Her verbal representation, therefore, is not comparable to her mathematical one. Using her verbal cues, she then goes on to draw a representation that corresponds to the multiplication problem, rather than to the division one with which she had started. Borko and her colleagues consider the cause of this failure to be a problem both in the teacher's knowledge and in her planning practices.

Representations in history are more ambiguous than their counterparts in mathematics. For example, one can find analogical representations that support reasoning about historical issues and representations of history as a domain itself. For now, we consider only the issues associated with the former. Of the many ways in which an analogical representation can be used, perhaps the most powerful, if problematic, is the use of a direct historical analogy—comparing two events, such as the battles of the Gulf of Tonkin and the Gulf of Sidra, or two structures, such as the Great Society Program and the New Deal. What is analogically powerful for the explanation is the way a teacher and students can unpack elements of a known historical event or concept and map them to a new and unknown one. What is risky is that the material can be oversimplified and grossly distorted (see the discussions of this problem in Seixas, 1994; Young & Leinhardt, 1998a).

The positive and negative potentials of using historical analogies can be seen in the Great Society-New Deal example. The New Deal, on the one hand, took place in the context of the Great Depression, the worst financial and social disaster the United States had ever experienced and one that threatened to totally destroy the institutions and social systems of the country. The Great Society programs, on the other hand, took place in a time of relative prosperity that was accompanied by an increasing discrepancy between those who were making headway in the social system and those who were being held back because of poverty and discrimination. The core laws that supported the two programs were dramatically different. The populace and the courts treated the two programs quite differently. But students can benefit by considering these differences and similarities carefully in the service of an ongoing explanation—for example, an explanation of the role, obligation, or constitutionality of government in rearranging the social landscape of its population.

Representations are a supporting pedagogical mechanism in explanations. They can be powerful and useful, but, like examples, they have to be carefully considered and unpacked. The tradition in mathematics education and also in science education is to work with a limited set of representations and to require them to fit reasonably closely to the subject matter at hand. The tradition in history teaching is to be very wary of false analogies and, to some extent, to deny their usefulness in teaching. However, empirical data suggests that classroom history discussions are as replete with analogies as are science meetings (Dunbar, 1995; Young & Leinhardt, 1998a, p. 168). Learning how to build, select, critique, and refine representations is critical to effective teaching.

Completion

I have contrasted brief instances of explanatory moments in mathematics with those in history to trace ways in which instructional explanations can help to point out the distinctions between the teaching practices involved in two subjects. Explanations that are helpful make clear the core questions, use a range of examples, and select representations and analogies wisely. In enacting these explanatory features, teachers and their students are engaging in knowledge transformation in ways that support teaching and learning (Grossman, 1989; Shulman, 1986). But when are instructional explanations complete?

At the simplest level, an instructional explanation is complete when the various systems that have been put into place to support the explanations—the examples, questions, principles, and verbal discussion—are complete and coordinated, and the interconnections are shown. Frequently, new teachers manage to work through one part of an explanation—say, using a particular representation—but are unable to complete or coordinate with the other parts of the explanation—such as the verbal discussion. This lack of completion can occur either because they run out of time or because they do not see the connections themselves. In terms of the disciplines and the pedagogy, rules for completion in mathematics are dramatically different from those in history.

Explanations in mathematics seem to combine invoking the right range of principles needed for the explanation with a convergence of evidence. Frequently, talented mathematics teachers will lead students to examine a problem from several angles and to use a variety of methods in order to prove the validity of the solution and show how the discipline fosters multiple solution paths. When equivalent methods produce the same result—when there is convergence—then the explanation achieves a sense of completeness. The end point for an historical explanation, however, is more vague. In some sense, the discussion could always continue. An instructional explanation in history can be seen to be complete when one has examined the evidential record (whether that is a textbook account or source documents or artifacts) and has found that, for the moment, no dangling pieces remain in the constructed narrative of how something occurred, what its outcomes were, how different groups related to one another and why, the ways in which concepts of power were enacted, and the degree to which an hypothesis has been supported.

In addition to coordinating the various systems in an explanation so that completion can be accomplished, support for a completed explanation comes from enacting other goals, such as formally connecting new information to prior knowledge in ways that flag both what is new and what has been added. The enactment of this goal serves not only to attach the new ideas that are developed in the discussion to prior information but also to show the similarities and differences between them (e.g., how

the Chinese Revolution of 1949 was like and unlike the French Revolution or how considering the average number of people in a class who have cats versus dogs is different from considering the average number of cats and dogs owned by the class).

Another goal that moves an explanation toward completion is the goal that limits the range of the explanation and indicates the borders and boundaries as well as the conditions under which the new idea, procedure, or concept is applicable. For example, if an historical explanation of the Civil War suggests that the war was the result of conflicting economic factors, then developing the counter-idea that other causes were also possible (such as belief systems that emerged from philosophical rather than economic roots), would contribute to showing the limitations of the original explanation.

In mathematics, if one is learning how to add a percent to an original value, then it is important for an explanation to include the boundary or limitation that one cannot undo the addition of 25% to an original value by subtracting 25% from the new value. This idea is counterintuitive and results from the fact that, although addition and subtraction are complementary operations, something else about percents overrides that feature—namely, that percents are fundamentally multiplicative in nature despite their additive language.

Finally, it is important that explanations include ways of working through an understanding of errors in terms of core principles within the discipline. In some cases, this goal may be achieved simply by making a direct appeal to a rule while, in other cases, it may involve the careful presentation of a sequence of increasingly contradictory evidence. The actions that are required to meet this goal involve the thoughtful response to students' spontaneously generated errors, the development of examples that are themselves likely to produce an error or misconception so that it can be dealt with, or both. Some teachers deliberately avoid making direct corrections to student-generated errors (Ball & Lampert, 1999; Lampert, 1986, 1990, 1998; Lampert & Ball, 1998), but that does not mean the explanations that they orchestrate leave misconceptions standing as though they were truth. Rather, it means that errors are invitations to thoughtful discussions that gradually allow both corrections and an expansion of everyone's understanding.

In both history and mathematics, the completion of an instructional explanation is tied to the discipline's epistemology and the metasystems that undergird evidence and proof in that domain.

Summary

To recapitulate, the teaching of one subject area differs from the teaching of another because the fundamental structure of each discipline differs in important ways, enough so that the specific features of a discipline must be known by the teacher. Furthermore, by examining quite closely one instructional moment of significance—instructional explanations—we can learn both what is unique about the subjects and what is general. What I present above is a sketch of a model for critical components of an instructional explanation. In the next section, I will look at an example of an instructional explanation—in the form of text from a classroom—and then analyze it by looking at it through the lens of the explanatory model.

An Example from an AP History Class

My example comes from one of several highly accomplished AP (Advanced Placement) history teachers whom we have studied (Leinhardt, Stainton, & Virji, 1994). The particular teacher, Peterbene (pseudonym), was initially selected because of his student-centered approach to teaching that provided an interesting contrast in pedagogical style to teachers who were more disciplinary-based in their approaches. His emphasis was on the development of the adolescent mind. His classes had a unique rhythm, in part no doubt, because he had two double periods a week in addition to the regular three single periods, for a total of seven periods a week. This schedule gave him more time to explore important issues with students (than did the schedules of other AP teachers we have observed).

In general, Peterbene would pose a question on the blackboard and have students respond. The discussion by the students would be allowed to continue pretty much uninterrupted for a substantial part of the period. Then Peterbene would summarize the comments up to that point and call for further discussion or rephrasing, or he would move the discussion toward a conclusion. This pattern of posing questions, allowing lengthy student-directed discussion, and providing a summary and redirection was typical.

The portions of the lessons we are working with here came from a unit on the 1960s. The class had been working for several days on the Johnson era and the Great Society Programs, contrasting them to Wilson's and Franklin D. Roosevelt's (FDR's) social policies, when the discussion moved on to the Vietnam era. Peterbene chose to open a part of the Vietnam discussion with a question written on the board: To what extent can Lyndon Johnson be held accountable for the Vietnam tragedy? The ensuing discussion occupied four class periods over three days. It yielded more than 150 pages of typed protocol.

Because the purpose of this example is to illustrate how an explanation develops, I will focus on the more coherent and easy-to-follow sections of the teacher's talk. We must realize that many "facts" about the events leading up to and during the Vietnam engagement were discussed and examined quite closely by the students. To appreciate the length of this multi-day discussion, readers might find it helpful to know that the transcript for each lesson averaged approximately 1,100 lines of text. In general, student-based discussion took up about 66% of each transcript. This example examines a subset of the remaining 33%. The terms that are italicized indicate elements in the model of an explanation that can be seen in various parts of the lesson.

On the blackboard, the question is written: To what extent can Lyndon Johnson be held accountable for the Vietnam tragedy?

The core question or problem is stated in writing and restated verbally.

Teacher: Lyndon Johnson's at fault. He has the principal responsibility for this tragedy. Your arguments please. (Starts at line 450)

A long debate ensues (lines 450–677) between students on both sides of the issue who throw in various facts from the time period. The discussion drifts toward the issue of what more the United States could have done to win the war and drifts away from the core question. The teacher points this digression out and requests that they return to the issue. As a way of redirecting the discussion, Peterbene reminds them of Barry Goldwater's charges in the campaign that Johnson and the Democrats were soft on communism.

Conditions of use and connection to the principle of forming a coherent argument. Not all facts are relevant, and the discussion of other ways to win the war—although often mentioned in commentary on the period—is not germane to this discussion of blame. Class discussion continues, and then Peterbene rephrases a student comment:

Teacher: Let's blow them out of the water. Let's use nuclear weapons if we have to. And now is it possible that that kind of rhetoric during the campaign had some impact on Johnson's foreign policy with regard to North Vietnam?

The example connects to prior knowledge. Peterbene uses the previous paraphrase as an example that will help students connect to their prior knowledge. Students were aware of the political campaigns of the era.

Teacher: Highly likely. And one of the things suggested, you said a few minutes ago, was that . . . this plan that was implemented during 1964 by the Johnson administration was in fact, seemingly at least, a response to some of that criticism that he had been "soft on communism" in general, and that this particular set of policies that the United States seemed to be pursuing was simply an indication that he was soft on communism. Reminder too, that this plan A-34 [writes A-34 on the black board] was in fact a reversal of Kennedy's plan that had been drawn up in 1963 before he was assassinated. His plan was to do what with regard to American advisors in South Vietnam? . . . Pull them out. . . . Gradual withdrawal. Remember by the end of '63 we've got about 10,000 quote–unquote advisors in South Vietnam. Johnson changes that. Folks, one, one of the things that we're trying to suggest here is that, in fact, one of those factors that seem to be leading, directing American foreign policy in 1964 is what gets said and what happens in this campaign, in part.

The problem or query is understood. Peterbene points to progress on the as-yet-unstated goal of making an appropriate historical argument.

Teacher: To what extent is Johnson responsible then? If it's the campaign—what's the implication here?

A long discussion among students (lines 714–839) raises issues of Goldwater's responsibility, the role of Vietnamization of the war, the alliances between the United States and various groups in Vietnam since World War II, and the cancellation of the elections in Vietnam, which suggested that the Vietnamese would have voted against the Western powers.

An example is provided. A major example of the canceled election is being posted in the argument-explanation.

Teacher: Let's go back for some detail. . . . Emily, you mentioned that there were supposed to be elections in Vietnam. What was it that provided for those elections? . . . At the Geneva Conference in 1954, there was a decision made that there would be elections in South Vietnam. There were none held, and in part, the United States acquiesces to that lack of elections. And what impact does that have on the Vietnamese people in general would you say? . . . For what other reason might the U.S. be aligned with South Vietnam?

The example connects. This previous example connects the core explanation to the larger context of interventions. Students discuss the idea of containment (lines 850–902). Peterbene says, "[I]t appears as though Lyndon Johnson may have had some responsibility" and lists a summary of students' points—containment, campaign, American public support—as reasons for increased involvement. Students discuss the fact that Johnson uses support of the people, but when popular opinion goes against the war, Johnson assumes that people do not know enough and so continues as a "Lone Cowboy."

Representation is provided. A student introduces the analogical representation of Johnson as Lone Cowboy—a representation designed to further the Johnson-as-solely-responsible part of the argument. Peterbene responds.

Teacher: Look, wait a minute now. Is he a lone cowboy? Is this an accurate statement? [Note that the representation of Johnson as Lone Cowboy is used to move the argument by both the students and the teacher.] . . . We've already suggested the American public is behind him. Is he getting support from anywhere else?

Another long, student-led discussion ensues until the congressional vote on the Gulf of Tonkin is mentioned (lines 908–946).

Teacher: Johnson says to Congress, "I need your support. I need you to tell me I can do what I need to do in order to prevent this kind of thing from happening again and to let the North Vietnamese know that we mean business. They should never attack our ships again." And what do they do? By overwhelming numbers, Congress supports the president—gives him a blank check to do pretty much what he needs. Lyndon Johnson is a lone cowboy in this?

No discussion occurs in the texts or in class about the idea that the Gulf of Tonkin incident might have been manufactured. Note the specific unpacking of the "lone cowboy" analogy. This approach works at two levels—it advances the posted argument of Johnson as responsible or not, and it also critiques the form of historical argumentation.

Students discuss the international scene at the time and the U.S. role or lack thereof in other interventions (lines 957–1036).

Teacher: I want you to see one other thing, that as far as this attack is concerned on our two destroyers—or at least one, the Maddox—these attacks occur . . . before the election in November. I don't think we can stress, although Bailey and Schlesinger and the texts do not do this heavily, I don't think there is much question that this campaign in fact influenced the extent to which Johnson went to put down this threat. Because when he tried to do that, and the response not only by Congress but from the American public was so positive, supportive of him, what does that suggest to a presidential candidate? . . . [T]his man is pursuing these policies not only be-

cause of an anticommunist stance, but I think as well because he wants to be elected. Now there are incidents afterward—not only in the Dominican Republic, but in Southeast Asia as well—that continue to influence American foreign policy, whether it's the attack on our military installations or the behavior on the part of the North Vietnamese. Of course, all of these have a dramatic impact on the kinds of decisions that we made with regard to South Vietnam and North Vietnam. And we'll talk more about these tomorrow. Please . . . be prepared to conclude this discussion, thinking once again about what additional information we ought to plug in as part of our argument.

A new goal or problem is set and is connected to principles. Because this is both an argument about Johnson and a case of argument in history, a new goal or problem is set, which connects what is being learned to principles of historical reasoning.

Peterbene opened the next lesson with a student's lengthy discussion (approximately 500 lines) of a book about Ford's presidency. Then, after reviewing the arguments made the previous day, Peterbene asks whether the class had assigned blame for "the Vietnamese tragedy" to Johnson. The students discuss the election process as one cause of U.S. involvement in Vietnam and Peterbene concurs. The students continue reviewing the conclusions, and about halfway through the first period (it is a double-period day), Peterbene asks directly for opinions that defend Johnson. This request, in turn, leads to a discussion of the various ways that the peace initiatives to the North can be interpreted.

Teacher: History isn't always just one answer to a question. It *can't* always be just one answer. Because when we look at a person's point of view about what goes on in the Ford administration, no matter what other sources that person may use to defend his particular idea or thesis, we have got to recognize that bias is a part of that—that that person is looking at the daily goings on with a particular frame of reference that may be different from somebody else's. That's why history bothers some people, I think, because it's not always just cut and dry.

Note the use of the Ford example from the beginning of class to integrate the Ford and Johnson discussions. Note, too, the various analogies inside the language. The discussion is moving toward completion by answering the posed questions or problems—Johnson's responsibility and how to build an historical argument.

Teacher: It is always to some extent interpretive. And what I am looking for you folks to be able to do, and I think you are getting better and better at it, is defending a particular argument with specific evidence that you are aware of. . . . [Note the idea of *setting the problem*—of establishing an argument with evidence that is interpreted for the purpose of the stance being taken.] What role do other Southeast Asian countries play in South Vietnam? What role do other countries play?

Students continue the discussion with a summary by Peterbene that points to the ambiguity of the United States being invited in and also being asked to leave different countries that were perceived as being vulnerable to communism.

The selection of these transcript excerpts (Peterbene, 4/10 & 4/11) is designed to give at least a partial sense of what is meant by analyzing an instructional explanation. This particular set of discussions can also be analyzed in many other ways—in terms of (a) who advances the ideas, (b) when the course of the discussion switches from attack to defense of Johnson, or (c) what the ratio of student-to-teacher talk is—but here, the point is to show how various explanatory goals are met over several days of discussion. First, two core questions or problems are being explained. One is stated at the very beginning: Can Johnson be held accountable? The other is hinted at during the discussion, becoming explicit in the middle: What do we need to do to construct a good argument? The discussion abounds with examples, a few of which are directly flagged by the teacher; indeed, much of the reasoning is example based. How could this discussion have looked different, covered the same material, and not been an explanation? Or is everything an explanation?

Imagine the following opening "query" for a classroom discussion: List at least three factors that show why we were involved and continued to be involved in Vietnam after the Kennedy assassination. The "answer" could be arrived at in less than five minutes of discussion: the Goldwater/Johnson election, the policy of containment of communism, strong public support of intervention, and international instability following the end of colonialism. Students could expect a short-answer question on their unit tests that would ask almost the same question, and if they had studied appropriately, they might be able to answer it. But these fragments of information would constitute only an isolated island of knowledge for students, unconnected to the full historical context. An explanation, to be effective, needs to be attached not only to a single question but also to a system of questions that are important and valued by the discipline and by the students.

Throughout the above abbreviated section of the Peterbene transcript, we find evidence of the teacher tying the discussion back to both the stated historical problem and the more general problem of how to make a valid historical argument. Both explanations are working in tandem, using examples and representations as well as linking statements back to the core underlying principles of the discipline.

Connecting to Current Educational Ideologies

The example of the three-day, four-lesson discussion about Vietnam could be seen as fitting in or as not fitting in with reform ideas, or it could be seen as "acquisitional," "participatory," or neither (Sfard, 1998). Students are trying to acquire the skills of good historical argument so they will do well on a particular form of examination. But they are also in the process of building and sustaining an intellectual community that has found ways to discuss highly charged and significant ideas using particular tools of historical discourse. From the perspective of the underlying psychology of constructivism, namely, that we learn things only when we construct meaning of them ourselves, the discussion is constructive. From the point of view of participation, the majority of the students were involved in the discussion that lasted over several days, and their discussions became more elaborate and more productive. Students constantly used the opportunity to integrate facts and details into a larger coherent picture. Because this discussion was in an AP class, students were aware of the need to master the idea of building an historical argument and were trying out various ways of accomplishing that goal. The students were in the active process of building a community and of elaborating their own practices.

Peterbene is very visible in this discussion. The discussion, while lengthy and open-ended, is refocused by the teacher on several occasions. The specific topic or question was chosen by the teacher, not by the students. No particular effort was made to relate these discussions to the personal views or experiences of the students, although the students were definitely passionate about their positions on the subject. The sense of what makes an argument work was defined not through negotiation with the students but by the teacher as a low-keyed but real evaluator.

So what are we to make of this? Is explaining by definition an act of imposition that puts teaching at odds with current views of what good instruction should be like, whether the speakers are the teacher or the students? Obviously, I do not think this is the case. Disciplines have special—and sometimes overlapping—epistemologies. They are made up of facts, ideas, and concepts; they have both particular ways of adding to their domains and particular ways of deleting or correcting information. In learning about these ways of reasoning in a particular discipline and in learning to participate in them, students can be invited to build up their own meanings and values, but they can do this building with a guide.

Instructional explanations deal with both the content of the domain and its epistemology. Wineburg and Wilson (1991), in their chapter in Brophy's *Advances in Research on Teaching,* point to the idea that any act of teaching presents both the content of a domain and a representation of the domain. Cues to the unique discourse register of any domain can most easily be understood by participating systematically in a community of discourse in which the serious and real ideas of the domain are under discussion. Wineburg and Wilson suggest that the representation of the domain emerges from the teacher's own understanding of the subject itself combined with his or her understanding of the ways in which students are seeing the issues in the domain (Wineburg & Wilson, 1991, p. 333; see also Wood, Cobb, & Yackel, 1991).

I concur, and I suggest that explanations inside of a domain are an appropriate location for examining both content and epistemology. Students can and do become meaningfully engaged in explanation, but they are also pressed to expand beyond what they already know and already feel. The formalisms of historical argument can be seen, I think, as tools for expressing deeply held beliefs and for challenging those beliefs, not as mindless tricks to be mastered. In our Peterbene example and in the examples quoted by Wineburg and Wilson (1991) and by Walvoord and Breihan (1990), the teachers are supporting students and are constructing understanding and knowledge about the content and epistemology with them, not imposing it on them.

Another way to approach this argument—that of the role of the teacher in "teaching"—is to consider the message being sent if the teacher is excluded from the explanatory discourse. It is unseemly to place a human being in a social context and then assign to that person the role of being invisible out of a fear that their every breath may contaminate the creativity and authentic desires of the rest of the group.

I am arguing that the teacher does have a role as teacher in the classroom. This role is recognized both by the sociocultural views of the world and by the constructivist and emergent views of the world (Cobb & Yackel, 1996). As Cobb and Yackel point out, in the former view, the teacher is seen as the carrier and transmitter of appropriate cultural norms—such as mathematical reasoning—while in the latter, the teacher is viewed as a responsible coconstructor of such classroom reasoning norms. The particular practices of teaching can and should vary. As Ball and Lampert point out in many of their writings, they choose not to make moves to explicitly correct or clarify; but, because they deeply value meaning making, they make many implicit moves to do so. Further, Ball and Lampert both work extremely hard to keep the nature of the intellectual conversations focused and meaningful both to the students and to the practice of mathematics (Ball, 1993; Ball & Lampert, 1999; Lampert, 1986, 1990, 1992; Lampert & Ball, 1998). Likewise, Wineburg and Wilson (1991) describe two good but very different teachers: one who is (for the teaching episode that they choose to identify) invisible and discretely evocative and one who is dramatically directive.

The Value of Looking Closely

At the beginning of this chapter, I suggested that two kinds of questions were on the table: one that asks what we know about the practice of teaching in the subject areas and another that asks what we know about studying the practice of teaching in the subject matters. Many new trends—some might say fads—have developed in the time since the last *Handbook of Research on Teaching*. One trend seems to have considerable staying power: a steady and unrelenting demand that teachers, students, and researchers make sense of and build meanings from what they are doing. Lists of unrelated variables thrown into a mindless factoring program are not acceptable in research on teaching—and doubtfully will be ever again. Lengthy tales of researchers' personal experiences in classrooms, tales that focus exclusively on the hidden agenda while ignoring the intended agenda and that are unrelated to the content of what is being learned—old-styled ethnographies—are likewise unacceptable in research on teaching and are unlikely to return to fashion.

The issue is not one of methodology, it is one of meaning. The requirement is the same for researchers as it is for the teachers and students, namely, that researchers connect carefully with the form and content of what they are studying. The work here emphasizes the idea that looking closely and over a long period of time at some specific portion of the teaching and learning enterprise has value, because doing so affords the opportunity for the researcher to make sense of what is being seen (van Zee & Minstrell, 1997). The complexity lies in selecting something that has both a sense of universality and a sense of richly textured variability. By pulling apart instructional explanations, I have tried to locate places where the dynamics of teaching and learning can be seen and where the ways in which the social system of the classroom operates can be observed,

whether or not that classroom is part of the modern reforms and is consciously coconstructing rules of behavior, norms, and routines for intellectual development.

Future Paths for Research

What should future research look like? Research that is designed to help us understand more about effectively designing classroom experiences must take into account the unique social system in the classroom and the ways in which particular activities are construed, redefined, and pressed into service for new purposes. Such research must also be mindful both of the significance of the cultural differences among different subject matters—not just among students—and of the way those differences are played out in the classroom. Future research that attempts to identify ways in which we can best support the learning of teachers must likewise be willing to put aside old divisions within the domain of teacher education and link more realistically to the worlds of practice and the situations of content. Not only must future research account for the larger social systems, but also it must select boundaries—neither too small and confining nor too large and global—within which the researcher will observe closely and record carefully the details of what is understood. Only through understanding these specifics can we build general understandings.[7] The selection of the moments to be observed and the level of detail with which to observe them will be—like explanations in the classroom—a socially negotiated practice.

REFERENCES

Adams, A. (1983). *Examples: The making of forty photographs.* Boston: Little, Brown.

Anzai, Y., & Simon, H. A. (1979). The theory of learning by doing. *Psychological Review, 86*(2), 124–140.

Ball, D. L. (1993). With an eye on the mathematical horizon: Dilemmas of teaching elementary school mathematics. *Elementary School Journal, 93*(4), 373–397.

Ball, D. L., & Lampert, M. (1999). Multiples of evidence, time, and perspective: Revising the study of teaching and learning. In E. C. Lagemann & L. S. Shulman (Eds.), *Issues in education research: Problems and possibilities* (pp. 371–398). San Francisco: Jossey-Bass.

Barr, A. S. (1929). *Characteristic differences in the teaching performance of good and poor teachers of the social studies.* Bloomington, IL: Public School Publishing.

Beck, I. L., McKeown, M. G., & Gromoll, E. (1989). Learning from social studies texts. *Cognition and Instruction, 6*(2), 99–158.

Beck, I. L., McKeown, M. G., Hamilton, R. L., & Kucan, L. (1997). *Questioning the Author: An approach for enhancing student engagement with text.* Newark, DE: International Reading Association.

Berliner, D. C. (1983). Developing conceptions of classroom environments: Some light on the T in classroom studies of ATI. *Educational Psychologist, 18,* 1–13.

Berliner, D. C. (1986). In pursuit of the expert pedagogue. *Educational Researcher, 15*(7), 5–13.

Berliner, D. C. (1992). Commentary on Chapter 7. In J. H. Shulman (Ed.), *Case methods in teacher education* (pp. 146–147). New York: Teachers College Press.

Borko, H., Eisenhart, M., Brown, C. A., Underhill, R. G., Jones, D., & Agard, P. C. (1992). Learning to teach hard mathematics: Do nov-

---

[7] I am indebted to Suzanne Wilson (personal communication, August 16, 1998) for pointing out to me that going from the general to the specific is not possible.

ice teachers and their instructors give up too easily? *Journal for Research in Mathematics Education, 23*(3), 194–222.

Borko, H., & Livingston, C. (1989). Cognition and improvisation: Differences in mathematics instruction by expert and novice teachers. *American Educational Research Journal, 26*(4), 473–498.

Bossert, S. (1979). *Tasks and social relationships in classrooms: A study of instructional organization and its consequences.* Cambridge, UK: Cambridge University Press.

Brownell, W. A. (1948). Learning theory and educational practice. *Journal of Educational Research, 41*(7), 481–497.

Callanan, M. A., & Oakes, L. M. (1992). Preschoolers' questions and parents' explanations: Causal thinking in everyday activity. *Cognitive Development, 7,* 213–233.

Callanan, M. A., Shrager, J., & Moore, J. L. (1995). Parent-child collaborative explanations: Methods of identification and analysis. *The Journal of the Learning Sciences, 4*(1), 105–129.

Carlsen, W. S. (1991). Subject-matter knowledge and science teaching: A pragmatic perspective. In J. Brophy (Ed.), *Advances in research on teaching: Volume 2. Teachers' knowledge of subject matter as it relates to their teaching practice* (pp. 115–143). Greenwich, CT: JAI Press.

Carroll, L. (1962). *The annotated Snark.* (M. Gardner, Annotator) New York: Simon and Schuster.

Cazden, C. B. (1986). Classroom discourse. In M. C. Wittrock (Ed.), *Handbook of research on teaching* (3rd ed., pp. 432–463). New York: Macmillan.

Chi, M. T. H. (2000). Self-explaining expository texts: The dual processes of generating inferences and repairing mental models. In R. Glaser (Ed.), *Advances in instructional psychology* (Vol. 5, pp.161–238). Mahwah, NJ: Lawrence Erlbaum Associates.

Cobb, P. (1994). Where is the mind? Constructivist and sociocultural perspectives on mathematical development. *Educational Researcher, 23*(7), 13–20.

Cobb, P., & Yackel, E. (1996). Constructivist, emergent, and sociocultural perspectives in the context of developmental research. *Educational Psychologist, 31*(3/4), 175–190.

Crowley, K., & Callanan, M. A. (1998). Describing and supporting collaborative scientific thinking in parent-child interactions. *Journal of Museum Education, 23*(1), 12–17.

Doyle, W. (1979). *The tasks of teaching and learning in classrooms* (R & D Rep. No. 4013). Austin: University of Texas, Research and Development Center for Teacher Education.

Doyle, W. (1983). Academic work. *Review of Educational Research, 53*(2), 159–199.

Doyle, W. (1992). Curriculum and pedagogy. In P. W. Jackson (Ed.), *Handbook of research on curriculum* (pp. 486–516). New York: Macmillan.

Doyle, W., & Carter, K. (1984). Academic tasks in classrooms. *Curriculum Inquiry, 14*(2), 129–149.

Duesterberg, L. M. (1998). Rethinking culture in the pedagogy and practices of preservice teachers. *Teaching and Teacher Education, 14*(5), 497–512.

Dunbar, K. (1995). How scientists really reason: Scientific reasoning in real-world laboratories. In R. J. Sternberg & J. E. Davidson (Eds.), *The nature of insight* (pp. 365–395). Cambridge, MA: MIT Press.

Durkheim, E. (1961). *Moral education: A study in the theory and application of the sociology of education.* New York: Free Press of Glencoe. (Original work published 1925)

Eicholz, R. E., O'Daffer, P. G., Charles, R. I., Young, S. L., Barnett, C. S., & Fleenor, C. R. (1991). *Addison-Wesley mathematics, Grade 6.* Menlo Park, CA: Addison-Wesley.

Eisenhart, M., Borko, H., Underhill, R., Brown, D., Jones, D., & Agard, P. (1993). Conceptual knowledge falls through the cracks: Complexities of learning to teach mathematics for understanding. *Journal for Research in Mathematics Education, 24*(1), 8–40.

Even, R. (1993). Subject-matter knowledge and pedagogical content knowledge: Prospective secondary teachers and the function concept. *Journal for Research in Mathematics Education, 24*(2), 94–116.

Fenstermacher, G. D., & Richardson, V. (1994). Promoting confusion in educational psychology: How is it done? *Educational Psychologist, 29*(1), 49–55.

Fenstermacher, G. D., & Soltis, J. F. (1986). *Approaches to teaching.* New York: Teachers College Press.

Gentner, D. (1989). The mechanisms of analogical learning. In S. Vosniadou & A. Ortony (Eds.), *Similarity and analogical reasoning* (pp. 199–241). New York: Cambridge University Press.

Greene, M. (1994). Epistemology and educational research: The influence of recent approaches to knowledge. In L. Darling-Hammond (Ed.), *Review of research in education* (Vol. 20, pp. 423–464). Washington, DC: American Educational Research Association.

Gregg, M., Ellis, E. S., Casareno, A., Rountree, B., Schlichter, C., & Mayfield, P. (1997). The Multiple Abilities Program at the University of Alabama: Preparing teachers to meet all students' needs. In L. P. Blantz, C. Griffin, J. A. Winn, & M. C. Pugach (Eds.), *Teacher education in transition: Collaborative programs to prepare general and special educators* (pp. 106–127). Denver, CO: Love Publishing.

Grice, P. (1989). *Studies in the way of words.* Cambridge, MA: Harvard University Press.

Grossman, P. L. (1989). A study in contrast: Sources of pedagogical content knowledge for secondary English. *Journal of Teacher Education, 40*(5), 24–32.

Grossman, P. L. (1991). What are we talking about anyway? Subject-matter knowledge of secondary English teachers. In J. Brophy (Ed.), *Advances in research on teaching: Volume 2. Teachers' knowledge of subject matter as it relates to their teaching practice* (pp. 245–264). Greenwich, CT: JAI Press.

Grossman, P. L., & Stodolsky, S. S. (1994). Considerations of content and the circumstances of secondary school teaching. In L. Darling-Hammond (Ed.), *Review of research in education* (Vol. 20, pp. 179–221). Washington, DC: American Educational Research Association.

Gudmundsdottir, S. (1991). Pedagogical models of subject matter. In J. Brophy (Ed.), *Advances in research on teaching: Volume 2. Teachers' knowledge of subject matter as it relates to their teaching practice* (pp. 265–304). Greenwich, CT: JAI Press.

Gutierrez, K., Rymes, B., & Larson, J. (1995). Script, counterscript, and underlife in the classroom: *James Brown v. Board of Education. Harvard Educational Review, 65*(3), 445–471.

Hashweh, M. Z. (1985). *An exploratory study of teacher knowledge and teaching.* Unpublished doctoral dissertation, Stanford University, Palo Alto, CA.

Henningsen, M., & Stein, M. K. (1997). Mathematical tasks and student cognition: Classroom-based factors that support and inhibit high-level mathematical thinking and reasoning. *Journal for Research in Mathematics Education, 28*(5), 524–549.

Holyoak, K. J., & Thagard, P. (1995). *Mental leaps: Analogy in creative thought.* Cambridge, MA: MIT Press.

Jackson, P. W. (1968). *Life in classrooms.* New York: Holt, Rinehart and Winston.

Jones, M. G., & Vesilind, E. (1995). Preservice teachers' cognitive frameworks for class management. *Teaching and Teacher Education, 11*(4), 313–330.

Joshua, S., & Dupin, J. J. (1987). Taking into account student conceptions in instructional strategy: An example in physics. *Cognition and Instruction, 4*(2), 117–135.

Judd, C. H. (1915). *The psychology of high school subjects.* Boston: Ginn.

Judd, C. H. (1936). *Education as the cultivation of the higher mental processes.* New York: Macmillan.

Kanigel, R. (1991). *The man who knew infinity: A life of the genius, Ramanujan.* New York: C. Scribner's .

Kemper, D. (1992). Commentary on Chapter 7. In J. H. Shulman (Ed.), *Case methods in teacher education* (pp. 147–149). New York: Teachers College Press.

Kieran, C. (1992). The learning and teaching of school algebra. In D. A. Grouws (Ed.), *Handbook of research on mathematics teaching and learning* (pp. 390–419). New York: Macmillan.

Kindervater, A., & von Borries, B. (1997). Historical motivation and historical-political socialization. In M. Angvik & B. von Borries (Eds.), *A comparative European survey on historical consciousness and political attitudes among adolescents* (Vol. A, pp. 62–105). Hamburg: Körber-Stiftung.

Lampert, M. (1985). How do teachers manage to teach? Perspectives on problems in practice. *Harvard Educational Review, 55,* 178–194.

Lampert, M. (1986). Teaching multiplication. *The Journal of Mathematical Behavior, 5*(3), 241–280.

Lampert, M. (1989). Choosing and using mathematical tools in classroom discourse. In J. Brophy (Ed.), *Advances in research on teaching* (Vol. 1, pp. 223–265). Greenwich, CT: JAI Press.

Lampert, M. (1990). When the problem is not the question and the solution is not the answer: Mathematical knowing and teaching. *American Educational Research Journal, 27,* 29–63.

Lampert, M. (1992). Teaching and learning long division for understanding in school. In G. Leinhardt, R. Putnam, & R. A. Hattrup (Eds.), *Analysis of arithmetic for mathematics teaching* (pp. 221–282). Hillsdale, NJ: Lawrence Erlbaum Associates.

Lampert, M., & Ball, D. L. (1998). *Mathematics, teaching, and multimedia: Investigations of real practice.* New York: Teachers College Press.

Lane, H. C. (1998). *Using the student model to govern explanation in an intelligent tutoring system.* Unpublished manuscript, University of Pittsburgh, Learning Research and Development Center, Pittsburgh, PA.

Larreamendy-Joerns, J. (1996). *Learning science from text: Effects of theory and examples on college students' ability to construct explanations in evolutionary biology.* Unpublished doctoral dissertation, University of Pittsburgh, Pittsburgh, PA.

Lehrer, R., & Romberg, T. (1996). Exploring children's data modeling. *Cognition and Instruction, 14*(1), 69–108.

Leinhardt, G. (1986). Expertise in mathematics teaching. *Educational Leadership, 43*(7), 28–33.

Leinhardt, G. (1987). Development of an expert explanation: An analysis of a sequence of subtraction lessons. *Cognition and Instruction, 4*(4), 225–282.

Leinhardt, G. (1988). Expertise in instructional lessons: An example from fractions. In D. A. Grouws & T. J. Cooney (Eds.), *Perspectives on research on effective mathematics teaching* (Vol. 1 in a series of monographs from conferences of the National Council of Teachers of Mathematics, pp. 47–66). Hillsdale, NJ: Lawrence Erlbaum Associates.

Leinhardt, G. (1989). Math lessons: A contrast of novice and expert competence. *Journal for Research in Mathematics Education, 20*(1), 52–75.

Leinhardt, G. (1990). A contrast of novice and expert competence in math lessons. In J. Lowyck & C. Clark (Eds.), *Teacher thinking and professional action* (pp. 75–97). Leuven, Belgium: Leuven University Press.

Leinhardt, G. (1993a). Instructional explanations in history and mathematics. In W. Kintsch (Ed.), *Proceedings of the Fifteenth Annual Conference of the Cognitive Science Society* (pp. 5–16). Hillsdale, NJ: Lawrence Erlbaum Associates.

Leinhardt, G. (1993b). On teaching. In R. Glaser (Ed.), *Advances in instructional psychology* (Vol. 4, pp. 1–54). Hillsdale, NJ: Lawrence Erlbaum Associates.

Leinhardt, G. (1993c). Weaving instructional explanations in history. *British Journal of Educational Psychology, 63,* 46–74.

Leinhardt, G., & Greeno, J. (1986). The cognitive skill of teaching. *Journal of Educational Psychology, 78*(2), 75–95.

Leinhardt, G., Putnam, R. T., Stein, M. K., & Baxter, J. (1991). Where subject knowledge matters. In J. Brophy (Ed.), *Advances in research on teaching: Volume 2. Teachers' knowledge of subject matter as it relates to their teaching practice* (pp. 87–113). Greenwich, CT: JAI Press.

Leinhardt, G., & Schwarz, B. B. (1997). Seeing the problem: An explanation from Pólya. *Cognition and Instruction, 15*(3), 395–434.

Leinhardt, G., Stainton, C., & Virji, S. (1994). A sense of history. *Educational Psychologist, 29*(2), 79–88.

Leinhardt, G., Weidman, C., & Hammond, K. M. (1987). Introduction and integration of classroom routines by expert teachers. *Curriculum Inquiry, 17*(2), 135–176.

Leinhardt, G., Young, M. K., & Merriman, J. (1995). Integrating professional knowledge: The theory of practice and the practice of theory. *Learning and Instruction, 5,* 401–408.

Mathematical Association of America. (Producer). (1965). *Let us teach guessing* [Film]. (Available from MAA, 1529 18th Street NW, Washington, DC, 20036)

McDermott, R. P. (1977). Social relations as contexts for learning in school. *Harvard Educational Review, 47*(2), 198–312.

McQuaide, J., Fienberg, J., & Leinhardt, G. (1991). *Transcript of "Pólya: Let us teach guessing"* (Tech. Rep. No. CLIP-91–01). Pittsburgh, PA: University of Pittsburgh, Learning Research and Development Center.

Mehan, H. (1979). *Learning lessons.* Cambridge, MA: Harvard University Press.

Moore, J. D. (1995). *Participating in explanatory dialogues.* Cambridge, MA: MIT Press.

Ohlsson, S. (1992). The cognitive skill of theory articulation: A neglected aspect of science education? *Science and Education, 1,* 181–192.

Parker, M., & Leinhardt, G. (1995). Percent: A privileged proportion. *Review of Educational Research, 65*(4), 421–481.

Perfetti, C. A., Britt, M. A., Rouet, J-F., Georgi, M. C., & Mason, R. A. (1994). How students use texts to learn and reason about historical uncertainty. In M. Carretero & J. F. Voss (Eds.), *Cognitive and instructional processes in history and the social sciences* (pp. 257–283). Hillsdale, NJ: Lawrence Erlbaum Associates.

Peterson, P. L., Fennema, E., Carpenter, T. P., & Loef, M. (1989). Teachers' pedagogical content beliefs in mathematics. *Cognition and Instruction, 6*(1), 1–40.

Pólya, G. (1968). *Mathematics and plausible reasoning: Vol. 1. Induction and analogy in mathematics.* Princeton, NJ: Princeton University Press. (Original work published 1954)

Pontecorvo, C. (1993a). Introduction: Forms of discourse and shared thinking. *Cognition and Instruction, 11*(3 & 4), 189–196.

Pontecorvo, C. (Ed.). (1993b). Discourse and shared reasoning [Special issue]. *Cognition and Instruction, 11*(3 & 4).

Putnam, R. T. (1985). Teacher thoughts and actions in live and simulated tutoring of addition (Doctoral dissertation, Stanford University, 1985). *Dissertation Abstracts International, 46,* 933A–934A.

Raghavan, K., Sartoris, M. L., & Glaser, R. (1998). Impact of the MARS curriculum: The mass unit. *Science Education, 82*(1), 53–91.

Resnick, L. B., (1986). The development of mathematical intuition. In M. Perlmutter (Ed.), *Perspectives on intellectual development: The Minnesota symposium on child psychology* (pp. 159–194). Hillsdale, NJ: Lawrence Erlbaum Associates.

Resnick, L. B., Salmon, M., Zeitz, C. M., Wathen, S. H., & Holowchak, M. (1993). Reasoning in conversation. *Cognition and Instruction, 11*(3 & 4), 347–364.

Rissland, E. L. (1991). Example-based reasoning. In J. F. Voss, D. N. Perkins, & J. W. Segal (Eds.), *Informal reasoning in education* (pp. 187–208). Hillsdale, NJ: Lawrence Erlbaum Associates.

Rust, F. O. (1994). The first year of teaching: It's not what they expected. *Teaching and Teacher Education, 10*(2), 205–230.

Sabers, D. S., Cushing, K. S., & Berliner, D.C. (1991). Differences among teachers in a task characterized by simultaneity, multidimensionality, and immediacy. *American Educational Research Journal, 28*(1), 63–88.

Schama, S. (1995). *Landscape and memory.* New York: Random House.

Schoenfeld, A. H. (1983). Beyond the purely cognitive: Belief systems, social cognitions, and metacognitions as driving forces in intellectual performance. *Cognitive Science, 7,* 329–363.

Schoenfeld, A. H. (1998). Toward a theory of teaching-in-context. *Issues in Education, 4*(1), 1–94.

Schwab, J. J. (1978). The practical: Arts of eclectic. In I. Westbury & N.J. Wilkof (Eds.), *Science, curriculum, and liberal education: Selected essays* (pp. 322–364). Chicago: University of Chicago Press.

Seixas, P. (1993, April). *Young people's understanding of historical significance.* Paper presented at the annual meeting of the American Educational Research Association, Atlanta, GA.

Seixas, P. (1994). Confronting the moral frames of popular film: Young people respond to historical revisionism. *American Journal of Education, 102,* 261–285.

Sfard, A. (1991). On the dual nature of mathematical conceptions: Reflections on processes and objects as different sides of the same coin. *Educational Studies in Mathematics, 22,* 1–36.

Sfard, A. (1998). On two metaphors for learning and the dangers of choosing just one. *Educational Researcher, 27*(2), 4–13.

Shulman, L. S. (1974). The psychology of school subjects: A premature obituary? *Journal of Research in Science Teaching, 11*(4), 319–339.

Shulman, L. S. (1986). Paradigms and research programs in the study of teaching: A contemporary perspective. In M. C. Wittrock (Ed.), *Handbook of research on teaching* (3rd ed., pp. 3–36). New York: Macmillan.

Shulman, L. S. (1987). Knowledge and teaching: Foundations of the new reform. *Harvard Educational Review, 57*(1), 1–22.

Shulman, L. S. (1992). Toward a pedagogy of cases. In J. Shulman (Ed.), *Case methods in teacher education* (pp. 1–30). New York: Teachers College Press.

Shulman, L. S., & Quinlan, K. M. (1996). The comparative psychology of school subjects. In D.C. Berliner & R. C. Calfee (Eds.), *Handbook of educational psychology* (pp. 399–422). New York: Macmillan Library Reference USA.

Simon, H. A., & Chase, W. G. (1973). Skill in chess. *American Scientist, 61,* 394–403.

Smith, M. J. (1995). *Pedagogical challenges of instructional assessment in middle school earth science: Two case studies.* Unpublished doctoral dissertation, University of Pittsburgh, Pittsburgh, PA.

Sobel, D. (1995). *Longitude: The true story of a lone genius who solved the greatest scientific problem of his time.* New York: Walker and Company.

Stein, M. K., Grover, B. W., & Henningsen, M. (1996). Building student capacity for mathematical thinking and reasoning: An analysis of mathematical tasks used in reform classrooms. *American Educational Research Journal, 33*(2), 455–488.

Stodolsky, S. S. (1988). *The subject matters: Classroom activity in math and social studies.* Chicago: University of Chicago Press.

Tamir, P. (1988). Subject matter and related pedagogical knowledge in teacher education. *Teaching and Teacher Education, 4,* 99–110.

Tamir, P. (1991). Professional and personal knowledge of teachers and teacher educators. *Teaching and Teacher Education, 7*(3), 263–268.

Teel, K. M., Debruin-Parecki, A., & Covington, M. V. (1998). Teaching strategies that honor and motivate inner-city African-American students: A school/university collaboration. *Teaching and Teacher Education, 14*(5), 479–496.

Thagard, P. (1992). *Conceptual revolutions.* Princeton, NJ: Princeton University Press.

Thorndike, E. L. (1922). *The psychology of arithmetic.* New York: Macmillan.

van Zee, E., & Minstrell, J. (1997). Using questioning to guide student thinking. *The Journal of the Learning Sciences, 6*(2), 227–269.

Walvoord, B. E., & Breihan, J. R. (1990). Arguing and debating: Breihan's history course. In B. E. Walvoord (Ed.), *Thinking and writing in college* (pp. 97–143). Urbana, IL: National Council of Teachers of English.

White, B. Y. (1993). Intermediate causal models: A missing link for successful science education? In R. Glaser (Ed.), *Advances in instructional psychology* (Vol. 4, pp. 177–252). Hillsdale, NJ: Lawrence Erlbaum Associates.

Wineburg, S. S. (1998). Reading Abraham Lincoln: An expert/expert study on the interpretation of historical texts. *Cognitive Science, 22*(3), 319–346.

Wineburg, S. S., & Wilson, S. M. (1988). Models of wisdom in the teaching of history. *Phi Delta Kappan, 70,* 50–58.

Wineburg, S. S., & Wilson, S. M. (1991). Subject-matter knowledge in the teaching of history. In J. Brophy (Ed.), *Advances in research on teaching: Volume 2. Teachers' knowledge of subject matter as it relates to their teaching practice* (pp. 305–348). Greenwich, CT: JAI Press.

Wisconsin Center for Education Research, & Freudenthal Institute (1998). *Mathematics in context.* Chicago: Encyclopedia Britannica Educational Corporation.

Wood, T., Cobb, P., & Yackel, E. (1991). Change in teaching mathematics: A case study. *American Educational Research Journal, 28*(3), 587–616.

Young, K. M. (1998). *Models and examples in teaching and learning writing: A reconsideration.* Unpublished manuscript, University of Pittsburgh, Learning Research and Development Center, Pittsburgh, PA.

Young, K. M., & Leinhardt, G. (1998a). Wildflowers, sheep, and democracy: The role of analogy in the teaching and learning of history. In M. Carretero & J. G. Voss (Eds.), *Learning and reasoning in history* (pp. 154–196). London: Woburn Press.

Young, K. M., & Leinhardt, G. (1998b). Writing from primary documents: A way of knowing in history. *Written Communication, 15*(1), 25–68.

Zaslavsky, O., & Peled, I. (1996). Inhibiting factors in generating examples by mathematics teachers and student teachers: The case of binary operation. *Journal for Research in Mathematics Education, 27*(1), 67–78.

Zhu, X., & Simon, H. A. (1987). Learning mathematics from examples and by doing. *Cognition and Instruction, 4*(3), 137–166.

20.

The Teaching of Second Languages: Research Trends

Charles R. Hancock
Ohio State University

> *In a time of increasingly technical language, bureaucratic formulations, simulation games, and a lingua franca deriving from the media, it may become more and more necessary for teachers to create the kinds of speech situations in which and through which learners can open themselves to their lived worlds, to one another, and to themselves.*

> (Maxine Greene)

Chapter Overview

The chapter is divided into the following sections:

Descriptive Demographics: Figures and Tables
Second Language Acquisition (SLA) Theory and Research
Important Research Areas for the Next Decade
    Role of Grammar in L2 Teaching: Two Opposing Perspectives (to Correct or Not to Correct L2 Learner Errors)
    Task-Based L2 Learning: Some Promising Research Perspectives
    Technology and Language Learning: Some Preliminary Findings
Facing the New Millennium in L2 Teaching and Research: A Modest Proposal
Conclusion

Any one of the above topics alone could have been the focus of this entire chapter, given their importance to the second language (L2) profession. However, it seemed more appropriate to explore several key areas and their interactions, rather than focus on a single topic. Additionally, many experienced members of the L2 profession will concur that the past 25 or more years have seen a fragmentation of research based on individual researchers' agendas, rather than a broad-based, collective one. The overall goal of this chapter is to analyze key trends in the mid- and late-1990s, considering, whenever possible, the perspectives of L2 professionals in both the classroom instructor and researcher camps.

Introduction

Estimates of the world's current population set the number at 4 billion people; they speak thousands of languages and dialects. Similarly, estimates of the number of second language learners run in the millions worldwide.[1] In formal school settings, students throughout the world study languages other than their own, either as a requirement in their academic programs of study or for personal reasons. In informal naturalistic set-

The author would like to acknowledge the helpful comments and perspectives shared by the following individuals: William E. DeLorenzo (University of Maryland, College Park), Ange-Marie Hancock (University of North Carolina at Chapel Hill), Anthony Mistretta (South Colonie, New York, School District), Zena Moore (University of Texas at Austin), and colleagues and students at The Ohio State University, including: Cora Kaylani, Jun Liu, Debbie Robinson, Mark Warner, and others who reacted to the manuscript.

[1] For ease of communication, the terms foreign language, second language, world language, global language, target language, nonnative language, and language of wider communication are all used synonymously in this manuscript, despite the important connotations of each term. Second

tings, the number of second language (SL) learners is virtually incalculable. Language students range in age from the proverbial birth to the grave.

After years of school-based study, L2 students, their parents, and the policymakers who make important decisions about the inclusion or elimination of L2 language study as part of school-based and higher education curricula usually want information on achievement outcomes. To what extent can L2 learners use the language they have studied (e.g., read a document, write a summary of it, understand or leave a phone message, or use the language for their own purposes)? L2 professionals are often confronted with very basic questions for which the field does not have clear-cut answers: What helps a student to succeed in learning a second language? What hinders such success? Can individuals improve their ability to master an L2? If so, how? If not, why not? Does aptitude for L2 learning exist? Is there an ideal age for starting to learn a language? Is it ever too late to start studying an L2? Can children really learn an L2 better than adults? What is the role of technology in learning and maintaining an L2? What does it mean to master an L2? Which students best learn what aspects of language in what instructional settings and with what media? Should grammar be taught to L2 students when they need it to accurately communicate their own meanings? What is language loss? How does it occur? And the list goes on.

When answering these types of questions, L2 specialists typically answer by referring to the prevailing canons: advance organizers; instrumental versus integrative motivation; L2 aptitude; opportunity for practice; contrastive analysis of similarities between native language (L1) and L2; critical period hypothesis; oral proficiency testing; comprehensible input, interaction, and output; error analysis; variability; interlanguage; fossilization; learner strategies; communicative competence; autonomy; and task-based L2 learning. Within the L2 profession, it has been difficult to establish principled answers to such questions because of differing epistemologies and even because of oppositional theories. However, despite pendulum swings in language teaching during the past few decades, a few trends would likely be widely acceptable to many L2 professionals: (a) There is no one best method for L2 teaching or learning; (b) learners should be empowered to take charge of their own learning, with the eventual aim of autonomous lifelong learning; (c) L2 learning involves four interconnected language skills (i.e., listening, speaking, reading, and writing), which coexist during L2 acquisition, particularly in formal language settings; (d) while constructivist theories are increasing at the end of the 1990s within the L2 profession, behaviorist theories in L2

learning-teaching are popular among learners and instructors; and, finally, (e) L2 research needs to be conducted in both the rationalistic and the naturalistic paradigms by using both quantitative and qualitative methodologies if the complex L2 learning process is to be understood.

According to Lynch (1996), L2 research can fall into both the rationalistic, quantitative paradigm and the naturalistic, qualitative paradigm. For example, naturalistic researchers, who tend to associate themselves primarily with a qualitative orientation, may indeed study, classify, and quantify various phenomena. Given the very embryonic nature of L2 research into second language acquisition broadly defined, formal research is needed from multiple perspectives. To limit L2 research to one paradigm would not serve the needs of the profession.

The truth is that the L2 profession, with its many dichotomies (e.g., bilingual education versus English as a second language, foreign versus second language, immersion versus foreign language in the elementary schools, school-based versus natural settings), does not currently have answers to some basic questions posed by students, parents, and policymakers. The L2 acquisition (SLA) process has been and continues to be the focus of important L2 research. This chapter synthesizes our current understanding of the process of L2 learning and teaching, particularly in school settings. Although research-based findings in technology-related L2 education are still somewhat preliminary, the topic is included in this analysis because of a growing need to deal with this area. The chapter summarizes some key aspects of our current understanding as well as posits ways of integrating SLA research with L2 instruction (Hancock, 1994).

The prevailing canons of L2 teaching suggest that second language study appropriately includes all of the following: phonology, lexicon, syntax, semantics, and semiotics. In addition, recent findings suggest that sociolinguistics, psycholinguistics, and pragmatics, as well as both verbal and nonverbal communication, are also an integral part of L2 study in school settings. The above categories all assume a culturally authentic base. Given the wide range of perspectives about what second language teaching involves, it is assumed in this chapter that all of the aspects listed above are indeed part of the study of a second language. The prevailing canons, it can be argued, are reflected in the recent research published in the major journals of the profession. A recent L2 professional journal search for the years 1994 to 1997 revealed a range of research themes and methodologies in the major journals.[2] Table 20.3 describes the results of the journal search.

---

language (SL) is the term used herein to connote any additional language(s) taught, either in part or in full. in a formal school setting anywhere from preschool to graduate study.

[2] *The Modern Language Journal* regularly carries a section titled "In Other Professional Journals," which served as the main source of journals for the present search. The search was limited to 20 L2-related professional journals written in English that are widely disseminated nationally and internationally and that were deemed to be key journals with multiple years of publication. These journals regularly publish research on either SL acquisition or pedagogy, and they are believed to be read regularly by second language professionals, particularly those interested in research. The 1994–1997 issues of the following journals were searched: (a) *Association of Departments of Foreign Languages (ADFL) Bulletin,* (b) *Applied Language Learning (ALL),* (c) *Applied Linguistics (AL),* (d) *CALICO Journal,* (e) *English for Specific Purposes (ESP),* (f) *English Language Teaching Journal (ELT),* (g) *Foreign Language Annals,* (h) *French Review (FR),* (i) *German Quarterly (GQ),* (j) *Hispania (H),* (k) *International Association of Language Laboratory Directors Journal (IALL),* (l) *Language Learning (LL),* (m) *Language Testing (LT),* (n) *The Modern Language Journal (MLJ),* (o) *Second Language Research (SLR),* (p) *Slavic and East European Languages Journal (SEEJ),* (q) *Studies in Second Language Acquisition (SSLA),* (r) *System (S),* (s) *Teaching English to Speakers of Other Languages Journal (TESOL J),* (t) *Teaching English to Speakers of Other*

Given the wide diversity of topics currently researched and published in the main journals by L2 researchers, coupled with the need for greater collaboration to answer complex questions facing the profession in the next decade or so, it is important to identify the primary assumptions upon which this chapter is based.

Assumptions

The basic assumptions that have guided the conceptualization of this chapter are presented as background information for readers and to provide context for the chapter contents. The list is not meant to be exhaustive:

1. Second language study is a complicated process that involves the intentions of students (and their parents or guardians), teachers, and policymakers; it cannot be presented in a single, simplified matrix. Yet, its elements need to be continuously researched.
2. Meaning is context specific, constructed by participants, and therefore teachers and learners of any discipline (including the L2 discipline) must allow opportunities for the exploration of novel and creative insights that may be unique to the individuals within the speech community (e.g., the classroom). In other words, research must give voice to the various constituencies within the profession if it is to serve the needs of all L2 learners.
3. The L2 discipline may be unique in that learners both in classrooms and in naturalistic settings are often children, adolescents, or adults, who are highly proficient in their LI and have (deep) meanings, which they wish to communicate but are unable to communicate because of limited proficiency in listening, speaking, reading, and writing in their L2. Unlike many other disciplines, a high attrition rate occurs in L2 before learners are able to reach a satisfactory balance between their L2 proficiency and the expression of their own meanings.
4. Second language as a discipline is linked to linguistic science, and the constructs that define second language include areas such as contrastive analysis, discourse analysis, psycholinguistics, sociolinguistics, pragmatics, and semantics.
5. Clearly, L2 study occurs worldwide and typically involves unique local conditions in each area in which languages are learned and taught. Whether the context is China, where Mandarin plus Cantonese, Taiwanese, and other dialects may be learned by children and adults alike, or whether the setting is Canada, where French and English are considered native languages in different parts of the country, multilingualism is seen as a valuable asset. Readers will certainly recognize a major limitation of this chapter: a U.S. focus and perspective permeating the chapter. Given the U.S. history of monolingualism, compared with the sit-

uation in many countries of the world, where multilingual traditions exist (e.g., in Senegal, West Africa, where individuals may learn functional French, Oulof, and an additional local language or two), we could well see the value of taking another perspective. Conversely, the reality is that the United States is, in fact, composed of many vibrant language communities (e.g., native speakers of Spanish live throughout the nation and are also concentrated in particular regions and cities, while there also are many thriving ethnic language communities in major U.S. cities). The decision to focus the chapter on a U.S.-American perspective was a conscious one.

Descriptive Demographics: Figures and Tables

The enrollment figures of students at all ages studying an L2 in the United States reveal a complex profile. And yet the figures can serve as a context from which to investigate both the complexity and the vastness of L2 learning and teaching. In other words, the use of a worldwide context would have far too many complications, so it makes sense to focus on a single country for our analysis with the expectation that some possible applications may eventually be made to other contexts. Thus, enrollment data from the United States are presented in Tables 20.1 and 20.2 and in Figure 20.1. The data provide selected, descriptive statistics for the United States. Space constraints dictate that summary statistics be used here mainly as examples.

Figure 20.1 is based on data from the Modern Language Association (MLA) of America and describes enrollment trends for L2 study at the higher education level from 1960 to 1995 in

Table 20.1. Fall 1990 and 1995 Foreign Language Registrations in U.S. Institutions of Higher Education

Language	1990	1995	Percentage Change
Arabic	3,475	4,444	+27.9
Chinese	19,490	26,471	+35.8
French	272,472	205,351	−24.6
German	133,348	96,263	−27.8
Ancient Greek	16,401	16,272	−0.8
Hebrew[a]	12,995	13,127	+1.0
Italian	49,699	43,760	−11.9
Japanese	45,717	44,723	−2.2
Latin	28,178	25,897	−8.1
Portuguese	6,211	6,531	+5.2
Russian	44,626	24,729	−44.6
Spanish	533,944	606,286	+13.5
Other Languages	17,544	24,918	+42.0
Total	1,184,100	1,138,772	−3.8

[a]The 1995 total comprises 5,648 registrations in Biblical Hebrew and 7,479 in Modern Hebrew. The equivalent figures for fall 1990 are 5,724 and 7,271, respectively. The above data were taken from enrollment surveys by the Modern Language Association of America.

Languages Quarterly (TESOL Q). It is recognized, of course, that many other excellent publications exist and should be included in a complete analysis (e.g., journals written in languages other than English; special research publications, including festschrifts; documents disseminated locally; theses and dissertations; publications available only electronically; and materials found in databases such as the Educational Resources Information Center (ERIC). However, it is assumed that the professional journals listed above constitute a meaningful sample of journals that are regularly read by L2 professionals and were, therefore, appropriate for the current purpose of surveying L2 journals for research content.

Table 20.2. Foreign Language Enrollments in Public High Schools, 1890–1994

Year	HS Enr.	Modern FL		Spanish		French		German		Italian		Japanese		Russian		Latin		Total FL	
		Enr.	%	Enr.	%	Enr.	%	Enr.	%	Enr.	%	Enr.	%	Enr.	%	Enr.	%	Enr.	%
1890	202,963	33,089	16.3			11,722	5.8	21,311	10.5							70,429	34.7	103,518	51.0
1895	350,099	62,685	17.9			22,757	6.5	39,911	11.4							153,693	43.9	216,378	61.8
1900	519,251	114,765	22.1			40,503	7.8	74,252	14.3							262,752	50.6	377,517	72.7
1905	609,702	199,153	32.7			61,852	10.1	137,299	22.5							341,215	56.0	540,368	88.6
1910	915,061	313,890	34.3	6,406	0.7	90,591	9.9	216,869	23.7							448,383	49.0	762,273	83.3
1915	1,328,984	477,110	35.9	35,882	2.7	116,957	8.8	324,272	24.4							495,711	37.3	972,821	73.2
1922	2,230,000	611,025	27.4	252,000	11.3	345,650	15.5	13,385	0.6							613,250	27.5	1,224,275	54.9
1928	3,354,473	845,338	25.2	315,329	9.4	469,626	14.0	60,381	1.8							737,984	22.0	1,583,322	47.2
1934	5,620,626	1,096,022	19.5	348,497	6.2	612,648	10.9	134,897	2.4							899,300	16.0	1,995,322	35.5
1948	5,399,452	740,800	13.7	442,755	8.2	253,781	4.7	43,195	0.8							429,174	7.9	1,169,974	21.7
1958	7,897,232	1,295,944	16.4	691,024	8.8	479,769	6.1	93,054	1.2	22,133	0.3			4,044	0.1	617,500	7.8	1,913,444	24.2
1959	8,155,573	1,564,883	19.2	802,266	9.8	603,733	7.4	123,581	1.5	21,118	0.3			7,055	0.1	639,776	7.8	2,204,659	27.0
1960	8,649,495	1,867,358	21.6	933,409	10.8	744,404	8.6	150,764	1.7	20,026	0.2			9,722	0.1	654,670	7.6	2,522,028	29.2
1961	9,246,925	2,192,207	23.7	1,054,730	11.4	908,082	9.8	184,820	2.0	22,277	0.2			13,224	0.1	695,297	7.5	2,887,504	31.2
1962	9,891,185	2,391,206	24.2	1,137,757	11.5	996,771	10.1	211,676	2.1	21,654	0.2			15,832	0.2	702,135	7.1	3,093,341	31.3
1963	10,750,081	2,781,737	25.9	1,336,105	12.4	1,130,987	10.5	260,488	2.4	23,250	0.2			21,552	0.2	680,234	6.3	3,461,971	32.2
1964	11,075,343	2,898,665	26.2	1,362,831	12.3	1,194,991	10.8	285,613	2.6	24,735	0.2			20,485	0.2	590,047	5.3	3,488,712	31.5
1965	11,611,197	3,067,613	26.4	1,426,822	12.3	1,251,373	10.8	328,028	2.8	25,233	0.2			26,716	0.1	591,445	5.1	3,659,058	31.5
1968	12,721,352	3,518,413	27.7	1,698,034	13.3	1,328,100	10.4	423,196	3.3	26,920	0.2			24,318	0.2	371,977	2.9	3,890,390	30.6
1970	13,301,883	3,514,053	26.4	1,810,775	13.6	1,230,686	9.3	410,535	3.1	27,321	0.2			20,162	0.2	265,293	2.0	3,779,346	28.4
1974	13,648,906	3,127,336	22.9	1,678,057	12.3	977,858	7.2	392,983	2.9	40,233	0.3			15,148	0.1	167,165	1.2	3,294,501	24.1
1976	13,952,058	3,023,498	21.7	1,717,023	12.3	888,351	6.4	352,690	2.5	45,587	0.3			11,252	0.1	150,470	1.1	3,173,968	22.7
1978	13,941,369	3,048,331	21.9	1,631,375	11.7	855,998	6.1	330,637	2.4	45,518	0.3			8,789	0.1	151,782	1.1	3,200,113	23.0
1982	12,879,254	2,740,198	21.3	1,562,789	12.1	857,984	6.7	266,901	2.1	44,114	0.3			5,702	0.0	169,580	1.3	2,909,778	22.6
1985	12,466,506	3,852,030	30.9	2,334,404	18.7	1,133,725	9.1	312,162	2.5	47,289	0.4			6,405	0.1	176,841	1.4	4,028,871	32.3
1990	11,099,648	4,093,002	36.9	2,611,367	23.5	1,089,355	9.8	295,398	2.7	40,402	0.4	25,123	0.23	16,491	0.2	163,923	1.5	4,256,925	38.4
1994	11,847,469	4,813,031	40.6	3,219,775	27.2	1,105,857	9.3	325,964	2.8	43,838	0.4	42,290	0.36	16,426	0.1	188,833	1.6	5,001,864	42.2

Data in this table come from an enrollment study done by the American Council on the Technology of Foreign Languages (ACTFL).
HS Enr., total public high school enrollment; FL, foreign language; %, enrollment percentage of total U.S. public high school students reported in survey.

the United States for modern languages. Figure 20.1 shows that 1990 and 1995 were the highest student enrollment years, while 1960 and 1980 were the lowest. In the 4 highest years, more than a million U.S. students each year were enrolled in modern language study.

Table 20.1 shows foreign language registrations in colleges and universities in the United States for the most frequently selected languages for the years 1990 and 1995 and shows the percentage change between the two years in either a positive or a negative direction. Spanish, French, and German continued in the 2 comparison years to represent the largest number of registrations, but, while Spanish increased by 13.5%, both French and German showed a decrease in the 25% range for the 2 comparison years. Russian experienced a decline of 44.6%. Arabic and Chinese showed a gain of approximately 28% and 36%, respectively.

Table 20.2 shows selected foreign language enrollments in U.S. public schools for selected years from 1890 to 1994. Approximately 5 million high school students were studying foreign languages in public schools in 1994, with roughly 3.2 million of the students studying Spanish (approximately 27% of the total high school enrollment). Roughly 1.1 million (approximately 9%) of high school students were enrolled in French, which registered the second highest enrollment in 1994. The data for more recent years were not available, but Table 20.2 is reprinted by permission of the American Council on the Teaching of Foreign Languages (ACTFL).

The MLA of America publishes figures from its periodic survey of foreign language enrollment based on college-course registrations in U.S. institutions of higher education. The latest survey is the 18th in a series conducted since 1958; it describes enrollment data for languages taught in U.S. colleges and universities, noting patterns and trends. Table 20.1 was published in a report by the MLA of America and describes enrollment trends for L2 study in U.S. higher education from 1960 to 1995. Both Figure 20.1 and Table 20.1 are used with permission of the MLA of America.

Table 20.1 is based on responses from 2,399 (86.5%) institutions (out of 2,772 mailed surveys to separate institutions), which reported fall 1995 registrations in at least one language other than English. Of these responses, 897 (37%) came from 2-year colleges, while 1,502 came from 4-year institutions. Brod and Huber (1997) reported that, although the total number of registrations recorded for fall 1995 was almost 4% lower than the 1990 total, the figure exceeded the 1986 total (not reported in Table 20.1) by 13.5% and the 1980 total (not reported in Table 20.1) by 23%. In other words, there have been fluctuations in the enrollment data, with both negative and positive percentages of change. Table 20.1 also shows that the descending rank order of languages for the 1995 data are Spanish, French, German, Japanese, Italian, Chinese, Latin, Russian, Ancient Greek, Hebrew (biblical and modern), Portuguese, and Arabic. Table 20.1 suggests that registrations in different languages moved in either a positive or a negative direction between 1990

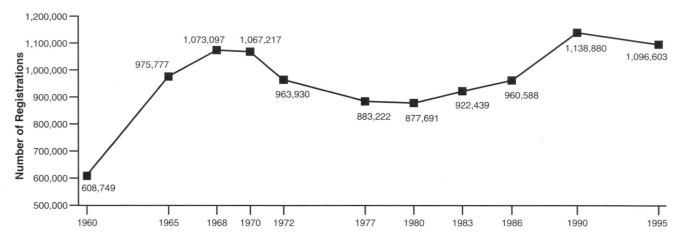

Note: The above numbers include all registrations except those in Latin and ancient Greek.

Figure 20.1. Modern foreign language registrations by year.

and 1995. Registrations in Greek, Hebrew, and Latin remained essentially unchanged. Registrations in both Spanish and Portuguese showed slight increases, with Arabic, Chinese, and Hebrew also showing higher registrations for 1995 than in 1990. The "other" category includes four languages that account for the increased registrations; they are American Sign Language, Korean, Vietnamese, and Hawaiian.

The profile provided above includes students of various ages who study different foreign and second languages at varying instructional levels in a variety of school settings. These variables make it impossible to arrive at a simple answer to the guiding question of this article: What factors most affect the outcomes of foreign and second language study? One indication of what language educators think is important concerns the topics they choose to research. Factors such as themes and independent variables of published articles in key language journals (e.g., age, teaching method, gender issues, language proficiency) can give an indication of what is considered important in the profession. While a conscious effort was made to include international publications in the search, it is recognized that these journals may not include important publications produced in some areas of the world. Finally, it is assumed that the years selected for this analysis, 1994 to 1997, are representative of the types of articles frequently published in the particular journals. To reiterate, this analysis shows major themes published by researchers within the profession during the middle years of the 1990s.

Table 20.3 is based on a recent search of key journals in which L2 researchers publish. It shows that L2 professionals frequently study linguistic topics such as structural linguistics, morpheme studies, syntax, sociolinguistics, and so forth. Chomsky (1992) continues to have an effect in the L2 field. His work emphasized formalist syntactic frameworks such as government-binding (GB) and theory-based linguistic analyses. Table 20.4 shows the number of articles in key journals that deal with conventional language skills (i.e., listening, speaking, reading, writing, or a combination of skills) from 1994 to 1997. Table 20.5 identifies the second languages reported as the focus of L2 research in the same key journals for the same time period. That table shows that English and Spanish, respectively,

were the most researched second languages for the sample years.

Second Language Acquisition (SLA) Theory and Research

It is fitting to begin this section with Hymes's work (1974, 1982) for two reasons: His theories have provided the foundation for much of the focus on communicative competence in the field of L2 during the last few decades, and his perspectives on classroom discourse will likely continue to permeate the L2 field during the next few decades. Members of the L2 profession are familiar with Hymes's (1972) contribution to the widely popular communicative methodology of the 1980s and 1990s but perhaps less so with respect to his views about the construct of context. If a bridge is to be built between pure linguistic research and classroom applications (as this author believes it should be built), it will be important to pay special attention to Hymes's views about the importance of context. He wrote that incorporating "the analysis of context into linguistics would transform linguistics, making it a realization of the program of the 'ethnography of speaking,' or other sociolinguistic perspectives" (1982, p. 14).

Research in L2 currently recognizes the importance of context as the overarching concept under which ethnography of speaking in both classroom and natural settings is viewed. Kramsch (1995) wrote convincingly about the notion of L2 context, often with emphasis on classroom contexts and the need to redefine the boundaries of language study. Her work can be viewed as a part of the larger construct of pragmatics. Spolsky (1990) proposed a comprehensive set of conditions for developing a theory of SLA. These researchers argued that context is an important variable in L2 acquisition, a variable that needs further illumination based on empirical research. The work of Saville-Troike (1989) is also important in this area. She combined an anthropological and a sociolinguistic perspective in addressing the study of communicative behavior in various cultural contexts.

A well-known (and often controversial) SLA researcher,

Table 20.3. Number of Journal Articles Found Based on Linguistic Categories

Journal	General Second Language Acquisition	Discourse	Code-switching	Linguistics-Structural Analysis	Psycholinguistics	Sociolinguistics	Pragmatics	Semantics
Assoc of Depts of Foreign Langs Bulletin	—	1	1	—	—	—	1	1
Applied Lang Learning	—	2	—	1	—	—	—	—
Applied Linguistics (AL)	12	3	—	3	—	2	2	1
CALICO Journal	2	—	—	—	—	—	—	—
English for Spec Purposes (ESP)	1	—	—	—	—	—	—	—
English Lang Teaching Journal (ELT)	1	3	3	—	—	—	—	—
French Review	—	—	—	1	—	—	—	—
German Quarterly	1	—	—	—	—	—	—	—
Hispania	1	—	—	1	—	—	1	1
Int Assoc of Learning Labs J (IALL)	—	1	1	4	—	2	—	—
Language Learning (LL)	2	—	—	—	—	—	—	—
Language Testing (LT)	14	—	2	7	1	2	—	—
The Modern Language Journal (MLJ)	3	1	—	2	—	—	1	—
Second Language Research (SLR)	1	—	—	—	—	—	—	—
Studies in Second Language Acquisition (SSLA)	13	1	—	1	—	—	—	—
System	19	5	—	1	4	—	—	—
TESOL Journal	1	—	—	—	—	—	—	—
TESOL Quarterly	1	1	—	—	—	—	—	1
Total	72	18	7	21	5	6	5	4

Note: Dash (—) indicates no items were found in journal search for the years searched.

Table 20.4. Number Language Skills-Related Articles in Foreign Language Journals

Journal	Listening	Speaking	Reading	Writing	Combination of Skills
Assoc of Depts of Foreign Langs Bulletin	—	—	—	—	—
Applied Lang Learning	—	2	2	1	—
Applied Linguistics (AL)	1	3	3	6	—
CALICO Journal	1	—	1	1	2
English for Spec Purposes (ESP)	—	—	—	—	—
English Lang Teaching Journal (ELT)	2	2	7	12	—
French Review	—	9	4	2	1
German Quarterly	—	—	2	1	1
Hispania	—	1	—	—	—
Int Assoc of Learning Labs J (IALL)	1	7	3	6	2
Language Learning (LL)	—	—	—	—	—
Language Testing (LT)	—	1	5	2	—
The Modern Language Journal (MLJ)	4	5	6	2	1
Studies in Second Language Acquisition (SSLA)	—	—	1	—	—
System	2	5	1	2	—
TESOL Journal	1	—	—	—	—
TESOL Quarterly	—	—	4	10	—
Total	12	35	39	45	7

Note: Dash (—) indicates no items were found in journal search for the years searched.

Krashen (Krashen,1981, 1982, 1987; Krashen & Terrell, 1983), despite the controversy surrounding his work, has had a major effect on the L2 profession since his introduction of a set of hypotheses dealing with constructs such as comprehensible input, i+1 affective filter, and monitor model. Krashen also worked with Terrell (1983) on the topic of grammar within the L2 context. Krashen indeed has been a key player in SLA research, and his work is frequently cited and analyzed within the L2 profession. He is considered to be a naturalistic SLA advocate.

Table 20.5. Number of Journal Articles Dealing with a Specific Language

Journal	Arabic	Chinese	English (L2)	French	German	Greek	Italian	Japanese	Russian	Spanish	Other
Applied Lang Learning (ALL)	1	—	—	—	—	—	—	—	—	—	5
Applied Linguistics (AL)	1	—	7	2	1	—	—	—	—	—	5
CALICO	—	—	1	1	2	—	—	—	—	—	—
English for Spec Purposes	—	—	—	—	—	—	—	—	—	—	—
English Lang Teaching Journal (ELT)	—	—	11	1	—	—	—	—	—	—	—
French Review	—	—	—	8	—	—	—	—	—	—	—
Hispania	—	—	—	—	—	—	—	—	—	33	—
Int Assoc of Learning Labs J (IALL)	—	—	20	—	—	—	—	—	—	—	—
Language Learning (LL)	—	—	—	—	—	—	—	—	—	—	—
Language Testing (LT)	2	7	1	—	1	1	2	—	2	3	—
The Modern Language Journal (MLJ)	—	1	7	—	—	—	—	—	—	3	1
Studies in Second Language Acquisition (SSLA)	—	—	4	2	4	—	—	2	—	—	—
System	—	2	3	—	—	—	2	—	—	—	1
TESOL Journal	—	—	2	—	—	—	—	—	—	—	—
TESOL Quarterly	—	—	12	—	—	—	—	—	—	—	—
Total	4	10	68	14	8	1	4	2	2	39	7

Note: Dash (—) indicates no items were found in journal search for the years searched.

The seminal work of Rod Ellis (1987, 1994, 1995) and an effect during the past decade, particularly in the area of connecting SLA research to pedagogy. Ellis advocated the empowerment of both theoretical SLA researchers and classroom teacher-researchers who need to collaboratively study the SLA process, each contributing to the development of a broad-based profile of what this complex process entails for L2 acquirers. Accepting the importance of context in SLA, Ellis (1987, p. 3) proposed two different approaches to SLA. The first approach dealt with the question: How can the study of the context of SLA throw light on the acquisition of the linguistic code? And the process of developing linguistic competence on the part of L2 learners is the focus. The second approach dealt with the question: What can the social context reveal about how L2 learners develop facility in communicating their ideas in the L2? The focus in the second approach was not solely on the language but also on the competence that the learner develops in using the L2 for unique social purposes. Ellis is considered to be a main proponent of instructed SLA.

Gardner (1985) also emphasized the importance of context. His focus was the involvement of the community, including parents, in the development of attitudes of learners on processes such as SLA. He stated, "Beliefs in the community concerning the importance and meaningfulness of teaming the language, the nature of the skill development expected, and the particular role of various individual differences in the language learning process will affect second language acquisition" (p. 146). In essence, the value placed on language acquisition by the community can affect the SLA process of individual language learners, according to Gardner. His work emphasized the form of SLA, and he is considered to be a causal-process advocate.

Lantolf (1996) wrote an overview of SLA theory building in a review article for *Language Learning* in which he called for an acceptance of varying notions of SLA theory. He called his analysis a postmodernist (Lather, 1992) critical analysis of SLA theory-building literature. Lantolf primarily addressed the work of Beretta (1993), Beretta and Crookes (1993), Eubank and Gregg (1995), Gregg (1993), Long (1990, 1991, 1993), and

Long and Sato (1984). Lantolf stated that he wished "to address the literature whose concern is to imbue the field with a *proper* sense of theory, and, consequently, science" (p. 714), taking the position (p. 721) that language and linguistically construed concepts and discourse impose structure on the mind. This contrasted, Lantolf concluded, with Chomsky's and Crookes's positions that the mind imposes structure on thought via language. Lantolf argued for the possibility that a single theoretical perspective for all SLA is neither valid nor recommended, despite the merits of individual theories such as those of Chomsky, Crookes, Gregg, Eubank, Long, and others. These linguists have, in turn (and rightly so, in my opinion), rejected the notion that they collectively represent a single theoretical perspective for SLA. Schumann (1995) wrote a critique of the work of Eubank and Gregg. Long (1990, 1997) wrote his own position on the issue of theory building in SLA. Odlin (1994, 1997) researched language transfer and advocated the need for this concept to be included in SLA models. Thus, research and investigations into SLA must continue to define and refine issues related to scope, source, and type of SLA. One interesting study is described below.

Donato, Antonek, and Tucker (1996) described an interesting longitudinal study in which they reported the results of an evaluation of an innovative Japanese-as-a-foreign-language elementary school (FLES) program for Grades Kindergarten through 5. With an enrollment of 195 participants, the program permitted these researchers to study both the ambiance within which the program existed (including descriptions of parents, teachers, and staff members) and the surrounding community in which the program was set. They also focused on the individual children, who were L2 learners of Japanese, examining language development in the context of an elementary school. Regarding stakeholder satisfaction, they reported that adults felt that the children were making reasonable gains and that these adults would like to see Japanese language study continue. In addition, learners reported using Japanese outside of the L2 classroom as well as their willingness to demonstrate their linguistic competence in Japanese. Their attitudes and perceptions were reported to be positive. Data on language achievement suggested a "steady growth in the children's ability to express themselves verbally, acquire vocabulary, and expand their control of specific syntactic features of Japanese" (p. 524). The research also showed that "younger is better from the perspective of overall receptivity and positive affective reactions to language learning" (p. 524). This research project is an excellent model of SLA within a conventional elementary school setting.

To conclude this SLA section of the chapter, it is important to note that the debate continues with respect to L2 instruction and SLA. The work of Firth and Wagner (1997) showed promise of a needed reconceptualization of SLA research that would enlarge the ontological and empirical parameters of the field. By way of summary, however, I have opted to highlight Ellis's work (1987, 1990, 1994, 1995). With respect to its scope, Ellis's research came primarily from the perspective of instructed SLA as opposed to naturalistic SLA, which was the perspective of Schumann (1995), or a metalinguistic perspective, as described by Bialystok (1990). Ellis's work in SLA suggested the following applications categorized broadly as:

Syllabus Design

A variability model of SLA supports both a product (e.g., a structural or a notional-functional) syllabus and a process (e.g., a procedural or task-based syllabus). Prabhu (1987) argued that forms of language can best be learned when learners focus on meaning. However, since both types of syllabi are needed, Ellis recommended a parallel syllabus design in which both forms (product) and meaning (process) can be sequenced and integrated in course designs. Language forms should be presented in different linguistic contexts and recycled later for incremental learning. Decisions about course design must, of course, be informed by course purposes, learner needs, and available resources for implementation.

Language Teaching Materials

Language variability research has provided some limited guidance in the area of L2 instructional materials. Purpose is a key in terms of the development and selection of teaching materials in any syllabus. In a parallel syllabus model, learners need to have instruction on the forms of the language as well as opportunities to practice the forms in context, which Ellis calls "focused materials." In addition, the process aspect of the syllabus needs to be addressed via teaching materials related to "unfocused activities" (e.g., negotiated meanings between different learners in group work, solving problems, emphasis on message rather than form). Language teaching materials should be seen as resources on a continuum from "focused" to "unfocused" materials, rather than as parts of a dichotomy.

Classroom Practices

Language variability from an SLA perspective assumes a multifaceted language classroom interaction. Depending on the course syllabus and teaching materials, roles of teachers and students are likely to change periodically, ranging from planned

typical classroom discourse of the initiate-response-feedback (IRF) type researched by Wells (1993) to the unplanned communicative types (Swain, 1984, 1985). A variability model of SLA also assumes that teachers should expect learner output to range from correct to incorrect, authentic to nonauthentic, and from controlled usage to "trying out" variations of language. The notion here is practical inquiry, a process that helps define conceptions of the nature of good and effective teaching. Finally, teachers need to design both instruction and complementary assessments with a balance of expectations that learner performance may vary, depending on the different tasks in the L2 classroom.

Important Research Areas for the Next Decade

L2 researchers have set agendas, formed groups for collaborative research, and continue to conduct research on all aspects of L2 learning. The work of particular SLA researchers has been referenced above as examples of contemporary L2 research as well as suggestions for the types of research priorities that will be needed in the future. From the perspective of an L2 professional with many years of experience in various educational settings, I wanted to take this opportunity to recommend several key areas of needed research, particularly for the benefit of readers who may be exploring research agendas of their own or who wish to establish cooperative projects with other researchers inside and outside of the L2 field. Several areas of needed formal research and practical inquiry are listed below.

Role of Grammar in L2 Teaching: Two Opposing Perspectives (to Correct or Not to Correct L2 Learner Errors)

Researchers such as Eubank and Beck (1993), Garrett (1986), Rounds and Schachter (in Schachter & Gass, 1996), Rutherford (1987), Truscott (1996), and VanPatten (1996), as well as many L2 classroom practitioners, continue to view grammar as an important topic. Although definitions differ on what grammar is, many consider it to be one of the areas of competency that is linked to successful use of the L2 by learners. However, despite available research over the years on the topic of grammar instructions, fundamental questions remain about the relationship of formal grammar study to the development of L2 communicative ability. Research within certain skill areas (e.g., error correction in compositions) has frequently been conducted (Ferris, 1995). Questions remain about whether or not to "correct" learners' grammar and, if so, at what point and how to do so. In addition, questions remain about how to effectively instruct students to acquire the structures (forms) needed to express their own personal ideas authentically and correctly in the L2. Clearly, grammar is a topic deserving further study in the years ahead. Grammar instruction is certainly a topic that persists and has occupied the attention of L2 professionals in the past. In the case of some native speakers of languages in language programs (e.g., native speakers of Spanish in the United States), the need for research-based answers is urgent, because employment may be linked to the ability to read and write a version of Spanish that is not the one spoken at home or in the community among peers. Computers may offer an untapped possibility for grammar instruction linked to L2 student learning style. Further research will illuminate this area.

Task-Based L2 Learning: Some Promising Research Perspectives

Chaudron (1988); Crookes and Gass (1993a, 1993b); De Bot (1996); Doughty and Williams (1998); Ellis (1987, 1990); Gass and Varonis (1985); Long (1991, 1997); Nunan (1989); Pica (1994); Pica, Kanagy, and Falodun (1993); Schachter and Gass (1996); Schmidt (1993); and others have conducted needed research in the area of task-based L2 instruction. This promising area of research has the potential to be a central unifying theme for much L2 instruction and should continue to receive the attention it is getting. From an interactionist perspective, the research on tasks is likely to also serve as a promising way to deal with language maintenance of bilinguals. (See Lemke, 1985; Odlin, 1997; Pica and Doughty, 1985; Sheen, 1994; Yates and Ortiz, 1983; and Wong-Fillmore & Valadez, 1986.)

Student Factors in L2 Learning: Shifting Toward Learners

Research on student factors is desperately needed in L2, notwithstanding the excellent past research of Gardner (1985) and of those who followed his lead. Motivation, attitudes, and learning styles are at the heart of a renewed effort to respond to the individual needs of L2 learners. Nyikos and Oxford's (1997) publication was an excellent effort to include a cross-cultural perspective in research on strategies. The importance of affective factors is an important area of needed future research in the L2 field.

Technology and Language Learning: Some Preliminary Findings

L2 research in the area of technology is in its infancy. Several promising research areas are noteworthy, however, as the L2 profession identifies various roles for technology (e.g., technology as a "tool," a "tutor," a "teacher"). The work of Kern (1995), Kroonenberg (1994/ 1995), and Warschauer (1995, 1997) on electronic classrooms and use of the Internet as a resource will continue to refine the principled use of technology in general and computers in particular in L2 instruction.

Facing the New Millennium in L2 Teaching and Research: A Modest Proposal

An analysis of the current research efforts of many individuals and groups of researchers suggests that the need exists in the field of L2 for a culling of myriad independent projects and the setting of a broad-based research agenda for the profession during the next few decades. This idea was also recommended, in principle, by Clark and Davidson (1993). They called, with appropriate cautions, for a Research Consolidation Project (RCP) that would aim toward establishing solid data-based responses to empirical questions such as those posed at the outset of this chapter (e.g., Which students best learn what aspects of language in what instructional settings via what media?). The col-

laborative, broad-based empirical research paradigm advocated by Clark and Davidson would provide a model to conduct empirical research on L2 learning in the United States and beyond. I repeat their proposal here because it makes intuitive sense and would move L2 research to a meta-analysis level with an international focus, rather than a localized one. In essence, the proposal contains three parts:

1. A collaborative approach to L2 research has the potential to provide quality, robust, large-scale, longitudinal national research as a complement to independent research efforts currently under way.
2. A solid theoretical basis for launching the collaborative research initiative proposed by Clark and Davidson is needed. Spolsky's "conditions of learning" model is recommended as such a base since it is comprehensive. However, as was indicated in the SLA theory building studies described earlier in this chapter, no single formulation for L2 language learning presently accommodates all aspects of this complex process.
3. Successful networking for collaborative research purposes is possible in the late 1990s because of major advances in technology and information-processing theory development; the potential for the storage, retrieval, and dissemination of data; and the need for empirical research answers to important L2 learning questions. Current computer-based information storing and retrieval as well as widespread access via the Internet, for example, provide a strong rationale for embarking on this venture at this time.

The future of L2 instruction and research is likely to be strongly linked to the national standards movement (in the United States), enhanced research involving classroom teachers as researchers (Nunan, 1989, 1990), and shifts toward a more constructivist orientation in L2 instruction, as can be seen in the work of Chamot and O'Malley (1987); De Bot (1996); Firth and Wagner (1997); Freire (1970); Garcia (1990); Hall (1997); Lantolf and Appel (1994); Larsen-Freeman and Long (1988); Leontiev (1981); Long and Sato (1984); Markee (1997); Moll (1990); Rampton (1997); and Van Els, De Bot, and Weltens (1991).

Conclusion

This chapter on L2 research has summarized some of the major research conducted during the past few decades, a preponderance of which could be identified with process-product (i.e., observable teacher behaviors) that are statistically associated with student achievement. It is important to note that the dominant paradigm for L2 research is shifting, however, and that more ethnographic and qualitative research is being conducted in the L2 field during the latter part of the 1990s.

Omaggio-Hadley (1993) wisely identified an important need in the L2 profession back in 1993, which was still true in 1998, when she cautioned that a mere proliferation of studies may lead to confusion if there is no integration of the results and if there is a lack of effective communication among researchers in L2 (i.e., foreign language and English as second language studies) without the systematic inclusion of practitioners in such research. The central aims of this chapter have been the identification of selected examples of important L2 research in the 1990s, the synthesis of trends and priorities, and the forecasting of a needed collaborative approach to L2 research. While no convergence of agreement on the various types of research in L2 is found at this time, it is clear that the profession as a whole needs greater levels of involvement of L2 classroom practitioners in systematic, formative ways to help shape, implement, and draw appropriate inferences from both formal research and practical classroom perspectives.

REFERENCES

Beretta, A. (1993). As God said, and I think, rightly: Perspectives on construction in SLA: An introduction. *Applied Linguistics 14*(22), 1.

Beretta, A., & Crookes, G. (1993). Cognitive and social determinants of discovery in SLA. *Applied Linguistics, 14,* 250–275.

Beretta, A., Crookes, G., Gregg, K. R., & Long, M. H. (1993). A comment on some contributors to volume 14, issue 3. *Applied Linguistics, 15 ,* 16–25.

Bialystok, E. (1990). The competence of processing: Classifying theories of second language acquisition. *TESOL Quarterly, 24,* 635–648.

Brod, R., & Huber, B. J. (1996). The MLA survey of foreign language entrance and degree requirements 1994–95. *ADFL Bulletin, 28,* 35–43.

Brod, R., & Huber, B. J. (1997). Foreign language enrollments in U.S. institutions of higher education, fall 1995. *ADFL Bulletin 28,* 55–61.

Chamot, A. U., & O'Malley, J. M. (1987). The cognitive academic language learning approach: A bridge to the mainstream. *TESOL Quarterly, 21,* 227–249.

Chaudron, C (1988). *Second language classrooms: Research on teaching and learning.* Cambridge, UK: Cambridge University Press.

Chomsky, N. (1992). *A minimalist program for linguistic theory.* Cambridge, MA: Massachusetts Institute of Technology, Department of Linguistics and Philosophy.

Clark, J. L. D., & Davidson, F. (1993). Language-learning research: Cottage industry or consolidated enterprise? In A. Omaggio-Hadley (Ed.), *Research in language learning: principles, processes, and prospects.* Lincolnwood, IL: National Textbook Company.

Crookes, G. (1989). Planning and interlanguage variation. *Studies in Second Language Acquisition, 11,* 367–387.

Crookes, G., & Gass, S. M. (Ed.). (1993a). *Tasks and language learning: Integration theory and practice.* Philadelphia: Multilingual Matters, Ltd.

Crookes, G., & Gass, S. M. (Eds.). (1993b). *Tasks in pedagogical context: Integrating theory and practice.* Philadelphia: Multilingual Matters, Ltd.

De Bot, K. (1996). Review article: Psycholinguistics of the output hypothesis. *Language Learning, 46,* 529–555.

De Bot, K., Ginsberg, R. B., & Kramsch, C. (Eds.). (1991). *Foreign language research in cross-cultural perspective.* Amsterdam/Philadelphia: John Benjamins Publishing Company.

Donato, R., Antonek, J. L., & Tucker, G. R. (1996). Monitoring and assessing a Japanese FLES program: Ambiance and achievement. *Language Learning, 46,* 497–528.

Doughty, C. (1991). Second Language Instruction does make a difference: Evidence from an empirical study of SL relativization. *Studies in Second Language Acquisition 13,* 431–469.

Doughty, C., & Williams, J. (Eds.). (1998). *Focus on form in classroom second language acquisition.* Cambridge, UK: Cambridge University Press.

Ellis, R. (Ed.). (1987). *Second language acquisition in context.* Englewood Cliffs, NJ: Prentice-Hall International.

Ellis, R. (1990). *Instructed second language acquisition.* Oxford, UK: Blackwell.

Ellis, R. (1994). *The study of second language acquisition.* Oxford, UK: Oxford University Press.

Ellis, R. (1995). Appraising second language acquisition theory in relation to language pedagogy. In G. Cook & B. Seidlhofer (Eds.), *Principles and practice in applied linguistics: Studies in honor of H. G. Widdowson* (pp. 73–90). Oxford, UK: Oxford University Press.

Eubank, L., & Beck, M. (1993). Generative research in second-language learning. In A. Omaggio-Hadley (Ed.), *Research in language learning: Principles, processes, and prospects.* Lincolnwood, IL: National Textbook Company.

Eubank, L., & Gregg, K. R. (1995). Et in amygdala egoî UG, (S)LA, and neurobiology. *Studies in Second Language Acquisition, 17,* 35–57.

Ferguson, C. A., & Huebner, T. (1991). Foreign language instruction and second language acquisition research in the United States. In K. De Bot, R. B. Ginsberg, & C. Kramsch. (Eds.), *Foreign language research in cross-cultural perspective* (pp. 3–19). Philadelphia: John Benjamins Publishing Company.

Ferris, D. (1995). Student reactions to teacher response in multiple draft composition classrooms. *TESOL Quarterly, 29*(1), 33–54.

Firth, A., & Wagner, J. (1997). On discourse, communication, and (some) fundamental concepts in SLA research. *The Modern Language Journal, 81,* 285–300.

Fishman, J. A., & Lovas, J. (1970). Bilingual education in a sociolinguistic perspective. *TESOL Quarterly, 4*(3), 215–222.

Freire, P. (1970). *Pedagogy of the oppressed.* New York: The Seabury Press.

Garcia, E. E. (1990). Educating teachers for language minority students. In W. R. Houston (Ed.), *Handbook of research on teacher education.* New York: Macmillan.

Gardner, R. C. (1985). *Social psychology and second language learning: The role of attitudes and motivation.* Baltimore: Edward Arnold.

Garrett, N. (1986). The problem with grammar: What kind can the language learner use? *The Modern Language Journal, 70,* 133–148.

Gass, S. M., & Varonis, E. M. (1985). Task variation and nonnative/native negotiation of meaning. In S. M. Gass & C. G. Madden (Eds,), *Input in second language acquisition.* New York: Newbury House.

Genesee, F., Tucker, G. R., & Lambert, W. E. (1978). The development of ethnic identity and ethnic role taking skills in children from different school settings. *International Journal of Psychology. 13,* 39–57.

Graves, M. F., & Graves, B. B. (1994). *Scaffolding reading experiences to promote success.* Norwood, MA: Christopher Gordon Publishers.

Gregg, K. R. (1993). Taking explanation seriously: Or, let a couple of flowers bloom. *Applied Linguistics 14,* 276–294.

Greene, M. (1986). Philosophy and teaching. In M. C. Wittrock (Ed.), *Handbook of research on teaching,* (3rd ed., pp. 279–501). New York: Macmillan.

Hall, J. K. (1997). A consideration of SLA theory as a theory of practice: A response to Firth and Wagner. *The Modern Language Journal, 81,* 301–306.

Halliday, M. A. K. (1993). Toward a language-based theory of learning. *Linguistic and Education, 5,* 93–116.

Halliday, M. A. K., & Hasan, R. (1985). *Language. context, and text: Aspects of language in a social-semiotic perspective.* Geelong, Victoria, Australia: Deakin University Press.

Hancock, C. R.(Ed.). (1994). *Teaching, testing, and assessment: Making the connection.* Reports of the Northeast Conference on Language Teaching. Lincolnwood, IL: National Textbook Company.

Hasan, R. (1985). The structure of a text. In M. A. K. Halliday & R. Hasan (Eds.), *Language, context, and text: Aspects of language in a social-semiotic perspective* (pp. 52–69). Geelong, Victoria, Australia: Deakin University Press.

Hymes, D. H. (1972). On communicative competence. In J. B. Pride (Ed.), *Sociolinguistics* (pp. 263–293). London: Cambridge University Press.

Hymes, D. H. (1974). *Foundations of sociolinguistics: An ethnographic approach.* Philadelphia, University of Pennsylvania Press.

Hymes, D. H. (1982, April). *Ethnolinguistic study of classroom discourse* (final report, ED 217 710). London: National Institute of Education.

Johnson, D. M. (1992). *Approaches to research in second language learning.* White Plains, NY: Longman Publishing Group.

Johnson, D. M. (1993). Classroom-oriented research in second-language learning. In A. Omaggio-Hadley (Ed.). (1993). *Research in language: Learning: principles, processes, and prospects* (pp. 1–23). Lincolnwood, IL: National Textbook Company.

Kagan, D. (1993). *Laura and Jim and what they taught me about the gap between educational theory and practice.* New York: State University of New York Press.

Kelm, O. (1992). The use of synchronous computer networks in second language instruction: A preliminary report. *Foreign Language Annals, 25,* 441–454.

Kern, R. (1995). Restructuring classroom interaction with networked computers: Effects on quantity and quality of language production. *The Modern Language Journal, 79,* 457–476.

Kramsch, C. (Ed.). (1995). *Redefining the boundaries of language study.* Boston: Heinle.

Krashen, S. D. (1981). *Second language acquisition and second language learning.* Oxford, UK: Pergamon.

Krashen, S. D. (1982). *Principles and practice in second language acquisition.* Englewood Cliffs, NJ: Prentice-Hall.

Krashen, S. D. (1987). Applications of psycholinguistic research to the classroom. In M. H. Long & J. Richards (Eds.), *Methodology in TESOL: A book of readings* (pp. 33–44). New York: Newbury House.

Krashen, S. D., & Terrell, T. D. (1983). *The natural approach.* Englewood Cliffs, NJ: Alemany Press.

Kroonenberg, N. (1994/1995). Developing communicative and thinking skills via electronic mail. *TESOL Journal,* 24–27.

Lafayette, R. C. (Ed.) (1996). *National standards: A catalyst for reform.* Lincolnwood, IL: National Textbook Company.

Lambert, W. E., & Tucker, G. R. (1972). *Bilingual education of children: The St. Lambert experiment.* Rowley, MA: Newbury House.

Lantolf, J. P. (1996). Review article, SLA theory building: Letting all the flowers bloom. *Language Learning, 46,* 713–749.

Lantolf, J. P., & Appel, G. (1994). *Vygotskayan approaches to second language research.* Norwood, NJ: Ablex.

Larsen-Freeman, D., & Long, M. H. (1988). *Research priorities in foreign language learning and teaching.* Paper presented at the National Foreign Language Center, The Johns Hopkins School for Advanced International Studies, Washington, DC.

Lather, P. (1992). Postmodernism and the human sciences. In S. Kvale (Ed.), *Psychology and postmodernism* (pp. 1–25). London: Sage.

Lemke, J. L. (1985). *Using language in the classroom.* Geelong, Victoria, Australia: Deakin University Press.

Leontiev, A. N. (1981). The problem of activity in psychology. In J. V. Wertsch (Ed.), *The concept of activity in Soviet psychology* (pp. 37–71). Armonk, NY: Sharpe.

Long, M. H. (1990). The least a second language acquisition theory needs to explain. *TESOL Quarterly, 24,* 649–666.

Long, M. H. (1991). Focus on form: A design feature in language teaching methodology. In K. De Bot, R. Ginsburg, & C. Kramsch (Eds.), *Foreign language research in cross-cultural perspective* (pp. 39–42). Amsterdam/Philadelphia: John Benjamins Publishing Company.

Long, M. H. (1993). Assessment strategies for second language acquisition theories. *Applied Linguistics, 14,* 225–249.

Long, M. H. (1997). Authenticity and learning potential in L2 classroom discourse. In G. M. Jacobs (Ed.), *Language classrooms of tomorrow: Issues and responses* (pp. 148–169). Singapore: SESMEO Regional Language Center.

Long, M. H., & Sato, C. J. (1984). Methodological issues in interlanguage studies: An interactionist perspective. In A. Davies, C. Criper, & A. Howatt (Eds.), *Interlanguage* (pp. 253–279). Edinburgh, Scotland: Edinburgh University Press.

Lynch, B. (1996). *Language program evaluation: Theory and practice.* Cambridge, UK: Cambridge University Press.

Markee, N. (1997). Second language acquisition research: A resource for changing teachers' professional cultures? *The Modern Language Journal. 81,* 80–93.

Moll, L. C. (Ed.). (1990). *Vygotsky and education: Instructional implications and applications of sociohistorical psychology.* Cambridge, UK: Cambridge University Press.

Nunan, D. (1989). *Understanding language* New York: Prentice Hall Publishers.

Nunan, D. (1990). Action research in the language classroom. In J. C. Richards, & D. Nunan (Eds.), *Second language teacher education.* Cambridge, UK: Cambridge University Press.

Nyikos, M., & Oxford, R. (Eds.). (1997). Interaction, collaboration, and cooperation: Learning languages and preparing language teachers. *The Modern Language Journal, Special Issue.*

Odlin, T. (Ed.). (1994). *Perspectives on pedagogical grammar.* Cambridge, UK: Cambridge University Press.

Odlin, T. (1997). *Language transfer.* Lecture presented in a doctoral seminar at The Ohio State University, November 17, 1997.

Omaggio-Hadley, A. (Ed.). (1993). *Research in language learning: Principles, processes, and prospects.* Lincolnwood, IL: National Textbook Company.

Oxford, R. (Ed.). (1996). *Language learning strategies around the world: Cross-cultural perspectives.* Honolulu, HI: University of Hawaii Press.

Oxford, R. (1997). Cooperative learning, collaborative learning, and interaction: Three communicative strands in the language classroom. *The Modern Language Journal, 81.* 443–456.

Pica, T. (1994). Research on negotiation: What does it reveal about second language learning conditions, processes, and outcomes? *Language Learning, 44,* 493–527.

Pica, T., & Doughty, C. (1985). Input and interaction in the communicative language classroom: A comparison of teacher-fronted and group activities. In S. M. Gass & C. G. Madden (Eds.), *Input and second language acquisition* (pp. 115–132). New York: Newbury House.

Pica, T., Holliday, L., Lewis, N., & Morgenthaler, L. (1989). Comprehensible output as an outcome of linguistic demands on the learner. *Studies in Second Language Acquisition, 11,* 63–90.

Pica, T., Kanagy, R., & Falodun, J. (1993). Choosing and using communication tasks for second language instruction and research. In G. Crookes & S. M. Gass (Eds.), *Tasks and language learning: Integrating theory and practice* (pp. 9 –34). Clevedon, UK: Multilingual Matters, Ltd.

Prabhu, N. S. (1987). *Second language pedagogy.* Oxford, UK: Oxford University Press.

Rampton, B. (1997). A sociolinguistic perspective on L2 communication strategies. In G. Kasper & E. Kellerman (Eds.), *Communication strategies: Psycholinguistic and sociolinguistic perspectives.* London: Longnian.

Ritchie, W. C., & Bahia, T. K. (Eds.). (1996). *Handbook of research on language acquisition: Vol. 2. Second-language acquisition.* New York: Academic Press.

Rutherford, W. (1987). *Second language grammar: Learning and teaching.* New York: Longman.

Saville-Troike, M. (1989). *The Ethnography of communication: An introduction* (2nd ed.). Oxford, UK: Basil Blackwell.

Schachter, J., & Gass, S. (1996). *Second language classroom research: Issues and opportunities.* Mahwah, NJ: Lawrence Erlbaum Associates.

Schmidt, R. (1993). Awareness and second language acquisition. *Annual Review of Applied Linguistics, 13,* 206–226.

Schumann, J. H. (1995). Ad minorem theoriae gloriam: A response to Eubank and Gregg. *Studies in Second Language Acquisition, 17,* 59–63.

Sheen, R. (1994). A critical analysis of the advocacy of the task-based syllabus. *TESOL Quarterly, 28,* 127–151.

Shulman, L. S. (1986). Paradigms and research programs in the study of teaching: A contemporary perspective. In M. C. Wittrock (Ed.), *Handbook on research in teaching* (3rd ed., pp. 3–36). New York: Macmillan Publishing Company.

Spolsky, B. (1989). *Conditions for second language learning.* Oxford, UK: Oxford University Press.

Spolsky, B. (1990). Introduction to a colloquium: The scope and form of a theory of second language learning. *TESOL Quarterly, 24,* 609–616.

Su, C.-W. (1995). Report on the CLASS survey of Chinese language programs in America's secondary and elementary schools. *CLASS (Chinese Language Association of Secondary-Elementary Schools) Journal, 1,* 13–24.

Swaffer, J. K., Arens, K., & Morgan, M. (1982). Teacher practices: Redefining method as task hierarchy. *The Modern Language Journal, 66,* 24–33.

Swain, M. (1984). A review of immersion education in Canada: Research and evaluation studies. *Studies on immersion education: A collection for United States educators* (pp. 1–35). Sacramento, CA: California State Department of Education.

Swain, M. (1985). Communicative competence: Some roles of comprehensible input and comprehensible output in its development. In S. Gass & C. Madden (Eds.), *Input in second language acquisition* (pp. 235–253). Rowley, MA: Newbury House.

Swain, M., & Lapkin, S. (1995). Problems in output and the cognitive process they generate: A step toward second language learning. *Applied Linguistics, 16,* 371–391.

Tremblay, P. F., & Gardner, R. C. (1995). Expanding the motivation construct in language learning. *The Modern Language Journal, 79,* 505–518.

Truscott, J. (1996). Review article: The case against grammar correction in L2 writing classes. *Language Learning, 46,* 327–369.

Van Els, T., De Bot, K., & Weltens, B. (1991). Empirical foreign language research in Europe. In K. De Bot, R. B. Ginsberg, & C. Kramsch. (Eds.), *Foreign language research in cross-cultural perspective* (pp. 3–19). Amsterdam/Philadelphia: John Benjamins Publishing Company.

Van Lier, L. (1988). *The classroom and the language learner.* New York: Longman.

Van Lier, L. (1994). Forks and hope: Pursuing understanding in different ways. *Applied Linguistics, 15,* 328–346.

VanPatten, B. (1996). *Input processing and grammar instruction in second language acquisition.* Norwood, NJ: Ablex.

Vygotsky, L. S. (1962). *Thought and language.* Cambridge, MA: MIT Press.

Warschauer, M. (Ed.). (1995). *Virtual connections: Online activities and projects for networking language learners.* Honolulu, HI: University of Hawaii, Second Language Teaching and Curriculum Center.

Warschauer, M. (1997). Computer-mediated collaborative learning: Theory and practice. *The Modern Language Journal, 81,* 470–481.

Wells, G. (1993). Reevaluating the IRF sequence: A proposal for the articulation of theories of activity and discourse for the analysis of teaching and learning in the classroom. *Linguistics and Education, 5,* 1–37.

Wertsch, J. V. (1985). *Culture, communication, and cognition: Vygotskian perspectives.* Cambridge, UK: Cambridge University Press.

Wong-Fillmore, L., & Valadez, C. (1986). Teaching bilingual learners. In M. C. Wittrock (Ed.), *Handbook of research on teaching,* 3rd ed. (pp. 648–685). New York: Macmillan.

Yates, J. R., & Ortiz, A. A. (1983). Baker-deKanter review: Inappropriate conclusions on the efficacy of bilingual education. *NABE Journal, 7*(3), 75–84.

21.
Research on Writing

Melanie Sperling
University of California, Riverside

Sarah Warshauer Freedman
University of California, Berkeley

In the decade that has passed since the last *Handbook of Research on Teaching* was published, research on writing and writing instruction has proliferated. Writing research has been girded by national reform movements such as the Annenberg Challenge, Schools for Thought, and Accelerated Schools, which recognize writing as a key factor in students' academic lives; by the National Writing Project, the one major professional development movement that continues after more than 25 years to influence writing curriculum, instruction, and evaluation internationally; and by the establishment of the National Center for the Study of Writing, which from 1985 to 1995 focused on conducting writing and literacy research. During this time, increasing attention has been paid to a range of writers from preschool to adulthood in varied in-school and out-of-school contexts. Not least, theories about writing and learning to write have evolved as social and cultural perspectives on teaching, learning, and language have achieved prominence and become integrated with the cognitive perspective that dominated writing research in the 1970s and early 1980s. The research that we review in the body of this chapter reflects these changes.

As is the case for research in general, the questions writing researchers have asked, the methods they have employed, the theoretical conceptions they have brought to their work, and, perhaps most important, the way their research has been perceived, interpreted, and valued in the writing and literacy research community have reflected the social and political climate in which the research has been conducted (see Calfee & Drum, 1986). An important characteristic of the climate surrounding writing research has been the recognition of the growing diversity of the student population, from kindergarten through university. In the context of student diversity, we have witnessed

mounting academic and popular concern for the writing and literacy skills of students from varied linguistic, cultural, and ethnic backgrounds. Fueling this concern have been National Assessment of Educational Progress (NAEP) writing achievement data, which revealed that bottom-performing schools in writing achievement were characterized by an ethnic and racial diversity not seen in top-performing schools and that white students outperformed students of color on most writing tasks (Applebee, Langer, Mullis, Latham, & Gentile, 1994). Such statistics have raised questions about who or what to blame for disparities in both teaching and learning in contexts of student diversity and have pointed to critical instructional needs as yet unmet and, frequently, contestably defined.

Researchers have also worked amidst a hovering political anxiety about the United States' educational standing in the international community. With implications especially for the place of the United States in the global economy, being first and best in academic skills and knowledge has been a national goal, energized by the popular media. With a general apprehension that the United States is lagging behind in the international race with respect to writing and literacy, concerns have been voiced about whether U.S. educators are teaching writing well compared to their counterparts in other nations. Often missing from this conversation have been the questionable means of making comparisons. In fact, the one major research project to emerge in the past decade that tried to compare students' writing achievement cross-nationally, initiated by the International Association for the Evaluation of Educational Achievement, was deemed a failure by one of its directors because of the difficulty in obtaining reliable cross-national judgments of writing (Purves, 1992).

Not least in the social-political climate has been the ongoing

The authors wish to thank the following reviewers of the chapter; Arthur Applebee, State University of New York at Albany; and Linda S. Flower, Carnegie Mellon University.

technological revolution, which has considerably upped the ante on the writing and literacy skills deemed necessary for students to participate fully in private, academic, and civic life. Computers have continued to introduce not only new ways of generating and organizing written text but, through the electronic "superhighway," have also introduced a new textual component to human relationships. The popular and academic urge to predict the long-term effects of this technology on the teaching and learning of writing and literacy along with an academic push to understand the place of advancing communications within larger theories of language, literacy, and culture have been strong.

While certain core questions have always motivated writing research—in particular, how different students learn to write, how best to teach writing in different situations, how students' writing stands up evaluatively in different contexts—in the current research climate writing researchers have been challenged to incorporate as central to these issues the perspective that the acts of writing and writing instruction reflect broader social and cultural processes at work. In a related way, this decade of writing research has witnessed an exciting conceptual evolution, marked by theories of writing and learning that integrate more fully than in previous decades the cognitive and social-cultural perspectives on writing and learning to write. Such integrated perspectives have helped researchers to understand writers not only as individuals but also as members of broader social and cultural communities. Indeed, during the past decade it has been difficult not to speak of writers' individuality and their social-cultural communality in the same breath.

Research Coherence

Given the fact that just ten years ago writing was newly recognized as a serious area of study in education (see Dyson & S. W. Freedman, 1991; S. W. Freedman, Dyson, Flower, & Chafe, 1987; Langer & Allington, 1992; Nystrand, Greene, & Wiemelt, 1993), few are surprised that the last *Handbook* was the first to include a review on the topic of writing and that this review pointed to a lack of coherence in the field (Scardamalia & Bereiter, 1986). Although writing remains a relatively new field of study, a growing coherence has marked the past decade.

This coherence is reflected, in part, in the shared assumption of most writing researchers that writing is inseparable from broader linguistic, communicative, and literate processes. Moreover, whereas ten years ago researchers wondered about the theoretical principles that guided research on writing and discussed the lack of a guiding theoretical base (e.g., Gere, 1986), one of the more defining developments of the past ten years has been the growing consciousness and explicit airing among researchers of the situated nature of their own work and of the parallels between their motivating theories and broader intellectual tendencies.

Nystrand et al. (1993) have charted an intellectual movement in writing research from the 1940s to the present day that parallels similar evolutions in the study of language and in critical theory. This movement flows from formalist epistemology and an associated focus on issues of text to structuralist theories and a focus on underlying processes to, presently, more dialogic theories and a focus on text and process intertwined with social

and cultural contexts. This intellectual progression—and the sociocultural frameworks for writing and learning that have emerged in its wake—reflects, in large part, the demographic changes that have occurred in the United States in the latter part of this century. The progression also reflects a more general shift in educational theories and research to postmodern ideologies. The desirability and need to recognize writing's embeddedness in the broader literate-communicative system also accounts for writing research's often diverse family of researchers, who have followed different disciplinary roads to study writing and who come mainly from anthropology, education, English, linguistics, psychology, and rhetoric.

With the growing number of researchers interested in issues of writing and literacy, a number of reviews of writing research have been written in the last ten years, not surprisingly to establish coherent perspectives on particular areas of the field. While different reviewers with different purposes for writing their reviews have found a variety of points of entry for examining writing research, they have generally developed two related assumptions about writing: (a) writing is a cognitive and social process and (b) critical relationships exist between writing and other language processes. When emphasizing these assumptions, reviewers have reflected interests in broad-based instructional philosophies, especially variations of "writing process" curriculum and instruction (e.g., Hillocks, 1986) and particular practices to promote students' writing and learning such as using computers (e.g., Cochran-Smith, 1991) or peer response groups (e.g., DiPardo & S. W. Freedman, 1988). Research reviews of this sort also have allowed researchers to address notions of generalizability in writing research, with the position ascendant—influenced largely by socially cast theories of thinking and learning—that one can fully understand neither an instructional philosophy nor a method apart from the ways particular teachers work in particular instructional contexts. One research trend has been for comparisons of control and experimental classes to be supplemented by, if not often replaced in favor of, ethnography, case study, and teacher research.

Overview

The rest of this chapter is divided into two main sections, which correspond to the two critical assumptions about writing and writing pedagogy that have developed in the field. In the first section, we discuss writing as a cognitive and social process. We begin this section by discussing cognitive perspectives on the writing process, which gave much of the initial impetus to writing research and to process-oriented instruction. We summarize what we know about composing and pedagogy from these perspectives. We then explore social and cultural perspectives, which have helped to expand our conceptions of writing. This discussion serves in part as a theoretical base for the second section. In the second section, we discuss connections between writing and other communicative and literate processes. We focus specifically on connections between writing and speaking and writing and reading, and we explore what is known about these connections in relation to students' learning and classroom practice. We end the chapter with some thoughts on the next decade of writing research.

Writing Processes

Beginning with Cognition

Encapsulating the strong cognitive perspective on writing that dominated in the 1970s and 1980s, Flower and Hayes asserted in 1981 that "the process of writing is best understood as a set of distinctive thinking processes which writers orchestrate or organize during the act of composing" (p. 366). This perspective on writing reflected the general "cognitive revolution" that has continued to motivate much educational research over the past 2 to 3 decades and that established a cognitive paradigm for understanding teaching and learning. This paradigm continues to prevail in many domains—teaching students how to think and how to engage in problem solving through reasoning and critique remains, after all, a central concern of the schooling enterprise in diverse subjects such as literature, mathematics, biology, and history.

In writing research, cognitive perspectives on learning and performance yielded models of writers' thinking during composing, which have critically guided both research and classroom practice. The most enduring and influential of these models, created by Flower and Hayes (e.g., Flower & Hayes, 1981; Hayes & Flower, 1980), suggested that writing does not progress through linearly ordered stages but, rather, flows recursively through a set of subprocesses that includes *planning* (generating ideas, setting goals, and organizing), *translating* (turning plans into written language), and *reviewing* (evaluating and revising). Writers routinely interrupt one subprocess to cycle into another, with the interruptions coming and the subprocesses occurring in no fixed order (Hayes & Flower, 1980). This composing process is constrained by what Hayes and Flower called the writer's task environment (topic, audience, rhetorical exigencies, and evolving text) and the writer's memory. Above all, according to the Hayes and Flower model, the composing process is a goal-directed, problem-solving process. Writing proceeds as writers create and change their goals in the act of writing and solve various rhetorical problems related to their goals.

One sees the links between this model and process-oriented writing pedagogy, especially in approaches that serve students' planning—for example, through brainstorming ideas and strategies—and that serve students' reviewing— for example, through teacher and peer feedback. Important for research, both the Hayes and Flower model and other cognitive models of the composing process have served as objects of study in their own right and as frameworks for research on the composing process and how that process is taught and learned among different writers.

WRITERS' COMPOSING

To elaborate on the Hayes and Flower model and to explore its implications for teaching and learning, early researchers of the writing process examined how expert writers compose—with the goal of teaching novices the processes that experts use. Mainly, they studied the various rhetorical problems that various types of native-speaking writers attempt to solve and found that adult novices and experts tackle different problems. In particular, experts think about their readers more than novices,

who think more about themselves (Flower, 1979); when revising, experts reorganize and reconceptualize large chunks of text while novices tend to revise at the word and sentence levels (Hayes, Flower, Schriver, Stratman, & Carey, 1987; Sommers, 1980); and experts make global plans while novices make local plans, thinking most about what comes next (Bereiter & Scardamalia, 1987; Flower & Hayes, 1981). Although these studies explain expert processes, they do not provide information about the route writers travel as they learn to attain those abilities— the journey from the state of being and behaving like a novice to the state of being and behaving like an expert.

Recently, studies of writers' cognitive processes have begun to focus on nonnative speakers of English, although the scope of extant second language (L2) studies is still limited. Krapels (1990) reviewed a number of such studies, finding mostly case studies, which altogether only included 100 subjects—many of whom were subjects of convenience, usually the researcher's students, and usually competent writers at the university level. These studies, which focus on intermediate and advanced learners rather than on students initially learning their second language, emphasize the similarities of the processes of native and nonnative speakers and, essentially, repeat, for a population that speaks a second language, the findings about those writing in their native language.

Differences when composing in a second language begin to emerge, however, when light is trained on the differences between unskilled L1 (native language) and L2 writers or between unskilled and skilled L2 writers. Raimes (1983), for example, found that unskilled, L2 writers, that is, those who scored poorly on a holistically scored university-administered writing sample, wrote more and showed more commitment to their writing tasks than L1, basic-level writers. These L2 writers did not worry about making errors when they were composing and were not inhibited by error correction once they had written, unlike their native speaking counterparts. For L2 writers, a critical part of the writing process may be the way in which they use their own native languages. Evidence shows that differences among writers using native languages correspond to students' writing proficiency in second languages. In her review, Krapels found stronger L2 writers to be more skilled at using their native languages when composing; increased native-language usage in L2 writing correlated with stronger writing, not weaker writing. In these studies, a native language was often used during planning, especially when the topic was culture bound and related to situations the writer normally experienced in the native language. Writers, writing in a second language, also found their native languages useful when they needed vocabulary in the second language that they did not have; the native language allowed a writer to move forward with the flow of the writing and find the word later. In spite of these observations about different L2 writers, however, the research on writing processes in a second language has barely touched the great variety within populations using second languages.

WRITERS' COGNITIVE PROCESSES: IMPLICATIONS FOR THE CLASSROOM

In the early 1970s, simultaneous with the initial L1 studies of the writing process, many people in the teaching profession were rethinking the nature of writing and the teaching of writing. In 1972, the Bay Area Writing Project, soon to become the National Writing Project (NWP), began bringing together teacher leaders to share their skills and to develop workshops for other teachers. The NWP, which was destined to become a major force in teacher professionalization efforts and which has influenced and continues to influence millions of writing teachers around the world, embraced the writing process studies early on. The NWP, especially in the beginning, focused mostly on writing for native speakers. The L2 community, independently of the NWP, began to make important changes in their classrooms by the early 1980s as research on L2 writing processes began to emerge (Krapels, 1990).

As the results of research on the writing process reached both L1 and L2 teachers, they began not only to assign more writing but also to restructure their classes to support their students through an elaborate writing process, taking into account the fact that their students would benefit from help with planning, writing, and revising. This change in research and teaching was so monumental that, borrowing from Kuhn (1963), Hairston (1982) called it a "paradigm shift," suggesting that old conceptual models were overturned in favor of new ones. Just one year later, Hairston's language of a paradigm shift was picked up by Raimes (1983) for the L2 community.

In spite of the changes that were occurring inside classrooms, studies of these changes revealed that although the research on the writing process was being widely implemented, it was often misinterpreted and misapplied. Taking a different view of the changes than Hairston, Applebee (1986) argued that the new research findings were being transformed to fit old paradigms for teaching. The difficulties in implementing writing process research seemed related to the realities of teachers' and students' lives inside schools, which forced compromises that researchers had not anticipated. With larger classes, increased numbers of classes, and more extracurricular duties, teachers had little time to support individual students' thinking or to explicitly guide them in solving their particular writing problems. Yet once teachers assigned more writing, they had to figure out how to handle the load. So although teachers stressed the writing process, it was rarely taught as recursive but rather as a set of ordered stages—first plan, then write, then revise. Help with planning often involved students in whole-class brainstorming activities, after which everyone would write and then revise whether they needed to or not. The problem-solving focus of the research often seemed to get lost in the translation. Further, what went under the label of writing process pedagogy could be vastly divergent from one classroom to the next for both L1 students (Applebee, 1986) and L2 students (Gutierrez, 1992; Reyes, 1991). Finally, the process received so much attention, fears grew that the quality of students' written products was being neglected (see review in S. W. Freedman et al., 1987).

As teachers experimented with new classroom practices, researchers began to compare the effectiveness of varied kinds of writing instruction on writing improvement. Looking primarily at classrooms serving native speakers, Hillocks (1986) conducted a meta-analysis in which he examined all experimental studies conducted between 1963 and 1982 that compared the effectiveness of different classroom practices on the quality of student writing. Using statistical procedures to cumulate the results across studies, Hillocks presented the first comprehensive look at the effectiveness of the new emphasis on process. He included only studies in which there was some control for teacher bias, for the validity and reliability of ratings of student writing, and for differences in students in control and treatment groups. He compared four approaches: (a) a natural process mode, in which teachers have general objectives, students write freely for the response of their peers on topics that interest them, and teachers provide opportunities for students to revise; (b) a traditional presentational mode, in which teachers have specific objectives and present information to students about grammar or about model texts, assign writing that generally involves imitating a pattern that has been taught, and give feedback on the writing; (c) an environmental mode, designed by Hillocks himself, in which teachers have clear and specific objectives and in which they help students solve writing problems in small groups; and (d) an individualized mode, in which teachers provide students with programmed instruction or with one-on-one writing conferences. The environmental mode, which was mostly the subject of Hillocks' own studies, proved to be the most successful, followed by a tie for the natural process and individualized modes. The presentational mode was relatively ineffective.

These findings are interesting in relation to the research on the writing process and its applications in the classroom. The most successful environmental mode, with its clear attention to guided problem solving, not the natural process mode, follows most consistently from the writing process research. In contrast, the natural process mode, as defined by Hillocks, seems like a typical misapplication of writing process research, similar to the misguided instruction that Applebee observed. Unfortunately, to interpret findings regarding the third-ranking individualized mode is difficult, because it included two disparate practices, one that should theoretically promote the findings of the process research—one-on-one conferences—and the other that would likely not promote the findings—programmed instruction.

Social and Cultural Perspectives

Over the past decade, newer—or newly recognized—social and cultural perspectives on language and learning have forced many writing researchers to extend or offer alternatives to the cognitive theories of composing that attracted so much research attention in the 1970s and 1980s (see Durst, 1990; Dyson & S. W. Freedman, 1991; S. W. Freedman et al., 1987; Nystrand et al., 1993; Sperling, 1996). In particular, scholars have attempted to bring together cognitive, social, and cultural strands of research on writing and literacy to suggest sociocognitive (social cognitive) and sociocultural (social cultural) theories that may better explain the writing and learning experiences of diverse students working across diverse literacy and learning contexts (S. W. Freedman, 1996). The general acceptance of social and cultural accounts of writing and literacy was foreshadowed, in large part, by Scribner and Cole's accounts of literacy in Liberia (e.g., 1981), which showed that literacy and the thinking associated with literacy was closely linked to the functions and purposes of literacy in different contexts.

In fact, scholars have been pushed to elaborate existing cognitive theories by research that was conducted in a broad spectrum of social and cultural contexts wherein writing served varied functions and purposes, ranging from communicating among family members to conducting business in the workplace and community and from reflecting privately on personal experience to reporting publicly on civic events. Such research has been important for exploring how writing is learned across varied populations and for understanding the roles and relationships of writers and readers in different contexts, including the norms, assumptions, values, and beliefs that influence them. Theories of writing have needed to account for the extent to which writers act as individual agents, executing their own goals and visions for what and how to communicate in written language, and the extent to which their literate practices are shaped and situated within broader social and cultural contexts. Differences in conceptualizing the writer in context mark much of the current theoretical debate.

Despite their differences, however, social and cultural perspectives on writing and learning to write generally have owed in common a debt of thanks to the language theories of Lev Vygotsky and Mikhail Bakhtin, both of whom reflect a Russian scholarly tradition concerned with the links between psychological development and societal context (Forman, Minick, & Stone, 1993). In particular, for both Vygotsky and Bakhtin, language development is seen as a process rooted in and inseparable from relationships forged in the social world.

VYGOTSKY'S CONTRIBUTION TO WRITING THEORY

Vygotsky's theories of learning and development have forced writing researchers to pay attention not only to individuals learning to write but also to the social interactions through which, Vygotsky argues, such learning occurs. He asserts that the social interactions between the child and others become, for the child, the raw material of thought. "Human learning," Vygotsky notes, "presupposes a specific social nature and a process by which children grow into the intellectual life of those around them" (1978, p. 88).

To explain this process of learning and development, Vygotsky uses the metaphor of buds or flowers that, with assistance, will fruit into independent accomplishments (p. 86). These buds or flowers, Vygotsky claims, need to be nourished in the classroom through classroom interactions. Vygotsky's theory of learning and development explains that these interactions occur within "the zone of proximal development: the distance between the actual developmental level as determined by independent problem solving and the level of potential development, as determined through problem solving under adult guidance or in collaboration with more capable peers" (p. 86). Put another way, by interacting with an able assistant, individuals can carry out certain tasks in the social world that they would not be able to carry out alone.

Following Vygotsky's theories, scholars have suggested that the learning process is one in which an adult or more capable peer, interacting with the learner, provides a scaffold (Bruner, 1978; Wood, Bruner, & Ross, 1976) to aid learning and development. Acting as a scaffold, the adult or peer may perform part of the task for the learner, model the task, or in other ways offer guidance. The scaffold is gradually withdrawn as the learner

takes over the task. In this way, learners begin to "appropriate modes of speaking, acting, and thinking" (Forman et al., 1993) that represent their growth into the life around them.

The implication of Vygotsky's theory for writing pedagogy is that to learn and develop as writers—to "appropriate" the information, skills, and values associated with writing—students need to be engaged in social interactions. These interactions center around aspects of the task of writing (including generating ideas, selecting language, shaping and reshaping text) that they cannot accomplish alone but that they can accomplish with assistance.

Over the past decade or so, the metaphor of scaffolding has caught on, particularly for presenting a vision of classroom practice. One likely reason for its acceptance is that, conceptually, the construct matches general curricular and reform goals of socializing students into the critical writing life of both school and civic culture. However, the metaphor is limited insofar as it does not convey the subtleties of the teaching and learning process that followers of Vygotsky, closely studying instructional interactions, have identified. One criticism is that the scaffold metaphor tends to highlight the teacher's role more than the student's in the learning interaction (see Cazden, 1988) and to suggest that the student somewhat magically internalizes teacher-student interchanges (Stone, 1993). According to Stone (1993), the metaphor ignores the multiple communicative mechanisms that learners, along with teachers, employ in order for teaching and learning to take place. In particular, Stone singles out the linguistic and semiotic mechanisms of inferencing through which learners come to share teachers' perspectives, the nature of teacher-student interpersonal relations, and, relatedly, the social value teachers and students attach to particular learning situations.

In spite of sometimes poorly realized interpretations, Vygotsky's interest in the interaction between learner and other in the "zone of proximal development" has, perhaps more than any other single influence over the past decade or so, attracted writing researchers to study specific interactive contexts of writing life in classrooms in order to understand their potential for students' learning and development as writers. These interactive contexts include teacher-writer interactions as seen in teacher-student writing conferences and peer-writer interactions as seen in various peer collaborations around students' texts. Unlike other domains that draw on Vygotsky's theories, writing research frequently has assumed that, as student writers interact with others to explore and get feedback on their writing, they in effect make explicit the relationship between writer and reader that is implicit in and critical to the composing process. Put another way, when the student writer interacts with a capable reader regarding a writing activity, the expectations and assumptions of the reader are exposed and made available for teaching and learning (S. W. Freedman, with Greenleaf & Sperling, 1987).

How effective such interactions are for all students' learning, however, has been the topic of some debate. The theoretical ideal is not always realized, especially in cross-cultural situations where teachers and students may bring different assumptions and values related not only to writing and literacy but also to the instructional process itself (see, e.g., Au, 1980; Cazden, 1988; Delpit, 1986, 1995). Indeed, attention to the range of students who work with a single teacher in any classroom has forced researchers to address what kind of learning interactions teachers and different students coconstruct. Highlighting the social, cultural, and political-historical threads of which this teaching and learning fabric is woven, Forman et al. (1993) assert:

> . . . [E]ducationally significant human interactions do not involve abstract bearers of cognitive structures but real people who develop a variety of interpersonal relationships with one another in the course of their shared activity in a given institutional context. Within educational institutions, for example, the sometimes conflicting responsibilities of mentorship and evaluation can give rise to distinct interpersonal relationships between teachers and pupils that have important influences on learning. For example, appropriating the speech or actions of another person requires a degree of identification with that person and the cultural community he or she represents. Educational failure, in this perspective, can represent an unwillingness to subordinate one's own voice to that of another rather than an inability to learn. (1993, p. 6)

Insofar as appropriating the information, skills, and values of a particular written language is tantamount to appropriating a particular sociocultural voice, extending Vygotsky's theories has been critical to incorporate more strongly a sociocultural perspective. Bakhtin extends these theories; he suggests the need to situate such learning events within cultural, institutional, and historical contexts (Wertsch, 1991).

BAKHTIN'S CONTRIBUTION TO WRITING THEORY

Like Vygotsky, Bakhtin (1986) assumes the centrality of social interactions in language and thought but emphasizes the overlapping, intertwining, and "interpenetrating" nature of these interactions in a broader sociocultural structure:

> Our thought itself—philosophical, scientific, and artistic—is born and shaped in the process of interaction and struggle with others' thought, and this cannot but be reflected in the forms that verbally express our thought as well. . . . The utterance proves to be a very complex and multiplanar phenomenon if considered not in isolation and with respect to its author (the speaker) only, but as a link in the chain of speech communication and with respect to other, related utterances. (1986, pp. 92–93)

Addressing, in particular, the way language is learned, Bakhtin adds:

> We know our native language—its lexical composition and grammatical structure—not from dictionaries and grammars but from concrete utterances that we hear and that we ourselves reproduce in live speech communication with people around us. *We assimilate forms of language only in forms of utterances.* [emphasis added] (1986, p. 95)

In other words, language, by its nature, comprises the social and cultural history of its users: Language is nothing if not connotative, and it is learned as such. This linguistic premise forms the basis for Bakhtin's term "voice." As Cazden (1993b) explains,

> *Voice* is Bakhtin's term for the "speaking consciousness": the person acting—that is, speaking or writing in a particular time and place to known or unknown others. "Voice" and its utterances always express a point of view, always enact particular values . . . [while] taking account of the voices being addressed, whether in speech or writing. (p. 198)

In this sense, words are laden with the voices of exigent contexts.

In this sense, too, language is, in Bakhtin's view, dialogic. According to Morson (1986), who explains this dialogic quality,

> Bakhtin understands discourse to be not an individual writer's or speaker's instantiating of a code but, instead, the product of a complex social situation in which real or potential audiences, earlier and possible later utterances, habits and "genres" of speech and writing, and a variety of other complex social factors shape all utterances from the outset. . . . The only way in which the individual speaker can be sole author of an utterance, according to Bakhtin, is in the purely physiological sense. (1986, p. 83)

For Bakhtin, then, each piece of writing is composed of the writer's past interactions with the thoughts of others and of anticipated future interactions.

Taking Bakhtin's theories to the writing classroom, we may assume that students' speech and writing are imbued with the viewpoints and values of multiple and sometimes competing voices. For example, as Cazden (1993b) points out, student writers are always faced with negotiating the "dual audience" of teacher and peers (p. 204), with the teacher being the usual primary audience and therefore the student's main addressee but with peers playing the role of what Cazden calls "ratified auditors" (p. 204). Students, in both their speech and writing, choose language that asserts their relationships to and acknowledges both of these influences. Similarly, Dyson (1993) identifies three "social spheres of interest" (p. 13) for students communicating in classroom contexts: the official school world, the unofficial peer world, and the sociocultural community as realized in the classroom—"each world with its own social beliefs and language values" (p. 13). Looking beyond the classroom, Brandt (1992), by implication, extends the notion of ratified auditorship and suggests additional spheres of interest for student writers when she indicates that all writers relate not only to readers' needs and expectations but also—and, Brandt suggests, perhaps primarily—to their "affiliations with the sense-making practices of a particular group, say, feminists, the Roman Catholic Church, or AT & T" (p. 330). Sperling (1995, 1998), accounting for these embedded social and cultural worlds in language and learning, suggests that students as writers participate in a "role complex," their voices reflecting the multiple stances they assume in relationship to multiple others both inside and outside of school.

A major implication of Bakhtin's theories for classrooms is that, in the theoretical ideal, students' thinking and their written texts move inexorably toward reflecting the voices valued in that context. It follows that students' thinking and texts will be richer in learning contexts where multiple voices and multiple ways of voicing are welcomed (see S. W. Freedman, 1994; Knoeller, 1998).

To achieve such a learning context, teachers may need to open up their classrooms both to conventional academic texts and to texts that conventionally do not get fostered in academic settings—incorporating various literary and nonliterary discourses from western and nonwestern cultures, ranges of genres reflecting students' social and cultural diversity, and nonverbal symbolic media (including gesturing, drawing, and signing). Toward this end, research in nonacademic contexts helps us to see beyond classroom genres, to define discourses and texts broadly, and to see both younger and older writers using combinations of verbal and nonverbal signs to make meaning (see, e.g., Witte, 1992). In the next decade, writing research needs to press on the implications for communication, teaching, and learning and on the implications of incorporating broadly defined discourses into the established literate meaning-making practices of school. As Delpit (1995) argues, teachers will need to lead students to acquire the dominant discourse but, in the process, to find their own place within it. Teachers must "saturate the dominant discourse with new meanings, must wrest from it a place for the glorification of their students and their forebears" (p. 164). Research not only needs to probe the value of such practices across students but also to explore how to implement them to advantage in different school settings. Such exploration is important if writing curriculum and policy are to keep pace with the social and cultural diversity of our students and with rapidly expanding technologies, both of which are adding new and varying discourses to social intercourse.

Research and Theory Bringing Together the Cognitive with the Social and Cultural

Flower's (1989, 1994) recent work has become a widely cited illustration of one kind of sociocognitive position. In this work, Flower has extended her early composing model to better account for (a) the influence on writers of their social and cultural contexts and (b) the reader's role in contributing to the meaning of writers' texts. Flower presents not a model of "composing" but rather of "discourse construction" and, in doing so, recognizes that no composing or meaning making occurs apart from the way writers function in different sociocultural contexts (Figure 21.1).

A critical difference between this model of discourse construction and earlier cognitive models of the composing process lies in the data sources that led to them. Whereas earlier models of composing were based on relatively homogeneous groups of mainstream writers composing under laboratory conditions, Flower's model of discourse construction is based on the reading and writing activities of diverse students working in natural reading and writing situations. As such, it emphasizes both individual diversity and the contexts in which individuals function.

As seen in Figure 21.1 and according to Flower,

. . . both writers and readers construct meaning within the broader context of a social and cultural context, of language, of discourse conventions (a trio that was meant to be suggestive, rather than exclusive). These form an outer circle of influence in conjunction with and often produced through a more immediate circle of gen-

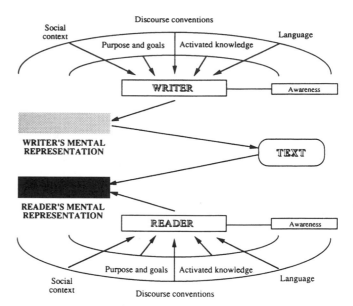

Figure 21.1. A model of discourse construction (from Flower, 1990).

eral purposes, specific goals, and activated knowledge linked to the task at hand. In the model, both readers and writers build socially shaped, individually formed meanings. (1994, pp. 52–53)

In the discourse construction process, writers and readers build internal representations of text, and, according to Flower, these internal representations are linked to differences among writers in their interpretations of such influences as social expectations, the task, conventions, or teacher's response. Writers' and readers' internal text representations, moreover, also include questions, dilemmas, contradictions, and alternative strategies that they either are considering or have discarded—in Flower's words, "forces in conflict and roads not taken" (1994, p. 53). In this way, "outer forces translate themselves into inner voices" (p. 54) that writers and readers must negotiate as they attempt to produce or make meaning of text. The "awareness" box in Figure 21.1 indicates that writers and readers can be more or less aware of this discourse construction process.

One of the criticisms levied against the earlier Hayes and Flower composing model (Flower & Hayes, 1981; Hayes & Flower, 1980) was that, as Bizzell (1986) asserted, the writer's context (or "task environment") was depicted as merely a frame for the activities inside the writer's head, which composed the main interest. The same cannot be said for the more current model of discourse construction in which writing does not exist apart from the circumstances surrounding it, including its eventual reading. Yet the model does not dismiss or even downplay individual cognition. Rather, it emphasizes how context cues cognition—note the multiple arrows leading from context to writer, which in turn lead to the writer's mental representation in Figure 21.1. The model emphasizes, too, how cognition—the writer's mental representation—mediates between context and text. Critical to this conception of discourse construction, then, are the dilemma-driven, goal-directed writer and reader who are working together to make meaning happen. Key to instruction is making these writers and readers explicit and available for students to consider.

Flower's model includes elements that have become key in current theoretical debates, namely, context, the relationship of context to writer and reader, and the nature of the writer-reader relationship itself. A central question encompassing all these elements (see, e.g., Nystrand et al., 1993) is whether context is an exterior influence that acts upon writers and readers or whether it is accomplished by writers and readers working dialogically (see Brandt, 1992). In contrast to Flower's conception that context cues cognition, some theorists emphasize the dialogical relationship between writer and reader as the central contextualizing act. Criticizing Flower's sociocognitive theory, which she sees as cognitive theory somehow made "context sensitive," Brandt (1992) asserts that the social world (i.e., context) should not be "treated as something that is *taken in* as a kind of raw material, mixed with the ingredients of long-term memory and rhetorical purpose, and put through the recursive mental operations of goal setting, planning, organizing, and so on" (p. 324). Rather, context should be seen to be "created and justified" (Nystrand et al., 1993) in writing and reading. What these theorists suggest, then, is that written discourse is not just "situated" but is also "situating" (Brandt, 1992; Nystrand, 1986; Nystrand et al., 1993). This dialogic perspective on discourse begins to reveal the fuzzy boundary between sociocognitive and sociocultural views. From a sociocultural perspective, too, writing is situating, helping to shape and maintain roles and relationships that are ratified in the broader social and cultural world.

With social and cultural perspectives on writing and writing processes well established in shaping current theoretical debates, some writing researchers have recently articulated shortcomings of these perspectives and have called for a theory that integrates material factors into cognitive, social, and cultural factors to account for the writing process and its teaching and learning (Bracewell & Witte, 1997; Witte, 1992). According to Bracewell and Witte (1997), critical for understanding the influences on and development of the literate mind is perceiving how writing is "grounded in the material world" (p. 1). They suggest three ways in which writing may be so grounded: (a) "the writer communicates using material objects (letters, pen, paper, word processor, internet) which in turn shape the writing;" (b) "the product of writing—that is, the text—is a material object in itself;" and (c) "the text also influences events in the material world" (p. 1). This material aspect of writing—and what it may mean for the teaching and learning of writing in classroom contexts—has as yet been studied little empirically. However, a theory that considers the material either as a separate factor in writing or as an aspect of social or cultural context, may be particularly useful in the coming years and may shed light on the ways that writing technology changes the significance and meaning of writing in school and is linked to students' acquisition and development of the information, skills, and values associated with written language.

What all these scholars illustrate is the intense focus in recent years on writing as a meaning-making process undertaken by writers in conjunction with others in the social (cultural and material) world and, perhaps, especially including readers (we note that the reader is sometimes also the writer). Both writers and readers are bound to the contexts that give meaning and significance to texts and to the acts of writing and reading them. As differing perspectives on this process indicate, how best to think of writing as a literate act—what a literate act is and how we might best teach and learn it—may not be a question that has one grand solution. Still, social and cultural perspectives on writing are critical to conceive of students' diverse experiences as writers and, in turn, to develop ways that foster those experiences in various social arrangements within classrooms and schools.

Writing Connections

Over the past decade, the tendency has been to extend the list of broader literacy and learning processes of which writing is seen as an instantiation. Just as cognitive studies focus on writing as an instantiation of problem solving, for example, so sociocognitive and sociocultural perspectives focus on the way writing instantiates such processes as literate action, symbolic performance, and sense making. Evolving theories have put the spotlight on this bigger language and learning picture, often demanding that we know just what the bigger picture is or needs to be if our work is to help teachers teach and children learn. How writing fits into this bigger picture is what we now turn to.

Writing and Speaking

The connection between writing and speaking has been a topic of interest not only for educators but also for linguists, psychologists, and anthropologists who have sought to understand the nature of language, processes of language acquisition and development, and the ways language functions in the social world (see, e.g., reviews by Chafe & Tannen, 1987; Horowitz & Samuels, 1987; Sperling, 1996). These interests have fueled the question that asks how teachers can connect their knowledge of oral and written language processes to the teaching of writing.

We know that while writing and speaking are each modes of communication, speakers customarily have the advantage of communicating with others who are present while writers, in contrast, usually work in relative physical isolation. Speakers and their interlocutors can help one another shape messages as they unfold, but for writers, the burden to shape messages lies within themselves as they—without contingent and present help—in effect, communicate with "absent others" (on the cognitive ramifications of these differences, see review by Scardamalia & Bereiter, 1986; and on the limitations of the cognitive perspective see Gee, 1990; Street, 1984). Thus, writers and speakers operate within often differing cognitive constraints and cultural conventions for communicating in one mode or the other. We do not mean to imply that a variety of communicative circumstances do not exist in which speakers find themselves relatively isolated (for example, when radio announcers speak to unseen audiences), when writers' audiences are physically present (for example, when individuals write out answers to spoken questions), or in which a host of variations occur on the speaking and writing continuum. However, the physical absence of an interlocutor or audience customarily distinguishes writing from speaking.

These conditions of writing and speaking have helped to establish two general conceptions of writing and speaking connections, both of which can motivate writing research and practice: (a) writing and speaking are distinct though sometimes comparable discourse modes; and (b) speaking to others who are present can support writing in practical learning contexts. These perspectives lead to two corollary questions: (a) When students shift from speaking to writing, what do they need to learn and unlearn about language? and (b) What spoken language experiences in the classroom foster students' development of written language?

WRITING AND SPEAKING AS DISTINCT DISCOURSE MODES

Over the last several decades, a prodigious body of research has accumulated that distinguishes spoken from written language or that considers one with reference to the other (see review in Chafe & Tannen, 1987). Until relatively recently, however, much of this research has focused on formal features of oral and written texts, with particular attention paid to the features of spoken and written syntax. Research comparing spoken and written syntax generally shows how writing is syntactically more complex than speaking. Writing, for example, is characterized by more subordinations, clausal elaborations, embeddings, passive verb forms, and a variety of sentence-combining transformations. Mastery over these forms has been seen to distinguish mature from immature writing (Hunt, 1965; Loban, 1976).

As the focus has shifted from describing the syntactic features of writing and speaking to understanding the social contexts in which writing and speaking are used, however, it has become clear that language features do not exist independent of these contexts. Not only syntax but also other aspects of language such as what is said and what is taken for granted or what is developed and in what ways reflect speakers' and writers' purposes and listeners' and readers' expectations for how and what to communicate in particular situations (see, e.g., Gee, 1990). Even very young children learn without formal instruction to distinguish the demands of certain written from spoken contexts, in particular, producing either oral- or written-like stories when it is appropriate to do so (see review in Sperling, 1996).

What is not so clear, and what we have yet fully to understand, however, is how individuals over the course of their development learn to distinguish the range of written-like from spoken-like strategies that they encounter both inside and outside school, especially when formal schooling influences what and how students think about writing and speaking. We also do not know fully how this learning process might differ for those who develop mastery over written strategies in academic settings and for those who do not.

We do know that students at all levels demonstrate, if not mastery, at least a certain acquaintance with the distinct nature and function of written academic discourse, and evidence to this effect has kindled questions about the role of social and cultural knowledge in the process of learning how to write. For example, basic writing students, deemed to have few viable skills for producing academic papers, have demonstrated, nonetheless, some understanding of written discourse, as Shaughnessy (1977) found in her now-classic examination of 4,000 placement essays written by open-admissions freshmen at the City University of New York. These writers attempted a number of characteristically written-like forms (e.g., nominalizations, passive verbs, and complex, integrated syntax) and, in many cases, appeared to use such language in an attempt to convey learned perspectives on everyday topics, a stance consistent with writing in university settings. However, in contrast to skilled writers, these writers often mixed into their writing strategies that are natural to speech (e.g., redundancy, fragmentation, and loose sequencing). It appears that even when basic writers have mastered few written discourse skills, they may, nonetheless, demonstrate an approximate sense of how written discourse conventionally appears and sounds (see reviews in Goen, 1997; Sperling, 1996).

In contrast to the textual evidence from basic L1 writers, text data on L2 writers of different ages suggest that these writers often fall back on spoken-like English strategies when they write in English as their second language (for example, using much coordination, shorter T units [an independent clause plus all its dependent structures], unmodified nouns and verbs, and fewer prepositional phrases) and apparently do not attempt counterpart written-like forms, even though such forms are more appropriate to the writing tasks (see review of text data in Silva, 1993). A commonsensical explanation for this situation is that some L2 writers who lack sufficient mastery over English written-like strategies may draw on those English spoken-language strategies that they are certain of. However, we do not know what strategies L2 writers use when their written language development is more advanced than their oral language development. We also do not fully know how beginning L2 writers might contrast to L1, basic-level writers, for whom much social currency appears to come from sounding written-like and academic, even when they have little mastery over such language themselves. Comparative studies of L1, basic-level writers and beginning L2 writers could help reveal the kinds of knowledge this range of writers leans on, including not only knowledge of text features that can be gained from exposure to books but also the kinds of social and cultural knowledge that fosters linguistic strategies in academic settings.

How students might acquire and develop social and cultural background knowledge along with the written language features that reflect this knowledge is the topic of some debate among both researchers and practitioners. A growing, though not always empirically based, perspective among many language educators is that when dominant mainstream discourses appear particularly congenial for certain students (usually white, middle-class students), these students can implicitly acquire writing strategies valued in academic settings. This implicit learning process is largely one of acculturation and occurs, in part, as students are immersed in reading and writing different kinds of mainstream texts (Berkenkotter & Huckin, 1993; Gee, 1990). In contrast, students whose social or cultural backgrounds are linked to languages or discourses different from those favored by mainstream groups may need more explicit instruction in the text structures encountered in school and other mainstream settings (Cope & Kalantzis, 1993; Delpit,

1986; A. Freedman, 1993). Delpit (1986), for example, protests what she sees as the neglect of students' explicit learning of mainstream written language structures by many process-oriented writing teachers and calls for direct and explicit instruction of standard written or edited English to be provided for students who, because of their social, cultural, or ethnic backgrounds, speak a dialect of English (e.g., African-American English vernacular) that does not form an easy springboard for acquiring standard written or edited forms.

Genre-based pedagogy, which more strongly reacts against process approaches to writing instruction, is popular especially in Australia and Canada and emphasizes the importance of making written language structures explicit to students as part of teaching them to write different kinds of texts. Scholars of this approach (see reviews in Cope & Kalantzis, 1993) argue that knowledge of written language, in contrast to knowledge of spoken language, does not develop naturally but, rather, develops through instruction in formal learning settings. The function of schooling is to make such knowledge explicit to students as they learn to read and write.

The focus of genre-based pedagogy is on the nature of texts to do things in the world and on the ways in which these texts reflect what they do in their forms. Genre, then, is defined as the relationship between textual features—ranging from global rhetorical to sentence-level syntactic features—and a text's social function and purpose (Cope & Kalantzis, 1993). In the theoretical ideal, genre-based teaching explicates the links among form, function, and social context, helping learners to develop mastery over a range of text types. In Australia, especially, this ideal extends to teaching genre critically, leading students to challenge cultural assumptions found in different mainstream texts, for example, the tendency to evacuate the author's voice or presence in certain kinds of scientific writing. Thus literacy instruction as socialization is balanced with literacy instruction as critique (Cazden, 1993a).

One problem with genre-based pedagogy is that scholars themselves are still debating what it is or should be. This problem is reflected in the concern for whether actual teaching can be true to the theoretical ideal. If, for example, text structures are taught in relationship to social and linguistic context, one might question the value of explicating these structures out of context. Relatedly, we do not know whether genre-based instruction gives students transferable knowledge of language structures, a question that has been raised for both L1 learners (see review in Smagorinsky & Smith, 1992) and L2 learners (Widdowson, 1993). In practice, too, teaching that is genre based has been seen often to focus more on formal text characteristics such as global rhetorical structures or lexical and grammatical features than on the sociocultural assumptions linking such features to contexts (see review in Hyon, 1996).

Unfortunately, little empirical research—and no large-scale studies—show the impact of genre-based pedagogy in writing classrooms (see review in Hyon, 1996). Some English as a Second Language (ESL) research suggests that explicit teaching of rhetorical structures benefits ESL writing development (Swales, 1990). Similarly, evidence from interview data and writing samples in an examination of socially and culturally heterogeneous fifth- and sixth-grade students' writing showed that focusing teaching on the rules and patterns of global discourse characteristics was effective when students also learned about the broader contexts of writing audiences and purposes (Raphael, Englert, & Kirschner, 1986; Raphael, Kirschner, & Englert, 1986). Flower (1994), however, has complicated this picture with case-studies of college freshman writers, concluding that while teaching about written text structures in the context of their broader academic functions is possible, learning in the academy is strongly shaped by each student's own prior knowledge and goals, immediate competing social realities, and the constraints of doing writing for a teacher.

At this point, we do not adequately understand how much explicit knowledge about structure at any level is helpful, to which writers explicit knowledge would be helpful, or under what circumstances it might be helpful. In the coming years, writing researchers will need to address the value of explicit instruction to foster students' acquisition and development of standard edited English. For example, the issues of explicit teaching likely differ depending on what language structures are being learned, that is, whether students are learning about rhetorical structures, syntactic structures, or lexical structures. Teachers always run the risk of formulaic teaching when explicating features and rules, but the danger seems greater as one teaches increasingly higher levels of discourse. One complication is that at higher levels of discourse, structures become less stable over contexts. Spelling, for example, is relatively stable over differing writing situations. Syntax is not so stable, and global rhetorical structures are (ipso facto) the least stable of all. We need research that addresses these distinctions. We also need research that can test explicit teaching methods over diverse learning settings and that can allow for examining how and if students' structural knowledge and skills build and grow across semesters and years under different teaching methods. More importantly, we need continually to ask how we might create learning contexts that, over time, will foster diverse students' acquisition of written language structures.

Some lessons can be learned about teaching formal structures from an already-solid research base in the teaching and learning of spelling and of sentence-level grammar and syntax. A substantial research base has developed in particular on the nature and development of spelling knowledge and skills, especially among preschoolers and primary-grade students. Young students' acquisition of spelling appears to follow a developmental trajectory, as students who are learning to read and write can, without formal spelling instruction, produce spelling forms that increasingly come to match English spelling conventions (see seminal work by Read, 1971; see review in Hodges, 1991). These invented spellings reflect children's attempts to organize sound and letter correspondences and are seen to be an important part of the spelling acquisition process as children discover, through their own spellings, the ways that sounds map onto written words. In this process, the spelling errors that writers make can provide clues to their personal system of phonographemic rules, which teachers can use to help students acquire standard forms. Generally, the studies suggest a balanced teaching approach that recognizes students' invented spellings while leading them in the direction of standard forms. Most of this research, however, is with culturally mainstream students and L1 students. We do not have as much information on culturally diverse writers and L2 writers.

The research on grammar instruction is almost as unequivocal as that on spelling, yet as with research on spelling, much of what we know we have learned from white, middle-class students and L1 students. For example, we have been told from years of research on the teaching of sentence-level grammar that a focus on teaching formal grammar and usage apart from meaningful contexts does not improve students' writing (see meta-analysis by Hillocks, 1986). Grammar instruction has often been associated with worksheet exercises and memorizing rules, thereby displacing other kinds of practice with extended writing. Sentence-combining—the practice of revising two or more short declarative sentences into one larger compound or complex structure—often stresses that students compose their own sentences rather than work with those from a worksheet, yet this practice, too, emphasizes writing at the sentence level, divorced from the context of students' extended pieces. In contrast, teaching that links grammar to students' genuine communicative needs as they attempt to write for real readers appears to benefit students' writing and learning (see review in Sperling, 1996). However, researchers, over time, have not tested any kind of systematic grammar instruction through empirical studies that builds on this assumption. Nor have researchers systematically addressed issues of cultural or language diversity.

WRITING AND SPEAKING INTERTWINED

Dyson and S. W. Freedman (1991) remind us that "in the schools, writing is taught as teachers and students talk about writing" (p. 757). In fact, talk can be an integral instructional support for writing and is widely recognized as such, largely because through talk writers have the opportunity to discuss ideas and strategies with others. Some supportive talk of this sort occurs in one-on-one or small group conversations, as seen in teacher-student writing conferences (private conversations between the teacher and student about the student's writing or writing process) and in student pairs or peer groups designed around a collaborative goal (see reviews in DiPardo & S. W. Freedman, 1988; Sperling, 1996). Dynamics in such configurations can reflect almost prototypically Vygotsky's notions of learning through social interaction: Dyadic or small group contexts allow students and their interlocutors to build on one another's input and help shape writing ideas and strategies through the conversational process. The interactions also reflect Bakhtin's notions that texts are multivoiced, as ideas and strategies for writing become imbued with the collaborative efforts of the writer in dialogue with others (see Dyson & S. W. Freedman, 1991; Nystrand et al., 1993; Sperling, 1996). While they are theoretically appealing, however, the effectiveness of such conversations for students' writing development can be mixed (see reviews in DiPardo & S. W. Freedman, 1988; Sperling, 1996).

Teacher-student writing conferences, rather than conventional classroom I-R-E exchanges (in which the teacher *initiates* by asking a question or providing a prompt, the student *responds,* and the teacher *evaluates* the response), appear to be the most valuable, especially for students to explore and develop their ideas. In Sperling's (1990) case study of writing conferences among ninth-grade students and their teacher, conferences became more conversationally interactive and less like teacher-led classroom exchanges over the course of the semester, in part, because students in this classroom had many opportunities to confer with their teacher and got used to doing so. In these conferences, too, instructional purposes varied, from planning unwritten texts to revising already-written drafts to clarifying the teacher's written comments, which gave individual students opportunities to interact when the purpose was important to them. Such multiple and varied teacher-student conversations, however, do not always occur in writing classrooms. Further, writing conference conversations can be marked by miscommunication and "missed opportunities for learning" (see review of college-level conferences, Prior, 1998) or more resemble teacher monologues than dialogues, especially when teachers press to get across their own agendas for students' work (see review in Sperling, 1996).

Taken together, the studies on writing conferences suggest that problems occur in conferences when certain conversational conditions are not met: when teachers and students assume the kinds of conventional classroom roles that allow teachers to dominate conference talk; when, for experiential or cultural reasons, students and teachers follow inconsistent rule systems for teacher-student interaction; and when conferences do not take place within otherwise supportive classrooms.

Group conversations among peers work best when student writers talk as equals and do tasks that allow them to take on the natural roles that they are comfortable assuming with one another (S. W. Freedman, 1992). In case studies, Freedman found that under these circumstances, peers can provide helpful feedback that is qualitatively different from the teacher's and that peers can work especially well together when solving a jointly owned problem, as was the case when they composed collaboratively or when they generated ideas for everyone to use. This finding is consistent with more general findings on how groups function in the classroom (e.g., see work on cooperative learning groups, Sharon, 1984; Slavin, 1980). However, when peers are asked to take on roles that require them to assume power over one another or when the teacher controls the conversation in the peer group through explicit directives and evaluation of peer activity, peers have difficulty helping one another. For example, teachers commonly ask group members to evaluate one another and thereby take on the role of expert. They also commonly attempt to control the activity by asking group members to complete evaluation forms on each piece of writing and to turn in those forms to the teacher. In such cases, group members have to balance pleasing the teacher with maintaining their friendships with their peers, goals that often work at cross-purposes. These conflicting roles, not surprisingly, can create interactional difficulties. Students also run into difficulty when they are expected to act as experts in relation to one another because they often are not expert enough to provide helpful advice (S. W. Freedman, 1992; see also review in DiPardo & S. W. Freedman, 1988).

In sum, it is important for teachers to think carefully about the roles they are asking students to assume and the kinds of tasks they are asking them to perform in peer response groups. Also important is the need for teachers to align roles and tasks so they are comfortable for the students and will enable them to advance their learning. Such an environment is flexible and attentive to individual differences and fosters communication about issues of genuine significance to students—a workplace organized and guided by a teacher, but one that offers writers opportunities to solicit feedback from peers and from the teacher in support of their evolving, individual needs (Di-Pardo & S. W. Freedman, 1988). In such a collaborative classroom, teaching can spring free of its traditional connotations—including the urge to dominate—in favor of a less intrusive monitoring and shaping approach. It appears that if peer interactions around writing are to take root and flourish, they must be grounded in a theoretic foundation that embraces this Deweyan (Dewey, 1938) vision of the teaching and learning process.

Interactional patterns in the classroom also affect what L2 writers learn in ways that are consistent with the effects on L1 learners. Gutierrez (1992) studied whole-class interactions in 7 second- and third-grade "writing process" classrooms with large numbers of Latino students. She found that the same activity (e.g., journal writing, author's chair, and peer response groups) differed depending on the more general interactional patterns of the classroom. In the mostly recitation classrooms, teachers kept rigid control of the conversation, giving students little room to participate meaningfully. Talk was characterized by teachers asking known-answer questions, with a focus on getting students to give the right answer and on transmitting information. The use of the I-R-E structure in classrooms predominated. This type of classroom proved least successful as measured both by student participation and by student writing. At the other pole, the mostly responsive and collaborative classroom, having features consistent with the kind of classroom described by DiPardo and S. W. Freedman, proved most successful for language learning, particularly for learning oral language.

Writing and Reading

Scholars have made serious calls over the last decade or so for research and practice to emphasize writing and reading connections (see, e.g., Dyson, 1986; S. W. Freedman et al., 1987; Langer & Allington, 1992; Nelson & Calfee, 1998; Tierney & Shanahan, 1991). In their review of research on writing-reading relationships, Tierney and Shanahan call specifically for integrating writing and reading under the rubric of "literacy."

Given the prodigious body of historical and anthropological accounts of literacy in the United States and elsewhere that encompasses both writing and reading, such suggestions seem remarkable insofar as they have to be made at all. Yet, historically, writing and reading have followed different paths in both curriculum and research (for accounts of these divergent paths, see Clifford, 1986; review by Langer & Allington, 1992; Nelson & Calfee, 1998). Relatedly, pedagogical philosophies based on "integrated language arts," an idea with a relatively long philosophical history, remain the topic of much discussion among theorists and practitioners alike, with whole language and writing process philosophies likely the most talked-about present-day examples. In fact, surveys of writing and reading practices across U.S. schools indicate that a large portion of classrooms still ignore integrated approaches (see reports of the NAEP: Applebee, Langer, Mullis, Latham, & Gentile, 1994), and research has yet to develop a comprehensive theory of writing and reading that can guide such approaches across diverse learning settings.

Still, research has been able to refine the conceptual connection between writing and reading, leading to two generalizations on this topic: (a) writing and reading are distinct but related processes, and (b) writing and reading are intertwined and interconnected in day-to-day practice. These generalizations suggest two related questions: (a) "What can we learn about writing and writers through comparisons to reading and readers?" and (b) "In what ways is writing part of a broader literate landscape?"

WRITING AND READING COMPARED

Two common approaches to connecting writing and reading conceptually are either to compare students' writing and reading performances or to compare students' cognitive processes as they write and read different types of texts. The first route puts a good deal of focus on students' writing and reading test scores or evaluations, taking these as indicators of students' skills and knowledge, while the second depends on think-aloud protocols to trace and describe students' thinking as they write and read. Generally, however, the research has been inconclusive (see review in Tierney & Shanahan, 1991).

Early work such as Loban's (1976) longitudinal study of students' writing and reading performances at multiple grade levels suggested a correlation between the quality of students' writing and their reading comprehension. However, later studies of students' writing and reading skills suggested that there were no easy correlations between the two. In particular, students, who on different measures were deemed good readers, were not necessarily deemed good writers—an observation that, from a commonsensical perspective, was not all that surprising. What was surprising, however, were those studies that showed good writers were not necessarily good readers. Unreliable measures and cross-study inconsistency mars many of these findings, however, and such research raises one question: Do we help students by relying on product-based measures while ignoring students' underlying thinking processes as they write and read (see review in Tierney & Shanahan, 1991)?

Unlike performance-based research, explorations of cognitive processes not only are able to capture writing and reading comparatively but also can test and contribute to cognitive models of the writing and reading process (e.g., de Beaugrande, 1984; Flower et al., 1990; Kucer, 1985; Martin, 1987; Squire, 1984; Tierney & Pearson, 1983; Wittrock, 1984). As Tierney and Shanahan point out, these models, with their focus on writing and reading as meaning-making activities, generally suggest that writing and reading can be defined in terms of the same general cognitive processes. For example, the Tierney and Pearson model includes for both writing and reading the strategies of goal setting, knowledge mobilization, projection, perspective-taking, refinement, review, self-correction, and self-assessment; the Martin model includes monitoring, phrasing content, invoking knowledge of content and text form, rereading, questioning, inferencing, and making connections. In such models, differences between writing and reading are said to reside in the extent to which students invoke various strategies at different times in the writing and reading process. However, after studying the story and report writing and reading of 67 third-, sixth-, and ninth-grade students, Langer (1986) concluded that although writers and readers may share certain strategies, writing and reading are each too complex, with patterns of cognitive behavior differing substantially within each, to assume they are similar activities.

Considering writing and reading within real instructional contexts helps to reveal this complexity and to highlight the connection between literate processes and contextual variables (see review in Greene & Ackerman, 1996). The consideration of context, in fact, highlights the ways writing and reading are intertwined as thinking processes and interwoven in everyday practice.

WRITING AND READING INTERTWINED

The many ways writing and reading are intertwined are revealed in the research laboratory and observed in classroom activity. From research, especially, we know that writers must read their own texts in the process of writing and revising and that writers must anticipate and incorporate the reading of others as they make their texts sensible in particular literate contexts. By observing what occurs in classrooms, we know that students often are asked to read and interpret others' texts in order to create their own—a process that Flower and her colleagues (Flower et al., 1990) call "reading-to-write"—and writing is often used to foster students' learning from others' texts (see review in S. W. Freedman et al., 1987). Given these various connections between writing and reading, how these relationships play out for different students in different school contexts is of particular interest.

READING AS PART OF THE WRITING PROCESS

A major component of both early and recent models of the writing process (e.g., Flower, 1994; Hayes & Flower, 1980; Kucer, 1985) is the influence on the writer of text already written. On the basis of their already-written texts, writers read and write or read and revise throughout the writing process.

We know that adult expert writers, when compared to adult novices, read and reflect more on their own emerging texts. The critical components in this discrepancy between novice and expert seem to be that, in rereading their texts, skilled writers are shaping their evolving texts to meet readers' needs and to fulfill the purposes of the assignment. Through also rereading their assignment, these writers often build progressive representations of their audience, spending much time thinking about how they want to affect it (on the effects of reading representations on writing, see Flower & Hayes, 1981, 1984; Hayes & Flower, 1980; Sommers, 1980; see also, review in Scardamalia & Bereiter, 1986; on the effects of readers' rhetorical representations on comprehension, see Haas & Flower, 1988).

Along with the generous number of L1 studies yielding information on this writing and reading connection, researchers recently have begun to put together a picture of this connection from an L2 perspective. Some evidence has been found that L2 writers less frequently reread and reflect on their written texts than L1 writers and that, in spite of reading their evolving texts less often, they revise them more. L2 students, unlike L1 students, appear not to revise based on how their texts sound, but, rather, by invoking rules of grammar, surely a more arduous

and self-conscious reading and reviewing process (see review in Silva, 1993; see also, Perl, 1979). Hull (1987) found a similar pattern among less skilled college writers. These observations should not suggest that, as L2 writers read and reflect on their writing, they are no different from the novice L1 writers seen in earlier studies. Yet to fully understand this distinction, we need to investigate how the special circumstances of and constraints on reading while composing in a second language may alter the writing process for L2 writers such that the process becomes a more laborious undertaking.

ANTICIPATING AND INCORPORATING THE READING OF OTHERS

Students who are taught to consider their readers have been found to write better than those who are not, and writing that reveals reader-directed adaptations has generally been perceived to be of higher quality than writing that does not (see reviews in Sperling, 1996; Tierney & Shanahan, 1991). Adaptations are usually gleaned from features such as syntactic complexity and rhetorical structuring, including strategies such as elaborating and giving orienting information through which writers establish a shared background and perspective with their readers.

Generally, older and more proficient writers control such strategies differently than younger or less proficient writers. For example, basic writers, even at the college level, often make implicit and erroneous assumptions about the kinds of information and language that their readers will be able to follow when reading their texts. As a result, writing that is fully comprehensible to the writer may seem, in one way or another, elliptical to readers. Such writing is said to reflect the writer's difficulty in taking a point of view (the reader's) that may differ from the writer's. Flower (1979) dubbed this kind of writing "writer-based prose."

The prodigious amount of research on L1 writing, especially at the college level, overwhelms the scant work as yet reported and reviewed for L2 writing. The little evidence presented on L2 strategies, however, suggests that many L2 writers may approach readers quite differently than L1, basic-level writers. One study (Scarcella, 1984) found that L2 writers produced longer reader orientations (defined as material preceding the introduction of a thesis statement), used more clarifying devices to help readers understand their themes, and, in doing so, included more obvious information that appeared to underestimate their readers' knowledge. Another study of native Arabic speakers (Atari, 1983) found that students included introductory statements that were too broadly orienting and general for the essay. The studies do not tell us, however, the extent to which these strategies are conscious and deliberate (see review in Silva, 1993).

L1 and L2 writers may exhibit different approaches to anticipating their readers, yet a single critical aspect of the writing process likely explains the gap between them, namely the central role in their writing played by social and cultural knowledge and background. In particular, whereas L1, basic-level writers may tend to assume too readily that they and their readers share knowledge and background, thus leaving much left unsaid or implicit in their writing, L2 writers, on the other hand, may be unsure of such shared understanding and over-compensate by saying too much. Unfortunately, we have too few studies of L2 writers to firmly support this intellectually appealing polarity.

Learning to Anticipate Readers. Students can successfully be taught to anticipate their readers as part of the writing process. One way to heighten students' sense of their readers is to manipulate assignments to specify audience; another way is to focus instruction so students discuss and learn about their readers. Much of the research in teaching audience awareness was conducted in the late 1980s on L1 writing and followed experimental designs comparing treatment groups. These studies show that (a) assignments for real audiences affect writers' composing more than assignments directed at imaginary audiences or no audiences at all, (b) the teacher-as-audience likely has less effect on writing than audiences other than the teacher, and (c) sensitivity to audience is enhanced when the writer is given information on the reader's viewpoint or has experience with the kinds of problems readers encounter. This research has tended to focus on older writers, however, and though some investigators have compared better and poorer writers, they have generally not addressed writers' experiential or cultural background in this work (see reviews in Sperling, 1996; Tierney & Shanahan, 1991).

Learning from Reader Response. Writers also develop a sense of readership by receiving response from readers to texts already completed or in various stages of planning and drafting. In classrooms, such response comes primarily from teachers but often, also, from peers. The practice of giving writers response follows from the psycholinguistic premise that feedback is key to language acquisition and development, including both written and spoken language. Response practice is also consistent with Vygotskian and Bakhtinian conceptions of the social nature of language wherein individuals learn language by using it in social contexts. In classrooms, response traditionally comes in the form of teachers' written comments on students' papers, but, less traditionally, it also emerges in conversations with teachers and peers meant to help students with their writing. Given at various stages of writing and revising, such response figures importantly in writing process classrooms. All forms of response, however, are not equally effective in all writing situations.

TEACHERS' WRITTEN COMMENTS. If given unaccompanied by other kinds of response, written comments by the teacher may be especially problematic (see review in Hillocks, 1986). In general, investigators have found that comments on mechanics and form tend to dominate or overshadow comments on ideas, knowledge, or disciplinary values; comments often carry more meaning for the teacher who is writing them than for the student who must interpret and use them; comments often function more to justify a grade than to serve students' writing development; comments tend to become formulaic, telegraphic, or full of jargon as teachers face large paper loads and have to make do with responding in the most efficient ways to the greatest number of students; and students often discount comments, seeing them as reflections of their teachers' "confused read-ings" rather than their own writing weaknesses (see reviews in Dyson & S. W. Freedman, 1991; Hillocks, 1986; Prior, 1998; Sperling, 1996, 1998). Further, comments tend to make the teacher's reading paramount, leaving students little opportunity to practice evaluating their own progress (Dyson & S. W. Freedman, 1991).

Taken together, the many studies suggest that teachers' written comments cannot stand on their own in conveying to students how teachers read their work. One problem with written comments is that, as an abbreviated medium of communication, they easily accommodate conventionalized editorial or prescriptive response. Even when teachers transcend such response, however, students may misinterpret teachers' comments or ignore them altogether, because a shared interpretive context does not always exist when teachers write and students read the comments, (see review in Sperling, 1998).

Preconceptions of students' capabilities can unduly influence student performance and teachers' assessments of students' performance; this is not recent news among educators (Weinstein, 1989). Not surprisingly, such preconceptions can affect the ways teachers interpret (or misinterpret) students' texts and can result in problematic written responses. The most convincing evidence of such teacher misinterpretations comes from case studies of response, including evidence that this problem can be particularly acute for culturally diverse students whose teachers do not share their cultural backgrounds and, thus, misinterpret and respond inappropriately to their communicative practices (e.g., Hull, Rose, Fraser, & Castellano, 1991; see also, review in Prior, 1998).

Sperling (1994) extends such observations, offering a framework for describing the teacher as a reader of students' writing. According to this framework, teacher response can reflect a teacher's different social roles in relationship to different students (e.g., literary scholar, friend, editor); the different interpretive lenses a teacher brings to students' texts (personal, cultural, popular, academic); a teacher's cognitive and emotive reactions to different students and their texts; a teacher's pedagogical purposes for different students and for giving particular assignments; and a teacher's evaluative stances (positive, negative). All these components feed into the response process, yet in Sperling's case study, the latter two, especially, dominated students' interpretations of their teachers' written comments. Students tended to see their teachers' responses as reflecting, above all, a school-based authority to exact particular writing behaviors and to reward good writing or punish poor writing through grades. This situation is corroborated in a number of other studies (see reviews in Dyson & S. W. Freedman, 1991; S. W. Freedman, with Greenleaf & Sperling, 1987; Nystrand et al., 1993).

TEACHER–STUDENT WRITING CONFERENCES. Given the constraints on reader response seen in teacher-written comments, the impetus has been strong to explore the potential of teacher-student writing conferences to provide responses to writing. These face-to-face conversations hold the promise of allowing writers and readers to establish a shared context for communication. Ideally, during conferences, students and their teacher readers can continually shape and reshape meanings and clarify meanings for one another, and the teacher's response to a student's text can evolve through this interaction (see earlier discussion of writing conferences in the section on writing and speaking).

This conceptual ideal is supported by a variety of studies from elementary level through college (see review in S. W. Freedman et al., 1987). Conferences have the effect of allowing students, especially higher achieving students, to talk about ideas rather than mechanics and of allowing students and teachers to collaborate in thinking about the students' text. However, as we indicated earlier, even in conferences, students can find it difficult to see their teacher-reader as more than a directive teacher-evaluator unless teachers and students shift their talk from conventional I-R-E routines to more fully interactive and spontaneous discussion. This shift may be particularly difficult and also culturally inappropriate when students bring diverse experiential and cultural backgrounds to such conversations.

PEER RESPONSE. In part because the teacher is really only one reader and a powerful presence in the classroom, studies of peer response have sought to examine the kinds of roles peers can play in providing response, both within and outside the classroom. Peers generally are expected to broaden and emphasize the audience for writing. In most cases, when peers serve as readers and responders, the writers take their turns at responding to the writing of others. This reciprocal opportunity for response ideally allows students to take new points of view on their own writing and to see more clearly its strengths and weaknesses.

Inside classrooms, some research shows that groups work well to help students revise, leading writers to reconceptualize their ideas and focus on the substance of what they want to communicate, while other studies uncover problems with peer response. For example, Gere and Stevens (1985) found that high school students, unlike their teachers, were not inclined to ask writers to conform to an ideal of good writing but, rather, were more inclined to engage with the content of the writing. Similarly, at the college level, Nystrand (1986) found that peers engaged with what a writer tried to say, often leading writers to reconceptualize their ideas. By contrast, Newkirk (1984), also working with college students, found that the students he studied engaged with content but that they had difficulty putting aside their own idiosyncratic ideas and listening to what the writer was trying to say. Berkenkotter (1984) showed that peer feedback was confusing to writers. In the end, it seems that the ways groups are organized and the context in which they are enacted exert powerful influences on the kinds of feedback students give and on the effectiveness of that feedback. Possibly for this reason S. W. Freedman (S. W. Freedman, with Greenleaf & Sperling, 1987) found that expert teachers were deeply divided about the usefulness of peer response. More research is needed on the ways classroom structures and teachers' philosophies relate to peer structures and ultimately to the effectiveness of peer response.

In contrast to response that comes from classroom peer groups, response that comes from students outside the classroom is generally less direct and often comes as an aside to other, more central between-class activities. For example, S. W. Freedman (1994) describes writing exchanges between second-

ary school classes in the United States paired with secondary school classes in Great Britain. As part of the U.S.-British exchanges, the students in each country sometimes responded spontaneously to one another's writing. These responses were embedded in the students' own writing and addressed what students from the paired class had to say. Sometimes these responses were directed to individual students, but more often they took the form of comments to an entire set of papers. Students' reactions to papers written by students from the paired class influenced their attention to details such as mechanics and form in their own writing. In addition, there were times when teachers asked students in their classes to study the writing of their peers from abroad and to analyze what made writing appealing and accessible. Exchanges of this sort have also been studied by Heath and Branscombe (1985), who set up a situation in which older students responded to the writing of younger students, essentially playing the role of teacher. In this exchange, the younger students were influenced by the model letters the older students wrote and by the explicit feedback directed toward them. More research is needed on the effects of broadening the audience for response to student writing and on the role of direct and teacher-like response versus the kind of natural response that occurs as students attempt to communicate through writing.

READING AND INTERPRETING OTHERS' TEXTS

Writing in school contexts means, primarily, personal experience narratives at the elementary level and expository or argumentative writing at the secondary and postsecondary levels (S. W. Freedman, 1994; Vahapassi, 1988). In high school, the most frequent writing (though not necessarily the focus of writing instruction) is writing about literature as students read and interpret other authors' texts. In college, argumentative essays can be the mainstay of both composition and content area courses. Here, typical writing assignments emphasize reading and interpreting other authors' texts in order to advance one's own stance on a topic (see Flower et al., 1990).

Multiple factors distinguish writing that involves interpreting others' texts from other kinds of writing and make such text-interpretive writing especially difficult for some students (see review in Greene & Ackerman, 1996). In such writing, writers must synthesize and restructure outside text information to make it useful to their own writing purposes, the primary purpose being to connect outside texts to their own. When making these connections, they must consider the discipline's expectations for acceptable discourse content and structure. And they must decide on their abilities and rights as students to contribute unique perspectives on topics that others, usually experts, have written about. Greene and Ackerman see this process to be a critical intellectual step, marking students' entry into the kind of academic conversation that is central to postsecondary education. Not surprisingly, older students and students considered to be more mature readers have been seen in correlational studies to better succeed in this process: They write more sophisticated argumentative papers, which include incorporating greater amounts of source text information, pinpointing ideas better, and integrating and elaborating more on different levels of ideas (see review in Tierney & Shanahan, 1991).

Flower and her colleagues (Flower et al., 1990) suggest that often students go about interpreting, synthesizing, and restructuring texts in vastly different ways. Their research examined the writing processes of 72 college writers faced with an assignment specifically asking them to advance an argument based on their interpretations of source texts. Students in only a few cases analyzed the source texts in order to make an original argument, as the assignment intended. Many opted instead to write straightforward summaries of the texts they read or to use the readings as springboards for focusing on their own ideas. Interestingly, just as students have been seen to interpret such assignments differently, instructors have been seen to represent such assignments differently in class (see review in Prior, 1998).

Taken together, the studies indicate that producing expository essays from reading is influenced only partly by reading ability or the writing task itself. This writing is also—and perhaps especially—influenced by a number of other factors, including topic knowledge, knowledge of the discourse conventions of different disciplines, and beliefs about what counts and what works when ideas are linked to those found in other texts. The latter two factors, especially, draw on culturally and experientially influenced notions of appropriate academic discourse.

Evidence has surfaced from a handful of studies, many of them case studies, that these factors may have particular implications for basic writers, students from diverse cultural backgrounds, and L2 writers (these groups often overlap). In a case study of one college-level basic writer, Hull and Rose (1990) found that the student's particular beliefs about what constituted plagiarism, based on years of warnings about plagiarism in low-level writing courses, greatly constrained her strategies for writing based on reading. The student so restructured the content and wording of the source text in order to write about it that she effectively derailed her own writing. Other case studies show that basic writers and writers from different cultures are reluctant to exert their own authority on a topic when their writing draws on outside texts written by experts, even when that authority shows up in other classroom situations (Goen, 1997; Greene, 1995).

L2 students may have particular difficulties with when and how to incorporate source text information in their writing, yet evidence to this effect comes primarily from text analyses, making it impossible to tell whether the students' writing problems stem from not knowing certain written conventions such as where to include source text information and how to ground it or, rather, whether students do not know how or when to express their own ideas in relation to others in the social and cultural contexts of writing in school (see review in Silva, 1993).

USING WRITING TO LEARN FROM TEXTS

A widely embraced view connecting writing and reading is that writing fosters text-based learning: In particular, writing aids in comprehending and recalling text and in learning new text material. This view is motivated in part by a large body of research conducted primarily in the 1960s and 1970s showing that when students actively manipulate or elaborate on the texts they read, their text understanding increases as does their text memory (see review in Applebee, 1984). This conclusion and its companion view that, through writing, students can more thought-fully explore text-based ideas and situations has been supported by a number of studies, including studies focused on writing about literature and studies exploring writing's connection to learning from science or social science texts (e.g., Langer & Applebee, 1987; see review in Tierney & Shanahan, 1991).

In taking this view, researchers have distinguished between different functions of writing and the ways those functions variably affect learning from texts. The concept of writing functions is taken largely from the work of James Britton (1970; Britton, Burgess, Martin, McLeod, & Rosen, 1975), who suggested that writing could be classified according to writers' cognitive processes and writers' social contexts for writing, rather than according to more traditional distinctions based on the form of the finished product (narration, description, exposition, or argument). Britton offered three such categories of writing functions: (a) transactional writing—writing that serves to transact business and provide information (including essays and reports); (b) expressive writing—writing that, with formal rules relaxed, allows the writer to think through ideas much as one would in informal talk among friends (including journal writing and diaries); and (c) poetic writing—writing that functions literarily (including poetry, story, and drama).

To study the effects that different writing functions have on learning, researchers have generally focused on the transactional category: restricted school writing tasks such as short answers written to text-based questions, the kind that students typically encounter at the ends of chapters to aid studying; and different kinds of extended writing tasks, also typically encountered in school, including note-taking, text summary, and text analysis. All extended transactional writing is more effective than restricted writing for gathering, consolidating, and reviewing relevant information and ideas. Extended analytic writing, in particular, has been associated with examining the relationships among ideas and is seen by many researchers to entail more complex subject-matter understanding than other transactional writing tasks—although analytic writing involves focusing on a generally narrower range of text content when compared to other transactional tasks (see reviews in Durst & Newell, 1989; Newell, 1998; Tierney & Shanahan, 1991).

Despite a body of research showing links between the functions of students' writing and their learning from texts, the picture is more complex than research sometimes suggests. For example, learning from texts also depends on individual differences among learners (see review in Tierney & Shanahan, 1991). One individual difference that matters a great deal in students' learning is the prior knowledge they bring to writing and learning tasks (see review in Newell, 1998).

Questioning claims that writing leads to learning, Ackerman (1993)—after reviewing 35 frequently cited studies—critiques the writing and learning research on a number of grounds. In particular, he questions whether writing tasks, claimed to be extended, really are; whether learning is always soundly operationalized (for example, many studies equate learning with remembering); and whether the researchers don't expect to find a writing and learning connection, thus biasing their interpretations of findings which may not always support this connection. Ackerman also questions whether many writing and learning studies adequately consider the range of academic variables that can affect writing and learning connections. For example, writing-to-learn studies have often ignored the diverse ways of knowing and doing that are associated with different academic disciplines and fields (Newell, 1998; Sperling, 1996).

Behind the writing and learning research, of course, is a fundamental belief that particular kinds of writing can be exploited for students' cognitive growth and development. Yet many scholars have suggested that cultural biases lie behind this strong claim. Writing practices (e.g., personal writing, writing that challenges authority, and writing that explores new ideas) carry cultural values, and writing cannot in and of itself lead to learning without some congruity of values between the writer and the writing task (see review in Newell, 1998). Such biases might better be understood were researchers to study the issue of writing and learning connections across different cultural contexts and among students from diverse cultural backgrounds who may bring various approaches to literacy learning in school.

The Future: Research and Practice

Over the years, arguments surface that writing cannot be taught, that gifted writers, just as gifted orators, musicians, and visual artists, inherit their gifts. The best that the public schools can do is nurture those with special talents by providing elective creative writing classes. Just a few decades ago, before the writing process movement helped to make writing a curricular focus, sustained writing was rarely expected outside the English class; and even in the usual English class, the teacher did not attempt to teach writing beyond assigning essays to test how well students could interpret a piece of literature. The main feedback students received came in the form of teachers' corrections, usually written in red pen, usually focused on grammar, and usually formulated to justify the grade more than to teach the student (see review in Sperling, 1998). In spite of research findings to the contrary (see reviews in Braddock, Lloyd Jones, & Shoer, 1963; Hillocks, 1986), teachers also believed that students would improve their writing by studying formal grammar. Hence, writing instruction consisted largely of assigning and correcting papers coupled with grammar drills.

Important findings from writing research, combined with social pressures to include writing as a prominent part of the curriculum, however, have revolutionized classroom practices over the past several decades. In our best schools today, children write extended stories in the early grades; as they grow older, they use writing to learn across the curriculum—from social studies and English classes to math and science; and across the grades, they write in varied ways, for varied purposes, and for varied audiences. We are making progress, and classroom practice is charting out new directions. Nonetheless, we still have a long way to go before all our students have adequate writing and literacy skills. The need only increases for research that addresses the range of students and the range of contexts in which their writing and literacy skills will develop.

Research grounded in sociocognitive and sociocultural perspectives, which has been especially prevalent in the past decade, has gone a long way to connect our thinking about writing to this student range, especially to students' linguistic and cultural diversity, and to connect our thinking about writing instruction and learning to the range of language and literacy practices that shape students as writers and as learners in school. With the research evidence gleaned from this past decade, we have learned that trying to generalize the writing and literacy learning experience for all of our students adds little value.

In the next decade, writing researchers will have to continue focusing on issues related to writing and literacy learning in light of students' language and cultural diversity and, in doing so, will have to grapple with three challenging tasks: (a) refining principles of writing and learning to write so they transcend sociocultural and linguistic contexts, (b) understanding patterns in writing and learning to write that are influenced by particular differences in these contexts, and (c) understanding how (a) and (b) are related to and inform one another. Thus, it will be necessary continually to assess and reassess notions of writing competency across grade levels and how grade level intersects with experiential differences, with the English language, and with written discourse. Relatedly, we will need to keep enlarging our notions of writing instruction and learning in ways that recognize the role of writing in the context of language and literacy practices that are valued in schools and in other social contexts. We believe that the focus of this review on the connections between writing and broader language and literacy practices provides both a reasonable and an exciting synthesis for helping to launch the next decade of writing research.

REFERENCES

Ackerman, J. M. (1993). The promise of writing to learn. *Written Communication, 10*(3), 334–370.

Applebee, A. N. (1984). Writing and reasoning. *Review of Educational Research, 54*(4), 577–596.

Applebee, A. N. (1986). Problems in process approaches: Toward a reconceptualization of process instruction. In A. Petrosky & D. Bartholomae (Eds.), *The Teaching of Writing, 85th Yearbook of the National Society for the Study of Education* (Part II, pp. 95–113). Chicago: University of Chicago Press.

Applebee, A. N., Langer, J. A., Mullis, I. V. S., Latham, A. S., & Gentile, C. A. (1994). *NAEP 1992 writing report card* (Report No. 23-W01). Washington, DC: Office of Educational Research and Improvement, U.S. Department of Education.

Atari, O. (1983). A contrastive analysis of Arab and American university students' strategies in accomplishing written English discourse functions. (Doctoral dissertation). *Dissertation Abstracts International, 44* (11), 3307A.

Au, K. (1980). Participation structures in a reading lesson with Hawaiian children: Analysis of a culturally appropriate instructional event. *Anthropology and Education Quarterly, 11,* 91–115.

Bakhtin, M. M. (1986). *Speech genres and other late essays.* Austin, TX: University of Texas Press.

Bereiter, C., & Scardamalia, M. (1987). *The psychology of written composition.* Hillsdale, NJ: Lawrence Erlbaum Associates.

Berkenkotter, C. (1984). Student writers and their sense of authority over text. *College Composition and Communication, 35*(3), 312–319.

Berkenkotter, C., & Huckin, T. (1993). Rethinking genre from a sociocognitive perspective. *Written Communication, 4*(4), 475–509.

Bizzell, P. (1986). Composing processes: An overview. In A. Petrosky & D. Bartholomae (Eds.), *The Study of the teaching of writing: 85th yearbook of the National Society for Education* (Part II, pp. 49–70). Chicago: University of Chicago Press.

Bracewell, R. J., & Witte, S. P. (1997, March). *The implications of activity, practice, and semiotic theory for cognitive constructs of writing.* Paper presented at the annual meeting of the American Educational Research Association, Chicago, IL.

Braddock, R., Lloyd Jones, R., & Shoer, L. (1963). *Research in written composition.* Urbana, IL: National Council of Teachers of English.

Brandt, D. (1992). The cognitive as the social: An ethnomethodological approach to writing process research. *Written Communication, 9*(3), 315–355.

Britton, J. (1970). *Language and learning.* Middlesex, England: Penguin.

Britton, J., Burgess, T., Martin, N., McLeod, A., & Rosen, H. (1975). *The development of writing abilities (11–18).* London: Macmillan.

Bruner, J. (1978). The role of dialogue in language acquisition. In A. Sinclair, R. J. Jarvella, & W. Levelt (Eds.), *The child's concept of language* (pp. 241–255). New York: Springer-Verlag.

Calfee, R., & Drum, P. (1986). Research on teaching reading. In M. C. Wittrock (Ed.), *Handbook of research on teaching* (3rd ed., pp. 804–849). New York: Macmillan.

Cazden, C. B. (1988). *Classroom discourse: The language of teaching and learning.* Portsmouth, NH: Heinemann.

Cazden, C. B. (1993a). Foreword. In B. Cope & M. Kalantzis (Eds.), *The powers of literacy: A genre approach to teaching writing* (pp. ix–x). London: Falmer Press.

Cazden, C. B. (1993b). Vygotsky, Hymes, and Bakhtin. In E. A. Forman, N. Minick, & C. A. Stone (Eds.), *Contexts for learning: Sociocultural dynamics in children's development* (pp. 197–212). New York: Oxford University Press.

Chafe, W., & Tannen, D. (1987). The relation between written and spoken language. *Annual Review of Anthropology, 16,* 383–407.

Clifford, G. J. (1986). A Sisyphean task: Historical perspectives on writing and reading instruction. In A. H. Dyson (Ed.), *Collaboration through writing and reading: Exploring possibilities* (pp. 25–83). Urbana, IL: National Council of Teachers of English.

Cochran-Smith, M. (1991). Word processing and writing in elementary classrooms: A critical review of related literature. *Review of Educational Research, 61*(1), 107–155.

Cope, B., & Kalantzis, M. (Eds.). (1993). *The powers of literacy: A genre approach to teaching writing.* London: Falmer Press.

de Beaugrande, R. (1984). *Text production: Toward a science of composition.* Norwood, NJ: Ablex.

Delpit, L. (1986). Skills and other dilemmas of a progressive black educator. *Harvard Educational Review, 56*(4), 379–385.

Delpit, L. (1995). *Other people's children.* New York: New Press.

Dewey, J. (1938). *Experience and education.* New York: Collier Books, Macmillan.

DiPardo, A., & Freedman, S. W. (1988). Peer response groups in the writing classroom: Theoretic foundations and new directions. *Review of Educational Research, 58*(2), 119–149.

Durst, R. K. (1990). The mongoose and the rat in composition research: Insights from the RTE annotated bibliography. *College Composition and Communication, 41*(4), 393–408.

Durst, R. K., & Newell, G. E. (1989). The uses of function: James Britton's category system and research on writing. *Review of Educational Research, 59*(4), 375–394.

Dyson, A. H. (Ed.). (1986). *Collaboration through writing and reading: Exploring possibilities.* Urbana, IL: National Council of Teachers of English.

Dyson, A. H. (1993). *Social worlds of children learning to write in an urban primary school.* New York: Teachers College Press.

Dyson, A. H., & Freedman, S. W. (1991). Writing. In J. Flood, J. Jensen, D. Lapp, & J. Squire (Eds.), *Handbook of research on teaching the English language arts* (pp. 754–774). New York: Macmillan.

Flower, L. S. (1979). Writer-based prose: A cognitive basis for problems in writing. *College English, 41*(1), 19–37.

Flower, L. S. (1989). Cognition, context, and theory building. *College Composition and Communication, 40*(3), 282–311.

Flower, L. S. (1994). *The construction of negotiated meaning: A social cognitive theory of writing.* Carbondale, IL: Southern Illinois University Press.

Flower, L. S., & Hayes, J. R. (1981). A cognitive process theory of writing. *College Composition and Communication, 32*(4), 365–387.

Flower, L. S., & Hayes, J. R. (1984). Images, plans, and prose: The representation of meaning in writing. *Written Communication, 1*(1), 120–160.

Flower, L. S., Stein, V., Ackerman, J. M., Kantz, P., McCormick, K., & Peck, W. (1990). *Reading to write: Exploring a cognitive and social process.* New York: Oxford University Press.

Forman, E. A., Minick, N., & Stone, C. A. (1993). *Contexts for learning: Sociocultural dynamics in children's development.* New York: Oxford University Press.

Freedman, A. (1993). Show and tell? The role of explicit teaching in the learning of new genres. *Research in the Teaching of English, 27*(3), 222–251.

Freedman, S. W. (1992). Outside-in and inside-out: Peer response groups in two ninth-grade classes. *Research in the Teaching of English, 26*(1), 71–107.

Freedman, S. W. (1994). *Exchanging writing, exchanging cultures: Lessons in school reform from the United States and Great Britain.* Urbana, IL: National Council of Teachers of English, and Cambridge, MA: Harvard University Press.

Freedman, S. W. (1996). Moving writing research into the 21st century. In L. Z. Bloom, D. A. Daiker, & E. M. White (Eds.), *Composition in the twenty-first century: Crisis and change* (pp. 183–193). Carbondale, IL: Southern Illinois University Press.

Freedman, S. W., Dyson, A. H., Flower, L. S., & Chafe, W. (1987). *Writing research: Past, present, future* (Technical Report No. 1). Berkeley, CA: Center for the Study of Writing.

Freedman, S. W., with Greenleaf, C., & Sperling, M. (1987). *Response to student writing* (Research Report No. 23). Urbana, IL: National Council of Teachers of English.

Gee, J. (1990). *Social linguistics and literacies: Ideology in discourses.* London: Falmer Press.

Gere, A. R. (1986). Teaching writing: The major theories. In A. Petrosky & D. Bartholomae (Eds.), *The teaching of writing: 85th yearbook of the National Society for the Study of Education* (Part II, pp. 30–48). Chicago: University of Chicago Press.

Gere, A. R., & Stevens, R. (1985). The language of writing groups: How oral response shapes revision. In S. W. Freedman (Ed.), *The acquisition of written language: Response and revision* (pp. 85–105). Norwood, NJ: Ablex.

Goen, S. (1997). *Re-considering remediation: A case study of basic writing in the California State University.* Unpublished doctoral dissertation, Stanford University, Stanford, CA.

Greene, S. (1995). Making sense of my own ideas: Problems in authorship in a beginning writing classroom. *Written Communication, 12*(2), 186–218.

Greene, S., & Ackerman, J. M. (1996). Expanding the constructivist metaphor: A rhetorical perspective on literacy research and practice. *Review of Educational Research, 65*(4), 383–420.

Gutierrez, K. D. (1992). A comparison of instructional contexts in writing process classrooms with Latino children. *Education and Urban Society, 24*(2), 244–262.

Haas, C., & Flower, L. S. (1988). Rhetorical reading strategies and the construction of meaning. *College Composition and Communication, 39*(2), 167–183.

Hairston, M. (1982). The winds of change: Thomas Kuhn and the revolution in the teaching of writing. *College Composition and Communication, 33*(1), 76–88.

Hayes, J. R., & Flower, L. S. (1980). Identifying the organization of writing processes. In L. W. Gregg & E. R. Steinberg (Eds.), *Cognitive processes in writing* (pp. 31–50). Hillsdale, NJ: Lawrence Erlbaum Associates.

Hayes, J. R., Flower, L. S., Schriver, K. A., Stratman, J., & Carey, L. (1987). Cognitive processes in revision. In S. Rosenberg (Ed.), *Advances in applied psycholinguistics: Vol. II. Reading, writing, and language processing* (pp. 176–240). Cambridge, UK: Cambridge University Press.

Heath, S. B., & Branscombe, A. (1985). "Intelligent writing" in an audience community: Teacher, students and researchers. In S. W. Freedman (Ed.), *The acquisition of written language: Response and revision* (pp. 3–32). Norwood, NJ: Ablex.

Hillocks, G. (1986). *Research on written composition: New directions for teaching.* Urbana, IL: ERIC Clearinghouse on Reading and Communication Skills.

Hodges, R. E. (1991). The conventions of writing. In J. Flood, J. Jensen,

D. Lapp, & J. Squire (Eds.), *Handbook of research on teaching the English language arts* (pp. 775–786). New York: Macmillan.

Horowitz, R., & Samuels, S. J. (1987). Comprehending oral and written language: Critical contrasts for literacy and schooling. In R. Horowitz & S. J. Samuels (Eds.), *Comprehending oral and written language* (pp. 1–52). San Diego, CA: Academic Press.

Hull, G. (1987). The editing process in writing: A performance study of more skilled and less skilled college writers. *Research in the Teaching of English, 21*(1), 8–29.

Hull, G., & Rose, M. (1990). Toward a social-cognitive understanding of problematic reading and writing. In A. A. Lunsford, H. Moglen, & J. Slevin (Eds.), *The right to literacy* (pp. 235–244). New York: Modern Language Association.

Hull, G., Rose, M., Fraser, K. L., & Castellano, M. (1991). Remediation as social construct: Perspectives from an analysis of classroom discourse. *College Composition and Communication, 42*(3), 299–329.

Hunt, K. (1965). A synopsis of clause-to-sentence length factors. *English Journal, 54*(2), 300, 305–309.

Hyon, S. (1996). Genre in three traditions: Implications for ESL. *TESOL Quarterly, 30*(4), 693–722.

Knoeller, C. (1998). *Voicing ourselves: Whose words we use when we talk about books.* Albany, NY: State University of New York Press.

Krapels, A. (1990). An overview of second language writing process research. In B. Kroll (Ed.), *Second language writing: Research insights for the classroom* (pp. 37–56). Cambridge, UK: Cambridge University Press.

Kucer, S. L. (1985). The making of meaning: Reading and writing as parallel processes. *Written Communication, 2*(3), 317–336.

Kuhn, T. (1963). *The structure of scientific revolutions.* Chicago: University of Chicago Press.

Langer, J. A. (1986). *Children reading and writing: Structures and strategies.* Norwood, NJ: Ablex.

Langer, J. A., & Allington, R. (1992). Curriculum research in writing and reading. In P. W. Jackson (Ed.), *Handbook of research on curriculum* (pp. 687–725). New York: Macmillan.

Langer, J. A., & Applebee, A. N. (1987). *How writing shapes thinking.* Urbana, IL: National Council of Teachers of English.

Loban, W. (1976). *Language development: Kindergarten through grade twelve.* Urbana, IL: National Council of Teachers of English.

Martin, N. (1987, December). *The meaning-making strategies reported by readers and writers.* Paper presented at the meeting of the National Reading Conference, St. Petersburg, FL.

Morson, G. S. (1986). Dialogue, monologue, and the social: A reply to Ken Hierchkop. In G. S. Morson (Ed.), *Bakhtin: Essays and dialogues on his work* (pp. 73–88). Chicago: University of Chicago Press.

Nelson, N., & Calfee, R. (Eds.) (1998). *The reading-writing connection: Yearbook of the National Society for the Study of Education.* Chicago University of Chicago Press.

Newell, G. E. (1998). "How much are we the wiser?" Continuity and change in writing and learning in the content areas. In N. Nelson & R. Calfee (Eds.), *The reading-writing connection: Yearbook of the National Society for the Study of Education* (pp. 178–202). Chicago: University of Chicago Press.

Newkirk, T. (1984). How students read student papers: An exploratory study. *Written Communication, 3*(3), 283–305.

Nystrand, M. (1986). *The structure of written communication: Studies in reciprocity between writers and readers.* Orlando, FL: Academic Press.

Nystrand, M., Greene, S., & Wiemelt, J. (1993). Where did composition studies come from? An intellectual history. *Written Communication, 10*(3), 267–333.

Perl, S. (1979). The composing processes of unskilled college writers. *Research in the Teaching of English, 13*(4), 317–336.

Prior, P. (1998). Contextualizing instructors' responses to writing in the college classroom. In N. Nelson & R. Calfee (Eds.), *The reading-writing connection: Yearbook of the National Society for the Study of Education* (pp. 153–177). Chicago: University of Chicago Press.

Purves, A. (1992). Reflections on research and assessment in written composition. *Research in the Teaching of English, 26*(1), 108–122.

Raimes, A. (1983). Tradition and revolution in ESL teaching. *TESOL Quarterly, 17*(4), 535–552.

Raphael, T. E., Englert, C. S., & Kirschner, B. W. (1986). *The impact of text structure instruction and social context on students' comprehension and production of expository text* (Research Series No. 177). East Lansing, MI: Michigan State University, Institute for Research on Teaching.

Raphael, T. E., Kirschner, B. W., & Englert, C. S. (1986). *Students' metacognitive knowledge about writing* (Research Series No. 176). East Lansing, MI: Michigan State University, Institute for Research on Teaching.

Read, C. (1971). Preschool children's knowledge of English phonology. *Harvard Educational Review, 41*(1), 1–34.

Reyes, M. de la Luz. (1991). A process approach to literacy using dialogue journals and literature logs with second language learners. *Research in the Teaching of English, 25*(3), 291–313.

Scarcella, R. (1984). How writers orient their readers in expository essays: A comparative study of native and non-native English writers. *TESOL Quarterly, 18*(4), 671–688.

Scardamalia, M., & Bereiter, C. (1986). Research on written composition. In M. C. Wittrock (Ed.), *Handbook of research on teaching* (3rd ed., pp. 778–803). New York: Macmillan.

Scribner, S., & Cole, M. (1981). *The psychology of literacy.* Cambridge, MA: Harvard University Press.

Sharon, S. (1984). *Cooperative learning.* Hillsdale, NJ: Lawrence Erlbaum Associates.

Shaughnessy, M. (1977). *Errors and expectations: A guide for the teacher of basic writing.* New York: Oxford University Press.

Silva, T. (1993). Toward an understanding of the distinct nature of L2 writing: The ESL research and its implications. *TESOL Quarterly, 27*(4), 657–677.

Slavin, R. E. (1980). Cooperative learning. *Review of Educational Research, 50*(3), 315–342.

Smagorinsky, P., & Smith, M. (1992). The nature of knowledge in composition and literary understanding: The question of specificity. *Review of Educational Research, 62*(3), 279–305.

Sommers, N. (1980). Revision strategies of student writers and experienced writers. *College Composition and Communication, 31*(4), 378–388.

Sperling, M. (1990). I want to talk to each of you: Collaboration and the teacher-student writing conference. *Research in the Teaching of English, 24*(3), 279–321.

Sperling, M. (1994). Constructing the perspective of teacher-as-reader: A framework for studying response to student writing. *Research in the Teaching of English, 28*(2), 175–207.

Sperling, M. (1995). Uncovering the role of role in writing and learning to write: One day in an inner-city classroom. *Written Communication, 12*(1), 93–133.

Sperling, M. (1996). Revisiting the writing-speaking connection: Challenges for research on writing and writing instruction. *Review of Educational Research, 66*(1), 53–86.

Sperling, M. (1998). Teachers as readers of student writing. In N. Nelson & R. Calfee (Eds.), *The reading-writing connection: Yearbook of the National Society for the Study of Education* (pp. 131–152). Chicago: University of Chicago Press.

Squire, R. J. (1984). Composing and comprehending: Two sides of the same basic processes. In J. M. Jensen (Ed.), *Composing and comprehending* (pp. 23–31). Urbana, IL: National Council of Teachers of English.

Stone, C. A. (1993). What is missing in the metaphor of scaffolding? In E. A. Forman, N. Minick, & C. A. Stone (Eds.), *Contexts for learning: Sociocultural dynamics in children's development* (pp. 169–183). New York: Oxford University Press.

Street, B. (1984). *Literacy in theory and practice.* Cambridge, UK: Cambridge University Press.

Swales, J. M. (1990). *Genre analysis: English in academic and research settings.* Cambridge, UK: Cambridge University Press.

Tierney, R. J., & Pearson, P. D. (1983). Toward a composing model of reading. *Language Arts, 60,* 568–580.

Tierney, R. J., & Shanahan, T. (1991). Research on reading-writing relationships: A synthesis and suggested directions. In R. Barr, M. Kamil, P. Mosenthal, & P. D. Pearson (Eds.), *Handbook of reading research* (Vol. 2, pp. 246–280). New York: Longman.

Vahapassi, A. (1988). The domain of school writing. In T. P. Gorman,

A. C. Purves, & R. E. Degenhart (Eds.), *International studies in educational achievement, Vol. 5. The IEA study of written composition I: The international writing tasks and scoring scales* (pp. 15–40). Oxford, UK: Pergammon.

Vygotsky, L. S. (1978). *Mind in society: The development of higher psychological processes.* Cambridge, MA: Harvard University Press.

Weinstein, R. S. (1989). Perception of classroom processes and student motivation: Children's views of self-fulfilling prophecies. In R. Ames & C. Ames (Eds.), *Research on motivation in education* (Vol. 3, pp. 187–221). Orlando, FL: Academic Press.

Wertsch, J. (1991). *Voices of the mind.* Cambridge, MA: Harvard University Press.

Widdowson, H. G. (1993). The relevant conditions of language use and learning. In M. Krueger & F. Ryan (Eds.), *Language and content: Discipline and content-based approaches to language study* (pp. 27–36). Lexington, MA: D.C. Heath and Company.

Witte, S. P. (1992). Context, text, intertext: Toward a constructivist semiotic of writing. *Written Communication, 9*(2), 237–308.

Wittrock, M. C. (1984). Writing and the teaching of reading. In J. M. Jensen (Ed.), *Composing and comprehending* (pp. 77–83). Urbana, IL: National Council of Teachers of English.

Wood, D., Bruner, J., & Ross, G. (1976). The role of tutoring in problem solving. *Journal of Child Psychology and Psychiatry, 66,* 181–191.

22.
Research on the Teaching of Reading

Rebecca Barr
National-Louis University

During the past decade, major shifts have occurred in how classroom teaching of reading is envisioned and studied. The purpose of this chapter is to describe how researchers from the field of reading think about and study teaching. There are several reasons why it is important for us to reflect on our research activity. First, a careful look at the research on teaching reading will provide a description of research approaches and an indication of how ways to study teaching have changed over time. Second, detailed analyses can provide the basis for understanding the advantages and limitations of certain ways of looking at teaching, and for judging whether we are learning what we need to know. In the end, we study teaching not only to know more about the process in a theoretical sense, but for its assumed utilitarian value—to inform teachers so they may be able to help all children become literate.

This purpose can be approached in several different ways. The one I have selected is to look carefully at a set of studies representing diverse theoretical and methodological perspectives. After reviewing the literature on reading that pertains to teaching reading, several "active" areas became apparent.[1] Some of these areas, such as beginning reading methods, are of long-standing interest; others, such as emergent literacy environments in preschool classrooms and teacher inquiry, are more recent; still others, such as comprehension strategy instruction, have preoccupied a majority of researchers in the field. The problem of delineating "active" areas of research is *not* for the purpose of a representative sampling of the field; instead, my

analytic need was to obtain a diverse set of studies to demonstrate differences in perspective.

In the end, I selected the following four thematically related areas: (a) emergent literacy, (b) early reading instruction, (c) facilitating comprehension, and (d) teaching situated in classrooms. Studies of emergent literacy typically place importance on the developmental characteristics of children, whereas those on early reading instruction usually give priority to teachers' instructional methods. Comprehension instruction to facilitate strategy development also emphasizes teachers' instructional methods; in contrast, response-to-literature approaches feature the characteristics of literature as well as the personal responses of readers to them. Finally, studies by teachers and by university researchers working with teachers offer a perspective that privileges the culture of classrooms and the perspectives of teachers. Obviously, other areas than these four could have been selected, but these areas are useful for the purpose of revealing differences in theoretical perspectives on teaching and research methods.

In each thematic cluster, I selected two topics, each offering a different research perspective and approach as shown in Table 22.1. Other areas might have been selected, but for my purpose of obtaining a diverse set of studies, these topical clusters will serve. Moreover, my general review of the research literature showed that this set illustrates most approaches to research on teaching reading.

Finally, in each topical area I selected a study for detailed

Many persons provided support to me during the writing of this chapter. I wish to thank Susan Kajiwara Ansai and Deborah Gurvitz for their thorough search of the research literature; and Donna Alvermann (University of Georgia), Eileen Ball (University of Massachusetts at Dartmouth), Camille Blachowicz (National-Louis University), Roberta Buhle (Manheim School District), Robert Dreeben (University of Chicago), James Hoffman (University of Texas–Austin), Catherine Lacey (Spencer Foundation), Susan Lytle (University of Pennsylvania), and William Teale (University of Illinois–Chicago) for their insightful, provocative, and encouraging comments on various drafts of the manuscript. The chapter is much better for their wise counsel; errors of omission and commission are, of course, mine.

[1] I conducted ERIC searches, surveyed major literacy journals, examined studies listed in the *Annual Summary of Investigations Relating to Reading,* considered studies published in the annual National Reading Conference Yearbooks, and consulted with colleagues. To bring studies of teaching into sharper focus, I identified all reports appearing in the *Reading Research Quarterly* and the *Journal of Reading Behavior* (now titled *Journal of Literacy Research*) from 1985 to 1997 that pertained to teaching and classified them in terms of topical focus. On the basis of these various reviews, I identified the topical areas in which substantial numbers of studies occurred as well as several emerging.

Table 22.1. Themes and Topics Related to Teaching Reading

Themes	Topical Focus	Exemplary Research
Emergent Literacy	Literacy Environments	Kantor, Miller & Fernie (1992)
	Storybook Reading	Dickinson & Smith (1994)
Early Reading Instruction	Phonemic Awareness	Blachman, Ball, Black & Tangel (1994)
	Whole Language vs. Traditional Approaches	Dahl & Freepon (1995)
Facilitating Comprehension	Strategy Instruction	Dole, Brown & Trathen (1996)
		Beck, McKeown, Sandora, Kucan, Worthy (1996)
	Response to Literature	Eeds & Wells (1989)
Teaching Situated in Classrooms	Studying and Changing Teaching Practice	Moje (1996)
	Teacher Inquiry	Maher (1994)

analysis (two for Strategy Instruction to reveal changes in approach in the area). This approach yielded a manageable set; more studies from each area would have made the analytic task unwieldy. Most studies were similar to others in the same area, although representativeness was not the issue for me. I was not attempting to nor could I have selected a single study that would resemble and represent all others in a particular topical area. Important for my analytic purposes was the derivation of a diverse *set of studies* that collectively would reveal different ways to think about and study reading instruction. I selected these illustrative studies with two criteria in mind: (a) conceptual and methodological diversity and (b) useful analyses of literacy, research approaches, and views of teaching. For every study selected, others in the same area could have done as well; but, in the end, these research cases provided the conceptual tensions needed for an instructive analysis.

In representing each study, I attempted to provide a summary overview that was true to the way the study was framed and pursued. Yet, as in any selective process, choices were made; the summary is *my* rendering, not the author's. Thus, readers are encouraged to read the nine studies to become familiar with the research and to judge the degree of fidelity I was able to achieve.

Three questions guided my analysis of each study. First, what underlying theoretical perspectives on literacy and learning informed the research? Second, what view of teaching is developed? Third, how might the knowledge developed about teaching be useful to both experienced teachers and those learning how to teach?

As I looked at my analyses of studies, it became clear that a reader needed contextual information about other studies in each area and about the major issues pursued. I decided, then, to frame each analysis with a brief summary of the literature. These summaries should not be taken as comprehensive literature reviews. For a discussion of findings from each body of research, I refer the reader to existing comprehensive reviews. For my purposes, each brief review sets the stage for the de-

tailed analysis and lets the reader learn about other ways in which the topic is pursued empirically.

This examination of literacy teaching was organized according to those eight topical areas. I began with a brief description of trends in the literature over the past decade. Next, I provided a detailed description of the selected study. Finally, I summarized my thinking in response to the three guiding questions. I concluded the chapter with a reflective essay on how literacy research informs us about the teaching of reading.

It may also be useful to state what is outside the scope of this chapter. This study is not a traditional literature review. I have not attempted to represent research findings nor to summarize what generalizations about teaching reading are empirically warranted (see, for example, Hoffman, 1991; Roehler & Duffy, 1991). Nor have I attempted to provide a treatment of studies that is representative of the existing literature, either conceptually, empirically, or methodologically; in other words, the selection of studies was purposive not representative, and was aimed to build strategic comparisons among cases to draw conceptual distinctions about teaching.

Beyond that, the review was limited in scope to studies of reading. For the most part, I have not examined studies of writing and literature instruction because these topics are addressed in other chapters of the *Handbook.* Yet these boundaries are difficult to establish; during the past decade, writing has become an integral part of reading instruction, and literature is frequently used as a basis for teaching reading. The focus of the review is on *teaching.* Yet here again, as teaching and learning are increasingly viewed as integrally connected, the boundaries are difficult to establish. The time span of this review captured recent trends in the field since the last review of reading research in the *Handbook of Research on Teaching,* Third Edition, by Calfee and Drum (1986).

Emergent Literacy

Creating Literacy Environments

OVERVIEW AND ISSUES

A general consensus exists among researchers about the importance of creating print and language-rich environments. It is believed that establishing literacy-rich environments, similar to those of highly supportive families (Taylor, 1983), will enhance the development of preschoolers' understanding the forms and functions of literacy. And interventions into preschool classes (Morrow & Rand, 1991; Neuman & Roskos, 1992 1993) and kindergartens (Taylor, Blum, & Logsdon, 1986) to create language and print-rich environments are found to enhance the frequency and complexity of children's literacy activity and learning. Rowe's research (1989) pointed to the role of social interaction and language use in literacy learning. However, McGill-Franzen and Lanford (1994) documented wide variation in preschool environments and in children's related understandings (see also Morrow, 1991).

Debate focuses on the balance between creating print-rich environments and the need for more direct instruction. This debate between child-centered approaches and direct instruction is one that occurs in various forms in other sections of this chapter. On the side of more structured instruction, some observers reported little change in children's literacy actions and routines in stimulating environments over time (Neuman & Roskos, 1997), and others observed that teacher guidance can have a marked influence on children's engagement in literacy activities (Morrow & Rand, 1991). It may be that a stimulating setting is a necessary but not sufficient condition. Research, however, tends to focus either on the nature of literacy activity initiated by children in conducive environments (e.g., Kantor, Miller, & Fernie, 1992; Neuman & Roskos, 1997) or on the influence of teaching strategies on learning (e.g., Morrow & Rand, 1991).

Selecting a study for detailed analysis posed a dilemma, that is, whether to select one analysis that assessed the effectiveness of more direct forms of instruction or one that represented more informal, child-centered forms of literacy learning. Although I selected the ethnography by Kantor et al. (1992) for its detailed representation of life in the preschool classroom and because the perspective of a teacher-researcher is represented, the reader should keep in mind that other studies might have provided a different take on preschool literacy.

DESCRIPTION OF THE
KANTOR, MILLER, AND FERNIE STUDY

Kantor et al. (1992), influenced by the studies of Cochran-Smith (1984), Dyson (1989), and Rowe (1989), conceptualized teaching and learning as connected and evolving opportunistically. They examined literacy activities in a university laboratory preschool over a school year. Participants included 18 largely middle-class 3- and 4-year-olds of diverse ethnicity and their two teachers. The curriculum was constructed jointly by teachers and children. Children were encouraged to create, question, and solve problems in planned classroom activities and to play with peers. Teachers believed that through countless informal literacy experiences, children begin to understand the power and functions of print.

Kantor, Miller, and Fernie addressed the following questions: "(a) What are the different ways in which literacy is constructed by children and teachers of the preschool in the course of their daily life? (b) What kinds of literacy or literacies are constructed within and across peer culture or school culture events? and (c) Within these events, how do children and teachers participate in and use literacy?" (Kantor et al., 1992, p. 188). They pursued a cyclical and recursive ethnographic study that employed videotapes taken during the first 2 weeks of each of 3 quarters, field notes written daily, interviews with children and their parents, retrospective journals kept by the two teachers, and notes made during weekly meetings of the research team. Literacy was judged to occur whenever a teacher or child referred to or introduced reading and writing, or constructed print.

Data analysis proceeded in two phases. The first analysis, based on an overview of videotapes and conversations with teachers, revealed that print was an integral part of preschool life woven into a variety of ongoing events throughout the day. Four contexts were selected for more detailed analysis in the second phase of the study; two included teacher-planned small group activities for 3-year-olds (Donna's small group)

4-year-olds (Rebecca's small group), and two were directed by peer culture concerns (the block area and the art activity tables). In each of the four settings, Kantor and colleagues identified all events that involved literacy and characterized them in terms of "structure" (who initiated the literacy event, who authored the message, who recorded it); "ways to do literacy" (e.g., journal writing; inviting children to label, identify, talk about their work); and "uses of literacy" (e.g., describe your art or construction). For the two settings involving teacher-planned activities, those for 3-year-olds focused on learning how to be a group and those for 4-years-olds focused on skills to collaborate in groups. One theme running through all interpretations was that literacy was integrated into activities to achieve these social purposes rather than being a focus itself. A second theme, illustrated through vignettes, was that teachers' offers to support literacy were sometimes not taken up by children; and when they were, children did not always treat them as the teacher intended.

Findings presented for the four group settings consisted of a description of telling episodes and an analysis of how literacy developed and its purposes. The vignettes showed that by using print in play children learned that printed language held power to mediate social issues. The analysis of Rebecca's small group of 4-year-olds illustrates the findings. Some activities, such as journal writing, offering to take dictation of words, and encouraging children to take control of their writing, were planned events initiated by the teacher through comments such as, "Let's find out about this and write it down." Others, such as labeling Lego constructions and writing rules for using tools safely, occurred opportunistically, coming about through suggestions from Rebecca such as, "We can write your words and tell about your piece" (p. 193).

In terms of structural characteristics, children in both teacher-led groups initiated most of the print interactions and authored the messages, but the teachers did most of the writing. In contrast, the teachers actively initiated literacy activities at the Activity Table Area (50% of the time) and in the Block Area (83% of the time). While teachers assumed technical control of most writing in the Block Area, surprisingly, they did so only 12% of the time at the Activity Table. This Activity Table apparently became a setting in which children asserted their ability to write their names and other messages autonomously. These analyses provide a glimpse of how literacy is woven through the fabric of classroom life, first through teacher responsiveness that attaches language to physical experience, and then through student appropriation of literacy activities as solutions to their problems. Kantor and colleagues showed how countless informal writing experiences develop an interest in and a knowledge of literacy and its various forms and functions.

ANALYSIS

What broader conceptualization of literacy and learning framed this research? A sociocultural perspective informs the ethnographic methods used to collect and analyze the data, as well as the philosophy of the preschool program (Piaget, 1926/1959; Vygotsky, 1978). Literacy is viewed as socially constructed in different ways. It is "constructed by children and teacher" and "children and teachers participate in and use literacy." Literacy activities are tied to and serve the broader social development goals of the teachers. They arise out of activities and are frequently initiated by children. The research questions reflect an organic view of how teaching is connected to learning. The classroom was chosen in which teachers shared this view of teaching, and ethnographic methods were used to represent the fluid nature of the interaction.

Consistent with this view, teaching is not conceptualized in its own terms but rather as embedded in child-centered activities. Thus, empirically, teaching is not focused on as an activity separate from its interactive context. In fact, daily events in which literacy teaching occurred as a more formal activity, such as storytime, were not included in the study. Instead, the researchers chose to focus on the "many instances of literacy [that] were constructed opportunistically" (p. 189). This focus is consistent with their purpose, but the partial portrayal of literacy teaching and learning precludes a complete view of literacy activities and does not allow consideration of the relation between informal and more formal literacy activities. How the different forms of teaching within these activities reinforced each other cannot be known.

How might this perspective on teaching be useful to other teachers? The research provided a rich portrayal of how informal literacy teaching and learning occur in the classroom. A partial view of teaching entailing opportunistic responsiveness was represented. A subtle argument against direct forms of instruction seemed to exist, overtly through the choice not to look at formal literacy activities, and implicitly in how the study was framed. If the purpose had been to understand the contributions of teaching to children's literacy learning, they might have focused on what they call teaching *formats* ("Let's find out about this and write it down") and *invitations* ("We can write your words and tell about your piece") as a way of clarifying for other teachers how "opportunistic" instruction works. However, not only would this analytic focus have been at odds with their overall purpose of demonstrating the embedded nature of teaching, but also it would have failed to respect the integrity of other class settings. The authors suggested that this "specific description of multiple literacies does not imply a specific literacy curriculum for other preschool programs. The broader implication is that a literacy curriculum must respect and reflect the nature of daily life within a particular setting" (pp. 199–200). They might argue that the usefulness of this documentation for other teachers lies in its portrayal of an approach unlike more direct forms of instruction.

Storybook Reading

OVERVIEW AND ISSUES

In contrast to the limited number of studies of preschool literacy environments, storybook reading has been the focus of extensive research. Sulzby and Teale (1991) in their review of this literature emphasized several characteristics of storybook reading, including its social nature. That is, the words being read from text do not occur by themselves but are elaborated through explanations, comments, and questions. These social-interactional patterns differ for parents and for teachers, but, for any particular individual, a pattern that is quite stable can

be identified (Martinez & Teale, 1993; Morrow, 1988; Teale, Martinez, & Glass, 1989). Indeed, it has been argued that it is the predictable and recurring pattern of storybook reading that enables children to participate (Ninio & Bruner, 1978; Snow & Ninio, 1986; Sulzby & Teale, 1991). Descriptive studies also show that interactional patterns are responsive to such characteristics of children as their age and development (Snow, 1983; Teale et al., 1989) and their past experience with storybook reading (Anderson-Yockel & Haynes, 1994; Bus & van IJzendoorn, 1988, 1995), as well as to the type of book being read, and the familiarity of children with particular stories (Martinez & Roser, 1985; Pelligrini, Perlmutter, Galda, & Brody, 1990; Phillips & McNaughton, 1990).

Many investigations of storybook reading focus on parent–child storybook reading and explore its consequence for the literacy development of children. It is widely believed that storybook reading has strong effects on later literacy development (Anderson, Hiebert, Scott, & Wilkinson, 1984). Yet, two recent reviews of the research literature offer conflicting conclusions on how the frequency of storybook reading affects the oral language and emergent literacy of children. Scarborough and Dobrich (1994), based on their narrative review, concluded that the association between storybook reading and the development of child language and literacy skills is modest. Bus, van IJzendoorn, and Pelligrini (1995), in contrast, using a meta-analysis of many of the same studies, concluded that parent–child storybook reading does have significant consequence for language growth, emergent literacy, and reading achievement. Recent research (e.g., Senechal, LeFevre, Hudson, & Lawson, 1996; Senechal, LeFevre, Thomas, & Daley, 1998), continues to address this issue to clarify the impact of storybook reading on aspects of language and literacy development.

From this large body of research on storybook reading, I am particularly concerned with those studies conducted in preschool and primary school classrooms. Some explore *how* the interactive process of storybook reading works (Golden & Gerber, 1990; Martinez & Teale, 1993). Teale et al. (1989), for example, developed a system for describing group storybook reading in classrooms that accounted for the roles of all participants in the event, including the teacher, the students, and the text. Green, Harker, and Golden (1986) explored storybook interaction from three perspectives: sociolinguistic and discourse analysis, semantic analysis and comprehension of text, and text analysis and reader response theory. These multiple perspectives combined revealed how the two teachers established different instructional and social frames for their lessons. These frames, in turn, required students to attend to different types of information and respond in specific ways.

Other studies focus more directly on how storybook discussions affect children's learning about language and literacy. When teachers offer explanations, for example, vocabulary acquisition tends to be enhanced (e.g., Dickinson & Smith, 1994; Elley, 1989). When they make comments rather than asking specific questions, children respond with more complex comments (Kertoy, 1994), and the children's listening comprehension and expressive language improves (e.g., Dickinson & Keebler, 1989; Feitelson, Goldstein, Iraqi, & Share, 1993; Morrow, O'Connor, & Smith, 1990; Roser & Martinez, 1985). Particularly among children of low socioeconomic status, it seems better to read the same books repeatedly over time than to read many different books (e.g., Morrow, 1988; Nielsen, 1993). Moreover, when children also read the books their teachers have read aloud to them, their understanding of written language and story structure tends to be enhanced (e.g., Eller, Pappas, & Brown, 1988; Feitelson, Kita, & Goldstein, 1986; Mason, Kerr, Sinha, & McCormick, 1990; Mason, Peterman, Powell, & Kerr, 1989).

From this body of research, I selected the study by Dickinson and Smith (1994) for detailed consideration. I chose this study because it (a) focuses on the storybook reading as it naturally occurred in the rooms of a large sample of preschool teachers, (b) delineates patterns of discourse that characterize their storybook reading, and (c) examines the relations between characteristics of discourse and student learning.

DESCRIPTION OF THE DICKINSON AND SMITH STUDY

As part of a larger study on home–school relations, Dickinson and Smith (1994) examined storybook reading in preschool classrooms and the effect of patterns of talk on learning. Their study viewed teaching from a Vygotskian perspective through the lens of discourse. They asked, "Are there identifiable patterns of teacher–child interaction during book reading in preschool classrooms?" (p. 105). On the basis of a sample of videotaped interactions between 25 teachers and their students reading a single storybook, they classified utterances by when they occurred (before, during, or after storybook reading), the nature of the requests (e.g., requests for information, responses to requests), and content (e.g., talk about vocabulary, evaluative responses to the story). These categories were reduced to a set of 21 variables. Comments made spontaneously by children and teachers showing analysis, prediction, and concern with vocabulary were of greatest interest to Dickinson and Smith.

A cluster analysis with the variables along with a holistic reading of the transcripts revealed three patterns of talk. In the first pattern, occurring in five classrooms, teachers and children engaged in high amounts of talk during book reading. In addition, many analytic and clarifying comments occurred as part of extended and conceptually challenging conversations (co-construction). This pattern was illustrated by a class reading *There's a Nightmare in My Closet* by Mercer Mayer. On finishing reading a page, the teacher pointed to one of the pictures (Dickinson & Smith, 1994, p. 112):

Child: He's sad, he's sad.
Teacher: Why do you think he's sad, Jake?
Child: He's sad because he wants the teddy bear.
Teacher: You think so?
Child: Yeah.
Teacher: But how can you tell that he's sad?
Child: By his face.
Teacher: Oh, his face is telling you?
Child: [nods]

In the second pattern, occurring in 10 classrooms, children engaged in limited amounts of talk, either before, after, or during book reading. Children tended to respond either to questions about factual details or to produce portions of the text in chorus (didactic-interactional). This sort of recitational pattern was exemplified in the following exchange involving the factual book *Robins*. The teachers pointed to a male robin and a female robin on the page (Dickinson & Smith, 1994, p. 113):

Teacher: What was the male robin doing?
Teacher: Raise a quiet hand and tell me.
Teacher: What was he doing?
Teacher: Uh, Brian?
Child: Uh, sittin' there on the tree.
Teacher: No.
Teacher: What was he doing, Lauren?
Child: Singing.
Teacher: He was singing.

In the third pattern, occurring in 10 classrooms, books were introduced through extended discussion, the text was read with selective, limited discussion, and the reading was followed by extended discussion (performance-oriented). These discussions often focused on predictions and personal connections, a consideration of characters, or an analysis of vocabulary. This patterns was illustrated by the discussion during the reading of *Nicholas, Where Have You Been?* by Leo Lionni (Dickinson & Smith, 1994, p. 114):

Teacher: What's "the mother bird's soft down"? Does anyone know what that is?
Child: It's lying down.
Teacher: Well, it's not lying down.
Teacher: They call it "against her down."
Teacher: The down is her feathers, her soft feathers.
Child: Cuddle, cuddle.
Teacher: They cuddle against her down; the down is her feathers.

Dickinson and Smith also asked about the consequence of these patterns: "Do the ways teachers read books to 4-year-olds have effects on children's language and literacy development that can be detected 1 year later?" (Dickinson & Smith, 1994, p. 105). The measures used to explore children's language and literacy development were tests of vocabulary (PPVT-R) and story understanding administered when the children were 5 years old. Similar tests were not administered at the beginning of the preschool year so no basis existed to determine whether the classrooms were similar at the onset.

Two forms of analysis yielded significant relations between storybook reading discourse and the two measures. The first, using analysis of variance, found that the three patterns were significantly related to the level of vocabulary development; no significant differences were found in relation to story understanding. Children in the performance-oriented classrooms realized significantly higher vocabulary development than those from the didactic-interactional classrooms, with those from the co-constructive approach falling in between (possibly because of the small number of classes representing this pattern).

Dickinson and Smith also examined the predictive effectiveness of variables they had derived from their more detailed analysis at the level of utterances. One combined variable involving analysis, prediction, and vocabulary discussion by children and teachers during reading out performed the others. Those children most involved in this form of talk performed higher in vocabulary (adjusted R^2 0.51) and somewhat higher in story understanding (adjusted R^2 0.25) than their peers exposed to less analytic forms of storybook reading.

ANALYSIS

The Vygotskian perspective framing the study focused on the cognitive and linguistic operations that children develop through social interaction. Teaching is viewed as part of a responsive social environment in which a more knowledgeable adult scaffolds the constructive processes of children who gradually achieve autonomy in their performance. Dickinson and Smith focused on one aspect of instruction, interactional patterns during storybook reading. The analysis considered the content of the exchange as well as its form. We learn, for example, about the sorts of reflective thought some teachers elicited from children, while others (didactic-interactional) encourage memory for stated details and choral response.

What picture of teaching does this analysis provide? Comparisons across a set of classrooms enabled Dickinson and Smith to see commonalities as well as differences in how teachers read stories. Some develop conceptually rich exchanges with their students, while others firmly control the discussion and encourage memory for stated details. However, studying a large number of teachers instead of one or two in depth means that aspects of teaching have been selected out for scrutiny while other parts are not examined. We do not learn much about the children participating in the story reading; they are viewed as a "collective" child. Dickinson and Smith noted that some books seemed to lead to more conceptually stimulating dialogue than others. They observed, for example, that "performance-oriented" teachers, particularly those with high levels of choral response, "often used books with limited vocabulary and minimal plot" (Dickinson & Smith, 1994, p. 117). Yet, in contrast with studies including fewer teachers (e.g., Teale et al., 1989), their analysis did not systematically examine such inter-textual dimensions. Finally, the analysis was limited to one point in time. We cannot know how representative the patterns are and whether they recur, nor do we gain a view of the context of story reading and range of other literacy activities that occur in the class. Studying many teachers in a more limited way leads to more qualified generalizations, and some uncertainty as to whether the recommended patterns would be effective in other contexts.

As discussed by Dickinson and Smith, what may be of use to teachers is the description of alternative discourse patterns and how they seem to work. Identifying patterns alerts teachers to how other teachers structure storybook reading. The correlational evidence suggests that certain patterns and types of utterances may support learning about literacy. Yet, some caution is appropriate because we cannot be certain that a particular story reading pattern is *the* effective condition, or whether teachers using these patterns also initiate other forms of responsive instruction that in combination lead to enhanced literacy development.

Early Reading Instruction

Phonemic Awareness

OVERVIEW AND ISSUES

What do children need to know to learn to read? Ehri (1991) and Juel (1991), in their reviews of studies of beginning reading, proposed developmental models that include phonemic awareness as an important precursor to reading acquisition. Although correlational studies using cognitive measures suggest the importance of children becoming aware of phonemes in speech, Bradley and Bryant's (1983) landmark study supported the causal nature of the relationship experimentally. Their study spawned a substantial body of research exploring the effect of phonemic awareness training on learning to read. Most studies, similar to the Bradley–Bryant research, compare two or more groups of children who differ in instructional support.

This body of experimental research varies along a number of dimensions. Some studies are of short duration (e.g., Ehri & Wilce, 1987; Weiner, 1994), but most extend over at least several months. Many are conducted in laboratory or tutorial settings, not classrooms (Ball & Blachman, 1988, 1991; Bruck & Treiman, 1992; Byrne & Fielding-Barnsley, 1991; Cunningham, 1990; Ehri & Wilce, 1987; Torgesen, Morgan, & Davis, 1992). For the few studies in classrooms, researchers typically provided the instruction to control its form and content (Lundberg, Frost, & Petersen, 1988; McGuinness, McGuinness, & Donohue, 1995; Reutzel, Oda, & Moore, 1989; Uhry & Shepherd, 1993). The phoneme awareness training is not an integral part of language arts instruction; rather, the instruction is a self-contained supplement to ongoing instruction.

Studies that focus on developing phoneme awareness without reference to print (see, e.g., Cunningham, 1990; Lundberg et al., 1988) confirmed that such instruction enhances reading achievement. Evidence also shows that reading achievement is higher when children receive explicit letter–sound training along with phoneme awareness than when only phoneme awareness training is provided (Bradley & Bryant, 1983, 1985). Training in letter–sound association itself, without phoneme awareness training, is also less effective than when combined with phoneme awareness (Ball & Blachman, 1991). Children generally profit from combinations of both forms of instruction (however, see Weiner, 1994, showing differences between experimental and control groups in phoneme awareness but not in reading achievement).

Although most studies are experimental in design, a few classroom studies followed a different approach (French & Feng, 1992; Windsor, 1990; Windsor & Pearson, 1992) by describing children as they learn about speech and print. As part of these case studies, descriptions of phoneme awareness instruction were developed that showed differences among classroom teachers in the duration and type of activities their students pursue.

I selected the Blachman, Ball, Black, and Tangel (1994) study because it involved teachers' classroom instruction. Blachman and colleagues noted that most studies of phoneme awareness training have been conducted outside the classroom by specially trained teachers or clinicians. They argued that "if educators are going to heed the advice of numerous researchers to provide instruction in phoneme awareness in regular classrooms, . . . we need more direct evidence that this model of instruction is effective" (Blachman et al., 1994, p. 5).

DESCRIPTION OF THE
BLACHMAN, BALL, BLACK, AND TANGEL STUDY

Blachman et al. (1994) studied phonemic awareness in 10 classrooms in two low-income, inner-city schools. The 84 children in the sample were taught by their teachers in groups of four or five, 4 days a week for about 15 to 20 minutes for 11 weeks from March until May. Each lesson consisted of the following three parts: (a) segmentation activities teaching children to represent the sounds of words by moving disks; (b) segmentation-related activities including, for example, grouping words on the basis of rhyme or alliteration and marking letters in simple three-letter words (Elkonin, 1973); and (c) instruction in letter names and sounds using games such as Bingo with more emphasis on letters during the final 3 weeks.

Training for the teachers included seven 2-hour sessions to learn the activities for the three parts of each lesson. A theoretical framework was developed, and teachers were given time to practice activities and ask questions. The report provided no evidence, however, on how the teachers or their assistants actually implemented the program. We do not even learn, for example, whether the assistant or the teachers did most of the teaching.

The experimental groups were compared with children comparable in terms of pretest measures from two other schools. Results from pretests and posttests indicated that instruction involving phoneme segmentation and connecting the phonemic segments to alphabet letters significantly enhanced the early reading and spelling of children in the phoneme awareness group not only on measures of phoneme awareness and letter–sound knowledge but also on reading and spelling measures. The flavor of the results is captured by differences in developmental spelling scores; whereas 51% of the experimental children were in the top third of the sample, only 17% of the control children were. These findings show that instruction in phoneme awareness coupled with letter–sound training leads to higher reading and spelling achievement, and that this instructional support can be effectively offered in kindergarten classrooms by teachers or their assistants.

ANALYSIS

A cognitive psychology perspective informed this research; the prior knowledge of children was viewed as a main influence on literacy acquisition. This knowledge is believed to be "trainable" through a series of relevant activities and experiences that teachers can provide. The Blachman study was concerned with not only whether a group of children receiving the designated training improved its phoneme awareness more than an untrained group, but also whether this experience, in turn, influenced learning to read, beyond that realized by the control group. Instruction was viewed as a self-contained package to be compared with alternatives. The instruction was "scripted."

Whereas the instructional script might originally be developed to be responsive to the characteristics of children of a particular age, it was not modified during the course of instruction in response to the learning of individual children. That is, instructional scripts will not change to include new components or approaches or to eliminate components. Instruction was predesigned and conveyed by the teacher, rather than being formed through the joint construction of students with the teacher.

The research question and its implicit view of teaching have consequence for how the inquiry proceeds. The question called for a comparison, not an exploration into *how* something works. The focus was on experimentally contrasting the experimental and control approaches. Because of assumptions about the predefined nature of the instruction, no observational evidence was collected during the course of instruction that would document the sequence of activities over time, the nature of the ongoing dialogue, and differences among teachers in their approaches. This work created a map of reality with individual features omitted. The general characteristics of a situation are assumed to be more important than specific nuances. The conception of influence was linear.

The advantage of this way of viewing teaching derives from the results—they provide guidance for teachers about the importance of phonemic awareness instruction in supporting literacy development. And yet, the absence of nuanced descriptions of how individual teachers work out their teaching limits the understanding. Scripts provide an idealized overview of instruction without including the contextual conditions and dilemmas posed by instruction of diverse classes of students. Accordingly, scripted descriptions are limited as models from which teachers can learn.

Whole Language versus Traditional Instruction

OVERVIEW AND ISSUES

Disputes over the most effective way to teach children to read extend back into the 18th and 19th centuries (Matthews, 1966) and have continued into the 20th century (Bond & Dykstra, 1967; Chall, 1968/1983; Dykstra, 1968). Similar to the studies just considered, teaching methods have tended in the past to be characterized in global terms, with little documentation of instructional approaches in individual classrooms. Consequently, it has not been possible to see how different teachers using the same approach developed their instruction in different ways nor to identify patterns of instruction associated with the huge differences observed among teachers using the same approach.

A variation of this debate emerged in the 1980s over the value of "whole language" versus traditional approaches. Some researchers responded by making global comparisons in ways not unlike the studies of the 1960s (e.g., Boljonis & Hinchman, 1988; Dewalt, Rhyne-Winkler, & Rubel, 1993; Eldredge, 1991; Gambrell & Palmer, 1992; Hagerty, Hiebert, & Owens, 1989; Holland & Hall, 1989; Klesius, Griffith, & Zielonka, 1991; Mervar & Hiebert, 1989; Milligan & Berg, 1992; Morrow, 1992; Reutzel & Cooter, 1990). The results were similar to the earlier methods–comparison research, with some studies reporting differences favoring the new methods, but many others finding no differences (for reviews of this literature, see Pressley, 1994; Stahl, McKenna, & Pagnucco, 1994; Stahl & Miller, 1989).

Others during this period used more qualitative forms of research to document instruction (e.g., Dahl & Freppon, 1995; Fisher & Hiebert, 1990; Milligan & Berg, 1992; Turner, 1993). Some conducted case studies of whole language or variants of more traditional instruction (e.g., Allen et al., 1989; Bergiloff, 1993; Cunningham, Hall, & Defee, 1991; Dahl, 1993; Morrow & Sharkley, 1993). Moreover, many explored how special groups of children learn. Perez (1994), Goldenberg (1994), Goldenberg and Gallimore (1991), and Orellana (1995), for example, studied literacy development among Spanish-speaking children. Purcell-Gates and Dahl (1991), Freppon (1995), and Morrow (1992) investigated how beginning reading methods influence how low-income and minority children learn.

A shift has also occurred in thinking about the effectiveness of instructional methods. Before the 1980s, methods were usually judged to be effective in terms of relative increases in reading achievement. More recently, affective measures as well as those pertaining to reading and writing achievement have been used (e.g., McKenna, Stratton, Grindler, & Jenkins, 1995). Stahl et al. (1994) in their review of methods–comparison studies from 1988 to 1993 found that slightly less than half of the 45 studies they examined used measures of reading achievement, a third used measures of writing development, and about half assessed differences using affective measures. Several researchers have explored the perspectives of participants (e.g., Boljonis & Hinchman, 1988; Dahl & Freppon, 1995; Freppon, 1991, 1995; Gambrell & Palmer, 1992; Hagerty et al., 1989; Purcell-Gates, 1995), book selection strategies (Mervar & Hiebert, 1989), and their motivational behaviors related to reading strategies, learning strategies, persistence, and attention control (Turner, 1993, 1995). A more interactive view of outcomes was developed by Purcell-Gates and Dahl (1991; see also Purcell-Gates, 1995) who classified children into groups on the basis of their knowledge about literacy when they entered kindergarten and explored their learning paths during kindergarten and first grade (also see McIntyre, 1992).

Dahl and her colleagues conducted two ethnographic inquiries, the first in three inner-city schools where children experienced traditional skills-based programs (Purcell-Gates & Dahl, 1991) and the second inquiry, following a similar research approach, in two inner-city schools where children learned to read and write in whole language classrooms (Dahl, 1993; Dahl & Freppon, 1991; Freppon & Dahl, 1991). I selected the Dahl and Freppon (1995) study for more detailed analysis because it captured the flavor of recent ethnographic research and because it departed from more typical methods–comparison studies in its representation of how children make sense of alternative instructional approaches.

DESCRIPTION OF THE DAHL AND FREPPON STUDY

Dahl and Freppon (1995) in a comparative analysis based on their two ethnographic studies pursue two issues: "first, how inner-city children in the United States make sense of and interpret their beginning reading and writing instruction in the early grades of school, and second, how learners' interpretations may differ when they experience skills-based or whole language classroom programs." (p. 50). The samples of children studied included African-American and White Appalachian students.

In the comparative analysis, Dahl and Freppon reported on four class groups as they progress from kindergarten through first grade. Twelve children were randomly selected from each class group for a total of 48 children responding to written language knowledge measures at the beginning and end of the study. From this set, Dahl and Freppon selected focal children, eight from the skill-based and 12 from the whole language classrooms. In twice weekly observations in kindergarten and first grade, one focal child, on a rotating basis, wore a remote microphone during the 2-hour observation period and responded to questions such as "What are you doing now?" and "Tell me about that." Data were gathered through field notes, audio recordings of reading and writing episodes, student papers, as well as the pre- and postmeasure of written language knowledge.

Case studies of focal children were developed; common patterns across groups of children were identified and compared across the two instructional settings. In both settings, focal children were concerned about accuracy, even those from whole language classrooms where accuracy was not emphasized. Both groups progressed in their understanding of letter–sound relations, but whole language learners used strategies demonstrating their application of this knowledge. Learners in both groups enjoyed literature, but only whole language children pursued intertextual comparisons across stories. The least proficient readers and writers from whole language classes demonstrated a greater range of coping strategies and greater persistence when working independently than their counterparts from skill-based classrooms.

Analyses were also made of the beginning and end-of-year scores on the measures of written language knowledge. Few significant differences were noted when children from the two instructional settings were compared. Whole language learners showed an advantage in one area: the test assessing student knowledge of written narratives.

Given the purpose of the study to detail learner interpretations across instructional settings, further description of instruction might have been unnecessary. Dahl and Freppon emphasized that they were interested in understanding the children's learning rather than teachers' thinking and activities. Indeed, they assert, "We have been asking the wrong questions. The important issue was not how children were taught in school-based settings, but rather what sense they could make" (p. 70). If they had stopped at this point, the design of their study would be reminiscent of earlier methods–comparison studies of the 1960s in which instructional contrasts remained unexplored.

But Dahl and Freppon did proceed to identify important instructional differences on the basis of their ethnographies. Teaching approaches are represented as learning opportunities in whole language and traditional classrooms in phonics, writing, and response to literature. They describe phonics learning opportunities in skills-based classrooms as follows: "Letter–sound relations were addressed in skill lessons. Teachers showed how to sound out words, and learners sounded out words as they read aloud. Worksheets about phonics were required as seatwork. Boardwork asked learners to copy words grouped by letter–sound patterns" (p. 68). In whole-language classrooms, "Teachers demonstrated sounding out during whole-group instruction with big books. In reading lessons letter–sound relations were one of the cueing systems that learners used to figure out words. Writing workshops included help for individual learners grappling with what letters to write for their intended meaning. Peers provided letter–sound information during daily writing" (p. 68). Few opportunities were available for extended writing in the skill-based curriculum. The most striking differences occurred in children's exposure to and individual response to literature. These descriptions of instruction were, however, global in nature; variations among teachers within instructional approach were not described.

These descriptive summaries suggest that both sets of teachers *taught* phonics but did so in different ways. Skills-based teachers addressed letter–sound relations in skill lessons by showing students how to sound out words and having students sound out words as they read aloud. Practice was provided through worksheets about phonics and boardwork involving word families. Whole-language teachers also demonstrated sounding out procedures during whole-group instruction with big books and provided practice on letter–sound relations during reading and writing. Both sets of teachers included writing and literature but did so in different ways.

ANALYSIS

Similar to Kantor et al., Dahl and Freepon (1995) used ethnographic methods to study literacy development, focusing their description on children, particularly on a subset whose learning they explore in depth. They view learning as a constructive process in which learners modify their knowledge through transactions in social and cultural contexts, including programs of instruction. Their view of learning took center stage in their analysis, and teaching was treated as a contextual condition.

Dahl and Freepon characterized teaching in general terms. The skill-based curriculum was described as "based on the idea that written language is learned through teacher-directed lessons and practiced as discrete skills that are taught sequentially" (p. 53). More compatible with their view of teaching and learning were the meaning-centered activities of whole language classrooms in which "the teacher 'leads from behind,' demonstrating reading and writing behaviors, instructing directly, and supporting children's efforts to learn" (p. 53). Although one may be concerned that their view of learning with its implicit view of teaching is at odds with that in skill-based classes, this was not a problem for Dahl and her colleagues. Their focus was clearly on learner interpretations of their literacy experiences, and they adopted a sociocultural perspective to explore how the dynamics of alternative learning environments shaped the motivation and knowledge construction of children.

For my purpose, however, what was missing was a nuanced portrayal of teaching, though providing one was not Dahl and Freepon's purpose. We learn, in spite of their limited treatment of teaching, about how teachers following different approaches organize different instructional activities. We do not gain an understanding from these global descriptions of how teachers using the same approach differ or learn about how teachers

think—what guided their participation and how they evolved instructional patterns that differ in unique ways from other teachers espousing similar philosophical perspectives. Studies that focus on learner response provide the basis for understanding learners, but they are not useful in developing an understanding of how teachers think and act. The descriptions of how children make sense of their instruction would be of interest to new and experienced teachers, but the description might be more informative with a more elaborated representation of teaching. The assumption that researchers must choose between a focus on teaching and learning can be questioned; we learn most when both aspects of this interactive whole are represented.

Facilitating Comprehension

Strategy Instruction

OVERVIEW AND ISSUES

Most studies of teaching in the field of reading focus on strategies to develop comprehension and vocabulary. These investigations have their roots in the cognitive research of the 1960s and 1970s. On the basis of the reading processes shown by proficient readers compared to the less proficient, researchers in the 1970s and 1980s explored *how* relevant knowledge and effective strategies could be taught. Strategy research has focused on preparing students to read prior to reading, encouraging them to monitor their reading while reading, and helping them remember what they have read. The approach, similar to that in studies of phonemic awareness, has been experimental; typically an innovative strategy is compared with traditional instruction (for reviews of this literature, see Alvermann & Moore, 1991; Beck & McKeown, 1991; Paris, Wasik, & Turner, 1991; Pearson & Fielding, 1991; Raphael & Brock, 1997).

Teachers who provide students with relevant background knowledge find that comprehension is improved (Dole, Valencia, Greer, & Wardrop, 1991; Stahl, Jacobson, Davis, & Davis, 1989; Wixson, 1986). Teachers who activate prior knowledge through interactive discussions (e.g., Rinehart, Barksdale-Ladd, & Paterson, 1994) and encourage integration of new information (DeWitz, Carr, & Patberg, 1987) have students who comprehend more than those without such preparation. But prior knowledge is not always a reliable source to guide comprehension, particularly when students have misconceptions. Guzzetti, Snyder, Glass, and Gamas (1993) in their review of research on science instruction found that teaching designed to promote cognitive conflict was more effective in promoting learning and clarifying misconceptions than less intrusive forms.

Many instructional interventions encourage students to be more aware of their reading processes. Such interventions include training students to think aloud about passage meaning (Baumann, Jones, & Siefert-Kessell, 1993; Baumann, Siefert-Kessell, & Jones, 1992), use mnemonic imagery (Peters & Levin, 1986), use metacognitive strategies reinforced with self-control training (Lundeberg, 1987), resolve anaphoric ambiguities (Baumann, 1986), use writing strategies to aid comprehension (Konopak, Martin, & Martin, 1990), and highlight key vocabulary to suggest inferences (Reutzel & Hollingsworth, 1988). Instructional efforts to enhance learning from text involve such strategies as summarizing text (Rinehart, Stahl, & Erickson, 1986), outlining and constructing graphic organizers (Bean, Singer, Sorter, & Frazee, 1986; Darch, Carnine, & Kameenui, 1986), mapping stories (Baumann & Bergeron, 1993; Scevak, Moore, & Kirby, 1993), and examining the nature of text organization (Berkowitz, 1986).

Experimental research of this sort continued into the 1990s, although at a somewhat diminished level than in prior years. Many current studies focused on the learning of special populations, including students identified as learning disabled, "at-risk," and bilingual (e.g., Borkowski, Weyhing, & Carr, 1988; Chan, Cole, & Morris, 1990; Dole, Brown, & Trathen, 1996; Kearn, 1989; Pressley, Brown, El-Dinary, & Afflerbach, 1995; Schunk & Rice, 1991, 1993).

In addition, the nature of experimental study has shifted substantively and methodologically. Changes have occurred in (a) *focus,* (b) *setting,* and (c) *research approach.* The focus of research has shifted from single strategies to combinations of strategies and in setting from unrelated sets of texts to classroom programs in content areas. Beginning with the seminal work of Palinscar and Brown (1984) and Duffy and colleagues (1986, 1987), researchers have increasingly developed content-specific strategy programs in the areas of literacy, social studies, history, science, and math (e.g., Bereiter & Bird, 1985; Gaskins, Anderson, Pressley, Cunicelli, & Satlow, 1993; Guthrie et al., 1996; Morrow, Pressley, Smith, & Smith, 1997; Paris & Oka, 1986; Pressley et al., 1992; Siegel & Fonzi, 1995). In these approaches, teachers are introduced to a variety of strategies that they introduce one at a time through direct instruction and revisit on a regular basis as appropriate throughout the year.

The long-term collaborations between university-based researchers and classroom teachers have prompted new ways of thinking about comprehension instruction. Because of the responsive nature of this teaching, Pressley et al. (1992) referred to this instruction as "transactional strategy instruction," marking a shift from older behavioral formulations of teaching to sociocognitive perspectives. The collaborative work has also shifted the focus of researchers from a preoccupation with student learning to an additional focus on the learning of teachers (Duffy et al., 1986, 1987; El-Dinary, Pressley, & Schuder, 1992; Hoffman, 1991; Roehler & Duffy, 1991). The strategy instruction introduced by teachers was evaluated through quasi-experimental designs involving comparison of students engaged in the strategy program with students from comparable classes receiving traditional instruction.

The approach has changed in some research to include descriptions of instruction in addition to experimental comparison. Recognizing the limitations of the skeletal descriptions of instruction in past research, qualitative research involving interviews and observation has become more common (e.g., Alvermann, O'Brien, & Dillon, 1990; Gaskins et al., 1993; Goldenberg, 1992; Guzzetti, & Williams, 1996; Lemke, 1990; Pressley et al., 1992; Saunders, O'Brien, Lennon, & McLean, 1998).

Because of the large number of studies pertaining to strategy instruction, relative to the other topical areas considered, two illustrative studies are considered in this section. The first by Dole et al. (1996) compared the effectiveness of two approaches, each consisting of several strategies, with traditional instruction on the learning of at-risk students. The second by Beck, McKeown, Sandora, Kucan, and Worthy (1996) entailed qualitative description of strategy instruction. The first is similar to many other studies of strategy and shows the application of the research approach to a special group of readers. The second shows the evolution of the research community into more qualitative forms of research.

DESCRIPTION OF THE DOLE, BROWN, AND TRATHEN STUDY

Dole et al. (1996) used an experimental comparison to assess the best approach to help at-risk students develop comprehension strategies. They argued that two major approaches have been shown to be effective. The first approach, *story content instruction,* is derived from a schema-theoretic perspective. By activating the prior knowledge of children and further developing their declarative knowledge, students are expected to show increases in their comprehension. The second approach, which they refer to as *strategy instruction,* is based in the literature on metacognition. In this approach, students are taught procedural and conditional knowledge; that is, how and when to use different strategies.

The question Dole and her colleagues pursued was "Which instructional approach is better for at-risk upper elementary students?" In particular, which is more effective in terms of (a) immediate story comprehension and (b) independent story reading? They also attempted to determine if these innovative approaches were more effective than the basal instruction used in the school (*basal control instruction*).

They selected 24 narratives, developed scripts for the three forms of instruction, randomly assigned 75 fifth and sixth graders to the three groups, and provided instruction over a 20-day (5 weeks) period. Instruction was offered during 50-minute periods to the three groups on a rotating basis by a Chapter 1 teacher, a graduate student, and one of the researchers. The story-content instructional script introduced vocabulary central to the story, provided a historical context for the story, and explained concepts and processes central to understanding it. The strategy instructional script encouraged self-monitoring, such as examining title and picture clues to get ideas about the story before reading and picking out the main character and identifying the problem while reading. The teacher was encouraged to stop periodically during the story to model reflection on what had been learned. The instructional script for the basal lesson recommended introducing vocabulary, developing background experiences, and asking comprehension questions that were included in the teacher's manual.

To assess comprehension, six passages with open-ended comprehension questions were developed, two administered at the beginning of the study, two at the end of 5 weeks following instruction, and two 7 weeks later. During each testing, one selection was read independently and one was read following instructional support of the sort experienced during the 5-week instructional period. The two experimental groups and the basal control did not differ in their comprehension when instructional support was offered. In contrast, students receiving strategy instruction performed significantly better than those who received story content and basal instruction when they read on their own without teacher support.

ANALYSIS

Dole and colleagues described two related cognitive perspectives that frame this research. The "schema-theoretic" perspective focused on activating and developing prior knowledge, whereas the "strategy" perspective focused on procedural and conditional knowledge about how and when to use different strategies. A difference existed in the way students and teachers were viewed. Students were viewed as active constructors of knowledge, whereas teachers were viewed as passively following scripts. Similar to the research on phonemic awareness, teaching emanates from a script to be faithfully followed, rather than from the joint construction of teacher and students.

In keeping with the experimental method and instructional treatments predefined by researchers, no attempt was made to document how instruction works. Evidence on the sequence of activities and the nature of the dialogue over time and across teachers was not collected. Potential variation in methods was not of interest because the research contrasts the generic approaches themselves. A chain of effects was assumed, that is, from a specified form of instruction, through teaching to supported learning, and then to unsupported literacy. The conception of teaching influence is linear.

How might this research be useful to teachers? It is useful to know that instruction focused on metacognitive strategies has an advantage for at-risk students when they read on their own. The generic descriptions of teaching may be instructive to both beginning and experienced teachers who are struggling to help their students become independent learners. Yet, the image presented fails to represent the interactive character of teaching, with its unpredictable aspects, and does not describe how different teachers work out the generic script.

DESCRIPTION OF THE BECK, MCKEOWN, SANDORA, KUCAN, AND WORTHY STUDY

Beck et al. (1996) developed an instructional approach, "Questioning the Author," that combines several strategies to enhance learning in the content areas of history and language arts. They referred to it as a deceptively simple approach in which "students grapple with and reflect on what an author is trying to say in order to build a representation from it" (p. 387). In this study, they assessed the developmental phase of the intervention by documenting the discussion and the perceptions of participants as well as student learning.

Teachers learning the approach were taught how to structure the whole class discussion actively. Two forms of support were provided; the first was a protocol teachers could use to model how a reader might respond to ideas in a text in an effort to develop understanding, and the second was a set of queries to guide discussion. These queries were subject matter specific and for expository texts included such as the following questions: "What is the author trying to say?" "That's what the author says, but what does it mean?" "How does that connect with what the author already told us?" "Did the author explain that clearly?" A modified version was developed for narratives.

The study documenting this approach occurred in a small, predominantly African-American parochial school and involved a language arts teacher, a social studies teacher, and their 23 inner-city fourth grade students. Beck and her colleagues provided support for the teachers through ongoing observations and discussions and weekly meetings. Data sources included frequent classroom observation and weekly videotaping, beginning in the spring of the year to establish a base condition and continuing from September to May of the subsequent year. Teachers were interviewed frequently, kept journals, and observed each other's teaching. Students were interviewed and responded to individual comprehension tasks in September and May.

Questions focused on describing changes in lessons from the beginning to the end of the study as evidenced by changes in (a) classroom talk, (b) teacher and student perceptions, and (c) student comprehension. A class lesson was documented during the baseline period, and five lessons were observed during the year (September, November, January, March, and May). Yet, instead of showing trends over time during the period of the intervention, simple comparisons were made between the base lesson and an average of the five Questioning-the-Author lessons.

Analysis focused on the nature of teacher questions and the amount of teacher versus student talk during the baseline lesson compared to the average of the intervention lessons. Teachers shifted away from an emphasis on questions to retrieve information during the base lesson to an increase in questions promoting construction of the message and extension of the discussion, particularly for the social studies instruction. Both teachers made more comments that made student contributions public through refinement as opposed to simply repeating comments. For both teachers, the proportion of teacher talk decreased and the proportion of student talk, including the number of student initiated questions and comments, increased during Questioning the Author. Whether improvement occurred during the course of the school year cannot be known because a single average score was used.

The comments of the teachers and students about the instruction revealed the changes they experienced. Student learning assessed by a comprehension task showed higher levels of constructive activity and successful monitoring at the end of the year than at the beginning. No control condition was included in the study. Beck and colleagues suggested that conclusions about students' abilities to construct meaning and monitor their understanding must be limited: "The extent to which these results are due to students' experience with Questioning the Author cannot be said with certainty because of the lack of a control condition" (p. 408).

ANALYSIS

Similar to the study by Dole et al., Beck and colleagues also worked from a cognitive perspective. They assumed, however, that the meaning construction of students was similar to the meaning construction of teachers during responsive instruction. Their approach reflected a belief in the power of social interaction as a catalyst to meaning making and learning. The instructional approach was much more flexible than scripted approaches that specify teaching activity and language more completely. Teachers were expected to monitor the content of discussion to discover what queries are appropriate. In sum, the implicit views of teaching and learning conformed more closely to a social-constructivist perspective than did those involving scripted interventions.

The process of teaching was viewed as constructive, and thus, understanding how instruction specifically gets worked out on a daily basis was important. From the descriptive research, we see how the nature of teacher questions, as well as the comments and questions of children, shifted with the implementation of the new approach. In its focus on discourse, Beck's study was similar to Dickinson's. They both valued discourse as a key aspect of instruction. Other aspects of classroom activity, however, were not explored (writing, other language art activities) even through they may influence how teaching and learning occur. Moreover, the characteristics of text were not examined in relation to discourse. For Beck's study, in particular, relating complexities of text, as well as students comments, to the queries of teachers would provide evidence on the appropriateness of teacher comments. Analysis similar to that of Dickinson where classes were characterized in terms of distinctive discourse patterns could not be pursued in Beck's research because of the small number of teachers studied. The evidence presented by Beck and colleagues, nevertheless, showed that the nature of Questioning the Author discourse differed from traditional recitational instruction.

The qualitative evidence on student and teacher perceptions of the program and its implementation complemented the discourse evidence; together they offered a textured portrayal of the program. Particularly from the comments of teachers, one gains an appreciation of the complexities inherent in changing mental habits that alter the balance of power in a classroom. Beck's research, and other similar studies, have shifted the focus of research from student learning with teaching as a "black box" to a focus on teaching as well as learning.

Response to Literature

OVERVIEW AND ISSUES

Research on response to literature has its origins in the theoretical and empirical work of scholars from the field of English; it arises, then, from quite different traditions than the research on reading strategies. The conceptual center of the field continues to be on the response of individuals to literature (e.g., Beach & Hynds, 1991; Galda, Shockley, & Pellegrini, 1995; Hynds, 1989; Langer, 1992; 1995; Marshall, Smagorinski, & Smith, 1995), although interest in contextual influences (e.g., Almasi, McKeown, & Beck, 1996; Hickman, 1983; Marshall, 1987), cultural and linguistic background (e.g., Brock, 1997; Lee, 1993; 1995), and in strategy instruction (e.g., Block, 1993; McGee, Courtney, & Lomax, 1994; Newell, 1996) has risen along with theoretical developments emphasizing the social nature of constructed response (see chapter 23 for further description of this literature).

The challenge for researchers interested in classroom instruction is to find teachers who organize their instruction so that students have a chance to respond to literature; this is not easy,

given the predominance of recitations or "gentle inquisitions" in which students' responses tend to be literal and limited. Two main solutions are followed (a) finding exemplary teachers who encourage "grand conversations" around literature and are willing to be studied (e.g., McMahon, 1992, McMahon & Raphael, 1997) and (b) supporting teachers willing to learn new strategies and documenting their effect on the conversations of students (Almasi, 1995; Eeds & Wells, 1989; Rogers, 1991). In addition, some researchers provide the instruction themselves, as well as supporting the instruction of other teachers (Lee, 1993; 1995).

In addition to studies of teacher-led discussions, others examine conditions under which productive discussions occur, documenting student participation in peer-led groups, sometimes in comparison with those led by teachers (Almasi, 1995; Evans, 1996; Knoeller, 1994; McGee, 1992). It is not always true that student discussions are productive (McMahon, 1992; Raphael et al., 1992). Finally, the approach used to study students' response to literature is also used to explore students' response to content area text. Alvermann and colleagues (1996) found, for example, that students could articulate the norms and expectations for peer-led and whole-class discussions and were aware of how such discussions helped them understand content area texts.

The research literature consists mainly of case studies that focus on the discourse of groups to identify indices of rich discussions and to trace how individual perspectives shape interpretation. Some researchers, working from the perspective of feminist theories, examine the struggles over identity and the contradictions that emerge in the language of discussions and the language of literature (e.g., Alvermann, Commeyras, Young, Randall, & Hinson, 1997; Crawford & Chaffin, 1986; Nielson, 1997). Alvermann's (1996) case study in which she examined her own teaching and students' response to literature, for example, applies a feminist framework to understanding the response of students to literature and her own feelings about their comments and her response to them. Others explore the relations between literature discussions and cultural identity (e.g., Encisco, 1994; Raphael & Brock, 1993).

DESCRIPTION OF THE EEDS AND WELLS STUDY

Eeds and Wells (1989) in their study of grand conversations sought to describe patterns of classroom discussion and how teachers and students responded to text and to each other. Instead of studying existing classes, Eeds and Wells created heterogeneous study groups composed of four to eight fifth and sixth grade students. These groups were led by teachers-in-training, participating in a practicum taught by one of the researchers. The teachers-in-training were encouraged not only to let meaning emerge from group discussion but also to seize "teachable moments" as they occurred. The teachers met with their groups of students twice a week over a 4- to 5-week period and kept journals of their experiences. The researchers assumed the role of participant observers, taking extensive field notes and audio taping all sessions.

From a total of 17 study groups, 15 yielded complete, intelligible, and transcribable audio data. On the basis of a reading of all discourse transcripts, the following four group cases were selected for in-depth analysis: two groups believed to be extremely successful (*Tuck Everlasting* and *After Goat Man*) and two groups thought to be less successful (*Harriet the Spy* and *The Dark Angel*), according to Eeds and Wells' perception that the latter teachers talked too much, emphasized literal meaning, and failed to respond to teachable moments. To test these impressions, they examined the number and nature of comments during group discussion. Contrary to their first impression, they found that the teacher of *Harriet the Spy* talked less than did her students and relatively less than the other three teachers, while the teacher of *After Goat Man* talked the most. Also contrary to expectations, interpretative and evaluative comments exceeded literal ones for all teachers, but the group they viewed positively, reading *Tuck Everlasting,* made fewer literal comments than the other three.

On the basis of their detailed analysis of discourse, Eeds and Wells continued to view the discussion of *Tuck Everlasting* as more successful and that of *The Dark Angel* as less successful, with the other two groups falling in between. The results suggested that first impressions may be deceiving. They found the conversation of the *Harriet the Spy* group to be of higher quality than they had first thought. At the same time, they noted that the group leader of *The Dark Angel* encouraged students less than the other leaders, made fewer synthetic comments, and focused more on general conversational maintenance through requests for agreement, nominations for turns, and initiations. Regarding the success of the discussion of *Tuck Everlasting,* Eeds and Wells speculated that the generalization comments, when students analyzed the author's intended message or discussed their perception of the theme, accounted for the exciting nature of the group discussion.

Yet all groups looked more alike than different on the basis of the quantitative findings from the discourse analysis. Eeds and Wells suggested that these patterns reflected generic features of all group discussions and, in this capacity, were not particularly useful in understanding the qualitative differences related to an aesthetic reading of literature. They suggested that a more appropriate focus may be how often teachers seized teachable moments by calling attention "to the literary element that was being discussed (characterization or style, for example)" (p. 10). To do this, the teacher must be aware of the characteristics of the literary selection being discussed, as well as the substance of the discussion. The total number of teachable moment opportunities varied among groups from 25 to 48, and teachers differed considerably in taking advantage of these moments. The two teachers initially thought to be most successful showed a high degree of responsiveness (*Tuck Everlasting,* 44%, and *After Goat Man,* 85%) as did the teacher of *Harriet the Spy* (55%). The teacher of *The Dark Angel* was least successful (6%).

To examine qualitative differences further, Eeds and Wells shifted to a different set of categories to "address the essence of what occurred in these literature study groups" (p. 14). They identified four categories. The first category, constructing simple meaning, referred to the talk following the initial reading when group members "lived the action and then shared their impressions and ideas and problems or difficulties they encountered in constructing meaning" (p. 15). The second category, personal involvement, entailed sharing personal stories triggered by the story or the discussion. The third category, inquiry, involved hypothesizing about meaning, extending interpretations, and verifying their speculations. The final category, critique, addressed what was liked and valued and why. Eeds and Wells presented excerpts from group discussions to exemplify these exchanges.

The personal journals of the group leaders revealed how difficult it was for them to shift from the recitational tradition of gentle inquisitions to real discussions. Yet, in spite of this, Eeds and Wells noted that children as young as 10, different in ability, constructed simple meanings based on their readings, shared personal experiences, predicted and speculated about their understandings, and critiqued the stories—evidence that the teachers were successful in promoting rich discussions.

ANALYSIS

What broader conceptualization of literacy and learning framed this research? In keeping with disciplinary influences from the field of English, Eeds and Wells were influenced by reader response theory. They compared what actually occurred in groups with an idealized model that they referred to as grand conversation. By a grand conversation they meant the construction and disclosure of "deeper meaning, enriching understanding for all participants" (Eeds & Wells, 1989, p. 5). They were interested in documenting how teachers and students responded to text and to each other. They were also interested in teachers seizing the teachable moments by calling attention "to the literary element being discussed (characterization or style, for example)" (p. 10). To do this, the teacher must be aware of the characteristics of the literary selection, as well as the substance of the discussion. Although Eeds and Wells mentioned the work of Vygotsky and the importance of interacting with peers, sociocognitive theories did not appear to have had a major influence on their research; their interpretations derived mainly by the values and assumptions of response theory.

Eeds and Wells' view of teaching was clearly on the side of resisting gentle inquisitions, in favor of promoting discussions that disclosed the deeper meaning of literature. Following their empirical analysis of group discourse, they rejected a discourse view of teaching as being not particularly useful in understanding the qualitative differences related to an aesthetic reading of literature. The set of four categories they developed retained the essence of response to literature as a dynamic process in which action is lived, impressions are shared, problems of construction are discussed, and personal stories are shared. Teaching was viewed as highly contextualized by the literature being read and the responses of other readers.

How might this perspective on teaching be useful to other teachers? Through observation; audio and video taping of the discussions; journals kept by the researcher, teachers, and students; and interviews with participants, they developed portraits of each of the 15 groups. They questioned, however, whether their more systematic analysis of the discourse in four of the groups was of value, choosing instead to develop a scheme that more directly derives from response theory. What may be of particular value to teachers were their view of interpretive processes and the goals of grand conversations. Teachers may use this perspective to reflect on their own practice in teaching literature and finding teachable moments.

Teachers and Teaching

Understanding and Changing Teaching

OVERVIEW AND ISSUES

A different perspective on teaching builds on anthropological and sociological traditions to describe and interpret the processes of literacy instruction *as situated* in classrooms and schools. Researchers seek to understand teaching and learning as shaped by cultural, motivational, material, and temporal conditions (Gee, 2000; Green & Bloome, 1997; Roehler & Duffy, 1991). They emphasize the social and situationally embedded nature of reading and reading instruction and argue that attempts to change instruction must begin with an understanding of teaching as it exists. Only then can changes be made that are compatible with existing conditions (Barr, 1986).

Several ethnographies, focusing mainly on classroom activities, ask about how the classroom culture is socially constructed through the content and form of language (Bloome, 1987; Bloome & Green, 1984; Santa Barbara Discourse Group, 1992, 1995). Some researchers describe the relations between curricular materials, teacher goals, and classroom language (e.g., Alvermann et al., 1990; Alvermann & Hayes, 1989; Alvermann, O'Brien, Dillon, & Smith, 1985; Barr, 1987; Dillon, 1989; Dillon, O'Brien, Moje, & Steward, 1994; Kamberelis, & de la Luna, 1996). Others consider the culture of students' families and communities in relation to their schooling (e.g., Heath, 1983; Moll, 1992; Moll & Gonzales, 1994). What these studies have in common is seeking to understand classrooms and the perspectives of classroom participants in their own terms.

Over the past decade, literacy research continues to provide a conceptual representation of classroom culture. But some studies explore how teaching and learning in the classroom can be changed. Initiatives for change come from researchers or teachers or both seeking to align instruction more closely with the cultural understandings of students. In a classic precursor to current research, Au (1980) worked with teachers in the Kamehameha School to develop a new form of reading instruction, "talk" story based on classroom discourse and Hawaiian family language patterns. Similarly, Moll and Gonzales (1994) showed that some teachers build on an increased understanding of their students' family and community experiences directly, whereas others incorporate such knowledge in indirect ways (see also Kamberelis & de la Luna, 1996; Lee, 1995).

Other initiatives for change come from socioconstructivist perspectives of teaching and learning that have implications for the roles and social interaction among participants in the classroom. Many teachers working closely with university researchers during the past decade have sought to implement and reflect on literature-based reading instruction (e.g., Allen, Cary, & Delgado, 1995; Bruneau, 1992; Hoffman et al., 1996; Raphael & Goatley, 1994; Scharer, 1992, 1996; Solsken, 1993; Stewart, Paradis, & Van Arsdale, 1995). The resulting case studies describe the ongoing collaborative process of identifying approaches to be used and the challenges inherent in establishing new roles and classroom patterns.

Radical change in classroom practice is complex and demanding. As Richardson and colleagues argued, an exploration of beliefs is pivotal in changing practice (Fenstermacher, 1994; Richardson, 1990, 1994; Tidwell, 1995). In their study of the relations between teachers' beliefs about teaching reading comprehension and their classroom practices in Grades 4, 5, and 6, Richardson, Anders, Tidwell, and Lloyd (1991) found a close relation between beliefs and practice. On the basis of the discrepant case of a teacher whose beliefs did not correspond to practice, they found that changes in belief preceded those in practice.

Not all desired changes, however, are easily made. Alvermann and Hayes (1989), for example, explored whether five high school teachers with whom they worked could modify aspects of their practice that they wanted to change. Four teachers were able to change the types of references they made to text so that the student inferences became more closely related to textual evidence. In contrast, patterns of verbal interaction in all classrooms continued to be dominated by teacher talk even though all teachers had hoped to increase student contributions, particularly from the silent majority of each class. Difficulties inherent in change are instructive because they reveal the complexity of relating a range of beliefs and goals, some of which may be in conflict, to classroom practice.

DESCRIPTION OF THE MOJE STUDY

Moje's (1996) ethnography of a high school basic chemistry class grew from her desire to understand why many high school teachers either resist using or inconsistently use content literacy practices (O'Brien, Stewart, & Moje, 1995). She posed the following four questions: "(a) What is the nature of the literacy events and practices in one chemistry classroom? (b) How do students and the teacher make decisions about using literacy to learn chemistry? (c) How are these decisions about literacy events and practices shaped by the teacher's and students' life experiences and histories? and (d) How are these decisions shaped by classroom interactions? How do the decisions shape interactions?" (Moje, 1996, p. 172). As the questions suggest, she views literacy practices as socially constructed within specific contexts and for certain purposes. Her goal was to explore how an exemplary teacher used literacy to help her students learn chemistry.

Although the study was conducted over a 2-year period, the analysis was based mainly on data collected with the teacher, Ms. Landy, during the second year of the study with a class of 22 students. Ms. Landy, a 20-year veteran, was selected because she reported using literacy activities to teach her students. Seven students were selected as key informants because of their unique interactions with Ms. Landy and their differing achievement levels. Primary sources of data included daily field note observations, seven structured interviews with the teacher, 15 interviews with the key student informants, and daily informal interviews with participants. On the basis of reading and rereading these observational interview notes, recurring categories were identified and related. The results support two related assertions: (a) "In this chemistry classroom, literacy was practiced as a tool for organizing thinking and learning in the context of a relationship built between the teacher and her students" (p. 180), and (b) "The practice of literacy as an organizational tool was encouraged and supported by the relationship that had been built in the classroom culture" (p. 181). The first assertion summarized those reports and observations showing that literacy was used as a tool in the class and how it was used. The second summarized data showing that students believed Landy cared about them and used literacy activities to help them learn chemistry; hence their use of the literacy activities.

One part of the report presented observations and comments corresponding to the first assertion. Moje began by providing a holistic picture of classroom interaction, with examples showing how literacy was used in the classroom. In a description of a lesson at the beginning of the semester, she noted that "Homework" (including use of a study strategy, SQ3R) and "Do now" assignments were listed on the board. The illustrative lesson began with Landy's elicitation of definitions of observation and the discussion focused on the meaning of observation versus inference. Landy then prepared a science demonstration, filling two beakers with unknown liquid(s) and dropping a blue-colored cube in each beaker. She asked students in turn to share their observations, as one student recorded them on the board, and then to review their observations to decide if what was written was an observation or an inference.

Moje followed this description with interpretive summaries. With respect to Landy's literacy practices, Moje noted that she used mainly textbook readings with some secondary source reading, and that she introduced reading strategies (e.g., concept mapping), note-taking strategies (e.g., split-page notes), and study strategies (e.g., SQ3R) to help students organize their understanding of the text. Moje presented interview evidence that Landy treated science metaphorically as organization:

Sometimes if a student raises a question in discussion, you know, in term of organization, I'm flexible. In terms of that, where I'd maybe not teach what's in the lesson but take something that comes off or stems from the side, but basic organization skills . . . that's what chemistry is. (Interview, November 21, 1991, p. 184)

With regard to her interactions with students, Landy engaged students in activities that developed meaningful distinctions about science and involved them in informal banter to bring interest and humor to the discussion.

To understand the teacher–student relationships that developed in the class, Moje developed a historical narrative of Landy's family and teaching experiences, tracing their relation to her beliefs and decisions. Similarly, on the basis of interviews with the seven students, Moje explored their beliefs about teachers, success in learning, construction of classroom interactions, and reasons for following the literacy strategies Landy introduced. Most interesting, Moje reported that although students learned and used literacy strategies in the chemistry class, they did not transfer them to other classes. She interpreted this finding as showing that

the strategies were shaped by and served the social practices of that chemistry classroom. Organization was the operating metaphor for the classroom culture, and every strategy that was used supported organized learning and teaching in some way. Thus, a strategy like SQ3R seemed inappropriate to students in classrooms where social and academic practices were not shaped by organization but were shaped by ambiguity or creativity. (p. 190)

The use of literacy practices were supported by the complex set of relationships formed in this particular classroom. Moje drew the following two main implications: (a) subsequent research needs to focus on instruction as embedded in classroom and school contexts and (b) teacher beliefs need to be represented more broadly in terms of their beliefs about their content area, students and the social and political context of the school, in addition to their beliefs about literacy.

ANALYSIS

In developing the theoretical framework for this study, Moje drew on sociocultural theories of literacy, teaching, and learning to interpret how the beliefs and experiences of participants influence their interaction in the classroom and their learning. We have here a probing of the interface between the past histories and perspectives of participants and the organizational structure of science instruction. Moje's ethnographic focus was on understanding the social interactions in the classroom and the meanings that the teacher and students ascribe to them. Through long-term involvement in the classroom, Moje pursued a representation of literacy *as situated* in classrooms to understand how teaching and learning were shaped by cultural, motivational, material, and temporal conditions.

Similar to Kantor and her colleagues, Moje treated teaching as an integrated system that evolves over time, responsive to the knowledge and past experiences of teachers and the beliefs, experiences, and initiatives of students. Accordingly, strategies cannot be easily inserted into a classroom unless the web of established relations and the teacher's conception of the work of the class support such incorporation. This view contrasts markedly with those of interventions in phonemic awareness and strategy instruction that assume a script, predefined or interactive, can be added into an existing instructional system; in the latter form of intervention, instructional sequences are assumed to hold for all situations in spite of different classroom conditions. Moje's study also goes beyond thinking of teaching in terms of what teachers say (discourse) to include an understanding of meanings ascribed in the context of subject matter learning.

The knowledge developed about teaching through this research and similar studies might be of value to teachers who contemplate including literacy practices to support content learning. The beliefs and experiences of the teacher and her students and how they view classroom interaction are described in rich detail. And yet, more attention is focused on the social than on the academic aspect of the work of the classroom. An ethnography permits visions of classroom teaching and learning from a variety of perspectives, and Moje chose to focus on teacher–student relationships as contexts for literacy more than on Landy's subject matter decision making and practice. We learn relatively little from the case about how Landy's metaphorical thinking about chemistry as "organization" evolved, and what its implications were for the selection of class activities, assignments, and literacy strategies. Perhaps, the reason why Landy can focus on relationships and content in such a flexible manner is that she has already developed an understanding of which science activities create useful problematic situations for learning, which literacy strategies support student learning, and what she wants students to learn.

Teacher Inquiry

OVERVIEW AND ISSUES

The history of teacher inquiry is long; what distinguishes the current period is the large number of teachers who are looking at their practice and writing about their inquiries (Baumann, Bisplinghoff, & Allen, 1997; Lytle & Cochran-Smith, 1994). Much current writing comes from teacher research communities that emerged from writing projects or university partnerships (e.g., Allen et al., 1995; Beyer, 1996; Bissex & Bullock, 1987; Cochran-Smith & Lytle, 1993; Gitlin et al., 1992; Goswami & Stillman, 1987; Wells, 1994).

What is important about and unique to this work is that teachers intimately familiar with the workings of the classroom, its participants, its history, and its culture are writing about their sense of what occurs there. They ask questions that arise from their practice: Who are their students and what are the implications of their background experiences for teaching and learning? Is the curriculum the best it could be; what is taken up by students and what is unheard? What political power relations and policies exist in the school; who do they serve and who do they marginalize? Through systematic observation and reflection concerning such questions as these, teachers refine their practical theory of teaching and share their ideas with others.

Many studies focus on children's learning and development (e.g., Buchanan, 1993; Gallas, 1994; Strieb, 1993). Others address a variety of issues, including assessing learning (Bailey, 1995; Morrison & Kieffer, 1995), creating democratic classrooms (Cunat, 1996; Gitlin et al., 1992; Jaddaoui, 1996; Shah, 1996), developing home–school connections (White, 1995), incorporating drama (Kieffer, 1995), examining gendered roles (e.g., Waff, 1995), including special needs students (Kimbrell-Lee & Wood, 1995), responding to diversity (e.g., Colgan-Davis, 1993), supporting reader response (e.g., Atwell, 1987; Kauffman, Short, Crawford, Kahn, & Kaser, 1996; Swartz, 1994), developing literature-based programs (Gallas, 1994; Maher, 1994), and understanding text genre (e.g., Donovan, 1996; Feldgus, 1993). University professors also report on their teaching experiences in public schools (e.g., Baumann, 1996; Rowe, 1994) and universities (e.g., Alvermann, 1966; Bullion-Mears, 1994; Deegan, 1995; Fey, 1994; Mosenthal, 1994, 1995).

Studies by teacher researchers are not of a type. Some are empirical inquiries in classrooms, others involve journal reflections over time, and still others are reflective essays (Cochran-Smith & Lytle, 1993; Patterson, Santa, Short, & Smith, 1993). Those teacher researchers pursuing empirical questions typically collect and analyze samples of students' work, journals,

observational notes, and audiotapes or videotapes. More conceptual inquiries entail analyses of selected aspects of classroom life to reveal hidden assumptions and complex understandings of teaching and learning. As noted by Baumann and colleagues (1997), the struggle of teachers in pursuing their questions is to find methods that are doable, true to the intent of the inquiry, and non-preemptive of the teacher's first priority to teach students.

Because of ongoing responsibilities and involvement, teachers have a unique opportunity to develop contextualized insights and knowledge. At the same time, this involvement may make it particularly difficult for them as "insiders" to discern and understand taken-for-granted aspects of everyday experience (Erickson, 1986). Huberman (1996) in his reflections on teacher inquiry believed the following four activities are needed for this line of research to realize its potential: "staying intimate with local knowledge . . . keeping close to the community of people interested in the same issues . . . elaborating a robust yet tailored methodological repertoire . . . [and] conceptual mastery over the visible and unseen processes that account for pupils' learning" (p. 138).

Selecting an appropriate illustrative study for detailed analysis was difficult because of the diversity in teacher research topics and approaches. I chose the study by Maher because of her desire to understand processes accounting for the learning of her pupils.

DESCRIPTION OF THE MAHER STUDY

Maher's inquiry (1994) entailed a progressive delineation of what she took as problematic aspects of her classroom literacy program, and her attempted solutions and further refinements. As she noted, "As is often the case with action research, it took me some time to discover the full import of where my inquiry was leading" (p. 96). Her study, based in her Grade 4/5 classroom, was precipitated by her unease with her teacher-directed form of reading instruction in which she worked on a daily basis with a small group of eight to ten students while the remaining students read other material independently. She was concerned by the superficial discussions occurring in the groups and the limited amount of time that students had to read. She assessed the situation as requiring a new structure where students had more control over what they read and the time and opportunity to respond to what they read "in a comfortable and natural manner."

She met with her students to tell them of her concern and her plan to have them read books of their choice two periods a week, while they would have directed group reading the other three periods. The children agreed. But the plan raised questions for Maher about how she would hear students read, evaluate their comprehension, and talk with them about the books they were reading. She decided to have them begin by using reading journals. After reading their journal entries, however, she became concerned about their impersonality. Through her personal response to students in the form of letters with questions, she began over time to see the personal voice of students appear.

She noted a second problem in the journals—the lack of immediacy in conversation arose because journal exchanges were infrequent. She contemplated ways to encourage vivid conversations. During a basal reading lesson when she had been called away, she returned to find that the students were dramatizing the story. This experience, in addition to the encouragement she received from a conference speaker and a book she read about teacher experiences with literature-based reading programs, gave her the resolve to give up directed reading instruction and shift to an independent reading approach.

She initiated the independent reading with a conversation about some aspect of the books she and her students were reading. On the first day, she read the first sentence from the detective novel she was reading. From Dickens, a child read the first line, "Marley was dead to begin with," which set off a lively discussion about writers' techniques. Each day, the class began the period with what they called "conversations about books," followed by 20 to 30 minutes of silent reading. During the latter portion of this period, she met with students individually and kept a record of their discussion, what they were reading, and how they felt about it. She also recorded some of the conferences to reflect further on the quality of the conversation. In addition, she organized weekly small group meetings in which children shared their reactions to their books with each other. These discussions complemented more informal student discussion that punctuated the ongoing events in the class.

To take stock, she invited the children to comment on their reading experiences with the new program. Their comments included "'I like people to talk about my books.' 'And then we have lots more books cause some kids bring some in to share.' and 'Yeah, you get to learn about more books and read more books and get to find out about more books'" (p. 93). In addition, she reflected on what she had learned. She noted that "what started as simply a concern with the reading component of my programs has naturally spread into all areas of linguistic-meaning making" (p. 86). Reflecting on the changes for students, she commented that she "needed the time and opportunity to experience, first-hand, their responses to these changes. Their genuine interests in, and enthusiasm for, our conversations about books convinced me that my program was becoming more successful" (p. 87).

ANALYSIS

Maher's perspective was based in whole language philosophy. Her approach to change entailed action research in which she identified a problem, enlisted the class in a solution, implemented the agreed-upon change, collected student written and oral work, and evaluated the results. The evaluation phase then began the cycle again, either toward increased refinement of an activity or identification of a new aspect of literacy to be modified. In her study, Maher considered existing circumstances, but perhaps because these circumstances were so familiar to her, a precise description was not provided. She drew on her assessment of student work and on ideas from the whole language literature to define appropriate activities. The approach entailed progressive refinement in which the activities of students conformed more closely over time to the ideal she had in mind. The process was lengthy and cyclical, and through her reflection on students' responses to instructional activities, she continued to develop an increasingly more complex understanding of teaching and learning.

The view of teaching was similar to that portrayed in collaborative studies of change in teaching practice. That is, teaching consists of creating a culture for a specific group of children. Maher's report demonstrated how she refined a vision for the thoughtful reading and writing she wished her students to do. It described not only the instructional structures she established but also the resulting quality of students' comments and writing. The documentation focused mainly on student work and less on her role in establishing these new activities—what she said, how the room was organized, how she thought about time, and what she needed to know about the materials.

Reports from teacher researchers are valuable to other teachers who also reflect on their practice, reconceptualize it, and contemplate changes. Studies are useful if they raise provocative questions, suggest rich conceptual frameworks for understanding students' and classroom life, and thus can inform a teacher's further inquiry into his or her own practice. The number of rich, detailed case studies of teacher inquiry in the literature is increasing. The studies provide a window into other classrooms and into the minds of other teachers that can inform practice.

Summary and Discussion

The dominant paradigm for exploring teaching literacy before 1985 involved experimental comparison of new methods with traditional approaches with a smattering of ethnographic and sociological studies. A striking departure from the past decade is the increased amount of literacy research about teaching and learning in classrooms. Experimental studies previously conducted in laboratories and other settings are now usually pursued in classrooms. Ethnographic, sociolinguistic, and other descriptive classroom studies have become common. Moreover, collaborative studies by university and school-based teachers and inquiries by teachers have added an insider perspective on teaching and learning.

Most current literacy researchers were trained in the social sciences, typically with emphasis on psychological perspectives. Almost all the research reviewed falls within the scientific traditions of inquiry in which claims are justified in relation to a body of empirical knowledge on the nature of teaching and learning (e.g., Darling-Hammond & Snyder, 1992). Yet, particularly for descriptive research, a greater variety of interpretive frames are now applied than in the past, including those from humanistic traditions that seek to understand phenomena with reference to more purely philosophical or humanistic values and beliefs (Lincoln, 1992). This tendency is especially marked in studies of response to literature.

Classroom studies differ in how much they address teaching. Some do so in a limited way. Experimental designs, in particular, treat teaching as a variable, an activity introduced to observe its effect on some outcome, rather than as something to study in its own right. This is true for much research on phonemic awareness and reading strategies, and some on beginning reading methods. The recent inclusion of descriptive research, shown most clearly in studies of strategies, complements research on effectiveness by revealing *how* an instructional approach works and how teachers differ in using it. This documentation shows not only whether the intended model is realized, but also how teachers respond and build on the comments of students.

Beck and her colleagues' description of strategy instruction was similar to the studies of Dickinson and Smith and Eeds and Wells in their focus on language. The three represent a useful contrast for thinking about how research on discourse informs our conceptualization of teaching. Their purposes are similar, that is, to identify patterns of teacher–child interaction during book reading (Dickinson), to describe changes in discourse during lessons (Beck), and to describe how teachers and students respond to text and to each other (Eeds). Transcripts of discourse reveal the dynamic quality of language and convey primary aspects of teaching and learning that are lost through coding abstractions. At the same time, discourse analyses deepen our understanding of categories of teaching and learning that may not be obvious through direct observation or first impressions from transcripts. Both Beck and Eeds and their colleagues depicted a responsive quality on the part of teachers to the specific comments of students; both are concerned with shared power, decreasing teacher talk, and increasing the complexity of discussions. Yet, as Eeds and Wells argued, these categories may not adequately represent important aspects of discussions, particularly about literature. Although these three groups of researchers acknowledged the importance of materials, none represented their effect systematically on classroom discussion through intertextual relations. What we have in these analyses of discourse is a partial rendering of an essential aspect of teaching, but what is lacking is a broader formulation of teaching of which discourse is a part.

One focus of this analysis has been on the methodological changes that have occurred in the study of literacy teaching. These methodological shifts are symptomatic of underlying changes in how we think about teaching and learning. Theoretically, this shift from behavioristic to socioconstructivist formulations marks a change from thinking of teaching and learning as separate processes to those that are tied together, from viewing the teaching–learning process as unidirectional to interactive, from believing what is taught is also learned to understanding that what is taught may not be what is learned, from viewing learning as an individual process to one that is social. The theoretical shift incorporates the active role of learners in the process of learning. Correspondingly, we see in the research on strategies a shift from preoccupation with scripts to guide teaching, to a focus on responsive, interactive forms of socially constructed activity. Analyses of discourse reveal the dynamic nature of this interaction and allow us to trace how what is provided by the teacher, student, or materials is taken up, changed, and elaborated by students and teacher. Does this unified view of teaching and learning mean that we cannot focus on teaching or on learning to understand their separate contributions to the process?

Dahl and Freppon along with Kantor and her colleagues exemplified somewhat different answers to this question. Dahl and Freppon, for example, argued that the important issue was "not how children were taught in school-based settings, but rather what sense they could make;" in other words, they believe that "looking at teaching reflects asking the wrong question" (p. 70). They seemed to say that because children take up instruction in different ways, there is no practical benefit in describing or understanding teaching. Yet, their documentation of the influence of whole-language and skills-based teaching on the sense children make of literacy suggested, to the contrary, the importance of teaching. Children, depending on the nature of their instruction, participate in different activities and learn to think about literacy differently.

Kantor and colleagues made no distinction between teaching and learning in the first place. They believed that literacy activities should be designed to achieve social purposes; through participation in countless informal literacy experiences, children begin to understand the power and functions of print. They observed that teachers' efforts to support literacy were sometimes not taken up by children; and when they were, children did not always treat them as the teacher intended. Similar to Dahl and colleagues, their purpose was not to explore the nature of teaching. Perhaps to do so would work against their characterization of literacy activities as carefully orchestrated interactions between students and teachers. But the teacher does the orchestrating, and similar to experiencing a symphony, it is possible to focus on the role of a player or conductor. Knowing the symphony as a whole furthers understanding a particular role. For teachers wishing to teach the ways Kantor and colleagues described, an analysis of teaching that shows the main considerations teachers make in establishing this environment, as well as the nature of "formats" and "invitations," would be helpful.

Most literacy researchers have shifted to a socioconstructivist view of literacy teaching and learning. Yet ambivalence remains, which is shown most clearly by those who seek representations of practice to guide the professional development of experienced and novice teachers. The development of instructional scripts and sets of instructional activities may be an effective way to represent instruction, but implicit in this approach is a view of teaching that is unidirectional in influence and not responsive to the needs and contributions of students. Even more responsive forms, such as exemplified in the Beck study, model a particular way of reading text and guide teachers to ask certain types of questions. Similarly, Dickinson's identification of storybook reading patterns provides guidance for educating preschool teachers, but at the same time, a patterned conception of teaching becomes reified. However, Kantor's choosing not to focus on the teaching aspect of the interaction provides less guidance for teacher education. The important question remains: How do teachers learn and how can teacher educators foster this process?

Part of the problem may derive from our current theories of teaching and learning. Most literacy researchers claim to be guided by a Vygotskian formulation. A Vygotskian perspective features the role of a teacher in assessing student knowledge and providing activities that appropriately challenge a student. The nature of the learning is social with the teacher listening carefully to student constructions and refining the task to further student problem solving. This Vygotskian formulation of teaching and learning is, however, based on tutorial interaction and accordingly provides only limited guidance for thinking about classroom teachers. Whether one can expand a tutorial formulation to account for teaching and learning in classrooms is an interesting question. Vygotskian thinking may serve as a springboard to develop a new perspective for classroom instruction, not as an elaborated view of Vygotsky, but a totally new formulation.

Alternatively, the formulation may be applied so as to pursue a restricted view of classroom teaching and learning. That focus may include the teacher, the class treated as a collective child, and the activity interaction among them represented through an analysis of discourse. Instructional materials currently used and those used in the past are not typically represented as part of the interaction. A tendency exists to think ahistorically about teaching and learning, even through teachers and their students develop a shared history. The question remains whether applying a Vygotskian perspective can usefully represent more than a limited, albeit important, aspect of classroom teaching and learning.

What are the alternatives for conceptualizing teaching? One way to look at the studies reviewed in this chapter is as a collection of answers. But to what *questions* do they respond? They are not the problems that teaching poses for teachers. For some, the approach is more in the realm of coming up with a better solution to a researcher's problem. Scripts and discourse routine respond to what researchers think teachers need to know (say and do) to facilitate learning. Such solutions do not arise from a view of teaching with its defining parameters but from research on individual reading processes. Because of the overriding influence of contextual conditions, a strategy may prove effective in one programmatic setting but not in another. What we need is a more general conceptualization of teaching that describes the key choices teachers make in establishing literacy programs and in altering them.

Even those studies providing a broader view of teaching and learning do not attempt to identify the basic realities of teaching, such as the theoretical perspective of the teacher, collective character of the class, extension over long periods of time, inclusion of multiple activities, and unanticipated events. We will continue to proceed in a piecemeal fashion if we focus on each new program or approach as it comes along without also considering the basic parameters of the complex phenomena into which the program or approach is introduced.

The contrast between traditional literacy research, whether reflecting teacher-imposed or interactive solutions, and recent research with and by teachers is striking. In the first, little effort is made to describe classroom processes beyond the program or approach being studied. In the latter, an attempt is made to depict and understand the nature of classroom processes. Moje's study of practice, similar in many respects to that of Kantor and colleagues, conforms to a long anthropological and sociological tradition of research that seeks to document existing conditions of class instruction and to examine how the past experiences and beliefs of teachers interact with those of their students to form unique cultures. We gain a sense of the shared history of teaching and learning and insight into some aspects of the nature of the work of teaching. As previously suggested, the flexible manner in which Landy interacted with her class may have been made possible by her well-developed knowledge of teaching chemistry. Mastery of a set of routines frees a teacher to direct activities, interact with students to clarify their thinking, assess student knowledge, and deal with unexpected problems.

Mayer's study also represents fertile ground for thinking about the nature of teaching. Her mapping of her own thinking and concerns as she attempted to change her reading program reveals a view of teaching that has implications for how she interweaves activities (or tasks), groups of students, and control of activities in real time. Her writing reveals an implicit formulation of teaching. The detailed documentation typical of ethnographic work does not appear in this report, but the main outlines of how she changed instruction are clear.

Members of occupations over a period of time benefit from defining the nature of their work, determining which aspects are stylistic or idiosyncratic, and which are central. Formulations of practice have been developed by other professional groups (see, for example, Abbott, 1988).[2] These formulations enhance communication among professionals, influence the induction of new members, and focus research on the nature and improvement of the work. An analysis of the central tasks of literacy teaching would be useful. Such conceptualization needs to be based on an understanding of the core activities of teaching *as they occur* in classrooms. Recent descriptions suggest that some core activities pertain to selecting appropriate materials, developing and using assessment systems, developing a productive balance of reading and writing activities, responding to the special needs of a diverse group of students, and sharing power with students.[3]

Conceptualizing the nature of teaching literacy needs to be done by members of the profession who are intimately familiar with its complexities; yet immersion in the particularities of practice may make it difficult to discern the broad strokes

---

[2] In *The System of Professions,* Andrew Abbott (1988) developed a theory about how and why professions evolve. Although professions are typically treated one at a time, Abbott saw them as existing in a system in which one profession could preempt the work of another or split into several occupations. In the area of the information professions, for example, he described the early work of librarians as involving three core types of work (a) access to and the retrieval of information desired by users, (b) education, and (c) entertainment. Given various other professions competing for the same functions and the technical developments of the Dewey decimal system toward scientific management, the first activity came to dominate the work of the profession.

[3] The interactions between the core activities of pedagogy, curriculum development, and assessment are particularly interesting. Whether because of the movement toward "efficient education" between 1890 and 1920 (Callahan, 1962; Tyack, 1974), the increased dominance of publishing firms (Shannon, 1989), or the historical development of teaching as an occupation in American culture (Herbst, 1989), school administrators in the United States have had more control over the curriculum than have teachers. Assessment, also controlled by administrators, has been a means of enforcing curricular adherence. One way to view recent initiatives by teachers is as an effort to regain control over curriculum and assessment decisions. Teacher researchers write about how pedagogy is constrained when the curriculum and assessment are uniformly specified by others (see, for example, Garlock, 1996). Abbott (1988) would view this struggle between educational administrators and teachers as an effort on the part of teachers to seek a broadened definition of their work.

of the work. A second pair of eyes, particularly those of university-based researchers who collaborate with teachers and who describe the complexities of classroom as observed, have a contribution to make.

How might such a representation of professional knowledge be useful? A portrayal of literacy teaching and learning may make it easier for teachers to discuss the nature of their work. Like the metaphor of "symphony," a formulation of teaching may clarify for teachers how certain strategies or discourse patterns fit into the broader set of activities we refer to as classroom teaching and learning. Being able to think more clearly about the core activities of teaching literacy will have implications for how research is conceptualized and approached, for teachers learning about the nature of their craft, and for teacher educators supporting the induction of new teachers. In the end, however, it is children learning to read and write who will benefit from our performing this conceptual task well.

REFERENCES

Abbott, A. (1988). *The system of professions: An essay on the division of expert labor.* Chicago: University of Chicago Press.

Allen, J., Cary, M., & Delgado, L. (1995). *Exploring blue highways: Literacy reform, school change, and the creation of learning communities.* New York: Teachers College Press.

Allen, J., Clark, W., Cook, M., Crane, P., Fallon, I., Hoffman, L., Jennings, K. S., & Sours, M. A. (1989). Reading and writing development in whole language kindergartens. In J. Mason (Ed.), *Reading and writing connections* (pp. 121–146). Boston: Allyn & Bacon.

Almasi, J. F. (1995). The nature of fourth graders' sociocognitive conflicts in peer-led and teacher-led discussion of literature. *Reading Research Quarterly, 30,* 314–351.

Almasi, J. F., McKeown, M. G., & Beck, I. L. (1996). The nature of engaged reading in classroom discussions of literature. *Journal of Literacy Research, 28,* 107–146.

Alvermann, D. E. (1996). Introducing feminist perspectives in a content literacy course: Struggles and self-contradictions. In D. J. Leu, C. K. Kinzer, & K. A. Hinchman (Eds.), *Literacies for the 21st century: Research and practice* (pp. 124–133). Chicago: National Reading Conference.

Alvermann, D. E., Commeyras, M., Young, J. P., Randall, S., & Hinson, D. (1997). Interrupting gendered discursive practices in classroom talk about texts: Easy to think about, difficult to do. *Journal of Literacy Research, 29,* 73–104.

Alvermann, D. E., & Hayes, D. A. (1989). Classroom discussion of content area reading assignments: An intervention study. *Reading Research Quarterly, 24,* 305–335.

Alvermann, D. E., & Moore, D. W. (1991). Secondary school reading. In R. Barr, M. Kamil, P. Mosenthal, & P. D. Pearson (Eds.), *Handbook of reading research* (Vol. II, pp. 951–983). New York: Longman.

Alvermann, D. E., O'Brien, D. G., & Dillon, D. R. (1990). What teachers do when they say they're having discussions of content area reading assignments: A qualitative analysis. *Reading Research Quarterly, 25,* 296–322.

Alvermann, D. E., O'Brien, D. G., Dillon, D. R., & Smith, L. C. (1985). The role of the textbook in discussion. *Journal of Reading, 29,* 50–57.

Alvermann, D. E., Young, J. P., Weaver, D., Hinchman, K. A., Moore, D. W., Phelps, S. F., Thrash, E. C., & Zalewski, P. (1996). Middle and high school students' perceptions of how they experience text-based discussions: A multicase study. *Reading Research Quarterly, 31,* 244–267.

Anderson, R. C., Hiebert, E. H., Scott, J. A., & Wilkinson, I. A. (1984). *Becoming a nation of readers: The report of the Commission on Reading.* Washington, DC: National Institute of Education.

Anderson-Yockel, J., & Haynes, W. O. (1994). Joint book-reading strategies in working-class African American and white mother-toddler dyads. *Journal of Speech and Hearing Research, 37,* 583–593.

Atwell, N. (1987). *In the middle: Writing, reading, and learning with adolescents.* Upper Montclair, NJ: Boynton/Cook.

Au, K. H. (1980). Participant structures in a reading lesson with Hawaiian children. Analysis of a culturally appropriate instructional event. *Anthropology and Education Quarterly, 11,* 91–115.

Bailey, G. (1995). A schoolwide study of assessment alternatives. In J. Allen, M. Cary, & L. Delgado (Eds.), *Exploring blue highways: Literacy reform, school change, and the creation of learning communities* (pp. 99–108). New York: Teachers College Press.

Ball, E. W., & Blachman, B. A. (1988). Phoneme segmentation training: Effect on reading readiness. *Annals of Dyslexia, 38,* 208–225.

Ball, E. W., & Blachman, B. A. (1991). Does phoneme segmentation training in kindergarten make a difference in early word recognition and developmental spelling? *Reading Research Quarterly, 26,* 49–66.

Barr, R. (1986). Studying classroom reading instruction. *Reading Research Quarterly, 21,* 231–236.

Barr, R. (1987). Classroom interaction and curricular content. In D. Bloome (Ed.), *Literacy, language, and schooling: New directions.* Norwood, NJ: Ablex.

Baumann, J. F. (1986). Teaching third-grade students to comprehend anaphoric relationships: The application of a direct instruction model. *Reading Research Quarterly, 21,* 70–90.

Baumann, J. F. (1996). The inside and outside of teacher research: Reflections on having one foot in both worlds. In D. J. Leu, C. K. Kinzer, & K. A. Hinchman (Eds.), *Literacies for the 21st century: Research and practice* (pp. 500–511). Chicago: National Reading Conference.

Baumann, J. F., & Bergeron, B. S. (1993). Story map instruction using children's literature: Effects on first graders' comprehension of central narrative elements. *Journal of Reading Behavior, 25,* 407–437.

Baumann, J. F., Bisplinghoff, B. S., & Allen, J. (1997). Methodology in teacher research: Three cases. In J. Flood, S. B. Heath, & D. Lapp (Eds.), *Handbook of research on teaching literacy through the communicative and visual arts* (pp. 121–143). New York: Macmillan.

Baumann, J. F., Jones, L. A., & Siefert-Kessell, N. (1993). Using think alouds to enhance children's comprehension monitoring abilities. *The Reading Teacher, 47,* 184–193.

Baumann, J. F., Siefert-Kessell, N., & Jones, L. A. (1992). Effect of think-aloud instruction on elementary students' comprehension monitoring abilities. *Journal of Reading Behavior, 24,* 143–172.

Beach, R., & Hynds, S. (1991). Research on response to literature. In R. Barr, M. Kamil, P. Mosenthal, & P. D. Pearson (Eds.), *Handbook of reading research* (Vol. II. pp. 453–489). New York: Longman.

Bean, T. W., Singer, H., Sorter, J., & Frazee, C. (1986). The effect of metacognitive instruction in outlining and graphic organizer construction on student comprehension in a tenth-grade world history class. *Journal of Reading Behavior, 18,* 153–169.

Beck, I. L., & McKeown, M. G. (1991). Conditions of vocabulary acquisition. In R. Barr, M. Kamil, P. Mosenthal, & P. D. Pearson (Eds.), *Handbook of reading research* (Vol. II, pp. 789–814). New York: Longman.

Beck, I. L., McKeown, M. G., Sandora, C., Kucan, L., & Worthy, J. (1996). Questioning the author: A yearlong classroom implementation to engage students with text. *Elementary School Journal, 96,* 385–414.

Bereiter, C., & Bird, M. (1985). Use of thinking aloud in identification and teaching of reading comprehension strategies. *Cognition and Instruction, 2,* 131–156.

Bergiloff, B. (1993). Moving toward aesthetic literacy in the first grade. In D. J. Leu & C. K. Kinzer (Eds.), *Examining central issues in literacy research, theory, and practice* (pp. 217–226). Chicago: National Reading Conference.

Berkowitz, S. J. (1986). Effects of instruction in text organization on sixth-grade students' memory for expository reading. *Reading Research Quarterly, 21,* 161–178.

Beyer, L. E. (Ed.). (1996). *Creating democratic classrooms: The struggle to integrate theory and practice.* New York: Teachers College Press.

Bissex, G. L., & Bullock, R. H. (Eds.). (1987). *Seeing for ourselves: Case-study research by teachers of writing.* Portsmouth, NH: Heinemann.

Blachman, B. A., Ball, E. W., Black, R. S., & Tangel, D. M. (1994).

Kindergarten teachers develop phoneme awareness in low-income, inner-city classrooms. Does it make a difference? *Reading and Writing: An Interdisciplinary Journal, 6,* 1–18.

Block, C. C. (1993). Strategy instruction in a literature-based reading program. *The Elementary School Journal, 94,* 139–151.

Bloome, D. (1987). Reading as a social process in a middle school classroom. In D. Bloome (Ed.), *Literacy and schooling* (pp. 123–149). Norwood, NJ: Ablex.

Bloome, D., & Green, J. (1984). Directions in the sociolinguistic study of reading. In P. D. Pearson, R. Barr, M. Kamil, & P. Mosenthal (Eds.), *Handbook of reading research* (Vol. II, pp. 395–422). New York: Longman.

Boljonis, A., & Hinchman, K. (1988). First graders' perceptions of reading and writing. In J. E. Readence & R. S. Baldwin (Eds.), *Dialogues in reading research: Thirty-seventh yearbook of the National Reading Conference* (pp. 107–114). Chicago: National Reading Conference.

Bond, G. L., & Dykstra, R. (1967). The Cooperative Research Program in first-grade reading instruction. *Reading Research Quarterly, 2,* 5–142.

Borkowski, J. G., Weyhing, R. S., & Carr, M. (1988). Effects of attributional retraining on strategy-based reading comprehension in learning-disabled students. *Journal of Educational Psychology, 80,* 46–53.

Bradley, L., & Bryant, P. E. (1983). Categorizing sounds and learning to read: A causal connection. *Nature, 301,* 419–421.

Bradley, L., & Bryant, P. E. (1985). *Rhyme and reason in reading and spelling.* Ann Arbor, MI: University of Michigan Press.

Brock, C. (1997). Exploring the use of Book Club with second-language learners in mainstream classrooms. In S. I. McMahon & T. E. Raphael (Eds.), *The Book Club connection: Literacy learning and classroom talk* (pp. 141–158). New York: Teachers College Press.

Bruck, M., & Treiman, R. (1992). Learning to pronounce words: The limitations of analogies. *Reading Research Quarterly, 27,* 374–388.

Buchanan, J. (1993). Listening to the voices. In M. Cochran-Smith & S. L. Lytle (Eds.), *Inside/outside: Reader research and knowledge* (pp. 212–220). New York: Teachers College Press.

Bullion-Mears, A. (1994). Developing collaboration and teacher reflection in a college curriculum class. In C. K. Kinzer & D. J. Leu (Eds.), *Multidimensional aspects of literacy research, theory, and practice* (pp. 380–386). Chicago: National Reading Conference.

Bruneau, B. J. (1992). Implementing whole-language instruction for young children: Cases of teacher development and change. In C. K. Kinzer & D. J. Leu (Eds.), *Multidimensional aspects of literacy research, theory, and practice* (pp. 225–233). Chicago: National Reading Conference.

Bus, A. G., & van IJzendoorn, M. H. (1988). Mother-child interactions, attachment, and emergent literacy: A cross-sectional study. *Child Development, 59,* 1262–1272.

Bus, A. G., & van IJzendoorn, M. H. (1995). Mothers reading to their 3-year-olds: The role of mother-child attachment security in becoming literate. *Reading Research Quarterly, 30,* 998–1015.

Bus, A. G., van IJzendoorn, M. H., & Pelligrini, A. D. (1995). Joint book reading makes for success in learning to read. A meta-analysis on intergenerational transmission of literacy. *Review of Educational Research, 65,* 1–21.

Byrne, B., & Fielding-Barnsley, R. (1991). Evaluation of a program to teach phonemic awareness to young children. *Journal of Educational Psychology, 83,* 451–455.

Calfee, R., & Drum, P. (1986). Research on teaching reading. In M. C. Wittrock (Ed.), *Handbook of Research on Teaching* (3rd ed., pp. 804–849). New York: Macmillan.

Callahan, R. E. (1962). *Education and the cult of efficiency.* Chicago: University of Chicago.

Chall, J. S. (1983). *Learning to read: The great debate.* New York: McGraw-Hill. (Original work published in 1968).

Chan, L. K. S., Cole, P. G., & Morris, J. N. (1990). Effects of instruction in the use of a visual-imagery strategy on the reading-comprehension competence of disabled and average readers. *Learning Disability Quarterly, 13,* 2–11.

Cochran-Smith, M. (1984). *The making of a reader.* Norwood, NJ: Ablex.

Cochran-Smith, M., & Lytle, S. L. (1993). *Inside/outside: Reader research and knowledge.* New York: Teachers College Press.

Colgan-Davis, P. (1993). Learning about learning diversity. In M. Cochran-Smith & S. L. Lytle (Eds.), *Inside/outside: Reader research and knowledge* (pp. 163–169). New York: Teachers College Press.

Crawford, M., & Chaffin, R. (1986). The reader's construction of meaning: Cognitive research on gender and comprehension. In E. A. Flynn & P. P. Schweickart (Eds.), *Gender and reading* (pp. 3–30). Baltimore: Johns Hopkins University Press.

Cunat, M. (1996). Vision, vitality, and values: Advocating the democratic classroom. In L. E. Beyer (Ed.), *Creating democratic classrooms: The struggle to integrate theory and practice* (pp. 127–149). New York: Teachers College Press.

Cunningham, A. E. (1990). Explicit vs. implicit instruction in phonemic awareness. *Journal of Experimental Child Psychology, 50,* 429–444.

Cunningham, P., Hall, M., & Defee, C. (1991). Non-ability grouped, multi-level instruction: A year in a first-grade classroom. *The Reading Teacher, 44,* 566–571.

Dahl, K. L. (1993). Children's spontaneous utterances during early reading and writing instruction in whole-language classrooms. *Journal of Reading Behavior, 25,* 279–294.

Dahl, K. L., & Freppon, P. A. (1991). Literacy learning in whole-language classrooms: An analysis of low socioeconomic urban children learning to read and write in kindergarten. In J. Zutell & S. McCormick (Eds.), *Learner factors/teacher factors: Issues in literacy research and instruction* (pp. 149–158). Chicago: National Reading Conference.

Dahl, K. L., & Freppon, P. A. (1995). A comparison of inner-city children's interpretations of reading and writing instruction in the early grades in skills-based and whole language classrooms. *Reading Research Quarterly, 30,* 50–74.

Darch, C. B., Carnine, D. W., & Kameenui, E. J. (1986). The role of graphic organizers and social structure in content area instruction. *Journal of Reading Behavior, 18,* 275–295.

Darling-Hammond, L., & Snyder, J. (1992). Curriculum studies and the traditions of inquiry: The scientific tradition. In P. W. Jackson (Ed.), *Handbook of research on curriculum* (pp. 41–78). New York: Macmillan.

Deegan, D. H. (1995). Taking it up/taking it seriously: Critical literacy in preservice teacher education. In K. A. Hinchman, D. J. Leu, & C. K. Kinzer (Eds.), *Perspectives on literacy research and practice* (pp. 342–348). Chicago: National Reading Conference.

Dewalt, M., Rhyne-Winkler, M. C., & Rubel, S. (1993). Effects of instructional method on reading comprehension. *Reading Improvement, 30,* 93–100.

DeWitz, R., Carr, E. M., & Patberg, J. P. (1987). Effects of inference training on comprehension and comprehension monitoring. *Reading Research Quarterly, 22,* 99–121.

Dickinson, D., & Keebler, R. (1989). Variation in preschool teachers' styles of reading books. *Discourse Processes, 12,* 353–375.

Dickinson, D. K., & Smith, M. W. (1994). Long-term effects of preschool teachers' book readings on low-income children's vocabulary and story comprehension. *Reading Research Quarterly, 29,* 104–122.

Dillon, D. R. (1989). Showing them that I want them to learn and that I care about who they are: A microethnography of the social organization of a secondary low-track English-reading classroom. *American Educational Research Journal, 26,* 227–259.

Dillon, D. R., O'Brien, D. G., Moje, E. B., & Steward, R. A. (1994). Literacy learning in secondary school science classrooms: A cross-case analysis of three qualitative studies. *Journal of Research in Science Teaching, 31,* 345–362.

Dole, J. A., Brown, K. J., & Trathen, W. (1996). The effects of strategy instruction on the comprehension performance of at-risk students. *Reading Research Quarterly, 31,* 62–85.

Dole, J. A., Valencia, S. W., Greer, E. A., & Wardrop, J. L. (1991). Effects of two types of prereading instruction on the comprehension of narrative and expository text. *Reading Research Quarterly, 26,* 142–159.

Donovan, C. A. (1996). First graders' impressions of genre-specific elements in writing narrative and expository texts. In D. J. Leu, C. K. Kinzer, & K. A. Hinchman (Eds.), *Literacies for the 21st century:*

Research and practice (pp. 183–194). Chicago: National Reading Conference.

Duffy, G. G., Roehler, L. R., Meloth, M., Vavrus, L., Book, C., Putnam, J., & Wesselman, R. (1986). The relationship between explicit verbal explanation during reading skill instruction and student awareness and achievement: A study of reading teacher effects. *Reading Research Quarterly, 21,* 237–252.

Duffy, G. G., Roehler, L. R., Sivan, E., Rackliffe, G., Book, C., Meloth, M., Vavrus, L., Wesselman, R., Putnam, J., & Bassiri, D. (1987). Effects of explaining the reasoning associated with using reading strategies. *Reading Research Quarterly, 22,* 347–368.

Dykstra, R. (1968). Summary of the second grade phase of the Cooperative Research Program in primary reading instruction. *Reading Research Quarterly, 4,* 49–70.

Dyson, A. H. (1989). *Multiple worlds of child writers: Friends learning to write.* New York: Teachers College Press.

Eeds, M., & Wells, D. (1989). Grand conversations: An explanation of meaning construction in literature study groups. *Research in the Teaching of English, 23,* 4–29.

Ehri, L. C. (1991). Development of the ability to read words. In R. Barr, M. Kamil, P. Mosenthal, & P. D. Pearson (Eds.), *Handbook of reading research* (Vol. II, pp. 383–417). New York: Longman.

Ehri, L., & Wilce, L. (1987). Does learning to spell help beginners learn to read words? *Reading Research Quarterly, 12,* 47–65.

El-Dinary, P. B., Pressley, M., & Schuder, T. (1992). Teachers learning transactional strategies instruction. In C. K. Kinzer & D. J. Leu (Eds.), *Literacy research, theory, and practice: Views from many perspectives* (pp. 453–462). Chicago: National Reading Conference.

Eldredge, J. L. (1991). An experiment with a modified whole language approach in first-grade classrooms. *Reading Research and Instruction, 30,* 21–38.

Elkonin, D. B. (1973). U.S.S.R. In J. Downing (Ed.), *Comparative reading* (pp. 551–580). New York: Macmillan.

Eller, R. G., Pappas, C. C., & Brown, E. (1988). The lexical development of kindergartners: Learning from written context. *Journal of Reading Behavior, 20,* 5–24.

Elley, W. B. (1989). Vocabulary acquisition from listening to stories. *Reading Research Quarterly, 24,* 174–187.

Encisco, P. E. (1994). Cultural identity and response to literature: Running lessons from Maniac Magee. *Language Arts, 71,* 524–533.

Erickson, F. (1986). Qualitative methods in research on teaching. In M. C. Wittrock (Ed.), *Handbook of research on teaching* (3rd ed., pp. 119–161). New York: Macmillan.

Evans, K. S. (1996). Creating spaces for equity? The role of positioning in peer-led literature discussions. *Language Arts, 73,* 194–202.

Feitelson, D., Goldstein, Z., Iraqi, J., & Share, D. L. (1993). Effects of listening to story reading on aspects of literacy acquisition in a diglossic situation. *Reading Research Quarterly, 28,* 70–79.

Feitelson, D., Kita, B., & Goldstein, Z. (1986). Effects of listening to series stories on first graders' comprehension and use of language. *Research in the Teaching of English, 20,* 339–356.

Feldgus, E. G. (1993). Walking to the words. In M. Cochran-Smith & S. L. Lytle (Eds.), *Inside/outside: Reader research and knowledge* (pp. 170–177). New York: Teachers College Press.

Fenstermacher, G. D. (1994). The place of practical arguments in the education of teachers. In V. Richardson (Ed.), *A theory of teacher change and the practice of staff development: A case in reading instruction* (pp. 23–42). New York: Teachers College Press.

Fey, M. (1994). Transforming the literacy classroom through reader response and computer networking. In C. K. Kinzer & D. J. Leu (Eds.), *Multidimensional aspects of literacy research, theory, and practice* (pp. 296–305). Chicago: National Reading Conference.

Fisher, C. W., & Hiebert, E. H. (1990). Characteristics of tasks in two approaches to literacy instruction. *Elementary School Journal, 91,* 3–18.

French, V. L., & Feng, J. (1992). Phoneme awareness training with at-risk kindergarten children: A case study. Statesboro, GA: Georgia Southern University. (ERIC Document Reproduction Service No. ED 361 120).

Freppon, P. A. (1991). Children's concepts of the nature and purpose of reading in different instructional settings. *Journal of Reading Behavior, 23,* 39–163.

Freppon, P. A. (1995). Low-income children's literacy interpretations in a skills-based and a whole-language classroom. *Journal of Reading Behavior, 27,* 505–533.

Freppon, P. A., & Dahl, K. L. (1991). Learning about phonics in a whole language classroom. *Language Arts, 68,* 190–197.

Galda, L., Shockley, B., & Pellegrini, A. D. (1995). *Talking to read and write: Opportunities for literate talk in one primary classroom.* Athens, GA: National Reading Research Center.

Gallas, K. (1994). *The languages of learning: How children talk, write, dance, draw, and sing their understanding of the world.* New York: Teachers College Press.

Gambrell, L. B., & Palmer, B. M. (1992). Children's metacognitive knowledge about reading and writing in literature-based and conventional classrooms. In C. K. Kinzer & D. J. Leu (Eds.), *Literacy research, theory, and practice: Forty-first yearbook of the National Reading Conference* (pp. 215–223). Chicago: National Reading Conference.

Garlock, J. (1996). The rock house: Barriers in education and their demolition. In L. E. Beyer (Ed.), *Creating democratic classrooms: The struggle to integrate theory and practice* (pp. 62–72). New York: Teachers College Press.

Gaskins, I. W., Anderson, R. C., Pressley, M., Cunicelli, E. A., & Satlow, E. (1993). Six teachers' dialogue during cognitive process instruction. *Elementary School Journal, 93,* 277–304.

Gee, J. P. (2000). Discourse and sociocultural studies in reading. In M. Kamil, P. Mosenthal, P. D. Pearson, & R. Barr (Eds.), *Handbook of reading research* (Vol. III). Mahwah, NJ: Lawrence Erlbaum Associates.

Gitlin, A., Bringhurst, K., Burns, M., Cooley, V., Myers, B., Price, K., Russell, R., & Tiess, P. (1992). *Teachers voices for school change.* New York: Teachers College Press.

Golden, J. M., & Gerber, A. (1990). A semiotic perspective of text: The picture story book event. *Journal of Reading Behavior, 22,* 203–219.

Goldenberg, C. (1992). Instructional conversations: Promoting comprehension through discussion. *Reading Teacher, 46,* 316–326.

Goldenberg, C. (1994). Promoting early literacy development among Spanish-speaking children: Lessons from two studies. In E. H. Hiebert & B. M. Taylor (Eds.), *Getting reading right from the start: Effective early literacy interventions.* Boston: Allyn & Bacon.

Goldenberg, C., & Gallimore, R. (1991). Local knowledge, research knowledge, and educational change: A case study of first grade Spanish reading improvement. *Educational Researcher, 20,* 2–14.

Goswami, D., & Stillman, P. (1987). *Reclaiming the classroom: Teacher research as an agency for change.* Upper Montclair, NJ: Boynton/Cook.

Green, J., & Bloome, D. (1997). Ethnography and ethnographers of and in education: A situated perspective. In J. Flood, S. B. Heath, & D. Lapp (Eds.), *Handbook of research on teaching literacy through the communicative and visual arts* (pp. 181–202). New York: MacMillan.

Green, J. L., Harker, J. O., & Golden, J. M. (1986). Lesson construction: Differing views. In G. W. Noblit & W. T. Pink (Eds.), *Schooling in social context: Qualitative studies* (pp. 46–77). Norwood, NJ: Ablex.

Guthrie, J. T., Van Meter, P., McCann, A. D., Wigfield, A., Bennett, L., Poundstone, C. C., Rice, M. E., Faibisch, F. M., Hunt, B., & Mitchell, A. M. (1996). Growth of literacy engagement: Changes in motivations and strategies during concept-oriented reading instruction. *Reading Research Quarterly, 31,* 306–332.

Guzzetti, B. J., Snyder, T. E., Glass, G. V., & Gamas, W. S. (1993). Promoting conceptual change in science: A comparative meta-analysis of instructional interventions from reading education and science education. *Reading Research Quarterly, 28,* 116–159.

Guzzetti, B. J., & Williams, W. O. (1996). Gender, text, and discussion: Examining intellectual safety in the science classroom. *Journal of Research in Science Teaching, 22,* 5–20.

Haggerty, P. J., Hiebert, E. H., & Owens, M. K. (1989). Students' comprehension, writing, and perceptions in two approaches to literacy instruction. In S. McCormick & J. Zutell (Eds.), *Cognitive and social perspectives for literacy research and instruction* (pp. 453–459). Chicago: National Reading Conference.

Heath, S. B. (1983). *Ways with words: Language, life, and work in communities and classroom.* Norwood, NJ: Ablex.

Herbst, J. (1989). *And sadly teach: Teacher education and professionalization in American culture.* Madison, WI: University of Wisconsin Press.

Hickman, J. (1983). Everything considered: Response to literature in an elementary school setting. *Journal of Research and Development in Education, 16,* 8–13.

Hoffman, J. V. (1991). Teacher and school effects in learning to read. In R. Barr, M. Kamil, P. Mosenthal, & P. D. Pearson (Eds.), *Handbook of reading research* (Vol. II, pp. 911–950). New York: Longman.

Hoffman, J. V., McCarthey, S. J., Elliott, B., Price, D., Bayles, D., Ferree, A., Rehders, S., & Abbott, J. (1996). Literature-based reading instruction: Problems, possibilities, and polemics in the struggle to change. In D. J. Leu, C. K. Kinzer, & K. A. Hinchman (Eds.), *Literacies for the 21st century: Research and practice* (pp. 359–372). Chicago: National Reading Conference.

Holland, K. W., & Hall, L. E. (1989). Reading achievement in the first grade classroom: A comparison of basal and whole language approaches. *Reading Improvement, 26,* 323–329.

Huberman, M. (1996). Moving mainstream: Taking a closer look at teacher research. *Language Arts, 73,* 124–140.

Hynds, S. D. (1989). Bring life to literature and literature to life: Social constructs and contexts of four adolescent readers. *Research in the Teaching of English, 23,* 3061.

Jaddaoui, N. H. (1996). Building bridges toward democracy. In L. E. Beyer (Ed.), *Creating democratic classrooms: The struggle to integrate theory and practice* (pp. 73–86). New York: Teachers College Press.

Juel, C. (1991). Beginning reading. In R. Barr, M. Kamil, P. Mosenthal, & P. D. Pearson (Eds.), *Handbook of reading research* (Vol. II, pp. 759–788). New York: Longman.

Kamberelis, G., & de la Luna, L. C. (1996). Constructing multiculturally relevant pedagogy: Signifying on the basal. In D. J. Leu, C. K. Kinzer, & K. A. Hinchman (Eds.), *Literacies for the 21st century: Research and practice* (pp. 329–344). Chicago: National Reading Conference.

Kantor, R., Miller, S., & Fernie, D. (1992). Diverse paths to literacy in a preschool classroom: A sociocultural perspective. *Reading Research Quarterly, 27,* 184–201.

Kauffman, G., Short, K. G., Crawford, K. M., Kahn, L., & Kaser, S. (1996). Examining the roles of teachers and students in literature circles across classroom contexts. In D. J. Leu, C. K. Kinzer, & K. A. Hinchman (Eds.), *Literacies for the 21st century: Research and practice* (pp. 373–384). Chicago: National Reading Conference.

Kearn, R. G. (1989). Second language reading strategy instruction: Its effects on comprehension and word inference ability. *The Modern Language Journal, 73,* 135–149.

Kertoy, M. K. (1994). Adult interactive strategies and the spontaneous comments of preschoolers during joint storybook readings. *Journal of Research in Childhood Education, 9,* 58–67.

Kieffer, C. C. (1995). Being somebody else: Informal drama in the fourth grade. In J. Allen, M. Cary, & L. Delgado (Eds.), *Exploring blue highways: Literacy reform, school change, and the creation of learning communities* (pp. 68–83). New York: Teachers College Press.

Kimbrell-Lee, J., & Wood, T. (1995). Teaching, learning, and partnerships: Strategies for including special needs students. In J. Allen, M. Cary, & L. Delgado (Eds.), *Exploring blue highways: Literacy reform, school change, and the creation of learning communities* (pp. 55–67). New York: Teachers College Press.

Klesius, J. P., Griffith, P. L., & Zielonka, P. (1991). A whole language and traditional instruction comparison: Overall effectiveness and development of the alphabetic principle. *Reading Research and Instruction, 30,* 47–61.

Knoeller, C. P. (1994, April). Negotiating interpretations of text: The role of student-led discussions in understanding literature. *Journal of Reading, 37,* 572–580.

Konopak, B. C., Martin, S. H., & Martin, M. A. (1990). Using a writing strategy to enhance sixth-grade students' comprehension of content material. *Journal of Reading Behavior, 22,* 19–37.

Langer, J. A. (1992). Rethinking literature instruction. In J. A. Langer (Ed.), *Literature instruction: A focus on student response* (pp. 35–53). Urbana, IL: National Council of Teachers of English.

Langer, J. A. (1995). *Envisioning literature: Literary understanding and literature instruction.* New York: Teachers College Press.

Lee, C. D. (1993). *Signifying as a scaffold for literary interpretation. The pedagogical implications of an African American discourse genre* (NCTE Research Report No. 26). Urbana, IL: National Council of Teachers of English.

Lee, C. D. (1995). A culturally based cognitive apprenticeship: Teaching African American high school students skills in literary interpretation. *Reading Research Quarterly, 30,* 608–630.

Lemke, J. (1990). *Talking science: Language, learning, and values.* Norwood, NJ: Ablex.

Lincoln, Y. S. (1992). Curriculum studies and the traditions of inquiry: The humanistic tradition. In P. W. Jackson (Ed.), *Handbook of research on curriculum* (pp. 79–97). New York: Macmillan.

Lundberg, I., Frost, J., & Petersen, O. (1988). Effects of an extensive program for stimulating phonological awareness in preschool children. *Reading Research Quarterly, 23,* 263–284.

Lundeberg, M. A. (1987). Metacognitive aspects of reading comprehension: Studying understanding in legal case analysis. *Reading Research Quarterly, 22,* 407–432.

Lytle, S. L., & Cochran-Smith, M. (1994). Teacher-research in English. In A. C. Purves (Ed.), *Encyclopedia of English studies and language arts* (pp. 1153–1155). New York: Scholastic.

Maher, A. (1994). An inquiry into reader response. In G. Wells (Ed.), *Changing schools from within: Creating communities of inquiry* (pp. 81–97). Portsmouth, NH: Heinemann.

Marshall, J. D. (1987, February). The effects of writing on students' understanding of literary texts. *Research in the Teaching of English, 21,* 30–63.

Marshall, J. D., Smagorinski, P., & Smith, M. W. (1995). *The language of interpretation: Patterns of discourse in discussion of literature.* Urbana, IL: National Council of Teachers of English.

Martinez, M., & Roser, N. (1985). Read it again: The value of repeated readings during storytime. *Reading Teacher, 38,* 782–786.

Martinez, M., & Teale, W. (1993). Teacher storybook reading style: A comparison of six teachers. *Research in the Teaching of English, 27,* 175–199.

Mason, J. M., Kerr, B. M., Sinha, S., & McCormick, C. (1990). Shared book reading in an early start program for at-risk children. In J. Zutell & S. McCormick (Eds.), *Literacy theory and research: Analyses from multiple paradigms. Thirty-ninth yearbook of the National Reading Conference* (pp. 189–198). Chicago: National Reading Conference.

Mason, J. M., Peterman, C. L., Powell, B. M., & Kerr, B. M. (1989). Reading and writing attempts by kindergartners after book reading by teachers. In J. M. Mason (Ed.), *Reading and writing connections* (pp. 105–120). Boston: Allyn & Bacon.

Matthews, M. M. (1966). *Teaching to read: Historically considered.* Chicago: University of Chicago Press.

McGee, L. M. (1992). An exploration of meaning construction in first graders' grand conversations. In C. K. Kinzer & D. J. Leu (Eds.), *Literacy research, theory, and practice: Views from many perspectives* (pp. 177–186). Chicago: National Reading Conference.

McGee, L. M., Courtney, L., & Lomax, R. G. (1994). Teachers' roles in first graders' grand conversations. In C. K. Kinzer & D. J. Leu (Eds.), *Multidimensional aspects of literacy research, theory, and practice* (pp. 517–526). Chicago: National Reading Conference.

McGill-Franzen, A., & Lanford, C. (1994). Exposing the edge of the preschool curriculum: Teachers' talk about text and children's literary understandings. *Language Arts, 71,* 264–273.

McGuinness, D., McGuinness, C., & Donohue, J. (1995). Phonological training and the alphabet principle: Evidence for reciprocal causality. *Reading Research Quarterly, 30*(4), 830–852.

McIntyre, E. (1992). Young children's reading behaviors in various classroom contexts. *Journal of Reading Behavior, 24,* 339–371.

McKenna, M. C., Stratton, B. D., Grindler, M. C., & Jenkins, S. J. (1995). Differential effects of whole language and traditional instruction on reading attitudes. *Journal of Reading Behavior, 27,* 19–44.

McMahon, S. I. (1992). Book Club: A case study of a group of fifth graders as they participate in a literature-based reading program. *Reading Research Quarterly, 27,* 292–294.

McMahon, S. I., & Raphael, T. E. (Eds.). (1997). *The Book Club connection: Literacy learning and classroom talk.* New York: Teachers College Press.

Mervar, K., & Hiebert, E. F. (1989). Literature selection strategies and amount of reading in two literacy approaches. In S. McCormick & J. Zutell (Eds.), *Cognitive and social perspectives for literacy research and instruction: Thirty-eighth yearbook of the National Reading Conference* (pp. 529–535). Chicago: National Reading Conference.

Milligan, J. L., & Berg, H. (1992). The effect of whole language on the comprehending ability of first grade children. *Reading Improvement, 29,* 146–154.

Moje, E. B. (1996). "I teach students, not subjects": Teacher-student relationships as contexts for secondary literacy. *Reading Research Quarterly, 31,* 172–195.

Moll, L. C. (1992). Literacy research in community and classrooms: A sociocultural approach. In R. Beach, J. Green, M. Kamil, & T. Shanahan (Eds.), *Multidisciplinary perspectives in literacy research* (pp. 211–244). Urbana, IL: National Conference on Research in English.

Moll, L. C., & Gonzales, N. (1994). Lessons from research with language minority students. *Journal of Reading Behavior, 26,* 439–461.

Morrison, L., & Kieffer, R. (1995). Developing portfolio processes: "If you don't have anything in there, you can't do this." In J. Allen, M. Cary, & L. Delgado (Eds.), *Exploring blue highways: Literacy reform, school change, and the creation of learning communities* (pp. 109–124). New York: Teachers College Press.

Morrow, L. M. (1988). Young children's responses to one-to-one story readings in school settings. *Reading Research Quarterly, 23,* 89–107.

Morrow, L. M. (1990). Preparing the classroom environment to promote literacy during play. *Early Childhood Research Quarterly, 5,* 537–554.

Morrow, L. M. (1991). Relationships among physical designs of play centers, teachers' emphasis on literacy in play, and children's literacy behaviors during play. In J. Zutell & S. McCormick (Eds.), *Learner factors/teacher factors: Issues in literacy research and instruction* (pp. 127–140). Chicago: National Reading Conference.

Morrow, L. M. (1992). The impact of a literature-based program on literacy achievement, use of literature, and attitudes of children from minority backgrounds. *Reading Research Quarterly, 27,* 250–275.

Morrow, L. M., O'Connor, E. M., & Smith, J. K. (1990). Effects of a story reading program on the literacy development of at-risk kindergarten children. *Journal of Reading Behavior, 22,* 255–275.

Morrow, L. M., Pressley, M., Smith, J. K., & Smith, M. (1997). The effect of a literature-based program integrated into literacy and science instruction with children from diverse backgrounds. *Reading Research Quarterly, 32,* 55–76.

Morrow, L. M., & Rand, M. (1991). Preparing the classroom environment to promote literacy during play. In J. F. Christie (Ed.), *Play and early literacy development* (pp. 141–165). Albany, NY: State University of New York Press.

Morrow, L. M., & Sharkley, E. A. (1993). Motivating independent reading and writing in the primary grades through social cooperative literacy experiences. *The Reading Teacher, 47,* 162–165.

Mosenthal, J. (1994). Constructing knowledge and expertise in literacy teaching: Portfolios in undergraduate teacher education. In C. K. Kinzer & D. J. Leu (Eds.), *Multidimensional aspects of literacy research, theory, and practice* (pp. 407–417). Chicago: National Reading Conference.

Mosenthal, J. (1995). A practice-oriented approach to methods coursework in literacy teaching. In K. A. Hinchman, D. J. Leu, & C. K. Kinzer (Eds.), *Perspectives on literacy research and practice* (pp. 358–367). Chicago: National Reading Conference.

Neuman, S. B., & Roskos, K. (1992). Literacy objects as cultural tools: Effects on children's literacy behaviors in play. *Reading Research Quarterly, 27,* 202–225.

Neuman, S. B., & Roskos, K. (1993). Access to print for children of poverty: Differential effects of adult mediation and literacy-enriched play settings on environmental and functional print tasks. *American Educational Research Journal, 30,* 96–122.

Neuman, S. B., & Roskos, K. (1997). Literacy knowledge in practice:

Contexts of participation for young writers and readers. *Reading Research Quarterly, 32,* 10–32.

Newell, G. E. (1996). Reader-based and teacher-centered instructional tasks: Writing and learning about a short story in middle-track classrooms. *Journal of Literacy Research, 28,* 147–172.

Nielsen, D.C. (1993). The effects of four models of group interaction with storybooks on the literacy growth of low-achieving kindergarten children. In D. J. Leu & C. K. Kinzer (Eds.), *Examining central issues in literacy research, theory, and practice* (pp. 279–287). Chicago: National Reading Conference.

Nielson, L. (1997). Re-making sense, re-shaping inquiry: Feminist metaphors and a literacy of the possible. In J. Flood, S. B. Heath, & D. Lapp (Eds.), *Handbook of research on teaching literacy through the communicative and visual arts* (pp. 203–214). New York: Macmillan.

Ninio, A., & Bruner, J. (1978). The achievement and antecedents of labeling. *Journal of Child Language, 5,* 1–15.

O'Brien, D. G., Stewart, R. A., & Moje, E. B. (1995). Why content literacy is difficult to infuse into the secondary curriculum: Strategies, goals, and classroom realities. *Reading Research Quarterly, 30,* 442–463.

Orellana, M. F. (1995). Literacy as a gendered social practice: Tasks, texts, talk, and take-up. *Reading Research Quarterly, 30,* 674–708.

Palincsar, A. S., & Brown, A. L. (1984). Reciprocal teaching of comprehension-fostering and comprehension-monitoring activities. *Cognition and Instruction, 1,* 117–175.

Paris, S. G., & Oka, E. R. (1986). Children's reading strategies, metacognition, and motivation. *Developmental Review, 6,* 25–56.

Paris, S. G., Wasik, B. A., & Turner, J. C. (1991). The development of strategic readers. In R. Barr, M. Kamil, P. Mosenthal, & P. D. Pearson (Eds.), *Handbook of reading research* (Vol. II, pp. 609–640). New York: Longman.

Patterson, L., Santa, C. M., Short, C., & Smith, K. (1993). *Teachers are researchers: Reflection and action.* Newark, DE: International Reading Association.

Pearson, P. D., & Fielding, L. (1991). Comprehension instruction. In R. Barr, M. Kamil, P. Mosenthal, & P. D. Pearson (Eds.), *Handbook of reading research* (Vol. II, pp. 815–860). New York: Longman.

Pelligrini, A. D., Perlmutter, J. C., Galda, L., & Brody, G. H. (1990). Joint reading between black Headstart children and their mothers. *Child Development, 61,* 443–453.

Perez, B. (1994). Spanish literacy development: A descriptive study of four bilingual whole-language classrooms. *Journal of Reading Behavior, 26,* 75–94.

Peters, E. E., & Levin, J. R. (1986). Effects of a mnemonic imagery strategy on good and poor readers' prose recall. *Reading Research Quarterly, 21,* 179–192.

Phillips, G., & McNaughton, S. (1990). The practice of storybook reading to preschool children in mainstream New Zealand families. *Reading Research Quarterly, 25,* 196–212.

Piaget, J. (1959). *The language and thought of the child* (M. Gabain, Trans.). London: Routledge & Kegan Paul. (Original work published 1926)

Pressley, M. (1994). State-of-the-science primary-grades reading instruction or whole language? *Educational Psychologist, 29,* 211–215.

Pressley, M., Brown, R., El-Dinary, P. B., & Afflerbach, P. (1995). The comprehension instruction that students need: Instruction fostering constructively responsive reading. *Learning Disabilities Research and Practice, 10,* 215–224.

Pressley, M., El-Dinary, P. B., Gaskins, I., Schuder, T., Bergman, J., Almasi, L., & Brown, R. (1992). Beyond direct explanation: Transactional instruction of reading comprehension strategies. *Elementary School Journal, 92,* 511–554.

Purcell-Gates, V. (1995). *Other people's words: The cycle of low literacy.* Cambridge, MA: Harvard University Press.

Purcell-Gates, V., & Dahl, K. L. (1991). Low-SES children's success and failure at early literacy learning in skills-based classrooms. *Journal of Reading Behavior, 23,* 1–34.

Raphael, T. E., & Brock, C. (1993). Mei: Learning the literacy culture in an urban elementary school. In D. J. Leu & C. K. Kinzer (Eds.), *Examining central issues in literacy research, theory, and practice* (pp. 179–189). Chicago: National Reading Conference.

Raphael, T. E., & Brock, C. H. (1997). Instructional research in literacy: Changing paradigms. In C. K. Kinzer, K. A. Hinchman, & D. J. Leu (Eds.), *Inquiries in literacy theory and practice: Forty-fifth yearbook of the National Reading Conference* (pp. 13–36). Chicago: National Reading Conference.

Raphael, T. E., & Goatley, V. J. (1994). The teacher as "more knowledgeable other": Changing roles for teachers in alternative reading instruction programs. In C. K. Kinzer & D. J. Leu (Eds.), *Multidimensional aspects of literacy research, theory, and practice* (pp. 527–536). Chicago: National Reading Conference.

Raphael, T. E., McMahon, S. I., Goatley, V. J., Bentley, J. L., Boyd, F. B., Pardo, L. S., & Woodman, D. A. (1992). Research directions: Literature and discussion in the reading program. *Language Arts, 69,* 54–61.

Reutzel, D. R., & Cooter, R. B. (1990). Whole language: Comparative effects of first grade reading achievement. *Journal of Educational Research, 83,* 252–257.

Reutzel, D. R., & Hollingsworth, P. M. (1988). Highlighting key vocabulary: A generative-reciprocal procedure for teaching selected inference types. *Reading Research Quarterly, 23,* 358–378.

Reutzel, D. R., Oda, L. K., & Moore, B. H. (1989). Developing print awareness: The effect of three instructional approaches on kindergartners' print awareness, reading readiness, and word reading. *Journal of Reading Behavior, 21,* 197–217.

Richardson, V. (1990). Significant and worthwhile change in teaching practice. *Educational Researcher, 19,* 10–18.

Richardson, V. (Ed.). (1994). *A theory of teacher change and the practice of staff development: A case in reading instruction.* New York: Teachers College Press.

Richardson, V., Anders, P., Tidwell, D., & Lloyd, C. (1991). The relationship between teachers' beliefs and practices in reading comprehension instruction. *American Educational Research Journal, 28,* 559–586.

Rinehart, S. D., Barksdale-Ladd, M. A., & Paterson, J. J. (1994). Story recall through prereading instruction: Use of advance organizers combined with teacher-guided discussion. In E. G. Sturtevant & W. M. Linek (Eds.), *Pathways for literacy: Learners teach and teachers learn* (pp. 237–247). Pittsburgh, KS: College Reading Association.

Rinehart, S. D., Stahl, S. A., & Erickson, L. G. (1986). Some effects of summarization training on reading and studying. *Reading Research Quarterly, 21,* 422–438.

Roehler, L. R., & Duffy, G. G. (1991). Teachers' instructional actions. In R. Barr, M. Kamil, P. Mosenthal, & P. D. Pearson (Eds.), *Handbook of reading research* (Vol. II, pp. 861–883). New York: Longman.

Rogers, T. (1991). Students as literary critics: The interpretive experiences, beliefs, and processes of ninth-grade students. *Journal of Reading Behavior, 23,* 391–423.

Roser, N., & Martinez, M. (1985). Roles adults play in preschoolers' response to literature. *Language Arts, 62,* 485–490.

Rowe, D. W. (1989). Author/audience interaction in the preschool: The role of social interaction in literacy learning. *Journal of Reading Behavior, 21,* 311–349.

Rowe, D. W. (1994). Learning about literacy and the world: Two-year-olds' and teachers' enactment of a thematic inquiry curriculum. In C. K. Kinzer & D. J. Leu (Eds.), *Multidimensional aspects of literacy research, theory, and practice* (pp. 217–229). Chicago: National Reading Conference.

Santa Barbara Classroom Discourse Group. (1992). Constructing literacy in classrooms: Literate action as social accomplishment. In H. H. Marshall (Ed.), *Redefining student learning: Roots of educational change* (pp. 119–150). Norwood, NJ: Ablex.

Santa Barbara Classroom Discourse Group. (1995). Two languages, one community: An examination of educational opportunities. In R. Macias & R. Garcia (Eds.), *Changing schools for changing students: An anthology of research on language minorities* (pp. 63–106). Santa Barbara, CA: Linguistic Minority Research Institute.

Saunders, W., O'Brien, G., Lennon, D., & McLean, J. (1998). Making the transition to English literacy successful: Effective strategies for studying literature with transition students. In R. Gersten & R. Jimenez (Eds.), *Effective strategies for teaching language minority students.* Monterey, CA: Brooks Cole.

Scarborough, H. S., & Dobrich, W. (1994). On the efficacy of reading to preschoolers. *Developmental Review, 14,* 245–302.

Scevak, J. J., Moore, P. J., & Kirby, J. R. (1993, October). Training students to use maps to increase text recall. *Contemporary Educational Psychology, 18,* 401–413.

Scharer, P. L. (1992). Teachers in transition: An exploration of changes in teachers and classrooms during implementation of literature-based reading instruction. *Research in the Teaching of English, 26,* 408–445.

Scharer, P. L. (1996). "Are we supposed to be asking questions?": Moving from teacher-directed to student-directed book discussions. In D. J. Leu, C. K. Kinzer, & K. A. Hinchman (Eds.), *Literacies for the 21st century: Research and practice* (pp. 420–429). Chicago: National Reading Conference.

Schunk, D. H., & Rice, J. M. (1991). Learning goals and progress feedback during reading comprehension instruction. *Journal of Reading Behavior, 23,* 351–364.

Schunk, D. H., & Rice, J. M. (1993). Strategy fading and progress feedback: Effects on self-efficacy and comprehension among students receiving remedial reading services. *Journal of Special Education, 27,* 257–276.

Senechal, M., LeFevre, J., Hudson, E., & Lawson, E. P. (1996). Knowledge of storybooks as a predictor of young children's vocabulary. *Journal of Educational Psychology, 88*(3), 520–536.

Senechal, M., LeFevre, J., Thompson, E. M., & Daley, K. E. (1998). Storybook exposure and parent teaching. *Reading Research Quarterly, 33,* 96–116.

Shah, U. (1996). Creating space: Moving from the mandatory to the worthwhile. In L. E. Beyer (Ed.), *Creating democratic classrooms: The struggle to integrate theory and practice* (pp. 41–61). New York: Teachers College Press.

Shannon, P. (1989). *Broken promises: Reading instruction in twentieth-century America.* New York: Bergin & Garvey.

Siegel, M., & Fonzi, J. M. (1995). The practice of reading in an inquiry-oriented mathematics class. *Reading Research Quarterly, 30,* 632–673.

Snow, C. (1983). Literacy and language: Relationships during the preschool years. *Harvard Educational Review, 53,* 165–189.

Snow, C. E., & Ninio, A. (1986). The contracts of literacy: What children learn from learning to read books. In W. H. Teale & E. Sulzby (Eds.), *Emergent literacy: Writing and reading.* Norwood, NJ: Ablex.

Solsken, J. W. (1993). *Literacy, gender, & work in families and in school.* Norwood, NJ: Ablex.

Stahl, S. A., Jacobson, M. G., Davis, C. E., & Davis, R. L. (1989). Prior knowledge and difficult vocabulary in the comprehension of unfamiliar text. *Reading Research Quarterly, 24,* 27–43.

Stahl, S. A., McKenna, M. C., & Pagnucco, J. R. (1994). The effects of whole-language instruction: An update and a reappraisal. *Educational Psychologist, 29,* 175–185.

Stahl, S. A., & Miller, P. D. (1989). Whole language and language experience approaches for beginning reading: A quantitative research synthesis. *Review of Educational Research, 59,* 87–116.

Stewart, R. A., Paradis, E. E., & Van Arsdale, M. (1995). Mrs. Van's story: An exploration of the meaning changes in a teacher's professional life. In K. A. Hinchman, D. J. Leu, & C. K. Kinzer (Eds.), *Perspectives on literacy research and practice* (pp. 438–447). Chicago: National Reading Conference.

Strieb, L. Y. (1993). Visiting and revisiting the trees. In M. Cochran-Smith & S. L. Lytle (Eds.), *Inside/outside: Reader research and knowledge* (pp. 121–130). New York: Teachers College Press.

Sulzby, E. & Teale, W. (1991). Emergent literacy. In R. Barr, M. Kamil, P. Mosenthal, & P. D. Pearson (Eds.), *Handbook of reading research* (Vol. II, pp. 727–757). New York: Longman.

Swartz, L. (1994). Reading response journals: One teacher's research. In G. Wells (Ed.), *Changing schools from within: Creating communities of inquiry* (pp. 99–127). Portsmouth, NH: Heinemann.

Taylor, D. (1983). *Family literacy: The social context of learning to read and write.* Portsmouth, NH: Heinemann Educational Books.

Taylor, N. E., Blum, I. H., & Logsdon, D. M. (1986). The development of written language awareness: Environmental aspects and program characteristics. *Reading Research Quarterly, 21,* 132–149.

Teale, W., Martinez, M., & Glass, W. (1989). Describing classroom storybook reading. In D. Bloome (Ed.), *Classrooms and literacy* (pp. 158–188). Norwood, NJ: Ablex.

Tidwell, D. L. (1995). Practical argument as instruction: Developing an inner voice. In K. A. Hinchman, D. J. Leu, & C. K. Kinzer (Eds.), *Perspectives on literacy research and practice* (pp. 368–373). Chicago: National Reading Conference.

Torgesen, J. K., Morgan, S. T., & Davis, C. (1992). Effects of two types of phonological awareness training on word learning in kindergarten children. *Journal of Educational Psychology, 84,* 364–370.

Turner, J. C. (1993). Situated motivation in literacy instruction. *Reading Research Quarterly, 28,* 288–290.

Turner, J. C. (1995). The influence of classroom contexts on young children's motivation for literacy. *Reading Research Quarterly, 30,* 410–441.

Tyack, D. (1974). *The one best system.* Cambridge, MA: Harvard University Press.

Uhry, J. K., & Shepherd, M. J. (1993). Segmentation/spelling instruction as part of a first-grade reading program: Effects on several measures of reading. *Reading Research Quarterly, 28,* 218–233.

Vygotsky, L. S. (1978). *Mind and society.* Cambridge, MA: Harvard University Press.

Waff, D. R. (1995). Romance in the classroom: Inviting discourse on gender and power. *National Writing Project Quarterly, 17,* 15–18.

Weiner, S. (1994). Effects of phonemic awareness training on low- and middle-achieving first graders' phonemic awareness and reading ability. *Journal of Reading Behavior, 26,* 277–300.

Wells, G. (1994). *Changing schools from within: Creating communities of inquiry.* Portsmouth, NH: Heinemann.

White, J. (1995). A communication triple crown: Making home-school connections among parents, students and teachers. In J. Allen, M. Cary, & L. Delgado (Eds.), *Exploring blue highways: Literacy reform, school change, and the creation of learning communities* (pp. 145–158). New York: Teachers College Press.

Windsor, P. J. T. (1990). *Developing phonemic awareness: Knowledge and practice in holistic instruction.* Paper presented at the 40th Annual Meeting of the National Reading Conference, Miami, FL. (ERIC Document Reproduction Service No. ED 329 933)

Windsor, P. J. T., & Pearson, P. D. (1992). *Children at risk: Their phonemic awareness development in holistic instruction.* Sponsored by the Office of Educational Research and Improvement, Washington, DC. (ERIC Document Reproduction Service No. ED 345 209)

Wixson, K. K. (1986). Vocabulary instruction and children's comprehension of basal stories. *Reading Research Quarterly, 21,* 317–329.

23.

Research on the Teaching of Literature: Finding a Place

Pamela L. Grossman
University of Washington

The first appearance of a chapter on the teaching of literature in the fourth *Handbook of Research on Teaching,* while cause for celebration, calls attention to the changes in the fields of research on teaching and English education. Early research on teaching focused more on the search for generalizations about teaching that transcended subject matter and grade levels (Shulman, 1986). Yet even as the field began to recognize the importance of subject-specific research, the teaching of literature still sat on the sidelines. The third edition of *Handbook of Research on Teaching,* for example, devoted chapters to the teaching of reading and the teaching of writing, but literature does not appear even in the index. In part, this reflects the concerns of the field of English education, which spent much of the past two decades studying the processes of writing and how writing might be taught. During this period, relatively little attention was paid to the reading and understanding of literature.

The relative paucity of research on the teaching of literature is surprising. Literature has long been at the center of the secondary English and language arts curriculum (Applebee, 1974, 1993). The teaching and learning of literature also provide opportunities to study the intersection of everyday and disciplinary knowledge and complex knowledge acquisition in an ill-structured domain. As Susan Hynds commented, "By its very indeterminacy, complexity, and relative unfamiliarity, literature presents a whole host of possibilities and interpretive problems for students to explore. The very act of literary reading demands a tolerance for the multiple tensions and disruptions in-

herent in the literary encounter" (1991, p. 124). Perhaps the very complexity and range of possibilities help explain the lack of research in this area. Literature is an inherently messy field, ill-structured, as much aesthetic as cognitive. Researchers and literary critics have struggled to define literary understanding and to devise measures to assess its attainment (Beach & Hynds, 1991). Literature has also been the site for fiery academic debates in the past decade, and researchers who enter the fray risk getting caught in the cross fire. Despite the vagaries and vagueness of the field, however, research on the teaching and learning of literature has proliferated in the last decade.

This chapter will review the existing research in the areas of students' responses to literature, the literature curriculum, and literature instruction, with particular emphasis on research done in the past 20 years.[1] In this chapter, I take a perspective that spans kindergarten through high school, with occasional forays into college. This perspective masks the division that exists between two distinct research communities, one focused primarily on elementary school and one that investigates secondary school and college.

The chapter opens with a brief account of the evolution of literary theory over the past few decades and how these theories have informed the research agenda. I then turn to a review of the research on students' responses to literature, by far the most robust body of literature reviewed in this chapter, followed by research on approaches to teaching literature. The chapter then provides an overview of research on teachers of literature and the literature curriculum.

I would like to thank Judith Langer, James Marshall, and Peter Smagorinsky for their thorough and thoughtful responses to an earlier version of this chapter. I have benefited greatly from their collective wisdom, while accepting final responsibility for the interpretations expressed in the chapter.

[1] I have relied primarily on published work and dissertations for this review, while recognizing that this decision rule may result in a potential "publication bias." I have chosen not to include technical reports or conference presentations as part of this review.

Literary Theory: A Brief Account[2]

Reading is too rich and many-faceted an activity to be exhausted by a single theory. (Suleiman, 1980, p. 31)

A comprehensive treatment of literary theories and the accompanying skirmishes in the field is well beyond the scope of this chapter. However, as foolhardy as it may be to try to treat the subject briefly, an understanding of how literary theories have evolved in the past 30 years provides a critical context for exploring how the teaching of literature has been studied. What follows is a necessarily simplified account of some of the major schools of literary theory and how each conceptualized the roles of the reader, the text, and the context in the reading of literature.

One of the most influential theories to gain a solid foothold in the schools was New Criticism (Brooks, 1947; Wimsatt, 1954), as represented by a group of critics from the 1950s. Modeling the practice of literary work on inquiry in the hard sciences, these critics sought to establish the primary importance of the text as the object of study. What was most important, from their perspective, was the interrelationship of parts to whole, of form and technique to meaning. Trying to understand the author's initial intent and the influence of the author's biography on a text were considered fallacies of interpretation, as were considerations of the emotional or affective responses of the reader (Wimsatt, 1954). This school of criticism advocated close readings of individual texts, with an emphasis on how the form, language, and literary technique all contributed to its meaning.

New Criticism was enormously successful in permeating the classroom practices of myriad secondary school teachers of literature. Part of this success reflects the tendency of teachers to replicate the instructional practices they have observed in their own schooling. In addition, however, the New Critics, particularly Brooks and Warren, took seriously the pedagogical implications of their theory. They coauthored a popular textbook, *Understanding Poetry,* that modeled the kinds of questions New Critics might ask of poems. Teachers could then adopt this critical apparatus for the teaching of other texts as well. Eagleton (1983), however, argued that the popularity of New Criticism owed more to its political detachment than its pedagogical apparatus. For whatever reasons, New Criticism flourished in the secondary English classrooms for many years, where the emphasis on close readings and analysis of literary technique predominated (Gallagher, 1997).

In reaction to this focus on the text as an object in and of itself, other critics began to refute the "affective fallacy" by arguing for the legitimate role of the reader in the interpretive process. A variety of schools of literary criticism have addressed the role of the reader. Before the emergence of the New Critics, for example, Rosenblatt (1938/1968) had argued for a reconsideration of reading as a transaction between readers and texts. According to Rosenblatt, meaning does not reside either wholly in texts or wholly in the reader's mind but in the transaction that occurs between them. The interpretation created by a reader is essentially a new text, or poem, as Rosenblatt (1978) referred to it in her work, *The Reader, the Text, and the Poem.*[3]

Reader-response theorists, who came to the forefront in the 1970s and 1980s, differ in where they fall in this space between the text and the reader (see Suleiman, 1980, for one mapping of the terrain; Eagleton, 1983, for another; and Tompkins, 1980, for yet another). Reception theorists, such as Wolfgang Iser (1978), emphasized the features of the literary text that force readers to focus on the literary codes necessary to understand a text. Readers encounter "gaps" in literary texts that push them to make inferences and construct meaning. Within this theory, both the nature of the text and the understandings and strategies of the reader contribute to an individual's interpretation. This work hypothesizes the activities of skilled readers as they make their way through a necessarily indeterminate text. Other theorists identified with subjective criticism (Bleich, 1978; Holland, 1975) focused more on the subjective or psychological dimensions of the reader and how these dimensions affected their transactions with texts. From this perspective, a reader's interpretation of text reveals his or her own psychological makeup as much as it reveals about the text itself. Reader-response theories, and their implicit pedagogical practice of focusing on the reader's experience and reactions to texts, have found their way into the practice of teaching literature at all grade levels.

While critics of the various reader-response schools might vary in the importance they attach to the role of reader and text, few debate the presence of a text to be read. By attacking the very concept of a "text," deconstructionists call into question the possibility of a unified text (de Man, 1979; Derrida, 1976; Miller, 1976). Within this theoretical framework, the text is something to be deconstructed, its instability exposed. As J. Hillis Miller wrote, "Deconstruction is not a dismantling of the structure of a text but a demonstration that it has already dismantled itself. Its apparently solid ground is no rock but thin air" (1976, p. 341). Despite the attention deconstruction garnered in the university setting and in the media, relatively few traces of this theoretical apparatus can be found in K–12 classrooms.

Most recent theories have focused most of their attention on

---

[2] Eagleton (1983) provides a lively and concise history of literary theory from the early days of English as an university subject, as defined by F. R. Leavis in the 1920s and 1930s through the intricacies of poststructuralism and political theory. Another indispensable book is Gerald Graff's *Professing Literature,* which provides a more institutional account of how literature has been defined and taught from 1828 through the current emphasis on literary theory. From a different perspective, John Guillory addresses the current debates over the canon by using Bordieu's concept of cultural canon to examine three distinct periods of canon formation.

[3] The absence of Rosenblatt's work from so many discussions of literary criticism is puzzling. In her introduction to *The Reader in the Text,* Suleiman concluded with a footnote on Rosenblatt's work, apologizing that she learned of the work too late to include it in the collection. Her absence from this volume speaks volumes on the gaps that have existed between criticism and pedagogy. Robert Scholes, author of *Textual Power,* has tried to address this gap with his admonition that all teaching is implicitly theoretical. All theories may also be implicitly pedagogical, but too often the voice of pedagogy is silent.

the contexts surrounding the reader and text. Fish's work (1980) called attention to the "interpretive communities" that surround both the writer and reader of text. Any claims about the meaning of a text are made from within an interpretive community and would be inexplicable outside of this context. The work of Bakhtin drew attention to the multiple voices that constitute both fictional works and the mind of the reader, suggesting the necessarily dialogical nature of reading and interpretation (Bakhtin, 1981). Postmodern critics have also focused on how the racial, ethnic, gendered, and political identities of both readers and writers necessarily influence their transactions with texts (Butler, 1990; Said, 1983). Part of the critical effort, within these theoretical orientations, is to clarify these various positions and how they encompass our readings of text.

The research literature has followed these changes in literary theory. Early research focused on students' difficulties in reading and understanding literary texts with the text representing a more or less fixed set of meanings (compare Hartley, 1930; Richards, 1929). As literary theory shifted from a primary focus on the meanings contained within the text to greater attention to the role readers play in interpretation (Rosenblatt, 1938/1968, 1978; Suleiman & Crosman, 1980; Tompkins, 1980), research began to focus more on students' responses to literature and how individual differences among students shaped their differing responses (compare Bleich, 1978; Holland, 1975). More recent research has focused less on the individual reader and more on the interpretive communities (Fish, 1980) and the sociocultural influences (Bakhtin, 1981) that frame the act of reading. From this perspective, readers negotiate meaning based on interactions with others; reading is always a dialogue. This perspective has led to more studies of groups of readers and the ways in which social and cultural contexts shape the activity of reading and the negotiation of meaning.

Each of these theories contains within it its own unit of analysis (the text, the reader, the social group, the cultural context), preferred methodology, and pedagogical implications. The empirical study of these theories has also depended on existing research paradigms and methodological tools. Just as early research borrowed from psychometric traditions (compare Hartley, 1930), recent research has borrowed from anthropology, discourse analysis, and cognitive psychology.

The multiplicity of theories and methods has led to a necessary and perhaps healthy eclecticism in research on the teaching and learning of literature. However, this eclecticism carries its own methodological and hermeneutic risks. Some fear that without fully understanding the disciplinary traditions that underlie particular research approaches, researchers may end up violating both the spirit and the very principles of the disciplinary tradition they have adopted (compare Athanases & Heath, 1995). Another risk is that, given the diversity of theoretical and methodological approaches, researchers may find it difficult to communicate with each other or to aggregate findings, in part because they are working within divergent discourse communities.

Students' Responses to Literature

By far the largest research literature exists on how students read and respond to literary texts (see reviews by Beach & Hynds,

1991; Probst, 1991). The early work of I. A. Richards (1929) introduced the technique of having students read a set of literary texts and write about their responses. His work marked a shift from speculation about how students read to empirical investigations of the process of reading itself. In his study of Cambridge undergraduates, he deplored the difficulty students had in reading literary texts and noted a number of common barriers to understanding, including what he termed "stock responses" and "preconceptions." Although he remarked on the variability of individual readers' responses to different poems, he did not trace this variation, choosing to focus instead on the general portrait of undergraduates' understanding. In many ways, Richards' work showed remarkable prescience; a number of the issues he identified have continued to occupy researchers in the area of student response to literature. He also identified the need to look more closely at the instruction that could support the development of students' responses to literature, observing that literary understanding can be explicitly taught.

> This construing, we must suppose, is not nearly so easy and "natural" a performance as we tend to assume. It is a craft, in the sense that mathematics, cooking, and shoe-making are crafts. It can be taught. And though some gifted individuals can go far in the strength of their own sagacity alone, instruction and practice are very necessary for others. The best methods of instruction remain to be worked out. (Richards, 1929, p. 294)

Richards also challenged the discipline of psychology to focus its attention on the subject matter of literature.

An early and influential study by Norman Holland took a psychological perspective to explain how readers differed in their readings of common literary texts (Holland, 1975). Not only did he use the psychological methods suggested by Richards, but he also studied the variability of individual readers noted but not explored in Richards's study. In investigating how five readers made sense of a common text, Holland outlined how readers' responses reflected their own identities and psychological struggles. Holland believed that "a reader responds to a literary work by using it to re-create his own characteristic psychological processes" (Holland, 1975, p. 40). His work focused on the issues and feelings the texts evoked in readers rather than on the actual processes of reading, a strategy followed by other researchers in this area as well (Petrosky, 1977). A related study (Dillon, 1982) identified three general styles of reading. Character–action–moral style treats meaning as more or less evident in a text and assumes that the world of the text is simply an extension of the real world. This style of reading does not question the artifice of the text or the role of the author. The "digger for secrets" style of reading focuses on looking for the symbolism concealed in the text. Finally, the "anthropologists' style" focuses on the cultural backdrop to the work and identifies the cultural values that help explain characters' actions. Dillon suggested that these styles captured individuals' characteristic responses to literary texts. Other research has also documented students' preferred responses to literary texts and how these preferences affect their responses to text (Golden & Guthrie, 1986).

Other theorists have focused more on the process of readers' transactions with literature than on the products of these transactions. The influential work of Louise Rosenblatt (1938/1968, 1978) offers a conceptualization of the transactional quality of students' engagement with literary texts. Rosenblatt distinguished between efferent readings of texts, or reading for information, as one reads expository texts, and aesthetic readings focused more on the experiential and literary aspects of reading. In her work, she highlighted the centrality of the transactions between the reader and text, and the ways in which readers use their own experiences and background knowledge to make sense of literary works. Britton (1990) made a similar distinction between participant and spectator stances in the uses of language; the spectator stance focuses on the more aesthetic uses of language, while the participant stance is used for more utilitarian ends—to inform, persuade, request. Both of these frameworks have been used extensively in the study of students' responses to literature.

One of the most widely used approaches to analyzing responses to literature has been the Purves–Rippere (1968) framework. The elements include four major categories and 139 elements overall. The major categories of response include engagement–involvement (statements of emotional reaction and interest), perception (descriptive statements about a text, including literal retellings, summaries), interpretation (comments in which the readers ascribe meaning to the text and try to generalize beyond it), and evaluation (judgments of quality). In reviewing a number of studies that used this framework, Applebee (1977) noted the consistent finding that age matters. Younger children focus primarily on perception, while adolescents engage in more interpretation. The range of responses also increased with age. (See Applebee, 1977, for an overview of studies using this system of analysis.)

Subsequent empirical work has begun to create a variety of accounts of students' literary responses. Recent work has borrowed cognitive techniques such as think-aloud protocols to gain access to student' on-line responses and analyses of literary texts. In this respect, research on students' literary thinking has built on the methods used in research on students' writing processes (Flower & Hayes, 1980).

The focus of research has also followed trends within the development of psychology (Gardner, 1985). As cognitive psychology replaced the more psychoanalytical tradition used by Holland, research began to focus more on students' prior knowledge (Harker, 1994), cognitive activity, analogical reasoning, perception (Kintgen, 1983), and interpretive strategies (Earthman, 1992; Langer, 1990; Shimron, 1980; Svensson, 1990). A more developmental line of research has focused on the development of literary understanding and response in students of different ages (e.g., Applebee, 1974; Beach & Wendler, 1987; Hardy-Brown, 1979; Svensson, 1990).

The studies focusing on the interpretative strategies and experiences of readers have blended literary theory with the methodological tools of cognitive psychology. These studies typically have used think-aloud protocols (e.g., Flower & Hayes, 1980) to gain access to readers' on-line transactions with texts (Earthman, 1992; Harker, 1994; Kintgen, 1983; Langer, 1990; Shimron, 1980). This approach allows researchers to follow a readers' first responses and tentative construals of a work and to trace emerging questions and revised understandings through to the final interpretation. While think-aloud methods may also

create an artificial context for reading and compromise the ecological validity of the task (Cooper & Holtzman, 1983), they are better suited to documenting the exploratory nature of literary transactions than written or verbal retrospective self-reports of readers' encounters with literature, which may feature final conclusions or evaluations of texts.

Langer (1995) has used this method to create a portrait of students' encounters with literary works. Building from her research on 36 middle school and high school students' readings of literary works, Langer describes the four stages of building "envisionments" of literary texts. She describes the process of envisionment building, her term for creating an interpretation, as beginning with stepping into an envisionment in which readers search for clues to orient themselves to a text. At this stage, readers are still creating a broad and somewhat superficial understanding of the work. In another stance, which Langer calls "being in and moving through" an envisionment, readers call on both personal and textual knowledge to question a text. During this stage, readers are immersed within the world of text and are building understandings of its meanings. A third stance, "stepping out and rethinking what one knows," focuses more on how the text can illuminate readers' lives and contribute to their understanding of the world. A fourth stance, "stepping out and objectifying the experience," is more explicitly analytic, as readers begin to focus on the author's craft, on features of the literary text that contribute to its power, and on the texts' connection to other literary works. Langer emphasized that these stances are not linear but recursive. At various points in transactions with texts, readers may move back and forth between these stances.

Building on Langer's framework, Purcell-Gates (1991) investigated more specifically how remedial readers engaged in the process of making meaning from text. By using similar think-aloud protocols with six students designated as remedial readers, Purcell-Gates found that the students spent most of their time either trying to get into the text or failing to move beyond a restatement of the words of the text. In his studies of his own students, Wilhelm (1997) also found that reluctant readers had difficulty entering the world of a text. Reluctant readers also engaged in fewer dimensions of response, compared to the more engaged readers in the class. These portrayals of the readings of weaker readers suggest that instruction needs to be focused on first helping them enter the world of the text.

With the conceptual work of Iser and Rosenblatt as a foundation, Earthman (1992) used a modified expert–novice design to study the transactions of more- and less-experienced readers with four literary works. She focused particularly on the ways in which graduate students in English and college freshmen acknowledged and filled gaps in a text, used the repertoire of a text to create an interpretation, and assumed multiple perspectives with which to view a literary work. If Langer's study provided a broader overview of the interpretive process, Earthman's study investigated microprocesses within this process. She found that freshmen had great difficulty in assuming multiple perspectives on a text; once they had decided on a perspective, they were reluctant to rethink it. Graduate students were much more comfortable with multiple perspectives and the resulting ambiguity and were more likely to revise their opinions as their readings progressed. In a similar study, Peskin (1998) examined the difference between eight novices and eight experts as they read two period poems. In contrast to the novices, experts relied on productive strategies for interpreting poetry and possessed greater domain knowledge that provided access into the specific poems. Novices experienced great difficulty in making sense of the poems, which ultimately affected their appreciation.

While the differences between more- and less-experienced readers are not surprising, they do offer a picture of some of the strategies experienced readers use in transactions with literature (see Wineburg, 1991, for a similar approach to studying historical thinking). In his study of 15 10th graders identified as able readers of literature, Harker (1994) came to a similar conclusion. The students read the poems searching for the "plain sense" or what the poem "meant." While students continued to refine their initial responses to a poem, they were unlikely to substantially revise their first conclusions. One interpretation both Harker and Earthman offered for students' inability to look for multiple perspectives or revise initial responses was developmental. Another line of research has pursued a developmental agenda to trace changes in children's and adolescents' understandings and responses to literature.

A number of studies have found that preadolescents focus primarily on literal elements of a story, while adolescents are more likely to engage in interpretation (Applebee, 1977). Applebee's own study of developmental differences in responses to stories looked across 6-, 9-, 13-, and 17-year-olds (Applebee 1978). The younger children focused primarily on story action and relied on retellings or summaries to organize their responses. The youngest students also offered relatively global responses to stories. In contrast, the 13- and 17-year-olds were more concerned with developing themes and generalizations from the stories, and their evaluations of quality were tied more to their analyses. A number of subsequent studies have supported Applebee's findings (Cullinan, Harwood, & Galda, 1983; Galda, 1982; Lehr, 1988; Many, 1991). Applebee contends that the differences reflect changes in cognitive development, a central premise of the work of Hardy-Brown (1979).

In a study that compared eighth graders, 11th graders, college freshmen, and college juniors in terms of their response to a story, Beach and Wendler (1987) found that the college students were much more likely to focus on social and psychological aspects of characters as opposed to their actions. Svensson (1990) had 72 students at three age levels (11, 14, and 18) read four poems that were open to both symbolic and more literal interpretations. Students listened to the poems on tape and were asked to talk about what the poem was about. He found that older students were significantly more likely to offer symbolic responses to the poems and that students' backgrounds in reading also affected the nature of their responses, confirming the findings of other studies in this area.

While this research demonstrated that responses to literature develop with age, some of the literature also suggested that children's own backgrounds with literature affect their responses. For example, Lehr (1988) found that students with the greatest exposure to literature were better able to generate thematic statements, even though this was not generally characteristic of their age group. The work on children's responses to familiar stories (Martinez & Roser, 1991) also found that very young students offered more complex responses to familiar stories and that their responses deepened with re-readings. Development alone cannot explain the changes in children's responses to literature; as much of the research suggests, parents and teachers play a critical role in developing students' literary responses (Cochran-Smith, 1984; Kiefer, 1982; Morrow, 1992).

While these studies have contributed enormously to our understanding of how readers actually interact with texts, the research paradigm itself has also perpetuated the image of a solitary reader reading, rather than a community of readers engaged in making meaning together. Another line of research on students' understanding of literature has tried to look at the influences of social and textual resources on students' readings of texts.

One sociocognitive set of studies looked at the ways in which readers brought social knowledge, specifically knowledge of interpersonal relationships, to their reading of literature (Hynds, 1985, 1989). With the use of a variety of response modes to elicit student readings, including think-aloud methods, interviews, written responses, and questionnaires, Hynds studied how 56 high school seniors responded to five stories, all of which represented interpersonal conflict and opportunities to reflect on characters' motivations and actions. Students were assessed on their interpersonal cognitive complexity through questionnaires that were coded according to the number of different ways a character might be described.

These questionnaires were used both with short stories and with students' description of peers. From the 56 students, four students were selected for case studies. Hynds found that these readers used their understanding of characters to make predictions about a story, to reflect on their own lives, or to generalize from the text to the world. Students who were able to make these kinds of predictions or speculations about peers, however, were not always able to use this knowledge in their responses to literature. The students who were best able to move between the text and their personal lives were those who had strong home support for reading and who found reading intrinsically motivating.

A number of studies have explored the role that intertextuality plays in readers' understandings of literature. Kristeva (1974) first coined the term intertextuality to describe how readers move from one text to another in their readings, at times transposing texts, at other times assimilating one text into another, but always using their knowledge of other texts as they read. In his study of intertextuality among eight readers, Hartman (1995) defined intertextuality as connecting or assembling meanings from different knowledge sources. He looked at eight proficient readers as they read through five passages all connected to the theme of war and dying. Students were taught to think aloud and then to use the think-aloud procedure while reading these five passages. Hartman identified three textual resources students drew on in their readings: primary endogenous (within the passage students were currently reading), secondary endogenous (passages read previously in the study), and exogenous (texts from outside the study). Students tended to rely on the primary endogenous links when a passage was oblique. Hartman also identified different profiles of readers. The intratextual reader made connections to other passages only when the reading was concluded, not in the process of working through an understanding. Hartman identified this as "post-hoc" linking. Intertextual readers continually referred to other passages and allowed these prior texts to influence their understandings of the current text. Finally, the extratextual reader made connections to personal experience, rarely, if ever, making connections to other texts.

Not surprisingly, researchers have found that more experienced readers are better able to use intertextual links. The experienced readers of poetry in Kintgen's (1983) study, for example, used their knowledge of other poetic texts to make sense of new poems. The more able readers in another study (Beach, Appleman, & Dorsey, 1990) were also more likely to make specific links among literary texts. Rather than a particular style of reading that distinguishes between individuals, the ability to use intertextuality may depend on experience and instruction.

Much of the research on how students engaged in the reading of literature seems detached from considerations of how they were taught to read by parents and teachers. Yet as Purves (1993) has observed, habits of reading are a product of both schooling and national culture.

> The school reader exists in a field of school reading that has developed in that reader a set of habits of mind about how to read and how to talk about what has been read. . . . Students in the United States differ from students in other countries who have acquired different habits of reading and articulating their response to what they have read. . . . Their habits, like those of the Italian students who focus on history or the British students who focus on image and metaphor, are the products of an educational system that trains the mind. (Purves, 1993, p. 351)

In investigating students' responses to literature, one is inevitably also studying how they have been taught to respond by parents, teachers, and communities. The following section will examine research on different approaches to teaching literature.

Approaches to Teaching Literature

Despite the wide-reaching changes in literary theories, literature instruction in the schools has changed relatively little since Dora Smith (1933) documented the prevalence of teacher-led recitations in literature classrooms (Applebee, 1982; Applebee & Purves, 1992). Just as a curriculum script has predominated in the teaching of mathematics, (homework check followed by introduction of new materials, followed by guided practice) (Leinhardt & Putnam, 1987), so a script seems to underlie much of the teaching of literature. In this script, teachers ask questions about the texts, and students offer short responses, usually followed by teachers' evaluations and elaborations (Applebee, 1993; Barnes, Barnes, & Clarke, 1984; Marshall, Smagorinsky, & Smith, 1995). Teachers' questions are designed either to elicit students' responses to the literature or to help students develop the skills of "close reading." Often questions regarding students' responses to a work serve as a motivational strategy to help students become engaged in a text before moving on to analysis (Applebee, 1993).

Relatively little research has looked closely at the benefits of different instructional approaches for the teaching of literature, a situation Applebee attributed to the lack of a coherent conceptual framework for linking the goals of literature instruction with particular approaches (Applebee, 1982). While isolated studies compared different approaches to the teaching of literature, these studies did not constitute a coherent research program. In fact, many studies on the teaching of literature could be described as distinctly idiosyncratic in nature (e.g., Folta, 1981; Lennox, Small, & Keeling, 1978). These studies generally used an experimental design to test the effectiveness of a particular strategy for teaching literature. However, the strategies described in these early studies were rarely rooted in a larger conceptual framework. This line of research suggested, however, that students can be taught a variety of ways of responding to literature, including using drama, visual strategies, and media.

A more recent line of research on the teaching of literature has attempted to build instructional models based on theoretical analyses of how readers make meaning from text. One study, building on the relationship between writing and learning, looked at how different writing tasks shaped students' responses to literature (Marshall, 1987); the study found that different assignments led to varying responses to literature. A particularly powerful finding was the endurance of these effects of writing task on response in a later posttest. As Marshall concluded, "In general, regardless of the time elapsed, when students had first written extensively about a story in either a personal analytic or formal analytic mode, they were better able to recall and interpret its features than when they had written in a restricted mode" (Marshall, 1987, p. 57).

Another study that built on a theoretical framework of how students make meaning from text is Smith's (1989) study of different approaches to the teaching of irony in poetry. By building on Wayne Booth's (1974) analysis of how readers detect irony in literary texts, Smith devised an instructional unit that explicitly taught students to recognize five clues to ironic meaning. Smith hypothesized that teaching students strategies for recognizing irony would result in greater ability to interpret ironic meanings. He contrasted the direct approach of strategy instruction with what he termed a tacit approach in which students were provided with extensive examples of ironic texts and were asked to interpret these texts on their own. In this approach, irony was not mentioned directly nor were students taught Booth's five strategies. Both of these approaches were contrasted to no instruction in irony.

Not surprisingly, students in both direct and tacit approaches outperformed the students who had received no instruction at all. However, the differences between the direct and tacit approaches were not significant across all students. The direct approach, in which students were given the tools for detecting and interpreting ironic meaning, seemed most beneficial to the ninth graders, the least experienced readers in the study. While the study offered a promising direction for future research, the lack of difference between approaches suggested that we need to learn more about how students actually develop skills of literary interpretation; the success of both methods suggested that there are likely to be multiple ways. The finding that the least experienced readers benefited most from the direct approach also suggested the importance of instructional scaffolding for inexperienced readers. Conversely, the success of the tacit approach for more experienced readers supported the value of textual experiences and immersion. This study also rested on the assumption that ironic meanings are stable and different readers can agree on the ironic meaning. This assumption may be questioned by theorists who concentrate on what readers bring to texts and how readers' backgrounds affect their interpretations.

The importance of this study lies in its attempt to provide a theoretical basis for literature instruction, based on knowledge from literary criticism. This work resembled the work in reading, which built instruction about metacognitive strategies used by skilled readers (Palinscar & Brown, 1984); the work in mathematics, which devised cognitively guided instruction based on research on young children's counting strategies (Carpenter, Fennema, Peterson, & Carey, 1988); or the work in physics, which has devised instructional models based on common student misconceptions. By attending to the common difficulties readers face while reading specific kinds of texts, this study heeded Richards' (1929) admonition that we "cease to regard a misinterpretation as a mere unlucky accident. We must treat it as the normal and probable event" (p. 315).

In another study that used instructional scaffolding, Carol Lee created a literature unit that built on the African-American discourse genre of signifying (Gates, 1988; Lee, 1993). Lee's work was especially significant as it bridged the research on culturally responsive pedagogy, which is often generic with regard to subject matter, with research on the teaching of literature. Other studies have investigated the relationship between cultural knowledge and literary understanding. One study of the relationship between the ability to understand figurative language and African-American children's experience with "sounding" or "playing the dozens" demonstrated a positive relationship between children's own experiences with sounding and their ability to understand figurative language (Ortony, Turner, & Larson-Shapiro, 1985). By building on this relationship, Lee created an instructional unit that helped students use their cultural knowledge of signifying to understand complex literary texts. She contrasted four experimental classes with two control classes. Students were given pretests on reading skills, on knowledge of signifying, and on prior social knowledge and a posttest on reading skills. Both the pretest and the posttest of reading skills gave students stories they had not encountered before.

Lee found that while all students made gains during the unit, students in the experimental group made significantly greater gains on the posttest of reading skills. Lee also found that both prior social knowledge and knowledge of signifying predicted students' scores on both the pretest and the posttest. Students in the experimental groups with the least prior knowledge gained the most.

As Lee acknowledged, the design of the study made it impossible to separate out the effects of the mode of instruction in the experimental classes, which used an inquiry approach, from the use of culturally congruent literary texts. In this sense, the study altered both curriculum and instruction within the experimental classes. Lee also recognized that the data made it difficult to understand the actual processes through which students drew on their prior knowledge of a social world and of signifying in their interpretations of the novel. However, her study provided us with an important model of the power of careful instructional scaffolding for the reading of complex literary texts; in addition, her study provided an image of a culturally congruent literature curriculum that draws on students' so-

cial and cultural background to enable them to become more skilled readers of literary texts.

Work at the elementary level has documented the differential effects of different approaches to the teaching of literature. A study of third-grade readers designed an instructional intervention based on Rosenblatt's (1938/1968) distinction between efferent and aesthetic readings of text (Many & Wiseman, 1992). In comparing the consequences of different forms of instruction, researchers found that students who were taught with an approach based on literary analysis were more likely to focus on literary elements in their responses to stories, while students taught from an approach based on literary experience responded more personally to the stories, making more connections between the text and life. Students who did not participate in any discussions of the stories were more likely to retell the text. These findings lend additional support to Purves's (1993) contention that children's responses to literature are shaped by instruction and teachers' approaches to reading.

Another line of research has focused on incorporating alternative modes of response into the literature classroom. By building on a framework of how students make meaning from text (Benton, 1992; Langer, 1990), Wilhelm (1997) experimented with the use of drama and art in the literature classroom to help students enter the world of a literary text. With the use of his own middle school classroom as a research site, Wilhelm used a variety of dramatic activities to help students move from passive and literal readings of text, including dramatic reenactments of the text and guided imagery. These activities, according to Wilhelm, helped students envision the world of the text and understand the feelings and motivations of the characters. He also used visual art activities, including picture mapping, illustration, and collage, to help students see the events of the story and represent their responses. The use of drama and art served to help most of the readers, but particularly the weaker readers develop a greater variety of strategies for reading literary text and to move beyond decoding to engagement and meaning making.

Other studies have also examined the uses of alternative modes of response to literature, including theater and dance (Smagorinsky & Coppock, 1995; Wolf, 1994). If, as both Wilhelm and Purcell-Gates (1991) found, poor readers find themselves all too often "on the outside looking in," activities such as drama and art can help those students envision and inhabit the world of a text, a critical prerequisite for responding to literature (Benton, 1992; Langer, 1990). Such activities also shift the roles of students and teachers in classrooms, making students more active participants and evading the powerful but invisible script of classroom discourse, a script that underlies most typical classroom discussions of literature. These studies also suggest why earlier studies on the use of art or drama in the teaching of literature found a positive relationship between such activities and students' response to literature (e.g., Folta, 1981).

Discussions of Literature

Because the dominant instructional model is whole class discussion of a common text, perhaps it is not surprising that a variety of researchers have focused on discussions of literature. One line of research has been primarily descriptive in nature, looking for ways in which classroom discussions provide opportunities for transactions between readers and texts and foster specific ways of talking and thinking about literature (e.g., Marshall et al., 1995; Rogers, 1991). Yet another line of research has tried to link features of classroom discussion to student achievement (Nystrand & Gamoran, 1991).

In his study of classroom discussions of literature at the high school level, Marshall (Marshall et al., 1995) studied 16 classrooms, which included high, middle, and low tracks. The teachers' goals for the classroom discussions reflected a dual emphasis on close readings of texts and students' responses. After careful coding of videotapes of the discussions, Marshall and his colleagues found that teachers tend to dominate large-group discussions, with teacher turns lasting two to five times as long as student turns. Teachers controlled the pace and direction of the discussions, with students' role confined to responding to teachers' questions. Overall, the researchers found relatively few opportunities for students to develop their own interpretations of text in these discussions. While there were differences in teachers' goals for different tracks, the overall picture of classroom discussions of literature remained similar across tracks. These findings confirm the portrait of teacher-dominated classrooms found in other research on literature instruction (Barnes et al., 1984; Hillocks, 1989) as well as large-classroom studies across subject areas (e.g., Goodlad, 1984). In a study that contrasted two approaches to the discussion of literary text in ninth grade (Rogers, 1991), the teacher-led discussion followed a similar pattern to that documented by Marshall. The teacher directed the discussion as a way to review the story and to develop a particular interpretation; students were given few opportunities to develop their own interpretive responses. In the researcher-led discussion, explicitly designed to develop students' interpretive skills, students were encouraged to elaborate on their initial responses and to make intertextual connections. The study also found an interaction between students' own interpretive preferences and their responses to the instructional approach. A study of a second-grade classroom (Commeyras & Sumner, 1998) found that children were more engaged in literature discussions when they generated the topics.

While researchers may not have seen productive discussions occurring in the majority of classrooms, students seem aware of what makes a good text-based discussion in their classes. In a study that asked students for their perceptions of classroom discussions, Alvermann et al. (1996) found that middle school and high school students are well aware of the conditions they believe support good discussions. Researchers videotaped discussions from five different classrooms and then showed the videotapes to focal students to stimulate their thinking about text-based discussions. Students were clearly aware of the norms and responsibilities that contribute to productive discussions, including the importance of each individual contributing to the group talk. Most students preferred the small-group format for discussion as it allowed greater opportunities for participation and for more exploratory talk. Students also believed that the nature of the tasks assigned by teachers strongly influenced their participation in discussions.

SMALL-GROUP DISCUSSIONS OF LITERATURE

Proponents of more student-centered instruction have often urged that teachers use small groups to encourage more student engagement, and a number of researchers have demonstrated the relationship between small-group communication and learning (Barnes, 1976; Dias, 1979). The specific roles of teachers and students in these small groups, however, may be critical to the quality of both the conversation and the learning. In his study of children's discussions, Barnes (1976) suggested the central importance of the teacher's view of knowledge and of the teacher's own role in supporting or directing student learning. Where teachers maintain strict control over the content that can be discussed, students are much less free to engage in the exploratory talk that is central to constructing an interpretation. At the same time, Barnes demonstrated that students are not necessarily free to engage in this kind of talk in peer groups, without careful scaffolding by the teacher.

More current research seems to support Barnes's contention. In their study of small-group discussions led by prospective teachers, Eeds and Wells (1989) found that it was the quality of teachers' talk that distinguished the more- and less-effective small-group discussions. In the most-effective discussions, the adults picked up on "teachable moments," built on students' interpretations, and synthesized children's contributions to the discussion. In a study of small-group discussion in four classrooms, Smagorinsky (in Marshall et al., 1995) found that even during small-group discussion, too little emphasis was placed on students' constructions of literary interpretation. The small-group discussions in these classrooms tended to mirror the discourse of large-group discussions. If students were not given opportunities to create meaning within the large-group discussions, they did not exercise their interpretive powers in small groups.

Other work also suggested the difficulty of getting students to engage in interpretive conversations about literature in small groups. In a study of teacher-led small-group discussion of literature among sixth graders, only the higher-ability students were able to develop a conversation in which students actively contributed (Wollman-Bonilla, 1994). In the group of less-able readers, students rarely engaged in lively conversations about literature but looked to the teacher to provide both the questions and answers. All of these studies suggested that the defined roles of teacher and students affect the quality of the small-group experience for students.

Other research has looked explicitly at student-led small-group discussions of literature. In her comparison of peer-led and teacher-led discussions of literature with fourth graders, Almasi (1995) found that the discourse differed in student-led and teacher-led groups as did the students' ability to recognize and to resolve conflicts. In peer-led groups, students were better able to recognize and resolve conflicts. She also found that students were more likely to expand on their ideas and direct the course of the conversation in peer-led groups. One study of a fifth grade "book club" (Goatley, Brock, & Raphael, 1995) investigated students' discussions of a novel in a heterogeneous group that included students who qualified for services in special education, Chapter 1, and English as a second language. All students participated in the discussions of literature, sharing leadership roles and providing resources for solving interpretive challenges. The authors pointed out that all of the students found the text challenging, not just the students who qualified for special help, and all students in the group were able to have access to the range of interpretive strategies needed to comprehend literary texts. The success of the students may be related to their age, as another study found that older elementary students were much better able to draw on ideas and information offered by peers during peer-group discussions of literature (Leal, 1992).

Other studies of student-led small groups, however, have shown that such small-group discussions can exacerbate existing status differences among students. In a study that analyzed the uses of power wielded in peer-led discussions, Lewis (1997) showed how students with more social power within the classroom tended to dominate peer-led discussions. In her ethnographic study of peer-led literature discussions in a fifth- and sixth-grade classroom, she found that social roles within the classroom were both constructed and solidified by interactions during small-group discussions. From this perspective, peer-led discussions can replicate the inequitable patterns of discourse that exist within large-group discussions.

In search of models for the grand conversations about literature teachers hope to instigate among students, one researcher studied adult book clubs. Smith (in Marshall et al., 1995) audiotaped and analyzed discussions held in two voluntary adult reading groups, one all male and one all female. In contrast to portraits of school discussions of literature, the book-club discussions featured more examples of cooperative turns in which members worked together to construct an understanding. More references were made to personal experiences than were found in high school discussions of literature, as well as many fewer evaluative comments. Smith identified the importance of the social contexts for literature discussion, including the voluntary nature of book clubs and involuntary nature of school, the equality among members in an adult book club, and the spirit of cooperation that characterized book-club discussions as significant reasons for the differences in discourse.

More research needs to investigate small-group discussions of literature, with careful attention given to the roles of teachers and students in the small groups, and the ways in which discourse is modeled in whole-class discussions and its relationship to how discourse unfolds in small groups. Lewis's (1997) research suggested the negative side effects of relatively unstructured small-group discussions and the need to counteract status differences more explicitly in the design of group work. Future research will also need to look more carefully at the nature of activities or tasks that are assigned to small groups and at how these tasks embody the interpretive skills for discussing literature and allow diverse students to contribute to the construction of meaning. Finally, we need more studies of what students are actually learning in small-group discussions of literature.

DISCUSSION AND STUDENT ACHIEVEMENT

Relatively little research has tried to connect instructional models with students' achievement in literature, in part because of the complexity of defining what we mean by achievement in literature. One exception to this rule has been the work of Nystrand and Gamoran (1991). In their study of 58 eighth-grade English classrooms, they described features of classroom discussions of literature that indicate disengagement, procedural engagement, and substantive engagement. The features that describe substantive engagement include teachers' use of open-ended questions (which they term authentic questions) to which

there are no prespecified answers; teachers' use of uptake, or follow-ups to student responses that incorporate students' words and concerns; and teacher evaluation that is both positive and uses a student response to direct further discussion. Literature achievement was measured by a test of students' understanding of five pieces of fiction that they had read in class. While substantive engagement in discussion was relatively rare in the classrooms studied, these indicators were related strongly and positively to students' achievement in literature. In classrooms characterized by greater uptake and more authentic questions, students scored higher on the literature test. Contrary to the researchers' expectations, however, time spent in small groups correlated negatively with achievement. The researchers attributed this negative relationship to the relatively low quality of group assignments. While this study is suggestive, future research might look more broadly not only at what teachers do in classroom discussion but also at students' talk as well.

The existing research suggests that most classroom discussions of literature closely resemble the recitations that characterize much of school life (Britton, Burgess, Martin, & Rosen, 1975). While most English teachers want students to engage with the texts and make connections between literature and their own lives (Marshall et al., 1995; Zancanella, 1991), classroom discussions of literature most resemble "gentle inquisitions" (Eeds & Wells, 1989) that ultimately stifle students' opportunities to follow their own thinking or to create interpretations for themselves. Marshall et al. (1995) attributed the lifeless discussions that often take place despite the teachers' best intentions to the prevalence of a speech genre of classroom discourse in which both teachers and students are trapped. They suggested the importance of developing new activities for the classroom that cast teachers and students in different roles in which teachers trade in the role of examiner for co-explorer.

Abdicating authority to small-group work does not solve the problem of lifeless discussions. The mixed picture of student talk in small groups that emerges from the research suggests the need to understand more clearly how the nature of the group activity, student and teacher roles within the group, the nature of the text and assigned task, and prior instruction all affect the quality of small-group discussions of literature (Smagorinsky & O'Donnell-Allen, 1998). Careful scaffolding of approaches to interpretation is still the responsibility of the teacher. Whether this scaffolding takes place in whole-group instruction or in small-group activities, the quality of group activity and the relationship of activities to interpretive processes and tasks are crucial (Hamel & Smith, 1998). The relationship between participation in small-group discussions and students' social position within the classroom also suggests that teachers who use group work must understand the literature on how groups can exacerbate existing status differences among group members and must structure tasks to distribute the intellectual leadership of the groups more equitably (Cohen, 1986).

LITERATURE LEARNING AT HOME

An entirely different line of research has studied what children learn about literature in the home environment. By using primarily ethnographic methods, such studies have tried to portray the everyday interactions children have with literature in their homes and communities, and the ways in which this experience does, and does not, articulate with the culture of the school. While not focusing specifically on literature, Shirley Brice Heath's book, *Ways with Words* (1983) documented different communities' connections to ways of speaking and interacting with text and provided an exemplary model of this line of research. By documenting the early literary encounters of her two daughters, Shelby Wolf (Wolf & Heath, 1992) used her dual roles as researcher and mother to provide an intimate portrait of all the ways in which literature infuses the lives of her children. This work suggested the power of literature in children's lives and the possibilities for future learning. Finders's (1996) work on early adolescent girls focused on the roles that a variety of literacy activities play in these girls' lives and their connection to the roles of literacy in their homes and communities.

Perhaps the most general conclusion that can be drawn from research on the teaching of literature is that students learn to read and respond to literature as they are taught. From early childhood through secondary school, students acquire ways of reading and paying attention to texts from their parents and teachers (Finders, 1996; Roser & Martinez, 1985; Wolf & Heath, 1992). Work on small-group discussions suggested that students bring these ways of responding to literature into their discussions with peers. Given the predominant script for teaching literature, which features teachers asking relatively low-level questions, perhaps we should not be surprised by students' difficulty in making inferences in literary texts (Hillocks, 1989; Mullis, Campbell, & Farstrup, 1993). According to the picture that emerges from the research, students are given relatively few opportunities to construct interpretations on their own or to argue about competing interpretations. Future research needs to explore instructional models that allow students to take on the primary work of constructing meaning and to illustrate how teachers can help students grow in their interpretive powers.

Another crucial line of research needs to address how teachers can change from the teacher-dominated recitations that currently comprise most literature instruction to more open-ended discussions of literature. What do teachers need to know and believe in order to make such a pedagogical shift? What models of professional development can best support teachers as they make changes in their practice? These questions will be addressed later in this chapter.

The Literature Curriculum: A Still Life

Despite the dramatic changes occurring in literary theory within the academy (Eagleton, 1983) and concomitant reconsideration of the literary canon (Gates, 1992), the literature curriculum in secondary schools has remained remarkably stable (Applebee, 1993; Applebee & Purves, 1992). As Applebee has amply documented in a large-scale survey, little has changed either in the titles of courses that compose the secondary literature curriculum or in the titles of books read in these courses. Despite the expansion of the canon in the academy, the top 10 works required in grades 9 to 12 across the 322 public schools studied by Applebee and his colleagues (Applebee, 1993) continued to include *Romeo and Juliet, Macbeth, Huckleberry Finn, Julius Caesar, To Kill a Mockingbird, Scarlet Letter, Of Mice and Men, Hamlet, The Great Gatsby,* and *Lord of the Flies.* The

selections remained virtually identical across the Catholic and independent schools included in the sample. Since 1963, the only work to be dropped from the top 10 list was *Silas Marner,* ironically, one of the few texts written by a woman, as Applebee notes.

If book-length works have failed to reflect the expansion of a literary canon, the contents of literature anthologies have shifted to include more works by women and minorities (Applebee, 1993). In fact, Applebee suggested that students' best opportunity to experience texts written by writers of different races, cultures, and ethnicities comes from anthologies. While advocates have urged that students study literature that more accurately reflects America's multicultural composition (Graff, 1992; Stotsky, 1991), the actual curriculum has been slow to change. The overall picture of the literature curriculum at the secondary level is one of a still life, with subtle changes around the edges rather than at the core.

Efforts such as the Pacesetter curriculum (Scholes, 1995; Wolf, 1995) have tried to revitalize the secondary literature curriculum by putting language use and culture at the forefront of the curriculum, with literature as one of many opportunities to explore the uses of language in a variety of both print and nonprint texts. Future research will need to examine how the ideas of this course are received and modified by classroom teachers, and how the selection of texts at the local level corresponds to the initial vision of the developers.

Greater change in the literature curriculum has appeared at the elementary level, as schools have begun to adopt literature-based reading programs rather than relying solely on basal readers, which often excerpted longer works. Work by several researchers suggested that most elementary schools are beginning to balance basal readers and trade books in the reading curriculum (Allington & Guice, 1997; Hoffman, Roser, & Battle, 1993). Data from the National Assessment of Educational Progress (NAEP) (Mullis, Campbell, & Farstrup, 1993) indicated that half of the fourth-grade teachers in the sample reported a heavy emphasis on literature-based reading instruction. Reflecting this emphasis, half of the fourth graders reported having daily time to read a book of their choice during class. NAEP data also showed that students of those teachers reporting greater emphasis on literature-based reading also scored higher on the assessments.

These reports all suggest that elementary teachers have begun to incorporate more literature within their reading curriculum. However, as Allington, Guice, Michaelson, Baker, and Li (1996) pointed out, literature is more likely to be used as part of an independent reading program or in conjunction with read-aloud activities than as a primary focus of instruction. They concluded that

> while it does seem that children's literature has made inroads in American classrooms, few teachers seem to actually use children's books in many of their lessons. Literature is more likely to be used in either read-aloud events or independent reading activities than to be used as a part of an instructional episode or integrated curriculum. (Allington et al., 1996, p. 73)

Some research has begun to investigate changes that accompany the curricular tilt toward literature. Reports suggest that children read and write more frequently in literature-based classrooms (Mervar & Hiebert, 1989; Walmsley, 1992) and that talk between teachers and students differed in these classes (Hiebert & Colt, 1989). However, it is not clear if these changes are due to the curriculum or characteristics of the teachers who have adopted literature-based reading programs. In their study of 54 classrooms in six high-poverty schools, Allington et al. (1996) found that, although most children had opportunities to read each day, teachers still tended to control the literature being read. They also found few connections between reading and writing in these classes. They concluded that, while there was certainly more inclusion of literature, very few classrooms offered a comprehensive literature program.

Other researchers who have studied classroom practice question whether or not there is actually a literature curriculum to accompany the trade books or literature anthologies that have been adopted. One report suggested that, while a number of schools have implemented literature-based instruction, few schools have really developed a curriculum to teach literature. Most teachers report using the literature to teach an enjoyment of reading and to reinforce reading skills rather than to teach literature as a separate area (Walmsley & Walp, 1990). The study of literature-based reading instruction in high-poverty schools found relatively limited knowledge of children's books among the teachers they studied (Allington et al., 1996), but the study also noted that none of the schools had provided any opportunities for teachers to gain a wider knowledge of children's literature. The study highlighted the central importance of teachers to any curricular innovation. While elementary teachers have generally responded positively to the movement toward a literature-based curriculum, few have been offered much preparation either in literature or in literature instruction.

Teachers of Literature

What is striking in the research on the teaching of literature is the general lack of research on the teachers of literature (see Travers, 1984, for review of research on teachers of poetry). In the section on literature in the *Handbook of Research on Teaching the English Language Arts,* two chapters are dedicated to students' responses to literature: a chapter on students' reading preferences and a chapter on promoting voluntary reading among students. The chapters on the preparation of language arts teachers are embedded within a section on research on language learners. As mentioned in the section on students' responses to literature, studies of response in the classroom have begun to demonstrate the power of teachers in shaping students' responses. However, relatively little research has explored how teachers themselves develop preferred responses to literature. Perhaps even more importantly, given the critiques of literature instruction, little research has tried to understand how teachers can change their patterns of teaching literature to engage students more actively in the process of making meaning from texts.

In general, existing research presents a somewhat mixed picture regarding the subject matter preparation of English teachers. According to the national survey conducted recently by the Center for Research on the Teaching and Learning of Literature, approximately 95% of secondary English teachers received degrees in English or a related major (Applebee, 1993). This

statistic represents a significant improvement over the findings of 1964 in which only 73% of teachers had received direct preparation in English (NCTE, 1964, as cited in Squire & Applebee, 1968). However, another study (Ingersoll, 1998) found that nearly one quarter of high school English teachers held neither a major nor a minor in English or related areas. Elementary teachers are much less likely to have specific preparation in literature. In a national survey from the 1970s, Purves (1981) found that only 11% of elementary teachers had majored in English. What is less clear is what a major in English represents as preparation for the teaching of literature.

Recent research has studied teachers' knowledge and beliefs about literature and their influence on classroom instruction. In general, this research has confirmed the influence of teachers' own orientations to literature on what actually happens in classroom instruction (Travers, 1984). Zancanella (1991) identified teachers' primary orientations to literature, distinguishing between text-centered orientations and reader-centered orientations. He illustrated how these orientations shaped teachers' goals for classroom instruction and student learning. He found that most teachers shared a personal approach to reading. However, similar to the research on the teaching of literature, he found that most teachers reverted to "a school approach" to teaching literature, which emphasized surface comprehension and the learning of literary terms and concepts. He identified the tensions between teachers' goals for teaching literature as imaginative experience and the school context, which emphasized teaching a body of information about literature.

A study by Grossman (1991) contrasted two teachers with similar backgrounds in literature but strikingly different theoretical orientations. The teacher with an orientation toward the text planned her classroom lessons around close textual analysis and attention to the uses of language in a text. Her goals for students mirrored her own orientation. In contrast, the teacher with a strong reader-response orientation planned her lessons around evoking students' responses to literary text and hoped that students would focus more on their reactions to literary texts than on "correct interpretations." Both teachers shared a goal that students gain confidence in their literary interpretations, but what they each meant by literary interpretation differed. Clift (1991) reported similar results in her study of beginning English teachers. While these studies looked at specific orientations to literature, an earlier study (Peters & Blues, 1978) looked at the effect of a teacher's intellectual style on students' interpretations. The researchers found that college students of professors with more tolerance of ambiguity tended to make fewer misinterpretations of literature, using Richards' (1929) categories.

These qualitative research studies supported the findings of an earlier large-scale survey conducted under the auspices of the International Association for the Evaluation of Educational Achievement (Purves, 1981). A factor analysis of questionnaires filled out by secondary English teachers indicated the existence of two primary responses to literature. The first approach focused on the text and its literary devices, while the second approach focused much more on the reader's responses to the text. A more recent study confirmed this pattern (Applebee, 1993), finding that roughly half of the teachers surveyed reported an approach to literature based in New Criticism and half reported a more reader-response orientation. What is perhaps more surprising is the relative absence of more critical orientations to the teaching of literature that mirror changes occurring in literary theory. As Hynds and Appleman (1997), among others, suggested, both New Criticism and reader-response frameworks share a lack of concern for the larger societal, cultural, and political influences that shape both texts and readers' responses to these texts. While theorists and researchers promote more critical approaches to teaching literature (Slevin & Young, 1996), 72% of teachers reported little or no familiarity with contemporary literary theory, according to this national survey (Applebee, 1993). These data provide further testimony to the finding that what teachers know, and do not know, about literature will inevitably shape their classroom practice.

As the work of Marshall and others (Burroughs, 1995; Marshall et al., 1995; McAlpine, 1995) suggested, these are not mutually exclusive orientations in practice. Teachers may hold goals that reflect both an orientation toward the reader's response and an orientation to textual analysis. In addition, the nature of students in the classroom may affect the dominant orientation in the classroom, with higher-track classrooms focused more on the text and lower-track classes emphasizing student response.

Given the importance of teachers' own orientations to literature, a number of teacher educators have recommended that these orientations be made explicit during teacher preparation (Burroughs, 1995; Clift, 1987; Fox, 1995; Grossman, 1990; Sperling, 1994), so that prospective teachers can begin to examine the pedagogical implications of their stances toward literature. A number of English educators have studied the effects of a variety of approaches to eliciting prospective teachers' beliefs and orientations, from literacy autobiographies to the use of reflective journals and examination of teaching metaphors (e.g., Agee, 1998; Fox, 1995; Hermann & Sarracino, 1993; Pultorak, 1993; Sperling, 1994; Stansell, 1994; White & Smith, 1994).

The widespread adoption of trade books at the elementary level without a curriculum for teaching literature available places greater demands on elementary teachers' knowledge of how to select and teach literature. Early work in this area (Scharer, Freeman, Lehman, & Allen, 1993; Walmsley, 1992) suggested that elementary teachers rarely have a solid foundation in the teaching of literature. Their goals for teaching literature are primarily to encourage a love of reading rather than to develop literary understanding. In a study of a literature-based reading program, elementary school teachers themselves felt they had limited knowledge about literature to draw on and an equally limited repertoire for the teaching of literature (Allington et al., 1996; Scharer, 1992). Given the importance of teachers' own knowledge and beliefs about teaching literature in shaping students' opportunities to learn in the classroom, more research needs to look closely at this issue among elementary teachers (Vali, 1994). One study documented changes in prospective elementary teachers' expectations for children's responses to literature as a result of their involvement in a children's literature course (Wolf, Corey, & Mieras, 1996). As part of the course, preservice teachers were asked to read with a child over the quarter and keep careful field notes on their experiences. Their final case studies of their experience revealed

shifts in their expectations for children's literary engagement, with most preservice teachers surprised by the students' abilities to make connections across texts and to engage in interpretive conversations about literature. This work suggested that teacher education and professional development need to address teachers' opportunities to learn more not only about literature but also about children's capacities to respond to and analyze literature.

Future Directions in Research on Teaching Literature

Although many vigorous lines of research exist within the areas of students' response to literature, the specific area of research on the teaching of literature is still relatively inchoate. What follows is one version of an agenda for future research in this area.

The research is fairly unanimous on teachers' influences on students' responses to literature. Much more research, however, needs to look carefully at how teachers support students' literary encounters and how they scaffold the continuing development of students' abilities. The critical link between teachers' classroom practices and students' developing understanding of literature deserves closer scrutiny. Much of the existing research that has tried to explicate this connection has focused on the number of questions teachers ask, the types of questions asked, the percentages of teacher and student talk, and the frequency of teachers' responses to student ideas. Future research will need to fine-tune existing methodological tools for observing and describing classroom interactions between teachers and students, as well as among students, that support literary understanding. Ultimately, we will also need more powerful conceptual tools for explaining, in general terms, the kinds of interactions that support the continual development of students' interpretive powers.

Part of the lack of clarity in existing research has been the field's difficulty in defining clearly what it means by learning and achievement in literature. What do we mean by literary understanding? How do personal responses and textual analysis contribute to a description of literary achievement? What kinds of analytic strategies might be expected, for example, of high school seniors? How do we assess the full range of textual power in responses to literature (Scholes, 1985)? As a field, English education needs to become clearer about the disciplinary tools and habits of mind that lead to deeper and more fully realized readings of literary works (e.g., Applebee, 1996). The implicit dichotomy drawn between response and analysis, with recent emphasis on response, has hampered our ability to depict a more balanced and complex portrait of literary understanding in which response and analysis can coexist. Just as personal responses to literature are essential for gaining entry into a literary world, so can analytic strategies help readers develop more complex readings of a work, which, in turn, may affect their subsequent responses. As Langer's work on envisionments suggests, the process of literary understanding is many layered and recursive. The emergence of critical and postmodern theories poses further challenges to our definitions of achievement in literature. What kinds of performances would demonstrate an understanding of critical approaches to literature? To what extent, in defining literary achievement, must we choose among the theoretical stances that compose literary study?

Another lacuna in research on literary response has to do with the issue of the readers included, and not included, in studies of reader response. Many of the studies of reader response have been conducted with middle-class Caucasian students. To what extent can this research help us understand how racial or ethnic identities shape readings of text? How do second-language learners respond to literary texts in both their native language and in a second language? Understanding the "funds of knowledge" that second-language learners and other non-mainstream students bring to literature (Moll & Gonzalez, 1994; Rose, 1989) can help teachers reconsider classroom practices that can enable more students to join the conversation. One way to address this issue is to bring more multicultural and multilingual texts into the classroom. Carol Lee's work represents an example of how African-American students' knowledge of discourse in their own communities provides a valuable entrance into literary texts. By broadening the array of texts in the classroom, the class will need to draw on the diverse knowledge of language and community that students hold (Athanases, 1998).

The challenge of incorporating more multicultural literature into the classroom also deserves further research. If teachers are not given opportunities to continue to develop their own knowledge of literature from different cultures, why are we surprised to find the literature curriculum stubbornly unchanged? Teaching multicultural literature within classrooms of racially and ethnically diverse classrooms also poses new risks and dilemmas for teachers (Hynds & Appleman, 1997; Rogers & Soter, 1997). How do we prepare teachers to accept and use the conflicts that will inevitably erupt as students grapple with diverse perspectives?

Research on the teaching of literature also needs to examine more carefully how different approaches work with ethnically and linguistically diverse students. An emerging line of research suggests that recommended approaches such as literature logs (Reyes, 1992) and literature circles (Lewis, 1997) do not work equally well for different student populations. In their critique of process-oriented approaches in bilingual classrooms, both Reyes (1992) and Gutierrez (1992) argued for the need to modify activities to better serve second-language learners. How do we ensure that English-language learners have opportunities to develop skills of literary analysis and interpretation as they learn English? Future research will need to examine carefully how efforts to create culturally relevant pedagogy in literature classrooms affect student learning and engagement with literature.

The paucity of work on teacher preparation and development noted by O'Donnell (1979) continues to exist. While there is an emerging line of research on the preparation of language arts teachers, the focus of this research needs to be broadened (see Grossman, Valencia, & Hamel, 1997, for a review of work in this area). For example, given the importance of teachers' existing orientations toward literature, what more can we say about how these orientations develop? This line of research must include studies of teaching and learning in literature courses in the undergraduate English major. While we have broad overviews of the historical shifts in the teaching of literature in higher education (Graff, 1987; Ohmann, 1976), only now are researchers going into undergraduate classrooms to investigate how prospective teachers are actually taught (Marshall & Smith, 1997; Norell, 1994). Such studies can help us understand how academic majors represent, both explicitly and implicitly, the pedagogy entangled with literary theory (Scholes, 1985; Willinsky, 1991). For example, how aware are prospective teachers of the pedagogical implications of the theories they encounter? To what extent have their own professors considered the pedagogical implications of their theoretical positions? What is the articulation between theoretical orientations either espoused or enacted in English departments and the pedagogical orientations proposed within teacher-education programs? Studies such as that of Marshall and Smith (1997) can illuminate why the newer critical theories have failed to have much impact on high school teaching.

These questions, however, are focused primarily on secondary teachers who spend extended time in English departments. We know even less about the preparation of elementary teachers. How are elementary teachers being prepared to teach literature? Do they hold goals for teaching literature that are distinct from the teaching of reading? To what extent do they see literature as a distinctive subject matter or simply as a convenient vehicle for teaching other subjects? Where do they encounter opportunities to develop their own literary understandings during teacher preparation?

Perhaps one of the biggest lacuna within research on the teaching of literature concerns the professional development of practicing teachers. While models exist within the area of writing, such as the National Writing Project, no corresponding models have been developed for teachers of literature. If reports of current practice were sanguine about the teaching of literature, there would be little impetus for developing models of professional learning. Given the litany of laments about the nature of classroom interactions around literature, however, the paucity of research or practical models in this area is troublesome. As Allington et al. (1996) noted, even as teachers were urged to adopt literature-based curricula, few opportunities existed for the practicing teachers in their study to develop their knowledge and skills about the teaching of literature.

What is required to orchestrate deep and engaging discussions of a literary work? If the ability to listen carefully to students' ideas and to build on them is one characteristic of a skillful discussion leader, how do experienced teachers develop such skills? What kinds of experiences would help them learn to listen differently, not for right answers but for the kernels of powerful interpretations? Just as elementary school teachers studied their own students' counting strategies in the work on Cognitively Guided Instruction (Carpenter et al., 1988), could literature teachers study a range of student responses to a single work and explore the potential of each response? How do teachers learn to assess learning as it emerges in classroom discussions? Could teachers study transcripts or videotapes of their own classroom discussions to see the emergence of understanding through discourse? How might such activities come to influence classroom practices and, ultimately, student learning?

Another model of professional development might focus more on teachers' continuing engagement with literature through teacher book clubs. Just as the National Writing Project and its affiliates assumed that teachers of writing needed to be actively involved in their own writing, so do teachers of literature need continuing experiences in reading and discussing of texts. One model of professional development has tried to create a community of learners among English and social studies teachers at an urban comprehensive high school (Grossman, Wineburg, & Woolworth, in press). At the core of this community is a book-club environment in which teachers read roughly a book a month, with texts drawn from literature, history, memoir, and pedagogy. This opportunity has reminded teachers of the wide diversity of responses even among very experienced readers and the need to be more attentive to this diversity within their own classrooms.

Other efforts have tried to introduce elementary teachers to cultural issues through book clubs that focus on autobiographies of ethnic and racial minorities (Florio-Ruane & de Tar, 1995; Florio-Ruane, 1994). Such book-club experiences are likely to be even more important for elementary school teachers, who may or may not have had the opportunity to engage in rich, wide-ranging discussions of literature. Before teachers can orchestrate such discussions in their classrooms, they must know from their own experience what such a discussion might look like.

Just as theory has focused less on the individual reader and more on readers in contexts, future programs of research on literature teachers will also need to address not only the individual teacher but also teachers as members of distinct communities. How teachers teach literature is likely to be framed not only by their individual orientations to literature but also by the departments, schools, teams, and districts in which they work. Some work has already begun to investigate the influence high school departments have on classroom practices in English (Burroughs, 1995; Grossman & Stodolsky, 1995; Newell & Holt, 1997). These institutional contexts offer only a first layer of investigation. We will also need to learn more about how teachers' membership in cultural, racial, linguistic, and gendered communities shapes their reading and teaching of literature.

Future research, however, must also question the place of literature within the curriculum and how the study of literature connects to the more overarching goals of English and language arts. The virtues of literature, whether ethical, moral, intellectual, or cultural, can no longer be assumed nor can the power of literature to speak for itself. As a number of critiques makes clear (Scholes, 1997; Willinsky, 1991; Yagelski, 1994), literature's place at the center of an English curriculum is under scrutiny, if not attack. Willinsky (1991) argued that the study of literature has succeeded in displacing students' more active involvement in literate activities in the world. In his latest book, tellingly titled *The Rise and Fall of English,* Robert Scholes (1997), a passionate writer on the interrelationships of theory and pedagogy, argued eloquently that English as a field of study can no longer afford to retain literature as the centerpiece of instruction. Both of these writers argued, from different positions, for an emphasis on textual study, for classrooms that engage students in the active critique and production of the multiple forms of text that exist in the world. Much of the existing research on the teaching of literature reviewed in this chapter assumes, rather than questions, literature's place in the classroom. Yet, as histories of our field remind us (Applebee, 1974; Graff, 1987; Scholes, 1997), the field of English education is still relatively new and constantly changing. As our definitions of

both literacy and literature evolve, as the literary canon is debated and expanded, research in this area must necessarily evolve as well.

These questions of literature's place in the classroom are not merely academic. As policymakers and parents alike have begun to question which literature belongs in the classroom, issues regarding the teaching of literature have become increasingly political in nature. At the elementary level, where literature is just finding its place, literature-based curricula are being pitted against more skill-based approaches to teaching reading. At the secondary level, efforts to expand the literature to be read are met with resistance. I opened this chapter by remarking on the significance of this first chapter on the teaching of literature in the *Handbook of Research on Teaching.* If this first chapter is not to be the last, researchers and teachers of literature alike will need to make their voices heard in the debate over the place of literature in and out of school.

REFERENCES

Agee, J. (1998). Negotiating different conceptions about reading and teaching literature in a preservice literature class. *Research in the Teaching of English, 33,* 85–124.
Allington, R. L., & Guice, S. (1997). Literature curriculum: Issues of definition and control. In J. Flood, D. Lapp, & S. B. Heath (Eds.), *Handbook of research on teaching literacy through the communicative and visual arts* (pp. 727–734). New York: Macmillan.
Allington, R. L., Guice, S., Michaelson, N., Baker, K., & Li, S. (1996). Literature-based curricula in high-poverty schools. In *The first R: Children's right to read* (pp. 71–94). New York: Teachers College Press.
Almasi, J. (1995). The nature of 4th graders' sociocognitive conflicts in peer-led and teacher-led discussions of literature. *Reading Research Quarterly, 30,* 314–351.
Alvermann, D. E., Young, J. P., Weaver, D., Hinchman, K. A., Moore, D. W., Phelps, S. F., Thrash, E. C., & Zalewski, P. (1996). Middle and high school students' perceptions of how they experience text-based discussions: A multicase study. *Reading Research Quarterly, 31,* 244–267.
Applebee, A. N. (1974). *Tradition and reform in the teaching of English.* Urbana, IL: National Council of Teachers of English.
Applebee, A. N. (1977). ERIC/RCS report: The elements of a response to a literary work: What we have learned. *Research in the Teaching of English, 11,* 255–271.
Applebee, A. N. (1978). *The child's concept of story.* Chicago: University of Chicago Press.
Applebee, A. N. (1982). Literature. In H. Mitzel (Ed.), *Encyclopedia of education research* (5th ed., Vol. 3, pp. 1105–1108). New York: Macmillan.
Applebee, A. N. (1993). *Literature in the secondary school: Studies of curriculum and instruction in the United States* (NCTE Research Report No. 25). Urbana, IL: National Council of Teachers of English.
Applebee, A. N. (1996). *Curriculum as conversation.* Chicago: University of Chicago Press.
Applebee, A. N., & Purves, A. C. (1992). Literature and the English language arts. In P. W. Jackson (Ed.), *Handbook of research on curriculum* (pp. 726–748). New York: Macmillan.
Athanases, S. Z. (1998). Diverse learners, diverse texts: Exploring identity and difference through literary encounters. *Journal of Literacy Research, 30,* 273–296.
Athanases, S. Z., & Heath, S. B. (1995). Ethnography in the study of the teaching and learning of English. *Research in the Teaching of English, 29,* 287.
Bakhtin, M. M. (1981). *The dialogic imagination: Four essays of M. M. Bakhtin* (C. Emerson & M. Holquist, Trans.). Austin, TX: University of Texas Press.

Barnes, D. (1976). *From communication to curriculum.* Middlesex, UK: Penguin Books.

Barnes, D., Barnes, D., & Clarke, S. (1984). *Versions of English.* London: Heineman Press.

Beach, R., Appleman, D., & Dorsey, S. (1990). Adolescents' use of intertextual links to understanding literature. In R. Beach & S. Hynds (Eds.), *Developing discourse patterns in adolescence and adulthood* (pp. 224–245). Norwood, NJ: Ablex.

Beach, R., & Hynds, S. (1991). Research on response to literature. In R. Barr, M. L. Kamil, P. Mosenthal, & P. D. Pearson (Eds.), *Handbook of reading research* (Vol. II, pp. 453–489). New York: Longman.

Beach, R., & Wendler, L. (1987). Developmental differences in response to a story. *Research in the Teaching of English, 21,* 286–297.

Benton, M. (1992). *Secondary worlds: Literature teaching and the visual arts.* Buckingham, England: Open University Press.

Bleich, D. (1978). *Subjective criticism.* Baltimore: Johns Hopkins University Press.

Booth, W. C. (1974). *The rhetoric of irony.* Chicago: University of Chicago Press.

Britton, J. (1990). *The place of literature.* Portsmouth, NH: Heinemann.

Britton, J., Burgess, T., Martin, N., & Rosen, H. (1975). *The development of writing abilities, 11–18.* London: Macmillan.

Brooks, C. (1947). *The well wrought urn: Studies in the meaning of poetry.* New York: Harcourt Brace.

Burroughs, R. S. (1995). Teacher change and teacher socialization: A study of subject matter knowledge in the context of schooling. *Dissertation Abstracts International, 56*(10), 3861.

Butler, J. (1990). *Gender trouble: Feminism and the subversion of identity.* New York: Routledge.

Carpenter, T., Fennema, E., Peterson, P., & Carey, D. (1988). Teachers' pedagogical content knowledge of students' problem solving in elementary arithmetic. *Journal of Research in Mathematics Education, 19,* 385–401.

Clift, R. T. (1987). English teacher or English major: Epistemological differences in the teaching of English. *English Education, 19,* 229–236.

Clift, R. T. (1991). Learning to teach English—maybe: A study of knowledge development. *Journal of Teacher Education, 42,* 357–372.

Cochran-Smith, M. (1984). *The making of a reader.* Norwood, NJ: Ablex.

Cohen, E. (1986). *Designing groupwork.* New York: Teachers College Press.

Cooper, M., & Holzman, M. (1983). Talking about protocols. *College Composition and Communication, 34,* 284–293.

Commeyras, M., & Sumner, G. (1998). Literature questions children want to discuss: What teachers and students learned in a second-grade classroom. *Elementary School Journal, 99,* 129–152.

Cullinan, B., Harwood, K., & Galda, L. (1983). The reader and the story: Comprehension and response. *Journal of Research and Development in Education, 16*(3), 29–38.

de Man, P. (1979). *Allegories of reading: Figural language in Rosseau, Nietzsche, Rilke, and Proust.* New Haven, CT: Yale University Press.

Derrida, J. (1976). *Of grammatology* (G. C. Spivak, Trans.). Baltimore: Johns Hopkins University Press.

Dias, P. X. (1979). Developing independent readers of poetry. *McGill Journal of Education, 14*(2), 199–213.

Dillon, G. L. (1982). Styles of reading. *Poetics Today, 3*(2), 77–88.

Eagleton, T. (1983). *Literary theory.* Minneapolis, MN: University of Minnesota Press.

Earthman, E. A. (1992). Creating the virtual work: Readers' processes in understanding literary texts. *Research in the Teaching of English, 26,* 351–384.

Eeds, M., & Wells, D. (1989). Grand conversations: An exploration of meaning construction in literature study groups. *Research in the Teaching of English, 23,* 4–29.

Finders, M. (1996). *Just girls.* New York: Teachers College Press.

Fish, S. (1980). *Is there a text in this class? The authority of interpretive communities.* Cambridge, MA: Harvard University Press.

Florio-Ruane, S. (1994). The future teachers' autobiography club: Preparing educators to support literacy learning in culturally diverse classrooms. *English Education, 26,* 52–66.

Florio-Ruane, S., & de Tar, J. (1995). Conflict and consensus in teacher candidates' discussions of ethnic autobiography. *English Education, 27,* 11–39.

Flower, L. S., & Hayes, J. R. (1980). The dynamics of composing: Making plans and juggling constraints. In L. Gregg & E. Steinberg (Eds.), *Cognitive processes in writing* (pp. 31–50). Hillsdale, NJ: Lawrence Erlbaum Associates.

Folta, B. (1981). Effects of three approaches to teaching poetry to sixth grade students. *Research in the Teaching of English, 15,* 149–161.

Fox, D. L. (1995). From English major to English teacher: Two case studies. *English Journal, 84*(2), 17–25.

Galda, L. (1982). Assuming the spectator stance: An examination of the responses to three young readers. *Research in the Teaching of English, 16,* 1–20.

Gallagher, C. (1997). The history of literary criticism. *Daedalus, 126*(1), 133–153.

Gardner, H. (1985). *The mind's new science.* New York: Basic Books.

Gates, H. L., Jr. (1988). *The signifying monkey: A theory of Afro-American literary criticism.* New York: Oxford University Press.

Gates, H. L., Jr. (1992). *Loose canons: Notes on the culture wars.* New York: Oxford University Press.

Goatley, V. J., Brock, C. H., & Raphael, T. E. (1995). Diverse learners participating in regular education "Book Clubs." *Reading Research Quarterly, 30,* 352–380.

Golden, J., & Guthrie, J. T. (1986). Convergence and divergence in reader response to literature. *Reading Research Quarterly, 20,* 408–421.

Goodlad, J. (1984). *A place called school.* San Francisco: Jossey-Bass.

Graff, G. (1987). *Professing literature: An institutional history.* Chicago: University of Chicago Press.

Graff, G. (1992). *Beyond the culture wars: How teaching the conflicts can revitalize American education.* New York: W. W. Norton.

Grossman, P. L. (1990). *The making of a teacher: Teacher knowledge and teacher education.* New York: Teachers College Press.

Grossman, P. L. (1991). What are we talking about anyhow? Subject matter knowledge of secondary English teachers. In J. Brophy (Ed.), *Advances in research on teaching: Vol. 2. Subject matter knowledge.* Greenwich, CT: JAI Press.

Grossman, P. L., & Stodolsky, S. S. (1995). Content as context: The role of school subjects in secondary school teaching. *Educational Researcher, 24*(8), 5–11.

Grossman, P. L., Valencia, S. W., & Hamel, F. (1997). Preparing language arts teachers in a time of reform. In J. Flood, D. Lapp, & S. B. Heath (Eds.), *Handbook of research on teaching literacy through the communicative and visual arts* (pp. 407–416). New York: Macmillan.

Grossman, P., Wineburg, S., & Woolworth, S. (in press). Toward a theory of teacher community. *Teachers College Record.*

Gutierrez, K. (1992). A comparison of instructional contexts in writing process classrooms with Latino children. *Education and Urban Society, 24,* 244–262.

Hamel, F., & Smith, M. W. (1998). You can't play if you don't know the rules: Interpretive conventions and the teaching of literature to students in lower-track classes. *Reading and Writing Quarterly, 14,* 355–377.

Hardy-Brown, K. (1979). Formal operations and the issue of generalizability: The analysis of poetry by college students. *Human Development, 22,* 127–136.

Harker, W. J. (1994). "Plain sense" and "poetic significance": 10th grade readers reading two poems. *Poetics, 22,* 199–218.

Hartley, H. W. (1930). *Tests of the interpretive reading of poetry for teachers of English: Contributions to education, no. 433.* New York: Teachers College.

Hartman, D. K. (1995). 8 readers reading: The intertextual links of proficient readers reading multiple passages. *Reading Research Quarterly, 30,* 520–561.

Heath, S. B. (1983). *Ways with words: Language, life, and work in communities and classrooms.* Cambridge, UK: Cambridge University Press.

Hermann, B. A., & Sarracino, J. (1993). Restructuring a preservice literacy methods course: Dilemmas and lessons learned. *Journal of Teacher Education, 44,* 96–106.

Hiebert, E. H., & Colt, J. (1989). Patterns of literature-based reading instruction. *The Reading Teacher, 43*, 14–20.

Hillocks, G. (1989). Literary texts in classrooms. In P. Jackson & S. Haroutonian-Gordon (Eds.), *From Socrates to software: The teacher as text and the text as teacher* (pp. 135–158). Chicago: National Society for the Study of Education.

Hoffman, J. V., Roser, N. L., & Battle, J. (1993). Reading aloud in classrooms: From the modal to a "model." *The Reading Teacher, 46*, 496–505.

Holland, N. (1975). *5 readers reading.* New Haven, CT: Yale University Press.

Hynds, S. (1985). Interpersonal cognitive complexity and the literary response processes of adolescent readers. *Research in the Teaching of English, 19*, 386–404.

Hynds, S. (1989). Bringing life to literature and literature to life. Social constructs and contexts of four adolescent readers. *Research in the Teaching of English, 23*, 30–61.

Hynds, S. (1991). Questions of difficulty in literary reading. In A. C. Purves (Ed.), *The idea of difficulty in literature* (pp. 117–139). New York: SUNY Press.

Hynds, S., & Appleman, D. (1997). Walking our talk: Between response and responsibility in the literature classroom. *English Education, 29*, 272–294.

Ingersoll, R. M. (1998). The problem of out-of-field teaching. *Phi Delta Kappan, 79*(10), 773–776.

Iser, W. (1978). *The act of reading.* Baltimore: Johns Hopkins University Press.

Kiefer, B. Z. (1982). *The response of primary children to picture books.* Unpublished dissertation, The Ohio State University, Columbus, OH. *Dissertation Abstracts International, 43*(08), 2580.

Kintgen, E. R. (1983). *The perception of poetry.* Bloomington, IN: Indiana University Press.

Kristeva, J. (1974). *Revolution in poetic language* (M. Wallter, Trans.). New York: Columbia University Press.

Langer, J. A. (1990). The process of understanding: Reading for literary and informative purposes. *Research in the Teaching of English, 24*, 229–260.

Langer, J. A. (1995). *Envisioning literature: Literary understanding and literature instruction.* New York: Teachers College Press.

Leal, D. J. (1992). The nature of talk about three types of text during peer group discussion. *Journal of Reading Behavior, 24*, 313–338.

Lee, C. D. (1993). *Signifying as a scaffold for literary interpretation: The pedagogical implications of an African-American discourse genre* (NCTE Research Report No. 26). Urbana, IL: National Council of Teachers of English.

Lehr, S. (1988). The child's developing sense of theme as a response to literature. *Reading Research Quarterly, 23*, 337–357.

Leinhardt, G., & Putnam, R. T. (1987). The skill of learning from classroom lessons. *American Educational Research Journal, 24*, 557–587.

Lennox, W. H., Small, L. L., & Keeling, B. (1978). An experiment in teaching poetry to high school boys. *Research in the Teaching of English, 12*, 307–320.

Lewis, C. (1997). The social drama of literature discussions in a fifth/sixth grade classroom. *Research in the Teaching of English, 31*, 163–204.

Many, J. E. (1991). The effects of stance and age level on children's literary response. *Journal of Reading Behavior, 23*, 61–85.

Many, J. E., & Wiseman, D. L. (1992). The effect of teaching approach on third grade students' response to literature. *Journal of Reading Behavior, 24*, 265–287.

Marshall, J. D. (1987). The effects of writing on students' understanding of literary texts. *Research in the Teaching of English, 21*, 30–63.

Marshall, J., & Smith, J. (1997). Teaching as we're taught: The university's role in the education of English teachers. *English Education, 29*, 246–268.

Marshall, J. D., Smagorinsky, P., & Smith, M. W. (1995). *The language of interpretation: Patterns of discourse in discussions of literature* (NCTE Research Report No. 27). Urbana, IL: National Council of Teachers of English.

Martinez, M. G., & Roser, N. L. (1991). Children's responses to literature. In J. Flood, J. M. Jensen, D. Lapp, & J. R. Squire (Eds.), *Handbook of research on teaching the English language arts* (pp. 643–654). New York: Macmillan.

McAlpine, C. G. (1995). *An analysis of the new criticism and reader-response theories of criticism with implications for teaching literature in the secondary schools.* Unpublished dissertation, University of Virginia, Charlottesville, VA. *Dissertation Abstracts International, 56*(04), 1277.

Mervar, K., & Hiebert, E. H. (1989). Literature-selection strategies and amount of reading in two literacy approaches. In S. McCormick & J. Zutell (Eds.), *Cognitive and social perspectives for literacy research and instruction: Thirty-eighth yearbook of the National Reading Conference* (pp. 529–535). Chicago: National Reading Conference.

Miller, J. H. (1976). Stevens' rock and criticism as cure, II. *The Georgia Review, 30*, 340–348.

Moll, L. C., & Gonzalez, N. (1994). Lessons from research with language-minority children. *Journal of Reading Behavior, 26*, 439–456.

Morrow, L. M. (1992). The impact of a literature-based program on literacy achievement, use of literature, and attitudes of children from minority backgrounds. *Reading Research Quarterly, 27*, 250–276.

Mullis, I. V. S., Campbell, J. R., & Farstrup, A. E. (1993). *NAEP 1992 reading report card for the nation and states.* Washington, DC: U.S. Department of Education.

Newell, G. E., & Holt, R. A. (1997). Autonomy and obligation in the teaching of literature: Teachers' classroom curriculum and departmental consensus. *English Education, 29*(1), 18–37.

Norell, M. H. (1994). *Sources of critical theory for secondary English teachers: Levels of authority in college literature classrooms.* Unpublished dissertation, George Mason University, Fairfax, VA. *Dissertation Abstracts International, 55*(05), 1201.

Nystrand, M., & Gamoran, A. (1991). Instructional discourse, student engagement, and literature achievement. *Research in the Teaching of English, 25*, 261–290.

O'Donnell, R. C. (1979). Research in the teaching of English: Some observations and questions. *English Education, 10*, 181–182.

Ohmann, R. (1976). *English in America: A radical view of the profession.* New York: Oxford University Press.

Ortony, A., Turner, T. J., & Larson-Shapiro, N. (1985). Cultural and instructional influences on figurative language comprehension by inner city children. *Research in the Teaching of English, 19*, 25–36.

Palinscar, A. S., & Brown, A. L. (1984). Reciprocal teaching of comprehension-fostering and comprehension-monitoring activities. *Cognition and Instruction, 1*, 117–175.

Peskin, J. (1998). Constructing meaning when reading poetry: An expert-novice study. *Cognition and Instruction, 16*, 235–263.

Peters, W. H., & Blues, A. G. (1978). Teacher intellectual disposition as it relates to student openness in written response to literature. *Research in the Teaching of English, 12*, 127–136.

Petrosky, A. (1977). Genetic epistemology and psychoanalytic ego psychology: Clinical support for the study of response to literature. *Research in the Teaching of English, 11*, 28–38.

Probst, R. (1991). Response to literature. In J. Flood, J. M. Jensen, D. Lapp, & J. R. Squire (Eds.), *Handbook of research on teaching the English language arts* (pp. 655–663). New York: Macmillan.

Pultorak, E. G. (1993). Facilitating reflective thought in novice teachers. *Journal of Teacher Education, 44*, 288–295.

Purcell-Gates, V. (1991). On the outside looking in: A study of remedial readers' meaning-making while reading literature. *Journal of Reading Behavior, 23*, 235–253.

Purves, A. C. (1981). *Reading and literature: American achievement in international perspective.* Urbana, IL: National Council of Teachers of English.

Purves, A. C. (1993). Toward a reevaluation of reader response and school literature. *Language Arts, 70*, 348–361.

Purves, A. C., & Rippere, A. (1968). *Elements of writing about a literary work: A study of response to literature.* Urbana, IL: National Council of Teachers of English.

Reyes de la Luz, M. (1992). Challenging venerable assumptions: Literacy instruction for linguistically different children. *Harvard Educational Review, 62*, 427–446.

Richards, I. A. (1929). *Practical criticism*. New York: Harcourt Brace & Co.

Rogers, T. (1991). Students as literary critics: The interpretive experiences, beliefs, and processes of ninth-grade students. *Journal of Reading Behavior, 23*, 391–423.

Rogers, T., & Soter, A. O. (1997). *Reading across cultures: Teaching literature in a diverse society*. New York: Teachers College Press.

Rose, M. (1989). *Lives on the boundary*. New York: Penguin.

Rosenblatt, L. M. (1968). *Literature as exploration*. New York: Modern Language Association. (Original work published 1938).

Rosenblatt, L. M. (1978). *The reader, the text, and the poem: The transactional theory of the literary work*. Carbondale, IL: Southern Illinois University Press.

Roser, N., & Martinez, M. (1985). Roles adults play in preschoolers' response to literature. *Language Arts, 62*, 485–490.

Said, E. W. (1983). *The world, the text, and the critic*. Cambridge, MA: Harvard University Press.

Scharer, P. L. (1992). Teachers in transition: An exploration of changes in teachers and classrooms during implementation of literature-based reading instruction. *Research in the Teaching of English, 26*, 408–443.

Scharer, P. L, Freeman, E. B., Lehman, B. A., & Allen, V. G. (1993). Literacy and literature in elementary classrooms: Teachers' beliefs and practices. In D. J. Leu & C. K. Kinzer (Eds.), *Examining central issues in literacy research, theory, and practice* (pp. 359–366). Chicago: National Reading Conference.

Scholes, R. (1985). *Textual power: Literary theory and the teaching of English*. New Haven, CT: Yale University Press.

Scholes, R. (1995, January). An overview of Pacesetter English. *English Journal, 84*(1), 69–75.

Scholes, R. (1997). *The rise and fall of English*. New Haven, CT: Yale University Press.

Shimron, J. (1980). Psychological processes behind the comprehension of a poetic text. *Instructional Science, 9*, 43–66.

Shulman, L. S. (1986). Those who understand: Knowledge growth in teaching. *Educational Researcher, 15*(2), 4–14.

Slevin, J. F., & Young, A. (Eds.). (1996). *Critical theory and the teaching of literature*. Urbana, IL: National Council of Teachers of English.

Smagorinsky, P., & Coppock, J. (1995). The reader, the text, and the context: An exploration of a choreographed response to literature. *Journal of Reading Behavior, 27*, 271–298.

Smagorinsky, P., & O'Donnell-Allen, C. (1998). The depth and dynamics of context: Tracing the sources of engagement and disengagement in students' responses to literature. *Journal of Literacy Research, 30*, 515–559.

Smith, D. V. (1933). *Instruction in English* (National Survey of Secondary Education Monograph No. 20). Washington DC: Government Printing Office.

Smith, M. W. (1989). Teaching the interpretation of irony in poetry. *Research in the Teaching of English, 23*, 254–272.

Sperling, M. (1994). Moments remembered, moments displayed: Narratization, metaphor, and the experience of teaching. *English Education, 26*, 142–156.

Squire, J. R., & Applebee, R. K. (1968). *High school English instruction today*. New York: Appleton-Century-Crofts.

Stansell, J. C. (1994). Reflection, resistance, and research among preservice teachers studying their literacy histories: Lessons for literacy teacher education. In C. K. Kinzer & D. J. Leu (Eds.), *Multidimensional aspects of literacy research, theory, and practice: Forty-third Yearbook of the National Reading Conference*. Chicago: National Reading Conference.

Stotsky, S. (1991, December). Whose literature? America's! *Educational Leadership, 49*(4), 53–56.

Suleiman, S. R. (1980). Introduction: Varieties of audience-oriented criticism. In S. R. Suleiman & I. Crosman (Eds.), *The reader in the text: Essays on audience and interpretation*. Princeton, NJ: Princeton University Press.

Suleiman, S. R., & Crosman I. (Eds.). (1980). *The reader in the text: Essays on audience and interpretation*. Princeton, NJ: Princeton University Press.

Svensson, C. (1990). The development of poetic understanding in adolescence. In R. Beach & S. Hynds (Eds.), *Developing discourse patterns in adolescence and adulthood* (pp. 136–160). Norwood, NJ: Ablex.

Tompkins, J. (Ed.). (1980). *Reader-response criticism*. Baltimore: Johns Hopkins University Press.

Travers, D. M. M. (1984). The poetry teacher: Beliefs and attitudes. *Research in the Teaching of English, 18*, 367–384.

Vali, C. L. (1994). *What does the story mean? A study of theme in the third-grade classroom*. Unpublished dissertation, Stanford University, Palo Alto, CA. *Dissertation Abstracts International, 54*(12), 4396.

Walmsley, S. A. (1992). Reflections on the state of elementary literature instruction. *Language Arts, 69*, 508–514.

Walmsley, S. A., & Walp, T. P. (1990). Integrating literature and composing into the language arts curriculum: Philosophy and practice. *Elementary School Journal, 90*, 251–274.

White, B., & Smith, M. W. (1994). Metaphors in English education: Putting things in perspective. *English Education, 26*(3), 157–176.

Wilhelm, J. D. (1997). *"You gotta BE the book": Teaching engaged and reflective reading with adolescents*. New York: Teachers College Press.

Willinsky, J. (1991). *The triumph of literature/the fate of literacy: English in the secondary school curriculum*. New York: Teachers College Press.

Wimsatt, W. E. (1954). *The verbal icon: Studies in the meaning of poetry*. Lexington, KY: University of Kentucky Press.

Wineburg, S. S. (1991). On the reading of historical texts: Notes on the breach between school and academy. *American Educational Research Journal, 28*, 495–519.

Wineburg, S. S., & Grossman, P. L. (1998). Building a community of learners among high school teachers. *Phi Delta Kappan, 79*(5), 350–353.

Wolf, D. P. (1995, January). Of courses: The pacesetter initiative and the need for curriculum-based school reform. *English Journal*, 60–68.

Wolf, S. A. (1994). Learning to act/Acting to learn: Children as actors, characters, and critics in classroom theater. *Research in the Teaching of English, 28*, 7–44.

Wolf, S. A., Corey, A. A., & Mieras, E. L. (1996). "What is this literachurch stuff anyway?": Preservice teachers' growth in understanding children's literary response. *Reading Research Quarterly, 31*, 130–157.

Wolf, S. A., & Heath, S. B. (1992). *The braid of literature: Children's worlds of reading*. Cambridge, MA: Harvard University Press.

Wollman-Bonilla, J. E. (1994). Why don't they "just speak?" Attempting literature discussions with more and less able readers. *Research in the Teaching of English, 28*, 231–258.

Yagelski, R. P. (1994). Literature and literacy: Rethinking English as a school subject. *English Journal, 83*(3), 30–36.

Zancanella, D. (1991). Teachers reading/Readers teaching: Five teachers' personal approaches to literature and their teaching of literature. *Research in the Teaching of English, 25*, 5–32.

24.

Research on Teaching Mathematics: The Unsolved Problem of Teachers' Mathematical Knowledge

Deborah Loewenberg Ball
University of Michigan

Sarah Theule Lubienski
Iowa State University

Denise Spangler Mewborn
University of Georgia

Why does it work to add a zero on the right when multiplying by 10, or two zeros when multiplying by 100? Why, when the number includes a decimal, do we move the decimal point over instead of adding zeros? Is zero a number? If it is a number, is it even or odd? What does it mean to divide *by* one-half? What is an irrational number? Is a square a rectangle? What is the probability that in a class of 25, two people will share a birthday?

For all the rhetoric about the centrality of mathematics to the life and progress of this new century, we did not manage to achieve high levels of mathematical competence among most American adults by the end of the past century. Most well-educated adults cannot comfortably answer the questions in the previous paragraph. They cannot make judgments about orders of magnitude, cannot reasonably estimate the likelihood of particular events, and cannot reason skillfully about quantitative relationships.

That many people leave their formal experience of learning mathematics both uninterested in and unskillful with the subject has long been a matter of concern. Problems with mathematics education are not new. Why does formal schooling in the United States manage to help so many people learn to read and to write successfully and yet fail with so many others in developing a similar level of mathematical proficiency?

Although the reasons for this failing and its consequent effect on adults' mathematical proficiency are many, we focus in this chapter on one: our insufficient understanding of the mathematical knowledge it takes to teach well. This insufficient understanding has meant inadequate opportunities for teachers to develop the requisite mathematical knowledge and the ability to use it in practice. Without such knowledge, teachers lack resources necessary for solving central problems of their work—for instance, using curriculum materials judiciously, choosing and using representations and tools, skillfully interpreting and responding to their students' work, and designing useful homework assignments. Because what teachers and students are able to do together with mathematics in classrooms is at the heart of mathematics education, the problem we set out to investigate in this chapter is, we argue, central to improving such education.

The ideas in this chapter have been significantly influenced by the thinking and writing of Suzanne Wilson, David Cohen, Magdalene Lampert, Hyman Bass, Lee Shulman, Joan Ferrini-Mundy, Daniel Chazan, Deborah Schifter, and Jeremy Kilpatrick. The authors also acknowledge, gratefully, Mark Hoover's and Eric Siegel's assistance across many phases of the work and Kara Suzuka's help in the final preparation of the manuscript. Work on this chapter was supported, in part, by the Spencer Foundation for the project, "Crossing Boundaries: Probing the Interplay of Mathematics and Pedagogy in Elementary Teaching" (MG #199800202, Deborah Ball). The order of coauthorship is alphabetical. Both coauthors contributed significantly to the development of this chapter along with the lead author.

Why Focus on Mathematical Knowledge for Teaching?

We chose to focus on teachers' knowledge of mathematics for a chapter about research on mathematics teaching for three reasons. First, the history of research in the past 15 years reveals an overwhelming focus on teachers' knowledge and beliefs. In our perusal of articles published between 1986 and 1998 in 48 educational research journals, we identified 354 articles that dealt specifically with mathematics teaching and learning (i.e., focused on teachers, students, curriculum, or interactions among any of these).[1] Almost half of those pieces focused on mathematics *teachers* alone, and many others included teachers' knowledge and beliefs in their central questions and analyses.[2] As we had expected, teachers and teacher knowledge had been a significant focus of research since the publication of the *Handbook of Research on Teaching, Third Edition* (Wittrock, 1986).

Researchers, who turned inward to investigate teachers' reasoning, have greatly added to our knowledge of what teachers know and believe, as well as to our ideas about the frameworks for asking such questions. Because the present *Handbook* represents an opportunity to take stock of where we are as a field and because, in the last 15 years, so much effort has been aimed at questions about teachers, the focus on teachers in this chapter seemed appropriate.

A second reason for choosing this focus on teachers was less internal to the field, less exclusively about research. We also considered the continuing public concern with improving mathematics education. Amid frequent claims about how to improve teachers (or improve teaching), we found that research, policy, practice, and advocacy are deeply intertwined when it comes to questions of teaching and learning mathematics. Researchers and policymakers, mathematicians and practitioners, politicians and parents are in the mix as they make claims and recommend courses of action. Appraising what we know—and what we do not—as well as where we need to head with respect to teachers' knowledge seemed timely. For example, although 15% of the articles we reviewed focused on teachers' knowledge and beliefs, only 5% probed how teachers' mathematical understanding affected their practice, and only 2% examined how it affected students' learning. We still face a gap in the knowledge needed to guide policy and practice.

A third reason for choosing to focus our chapter on teachers' knowledge of mathematics was theoretical. We saw in this topic the opportunity to integrate and to investigate comparatively what have been very different kinds of work. We saw an opportunity to lay the foundations for a programmatic agenda focused on mathematical knowledge for teaching, an agenda that would combine theory, practice, and empirical inquiry in research on mathematics teaching and teacher learning.

Before we examine the problems associated with understanding, studying, and developing the mathematical knowledge needed for teaching, we step back to situate this chapter in the broader context of contemporary mathematics education. We trace briefly other explanations offered for so many American adults' lack of mathematical proficiency.[3]

Why Are So Few American Adults Mathematically Proficient?

The school mathematics experience of most Americans is and has been uninspiring at best, and intellectually and emotionally crushing at worst. "Mathematical presentations, whether in books or in the classroom, are often perceived as authoritarian" (Davis & Hersh, 1981, p. 282). Ironically, the most logical of the human disciplines of knowledge is transformed through misrepresentative pedagogy into a body of precepts and facts to be remembered "because the teacher said so."

Despite its power, rich traditions, and beauty, mathematics is too often encountered in ways that lead to its being misunderstood and unappreciated. Many pupils spend their time in mathematics classrooms where mathematics is no more than a set of arbitrary rules and procedures to be memorized. Davis and Hersh (1981) describe the pattern of the "ordinary math class" in which many readers of this chapter were likely raised:

> The program is fairly clear-cut. We have problems to solve, or a method of calculation to explain, or a theorem to prove. The main work will be done in writing, usually on the blackboard. If the problems are solved, the theorems proved, or the calculations completed, then the teacher and the class know they have completed the daily task. (p. 3)

When students don't "get it," their confusions are addressed by the teacher's repeating the steps in "excruciatingly fine detail," more slowly, and sometimes even more loudly (Davis & Hersh, 1981, p. 279).

Improving Mathematics Teaching and Learning: Why Has It Been So Difficult?

The past 40 years have seen several waves of mathematics reform, each entailing serious efforts to improve mathematics learning. Each wave has attempted to upgrade what counts as "mathematics" in school, to alter students' mathematical experiences, and to improve their grasp of fundamental ideas and skills. Yet change has been difficult, and many students experience their math classes much like those described in the previous section.

In fact, much about mathematics education has remained the same as it was in 1950 or even 1900. Students still practice pages of sums and products and are still asked to solve improbable

---

[1] We included in our perusal those journals that contained at least some mathematics education–related research, were national or international in scope, and were accessible through ERIC. The lists used for the annual reviews of research in mathematics education were a starting point for creating the pool of journals. Several entries on the annual review lists did not meet those criteria and were deleted, and a few missing journals that were obviously relevant were added to the list (e.g., the new *Hiroshima Journal of Mathematics Education*).

[2] Fewer than a third of the articles focused on curriculum, and most of those focused on how technology might be used in classrooms. Just over a fifth of the articles focused on students; only 4% (14) of the articles examined interactions of students, curriculum, and teaching.

[3] John Allen Paulos (1988) describes in detail the nature of this "illiteracy" and, in so doing, provides rich examples of what it might mean to be mathematically literate.

story problems. Students are still told to "invert and multiply" to divide fractions and to use "My dear Aunt Sally" (MDAS) to remember to multiply and divide before adding and subtracting in an expression. Teachers still explain how to do procedures, offer rules of thumb, give tests on definitions and procedures, and provide applications. Those practices in and of themselves are not necessarily unhelpful. However, the prevalence of instruction that consists only of such practices helps to explain why the number of students who leave school as proficient with mathematics as they are literate with English remains small.

No single cause can account for the failure of past reform efforts to change the face of mathematics teaching in American classrooms. Yet the patterns of the "ordinary" mathematics class have dominated. And despite contemporary rhetoric and debate, they continue to prevail. The failure of reforms to penetrate core practice has preoccupied many scholars (Berman & McLaughlin, 1975; Cohen & Ball, in press; Cohen, 1989; McLaughlin, 1990; McLaughlin & Marsh, 1978; Sarason, 1971; Tyack & Cuban, 1995). Dominant explanations for this failure of past reform efforts suggest factors that impede progress. Among the most frequent explanations are the misrepresentation of mathematics; culturally embedded views of knowledge, learning, and teaching; social organization of schools and teaching; curriculum materials and assessments; and teacher education and professional development.

In this chapter, we focus on a problem that underlies all of those explanations: our understanding of the mathematical knowledge that is needed to teach mathematics well. We begin with a brief examination of the other explanations, however, because we argue that each of them contributes to the difficulties in solving the problem that is the focus of this chapter— mathematical knowledge for teaching.

The Misrepresentation of Mathematics

Alfred North Whitehead (1911/1948) saw one root of mathematical illiteracy in the fact that, as mathematics is usually taught, the elegance and power of mathematics are not exposed to students as they are helped to acquire skills and tools. Whitehead described the encounters that most people have with mathematics:

> The study of mathematics is apt to commence in disappointment. The important applications of the science, the theoretical interest of its ideas, and the logical rigour of its methods, all generate the expectation of a speedy introduction to processes of interest. . . . Yet, like the ghost of Hamlet's father, this great science eludes the efforts of our mental weapons to grasp it. . . . The reason for this failure of the science to live up to its great reputation is that its fundamental ideas are not explained to the student disentangled from the technical procedure which has been invented to facilitate their exact presentation in particular instances. Accordingly, the unfortunate learner finds himself struggling to acquire a knowledge of a mass of details which are not illuminated by any general conception. (Whitehead, 1911/1948, pp. 1–2)

Too often, the curriculum and teaching methods used in school inundate students with skills and procedures without allowing them to develop an appreciation for the power of mathematics

as a system of human thought. Most adults graduate from school never having experienced any of the power, elegance, and beauty of the subject. Their interest has not been captured, and many conclude that they neither can do nor need mathematics.

Views of Knowledge and Learning

A second explanation for the resilience of the common patterns of mathematics instruction in the United States reflects what Jackson (1986) calls the "mimetic" tradition, which is at odds with the more ambitious instruction that is advocated by reformers. Knowledge is fixed; teachers give knowledge to pupils who store and remember it. This tradition is firmly embedded in Western culture. Cohen (1989) writes that, as many as 300 years ago,

> most teaching proceeded as though learning was a passive process of assimilation. Students were expected to follow their teachers' directions rigorously. To study was to imitate: to copy a passage, to repeat a teacher's words, or to memorize some sentences, dates, or numbers. Students may have posed questions in formal discourse, and perhaps even embroidered the answers. But school learning seems to have been a matter of imitative assimilation. (pp. 42–43)

Cohen (1989) argues that innovative approaches to teaching and learning often embody assumptions about knowledge as well as about teaching and learning that are "a radical departure from inherited ideas and practices" in this culture. These new approaches fly in the face of centuries-old intellectual traditions, not only in mathematics but also in all disciplines. Those intellectual traditions also live outside the school institutions, in the everyday occasions for informal teaching— occasions involved in parenting, for example. The views that knowledge is fixed, that teaching is achieved through transmission, and that teachers are authorities run very deep in U.S. culture. By contrast, Stigler and Hiebert (1999) provide portraits of Japanese mathematics instruction and argue that the differences highlight the ways in which teaching is a cultural activity, embedded in and reflective of the culture in which it takes place.

Organizational Factors

A third common explanation for the failure of mathematics reform involves institutional and organizational factors in schools. Schools are charged with multiple and competing goals. The push to standardize and to avoid risks or experiments is great in light of those pressures (Ball & Cohen, 1999; Cohen & Neufeld, 1981; Goodlad, 1984). Administrators and school board members, who are preoccupied with test scores, put pressure on teachers to emphasize "basic skills"—computation and memorization of "facts." Teachers are generally responsible for a curriculum that is both traditional and warranted by those very traditions.

The structure of the school day means that teachers are isolated from one another and have little time or support for learning or trying out innovations. Time is segmented into 55-minute blocks, content must be covered, and pupils must be prepared not only for tests but also for the next level. Moreover, working with groups of 30 children makes experimenting with pedagogy risky for teachers who must also maintain order and routines. Elementary teachers must teach many other subjects in addition to mathematics; secondary teachers must teach many more students.

The incentives to work on more complex content and to press for higher performance are not necessarily present. Teachers often do not have time to plan and organize rich experiences for pupils, and they cannot afford the looseness of more exploratory curricula. They feel pressure to make sure that pupils master required content. For example, the time required for students to "get inside" a topic like measurement may seem to conflict with the time needed to ensure that students also get to everything else. The pull toward neat, routinized instruction is very strong. Teaching measurement by giving out formulas—$l \times w =$ some number of square units and $l \times w \times h =$ some number of cubic units—may seem much more efficient than hauling out containers, blocks, and rulers and having students explore the different ways to answer questions of "how big" or "how much." With focused, bounded tasks, students get the right answers, and everyone can think that they are successful. The fact that these bounded tasks sometimes results in sixth graders who think that you measure water with rulers may, unfortunately, go unnoticed.

Such features of school organization and of teaching conditions are part of the environments within which reforms must operate (Cohen & Ball, in press; Cuban, 1984; Sarason, 1971). Sarason (1971) argues that one important reason the New Math curriculum failed was that the reformers generally failed to take a sufficiently broad perspective of the "regularities" of the school setting and the culture of the school—teachers had little access to professional development or few opportunities to work together on curriculum, for instance.[4]

These regularities of schooling and the culture of the school are among the many other elements of the surrounding environments in which teaching and learning take place: policies, state mandates, assessments, parents, communities, districts, and the like. If the environments of teaching and learning are ignored, then change—if it occurs at all—is likely to be superficial: for example, changing textbooks but not the mode of instruction (Sarason, 1971).

These environments influence the course of innovation through the many ways in which they permeate instruction (Cohen & Ball, in press). This perspective challenges the very concept of "implementation" itself (Cohen & Ball, 1999; Farrar, Descantis, & Cohen, 1980; Giadomenico & Wildavsky, 1984). Sarason would argue that reformers who do not consider what schools are like will operate under the misguided impression that changes can be simply "put into place." Quite to the contrary, innovations are interpreted and adapted by teachers; the intent, the enactment, and the effect of an innovation changes in the translation (Berman & McLaughlin, 1975; Cohen & Ball, in press; McLaughlin, 1990; McLaughlin & Marsh, 1978; Sarason, 1971). The expectation that reforms can be instituted faithfully from the top down is a fantasy that ignores the loose connections between official authority and actual practice. American teachers, in fact, have considerable elbow room at the classroom level and typically "[arbitrate] between their own priorities and the implied priorities of external policies" (Schwille et al., 1983, p. 387).

Curriculum Materials and Assessments

In the past, a fourth explanation for the continuity and conservatism of mathematics teaching has been the conservative nature of the materials from which teachers teach and the confining effects of traditional assessments. Stodolsky's (1988) analysis of elementary mathematics textbooks suggests that concepts and procedures were often inadequately developed, with just one or two examples given, and that the textbooks emphasized "hints and reminders" to students about what to do. For example, in her study, Stodolsky found that area and perimeter (the content of the example in the preceding section) were presented in terms of the formulas—$l \times w$ and $2 \times l + 2 \times w$—with, perhaps, some pictures to illustrate. The books provided practice in calculating the area and perimeter of some rectangles, with reminders to state the answers to area problems in terms of "*square* units." Multiplication by 10 was explained in terms of "adding a zero," algebra texts claimed that vertical lines have "no slope," and rectangles were represented as figures with two long and two shorter sides.

Until the past decade, geometry below tenth grade was scant, measurement was more procedural than conceptual, and probability investigations were relegated to the little "Time Out" boxes on a few random pages. The curriculum analyses conducted by researchers for the Third International Mathematics and Science Study (TIMSS) revealed a portrait of U.S. textbooks as recycling the same topics year after year, covering a vast number of topics, and not developing any topic deeply (Schmidt, McKnight, & Raizen, 1997; Schmidt, McKnight, Valverde, Houang, & Wiley, 1997a; Schmidt, McKnight, Valverde, Houang, & Wiley, 1997b).

In the past 10 years, however, curriculum materials once again have been a major lever of reform. The National Science Foundation invested millions of dollars in new curricula, and many new mathematics curriculum materials have appeared. Their developers, like the predecessors in the 1960s, seek to improve teaching and learning by effecting significant changes in the mathematics curriculum. Whether and how these curriculum materials will fare differently in their aim to permeate teaching and learning remain to be seen.

Some early studies of teachers who are using new curriculum materials suggest that teachers' knowledge and beliefs continue to shape their interpretations and uses of those materials. Significant questions about the interplay of guidance and opportunity to learn will emerge, as before, in the enactment of new materials (Collopy, 1999; Remillard, 1999a, 1999b; Rickard, 1993).

---

[4] The "New Math" is the name commonly given to the curriculum reforms of the 1960s, which emphasized mathematical structure, and focused on improving the curriculum for college-bound students, but which also spread to middle and elementary schools. See Romberg (1992) for an insightful analysis of the New Math and its successes and disappointments.

Teacher Education and Professional Development

A final focus of analysis has been the weak impact of professional education on teachers. Critics observe that preservice teacher education typically has a weak effect on teachers' knowledge and beliefs and that whatever prospective teachers learn at the university tends to be "washed out" once they get to schools (Zeichner & Tabachnick, 1981). In fact, it is rather unsurprising that a handful of university courses often fails to substantially alter the knowledge and assumptions that prospective teachers have had "washed in" through years of first-hand observations of teachers. By the time they begin professional education, teachers have already clocked more than 2,000 hours in a specialized "apprenticeship of observation" (Lortie, 1975, p. 61), which not only has instilled traditional images of teaching and learning but also has shaped their understanding of mathematics (Ball, 1988). Because this understanding of mathematics is the mathematics they will *teach*, what they have learned about the subject matter in elementary and high school turns out to be a significant component of their preparation for teaching.

Professional education is also the target of frequent criticism for its fragmented, episodic, and superficial nature. Although a good deal of money is spent on "staff development" in the United States and although there is no shortage of in-service "training" for teachers, most training money is spent on sessions and workshops that are often intellectually superficial, disconnected from deep issues of curriculum and learning, fragmented, and noncumulative (Cohen & Hill, 2000; Heaton, 1992; Little, 1993; Wilson, Lubienski, and Mattson, 1996). Rarely do these inservice opportunities seem based on a curricular view of teachers' learning (Ball & Cohen, 1999). Teachers are thought to need "updating" rather than opportunities for serious and sustained learning about curriculum, students, and teaching.

Because professional development is rarely seen as a continuing enterprise for teachers, it is only occasionally truly *developmental*. One reason is that many people see teaching as mostly commonsense, and they perceive little need for professional learning. Another reason is that teaching has been seen and organized as a career in which sustained learning is not required for adequate performance. Still another reason is that no coherent infrastructure exists for professional development. In other words, no easily identifiable group or agency is responsible for professional development, and so it happens everywhere—and, consequently, lacks consistency and coherence. A final reason is that professional development lacks a curriculum for teachers' learning, a curriculum that considers the practices they are being asked to enact, the mathematical knowledge that such practice entails, and the attention to what they already know and believe—that is, what they bring to the undertaking (Heaton, 2000).

The Role of Knowledge of Mathematics for Teaching

Another factor that is often cited to explain the weaknesses of U.S. mathematics education is U.S. teachers' knowledge of mathematics. Observers note that interpreting reform ideas, managing the challenges of change, using new curriculum materials, enacting new practices, and teaching new content all depend on teachers' knowledge of mathematics. What many assume, however, is that this mathematical knowledge is shallow and relatively transparent, that the problem faced is one of current U.S. teachers' intellectual weaknesses. Few have looked closely at the practice of elementary or secondary mathematics teaching to consider the nature of its mathematical entailments.

Consider the mathematical understanding entailed in teaching the multiplication of decimals. To enhance appreciation of the complexity and subtlety of the mathematical understanding required, we peek in on a classroom where a teacher is helping her students learn to multiply decimals.[5] When she taught multiplication of whole numbers, she used repeated addition as a model (e.g., $6 \times 7 = 7 + 7 + 7 + 7 + 7 + 7$), but she had introduced area representations as well. She begins the lesson on multiplying decimals by reviewing an example with whole numbers:

"If the unit is one little square," asks the teacher, "how could you show 7×6 with the tiles?" Michael volunteers. He goes over to the overhead, carefully lays out seven tiles, and then makes six rows of them to form a rectangle:

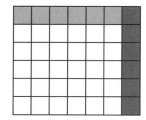

"I have 7 times 6," he explains, and he counts each tile carefully across the top row: "One, two, three, four, five, six, seven." Then, he points down the right-hand column, "One, two, three, four, five, six."

"How much is that altogether?" asks the teacher.

"Forty-two," he replies, confidently, pointing at the squares filling his rectangular array. He counts the tiles quickly to show that he is right, and several children chime in, "1, 2, 3, 4, 5, 6, 7, . . . 38, 39, 40, 41, *42!*"

The teacher is pleased. She knows that using the area representation will help to demystify the rule for multiplication of decimals: (a) multiply as with whole numbers, (b) then count the number of decimal places in the numbers being multiplied, (c) count over that combined number of places in the answer, and (d) place the decimal point there.

For years, students would ask, "Why does that work? When we add decimals, you tell us to keep the decimal place lined up. Why, when we multiply, do we move the decimal point?" At those times, she had felt a kind of despair at teaching meaningless rules. Using the area model for multiplication, she now thought, would help to make the procedure make sense.

---

[5] This example is constructed on the basis of a composite of several lessons taught by Deborah Ball.

"Good job, Michael. We're going to try something a little harder now," the teacher announces to the fourth graders. She holds up a large square, scored 10 by 10 into 100 little squares. "Instead of the little square being the unit, the *large* square is going to be the unit. So, first, what is the little square now?"

Several children call out, "One hundredth."

"How do you know?" asks the teacher.

Jamie breaks out, "Because there are 100 of them in the big square, so one of them is one hundredth." Other children nod.

The teacher holds up the rod composed of 10 little squares:

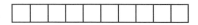

"So what is this, then?" she asks. There is a pause.

"It's 10," says one boy. "Wait, no, wait, it's not. It's one *tenth* because there are 10 of those in the whole square."

The teacher nods. "Now try showing this problem with the tiles," she says, and she writes: .3 × .7.

The children go to work at their desks, many using the little squares. Their arrays look like Figure 24.1. The area of these shapes is 21 *hundredths* or .21, as expected. Suddenly, the teacher notices that these arrays are constructed with three *hundredths* or .03 on one side and seven *hundredths* or .07 on the other, because the little squares are each one hundredth. The children were supposed to be multiplying three *tenths* times seven *tenths*. What is going on? Shouldn't they be using the tenths, the long rods, to build the arrays? She looks in the teacher's guide, slightly unsettled, and sees that the arrays look like those her students are making. She feels a little relieved but still wonders what is going on. These rectangles show the right answer, but where are .7 and .3, the original numbers? Looking closely, she sees that one can interpret the arrays as 7 × .03 by adding each column together (.03 + .03 + .03 + .03 + .03 + .03 + .03 = .21). Moreover, she can also see 3 × .07 by counting the rows. What is being represented here? Is it .03 × .07? 3 × .07? 7 × .03? Or is it .3 × .7, as she had posed? This sudden loss of mathematical footing is unsettling.

The teacher sees that, over on the side of the room, two boys have constructed a different proposed solution. Using the long rods, which correspond to tenths when the square is the unit, they have built an array (see Figure 24.2).

She sees that they have built a contiguous array of rods that represents tenths—three groups of seven tenths. But something is definitely wrong here because, in total, this array represents 2.1 (see Figure 24.3), and the product of .7 × .3 is .21, not 2.1. She quickly realizes that these students have indeed worked with tenths, but that the product they have represented is *three* times seven tenths, not *three-tenths* times seven-tenths, hence the answer of 2.1.

She considers again the area represented by the 21 hun-

dredths (see Figure 24.1). Suddenly she realizes that this array *does* represent three tenths times seven tenths. Each small square has a *side length* of one tenth. The side of the unit square has a length of 1, and so the side of each of the little squares is one-tenth of 1, or 0.1 (see Figure 24.4). If each little square has a side length of one-tenth, then it makes sense, she sees, that each square has an area of one-hundredth of a unit, that is, one-tenth times one-tenth (see Figure 24.5).

Given all that, the rectangle formed by 21 little squares *does* represent .3 length along one side and .7 length along the other, and hence, the area product of .3 × .7. She realizes, with interest, that the same array can be used to represent 3 × .07 or 7 × .03 but that, in these products, the numbers do not correspond to lengths. Instead, those arrays are examples that iterate the addition of rows or columns. In this representation of repeated addition, one number represents the number of iterations while the other number represents the area units being iterated. In 7 × .03, the seven represents how many units of three-hundredths are added together. Three-hundredths corresponds to a unit of area, and seven corresponds to the number of such units.

In the classroom example we have just examined, what was the content? Multiplication of decimals. This teacher knew that 3 × 7 was 21, and she knew that .3 × .7 was .21. She knew that when you multiply tenths, you get hundredths—hence the rule for moving over the decimal point. And her textbook provided guidance for using the area model for helping students understand procedures for multiplying decimals. But in this lesson, she realized afresh how subtle and yet how important the mathematical ideas underlying this lesson were. When one multiplies whole numbers with the area model and counts the unit square as 1, it is easy to overlook the fact that what is being multiplied are the lengths of the sides—which are linear measures—and that what is being produced are areas. In the whole number example, both the length and the area of the little unit are 1 in this model, so one can easily miss this important distinction. And yet this distinction becomes much clearer with the multiplication of tenths because then the areas of the little squares are hundredths, and their side lengths are, therefore, tenths. If all one does is count the areas, it can appear that what is being multiplied are hundredths, yielding hundredths as well.

Knowing this web of ideas is important for teaching the multiplication of decimals. Understanding the ideas connected to a particular mathematical topic matters in any approach to teaching, whether the teacher provides the explanation and asks students to practice, or whether, as in this example, she engages students in tasks and discussions of those tasks. Without question, being able to multiply whole numbers and decimals constitutes necessary but insufficient knowledge for teaching that skill well. This teacher needed to have a refined and explicit understanding of the meaning of multiplication, combined both as iterated addition and as the product of two linear units that yield an area, together with the correspondences between these models. She needed to understand how the model she was using worked and how it corresponded to the symbolic form of .3 × .7 = .21. She also needed confidence in her own mathematical knowledge to be able to analyze the problem and its representation "on the fly" when she realized that she was unclear about what was being modeled with the blocks. In this case, the

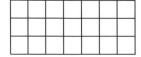

Figure 24.1 A typical arrangement of tiles to show .3 × .7.

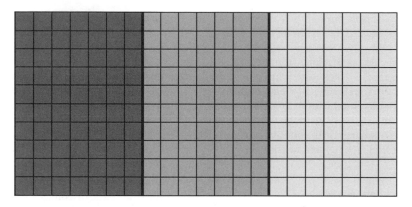

Figure 24.2. A representation of 3 × .7 using three groups of seven rods.

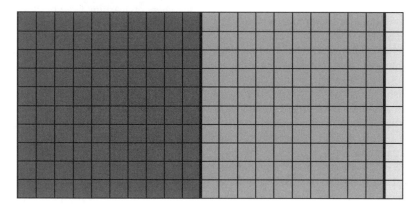

Figure 24.3. Three groups of seven rods reorganized as two large squares and one tenth of a large square.

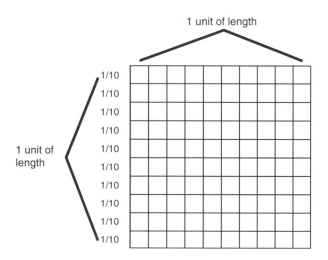

Figure 24.4. The relationship between side *lengths* of the little squares and the large square.

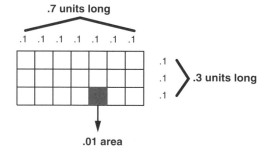

Figure 24.5. The relationship between side *lengths* (in tenths) and *area* (in hundredths) for .3 × .7.

teacher needed to be able to reason through her confusion as the lesson unfolded so she could keep the lesson on track mathematically.

With this glimpse of mathematics teaching in mind, we return to our problem. The search to delineate what it is that teachers *do* need to know in order to teach has been a challenging one. In this chapter, we trace the history of the efforts to determine the relative role of teachers' mathematical knowledge in teaching, to explore changing ideas about what counts as mathematical knowledge for teaching, and to consider what we need to learn.

Teacher knowledge is not a new issue and is not one tied exclusively to reform. Questions about the knowledge that teachers need to know, how it affects their teaching, and how they can be helped to develop it have preoccupied professional developers, policymakers, and researchers alike for more than four decades. Teachers' knowledge of mathematics was one of the first variables investigated by researchers on teaching in the 1960s. Those researchers asked questions about how teachers' knowledge influenced the teachers' effectiveness (Begle, 1972, 1979). And teachers' mathematical knowledge has continued to be a much-discussed problem in the contemporary debates about the improvement of mathematics teaching and learning.

In 1999, Liping Ma published *Knowing and Teaching Elementary Mathematics,* a book that has attracted renewed and much wider interest in this issue. In her study, Ma compared Chinese and U.S. elementary teachers' mathematical knowledge. Producing a portrait of dramatic differences between the two groups, Ma used her data to develop a notion of "profound understanding of fundamental mathematics," an argument for a kind of connected, curricularly structured, and longitudinally coherent knowledge of core mathematical ideas.

Ma's book has broadened and reignited discussions around teachers' mathematics knowledge and its contributions to instruction. Research mathematicians, deeply concerned about what some perceived as the morass of K–12 mathematics education, have taken note. They were suddenly struck with how central teachers' mathematical knowledge is to effective teaching and to improvement. Roger Howe (1999) reflected the reactions of many mathematicians when he wrote:

> [Ma's work] gives us new perspectives in the problems of improving mathematics education in the United States. For example, it strongly suggests that without a radical change in the state of mathematical preparedness of the American teaching corps, calls such as those contained in the NCTM Standards, are simply doomed. (p. 884)

Although many researchers, teachers, policymakers, and teacher educators have recognized the importance of teachers' mathematical knowledge, understanding the nature and role or mathematical knowledge for teaching—plus developing it effectively—remains an unsolved problem for the improvement

of mathematics teaching and learning. We move next to trace where the field has been in seeking to define and solve this problem. We describe what we know—and do not know—from research, and we frame directions for where work on this problem needs to head.

Mathematics Knowledge for Teaching: A Problem for Practice, Policy, and Research

First, we take a look back. In the previous edition of *Handbook of Research on Teaching,* Romberg and Carpenter (1986) surveyed research in mathematics education and worried about what they saw as a disconnect between research on teaching and research on learning. They noted that, despite big gains in understanding students' mathematical conceptions and development, the findings from research on teaching were unaligned with questions arising from research on learning.[6] While researchers on learning were producing portraits of the complexity of developing conceptions of rational numbers, or area, or multidigit subtraction, research on teaching was investigating whether students involved in cooperative learning within small group settings were indeed behaving cooperatively and were more productive than students in noncooperative small group settings. How research on teaching related to mathematical work was often invisible, leaving unprobed many questions about the critical relationships between teaching and learning.

Looking ahead to the next 10 years, the authors urged researchers to integrate studies of learning with studies of teaching to "bridge the learning–teaching gap" (Romberg & Carpenter, 1986, p. 868). Mathematics should be at the center of such studies, they urged, with increased refinement and detail when considering the role of content in teaching and learning. Without this increasing integration of mathematical content and without greater coordination between research on teaching and research on learning, knowledge useful for improving instruction would continue to be elusive. Romberg and Carpenter's argument was an important one. Our examination of the literature suggests that researchers *have* turned more toward instruction, as Romberg and Carpenter had urged.

Solving the Problem of Mathematical Knowledge for Teaching: From Teachers to Teacher Knowledge

The assertion that teachers' own knowledge of mathematics is an important resource for teaching is so obvious as to be trivial. Commonplace are statements such as: "A thorough grounding in college-level subject matter and professional competence in professional practice are necessary for good teaching. . . . The data are unequivocal: students learn more mathematics when their teachers report having taken more mathematics" (American Council on Education [ACE], 1999, p. 6). The ACE report goes on to cite evidence that earning a college degree in mathe-

---

[6] One example was the robust finding that the amount of time devoted to mathematics instruction was found to be positively related to student achievement. Time on task, argued Romberg and Carpenter (1986), was inadequate as a useful measure without data on what students were engaged in doing. Academic tasks differ markedly in mathematical scope and cognitive demand, and task enactment in class further differentiates the nature of the work. As such, the amount of time spent engaged in work was an imprecise measure of learning opportunity and was certainly too imprecise to be useful for improving classroom learning.

matics, being certified in mathematics, and being mathematically skillful "all contribute to effective teaching of mathematics" (p. 6). The warrant is, however, much weaker than the ACE authors would like.

The claim that teachers' knowledge matters is commonsense. However, the empirical support for this "obvious" fact has been surprisingly elusive. "No one questions the idea that what a teacher knows is one of the most important influences on what is done in classrooms and, ultimately, on what students learn," assert Fennema and Franke (1992, p. 147). And yet, as those authors explain, no consensus exists on the mathematical knowledge that is required to teach. This lack of consensus is a problem for policymakers and teacher educators alike. If we are to identify what teachers need to know or to learn, then an important matter is how much knowledge of mathematics it takes to teach. It matters for teacher certification requirements, it matters for teacher education policy and practice, it matters for recruiting and hiring teachers, and it matters for curriculum development.

Three approaches have dominated efforts to solve the problem of teachers' mathematical knowledge. One approach is a policy response; two approaches involve research. The policy response to resolving this problem of what teachers need to know has been to work logically and to create documents and lists of what teachers should know. Some documents are general; others, much more specific. The general documents (ACE, 1999; Interstate New Teacher Assessment and Support Consortium [INTASC], 1993; National Board for Professional Teaching Standards, 1991; National Commission on Teaching and America's Future, 1996) simply call for teachers to know their content well and are not particular to mathematics. They extol qualities of the requisite knowledge: it should be deep, connected, and conceptual and should include knowledge of the epistemology of the field.

In the more specific documents, experts identify the mathematical knowledge by considering the topics in the curriculum and by assuming, quite reasonably, that teachers need to know that which they have to teach (e.g., Conference Board of the Mathematical Sciences, 2000; Leitzel, 1991; National Council of Teachers of Mathematics, 1991). Those documents produce lists of mathematical topics. As they recognize the need for teachers to have mathematical perspective about the connections among ideas, such lists usually identify topics beyond the curriculum. This approach to specifying knowledge for teaching is rooted primarily in policy deliberations and often does not reflect research evidence.

Although this approach has been an important one, in our analysis, we focus on two other approaches that researchers have used to solve or at least to better understand the problem of mathematical knowledge for teaching. How the problem has been defined has influenced the manner in which it has been approached by researchers. Those approaches are distinguished by more than differences in their orientation and focus: they also entail particular stances on measurement and teacher education. Each approach has relied on measuring mathematical knowledge for teaching in particular ways and is associated with particular perspectives on how to help teachers develop the requisite knowledge for teaching.

The first research approach, which centers on looking at

characteristics of *teachers,* is associated with the assumption that knowledge of and skill with mathematics content is essential to teaching. It assumes, further, that indicators such as the courses taken, degrees earned, or certification received will represent the requisite knowledge and that teacher knowledge can be measured using such relatively straightforward indices. Thus, research in this domain focuses largely on description and analysis of teacher characteristics, particularly the amount of mathematics that teachers have taken.

The second research approach, which focuses on teachers' *knowledge,* builds on the first approach in that it acknowledges the importance of the content of teachers' mathematical knowledge, but it also prominently includes a qualitative focus on the nature of teachers' knowledge. This approach is based, in part, on the notion of pedagogical content knowledge as an intertwining of knowledge about how ideas might be represented, how students learn, and what they find difficult (Shulman, 1986, 1987; Wilson, Shulman, & Richert, 1987). This second approach to research does not replace but builds on the first: the first emphasizes *teachers;* the second emphasizes teachers' *knowledge.* Although the second approach has a strong contemporary following among researchers and teacher educators, the first approach is attractive to policymakers. We argue in this chapter that each approach has merit. We propose, further, that these two approaches be reconnected in the next steps to solve the problem of what mathematical knowledge is necessary to teach well.

An alternative approach, with which the chapter concludes, builds on both lines of prior work—on *teachers* and on *knowledge*—but shifts to a greater focus on *teaching* and on *teachers' use of mathematical knowledge.*

Looking at Teachers

In the earliest approach to answering questions about the mathematical knowledge that is necessary for teaching, researchers attempted to validate empirically the common maxim that the more mathematical knowledge teachers have, the more mathematical knowledge their students will have. This foundational assumption led researchers to count the courses teachers had taken and to analyze relationships between the extent of their mathematics course work and their students' learning. The approach to measuring teachers' knowledge is straightforward: count the courses taken, the credits earned, and the degrees attained. Each of those totals is considered to be a representation of teachers' mathematical knowledge. This approach still holds considerable interest (e.g., Darling-Hammond, 1999; Monk, 1994). Similarly, in terms of teacher preparation, this approach to teacher knowledge leads to stipulations of credit and course requirements but pays little attention to content, scope or the nature of mathematics. Teachers' exposure to and development of mathematical content is assumed to equip them with the resources needed for effective teaching.

Perhaps best known among the early work in this approach was Edward Begle's (1979) meta-analysis of studies conducted between 1960 and 1976 that probed the effects of teacher variables on student performance. Convinced that mathematics education was suffering from too much opinion and not enough careful empirical work, Begle initiated the National Longitudinal Study of Mathematical Abilities as a forum for examining factors that affect mathematics learning. In offering his analysis of teacher effects, Begle (1979) commented:

> There is no doubt that teachers play an important role in the learning of mathematics by their students. However, the specific ways in which teachers' understanding, attitudes, and characteristics affect their students are not widely understood. In fact, there are widespread misconceptions, on the part not only of laypeople but also of mathematics educators, about the ways in which teachers influence mathematics learning by their students. (p. 27)

Begle's analysis of the relationship between the number of courses teachers had taken past calculus and student performance produced a surprise to many. He found that the extent of teachers' mathematics course taking produced positive main effects on students' achievement in only 10% of the cases and, perhaps more jolting, negative main effects in 8%.[7] This latter result has been the topic of much speculation. It is an interesting result because the negative main effects are not easily explained by the ubiquitous criticism that mathematics courses past calculus are not relevant to teaching or that taking courses is a poor proxy for teachers' actual mathematical knowledge. Those claims support finding no effects.

But how might such variables be associated with negative effects? One explanation might rest with the increasing compression of knowledge that accompanies increasingly advanced mathematical work, a compression that may interfere with the unpacking of content that teachers need to do (e.g., Ball & Bass, 2000; Cohen, in preparation). Another explanation might be that more course work in mathematics is accompanied by more experience with conventional approaches to teaching mathematics. Such experience may imbue teachers with pedagogical images and habits that do not contribute to their effectiveness with young students (Ball, 1988). What underlies those negative main effects is not known but is worth further exploration.

Begle (1979) also examined other teacher knowledge variables. For example, his analysis of the relationship of teachers' course taking and their students' performance revealed that majoring or minoring in mathematics yielded positive main effects in 9% of the cases and negative main effects in 4%. A less-often reported result was that the greatest number of positive main effects was produced from the analysis of the relationship between the number of credits in mathematics *methods* courses and student performance—49, or 23%. This analysis yielded only 12 negative main effects (5%).

Begle (1979) concluded from these results that the belief stated as "the more a teacher knows about his subject matter, the more effective he will be as a teacher" demanded "drastic modification" (p. 51). On the basis of his finding, he claimed that advanced mathematical understanding contributed little to teacher effectiveness. He noted that, although "it seems to be taken for granted that it is important for a teacher to have a

thorough understanding of the subject matter being taught," the question of what should be meant by "thorough" was never examined in these studies (p. 28). He concluded that future analyses of the amount of mathematics taken by teachers were not likely to produce significant effects, and that further research of this sort was not needed until the ways in which teacher knowledge might affect student achievement were better understood. A clue may have been buried within his own results—the relative strength of the relationship between credits in mathematics methods and student performance.[8]

The interest in teachers has continued, however. In 1996, the National Commission on Teaching and America's Future (NCTAF) released its report, which proposed a series of strong recommendations for improving the nation's schools. It consisted of "a blueprint for recruiting, preparing, and supporting excellent teachers in all of America's schools" (p. vi). Asserting that what teachers know and can do has the most important influence on what students learn, the report argues that teachers' knowledge affects both students' opportunities to learn and their actual learning. Teachers must know the content thoroughly to be able to present it clearly, to make the ideas accessible to a wide variety of students, and to engage students in challenging work.

The report's authors cite a number of studies showing that teacher knowledge makes a substantial contribution to student achievement. They argue that "differences in teacher qualifications accounted for more than 90% of the variation in student achievement in reading and mathematics" (Armour-Thomas, Clay, Domanico, Bruno, & Allen, 1989, cited in National Commission on Teaching and America's Future, 1996, p. 8). Challenging some reformers' designs, the NCTAF report takes the position that neither curriculum materials, standards, nor assessments can make an impact unless teachers understand them and can make productive use of them with students. It is a document decidedly focused on teachers and on the importance of their qualifications.

To investigate empirically the relationship of teachers' subject matter preparation and student achievement, Monk (1994) analyzed data from the Longitudinal Study of American Youth (LSAY).[9] Teacher preparation was measured by a survey administered to teachers in which they reported the number of mathematics and science courses they took as undergraduates and in graduate programs. Surveys were used to document teachers' overall education level (bachelor's degree, master's, or master's plus additional credits) and years of teaching experience. In general, Monk reached a similar conclusion to that reached by Begle—namely, that the number of mathematics courses makes a difference, but only up to a point. In his analysis, he found that five courses in mathematics, independent of the specific content covered, was the threshold beyond which few effects accrue.

Interestingly, Monk's analysis also showed that each under-

---

[7] A positive main effect would mean that more credits of mathematics were associated with greater student performance; a negative main effect would mean that more credits of mathematics were associated with lower levels of achievement.

[8] Darling-Hammond (1999) claims that education course work matters more than content knowledge, especially in terms of predicting teacher performance: 16.5% of the variance in student achievement is accounted for by teachers' course work in education.

[9] The Longitudinal Study of American Youth (LSAY) was conducted in the late 1980s and early 1990s with high school sophomores and juniors. Student achievement data were based on items developed by the National Assessment of Educational Progress (NAEP).

graduate mathematics education course a teacher takes is associated with a .04% gain in student achievement. Monk also investigated more traditional measures of teacher preparation such as having a mathematics major and holding a master's degree. As with earlier studies, whether a teacher had majored in mathematics had no effect on student performance. Whether a teacher had completed additional mathematics course work at the graduate level had either no effect or a negative effect on student performance. Monk notes that many of the relationships that he did find were nonlinear, suggesting that effects are diminished over time or that there are some threshold effects. In addition, where teacher characteristics are associated with pupil gains, the gains are of a rather minor magnitude. Finally, as in Begle's analysis, Monk uncovered significant effects of courses in undergraduate mathematics pedagogy. Such courses, he found, "contribute more to pupil performance gains than do courses in undergraduate mathematics" (p. 130).[10]

Much of the work examining the relationship between teacher characteristics (educational level, courses taken, intelligence, etc.) and student performance is not focused on mathematics. One widely cited example is the work done by Ferguson (1991). In his analysis of factors that predict student achievement, he found that, when he controlled for family and community background influences, teachers' scores on the state certification exam (Texas Examination of Current Administrators and Teachers [TECAT]) accounted for about 20–25% of the variation in students' average scores on the state competency examination in mathematics and reading. Moreover, between third and seventh grade, teachers' scores also predicted changes in students' average scores over time.

In interpreting those results, Ferguson is careful to note that the analyses do not reveal what high-scoring teachers do that affects their students' learning. It may be, he acknowledges, that teachers with high scores attended better teacher education programs, or they may simply have better thinking skills that influence their pedagogical reasoning or their articulateness as teachers. Ferguson's analysis is still rather remote from the specific question of mathematical knowledge for teaching because the TECAT measures basic literacy skills, which offer neither a reliable proxy for mathematical history nor an estimate of knowledge. Still, this study provides support for the continuing assumption that teachers' ability and achievement are factors in their effectiveness, and it has been widely used to support the importance of teachers to students' achievement (Darling-Hammond, 1999).

Although many of the studies in this approach have been criticized for equating simple indicators such as course taking with mathematical knowledge and although the equivocal findings of those studies seem to lack promise for guiding our thinking about the knowledge needed for teaching, it is impossible to entirely dismiss this approach to the problem. It is intuitively logical and inherently reasonable to believe that a teacher's knowledge and mathematical proficiency, as developed through opportunities for formal study, do matter. Still, the correspondences are often difficult to map.

For example, how might research that focuses on teachers inform our earlier example of teaching decimal multiplication? Knowing how many mathematics courses a teacher had taken does not enable us to predict whether the teacher would be able to untangle the mathematical complexities that arise in this lesson. Simply counting courses does not permit an examination of whether the teacher has the mathematical knowledge needed for this lesson. In fact, even if the data permitted us to learn exactly what courses a teacher had taken, it would not be easy to identify what sort of course would offer opportunities to learn about the nature of the number system and its properties, as needed in this example and its adjacent lessons. Some of this content might arise in a modern algebra course or in a course in real analysis, typically studied by advanced undergraduate mathematics majors, and yet, most of the evidence suggests that advanced courses have no effects or even negative effects. Probably the best course would be an outstanding fifth grade mathematics class, complemented by a later study to extend and make more explicit a global and overarching perspective on the number system. In fact, typical advanced mathematics courses do not provide this perspective nor do typical courses for teachers.

A focus on teachers and their mathematical qualifications and experience affords certain clarity for policy; it leaves obscured, however, the nature of teachers' mathematical knowledge. This chasm between data on teachers and questions about teacher knowledge has given rise to the second approach to solving the problem of the mathematical knowledge that matters for teaching— an approach that preserves the focus on teachers but that adds a closer, more probing analysis of mathematical knowledge.

Looking at Teachers' Knowledge

Dissatisfied with studies of teachers that did not probe the nature of the knowledge being measured, many researchers were convinced that teachers' knowledge of mathematics content mattered in ways that were masked by counting numbers of courses. They turned to a closer probing of mathematical knowledge rather than measuring second-order indicators of knowledge. Some of the precipitants for this shift were the substantial reforms being advocated. Kennedy (1997) explains the contextual factors that also influenced the field:

> Because the main goal of [current] reformers is to instill a deeper understanding in students of the central ideas and issues in various subjects and to enable students to see how these ideas connect to, and can be applied in, real world situations, it therefore makes sense to require that teachers themselves also understand the central ideas of their subjects, see these relationships, and so forth. (p. 6)

A host of descriptive studies of teachers' knowledge appeared. Most were oriented to this more probing approach. One significant distinction is that those studies focus on specific mathematical topics rather than on global conceptions of math-

---

[10] "A statistical test of the difference between the coefficients estimated for undergraduate mathematics courses and undergraduate mathematics education courses indicated . . . that the difference is significant at better than the 0.01 level" (Monk, 1994, p. 130).

ematical knowledge. A second is that many of the studies are qualitative, using interviews to probe teachers' knowledge. A third and, perhaps, most important distinction has been the opening up of the idea of *mathematical knowledge for teaching.* Unwilling to accept general notions of mathematical background as sufficiently equivalent to the mathematical knowledge needed for teaching, researchers have explored the knowledge that they thought would matter in teaching.

In developing methods for this work, researchers grappled with the question of what would constitute conceptual understanding for teachers (Ball, 1991a, 1991b; Kennedy, 1997; Ma, 1999; Shulman, 1986; Wilson, 1988; Wilson, Shulman, & Richert, 1987) and have designed new ways to probe teachers' knowledge. The analytic work of defining mathematical knowledge for teaching went hand in hand with the development of new approaches to measuring teacher knowledge (Grossman, Wilson, & Shulman, 1989; Kennedy, Ball, & McDiarmid, 1993; Post, Harel, Behr, & Lesh, 1991; Wilson, 1988). How researchers conceived of content knowledge for teaching shaped the tools they created to probe it. Those new measures, in turn, have profoundly influenced what the studies have produced.

Central to this work has been a focus on propositional and procedural knowledge *of* mathematics—that is, understandings of particular topics (e.g., fractions and trigonometry), procedures (e.g., long division and factoring quadratic equations), and concepts (e.g., parallelism and infinity) as well as the relationships among such topics, procedures, and concepts (R. Davis, 1986; Hiebert & Lefevre, 1986; Skemp, 1978). This *substantive knowledge of mathematics* is most easily recognized by others as "subject matter knowledge," or "content knowledge" (Ball, 1991a; Grossman, Wilson, & Shulman, 1989).

A second dimension, however, has been a focus on knowledge *about* mathematics (Ball, 1991a). This focus includes understandings about the nature of knowledge in the discipline—where it comes from, how it changes, and how truth is established. Knowledge about mathematics also includes what it means to know and to do mathematics, what is the relative centrality of different ideas, what is arbitrary or conventional versus what is necessary or logical, and what is key to having a sense of the philosophical debates within the discipline.[11]

Researchers working in this approach often use methods that probe teachers' knowledge and that situate the questions in and around questions that might arise in teaching. Such questions respond to a student's confusion, explain a mathematical procedure whose meaning is buried inside rules of thumb, or consider the connections among ideas. Those questions create conditions where teachers have to make explicit their understanding of the mathematical ideas and procedures behind the questions.

An overwhelming majority of the studies associated with this approach to teacher knowledge have been conducted with preservice elementary teachers. Three reasons help to explain the preponderance of work on preservice teachers. One is that researchers have easier access to prospective teachers who are right there on campus. Second, researchers, usually teacher educators themselves, are curious about their own students'

knowledge. Finally, ethical and relational issues around "testing" teachers have plagued researchers interested in examining experienced teachers' knowledge. However, some studies have focused on the mathematical knowledge of practicing teachers. Why research has focused on elementary teachers reflects a continuing assumption that content knowledge is not a problem for secondary teachers, who, by virtue of specialized study in mathematics, know their subjects. However, research on secondary teachers repeatedly reveals the fallacy of this assumption (e.g., Ball, 1988, 1990b; Even, 1993; Steinberg, Haymore, & Marks, 1985).

An overview of those studies of teachers' mathematical knowledge—elementary and secondary, preservice and experienced—reveals pervasive weaknesses in U.S. teachers' understanding of fundamental mathematical ideas and relationships. Although numerous mathematical topics have been investigated, many have not been studied with any depth.

We summarize here the research that is focused on the topics of whole number multiplication and place value, division, rational numbers, functions, geometry and measurement, and proofs as a representative sample of the research that has been conducted.

MULTIPLICATION AND PLACE VALUE

Research that studies teachers' knowledge of multiplication has focused primarily on the algorithm for performing computations with multidigit numbers as a strategy to probe teachers' understanding of the place value concepts that underlie the procedure. By and large, studies show that the teachers interviewed were able to accurately perform the multiplication algorithm to achieve correct answers. However, they often were not able to provide explanations of the place value concepts that underlie the algorithm. For example, Ball (1988) interviewed 19 prospective elementary and secondary teachers on the topic of multidigit multiplication. She posed the following task:

Some eighth-grade teachers noticed that several of their students were making the same mistake in multiplying large numbers. In trying to calculate

$$\begin{array}{r} 123 \\ \times\ 645 \end{array}$$

the students seemed to be forgetting to "move the numbers" (i.e., the partial products) over on each line. They were doing this:

$$\begin{array}{r} 123 \\ \times\ \ 645 \\ \hline 615 \\ 492 \\ 738 \\ \hline 1{,}845 \end{array}$$

instead of this:

---

[11] Schwab (1961/1978) refers to these kinds of understandings as knowledge of the "substantive" and "syntactic" structures of a discipline—in this case, the discipline of mathematics.

$$
\begin{array}{r}
123 \\
\times \quad 645 \\
\hline
615 \\
492 \\
738 \\
\hline
79{,}335
\end{array}
$$

While these teachers agreed that this stacking was a problem, they did not agree on what to do about it. What would you do if you were teaching eighth grade and you noticed that several of your students were doing this? (p. 123)

This question is prototypical of many of the research tasks used in this approach to studying teachers' knowledge. Ball (1988) explains:

Since place value (and its root idea, grouping) is a fundamental mathematical idea and since pupils often find it difficult, it seemed a critical area of teachers' knowledge to investigate. I embedded place value concepts in two different interview tasks: one a classroom scenario focused on student difficulties with the multiplication algorithm, the other a structured planning–teaching–assessment exercise on subtraction with regrouping ("borrowing"). Although place value is the underlying foundation of these conventional procedures, adults can perform the procedures competently without thinking about place value at all. I wanted to examine how well the prospective teachers' adult operational knowledge of numbers equipped them to help pupils make sense of the meaning of written numerals and the meanings of these operations with them. (p. 49)

Consider what is going on inside this question. The algorithm for multiplying large numbers is derived from the process of decomposing numbers into "expanded form" and multiplying them in parts. To understand this process, one must understand decimal numerals as representations of numbers in terms of hundreds, tens, and ones—namely, that in the numeral 123, the 1 represents one *hundred,* the 2 represents two *tens,* and the 3 represents three *ones.* In this example, 123 × 645, one first multiplies 5 × 123,

$$
\begin{array}{r}
123 \\
\times \quad 5 \\
\hline
615
\end{array}
$$

then 40 × 123,

$$
\begin{array}{r}
123 \\
\times \quad 40 \\
\hline
4{,}920
\end{array}
$$

and then 600 × 123.

$$
\begin{array}{r}
123 \\
\times \quad 600 \\
\hline
73{,}800
\end{array}
$$

In the final step, one adds the results of these three products

$$
\begin{array}{r}
123 \\
\times \quad 645 \\
\hline
615 \\
4{,}920 \\
73{,}800
\end{array}
$$

In effect, one is putting the results of the parts, or steps, of the operation back together—that is, 645 × 123 = (600 × 123) + (40 × 123) + (5 × 123). Few people write their computations out this way. Most "shortcut" it by writing

$$
\begin{array}{r}
123 \\
\times \ 645 \\
\hline
615 \\
492 \\
738
\end{array}
$$

This shortcut, in effect, hides the conceptual base of the procedure. Furthermore, people can learn the shortcut without learning the conceptual foundation of the procedure. This procedure, which depends conceptually on place value and the distributive property, is thus a strategic site for exploring knowledge of place value.

The teachers in Ball's study (1988, 1990a) explained the algorithm, particularly the need to begin the second partial product in the tens place rather than the ones place, using language such as "lining it up correctly," "moving the numbers over," "adding a zero," and "using zero as a place holder." In some cases, the preservice teachers clearly had only partial or incomplete understanding of the role of place value in multiplication. In other cases, it was less clear whether they lacked understanding or whether they lacked the ability to make that understanding explicit for the interviewer.

Using this same task, Ball studied practicing teachers and obtained similar results. Later, Ma (1999) reanalyzed these same data and reported that the teachers tended to give "pseudo-explanations" for the algorithm, using much of the same language as the preservice teachers in Ball's (1988) study. For example, teachers spoke of the "tens place" or the "hundreds place" but were referring primarily to the location of digits, not to the essential features of place *value.* Some of the teachers even used nonmathematical symbols, such as asterisks, for place-holders in the algorithm. When Ma used this same question with 72 Chinese teachers, however, she found that they provided explanations of the multiplication algorithm that used the distributive property to explain the role of place value in the partial products. Using the same questions, Ma's interviews produced portraits of teacher knowledge that were distinctly different from those revealed in many of the previous studies.

Studies of secondary teachers revealed, to some people's surprise, that these teachers' knowledge was much thinner and less robust than most assumed, despite the fact that they—unlike their elementary counterparts—usually major in mathematics. Indeed, in studies at several major universities, mathematics majors stumbled over similar concepts and had difficulty justifying similar procedures and solutions as did elementary teachers (e.g., Ball, 1988, 1990a; Ball & Wilson, 1990; Steinberg, Haymore, & Marks, 1985). Studies comparing the mathematical knowledge of prospective elementary and secondary teachers show that secondary teachers' conceptual knowledge of elementary mathematics is not significantly stronger than that of their elementary counterparts.

In particular, Ball (1991b) compared the mathematical knowledge of preservice elementary education majors and preservice secondary mathematics education majors using the multiplication problem noted above. Although the mathematics majors were more successful at obtaining correct answers than the elementary majors, they were not adept at explaining the reasons behind the rules they invoked, and their knowledge was not connected across various contexts. Thus, Ball concluded that although the secondary preservice teachers who were mathematics majors had successfully completed a number of advanced mathematics courses, this academic preparation did not provide them with "the opportunity to revisit or extend their understandings of arithmetic, algebra, or geometry, the subjects they will be teaching" (p. 24). This finding lends further credence to the claim noted earlier that simply requiring teachers to take more mathematics classes without paying attention to the specific content of those classes is unwarranted.

DIVISION

Research on teachers' knowledge of division has revealed that teachers use a predominantly partitive (sharing) conception of division (Ball, 1990a, 1990b; Graeber, Tirosh, & Glover, 1989; Simon, 1993; Tirosh & Graeber, 1990). Because those teachers did not tend to use the quotitive (measurement) interpretation of division, they often were not able to reason through problems involving division by zero, division of fractions and decimals, or dividing a smaller number by a larger number. For example, Simon (1993) posed the following problems to 33 prospective elementary teachers:

> Write three different story problems that would be solved by dividing 51 by 4 and for which the answers would be, respectively,
> (a) 12 $\frac{3}{4}$ (b) 13   (c)12
> You should have three realistic problems. (p. 239)

> Write a story problem for which 3/4 divided by 1/4 would represent the operation used to solve the problem. (p. 240)

In the first task, 74% of the story problems generated by the prospective teachers reflected a partitive interpretation of division, and 17% of the problems reflected a quotitive interpretation. The teachers found part (b) of the task to be the most difficult, and only those who produced quotitive problems were successful in obtaining a realistic problem for which the answer would be 13. For the fraction division task, 73% of the prospective teachers gave inappropriate problems. The most common incorrect problem reflected a multiplication situation. When asked to generate a word problem involving division by a fraction, teachers across many studies provided a problem that represented a multiplication situation instead (Ball, 1990a; Ball & Wilson, 1990; Borko, Eisenhart, Brown, Underhill, Jones, & Agard, 1993; Ma, 1999). Researchers hypothesize that a teacher's tendency to rely on partitive models for division may lead to conceptual difficulty when using fractional divisors. (For a

thorough explanation of the meaning of division, particularly in the context of fractions, see Ball, 1990a.)

Few teachers (at any level) were able to convincingly explain why division by zero is undefined. In some cases, teachers were not aware that division by zero presented a significant issue. For example, Ball (1988, 1990a) found that 12 of 19 teacher candidates (elementary and secondary) relied on a memorized rule to answer and to explain the calculation 7 divided by zero. Of those 12 responses, five invoked the wrong rule, saying that 7 divided by zero was zero. Two teacher candidates could not remember a rule at all and were unable to provide an answer to the question.

Simon (1993) found that not one of the 33 prospective elementary teachers in his study was able to explain why the steps of the long division algorithm result in a correct solution. Their explanations focused on the computational aspects of the algorithm (e.g., checking to see if the number remaining is smaller than the divisor) and made no references to the iterative process of making groups of a particular size and removing a certain number of those groups.

In another study, Tirosh and Graeber (1990) found that elementary preservice teachers incorrectly applied their procedural knowledge of division of whole numbers to situations involving division of decimals. For example, the majority of participants thought that division resulted in a quotient that is smaller than the dividend, even when dividing by a decimal between zero and one. When the participants carried out the correct computational procedure and arrived at a quotient larger than the dividend, some were still inclined to rely on their previous experiences with whole numbers and to dismiss the results of the algorithm, perhaps because they lacked an understanding of the equivalence-preserving effect of moving the decimal point in the divisor and the dividend.

RATIONAL NUMBERS

Studies that focus on teachers' knowledge of rational numbers suggest that teachers are considerably less confident and less successful in the area of rational numbers than they are in the domain of whole numbers. Post et al. (1991) administered to 218 practicing middle school teachers a written survey containing both content items and pedagogical items related to rational numbers. Follow-up interviews were conducted with 15 teachers. Examples of content items included the following:

> What number is one-third of [the] way from 1/2 and 7/8? (p. 188)

> What will happen to the value of the fraction a/b if "a" is increased four times and "b" is halved? (p. 188)

> Given 9 circles of equal size, which represent 3/4 of [the total], determine [the number] of circles in 2/3 of [the] same unit. (p. 189)

> Marissa bought 0.46 of a pound of wheat flour for which she paid $0.83. How many pounds of flour could she buy for one dollar? (p. 193)

Participants were asked to solve approximately 60 of these

types of problems on the written survey. For six items, they were asked to provide thorough explanations of their thought processes and solution procedures. Some of the items also asked for an explanation of how the information could be taught to children. The interviews probed the participants' responses on both the written survey and the pedagogical items.

Post et al. (1991) found that 10–25% of the teachers struggled with basic computation with fractions. Approximately half of the teachers were unable to find a decimal from two given decimals, to find a number one-third of the way from two given fractions, to solve a simple proportion, and to solve word problems given on the National Assessment of Educational Progress tests for 13-year-old and 17-year-old students. The overall mean for the written test was between 60% and 70%. A significant number of teachers (20–30%) scored below 50% on the written instrument.

The follow-up interviews showed that even when the teachers were able to provide computationally sound solutions to problems, they were unable to provide pedagogically sound explanations for their solutions. Although the authors did not provide a detailed explanation of what they considered a pedagogically adequate explanation, they did delineate the types of responses the teachers gave in general terms. For example, in the proportional reasoning problem given above, only 10.5% of the teachers gave an adequate explanation. Many gave partial or sketchy explanations that were on the correct path, while others gave explanations that were garbled, confusing, or difficult to follow. Still others gave vague explanations or gave no explanation at all. Approximately 30% of the teachers gave only procedural explanations, and 28% gave explanations that made partial use of both procedural and conceptual explanations. Two-thirds of the teachers did not use diagrams in their explanations, and only 5% used estimation to check their answers.

Other studies showed that teachers tended to overgeneralize their knowledge of whole numbers when working in the domain of rational numbers (Tirosh, Fischbein, Graeber, & Wilson, 1999), which led to misconceptions and impoverished ideas about rational numbers. For example, Leinhardt and Smith (1985) observed classroom teachers who thought that multiplication always resulted in a product that is larger than either of the two factors (true for whole numbers but false for rational numbers). Those teachers also failed to recognize the use of the identity element for multiplication when creating equivalent fractions. Thus, in teaching their students to make equivalent fractions or to simplify fractions, they told their students that the resulting fraction was actually larger (in the case of equivalent fractions) or smaller (in the case of simplified fractions) than the original fraction.

FUNCTIONS

Functions are a fundamental topic in the secondary mathematics curriculum and are one more mathematical area that has received considerable focus in this approach to research on teachers' knowledge. Even (1993) used questionnaires and interviews to assess 162 prospective secondary teachers' understanding of functions. The prospective teachers came from eight universities and were in the final stage of their preparation pro-

grams. Those teachers thought that functions should be represented by algebraic equations and that the graphs of functions should be smooth and continuous. Although most of the participants knew that the vertical line test could be used to determine if a particular graph represents a function, most also thought that all functions must be one-to-one and onto. Few teachers seemed to understand that functions need not satisfy these properties, nor were they able to explain why it is necessary to be able to distinguish between functions and relations.

GEOMETRY AND MEASUREMENT

Several studies have used the van Hiele levels to characterize teachers' knowledge of geometry. For example, Mayberry (1983) found that more than 70% of the preservice elementary teachers in her study performed at either the recognition or the analysis van Hiele levels before instruction. Similarly, Swafford, Jones, and Thornton (1997) found that 80% of the practicing middle school teachers in their study were functioning at or below the van Hiele level of informal deduction.

A particular area of geometry and measurement that has been investigated is teachers' understanding of the relationship between area and perimeter. Such studies suggest that teachers frequently assume that there is a direct relationship between area and perimeter so that as perimeter increases, area increases also (Ball, 1988; Ball & Wilson, 1990; Baturo & Nason, 1996; Heaton, 1992; Ma, 1999). Further, teachers often do not use appropriate units when computing area and perimeter, commonly failing to use square units when reporting measures of area (Baturo & Nason, 1996; Heaton, 1992; Simon & Blume, 1994).

PROOF

A few studies have investigated teachers' knowledge of proof. The evidence from those studies suggests that teachers are prone to accept inductive evidence, such as a series of empirical examples or a pattern, as being sufficient to establish the validity of a claim (Ball & Wilson, 1990; Ma, 1999; Martin & Harel, 1989; Simon & Blume, 1996). Several researchers (Ball, 1988; Ma, 1999; National Center for Research on Teacher Learning, 1993) presented teachers with the claim that, as the perimeter of a rectangle increases, the area increases. The claim was framed as a conjecture that was developed by a student and was accompanied by drawings of two rectangles that fit the conjecture—one 4 cm long and 4 cm wide and another 8 cm long and 4 cm wide. Teachers were asked how they would respond to the student.

In Ma's (1999) analysis of this item, among 23 U.S. teachers and 72 Chinese teachers, 9% of the U.S. teachers and 8% of the Chinese teachers accepted the claim on the basis of those examples with no further verification. Another 22% of the U.S. teachers said that they would need to look in a book to determine if the claim was true and placed no burden on themselves to investigate further. More than half (56%) of the U.S. teachers wanted to see more examples to investigate the claim. Although they recognized that one example was not sufficient to establish the validity of the claim, they did not seem to realize that a finite number of examples would also be insufficient. Among the Chinese teachers who investigated the claim, either by using examples or by using the formulas for area and perimeter, 22% erroneously concluded that the student's conjecture was correct. Thirteen percent of the U.S. teachers and 69% of the Chinese teachers were able to explore the problem and produce counterexamples to show that the conjecture was false.

Many teachers seemed to have little propensity to search for alternative solutions or to verify their solutions using alternative methods (Baturo & Nason, 1996; Ma, 1999). However, Ma (1999) found that the Chinese teachers tended to provide multiple solutions to problems, often searching for more efficient and elegant solutions without external prompting.

Simon and Blume (1996) studied a group of 26 preservice elementary teachers in a mathematics content course and documented the process by which the group developed as a mathematical community. They noted tendencies on the part of the preservice teachers that were similar to those described for the groups studied by Ma. Namely, the preservice teachers were not initially inclined to question the validity of explanations offered by classmates, and they tended to accept inductive evidence as sufficient justification. Simon and Blume paint a vivid picture of the challenges and opportunities of trying to engage this group of students in mathematical arguments. In particular, they noted that each participant's knowledge of the mathematics at hand affects his or her interpretation of peers' use of justification. The preservice teachers' mathematical knowledge limited their ability to make sense of peers' arguments.

Revising Conceptions of Teacher Knowledge: Pedagogical Content Knowledge

This rapid growth of research on teacher knowledge yielded more than mountains of data on teachers' understanding of particular topics. One of the most significant contributions within this closer focus on teacher knowledge has been a powerful and convincing new conception of subject matter knowledge for teachers called "pedagogical content knowledge" (Grossman, 1990; Shulman, 1986, 1987; Wilson, Shulman, & Richert, 1987). With the introduction of *pedagogical content knowledge* to the lexicon of research on teaching and teacher education, Lee Shulman and his colleagues called attention to a special kind of teacher knowledge that linked content and pedagogy. In addition to general pedagogical knowledge and knowledge of the content, argued Shulman and his colleagues, teachers need to know things like what topics children find interesting or difficult and what the representations are that are most useful for teaching a specific content idea. Pedagogical content knowledge is a unique kind of knowledge that intertwines content with aspects of teaching and learning.

The introduction of the notion of pedagogical content knowledge brought to the fore questions about the content and nature of teachers' subject matter understanding in ways that the previous focus on teachers' course taking had not. It also led to

the crucial insight that even expert personal knowledge of mathematics often could be surprisingly inadequate for teaching. Knowing mathematics in and for teaching requires one to transcend the tacit understanding that characterizes much personal knowledge (Polanyi, 1958). It also requires a unique understanding that intertwines aspects of teaching and learning with content.

Consider our earlier example on multiplication of decimals. The teacher had to know more than how to multiply decimals correctly herself. She had to understand why the algorithm for multiplying decimals works and what might be confusing about it for students. She had to understand multiplication as iterated addition and as area, and she had to know representations for multiplication. She had to be familiar with base-ten blocks and to know how to use them to make such ideas more visible to her students. Place value and the meaning of the places in a number were at play here as well. She needed to see the connections between multiplication of whole numbers and multiplication of decimals in ways that enabled her to help her students make this extension. She also needed to recognize where the children's knowledge of multiplication of whole numbers might interfere with or obscure important aspects of multiplication of decimals. And she needed to clearly understand and articulate why the rule for placing the decimal point in the answer—that one counts the number of decimal places in the numbers being multiplied and counts over that number of places from the right—works. In addition, she needed an understanding of linear and area measurement and of how they could be used to model multiplication.[12] She even needed to anticipate that a fourth-grade student might ask why one does not do this magic when adding or subtracting decimals and to have in mind what she might say. All this represents an intertwining of content and pedagogy, or pedagogical content knowledge.

The kind of knowledge and sensibility described above highlights quintessential elements of pedagogical content knowledge. Such knowledge is not something a mathematician would have by virtue of having studied advanced mathematics. Neither would it be part of a high school social studies teacher's knowledge by virtue of having teaching experience. Rather, it is knowledge special to the teaching of mathematics. Pedagogical content knowledge—representations of particular topics and of how students tend to interpret and use them, for example, or ideas or procedures with which students often have difficulty—describes a unique subject-specific body of pedagogical knowledge that highlights the close interweaving of subject matter and pedagogy in teaching. Bundles of such knowledge are built up over time by teachers as they teach the same topics to children of certain ages and by researchers as they investigate the teaching and learning of specific mathematical ideas.

Liping Ma's (1999) work contributes to the notion of pedagogical content knowledge by describing something she calls "profound understanding of fundamental mathematics." Ma describes the "knowledge packages" that are part of the knowledge of the 72 Chinese elementary teachers whom she inter-

---

[12] This point is not a trivial one. See Simon and Blume (1994) for a detailed explanation of the conceptual complexity underlying the area model for multiplication.

viewed. Those knowledge packages constitute a refined sense of the organization and development of a set of related ideas in an arithmetic domain. The Chinese teachers whom Ma studied clearly articulated ideas about "the longitudinal process of opening up and cultivating such a field in students' minds" (Ma, 1999, p. 114). Their knowledge packages consisted of (a) key ideas that "weigh more" than other ideas in the package, (b) sequences for developing the ideas, and (c) "concept knots" that link crucially related ideas. Ma's notion of knowledge packages represents a particularly generative form of and structure for pedagogical content knowledge. Key in her notion of mathematical knowledge for teaching is a kind of culturally situated and curricular structuring of the content that readies it for teaching by identifying central ideas and their connections, as well as the longitudinal trajectories along which ideas can be effectively developed.

This approach to the study of teacher knowledge takes several important steps toward solving the problem of mathematical knowledge for teaching. First, it fills in gaps left when the focus is on only teachers' credentials. This approach probes the intricacies of mathematical knowledge to explore and identify what there is to know inside the school curriculum, inside the ideas and procedures that teachers must help others learn.

Second, the idea of pedagogical content knowledge substantially improves our understanding of the knowledge required for teaching. The concept implies that not only must teachers know content deeply, know it conceptually, and know the connections among ideas, but also must know the representations for and the common student difficulties with particular ideas. That concept makes clear that knowledge of mathematics for teaching encompasses more than what is taught and learned in conventional mathematics courses. The concept of pedagogical content knowledge helps to explain Begle's (1979) and Monk's (1994) findings that courses in mathematics methods had more effect on student performance than did typical mathematics courses. Because the curriculum of methods courses often focuses on pedagogical content knowledge, taking such courses may offer teachers the opportunity to develop this kind of knowledge.

Third, this approach to teacher knowledge has produced a constellation of new methods for probing what teachers know and, in so doing, has yielded portraits of highly developed teacher knowledge such as that contributed by Ma (1999).

However, this approach also leaves gaps in efforts to solve the problem of mathematical knowledge for teaching. One kind of gap emerges from the limits of repeatedly documenting teachers' lack of knowledge—or even, in some cases, what they do know. Such portraits do not necessarily illuminate the knowledge that is critical to good practice. What they do reveal is the content and structures of teachers' mathematical knowledge, and they help to substantiate the idea that teachers' knowledge is different from mathematicians' knowledge in some significant ways.

The second gap centers on the remaining distance between studies of teacher knowledge and of teaching itself. To understand the mathematical work of teaching would require a closer look at practice, with an eye to the mathematical understanding that is needed to carry out the work.

We turn our attention now to those gaps and to a promising approach with which we can address them in the next, and final, section of this chapter. It is the recognition of those gaps that has pressed the field toward a new approach to solving the problem of mathematical knowledge for teaching, an approach built on and extending the previous two research approaches.

Redefining the Problem: From Teachers' Mathematics Knowledge to Knowledge of Mathematics in and for Teaching

Before moving ahead, we will recapitulate the two approaches that have been dominant in research on teachers' knowledge. First, looking at teachers and their characteristics, as well as asking questions about how their qualifications relate to student learning, leaves a gap. What knowledge of mathematics do they have? What is the nature of that knowledge? Without this finer probing of the nature of teachers' knowledge, efforts to solve the problem of the mathematical knowledge that could enable better teaching and learning will run aground. Little evidence can be found to support the contributions of mathematics course work or mathematical credentials to teacher effectiveness. And even when such evidence emerges in a few cases, it is not helpful in deciding what mathematics teachers might need to learn.

A second approach to the problem, then, engages researchers in closely analyzing the nature of teachers' mathematical knowledge. However, such an analysis is still conducted at some distance from practice. Findings about what teachers know, as well as how they think about mathematics teaching and learning or about particular mathematical topics, still describe teachers and teachers' knowledge more than they describe teaching. Studying teachers, although valuable, is incomplete because results deduce teaching's mathematical demands from teachers' accounts of what they think or would do. Without our knowing whether the teachers interviewed are actually effective, however, what they report remains in some significant ways unwarranted.

The problem of the mathematical knowledge needed in and for practice remains, therefore, unsolved in significant ways. Given all the work in this area, why do we make this claim? First, many studies reveal portraits of U.S. teachers—experienced and preservice, elementary and secondary—whose fundamental understandings are shallow. On the one hand, discussions of those findings sometimes become mired in criticism and despair about the current teaching force. Observers are tempted to think that the solution is to recruit "smarter" people into teaching rather than to appreciate the subtle and complex content knowledge required for teaching (and to acknowledge the fact that most adults—not just teachers—find these subject matter questions difficult to answer). On the other hand, taking seriously the significance of the findings yields a substantial challenge: How can teachers' mathematical knowledge be developed in ways that would more closely correspond to what Ma (1999) found among Chinese teachers or would more satisfactorily "fulfill" the questions that researchers are using?

Although those questions are important and the issues are serious, no one question completely penetrates the central problems of practice. Although teaching depends on knowledge, knowing is not synonymous with teaching. Approaches that focus on teachers rather than on teaching can foreclose opportunities to examine closely the mathematical territory and demands of the work.

Consider, for example, Lampert's research on teaching (e.g., Lampert, 1986, 1989, 1990, 1992). Her writing, not about the teacher but about practice, reveals vividly the mathematical reasoning involved in choosing and using particular representations, in managing a complex classroom discussion, and in designing a problem or in figuring out how to formulate a good question. Her work shows some of the mathematics needed in teaching as well as where and how those mathematics have to be put to use.

A key distinction is worth making: whether studies of knowledge are or are not studies of knowing *in* teaching. New subtleties are added to the problem of mathematics knowledge: namely, what matters ultimately is not only what courses teachers have taken or even what they know, but also whether and how teachers are able to *use* mathematical knowledge in the course of their work.

Knowing Mathematics in Teaching

We turn first to instances in which researchers have been doing more than talking with teachers about mathematics or even about teaching and learning. Instead, researchers have been watching teachers who seek to use mathematical knowledge in the course of their work. What emerges from these observations is that being able to talk about mathematics is different from doing it.

Despite the fact that the work on teachers' knowledge has developed innovative means of probing teachers' knowledge of mathematics for teaching—through scenarios and situated examples—responding to such grounded situations is not fully equivalent to the on-line work of teaching. How it is different is only vaguely emergent, but the deeply cognitive orientation of research on teacher knowledge does not adequately take up the mathematical problem solving that teachers do as they engage in the activities of their work.

What becomes clearer across those studies is that studying what teachers know, or defining the knowledge that teachers should know, is insufficient to solving the problem of understanding the knowledge that is needed for teaching. What is missing with all the focus on teachers is a view of mathematical knowledge in the context of teaching. It is toward this aspect of the problem that the field is currently heading. A few examples help to illuminate this direction and to show what sort of new knowledge is needed.

Swafford, Jones, and Thornton (1997) report on 49 middle school teachers who completed a summer course in geometry where the work was situated in the practical situations in which they would use the mathematics. Those teachers showed significant gains in their geometry content knowledge as measured by a pretest and posttest. Among the teachers, 72% increased one van Hiele level, and more than 50% increased two van Hiele levels. Eight teachers who were selected for classroom observations and interviews during the following school year reported that they spent more time on geometry, were willing to try new

ideas, were more likely to take risks to enhance student learning, and were more confident in their abilities to elicit and respond to higher levels of geometric thinking as a result of their experience in the geometry course.

Similarly, Sowder, Philipp, Armstrong, and Schappelle (1998) describe a 2-year teacher enhancement and research project with five middle school teachers in the areas of rational numbers, quantity, and proportional reasoning. Like Swafford and her colleagues, these researchers documented increases in the teachers' content knowledge and changes in their classroom practice. Sowder et al. report that as the teachers' content knowledge increased and deepened, the teachers were more willing to try new mathematics with their students, saw their students as more capable mathematically, encouraged and expected more conceptual explanations of material, became less dependent on prescribed curricula, and tended to probe students' thinking more often. This result suggests that there may have been something that these teachers were able to do in their work with students that was shaped by their new knowledge or by the experiences that they had in the project. In addition to the teachers' changed attitudes toward the content and toward their students, growth in students' knowledge of these topics was documented with pretest and posttest data. The evidence from student data suggested that students' knowledge of fractions did increase. The authors suggest that this increase is linked to the teachers' increased content knowledge.

Getting still closer to teaching practice, studies of the Cognitively Guided Instruction program (Carpenter, Fennema, Peterson, & Carey, 1988) have encouragingly shown that teachers who know problem types for addition and subtraction, the relationship between the two operations, and common strategies used by students in solving such problems are successful in engaging students in rich discourse about mathematics and in facilitating students' constructions of multiple solutions to problems (Fennema & Franke, 1992). Two things seem important here. One has to do with what mathematical knowledge matters (classification of problem types within addition and subtraction) and the other has to do, mostly implicitly, with uses to which teachers must put such knowledge (managing productive discussions in class and helping students develop multiple solutions to problems).

Making use of mathematical knowledge in the practice of teaching is challenging. Some work has probed deeply enough to begin to illuminate that challenge. Thompson and Thompson (1994), for example, highlight the crucial role played by language. They vividly describe the situation of one teacher who, although he understood the concept of rate himself, was restricted in his capacity to express or discuss the ideas in everyday language. He was satisfied with computational language for his own purposes, but when this language did not help students understand, he was not able to find other means of expressing key ideas.

Another clear example is cogently articulated by Schram, Wilcox, Lanier, and Lappan (1988). Reporting some success in helping preservice teachers expand their conceptual understanding during the mathematics content courses, those researchers found that the preservice teachers developed a deeper understanding of many of the facts, formulas, and rules that they had previously memorized. This deeper understanding resulted from taking a course that emphasized problem solving, reasoning, discourse, group work, and the use of multiple representations. However, when researchers followed the teachers into their first year of teaching, they found that many of the preservice teachers did not attempt to work with such ideas in their own practice. The experience of the carefully developed mathematical courses in which the teachers had participated did not automatically equip them with the understanding or skill to do similar work with children. The researchers (Wilcox, Lanier, Schram, & Lappan, 1992) were led to conclude the following:

> Disciplinary study is necessary to develop in novice teachers a set of intellectual tools and a disposition to engage in mathematical inquiry themselves. But disciplinary study alone may be insufficient . . . to develop in beginning teachers the knowledge, skills, and beliefs to conceive of teaching as something other than telling or as more than a matter of technical competence. (p. 23)

This example lends further credence to the argument that a number of different types of knowledge interact when a teacher makes decisions. Although the teachers possessed some level of desirable substantive knowledge of mathematics, they lacked adequate knowledge of mathematics as a discipline, as pedagogical content knowledge or as both to enable them to teach mathematics in ways consistent with current reform efforts. Clearly, knowing mathematics for oneself is not the same as knowing how to teach it.

In one of the most astonishing—but not anomalous—cases depicting the challenges of using mathematical knowledge in teaching, Eisenhart, Borko, Underhill, Brown, Jones, and Agard (1993) describe the case of a middle school student teacher, Ms. Daniels, who was asked by a child to explain why the invert-and-multiply algorithm works. Ms. Daniels tried to create a word problem for three-fourths divided by one-half by saying that three quarters of a wall was unpainted. However, there was only enough paint to cover one-half of the unpainted area. As she drew a rectangle to represent the wall and began to illustrate the problem, she realized that something was not right. She aborted the problem and her explanation in favor of telling the children to "just use our rule for right now" (p. 198).

Despite having taken two years of calculus, a course in proof, a course in modern algebra, and four computer science courses, Ms. Daniels was unable to provide a correct representation for division of fractions. She, in fact, provided a representation—orally and pictorially—of multiplication, rather than the division, of fractions. What is important to note here and what distressed the research team is that Ms. Daniels had had opportunities to develop conceptual understanding of division of fractions, including different interpretations of division (quotitive, partitive), as well as representations of the concept. The researchers had, in fact, documented Ms. Daniels' learning about division of fractions and had interviewed her about the topic. That she had such difficulty making sense of division of fractions when she encountered it in practice was a sign of the need to redefine the problem of teacher knowledge. Researchers needed to turn from looking at teachers and their knowledge to looking more closely at teaching and to probing the mathematical entailments of practice (Ball, 1999).

In yet another case, Heaton (2000) studied her own mathematics teaching practice as she worked to change her approach. Her work offers insight into the challenges of knowing and using mathematics in context. For example, in a lesson involving composition of functions, Heaton asked her students to identify patterns they saw in tables as she hoped to help them articulate a generalization about the composition of two functions. When her students began identifying random, interesting occurrences rather than meaningful patterns, Heaton realized that she was unsure how to decide what constituted a mathematically relevant pattern and that she did not know how to use the idea of composition of functions with this problem. In reflecting on the lesson, Heaton came to realize that because she did not really understand how composition of functions was relevant to the rest of the elementary mathematics curriculum, she had no purpose or direction for her lesson or for the questions she asked during her lesson. Thus, she was unable to help children make sense of each other's ideas or to ask questions that would lead to productive discourse. Heaton's story offers a clue: knowing mathematics in practice is not simple; yet, knowing mathematics is what ultimately matters.

These examples reveal the additional—and central—problem of mathematical knowledge in use. They suggest a set of important questions for research that would enable a closer connection of knowledge and practice, the very connection that prompted work on this problem in the first place. A recent finding provides a glimpse of the important distinction between knowing how to do mathematics and knowing mathematics in ways that enable its use in practice.

In their analysis of data from the National Education Longitudinal Study of 1988, Rowan, Chiang, and Miller (1997) report strong positive correlations between teachers' responses to items that are designed to measure the use of mathematical knowledge in teaching and their students' performance.[13] Although teachers' mathematical knowledge has rarely shown any significant effects on student performance, this analysis provides some confirmation that understanding the *use* of mathematics in the work of teaching is a critical area ripe for further examination. It is not only what mathematics teachers know but also how they know it and what they are able to mobilize mathematically in the course of teaching (Cohen & Ball, in press). Although less easily quantified than other indices such as the type and number of courses taken, it is this pedagogically functional mathematical knowledge that seems to be central to effective teaching.

Ultimately, teachers must be able to know and use mathematics in practice, not merely do well in courses or answer pedagogically contextualized questions in interviews. This conclusion

---

[13] These items were developed at the National Center for Research on Teacher Learning, Michigan State University. See Kennedy, Ball, and McDiarmid (1993).

suggests the need to redefine the problem from one about *teachers* and *what teachers know* to one about *teaching and what it takes to teach*. What mathematical knowledge is actually entailed in teaching? How is it used?

What Is Mathematically Entailed by Teaching the Multiplication of Decimals?

To begin to unpack this question of practice and its mathematical demands, we return once more to our example of teaching the multiplication of decimals. We note the mathematical depth of the task and its surrounding territory of investigation. What mathematical demands are created by the enactment of this lesson? Underlying this basic procedure—the multiplication of decimals—are several critical mathematical notions: the importance of the idea of the units (often tacitly understood) that numbers carry, the transitions between linear and area representations of number, and the difference and correspondences between the area and iterated addition models for multiplication.

One demand of teaching this topic is to be able to handle the predictable questions. Why *does* the rule for placing the decimal point in the answer—that one counts the number of decimal places in the numbers being multiplied and then counts over that number of places from the right—work? Why does one not do this "magic" when adding or subtracting decimals?

Another mathematical entailment of teaching this topic is to be sure-footed in its complex substantive and representational territory. Whereas discussions of pedagogical content knowledge have made representations a central component, this small example illuminates the mathematical work of using representations in particular contexts. Using and managing the mathematical correspondences and pedagogical challenges of these geometric representations of multiplication, and of place value, requires considerable mathematical depth and flexibility. As our teacher contemplated the area representations that her students were constructing, she noticed that the rectangles were constructed with seven hundredths along the top and three hundredths along the side, and she had to think, "How did this arrangement correspond to the problem .3 × .7?" (see Figure 24.6).

When she saw that this same representation could be used to model 3 × .07 or 7 × .03, she had to make a clear distinction between numbers interpreted as products of lengths in the .3 × .7 version and as iterations of area units in the 3 × .07 or 7 × .03 version. Looking at her students' construction using the rods that represented tenths (of area units), she had to be clear with herself that they were modeling *three* times seven-tenths, a different problem. Using the representation competently requires more than knowing how to show it oneself.

In addition, our teacher was aware that the tenths could be used to model .3 × .7 by superimposing the two rectangular arrays as pictured in Figure 24.7.

Although she did not use it in this instance, this representation was part of her repertoire. Because the problem asks about multiplication of tenths, a student might try to construct a representation starting with tenths. Understanding this representation helps the teacher be prepared to discriminate between this representation and the one depicted in Figure 24.2. Like the

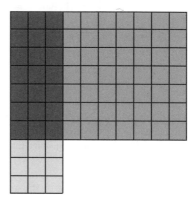

Figure 24.6. A typical arrangement of tiles to show .3 × .7.

basic area model represented in Figure 24.2, this figure shows a rectangle with sides having lengths of .7 and .3 (see dark shaded region in Figure 24.7). However, unlike Figure 24.2, which is constructed directly out of hundredths, Figure 24.7 starts with tenths, corresponding to the problem .7 × .3.

Crisscrossing the tenths affords a view of the interpretations "seven-tenths of three-tenths" and "three-tenths of seventenths." (Focusing on the three tenths, one can see the overlapped area as demarcating seven tenths of the three tenths. And focusing on the seven tenths, one can see the overlap as marking off three-tenths of the seven tenths.) This model (Figure 24.7), like the other one (Figure 24.2), affords a view of both the iterated addition interpretation (e.g., seven-tenths of three tenths), as well as the area model (e.g., constructing a rectangle with side lengths of .7 and .3).

Being able to manage the confusions into which students stumble, to keep one's mathematical bearings, to have a sense of the relationships between the multiplication of whole numbers and the multiplication of decimals, and to be skillful in putting the base-ten blocks into flexible use—each of these activities requires particular kinds of mathematical knowledge and ways of reasoning. Looking inside classroom lessons, plus developing mathematical topics over time, helps to unearth the mathematical entailments of practice.

Starting with Practice in Order to Uncover Knowledge

This redefinition of the problem of mathematical knowledge for teaching reverses the usual approaches. The other approaches begin with knowledge, or with teachers, to identify the knowledge needed to teach. Most approaches identify the mathematical knowledge that is needed for teaching by analyzing the curricula that teachers use or by interviewing teachers to learn what they know. After one has decided what teachers need to know, the problem has been to try to get teachers to know those things. When they do, another familiar problem arises: knowledge and practice are not seamlessly connected. On the one hand, teachers cannot always use what they know. On the other hand, what they know may not fully accommodate the demands of their work in context. For both of these reasons, researchers working in this third approach would begin instead with an examination of practice itself.

This approach would entail mathematical analyses of core activities of mathematics teaching. Those core activities include things such as figuring out what students know; choosing and managing representations of mathematical ideas; appraising, selecting, and modifying textbooks; deciding among alternative courses of action; and steering a productive discussion. Identifying the mathematical resources entailed by these teacher activities would be an important step in this approach.

For example, teachers design tasks. What does it take to discriminate between different possible examples of the multiplication of decimals? Consider, for example, the differences between assigning 0.2×0.5 versus 0.3×0.7 in our example. Similarly, what difference would it make for students' work if the teacher chose 2.3×3.7? Considering with precision the often subtle ramifications of different numerical parameters in a mathematical task is an example of crucial mathematical problem solving in the context of practice.

What mathematical insights does such work take? What are the mathematical ideas that it requires, and what is the nature of the reasoning entailed? Clearly, this work involves more than being able to multiply decimals oneself. Again, the focus in this definition of the problem is on teaching practice, its sites of work, and its demands, as well as on what mathematical knowledge it entails, and how it is used—not merely on what teachers do or do not know.

What mathematical work is entailed in other core activities of teaching, such as sizing up students' ideas and responding? Responding is also a complex—and not wholly generic—task. It requires being able to hear and interpret what the student is saying, and it includes being able to skillfully probe in cases where the student's idea is not clear. It may entail designing and posing a question, answering a query, or pointing out an incongruity or connection. That this is mathematical, not simply pedagogical, reasoning becomes clearer the more closely one looks. When a teacher decides to ask, "How do you know that those are hundredths?" or "Is that the only solution to this problem?" or "How would you convince someone else of what you are seeing?" then she is engaged in mathematical work, is considering the problems and ideas at hand, and is working to orchestrate more than her own thinking about the subject matter.

This approach to research on mathematical knowledge in and for teaching would also respond to the fact that teaching is a practice embedded with both regularities and endemic uncertainties. That it involves regularities gives rise to certain sorts of knowledge used to anticipate, prepare for, and manage the predictable. For example, some topics—such as arithmetic with integers, probability, and fractions—are quite often difficult for students. Certain ways of approaching these topics—particular representations and methods of development—can help medi-

ate such difficulties. Often-used mathematical tasks can be mapped by the range of typical approaches used by students of a given age (Stigler & Hiebert, 1999). Being prepared for these regularities of practice is enabled by pedagogical content knowledge, which involves bundles of understanding that combine knowledge of mathematics, of students, and of pedagogy. Pedagogical content knowledge is a special form of knowledge that bundles mathematical knowledge with knowledge of learners, learning, and pedagogy. Those bundles offer a crucial resource for teaching mathematics because they can help the teacher to anticipate what students might have trouble learning and to have ready alternative models or explanations to mediate those difficulties.

One big challenge of teaching is to integrate many kinds of knowledge in the context of particular situations. That there are patterns in and predictability to what students might think, and that there are well-tried approaches to develop certain mathematical ideas, can help researchers manage this challenge. However, possessing a body of such bundled knowledge may not always equip the teacher with the flexibility needed to manage the complexity of practice. Teachers also need to puzzle about the mathematics in an unanticipated idea or formulation proposed by a student, to analyze a textbook presentation, to decide to change the numerical parameters of a problem, to make up homework exercises, and to consider the relative value of two different representations in the face of a particular mathematical issue. These recurrent activities of teaching entail a kind of mathematical understanding that is pedagogically useful and ready, not simply bundled in advance with other considerations of students or learning or pedagogy.

Looking closely at teaching brings to the fore the nature of the work, both in planning and reflecting, as well as in the moment-to-moment work of enactment in class. An endless barrage of situations—of what can be freshly understood as mathematical problems to be solved in practice—entails an ongoing use of mathematical knowledge that is not visible until probed at the level of practice. What it takes *mathematically* to manage these both routine and nonroutine activities of practice is the focus of this third approach to understanding the relationship between mathematical knowledge and teaching. It is the need to unearth this kind of *pedagogically useful mathematical understanding* that gives rise to the need for this new work on knowledge of mathematics for teaching. Such a mathematical perspective on the work of teaching can extend what we currently understand about teachers, about the knowledge that they have and need, and about the role of such knowledge in practice. It is a timely shift from teachers to teaching that will push the field ahead in solving this central but complex problem. By making practice the focal point, researchers can bring mathematics and teaching into closer connection in ways that would be able to contribute to the improvement of teacher education, policy, and practice.

REFERENCES

American Council on Education (ACE). (1999). *To touch the future: Transforming the way teachers are taught. An action agenda for college and university presidents.* Washington, DC: American Council on Education.

Armour-Thomas, E., Clay, C., Domanico, R., Bruno, K., & Allen, B. (1989). *An outlier study of elementary and middle schools in New York City: Final report.* New York: New York City Board of Education.

Ball, D. L. (1988). *Knowledge and reasoning in mathematical pedagogy: Examining what prospective teachers bring to teacher education.* Unpublished doctoral dissertation, Michigan State University, East Lansing.

Ball, D. L. (1990a). The mathematical understandings that prospective teachers bring to teacher education. *Elementary School Journal, 90*(4), 449–466.

Ball, D. L. (1990b). Prospective elementary and secondary teachers' understandings of division. *Journal for Research in Mathematics Education, 21*(2), 132–144.

Ball, D. L. (1991a). Teaching mathematics for understanding: What do teachers need to know about subject matter? In M. Kennedy (Ed.), *Teaching academic subjects to diverse learners* (pp. 63–83). New York: Teachers College Press.

Ball, D. L. (1991b). Research on teaching mathematics: Making subject matter part of the equation. In J. Brophy (Ed.), *Advances in research on teaching* (Vol. 2, pp. 1–48). Greenwich, CT: JAI Press.

Ball, D. L. (1999). Crossing boundaries to examine the mathematics entailed in elementary teaching. In T. Lam (Ed.), *Contemporary Mathematics.* Providence, RI: American Mathematical Society.

Ball, D. L., & Bass, H. (2000). Interweaving content and pedagogy in teaching and learning to teach: Knowing and using mathematics. In J. Boaler (Ed.), *Multiple perspectives on the teaching and learning of mathematics.* Westport, CT: Ablex.

Ball, D. L., & Cohen, D. K. (1996). Reform by the book: What is—or might be—the role of curriculum materials in teacher learning and instructional reform? *Educational Researcher, 25*(9), 6–8, 14.

Ball, D. L., & Cohen, D. K. (1999). Developing practice, developing practitioners: Toward a practice-based theory of professional education. In G. Sykes & L. Darling-Hammond (Eds.), *Teaching as the learning profession: Handbook of policy and practice* (pp. 3–32). San Francisco: Jossey-Bass.

Ball, D. L., & Wilson, S. M. (1990). *Knowing the subject and learning to teach it: Becoming a mathematics teacher* (Research Report 90–7). East Lansing: Michigan State University, National Center for Research on Teacher Education.

Baturo, A., & Nason, R. (1996). Student teachers' subject matter knowledge within the domain of area measurement. *Educational Studies in Mathematics, 31,* 235–268.

Begle, E. G. (1972). *Teacher knowledge and student achievement in algebra* (SMSG Report No. 9). Palo Alto, CA: Stanford University.

Begle, E. G. (1979). *Critical variables in mathematics education: Findings from a survey of the empirical literature.* Washington, DC: Mathematical Association of America and National Council of Teachers of Mathematics.

Berman, P., & McLaughlin, M. W. (1975). *Federal programs supporting educational change: Findings in review* (Vol. 4). Santa Monica, CA: Rand.

Borko, H., Eisenhart, M., Brown, C., Underhill, R., Jones, D., & Agard, P. (1993). Learning to teach hard mathematics: Do novice teachers and their instructors give up too easily? *Journal for Research in Mathematics Education, 23,* 194–222.

Carpenter, T. P., Fennema, E., Peterson, P. L. and Carey, D. A. (1988). Teachers' pedagogical content knowledge of students' problem solving in elementary arithmetic. *Journal for Research in Mathematics Education, 19*(5), 385–401.

Cohen, D. K. (1989). Teaching practice: Plus que ça change. In P. W. Jackson (Ed.), *Contributing to educational change: Perspectives on research and practice* (pp. 27–84). Berkeley, CA: McCutchan.

Cohen, D. K. (in preparation). *Teaching practice and its predicaments.* Unpublished manuscript in preparation, University of Michigan, Ann Arbor.

Cohen, D. K., & Ball, D. L. (1999). *Instruction, capacity, and improvement* (CPRE Research Report No. RR–043). Philadelphia: University of Pennsylvania, Consortium for Policy Research in Education.

Cohen, D. K., & Ball, D. L. (in press). Making change: Toward a theory of instruction and instructional improvement. *Kappan.*

Cohen, D. K., & Hill, H. (2000). State policy and classroom performance: Mathematics reform in California. *Teachers College Record, 10*(2), 294–343.

Cohen, D. K., & Neufeld, B. (1981). The failure of high schools and the progress of education. *Daedalus, 110*(Summer), 69–89.

Collopy, R. M. B. (1999). *The educative potential of curriculum materials and their contribution to the learning of elementary mathematics teachers.* Unpublished doctoral dissertation, University of Michigan, Ann Arbor.

Conference Board of the Mathematical Sciences. (2000). *Mathematical Education of Teachers Project.* Available at <http://www/maa/org/metdraft/index.htm> (accessed April 2000).

Cuban, L. (1984). *How teachers taught: Constancy and change in American classrooms, 1890–1990.* New York: Teachers College Press.

Darling-Hammond, L. (1999). *Teacher quality and student achievement: A review of state policy evidence.* Seattle: University of Washington, Center for Teaching and Policy.

Davis, P., & Hersh, R. (1981). *The mathematical experience.* Boston: Houghton Mifflin.

Davis, R. (1986). Conceptual and procedural knowledge in mathematics: A summary analysis. In J. Hiebert (Ed.), *Conceptual and procedural knowledge: The case of mathematics* (pp. 265–300). Hillsdale, NJ: Lawrence Erlbaum Associates.

Eisenhart, M., Borko, H., Underhill, R. G., Brown, C. A., Jones, D., & Agard, P. C. (1993). Conceptual knowledge falls through the cracks: Complexities of learning to teach mathematics for understanding. *Journal for Research in Mathematics Education, 24*(1), 8–40.

Even, R. (1993). Subject-matter knowledge and pedagogical content knowledge: Prospective secondary teachers and the function concept. *Journal for Research in Mathematics Education, 24*(2), 94–116.

Farrar, E., Descantis, J., & Cohen, D. (1980). Views from below: Implementation research in education. *Teachers College Record, 82,* 77–100.

Fennema, E., & Franke, M. L. (1992). Teachers' knowledge and its impact. In D. A. Grouws (Ed.), *Handbook of research on mathematics teaching and learning* (pp. 147–164). New York: Macmillan.

Ferguson, R. F. (1991). Paying for public education: New evidence on how and why money matters. *Harvard Journal on Legislation, 28,* 465–498.

Gardner, M. (1978). *Aha! Insight.* New York: Scientific American.

Giadomenico, M., & Wildavsky, A. (1984). Implementation as evolution (1979). In J. Pressman & A. Wildavsky (Eds.), *Implementation* (3rd ed., pp. 163–180). Berkeley: University of California Press.

Goodlad, J. (1984). *A place called school: Prospects for the future.* New York: McGraw-Hill.

Graeber, A. O., Tirosh, D., & Glover, R. (1989). Preservice teachers' misconceptions in solving verbal problems in multiplication and division. *Journal for Research in Mathematics Education, 20*(1), 95–102.

Grossman, P. L. (1990). *The making of a teacher: Teacher knowledge and teacher education.* New York: Teachers College Press.

Grossman, P. L., Wilson, S. M., & Shulman, L. S. (1989). Teachers of substance: Subject matter knowledge for teaching. In M. C. Reynolds (Ed.), *Knowledge base for the beginning teacher* (pp. 23–36). New York: Pergamon.

Heaton, R. M. (1992). Who is minding the mathematics content? A case study of a fifth-grade teacher. *Elementary School Journal, 93*(2), 153–162.

Heaton, R. M. (2000). *Teaching mathematics to the new standards: Relearning the dance.* New York: Teachers College Press.

Hiebert, J., & Lefevre, P. (1986). Conceptual and procedural knowledge. In J. Hiebert (Ed.), *Conceptual and procedural knowledge: The case of mathematics* (pp. 1–27). Hillsdale, NJ: Lawrence Erlbaum Associates.

Howe, R. (1999). Knowing and teaching elementary mathematics: Review by Roger Howe. *Notices of the American Mathematical Society, 46*(8), 881–887.

Interstate New Teacher Assessment and Support Consortium (INTASC) Mathematics Subcommittee. (1993). *Model standards for beginning teacher licensing and development: A resource for state dialogue.* Washington, DC: Council for Chief State School Officers.

Jackson, P. (1986). *The practice of teaching.* New York: Teachers College Press.

Kennedy, M. (1997). *Defining optimal knowledge for teaching science and mathematics* (Research Monograph 10). Madison: University of Wisconsin, National Institute for Science Education.

Kennedy, M., Ball, D. L., & McDiarmid, D. (1993). *A study package for examining and tracking changes in teachers' knowledge* (Technical Series 93–1). East Lansing: Michigan State University, National Center for Research on Teacher Education.

Lampert, M. (1986). Knowing, doing, and teaching multiplication. *Cognition and Instruction, 3,* 305–342.

Lampert, M. (1989). Choosing and using mathematical tools in classroom discourse. In J. Brophy (Ed.), *Advances in research on teaching* (Vol. 1, pp. 223–264). Greenwich, CT: JAI Press.

Lampert, M. (1990). When the problem is not the question and the answer is not the solution: Mathematical knowing and teaching. *American Educational Research Journal, 27,* 29–63.

Lampert, M. (1992). Problems in teaching authentic mathematics. In F. Oser, D. Andreas, & J. Patry (Eds.), *Effective and responsible teaching: A new synthesis* (pp. 295–314). San Francisco: Jossey-Bass.

Leinhardt, G., & Smith, D. A. (1985). Expertise in mathematics instruction: Subject matter knowledge. *Journal of Educational Psychology, 77*(3), 247–271.

Leitzel, J. R. C. (1991). *A call for change: Recommendations for the mathematical preparation of teachers of mathematics.* Washington, DC: Mathematical Association of America.

Little, J. W. (1993). Teachers' professional development in a climate of educational reform. *Educational Evaluation and Policy Analysis, 15*(2), 129–151.

Lortie, D. (1975). *Schoolteacher: A sociological study.* Chicago: University of Chicago Press.

Ma, L. (1999). *Knowing and teaching elementary mathematics: Teachers' understanding of fundamental mathematics in China and the United States.* Hillsdale, NJ: Lawrence Erlbaum Associates.

Martin, W. G., & Harel, G. (1989). Proof frames of preservice elementary teachers. *Journal for Research in Mathematics Education, 20*(1), 41–51.

Mayberry, J. (1983). The van Hiele levels of geometric thought in undergraduate preservice teachers. *Journal for Research in Mathematics Education, 14*(1), 58–69.

McLaughlin, M. W. (1990). The Rand change agent study revisited: Macro perspectives and micro realities. *Educational Researcher, 19*(December), 11–16.

McLaughlin, M. W., & Marsh, D. D. (1978). Staff development and school change. *Teachers College Record, 80*(1), 69–94.

Monk, D. H. (1994). Subject area preparation of secondary mathematics and science teachers and student achievement. *Economics of Education Review, 13*(2), 125–145.

National Board for Professional Teaching Standards. (1991). *What teachers should know and be able to do.* Detroit: National Board of Professional Teaching Standards.

National Center for Research on Teacher Learning. (1993). *Findings on learning to teach.* East Lansing: Michigan State University, National Center for Research on Teacher Learning.

National Commission on Teaching and America's Future. (1996). *What matters most: Teaching for America's future.* New York: National Commission on Teaching and America's Future.

National Council of Teachers of Mathematics. (1991). *Professional standards for teaching mathematics.* Reston, VA: National Council of Teachers of Mathematics.

Paulos, J. (1988). *Innumeracy: Mathematical illiteracy and its consequences.* New York: Hill and Wang.

Polanyi, M. (1958). *Personal knowledge: Towards a post-critical philosophy.* Chicago: University of Chicago Press.

Post, T. R., Harel, G., Behr, M. J., & Lesh, R. (1991). Intermediate teachers' knowledge of rational number concepts. In E. Fennema, T. P. Carpenter, & S. J. Lamon (Eds.), *Integrating research on teaching and learning mathematics.* New York: State University of New York Press.

Remillard, J. T. (1999a). *Changing texts, teachers, and teaching: The role of textbooks in reform in mathematics education.* Unpublished doctoral dissertation, Michigan State University, East Lansing.

Remillard, J. T. (1999b). Curriculum materials in mathematics reform: A framework for examining teachers' curriculum development. *Curriculum Inquiry, 29*(3), 315–342.

Rickard, A. (1993). *Teachers' use of a problem-solving oriented sixth-grade mathematics unit: Two case studies.* Unpublished doctoral dissertation, Michigan State University, East Lansing.

Romberg, T. (1992). "New Math" was a failure—or was it? *UME Trends: News and Reports on Undergraduate Mathematics, 2*(6), 1, 3, 7.

Romberg, T., & Carpenter, T. (1986). Research on teaching and learning mathematics: Two disciplines of scientific inquiry. In M. Wittrock (Ed.), *Handbook of research on teaching* (3rd ed., pp. 850–873). New York: Macmillan.

Rowan, B., Chiang, F., & Miller, R. (1997). Using research on employees' performance to study the effects of teachers on students' achievement. *Sociology of Education, 70*(4), 256–284.

Sarason, S. B. (1971). *The culture of the school and the problem of change.* Boston: Allyn & Bacon.

Schmidt, W. H,, McKnight, C. C., & Raizen, S. (1997). *Splintered vision: An investigation of U.S. science and mathematics education.* Dordrecht, Netherlands: Kluwer.

Schmidt, W. H., McKnight, C. C., Valverde, G. A., Houang, R. T., & Wiley, D. E. (1997a). *Many visions, many aims: A cross-national investigation of curricular intentions in school mathematics* (Vol. 1). Dordrecht, Netherlands: Kluwer.

Schmidt, W. H., McKnight, C. C., Valverde, G. A., Houang, R. T., & Wiley, D. E. (1997b). *Many visions, many aims: A cross-national investigation of curricular intentions in school mathematics* (Vol. 2). Dordrecht, Netherlands: Kluwer.

Schram, P., Wilcox, S., Lanier, P., & Lappan, G. (1988). *Changing mathematics conceptions of preservice teachers: A content and pedagogical intervention* (Research Report 88–4). East Lansing: Michigan State University, National Center for Research on Teacher Learning.

Schwab, J. (1961/1978). *Science, curriculum, and liberal education: Selected essays.* Chicago: University of Chicago. (Original work published 1961)

Schwille, J., Porter, A., Belli, G., Floden, R., Freeman, D., Knappen, L., Kuhs, T., & Schmidt, W. (1983). Teachers as policy brokers in the content of elementary school mathematics. In L. S. Shulman & G. Sykes (Eds.), *Handbook of teaching and policy* (pp. 370–391). New York: Longman.

Shulman, L. S. (1986). Those who understand: Knowledge growth in teaching. *Educational Researcher, 15*(2), 4–14.

Shulman, L. S. (1987). Knowledge and teaching: Foundations of the new reform. *Harvard Educational Review, 57*(1), 1–22.

Simon, M. A. (1993). Prospective elementary teachers' knowledge of division. *Journal of Research in Mathematics Education, 24*(3), 233–254.

Simon, M. A., & Blume, G. W. (1994). Building and understanding multiplicative relationships: A study of prospective elementary teachers. *Journal for Research in Mathematics Education 25*(5), 472–494.

Simon, M. A., & Blume, G. W. (1996). Justification in the mathematics classroom: A study of prospective elementary teachers. *Journal of Mathematical Behavior, 15*(1), 3–31.

Skemp, R. (1978). Relational understanding and instrumental understanding. *Arithmetic Teacher, 26*(3), 9–15.

Sowder, J. T., Philipp, R. A., Armstrong, B. E., & Schappelle, B. P. (1998). *Middle-grade teachers' mathematical knowledge and its relationship to instruction: A research monograph.* New York: State University of New York Press.

Steinberg, R., Haymore, J., & Marks, R. (1985, April). *Teachers' knowledge and structuring content in mathematics.* Paper presented at the Annual Meeting of the American Educational Research Association, Chicago.

Stigler, J., & Hiebert, J. (1999). *The teaching gap: Best ideas from the world's teachers for improving education in the classroom.* New York: Free Press.

Stodolsky, S. S. (1988). *The subject matters: Classroom activity in math and social studies.* Chicago: University of Chicago Press.

Swafford, J. O., Jones, G. A., & Thornton, C. A. (1997). Increased knowledge in geometry and instructional practice. *Journal for Research in Mathematics Education, 28*(4), 467–483.

Thompson, P., & Thompson, A. (1994). Talking about rates conceptually, Part I: A teacher's struggle. *Journal for Research in Mathematics Education, 25,* 279–303.

Tirosh, D., Fischbein, E., Graeber, A. O., & Wilson, J. W. (1999). *Prospective elementary teachers' conceptions of rational numbers.* Available at <http://jwilson.coe.uga.edu/texts.folder/tirosh/pros.el.tchrs.html>.

Tirosh, D., & Graeber, A. O. (1990). Evoking cognitive conflict to explore preservice teachers' thinking about division. *Journal for Research in Mathematics Education, 21,* 98–108.

Tyack, D. B., & Cuban, L. (1995). *Tinkering toward utopia: A century of public school reform.* Cambridge, MA: Harvard University Press.

Whitehead, A. N. (1948). *An introduction to mathematics.* New York: Oxford University Press. (Original work published 1911)

Wilcox, S., Lanier, P., Schram, P., & Lappan, G. (1992). *Influencing beginning teachers' practice in mathematics education: Confronting constraints of knowledge, beliefs, and context.* (Research Report 92–1). East Lansing: Michigan State University, National Center for Research on Teacher Learning.

Wilson, S. M. (1988). *Understanding historical understanding: Subject matter knowledge and the teaching of American history.* Unpublished dissertation, Stanford University, Stanford, CA.

Wilson, S. M., Lubienski, S., & Mattson, S. (1996, April). *Where's the mathematics?: The competing commitments of professional development.* Paper presented at the annual meeting of the American Educational Research Association, New York.

Wilson, S. M., Shulman, L. S., & Richert, A. (1987). "150 different ways of knowing": Representations of knowledge in teaching. In J. Calderhead (Ed.), *Exploring teacher thinking* (pp. 104–124). Sussex, UK: Holt, Rinehart and Winston.

Wittrock, M. (1986). *Handbook of research on teaching* (3rd ed.). New York: Macmillan.

Zeichner, K., & Tabachnick, B. R. (1981). Are the effects of teacher education washed out by school experience? *Journal of Teacher Education, 32*(3), 7–11.

25.

The Revolution in Research on Science Teaching

Richard White
Monash University

To read Watson's (1963) chapter on science in the first edition of the *Handbook of Research on Teaching* is to return to a different world from the present: smaller, simpler, and far more limited. A few years after the commencement of the great surge in national curricula, Watson wrote of PSSC, BSCS, Chem Study, Nuffield, ASEP, and so forth. He commented on the scarcity of research, and criticized the few studies that had been done for their disregard of affective and psychomotor outcomes and their restriction of cognitive measures to recognition and recall. Watson cited 69 publications concerning teachers' behavior, laboratory work, learning from film and television, and programmed instruction. All of these works were published in the United States, nearly half of them in three journals: *Science Education,* the *Journal of Experimental Education,* and the *American Journal of Physics.* Watson had a limited field to draw upon: There were no European, Asian, African, Australian or South American journals dedicated to science education research, and the first volume of the *Journal of Research in Science Teaching* was a year away.

Watson's observations contrast with the present when there is enough research to support a handbook (Gabel, 1994) of 600 pages and an equally substantial *International Handbook of Science Education* (Fraser & Tobin, 1998), and there are active researchers in many countries. The change in the amount of research is sufficient alone to warrant the term *revolution,* but even more significant is its nature. When Nisbet (1974) reviewed a series of digests of research begun by Francis Curtis and covering the years from 1906 to 1957, he made a negative evaluation: "In each of the six volumes, it is possible to find much the same kind of study reported, so that a first impression from a quick glance through the series is that there has been no real development over the period" (p. 105). That conclusion does not apply to the research of the past two decades. There has

been a revolution in style. My purpose here is to consider the forces that drove this revolution, to chart its nature in detail, to look at its effect on practice, and to speculate on its future course. This purpose leads to a chapter that differs in nature from the ones on science teaching in the first three editions of the *Handbook of Research on Teaching.* The publication of the *Handbook of Research on Science Teaching* (Gabel, 1994) and the *International Handbook of Science Education* (Fraser & Tobin, 1998) remove the need for another review of that type. Instead, the chapter provides quantitative and qualitative analyses of changes in the topics and style of research since the revolution began to gather pace about 30 years ago.

Forces Impelling the Revolution

The revolution in research on science teaching is but one minor consequence of World War 2, which disrupted old ways of doing things, especially in Europe and Asia, and stimulated enormous expansion of national economies. The sharp increase in birth rates and large-scale migration that followed the war, doubling the populations of many countries, brought great changes to communities. The population rise alone would have increased the need for new schools, but the surging economies multiplied the need. New technologies and industries required a more educated workforce and opened opportunities for people to move from laboring to skilled jobs. This meant more people wanted to stay on at school, and secondary school enrollments rose even more sharply than elementary ones. Fortunately, the growing economies also provided governments with the funds to support the greater number of schools.

The massive growth in school populations and the shift to secondary education for all created new problems. The success of scientific research, evident from the war and the new indus-

The author thanks reviewers Paul Black (King's College, University of London) and Gaalen Erickson (University of British Columbia), and the many scholars who responded to his call for their views on the future of research.

tries that followed it, gave confidence that research could show how to solve social problems also. This confidence, together with greater demand and the positive economies, enabled the expansion of higher education. Between 1960 and 1993, enrollments in the third level of education per 10,000 inhabitants went up by 2.8 times in the United States, by 4 times in Australia, by 6 times in France, by 7.6 times in Canada, by 12 times in Korea, by 14 times in Peru, and by 22 times in Indonesia (UNESCO, 1971, 1995). In part, that expansion had to supply new teachers for the rapidly growing schools, so schools of education grew apace with them as did the number of researchers of education. Membership of the American Educational Research Association rose from 1,207 in 1955 to 12,191 in 1975 and to 21,777 in 1995.[1]

Both World War 2 and the new industries demonstrated the importance of science and technology, so the place of science in the curriculum was assured. The teaching of science and the research on science teaching then received specific stimulation from the Cold War and the space race associated with it. Although developments in science curricula began before Sputnik, the orbiting of that small satellite in 1957 had a powerful effect on attitudes to science. It generated much interest in science, especially physics, and produced greater support from governments for science teaching and related research than might otherwise have been given.

There has to be a time lag between the onset of forces that put researchers in place and their production of research. Once researchers are present, they can produce research for decades, if conditions permit. Among those conditions is stimulation. Whatever else they did, the Vietnam War, the student riots in Europe, the decolonization of Africa and Asia, and the rights movement in the United States stimulated individuals to action in many things, from the late 1960s through the 1970s and to the present. These have not been decades of stagnation, contentment, and apathy.

The social forces influenced a parallel intellectual development that has had consequences for research on science education. This is the move in psychology from behaviorism to cognition as the dominant model of learning. Without that shift, styles of research, now common, are unlikely to have developed, nor would research have addressed topics such as students' beliefs and conceptions of phenomena.

The revolution in research on science teaching is a worldwide phenomenon. The International Council of Associations of Science Education includes practitioners' and researchers' groups, but the fact that in 1996 it covered 135 organizations in 70 countries is an indication of the universal spread. This relates to the importance of communication as a factor in the revolution. In 1975 electronic mail did not exist, facsimile machines were rare, and although air travel was common it was not unusual for people to travel across the oceans by ship. Modern systems and the spread of English as an international language make it easy for geographically distant researchers to communicate. Interest in learners' alternative conceptions, for example, spread quickly to many countries in the mid-1980s, while a beginning 40 years earlier (Oakes, 1945) withered. An outcome that might be expected from easy communication is a greater number of studies that compare curricula, teaching, and learning in different countries. Few are evident, so there may be factors that inhibit them even more than communication permits them.

Nature of the Revolution

Revolutions become evident in a number of ways. For research, aspects of change are the questions and topics that investigations address, the style, the people who do the research, and the people who are its subjects. These aspects are related: Different questions require different methods, and new people are interested in new topics. Before considering their synthesis, however, we have to analyze each aspect separately.

Questions and Topics

Few studies are done now on cognitive preferences or advance organizers, which were popular topics 20 to 30 years ago. Which others have faded from attention, which have remained popular, and what new ones are appearing? These questions could be answered through forming a subjective impression from reading research reports, or, as in the following analysis, through a systematic and quantitative procedure. The analysis takes two forms: counting the numbers of summaries in the compilation of the Educational Resources Information Center (ERIC) that contain terms of interest, and categorizing the topics for a sample of journal articles.

COUNTS OF TERMS

The ERIC summaries include authors' names, titles of articles, year of publication, source, keywords, and abstracts. The number of summaries per year that contain the word *laboratory,* for example, is a measure of researchers' interest in laboratory work. Single year counts are possible, but in the present analysis the 30 years covered by ERIC are grouped into 5-year periods.

Any choice of the terms to count is subjective, but the choice here should be broad enough to illustrate the nature of the revolution in research.

ERIC covers all aspects of education. The counts reported here are for summaries that relate to science teaching. Each count is the number of reports in the intersection of the term with the union of teaching and education and the union of science, physics, chemistry, biology, botany, zoology, geology and earth science. Thus for the period 1966–1970, ERIC contains 62,650 reports, but only 4,887 are about teaching or education of the sciences. Of these, 521 mentioned *laboratory.*

Absolute numbers of reports mentioning *laboratory* would indicate a trend, but interpretation should take account of the total number of reports—the count for a term might rise, but at a lesser rate than the total amount of research on science education. Therefore, the absolute numbers have been converted to proportions in Table 25.1 to indicate the number of times the term appears per 10,000 reports connected with science teaching.

Table 25.1 shows that the number of reports in ERIC, both

---

[1] W. Russell, personal communication September 1996

Table 25.1. Numbers of Entries in ERIC Containing Terms per 10,000 Entries

	1966–70	1971–75	1976–80	1981–85	1986–90	1991–95
TOTAL ARTICLES	62,650	162,988	178,112	156,213	156,731	151,608
TOTAL SCIENCE ARTICLES	4,887	14,982	17,930	15,658	14,971	13,284
% SCIENCE ARTICLES	7.8	9.2	10.1	10.0	9.6	8.8
INCREASED						
action research	14	5	9	19	23	52
analogy or analogies	14	17	22	35	37	92
assessment	280	303	519	522	744	853
conceptions	14	10	23	66	83	123
conceptions or misconceptions	23	24	36	134	269	285
constructivist or constructivism	0	0	2	3	57	233
cooperative learning	0	1	5	50	140	204
critical thinking	153	59	53	73	188	196
epistemolog*	12	12	2	53	64	162
interview*	346	155	228	323	293	417
learning strategies	4	13	21	88	315	260
metacognition	0	0	1	11	33	47
metaphor*	4	7	12	23	32	71
misconceptions	8	14	13	116	226	285
peer teaching or tutoring	6	15	10	17	33	31
prior knowledge or learning	41	29	37	63	75	93
problem solving	354	317	409	541	681	761
reflection	18	19	21	19	51	81
sex or gender	266	231	399	512	511	585
teacher(s)	4,324	2,917	2,692	3,046	3,016	3,181
DECLINED						
audiotutorial	47	70	18	21	3	1
individual differences	61	29	57	68	23	20
IQ or intelligence	227	103	83	108	126	65
PEAKED						
classroom(s)	1,289	1,031	1,858	2,115	1,949	1,648
comput*	1,060	983	844	1,863	1,956	1,463
creationism	0	10	12	98	31	19
laboratory	1,066	1,326	1,154	1,019	1,058	583
Piaget*	45	77	140	84	92	55
science technology society	108	104	127	319	560	105
scientific literacy	94	58	76	142	252	209
society	518	489	523	847	1,383	824
technology	1,099	852	891	1,348	1,924	1,490
wait time	0	5	6	14	9	4
MAINTAINED						
ability or abilities	692	437	429	503	476	403
attitud*	1,107	964	888	1,036	1,063	1,234
creativity	117	63	57	80	78	74
curricul*	4,019	3,044	2,539	2,578	2,761	2,803
discovery	207	120	100	92	121	203
informal learning	10	3	4	4	11	6
inquiry	450	277	157	192	196	253
mastery	45	75	59	77	74	69
motiv*	344	268	220	264	330	319
museum(s)	96	44	51	80	72	90
questioning	98	86	66	83	72	77
values	344	321	370	326	344	346

Includes words that are extensions of the base, e.g. curricul includes curriculum, curricula, curricular

for all education and for science teaching, peaked during 1976–1980. The amount of research since the peak might have declined, or there could have been a change in ERIC procedures. It is perhaps more significant that the proportion that science teaching is of the whole also peaked at that time. Research into the cause of this would be useful.

There is no apparent reason why a procedural change by ERIC should affect one topic more than another, so the propor-

tion of the science teaching articles that mention a term should be a reasonable indication of the interest it holds for researchers. There are, however, several reasons for caution. First, the meaning or use of the term might have changed with time. Though this probably is not the case for *laboratory*, it could be for other terms such as *conceptions*. Second, a term might have gone out of fashion but be replaced by another with the same meaning. *Sex* and *gender* are such a pair. Third, the prominence of the term in the reports might have changed. References to *classrooms* in earlier reports could have been incidental, whereas in later studies classrooms may more often have been the central theme. Fourth, ERIC summaries include suggestions for practice, viewpoints and accounts of curricula that are descriptions or arguments rather than research. As Baker (1991) observed in relation to computers, there is more talk about teachers using them than actual research on their use and its effects. And finally, ERIC, though wide-ranging, does not cover all the relevant journals. It has a North American and English language bias. It does not, for instance, include the major British review journal *Studies in Science Education,* the Spanish *Ensenanza de las Ciencas,* the French *Didaskalia,* the German *Zeitschrift für Didaktik der Naturwissenschaften,* and, until 1995, the Australasian journal *Research in Science Education.* Since 1981 ERIC lists only 15 journal articles on science education in languages other than English. Despite these cautions, I take the frequency with which terms appear in ERIC as one valid indication of researchers' interest in them.

Table 25.1 shows both the overall popularity of terms and the patterns across periods. Perhaps the only surprises in the overall numbers are the high popularity of *interview* across the 30 years, and the low frequencies for *individual differences, metacognition, prior knowledge* or *prior learning,* and *questioning.* The analysis of style below suggests that *interview* may be one of the terms that has changed in prominence in reports.

Table 25.1 groups the terms into four broad patterns across periods. The greatest number of terms is in the "increasing" category. This is a consequence of the terms being chosen in 1996, when the chooser is aware of present interests but will have forgotten what was salient in past times. If this count were repeated in ten years' time, many of the terms in this category may be seen to have peaked during 1991–1995, as *creationism* did during 1981–1985 and *Piaget* did during 1976–1980.

The surge of interest in *classrooms, teachers,* and *interviews* indicates growth in concern for practice and the social dynamics of learning and, perhaps, a confidence lacking in earlier times that research on the complexities of classrooms is feasible.

Science, technology and society and *scientific literacy* rose in popularity through the 1980s, but fell away in the last five years. The social importance of these topics requires their future trends to be monitored, and the reasons behind the trends to be explored.

Interest in learning of specific content is an important feature of the revolution, evident in Table 25.1 in the incidence of *conceptions* and *misconceptions,* which increased sharply around 1980. This increase occurred in many countries, and was the focus for concentrated research programs such as the Learning in Science Project in New Zealand (Osborne & Freyberg, 1985) and the Children's Learning in Science Project in England (Driver, 1983). The ERIC system, though wide-ranging, is not fully comprehensive, especially for non-American sources, so the bibliography for research on conceptions compiled by Pfundt and Duit (1994) contains 3600 references, several times more than Table 25.1 indicates.

The simple counts in Table 25.1 do not show shifts in the nature of researchers' interest in a term. For instance, initial studies of misconceptions or, as many prefer to call them, alternative conceptions, concentrated on identification (e.g., Erickson, 1979); later studies concentrated on attempts to bring students' beliefs in line with scientists' (e.g., Hewson & Hewson, 1983); and still later ones concentrated on mapping the development of conceptions (e.g., Bliss & Ogborn, 1994). Simple counts also do not reveal connections between the terms. It can be argued that the research on alternative conceptions stimulated interest in constructivism and learning strategies. A further analysis, not attempted here, of the intersections between terms in the ERIC reports could test this hypothesis. Fensham, Gunstone, and White (1994) link constructivist theory with a theory of content and methods of teaching.

Though the absolute numbers are not great, the increase shown in Table 25.1 in the numbers of studies of learning strategies and metacognition has promise for change in classroom practice. One of the criticisms of traditional practice is that it often results in science being learned as propositions and drills that are not well understood, so that alternative conceptions persist despite teaching. Metacognition concerns purposeful and reflective learning, which should assist students to develop sophisticated conceptions. Lengthy classroom-based studies (e.g., Adey & Shayer, 1994; Baird, 1986; Baird & White, 1982) show that gains in metacognition are possible. The Project for Enhancing Effective Learning (Baird & Northfield, 1992; White & Mitchell, 1993) and the Cognitive Acceleration through Science Education project (Adey & Shayer, 1994; Shayer & Adey, 1993) are large-scale efforts to improve strategies of learning and metacognition. There should be further exploration of the relation between teaching styles, development of learning strategies, and adequacy of students' scientific conceptions.

Table 25.1 suggests other lines of research. One would be into causes of the patterns. Did interest in audiotutorials decline because there was nothing more to discover, or because this mode of teaching was seen to serve no useful purpose? What triggered the interest in alternative conceptions? Why was there a steep drop during 1991–1995 in the number of studies involving the laboratory, which up to then had attracted a stable level of interest? Another line would be on shifts in focus. Do studies on sex or gender have similar purposes across the years? How has research involving computers changed?

JOURNAL ARTICLES

Another way to study changes in questions and topics of research is to look at the themes of published articles. This examination provides a more weighted analysis than the count of words, for the latter does not discriminate between the term being the focus of a study or merely a passing reference in the abstract provided for ERIC. The journals chosen for this analysis are, from the United States, *Science Education* and the *Journal of Research in Science Teaching* (*JRST*); from Australia, *Research in Science Education* (*RISE*); and from Europe, the *International* (formerly *European*) *Journal of Science Education* (*IJSE*). They are published in English—convenient for this reviewer—provide some international spread, and are dedicated to research on science education. A new journal, *Research on Science and Technological Education,* could have been included but its relatively small number of articles would not have changed the indications from the chosen set. *Studies in*

Science Education is an important source of reviews and historical articles that provide another indication of trends but is not analyzed here. Other journals on science teaching such as *School Science and Mathematics, Journal of College Science Teaching, Physics Education, Journal of Chemical Education,* and *Journal of Biology Education* contain occasional research reports but, in the main, deal with unevaluated descriptions of practice or suggestions for curriculum development. General research journals such as the *American Educational Research Journal, Learning and Instruction,* and *Instructional Science* contain articles on science teaching, but these articles do not appear different in style from those in the chosen journals. Viglietta (1996) summarizes the functions of a number of science education journals.

Within each of the chosen journals, comparisons across the years display the ebb and flow of themes. Some, such as attitudes and laboratory work, are as common in the 1970s as they are in the 1990s, while others such as cognitive preferences disappear and the new themes of alternative conceptions, metacognition, situated cognition, technology and multimedia appear.

Method of instruction has always been a popular theme. Rowsey and Mason (1975) provide an example representative of 1975 in comparing the effects on achievement and retention of conventional lecture-laboratory teaching with those of audiotutorials in a university course in biology. As Table 25.1 shows, there was considerable interest in audiotutorials at this time. There is research of similar style in a factorial investigation by Watson and Marshall (1995) of the effects of incentives to cooperate and heterogeneous achievement groupings on achievement and interactions between students. Both studies involve the allocation of students to contrasting forms of teaching, followed by tests. Mean scores on the tests, checked for statistical significance of difference by t-test or analysis of variance or covariance, determine the relative success of the methods. Other examples of research on teaching from 1995, however, follow different styles for which there are no 1975 examples in the chosen journals such as case studies of a single teacher. Lee (1995) provides an example of a case study; she found that limited knowledge of science combined with values for control and discipline make the teacher depend on a textbook and avoid discussion and other whole-class activities. Differences in style are analyzed further in the next section.

Studies of learning overlap studies of teaching and also appear frequently across the decades. There is, however, a shift in focus within this broad topic. Piaget's stages of operational thinking dominated the 1975 research on learning and cognitive development, while most of the 1995 studies of learning are concerned with alternative conceptions, which Table 25.1 shows increased in popularity through the 1980s. Among the numerous 1995 examples that might be chosen are Demastes, Settlage and Good (1995), Galili (1995), Ginns and Watters (1995), Quilez-Pardo and Solaz-Portolés (1995), and Weller (1995). Za'rour (1975) provides a solitary example of 1975 research on alternative conceptions.

Many studies of learning and teaching and indeed all of those from the earlier period are concerned only with the form of instruction, and assume that other factors are balanced in any comparison of methods. Several 1995 studies, however, provide a fuller picture of learning environments in classrooms, through investigations of teachers' and students' perceptions of purpose of learning, interpersonal relations and patterns of power and control of behavior, balance between competition and cooperation, and so on. Examples are Dorman, Fraser, and McRobbie (1995); Fisher, Henderson, and Fraser (1995); McGinn, Roth, Boutonné, and Woszczyna (1995); and Ritchie, Tobin, and Hook (1995).

In the 1975 volumes of *JRST, Science Education,* and *RISE,* sex is a variable in several studies but is the major focus in only one, by Graybill (1975). In the third edition of the *Handbook of Research on Teaching,* White and Tisher (1986) omitted sex differences from their review of the previous decade of research on science teaching. In contrast, the *Handbook of Research on Science Teaching* has a whole chapter by Kahle and Meece (1994) on gender issues. The 1995 journals contain a number of studies of sex differences in achievement, attitudes, or engagement in science (e.g., Baker & Leary, 1995; Catsambis, 1995; Greenfield, 1995a, 1995b; Roychoudhury, Tippins, & Nichols, 1995; Seymour, 1995). Weinburgh (1995) provides a meta-analysis of research on sex differences in attitudes to science. In much of this work the focus is on girls with boys tending to be of interest only as a group for comparison. In this regard, the revolution in science education is part of a wider social movement, feminism.

A notable difference between 1975 and 1995 is in attention to epistemologies of science and teaching. This is one of the most common themes in 1995, with studies by Abrams and Wandersee (1995); Gurney (1995); Hammer (1995); Hewson, Kerby, and Cook (1995); Maor and Taylor (1995); and numerous others earlier in the 1990s including a special issue (1991, vol. 28 no. 9) of *JRST.* An important study by Lederman and Zeidler (1987) found little connection between teachers' conceptions of science and teaching behavior. This needs replication. During the 1970s, research on epistemology was less frequent and mostly involved multiple choice tests such as the Test of Understanding Science or, as in Billeh and Hasan (1975), of the researchers' own creation.

Table 25.1 reports increasing interest in analogies, metaphors and models, which is also apparent in themes of articles in each of *JRST* (Dagher, 1995; Gurney, 1995; Tobin & LaMaster, 1995; Williamson & Abraham, 1995), *Science Education* (Hafner & Stewart, 1995; review by Dagher, 1995), *RISE* (Milne & Taylor, 1995), and *IJSE* (Cosgrove, 1995; Thiele & Treagust, 1995). A special issue of *JRST* on analogies was published in December 1993.

Style

TYPES OF STUDY

Journal articles show how the style of research changed between 1975 and 1995. Style is an imprecise concept with diverse features. One feature is the degree of intervention by the researcher: a contrived intervention or merely the gathering of information; a new teaching method or a new curriculum. Some studies test a causal relation; others measure correlations. Some compare one naturally occurring group with another. In Table 25.2 the studies reported in *Science Education, JRST, RISE,* and *IJSE* in 1975, 1985, and 1995 are classed as experimental, evaluation of a curriculum, correlational, comparison of groups, descriptive, or test development. Horton et al. (1993) used a similar grouping, though with finer divisions of the experimental and descriptive categories, to analyze articles in the 1985, 1987, and 1989 issues of *JRST*. The journals also contain articles that do not report empirical research but are theoretical or argumentative viewpoints or reviews.

The most notable feature of Table 25.2 is the replacement of experiments and curriculum evaluations with descriptions (*IJSE* excepted). Descriptions include accounts of alternative conceptions and of classroom practices. This marked difference in style might be labeled as a shift from a psychological model to a historical or journalistic one. For a partial counter to the English language bias in the selection of journals, I invited Dr. Song Jinwoon to analyze reports in the 1995 volume of the *Journal of the Korean Association for Research in Science Education*. Overall, he found the proportions of the types of study to be about the same as those for the 1995 volumes of the Western journals.

TYPE OF VARIABLE

Another aspect of style is the variables in the research. Independent and dependent variables are used in experiments, evaluations of curricula, or comparisons of groups. Independent variables could include teaching method or curriculum, sex, age or educational level, ability, race, nationality or socioeconomic status. Dependent variables could include cognitive, affective, or physical. Tables 25.3 and 25.4 show the trends.

Interpretation of the trends for independent variables is complicated by the overall drop in experimental studies. Interest in comparisons of teaching methods appears to have declined more in America than in Australia or Europe. Another regional difference is in the dependent variables. Some research encompasses both cognitive and affective variables, so the numbers in Table 25.4 add to more than the actual number of studies. Though there is no clear pattern for affective variables, the American journals show a decrease in studies of cognitive variables, while the other two journals show an increase. If a more extensive analysis covering more years confirms this trend, re-

Table 25.2. Types of Research

	Science Education			JRST			RISE			IJSE	
	1975	1985	1995	1975	1985	1995	1975	1985	1995	1985	1995
Total articles	65	49	38	52	61	60	20	24	33	40	48
Experimental	16	8	5	22	20	15	4	5	4	6	11
Curriculum evaluations	2	2	2	6	0	0	4	0	1	1	2
Correlational	7	3	4	13	13	6	1	3	3	3	1
Comparison of groups	10	6	1	1	10	11	4	3	2	2	2
Descriptive	2	14	11	6	13	23	1	9	14	11	14
Test development	2	0	1	2	3	2	0	0	3	2	1
Viewpoint/review	31	15	17	2	3	4	4	5	5	15	17
Other	2	2	0	1	0	1	2	1	2	0	0

Note: Some articles were placed in more than one class.

Table 25.3. Independent Variables

	Science Education			JRST			RISE			IJSE	
	1975	1985	1995	1975	1985	1995	1975	1985	1995	1985	1995
Teaching method/curriculum	18	10	4	28	18	15	8	5	5	6	10
Sex	2	1	0	2	6	8	1	1	1	0	2
Age/educational level	2	2	1	1	3	3	2	2	2	2	1
Other	3	4	0	0	11	5	3	0	2	2	3

Table 25.4. Dependent Variables

	Science Education			JRST			RISE			IJSE	
	1975	1985	1995	1975	1985	1995	1975	1985	1995	1985	1995
Cognitive	22	17	12	37	42	21	10	12	15	14	22
Affective	10	15	6	12	20	18	8	5	8	3	6
Other	5	6	3	10	12	15	1	3	5	4	0

Table 25.5. Methods of Data Collection

	Science Education			JRST			RISE			IJSE	
	1975	1985	1995	1975	1985	1995	1975	1985	1995	1985	1995
Test or questionnaire	30	26	9	44	53	38	15	9	16	19	17
Interview	3	3	9	0	5	19	0	4	16	6	15
Observation	4	1	8	10	9	18	1	3	11	2	7
Other	1	4	4	0	1	6	0	4	4	2	6

Table 25.6. Numbers of Articles that Report Empirical Data Classified by Forms of Statistics

	Science Education			JRST			RISE			IJSE	
	1975	1985	1995	1975	1985	1995	1975	1985	1995	1985	1995
Inferential	25	17	7	46	50	27	10	6	4	9	8
Descriptive	6	11	6	1	7	11	5	9	11	13	12
None	0	6	8	3	1	21	0	4	13	2	11

search could be done to discover what lies behind it. That research would involve questioning researchers from different countries about their perceptions of what research is needed, and why they chose their current topic of study.

METHODS OF DATA COLLECTION AND ANALYSIS

Style includes the means by which data are collected: test or questionnaire (in which data often are hard to distinguish), interviews, observations, students' workbooks or drawings, or some other method (Table 25.5). There is also the way the researcher treated these data—through inferential or descriptive statistics, or no statistics at all (Table 25.6). How data are reported is another aspect of their treatment, especially the inclusion of verbatim quotes from observations of lessons or from interviews.

The main feature of Table 25.5 is the rise in the use of interviews and observations (almost always of classrooms). The American journals show decreases in the use of tests and questionnaires, though they remain the most common method of data collection. The 1995 studies use multiple methods more often than do the earlier ones, so that in many cases tests are supplemented by interviews and observations. Other methods, which Table 25.5 shows became more frequent by 1995, include students' drawings (e.g., Arnold, Sarge, & Worrall, 1995; Rennie & Jarvis, 1995; Strommen, 1995), context maps (Bloom, 1995), concept maps (Peterson & Treagust, 1995), tree graphs (Mohapatra & Parida, 1995), journal entries (Crawley & Salyer, 1995; Loughran, 1995; Pedretti & Hodson, 1995), and classroom artifacts (Demastes, Good, & Peebles, 1995). These methods provide research with a different quality of insight. In the Korean studies, tests are much more common than interviews or observations.

The increased use of interviews and observations is accompanied (except for *IJSE*) by much reporting of verbatim quotes or lesson extracts and a move away from inferential statistics.

These changes are in concert with the shift from experiments to descriptive studies shown in Table 25.2. Even when interviews were used in early research, the published reports (e.g., Hibbard & Novak, 1975) hardly ever included verbatim material. In *JRST* only one 1975 article, by Linn and Thier (1975), contains even a hint of what the participants wrote or said. In 1985, 6 of the 61 reports provide extracts, three of substantial length (Fisher, 1985; Ostlund, Gennaro, & Dobbert, 1985; Renner, Abraham, & Birnie, 1985). By 1995, the proportion has exceeded half—32 of 60 reports. Similar growth occurred in the other science journals: *Science Education* 0 (1975), 3 (1985), 14 (1995); *RISE* 1, 5, 21; *IJSE* —, 7, 23.

LENGTH

Change in style has led to a change in the nature of reports in journals. They are less formal in structure in the later years and longer. Descriptive studies and the introduction of verbatim extracts are responsible for the mean number of pages (omitting reference lists and appendices) of articles in *Science Education* increasing from 7.1 in 1975 to 15.0 in 1995, and in *JRST* from 6.9 in 1975 to 14.8 in 1995. *JRST* moved from 4 issues in 1975 to 10 in 1995, but the number of articles went up only from 52 to 60. Articles also became longer in *RISE* and *IJSE*.

REFERENCE LISTS

Change in style of research can make the increase in length of articles understandable, but it is not clear why it should be accompanied by a marked change in referencing. The mean number of references in a *Science Education* article went from 12 in 1975 to 35 in 1995; *JRST* from 12 (1975) to 39 (1995); *RISE* from 16 (1975) to 26 (1995); *IJSE* from 18 (1985) to 25 (1995). Of course by 1995 there was more to cite, but it is questionable whether there was markedly more that was relevant to the topic. No doubt it is helpful to readers to have what approaches a bibliography, but it is not clear how the author of the article benefits.

The proportion of foreign articles in reference lists is a measure of awareness of international research. For the two United States journals, the proportion of references that were published in another country increased considerably between 1975 and 1995. For *Science* Education, percentages of foreign citations were (1975) 8.6, (1985) 21.5, (1995) 24.8; for *JRST,* 7.7, 11.0, 17.0. Of course, some of this increase is due to greater numbers of foreign authors writing for *Science Education* and *JRST,* but if foreign authors are removed from the analysis, the U.S. authors still show an increasing awareness of foreign research. For U.S. authors, the percentages of foreign citations are as follows: *Science Education,* 2.8 (1975), 5.2 (1985), 10.1 (1995); *JRST* 3.0, 5.9, 6. 1. It is a matter of debate whether these values are appropriate. Authors from other countries show greater awareness of foreign work. They not only cite American publications frequently but also cite works from other countries. Percentages of the citations that foreign authors make for publications from neither the United States nor those authors' own countries are as follows: *Science Education* 15 (1975), 12 (1985), 34 (1995); *JRST* 12, 19, 21.

Many studies could be chosen to illustrate the change in style that Tables 25.2–25.6 summarize. In 1975 it was common to study the effects that two or more methods of instruction had on achievement and attitudes. This form of research was less common in 1995. The later researchers who compared teaching methods often gathered both qualitative and quantitative data. Houtz (1995) provides an example: She interviewed the teachers, principal, and consultant who took part in her study to discover which characteristics of the instructional treatments were likely to have produced the quantitative test results. Without the insights provided by the interviews, the test results would have been difficult to explain.

Baker and Leary (1995) provide another example of the concern evident in recent research to discover mechanisms behind effects. Their purpose was to find out why girls choose or do not choose to study science. Twenty or more years earlier, if this question were to be investigated at all, it most likely would have been by questionnaire. Instead, Baker and Leary interviewed 40 girls across grades 2, 5, 8, and 11 on their feelings for science, how it is taught, careers, and peer and parental support. They found that the key to the girls' attitudes was their notion of equity, which went with a preference for working in groups and a distaste for competition and hierarchical ratings of individuals. This result has direct implications for the conduct of lessons.

A researcher from an earlier period might criticize the Baker and Leary study as having too few subjects to give confidence in the conclusion. Replication is needed to counter this criticism. One or two more sets of interviews by other researchers in other contexts that found similar responses to those gathered by Baker and Leary would provide wider confidence.

Replication does not have to be identical in form. Generalization can follow from studies that, though different, produce similar insights. Seymour's (1995) ethnographic investigation of factors that contribute to undergraduates' dropping out of courses in science, mathematics and engineering supports the result of Baker and Leary that women, even more than men, prefer courses in which there is support and building of confidence.

To find out whether students' failure to develop inquiry-related thinking skills is due to their teachers' beliefs about the nature of knowledge, Maor and Taylor (1995) studied two teachers of contrasting styles. One was markedly transmissive, the other encouraged discussion. Researchers 20 years earlier most likely would have simply compared students' scores on a test of inquiry skills and ascribed any difference to teaching style. That ascription could then have been challenged as being caused by difference in competence, not style, of the teachers. Instead, Maor and Taylor began by interviewing the teachers about their epistemological beliefs, to discover the rationale each had regarding classroom style. They then observed 40 lessons of each teacher on a topic involving use of computer-based data. In the course of the participant observations the researchers looked for events that would disconfirm their assertion that "teacher epistemology mediates student-computer interactions; a constructivist pedagogy provides enhanced opportunities for the development of students' higher-level thinking skills." (p. 845). The extracts the researchers provide from interviews and lessons portray the distinct styles of the two teachers and support their assertion. In contrast with the norm of earlier times, the report includes no quantitative analysis of the lessons. This illustrates another characteristic of much recent research: The consumer has to take much on trust. Although the study has triangulation of data sources and methods of data generation, there is no independent check on the researchers' selection of observations or their interpretation of events. Of course independent checks on the quantitative experiments of the 1970s were rare, but the new style makes it even more imperative to attend to issues of acceptance of results, generalization, and criteria of quality in research. Maor and Taylor's search for disconfirming events is especially important, though as Laurence Sterne pointed out many years ago is difficult to maintain: "It is in the nature of a hypothesis, when once a man has conceived it, that it assimilates every thing to itself, as proper nourishment; and, from the first moment of your begetting it, it generally grows stronger by everything you see, hear, read, or understand" (Sterne, 1763, p. 177).

Table 25.5 shows that collection of data is one of the main differences between 1975 and 1995 in style of research. By 1995 tests had become supplemented by more intensive interactions with subjects. This change is related to a shift in the questions researchers are concerned to answer. Tests would not have helped Scruggs and Mastropieri (1995) determine how mentally retarded students coped with an inquiry-oriented, hands-on science course. Instead, the researchers observed classes for 2 years, taking field notes, making video and audio recordings, collecting products of students' work, and interviewing students.

To maintain the new style of research against criticisms of looseness and subjectivity, researchers must employ systematic procedures such as those detailed by Guba and Lincoln (1981) and Miles and Huberman (1984). Among these procedures are analyses of transcripts of interviews and lessons. Hewson et al. (1995) set out five steps for processing a transcript and an asso-

Table 25.7. Numbers of Authors Classified by Sex

	Science Education			JRST			RISE			IJSE	
	1975	1985	1995	1975	1985	1995	1975	1985	1995	1985	1995
Male	87	61	38	79	87	67	25	25	47	34	47
Female	16	19	18	12	29	48	3	9	20	16	26
Unknown	10	1	6	1	6	10	3	2	2	25	23

ciated procedure for extracting themes. Their example applies the system to interviews with teachers to reveal themes in conceptions of teaching science.

The Researchers

Table 25.7 shows that an increasing number of women are publishing research in science education. Although they do not yet make up half the number of authors, their proportion may well match the proportion of women in academic posts where research is expected. It is open to speculation and further analysis whether the increased involvement of women is related causally, in either direction, to the changes in style of research.

Some of the changes in style such as the move to descriptions of classrooms and the probing of alternative conceptions should make it easier for schoolteachers to do research. Unfortunately, the conditions under which schoolteachers work rarely provide them with the time or, perhaps more crucially, the collegial support that research requires. Doing research might not bring them professional recognition or advancement. Whatever the reasons, Table 25.8 shows that few publish research in *Science Education, JRST, RISE,* or *IJSE.* Their numbers may be disguised because they may list an affiliation to universities where they are enrolled for postgraduate degrees rather than to their schools, but it does seem that teachers continue to be the subjects rather than the authors of research. They might be publishing research accounts in journals of local science teacher associations, but the evidence from the journals analyzed here is that research is still done on teachers more often than by or with them.

The Subjects of Research

Of course, students are even more the focus of research than are teachers. In most countries the formal study of science as a separate subject begins in secondary school, so one would expect secondary school pupils to be the most common subjects of science education research. Table 25.9 shows this to be so, although for Australasia and Europe the number of studies on elementary school students increased, in the main by research on alternative conceptions.

A high proportion of studies have been conducted at the college level. For many of these, the subjects were enrolled in courses of training for elementary school teaching, presumably at the researchers' own institutions, constituting samples of convenience. In contrast, preschoolers and the general public are populations of inconvenience, hard to recruit for a study,

Table 25.8. Numbers of Articles Where an Author's Affiliation Is to a School

	1975	1985	1995
Science Education	7	4	1
JRST	3	3	3
RISE	1	1	1
IJSE	—	1	3

and so are rarely the subjects of research. This is unfortunate, because they hold information on key issues in science teaching. Research on preschoolers could reveal how early experience builds up the complex, established alternative conceptions that later inhibit assimilation of scientists' explanations. Evaluation of long-term outcomes of science teaching, especially those to do with understanding of issues in science, technology and society, or scientific literacy requires assessment of out-of-school populations.

Purposes

The changes in style evident in the tables and the illustrative examples reflect researchers' growing awareness of the complexity of interactions in teaching and learning and a consequent shift in their purposes over the years between 1975 and 1995. At the beginning of this period, most studies of teaching were evaluations of predetermined methods, developed and controlled by the researcher. Often the method of interest to the researcher was termed "experimental" and was compared with another, less favored method, which was then termed "control." Each was taken to be a representative instance of a class of similar methods. Researchers intended that teachers and curriculum designers would note their conclusions about the methods and apply them. Largely, they were disappointed. Eventually, this disappointment spurred the revolution: Researchers realized that for their studies to influence practice they must take account of the complex nature of teaching and learning. They turned to describing the complexity in order to understand it before trying to manage it.

A major element in the complexity of teaching and learning is the variation between individuals—whether students or teachers—and between situations. In 1975 researchers saw individual differences as a nuisance, increasing the spread of scores within a group and so making it more difficult to show a statistically significant difference between instructional treatments. Often in statistical tables they labeled the variance

Table 25.9. Subjects of Research

	Science Education			JRST			RISE			IJSE	
	1975	1985	1995	1975	1985	1995	1975	1985	1995	1985	1995
Preschoolers	0	1	0	4	1	0	0	0	0	1	1
Elementary School Students	6	6	2	12	6	6	2	3	6	1	7
Secondary School Students	16	16	10	19	31	22	8	13	10	19	11
College Students	11	10	6	14	16	17	5	6	10	3	14
Teachers	8	6	4	4	3	15	2	0	3	2	5
Others	0	0	1	2	2	2	0	0	0	0	0

within groups as "error." By 1995, however, individual differences were the focus of research. In 1975 the learner was considered to be wax in the hands of the experimenter; in 1995 researchers appreciated the active role learners play in forming the situation, so they turned to interviews to discover participants' beliefs, feelings, and purposes.

Piaget's studies of children's beliefs about the world alerted researchers to the importance of individual differences, and prepared the way for the research on alternative conceptions of natural phenomena that is a significant feature of the revolution. In most of the 1975 studies, the content that students were asked to learn was only a vehicle; the teaching method was the prime concern, and its interaction with the subject matter was ignored. In contrast, through the 1980s, researchers' interest in comparisons of teaching methods diminished while their interest in individuals' understanding of specific context grew. Books by Osborne and Freyberg (1985); Driver (1983); and Driver, Guesne, and Tiberghien (1985) summarized and promoted this development.

Knowledge of information processing and constructivist theories of learning spread through the 1970s. These theories provided a more useful basis than behaviorism for depicting the complexity of learning. Osborne and Wittrock (1983) and White (1988) provide accounts of their specific application to science. While researchers found that these theories accommodated to a degree their appreciation of the complex nature of teaching and learning, the theories did not illuminate the social context. To fill the gap, researchers began lengthy observations of the interpersonal dynamics occurring in science lessons.

Continuation of this interest in social context should include comparisons of societies or cultures with respect to what science content they teach, how classrooms are organized, and how students learn. These comparisons would go beyond the simple assessments made in large-scale evaluations such as the Second International Mathematics and Science Study. The reasons behind differences (or similarities) need to be discovered. Although simple assessments continued in the Third International Mathematics and Science Study, the project was expanded to collect a wider and more useful range of information, of textbooks and curriculum materials, and of questionnaires on classroom procedures completed by teachers and pupils. Schmidt et al. (1996) summarize this information, and add illustrative examples of science lessons from six countries.

Distance and differences of language and school organization make cross-national studies difficult. Even with no language barrier, there are hardly any comparisons, other than the International Mathematics and Science Studies, of science teaching outcomes between the United States, Canada, the United Kingdom, and Australia, or even between educational systems within each of these countries. The few studies that have been done are of great interest.

Mattheis et al. (1992) compared several thousand United States and Japanese high school students on logical thinking and science process skills. The Japanese students performed markedly better. Lawson (1990) discusses possible causes of the result. In another study that involved thousands of high school students, Lynch, Chipman, and Pachaury (1985a, 1985b) compared Indians and Australians on ability to recognize definitions of science concepts and on preferential thinking style. Watson, Prieto, and Dillon (1995) relate differences between English and Spanish students in their understanding of combustion to differences in styles of teaching and learning. While they found that the laboratory-based curriculum in England made students more aware of the presence of gases in combustion, the students did not use this knowledge in their explanations of combustion. There was insufficient integration of personal and teacher-given explanations, which has been commonly observed in relation to alternative conceptions.

Similarities between countries are as revealing as differences. The finding by Shipstone et al. (1988) that students from five European countries displayed the same patterns of difficulties in understanding of electricity implies that the source of alternative conceptions is independent of language and the specifics of the curriculum and derives from either general social transmission or a common developmental experience. In another example, Ogunniyi, Jegede, Ogawa, Yandila, and Oladele (1995) found that science teachers in Botswana, Indonesia, Japan, Nigeria, and the Philippines held essentially identical beliefs about the nature of reality and how people acquire knowledge of it. They speculate that this might follow from the teaching of physical science as value free, universal and independent of culture.

Black and Atkin (1996) made a subtle comparison of science education in 13 countries from Europe, North America, Asia, and Australia. Through 23 case studies of innovations in science, mathematics, and technology, the authors derive features that are important for reform in curriculum design and teaching. These features include shifts in perceptions of the aims of science and of the function of assessment, the crucial natures of communication with parents, key teachers as agents of change, and collegiality among teachers.

Other comparative studies include the finding of differences in epistemology of science between teachers from Italy and

Latin America (Ruggieri, Tarsitani, & Vicentini, 1993) and between preservice teachers from Nigeria and the United States (Cobern, 1989), the treatment of evolution in texts from China, the United States, and the former USSR (Swarts, Anderson, & Swetz, 1994), and the comparison within the United States by Baird, Prather, Finson, and Oliver (1994) of the perceptions of needs held by science teachers from rural and nonrural districts.

Within the theme of social context is the relation of the science learned in school to society and self. It includes assessments of the perception adults have of the usefulness of what they learned, and how much of it they retain. Though crucial in determining the worth of the science curriculum, evaluations of these outcomes are uncommon. In a long review of science teaching that includes a section titled "Adult Science Literacy," Walberg (1991) cites only one study of lay knowledge of science. The few results that relate to adults' knowledge of science are not encouraging: In a large survey of adults, Lucas (1987) found little difference in knowledge of key biological facts between those who had studied biology to advanced level in school and those who had not. In a less direct but equally revealing method, Eijkelhof and Millar (1988) analyzed newspaper reports of the Chernobyl nuclear power station accident to demonstrate differences between lay and expert understanding of radiation. Eijkelhof, Klaassen, Lijnse, and Scholte (1990) used a Delphi-study to obtain from radiation experts the misconceptions they encounter most freely in exchanges with lay people. Millar and Wynne (1988) argue that there should be as much concern for public understanding of the epistemology of science as for specific content. There is a need for development and trials of innovative programs that aim to increase public understanding of science. Furnham (1992) provides an extensive discussion of lay understanding.

Effect of social relations on learners is part of the theme. Research is needed on how beliefs form about appropriate classroom behavior. Some of the recent studies of single classrooms (e.g., Flick, 1995; McRobbie & Tobin, 1995; Moje, 1995; Wildy & Wallace, 1995) are a beginning. Associated with this research would be probes of beliefs about the purpose of schooling, and the reasons for learning science.

Another aspect of social context is the acquisition of foundations for conceptions of the physical world, alluded to above, which requires longitudinal studies beginning in early childhood. A longitudinal application of Piaget's cohort studies of young children would be exceptionally valuable. Longitudinal studies of any sort are rare. Arzi (1988) found only 34 examples in *Science Education, JRST, RISE,* and *IJSE* for the 25 years from 1963 to 1987. About half were concerned with learning; attitudes and teaching style followed next in popularity. Since Arzi's review, the rate of appearance in these journals of longitudinal studies has changed little. Among the few examples are the studies of secondary school students by Bliss, Morrison, and Ogborn (1988) with respect to concepts of dynamics; by Oliver and Simpson (1988) on affect and achievement; by Mulkey and Ellis (1990) on minority groups' involvement and achievement in science; by Adey and Shayer (1994) on cognitive development and achievement; by Gunstone, Gray, and Searle (1992) on awareness of conceptual change; and by Helldén (1995) on understanding among pupils ages 9–15 years of organic decomposition. Longitudinal studies of preservice science teachers are by Mason (1992) and Gunstone, Slattery, Baird, and Northfield (1993); of teachers by Constable and Long (1991); of science talent search winners by Subotnik, Duschl, and Selmon (1993); and of former Exploratorium explainers by Diamond, St. John, Cleary, and Librero (1987). Rarity is associated with difficulty, particularly of maintaining availability of subjects. Researchers need to be confident that the question instigating the research will remain of interest to the end. Some of these problems are solved for individual researchers by large national surveys such as the National Educational Longitudinal Study (e.g., Catsambis, 1995) and the Longitudinal Study of American Youth (e.g., Wang & Wildman, 1995).

While it is important to explicate the complexity of teaching and learning, it is incomplete as a research agenda. Education is interventionist: It concerns ways of changing people's beliefs, feelings, and skills. A major function of educational research is to discover how to intervene effectively. The experiments of the 1960s, for example, comparing discovery with transmissive teaching had that purpose, but because they were based on too simple a model of learning, they were premature. The next phase of the revolution could see the return of experiments as the dominant form of research, though in a more subtle and complex character than those of the earlier period.

The effects on practice of both descriptions and experiments need to be evaluated. There should be research on research. We need to know the long-term influence of research on curricula, the nature of texts, and teaching methods. The distinction evident in Table 25.8 between researchers and schoolteachers must restrict the influence research has on elementary and secondary classrooms. Of course, many researchers teach in colleges or universities, and some might also teach from time to time in schools, though published instances are rare. Among them are Featherstonhaugh (Featherstonhaugh & Treagust, 1992), Hammer (1995), Northfield (Loughran & Northfield, 1996; Northfield and Gunstone 1985), Roth (1995), and Russell (1995).What are teachers' perceptions of the value of research? What would teachers want research to do? Evaluations of teachers' awareness of research might be salutary, not in order to blame teachers for any ignorance revealed, but to improve programs of training and to discover effective means of disseminating research results.

Many parallel studies must be conducted before their cumulated results establish widely accepted principles of teaching and learning, and then it takes decades to disseminate these principles to a dispersed teaching profession. Consequently, the influence of research on practice appears indirect and slow. Evaluation of that influence therefore requires historical investigation. An outstanding early example is Layton's (1973) *Science for the People,* with more recent work by McCulloch, Jenkins, and Layton (1985) and Montgomery (1994). *Studies in Science Education* frequently publishes historical and philosophical articles. The commencement in 1992 of the journal *Science and Education* indicates growing appreciation of the importance of this research, which among other topics should address the reasons for particular reforms or curriculum movements and the factors that drive trends in research.

Throughout the revolution, most researchers in science education have been content to use new methods of investigation without pausing to debate their merits. There are exceptions. Eylon and Linn (1988) provide an extensive review of research methods in science teaching; Feldman (1994) discusses validity in action research; Muralidhar (1993) explores ways of linking diverse sources of information to provide more complete accounts of classroom events; and Brickhouse (1992) and Tobin (1992) discuss ethical issues in classroom research. In addition, editorials analyzing research methods appear in *JRST* by Krockover and Shepardson (1995) and Adams and Tillotson (1995) as do brief articles by Kyle, Abell, Roth, and Gallagher (1992) and Roth (1993) with rejoinders by Lawson (1993), Richardson (1994), and French (1995).

The relevance of debate about research methods extends beyond research itself. Shymansky and Kyle (1992) and Hurd (1993) argue that new forms of research are essential for curriculum reform. Robottom and Hart (1993) call for consideration of the relations between tacit assumptions underlying research and the professionalism of teachers and curriculum development.

Revolutions do not go on forever; sooner or later the pace of change slows. Periods of activity and change end with the conditions that stimulate and support them. Among the conditions that are positive for the revolution are the high interest people find in current research, part of which lies in relevance to practice; the opportunity the new style provides for teachers to do research; and the development of rapid and common means of communication.

Interest is subjective. Some people, probably a minority, are fascinated by complex statistics and delight in a fine analysis of covariance or a table of eigenvalues; but most people in education are interested in other people and prefer to reflect on the richness of individual differences rather than on cell means. This preference lies behind the shift, evident in Table 25.6, away from statistics and towards quotes from interviews and transcripts of lessons. Many may believe that the quotes convey more directly the life of a classroom or the thinking of an individual and so give them a better understanding than numbers do. This belief is another piece of subjectivity. Quotes and numbers both carry meaning. Revolutions must advance, or they cease to be revolutions. Synthesis of words and numbers might be the appropriate direction for this revolution. Statistics and quotes would go together, rather than be exclusive alternatives.

The conditions of teachers' work and a long period when educational research was more common in psychology laboratories than in schools made teaching one of the professions least in touch with research. The change in style has removed the second of these obstacles. Research is now needed to assess how aware teachers are of this change and to determine the factors that facilitate or inhibit their acquaintance with research and those factors that support or prevent their application of research results in their work.

For research to have a real, long-term effect on practice, it may be necessary to involve more teachers in it. For that reason, it is disappointing to find so few authors in the research journals who state affiliation with a school. There are implications here for the conditions of teachers' work, for the training of teachers, and for the formation of partnerships between teachers and academics.

Certain factors can have a negative effect, bringing the revolution to its end. An important one is the state of national economies. When economies stagnate, funds become tight in schools and universities, both state-supported and private. Class sizes rise, and innovations become less probable. The morale of teachers falls, intrusions into their classrooms become less welcome, and their energy and interest in doing research decline. Universities make fewer faculty appointments, there are fewer research students, and the supply of new researchers dries. Teaching and administrative loads increase, so the academics have less time for research. Departmental funds and individual careers become even more tightly connected to research output, so that although this appears to stimulate research, there is a negative effect on quality. Funding arrangements press academics to obtain large grants, which are used to hire research assistants. The assistants spend the time in the classrooms and gather the qualitative data predetermined by the researcher. As in the experiments of the psychology laboratory, the researcher who obtained the grant is divorced from the complexity of the classroom, and becomes a content analyst of the data instead of an observer of actual events. Excessive pressure to publish encourages poor research and limits the range of styles. Attempts to promote metacognition, detailed studies of the dynamics and social relations in a science classroom, or longitudinal studies of the development of conceptions take much time and effort; briefer, but less useful, studies may bring in as much money. The danger is not of a return to irrelevant, psychological-laboratory-style studies but of a degradation of the descriptive style that Table 25.2 shows has become popular. The descriptions could become shallow. There is a need for criteria of quality in descriptive research. There is also a need to promote conditions that allow experiments of a subtlety sufficient to capture the complexity of the teaching and learning of science. Such experiments are necessary if research is to capture the attention of teachers and administrators and to improve the quality of practice.

REFERENCES

Abrams, E., & Wandersee, J. H. (1995). How does biological knowledge grow? A study of life scientists' research practices. *Journal of Research in Science Teaching, 32,* 649–663.

Adams, P. E., & Tillotson, J. W. (1995). Why research in the service of science teacher education is needed. *Journal of Research in Science Teaching, 32,* 441–443.

Adey, P., & Shayer, M. (1994). *Really raising standards: Cognitive intervention and academic achievement.* London: Routledge.

Arnold, P., Sarge, A., & Worrall, L. (1995). Children's knowledge of the earth's shape and its gravitational field. *International Journal of Science Education, 17,* 635–641.

Arzi, H. J. (1988). From short- to long-term: Studying science education longitudinally. *Studies in Science Education, 15,* 17–53.

Baird, J. R. (1986). Improving learning through enhanced metacognition: A classroom study. *European Journal of Science Education, 8,* 263–282.

Baird, J. R., & Northfield, J. R. (Eds.). (1992). *Learning from the PEEL experience.* Melbourne: Authors.

Baird, J. R., & White, R. T. (1982). Promoting self-control of learning. *Instructional Science, 11,* 227–247.

Baird, W.-E., Prather, J. P., Finson, K. D., & Oliver, J. S. (1994). Comparison of perceptions among rural versus nonrural secondary science teachers: A multistate survey. *Science Education, 78,* 555–576.

Baker, D. R. (1991). A summary of research in science education—1989. *Science Education, 75,* 255–402.

Baker, D., & Leary, R. (1995). Letting girls speak out about science. *Journal of Research in Science Teaching, 32,* 3–27.

Billeh, V. Y., & Hasan, O. E. (1975). Factors affecting teachers' gain in understanding the nature of science. *Journal of Research in Science Teaching, 12,* 209–219.

Black, P., & Atkin, J. M. (Eds.) (1996). *Changing the subject: Innovations in science, mathematics and technology education.* London: Routledge.

Bliss, J., Morrison, I., & Ogborn, J. (1988). A longitudinal study of dynamics concepts. *International Journal of Science Education, 10,* 99–110.

Bliss, J., & Ogborn, J. (1994). Force and motion from the beginning. *Learning and Instruction, 4,* 7–25.

Bloom, J. W. (1995). Assessing and extending the scope of children's contexts of meaning: Context maps as a methodological perspective. *International Journal of Science Education, 17,* 167–187.

Brickhouse, N. W. (1992). Ethics in field-based research: Ethical principles and relational considerations. *Science Education, 76,* 93–103.

Catsambis, S. (1995). Gender, race, ethnicity, and science education in the middle grades. *Journal of Research in Science Teaching, 32,* 243–257.

Cobern, W. W. (1989). A comparative analysis of NOSS profiles on Nigerian and American preservice, secondary science teachers. *Journal of Research on Science Teaching, 26,* 533–541.

Constable, H., & Long, A. (1991). Changing science teaching: lessons for a long-term evaluation of a short in-service course. *International Journal of Science Education, 13,* 405–420.

Cosgrove, M. (1995). A study of science-in-the-making as students generate an analogy for electricity. *International Journal of Science Education, 17,* 295–310.

Crawley, F. E., & Salyer, B. A. (1995). Origins of life science teachers' beliefs underlying curriculum reform in Texas. *Science Education, 79,* 611–635.

Dagher, Z. R. (1995). Analysis of analogies used by science teachers. *Journal of Research in Science Teaching, 32,* 259–270.

Demastes, S. S., Good, R. G., & Peebles, P. (1995). Students' conceptual ecologies and the process of conceptual change in evolution. *Science Education, 79,* 637–666.

Demastes, S. S., Settlage, J., & Good, R. (1995). Students' conceptions of natural selection and its role in evolution: Cases of replication and comparison. *Journal of Research in Science Teaching, 32,* 535–550.

Diamond, J., St. John, M., Cleary, B., & Librero, D. (1987). The Exploratorium's explainer program: The long-term impacts on teenagers of teaching science to the public. *Science Education, 71,* 643–656.

Dorman, J. P., Fraser, B. J., & McRobbie, C. J. (1995). Associations between school-level environment and science classroom environment in secondary schools. *Research in Science Education, 25,* 333–351.

Driver, R. (1983). *The pupil as scientist?* Milton Keynes, UK: Open University Press.

Driver, R., Guesne, E., & Tiberghien, A. (Eds.). (1985). *Children's ideas in science.* Milton Keynes, UK: Open University Press.

Eijkelhof, H. M. C., Klaassen, C. W. J. M., Lijnse, P. L., & Scholte, R. L. J. (1990). Perceived incidence and importance of lay-ideas on ionizing radiation: Results of a Delphi-study among radiation experts. *Science Education, 74,* 183–195.

Eijkelhof, H., & Millar, R. (1988). Reading about Chernobyl: The public understanding of radiation and radioactivity. *School Science Review, 70*(251), 35–41.

Erickson, G. L. (1979). Children's conceptions of heat and temperature. *Science Education, 63,* 221–230.

Eylon, B.-S., & Linn, M. C. (1988). Learning and instruction: An examination of four research perspectives in science education. *Review of Educational Research, 58,* 251–301.

Featherstonhaugh, T., & Treagust, D. F. (1992). Students' understanding of light and its properties: Teaching to engender conceptual change. *Science Education, 76,* 653–672.

Feldman, A. (1994). Erzberger's dilemma: Validity in action research and science teachers' need to know. *Science Education, 78,* 83–101.

Fensham, P. J., Gunstone, R. F., & White, R. T. (Eds.). (1994). *The content of science: A constructivist approach to its teaching and learning.* London: Falmer Press.

Fisher, D., Henderson, D., & Fraser, B. (1995). Interpersonal behaviour in senior high school biology classes. *Research in Science Education, 25,* 125–133.

Fisher, K. M. (1985). A misconception in biology: Amino acids and translation. *Journal of Research in Science Teaching, 22,* 53–62.

Flick, L. B. (1995). Navigating a sea of ideas: Teacher and students negotiate a course toward mutual relevance. *Journal of Research in Science Teaching, 32,* 1065–1082.

Fraser, B. J., & Tobin, K. G. (Eds.) (1998). *International Handbook of Science Education,* Dordrecht, Netherlands: Kluwer.

French, M. J. (1995). Toward a mature discipline revisited. *Journal of Research in Science Teaching, 32,* 885–886.

Furnham, A. (1992). Lay understanding of science: Young people and adults' understanding of scientific concepts. *Studies in Science Education, 20,* 29–64.

Gabel, D. L. (Ed.). (1994). *Handbook of research on science teaching and learning.* New York: Macmillan.

Galili, I. (1995). Interpretation of students' understanding of the concept of weightlessness. *Research in Science Education, 25,* 51–74.

Ginns, I. S., & Watters, J. J. (1995). An analysis of scientific understandings of preservice elementary teacher education students. *Journal of Research in Science Teaching, 32,* 205–222.

Graybill, L. (1975). Sex differences in problem-solving ability. *Journal of Research in Science Teaching, 12,* 341–346.

Greenfield, T. A. (1995a). An exploration of gender participation patterns in science competitions. *Journal of Research in Science Teaching, 32,* 735–748.

Greenfield, T. A. (1995b). Sex differences in science museum exhibit attraction. *Journal of Research in Science Teaching, 32,* 925–938.

Guba, E. G., & Lincoln, Y. S. (1981). *Effective evaluation.* San Francisco: Jossey-Bass.

Gunstone, R. F., Gray, C. M. R., & Searle, P. (1992). Some long-term effects of uninformed conceptual change. *Science Education, 76,* 175–197.

Gunstone, R. F., Slattery, M., Baird, J. R., & Northfield, J. R. (1993). A case study exploration of development in preservice science teachers. *Science Education, 77,* 47–73.

Gurney, B. F. (1995). Tugboats and tennis games: Preservice conceptions of teaching and learning revealed through metaphors. *Journal of Research in Science Teaching, 32,* 569–583.

Hafner, R., & Stewart, J. (1995). Revising explanatory models to accommodate anomalous genetic phenomena: Problem solving in the "Context of Discovery". *Science Education, 79,* 111–146.

Hammer, D. (1995). Epistemological considerations in teaching introductory physics. *Science Education, 79,* 393–413.

Helldén, G. (1995). Environmental education and pupils' conceptions of matter. *Environmental Education Research, 1,* 267–277.

Hewson, M. G., & Hewson, P. W. (1983). Effect of instruction using students' prior knowledge and conceptual change strategies on science learning. *Journal of Research in Science Teaching, 20,* 731–743.

Hewson, P. W., Kerby, H. W., & Cook, P. A. (1995). Determining the conceptions of teaching science held by experienced high school science teachers. *Journal of Research in Science Teaching, 32,* 503–520.

Hibbard, K. M., & Novak, J. D. (1975). Audio-tutorial elementary school science instruction as a method for study of children's concept learning: Particulate nature of matter. *Science Education, 59,* 559–570.

Horton, P. B., McConney, A. A., Woods, A. L., Barry, K., Krout, H. L., & Doyle, B. K. (1993). A content analysis of research published in the *Journal of Research in Science Teaching* from 1985 through 1989. *Journal of Research in Science Teaching, 30,* 857–869.

Houtz, L. E. (1995). Instructional strategy change and the attitude and achievement of seventh- and eighth-grade students. *Journal of Research in Science Teaching, 32,* 629–648.

Hurd, P. D. (1993). Comment on science education research: A crisis of confidence. *Journal of Research in Science Teaching, 30,* 1009–1011.

Kahle, J. B., & Meece, J. (1994). Research on gender issues in the classroom. In D. L. Gabel (Ed.), *Handbook of research on science teaching* (pp. 542–557). New York: Macmillan.

Krockover, G. H., & Shepardson, D. P. (1995). The missing links in gender equity research. *Journal of Research in Science Teaching, 32,* 223–224.

Kyle, W. C., Abell, S. K., Roth, W.-M., & Gallagher, J. J. (1992). Toward a mature discipline of science education. *Journal of Research in Science Teaching, 29,* 1015–1018.

Lawson, A. E. (1990). Science education in Japan and the United States: Are the Japanese beating us at our own game? *Science Education, 74,* 495–501.

Lawson, A. E. (1993). Constructivism taken to the absurd: A reply to Roth. *Journal of Research in Science Teaching, 30,* 805–807.

Layton, D. (1973). *Science for the people: The origins of the school science curriculum in England.* London: Allen & Unwin.

Lederman, N. G., & Zeidler, D. L. (1987). Science teachers' conceptions of the nature of science: Do they really influence teaching behavior? *Science Education, 71,* 721–734.

Lee, O. (1995). Subject matter knowledge, classroom management, and instructional practices in middle school science classrooms. *Journal of Research in Science Teaching, 32,* 423–440.

Linn, M. C., & Thier, H. D. (1975). The effect of experiential science on development of logical thinking in children. *Journal of Research in Science Teaching, 12,* 49–62.

Loughran, J. J. (1995). Practising what I preach: Modelling reflective practice to student teachers. *Research in Science Education, 25,* 431–451.

Loughran, J. J., & Northfield, J. R. (1996). *Opening the classroom door.* London: Falmer Press.

Lucas, A. (1987). Public knowledge of biology. *Journal of Biological Education, 21,* 41–45.

Lynch, P. P., Chipman, H. H., & Pachaury, A. C. (1985a). The language of science and the high school student: The recognition of concept definitions: A comparison between Hindi speaking students in India and English speaking students in Australia. *Journal of Research in Science Teaching, 22,* 675–686.

Lynch, P. P., Chipman, H. H., & Pachaury, A. C. (1985b). The language of science and preferential thinking styles: A comparison between Hindi speaking students (in India) and English speaking students (in Tasmania). *Journal of Research in Science Teaching, 22,* 699–712.

Maor, D., & Taylor, P. C. (1995). Teacher epistemology and scientific inquiry in computerized classroom environments. *Journal of Research in Science Teaching, 32,* 839–854.

Mason, C. L. (1992). Concept mapping: A tool to develop reflective science instruction. *Science Education, 76,* 51–63.

Mattheis, F. E., Spooner, W. E., Coble, C. R., Takemura, S., Matsumoto, S., Matsumoto, K., & Yoshida, A. (1992). A study of the logical thinking skills and integrated process skills of junior high school students in North Carolina and Japan. *Science Education, 76,* 211–222.

McCulloch, G., Jenkins, E., & Layton, D. (1985). *Technological revolution? The politics of school science and technology in England and Wales since 1945.* London: Falmer Press.

McGinn, M. K., Roth, W.-M., Boutonné, S., & Woszczyna, C. (1995). The transformation of individual and collective knowledge in elementary science classrooms that are organised as knowledge-building communities. *Research in Science Education, 25,* 163–189.

McRobbie, C., & Tobin, K. (1995). Restraints to reform: The congruence of teacher and student actions in a chemistry classroom. *Journal of Research in Science Teaching, 32,* 373–385.

Miles, M. B., & Huberman, A. M. (1984). *Qualitative data analysis: A sourcebook of new methods.* Beverly Hills, CA: Sage.

Millar, R., & Wynne, B. (1988). Public understanding of science: From contents to process. *International Journal of Science Education, 10,* 388–398.

Milne, C., & Taylor, P. C. (1995). Metaphors as global markers for teachers' beliefs about the nature of science. *Research in Science Education, 25,* 39–49.

Mohapatra, J. K., & Parida, B. K. (1995). The location of alternative conceptions by a concept graph technique. *International Journal of Science Education, 17,* 663–681.

Moje, E. B. (1995). Talking about science: An interpretation of the effects of teacher talk in a high school science classroom. *Journal of Research in Science Teaching, 32,* 349–371.

Montgomery, S. L. (1994). *Minds for the making: The role of science in American education, 1750–1990.* New York: Guilford.

Mulkey, L. M., & Ellis, R. S. (1990). Social stratification and science education: A longitudinal analysis, 1981–1986, of minorities' integration into the scientific talent pool. *Journal of Research in Science Teaching, 27,* 205–217.

Muralidhar, S. (1993). The role of multiple data sources in interpretive science education research. *International Journal of Science Education, 15,* 445–455.

Nisbet, J. (1974). Fifty years of research in science education. *Studies in Science Education, 1,* 103–112.

Northfield, J., & Gunstone, R. (1985). Understanding learning at the classroom level. *Research in Science Education, 15,* 18–27.

Oakes, M. E. (1945). Explanations of natural phenomena by adults. *Science Education, 29,* 137–142, 190–201.

Ogunniyi, M. B., Jegede, O. J., Ogawa, M., Yandila, C. D., & Oladele, F. K. (1995). Nature of worldview presuppositions among science teachers in Botswana, Indonesia, Japan, Nigeria, and the Philippines. *Journal of Research in Science Teaching, 32,* 817–831.

Oliver, J. S., & Simpson, R. D. (1988). Influences of attitude toward science, achievement motivation, and science self concept on achievement in science: A longitudinal study. *Science Education, 72,* 143–155.

Osborne, R. J., & Freyberg, P. (1985). *Learning in science: The implications of children's science.* Auckland: Heinemann.

Osborne, R. J., & Wittrock, M. C. (1983). Learning science: A generative process. *Science Education, 67,* 489–508.

Ostlund, K., Gennaro, E., & Dobbert, M. (1985). A naturalistic study of children and their parents in family learning courses in science. *Journal of Research in Science Teaching, 22,* 723–741.

Pedretti, E., & Hodson, D. (1995). From rhetoric to action: Implementing STS education through action research. *Journal of Research in Science Teaching, 32,* 463–485.

Peterson, R., & Treagust, D. (1995). Developing preservice teachers' pedagogical reasoning ability. *Research in Science Education, 25,* 291–305.

Pfundt, H., & Duit, R. (1994). *Bibliography: Students' alternative frameworks and science education* (4th ed.). Kiel, Germany: Institute for Science Education, University of Kiel.

Quilez-Pardo, J., & Solaz-Portolés, J. J. (1995). Students' and teachers' misapplication of Le Chatelier's principle: Implications for the teaching of chemical equilibrium. *Journal of Research in Science Teaching, 32,* 939–957.

Renner, J. W., Abraham, M. R., & Birnie, H. H. (1985). The importance of the *form* of student acquisition of data in physics learning cycles. *Journal of Research in Science Teaching, 22,* 303–325.

Rennie, L. J., & Jarvis, T. (1995). Children's choice of drawings to communicate their ideas about technology. *Research in Science Education, 25,* 239–252.

Richardson, L. (1994). Comment: The maturity of science education research. *Journal of Research in Science Teaching, 31,* 319–320.

Ritchie, S. M., Tobin, K., & Hook, K. S. (1995). Exploring the boundaries: A study of multiple classroom learning environments. *Research in Science Education, 25,* 305–322.

Robottom, I., & Hart, P. (1993). Towards a meta-research agenda in science and environmental education. *International Journal of Science Education, 15,* 591–605.

Roth, W.-M. (1993). In the name of constructivism: Science education research and the construction of local knowledge. *Journal of Research in Science Teaching, 30,* 799–803.

Roth, W.-M. (1995). Affordances of computers in teacher-student interactions: The case of interactive physics. *Journal of Research in Science Teaching, 32,* 329–347.

Rowsey, R. E., & Mason, W. H. (1975). Immediate achievement and retention in audio-tutorial versus conventional lecture-laboratory instruction. *Journal of Research in Science Teaching, 12,* 393–397.

Roychoudhury, A., Tippins, D. J., & Nichols, S. E. (1995). Gender-inclusive science teaching: A feminist-constructivist approach. *Journal of Research in Science Teaching, 32,* 897–924.

Ruggieri, R., Tarsitani, C., & Vicentini, M. (1993). The images of science of teachers in Latin countries. *International Journal of Science Education, 15,* 383–393.

Russell, T. (1995). Returning to the physics classroom to re-think how one learns to teach physics. In T. Russell & F. Korthagen (Eds.), *Teachers who teach teachers: Reflections on teacher education* (pp. 95–109). London: Falmer Press.

Schmidt, W. H., Jorde, D., Cogan, L. S., Barrier, E., Gonzalo, I., Moser, U., Shimizu, K., Sawada, T., Valverde, G. A., McKnight, C., Prawat, R. S., Wiley, D. E., Raizen, S. A., Britton, E. D., & Wolfe, R. G. (1996). *Characterizing pedagogical flow: An investigation of mathematics and science teaching in six countries.* Dordrecht, The Netherlands: Kluwer.

Scruggs, T. E., & Mastropieri, M. A. (1995). Science and students with mental retardation: An analysis of curriculum features and learner characteristics. *Science Education, 79,* 251–271.

Seymour, E. (1995). The loss of women from science, mathematics, and engineering undergraduate majors: An explanatory account. *Science Education, 79,* 437–473.

Shayer, M., & Adey, P. S. (1993). Accelerating the development of formal thinking in middle and high school students IV: Three years after a two-year intervention. *Journal of Research in Science Teaching, 30,* 351–366.

Shipstone, D. M., von Rhöneck, C., Jung, W., Kärrqvist, C., Dupin, J.-J., Johsua, S., & Licht, P. (1988). A study of students' understanding of electricity in five European countries. *International Journal of Science Education, 10,* 303–316.

Shymansky, J. A., & Kyle, W. C. (1992). Establishing a research agenda: Critical issues of science curriculum reform. *Journal of Research in Science Teaching, 29,* 749–778.

Sterne, L. (1763). *The life and opinions of Tristram Shandy, gentleman* (5th ed., Vol. 2). London: R. & J. Dodsley.

Strommen, E. (1995). Lions and tigers and bears, Oh my! Children's conceptions of forests and their inhabitants. *Journal of Research in Science Teaching, 32,* 683–698.

Subotnik, R. F., Duschl, R. A., & Selmon, E. H. (1993). Retention and attrition of science talent: A longitudinal study of Westinghouse Science Talent Search winners. *International Journal of Science Education, 15,* 61–72.

Swarts, F. A., Anderson, O. R., & Swetz, F. J. (1994). Evolution in secondary school biology textbooks of the PRC, the USA, and the latter stages of the USSR. *Journal of Research in Science Teaching, 31,* 475–505.

Thiele, R. B., & Treagust, D. F. (1995). Analogies in chemistry textbooks. *International Journal of Science Education, 17,* 783–795.

Tobin, K. (1992). Ethical concerns and research in science classrooms: Resolved and unresolved dilemmas. *Science Education, 76,* 105–117.

Tobin, K., & LaMaster, S. U. (1995). Relationships between metaphors, beliefs, and actions in a context of science curriculum change. *Journal of Research in Science Teaching, 32,* 225–242.

UNESCO (1971). *Statistical yearbook 1970.* Paris: UNESCO Publishing & Bernan Press.

UNESCO (1995). *Statistical yearbook 1995.* Paris: UNESCO Publishing & Bernan Press.

Viglietta, L. (1996). Science education journals: From theory to practice. *Science Education, 80,* 367–394.

Walberg, H. J. (1991). Improving school science in advanced and developing countries. *Review of Educational Research, 61,* 25–69.

Wang, J., & Wildman, L. (1995). An empirical examination of the effects of family commitment in education on student achievement in seventh grade science. *Journal of Research in Science Teaching, 32,* 833–837.

Watson, F. G. (1963). Research on teaching science. In N. L. Gage (Ed.), *Handbook of research on teaching* (pp. 1031–1059). Chicago: Rand McNally.

Watson, R., Prieto, T., & Dillon, J. S. (1995). The effect of practical work on students' understanding of combustion. *Journal of Research in Science Teaching, 32,* 487–502.

Watson, S. B., & Marshall, J. E. (1995). Effects of cooperative incentives and heterogeneous arrangement on achievement and interaction of cooperative learning groups in a college life science course. *Journal of Research in Science Teaching, 32,* 291–299.

Weinburgh, M. (1995). Gender differences in student attitudes toward science: A meta-analysis of the literature from 1970 to 1991. *Journal of Research in Science Teaching, 32,* 387–398.

Weller, H. G. (1995). Diagnosing and altering three Aristotelian alternative conceptions in dynamics: Microcomputer simulations of scientific models. *Journal of Research in Science Teaching, 32,* 271–290.

White, R. T. (1988). *Learning science.* Oxford: Blackwell.

White, R. T., & Mitchell, I. J. (1993, September). *The promotion of good learning behaviours.* Paper given at the conference of the European Association for Research on Learning and Instruction, Aix-en-Provence.

White, R. T., & Tisher, R. P. (1986). Research on natural sciences. In M. C. Wittrock (Ed.), *Handbook of research on teaching* (3rd ed., pp. 874–905). New York: Macmillan.

Wildy, H., & Wallace, J. (1995). Understanding teaching or teaching for understanding: Alternative frameworks for science classrooms. *Journal of Research in Science Teaching, 32,* 143–156.

Williamson, V. M., & Abraham, M. R. (1995). The effects of computer animation on the particulate mental models of college chemistry students. *Journal of Research in Science Teaching, 32,* 521–534.

Za'rour, G. I. (1975). Science misconceptions among certain groups of students in Lebanon. *Journal of Research in Science Teaching, 12,* 385–391.

26.
School Health Education

Liane M. Summerfield

Marymount University, School of Health Professions

Education for the preservation and improvement of health has been promoted in the United States since the mid-1800s, when what we now know as health education was called hygiene and focused almost exclusively on cleanliness, good health habits, and prevention of the spread of disease. The past 30 years have been particularly significant in the metamorphosis of school health and hygiene into the discipline known today as comprehensive school health education (Gold, 1994). Health education is supported by hundreds of research studies and now has a body of terminology (Joint Committee, 1990), a credentialing process for entry-level health educators (National Commission, 1994), and national standards (Joint Committee, 1995). Today, widespread support for school health education exists among parents, school administrators, and students (Seffrin, 1994); national organizations, such as the American Medical Association (1990), Council of Chief State School Officers (1991), the National Association of State Boards of Education (National Commission, 1990), and the National School Boards Association (1991); and federal agencies concerned with health and education (U.S. Department of Education, 1991; U.S. Department of Health and Human Services, 1990). Good health is recognized to be a desirable endpoint of education as well as a quality that serves society in a variety of ways—reduced health care costs, improved productivity, and enhanced quality of life.

Yet, the teaching of health is still considered in many schools as a frill and not on a par with so-called core subjects, such as reading, math, and science. This is partly because of the nature of health and partly because of the nature of health education. Health is something that most people purport to value but are not entirely sure how to attain. Only relatively recently have people begun to think of their health as something over which they have control, although their reasons for adopting healthy behaviors may have little to do with their health. Health education, unlike other school subjects, includes material considered by some to be sensitive and controversial, is best taught through nontraditional methods, and is not effectively assessed through traditional tests. In addition, and perhaps what distinguishes it most from other core subjects, the content of health instruction is usually left up to local or district officials, rather than following a national standard, and parents may opt their children out of all or part of health instruction in most states and localities.

Research has established that health education is effective in improving students' knowledge and motivation. Less clear-cut is the capacity of school health education to have an immediate or long-term effect on health behavior. This chapter examines some of the rich body of research in school health education. Although space does not permit a thorough discussion of all aspects of health research, the author has attempted to synthesize findings from several of the major studies of comprehensive school health education and the categorical areas of tobacco, alcohol, and drug education; nutrition and cardiovascular health; sexuality education; and HIV/AIDS prevention education.

The Need for School Health Education

Health Status of Children and Youth

A number of large-scale surveys of the health knowledge, attitudes, and practices of children have been conducted and have established a need and a direction for school health education. These surveys include the School Health Education Study (Sliepcevich, 1964), the National Adolescent Student Health Survey (American School Health Association, 1989), the Centers for Disease Control and Prevention's (CDC) Youth Risk Behavior Surveillance System (YRBSS) (Kann et al., 1995), and the National Children and Youth Fitness Study (Ross, Delpy, Christenson, Gold, & Damberg, 1987; Ross, Pate, Delpy, Gold, & Svilar, 1987). These surveys point to a pressing need for early and sustained school health education.

Despite the fact that 90% of U.S. children are born healthy

The author wishes to thank reviewers Lawrence F. Locke (University of Massachusetts) and James McKenzie (Ball State University).

and enter school healthy, by adolescence, and largely because of choices made by the child or caregiver, perhaps as many as one half of 10- to 17-year-olds are at moderate to high risk of health problems (Dryfoos, 1990; Seffrin, 1990). Almost 50% of 9th- through 12th-graders consume alcohol regularly, 33% smoke cigarettes, 18% use marijuana, and almost 40% are currently sexually active (Kann et al., 1995). Between 5% and 20% of children and young adults have cardiovascular risk factors (Berenson, Arbeit, Hunter, Johnson, & Nicklas, 1991), the prevalence of being overweight among 6- to 17-year-olds in the United States has more than doubled in the past 30 years, and approximately 11% of children are seriously overweight (Centers for Disease Control and Prevention, 1996). Thus, the CDC considers the most significant contributors to morbidity in children and youth to be alcohol and other drug abuse, smoking, sexual behaviors leading to unintended pregnancy and sexually transmitted diseases, and poor diet and exercise habits.

Exposure to health risks starts early. The average ages for initial experimentation with alcohol and marijuana are 12.9 years and 13.9 years respectively (Public Health Service, 1994a), and the majority of adolescents who initiate smoking do so between Grades 6 and 9 (Perry, Kelder, Murray, & Klepp, 1992). The average age at initial intercourse is 16 for males and 17 for females (Haffner, 1995), although 33% of 14- to 15-year-olds has had sexual intercourse (Adams, Schoenborn, Moss, Warren, & Kann, 1995), and approximately 12.5% of 13- to 19-year-olds contracts a sexually transmitted disease annually (Coyle et al., 1996).

An excellent synthesis of 25 significant reports directed at the health needs of children and youth was developed by the Harvard School Health Education Project (Lavin, Shapiro, & Weill, 1992) and concluded that (a) education and health are interrelated; (b) social morbidities (preventable health problems) are the biggest threats to health; (c) a comprehensive, integrated approach to prevention is needed; (d) the school should be the central point for health promotion and education; and (e) prevention is cost-effective.

Relationship Between Education and Health

Education plays a key role in improving children's health, and healthier children are better able to benefit from education. Available evidence suggests that poor health practices, such as sedentary lifestyle, inadequate diet, and stress, can have a severe impact on a child's school performance and cognitive development (Centers for Disease Control and Prevention, 1996; Kolbe et al., 1986). Encouragingly, a small body of evidence indicates that health instruction programs that target multiple risk behaviors may be somewhat effective in raising students' grades, preventing delinquency, or dropping out of school (Devaney, Schochet, Thornton, Fasciano, & Gavin, 1994).

In addition, school health education programs have been shown to positively affect students' health knowledge and attitudes (Connell, Turner, & Mason, 1985). Recently, several large-scale, longitudinal studies have confirmed that school health education can also change some students' health practices, and that these improved health behaviors are maintained for many years (Luepker et al., 1996; Perry et al., 1996; Ross, Gold, Lavin, Errecart, & Nelson, 1991). Comprehensive school

health education is considered to be the most effective type of health education for achieving this kind of long-term effect on children's health (Gold, 1994; Schall, 1994).

The Concept of Comprehensive School Health Education

Schools serve multiple roles in promoting the health of children. Gingiss (1997) offers a model that integrates primary, secondary, and tertiary prevention in school health education. Primary prevention, the prevention of problem behaviors before they occur, is the role of health education most typically attributed to schools. For most elementary-age children and that half of 10- to 17-year-olds who are not engaged in risky health behaviors, primary prevention is the school's principal role. For the 25% of youths who are engaged in some risky behaviors, the school may also serve a critical role in secondary prevention, which includes screening, detection, and treatment activities to prevent the further escalation of risk. An additional 25% of young people are engaged in a high level of risky health practices, and for these individuals the school may be a site for tertiary prevention, including treatment to restore health and prevent secondary complications. Tertiary prevention may also be needed for children born with diseases and conditions requiring special educational, health, social, and psychological services, such as HIV/AIDS, fetal alcohol syndrome, and addiction to drugs.

The comprehensive school health program (CSHP) is a concept that developed in recognition of the school's broad role in the promotion of health. Recognizing that the classroom by itself cannot address secondary and tertiary prevention, the CSHP includes school health services; food service; the physical and psychosocial environment; health programs for faculty and staff; counseling and psychological services; physical education; and integrated school, family, and community health promotion activities; as well as comprehensive school health education (CSHE) (Allensworth & Kolbe, 1987). CSHE is a planned, sequential program of learning experiences taught by trained staff that addresses multiple health topics for the purpose of giving children in prekindergarten through Grade 12 the knowledge and skills to maintain and improve their health (Allensworth & Kolbe, 1987; Kolbe, 1993).

National health education standards were published in 1995, describing the knowledge and skills needed to be health literate. While the standards are not content oriented, they may be applied to any health topic area, such as the 10 content areas suggested by the National Professional School Health Education Organizations (1984), or the six priority health behaviors identified by the CDC. Figure 26.1 illustrates the interrelationship between health content areas, health education standards, and health risk factors, which could serve as a model for CSHE program design.

Evaluations of Comprehensive School Health Education

The first definitive evidence on the effectiveness of school health education taught by regular classroom teachers was provided by the School Health Education Evaluation (SHEE). Conducted over 3 years in the early 1980s, SHEE assessed the effects of the School Health Curriculum Project (now known as

---

National Health Education Standards

- Students will comprehend concepts related to health promotion and disease prevention.
- Students will demonstrate the ability to access valid health information and health-promoting products and services.
- Students will demonstrate the ability to practice health-enhancing behaviors and reduce health risks.
- Students will analyze the influence of culture, media, technology, and other factors on health.
- Students will demonstrate the ability to use interpersonal communication skills to enhance health.
- Students will demonstrate the ability to use goal-setting and decision-making skills to enhance health.
- Students will demonstrate the ability to advocate for personal, family, and community health.

Health Education Content Areas	**Centers for Disease Control and Prevention: Adolescent Risk Behaviors**
Community health Consumer health Environmental health Family life Mental and emotional health Injury prevention and safety Nutrition Personal health Prevention and control of disease Substance use and abuse	Tobacco use Dietary patterns that contribute to disease Sedentary lifestyle Sexual behaviors that result in HIV infection/other STDs and unintended pregnancy Alcohol and other drug use Behaviors that result in intentional and unintentional injury

Figure 26.1. This figure represents the work of the Joint Committee on National Health Education Standards. Copies of the *National Health Education Standards: Achieving Health Literacy* can be obtained through the American School Health Association, the American Association for Health Education, or the American Cancer Society.

Growing Healthy) and three other health curricula on more than 30,000 children in 1,071 Grade 4 through 7 classrooms in 20 states (Connell et al., 1985).

Students in classrooms that received health programs showed significant gains in health knowledge, attitudes, and self-reported practices, and knowledge gains were the largest. Students required at least 40 hours of classroom instruction to demonstrate small gains in knowledge, attitudes, and practices, with gains stabilizing at 50 hours of instruction. Teacher training was critical to program success. Teachers having more hours of in-service training implemented the health education program with greater fidelity than those with fewer in-service hours did. In addition, a substudy of SHEE found teachers implementing the School Health Curriculum Project (SHCP) for the second time were able to effect even greater changes in knowledge, attitudes, and practices and to do so with fewer classroom hours (Connell & Turner, 1985). Regardless of grade level, a second substudy found a cumulative effect of health education, with students benefiting from an additional year of SHCP by

further gains in knowledge, attitudes, and practices (Connell & Turner, 1985).

Additional evidence of the effectiveness of CSHE came from the 1986 to 1989 evaluation of the Teenage Health Teaching Modules (THTM), funded by CDC (Nelson, Cross, & Kolbe, 1991). Two evaluation environments were used: a controlled, experimental setting with users who adopted THTM solely for the evaluation and a less well-controlled naturalistic setting with users who had thoroughly adopted THTM before the study. Same-school control groups in both settings did not receive health education. A total of 4,806 junior high school or middle school and high school students (54% male, 75% white) from more than 300 classrooms in seven states completed the evaluation (Ross et al., 1991).

Students who received THTM, particularly in junior high school or middle school, were more knowledgeable about health than control students (Errecart et al., 1991). THTM had little effect on attitudes of junior high school or middle school students, but, because of deterioration in health attitudes of control group senior high students, THTM-group high school students had significantly better health attitudes. Health practices significantly improved in all THTM groups, particularly self-reported smoking and use of illegal drugs, except for junior high school or middle school students in naturalistic settings.

These two large-scale studies, as well as others not discussed here (Bush et al., 1989; Walter, 1989), provide a sound rationale for CSHE. CSHE, provided by trained classroom teachers, can improve health knowledge, attitudes, and practices of children.

The Extent of Health Education in U.S. Schools

Few children receive a program of health instruction that is comprehensive or sustained enough to yield those results. Although 90% of the states require school health education, a separate health course is mandated at the elementary level by 9.8% of the states, at the middle school or junior high school level by 27.5% of the states, and at the high school level by 55% of the states (Collins et al., 1995). Rarely are required health courses more than one semester long, and 75% of schools permit student exemption from all or part of health courses, mainly because of parental request (Collins et al., 1995).

State health education requirements tend to be categorical rather than comprehensive, and specified curricular areas in which instruction is required mirror areas in which federal funding is available. For example, 72% or more of the states require instruction in HIV/AIDS prevention, alcohol and other drugs, and tobacco, whereas fewer than half require instruction in human sexuality and pregnancy prevention (Collins et al., 1995). Yet, many health behaviors are linked. Young people who practice one high-risk behavior tend to be involved in others, suggesting a rationale for a comprehensive approach. For example, use of alcohol and other drugs has been linked to increased morbidity and mortality from accidents, homicides, and suicides; to school failure; and to risky sexual behaviors (Kandel & Logan, 1984). In addition, adolescent smokers are considerably more likely than experimenters or never-smokers to have consumed alcohol recently, engaged in binge drinking, used marijuana, carried a weapon, engaged in a physical fight, or had sexual intercourse (Willard & Schoenborn, 1995).

Evaluations of Categorical Health Education Programs

Because of the prevalence of categorical health education programs, this section of the chapter reviews the most common programs: tobacco, alcohol, and drug education; nutrition and cardiovascular health; sexuality education; and HIV/AIDS prevention education. Typically, each category of program stands alone, but occasionally they are imbedded into CSHE and some target multiple health behaviors.

Tobacco, Alcohol, and Other Drug (TAOD) Prevention Education

More large-scale longitudinal studies of substance abuse prevention programs have been conducted than any other categorical health education area (Hansen, Tobler, & Graham, 1990). While most would agree that use and abuse of tobacco, alcohol, and other drugs by adolescents must be prevented,

cultural norms in this country are generally accepting of adult alcohol use and only recently somewhat discouraging of adult tobacco use. Educational messages of "no use" for adolescents conflict sharply with widespread availability, advertising, promotion, and consumption of these legal psychoactive drugs by adults.

EFFECT OF TAOD PREVENTION PROGRAMS ON CHANGING BEHAVIOR

Most substance abuse prevention research has occurred within the past 20 to 30 years, and the following four approaches to substance abuse prevention education have predominated (Botvin & Dusenbury, 1992; Bruvold, 1993; Hansen, 1992; Moskowitz, 1989):

1. Providing information about drugs and the consequences of using drugs, often using scare tactics (information approach). This approach is based on the premise that increased knowledge about TAOD will promote negative attitudes toward drugs, thereby reducing the likelihood of their use.
2. Promoting decision-making and interpersonal skills and self-esteem building, with minimal information about drugs (affective approach). The premise is that greater self-awareness and improved self-image will lead to more responsible behavior.
3. Providing opportunities for participation in youth activities that can substitute for drug use, such as volunteering and participating in adventure recreation (alternatives approach).
4. Developing resistance skills to counteract peer and media influences on drug use (social pressures, or inoculation, approach), often coupled with generic personal and social skills for problem solving, decision making, stress management, assertiveness, and enhancing self-esteem (life skills approach).

Most drug education programs developed since 1980 used several modalities (Elmquist, 1995; Hansen, 1992; Tobler, 1986), although the information approach is the most common (Perry & Kelder, 1992). With a few notable exceptions, particularly tobacco programs, most TAOD prevention education programs have been ineffective in preventing misuse and changing behavior (Botvin & Dusenbury, 1992; LaMarine, 1993; Moskowitz, 1989).

Tobler's 1986 meta-analysis of 98 research studies conducted between 1972 and 1984 that used 143 different program modalities showed clearly that knowledge improved following substance abuse prevention education at the secondary level. Knowledge gains did not, however, readily translate into attitudinal or behavioral changes. In fact, Tobler found sufficient evidence from her work to recommend that information-only or affective-only programs be discontinued.

Bangert-Drowns (1988) used more stringent criteria than Tobler in a meta-analysis of 33 published reports of school-based drug and alcohol education programs conducted from 1968 to 1986, yet some findings were similar. Knowledge gains did not lead to comparable changes in attitudes toward drugs or drug use. Peer instruction was more effective than adult instruction in changing behaviors, particularly when adults used lecture format.

One of the most widely used drug education curricula in U.S. schools is Project DARE (Drug Abuse Resistance Education), which has been adopted by half of local school districts (Ennett, Tobler, Ringwalt, & Flewelling, 1994). The 1986 Drug-Free Schools and Communities Act provided set-aside funding for programs like DARE, which explains its wide dissemination. The 17-session, primarily lecture-based curriculum is aimed at late elementary-age students and taught by trained police officers. A meta-analysis of eight published evaluations of DARE that met specific methodological criteria found moderate effects on substance abuse knowledge, social skills, and attitudes toward the police and slight effects on drug use; only effects on smoking were statistically significant (Ennett et al., 1994). The authors noted, "DARE's limited influence on adolescent drug use behavior contrasts with the program's popularity and prevalence" (p. 1399).

EXAMPLES OF SUCCESSFUL PROGRAMS

Hansen (1992) found the most positive program outcomes occurred among TAOD programs that incorporated multiple modalities. Several examples of such programs are discussed in this section: the Life Skills Training (LST) Program (Botvin, Baker, Dusenbury, Tortu, & Botvin, 1990); Project STAR (Students Taught Awareness and Resistance) (Pentz et al., 1990; Pentz, Brannon, et al., 1989); a smoking prevention program in Minnesota (Murray, Johnson, Luepker, & Mittelmark, 1984); the Class of 1989 Study (Perry et al., 1992); and Project Northland (Perry et al., 1996).

The Midwestern Prevention Project (MPP), begun in 1984, evaluated effects of a school-based drug education program called Project STAR that included parent involvement and community supports (Pentz, Brannon, et al., 1989). For 2 years, sixth and seventh graders from over 50 midwestern schools received regular health education or participated in Project STAR, consisting of 10 in-school resistance skills training sessions and 10 family homework sessions; both groups were exposed to mass media coverage and community supports. At the end of the program, self-reported drug use among intervention schools had slowed in comparison to control schools, and these effects were maintained at 2-year follow-up. Effects on marijuana and tobacco use were sustained at 3rd-year follow-up, but the effect on alcohol use had eroded by then (Johnson et al., 1990).

The LST Program was tested in seventh grade New York state classrooms (Botvin, Baker, Dusenbury, et al., 1990). The program consisted of information about smoking, drinking, and other drug use, as well as activities for self-esteem building, resistance of media influences, anxiety management, communication skills, relationship skills, and assertiveness, conducted over 15 class sessions. Intervention students were given 10 booster sessions in eighth grade and 5 in ninth grade. Results at the end of ninth grade indicated significantly less smoking and marijuana use among students in intervention schools than in control schools. No significant differences were found in frequency of alcohol use. Intervention groups showed significantly higher knowledge about substance abuse and interpersonal skills. At the end of the 12th grade, students were surveyed again (60% of the original sample participated), and the intervention groups were found to have a significantly lower prevalence of smoking, problem drinking, and alcohol use (Botvin, Baker, Dusenbury, Botvin, & Diaz, 1995). The LST approach has shown promise in reducing smoking among adolescents in treatment schools that were predominantly White (Botvin, Tortu, Baker, & Dusenbury, 1990), Black (Botvin, Batson, et al., 1989), and Hispanic (Botvin, Dusenbury, Baker, James-Ortiz, & Kerner, 1989).

Minnesota seventh graders who participated in either an adult-led, information-based program emphasizing long-term consequences of tobacco use or in a peer-led or adult-led intervention emphasizing short-term consequences, resistance skills, and correcting normative expectations about prevalence of tobacco use (social pressures approach) had lower smoking rates at posttest and 1-year follow-up than comparison groups (Murray et al., 1984). Most effective programs were the peer-led interventions for students who were not yet smokers. By the junior or senior year of high school, program effects had faded, although a weak positive effect was still seen among those students who had participated in one of the peer-led social influences interventions (Murray, Davis-Hearn, Goldman, Pirie, & Luepker, 1988).

Two recent studies offer additional hopeful evidence for the long-term effects of school-based smoking prevention coupled with community supports. A substudy of the 1980 to 1993 community-wide Minnesota Heart Health Program (MHHP), the Class of 1989 Study, followed sixth graders in two similar Midwestern communities through high school graduation. Students in one community not only were exposed to MHHP school health programs but also participated in the Minnesota Smoking Prevention Program, a social influences program, in seventh grade. In all follow-up years through high school graduation, lower smoking rates were recorded for intervention students (Perry et al., 1992). Seniors in the intervention community had a 40% lower risk of being a smoker than seniors in the comparison community. Flynn et al. (1992) found similar reductions in smoking at 4-year follow-up for students who received what the authors described as intensive smoking prevention education in Grades 4, 5, and 6, coupled with mass media interventions (television and radio spots) during the 4-year follow-up period. Two years after the mass media interventions ended, significant treatment effects were still apparent (Flynn et al., 1994).

Recent results from Project Northland, a communitywide alcohol use prevention program in Minnesota, were also encouraging. Project Northland involved sixth graders from 24 school districts randomly assigned to intervention or reference conditions (Perry et al., 1996). Beginning in fall 1991 and through the eighth grade, these students received a behaviorally based alcohol education program including parent involvement, peer leadership, and community activities that supported changes in the environment to discourage alcohol use. At the end of 3 years, the intervention group reported significantly lower recent alcohol use than the reference group, especially among those who were nonusers at the beginning of Grade 6.

CHARACTERISTICS OF EFFECTIVE TAOD PROGRAMS

TAOD prevention programs have varied greatly in setting, participants, breadth of curriculum, teaching methods, number of sessions, and approach, making generalizations about characteristics of effective programs difficult (Bangert-Drowns, 1988; Best, Thomson, Santi, Smith, & Brown, 1988). Further, most evaluated school-based programs have used predominantly middle-class, White samples, so application to other groups may be limited. Nevertheless, certain characteristics stand out in evaluated programs that have reported at least a modest degree of success.

1. Because of the interaction between social and intrapersonal factors in initiating drug and alcohol use, prevention programs that are most effective use a life skills approach and include social competence skills such as decision making and independent thinking; media and advertising influences; the improvement of self-image; coping skills for stress and anxiety; communication, social interaction, and assertiveness skills; and refusal skills to resist pressures to use drugs (Botvin, Baker, Dusenbury, et al., 1990; *Making the Grade,* 1996; Perry & Kelder, 1992).

2. Conservative norms, accurately characterizing the extent of drug use among young people, are communicated so students understand that not everyone uses drugs (Botvin, Baker, Dusenbury, et al., 1990; Dusenbury & Falco, 1995). Initial results from the Adolescent Alcohol Prevention Trial, an 8-year project initiated in 12 Los Angeles area junior high schools, indicated that alcohol, tobacco, and marijuana use were lower among students who received a program to establish conservative norms about drug use, compared with students who received only resistance training (Hansen & Graham, 1991).

3. Student-centered, active learning approaches that use small group activities and are led by credible sources, in particular by older or same-age peers, are considered particularly effective (Bangert-Drowns, 1988). Botvin, Baker, Filazzola, and Botvin (1990) compared eighth-grade booster sessions, which were either led by adults or older peers as part of the LST program, and found that peer-led sessions were more effective than adult-led sessions in reducing substance use and influencing knowledge, attitudes, and interpersonal skills. Ennett et al. (1994) postulated that the traditional teaching style used by DARE officers, not program content, might explain the program's minimal effect on drug use behaviors.

4. Messages conveyed are appropriate for the audience. Goodstadt (1986) observed that, "Drug education proceeds as though classes are comprised exclusively of nonusers" (p. 278). Rather than offering one theme of "no use," programs might provide abstainers and infrequent users with refusal, coping, and decision-making skills (primary prevention), while aiming secondary prevention messages, such as avoidance of dangerous drugs like PCP and crack, consequences of driving under the influence, and skills for avoiding unprotected sex, at frequent users or drug abusers (Gutierres, Molof, & Ungerleider, 1994).

5. Instruction is offered from Grades K–12, but at least be-

ginning by Grade 6 and intensifying in middle school, followed by booster sessions in high school. Most TAOD programs are limited to students in Grades 5 through 8, assuming that if drug use is curtailed during this age of experimentation that drug use will not be initiated in high school (Resnicow & Botvin, 1993). No evidence supports this assumption. An evaluation of Project ALERT, a comprehensive junior high school drug education program, found students followed for 6 years maintained knowledge gains but lost resistance self-efficacy as they entered high school, suggesting a need for continual reinforcement (Ellickson, Bell, & McGuigan, 1993). Given that young people who avoid becoming smokers at any point through high school are unlikely to become smokers as adults (Public Health Service, 1994b), it is imperative that smoking education programs continue into high school. A National Cancer Institute expert panel (Glynn, 1990) and the CDC (Guidelines, 1994) recommend that smoking prevention programs include 10 sessions per year for 3 years, but at least five classroom sessions in each of 2 years, with booster sessions in subsequent years. Programs that failed to produce long-term effects on smoking (Flay et al., 1989; Vartiainen, Fallonen, McAlister, & Puska, 1990) did not include booster sessions through high school.

6. Some experts have suggested that family influences are far more significant than peer influences in controlling alcohol and other drug use (Young & West, 1985). Broader based programs that involve families, either minimally (parents help children complete homework assignments) or more comprehensively (programs aimed at parents to improve parenting skills or to alter parental TAOD behaviors), have been suggested but have not been widely implemented or evaluated (Elmquist, 1995).

7. The broader community is involved. Effective community approaches include changing policies so access to cigarettes and alcohol by adolescents is limited, enforcement of laws related to driving under the influence and to the sale of alcohol and tobacco to minors, promoting alcohol-free youth events, and educating those who sell or serve alcohol. Two long-term projects are currently under way to test community alcohol-use prevention initiatives—Project Northland (Perry et al., 1996) and Communities Mobilizing for Change on Alcohol (CMCA) (Wagenaar & Perry, 1994).

8. Regular classroom teachers who receive at least some training can successfully implement TAOD programs (Botvin et al., 1995; Pentz et al., 1990; Smith, McCormick, Steckler, & McLeroy, 1993). Both time commitment to drug education and teacher fidelity to implementing a curriculum are critical to the success of drug education efforts. Better trained teachers, and those who receive periodic in-service training, may devote more time to a curriculum and implement it with greater fidelity. A high level of program implementation, which resulted in more exposure to drug education, was associated with a significantly greater effect on reducing substance abuse in the MPP (Pentz et al., 1990) and the LST studies (Botvin, Baker, Dusenbury, et al., 1990). Botvin, Baker, Dusenbury, et al. (1990) observed that teachers' coverage of material ranged from a low of

27% to a high of 97% (mean of 68%). The strongest effects on reducing substance abuse were seen in students who received at least 60% of program material ("high fidelity" sample) in 9th grade, and effects persisted through 12th grade (Botvin et al., 1995).

Nutrition and Cardiovascular Health Programs

Cardiovascular disease is the leading cause of death among adults in the United States and most other developed nations, and cancer is the second. Various dietary practices modify the risk of cardiovascular disease, cancer, obesity, diabetes, and other disorders. Both the U.S. Department of Health and Human Services and the U.S. Department of Agriculture encourage school-based nutrition education, coupled with physical activity, starting in preschool and continuing through Grade 12 (CDC, 1996).

EFFECT OF NUTRITION AND CARDIOVASCULAR HEALTH PROGRAMS ON CHANGING BEHAVIOR

Cardiovascular health interventions for schoolchildren have varied greatly in design, number of sessions, family involvement, and participant characteristics. Research has established that school-based nutrition education programs can improve knowledge (Lytle, 1994). Because the relationship between knowledge gain and behavior change is weak, recent investigations have focused specifically on behavioral outcomes resulting from nutrition programs, with mixed results.

The largest multisite school-based health promotion intervention ever funded is the Child and Adolescent Trial for Cardiovascular Health (CATCH) (Luepker et al., 1996). The 3-year study involved 5,106 initially third-grade students from ethnically diverse backgrounds in 96 public schools located in four states. Students from 56 randomly selected schools received an intervention that included modification of school food services, increased physical education, and skills-based health education curricula, lasting through Grade 5; 28 of the intervention schools also received a family-based program. All 96 schools maintained their involvement in the project for 3 years, and 79% of students were contacted for fifth-grade follow-up. Classroom observations documented a high degree of fidelity by classroom teachers in implementing the program.

At the conclusion of the study, no significant differences were found in serum cholesterol levels between students in intervention and control schools. This difference is consistent with findings of other large-scale cardiovascular health programs, such as the Pawtucket Heart Health Program (Carleton et al., 1995) and the MHHP (Luepker et al., 1994). However, CATCH intervention schools demonstrated significant reductions in fat content of school lunches and increases in physical education class time devoted to moderate-to-vigorous physical activity. Student self-reports of physical activity and eating patterns showed significant reductions in fat intake and daily vigorous activity among those in intervention schools. Intervention schools having the family component showed only modest improvements in dietary knowledge over intervention schools having no family component.

The Stanford Adolescent Heart Health Program (Killen et al., 1989) consisted of health intervention sessions presenting information about cardiovascular disease, physical activity, nutrition, cigarette smoking, and stress. The program was conducted during regularly scheduled 10th-grade physical education classes 3 days per week for 7 weeks at two senior high schools (two high schools in the same districts served as controls). Lecture, discussion, role-playing, videos, problem solving, self-monitoring, and goal setting were used. Students who received the program showed significant knowledge gains, lower resting heart rates, and reductions in body fat. Daily smokers did not change smoking behavior, although experimental smokers in the treatment group reported a higher quit rate than controls. Blood pressures did not change. At the present time, longitudinal data are insufficient to conclude that behavioral changes seen in childhood translate into desirable behaviors and reduced morbidity and mortality in adulthood (Lytle, 1994).

CHARACTERISTICS OF EFFECTIVE NUTRITION AND CARDIOVASCULAR HEALTH PROGRAMS

In addition to the studies discussed above, reviews of nutrition education programs for school-aged children (Contento, Manning, & Shannon, 1992; Lytle, 1994) and findings from an expert panel recently convened by the CDC (1996) suggest the following characteristics of effective nutrition and cardiovascular health programs:

1. Behaviorally based programs that target specific dietary behaviors are the most likely to effect change. Lytle's (1994) review of 17 nutrition education articles noted that the majority of studies did not cite a theoretical base.
2. Family and community involvement is present.
3. A coordinated school nutrition policy exists that ensures consistency between classroom lessons and a supportive school environment, including supports for healthy school lunches, vending machines, and opportunities for physical activity.
4. Training for teachers and other school staff is provided.
5. Programs of longer duration have greater impact.

Sexuality Education

Sexuality education has been defined as a formal, comprehensive course of study, ideally occurring from kindergarten through college, which includes information and skills to help children develop a positive view of sexuality, take care of their sexual health, and make decisions (Haffner, 1995; Jacobs & Wolf, 1995). In practice, sexuality education rarely is comprehensive, offered in elementary grades, or a stand-alone course. It may exist as part of health education (44 states), home economics (30 states), HIV/AIDS education (29 states), science (19 states), or physical education (13 states); and, therefore, it may be taught by a multitude of teachers, although most commonly by health education teachers in middle school and high school and, when offered, by elementary teachers in earlier grades (Gambrell & Haffner, 1993).

Almost 90% of adults approve of school-based sexuality education (Gallup, 1985; Sex in America, 1991). The most recent survey of state requirements for sexuality education (Gambrell & Haffner, 1993) found that just 35 states have sexuality education guidelines and only 17 have curricula. The only sexual behavior topic universally covered is abstinence. Refusal and communication skills are less typically covered; and controversial topics, such as abortion and sexual orientation, are rarely presented. Most programs described as "sexuality education" are brief interventions, often focusing on a single topic, such as pregnancy prevention or HIV/AIDS (Jacobs & Wolf, 1995). The Sexuality Information and Education Council of the United States (SIECUS) estimates that less than 10% of U.S. schoolchildren receive comprehensive sexuality education (Gambrell & Haffner, 1993).

EFFECT OF SEXUALITY EDUCATION PROGRAMS ON CHANGING BEHAVIOR

Postponing sexual involvement until young people are cognitively and emotionally mature is extremely important for good health (Haffner, 1995). Available research to date indicates that sexuality education programs do not promote promiscuity or result in an earlier onset of intercourse (Holtgrave et al., 1995; Kirby et al., 1993), and some data indicate that the opposite is true (Jemmott, Jemmott, & Fong, 1992; Zabin, Hirsch, Smith, Streett, & Hardy, 1986). Comprehensive sexuality education programs appear to have their greatest effect on sexual behaviors of adolescents who are not yet sexually active, so timing interventions to begin before sexual activity is initiated (no later than seventh grade) will be most effective (Eisen, Zellman, & McAlister, 1990; Howard & McCabe, 1990; Kirby, Barth, Leland, & Fetro, 1991).

The 1981 Adolescent Family Life Act (AFLA) provided federal funding for abstinence-based pregnancy prevention programs. Few AFLA projects have been evaluated, and no AFLA project has included long-term evaluation. Evaluated abstinence-based programs have demonstrated short-term positive effects on attitudes toward abstinence (Donahue, 1987; Olsen, Weed, Ritz, & Jensen, 1991), with students who were not currently sexually active more likely to adopt positive attitudes toward abstinence than those who were sexually active before the program began (Christopher & Roosa, 1990). The limited evidence from abstinence-based programs is insufficient to conclude that such programs delay the initiation of sexual intercourse, reduce the frequency of intercourse, or decrease adolescent pregnancy rates (Kirby et al., 1994; Roosa & Christopher, 1990).

Comprehensive sexuality education programs have been more rigorously evaluated, although these programs vary significantly in their goals, content, timing, and length. Such programs, which typically include information about contraception, decision making, and sexually transmitted diseases (STDs), do not appear to hasten the initiation of sexual intercourse (Eisen et al., 1990; Howard & McCabe, 1990; Kirby et al., 1991). The only school-based, comprehensive curriculum that has been evaluated over an extended period of time is *Reducing the Risk: Building to Prevent Pregnancy (RTR),* a skills-based program grounded in social learning theory that emphasizes avoidance of unprotected intercourse by abstinence or use of contraceptives (Kirby et al., 1991). *RTR* is widely regarded as having a significant effect on behavior, particularly on delaying the initiation of intercourse, among students who were not yet sexually active and on increasing use of contraception by certain groups of students who were already sexually active (Kirby & DiClemente, 1994; Main et al., 1994). Eighteen months following *RTR,* 29% of participants and 38% of nonparticipants had initiated sexual intercourse, a significant difference (Kirby et al., 1991).

Although knowledge about contraception and STDs increases following participation in sexuality education programs, a reduction in high-risk behaviors does not necessarily follow for all program participants (Kirby & DiClemente, 1994). Some programs have found an increase in contraceptive use by sexually inexperienced but not by experienced adolescents (Howard & McCabe, 1990), by sexually experienced females and low-risk teens but not by males and higher-risk youth (Kirby et al., 1991).

CHARACTERISTICS OF EFFECTIVE SEXUALITY EDUCATION PROGRAMS

In 1991, a national task force of 20 professionals representing medical, health, and education organizations developed *Guidelines for Comprehensive Sexuality Education* (National Guidelines Task Force, 1991), which proposed six key concepts for age-appropriate sexuality education at early elementary, upper elementary, middle school or junior high school, and high school levels. The recommended key concepts and their associated topics are (a) human development (reproductive anatomy, reproduction, puberty, sexual identity and orientation); (b) relationships (families, friends, love, dating, marriage and lifetime commitments, parenting); (c) personal skills (values, decision making, communication, assertiveness, negotiation, finding help); (d) sexual behavior (sexuality throughout life, masturbation, shared sexual behavior, abstinence, human sexual response, fantasy, sexual dysfunction); (e) sexual health (contraception, abortion, STDs and HIV/AIDS, sexual abuse, reproductive health); and (f) society and culture (gender roles, law, religion, the arts, the media, diversity). Under these guidelines, SIECUS has identified four states—Alaska, Iowa, Kansas, and Rhode Island—as having exemplary programs (Gambrell & Haffner, 1993).

Other research suggested that sexuality education programs do not have to be this comprehensive to achieve the goals of delaying the onset of sexual intercourse and reducing unprotected intercourse. In an extensive review of programs, Kirby and colleagues (1994) cited the following six characteristics of effective sexuality education programs:

1. Health behavior theory, particularly social learning theory, is the foundation.
2. Goals are centered in reducing high-risk sexual behaviors.
3. Basic, accurate information on the risks of unprotected sex and avoiding these risks is conveyed by using active learning techniques that help students to personalize the information.
4. Information is included about social influences on sexual activity.
5. An effort is made to change or reinforce group norms, using age- and experience-appropriate activities that re-

inforce beliefs and values in favor of delaying intercourse and against unprotected sex. Peer instructors may be helpful in this regard, as well as providing accurate information about the prevalence of sexual behaviors and the risk associated with such activities. This information may reinforce the notion that *not* everybody is "doing it," and that certain risks are unacceptably high.

6. Content includes skills-based training for decision making and negotiation. Both *Reducing the Risk* and a related program, *Safer Choices* (Coyle et al., 1996), offer students opportunities for role-play activities to improve refusal skills and condom negotiation skills.

HIV/AIDS Prevention Education

By October 31, 1995, 501,310 cases of AIDS had been recorded in the United States, nearly half of which were reported since 1993 (First 500,000, 1995). Since 1981, when AIDS data were first collected, the proportion of cases among Whites has decreased from 60% to 43%, and an increasing proportion of cases had occurred among African Americans (from 25% in 1981–1987 to 38% in 1995) and Hispanics (14% to 18%). Women now represent 18% of AIDS cases. While homosexual intercourse remains the primary mode of transmission, 27% of AIDS cases occur among injecting-drug users (17% of cases in 1981–1987), and 10% of cases were transmitted through heterosexual contact (3% in 1981–1987). Worldwide, estimates project that there are 4.5 million people with AIDS (World Health Organization, 1995).

Among 18- to 45-year-olds in the United States, AIDS is the leading cause of death in men and the fourth leading cause of death in women (Kelly, 1995). With an approximate 10-year incubation period between infection with HIV and development of AIDS, the likelihood that many of these individuals were infected in adolescence is high. Although the actual number of 5- to 19-year-olds with AIDS is small, the number has increased from 299 reported cases in 1981–1987 to 1,959 reported cases in 1993–1995 (First 500,000, 1995). Seropositivity (the marker of HIV infection) ranges from 1% in the general adolescent population to 12% among high-risk adolescent subgroups (Rotheram-Borus, Mahler, & Rosario, 1995).

Even young children are aware of AIDS and know that it is a disease (Hoppe, Wells, Wilsdon, Gillmore, & Morrison, 1994; Schonfeld et al., 1995; Smith, Minden, & Lefevbre, 1993). High school students' HIV-related knowledge, beliefs, and behaviors were first measured in a national, school-based survey in 1989 (Kann et al., 1991). The Secondary School Student Health Risk Survey found generally high levels of knowledge about HIV/AIDS, but some beliefs (you can tell people are infected with HIV by looking at them) and practices (3% had injected drugs; 59% had had sexual intercourse) put them at risk. Another survey found sexually active seventh and eighth graders to have less knowledge about HIV/AIDS, less intent to engage in less risky behaviors, and more associated risk behaviors than abstinent seventh and eighth graders (Brown, DiClemente, & Beausoleil, 1992).

Many adolescents are sexually active. The latest YRBSS indicated that 53% of high school students have had sexual intercourse at least once, and 37.6% are currently sexually active (had sexual intercourse during the preceding 3 months). Almost 19% had had four or more sex partners (Kann et al., 1995). Prevention or modification of risk behaviors that lead to HIV infection is presently the only course of action available to reduce the morbidity and mortality from HIV/AIDS. Most adolescents become infected with HIV through unprotected sexual intercourse (Rotheram-Borus et al., 1995). Slightly more than half of sexually active students (52.8%) used a condom at last intercourse (Kann et al., 1995), although other studies suggest that as few as 10 to 20% of adolescents consistently use condoms (Sells & Blum, 1996). A study of sexually active minority junior high school students found that 36.6% rarely or never used condoms and that those with the most sex partners had the lowest frequency of condom use (DiClemente et al., 1992).

THE ROLE OF HEALTH EDUCATION PROGRAMS IN CONTROLLING THE SPREAD OF AIDS

The threat of AIDS has brought schools to the forefront as the points for HIV prevention education. Although HIV/AIDS education is not without controversy, both parents and teachers believe that the school is an appropriate place for HIV/AIDS education, even for elementary children (McQueen, Fassler, Copeland, & Duncan, 1992; Smith, Minden, et al., 1993). A recent survey of U.S. residents reported that 95% believed schools should provide information about AIDS (Kaiser Family Foundation, 1996).

School-based HIV/AIDS education programs are confined by several factors. First, federal, state, and district policymakers have shown a clear preference for abstinence-based education, despite insufficient evidence that "just say no" programs delay initiation of sexual activity. Because HIV is primarily transmitted through sexual behavior, prevention programs must either effectively prevent sexual intercourse or provide sexually active individuals with the knowledge and skills to adopt safer sex behaviors. As discussed in the previous section, education programs are available that can help prevent the spread of AIDS, but few schools use such programs. Second, even when effective programs are in place, the heterogeneity of students in a given classroom will affect program outcomes. Differences in HIV-related knowledge, attitudes, and behaviors found between sexually active and abstinent seventh and eighth graders in one study suggested that program content might appropriately differ between these groups (Brown et al., 1992). When programs are offered only to older adolescents, many of whom are already sexually active, changing well-established behaviors will be very difficult.

EFFECT OF AIDS EDUCATION PROGRAMS ON CHANGING KNOWLEDGE AND BEHAVIOR

Very few HIV/AIDS prevention programs have been rigorously evaluated to determine their effectiveness (Choi & Coates, 1994; Janz et al., 1996; Oakley, Fullerton, & Holland, 1995). Of the 815 HIV/AIDS prevention interventions examined in one review, only 68 were judged to be outcome evaluations, and, of those, just 18 were considered methodologically sound (Oakley et al., 1995). However, most of the sound interventions were found to be at least partly effective.

Knowledge gains resulting from HIV/AIDS prevention education have been evaluated more consistently than behavior change. Information-based programs have largely succeeded in increasing students' knowledge about HIV/AIDS (Ashworth, DuRant, Newman, & Gaillard, 1992; Hamalainen & Keinanen-Kiukaanniemi, 1992; Holtzman, Lowry, Kann, Collins, & Kolbe, 1994; Kirby & DiClemente, 1994). Even children in kindergarten through Grade 6 have been shown to gain knowledge about the causes and prevention of AIDS following an educational program (Schonfeld et al., 1995).

Some HIV/AIDS education programs have succeeded in changing attitudes about people with AIDS. It is particularly important that programs affect attitudes, because if people with AIDS are seen as "different," then denying one's own susceptibility to infection is much easier. Handler et al. (1994) found high correlation between knowledge about AIDS and favorable attitudes toward people with AIDS among predominantly minority seventh to ninth graders. When six intervention and six nonintervention classes in San Francisco middle and high schools participated in a three-session AIDS lesson plan (or no instruction), knowledge about AIDS was increased and fears about having HIV-positive classmates were reduced in the intervention classes (DiClemente et al., 1989). Two studies of one-session AIDS education programs, however, found no differences in attitudes toward persons with AIDS or perceived susceptibility to HIV infection among 11th and 12th graders (Ashworth et al., 1992) and only small changes in attitudes toward persons with AIDS among ninth graders (Hamalainen & Keinanen-Kiukaanniemi, 1992).

Despite steady knowledge gains and some improvements in attitudes about HIV/AIDS, sexual behaviors among adolescents and young adults, including the consistent use of condoms, have changed very little over the years (DiClemente et al., 1992; Kegeles, Adler, & Irwin, 1988; Kelly, 1995). In one study, over 80% of younger adolescents were knowledgeable about the role of condoms in reducing the risk of HIV infection; yet 70% of the knowledgeable adolescents were undecided about which preventive practices they would adopt (Barling & Moore, 1990).

Three excellent studies illustrate the knowledge-behavior dilemma. In one study (Main et al., 1994), experienced teachers who received additional training presented a 15-session skills-based HIV/AIDS program to ethnically diverse students in 10 Colorado secondary schools (students in seven control schools received their regular AIDS education program). The program aimed to change HIV risk behaviors and did achieve some of its objectives. Knowledge about HIV/AIDS was significantly higher in intervention students following the program. At 6-month follow-up, intervention school students demonstrated significant differences in several practices, such as purchasing and using condoms and having fewer sexual partners. However, the program did not succeed in postponing the initiation of sexual intercourse, altering use of alcohol and other drugs before intercourse, or reducing frequency of intercourse.

The second study included predominantly minority 9th and 11th graders from four high schools in a New York City borough who received a six-session information and skills-based AIDS prevention curriculum taught by specially trained classroom teachers, or no program (Walter & Vaughan, 1993). At completion of the program and 3-month follow-up, the intervention group demonstrated significantly greater knowledge and trends toward reducing high-risk behaviors, but no significant differences in behavior was found in the control group.

Finally, the third study compared knowledge, attitudes, and behaviors of male, African-American adolescents who participated in a 1-day AIDS instruction and skills training program with those who received a 1-day career training program (Jemmott et al., 1992). Both programs took place at a school on a Saturday. The AIDS intervention group not only gained AIDS knowledge but also had more negative attitudes toward engaging in risky sexual behaviors. At 3-month follow-up, the intervention adolescents were engaging in sexual intercourse less than the control group, with fewer sexual partners, and with greater use of condoms.

The discrepancy between knowledge and behavior is an area of great interest to AIDS education researchers. An individual's beliefs about HIV transmission may be one determinant of the magnitude of the discrepancy. Among the beliefs that have been identified as critical to the adoption of safer practices are belief in one's ability to effect a change in behavior (perceived self-efficacy); possessing a sense of support by peers, community, and family; a belief that one has self-control in sexual situations; and perception of AIDS as a threat (Stevenson, Davis, Weber, Weiman, & Abdul-Kabir, 1995). Many data suggest that adolescents simply do not believe themselves to be at personal risk of contracting HIV (Boyer & Kegeles, 1991; Strunin, 1991). With a disproportionately large number of HIV-infected adolescents being African American and Hispanic, cultural beliefs are also significant. Some racial and ethnic differences in perceived vulnerability to AIDS have been identified (Strunin, 1991).

CHARACTERISTICS OF EFFECTIVE HIV/AIDS PREVENTION EDUCATION PROGRAMS

Provision of information about HIV/AIDS is a necessary first step in HIV/AIDS education. Particularly for young children, factual information about the differences between communicable and noncommunicable diseases, the immune system, symptoms and treatment of illness, and HIV/AIDS is important to correct misconceptions and reduce anxiety (Hoppe et al., 1994; Schonfeld et al., 1995). However, behavior change through educational programs is unlikely when information alone is the program's focus.

Various authors (Holtgrave et al., 1995; Kelly, 1995; Main et al., 1994; Oakley et al., 1995; Rotheram-Borus et al., 1995; St. Lawrence, Brasfield, Jefferson, Alleyne, & O'Bannon, 1995) have suggested the most effective interventions in changing both HIV/AIDS knowledge and preventive behaviors among adolescents have the following characteristics:

1. The programs are grounded in health behavior theory, particularly social learning theory. Literature reviews have identified social learning theory and the theory of reasoned action as used most frequently in HIV/AIDS program development (Kirby et al., 1994; Main et al., 1994; Stevenson et al., 1995), with some use of the health belief model (Rosenstock, Strecher, & Becker, 1994).

2. Goals are clearly relevant to the target population and are

developmentally and culturally appropriate. Programs may need different interventions for youth from different minority groups, because sexual behaviors vary considerably (Rotheram-Borus et al., 1995), and because knowledge (Stevenson, Gay, & Josar, 1995) and beliefs (Stevenson et al., 1995) about HIV and AIDS differ. Even within the same minority classification, significant differences may exist. For example, Horan and DiClemente (1993) found differences in HIV/AIDS knowledge, ability to communicate about HIV, and sexual activity levels between Chinese- and Filipino-Americans in San Francisco high schools. Stevenson, Gay, et al. (1995) identified significant differences in AIDS knowledge gains following a video intervention between African-American teenagers who characterized themselves as knowing some, knowing a little, or knowing a lot about AIDS before the intervention. Guidelines for choosing culturally responsive HIV educational materials have been proposed by Walters, Canady, and Stein (1994).

3. Accurate information about HIV transmission and prevention is provided. Children need accurate information about cause, mechanisms of transmission, and prevention of HIV and AIDS, as well as access to resources to dispel myths and misconceptions (Boyer & Kegeles, 1991; Kelly, 1995; Rotheram-Borus et al., 1995). Adolescents in particular need a frame of reference that can be provided by putting AIDS education into the context of other STDs, which are perhaps more familiar to them (DiClemente, Boyer, & Mills, 1987).

4. Active, skills-based learning techniques are used, including activities for development of communication, decision-making, negotiation, and refusal skills, which are consistent with the interpersonal nature of HIV transmission. Peer-led AIDS education programs have enhanced knowledge, attitudes, and behaviors (Rickert, Jay, & Gottlieb, 1991).

5. Programs give consideration to motivational factors in behavior, such as peer influences and the role of drugs and alcohol. It is relatively easy to teach people practices for safe sex. Social cognitive theory acknowledges the difficulty in changing people's self-beliefs and behaviors so they can resist real-life situations that are fraught with interpersonal pressures and situational enticements and limitations (Bandura, 1994). The Botvin and Dusenbury (1992) program is an example of one that teaches resistance to social pressures.

6. Abstinence and acknowledgment of lower-risk sexual practices for individuals who are not willing to be abstinent are promoted.

Factors that Increase Effectiveness of School Health Education

The comprehensive and categorical health education programs discussed thus far suggest several commonalities among effective programs. This section briefly reviews factors that are widely considered to make school health programs more effective.

Sound Theoretical Basis for the Program

Numerous researchers have observed that health education programs that work are theory based, whether in cardiovascular health (Killen et al., 1989; Lytle, 1994; Stone, Perry, & Luepker, 1989), HIV prevention (Holtgrave et al., 1995), sexuality education (Kirby et al., 1994), or alcohol and other drug education (Perry et al., 1996). Theoretical models help explain behavior and suggest program components to modify behavior. This section briefly discusses three models most commonly applied to school health education. Other authors provide a thorough review of all the theoretical models applicable to school health (Elder, Geller, Hovell, & Mayer, 1994; Parcel, 1984).

HEALTH BELIEF MODEL

The health belief model (HBM) proposes that a person's beliefs about four factors determine his or her health behavior: (a) susceptibility to a disease, (b) seriousness of the disease, (c) benefits of health actions, and (d) barriers to action. In addition, self-perception of capacity for carrying out actions (self-efficacy) is important (Rosenstock, 1990). Although the model was originally developed in an environment of preventing contagious diseases and promoting immunizations, it can also be applied to promoting preventive health behaviors that reduce the risk of chronic diseases (Janz & Becker, 1984).

Limitations of the HBM have been discussed by others (Brown, DiClemente, & Reynolds, 1991; Bush & Iannotti, 1990; Janz & Becker, 1984; Rosenstock, 1990; Stevenson, Gay, et al., 1995). Nonetheless, some consider the HBM to be an appropriate model for various aspects of health education, including HIV/AIDS education (Eisen et al., 1990; Kipke, Boyer, & Hein, 1993). Rosenstock et al. (1994) conducted a selective literature review to determine the usefulness of the model in predicting HIV-preventive behaviors and found ample evidence to warrant the recommendation that health-belief variables (perceived susceptibility to AIDS, belief in severity of the problem, benefits of AIDS-preventive behaviors) be used in program planning.

SOCIAL LEARNING THEORY AND SOCIAL COGNITIVE THEORY

Social learning theory (SLT) proposes that people will adopt a health behavior if they believe the behavior will have the desired result and if they believe they can perform the behavior (Bandura, 1994). Reciprocal interactions between personal, behavioral, and environmental factors affect behavior change. Personal factors that influence health include the individual's knowledge, attitudes, and values and beliefs in his or her ability to change. Behavioral factors include skills for health behavior change and the individual's ability to use those skills. And environmental factors include social supports and role models in the individual's environment. Central to SLT is the concept of self-efficacy, which influences every stage of health behavior change, from the earliest thoughts about making a change, to the efforts one puts into changing, to the level of behavior change ultimately achieved and sustained (Bandura, 1994).

Therefore, health education curricula based on SLT should include four components: (a) information, (b) opportunities for development of prevention skills, (c) opportunities for skills practice, and (d) social supports. SLT has been successfully applied to elementary-level diet and exercise (Parcel, Simons-Morton, O'Hara, Baranowski, & Wilson, 1989), cardiovascular health (Berenson et al., 1991; Prokhorov, Perry, Kelder, & Klepp, 1993), violence prevention (Weiler & Dorman, 1995), HIV/AIDS education (Handler et al., 1994; Kipke et al., 1993), alcohol education (Perry et al., 1996), smoking cessation, contraceptive behavior, and exercise (Parcel, Taylor, et al., 1989).

THEORY OF REASONED ACTION

This theory states that a person's intention to perform a specific behavior is the best determinant of whether the person will actually adopt the behavior. Intention to perform the action is influenced by (a) the person's general attitude toward the behavior and (b) the person's view of the social expectations regarding the behavior (beliefs regarding what people who are valued think he or she should do) (Fishbein, Middlestadt, & Hitchcock, 1994).

According to the theory of reasoned action, behavioral interventions must target specific behaviors and influence a person's behavioral intent. The theory has formed the basis for changing social norms in smoking, alcohol (Bruvold, 1993), and contraceptive programs (Parcel, 1984) and has been proposed for HIV/AIDS education (Fishbein et al., 1994; Stevenson et al., 1995; Warden & Koballa, 1995). Critics of the theory contend that attitudes may not influence behavioral intent in as rational a way as the theory implies, particularly with respect to adolescent drug and alcohol use (Moskowitz, 1989).

Program Content Based on Priority Health Behaviors

The 10 core content areas for school health education recommended by the National Professional School Health Education Organizations, listed previously in this chapter, were suggested in 1984 as guidelines for health content. Several authorities have recommended modifying health content to reflect nationwide health trends and priority health behaviors (Allensworth, 1994; Pigg, 1989). The CDC targets six priority behaviors that most influence health, and data from the ongoing YRBSS support the need for health education to address these behaviors. The priority behaviors that have been identified are behaviors that contribute to intentional and unintentional injuries, tobacco use, alcohol and other drug use, sexual behaviors contributing to unintended pregnancy and STDs (including HIV), dietary behaviors, and physical activity. An excellent resource for the systematic selection or development of curricula is that written by English, Sancho, Lloyd-Kolkin, and Hunter (1990).

Sufficient Program Time

On the basis of the work of Connell et al. (1985), the American School Health Association recommended that elementary and middle school children receive 50 hours of health instruction per year and that high school students receive at least 150 hours

of health instruction provided by certified health teachers (Allensworth, 1993). More lasting effects on health behaviors are seen when interventions are sustained. For example, Rotheram-Borus, Koopman, Haignere, and Davies (1991) reported that consistent condom use almost doubled at 6-month follow-up among runaway adolescents who attended more (at least 15) intervention sessions, and the Metropolitan Life Foundation (1988) reported less frequent alcohol use and smoking among students with 3 years of health education versus 1 year of health education.

The most effective health education programs begin before children have initiated unhealthy behaviors. Sexuality education programs seem most successful when they are initiated before first intercourse (Choi & Coates, 1994). Information about alcohol, nicotine, and marijuana is most effective when introduced 2 years before the age of first use (Ames, Trucano, Wan, & Harris, 1992). In addition, research examining clustering of both positive and negative health behaviors supports the early development of as many positive health behaviors as possible, to thwart consolidation of negative behaviors (Lytle, Kelder, Perry, & Klepp, 1995).

Transitions from one level of schooling to another are particularly critical times for health education, particularly from elementary to middle school. A softening of attitudes toward smoking was seen in nonsmoking sixth graders during Grades 7 and 8, but an inoculation approach to smoking prevention initiated in Grade 7 had a modest effect on preventing smoking for a year, particularly among students with low self-esteem (Pfau & Van Bockern, 1994). Reintroducing the same health topic in different grade levels not only reinforces and reviews prior health content, but it also acknowledges that children gain different dimensions of understanding as they mature cognitively.

Skills-Based Approach to Education

The purposes of health instruction are not distinct or different from the broad purposes of education, that is, to promote certain values, such as responsibility and quality of life; to improve students' knowledge, skills, and competence; and to enhance students' abilities to locate and use new information (Lohrmann, Gold, & Jubb, 1987). Years of research have established that health instruction can improve students' health knowledge. However, knowledge gain alone is insufficient for development of health promoting skills for behavior change.

Whatever the health content area, several generic skills can be useful to students—problem solving, decision making, refusal and assertiveness, communication, and behavior contracting. Such general prevention education skills can be used in health education programs that cover any topic area. Oakley et al. (1995) noted than most health education interventions have not been well evaluated, but of those with a strong evaluation component, the skills-based interventions worked best.

Certain health behaviors tend to cluster in youth. Links have been observed between substance abuse, sexual intercourse, and STDs (Fortenberry, 1995). Lytle et al. (1995) cited research linking smoking, alcohol, and other drug use; links between exercise, dietary habits, and oral health; and their own findings of relationships between physical activity, smoking prevalence, and healthy food choices. Thus, the same intervention strategy might be used for these clusters of behavior, teaching skills and providing students the opportunity to practice skills and receive feedback. Comprehensive health education programs, more so than categorical programs, allow an opportunity for an integrated and progressive approach to these skills.

Instructional methods used in health education should be based on the outcome desired. When increased awareness is the goal, appropriate teaching methods may include lecture and media; when improved decision making is the goal, ranking, role-playing, simulations, and problem-solving activities will be appropriate; for behavior change, self-monitoring, behavior contracting, peer instruction, skill building, and family and community involvement activities will be needed (Allensworth, 1994). Teachers who use a balance of both cognitive and affective teaching methods have been found to enhance student knowledge and skill acquisition (Lohrmann & McClendon, 1987; Tappe, Galer-Unti, & Bailey, 1995). Unfortunately, most teachers do not have a high level of comfort, confidence, and ability to use skills-based instructional techniques (Botvin, Tortu, et al., 1990; Killen et al., 1989). Botvin, Baker, Filazzola, et al. (1990) observed regular classroom teachers to implement cognitive portions of a drug education curriculum with greater fidelity than the skills-training component.

Active Student Involvement

Peer-led health education programs have been described as "the most underutilized prevention strategy" (DiClemente, 1993, p. 761). The value of peer-led programs stems from the ability of peers, who share program participants' values and beliefs, to exert numerous influences, such as eliciting greater involvement from participants, serving as positive behavior models, increasing adolescents' sense of perceived vulnerability to disease or health conditions, communicating in a way that is clear to other adolescents, and providing a realistic appraisal of peer group norms (DiClemente, 1993; Janz et al., 1996; Murray et al., 1984; Sciacca & Appleton, 1996).

Several health education programs have demonstrated the effectiveness of peer leaders, although few long-term studies have been conducted. For example, Botvin, Baker, Filazzola, et al. (1990) observed peer-led booster sessions to be more effective in influencing substance use than adult-led booster sessions. At 4-year follow-up, a seventh grade smoking prevention program taught by same-age peers and classroom teachers still had modest effects in reducing smoking incidence (Murray et al., 1988). A peer-led sexuality education program delayed the onset of intercourse at 1-year follow-up among high-risk, low-income students (Howard & McCabe, 1990).

Supportive School, Community, and Family

In social cognitive theory, the environment is a mediating factor in personal change (Bandura, 1994). When a message taught in school is further reinforced at home or in the community, behavior change is facilitated. Health education programs with a family and community base have been successful in improving health knowledge (Hopper, Gruber, Munoz, & MacConnie, 1996; Luepker et al., 1996) and in modifying high-risk behaviors, such as those associated with HIV infection (Choi & Coates, 1994), eating and physical activity patterns (Luepker et al., 1996), diet (Perry et al., 1988), alcohol use (Perry et al., 1996), and drug use (Johnson et al., 1990).

In addition, environmental supports within the school itself that demonstrate administrative commitment to health, such as school policies that promote a healthy school environment; inservice training time for teachers; and integrated school, family, and community health promotion activities, can complement classroom health instruction (Allensworth, 1994; Gingiss, Gottlieb, & Brink, 1994). School no-smoking policies have been associated with a decrease in adolescent smoking (Pentz, Brannon, et al., 1989). In addition, school administrators who support health education are able to resolve scheduling issues, advocate the curriculum to higher levels of administration, and provide teachers with time and resources to implement the program appropriately. A study of implementation of tobacco prevention curricula found administrative support to be a critical determinant of program implementation (Smith, McCormick, et al., 1993).

English (1994) observed that, despite federal, state, and local mandates for school–family alliances, most schools are ill-equipped to do form such alliances. Among the ways that schools can encourage family involvement in school health education is to provide homework activity packets completed by parent and child, to establish school–parent involvement advisory groups, to create parent peer support groups, to offer parent volunteer opportunities, and to provide materials for parents to create a home environment supportive of health.

Trained Teachers

Since the School Health Education Evaluation was started (Connell & Turner, 1985), it has been clear that teacher training plays a pivotal role in the delivery of effective school health education. Studies of the diffusion of effective health education curricula have repeatedly demonstrated that program failures result more often from inadequate program implementation than from a flaw in program design (McCormick, Steckler, & McLeroy, 1995; Tortu & Botvin, 1989). A key factor in program implementation is the classroom teacher, whose skills and behavior directly affect the quality and quantity of health instruction (Botvin, Dusenbury, et al., 1989; Smith, McCormick, et al., 1993; Tortu & Botvin, 1989).

Berenson et al. (1991) noted that "Elementary school teachers have a greater potential influence upon the health of a child, outside of the home, than any other group" (p. 306). Only 6% of the states require that elementary health teachers be certified in health (Collins et al., 1995), and elementary school teachers in just 31 states are required to have some health coursework (Stone & Perry, 1990). At the secondary level, 69% of the states require health certification for health teachers, although certification does not necessarily require majoring in health; in fact, over one third of secondary health teachers majored in a field other than health or science (Collins et al., 1995).

Preservice training in health is valuable to enhance teachers' knowledge about health education subject matter and teaching methods. Teachers are more likely to use teaching methods with which they are knowledgeable and comfortable (Gingiss & Hamilton, 1989). Preservice preparation can also have a positive effect on teacher attitudes about health and increase the probability of continuing to teach health subjects (Levenson-Gingiss & Hamilton, 1989), particularly as teachers move beyond primary prevention to secondary prevention.

For many teachers, because of a lack of comprehensive preservice preparation, in-service is the principal method of training in health education. Like preservice training, in-service has been found to improve teachers' self-assurance and their attitudes toward teaching health (Tricker & Davis, 1988). In-depth tobacco education training was significantly associated with greater implementation of the curriculum by teachers from 21 North Carolina school districts (McCormick et al., 1995), similar to findings from the THTM evaluation study. Teachers with more training in THTM had more positive effects on student health knowledge and attitudes than did untrained teachers (Gold et al., 1991).

Teacher experience affects the kinds of information teachers need for presenting effective health education programs. When regular classroom teachers were given training to implement a K–12 drug and alcohol education program called *Here's Looking at You, Two,* inexperienced teachers required more training about drugs, program content, and teaching methods than experienced teachers (Tricker & Davis, 1988).

Interestingly, teacher training for a specific program does not have to be intensive for a program to be successful. Botvin et al. (1995) developed a drug education program for which regular classroom teachers were trained in either a 1-day workshop with feedback or by videotaped instruction, and both groups of teachers presented a curriculum that was effective in reducing substance abuse at ninth grade and through high school. Participation in a 6-hour communication skills training program for parents, teachers, and youth leaders was associated with significantly reduced initiation of cigarette smoking by students in communities where the ratio of program participants to students was highest (Worden et al., 1987). One-year follow-up revealed that adult participants continued to use skills and techniques developed in the program.

Tortu & Botvin (1989) suggested that in-service training be viewed as a process rather than a single event. They recommended a five-component training program for any health curriculum to include (a) presentation of the theoretical foundation of the program, (b) demonstration of instructional skills used in effective health curricula, (c) opportunities for practice in small groups and simulated classroom situations, (d) written feedback immediately following practice, and (e) coaching during classroom visits.

Conclusion

The research reviewed and referred to in this chapter confirmed that a broad scientific base for school health education has been established, principally in the area of primary prevention. McKinlay, Stone, and Zucker observed in 1989 that school health education research had progressed through three generations of studies and is presently in the fourth generation. In the first generation, sample sizes were small, methodology was weak, and outcome measures looked mainly at knowledge and attitude gains. The second generation of research began to measure behavior change in subjects, but this measurement was generally over the short term, and many studies continued to have methodological weaknesses. The third generation included randomized research designs and a broader array of outcome measures. And, finally, the fourth generation is characterized by multisite studies having more sophisticated methodology and with long-term follow-up of behavior change.

Most major funded health research done today meets the criteria for methodologically sound investigation and has shown that the school is an appropriate site for health education; schoolchildren can gain an understanding of the nature of priority health behaviors and factors that reduce risk; skills needed to improve health practices and avoid high-risk health behaviors can be taught, learned, and maintained for many years; and a supportive school environment, coupled with family and community supports, will strengthen effects of classroom health instruction. Health education programs having a sound theoretical foundation, adequate class time, skills-based educational approach, peer leadership, community and family involvement, and trained teachers can affect children's health knowledge, attitudes, and practices.

Nevertheless, while many American schoolchildren receive health education that is adequate to enhance knowledge, few receive the kind of health education needed to prevent risky health practices (primary prevention) or to modify already existent practices (secondary prevention) or health conditions (tertiary prevention). Among the challenges ahead for school health education will be bringing strong national efforts toward CSHE to state and local levels, increasing the effectiveness of health education interventions by improved teacher preparation, diffusing successful curricula and approaches to different schools, and developing more effective ways to create a culture supportive of health change.

REFERENCES

Adams, P. F., Schoenborn, C. A., Moss, A. J., Warren, C. W., & Kann, L. (1995). Health risk behaviors among our nation's youth: United States, 1992. *Vital and Health Statistics, 10*(192).

Allensworth, D. D. (1993). Health education: State of the art. *Journal of School Health, 63*(1), 14–20.

Allensworth, D. D. (1994). The research base for innovative practices in school health education at the secondary level. *Journal of School Health, 64*(5), 180–187.

Allensworth, D. D., & Kolbe, L. J. (1987). The comprehensive school health program: Exploring an expanded concept. *Journal of School Health, 57*(10), 409–412.

American Medical Association. (1990). *America's adolescents: How healthy are they?* Chicago: American Medical Association, Department of Adolescent Health.

American School Health Association, Association for the Advancement of Health Education, & Society for Public Health Education, Inc. (1989). *The National Adolescent Student Health Survey: A report on the health of America's youth.* Oakland, CA: Third Party Publishing.

Ames, E. E., Trucano, L. A., Wan, J. C., & Harris, M. H. (1992). *Designing school health curricula.* Dubuque, IA: William C. Brown Publishers.

Ashworth, C. S., DuRant, R. H., Newman, C., & Gaillard, G. (1992). Evaluation of a school-based AIDS/HIV education program for high school students. *Journal of Adolescent Health, 13*(7), 582–588.

Bandura, A. (1994). Social cognitive theory and exercise of control over HIV infection. In R. J. DiClemente & J. L. Peterson (Eds.), *Pre-*

venting AIDS: Theories and methods of behavioral interventions (pp. 25–59). New York: Plenum Press.

Bangert-Drowns, R. L. (1988). The effects of school-based substance abuse education—A meta-analysis. *Journal of Drug Education, 18*(3), 243–264.

Barling, N. R., & Moore, S. M. (1990). Adolescents' attitudes towards AIDS precautions and intention to use condoms. *Psychological Reports, 67*, 883–890.

Berenson, G. S., Arbeit, M. L., Hunter, S. M., Johnson, C. C., & Nicklas, T. A. (1991). Cardiovascular health promotion for elementary school children: The Heart Smart program. *Annals of the New York Academy of Sciences, 623*, 299–313.

Best, J. A., Thomson, S. J., Santi, S. M., Smith, E. A., & Brown, K. S. (1988). Preventing cigarette smoking among school children. *Annual Reviews of Public Health, 9*, 161–201.

Botvin, G. J., Baker, E., Dusenbury, L., Botvin, E. M., & Diaz, T. (1995). Long-term follow-up results of a randomized drug abuse prevention trial in a white middle-class population. *Journal of the American Medical Association, 273*(14), 1106–1112.

Botvin, G. J., Baker, E., Dusenbury, L., Tortu, S., & Botvin, E. M. (1990). Preventing adolescent drug abuse through a multimodal cognitive-behavioral approach: Results of a 3-year study. *Journal of Consulting and Clinical Psychology, 58*(4), 437–446.

Botvin, G. J., Baker, E., Filazzola, A. D., & Botvin, E. M. (1990). A cognitive-behavioral approach to substance abuse prevention: One-year follow-up. *Addictive Behaviors, 15*, 47–63.

Botvin, G. J., Batson, H. W., Witts-Vitale, S., Bess, V., Baker, E., & Dusenbury, L. (1989). A psychosocial approach to smoking prevention for urban black youth. *Public Health Reports, 104*(6), 573–582.

Botvin, G. J., & Dusenbury, L. (1992). Substance abuse prevention: Implications for reducing risk of HIV infection. *Psychology of Addictive Behaviors, 6*(2), 70–80.

Botvin, G. J., Dusenbury, L., Baker, E., James-Ortiz, S., & Kerner, L. (1989). A skills training approach to smoking prevention among Hispanic youth. *Journal of Behavioral Medicine, 12*(3), 279–296.

Botvin, G. J., Tortu, S., Baker, E., & Dusenbury, L. (1990). Preventing adolescent cigarette smoking: Resistance skills training and development of life skills. *Special Services in the Schools, 6*(1/2), 37–61.

Boyer, C. B., & Kegeles, S. M. (1991). AIDS risk and prevention among adolescents. *Social Science and Medicine, 33*(1), 11–23.

Brown, L. K., DiClemente, R. J., & Beausoleil, N. I. (1992). Comparison of human immunodeficiency virus related knowledge, attitudes, intentions, and behaviors among sexually active and abstinent young adolescents. *Journal of Adolescent Health, 13*, 140–145.

Brown, L. K., DiClemente, R. J., & Reynolds, L. A. (1991). HIV prevention for adolescents: Utility of the health belief model. *AIDS Education and Prevention, 3*(1), 50–59.

Bruvold, W. H. (1993). A meta-analysis of adolescent smoking prevention programs. *American Journal of Public Health, 83*(6), 872–880.

Bush, P. J., & Iannotti, R. J. (1990). A children's health belief model. *Medical Care, 28*(1), 69–86.

Bush, P. J., Zuckerman, A. E., Taggert, V. S., Theiss, P. K., Peleg, E. O., & Smith, S. A. (1989). Cardiovascular risk factor prevention in black school children: The 'Know Your Body' evaluation project. *Health Education Quarterly, 16*(2), 215–227.

Carleton, R. A., Lasater, T. M., Assaf, A. R., Feldman, H. A., McKinlay, S., & the Pawtucket Heart Health Program Writing Group. (1995). The Pawtucket Heart Health Program: Community changes in cardiovascular risk factors and projected disease risk. *American Journal of Public Health, 85*(6), 777–785.

Centers for Disease Control and Prevention. (1996). Guidelines for school health programs to promote lifelong healthy eating. *Morbidity and Mortality Weekly Report, 45*(No. RR-9), 1–42.

Choi, K.-H., & Coates, T. J. (1994). Prevention of HIV infection. *AIDS, 8*(10), 1371–1389.

Christopher, F. S., & Roosa, M. W. (1990). An evaluation of an adolescent pregnancy prevention program: Is 'Just Say No' enough? *Family Relations, 39*, 68–72.

Collins, J. L., Small, M. L., Kann, L., Pateman, B. C., Gold, R. S., & Kolbe, L. J. (1995). School health education. *Journal of School Health, 65*(8), 302–311.

Connell, D. B., & Turner, R. R. (1985). The impact of instructional experience and the effects of cumulative instruction. *Journal of School Health, 55*(8), 324–331.

Connell, D. B., Turner, R. R., & Mason, E. F. (1985). Summary of findings of the School Health Education Evaluation: Health promotion effectiveness, implementation, and costs. *Journal of School Health, 55*(8), 316–321.

Contento, I. R., Manning, A. D., & Shannon, B. (1992). Research perspectives on school-aged nutrition education. *Journal of Nutrition Education, 24*(5), 247–260.

Council of Chief State School Officers. (1991). *Beyond the health room.* Washington, DC: Resource Center on Educational Equity.

Coyle, K., Kirby, D., Parcel, G., Basen-Engquist, K., Banspach, S., Rugg, D., & Weil, M. (1996). Safer choices: A multicomponent school-based HIV/STD and pregnancy prevention program for adolescents. *Journal of School Health, 66*(3), 89–94.

Devaney, B., Schochet, P., Thornton, C., Fasciano, N., & Gavin, A. (1994). *Evaluating educational outcomes of school health programs.* Washington, DC: U.S. Department of Health and Human Services, Office of Disease Prevention and Health Promotion.

DiClemente, R. J. (1993). Preventing HIV/AIDS among adolescents: Schools as agents of behavior change. *Journal of the American Medical Association, 270*(6), 760–762.

DiClemente, R. J., Boyer, C. B., & Mills, S. J. (1987). Prevention of AIDS among adolescents: Strategies for the development of comprehensive risk-reduction health education programs. *Health Education Research: Theory & Practice, 2*(3), 287–291.

DiClemente, R. J., Durbin, M., Siegel, D., Krasnovsky, F., Lazarus, N., & Comacho, T. (1992). Determinants of condom use among junior high school students in a minority, inner-city school district. *Pediatrics, 89*(2), 197–202.

DiClemente, R. J., Pies, C. A., Stoller, E. J., Straits, C., Olivia, G. E., Haskin, J., & Rutherford, G. W. (1989). Evaluation of school-based AIDS education curricula in San Francisco. *Journal of Sex Research, 26*(2), 188–198.

Donahue, M. (1987). *Technical report of the national demonstration project field test of human sexuality: Values and choices.* Minneapolis, MN: Search Institute.

Dryfoos, J. G. (1990). *Adolescents at risk: Prevalence and prevention.* New York: Oxford University Press.

Dusenbury, L., & Falco, M. (1995). Eleven components of effective drug abuse prevention curricula. *Journal of School Health, 65*(10), 420–425.

Eisen, M., Zellman, G. L., & McAlister, A. L. (1990). Evaluating the impact of a theory-based sexuality and contraceptive education program. *Family Planning Perspectives, 22*(6), 261–271.

Elder, J. P., Geller, E. S., Hovell, M. F., & Mayer, J. A. (1994). *Motivating health behavior.* Albany, NY: Delmar Publishers.

Ellickson, P. L., Bell, R. M., & McGuigan, K. (1993). Preventing adolescent drug use: Long-term results of a junior high program. *American Journal of Public Health, 83*(6), 856–861.

Elmquist, D. L. (1995). Alcohol and other drug use prevention for youths at high risk and their parents. *Education and Treatment of Children, 18*(1), 68–88.

Ennett, S. T., Tobler, N. S., Ringwalt, C. L., & Flewelling, R. L. (1994). How effective is drug abuse resistance education: A meta-analysis of Project DARE outcome evaluations. *American Journal of Public Health, 84*(9), 1394–1401.

English, J. (1994). Innovative practices in comprehensive health education programs for elementary schools. *Journal of School Health, 64*(5), 188–191.

English, J., Sancho, A., Lloyd-Kolkin, D., & Hunter, L. (1990). *Criteria for comprehensive health education curriculum.* Los Alamitos, CA: Southwest Regional Laboratory.

Errecart, M. T., Walberg, H. J., Ross, J. G., Gold, R. S., Fiedler, J. L., & Kolbe, L. J. (1991). Effectiveness of Teenage Health Teaching Modules. *Journal of School Health, 61*(1), 26–30.

First 500,000 AIDS cases—United States, 1995. (1995, 24 November). *Morbidity and Mortality Weekly Report, 44*(46), 849–853.

Fishbein, M., Middlestadt, S. E., & Hitchcock, P. J. (1994). Using information to change sexually transmitted disease-related behaviors: An analysis based on the theory of reasoned action. In R. J. DiClemente & J. L. Peterson (Eds.), *Preventing AIDS: Theories and methods of behavioral interventions* (pp. 61–78). New York: Plenum Press.

Flay, B. R., Koepke, D., Thomson, S. J., Santi, S., Best, J. A., & Brown, K. S. (1989). Six-year follow-up of the first Waterloo school smoking prevention trial. *American Journal of Public Health, 79*(10), 1371–1376.

Flynn, B. S., Worden, J. K., Secker-Walker, R. H., Badger, G. J., Geller, B. M., & Costanza, M. C. (1992). Prevention of cigarette smoking through mass media intervention and school programs. *American Journal of Public Health, 82*(6), 827–834.

Flynn, B. S., Worden, J. K., Secker-Walker, R. H., Pirie, P. L., Badger, G. J., Carpenter, J. H., & Geller, B. M. (1994). Mass media and school interventions for cigarette smoking prevention: Effects 2 years after completion. *American Journal of Public Health, 84*(7), 1148–1150.

Fortenberry, J. D. (1995). Adolescent substance use and sexually transmitted diseases risk: A review. *Journal of Adolescent Health, 16,* 304–308.

Gallup, A. M. (1985). The 17th annual Gallup poll of the public's attitudes toward the public schools. *Phi Delta Kappan, 67*(22), 35–47.

Gambrell, A. E., & Haffner, D. (1993). *Unfinished business: A SIECUS assessment of state sexuality education programs.* New York: Sex Information and Education Council of the United States.

Gingiss, P. L. (1997). *Building a future without HIV/AIDS: What do educators have to do with it?* Washington, DC: American Association of Colleges for Teacher Education.

Gingiss, P. L., Gottlieb, N. H., & Brink, S. G. (1994). Increasing teacher receptivity toward use of tobacco prevention education programs. *Journal of Drug Education, 24*(2), 163–176.

Gingiss, P. L., & Hamilton, R. (1989). Teacher perceptions after implementing a human sexuality education program. *Journal of School Health, 59*(10), 437–441.

Glynn, T. J. (1990). *School programs to prevent smoking: The National Cancer Institute guide to strategies that succeed.* Bethesda, MD: U.S. Department of Health and Human Services, National Institutes of Health.

Gold, R. S. (1994). The science base for comprehensive health education. In P. Cortese & K. Middleton (Eds.), *The comprehensive school health challenge: Promoting health through education* (Vol. 2, pp. 545–573). Santa Cruz, CA: ETR Associates.

Gold, R. S., Parcel, G. S., Walberg, H. J., Luepker, R. V., Portnoy, B., & Stone, E. J. (1991). Summary and conclusion of the THTM evaluation: The expert work group perspective. *Journal of School Health, 61*(1), 39–42.

Goodstadt, M. S. (1986). School-based drug education in North America: What is wrong? What can be done? *Journal of School Health, 56*(7), 278–281.

Guidelines for school health programs to prevent tobacco use and addiction. (1994). *Journal of School Health, 64*(9), 353–360.

Gutierres, S. E., Molof, M., & Ungerleider, S. (1994). Relationship of 'risk' factors to teen substance use: A comparison of abstainers, infrequent users, and frequent users. *International Journal of the Addictions, 29*(12), 1559–1579.

Haffner, D. W. (Ed.). (1995). *Facing facts: Sexual health for America's adolescents.* New York: Sexuality Information and Education Council of the United States.

Hamalainen, S., & Keinanen-Kiukaanniemi, S. (1992). A controlled study of the effect of one lesson on the knowledge and attitudes of schoolchildren concerning HIV and Aids [sic]. *Health Education Journal, 51*(3), 135–138.

Handler, A., Lampman, C., Levy, S., Weeks, K., Rashid, J., & Flay, B. (1994). Attitudes toward people with AIDS and implications for school-based youth AIDS education. *AIDS Education and Prevention, 6*(2), 175–183.

Hansen, W. B. (1992). School-based substance abuse prevention: A review of the state of the art in curriculum, 1980–1990. *Health Education Research: Theory & Practice, 7*(3), 403–430.

Hansen, W. B., & Graham, J. W. (1991). Preventing alcohol, marijuana, and cigarette use among adolescents: Peer pressure resistance training versus establishing conservative norms. *Preventive Medicine, 20,* 414–430.

Hansen, W. B., Tobler, N. S., & Graham, J. W. (1990). Attrition in substance abuse prevention research: A meta-analysis of 85 longitudinally followed cohorts. *Evaluation Review, 14*(6), 677–685.

Holtgrave, D. R., Qualls, N. L., Curran, J. W., Valdiserri, R. O., Guinan, M. E., & Parra, W. C. (1995). An overview of the effectiveness and efficiency of HIV prevention programs. *Public Health Reports, 110*(2), 134–146.

Holtzman, D., Lowry, R., Kann, L., Collins, J., & Kolbe, L. J. (1994). Changes in HIV-related information sources, instruction, knowledge, and behaviors among U.S. high school students, 1989 and 1990. *American Journal of Public Health, 84*(3), 388–393.

Hoppe, M. J., Wells, E. A., Wilsdon, A., Gillmore, M. R., & Morrison, D. M. (1994). Children's knowledge and beliefs about AIDS: Qualitative data from focus group interviews. *Health Education Quarterly, 21*(1), 117–126.

Hopper, C. A., Gruber, M. B., Munoz, K. D., & MacConnie, S. (1996). School-based cardiovascular exercise and nutrition programs with parent participation. *Journal of Health Education, 27*(Suppl. 5), S32–S39.

Horan, P. F., & DiClemente, R. J. (1993). HIV knowledge, communication, and risk behaviors among white, Chinese- and Filipino-American adolescents in a high-prevalence AIDS epicenter: A comparative analysis. *Ethnicity & Disease, 3,* 97–105.

Howard, M., & McCabe, J. B. (1990). Helping teenagers postpone sexual involvement. *Family Planning Perspectives, 22*(1), 21–26.

Jacobs, C. D., & Wolf, E. M. (1995). School sexuality education and adolescent risk-taking behavior. *Journal of School Health, 65*(3), 91–95.

Janz, N. K., & Becker, M. H. (1984). The health belief model: A decade later. *Health Education Quarterly, 11*(1), 1–47.

Janz, N. K., Zimmerman, M. A., Wren, P. A., Israel, B. A., Freudenberg, N., & Carter, R. J. (1996). Evaluation of 37 AIDS prevention projects: Successful approaches and barriers to program effectiveness. *Health Education Quarterly, 23*(1), 80–97.

Jemmott, J. B., Jemmott, L. S., & Fong, G. T. (1992). Reductions in HIV risk-associated sexual behaviors among black male adolescents: Effects of an AIDS prevention intervention. *American Journal of Public Health, 82,* 372–377.

Johnson, C. A., Pentz, M. A., Weber, M. D., Dwyer, J. H., Baer, N., MacKinnon, D. P., & Hansen, W. B. (1990). Relative effectiveness of comprehensive community programming for drug abuse prevention with high-risk and low-risk adolescents. *Journal of Consulting and Clinical Psychology, 58,* 447–456.

Joint Committee on Health Education Terminology. (1990). Report of the joint committee on health education terminology. *Journal of Health Education, 22*(2), 97–108.

Joint Committee on National Health Education Standards. (1995). *National health education standards.* Atlanta, GA: American Cancer Society.

Kaiser Family Foundation. (1996). *The Kaiser survey on Americans and AIDS/HIV.* Menlo Park, CA: Kaiser Family Foundation.

Kandel, D. B., & Logan, S. A. (1984). Problems of drug use from adolescence to young adulthood: Periods of risk initiation, continued use, and discontinuation. *American Journal of Public Health, 74,* 660–666.

Kann, L., Anderson, J. E., Holtzman, D., Ross, J., Truman, B. I., Collins, J., & Kolbe, L. J. (1991). HIV-related knowledge, beliefs, and behaviors among high school students in the United States: Results from a national survey. *Journal of School Health, 61*(9), 397–401.

Kann, L., Collins, J. L., Pateman, B. C., Small, M. L., Ross, J. G., & Kolbe, L. J. (1995). The School Health Policies and Programs Study (SHPPS): Rationale for a nationwide status report on school health programs. *Journal of School Health, 65*(8), 291–294.

Kegeles, S. M., Adler, N. E., & Irwin, C. E., Jr. (1988). Sexually active adolescents and condoms: Changes over one year in knowledge, attitudes and use. *American Journal of Public Health, 78*(4), 460–461.

Kelly, J. A. (1995). Advances in HIV/AIDS education and prevention. *Family Relations, 44,* 345–352.

Killen, J. D., Robinson, T. N., Telch, M. J., Saylor, K. E., Maron, D. J., Rich, T., & Bryson, S. (1989). The Stanford Adolescent Heart Health Program. *Health Education Quarterly, 16*(2), 263–283.

Kipke, M. D., Boyer, C., & Hein, K. (1993). An evaluation of an AIDS risk reduction education and skills training (Arrest) program. *Journal of Adolescent Health, 14*(7), 533–539.

Kirby, D., Barth, R. P., Leland, N., & Fetro, J. V. (1991). Reducing the risk: Impact of a new curriculum on sexual risk-taking. *Family Planning Perspectives, 23,* 253–262.

Kirby, D., & DiClemente, R. J. (1994). School-based interventions to prevent unprotected sex and HIV among adolescents. In R. J. DiClemente & J. L. Peterson (Eds.), *Preventing AIDS: Theories and methods of behavioral interventions* (pp. 117–139). New York: Plenum Press.

Kirby, D., Resnick, M. D., Downes, B., Kocher, T., Gunderson, P., Potthoff, S., Zelterman, D., & Blum, R. W. (1993). The effects of school-based health clinics in St. Paul on school-wide birthrates. *Family Planning Perspectives, 25,* 12–16.

Kirby, D., Short, L., Collins, J., Rugg, D., Kolbe, L., Howard, M., Miller, B., Sonenstein, F., & Zabin, L. S. (1994). School-based programs to reduce sexual risk behaviors: A review of effectiveness. *Public Health Reports, 109*(3), 339–360.

Kolbe, L. J. (1993). An essential strategy to improve the health and education of Americans. *Preventive Medicine, 22,* 1–17.

Kolbe, L. J., Green, L., Foreyt, J., Darnell, L., Goodrick, K., Williams, H., Ward, D., Korton, A. S., Karacan, I., Widmeyer, R., & Stainbrook, G. (1986). Appropriate functions of health education in schools: Improving health and cognitive performance. In N. A. Krasnegor, J. D. Arasteh, & M. F. Cataldo (Eds.), *Child health behavior: A behavioral pediatrics perspective* (pp. 171–216). New York: John Wiley & Sons.

LaMarine, R. J. (1993). School drug education programming: In search of a new direction. *Journal of Drug Education, 23*(4), 325–31.

Lavin, A. T., Shapiro, G. R., & Weill, K. S. (1992). *Creating an agenda for school-based health promotion: A review of selected reports.* Boston: Harvard School of Public Health.

Levenson-Gingiss, P., & Hamilton, R. (1989). Determinants of teachers' plans to continue teaching a sexuality education course. *Family and Community Health, 12*(3), 40–53.

Lohrmann, D. K., Gold, R. S., & Jubb, W. H. (1987). School health education: A foundation for school health programs. *Journal of School Health, 57*(10), 420–425.

Lohrmann, D. K., & McClendon, E. J. (1987). A preliminary study of assumptions underlying school health instruction. *Health Education Research: Theory & Practice, 2*(2), 131–44.

Luepker, R. V., Murray, D. M., Jacobs, D. R., Jr., Mittelmark, M. B., Bracht, N., Carlaw, R., Crow, R., Elmer, P., Finnegan, J., Folsom, A. R., Grimm, R., Hannan, P. J., Jeffrey, R., Lando, H., McGovern, P., Mullis, R., Perry, C. L., Pechacek, T., Pirie, P., Sprafka, M., Weisbrod, R., & Blackburn, H. (1994). Community education for cardiovascular disease prevention: Risk factor changes in the Minnesota Heart Health Program. *American Journal of Public Health, 84*(9), 1383–1393.

Luepker, R. V., Perry, C. L., McKinley, S. M., Nader, P. R., Parcel, G. S., Stone, E. J., Webber, L. S., Elder, J. P., Feldman, H. A., Johnson, C. C., Kelder, S. H., & Wu, M. (1996). Outcomes of a field trial to improve children's dietary patterns and physical activity. *Journal of the American Medical Association, 275*(10), 768–776.

Lytle, L. A. (1994). *Nutrition education for school-aged children: A review of research.* Alexandria, VA: U.S. Department of Agriculture, Food and Consumer Service.

Lytle, L. A., Kelder, S. H., Perry, C. L., & Klepp, K.-I. (1995). Covariance of adolescent health behaviors: The Class of 1989 study. *Health Education Research: Theory & Practice, 10*(2), 133–146.

Main, D. S., Iverson, D.C., McGloin, J., Banspach, S. W., Collins, J. L., Rugg, D. L., & Kolbe, L. J. (1994). Preventing HIV infection among adolescents: Evaluation of a school-based education program. *Preventive Medicine, 23*(4), 409–417.

Making the grade: A guide to school drug prevention programs. (1996). Washington, DC: Drug Strategies.

McCormick, L. K., Steckler, A. B., & McLeroy, K. R. (1995). Diffusion of innovations in schools: A study of adoption and implementation of school-based tobacco prevention curricula. *American Journal of Health Promotion, 9*(3), 210–219.

McKinlay, S. M., Stone, E. J., & Zucker, D. M. (1989). Research design and analysis issues. *Health Education Quarterly, 16*(2), 307–313.

McQueen, K., Fassler, D., Copeland, L., & Duncan, P. (1992). Attitudes about AIDS education for young children among parents and teachers. *Children's Health Care, 21*(1), 26–30.

Metropolitan Life Foundation. (1988). *An evaluation of comprehensive school health education in American public schools.* New York: Louis Harris and Associates.

Moskowitz, J. M. (1989). The primary prevention of alcohol problems: A critical review of the research literature. *Journal of Studies on Alcohol, 50*(1), 54–88.

Murray, D. M., Davis-Hearn, M., Goldman, A. I., Pirie, P., & Luepker, R. V. (1988). Four- and five-year follow-up results from four seventh grade smoking prevention strategies. *Journal of Behavioral Medicine, 11*(4), 395–405.

Murray, D. M., Johnson, C. A., Luepker, R. V., & Mittelmark, M. B. (1984). The prevention of cigarette smoking in children: A comparison of four strategies. *Journal of Applied Social Psychology, 14*(3), 274–288.

National Commission for Health Education Credentialing, Inc. (1994). A framework for the development of competency-based curricula for entry level health educators. In P. Cortese & K. Middleton (Eds.), *The comprehensive school health challenge: Promoting health through education* (Vol. 2, pp. 933–939). Santa Cruz, CA: ETR Associates.

National Commission on the Role of the School and the Community in Improving Adolescent Health. (1990). *Code blue: Uniting for healthier youth.* Alexandria, VA: National Association of State Boards of Education.

National Guidelines Task Force. (1991). *Guidelines for comprehensive sexuality education: Kindergarten–12th grade.* New York: Sexuality Information and Education Council of the United States.

National Professional School Health Education Organizations. (1984). Comprehensive school health education—A definition. *Journal of School Health, 54*(8), 312–315.

National School Boards Association. (1991). *School health: Helping children learn.* Alexandria, VA: National School Boards Association.

Nelson, G. D., Cross, F. S., & Kolbe, L. J. (1991). Introduction: Teenage Health Teaching Modules evaluation. *Journal of School Health, 61*(1), 3–4.

Oakley, A., Fullerton, D., & Holland, J. (1995). Behavioural interventions for HIV/AIDS prevention. *AIDS, 9*(5), 479–486.

Olsen, J. A., Weed, S. E., Ritz, G. M., & Jensen, L. C. (1991). The effect of three abstinence sex education programs on student attitudes toward sexual activity. *Adolescence, 26*(103), 631–641.

Parcel, G. S. (1984). Theoretical models for application in school health education research. *Journal of School Health, 54,* 39–49.

Parcel, G. S., Simons-Morton, B., O'Hara, N. M., Baranowski, T., & Wilson, B. (1989). School promotion of healthful diet and physical activity: Impact on learning outcomes and self-reported behaviors. *Health Education Quarterly, 16*(2), 181–199.

Parcel, G. S., Taylor, W. C., Brink, S. G., Gottlieb, N., Engquist, K., O'Hara, N. M., & Eriksen, M. P. (1989). Translating theory into practice: Intervention strategies for the diffusion of a health promotion innovation. *Family and Community Health, 12*(3), 1–13.

Pentz, M. A., Brannon, B. R., Charlin, V. L., Barrett, E. J., MacKinnon, D. P., & Flay, B. R. (1989). The power of policy: The relationship of smoking policy to adolescent smoking. *American Journal of Public Health, 79*(7), 857–862.

Pentz, M. A., Dwyer, J. H., MacKinnon, D. P., Flay, B. R., Hansen, W. B., Wang, E. Y. I., & Johnson, C. A. (1989). A multicommunity trial for primary prevention of adolescent drug abuse. *Journal of the American Medical Association, 261*(22), 3259–3266.

Pentz, M. A., Trebow, E. A., Hansen, W. B., MacKinnon, D. P., Dwyer, J. H., Johnson, C. A., Flay, B. R., Daniels, S., & Cormack, C. (1990). Effects of program implementation on adolescent drug use behavior. The Midwestern Prevention Project (MPP). *Evaluation Review, 14*(3), 264–289.

Perry, C. L., & Kelder, S. H. (1992). Models for effective prevention. *Journal of Adolescent Health, 13,* 355–363.

Perry, C. L., Kelder, S. H., Murray, D. M., & Klepp, K.-I. (1992). Communitywide smoking prevention: Long-term outcomes of the Minnesota Heart Health program and the class of 1989 study. *American Journal of Public Health, 82*(9), 1210–1216.

Perry, C. L., Luepker, R. V., Murray, D. M., Kurth, C., Mullis, R., Crockett, S., & Jacobs, D. R., Jr. (1988). Parent involvement with children's health promotion: The Minnesota Home Team. *American Journal of Public Health, 78*(9), 1156–1160.

Perry, C. L., Williams, C. L., Veblen-Mortenson, S., Toomey, T. L., Komro, K. A., Anstine, P. S., McGovern, P. G., Finnegan, J. R., Forster, J. L., Wagenaar, A. C., & Wolfson, M. (1996). Project Northland: Outcomes of a communitywide alcohol use prevention program during early adolescence. *American Journal of Public Health, 86*(7), 956–965.

Pfau, M., & Van Bockern, S. (1994). The persistence of inoculation in conferring resistance to smoking initiation among adolescents: The second year. *Human Communication Research, 20*(3), 413–430.

Pigg, R. M., Jr. (1989). The contribution of school health programs to the broader goals of public health: The American experience. *Journal of School Health, 59*(1), 25–30.

Prokhorov, A. V., Perry, C. L., Kelder, S. H., & Klepp, K.-I. (1993). Lifestyle values of adolescents: Results from Minnesota Heart Health youth program. *Adolescence, 28*(111), 637–47.

Public Health Service. (1994a). *Healthy People 2000 progress report for: Alcohol and other drugs.* Washington, DC: U.S. Department of Health and Human Services, Office of Disease Prevention and Health Promotion.

Public Health Service. (1994b). *Healthy People 2000 progress report for: Tobacco.* Washington, DC: U.S. Department of Health and Human Services, Office of Disease Prevention and Health Promotion.

Resnicow, K., & Botvin, G. (1993). Commentary. School-based substance use prevention programs: Why do effects decay? *Preventive Medicine, 22*(4), 484–490.

Rickert, V. I., Jay, M. S., & Gottlieb, A. (1991). Effects of a peer-counseled AIDS education program on knowledge, attitudes, and satisfaction of adolescents. *Journal of Adolescent Health, 12*(1), 38–43.

Roosa, M. W., & Christopher, F. S. (1990). Evaluation of an abstinence-only adolescent pregnancy prevention program: A replication. *Family Relations, 39,* 363–367.

Rosenstock, I. M. (1990). The health belief model: Explaining health behavior through expectancies. In K. Glanz, F. M. Lewis, & B. K. Rimer (Eds.), *Health behavior and health education* (pp. 39–62). San Francisco: Jossey-Bass.

Rosenstock, I. M., Strecher, V. J., & Becker, M. H. (1994). The health belief model and HIV risk behavior change. In R. J. DiClemente & J. L. Peterson (Eds.), *Preventing AIDS: Theories and methods of behavioral interventions* (pp. 2–24). New York: Plenum Press.

Ross, J. G., Delpy, L. A., Christenson, G. M., Gold, R. S., & Damberg, C. L. (1987). The National Children and Youth Fitness Study II: Study procedures and quality control. *Journal of Physical Education, Recreation, and Dance, 58*(9), 57–62.

Ross, J. G., Gold, R. S., Lavin, A. T., Errecart, M. T., & Nelson, G. D. (1991). Design of the Teenage Health Teaching Modules evaluation. *Journal of School Health, 61*(1), 21–25.

Ross, J. G., Pate, R. R., Delpy, L. A., Gold, R. S., & Svilar, M. (1987). National Children and Youth Fitness Study II: New health-related fitness norms. *Journal of Physical Education, Recreation, and Dance, 58*(9), 66–70.

Rotheram-Borus, M. J., Koopman, C., Haignere, C., & Davies, M. (1991). Reducing HIV sexual risk behaviors among runaway adolescents. *Journal of the American Medical Association, 266*(9), 1237–1241.

Rotheram-Borus, M. J., Mahler, K. A., & Rosario, M. (1995). AIDS prevention with adolescents. *AIDS Education and Prevention, 7*(3), 320–336.

Schall, E. (1994). School-based health education: What works? *American Journal of Preventive Medicine, 10*(Suppl. 1), 30–32.

Schonfeld, D. J., O'Hare, L. L., Perrin, E. C., Quackenbush, M., Showalter, D. R., & Cicchetti, D. V. (1995). A randomized, controlled trial of a school-based, multi-faceted AIDS education program in the elementary grades: The impact on comprehension, knowledge and fears. *Pediatrics, 95*(4), 480–486.

Sciacca, J., & Appleton, T. (1996). Peer helping: A promising strategy for effective health education. *Peer Facilitator Quarterly, 13*(2), 22–28.

Seffrin, J. R. (1990). The comprehensive school health curriculum: Closing the gap between state-of-the-art and state-of-the-practice. *Journal of School Health, 60*(4), 151–155.

Seffrin, J. R. (1994). America's interest in comprehensive school health education. *Journal of School Health, 64*(10), 397–399.

Sells, C. W., & Blum, R. W. (1996). Morbidity and mortality among U.S. adolescents: An overview of data and trends. *American Journal of Public Health, 86*(4), 513–519.

Sex in America. (1991). *Gallup Poll Monthly, 56,* 1–9, 71.

Sliepcevich, E. M. (1964). *School health education study: Summary report.* Washington, DC: School Health Education Study.

Smith, D. W., McCormick, L. K., Steckler, A. B., & McLeroy, K. R. (1993). Teachers' use of health curricula: Implementation of Growing Healthy, Project SMART, and the Teenage Health Teaching Modules. *Journal of School Health, 63*(8), 349–354.

Smith, M. L., Minden, D., & Lefevbre, A. (1993). Knowledge and attitudes about AIDS and AIDS education in elementary school students and their parents. *Journal of School Psychology, 31*(2), 281–292.

St. Lawrence, J. S., Brasfield, T. L., Jefferson, K. W., Alleyne, E., & O'Bannon, R. E., III. (1995). Cognitive-behavioral intervention to reduce African American adolescents' risk for HIV infection. *Journal of Consulting and Clinical Psychology, 63*(2), 221–237.

Stevenson, H. C., Davis, G., Weber, E., Weiman, D., & Abdul-Kabir, S. (1995). HIV prevention beliefs among urban African-American youth. *Journal of Adolescent Health, 16,* 316–232.

Stevenson, H. C., Gay, K. M., & Josar, L. (1995). Culturally sensitive AIDS education and perceived risk knowledge: Reaching the 'know-it-all' teenager. *AIDS Education and Prevention, 7*(2), 134–144.

Stone, E. J., & Perry, C. L. (1990). United States: Perspectives in school health. *Journal of School Health, 60*(7), 363–369.

Stone, E. J., Perry, C. L., & Luepker, R. V. (1989). Synthesis of cardiovascular behavioral research for youth health promotion. *Health Education Quarterly, 16*(2), 155–169.

Strunin, L. (1991). Adolescents' perceptions of risk for HIV infection: Implications for future research. *Social Science and Medicine, 32*(2), 221–228.

Tappe, M. K., Galer-Unti, R. A., & Bailey, K. C. (1995). Long-term implementation of the Teenage Health Teaching Modules by trained teachers: A case study. *Journal of School Health, 65*(10), 411–415.

Tobler, N. S. (1986). Meta-analysis of 143 adolescent drug prevention programs: Quantitative outcome results of program participants compared to a control or comparison group. *Journal of Drug Issues, 16*(4), 537–567.

Tortu, S., & Botvin, G. J. (1989). School-based smoking prevention: The teacher training process. *Preventive Medicine, 18,* 280–289.

Tricker, R., & Davis, L. G. (1988). Implementing drug education in schools: An analysis of the costs and teacher preparation. *Journal of School Health, 58*(5), 181–185.

U.S. Department of Education. (1991). *America 2000: An education strategy.* Washington, DC: U.S. Department of Education.

U.S. Department of Health and Human Services. (1990). *Healthy people 2000: National health promotion and disease prevention objectives.* Washington, DC: Superintendent of Documents, U.S. Government Printing Office.

Vartiainen, E., Fallonen, U., McAlister, A. L., & Puska, P. (1990). Eight-year follow-up results of an adolescent smoking prevention program: The North Karelia Youth Project. *American Journal of Public Health, 80*(1), 78–79.

Wagenaar, A. C., & Perry, C. L. (1994). Community strategies for the reduction of youth drinking: Theory and applications. *Journal of Research on Adolescence, 4*(2), 319–345.

Walter, H. J. (1989). Primary prevention of chronic disease among children: The school-based 'Know Your Body' intervention trials. *Health Education Quarterly, 16*(2), 201–214.

Walter, H. J., & Vaughan, R. D. (1993). AIDS risk reduction among a multiethnic sample of urban high school students. *Journal of the American Medical Association, 270*(6), 725–730.

Walters, J. L., Canady, R., & Stein, T. (1994). Evaluating multicultural approaches in HIV/AIDS educational material. *AIDS Education and Prevention, 6*(5), 446–453.

Warden, M. A., & Koballa, T. R., Jr. (1995). Using students' salient beliefs to design an instructional intervention to promote AIDS compassion and understanding in the middle school. *AIDS Education and Prevention, 7*(1), 60–73.

Weiler, R. M., & Dorman, S. M. (1995). The role of school health instruction in preventing interpersonal violence. *Educational Psychology Review, 7*(1), 69–91.

Willard, J. C., & Schoenborn, C. A. (1995). *Relationship between cigarette smoking and other unhealthy behaviors among our nation's youth: United States, 1992* (Advance data from vital and health statistics; no. 263). Hyattsville, MD: National Center for Health Statistics.

Worden, J. K., Flynn, B. S., Brisson, S. F., Secker-Walker, R. H., McAuliffe, T. L., & Jones, R. P. (1987). An adult communication skills program to prevent adolescent smoking. *Journal of Drug Education, 17*(1), 1–9.

World Health Organization. (1995). *The current global situation of the HIV/AIDS pandemic.* Geneva, Switzerland: World Health Organization.

Young, K. R., & West, R. P. (1985). *Factors influencing the onset of substance abuse: A chronological review of the literature, 1973–1983.* Logan, UT: Family Skills Development Project.

Zabin, L. S., Hirsch, M. B., Smith, E. A., Streett, R., & Hardy, J. B. (1986). Evaluation of a pregnancy prevention program for urban teenagers. *Family Planning Perspectives, 18*(3), 119–126.

27.

Research on Teaching in Physical Education

Kim C. Graber
University of Illinois

Although there have been reviews that have focused on subsets of the literature on teaching in physical education (e.g., Bain, 1997; Lee, 1996; Rink, 1996a; Silverman, 1991), several decades have passed since the last effort to prepare a comprehensive status report for this area of always zesty but rarely systematic inquiry (Nixon & Locke, 1973). Accordingly, I have taken that interval as license to begin from scratch by ignoring other efforts and simply inventing a framework for organizing the literature as I understand it and for readers as I imagine them (see Figure 27.1). The framework that guides this chapter was developed as a vehicle to (a) organize research reports into categories that will be easily comprehensible to readers, (b) display primary topics of inquiry, (c) maintain some sense of the connection between research questions and forms of inquiry, and (d) portray, in a general way, the evolution of pedagogical research in this subject field.

Given the restrictions of a *Handbook* chapter, any ambition to be comprehensive has to be tempered by reality. Some areas of considerable activity have been given only small and subordinate status in the framework. Others, of course, will be named in the text, but not awarded the attention of display in the graphic organizer. All such decisions bring the risk of being perceived as neglectful, prejudiced, or intentionally invidious (Dunkin, 1996). I hope that none of my decisions are perceived in this way. A host of considerations, including the availability of more specialized reviews, and my own sense of priorities within the research enterprise were what conditioned the pruning process.

Finally, whatever one's position in our profession's long conversation about, "For whom is research really done, and to whom should it be addressed?" it must be understood that this chapter was written by a researcher—primarily for consumption by other researchers and their graduate students. That separation of the academy from the world of practice can be viewed as arrogance (Metzler, 1992). My only response to that accusation lies in the nature of what follows. At every point, my goal has been to organize and write as clearly as possible, allowing nothing that seemed unessential to obscure access to what investigators have attempted and discovered. I am content to leave judgments about success or failure to you, the reader.

The model that guides this review consists of nine separate categories that are serially ordered around the logical operations of teaching. The model begins with studies describing the characteristics and competencies of teachers and progresses to research on teacher behaviors that predominantly occur prior to the teaching act. Within the circle representing the instructional context, studies describing the workplace are reviewed along with research that documents teacher behaviors associated with student learning and student behaviors that mediate instruction. The categories toward the bottom of the model provide a description of student characteristics that influence learning, a discussion of the outcomes of instruction, and, finally, a description of research as it relates to teacher behaviors that usually follow instruction. Although I do not regard research on teaching as coterminous with research on teacher education, some attention is given to the latter in cases where there is direct implication for the former. Finally, the diagram is not intended to have perfect verisimilitude. Some of the research reviewed for topics that fall outside of the circle repre-

The author wishes to acknowledge the significant contributions of Amelia M. Lee and Lawrence F. Locke who served as the primary reviewers for this chapter, the input of Patt Dodds whose comments provided vital encouragement, the retrieval efforts of Prithwi Raj Subramaniam, and the substantial assistance given by many colleagues and graduate students during the development and editing of the manuscript. Special thanks are extended to Virginia Richardson for her support and encouragement.

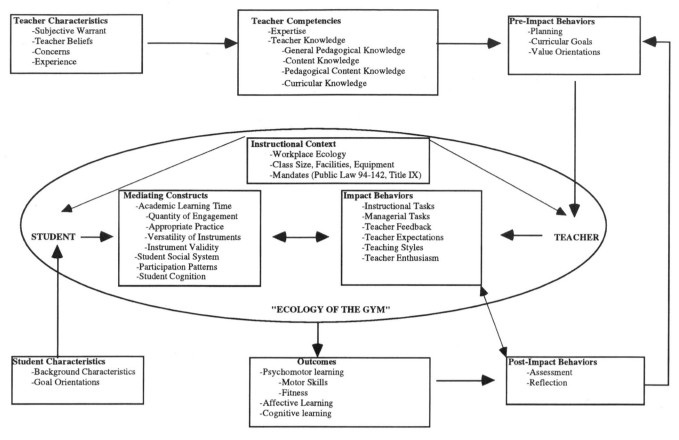

Figure 27.1. A conceptual model of areas of research on teaching.

senting the instructional context may have equal significance for events that occur within that domain. It is not possible, however, to address every conceivable relationship within the confines of a single diagram.

Teacher Characteristics

The study of teacher characteristics, sometimes referred to as *presage variables,* continues to represent a popular area of research, albeit with a considerable change in focus. Although the research literature through the 1970s is replete with studies of presage variables such as those designed to correlate teacher personality characteristics with student learning, the results have been varied, inconclusive, and generally insignificant (Siedentop, 1995). The Dunkin and Biddle (1974) model of teaching that has been heavily referenced as a means of classifying research no longer is adequate to describe the full range of studies involving teacher characteristics. Recent studies have relied less on psychometric instrumentation and increasingly on interviews and other data collection techniques associated with qualitative research. The trend has been away from examining teacher formative experiences and teacher properties and toward an understanding of (a) the subjective warrant, (b) teacher beliefs, and (c) teacher concerns.

Subjective Warrant

Most early research that examined the reasons for why individuals elected to become physical education teachers employed designs that provided only limited insight into teacher characteristics. As scholars began to examine teacher characteristics with new methodological approaches, and particularly prior to formal training, new insights emerged. A primary area of interest has been studying teacher characteristics from the perspective of teacher socialization. By building on initial insights from other scholars (Lortie, 1975; Pooley, 1972), Lawson (1983a) introduced the concept of the subjective warrant within the sphere of physical education. The subjective warrant, developed through years of socialization, represents recruits' perceptions about the requirements and belief systems that characterize a given profession. It is against the subjective warrant that recruits match their personal characteristics, abilities, and aspirations. In one of the only studies designed to examine different variables associated with the subjective warrant (personal attributes, sport background, and influence of others on occupational choice), investigators compared physical education recruits with preservice students enrolled in other sport-related fields (Dodds et al., 1992). Although the two groups shared a number of characteristics, some differences did exist and were explained within a social-systems framework. Despite the insights that might have been gleaned from further studying the many facets of the subjective warrant, most scholarly activity has continued to take the form of theorization (Dewar, 1989; Dewar & Lawson, 1984; Lawson, 1983a; Schempp & Graber, 1992), rather than of empirical inquiry.

One aspect of the subjective warrant that has received some attention is the affinity for coaching that characterizes many teacher education recruits in physical education (Bain & Wendt, 1983). With only limited exception (Belka, Lawson, & Lipnickey, 1991), research results overwhelmingly indicate that future teachers perceive teaching as the bridge to coaching (Chu, 1984; Hutchinson, 1993; Templin, Woodford, & Mulling, 1982). Other aspects of the subjective warrant, however, remain unexplored. For example, what other aspirations and abilities are characteristic of those who seek entry into the profession, and how do they blend or conflict upon formal entry into teacher education and employment?

Teacher Beliefs

Beliefs are not easily defined, and because they can only be inferred, pose great measurement difficulties (Pajares, 1992). As commonly described, beliefs represent what is true and what is false to the believer, are developed through personal experience, and form the substance for an opinion or point of view. According to Ajzen (1988), "Some beliefs may persist over time, others may weaken or disappear, and new beliefs may be formed" (p. 33). The past decade has seen constant reference to the work of Lortie (1975) who postulated that over 13,000 hours of pretraining in the public schools, commonly referred to as an apprenticeship of observation, instills beliefs in recruits that are well developed and difficult to alter. In physical education, the years spent in the student role (K–12) have been referred to as a time in which future teachers become acquainted with the task of teaching but in which there is no opportunity to practice or master pedagogical skill (Schempp, 1989). Although some beliefs contradict the goals of professional and organizational socialization in relatively benign ways, others have more serious implications for the act of teaching. As Hutchinson (1993) discovered in her study of high school students, future teachers may believe that physical education accommodates athletes, is primarily designed for fun, and is an environment in which all students can be successful (with a minimum amount of instruction) if they simply exert enough effort.

There is evidence that recruits enter teacher education with a broad spectrum of beliefs about the purpose for physical education (Goc-Karp, Kim, & Skinner, 1985; Loucks, 1979; Placek et al., 1995). It is interesting to note, however, that the data generated from one of these investigations led the researchers to conclude that a "national curriculum" for physical education exists in the United States (Placek et al., 1995). That is, during pretraining most recruits had experienced a curriculum that included traditional activities such as team sports, fitness activities, and movement skills. Notwithstanding that common background, based on the results of a case analysis in which both participants' beliefs about the purposes of physical education and their beliefs about good teaching were tracked from train-

ing program entry to exit, it was apparent that sharp differences had existed from the outset (Doolittle, Dodds, & Placek, 1993). In part, those differences could be attributed to the points in time at which the individuals elected to become teachers (early as opposed to late deciders). Although some beliefs became more sophisticated over time, differences in initial beliefs tended to persist throughout training—due, in part, to a professional preparation program that in many ways treated all recruits as the same.

In one of the few studies to contrast the beliefs of different groups of individuals associated with the same training program (prospective teachers, student teachers, and cooperating teachers), it was demonstrated that beliefs held by prospective teachers were different from the beliefs of the individuals in the remaining two groups (Graham, Hohn, Werner, & Woods, 1993). Supporting the work of Lortie (1975), prospective teachers had acquired beliefs during pretraining that were limited, based largely on imagination, grounded within the individual personalities of the recruits, and, as confirmed by Dodds and Locke (1995), often situationally dependent and contradictory. Participants in the remaining two groups maintained an orientation about teaching that was similar to the teacher education program with which they were currently associated. In an investigation comparing one teacher's beliefs about the purpose of physical education with beliefs on that topic held by her students, Parker (1996) discovered views that were completely different. That students never understood their teacher's beliefs about the importance of the subject matter could be explained by the fact that those beliefs never were publicly shared with the class.

As prospective teachers progress along the career continuum, some beliefs will be modified. This does not, however, imply that prospective teachers are blank slates (Zeichner, 1979) waiting to be filled with information about effective teaching. Instead, as prospective teachers advance from one career stage to another, they will filter new information through a screen of experiences and beliefs acquired during the apprenticeship period. When conflict emerges between old beliefs and new knowledge, a dialectic occurs (Schempp & Graber, 1992). Although further discussion of the dialectic is better suited for a review of research on teacher education or teacher socialization, it is interesting to consider why some beliefs are more easily modified than others. For example, why do prospective teachers who enter teacher education with a custodial orientation gradually shift toward a more humanistic orientation, and eventually revert back to a custodial orientation upon reentry into the public schools (Dodds, 1989; Locke, 1984; Templin, 1979)?

Concerns

A number of investigations in physical education have been undertaken as a means of identifying teacher concerns at various career stages. Many have relied on Fuller's (1969) concerns theory for the development of study design. The results, for example, indicate that student teachers experience "phases of concern" that emerge at different points during student teaching and range from planning anxieties to concerns about the worth of physical education as a career (Boggess, McBride, & Griffey, 1985). Although a few investigations have resulted in some support for Fuller's (1969) three-stage model of development (McBride, Boggess, & Griffey, 1986), other investigations have resulted in cautions concerning use of the model because it could not be fully substantiated with physical education teachers (Behets, 1990; Boggess et al., 1985; Meek, 1996; Wendt & Bain, 1989; Wendt, Bain, & Jackson, 1981). Such discrepancies may have more to do with the need to develop instruments for measuring concerns that are specific to physical educators than with the reality of teachers' concerns. It also suggests that other instruments such as the Stages of Concern Questionnaire (Hall, George, & Rutherford, 1979), utilized by Faucette (1987) to assess concerns of teachers as they progressed through an inservice program, or the TCQ-PE, developed by McBride (1993) and confirmed as valid and reliable by Conkle (1996), may provide useful measurement alternatives.

Despite wide recognition of the need, the literature contains few evaluation studies of interventions designed to alleviate concerns of new and experienced teachers. As McBride (1984) demonstrated in one small scale study, systematic intervention may reduce concerns. There remain, however, many unanswered questions concerning how interventions should occur, at what points in time, and for what duration.

Experience

A number of scholars have emphasized that teaching experience and teaching expertise are often incorrectly treated as synonyms in the research literature (Dodds, 1994; Siedentop & Eldar, 1989). In earlier studies this could be attributed to the absence of criteria with which to separate experienced teachers from experts. In recent years, researchers have developed a framework for distinguishing between the two, recognizing that experience is only one of many variables characterizing expertise. As such, experience guarantees neither expertise nor competence. With that reservation aside, teaching experience refers to the accumulated work-related memories and dispositions that teachers acquire as they progress from pretraining through the remainder of their careers. It represents one way of distinguishing among teachers with different employment histories. The research that examines how experience influences teacher development, both over time and as a result of specific encounters, conclusively demonstrates that experience has the potential to enhance the quality of teachers' work. "Experience is not a sufficient condition for effectiveness in teaching, but familiarity with the complexity of instructional settings is necessary for effective teaching behaviors to be employed appropriately" (Griffey & Housner, 1991, p. 202).

The results from one study comparing preservice teachers with experienced teachers, indicates that experienced teachers made more instructional decisions when planning lessons, focused on individual student performance (not catering to the interest level of the entire class), and possessed knowledge structures that were rich in strategies associated with effective teaching (Housner & Griffey, 1985). Further, experienced teachers had more contingency concerns when planning, fewer instances of student off-task behavior during the lesson, and

much less class time spent with students waiting (Griffey & Housner, 1991). These results support those of Byra and Sherman (1993) who characterized experienced teachers as making more requests for information when planning, and being less constrained in making adjustments when the lesson did not proceed as planned. In another study, novice teachers showed greater reliance on textbooks and demonstrated more concern about which learning tasks would result in success than experienced teachers (Graham, Hopple, Manross, & Sitzman, 1993).

Regardless of the evidence suggesting that experience does differentiate novices from veterans, there are some studies in which such contrasts are minimized. For example, in a comparative study of public school teachers with varying degrees of experience, competence, and expertise, differences in teaching behaviors across years of experience were less than might have been expected (van der Mars, Vogler, Darst, & Cusimano, 1995). During an investigation of visual retention and knowledge of selected sport skills, undergraduate physical education teachers exhibited greater gains from pretest to posttest than their more experienced counterparts after both groups participated in a 30-hour treatment (Beveridge & Gangstead, 1988). Such results suggest that researchers have only begun to understand the role of experience in the development of teaching skills.

Teacher Competencies

The construct of *teaching competencies* refers to the skills and knowledge that teachers develop and that are necessary for the teaching of physical education. Competencies represent one way of identifying teachers along a continuum of professional growth from novice to journeyperson and, sometimes, to expert.

Expertise

Debate concerning the definition of expertise in teaching has been given much recent attention (e.g., Dodds, 1994; Schempp & De Marco, 1996; Siedentop & Eldar, 1989), however, scholars in physical education have produced little data for consideration. The problem for inquiry appears to reside with the definition of expertise. Although it is easy to construct a list of factors that we imagine to be associated with expertise—peer recognition, great flexibility and large repertoires of response, high rates of success, and the like—these do not readily provide a reliable theoretical framework within which study questions can be grounded.

Berliner (1988) proposed that expertise was developmental, gradually maturing as teachers progress through five different stages. Others have suggested that expertise is rooted within high levels of personal performance in the subject field. For example, the performance of individuals in highly technical domains such as chess (de Groot, 1965, 1966), figure skating (Deakin, 1987), and tennis (Langley & Knight, 1996) has been studied as a means of identifying properties associated with teaching competence. Dodds (1994) has suggested that although performance ability may contribute to pedagogical knowledge, it is neither sufficient nor necessary as a characteristic of someone who can be classified as an expert teacher. Instead, other skills are equally, if not more, important.

O'Sullivan and Doutis (1994) equate expertise with the term *virtuoso*, referring to teachers who not only can manipulate subject matter and pedagogical knowledge, but who also are sensitive to the social and moral agenda of education. Many emphasize that expertise is domain specific (Glaser & Chi, 1988; Siedentop & Eldar 1989; Tan, 1997). Housner and French (1994) state: "Research indicates that the nature of expertise in teaching physical education is best characterized by its multidimensionality. Expertise in teaching is contingent on the acquisition and application of a complex amalgamation of knowledge and beliefs" (p. 241). Finally, the study of expertise is rooted in cognitive psychology and schemata theory. In essence, as individuals acquire experiences and develop knowledge, they develop more complex schemata about the act of teaching physical education, partially because they can rely on information stored in long-term memory (Dodds, 1994). They have what Bloom (1986) refers to as automaticity. It appears that when compared to expert teachers the schemata of novice teachers are incomplete (Borko & Livingston, 1989). For example, in one study that employed three comparison groups (beginning preservice students, experienced preservice students, and expert teacher educators), the schemata of beginning students were clearly less developed than individuals in either of the two remaining groups (Graham, French, & Woods, 1993). While this finding supports the significance of experience, it was the experts who distinguished themselves as having the most insightful instructional observations and the disposition to evaluate lessons based on student performance.

In a novel attempt to explore expertise, Siedentop and Eldar (1989) studied seven teachers they regarded as effective—three of whom they classified as having expertise. Although teaching experience had been essential to the development of their high level of pedagogical competence, those regarded as expert also had high subject matter competence—which the authors propose is often acquired primarily through personal experiences such as involvement in athletics.

Field systems analysis (Sharpe & Hawkins, 1992a) and sequential behavior analysis (Sharpe, 1997) have been used as vehicles for distinguishing expertise. For example, using field systems analysis to compare the behaviors of two teachers (both characterized as effective), one at the novice stage and the other with considerably more experience, distinguishing differences between the two were discovered (Sharpe & Hawkins, 1992b). The novice had less command of subject matter and taught with a more managerial orientation than the expert. In a recent dissertation study (England, 1994), five subject matter experts were studied during tutorial tennis instruction. The resulting protocols indicate that despite engaging in some unsurprising behaviors that are commonly associated with effective teaching, other strategies differed from those used in typical physical education classes. When refining initial skill performances, for example, experts employed "behavior chaining which linked prompts to tasks before and after most learner responses" (p. 2943-A). Finally, the results from two different investigations comparing the visual search patterns of novice and expert teachers (Petrakis, 1986, 1987) suggest that the path and pattern of their eye scans differ when observing live performance—confirming the supposition that experts actually see the world differently.

Teacher Knowledge

Shulman (1986, 1987) has posited that the knowledge related to teaching exists in different forms. Based on his description and the conceptual frameworks employed in studies of knowledge over the past decade, four forms of knowledge are briefly described below and illustrated with representative findings. Although much remains to be discovered in both general education (Carter, 1990) and physical education, research already has made some contribution to the understanding of knowledge forms in teaching. If the results of a study by Vertinsky (1989) prove to be generally true, teachers who enjoy teaching and believe they know more about it will be more predisposed to acquire additional knowledge than those who believe they know less. Thus, knowledge acquisition may invigorate teachers and generate in them an even greater desire to learn. The type of knowledge that teachers may seek to acquire, however, remains less clear. Among physical education teachers, some evidence suggests that there may be a strong preference for acquiring knowledge that has a direct application to instruction (Schempp, 1993).

Research employing designs such as concept mapping and stimulated recall interviews suggests that knowledge concepts and structures become more advanced as individuals gain training and experience (Ennis, Mueller, & Zhu, 1991; Walkwitz & Lee, 1992), and are influenced by both teacher educators (Housner, Gomez, & Griffey, 1993a, 1993b) and individual teacher education programs (Rink, French, Lee, Solmon, & Lynn, 1994). It also has been observed that within the context of a well-developed, field-based methods course, in which future teachers are guided by teacher educators, problematic prior knowledge can be recognized and restructured (Rovegno, 1991).

General pedagogical knowledge represents what a teacher understands about the principles and strategies that are designed to guide class instruction, organization, and management (Shulman, 1987). This form of knowledge is generic to teaching and is not specific to subject matter. Although it has received less attention than other forms of teacher knowledge, it is central to the development of expertise (Berliner, 1988; Dodds, 1994; Siedentop & Eldar, 1989), and it matures with experience (Housner & Griffey, 1985). The degree to which it is incorporated into lessons may be influenced by teaching context and significant individuals such as the pupils whom the teacher encounters (Graber, 1995).

Content knowledge describes what a teacher understands about the subject matter of physical education (dance, sports, games, exercise). Regrettably, investigations into this critical form of teacher knowledge are largely absent from the literature, yet dialogue continues about what forms of content knowledge are most significant for the preparation of teachers, albeit without much data (see Bain, 1990). With the exception of surveys of course requirements in preparation programs and state certification exams that typically lack both breadth and depth, there is little evidence on which to estimate the quality and extent of what physical education teachers know about their subject matter. In the only study located, Hastie (1996a) employed an ecological paradigm in which the teaching behaviors of nine high school teachers, who were classified as having either high or low subject matter knowledge, were compared. Data revealed that those with higher content knowledge had less off-task student behavior, used more instructional tasks, and created a higher degree of student accountability than those with less subject matter knowledge. Clearly, this is an area of inquiry that demands further attention.

Pedagogical content knowledge "includes overarching conceptions of what it means to teach a particular subject, knowledge of curricular materials and curriculum in a particular field, knowledge of students' understanding and potential misunderstanding of a subject area, and knowledge of instructional strategies and representations for teaching particular topics" (Grossman, 1989, p. 25). In Shulman's words (1986), pedagogical content knowledge describes "ways of representing and formulating the subject that make it comprehensible to others" (p. 9). Some of the initial studies in physical education (Graber, 1995; Walkwitz & Lee 1992) have been criticized for lacking in specificity, however, increasingly refined study design and stronger conceptual understandings are beginning to create greater insight into this form of knowledge.

In an award-winning study, Barrett and Collie (1996) demonstrated that it was possible to uncover pedagogical content knowledge by analyzing the movement patterns of children in relation to the actions of teachers who were learning (from experts) to teach lacrosse. Rovegno has conducted a series of studies focusing on pedagogical content knowledge, exploring how recruits acquire this form of knowledge and come to view it as salient to teaching (Rovegno, 1992b). She has observed student teachers who, when confronted by the different realities of high school student culture, retreated into a "curricular zone of safety" (Rovegno, 1994). That search for what is safe to teach in the gymnasium can lead novice teachers to make task and progression decisions on the basis of an increasingly narrow conception of the relevant content knowledge (Rovegno, 1995).

Curricular knowledge is defined as the ability to select, understand, transform, convey, and implement appropriate content into lessons, units, and programs. Ennis (1994a) describes curricular expertise as "reflected in teachers' abilities to select and convey content appropriate to the learner within a particular contextual setting and situation" (p. 164). This form of knowledge, like the others, has not been widely investigated within physical education. In fact, despite the many curricular options now available to teachers, researchers have not shown interest in understanding how teachers learn about curriculum or the degree to which they have sufficient knowledge to implement the various models correctly. The only enthusiasm exhibited has been in relation to the movement approach. In this case, it is clear that even when taught within an exemplary teacher education program, this form of curriculum conflicts with students' notions about curriculum acquired during pretraining, and elicits inaccurate conceptions as novices initially learn to implement the approach (Rovegno, 1993). Investigating teacher knowledge about different curricular models is worthy of further investigation, especially for purposes of understanding the successes and failures of particular approaches.

Preimpact Behaviors

Teachers' preimpact behaviors occur during the time that precedes teaching—over a span ranging from a few minutes to a year or more. It is then that teachers set goals and make planning decisions.

Planning

Three findings have consistently emerged from research on teacher planning. The first indicates that planning promotes more frequent use of behaviors associated with active teaching in novice teachers (e.g., Twardy & Yerg, 1987). In a study describing the teaching behaviors of a group of preservice teachers who planned a lesson compared with a group who did not, there were fewer instances of silence and greater use of equipment from those who planned (Imwold et al., 1984). In a similar investigation comparing two lessons taught by the same individuals, one planned and one unplanned, planned lessons were characterized as having fewer instances of off-task student behavior, less time spent in lines, and greater instructional time (Byra & Coulon, 1994).

The second finding indicates that planning changes with experience. Not surprisingly, experienced teachers ask more questions prior to planning and show greater concern for contingencies that may occur during the lesson (Griffey & Housner, 1991). Planning, however, also changes in other less predictable ways. For example, during a case study of one teacher who was followed from preservice into her first year of teaching, the quantity of information to appear on written plans was reduced as she gained experience, shifting in focus away from the orientation promoted during teacher education (Barrett, Sebren, & Sheehan, 1991). The same shift in focus was observed during a study of student teachers (McCarriar, 1992). Reduction in written planning has also been observed by other investigators. For example, Placek (1984) described experienced teachers who predominantly relied on mental planning and were primarily interested in keeping students "busy, happy, and good" (Placek, 1983). Finally, results from a random sampling of physical education teachers in 20 secondary schools indicated that a large percentage of teachers did not use formal planning procedures of any kind (Kneer, 1986).

A third finding that has appeared in the planning literature suggests that teachers who are characterized as effective may plan differently than either novices or other experienced teachers who are not so characterized. In a study of the "blueprints" of seven effective elementary teachers, the majority adhered to Tyler's model (1949) of planning (Stroot & Morton, 1989). Contrary to the findings in previous studies (Goc-Karp & Zakrajsek, 1987; Placek, 1984; Twardy & Yerg, 1987), whereby teachers were primarily concerned about planning activities as opposed to devising sound learning objectives, participants who were characterized as effective by Stroot and Morton (1989) considered objectives prior to determining activities. Further, the effective teachers were less plan dependent while engaged in the act of teaching—a behavior that the investigators attributed to greater confidence. It may be that in the case of the teachers selected for this study (Stroot & Morton, 1989), what was considered to be effective behavior is sufficiently distinctive to constitute genuine expertise.

Curricular Goals

Goals are statements of what teachers intend as an outcome of instruction. Although in purely logical terms a linear relationship between goals and instruction should be apparent, studies show that in the gymnasium the two may be unrelated or even in conflict (Lambdin & Steinhardt, 1992; Romar, 1995; Steinhardt, Lambdin, Kamrath, & Ramirez, 1993). That is, sharp differences may exist between what teachers espouse as educational goals and what they ultimately enact as instruction.

The written, verbal, and enacted curriculum that teachers develop should enable outsiders to draw conclusions about teacher goals for instruction. For example, if asked, high school teachers who utilize a traditional physical education curriculum (multiunit programs) may respond that their primary goal is to develop lifetime interest in sports. Direct observation of what transpires in actual classes, however, may reveal that there is little connection between encouraging lifelong participation and the content and processes of the curriculum (Siedentop, Panayotis, Tsangaridou, Ward, & Rauschenbach, 1994).

Although this review will not give direct attention to research on curriculum (for a useful review see Steinhardt, 1992) because fully explicated curriculum models have direct and sometimes detailed implications for the pedagogy to be employed, a cursory overview is provided. For example, Siedentop's (1994) sport education curriculum represents an alternative and potentially promising form of physical education that is undergoing close empirical scrutiny (Alexander, Taggart, & Medland, 1993; Alexander, Taggart, & Thorpe, 1996; Hastie, 1996b; Ormond, DeMarco, Smith, & Fisher, 1995; Pope & Grant, 1996). Adventure education and health and fitness (wellness) also represent curricular models. These have accumulated substantial bodies of research that attend, in some part, to the pedagogies involved (Dyson, 1995; see McKenzie & Sallis, 1996). Laban's approach to movement education and the many versions thereof (e.g., Logsdon et al., 1984) continues to remain an option for elementary school physical education (e.g., Ennis, 1990). Finally, although it may be enacted least frequently in public schools, the Purpose Process Curriculum Framework, initially developed by Jewett & Mullan (1977), remains an alternative (Ennis & Hooper, 1990; Jewett & Bain, 1987).

Other recent innovations in physical education curriculum involve goals that are more limited or that deal more centrally with teaching processes than with content. These too provide opportunity for inquiry about teaching. First, Hellison (1978, 1985, 1995) has been an advocate for a social development model of teaching. Although recognized for its potential (Kirk, 1993), it is supported by little data (e.g., DeBusk & Hellison, 1989). Second, cooperative learning has received buzzword status but limited research attention (e.g., Dyson & Harper, 1997; Johnson, Bjorkland, & Krotee, 1984; Smith, Markley, & Goc-Karp, 1997; Sparapani, Abel, Easton, Herbster, & Edwards, 1994; Strachan & MacCauley, 1997). Third, teaching for understanding (Berkowitz, 1996; Bunker & Thorpe, 1982; Chandler, 1996; Curtner-Smith, 1996; Griffin, 1996; Mitchell, 1996; Oslin, 1996b; Rauschenbach, 1996; Sariscsany, 1996; Thorpe, Bunker, & Almond, 1986; Werner, Thorpe, & Bunker, 1996), which emphasizes strategic development as an addition to traditional skill development, has been subject to empirical examination and review (e.g., Mitchell, Griffin, & Oslin, 1994; Mitchell, Os-

lin, & Griffin, 1995; Rink, 1996b; Turner, 1996; Turner & Martinek, 1993, 1995). Although conflicting results have emerged, they often can be attributed to differences in study design (Rink, French, & Tjeerdsma, 1996).

Value Orientations

Teacher value orientations "constitute belief structures or philosophical positions that can be defined operationally in educational settings. They represent educational perspectives that influence the teachers' relative emphasis on the learner, the context, and the body of knowledge" (Ennis, Ross, & Chen, 1992, p. 38). Unquestionably, the most active researcher in this area of study has been Catherine Ennis. Not only is she one of the few investigators in physical education pedagogy to have developed and persisted with a clearly defined and sequential line of inquiry, but by artfully combining multiple research methodologies, she also has convincingly demonstrated that qualitative and quantitative inquiry can be blended to produce portraits of educational settings that are rich in both reliable data and descriptive information. The research presented here provides not only a brief overview of her work, but also a demonstration of how a well-developed line of inquiry can produce a domino effect in knowledge acquisition.

Early investigations by Ennis relied predominantly on the Value Orientation Inventory (Ennis & Hooper, 1988). The results demonstrate the flexibility of the instrument for measuring issues that range from determining consistency between teacher goal decisions and value orientations (Ennis & Zhu, 1991) to investigating the "extent to which teachers' value orientations mediate their responses to inservice training" as measured by change in lesson planning skills (Ennis, Mueller, & Hooper, 1990, p. 360). The inventory now has been revised (Ennis & Chen, 1993), with changes that include greater sensitivity to the orientation of teachers toward social responsibility.

More recent studies, employing multiple data collection techniques, are represented as two branches. The first branch is based on the theory that environmental constraints may affect the degree to which values can be operationalized (Ennis, 1992; Ennis, Ross, & Chen, 1992). That is, when conflict between values and environment emerge, value orientations may not be reflected in goals or practice. The second branch of research has focused on examining particular contexts of instruction. The results indicate that teachers in urban schools may have different orientations than their counterparts in rural schools (Ennis & Chen, 1995), with urban teachers having a propensity toward social reconstruction (Ennis, Chen, & Ross, 1992). It also appears that the context of an urban environment facilitates consistency between teacher decisions and concern for social responsibility (Ennis, 1994b; Ennis, 1994c).

Instructional Context

The significance of instructional context for teaching behaviors and student learning cannot be underestimated. When a fit exists between teachers' expectations and the instructional context, teachers are likely to be satisfied employees. When students are provided with such contextual elements as clean and attractive facilities, ample equipment, classes of reasonable size, a thoughtfully devised schedule, an appropriate degree of choice among activity offerings, a friendly and businesslike class atmosphere, and opportunities to learn and perform—at the least, they will approach physical education with the impression that the school values the subject and expects both effort and achievement. The research literature focusing on instructional context has been growing slowly and already is bearing fruit. What follows is a description of some of the most interesting questions to be addressed within that effort.

Workplace Ecology

Research on workplace ecology has relied predominantly on qualitative inquiry, with case studies representing a sizable portion of studies. The literature generally characterizes work environments in physical education as places of struggle (Locke & Griffin, 1986), where the subject matter is socially and politically marginalized (Hendry, 1975; Lock, Telljohann, & Price, 1995; Solmon, Worthy, & Carter, 1993; Sparkes & Templin, 1992; Templin, 1989; Templin, Sparkes, Grant, & Schempp, 1994). Teachers grapple with a host of conflicts between personal and professional concerns (Lambdin, 1993), moonlight in outside jobs in response to frustration with contextual inadequacies (Williams, 1992, 1993), juggle role responsibilities (Locke & Massengale, 1978), devise situational adjustments (Moreira, Sparkes, & Fox, 1995), lack control of significant portions of their work life (Pinkham, 1994), confront the difficult ecology of secondary school culture (see Griffey, 1987; Locke, 1992; O'Sullivan, 1994; Siedentop, 1987, 1992), encounter homophobic colleagues (Sparkes, Templin & Schempp, 1993; Woods, 1992), cope with the negative aspects of the environment by emphasizing their gratitude for employment (Schempp, Sparkes, & Templin, 1993), or simply leave the teaching profession out of dissatisfaction (Macdonald, 1995).

Induction into the workplace can be characterized as the crossing of a threshold, and "all such boundary passages are points at which socialization promises to be most potent" (Lawson, 1983b, p. 3). Research has shown that some new teachers find immediate dissatisfaction and will leave the profession, citing curricular concerns, discontent with administrative procedures, and dissatisfaction with colleagues (Hutchins & Macdonald, 1993). Induction, however, has also been observed as a period of smooth transition, in which success is attributed to strong beginnings (O'Sullivan, 1989). Although induction assistance is often limited (Smyth, 1995), it may have a powerful positive influence if well executed (Napper-Owen & Phillips, 1995). Unfortunately, as teachers gain experience, assistance often does not continue (e.g., Pissanos, 1995), even though the need is obvious (Locke, 1983; Oliver, 1987) and despite research, which illustrates that teachers may benefit from interventions designed to promote skills such as accurate self-monitoring of daily teaching practices (Sharpe, Spies, Newman, & Spickelmier-Vallin, 1996).

The best hope for establishing positive work environments may reside in examining those programs that are characterized as outstanding in the minds of field-based professionals. In one long-term study, Anderson and his colleagues (1994) accomplished exactly that. Results indicate four key factors in program building: (a) supportive teacher relationships, (b) teacher knowledge and reflection, (c) program credibility, and (d) ad-

ministrative support. As also articulated by others (Stroot, Collier, O'Sullivan, & England, 1994; Templin, 1988), developing collegial support appears to be one of the most critical components in program development (Gay & Ross, 1994).

Class Size, Facilities, and Equipment

Related to workplace conditions are variables that have the potential to either enhance or restrict student learning. With the exception of only a few efforts (Hastie & Saunders, 1991; Silverman, 1988), one variable, class size, has received little direct attention in the physical education literature over the past decade. The significance of class size, however, cannot be overestimated. Larger classes often result in fewer opportunities for students to participate (less equipment and space per student and more waiting in lines), reduced individual contact with teachers, plus more complex managerial problems in the design of effective instruction (see Tyson, 1996). While teachers continue to voice dissatisfaction about class size and time available for instruction (e.g., Jones, Tannehill, O'Sullivan, & Stroot, 1989; Solmon, Worthy, & Carter, 1993; Templin, 1989), few attempts have been made to directly correlate learning with class size. Perhaps this is because such an undertaking would only represent a "study of the obvious."

Other variables such as facilities and equipment have received some attention in the physical education literature, but the vast majority of research on equipment modification and student learning has been conducted within the subdiscipline of motor learning. For example, studies of equipment modification have demonstrated that making minor adjustments such as lowering the basket height in basketball (e.g., Chase, Ewing, Lirgg, & George, 1994) and decreasing the ball weight in volleyball (Pellett, Henschel-Pellett, & Harrison, 1994b) can enhance student learning. Opportunities are rare, however, to purchase such specialized learning materials. The norm is that budgets are not adequate to maintain even basic equipment and facilities in quality and quantities that do not restrict curriculum or reduce teaching efficiency (Siedentop, Doutis, Tsangaridou, Ward, & Rauschenbach, 1994), particularly in urban environments (see Griffin, 1985c).

Mandates

Several legislative mandates at the federal level have had major implications for the manner in which physical education is conducted, influencing the instructional context in significant ways. The first, Public Law 94-142, mandates that children with disabilities receive physical education. Given the volume of research conducted on adaptive physical education, mainstreaming, and inclusion, it is not possible within the confines of this review to discuss results and implications. For current and comprehensive synopses, readers are referred to other reviews (e.g., DePauw, 1996; Heikinaro-Johansson & Vogler, 1996) and specialized journals (e.g., *Adapted Physical Activity Quarterly*).

The second mandate, Title IX, was designed as a vehicle for creating more equitable treatment of females in educational environments (see Williamson, 1996). The result was a regulation requiring sex-integrated rather than single-sex classes (the actual extent of compliance with this regulation, however, remains unknown). Despite the many positive advances associated with Title IX such as greater opportunities for female participation in sport, research has demonstrated that inequities continue to exist in both sport and physical education (American Association of University Women, 1992). Classroom research indicates that girls in coeducational classes have lower opinions of their abilities (Campbell, 1986; Mahony, 1985) and are often treated with less favor than their male counterparts (Grossman & Grossman, 1994; Morrison, 1979). In physical education, boys are the primary source of negative peer treatment for girls (Kunesh, Hasbrook, & Lewthwaite, 1992), and gender differences exist in participation rates (Eccles & Harold, 1991), practice opportunities (Solomons, 1980), and self-confidence (Lirgg, 1994). These results are particularly bleak given that biological differences may appear less significant in determining performance than societal expectations (Carlson, 1994; Greendorfer & Brundage, 1987), particularly prior to puberty (Thomas & French, 1985; Thomas & Thomas, 1988). There is some evidence, however, indicating that when teachers are trained with specific skills for instructing coeducational classes, they can promote a more equitable environment (Dunbar & O'Sullivan, 1986; Griffin, 1985b).

Impact Behaviors

Teacher actions occurring within the confines of the instructional context that are intended to influence pupil actions are referred to here as *impact behaviors.* Within the past two decades, impact behaviors have been studied predominantly within the descriptive research paradigm, which places less emphasis on testing hypotheses (Silverman, 1991) and more emphasis on describing teacher behaviors within particular contexts of instruction. Initial efforts by Anderson (Anderson, 1975; Anderson & Barrette, 1978), who developed a series of studies based on a data bank, served as a framework for other scholars who quickly perceived the potential of this form of research. Process-product designs that examined the relationship between teacher and student behaviors—and learning—were added to purely descriptive-analytic studies. All of this activity produced a variety of new research methods, the most notable being systematic observation (see Darst, Zakrajsek, & Mancini, 1989), which spurred the development of more than 50 different data collection instruments (De Marco, Mancini, Wuest, & Schempp, 1996). These instruments provide reliable data with which to inform researchers about teacher behaviors. In addition, systems of observation such as Cheffers' Adaptation of Flanders' Interaction Analysis System (CAFIAS) (Cheffers, 1973; Cheffers & Mancini, 1989) also have been used to encourage change in the behavior of teachers (e.g., Mancini, Wuest, & van der Mars, 1985). A number of investigators studying impact behaviors have also utilized experimental teaching units (Piéron & Graham, 1984) as an alternative to large scale studies employing the process-product paradigm (see Piéron, 1994).

Many studies involving impact behaviors are classified as teacher effectiveness research. Although there remains no one universal description of effective physical education teachers, there now are generally agreed-upon characteristics of effective teaching. As emphasized by a number of scholars (Graham,

1993; Rink, 1996a), most knowledge about effective teaching is rooted in the work of classroom researchers (e.g., Brophy & Good, 1986; Emmer, Evertson, & Anderson, 1980). Despite significant differences in context and subject matter, scholars in physical education also have been successful in identifying some of the behaviors of effective teachers (e.g., Siedentop, 1989) and in distinguishing among behaviors that tend to promote learning and those that do not. Nonetheless, there remain inherent difficulties in studying teacher effectiveness, whereby researchers must grapple with issues such as selecting variables and measurement procedures, characterizing learners and teachers, and accounting for their developmental differences (Dodds & Placek, 1991). In addition, although this section will focus primarily on assertions about effective teaching that are based on research, it must be emphasized that both future teachers and inservice teachers have strong views about effective teaching that are grounded in experience (craft knowledge) and are no less real (whatever their validity) to those who hold them than are assertions supported by scholars (Arrighi & Young, 1987; Parker, 1995; Siedentop, 1991b).

Instructional Tasks

Rink (1994) employs the term *task presentation* to represent those tasks that involve communicating directions and instructions to learners. She divides task presentation into three stages of direct instruction: (a) set induction (communicating the meaning of what is being learned), (b) organizational conditions (organization of space, equipment, and practice time), and (c) goal of the practice (communicating focus or purpose of instructional task). Further, she posits that three types of instructional tasks (extension, refinement, and application) are necessary to content development (Rink, 1993). Studies examining task presentation (clarity of instruction) and content development (organization of tasks) have produced a number of interesting findings that are generally consonant with classroom research (e.g., Kennedy, Cruickshank, Bush, & Meyers, 1978).

In one case study describing effective teaching behaviors of teachers instructing students in jumping and landing skills, effective teachers employed full demonstration, used appropriate cues, and were characterized as possessing clarity (Werner & Rink, 1989). The Qualitative Measures of Teaching Performance Scale (Rink & Werner, 1989) used in this study and in subsequent investigations by others (e.g., Gusthart & Sprigings, 1989), suggests that there may be a positive correlation between a teacher's score on the instrument and student learning (Gusthart, Kelly, & Rink, 1997). Kwak (1994) discovered that students in a treatment group who were exposed to instructional procedures consistent with full demonstration, summary cues, and verbal/visual rehearsal became more skilled in overhand throwing than students not exposed to those conditions. Studies comparing student learning with different ways of structuring tasks indicate the importance of providing students with opportunities to practice refinement tasks (Masser, 1987; Pellett & Harrison, 1995; Rink, French, Werner, Lynn, & Mays, 1992) and with explicit instructions about task performance (Silverman, Kulinna, & Crull, 1995). The manner in which content is structured (part training, simplification, criterion) also has been found to influence student learning in dramatic ways

500 KIM C. GRABER

(Hebert, 1996). Time spent practicing may be even less important than providing students with a progression of increasingly difficult tasks (French et al., 1991). Providing appropriate instruction, however, for students with large differences in skill level is a complex endeavor (Graham, 1987). Further, possessing an appropriate degree of content knowledge is a necessary precursor to effective task presentation and proper content development (Werner & Rink, 1989).

Managerial Tasks

If instructional tasks are to be implemented effectively, they must be supported by appropriate managerial responses such as maintaining order and organizing students into groups. They represent teachers' responsibilities that are noninstructional in nature (Siedentop, 1991a). Management represents the ability of the teacher both to maintain the learning environment and to effectively organize (Rink, 1996a). Research conducted in physical education has focused on a number of different variables associated with management. In all cases, it is clear that effective management is a necessary condition for effective instruction. The inherent complexity of maintaining order effectively (Locke, 1975) is compounded by students who exert a significant degree of control as socializing agents for new teachers (Templin, 1981), even to the extent of influencing curricular decisions (Ennis, 1996). Nevertheless, research has demonstrated that once effective management routines are established, the result is an increased opportunity for student learning.

The first line of research on management focuses on examining how teachers develop routines for organizing the class (placing students into groups, distributing equipment, etc.). During an investigation of seven effective elementary teachers (Fink & Siedentop, 1989), researchers observed that teacher routines were clearly described, practiced, and supported with feedback. Even the first-year teachers in the group were not overwhelmed by managerial concerns because they had acquired skills during teacher education, unlike the novices described in other studies (Fernández-Balboa, 1989; Ratliffe, 1987). In another study of 11 high school teachers, participants believed they had few instances of off-task behavior because routines had been introduced early and practiced frequently (O'Sullivan & Dyson, 1994). The same teachers, however, also believed they had progressively reduced their demands for managerial compliance over the years as they perceived students to be increasingly resistant to teacher authority and less motivated with regard to achievement. Other research indicates that differences in how teachers execute routines may, in part, be attributed to the contextual characteristics of the environment (Oslin, 1996a) and individual dispositions of the teacher (Henkel, 1991).

A second line of research on management focuses on teacher behaviors that are directed at maintaining appropriate student behavior. The limited research conducted in this area indicates that teachers who exhibit "withitness"—prompt, accurate, and appropriate teacher responses to student actions—(Kounin, 1970) appear to have greater student compliance (Johnson, 1995). For example, the manner in which teachers move about the gym may enhance their ability to actively supervise (van der Mars, Vogler, Darst, & Cusimano, 1994). Attending first to high-skilled and disruptive students may reduce the complexity of class management (Boggess, Griffey, & Housner, 1986). In-creasing the degree to which teachers praise students for appropriate behavior can reduce off-task behaviors (van der Mars, 1989). In fact, novice teachers can be taught skills such as the delivery of praise through techniques like audiocuing (van der Mars, 1987), and when provided with extended, clear, and specific feedback from other professionals, can reduce management time and promote increased levels of activity (Smith & Steffen, 1993; Ratliffe, 1986).

A third and relatively recent area of research interest in class management has been the behaviors teachers use in reaction to student misbehavior. It appears that strategies such as time-out are highly effective with elementary students (White & Bailey, 1990), whereas other techniques such as conferencing with students when reprimands prove ineffective may be more appropriate for high school students (O'Sullivan & Dyson, 1994). Unfortunately, novice teachers may believe there is little they can do to prevent discipline problems and will blame students, not themselves, when infractions occur (Fernández-Balboa, 1991). Further, there is some indication that teachers who know less about management will be less confident in their abilities to influence student learning (Duncan, 1993).

Teacher Feedback

The research on teacher feedback produced more conflicting results than any other area reviewed for this chapter. This may be partly attributed to the fact that researchers in physical education have yet to develop a solid research base. That is, whereas much of the research conducted on teacher responses in the classroom is transferable to the gymnasium, the same is not true for teacher feedback in response to motor performance—in part because gross movement skills represent a unique variable in instruction. Although motor-learning research has provided some guidance, the tightly controlled conditions of a laboratory are sharply different from the environment of a gymnasium filled with a large number of freely interacting students who have different abilities and levels of achievement. Motor-learning research, therefore, is often ignored in the pedagogical community (Locke, 1990).

Conducting research on feedback in physical education is complicated by (a) students who receive varying numbers of practice trials, (b) feedback behaviors that are difficult to isolate, (c) the nature of different learning tasks, (d) teacher variations such as subject matter knowledge, and (e) the brief duration of many investigations (Lee, Keh, & Magill, 1993). Further, differences in the type of feedback (knowledge of results as opposed to knowledge of performance) complicate the design of studies. Given the conflicting findings in physical education and the complexity of presenting a credible synopsis, only brief attention is given here to reviewing research on feedback. For more extensive treatment, readers are directed to reviews devoted to the topic (e.g., Lee et al., 1993; Magill, 1993, 1994; Silverman, 1994a).

Based on accumulated findings, some investigators have concluded that teacher feedback may be less important to motor skill learning than once believed (Silverman, 1994a). Perhaps because many different observational instruments have been employed, there remains more disagreement than agreement about teacher feedback. Some research, for example, has been encouraging, indicating that teacher feedback has positive results. For example, when provided with knowledge of performance, student performance improved during a rifle shooting task (Boyce, 1991), performance improved for elementary students who received "critical cues" while learning handstands and forward rolls (Masser, 1993), and improvements occurred among students instructed in a self-cuing technique for the tennis forehand (Cutton, 1994). Specialists may provide better quality feedback than nonspecialists (Cloes, Deneve, & Piéron, 1995), and rates of practice success have been shown to increase for low- and high-skilled students after receiving feedback (Pellett, Henschel-Pellett, & Harrison, 1994a).

Other research is less encouraging, suggesting that although feedback may increase the number of appropriate practice trials, it may not be directly related to achievement (Keh, 1993). Studies generated from one large data bank indicate that (a) students in physical education classes often receive relatively low amounts of feedback regardless of skill level (Silverman, Tyson, & Krampitz, 1993), (b) the success of feedback may be subject matter specific (Silverman, Tyson, & Krampitz, 1992), and (c) feedback may be less significant than practice for student achievement (Silverman, Tyson, & Morford, 1988). One study describes preservice teachers who provided feedback on a component of the overhand throw that students had already demonstrated at a high level of proficiency. Interestingly, these same teachers ignored less desirable aspects of performance because they were unable to correctly assess deficits (Stroot & Oslin, 1993). Some investigators report findings indicating feedback is often negative (Fishman & Tobey, 1978), whereas others find little evidence of negative feedback (Silverman et al., 1992). In fact, one study suggests that feedback may sometimes negatively affect performance (Yerg, 1981).

Although results on feedback are conflicting, several findings seem relatively secure. Teachers with higher levels of subject matter knowledge provide more content-related feedback (Lynn, Rink, & French, 1990; Solmon, Lee, & Hill, 1991), and coaching specialists are better able to diagnose errors and provide feedback than teachers (Piéron & Goncalves, 1987). Further, it has been demonstrated that preservice and inservice teachers can be trained to increase levels and appropriateness of feedback (Cusimano, 1987; Landin, Hawkins, & Wiegand, 1986; Nielsen & Beauchamp, 1992).

It seems likely that research into feedback will continue to produce conflicting results while differing designs, instruments, and definitions are employed. Further, it is certain that more sophisticated studies will be required before any firm conclusions can be developed. The difficult dimension of qualitative accuracy in the content of feedback also must be reliably assessed and factored into study designs. Finally, investigators must make distinctions in studies between the type of knowledge teachers have about subject matter as opposed to their ability to accurately convey that knowledge under appropriate circumstances.

Teacher Expectations

The terms *self-fulfilling prophecy* or *Pygmalion effect* are often used to describe teacher expectations (judgments or inferences made by teachers about students) that influence instructional behaviors, and subsequently student performance. Arguably, the topic of teacher expectations could have been placed in any

of several locations within the organizing framework for this chapter. Not only do teacher expectations characterize teachers as individuals, but they also are mediated within the learning environment by students. That is, the manner in which students interpret and respond to expectations influences student self-perception, engagement in learning tasks, and, ultimately, achievement. The topic has been placed here in the impact section of the chapter, however, because expectations are enacted primarily during the instructional process.

The leading scholar in the study of teacher expectations in physical education has been Thomas J. Martinek. By building on the initial insights of Robert Merton (1948) and Rosenthal and Jacobson (1968), Martinek has established a line of inquiry that has produced insight into the negative effects that expectations have on some learners. Initial research efforts established the existence of expectancy in physical education (e.g., Martinek & Karper, 1982), emphasizing that teachers respond differently to different students through such behaviors as offering greater amounts of praise to high expectancy as opposed to low expectancy students (Martinek & Johnson, 1979). Subsequent studies have demonstrated that (a) learning context (e.g., individualized as compared to competitive or cooperative settings) influences the amount and kind of feedback given to students of differing ability levels, with high ability students perceiving more supportive teacher behaviors than low ability students (Martinek & Karper, 1986); (b) competitive environments have a negative influence on the amount of effort exerted by low expectancy students (Martinek & Karper, 1984); (c) teachers expect attractive students to perform better and be more socially adept (Martinek, 1981); and (d) students of high ability are more likely than students of low ability to recount instances of teacher praise as compared to instances of reprimand (Martinek, 1988).

More recent efforts have been directed toward discussing and examining the influence of learned helplessness as a construct of attribution theory, a phenomenon that occurs when low ability students believe they are incapable of achievement because of negative past experiences and low teacher expectations for their performance (Martinek, 1989; Portman, 1992). The devastating effects of learned helplessness are witnessed when students exert little effort, rarely credit themselves for success, and concede to failure (Martinek & Griffith, 1993; Walling & Martinek, 1995). It appears that as students increase in age and experience, self-perceptions of students characterized as mastery-oriented and those characterized as learned helpless become increasingly distinct. For example, when comparing mastery-oriented students to students with learned helplessness, older students characterized by learned helplessness blame failure on lack of ability, whereas mastery-oriented students blame failure primarily on lack of effort (Martinek & Griffith, 1994). The powerful effects of learned helplessness have fortunately prompted recommendations for teachers working with learned-helpless students (Martinek & Griffith, 1993).

Teaching Styles

Although many alternative forms of instruction exist and are advocated in classroom research (constructivist, direct, and cooperative forms of instruction), the Spectrum of Styles as introduced by Mosston (1966) represents the most prominent framework of alternative styles in physical education. It was developed as a means of fostering student growth through instructional styles that progress gradually from teacher directed to student directed activities. Although the initial model has been modified (Mosston & Ashworth, 1994), scholarly interest in studying the effects of the different styles has grown from the time that Nixon and Locke (1973) initially suggested a complete program of inquiry. Although initial efforts were inconclusive and problematic (Paese, 1982), subsequent studies have confirmed that employing different instructional styles may enhance student achievement, and teachers trained in the different styles are more likely to engage learners, provide feedback, and alter instructional styles (Ashworth, 1984).

At this point, it appears that type of task and student ability level may be the critical elements in determining the appropriateness of a particular teaching style. For example, the command and practice styles have been documented as superior to the reciprocal style in college riflery classes (Boyce, 1992). In college volleyball classes, low-skilled students performed better with the command style when learning the set and with the practice style during the spike (Harrison, Fellingham, Buck, & Pellett, 1995). Average aptitude students responded best to the practice style while learning a hockey accuracy test; however, exceptional students (representing low and high aptitude) responded best to individualized instruction (perhaps because exceptional students respond better to flexible conditions) (Goldberger & Gerney, 1986). When comparisons were made between teacher-rotated circuits and learner-rotated circuits during teaching using a practice style, lower skilled learners profited more from the latter condition, although, overall, both modes of instruction were found to be effective (Goldberger & Gerney, 1990). The nature of the outcome measure also may make a difference in which style appears to be superior. Although college age students learning soccer juggling skills responded well to both practice and inclusion styles, students in the inclusion group scored better on a written exam (Beckett, 1991), supporting the assertion that the inclusion style requires greater cognitive involvement (Mosston & Ashworth, 1986).

Some scholars have compared the nuances of particular styles. For example, although the practice, reciprocal, and inclusion styles all produced improvement in student performance for a hockey accuracy test, the reciprocal style also appeared to enhance social development (Goldberger, Gerney, & Chamberlain, 1982). When examining the effects of how learners were paired during the reciprocal style, observers provided greater amounts of feedback to partners who were friends than those who were not. In turn, partners were more comfortable accepting feedback from friends than from classmates who were not (Byra & Marks, 1993). It also has been demonstrated that the reciprocal style may enhance a student's ability to analyze motor performance (Goldberger, 1995); however, gains in skill may be smaller in the reciprocal style than in the practice style (Goldberger, 1992). There is some evidence that students who are given decision-making responsibilities (a factor that underlies the structure of Mosston's Spectrum) are able to maintain a level of achievement that is equal to those not allowed to make decisions (Lydon & Cheffers, 1984), and may score higher on measures of creativity, motor skills, and self-concept (Schempp, Cheffers, & Zaichkowsky, 1983).

Although investigations to date are encouraging in comparisons of styles within the Spectrum, few studies have accounted for the variability in practice trials. Without greater control of this important variable, conclusions about the relative impact of particular styles may be premature. For example, cognitive ability improved for students in command and guided discovery groups, but there were no significant differences in skill improvement when these students were compared to a group receiving no instruction (Salter & Graham, 1985). The authors suggest that this may be attributed to the greater number of practice trials that the no instruction group received. Finally, despite some criticism of Mosston's Spectrum for its exclusive emphasis on teacher behavior (Hurwitz, 1985; Metzler, 1983), other style-based models such as the Hurwitz Instructional Strategy Model (Hurwitz, 1986) have yet to receive the same degree of scholarly attention.

Teacher Enthusiasm

One element of teaching that has been ignored by physical education researchers within the past decade is teacher enthusiasm. Although enthusiasm clearly is one means of characterizing teachers, it is placed under the impact section of the framework because it is a variable which has the potential to strongly influence the instructional environment. Despite an early review by Locke and Woods (1982) emphasizing that it clearly is possible to define enthusiasm, train teachers to emit enthusiastic behaviors, and reliably quantify those behaviors, researchers have been less than enthusiastic about exploring this variable in the instructional setting. Although only two studies have emerged in the literature, the results are encouraging. In one study, not only did teachers trained in the use of enthusiasm receive higher assessment ratings, but their students also displayed significantly greater achievement gains (Carlisle & Phillips, 1984). In another study, a clear relationship emerged between enthusiastic teaching behaviors and student performance (Rolider, Siedentop, & Van Houten, 1984). Based on those tantalizing results, it is surprising that teacher enthusiasm continues to be ignored as a variable in explorations of effective teaching.

Mediating Constructs

According to Doyle (1979), research employing the process-product paradigm has a powerful implicit assumption. That is, the direction of causality is from teacher to student. Doyle has found this unidirectional model inadequate because it does not account for a host of other variables such as how students influence the learning environment. Interpreting learning from a mediating-process paradigm may provide a better framework for understanding the learning environment because student behaviors and their understanding of tasks are considered significant variables that impact learning. With this paradigm, the major focus is on student process variables.

The purpose of this section is to describe the mediating-process paradigm and the research it has stimulated. As explained by Siedentop,

> . . . it had become clear by the mid-1970s that teacher behavior did not directly affect student outcomes; instead what was more likely

was that teachers, through their actions and strategies, influenced what students did in classes, and it was what the students did that influenced the outcome measures. (1995, p. 5)

In this paradigm students are treated as an intervening variable, mediating between the acts of instruction and the product of learning. The first part of this section focuses on Academic Learning Time (ALT) and a variety of related instrumentation which deals specifically with students' opportunities to respond in class, describing how teachers' use of time influences student work, and how student achievement ultimately is affected by both quality and quantity of that engagement. The second part describes how the students' own agendas, resultant student participation patterns, and the processes of student cognition serve to mediate instruction.

Academic Learning Time

In 1983, Siedentop characterized the construct of ALT as "a new kid on the block in teaching research in physical education" (p. 3). In a few years, ALT proved to be so robust as a construct and so valuable as a source of insight into teaching, it was widely adopted as a basic variable in pedagogical research. Given the number of studies that have been conducted since 1983, the growing sophistication in instrumentation, and the strong bodies of evidence that have been presented to date, Siedentop's new kid appears not only to have survived adolescent life on the block, but also to have matured swiftly into a productive adulthood.

Although time on task was established as an important instructional variable in classroom research (e.g., Berliner, 1979; Bloom, 1980, Carroll, 1963) prior to development of the first Academic Learning Time–Physical Education (ALT-PE) prototype, significant early work in physical education served as a prelude. Metzler (1989) describes the efforts of Costello and Laubach (1978) and Anderson (Anderson & Barrette, 1978) as fishing nets for catching elements of time on task. The leap forward in understanding the centrality of student time on task in physical education, however, was triggered by the development of standardized recording procedures in the form of an instrument (with protocols for use), ALT-PE, at The Ohio State University (Siedentop, Birdwell, & Metzler, 1979; Siedentop, Tousignant, & Parker, 1982). Subsequent instruments for measuring learning time and student opportunity to respond have been developed and successfully implemented in other studies (e.g., Buck & Harrison, 1990; Silverman et al.,1988).

QUANTITY OF ENGAGEMENT

The first study employing the ALT-PE instrument was conducted by Metzler (1979) whose ALT data revealed exactly how students in physical education spent their time. That study began what has become a sad litany of descriptions of classes in which students spend astonishingly little time in successful practice of learning tasks that fit the skill development level of the learner (e.g., Godbout, Brunelle, & Tousignant, 1983)—what has come to be called "appropriate practice." Further, research comparing student skill levels (using either ALT-PE or other related instrumentation) has indicated that high-skilled

students have greater opportunities for practice and often experience more success than low-skilled students (Buck & Harrison, 1990; Grant, Ballard, & Glynn, 1989; Piéron, 1982; Shute, Dodds, Placek, Rife, & Silverman, 1982; Telama, Varstala, Heikinaro-Johansson, & Utriainen, 1987). It also has become clear that student characteristics are important variables that should be accounted for in understanding time spent on learning tasks (Silverman, 1985b). Low-skilled students are often more profoundly influenced by both appropriate and inappropriate practice (Silverman, 1993), and while gender and skill level clearly are powerful mediating variables, the instructional setting of physical education is sufficiently complex to ensure that they do not always account for differences in learning time (Silverman, Dodds, Placek, Shute, & Rife, 1984).

APPROPRIATE PRACTICE

The most useful finding to be derived from the study of learning time goes beyond the unsurprising demonstration of a positive correlation between learning time and student learning of motor skills (see Metzler, 1989) to confirm that the functional relationship is between appropriate practice and student achievement. One of the first investigators to demonstrate the significance of appropriate practice with student achievement was Silverman (1985a). Others have subsequently documented this correlation (e.g., Ashy, Lee, & Landin, 1988; Buck, Harrison, & Bryce, 1990). Results from a recent dissertation study even suggest that teachers can be trained to push students to engage in higher levels of appropriate practice (Ward, 1994).

VERSATILITY OF INSTRUMENTS

Investigators also have used ALT-PE and variations of time-on-task instrumentation to demonstrate such things as (a) the significance of preactive planning as it relates to time on task (Metzler & Young, 1984), (b) the relationship between teacher expectations and academic learning time (Cousineau & Luke, 1990), (c) differences in amounts of learning time between classes taught by specialist and nonspecialist teachers (Placek & Randall, 1986) and more as opposed to less experienced teachers (Behets, 1997), (d) differences in achievement gains when comparing individual and reciprocal practice to practice occurring during scrimmage (Silverman et al., 1988), (e) teacher behaviors that are associated with high and low levels of student involvement (Hastie, 1994), (f) the influence of model/practice and verbal/rehearsal as they relate to on-task and off-task behavior (Sharpe, Hawkins, & Wiegand, 1989), and (g) the effectiveness of training/intervention as a means of increasing learning time (Grant, Ballard, & Glynn, 1990; Randall & Imwold, 1989).

ALT-PE INSTRUMENT VALIDITY

ALT-PE instrumentation, specifically, has seen the most widespread acceptance to the degree that it has been studied for validity as a process measure of achievement (Silverman, Devillier, & Ramírez, 1991), and for validity of interval recording periods (Stewart & Destache, 1992). With regard to the former, it has been suggested that discrete trials procedures may be a useful alternative to ALT-PE if the intent of the investigator is to measure behavior change (Siedentop et al., 1982; Alexander, 1983), because direct trials procedures measure change directly whereas ALT-PE only predicts such change. Silverman (1985a) suggests that number and difficulty level (appropriateness) of learning trials may be more accurate predictors of achievement than time on task. With regard to the validity of interval recording periods, no significant differences were found in a study comparing three different observe and record methods: 5-second record, 5-second observe; 5-second observe, 10-second record; 5-second observe, 20-second record (Stewart & Destache, 1992). Silverman and Zotos (1987), however, compared ALT-PE instrumentation with other methods and discovered that estimates of engaged time using ALT-PE instrumentation were higher than what was found using time sampling estimates or actual time. Further, investigators have compared versions I and II of ALT-PE (Rife, Shute, & Dodds, 1985), and presented batteries of new systems for measuring ALT (Metzler, De-Paepe, & Reif, 1985). Without doubt, ALT-PE will remain a staple for investigators in physical education. Researchers, however, have yet to seriously address Siedentop's (1983) suggestion that content-specific categories be developed for both the many different subject matter activities emphasized in physical education, and for the goals of particular learning environments. When that further refinement is available, ALT-PE may yet open new windows on life in the gymnasium.

Student Social System

Doyle (1979, 1981) emphasizes that teachers' work can be divided into instructional and managerial tasks. These were previously described and discussed in the "Impact Behaviors" section of this review because they represent tasks for which the teacher is responsible. A third category of events, those related to the student social system, falls within the domain of pupils, empowering them through behaviors that have the potential to modify the other two systems (Siedentop, 1991a, 1995). This system may be observed, for example, when students choose not to comply with the intentions of the teacher but, instead, pursue personal agendas in directing their class behaviors. Allen's (1986) study of the emergence of the student social system in the classroom, Tousignant's (1982) use of an ecological paradigm to study physical education classes, and Tousignant and Siedentop's (1983) early efforts to analyze task structures in physical education have served as useful templates for viewing the act of teaching as dual directional. That is, teachers exert control over students, and students often exert equally strong influence on teachers (counter control).

Subsequent research has demonstrated that management appears to be a key factor in reducing the potential for the student social system to emerge in negative ways. For example, in one study of the classes of two different physical education teachers with differing degrees of experience, teachers established the managerial system from the beginning as a means of gaining and maintaining student cooperation (Jones, 1992). Although the student social system emerged as a factor in student behavior, teachers found ways for it to be accommodated within the broader instructional and managerial systems. Thus, all three systems interacted to produce student learning. Even in secondary schools, management in the form of close teacher monitor-

ing has been shown to reduce off-task behavior to the degree of almost complete task involvement (Hastie & Saunders, 1990). For example, Hastie (1995) investigated the ecology of a secondary school outdoor adventure camp. In this case, although students were firmly held accountable for management, the student social system actually drove the instructional system. Similar results also emerged during an investigation of the effects of sport education, in which the managerial and instructional roles into which students had been placed became a part of the student social system (Carlson & Hastie, 1997). In the two latter cases it appears that the curricular focus, which encouraged the development of a positive student social system, resulted in internalized norms for both managerial compliance and high rates of on-task effort. That description is in sharp contrast with results from another study describing the negative effects of the student social system as it emerged in a secondary school dance class (Hastie & Pickwell, 1996). There, the teacher was willing to accept lower levels of participation in exchange for appropriate behavior—the consequent product being a nondisruptive group of students, predominantly composed of boys, who practiced little and learned less. Taken together, these studies underscore the importance of establishing a strong managerial task system in conjunction with a curriculum that allows the student social system to function in ways that are not counterproductive to learning.

Participation Patterns

Student participation patterns represent another form of mediating behaviors that have the potential to undercut the instructional and managerial task systems, influencing the degree to which students become actively involved in appropriate learning tasks. Griffin's classic studies (1984, 1985a) illustrate the degree to which participation patterns vary for boys and girls, ranging from girls who exhibit athletic prowess to girls who give up and from boys who are classified as "machos" to those described as "wimps" or "invisible players." This range significantly increases the complexity of the teaching role, requiring teachers to have skills for maintaining the interest of the highly skilled, while attempting to involve the lower skilled, all the while responding to individual student needs and personalities. Further, investigations that distinguish students by race, gender, social class, and participation have resulted in interesting observations. In a study of secondary school physical education, race and gender were found to be a major influence on student participation patterns and peer interaction, while social class distinctions led to the formation of cliques in which instruction was often considered low priority (Chepyator-Thomson, 1990). Studies investigating teacher responses to student characteristics have shown that teachers interact inequitably with students (Dunbar & O'Sullivan, 1986), and show instructional favor to boys (DeVoe, 1992; Macdonald, 1990) or those perceived as "high participants" (DeVoe, 1991). What remains less clear is the degree to which teacher responses to students are an outgrowth of their own biases (boys should receive greater attention because they are better skilled) or are the reflection of a belief about the relationship between gender and teaching (boys require greater attention if they are to remain on-task).

Student Cognition

A complex problem associated with studying cognition is selecting measures that have the potential to provide reliable information about events that reside within the human brain. As Lee and Solmon suggest, "Cognition is internal and cannot be observed, so in order to investigate student thoughts, researchers, by design, must rely on verbal self-reports of mental processes as data" (1992, p. 60). This alone presents major obstacles for researchers who must account in study design for variables such as student honesty, student ability to recall information, and the presence of artifacts produced by the recording process.

In that regard, researchers in physical education appear to have once again stumbled upon Locke & Jensen's early work (1974), as a template for considering how pupil thought processes mediate achievement. In that study, the investigators employed a thought sampling technique in which students reported thoughts immediately prior to a signal for response. Content analysis of the data revealed both the composition of student thoughts and the degree of attention to the motor task they were performing. Those variables, in turn, were related to the pedagogical situation created by the teacher at the time the sample was taken.

Recent investigations have employed several new variations of the thought-sampling strategy for uncovering how students' cognitive processing interacts with instruction. During a large-scale study of students enrolled in a university bowling course, Langley (1995b) employed audiotaped, think-aloud procedures to examine student thoughts as they completed practice trials. Interpreted within a theory of situated cognition, he described cognition as primarily task focused, in which students exhibited a high propensity toward concern about errors in performance. In another analysis, Langley (1995a) used narratives to depict the meanings that students constructed as they practiced and learned. These revealed the distinct individual experiences of participants in relation to personal goals, conflicts experienced during learning, and events leading to resolution of conflicts.

As interest in studying student cognition grows, unraveling such complex relationships may provide new insights into a previously closed area of the mediating paradigm. For example, during a stimulated recall interview with beginning students in tennis, those who reported having specific thoughts about technique during performance were observed to perform better during individualized practice (Lee, Landin, & Carter, 1992). After accounting for entry characteristics of students learning the forearm pass in volleyball, students with higher self-perceived competence and initial skill level did not pay close attention during instruction, but were able to detect errors and use time effectively, whereas low-skilled students appeared to pay more attention during instruction but wasted time or practiced inappropriately (Solmon & Lee, 1996).

Student Characteristics

One premise of the mediating paradigm is that individual student characteristics influence achievement. Research on student characteristics, not only as they relate to the mediating paradigm but also more generally as they play a part in other aspects of instruction (see Figure 27.1), has clearly demonstrated that it is impossible to completely understand student learning without accounting for what students bring to the learning environment.

Background Characteristics

Tyson's (1996) review of school context portrays a composite of students representing many different backgrounds, cultures, ethnicities, abilities, genders, and social classes. In response to concerns such as Griffin's (1985c) notion that schools are ill prepared for diverse clientele, scholars have publicly advocated for more than a traditional one-size-fits-all orientation (Lawson, 1993). Despite the fact that discussion of multicultural issues in the gymnasium has begun (DeSensi, 1995; Stanley, 1995), given projected increases in multicultural clientele over the next few decades along with the degree to which diversity can be expected to influence the learning environment, there have been surprisingly few published studies focusing primarily on those variables. Although an instrument has been developed for assessing teacher attitudes toward cultural diversity (Stanley, 1993) and despite an examination of the influence of cultural diversity training on future teachers (Sparks & Verner, 1995), little is known about the degree to which diversity influences learning in physical education—or about teacher behaviors directed toward diverse clientele. For example, there is no research in physical education on the instructional needs presented by students who suffer from inadequate nutrition, are raised in dysfunctional homes, are characterized as latchkey pupils, are addicted to drugs, or who are associated with gangs. Although there is abundant research from which to draw with regard to such topics (see Tyson, 1996; Summerfield, this volume), its applicability to the physical education class environment is not always clear.

In contrast, there has been a long history of substantial effort devoted to research on disability in physical education classes (see, for example, the journal *Adapted Physical Activity Quarterly;* DePauw, 1996; Heikinaro-Johansson & Vogler, 1996) and, more recently, issues related to gender (see Williamson, 1996). Such interest, in part, can be attributed to legislative mandates (Public Law 94–142 and Title IX) that have forced change in the instructional environment (see the "Mandates" section of this chapter). Concern about the health and fitness levels of students also has resulted in large numbers of investigations and research reviews (e.g., McKenzie, Sallis, & Nader, 1992; Sallis & McKenzie, 1991). Finally, the most widely investigated student characteristic is ability, and interest in that variable can be observed throughout this chapter.

Goal Orientations

Scholarly interest in understanding student goal orientations (motivation for achievement) in physical education has been generated as a result of research reviews and studies conducted in academic and youth sport settings (e.g., Ames, 1992; Ames & Archer, 1988; Duda, 1989; Roberts, Kleiber, & Duda, 1981; Treasure & Roberts, 1994). It is believed that by age 12, children can distinguish concepts such as luck, task difficulty, differences between ability and effort (Nicholls, 1984), and climate dimensions of performance and mastery (Biddle et al., 1995). The

conceptions they develop about themselves in relation to learning and performing motor skills translates into the formation of
one of two orientations. The first, task-involved orientation, is
characteristic of students who concentrate on learning and mastering tasks. The second, ego-involved orientation, refers to students who are primarily focused on competition, their relative
position in the class hierarchy of performance, and achieving
success with little effort (see Duda, 1992; Treasure & Roberts,
1995). Although it would be impossible for a teacher to directly
change such student orientations, it may be possible to so structure the instructional climate that it encourages the development of one orientation over another (Treasure & Roberts,
1995).

Results from a study exploring the goal perspectives of college students enrolled in beginning tennis indicate that students
with a task orientation (also referred to as mastery orientation)
selected more challenging learning tasks and responded to a
cognitive processes questionnaire in a way that significantly
predicted achievement (Solmon & Boone, 1993). It also has
been documented that students high in task orientation believe
success is achieved through a work ethic approach driven by
intrinsic sources of motivation (Walling & Duda, 1995). In the
only investigation that attempted to manipulate the motivational environment in physical education (Treasure, 1994), students were assigned to either a task-involved or ego-involved
treatment condition. The results indicate that students correctly
perceived the orientation of the class into which they had been
placed, thereby demonstrating the ability of teachers to manipulate the learning environment. In addition, students in the task
group preferred challenging tasks, whereas students in the ego
treatment resorted to deceptive practices. Encouraged by results from accumulating studies, scholars in physical education
have begun to suggest strategies for enhancing student motivation and facilitating a mastery-oriented learning environment
(Mitchell & Chandler, 1993). Finally, by highlighting goal and
motivation theories and the impact of Pygmalion effects and
class climate, conceptually more sophisticated and more complex research designs already have become the standard for inquiry in this area (e.g., Papaioannou, 1995).

Outcomes

All of the areas diagrammed in the model for this chapter (see
Figure 27.1) contain variables that can directly or indirectly
shape the extent and quality of the final product—student
learning—as an outcome of instruction in physical education.
Outcome here is defined as achievement in the psychomotor,
affective, and cognitive domains.

Psychomotor Learning

The research presented in this chapter suggests that student
achievement is influenced by teacher actions, however, that link
invariably is usually mediated by student variables such as practice. Although logic holds that some teaching variables will
have a significant and positive relationship with student learning, few studies have been undertaken to directly confirm that
assumption.

MOTOR SKILLS

Given that this chapter is devoted to research on the subject
matter of sports, games, dance, exercise, and physically active
forms of recreation, it is appropriate to begin with an overview
of studies that address how well students perform after having
been taught (e.g., the degree to which throwing ability improves
from pre- to post-instruction). In a recent review of instruction
and achievement, Silverman (1994b) concluded that the most
widely studied variables are the use of class time and student
practice (quality and quantity of engagement). Other efforts
have been directed at comparing the success of various instructional methods, with particular attention to the variables of task
structures, feedback, and student characteristics. Among the individual findings that have been particularly illuminating with
regard to the linkage between instruction and achievement have
been those that illustrate the complexity of teaching effectiveness (Rink, Werner, Hohn, Ward, & Timmermans, 1986), the
significance of appropriate practice (Ashy et al., 1988; Silverman, 1985a), the potential for mastery learning (Blakemore,
Hilton, Harrison, Pellett, & Gresh; 1992), the influence of content development (Hebert, 1996) and contextual variety (Wrisberg, 1991), and the importance of appropriate and progressive
sequencing of practice (French et al., 1991). In many of those
investigations, the design allowed examination of both gender
and student ability level as mediating variables.

FITNESS

Although physical education teachers historically have espoused physical fitness as a curricular objective, there is little
evidence to support the conclusion that it has often been
achieved (Taggart, 1985). The number of studies conducted on
either broad-health fitness or skill-specific performance fitness
would require extensive reviews of their own (see McKenzie &
Sallis, 1996; Pollock, Feigenbaum, & Brechue, 1995). Given,
however, the recognition that physical activity promotes both
improved quality of life and longevity, physical educators are
being encouraged to assist children in developing life-long commitment to regular physical activity at an early age (see Summerfield, this volume; also see U.S. Department of Health and
Human Services, 1990, 1994, 1996). There is some evidence of
a response within the physical education community to shift
the focus of public school curriculum away from the dominant
emphasis on development of sport-specific motor skills and traditional fitness components such as strength and speed to a
broader conceptual curriculum that also emphasizes such elements as weight control, nutrition, and moderate forms of exercise (Pate et al., 1995). Health-related fitness, defined in such
broad terms, is receiving increasing attention in the physical
education research literature and already shows promising results (see McKenzie & Sallis, 1996). For example, when compared to control groups, teachers trained to implement health-
related physical education programs were able to almost double
class time devoted to fitness activities (Simons-Morton, Parcel, & O'Hara, 1988). Gains in cardiorespiratory endurance and
reduction in body fat have also been observed (see McKenzie &
Sallis, 1996).

Affective Learning

There are two streams of research on affective learning in physical education. The first represents student achievement in sportsmanship, social responsibility, cooperation, and ethical behavior. There is evidence, albeit limited, to suggest that teachers can successfully influence student achievement in these less tangible areas by including them as a major curricular focus (see Wood, 1996). The second form of affective learning, on which discussion here will focus, refers to the dispositions students acquire about physical activity, their own capabilities, and the physical education class itself. Given that asking and recording responses are the primary means of surveying such student dispositions, data are derived primary from questionnaires and interviews. This, in itself, can be problematic, particularly if the researcher is inexperienced in the use of such techniques with children, or is naive to the problems presented by participants who, because of a strong desire to please or make socially desirable responses, consistently provide carefully sanitized data.

Those methodological difficulties aside, however, Graham (1995) has taken the position that if students are, in some sense, referred to as clients or customers, their voices of commentary on the product of physical education should be heard. In some studies, customer satisfaction seems high. One study, for example, clearly indicated that children in the lower elementary grades truly enjoyed physical education and looked forward to their classes (Solmon & Carter, 1995). Students surveyed in grades 6 through 12 of three urban communities valued physical education as an important curricular area, and although some voiced dissatisfaction about fitness activities, students perceived physical education to be fun and an enjoyable component of their schoolday (Tannehill & Zakrajsek, 1993). Female Australian students in Year 12 who elected to enroll for physical education did so because they valued acquiring new skills and enjoyed the activities that were offered (Browne, 1992). Students in other studies have expressed positive feelings toward new curricular innovations because the innovations encouraged challenge and inclusion (Dyson, 1995; Hastie, 1996b).

In studies that have examined particular subgroups of students, however, the voices of students have been much less positive. In one investigation, for example, alienated students disliked physical education because they believed they lacked physical ability and had to suffer public embarrassment (Carlson, 1995). In another study of 13 low-skilled sixth-grade students, all exhibited symptoms of learned helplessness and referred to the subject as barely tolerable (Portman, 1995). Smith and Goc-Karp (1996) observed marginalized students who were further victimized by teachers who supported the existence of power structures that excluded some members of the class, and students in one high school were described as living in a pervasive culture of alienation of which physical education classes were simply one more occasion for frustration and anger (Cothran & Ennis, 1996).

Such student attitudes have been observed to be influenced by variables that range as widely as curriculum, teacher behaviors, class context, self-perceptions, facilities, and peer behavior (Figley, 1985; Luke & Sinclair, 1991). This suggests that virtually every context for instruction in physical education provides at least some opportunity for teachers to create class environments that exert positive influence in shaping student dispositions.

Cognitive Learning

The least investigated area of learning in physical education is concerned with cognitive outcomes. What students come to know through 12 years of study about diverse knowledge contents such as rules, strategies, technical elements of skill learning and execution, sport history, personal fitness, and the many other broad topics of physical education remains largely unknown. Research efforts directed at uncovering the cognitive aspects of expert motor performance are an exception (see, for example, Thomas, 1994). One finding from such studies confirms the proposition that students may possess knowledge about proper skill execution, yet not be able to provide an appropriate motor response. There also is provocative evidence that curricula in physical education can be designed to promote student thinking skills (Ennis, 1991). Despite the negligible attention given to studying thinking in physical education (see review by McBride, 1991), the results from one study indicating that critical thinking strategies encouraged young students to generate a variety of solutions to movement problems do support further exploration of the topic (Cleland, 1994).

The degree to which students misconceive physical education content represents an area of inquiry with regard to student learning that has yet to receive attention in physical education. Despite growing interest by classroom researchers (e.g., Odom, 1995; Schoon, 1995), scholars in physical education can tell us nothing about the differences between the knowledge teachers intend and the knowledge students actually acquire.

Postimpact Behaviors

The final category of research represented in the framework (see Figure 27.1), postimpact behaviors, includes events that transpire both within and outside of the instructional context. Within the framework, postimpact behaviors are placed outside of the circle depicting the ecology of the gym because they typically transpire after the immediate instructional act. For example, assessment is often used as a means of evaluating student performance (for purposes of reporting progress to students and parents or for diagnosing the effectiveness of teaching). Reflection may occur during the pedagogical act itself, but most commonly occurs at the completion of instruction for purposes of improvement at a later date.

Assessment

It does not require elaborate research to document the fact that in physical education, teachers use assessment primarily for the purpose of evaluating students (determining grades or progress reports) rather than to critically examine the process of instruction, or the content of curriculum. Further, despite increasing pressure on teachers to be accountable for student learning

(Doolittle, 1996), there is a great discrepancy between how assessment is advocated in teacher education and how it is executed in the public schools (see Wood, 1996). Overall, many teachers (even those considered superior by some standards) do not employ formal measures of student achievement in their curriculum (Hensley et al., 1989; Imwold, Rider, & Johnson, 1982), blaming contextual factors such as overcrowded classes or lack of time, or inadequacies in their own knowledge or organizational ability (Veal, 1988, 1992). Student evaluations, therefore, are based less on any form of learning that may or may not have occurred and more on whether students participate in learning activities, comply with class rules for dress and demeanor, and attend on a regular basis (e.g., Wood, 1996; Matanin & Tannehill, 1994).

Authentic assessment, used as an alternative to traditional assessment, has attracted some interest as a means of promoting student accountability—placing responsibility on both the pupil and the teacher for student achievement (see review by Lund, 1992). This form of assessment, however, raises measurement concerns and may place greater demands on a teacher than traditional forms of assessment that have already proven to be problematic (Wood, 1996). Given the degree to which this form of student evaluation is increasingly being employed in public schools and advocated in professional service journals (Doolittle, 1996; Schwager, 1996; Smith, 1997), it is deserving of increased scholarly attention. A host of questions remain to be answered such as whether or not authentic assessment enhances students' desire to learn, motivates teachers to improve current curriculum, or usurps instructional time that might be better spent on other activities.

Reflection

Teacher reflection represents one of the most widely discussed yet least investigated (or evaluated) areas of inquiry in physical education. While the extent to which reflection is promoted in the literature is not particularly surprising, it is a painful example of data-free advocacy. Classroom researchers, on the other hand, have had a much more distinguished and productive history—making significant conceptual and theoretical strides—even to the degree that the evolution of different reflective traditions has allowed the promotion of distinct academic and social agendas (Zeichner & Tabachnick, 1991). In a recent review, for example, Tsangaridou and Siedentop (1995) describe reflection as having been conceptualized in several different forms (routine as opposed to thoughtful), at sharply contrasting levels (ranging from a purely technical focus to critical or moral examination), and as an event transpiring either during or outside of the "arena of endeavor" (p. 213). The authors note, particularly, the absence of long-term studies and express reservations about what serious evaluation ultimately may reveal in this area. They suggest future efforts be directed at "describing what, how, and under what conditions experienced teachers, with varying degrees of experiences and working in different settings, and prospective teachers, at different stages in their program, reflect on their teaching" (p. 231).

Research efforts on reflection in physical education have focused mainly on preservice teachers, with particular emphasis on recording, categorizing, and uncovering reflective thoughts and testing the effectiveness of different strategies for encouraging the processing of observations made during the act of teaching. Results have been interesting and varied. First, not all future teachers are comfortable with the notion of reflective teaching. At the least, it has been demonstrated that some individuals are more inclined to be reflective than others (Bolt, 1996; Gore, 1990; Rovegno, 1992a). Second, based on efforts to promote reflection in preservice teachers, it is clear that some of the skills required for reflection can be taught and the act itself at least encouraged—although some strategies have particular advantages over others (Byra, 1996; Tsangaridou & O'Sullivan, 1994). Finally, based on an investigation which employed reflection groups during preservice teacher education, Sebren (1995) suggests that reflection may promote connections within the knowledge structures of preservice teachers. Although the individuals in her study had not developed the ability to respond reflectively during instruction, they were able to effectively analyze the lesson after it had transpired—a result she attributes to the development of declarative knowledge, which naturally precedes the development of procedural knowledge.

Future Directions

In 1977, Lawrence F. Locke described research on teaching in physical education as a dismal science with "no cumulative body of knowledge about teaching motor skills or any of the cognitive and affective learnings which are adjunct to skill acquisition" (p. 2). Not only did that characterization provide a benchmark for future research efforts, but also his prediction that, taken together, new tools for gathering reliable data through systematic observation and the development of graduate programs grounded in distinctive research traditions "portend a genuine revolution" (p. 8), was an accurate foreshadowing of what was to come in the ensuing two decades. By 1986 a dismal science had matured into "cautious optimism" (Placek & Locke, 1986) in which it was finally "possible to describe elements in teaching that control a portion of the variance in student learning which is open to instructional influence" (Locke, 1987, p. 84). The past two decades have witnessed growing sophistication in research design, the evolution of qualitative research as a valued paradigm, increasing interest in theoretically driven (as opposed to methodologically driven) research, acceptance of student voice as a significant area of inquiry, and the definition of more sophisticated research questions concerning the improvement of instruction and enhancement of achievement.

Such improvement aside, the important question that remains is whether the tremendous effort expended on the studies noted in this chapter leave us better positioned to provide specific tools and advice for those who undertake the work of teaching and whether that substance is better than what was available when the last comprehensive status report was written (Nixon & Locke, 1973). My answer to that question is that in some cases we are much better positioned to make a difference for both teachers and students, while in other cases little progress has been made. For example, where it once seemed impossible to pinpoint behaviors associated with teacher effectiveness, it now is possible to link specific teacher actions with student achievement. In contrast, 25 years of work on the complex role of teacher feedback in student learning has left us, if anything, more confused than when we started.

With regard to future directions for research on teaching physical education, to understand how much remains to be achieved, one need only contrast what has been reviewed here with the content of the accompanying chapter dealing with research on health education. That contrast painfully makes clear how much of the pedagogical research literature in physical education is comprised of relatively low-powered forms of inquiry. For example, health education studies are far more commonly multisite, multivariate, longitudinal, large sample, and serial (in the sense of being embedded in a continuing line of inquiry). With the exception of a very small number of investigators, it is impossible to identify physical education researchers whose work persistently displays more than one of those powerful design characteristics.

Scholars in physical education often follow a pattern of individualistic "research wildcatting" in which the majority of resulting studies have inadequate logistic support (it is the long track record and not the novel enterprise that attracts the big money) and suffer the destiny of poor or absent follow-up—a common feature of opportunism as opposed to long-term planning. Examined closely, there is evidence in this review of a tendency among physical education researchers to jump on the latest educational fad without adequate attention to either proper conceptualization of the problem or development of reliable tools for data collection. The end results are that (a) too many intriguing results are abandoned, (b) valuable time and talent are wasted on predictable dead ends, and (c) too many findings are probably artifactual—the products of particular samples or unique research settings.

That there are exemplary individual exceptions to all of this is genuine cause for celebration, but it does not change a basic fact. If physical education is to keep pace, then its scholars must do better. That observation, in turn, leads to a consideration of how young researchers are trained, how professors of physical education are socialized, and how research productivity is rewarded in higher education—topics that might be at least as intriguing and, perhaps, even more informative than the present examination of the end products of physical education's research enterprise.

This chapter was designed to provide a map of how far research on teaching has come, where it is now, and where it must venture. One fundamental question, however, remains. To what extent and in what ways does research on teaching provide concrete and useful guidance to practitioners—to those who actually do work of teaching? Of course, it has had some influence on how teachers talk about and, perhaps, think about their work. Research-based constructs and research-based conceptions of effective instruction that are emphasized in teacher education programs throughout the nation eventually do trickle down into the discourse of practitioners. How much that process of indirect influence (through teacher educators and their programs) actually changes daily teacher practice is far less certain—and undocumented by research! If scholars intend that research provide a useful resource for the guidance of teachers, they have yet to create what is necessary to achieve that important goal. As the research enterprise ventures into the 21st century, once more raising the question, "For whom is research actually done?" may be the most important agenda of all.

REFERENCES

Ajzen, I. (1988). *Attitudes, personality, and behavior.* Chicago: Dorsey Press.

Alexander, K. (1983). Beyond the prediction of student achievement: Direct and repeated measurement of behavior change. In P. Dodds & F. Rife (Eds.), Time to learn in physical education: History, completed research, and potential future for academic learning time in physical education [Monograph]. *Journal of Teaching in Physical Education, Monograph 1,* 42–47.

Alexander, K., Taggart, A., & Medland, A. (1993). Sport education in physical education: Try before you buy. *Australian Council for Health, Physical Education and Recreation National Journal, 142,* 16–23.

Alexander, K., Taggart, A., & Thorpe, S. (1996). A spring in their steps? Possibilities for professional renewal through sport education in Australian schools. *Sport, Education and Society, 1*(1), 23–46.

Allen, J. D. (1986). Classroom management: Students' perspectives, goals, and strategies. *American Educational Research Journal, 23,* 437–459.

American Association of University Women (1992). *How schools shortchange girls: A study of major findings on girls in education.* Washington, DC: National Education Association.

Ames, C. (1992). Achievement goals, motivational climate, and motivational processes. In G. C. Roberts (Ed.), *Motivation in sport and exercise* (pp. 161–176). Champaign, IL: Human Kinetics.

Ames, C., & Archer, J. (1988). Achievement goals in the classroom: Students' learning strategies and motivation processes. *Journal of Educational Psychology, 80,* 260–267.

Anderson, W. G. (1975). Videotape data bank. *Journal of Physical Education and Recreation, 46*(7), 31–34.

Anderson, W. G. (Ed.). (1994). Building and maintaining outstanding physical education programs: Key factors. *Journal of Physical Education, Recreation & Dance, 65*(7), 22–57.

Anderson, W. G., & Barrette, G. T. (Eds.). (1978). What's going on in gym: Descriptive studies of physical education classes. *Motor Skills: Theory Into Practice, Monograph 1.*

Arrighi, M. A., & Young, J. C. (1987). Teacher perceptions about effective and successful teaching. *Journal of Teaching in Physical Education, 6,* 122–135.

Ashworth, S. (1984). Effects of training in Mosston's spectrum of teaching styles on the feedback of teachers. *Dissertation Abstract International, 45*(01), 0115A. (University Microfilms No. DA84-10120)

Ashy, M. H., Lee, A. M., & Landin, D. K. (1988). Relationship of practice using correct technique to achievement in a motor skill. *Journal of Teaching in Physical Education, 7,* 115–120.

Bain, L. L. (1990). Physical education teacher education. In W. R. Houston (Ed.), *Handbook of research on teacher education* (pp. 758–781). New York: Macmillan.

Bain, L. L. (1997). Sport pedagogy. In J. D. Massengale & R. A. Swanson (Eds.), *The history of exercise and sport science* (pp. 15–37). Champaign, IL: Human Kinetics.

Bain, L. L., & Wendt, J. C. (1983). Undergraduate physical education majors' perceptions of the roles of teacher and coach. *Research Quarterly for Exercise and Sport, 54,* 112–118.

Barrett, K. R., & Collie, S. (1996). Children learning lacrosse from teachers learning to teach it: The discovery of pedagogical content knowledge by observing children's movement. *Research Quarterly for Exercise and Sport, 67,* 297–309.

Barrett, K. R., Sebren, A., & Sheehan, A. M. (1991). Content development patterns over a 2-year period as indicated from written lesson plans. *Journal of Teaching in Physical Education, 11,* 79–102.

Beckett, K. D. (1991). The effects of two teaching styles on college students' achievement of selected physical education outcomes. *Journal of Teaching in Physical Education, 10,* 153–169.

Behets, D. (1990). Concerns of preservice physical education teachers. *Journal of Teaching in Physical Education, 10,* 66–75.

Behets, D. (1997). Comparison of more and less effective teaching behaviors in secondary physical education. *Teaching and Teacher Education, 13,* 215–224.

Belka, D. E., Lawson, H. A., & Lipnickey, S. C. (1991). An exploratory study of undergraduate recruitment into several major programs at one university. *Journal of Teaching in Physical Education, 10,* 286–306.

Berkowitz, R. J. (1996). Tactical approaches to teaching games. *Journal of Physical Education, Recreation & Dance, 67*(4), 44–45.

Berliner, D.C. (1979). Tempus Educare. In P. L. Peterson & H. J. Walberg (Eds.), *Research on teaching: Concepts, findings and implications* (pp. 120–135). Berkeley, CA: McCutchan.

Berliner, D.C. (1988). *The development of expertise in pedagogy.* Washington, DC: American Association of Colleges for Teacher Education.

Beveridge, S. K., & Gangstead, S. K. (1988). Teaching experience and training in the sports skill analysis process. *Journal of Teaching in Physical Education, 7,* 103–114.

Biddle, S., Cury, F., Goudas, M., Sarrazin, P., Famose, J., & Durand, M. (1995). Development of scales to measure perceived physical education class climate: A cross-national project. *British Journal of Educational Psychology, 65,* 341–358.

Blakemore, C. L., Hilton, H. G., Harrison, J. M., Pellett, T. L., & Gresh, J. (1992). Comparison of students taught basketball skills using mastery and nonmastery learning methods. *Journal of Teaching in Physical Education, 11,* 235–247.

Bloom, B. (1980). The new direction in educational research: Alterable variables. *Phi Delta Kappan, 61,* 382–385.

Bloom, B. S. (1986). Automaticity. *Educational Leadership, 43*(5), 70–77.

Boggess, T. E., Griffey, D.C., & Housner, L. D. (1986). The influence of teachers' perceptions of student temperament on managerial decision-making. *Journal of Teaching in Physical Education, 5,* 140–148.

Boggess, T. E., McBride, R. E., & Griffey, D.C. (1985). The concerns of physical education student teachers: A developmental view. *Journal of Teaching in Physical Education, 4,* 202–211.

Bolt, B. R. (1996). The influence of case discussions on physical education preservice teachers' reflection in an educational games class. *Dissertation Abstracts International, 57*(05), 1990A. (University Microfilms No. DA96-32124)

Borko, H., & Livingston, C. (1989). Cognition and improvisation: Differences in mathematics instruction by expert and novice teachers. *American Educational Research Journal, 26,* 473–498.

Boyce, B. A. (1991). The effects of an instructional strategy with two schedules of augmented KP feedback upon skill acquisition of a selected shooting task. *Journal of Teaching in Physical Education, 11,* 47–58.

Boyce, B. A. (1992). The effects of three styles of teaching on university students' motor performance. *Journal of Teaching in Physical Education, 11,* 389–401.

Brophy, J., & Good, T. L. (1986). Teacher behavior and student achievement. In M. C. Wittrock (Ed.), *Handbook of research on teaching* (3rd ed., pp. 328–375). New York: Macmillan.

Browne, J. (1992). Reasons for the selection and nonselection of physical education studies by year 12 girls. *Journal of Teaching in Physical Education, 11,* 402–410.

Buck, M., & Harrison, J. M. (1990). An analysis of game play in volleyball. *Journal of Teaching in Physical Education, 10,* 38–48.

Buck, M., Harrison, J. M., & Bryce, G. R. (1990). An analysis of learning trials and their relationship to achievement in volleyball. *Journal of Teaching in Physical Education, 10,* 134–152.

Bunker, D., & Thorpe, R. (1982). A model for the teaching of games in secondary schools. *Bulletin of Physical Education, 18*(1), 5–8.

Byra, M. (1996). Postlesson conferencing strategies and preservice teachers' reflective practices. *Journal of Teaching in Physical Education, 16,* 48–65.

Byra, M., & Coulon, S. C. (1994). The effect of planning on the instructional behaviors of preservice teachers. *Journal of Teaching in Physical Education, 13,* 123–139.

Byra, M., & Marks, M. C. (1993). The effect of two pairing techniques on specific feedback and comfort levels of learners in the reciprocal style of teaching. *Journal of Teaching in Physical Education, 12,* 286–300.

Byra, M., & Sherman, M. A. (1993). Preactive and interactive decision-making tendencies of less and more experienced preservice teachers. *Research Quarterly for Exercise and Sport, 64,* 46–55.

Campbell, P. B. (1986). What's a nice girl like you doing in a math class? *Phi Delta Kappan, 67,* 516–520.

Carlisle, C., & Phillips, D. A. (1984). The effects of enthusiasm training on selected teacher and student behaviors in preservice physical education teachers. *Journal of Teaching in Physical Education, 4,* 64–75.

Carlson, T. B. (1994). *Why students hate, tolerate, or love gym: A study of attitude formation and associated behaviors in physical education.* Unpublished doctoral dissertation, University of Massachusetts, Amherst.

Carlson, T. B. (1995). We hate gym: Student alienation from physical education. In G. Graham (Ed.), Physical education through students' eyes and in students' voices [Monograph]. *Journal of Teaching in Physical Education, 14,* 467–477.

Carlson, T. B., & Hastie, P. A. (1997). The student social system within sport education. *Journal of Teaching in Physical Education, 16,* 176–195.

Carroll, J. B. (1963). A model of school learning. *Teachers College Record, 64,* 723–733.

Carter, K. (1990). Teachers' knowledge and learning to teach. In W. R. Houston (Ed.), *Handbook of research on teacher education* (pp. 291–310). New York: Macmillan.

Chandler, T. (1996). Teaching games for understanding: Reflections and further questions. *Journal of Physical Education, Recreation & Dance, 67*(4), 49–51.

Chase, M. A., Ewing, M. E., Lirgg, C. D., & George, T. R. (1994). The effects of equipment modification on children's self-efficacy and basketball shooting performance. *Research Quarterly for Exercise and Sport, 65,* 159–168.

Cheffers, J. T. F. (1973). The validation of an instrument designed to expand the Flanders system of interaction analysis to describe nonverbal interaction, different varieties of teacher behaviour and pupil responses. *Dissertation Abstracts International, 34*(04), 1674A. (University Microfilms No. DA73-23327)

Cheffers, J. T. F., & Mancini, V. H. (1989). Cheffers' Adaptation of the Flanders' Interaction Analysis System (CAFIAS). In P. W. Darst, D. B. Zakrajsek, & V. H. Mancini (Eds.), *Analyzing physical education and sport instruction* (2nd ed., pp. 119–135). Champaign, IL: Human Kinetics.

Chepyator-Thomson, J. R. (1990). Stratification in an American secondary school: Issues of race, class, gender, and physical ability in physical education. *Dissertation Abstracts International, 51*(04), 1155A. (University Microfilms No. DA90-24757)

Chu, D. (1984). Teacher/coach orientation and role socialization: A description and explanation. *Journal of Teaching in Physical Education, 3*(2), 3–8.

Cleland, F. E. (1994). Young children's divergent movement ability: Study II. *Journal of Teaching in Physical Education, 13,* 228–241.

Cloes, M., Deneve, A., & Piéron, M. (1995). Inter-individual variability of teachers' feedback. Study in simulated teaching conditions. *European Physical Education Review, 1,* 83–93.

Conkle, T. (1996). Inservice physical educators' stages of concerns: A test of Fuller's model and the TCQ-PE. *The Physical Educator, 53,* 122–131.

Costello, J., & Laubach, S. A. (1978). Student behavior. In W. G. Anderson & G. T. Barrette (Eds.), What's going on in gym: Descriptive studies of physical education classes. *Motor Skills: Theory into Practice, Monograph 1,* 11–24.

Cothran, D. J., & Ennis, C. D. (1996, April). *"Nobody said nothing about learning stuff": High school students' perceptions of physical education.* Paper presented at the annual meeting of the American Educational Research Association, New York, NY.

Cousineau, W. J., & Luke, M. D. (1990). Relationships between teacher expectations and academic learning time in sixth grade physical education basketball classes. *Journal of Teaching in Physical Education, 9,* 262–271.

Curtner-Smith, M. D. (1996). Teaching games for understanding: Using games invention with elementary children. *Journal of Physical Education, Recreation & Dance, 67*(3), 33–37.

Cusimano, B. E. (1987). Effects of self-assessment and goal setting on verbal behavior of elementary physical education teachers. *Journal of Teaching in Physical Education, 6,* 166–173.

Cutton, D. M. (1994). The comparative effects of a cognitive learning strategy and movement sequence feedback during motor skill acquisition. *Dissertation Abstracts International, 54*(08), 2943A. (University Microfilms No. DA94-01514)

Darst, P. W., Zakrajsek, D. B., & Mancini, V. H. (Eds.). (1989). *Analyzing physical education and sport instruction* (2nd ed.). Champaign, IL: Human Kinetics.

Deakin, J. (1987). *Cognitive components of skill in figure skating.* Unpublished doctoral dissertation, University of Waterloo, ON, Canada.

DeBusk, M., & Hellison, D. (1989). Implementing a physical education self-responsibility model for delinquency-prone youth. *Journal of Teaching in Physical Education, 8,* 104–112.

de Groot, A. D. (1965). *Thought and choice in chess.* The Hague, Netherlands: Mouton.

de Groot, A. D. (1966). Perception and memory versus thought: Some old ideas and recent findings. In B. Kleinmuntz (Ed.), *Problem solving research, methods and theory* (pp. 19–50). New York: Wiley.

De Marco, G. M., Mancini, V. H., Wuest, D. A., & Schempp, P. G. (1996). Becoming reacquainted with a once familiar and still valuable tool: Systematic observation methodology revisited. *International Journal of Physical Education, 32*(1), 17–26.

DePauw, K. P. (1996). Students with disabilities in physical education. In S. J. Silverman & C. D. Ennis (Eds.), *Student learning in physical education* (pp. 101–124). Champaign, IL: Human Kinetics.

DeSensi, J. T. (1995). Understanding multiculturalism and valuing diversity: A theoretical perspective. *Quest, 47,* 34–43.

DeVoe, D. E. (1991). Teacher behavior directed toward individual students in elementary physical education. *Journal of Classroom Interaction, 26*(1), 9–14.

DeVoe, D. E. (1992). Teacher/student dyadic interaction of elementary physical education student teachers. *College Student Journal, 26,* 103–109.

Dewar, A. M. (1989). Recruitment in physical education teaching: Toward a critical approach. In T. J. Templin & P. G. Schempp (Eds.), *Socialization into physical education: Learning to teach* (pp. 39–58). Indianapolis: Benchmark.

Dewar, A. M., & Lawson, H. A. (1984). The subjective warrant and recruitment into physical education. *Quest, 36,* 15–25.

Dodds, P. (1989). Trainees, field experiences, and socialization into teaching. In T. J. Templin & P. G. Schempp (Eds.), *Socialization into physical education: Learning to teach* (pp. 81–104). Indianapolis: Benchmark.

Dodds, P. (1994). Cognitive and behavioral components of expertise in teaching physical education. *Quest, 46,* 153–163.

Dodds, P., & Locke, L. F. (1995, May). *Listening to recruits: Images of teaching reflected in the belief systems of prospective physical education teachers.* Paper presented at the annual meeting of the New England Educational Research Organization, Portsmouth, NH.

Dodds, P., & Placek, J. H. (1991). Silverman's RT-PE review: Too simple a summary of a complex field. *Research Quarterly for Exercise and Sport, 62,* 365–368.

Dodds, P., Placek, J. H., Doolittle, S., Pinkham, K. M., Ratliffe, T. A., & Portman, P. A. (1992). Teacher/coach recruits: Background profiles, occupational decision factors, and comparisons with recruits into other physical education occupations. *Journal of Teaching in Physical Education, 11,* 161–176.

Doolittle, S. (1996). Practical assessment for physical education teachers: Introduction. *Journal of Physical Education, Recreation & Dance, 67*(8), 35–37.

Doolittle, S. A., Dodds, P., & Placek, J. H. (1993). Persistence of beliefs about teaching during formal training of preservice teachers. *Journal of Teaching in Physical Education, 12,* 355–365.

Doyle, W. (1979). Classroom tasks and students' abilities. In P. L. Peterson & H. J. Walberg (Eds.), *Research on teaching: Concepts, findings and implications* (pp. 183–209). Berkeley, CA: McCuthan.

Doyle, W. (1981). Research on classroom contexts. *Journal of Teacher Education, 32*(6), 3–6.

Duda, J. L. (1989). The relationship between task and ego orientation and the perceived purpose of sport among male and female high school athletes. *Journal of Sport & Exercise Psychology, 11,* 318–335.

Duda, J. L. (1992). Motivation in sport settings: A goal perspective approach. In G. Roberts (Ed.), *Motivation in sport and exercise* (pp. 57–91). Champaign, IL: Human Kinetics.

Dunbar, R. R., & O'Sullivan, M. M. (1986). Effects of intervention on differential treatment of boys and girls in elementary physical education lessons. *Journal of Teaching in Physical Education, 5,* 166–175.

Duncan, C. A. (1993). The relationship between declarative behavior management knowledge, pupil control ideology, and teacher efficacy for middle-grade physical education teachers. *Dissertation Abstracts International, 53*(11), 3840A. (University Microfilms No. DA93-06030)

Dunkin, M. J. (1996). Types of errors in synthesizing research in education. *Review of Educational Research, 66,* 87–97.

Dunkin, M. J., & Biddle, B. J. (1974). *The study of teaching.* New York: Holt, Rinehart & Winston.

Dyson, B. P. (1995). Students' voices in two alternative elementary physical education programs. In G. Graham (Ed.), Physical education through students' eyes and in students' voices [Monograph]. *Journal of Teaching in Physical Education, 14,* 394–407.

Dyson, B. P., & Harper, M. L. (1997). Cooperative learning in an elementary physical education program. *Research Quarterly for Exercise and Sport, 68*(Suppl. 1), A–68.

Eccles, J. S., & Harold, R. D. (1991). Gender differences in sport involvement: Applying the Eccles' expectancy-value model. *Journal of Applied Sport Psychology, 3,* 7–35.

Emmer, E. T., Evertson, C. M., & Anderson, L. M. (1980). Effective classroom management at the beginning of the school year. *Elementary School Journal, 80,* 219–231.

England, K. M. (1994). Analysis of the instructional ecology in tutorial tennis settings. *Dissertation Abstracts International, 54*(08), 2943A. (University Microfilms No. DA94-01254)

Ennis, C. D. (1990). Analyzing curriculum as participant perspectives. *Journal of Teaching in Physical Education, 9,* 79–94.

Ennis, C. D. (1991). Discrete thinking skills in two teachers' physical education classes. *The Elementary School Journal, 91,* 473–487.

Ennis, C. D. (1992). Curriculum theory as practiced: Case studies of operationalized value orientations. *Journal of Teaching in Physical Education, 11,* 358–375.

Ennis, C. D. (1994a). Knowledge and beliefs underlying curricular expertise. *Quest, 46,* 164–175.

Ennis, C. D. (1994b). Urban secondary teachers' value orientations: Delineating curricular goals for social responsibility. *Journal of Teaching in Physical Education, 13,* 163–179.

Ennis, C. D. (1994c). Urban secondary teachers' value orientations: Social goals for teaching. *Teaching and Teacher Education, 10,* 109–120.

Ennis, C. D. (1996). When avoiding confrontation leads to avoiding content: Disruptive students' impact on curriculum. *Journal of Curriculum and Supervision, 11,* 145–162.

Ennis, C. D., & Chen, A. (1993). Domain specifications and content representativeness of the revised value orientation inventory. *Research Quarterly for Exercise and Sport, 64,* 436–446.

Ennis, C. D., & Chen, A. (1995). Teachers' value orientations in urban and rural school settings. *Research Quarterly for Exercise and Sport, 66,* 41–50.

Ennis, C. D., Chen, A., & Ross, J. (1992). Educational value orientations as a theoretical framework for experienced urban teachers' curricular decision making. *Journal of Research and Development in Education, 25,* 156–164.

Ennis, C. D., & Hooper, L. M. (1988). Development of an instrument for assessing educational value orientations. *Journal of Curriculum Studies, 20,* 277–280.

Ennis, C. D., & Hooper, L. M. (1990). An analysis of the PPCF as a theoretical framework for an instrument to examine teacher priorities for selecting curriculum content. *Research Quarterly for Exercise and Sport, 61,* 50–58.

Ennis, C. D., Mueller, L. K., & Hooper, L. M. (1990). The influence of teacher value orientations on curriculum planning within the parameters of a theoretical framework. *Research Quarterly for Exercise and Sport, 61,* 360–368.

Ennis, C. D., Mueller, L. K., & Zhu, W. (1991). Description of knowledge structures within a concept-based curriculum framework. *Research Quarterly for Exercise and Sport, 62,* 309–318.

Ennis, C. D., Ross, J., & Chen, A. (1992). The role of value orientations in curricular decision making: A rationale for teachers' goals and expectations. *Research Quarterly for Exercise and Sport, 63,* 38–47.

Ennis, C. D., & Zhu, W. (1991). Value orientations: A description of teachers' goals for student learning. *Research Quarterly for Exercise and Sport, 62,* 33–40.

Faucette, N. (1987). Teachers' concerns and participation styles during in-service education. *Journal of Teaching in Physical Education, 6,* 425–440.

Fernández-Balboa, J. (1989). Physical education student teachers' reflections, beliefs, and actions regarding pupil misbehavior. *Dissertation Abstracts International, 50*(07), 2020A. (University Microfilms No. DA89-17347)

Fernández-Balboa, J. (1991). Beliefs, interactive thoughts, and actions of physical education student teachers regarding pupil misbehaviors. *Journal of Teaching in Physical Education, 11,* 59–78.

Figley, G. E. (1985). Determinants of attitudes toward physical education. *Journal of Teaching in Physical Education, 4,* 229–240.

Fink, J., & Siedentop, D. (1989). The development of routines, rules, and expectations at the start of the school year. In D. Siedentop (Ed.), The effective elementary specialist [Monograph]. *Journal of Teaching in Physical Education, 8,* 198–212.

Fishman, S., & Tobey, C. (1978). Augmented feedback. In W. G. Anderson & G. T. Barrette (Eds.), What's going on in the gym: Descriptive studies of physical education classes. *Motor Skills: Theory into Practice, Monograph 1,* 51–62.

French, K. E., Rink, J. E., Rikard, L., Mays, A., Lynn, S., & Werner, P. (1991). The effects of practice progressions on learning two volleyball skills. *Journal of Teaching in Physical Education, 10,* 261–274.

Fuller, F. F. (1969). Concerns of teachers: A developmental conceptualization. *American Educational Research Journal, 6,* 207–226.

Gay, D. A., & Ross, J. R. (1994). Supportive relationships. *Journal of Physical Education, Recreation & Dance, 65*(7), 27–30.

Glaser, R., & Chi, M. T. H. (1988). Overview. In M. T. H. Chi, R. Glaser, & M. J. Farr (Eds.), *The nature of expertise* (pp. xv–xxviii). Hillsdale, NJ: Lawrence Erlbaum Associates.

Goc-Karp, G., Kim, D., & Skinner, P. (1985). Professor and student perceptions and beliefs about physical education. *The Physical Educator, 43,* 115–119.

Goc-Karp, G., & Zakrajsek, D. B. (1987). Planning for learning—theory into practice? *Journal of Teaching in Physical Education, 6,* 377–392.

Godbout, P., Brunelle, J., & Tousignant, M. (1983). Academic learning time in elementary and secondary physical education classes. *Research Quarterly for Exercise and Sport, 54,* 11–19.

Goldberger, M. (1992). The spectrum of teaching styles: A perspective for research on teaching physical education. *Journal of Physical Education, Recreation & Dance, 63*(1), 42–46.

Goldberger, M. (1995). Research on the spectrum of teaching styles. In R. Lidor, E. Eldar, & I. Harari (Eds.), *Proceedings of the 1995 AIESEP World Congress* (pp. 429–435). Wingate Institute, Israel: The Zinman College of Physical Education and Sport Sciences.

Goldberger, M., & Gerney, P. (1986). The effects of direct teaching styles on motor skill acquisition of fifth grade children. *Research Quarterly for Exercise and Sport, 57,* 215–219.

Goldberger, M., & Gerney, P. (1990). Effects of learner use of practice time on skill acquisition of fifth grade children. *Journal of Teaching in Physical Education, 10,* 84–95.

Goldberger, M., Gerney, P., & Chamberlain, J. (1982). The effects of three styles of teaching on the psychomotor performance and social skill development of fifth grade children. *Research Quarterly for Exercise and Sport, 53,* 116–124.

Gore, J. M. (1990). Pedagogy as text in physical education teacher education: Beyond the preferred reading. In D. Kirk & R. Tinning (Eds.), *Physical education, curriculum and culture: Critical issues in the contemporary crisis* (pp. 101–138). New York: Falmer Press.

Graber, K. C. (1995). The influence of teacher education programs on the beliefs of student teachers: General pedagogical knowledge, pedagogical content knowledge, and teacher education course work. *Journal of Teaching in Physical Education, 14,* 157–178.

Graham, G. (1995). Physical education through students' eyes and in students' voices: Introduction. In G. Graham (Ed.), Physical education through students' eyes and in students' voices [Monograph]. *Journal of Teaching in Physical Education, 14,* 364–371.

Graham, G., Hopple, C., Manross, M., & Sitzman, T. (1993). Novice and experienced children's physical education teachers: Insights into their situational decision making. *Journal of Teaching in Physical Education, 12,* 197–214.

Graham, K. C. (1987). A description of academic work and student performance during a middle school volleyball unit. *Journal of Teaching in Physical Education, 7,* 22–37.

Graham, K. C. (1993). Research and the improvement of practice in secondary school physical education. In J. E. Rink (Ed.), *Critical crossroads: Middle and secondary school physical education* (pp. 60–72). Reston, VA: National Association for Sport and Physical Education.

Graham, K. C., French, K. E., & Woods, A. M. (1993). Observing and interpreting teaching-learning processes: Novice PETE students, experienced PETE students, and expert teacher educators. *Journal of Teaching in Physical Education, 13,* 46–61.

Graham, K. C., Hohn, R. C., Werner, P. H., & Woods, A. M. (1993). Prospective PETE students, PETE student teachers, and clinical model teachers in a university teacher education program. *Journal of Teaching in Physical Education, 12,* 161–179.

Grant, B. C., Ballard, K. D. & Glynn, T. L. (1989). Student behavior in physical education lessons: A comparison among student achievement groups. *Journal of Educational Research, 82,* 216–226.

Grant, B. C., Ballard, K. D., & Glynn, T. L. (1990). Teacher feedback intervention, motor-on-task behavior, and successful task performance. *Journal of Teaching in Physical Education, 9,* 123–139.

Greendorfer, S. L., & Brundage, C. L. (1987). Gender differences in children's motor skills. In M. J. Adrian (Ed.), *Sports women* (pp. 125–137). New York: Karger.

Griffey, D.C. (1987). Trouble for sure: A crisis—perhaps. *Journal of Physical Education, Recreation & Dance, 58*(2), 20–21.

Griffey, D.C., & Housner, L. D. (1991). Differences between experienced and inexperienced teachers' planning decisions, interactions, student engagement, and instructional climate. *Research Quarterly for Exercise and Sport, 62,* 196–204.

Griffin, L. (1996). Improving net/wall game performance. *Journal of Physical Education, Recreation & Dance, 67*(2), 34–37.

Griffin, P. S. (1984). Girls' participation patterns in a middle school team sports unit. *Journal of Teaching in Physical Education, 4,* 30–38.

Griffin, P. S. (1985a). Boys' participation styles in a middle school physical education team sports unit. *Journal of Teaching in Physical Education, 4,* 100–110.

Griffin, P. S. (1985b). Teachers' perceptions of and responses to sex equity problems in a middle school physical education program. *Research Quarterly for Exercise and Sport, 56,* 103–110.

Griffin, P. S. (1985c). Teaching in an urban, multiracial physical education program: The power of context. *Quest, 37,* 154–165.

Grossman, H., & Grossman, S. H. (1994). *Gender issues in education.* Boston: Allyn & Bacon.

Grossman, P. L. (1989). A study in contrast: Sources of pedagogical content knowledge for secondary English. *Journal of Teacher Education, 40*(5), 24–31.

Gusthart, J. L., Kelly, I. M., & Rink, J. E. (1997) The validity of the Qualitative Measures of Teaching Performance Scale as a measure of teacher effectiveness. *Journal of Teaching in Physical Education, 16,* 196–210.

Gusthart, J. L., & Sprigings, E. J. (1989). Student learning as a measure of teacher effectiveness in physical education. *Journal of Teaching in Physical Education, 8,* 298–311.

Hall, G. E., George, A. A., & Rutherford, W. L. (1979). *Measuring stages of concern about the innovation: A manual for use of the SoC questionnaire* (2nd ed.). Austin, TX: R & D Center for Teacher Education, The University of Texas at Austin.

Harrison, J. M., Fellingham, G. W., Buck, M. M., & Pellett, T. L.

(1995). Effects of practice and command styles on rate of change in volleyball performance and self-efficacy of high-, medium-, and low-skilled learners. *Journal of Teaching in Physical Education, 14,* 328–339.

Hastie, P. A. (1994). Selected teacher behaviors and student ALT-PE in secondary school physical education. *Journal of Teaching in Physical Education, 13,* 242–259.

Hastie, P. A. (1995). An ecology of a secondary school outdoor adventure camp. *Journal of Teaching in Physical Education, 15,* 79–97.

Hastie, P. A. (1996a). The effect of teacher content knowledge on accountability in instructional tasks. *Research Quarterly for Exercise and Sport, 67*(Suppl. 1), A–81.

Hastie, P. A. (1996b). Student role involvement during a unit of sport education. *Journal of Teaching in Physical Education, 16,* 88–103.

Hastie, P. A., & Pickwell, A. (1996). Take your partners: A description of a student social system in a secondary school dance class. *Journal of Teaching in Physical Education, 15,* 171–187.

Hastie, P. A., & Saunders, J. E. (1990). A study of monitoring in secondary school physical education classes. *Journal of Classroom Interaction, 25*(1 & 2), 47–54.

Hastie, P. A., & Saunders, J. E. (1991). Effects of class size and equipment availability on student involvement in physical education. *Journal of Experimental Education, 59,* 212–224.

Hebert, E. P. (1996). Content development strategies in physical education: An exploratory investigation of student practice, cognition, and achievement. *Dissertation Abstracts International, 56*(11), 4318A. (University Microfilms No. DA96–09092)

Heikinaro-Johansson, P., & Vogler, E. W. (1996). Physical education including individuals with disabilities in school settings. *Sport Science Review, 5,* 12–25.

Hellison, D. (1978). *Beyond balls and bats.* Washington, DC: American Alliance of Health, Physical Education, Recreation and Dance.

Hellison, D. R. (1985). *Goals and strategies for teaching physical education.* Champaign, IL: Human Kinetics.

Hellison, D. R. (1995). *Teaching responsibility through physical activity.* Champaign, IL: Human Kinetics.

Hendry, L. B. (1975). Survival in a marginal role: The professional identity of the physical education teacher. *The British Journal of Sociology, 26,* 465–476.

Henkel, S. A. (1991). Teachers' conceptualization of pupil control in elementary school physical education. *Research Quarterly for Exercise and Sport, 62,* 52–60.

Hensley, L. D., Aten, R., Baumgartner, T. A., East, W. B., Lambert, L. T., & Stillwell, L. J. (1989). A survey of grading practices in public school physical education. *Journal of Research and Development in Education, 23,* 37–42.

Housner, L. D., & French, K. E. (1994). Future directions for research on expertise in learning, performance, and instruction in sport and physical activity. *Quest, 46,* 241–246.

Housner, L. D., Gomez, R., & Griffey, D.C. (1993a). A pathfinder analysis of pedagogical knowledge structures: A follow-up investigation. *Research Quarterly for Exercise and Sport, 64,* 291–299.

Housner, L. D., Gomez, R. L., & Griffey, D.C. (1993b). Pedagogical knowledge structures in prospective teachers: Relationships to performance in a teaching methodology course. *Research Quarterly for Exercise and Sport, 64,* 167–177.

Housner, L. D., & Griffey, D.C. (1985). Teacher cognition: Differences in planning and interactive decision making between experienced and inexperienced teachers. *Research Quarterly for Exercise and Sport, 56,* 45–53.

Hurwitz, D. (1985). A model for the structure of instructional strategies. *Journal of Teaching in Physical Education, 4,* 190–201.

Hurwitz, D. (1986). Application of the Hurwitz Instructional Strategy Model (HISM) to Mosston's Spectrum of Styles. *Journal of Teaching in Physical Education, 5,* 176–184.

Hutchins, C., & Macdonald, D. (1993). Beginning physical education teachers and early career decision-making. *Physical Education Review, 16,* 151–161.

Hutchinson, G. E. (1993). Prospective teachers' perspectives on teaching physical education: An interview study on the recruitment phase of teacher socialization. In S. Stroot (Ed.), Socialization into physi-

cal education [Monograph]. *Journal of Teaching in Physical Education, 12,* 344–354.

Imwold, C. H., Rider, R. A., & Johnson, D. J. (1982). The use of evaluation in public school physical education programs. *Journal of Teaching in Physical Education, 2*(1), 13–18.

Imwold, C. H., Rider, R. A., Twardy, B. M., Oliver, P. S., Griffin, M., & Arsenault, D. N. (1984). The effect of planning on the teaching behavior of preservice physical education teachers. *Journal of Teaching in Physical Education, 4,* 50–56.

Jewett, A. E., & Bain, L. L. (Eds.). (1987). The Purpose Process Curriculum Framework: A personal meaning model for physical education [Monograph]. *Journal of Teaching in Physical Education, 6,* 195–366.

Jewett, A. E., & Mullan, M. R. (1977). *Curriculum design: Purposes and processes in physical education teaching-learning.* Washington, DC: American Alliance of Health, Physical Education and Recreation.

Johnson, B. D. (1995). "Withitness": Real or fictional? *The Physical Educator, 52,* 22–28.

Johnson, R. T., Bjorkland, R., & Krotee, M. L. (1984). The effects of cooperative, competitive and individualistic student interaction patterns on the achievement and attitudes of students learning the golf skill of putting. *Research Quarterly for Exercise and Sport, 55,* 129–134.

Jones, D. L. (1992). Analysis of task systems in elementary physical education classes. *Journal of Teaching in Physical Education, 11,* 411–425.

Jones, D. L., Tannehill, D., O'Sullivan, M., & Stroot, S. (1989). The fifth dimension: Extending the physical education program. In D. Siedentop (Ed.), The effective elementary specialist [Monograph]. *Journal of Teaching in Physical Education, 8,* 223–226.

Keh, N. C. (1993). Students' use of teacher feedback during badminton instruction. *Dissertation Abstracts International, 53*(09), 3140A. (University Microfilms No. DA93-02906)

Kennedy, J. J., Cruickshank, D. R., Bush, A. J., & Meyers, B. (1978). Additional investigations into the nature of teacher clarity. *Journal of Educational Research, 72,* 3–10.

Kirk, D. (1993). Curriculum work in physical education: Beyond the objectives approach? *Journal of Teaching in Physical Education, 12,* 244–265.

Kneer, M. E. (1986). Description of physical education instructional theory/practice gap in selected secondary schools. *Journal of Teaching in Physical Education, 5,* 91–106.

Kounin, J. S. (1970). *Discipline and group management in classrooms.* New York: Holt, Rinehart & Winston.

Kunesh, M. A., Hasbrook, C. A., & Lewthwaite, R. (1992). Physical activity socialization: Peer interactions and affective responses among a sample of sixth grade girls. *Sociology of Sport Journal, 9,* 385–396.

Kwak, E. C. (1994). The initial effects of various task presentation conditions on students' performance of the lacrosse throw. *Dissertation Abstracts International, 54*(07), 2507A. (University Microfilms No. DA94-00234)

Lambdin, D. D. (1993). Elementary school teachers' lives and careers: An interview study of physical education specialists, other subject specialists, and classroom teachers. *Dissertation Abstracts International, 53*(10), 3441A. (University Microfilms No. DA93-05853)

Lambdin, D. D., & Steinhardt, M. A. (1992). Elementary and secondary physical education teachers' perceptions of their goals, expertise, curriculum, and students' achievement. *Journal of Teaching in Physical Education, 11,* 103–111.

Landin, D. K., Hawkins, A., & Wiegand, R. L. (1986). Validating the collective wisdom of teacher educators. *Journal of Teaching in Physical Education, 5,* 252–271.

Langley, D. J. (1995a). Examining the personal experience of student skill learning: A narrative perspective. *Research Quarterly for Exercise and Sport, 66,* 116–128.

Langley, D. J. (1995b). Student cognition in the instructional setting. *Journal of Teaching in Physical Education, 15,* 25–40.

Langley, D. J., & Knight, S. M. (1996). Exploring practical knowledge: A case study of an experienced senior tennis performer. *Research Quarterly for Exercise and Sport, 67,* 433–447.

Lawson, H. A. (1983a). Toward a model of teacher socialization in physical education: The subjective warrant, recruitment, and teacher education (Part 1). *Journal of Teaching in Physical Education, 2*(3), 3–16.

Lawson, H. A. (1983b). Toward a model of teacher socialization in physical education: Entry into schools, teachers' roles orientations, and longevity in teaching (Part 2). *Journal of Teaching in Physical Education, 3*(1), 3–15.

Lawson, H. A. (1993). School reform, families, and health in the emergent national agenda for economic and social improvement: Implications. *Quest, 45,* 289–307.

Lee, A. M. (1996). How the field evolved. In S. J. Silverman & C. D. Ennis (Eds.), *Student learning in physical education* (pp. 9–33). Champaign, IL: Human Kinetics.

Lee, A. M., Keh, N. C., & Magill, R. A. (1993). Instructional effects of teacher feedback in physical education. *Journal of Teaching in Physical Education, 12,* 228–243.

Lee, A. M., Landin, D. K., & Carter, J. A. (1992). Student thoughts during tennis instruction. *Journal of Teaching in Physical Education, 11,* 256–267.

Lee, A. M., & Solmon, M. A. (1992). Cognitive conceptions of teaching and learning motor skills. *Quest, 44,* 57–71.

Lirgg, C. D. (1994). Environmental perceptions of students in same-sex and coeducational physical education classes. *Journal of Educational Psychology, 86,* 183–192.

Lock, R. S., Telljohann, S. K., & Price, J. H. (1995). Characteristics of elementary school principals and their support for the physical education program. *Perceptual and Motor Skills, 81,* 307–315.

Locke, L. F. (1975). *The ecology of the gymnasium: What the tourists never see.* (Report No. SP-009-056). Amherst, MA: University of Massachusetts. (ERIC Document Reproduction Service No. ED 104 823)

Locke, L. F. (1977). Research on teaching in physical education: New hope for a dismal science [Monograph]. *Quest, 28,* 2–16.

Locke, L. F. (1983). Research on teacher education for physical education in the U.S.A., Part II: Questions and conclusions. In R. Telama, V. Varstala, J. Tiainen, L. Laakso, & T. Haajanen (Eds.), *Research in school physical education* (pp. 285–320). Jyväskylä, Finland: Foundation for Promotion of Physical Culture and Health, University of Jyväskylä.

Locke, L. F. (1984). Research on teaching teachers: Where are we now? *Journal of Teaching in Physical Education, Monograph 2.*

Locke, L. F. (1987). The future of research on pedagogy: Balancing on the cutting edge. In M. J. Safrit & H. M. Eckert (Eds.), *The cutting edge in physical education and exercise science research: American Academy of Physical Education Papers No. 20* (pp. 83–95). Champaign, IL: Human Kinetics.

Locke, L. F. (1990). Why motor learning is ignored: A case of ducks, naughty theories, and unrequited love. *Quest, 42,* 134–142.

Locke, L. F. (1992). Changing secondary school physical education. *Quest, 44,* 361–372.

Locke, L., & Griffin, P. (Eds.). (1986). Profiles of struggle: Introduction. *Journal of Physical Education, Recreation & Dance, 57*(4), 32–33.

Locke, L. F., & Jensen, M. K. (1974). Thought sampling: A study of student attention through self-report. *Research Quarterly, 45,* 263–275.

Locke, L. F., & Massengale, J. D. (1978). Role conflict in teacher/coaches. *Research Quarterly for Exercise and Sport, 49,* 162–174.

Locke, L. F., & Woods, S. E. (1982). Teacher enthusiasm! *Journal of Teaching in Physical Education, 1*(3), 3–14.

Logsdon, B. J., Barrett, K. R., Ammons, M., Broer, M. R., Halverson, L. E., McGee, R., & Roberton, M. A. (1984). *Physical education for children: A focus on the teaching process* (2nd ed.). Philadelphia: Lea & Febiger.

Lortie, D.C. (1975). *Schoolteacher: A sociological study.* Chicago: University of Chicago Press.

Loucks, H. D. (1979). New professionals reorder objectives. *Journal of Physical Education and Recreation, 50*(7), 64–65.

Luke, M. D., & Sinclair, G. D. (1991). Gender differences in adolescents' attitudes toward school physical education. *Journal of Teaching in Physical Education, 11,* 31–46.

Lund, J. (1992). Assessment and accountability in secondary physical education. *Quest, 44,* 352–360.

Lydon, M. C., & Cheffers, J. T. F. (1984). Decision-making in elementary school-age children: Effects upon motor learning and self-concept development. *Research Quarterly for Exercise and Sport, 55,* 135–140.

Lynn, S., Rink, J., & French, K. (1990, March). *The relation of content knowledge to instructional performance in preservice teachers.* Paper presented at the annual meeting of the American Alliance of Health, Physical Education, Recreation and Dance, New Orleans, LA.

Macdonald, D. (1990). The relationship between the sex composition of physical education classes and teacher/pupil verbal interaction. *Journal of Teaching in Physical Education, 9,* 152–163.

Macdonald, D. (1995). The role of proletarianization in physical education teacher attrition. *Research Quarterly for Exercise and Sport, 66,* 129–141.

Magill, R. A. (1993). *Motor learning: Concepts and applications* (4th ed.). Dubuque, IA: Brown and Benchmark.

Magill, R. A. (1994). The influence of augmented feedback on skill learning depends on characteristics of the skill and the learner. *Quest, 46,* 314–327.

Mahony, P. (1985). *Schools for the boys? Co-education reassessed.* London: Hutchinson.

Mancini, V. H., Wuest, D. A., & van der Mars, H. (1985). Use of instruction and supervision in systematic observation in undergraduate professional preparation. *Journal of Teaching in Physical Education, 5,* 22–33.

Martinek, T. J. (1981). Physical attractiveness: Effects on teacher expectations and dyadic interactions in elementary age children. *Journal of Sport Psychology, 3,* 196–205.

Martinek, T. J. (1988). Confirmation of a teacher expectancy model: Student perceptions and causal attributions of teaching behaviors. *Research Quarterly for Exercise and Sport, 59,* 118–126.

Martinek, T. J. (1989). Children's perceptions of teaching behaviors: An attributional model for explaining teacher expectancy effects. *Journal of Teaching in Physical Education, 8,* 318–328.

Martinek, T. J., & Griffith, J. B. (1993). Working with the learned helpless child. *Journal of Physical Education, Recreation & Dance, 64*(6), 17–20.

Martinek, T. J., & Griffith, J. B. (1994). Learned helplessness in physical education: A developmental study of causal attributions and task persistence. *Journal of Teaching in Physical Education, 13,* 108–122.

Martinek, T., & Johnson, S. (1979). Teacher expectations: Effects on dyadic interaction and self-concept in elementary age children. *Research Quarterly for Exercise and Sport, 50,* 60–70.

Martinek, T., & Karper, W. (1982). Canonical relationships among motor ability, expression of effort, teacher expectations and dyadic interactions in elementary age children. *Journal of Teaching in Physical Education, 1*(2), 26–39.

Martinek, T. J., & Karper, W. B. (1984). The effects of noncompetitive and competitive instructional climates on teacher expectancy effects in elementary physical education classes. *Journal of Sport Psychology, 6,* 408–421.

Martinek, T., & Karper, W. B. (1986). Motor ability and instructional contexts: Effects on teacher expectations and dyadic interactions in elementary physical education classes. *Journal of Classroom Interaction, 22*(2), 16–25.

Masser, L. (1987). The effect of refinement on student achievement in a fundamental motor skill in grades K through 6. *Journal of Teaching in Physical Education, 6,* 174–182.

Masser, L. S. (1993). Critical cues help first-grade students' achievement in handstands and forward rolls. *Journal of Teaching in Physical Education, 12,* 301–312.

Matanin, M., & Tannehill, D. (1994). Assessment and grading in physical education. In M. O'Sullivan (Ed.), High school physical education teachers: Their world of work [Monograph]. *Journal of Teaching in Physical Education, 13,* 395–405.

McBride, R. E. (1984). An intensive study of a systematic teacher training model in physical education. *Journal of Teaching in Physical Education, 4,* 3–16.

McBride, R. E. (1991). Critical thinking—An overview with implications for physical education. *Journal of Teaching in Physical Education, 11,* 112–125.

McBride, R. E. (1993). The TCQ-PE: An adaptation of the teacher concerns questionnaire instrument to a physical education setting. *Journal of Teaching in Physical Education, 12,* 188–196.

McBride, R. E., Boggess, T. E., & Griffey, D.C. (1986). Concerns of inservice physical education teachers as compared with Fuller's concern model. *Journal of Teaching in Physical Education, 5,* 149–156.

McCarriar, S. M. (1992). Undetermined outcomes: Student teachers and the heuristics of adjusting lesson plans to various ecological influences. *Dissertation Abstracts International, 53*(08), 2736A. (University Microfilms No. DA92-37701)

McKenzie, T. L., & Sallis, J. F. (1996). Physical activity, fitness, and health-related physical education. In S. J. Silverman & C. D. Ennis (Eds.), *Student learning in physical education* (pp. 223–246). Champaign, IL: Human Kinetics.

McKenzie, T. L., Sallis, J. F., & Nader, P. R. (1992). SOFIT: System for observing fitness instruction time. *Journal of Teaching in Physical Education, 11,* 195–205.

Meek, G. A. (1996). The teacher concerns questionnaire with preservice physical educators in Great Britain: Being concerned with concerns. *Journal of Teaching in Physical Education, 16,* 20–29.

Merton, R. K. (1948). The self-fulfilling prophecy. *Antioch Review, 8,* 193–210.

Metzler, M. W. (1979). *The measurement of Academic Learning Time in physical education.* Unpublished doctoral dissertation, The Ohio State University, Columbus, OH.

Metzler, M. W. (1983). On styles. *Quest, 35,* 145–154.

Metzler, M. (1989). A review of research on time in sport pedagogy. *Journal of Teaching in Physical Education, 8,* 87–103.

Metzler, M. (1992). Commentary on "Research on teaching in physical education." *Research Quarterly for Exercise and Sport, 63,* 205–206.

Metzler, M., DePaepe, J., & Reif, G. (1985). Alternative technologies for measuring academic learning time in physical education. *Journal of Teaching in Physical Education, 4,* 271–285.

Metzler, M. W., & Young, J. C. (1984). The relationship between teachers' proactive planning and student process measures. *Research Quarterly for Exercise and Sport, 55,* 356–364.

Mitchell, S. (1996). Improving invasion game performance. *Journal of Physical Education, Recreation & Dance, 67*(2), 30–33.

Mitchell, S. A., & Chandler, T. J. L. (1993). Motivating students for learning in the gymnasium: The role of perception and meaning. *The Physical Educator, 50,* 120–125.

Mitchell, S. A., Griffin, L. L., & Oslin, J. L. (1994). Tactical awareness as a developmentally appropriate focus for the teaching of games in elementary and secondary physical education. *The Physical Educator, 51,* 21–28.

Mitchell, S. A., Oslin, J. L., & Griffin, L. L. (1995). The effects of two instructional approaches on game performance. *Pedagogy in Practice, 1,* 36–48.

Moreira, H., Sparkes, A. C., & Fox, K. (1995). Physical education teachers and job commitment: A preliminary analysis. *European Physical Education Review, 1,* 122–136.

Mosston, M. (1966). *Teaching physical education.* Columbus, OH: Merrill.

Mosston, M., & Ashworth, S. (1986). *Teaching physical education* (3rd ed.). Columbus, OH: Merrill.

Mosston, M., & Ashworth, S. (1994). *Teaching physical education* (4th ed.). New York: Macmillan.

Napper-Owen, G. E., & Phillips, D. A. (1995). A qualitative analysis of the impact of induction assistance on first-year physical educators. *Journal of Teaching in Physical Education, 14,* 305–327.

Nicholls, J. (1984). Conceptions of ability and achievement motivation. In R. Ames & C. Ames (Eds.), *Research on motivation in education: Student motivation* (Vol. 1, pp. 39–73). New York: Academic Press.

Nielsen, A. B., & Beauchamp, L. (1992). The effect of training in conceptual kinesiology on feedback provision patterns. *Journal of Teaching in Physical Education, 11,* 126–138.

Nixon, J. E., & Locke, L. F. (1973). Research on teaching in physical education. In R. M. W. Travers (Ed.), *Second handbook of research on teaching* (pp. 1210–1242). Chicago: Rand McNally.

Odom, A. L. (1995). Secondary & college biology students' misconceptions about diffusion & osmosis. *The American Biology Teacher, 57,* 409–415.

Oliver, B. (1987). Teacher and school characteristics: Their relationship to the inservice needs of teachers. *Journal of Teaching in Physical Education, 7,* 38–45.

Ormond, T., DeMarco, G., Smith, R., & Fisher, K. (1995). Comparison of the sport education model and the traditional unit approach to teaching secondary school basketball. *Research Quarterly for Exercise and Sport, 66*(Suppl. 1), A–66.

Oslin, J. L. (1996a). Routines as organizing features in middle school physical education. *Journal of Teaching in Physical Education, 15,* 319–337.

Oslin, J. L. (1996b). Tactical approaches to teaching games: Introduction. *Journal of Physical Education, Recreation & Dance, 67*(1), 27.

O'Sullivan, M. (1989). Failing gym is like failing lunch or recess: Two beginning teachers' struggle for legitimacy. In D. Siedentop (Ed.), The effective elementary specialist [Monograph]. *Journal of Teaching in Physical Education, 8,* 227–242.

O'Sullivan, M. (Ed.). (1994). High school physical education teachers: Their world of work [Monograph]. *Journal of Teaching in Physical Education, 13,* 324–441.

O'Sullivan, M., & Doutis, P. (1994). Research on expertise: Guideposts for expertise and teacher education in physical education. *Quest, 46,* 176–185.

O'Sullivan, M., & Dyson, B. (1994). Rules, routines, and expectations of 11 high school physical education teachers. In M. O'Sullivan (Ed.), High school physical education teachers: Their world of work [Monograph]. *Journal of Teaching in Physical Education, 13,* 361–374.

Paese, D. G. (1982). Current status and application of instructional strategy research. *Journal of Teaching in Physical Education, 1*(3), 31–38.

Pajares, M. F. (1992). Teachers' beliefs and educational research: Cleaning up a messy construct. *Review of Educational Research, 62,* 307–332.

Papaioannou, A. (1995). Differential perceptual and motivational patterns when different goals are adopted. *Journal of Sport & Exercise Psychology, 17,* 18–34.

Parker, J. (1995). Secondary teachers' views of effective teaching in physical education. *Journal of Teaching in Physical Education, 14,* 127–139.

Parker, J. (1996). *Teacher and student beliefs: A case study of a high school physical education class.* Unpublished doctoral dissertation, University of Massachusetts, Amherst, MA.

Pate, R. R., Small, M. L., Ross, J. G., Young, J. C., Flint, K. H., & Warren, C. W. (1995). School physical education. *Journal of School Health, 65,* 312–318.

Pellett, T. L., & Harrison, J. M. (1995). The influence of refinement on female junior high school students' volleyball practice success and achievement. *Journal of Teaching in Physical Education, 15,* 41–52.

Pellett, T. L., Henschel-Pellett, H. A., & Harrison, J. M. (1994a). Feedback effects: Field-based findings. *Journal of Physical Education, Recreation & Dance, 65*(9), 75–78.

Pellett, T. L., Henschel-Pellett, H. A., & Harrison, J. M. (1994b). Influence of ball weight on junior high girls' volleyball performance. *Perceptual Motor Skills, 78,* 1379–1384.

Petrakis, E. (1986). Visual observation patterns of tennis teachers. *Research Quarterly for Exercise and Sport, 57,* 254–259.

Petrakis, E. (1987). Analysis of visual search patterns of dance teachers. *Journal of Teaching in Physical Education, 6,* 149–156.

Piéron, M. (1982). Behaviors of low and high achievers in physical education. In M. Piéron & J. Cheffers (Eds.), *Studying the teaching in physical education* (pp. 53–60). Liege, Belgium: Association Internationale des Ecoles Superieures d'Education.

Piéron, M. (1994). Studying the instruction process in teaching physical education. *Sport Science Review, 3,* 73–82.

Piéron, M., & Goncalves, C. (1987). Participant engagement and teacher's feedback in physical education teaching and coaching. In G. T. Barrette, R. S. Feingold, C. R. Rees, & M. Piéron (Eds.), *Myths, models, and methods in sport pedagogy* (pp. 249–254). Champaign, IL: Human Kinetics.

Piéron, M., & Graham, G. (1984). Research on physical education teacher effectiveness: The experimental teaching units. *International Journal of Physical Education, 21*(3), 9–14.

Pinkham, K. M. (1994). The school as a workplace: The perspectives of secondary school physical educators. *Dissertation Abstracts International, 55*(03), 506A. (University Microfilms No. DA94-20677)

Pissanos, B. W. (1995). Providers of continued professional education: Constructed perceptions of four elementary school physical education teachers. *Journal of Teaching in Physical Education, 14,* 215–230.

Placek, J. H. (1983). Conceptions of success in teaching: Busy, happy and good? In T. J. Templin & J. K. Olson (Eds.), *Teaching in physical education* (pp. 46–56). Champaign, IL: Human Kinetics.

Placek, J. H. (1984). A multi-case study of teacher planning in physical education. *Journal of Teaching in Physical Education, 4,* 39–49.

Placek, J. H., Dodds, P., Doolittle, S. A., Portman, P. A., Ratliffe, T. A., & Pinkham, K. M. (1995). Teaching recruits' physical education backgrounds and beliefs about purposes for their subject matter. *Journal of Teaching in Physical Education, 14,* 246–261.

Placek, J. H., & Locke, L. F. (1986). Research on teaching physical education: New knowledge and cautious optimism. *Journal of Teacher Education, 37*(4), 24–28.

Placek, J. H., & Randall, L. (1986). Comparison of academic learning time in physical education: Students of specialists and nonspecialists. *Journal of Teaching in Physical Education, 5,* 157–165.

Pollock, M. L., Feigenbaum, M. S., & Brechue, W. F. (1995). Exercise prescription for physical fitness. *Quest, 47,* 320–337.

Pooley, J. C. (1972). Professional socialization: A model of the pretraining phase applicable to physical education students. *Quest, XVIII,* 57–66.

Pope, C. V., & Grant, B. C. (1996). Student experiences in sport education. *Waikato Journal of Education, 2,* 103–118.

Portman, P. A. (1992). The experience of low-skilled students in public school physical education: The significance of being chosen last. *Dissertation Abstracts International, 53*(06), 1850A. (University Microfilms No. DA92-33134)

Portman, P. A. (1995). Who is having fun in physical education classes? Experiences of sixth-grade students in elementary and middle schools. In G. Graham (Ed.), Physical education through students' eyes and in students' voices [Monograph]. *Journal of Teaching in Physical Education, 14,* 445–453.

Randall, L. E., & Imwold, C. H. (1989). The effect of an intervention on academic learning time provided by preservice physical education teachers. *Journal of Teaching in Physical Education, 8,* 271–279.

Ratliffe, T. (1986). The influence of school principals on management time and student activity time for two elementary physical education teachers. *Journal of Teaching in Physical Education, 5,* 117–125.

Ratliffe, T. (1987). Overcoming obstacles beginning teachers encounter. *Journal of Physical Education, Recreation & Dance, 58*(4), 18–23.

Rauschenbach, J. (1996). Charge! and catch coop: Two games for teaching game play strategy. *Journal of Physical Education, Recreation & Dance, 67*(5), 22–24.

Rife, F., Shute, S., & Dodds, P. (1985). ALT-PE versions I and II: Evolution of a student-centered observation system in physical education. *Journal of Teaching in Physical Education, 4,* 134–142.

Rink, J. E. (1993). *Teaching physical education for learning* (2nd ed.). St. Louis, MO: Mosby.

Rink, J. E. (1994). Task presentation in pedagogy. *Quest, 46,* 270–280.

Rink, J. E. (1996a). Effective instruction in physical education. In S. J. Silverman & C. D. Ennis (Eds.), *Student learning in physical education* (pp. 171–198). Champaign, IL: Human Kinetics.

Rink, J. E. (Ed.). (1996b). Tactical and skill approaches to teaching sport and games [Monograph]. *Journal of Teaching in Physical Education, 15,* 397–519.

Rink, J. E., French, K., Lee., A. M., Solmon, M. A., & Lynn, S. K. (1994). A comparison of pedagogical knowledge structures of preservice students and teacher educators in two institutions. *Journal of Teaching in Physical Education, 13,* 140–162.

Rink, J. E., French, K. E., & Tjeerdsma, B. L. (1996). Foundations for the learning and instruction of sport and games. In J. Rink (Ed.), Tactical and skill approaches to teaching sport and games [Monograph]. *Journal of Teaching in Physical Education, 15,* 399–417.

Rink, J. E., French, K. E., Werner, P. H., Lynn, S., & Mays, A. (1992). The influence of content development on the effectiveness of instruction. *Journal of Teaching in Physical Education, 11,* 139–149.

Rink, J. E., & Werner, P. H. (1989). Qualitative measures of teaching performance scale (QMTPS). In P. W Darst, D. B. Zakrajsek, & V. H. Mancini (Eds.), *Analyzing physical education and sport instruction* (2nd ed., pp. 269–275). Champaign, IL: Human Kinetics.

Rink, J. E., Werner, P. H., Hohn, R. C., Ward, D. S., & Timmermans, H. M. (1986). Differential effects of three teachers over a unit of instruction. *Research Quarterly for Exercise and Sport, 57,* 132–138.

Roberts, G. C., Kleiber, D. A., & Duda, J. L. (1981). An analysis of motivation in children's sport: The role of perceived competence in participation. *Journal of Sport Psychology, 3,* 206–216.

Rolider, A., Siedentop, D., & Van Houten, R. (1984). Effects of enthusiasm training on subsequent teacher enthusiastic behavior. *Journal of Teaching in Physical Education, 3*(2), 47–59.

Romar, J. (1995). *Case studies of Finnish physical education teachers: Espoused and enacted theories of action.* Åbo, Finland: Åbo Akademi University Press.

Rosenthal, R., & Jacobson, L. (1968). *Pygmalion in the classroom: Teacher expectation and pupils' intellectual development.* New York: Holt, Rinehart & Winston.

Rovegno, I. (1991). A participant-observation study of knowledge restructuring in a field-based elementary physical education methods course. *Research Quarterly for Exercise and Sport, 62,* 205–212.

Rovegno, I. (1992a). Learning to reflect on teaching: A case study of one preservice physical education teacher. *The Elementary School Journal, 92,* 491–510.

Rovegno, I. C. (1992b). Learning to teach in a field-based methods course: The development of pedagogical content knowledge. *Teaching and Teacher Education, 8,* 69–82.

Rovegno, I. (1993). The development of curricular knowledge: A case of problematic pedagogical content knowledge during advanced knowledge acquisition. *Research Quarterly for Exercise and Sport, 64,* 56–68.

Rovegno, I. (1994). Teaching within a curricular zone of safety: School culture and the situated nature of student teachers' pedagogical content knowledge. *Research Quarterly for Exercise and Sport, 65,* 269–279.

Rovegno, I. (1995). Theoretical perspectives on knowledge and learning and a student teacher's pedagogical content knowledge of dividing and sequencing subject matter. *Journal of Teaching in Physical Education, 14,* 284–304.

Sallis, J. F., & McKenzie, T. L. (1991). Physical education's role in public health. *Research Quarterly for Exercise and Sport, 62,* 124–137.

Salter, W. B., & Graham, G. (1985). The effects of three disparate instructional approaches on skill attempts and student learning in an experimental teaching unit. *Journal of Teaching in Physical Education, 4,* 212–218.

Sariscsany, M. J. (1996). Turning ideas into practices: A teacher development workshop. *Journal of Physical Education, Recreation & Dance, 67*(3), 38–40.

Schempp, P. G. (1989). Apprenticeship-of-observation and the development of physical education teachers. In T. J. Templin & P. G. Schempp (Eds.), *Socialization into physical education: Learning to teach* (pp. 13–38). Indianapolis: Benchmark.

Schempp, P. G. (1993). Constructing professional knowledge: A case study of an experienced high school teacher. *Journal of Teaching in Physical Education, 13,* 2–23.

Schempp, P. G., Cheffers, J. T. F., & Zaichkowsky, L. D. (1983). Influence of decision-making on attitudes, creativity, motor skills, and self-concept in elementary children. *Research Quarterly for Exercise and Sport, 54,* 183–189.

Schempp, P. G., & De Marco, G. M. (1996). Instructional theory in sport pedagogy (1994–1995). *International Journal of Physical Education, 32*(1), 4–8.

Schempp, P. G., & Graber, K. C. (1992). Teacher socialization from a dialectical perspective: Pretraining through induction. *Journal of Teaching in Physical Education, 11,* 329–348.

Schempp, P. G., Sparkes, A. C., & Templin, T. J. (1993). The micropolitics of teacher induction. *American Educational Research Journal, 30,* 447–472.

Schoon, K. J. (1995). The origin and extent of alternative conceptions in the earth and space sciences: A survey of pre-service elementary teachers. *Journal of Elementary Science Education, 7*(2), 27–46.

Schwager, S. (1996). Getting real about assessment: Making it work. *Journal of Physical Education, Recreation & Dance, 67*(8), 38–40.

Sebren, A. (1995). Preservice teachers' reflections and knowledge development in a field-based elementary physical education methods course. *Journal of Teaching in Physical Education, 14,* 262–283.

Sharpe, T. (1997). Research note: An introduction to sequential behavior analysis and what it offers physical education teacher education researchers. *Journal of Teaching in Physical Education, 16,* 368–375.

Sharpe, T., & Hawkins, A. (1992a). Field systems analysis: A tactical guide for exploring temporal relationships in classroom settings. *Teaching and Teacher Education, 8,* 171–186.

Sharpe, T., & Hawkins, A. (1992b). Study III expert and novice elementary specialists: A comparative analysis. In A. Hawkins & T. Sharpe (Eds.), Field Systems Analysis: An alternative for the study of teaching expertise [Monograph]. *Journal of Teaching in Physical Education, 12,* 55–75.

Sharpe, T. L., Hawkins, A., & Wiegand, R. (1989). Model/practice versus verbal/rehearsal introductions of systems skills within an individually prescribed instructional system. *Journal of Teaching in Physical Education, 9,* 25–38.

Sharpe, T., Spies, R., Newman, D., & Spickelmier-Vallin, D. (1996). Assessing and improving the accuracy of in-service teachers' perceptions of daily practice. *Journal of Teaching in Physical Education, 15,* 297–318.

Shulman, L. S. (1986). Those who understand: Knowledge growth in teaching. *Educational Researcher, 15*(2), 4–14.

Shulman, L. S. (1987). Knowledge and teaching: Foundations of the new reform. *Harvard Educational Review, 57,* 1–22.

Shute, S., Dodds, P., Placek, J., Rife, F., & Silverman, S. (1982). Academic learning time in elementary movement education: A descriptive-analytic study. *Journal of Teaching in Physical Education, 1*(2), 3–14.

Siedentop, D. (1983). Academic learning time: Reflections and prospects. In P. Dodds & F. Rife (Eds.), Time to learn in physical education: History, completed research, and potential future for academic learning time in physical education [Monograph]. *Journal of Teaching in Physical Education, Monograph 1,* 3–7.

Siedentop, D. (1987). High school physical education: Still an endangered species. *Journal of Physical Education, Recreation & Dance, 58*(2), 24–25.

Siedentop, D. (Ed.). (1989). The effective elementary specialist study [Monograph]. *Journal of Teaching in Physical Education, 8,* 187–270.

Siedentop, D. (1991a). *Developing teaching skills in physical education* (3rd ed.). Mountain View, CA: Mayfield.

Siedentop, D. (1991b). The mountain yet to be climbed. In G. M. Graham & M . A. Jones (Eds.), *Collaboration between researchers and practitioners in physical education: An international dialogue* (pp. 3–9). International Association of Physical Education Schools in Higher Education.

Siedentop, D. (1992). Thinking differently about secondary physical education. *Journal of Physical Education, Recreation & Dance, 63*(7), 69–72, 77.

Siedentop, D. (1994). *Sport education.* Champaign, IL: Human Kinetics.

Siedentop, D. (1995, April). *The 1995 Alliance Scholar Lecture: Teaching effectively.* Paper presented at the annual meeting of the American Alliance of Health, Physical Education, Recreation and Dance, Portland, OR.

Siedentop, D., Birdwell, D., & Metzler, M. (1979, March). *A process approach to measuring teaching effectiveness in physical education.* Paper presented at the annual meeting of the American Alliance of Health, Physical Education, Recreation and Dance, New Orleans, LA.

Siedentop, D., Doutis, P., Tsangaridou, N., Ward, P., & Rauschenbach, J. (1994). Don't sweat gym! An analysis of curriculum and instruction. In M. O'Sullivan (Ed.), High school physical education teachers: Their world of work [Monograph]. *Journal of Teaching in Physical Education, 13,* 375–394.

Siedentop, D., & Eldar, E. (1989). Expertise, experience, and effectiveness. In D. Siedentop (Ed.), The effective elementary specialist study [Monograph]. *Journal of Teaching in Physical Education, 8,* 254–260.

Siedentop, D., Tousignant, M., & Parker, M. (1982). *Academic learning time—physical education, 1982 revision: Coding manual.* Columbus, OH: School of Health, Physical Education and Recreation, The Ohio State University.

Silverman, S. (1985a). Relationship of engagement and practice trials to student achievement. *Journal of Teaching in Physical Education, 5,* 13–21.

Silverman, S. (1985b). Student characteristics mediating engagement-outcome relationships in physical education. *Research Quarterly for Exercise and Sport, 56,* 66–72.

Silverman, S. (1988). Relationships of selected presage and context variables to achievement. *Research Quarterly for Exercise and Sport, 59,* 35–41.

Silverman, S. (1990). Linear and curvilinear relationships between student practice and achievement in physical education. *Teaching and Teacher Education, 6,* 305–314.

Silverman, S. (1991). Research on teaching in physical education. *Research Quarterly for Exercise and Sport, 62,* 352–364.

Silverman, S. (1993). Student characteristics, practice, and achievement in physical education. *Journal of Educational Research, 87,* 54–61.

Silverman, S. (1994a). Communication and motor skill learning: What we learn from research in the gymnasium. *Quest, 46,* 345–355.

Silverman, S. (1994b). Research on teaching and student achievement. *Sport Science Review, 3*(1), 83–90.

Silverman, S., Devillier, R., & Ramírez, T. (1991). The validity of academic learning time—physical education (ALT-PE) as a process measure of achievement. *Research Quarterly for Exercise and Sport, 62,* 319–325.

Silverman, S., Dodds, P., Placek, J., Shute, S., & Rife, F. (1984). Academic learning time in elementary school physical education (ALT-PE) for student subgroups and instructional activity units. *Research Quarterly for Exercise and Sport, 55,* 365–370.

Silverman, S., Kulinna, P. H., & Crull, G. (1995). Skill-related task structures, explicitness, and accountability: Relationships with student achievement. *Research Quarterly for Exercise and Sport, 66,* 32–40.

Silverman, S., Tyson, L. A., & Krampitz, J. (1992). Teacher feedback and achievement in physical education: Interaction with student practice. *Teaching and Teacher Education, 8,* 333–344.

Silverman, S., Tyson, L. A., & Krampitz, J. (1993). Teacher feedback and achievement: Mediating effects of initial skill level and sex. *Journal of Human Movement Studies, 24,* 97–118.

Silverman, S., Tyson, L. A., & Morford, L. M. (1988). Relationships of organization, time, and student achievement in physical education. *Teaching and Teacher Education, 4,* 247–257.

Silverman, S., & Zotos, C. (1987). Validity of interval and time sampling methods for measuring student engaged time in physical education. *Educational and Psychological Measurement, 47,* 1005–1012.

Simons-Morton, B. G., Parcel, G. S., & O'Hara, N. M. (1988). Implementing organizational changes to promote healthful diet and physical activity at school. *Health Education Quarterly, 15,* 115–130.

Smith, B. T., & Goc-Karp, G. (1996). Adapting to marginalization in a middle school physical education class. *Journal of Teaching in Physical Education, 16,* 30–47.

Smith, B., Markley, R., & Goc-Karp, G. (1997). The effect of a cooperative learning intervention on the social skill enhancement of a third grade physical education class. *Research Quarterly for Exercise and Sport, 68*(Suppl. 1), A–68.

Smith, M. D., & Steffen, J. P. (1993). The effect of different schedules of managerial feedback on the instructional time of student teacher. *International Journal of Physical Education, 30*(4), 11–24.

Smith, T. K. (1997). Authentic assessment: Using a portfolio card in physical education. *Journal of Physical Education, Recreation & Dance, 68*(4), 46–52.

Smyth, D. M. (1995). First-year physical education teachers' perceptions of their workplace. *Journal of Teaching in Physical Education, 14,* 198–214.

Solmon, M. A., & Boone, J. (1993). The impact of student goal orientation in physical education classes. *Research Quarterly for Exercise and Sport, 64,* 418–424.

Solmon, M. A., & Carter, J. A. (1995). Kindergarten and first-grade students' perceptions of physical education in one teacher's classes. *The Elementary School Journal, 95,* 355–365.

Solmon, M. A., & Lee, A. M. (1996). Entry characteristics, practice variables, and cognition: Student mediation of instruction. *Journal of Teaching in Physical Education, 15,* 136–150.

Solmon, M. A., Lee, A. M., & Hill, K. (1991, April). *The role of content knowledge in teaching physical education.* Paper presented at the annual meeting of the American Alliance of Health, Physical Education, Recreation and Dance, San Francisco, CA.

Solmon, M. A., Worthy, T., & Carter, J. A. (1993). The interaction of school context and role identity of first-year teachers. *Journal of Teaching in Physical Education, 12,* 313–328.

Solomons, H. H. (1980). Sex role mediation of achievement behaviors and interpersonal interactions in sex-integrated team games. In E. A. Peditone (Ed.), *Children in cooperation and competition: Toward a developmental social psychology* (pp. 321–364). Lexington, MA: Lexington Books.

Sparapani, E. F., Abel, F. J., Easton, S. E., Herbster, D. L., & Edwards, P. (1994, February). *Cooperative learning: What teachers know about it and when they use it.* Paper presented at the annual meeting of the Association of Teacher Educators, Atlanta, GA.

Sparkes, A. C., & Templin, T. J. (1992). Life histories and physical education teachers: Exploring the meanings of marginality. In A. C. Sparkes (Ed.), *Research in physical education and sport: Exploring alternative visions* (pp. 118–145). London: Falmer Press.

Sparkes, A. C., Templin, T. J., & Schempp, P. G. (1993). Exploring dimensions of marginality: Reflecting on the life histories of physical education teachers. In S. Stroot (Ed.), Socialization into physical education [Monograph]. *Journal of Teaching in Physical Education, 12,* 386–398.

Sparks, W. G., & Verner, M. E. (1995). Intervention strategies in multicultural education: A comparison of pre-service models. *The Physical Educator, 52,* 170–180.

Stanley, L. S. (1993). The development of an instrument to assess the attitudes toward cultural diversity and cultural pluralism among preservice physical education majors. *Dissertation Abstracts International, 53*(09), 3142A. (University Microfilms No. DA93-01225)

Stanley, L. S. (1995). Multicultural questions, action research answers. *Quest, 47,* 19–33.

Steinhardt, M. A. (1992). Physical education. In P. W. Jackson (Ed.), *Handbook of research on curriculum* (pp. 964–1001). New York: Macmillan.

Steinhardt, M., Lambdin, D., Kamrath, M., & Ramirez, T. (1993). An analysis of student teachers' intentional, perceived, and operational motor skills and physical fitness curriculum. *Journal of Teaching in Physical Education, 12,* 134–148.

Stewart, M. J., & Destache, D. (1992). Validity of interval recording in measuring classroom climates in physical education. *Journal of Teaching in Physical Education, 11,* 315–323.

Strachan, K., & MacCauley, M. (1997). Cooperative learning in a high school physical education program. *Research Quarterly for Exercise and Sport, 68*(Suppl. 1), A–69.

Stroot, S. A., Collier, C., O'Sullivan, M., & England, K. (1994). Contextual hoops and hurdles: Workplace conditions in secondary physical education. In M. O'Sullivan (Ed.), High school physical education teachers: Their world of work [Monograph]. *Journal of Teaching in Physical Education, 13,* 342–360.

Stroot, S. A., & Morton, P. J. (1989). Blueprints for learning. In D. Siedentop (Ed.), The effective elementary specialist study [Monograph]. *Journal of Teaching in Physical Education, 8,* 213–222.

Stroot, S. A., & Oslin, J. L. (1993). Use of instructional statements by preservice teachers for overhand throwing performance of children. *Journal of Teaching in Physical Education, 13,* 24–45.

Taggart, A. (1985). Fitness—direct instruction. *Journal of Teaching in Physical Education, 4,* 143–150.

Tan, S. K. (1997). The elements of expertise. *Journal of Physical Education, Recreation & Dance, 68*(2), 30–33.

Tannehill, D., & Zakrajsek, D. (1993). Research note: Student attitudes

towards physical education: A multicultural study. *Journal of Teaching in Physical Education, 13,* 78–84.

Telama, R., Varstala, V., Heikinaro-Johansson, P., & Utriainen, J. (1987). Learning behavior in PE lessons and physical and psychological responses to PE in high-skill and low-skill pupils. In G. T. Barrette, R. S. Feingold, C. R. Rees, & M. Piéron (Eds.), *Myths, models, and methods in sport pedagogy* (pp. 239–248). Champaign, IL: Human Kinetics.

Templin, T. J. (1979). Occupational socialization and the physical education student teacher. *Research Quarterly, 50,* 482–493.

Templin, T. J. (1981). Student as socializing agent. *Journal of Teaching in Physical Education, Introductory Issue,* 71–79.

Templin, T. J. (1988). Teacher isolation: A concern for the collegial development of physical educators. In T. J. Martinek and P. G. Schempp (Eds.), Collaboration for instructional improvement: Models for school-university partnerships [Monograph]. *Journal of Teaching in Physical Education, 7,* 197–205.

Templin, T. J. (1989). Running on ice: A case study of the influence of workplace conditions on a secondary school physical educator. In T. J. Templin & P. G. Schempp (Eds.), *Socialization into physical education: Learning to teach* (pp. 165–197). Indianapolis: Benchmark.

Templin, T. J., Sparkes, A., Grant, B., & Schempp, P. (1994). Matching the self: The paradoxical case and life history of a late career teacher/coach. *Journal of Teaching in Physical Education, 13,* 274–294.

Templin, T., Woodford, R., & Mulling, C. (1982). On becoming a physical educator: Occupational choice and the anticipatory socialization process. *Quest, 34,* 119–133.

Thomas, K. T. (1994). The development of sport expertise: From Leeds to MVP legend. *Quest, 46,* 199–210.

Thomas, J. R., & French, K. E. (1985). Gender differences across age in motor performance: A meta-analysis. *Psychological Bulletin, 98,* 260–282.

Thomas, J. R., & Thomas, K. T. (1988). Development of gender differences in physical activity. *Quest, 40,* 219–229.

Thorpe, R., Bunker, D., & Almond, L. (1986). *Rethinking games teaching.* Loughborough, UK: University of Technology, Department of Physical Education and Sport Science.

Tousignant, M. G. (1982). Analysis of the task structures in secondary physical education classes. *Dissertation Abstracts International, 43*(05), 1470A. (University Microfilms No. DA82-22191)

Tousignant, M., & Siedentop, D. (1983). A qualitative analysis of task structures in required secondary physical education classes. *Journal of Teaching in Physical Education, 3*(1), 47–57.

Treasure, D.C. (1994). A social-cognitive approach to understanding children's achievement behavior, cognitions, and affect in competitive sport. *Dissertation Abstracts International, 54*(11), 4032A. (University Microfilms No. DA94-11802)

Treasure, D.C., & Roberts, G. C. (1994). Cognitive and affective concomitants of task and ego goal orientations during the middle school years. *Journal of Sport & Exercise Psychology, 16,* 15–28.

Treasure, D.C., & Roberts, G. C. (1995). Applications of achievement goal theory to physical education: Implications for enhancing motivation. *Quest, 47,* 475–489.

Tsangaridou, N., & O'Sullivan, M. (1994). Using pedagogical reflective strategies to enhance reflection among preservice physical education teachers. *Journal of Teaching in Physical Education, 14,* 13–33.

Tsangaridou, N., & Siedentop, D. (1995). Reflective teaching: A literature review. *Quest, 47,* 212–237.

Turner, A. (1996). Teaching for understanding: Myth or reality? *Journal of Physical Education, Recreation & Dance, 67*(4), 46–48.

Turner, A. P., & Martinek, T. J. (1993). A comparative analysis of two models for teaching games (technique approach and game-centered (tactical focus) approach). *International Journal of Physical Education, 29*(4), 15–31.

Turner, A. P., & Martinek, T. J. (1995). Teaching for understanding: A model for improving decision making during game play. *Quest, 47,* 44–63.

Twardy, B. M., & Yerg, B. J. (1987). The impact of planning on inclass interactive behaviors of preservice teachers. *Journal of Teaching in Physical Education, 6,* 136–148.

Tyler, R. (1949). Basic principles of curriculum and instruction. Chicago: University of Chicago Press.

Tyson, L. (1996). Context of schools. In S. J. Silverman & C. D. Ennis (Eds.), *Student learning in physical education* (pp. 55–79). Champaign, IL: Human Kinetics.

U. S. Department of Health and Human Services. (1990). *Healthy people 2000: National health promotion and disease prevention objectives.* Washington, DC: Superintendent of Documents, U.S. Government Printing Office.

U. S. Department of Health and Human Services. (1994). *Evaluating educational outcomes of school health programs.* Washington, DC: Office of Disease Prevention and Health Promotion.

U. S. Department of Health and Human Services. (1996). *Surgeon General's report on physical activity and health.* Atlanta, GA: Centers for Disease Control and Prevention.

van der Mars, H. (1987). Effects of audiocuing on teacher verbal praise of students' managerial and transitional task performance. *Journal of Teaching in Physical Education, 6,* 157–165.

van der Mars, H. (1989). Effects of specific verbal praise on off-task behavior of second-grade students in physical education. *Journal of Teaching in Physical Education, 8,* 162–169.

van der Mars, H., Vogler, B., Darst, P., & Cusimano, B. (1994). Active supervision patterns of physical education teachers and their relationship with student behaviors. *Journal of Teaching in Physical Education, 14,* 99–112.

van der Mars, H., Vogler, E. W., Darst, P. W., & Cusimano, B. (1995). Research note: Novice and expert physical education teachers: Maybe they think and decide differently . . . but do they behave differently? *Journal of Teaching in Physical Education, 14,* 340–347.

Veal, M. L. (1988). Pupil assessment perceptions and practices of secondary teachers. *Journal of Teaching in Physical Education, 7,* 327–342.

Veal, M. L. (1992). School-based theories of pupil assessment: A case study. *Research Quarterly for Exercise and Sport, 63,* 48–59.

Vertinsky, P. (1989). Information source utilization and teachers' attributes in physical education: A preliminary test of a rational paradigm. *Research Quarterly for Exercise and Sport, 60,* 268–279.

Walkwitz, E., & Lee, A. (1992). The role of teacher knowledge in elementary physical education instruction: An exploratory study. *Research Quarterly for Exercise and Sport, 63,* 179–185.

Walling, M. D., & Duda, J. L. (1995). Goals and their associations with beliefs about success in and perceptions of the purposes of physical education. *Journal of Teaching in Physical Education, 14,* 140–156.

Walling, M. D., & Martinek, T. J. (1995). Learned helplessness: A case study of a middle school student. In G. Graham (Ed.), Physical education through students' eyes and in students' voices [Monograph]. *Journal of Teaching in Physical Education, 14,* 454–466.

Ward, P. C. (1994). An experimental analysis of skill responding in high school physical education. *Dissertation Abstracts International, 54*(08), 2950A. (University Microfilms No. DA94-01382)

Wendt, J. C., & Bain, L. L. (1989). Concerns of preservice and inservice physical educators. *Journal of Teaching in Physical Education, 8,* 177–180.

Wendt, J. C., Bain, L. L., & Jackson, A. S. (1981). Fuller's concerns theory as tested on prospective physical educators. *Journal of Teaching in Physical Education, Introductory Issue,* 66–70.

Werner, P., & Rink, J. (1989). Case studies of teacher effectiveness in second grade physical education. *Journal of Teaching in Physical Education, 8,* 280–297.

Werner, P., Thorpe, R., & Bunker, D. (1996). Teaching games for understanding: Evolution of a model. *Journal of Physical Education, Recreation & Dance, 67*(1), 28–33.

White, A. G., & Bailey, J. S. (1990). Reducing disruptive behaviors of elementary physical education students with sit and watch. *Journal of Applied Behavior Analysis, 23,* 353–359.

Williams, J. A. (1992). Moonlighting: The norm for physical educators. *The Physical Educator, 49,* 14–22.

Williams, J. A. (1993). Teacher moonlighting: Interviews with physical educators. *Journal of Teaching in Physical Education, 13,* 62–77.

Williamson, K. M. (1996). Gender issues. In S. J. Silverman & C. D. Ennis (Eds.), *Student learning in physical education* (pp. 81–100). Champaign, IL: Human Kinetics.

Wood, T. M. (1996). Evaluation and testing: The road less traveled. In S. J. Silverman & C. D. Ennis (Eds.), *Student learning in physical education* (pp. 199–219). Champaign, IL: Human Kinetics.

Woods, S. E. (1992). Describing the experience of lesbian physical educators: A phenomenological study. In A. C. Sparkes (Ed.), *Research in physical education and sport: Exploring alternative visions* (pp. 90–117). London: Falmer Press.

Wrisberg, C. A. (1991). A field test of the effect of contextual variety during skill acquisition. *Journal of Teaching in Physical Education, 11,* 21–30.

Yerg, B. J. (1981). The impact of selected presage and process behaviors on the refinement of a motor skill. *Journal of Teaching in Physical Education, 1*(1), 38–46.

Zeichner, K. M. (1979, December). *The dialectics of teacher socialization.* Paper presented at the annual meeting of the Association for Teacher Educators, Orlando, FL.

Zeichner, K. M., & Tabachnick, B. R. (1991). Reflections on reflective teaching. In B. R. Tabachnick & K. M. Zeichner (Eds.), *Issues and practices in inquiry-oriented teacher education* (pp. 1–21). London: Falmer Press.

28.

Classroom Research in the Visual Arts

Cynthia Colbert
University of South Carolina

Martha Taunton
University of Massachusetts, Amherst

Numerous reviews and summaries have been done of research and research methodologies in visual arts education (Colwell, 1995; Davis, 1971; Eisner, 1969, 1973; Hardiman & Zernich, 1976; Hausman, 1963; La Pierre & Zimmerman, l997). These reviews reflect significant issues and concerns prevalent in the field, reveal insights gained from the accumulation of studies, offer directions for change, and suggest areas for new research. Reviews of research reflect the issues, trends, and concerns at particular points of time in our history. Each review carries with it the stance of its writer. At best, research reviews show us new directions for research and change. This review will focus on the accumulating research done on site in school classrooms and particularly on the teaching–learning process in the visual arts. It is not intended to be an all-inclusive compendium of art educational classroom research but includes studies that represent the genre and that illustrate pertinent areas of research. The role of the teacher is pervasive in this review as it is in most of the research. Three areas of classroom research are delineated in this review: social context of art classrooms, portraits of teachers and students, and planned instructional interventions.

Social Contexts of the Art Classroom

Art Classrooms as Learning Communities

Classroom researchers have looked closely at the context of the classroom and the teaching–learning process. Believing that knowledge is constituted through social interaction, that knowledge involves culturally appropriate meanings and interpretations, and that knowledge is internalized in human consciousness, Johnson (1985) conducted a number of studies to ascer-

tain what knowledge was being transmitted in the art classroom. In her 1985 study of an eighth-grade art class, Johnson gathered data through participant–observation, interviews, and a questionnaire. Johnson's particular interest is how the teacher selects content, how the knowledge is communicated to students, what knowledge students have, what students think about as they are engaged in making and responding to art, and what teachers think about as they teach. Johnson found the teacher to be very interested in the "basics." By basics, Johnson meant the elements of art and the principles of design, or formalist approaches to teaching art. Students brought a wide variety of views of art to the classroom. Some found it irrelevant, others held formalist, humanist, aesthetic, expressionist, and nihilistic views.

Johnson (1986) observed a high school art class to study socialization. She sought to learn more about the process of building art knowledge, to identify the art teacher's sources for lessons in art, and to discover what knowledge students had about art in general. The drawing and painting course Johnson observed ascribed to traditional kinds of concepts about art forms and art media. The teacher's approach to planning instruction was both deliberate and spontaneous. It reflected a problem-solving approach similar to those of many secondary and postsecondary teachers of studio art. The teacher used information about several artists from the past in the classroom, but the teacher did not incorporate a plan for instruction in art history or art criticism in the course. Students were evenly divided between intuitive and observational approaches toward ideas for their work. Students were mostly left to their own to develop strategies for solving the teacher's problem. Making art was learned primarily through trial and error. Occasional interventions from the teacher included suggesting sources for imagery, making sketches, or pointing out

The authors and editor wish to thank the following chapter reviewers: Laura Chapman and Craig Kridel.

to students what was not working in the artworks they were developing.

Stokrocki (1988) found that when middle school students were engaged in studio activities, immediate interruption for correction has more impact, has more specificity, and is more effective, than waiting until the work is completed and using a final critique. Stokrocki also suggested that the student and teachers need to reflect on the completed work as a whole to improve skills in aesthetics and criticism.

In another research study on classroom context and the impact of student–student conversations and teacher–student exchanges, Taunton (1986) looked at the ways aesthetic values are learned and taught in the classroom in an elementary school setting. Her descriptive study is based on classroom observations, recordings, and transcripts of lessons and conversations within the classroom. She found the process to be spontaneous during art activities with children. Taunton found that peers, as well as teachers, played a role in determining standards for the artwork produced. The children were aware of the teacher' standards and also aware of differences between their personal criteria and those of their teacher. The teacher, too, showed an awareness that students did not always choose to use his criteria for their work.

In a study that took place in a preschool setting, Swann (1986) recorded the child and adult interactions during art activities. This year-long study used naturalistic methods in recording the interactions between 15 children and adults who supervised the art activities in the classroom. Swann found a pattern of "achievement seeking" among the children who sought to conform to the teacher's cues and directions and whose verbal responses indicated aspiring behaviors as children sought to please adults. Adults in the classroom frequently asked the children, "What is that?" Adults also triggered responses by suggesting that children's work was a representation of a particular object. Children responded by calling out names for their paintings to arouse the adults' interest in their work. Some children picked up these cues from other children, as well as from the adults. Swann's findings suggested that children seemed to strive for more difficult solutions in elicited and structured art activities. Children may have been encouraged to create elaborate meanings for their paintings more as a result of achievement rewards and peer competition than from meanings inherent to the nature of their paintings. The consequences of the social context of the adult influences and the public declarations of content in this classroom shaped children's behavior. At other times, in other settings, Swann believed that these children may have pursued more private meanings for their work and, as a result, described the same paintings quite differently.

Studies concerned with the context in which art learning takes place have shown the importance of the combined influences of teachers and peers in the standards for art learning behaviors and artwork produced. Certain kinds of teacher comments and teacher behaviors were found to trigger specific kinds of responses from students. The effects of student–student interactions were found to be as important as student–teacher interactions. Teachers of art need to listen to the comments and gage the reactions of students to what they say in class as well as how they say it. Art teachers are advised to give serious con-

siderations to the role peers play in the art learning that occurs in their classrooms and the artistic standards that are set by student–student interactions.

Critical Classroom Conversations

Researchers have also examined the social and contextual influences on art learning in the early childhood classroom. We know that dialogues in classrooms are pivotal in learning. Teachers are primary shapers of rehearsed and unrehearsed dialogue through their classroom structure, space, and their assignments. Rosario and Collazo (1981), Taunton (1983), Cocking and Copple (1979), and Alexander (1984) reported on spontaneous socialization in the classroom as it revealed conceptions about art and shaped art content.

Rosario and Collazo (1981) observed art activities in two preschool classrooms. They found that a "reproductive aesthetic code" was present in both classrooms where teachers' expectations for naturalistic art products were transmitted to children. This transmission of teachers' expectations for naturalistic products was found in teacher dialogue, in the structure of the art tasks, in their use of objective models for art to be made by children, in setting explicit criteria addressing representational work, in praise for selected artwork, and in the materials made available to children for art making.

Taunton (1983) observed art activities in three preschool classrooms, focusing on verbal interactions of adults and children. Her study indicated that classroom discussion of art and young children's learning of art concepts and behaviors were dependent on multiple factors determined by the teacher. These factors included the amount of time allowed for art, the manipulative complexity of the art task, the children's choice of art versus other activities, and the type of verbal interaction initiated by adults. Cocking and Copple (1979) studied the verbal exchanges of preschoolers in drawing sessions to gain information about social regulation of representational competence. Their work indicated that four-year-old children who were self-conscious about their own and other's representations were influenced by peers in the evaluative and reflective processes.

Alexander (1984) also described peer interactions by comparing first-grade children's classroom conversations occurring during a structured portrait painting lesson and during unstructured drawing activities. She indicated that social conversations occurred during both structured and unstructured lessons. Fantasy and play discussions occurred more frequently during the unstructured drawing activity. Media and procedure conversations and verisimilitude and likeness conversations were more frequent during the structured portraits. Alexander found two subcategories in these comments: (a) negative assessments, or complaints about the shortcomings of their work, and (b) positive statements, including compliments on the work of others. These conversations differed in content from those of children engaged in unstructured art activities.

The research reviewed in relation to classroom discourse underscores that the construction of the meanings of and about art in schools is a jointly shared social enterprise, directed by the teacher, but certainly influenced by the students. It is social as children work together, it is social in that the content taught is a result of teachers' ideas that are mediated and negotiated at the art table and in the flux of classroom and school life. It is social that both the teachers' and the students' understandings about art brought into the classroom setting are generated from previous experiences and they meet on the classroom stage.

Portraits of Teachers and Students

The Role of Visual Arts Teachers in Student Learning

Characteristics of effective teachers are often given in qualitative dimensions. In the teaching of art, as in other subject areas, good teachers are clear, enthusiastic, interested in students, knowledgeable, and committed to their discipline. We know from studies of classrooms that teachers in art play multiple roles; orchestrate subtle and complex events in very short time periods; are "idiosyncratic" in their presentations; and create spaces, experiences, and dialogues that entertain, challenge, frustrate, perplex, and engage their students as they teach and learn about art. We also know that there is no one measure of an effective teacher. Teachers are multidimensional, and they must be viewed as such by researchers in order to capture what makes them so effective.

Interest in what makes a teacher of art effective in the classroom has taken researchers into schools to document their methods, communication skills, content, and style. Several researchers presented portraits of teachers that are illustrative of exceptional teaching and are engaging representations in their detail and focus. Stokrocki (1986) described an elementary art teacher who is seen as an outstanding teacher by other professionals because she is an effective manager of the 30-minute allotted art period for second graders in an unwieldy physical space. Pariser (1981) described, in a personal reflection of his own teaching, how he negotiated the subject of art, the structure of lesson planning, and the institution of schooling. He described the well-defined tasks that he gave to the children as a "directive approach" that reflected the work ethic of the school, led to less discipline problems, and adhered to conventional ideas of teachers and lessons. He considered that he often was teaching an artisan approach to art and used his environment to offset that approach, to generate unplanned learning as students responded to their encounters with a collection of objects he made available to them for personal explorations. Pariser's observations of what he refers to as "unplanned learning," show his interest in student-initiated learning stemming from objects in the classroom.

Alexander presented two renderings of high school teachers. She describes William, a high school art history teacher, as a performer and a shaman, who challenges his students' beliefs about art and art history through the vehicle of performance art. Her picture of William invites consideration of the adventures possible in teaching and the consequences of risk taking in your classroom and your teaching (Alexander, 1983). She also introduces us to Mr. Jewel, a teacher who models enthusiasm and interest in his students and subject and who makes students comfortable in his classroom. Mr. Jewel talks about art in the classroom in ways that his students emulate (Alexander, 1980).

Sevigny (1977) conducted a study of how drawing is taught at the undergraduate level. Sevigny attended a university undergraduate drawing class, posing as a student. He reported his findings through multiple perspectives, his own and those of his student peers, on the teacher's interactions and performance in the classroom setting. Sevigny's study offers insights into classrooms not often studied and data from multiple perspectives, his own and those of his student peers. Sevigny's findings suggest that in studio art instruction, teachers' intended instructional goals and objectives are interpreted by the adult students in ways other than anticipated. The student's interpretation of what the teacher says has a strong effect on the outcome of the instruction.

Zimmerman (1992) reported on a comparative study of two painting teachers of talented young adolescents to compare their characteristics in the classrooms and their successes there. The two teachers Zimmerman studied showed contrasts in their curricular concerns and in the time spent and methods used in substantive instruction. Both teachers spent almost half the class period critiquing in-process student work. They differed in their approaches to critiquing finished work. One spent much more class time in group critiques than the other. Both teachers seemed to meet the students' needs in helping them develop skills and techniques, but the teacher who spent more time in group critiques was also able to encourage students to think reflectively about the ideas and choices they made in their work.

In these and other qualitative portraits of individual teachers, we see differences in views of students, in the learning process in art, and in the mission of teaching. These individual presentations necessarily do not allow generalizations about what is effective teaching. But in these strong characterizations we can consider the many permutations that effective teaching can take. A study of these portraits requires us, as researchers of art teaching, to look closely. The act of looking, discussing, and reflecting about the teachers portrayed may prompt insight about the diversity of effective teaching and may offer clues to our own teaching styles.

Classroom Landscapes

The classrooms that teachers design have their own teaching presence. Like installation art, the classrooms invite us into a space to learn about art and about being an artist. Studies show that teachers plan spaces for discussion, walls for critiques, and areas for supplies. In the use of these spaces by teachers and students, the spaces and artifacts take on meanings and shape art content and behaviors. Work displayed illustrates the teacher's endorsement of aesthetic values and serves as a catalyst for the informal discussions by students, extending the art learning in new directions, perhaps intended, but not managed by the teacher. The importance of consciously using classroom space as a teaching consideration is discussed by Araca (1990) and Susi (1990).

Pariser (1981) also explored the issue of classroom space as he described how he used the art room as a space for the cluttered collection and display of interesting objects, art reproductions, and children's finished and unfinished work. Such an environment, he felt, offered a change from his conventional lessons and prompted nonlinear and spontaneous learning. The planned space and objects initiated the unplanned learning about art in his classroom that was often more meaningful to student and teacher than the structured lessons.

Students as Learners in the Art Classroom

Portraits of learners in the visual arts are less prevalent than portraits of effective teachers. Students may be well described in research on effective teaching, but they often serve as a backdrop to the story of the teacher. Classroom research tells little about the developmental aspects of learners and more about the art processes, the classroom talk about art, and the students' interactions among themselves and with adults in the classroom. Many classroom researchers in the visual arts have focused their work on special populations of students.

In one such study, Twiggs (1970) sought to find the effectiveness of teaching a method of art criticism and aesthetics to junior high school students who were described as disadvantaged. With the use of Feldman's work in art criticism and by employing Feldman's sequence of description, formal analysis, interpretation, and evaluation, Twiggs found that junior high school students were successful in using art criticism. Regans (1971) used Feldman's work in criticism to test the effects of instruction on criticism to responses to art objects with first-grade children. The first graders in Regans's study developed competencies to use this method of criticism.

In a study of self-concept in African-American students and the enhancement of self-concept through a discipline-based multicultural curriculum in art, Floyd (1997) used a quasi-experimental design to study 238 fourth- and fifth-grade students from two public schools. Quantitative and qualitative measures and recordings of data were taken. Floyd's interest in this approach stemmed from her observations that African-American children often fail to add skin-tone color to their self-portrait drawings. Floyd's qualitative results indicated that as a result of the multicultural art experiences, students became more aware of using skin-tone color in their self-portrait drawings. Floyd anticipated that the multicultural art curriculum would enhance African-American children's self-concepts. No significant effects were found in the statistical analysis of the quantitative data. Floyd recommended the qualitative approach to recording concepts of self by minority children over longer time periods and the use of art curricula that are culturally and personally relevant to the students' lives.

In a case-study approach, Emery (1989) observed 10 children who were students within a class of 35. Emery sought to make observations of the thinking processes used by children engaged in making tasks in art. Emery found that when children engaged in artistic tasks, they had three main decisions to make. They made decisions about (a) making something their peers and teachers would like, (b) how to go about constructing it, and (c) what ideas the work would represent. Overlying the three parts of the art-making process, Emery discussed the role of the child's belief in the artistic search. The belief of the child

included that some problem needs to be solved; that the process of solution requires the child to make a commitment to define it and to establish intentions for art making in which the child engages in the artistic search process; and that the child engages in imaginative, interpretive, and expressive ways of responding to the problem. Emery noted that when children work expressively, they were not content to use ready-made clichés, wanting something more personal or more uniquely their own. Belief was determined to be a central ingredient for children's art making and thinking. Emery described "Artistic Believers" as being socially independent children who display commitment to the artistic search and who attained social, cognitive, and sensory mobility in their work.

Students' responses to and preferences for specific materials used in creating art have also been the focus of research. In a study of students' reposes to art media, May (1987) explored media preference and students' expressed reasons for preferences. Participant observation was the data-gathering method used in this study. May found that students enjoyed exploring and manipulating different media, especially when they could experiment. Pencils, crayons, scissors, and glue or paste ranked low in student preference, perhaps because of student familiarity with these items. Clay ranked high because of its potential for flexibility of ideas. Three-dimensional materials were more highly regarded than two-dimensional ones. May devised categories for the reasons given for media preferences by 164 third-grade subjects. The highest percentages of these categories fell into the qualities of the medium—how the material was manipulated or what sensory qualities are stimulated, the generic pleasure derived from the material, the product outcomes from using a material, and the flexibility of ideas or expressive potential of the material. Ability to control the media was also an important factor, especially for fourth graders.

In studies of students as learners, researchers have focused on many attributes of the leaner, the environment of learning, the special attributes of learners, the content of what is offered to the learner, and the materials available to the learner. Art teachers need to know what students are capable of learning and when it is appropriate to teach it. Research on special populations of students with particular backgrounds, experiences, or abilities helps inform the practice of teaching students with a variety of needs and offers some insights into how what we choose to teach and the materials we offer in teaching affect students.

Planned Instructional Interventions

Research studies included in this section are predominately quantitative in format, offer valuable information about teaching, and are complementary to the qualitative studies. These studies are often concerned with the development of a teaching strategy or an approach to teaching or curriculum and how these approaches may be manifested in student knowledge, usually as shown in a product or through another form of student assessment. In these studies, strategy is often scripted. Students' art products may be rated on scales specific to the researchers' hypotheses and research questions. Pretests and posttests may be given. Classroom research has been conducted on the effectiveness of instruction in art, the impact of teachers on development of students' abilities in creating and discussing art, and the effects of teachers' expectations on students' art products. Notable are the studies of Douglas and Schwartz (1967), Sharp (1981), Smith (1985), Neperud (1966), Brewer and Colbert (1992), Grossman (1980), Davis (1969), Day (1969), Thompson (1991), and Haanstra (1994).

Douglas and Schwartz (1967) studied the effect of planned adult-child interaction during art activities in the classroom. Preschool teachers were trained to encourage children to observe artworks carefully as well as to discuss artwork and art concepts with children. Douglas and Schwartz reported that the teachers and the children in these classrooms used more art vocabulary and more art process and action-related words than did children in the classrooms of untrained teachers. Similarly, Sharp (1981) reported that as trained kindergarten teachers increased the quantity and the quality of their talk about aesthetics qualities of works of art, similar increases were observed in their students' vocabularies.

Classroom studies of drawing are often psychologically based and data are collected using experimental, or quasi-experimental methods. In 1985, Smith's study of five outstanding teachers of elementary art had two goals: teaching children the process of drawing from observation with attention to the meaningful quality of the process and the product. Smith and her teacher colleagues believed that drawing should be taught with attention to children's development of drawing strategies and systems. The data from this study showed changes in children's intentions for how to depict the object drawn. These intentions included discursive or narrative, fantasy, and figural descriptions of the object. The data also yielded two categories of translation processes: basic object definition and drawing the third dimension. Smith suggested that observational drawing is a search for the perceptual, aesthetic, and empathetic meaning of objects and that it can be taught with rigor without teachers being authoritarian.

Research about the effectiveness of instruction was conducted by Neperud (1966). In his study of fifth-grade students' drawings, Neperud found that direct instruction and intervention by teachers during the process of working on drawings led to a higher level of drawing skill than offering feedback at the completion of the drawing.

Brewer and Colbert (1992) conducted a study of seventh graders' ceramic vessels, contrasting three unique types of teaching in three intact classes. Like Neperud, Brewer and Colbert found that direct, studio-based instruction positively affected students' performance levels in constructing with clay. Using a combination of analytical and holistic forms of assessment of student's pretest and posttest ceramic vessels, significant gains were found across all treatment groups. When groups were compared, the studio or technical and historical or cultural instruction strategies resulted in student production of ceramic vessels that were judged to be of higher quality than those produced in the questioning or discussion group.

Grossman (1980) studied the effect of instructional experiences in clay-modeling skills and the representation of the human figure modeled by preschool children. Grossman was also interested in transfer of learning from the modeling of human figures in clay to drawn representations of the figure. Grossman studied six intact classes and trained the teachers of those

classes to teach 15 clay-modeling lessons that centered on the basics of manipulating and joining clay. Using experimental and control groups in a quasi-experimental design, Grossman found significant differences in the formal elements, structure, and details of the modeled figures of the children who had received the 15 modeling lessons in the experimental treatment. No significant differences were found between the performance of girls and boys on modeling the human figure nor was a cross-media transfer to drawing abilities noted as the result of the experimental treatment.

In a study conducted in 1969 in college classrooms, Davis reported his findings on the effects of depth and breadth approaches to art instruction on creative-thinking abilities, attitudes about art, and the aesthetic qualities of art products produced by art students beginning postsecondary instruction. His purpose was to compare two teaching methods in art, one emphasizing a breadth approach and the other a depth approach to the subject. The results of his study raised some important questions about the superiority of either method of teaching, as his findings showed no significant differences in student performance and learning when the two approaches were compared. His findings also raised questions about the relationship of art instruction as a way to promote general creativity, as no increases in creativity were noted in either subject group.

Day (1969) studied different methods for teaching art history in two junior high school art classes. Specifically, he studied contrasting instructional strategies for teaching young adolescents about Cubism. Contrasting the traditional lecture–slide instruction to instruction integrating of hands-on art activities with the traditional lecture–slide approach, Day found that students who received the combined hands-on and lecture–slide instruction performed significantly better on the Cubism knowledge exam. Subjective evaluations of the students' progress produced by two participating art teachers supported the statistical comparisons. The art teachers also noted that the artwork produced under the experimental treatment was above average in terms of originality and quality.

Research on how the study of the visual arts affects student achievement in other subjects and how students' art performances are affected by interdisciplinary approaches linking the visual arts with other subjects may offer insights into new ways to organize the art curriculum. Thompson (1991) conducted classroom research in the middle school, contrasting two approaches of instruction in art. In one approach, art was taught as an interdisciplinary study along with science. In the second approach, art was taught alone. Thompson found that when art was taught alone, student's enthusiasm was greater, and scores on creativity and thinking-skills measures, as well as on specific projects and basic art skills, were higher.

Haanstra (1994) compiled studies from three computer databases to review classroom research that compared studio approaches to learning with the students' abilities to respond aesthetically to works of art. Using 30 studies on visual–spatial abilities and 39 studies on aesthetic perception, Haanstra's meta-analyses indicated that when studio education is solely performance based, it has no effect on students' visual–spatial abilities and only modest effects on students' abilities to perceive and to respond aesthetically.

Each of these studies has implications for teaching and curriculum strategies. Unfortunately, many studies of this type were not expanded to include different age groups nor were they conducted in additional classroom settings or formulated into more cohesive research questions. Classroom practices can be shaped by the ideas and findings of these studies, but more research is needed.

Conclusions

A primary reason for reviewing previous research is to understand if our practice of teaching art has been informed by research and to consider if classroom practices in visual arts education can be influenced by the findings of research. Hardiman and Zernich said in 1976 that we could take away the last 10 years of research and see no effect on art classrooms. From the number of research studies conducted in art classrooms since that statement, one might surmise that we do have much more information about art teaching. Yet, the question about the effect of research on teaching practice still remains.

Today we have schools built around the ideas and findings of research. In these schools, art instruction has been influenced by research findings. We find magnet schools with focuses on multiple intelligence, multicultural education, inquiry-based education, international education, arts education, mathematics, science, and interdisciplinary-based instruction. In these schools, visual arts instruction is influenced by the research on which the school was created.

It is difficult to tell what influences research findings have on art instruction. Art instruction is offered by certified art teaching specialists in some geographic locations and by classroom teachers with an average of 3 semester hours of visual arts credit in others. Many of the research studies reviewed here were conducted in isolation and have not been replicated in settings with different age groups and in different kinds of schools. These limitations are faced in applying the findings to other classroom climates, students, and school settings.

The question about whether research has changed practice might be rephrased to question whether research informs practice and what is the process of change. Stokrocki (1993) commented that cross-site research is designed to build theory rather than generalize and to analyze for critical problems and to do further study. The mercurial nature of the classroom requires such a perspective for research on teaching. If we regard our cumulative research as sketches that leave areas unresolved and offer particular views through which we clarify our multiple visions of teaching, then classroom research has much to tell us about teaching.

REFERENCES

Alexander, R. R. (1980). Mr. Jewel as a model: An educational criticism. *Studies in Art Education, 21*(3), 20–30.

Alexander, R. R. (1983). Teacher as shaman: An educational criticism. *Studies in Art Education, 25*(1), 50–57.

Alexander, R. R. (1984, April) *First graders' classroom conversations about art making: Social life, fantasy and play, verisimilitude, and medial procedures.* Paper presented at the meeting of the American Educational Research Association Meeting, New Orleans, LA.

Araca, A. (1990). Environment of middle and secondary art classrooms: Becoming aware of, designing, and implementing changes in the furniture, facilities, and spaces. In B. E. Little (Ed.), *Secondary art education: An anthology of issues* (pp. 69–92). Reston, VA: National Art Education Association.

Brewer, T. M., & Colbert, C. B. (1992). The effect of contrasting instructional strategies on seventh-grade students' ceramic vessels. *Studies in Art Education, 34*(1), 18–27.

Cocking, R. R., & Copple, C. E. (1979). Change through exposure to others: A study of children's verbalizations as they draw. In M. K. Poulsen & G. Lubin (Eds.), *Piagetian theory and its implications for the helping professionals* (pp. 124–132). Los Angeles: University of California.

Colwell, R. (1995). The arts. In G. Cawelti (Ed.), *Handbook of research on improving student achievement* (pp. 21–42). Arlington, VA: Educational Research Service.

Davis, D. J. (1969). The effects of depth and breadth methods of art instruction upon creative thinking, art attitudes, and aesthetic quality of art products in beginning college art students. *Studies in Art Education, 10*(2), 27–40.

Davis, D. J. (1971). Research in art education: An overview. *Art Education, 8*(2), 2–9.

Day, M. (1969). The compatibility of art history and studio art activity in the junior high school art program. *Studies in Art Education, 10*(2), 57–65.

Douglas, N., & Schwartz, J. (1967). Increasing awareness of art ideas of young children through guided experience in ceramics. *Studies in Art Education, 8*(2), 2–9.

Eisner, E. (1969). Art education. In R. Ebel (Ed.), *Encyclopedia of educational research* (pp. 76–86). New York: Macmillan.

Eisner, E. (1973). Research on teaching in the visual arts. In R. Travers (Ed.), *Second handbook on Teaching* (pp. 1196–1209). Chicago: Rand McNally.

Emery, L. (1989). Believing in artistic making and thinking. *Studies in Art Education, 30*(4), 237–248.

Floyd, M. B. (1997). *The enhancement of self-concept in African-American students through discipline-based multicultural art curriculum.* Unpublished doctoral dissertation, Florida State University, Tallahassee.

Grossman, E. (1980). Effects of instructional experiences in clay modeling skills on modeled human figure representation in preschool children. *Studies in Art Education, 22*(1), 51–59.

Haanstra, F. (1994). *Effects of art education on visual–spatial ability and aesthetic perception: Two meta analyses.* Amsterdam, The Netherlands: Thesis Publishers.

Hardiman, G., & Zernich, T. (1976). Research in art education 1970–74: Portrayal and interpretation. *Art Education, 29,* 23–26.

Hausman, J. (1963). Research on teaching in the visual arts. In N. L. Gage (Ed.), *Handbook on Teaching* (pp. 1101–1117). Chicago: Rand McNally.

Johnson, N. (1985). Teaching and learning in art: The acquisition of art knowledge in an eighth grade class. *AERA: Arts and Learning Special Interest Group Proceedings* (pp. 14–25). Washington, DC: American Educational Research Association.

Johnson, N. (1986). Teaching and learning art: Socialization in a high school art class. *Arts and Learning Research, 4,* 64–72.

La Pierre, S., & Zimmerman, E. (1997). *Research methods and methodologies for art education.* Reston, VA: National Art Education Association.

May, W. T. (1987). Student responses to media: Implications for elementary art curriculum. *Studies in Art Education, 28*(2), 105–117.

Neperud, R. W. (1966). An experimental study of visual elements, selected art instruction methods, and drawing development at the fifth grade level. *Studies in Art Education, 7*(2), 3–13.

Pariser, D. (1981). Linear lessons in a centrifugal environment: An ethnographic sketch of an art teaching experience. *Review of Research in Visual Arts Education, 9,* 81–90.

Regans, R. (1971). *The effects of instruction in a technique of art criticism upon the responses of elementary students to art objects.* Unpublished doctoral dissertation. University of Georgia, Athens.

Rosario, J., & Collazo, E. (1981). Aesthetic codes in context: An exploration in two preschool classrooms. *Journal of Aesthetic Education, 15*(1), 71–82.

Sevigny, M. (1977). *A descriptive study of instructional interaction and performance appraisal in a university studio art setting: A multiple perspective.* Unpublished doctoral dissertation. The Ohio State University, Columbus.

Sharp, P. (1981). *The development of aesthetic response in early educa-*

tion. Unpublished doctoral dissertation, Stanford University, Stanford, CA.

Smith, N. R. (1985). Observation drawing: Changes in children's intention and translation methods grades K–6. *AERA: Arts and Learning Special Interest Group Proceedings* (pp. 47–62). Washington, DC: American Educational Research Association.

Stokrocki, M. L. (1986). A portrait of an effective art teacher. *Studies in Art Education, 27*(2), 82–93.

Stokrocki, M. L. (1988). Teaching preadolescents during a nine-week sequence: The negotiator's approach. *Studies in Art Education, 30*(1), 39–46.

Stokrocki, M. (1993). Participant observation research on pedagogy and learning. *Translations, 3*(1), 1–5.

Susi, F. D. (1990). The art classroom as a behavior setting. In B. E. Little (Ed.), Secondary art education: An anthology of issues (pp. 93–105). Reston, VA: National Art Education Association.

Swann, A. (1986). Child/adult interaction during art activities in a pre-school setting: An achievement seeking response. *Arts and Learning Research, 4,* 73–79.

Taunton, M. (1983). Ways to talk and what to say: A study of art conversations among young children and adults in pre-school settings. *Conference Proceedings, AERA/Arts and Learning Special Interest Group, 1,* 1–14.

Taunton, M. (1986). The conveyance of aesthetic values during art activities in grades one through three. *Journal of Multicultural Research in Art Education, 2,* 10–16.

Thompson, K. (1991). *Assessing the creative effectiveness of two approaches to teaching art at the middle school level.* Unpublished doctoral dissertation. University of Georgia, Athens.

Twiggs, L. F. (1970). *The effects of teaching a methods of art criticism on the aesthetic responses of culturally disadvantaged junior high school students.* Unpublished doctoral dissertation. University of Georgia, Athens.

Zimmerman, E. (1992). A comparative study of two painting teachers of talented adolescents. *Studies in Art Education, 33*(3), 174–185.

29.
Research on History Teaching

Suzanne M. Wilson
Michigan State University

The research base for the teaching and learning of history is thin and uneven. Much of the professional literature about history teaching consists of either descriptions of exemplary practices, usually reports from the teachers who developed the approach or the method or untried prescriptions for effective teaching. Claims for the exemplary nature of the methods being recommended are seldom supported by evidence of what or how much student learning took place.
(Downey & Levstik, 1991, p. 400)

"There is a dearth of research on history teaching," Downey and Levstik conclude in their introduction to the chapter titled "Teaching and Learning History," one of 53 chapters in the *Handbook of Research on Social Studies Teaching and Learning* (Shaver, 1991). Until recently, their claim seemed well grounded. As testimony to their claim, the chapter on research on social studies in the third edition of the *Handbook of Research on Teaching* (Wittrock, 1986) was the shortest in the book—eight pages of prose—with nary a reference to history teaching.

But by the time Wineburg (1996) reviewed the literature on history teaching and learning for the *Handbook of Educational Psychology,* this void of references to history teaching existed no longer. In the past 10 years, we have witnessed a surge in subject-specific studies of teaching (and learning) in the field of history teaching. Building on earlier work in Great Britain (e.g., Booth, 1980, 1983, 1987, 1994; Dickinson & Lee, 1978; Dickinson, Lee, & Rogers, 1984; Elton, 1970; Hallam, 1967, 1970, 1971) that Wineburg (1996) has reviewed, researchers in the United States and Europe have enthusiastically pursued a range of significant questions concerning history education. A handful of books have appeared (Brophy & VanSledright, 1997; Carretero & Voss, 1994; Husbands, 1996; Leinhardt, Beck, & Stainton, 1994; Stearns, Seixas, & Wineburg, 2000; Voss & Carretero, 1999) with others, no doubt, on the way. Articles about history education have appeared in journals whose audiences go well beyond social studies educators (e.g., Bain, 1995; Fournier & Wineburg, 1997; Gardner & Boix-Mansilla, 1994; Wilson & Wineburg, 1988). Several journals—*Cultural Psychology, Educational Psychologist,* and the *International Journal of Educational Research*—have had special issues devoted to the teaching and learning of history. And history-related articles appear more frequently in social studies research journals like *Theory and Research in Social Education.*

This flurry of scholarship includes many voices: historians, teachers, teacher educators, curriculum developers, educational and cognitive psychologists, and reformers. Although the scholarship shares the signifier "history," the focus and substance shifts considerably with each author. At times, researchers attempt to understand students' historical understanding; at other times, they explore teachers' subject matter knowledge. Some researchers describe instructional strategies; others, how prospective history teachers learn to teach. Some relevant reading is not "research based": Curriculum mandates that are based, in part, on research but more on collective opinion and hope describe what students should learn and what teachers should know (Center for Civic Education, 1995; National Center for History in the Schools, 1996; National Council for Social Studies, 1994). A very different source of readings includes personal accounts by historians, teacher educators, and teachers about their experiences with teaching history or with reforming history education. Bailyn (1994), for example, writes about the

Samuel S. Wineburg, Peter Seixas, and Philip A. Cusick offered insightful feedback at critical times. Conversations with Gaea Leinhardt, Cindy Hartzler-Miller, and Shari Levine Rose also contributed enormously to the piece. Factual and interpretative errors that remain are my own.

teaching and writing of history; Holt (1990) explains how he helps undergraduates learn to read and write history. Cornbleth and Waugh (1995) tell stories of social studies curricular reform in California and New York in the past decade; Nash, Crabtree, and Dunn (1997) report on what happened to the national history standards at the same time. Bain (1995), a high school teacher from Ohio at the time, recounts the experience of sitting on the panels that developed and reviewed such standards. Dow (1991) tells the story of MACOS (Man: A Course of Study), an earlier reform effort. Husbands (1996) weaves together personal experiences and observations of other teachers and students. And Levstik and Barton (1997) have published an unusual teacher's manual that integrates research on history teaching and learning, writing by historians, and practical tips. Each of these documents—research, reform rhetoric, personal accounts, and innovative curricula (for students and teachers)—holds promise for informing our view of teaching history.

Underlying this flurry of activity are varied assumptions about history, teaching, and learning, assumptions that shape the work. As Voss (1997) points out, considerations of history teaching and learning cannot be "considered in a vacuum":

> They force from the conceptual bushes the emergence of questions such as: What is the purpose of teaching history? What does it mean to "explain" and/or "understand" historical events? What is the role of narrative in history? How does causation take place in history? How should history be taught? (p. 187)

Anyone who has even flirted with the study of history as a discipline or with social studies as a curricular field knows of the endless (often acrimonious) debates concerning these questions (e.g., Hertzberg, 1982; Ravitch, 1985). Most recently, these debates surfaced in response to the release of the national history standards. Rush Limbaugh told his audience that the standards were "a bunch of p. c. crap," explaining,

> History is real simple. You know what history is? It's what happened. . . . The problem you get into is when guys like this try to skew history by [saying], "Well, let's interpret what happened because maybe we can't find the truth in the facts, or at least we don't like the truth as it's presented. So let's change the interpretation a little bit so that it will be the way we wished it were." Well, that's not what history is. History is what happened, and history ought to be nothing more than the quest to find out what happened. (Nash, Crabtree, & Dunn, 1997, p. 6)

Limbaugh is an extreme, and I cite him with caution: his position might be considered a caricature. But in his willingness to be explicit, Limbaugh captures the essence of popular belief: History is settled, and there is only one; history's purposes are to make us proud Americans, not critical ones (Gitlin, 1995).

In contrast, the authors of the national standards attempted to write a multiperspectival account of history. Their history would tell many stories, celebratory and critical. This history would reflect the intellectual developments of the field (Novick, 1988), acknowledging the varied experiences of American citizens: Native Americans, African Americans, immigrants, or—as Hughes (1994) puts it—"history from the bottom." This version of history—a sometimes uncomfortable cobbling together of multiple perspectives, opinions, voices, and judgments—

reignited an age-old debate about the role of history education. Where was *the* American story? critics asked,

> . . . insist[ing] that historical certitudes be reaffirmed, especially the stories and traditional truths that accord with the nation's self-image as great, good, and free. (Nash, Crabtree, & Dunn, 1997, p. 40)

Discussions about history and social studies curricula always reflect our own divided beliefs about the nature of history and the role of historical knowledge in society. So, not surprisingly, as some critics railed against the national standards for those standards' failure to honor a single, true history, other critics in California claimed that the state standards for history teaching were not multicultural enough and that they were racist "Eurocentric pap" (Gitlin, 1995).

These debates, deeply rooted in our conflicted American goals of equality and liberty, are complex and deserve more attention and analysis than I offer here. However, it is important to note that the backdrop for contemporary research on history teaching includes a heated political, ideological, and intellectual debate about the content of the American curriculum. Criticisms of national standards in mathematics, history, and language arts have brought to the surface serious and, as of yet, unresolved issues about U.S. education. The issues are many and include—but are not limited to—the purposes of American education (Cohen & Neufeld, 1981; Labaree, 1997), the "liberal orthodoxy" of many standards (Gitlin, 1995), and the misinterpreted, sometimes negative heritage of Dewey's progressive ideals (Dewey, 1938; Hirsch, 1996).

The argument is not unique to the United States. One sees similar arguments in debates over national curricula in Great Britain, Israel, Estonia, Spain, and Russia (e.g., Husbands & Pendry, 1992; Marriott, 1990; Slater, 1990). As McKiernan (1993) notes, political shifts—Taiwan's democratization, the European move to a single currency, the deconstruction of the former USSR—that involve reconsideration of the meaning of *nation* all have direct consequences for the idea of a national curricula. Chou (1999), for instance, tells the story of how social studies curricula become the battleground for ideological and political differences in Taiwan, a "nation" conflicted about its own boundaries.

The debate over history education does not stop there. In the United States, an age-old conflict rages between those who advocate a social studies, rather than a history, education. Some social studies educators worry that history instruction will only focus on the acquisition of factual knowledge and does not prepare students to deal with social, economic, and political problems. Seixas (1993b) and Whelan (1992) argue that these critics possess stale conceptions of the discipline and assume that history is inherently conservative and stultifying, as did many progressive educators who first called for the development of a social studies curriculum. Evans (1990) declares himself "a critic of the revival of history," seeing it as a "new conservatism." Likewise, Cornbleth and Waugh (1995) make a similar assumption when they clump all educators with interests in the teaching and learning of history (as opposed to social studies or multiculturalism) into what they call a "neonativist network."

Such pigeonholing becomes increasingly difficult to justify.

One has only to browse the history shelves in any bookstore to notice that the field is neither monolithic nor univocal. Laurel Ulrich (1990), using evidence that had previously been dismissed by political historians, reconstructs the life of a midwife and, in so doing, makes a different argument for the structure of the colonial community and economy. Daniel Goldhagen (1997) writes a disquieting argument in *Hitler's Willing Executioners,* while David Oshinsky (1997) pens a harrowing tale of Parchman Farm, a state penitentiary in Mississippi that was dedicated to "keeping the ex-slaves in line." Readers of these histories leave shaken; these historians do not intend to communicate a glorified vision of the past but, instead, a realistic one that is intended to help us see humanity in its depth and frailty, wisdom and cruelty. These histories are not meant to conserve but to push, prod, and make us question our commitments and limitations.

Further, the heated and diverse reactions to such histories in the *New York Review of Books,* the *New Yorker,* and *The Economist* demonstrate that the discipline itself contains multitudes. In a survey of the profession, Bender (1994) found that

> The single quality of the profession most valued by historians is its diversity of topics, methods, and practitioners. Yet the greatest worry expressed by the respondents concerns a tendency toward balkanization, or "lack of community," which is attributed to excessive specialization, narrow careerism, and ideological blinders, including those of race, gender, and class. The profession, it seems, is either divided or confused. (p. 994)

So when critics of history teaching treat all researchers or advocates as a monolithic camp called "neonativists" or "conservatives," they fail to recognize the diverse conceptions of what history is and why we ought to teach it that currently exist in the academy. As this review will reveal, researchers—holding diverse views on teaching, learning, history, and purposes—have not postponed their investigations until those issues are resolved. (Of course, resolution is not likely to be either attainable or attractive; a healthy and self-critical democracy depends on such debate.) I begin this chapter by sidestepping these differences and offering an account of the current state of the research of history teaching. But I return to the field's diversity in the end, for it has serious consequences for our research and discourse.

As an initial structure for this analysis, I consider three questions: (a) What is traditional history teaching like?; (b) What are researchers learning about "accomplished" history teaching?; and (c) What explains good teaching? After reviewing representative samples of this literature, I briefly review emerging research on students' learning of history before suggesting some for new directions in the field.

Researchers' Portraits of Traditional History Teaching

In their review of the then extant literature, Downey and Levstik (1988) claim that we know quite a bit about traditional history teaching: the heavy reliance on textbooks (Goodlad, 1984; Shaver, Davis, & Helburn, 1980); a dominance of teacher lecture and recitation (Cuban, 1991; McNeil, 1986; Ravitch & Finn, 1987); and the weekly quizzes and individual assignments

that are interrupted sporadically with a film (Cuban, 1991). Indeed, images of the prototypical history class abound (Cuban, 1984; Goodlad, 1984; Hoetker & Ahlbrand, 1969; Shaver, Davis, & Helburn, 1980; Sirotnik, 1983).

Furthermore, those images seem woven into the fabric of American culture, part of the folklore of schooling. School history, in fact, has an international reputation for being universally mind-numbing. A Scottish lay historian wrote:

> Let there be no mistake about this—I am not setting out to write a history-book. For one thing, I am not a qualified historian—only a story-teller with an interest in history. For another, all too often history-books are dull, dull—that in my eyes is a crime. How anyone can make history dull and boring is beyond my conception . . . for history is in fact the most dramatic, colourful and exciting subject under the sun, the very essence of mankind's greatness and weakness, efforts and failures, heroics and cowardices, ambitions, knaveries, and follies—indeed everything which story-telling is based upon, the very raw materials of drama, tragedy, comedy, farce. Yet generation after generation of academic historians *have* somehow managed to make history dull for millions of folk, in book and classroom. (Tranter, 1987)

Ennui, presumed to be part of most history classrooms, is a refrain heard in the introductions of most contemporary research. Onosko (1990) begins with claims about schools as "landscapes of mindlessness" (p. 443). Spoehr and Spoehr (1994) evoke images of Dickens's Mr. Gradgrind when they assert that

> Focusing exclusively on facts is what makes history study so deadly dull for so many students in so many schools; students get the idea that history is just one damn thing after another, and that their job is to memorize as many facts as possible, preferably in chronological order. (p. 71)

Joyce Cruse (1994), a high school teacher, begins an essay by quoting her students:

> "I hate American history, it's boring." "Who wants to learn about dead people?" "I flunked the Constitution test twice; I couldn't remember all those amendments." "I'm sick of memorizing facts and dates, what does this have to do with real life?" (p. 1064)

And Paxton and Wineburg (2000) begin their review of the recent literature with a scene from the movie *Ferris Bueller's Day Off.* The first period of the day, 35 high school students listen as their history teacher begins class:

> In 1930, the Republican-controlled House of Representatives endeavored to alleviate the effects of the—anyone? anyone?—Great Depression. Pass the—anyone? anyone?—the tariff bill. The Hawley-Smoot Tariff Act, which—anyone? raised or lowered?—raised tariffs in an effort to collect more revenues for the federal government. Did it work? Anyone? (p. 855)

> This satire portrays our collective sense of history teaching: the senseless march through dusty facts, the absurd and trite "Socratic" monologues; the silenced students who alternate between scribbling notes and nodding off to sleep; teachers—sometimes frantically, sometimes farcically—trying to engage students in "discussions" in which students belligerently close down the teacher's attempt at con-

versation or in which teachers ignore students' fragile efforts to volunteer ideas.

Yet when he reviewed the empirical literature, Cuban (1991) found only a dozen studies spanning the period from 1900 to 1980. Few projects actually sent researchers into classrooms to witness and document actual teaching practices. In one such study, Shaver, Davis, and Helburn (1980), studying the state of social studies teaching in the wake of 1960s and 1970s reforms, noted that "there has been great stability in the social studies curriculum."

Social studies classes will be strikingly similar to those that many of us experienced as youngsters: textbook assignments followed by recitation led by a teacher who, in his or her own way, likes students and tries to show concern for them—and avoids controversial issues, but tries to pitch the class at the students' level. (p. 7)

Goodlad's (1984) "A Study of Schooling" drew similar conclusions about the 38 schools that served as the basis of that work. Researchers in that study found an amorphous curriculum (especially at the elementary level) and "a preponderance of classroom activity involving listening, reading textbooks, completing workbooks and worksheets, and taking quizzes" (p. 213).

Applebee, Langer, and Mullis (1987), using national survey data, found that students' self-reports echoed this message: Classrooms were teacher centered. Students reported that they memorized information (83%), used the textbook weekly (89%), and saw films weekly (33%). They never visited museums (93%) or wrote long reports for class (68% of the 11th graders), but students did report that they participated in whole-group lectures at least some of the time (97%) (see also Ravitch & Finn, 1987, for complementary results).

McNeil's (1986) research buttresses this view. In her ethnography of high school social studies teaching, McNeil found that our educational bureaucracy has "placed the 'smooth running' of schools ahead of 'literate' or 'intellectual' education. . . ." (p. 161). Learning takes a backseat to order, and teachers respond to these priorities, "simplify[ing] content and reduc[ing] demands on students in return for classroom order and minimal student compliance." Teachers do this, she argued, by "teaching defensively" (p. 158).

McNeil posited several types of defensive teaching. The first she calls "fragmentation," which is

. . . the reduction of any topic to fragments or disjointed pieces of information—lists. A list lets a teacher avoid having to elaborate or show linkages. . . . No one is called upon to synthesize or give a picture of interrelationships. (p. 167)

Such lists can become the educational end rather than the educational means. A list, then, does not function as a mere aide to memory or to foster understanding of complicated ideas, the list "*is* the study of the topic" (p. 168). The second defensive strategy is called "mystification," which occurs when teachers "surround a controversial or complex topic with mystery to close off discussion of it" (p. 169). The third is called

"omission" whereby teachers omit difficult or complicated issues from discussion or redirect conversation away from difficult topics or questions. The fourth strategy, called "defensive simplification," occurs when "teachers . . . win the students' compliance on a lesson by promising that it will not be difficult and will not go into any depth" (p. 174). Teachers use this strategy when they doubt students' interest or abilities to understand the topic. Adequate treatment of the topic would be difficult, would take time, and would make it difficult to cover the curriculum efficiently. "Topics introduced 'defensively'," McNeil claimed, "tended to be topics that needed a great deal of unpackaging to be grasped, topics not amenable to reduction to items in a list" (p. 175).

So what did these studies reveal? Diverse in their methods, the collective story these studies tell is nonetheless coherent: little intellectual engagement, a dominance of teachers and textbooks, and minimal problem solving or critical thinking. Moreover, Goodlad found that students consistently ranked social studies as less important than mathematics, English, vocational or career education, and science. Students also consistently reported social studies to be less likable than art, physical education, mathematics, and English. These findings, combined with the folklore of history teaching, suggests that we know enough about typical history teaching.

In the late 1980s, researchers began searching for alternative questions to ask about the content and character of history teaching. Shulman (1983) argued for such a move when he claimed that we needed research of both the "possible" and the "probable" in teaching. Three years later, Shulman (1986) added subject matter to the research equation, arguing that for far too long, research on teaching had treated instruction as a generic phenomenon. Subsequently, a growing number of researchers—from varied disciplinary perspectives—began studies of history teaching. Although traditionally the territory of social studies educators with an interest in history, history teaching began to attract the attention of cognitive psychologists, historians, and others.

With this shift, we are learning a great deal about what happens in the classes of accomplished history teachers, about what it takes to teach well, and about what it takes to prepare teachers well.[1] We are also learning about student learning, about not only what they bring to school but also how they experience instruction. Although, not strictly within the boundaries of a traditional review of research on teaching, research on students ought to inform our thinking about research on teaching. In that spirit, I also include a brief summary of some intriguing research in the area of students' ideas and thinking about history.

This is not a comprehensive review. A happy consequence of the explosion of interest in history teaching and learning is that too much research is now available to review adequately in such a short space. To review all the research, one would have to succumb to the problem that plagues most history curricula: So much "content" is summarized that the listing obscures an emergent argument. Instead, I opt for a review of representative

---

[1] The very presence of two chapters—one about social studies and one about history teaching—in this volume suggests a shift toward greater subject-specificity in research on this realm of teaching.

research that sheds light on the current state of the field and that points to prospective new directions for research.

Research on Accomplished Practice

The 1980s witnessed a surge in studies of good teachers and teaching. The language used varies: Some researchers study expert teachers, others, accomplished or exemplary teachers. One line of this work had its roots in Shulman's (1986) attempts to understand subject-specific aspects of teaching. Researchers in both the Knowledge Growth in a Profession Project and the subsequent Teacher Assessment Project used in-depth interviews, longitudinal classroom observations, and cognitive tasks to investigate the role of subject matter knowledge in teaching. As part of that effort, Wineburg and I published a series of studies concerning the knowledge and skill of beginning and experienced teachers. In Wilson and Wineburg (1988), we analyzed the differences in the perspectives of four beginning history teachers who had different undergraduate preparation. The nonhistory majors had naive and narrow views of history. Largely, they saw history in the same ways that high school students report: factual and dull. In their eyes, other fields—political science and anthropology, for instance—used historical facts in the service of more interesting interpretations. When asked to talk about how they would teach history, these teachers described lessons that did not capture the epistemological complexity of history.

In another study (Wineburg & Wilson, 1991), we contrasted two experienced teachers, Elizabeth Jensen and John Price. When we observed Jensen's teaching, she was largely invisible. During our observations, students were engaged in a debate as loyalists and rebels who were discussing the resolution, "The British government possesses the legitimate authority to tax the American colonies." Jensen sat on the sidelines, scribbling notes, smiling, occasionally reminding the judges to maintain order. For days, Jensen had assigned readings, facilitated discussions, and gathered students into research groups to set the stage for this debate.

Price offered a very different image. As discussion leader, he dominated; in five minutes, he uttered 770 words versus the 26 words contributed by a subset of his students. At one point, Price referred to his teaching as a "lion-taming act":

> I had a lion-taming act back in the late 60s. . . . You either got the whole group's attention and you kept them interested in something or you had [fighting] going on constantly. The fighting was difficult to control. . . . So the way I did it was just bowl them over with interesting stuff so that they are sitting there with their mouths open and they don't have time to be clawing away at each other. And that was a survival technique that I developed. Over the years, of course, I have loosened it up. (p. 325)

Price, too, set the stage for his performances. Students learned about background information and a theory of revolution. He defined terms, asked them to consider points of view, and introduced multiple interpretations.

Even though differences in their teaching seemed obvious, we found that these two teachers were more similar than different. Each thought of history as both fact and interpretation, each strove to create educational opportunities that capture those as-

pects of historical knowledge. Both Price and Jensen treated the textbook as an intellectual companion—not master—in classwork, and both teachers had in their repertoire a variety of instructional strategies to use for different topics and purposes. Both teachers were also lifelong students of history, restless in their search for new interpretations and insights into the events and characters that they had spent their careers discussing with students.

Simultaneously, Leinhardt and her colleagues, continuing the work that they had started on instructional explanations in mathematics (Leinhardt, 1985, 1990; Leinhardt & Greeno, 1986), began documenting cases of exemplary history teachers (Leinhardt, 1993, 1997; Leinhardt, Stainton, Virji, & Odoroff, 1994). Distinguishing instructional explanations from other sorts of explanations (discipline-based and self-referential, for example), Leinhardt (1993) found considerable variance in the use of explanations in history classes. Two distinct types of explanations occurred—blocked and ikat—and teachers' use of these explanations varied according to historical occasion and instructional goals. Blocked explanations were self-contained, coherent, and could stand alone. Ikat explanations were woven into class discussions. Much like the weaving method for which Leinhardt named these explanations, these explanations were threaded into instruction over time, appearing sometimes, only to disappear again. These explanations took more time to develop, were more context dependent, and had a coherence that emerged over time.

Looking closer, Leinhardt (1993) found that teachers' explanations were about different kinds of content. In an analysis of 10 randomly selected lessons, 25% of teachers' explanations — both blocked and ikat—were about themes, 22% were event-theme combinations, 20% were about events, 4% about structures (e.g., forms of government, rules of politics and economics), and 5% were about metasystems (tools of analysis, synthesis, hypothesis generation, interpretation, and the like). Explanations of events and structures were often blocked explanations whereas explanations of themes and metasystems often took the form of ikat explanations. This pattern makes intuitive sense: If themes develop over time, so too might their explanations. Moreover, history's metasystems, tools of analysis, and interpretative strategies are not readily or easily packaged and delivered. Instead, these tools take time to develop, explain, and hand over to student apprentices who are learning to acquire those skills and tools themselves.

Although Ms. Sterling, the teacher in Leinhardt's study, generated most of the explanations, the majority of the explanations were partially shared by the teacher and her students. The class, though teacher-centered, consistently included the active participation of students who were learning to generate their own explanations. In fact, in her analysis of student-to-teacher talk ratios, Leinhardt found a steady increase in student talk over time. Investigating the nature of that talk, Leinhardt found that student discourse early in the term focused on organizational issues (Do we use textbooks?) and well-intentioned but fumbling answers to the teacher's substantive questions about the content. Later in the term, those same students offered explanations that were long, detailed, and complex, reflecting many of the characteristics of the teacher's explanations while still containing awkwardnesses and flaws that signaled the students' novice status. Nonetheless, these discussions are strikingly different from the all-too-familiar caricature portrayed in *Ferris Bueller's Day Off* or in *Teachers.*

Leinhardt's work was among the first to reflect and integrate cognitive science into studies of history teaching. Using micro-analyses of instructional processes, Leinhardt and her colleagues searched for ways to understand how history instruction manifests itself in teacher and student performances. Other researchers use different methods. Although previous works have offered descriptions, VanSledright (1996) begins one chapter about history teaching by claiming that the "history education literature suffers from the paucity of finely textured teaching examples" (p. 259). He then goes on to offer a chronologically arranged inventory of 35 lessons that formed a unit of instruction of one experienced teacher, Dr. Reese, who recently earned a PhD in history. Although the teacher had learned about current debates within the field of history concerning interpretation, knowledge, and the role of the historian, very little of that knowledge seeped into her practice. VanSledright offers three "buffers" that "mitigate a full translation of Reese's knowledge from discipline to school" (p. 282), proposing that the relationship between teachers' knowledge of the discipline and what is taught is not straightforward. Echoing earlier claims made by other researchers, VanSledright suggests that what teachers teach (in contrast to what they know) might well be shaped by forces like beliefs about students and curriculum mandates. Dr. Reese, for example, felt that she had a responsibility to teach the school's curriculum (albeit with some latitude), even though it represented a view of history void the epistemological debates characterizing the field.

Across a number of articles that culminated in a book, Brophy and VanSledright (1997) offer additional "contextualized research portraits" of three experienced fifth-grade social studies teachers who have been nominated as good teachers. Using Evans's (1989) categories, the researchers claim that each teacher serves as an exemplar of storyteller, scientific historian, and reformer and that no one teacher is better than the others. The portraits are largely summaries or excerpts from lesson transcripts. By far, the most extensive case is that of Mary Lake, a storyteller who strove to engage students in learning history by telling them stories about the past and embedding within those stories significant historical ideas and concepts. Another teacher, Ramona Palmer—a scientific historian—taught students about the discipline of history, the use of evidence, the role of cause and effect. Sara Atkinson, a reformer, approached her teaching in ways that helped students see the relevance of the past to current events and that prepared them to be critical readers, sometimes even "principled social activists."[2]

The presentation of observational and interview data in this book by Brophy and VanSledright is considerable. In the Mary Lake case, for instance, it is not unusual for the authors to present three uninterrupted pages of transcript. These transcripts highlight the dominant role played by Mary Lake because—as storytellers do—she monopolized the floor. But readers may leave puzzled over what makes this "good" practice; the portrait of Mary Lake can be read as a portrait of the traditional practice that so many students, reformers, and teachers have criticized. As the authors themselves note, "Her students did not get many opportunities for extended discussion or debate during whole-class activities (where her discourse patterns were mostly limited to review and recitation)" (p. 68).

The authors very carefully portray the variety of kudos and criticism such teaching can invite. For instance, they note that some educators "would want to see less recitation and more dialogue, debate, or other sustained discussion (Newmann, 1990)" (p. 70). After summarizing the various criticisms and concerns about different views of teaching, the authors nevertheless conclude that all three teachers taught well. The researchers do so by showing how teaching's "goodness" varies according to one's frame of reference. Theirs is a functional analysis (Stinchcombe, 1968) because they claim a "uniformity of consequences"—good teaching—although a wide variety of behaviors led to those consequences.

Others take a different stance, arguing that not all functional teaching leads to high quality student learning. Consider, for example, the work of Newmann, Onosko, and their colleagues, who observed and interviewed teachers and students, administered questionnaires, and developed a scheme for understanding the qualities of teaching for higher-order thinking (Newmann, 1990a, 1990b; Onosko, 1989, 1990). In one analysis that contrasted teachers across dimensions of thoughtfulness, Onosko (1990) reported that higher-scoring teachers discussed fewer topics, presented students with significantly more challenging tasks, displayed significantly more substantive coherence in their lessons, and modeled thoughtfulness. Significant differences were also found between higher- and lower-scoring teachers on dimensions that related to students giving reasons and explanations for their statements and the teacher engaging students in careful consideration of those reasons and explanations. An image of thoughtful classroom practice—quite different from Brophy and VanSledright's ecumenical acceptance of multiple visions—emerged from this analysis:

> High scorers construct lessons that address fewer topics, and they discuss the topics in a more coherent manner. The problems and tasks posed during the lesson are more challenging given the ability levels of students, and students are more likely to share their reasoning. The teacher is more likely to model thoughtfulness, particularly by sharing his/her reasoning and complimenting students on their thinking. In addition, reasons and explanations entertained during lessons are more likely to be carefully considered. This may be in part due to high scorers' more frequent use of Socratic dialogue. Finally, students in high scorers' classes are more often exposed to the competing views of authoritative sources. (Onosko, 1990, p. 452)

When they then examined the instructional strategies used by these teachers, the researchers found that high scorers' lessons typically included both note taking by students and teacher-centered, whole-group discussions. The more thoughtful teach-

---

[2] I should note here that Evans' categorization of teachers were the product of an exploratory study that the author argues is not generalizable. Furthermore, Evans noted that many teachers were not so easily categorized and that 22.5% of teachers had no central tendency, preferring an eclecticism in their teaching in which they mix practices rather than adhere to one.

ers relied less on textbooks and more on primary sources and teacher-generated materials. Teachers' lessons that scored lower tended to take the form of lectures and recitations, a frequent use of textbooks, and an infrequent use of teacher-centered, whole-group discussions, precisely the features of Brophy and VanSledright's Mary Lake. The fact that researchers can—and do—draw opposite conclusions about the quality of a teacher's practice is a point that I will return to later in this chapter.

These studies are but a sample of the growing body of work that attempts to capture—some in broad strokes, others in fine detail—the nature of accomplished history teaching. Another kind of description of good teaching consists of teachers describing their practices. The exemplar for this is the work of Holt (1990), a professional historian who teaches at the University of Chicago. In *Thinking Historically: Narrative, Imagination, and Understanding,* Holt describes his work—not as historian but as teacher—with undergraduates. He argues for a version of history teaching that engages students in asking questions, thinking critically, and using their imaginations. He then describes History 413, a course he has designed to make the work of history "visible and open to students" and illustrates his points with excerpts of students' work to show how understandings develop over time. The reader leaves wishing to take such a course because the readings, discussions, and room for interpretation and thought—as illustrated in the following quote—are appealing:

> For the next day's discussion, [students] were presented a second set of documents clustered around a particular set of closely spaced events in a such a way as to help them grasp the narrative aspect of history. The first was a letter written by freedmen stating in their own terms precisely what they expected freedom to mean. The second was written by a Freedman's Bureau agent, almost as if in reply to the first (though it was not), and represents the view of many northerners committed to the ideology of free wage labor, or at least one variant of it. The final document was a report on the views of an African American Bureau agent who articulated a more radical view of what freedom requires. Each of these documents, as part of this larger whole, was also chosen to help students understand one moment in history as the interplay of many lines of action, conflicting desires, and dramatically different conceptions of what freedom should bring.
>
> Having worked with these and similar documents, I entered the class with a number of preconceptions about their meaning and the narrative I expected students to extract from or construct about emancipation's aftermath. But materials like these are "live," that is, they allow the students direct access to see and hear for themselves and thus to formulate their own questions and answers. Such questions arise in the space between the document itself and the reader's experience, what he or she *brings to* the material. Consequently, one should not be surprised when they do find new and unexpected meaning or raise fresh questions that are sometimes not immediately answerable. In fact, the most successful discussions are neither predictable, controllable, nor closable. And that is as it should be. (Holt, 1990, p. 19)

This class bears no resemblance either to school history's familiar caricatures or to charges of "nativism" or perspectival insularity. Similarly, the classroom of Bain (1997), a now-former high school teacher from Beechwood, Ohio, also does not resemble the caricatures or the charges. In Bain's "Teaching History as an Epistemic Act: Notes from a Practitioner," we see a high school teacher using emergent research results to inform his practice. For example, as a member of a committee charged with a critical review of the national history standards, Bain used his knowledge of research on history teaching and learning to critique the generic assumptions about learning and understanding that were embedded in the standards. He noted that Bloom's taxonomy—"an important cultural tool of American educators" (Bain, 1997, p. 9)—dominated the standards. This view is problematic from his perspective because the taxonomy assumes all knowledge to be hierarchical, similar across disciplines. Yet the unique character of historical knowledge gets lost with such generic language:

> There are problems with an unacknowledged, uncritical (reified?) use of the taxonomy. Its hierarchical structure creates the impression that elements of disciplined thought are discrete and linear. Thinking appears flat and one dimensional. . . . More relevant to this paper, the taxonomy appears to be discipline neutral, describing universal processes. (Bain, 1997, pp. 10–11)

Bain argues that the standards should reflect, instead, current knowledge. The standards could refer to sourcing, corroborating, and contextualizing—three strategies that Wineburg (1991) noted in the reading of historians—or they could differentiate between events, themes, metasystems when talking about the focus of instruction—distinctions that Leinhardt and her colleagues have made.

Also interesting is Bain's application of research to his teaching. He writes of teaching ninth graders to distinguish between history as an account and history as an event, and of constructing with them a graphic representation of the different forms history takes. In so doing, Bain begins to help students differentiate events from remaining evidence, authors from their arguments. He also writes of the different instructional strategies he uses to make both his and his students' thinking more public, including journals and structured interactions. These efforts all are designed to foster students' metacognitive awareness about their assumptions and beliefs about history. He ends his paper with questions for researchers: Do these practices "plausibly apply contemporary research to practice"? How do students and teachers negotiate epistemological differences? Are there patterns in how students learn about history and historical knowledge when engaging in these kinds of activities?

This sort of writing, coming as it does from teachers, is unlike the traditional "good practice" columns featured in practitioner journals that Downey and Levstik (1991) discuss. Although not traditional research, these accounts are nevertheless scholarly and continue a teacher–scholar tradition that was pioneered by Lampert (1985), Paley (1981), Duckworth (1987), and others.

Across the research and self-report, three themes emerge that correspond to the commonplaces of this review: research, teaching, and history. First, there are different views of how one conducts research. Methods for data collection and analysis include surveys and observational studies, ethnographies and semantic nets. Such diversity (when disciplined) can only help the field. Second, one sees very different conceptions of "good" his-

tory teaching, ranging from Brophy and VanSledright's willingness to embrace a full range of models to Newmann's, Onosko's,
and others' attempts to stipulate a normative frame. Although
such diversity is also probably quite healthy, it complicates discourse and analysis in the field because we are using the same
language—in this case, "good" or "accomplished" teaching—
to describe very different phenomena.

A third theme concerns the variation in how researchers conceptualize history. Although not always explicated by researchers, history sometimes appears to be defined relatively narrowly
as a list of significant dates, events, actors, and eras. In other
research, history is portrayed as a contested terrain. Researchers also vary in terms of whether they include the "hows," or
processes (skills of analysis and interpretation, methods of inquiry, the use of evidence), as part of the content of history.
Again, this variation complicates our discourse because the
claims we make about teaching history depend heavily on what
is being taught. The problems presented by this predictable
multiplicity and variation will echo throughout this review.

Explaining Good Teaching

Most research does not stop at portraits of teaching or learning
because, as teachers and scholars, we have an obligation first to
describe but then to explain what we have witnessed. Researchers, then, have also tried to answer the question: What does it
take to be a good history teacher? Current research seems to
cluster in two distinct explanatory camps: One searches for an
explanation of good teaching in the behaviors that teachers exhibit; the other explores the potential influence of teachers'
knowledge and beliefs and how these effect classroom instruction.

Explanations That Look to Teachers' Behaviors

Clearly, Leinhardt and her colleagues were interested in examining the features of instruction that made Ms. Sterling's teaching exemplary. The analyses of different kinds of explanations
(ikat and blocked) provide researchers with a lens through
which to examine instruction. In further analyses of these explanations, Leinhardt (1997) also unpacked—using semantic
nets (a tool borrowed from cognitive science)—the concepts
that emerged during these various explanations, documenting
the devices that Ms. Sterling used to support students' attempts
to participate in the joint construction of instructional explanations. For example, in one explanation (that took four days
to build), Sterling posed framing questions that modeled historical heuristics that students were learning to use. She modeled
the use of evidence in explanation-building and consistently
checked for students' prior knowledge. She moved between the
first and third person voice to help students understand where
they were in relation to the question they were investigating,
"pulling the students into the problem space" (p. 231). And she
was always careful to summarize—signaling to students that
she was about to move on to another part of the explanation—
reviewing what had gone on, foreshadowing what was to come.

The logic of Leinhardt's analysis goes something like this:
Ms. Sterling is a good teacher; her teaching has these features;
these features might then be characteristics of good teaching.

Newmann, Onosko, and their associates take a slightly

different route. They began by reviewing the extant literature
on effective teaching and schools as well as the literature on
higher-order thinking. They viewed videotapes and talked with
experienced teachers. They agreed that their initial framework
should consist of observable teacher and student behaviors.
Eventually, their framework consisted of 17 dimensions:

General
1. There was sustained examination of a few topics rather than
   superficial coverage of many.
2. The lesson displayed substantive coherence and continuity.
3. Students were given an appropriate amount of time to think,
   that is, to prepare responses to questions.

Teacher behavior
4. The teacher asked challenging questions and/or structured challenging tasks (given the ability level and preparation of the students).
5. The teacher carefully considered explanations and reasons for
   conclusions.
6. The teacher pressed individual students to justify or to clarify
   their assertions in a Socratic manner.
7. The teacher encouraged students to generate original and unconventional ideas, explanations, or solutions to problems.
8. The teacher showed an awareness that not all assertions emanating from authoritative sources are absolute or certain.
9. Students' personal experience (where relevant) was integrated
   into the lesson.
10. The teacher was model of thoughtfulness.

Student behavior
11. Students offered explanations and reasons for their conclusions.
12. Students generated original and unconventional ideas, explana-
    tions, hypotheses or solutions to problems.
13. Students assumed the roles of questioner and critic.
14. Student contributions were articulate, germane to the topic and
    connected to prior discussion.
15. What proposition of students participated verbally in the
    lesson?
16. What proportion of time did students spend engaged in
    thoughtful discourse with one another?
17. What proportion of students showed genuine involvement in
    the topics discussed? (Newmann, 1990a)

After conducting extensive fieldwork to test these original
dimensions, the researchers proposed six minimal criteria for
"thoughtful lessons":

• Sustained examination of a few topics rather than superficial cov-
  erage of many
• Substantive coherence and continuity
• Appropriate amount of time given to students to think and re-
  spond
• Challenging questions or tasks presented by teacher
• Thoughtfulness modeled by teacher
• Explanations and reason for their conclusions offered by students
  (Newmann, 1990b)

The logic in this research follows this line of reasoning: Research suggests that these features are relevant to thoughtful
teaching. When we observed teachers, we found that six were
most clearly associated with students' higher-order thinking.
These dimensions, then, might be those of thoughtful practice.

Brophy and VanSledright characterize good teaching in yet

another way. They portray each teacher by sharing with the reader transcripts of class discussions and interview excerpts of teacher-student interactions. Following each description is a three- or four-page section that "assesses" the case. Here, the authors argue that the teaching would be judged "effective" by certain criteria and criticized by other perspectives. The assessment is done holistically, matching claims about the data offered in the unedited transcripts with claims about principles of instruction that have emerged from the literature. For instance,

> Lake's teaching also would be judged as effective according to a variety of other criteria. First, she exemplified virtually all of the personal qualities and general teaching strategies that process-outcome research has identified as correlates of student achievement gain (Brophy & Good, 1986). She was extraordinarily good at establishing her classroom as a learning environment in which students spend most of their time engaged in ongoing academic activities. Activities got started briskly, transitions were brief and orderly, and very little time was lost getting organized or dealing with disruptive behavior. She presented material with enthusiasm and structured it around main ideas that were emphasized during presentations and followed up using key word cards, story maps, study guides, and related techniques for engaging students in meaningful learning of connected content rather than rote memorizing of isolated facts. She used an active teaching approach . . . she made sure that students knew what to do . . . she circulated to monitor and assist students. (pp. 68–69)

The logic of the Brophy and VanSledright explanation is more hands-off: Come into these classrooms with us and watch these teachers. Notice what you will. Afterwards, we will show you that these teachers demonstrate characteristics seen in the literature on effective teaching. Thus, each teacher is good, depending on one's frame of reference.

In summary, one way to characterize these diverse research projects is that all of the researchers are attempting to build a theory of good instruction: They closely study the pedagogical moves of teachers whose students do well. They then use those studies to conceptualize good history instruction. In some cases, they connect studies of teaching to some evidence of student achievement.

Explanations That Look to Teachers' Beliefs and Knowledge

A second sort of explanation involves attempts to explore different kinds of teacher knowledge and belief. Some researchers have examined the relationship between teachers' beliefs about the nature of history and their ideas about teaching. As part of our work on the Knowledge Growth in a Profession Project, for instance, Wineburg and I (Wilson & Wineburg, 1988) interviewed first-year social studies teachers and found striking differences in their orientations toward the subject matter. One novice teacher, who had majored in political science, saw history as "the facts," reserving interpretation for fields like political science. Another novice, who had an undergraduate degree in anthropology, also saw history as factual, echoing those familiar caricatures of history.

Yet, we also interviewed a new teacher who had majored in social history and whose ideas about history teaching were much like the experienced teachers Jensen and Price. For her, history was both fact and interpretation, and the study of history was full of life, music, art, drama. She sought to communicate that intellectual excitement to students, both through how and what she taught. For the nonhistory majors who became history teachers, however, history and its teaching was much more likely to be viewed as arcane, dusty, and dull. Although they, too, wanted their students to enjoy social studies classes, these teachers saw the study of history as a necessary evil. Once dispensed with, teachers might then move on to more interesting schoolwork.

When we then sought to explain the differences in how these novice teachers thought about teaching, Wineburg and I argued that their beliefs about the nature of history shaped their beliefs about what they should teach. We also followed our informants into their classrooms and watched their practice. Differences in knowledge and beliefs were associated with differences in instruction. Beginning teachers who saw history as interpretative and exciting crafted instruction to communicate those aspects of the discipline; teachers who saw history as "the facts" or who had little historical knowledge fell into age-old routines of uninspired history teaching.

Evans (1990) explored the relationships between teachers' conceptions of history and their teaching style as well as background factors that may influence those conceptions. Interviewing and surveying 30 teachers, Evans did in-depth work with 5 teachers whom he interviewed and observed. He also interviewed their students.

Evans proposed five admittedly overlapping categories for teachers' conceptions of history teaching: storyteller, scientific historian, relativist-reformer, cosmic philosopher, and eclectic. Most of his informants displayed a dominant philosophy about the purposes of teaching history, but they also exhibited features of other categories. Storytellers ran teacher-centered classrooms where teacher talk dominated and storytelling was used as the common mode of that form of communication. Scientific historians

> suggest that historical explanation and interpretation makes history most interesting and argue that understanding historical processes and gaining background knowledge for understanding current issues are the key reasons for studying history. (p. 13)

Relativist-reformers emphasized the relation of past problems to present problems; cosmic philosophers saw generalizations or "laws" as the most interesting aspect of history, intrigued with patterns that they noticed over time. Eclectics did not fall into any of those categories comfortably.

Evans then hypothesized that these differences in belief play out in classroom practice. Storytellers, according to Evans, are "essentialists," scientific historians are more progressive, reformers are reconstructionists. Storytellers and scientific historians have a close tie between their beliefs about history and how they teach: Storytellers weave narratives; scientific historians have students engage in inquiry.

Although the work by Evans and others suggests that novice and practicing teachers have varying views of historical knowledge, the researchers left unanswered the question of how things got that way. Yeager and Davis (1995) found that prospective teachers without extensive history education resembled the students that Wineburg and I interviewed and went on to argue that those prospective teachers would benefit from more study of history. However, they also noted that taking more courses will not necessarily lead to new conceptions of history, because history courses that are traditionally taught will reproduce familiar ideas about the subject matter and its pedagogy, not inspire innovative practice.

Quinlan's (1999) work supports this hunch. In one history department that she uses as a focal case, Quinlan heard multiple tales of intergenerational tension within the department, where decisions often split along old- and new-guard lines. Quinlan found some emerging differences in pedagogical emphasis: Some professors wanted to teach students about history as detective work and to emphasize themes; others were concerned with covering the content and providing students in survey courses with basic knowledge. Despite these tensions, she also found remarkable consistency in professors' (a) goals for history education (to create a historically contextualized awareness of the present, to develop critical thinking skills, to make connections), (b) perceptions of students (they have short attention spans, need structure, and lack motivation), and (c) teaching method (teachers did most of the talking). If this is the stuff of undergraduate history courses, it is little wonder that prospective teachers often hold on to staid and narrow beliefs about history.

McDiarmid, in collaboration with a historian colleague, Vinten-Johansen, chose to use an undergraduate historiography seminar as a site to investigate prospective teachers' learning of history (McDiarmid, 1994; McDiarmid & Vinten-Johansen, 1993). They documented the opportunities students had to learn throughout Vinten-Johansen's course and collected data on volunteers, interviewing them several times. When undergraduates entered the course, the majority had a rather cynical view of the development of historical knowledge: The personal circumstances of the individual historian—gender, race, values, home region—inevitably skewed historical accounts. By the end of the course, however, the majority developed a more tempered view that acknowledged the inevitability of the constructed and tentative nature of historical knowledge.

Although McDiarmid and Vinten-Johansen found that students' ideas about history might shift over time, their views of teaching history did not. Most saw learning history as unproblematic: Students need to be told what to know, and teachers need to lecture frequently. Despite the fact that all but three of the informants identified the historiography seminar as the best history class they had ever taken (in which very little traditional history teaching took place), the informant's views of history teaching and learning remained unshaken. And much like VanSledright noted of Dr. Reese, the undergraduates' views of historical knowledge appeared compartmentalized, "cut off from [their] beliefs about teaching and learning history" (p. 179). This research suggests that teachers' beliefs about the nature of historical knowledge are not sufficient to predict or explain their instructional choices—although other scholars continue to aver that teachers must understand the interpretive nature and teach that to their students (e.g., Blanco & Rosa, 1997).

If understanding teachers' epistemologies is not sufficient to explain the differences between teachers' classroom practice, what other variables might matter? Some researchers have sought to find an explanation in other aspects of teacher knowledge. In Wineburg and Wilson (1991), we reported on studies of what Shulman (1987) called the "wisdom of practice," the capacities and commitments that experienced and able teachers develop over the course of their careers. Using the cases of Price and Jensen, we proposed that their teaching was, in part, informed by a vision of history as human construction, their epistemologies if you will.

However, we also claimed that both teachers re-present the subject matter in ways that attend to both epistemological issues (the ways of knowing history) and contextual issues (specific concepts, ideas, and events). For example, Jensen first needed to cajole students into taking the side of the loyalists. (After all, who would ever sympathize with the Tories?) But after a careful examination of primary and secondary documents, students came to see that the Tories had a reasonable position. Neither cowards nor reactionaries, they were, as Wallace Brown (1969) portrayed them, "good Americans" (Wineburg & Wilson, 1991, p. 335). It was Jensen's substantial knowledge of the subject matter, we argued, that both drove and enabled her to help her students learn to think differently about the Tories. And in their comments on our work, the teachers themselves reemphasized the need to continually update their subject matter knowledge. Consider Price's comments:

> I wrestle continually with the awareness that I may not be completely accurate, and I am constantly seeking new sources and testing the version of history that I am relating to my students. Incidentally, I make my students fully aware of this concern. I might say to them, for example, "I used to go along with a number of historians and most of my colleagues on this floor in portraying President Eisenhower as a relatively uninspiring, detached, mediocre intellect who cared more about reading western novels and playing golf than the hard work of active presidential leadership. I now believe that when I taught about Eisenhower that way, I was quite wrong. Let's look at the work of Professor Fred Greenstein who found some remarkable things about Ike in writing a book called *Hidden Hand Presidency*. (John Price commentary in Wineburg & Wilson, 1991, p. 338)

So we offered our explanation of good teaching: Here are two teachers nominated as exceptional. Although their teaching differed, both teachers possessed considerable subject matter knowledge. When they taught, they represented the subject matter in ways to help students see the complexity of historical understanding. Those representations were shaped by other kinds of knowledge and beliefs—what students know and care about, what curricular resources are available, what parents expect of schools. Thus, we argue, perhaps good teaching is shaped by teachers' knowledge and beliefs. VanSledright (1996) adds other factors to the conceptual landscape, suggesting that barriers—external to teachers' knowledge and commitments—also shape instruction.

This group of researchers, then, attempt to explain good teaching by looking to teachers' knowledge and beliefs, as well as the myriad contexts of education—students, schools, policy mandates, curriculum reforms, and so forth. This line of research entails building a different theory, one that focuses on presage and contextual variables rather than on the act of teaching itself.

Although different, both camps of explanation and theory building suffer from two problems. The first problem concerns the theories' lack of explanatory power; the second concerns their circularity. First, neither emergent theory—(a) good instruction and presage (teacher knowledge and beliefs) nor (b) contextual variables (school conditions, curricular mandates, community expectations)—has much power. Why do those particular teaching behaviors lead to good teaching? By what mechanisms do they work? Why are certain teacher beliefs and knowledge associated with good teaching? How—exactly—does certain knowledge trigger good teaching?

In part, this lack of power is rooted in the second problem from which the research literature suffers—a circularity in reasoning. For example, here is a good teacher; now I will describe her teaching or his knowledge; because this good teacher taught in these ways or knows these things, I will claim that they are characteristics of good teaching or teachers. Very little research goes back to test the original assumption that these were good teachers. While Newmann and Leinhardt and their associates as well as Brophy and VanSledright attempt to anchor their arguments with data on student learning, researchers' reasoning—for the most part—remains more circular than not.

I conclude this chapter by making a case for research that attempts to link teaching and learning. Before doing so, however, I briefly introduce emerging research on students' historical knowledge and reasoning, for this research has important implications for the future of research on history teaching.

Research on Students' Historical Knowledge and Reasoning

Some research has compared the thinking and reading of historians to that of novices, be they K–12 students or undergraduates (Wiley & Voss, 1996; Wineburg, 1991, 1994).[3] Other researchers have investigated how students learn and reason with texts (Britt, Rouet, Georgi, & Perfetti, 1994; Perfetti, Britt, Rouet, Georgi, & Mason, 1994; Voss & Silfies, 1996). Still, others examine students as authors of history (Greene, 1994a, 1994b; Voss & Wiley, 1997; Young & Leinhardt, 1998).

Another line of research concerns the historical sense making of students. Lee, Dickinson, and Ashby (1997) investigated the maturity of elementary school students' historical reasoning, concluding that children are capable of historical thought and that there is a developmental progression of rational understanding in history. Voss and his colleagues have documented student perceptions of history and historical concepts (Voss, Wiley, & Kennet, 1999). Furnham (1994) has investigated students' understanding of politics, and Berti (1994) examined children's conceptions of state. Seixas has investigated aspects of adolescents' historical understanding: their understanding in multicultural settings (Seixas, 1993a), their moral frames (Seixas, 1994), and their understanding of significance in world history (Seixas, 1998). Fournier and Wineburg (1997), using children's drawings about historical topics, examined how gen-

der stereotypes influence children's thinking. Torney-Purta (1995) has also studied adolescents' thinking about political and historical issues, and Delval (1994) proposes stages in children's conceptions of social knowledge. Epstein (1998, 2000) has investigated how African-American high school students make sense of the history they learn in school and argues persuasively that adolescents' historical understandings are shaped by the "lived experiences of the adolescents themselves and family members" (1998, p. 397). The massive survey conducted under the auspices of the Youth and History Project (Angvik & von Borries, 1997), documented the historical ideas and political attitudes of 32,000 ninth graders in 27 European countries.

In one longitudinal line of research, Beck and McKeown investigated elementary students' reading and intellectual engagement. They analyzed elementary social studies textbooks (Beck, McKeown, & Grommoll, 1989) and found that curricula were not organized to present history as a coherent chain of events. The researchers found that textbook authors assumed varied and unrealistic background knowledge among students and provided no coherence in the presentation of events and concepts.

The researchers then went on to investigate student thinking. McKeown and Beck (1990) found that fifth graders' relevant knowledge about historical events was often confused and almost always limited to simple associations. Relying on their analyses of textbooks and student knowledge, the researchers then designed a series of interventions to experiment with ways to help students get more actively involved in learning history (Beck, McKeown, Sinatra, & Loxterman, 1991; McKeown & Beck, 1994).

Levstik and Barton also engaged in a longitudinal study of elementary students' sense making (Levstik, 1992, 1993). In one study, the researchers (Barton & Levstik, 1996) used photographs while interviewing 58 children (K–6) to determine their conceptions of history and historical time. The researchers found that children of all ages had a sense of how to appropriately order the pictures, indicating that children might have a significant capacity to grasp historical chronology. Even though the younger children were confused over dates, the researchers found that "children develop important historical understandings prior to—and to some extent independently of—their use of dates and other adult vocabulary" (p. 445). The researchers suggest that teachers might capitalize on this ability and help students "refine and extend" their historical knowledge.

In a year-long study of two elementary school classrooms, Barton (1999) found that children—over the course of the year—became more sophisticated in their judgments about what kinds of evidence inform historical accounts and how reliable those sources are. Barton concludes:

> Students' experiences with disagreements, with bias, and with memory—all developed outside of the context of school history—equipped them with the critical skills needed for sound historical reasoning. But just as importantly, these students regarded texts so

---

[3] Outside of the purview of this review is the fascinating work by Leinhardt and Young (1996) and Wineburg (1998b) that examines the nature of historians' textual interpretations.

critically they considered them pure fiction. Faced with conflicting sources, students despaired of establishing any reliability and they rejected them all. (p. 19)

Rose (1999), in a study of third and fourth graders' historical reasoning, found somewhat conflicting evidence. Conducting a design experiment in which she taught an elementary school social studies class for a year, Rose began the year by asking students to consider two different textbooks in which the "facts" differed. Using these differences to help students develop their capacities to be critical of textbooks, Rose had students rewrite the textbooks so they might begin learning about the interpretive nature of historical knowledge and their own use of tentative language to circumscribe claims. Like many students, Rose's students did what they were told. But the next day when she asked them to read another part of one of the textbooks,

> Timmy did not want to use the book. He boldly told me that I "should get a true book, a book that has true facts" because "this book is not true." Vanessa expressed similar concerns. She wondered how the people who wrote the book "got these facts." Like Timmy, she wanted to know the "real facts." For her, this book clearly no longer offered that. She worried that "kids could have drew these pictures or made these arrowheads" and that the author "didn't really know the real facts." Skeptical of the textbook's authority, their belief that they could acquire the "real facts" remained unshaken. They simply believed that they needed to find a better book. (p. 88)

Encountering an experience similar to what Barton observed, Rose—as the teacher—was, nevertheless, able to continue working with her students, documenting how their attitudes toward texts and their capacities to interpret and construct narratives changed over time. By the end of the year, students were no longer looking for the perfect textbook because they had developed an understanding of texts as being both interpretative and potentially flawed. They had also developed the capacity to read those texts critically without rejecting them out of hand.

Although Rose and Barton differ on how sophisticated elementary schoolchildren can be in their historical reasoning, the researchers do agree, as do other researchers like Lee, Dickinson, and Ashby (1997; see also Dickinson, Lee, & Rogers, 1984) and Wineburg (2000), that the capacity students have for historical thought is quite extensive.

A recent related development has been a growing interest among researchers in understanding historical consciousness outside of schools (e.g., von Borries, 1994). As Becker (1932) taught us in his classic essay, every one of us is compelled to be a historian, to understand our past, and to act as historical actors, even when we are not aware of it. Barton and Levstik (1996), in fact, chide researchers for comparing children to historians: Such a comparison sets up a deficit model for thinking about what children do not do. They—and a growing number of researchers—argue that we ought to start by asking what students do bring by way of historical knowledge, beliefs, and skills that might influence teaching. Wertsch (1994) examined the historical representations of lay adults (nonhistorians).

In the case of U.S. adults who were asked to account for the origins of the country, the lay historians told a "story of the motivations and agency of European settlers as they carried out a basic set of events" (p. 334). The "monological" or "univocal" nature of their accounts was only occasionally broken by a hint that some adults were dissatisfied with this singular narrative. Where did this story comes from? Perhaps school, perhaps a lack of opportunities to engage in critical reading of historical accounts, perhaps from the larger culture. Wertsch hypothesizes that the informants were using a single cultural tool and that the lack of variation in their narratives was because they did not have experience with other, alternative narratives.

The recent work by Wineburg (2000) on students' historical sense making pursues similar questions. In one analysis, Wineburg—having interviewed high school students and their families over the course of two and one-half years—describes how students' views of history are embedded in family discourse and are alternatively fueled by school, movies, and personal experience. Rose (1999), too, found that fourth graders bring beliefs about equality and progress that shape how they view the evidence and the narratives they are compelled to construct. Angvik and von Borries (1997) document the political viewpoints and interests of European teenagers.

Of course, not all researchers are so hopeful about students' capacity to work with and understand complex historical ideas and materials. Brophy and VanSledright (1997), for example, also include "qualitative analyses" of Mary Lake's fifth graders. Their conclusions are less optimistic:

> The students' learning was insightful in many ways but also replete with naive conceptions that serve as reminders that fifth graders are children whose cognitive structures are still developing. This raises questions about the degree to which it is desirable and feasible to replace oversimplified and romanticized treatments of topics with more realistic and analytic ones. (p. 142)

One would expect such disagreement as the field expands. One would also expect such disagreement within a field that operates with multiple views of good teaching, good research, and history. Brophy and VanSledright, for example, operationally define historical knowledge as lists of facts, names, and events. Beck and McKeown use a similar implicit definition, relying on school curricula as the operational definition of historical knowledge. Angvik and von Borries, in contrast, define history as both an account of the past and accounts of present perspectives on the past. Rose defines historical understanding more broadly as knowledge of facts, skills of historical reasoning and analysis, and norms of discourse in a community of learners. When the meaning of history is so varied, it is difficult to synthesize across researchers' claims that students understand or do not understand history.

The conceptual landscape becomes more complicated when student learning is studied in the context of "good teaching." Rose conceptualizes good teaching in a reform-oriented manner—acting as facilitator and guide, requiring children to voice and defend their ideas publicly, and directing the conversation strategically as the leader. Mary Lake's teaching seems more traditional. Children speak infrequently, and their terse contributions are aimed at the teacher, not at other students. Leinhardt's Ms. Sterling also seems different, as do the teachers in the Newmann and Onosko work.

Studies of students learning history—when done in the naturalistic context of school classrooms—are very much dependent on the kind of teaching found in those classrooms. Claims about what students may or may not learn and about what they can and cannot do are situated within the opportunities they have had to learn history. Much like educational psychologists who were concerned about aptitude-treatment interactions (Cronbach, 1975), researchers in our field must be concerned about learning-teaching interactions. But recall my earlier observation that research on history teaching varies both in terms of how history is conceptualized and how good teaching is conceptualized. These variations muddy the water considerably, because difficult as it might be to explore such interactions, doing so becomes nearly impossible when the primary constructs of the research—knowledge, history, learning, teaching—are conceptualized and operationally defined in such strikingly different ways.

Where to Now?

It is time to take stock. The field of research on history teaching is alive and well—as is the field of research on students' historical knowledge and reasoning. My tentative claims about the challenges facing the field include the following:

- Our conceptions of history, good teaching, student learning, and research vary. These variations correspond to differences in our respective scholarly communities: historians, philosophers, psychologists, and the public.
- Our explanations for good history teaching lack explanatory power.
- Little work has linked history teaching to student learning.
- Students' historical understanding interacts with history teaching in ways we have yet to understand.

There are, of course, exceptions to these claims. Researchers have indicated a commitment to move toward more powerful explanations. Young and Leinhardt (1998), for example, explore Ms. Sterling's pedagogical moves as she teaches students to prepare for documents analysis questions on the Advanced Placement examination at the same time that they describe students' learning over time. Newmann, Onosko, and their colleagues correlate features of teaching with students' capacity to think in higher-order ways. Brophy and VanSledright (1997) include analyses of student learning with portraits of practice. Researchers who investigate teacher knowledge track the kinds of knowledge that teachers possess and try to untangle the influence that knowledge has on these teachers' ideas about history and their capacity to teach it.

In short, the research community seems to be creeping toward the construction of more powerful explanations. At the very least, many people are collecting the kinds of data we need. But we have not—yet—built theories that explain either the mechanisms by which some teaching leads to significant student learning or how some beliefs influence future learning. Perhaps this is our next, greatest challenge.

Several critical factors will shape those future endeavors. I nominate a brief list of issues here: (a) rethinking the concept of an accomplished teacher, (b) attending to the links between teaching and learning, and (c) strategically reducing some variation.

Rethinking the Concept of an Accomplished Teacher

My first issue questions the premise of the accomplished teacher. As a teacher, I know that I have moments of clarity when I make certain pedagogical moves and some of my students learn something important. These moments of expertise do not mean that everything I do is equally accomplished. The variation in my practice is circumstantial (the subject I am teaching, the students and context in which I am working, and my knowledge, for instance, are all significant variables). As a teacher, I also know that what works for one student does not work for all. Perhaps in our enthusiasm to study good teaching, we collectively forgot that good teachers have good and bad days, good and not-so-good practices. Consequently, we have lost the opportunity to examine variability within our cases. We could, however, begin to look for variation within cases of accomplished teaching and note when a teacher's teaching was more or less accomplished. Other research might contrast accomplished instances of teaching with more ordinary ones. Contrasts help us to confirm and falsify. Such contrasts might lead us to more powerful explanations for (a) why some teaching leads to student learning and (b) why some teacher knowledge and belief matters.

Attending to the Links between Teaching and Learning

My second issue concerns the need to link studies of teaching to studies of learning so that we might better understand each. Such research might help us begin understanding, for example, the mechanisms by which instructional choices increase children's opportunities to learn or how particular kinds of teacher knowledge improve practice. Brophy and Alleman (1999) have begun documenting children's notions of social studies concepts like shelter, food, clothing, transportation. They are then using that knowledge of children to design less trite, more powerful curricula.

But as the research on student historical understanding suggests, children's knowledge is a slippery phenomenon. Claims about what children do and can know depend, in part, on the education they have experienced and on the contexts in which they live. The emerging work on students' historical consciousness and the power of contemporary, sometimes popular, culture to shape students' historical ideas lend credence to the claim that children enter school with knowledge and beliefs as well as conceptions and misconceptions that are related to history curricula. They come with ideas and values about particular events like Vietnam (Wineburg, 2000); about the origins of the United States (Wertsch & O'Connor, 1999); about concepts such as equity and human agency (Rose, 1999) or shelter (Brophy & Alleman, 1999); or about the knowledge and authority of textbooks (Rose, 1999; Wineburg, 1991).

What happens in classrooms is shaped by these entering ideas, by the teachers' knowledge and beliefs that other researchers have documented, and by various educational opportunities students encounter. McNeil's work stands out as a vivid reminder: What happens in classrooms is shaped by forces that extend far beyond the psychology of teachers and their students. We would do well to begin exploring a fuller range of factors that shape teaching: The connection between teaching and teacher beliefs and learning and student beliefs remains a black hole in our research landscape.

Future research on teaching might launch into this black hole. As many historians would argue, what happens in any given classroom is itself a potentially historical event and, as such, cannot be reduced to a simple cause and effect equation. Therefore, I am not arguing for traditional, quasi-experimental research on teaching that links certain teaching moves to the development of certain kinds of student understanding. Rather, I am suggesting that we need a more detailed portrait that attempts to fill in some of the gaps left by the research reviewed here. Cronbach (1975) argued that pinning down interaction effects would require huge amounts of data that were likely to lose their validity over time. "Some effects in the network will change in form," he wrote, ". . . even before qualifying clauses have been added to describe the effect accurately" (p. 126). He concludes, "Though our sketch of man may become more elaborate, it will remain a sketch" (p. 126). I argue here for a more elaborate sketch of the relationship between history teaching and learning that includes (a) details concerning students' entering and unfolding beliefs; (b) teachers' entering and changing knowledge, skills, and beliefs; (c) the consequences and correlates of particular pedagogical moves; (d) the emerging discourse patterns of communities of learners; and (e) the influence of cultural and organizational structures.

Strategically Reducing Some Variation

Drawing the portrait will remain impossible, however, if we do not search for some ways to reduce unnecessary or unproductive variation. The field is awash with confusing differences. We differ in our conceptions of accomplished teaching, of history, of learning. Many such differences are part of any healthy discourse community, but not all are necessary. My hunch is that we have two means by which to discriminate healthy and unnecessary variation. The first way involves a more systematic examination of the role of our own beliefs; the second entails recreating research so that it is genuinely subject-specific.

Personal, professional, and political values are everywhere in our work. Consider our multiple conceptions of "good" teaching. Lake, Price, Jensen, Sterling, and the teachers in McNeil's study have taught for a long time. Their teaching has persistence; it serves a purpose (or several). But one researcher's functionalism may very well be another researcher's dysfunctionalism. With the explosion of interest and participation in research on history teaching, we have increased the likelihood that we will encounter such differences in values.

Using different methods and intellectual frames, we have pursued the same goal: understanding the nature of quality history teaching. Nevertheless, the teachers we each nominate as exemplary draw questions of quality—despite our good intentions—from our colleagues. Wineburg (1998a), for example, raises questions about the knowledge of Brophy and VanSledright's teachers and objects to the claim that these teachers are accomplished. Similarly, Brophy (personal communication, 1990, 1998) and Evans (personal communication, 1990) have raised

questions about the quality of my teaching of third graders (Wilson, 1990).

The debates that characterize and, unfortunately, all too often paralyze the field are, in part, debates about values. We tend, like many educators, to avoid discussing these value differences in public arenas, opting instead to bury them in personal letters or vindictive asides, even though they profoundly shape our work. For example, Brophy and VanSledright (1997) spend most of their time describing the teaching of Mary Lake and the learning of her students. As it turns out, she is the model of effective teaching, a field that Brophy had an important role in shaping:

> First, she exemplified virtually all of the personal qualities and general teaching strategies that process-outcome research has identified as correlated of student achievement gain (Brophy & Good, 1986). (Brophy & VanSledright, 1997, p. 68)

In contrast, Wineburg and I were socialized into a very different way of thinking about teaching, given, in part, our intellectual histories and, in part, our experiences in graduate school with Lee Shulman. And Leinhardt, in a careful review of our work, once reminded us to be more self-conscious about the influence of our own training and education on our valuing of teaching. In response to that criticism, we eventually explained our perspective in another analysis of history teaching:

> It would be disingenuous to claim that we did not find ourselves favoring Kelsey's responses over Barnes's. Nor would we suggest that our affirmation of one teacher over the other was a coincidence or historical accident. Indeed, the differences we found between these two teachers represent major shifts in how we, as individuals and as members of academic communities, conceptualize teaching, learning, and the discipline of history. Ms. Kelsey studied to be a teacher at a time, 1984, and a place, a prestigious research university, where the effects of the cognitive revolution were being felt as never before. . . . Similarly, her understanding of history reflected some of the recent developments in that discipline. . . . As researchers with feet in the educational, psychological, and historical communities, both of us learned to frame our thinking in ways similar to those we lay out [here]. (Wilson & Wineburg, 1993, pp. 755–756)

We are all prisoners of our world views, a fundamental challenge in social inquiry. Here, too, we might look to our subject matter—history—for insights. Historians have long known that their world views shape the narratives they write. Our goal need not be to reconcile our diverse values but, rather, to make them public and, in so doing, enable better access to our work. To understand a piece of research on history teaching, one needs to know the author's conceptions of history, of good teaching, of understanding.

Revealing our normative conceptions might help us reinvent our scholarship along the lines that Wineburg (1996) imagined when he called for a new kind of research—applied epistemology. As a group, we have a long way to go before we do deeply subject-specific work (Shulman, 1983). Such work is not simply the product of psychologists reading a few books by historians or historians learning to think and talk about curriculum and instruction. Largely, what the field has done thus far, acquiring new knowledge—of history, of context, of teaching—and fitting it into our existing knowledge base, is more similar to a Piagetian assimilation.

However, applied epistemology would require an even larger leap, a leap in which we shift our cognitive structures and reorient our concepts, values, questions, and methods. Such a leap requires that we locate ourselves at the intersection of multiple discourses that seldom meet: the discourse of historians and philosophers of history, the discourse of educational researchers, and the discourse of classrooms. Such a leap also requires that we develop a colloquy among those discourses, working back and forth between them, using one to understand and conceptualize the other. I offer a thought experiment here. First, let us consider two definitions of understanding that were published in the same year. The first was crafted by an educational psychologist:

> Deep content understanding is hypothesized to encompass three core components: (a) the larger schemata or major principles by which detailed knowledge is organized (Chi & Glaser, 1988), (b) the encoding of text or other new knowledge to be acquired, and (c) the integration of new knowledge into extant representation as modified by the goals and expectations of the learner related to his or her intentions regarding the text (Glaser, 1992; Glaser, Raghaven, & Baxter, 1992). (Baker, 1994, p. 99)

The second definition of understanding was developed by a historian:

> The lush, vast delta of Bangladesh is spattered with small shrines. Occupying the present, mute features of daily experience, these objects provoke questions. The answers are historical. The men who tend the shrines, as archivists care for documents, keeping them from decay, tell stories that explain their existence. Separate on the landscape, the shrines, once explained, join in the mind as episodes in the epic of the arrival of Islam. The biography of the saint venerated at the shrine invests the building with meaning, and the circle of significance is entered when the shrine's ritual is enacted. Manir Uddin, keeper of the shrine, instructs the pilgrim to pray while placing a burned clay horse beside the tomb of Ghora Pir in remembrance of one of the holy horsemen who brought the faith of the one God to Bengal. In ritual, a social unit is momentarily constituted, fused in a oneness of observance. Then through repetitive enactment, the ritual, cued by an object, founded upon historical narrative, consolidates a small community of devotees while, simultaneously, tightening the bonds that connect them into the international congregation of a great religion.
>
> Nothing is set, foregone. The shrine could be left to rot, the story forgotten. But preserved, the little building invites a question. The answer yields an explanation, producing understanding. Understanding invites participation in a customary activity. Repeated enactment invites committed participation, the formation of an ongoing social order, history's conspicuous purpose. A holy shrine, it could have been a book, a faded photograph, an old war story; it might have been fireworks on the Fourth of July, interrupting the night sky to prompt a tale that requests social commitment through new historical understanding. (Glassie, 1994, p. 961).

Glassie continues his explanation of history:

> The transformational sequence in historical awareness steps from query to explanation, from understanding through validation to commitment. It is history's purpose to preserve things that prompt questions as much as to supply answers that inspire action. (p. 963)

An applied epistemology requires that the psychologist and the historian, working together, would talk about their ideas, ask questions about their assumptions, explore the intersection of their beliefs. What is a schema? Is it a phenomenon that exists in the world of historical analyses? Do historians use schemas as they create their historical narratives and as they participate in and shape the "ongoing social order" that invites explanation, understanding, commitment, and participation? Perhaps as a consequence of such dialogue, the historian and the psychologist would reorganize their intellectual universes and find a new language with which to talk about history teaching and learning.

An applied epistemology would also require that the historian and the psychologist listen to classrooms in new ways. As they do so, their own understanding might continue to unfold, as the words of a child or the discourse of a classroom send them back to history and psychology in search of resonant ideas. They might see in a child's words central historical concepts like the role of human agency. They might hear in a student's reasoning echoes of historians' accounts of how they reason. An applied epistemology would require a Piagetian-like accommodation rather than the safer assimilation that the field has done thus far. We ought not be defining historical knowledge generically, as Bain (1997) points out. Instead, we ought to become students of history so that we might better understand the phenomena we study.

The fact that such an explosion of interest in the research on history teaching has occurred across countries and across disciplines holds promise for the conversations and collaborations such work would entail. Through that work, we might aim to reduce unnecessary variation, thus, developing more disciplinary and disciplined constructs with which to frame our work. These efforts would not erase all of our diversity but would help us to take advantage of healthy differences that could push the field forward. As Glassie (1994) notes

> Disorderly, fragmentary, malleable, history leaves room for diverse participation. The professionals cannot do it perfectly, so all can take a turn. They must. Everyone is obliged . . . to act like a historian. (p. 966)

The challenge that future research on history teaching faces is to help the historian act like a psychologist or sociologist while helping the educational researchers learn to act—and think—like historians so we might draw a better sketch.

REFERENCES

Angvik, M., & von Borries, B. (Eds.). (1997). *Youth and history: A comparative European survey on historical consciousness and political attitudes among adolescents.* Hamburg: Körber-Stiftung.

Applebee, A., Langer, J., & Mullis, I. (1987). *The nation's report card: Literature and U.S. history.* Princeton, NJ: Educational Testing Service.

Bailyn, B. (1994). *On the teaching and writing of history.* Hanover, NH: University Press of New England.

Bain, R. B. (1995). The world-history standards: A teacher's perspective. *Education Week, Feb. 22,* 34, 36.

Bain, R. B. (1997, January). *Teaching history as an epistemic act: Notes from a practitioner.* Paper presented at the annual meeting of the American Historical Association, New York, NY.

Baker, E. (1994). Learning-based assessments of history understanding. *Educational Psychologist, 29,* 97–106.

Barton, K. C. (1999). "I just kinda know": Elementary students' ideas about historical evidence. *Theory and Research in Social Education, 25,* 407–430.

Barton, K. C., & Levstik, L. S. (1996). "Back when God was around and everything": Elementary children's understanding of historical time. *American Educational Research Journal, 33,* 419–454.

Beck, I. L., McKeown, M. G., & Grommoll, E. W. (1989). Learning from social studies texts. *Cognition and Instruction, 6,* 99–158.

Beck, I. L., McKeown, M. G., Sinatra, G. M., & Loxterman, J. A. (1991). Revising social studies text from a text-processing perspective: Evidence of improved comprehensibility. *Reading Research Quarterly, 26,* 251–276.

Becker, C. L. (1932). Everyman his own historian. *American Historical Review, 37,* 221–236.

Bender, T. (1994). "Venturesome and cautious": American history in the 1990s. *The Journal of American History,* 992–1003.

Berti, A. E. (1994). Children's understanding of the concept of state. In M. Carretero & J. F. Voss (Eds.), *Cognitive and instructional processes in history and the social sciences* (pp. 49–75). Hillsdale, NJ: Lawrence Erlbaum Associates.

Blanco, F., & Rosa, A. (1997). Dilthey's dream: Teaching history to understand the future. *International Journal of Educational Research, 27,* 189–200.

Booth, M. (1980). A modern world history course and the thinking of adolescent pupils. *Educational Review, 32,* 245–257.

Booth, M. (1983). Skills, concepts, and attitudes: The development of adolescent children's historical thinking. *History and Theory, 22,* 101–117.

Booth, M. (1987). Ages and concepts: A critique of the Piagetian approach to history teaching. In C. Portal (Ed.), *The history curriculum for teachers* (pp. 22–38). London: Falmer Press.

Booth, M. (1994). Cognition in history: A British perspective. *Educational Psychologist, 29,* 61–69.

Britt, M. A., Rouet, J. F., Georgi, M. C., & Perfetti, C. A. (1994). Learning from history texts: From causal analysis to argument models. In G. Leinhardt, I. L. Beck, & C. Stainton (Eds.), *Teaching and learning history* (pp. 47–84). Hillsdale, NJ: Lawrence Erlbaum Associates.

Brophy, J., & Alleman, J. (1999). *Primary-grade students' knowledge and thinking about shelter as a cultural universal.* Unpublished manuscript. East Lansing, MI: College of Education.

Brophy, J., & VanSledright, B. (1997). *Teaching and learning history in elementary schools.* New York: Teachers College Press.

Brown, W. (1969). *The good Americans: The loyalists in the American Revolution.* New York: Morrow.

Carretero, M., & Voss, J. F. (Eds.). (1994). *Cognitive and instructional processes in history and social sciences.* Hillsdale, NJ: Lawrence Erlbaum Associates.

Center for Civic Education. (1995). *National standards for civic and government.* Calabasas, CA: Author.

Chou, P. M. (1999). *The democratization of the Taiwanese social studies curriculum: A study of practice.* Unpublished doctoral dissertation, Michigan State University, East Lansing.

Cohen, D. K., & Neufeld, B. (1981). The failure of high schools and the progress of education. *Daedelus, 110,* 69–89.

Cornbleth, C., & Waugh, D. (1995). *The great speckled bird: Multicultural politics and education policymaking.* New York: St. Martin's Press.

Cronbach, L. J. (1975). Beyond the two disciplines of scientific psychology. *American Psychologist, 30,* 116–127.

Cruse, J. (1994). Practicing history: A high school teacher's reflections. *The Journal of American History, 81,* 1064–1074.

Cuban, L. (1984). *How teachers taught: Constancy and change in American classrooms: 1890–1980.* New York: Longman.

Cuban, L. (1991). History of teaching in social studies. In J. P. Shaver (Ed.), *Handbook of research on social studies teaching and learning* (pp. 197–209). New York: Macmillan.

Delval, J. (1994). Stages in the child's construction of social knowledge.

In M. Carretero & J. F. Voss (Eds.), *Cognitive and instructional processes in history and the social sciences* (pp. 77–102). Hillsdale, NJ: Lawrence Erlbaum Associates.

Dewey, J. (1938). *Experience and education.* New York: Collier Books.

Dickinson, A. K., & Lee, P. J. (1978). *History teaching and historical understanding.* London: Heinemann.

Dickinson, A. K., Lee, P. J., & Rogers, P. J. (Eds.). (1984). *Learning history.* London: Heinemann.

Dow, P. (1991). *Schoolhouse politics: Lessons from the Sputnik era.* Cambridge, MA: Harvard University Press.

Downey, M. T., & Levstik, L. S. (1988). Teaching and learning history: The research base. *Social Education, 52,* 336–342.

Downey, M. T., & Levstik, L. S. (1991). Teaching and learning history. In J. P. Shaver (Ed.), *Handbook of research on social studies teaching and learning* (pp. 400–410). New York: Macmillan.

Duckworth, E. (1987). *"The having of wonderful ideas" and other essays on teaching and learning.* New York: Teachers College Press.

Elton, G. R. (1970). What sort of history should we teach? In M. Ballard (Ed.), *New movements in the study and teaching of history.* London: Temple Smith.

Epstein, T. (1998). Deconstructing differences in African-American and European-American adolescents' perspectives on U.S. history. *Curriculum Inquiry, 28,* 397–423.

Epstein, T. (2000). Adolescents' perspectives on racial diversity in U.S. history: Case studies from an urban classroom. *American Educational Research Journal, 37,* 185–214.

Evans, R. W. (1989). Teacher conceptions of history. *Theory and Research in Social Education, 17,* 210–240.

Evans, R. W. (1990). History, ideology, and social responsibility. *Social Science Record, 27*(2), 11–17.

Fournier, J. C., & Wineburg, S. S. (1997). Picturing the past: Gender differences in the depiction of historical figures. *American Journal of Education, 105,* 160–185.

Furnham, A. (1994). Young people's understanding of politics and economics. In M. Carretero & J. F. Voss (Eds.), *Cognitive and instructional processes in history and the social sciences* (pp. 17–47). Hillsdale, NJ: Lawrence Erlbaum Associates.

Gardner, H., & Boix-Mansilla, V. (1994). Teaching for understanding in the disciplines—and beyond. *Teachers College Record, 96*(2), 198–218.

Gitlin, T. (1995). *The twilight of common dreams: Why America is wracked by culture wars.* New York: Henry Holt.

Glassie, H. (1994). The practice and purpose of history. *The Journal of American History,* 961–968.

Goldhagen, D. J. (1997). *Hitler's willing executioners: Ordinary Germans and the Holocaust.* New York: Vintage Books.

Goodlad, J. (1984). *A place called school: Prospects for the future.* New York: McGraw-Hill.

Greene, S. (1994a). The problems of learning to think like a historian: Writing history in the culture of the classroom. *Educational Psychologist, 29,* 89–96.

Greene, S. (1994b). Students as authors in the study of history. In G. Leinhardt, I. L. Beck, & C. Stainton (Eds.), *Teaching and learning history* (pp. 137–170). Hillsdale, NJ: Lawrence Erlbaum Associates.

Hallam, R. N. (1967). Logical thinking in history. *Educational Review, 19,* 183–202.

Hallam, R. N. (1970). Piaget and thinking in history. In M. Ballard (Ed.), *New movements in the study and teaching of history*. London: Temple Smith.

Hallam, R. N. (1971). Thinking and learning in history. *Teaching History, 2,* 337–346.

Hertzberg, H. W. (1982). The teaching of history. In M. Kammen (Ed.), *The past before us: Contemporary historical writing in the United States* (pp. 474–504). Ithaca, NY: Cornell University Press.

Hirsch, E. D., Jr. (1996). *The schools we need and why we don't have them.* New York: Doubleday.

Hoetker, J., & Ahlbrand, W. (1969). The persistence of recitation. *American Educational Research Journal, 6,* 145–167.

Holt, T. (1990). *Thinking historically: Narrative, imagination, and understanding.* New York: College Entrance Examination Board.

Hughes, R. (1994). *Culture of complaint : A passionate look into the ailing heart of America.* New York: Warner.

Husbands, C. (1996). *What is history? Language, ideas, and meaning in learning about the past.* Buckingham, UK: Open University Press.

Husbands, C., & Pendry, A. (1992). *Whose history? School history and the national curriculum.* East Anglia, UK: History Education Group.

Labaree, D. F. (1997). Public goods, private goods: The American struggle over educational goals. *American Educational Research Journal, 34,* 39–81.

Lampert, M. (1985). How do teachers manage to teach: Perspectives of problems in practice. *Harvard Educational Review, 55,* 178–194.

Lee, P., Dickinson, A., & Ashby, R. (1997). "Just another emperor": Understanding action in the past. *International Journal of Educational Research, 27*(3), 233–244.

Leinhardt, G. (1985). *The development of an expert explanation: An analysis of a sequence of subtraction lessons.* Pittsburgh: University of Pittsburgh, Learning Research Development Center.

Leinhardt, G. (1990). *Towards understanding instructional explanations* (Tech. Rep. No. CLIP-90–03). Pittsburgh: University of Pittsburgh, Learning Research Development Center.

Leinhardt, G. (1993). Weaving instructional explanations in history. *British Journal of Educational Psychology, 63,* 46–74.

Leinhardt, G. (1997). Instructional explanations in history. *International Journal of Educational Research, 27,* 221–232.

Leinhardt, G., Beck, I. L., & Stainton, C. (Eds.). (1994). *Teaching and learning history.* Hillsdale, NJ: Lawrence Erlbaum Associates.

Leinhardt, G., & Greeno, J. G. (1986). The cognitive skill of teaching. *Journal of Educational Psychology, 78,* 75–95.

Leinhardt, G., Stainton, C., Virji, S. M., & Odoroff, E. (1994). Learning to reason in history: Mindlessness to mindfulness. In M. Carretero & J. F. Voss (Eds.), *Cognitive and instructional processes in history and the social sciences* (pp. 131–158). Hillsdale, NJ: Lawrence Erlbaum Associates.

Leinhardt, G., & Young, K. M. (1996). Two texts, three readers: Distance and expertise in reading history. *Cognition and Instruction, 14,* 441–486.

Levstik, L. S. (1992). "I wanted to be there": History and narrative in the elementary curriculum. In M. Tunnell & R. Ammon (Eds.), *The story of ourselves: Teaching history through children's literature* (pp. 65–77). Portsmouth, NH: Heinemann.

Levstik, L. S. (1993). Building a sense of history in a first grade classroom. In J. Brophy (Ed.), *Advances in research on teaching: Volume 4. Research in elementary social studies* (pp. 1–31). Greenwich, CT: JAI Press.

Levstik, L. S., & Barton, K. C. (1997). *Doing history: Investigations with children in elementary and middle schools.* Mahwah, NJ: Lawrence Erlbaum Associates.

Slater, J. (1990). History in the national curriculum: An agenda for the future. *Discoveries: A Journal for History Teachers, 2,* 11–13.

McDiarmid, G. W. (1994). Understanding history for teaching: A study of the historical understanding of prospective teachers. In M. Carretero & J. F. Voss (Eds.), *Cognitive and instructional processes in history and the social sciences* (pp. 159–185). Hillsdale, NJ: Lawrence Erlbaum Associates.

McDiarmid, G. W., & Vinten-Johansen, P. (1993). *Teaching and learning history—from the inside out* (Special Report). East Lansing: Michigan State University, National Center for Research on Teacher Learning.

McKeown, M. G., & Beck, I. L. (1990). The assessment and characterization of young learners' knowledge of a topic in history. *American Educational Research Journal, 27,* 688–726.

McKeown, M. G., & Beck, I. L. (1994). Making sense of accounts of history: Why young students don't and how they might. In G. Leinhardt, I. L. Beck, & C. Stainton (Eds.), *Teaching and learning history* (pp. 1–26). Hillsdale, NJ: Lawrence Erlbaum Associates.

McKiernan, D. (1993). History in a national curriculum: Imagining the nation at the end of the 20th century. *Journal of Curriculum Studies, 25,* 33–51.

McNeil, L. (1986). *Contradictions of control.* New York: Routledge & Kegan Paul.

Nash, G. B., Crabtree, C., & Dunn, R. E. (1997). *History on trial: Culture wars and the teaching of the past.* New York: Alfred A. Knopf.

National Center for History in the Schools. (1996). *National standards for history.* Los Angeles, CA: Author.

National Council for Social Studies. (1994). *Expectations for excellence: Curriculum standards for social studies.* Washington, DC: Author.

Newmann, F. M. (1990a). Higher order thinking in teaching social studies. *Journal of Curriculum Studies, 22,* 41–56.

Newmann, F. M. (1990b). Qualities of thoughtful social studies classes: An empirical profile. *Journal of Curriculum Studies, 22,* 253–275.

Novick, P. (1988). *That noble dream: The "objectivity question" and the American historical profession.* Cambridge: Cambridge University Press.

Onosko, J. J. (1989). Comparing teachers' thinking about prompting students' thinking. *Theory and Research in Social Education, 17,* 174–195.

Onosko, J. J. (1990). Comparing teachers' instruction to promote students' thinking. *Journal of Curriculum Studies, 22,* 443–461.

Oshinsky, D. M. (1997). *"Worse than slavery": Parchman Farm and the ordeal of Jim Crow justice.* New York: Free Press.

Paley, V. G. (1981). *Wally's stories: Conversations in the kindergarten.* Cambridge, MA: Harvard University Press.

Paxton, R. J., & Wineburg, S. S. (2000). Expertise and the teaching of history. In B. Moon, M. Ben Peretz, & S. Brown (Eds.), *Routledge international companion to education* (pp. 855–864). London: Routledge.

Perfetti, C. A., Britt, M. A., Rouet, J. F., Georgi, M. C., & Mason, R. A. (1994). How students use texts to learn and reason about historical uncertainty. In M. Carretero & J. F. Voss (Eds.), *Cognitive and instructional processes in history and the social sciences* (pp. 257–283). Hillsdale, NJ: Lawrence Erlbaum Associates.

Quinlan, K. M. (1999). Commonalities and controversy in context: A study of academic historians' educational beliefs. *Teaching and Teacher Education, 15,* 447–463.

Ravitch, D. (1985). *The schools we deserve: Reflections on the educational crises of our time.* New York: Basic Books.

Ravitch, D., & Finn, C. E. (1987). *What do our 17-year-olds know? A report on the First National Assessment of History and Literature.* New York: Harper and Row.

Rose, S. L. (1999). *Understanding children's historical sense-making: A view from the classroom.* Unpublished manuscript, College of Education, Michigan State University, East Lansing.

Seixas, P. (1993a). Historical understanding among adolescents in a multicultural setting. *Curriculum Inquiry, 23,* 301–327.

Seixas, P. (1993b). Parallel crises: History and the social studies curriculum in the USA. *Journal of Curriculum Studies, 25,* 235–250.

Seixas, P. (1994). Confronting the moral frames of popular film: Young people respond to historical revisionism. *American Journal of Education, 102,* 261–285.

Seixas, P. (1998). Mapping the terrain of historical significance. *Social Education, 61*(1), 22–27.

Shaver, J. P. (Ed.). (1991). *Handbook of research on social studies teaching and learning.* New York: Macmillan.

Shaver, J., Davis, O., & Helburn, S. (1980). The status of social studies education: Impressions from three National Science Foundation studies. In *What are the needs in precollege science, mathematics, and social science education?* Washington, DC: National Science Foundation.

Shulman, L. S. (1983). Autonomy and obligation. In L. S. Shulman & G. Sykes (Eds.), *Handbook of teaching and policy* (pp. 484–504). New York: Longman.

Shulman, L. S. (1986). Paradigms and research programs in the study of teaching: A contemporary perspective. In M. C. Wittrock (Ed.), *Handbook of research on teaching* (3rd ed., pp. 3–36). New York: Macmillan.

Shulman, L. S. (1987). Knowledge and teaching: Foundations of the new reform. *Harvard Educational Review, 57,* 1–22.

Sirotnik, K. (1983). What you see is what you get—constancy, persistency, and mediocrity in classrooms. *Harvard Educational Review, 53,* 16–31.

Slater, J. (1990). History in the national curriculum: An agenda for the future. *Discoveries: A Journal for History Teachers, 2,* 4–10.

Spoehr, K. T., & Spoehr, L. W. (1994). Learning to think historically. *Educational Psychologist, 29,* 71–77.

Stearns, P., Seixas, P., & Wineburg, S. S. (Eds.). (2000). *Teaching and learning history in a national and international context.* New York: New York University Press.

Stinchcombe, A. L. (1968). *Constructing social theories.* New York: Harcourt, Brace, & World.

Torney-Purta, J. (1995). Dimensions of adolescents' reasoning about political and historical issues: Ontological switches, developmental processes, and situated learning. In M. Carretero & J. F. Voss (Eds.), *Cognitive and instructional processes in history and the social sciences* (pp. 103–128). Hillsdale, NJ: Lawrence Erlbaum Associates.

Tranter, N. (1987). *The story of Scotland.* London: Routledge & Kegan Paul.

Ulrich, L. T. (1990). *A midwife's tale: The life of Martha Ballard, based on her diary, 1785–1812.* New York: Vintage Books.

VanSledright, B. (1996). Closing the gap between school and disciplinary history: Historian as high school history teacher. In J. Brophy (Ed.), *Advances in research on teaching* (Vol. 6, pp. 257–289). Greenwich, CT: JAI Press.

von Borries, B. (1994). (Re)constructing history and moral judgment: On relationships between interpretations of the past and perceptions of the present. In M. Carretero & J. F. Voss (Eds.), *Cognitive and instructional processes in history and the social sciences* (pp. 339–355). Hillsdale, NJ: Lawrence Erlbaum Associates.

Voss, J. F. (1997). Introduction. *International Journal of Educational Research, 27,* 187–188.

Voss, J. F., & Carretero, M. (Eds.) (1999). *Learning and reasoning in history* (International review of history education, vol. 2). London: Woburn Press.

Voss, J. F., & Silfies, L. N. (1996). Learning from history text: The interaction of knowledge and comprehension skill with text structure. *Cognition and Instruction, 14,* 45–68.

Voss, J. F., & Wiley, J. (1997). Developing understanding while writing essays in history. *International Journal of Educational Research, 27,* 255–265.

Voss, J. F., Wiley, J., & Kennet, J. (1999). Student perceptions of history and historical concepts. In J. F. Voss, & M. Carretero (Eds.), *Learning and reasoning in history.* London: Woburn Press.

Wertsch, J. V. (1994). Struggling with the past: Some dynamics of historical representation. In M. Carretero & J. F. Voss (Eds.), *Cognitive and instructional processes in history and the social sciences* (pp. 323–338). Hillsdale, NJ: Lawrence Erlbaum Associates.

Wertsch, J. V., & O'Connor, K. (1999). Multivoicedness in historical representation: American college students' accounts of the origins of the U.S. *Journal of Narrative and Life History, 4*(4), 295–309.

Whelan, M. (1992). History and the social studies: A response to the critics. *Theory and Research in Social Education, 20*(1), 2–16.

Wiley, J., & Voss, J. F. (1996). The effects of "playing historian" on learning in history. *Applied Cognitive Psychology, 10* (special issue), 563–572.

Wilson, S. M. (1990). *Mastodons, maps, and Michigan: Exploring uncharted territory while teaching elementary school social studies* (Elementary Subjects Center Series No. 24). East Lansing, MI: Institute for Research on Teaching, Michigan State University.

Wilson, S. M., & Wineburg, S. S. (1988). Peering at history from different lenses: The role of disciplinary perspectives in the teaching of American history. *Teachers' College Record, 89,* 525–539.

Wilson, S. M., & Wineburg, S. S. (1993). Wrinkles in time and place: Using performance assessments to understand the knowledge of history teachers. *American Educational Research Journal, 30,* 729–769.

Wineburg, S. S. (1991). Historical problem solving: A study of cognitive processes used in the evaluation of documentary and pictorial evidence. *Journal of Educational Psychology, 83,* 73–87.

Wineburg, S. S. (1994). The cognitive representation of historical texts. In G. Leinhardt, I. L. Beck, & C. Stainton (Eds.), *Teaching and learning in history* (pp. 85–136). Hillsdale, NJ: Lawrence Erlbaum Associates.

Wineburg, S. S. (1996). The psychology of learning and teaching history. In D.C. Berliner, & R. C. Calfee (Eds.), *Handbook of educational psychology* (pp. 423–437). New York: Simon & Schuster Macmillan.

Wineburg, S. S. (1998a). A partial history: An essay review of teaching and learning history in elementary schools. *Teaching and Teacher Education, 14,* 233–243.

Wineburg, S. S. (1998b). Reading Abraham Lincoln: An expert/expert study in the interpretation of historical texts. *Cognitive Science, 22,* 319–346.

Wineburg, S. S. (2000). Making historical sense. In P. Stearns, P. Seixas, & S. S. Wineburg (Eds.), *Teaching and learning history in a national and international context.* New York: New York University Press.

Wineburg, S. S., & Wilson, S. M. (1991). Subject-matter knowledge in the teaching of history. In J. Brophy (Ed.), *Advances in research on teaching* (Vol. 2, pp. 305–347). JAI Press.

Wittrock, M. C. (Ed.). (1986). *Handbook of research on teaching* (3rd ed.). New York: Macmillan.

Yeager, E., & Davis, O. L., Jr. (1995). Between campus and classroom: Secondary student-teachers' thinking about historical texts. *Journal of Research and Development in Education, 29*(1), 1–8.

Young, K. M., & Leinhardt, G. (1998). Writing from primary documents: A way of knowing in history. *Written Communication, 15,* 25–68.

30.

Review of Research on Social Studies

Peter Seixas
University of British Columbia

Reviewing a section of the *Handbook of Research on Social Studies Teaching and Learning* (Shaver, 1991), Wilma Longstreet expressed a note of despair about research in social studies: "[O]ne could have dropped out of the field for 20 years, only to return to a set of essentially unchanged dilemmas" (1990, p. 247). I completed my own preservice teacher education in 1970 amid vibrant debates about the field and, like most teachers, I found little time or support immediately thereafter for reading social studies research. When my teaching career opened up enough space for me to pursue graduate degrees, I chose to do so in history. Then in 1990, appointed to a university position in social studies education, I lived the exact experience that Longstreet had posed hypothetically. Reimmersing myself in the social studies literature, I was struck by the absence of significant advances since my last systematic reading in the teacher education program 20 years earlier. The excitement of the historiographic revolution that had charged my graduate studies during the late 1970s and the 1980s seemed to have bypassed social studies scholarship. Moreover, as I read new literature on teaching and learning in the subjects and disciplines, I found that social studies (with the exception of history education) had participated only marginally and sporadically. This review of social studies research takes this commonly acknowledged problem as a starting point.

In the last three editions of the *Handbook of Research on Teaching,* there has been a chapter on social studies (Armento, 1986; Metcalf, 1963; Shaver & Larkins, 1973). The inclusion of such a chapter is supported by the existence of a school subject of social studies in most jurisdictions in North America, a professional organization (the National Council for Social Studies—NCSS), and a group of educational researchers who affiliate themselves with social studies curriculum and instruction. But social studies is problematic both as a school subject and as a research field. In a study comparing high school subject areas, Siskin (1994, p. 164) characterized social studies as a sub-

ject area where "contests are frequent, and where everything must be locally negotiated, since there are few standardized assumptions about how things must be." Moreover, she noted that there was a marked "difficulty of connecting this amorphous subject to the immediate needs of students" (Siskin, 1994, p. 165; see also Little, 1990; Stodolsky & Grossman, 1995). Indeed, as many commentators have noted, social studies educators (and by this term, I refer to university-based researchers, theorists, and teacher educators) write more about defining social studies than about any other aspect of the field, with remarkably little progress (Longstreet, 1990, p. 246; Marker & Mehlinger, 1992). Two researchers complained recently that "the vagueness with which social studies education is defined makes it difficult to identify research . . . directed to social studies education" (Preissle-Goetz & LeCompte, 1991, p. 62).

The definition of social studies knowledge—and thus teaching and learning—would be simpler if there were an easy correspondence between school social studies and academic disciplines (see Shaver & Larkins, 1973, p. 1244). But this relationship is unclear, and it is nowhere more unclear than on the question of history and social studies (Nelson, 1990; Seixas, 1993; Thornton, 1994; Whelan, 1992; Wraga, 1993). In practice, much of social studies concerns historical knowledge. Yet social studies theorists generally eschew disciplinary definitions for the school subject and specifically reject history as its core (e.g., NCSS, 1994). In the past decade Ravitch and Finn (1987), the National History Standards (National Center for History in the Schools, 1994), the Bradley Commission (Gagnon & the Bradley Commission, 1989), and others have stimulated widespread public debate about the teaching of history in the schools. At the same time, there has also been a dramatic growth of research in history education. In this context, the editor of this volume has made a significant but controversial choice to devote a separate chapter for the first time to research on teaching history (Wilson, this volume). The chapter stands as a recogni-

The author would like to acknowledge the helpful critiques and thoughtful suggestions of the reviewers, Roland Case and William Stanley, as well as Beverly Armento, Larry Cuban, Carole Hahn, Walt Werner, and Sam Wineburg. The author has necessarily been selective in taking those suggestions, and takes full responsibility for what remains.

tion of the degree to which a disciplinary framework for the school subject has advanced in the years since the last edition. In an attempt to avoid duplication, this chapter on social studies will not include the research that deals specifically with history education. An important question confronting this chapter—and the field—is what is left over in research on teaching of the subject of social studies once research on teaching history is removed.

If the subject area of social studies largely refuses a disciplinary definition, then the boundaries of the subject area become exceptionally porous. Much of the research undertaken in social studies classrooms examines problems that apply across the subjects. Social studies curriculum as education for citizenship, broadly defined, takes on virtually all of schooling (Engle & Ochoa, 1988). Likewise, problems of teaching for higher order thinking (Newmann, 1990a), moral education (Leming, 1995; Scott, 1991), and practical competence (Whitson & Stanley, 1996), which apply to all of schooling, create problems in defining where to draw the line. Though I do not exclude the literature in these areas, I consistently interrogate it from the perspective of asking what it contributes to social studies as a school subject, since its other contributions should be covered elsewhere in this volume.

This chapter extends to North American literature published in English since the appearance of the last *Handbook of Research on Teaching* (Wittrock, 1986). In that period of time, several major reviews of social studies research have appeared, most comprehensively the *Handbook of Research on Social Studies Teaching and Learning* (Shaver, 1991). Rather than repeating the reviews that have already been undertaken, this chapter focuses on the syntheses themselves, along with some of the larger research programs.

The first part of this review sets a context for the examination of social studies research on teaching in the past decade. This is established through (a) a review of two significant developments in research on teaching and (b) an analysis of changes in the disciplines that underlie social studies knowledge and that might have an impact on conceptions of social studies theory and practice. The second part examines how, and to what extent, social studies researchers have participated in and contributed to these developments. A final section proposes an avenue that might lead to promising and productive lines of research, teaching, and theory in the coming decade.

Part I: The Research Context

A. Relevant Developments in Research on Teaching

In the last edition of the *Handbook,* Armento (1986, p. 945) decried the "noticeable absence of any well-articulated theoretical framework for studying teaching and learning" in social studies. Since that time, two developments outside of social studies appeared to offer the basis for such a framework. Both of these programs of research on teaching took special interest in the problem of the school subjects, the disciplines, or both.

Shulman's (1986) "Those Who Understand: Knowledge Growth in Teaching" was published in the same year as Armento's (1986) review chapter, seemingly offering a theoretical framework to fill the void she (among many others) had identified. Shulman's research program is particularly important for any focus on the teaching of subject matter, since it provides a theoretical framework for understanding the connections between "content" and "pedagogy." Indeed, it was developed to restore a place for the sustained consideration of "content" within the purview of pedagogical research, a place that had been largely eclipsed by generic process-product research of the 1980s. This was the first, and arguably the most important to date, of research programs arching across subject areas and disciplines, which also took the distinctiveness of subjects and disciplines as serious objects of study.

Of Shulman's types of teacher knowledge, the one that inspired the greatest volume of subsequent research literature was the one that intersected content and pedagogy: pedagogical content knowledge (Grossman & Yerian, 1992; also see Fenstermacher, 1994, pp. 14–15). Research programs were developed in the teaching of English (e.g., Grossman, 1991), mathematics (e.g., Lampert, 1990), history (e.g., Wilson & Wineburg, 1993), and science. The definition of the project posed problems, however, for social studies educators. Shulman's research program was concerned with how student teachers learned to teach in high schools what they had studied in college. The ambivalent relationship of social studies to the academic disciplines of history and social science made this conception of research on teaching less attractive. Not being a "subject studied in college," social studies was not the starting point for student teachers in the way that the study of literature or history could be. The knowledge systems—however diffuse, contested, and permeable—that compose the other academic school subjects provided a more potent basis for this research paradigm.

Armento (1986, p. 946), herself, pointed to the second promising "emerging research focus": constructivism. In doing so, she called for "much more work . . . to illuminate the unique conceptual properties of the knowledge and processes of social studies, and to identify the psychological processes students at various developmental stages employ as they construct and restructure images of the social world and deal with social issues." (Armento, 1986, p. 948). There are two aspects of this injunction: the "conceptual properties" of the subject area and the "psychological processes" of students engaged in learning. There has been some deflation in the promise of generic developmental stages to tell us much about learning in particular subject areas other than those from which the generic understandings were developed. Nevertheless, the focus on children's prior understandings, their misconceptions or stereotypes, and the processes through which they revise and build their understandings have born fruit in a number of areas outside of social studies, as well as in history education, and in some of the disciplinary components of social studies (Avery & Gamradt, 1991; Carretero & Voss, 1994; Steffe & Gale, 1995; Williams, 1996; see also Hughes & Sears, 1996). But the ambivalent relationship of social studies to its component academic disciplines poses a problem for this research program. Without models drawn from the disciplines of history and the social sciences, potential frameworks for studying the development of students' ideas remain murky.

Some of the most cogent arguments for taking disciplinary knowledge seriously come from Howard Gardner and his associates. Gardner (1991, p. 11) explains the importance of disciplinary expertise (as opposed to the knowledge of what he calls the "intuitive learner" and the "traditional student"): "The understandings of the disciplines represent the most important cognitive achievements of human beings. It is necessary to come to know these understandings if we are to be fully human, to live in our time, to be able to understand it to the best of our abilities, and to build upon it."

Building on this conception of disciplinary knowledge as cultural achievement, Boix-Mansilla and Gardner (1998) use examples of students learning biology and history to develop a framework for understanding students' understanding across the disciplines. They define expertise in an area along four dimensions: knowledge of the field (the flexible mastery of concepts and details, generalizations, and examples), methods for building and validating knowledge in the field, purposes for which knowledge is used, and forms in which knowledge is expressed. Constructivist educational research derives its strength as an orientation, not only from attending to the structures of ideas and beliefs that students entertain, but by positing some notion of expertise toward which students can move. In the absence of such models of expertise, constructivist research becomes very difficult. In the absence of the disciplines (their knowledge, epistemologies, and methodologies) models of expertise become either highly complex or unsatisfactorily vague (see Langer & Applebee, 1988; Langer, 1992).

Constructivism and pedagogical content knowledge have both inspired major programs of research on teaching and learning during the past decade. Both have steered educational researchers away from generic pedagogical research toward concerns framed by particular subjects. But, unless one looks at its component disciplines like history, geography, or civics, the subject of social studies has not been home to a substantial new body of research based on either constructivism or pedagogical content knowledge.

B. Changes in History and the Social Sciences

Broad shifts in the focus of academic history and the social sciences have rendered problematic the status of knowledge across the disciplines that have traditionally composed the academic correlates of "the social studies." While these changes certainly have roots deeper than the last decade, they have reached a pervasiveness in most recent years that is dramatic if not revolutionary. Rooted in the "condition of postmodernity," the changes are characterized by several broad features across the disciplines (Harvey, 1989). First, the relationship between the knower and the known has come under scrutiny in an intensified way. Epistemology is a growth industry across the social sciences, with various forms of antifoundationalism offering accounts of the nature of knowledge. "Positionality" emerged as a major concern, posing major challenges to older ideals of objectivity, particularly in relation to the social locations of race, gender, and class. At the same time, interdisciplinary initiatives in gender and women's studies, queer theory, and postcolonial and cultural studies confront traditional disciplinary practices. Questions about the positioned, autobiographical and linguistic dimensions of "objective" scholarly practice have generated new forms of writing that self-consciously declare their positioned, autobiographical and linguistic nature (e.g., Clifford & Marcus, 1986; de Certeau, 1988; hooks, 1988).

The Gulbenkian Commission on the Restructuring of the Social Sciences, a high profile, international group of 10 scholars under the leadership of Immanuel Wallerstein, traced the beginnings of the recent breakdown in disciplinary boundaries among the social sciences to the immediate post-World War II period (Gulbenkian Commission on the Restructuring of the Social Sciences, 1996). By the late 1960s, according to the commission, the question of Eurocentric parochialism hidden underneath the social sciences' claims to objectivity and universality, had become more pressing (p. 48). On one level, the universalist claims of social science demanded the inclusion of the "other" in the ranks of academe. But that very inclusion led to more fundamental challenges about the theoretical and epistemological bases for social scientific investigation. "The call for inclusion, the call for elucidation of theoretical premises has been a call for decolonization, that is, for a transformation of the power relationships which created the particular form of institutionalization of the social sciences that we have known" (p. 56).

The upheaval in the academic disciplines is widespread and multifaceted. Two widely discussed works both describe and exemplify the upheaval. These are two recent histories of the disciplines most frequently understood as central to social studies: history and geography. The book by Peter Novick (1988) titled *That Noble Dream: "The Objectivity Question" and the American Historical Profession* appeared after 2 decades of "the new social history" had transformed historical studies in North America, introducing "history from the bottom up"; generating a burst of activity in women's, African-American, working-class and immigration history; and spawning new journals, more self-conscious theorizing, and innovative methodologies (see Seixas, 1993). Yet, the crisis that Gertrude Himmelfarb (1989; see also 1994) labeled "the new, new history," was still taking shape. Indeed, Novick's monograph helped to give it form. On the one hand, he eschewed explicit discussion of his own epistemological stance and offered what had, on the surface, all of the formal attributes of a traditional history: a narrative emplotment, thorough archival research, copious footnotes—indeed, a story primarily about dead White men. On the other hand, at a deeper level, his accomplishment was to bring the practice of history under the same gaze that historians habitually focus on others; that is, he historicized the practice of history. The study argued persuasively how the ideal of objectivity and the methodologies that were supposed to produce it, the foundations upon which the profession had staked its claim to knowledge, were flawed and contested from the outset and were increasingly problematic. At the same time, the new movements shaking all of the humanities and social sciences made vigorous entries into subsequent professional meetings and journals of North American historians (see Hunt, 1989; Kernan, 1997). The point here is that the postmodern insurgency was alive and well within the disciplinary communities of academia, notwithstanding its close links to ideological, political, economic, and demographic changes beyond the university.

The book by Derek Gregory (1994) titled *Geographic Imaginations* bears a somewhat different relationship to its disciplinary roots, in part because it was published 6 crucial years later, and in part because of the different disciplinary practices that Gregory interrogates. And yet it is similar to Novick's work in that it offers an explanation of the current state of inquiry in geographic discourse by tracing its evolution. This, in any case, is the structure of the first half of the book. (The second half is less pertinent to the discussion here.) Gregory shows both how geography has intertwined with other disciplinary practices throughout its history and how, in the current moment of epistemological upheaval in the humanities and social sciences, space, place, and landscape have become central concerns across the humanities and social sciences. In the volume's first essay, Gregory argues that geography was tied to anthropology in the 18th century, sociology in the 19th, and economics at the turn of the 20th. In the second essay, dealing with the more recent past, he reverses the order of association, moving from political economy, through social theory, to cultural studies (Gregory, 1994, p. 5). Questions of power and knowledge, representer and represented, West and East, pervade the entire analysis. So, while the concerns of geographers are central throughout the book, the impact is to question every aspect of their practice. Gregory's postmodernism is, as he puts it "the disorientation of Occidentalism" (p. 139). He mobilizes the theorists of postcolonialism, poststructuralism, and cultural studies in order to "displace" and "dislocate" the unselfconscious pose of geographic objectivity that underlay the West's mapping of the world (p. 135).

Novick and Gregory challenge the foundations of their own disciplines in terms similar to challenges that have been mounted across the humanities and social science. The concerns of gender, non-Eurocentric approaches, and the destabilization of the metanarrative of progress (in both technology and knowledge) underlie not only these accounts, but the explosion of cultural studies across the humanities and social sciences (Gulbenkian Commission, 1996, p. 64). Of course, some disciplines are probably less transformed than others (see, e.g., Alway, 1995).

What do these developments mean for research on teaching social studies? Those who write on the foundations of educational research have been as affected as any of the other social sciences ("Foundations" chapters, this volume). But this chapter opens an additional question, specifically in the subject of social studies: What are the implications of these fundamental transformations in conceptions of social and cultural knowledge for the school subject that is most directly in line to teach this knowledge? To what extent have researchers incorporated the new developments in humanities and social scientific knowledge in their frameworks for examining the teaching and learning of social studies?

Part II: Research on Social Studies Teaching

A. Writing on the Meanings and Purposes of Social Studies Teaching

In the last edition of this *Handbook,* Armento (1986, p. 944) expressed concerns "about the focus of most of the research on isolated and minor questions, the atheoretical nature of much of the current work, and the lack of accumulated knowledge

after years of inquiry." Others express weariness with the very attempt to come up with a definition and rationale for social studies: "With the exception of articles on teaching methods . . . more is written about the 'nature' of the social studies, its purpose, what it is, is not, and must become than about any other social studies topic" (Marker & Mehlinger, 1992, p. 831). Nevertheless, it is impossible to sidestep the issue. Research on teaching social studies implicitly or explicitly involves conceptions on the part of researchers and teachers about what should be taught. Thus, attempts to articulate the purposes and practices of social studies (however tiresome) are the subject of this section.

Education for citizenship continues to be a fundamental part of the definition of social studies (Anderson, Avery, Pederson, Smith, & Sullivan, 1997; Gross & Dynneson, 1991; McLeod, 1989). Sears (1994) flags the differences between conceptions of citizenship between the United States and Canada at the same time as he remarks on the lack of consensus on the characteristics of the "good" citizen in either jurisdiction. But this is only one part of the problem. O. L. Davis calls citizenship a dead and burdensome metaphor. "Both as a legitimation and as slogan, the term misleads social studies pupils and practitioners. It also confuses the public and other educational professionals" (Davis, 1991, p. 33). Marker and Mehlinger (1992, p. 832) offer three "obvious" reasons for the failure of the goal of citizenship to define the social studies:

1. It is too broad: Everyone can subscribe to it, even those with diametrically opposing views.
2. Citizenship education is a goal of schooling itself; thus, "there is no simple way to distinguish easily the contributions social studies is to make to the education of youth that is separate from the broad socialization role of schools generally."
3. "There is no organized, agreed-upon body of knowledge for citizenship education."

Like all educational researchers in curriculum subject areas, social studies researchers are positioned between practicing teachers and academics (in the case of social studies, in the humanities and social sciences). But their theoretical stances and research practices can either exacerbate or ameliorate the problems entailed in this location. Three problematic aspects of social studies theory stand out in the writing of the past decade: (a) The rejection of academic work in general as having relevance for the school subject; (b) the rejection of disciplinary investigation as a method for generating social knowledge significant for school-age children, and (c) most specifically, the characterization of social science methodology as being disengaged, "academic," value-neutral and therefore irrelevant for school students (see, e.g., Martorella, 1991; Stanley, 1992, p. 69; Wraga, 1993).

Ambivalence about the disciplinary status of social studies underlies the tripartite scheme that continues, after 20 years and with a number of variations, to provide much of the theoretical foundation for social studies. Developed by Barth and Shermis (1970) and elaborated by Barr, Barth, and Shermis (1977), the three rationales include citizenship transmission (the inculcation of knowledge, skills, and values), social sciences simplified for pedagogical purposes, and critical or reflective inquiry (see Stanley, 1992, pp. 63–83; Brophy, 1990).

Thornton's (1994) review of social studies provides an opportunity to examine a recent recapitulation of the Barr, Barth, and Shermis scheme. Thornton structured his chapter around the three social studies orientations, but he then also appended two additional sections to deal with pressing themes (the growth of history education and considerations of diversity and inclusion) that could not otherwise be incorporated satisfactorily. The normative and ideological dimensions of the framework (transmission bad, social sciences better, critical inquiry best) are explicit. The first orientation, transmission, is generally associated with low-level and uncritical memorization and recitation (p. 226), while the third orientation, reflective or critical thinking, is "transformative" (p. 233). Social studies educators who subscribe to the model see their job as moving teaching from the first, predominant (as established by Shaver, Davis, & Helburn, 1980) transmission tradition and toward the transformative, critical, or reflective approach.

The second, intermediate orientation is "social sciences [including history] simplified for pedagogical purposes." In assessing the import of this second orientation, Thornton draws a sharp distinction between "scholarly" social science interests and "broader conceptions of citizenship education." The former, according to Thornton, put the social science orientation into the "mimetic" camp, while the latter put it into the "transformative" camp. Thornton's dichotomous treatment of the second orientation demands close scrutiny. A lot hinges on it, because it is the one category of the three that holds a promise of drawing relationships between the growth of knowledge among disciplinary specialists and the growth of knowledge among school children, as framed by Gardner (1991). It is the conception of the subject that puts it in the best position to benefit from the constructivist and pedagogical content knowledge research programs outlined above. What are the implications of dismissing how anthropologists think and work, as having relevance for how we want students to think and learn about other cultures? Do the practices of historians have any relevance for the ways that students should think and learn about the past (Bruner, 1996, pp. 91–92; Gardner & Boix-Mansilla, 1994; Shulman, 1986, 1987)?

According to Thornton, "it is not at all clear that disciplinary knowledge constitutes the best education for citizens. Unless the social science approach involves students in the active construction of knowledge and analysis of values, it both falls short of social studies goals . . . and becomes, like the transmission approach, what Whitehead . . . called 'inert ideas'" (p. 232). Contrary to Thornton, it is unclear how teachers could have students engage in the practices of social science without "active construction of knowledge and analysis of values," since that is exactly what social science does. Having students examine only the products of social science research, without participating in a critical examination of their production (too often what is done in school) would hardly be participating in "the practices of social science." Conversely, it is unclear how teachers could provide valid models for students' "active construction of knowledge" without using those derived from scholarly practice. Critical analysis, which social studies educators generally reserve for their third orientation, is the foundation of academic work in the social sciences. The achievements of academic disciplinary communities are, precisely, those conceptual and procedural frameworks (growing, shifting and self-critical, but nevertheless building upon past scholarship) that provide the scaffolding for growth in knowledge. Like the analysis provided by Thornton, much of the other theorizing about social studies rests on problematic formulations of the character of the social science disciplines.

The ongoing uneasiness about the relationship of social studies to disciplinary knowledge was expressed in a special issue of the *International Journal of Social Education,* titled "Social Studies as a Discipline" (6,2, Autumn, 1991). Barth (1991, p. 19) offers the following definition: "Social studies is the interdisciplinary integration of social science and humanities concepts for the purpose of practicing citizenship skills on critical social issues." He decries "fragmented" knowledge, which apparently characterizes such disciplines as history and geography, and calls social studies the one school subject that "intends to integrate knowledge" (p. 20).

Jack L. Nelson (1991) offers an ideological critique of the disciplines. He understands the disciplines in social studies (and disciplinary knowledge in general) as being politically conservative. Thus, eliminating the remnants of the disciplines constitutes a move, for Nelson, toward emancipatory pedagogy. For him, disciplines are "the result of historical accident and vested interests" (Nelson, 1991, p. 45).

The disciplines are, of course, historically contingent; that is to say, there is nothing a priori about the objects or methods of their studies. Their substantive and syntactic structures change and develop over time, in an interplay with shifting ideological and political economic forces. Yet the shifting, evolving disciplines—their structures as well as the procedures for critiquing, adding to, and renovating those structures—are, as Gardner (1991) explained, the only knowledge tools that we have as a culture. Historians, geographers, anthropologists, and sociologists are (as I have argued above) at the forefront of analyzing how "vested interests" have shaped their disciplines in the past and of transforming their own practices in the process.

Given his blanket rejection of disciplined knowledge, Nelson seeks "to bring caution to the effort to define social studies as a discipline" (p. 43). Wilma Longstreet (1991) takes the opposite tack in another article in the series. Longstreet acknowledges that the definitions of citizenship that have been used in the field of social studies have been inadequate. The field of social studies, based on an inadequate conception of citizenship, might be fixed by conceptualizing it more rigorously, by, in her words, turning "citizenship into a discipline." But precisely because of the very historical nature of disciplines, with their legitimacy built through a process of mutual and public critique undertaken with the goal of generating socially valued knowledge, it is unclear exactly what this prescription means.

Claire W. Keller (1991) offers a rejoinder: "The time has come to give up the mythology that social studies exists as a discipline and concentrate on the failure to teach better history and social science" (p. 75). Who, Keller asks, "would be prepared to teach such courses requiring a difficult synthesis of several disciplines? Where would teachers be trained or retrained for such courses? . . . The NCSS standards on teacher certification for all levels call for training in history and the social sciences, not social studies. . . . Textbooks, the dominant determiner of what teachers teach, are now and always have been written as history or social science texts. Where can teachers acquire adequate material for such courses?" (pp. 74–75). Keller calls for the elimination of "social studies" as a school subject and for the substitution of history and social sciences (see Social Sciences Education Consortium, 1996).

The rejection of social science by social studies educators is often based on the notion that social science is neutral and objective and that it has nothing to do with human choices or human values. Stanley (1992, p. 69) notes, "the social science tradition [among social studies educators] emphasizes value neutrality (except for the valuing of the scientific method itself)" (also see Martorella, 1991). Though seemingly accepted among social studies educators as a description of social science, this characterization ill fits contemporary social scientists' engagement in broad questions of value, politics, power, and change. Indeed, given the seriousness and ferment with which academics in the humanities and social sciences have pursued questions of voice, representation, social action, and political change (to mention just a few), the failure of social studies educators to draw important relationships to academic knowledge for the purposes of "reflective inquiry" is unfortunate.

Banks (1993, 1995) is one of the few researchers who has made an attempt to deal with the implications of these changes for social studies. He contrasts "mainstream" with "transformative" academic knowledge. The former, he claims, rests on the notion that "a set of objective truths . . . can be discovered and verified through rigorous and objective research procedures that are uninfluenced by human interests, values, and perspectives" (Banks, 1995, p. 4). "Transformative academic knowledge," in contrast, rests on the assumption that "all knowledge reflects the power and social relationships within society, and that an important purpose of knowledge construction is to help people improve society" (Banks, 1995, p. 6). Leaving aside Banks's excessively broad strokes in this contrast as well as his neglect of the progressive roots of much traditional social science, the categories of "mainstream" and "transformative" academic knowledge imply that the changes in history and social sciences have been marginal, rather than reaching, as they have, to the core of these disciplines.

One of the major recent attempts to define the work of the social studies was the National Commission on Social Studies, formed in 1986 as a joint project of the American Historical Association, the National Council for Social Studies, the Organization of American Historians, and the Carnegie Foundation. The commission ran headlong into accusations from social studies educators that historians had been too influential in the process. The commission's reports included *Charting a Course: Social Studies in the 21st Century* (National Commission on Social Studies in the Schools, 1989) and *Voices of Teachers: Report of a Survey on Social Studies* (National Commission on Social Studies in the Schools, 1991). A third publication by David Jenness (1990), *Making Sense of Social Studies,* was undertaken in part, as "a history of the social studies movement, with particular attention to the efforts of the disciplines at various stages to influence the process" (p. xv).

Jenness, an "outsider" in the field of social studies, based his work both on interviews with researchers in the field and on their published work. Much of the book is organized around social studies as a series of social sciences, with a nod to the importance of blurring their boundaries. Jenness noted that "most observers report relatively little evidence in classrooms for concerted work on higher-order thinking" of any kind (p. 379). The practices observed in the National Science Foundation studies 2 decades earlier—an emphasis on factual recall and recitation—remained pervasive. Social studies was not seen as a serious or challenging subject by many teachers and many students, elementary and secondary (pp. 382–383).

Jenness's chapter on "Higher Order Thinking" provides another example of the problematic persistence of the Barr, Barth, and Shermis conception of social science. In the introduction to the chapter, Jenness attempts to bring developments in cognitive theory, particularly schema theory, to bear on social studies. Using Barr, Barth, and Shermis's distinction between social science teaching and reflective inquiry, Jenness summarizes what he sees as a central dilemma for social studies classrooms:

> For the school curriculum, much depends on whether students should be led through the actual steps or logic of discovery within specific fields or frameworks or whether, other things being equal, time and effort are better spent on learning how to use the fruits of organized knowledge in a responsible, critical, appreciative, confident way in a messy, decision-laden world. (Jenness, 1990, p. 373)

Much like Thornton's discussion of social science, this dichotomous formulation follows directly from the Barr, Barth, and Shermis typology. It fails to understand the project of academic social science, where each discipline must use the fruits of earlier inquiry to guide new explorations in a "messy" world. And, consequently, it fails to envision students' parallel activities, in using "the fruits of organized knowledge" to develop new responsible, critical, positioned stances themselves. In other words, the apparent dichotomy ("whether students should . . . or whether time and effort are better spent . . .") misunderstands the nature of inquiry, which must both build on the "fruits of organized knowledge" and have a valid method to build and use new knowledge.

The responses to Jenness (1990) and to the commission's other major publication, *Charting a Course: Social Studies for the 21st Century* (National Commission on Social Studies in the Schools, 1989), were largely negative among social studies educators, but short-lived. Shirley Engle (1990, p. 432) wrote: "Surely a basic change in what is taught in the social studies and how it is taught is urgently needed." The commission offered, instead, more of the same. *Charting a Course* included statements from social science organizations about their own disciplines. But, as Cleo Cherryholmes (1990) pointed out, these statements reflected very poorly the current practices in the social science fields in 1989. Rather, they seemed drawn from an earlier, positivist paradigm, the challenges to which barely surfaced in the document. Perhaps, just as social studies educators' nods to social science produce inadequate conceptions of their purposes and practices, social scientists' engagement with precollegiate education is similarly cursory.

The commission publications were followed by a series of high-profile discussions of public policy documents in the areas of social studies education (Gagnon & the Bradley Commission, 1989; Geography Education Standards Project, 1994; National Center for History in the Schools, 1994; National Council for Social Studies, 1994). Consequently, Nelson's (1990, p. 437) hope that the report "be forgotten quickly" was largely realized.

Publication of major volumes in the social studies continued in these years with the appearance of the first *Handbook of Research on Social Studies Teaching and Learning* (Shaver, 1991). As a handbook, it was intended to be definitive of the field. Unlike the commission's publications, the work was produced by a large group of social studies educators. If there is a community of inquiry in the social studies, the *Handbook* is its most compact documentary expression, on a different scale from previous multiauthor reviews of the field (e.g., Stanley, 1985). A comprehensive review in this chapter is neither possible nor appropriate: I will examine the chapters that focus centrally on teachers and teaching. Each of its sections was reviewed (prepublication) in a special issue of *The Social Studies* (Nov.–Dec., 1990). As Byron Massialas (1990) noted in his editorial introduction, "The subject of social studies . . . has suffered for a long time from a dearth of quality research. . . . [R]eview after review stated, with monotonous regularity, that because of its questionable quality, whatever scant research was conducted in the field had little value for either practitioners or researchers" (p. 237). Could the *Handbook* contribute to improvement?

Four years after its appearance, Leming and Nelson (1995) conducted an analysis of the citations in the *Handbook*. Among other things, they found a heavy preponderance of citations from the two journals published by the National Council for Social Studies: 285 citations of *Theory and Research in Social Education,* and 138 of *Social Education.* The next most frequently cited journal was *American Educational Research Journal,* with 43, and they dropped off steeply subsequently. References to history and social science journals outside of psychology were "scattered." The authors concluded that the field "largely relies upon its own scholarship, rather than drawing upon the social sciences for its knowledge base" (p. 169). Given that their study was based on reviews of social studies research, one might expect primarily citations from social studies journals. But it does raise the ironic question of whether a community of scholars who worry about "the perils of disciplinarity" is actually quite inward-looking and fails to draw widely from related literature in the humanities and social sciences, at the exact moment when scholars in the disciplines social studies educators see as narrow and boundaried are increasingly exploring each others' work (see Wraga, 1993).

Armento (1991, p. 185) introduces her chapter with a refreshing "sense of optimism." Acknowledging the minimal impact at the time she was writing, Armento sought "to describe and document the emerging quiet revolution in the research on teaching social studies," so that its impact might be extended (1991, p. 186). Her optimism comes in part from the large-scale research programs of Newmann, Brophy, Shulman, and Voss. Research in social studies, she wrote, is also "benefiting from the cognitive psychology movement which prompted changes in the research on teaching reading, mathematics, and science . . ." (1991, p. 185). She identifies five fundamental shifts in the research on teaching social studies:

1. New epistemological traditions (including interpretive and critical analyses).

2. Multidimensional and complex conceptualizations of teachers' roles.
3. Units of analysis, which include larger holistic structures [e.g., the classroom, the department, the school] as well as teachers' belief and knowledge schemata.
4. Shifting focus from isolated elements toward more integrative analyses [i.e., from behaviorist to cognitive investigations].
5. Changes in the conceptualization of social studies itself.

Armento's chapter is an attempt to identify hopeful new directions, to document their sources, often in other fields, to cite those social studies researchers who have begun to pursue these directions, and to encourage more. To some extent, her sense of change may be wishful thinking: Much of the research she cites has not specifically grown out of, nor been applied to, social studies research. The section supporting new conceptualizations of social studies, for example, draws mainly on the work of historians and history education researchers. Yet it is difficult not to support the directions that she hopes the field will move.

Stanley's chapter, too, tries to put the best face on the field. He defines three major research traditions that offer conceptions of teacher competence in social studies: the generic educational process-product research, a reaction that emphasized "content and context," and a critical approach, "which is a rejection of many of the assumptions and guidelines prescribed by the other two mainstream approaches" (Stanley, 1991, p. 249; compare with Popkewitz, 1986). He argues that "in the move from the teacher effectiveness approach to the teacher content-knowledge approach and, finally, to the critical approach to competence, social studies is successively taken more seriously as an area of curriculum with unique attributes and goals" (Stanley, 1991, p. 249). What, precisely, is the relationship between these shifts in research orientation and the legitimacy of social studies as a school subject with "unique attributes and goals"?

Little of the teacher effectiveness research actually involved social studies, but, because of its generic nature, it could be applied to social studies. But Stanley is actually more interested in the multiple critiques of the teacher effectiveness literature. One central problem is that, until desirable outcomes are agreed upon for social studies, it is not clear what measure of student performance will count as effectiveness. Citing Armento (1986) he argues that the "focus on isolated teacher and student behaviors promotes a narrow view of instruction, knowledge, and understanding that ignores the interrelationships among forms of knowledge and the social and affective dimensions of teaching" (Stanley, 1991, p. 251). As noted in virtually all of the reviews of research since 1986, the positivist assumptions that undergirded the process-product research have been increasingly rejected by educational researchers.

Stanley's second research tradition, "competence related to teacher knowledge of subject matter," focuses directly on Shulman's research program. He notes not only the basic shift in the research questions but also the shift in methodology to small-scale ethnographic and case study research, and particularly that which looks at expert teachers. "The more knowledgeable teachers not only knew more about subject matter but also knew more about the relationship among the parts of this knowledge; how this discipline or field related to other areas of knowledge; and, equally important, how best to represent this knowledge so students would come to understand it" (Stanley, 1991, p. 253). The strengths that Stanley observes in these studies echo Armento's assessment. But importantly, and again echoing Armento, none of the research explored in this section of the chapter defines the relevant field or discipline as "social studies," but rather as "history." It is difficult, then, to understand how this research program has contributed to "social studies" as a subject (as opposed to history) being "taken more seriously as an area of curriculum with unique attributes and goals" (p. 249).

Stanley's third research tradition, based on critical thinking and critical pedagogy, is an uneasy amalgam of three schools of thought: critical thinking, including Newmann's (1990a) research on higher-order thinking, Giroux's (1988) critical pedagogy, and Stanley's own "practical competence" (Whitson & Stanley, 1988). What stands out here, particularly in its placement after the subject-matter research, is the generic nature (with respect to school subjects) of this body of work. To define teaching social studies in terms of critical thinking, critical pedagogy, or practical competence is problematic in the same way as defining it as citizenship education: These are goals for all of schooling, not for any one subject area. Admittedly, Newmann's research has been carried out in the context of social studies classes, and "higher order thinking" would presumably look quite different in the context of a mathematics class. But none of his research aims to pinpoint how it would look different. Again, it is thus difficult to see how this research tradition can contribute to an understanding of social studies teaching as an enterprise with "unique attributes and goals."

In reviewing all six essays in the *Handbook* on research on teaching social studies, Zevin (1990, p. 262) observed: "The shocking conclusion that must be drawn from these six elaborate and rich essays on teaching in social studies is the impoverished nature of the research that is available for review and reexamination. Most shocking of all is the lack of direct observations of classrooms, of primary documentation from or about teachers at all levels, and the dearth of significant and reliable major studies conducted on a regional scale in accord with well-known research standards."

B. What Do Social Studies Teachers Know and Believe?

Notwithstanding Zevin's concerns, since the publication of the *Handbook* there have been a number of studies that enter classrooms and attempt to give us some picture of teacher's beliefs, knowledge, and decision making. Again, I have excluded the rapidly accumulating studies of teachers engaged in history education.

Brophy's series, *Advances in Research on Teaching,* has attended more to social studies than to any other school subject. Volume Four (Brophy, 1993a) is entirely given over to case studies in social studies. At times, Brophy's introduction (p. ix) has a tone rooted in the process-product research paradigm: "Most contributions to the series link information about teaching processes with information about presage variables (especially teacher knowledge and beliefs), context variables, or student outcome variables." Yet, acknowledging the relative dearth of research on social studies teaching, Brophy's aim is to provide thick descriptions of good social studies teaching: both "to highlight exemplary teachers as models and to clarify some of the dilemmas involved in learning to teach the subject well" (p. x). All of the studies reflect a concern with the way in which teachers' knowledge and beliefs shape their teaching and their classrooms.

This volume raises a number of important questions for research on social studies teaching. How do the researchers theorize or generalize, based on "thick description?" What are the contributions and the limits of this research methodology? What is the range of researcher-teacher relationships in such cases? On the one hand, what light will such studies shed on the relationship between the knowledge and beliefs of teachers and, on the other hand, on the way their classrooms look? The contributions to this volume offer food for thought on these issues. The cases also offer exemplary opportunities to see how the subject "matters" (Levstik, 1993; compare with Stodolsky, 1988).

Evans's (1993) model is one way of dealing with what classroom observations mean: He constructs a typology according to teachers' "ideologies." Evans observes, "Because it is exploratory, this study will provide few generalizable answers. Instead it will provide grounded insights into what is happening in particular classrooms with particular teachers and their students. From these classrooms we can all learn" (Evans, 1993, p. 182). Exactly how we can learn all is perhaps still somewhat vague. Thornton (1993, p. 160), quoting Shulman, notes: "The well-crafted case instantiates the possible, not only documenting that it can be done but also laying out at least one detailed example of how it was organized, developed, and pursued."

Case studies such as those presented in the Brophy volume offer a critical opportunity to reconsider the relationships between researchers and teachers. What are the researchers' responsibilities to the teachers they write about? Particularly when teachers are working in ways that researchers see as exemplary, when they provide models of wisdom, they have a very active role in the construction of the knowledge presented as the case study. The inclusion of the teacher subject as a coauthor in the chapter by White (with Rumsey, 1993) offers an important alternative to the anonymous teacher subject. It also appears to speak directly to the work of Marker and Mehlinger (1992, p. 846) musing: "One must wonder if social studies research were conducted by practitioners or by teams of practitioners and professors whether the research topics would be more closely related to practice and whether the research results would be used more often by those who are responsible for curriculum decisions."

Thornton emphasizes the organizing framework for the whole volume: case studies of good teaching. In reviewing the literature to date, he concludes that there is no single best model, but multiple models of good teaching. But these bear a complex relationship to teachers' beliefs. He notes the accumulating evidence of the disjunction between what social studies teachers say they want to do and what they actually do. As John Goodlad (1984, p. 212) observed, the articulated goals of social studies tell us little about what actually transpires, because "something strange seems to have happened to them on the way to the classroom."

Goodlad's observation is not, however, to dismiss the importance of well-articulated beliefs about a subject in the formulation of teaching goals. As Brophy (1993b, p. 223) notes in his final summary: "If teachers are to become more goal-directed in their instructional planning in social studies they will need to acquire a vision of the subject as a coherent curriculum component designed to accomplish unique citizen education purposes and goals, not merely as a collection of miscellaneous content to be covered. A coherent orientation toward the field does not guarantee successful social studies teaching . . . but it is probably a necessary precondition" (p. 223). In order to provide an overarching coherence, Brophy (1993b, p. 22) returns to the Barr, Barth, and Shermis (1977) model of social studies with the revision by Martorella (1985). Brophy uses them only to point to the conclusion that "most scholars view the diversity of opinion about social studies purposes and goals as healthy, signifying the field's vitality, even though it complicates attempts to define and study effective teaching" (p. 221).

Other studies are further from the classroom but still focus on teachers' beliefs as significant explanatory factors in explaining the contours of social studies instruction. Nelson and Drake (1994) used life-story interviews to explore the beliefs of 29 veteran social studies teachers. Their subjects were mainly White, male teachers from suburban or rural school districts in Maine and Illinois. They placed these life stories "within the social and political context of a particular time frame" (p. 47). In so doing, they attempt to explain teachers' responses to a variety of social issues and educational reforms from the 1950s to the 1970s. The ubiquitous Barr, Barth, and Shermis (1977) framework provides many of the researchers' questions and analysis. A rich, disturbing, but not particularly surprising picture emerges. The authors emphasize the ideological gulf between social studies educators and these teachers, the difficulty the latter had with teaching controversial issues, and the distance they maintained from the New Social Studies reforms of the late 1960s and 1970s. Interestingly, "only two of the interviewees referred to themselves as social studies teachers, and identification as such was avoided. Social studies per se was regarded as an illegitimate and demeaning label" (Nelson & Drake, 1994, p. 60). Despite its distance from classroom observation, this kind of research provides a sense of the meanings of teaching, curricular change, and sociopolitical context, as experienced by teachers themselves.

Makler's interviews with 18 classroom teachers offers an in-depth understanding of how they conceptualize and teach about justice (Makler, 1994). She found three major themes: justice as right and wrong, as fairness, and as an ideal or standard. Makler attributes teachers' unwillingness to confront their students' radical relativism in relation to issues of justice, to insecurities stemming from their unfamiliarity with academic work in the field. She found no significant differences in conceptualizations of justice along gender lines. Like researchers who draw on expert thinking in history to frame their studies of history education, Makler mobilizes the philosophical literature on justice in order to frame her own study of justice. Her willingness and ability to draw on relevant academic literature for concepts and theories of justice provide depth to her models of teacher thinking.

Nuanced understandings of classroom thinking and decision making in social studies are apparent in Kon's (1995) study of seven fifth-grade teachers' decisions about a new social studies textbook and in Grant's (1996) study of teacher's thinking and practice (drawing on Thornton, 1991). In the former, Kon demonstrates significant variation among teachers' strategies, arguing that the textbook was much less determinative of classroom activity than other research has suggested (or assumed). In the latter, Grant ascertains how teachers think about authority over their teaching decisions (divided by Grant into content and pedagogy), by studying 11 teachers, and the mix of personal, organizational, and policy influences on their decision making.

An important difference between Makler's study and those of Kon and Grant is the relationship of the research to the subject of social studies. The questions raised by Kon and Grant are important for social studies classes, and they look like social studies research because the specific cases they discuss involve social studies texts and curricula. However, their generic questions could be addressed equally well across the school subjects; unlike Makler's they have no exclusive relevance to social studies, which is not to say that they are not important. But until researchers investigate them in comparative work across the subjects, they only tangentially contribute to a specific body of knowledge about social studies teaching and learning. There are, fortunately, a new and growing number of studies that do compare teachers' thinking and teachers' practices across different subjects (e.g., Brown, 1996; Grant, 1995; Stodolsky, 1988; Stodolsky & Grossman, 1995). In her study of student teachers, Grant (1995) found that the dominant concern of those planning to teach mathematics was "How do I get these kids to learn mathematics?" while that of those preparing for social studies teaching was "What do I teach kids?" The comparison opens up important questions about each subject's organization of knowledge.

Since the *Handbook* (Shaver, 1991) appeared, there has been a fairly steady flow of small-scale, qualitative studies looking at the knowledge and attitudes of teachers, even outside of the growth industry of history education. The shift from quantitative methodologies to various forms of qualitative research, called for by Shaver, Davis, and Helburn (1980), has become even more pronounced since the publication of the *Handbook* (and not only in the study of teacher's thinking, but across social studies education). Armento (1996), reviewing research on social studies teacher education, in fact, complains that there is virtually no quantitative research under way that can provide a needed overview (for contrast in Canada, compare with Sears, 1994; and, perhaps more predictably, in economics education, Watts & Highsmith, 1992).

The National Commission on Social Studies in the Schools (1991) did attempt to ascertain, as part of the basis for its curriculum recommendations, a broad view of the ideas of social studies teachers across the United States. Through professional bodies and journals, it issued an invitation for teachers to become involved in the commission's work as "adviser-responders." A series of questionnaires was then sent to the 777 teachers who agreed to do so. While the group did not constitute a scientific sample of social studies teachers in general, the commission nevertheless put some weight on their opinions. Among other findings, more than half (53.4%) of those surveyed responded that history should form either the core or the sole focus of social studies (p. 41). At the same time, a majority (55.2%) saw the main purpose of social studies as "developing skills for well-informed citizens" (p. 42). The published report does not reveal which of the questions were open-ended and which were multiple choice, nor does it discuss any measures taken to ensure reliable coding of the former. Thus, while it is of some interest as a high-profile national effort, the report itself constitutes a questionable contribution to the research literature.

Methodologically more sophisticated was a "Q-sort" investigation of teachers attitudes toward citizenship education and social studies (Anderson et al., 1997). Reported as a study of "divergent perspectives on citizenship education," the researchers analyzed patterns of social studies teachers' rankings of a set of statements about citizenship education. A small national sample yielded the following categories: critical thinkers, legalists, cultural pluralists, and assimilationists. These results were then used to frame a large-scale national survey: 800 randomly sampled members of the National Council for Social Studies (with 45% or 361 responding). This study provides a textured and nuanced confirmation of the lack of consensus about citizenship education. The authors concluded that social studies teachers disagree about some of its most central elements, and occasionally their views are in significant conflict (p. 352).

C. Social Studies Teachers in Classrooms and Departments

Moving beyond what teachers know and believe, we come upon a second growing body of research on social studies teaching, that on the nature of student-teacher interactions, classroom dynamics, classroom climate, and the departmental context. This research is based on two premises: first, that the core of social studies is teaching for democratic citizenship; and second, that how a class is run is a good part of what is being taught to students (see Engle & Ochoa, 1988). In other words, the division between "content" and "pedagogy" is an oversimplification.

Though these premises are as old as social studies itself, Cuban's (1991) history of research on social studies teaching underscores just how new the investigation of their relationship in the classroom is. He found numerous articles on what social studies should be, but he found very few sources from which to construct a picture of what actually happened in social studies classrooms. Like that in his earlier study of stability and change in classrooms over time, his central concern is the question of teacher-centered vs. student-centered classrooms. (Cuban, 1984). He found that, in the three editions of the *Handbook of Research on Teaching,* covering 3 decades of research, there were no studies of the classroom behavior of social studies teachers (Cuban, 1991, p. 199). Only 3 of 221 articles published in *Theory and Research in Social Education* since 1973 dealt with teaching behaviors: two on elementary teachers, and one on Australian high school teachers. In spite of the lack of research, Cuban paints a broad picture of persistence of social studies characterized by "tedium, uselessness, and forgettability" (Cuban, 1991, p. 205). He asks why such problems persist,

given substantial improvement in the professional conditions of teaching over the century. Without offering a conclusive response, he offers a "quasi-speculative answer," combining elements of individual, setting, and environments external to the setting.

Newmann's long-term research on higher order thinking in social studies provides almost a direct response to Cuban's complaints about research (Newmann, 1990a, 1990b, 1991a, 1990b; Onosko, 1991; compare with Wilen & White, 1991). The research was framed around two central questions, with social studies departments as the unit of study. These questions were (a) "To what extent is it possible for high school social studies departments to promote higher-order thinking?" and (b) "How are the apparent barriers overcome in more successful departments?" Newmann's conception of higher-order thinking is an attempt to embrace features of all of the conceptions of the teaching of thinking in social studies (Newmann, 1990a, p. 42). But he quickly moves to what he sees as the deeper issue: "The more serious problem . . . is not the failure to teach some specific aspect of thinking, but the profound absence of thoughtfulness in U.S. classrooms" (Newmann, 1990a, p. 44). His general conception of high-order thinking has at its core, the posing and solving of nonroutine problems. He aims for "a framework that is responsive both to the general literature on thinking and to the particular content of social studies" (1990a, p. 43). While making an important contribution, it too is far more oriented toward the "general" than toward particular social studies knowledge. Newmann's interest happens to be social studies classes, but, in the end, no conceptual link is made between this definition of higher-order thinking and the subject matter of social studies. Indeed, this conception of higher-order thinking "encompasses problem solving in a wide range of school subjects as well as in nonacademic areas" (Newmann, 1990a, p. 48).

Angela Harwood (1992) traces the roots of the interest of social studies in the relationship between classroom climate and civic education to research on political socialization. In so doing, she uncovers a far more substantial body of relevant literature than Cuban did. She notes two early (1930s) lines of research on classroom climate, distinguished by their sources of data: those based on observations of teachers' behaviors and those drawn from students' perceptions. The seminal work of Almond and Verba (1963) provided the possibility of theoretical links to political socialization literature. A substantial body of work by Ehman, Torney-Purta, and others examined school and classroom practices for their impact on students' sense of political efficacy, understanding of democratic processes, and political attitudes. More recently, qualitative studies have underscored the complexity of classroom climate formation, the problems associated with survey methodologies, and the need for further research using qualitative methods (Harwood, 1992, p. 77). Harwood notes the mixed picture presented by the research and the difficulty in generalizing across studies that use different variables and definitions of those variables. And yet, despite her warnings to reviewers who have overstated the research findings on the effects of classroom climate, she finds "glimmers of hope": "The consistent relationships between classroom climate and political interest, efficacy, and confidence

... suggest that what happens in social studies classrooms is indeed related to what students think about politics" (Harwood, 1992, p. 78; see also Harwood, 1991).

Research on political socialization in Canada points in similar directions, but has been very limited in recent years. Sears (1994, p. 21) reviews only two quasi-experimental studies, both of which supported claims that inquiry-based approaches fostered the development of democratic attitudes but which may have limited generalizability. Beyond research focused specifically on classrooms, political socialization research offers sophisticated models of investigation that might be further mined by social studies educators. The field has broadened its own definition of political socialization to include varieties of activity in voluntary organizations, the workplace, and the family (Ichilov, 1990, p. 2).

Judith Torney-Purta (1990) has attempted to incorporate some of the theoretical advances from cognitive psychology into the research on political socialization. In particular, she discusses the advantages of using schema theory to understand how students learn about solving social scientific problems. She contrasts models of problem solving in science, math, and logic with those in the ill-defined social sciences (1990, p. 105). Incorporating some of the cognitive research on social scientific problem solving conducted by Voss, Tyler, and Yengo (1983), she argues that think-aloud protocols can provide the basis for diagrams representing students' schemata.

Torney-Purta's contributions are closely related to cognitive research on other disciplines within social studies, including research on the development of children's understanding of economics, politics, and social institutions and stratification and mobility (Carretero & Voss, 1994). Operating in a field initially shaped by Piaget, and attempting to theorize children's progression in these domains, cognitive researchers often use the notion of stages of growth, though not uncritically. They attempt to define stages and to identify developmental, environmental, and instructional factors that contribute to or retard development. Such cognitive research may well be a prerequisite or corequisite for research on teaching and for research-based curricular reform.

The links among a definition of a discipline, conceptions of disciplinary reasoning, cognitive research on young people's learning, and research on teaching the discipline are explicitly drawn by Gregg and Leinhardt (1994) in their major review of research in geography education. If this review provides a model for the corequisites of research on teaching school subjects (and I believe it does), then it also provides some insight into the reasons why research on social studies teaching per se remains so underdeveloped. The authors take on the thorny problem of defining the "core knowledge structures [of geography] in terms of principles and concepts, as well as in terms of actions that geographers perform" (p. 317). Despite their broad definition of geography (not broad enough, albeit, to introduce the kinds of concerns raised by Gregory, 1994), they note the paucity of research both on learning and on teaching geography, other than that focused on reading maps, including a "vast literature" on teaching map skills (Gregg & Leinhardt, 1994, pp. 330, 344). Written before the publication of *Geography for Life: National Geography Standards* (Geography Edu-

cation National Standards Project, 1994), Gregg and Leinhardt summarize critiques of their precursor, the five themes of the Geography Education National Implementation Project (1987, 1989), but note the relative absence of empirical research on their effectiveness for informing geography teaching and learning. "What is needed," they suggest, "is a way of helping teachers acquire both the core epistemological themes and concepts of geography and knowledge about the problems that students face as learners. Without this kind of understanding of what geography is supposed to teach, the five themes are of limited use" (Gregg & Leinhardt, 1994, p. 350).

Research in the teaching of economics has a comparable profile. An institutional, publication (*Journal of Economic Education*), and research infrastructure that includes both economists and educators, have enabled progress toward defining both characteristics of economic thinking and some core concepts in the field (Schug & Walstad, 1991, p. 412). At the same time, there is a small but growing body of research on children's economic ideas (e.g., Berti & Bombi, 1988). Perhaps predictably, the research on teaching economics remains dominated almost exclusively by quantitative methodologies, much of it based on a data set generated as the National Assessment of Economic Education (Becker, Greene, & Rosen, 1990). Multiple choice tests and surveys remain the instruments of choice. They have shown that the teacher makes a difference in students' economics test performance (beyond differences in student abilities, school, etc.) but little about what teachers actually do to make a difference (Bosshardt & Watts, 1994). Bosshardt and Watts (1994, p. 205) did show that the most effective teachers in elementary and junior high schools taught more concentrated units on economics rather than infusing economic concepts throughout the year. And Becker, Greene, and Rosen (1990, p. 234) detected a positive correlation between teachers' knowledge of economics and student learning. "Clearly," they concluded, "there is more to learn about the role of teachers in economic education." Schug and Walstad (1991, pp. 416–417) located no studies involving formal observations of the teaching of economics at the elementary or secondary school levels and recommended that "more effort be devoted to observing actual instruction." They suggested that studies be undertaken to examine the effectiveness of particular modes of instruction in teaching particular economic ideas at particular grade levels, for example, "What analogies best illustrate the concept of GNP to students at Grade 11?" (p. 317). The groundwork for such studies is laid through the existence of a disciplinary core of economics, even if economics educators have not yet taken up the challenge.

Researchers like Gregg and Leinhardt, Carretero and Voss, Torney-Purta, and others discussed above use cognitive approaches to teaching and learning in relation to concepts and procedures embedded in the practices of the social science disciplines. Their disciplinary frameworks stand in contrast to much of the social studies literature. Discussing knowledge acquisition in the social studies, for example, Martorella (1991, p. 371) argued that disciplines are irrelevant, since "disciplinary parameters normally do not parallel the patterns of data construction that learners employ in their knowledge acquisition. . . ." While it is certainly the case that children follow other than disciplinary practices in thinking about the world or solving problems, it is also true that the most powerful conceptual, theoretical, and procedural tools for thinking about, talking about, and acting on politics, economics, international relations or social phenomena have been developed through the academic disciplines. Without those tools, children must rely on their intuitive understandings, subject to misconceptions, rigidly applied algorithms, stereotypes, and simplifications (Gardner, 1991, p. 151).

Hahn (1996a) built upon the strengths of political socialization research, though she was less cautious than Harwood in concluding the strong effects of classroom climate. Moreover, she and a large group of social studies educators have attempted to parlay the substantial research on political socialization into a rationale for the far more ephemeral "issues-centered education" (Evans & Saxe, 1996). In her review of research on the latter, Hahn (1996a) defined it as "a teaching approach that uses social issues to emphasize reflective and often controversial questions in contemporary and historic contexts as the heart of social studies," drawing links to Quillen and Hanna's (1948) "problems approach," Hunt and Metcalf's (1955) "reflective inquiry," and Oliver and Shaver's (1966) "jurisprudential approach" (p. 25; see Evans, Newmann, & Saxe, 1996; also compare issues-centered education to problem-based learning, Savoie, 1995). While admitting that "the research base for issues-centered instruction relies on studies of an amorphous dynamic 'independent variable,'" her review was nevertheless presented as support for this conception of social studies. "Remarkably," she claimed, "the research reviewed in this chapter stands in stark contrast to [the] negative litany [of most social studies research]. . . . it reveals that issues-centered social studies instruction, in particular . . . holds much promise" (Hahn, 1996b, p. 26).

Hahn identified three aspects of teaching that were required for issues-centered education and that were investigated by researchers: content, pedagogy, and climate. In issues-centered education, content should include diverse positions; the tasks provided for students should encourage them to research, discuss, and present in such a way that differing views confront each other; and the classroom climate should be open and supportive of conflict, diversity, and the expression of diverse views. In a section on characteristics of issues-centered classes and teachers, Hahn reviewed five studies. Only two actually used "issues" or "conflict" as a framework for the study. The other three studies examined pedagogical content knowledge in the discipline of history, using theoretical frameworks based directly on Shulman's research program. Thus, while controversial issues, active students, and an open climate did characterize these classrooms, the researchers themselves had conceptualized their studies around a theoretical framework that went considerably beyond these aspects of teaching (in contrast, see Rossi, 1993, 1995).

Though Fine (1993) does not articulate the problem in the same way, the links among content, pedagogy, and climate are present in her study of conflicts in a diverse seventh-eighth grade class during their engagement with a study of the Holocaust "Facing History and Ourselves," used as a springboard to discuss various related contemporary issues. After daily classroom visits over a 4-month period, she was able to paint a finely grained portrait of the classroom interactions. Although she observed, alternatively, subordination and privilege among the students, she concluded that students were learning to handle the difficulties of ambiguity and conflicting viewpoints, without succumbing to either indoctrination or moral relativism. Fine's (1995) larger study of the same curriculum expands the research lens to set her case in the context of national political debates over education. When Wade (1992) worked in an elementary school class studying human rights, she also examined students' peer relations. Though she found increased understanding and interest in human rights issues as a result of the teaching, there was no significant change in students' peer relations.

However important the issues of classroom climate and intergroup relations, there are dangers (for researchers) associated with conceptualizing these as part of the subject matter of social studies. In a guest-edited theme issue of *Theory into Practice,* Bickmore (1997) examines conflict and conflict resolution per se, both in the social studies classroom and beyond. In her lead article, she presents two cases of conflict resolution. The first was an extracurricular peer mediation program, "Anti-Violence," whose training process and school impact she assessed in two elementary schools and a middle school. On the basis of observations and interviews, she concludes that there was less violence and students took more responsibility for handling problems in the three schools. The article juxtaposes this program with two social studies classrooms where conflict was introduced as a part of the academic curriculum. The two teachers "believed that democracy (and thus democratic education) thrives on conflict" (Bickmore, 1997, p. 5). According to Bickmore, conflict was introduced into the classroom in three ways: through current events involving conflict, through historical problems involving contrasting viewpoints, and through the active participation of all students in discussing cultural and ideological differences. "Directly and indirectly, Tom Clark's students were taught that human history is a dynamic and conflictual process in which all of them were already participants. They practiced, and (importantly) were tested and graded upon, citizenship behavior based on inquiry and reasoning" (Bickmore, 1997, p. 7). The teachers used straw votes and affirmed "that each person's opinion was valid" (Bickmore, 1997, p. 6).

Bickmore's two-faceted study links curricular concerns in the classroom to problems of violence confronting students outside of the classroom. However worthy each of these activities, her use of the concept of conflict to link two disparate phenomena needs scrutiny. Outside of the classroom, the central aim was to mediate school conflicts in the interests of resolving them nonviolently. Within the classroom, controversy is part of an epistemological project, a contribution to the growth of knowledge. In this context, mediation as a means of resolving differences is irrelevant, if not counterproductive. Rather, the classroom should attempt, for example, to provide clarification of good grounds for holding a position, articulation of assumptions lying behind a particular position, and the development of relevant evidence to support a position. The use of straw votes and the affirmation of everyone's opinion as valid do not move this essentially epistemological project forward, however much they may "enhance individual students' opportunities to practice managing conflict" (p. 8). Looking for and stimulating "conflict" and "issues" should be widespread as researchers attempt to identify and promote thoughtful classes. On the one hand, they are necessary for building knowledge. On the other hand, they are not sufficient (see Bickmore, 1991).

Issues of inclusion and equity sprawl across the same divide that Bickmore tried to span. On the one hand, they present pressing issues at the level of school policy; on the other hand, they are (or should be) on the curricular agenda for teachers of social studies. To what degree has social studies research been transformed by concerns of inclusion? How have questions about ethnicity, gender, class, and race broadened or changed the kinds of questions asked about the nature of student-teacher interactions, classroom dynamics, classroom climate, and the departmental context? In educational research in general, of course, these questions have received considerable attention in recent years. Again, for the purposes of this chapter, the question concerns research on teaching social studies.

A substantial literature, much of it focused on history education, advocates a more inclusive social studies curriculum. In respect to the issue of gender, Tetreault defined a simple scheme for categorizing curriculum and teaching, which she called "feminist phase theory" (Tetreault, 1997; compare Scott, 1988). The progression starts with male-defined curriculum and moves through contribution curriculum, bifocal curriculum, mad women's curriculum to gender-balanced curriculum. Tetreault cautioned against seeing the scheme as a simple linear progression, and yet the analysis is clearly a look backward from the stance of the gender-balanced curriculum, which Maher and Tetreault (1994) explored in depth at the post-secondary level. Other feminist theorists have attempted to reconceptualize "citizenship" and to rethink the boundaries between public and private in such a way as to transform fundamentally the aims of social studies (Martin, 1992; Noddings, 1992). But there is little if any evidence of impact beyond theoretical debates; there exists little research on "feminist classrooms" in elementary or high school social studies (see Bernard-Powers, 1995; Singer, 1995).

Continuing to investigate questions of political socialization, Hahn (1996b) brought the lens of gender to a review of this aspect of social studies teaching and learning. She noted that "almost no research on gender and political learning has been reported in the social studies research literature" (Hahn, 1996a, p. 9). She found a preponderance of existing studies showing male students demonstrating a higher level of knowledge and interest in the world of politics. At the same time, a few large-scale studies showed no gender differences. Existing studies revealed no gender differences in respect to students' sense of trust and political efficacy, whereas several large-scale studies showed girls as more supportive than boys of the idea of women as politicians. Most significant for the purposes of this chapter were Hahn's observations about the research on teaching: "Although some authors suggest that the content of social studies classes might contribute to gender differences in political attitudes and to future voters' support of women in political office, little research is available that addresses this hypothesis" (Hahn, 1996a, p. 15).

Hahn's own study of students in two civics classes, reported in the same article, draws a profile of political attitudes and behavior roughly similar across the gender divide. Moreover, in these classes, "gender simply was not dealt with as a political issue, nor was the role of women in politics explored in either class" (Hahn, 1996a, p. 23). Even where their textbook provided material and opportunity for the discussion of gender and politics, the topic was bypassed by the teachers (one male and one female). This absence suggests a large and fruitful set of research questions on the impact of various approaches to (and neglect of) the issue of gender and politics on students' attitudes.

In transforming social studies through racial and ethnic inclusion, we can look beyond theoretical literature to the National Council for Social Studies' policy document, "Curriculum Guidelines for Multicultural Education" (NCSS, 1992). A policy statement suggests two things: It indicates that there may be sufficient support or consensus to bring the policy to publication and that, until conflicting or negating policies are published, it may exercise some influence in the field. To what degree, in what ways, and with what impact multicultural education has actually been incorporated into social studies classes can only be ascertained through research reports. To what degree new teaching practices have had an impact on students' knowledge, beliefs, and activities, again, can only be answered through empirical research. As Banks (1991, p. 459) noted, there is a paucity of research describing these effects.

In Canada, though there are insistent calls for more research, there are also annual research reviews that summarize "the state of the art" (McLeod, 1993, 1995, 1996). The overarching orientation of the studies is the assessment of racial prejudice—either of students or of teachers—and of programs for its reduction. Much of the research is quasi-experimental, revolving around the effects of multicultural or antiracist treatments of various student and teacher populations. This quantitative research approach is exemplified by McGregor and Ungerleider's (1993) meta-analysis of research on programs for teachers. Perhaps most troubling in the latter was the finding of 28% negative effect sizes across the 19 studies they examined: A substantial number of the interventions intended to reduce racial prejudice produced the opposite effect. Subsequent volumes in the series include diverse studies but focus on language programs as one aspect of multiculturalism (McLeod, 1995) and on changes in Canadian multicultural policy and the impact of these changes on schools and classrooms (McLeod, 1996).

Like Tetreault (1997), Banks and Banks (1995) proposed a hierarchical framework of multicultural curriculum reform, from "contributions," through "additive" and "transformation," to an "action approach." Like Tetreault's scheme, this framework provides a descriptive categorization, within which research might take place (Mehan, Okamoto, Lintz, & Wills, 1995). Whether it can provide anything more analytically potent remains unproven.

Part III: For a Transformed Social Studies

The findings of Shaver, Davis, and Helburn (1980) about teaching social studies might be used, with minimal revision, as a guide to the current malaise in the field:

1. Knowing for the student is largely a matter of having information, and the demonstration of the knowledge frequently involves being able to reproduce the language of the text in class discussions or on tests (p. 6).

2. On the whole, social studies courses are not organized sequentially; one social studies course is rarely "more advanced" than another (p. 7).
3. The teachers' view of the textbook as authoritative undoubtedly stands in the way of their involving students in inquiry. Another factor is that they are not likely to be model inquirers themselves (p. 8).
4. The teacher's beliefs and the demands of the school as a social system are largely incompatible with the norms of the university scholarship system and with the norms of teaching espoused by trainers of teachers (p. 11).

Other than being so constant over the past 20 years (see, e.g., Jenness, 1990; Sears, 1994, p. 33), the other notable aspect of this list is how closely related the problems are. Underlying each is an impoverished conception of knowledge as recall and recitation of information. In number 1, the implication is that recall and recitation demonstrates "knowing." Knowledge here is simply remembering information, in much the same sense that we might "know" someone's phone number.

Number 2 follows from the view of knowledge uncovered in number 1. If knowledge is merely information (to be believed simply because the textbook or the teacher said it), then taking additional courses can serve only the ends of accumulating more information. Number 3 is part of the same epistemology. The textbook, the source of "knowledge," is viewed as a compendium of unquestioned facts. Number 4 tells us that the "university scholarship system" and trainers of teachers are after something different, that is., knowledge as understanding. The nature of social studies "knowledge," as found by Shaver, Davis, and Helburn (1980) was largely consistent across student tasks, student understandings, teachers' understandings, and curriculum sequencing.

In the years since 1980, social studies educators, though well aware of these problems, have, as we have seen, been unable to develop a robust conception of their school subject that would convincingly address these problems, despite important, and sometimes large-scale efforts. The Shulman research program has led researchers away from social studies altogether, toward definitions of school subjects more closely aligned to the disciplines. Newmann and others have defined the aims of social studies in ways that fail to distinguish them from the goals of all school subjects. A leading researcher can still affirm the following as a "basic principle of curriculum construction": "Content is not included as a self-justifying end in itself; instead, content is selected as a means of accomplishing larger purposes and goals. Whatever coherence social studies curricula possess is rooted in these larger purposes and goals" (Brophy, 1990, p. 4). If "content" is merely information (i.e., the inert knowledge observed by Shaver, Davis, & Helburn, 1980), and only if so, then this statement makes sense. But if content is deep knowledge and understanding, then it is a troubling assertion. Indeed, the statement is a reflection of epistemological trouble in the field.

A major theme in social studies education is the search for depth, for engagement, for understanding, for "higher-order thinking," for promoting teaching that goes beyond the dominance of factual memorization, recall, and recitation as its dominant orientation (Perkins, 1992). For reasons that go beyond the scope of this review, many social studies researchers have not taken seriously the disciplinary tools the use of which make higher-order thinking possible. They prefer instead to grapple with generic constructs like higher-order thinking; critical thinking; and reflective, transformative and issues-based teaching.

The nature of social studies knowledge thus lies close to the core of the malaise. Armento (1991), Stanley (1991, 1992), Thornton (1994), Longstreet (1990), Banks (1995), Cherryholmes (1991), and Popkewitz and St. Maurice (1991), among others, have called for the incorporation into social studies research of the issues and insights raised by new epistemological movements. In this section, I explore what it might mean to do so, in order to shed light on some of the limitations of social studies theory and research over the past 10 years, and suggest some possibilities for the future. How might the intellectual challenges that have swept academic humanities and social sciences push social studies researchers toward a deeper and richer conception of the knowledge that should lie at the core of the subject?

At the time that social studies was being formed in progressive America, the word "social" captured the imagination of both academics and reformers: "Sociology" and the other young social sciences dwelled on "social" bonds; social work was born out of charity work; campaigns for social insurance, social efficiency, and social welfare gathered strength; and "social studies" had an attractive ring to the reform ear (Hertzberg, 1989; Lybarger, 1980, 1987; Rodgers, 1982; Seixas, 1987). Indeed, Rodgers (1982) considers concern with the language of the "social" one of the defining marks of Progressive ideology. Liberally employed as it was, it provided an implicit critique of laissez-faire individualism, emphasizing interdependence from psychology to economics to politics.

Today, "cultural" is in comparable fashion, and it bears an analogous (though different) message. Because the concept of "culture" entails examination of peoples' ways of making meaning, the introduction of the cultural across the humanities and social sciences signals a new level of epistemological self-consciousness. At one time the defining concept of anthropology, "culture" is now central to new work across the disciplines, from the "new cultural history" (Hunt, 1989), to psychology (e.g., Bruner, 1996) to cultural studies, which Giroux (1994, p. 278) enthusiastically calls "about the hottest thing in humanities and social-science research right now" (see Dirks, Eley, & Ortner, 1994; During, 1993; Grossberg, Nelson, & Treichler, 1992). While the "social" deals with problems of interdependence in the world out there, without necessarily examining how we know that world, the "cultural" raises questions about the relationship between the knower and the known. Whose meaning are we talking about? What is beautiful (or true or real) in the eye of which beholder? These questions thread back and forth across the academic disciplines building on concerns of "the social," but adding a now-inescapable layer of epistemological self-consciousness to "social" inquiry. These movements have profound implications not only for academic knowledge, but also for the relationship between academic knowledge and the world beyond, including schools (Kernan, 1997; Readings, 1996). Social studies educators might draw out these implications in order to construct a more sophisticated, potent understanding of knowledge for teaching and learning in the schools.

Two features stand out as we compare new academic trends in the humanities and social sciences in the university and the school subject of social studies. First, they attempt to address and encompass roughly the same realms of human knowledge. But the former do so with an epistemological self-consciousness that has typically been absent in social studies teaching. The new humanities and social sciences thus raise, as an integral part of any investigation, questions about the nature of their knowledge; the relationship between knowledge and power; and the contingent, positioned, and historicized nature of all knowledge claims. Their epistemological practices may help to disrupt constructively the impoverished notion of knowledge as information that pervades social studies practice and theory. Secondly, comparing academic humanities and social sciences with school social studies necessarily raises questions about universities and schools and about the nature of knowledge generated in each. While social studies researchers will find a surface familiarity in academics' move toward interdisciplinarity, the problems raised by the latter will also force new and potentially deeper confrontations with the nature of disciplinary knowledge.

Because academic inquiry always presupposes public scrutiny and critique, it has traditionally made public the grounds for its claims, the sources of its knowledge. The new movements in humanities and social sciences add consciousness of the position of the inquirer as an important aspect of contextualizing knowledge claims. In the best of social studies classes, there are not only textbooks, maps, displays, films, videos, but also websites, guest speakers, field trips, simulations, role plays, and so on, all of which provide representations of the world. A transformed social studies would turn all of these from mere sources of information, to texts to be interpreted as active forces in cultural construction. Good social studies teachers discuss the "bias" of sources, but the focus in a transformed social studies would be different. Rather than eliminating bias or biased sources, the object would be to study the perspective that is embodied in every textual source, in an attempt to see not only what the text says, but what it does, how it works. (Such an approach would simultaneously demand and promote the introduction of a much broader range of textual representations into the classroom.) The result would help students begin to achieve an understanding of what Giroux (1994, p. 279) has called the "critical relationship among culture, knowledge, and power."

Central to the new epistemological self-consciousness are the concepts of text and discourse (e.g., Berkhofer, 1995; Luke, 1995). Bowen and Shapiro (1997, p. vii) remind us that "close reading and interpretation of texts" lies close to the core of humanistic scholarship. Nor can such reading be dismissed as merely "academic." Luke (1995, pp. 6–7) reminds us of the pedagogical imperative to teach about texts:

> The 21st century citizen will work in media-, text-, and symbol-saturated environments. For the unemployed, underemployed, and employed alike, a great deal of service and information-based work,

consumption, and leisure depends on their capacities to construct, control, and manipulate texts and symbols." (Allan Luke, 1995, pp. 6–7)

We can think of "texts" in the broadest sense: representations of meaning in a relatively permanent form (Wells, 1990, p. 370). Yet a text's relative permanence in form does not imply a fixed meaning. No representation is an unmediated, neutral, and transparent lens through which to view the world. Luke (1995, p. 18) calls language "refractive rather than . . . transparent, . . . mediating interpreting, and reconstructing versions of the natural and social world, identity and social relations" (see also Luke & Walton, 1995). Nor can any reading be free from the discursive frames of the reader. As social studies students and teachers examine textual representations of other times, other people, other cultures, we need to be aware of how far away we are from that which is represented. We need constantly to ask about the circumstances of the textual construction, as well as about our own discursive positions as interpreters.

The texts we read both construct, and are constructed by, their contexts. As Giroux (1994, p. 300) notes, citing Stuart Hall, "it is not that there is a world outside, 'out there,' which exists free of the discourse of representation. What is 'out there' is, in part, constituted by how it is represented." Asking teachers and students to interrogate texts in this way brings classroom, school, students, teachers—and researchers—into a new, self-conscious interplay with the world outside. Furthermore, it changes the parameters for choosing the kinds of texts most appropriate for the classroom, from those whose authors are invisible and seemingly positionless (and thus most difficult to interrogate and engage), to those written from clear positions and perspectives. In history, for example, textbooks would have a much smaller role, and primary sources, fiction, art, and film a much larger one (but not, obviously, simply as the "story well told").

Claims about the interplay of knowledge and power challenge any easy formula for increased curricular representation of women or people of color (Banks, 1995; Bickmore, 1993; Noddings, 1992). Here, the "other" world, which has been the object of study in (the best of) social studies, looks back at the platform from which that gaze was constructed. Thus, bell hooks (1992) articulates what "Whiteness" looks like in the Black imagination (compare with Bhabha, 1994). Furthermore, the purportedly objective or transparent texts, which provided the lens for the White, male gaze on the rest of the world, now, themselves become the subject of analysis (e.g., Said, 1993; Willinsky, 1998).

Twenty years ago, in the wake of the "new social studies," a notion of the "social science disciplines" as objective, disengaged, value-free, strongly boundaried academic pursuits based on science-like hypothesis testing, was built into the social studies literature. The legacy of this understanding of social science continues, each time the Barr, Barth, and Shermis typology (or its recent variations) is redeployed. Given the upheaval in the humanities and social sciences during the same period, this characterization leads in entirely mistaken directions (e.g., Eagleton, 1983; Novick, 1988; Polkinghorne, 1988). Whitson and Stanley (1996) break down some of the barriers erected by social studies literature, around the "social science disciplines" as if they were ends in themselves or simply a part of a world of academe entirely separate from the rest of the world. Whitson and Stanley (1996, p. 330) urge that we understand "disciplinary capabilities as aspects of practical competence," which enable people to deal most thoughtfully and knowledgeably with the world. In their insights about "the condition of postmodernity," the transformed disciplines offer insights and perspectives that social studies can ill-afford to ignore (Harvey, 1989).

The trend toward interdisciplinary exploration in the academy sounds similar to the notions that lie behind integrated social studies, and yet there are important differences. Academic disciplines serve as knowledge communities: they share a history, a set of achievements, a set of methods for generating new knowledge. However contested and shifting each of these is, new movements are never accomplished without reference to what has gone before. The very ability to construct such references is made possible by the existence of a disciplinary literature and community. Indeed, when Giroux (1994, p. 299) advocates "post-disciplinary studies," he points, in spite of himself, to the degree to which the new studies have been based upon transformations within the disciplines themselves. Moreover, the new areas—if they survive—are likely to reconstitute themselves in discipline-like communities, since, as Stanley Fish (1994, p. 237) has argued, "the blurring of existing authoritative disciplinary lines and boundaries will only create new lines and new authorities: The interdisciplinary impulse finally . . . merely redomiciles us in enclosures that do not advertise themselves as such."

In what ways might the academic disciplines' current dynamism, self-consciousness, and sense of crisis invigorate social studies theory, research, and practice? Perhaps we can achieve a synoptic view through a review of *Reading National Geographic* (Lutz & Collins, 1993), an examination of the Third World, as constructed through the magazine. Like social studies classes, *National Geographic* presents a picture of the world beyond the school and North America. Also like social studies classes and their textual materials, *National Geographic* presents a refracted vision. Indeed, Lutz and Collins tell us, their work is a book not about the Third World at all, but about how Americans construct the Third World through their texts. Many of the dilemmas of teaching about the world are faced by the editors, writers, and photographers at the magazine: how to deal with controversy, how much negativity its consumers can handle, how to present coherent stories of ill-defined phenomena. Lutz and Collins offer an interpretation of the cultural product, using historical analysis of the publication, textual analysis of the photographs, and an inquiry into readers' responses to the images. Imported directly into the classroom, their view of the construction of geographic knowledge would bring students face to face, not only with questions of universality and difference, but also with the social construction of texts and of our knowledge about others. It would make possible the exploration of relationships between students and teachers in schools, between Americans and the objects of their studies, between the authors of texts and their readers, among different groups of students in the school. And the texts would be understood not

merely as reflective, but also as constructive of those relationships. If social studies had the responsibility of teaching students to read and write texts in this way, a large theoretical literature, already used for the reading of historical texts, might be mobilized (e.g., Boyarin, 1993; Heap, 1991; Langer, 1992; Wells, 1990; Wineburg, 1991; Young & Leinhardt, 1998).

These insights and conceptions might refocus the work of social studies researchers. In broad terms, I am suggesting that researchers frame their questions keeping in mind the potential of productive interactions between academic knowledge and school knowledge in the humanities and social sciences. On the one hand, this strategy seems obvious, and, on the other hand, it is radically unorthodox. For those who greet such a suggestion with the accusation that it is a call for an elitism foisted upon the schools, I respond that I am calling for drawing upon the most democratic and egalitarian (or what Banks would call transformative) currents from the contemporary academy.

Those who define social studies in terms of citizenship and decision making might object that my suggestions would turn social studies from its goals of preparing students to act in the world to teaching the reading and writing of interpretations about the world. To this objection, I would respond that the former orientation has always been mediated by the latter. The latter orientation would, however, make the interplay between language and practice and between text and world explicit and self-conscious.

As the core of the school subject, the ability of students to read and interpret various forms of text and to construct their own representations of the social world will have a very different emphasis from the content of social studies either as information (the dominant classroom practice) or as a tool for teaching democratic citizens how to make decisions (the dominant theoretical stance). This conception of the subject makes possible the construction of models of growth in students' abilities and understanding, in much the same way that history education researchers have started to do. Such a conception opens up for investigation the problems of students' reading of, for example, documentary film, historical photographs, urban landscapes, and contemporary clothing fashions. Are there more or less sophisticated readings of these texts? How do students' readings and representations compare with those of experts? What counts as progress in a students' interpretations of these texts? How do students' social locations lead to different readings? By what criteria should students' representations and performances be judged? (See Boix-Mansilla & Gardner, 1998.) These kinds of questions would allow social studies research to build on the disciplinary strengths of history and literature, with the possibility of expanding into some of the contentious arenas opened up in interplay with new work in the social sciences.

With a more workable conception of students' progress and the articulation of models of expertise, the question of knowledge for teaching would become open to investigation. The issue of pedagogical content knowledge, which has rarely been engaged by social studies researchers outside of history education, could begin to be addressed. What kinds of texts do teachers, themselves, know how to read critically? What do teachers know about teaching students how to do so? How does contextual knowledge frame teachers' reading of texts? What guides their choices of teaching texts? How and when do they challenge students; how and when do they define interpretive limits? How do they construct interpretive communities in the classroom, and what kinds of backgrounds and experiences enable them to do so? What are the possibilities for the construction of communities that include both teachers and academics? Investigation of these questions could provide important insights for teacher education and development.

Finally, insights from the new humanities and social sciences would call upon researchers to understand the texts they produce as part of the exercise of power, that is, how their own practice constructs teachers, student-teachers, and students. Such understandings should lead to critical scrutiny of teacher-researcher relations, and from such scrutiny potentially could lead to more collaborative research, as well as to other creative challenges to the traditionally separate and distinct roles of teachers and researchers.

Conclusion

The academic disciplines in the humanities and social sciences are undergoing profound change and are facing crisis, challenge, excitement, and renewal. It would be difficult to make the same statement about theory and research on the school subject that bears the closest relationship to these disciplines. Leming and Nelson (1995, p. 180) remark that "many once highly visible and influential doctoral programs in social studies education are now moribund." Reviewers of research regularly complain about the state of the field. At the same time, the related field of history education has enjoyed remarkable growth, enriched both by insights from the new historiography and by insights from cognitive and constructivist perspectives on teaching and learning. Far from being limited by the discipline of history, educators have found, as the field of history has explored its connections with literature, anthropology, and psychology, that these have posed new kinds of questions for history education research.

The field of social studies has remained too distant from the academic ferment that might give it life. The insights of the new academic humanities and social science, if they could be appropriately expressed for schools and curricula, would draw the subject into closer relationship to the diverse and divided world outside the classroom. The critical tasks of knowledge-building take place within communities of inquiry that have largely been defined by disciplines. The recent critical work that has helped to redefine academic disciplines in the humanities and social sciences, blur their lines, and usher in cultural studies, has touched social studies education only peripherally (Leming & Nelson, 1995, p. 176). A transformed social studies would allow educators to leave behind conceptualizations of the field which have prevented full utilization of new theoretical perspectives. It would bring to the foreground the problems of knowledge, power, culture, and difference that have animated the humanities and social sciences over the past 20 years, and, along with them, the complex and theoretically rich tasks of teaching students how to read the texts that structure their lives, and write the ones that might restructure the world.

REFERENCES

Almond, G., & Verba, S. (1963). *The civic culture.* Princeton, NJ: Princeton University Press.

Alway, J. (1995). The trouble with gender: Tales of the still-missing feminist revolution in sociological theory. *Sociological Theory, 13*(3), 209–228.

Anderson, C., Avery, P. G., Pederson, P. V., Smith, E. S., & Sullivan, J. L. (1997). Divergent perspectives on citizenship education: A Q-method study and survey of social studies teachers. *American Educational Research Journal, 34*(2), 333–364.

Armento, B. (1986). Research on teaching social studies. In M. C. Wittrock (Ed.), *Handbook of research on teaching* (3rd ed., pp. 942–951). New York: Macmillan.

Armento, B. (1991). Changing conceptions of research on the teaching of social studies. In J. P. Shaver (Ed.), *Handbook of research on social studies teaching and learning* (pp. 185–196). New York: Macmillan.

Armento, B. (1996). The professional development of social studies educators. In J. Sikula, T. J. Buttery, & E. Guyton (Eds.), *Handbook of research on teacher education* (pp. 485–502). New York: Macmillan.

Avery, P. G., & Gamradt, J. A. (1991). Students' geopolitical perspectives. *Social Education, 55*(5), 320–325.

Banks, J. A. (1991). Multicultural education: Its effects on students' racial and gender role attitudes. In J. P. Shaver (Ed.), *Handbook of research on social studies teaching and learning* (pp. 459–469). New York: Macmillan.

Banks, J. A. (1993). The canon debate, knowledge construction, and multicultural education. *Educational Researcher, 22*(5), 4–14.

Banks, J. A. (1995). Transformative challenges to the social science disciplines: Implications for social studies teaching and learning. *Theory and Research in Social Education, 23*(1), 2–20.

Banks, J. A., & Banks, C. A. M. (Eds.). (1995). *Handbook of multicultural education.* New York: Macmillan.

Barr, R., Barth, J. L., & Shermis, S. S. (1977). *Defining the social studies.* Arlington, VA: National Council of Social Studies.

Barth, J. L. (1991). Disciplined thinking about social studies: A comparative study of United States, Nigerian, Egyptian, and Japanese responses. *International Journal of Social Education, 6*(2), 78–87.

Barth, J. L., & Shermis, S. S. (1970). Defining the social studies: An exploration of three traditions. *Social Education, 34,* 745–751.

Becker, W., Greene, W., & Rosen, S. (1990). Research on high school economic education. *Journal of Economic Education, 21*(3), 231–245.

Bennett, C., & Spalding, E. (1992). Teaching the social studies: Multiple approaches for multiple perspectives. *Theory and Research in Social Education, 22*(3), 263–292.

Berkhofer, R. F. (1995). *Beyond the great story: History as text and discourse.* Cambridge, MA: Harvard University Press/Belknap.

Bernard-Powers, J. (1995). Out of the cameos and into the conversation: Gender, social studies, and curriculum transformation. In J. Gaskell & J. Willinsky (Eds.), *Gender in/forms curriculum: From enrichment to transformation* (pp. 191–208). New York: Teachers College Press.

Berti, A. E., & Bombi, A. S. (1988). *The child's construction of economics.* Cambridge, UK: Cambridge University Press.

Bhabha, H. K. (1994). The other question: Stereotype, discrimination and the discourse of colonialism. In *The location of culture* (pp. 66–84). London: Routledge.

Bickmore, K. (1991). *Practicing conflict: Citizenship education in high school.* Unpublished doctoral dissertation, Stanford University, Stanford, CA.

Bickmore, K. (1993). Learning inclusion/inclusion in learning: Citizenship education for a pluralistic society. *Theory and Research in Social Education, 21*(4), 341–384.

Bickmore, K. (1997). Preparation for pluralism: Curricular and extracurricular practice with conflict resolution. *Theory into Practice, 36*(1), 3–10.

Boix-Mansilla, V., & Gardner, H. (1997). Of kinds of disciplines and kinds of understanding. *Phi Delta Kappan* (Jan.), 381–386.

Boix-Mansilla, V., & Gardner, H. (1998). What are the qualities of understanding? In M. S. Wiske (Ed.), *Teaching for understanding:*

Linking research with practice (pp. 161–196). San Francisco: Jossey-Bass.

Bosshardt, W., & Watts, M. (1994). Instructor effects in economics in elementary and junior high schools. *Journal of Economic Education, 25*(3), 195–211.

Bowen, W. G., & Shapiro, H. T. (1997). Foreword. In A. Kernan (Ed.), *What's happened to the humanities?* (pp. vii–viii). Princeton, NJ: Princeton University Press.

Boyarin, J. (Ed.). (1993). *The ethnography of reading.* Berkeley, CA: University of California Press.

Brophy, J. (1990). Teaching social studies for understanding and higher-order applications. *The Elementary School Journal, 90*(4), 351–417.

Brophy, J. (Ed.). (1993a). *Advances in research on teaching: Case studies of teaching and learning in social studies, 4.* Greenwich, CT: JAI Press.

Brophy, J. (1993b). Findings and issues: The cases viewed in context. In J. Brophy (Ed.), *Advances in research on teaching: Case studies of teaching and learning in social studies, 4* (pp. 219–232). Greenwich, CT: JAI Press.

Brown, J. E. P. (1996). *Writing in eighth-grade science and social studies classes.* Unpublished doctoral dissertation, University of Alabama, Birmingham, AL.

Bruner, J. (1996). *The culture of education.* Cambridge, MA: Harvard University Press.

Carretero, M., & Voss, J. F. (Eds.). (1994). *Cognitive and instructional processes in history and the social sciences.* Hillsdale, NJ: Lawrence Erlbaum Associates.

Cherryholmes, C. (1990). Social studies for which century? *Social Education, 54*(7), 438–446.

Cherryholmes, C. (1991). Critical research and social studies education. In J. P. Shaver (Ed.), *Handbook of research on social studies teaching and learning* (pp. 41–55). New York: Macmillan.

Chilcoat, G. W., & Ligon, J. A. (1994). Developing democratic citizens: The Mississippi Freedom Schools as a model for social studies instruction. *Theory and Research in Social Education, 22*(2), 128–175.

Clifford, J., & Marcus, G. (1986). *Writing culture: The politics and poetics of ethnography.* Berkeley, CA: University of California Press.

Cobb, S. L., & Foeller, W. H. (1992). An organizational analysis of teacher attitudes about teaching high school economics. *Theory and Research in Social Education, 20*(4), 421–439.

Cornbleth, C. (Ed.). (1986). *An invitation to research in social education.* Washington, DC: National Council for the Social Studies, Bulletin No. 77.

Crismore, A. (1991). Rethinking language, rhetoric, knowledge, and social studies: Classroom implications. *Southern Social Studies Journal, 16*(2), 49–78.

Cuban, L. (1984). *How teachers taught: Constancy and change in American classrooms, 1890–1980.* New York: Longman.

Cuban, L. (1991). History of teaching in social studies. In J. P. Shaver (Ed.), *Handbook of research on social studies teaching and learning* (pp. 197–209). New York: Macmillan.

Davis, O. L., Jr. (1991). Citizenship education as the central purpose of the social studies: The heavy load of a dead metaphor. *The International Journal of Social Education, 6*(2), 33–36.

de Certeau, M. (1988). *The writing of history* (Tom Conley, Trans.). New York: Columbia University Press.

Dirks, N. B., Eley, G., & Ortner, S. B. (Eds.). (1994). *Culture/power/history: A reader in contemporary social theory.* Princeton NJ: Princeton University Press.

During, S. (Ed.). (1993). *The cultural studies reader.* London: Routledge.

Eagleton, T. (1983). *Literary theory: An introduction.* Minneapolis, MN: University of Minnesota Press.

Egan, K. (1983). Social studies and the erosion of education. *Curriculum Inquiry, 13*(2), 195–214.

Engle, S. H. (1990). The Commission report and citizenship education. *Social Education, 54*(7), 431–434.

Engle, S. H., & Ochoa, A. (1988). *Education for democratic citizenship: Decision making in the social studies.* New York: Teachers College Press.

Evans, R. (1993). Ideology and the teaching of history: Purposes, practices, and student beliefs. In J. Brophy (Ed.), *Advances in research on teaching: Case studies of teaching and learning in social studies, 4* (pp. 179–218). Greenwich, CT: JAI Press.

Evans, R., Newmann, F., & Saxe, D. W. (1996). Defining issues-centered education. In R. Evans & D. W. Saxe (Eds.), *Handbook on teaching social issues* (pp. 2–5). Washington, DC: National Council for Social Studies, Bulletin No. 93.

Evans, R., & Saxe, D. W. (Eds.). (1996). *Handbook on teaching social issues.* Washington, DC: National Council for Social Studies, Bulletin No. 93.

Fenstermacher, G. (1994). The knower and the known: The nature of knowledge in research on teaching. *Review of Research in Education, 20,* 3–56.

Fine, M. (1993). "You can't just say that the only ones who can speak are those who agree with your position": Political discourse in the classroom. *Harvard Educational Review, 63*(4), 412–433.

Fine, M. (1995). *Habits of mind: Struggling over values in America's classrooms.* San Francisco: Jossey-Bass.

Fish, S. (1994). Being interdisciplinary is so very hard to do. In *There's no such thing as free speech* (pp. 231–242). New York: Oxford University Press.

Fiske, J. (1989). *Reading the popular.* Boston: Unwin Hyman.

Gagnon, P., & the Bradley Commission on History in the Schools (Eds.). (1989). *Historical literacy: The case for history in American education.* New York: Macmillan.

Gardner, H. (1991). *The unschooled mind.* New York: Basic Books.

Gardner, H., & Boix-Mansilla, V. (1994). Teaching for understanding in the disciplines—and beyond. *Teachers College Record, 96*(2), 198–218.

Gaskell, J., & Willinsky, J. (Eds.). (1995). *Gender in/forms curriculum: From enrichment to transformation.* New York: Teachers College Press.

Geography Education National Implementation Project. (1987). *K–6 geography: Themes, key ideas, and learning opportunities.* Indiana, PA: National Council for Geographic Education, Indiana University of Pennsylvania.

Geography Education National Implementation Project. (1989). *7–12 geography: Themes, key ideas, and learning opportunities.* Indiana, PA: National Council for Geographic Education, Indiana University of Pennsylvania.

Geography Education Standards Project (1994). *Geography for life: National geography standards.* Washington, DC: National Geographic.

Giroux, H. A. (1988). *Schooling and the struggle for public life: Critical pedagogy in the modern age.* Minneapolis, MN: University of Minnesota Press.

Giroux, H. A. (1994). Doing cultural studies: Youth and the challenge of pedagogy. *Harvard Educational Review, 64*(3), 278–308.

Giroux, H. A. (1995). Is there a place for cultural studies in colleges of education? *Review of Education/Pedagogy/Cultural Studies, 17*(2), 127–142.

Goodlad, J. (1984). *A place called school.* New York: McGraw-Hill.

Gordon, D. (1988). Education as text: The varieties of educational hiddenness. *Curriculum Inquiry, 18*(4), 425–449.

Grant, S. G. (1996). Locating authority over content and pedagogy: Cross-current influences on teachers' thinking and practice. *Theory and Research in Social Education, 24*(3), 237–272.

Grant, T. J. (1995). *Preservice teacher planning: An analysis of the journey from learner to teacher in mathematics and social studies.* Unpublished doctoral dissertation, University of Delaware, Newark, DE.

Gregg, M., & Leinhardt, G. (1994). Geography: An example of epistemology and education. *Review of Educational Research, 64*(2), 311–361.

Gregory, D. (1994). *Geographical imaginations.* Cambridge, MA: Blackwell.

Gross, R., & Dynneson, T. (Eds.). (1991). *Social science perspectives on citizenship education.* New York: Teachers College Press.

Grossberg, L., Nelson, C., & Treichler, P. (Eds.). (1992). *Cultural studies.* London: Routledge.

Grossman, P. L. (1991). *The making of a teacher: Teacher knowledge and teacher education.* New York: Teachers College Press.

Grossman, P. L., & Stodolsky, S. S. (1994). Considerations of content and the circumstances of secondary school teaching. *Review of Research in Education, 20,* 179–122.

Grossman, P. L., & Yerian, S. Y. (1992). *Pedagogical content knowledge: The research agenda.* Paper presented at the annual meeting of the American Educational Research Association, San Francisco, CA.

Gulbenkian Commission on the Restructuring of the Social Sciences. (1996). *Open the social sciences: Report of the Gulbenkian Commission on the restructuring of the social sciences.* Stanford, CA: Stanford University Press.

Hahn, C. L. (1996a). Gender and political learning. *Theory and Research in Social Education, 24*(1), 8–35.

Hahn, C. L. (1996b). Research on issues-centered social studies. In R. W. Evans & D. W. Saxe (Eds.), *Handbook on teaching social issues* (pp. 25–41). Washington, DC: National Council for Social Studies, Bulletin No. 93.

Harvey, D. (1989). *The condition of postmodernity.* Cambridge, MA: Blackwell.

Harwood, A. M. (1991). *Social studies classroom climates and students' political attitudes: Views from three high school civics classes.* Unpublished doctoral dissertation, Emory University, Atlanta, GA.

Harwood, A. M. (1992). Classroom climate and civic education in secondary social studies research: Antecedents and findings. *Theory and Research in Social Education, 22*(1), 47–86.

Heap, J. L. (1991). Reading as cultural activities: Enabling and reflective texts. *Curriculum Inquiry, 21*(1), 11–39.

Hertzberg, H. (1989). History and progressivism: A century of reform proposals. In P. Gagnon & the Bradley Commission on History in the Schools (Eds.), *Historical literacy: The case for history in American education* (pp. 69–99). New York: Macmillan.

Himmelfarb, G. (1989). Some reflections on the new history. *American Historical Review, 94*(3), 661–670.

Himmelfarb, G. (1994). *On looking into the abyss: Untimely thoughts on culture and society.* New York: Vintage.

hooks, b. (1988). *Talking back: Thinking feminist, thinking black.* Toronto, Canada: Between the Lines.

hooks, b. (1992). Representing whiteness in the black imagination. In L. Grossberg, C. Nelson, & P. Treichler (Eds.), *Cultural studies* (pp. 338–346). London: Routledge.

Hope, W. (1996). It's time to transform social studies teaching. *The Social Studies, 87*(4), 149–151.

Hughes, A. S., & Sears, A. M. (1996). Macro and micro level aspects of a programme of citizenship education research. *Canadian and International Education, 25*(2), 17–30.

Hunt, L. (Ed.). (1989). *The new cultural history.* Berkeley, CA: University of California Press.

Hunt, M. P., & Metcalf, L. E. (1955). *Teaching high school social studies: Problems in reflective thinking and social understanding.* New York: Harper & Row.

Ichilov, O. (Ed.). (1990). Introduction. In *Political socialization, citizenship education, and democracy* (pp. 1–9). New York: Teachers College Press.

Janzen, R. (1995). The social studies conceptual dilemma: Six contemporary approaches. *The Social Studies, 86,* 134–140.

Jenness, D. (1990). *Making sense of social studies.* New York: Macmillan.

Keller, C. W. (1991). It is time to abolish the mythology that the social studies constitute a discipline. *International Journal of Social Education, 5*(1), 69–77.

Kernan, A. (Ed.). (1997). *What's happened to the humanities?* Princeton, NJ: Princeton University Press.

Kon, J. H. (1995). Teachers' curricular decision making in response to a new social studies textbook. *Theory and Research in Social Education, 23*(2), 88–120.

Lampert, M. (1990). When the problem is not the question and the solution is not the answer. *American Educational Research Journal, 27*(1), 29–63.

Langer, J. A. (1992). Speaking of knowing: Conceptions of learning in academic subjects. In A. Herrington & C. Moran (Eds.), *Writing, teaching, and learning in the disciplines* (pp. 69–85). New York: The Modern Language Association of America.

Langer, J. A., & Applebee, A. N. (1988). Speaking of knowing: Conceptions of learning in academic subjects. *Final report, academic learning in high school subjects.* U.S. Department of Education, OERI, Grant G008610967.

Leming, J. S. (1992). The influence of contemporary issues curricula on school-age youth. *Review of Research in Education, 18,* 111–161.

Leming, J. S. (1995). Reflections on thirty years of moral education research. *Moral Education Forum, 20*(3), 1–9.

Leming, J. S., & Nelson, M. (1995). A citation analysis of the *Handbook of research on social studies teaching and learning. Theory and Research in Social Education, 23*(2), 169–182.

Levstik, L. (1993). Building a sense of history in a first-grade classroom. In J. Brophy (Ed.), *Advances in research on teaching: Case studies of teaching and learning in social studies, 4* (pp. 1–32). Greenwich, CT: JAI Press.

Little, J. W. (1990). Conditions of professional development in secondary schools. In M. W. McLaughlin, J. E. Talbert, & N. Bascia (Eds.), *The contexts of teaching in secondary schools* (pp. 187–223). New York: Teachers College Press.

Longstreet, W. (1990). The social studies: In search of an epistemology. *The Social Studies, 81*(6), 244–248.

Longstreet, W. (1991). Reflections on a discipline of the social studies. *The International Journal of Social Education, 6*(2), 25–32.

Luke, A. (1995). Text and discourse in education: An introduction to critical discourse analysis. *Review of Research in Education, 21,* 3–48.

Luke, A., & Walton, C. (1995). Critical reading: Teaching and assessing. In L. W. Anderson (Ed.), *International encyclopedia of teaching and teacher education* (2nd ed., pp. 467–471). Oxford, UK: Elsevier.

Lutz, C. A., & Collins, J. L. (1993). *Reading National Geographic.* Chicago: University of Chicago Press.

Lybarger, M. B. (1980). The political context of the social studies: Creating a constituency for municipal reform. *Theory and Research in Social Education, 8*(3), 1–28.

Lybarger, M. B. (1987). Need as ideology: A look at the early social studies. In T. S. Popkewitz (Ed.), *The formation of the school subjects: The struggle for creating an American institution* (pp. 176–180). New York: Falmer.

Maher, F., & Tetreault, M. K. T. (1994). *The feminist classroom.* New York: Basic Books.

Makler, A. (1994). Social studies teachers' conceptions of justice. *Theory and Research in Social Education, 22*(3), 281–304.

Mani, L. (1992). Cultural theory, colonial texts: Reading eyewitness accounts of widow burning. In L. Grossberg, C. Nelson, & P. Treichler (Eds.), *Cultural studies* (pp. 392–408). London: Routledge.

Marker, G., & Mehlinger, H. D. (1992). Social studies. In P. Jackson (Ed.), *Handbook of research on curriculum* (pp. 830–851). New York: Macmillan.

Martin, J. R. (1992). *Schoolhome: Rethinking schools for changing families.* Cambridge, MA: Harvard University Press.

Martorella, P. (1985). *Elementary social studies: Developing reflective, competent, and concerned citizens.* Boston: Little, Brown.

Martorella, P. H. (1991). Knowledge and concept development in social studies. In J. P. Shaver (Ed.), *Handbook of research on social studies teaching and learning* (pp. 370–384). New York: Macmillan.

Massialas, B. (1990). The state of research in social studies: An introduction. *The Social Studies, 81*(6), 237–238.

McGregor, J., & Ungerleider, C. (1993). Multicultural and racism awareness programs for teachers: A meta-analysis of the research. In K. A. McLeod (Ed.), *Multicultural education: The state of the art national study Report #1* (pp. 59–63). Toronto, Canada: Canadian Association of Second Language Teachers.

McLeod, K. A. (Ed.). (1989). *Canada and citizenship education.* Toronto, Canada: Canadian Education Association.

McLeod, K. A. (Ed.). (1993). *Multicultural education: The state of the art national study Report #1.* Toronto, Canada: Canadian Association of Second Language Teachers.

McLeod, K. A. (Ed.). (1995). *Multicultural education: The state of the art: Studies of Canadian heritage.* Toronto, Canada: Canadian Association of Second Language Teachers.

McLeod, K. A. (Ed.). (1996). *Multicultural education: The state of the art national study Report #4.* Toronto, Canada: Canadian Association of Second Language Teachers.

McNeil, L. (1988). *Contradictions of control.* New York: Routledge.

Mehan, H., Okamoto, D., Lintz, A., & Wills, J. S. (1995). Ethnographic studies of multicultural education in classrooms and schools. In J. Banks & C. M. Banks (Eds.), *Handbook of multicultural education* (pp. 129–144). New York: Macmillan.

Menand, L. (1997). The demise of disciplinary authority. In A. Kernan (Ed.), *What's happened to the humanities?* (pp.?) Princeton, NJ: Princeton University Press.

Metcalf, L. E. (1963). Research on teaching the social studies. In N. L. Gage (Ed.), *Handbook of research on teaching* (pp. 929–965). Chicago: Rand McNally.

National Center for History in the Schools. (1994). *National standards for United States history: Exploring the American experience*. Los Angeles: Author.

National Commission on Social Studies in the Schools. (1989). *Charting a course: Social studies for the 21st century*. Washington, DC: Author.

National Commission on Social Studies in the Schools. (1991). *Voices of teachers: Report of a survey on social studies*. Dubuque, IA: Kendall/Hunt Publishing Co.

National Council for Social Studies. (1992). Curriculum guidelines for multicultural education. *Social Education, 56*(5), 274–294.

National Council for Social Studies. (1994). *Expectations of excellence: Curriculum standards for social studies*. Washington, DC: Author.

Nelson, J. L. (1990). Charting a course backward: A response to the National commission's nineteenth century social studies program. *Social Education, 54*(7), 434–437.

Nelson, J. L. (1991). Discipline, knowledge, and social education. *The International Journal of Social Education, 6*(2), 41–50.

Nelson, J. L. (1994). Contemporary social education literature: An essay review. *Theory and Research in Social Education, 22*(4), 461–481.

Nelson, L. R., & Drake, F. D. (1994). Secondary teachers' reactions to the new social studies. *Theory and Research in Social Education, 22*(1), 44–73.

Newmann, F. M. (1990a). Higher order thinking in teaching social studies: A rationale for the assessment of classroom thoughtfulness. *Journal of Curriculum Studies, 22*(1), 4156.

Newmann, F. M. (1990b). Qualities of thoughtful social studies classes: An empirical profile. *Journal of Curriculum Studies, 22*(2), 253–275.

Newmann, F. M. (1991a). Promoting higher order thinking in social studies: Overview of a study of sixteen high school departments. *Theory and Research in Social Education, 19*(4), 324–340.

Newmann, F. M. (1991b). Classroom thoughtfulness and students' higher order thinking: Common indicators and diverse social studies courses. *Theory and Research in Social Education, 19*(4), 410–433.

Noddings, N. (1992). Social studies and feminism. *Theory and Research in Social Education, 20*(3), 230–241.

Novick, P. (1988). *That noble dream: "The objectivity question" and the American historical profession*. New York: Cambridge University Press.

Oliver, D. W., & Shaver, J. P. (1966). *Teaching public issues in the high school*. Boston: Houghton Mifflin.

Onosko, J. J. (1991). Barriers to the promotion of higher order thinking. *Theory and Research in Social Education, 19*(4), 341–366.

Palonsky, S. (1993). A knowledge base for social studies teachers. *International Journal of Social Education, 7*(3), 7–23.

Parker, W. (Ed.). (1995). *Educating the democratic mind*. Albany, NY: State University of New York Press.

Perkins, D. (1992). *Smart schools: From training memories to educating minds*. New York: The Free Press.

Polkinghorne, D. E. (1988). *Narrative knowing and the human sciences*. Albany, NY: State University of New York Press.

Popkewitz, T. (1986). Paradigm and purpose. In C. Cornbleth (Ed.), *An invitation to research in social education* (pp. 10–27). Washington, DC: National Council for the Social Studies.

Popkewitz, T. S., & St. Maurice, H. (1991). Social studies education and theory: Science, knowledge, and history. In J. P. Shaver (Ed.), *Handbook of research on social studies teaching and learning* (pp. 27–40). New York: Macmillan.

Preissle-Goetz, J., & LeCompte, M. D. (1991). Qualitative research in social studies education. In J. P. Shaver (Ed.), *Handbook of research on social studies teaching and learning* (pp. 56–66). New York: Macmillan.

Quillen, I. J., & Hanna, L. A. (1948). *Education for social competence*. New York: Scott, Foresman.

Ravitch, D., & Finn, C. (1987). *What do our 17-year olds know?* New York: Harper & Row.

Readings, B. (1996). *The university in ruins*. Cambridge, MA: Harvard University Press.

Rodgers, D. T. (1982). In search of progressivism. *Reviews in American History, 10*(4), 113–132.

Rossi, J. A. (1993). *The practice of in-depth study in the secondary social studies classroom*. Unpublished doctoral dissertation, University of Wisconsin, Madison, WI.

Rossi, J. A. (1995). In-depth study in an issues-oriented social studies classroom. *Theory and Research in Social Education, 23*(2), 88–120.

Said, E. W. (1993). *Culture and imperialism*. New York: Knopf.

Savoie, J. M. (1995). *Problem based learning in social studies: Results of a field trial with adolescents*. Unpublished dissertation, University of New Brunswick, Canada.

Schug, M. C., and Walstad, W. B. (1991). Teaching and learning economics. In J. P. Shaver (Ed.), *Handbook of research on social studies teaching and learning* (pp. 411–426). New York: Macmillan.

Scott, J. W. (1988). *Gender and the politics of history*. New York: Columbia University Press.

Scott, K .P. (1991). Achieving social studies affective aims: Values, empathy, and moral development. In J. P. Shaver (Ed.), *Handbook of research on social studies teaching and learning* (pp. 357–369). New York: Macmillan.

Sears, A. (1994). Social studies as citizenship education in English Canada: A review of research. *Theory and Research in Social Education, 22*(1), 6–43.

Seixas, P. (1987). Lewis Hine: From "social" to "interpretive" photographer. *American Quarterly, 39*(3), 381–409.

Seixas, P. (1993). Parallel crises: History and the social studies curriculum in the USA. *Journal of Curriculum Studies, 25*(3), 235–250.

Selwyn, D. (1995). *Arts and humanities in the social studies*. Washington, DC: National Council for Social Studies.

Shaver, J .P. (Ed.). (1991). *Handbook of research on social studies teaching and learning*. New York: Macmillan.

Shaver, J. P., Davis, O. L., & Helburn, S. (1980). An interpretive report on the status of pre-collegiate social studies based on three NSF-funded studies. In *What are the needs in precollege science, mathematics, and social science education? Views from the field*. Washington, DC: National Science Foundation.

Shaver, J. P., & Larkins, A. G. (1973). Research on teaching social studies. In R. M. W. Travers (Ed.), *Second handbook of research on teaching* (pp. 1243–1262). Chicago: Rand McNally.

Shulman, L. (1986). Those who understand: Knowledge growth in teaching. *Educational Researcher, 15*(7), 4–14.

Shulman, L. (1987). Knowledge and teaching: Foundation of the new reform. *Harvard Educational Review, 57*(1), 1–22.

Singer, A. (1995). Challenging gender bias through a transformative high school social studies curriculum. *Theory and Research in Social Education, 23*(3), 234–259.

Siskin, L. (1994). *Realms of knowledge: Academic departments in secondary schools*. Washington, DC: Falmer Press.

Social Sciences Education Consortium. (1996). *Teaching the social sciences and history in secondary schools: A methods book*. Belmont, CA: Wadsworth.

Stanley, W. B. (Ed.). (1985). *Review of research in social studies education*. Washington, DC: National Council for the Social Studies.

Stanley, W. B. (1991). Teacher competence for social studies. In J. P. Shaver (Ed.), *Handbook of research on social studies teaching and learning* (pp. 249–262). New York: Macmillan.

Stanley, W. B. (1992). *Curriculum for utopia: Social reconstructionism and critical pedagogy in the postmodern era*. New York: State University of New York Press.

Steffe, L. P., & Gale, J. (Eds.). (1995). *Constructivism in education*. Hillsdale, NJ: Lawrence Erlbaum Associates.

Stodolsky, S. S. (1988). *The subject matters: Classroom activity in math and social studies*. Chicago: University of Chicago Press.

Stodolsky, S. S., & Grossman, P. (1995). The impact of subject matter on curricular activity: An analysis of five academic subjects. *American Educational Research Journal, 32*(2), 227–249.

Tetreault, M. K. T. (1997). Classrooms for diversity: Rethinking curriculum and pedagogy. In J. Banks & C. M. Banks (Eds.), *Multicultural education: Issues and perspectives* (3rd. ed., pp. 150–170). Boston: Allyn & Bacon.

Thornton, S. J. (1991). Teacher as curricular-instructional gatekeeper in social studies. In J. P. Shaver (Ed.), *Handbook of research on social studies teaching and learning* (pp. 237–248). New York: Macmillan.

Thornton, S. (1993). Toward the desirable in social studies teaching. In J. Brophy (Ed.), *Advances in research on teaching: Case studies of teaching and learning in social studies, 4* (pp. 157–178). Greenwich, CT: JAI Press.

Thornton, S. (1994). The social studies near century's end: Reconsidering patterns of curriculum and instruction. *Review of Research in Education, 20,* 223–254.

Torney-Purta, J. (1990). From attitudes and knowledge to schemata: Expanding the outcomes of political socialization research. In O. Ichilov (Ed.), *Political socialization, citizenship education, and democracy* (pp. 98–115). New York: Teachers College Press.

Voss, J. F., Tyler, S, & Yengo, L. (1983). Individual differences in the solving of social science problems. In R. Dillon & R. Schmeck (Eds.), *Individual differences in problem solving* (pp. 205–232). New York: Academic Press.

Wade, R. C. (1992). *Human rights education in the elementary school: A case study of fourth graders' responses to a democratic, social action oriented human rights curriculum (democratic classroom practices).* Unpublished doctoral dissertation, University of Massachusetts, Amherst, MA.

Watts, M., & Highsmith, R. J. (1992). International economics in U.S. high schools: Results from a national survey. *Journal of Economic Education, 23*(Fall), 291–315.

Wells, G. (1990). Talk about text: Where literacy is learned and taught. *Curriculum Inquiry, 20*(4), 369–405.

Whelan, M. (1992). History and the social studies: A response to the critics. *Theory and Research in Social Education, 20*(1), 2–16.

White, J. J. (with S. Rumsey). (1993). Teaching for understanding in a third-grade geography lesson. In J. Brophy (Ed.), *Advances in research on teaching: Case studies of teaching and learning in social studies, 4* (pp. 33–70). Greenwich, CT: JAI Press.

Whitson, J. A., & Stanley, W. (1988). *Practical competence: A rationale for social education.* Paper presented at the meeting of the National Council for Social Studies, Orlando, FL.

Whitson, J. A., & Stanley, W. (1996). "Re-minding" education for democracy. In W. Parker (Ed.), *Educating the democratic mind* (pp. 309–336). Albany, NY: State University of New York Press.

Wilen, W. W., & White, J. J. (1991). Interaction and discourse in social studies classrooms. In J. P. Shaver (Ed.), *Handbook of research on social studies teaching and learning* (pp. 438–495). New York: Macmillan.

Williams, M. (Ed.). (1996). *Understanding geographical and environmental education: The role of research.* London: Cassell.

Willinsky, J. (1998). *Learning to divide the world: Education at empire's end.* Minneapolis, MN: University of Minnesota Press.

Wilson, S., & Wineburg, S. S. (1993). Wrinkles in time: Using performance assessments to understand the knowledge of history teachers. *American Educational Research Journal, 30*(4), 729–769.

Wineburg, S. S. (1991). On the reading of historical texts: Notes on the breach between school and academy. *American Educational Research Journal, 28*(3), 495–519.

Wittrock, M. C. (Ed.). (1986). *Handbook of research on teaching* (3rd ed.). New York: Macmillan.

Wraga, W. G. (1993). The interdisciplinary imperative for citizenship education. *Theory and Research in Social Education, 21*(3), 201–231.

Young, K. M., & Leinhardt, G. (1998). Writing from primary documents: A way of knowing in history. *Written Communication, 15*(1), 25–86.

Zevin, J. (1990). Teachers in social studies education. *The Social Studies, 81*(6), 254–263.

31.
Teaching and Schooling Effects on Moral/Prosocial Development

Daniel Solomon, Marilyn S. Watson, and Victor A. Battistich
Developmental Studies Center, Oakland, California

There are widely varying beliefs about the proper roles of schools in fostering students' moral development—or indeed about whether they should have *any* role. While some feel that moral education is the domain of home and church and not schools, others feel that schools play a continual and inescapable role, even when unplanned and inadvertent. Durkheim (1925/1961) felt that the school (or, more specifically, the classroom) played an essential role in moral socialization, as the "intermediary between the affective morality of the family and the more rigorous morality of civic life" (p. 149). More recent writers have stressed the ethical issues, decisions, and examples that abound in everyday school life and that are likely to influence various aspects of students' moral development, including their notions of justice, the importance of interpersonal concern and mutual responsibility, and the connection of the individual to the larger group (Bryk, 1988; Goodlad, Soder, & Sirotnik, 1990; Hansen, 1993, 1996; Jackson, Boostrom, & Hansen, 1993; Oser, 1994; Oser & Althof, 1993).

A great deal has been written about moral development and about moral education. However, while many aspects of moral development have been extensively researched, there is still relatively little research that touches directly on the effectiveness of various approaches to moral education or on the associations of the broad range of existing educational practices or school or classroom atmospheres with moral development. In this chapter we will focus on this research. We will briefly describe the various school-based approaches to moral education, but we will attend most to those that have reported evaluation findings. We will also describe background research on moral development conducted in noneducational settings, but which has

relevance for education. First, however, it is necessary to give some indication of the domain we are considering.

Conception of a "Moral Person"

Conceptual differences in definitions of morality and in theories about how one becomes a moral person underlie the various approaches to moral education. These approaches differ according to whether the emphasis is on the learning of specific behaviors, the internalization of specific values or character traits, the internalization of mental constructs (e.g., conscience), or the development (construction) of a personal understanding of moral values. The assumed processes of acquisition vary in parallel ways. When the emphasis is on learning of specific behaviors, the presumed determinants and mechanisms (as promulgated by learning theory and social learning theory) include direct teaching; exhortation; positive and negative reinforcement; and imitation of powerful, competent, rewarding, or successful models (Jones, 1936, as cited in Turiel, 1973; Aronfreed, 1969; Bandura, 1969; Grusec, 1979; Grusec, Kuczynski, Rushton, & Simutis, 1979). When the emphasis is on internalization of cultural values, character traits, or mental constructs, the major presumed antecedents are parent-child relationship and identification with parents (from psychoanalytic and related approaches: Hoffman & Saltzstein, 1967; Peck & Havighurst, 1960; Sears, Maccoby, & Levin, 1957; Sears, Rau, & Alpert, 1965). When the emphasis is on personal construction of moral values and principles, the role of adults is to provide experiences and opportunities that will enhance this personal construction (most often through discussions, negotia-

Preparation of this chapter has been aided by grant funds from the William and Flora Hewlett Foundation, the San Francisco Foundation, the Robert Wood Johnson Foundation, the Danforth Foundation, Stuart Foundations, the Pew Charitable Trusts, the John D. and Catherine T. MacArthur Foundation, the Annenberg Foundation, Spunk Fund Inc., DeWitt Wallace-Reader's Digest Fund Inc., Louise and Claude Rosenberg Jr., and the Center for Substance Abuse Prevention of the U.S. Department of Health and Human Services. The authors would also like to acknowledge valuable help from Marlene Tonai in tracking down and organizing references, and from Rosa Zubizaretta in translating and summarizing Spanish papers and reports.

tions, and confrontations with others: Blatt & Kohlberg, 1975; Piaget, 1932/1965). In this latter view, usually described as the "cognitive-developmental" approach, moral development is seen as involving a series of universal stages that "define the ways in which the child actively organizes his own experiences, and it is out of efforts at active organization of experience" that the child reaches higher stages of moral thought (Turiel, 1973, p. 732).

There are also differences in the assumed instigation or motivation for moral-prosocial behavior. It is sometimes defined as compliance with a norm established by a model or by a verbal directive or exhortation and sometimes as behavior in accordance with an internalized norm. This distinction, applied to altruistic behavior, is referred to by Rosenhan (1970) as being between "autonomous altruism" (help that is internally directed), and "normative altruism" (help that is more externally controlled, particularly by the prospect of rewards or punishment).

Although each of these approaches focuses on a particular aspect of morality (e.g., moral behavior, moral values, internal mental constructions), most recognize the importance of additional aspects for a complete conception of morality. Rest (1983) has constructed a useful typology that identifies four fundamental functional psychological processes that he believes must combine to produce moral behavior. These are *moral sensitivity* (awareness of the potential effects of one's actions on others), *moral judgment* (judging the moral justification for various potential actions), *moral motivation* (the importance one assigns to moral, as opposed to other, values), and *moral character* (determination and ability to follow through on moral actions judged to be appropriate). Educational goals, strategies, and specific variables related to each of these processes have been proposed by Bebeau, Rest, and Narvaez (1995).

The domain has been laid out somewhat differently by Eisenberg (1986), Staub (1978), and Solomon et al. (1985). These approaches focus on autonomous prosocial behavior (e.g., helping, sharing) and on the factors assumed to be, in combination, the proximate determinants of that behavior. These antecedent factors include *cognitive variables,* such as interpersonal understanding; *affective-motivational variables,* such as empathy and concern for others; *behavioral competencies,* such as communication skills; and *personality factors,* such as assertiveness and sense of efficacy. The general expectation is that particular combinations of these variables increase the likelihood of autonomous prosocial action. Thus social understanding can be used to facilitate either prosocial or antisocial behavior; for it to result in increased prosocial behavior it must be combined with the appropriate motivational variables, such as concern for others, and the behavioral competencies necessary for performing the actions. It is assumed that personality factors such as assertiveness and sense of efficacy make prosocial behavior more likely, because the individual with these characteristics feels more confident that such action will be effective.

Each of the areas thus fills a characteristic function in the production of prosocial-moral-ethical behavior: Cognitive variables provide the necessary awareness and understanding, affective-motivational variables the necessary inclinations or desires, behavioral competencies variables the necessary social

and behavioral skills, and personality variables the necessary confidence and persistence. While the relationships implied by this model have not been systematically investigated, there is evidence linking moral or prosocial behavior with some of the above "internal" factors, including moral reasoning (Blasi, 1980; Carlo, Koller, Eisenberg, Da Silva, & Frohlich, 1996; Kohlberg & Candee, 1984; Eisenberg & Mussen, 1989; Miller, Eisenberg, Fabes, & Shell, 1996), moral motivation (Asendorpf & Nunner-Winkler, 1992), social understanding (Krebs & Sturrup, 1981; Bengtsson & Johnson, 1992; Carlo, Knight, Eisenberg, & Rotenberg, 1991; Underwood & Moore, 1982), affective perspective-taking (Denham, 1986), and empathy (Bengtsson & Johnson, 1992; Eisenberg & Miller, 1987, Eisenberg et al., 1990; Krevans & Gibbs, 1996; Roberts & Strayer, 1996).

Approaches that look at the "whole child" typically combine all of these aspects. A number of studies investigating parent socialization have produced converging conceptions of psychologically healthy children with good character—conceptions that can also be taken to reflect the ideal "moral person." Peck and Havighurst (1960) label such children "rational-altruistic" as opposed to "amoral," "expedient," "conforming," or "irrational-conscientious." Baumrind describes them as "agentic and communal" (that is, "socially assertive" and "socially responsible," Baumrind, 1989, p. 359), and Pitkanen-Pulkkinen (1980) labels them "constructive" as opposed to submissive, anxious, or aggressive.

In this chapter we will consider variables from all of these domains, with an emphasis on those that seem capable of being influenced by an educational program (or that have been demonstrated to have been so influenced); thus, there is little emphasis on personality factors, because these are generally considered to be less easily altered by school programs. We will include discussions of research on some variables that cannot be considered indicators of morality in themselves but are considered to be important or essential aspects, components, or conditions for morality (e.g., empathy, conflict resolution skill, interpersonal understanding).

Research on Processes with Implications for Education

Much of the knowledge and speculation that has been applied to the development of educational programs has derived from research conducted on families or in experimental (nonschool) settings. We will review this research briefly before turning to the studies specifically focused on educational settings.

Parental Socialization

In considering the relevant research on home environments, we will focus on a set of three comprehensive longitudinal studies that, despite variation with respect to their theoretical bases and the socioeconomic classes, cultures, and ages of children investigated, have embodied similar broad conceptions of moral maturity and have produced a remarkably consistent set of findings as to its family antecedents or correlates. These studies (Baumrind, 1989; Peck & Havighurst, 1960; Pitkanen-Pulkkinen, 1980) each included multiple data points, relatively large samples, and multifaceted assessments of children's moral orientations that involved the convergence of several types of data (self-reports, assessments by others, psychological inventories, projective assessments, etc.). We will concentrate on the findings of these studies but will include parallel information from some other studies as well.

Descriptions of the home environments of those children who are classified in these studies as "morally mature" suggest that many of the factors that various theories argue are important for moral development have been consistently part of these children's socialization experiences. We will describe what appear to be the most important aspects of these experiences, but it should be borne in mind that these aspects are not found in isolation but are interrelated parts of a total coherent pattern. (For comprehensive reviews of research linking parent socialization practices to children's moral-prosocial development, see Maccoby & Martin, 1983, and Radke-Yarrow, Zahn-Waxler, & Chapman, 1983.)

CLOSE, RESPONSIVE, AND TRUSTING RELATIONSHIP WITH THE CHILD

These and other studies have found a cluster of related parental practices associated with the development of children who show mature moral-prosocial behavior and orientations. Parents of such children tend to be sensitive and responsive to the child's needs (Ainsworth, Blehar, Waters, & Wall, 1978; Baumrind, 1967; Baumrind, 1989; Peck & Havighurst, 1960; Pitkanen-Pulkkinen, 1980; Roche Olivar, undated; Main & Weston, 1981; Sroufe, 1988); emotionally involved with, as opposed to distant from, their child (Main & Weston, 1981; Sroufe, 1988; the Fels longitudinal study, as described in Baldwin, 1955; Baumrind, 1989; Roche Olivar, undated); affective caregiving (Zahn-Waxler & Radke-Yarrow, 1979); trusting of the child (Peck & Havighurst, 1960; Pitkanen-Pulkkinen, 1980); aware and encouraging of the child's activities (Pitkanen-Pulkkinen, 1980); and accepting of the child's individuality (Baumrind, 1989; Peck & Havighurst, 1960). Children who are actively disliked and rejected by their parents tend to be aggressive (Olweus, 1980) and "amoral" (Peck & Havighurst, 1960).

A DEMOCRATIC ENVIRONMENT IN WHICH CHILDREN CAN EXERT EFFECTIVE INFLUENCE; USE OF REASONING AND INDUCTION

These variables are considered together, because the use of reasoning is part of a "democratic" home environment— although it has also been considered separately. A democratic home environment is one in which parents encourage verbal give and take (Baumrind, 1989; Pitkanen-Pulkkinen, 1980); listen to children's opinions and allow them to influence decisions (Baldwin, 1955; Baumrind, 1989; Pitkanen-Pulkkinen, 1980; Peck & Havighurst, 1960); provide reasons for rules, directives, and restrictions (Baldwin, 1955; Baumrind, 1989; Hoffman & Saltzstein, 1967; Pitkanen-Pulkkinen, 1980); and use little power assertive punishment (hitting, yelling, withdrawing love or privilege: Baldwin, 1955; Hoffman & Saltzstein, 1967; Kochanska, 1991; Peck & Havighurst, 1960; Pitkanen-Pulkkinen, 1980). Although parents exercise a degree of "reasonable control," they

also allow the child the freedom to assume some responsibility (Baldwin, 1955; Peck & Havighurst, 1960; Pitkanen-Pulkkinen, 1980). Peck and Havighurst state

> . . . parental control which is at once consistent, trustful of the child, and allows him to practice making decisions together with the rest of his family produces mature, genuinely self-disciplined moral behavior. The parents who use this kind of discipline are rarely or never severe about it, and some of them are very lenient in their control without adverse effect on the child's behavior. (p. 125)

Hoffman and Saltzstein (1967) found parental use of "induction" (pointing out the potential effects of the child's actions on others) important for children's moral development. They saw children's empathy as an important conditioning or mediating factor in this relationship and reasoned that induction produced its effects by tapping the child's "capacity for empathy." The importance of induction for children's moral or prosocial development has also been demonstrated in other work by these researchers and others (e.g., Dekovic & Janssens, 1992; Dunn, 1987; Hoffman, 1970, 1975; Roche Olivar, undated; Saltzstein, 1976; Rollins & Thomas, 1979; Zahn-Waxler, Radke-Yarrow, Wagner, & Chapman, 1992; Krevans & Gibbs, 1996). Parents' use of reasoning (a closely related concept) was found to be related to the development of children's conscience in research by Sears, Maccoby, and Levin (1957), while Dunn, Brown, and Maguire (1995) found mothers' use of other-oriented arguments in conflict management situations to be related to young children's moral orientations.

OPPORTUNITIES FOR MORAL CONVERSATIONS OR MORAL DISCOURSE

In democratic home environments, children participate in discussions about various family issues with their parents. The importance of open discourse and of "ordinary conversations" with caring others have been stressed by Oser (1986) and Noddings (1994). The parents of morally mature children, as described in the above studies, discuss various issues with their children, seriously consider the children's opinions, and explain their values and their reasoning to their children (Pitkanen-Pulkkinen, 1980; Baumrind, 1989). Peck and Havighurst, who present the most extensive data on family interactions and conversations, note that the "rational altruistic" children in their study frequently contribute to family decision making, share confidences with their parents, and have "the opportunity to . . . develop and trade ideas, unafraid, with parents and other family members" (p. 177).

Consistent results were obtained in a focused study by Walker and Taylor (1991) in which parents and children were observed discussing hypothetical and "real-life" moral dilemmas. Children's gains in moral reasoning (between an assessment conducted with the Kohlberg Moral Judgment Interview at the same time and again 2 years later) were related to parent discussion styles that were both highly "representational" (involving asking for and attending to the child's opinions, asking clarifying questions, paraphrasing, checking for understanding) and highly "supportive" (involving praise, encouragement to participate, and humor).

STABILITY OF HOME ENVIRONMENT

Peck and Havighurst (1960) and Pitkanen-Pulkkinen (1980) both found unstable living conditions (e.g., lack of regularity in the home, inconsistent—and therefore unpredictable—parental behavior, frequent moves, frequent changes in child-care arrangements, unpredictable parent work schedules) to be negatively correlated with "maturity of character" (Peck & Havighurst) or positively correlated with anxiety and aggressiveness (Pitkanen-Pulkkinen). Marked inconsistency in the way their parents respond to them was the most important predictive factor for children who were found to be "amoral" (that is impulsive, hostile, and selfish, acting without regard to moral principles) in Peck and Havighurst's study. This inconsistency was generally coupled with a lack of trust in and a lack of positive regard for the child.

SENSITIVE FIRM CONTROL AND HIGH DEMANDS

Baumrind (1989) calls this dimension "demandingness," and it is part of the constellation of behaviors that she has labeled "authoritative parenting"—a style that balances demandingness with responsiveness to the child. This was the most common successful child-rearing style in Baumrind's data. Related findings have been reported by Dekovic and Janssens (1992), Pitkanen-Pulkkinen (1980), Peck and Havighurst (1960), and Sears, Rau, and Alpert (1965), but there is also suggestive evidence that responsiveness may be the more important element of this constellation. (See Lewis, 1981)

CARING RELATIONSHIPS; PARENTAL WARMTH; MORAL-PROSOCIAL MODELS

The importance of parental warmth and of parents' functioning as positive models are often discussed separately but are difficult to distinguish empirically, because the same behaviors (e.g., parental nurturance) may fill both functions. Noddings (1988, 1992), Gilligan (1982), Kerr (1996), and others have argued that a commitment to care is central to morality and that children learn to become caring by being in caring relationships. Staub (1981) cites "extensive research" showing that adult warmth, affection, nurturance, and love promotes positive behavior in children, while hostility and anger relates to negative behavior and aggression. Zahn-Waxler, Radke-Yarrow, Wagner, and Chapman (1992), for example, found mothers' empathic caregiving to be positively related to children's altruism and reparations for transgressions.

Social learning theorists such as Bandura (1969) and Aronfreed (1969) stress the importance of modeling for acquiring new behavior. In one study of prosocial behavior, Eisenberg et al. (1993) found mothers' modeling of perspective taking to be related to girls' subsequent comforting behavior. Parents of the morally mature children in the core studies mentioned above clearly were both warm and caring and also provided consistent examples of prosocial behavioral styles. Combinations of parental warmth and parental modeling of committed prosocial activity or moral character have also been found to be consistent antecedents of prosocial activity by civil rights volunteers

or by "rescuers" in retrospective studies by Rosenhan (1970), Clary and Miller (1986), Oliner and Oliner (1988), and London (1970). (Colby & Damon, 1992, in a discussion of the latter two studies, point out, however, that many nonrescuers had similar backgrounds and question whether such factors can really account for long-term and intense moral commitment, which, in their research, appeared to involve a continual process of personal development.)

OPPORTUNITIES TO BE RESPONSIBLE OR TO ENGAGE IN PROSOCIAL ACTION

Staub (1975) and others have postulated that having opportunities to take responsibility in the home is an important precursor of later prosocial dispositions. Such opportunities also appear to have been part of the "morally mature" constellation cited above—the children were generally expected to be responsible for performing some significant family chores. The importance of giving children significant responsibilities in the home has also been demonstrated in cross-cultural research by Whiting and Whiting (1975). That the kind of activity children engage in is also important has been demonstrated in research by Grusec, Goodnow, and Cohen (1996). They found a positive correlation for 14-year-olds (but not 9-year-olds) between participating in routine (as opposed to specifically requested) chores that involved helping others and a measure of concern for others, while participating in requested household chores or self-help chores (e.g., making one's own bed) showed no such relationship.

ROLE-TAKING OPPORTUNITIES

Theorists from a cognitive or structural developmental perspective argue that role-taking opportunities are essential to the development of full moral capacity (e.g., DeVries & Zan, 1994; Kohlberg, 1969; Piaget, 1932/1965; Turiel, 1973). While never explicitly using the language of role-taking, descriptions of the home environments of the "morally mature" children and adolescents in the above studies indicate that they were rich in role-taking opportunities.

EXHORTATION AND MORALIZING

Ryan (1989), Lickona (1991), Wynne (1989), and other researchers in the domain of character education have argued for the importance of exhortation and moralizing in promoting children's character development. The authoritarian families in Baumrind's and Peck and Havighurst's studies clearly engaged in considerable exhortation and moralizing. Children from these family environments tended to be rule-conforming but not to be autonomous moral individuals. It seems likely that the parents in the families that produced the most morally mature children also engaged in some exhortation and moralizing but that this approach was greatly tempered by an appeal to reason and explanation and a tendency not to insist on rigid compliance.

HYPOTHESES ABOUT SOCIOCULTURAL DIFFERENCES IN SOCIALIZATION PRACTICES AND THEIR EFFECTS

Delpit (1995), among others, has suggested that children from different cultural backgrounds are accustomed to different socialization styles and are most likely to respond well to styles with which they are familiar. This suggestion implies that the findings summarized above—which were derived primarily from studies of White European-American or European and largely middle class families—may not generalize to children from all sociocultural groups. While between-group differences in parental socialization practices have been documented repeatedly (e.g., by Baumrind, 1972; Davis & Havighurst, 1946; Hess & Shipman, 1965), evidence on the effects of these differences is somewhat mixed. Some parental variables seem to have similar effects across groups. There is consistent evidence, for example, that harsh and aversive parental discipline is associated with poor outcomes in children, including aggressiveness (e.g., Dodge, Pettit, & Bates, 1994) and low levels of achievement (Blau, 1981).

The effects of other variables are more differentiated according to group circumstances. Steinberg, Dornbusch, and Brown (1992) found "authoritative" parenting to be positively related to achievement for White and Hispanic students but not for African-American or Asian students; for the latter two groups the degree to which peers supported achievement efforts was a more important determinant of achievement than parent behavioral style. Baldwin, Baldwin, and Cole (1990) examined the relationships of parenting practices to "cognitive outcomes" for students in "high-risk" and "low-risk" groups (with risk being a composite composed of parent education, parent occupation, minority status, and father absence). They found that the high-risk parents were much less democratic than the low-risk parents and that parental restrictiveness and clarity of policy were strongly positively correlated with the cognitive outcomes for the high-risk sample, while democracy of policy was the strongest predictor for the low-risk sample. They argue that the pressures and dangers of the environment for the high-risk families make parental control more necessary. Further analyses showed, similarly, that parental restrictiveness was positively related to cognitive outcomes in high-crime areas and negatively related in low-crime areas. Baldwin and others (1990) argue that such findings indicate that the effectiveness of parental behavior is largely determined by its appropriateness to the particular circumstances facing the child and the family. When restrictiveness can be seen by the child as reasonable and necessary (e.g., in high-crime areas), it relates to positive cognitive outcomes; when it appears to the child as arbitrary and unnecessary, it is more likely to result in resistance and negative cognitive outcomes.

That the effectiveness of parent behavior is mediated by the child's perception of that behavior is also suggested by findings of Pitkanen-Pulkkinen (1980). In her study, one of the most important socialization variables predicting moral maturity was not how much control the parent exercised but whether the child saw that control as being exercised for the child's welfare. Thus, it may be that, regardless of class, risk level, or cultural group, the same communicated parenting *intentions* are required for good social or cognitive outcomes (intentions focused on protecting and meeting the needs of the child), although the specific parental behaviors that are effective may vary according to the requirements of the situation.

These investigations of differential effects of socialization practices have not been extended to prosocial-moral outcomes (with the exception of aggressiveness, which can be considered the inverse of prosocial behavior). It seems most likely that further investigations in the moral-prosocial domain would show results similar to those summarized here, with some variables having generally similar effects across groups and others being more differentiated. In particular, few studies have looked beyond the specific parental behaviors to investigate the parents' intentions and the child's perceptions of those intentions across sociocultural groups and environmental circumstances. These factors could have particular importance in the moral-ethical domain, since intention is an important component of the moral meaning of an act and thus may determine whether a given parent behavior is seen as modeling, for example, caring and moral responsibility versus selfishness and lack of self-control, from the child's perspective.

EDUCATIONAL IMPLICATIONS OF FAMILY RESEARCH

The home environments of "morally mature" children and adolescents—as described in the three focal studies referred to above and in additional supportive research—form a coherent picture of families in which parents have close, warm, stable, and trusting relationships with their children; in which children have many opportunities to express themselves, to exert effective influence within the family, and to take on responsibilities; and in which there is an emphasis on the use of reason, coupled with clear and consistent parental guidance, and the communication of benevolent parental goals and intentions concerning their children. All of these variables (plus the others listed above) have relevance for education, and most have been represented in educational programs and research related to moral development, as will be seen below.

Experimental Research on Promoting Moral-Prosocial Development

Much of the experimental research focuses on understanding conditions that result in increased positive *behavior* and therefore reveals little or nothing about the child's motives or strength of conscience or the way the child reasons about moral situations. If altruism is defined as behavior motivated by a concern for the welfare of others or a desire to uphold principles of care and justice, then an increase in "altruistic" acts following some experimental manipulation is insufficient evidence that true altruism—or morality or character—has been enhanced. Nevertheless, experimental research can provide information about the conditions likely to produce actions that have the appearance of being altruistic or prosocial. When combined with interviews and naturalistic data, such information can lead to a better understanding of the meaning of these behaviors and hence of ways to promote moral-prosocial development in schools.

From an associationist learning perspective (e.g., Gewirtz, 1969) prosocial behavior should increase if and only if it is rewarded—directly or vicariously. The effects of positive reinforcement on children's prosocial behavior has been demonstrated in a few studies (Doland & Adelberg, 1967; Gelfand, Hartmann, Cromer, Smith, & Page, 1975; Barton & Ascione, 1979). Marantz (1988) in a review of several studies conducted with young children, concludes that they "at best document the immediate impact of positive reinforcement on prosocial behaviour" (p. 30). Rosenhan (1972) and Eisenberg and Mussen (1989) have pointed out the paradox of linking reinforcement to altruistic behavior: If altruism is defined as acting to benefit another without thought for, or expectation of, personal gain, then reinforcement, which explicitly provides such gain, would seem to be the antithesis of altruism and therefore unlikely to enhance it. In fact, a number of studies have shown that the use of rewards for prosocial or moral behavior can undermine later performance of that behavior or people's perceptions of themselves as being helpful or altruistic (Kunda & Schwartz, 1983; Batson, Coke, Jasnoski, & Hanson, 1978; Smith, Gelfand, Hartmann, & Partlow, 1979). Parents' use of rewards to their 7- to 11-year-old children in a helping task was experimentally manipulated in a study by Fabes, Fultz, Eisenberg, May-Plumlee, and Christopher (1989). While children's helping was enhanced by rewards in the immediate situation, it was inhibited by rewards in a later free-choice situation, but only for children whose mothers approved of rewards. The authors' explanation was that rewards were more salient for these children; therefore their absence had more of an effect. They also reported that mothers who generally favored using rewards had less prosocial children than those who did not, possibly, according to the authors, because of a generally undermining effect of rewards.

According to Lepper (1983), Grusec (1991), and others, external forms of control, when strong and insistent, are relatively ineffective for promoting internalization of moral standards, because they lead the child to disclaim personal responsibility for his or her actions; while subtler influence techniques (including induction) allow or encourage the child to attribute actions to internal dispositions. Socialization agents can also contribute to this process by explicitly attributing children's actions to benevolent motives, intentions, or character traits. Studies supporting this supposition have been reported by Grusec, Kuczynski, Rushton, and Simutis (1979) and Grusec and Redler (1980).

EXPERIMENTS INVOLVING "PREACHING" OR MODELING

A recurrent question about moral socialization concerns the relative effectiveness of moral exhortations as opposed to moral examples. Advocates of moral indoctrination approaches to character education assume that both are important, but there has been skepticism about the efficacy of moral exhortation at least since the publication of the Hartshorne and May works, in which moral exhortation was reported to have little or no effect on moral behavior (Hartshorne & May, 1928; Hartshorne, May, & Maller, 1929; Hartshorne, May, & Shuttleworth, 1930). (These works are discussed in a later section.)

Modeling effects on children's moral judgments were shown in studies by Bandura and McDonald (1963) and by Cowan, Langer, Heavenrich, and Nathanson (1969), although their interpretations of the implications of the obtained relationships differed. Grusec (1979) and Rushton (1975) reported positive effects on children's donating behavior for both modeling and preaching, with stronger effects for modeling. Effects of modeling on donating behavior have also been reported by Rosenhan and White (1967). Several studies have shown that characteristics of the model enhance their effectiveness—such characteristics as competence (Eisenberg-Berg & Geisheker, 1979), nurturance (Yarrow, Scott, & Waxler, 1973), warmth (Midlarsky & Bryan, 1967) and charitability (Midlarsky, Bryan, & Brickman, 1973).

A few studies have shown that the effectiveness of preaching depends on its content. Eisenberg-Berg and Geisheker (1979) found children's generosity to be positively influenced by "empathic" preaching (pointing out the needs and feelings of potential recipients) but not by "normative" preaching (pointing out the moral imperative—"sharing is the right thing to do"), except in a condition where the children thought the normative preacher might be their teacher in the following year. Perry, Bussey, and Freiberg (1981) found that an "inductive" exhortation to share (emphasizing effects on another's well-being) was more effective than a "power assertive" one (emphasizing punishment for not sharing) among third- and fourth-grade children.

Dressel and Midlarsky (1978) found junior high school students' donations to charity to be influenced by the moral exhortations (for charity or for greed), exemplary behavior (charitable or greedy), and specific demands ("give to the poor" versus "keep your money") of an adult female model. Although all three variables were influential, demands were the most important of the three. Staub (1971b) found some negative (or "reactance") effects of preaching about the importance of helping, at least in the short term.

Imitation of the altruistic behavior of models and, in some cases, effects of their direct verbal instruction, has been shown in a number of other studies, including Bryan and Walbeck (1970), Elliott and Vasta (1970), Grusec and Skubiski (1970), Israel and Raskin (1979), Rice and Grusec (1975), Rutherford and Mussen (1968), Sagotsky, Wood-Schneider, and Konop (1981), Staub, (1971a), and Yarrow and Scott (1972).

PERSPECTIVE-TAKING EXPERIENCES

Sensitive and effective altruistic behavior requires an understanding of the situation and experiences of the other person (Krebs & Sturrup, 1981; Krebs & Van Hesteren, 1994). The dependence of moral thinking on role-taking ability has been demonstrated by Selman (1971). Staub (1971b) showed that kindergarten children who were trained in the roles of both helper and child who needed help later showed more helping and sharing than those without such training. Iannotti (1978) showed that role-taking and role-switching training had positive effects on the role-taking proficiency of both 6- and 9-year olds; it also had positive effects on the altruistic behavior (donating candy to needy children) of the 6-year-olds but not the

9-year-olds. Positive effects of role-taking training has also been shown for adolescents by Marsh, Serafica, and Barenboim (1980), for socially maladjusted girls by Chalmers and Townsend (1990), for delinquent males by Chandler (1973), and for emotionally disturbed youths by Chandler, Greenspan, and Barenboim (1974).

ATTRIBUTION OF PROSOCIAL CHARACTERISTICS

A central assumption of attribution theory is that people tend to behave in ways that are consistent with their self-attributions and that, therefore, helping them to acquire or to change attributions is a way to change their patterns of behavior. Research testing this assumption with respect to children's prosocial characteristics is reviewed by Grusec (1981). She cites several studies in which telling children that they helped or shared because they were helpful people led to more helping or sharing behavior than conditions in which they were not given such attributions. Because a positive attribution could be seen as having social reinforcement qualities, a study was conducted (Grusec & Redler, 1980) to test the relative effect of attribution (". . . you are a very nice and helpful person") versus social reinforcement (". . . that was a nice and helpful thing to do"). Although both conditions facilitated donation in an initial task, this behavior generalized to other tasks only for the attribution condition.

PARTICIPATING IN PROSOCIAL BEHAVIOR

As indicated above, this variable has figured in some of the family research. A number of experimental studies (summarized in Staub, 1979) have also shown that having children engage in positive, prosocial activities increases the likelihood that they will engage in similar subsequent activities voluntarily, although the way in which the initial participation is induced is important. Various studies have coupled participation with direct instruction, exhortation, modeling, reinforcement, or attributions, as described above. These have shown that processes that help the child see the initial participation as voluntary, as a reflection of the kind of person one is, or as a way of being like one with whom one identifies, are likely to be the most effective for producing long-lasting effects.

FACTORS INFLUENCING GROUP ATTRACTIVENESS
AND COHESIVENESS

Perhaps the most distinctive feature of schooling is that it occurs in a group setting (Goodenow, 1992). Research on groups thus has great potential relevance for the classroom. Although there is little group research conducted outside of classrooms that focuses on moral-prosocial outcomes, there are a number of investigations (summarized in Cartwright, 1968) that identify factors that enhance the attractiveness of groups to their members. These include opportunities for interaction, group goals that are personally important to the members, clarity of paths for reaching the goals, cooperative interdependence, democratic and participatory leadership (with widespread opportunity to participate in decision making), decentralized communication networks, and an atmosphere of acceptance and support. A

number of these variables have been important in several strands of educational research (discussed below), under the general assumption that students who are in supportive and cohesive classrooms are most likely to become actively engaged and to try to abide by the norms and values of the school and classroom.

In their classic research investigating the effects of experimentally manipulated "democratic," "autocratic," and "laissez-faire" climates in boys' clubs, Lewin, Lippitt, and White found that boys in the democratic groups behaved more cooperatively and less aggressively during club meetings, showed greater interpersonal affiliation and friendliness and a greater sense of fairness, made more "group-minded" suggestions to the leader, and, in general, were more attracted to the group than those who experienced the other climates (Lewin, 1938; Lewin, Lippitt, & White, 1939; Lippitt & White, 1952).

EDUCATIONAL IMPLICATIONS OF EXPERIMENTAL RESEARCH

The experimental research summarized above (see also Krebs & Miller, 1985) indicates that children's prosocial behavior can be enhanced by modeling (particularly if the model has positive characteristics), by "preaching" under certain conditions, by participation in role-taking experiences, by receiving prosocial attributions for one's behavior, by performing prosocial activities, and by having opportunities to participate in a supportive and democratic group environment. The role of rewards or praise is ambiguous—there is some evidence of short-term effects, but there is also evidence of undermining later prosocial performance or self-attributions.

As will be seen in the following sections, most of the variables that have been emphasized in the parent socialization and the experimental research have also figured in the research on moral-prosocial education. They have been combined in different ways and with different emphases, depending on the particular approach, but the most consistently applied variables include children's opportunity for influence, student opportunities for interaction and discussion, student autonomy and the exercise of responsibility, supportive and trusting relationships, reinforcement, adult modeling, and moral exhortation. A few variables, such as environmental stability and the use of exemplary literature, have been advocated or included in some programs, but they have not been investigated.

Effects of Schooling on Moral Development

Historically, approaches to moral development and character education have vacillated between two general approaches. The traditional or "direct" approach emphasizes adult transmission of specific moral values (e.g., honesty, conscientiousness) through direct teaching and exhortation and the shaping of children's conduct through use of reward and punishment. This approach is often identified with the theoretical views of Emile Durkheim, and its practices are consistent with behaviorist and social learning theories. Moral development from this perspective is seen as a process of internalizing societal norms and values and the development of internal mechanisms for regulating one's behavior.

The alternative, "indirect" approach to character education

emphasizes children's active construction of moral meaning and development of a personal commitment to principles of fairness and concern for the welfare of others through processes of social interaction and moral discourse. This approach is most closely identified with the theoretical views and educational practices of John Dewey and, more recently, of Lawrence Kohlberg, and its practices are consistent with cognitive developmental theory.

The direct approach was predominant in American education from the end of the 19th century through the first 2 decades of the 20th century. Although its popularity as an approach to moral or character education apparently declined in the 1930s, its practices and emphases (i.e., direct instruction, use of reward and punishment, emphasis on teacher authority and student compliance) are still characteristic of most schools to this day, and there has recently been a resurgence of direct approaches to character education. The indirect approach was part of the "progressive education" movement in the early part of the century and reemerged during the 1960s as an approach to moral education.

A parallel distinction can be drawn between formal and informal approaches to moral or character education. While the level of explicit attention to deliberate or formal approaches has fluctuated during this century in American public schools, educational thinkers since at least Dewey (1916/1966) and Durkheim (1925/1961) have consistently pointed out how various aspects of school and classroom organization have moral implications and convey moral lessons, including teacher-controlled grading systems and the patterns of subordinate-superordinate relationships (Deutsch, 1985), the uses of power and authority (Hansen, 1993), the pervasiveness of "organized dependency" (Schwartz, Merton, & Bursik, 1987), and the character of the school's structural arrangements and normative climates (Hawley, 1976; Serow, 1983). Schooling thus always involves moral and character education, even if this type of education is relegated to the "hidden curriculum."

The Character Education Inquiry

As noted, the direct approach to character education was pervasive in American schools during the early part of the century but disappeared rapidly—at least with respect to published accounts—in the 1930s, and was virtually absent through the 1950s. This decline may have been caused, at least in part, by the publicized conclusions of a major research project conducted by Hugh Hartshorne and Mark May in the 1920s to identify factors that contributed to the formation of character. The Hartshorne and May studies, published in the late twenties, concluded that children generally did not evidence stable, cross-situational consistencies in their tendencies to behave virtuously, and that inculcation methods were ineffective. Although these were the conclusions that were most attended to, they were not their only conclusions and perhaps not their major ones.

Hartshorne and May's overall undertaking was large, but it included many small studies. In one, they examined a small number of religious schools and found no general relationship between the length of time students spent in the school and measures of honesty (Hartshorne & May, 1928). Another con-

sisted of a small experiment in which seventh-, eighth-, and ninth-grade students were given 15 minutes of daily instruction with *The Honesty Book,* but no differences in student honesty were found in comparison with a control group that did not receive the instruction. Another experiment compared reactions to cheating opportunities among students with and without religious instruction. The experimenter wrote "Honesty is the best policy" on the board before leaving the room in one condition, and "God loves an honest man" in another. Students who had received religious instruction showed more honesty than students who had not only in the condition in which God was mentioned. Another small experiment with sixth and seventh graders (reported in Hartshorne et al., 1929) showed short-term positive effects of a condition in which teachers read and had students discuss stories about helping and cooperation on students' group orientation and cooperation. In spite of these modest positive effects, the authors' overall conclusion was "as in the case of tendencies to deceive, it is apparent that such efforts to train children in forms of charitable and cooperative behavior as are ordinarily used in school have very little, if any, effect" (p. 273, Book One).

Although Hartshorne and May found little evidence for the effectiveness of direct teaching on moral-prosocial outcomes, they did report evidence that there were general positive effects of school and classroom atmosphere and "morale." In Volume I (Hartshorne & May, 1928), they presented evidence that deceit and cheating were greater in public than in private schools and less in "progressive" than "traditional" schools (with similar student populations). They also found consistent differences between class groups and suggested that each class built up a "habit system, which, without much consciousness on the part of the individual members, operates to differentiate it from other groups" (p. 338, Book One). They concluded:

> The main attention of educators should be placed not so much on devices for teaching honesty or any other "trait" as on the reconstruction of school practices in such a way as to provide not occasional but consistent and regular opportunities for the successful use by both teachers and pupils of such forms of conduct as make for the common good. (p. 414, Book One)

Following their observations on the distinctiveness and consistency of the moral norms and atmosphere of the school and the class group, they drew the implication that "the normal unit for character education is the group or small community, which provides through cooperative discussion and effort the moral support required for the adventurous discovery and effective use of ideals in the conduct of affairs" (Hartshorne et al., 1930, p. 379). It appears that their message about the ineffectiveness of direct instruction was "heard," but the message that implied a need for more general changes in school atmosphere and in the opportunities for students to participate in "cooperative discussion" was largely ignored.

Investigations Focusing on "Democratic" or "Progressive" Approaches

It is intriguing that Hartshorne and May's calls for "cooperative discussion and effort" and "reconstruction" of school practices to provide "consistent and regular opportunities" for the practice of "such forms of conduct as make for the common good" are reminiscent of Dewey's approach to education. Dewey believed that moral education should not (indeed, could not) be divorced from the school as a mode of social life and was best achieved through cooperative social interaction in a democratic community.

> It may be laid down as fundamental that the influence of direct moral instruction, even at its very best, is *comparatively* small in amount and slight in influence, when the whole field of moral growth through education is taken into account. This larger field of indirect and vital moral education, [is] the development of character through all the agencies, instrumentalities, and materials of school life. (Dewey, 1909/1975, p. 4; emphasis in original)

Angell (1991), comparing the approaches to democratic education of Dewey (1916/1966); Dreikurs, Grunwald, and Pepper (1971); and Kohlberg (1975), found "strong common themes" in the descriptions of the classroom conditions likely to promote democratic citizenship among students. These conditions included: "(a) peer interaction in cooperative activities, (b) free expression, (c) respect for diverse viewpoints, and (d) equal student participation in democratic deliberations and decision making" (p. 249). While some have questioned whether classrooms can ever be truly "democratic" when teachers and students always and necessarily have unequal power and influence and schools are essentially authoritarian institutions, it can be seen as a matter of degree rather than in absolute terms. As Gutmann (1987) points out, "the most internally democratic schools typically balance the participatory and the disciplinary purposes of education, leaving some significant educational decisions . . . largely (but often not entirely) to the determination of teachers and administrators" (p. 93). As shown by Moos (1979) and by Goodlad (1984), very few schools stray far from the authoritarian-controlling pole of this dimension. It is likely that even relatively limited opportunities for democratic participation may be important for students' development of democratic attitudes, values, and habits. As Gutmann argues, "a substantial degree of democracy within schools will be useful, probably even necessary (although undoubtedly not sufficient), to creating democratic citizens" (p. 94).

Democratic participation involves open discussion and negotiation among students. The importance of interpersonal confrontations and negotiations with peers for the development of children's ability to take the perspectives of others and for learning to accommodate and balance their own needs and desires with those of others—and indeed for the very development of personality—has been emphasized by Youniss (1980) in comparing and integrating the views and approaches of Piaget (1932/1965) and Sullivan (1953).

Thus, while arguably not a "formal" approach to moral and character education, the findings from studies of democratic and progressive education and related approaches to schooling could potentially be quite informative. There are a number of educational approaches that differ in some particulars but have common emphases on the role of students' active democratic participation and engagement. Although much of the research

dealing with these approaches has focused on academic outcomes and related motivations, a number of studies have examined effects on moral-prosocial variables, either as a major or secondary focus.

COMPARISONS OF "TRADITIONAL" AND "PROGRESSIVE" EDUCATION

One of the first comparative studies of school effects on students' moral development was conducted by Minuchin, Biber, Shapiro, and Zimiles (1969). They compared various schooling effects for students in two "traditional" schools and two "modern" schools (one more modern than the other). The modern schools more strongly emphasized stimulation of students' intellectual processes (active exploration and discovery, critical questioning and probing involving higher-order concepts, searching for varied solutions to problems); used a greater variety of learning modes (involving creative expression and the integration of expressive and analytic modes), and focused more on encouraging students' intrinsic motivation, spontaneity, and curiosity. In addition,

> The modern schools emphasized flexibility in rules and regulations, veered away from being overrestrictive, were oriented more to correction than punishment, and expected the child's acceptance of authority to come gradually in response to rational treatment by adults and to involve a growing awareness of its functional necessity. The traditional schools established clear rules and regulations, regarded punishment as the necessary, logical sequel to infractions, and extolled compliance and obedience both as desirable behavior and as essential elements of a moral system in childhood. (p. 264)

They examined effects on students in a broad range of areas—including moral development—with a sample of 9-year-old children who had been in their respective schools for at least 3 years. They found that students in the modern schools felt more positive toward school. Students in the most modern of the four schools developed "an image of school authority that was rational and functional" (p. 270). Students' "codes of right and wrong" were assessed from a sentence completion task, interview questions, and moral judgment questions. Students at the most modern school were more likely to evaluate behavior in terms of general moral principles and to invoke issues of conscience and individual responsibility, and these students were less preoccupied with determining what was acceptable to school authority, and how to avoid punishment.

Studies by McCann and Bell (1975) and Clinchy, Lief, and Young (1977) also found effects of school approaches on children's moral development. In the McCann and Bell study, comparing "Freinet" progressive elementary schools—in which students were encouraged to have open discussions, help determine school rules, and participate in choices about selection and scheduling of learning activities and in which students experienced consensus-based and inductive discipline—with more traditional Catholic schools, students in the former schools showed higher levels of moral reasoning (McCann & Bell, 1975). Clinchy, Lief, and Young (1977) compared students in a traditional high school with those in a progressive high school—in which students participated in discussions about curriculum and school governance, students and teachers had cooperative relationships, and open class discussions were encouraged. When sophomores and seniors were compared across schools, it was found that sophomores did not differ across schools in level of moral reasoning, while seniors in the progressive school showed more advanced levels, suggesting that increased experience in the contrasting school environments produced the differences. A study by Whiteman and Kosier (1964) found that children assigned to ungraded, combined classrooms in which there was much cross-age interaction—features commonly included in "progressive" approaches—showed greater advances in moral judgment than those in conventional classes.

"CONSTRUCTIVIST" PRACTICES

The effects of varying classroom atmospheres and practices on the moral-prosocial development of young children has been investigated in a few studies with cognitive-developmental perspectives. Golub and Kolen (1976) found that kindergarten children from "constructivist" classrooms, as compared to those in more traditional ones, showed more social interaction that was more collaborative and more independent of adults. Long-term effects of the High/Scope cognitive-developmental preschool program on adolescents' delinquency, family relations, and helpfulness to others with problems have also been reported by Schweinhart, Weikart, and Larner (1986), although these findings have been disputed (Bereiter, 1986; Gersten, 1986).

Two studies by DeVries and colleagues have examined the "enacted" interpersonal understanding of children in constructivist and contrasting preschool settings. The constructivist classroom, as described by DeVries, Haney, and Zan (1991) emphasizes students' pursuit of their own interests, experimentation and self-correction, active reasoning, and participation in classroom decision making and collective activities; a teacher role as "a warm and supportive collaborator, a companion-guide who minimizes the exercise of adult authority without, however, being permissive" (p. 452); and the importance of establishing a "feeling of community characterized by a spirit of fairness, mutual concern, friendship and positive shared experience" (p. 452). In an initial study, DeVries and Goncu (1987) compared negotiation strategies of children from constructivist and Montessori preschools in experimental tasks and found that children from the constructivist classrooms had fewer interpersonal conflicts and resolved a larger proportion of them and that they used a higher proportion of negotiation strategies that reflected consideration of the other person's needs or wishes. In a second study (DeVries, Reese-Learned, and Morgan, 1991), the behavior of children from three different preschool programs was compared—constructivist, direct-instruction (DISTAR), and an "eclectic" program that combined features of the other two (but was closer to the direct instruction program). Again, children from the constructivist program exhibited greater use of negotiation strategies and "shared experiences" that attended to others' needs in experimental task sessions, while those from the direct instruction program showed the least.

OPEN EDUCATION

The "open education" approaches that were explored mainly in the 1960s and 1970s involved several aspects of democratic climate, as defined above, particularly the encouragement of student collaborative activities, the minimization of direct teacher control, and active student participation in decision making. These approaches also emphasized student intrinsic motivation, student exploration and self-guided learning, teachers functioning as resources or consultants to students, and the use of diverse and stimulating materials. In a study comparing three "open" and three "traditional" fourth-grade classrooms, Solomon and Kendall (1976) found that students in the open classrooms scored higher on a factor, derived from teacher ratings, representing democratic and cooperative behavior. Fry and Addington (1984) found greater social problem-solving skills among third-grade children who had attended open classrooms for 3 years than children who had attended traditional classrooms for 3 years. Hallinan (1976) found that students produced more even distributions of student sociometric choices in open atmospheres; while Allman-Snyder, May, and Garcia (1975) found that fifth-grade (but not first-grade) students in open classrooms were more likely than those in traditional classrooms to choose democratic methods for settling conflicts, while students in both first- and fifth-grade traditional classrooms (particularly first grade) were more likely to choose authoritarian methods.

A longitudinal study of high school students by Ehman, (1980b) showed student perceptions of the degree to which their teachers exposed them to controversial issues, allowed all sides of issues to be presented and discussed, and encouraged students to express their own opinions were positively related to both school-related and political attitudes (interpersonal trust, integration with one's social environment, and political interest), but negatively related to students' sense of political confidence or efficacy (possibly because hearing all sides of controversial issues makes one more aware that there are actively contending sides to many issues and hence less certain that actions in support of one position will be effective). In a review of research in high schools, (Ehman, 1980a) summarizes evidence indicating that open classroom and school climates are important for promoting growth in democratic values and attitudes.

EDUCATION IN CITIZENSHIP AND LAW

A comprehensive middle-school curriculum designed to (a) increase students' knowledge of their community, concepts of community governance, and the role of law and public institutions in managing conflict; (b) to enhance their cognitive, social, and citizenship participation skills; and (c) to help them develop positive attitudes toward self, family, school, and community has been developed by the Center for Civic Education and the Constitutional Rights Foundation (undated). A preliminary evaluation of this curriculum, conducted in a single intermediate school during one year and involving preassessments and postassessments of students in experimental and control groups reported positive effects of the program on participating students' attitudes toward authority, prosocial behavior, self-control, cooperation, and attitudes toward community (Center for Civic Education, 1996). There was also some indication that these effects were greatest for students in classrooms of teachers who most adequately implemented the curriculum.

Investigations of Specific Practices

Although research on the effects of traditional and nontraditional educational approaches on students' moral development is relatively sparse, there are extensive bodies of experimental research on two of the practices that characterize most "progressive" approaches: cooperative learning and student discourse. There is less research on specific teacher practices (although such research has figured heavily in "process-product" research focused on student achievement; see Brophy & Good, 1986), and virtually none on a set of practices considered potentially important by advocates of various theoretical persuasions—centered around the use of literature or narrative.

COOPERATIVE ACTIVITIES IN CLASSROOMS

A number of the essential features of democratic classrooms are involved in cooperative learning approaches. (See Slavin, 1990; Johnson & Johnson, 1989; Sharan, 1990.) A substantial amount of research on various approaches to cooperative learning has been conducted over the past 2 plus decades, and, while much of it, particularly more recently, has concentrated on strictly academic outcomes (which are generally found to be positively influenced), there have also been a number of investigations of the effects of cooperative learning on interpersonal and prosocial attitudes, behaviors, values, and skills.

Cooperative Learning and Intergroup Relations. Some of these approaches (e.g., Weigel, Wiser, & Cook, 1975) were developed with the specific intent of creating the conditions for promoting positive intergroup attitudes and relations specified in the "contact hypothesis" promulgated by Allport (1954) and Williams (1947)—namely, equal status contact and cooperative effort toward common goals. Weigel et al. (1975) conducted a cooperative learning experiment in newly desegregated junior and senior high schools. They established small interdependent student work groups composed of White, Black, and Mexican-American students who worked collaboratively toward common goals. Rewards were provided to "winning" groups, thus setting up a situation of competition between groups. The experiment included control classrooms (with similar ethnic distributions) in each school; there was much more whole-class instruction in the control classrooms. The results indicated less overall and cross-ethnic conflict in the experimental classrooms and more cross-ethnic helping behavior. They also found that these activities produced greater relative respect and liking for Mexican-American classmates among White students and more frequent friendship choices for Mexican-Americans by Whites. In discussing the findings, they consider the possibility that using intergroup competition may have been counterproductive, since some groups failed, causing negative feelings not only between groups but also within losing groups. (They apparently

did not consider the possibility of not using rewards at all, however.)

Slavin and Madden (1979) used questionnaire data collected in 51 high schools to examine relationships between school practices and improved racial attitudes and behaviors in desegregated schools. They found that working on tasks in biracial groups and participating on biracial teams had strong positive effects on both White and Black students' racial attitudes and cross-race behaviors, while class discussions about race and teacher workshops on race relations had weaker effects. They concluded that the essential practices are those that promote intergroup interaction:

> . . . The practices that most consistently affect interracial attitudes and behavior are those that directly involve students, as opposed to teachers, and more specifically structure black-white interaction. . . . The only independent variables to have positive effects on attitudes are those that require racial interaction; the variables directed at student attitudes, such as "discussions of race relations" and "minority history," do not have such effects. . . . To train teachers to foster interracial interaction, teacher workshops should be focused not on understanding intergroup relations but on specific teaching methods that promote student interaction. (p. 179)

Hansell and Slavin (1981) compared the number and patterning of cross-race friendships (as indicated by sociometric questionnaires) among seventh and eighth graders whose language arts classrooms were organized into cooperative teams with those in traditional classrooms in inner-city schools. They found that the cooperative treatment did increase cross-race friendships, and did so equally across sexes, races, and achievement levels.

Johnson and Johnson (1981) found that fourth grade students in a cooperative learning condition showed more overall interethnic interaction and cross-ethnic helping in both instructional and free-time activities, more interpersonal academic support, and greater group cohesion and cooperation than those in an individualistic condition.

Warring, Johnson, Maruyama, and Johnson (1985) found that sixth-grade students who participated in cooperative activities (in either of two conditions—cooperative controversy or cooperative debate) showed more positive cross-sex and cross-ethnic interaction in other settings than did students in an individualistic condition. In a second study, two cooperative conditions were compared for fourth-grade students—one involving intergroup cooperation, the other involving intergroup competition. Students in the intergroup cooperation condition reported more positive cross-sex and cross-ethnic relationships in other settings than those in the intergroup competition condition.

Several studies investigating the effects of participation in cooperative activities on interethnic interaction and relations have been conducted in Israel, generally involving situations in which "Western" Jewish students are in classrooms with "Middle Eastern" Jewish students. Sharan and Rich (1984) describe two studies using cooperative learning in ethnically mixed junior high schools. In the first study, three conditions were compared—whole class learning, Jigsaw (a condition based on "structured interdependence," in which lessons are broken into units, each of which is learned by an "expert," who then teaches it to the rest of the group), and Group Investigation (G-I—in which students work cooperatively on long-term projects that they themselves devise, plan, and carry out). Students in the G-I condition increased in cross-ethnic sociometric choices, and in the number of Middle Eastern students who were sociometric "stars." Cross-ethnic evaluations of other students became more equal in the G-I condition, but more polarized with Jigsaw. These results are explained as being due to the G-I class creating a

> relaxed and cooperative social climate, whereas the Jigsaw class promoted achievement, accompanied by increased stress, because each pupil must tutor all his groupmates simultaneously on a given portion of the learning task . . . this creates tension over one's own performance and the demand by others to perform well. Apparently, cross-ethnic relations do not benefit from this kind of stimulation. (p. 201)

In a second study described in this work (and also, in more detail, in Sharan et al., 1984) the relative effects of G-I, Student Teams Achievement Divisions (STAD—a cooperative approach in which the class is divided into teams that work cooperatively internally and compete against one another), and traditional whole-class teaching were compared. Both cooperative methods produced more small-group cooperation than whole-class teaching (which produced more competition). G-I students were equally cooperative within and across ethnic groups, while STAD produced unbalanced interaction (more cooperation within than across). Cross-ethnic attitudes worsened over the course of the year in the whole-class classrooms, and didn't change in either cooperative method. Sociometric data did not show differential effects by condition, nor did measures of friendship or classroom social relations.

In another study, involving eighth-grade classrooms, Sharan and Shachar (1988) compared the effectiveness of the G-I approach with that of whole-class organization in promoting positive interethnic interaction. In addition to observing classes and assessing achievement, they had students do standard tasks in small groups out of the classroom. They found that students in the G-I condition showed greater equality in the number of cooperative statements directed to Western and Middle Eastern students as well as in the number of turns students from each background had to speak.

In reviewing some of this research, Slavin (1985) concludes that cooperative learning methods generally produce positive effects on intergroup relations and that "when the conditions of contact theory are fulfilled, some aspect of friendship between students of different ethnicities improves" (p. 53). While we generally agree with this conclusion, there is also evidence, from the studies comparing different approaches, that intergroup relations are more enhanced by approaches that involve intergroup cooperation than by those involving intergroup competition.

Cooperative Learning and Prosocial-Moral Development. Cooperative learning activities, if accompanied by appropriate levels of teacher guidance (neither so little that groups flounder unproductively nor so much that they have no autonomy), provide students with the opportunity and necessity to interact and negotiate with others. Through the give and take of this interaction they can learn the importance of hearing and understanding the viewpoints of others, of asserting one's opinions but also of being willing to compromise, the benefits of interpersonal support, and the importance of playing a responsible role in an interdependent group. The potential importance of cooperative interaction for children's prosocial development has been emphasized by Brown and Solomon (1983), who hypothesized that it should promote the development of various related processes and factors, including children's social understanding; skill in compromising, cooperating, and negotiating; tendencies to make prosocial self-attributions and expectations; empathy; prosocial values and norms; moral judgments; and motives.

> A general cooperative atmosphere and normative structure may help the child to develop norms, expectations, and values concerning helping and cooperation. Repeated and routine cooperation should prompt the child to attend to, be concerned about, and try to accommodate to the needs and values of others. (p. 301)

Evidence consistent with these expectations has been provided in several studies. Aronson, Bridgeman, and Geffner (1978) summarize research using the Jigsaw cooperative procedure as showing positive effects on students' interethnic perceptions, liking for classmates, and role-taking abilities, as well as their academic performance and self-esteem. A study by Bridgeman (1981), for example, examined the effects of Jigsaw cooperative learning on role-taking and moral reasoning among fifth-grade students. Classrooms using cooperative peer-initiated group learning were compared with other innovative and more traditional teacher-centered methods. Role-taking was assessed by using Chandler's (1973) cartoon series. Moral reasoning was determined through the use of Kohlberg's Moral Judgment Interview. Two experimental classrooms used the Jigsaw method, two control classrooms used "noninterdependent" group methods, and two other control classrooms used more competitive, conventional approaches. They did not directly train students in role-taking skills, but they provided such training indirectly in the context of the regular classroom routine. Role-taking scores improved for the Jigsaw but not for the other two conditions. There were no differential effects on moral reasoning; students in all groups improved to about the same degree. Bridgeman suggested a set of distinctive aspects of the Jigsaw classrooms that may have accounted for the role-taking effect:

1. required interdependence and social reciprocity,
2. consistent opportunity to be an expert, "which allows for a better developed sense of self" (p. 1236),
3. integration of varied perspectives,
4. equal-status cooperative interaction, and
5. a highly structured process.

These findings seem somewhat inconsistent with the increased polarization found in Jigsaw classrooms by Sharan and Rich (1984), as described above, but may be due to differences in the way the Jigsaw program was implemented in the two projects.

Hertz-Lazarowitz, Sharan, and Steinberg (1980; also described in Hertz-Lazarowitz & Sharan, 1984) used the G-I method to help create classrooms designed to promote students' prosocial development. Assuming that a distinctive feature of socialization in the classroom is that "a classroom is a *peer society* and the nature and quality of peer interactions in the classroom are the critical variables that facilitate prosocial behavior among children" (p. 424), they helped teachers create classrooms centered around planned prosocial peer interaction. The teacher

> has to promote a positive classroom climate, where warmth and respect for child autonomy are an explicit set of norms. In order to become a "cooperative classroom teacher," every teacher had to learn gradually to relinquish his total control over student behavior in order to allow for direct interaction and communication among students. Teachers also had to undergo basic changes in attitudes toward competition and cooperation in the classroom. (p. 432)

The attitudes of teachers in these classrooms did shift toward providing students more autonomy, and the classroom social climates—as perceived by students—improved in the experimental classrooms and declined in the control. They found that third- to seventh-grade elementary school students who spent extended periods of time in these cooperative classrooms (using the Group Investigation procedure) behaved more cooperatively and made more altruistic and cooperative choices and judgments—and less competitive and "vengeful" ones—in experimental sessions conducted away from the class (and with students other than their group-partners in class) than students in traditional classrooms using whole-class instruction. They pointed out that ". . . the implementation of prosocial behavior on both the teacher and the peer levels was achieved without direct teaching of moral or prosocial principles, but rather through experiential learning and participation involving both social and cognitive elements" (p. 439).

Johnson, Johnson, Johnson, and Anderson (1976) similarly found that children who participated in cooperative learning activities made more altruistic choices and made more accurate identification of feelings (in taped conversations) than those who participated in individualistic or competitive activities. Ryan and Wheeler (1977) found that students with cooperative learning experience—as compared with those with competitive learning experience—made more cooperative and more helpful decisions in a simulation task. Kagan, Zahn, Widaman, Schwarzwald, and Tyrell (1985), in a study using cooperative learning procedures that involve between-group competition, also found positive effects on interpersonal cooperativeness.

Reviews of this research have been published by Slavin (1990); Sharan (1980); and Johnson, Johnson, and Maruyama (1983, 1984). Although the evidence is somewhat sparse in some areas, the preponderance of findings indicate that experience with other students in cooperative groups generally has positive effects on students' role-taking skills, cooperative actions and inclinations, altruistic behavior, feelings of acceptance, and interpersonal attraction. The 1983 review by Johnson, Johnson, and Maruyama indicates that cooperation without intergroup competition produces greater interpersonal attraction than cooperation with intergroup competition but that both of these conditions are superior to interpersonal competitive or individualistic conditions.

The essential element of cooperative classroom activities is that they provide students many opportunities to interact in a generally positive and supportive climate. The importance of student interaction for various aspects of development—including the socialization of values, the learning of social competencies, and the development of perspective-taking abilities—has been emphasized by Johnson (1981). In addition to its central role in most approaches to cooperative learning, student interaction—student discussion in particular—has also been studied separately.

STUDENT PARTICIPATION IN DISCUSSIONS

Linkages between student opportunities to participate in open classroom discussions and prosocial-moral outcomes have been demonstrated in several studies. Torney, Oppenheim, and Farnen (1975), in a 10-nation study of civic attitudes in which assessments of classroom practices and student attitudes and behaviors were obtained from questionnaires administered to 10-year-old, 14-year-old, and preuniversity students, found—fairly consistently across countries—that students' democratic values (in particular antiauthoritarianism and participation in political discussion) were greatest in classrooms that stressed the fostering of students' independent thought and "free discussion" and that minimized the use of drill and rote learning.

The importance of active student participation in discussion and negotiation for adherents of progressive education has been stated by Nicholls (1989): "Negotiation of meanings and purposes—itself the mark of a democratic society—is, for progressives, the means of developing the individual initiative, independence of judgment, and social commitment on which democracy in turn depends" (p. 167). Ehman (1980a), in a review of research on political socialization in high school, similarly concludes that positive political attitudes are most likely to develop in classrooms where students have opportunities to discuss controversial issues in "open classroom climates" where students have influence and are encouraged to express alternative viewpoints.

Approaches that emphasize the importance of active participation in discussion for moral-prosocial development, which Oser (1986) considers under the general category of "discourse," include the use of "constructive controversy" (Johnson & Johnson, 1994) and discussions of moral dilemmas (Kohlberg, 1978).

In his analysis of the field of moral education, Oser (1986) considered moral discourse to be the "common denominator" that underlies various approaches. Engaging children in moral discourse implies a trust in their social and moral capabilities. The moral education situation is one in which the underlying rules and principles of justice and respect are acquired through participating in discourse that involves rational discussion of dilemmas or situations in which the participants are usually not personally involved (e.g., through using hypothetical moral dilemmas), to ensure that their own involvement and commitment will not interfere with the ability to examine all sides of an issue. The aim is that the "child should learn to develop his or her personal point of view and at the same time to consider the other's point of view" (p. 920).

Oser distinguishes between several types or elements of moral discourse, including (a) *discourse entailing moral-cognitive conflict* (in which confronting more advanced modes of moral thinking leads to the reconstruction and reorganization of one's moral judgments), (b) *discourse aimed at role-taking and empathy* (involving role-taking exercises and discussions of others' perspectives and situations that are designed to enhance children's sensitivity to the needs and feelings of others), (c) *discourse directed at moral action* (in which the focus is on possible actions and decision making), (d) *discourse focused on shared norms and the moral community* (exemplified by the "Just Community" program described below), (e) *discourse involving the analysis of moral values in texts and other sources,* (f) *discourse aimed at bringing about personal change,* and (g) *discourse to increase theoretical moral knowledge* (i.e., one's knowledge *about* moral theories and values).

The use of discussion is an important part of several of the moral education programs described below. It has also been investigated by itself in two specific programs of research: one on the use of structured controversy and the other on moral dilemma discussions.

Structured Controversy. This approach begins with the assumption that participating in disputes, under the appropriate conditions, can have important benefits, both academic and interpersonal. It can help students learn to consider all evidence carefully before coming to conclusions, to learn to present one's case and to attend to that of one's opponent, and to understand and to respect the perspectives of all involved parties. Thus, it fulfills several of the functions described by Oser, as listed above. Much of the work in this area has been conducted by David and Roger Johnson and their colleagues (Johnson & Johnson, 1992; 1994; 1989). They emphasize the importance of the "appropriate conditions," pointing out, with Deutsch (1973) that controversy is most beneficial if conducted in a cooperative—as opposed to a competitive—context. Evidence confirming the importance of a cooperative context for realizing the benefits of controversy is summarized by Johnson and Johnson (1989, p. 103).

In addition to a cooperative context, the Johnsons' approach to controversy involves the use of structured discussion tasks with at least two well-documented positions. Students work in four-person groups, divided into pairs, each of which is given materials, including arguments and background information, supporting both a pair's assigned position and the opposed position. Each pair works up the material favoring a position and prepares a persuasive argument, giving the other pair any information discovered that supports *their* position. The pairs then argue their positions, with instructions to listen carefully to the opposing arguments. This presentation of arguments is followed by an open discussion in which each pair probes and discusses the other's arguments and conclusions. The pairs then reverse perspectives and each pair argues the other pair's position. Finally, the two pairs discuss the issue further until they reach a consensus, then prepare a report that presents the joint conclusion and its rationale. The discussions are conducted with certain guidelines (e.g., "being critical of ideas, not people") that represent social skills that need to be taught—if they are not already present—before these activities can be conducted in their intended way. (For more details about these procedures and their theoretical background, see Johnson & Johnson, 1992, 1994).

While the benefits of controversy have most often been discussed in terms of academic-intellectual outcomes, a few studies have also focused on interpersonal or prosocial ones. Research conducted within the above paradigm has shown that engaging in controversy produces positive effects on participants' liking for one another, perceived peer task support (e.g., Johnson & Johnson, 1985), and cognitive perspective taking (i.e., understanding others' positions; e.g., Tsjovold & Johnson, 1977).

Discussions of Moral Dilemmas. Another approach that involves the constructive use of conflict and controversy developed out of the Kohlberg approach to moral development, itself strongly influenced by Piaget's (1932/1965) cognitive-developmental approach to moral development. On the assumption that cognitive growth is triggered by the need to reconcile conflicts and to take account of the perspectives of others, subjects participated in experiments involving moral dilemma discussions in which they were exposed to moral arguments one or more stages above their own current level (e.g., Blatt & Kohlberg, 1975). These discussions were expected to stimulate change through moral-cognitive conflict. They were conducted in various settings in different studies. The higher-stage arguments were sometimes presented by a teacher or experimenter, they sometimes emerged in the course of a larger group discussion, and they sometimes took the form of dyadic conversations. In the latter paradigm, pairs of subjects were given series of moral dilemmas to discuss and were asked to reach consensus. The pairs were set up so that one member was typically at a higher moral "stage" (as assessed by the Kohlberg Moral Judgment Interview) than the other. The dilemma discussion would thus expose the member at the lower stage to reasoning at a higher stage and allow that member gradually to generate the principles of the higher stage (the interventions sometimes lasted as long as 32 weeks). Reviews of this research, which was mostly conducted in the 1970s, have been published by Berkowitz (1981), Lockwood (1978), Leming (1981, 1993), and Turiel (1973) and have generally shown that there is a small positive effect, with average upward movement of one-third to one-half a stage. Leming (1981) points out, however, that not everyone was so affected—between 30% and 50% of the subjects (depending on the study) show no upward movement as a result of the treatment. There was also evidence that arguments more than one stage above a subject's current level were ineffective in stimulating stage growth—presumably because they were too distant from the subject's current level of understanding to be meaningful (Turiel, 1973). A review by Schaefli, Rest, and Thoma (1985), based on studies using Rest's "Defining Issues Test" (a measure based on Kohlberg's Moral Judgment Interview, but using a multiple-choice questionnaire format; Rest, 1979), also finds evidence of positive—but generally small—effects of dilemma discussions on the level of moral reasoning with students ranging from junior high school to college.

In attempting to understand the mechanisms of such change, Berkowitz and Gibbs (1983) analyzed the content of discussions of dyads that, in an earlier study (Berkowitz, Gibbs, & Broughton, 1980), either had or had not shown change in the level of moral reasoning. They coded statements from these discussions into two general categories: "representational transacts" and "operational transacts." The former statements merely restate or elicit the other person's reasoning; the latter operate on or transform it. They found that operational transacts were significantly more frequent in the discussions of dyads that changed than those that did not and, in a regression analysis, that the frequency of operational transacts accounted for more of the variance than the disparity between the two members of the dyad in initial moral reasoning levels (which also accounted for a sizable portion of the variance, however) or the frequency of representational transacts (which accounted for a negligible portion). They pointed out as a major implication the importance of attending to the nature and quality of the discussion process in moral education efforts (as the Johnsons did in the "constructive controversy" approach described above).

Damon and Killen (1982) found similar process variables in small group discussions to be related to gains in moral reasoning about fairness, sharing, and distributive justice among students in Grades K-3, particularly for children at lower initial levels. Children at these levels who made reciprocal statements that reflected "co-construction" (accepting or transforming peers' statements through compromise or collaboration) showed the greatest gains. Other discussion process variables (the frequency of commands, off-task joking or talking, and verbal aggression) were shown to be important determinants of third- and sixth-grade children's group decisions—leading to less prosocial group choices in discussions of altruism and honesty dilemmas—in research by Berndt, McCartney, Caparulo, and Moore (1983–84).

In a recent paper summarizing what is known about the conditions under which moral dilemma discussions can be expected to produce positive effects, Berkowitz (1996) suggested that discussion groups (a) should "manifest some heterogeneity in moral reasoning," (b) should be varied according to participants' levels of development, (c) should be clearly structured by teachers (or others with "a certain level of maturity"), (d) should involve instructions to reach consensus, (e) should involve dilemmas with a diversity of opinions on preferred behavioral solutions, (f) should be part of a relatively lengthy intervention (probably 3–12 weeks), (g) should involve students who are cognitively "ready" for change (i.e., with appropriate logical and perspective-taking skills), and (h) should involve some cognitive conflict.

Discussions have also been shown to be effective for variables other than moral judgment stage scores. Fifth graders who had dilemma discussions after viewing evocative films were found by Parish (1981) to show greater increases in their "altruistic" behavior (giving some of their own candy to "children in another class") than children in a control group who neither saw the films nor discussed them (making it impossible to determine whether the effect was produced by viewing the films or by both viewing and discussing them). Jensen and Larm (1970) found that kindergarten students' use of intentionality (versus consequences) and maturity of explanation in moral judgments about stories increased more for students in a condition involving discussions about intentionality (following the presentations of several stories) than for students in a control group or a condition of reinforced discrimination. Crowley (1968), however, in another study of intentionality, found that a condition in which correct responses were "labeled" by the experimenter and also

discussed, led to judgments that were no more mature than a condition that involved labeling alone, while both conditions were superior to a control condition. Selman and Lieberman (1975) found that second-grade children who participated in "semistructured" group discussions of moral dilemmas (with debate encouraged) subsequently used the concept of moral intentionality to a greater extent than those in a control group.

A study by Lourenco (undated), which was conducted with 5-year-olds in Lisbon, was designed to use discussions to change children's views of altruistic behavior. Children in an experimental group—who were exposed to others' (older children in some sessions, an adult in others) views of the gains for the helper inherent in altruistic actions (including physical gain, psychological gain, and ethical gain)—increased their use of these cognitions themselves and, to some degree, their altruistic behavior.

Intensive intragroup and intergroup discussions, along with small group activity, were part of several programs involving "influential" Jewish and Palestinian teenagers conducted by the "School for Peace" in Israel (Bar & Bargal, 1987). The discussions were focused on helping participants to develop understanding of their own and the other group's culture and on exploring the aspects of background, social position, history, and so forth that related to each group's views on the Arab-Israeli conflict. A major goal was to have participants emerge with a complex rather than unidimensional (uniethnic) and stereotypic understanding of the conflict. The intervention groups in these projects (vis-à-vis comparison groups composed of other students at the same schools who did not participate in these activities) were, as a result of the intervention, more likely to want to maintain contact with members of the other ethnicity. Members of the intervention groups also became more aware of the complexity of the intergroup issues and showed less intergroup discrimination in their behavior (but not in their questionnaire responses). The relative importance of the specific content of the discussions versus the process of participating in the discussions could not be determined because both factors were part of the treatment. It also appears that there was less overall intergroup contact among students in the comparison groups, so it is possible that the results were due to the amount of intergroup contact *per se*.

Nonexperimental Research on Teaching Practices and Approaches

TEACHING PRACTICES RELATED TO STUDENTS' "SENSE OF COMMUNITY"

A study conducted in 24 elementary schools in various parts of the United States showed linkages between several aspects of teacher practices, students' classroom behavior, students' "sense of community" in the classroom, and several variables reflecting moral-prosocial characteristics. These findings were derived from the baseline phase of an intervention project. (The intervention and some of its effects will be described in a later section.) Sense of community—defined as including two elements: students' perceptions that their classmates are supportive and mutually concerned and perceptions that students actively participate in classroom decision making and norm-setting—was considered the critical variable in this research. One part of the study (described in Solomon, Battistich, Kim, & Watson, 1997) showed support for a model that linked students' sense of the classroom as a community to three aspects of students' classroom behavior: positive interpersonal behavior, active engagement, and exertion of effective influence; and that in turn linked these aspects of student behavior to several teacher practices—in particular, the use of cooperative learning activities, teacher warmth and supportiveness, and emphases on prosocial values and interpersonal understanding. Another set of analyses (described in Battistich, Solomon, Kim, Watson, & Schaps, 1995) showed the measure of sense of community to be positively related to a variety of other student measures, including concern for others, conflict resolution skill, acceptance of "outgroups," intrinsic prosocial motivation, democratic values, and self-reported altruistic behavior. These findings obtained across a wide range of poverty levels of school populations. The general conclusion was that teacher practices that stimulated and encouraged active student engagement and participation and that modeled positive and concerned interpersonal behavior were critical in this process. Students' sense of community was also related to reduced drug use and delinquent activity (Battistich & Hom, 1997). Although these findings were correlational, they were generally confirmed in the later analyses of the intervention phase of this project, which is described later in this chapter.

The sense of community was also a central concern in research by Wehlage, Rutter, Smith, Lesko, and Fernandez (1989), who studied 14 alternative high school programs for at-risk students throughout the United States. They focused on the importance of *social bonding,* defined as including four components: (a) *attachment* (social and emotional ties to others), (b) *commitment* (rational calculation of what is needed to achieve goals), (c) *involvement* (engagement in school activities, which are seen as legitimate and valuable), and (d) *belief* (faith in the institution). They hypothesized that

> School membership is promoted by . . . (i) active efforts to create positive and respectful relations between adults and students; (ii) communication of concern about and direct help to individuals with their personal problems; (iii) active help in meeting institutional standards of success and competence; and (iv) active help in identifying a student's place in society based on a link between self, school and one's future. In exchange for this energetic and active commitment from the institution, students are to make a reciprocal commitment that involves: (i) behaviors that are positive and respectful toward adults and peers; and (ii) educational engagement, that is, a level of mental and physical effort in school tasks that makes their own achievement likely and makes the commitment of adults rewarding. (p. 120)

Enabling school structures shared some common features: small size (allowing one-on-one relations with students) and school autonomy, flexibility, and control. The teacher culture and structural aspects of the school combine to create "a culture and structure of support." The investigators used both quantitative and qualitative indices to assess effects on students of schools varying in the degree to which they constituted "communities." Seven of the 14 programs studied had school membership as an explicit goal. Six of these "showed notable

improvements in student attitudes." Four had sizable effects on "sense of social bonding and sociocentric reasoning." (Sociocentric reasoning refers to children's concerns for the rights and feelings of others and for one's obligations to them.) More traditionally structured programs showed much smaller gains on these measures.

Although the correlates of sense of community in schools have been examined by several other researchers (e.g., Bryk & Driscoll, 1988; Shouse, 1996), and it would seem to relate very directly to the moral atmosphere of the school or classroom, these other studies have generally focused on academic and related variables only, and have not examined relationships with indices of moral and prosocial development.

RESEARCH ON OTHER TEACHER VARIABLES

Teacher Use of Induction Versus Behavior Modification. Rohrkemper (1984) identified eight exemplary elementary school teachers, four of whom used a consistent inductive approach to classroom discipline and four of whom used a consistent behavior modification approach. Vignettes describing fictional problematic students were presented to the students in each of the teachers' classrooms in interviews. Among other areas (e.g., their perceptions of how their teachers would react to the fictional students), students were asked how they themselves would react and feel. Students with the inductive teachers expressed more positive regard for the problematic students, more altruistic motives, and less self-interested motives than those with the behavior modification teachers.

Teacher Warmth and "Modeling". A few studies of desegregated schools have provided evidence that teachers' behavior is modeled in their students' patterns of intergroup interaction. St. John and Lewis (1973) and Gerard and Miller (1975) both found that teachers' behavior toward minority group children was subsequently reflected in intergroup sociometric patterns. In a study of 90 desegregated elementary school classrooms, Serow and Solomon (1979) found students' general positive intergroup interaction to be positively related to teachers' warmth and acceptance and negatively related to businesslike classroom atmospheres and strictly academic teacher-student interaction, while teacher patience, persistence, and diversity in classroom structure and activity were positively associated with intergroup helping and cooperation. Cohen (e.g., Cohen, Lotan, & Catanzarite, 1990) has written extensively on the potentially undermining effects of status differentials in classrooms with diverse student bodies; it seems likely that this process was operating to produce the negative relationships with teachers' academic interaction and businesslike atmospheres. These emphases may have made salient—and therefore exacerbated—preexisting achievement status differences between the groups, thereby reducing the potential for positive intergroup contact and positive feelings.

SUMMARY

The educational approaches and practices reviewed in the first part of this section, although clearly not identical, differ from "traditional" approaches in several ways: several of them represent more open and participatory school or classroom environments that (a) emphasize student interaction, collaboration, and negotiation; (b) actively involve students in their learning and the social life of the classroom and school; (c) minimize direct teacher control; and (d) provide students with greater autonomy and opportunities to participate in discussion, deliberation, and decision making. Implicitly or explicitly, most of them also attempt to establish a supportive classroom environment characterized by mutual respect and concern. The element common to all of them is the emphasis on the importance of active student participation in discussion and interaction. The studies that examined prosocial and moral outcome variables, while relatively small in number, consistently suggest that approaches that involve this, along with other aspects defined as part of "progressive" or "democratic" schooling, have more positive effects on students' social and moral development than "traditional" approaches.

Much less research has been conducted on the effects of specific patterns of teacher behavior on prosocial-moral outcomes for students, but there is some evidence (a) that students imitate their teachers' prosocial behavior under certain conditions, (b) that teacher warmth and patience may be important in this regard, (c) that teacher use of induction can promote students' altruistic orientations (as compared with teacher use of behavior modification techniques), and (d) that teacher practices that promote students' sense of community (including teacher warmth, concern, and use of cooperative learning activities) relate positively to various moral-prosocial indices among students. More research examining these and other effects of specific teaching styles and practices on such outcomes would be useful.

Specific Programs

The field of moral and character education at the turn of the century is more reminiscent of the beginning than the middle of the 20th century. Dramatic increases in the incidence of social problems among youths since the 1950s (e.g., illicit drug use, violence) led to increasing calls, beginning in the 1970s and continuing through the present, for schools to once again explicitly "teach values" to students. Also, as in the early decades of the 20th century, there is considerable diversity of opinion about how to accomplish this goal, and there are vocal proponents and a number of programs representing both "direct" and "indirect" approaches. For example, a recent paper by Ryan (1996) "embraces indoctrination as an educational practice and makes the case that a failure to inculcate children with the values of adult society is an abdication of one of the primary responsibilities adults have to children" (p. 75). He advocates using many means to instill the "basic" moral virtues, including modeling virtuous behavior, use of stories with heroes and heroines, direct study of the virtues, giving students opportunities to learn to reason and to be of service, learning to live in a civil, task-oriented environment, and engaging students in "their own formation of good character" (p. 83). He says that adults should decide which moral values, knowledge, and skill students are to learn. They should then be taught, using "well-established principles of instruction": matching the topic and level with developmental capacities, giving students opportunities to under-

stand and apply the learning, establishing strong incentives, evaluating growth with formal and informal means, and rewarding success and admonishing failure.

The approach advocated by Kohn (1997) is diametrically different. He believes that the term "character education" should be used broadly to refer to anything schools do other than academics (especially if it is aimed at helping children develop ethically), but that it has been taken to refer, more narrowly, to a particular style of moral training involving exhortations and extrinsic inducements (with drilling and indoctrination). He believes the goal of character education should be to help children become active participants in democratic society and develop into principled and caring community members, rather than learning to conform to conventional norms of good behavior (which he sees as the goal of the "narrow" view of character education). Thus, his view of appropriate character education includes regular and meaningful class meetings, opportunities for students to practice perspective taking, the use of literature to stimulate moral discussion, thinking, and reflection; and a general increase in the level of student autonomy and participation.

Clearly, both direct and indirect (or "traditional" and "progressive") approaches are alive and well in contemporary moral education. In practice, of course, many programs tend to fall somewhere in between these two opposing viewpoints (or to include some elements of each). We will review the moral-prosocial education programs in this section, grouping them according to whether they lean more toward the "direct" or the "indirect" approach. In addition, a number of programs, while not explicitly concerned with moral development *per se,* focus on the development of specific skills considered central to prosocial and moral behavior (e.g., empathy). These programs will be reviewed as well.

CONTEMPORARY PROGRAMS EMPHASIZING THE DIRECT APPROACH

The STAR Program. The STAR (Stop, Think, Act, Review) program, developed by the Jefferson Center for Character Education and adopted in a number of school districts nationwide, is designed to foster respect and responsibility in students and to create positive school climates. The program and its evaluation are described in McQuaide, Fienberg, and Leinhardt (1994). The program has monthly themes, specific lessons, and specific character education messages, but teacher flexibility in instructional methods is encouraged.

> Although the Jefferson Center provides lesson plans for each STAR concept, teachers are free to choose lessons that they believe will be most effective for the group of children in their classrooms. Some teachers choose to present the character education messages for approximately 10 minutes at the beginning of the day; others choose a 20-minute, once-a-week lesson. (p. 10)

Basic materials include (a) 10 classroom/school posters and banners that correspond to monthly themes (e.g., How can I be of service to others? How can I show respect for myself? How can I reward myself for being responsible?); (b) a principal's handbook with step-by-step implementation guidelines; (c) messages for morning announcements, lesson suggestions,

it aims neither to inculcate specific values nor to build students' commitment to moral principles. The program, described in Raths, Harmin, and Simon (1978), consists of a series of classroom exercises designed to help students become clear about what they value without being influenced by the teacher, whose role is to facilitate but not express personal opinions. The major goal of the program is to increase students' certainty about their values, thus making their behavior more confident, purposeful, and enthusiastic. The program is thus more about valuing than about values, and it is explicitly morally neutral and relativistic, in contrast to the other "indirect" programs reviewed below.

Research on the Values Clarification program has been reviewed by Lockwood (1978) and Leming (1981, 1985). As Leming (1985) points out, most of the research has been in the form of dissertations, and the programs evaluated have varied considerably in the specific classroom practices used, thus making cumulative summaries somewhat questionable. The general conclusion in these reviews is that the program developers' hypotheses have not been confirmed. In Leming's review of studies conducted between 1975 and 1984, for example, only 4 out of 10 studies that examined it showed positive effects on the clarity of students' value-related thinking, while 3.5 (one showing mixed results) out of 17 (21%) showed shifts in the content of values, 3 out of 9 showed changes in value-related behavior, and 3 out of 17 (18%) showed positive changes in self-concept. Oser (1986) comments on the values clarification approach: "The lack of stress on truth and rightness makes morality little more than a part of the domain of aesthetic judgment . . . claims are made only on a private level without discussing validity claims seriously" (p. 932).

CONTEMPORARY PROGRAMS EMPHASIZING THE INDIRECT APPROACH

Just Community. The collective norms and moral atmosphere of the school (or often a "school within a school") are the explicit foci of the "Just Community" programs initiated by Kohlberg and his colleagues (Higgins, Power, & Kohlberg, 1984; Kohlberg, 1975, 1985; Kohlberg, Lieberman, Powers, Higgins, & Codding, 1981; Kohlberg & Higgins, 1987; Power, 1988; Power & Makogon, 1996). These programs grew out of—and greatly extended—the earlier Kohlberg approach, described above, of having students discuss hypothetical moral dilemmas. While engaged discussions on moral issues are a common feature of both approaches, the Just Community adds, as its central focus, the creation of a participatory, functioning, collective moral atmosphere in the school. The approach has been used most often, but not exclusively, in high schools. (For a description of an elementary school application that produced positive effects on children's reasoning about justice, see Kubelick, 1982.) In a Just Community program, all community members—students and faculty alike—participate in establishing and maintaining community norms, through periodic community meetings. Because the Just Community approach requires active participation by all community members, relatively small communities must be established. This has been done in large urban schools by creating schools within schools or dividing the schools into "clusters" of 60–100 students and 4 or 5 teachers.

Typically, the full community meets weekly to discuss and determine rules, to set policies, and to plan activities. The focus is on issues of community welfare and fairness; the group does not deal with issues of school administration or curriculum. "At the core of this practice is the idea of participatory democracy—one person—one vote—whether student or teacher" (Kohlberg & Higgins, 1987, p. 104).

Students are encouraged to develop and present their own perspectives, but they are also encouraged to accept the group's majority decisions as binding. The teachers function as collaborators, facilitators, and guides:

> The teachers obviously have special authority by virtue of their position, but they try to operate as formally equal members of a democratic group and exercise authority by virtue of their wisdom and expertise and by means of consent rather than by virtue of their position of authority and by means of coercion. Teachers must walk between excessive advocacy—approaching indoctrination—and excessive permissiveness. (Kohlberg & Higgins, 1987, pp. 104–105)

Teachers act as process facilitators by encouraging role-taking, focusing on issues of fairness and morality, and highlighting or articulating "higher-stage" reasoning. They act as advocates by raising issues, helping the chair ensure full participation, and advocating positions "that will develop the group's expectations of justice and community" (Kohlberg & Higgins, 1987, p. 122). "In particular, our approach relies on the teacher to aid in establishing the mutual moral respect and the constitutive rules of a fair morality" (p. 121).

The community members also meet in smaller groups each week. Advisory groups composed of 10–15 students and 1 teacher-adviser prepare for the community meetings by having discussions of the most important topics on the community meeting agenda. One of the groups each week selects two members to chair the community meeting and plans the organization of the meeting. A discipline or fairness committee also meets weekly to determine fair consequences for members who have broken the community's rules.

> In each Just Community program the discipline or fairness committee's roles and duties develop over time. Because the committee is acting for the school or program, it becomes clear that the individuals who compose the committee are fulfilling a school- or program-wide responsibility. In this sense, membership becomes viewed as a duty, not just something to be volunteered for out of interest. This means that most students and staff will serve on this committee for some period during each academic year. (Kohlberg & Higgins, 1987, p. 106)

Kohlberg and Higgins (1987) describe their approach to the Just Community as a revision and integration of the perspectives of Piaget and Durkheim:

> For Piaget, the development of moral autonomy and moral maturity emerges from the spontaneous dialogue and cooperation between individuals who are peers having attributes of mutual respect and collective solidarity with one another. We believe, however, (1) that such interaction rests largely on the development of the collectivity of a set of group norms and an atmosphere of group solidarity conducive to dialogue with mutual respect, and (2) that this collective development is one that the teacher must help structure and advo-

cate. . . . Thus the opposition between Piaget's focus on interindividual dialogue and exchange and Durkheim's emphasis on collective norms and solidarity is for us not opposed but complementary to our theory of democratic social interaction. (p. 111)

For Durkheim, a sense of moral obligation to a norm rests on a sense of the norm as being shared by a group whose authority the individual accepts and of which he or she feels himself or herself to be a member. As distinct from obligations to rules and norms (the spirit of discipline), Durkheim views an equally important part of morality to be the more spontaneous spirit of altruism, or caring for other members of the community and the community as a whole. (p. 113)

We believe that, rather than relying entirely on spontaneous social interaction to develop an attitude of mutual respect and solidarity . . . and constitutive rules of dialogue and fair exchange, the educator and educational system must take a role in developing these conditions of peer interaction. (p. 121)

Findings from initial attempts to establish Just Community schools are described in Higgins (1980), Reimer and Power (1980), and Higgins, Power, and Kohlberg (1984). Higgins presents evidence (from the "Cluster School" in Cambridge, Massachusetts) that participating in the school increased students' moral reasoning scores, with greatest gains in the first year of participation. There was also evidence of gains in "school values" (community, democracy, fairness, and order). The development of norms in the same school, assessed by analysis of the content of community meetings, interviews with community members, and observations of social interactions, are described by Reimer and Power (1980). They report increases for norms of integration (expectation that students from diverse backgrounds would mix and be friendly) and attendance, and mixed results for norms concerning drug use and property. Higgins, Power, and Kohlberg (1984) describe additional findings from Cambridge—along with those from a Just Community project in Brookline—focusing on students' individual moral judgments and choices and on the perceived "moral atmospheres" in these schools, as compared with those in control schools. Measures were derived from individual interviews focusing on "practical," school-related dilemmas; questions about one's own reactions produced the individual scores, while questions about how the other students in the school would respond produced the school moral atmosphere measures. Students from the Just Community schools scored higher than those in the comparison schools on the measures of individual judgments and of the perceived school atmospheres. Their moral reasoning scores were higher, they more frequently made judgments invoking "responsibility," they were more likely to see both themselves and their classmates as making prosocial choices, and they were more likely to value the school as a community and to see the community norms as collectively shared.

Participating in Just Community schools in another project (in Scarsdale, New York) also resulted in significant moral reasoning gains for students (Kohlberg et al., 1981). The authors also present evidence that schoolwide community norms developed around issues of caring, limiting drug use during retreats, and building trust concerning property.

Schools based on the Just Community paradigm have been developed in other countries. Kohlberg modeled the Just Community in part on Israeli kibbutzim, and, while they cannot be considered investigations of Just Communities *per se,* a few studies have compared children in kibbutz versus other settings. Fuchs, Eisenberg, Hertz-Lazarowitz, and Sharabany (1986) found that Israeli kibbutz third graders scored higher than either Israeli or American urban third graders on several measures of prosocial reasoning, including reciprocity; affectional relationships; concern with "humanness"; and concern for norms, rules, and values. Snarey, Reimer, and Kohlberg (1985) found kibbutz adolescents to place greater emphasis on the importance of keeping promises and of collective moral principles than those in American or Turkish samples. A paper summarizing research in the Kibbutz that provided a model for the original Just Community approach (Dror, 1995) showed that kibbutz students (including those at low socioeconomic status levels) showed greater gains in level of moral reasoning than comparable urban counterparts.

An attempt to establish Just Community schools in Hungary was recently reported (Vari-Szilagyi, 1995). Following the end of the communist regime, the Hungarian government saw a need for democratic moral education in Hungarian schools, which had previously followed the Prussian model, which was highly centralized and strongly emphasized strict discipline. A project was conducted in a number of elementary and secondary schools (students aged 11–16), with selected, receptive teachers and schools with supportive headmasters. The approach developed there focused on class discussions but did not use the committees described in other Just Community settings. Discussion topics included developing self-evaluations or self-portraits of classes, putting together ideas about the ideal classroom, expression of student interests and wishes, and negotiation of school rules, regulations, and sanctions. Students preferred discussing "real-life" dilemmas to prepared hypothetical ones. Reported results were preliminary, but there were indications of growing tolerance and individual and group responsibility in the classes.

Three schools in Germany participated in a Just Community Project called "Democracy and Education in the School" (DES), beginning in 1987, which was described in Althof (1992). Somewhat different approaches developed in each school, and all differed from most previous Just Community projects in that they involved younger children, and, in addition to the Just Community meetings, had frequent moral dilemma classroom discussions included as part of the regular curriculum (whereas classroom moral dilemma discussions, which have occurred in some of the American projects, were not part of the regular curriculum). The German project did include agenda and fairness committees, however. (See Oser, 1992.) Although the study had no control groups (they were impossible to obtain), evidence of gains are reported in perceived school atmosphere (particularly teacher openness and supportiveness), perception of the school as a community, opportunities for students to participate in decision making, moral judgment level, and moral competence. The gain in moral competence was found to be greater than that in a nonintervention study conducted during the same period and using the same measure; that is, it was judged to represent substantially more than the effect of normal schooling (Lind & Althof, 1992).

Child Development Project (CDP). The CDP is a comprehensive elementary school program designed to influence children's social, ethical, and intellectual development. It was initiated in the early 1980s in a suburban school district near San Francisco. The program attempted to combine principles and practices derived from the research and theory on the determinants of prosocial and ethical behavior, as described above. The program included elements of both the "indirect" and the "direct" orientations—on the assumption that students need to make their own meaning in both the social-ethical and the intellectual realms, but that teacher experience and accumulated knowledge is an important and necessary guide in such explorations (see Watson, Solomon, Battistich, Schaps, & Solomon, 1989). (A shorthand term to describe this approach is "guided autonomy.") Thus, the major activities in the initial realization of the program attempted to incorporate inductive discipline; student autonomy and self-direction; student interaction, discussion, participation, collaboration and negotiation; student participation in positive ("prosocial") activities; clear adult direction and guidance; and a warm and supportive classroom and school environment. The program approach was designed to influence both (a) the overall atmosphere of the classroom (through an explicit emphasis on the importance of positive interpersonal values and attitudes, and an approach to classroom management that emphasized student autonomy, self-direction, and participation in classroom decision making—in class meetings and in other ways), and (b) the provision of specific classroom activities (collaborative learning activities, helping activities, social understanding activities). (The linkage between principles and activities in the initial program are described in Solomon et al., 1985, and Battistich, Watson, Solomon, Schaps, & Solomon, 1991.) Although the major emphasis was on the classroom program, the project also included schoolwide and family involvement activities.

The first effort to pilot and longitudinally evaluate the CDP program occurred in San Ramon, California, beginning in the 1982–83 school year and continuing through the 1988–89 session. The program was conducted by teachers in three program schools, one grade level at a time. The evaluation followed a cohort of students receiving the program from kindergarten through sixth grade and then into eighth grade in a 2-year follow-up assessment in intermediate school. The evaluation also included teachers and students in three demographically similar comparison schools in the same district.

Classroom observations conducted each year showed that the program was well implemented, with program teachers scoring higher than comparison teachers on all the various indices of program implementation (Solomon, Watson, Delucchi, Schaps, & Battistich, 1988). A comprehensive set of assessments—obtained with classroom observations, individual interviews, and student questionnaires—revealed positive effects of the program on students' interpersonal behavior in the classroom (Solomon et al., 1988), social problem solving and conflict resolution skills (Battistich, Solomon, Watson, Solomon, & Schaps, 1989), democratic values and interpersonal understanding (Solomon, Watson, Schaps, Battistich, & Solomon, 1990), social adjustment (Battistich, Solomon, & Delucchi, 1990), and loneliness in school and social anxiety (both reduced—Solomon, Watson, Battistich, Schaps, & Delucchi, 1992, 1996).

Program students also were more likely to see their classrooms as *communities* (assessed with a questionnaire measure), and this sense of community was itself related to a broad set of other positive characteristics among students (e.g., self-esteem, social competence, empathy, achievement motivation, reading comprehension) and also helped to enhance a number of the effects listed above (Solomon et al., 1992, 1996). One set of analyses suggested that the sense of community led students to adhere to the values that were most salient in the classroom. Thus students in program classrooms—which emphasized student autonomy, participation in classroom decision making, and interpersonal concern—responded to hypothetical prosocial dilemmas with autonomous and other-oriented moral reasoning, while students in comparison classrooms—which emphasized teacher control and student compliance—responded with heteronomous and reward-and-punishment-related reasoning (Solomon et al., 1992, 1996).

Students from four of the schools—two program and two comparison—entered the same intermediate school for seventh and eighth grades. Former program students scored higher than former comparison students at the eighth-grade level in conflict resolution skill and self-esteem, were rated by teachers as more assertive and popular, and reported having friends who were more involved in positive activities. Results were more mixed for the same cohort of students at the seventh-grade level: The former program students were more involved in school activities but also reported getting in trouble more and reading for pleasure less, possibly indicating that the former program students had greater initial difficulty adjusting to the more regimented atmosphere of the intermediate school but that the positive effects of the program manifested themselves after they had had time to become acclimatized to the new environment (Developmental Studies Center, 1998; Solomon, Battistich, & Watson, 1993).

A subsequent phase of the project was conducted in six districts—three in California and three in the eastern half of the United States. The program included many of the same elements as in the initial trial but was focused more explicitly on promoting students' intrinsic motivation while minimizing the use of external forms of control (reward and punishment), on the use of literature as a vehicle for exploring social and interpersonal issues, and on creating a sense of community among students and teachers.

An evaluation involved two demonstration and two demographically similar (matched but not randomly assigned) comparison schools in each district. Baseline data were collected in the 1991–92 school year, the year before the start of program implementation. Data collection continued in the following 3 years, during which the program was being implemented.

Reports of findings of this project have focused on testing a model that includes students' sense of community as a critical intervening variable. These have shown that participation in the program produced positive effects on students' sense of community and that the sense of community, in turn, related positively to gains in various questionnaire-assessed student outcomes, including concern for others, prosocial conflict resolution skill, intrinsic prosocial motivation, altruistic behavior, enjoyment of helping others learn, and trust in and respect for teachers, as well as students' observed positive interpersonal behavior and engagement in class (Developmental Studies Center, 1998; Solomon, Battistich, Watson, Schaps, & Lewis, 2000; Watson, Battistich, & Solomon, 1998). Other analyses have shown that significant gains in program implementation (as assessed by classroom observations and teacher questionnaires) were made in about half of the program schools and that students in these schools showed positive effects of the program on their sense of community and on a broad set of prosocial variables (including intrinsic prosocial motivation, concern for others, prosocial conflict resolution skill, democratic values, outgroup acceptance, altruistic behavior, alcohol and marijuana use (both reduced), and some delinquent behaviors (also reduced) (Developmental Studies Center, 1998; Battistich et al., 2000; Solomon et al., 2000; Watson et al., 1998).

The Responsive Classroom. The Responsive Classroom is an elementary school program designed to reflect developmentally appropriate practice and to create a sense of community (Wood, 1994). Its aim is to influence a specific set of social skills—cooperation, assertion, responsibility, empathy, and self-control—through use of a set of structured techniques, including modeling, role-playing, teacher reinforcement, reminders, and redirection. The program includes the provision of active interest areas for students; displays of student work; a mix of individual, group, and whole-class activities; morning meetings involving greetings, conversation, sharing, and problem solving; children's participation in the development of classroom rules and "logical consequences"; a free-choice period each day; an emphasis on "guided discovery"; and procedures for assessment and reporting to parents. An initial evaluation of this project, conducted in one school new to the program, one that had been doing it for some years, and one comparison school (Elliott, 1992), produced evidence that the program was related to gains in elementary school students' social skills and academic competence and to declines in their problem behaviors, all as reflected in behavioral ratings made by teachers, parents, and students. Similar findings were obtained for students at all elementary grades in a second evaluation (Elliott, 1995), with clearest effects on gains in students' rated cooperative and assertive behaviors.

Other Multifaceted Programs Aimed at Promoting General Prosocial Development. Three elementary school programs have been developed in Spain that are designed to have a general impact on children's prosocial development. One, which was developed by Roche Olivar and colleagues (described in Roche Olivar, 1990), has been used in a number of schools in Catalonia, starting in 1985. This program is aimed at fostering prosocial motives and behavior, and combines an emphasis on supportive, accepting, and affectionate teacher behavior involving the use of inductive discipline with such practices as attribution of prosocial intentions to children, exhortation to prosocial behavior, reinforcing prosocial behavior, and various classroom activities focused on prosocial themes, including lessons, readings, models, literature, debates, writing activities, structured exercises, murals, homework, and so forth. Specific prosocial values are presented explicitly to students at the start and throughout the program. Evaluations of this program have been initiated but as yet are partial and incomplete.

Another program, based in Malaga, Spain, and developed by Trianes Torres (described in Trianes Torres, 1994, 1996, and Trianes Torres, Munos Sanchez, & Sanchez Sanchez, 1995) is called "Program of Social and Affective Development." Teachers use a nonauthoritarian approach and try to develop a supportive and trusting classroom climate in which students participate actively and share responsibility, develop autonomy, and have opportunities for emotional expression and for developing close social relationships. Students participate in classroom norm development and are given exercises in conflict resolution skills. The program is divided into three modules:

1. *improving classroom climate* (focusing on social skills, norm setting, community building, and class meetings for problem solving);
2. *resolving interpersonal problems* (focusing on discussions about feelings and understanding others, perspective taking, negotiation skills, role playing conflicts, and problem solving); and
3. *learning to help and cooperate* (focusing on cooperative learning, development of attitudes and skills concerning helping and sharing, cooperative skills, and roles within groups).

An interim report of an evaluation of this program applied to compensatory education classrooms, where social competence and prosocial behavior were considered particularly problematical, showed somewhat mixed results (Trianes Torres, 1994). There was evidence that students benefited in classrooms where the program was well implemented, however. This benefit was particularly evident for measures of social skills. A second evaluation, conducted with sixth graders (Trianes Torres et al., 1995) focused on the impact of Module 1. Students who participated in the program, as compared with a control group, showed positive effects on teacher-assessed sociability (cooperation, friendliness, classroom affiliation) and teacher- and self-assessed social skills, with some evidence of cumulative effects. Inappropriate assertiveness and jealousy (self-assessed) increased for the control group but not the program group, suggesting that the program may have had some preventive effects.

A third Spanish program (Etxebarria et al., 1994) was designed to enhance students' prosocial-altruistic behavior through activities focusing on empathy, perspective taking, cooperation, and conceptions of people (i.e., views of others as benevolent versus self-centered). Students (10- to 12-year-olds), divided into groups of 7–10, participated in teaching units on each of these areas in 15 weekly 1-hour sessions. The sample comprised 110 subjects, aged between 10 and 12 years, from 4 class groups. Each teaching unit included 4 steps:

1. introductory and motivational activities explaining and defining the concept;
2. dramatizing (and videotaping) examples and counterexamples of the concept;
3. tasks involving relating the concept to everyday life (including writing examples, videotaping, and discussing relevant situations); and
4. games designed to develop cooperation, nonverbal communication skill, and role-taking skill.

Pretest-posttest comparisons showed a significant increase in prosocial-altruistic behavior (measured by a sociogram on "consoling and defending" behavior and a questionnaire on prosocial behavior), as well as improvements in students' perspective taking and in classroom climate. There was, however, no control group, so the change cannot unambiguously be attributed to the program experience.

A project based on that of Roche Olivar—the "Ethical Education Project" (Lencz, 1994) has been introduced into primary and secondary schools throughout Slovakia in recent (post-Communist) years. The project, which emphasizes the development of prosocial values, was begun in 20 schools in 1990 and has since been introduced into all schools in Slovakia. The project uses active, dialogue-based, learner-centered educational methods, with an emphasis on 10 factors (from Roche Olivar): communication, self-esteem, positive evaluation of others, creativity, ability to express one's feelings, empathy, assertiveness, prosocial models, prosocial behavior, and comprehensive prosocialness in public life. Further factors refer to the behavior of educators: unconditional acceptance of the student, attribution of prosociality and willingness to cooperate, positive discipline, encouragement of prosocial behavior, and "careful use of reward and punishment." The program begins with training in "preconditions": personal qualities (self-esteem) and skills (particularly communication) needed to foster a "structured process of moral maturation." It emphasizes the development of social skills and of identity (the two are considered inseparable), as well as the necessary grounding for acquiring the general and universally accepted values of prosocialness and cooperation. Informal evaluation of a pilot project indicated that students developed trust in teachers; had fewer arguments and disputes; had more positive attitudes toward unattractive, isolated, or minority children (e.g., gypsies); and developed friendly, social, and relaxed school atmospheres. After 1992, the government made this program compulsory for all primary and secondary schools (as an alternative to religion).

A program developed by Adalbjanardóttir (1992, 1993) and used by a group of Icelandic teachers, was designed to promote the social-cognitive competence and skills of elementary school children. It was conducted during 4 weeks in the fall of a school year, when the focus was on friendship, and 10 weeks in the spring, when the focus was on recess events (conflicts between students) and classroom interactions (interstudent interaction and teacher-student differences of opinion). The program included discussions of hypothetical interpersonal dilemmas—and of actual conflicts that occurred in the class—with the whole class and within student small groups and pairs. The program tried to create a comfortable classroom atmosphere that would promote student freedom of discussion and would help them to "face and define different perspectives in the process of solving interpersonal conflicts." In addition to these discussions, with focused teacher questioning, the program also had students write stories and poems, draw, paint, and role-play. All children were interviewed about interpersonal dilemmas and were observed (for social behavior) at the beginning and end of the year. The interviews were scored for their use of Interpersonal Negotiation Strategies (INS) levels (after Selman, 1980), while student behavior was scored for the parallel developmental levels of perspective coordination (impulsive, unilateral, reciprocal, or collaborative). The program was found to produce gains in INS thought level as well as in INS observed ac-

tion for student interaction with peers (but not with teachers); children who participated in the program showed greater progress in reciprocity. While both boys and girls showed program effects on thought level, the gains in action level were greater for boys than for girls (for whom the program and control group gains did not differ).

SOCIAL SKILLS TRAINING PROGRAMS

A number of training programs have focused directly on enhancing students' interpersonal orientations, understanding, and skill. The ability and inclination to understand and attend to the perspectives and situations of others is a common element in these and is considered by many to be critical for moral and prosocial development in general. As indicated earlier, a number of studies have shown a direct linkage between social understanding and prosocial behavior. Aside from their relationship with prosocial behavior, however, interpersonal skills and understanding can be considered essential ingredients of moral-prosocial orientations.

Empathy Training. A program designed to enhance empathy in preschool and elementary school children has been developed by Norma and Seymour Feshbach (Feshbach, 1979, 1984; Feshbach & Cohen, 1988; Feshbach & Feshbach, 1982). Along with Hoffman (1978) and Staub (1971a), they consider empathy a "key mediating mechanism" that both promotes prosocial behavior and inhibits aggression. Their approach to empathy includes both affective and cognitive aspects, and it "views empathy in children as a shared emotional response that the child experiences on perceiving another person's emotional reaction" (Feshbach, 1979, p. 237). They propose a three-component model that includes two cognitive factors—*discriminative skill* (ability to discriminate affective states of others) and *social comprehension, or other person role perspective* (ability to assume the perspective and role of another)—and one affective factor— *emotional responsiveness* (ability to experience the negative or positive emotions of another). They assume that an empathic person will be less likely to be aggressive because of being more aware—both cognitively and affectively—of the possible effects of that aggression on others.

In one study they developed training materials and activities for small groups of children in Grades 3 to 5. The activities took place in 45-minute sessions outside the classroom, meeting three times a week for 10 weeks. One condition emphasized both affective and cognitive components and included problem-solving games, storytelling, listening to and making tape recordings, written exercises, group discussions, and other tasks. In some tasks children were asked to identify emotions in pictures of facial expressions, tape recordings of conversations, and videotaped pantomimes. There were also role-playing exercises and perspective-taking tasks. A second condition was cognitive only, focusing on nonemotional aspects of social interaction; exercises included discrimination of social cues about thoughts, intentions and probable future behavior of others.

In a pilot experiment, third- and fourth-grade children, some of them highly aggressive, who received the affective-cognitive treatment showed positive effects on teacher ratings of aggressiveness and on prosocial behavior. In a later study with a larger sample, children in the empathy-training condition—as compared with those in two control conditions—showed gains in social sensitivity to others' feelings, and prosocial behavior. They also showed declines in aggressiveness that were greater than those in a nonparticipating control group but not in a control group with an alternative set of activities.

Another study, conducted with preschool- and kindergarten-age children (Feshbach & Cohen, 1988) produced more equivocal results. In this case, the experimental training sessions focused on recognition of emotional cues and attention to how other people feel in various situations, and the control training curriculum was addressed to the understanding of television advertisements. Although there were significant effects of the training on children's affect identification at the conclusion of the training, differences with the control group were no longer significant 1 week later.

"Second Step" is another social skills training program, aimed at violence prevention among elementary and middle school children, which also includes empathy training as a core element along with training in impulse control and anger management—conducted in 30 brief, focused lessons. An evaluation of this program (Grossman et al., 1997) with second- and third-graders in 12 schools (half randomly assigned to the intervention and half to a control group) showed that it produced modest reductions in observed aggressive behavior and increases in observed prosocial-neutral behavior ("prosocial" and "neutral" behavior categories were combined because observers were unable to distinguish between them reliably in the field). Ratings of the children's behavior by teachers and parents did not show parallel changes, however.

Social Problem-Solving Training Programs. Several programs have been developed to enhance children's social problem-solving skills. Spivack and Shure and colleagues have developed such programs for children from kindergarten through fifth grade as well as for psychiatric patients and young adults (Spivack, Platt, & Shure, 1976; Shure & Healey, 1993; Shure & Spivack, 1982). The general approach is to help the children (or others) to recognize problems, to generate multiple possible solutions to the problems, and to be able to predict the most likely outcomes of the various solutions. These functions are taught explicitly in structured sequences of activities, with direct questions and "guided dialogue," focused on both hypothetical and actual problem situations. Problem-solving thinking is assessed through responses to descriptions of hypothetical interpersonal problem situations. Behavior is assessed with ratings by peers, teachers, and other observers. The program is reported to have improved problem-solving thinking and reduced "behavioral difficulties" among kindergartners in school programs; to have improved alternative thinking skills and classroom adjustment; and to have increased respect and concern for others, attentiveness, and engagement in class among fourth and fifth graders. The program is also reported to have increased problem-solving skills and prosocial behaviors among fifth and sixth graders and enhanced young children's problem-solving skills and behavior in a program conducted by trained mothers with their own children.

Although the generality and stability of these findings has been questioned (Durlak, 1983) and early attempts to replicate them produced somewhat mixed or ambiguous conclusions (Urbain & Kendall, 1980), which may have been caused by variations in the quality of research and the consistency of implementation, a number of additional programs have been developed—based largely on the Spivack-Shure approach—which have found generally positive results. A number of these are described in Cowen et al. (1996). An elementary school lesson sequence described by Weissberg, Gesten, Liebenstein, Schmid, and Hutton (1980) included—as a major element—training in recognition of feelings in others as well as oneself, along with units on the identification of interpersonal problems, generation of alternative solutions, consideration of consequences and integration of problem-solving behavior. The importance of empathy was demonstrated in a study by Work and Olsen (1990) that showed that a child's initial level of empathy was an important determinant of the acquisition of social problem-solving skills in one of these programs. Evaluations of several versions of this program, as summarized by Cowen et al. (1996) generally indicated that children gained the social problem-solving skills emphasized as a result of experiencing the program.

In a similar approach, Elias et al. (1986) had teachers train fifth-grade students in an explicit set of social problem-solving skills—interpersonal sensitivity, means-ends thinking, and planning and anticipation of results—during the first half of a school year and in the application of these skills in specific situations in the second half of the year. Students who received this training, as compared with controls, reported that they were better able to cope with the stresses of entering middle school in the subsequent year. Further analyses indicated that this relationship was mediated by students' social problem-solving skill. (The authors do not indicate, however, whether the training also had a direct effect on social problem-solving skill, but such effects have been reported for this program elsewhere: Elias & Clabby, 1989). In another study (Elias, Gara, Schuyler, Branden-Muller, & Sayette, 1991), children who had received the same program in fourth and fifth grade were followed up 6 years later, in high school (Grades 9–11). A number of dependent variables were significantly differentiated between the program students and a control group. The experimental group students performed better on questionnaire measures of behavioral social competence, self-efficacy, and depression. Other positive effects showed different patterns for boys and girls. Experimental group boys showed superior performance (vis-à-vis those in the control group) on measures of violent behavior, providing alcohol for others, and identity problems; while experimental group girls did so on measures of on-the-job performance, use of tobacco, and vandalism of parental property. (For a detailed description of these and related programs, see Elias and Tobias, 1996.)

A middle-school program designed to enhance social problem-solving (Weissberg, Caplan, & Benetto, 1988) focused on stress management and impulse control, social information processing, and behavioral social skills training, using role-playing, modeling, didactic presentations, discussions, and games. All of these activities focused on learning and applying a sequential approach to responding to interpersonal problems (think before acting, describe the problem and one's own feelings, set a goal, generate multiple solutions, anticipate consequences, and try the best plan). Students who received this training during 2 successive years gained significantly more than those with no training in their ability to generate planful and cooperative solutions to hypothetical problems, their selection of assertive and cooperative strategies for solving interpersonal problems, and in teacher ratings of adjustment (Weissberg & Caplan, 1989).

A similar training program focused more explicitly on promoting students' emotional understanding and generalization to new situations, but it also included training in a series of sequential problem-solving steps (Greenberg, 1996). An evaluation of a 60-lesson version of this program (called PATHS—Promoting Alternative THinking Strategies), comparing samples of normally adjusted and behaviorally at-risk first- to third-graders who received the program with control groups, found positive effects on emotional fluency and understanding, as well as the ability to develop effective solutions to hypothetical interpersonal problems (all assessed with interview procedures) for both groups of students. However, the students' sense of initiative and efficacy for carrying out such solutions was affected only for the normally adjusted sample (aspects that were less emphasized in the at-risk group's lessons).

The relative effectiveness of different approaches to social problem-solving training was examined in a study by Elias and Allen (1992). They compared (a) a "directed" approach (in which students are expected to learn and internalize problem-solving strategies through observing adult models, verbally rehearsing rules and strategies explicitly taught or demonstrated, and using verbal labels); (b) a "discovery" approach (in which students are expected to generate problem-solving rules inductively through the use of guided questioning, exposure to, and experiences in relevant situations and participation in reflective classroom discussions); and (c) a "mixed" approach combining elements of both of these. The relative effectiveness of each of these approaches for students at different initial levels of social adjustment was also examined. Gains in social problem-solving skills were found for all three conditions, with some indication that longer-term generalization to other kinds of situations was greater with the two coherent programs than the mixed one. (Teachers also expressed preferences for programs in which theoretical underpinnings and program activities were well integrated.) While there were a few interactions between program type and students' level of social adjustment, most of the results did not show such interactions; that is, the gains occurred for students at all social adjustment levels. The fact that the programs were effective in helping students with poor social adjustment was considered particularly important.

A number of school programs designed to promote social problem solving, conflict resolution skills, other social skills, and "civic values" have been developed by Quest International, in collaboration with Lions Clubs International. A recent report (Laird, Syropoulos, & Black, 1996) described an evaluation of two of these programs—*Skills for Adolescence* and *Working Toward Peace.* The first of these works to promote students' responsibility, decision-making skills, communication skills, and avoidance of drug and alcohol use. The second focuses on conflict management, negotiation, and communication skills (and includes a service-learning component). About 1,900 adolescents participated in a 2-year evaluation of these programs,

comparing those in three groups of classes: those using *Skills for Adolescence* alone, those using *Skills for Adolescence* supplemented by *Working Toward Peace,* and those in control classes using neither of these curricula. The material in the two programs was taught in 45-minute sessions twice a week. In general, the greatest gains were found for students in the classes that included *Working Toward Peace* and, among these, with the teachers who did the best jobs of implementing the program. Students who received the combined *Skills for Adolescence* and *Working Toward Peace* curricula showed the greatest gains in knowledge about resolving conflicts and handling anger, the greatest decreases in "violence-related referrals," and the greatest increases (by far) in observed prosocial interactions. Program-related gains in academic achievement were also reported (particularly math achievement scores in the classes of "high fidelity" teachers).

Conflict Resolution-Mediation Training Programs. Another approach to interpersonal problem-solving focuses specifically on conflict. Several programs to help students find positive and constructive ways to mediate and resolve interpersonal conflicts have been developed in recent years, but few have been systematically evaluated. Johnson and Johnson (1996) recently completed a comprehensive review of the research on conflict mediation programs. Evaluations of a "Teaching Students to Be Peacemakers" program (Johnson & Johnson, 1995)—which involves teaching students the steps of "integrative negotiations" (stating one's own wants, feelings, and underlying reasons; understanding the other's wants, feelings, and reasons; generating potential arguments to maximize joint gain; agreement on solutions) and "procedures for mediation" (ending hostilities, ensuring commitment to the mediation process, facilitating integrative negotiations, and formalizing the agreement)—have shown that participants acquired knowledge of the negotiation steps and mediation procedures as well as conflict resolution skills (observed). There is also evidence that the knowledge and skills are retained several months after the training and that these skills continue to be applied to actual conflicts in school and nonschool settings, using integrative negotiating and compromising procedures. Evaluations of other conflict mediation programs (e.g., Sadalla, Holmberg, & Halligan, 1990) have reported reductions in conflicts, suspensions, and referrals.

One conflict mediation and resolution program that has been widely implemented in elementary and secondary schools, "Resolving Conflict Creatively" (Lantieri & Pati, 1996), embeds focused conflict resolution skills training within a comprehensive schoolwide curriculum that uses such techniques as role-playing, discussing in groups, and brainstorming to promote such interpersonal skills as active listening, empathy, perspective taking, cooperation, negotiation, appropriate expressions of feelings, and assertiveness. One evaluation of this program (Metis Associates, 1990, as cited in Lantieri & Pati, 1996) reported positive assessments by teachers and administrators. They saw improvements in levels of classroom violence and the spontaneous use of conflict resolution skills, as well as "increases in self-esteem, empowerment, awareness of and verbalization of feelings, caring behavior, and acceptance of differences" (Lantieri & Pati, 1996, p. 31). Participating students also reported less fighting and more cooperating, and they learned the meaning of relevant concepts (e.g., "conflict," "mediation") more than students in a control group. A more comprehensive evaluation is in process.

COMMUNITY SERVICE PROGRAMS

As mentioned earlier, there is evidence—from both experimental (e.g., Staub, 1975) and cross-cultural (e.g., Whiting & Whiting, 1975) research—that participating in helpful activities or being given responsibility to perform a helpful role for extended periods of time can promote individual dispositions to be helpful to others. Staub (1979) describes this process as "natural socialization," in that the desired behavior is not directly taught by socializing agents but is learned by the child from participation in the activity. These principles have been applied to education through the institution of community service programs, particularly in high schools and colleges. These programs are sometimes voluntary and sometimes required. While a large number probably exist, only a few have been evaluated, to our knowledge. (For additional rationales and summaries of work in this area, see Conrad & Hedin, 1991; Schine, 1997; Youniss, McLellan, & Yates, 1997, and Youniss & Yates, 1997.)

Some of the research on the effects of community service has focused on descriptive or qualitative assessments and self-reports. These researchers generally report positive findings (see Conrad & Hedin, 1991, for a summary of some). Youniss and Yates, for example, provide evidence that a program that involved helping in a soup kitchen, combined with a class in social justice, positively influenced high school students' sense of personal agency and social responsibility (as determined by analyzing essays and discussions; Youniss and Yates, 1997), as well as their understanding of the moral and political issues involved in the problems they were confronting (Yates & Youniss, 1996).

Giles and Eyler (1994) examined the effects on college students of participating in a "community service laboratory" (required within a Human Organization and Development major) over the course of a semester. After spending 5 weeks in seminar groups talking with representatives of social service agencies, students selected one and then did volunteer work 3 hours a week for 8 weeks. Participating students increased significantly their self-reported feelings of general efficacy (i.e., feeling that most people can make a difference) and their belief in the importance of involvement in the community. This study did not include a control group, but the authors presented an interesting within-group comparison: While most of those in the study had participated in similar service activities when in high school, only 39% had done so in the prior semester in college (where the extensive linkages with students' home communities that had existed in high school no longer existed for most). After participating in the volunteer program, 98% expressed an intention to continue to do so after the end of the program. Participating students also became less likely to blame social service clients for their own misfortunes and more likely to stress a need for equal opportunity. They indicated that their experience had led them to more positive perceptions of the people with whom they worked.

Hamilton and Fenzel (1988) found modest gains in a measure of social responsibility among adolescents who volunteered for either child care or community improvement work, with greater gains and a stronger commitment to future volunteering among the community improvement volunteers. This study also did not include a control or comparison group, however, so it is not possible to conclude definitively that the changes were produced by participation in the program.

Other studies have involved more controlled assessments and findings. Markus, Howard, and King (1993) found that college students who were assigned (randomly) to "community service" sections of a "Contemporary Political Issues" course showed greater gains than students in other sections on questionnaire measures of the importance of helping others and commitment to continue being helpful, and greater (self-rated) feelings of general efficacy and tolerance and appreciation of others.

Switzer, Simmons, Dew, Regalski, and Wang (1995) conducted an evaluation of a mandatory helping program developed by the National Center for Service Learning (NCSL) located at the City University of New York. This study involved students in seventh-grade home room classes who were randomly assigned to either a helping condition or a control condition. Those in the helping condition were required to do helping activity from late fall through the rest of the school year; some were part of a formal helping program involving being tutors or helpers at a senior center (also involving a weekly seminar and maintaining a journal). Others selected their own service projects. Using preintervention and postintervention assessments, positive effects were found for boys on several variables—self-esteem, depressive affect, involvement in school and community activities, and problem behavior. Similar effects were not found for girls. This difference is attributed by the authors to differential prior socialization: girls, having already been socialized to be nurturing and helpful, were less affected by a helping program than boys, for whom it was "outside their normal realm of experience" (p. 447).

An evaluation of high school community service programs was described by Newman and Rutter (1983). They studied eight public schools with community service programs, using control groups of students who either were not in the programs or planned to do them later. They examined effects of the programs on students' sense of responsibility and concern for the welfare of others, competence and efficacy in dealing with adults and with collective tasks, and anticipated participation in adult groups and politics, and found little evidence of change on most variables. The authors suggested that the results may have been meager because students spent relatively little time in the programs, and the programs were more oriented toward personal development than social responsibility.

Conrad and Hedin (1981) evaluated a group of 27 experiential high school programs, 10 of which involved community service (the others involved internships, community study, and outdoor adventure). There were positive effects of participating in the programs on several variables, including personal and social responsibility, attitude toward adults, attitude toward being active in the community, self-esteem, empathy, and feelings of personal competence.

Thus, while the findings are somewhat mixed, there is some evidence that community service programs can produce positive effects on students' prosocial orientations, attitudes, and commitments.

Conclusions

The classroom is a distinct social setting that differs in several ways from the settings for the research from which many of the variables incorporated in prosocial-, moral-, or character-education programs have been derived: (a) from families—in the timing of initial influence, the strength and nature of the ties between children and socializing agents, and the presence and importance of peers; (b) from laboratory investigations of modeling, preaching, reinforcement, and so forth—in the duration and nature of the tasks, the presence or roles of peers, and the general complexity of the environment; and (c) from the groups involved in small group research—in the role of adults, and in the nature and duration of the usual tasks. Thus, while the variables shown to be related to moral-prosocial characteristics in such research are good candidates for showing similar relationships in classrooms, there are also reasons for uncertainty that they should generalize to the particular situation of the classroom. We will briefly characterize the results of the educational research relating to each of the major clusters of predictor variables separately. (Although it should be remembered that in the case of program evaluations several of them are usually combined, making it difficult or impossible to ascertain their individual or unique effects.)

We should also point out that different programs or approaches differ in their emphases on different sets of outcomes and hypothesized mediating variables, making it difficult to compare their effects. Cognitive-developmental-constructivist approaches such as Just Community, for example, focus more on promoting students' moral-prosocial reasoning and thinking, while direct approaches focus more on the acquisition of particular skills or behaviors and knowledge of the accepted values of society.

The Major Variables

STUDENT AUTONOMY, SELF-DIRECTION, INFLUENCE

This cluster of variables was found to be important in much of the parent socialization literature. It has also been involved in much of the research on moral and character education where it has been investigated almost always as part of more general programs or approaches. It plays a major role in the research on progressive education, open education, constructivist classrooms, and cooperative learning, and in a number of specific programs (including Just Community and CDP). These programs and approaches have shown positive effects on students' sense of community, moral reasoning, democratic values, and positive interpersonal behavior, but the relative contribution of this set of independent variables to the overall effects of the programs cannot be determined.

STUDENT INTERACTION, COLLABORATION, PARTICIPATION IN OPEN DISCUSSION

This cluster of variables derives in part from small-group research and in part from approaches to child development that emphasize the importance of interaction with peers (e.g., Youniss, 1980). The same educational approaches and programs that emphasize student autonomy and influence, for the most part, also emphasize student interaction and discussion. Other approaches, such as moral dilemma discussion, focus on these interaction processes by themselves and have shown small but consistent effects on moral reasoning. Thus, along with student autonomy-influence, student interaction and active participation in discussions has been shown to help bring about various outcomes in a broad range of studies.

TEACHER WARMTH-ACCEPTANCE-SUPPORT, AND MODELING

While the importance of this complex of variables seems almost self-evident and has been demonstrated in a number of parent socialization studies, it has been explicitly included in only a few studies relating teacher practices to moral-prosocial outcomes in students. Positive relationships with positive student interaction and other prosocial variables have been found in those studies, but they have been found in too few studies to draw definitive conclusions.

TRAINING IN SOCIAL SKILLS

Social skills training programs have used a variety of teaching approaches, deriving from both the educational and the clinical fields. Evaluations of these programs usually report at least short-term positive effects on the relevant skills and related knowledge, whether empathy, social problem solving, or conflict resolution skills. A few have also reported positive effects on social understanding and on prosocial behavior.

HELPING

The importance of this variable has been demonstrated in both family socialization studies (focusing on performance of household chores) and in some experimental research. Some of the prosocial development programs described above (particularly CDP) include participation in helping activities in the classroom, school, and wider community as an important element, but its most direct application has been in the form of community service programs, which have shown some positive effects on interpersonal attitudes and beliefs and commitment to further helpful action.

DIRECT TEACHING

A common cluster of variables appears to be included in most of the "direct" approaches. These variables—derived primarily from learning theory and social learning theory and from traditional approaches to education—include direct teacher control (involving the use of reward and punishment); explicit teaching of moral principles and prosocial values; use of specific, targeted lessons; use of moral exemplars in literature and elsewhere; use of directed discussions (where the desired responses and outcomes are predetermined by the teacher); use of competition within and between classrooms; and an emphasis on school and class symbols, pride, and identification. Unfortunately, while some of these programs are in use in multiple sites, the research evaluating them is quite meager. Some positive results have been reported, but they are based mostly on anecdotal evidence and are mostly focused on effects on students' value-consistent behavior without regard for the reasoning or motivation underlying the behavior.

Theoretical Approaches to Moral-Prosocial Education

We have described the existing educational programs under two general categories, "direct" and "indirect." When we examine the theories about the origins of moral character (and the critical components of the corresponding definitions of moral character), however, it may be useful to think of three general theoretical approaches—one corresponding to the "direct" approach, as described above; and two that underlie most of the programs we have labeled as "indirect": one focused on cognitive development, and the other on the development of caring orientations. The goals, recommended teacher practices and proposed mediating variables differ in the three approaches, at least in their purest forms.

The direct approach aims at the transmission, acquisition, and exercise of what are seen as the accepted moral values of the culture (such as honesty and responsibility). It emphasizes the principles of learning and social learning theory, as promulgated by Bandura and others, and the importance of adult guidance and direction. In this approach, teachers directly teach principles and values, use reward and punishment to obtain compliance, use exemplary literature, and promote students' identification with and pride in the school or classroom. It is hypothesized that these practices will produce compliant students who are motivated to gain rewards and avoid punishments, and who will learn and internalize the taught principles and values both because they are rewarded for doing so and because it is seen as a way of complying with the norms of the school and classroom with which they identify.

The cognitive developmental approach—as expounded in the work of Piaget, Kohlberg, and others—stresses the importance of noncoercive interpersonal interaction with peers and of confronting challenges to one's accustomed ways of thinking. These features are expected to help students to construct personal moral meaning and to progress to higher stages of moral-prosocial reasoning, as well as to apply this reasoning in relevant situations. The approach emphasizes classroom practices that promote students' reflection and participation in open-ended discussions of moral issues (both hypothetical and "practical"), their opportunities for equal-status cooperative interactions, and their participation in decision making about issues important to the group. It is assumed that these practices, in combination, will help students to feel that they are part of a moral community and to understand the necessity for reciprocity in human interaction, eventually leading them to commitment to the universal moral principles of justice.

The caring approach, promoted in the work of Noddings and Gilligan, stresses the importance of experiencing and participating in close, mutual, and reciprocal caring relationships—with adults primarily, but also with peers. The approach involves meaningful dialogue between and among students and teachers, responsive teacher guidance, and a supportive and caring community, all of which are expected to help students learn the importance of caring for others and to develop caring orientations.

The caring approach overlaps with the other two in some respects. It shares with the direct approach an emphasis on the importance of the teacher-student relationship and, perhaps, on adult guidance and modeling (although the character of the relationship, the extent of the guidance, and the content of the behavior to be modeled differs between the two approaches). It shares with the cognitive developmental approach an emphasis on the importance of dialogue and of participating in a shared community (although the emphasis is more strictly focused on the affective-supportive aspects of both the dialogue and the community in the caring approach).

While the distinctions are fairly clear in theory, most of the existing comprehensive school programs (perhaps all of them) combine several of these goals and processes. Thus, the Just Community approach, for example, emphasizes cognitive development, but also stresses the role of adult guidance (particularly in the more recent formulations) and in this way contains some elements of the direct approach. The Child Development Project, for another example, includes aspects of all three approaches: clear, direct teacher guidance, emphasis on explicit moral principles and use of exemplary literature (from the direct approach); emphasis on collaboration, discussion of moral issues, and interaction with peers (from the cognitive developmental approach); and emphasis on developing close and supportive relationships between teachers and student, and among students (from the caring approach).

Needed Research

In general, the quality of the research that has been conducted in moral-character education, broadly defined, particularly that evaluating programs, is quite uneven. Many studies have little more than anecdotal evidence of effects, many are without control or comparison groups (making it impossible to attribute obtained changes to the influence of the program), and many reports do not give clear descriptions of the program or the evaluation design and procedures. There are also problems with the assessments of outcomes. Many studies investigate only short-term outcomes; assess outcomes in only one setting and by only one procedure; are limited to one set of variables (behaviors, or moral reasoning, or moral motivation, etc., but usually not all of these together); and thus do not provide a convincing picture of students' "moral character."

The outcomes in this area are inherently complex and difficult to assess in a meaningful way, particularly if one is interested in assessing the development of enduring moral-prosocial characteristics. Determining whether a particular program or sequence of educational experiences has produced such enduring effects will require long-term, longitudinal studies, but the few longitudinal follow-up studies that have been conducted (e.g., Solomon et al., 1993; Weed, 1995) have extended only a few years beyond the end of the investigated programs. (Longer-term longitudinal studies have been conducted in studies of moral development—the most notable being the continuing investigations of the development of moral reasoning in the sample originally assessed as teenagers for Kohlberg's dissertation: Kohlberg, 1958.)

While there are disagreements about the processes most important to the development of moral character and even about which domains of behavior are to be considered relevant to moral character (e.g., consensual sexual behavior outside of marriage), there is a consensus that moral character is multifaceted. For an act to be considered moral, it must be done for moral reasons. Returning a lost item in order to obtain a reward or recognition, for example, would not be considered moral, because it lacks moral motivation; that is, it is based not on a desire to help others or to uphold moral principles but rather to achieve personal gain or avoid personal pain. As suggested by Rest (1983) and others, a person considered "moral" must be able to think clearly about the best course of action, must see that a moral action is called for, must know what the reasonable action is, must wish to engage in the action for moral reasons, must have the will or self-control to engage in the action even at some personal expense, and must have the skills to accomplish the moral action. Virtually no studies of school-based moral education programs have assessed all these aspects of moral character.

A few of the earlier, general studies used multidimensional, intensive assessments involving several data sources (e.g., self-reports, teacher ratings, open-ended interviews, projective assessments) and ranged over several settings and time periods. These studies give one a feeling of confidence that the moral-prosocial characteristics of the study participants—in all their depth, complexity, and subtlety—are being represented (Minuchin et al., 1969; Peck & Havighurst, 1960). Unfortunately, such assessments are labor intensive and therefore difficult and expensive to do in a large-sample study. Yet, surely the goal of moral education programs is to help produce people who develop such complex orientations and tendencies and maintain them over long periods of time. A recent step toward representing this complexity has been taken by Bebeau (1994), who has developed assessments representing three of the four categories proposed by Rest and has used them to assess effects of an ethical training program for dentists.

Studies comparing the predictions of the three theoretical approaches described above would be instructive. It would be important to examine a common set of variables for each (including those representing the specific goals of each program) in order to determine and compare the patterning of results for each. A few studies have taken steps in this direction (e.g., DeVries et al., 1991; Benninga et al., 1990; Sharan & Rich, 1984), but, if we are to reach definitive conclusions, more systematic and comprehensive research involving larger samples is required. It would also be important to compare the short- and long-term effects of each program or approach in such studies.

Evaluations of programs typically compare a total program—representing a combination of components—in one set of classrooms, with the absence of the program in another set. While this comparison can produce valuable initial evidence, it does not provide information about the optimal combination of the program components—that is, whether all the elements are required for producing the intended effects or some subset might be equally or more effective. If programs have more than a few components, studies incorporating systematic variations involving even the most likely combinations would be prohibitively complex. With a large sample of schools or classrooms, however, it would be possible to examine the natural variation in the actual use of the program components among teachers

implementing the program and to use regression or structural equations modeling procedures to identify and compare the relative contribution of various groupings of components to each intervening and outcome variable. Cluster-analytic approaches can also be used to identify groups of teachers with distinct profiles of program components; results can then be compared for each of these implementation "types."

It is also important to examine the level of implementation achieved. Many program evaluations (in this and other areas) either assume that those assigned to a program group (and given training) are actually doing the program, or make only a cursory attempt to assess fidelity of implementation. Yet, variations in implementation are inevitable and should therefore be incorporated and exploited in program evaluations. If implementation is assessed thoroughly and systematically, it can provide valuable information on effects achieved with different levels of implementation, the level of implementation that may be a "threshold" for various effects (i.e., the minimum level needed to achieve them), and, as above, optimal combinations of implemented components.

In addition to improved and expanded evaluations of specific programs, research is needed that further assesses the hypothesized impact on moral-prosocial development of various aspects of teacher practices and teacher-student relationships. Associations of such practices and relationships with student achievement have been investigated extensively—as documented in this and earlier editions of the Handbook—but have been done so in only a limited way in the moral education arena. Such research could examine the hypothesized impact of the "hidden curriculum" embodied in the social-structural arrangements and nature of interpersonal relationships in classrooms and schools, as mentioned earlier. (Their presumed effects have been much discussed but little researched.) It could also examine the impact of practices that are explicitly aimed at moral development. For example, studies conducted by Nucci and colleagues (e.g., Nucci & Turiel, 1978) have shown that teachers generally react to students' transgressions in the moral and conventional domains in "domain-appropriate" rather than "domain-inappropriate" ways (i.e., focusing on others' feelings and the effects of the acts on others in the moral domain and on social expectations and the normative order in the conventional domain) and that students prefer "domain-appropriate" responses (Nucci, 1984). In one study (Elardo, 1978), teachers using a behavior modification approach responded in the same ways to transgressions in both domains. While Nucci's expectation is that moral development will be enhanced by the consistent use of "domain-appropriate" responses, this expectation has not as yet been tested empirically in classrooms, to our knowledge.

There is also a need for investigations of the occurrence and effects of the specific dimensions and variables that have emerged from the family socialization and experimental research summarized earlier, many of which have been incorporated in programs but have not been investigated separately when not part of a defined program. Rohrkemper's (1984) comparison of the effects of inductive and behavior-modification teaching styles is one example of this kind of research. It would be useful to examine further effects of these and other aspects of teaching styles, including effects on students' moral reasoning, interpersonal understanding, and actual interpersonal behavior. The role of environmental stability, in particular, warrants careful examination. This variable, which appeared to be an important precursor of moral maturity in a number of the family studies, has clear implications for schools. It also would appear to be a way to achieve the close and caring relationships advocated by Noddings and others and the sense of community seen as critical by Kohlberg, the developers of the Child Development Project, and others. Consistency of experience can be established through having similar approaches used throughout a school or through having students remain with a teacher over a period of several years. Such practices have been advocated and occasionally used. However, they are not an integral aspect of any of the moral education programs we have reviewed, and they do not appear to have been the subject of systematic research related to moral-prosocial development.

Earlier, we discussed the question of the generality of parent socialization findings across sociocultural groups. These issues of generality have only been touched on in studies of moral-character education. There is evidence that at least some variables have effects that generalize across groups. It has been shown, for example, as noted earlier, that being in a school that one experiences as a "community" is as strongly related to prosocial characteristics of children in high-poverty as those in low-poverty communities (Battistich et al., 1995). Further research thoroughly examining the generality of the effects of the variables and practices described in this chapter—and, in particular, identifying the practices, styles, and approaches that have similar effects across groups, as well as those which are more differentiated—is very much needed. It would be particularly valuable to investigate the degree to which the effectiveness of particular educational programs or practices is determined or conditioned by the social-cultural-environmental circumstances of the students and by their perceptions of their teachers' goals and intentions.

More generally, as noted above, the various approaches to moral-character education have been unevenly investigated with respect to many critical dimensions, including but not limited to, the target populations. While some approaches have been the subject of considerable amounts of research (e.g., the Just Community approach), others have not. It seems particularly paradoxical that the "direct" approach, which is probably the most widely used, has not been widely and comprehensively evaluated. One particular aspect of this approach—the use of literature to convey and transmit moral messages—has been strongly emphasized by many character educators (e.g., Bennett, 1991), but, as Leming (1993) points out, the impact of morally inspiring literature on moral development has not been investigated. Vitz (1990) argues for the importance of "narrative thought" for these ends and the consistency of such use with theories of moral development. Vitz suggests that the most effective way to use narrative would be to combine it with reflective discussions led by teachers. This approach seems fairly similar to the discussion of moral dilemmas that have been investigated in many studies (if the dilemmas can be considered a form of narrative text) or to the discussions of the moral implications of literature, as used in the Child Development Project. Dilemma discussions have been shown to be effective, as described above; but the effects of the CDP use of literature and

literature discussions have not as yet been evaluated by themselves, beyond their contribution to the overall implementation of the program.

For the various reasons discussed above—paucity of research, inadequate research designs, unevenness of research coverage, restrictions of samples, limitations in ranges of outcome variables assessed, lack of consensus on appropriate outcome measures, short time frames of studies, and so forth—little can be said to have been definitively established about the effectiveness of various approaches to moral-prosocial education, although there are certain clusters of variables, as mentioned, that seem particularly promising for certain outcomes (e.g., the role of active student participation in open-ended discussions). There is a need for research that examines all the relevant dimensions in several settings and with various populations (to determine their generality), by several procedures (to establish validity), and across several time periods (to examine stability and durability).

There is, in particular, a need for long-span longitudinal studies that assess the effects of various sequences of school experiences—either as part of defined programs or in the normal course of students' school careers—on the development of students' moral character, defined and assessed comprehensively. It is undoubtedly the case that moral character is produced and shaped by complex combinations of socialization experiences extending from earliest childhood through (at least) young adulthood. Schooling occurs during most of this period and thus has great potential for producing a significant impact, although it obviously is not the only source of moral character. Well-designed, theoretically grounded, multifaceted, multiyear investigations would add much to our knowledge of the normal course of moral development and ways that educational programs might enhance it.

REFERENCES

Adalbjanardóttir, S. (1992). Fostering children's social conflict resolutions in the classroom: A developmental approach. In F. K. Oser, A. Dick, & J.-L. Patry (Eds.), *Effective and responsible teaching: The new synthesis* (pp. 397–412). San Francisco: Jossey-Bass.

Adalbjanardóttir, S. (1993). Promoting children's social growth in the schools: An intervention study. *Journal of Applied Developmental Psychology, 14,* 461–484.

Ainsworth, M., Blehar, M., Waters, E., & Wall, S. (1978). *Patterns of attachment.* Hillsdale, NJ: Lawrence Erlbaum Associates.

Allman-Snyder, A., May, M. J., & Garcia, F. C. (1975). Classroom structure and children's perceptions of authority: An open and closed case. *Urban Education, 10,* 131–149.

Allport, G. (1954). *The nature of prejudice.* Reading, MA: Addison-Wesley.

Althof, W. (Ed.). (1992). Three paths toward a just community: The German experience. *Moral Education Forum, 17*(2), 1–36.

Angell, A. V. (1991). Democratic climates in elementary classrooms: A review of theory and research. *Theory and Research in Social Education, 19*(3), 241–266.

Aronfreed, J. (1969). The concept of internalization. In D. Goslin (Ed.), *Handbook of socialization theory and research* (pp. 263–323). Chicago: Rand McNally.

Aronson, E., Bridgeman, D. L., & Geffner, R. (1978). The effects of a cooperative classroom structure on student behavior and attitudes. In D. Bar-Tal & L. Saxe (Eds.), *Social psychology of education: Theory and research* (pp. 257–272). New York: Wiley.

Asendorpf, J. B., & Nunner-Winkler, G. (1992). Children's moral motive strength and temperamental inhibition reduce their immoral behavior in real moral conflicts. *Child Development, 63*(5), 1223–1235.

Baldwin, A. L. (1955). *Behavior and development in childhood.* New York: Dryden.

Baldwin, A. L., Baldwin, C., & Cole, R. E. (1990). Stress-resistant families and stress-resistant children. In J. Rolf, A. S. Masten, D. Cicchetti, K. H. Nuechterlein, & S. Weintraub (Eds.), *Risk and protective factors in the development of psychopathology* (pp. 257–280). Cambridge, UK: Cambridge University Press.

Bandura, A. (1969). Social learning theory of identificatory processes. In D. Goslin (Ed.), *Handbook of socialization theory and research* (pp. 213–262). Chicago: Rand McNally.

Bandura, A., & McDonald, F. J. (1963). Influence of social reinforcement and the behavior of models in shaping children's moral judgments. *Journal of Abnormal and Social Psychology, 67,* 274–281.

Bar, H., & Bargal, D. (1987). *The school for peace at Neve Shalom— 1985: Description and assessment of a longitudinal intervention among trainees and staff.* Jerusalem, Israel: The Israel Institute of Applied Social Research.

Barton, E. J., & Ascione, F. R. (1979). Sharing in preschool children: Facilitation, stimulus generalization, response generalization, and maintenance. *Journal of Applied Behavior Analysis, 12,* 417–430.

Batson, C. D., Coke, J. S., Jasnoski, M. L., & Hanson, M. (1978). Buying kindness: Effect of an extrinsic incentive for helping on perceived altruism. *Personality and Social Psychology Bulletin, 4*(1), 86–91.

Battistich, V., & Hom, A. (1997). The relationship between students' sense of their school as a community and their involvement in problem behaviors. *American Journal of Public Health, 87*(12), 1997–2001.

Battistich, V., Schaps, E., Watson, M., Solomon, D., & Lewis, C. (2000). Effects of the Child Development Project on students' drug use and other problem behavior. *Journal of Primary Prevention, 21*(1), 75–99.

Battistich, V., Solomon, D., & Delucchi, K. (1990). *Effects of a program to enhance prosocial development on adjustment.* Presented at meeting of American Psychological Association, Boston, MA.

Battistich, V., Solomon, D., Kim, D., Watson, M., & Schaps, E. (1995). Schools as communities, poverty levels of student populations, and students' attitudes, motives, and performance: A multilevel analysis. *American Educational Research Journal, 32*(3), 627–658.

Battistich, V., Solomon, D., Watson, M., Solomon, J., & Schaps, E. (1989). Effects of an elementary school program to enhance prosocial behavior on children's social problem-solving skills and strategies. *Journal of Applied Developmental Psychology, 10,* 147–169.

Battistich, V., Watson, M., Solomon, D., Schaps, E., & Solomon, J. (1991). The child development project: A comprehensive program for the development of prosocial character. In W. M. Kurtines & J. L. Gewirtz (Eds.), *Handbook of moral behavior and development: Vol. 3. Application* (pp. 1–34). Hillsdale, NJ: Lawrence Erlbaum Associates.

Baumrind, D. (1967). Child care practices anteceding three patterns of preschool behavior. *Genetic Psychology Monographs, 75,* 43–88.

Baumrind, D. (1972). An exploratory study of socialization effects on black children: Some black-white comparisons. *Child Development, 43*(1), 261–267.

Baumrind, D. (1989). Rearing competent children. In W. Damon (Ed.), *Child development today and tomorrow* (pp. 349–378). San Francisco: Jossey-Bass.

Bebeau, M. J. (1994). Influencing the moral dimensions of dental practice. In J. R. Rest & D. F. Narvaez (Eds.), *Moral development in the professions: Psychology and applied ethics* (pp. 121–146). Hillsdale, NJ: Lawrence Erlbaum Associates.

Bebeau, M. J., Rest, J. R., & Narvaez, D. (1995). *A plan for moral education.* Presented at meeting of Association for Moral Education, New York, NY.

Bengtsson, H., & Johnson, L. (1992). Perspective-taking, empathy, and prosocial behavior in late childhood. *Child Study Journal, 22,* 11–22.

Bennett, W. J. (1991). Moral literacy and the formation of character. In J. S. Benninga (Ed.), *Moral, character, and civic education in the elementary school* (pp. 131–138). New York: Teachers College Press.

Benninga, J. S. (1991). Moral and character education in the elemen-

tary school: An introduction. In J. S. Benninga (Ed.), *Moral, character, and civic education in the elementary school* (pp. 3–20). New York: Teachers College Press.

Benninga, J. S., Tracz, S. M., Sparks, R. K., Jr., Solomon, D., Battistich, V., Delucchi, K. L., Sandoval, R., & Stanley, B. (1990). Effects of two contrasting school task and incentive structures on children's social development. *Elementary School Journal, 92*(2), 149–167.

Bereiter, C. (1986). Does direct-instruction cause delinquency? *Early Childhood Research Quarterly, 1,* 289–292.

Berkowitz, M. W. (1981). A critical appraisal of the educational and psychological perspectives on moral discussion. *Journal of Educational Thought, 15,* 20–33.

Berkowitz, M. W. (1996). *The "plus one" convention revisited . . . and beyond.* Presented at meeting of Association for Moral Education, Ottawa, Canada.

Berkowitz, M. W., & Gibbs, J. C. (1983). Measuring the developmental features of moral discussion. *Merrill-Palmer Quarterly, 29*(4), 399–410.

Berkowitz, M. W., Gibbs, J. C., & Broughton, J. M. (1980). The relation of moral judgment stage disparity to developmental effects of peer dialogues. *Merrill-Palmer Quarterly, 26,* 341–357.

Berndt, T. J., McCartney, K., Caparulo, B. K., & Moore, A. M. (1983–84). The effects of group discussions on children's moral decisions. *Social Cognition, 2*(4), 343–359.

Blasi, A. (1980). Bridging moral cognition and moral action: A critical review of the literature. *Psychological Bulletin, 88*(1), 1–45.

Blatt, M., & Kohlberg, L. (1975). The effects of classroom discussion upon children's level of moral judgment. *Journal of Moral Education, 4,* 129–161.

Blau, Z. S. (1981). *Black children/white children: Competence, socialization, and social structure.* New York: The Free Press.

Bridgeman, D. L. (1981). Enhanced role taking through cooperative interdependence: A field study. *Child Development, 52,* 1231–1238.

Brophy, J. E., & Good, T. L. (1986). Teacher behavior and student achievement. In M. C. Wittrock (Ed.), *Handbook of research on teaching* (3rd ed., pp. 328–375). New York: Macmillan.

Brown, D., & Solomon, D. (1983). A model for prosocial learning: An in-progress field study. In D. L. Bridgeman (Ed.), *The nature of prosocial development: Interdisciplinary theories and strategies* (pp. 273–307). New York: Academic Press.

Bryan, J. H., & Walbeck, N. (1970). Preaching and practicing generosity: Children's actions and reactions. *Child Development, 41,* 329–353.

Bryk, A. S. (1988). Musings on the moral life of schools. *American Journal of Education, 96*(2), 256–290.

Bryk, A. S., & Driscoll, M. E. (1988). *The school as community: Theoretical foundations, contextual influences, and consequences for students and teachers.* Madison, WI: National Center on Effective Secondary Schools, University of Wisconsin.

Cahill, R. J., & Handy, H. W. (1974). *Character education: Summative evaluation of the first generation curriculum developed by the American Institute for Character Education.* Pittsburgh, PA: American Institutes for Research.

Carlo, G., Knight, G. P., Eisenberg, N., & Rotenberg, K. J. (1991). Cognitive processes and prosocial behaviors among children: The role of affective attributions and reconciliations. *Developmental Psychology, 27*(3), 456–461.

Carlo, G., Koller, S. H., Eisenberg, N., Da Silva, M. S., & Frohlich, C. B. (1996). A cross-national study on the relations among prosocial moral reasoning, gender role orientations, and prosocial behaviors. *Developmental Psychology, 32*(2), 231–240.

Cartwright, D. (1968). The nature of group cohesiveness. In D. Cartwright & A. Zander (Eds.), *Group dynamics: Research and theory* (3rd ed., pp. 91–109). New York: Harper & Row.

Center for Civic Education. (1996). *Impact assessment study of citizenship/law-related education on violent and antisocial behavior: Year one evaluation, Bell Gardens Intermediate School. Executive summary.* Calabasas, CA: Author.

Center for Civic Education and Constitutional Rights Foundation. (Undated). *Youth for justice: National coordinated law-related education program.* Los Angeles: Author.

Chalmers, J. B., & Townsend, M. A. R. (1990). The effects of training in social perspective taking on socially maladjusted girls. *Child Development, 61*(1), 178–190.

Chandler, M. J. (1973). Egocentrism and antisocial behavior: The assessment and training of social perspective taking skills. *Developmental Psychology, 9,* 326–332.

Chandler, M. J., Greenspan, S., & Barenboim, C. (1974). Assessment and training of role taking and referential communication skills in institutionalized emotionally disturbed children. *Developmental Psychology, 10,* 546–553.

Clary, E. G., & Miller, J. (1986). Socialization and situational influences on sustained altruism. *Child Development, 57*(6), 1358–1369.

Clinchy, B., Lief, J., & Young, P. (1977). Epistemological and moral development in girls from a traditional and a progressive high school. *Journal of Educational Psychology, 69,* 337–343.

Cohen, E. G., Lotan, R., & Catanzarite, L. (1990). Treating status problems in the cooperative classroom. In S. Sharan (Ed.), *Cooperative learning: Theory and research* (pp. 203–229). New York: Praeger.

Colby, A., & Damon, W. (1992). *Some do care: Contemporary lives of moral commitment.* New York: The Free Press.

Conrad, D., & Hedin, D. (1981). *Executive summary: Experiential education evaluation project.* St. Paul, MN: Center for Youth Development and Research, University of Minnesota.

Conrad, D., & Hedin, D. H. (1991). School-based community service: What we know from research and theory. *Phi Delta Kappan, 72,* 743–749.

Cowan, P. A., Langer, J., Heavenrich, J., & Nathanson, M. (1969). Social learning and Piaget's cognitive theory of moral development. *Journal of Personality and Social Psychology, 11*(9), 261–274.

Cowen, E. L., Hightower, A. D., Pedro-Carroll, J. L., Work, W. C., Wyman, P. A., & Haffey, W. G. (1996). *School-based prevention for children at risk: The Primary Mental Health Project.* Washington, DC: American Psychological Association.

Crowley, P. M. (1968). Effect of training upon objectivity of moral judgment in grade-school children. *Journal of Personality and Social Psychology, 8*(3), 228–232.

Damon, W., & Killen, M. (1982). Peer interaction and the process of change in children's moral reasoning. *Merrill-Palmer Quarterly, 28*(3), 347–369.

Davis, A., & Havighurst, R. S. (1946). Social class and color differences in child-rearing. *American Sociological Review, 11,* 698–710.

Dekovic, M., & Janssens, J. M. A. M. (1992). Parents' child-rearing style and child's sociometric status. *Developmental Psychology, 28*(5), 925–932.

Delpit, L. (1995). *Other people's children: Cultural conflict in the classroom.* New York: The New Press.

Denham, S. A. (1986). Social cognition, prosocial behavior, and emotion in preschoolers: Contextual validation. *Child Development, 57*(1), 194–201.

Deutsch, M. (1973). *The resolution of conflict.* New Haven, CT: Yale University Press.

Deutsch, M. (1985). *Distributive justice.* New Haven, CT: Yale University Press.

Developmental Studies Center. (1998). *The Child Development Project: Summary of the project and findings from three evaluation studies.* Oakland, CA: Author.

DeVries, R., & Goncu, A. (1987). Interpersonal relations between four-year-olds in dyads from constructivist and Montessori classrooms. *Applied Developmental Psychology, 8,* 481–501.

DeVries, R., Haney, J. P., & Zan, B. (1991). Sociomoral atmosphere in direct-instruction, eclectic, and constructivist kindergartens: A study of teachers' enacted interpersonal understanding. *Early Childhood Research Quarterly, 6,* 449–471.

DeVries, R., Reese-Learned, H., & Morgan, P. (1991). Sociomoral development in direct-instruction, eclectic, and constructivist kindergartens: A study of children's enacted interpersonal understanding. *Early Childhood Research Quarterly, 6,* 473–517.

DeVries, R., & Zan, B. (1994). *Moral classrooms, moral children: Creating a constructivist atmosphere in early education.* New York: Teachers College Press.

Dewey, J. (1975). *Moral principles in education.* Carbondale, IL: Southern Illinois University Press. (Original work published in 1909)

Dewey, J. (1966). *Democracy and education.* New York: The Free Press. (Original work published in 1916)

Dodge, K. A., Pettit, G. S., & Bates, J. E. (1994). Socialization mediators of the relation between socioeconomic status and child conduct problems. *Child Development, 65*(2), 649–665.

Doland, D. J., & Adelberg, K. (1967). The learning of sharing behavior. *Child Development, 38,* 695–700.

Dreikurs, R., Grunwald, B. B., & Pepper, F. C. (1971). *Maintaining sanity in the classroom: Illustrated teaching techniques.* New York: Harper & Row.

Dressel, S., & Midlarsky, E. (1978). The effects of model's exhortations, demands, and practices on children's donation behavior. *Journal of Genetic Psychology, 132,* 211–223.

Dror, Y. (1995). The Anne Frank haven in an Israeli kibbutz. *Adolescence, 30*(119), 617–629.

Dunn, J. (1987). The beginnings of moral understanding: Development in the second year. In J. Kagan & S. Lamb (Eds.), *The emergence of morality in young children* (pp. 91–112). Chicago: University of Chicago Press.

Dunn, J., Brown, J. R., & Maguire, M. (1995). The development of children's moral sensibility: Individual differences and emotion understanding. *Developmental Psychology, 31*(4), 649–659.

Durkheim, E. (1961). *Moral education: A study in the theory and application of the sociology of education.* New York: The Free Press. (Original work published in 1925)

Durlak, J. (1983). Social problem-solving as a primary prevention strategy. In R. Felner, L. Jason, J. Moritsugu, & S. Farber (Eds.), *Preventive psychology: Theory, research, and practice* (pp. 31–48). New York: Pergamon.

Ehman, L. H. (1980a). The American school in the political socialization process. *Review of Educational Research, 50,* 99–119.

Ehman, L. H. (1980b). Change in high school students' political attitudes as a function of social studies social climate. *American Educational Research Journal, 17*(2), 253–265.

Eisenberg, N. (1986). *Altruistic emotion, cognition, and behavior.* Hillsdale, NJ: Lawrence Erlbaum Associates.

Eisenberg, N., Fabes, R. A., Carlo, G., Speer, A. L., Switzer, G., Karbon, M., & Troyer, D. (1993). The relations of empathy-related emotions and maternal practices to children's comforting behavior. *Journal of Experimental Child Psychology, 55,* 131–150.

Eisenberg, N., Fabes, R. A., Miller, P. A., Shell, R., Shea, C., & May-Plumlee, T. (1990). Preschoolers' vicarious emotional responding and their situational and dispositional prosocial behavior. *Merrill-Palmer Quarterly, 36,* 507–529.

Eisenberg, N., & Miller, P. (1987). The relation of empathy to prosocial and related behaviors. *Psychological Bulletin, 101,* 91–119.

Eisenberg, N., & Mussen, P. H. (1989). *The roots of prosocial behavior in children.* New York: Cambridge University Press.

Eisenberg-Berg, N., & Geisheker, E. (1979). Content of preachings and power of the model/preacher: The effects on children's generosity. *Developmental Psychology, 15*(2), 168–175.

Elardo, R. (1978). Behavior modification in an elementary school: Problems and issues. *Phi Delta Kappan, 59,* 334–340.

Elias, M. J., & Allen, G. J. (1992). A comparison of instructional methods for delivering a preventive social competence/social decision-making program to at-risk, average, and competent students. *School Psychology Quarterly, 6,* 257–272.

Elias, M. J., & Clabby, J. F. (1989). *Social decision-making skills: A curriculum guide for elementary grades.* Rockville, MD: Aspen.

Elias, M. J., Gara, M. A., Schuyler, T. F., Branden-Muller, L. R., & Sayette, M. A. (1991). The promotion of social competence: Longitudinal study of a preventive school-based program. *American Journal of Orthopsychiatry, 61*(3), 409–417.

Elias, M. J., Gara, M. A., Ubriaco, M., Rothbaum, P. A., Clabby, J. F., & Schuyler, T. (1986). Impact of a preventive social problem-solving intervention on children's coping with middle-school stressors. *American Journal of Community Psychology, 14*(3), 259–275.

Elias, M. J., & Tobias, S. E. (1996). *Social problem solving: Interventions in the schools.* New York: Guilford.

Elliot, R., & Vasta, R. (1970). The modeling of sharing: Effects associated with vicarious reinforcement, symbolization, age, and generalization. *Journal of Experimental Child Psychology, 10,* 8–15.

Elliott, S. N. (1992). *Caring to learn: A report on the positive impact of a social curriculum.* Greenfield, MA: Northeast Foundation for Children.

Elliott, S. N. (1995). *The Responsive Classroom approach: Its effectiveness and acceptability. Final evaluation report.* Washington, DC: Center for Systemic Educational Change, District of Columbia Public Schools.

Etxebarria, I., Apodaka, P., Eceiza, A., Ortiz, M. J., Fuentes, M. J., & Lopez, F. (1994). Design and evaluation of a programme to promote prosocial-altruistic behavior in the school. *Journal of Moral Education, 23*(4), 409–425.

Fabes, R. A., Fultz, J., Eisenberg, N., May-Plumlee, T., & Christopher, F. S. (1989). Effects of rewards on children's prosocial motivation: A socialization study. *Developmental Psychology, 25*(4), 509–515.

Feshbach, N. D. (1979). Empathy training: A field study in affective education. In S. Feshbach & A. Fraczek (Eds.), *Aggression and behavior change: Biological and social processes* (pp. 234–249). New York: Praeger.

Feshbach, N. D. (1984). Empathy, empathy training, and the regulation of aggression in elementary school children. In R. M. Kaplan, V. J. Konecni, & R. W. Novaco (Eds.), *Aggression in children and youth* (pp. 192–208). The Hague, Netherlands: Martinus Nijhoff Publishers.

Feshbach, N. D., & Cohen, S. (1988). Training affect comprehension in young children: An experimental evaluation. *Journal of Applied Developmental Psychology, 9*(2), 201–210.

Feshbach, N. D., & Feshbach, S. (1982). Empathy training and the regulation of aggression: Potentialities and limitations. *Academic Psychological Bulletin, 4,* 399–413.

Fry, P. S., & Addington, J. (1984). Comparison of social problem solving of children from open and traditional classrooms: A two-year longitudinal study. *Journal of Educational Psychology, 76*(1), 318–329.

Fuchs, I., Eisenberg, N., Hertz-Lazarowitz, R., & Sharabany, R. (1986). Kibbutz, Israeli city and American children's moral reasoning about prosocial moral conflicts. *Merrill-Palmer Quarterly, 32*(1), 37–50.

Gelfand, D. M., Hartmann, D. P., Cromer, C. C., Smith, C. L., & Page, B. C. (1975). Effects of instructional prompts and praise on children's donation rates. *Child Development, 46,* 980–983.

Gerard, H. B., & Miller, N. (1975). *School desegregation.* New York: Plenum.

Gersten, R. (1986). Response to "Consequences of three preschool curriculum models through age 15." *Early Childhood Research Quarterly, 1,* 293–302.

Gewirtz, J. (1969). Mechanisms of social learning: Some roles of stimulation and behavior in early human development. In D. Goslin (Ed.), *Handbook of socialization theory and research* (pp. 57–212). Chicago: Rand McNally.

Giles, D. E., Jr., & Eyler, J. (1994). The impact of a college community service laboratory on students' personal, social, and cognitive outcomes. *Journal of Adolescence, 17,* 327–339.

Gilligan, C. (1982). *In a different voice.* Cambridge, MA: Harvard University Press.

Goble, F. G., & Brooks, B. D. (1983). *The case for character education.* Ottawa, IL: Green Hill Publishers.

Golub, M., & Kolen, C. (1976). *Evaluation of a Piagetian kindergarten program.* Presented at Sixth Annual Symposium of the Jean Piaget Society, Philadelphia.

Goodenow, C. (1992). Strengthening the links between educational psychology and the study of social contexts. *Educational Psychologist, 27*(2), 177–196.

Goodlad, J. (1984). *A place called school: Prospects for the future.* New York: McGraw-Hill.

Goodlad, J. I., Soder, R., & Sirotnik, K. A. (1990). *The moral dimensions of teaching.* San Francisco: Jossey-Bass.

Greenberg, M. T. (1996). *Final report to NIMH. The PATHS project: Preventive intervention for children.* Seattle, WA: Department of Psychology, University of Washington.

Grossman, D.C., Neckerman, H. J., Koepsell, T. D., Liu, P.-Y., Asher, K. N., Beland, K., Frey, K., & Rivara, F. P. (1997). Effectiveness of a violence prevention curriculum among children in elementary school: A randomized controlled trial. *Journal of the American Medical Association, 277*(20), 1605–1611.

Grusec, J. E. (1979). The role of example and moral exhortation in the training of altruism. *Child Development, 49*(3), 920–923.

Grusec, J. E. (1981). Socialization processes and altruism. In J. P. Rushton & R. M. Sorrentino (Eds.), *Altruism and helping behavior* (pp. 65–90). Hillsdale, NJ: Lawrence Erlbaum Associates.

Grusec, J. E. (1991). The socialization of altruism. In M. S. Clark (Ed.), *Prosocial behavior: Vol. 12* (pp. 9–33). Newbury Park, CA: Sage.

Grusec, J. E., Goodnow, J. L., & Cohen, L. (1996). Household work and the development of concern for others. *Developmental Psychology, 32*(6), 999–1007.

Grusec, J. E., Kuczynski, L., Rushton, J. P., & Simutis, Z. M. (1979). Modeling, direct instruction, and attributions: Effects on altruism. *Developmental Psychology, 14,* 51–57.

Grusec, J. E., & Redler, E. (1980). Attribution, reinforcement, and altruism: A developmental analysis. *Developmental Psychology, 16*(5), 525–534.

Grusec, J. E., & Skubiski, S. L. (1970). Model nurturance, demand characteristics of the modeling experiment, and altruism. *Journal of Personality and Social Psychology, 14,* 352–359.

Gutmann, A. (1987). *Democratic education.* Princeton, NJ: Princeton University Press.

Hallinan, M. T. (1976). Friendship patterns in open and traditional classrooms. *Sociology of Education, 49,* 254–264.

Hamilton, S. F., & Fenzel, L. M. (1988). The impact of volunteer experience on adolescent social development: Evidence of program effects. *Journal of Adolescent Research, 3*(1), 65–80.

Hansell, S., & Slavin, R. E. (1981). Cooperative learning and the structure of interracial friendships. *Sociology of Education, 54,* 98–106.

Hansen, D. T. (1993). From role to person: The moral layeredness of classroom teaching. *American Educational Research Journal, 30*(4), 651–674.

Hansen, D. T. (1996). Teaching and the moral life of classrooms. *Journal for a Just and Caring Education, 2*(1), 59–74.

Hartshorne, H., & May, M. A. (1928). *Studies in the nature of character. I. Studies in deceit. Book one: General methods and results. Book two: Statistical methods and results: Vol. 1.* New York: Macmillan.

Hartshorne, H., May, M. A., & Maller, J. B. (1929). *Studies in the nature of character. II. Studies in service and self-control. Book One: Studies in service. Book Two: Studies in self-control: Vol. 2.* New York: Macmillan.

Hartshorne, H., May, M. A., & Shuttleworth, F. K. (1930). *Studies in the nature of character. III. Studies in the organization of character: Vol. 3.* New York: Macmillan.

Hawley, W. D. (1976). *The implicit civics curriculum: Teacher behavior and political learning.* Durham, NC: Center for Policy Analysis, Duke University.

Hertz-Lazarowitz, R., & Sharan, S. (1984). Enhancing prosocial behavior through cooperative learning in the classroom. In E. Staub, D. Bar-Tal, J. Karylowski, & J. Reykowski (Eds.), *Development and maintenance of prosocial behavior: International perspectives on positive morality* (pp. 423–443). New York: Plenum Press.

Hertz-Lazarowitz, R., Sharan, S., & Steinberg, R. (1980). Classroom learning styles and cooperative behavior of elementary school children. *Journal of Educational Psychology, 72*(1), 99–106.

Hess, R. D., & Shipman, V. C. (1965). Early experience and the socialization of cognitive modes in children. *Child Development, 36*(4), 869–886.

Higgins, A. (1980). Research and measurement issues in moral education interventions. In R. L. Mosher (Ed.), *Moral education: A first generation of research and development* (pp. 92–107). New York: Praeger.

Higgins, A., Power, C., & Kohlberg, L. (1984). The relationship of moral atmosphere to judgments of responsibility. In W. M. Kurtines & J. L. Gewirtz (Eds.), *Morality, moral behavior and moral development* (pp. 74–106). New York: Wiley.

Hoffman, M. L. (1970). Moral development. In P. H. Mussen (Ed.), *Carmichael's manual of child psychology: Vol. 2* (pp. 261–360). New York: Wiley.

Hoffman, M. L. (1975). Moral internalization, parental power, and the nature of parent-child interaction. *Developmental Psychology, 11,* 228–239.

Hoffman, M. L. (1978). Empathy: Its development and prosocial implications. In C. B. Keasey (Ed.), *Nebraska Symposium on Motivation, 1977: Vol. 25* (pp. 169–217). Lincoln, NE: University of Nebraska Press.

Hoffman, M. L., & Saltzstein, H. D. (1967). Parent discipline and the child's moral development. *Journal of Personality and Social Psychology, 5,* 45–57.

Iannotti, R. J. (1978). Effect of role-taking experiences on role taking, empathy, altruism, and aggression. *Developmental Psychology, 14*(2), 119–124.

Israel, A. C., & Raskin, P. A. (1979). Directiveness of instructions and modeling: Effect on production and persistence of children's donations. *Journal of Genetic Psychology, 135,* 269–277.

Jackson, P. W., Boostrom, R. E., & Hansen, D. T. (1993). *The moral life of schools.* San Francisco: Jossey-Bass.

Jensen, L. C., & Larm, C. (1970). Effects of two training procedures on intentionality in moral judgments among children. *Developmental Psychology, 2*(2), 310.

Johnson, D. W. (1981). Student-student interaction: The neglected variable in education. *Educational Researcher, 10*(1), 5–10.

Johnson, D. W., & Johnson, R. T. (1981). Effects of cooperative and individualistic learning experiences on interethnic interaction. *Journal of Educational Psychology, 73*(3), 444–449.

Johnson, D. W., & Johnson, R. T. (1985). Classroom conflict: Controversy vs. debate in learning groups. *American Educational Research Journal, 22,* 237–256.

Johnson, D. W., & Johnson, R. T. (1989). *Cooperation and competition: Theory and research.* Edina, MN: Interaction Book Company.

Johnson, D. W., & Johnson, R. T. (1992). *Creative controversy: Intellectual challenge in the classroom.* Edina, MN: Interaction Book Company.

Johnson, D. W., & Johnson, R. T. (1994). Structuring academic controversy. In S. Sharan (Ed.), *Handbook of cooperative learning methods* (pp. 66–81). Westport, CT: Greenwood.

Johnson, D. W., & Johnson, R. T. (1995). *Teaching students to be peacemakers* (3rd ed.). Edina, MN: Interaction Book Company.

Johnson, D. W., & Johnson, R. T. (1996). Conflict resolution and peer mediation programs in elementary and secondary schools: A review of the research. *Review of Educational Research, 66*(4), 459–506.

Johnson, D. W., Johnson, R. T., Johnson, J., & Anderson, D. (1976). The effects of cooperative vs. individualized instruction on student prosocial behavior, attitudes toward learning, and achievement. *Journal of Educational Psychology, 68,* 446–452.

Johnson, D. W., Johnson, R. T., & Maruyama, G. (1983). Interdependence and interpersonal attraction among heterogeneous and homogeneous individuals: A theoretical formulation and meta-analysis of the research. *Review of Educational Research, 53*(1), 5–54.

Johnson, D. W., Johnson, R. T., & Maruyama, G. (1984). Goal interdependence and interpersonal attraction in heterogeneous classrooms: A meta-analysis. In N. Miller & M. Brewer (Eds.), *Groups in contact: The psychology of desegregation* (pp. 187–212). Orlando, FL: Academic Press.

Jones, V. (1936). *Character and citizenship training in the public schools.* Chicago: University of Chicago Press.

Kagan, S., Zahn, G. L., Widaman, K. F., Schwarzwald, J., & Tyrell, G. (1985). Classroom structural bias: Impact of cooperative and competitive classroom structures on cooperative and competitive individuals and groups. In R. E. Slavin, S. Sharan, S. Kagan, R. Hertz-Lazarowitz, C. Webb, & R. Schmuck (Eds.), *Learning to cooperate, cooperating to learn* (pp. 277–312). New York: Plenum.

Kerr, D. (1996). Democracy, nurturance, and community. In R. Soder (Ed.), *Democracy, education, and the schools.* San Francisco: Jossey-Bass.

Kochanska, G. (1991). Socialization and temperament in the development of guilt and conscience. *Child Development, 62*(6), 1379–1392.

Kohlberg, L. (1958). *The development of modes of moral thinking and choice in the years ten to sixteen.* Unpublished doctoral dissertation, University of Chicago, Chicago, IL.

Kohlberg, L. (1969). Stage and sequence: The cognitive-developmental approach to socialization. In D. Goslin (Ed.), *Handbook of socialization theory and research* (pp. 347–480). Chicago: Rand McNally.

Kohlberg, L. (1975). *The Just Community School: The theory and the Cambridge Cluster School experiment.* Collected papers from the Center for Moral Education (Chapter 29, pp. 21–77): (ERIC Document Reproduction Service No. ED 223 511).

Kohlberg, L. (1978). The cognitive-developmental approach to moral education. In P. Scharf (Ed.), *Readings in moral education* (pp. 36–51). Minneapolis, MN: Winston Press.

Kohlberg, L. (1985). The Just Community approach to moral education in theory and practice. In M. Berkowitz & F. Oser (Eds.), *Moral education* (pp. 27–87) . Hillsdale, NJ: Lawrence Erlbaum Associates.

Kohlberg, L., & Candee, D. (1984). The relationship of moral judgment to moral action. In W. M. Kurtines & J. L. Gewirtz (Eds.), *Morality, moral behavior, and moral development* (pp. 52–73). New York: Wiley.

Kohlberg, L., & Higgins, A. (1987). School democracy and social interaction. In W. Kurtines & J. Gewirtz (Eds.), *Moral development through social interaction* (pp. 102–128). New York: Wiley.

Kohlberg, L., Lieberman, M., Powers, C., Higgins, A., & Codding, J. (1981). Evaluating Scarsdale's "Just Community School" and its curriculum; implications for the future. *Moral Education Forum, 6*(4), 31–42.

Kohn, A. (1997). How not to teach values: A critical look at character education. *Phi Delta Kappan, 78*(6), 429–439.

Krebs, D. L., & Miller, D. T. (1985). Altruism and aggression. In G. Lindzey & E. Aronson (Eds.), *Handbook of social psychology* (3rd ed.). *Volume II: Special fields and applications* (pp. 1–71). New York: Random House.

Krebs, D. L., & Sturrup, B. (1981). Role-taking ability and altruistic behavior in elementary school children. *Journal of Moral Education, 11*(2), 94–100.

Krebs, D. L., & Van Hesteren, F. (1994). The development of altruism: Toward an integrative model. *Developmental Review, 14,* 103–158.

Krevans, J., & Gibbs, J. C. (1996). Parents' use of inductive discipline: Relations to children's empathy and prosocial behavior. *Child Development, 67,* 3263–3277.

Kubelick, C. (1982). Building a Just Community in the elementary school. In L. W. Rosenzweig (Ed.), *Developmental perspectives on the social studies: Vol. 66* (pp. 15–29). Washington, DC: National Council for the Social Studies.

Kunda, Z., & Schwartz, S. H. (1983). Undermining intrinsic moral motivation: External reward and self-presentation. *Journal of Personality and Social Psychology, 45*(4), 763–771.

Laird, M., Syropoulos, M., & Black, S. (1996). *Aggression and violence: The challenge for Detroit schools. Findings from an evaluation study of Lions-Quest Working Toward Peace in Detroit schools.* Newark, OH: Quest International.

Lantieri, L., & Pati, J. (1996). The road to peace in our schools. *Educational Leadership, 54*(1), 28–31.

Leming, J. S. (1981). Curricular effectiveness in moral/values education. *Journal of Moral Education, 10*(3), 147–164.

Leming, J. S. (1985). Research on social studies curriculum and instruction: Interventions and outcomes in the socio-moral domain. In W. B. Stanley (Ed.), *Review of research in social studies education: 1976–1983* (pp. 123–213). Boulder, CO, and Washington, DC: Social Science Education Consortium and National Council for the Social Studies.

Leming, J. S. (1993). In search of effective character education. *Educational Leadership, 51,* 63–71.

Leming, J. S., Henrick-Smith, A., & Antis, J. (1997). *An evaluation of the Heartwood Institute's "An Ethics Curriculum for Children."* Presented at meeting of American Educational Research Association, Chicago, IL.

Lencz, L. (1994). The Slovak Ethical Education Project. *Cambridge Journal of Education, 24*(3), 443–451.

Lepper, M. (1983). Social control processes, attributions of motivation, and the internalization of social values. In E. T. Higgins, D. N. Ruble, & W. W. Hartup (Eds.), *Social cognition and social development: A sociocultural perspective* (pp. 294–330). New York: Cambridge University Press.

Lewin, K. (1938). Experiments on autocratic and democratic atmospheres. *Social Frontiers, 4,* 316–319.

Lewin, K., Lippitt, R., & White, R. (1939). Patterns of aggressive behavior in experimentally created social climates. *Journal of Social Psychology, 10,* 271–299.

Lewis, C. C. (1981). The effects of parental firm control: A reinterpretation of findings. *Psychological Bulletin, 90,* 547–563.

Lickona, T. (1991). *Educating for character: How our schools can teach respect and responsibility.* New York: Bantam Books.

Lind, G., & Althof, W. (1992). Does the Just Community experience make a difference? Measuring and evaluating the effect of the DES project. *Moral Education Forum, 17*(2), 19–28.

Lippitt, R., & White, R. K. (1952). An experimental study of leadership and group life. In G. E. Swanson, T. M. Newcomb, & E. L. Hartley (Eds.), *Readings in social psychology* (Revised ed., pp. 340–355). New York: Henry Holt.

Lockwood, A. L. (1978). The effects of values clarification and moral development curricula on school-age subjects: A critical review of recent research. *Review of Educational Research, 48*(3), 325–364.

London, P. (1970). The rescuers: Motivational hypotheses about Christians who saved Jews from the Nazis. In J. Macaulay & L. Berkowitz (Eds.), *Altruism and helping behavior* (pp. 241–250). New York: Academic Press.

Lourenco, O. (Undated). *Promoting children's prosocial behavior: A Piagetian, gain-construction approach.* Unpublished manuscript, Lisbon, Portugal.

Maccoby, E. E., & Martin, J. A. (1983). Socialization in the context of the family: Parent-child interaction. In P. H. Mussen (Ed.), *Handbook of child psychology: Vol. 4. Socialization, personality, and social development* (pp. 1–101). New York: Wiley.

Main, M., & Weston, D. (1981). The quality of the toddler's relationship to mother and to father: Related to conflict behavior and the readiness to establish new relationships. *Child Development, 52,* 932–940.

Marantz, M. (1988). Fostering prosocial behaviour in the early childhood classroom: Review of the research. *Journal of Moral Education, 17*(1), 27–39.

Markus, G. B., Howard, J. P. F., & King, D.C. (1993). Integrating community service and classroom instruction enhances learning: Results from an experiment. *Educational Evaluation and Policy Analysis, 15*(4), 410–419.

Marsh, D. T., Serafica, F. C., & Barenboim, C. (1980). Effect of perspective taking training on interpersonal problem solving. *Child Development, 51,* 140–145.

McCann, J., & Bell, P. (1975). Educational environment and the development of moral concepts. *Journal of Moral Education, 5,* 63–70.

McQuaide, J., Fienberg, J., & Leinhardt, G. (1994). *The value of character: Final report on a study of the STAR program.* Pittsburgh, PA: Learning Research and Development Center.

Metis Associates. (1990). *The Resolving Conflict Creatively Program 1988–1989: A summary of significant findings.* New York: Author.

Midlarsky, E., & Bryan, J. H. (1967). Training charity in children. *Journal of Personality and Social Psychology, 5*(4), 408–415.

Midlarsky, E., Bryan, J. H., & Brickman, P. (1973). Aversive approval: Interactive effects of modeling and reinforcement on altruistic behavior. *Child Development, 44*(2), 321–328.

Miller, P. A., Eisenberg, N., Fabes, R. A., & Shell, R. (1996). Relations of moral reasoning and vicarious emotion to young children's prosocial behavior toward peers and adults. *Developmental Psychology, 32*(2), 210–219.

Minuchin, P., Biber, B., Shapiro, E., & Zimiles, H. (1969). *The psychological impact of school experience.* New York: Basic Books.

Moos, R. H. (1979). *Evaluating educational environments.* San Francisco: Jossey-Bass.

Newman, F. M., & Rutter, R. A. (1983). *The effects of high school community service programs on students' social development.* Madison, WI: Wisconsin Center for Education Research.

Nicholls, J. G. (1989). *The competitive ethos and democratic education.* Cambridge, MA: Harvard University Press.

Noddings, N. (1988). An ethic of caring and its implications for instructional arrangements. *American Journal of Education, 96*(2), 215–230.

Noddings, N. (1992). *The challenge to care in schools: An alternative approach to education.* New York: Teachers College Press.

Noddings, N. (1994). Conversation as moral education. *Journal of Moral Education, 23,* 107–118.

Nucci, L. P. (1984). Evaluating teachers as social agents: Students' ratings of domain appropriate and domain inappropriate teacher responses to transgressions. *American Educational Research Journal, 21*(2), 367–378.

Nucci, L. P., & Turiel, E. (1978). Social interactions and the development of social concepts in preschool children. *Child Development, 49*(2), 400–407.

Oliner, S. P., & Oliner, P. M. (1988). *The altruistic personality: Rescuers of Jews in Nazi Europe.* New York: The Free Press.

Olweus, D. (1980). Familial and temperamental determinants of aggressive behavior in adolescent boys: A causal analysis. *Developmental Psychology, 16*(6), 644–660.

Oser, F. K. (1986). Moral education and values education: The discourse perspective. In M. C. Wittrock (Ed.), *Handbook of research on teaching* (3rd ed., pp. 917–941). New York: Macmillan.

Oser, F. K. (1992). The pilot project "Democracy and Education in the School" (DES) in Northrine-Westphalia. *Moral Education Forum, 17*(2), 1–4.

Oser, F. K. (1994). Moral perspectives on teaching. In L. Darling-Hammond (Ed.), *Review of research in education: Vol. 20* (pp. 57–127). Washington, DC: American Educational Research Association.

Oser, F. K., & Althof, W. (1993). Trust in advance: On the professional morality of teachers. *Journal of Moral Education, 22*(3), 253–274.

Parish, T. S. (1981). The enhancement of altruistic behaviors in children through the implementation of dilemma discussion procedures. *Education, 102*(2), 154–158.

Peck, R. F., & Havighurst, R. J. (1960). *The psychology of character development.* New York: Wiley.

Perry, D. G., Bussey, K., & Freiberg, K. (1981). Impact of adults' appeals for sharing on the development of altruistic dispositions in children. *Journal of Experimental Child Psychology, 32,* 127–138.

Piaget, J. (1965). *The moral judgment of the child.* New York: The Free Press. (Original work published in 1932).

Pitkanen-Pulkkinen, L. (1980). The child in the family. *Nordisk Psykologi, 32*(2), 147–157.

Power, C. (1988). The Just Community approach to moral education. *Journal of Moral Education, 17*(3), 195–208.

Power, F. C., & Makogon, T. A. (1996). The Just-Community approach to care. *Journal for a Just and Caring Education, 2*(1), 9–24.

Radke-Yarrow, M., Zahn-Waxler, C., & Chapman, M. (1983). Children's prosocial dispositions and behavior. In P. H. Mussen (Ed.), *Handbook of child psychology: Vol. 2* (pp. 469–545). New York: Wiley.

Raths, L. E., Harmin, M., & Simon, S. B. (1978). *Values and teaching: Working with values in the classroom* (2nd ed.). Columbus, OH: Charles E. Merrill.

Reimer, J., & Power, C. (1980). Educating for democratic community: Some unresolved dilemmas. In R. J. Mosher (Ed.), *Moral education: A first generation of research and development* (pp. 303–320). New York: Praeger.

Rest, J. R. (1979). *Development in judging moral issues.* Minneapolis, MI: University of Minnesota Press.

Rest, J. R. (1983). Morality. In J. Flavell & E. Markman (Eds.), *Handbook of child psychology: Vol. 3. Cognitive development* (pp. 556–629). New York: Wiley.

Rice, M. E., & Grusec, J. E. (1975). Saying and doing: Effects on observer performance. *Journal of Personality and Social Psychology, 32,* 584–593.

Roberts, W., & Strayer, J. (1996). Empathy, emotional expressiveness, and prosocial behavior. *Child Development, 67*(2), 449–470.

Roche Olivar, R. (1990). *Psicologia y educacion de la prosocialidad: Optimización de las actitudes y comportamientos de generosidad ayuda, cooperación y solidaridad.* Unpublished manuscript, Barcelona, Spain.

Roche Olivar, R. (Undated). *Educative and family antecedents of prosocial behavior on children 13 and 14 years old.* Unpublished manuscript, Barcelona, Spain.

Rohrkemper, M. M. (1984). The influence of teacher socialization style on students' social cognition and reported interpersonal classroom behavior. *The Elementary School Journal, 85*(2), 246–275.

Rollins, B. C., & Thomas, D. L. (1979). Parental support, power, and control techniques in the socialization of children. In W. R. Burr, R. Hill, F. I. Nye, & I. L. Reiss (Eds.), *Contemporary theories about the family. Vol. 1: Research based theories* (pp. 317–364). New York: The Free Press.

Rosenhan, D. L. (1970). The natural socialization of altruistic autonomy. In J. Macauley & L. Berkowitz (Eds.), *Altruism and helping behavior* (pp. 251–268). New York: Academic Press.

Rosenhan, D. L. (1972). Learning theory and prosocial behavior. *Journal of Social Issues, 28*(3), 151–163.

Rosenhan, D. L., & White, G. M. (1967). Observation and rehearsal as determinants of prosocial behavior. *Journal of Personality and Social Psychology, 5*(4), 424–431.

Rushton, J. P. (1975). Generosity in children: Immediate and long-term effects of modeling, preaching, and moral judgment. *Journal of Personality and Clinical Psychiatry, 31*(3), 459–466.

Rutherford, E., & Mussen, P. (1968). Generosity in nursery school boys. *Child Development, 39,* 755–765.

Ryan, F., & Wheeler, R. (1977). The effects of cooperative and competitive background experiences of students on the play of a simulation game. *Journal of Educational Research, 70,* 295–299.

Ryan, K. (1989). In defense of character education. In L. Nucci (Ed.), *Moral development and character education: A dialogue* (pp. 3–17). Berkeley, CA: McCutchan.

Ryan, K. (1996). Character education in the United States: A status report. *Journal for a Just and Caring Education, 2*(1), 75–84.

Sadalla, G., Holmberg, M., & Halligan, J. (1990). *Conflict resolution: An elementary school curriculum.* San Francisco: Community Boards, Inc.

Sagotsky, G., Wood-Schneider, M., & Konop, M. (1981). Learning to cooperate: Effects of modeling and direct instruction. *Child Development, 52,* 1032–1042.

Saltzstein, H. D. (1976). Social influence and moral development: A perspective on the role of parents and peers. In T. Lickona (Ed.), *Moral development and behavior: Theory, research, and social issues* (pp. 253–265). New York: Holt, Rinehart & Winston.

Satnick, R. D. (1991). *The Thomas Jefferson Center Values Education Project: A survey of administrators in the Los Angeles Unified School District.* Van Nuys, CA: California Survey Research.

Schaefli, A., Rest, J. R., & Thoma, S. J. (1985). Does moral education improve moral judgment? A meta-analysis of intervention studies using the defining issues test. *Review of Educational Research, 55*(3), 319–352.

Schine, J. (Ed.). (1997). *Service learning: Ninety-sixth yearbook of the National Society for the Study of Education. Part I.* Chicago: University of Chicago Press.

Schwartz, G., Merton, D., & Bursik, R. J., Jr. (1987). Teaching styles and performance values in junior high school: The impersonal, nonpersonal, and personal. *American Journal of Education, 95,* 346–379.

Schweinhart, L., Weikart, D., & Larner, M. (1986). Consequences of three preschool curriculum models through age 15. *Early Childhood Research Quarterly, 1,* 15–46.

Sears, R. R., Maccoby, E. E., & Levin, H. (1957). *Patterns of child rearing.* Evanston, IL: Row, Peterson.

Sears, R. R., Rau, L., & Alpert, R. (1965). *Identification and child rearing.* Stanford, CA: Stanford University Press.

Selman, R. L. (1971). The relation of role taking to the development of moral judgment in children. *Child Development, 42*(1), 79–91.

Selman, R. L. (1980). *The growth of interpersonal understanding: Developmental and clinical analyses.* New York: Academic Press.

Selman, R. L., & Lieberman, M. (1975). Moral education in the primary grades: An evaluation of a developmental curriculum. *Journal of Educational Psychology, 67*(5), 712–716.

Serow, R. C. (1983). *Schooling for social diversity: An analysis of policy and practice.* New York: Teachers College Press.

Serow, R. C., & Solomon, D. (1979). Classroom climates and students' intergroup behavior. *Journal of Educational Psychology, 71,* 669–676.

Sharan, S. (1980). Cooperative learning in small groups: Recent methods and effects on achievement, attitudes and ethnic relations. *Review of Educational Research, 50,* 241–271.

Sharan, S. (Ed.). (1990). *Cooperative learning: Theory and research.* New York: Praeger.

Sharan, S., Kussell, P., Hertz-Lazarowitz, R., Bejarano, Y., Raviv, S., & Sharan, Y. (1984). *Cooperative learning in the classroom: Research in desegregated schools.* Hillsdale, NJ: Lawrence Erlbaum Associates.

Sharan, S., & Rich, Y. (1984). Field experiments on ethnic integration in Israeli schools. In Y. Amir & S. Sharan (Eds.), *School desegregation* (pp. 189–217). Hillsdale, NJ: Lawrence Erlbaum Associates.

Sharan, S., & Shachar, H. (1988). *Language and learning in the cooperative classroom.* New York: Springer-Verlag.

Shouse, R. C. (1996). Academic press and sense of community: Conflict, congruence, and implications for student achievement. *Social Psychology of Education, 1,* 47–68.

Shure, M. B., & Healey, K. N. (1993). *Interpersonal problem solving and prevention in urban school children.* Presented at meeting of American Psychological Association, Toronto, Canada.

Shure, M. B., & Spivack, G. (1982). Interpersonal problem solving in young children: A cognitive approach to prevention. *American Journal of Community Psychology, 10,* 341–356.

Slavin, R. E. (1985). Cooperative learning: Applying contact theory in desegregated schools. *Journal of Social Issues, 41*(3), 45–62.

Slavin, R. E. (1990). *Cooperative learning: Theory, research, and practice.* Englewood Cliffs, NJ: Prentice-Hall.

Slavin, R. E., & Madden, N. A. (1979). School practices that improve race relations. *American Educational Research Journal, 16*(2), 169–180.

Smith, C. L., Gelfand, D. M., Hartmann, D. P., & Partlow, M. E. Y. (1979). Children's causal attributions regarding help giving. *Child Development, 50*(1), 203–210.

Snarey, J. R., Reimer, J., & Kohlberg, L. (1985). Development of social moral reasoning among kibbutz adolescents: A longitudinal cross-cultural study. *Developmental Psychology, 21*(1), 3–17.

Solomon, D., Battistich, V., Kim, D., & Watson, M. (1997). Classroom practices associated with students' sense of community. *Social Psychology of Education, 1,* 235–267.

Solomon, D., Battistich, V., & Watson, M. (1993). *A longitudinal investigation of the effects of a school intervention program on children's social development.* Presented at meeting of Society for Research in Child Development, New Orleans, LA.

Solomon, D., Battistich, V., Watson, M., Schaps, E., & Lewis, C. (2000). A six-district study of educational change: Direct and mediated effects of the Child Development Project. *Social Psychology of Education, 4,* 3–51.

Solomon, D., & Kendall, A. J. (1976). Individual characteristics and children's performance in "open" and "traditional" classroom settings. *Journal of Educational Psychology, 68,* 613–625.

Solomon, D., Watson, M., Battistich, V., Schaps, E., & Delucchi, K. (1992). Creating a caring community: Educational practices that promote children's prosocial development. In F. K. Oser, A. Dick, & J.-L. Patry (Eds.), *Effective and responsible teaching: The new synthesis* (pp. 383–396). San Francisco: Jossey-Bass.

Solomon, D., Watson, M., Battistich, V., Schaps, E., & Delucchi, K. (1996). Creating classrooms that students experience as communities. *American Journal of Community Psychology, 24*(6), 719–748.

Solomon, D., Watson, M., Battistich, V., Schaps, E., Tuck, P., Solomon, J., Cooper, C., & Ritchey, W. (1985). A program to promote interpersonal consideration and cooperation in children. In R. Slavin, S. Sharan, S. Kagan, R. Hertz-Lazarowitz, C. Webb, & R. Schmuck (Eds.), *Learning to cooperate, cooperating to learn* (pp. 371–401). New York: Plenum.

Solomon, D., Watson, M., Delucchi, K., Schaps, E., & Battistich, V. (1988). Enhancing children's prosocial behavior in the classroom. *American Educational Research Journal, 25*(3), 527–554.

Solomon, D., Watson, M., Schaps, E., Battistich, V., & Solomon, J. (1990). Cooperative learning as part of a comprehensive program designed to promote prosocial development. In S. Sharan (Ed.), *Cooperative learning: Theory and research* (pp. 231–260). New York: Praeger.

Sparks, R. K., Jr. (1991). Character development at Fort Washington Elementary School. In J. S. Benninga (Ed.), *Moral, character, and civic education in the elementary school* (pp. 178–194). New York: Teachers College Press.

Spivack, G., Platt, J. J., & Shure, M. (1976). *The problem-solving approach to adjustment.* San Francisco: Jossey-Bass.

Sroufe, A. (1988). The role of infant-caregiver attachment in development. In J. Belsky & T. Nezworski (Eds.), *Clinical implications of attachment* (pp. 18–38). Hillsdale, NJ: Lawrence Erlbaum Associates.

St. John, N. H., & Lewis, R. G. (1973). Children's interracial friendships: An exploration of the contact hypothesis. (Cited in N. H. St. John, 1975, *School desegregation: Outcomes for our children.* New York: Wiley).

Staub, E. (1971a). A child in distress: The influence of nurturance and modeling on children's attempts to help. *Developmental Psychology, 5,* 124–132.

Staub, E. (1971b). The use of role playing and induction in children's learning of helping and sharing behavior. *Child Development, 42,* 805–816.

Staub, E. (1975). To rear a prosocial child: Reasoning, learning by doing, and learning by teaching others. In D. J. DePalma & J. M. Foley (Eds.), *Moral development: Current theory and research* (pp. 113–135). Hillsdale, NJ: Lawrence Erlbaum Associates.

Staub, E. (1978). *Positive social behavior and morality: Social and personal influences: Vol. 1.* New York: Academic Press.

Staub, E. (1979). *Positive social behavior and morality: Socialization and development: Vol. 2.* New York: Academic Press.

Staub, E. (1981). Promoting positive behavior in schools, in other educational settings, and in the home. In J. P. Rushton & R. M. Sorrentino (Eds.), *Altruism and helping behavior: Social, personality and developmental perspectives* (pp. 109–133). Hillsdale, NJ: Lawrence Erlbaum Associates.

Steinberg, L., Dornbusch, S. M., & Brown, B. B. (1992). Ethnic differences in adolescent achievement: An ecological perspective. *American Psychologist, 47*(6), 723–729.

Sullivan, H. S. (1953). *The interpersonal theory of psychiatry.* New York: Norton.

Switzer, G. E., Simmons, R. G., Dew, M. A., Regalski, J. M., & Wang, C.-H. (1995). The effect of a school-based helper program on adolescent self-image, attitudes, and behavior. *Journal of Early Adolescence, 15*(4), 429–455.

Torney, J. V., Oppenheim, A. N., & Farnen, R. F. (1975). *Civic education in ten countries: An empirical study.* New York: Wiley.

Triañes Torres, M. V. (1994). *Educacion de competencia para las relaciones interpersonales en niños de educacion compensatoria (Education for competence in interpersonal relations for children in compensatory education programs).* Presented at meeting of Educación y Sociedad (Education and Society), Madrid, Spain.

Triañes Torres, M. V. (1996). *Educacion y competencia social: Un programa en el aula.* Granada, Spain: Ediciones Aljibe.

Triañes Torres, M. V., Munos Sanchez, A., & Sanchez Sanchez, A. M. (1995). *A social competence program to prevent racism and xenophobia.* Presented at the Sixth European Conference for Research on Learning and Instruction, University of Nijmegen, Netherlands.

Tsjovold, D., & Johnson, D. W. (1977). The effects of controversy on cognitive perspective-taking. *Journal of Educational Psychology, 69,* 679–685.

Turiel, E. (1973). Stage transition in moral development. In R. M. W. Travers (Ed.), *Second handbook of research on teaching* (pp. 732–758). Chicago: Rand McNally.

Underwood, B., & Moore, B. (1982). Perspective-taking and altruism. *Psychological Bulletin, 91,* 143–173.

Urbain, E. S., & Kendall, P. C. (1980). Review of social-cognitive problem-solving interventions with children. *Psychological Bulletin, 88*(1), 109–143.

Vari-Szilagyi, I. (1995). *The Hungarian experimentation with the Just Community approach.* Presented at meeting of Association for Moral Education, New York.

Vitz, P. C. (1990). The use of stories in moral development: New psychological reasons for an old education method. *American Psychologist, 45*(6), 709–720.

Walker, L. J., & Taylor, J. H. (1991). Family interactions and the development of moral reasoning. *Child Development, 62*(2), 264–283.

Warring, D., Johnson, D., Maruyama, G., & Johnson, R. (1985). Impact of different types of cooperative learning on cross-ethnic and cross-sex relationships. *Journal of Educational Psychology, 77*(1), 53–59.

Watson, M., Battistich, V., & Solomon, D. (1997). Enhancing students' social and ethical development in schools: An intervention program and its effects. *International Journal of Educational Research, 27,* 571–586.

Watson, M., Solomon, D., Battistich, V., Schaps, E., & Solomon, J. (1989). The Child Development Project: Combining traditional and developmental approaches to values education. In L. Nucci (Ed.), *Moral development and character education: A dialogue* (pp. 51–92). Berkeley, CA: McCutchan.

Weed, S. E. (1995). *Alternative strategies for behavioral risk reduction in children: A character education approach to healthy behavior* (Report to the Thrasher Foundation). Salt Lake City, UT: The Institute for Research and Evaluation.

Wehlage, G. G., Rutter, R. A., Smith, G. A., Lesko, N., & Fernandez, R. R. (1989). *Reducing the risk: Schools as communities of support.* New York: Falmer Press.

Weigel, R. H., Wiser, P. L., & Cook, S. W. (1975). The impact of cooperative learning experiences on cross-ethnic relations and attitudes. *Journal of Social Issues, 31*(1), 219–245.

Weissberg, R. P., & Caplan, M. Z. (1989). *The evaluation of a social competence promotion program with young, urban adolescents.* Unpublished paper.

Weissberg, R. P., Caplan, M. Z., & Benetto, L. (1988). *The Yale-New Haven Social Problem-Solving (SPS) program for young adolescents.* New Haven, CT: Yale University.

Weissberg, R. P., Gesten, E. L., Liebenstein, N. L., Schmid, K. D., & Hutton, H. (1980). *The Rochester Social Problem-Solving (SPS) Program: A training manual for teachers of 2nd-4th grade children.* Rochester, NY: Primary Mental Health Project.

Whiteman, P. H., & Kosier, K. P. (1964). Development of children's moralistic judgment: Age, sex, IQ, and certain experimental variables. *Child Development, 35,* 843–850.

Whiting, B. B., & Whiting, J. W. M. (1975). *Children of six cultures: A psycho-cultural analysis.* Cambridge, MA: Harvard University Press.

Williams, R. M. (1947). *The reduction of intergroup tension.* New York: Social Science Research Council.

Wood, C. (1994). Responsive teaching: Creating partnerships for systemic change. *Young Children, 50*(1), 21–28.

Work, W. C., & Olsen, K. H. (1990). Development and evaluation of a revised social problem-solving curriculum for fourth graders. *Journal of Primary Prevention, 11,* 143–157.

Wynne, E. A. (1989). Transmitting traditional values in contemporary schools. In L. Nucci (Ed.), *Moral development and character education: A dialogue* (pp. 19–36). Berkeley, CA: McCutchan.

Wynne, E. A. (1991). Character and academics in the elementary school. In J. S. Benninga (Ed.), *Moral, character, and civic education in the elementary school* (pp. 139–155). New York: Teachers College Press.

Yarrow, M. R., & Scott, P. M. (1972). Imitation of nurturant and non-nurturant models. *Journal of Personality and Social Psychology, 23,* 259–270.

Yarrow, M. R., Scott, P. M., & Waxler, C. (1973). Learning concern for others. *Developmental Psychology, 8,* 240–260.

Yates, M., & Youniss, J. (1996). Community service and political-moral identity in adolescents. *Journal of Research on Adolescence, 6*(3), 271–284.

Youniss, J. (1980). *Parents and peers in social development: A Sullivan-Piaget perspective.* Chicago: University of Chicago Press.

Youniss, J., McLellan, J. A., & Yates, M. (1997). What we know about engendering civic identity. *American Behavioral Scientist, 40*(5), 620–631.

Youniss, J., & Yates, M. (1997). *Community service and social responsibility in youth.* Chicago: University of Chicago Press.

Zahn-Waxler, C., & Radke-Yarrow, M. (1979). Child rearing and children's prosocial initiations toward victims of distress. *Child Development, 50,* 319–330.

Zahn-Waxler, C., Radke-Yarrow, M., Wagner, E., & Chapman, M. (1992). Development of concern for others. *Developmental Psychology, 28*(1), 126–136.

32.

Vocational and Occupational Education: Pedagogical Complexity, Institutional Diversity

Frank Achtenhagen

Seminar für Wirtschaftspädagogik der Georg-August-Universität of Göttingen, Germany

W. Norton Grubb

David Gardner Chair in Higher Education
School of Education
University of California, Berkeley

> *It was the best of times, it was the worst of times, it was the age of wisdom, it was the age of foolishness, it was the epoch of belief, it was the epoch of incredulity . . .*
>
> Charles Dickens, *A Tale of Two Cities*

For vocational education, this is both an epoch of belief and an age of foolishness—belief in the occupational value of education, accompanied by institutional practices that often undermine the power of vocational teaching. In many countries, a renewed interest in the economic purposes of education have sent policymakers scurrying after more overtly vocational forms of education. In the United States, for example, *A Nation at Risk* (National Commission on Education, 1983) emphasized that "knowledge, learning, information, and skilled intelligence are the new raw materials of international commerce." Similarly, the European Commission has stressed that education and training will be central to "the need to strengthen European competitiveness in economic, technological, innovative scientific and organizational terms" (European Commission Study Group, 1997, p. 15). Comparable statements can be found for virtually all developed countries and also for many transitional and developing countries.

But the treatment of vocational education varies enormously among countries, and a substantial diversity exists in the institutional arrangements. In some countries—principally the German-speaking countries, as well as Denmark and Luxembourg—vocational education enjoys high status, substantial funding, and advanced teacher training. In many countries, however, vocational education suffers from relatively low status, low funding, and widespread ambivalence about its role in promoting individual mobility and social progress. Many countries would like to follow the German dual system, where apprentices spend about three years learning in both a vocational

This article was written when Norton Grubb was a site director of the former National Center for Research in Vocational Education, at the University of California at Berkeley. Erik Van Duzer provided invaluable research assistance. Richard Lynch and Cathy Stasz provided extremely helpful comments on an earlier draft. The authors received many helpful suggestions and references from Bill Bailey, Klaus Beck, Steven Billett, George Copa, Jim Gaskell, Andy Green, Rogers Hall, Phyllis Hudecki, Glynda Hull, Franz-Josef Kaiser, Wolfgang Lempert, Marcia Linn, Richard Lynch, Felix Rauner, Klaus Ruth, John Stevenson, Cathy Stasz, Judy Wagner, and Barbara White.

school and an enterprise, but such efforts have often been unsuccessful. The worldwide call for more occupational forms of education contrasts sharply with the continued neglect of vocational education in many countries.

Similar contrasts occur with teaching in vocational education. Theoretical developments have emphasized teaching "in context," problem-based instruction, cooperative learning, and the distinctive characteristics of apprenticeship—all common to occupational instruction. Vocational teaching proves to be unexpectedly rich: It uses a greater variety of teaching methods than does academic instruction, including modeling, simulation, and workshops, along with conventional classroom arrangements. Under the best conditions, it emphasizes a greater variety of competencies or "intelligences" (Gardner, 1983), including kinesthetic ("hands-on") skills, visual capabilities, aural and other perceptual abilities, and teamwork and other interpersonal skills. But the potential richness and complexity of vocational education have not been matched by comparable attention to teaching and learning. Research in most countries has concentrated on institutional and organizational problems, many of which cannot be generalized among countries (Achtenhagen, Nijhof, & Raffe, 1995; Evans et al., 1998). Analysis of teaching and learning, which is potentially more general, is sparse, and discussions about new approaches to pedagogy often have not reached vocational programs. In many countries, the preparation of vocational instructors does not match the complexity of practice. All too often, then, the institutional settings of occupational education undermine the potential power of its teaching.

In this chapter, we start to remedy the neglect of pedagogy[1] in vocational education, clarifying the varied practices in occupational teaching. Although the distinction is sometimes artificial, we examine pedagogy rather than content, the ways of teaching rather than the facts and procedures particular to any occupation. In addition to analyzing teaching practices, we also examine the institutional settings and national systems that influence teaching. As we clarify in section I, vocational education takes place not only in school settings but also in a variety of programs labeled "training" rather than "education," in employment itself, and in a variety of formal and informal settings. And the variation among countries is enormous. Inevitably, because of our backgrounds, we stress developments in the English-speaking countries and in the German tradition of a dual system. Fortunately, these two approaches capture the most important dimensions of market-oriented versus institutional approaches to vocational education, as we explain in section I. We neglect issues in developing countries even though they are often quite similar to those in developed countries (e.g., Foster, 1966; Middleton, Ziderman, & Van Adams, 1990; Psacharopoulos, 1987; World Bank, 1991; and the articles in Lauglo & Lillis, 1988, on the debates over expanding academic

versus vocational education) partly because of the lack of literature on pedagogical issues in such countries.

In this review, we face a paradox: While an overwhelming amount of material written on vocational education can be found—government reports, descriptions of new projects, efforts of teachers to cope with everyday teaching problems—much of this literature is fugitive, and little of it is rigorously empirical. For the United States alone, Worthington (1984) counted about 27,650 institutions involved in vocational education and training in some way, and a similar abundance of these institutions can be found in European countries, which have an "ever-changing kaleidoscope of special-purpose programs, most of them known by their acronyms" (Achtenhagen, Nijhof, & Raffe, 1995; Duke, 1990, p. 338). Vocational education, more than academic education, has had to concern itself with changing content as the work world changes; therefore, a vast literature that argues about curriculum revision (e.g., Arnold & Lipsmeier, 1995, for Germany; Copa & Bentley, 1992, for the United States; Nijhof & Streumer, 1994, for the Netherlands) has been generated, but this typically has little to do with teaching methods. In both Germany and the United States, the search for empirically verified models of practice (or *Modellversuche*) has shown the lack of useable results (Deutsche Forschungsgemeinschaft, 1990; Warnat, 1994, for tech-prep programs). Therefore, our analysis of teaching in vocational education must extrapolate from relatively few empirical sources, and we consider them exploratory.

In section I, we analyze the features of vocational education that distinguish it from academic instruction and influence the conditions of teaching. In section II, we present the common approaches to teaching, including innovative methods—simulations, modeling, workshop-based (or "hands-on") instruction—and more conventional approaches. Section III examines how different methods are used in practice, clarifying the many aspects of workshops and "hands-on" learning and the multiple competencies of occupational learning. Section IV briefly examines the issues in teacher training, which (like many other aspects of practice) differ substantially between countries with a dual system and those with a more market-oriented approach. In section V, we examine current debates and trends, clarifying the renewed interest in various reforms that institutional developments often undermine. Finally, in section VI, we clarify the potential role for policy and the expansion of research necessary to capitalize on the richness of vocational teaching.

I. Conceptualizing Vocational Education

Vocational education has always been differentiated from academic instruction, particularly by its purposes. Even though practical education is the oldest form of organized instruction, the *enkyklios paideia* that established philosophical and educa-

---

[1] In contrasting curriculum and content with pedagogical methods, we follow the terminology common in English. In most European and Scandinavian countries, the term *didactics* (or *Didaktik,* in German) describes the embedding of content in educational theory and practice and has a positive connotation rather than the negative connotation associated with lecturing. Shulman's (1986) term "pedagogical content knowledge" has the same flavor; see also Westbury, Hopmann, and Riquarts (1999). Thus, for vocational education, the *Fachdidaktik* of specific vocational areas (for example, *Wirtschaftspädagogik* for business and commerce) describes the combination of content and pedagogy that is central to the training of teachers.

tional theory was based on the education of the upper classes—the Pharaoh and high priests in ancient Egypt and politicians in Greece rather than craftsmen and slaves (Dolch, 1959; Weniger, 1994/1936)—and, therefore, defined vocational education as a minor subject. This distinction has been reaffirmed in many ways since then, though in ways that vary from country to country. But because the functions of the vocational sector also influence the students and purposes in academic education, it becomes impossible to understand the advantages and disadvantages of a particular education system without understanding vocational education.

The Subject Status of Vocational Education: Following the Dictates of the Labor Market

Vocational education prepares students for particular occupations, which may be broadly or narrowly defined. For example, the German Research Council defines vocational education as the "conditions, processes and consequences of the acquisition of professional qualifications and of personal and social attitudes for positions which appear significant for the execution of professionally organized work processes" (Deutsche Forschungsgemeinschaft, 1990, p. vii). This definition potentially covers a broad range of occupations including those (like law or medicine) that require postbaccalaureate education and those (like metal worker or baker) for which much less formal schooling is required.

This basic conception means that vocational education is an umbrella for multiple subjects and occupations rather than for a single subject. In developed countries with perhaps 20,000 to 30,000 occupations, different solutions have arisen to prepare for that many jobs. In Germany, about 360 well-defined apprenticeships exist, organized into six areas (trade and industry, handicrafts, the professions or *"freie Berufe,"* public services, agriculture, and navigation)—though some feel that this large number should be bundled into about 100 *Kernberufe,* or core occupations (Heidegger & Rauner, 1996). The National Vocational Qualifications (NVQs) in the United Kingdom cover more than 9,000 different occupations at different levels of preparation. In the United States, secondary-level vocational education has been an alliance of six broad occupational areas—business, marketing, agriculture, trades and industry, technical education, and home economics—though each is broken into narrower specialties with little in common. The tendency to divide vocational education into narrow specialties mirrors the labor market, of course, but it has thwarted the development of broader programs that could incorporate a wider variety of academic competencies. As jobs themselves have become broader and as multiple skills have become more common, older conceptions of specific vocational programs suited to a Taylorist division of labor have become obsolete, replaced by pressure for broader forms of vocational education (as we will see in section V).

Because vocational education encompasses multiple occupations, no single approach to teaching is applicable to all fields. Some subjects—business, for example, or construction management—can be taught in "academic" fashion, in classrooms with lectures and texts, though complex simulations and projects can also be used (as we see in section II). To teach other subjects—the automotive and machine trades, for example—is almost unthinkable without workshops or work settings where students practice with cars, farm equipment, or metalworking machines as appropriate. Agriculture requires still other contexts for practice, and some occupations—retail trade, tourism and hospitality, and many health occupations—require interactions with the public for which internships may be necessary. These varying practices, in turn, reflect the perception that the specific context of teaching matters a great deal (Achtenhagen, 1992; Engeström & Middleton, 1996; Lampert, 1992; Perkins & Salomon, 1989; Salomon, 1997; Stodolsky, 1988); purely general approaches are likely to break down, especially as the complexity and the realism of the educational setting increases (Gott, 1988). Therefore, precepts about teaching must be made specific to the occupational area being taught, and few of the teaching modes reviewed in section II are universally applicable.

The focus of vocational programs on occupations presents another challenge to teaching. At a faster rate than academic disciplines, job-specific occupational programs can quickly become out of date as occupations wax and wane and technologies change. In educational institutions geared to the slower evolution of academic disciplines, vocational instructors often feel overwhelmed by the pressure to keep up to date; the preparation time that academic instructors may devote to pedagogical innovation must be spent by occupational instructors to keep up with changes. Therefore, as we have already mentioned, many debates within vocational education have been concerned with curriculum changes rather than with pedagogy.

Recently, several dramatic shifts in employment have captured the attention of policymakers and educators alike. The driving forces behind these "megatrends," as Buttler (1992) has called them, include an increasing use of new information, communication, and research-based technologies. The consequences for employment include reduced hierarchy through lean production and lean management, jobs with a greater variety of skills, greater need for independence and initiative as supervisory levels have been reduced, more use of new technologies at almost every level of employment, and a greater integration of work within firms, which requires more sophisticated communication skills and understanding of complex systems. These "megatrends" have caused many countries to redefine the "core" or "key" competencies necessary at work so they can facilitate the transferability, flexibility, and mobility of employees. Many innovations and challenges that we discuss in section V have been developed to respond to the changing demands associated with these "megatrends." In addition, the shift from manufacturing to services has reduced jobs in traditional occupational areas that are related to manufacturing and construction—the crafts, metal-, and woodworking trades—and has increased the demand for computer-, business-, service-related, education, and health occupations, all of which have substantial knowledge bases and require more academic content.

The other challenges of these "megatrends" are more clearly pedagogical. Many traditional methods of vocational teaching (described in sections II and III) are poorly suited to teaching about complex situations in which workers are highly independent and perform a variety of tasks. Thus, changes in work may require not only new approaches to teaching but also changes in content (Berryman & Bailey, 1992). However, occupational teaching, teacher training, and research have not yet caught up to the problem; relatively little has been done to examine the teaching and learning processes necessary to develop transferability and mobility within a flexible system of production and trade.

The basic conception of vocational education immediately creates a divide between vocational and academic education—the first concerned with occupational preparation and forced to respond to employment conditions external to schools, the second concerned with the disciplines and changing relatively slowly. This conceptual divide has been reinforced, in most countries, by institutional practices that include creating separate schools or tracks within schools; allowing different forms of teacher preparation; often, establishing different funding streams; and supporting different research traditions. But this dichotomy is not inevitable. Indeed, in the United States, most vocational subjects in high schools have had both general and occupational components. For example, business education has been both a vehicle for teaching about the role of business in American life and a form of occupational preparation (Copa & Bentley, 1992); work experience has been not only a way of learning about the relation between school and adult life but also a way of teaching specific skills. An educational vision in which vocational programs also have intellectual or "academic" content was outlined by John Dewey (1916, especially chap. 23; Dewey, 1900/1990) 80 years ago in his vision of "education through occupations." As we will see in section V, this vision has reappeared in many countries seeking to integrate academic and vocational education.

The Special Characteristics of Occupational Teaching

In many respects, pedagogical issues in vocational education are similar to those in academic education. The debates about contrasting approaches to teaching; the appropriate mix of general or theoretical and specific or applied content; the particular roles of labs, workshops, or projects versus classroom instruction; the necessary training for instructors; and many other debates have counterparts in all areas of teaching. However, once vocational education is differentiated by its greater emphasis on preparation for occupations, a number of consequences follow: the competencies required are more varied, the needs of employers play a different role, the settings for vocational instruction are varied, and the purposes of students in vocational education are varied.

The competencies required are more varied. Most formal schooling within the conventions of the *enkyklios paideia* was established to teach literacy, and formal schooling still emphasizes linguistic and mathematical abilities over all others (Cook-Gumperz, 1986; Gardner, 1983). In contrast, successful work requires (in different proportions) manual or kinesthetic abili-

ties; visual abilities; perceptual facility, including the ability to respond to the sounds (and sometimes the smells) of work processes (Evans & Butler, 1992); interpersonal skills, including the ability to work in teams and to communicate appropriately with customers and superiors; and different personal characteristics including independence, initiative, and motivation.[2] However, the teaching of noncognitive abilities has received much less attention than has the teaching of linguistic and mathematical abilities, as we will clarify in section III. What little analysis is available is often intended for professions (architects and engineers, for example, described in Bromme & Tillema, 1995) and rarely makes its way to the prebaccalaureate level (Engeström, Engeström, & Kärkkäinen, 1995).

The needs of employers play a different role. While academic education has been susceptible to external pressures, particularly in attempts to define "core" skills that are responsive to changes in employment, external pressures from employers have more immediate effects on vocational education. Employers can refuse to hire from programs that fail to teach appropriate competencies, and advisory committees of local employers often represent their needs to vocational programs. In Great Britain, the National Vocational Qualifications (NVQs) are developed by industry groups, and, in turn, shape the content of vocational programs; similarly, in Germany, the *Prüfungen,* or tests that apprentices must pass, are controlled by chambers of industry and commerce or of handicrafts. Even in countries like the United States, with a largely unregulated employment system, many prebaccalaureate occupations, including health occupations, many building trades, and most jobs involving safety like aviation mechanics, require external exams.

These pressures generate at least three ambiguities, each with implications for teaching. Which employers or which particular jobs should govern the content of a particular program? In a world where individuals change jobs and where jobs change, the demands of initial jobs and those of subsequent jobs may be quite different. Vocational programs are often caught between conflicting demands—between small and medium-size local employers who are hiring individuals for entry-level employment and larger national and international firms who are more concerned about higher-order skills and the flexibility of the labor force over the longer run. Thus the "needs of employers" can justify either the narrowest forms of vocational education or the more general forms of integrated instruction.

The second ambiguity is related: If the needs of employers are important, what place is there to serve the needs of students, including the more general intellectual, political, and moral purposes of general education? While most vocational education incorporates both, some specialized programs—for example, short-term job-training programs in the United States, labor market programs in Australia, *Fördermassnahmen* in Germany, and firm-sponsored training in most countries—provide only job-related preparation. Germany represents a partial exception, where the idea has spread, based in part on Dewey's

---

[2] Of the many ways to categorize these abilities, we often follow the vocabulary developed by Gardner (1983) because it is comprehensive and because he establishes his seven "intelligences" on the same plane, rather than subordinate noncognitive capacities to cognitive abilities.

ideas (Wehle, 1964), that all work preparation should develop the intellectual and political capacities of students. But elsewhere, the balance of occupational and academic or intellectual content is the subject of continuing debate and efforts at reform that we explore in section V.

A final problem involves the question of who articulates the needs of employers. Countries vary enormously in how they do this. The German dual system relies on an elaborate tripartite deliberation involving unions, employers' associations, and governments. In Great Britain, the Tory government did not trust employers to state their own needs, so the National Center for Vocational Qualifications established its own procedures for NVQs and browbeat employers into following them. The United States, with its highly informal system, typically has no central forum for establishing the needs of employers, and often programs do this on their own through informal advisory committees. Where the procedures for articulating the demands of employers are unclear (as in the United States) or contentious (as in the United Kingdom), then the connections of vocational programs to employers may be confused and opaque to students, and the justification for teaching particular competencies may not be clear.

The settings for vocational instruction are varied. To prepare for certain occupations without some kind of work simulation or work itself—the vocational equivalent of science labs and academic projects—is virtually unthinkable. The most familiar instructional settings in the English-speaking countries are schools, typically including both classrooms and workshops or labs. Particularly in dual systems, the "workshop" component takes place at real work sites rather than at sites created for educational purposes. Sometimes in the dual system, employers create training centers where the work-based component takes place; as Bierhof and Prais (1996) point out, this is really a "triad" system. However, the multiple settings create special pedagogical demands for instructors: The variety of elements in classroom and workshop is substantial (as we will clarify in section III), and the consistency between classroom and workshop presents another challenge. Even within the German dual system, the coordination between learning in work-based settings (developed in a formalized process including chambers of industry and commerce, unions, and federal and state governments) and learning in the school-based settings of the *Berufschule* (developed and controlled by state ministries of education) is often unresolved (Heidegger & Rauner, 1996).

In many countries, vocational education takes place in separate schools, like the *Berufschule,* which is distinct from the academic *Gymnasium* in German-speaking countries, or in technical institutes and polytechnics, which are differentiated from academic universities. This reinforces the separation of vocational from academic education and may make it more difficult for students to transfer among tracks, but these institutions have the advantage of being devoted to occupational preparation, with special cost conditions and pedagogical requirements. In other countries—notably the United States, with its tradition of comprehensive high schools and community colleges, and other countries that have shifted away from specialized schools—occupational education is likely to fit awkwardly within academic institutions. Funding mechanisms are likely to be oriented to academic classes that have fewer requirements for expensive equipment and materials; the institutional incentives—to provide low-cost, high-enrollment programs—may undercut the commitment to expensive occupational programs; and academic administrators are unlikely to be familiar with the special teaching demands within vocational education. Each approach has its own drawbacks, therefore, with implications for teaching.

Vocational instruction also takes place in many settings outside the educational system. These include, for example, specialized area vocational schools, postsecondary technical institutes, adult education, short-term job-training programs, labor market programs for the unemployed, and employer-provided training. In many countries, a division has emerged between programs considered as education and those called "training"; job-training programs are generally shorter, limited to specific populations (like the long-term unemployed or welfare recipients), take place in a greater variety of informal settings, and often neglect broadly "educational" content including academic subjects, and the political and moral goals of education (Grubb, 1996a, pp. 1–8; Grubb & Ryan, 1999). Often, training is independent of the institutions most concerned with teaching; instructors are hired relatively casually, on a part-time basis, with no preparation in teaching; and little concern is demonstrated for the quality of teaching and staff development. In this review, we will not attempt to cover the teaching issues in this wide variety of settings, partly because even less literature can be found that describes what happens (except for some research on work-based learning included in section V). However, we note that the institutional conditions in many training programs are not conducive to carefully considered teaching, and we suspect that the neglect of teaching is one factor contributing to the ineffectiveness of short-term training (Grubb, 1996a; Grubb & Ryan, 1999).

The purposes of students in vocational education are varied. Some students are in occupational education to get initial preparation for entry into the labor force. Some have been employed but want to retrain for more promising occupations; others have become unemployed as the result of sectoral changes ("dislocated workers") and need retraining. Some seek upgrading of their abilities, particularly as occupations change and new skills become necessary (sometimes referred to as upgrade training or recurrent vocational education). And many countries have remedial training for the poor, welfare recipients, the long-term unemployed, and others with special problems making their way into employment. The competencies (including basic academic skills and interpersonal skills), interests, and motivation of these groups vary, complicating the conditions of teaching, and student-centered teaching that relies on the interests of students becomes difficult. Countries have resolved this problem in different ways: some have specialized programs for different populations, while others have more comprehensive programs that serve a variety of students—as do German job-training programs that incorporate both retraining and remedial training or U.S. comprehensive community colleges that enroll students for almost every purpose. Specialized programs may reduce the pedagogical complexity within these programs and allow particular teaching approaches to be used, but they may also complicate access to occupational education.

Institutional Versus Market-Oriented Approaches: The Status Issues in Vocational Education

The issues we have discussed so far are necessary complications in occupational teaching that are generated by its basic conception. However, other issues depend on the way a country organizes its vocational and academic education. Some countries—principally the German-speaking countries plus Denmark and Luxembourg—have developed a dual system that relies on both school-based and work-based components. In these cases, complex institutional arrangements have guaranteed access through the dual system to a wide variety of occupations, including well-paid positions that in other countries would be held by university graduates. Entry into many occupations and their wage and working conditions are regulated, assuring high economic benefits to vocational education. The provision of apprenticeships by many firms and the decision making by tripartite groups ensure that occupational preparation is a central concern of high-status groups rather than a marginal effort of the educational system. Even the terminology is different: The German conception of *Beruf* connotes a "calling" in English, an occupation that incorporates service to the community and to God rather than one that is a mere "vocation," and, therefore, *Berufsbildung,* the development of a calling, has more positive connotations than "vocational education."

In contrast, the English-speaking countries and several Scandinavian countries have followed a more free-market model in which relatively few interventions into labor markets have been made, and reliance on well-developed union, employer, and government bodies is reduced (Oulton & Steedman, 1994; Soskice, 1994). In these countries, vocational education usually leads to jobs of lower earnings and status and is itself of lower status than academic education (Wolf, 1993). The exceptions—the professions as distinct from prebaccalaureate occupations, many health professions, technical occupations linked to engineering, and some business occupations—have many of the same characteristics of vocational programs in German-speaking countries: they provide access to well-paid, stable occupations, with occupational education often required; they tend to involve employers more actively; and they also provide access to further baccalaureate-level education rather than being terminal programs.

These distinctions among countries affect many dimensions of vocational education. Where vocational education is of higher status, both vocational competencies and academic competencies can be of greater sophistication, as Bierhof and Prais (1996) have demonstrated for Switzerland: Students are much more likely to have chosen their program, the ambition of students is more heterogeneous, and the levels of both academic and vocational demands are greater, corresponding to the greater sophistication of the *Berufe.* In effect, national systems like those of the English-speaking countries that concentrate on a few students for the highest occupations neglect the education of an entire group of middle- and low-achieving students, de-

spite claims of treating all students equally; systems like those in the German-speaking countries, although they divide academic and vocational students relatively early, take preparation for middle-level employment seriously and end up with more equitable learning outcomes. This is a perfect example of our contention that to understand a country's system of education without understanding the role of vocational education is impossible.

In countries without a dual system, a basic source of the status differential is that the highest-status occupations are associated with academic education and with the political, moral, and intellectual purposes that dominated prior to vocationalism (e.g., Labaree, 1996, for the United States). The dominant competencies are linguistic and mathematical, defined by the *enkyklios paideia,* and are taught in a relatively abstract form oriented to symbolic systems (like writing and mathematical notation). The orientation of vocational programs to noncognitive competencies—which might be viewed in the adult worlds of employment and politics as pedagogical strengths of vocational education—means that vocational programs are considered second-class (Lewis, 1991, 1993): the literacy and mathematics they incorporate are more applied and the symbolic systems they include relate more to visual and kinesthetic abilities (in blueprints, electrical diagrams, and drafting) than to higher-status linguistic and mathematical abilities. One solution to this particular source of low status is to assert that vocational programs should incorporate the same high-status competencies as the academic track. Within the German system, for example, any vocational subject contains instructional content comparable to those in academic subjects. In other countries, efforts to integrate more academic content into vocational programs may have the same effects.

A related source of the status differential is that many countries without a dual system have created a single, high-status academic path through secondary school directly to a four-year college and to prestigious, well-paid employment, referred to in the United States as the "pipeline," or in Germany as the *Königsweg,* or "royal road" (Berliner & Biddle, 1996). Other clear examples are the rigid system of progress into the *grandes écoles* in France or the closed system from the university kindergarten to elite universities in Japan. Where a high-status "pipeline" or "royal road" exists, any deviation is of lesser status and is avoided by most parents. This is particularly the case when vocational education is "terminal"—when it does not provide opportunities for returning to the pipeline, particularly the baccalaureate degree. Then vocational education, which is one of these deviations, becomes the dumping ground for students who have missed the royal road, who have not done well in academic classrooms, and who are often disparaged as "manually minded" or "tactile."

Under these conditions, students in vocational programs do not necessarily choose to be there, and they may resist any teaching reminiscent of the academic track. As Claus's (1990) ethnographic study of a food preparation program clarifies, students' collective dislike of "book learning" and their low aspirations made it difficult for instructors to incorporate academic components, including the higher-order competencies necessary for more advanced work. The level of instruction is likely to be quite low because such programs focus on specific, entry-level jobs and because they conceive of academic competencies in remedial terms. These students suffer a triple deprivation: they have failed in the "royal road," because of these failures they reject the kind of learning that might enable them to succeed in demanding vocational programs, and their instructors lower their demands as well. In addition, the economic returns are likely to be low—as they have always been for secondary vocational education, for example, in the United States—because educational (or supply-side) considerations rather than labor market (or demand-related) conditions determine enrollments. The connection with employment, with the potential pedagogical advantages of work-based learning, is also likely to be missing. Under these conditions, the results are (as Evans et al., 1998, p. 1, have described them for England and Wales) "low expectations of what young people can achieve; an education system which produces young people who are disillusioned with formal learning; a widespread belief that many are destined for unemployment or low-skilled work; well-founded cynicism about the poor quality of government-financed training schemes."

The reasons for second-class status have been exacerbated in many countries by convention and even legislation (e.g., in the United States) that limit vocational education to schooling below the baccalaureate level, distinguishing it from professional education.[3] As a result of this distinction, vocational programs operate in a labor market where the value of formal schooling is uncertain because there are alternative ways to develop competencies including on-the-job training, experience, informal learning from parents or from a hobby, and military training. In the United States, for example, 72% of employees with a baccalaureate degree report that formal schooling is required for their jobs, but only 36% of those with some college and 15% of high school graduates report this requirement (Eck, 1993, Table 6); similar conclusions for Germany have been developed by Buttler (1992), and the same patterns prevail for other European countries. The uncertain economic returns in vocational education undermine the motivation to enroll compared to professional or academic education and to the guaranteed returns in the dual system.

Status also affects the material conditions of vocational teaching. In Germany, the budgets of specialized schools typically include special funding to reflect the higher costs of vocational programs. Buildings and equipment are financed by the districts or towns, which are usually proud of their vocational facilities and try to support them generously. When firms themselves do not have up-to-date equipment, the state pays for regional training centers run by chambers of handicraft. Where vocational education is of low status and academic education

structures the funding mechanisms, however, equipment, materials, and the time necessary to keep up to date are often neglected. And, as we will see in section IV, the differences between the training of instructors in countries with a high-status dual system and countries with more market-oriented systems are profound.

Finally, where vocational education has received little attention, research on occupational instruction has been a low priority, and other research that might be relevant to vocational education is often not applied. For example, in the United States, the research on engineering education (e.g., in *Engineering Education* and the *Journal of Engineering Education*)—which could be applied to technician training and to some traditional vocational subjects like machining[4]—remains within four-year colleges. A developing literature on problem-based learning, drawn from such areas as chemical engineering, medical education, and legal education (e.g., Wilkerson, 1996; Woods, 1996) bears no relationship to vocational education because of the division between professional and vocational education. The extensive literature in cognitive science on troubleshooting, electronics and computer programming, and arcane military applications—like the avionics of F-15 jets—(reviewed in Gott, 1988, 1995) has important implications for vocational education, though these connections are rarely made. But these limitations work the other way, too: The potential lessons from vocational education for academic subjects—about contextualized and applied instruction and project-based teaching, for example (Johnson, 1996), or about apprenticeship as a model of learning (Collins, Brown, & Newman, 1989)—have been neither well developed nor widely accepted. As a result, the separation of academic and occupational education impoverishes both.

By now, we have developed a more complex understanding of vocational education and determined a number of direct implications for teaching. Vocational teaching is particularly rich, because the settings—incorporating both classrooms and workshops or actual work—are more varied than they are in academic education. The range of competencies or "intelligences" is also more varied, as befits preparation for adult roles. But the institutional conditions for teaching vocational education are more challenging, in some ways, than academic instruction, particularly in countries with market-oriented approaches. Students vary enormously in their preparation and their goals, making student-centered instruction more complex. A great deal of vocational instruction takes place in institutions—not only in job-training programs and in firms but also in postsecondary institutions—with weaker commitments to the quality of teaching and less developed forms of instructor preparation. Throughout this review—and particularly when

---

[3] The distinction is evidently one about status and earnings, not about the characteristics of education required. In a review of professional education for the previous edition of this *Handbook,* Dinham and Stritter (1986) stated that "reliance on theory is among the most telling distinctions between a profession and a trade or craft" (p. 952)—and therefore between "professional" education and "vocational" education. However, their review concentrated on the practical elements in professional education including skills courses, apprenticeships, and internships—precisely the elements that distinguish vocational education from academic education. They concluded, as we do for vocational education, that practically no research has been done on the practical or clinical components of professional education except in the health professions.

[4] For example, Aglan and Ali (1996) propose the technique of mechanical dissection—dismantling a mechanical system or device, drawing the parts, and reassembling it—for baccalaureate engineering education. They then suggest applying it to secondary schools and two-year colleges, and report enthusiastic acceptance in classes of ninth- and eleventh-grade students.

we turn in section V to emerging reforms—we will ask whether the institutional arrangements of vocational education allow its richness and complexity to be realized or whether they present obstacles to improved teaching, particularly in a world of changing work.

II. The Methods of Teaching in Vocational Education

Because vocational education encompasses many different occupations, the dominant approaches to teaching vary also. The methods that are common in business and commerce, for example, include various games and simulations, which play the pedagogical role that workshops serve in more traditional agriculture and the trades. The newer technical occupations (like computer programming, electronics, and certain health occupations) require competencies and certain approaches to teaching that the traditional manufacturing occupations do not. Therefore, the teaching methods we review in this section are not applicable in all vocational fields. In addition, instructors in practice tend to use a mix of methods, incorporating some novel practices along with more traditional approaches. However, for analytic purposes, it is worthwhile distinguishing among conceptually distinct approaches to teaching. Finally, traditional methods are often fallback positions: Without institutional support and teacher training, vocational instructors are likely to fall back on traditional methods, just as academic teachers do.

The five approaches to vocational teaching that we include in this section have been more formally described in the German literature than in the English literature. All of these approaches are known also in the countries without a dual system (like the English-speaking countries), though the approaches often are embedded in teacher manuals, textbooks, and informal discussions among teachers and have been less carefully codified—a consequence of vocational education being less formalized and systematized in these countries.[5]

Traditional Vocational Teaching

Traditional teaching methods are those that have been more or less typical for vocational contexts (e.g., Flechsig, 1996; Joyce & Weil, 1972). In nearly all industrialized countries, the four-stage method is the dominant approach, both in school settings and at the worksite (Achtenhagen, 1997; Pätzold, 1996): preparation and planning; showing and explaining by the teacher; mimicking and explaining by the student; doing and working on one's own. (This four-stage model is sometimes caricatured as "showing and doing," the simplest form of vocational instruction that occurs when the stages of planning and explanation are truncated.) The advantage of this method, first proposed by Herbart (Connell, 1986), is that it can be learned easily and used by teachers because the instructional process is clearly structured. Nevertheless, this procedure has some weaknesses:

It is used mainly for teaching isolated skills in a rigid sequence; it fosters motivation and interest only at the first stage; and this method is less appropriate for occupations requiring increased levels of abstractness including business and commerce. Recent proposals enlarge the model to six stages, which are informing, planning, deciding, doing, controlling, and evaluating (Ott, 1997), but empirical evidence about the additional steps is not yet adequate (Achtenhagen, 1997).

Another traditional method, role play, involves students taking on roles in simulated situations, which helps students to develop an understanding of different motives at the worksite. This method can also bring a political dimension into education by clarifying the power relations at work. Normally, four phases are involved: preparation, including the choice of roles and necessary information about them; the role playing itself, where knowledge is developed; a summary of the results; and transfer of the insights to analogous situations. The main purpose is to develop the ability to understand complex situations in order to make appropriate decisions under relatively realistic conditions (Greenblatt; Streufert, Nogami, & Breuer, 1998).

The project method was developed in about 1850 for professional education at polytechnics in Germany. The United States also has a rich tradition with the project method, based upon the work of Dewey, Kilpatrick, Parkhurst, and others (Frey & Frey-Eiling, 1992; Lawrey, 1986). Normally, a project begins by defining the task in an open situation, without predefined goals. This is followed by structuring the task, organizing and distributing subtasks, working on the subtasks themselves, summarizing the results, and, finally, reflecting upon the project as a whole. The main advantages of project-based teaching are the ability to foster self-directed acting and learning, and the practice of working in teams under work-like conditions. However, the project method can break down if the planning and the activity stages are not carefully monitored. In addition, the nature of the projects themselves is critical; projects that are contrived, trivial, or otherwise distant from the conditions of real workplaces lose their educational value.

Teaching Methods in Commercial-Administrative Occupations

The use of learning tasks analogous to real work in business and commerce is based upon action and activity theory: students and apprentices carry out tasks and solve problems found in the worksite but without serious consequences for production (Achtenhagen et al., 1988a, 1988b). Routine tasks are consciously used to contextualize learning and to support the development of reasoning and metacognition (e.g., to understand the stages from inventory to balance in accounting, presented by Preiss & Tramm, 1996). Learning tasks are related to realistic models of enterprises, as in the virtual enterprise (Achtenhagen et al., 1997). Instructors thereby support teaching and learning

---

[5] For example, in the United States, the journal *Agriculture Education* has run a series of articles about effective teaching; the American Association for Vocational Instructional Materials has published a series of Performance-Based Teacher Education modules covering various pedagogical issues that are often skills oriented, competency based, and rely on the four-step model. However, these teaching-oriented materials are often hard to find, and the understanding of pedagogical issues is, at best, uneven. The recent reviews of vocational teacher preparation cited in section IV tend to present generic recommendations about teaching rather than practices specific to vocational education.

within the model enterprise and learning about the model enterprise by comparing the model to real enterprises.

The Office Learning Center (*Lernbüro*) is a model enterprise that combines theoretical knowledge and practical routines with a simulated office (Achtenhagen & Schneider, 1993; Kaiser, 1987; Kaiser, 1997; Kaiser & Weitz, 1990; Kaiser, Weitz, & Sarrazin, 1991; Schneider, 1996). In the past 300 years, office learning centers have been established throughout Europe, and by now nearly all commercial schools in middle Europe and Scandinavia have incorporated them. Students acquire basic economic knowledge, gain insight into the network structure of business, and improve their abilities to behave effectively in complex situations. Classes are divided into working groups that organize themselves, manage the tasks given them, solve problems (including ill-structured ones), and plan and carry out new tasks. Office learning centers typically encompass individual and group work, business activities, simulation and role play, and projects involving special plans (in the sense of business reengineering). The teacher's role changes from a person who imparts knowledge to a colleague of the students who advises and offers ideas in case students do not know how to proceed. Teachers must be aware of certain systemic problems, particularly those of balancing routine actions and new activities, practical work and theoretical reflection (Achtenhagen & Schneider, 1993; Kaiser, 1997; Schneider, 1996). Most of these problems can be solved through teacher training.

One drawback of office learning centers is that tasks can become artificial. This fundamental problem has favored the development of training firms (*Übungsfirma*), which carry out real production under special conditions (Tramm, 1997). All external activities are organized by a head office that coordinates all training firms, banks, tax offices, and courts. The head offices also organize sales catalogues and fairs to bring together the business activities of all training firms.[6] While the pedagogical advantages are substantial, the schools also have disadvantages: Many schools (particularly commercial schools meeting only 8 hours per week) find it difficult to complete the work required by other, full-time training firms within the time schedule.

At a somewhat greater level of complexity, a junior firm is a training firm (with both part-time and full-time models) that produces and sells goods for actual markets (Kutt, 1993, p. 33). While it is founded for the purposes of vocational education, a junior firm normally operates under the umbrella of the enterprise that developed it (Sommer & Fix, 1988). Normally, junior firms produce for the enterprise or for other junior firms (Kutt, 1993; for the United States Junior Achievement Movement see Brodersen, 1986). Students learn to behave as entrepreneurs and develop key competencies like teamwork, creativity, communications skills, and system-related thinking (Fix, 1989; Sommer & Fix, 1988). Junior firms have much in common with school-based enterprises in the United States (Stern, Stone, Hopkins, McMillion, & Crain, 1994), though such enterprises are often much less formal.

Simulation games, originating in the military sector, were systematically developed in the 17th and 18th centuries after a history of about 3,000 years. At the moment, simulation games (especially computer-based versions) are one of the most widely used teaching tools for business and economic education (Dinham & Stritter, 1986; Kaiser & Kaminski, 1994; Pieters & Brandsma, in press; Whitehead, 1984). Particularly in multiperiod models where decisions in one period affect subsequent periods, students can learn about planning in dynamic systems. Learners play distinct roles in making decisions and evaluating procedures; the final stage—examining results in subsequent periods to see how well a team has played—forms an essential part of the process. Through simulations, students acquire information about economic systems like markets, enterprises, production, and sales processes (Preiss, 1994). They learn to decide in uncertain and complex situations, especially when the models include thousands of variables (Dörner, Kreuzig, Reither, & Stäudel, 1983; Dörner & Pfeiffer, 1993). However, the effective use of simulations requires a great deal of teaching expertise because unreflective use of simulations results in performance below that of good frontal teaching (Achtenhagen, 1994; Fürstenau, 1994; Schunck, 1993).

Case studies materials offer real or simulated problems from business situations. This method, first introduced by the Harvard Business School in 1908 for future managers, can enhance the practical use of theoretical knowledge, decision-making behavior, and independent learning. Many different types of case studies can be found (Kaiser & Kaminski, 1994): *case study methods* emphasize analyzing presented facts, detecting hidden problems, and making appropriate decisions; *case problem methods* allow students more time for discussing alternative solutions and their unintended side-effects; *case incident methods* present incomplete cases and require students to collect missing information; and the *stated problem method* provides students with solutions and requires them to evaluate the solutions. For effective teaching with case studies, the realism of the case, its clarity, the personal significance for students, and possibilities for generalization must all be considered. The multitude of case studies on the market leads to highly varied practices for teaching via cases; like simulation games, case studies also require substantial pedagogical expertise before they can be used effectively (John, 1992).

Teaching Methods Used in Industrial-Technical Occupations

The task-centered learning method (*Leittextmethode*) is often used within the firm-based part of the dual system. It intends to provide students a more active role than the traditional four-stage method, and trainers serve more as advisers rather than as direct instructors (Hartmann, Gaevert, & Schleyer, 1990). At least six stages are involved (Kaiser & Kaminski, 1994; Pätzold, 1996): an initial stage of acquiring the necessary information; a

---

[6] These head offices are relatively large institutions: In Germany, the *"Zentrale des Deutschen Übungsfirmenrings"* governs about 1,000 training firms; in Austria, Denmark, and Luxembourg, all commercial schools are governed by one head office (Gramlinger, 1994). Comparable approaches can be found in Great Britain, France, Switzerland, the Ukraine, and Lithuania, and the trend is to establish a European head office corresponding to the European Union (EUROPEN Bulletin, No. 16, 1997).

planning phase; a decision-making stage about work processes; a stage of actual production; a stage for examining the results of production; and an evaluation stage that is conducted by trainers and apprentices together. This method is widely accepted because its instructional processes are well-organized and closely guided, especially for students with learning difficulties and little prior knowledge. In addition to the relatively high costs of materials, its problems include reduced attention to communicative behavior and social competence; the balance between teacher-guided instructional processes and the development of self-directed learning is also a common issue.

Apprentices' corners and workshops are the traditional form of work-based learning in the industrial-technical sector. Enterprises providing positions for apprentices generally allow them to work in close contact with normal production processes. Sometimes, however, apprentices work on subtasks that are away from the production line or function as "loan workers" in production itself (Dehnbostel, Holz, & Novak, 1992). One advantage of these approaches is that training can be made specific to the production process; but potential disadvantages include inflexible teaching, a lack of clarity about the underlying technical requirements, and a low level of complexity and of systemic knowledge (Laur-Ernst, 1993). Often, problems occur when tasks that are isolated from production for learning purposes are not reintegrated into production, preventing apprentices from understanding their purposes.

As an alternative, therefore, the concept of apprentices' islands has been developed, where teaching takes place in special "islands" within the usual production process. Apprentices learn within production itself, but with more time and control than other workers. This special treatment gradually vanishes until apprentices are completely integrated into production. The advantages include more serious tasks and communication with other workers, and better understanding of the complexity of production.

The concept of "study circles" (*Lernstatt*) was developed in the early 1980s, mainly to integrate foreign workers into employment (Härnsten, 1994; Holmstrand, Lindström, Löwstedt, & Englund, 1994). Since then, the practice has changed to develop the abilities of workers who do not have formal education and who are often functionally illiterate. Enterprises start with the learning and working experiences of participants; group processes are videotaped and discussed within the group. Then competencies necessary for work are introduced, adjusted to the goals and the prior knowledge of the participants. The first evaluation results show that study circle members increase motivation, improve the quality of their work, and reduce their absences (Paulsen & Stötzel, 1992).

Quality circles developed in Japan to increase the quality of products. Since the 1980s, this concept has been adopted by many Western countries to improve motivation and working conditions and to encourage further education and teamwork among employees (Bednarek, 1988; Holmstrand, Lindström, Löwstedt, & Englund, 1994). As in study circles, lower-level employees are usually involved; they concentrate on work-related problems and their solutions with the help of a moderator. Quality circles can focus on specific problems in particular departments, especially in production, but can also be extended to focus on larger problems of the enterprise. One major issue, however, is that effective quality circles often face legal, financial, personal, technical, and time-related constraints.

Computer-Assisted Learning Environments

The increased use of computer-based technologies has raised the question of how to include these techniques into vocational education.[7] Many efforts have emphasized computer-assisted learning environments that support self-directed learning. One strand includes constructivist approaches that offer multiple perspectives and contexts, but they must also be authentically related to actual work processes. A second strand includes self-directed learning via multimedia representations of worksite problems, with high levels of interaction between the system and the user. The role of the teacher or trainer, who has to shift from an active instructor to a "dynamic spectator," is critical (Brech, 1989, p. 163). At the moment, computer-based learning environments are still under development, and research is necessary to reconcile the technical possibilities and the teaching expertise of vocational instructors. As an example, Achtenhagen et al. (1997) developed effective teacher behavior using a computer-based virtual enterprise. The apprentices learned to solve problems within the virtual enterprise; then they solved the same tasks in their own real enterprise and contrasted their experiences of learning and working in both the commercial school setting and the workplace—something that could not be done without the computer environment because of the complexity and lack of transparency of the tasks in the real firm.

Learning at the Workplace

In countries with the dual system, vocational education has always encompassed both the work-based component and the school-based component. Evaluation studies generally show that workers attribute larger learning effects to work-based settings than to school settings that are separate from production (Kloas, 1992). However, such results should be interpreted carefully because the trainers' behavior at the workplace is critical; for example, Keck (1995) showed that the trainer's perception of apprentices and their interaction with apprentices decisively influenced the quality of education.

Work-based learning in dual systems takes place in a variety of actual work and work-like settings. In business and commercial education, office learning centers are simulations of offices, while training firms and junior firms operate under progressively more realistic conditions. Similarly, in industrial and technical occupations, apprentice corners, workshops, and islands facilitate learning during production, initially sheltered from some demands of production, but that increasingly be-

---

[7] In a large literature, see especially Anglin (1991); Dijkstra, Krammer, and van Merriënboer (1992); Dills and Romiszowski (1997); Gooler and Roth (1990); Jonassen (1988, 1996); Jones and Winne (1992); Merriënboer (1997); Pieters, Breuer, and Simons (1990); Rasmussen, Andersen, and Bernsen (1991); and Tuijnman (1996).

come like actual production. In many parts of Germany and Switzerland, the "dual" system is really a triad system because small- and medium-sized employers provide apprenticeships in cooperative workshops that are supervised by employers, but independent of production (Bierhof & Prais, 1996, p. 79; Heidegger & Rauner, 1996). Thus, work-based settings vary substantially in the extent to which they incorporate the conditions of production.

Even in countries without a dual system, a great deal of work-based learning still takes place, again falling along a continuum that includes work shadowing, internships, and cooperative education programs that can last anywhere from 1 week to 2 years (see Stern, Finkelstein, Stone, Latting, & Dornsife, 1995, and Urquiola et al., 1997, for the United States). In addition, schools often create school-based enterprises to engage in production under sheltered conditions (Stern et al., 1994). Recently, a number of countries have developed new interest in work-based learning, in most cases to overcome the problems of motivation, applicability, and datedness that occur when vocational education operates at a distance from production. (We will review several of these efforts in section V.) From a pedagogical perspective, they all involve similar questions: whether learning in a work-like setting conforms to the learning required at work or whether it is still contrived; whether learning is narrow or broad; whether teaching follows the rigid and sequential presentation of isolated skills or, instead, allows students to learn broader principles and systems. Despite the interest in work-based learning, work settings are not necessarily superior to school settings as places of learning. Indeed, in some technologically advanced firms, traditional on-the-job training largely has given way to classroom training and computer-based multimedia training (Quiñones & Ehrenstein, 1996a, p. 6), which suggests the limitations of on-the-job training in complex workplaces. Therefore, instructors in both settings need to understand the pedagogical complexity of vocational instruction to be effective (Berryman, 1995; Stasz & Kaganoff, 1997).

III. The Complexity of Vocational Teaching in Practice

The approaches outlined in section II indicate how varied vocational teaching can be, allowing instructors to choose from the most traditional to the newest methods involving computer-based simulations and hypermedia environments and from traditional school-based programs to those integrating work-based learning. A different dimension of complexity is the application of these different methods in practice—because virtually any method can be implemented in different ways. In addition, the richness of vocational teaching and learning environments means that what actually happens in educational settings often includes much more than what textbook approaches specify. To detect these complex dimensions of practice, we must rely on empirical studies of teaching, particularly observational studies. In this section, we describe several dimensions of practice that influence its effectiveness, including the special features of teaching in workshops and work-like settings, the ways the varied competencies required in work are taught, and the differences between skills approaches versus systems approaches.

As in section II, we often distinguish certain approaches to teaching (like skills approaches versus systems approaches) even though instructors in practice tend to use a mixture. Indeed, the most basic form of vocational instruction—the lecture/workshop in English-speaking countries, or the dual system with both classroom and work settings—specifically allows for mixed, or hybrid, teaching (Cuban, 1993) that includes both didactic, teacher-centered, fact-intensive instruction ("learning") and more practice-oriented, student- and project-centered, constructivist instruction ("doing"). We distinguish among different elements that are ordinarily combined for analytic reasons only. In addition, as is true for traditional approaches in vocational education, we suspect that untrained teachers tend to fall back on the most conventional and didactic approaches, ignoring the complexities presented in this section.

As we will see, evidence about effectiveness—about whether one approach to teaching is more effective than another as measured by outcomes like test scores, performance, rates of passing licensing exams, subsequent employment,[8] or any other measure of success—is largely missing, partly because existing studies tend to conceptualize approaches to teaching in different ways. A final dimension of complexity, then, is that conceptions of effectiveness in vocational teaching are so varied—so specific to different occupations and to the different settings in which vocational teaching takes place—that generalizations are difficult.

The Combination of Classroom and Workshop: The Meaning of "Hands-on" Teaching

In many areas of vocational education, not only workshops (or labs) but also classroom settings are common, sometimes in school settings and sometimes in work-based settings. Advocates for vocational education have long contended that vocational teaching is more active ("hands on") and less didactic than academic instruction and, therefore, has some intrinsic advantages—particularly for students who fare poorly under standard academic methods. Weber and Puleo (1988) and their colleagues compared 649 secondary vocational classes with 244 academic classes and found a variety of differences, many related to the greater use of workshops. Vocational teachers were much less likely to be lecturing and were more likely to model the performance required; students were more likely to have some control in carrying out activities and to work on complex, multipart tasks; "active" learning modes like student projects, student-to-student interaction, and diverse projects were used to a greater extent. Higher-order skills were more likely to develop in vocational than in academic classrooms. On the other hand, equipment tended to be out of date—a perennial issue related to cost differentials—and less time was devoted to reading. As in academic instruction, most teachers paid little explicit attention to higher-order competencies; instead, they focused on the specific knowledge and psychomotor skills nec-

---

[8] The large literature about the effects of vocational education on employment and earnings examines the quantity of vocational education or credentials received, not the content or teaching conditions within these programs.

essary to complete well-defined tasks in relatively specific ways, with little attention to the transferability of these skills.

A few other studies have examined the combination of classrooms and workshops (for the United States, Claus, 1990; Grubb et al., 1999; and Richardson, Fisk, & Okun, 1983, chap. 3; for Australia, McKavanaugh & Stevenson, 1994; for Great Britain, Harkin & Davis, 1996a, 1996b; Holloway, 1992). The classroom component allows the instructor to present the theory, the academic underpinnings, and the facts necessary for work, while the workshop or lab provides the applications and practice of material presented in the lecture. The combination exemplifies the Deweyan precept of "learning and doing":[9] it is neither, in most cases, merely repetitive practice in manipulative skills (as in many short-term job-training programs) nor is it all "theory" or classroom-based work, but rather a combination of the two.

To be sure, the separation of classroom and workshop can separate "learning" and "doing." In Claus's (1990) investigation of a secondary food preparation program—a good example of traditional vocational education—the first year was largely devoted to classroom instruction, a prerequisite for the second year when students did more cooking and ran a restaurant. But the students, harboring a distaste for academic work and unrelieved by any work-related component, disliked the bookwork of the first year; they resisted learning in the conventional, lecture- and textbook-driven format, and the teacher accommodated their low levels of participation by reducing her demands. The separation of learning from doing is a problem, even in countries with the dual system, where the content of school-based instruction is established by ministries of education while the work-based component is developed, with little coordination, by chambers of industry and commerce. The major problem is that teachers and trainers from vocational schools and firms have little routine contact, even within vocational schools themselves. Often, "theory" teachers (for the theoretical subjects) and "practice" teachers (for the workshop exercises within schools) do not cooperate (Heidegger & Rauner, 1996).

In other settings, the lectures and workshop components can be more closely integrated. While the lecture component can be as didactic and decontextualized as any academic lecture, it usually includes some discussion as well. Many questions in occupational classrooms are relatively simple, factual questions (What is an alloy? What is flux?), though occupational instructors tend to shift to more complex and diagnostic questions (What happens if I plug this filter?) and then to counterfactual and problem-posing questions (What would I do if I wanted x to happen? or What might be the cause of a breakdown?). In this way, skilled instructors move from simple recall to causal analysis to counterfactual analysis to problem solving, often within a very brief span of time.

But this does not always happen; the issue, for vocational as for academic instructors, is whether the instructor has sufficient command over teaching practices to shift between factual and higher-level questioning. In examining Further Education (FE) colleges in Great Britain, Harkin and Davis (1996a) determined that occupational instructors were somewhat less didactic than academic instructors, employing more small group work and student activity. However, occupational instructors still spent the majority of time managing instruction and motivating their students; discussion often consisted of formulaic responses and off-task chatting. In practice, then, instructors were not especially successful in moving away from directive modes of teaching.

In the workshop component of occupational programs, students typically work on projects—sometimes individually, often in small groups—that are similar to those that might arise in employment, though they may be simplified for purposes of instruction. The instructor circulates to answer questions, check on the progress of work, correct errors, and otherwise monitor performance. While such practices may seem obvious, the workshop, on closer examination, proves to be a complex setting that combines a number of conceptually distinct practices taking place almost simultaneously:

- *Showing and doing.* Showing is a teacher-centered activity that is normally followed within the workshop by doing, by the student mimicking what the instructor has just shown; the student activity, the doing, is usually the heart of the workshop. Sometimes there is only one right way to carry out a task, particularly in regulated occupations (like construction trades) or in practices related to health and safety; then student "doing" is entirely mimetic. However, in other cases, an instructor may present several ways of carrying out an operation or individual styles of working, allowing students to develop their own understanding of the requirements of successful work.

- *Developing noncognitive abilities.* The workshop is the locus of teaching the manipulative or kinesthetic abilities, the visual skills, and sometimes other perceptual skills (taste and smell in culinary classes, auditory response in various manufacturing occupations). Instructors vary in the extent to which they make explicit the teaching of noncognitive abilities. In the traditional crafts and trades, instructors spend a good deal of time showing the proper use of tools and correcting improper use; instructors in areas involving three-dimensional construction will often spend time on the process of visualization. However, in other cases, one can see instructors ignoring the development of these noncognitive abilities. For example, drafting instructors often teach CAD as a series of computer commands, ignoring the visual and conceptual process of moving between two and three dimensions; the welding instructors described by Evans and Butler (1992) ignored cognitive and perceptual skills and focused on manipulative skills only. In these cases, occupa-

---

[9] Dewey is often misquoted as advocating "learning by doing," but—given Dewey's antipathy to false dichotomies—this is not at all what he meant. Consistently he was in favor of combining "doing"—experience or project-based learning—and "learning"—more conventional instruction through texts, lectures, and (especially) considered reflection. He was particularly clear that "doing" without "learning"—without some reflection and understanding about experience—is ineffective. In *Schools of Tomorrow,* he and his wife explicitly stated that "Learning by doing does not, of course, mean the substitution of manual occupations or handwork for textbook studying" (Dewey & Dewey, 1915, p. 74), and they went on to clarify the complementarity between learning and doing.

tional instructors appear not to recognize that certain competencies are necessary on the job. In other cases, however, they face a common problem within occupational education: Little has been written about how best to develop these work-related, noncognitive abilities (Hacker & Skell, 1993), and many instructors have few colleagues to talk with or professional associations to contact. Particularly in countries without a well-developed teacher training program, vocational instructors are left to their own "natural" teaching approaches.

- *Student engagement.* Occupational instructors talk about workshops as being crucial to involving students actively. In the workshop, nonparticipation is obvious. Similarly, students who might be reluctant to ask questions in lectures are often forced, by the necessity to work on projects, to participate more actively. Sometimes, the students who select occupational programs for which the abstract lecture component cannot be absorbed unless accompanied by a concrete component (Holloway, 1992) show the greater motivation. While this may denigrate the needs of the "tactile" students in vocational education, a more positive interpretation is that it recognizes the variety of competencies required in employment.

- *Teaching problem solving, teamwork, and communications skills.* Workshops provide opportunities for problem solving that are often superior to those of the classroom. Often, workshops are based on problems: For example, many auto and electronics programs begin with nonfunctioning cars and circuits, and students must first diagnose the problem, based on their knowledge from the classroom and text, before they can fix it. Unlike classrooms, workshops can encompass the range of problems that occur on the job, which are usually more complex than textbook examples. In some cases, occupational instructors provide formulaic approaches to problems, fail to provide students with enough information and support to solve problems, or complicate simple problems before students have fully grasped the issues so that students are always confused. In contrast, the best instructors provide their students with alternative approaches and allow them to understand the reasons behind different approaches. Achtenhagen and his coworkers found that using workshops and simulations does not necessarily result in better learning; rather, instructors must handle these complex teaching settings as pedagogical experts (Achtenhagen, 1994; Achtenhagen et al., 1992).

  In workshops, the practice of having students work in teams is widespread, as a way of preparing students for the conditions of real work. The experience of teamwork also helps to develop communications among members of a team (Salas & Cannon-Bowers, 1996). As in academic classes, teamwork does not always work well, particularly if instructors fail to structure teams and their tasks appropriately; but under the right conditions, teams are vehicles for simultaneously accomplishing several pedagogical goals (Fürstenau, 1994; John, 1992).

- *Making the invisible visible and diagnosing errors.* Cognitive processes are invisible, and therefore observing them and diagnosing problems in student understanding can be difficult. But the workshop makes the invisible visible: The

progress on projects, the act of treating patients (or cows in agriculture programs), or the result of procedures in a construction or electronics workshop allows instructors to diagnose and correct errors. In many cases, the materials and projects impose their own corrections on students. If a circuit is not properly wired, it will not perform; if an auto part is not correctly installed, it will not function as intended; if bills are not booked or orders are not sent out, an office learning center does not function. The corrections come, at least some of the time, from the task or project itself; the instructor need not constantly personify authority or expertise.

In addition, vocational instructors generally stress learning from mistakes, in place of the error-free performance that is the goal of conventional, teacher-centered instruction. The process of circulating among students is intended to detect, discuss, and correct mistakes; discussion sessions after the workshop may be explicitly devoted to reviewing errors and problems during the workshop. The physical representation of learning in physical objects and visible procedures makes the detection of these errors and their correction easier than in the academic classroom.

- *Facilitating one-on-one instruction.* Like their academic peers, occupational instructors value the chance for one-on-one instruction. The projects in workshops lend themselves to one-on-one instruction, because the work is often individual (or done in small groups), and instructors typically spend time with individuals (or small groups) discussing their progress, their solutions, their thought processes, and the alternatives they might pursue. In a recent investigation, Zielke and Popp (1997) demonstrated the possibilities of individualization and differentiation within workshop-based training.

- *Facilitating "authentic" assessment.* In academic instruction, current debates often involve traditional forms of assessment—particularly, multiple-choice exams that tend to reinforce skills-oriented teaching—versus new or "authentic" assessment like open-ended exams, performance-based assessment, and portfolios that encourage more constructivist teaching. Vocational education has always had "authentic" assessments because workshops and simulations usually involve projects and performance-based assessment. In Technical and Further Education (TAFE) colleges in Australia, for example, classroom settings tend to rely on pen-and-paper exams that emphasize short answers, simple facts, and multiple-choice formats, while workshops use practice- or project-based assessment (Stevenson & Brown, 1994). Similarly, Weber and Puleo (1988) found a greater use of performance-based assessments in U.S. secondary vocational classes, with less use of multiple-choice exams. (However, many secondary vocational teachers still use conventional tests, even in vocational classes; Stecher, Rahn, Ruby, Alt, & Robyn, 1997, contrast more authentic assessments in secondary classes and workshops with conventional assessment practice.) Instructors in American community colleges also use various conventional tests in classrooms that examine students on information that has been covered and also performance-based assessments in workshops (Grubb et al., 1999, chap. 7). This hybrid approach allows vocational instructors to monitor students' performance relative to predetermined skills and standards, including those specified by competency-based approaches, but it also permits them to examine students for their deeper understanding of work processes.

- *Developing complex teaching-learning environments.* For those occupations without workshops—like business and commerce—complex teaching-learning environments have been developed to overcome the conventional structure of teaching and learning (Achtenhagen & John, 1992). These approaches use a systems approach to rearrange a linear curricular structure, making overt the underlying net structure found in enterprises (Achtenhagen, 1994, especially Figure 3; Preiss, 1994). Computer-based simulation games and case studies have also been introduced, and the new curricular structure is now part of the official apprenticeship for industrial clerks (Achtenhagen, et al., 1992). A further development led to a multimedia virtual enterprise (Achtenhagen et al, 1997). At the beginning, apprentices have to solve ill-structured problems (e.g., to decide on a delivery date for a certain product that is not in stock). After developing a solution by navigating through the virtual enterprise, they have to solve the same task within their real enterprise. The apprentices then present both their initial exploration and the solution in the firm to their classmates. The results show that the development of systems categories helps foster the understanding of workplaces, and apprentices can use their prior knowledge more appropriately in the classroom. This method provides a way of incorporating thinking and acting within systems into subjects where workshops would otherwise be impossible.

Workshops and their analogues in fields like business and commerce therefore embody several distinctive pedagogical practices. However, potential liabilities from hands-on instruction are also possible. The most obvious involves the differences between teaching workshops and real work: Workshops, with simpler, better-defined, and more clearly solved problems than the messy problems in real work, are inevitably somewhat out of date and less complex than real work settings. In conveying the lore of what work is really like, instructors frequently remind students about these differences. Whether these differences contribute to the educational power of workshops or simply detract from its realism and relevance is a subject of endless debate. In the hands of skilled instructors, however, the workshop can provide both learning within the workshop as a model of real work and learning about the workshop as a departure from realistic conditions (Achtenhagen et al., 1992; Tramm, 1997).

Another potential problem is that practice can take over a workshop so that it is left without any theory and no general learning; the purpose in such a workshop may be practice to gain automaticity and speed in low-level manipulative skills. This is the problem in the welding classes described by Evans and Butler (1992); in the United States, this approach is more common in short-term job-training programs like that observed by Hull (1993). Another problem with workshops is illustrated by Brereton, Sheppard, and Leifer (1995), who describe a mechanical dissection class for third- and fourth-year engineering students: Because students in this class tended to use experience

as their only source of reasoning, a workshop that does not require students to develop fundamental concepts may leave them with naive and incorrect conceptions of how things work— what Gardner (1983) calls intuitive learning.

A different problem, related to the balance between teacher-directed instruction and self-directed learning in the *Leittext-methode,* was illustrated by a secondary vocational classroom where Claus (1990) verified the greater use of experiential and project-based instruction. The loose structure of the workshop allowed students to avoid work; often the teacher provided the answers and carried out students' tasks, and Claus suggested that the greater popularity of vocational courses stemmed in part from the lower levels of demands on students. Similarly in Great Britain, the "new vocationalism" introduced more vocational options into secondary schools; students clearly preferred these alternatives, with their greater range of activities and experiences, to "normal lessons" (Hustler, 1988), but many found the programs a waste of time (Ghaill, 1988), and critics routinely charged the new programs with merely keeping students off the streets. Without careful structuring of workshops, the content of this kind of teaching can degenerate easily.

A final drawback to workshops was evident in the occupational courses observed by Grubb et al. (1999). Because the workshop is a rich environment, the large amount of information swirling around is not easy to retain. Unfortunately, students rarely take notes, and a great deal of information is lost. The lack of note taking suggests a separation between the classroom component and the workshop, which is largely an oral, kinesthetic, and visual culture where the literacy practices that aid learning are much less common. A more integrated form of instruction would introduce literacy practices into both the workshop and the classroom component.

The workshop—or the work-based setting—is therefore a complex place, where numerous practices take place simultaneously. Instructors can incorporate them explicitly or fail to acknowledge their value; each element can be carried out well or badly. And so the potential richness of vocational teaching depends in part on the skill of instructors in those settings that are unique to occupational education.

The Varied Competencies in Vocational Programs

The complexity of vocational teaching also emerges when examining the varied competencies required in employment—literacy in several forms, manual and visual skills, interpersonal abilities, the higher-order competencies associated with high performance workplaces, and various norms of employment. One persistent problem, common also to academic teachers, is whether instructors are explicit about what they are teaching. For example, vocational classes incorporate a variety of literacy practices, but vocational instructors vary in the extent to which they are explicit about their importance in the workplace (Worthen, 1997). Similarly, manual trades often involve blueprint reading and the manipulation of materials in three dimensions, but the visual skills necessary are usually embedded in tasks, rather than taught as a specific skill; the lore of the workplace is often conveyed in personal anecdotes and offhand comments, rather than being directly taught. One pedagogical question is whether vocational instruction would be more effective if teachers were explicit about the competencies required at work and developed them in the classroom.[10] In the absence of explicit teaching, certain skills may act as gatekeepers; for example, if a CAD program does not explicitly teach visual facility, then those students who already have certain visual competencies will do better than those who do not. The lack of explicit teaching also contributes to the perception that noncognitive competencies are innate, the result of aptitude rather than training.

The competencies required in employment are usually combined in ways particular to occupations; indeed, the unification of these different abilities is what makes a skilled worker. However, this mix may be neglected in vocational teaching. Drafting, for example, requires both spatial and mathematical competencies, and a certain logical facility for those using computer-assisted design (CAD) programs; but instructors sometimes merely treat the drafting task as a programming problem. Similarly, welding requires manipulative skills, cognitive skills (particularly in planning the weld), perceptual abilities, and the ability to respond to the perceptual information in the course of work; but instructors often stress manipulative skills (hands-on learning) to the exclusion of the cognitive and perceptual skills (Evans & Butler, 1992). How teacher preparation conveys the ability to recognize and balance different competencies is not clear. Again, Germany is a partial exception: There, vocational teachers have to finish at least one year in an occupation before starting studies in vocational teaching, and this sequence enables fledgling teachers to recognize and coordinate the various competencies necessary on the job.

LITERACY PRACTICES

From observations in workplaces (e.g., Dehnbostel, Holz, & Novak, 1992; Hacker & Skell, 1993; Hull, Jury, Ziv, & Katz, 1996), even relatively low-level occupations require literacy-related skills—particularly in high-performance workplaces that require communication with a variety of coworkers and customers, the reading of complex manuals and guides, and the ability to find information independently. Worthen (1997) found a greater variety and complexity of literacy practices in U.S. postsecondary occupational education than might be expected—reading complex texts, finding information quickly in repair manuals, interpreting government regulations, and presenting and writing reports to different audiences including customers, supervisors, and suppliers. While these literacy skills are no less sophisticated than those required in academic courses, they are often quite occupation-specific (Stevenson, 1996b) and are quite different from conventional academic competencies. Similarly, technical and business subjects often require sophisticated reasoning using elementary mathematical skills that are applied in complex sequences to solve poorly formulated problems, rather than the advanced skills with abstract concepts that

are taught in conventional math (Steen, 1997). Nothing prepares most occupational (or academic) instructors to teach these nonstandard forms of academic competencies, and occupational instructors often complain that academic courses provide little help with the reading, writing, and math demands of their occupational areas.

Despite these frustrations, many occupational instructors pay little explicit attention to literacy demands, because they do not regard teaching literacy as their job and may feel incompetent to teach language or math (Worthen, 1997). Therefore, some of the important cognitive abilities required in occupations are unlikely to be carefully taught. This problem has led to efforts in the English-speaking countries to integrate academic and occupational education (see section V). In Germany, one solution has been to prepare vocational teachers not only for commercial or technical content but also for literacy goals; the academic level of vocational teacher education corresponds to that of *Gymnasium* teachers.

KINESTHETIC OR MANUAL ABILITIES

Manual abilities are often central to occupational performance—sometimes in conjunction with other competencies like cognitive skills that help one understand how tools and materials should be used and perceptual skills that provide feedback (Gardner, 1983, chap. 9). Most vocational instructors pay considerable attention to the development of manual skills, including correct and incorrect ways of using tools and handling materials; they may devise drills—e.g., making various joints in carpentry classes, practicing different welds, or drawing objects in a manual drafting class. Instructors often provide substantial explanations for why certain manual procedures should be followed; in effect, they are providing students with the conceptual understanding necessary for skilled practice or the "device knowledge" about a particular tool that allows students to use it most effectively. In some cases, however—typified by Evans and Butler's (1992) welding instructors—an emphasis on manual skills may so dominate instruction that students fail to learn the rationale underlying different approaches.

The development of manual or kinesthetic skills has been given little explicit attention.[11] Often instructors assume that practice and drill—the hands-on approach—makes perfect, though some alternatives to rote and didactic instruction exist: In Germany, the *Leittextmethode* has students conceptualize practice, engage in workshop activities, and then analyze their successes and failures as a way of improving their abilities. The same practice sometimes takes place more informally in community colleges in the United States, where a few instructors present concepts of practice in the classroom, move to a workshop, and then move back into the classroom to evaluate the results (Grubb et al., 1999). Otherwise, with little systematic

---

[10] In the United States, Lisa Delpit (1986) has pointed out that, in the absence of explicit instruction, low-income black children may have no way to learn the linguistic styles of white middle-class people (and, by extension, of middle-class occupations). Worthen (1997) has clarified the profound differences between both academic and vocational instructors who are explicit about literacy practices and the majority who are not; without explicit attention, certain kinds of language use are likely never to be noticed by students.

[11] But see Hacker and Skell (1993), and Gardner's (1983, chap. 9) extensive review of "bodily kinesthetic intelligence." In this and other noncognitive abilities, Gardner views the acquisition of ability as a developmental process, but he is silent about the role of explicit instruction in developing such abilities.

discussion about ways of teaching manual skills, instructors appear to develop idiosyncratic approaches.

VISUAL AND SPATIAL ABILITIES

While many occupational areas require certain visual abilities, the extent to which visual abilities are explicitly taught in vocational classes varies substantially.[12] In some cases, as in the CAD class described previously, the specifically visual dimensions of practice are ignored in favor of an emphasis on procedures—for example, the necessary CAD computer instructions. Similarly, many engineers report that they have never been instructed in the spatial dimensions of their work (Bell & Linn, 1993), even though visual skills are thought to be highly important. If spatial abilities are necessary but not taught in occupational programs, then only those with innate spatial abilities will be proficient—and, therefore, tests of spatial ability will in fact predict who completes vocational and engineering programs, as Lohman (1988) reports.

But how should visual abilities be taught, once instructors accept the value of teaching them? Despite a large literature on spatial abilities (e.g., Gardner, 1983, chap. 8; Lohman, 1988), most investigations have taken place in the psychology lab, and the usefulness of these studies is limited. In particular, the evidence that visualizers (individuals who tend to see problems in purely visual terms) and verbalizers require different teaching strategies is weak and inconsistent. Bell and Linn (1993) distinguished holistic strategies for performing spatial tasks from both analytic strategies in which individuals focus on the details of an object (in performing spatial rotation, for example) and from a pattern strategy in which familiar parts of an object are rotated and then connected. Holistic strategies allow individuals to perform faster and get higher scores on tests of spatial reasoning, though expert engineers can be found in all three groups. Hsi, Linn, and Bell (1997) showed that explicit spatial instruction, using these three approaches, increased rates of passing an engineering course and reduced the differences between men and women. A computer program called Display Object, which permits the rotation of three-dimensional objects, is another method of making spatial thinking visible and concrete (Osborn & Agogino, 1992). Some techniques, then, can be identified for teaching visual abilities, though they are rarely incorporated into vocational and professional programs.

In addition, as Worthen (1997) has pointed out, occupational classes often incorporate literacy practices in which occupational phenomena are represented in notational systems that require visual skills—blueprints, electrical and refrigerant diagrams, and various maps. Students must learn to read these specialized notational systems accurately and fluidly. Some occupational instructors devote considerable time to teaching such competencies explicitly; for example, Achtenhagen et al. (1997) incorporated network displays, organizational diagrams, and aerial views of the real enterprise with other material in a multimedia virtual enterprise. By that the students are forced to switch over from one mode of representation to another. Others assume that students can pick them up along the way.

The work of Satchwell (1997) and Satchwell and Johnson (1992) with aviation electronics suggests that representational systems can be taught in different ways. When students used functional flow diagrams—diagrams illustrating electrical systems at a conceptual and causal level, rather than a collection of components with unknown causal connections—they did better on many (but not all) measures of performance. In a similar vein, while teachers often focus on developing simple "map skills"—interpreting a map's legend and understanding its scale, for example—document reading may be enhanced by teaching the dimensions of information represented in the underlying structure of diagrams; Mosenthal and Kirsch have examined documents incorporating visual information like maps, diagrams, and charts.[13] These results suggest that constructivist approaches may be the most effective approach to visual skills.

INTERPERSONAL RELATIONSHIPS AND MOTIVATION

Occupational instructors often incorporate interpersonal relationships and communications skills into their workshops through group discussion, supervised work experiences, and simulation and role play (Nelson & Nies, 1978). However, relatively little attention has been paid to flexibility and transfer (Achtenhagen, Nijhof, & Raffe, 1995). That is, modeling the personal relations after a particular occupation—or, often, after the instructor's own experiences—does not necessarily prepare students for different work settings, for fluid job changes, or for the flexible arrangements of the high-performance firm.

Schunck (1993) found that the development of motivation and interest depends upon the teacher's abilities. If vocational teachers behave as unreflective practitioners, the degree of motivation and interest among students decreases, with negative consequences for learning. A broad overview of motivational issues within the dual system shows that interest and motivation are higher within the enterprise than in the school-based component, but learning within the *Berufschule* is judged more important than that in the enterprise. Thus, the combination of school-based and work-based settings is necessary for both motivation and learning; a teacher's behavior toward students and the implementation of complex systems approaches are important to outcomes.[14]

---

[12] Smith and Douglas (1997) call these abilities "mathematical" rather than spatial and visual, signaling that even the categorization of various competencies is difficult. However, they stress, as we do, that the basic problem is one of schools not teaching the spatial and mathematical competencies required on the job.

[13] See the monthly series on "Understanding Documents" in the *Journal of Reading* from September 1990 to May 1991; see especially Mosenthal and Kirsch (1990, 1991).

[14] For research on commercial and business education, see Hardt, Zaib, Kleinbeck, and Metz-Göckel (1996); Prenzel, Kristen, Dengler, Ettle, and Beer (1996); Stark, Gruber, Graf, Renkl, and Mandl (1996); Straka, Nenniger, Spevacek, and Wosnitza (1996); and Wild and Krapp (1996). See also Stevenson (1998) for Australia.

COMPETENCIES FOR THE HIGH-PERFORMANCE WORKPLACE

Occupational instructors are usually more aware of trends in work and demands by employers than are academic instructors; many occupational programs have advisory committees that have brought the higher-order skills of the workplace to their attention. In Germany, higher-order skills are specified by the state curricula and by federal regulations for all apprenticeships; the new Qualifications and Curriculum Authority in the United Kingdom is also working in this direction, especially for post-16 education. However, the extent to which such competencies are incorporated into occupational classrooms remains unclear, and the appropriate teaching methods are not well established. In one study of American secondary education, Stasz et al. (1993; also Stasz, 1998) observed 8 classes (including 5 vocational classrooms) that were recommended by others as emphasizing these higher-order or generic skills. The most successful instructors stressed cooperative learning, self-managed groups, tasks and projects that reflected the complexities of real tasks, and intrinsic motivation based on student choices and individual responsibility.

In contrast, Stevenson and his colleagues (Stevenson, 1996a) concluded that higher-order competencies always have important context-specific elements. For example, reading within the tourism industry requires specific information about technical details like vocabulary, symbols, and abbreviations, but it also requires an understanding of the social relations of tourism. Because higher-order competencies may not be common among various occupations, Stevenson and colleagues recommend that these competencies should be taught in workplaces rather than in school settings, which often practice didactic instruction and do not attend to higher-order skills and context. (See also the examination of work-based learning in the United States by Stasz, Ramsey, Eden, Melamid, & Kaganoff, 1996.) To be sure, the conditions of work can be partially recreated through workshops, simulations, and school-based enterprises, as well as incorporated through work-based learning.

WORKPLACE NORMS AND LORE

The norms and informal practices of the workplace include ethical issues, ways of relating to coworkers and supervisors, and the norms governing contacts with customers. Often, instructors stress the differences between textbook solutions, which are sometimes contrived for teaching purposes, and the messy conditions of real work, which may require modifications of standard practice. Such teaching is often done covertly and implicitly. For example, Grubb and his colleagues (1999) and Hull (1993) found instructors making extensive use of personal stories, which can be powerful ways of teaching with important motivational effects. In other cases, instructors try to create conditions in workshops that mimic as nearly as possible the conditions at work: They set themselves up as bosses and have students form work teams responsible for production, wear uniforms, and receive discipline for various infractions. Role-play is a traditional way of allowing students to experience work-like relationships.

Of course, students often learn the informal norms governing work in work-based components like internships and coopera-tive education. However, as in school-based settings, these lessons are usually implicit rather than explicit, embedded in daily practice rather than explicitly taught or separately examined (Lave & Wenger, 1991; Stasz et al., 1996). One departure from this practice is the *Leittextmethode,* which includes an evaluative stage at the end. Similarly, a co-op program at one community college in the United States conducted seminars for students to analyze their work experiences, incorporating the constructivist (and Deweyan) practice of reflection along with experience. In practice, however, such seminars often turned into didactic sessions that concentrated on cognitive abilities required on the job (Grubb & Badway, 1998)—reflecting the likelihood that instructors without extensive training revert to didactic methods.

Another dimension of workplace norms involves power relations at work, including both workplace-specific issues like the rights of workers and larger political issues about the roles of unions; government regulation of the workforce; unemployment; and general economic policies. In countries with racially heterogeneous populations like the United States and Australia, racial discrimination is often a serious issue, and discrimination against women (including gender segregation by occupations and sexual harassment) has become a hotly debated topic. Many reformers—particularly critical theorists (e.g., Kincheloe, 1995; Lakes, 1994; Rehm, 1989; Shor, 1988a, 1988b; Simon, Dippo, & Schenke, 1987, 1991)—have argued that these political issues are widely ignored and recommend that they should be incorporated into all vocational programs.

Observing occupational instructors in U.S. community colleges, Grubb and his colleagues (1999) found that the political dimensions of work were almost universally ignored in classrooms and workshops. However, the reasons for such neglect were complex. Many instructors were small employers, so they took the perspectives of employers. Some had deliberately adapted authoritarian teaching styles, mimicking the authoritarian relations in many workplaces; they left little room for attention to the rights of workers. Some were so focused on the technical details of performance that they neglected other competencies (like cognitive and perceptual abilities) as well as political dimensions. Others were trying to instill a pride in their craft, and negative aspects of an occupation seemed counterproductive. And some didn't feel that they were justified in raising political issues in the classroom. To introduce critical perspectives requires that many issues about teaching in occupational education and the appropriate role of overtly political issues be resolved.

MORAL DEVELOPMENT AT WORK

Regarding political norms, many commentators assume that workplace norms influence moral development. Moral behavior at the worksite may differ from that in family settings, contrary to Kohlberg's assumption (Beck et al, 1996; Oser, 1986). The studies of Lempert (Corsten & Lempert, 1997; Lempert, 1994) for the technical field and of Beck et al. (1996; Lüdecke-Plümer Zirkel, & Beck, 1997) for the commercial field provide some evidence of differentiated moral judgment in different settings. The potential implications for teaching are numerous: Those at lower stages of moral development (based on Kohlberg's stages) may need knowledge of workplace rules and the motivation to conform to these rules; those at higher stages may need some mechanism to reconcile their independent moral codes with those of the workplace; and those who differentiate moral judgment in the workplace from that in the family and society may need to reconcile this kind of moral tension—including developing a greater tolerance for moral ambiguity. Although very few studies have investigated this problem in practice, the consequences for both workplace and social behavior may be substantial.

This brief discussion about teaching diverse competencies emphasizes a central dilemma of vocational teaching. The competencies required at work are complex and varied, and most are not taught in the conventional academic curriculum. But even in vocational programs, the ways of teaching these competencies are often informal and implicit; little systematic attention, in either research or the reform literature, has been paid to the question of how best to teach them. Indeed, no consensus has been reached about whether some of these competencies should be explicitly taught, and some—workplace norms and the politics of the workplace, for example—are quite controversial. The result is that the range of competencies required at work are not always incorporated into vocational education.

Skills Approaches Versus Systems Approaches

Some approaches to teaching—for example, the *Leittext-methode* with its emphasis on evaluating the results of production—and some ways of teaching noncognitive abilities—like Satchwell and Johnson's use of functional flow diagrams and Mosenthal and Kirsch's approach to document literacy—stress that students need a deep understanding of the processes and practices necessary in employment. Observing occupational workshops, a related division becomes apparent between a skills approach versus a systems approach. The distinction has much in common with the difference between part-to-whole teaching and skills-and-drills instruction in math or English—with its emphasis on small subskills (grammar, arithmetic facts)—on the one hand and the meaning-centered, constructivist, or holistic approach—with its emphasis on real writing, authentic problems, and whole-to-part instruction on the other hand. In general, the skills approach tends to teach a series of discrete skills and tasks, while the systems approach is more concerned with the conceptual understanding and mental models of machines, production processes, business procedures, and other dimensions of work. To be sure, instructors often use a variety of approaches because "there is no one way that students learn" (MacGraw & Peoples, 1996, interviewing TAFE instructors), but the distinction is still valuable to describe basic dimensions of occupational teaching.

The observations by Weber and Puleo (1988) of secondary vocational classrooms in the United States illustrate the differences: Most instructors focused on the specific knowledge and manipulative skills necessary to complete well-defined tasks, paying little explicit attention to higher-order skills including a conceptualization of the overall task. Among the community college instructors described by Grubb et al. (1999), those using a skills approach divided classes into small units of time and devoted each class to a particular skill. The alternative was to have students work on projects such as cars or electronic circuits with different problems. In a problem-driven approach, technical skills are learned in the process of developing solutions to larger problems—whole-to-part instruction. The systems approach is particularly critical in areas like the automotive trades because so many models of cars are produced that a program cannot possibly teach all of them; the only solution is to teach the generic operation of particular systems—transmissions, electrical and hydraulic systems, and the like—leaving the detail of specific models to on-the-job training. Similarly, in Germany a new "mechatronics" curriculum is being developed, which provides students with knowledge of an entire car and the interrelationships of its subsystems (electrical, hydraulic, power, etc.) so that students can understand where problems arise, rather than fix parts of a car as if they were independent.

The difference between skills and systems approaches is particularly evident with computer-based technology, as in word processing and CAD programs (Carroll, 1990, 1996; Jonassen, Mayes, & MacAlesse, 1993). Some systematic or skills-oriented instructors teach students to master a series of commands rather than to understand what the computer is supposed to accomplish; this enables students to operate a computer, but it blocks their conceptualization of any particular procedure. When students have little understanding of the underlying issues—for example, the mathematics of spreadsheet programs, the purpose of different word processing formats, the visual problems in moving from three to two dimensions in CAD—this approach can lead to serious error. The constructivist, minimalist, or systems approach has students learn the underlying purpose of a particular application and then teaches computer methods as the means to solve a problem at hand, using multiple approaches and learning from error.

Instructors often note that a systems approach is necessary for problem solving: If students do not know how a system works, they cannot identify what might cause a failure, and their search for the problem is random and inefficient (Glaser, Lesgold, & Gott, 1991; Quiñones & Ehrenstein, 1996b). Instructors who focus on problem solving teach students to understand the roles that different parts play in an overall system and to assess which parts are most likely to fail. More generally, a skills approach may be adequate for routine production under supervision, but for expert and nonroutine performance—the work expected in flexible and high-skilled workplaces—the conceptual knowledge and mental models of the systems approach are crucial (Evans & Butler, 1992).

The difference between skills and systems approaches has also emerged in research on troubleshooting in computer programming, electronics, and various military applications (Gott, 1988, 1995; Perez, 1991). Often, such applications involve a device of some kind (an avionics controller, an engine, an electronic device like the programmable logic controller, or a computer numerically-controlled (CNC) machine tool), and device knowledge, or knowledge about how the device works, is critical. One way to teach device knowledge and troubleshooting is a procedural one where trainees learn a series of specific procedures. Even in learning such procedures, students do better when they have a mental model that allows them to infer the internal structure and logic of a machine or device (Kieras & Bovair, 1984). However, as devices become more complex and as tasks become more like the messy, poorly structured work of the real world, the procedural approach becomes difficult to apply, and a deeper understanding of the device or system is necessary. In contrast, a purely theoretical approach is also clearly inadequate, as an older review of troubleshooting indicates (Morris & Rouse, 1985). Gott argues that an integration of procedural, device, and strategic control knowledge is necessary and requires a developmental approach in which the instructor leads the student through increasingly complex understandings. Indeed, some integration of theoretical and procedural knowledge, and of general procedures and context-specific information emerges as the most appropriate instructional approach. This underscores again the complexity of occupational teaching: The instructor must consistently integrate a number of elements in both class and workshop settings—rather than present competencies independently and *seriatim.*

The Effectiveness of Different Approaches to Teaching

Both the approaches to teaching reviewed in section I and the complexities in practice described in this section indicate that teaching vocational subjects and competencies can be done in many ways. However, evidence about effectiveness is sparse—much sparser than the evidence about academic subjects. Furthermore, the few studies that do exist conceptualize approaches to teaching in very different ways, study different populations, and suffer from small sample sizes and inadequate control variables (as in the literature on academic instruction[15]), so generalizations are hard to make.

For example, Rothenberger and Stewart (1995) found higher scores on a test of knowledge for secondary students with a greenhouse lab experience compared to students without the lab. In college-level automotive air conditioning programs, Cash, Behrman, Stadt, and Daniels (1997) contrasted the performance of 12 students in classes based on cognitive apprenticeship methods with 14 students in classes dominated by more conventional lecturing. Those in the cognitive apprenticeship-based classes improved their performance more on air conditioning information, performance on troubleshooting procedures, and applications of diagnostic skills. As we mentioned above, Satchwell (1997) found that students using functional flow diagrams that incorporated mental models rather than conventional, but highly abstract, schematic diagrams performed better in their technical understanding of the system and in their predictions, and had fewer misconceptions about the system's operation. On the other hand, Scott and Buffer (1983) contrasted a visual-spatial approach to an assembling task with a more verbal approach; women did significantly better in classes using a verbal approach while men did slightly better with the visual-spatial approach—but no pattern emerged with respect to different learning styles.

In the German context, Getsch (1990), Schunck (1993), and Fürstenau (1994, 1996) evaluated the effects of teaching via computer-based simulation games, and Weber (1994a, 1994b) differentiated these approaches by explicitly measuring the network structure of the students' prior knowledge and its change after teaching via simulation games. These investigations in the fields of commerce and business showed remarkable effects of a systems approach, as did studies in technical fields (for metal working, Tenberg, 1997; for electrical engineering, Glöggler 1997). Both understanding and practical knowledge increased among apprentices through network-based simulation.

In other settings, however, the lack of consistent research has made it impossible to formulate general theories about teaching and learning (Achtenhagen, 1990, p. 645 *ff.*), and attitudes toward teaching are therefore inconsistent with practice. For example, the German Bundesinstitut für Berufsbildung (BIBB) asked apprentices, trainers, and superiors which activities are most appropriate for differentiating training according to individual attributes like prior knowledge and school career (Zielke & Popp, 1997). On the average, the respondents reported no differences in the appropriate instructional materials and methods, except to cite the positive influence of the personal interaction between trainer and apprentice on learning outcomes. However, in contrast to these responses, "learning by doing"—the skills approach—led to reduced learning, less effective work behavior, lower motivation, and negative perceptions of both vocational training and the firm.

In the literature on troubleshooting in computer programming, electronics, and military applications, the emphasis has been on devising computer-based tutors rather than on alternative instructional methods (Gott, 1988). For example, the procedures-driven LISP tutor, designed to teach programming, lags behind human instruction, though both of these are superior to self-study. Adding information related to use on the job improves performance with highly procedure-driven methods, particularly for simpler tasks and for inexperienced technicians. A computer-based avionics tutor named Sherlock, which specifies the probable paths technicians follow in isolating faults, improved scores on troubleshooting tasks when compared to a control group with on-the-job training only; and Qualitative Understanding of Electrical System Troubleshootings (QUEST), an electronics tutor that embodies mental models of increasing complexity, improved the performance of seven high school students on their knowledge of circuit behavior and troubleshooting. These results suggest that adding knowledge about applications and system characteristics (particularly through increasingly complex and abstract models) improves performance.

What little evidence exists, therefore, suggests that systems approaches (including the incorporation of various mental models) are superior to highly proceduralized or skills approaches and that general approaches to problem-solving—heuristics intended to apply to a wide variety of situations—are less effective than context-sensitive methods. Overall, however, not much evidence has been generated about effectiveness. What little there is addresses very different types of instruction, and research has changed markedly over time as

---

[15] For the United States, see Good's (1996) review. Despite the volume of literature on effectiveness in academic teaching, differences in perspectives and methods make it difficult to derive many conclusions.

the approaches that were considered new and interesting have changed (Rowlett, 1964), making the accumulation of research results difficult.

IV. Teacher Preparation

We have already mentioned a number of institutional conditions that complicate vocational teaching. Particularly in countries with market-oriented systems, cost issues make it difficult for programs to keep up to date; the use of vocational education as a dumping ground for "manually minded" students and (in some countries) its location within academic institutions create other difficulties. But given the complexities of occupational teaching, one of the most crucial influences is the preparation of instructors. This issue provides a perfect illustration of the enormous variation in policy from country to country, as well as among settings within countries.

The Preparation of Vocational Instructors

In countries with a dual system like Germany, relatively high status and generous funding has led to substantial preparation of vocational teachers who have the ability to teach both academic and vocational competencies. Instructors in the school-based component complete an apprenticeship or at least one year of practical work; university studies related to vocational areas (like economics for the area of commerce, or electrical engineering for the technical areas of electronics and electricity) at the master's level; and a second academic subject out of a list that includes German and English. Then instructors finish a two-year, in-service program before they can teach independently. In the work-based component, larger firms tend to hire fully qualified vocational teachers as instructors. When firms hire masters of a skill who do not have academic preparation to teach, those masters complete at least an apprenticeship and a period as a journeyman, during which they take courses on how to teach in their vocational areas. Part-time instructors in enterprises, who perform their own job 80–90% of the time and instruct during the remaining time, are prepared through "train the trainer" programs run by the federal government with the chambers of industry and commerce. Thus, the largest firms have three distinct types of trainers, each with its own form of teacher preparation. Despite this, there remain questions about the quality of teaching; for example, Keck (1995; also Keck, Weymar, & Diepold, 1997; Zielke & Popp, 1997) showed that the double workload of part-time instructors leads to considerable variation in the quality of instruction.

In countries where vocational education suffers from second-class status, the preparation of vocational teachers is less thorough. In the United States at the secondary level, vocational instructors are prepared in teacher training institutions, in programs parallel to those for academic teachers. However, the separation of academic and vocational education after the turn of this century also differentiated vocational teacher preparation, which stressed experience in a trade as the foundation of vocational teaching. Charles Prosser, whose conception of relatively narrow and job-specific vocational education prevailed for many decades, encapsulated this approach in two of his much-cited "16 theorems" (Prosser & Quigley, 1949, cited in Lynch, 1997, p. 8):

- Vocational education will be effective in proportion as the instructor has had successful experience in the application of skills and knowledge to the operations and processes he undertakes to teach.
- The only reliable source of content for specific training in an occupation is the experiences of masters of that occupation.

Unfortunately, the emphasis on occupational experience—the equivalent to emphasis on subject mastery in academic education—may be misplaced. While some occupational experience improves the quality of teaching, studies over a 40-year period suggest that extensive experience does not further improve teaching; instead, formal postsecondary education is associated with desirable teacher and student outcomes (Lynch, 1997). Individuals who are experienced in their trades may lack the explicit understanding of expert practice to convey the range of competencies to their students (Evans & Butler, 1992, 1993); skilled practitioners may simply have forgotten the intermediate skills necessary in learning their occupations (Hutchins, 1996, chap. 7). This suggests that more formal preparation related to teaching would improve the quality of instruction. Unfortunately, recent efforts in the United States to reform vocational teacher training have stressed general principles of good teaching (e.g., "teachers are committed to their students") and mastery of subject matter ("teachers know the subjects they teach") but have failed to grapple with the issues specific to vocational teaching like the appropriate use of workshops or the integration of multiple competencies into instruction (Boesel, 1994; Frantz, 1997; Hartley & Wentling, 1996; Lynch, 1997; National Board for Professional Teaching Standards, 1997).

At the postsecondary level where the majority of vocational education now takes place, the standard practice has been to hire vocational instructors from business and industry. New teachers, both occupational and academic, commonly report that the dominant method of teacher training is "sink or swim," with no preparation for teaching (Grubb et al., 1999, chap. 2). This reinforces the notion, common in vocational education as in academic education, that mastery of one's subject (or craft) is the only prerequisite for good teaching, and it leads to approaches to teaching that are individual and idiosyncratic.

In some other countries, preparation is more extensive. In Australia, recent recommendations emphasize the need for pedagogical skills for occupational teaching, particularly for instructors coming out of practice (Chappell & Melville, 1995). In Great Britain, specific programs in further education colleges prepare instructors for teaching (e.g., Curzon, 1980; Kerry & Tollitt-Evans, 1992); but—as with the few such programs in the United States—these programs tend to be generic and to focus on the institutional and legal requirements of teaching rather than on the pedagogical complexity of occupational subjects. Overall, then, the preparation of vocational instructors in the English-speaking countries has been relatively neglected and tends to rely on expertise from prior experience.

In other settings for occupational education, the neglect of teaching is even more profound. In short-term job-training programs within both the United States and Europe, virtually no attention is paid to the preparation of instructors (Grubb 1996a; Grubb & Ryan, 1999)—even though the teaching challenges are especially difficult in remedial training where students usually require basic language and math skills. As we move away from countries with the dual system, then, and as we shift from programs considered "education" to those considered "training," the preparation of occupational instructors becomes even less thorough.

What approach to teaching do "natural"—that is, untrained—teachers adopt? Evidence from academic instruction suggests that such individuals revert to the ways they were taught and tend to think of subject mastery rather than of pedagogical alternatives as their dominant responsibility. This often leads to a concern with coverage of standard content, skills-oriented approaches, and didactic and teacher-centered forms of practice; as Keck (1995) found from interviews, untrained vocational instructors tend to use naive theories of effective teaching. Within vocational education, these pedagogical approaches are sometimes reinforced by a pride in craft among instructors who want students to "do it right" and by classrooms that are consciously modeled after workplace practices, recreating the authority relations of Taylorist workplaces where the teacher as "boss" gives orders to students as employees.

Of course, countervailing influences can be found as well, including the tradition of project-based teaching—or, in business and commerce, modeling and simulation along with classroom instruction. And, as in academic subjects, vocational teachers develop their approaches to teaching in individual ways, by trial and error and by watching what works; over time, this leads some instructors away from skills approaches to more constructivist methods (Grubb et al., 1999, chap. 2). But when training is lacking, good teaching develops idiosyncratically, not as a result of institutional support and policy.

In-service Training and Staff Development

A complement to preservice teacher training—or, where teacher training is weak, a substitute—is training during the initial periods of teaching, which can include mentoring for new teachers, staff development, and networks of teachers who share information about effective practice. The quality of in-service activities is related to the systematization of teacher training. In the German-speaking countries, one finds teachers' unions specifically for vocational teachers that have their own offices, journals, and staff development. In the English-speaking countries, however, these associations are relatively weak (especially at the postsecondary level) and tend not to discuss pedagogical issues. Most staff development within comprehensive institutions—like the community colleges in the United States and Further Education (FE) colleges in Great Britain—is relatively generic and provides little opportunity for vocational instructors to explore the issues specific to occupational teaching. In countries without extensive support for teachers, the feeling of beginning teachers that they must sink or swim or learn by trial and error is pervasive among both academic and occupational teachers. Some programs have been devised specifically for beginning vocational teachers in the United States (e.g., Camp & Heath, 1988; Camp & Heath-Camp, 1989), but they are not pervasive, and they provide sup-port only for secondary instructors, not for the postsecondary instructors and those in job training who now provide the majority of vocational education.

In Australia, Evans and Butler (1993) have documented the benefits of an alternative approach. They provided a single TAFE electrical instructor with a teaching model that emphasizes active student participation, development of conceptual knowledge and theoretical principles, and student self-monitoring of actions through feedback. An "experimental" group of students who were taught after receiving this guidance performed significantly better than a "control" group taught beforehand, showing that appropriate staff development can improve student performance. But even with an enthusiastic instructor, it proved difficult to change teaching through a short intervention, as is also true for academic teachers (e.g., Tharp & Gallimore, 1988, chap. 10). Changing teaching—a longer process that requires constant feedback—requires instructors to modify their conceptions of learning and their "teaching persona."

One other potentially useful form of staff development is the inspection process in Great Britain (Grubb, 2000). As this practice has developed in further education colleges, a team of external inspectors, including subject-area specialists plus a representative of the college, visits each college and spends a considerable amount of time observing classes. The inspection process generates a great deal of internal discussion about teaching and about institutional mechanisms of improvement to remedy any problems identified by the inspections team. In addition, subject-area specialists on inspection teams develop considerable expertise about teaching practices; these experiences have generated a series of booklets about teaching in specific areas (e.g., *Engineering*, 1996), which can also be used for improvement. With only the somewhat idiosyncratic (but replicable) example of inspection, then, and technical assistance provided for the reforms described in section V, vocational instructors in many countries have little access to in-service education that might help them improve their teaching.

V. Current Reforms in Vocational Education: The Contradictions of Innovation

The renewed interest in the broadly vocational purposes of education has led to many different reforms. Many reforms draw their inspiration from transformations in work. Following conventional wisdom about the skills necessary in high-performance workplaces, they generally promote more constructivist and systems-oriented teaching, make greater use of project- and experienced-based education including work experience, and replace relatively occupation-specific and skills-oriented vocational education with broader approaches.

However, the institutional developments in many countries are not necessarily conducive to pedagogical reform. Performance measures and competency-based assessments have added to the pressures for teaching discrete skills in place of systems approaches; competitive and fiscal pressures are causing educational institutions in many countries to be more market-oriented, reducing support for innovation in teaching. Overall, then, the major ideas about vocational teaching and the pressures from employment are driving pedagogy in one direction, while institutional developments and governmental policy often encourage a contrary direction.

Perspectives on Learning, Cognition, and Work

A number of educational theorists have taken their inspiration from apprenticeship as a particular model of learning (Raizen, 1994). In a widely read address, Resnick (1987) noted several differences between school learning and performance in nonschool contexts, especially work. Her implication was that, if schools are to prepare students for their lives outside of school, they should stress group instruction and performance rather than individual learning, learning with tools and other supports rather than pure cognition, context-specific reasoning and competencies rather than abstract and decontextualized learning. These recommendations support workshops and work-based learning in vocational education, as well as changes in academic instruction.

Others have drawn lessons from apprenticeship as the traditional form of preparation for work. Collins, Brown, and Newman (1989) noted that masters draw their apprentices gradually into work performance, provide "scaffolding" or support for initial efforts, coach and guide these early efforts, and gradually fade into the background as the apprentice gains facility. Furthermore, apprenticeships provide learners with the appropriate context for learning and incorporate both technical skills and nontechnical facilities, including the norms and values of the workplace. The notion of "cognitive apprenticeship," based on these observations, provides additional support for the teaching that is often observed in vocational education, but it also implies that academic teaching should be revised to provide "situated" or "applied" learning in which instruction is situated in real problems or realistic contexts (Brown, Collins, & Duguid, 1989; Lave & Wenger, 1991). These approaches are antidotes to conventional didactic teaching, which tends to be abstracted from applications, to present contrived and irrelevant exercises, and to truncate opportunities for students to search for solutions on their own.

To some extent, these authors have compared depictions of conventional teachers as didactic and unsupportive with idealized forms of apprenticeships (Achtenhagen, 1988)—ignoring the long history in which apprentices were trained in narrow ways or treated as cheap labor or abused by authoritarian masters (Douglas, 1921; Stratmann, 1967; Stratmann & Schlösser, 1990). Instead of being a necessarily superior setting for learning, work has pedagogical features similar to other educational settings (Berryman, 1995), and workplaces may suffer the disadvantages of routinized production and pedagogical stasis. The problems associated with employees moving from job to job and, therefore, with the transferability of competencies across settings—increasingly common in the modern economy (Achtenhagen, Nijhof, & Raffe, 1995)—has not been addressed by those writing about the superiority of apprenticeships. Similarly, others whose observations about work support the context-specificity of skills—for example, the Brazilian bookies who apparently carry out complex mathematical operations as described by Carraher, Carraher, and Schliemann (1985) or the warehouse workers studied by Scribner (1984)—describe individuals in narrow and stable contexts, not in complex settings.

Therefore, the other side of learning that is modeled on apprenticeship poses the problem of transferability—of performance in different contexts. Salomon and Perkins (1989) have stressed that "high-road" transfer can be achieved only if students are led, or "shepherded," (Perkins, 1992, chap. 5) to abstract general principles from a specific learning situation and to understand the possibility of multiple application. While "low-road" transfer can occur when individuals master procedures by rote and practice them to automaticity, this is a more uncertain route, especially in cases of "far" transfer where conditions are very unlike the original application. Similarly, research within TAFE colleges in Australia (Beven, 1994; Stevenson, McKavanaugh, & Middleton 1996) has stressed that students using higher-order procedures—conceptual knowledge and generalized problem-solving abilities—rather than the highly proceduralized knowledge of "low-road" transfer perform better on tasks involving "far" transfer. The implication is that occupational expertise initially requires "contextualized" instruction, embedded in some particular practice, but the ability to transfer instruction to other contexts requires a second stage of disembedding these competencies and abstracting them for other applications (Stevenson, 1994).

The process of embedded instruction and subsequent disembedding is obviously different from conventional academic instruction that emphasizes abstract principles. It also departs from simple recommendations for situated or applied learning because it stresses the necessary stage of abstraction, and it differs from conventional vocational teaching that is concerned with presenting skills and monitoring teacher-directed projects, which does not always include the problem-based approaches that can push students to transfer their learning to other contexts (Grubb et al., 1999; Harkin & Davis, 1996a; Holloway, 1992; Thomson, 1990). Thus, the insights drawn from apprenticeship, interpreted in a world of changing and flexible employment, imply that both traditional academic and traditional vocational teaching need reform.

Integrating Academic and Vocational Education: Toward "Education Through Occupations"

In several countries, a movement has developed to integrate vocational and academic education. In part, these efforts respond to demands for a skilled workforce for high-performance workplaces. The efforts also help to resolve status problems created by the separation of vocational from academic education. In effect, these reforms imply that both vocational education with its overly specific training and academic education with its tendency to become too abstract and decontextualized have abandoned the requirements of work.

In the United States, integration efforts begun during the 1980s were supported by federal legislation in 1990. Substantial experiments with many forms of integration have taken place in secondary schools (Grubb, 1995). At the postsecondary level, changes have been slower despite several exemplary practices (Badway & Grubb, 1997; Grubb, 1996b, chap. 5; Grubb & Kraskouskas, 1992), partly because community colleges do not usually support innovations in teaching. In Great Britain, the vocationalization of education after 1976, when Prime Minister Callahan highlighted the country's competitive problems, has led to a variety of experiments. One, the Technical and Vocational Education Initiative (TVEI), gave some teachers leeway to develop progressive approaches to vocationalism, though its main emphasis was relatively narrow (Dale et al., 1990). Pressure for more accountable forms of vocational education generated the narrowly vocational NVQs; then, in recognition that a broader approach that incorporated more academic skills was necessary, the General National Vocational Qualifications (GNVQs) were created in 1992, which incorporated several "core skills" (*Core Skills in GNVQs,* 1996). GNVQs were intended to reduce the "academic-vocational divide" and establish "parity of esteem" with academic credentials by providing credentials with both occupational value and academic content. To implement these plans, the Qualifications and Curriculum Authority was created.

In Australia, the 1993 Wiltshire report argued for the integration of academic and vocational education and emphasized creating different academic and vocational pathways through secondary schools while preserving options for postsecondary education. The articulation of key competencies has encouraged schools to adopt integrated programs; perhaps 40–60% of secondary schools now have such programs, usually parallel programs in which students take both academic and occupational courses, with little integration at the level of the classroom.[16] Integration practices are also appearing in Canada, particularly in locally developed programs of "applied academics" (Gaskell, 1997; Gaskell & Hepburn, 1997).

In the German-speaking countries, the father of the dual system, Georg Kerschensteiner, used Dewey's ideas about the integration of theoretical and applied learning as the foundation of the dual system (Achtenhagen, 1988; Prantl, 1917; Wehle, 1964; Wilhelm, 1957). More recently, Dewey's ideas for overcoming the false duality of reasoning and acting was a central starting point for action-oriented models—for example, Aebli's (1980, 1981) model of integrating action into learning processes. These ideas, combined with developments of Russian activity theory (Engeström, 1994), have been widely accepted in business and commercial education where they have been used for developing complex teaching-learning environments that are responsive to new challenges in workplaces (Achtenhagen & John, 1992; Achtenhagen, Tramm, Preiss, Seemann-Weymar, John, & Schunck, 1992; Arnold & Lipsmeier, 1995; Beck & Heid, 1996; Tramm, 1997). Germany has also developed pilot efforts, programs providing dual academic and occupational qualifications (Heidegger & Rauner, 1996). In practice, these too may be parallel rather than integrated approaches, though new approaches are being developed in both commercial and technical apprenticeships (Achtenhagen & John, 1992).

Approaches to integration vary widely (Lewis, 1994; see also the articles in Nijhof & Streumer, 1998). In some cases, voca-tional programs simply incorporate standard academic content—math drills, conventional reading comprehension, short essays—without integrating them with any vocational content or shifting to more constructivist teaching. GNVQs appear to be particularly susceptible to such "bolted-on" approaches: Despite a debate about embedding core skills in vocational applications versus nonembedded approaches (Green, 1996; Hodkinson, 1991; Spours, 1995), the key skills are taught as separate modules, by different instructors, using conventional materials drawn from academic instruction. This in turn undermines the purpose of "bridging the academic-vocational divide," because no bridging occurs within instruction itself.

More elaborated forms of integration include "applied academics" courses, which present the content of reading, writing, math, or basic science with their vocational applications. Still more substantial efforts involve matching academic and vocational instructors in "learning communities" where two or three academic and vocational instructors co-teach several related courses (e.g., Darling-Hammond, Ancess, & Falk, 1995, on reshaping the English curriculum with technical writing); matching them in schools-within-schools like career-oriented "academies" where several teachers teach the same students academic and vocational subjects (Stern, Raby, & Dayton, 1992); matching them in schools where all students elect one of several career-oriented majors or pathways (Grubb, 1995); and matching them in secondary schools where the entire school has a broad occupational emphasis. Not much evidence has been generated yet about effectiveness, but what little has been collected supports integrated approaches.[17]

In many small-scale efforts and in postsecondary reforms in the United States and Great Britain, the dominant purpose of integration is the incorporation of certain academic or higher-order competencies into occupational programs. However, the more substantial efforts in secondary schools in the United States—and perhaps in Australia[18]—represent a considerable transformation of both vocational and academic education, creating a new synthesis by using broadly defined occupations to provide the context for learning both academic and technical competencies. Such efforts need not be confined to the most obvious and utilitarian subjects—reading and writing, math, the science appropriate to certain occupations—but can extend to the more political and moral subjects like government (or civics), history, and literature (Koziol, 1992; Koziol & Grubb, 1995). This is similar to the proposal of Heidegger and Rauner (1996) in Germany for a system of double qualifications that combines both academic instruction and broad occupational preparation; similar developments have been proposed in other European countries (Manning, 1997).

Such schools exemplify the ideal of "education through occupations" that John Dewey articulated 80 years ago.[19] Dewey ar-

---

[16] Oral communication, Kim Bannikoff, Australian National Training Authority.

[17] In addition to the review by Stasz, Kaganoff, and Eden (1994), see especially Stern, Raby, and Dayton (1992) on the effectiveness of career academies; Crain, Heebner, Si, Jordan, and Kiefer (1992) on career-oriented magnet programs in New York City; and Roegge and Russell (1990) on an integrated approach to biology.

[18] See Seddon's (1994) analysis of vocationalism in Australia, which finds some hints at an integration of vocationalism and educational progressivism, particularly in the Mayer Report (Mayer, 1992).

[19] See in general Dewey (1916), chapters 15 and 23; Dewey (1900/1990), chapters I and VI. These are reviewed in Grubb (1995). Note that Dewey's conception of "occupation" is close to the German *Beruf.* The recent approaches to reform of vocational education in German-speaking countries, especially working with complex teaching-learning environments, refer explicitly to Dewey.

gued that academic and vocational education (or "learning" versus "doing," theory versus application) should not be separated, and that broadly occupational content provides the most appropriate materials for learning: "Education through occupations consequently combines within itself more of the factors conducive to learning than any other method" (Dewey, 1916, p. 309). His reasons sound remarkably modern: He argued that teaching should be contextualized ("exercised within activity which puts nature to human use") and should concentrate on the student as a social being rather than an autonomous individual, and that occupations provide the most powerful way of accomplishing both. He also argued that a broadly occupational focus would avoid passive, didactic teaching based on contrived "school" materials, and he feared that conventional schooling would otherwise narrow the education of those going into lower-skilled occupations.

Not surprisingly, curriculum integration faces substantial problems in implementation. In some countries, the second-class status of vocational education has discouraged efforts, and the need to retrain both academic and occupational instructors has been a recurrent problem (e.g., Schmidt, Finch, & Faulkner, 1995) External exams and assessments often reinforce standard academic practices, discouraging innovative efforts to teach "academic" competencies in new ways. As in so many areas, pedagogical innovations in vocational education are often thwarted by institutional norms and practices.

Renewed Interest in Work-Based Learning

Countries following the dual system have always incorporated work-based learning into vocational education, but recently efforts to encourage more work-based learning have also developed in other countries. In addition to the attractiveness of the German system (e.g., Bierhof & Prais, 1996; Hamilton, 1990; Hamilton & Lempert, 1996; Nothdurft, 1989), the argument of learning theorists about apprenticeship and other work-based methods has been influential. As the pace of technological change has accelerated, work-based learning seems to be the only way to keep up with the competencies necessary for high-productivity firms. And promoters of work-based learning cite other advantages including the motivational issues in employment, the value of work in clarifying career options, and the reinforcement of the value of cognitive competencies learned in school (e.g., Hamilton & Hamilton, 1997a).

In the United States, secondary schools and community colleges have adopted a variety of work-based programs including cooperative education and school-based enterprises (Stern et al., 1994, 1995; Urquiola et al., 1997). Interest in work-based learning culminated in the School-to-Work Opportunities Act of 1994, which provided federal funds for work-based components and for integrating academic and vocational education. In Great Britain, the Conservative government funded a program of mandatory work experience for the last year of compulsory education. Even though this experience is quite short—typically one week at the end of the last year of compulsory schooling—advocates claim that it has brought students new understandings about work, the role of schooling in preparation, and the alternatives available to them (Miller & Forrest, 1996). In Australia, a similar surge of interest in work-based learning has occurred, and a range of benefits has been asserted

for students (Cumming & Carbines, 1997). In addition, short-term job training is being replaced by work-based New Apprenticeships (Australian National Training Authority, 1997), resting on the presumed superiority of work-based preparation and its value in promoting user choice.

These efforts, taking place in countries without the traditions and institutions supporting work-based learning, have faced serious practical and logistical problems. The German system is not merely one in which work-based placements are "bolted on" to schooling. Instead, a complex of employer organizations, labor unions, government requirements, and educational institutions promotes and regulates the dual system. In countries without these supporting institutions, therefore, employer participation has been weak and the quality and duration of work-based placements remain difficult issues (see especially Jeong, 1995, on the failures in Korea). In addition, because schooling systems in these countries have been self-contained, coordinating work-based learning with school-based teaching proves to be difficult; in the United States and Great Britain, for example, the fledgling efforts have not yet been successful in establishing such links (Hershey, Hudis, Silverberg, & Haimson, 1997). If work-based learning and school-based teaching are independent or even contradictory, then the pedagogical value of work-based learning may be lost. As a result, Achtenhagen et al. (1997) developed an approach where the same problems and exploratory tasks are solved in both the vocational classroom and in firms, to coordinate the teaching activities in both settings.

A different problem is that the pedagogy of work-based learning has not been extensively addressed—not only in countries without the dual system (Quiñones & Ehrenstein, 1996a, p. 6) but even in Germany. Based on Australian experience, Billett (1993, 1994, 1996) has argued that firms can be rich environments for skill development and the cognitive apprenticeship model, but he acknowledges that workplaces are not always naturally good places for learning, and that vocational educators therefore have to participate in developing workplaces as learning environments. (See also Hamilton & Hamilton, 1997b, and Harris & Volet, 1997, on the characteristics necessary for work to be a learning experience.) The recognition is growing that rather than employing managers without any educational background or teachers without any workplace experience to teach, instructors in workplaces need specific preparation in adult learning (Spikes, 1995a, 1995b). By investigating the experiences of workers in three sectors, Billett (1993) found that most individuals valued the on-the-job learning more than school-based instruction; however, they also expressed concern about the ability of on-the-job learning to develop conceptual understanding of their work. Certain jobs—for example, those that are spatially or socially isolated from others—provide little potential for learning a wide array of competencies; and some work practices are difficult to see and understand, particularly those with computer and electronic processes. In addition, the knowledge acquired in a particular workplace may not be transferable to other settings. Similarly, Keck (1995; Keck, Weymar, & Diepold, 1997) investigated workplaces for industrial clerks and demonstrated that learning depends upon the interaction between trainer and apprentice; their mutual judgments about interest and "intelligence" govern the quality of tasks and the independence given to apprentices. Using Keck's instruments, Achtenhagen and Noss (1997) started a field study in a large bank; as a result, bank management will revise its training to meet new challenges, especially in the finance market. The overall finding, then, is that many work environments lack the conditions for effective learning. Gott (1995) has stressed that on-the-job training may be particularly inadequate for complex work where mental models and a deeper understanding of fundamental processes are most necessary.

To be sure, work-based learning that is devised specifically for educational purposes—as in internships and co-op programs—may be pedagogically more appropriate. The 17 organizations designed to encourage work-based learning that were studied by Harris and Volet (1997) provided a broad range of learning opportunities; they also incorporated a strategic approach to teaching, a clear recognition of expertise, and management commitment to learning. But this is not always the case. In the United States, Moore (1981) found no "rational pedagogy" being used in student internships. Similarly, Stasz and Kaganoff (1997) investigated three secondary programs integrating work-based learning. In some settings—particularly firms characterized by organizational openness and a high value on training—opportunities for learning and teaching strategies were carefully planned; in other cases, however, learning was limited, unplanned, and followed the didactic procedures of "show and tell." Stasz and Brewer (1998) investigated student perceptions of two secondary-level, work-based programs in the United States; only 15% of these students described their work as mentally challenging, and few used any higher-level reading, writing, or math competencies. Similarly, within short-term job-training programs in the United States, Kogan, Dickinson, Means, and Strong (1989) found that the training content of work experience is often weak or nonexistent—partly because these programs are short, poorly funded, and often devised to provide subsidized employees to firms rather than education and training.

Even in the dual system, consistent results about workplace learning are lacking. A recent survey to ascertain the teaching methods used for in-company training (Bundesministerium für Bildung und Wissenschaft, 1993, p. 87) revealed that the most effective methods—task-centered methods with reflection (Leittextmethode), project work, or work in simulated business enterprises—made up only 1% of training in small and medium-sized enterprises and about 4% in large-scale enterprises. In addition, Hamilton and Lempert (1996) reported that the German literature about apprenticeships defines "program quality" as well-equipped training centers, full-time instructors, and rotation through various positions—but provides little information about approaches to instruction. Implicitly, as in other countries, oblique references to low-quality placements acknowledge that many work settings are not especially educational.

Of course, work-based learning may have positive effects unrelated to its overt educational content: Work-based programs help students explore their preferences about work, and substantial economic benefits may be gained if the experience and training provided are valuable to employers.[20] But the instructional benefits of work-based learning depend on the content and pedagogy of these programs. Unless the teaching conditions can be carefully structured, work-based learning may be no more effective than its school-based analogue.

Defining Competency: Core Skills, Assessments, and Competency-Based Vocational Education

Given the "megatrends" that are changing employment in many developed countries, educators and policymakers in many countries have defined the competencies that are required in high-performance workplaces so they can be taught (Achtenhagen, Nijhof, & Raffe, 1995; Nijhof & Streumer, 1998)—competencies variously called "key qualifications" (in Germany, *Schlüsselqualifikationen,* and in Spain, *cualificaciones claves*) (Dörig, 1994; Echeverría Samanes, 1993), "key" or "core" skills in Great Britain and Australia, or "SCANS" skills in the United States, as described by the Secretary's Commission on Achieving Necessary Skills (Berryman & Bailey, 1992; Secretary's Commission for Achieving Necessary Skills, 1991, 1992). Then—particularly in countries like Great Britain and Germany, which enforce curricular objectives with mandatory assessments—these competencies have been embedded in tests and qualifications. These efforts have substantial implications for both the content and the pedagogy of vocational education, often in ways inconsistent with other trends.

In the United States, for example, the Secretary's Commission on Achieving Necessary Skills (SCANS, 1991) articulated the need for conventional academic capacities ("basic skills") of reading, writing, mathematics, and computation skills but also declared the importance of "thinking skills" such as decision making, problem solving, and knowing how to learn, along with personal qualities like responsibility, self-management, and sociability. It went on to declare five additional competencies—the use of resources, interpersonal relations, information, the understanding of systems, and technology—also essential for job performance. In Australia, the list is remarkably similar: *Skills for Australia* reinforced the importance of the "core disciplines of language, mathematics, and science," and went on to stress "the less measurable skills on which future prosperity depends—lifetime learning, enterprise and initiative, pursuit of excellence, communications skills, teamwork and responsibility" (Dawkins & Holding, 1987). Five years later, Mayer (1992) articulated seven "key competencies" relevant to work: collecting, analyzing, and organizing ideas and information; expressing ideas and information; planning and organizing activities; working with others and in teams; using mathematical ideas and techniques; solving problems; and using technologies.

In Great Britain, the idea of "core skills" emerged from a discussion during the 1970s and 1980s about unemployment and Britain's international standing (Green, 1996; Hodkinson, 1991). This led to the development of NVQs and, later, GNVQs (Dearing, 1996). The first concrete results were the six core skills for NVQs in communications, problem solving, application of numbers, information technology, working with others,

---

[20] However, in the United States with its market-oriented system, the literature attempting to verify economic benefits to co-op programs has been largely unsuccessful; see, for example, Stern, Finkelstein, Urquiola, and Cagampang (1997).

and improving one's own performance—a list slightly reworked for GNVQs. In Germany, lists of up to 500 key qualifications have been developed (Dörig, 1994; Reetz, 1990). Because 500 qualifications are too numerous to be useful, they have been reduced to a tripartite structure of individual competence, encompassing cognitive as well as emotional, motivational, and moral domains; professional competence, including domain-specific knowledge and procedural strategies; and social competence like teamwork, communications, complex problem solving, and empathy (Achtenhagen, 1998; Dörig, 1994; Reetz, 1990). In many countries, then, "key" or "core" skills are remarkably consistent.

Some educators have argued that the competencies necessary for high-performance workplaces can be taught only with certain pedagogical approaches. Teamwork skills may require small-group rather than whole-class instruction (Fürstenau, 1996); problem solving requires uncontrived problems and a process of constructing solutions; communications skills with a variety of audiences requires a deep sense of varied literacy practices (Berryman & Bailey, 1992; Stevenson, 1994, 1996a, 1996b). Similarly, the "generic skills" defined in Stasz et al. (1993) and Stasz (1998), quite similar to "core" skills, were best taught in classrooms that emphasized cooperative learning, self-managed groups, projects reflecting the complexities of real tasks, and intrinsic motivation based on student choices and individual responsibility.

However, these approaches to teaching have often been undermined by the realities of assessments. In Great Britain, the original core skills proved too complex to incorporate into the standardized assessment necessary for qualifications. In GNVQs, core skills were stripped to three required skills—communications skills, application of numbers, and information—and tested with conventional multiple-choice exams. Not only did this transformation eliminate the more complex competencies required for high-performance workplaces, but it also converted more complex understandings of certain competencies (like communications skills and mathematical reasoning) into conventional academic skills like arithmetic, reading comprehension, and factual recall. Elliott (1996) has documented the tension in FE colleges between the "pedagogic culture"—of instructors committed to student-centered approaches—versus the "managerial culture" that is represented by external exams and market-like mechanisms—which, over time, undermines the quality of teaching. Similarly in Germany, the institutes that were established by the Union of the Chambers of Industry and Commerce to evaluate tests have generally provided tests in multiple-choice formats, because more complex assessments cost time and money. While cheaper, the multiple-choice format fosters rote learning at relatively simple cognitive levels, and the tests have made it impossible to see whether key qualifications are being taught or not. In addition, the need for new test items each year has forced the central institute to formulate tests with special and sometimes abstruse questions, undermining their curricular validity and acceptability to employers. Thus, the technology of assessments has skewed the nature of core skills, and certain assessments also may undermine the quality of teaching.

In countries like the United States, where an academic pipeline is dominant, another assessment problem arises. Tests developed for academic programs and high school diplomas are poor ways of credentialing individuals for employment (Resnick & Wirt, 1996, pp. 2–13). Therefore, the development of alternative assessments for employment purposes, particularly in the form of skills standards for occupations, has been necessary. However, Bailey and Merritt's (1997) evaluation of 22 pilot projects revealed that none of them integrated the organizational and industry contexts of the job, and 15 followed a "skills components model" that depended on lists of discrete skills rather than on a "professional model" that integrated critical aspects of employment. While inattention to the varied competencies that are necessary for the flexible workplace is part of the problem (Glaser, Lesgold, & Gott, 1991), the inertia in assessment methods and the dominance of traditional certification systems are also to blame. New approaches to assessment are therefore necessary, illustrated by Darling-Hammond, Ancess, and Falk's (1995) example for a technical high school. Otherwise, narrow assessment procedures reinforce the skills approach to teaching rather than methods more appropriate to core competencies.

In many countries, a history of competency-based (or outcome-based) education has reinforced narrow conceptions of competencies and the skills approach to teaching in both academic and vocational teaching. This approach has been traced back to the task analysis first developed by Victor Della Vos in Moscow in the 1860s, which was based in part on Pavlov's research on conditioning; it was displayed at the 1876 Centennial Exposition in Philadelphia, where it made its way into the American movements for manual training and vocational education. Many curriculum developments have relied on competency-based approaches including the Modules of Employable Skills developed by the International Labor Office, the DACUM (Developing a Curriculum) process initiated in Canada, and the *serie metodica ocupacionis,* or shopwork methodological series, developed in Brazil and then spread throughout South America (Ducci, 1991; Wilson, 1990). Competency-based approaches have been widely supported in U.S. secondary schools since the 1960s and have been official policy in Australia since 1987 (Stevenson, 1993, 1996a, 1996b; Stevenson & Brown, 1994). They are also the basis for the NVQs in Great Britain (Burke, 1995; Hyland, 1993, 1994a, 1994b; Jessup, 1991; Levy, 1992; Levy, Mathews, Oates, & Edmond, 1989; Senker, 1996). Competency-based (CB) approaches are also consistent with behaviorist theories of academic curriculum development extending back to at least the 1930s (Kliebard, 1986, chap. 8), often associated with Ralph Tyler ("the first step in improving validity is to define clearly the types of behavior we are trying to teach").

Within vocational education, CB approaches usually begin with a task analysis in which a specific job is broken into the specific tasks necessary for successful performance. These tasks then become the competencies necessary in instruction. CB instruction is often an advance in emphasizing the competencies taught at work, rather than abstract theory, but it often leads to skills-based instruction because the competencies identified for specific jobs tend to be long lists of specific subskills. Modularization contributes to this problem, because workers taught in a modularized system are likely to have a random combination of fragmented skills, rather than coherent, Gestalt-oriented knowledge (Heidegger & Rauner, 1996). Competency-based instruction may also reinforce a static view of work, because it starts with a task analysis of a specific job at a particular moment. But in a world where multiskilling is increasingly common, where old job categories are becoming obsolete, and in which competencies change rapidly, the focus on specific jobs reinforces the age-old problem of keeping up to date.

The technology of assessment also has its problems. CB assessment tends to abstract competencies from the work settings in which they occur by asking students to perform isolated tasks on their own; therefore, the dimensions of teamwork, cooperation, and communications with others at different levels are neglected. The observation of performance usually emphasizes the routine accomplishment of specific tasks rather than the individual's understanding of the work process well enough to work independently, to respond appropriately as problems arise, or to generate new solutions to production problems. As Stevenson (1993, 1994, 1996a, 1996b) has argued, CB instruction may be appropriate to an older Taylorist world, but it is inadequate preparation for the high-skilled workplace with its demands for flexibility, autonomy, and problem solving abilities. And as Gott (1995, p. 35) contends, experts do not rely on long lists of detailed technical information, but instead rely on streamlined mental representations of the technical systems they operate as ways of simplifying their jobs and exercising judgment.

In Australia, for example, *Skills for Australia* was the origin of the government's competency-based approach to vocational teaching, enforced through competency standards, national qualifications for each industry, and assessment guidelines applicable across an industry. Overall, the emphasis on certain outcome measures and the neglect of teaching and teacher preparation in the competency-based approach have reinforced conventional didactic and teacher-centered instruction (Stevenson, 1996a, 1996b). In addition, competency-based approaches tend to de-skill occupational instructors. As an accounting teacher in a TAFE college described it (Mulcahy, 1996, pp. 48–49),

> everything is so very specified . . . I get handed a whole set of stuff and I have to teach to that. My concern is all the module documentation that we're now getting with CBT where everything is so very specified . . . I get handed a whole set of stuff and I have to teach to that almost letter by letter, word by word. And that's what my big concern with CBT is, that we are becoming very regimented, very disciplined, by somebody else if you don't have much input into it at all.

The review of the enormous competency-based education literature by Toohey, Ryan, McLean, and Hughes (1995) reveals a widespread consensus that competencies should be broadly defined, but in practice the tendency to assess only the most routine and easily measurable aspects of performance is likely to drive practice toward narrow skill training.

In Great Britain, the National Center for Vocational Qualifications (NCVQ) has insisted that several teaching approaches are consistent with any competencies (General National Vocational Qualifications, 1995). But without any illustration of alternative teaching methods or any technical assistance to occupational instructors, many observers feel that the NVQs encourage skills-oriented teaching (Hyland, 1994a, chap. 4). For engineering technicians, for example, NVQs reflect old forms of Taylorist production, with clearly delineated occupations and narrowly defined skills, but they are ill-suited to flexible production with multiple skills and fluid boundaries. Therefore, many employers prefer using older qualifications rather than the overly functionalist NVQs (Senker, 1996). More generally, NVQs have been adopted much more in lower-level clerical, secretarial, sales, and personal services and much less in professional, technical, and craft occupations (Robinson, 1996), suggesting again that these credentials have been less appropriate to employers in high-performance settings. Ironically, then, several countries have adopted competency-based systems precisely when they are least appropriate, given the changes in the nature of production.

The efforts to articulate core, key, or generic skills for the high-performance workplace have therefore been a mixed blessing. On the one hand, this discussion has supported those educators—both academic and vocational—and those employers who want schools and colleges to shift to more experiential and constructivist approaches to teaching. But on the other hand, the efforts to enforce these core skills through assessments and qualifications has led to pallid versions of these competencies and sometimes has undermined the teaching of vocational subjects.

The Pressures of Competition and Markets

The reforms and debates we have reviewed so far are particular to education. However, in many countries—developed and developing alike—international competition and market pressures are having far-reaching consequences for a number of public institutions including education. Within countries with market-oriented systems of vocational education, static or declining public funding for education and increased competition among institutions have become more prominent. Within the dual system, competition has undermined the willingness of employers to provide apprenticeships, and several fundamental practices of the dual system have come under attack. In this section, we examine the potential effects of these developments on teaching practice, because the reforms reviewed in this section depend on institutions with the resources to improve instruction.

In the United States, community colleges face static public funding while the demand for remedial education and English as a Second Language (ESL) has expanded. Fiscal pressures have also increased the numbers of part-time instructors and reduced staff development; both trends make it more difficult for colleges to experiment and innovate in teaching. These same pressures, as well as competition from private education, have caused many colleges to investigate computer-based instruction, distance learning, and other lower-cost technologies for teaching. But such approaches are often impossible in vocational education because of the need for workshops, and fiscal incentives for new approaches to teaching have generally reinforced conventional didactic instruction (Grubb et al., 1999, chap. 7). The most aggressive colleges have created more market-oriented divisions that provide training for specific employers; while these efforts are sensitive to the demands of employers, they are generally unconcerned with the nature of teaching (Grubb, Badway, Bell, Bragg, & Russman, 1997). The major institutional changes, therefore, have drawn attention away from teaching concerns and have made experimentation and innovation more difficult. (See Cuban, 1993, on the tendency toward managerialism among educational administrators.)

In Great Britain, Conservative governments since 1979 have introduced a bewildering variety of market-like mechanisms into education, intended to promote greater efficiency and responsiveness to the consumer. One subtle effect of competition is that administrators in FE colleges—like administrators in the United States—are increasingly concerned with enrollment, competition, public relations, and other entrepreneurial roles, rather than with educational issues (Finkelstein & Grubb, 2000; Gewirtz, Ball, & Bowe, 1995). Despite some countervailing pressures, the overall pattern has been to shift institutional concerns in the direction of survival and enrollment. Similarly, the Australian government has promoted greater competition among educational institutions. The existing consultation paper (Australian National Training Authority, 1996) stresses "freeing up and commercializing TAFE" rather than promoting its institutional development; the emphasis is on "defining the VET [Vocational Education and Training] product" and developing market elements like cost structures and consumer information, with no mention of instructional practices or teacher training. Competition has been especially difficult for TAFE colleges, which have become more concerned with enrollment and survival than with the quality of teaching.

Even in Germany, a crisis has challenged the dual system in several ways. The needs for more academic qualifications like communication skills have caused many firms to require higher education levels, and many enterprises, unable to teach the complex skills required in new forms of production, have offered fewer apprenticeship positions. In addition, regional imbalances (particularly in the former East Germany) have produced a lower supply of apprenticeships, and because of outdated equipment or uncompetitive goods, an increasing number of firms are unable to offer apprenticeships. Firms facing increased competition have become increasingly cost-conscious and less willing to offer apprenticeships, particularly in small and medium-sized firms and in the service sector (Bardeleben & Troltsch, 1997). In addition, the traditional part-time vocational schools (*Berufschule*) are now facing competition from new kinds of schools (*Berufsakademien*) and polytechnics, and from pressures being placed on students to enroll in academic universities. One result has been to strengthen conventional academic education at the expense of the dual system. In addition to these issues of funding and provision, a question has arisen whether the concept of *Beruf* as a center of identity is still valid, given substantial changes in workplaces. One response has been to restructure the experiences of employees to incorporate *Ganzheitlichkeit* (wholeness) into a redefinition of *Beruf*; in turn, this requires more systems-oriented teaching and the integration of both general and firm-specific knowledge (Beck & Dubs, 1998; Beck & Heid, 1996). While these developments can be interpreted as necessary adjustments to changes, they illustrate how susceptible the dual system can be to competitive pressures.

In several ways, then, declining public resources and the ideology of competition have driven institutional changes in many countries. But market-oriented approaches to education tend to downgrade the importance of teaching: Funds for teaching innovation and staff development are likely to dwindle, and institutional priorities are likely to drift toward noneducational goals like maintaining enrollments. These problems are particularly serious for vocational education because of its higher costs and complex teaching conditions. But both the external and internal demands on education—employer demands for the competencies necessary in high-performance workplaces as well as current discussions about the most appropriate pedagogical practices—require more innovation, not less, and more careful attention to the preparation of instructors.

VI. Implications for Research, Policy, and Practice

A central theme in this chapter has been the complexity of teaching in vocational education. The basic structure of vocational education, caught between broader educational goals and employer demands, is a recurring issue, and the variety of occupations and changing economic conditions adds further to the difficulties. The variety of teaching methods, the complexity of combining classroom-based and workshop (or work-based) instruction, and the variety of competencies in many occupations mean that vocational instructors must balance many conflicting demands.

Furthermore, changing economic conditions complicate vocational teaching. The competencies required by changes in work often require instruction that integrates both academic and vocational competencies, work-based learning, and more constructivist and systems-oriented teaching in place of the didactic, sequential, skills-centered methods that have dominated in the past. But the lack of teacher preparation in many countries, the technology of standardized assessments, the use of competency-based approaches (at least in the English-speaking countries), and the pressures of inadequate time and resources tend to undermine any commitment to innovative teaching. Just when innovative approaches to teaching are most necessary, they seem increasingly difficult to achieve.

Some implications of these dilemmas are obvious, though they may be difficult to correct in practice. Most obviously, a greater appreciation of the complexity of vocational teaching—of the special conditions that make occupational instruction different from academic instruction—is necessary. Particularly in countries where VET policies assume that experience is the only prerequisite for teaching, the pedagogical demands are often neglected, hidden by rhetoric about the value of hands-on teaching. Indeed, given the recent attention to the benefits of idealized apprenticeship methods as a metaphor for teaching, both academic and vocational instructors could benefit from a deeper understanding of occupational pedagogy.

A corollary is that more research about vocational teaching is necessary—in place of research that many countries have tended to focus on the institutional and curricular dimensions of vocational education. In particular, we see a great need to observe teaching practices because so little analysis has been conducted to understand what vocational instructors actually do—particularly in varied settings that include conventional classrooms and workshops, "training" programs as well as "education" programs, work-like settings such as internships and school-based enterprises, and work itself. Furthermore, the effectiveness of different practices, first in providing students with particular competencies and then in helping them gain access to employment, needs much more research.

As a greater understanding of the complex teaching conditions in vocational education is developed, the most important need will be to improve the ways teachers carry out their instruction, and therefore the preservice and further education of vocational teachers requires more attention. Particularly in those countries that provide little or no teacher preparation, this requires programs with both domain-specific knowledge and pedagogical knowledge. Expertise in practice alone is not necessarily sufficient, because evidence shows that some experts in a particular field who teach fail to recognize the important elements of expertise and don't understand the varied ways they can teach such expertise. In addition, vocational instructors need greater mastery of pedagogy, of the alternative approaches to teaching, of the ability to teach those competencies (including the noncognitive competencies like kinesthetic and visual abilities) necessary in particular occupations, and of the special demands of classrooms, workshops, and work-based settings. The development of ways to teach vocational instructors effectively is one of the central tasks for both research and policy, because it requires a better understanding of both the conditions of teaching and the policies—programs of teacher preparation, licensing requirements, attention to the preparation of instructors in both work-based settings and formal schooling—that might improve the quality of teaching.

The political difficulty of achieving these goals, particularly in countries where vocational education suffers from second-class status, illustrates the importance of national policies on vocational education and training. Many policies not only fail to support the quality of teaching, but they also actively work against it—for example, by promoting narrowly conceived competency-based approaches, by defining and assessing core competencies in limited ways, by subjecting public institutions to competitive pressures that undermine the commitment to teaching, or by providing inadequate funding for materials and equipment. Changing these policies obviously poses a series of difficult issues for policymakers and administrators of vocational programs. In some cases, for example integrating more academic or general content or incorporating more work-based learning, new policies will require the reshaping of basic institutions in which vocational education is provided. While the political support for these changes remains uncertain, the economic and pedagogical imperatives are clear.

REFERENCES

Achtenhagen, F. (1988). *Learning in school and out—General versus vocational education.* Paper presented at the annual meeting of the American Educational Research Association, New Orleans, LA.

Achtenhagen, F. (1990). How can we generate stable, consistent, and generalizable results in the field of research on teaching?—Theoretical considerations and practical tests. In H. Mandl, E. de Corte, N. Bennett, & H. F. Friedrich (Eds.), *Learning and instruction, Vol. 2.1* (pp. 645–662). Oxford, UK: Pergamon.

Achtenhagen, F. (1992). The relevance of content for teaching-learning processes. In F. Oser, A. Dick, & J.-L. Patry (Eds.), *Effective and responsible teaching* (pp. 315–328). San Francisco: Jossey-Bass.

Achtenhagen, F. (1994). How should research on vocational and professional education react to new challenges in life and in the workplace? In W. J. Nijhof & J. N. Streumer (Eds.), *Flexibility in training and vocational education* (pp. 201–247). Utrecht: Lemma.

Achtenhagen, F. (1997). Berufliche Bildung [Vocational education and training]. In F. E. Weinert (Ed.), *Psychologie des Unterrichts und der Schule* [Psychology of instruction and school] (pp. 603–657). Göttingen: Hogrefe.

Achtenhagen, F. (1998). General versus vocational education—Demarcation and integration. In W. J. Nijhof & J. N. Streumer (Eds.), *Key qualifications in work and education* (pp. 133–143). Dordrecht, The Netherlands: Kluwer.

Achtenhagen, F., Fürstenau, B., Getsch, U., John, E. G., Noss, M., Preiss, P., Siemon, J., & Weber, S. (1997). *Mastery Learning mit Hilfe eines multimedial repräsentierten Modellunternehmens in der Ausbildung von Industriekaufleuten* [Mastery learning via a virtual enterprise for a commercial apprenticeship]. Göttingen: Seminar für Wirtschaftspädagogik der Georg-August-Universität.

Achtenhagen, F., & John, E. G. (Eds.). (1992). *Mehrdimensionale Lehr-Lern-Arrangements* [Multidimensional teaching-learning arrangements]. Wiesbaden: Gabler.

Achtenhagen, F., John, E. G., Lüdecke, S., Preiss, P., Seemann, H., Sembill, D., & Tramm, T. (1988a). Handlungsorientierte Unterrichtsforschung in ökonomischen Kernfächern —Am Beispiel des Einsatzes einer arbeitsanalogen Lernaufgabe und eines Planspiels [Action-oriented instructional research on the core curriculum of business education—Exemplified for working-analogous working tasks and simulation games]. *Unterrichtswissenschaft, 16,* 23–37.

Achtenhagen, F., John, E. G., Lüdecke, S., Preiss, P., Seemann, H., Sembill, D., & Tramm, T. (1988b). Lernen, Denken, Handeln in komplexen ökonomischen Situationen—Unter Nutzung neuer Technologien in der kaufmännischen Berufsausbildung [Learning, reasoning, acting in complex economic situations—By using new technologies in the fields of business and commercial education]. *Zeitschrift für Berufs- und Wirtschaftspädagogik, 84,* 3–17.

Achtenhagen, F., Nijhof, W., & Raffe, D. (1995). *Feasibility study: Research scope for vocational education in the framework of COST social sciences.* European Commission, Directorate-General: Science, Research and Development. Brussels, Luxembourg: ECSC-EC-EAEC.

Achtenhagen, F., & Noss, M. (1997). *Förderungsmöglichkeiten selbstgesteuerten Lernens am Arbeitsplatz—Untersuchungen zur Ausbildung von Bank—bzw. Sparkassenkaufleuten* [Promotion of self-regulated learning at the workplace—investigations on vocational education and training in a bank]. Göttingen: Seminar für Wirtschaftspädagogik der Georg-August-Universität

Achtenhagen, F., & Schneider, D. (1993). *Stand und Entwicklungsmöglichkeiten der Lernbüroarbeit unter Nutzung der neuen Technologien* [Working and learning in office learning centers—Using new technologies]. Göttingen: Seminar für Wirtschaftspädagogik der Georg-August-Universität.

Achtenhagen, F., Tramm, T., Preiss, P., Seemann-Weymar, H., John, E. G., & Schunck, A. (1992). *Lernhandeln in komplexen Situationen* [Learn-acting in complex situations]. Wiesbaden: Gabler.

Aebli, H. (1980). *Denken: Das Ordnen des Tuns* [Reasoning: Putting in order the acting] (Vol. 1). Stuttgart: Klett-Cotta.

Aebli, H. (1981). *Denken: Das Ordnen des Tuns* [Reasoning: Putting in order the acting] (Vol. 2). Stuttgart: Klett-Cotta.

Aglan, H., & Ali, S. F. (1996). Hands-on experiences: An integral part of engineering curriculum reform. *Journal of Engineering Education, 85*(1), 1–3.

Anglin, G. J. (Ed.). (1991). *Instructional technology—Past, present, future.* Englewood, CO: Libraries Unlimited.

Arnold, R., & Lipsmeier, A. (Eds.). (1995). *Handbuch der Berufsbildung* [Handbook of vocational education and training]. Opladen: Leske + Budrich.

Australian National Training Authority (ANTA). (1997). *The report of the ANTA board on the implementation of new apprenticeships (including User Choice).* Brisbane: Author.

Badway, N., & Grubb, W. N. (1997, October). *A Sourcebook for reshaping the community college: Curriculum integration and the multiple domains of career preparation* (Vols. 1 and 2). Berkeley, CA: National Center for Research in Vocational Education, University of California at Berkeley.

Bailey, T., & Merritt, D. (1997). Industry skill standards and education reform. *American Journal of Education, 105,* 401–436.

Bardeleben, R. v., & Troltsch, K. (1997). Betriebliche Ausbildung auf dem Rückzug? Entwicklung der Ausbildungsbeteiligung von Betrieben im Zeitraum von 1985–1995 [Vocational training in enterprises on the withdrawal? Figures for the period 1985–1995]. *Berufsbildung in Wissenschaft und Praxis, 5,* 9–16.

Beck, K., Brütting, B., Lüdecke-Plümer S., Minnameier, G., Schirmer, U., & Schmid, S. N. (1996). Zur Entwicklung moralischer Urteilskompetenz in der kaufmännischen Erstausbildung—empirische Befunde und praktische Probleme [Development of moral judgment in commercial education and training—empirical results and practical problems]. In K. Beck & H. Heid (Eds.), *Lehr-Lern-Prozesse in der kaufmännischen Erstausbildung* [Teaching-learning processes in business and commercial education] (pp. 187–206). Stuttgart: Steiner.

Beck, K., & Dubs, R. (Eds.). (1998). *Kompetenzentwicklung in der Berufserziehung* [Development of competencies through vocational education and training]. Stuttgart: Steiner.

Beck, K., & Heid, H. (Eds.). (1996). *Lehr-Lern-Prozesse in der kaufmännischen Erstausbildung* [Teaching-learning processes in business and commercial education] (with English abstracts). Stuttgart: Steiner.

Bednarek, E. (1988). Lernstatt und Qualitätszirkel—Modelle der Organisationsentwicklung [Study circle and quality circle as models of organizational development]. In F. Ruppert & E. Frieling (Eds.), *Psychologisches Handeln in Betrieben und Organisationen* [Psychological acting in enterprises and organizations] (pp. 147–163). Bern: Huber.

Bell, J., & Linn, M. (1993). *Scaffolding novices in spatial reasoning and visualization for engineering.* Working paper. Berkeley, CA: School of Education, University of California at Berkeley.

Berliner, D.C., & Biddle, B. J. (1996). *The manufactured crisis* (5th ed.). Reading, MA: Addison-Wesley.

Berryman, S. (1995). Apprenticeship as a paradigm of learning. In W. N. Grubb (Ed.), *Education through occupations in American high schools: Vol. I. Approaches to integrating academic and vocational education.* New York: Teachers College Press.

Berryman, S., & Bailey, T. (1992). *The double helix of education and the economy.* New York: Institute on Education and the Economy, Teachers College, Columbia University.

Beven, F. (1994). Pressing TAFE learners into far transfer within a CBT framework. In J. Stevenson (Ed.), *Cognition at work: The development of vocational expertise* (pp. 217–243). Australia: National Centre for Vocational Research.

Bierhof, H., & Prais, S. J. (1996). *From school to productive work: Britain and Switzerland compared.* Cambridge, UK: Cambridge University Press.

Billett, S. (1993). *Learning is working when working is learning: A guide to learning in the workplace.* Brisbane: Griffith University, Centre for Skill Formation Research and Development.

Billett, S. (1994). Searching for authenticity: A socio-cultural perspective of vocational skill development. *Vocational Aspects of Education, 46,* 3–16.

Billett, S. (1996). The role of vocational educators in developing workplace curriculum. *Australian Vocational Education Review, 3,* 29–35.

Boesel, D. (1994). Teachers in vocational education. In D. Boesel, L. Hudson, S. Deitch, & C. Masten (Eds.), *Participation in and quality of vocational education* (Vol. II). Final report to Congress, National Assessment of Vocational Education. Washington, DC: Office of Educational Research and Improvement, U.S. Department of Education.

Brech, R. (1989). The educational challenge of business simulations. In J. H. G. Klabbers, W. J. Scheper, C. A. T. Takkenberg, & D. Crookhall (Eds.), *Simulation-Gaming: On the improvement of competence in dealing with complexity, uncertainty and value conflicts* (p. 163). Oxford, UK: Pergamon.

Brereton, M., Sheppard, S. D., & Leifer, L. (1995). *How students connect engineering fundamentals to hardware design.* Paper prepared for the International Conference on Engineering Design, Prague. Stanford University: Center for Design Research.

Brodersen, M. (1986). Junior achievement. In K. Kutt & R. Selka (Eds.), *Simulation und Realität in der kaufmännischen Berufsbildung* [Simulation and reality in commercial education] (pp. 271–291). Berlin: Beuth.

Bromme, R., & Tillema, H. H. (Eds.). (1995). Fusing experience and theory. *Learning and Instruction, 5,* 261–417.

Brown, J. S., Collins, A., & Duguid, P. (1989). Situated cognition and the culture of learning. *Educational Researcher, 18*(1), 32–42.

Bundesministerium für Bildung und Wissenschaft. (1993). *Berufsbildungsbericht 1993* [Federal report on vocational education and training, 1993]. Bonn: Bock.

Burke, J. (Ed.). (1995). *Outcomes, learning and the curriculum—Implications for NVQs, GNVQs and other qualifications.* London: Falmer Press.

Buttler, F. (1992). Tätigkeitslandschaft bis 2010. [Landscape of labor until 2010]. In F. Achtenhagen & E. G. John (Eds.), *Mehrdimensionale Lehr-Lern-Arrangements* [Multidimensional teaching-learning arrangements] (pp. 162–182). Wiesbaden: Gabler.

Camp, W., & Heath, B. (1988, December). *On becoming a teacher: Vocational education and the induction process* (Report No. MDS-018). Berkeley, CA: National Center for Research in Vocational Education, University of California at Berkeley.

Camp, W., & Heath-Camp, B. (1989). Structuring the induction process for beginning vocational teachers. *Journal of Vocational and Technical Education, 5*(2), 13–25.

Carraher, T. N., Carraher, D. W., & Schliemann, A. D. (1985). Mathematics in the streets and in schools. *British Journal of Developmental Psychology, 3,* 21–29.

Carroll, J. M. (1990). *The Nurnberg funnel: Designing minimalist instruction for practical computer skills.* Cambridge, MA: MIT Press.

Carroll, J. M. (1996). *Minimalism beyond the Nurnberg funnel.* Cambridge, MA: MIT Press.

Cash, J., Behrman, M., Stadt, R., & Daniels, H. (1997). Effectiveness of cognitive apprenticeship instructional methods in college automotive technology classrooms. *Journal of Industrial Teacher Education, 34*(2), 29–49.

Chappell, C., & Melville, B. (1995). *Professional competence and the initial and continuing education of NSW TAFE teachers.* Sydney: Research Centre for Vocational Education and Training, University of Technology.

Claus, J. (1990). Opportunity or inequality in vocational education? A qualitative investigation. *Curriculum Inquiry, 20,* 7–39.

Collins, A., Brown, J., & Newman, S. (1989). Cognitive apprenticeship: Teaching the craft of reading, writing, and mathematics. In L. B. Resnick (Ed.), *Knowing, learning, and instruction: Essays in honor of Robert Glaser* (pp. 453–494). Hillsdale, NJ: Lawrence Erlbaum Associates.

Connell, W. F. (1986). History of teaching methods. In M. J. Dunkin (Ed.), *The international encyclopedia of teaching and teacher education* (pp. 201–214). Oxford, UK: Pergamon.

Cook-Gumperz, J. (1986). Literacy and schooling: An unchanging equation? In *The social construction of literacy* (pp. 16–44). New York: Cambridge University Press.

Copa, G., & Bentley, C. (1992). Vocational education. In P. W. Jackson (Ed.), *Handbook of research in curriculum* (pp. 891–944). New York: Macmillan.

Core skills in GNVQs: Principles and practice. (1996). London: National Council for Vocational Qualifications.

Corsten, M., & Lempert, W. (1997). *Beruf und Moral* [Vocation and moral standards]. Weinheim: Deutscher Studien Verlag.

Crain, R. L., Heebner, A. L., Si, Y. P., Jordan, W. J., & Kiefer, D. R. (1992). *The effectiveness of New York City's career magnet schools: An evaluation of ninth grade performance using an experimental design.* Berkeley, CA: National Center for Research in Vocational Education, University of California at Berkeley.

Cuban, L. (1993). *How teachers taught: Constancy and change in American classrooms 1890–1990.* New York: Teachers College, Columbia University.

Cumming, J., & Carbines, B. (1997, March). *Reforming schools through workplace learning.* Ryde, New South Wales: National Schools Network.

Curzon, L. B. (1980). *Teaching in further education* (2nd ed.). London: Cassel.

Dale, R., Bowe, R., Harris, D., Leveys, M., Moore, R., Shilling, C., Sikes, P., Trevitt, J., & Valsecchi, V. (1990). *The TVEI story: Policy, practice and preparation for the work force.* Buckingham, UK: Open University Press.

Darling-Hammond, L., Ancess, J., & Falk, B. (1995). *Authentic assessment in action.* New York: Teachers College Press.

Dawkins, J. S., & Holding, A. C. (1987). *Skills for Australia.* Canberra: Australian Government Publishing Service.

Dearing, R. (1996). *Review of qualifications for 16–19 year olds.* Hayes, Middlesex: SCAA.

Dehnbostel, P., Holz, H., & Novak, H. (Eds.). (1992). *Lernen für die Zukunft durch verstärktes Lernen am Arbeitsplatz* [Learning for the future by learning at the workplace]. Berlin: Bundesinstitut für Berufsbildung.

Delpit, L. (1986). Skills and other dilemmas of a progressive black educator. *Harvard Educational Review, 56,* 379–385.

Deutsche Forschungsgemeinschaft. (1990). *Berufsbildungsforschung an den Hochschulen der Bundesrepublik Deutschland* [Research on vocational education and training at the German universities]. Weinheim: VCH.

Dewey, J. (1916). *Democracy and education: An introduction to the philosophy of education.* New York: The Free Press.

Dewey, J. (1990). *The school and society.* Chicago: University of Chicago Press. (Original work published in 1900).

Dewey, J., & Dewey, E. (1915). *Schools of tomorrow.* New York: E. P. Dutton.

Dijkstra, S., Krammer, H., & van Merriënboer, J. G. (Eds.). (1992). *Instructional models in computer-based learning environments.* Berlin: Springer.

Dills, C. R., & Romiszowski, A. J. (Eds.). (1997). *Instructional development paradigms.* Englewood Cliffs, NJ: Educational Technology Publications.

Dinham, S., & Stritter, F. (1986). Research on professional education. In M. C. Wittrock (Ed.), *Handbook of research on teaching* (3rd ed., pp. 952–970). New York: Macmillan.

Dörig, R. (1994). *Das Konzept der Schlüsselqualifikationen* [The concept of key-qualifications]. Hallstadt: Rosch.

Dörner, D., Kreuzig, H. W., Reither, F., & Stäudel, T. (1983). *Lohhausen—Vom Umgang mit Unbestimmtheit und Komplexität* [Lohhausen—About dealing with uncertainty and complexity]. Bern: Huber.

Dörner, D., & Pfeiffer, E. (1993). Strategic thinking, stress and intelligence. *Ergonomics, 36,* 1345–1361.

Dolch, J. (1959). *Lehrplan des Abendlandes—Zweieinhalb Jahrtausende seiner Geschichte* [Curriculum of occidental civilization—2500 years of its history]. Meisenheim: Henn.

Douglas, P. (1921). *American apprenticeship and industrial education* (Studies in History, Economics, and Law, Vol. 95, No. 2). New York: Columbia University.

Ducci, M. (1991). *Vocational training on the threshold of the 1990s* (Vol. II, Document No. PHREE/91/35, Interamerican Center for Research and Documentation for Vocational Training, CINTERFOR, and International Labour Organization, ILO). New York: World Bank, Education and Employment Division.

Duke, C. (1990). Educating and training the workforce. In N. Entwistle (Ed.), *Handbook of educational ideas and practices* (pp. 333–345). London: Routledge.

Echeverría Samanes, B. (1993). *Formación Profesional* [Vocational education]. Barcelona: Promociones y Publicaciones Universitarias.

Eck, A. (1993). Job-related education and training: Their impact on earnings. *Monthly Labor Review, 116*(10), 21–38.

Elliott, G. (1996). *Crisis and change in vocational education and training.* London: Jessica Kingsley Publisher.

Engeström, Y. (1994). *Training for change: New approach to instruction and learning in working life.* Geneva: International Labour Office.

Engeström, Y., Engeström, R., & Kärkkäinen, M. (1995). Polycontextuality and boundary crossing in expert cognition: Learning and problem solving in complex work activities. *Learning and Instruction, 5,* 319–336.

Engeström, Y., & Middleton, D. (Eds.). (1996). *Cognition and communication at work.* Cambridge, UK: Cambridge University Press.

Engineering: Curriculum area survey report. (1996). Report from the Inspectorate. Coventry, U.K.: Further Education Funding Council.

Evans, G., & Butler, J. (1992). Expert models and feedback processes in developing competence in industrial trade areas. *Australian Journal of TAFE Research and Development, 8,* 13–32.

Evans, G., & Butler, J. (1993). Use of a trade-practice model in teaching electrical installation procedures to apprentices. *Australian and New Zealand Journal of Vocational Education Research, 1*(2), 29–54.

Evans, K., Hodkinson, P., Keep, E., Maguire, M., Raffe, D., Rainbird, M., Senker, P., & Unwin, L. (1998). *Working to Learn. A work-based route to learning for young people* (Issues in People Management, No. 18). London: Institute of Personnel and Development.

Finkelstein, N., & Grubb, W. N. (2000). Making sense of education and training markets: Lessons from England. *American Educational Research Journal, 37*(3), 601–631.

Fix, W. (1989). *Juniorenfirmen—ein innovatives Konzept zur Förderung von Schlüsselqualifikationen* [Junior firms—An innovative concept for the promotion of key-qualifications]. Berlin: Schmidt.

Flechsig, K.-H. (1996). *Kleines Handbuch didaktischer Modelle* [Handbook of didactic models]. Eichenzell: Neuland.

Foster, P. (1966). The vocational school fallacy in development planning. In C. A. Anderson & M. J. Bowman (Eds.), *Education and economic development* (pp. 142–166). Chicago: Aldine.

Frantz, Jr., N. R. (1997). The identification of national trends and issues for workplace preparation and their implications for vocational teacher education. *Journal of Vocational and Technical Education,* [On-line], *14*(1). Available:

Frey, K., & Frey-Eiling, A. (1992). *Allgemeine Didaktik* [General didactics] (5th ed.). Zürich: VDF.

Fürstenau, B. (1994). *Komplexes Problemlösen im betriebswirtschaftlichen Unterricht* [Complex problem solving within business studies]. Wiesbaden: Gabler.

Fürstenau, B. (1996). Pupils' problem-solving: Evaluation of a complex teaching-learning arrangement. In W. B. Walstad (Ed.), *Secondary economics and business education* (pp. 285–294). London: The Economics and Business Education Association.

Gardner, H. (1983). *Frames of mind: The theory of multiple intelligences.* New York: Basic Books.

Gaskell, J. (1997). *Work, schoolwork, networks: Linking partners and courses in applied science.* Paper presented to the National Association of Research in Science Education, Chicago. Vancouver: University of British Columbia.

Gaskell, P. J., & Hepburn, G. (1997). Integration of academic and occupational curricula in science and technology education. *Science Education, 81,* 469–481.

General National Vocational Qualifications. (1995). *GNVQ Briefing: Information on the form, development and implementation of GNVQ's.* London: GNVQ Publishers.

Getsch, U. (1990). *Möglichkeiten einer Förderung von betriebswirtschaftlichem Zusammenhangswissen* [Possibilities of promoting a systems knowledge within business studies]. Göttingen: Seminar für Wirtschaftspädagogik der Georg-August-Universität.

Gewirtz, S., Ball, S., & Bowe, S. (1995). *Markets, choice, and equity in education.* Buckingham, UK: Open University Press.

Ghaill, M. M. (1988). The new vocationalism: The response of a sixth-form college. In A. Pollard, J. Purvis, & G. Walford (Eds.), *Education, training, and the new vocationalism: Experience and policy* (pp. 109–128). Milton Keynes, UK: Open University Press.

Glaser, R., Lesgold, A., & Gott, S. (1991). Implications of cognitive psychology for measuring job performance. In A. K. Wigdor & B. F. Green, Jr. (Eds.), *Performance assessment for the workplace: Vol. II. Technical issues* (pp. 1–26). Washington, DC: National Academy Press.

Glöggler, K. (1997). *Handlungsorientierter Unterricht im Berufsfeld Elektrotechnik* [Action-oriented instruction in the field of electrical engineering]. Frankfurt am Main: Lang.

Good, T. (1996). Teaching effects and teacher evaluation. In J. Sikula (Ed.), *Handbook of research on teacher education* (pp. 617–666). New York: Macmillan Library References.

Gooler, D. D., & Roth, G. L. (1990). *Instructional technology applications in vocational education: A notebook of cases.* Springfield, IL: Illinois State Board of Education.

Gott, S. P. (1988). Apprenticeship instruction for real-world tasks: The coordination of procedures, mental models, and strategies. In E. Rothkopf (Ed.), *Review of research in education* (Vol. 15, pp. 97–

169). Washington, DC: American Educational Research Association.

Gott, S. P. (1995). Rediscovering learning: Acquiring expertise in real-world problem-solving tasks. *Australian and New Zealand Journal of Vocational Education Research, 3*, 30–68.

Gramlinger, F. (1994). Die Übungsfirma als "Unterrichtsgegenstand" an allen kaufmännischen Schulen Österreichs [The training firms as official subject in all Austrian commercial schools]. *Wirtschaft und Erziehung, 46*, 404–408.

Green, A. (1996). *Core skills, general education and unification in post-16 education.* London: London University, Institute of Education.

Grubb, W. N. (1995). *Education through occupations in American high schools.* (Vols. I, II.) New York: Teachers College Press.

Grubb, W. N. (1996a). *Learning to work: The case for re-integrating job training and education.* New York: Russell Sage Foundation.

Grubb, W. N. (1996b). *Working in the middle: Strengthening education and training for the mid-skilled labor force.* San Francisco: Jossey-Bass.

Grubb, W. N. (2000). Opening classrooms and improving schools: Lessons from inspection systems in England. *Teachers College Record, 102*(4), 696–723.

Grubb, W. N., with Worthen, H., Byrd, B., Webb, E., Badway, N., Case, C., Goto, S., & Villenueve, J. C. (1999). *Honored but invisible: An inside look at teaching in community colleges.* New York: Routledge.

Grubb, W. N., & Badway, N. (1998, March). *Linking school-based and work-based learning: The implications of LaGuardia's co-op seminars for school-to-work programs* (Report No. MDS-1046). Berkeley, CA: National Center for Research in Vocational Education, University of California at Berkeley.

Grubb, W. N., Badway, N., Bell, D., Bragg, D., & Russman, M. (1997). *Workforce, economic, and community development: The changing landscape of the entrepreneurial community college.* Mission Viejo, CA: League for Innovation in the Community College.

Grubb, W. N., & Kraskouskas, E. (1992). *A time to every purpose: Integrating academic and occupational education in community colleges and technical institutes.* Berkeley, CA: National Center for Research in Vocational Education, University of California at Berkeley.

Grubb, W. N., & Ryan, P. (1999). *Plain talk on the field of dreams: The roles of evaluation in vocational education and training.* Geneva: International Labor Organization and London: Routledge.

Hacker, W., & Skell, W. (1993). *Lernen in der Arbeit* [Learning while working]. Berlin: Bundesinstitut für Berufsbildung.

Hamilton, M. A., & Hamilton, S. (1997b). When is work a learning experience? *Phi Delta Kappan, 78*, 682–689.

Hamilton, S. (1990). *Apprenticeship for adulthood: Preparing youth for the future.* New York: The Free Press.

Hamilton, S., & Hamilton, M. A. (1997a). When is learning work-based? *Phi Delta Kappan, 78*, 676–681.

Hamilton, S., & Lempert, W. (1996). The impact of apprenticeship on youth: A prospective analysis. *Journal of Research on Adolescence, 6*, 427–455.

Hardt, G., Zaib, V., Kleinbeck, U., & Metz-Göckel, H. (1996). Untersuchungen zu Motivierungspotential und Lernmotivation in der kaufmännischen Erstausbildung [Motivation and learning in basic business education]. In K. Beck & H. Heid (Eds.), *Lehr-Lern-Prozesse in der kaufmännischen Erstausbildung* [Teaching-learning processes in business and commercial education] (pp. 128–149). Stuttgart: Steiner.

Harkin, J., & Davis, P. (1996a). The communications styles of teachers in post-compulsory education. *Journal of Further and Higher Education, 20*, 25–34.

Harkin, J., & Davis, P. (1996b). The impact of GNVQs on the communications styles of teachers. *Research in Post-Compulsory Education, 1*, 97–107.

Härnsten, G. (1994). *The research circle—Building knowledge on equal terms.* Stockholm: The Swedish Trade Union Confederation.

Harris, L., & Volet, S. (1997). *Developing a learning culture in the workplace.* Murdoch, Western Australia: Murdoch University.

Hartley, N., & Wentling, T. (Eds.). (1996). *Beyond tradition: Preparing the teachers of tomorrow's workforce.* Columbia, MO: Instructional Materials Laboratory, University of Missouri.

Hartmann, M., Gaevert, S., & Schleyer, I. (1990). Neue Varianten des Lernens in Betrieb und Schule—z. B. Leittextmethode und Fallstudie [New variations of learning in enterprises and schools—task-centered method and case study]. In L. Reetz & T. Reitmann (Eds.), *Schlüsselqualifikationen* [Key-qualifications] (pp. 231–235). Hamburg: Feldhaus.

Heidegger, G., & Rauner, F. (1996). *Vocational education in need of reforms.* Expert Opinion to the Ministry of Labor, Health, and Social Affairs of North Rhine-Westphalia. Bremen: Institut Technik und Bildung, University of Bremen.

Hershey, A. M., Hudis, P., Silverberg, M., & Haimson, J. (1997). *Partners in progress: Early steps in creating school-to-work systems* Draft. (Contract No. EA95010001). Princeton, NJ: Mathematical Policy Research, Inc.

Hodkinson, P. (1991). Liberal education and the new vocationalism: A progressive partnership? *Oxford Review of Education, 17*, 73–88.

Holloway, I. (1992). Teaching catering: Catering lecturers' perspectives on students and classrooms. *Vocational Aspects of Education, 44*, 65–80.

Holmstrand, L., Lindström, K., Löwstedt, J., & Englund, A. (1994). *The research circle—A model for collaborative learning at work.* Manuscript. University of Uppsala.

Hsi, S., Linn, M., & Bell, J. (1997). The role of spatial reasoning in engineering and the design of spatial instruction. *Journal of Engineering Education, 85*(3), 151–158.

Hull, G. (1993). Critical literacy and beyond: Lessons learned from students and workers in a vocational program and on the job. *Anthropology and Educational Quarterly, 24*, 373–396.

Hull, G., Jury, M., Ziv, O., & Katz, M. (1996). *Changing work, changing literacy? A study of skill requirements and development in a traditional and restructured workplace.* Berkeley, CA: School of Education, University of California.

Hustler, D. (1988). "It's not like normal lessons: You don't have to wag school anymore." In A. Pollard, J. Purvis, & G. Walford (Eds.), *Education, training, and the new vocationalism: Experience and policy* (pp. 71–89). Milton Keynes, UK: Open University Press.

Hutchins, E. (1996). *Cognition in the wild.* Cambridge, MA: MIT Press.

Hyland, T. (1993). Vocational reconstruction and Dewey's instrumentalism. *Oxford Review of Education, 19*, 89–100.

Hyland, T. (1994a). *Competence, education and NVQs: Dissenting perspectives.* London: Cassell.

Hyland, T. (1994b). Silk purses and sows' ears. *Cambridge Journal of Education, 24*, 233–244.

Jeong, J. (1995). The failure of recent state vocational training policies in Korea from a comparative perspective. *British Journal of Industrial Relations, 33*, 237–252.

Jessup, G. (1991). *Outcomes: NVQs and the emerging model of education and training.* London: Falmer Press.

John, E. G. (1992). Fallstudien und Fallstudienunterricht [Instruction via case studies]. In F. Achtenhagen & E. G. John (Eds.), *Mehrdimensionale Lehr-Lern-Arrangements* [Multidimensional teaching-learning arrangements] (pp. 79–91). Wiesbaden: Gabler.

Johnson, S. (1996). Technology education as the focus of research. *The Technology Teacher, 55*, 47–49.

Jonassen, D. H. (Ed.) (1988). *Instructional designs for microcomputer courseware.* Hillsdale, NJ: Lawrence Erlbaum Associates.

Jonassen, D. H. (Ed.). (1996). *Handbook of research for educational communications and technology.* New York: Simon & Schuster Macmillan.

Jonassen, D. H., Mayes, T., & MacAlesse, R. (1993). A manifesto for a constructivist approach to use of technology in higher education. In T. M. Fuffy, J. Lowyck, D. H. Jonassen, & T. M. Walsh (Eds.), *Designing environments for constructivist learning* (pp. 230–248). New York: Springer.

Jones, M., & Winne, P. H. (Eds.). (1992). *Adaptive learning environments.* Berlin: Springer.

Joyce, B. R., & Weil, M. (1972). *Models of teaching.* Englewood Cliffs, NJ: Lawrence Erlbaum Associates.

Kaiser, F.-J. (Ed.). (1987). *Handlungsorientiertes Lernen in kaufmännischen Berufsschulen—Didaktische Grundlagen und Realisierungsmöglichkeiten für die Arbeit im Lernbüro* [Action-oriented learning in commercial schools—Theory and practice of office learning centers]. Bad Heilbrunn/Oberbayern: Klinkhardt.

Kaiser, F.-J. (1997). The office learning centre: Lernbüro (OLC)—A new approach in teaching office management in full-time commercial schools. *Economia, 7*(1), 13–18.

Kaiser, F.-J., & Kaminski, H. (1994). *Methodik des Ökonomie-Unterrichts* [Methods of economic education]. Bad Heilbrunn/Oberbayern: Klinkhardt.

Kaiser, F.-J., & Weitz, B. O. (1990). *Arbeiten und Lernen im Schulischen Modellunternehmen* [Working and learning in office learning centers] (Vol. 1). Bad Heilbrunn/Oberbayern: Klinkhardt.

Kaiser, F.-J., Weitz, B. O., & Sarrazin, D. (1991). *Arbeiten und Lernen im Schulischen Modellunternehmen* [Working and learning in office learning centers] (Vol. 2). Bad Heilbrunn/Oberbayern: Klinkhardt.

Keck, A. (1995). *Zum Lernpotential kaufmännischer Arbeitssituationen* [Learning potential of commercial work situations]. Göttingen: Seminar für Wirtschaftspädagogik der Georg-August-Universität.

Keck, A., Weymar, B., & Diepold, P. (1997). *Lernen an kaufmännischen Arbeitsplätzen* [Learning at commercial workplaces]. Bielefeld: Bertelsmann.

Kerry, T., & Tollitt-Evans, J. (1992). *Teaching in further education*. Oxford, UK: Blackwell Publishers.

Kieras, D. E., & Bovair, S. (1984). The role of mental models in learning to operate a device. *Cognitive Science, 8*, 255–273.

Kincheloe, J. L. (1995). *Toil and trouble: Good work, smart workers, and the integration of academic and vocational education*. New York: Peter Lang.

Kliebard, H. M. (1986). *The struggle for the American curriculum: 1893–1958*. Boston: Routledge & Kegan Paul.

Kloas, P.-W. (1992). Lernen an der Arbeit—Berufsbildung in Deutschland und Europa [Learning at the workplace—Vocational education and training in Germany and Europe]. In F. Achtenhagen & E. G. John (Eds.), *Mehrdimensionale Lehr-Lern-Arrangements* [Multidimensional teaching-learning arrangements] (pp. 196–211). Wiesbaden: Gabler.

Kogan, D., Dickinson, K., Means, B., & Strong, M. (1989). *Improving the quality of training under JTPA*. Oakland, CA: Berkeley Planning Associates and SRI International for the U.S. Department of Labor.

Koziol, K. (1992). *Novels and short stories about work: An annotated bibliography*. Berkeley, CA: National Center for Research in Vocational Education, University of California at Berkeley.

Koziol, K., & Grubb, W. N. (1995). Paths not taken: Curriculum integration and the political and moral purposes of education. In W. N. Grubb (Ed.), *Education through occupations in American high schools: Vol. II. The challenges of implementing curriculum integration* (pp. 115–140). New York: Teachers College Press.

Kutt, K. (1993). Juniorenfirmen [Junior firms]. *Berufsbildung, 47*, 31–34.

Labaree, D. (1996). Private goods, public goods: The American struggle over educational goals. *American Educational Research Journal, 34*, 39–81.

Lakes, R. (Ed.). (1994). *Critical education for work: Multidisciplinary approaches*. Norwood, NJ: Ablex.

Lampert, M. (1992). Practices and problems in teaching authentic mathematics. In F. Oser, A. Dick, & J.-L. Patry (Eds.), *Effective and responsible teaching* (pp. 295–314). San Francisco: Jossey-Bass.

Lauglo, J., & Lillis, K. (Eds.). (1988). *Vocationalizing education—An international perspective*. Oxford, UK: Pergamon.

Laur-Ernst, U. (1993). Das Zusammenspiel von Lernen und Arbeit [The interplay of learning and working]. In Bundesinstitut für Berufsbildung, *Umsetzung neuer Qualifikationen in die Berufsbildungspraxis* [New qualifications for the practice of vocational education and training] (pp. 149–156). Nürnberg:BW Bildung und Wissen.

Lave, J., & Wenger, E. (1991). *Situated learning: Learning peripheral participation*. Cambridge, UK: Cambridge University Press.

Lawrey, J. R. (1986). The project method. In M. J. Dunkin (Ed.), *The international encyclopedia of teaching and teacher education* (pp. 217–219). Oxford, UK: Pergamon.

Lempert, W. (1994). Moral development in the biographies of skilled industrial workers. *Journal of Moral Education, 23*, 451–468.

Levy, M. (1992). *Work based learning: Tools for transition*. Bristol: The Staff College.

Levy, M., Mathews, D., Oates. T., & Edmond, N. (1989). *A guide to work based learning terms*. Bristol: The Further Education Staff College.

Lewis, T. (1991). Difficulties attending the new vocationalism in the USA. *Journal of Philosophy of Education, 25*, 95–108.

Lewis, T. (1993). Valid knowledge and the problem of practical arts curricula. *Curriculum Inquiry, 23*, 175–202.

Lewis, T. (1994). Bridging the liberal/vocational debate: An examination of recent British and American versions of an old debate. *Oxford Review of Education, 20*, 199–217.

Lohman, D. (1988). Spatial abilities as traits, processes, and knowledge. In R. Sternberg (Ed.), *Advances in the psychology of human intelligence* (Vol. 4, pp. 181–248). Hillsdale, NJ: Lawrence Erlbaum Associates.

Lüdecke-Plümer, S., Zirkel, A., & Beck, K. (1997). Vocational training and moral judgment—Are there gender-specific traits among apprentices in commercial business. *International Journal of Educational Research, 27*, 605–617.

Lynch, R. (1997). *Designing vocational and technical teacher education for the 21st century: Implications from the reform literature* (Information Series No. 368). Columbus, OH: ERIC Clearinghouse on Adult, Career, and Vocational Education, Center on Education and Training for Employment.

MacGraw, J., & Peoples, M. (1996). *Mirror, mirror on the wall: Voices of VET teachers and trainers*. Canberra: Australian National Training Authority.

Manning, D. (Ed.). (1997). *Qualifications with a dual orientation towards employment and higher education. A collaborative investigation of selected issues in seven European Countries*. Berlin: Research Forum Education and Society.

Mayer, E. (1992). *Employment-related key competencies: A proposal for consultation*. Canberra, Australia: The Mayer Committee, Australian Education Council.

McKavanaugh, C., & Stevenson, J. (1994). Development of student expertise in TAFE colleges. In J. Stevenson (Ed.), *Cognition at work: The development of vocational expertise* (pp. 169–197). Australia: National Centre for Vocational Research.

Merriënboer, J. (1997). *Training complex skills*. Englewood Cliffs, NJ: Educational Technology Publications.

Middleton, J., Ziderman, A., & Van Adams, A. (1990). *Vocational education and training in developing countries*. Washington, DC: The World Bank.

Miller, A., & Forrest, G. (1996). *Work experience for the 21st century*. Coventry: University of Warwick, Centre for Education and Industry.

Moore, D. T. (1981). Discovering the pedagogy of experience. *Harvard Educational Review, 51*, 286–300.

Morris, N., & Rouse, W. (1985). Review and evaluation of empirical research in troubleshooting. *Human Factors, 27*, 503–530.

Mosenthal, P., & Kirsch, I. (1990). Understanding general reference maps. *Journal of Reading, 34*, 60–63.

Mosenthal, P., & Kirsch, I. (1991). Understanding mimetic documents through "knowledge modeling." *Journal of Reading, 34*, 552–558.

Mulcahy, D. (1996). Performing Competencies: Of training protocols and vocational education practices. *Australian and New Zealand Journal of Vocational Education Research, 4*, 35–67.

National Board for Professional Teaching Standards, Vocational Education Standards Committee (1997). *Draft report on standards for national board certification*. Detroit: Author.

National Commission on Excellence in Education. (1983). *A nation at risk: The imperative for educational reform*. Washington, DC: U.S. Government Printing Office.

Nelson, R., & Nies, J. (1978). Instructional techniques for teaching essential work skills. *Journal of Industrial Teacher Education, 16*, 24–32.

Nijhof, W. J., & Streumer, J. N. (1994). Flexibility in vocational education and training: An introduction. In W. J. Nijhof & J. N. Streumer (Eds.), *Flexibility in training and vocational education* (pp. 1–12). Utrecht: Lemma.

Nijhof, W. J., & Streumer, J. N. (Eds.). (1998). *Key qualifications in work and education*. Dordrecht, The Netherlands: Kluwer.

Nothdurft, W. (1989). *Schoolworks: Reinventing public schools to create the workforce of the future.* Washington, DC: The Brookings Institution.

Osborn, J., & Agogino, A. M. (1992). An interface for interactive spatial reasoning and visualization. *Proceedings of the ACM CHT92 Human Factors in Computing Systems Conference, 75–82.*

Oser, F. (1986). Moral education and values education: The discourse perspective. In M. C. Wittrock (Ed.), *Handbook of research on teaching* (3rd ed., pp. 917–941). New York: Macmillan.

Ott, B. (1997). *Grundlagen des beruflichen Lernens und Lehrens* [Foundations of vocational learning and teaching]. Berlin: Cornelsen.

Oulton, N., & Steedman, H. (1994). The British system of youth training: A comparison with Germany. In L. Lynch (Ed.), *Training and the private sector: International comparisons* (pp.). Chicago: University of Chicago Press.

Pätzold, G. (1996). *Lehrmethoden in der beruflichen Bildung* [Teaching methods for vocational education and training] (2nd ed.). Heidelberg: Sauer.

Paulsen, B., & Stötzel, B. (1992). Lernen und Arbeiten im Lernstatt-Modell [Learning and working by study circles]. In P. Dehnbostel, H. Holz, & H. Novak (Eds.), *Lernen für die Zukunft durch verstärktes Lernen am Arbeitsplatz* [Learning for the future by learning at the workplace] (pp. 333–345). Berlin: Bundesinstitut für Berufsbildung.

Perez, R. (1991). A view from troubleshooting. In M. Smith (Ed.), *Toward a unified theory of problem solving: Views from the content domains* (pp. 115–153). Hillsdale, NJ: Lawrence Erlbaum Associates.

Perkins, D. A. (1992). *Smart schools: From training memories to educating minds.* New York: The Free Press.

Perkins, D. N., & Salomon, G. (1989). Are cognitive skills context bound? *Educational Researcher, 18*(1), 16–25.

Pieters, J. M., & Brandsma, J. (Eds.). (in press). *Complex teaching-learning environments in education for business in Europe.* Utrecht: Lemma.

Pieters, J. M., Breuer, K., & Simons, P. R. J. (Eds.). (1990). *Learning environments.* Berlin: Springer.

Prantl, R. (1917). *Kerschensteiner als Pädagoge* [Kerschensteiner as pedagogue]. Unpublished doctoral dissertation, University of Würzburg, Germany.

Preiss, P. (1994). Schema-based modelling of complex economic situations. In W. J. Nijhof & J. N. Streumer (Eds.), *Flexibility in training and vocational education* (pp. 249–289). Utrecht: Lemma.

Preiss, P., & Tramm, T. (1996). Die Göttinger Unterrichtskonzeption des wirtschaftsinstrumentellen Rechnungswesens [The Göttingen model of accountancy]. In P. Preiss & T. Tramm (Eds.), *Rechnungswesenunterricht und ökonomisches Denken—Didaktische Innovationen für die kaufmännische Ausbildung* [Instruction of accountancy and economic reasoning—Didactical innovations for business education] (pp. 222–323). Wiesbaden: Gabler.

Prenzel, M., Kristen, A., Dengler, P., Ettle, R., & Beer, T. (1996). Selbstbestimmt motiviertes und interessiertes Lernen in der kaufmännischen Erstausbildung [Learning with interest and self-determination in vocational education]. In K. Beck & H. Heid (Eds.), *Lehr-Lern-Prozesse in der kaufmännischen Erstausbildung* [Teaching-learning processes in business and commercial education] (pp. 108–127). Stuttgart: Steiner.

Prosser, C., & Quigley, T. (1949). *Vocational education in a democracy.* Chicago: American Technical Society.

Psacharopoulos, G. (1987). To vocationalize or not to vocationalize: That is the curriculum question. *International Review of Education, 33,* 187–211.

Qualifications and Curriculum Authority. (1998). *Learning from work experience.* London: Author.

Quiñones, M. A., & Ehrenstein, A. (1996a). Introduction: Psychological perspectives on training in organizations. In M. A. Quiñones & A Ehrenstein (Eds.), *Training for a rapidly changing workplace* (pp. 1–10). Washington, DC: American Psychological Association.

Quiñones, M. A., & Ehrenstein, A. (Eds.). (1996b). *Training for a rapidly changing workplace. Applications of psychological research.* Washington, DC: American Psychological Association.

Raizen, S. A. (1994). Learning and work: The research base. In Organisation for Economic Co-Operation and Development, *Vocational*

education and training for youth: Towards coherent policy and practice (pp. 69–113). Paris: OECD.

Rasmussen, J., Andersen, H. B., & Bernsen, N. O. (Eds.). (1991). *Human-computer interaction—Research directions in cognitive science.* Hove: Lawrence Erlbaum Associates.

Reetz, L. (1990). Zur Bedeutung der Schlüsselqualifikationen in der Berufsausbildung [The importance of key-qualifications for vocational education and training]. In L. Reetz & T. Reitmann (Eds.), *Schlüsselqualifikationen* [Key-qualifications] (pp. 16–35). Hamburg: Feldhaus.

Rehm, M. (1989). Emancipatory vocational education: Pedagogy for the work of individuals and society. *Journal of Education, 171,* 109–123.

Resnick, L. B. (1987). Learning in school and out. *Educational Researcher, 16*(9), 13–20.

Resnick, L. B., & Wirt, J. G. (1996). The changing workplace. New challenges for education policy and practice. In L. B. Resnick & J. G. Wirt (Eds.), *Linking school and work* (pp. 1–19). San Francisco: Jossey-Bass.

Richardson, R., Fisk, E., & Okun, M. (1983). *Literacy in the open-access college.* San Francisco: Jossey-Bass.

Robinson, P. (1996). *Rhetoric and reality: Britain's new vocational qualifications.* London: Center for Economic Performance, London School of Economics.

Roegge, C., & Russell, E. (1990). Teaching applied biology in secondary agriculture: Effects on student achievement and attitudes. *Journal of Agricultural Education, 31,* 27–31.

Rothenberger, B., & Stewart, B. (1995). A greenhouse laboratory experience: Effects on student knowledge and attitude. *Journal of Agricultural Education, 36,* 24–30.

Rowlett, J. (1964). What research has to say for industrial education: Improving teaching. *Journal of Industrial Teacher Education, 11*(3), 20–30.

Salas, E., & Cannon-Bowers, J. A. (1996). Methods, tools, and strategies for team training. In M. A. Quiñones & A. Ehrenstein (Eds.), *Training for a rapidly changing workplace* (pp. 249–279). Washington, DC: American Psychological Association.

Salomon, G. (Ed.). (1997). *Distributed cognitions.* Cambridge, UK: Cambridge University Press.

Salomon, G., & Perkins, D. (1989). Rocky road to transfer: Rethinking mechanisms of a neglected phenomenon. *Educational Psychologist, 24,* 113–142.

Satchwell, R. (1997). Using functional flow diagrams to enhance technical systems understanding. *Journal of Industrial Teacher Education, 34,* 50–81.

Satchwell, R., & Johnson, S (1992). *The effect of conceptual diagrams on technical systems understanding of apprenticeship aircraft maintenance mechanics.* Berkeley, CA: National Center for Research in Vocational Education, University of California at Berkeley.

Schmidt, J., Finch, C., & Faulkner, S. (1995). The roles of teachers. In W. N. Grubb (Ed.), *Education through occupations in American high schools: Vol. II. The challenges of implementing curriculum integration* (pp. 82–191). New York: Teachers College Press.

Schneider, D. (1996). *Lernbüroarbeit zwischen Anspruch und Realität—Untersuchung zur Theorie und Praxis der Lernbüroarbeit an kaufmännischen Schulen unter fachdidaktischem Aspekt* [Working and learning in office learning centers between demand and reality]. Göttingen: Seminar für Wirtschaftspädagogik der Georg-August-Universität.

Schunck, A. (1993). *Subjektive Theorien von Berufsfachschülern zu einem planspielgestützten Betriebswirtschaftslehre-Unterricht* [Students' subjective theories about simulation game-based instruction in commercial full-time schools]. Göttingen: Seminar für Wirtschaftspädagogik der Georg-August-Universität.

Scott, M., & Buffer, J. (1983). The effects of visual-spatial and integrative instructional methodologies on the psychomotor achievement of male and female college students. *Journal of Industrial Teacher Education, 21,* 37–46.

Scribner, S. (1984). Vygotsky's use of history. In J. V. Wertsch (Ed.), *Culture, communication, and cognition: Vygotskyan perspectives.* Cambridge, UK: Cambridge University Press.

Secretary's Commission on Achieving Necessary Skills (SCANS). (1991). *What work requires of schools: A SCANS report for America 2000.* Washington, DC: U.S. Department of Labor.

Secretary's Commission on Achieving Necessary Skills (SCANS). (1992). *Learning a living: A SCANS report for America 2000.* Washington, DC: U.S. Department of Labor.

Seddon, T. (1994). Reconstructing social democratic education in Australia: Versions of vocationalism. *Journal of Curriculum Studies, 26,* 63–82.

Senker, P. (1996). The development and implementation of National Vocational Qualifications: An engineering case study. *New Technology, Work, and Employment, 11,* 83–95.

Shor, I. (1988a). *Critical teaching and everyday life.* Chicago: University of Chicago Press.

Shor, I. (1988b). Working hands and critical minds: A Paulo Freire model for job training. *Journal of Education, 170,* 103–121.

Shulman, L. S. (1986). Paradigms and research programs in the study of teaching: A contemporary perspective. In M. C. Wittrock (Ed.), *Handbook of research and teaching* (3rd ed., pp. 3–36). New York: Macmillan.

Simon, R. I., Dippo, D., & Schenke, A. (1987). What schools can do: Designing programs for work education that challenge the wisdom of experience. *Journal of Education, 169,* 101–116.

Simon, R. I., Dippo, D., & Schenke, A. (1991). *Learning work: A critical pedagogy of work education.* New York: Bergin & Garvey.

Smith, J., & Douglas, L. (1997). *Surveying the mathematical demands of manufacturing work: Lessons for educators from the automotive industry.* Paper presented at the annual meeting of the American Educational Research Association, Chicago.

Sommer, K.-H., & Fix, W. (1988). Juniorenfirmen als betriebspädagogisches Forschungsobjekt [Research on junior firms]. In M. Becker & U. Pleiss (Eds.), *Wirtschaftspädagogik im Spektrum ihrer Problemstellung* [Research scope of vocational education] (pp. 280–294). Baltmannsweiler: Pädagogischer Verlag Burgbücherei Schneider.

Soskice, D. (1994). Reconciling markets and institutions: The German apprenticeship system. In L. Lynch (Ed.), *Training and the private sector: International comparisons* (pp. 25–60). Chicago: University of Chicago Press.

Spikes, W. F. (1995a). Preparing workplace learning professionals. In W. F. Spikes (Ed.), *Workplace learning* (pp. 55–62). San Francisco: Jossey-Bass.

Spikes, W. F. (Ed.). (1995b). *Workplace learning.* San Francisco: Jossey-Bass.

Spours, K. (1995). *The strengths and weaknesses of GNVQ's: Principles of design* (Working paper 3). London: University of London, Institute of Education, Post-16 Education Centre.

Stark, R., Gruber, H., Graf, M., Renkl, A., & Mandl, H. (1996). Komplexes Lernen in der kaufmännischen Erstausbildung: Kognitive und motivationale Aspekte [Complex learning in basic business training: Cognitive and motivational aspects]. In K. Beck & H. Heid (Eds.), *Lehr-Lern-Prozesse in der kaufmännischen Erstausbildung* [Teaching-learning processes in business and commercial education] (pp. 23–36). Stuttgart: Steiner.

Stasz, C. (1998). Generic skills at work: Implications for occupationally oriented education. In W. J. Nijhof & J. N. Streumer (Eds.), *Key qualifications in work and education* (pp. 187–206). Dordrecht, The Netherlands: Kluwer.

Stasz, C., & Brewer, D. (1998). Work-based learning: Student perspectives on quality and links to schools. *Educational Evaluation and Policy Analysis, 20*(1), 31–46.

Stasz, C., & Kaganoff, T. (1997). *Learning how to learn at work: Lessons from three high school programs* (Report No. MDS-916). Berkeley, CA: National Center for Research in Vocational Education, University of California at Berkeley.

Stasz, C., Kaganoff, T., & Eden, R. (1994). Integrating academic and vocational education: A review of the literature, 1987–1992. *Journal of Vocational Education Research, 19*(2), 25–72.

Stasz, C., Ramsey, K., Eden, R., DaVanzo, J., Farris, H., & Lewis, M. (1993). *Classrooms that work: Teaching generic skills in academic and vocational settings.* Berkeley, CA: National Center for Research in Vocational Education, University of California at Berkeley.

Stasz, C., Ramsey, K., Eden, R., Melamid, E., & Kaganoff, T. (1996). *Workplace skills in practice.* Berkeley, CA: National Center for Research in Vocational Education, University of California at Berkeley.

Stecher, B., Rahn, M., Ruby, A., Alt, M., & Robyn, A. (1997). *Using alternative assessments in vocational education.* Santa Monica: RAND Corporation.

Steen, L. (1997). Preface: The new literacy. In L. Steen (Ed.), *Why numbers count: Quantitative literacy for tomorrow's America.* New York: College Entrance Examination Board.

Stern, D., Stone, J., Hopkins, C., McMillion, M., & Crain, R. (1994). *School-based enterprise: Productive learning in American high schools.* San Francisco: Jossey-Bass.

Stern, D., Finkelstein, N., Stone, J., Latting, J., & Dornsife, C. (1995). *School-to-work: Research on programs in the United States.* Bristol, PA: Falmer.

Stern, D., Finkelstein, N., Urquiola, M., & Cagampang, H. (1997). What difference does it make if school and work are connected? Evidence on co-operative education in the United States. *Economics of Education Review, 16,* 213–230.

Stern, D., Raby, M., & Dayton, C. (1992). *Career academies: Partnerships for reconstructing American high schools.* San Francisco: Jossey-Bass.

Stevenson, J. (1993). Competency-based training in Australia: An analysis of assumptions. *Australian and New Zealand Journal of Vocational Education Research, 1,* 87–204.

Stevenson, J. (1994). Vocational expertise. In J. Stevenson (Ed.), *Cognition at work: The development of vocational expertise* (pp. 217–243). Australia: National Centre for Vocational Research.

Stevenson, J. (1996a). *Learning in the workplace: Tourism and hospitality.* Queensland, Australia: Griffith University, Centre for Skill Formation Research and Development.

Stevenson, J. (1996b). The metamorphosis of the construction of competence. *Studies in Continuing Education, 18,* 24–42.

Stevenson, J. (1998). Performance of the cognitive holding power questionnaire in schools. *Learning and Instruction, 8,* 393–410.

Stevenson, J., & Brown, I. (1994). Australian TAFE assessment practices: Confusing relevance and responsiveness. *Australian Journal of Education, 38,* 118–138.

Stevenson, J., McKavanaugh, C., & Middleton, H. (1996). The transfer of emergency driving knowledge. *Australian Vocational Education Review, 3,* 35–45.

Stodolsky, S. (1988). *The subject matters: Classroom activity in math and social studies.* Chicago: University of Chicago Press.

Straka, G., Nenniger, P., Spevacek, G., & Wosnitza, M. (1996). Motiviertes selbstgesteuertes Lernen in der kaufmännischen Erstausbildung—Entwicklung und Validierung eines Zwei-Schalen-Modells [Motivated self-directed learning for primary business training—Developing and validating a two-shells model]. In K. Beck & H. Heid (Eds.), *Lehr-Lern-Prozesse in der kaufmännischen Erstausbildung* [Teaching-learning processes in business and commercial education] (pp. 150–162). Stuttgart: Steiner.

Stratmann, K. (1967). *Die Krise der Berufserziehung im 18. Jahrhundert als Ursprungsfeld pädagogischen Denkens* [The crisis of vocational education in the 18th century as the origin of pedagogical reasoning]. Ratingen: Henn.

Stratmann, K., & Schlösser, M. (1990). *Das Duale System der Berufsbildung* [The dual system of vocational education and training] (2nd ed.). Frankfurt am Main: G.A.F.B.

Streufert, S., Nogami, G. Y., & Breuer, K. (1998). *Managerial assessment in training.* Toronto: Hogrefe.

Tenberg, R. (1997). *Schülerurteile und Verlaufsuntersuchung über einen handlungsorientierten Metalltechnikunterricht* [Studies on action-oriented instruction in the field of metalworking]. Frankfurt am Main: Lang.

Tharp, R., & Gallimore, R. (1988). *Rousing minds to life: Teaching, learning, and schooling in social context.* New York: Cambridge University Press.

Thomson, P. (1990). Problem-solving and the transfer of skills. *Australian Journal of TAFE Research and Development, 6,* 66–77.

Toohey, S., Ryan, G., McLean, J., & Hughes, C. (1995). Assessing competency-based education and training: A literature review. *Australian and New Zealand Journal of Vocational Education Research, 3*(2), 86–117.

Tramm, T. (1997). *Lernprozesse in der Übungsfirma* [Learning processes in training firms]. Habilitation thesis. Göttingen: Georg-August Universität, Faculty of Economy and Business Studies.

Tuijnman, A. C. (Ed.). (1996). *International encyclopedia of adult education and training* (2nd ed.). Oxford, UK: Pergamon.

Urquiola, M., Stern, D., Horn, I., Dornsife, C., Chi, B., Williams, L., Merit, D., Hughes, K., & Bailey, T. (1997). *School to work, college and career: A review of policy, practice, and results, 1983–1993* (Report No. MDS-1144). Berkeley, CA: National Center for Research in Vocational Education, University of California at Berkeley.

Warnat, W. I. (1994). Tech prep education: An American innovation—linking high schools and community colleges. In Organisation for Economic Co-Operation and Development, *Vocational education and training for youth: Towards coherent policy and practice* (pp. 27–40). Paris: OECD.

Weber, J. M., & Puleo, N. F. (1988). A comparison of the instructional approaches used in secondary vocational and nonvocational classrooms. *Journal of Vocational Education Research, 3*(4), 49–70.

Weber, S. (1994a). Evaluation of knowledge structures by procedures of networking—in the context of commercial education. In D. Redman (Ed.), *AERA vocational education special interest group: Proceedings* (pp. 282–300). AERA Annual Meeting, New Orleans. Baton Rouge: Louisiana State University.

Weber, S. (1994b). *Vorwissen in der betriebswirtschaftlichen Ausbildung* [The role of prior knowledge within business studies]. Wiesbaden: Gabler.

Wehle, G. (1964). *Praxis und Theorie im Lebenswerk Georg Kerschensteiners* [Practice and theory in the work of Georg Kerschensteiner] (2nd ed.). Weinheim: Beltz.

Weniger, E. (1994). Zur Geistesgeschichte und Soziologie der pädagogischen Fragestellung [History and sociology of educational theory]. In H. Röhrs (Ed.), *Erziehungswissenschaft und Erziehungswirklichkeit* [Educational theory and practice] (pp. 346–373). Frankfurt am Main: Akademische Verlagsgesellschaft. (Original work published 1936).

Westbury, I., Hopmann, S., & Riquarts, K. (Eds.). (1999). *Teaching as a reflective practice: The German didaktik tradition.* Mahwah, NJ: Lawrence Erlbaum Associates.

Whitehead, D. J. (Ed.). (1984). *Handbook for economics teachers* (3rd ed.). London: Heinemann Educational Books.

Wild, K.-P., & Krapp, A. (1996). Lernmotivation in der kaufmännischen Erstausbildung [Learning motivation in primary vocational education]. In K. Beck & H. Heid (Eds.), *Lehr-Lern-Prozesse in der kaufmännischen Erstausbildung* [Teaching-learning processes in business and commercial education] (pp. 90–107). Stuttgart: Steiner.

Wilhelm, T. (1957). *Die Pädagogik Kerschensteiners* [The pedagogy of Kerschensteiner]. Stuttgart: Metzler, Poeschel.

Wilkerson, L. (1996). Tutors and small groups in problem-based learning: Lessons from the literature. *New Directions for Teaching and Learning, 68,* 23–32.

Wilson, D. (1990). Reform of technical-vocational education. *La Education, 197*(III), 77–115.

Wolf, A. (Ed.). (1993). *Parity of esteem: Can vocational awards ever achieve high status?* London: University of London, International Centre for Research on Assessment, Institute of Education.

Woods, D. (1996). Problem-based learning for large classes in chemical engineering. *New Directions for Teaching and Learning, 68,* 91–99.

World Bank. (1991). *Vocational and technical education and training.* A World Bank Policy Paper. Washington, DC: Author.

Worthen, H. (1997). *A comparison of literacy practices in occupational/technical and academic/liberal arts classrooms in community colleges.* Unpublished doctoral dissertation, University of California, Berkeley, CA.

Worthington, R. M. (1984). *Vocational education in the United States—Retrospect and prospect* (Occasional Paper No. 101). Columbus, OH: National Center for Research in Vocational Education, Ohio State University.

Zielke, D., & Popp, J. (1997). *Ganz individuell? Empirische Studien zur Individualisierung und Binnendifferenzierung in der betrieblichen Berufsausbildung* [Totally individual? Empirical studies on individualization and differentiation within entrepreneurial training]. Bielefeld: Bertelsmann.

Part 4
The Learner

33.

Consider the Difference: Teaching and Learning in Culturally Rich Schools

Mary E. Dilworth
American Association of Colleges for Teacher Education

Carlton E. Brown
Savannah State University

Teaching and learning as they occur in this nation's public schools are influenced by the socioeconomic, cultural, and political conditions that establish and support the public schools. Who is taught, what is taught, how it is taught, and by whom it is taught are governed in varying degrees by the temperament of the community at large. What we find today are societal dispositions and debates that seem to counter what teachers have come to understand as their mission. Specifically, there is a diminishment of the common purpose and agenda of public schools, that is, to educate all children well. As a consequence, there also is a growing disillusionment among practitioners of their ability to attain this goal. Simultaneously, the research has provided an increasingly rich repository of knowledge on teaching and learning that, if supported by public policy, embraced by teachers, and understood by students, shows great promise in the achievement of the nation's students.

Throughout the United States, the issues of race, culture, gender, and class are growing more complex and insidious. This complexity and insidiousness rings particularly loudly in the lives of children. It is, in fact, in the lives and experiences of children that the future of American diversity is fashioned. While we may debate the effect of events on the lives of adults and in the fortunes of the economy and political events; what happens to children fashions the views and experiences of the next generation of adults. Poor schooling opportunities, inadequate access to knowledge, inaccessible postsecondary educational opportunities, learnings about life chances, and viewpoints about the relative importance of effort determine the kind, disposition, and capability of the next generation of

adults (Kunjufu, 1984; Nieto, 1994; Oakes & Lipton, 1990). Thus, while children exhibit remarkable resiliency to the effect of schooling and other societal agencies; institutions and other agencies also exhibit a remarkable capacity to affect the lives of children in multiple and often very profound ways. It is a formidable task for the nation as a whole and educators specifically to shift the balance and delivery of education and services to include in a greater way groups that are currently disenfranchised.

In this chapter we begin by describing the racial-ethnic, linguistic, and socioeconomic diversity of the nation and its school population within the context of the emerging trends of societal conservatism and racism. In doing this, we hope to advance an understanding of how difference is too often perceived and addressed as a liability rather than as an asset. We further describe societal conditions external to the PK-12 school structure that, together with internal policies and practices, works against notions such as equal educational opportunity and that challenges the popular adage that "all children can learn." We go on to describe the school condition, that is, the variations in educational access, resources, and programmatic thrusts that influence the extent to which students from varying backgrounds are educated well. Issues of tracking, curriculum standards, and school reform initiatives are just a few of the factors that influence the opportunity of students to learn and to gain access to high-quality education. We then attempt to explain how students perceive the inequities that confront them in school and society and speak of the influence of practitioners' perceptions of difference on student learning. Finally, we go on to describe

---

The authors wish to thank Sonia Nieta of the University of Massachusetts, Amherst, for her thorough and helpful comments on drafts of this chapter.

various approaches that have been deemed appropriate in the research as good and essential learning styles and teaching practices for diverse learners and to describe the attributes and characteristics of teachers who, the research suggests, are culturally responsive.

Education and Diversity in Societal Context

Much attention has been devoted to the increasing diversity of American society and to how it will affect education, business, industry, health, and housing—virtually every segment of American life. As African-American; Hispanic, Asian- and Pacific-American; and Native-American populations increase, the White population decreases. This surge in racial, ethnic, and linguistic diversity is particularly apparent among school-age children. By the turn of the century, the White proportion of the population is projected to be less than 72%, with approximately 13% of African-American, 11% of Hispanic, 4% of Asian and Pacific-Islander, and less than 1% of Native American origin.[1] Estimates are that children of color will eclipse the number of children of Caucasian ancestry before the middle of the next century. These realities intensify the issues of race and culture in schooling in the United States, as they suggest securing and sharing a greater variety of educational resources for broader consumption.

A significant contribution to the nation's racial, ethnic, and linguistic diversity is immigration. Almost one-third of the current population growth is caused by net immigration. By 2000, the nation's population is projected to be 8 million larger than it would have been if there were no net immigration after July 1, 1992 (Cheeseman Day, 1995). A stark example may be found in the New York City Public Schools. In 1992, roughly 65,000 elementary school students were immigrants. While some 19% came from Mexico and from South and Central America, and an additional 42% came from islands in the Caribbean, 12% of the students came from Eastern European countries and 18% came from Asian countries such as China (Edwards, 1995). These data reveal that, while the turn of the century immigrants were overwhelmingly European, the largest concentrations of new immigrants to New York City come from the Caribbean basin, Latin America, and East Asia (Edwards, 1995, p. 73). Increasing immigration raises many issues for schools and educators, including, but not limited to, language differences, contexts for parent and community engagement, curriculum styles, learning, and diversity's value.

The debate among scholars persists regarding the school experiences and temperament of immigrant minorities and of those who are primarily African Americans whose ancestors came to the country involuntarily (Gibson & Ogbu, 1991). Yet, as Fuchs (1995) noted,

Universality in immigration policy is possible in the United States only because Americans are united by the principle of individual rights—rather than group rights—embodied in the 1st and 14th Amendments to the Constitution. Principles of individual rights enable Americans from dozens of different ancestral backgrounds to participate in a system of voluntary pluralism that allows them, if they choose, to carry forward in new and old ways important aspects of their ancestral cultures while participating in a civic culture that defines their shared American identity. (p. 293)

Fuchs further notes that the inclusive approach that prevailed with respect to Europeans throughout the 19th and in the early 20th centuries was never intended for newcomers of color. This being the case, we should not be surprised at the continuing resistance of Whites to others.

In addition to the increasing diversity brought about by immigration, other factors serve to increase and give the appearance of diversity. For instance, over the past 2 decades, the number of interracial marriages has escalated from 953,000 in 1989 to more than 1.3 million in 1998. The consequent mixed-race births have multiplied 26 times as fast as any other ethnic group's birthrate. Approximately 41% of all U.S. public schools report that they have students for whom the five standard federal categories of racial/ethnic origin are not accurately descriptive (Carey & Farris, 1996; U.S. Bureau of the Census, 1999).

As Takaki (1997) noted in a symposium on ethnicity and education,

[F]or the 2000 census there's a new group emerging now called multiracial. They say, 'Wait a minute; I'm not Black and I'm not White; I'm both. And for me to claim one or the other would be to deny one of my parents.' And I think this is kind of a fascinating devolvement in terms of deconstructing race. (p. 179)

As Nieto (1997) stated in the same symposium, "I see ethnicity as a step away from understanding the world in Black and White, a step closer to the real-life complexity of identity" (p. 176).

Religion also has implications for diversity in schools. Once a nation of Christians and Jews, the United States now has in-

---

[1] By 2050, the proportional shares shift quite dramatically, with less than 53% of White, 16% of Black, 23% of Hispanic origin 10% of Asian and Pacific Islander, and about 1% of American Indian, Eskimo, and Aleut origin. (Cheeseman Day, 1995, p. 2). Whites, the slowest-growing group, are likely to contribute less and less to the total population growth in this country. Although they make up almost 75% of the total population, they will contribute only 35% of the total population growth between 1990 and 2000. This percentage of growth will decrease to 23% between 2000 and 2010, and 14% from 2010 to 2030. Then the White population will contribute nothing to population growth after 2030, because it will be declining in size. It is further speculated that the Black population will increase almost 5 million by 2000, almost 10 million by 2010, and over 20 million by 2030. The African-American population will double its present size to 62 million by 2050. The fastest growing race group will continue to be the Asian and Pacific Islander population, with annual growth rates that may exceed 4% during the 1990s. By the turn of the century, the Asian and Pacific Islander population would expand to over 12 million, double its current size by 2010, triple by 2020. It will increase to more than 5 times its current size, to 41 million, by 2050. Growth of the Hispanic-origin population will probably be a major element of the total population growth. The Hispanic-origin population would be the largest growing group. By 2000, the Hispanic-origin population may increase to 31 million, double its 1990 size by 2015, and quadruple its 1990 size by the middle of the next century. In fact, the Hispanic-origin population will have contributed 32% percent of the nation's population growth from 1990 to 2000, 39% from 2000 to 2010, 45% from 2010 to 2030, and 60% from 2030 to 2050 (Cheeseman Day, 1995).

creasing numbers of youngsters from African-American and other backgrounds who are Muslim. The perceptions and accompanying approaches to learning for individuals with this background must be taken into consideration in teaching and learning as well (Lincoln, 1989; Parker-Jenkins, 1995).

Language is a key link in understanding the culture of students, their community, and, more importantly, their "ways of knowing" or learning. Educators in many localities, including Lowell, Massachusetts; DeKalb County, Georgia; and Fairfax County, Virginia, now are responsible for teaching children with limited or no English-language capacity in classrooms that include students who speak as many as 25 separate languages or more. More than 100 languages are spoken in the school systems of New York City, Chicago, Los Angeles, and Fairfax County (McDonnell & Hill, 1993). Also, teachers are continually challenged to place this language diversity into context. For instance, while 73% of Asian- and Pacific-American students and 76% of Hispanic students come from bilingual homes, only 27% and 39% of any of their teachers, respectively, understand them to be language-minority students. Frequently, teachers are unaware that a second language is spoken in a language-minority student's home, and, thus, they define these students as nonlanguage minority (Bradby, 1992).

An added and significant aspect to racial-ethnic and language diversity is socioeconomic status. It is an intervening factor that influences learning at all levels. Much has been written to substantiate and describe the conditions of youngsters in poverty (Finlay, 1996; Gonzalez, 1993; Knapp, 1995; Kozol, 1991; Shields, 1995). For instance, poor children are more likely to be sick and underweight as toddlers, are less likely to be ready for kindergarten, are more likely to fall behind as grade schoolers, and face a higher prospect of dropping out of high school (*Kids Count Data Book,* 1996, p. 5). At the same time, significant numbers of youngsters are from working, poor families. Specifically, 62% of poor children lived with at least one parent or relative who worked part time or full time. Actually, between the late 1970s and the early 1990s, the young child poverty rate grew at a far greater pace in the suburbs (59%) than in the cities (34%) (National Center for Children in Poverty, 1996–97). "Like the children of welfare families, the children of the working poor are less likely to be fully immunized, less likely to enter school ready to learn; and far more likely to experience academic failure and to drop out" (*Kids Count Data Book,* p. 6).

Thus, it becomes more and more likely that communities and school systems throughout the nation will be confronted with the realities of diversity of student race, culture, language, and social class and will be confronted with diversity in a larger number of combinations. This new profile of the nation's school students offers a new vitality to the breadth of knowledge and ideas that will help frame the nation as a whole as students enter society as thinking and working adults. At the same time, it challenges the skills, knowledge, and processes that currently exist to be more flexible without compromising high standards for achievement. This will require both new paradigms in the structure of schools and informed and culturally sensitive educators trained in a manner that will viably orchestrate the learning of children from various backgrounds.

While the increasing diversity of the nation's population rightly occupies a major heading on the education reform agenda, factors of intergroup tensions rarely emerge. Aronowitz (1997) contributed to understanding this phenomena by noting,

> [A]lthough the American ideology seems unshaken—most still believe they can "make it" if they really try—political scientists and sociologists claim people have increasingly discovered that their economic and political interest, as well as their cultural sentiments, may be expressed through the formation of ethnic blocs rather than through class affiliation. (p.195)

At the same time, a failed assumption exists that there is a homogeneity of thinking—attitudes and preferences that polarize Whites and "others"—and that "others" reside in a comfort zone between and among themselves. Reality clearly indicates that this is not the case. For instance, the divergence of the views of prominent African Americans W. E. B. Du Bois and Booker T. Washington at the beginning of this century that focused on the most propitious approach to the higher education of the "Negro" is a historical case in point (Washington, 1969, Du Bois, 1969).[2] Similarly, recent conflicts between the National Association for the Advancement of Colored People and the leadership of the Nation of Islam and the debates within Hispanic communities over the issues of language and bilingualism exemplify intragroup as well as intergroup tensions.

Perhaps the best known and most revealing of the manifestations of this debate is captured in the work of those who would claim a central and necessary American culture in the protection of the literary canon and the positing of multiculturalism as a detriment to the American intellect. Minority intellects and communities have themselves debated the realities of the condition of race and culture in America and of its meaning and appropriate resolve. Witness the suggestion of the end of racism by Thomas Sowell (1983, 1990) and Dinesh D'Souza's (1991) impassioned argument against affirmative action. Some African-American politicians, activists, and scholars continue to press for Afrocentrism in the affairs of the African-American community and in school curricula and activities (Gordon, 1993; Kunjufu, 1984; Murrell, 1993), while others are confident in what is understood to be basic, yet traditional curriculum (Collins & Tamarkin, 1990).

The debates within the African-American community are not different fundamentally from the differences between generations characterizing the views of Japanese Americans at an earlier point in history (Kitano, 1976). The Japanese in America have been touted as a largely adaptive culture in their response

---

[2] The debate between Booker T. Washington, founder and president of Tuskegee Institute, an African-American college, and W. E. B. Du Bois, one of the founders of the National Association for the Advancement of Colored People focused on the issue of the type of education the would be best for the then newly emancipated African Americans in this country. Washington contended that preparation should focus on skills and trades that would be useful in securing jobs, while Du Bois contended that the race would be advantaged by focusing on traditional academic knowledge and skills.

to life in the United States. Their adaptation to the values, goals, and public behaviors of the majority group have clearly played a role in the economic successes experienced by many Japanese Americans. Yet, members of different generations debate the question of the relative importance of maintaining or not maintaining a distinctive community and culture in the press for full participation in the society as well as the question of self-definition.[3]

The Mexican-American population experiences similar internal conflicts over relations with the larger "Anglo" world. Many Mexican Americans define themselves as American and may even be opposed to many of the open doors for illegal and legal immigration from Mexico. At an opposite extreme are those who view themselves in concert with the history of the Mexicans and therefore who perceive restrictions on immigration as a continuation of the racism, bias, and doctrines that led to the appropriation of the Mexican territories of Texas and California (Bartolome & Macedo, 1997). Still others take a cultural view and seek the maintenance and extension of a distinct Hispanic culture. The Mexican-American community also holds divergent viewpoints on the issue of bilingualism in education. Some hold that all education should be bilingual, others that bilingual education should be transitional, because—ultimately—all citizens must work in an English-speaking environment. Yet others argue that, given the size of the Hispanic population in the United States, the nation itself should become bilingual. These proponents cite many nations of the world that are successfully bilingual and even multilingual. Thus, while racial, ethnic, and linguistic diversity are frequently grouped together when considering issues of teaching and learning, they ought not be. Issues of immigration and intragroup-intergroup politics as well as socioeconomic conditions compel us to look at these issue with stronger and broader lens.

Issues of Race and Class

Since the late 1970s, increasing conservatism and backlash against the Civil Rights movement and affirmative action have steadily generated reactive views of America's diversity. Recent movements to eliminate affirmative action, race-based college scholarships, and majority-minority voting districts may be symptoms of a larger movement to deny the need of attention to race, class, and gender. The move to relativize cultural and racial symbols is also symptomatic. The 1996 Republican primary presidential candidate Patrick Buchanan suggested in South Carolina that "Dixie" and "We Shall Overcome" are equally meaningful in a democracy. The Commonwealth of Virginia has established the state holiday Lee-King-Jackson Day—a simultaneous honoring of the lead military general and the president of the Confederacy along with Martin Luther King, Jr.

Recent debates on political correctness and the multicultural

language codes are symptomatic of a nation attempting to hold to its meager cement in the face of increasing division. As concerns the political correctness debate, even the terminology "political correctness" trivializes the issues of diversity into a debate about speech codes as opposed to a debate about key national issues. Bartolome and Macedo (1997), in their analysis of mass media and recent news events, offered a compelling case of categorizing "language as racism" in a broader context. They stated, "As educators, we need to understand fully the interrelationship between symbolic violence produced through language and the essence of racism" (p. 225). In their view,

> [L]anguage not only produces cultural and social inequalities, but is also used by the dominant White ideology to distort and falsify realities. Take the proposition "school choice," which creates the illusion that all parents can equally exercise their democratic right to choose the "best schools for their children." In reality, "The illusion of choice also creates a pedagogy of entrapment that makes it undemocractic to argue against school choice." Thus school choice becomes part of a discourse the brooks no dissension or argument, for to argue against it is to deny democracy. (p. 233)

Many scholars have made compelling cases that racism continues to exist in American society (Bell, 1992; Brooks, 1990; Chavez-Chavez, 1995; Essed, 1991; West, 1993). Bartolome and Macedo (1997) posited, ". . . the racism and xenophobia we are witnessing in our society today are not isolated acts of individuals on the fringe" (p. 232). While the relative effect of personal-cultural racism and structural-political racism in the formula may have changed, only a handful of questioned scholars deny the existence of racism in the latter part of the 20th century (Perry & Fraser, 1993). The evidence that racism continues to exist and continues to affect the lives of members of the African-American, Hispanic, Asian-American, and Native-American communities can be seen in the continuing and growing income gaps between Whites and members of most racial and ethnic minority groups. Even where education can be held constant, the comparability between the income of White high school graduates and of Black and Hispanic college graduates, the growing relegation of non-Whites to the lower wage service sectors of the economy, and the increasing proportion of minority children living in poverty persists (Finlay, 1996).

The reality of race in America is pervasive to all students. Murrell (1997) aptly stated:

> Because the representations of race, gender, social class, and role in the social contexts of schooling deeply affect how children and adults think and act, a critical epistemology of schooling must make explicit what those representations are and how they may need to be pedagogically reconstructed in the school culture. It is an epistemology of schooling that pays careful attention to the social world of children while at the same time valuing deep critique and plain talk. (p. 55)

---

[3] Yet, the manner and extent to which various segments of this community have adapted remains an issue among members of this group. The Issei, the older generation, were largely adaptive, yet maintained significant elements of Japanese culture. The Nisei, while they have remained largely connected to and responsive to the Japanese community, have acculturated significantly. The Sansei by contrast are significantly adaptive (Kitano, 1976). While later writers, notably Suzuki, have taken issue with these clear distinctions, their works can be read as a disagreement more with the impression that earlier writers left of a very uniform response and with their omission of the continuing large groups of Asian poor.

Notwithstanding the debate even among African-American scholars about whether or not race continues to be a useful factor in the assessment of the issues affecting minority groups, some scholars have contended that the answer may be found within the intersections of race and class. As stated by Brooks (1990), "Certain societal hardships within [each] socioeconomic classes are manifested along racial [ethnic] lines, creating racial inequalities that form today's race problem" (p. 9). Still others (Pollard, 1996; Pollard & Avery, 1993) have suggested there continues to be a compelling interplay among race, gender, and class. Racism (as well as cultural bias) is an everyday reality and, therefore, is an everyday experience (Essed, 1991). Racism can show itself in the daily experiences of youths in a variety of ways. These experiences include rousting by police whenever a small group of minority youths congregates; close monitoring by store clerks; restrictions on entry by youths by one mall in a city frequented largely by minority youths, while another mall frequented by White youths does not institute these restrictions; targeting by guidance counselors of minority youths to community colleges and White youths to major institutions; and questioning of minority youths upon entry to an advanced placement class, while the entry of White youths is not questioned.

Legal race barriers were largely removed during the 1950–1980 period (Lee, 1984). Many legal supports to racism buttressed the several forms of economic, political and social discrimination that have always characterized American society. Removal of these barriers, it should be noted, removes neither other forms of structural racism nor the residual effects of a history of legalized racism. Additional supports to protect civil and human rights were invented in the forms of voting rights and affirmative-action protections (Smith, 1992). In the 1990s, we are witnessing the systematic erosion of these safeguards through the removal of affirmative-action legislation and majority-minority voting districts as well as the rolling back of court-ordered school desegregation. It should, thus, be noted that the power, viability, and hope experienced by many young members of minority groups in the 1960s and 1970s is not available to the minority youths of today.

The power and viability felt by young members of minority groups in the 1990s varies substantially by the social class origins and situation of parents. It may also be noted here that the aftermath of the Civil Rights movement has led to a distinct residential and lifestyle separation between the African-American and Hispanic lower classes and middle classes (Wilson, 1987). Thus, the identifiable models of success and behavior for achieving economic and lifestyle success in the terms of the larger society are no longer available to the lower socioeconomic classes. As a consequence, Goodlad (1990a) stated, "[T]here is a growing population of children, youths, and adults who simply will not manage to take advantage of the yellow brick road to an acceptable standard of living let alone fame and fortune" (p. 4).

Many groups of Americans who were previously employable are no longer employable educationally and structurally. African-American and other women of color in lower socioeconomic classes have been most affected by this. Given the lack of access to high-quality schooling of most poor children, the significance of large proportions of any racial group living in poverty has, and will continue to have, a staggering effect on the availability of opportunity—effectively locking subsequent generations of poor minority children into a permanent underclass. Additionally, although the working poor have always been with us, their ranks are growing and they are becoming a significant part of the population. A two-class society—the haves and the have-nots—has developed. A disproportionate number of African Americans, Hispanic Americans and Native Americans have joined a significant population of White Americans at the bottom of the economic structure. In many of our cities, intergenerational poverty has given rise to generations with no known family history of employment or independence as well as very little in the way of present models of personal success (Wilson, 1987). Many such families are the end result of several generations of babies born to adolescent mothers (Finlay, 1996).

This pattern is repeated in microcosm within communities of color. It was always the middle classes that sustained the supportive institutions in the African-American community. The growth and dispersion of the middle class African-American and Hispanic communities have left congregated communities without the full extent of the socioeconomic diversity of the racial group. This situation not only erodes the ability of traditional institutions—church, school, and community organizations—to provide cohesion, hope, and progressive values, but this absence also leaves the communities caught in a devastating market economy devoid of resources and of hope (Bell, 1992; Smith, 1992). Sight should not be lost of the fact that this also means a disconnection of teachers and administrators from the community of service. The rise and prestige of the violent and destructive trade in drugs and the escalating nature of crime in the African-American and Hispanic communities result from this radical structural change in the American economy and body politic.

Schools and other institutions have not effectively carried forward the socializing function of providing minority students with a high-quality sense of racial history and culture (Kunjufu, 1984, 1986). While the church is a continuing purveyor of culture, the church does not reach many segments of the needful minority groups. Thus, disconnected from the mainstream of societal understandings and expectations, separated from the minority middle classes that often provide some sense of at least family and community history and culture, and often alienated by the mainstream and middle-class teachings of schools, lower-class youths of color fail to gain the elements of social life that create a pressure toward and an expectation of success (Garibaldi, 1988; Kuykendall, 1992; Ogbu, 1987).

Many scholars and activists in both the African-American and Hispanic-American communities have responded to these realities with a very conservative brand of racialism designed to bolster the sense of pride and imaging of self and culture. Afrocentrism and its Hispanic counterpart are, according to Cornel West (1993), well-intentioned but divisive, spinning as they do on narrow and false notions of racial and cultural authenticity (p. 10). Acceptable racial and cultural behavior in these views is very narrowly defined and ignores the class and experiential diversity within the racial and cultural communities themselves. The most negative end of this thought process is manifested among African-American youths in many localities who view striving among their peers toward academic achievement and planning for the future as "acting White," a behavior that is to be eschewed and for which ostracism is an appropriate response. Part of the concerns giving rise to Afrocentric and other ethnocentric views grows from the structure and nature of the curriculum and the very mainstream nature of most curricular and text decisions (Castenell & Pinar, 1993; Garibaldi, 1992). Yet, one of the issues of race and class and school positioning is that not all children are provided equal access to critical social and skill knowledge (Goodlad & Keating, 1990; Graff, 1995).

Similar sentiments dominate in many Native-American communities, where many young people have left to pursue education and careers only to find themselves isolated and segregated in communities far from their home communities. Many tribes grapple with rebuilding cultures and traditions that their youths have never learned or experienced. On some reservations, the expression of culture is obvious to even casual observers. Driving through the Navajo reservation, car radios pick up a station on which DJs alternate effortlessly between English and Navajo (Boyer, 1997). In the Chienle School, educational reform is evident in each class, in the constructivist curriculum, and in teacher research and reflection, and yet the building architecture is designed around Navajo spiritual principles. As Deyhle (1995) reported, the church meeting captures the solidarity of the Navajo community and the cultural vitality of its people.

John Ogbu's early work showed differing responses of school personnel to students and parents based on race and social class (1974). In his research, he found that school personnel tended to address students and parents differentially on the basis of their societal status. Middle-class White parents were viewed by school personnel more as partners in the educational enterprise, while non-White and poorer parents were viewed as clients of the system. These differing views were manifested in different treatments in parental interactions with school personnel. Similar differences were found in the expectations of school personnel for children. Average achievement was viewed as acceptable for minority and poor children and as fully unacceptable for middle-class and White children.

Pang and Sablan (1998) also promoted these understandings as they explained teachers' attitudes toward African-American students. Their work indicated that racial attitudes do affect teacher efficacy beliefs. Specifically, they found that an alarming number of White teachers feel that they can not teach African-American students and that even a teacher with good teaching abilities may not reach African-American youths. A strong underlying belief seems to prevail that the African-American community does not support education (p. 66). At the same time, some parents have limited confidence in the schools' ability to teach and nurture their children.

In a study of Latino parents, researchers found that early childhood education that is promoted by policy and professional organization groups is not fully embraced by Latino families as it has been by White middle-class and African-American families. They found that Latino families viewed issues such as the scarcity of Spanish-speaking staff members and the absence of values and child-rearing practices that they hold sacred as sufficient justification to remain home from the workforce and nurture their youngsters at home (Fuller, Eggers-

Pie'rola, Holloway, Liang, & Rambaud, 1996). As Nieto (1997) stated,

> [T]eachers, in an attempt to be so-called color blind, want to say that they don't see any differences whether they are racial or cultural. . . . At the same time, I think that students' ethnicity, their culture, among other differences, and I would certainly include social class, is consciously or unconsciously used by schools and by teachers as an explanation for either their success or lack of success in school. (p. 185)

Bartolome and Macedo (1997) argue that one of the most pressing challenges facing educators in this nation is the specter of an "ethnic and cultural war." In their view, what we need is cultural peace—to determine how schools can be brokers in this peace process, or, in other words, how educators can ". . . forge cultural unity through diversity" (p. 242).

Schools as Deterrents to Learning

Despite the best efforts of many great thinkers and strategists, this nation has been unable or unwilling to craft a system of schooling whereby all children of compulsory school age are educated to their potential. Youngsters who are poor and who live in poor neighborhoods, children who are members of racial, ethnic or linguistically diverse groups and who are exceptional in their abilities—that is, those who rapidly compose the majority of children in schools—are slated more for failure in society than they are for success. While this situation is devastating to many, the nation as a whole allows it to persist. The National Commission on Teaching and America's Future commission report, *What Matters Most: Teaching for America's Future* (1996) cited an imperative to create schools that support learning for all children. The commission reported inconsistent expectations for students and unequal financial and material resources as impediments to quality instruction. "A haphazard hodgepodge of policies has left schools without clear, compelling standards connected to the means to achieve them" (p. 9). A range of solutions in the organization of schools has been tried and tested—for example, comprehensive service models, school choice options, alternative schools, and programs that are culturally focused with each community selecting what they feel will serve their community best. In the following discussion, we will discuss factors that disenfranchise students of color and explore ways to convert them to advantage all students' achievement and learning.

The conditions of schooling impinge heavily on the issues of difference in the American classroom. Historically, schools have served less as social leaveners and equalizers and more as social-control devices (Dryfoos, 1995; Katz, 1971; Kozol, 1985; Ogbu, 1974). While the outcomes of schooling are statistically predictable on the basis of race-ethnicity and class origin of students this is not a conclusive argument that the schools play a social control function. However, as the effective schools research of the early 1980s demonstrated, there are schools with identifiable characteristics in which this prediction paradigm does not hold (Edmonds, 1979; Lezotte & Bancroft, 1985).

As Greeley and Mizell (1993) posited, "Schools play a central role in perpetuating institutional racism and, likewise can play an equal role in combating it." And they continued, "When a school begins to engage in the process of multicultural, antiracist change, the expectations of all faculty, parents, and children are raised" (p. 215). Yet, school personnel respond inadequately to race, issues of intergroup conflict, diverse communities, and the consequent needs of children (Education Watch, 1996; Ladson-Billings, 1994).

For instance, in referring to Ahlquist (1991), Tettegah (1996) provided that frequently White teachers may claim or admit having racist attitudes toward persons in the general population, but they may profess that they have different attitudes toward students in their classrooms (p. 160). It is fair to say that, while issues of race and group are predominant in the consciousness of school children, at least of early adolescent age and higher, the majority of school personnel are reluctant to engage in these issues directly and consistently with children (Kunjufu, 1984, 1989). Studies, including the early work of Kenneth Clark, have provided evidence that children of color develop racial or group identities of many kinds much earlier than do White children. The differences in the life experiences of children and their parents leads to this earlier self-identification. Although many intergroup conflicts in schools develop along racial, class, and cultural divides, they are seldom resolved within these constructs.

One possible reason for inadequate attention to these issues is the growing distance between the school, on one hand, and families and communities, on the other hand; however, physical distance brought about by busing for desegregation is only a small part of this issue. The primary issues are the apparent lack of awareness of school personnel about the conditions and events occurring in the communities from which their students arrive each morning and the policies initiated at the point of desegregation that structurally allow school personnel to disregard community and family (Blackwell, 1991; Harry, 1992; Ogbu, 1974; Phelan, Davidson, & Yu, 1993).

It is also possible that part of this lack of attention resides in a mediocre sense of care and responsibility for others. The idea that majority America does not want to care for "other people's children," that is, those of color and varying ability, is substantiated in the research. (Delpit, 1988; Noddings, 1995; Pang & Sablan, 1998; Zimpher & Ashburn, 1992). In this regard, Goodlad (1990a) posited that many of us either turn our backs on what should be central to our personal and political lives or resort to a variety of modes of denial. "One of the most dangerous of these escapes is the narrowing of our sense of community to the family, social group, or religious sect, to the degree that self-interest no longer connects with the common weal" (p. 6). Noddings (1995) helped us to understand the importance of this approach and this tendency in the learning of children, when she noted "Caring implies a continuous search for competence. . . . Personal manifestations of care are probably more important in children's lives than any particular curriculum or pattern of pedagogy" (p. 676). As they advocated caring as one factor in countering the parochialism of prospective teachers, Zimpher and Ashburn (1992) concluded that the value of a caring community for the educational setting can be argued from several perspectives. Borrowing on the research of Etzioni (1983), Peck (1986), Ouchi (1981), Noddings (1986), and others, the authors commented that there is a psychological perspec-

tive that recognizes that we are social creatures who need each other for substance and meaning in our lives, that caring contributes to development and learning by allowing for a greater level of interaction and desire to learn to emerge, and that caring enhances productivity by addressing the social organization and learning (pp. 55–56).

Indeed, caring requires that we have a firm grasp on issues of morality, but, as McMannon (1995) asked, "What do normative words like 'morality,' 'equality,' 'democracy,' or even 'education' mean when applied to schools . . . ?" (p. 45). When people speak of morality in the schools, they often mean moral instruction or enforcement of moral behavior, with the anticipated outcome being harmonious interpersonal relations and societal efficiency—at any level of society from "the classroom to the nation" (p. 45).

Aronowitz (1997) argued that "Educational leaders and politicians have tolerance for the 'other' as long as she/he recognizes the practices of the dominant group as those to which all others must strive, regardless of the path they take to achieve them. The task for society remains that of assimilating potential or actual dissent into the prescribed public sphere . . ." (p. 192). He called attention to the manner in which artists and art forms, for instance, are legitimized or assimilated into Western culture. Jazz, for example, may be classified as "classical" music, and therefore may be acceptable in the distinguished concert halls of the nation, leaving little distinction, and drawing theoretical lines and connections between, individuals like Thelonius Monk, Charlie Parker, and John Coltrane as against Stravinsky or Schoenberg.

The arguments of Bartolome and Macedo (1997) were consistent with Aronowitz in a broader context when they stated that

> Multicultural analyses should not be limited to the study of the "other" in a way that makes the White cultural group invisible and beyond study. White invisibility is achieved partly through the very language we use to structure our discourse on race and ethnicity. For example, both White and non-White racial groups use the linguistic construction "people of color" to designate non-White individuals. The hidden assumption is that White is colorless, a proposition that is semantically impossible. By pointing out that White is also a color, we can begin to interrogate the false assumptions that strip White people of their ethnicity. (pp. 232–233)

The idea of cultivating educators and others to "care" seems to pale by comparison to critical issues of academic competence and pedagogical skill. Yet research (Schaps, Lewis, & Watson, 1995) has suggested that a caring, learning community does much to contribute to a student's academic achievement and social and ethical temperament. In regard to school reform efforts, they noted, "In order to provide a heightened sense of community, schools may need to make broad and deep change—in climate, structure, curricular content, and pedagogy" (p. 5). These changes are likely "to run against some of the most pervasive practices in American education: ability-grouping, adult-imposed rules and consequences, and motivation by competition" (p. 6).

When we consider the poor and the underachievement of students, there is a tendency to blame the victim. The general notion that there are "at-risk students" suggests that the young-sters are to blame. The reality is that these students are "placed at risk" by a host of socioeconomical factors over which the nation has taken little control. It is the feeling of hopelessness, or lack of caring for others, that allows too many students to be subject to nonconstructive events. Such events include teen pregnancy, drug abuse, homelessness, death and dying by disease such as HIV/AIDS, murders, and drive-by shootings and other random acts of violence. The tendency to set blame is perpetuated by many educators who feel comfortable in their biases against the parents and backgrounds of the students (Pang & Sablan, 1998).

Access to Knowledge

The shortcomings in what we provide school-aged youngsters are hardly disguised. Many indicators of school failure reside for the most part outside of the school. At the same time, many school systems fail to recognize and to craft learning conditions that will circumvent many of these barriers. As Garbarino opined (1997), we are educating children in a socially toxic environment. In his view, the social equivalents to lead and smoke in the air and to PCBs in the water are violence, poverty, and other economic pressures on parents and on their children. He included among these pressures disruption of family relationships and related trauma, despair, depression, paranoia, nastiness, and alienation—all contaminants that demoralize families and communities.

Kozol's (1991) observations were consistent. He concluded that the public often overlooks the inequalities in education when indicting schools, students, and their teachers. He stated that "none of the national reports I saw made even passing references to inequality or segregation. Low reading scores, high dropout rates, poor motivation—symptomatic matters seem to dominate the discussion" (p. 3).

Many factors have been identified as contributing to inequities in student access to high-quality teaching and learning, not the least of which are racism, classism, and the absence of caring for others. The nation's general disposition is toward individualism, which allows for otherwise well-meaning citizens to dismiss actions in the common good for those in favor of those focusing on individual advancement (Chavez-Chavez, 1995; Noddings, 1995).

Although history provides a clear picture of human difference used as a criteria for access and the application of education, the notion that public schools exist to moderate difference and allow all citizens to be contributing members of society persists. Yet, as social institutions, public schools are shaped by the deleterious effects of poverty, family disorganization, and racial and cultural isolation. Inequality in the life chances of children growing up in different socioeconomic environments is clearly evident in the schools they attend. Children from middle-class families who live in suburban communities with stable tax bases are more likely than low-income and students in urban areas to be offered challenging and progressive curriculum that is designed to prepare them for a range of postsecondary and career options (Wong, 1994).

Since school attendance is compulsory from ages 5 to 16, the issue of access is frequently blurred. There is a sense that, if a youngster has a school to attend and there is a teacher in the classroom, educational access has been achieved. Further, the concept of access has not been truly incorporated in the research either. As Grant and Millar (1992) noted, "'access' in the classroom as it is described in the literature doesn't necessarily include with it an analysis of race, class, gender, and disability and interactions that take into account curriculum, staffing, instruction, and other schooling factions that are critical to equitable education" (p. 15).

Opportunity to learn is a concept that extends beyond access and supports the popular notion that all children can learn. It considers the school and its environment, the type of training and understanding that the educational personnel bring, and the caliber of the curriculum, as well as the pedagogical techniques and resources that are available to the child. The general temperament is that equality may only be achieved through establishing high standards for all youngsters and by providing an appropriate environment for learning.

> Within states, a new priority has to be given to strengthening those districts that serve the highest concentrations of low-income and at-risk students. Within districts, priority must be given to improving those schools that have been least effective in achieving key learning benchmarks for all of their students. And within individual schools, a greater priority has to be placed on engagement and achievement by those students most likely to fall behind and fail. (*Kids Count Data Book,* 1996, p. 9)

Winfield and Manning (1992) specified a number of factors that contribute to problems of access to knowledge. Examples of these are teachers' beliefs, which influence their notion of personal responsibility for students' learning, and personnel assignments, which reflect management decisions regarding the allocation of resources. National programs that are designed to alleviate certain of these problems are incomplete. For instance, Sumberg (1991) reporting the Committee for Education Funding noted that programs such as Title 1 of the Elementary and Secondary School Act (ESEA) ought to closely consider the growing need for compensatory education, developmental education, nutrition, and health-care programs that prepare children for school and improve their future performance (p. 3). Indeed, the most recent legislation focusing on Title 1 (ESEA) programs aims more at producing good schools than just producing good programs. The legislation allows for staff development, curriculum enrichment, and organizational improvement (Wong, 1994).

Although education is a state and local responsibility, the basic tenets of PK-12 and postsecondary education are driven and guided by the reasoning of the nation as a whole. There is a presumption that, given the firm and well-stated commitment of the federal government to provide a quality education, states and localities will formulate policies and programs that, of necessity, will respond to the cultural realities of the communities they serve. If this were the case, we would expect to see better achievement across the board for all students, but we do not see better achievement. According to Wong (1994), this ineffectiveness is more a matter of incoherent policies than it is disregard for educational equality. He contended that specifically, federal policy has focused on special-needs populations but has paid limited attention to territorial disparity within states. States' territorial strategies are designed to equalize interdistrict fiscal capacity but are largely quiescent on how state aid should be used to address the needs of disadvantaged students in declining neighborhood schools. Local distribution policies not only fail to consider differing needs among student groups within the district but, with their focus on personnel allocation, [they also] widen the gap between declining and stable neighborhood schools. (p. 282)

As Parish and Aquila (1996) suggested,

In the past 30 years, federal, state, and local and private institutions have spent in excess of $40 billion designing and implementing more effective programs for urban and other schools. The schools' successful resistance to these efforts speaks volumes about the strength of cultural ways of schooling. (p. 304)

The authors went on to detail numerous reasons why the school culture remains, by and large, minimally responsive to educational reform notions that will enhance the quality and diversity of teaching and learning. Specifically, they suggested that there are few techniques available for imposing collaboration, or accountability, on teachers and principals. In their view, school-based educators empowering the formally powerless is not viable, as teachers and principals have no wish to be free, only to be in control of difference.

Perry and Fraser (1993) concurred that disparities in the condition of school and schooling do not solely reside in the federal or national arena. They stated that the local school ". . . cannot pursue policies in opposition to the aims of the school as a national institution in a democratic society. Schools must always pursue policies that support the education of all children for citizenship in a multiracial/multicultural democracy" (p. 16). In their view, schools should offer shared authority, based on questions such as the following (p. 9): "Who should be included in the school community?" "What criteria ought be used to determine what knowledge is worth pursuing?" "How should the past be represented?" "What should the vision of the future be?" "What metaphors would be useful to capture the past?" "What narratives are most important to pass on to youths?" "Who should be teachers?" "Who should hold authority?" "How should authority be exercised?"

Some school systems and programs seek to establish this democratic and equitable learning environment. A good example of a healthy condition for teaching and learning may be found in the binational school system in Deming and Columbus, New Mexico, wherein there appears to be a symmetry among the students, parents, teachers, and school administrators that seemingly provides a nurturing learning environment within a politically charged environment. In this vicinity, students from Palomas, Mexico, have traveled daily across the U.S. border to attend public school in Columbus and Deming, New Mexico. That this community is small and homogeneous, with primarily a Latino population, suggests that sameness of mind and purpose are critical components to achieving a fair and quality learning environment (Dilworth, 1995).[4]

There are virtually no public or private school reform initiatives that completely disregard the apparent imbalance of opportunity and achievement among students, However, the manner in which they address these issues varies. Anyon (1995) provided a poignant example of an educational reform initiative gone awry. She described how sociocultural differences between reformers, parents, and teachers and between reforms and the student population converged to the disadvantage of student learning and achievement. She spoke of reformers who, in the absence of necessary familiarity and sensitivity to community and class, alienate parents; administrators of color who have internalized beliefs about their students that mimic attitudes held by the White-dominated society, who fail through fear rather than through ignorance to incorporate curriculum that is culturally sensitive; teachers of all backgrounds who are frustrated with the system and, thus, who are abusive to the students; and students who are aware of the fact that ". . . they are in a situation in school that is hostile and aggressively rejecting of them" (p. 84). She stated that ". . . the structural basis for failure in inner-city schools is political, economic, and cultural. . . . Educational reform cannot compensate for the ravages of society" (p. 88). "Foremost among the things we need to insist on is a thoroughgoing reform of public education in America; a reform that reflects a basic reordering of the nation's education priorities" (*Kids Count Data Book,* 1996). All of this suggests a reordering of educational priorities.

What we find in many communities is a strategic, yet subtle, drive to exclude and isolate students of color while using difference as the criterion in determining who should and should not a have a high-quality education. This approach flies in the face of what some authors (Garbarino, 1997; Perry & Fraser, 1993) have suggested ought to be evident in a democratic society. The most recent and evident instances of using difference as a criteria for exclusion and isolation may be found in the recent politically charged California decision of Proposition 187, which precludes undocumented immigrant youngsters from an education, and a successor ruling, Proposition 209, which essentially ended affirmative action in that state. As Bartolome and Macedo (1997) stated,

The cultural condition that led to the passage of these laws, which were designed to control the flow of illegal immigrants and to end affirmative action in California, has had the effect of licensing institutional discrimination, whereby both legal and illegal immigrants materially experience the loss of their dignity, the denial of human citizenship, and, in many cases, outright violent and criminal acts committed to those institutions responsible for implementing the law. (p. 231)

---

[4] Although this decades-old arrangement seems to have served both communities well, the current political climate that argues against the immigration of Mexican Americans threatens to dissolve it. Youngsters who were born in the United States and are American citizens by birth but who simply moved to the Mexican side of the border will no longer be able to attend school on the American side without paying the costs of their education (LaFranchi & Harbison, 1996; Pressley, 1997).

The attempts to persuade us that children of immigrants ought be deprived of educational as well as other benefits, regardless of their innocence in being in this position, presents an ethical and moral dilemma for teachers, who have indicated a sensitivity to children by selecting the teaching profession. This temperament toward the "new immigrant," many of whom are of color, suggests that these undesirable children will be treated less well than others, even if they are "legal."

Olneck (1995) elaborated on this issue in noting that

> The encounter between immigrant children, families, and communities and the schools is conditioned by local school cultures; by perceptions relevant actors hold of one another and themselves; by diverse meanings immigrants and educators assign to schooling; by tacit as well as explicit pedagogical, curricular, and administrative practices degree of discontinuity that obtains between immigrant and school cultures; and by structural characteristics and cultural practices of immigrant communities. Immigrants have availed themselves of schooling as an avenue of social mobility, but not with equal success, and often as a hedge against discrimination, not as an affirmation of equal opportunity. (p. 315)

For instance, it is not necessarily important whether or not children arrive at the schoolhouse door with standard or nonstandard language skills. However, the preparation of many teachers predisposes them to believe (and act accordingly) that students who speak no or nonstandard English will be unable to perform as well academically as those who arrive speaking standard English (Denbo, 1982). The increasing language diversity in our society as well as the increasing diversity of nonstandard English speakers creates an untenable situation for the education of children if these biases are institutionalized through both teacher training and socialization and curriculum and school-enforced instructional practices (Kuykendall, 1992). Garibaldi (1988) and Kunjufu (1984) documented many of the serious disjunctions between the cultures of students of color and the school.

A different form of inequity is evident in the national educational system's approach to special education. Lipsky and Gartner (1996) suggested that "The history of education of students with disabilities runs parallel to that of other groups in the U.S. society who have been excluded from services, such as women, students of color, and those of 'minority' religions" (p. 763). They noted that

> . . . the system of special education, and the attitudes toward disability that undergird it, have harmful consequences for both those labeled "disabled" and those not. Among those labeled, their capacity is denied and, thus, expectations of them are limited. Those not labeled are encouraged to believe that people with disabilities are limited and, thus, they are encouraged to offer sympathy toward, but not to value the participation of persons with disabilities. Neither view provides a basis for a society of inclusion and equity. (p. 767)

Special education policy and procedure are significant issues in matters of race and class in schools (Harry, 1992; Kunjufu, 1984, 1986; Kuykendall, 1992; Ogbu, 1968). The fact that, in many localities, the majority of children receiving special education referral and placement are minority-group members belies the structural placement of the special education system.

The overwhelming majority of children so referred are placed in programs for the learning disabled, behaviorally disordered, or mentally retarded (Harry, 1992). Simultaneously, in many localities, the majority of children placed in settings for the emotionally disturbed are White. Some of the discrepancy in proportional referral and placement can be placed to the phrasing of the questions of special education. If a child's difficulty is examined in light of the adequacy of curriculum, instructional strategy, and preparation, a fundamentally different set of consequent actions result than when the search for the source of difficulty is focused on the child. Most unfortunate is the fact that students of color are often found in the placement categories of special education, wherein very few students are ever reintegrated into the mainstream (Harry, 1992).

The placement of students in effectual learning categories is not limited to youngsters with exceptionalities. In some measure, access to knowledge issues are deeply intertwined with formal and informal tracking (Goodlad & Keating, 1990; Oakes & Lipton, 1990). The instruction reserved for low-achieving children is generally dry and dull and is oriented toward preparation for unskilled or semiskilled workforce entry and consumer viability, that is, personal budgeting; rudimentary mathematics; and the ability to read instructions, technical directions, and the newspaper. Conversely, the instruction preserved for above-average students focuses on the primary issues of life and nation. Thus, above-average students are likely to come to know and understand the United States Constitution, the Declaration of Independence, the deeper aspects of history, and higher-order (and exciting) science and they are led to believe that they are actors on the human stage; while below-average-achieving students come to see themselves as dependent and to act dependently and are provided no tools for an understanding of daily events (Goodlad & Keating, 1990; National Commission on Teaching and America's Future [NCTAF], 1996). Clearly, within this paradigm, the vast majority of students of color would come into little or no meaningful contact with the history and achievements of their own racial or cultural group, thus leaving them to reformulate their self-understandings not in a vacuum, but within the social contexts of school and neighborhood without benefit of historical understanding or meaning (Kunjufu, 1984).

Tracking is a key factor in deterring equal access in schools and classrooms. Given the evidence against tracking supported by a number of critical court decisions, the fact that students of color and lower socioeconomic status are disproportionately placed in lower tracks and that these tracks block access to critical citizen knowledge for democracy and development begs the question of alternatives to tracking. Many schools use assignment to higher-level college preparatory and advanced classes as rewards to more effective teachers. Further, many upper-track classes are smaller and have additional instructional resources—thus, the apparent advantage to ability grouping or tracking is often actually an advantage of resource and expectation (Oakes & Lipton, 1990).

Finally, instructional methods and materials in low-ability classes are often based on rote and repetition and are staffed with less-well-qualified teachers (NCTAF, 1996; Oakes & Lipton, 1990). By contrast, the expectation structure of high-ability classes tend to lead to a stronger focus on problem solving, creativity, real-world issues, high-interest materials, and greater teacher-to-student engagement (Oakes & Lipton, 1990; Winfield & Manning, 1992). The structure of modern life and employment requires higher-order thinking and problem-solving abilities as well as self-directed learning capabilities from all citizens. Tracking clearly bars some children from the achievement of basic societal capabilities and knowledge. Therefore, as Oakes and Lipton asserted,

> These differences in learning opportunities portray significant schooling inequities, not to mention schooling's greatest irony: Those children who need more time to learn appear to get less; those who have the most difficulty succeeding have fewer of the best teachers; those who could benefit from classrooms with the richest intellectual resources get the poorest. (p. 195)

The data indicate that tracking provides no discernible benefit to any classification of children; tracking provides significant harm to children deemed to be of low ability; and tracking provides little-to-no benefit to high-ability or high-achieving children (Oakes & Lipton, 1990). In fact, some studies suggest that students of high ability actually gain enhanced achievement in heterogeneous groups (Madden & Slavin, 1983).

Davidson (1997) described the implications of tracking in a broader context:

> At the institutional level, disciplinary technology (isolating, ordering, systematizing practices) and serious speech acts (truth claims asserted by an expert in an area) are factors that work to enact power relations, primarily through contributing to a definition of what is "normal" in advance. Both can therefore be viewed as practices that "teach, or discipline" participants to the meaning of institutional (and social) categories such as prisoner, soldier, teacher, ESL student. In school, for example, the taken-for-granted, "objective" division of students into academic tracks can be viewed as a disciplinary technology that highlights differences and disciplines students and teachers to particular conceptions about the meaning of high and low achievement in students. (p. 18)

Caring for others, a resistance to categorize others, and the inclination to engage all youngsters to and beyond their potential will allow for equal access to knowledge and learning.

Students and Teachers within the School Culture

We frequently find that the sole responsibility of teaching disenfranchised students is placed on classroom teachers. Although teachers are indeed ultimately responsible for providing knowledge, skills, and abilities to their students, they are guided and restrained by a host of factors. State and local curriculum standards, assessments, prescribed programs of teaching techniques, classroom organization, student selection, types and kinds of resources, building organization, governance, and operations all influence the quality of instruction in both positive and negative ways. These approaches must be thoroughly understood by teachers in order to guide youngsters way from the maze of dysfunctional policies toward constructive learning environments.

For many children, particularly children of color, the meaning of events taking place in classrooms pales in comparison to the power and compelling nature of events in communities and

in their lives (Kunjufu, 1984; Perry & Fraser, 1993). The voices of such students who are grappling with tensions and demands of their worlds are clear in the book titled *Our America: Life and Death on the South Side of Chicago* (Jones & Newman, 1997), which was written by three African-American high school students in the inner city of Chicago. As one of the authors, Newman, stated:

> There's no kids from around here that we know who are doing OK in school past the second or third grade. But I bet if you take anybody from Donoghue [the school] out of this environment and put them in a suburban school, boy, they're going to hear some things they never heard of and think of some theories they never thought of. If you take them out of hearing gun shots everyday—POP!POP!-POP!—if you get 'em out of Vietnam-listening everyday, every night, and every second, you're going to see a big difference. These kids around here are looking at life from the inside out and not from the outside in, 'cause if they were looking from the outside in, they would see what they're doing and know that it's wrong. (p. 43)

The cultures of diverse communities, the cultures of youths, and the culture and norms of school are often in grave conflict (Garcia & McLaughlin, 1995; Pignatelli & Pflaum, 1993). For instance, a video study completed by Holmes Group personnel in Michigan documented children's descriptions of their lives in a Midwest city and their discussions of school experiences. Children described changes that they have been forced to make in their lifestyles within their own time brought about by the increasing level of urban violence and the increasing involvement of firearms. They no longer tarried or played on the street after school. They rushed to their homes, let themselves in, and did their homework with the windows closed and shades drawn. They had parental instructions to move under the table if they heard gunfire. These same children then described social studies classes as requirements to remember certain persons and ideas about group behavior and events in world and American history. We are significantly struck by the disjunction between the very powerful and compelling social studies that they lived and the very dry and meaningless social studies, that they were forced to learn. Social studies as presented in this school was not useful in enabling children to understand their own lives.

The views of children and youths on self, race, culture, and class are particularly revealing (Essed, 1991; Kunjufu, 1984, 1986; Nieto, 1994; People for the American Way, 1992; Phelan & Davidson, 1993). A national study of youths and youth attitudes conducted by People for the American Way (1992) was quite revealing. The majority of youths surveyed concluded that the nation has done quite poorly in its handling of race relations. African-American and Hispanic-American youths tend to hold the most negative perceptions. The rhetoric against affirmative action has resulted in White youths viewing themselves as equally vulnerable economically with minority youths. Youths of color, conversely, have a sharply different view through their own group experience. The study also finds that many White youths continue to harbor negative stereotypes of non-Whites as malingering welfare recipients, largely responsible for crime and significantly involved in drugs. The study also reveals a strong similarity among all youths on basic values of family, fair treatment for all, and belief in a God (pp. 17–19).

Student voices are also heard in a recent Metropolitan Life

Survey of the American Teacher (Leitman, Binns, & Steinberg, 1996). When 7th- through 12th-grade students were asked how well they were taught to be tolerant of others, 74% felt that their teachers were doing average or below average (p. 5). Further, only one-third believed their teachers reflected the ethnic backgrounds of their students. Among African-American students, a larger proportion (39%) believed their teachers' ethnic make-up was different from their students, and only 28% said that there was a similarity in background (p. 5). As Kozol (1991) noted, we have not "been listening much to children in these recent years of 'summit conferences' on education, of severe reports and omnibus prescriptions. The voices of children, frankly, had been missing from the whole discussion" (p. 5).

This assessment is consistent with the thinking of Nieto (1994), who advocates for "developing conditions in schools that let students know that they have a right to envision other possibilities beyond those imposed by traditional barriers of race, gender, or social class" (p. 422). Gresson (1997) noted the importance that students think of themselves as part of the problem or solution. In referring to a student's concern with cliquishness, he stated, "If such students cannot see themselves as actors in class oppression in racially homogeneous area schools, they are even less likely to identify themselves in the dramas portrayed in graphic discourses on 'They' who occupy the poor, urban communities and schools" (p. 343).

The attitudes of teachers toward race and culture are obviously important variables in the educational success of children of color as well as in the preparation of all students for life in a diverse society. It is extremely rare that teachers of any race exhibit clearly overt cultural and racial biases in diverse school settings. As Kendall (1983) indicated, negative racial and cultural attitudes have been pushed underground. Many citizens and politicians and even many scholars have concluded the end of racism as a major factor in American schooling. However, it is reasonable to conclude that as much racial attitude and practice exists in schools as exists anywhere else in the society. Racial and cultural bias is a deeply ingrained cultural and psychological factor (Farley & Allen, 1987), and, in many instances, individuals may not realize that their actions and beliefs are influenced by biases. This is as true for teachers as it is for any other citizen.

Tettegah (1996) concluded that the racist attitudes historically noted among the general population of the United States are just as common within its teacher populations. At the same time, she noted, "Quite often, however, White teachers may claim or admit having racist attitudes toward persons in the general population, but profess that their attitudes toward students in their classrooms are different" (p. 160). Conversely, Anyon (1995), in a study of an urban school reform effort, argued that issues of poverty, social class differences, and pressures to teach curriculum that are culturally insensitive can contribute to poor teacher behaviors, regardless of race or ethnicity, toward youngsters who are disenfranchised. She noted, "The desperate lives most of the children lead make many of them become restless and confrontational; many are difficult to teach, and to love" (p. 80).

Children are profoundly affected by teacher attitudes and actions (Kendall, 1983). Anyon (1995), Irvine (1990), and Kunjufu (1984) documented a number of areas of teacher attitude

that negatively affect students, their achievement based on race, and the attitudes of students toward each other. They detailed a variety of areas in which students are stunted in their growth and development and become detached from and denigrative of self and culture by teacher actions, attitudes, and beliefs. Ogbu's classic study (1974) of how school failure adaptation is achieved and maintained in an urban school is a classic case of the creation of negative expectation. Even when teachers are able to adjust racial views to a more positive outlook, there usually remain the very sticky and less concrete questions of cultural and class bias. To ascertain or develop a broader understanding, prospective teachers as well as teacher educators must craft methods to "interrogate their own constructions of issues" that are typically absent in their usual experiences (Chavez-Chavez, 1995; Cochran-Smith, 1995; Reyes, Capella-Santana, & Khisty, 1998; Vavrus & Ozcan, 1998).

Although research, discussed later in this chapter, provides instances where teachers' understanding of the background and culture of students precipitates a greater level of learning than is acquired under culturally insensitive conditions, we recognize that this is often not the prevailing practice. As Ladson-Billings (1997) noted, "Work on pedagogy by Shulman suggests that an important aspect of the knowledge base for teaching is the 'wisdom of practice.'. . . But missing from this dialogue on the wisdom of practice are issue of race and ethnicity. . . . Real life classrooms of teachers and students are racially constructed" (p. 133). Dilworth (1990) and Grant and Millar (1992) concurred, as they stated that the educational research typically excludes concepts of race-ethnicity, language, gender, and exceptionality when discussing school culture.

> Culture, regarding teachers, is typically defined introspectively from within schools, with certain faint recognition of external forces. Culture in the educational literature typically relates to the school and its environment and its actors (that is, to principals, students, parents, and peers) coupled with legitimate attention to gender. (Dilworth, 1990, p. 9)

What we find are many schools that do not form and maintain connections with their students within their social contexts. They shy away from issues of race, language, and culture. They emphasize issues of content and substance over consideration and viable usage of language and content used. Having no knowledge of the common vernacular, they narrow the margin for learning to standard English. And they fail to celebrate their students as individuals and as members of specific cultures, beyond limited placement of holidays events. There is little cultural synchronization among the school, its teachers, and its students (Chavez-Chavez, 1995; Cochran-Smith, 1995; Darling-Hammond, Dilworth, & Bullmaster, 1996; Dilworth, 1998; Irvine, 1992; Murrell, 1991; Nieto & Rolon, 1997).

Zimpher and Ashburn (1992) described the teaching population as "a largely female, White, monolingual, and locally raised group, who associate on campus with like groups of students and who prefer to teach average ability, middle-class pupils" (p. 43). As a consequence, it should come as no surprise that neophyte teachers cite reservations and reluctance in teaching students from groups and communities that are different from their own (American Association of Colleges for

Teacher Education [AACTE], 1990). We come to understand that there is a pervasive tendency in this nation to easily dispense with hard and difficult issues or things and people, as Lightfoot (1986) stated, "the messy, noisy world" that will require us to pursue something that on the face of it may be in our best interest and will ultimately require that we revisit that which we have come to know and understand as right.

The literature suggests that we may know more than we think and possibly not enough of what we ought to know. As Parish and Aquila (1996) noted, "Members of an organization learn its culture in a variety of "natural" ways, mostly through such hidden means as language, dress, tradition, covenants, history, structure, values, and rewards. Not knowing that our behavior is governed by these cultural ways, we often do not see the need for change even when such ways become dysfunctional and threaten the survival of our organization" (p. 299).

James A. Banks (1995) stated that "Among the variables that need to be examined in order to create a school culture that empowers students from diverse ethnic and cultural groups are grouping practices, labeling practices, the social climate of the school, and the staff expectations for student achievement" (p. 5). For example, Darling-Hammond (1995) noted that African-American, Latino, Native-American, and low-income students continue to be more likely than White or upper-income students to be placed in remedial and low-level courses. She went on to state that "Tracking endures in the face of growing evidence that it does not substantially benefit high achievers and tends to put low achievers at a serious disadvantage" (p. 473). Evidence suggests that teachers themselves are tracked—good teachers with good students and bad teachers with bad students.

Standards as Means and Assurance to Quality Teaching

These days the talk is tough: Standards must be higher and more exacting, outcomes must be measurable and comparable, accounting must be hard-edged and punitive, and sanctions must be applied almost everywhere—to students and teachers, especially—although not to those whose decisions determine the possibilities for learning in schools. (Darling-Hammond, 1996, p. 5)

Research (Darling-Hammond, 1995; Dilworth & Robinson, 1995) has shown that much of the difference in school achievement results from the effects of substantially different school opportunities, in particular greatly disparate access to high-quality teachers and teaching. Districts with the greatest concentration of poor children, children of color, and children of immigrants are also those in which incoming teachers are least likely to have learned contemporary child development or about how children grow, learn, and resolve difficulties. Unequal access to high-level courses and challenging curriculum explain much of the difference in achievement between poor students of color and White students (Dilworth & Robinson, 1995).

Contemporary teaching and teacher education promote the use of numerous techniques and a broad sense of subject matter content requiring a more flexible learning environment to practice than most systems allow. For instance, while the research suggests utility of student-centered learning and instruction and culturally responsive pedagogy and materials, the current organization of schools, with its many varying directives and achievement goals, tempers teachers' abilities to maximize these factors toward student achievement. Rather than incorporating the components of various cultures evenly throughout the mainstream of the learning process, we persist in separating or sorting students into groups that limit the opportunity to achieve. As Howe (1995) noted, "Twentieth-century U.S. education has wholeheartedly adopted the practice of sorting children into various tracts and special programs, awarding opportunities accordingly" (p. 526). At the same time, there are substantial data that indicate cultural differences in motivation and reward structures and pedagogical approaches. The challenge is to determine how to reconcile these difference within the K-12 school system (Cochran-Smith, 1995; Darling-Hammond & Bullmaster, in press; Dilworth, 1990; Dilworth & Robinson, 1995; Gadsden & Smith, 1994; Haney, 1993; Irvine, 1995; Nieto, 1994; Wells & Serna, 1996).

One reform mechanism for quality and equality has been the establishment of curriculum, program, licensing, and certification standards. Curriculum standards are intended to provide all students with similar skills and knowledge in various basic disciplines. However, the variation that exists among such standards nationally and locally serves to work against their intent. "Schools have rationed challenging curriculum—the kind that requires independent thinking, writing, planning and performance—to the 10% to 20% of students who were thought to be headed for intellectual pursuits" (NCTAF, 1996, p. 24). Although there is widespread use of standardized tests in this nation intended to gauge this knowledge, these tests often do not directly relate to the school curriculum, and they ignore many important kinds of learning. Textbooks and guides rarely reflect a powerful, coherent concept of curriculum and often do little to use the life experiences of disenfranchised youths to leverage their interest and motivation to learn (Garibaldi, 1992; NCTAF, 1996).

Heretofore, teachers have been trained, licensed, and certified, using a different set of standards than those imposed on students. Numerous professional development programs also exist, and they often are neither critical and valid nor are the teachers who are mandated to follow them truly trained or convinced of their merits (Anyon, 1995). The teachers' ability to be creative and to structure curriculum is greatly inhibited by existing standards. There is a high probability that the content that had been promoted during teacher training is inconsistent with the state curriculum standards for youngsters (Beckum, 1992). Needless to say, "Students will not be able to achieve higher standards of learning unless teachers are prepared to teach in new ways and schools are prepared to support high-quality teaching" (NCTAF, 1996, p. 27). Efforts have been made to align PK–12 curriculum, teacher preparation, licensing, and certification standards through such public and private initiatives as the National Education Goals Panel, the National Council for Accreditation of Teacher Education (NCATE), the Interstate New Teacher Assessment and Support Consortium (INTASC), and the National Board for Professional Teaching Standards (NBPTS). The fact that students who are from minority or poor communities are frequently taught by those who are less prepared for and understanding of those standards suggests that standards are not the great equalizers that they have been touted to be.

Culturally Responsive Learning Theories and Styles

The context for learning from the earliest developmental years is influenced by a number of factors, not the least of which would be what is most valued from that culture. While there is significant variation among racial, ethnic, and linguistic groups, there are also differences among us in socioeconomic conditions and in the experiences students are accustomed to and exposed to in their day-to-day living. Education in this nation is perceived as a means for improving the quality of life. However, the point of departure for students varies significantly. According to Irvine and York (1995) and Irvine (1990), the natural approaches to learning by students of color are often "incongruous with expected middle-class values, beliefs, and norms of schools. These cultural differences often result in cultural discontinuity or lack of cultural synchronization between the student and the school" (p. 489). Couple this with varying resources, expertise, and curriculum within schools, and we see clearly how skewed academic performance persists.

Educators tend to rely on learning-style theory to discern approaches for students from various racial-ethnic cultures. However, Irvine and York (1995) found that the research tends to prescribe in a few narrow areas. For instance, cooperative education and field-dependent teaching strategies seem to monopolize the literature when considering African-American, Hispanic, and Native-American students' ways of knowing. They concluded that reliance on these strategies as the primary mechanisms for academic achievement for students from these groups would be premature and conjectural. In interpreting field dependence-independence as "psychological constructs that define the ways individuals respond cognitively to confusing information or unfamiliar situations," the authors explained how such narrow interpretations are insufficient for learning styles in a culturally responsive teachers' repertoire of knowledge and skills. Allowing for "methodological, conceptual, and pedagogical problems in the learning-styles research" Irvine and York (1995) provided a summary of learning styles for several marginal groups. The following are some of their findings:

African-American learners tend to

> respond to things in terms of the whole instead of isolated parts;
> prefer inferential reasoning as opposed to deductive or inductive;
> approximate space and numbers rather than adhere to exactness or accuracy;
> focus on people rather than things;
> be more proficient in nonverbal than verbal communication.

Hispanic learners tend to

> prefer group learning situations;
> be sensitive to the opinions of others;
> be extrinsically motivated;
> prefer concrete representations to abstract ones.

Native-American learners tend to

> prefer visual, spatial, and perceptual information rather than verbal;
> learn privately rather than in public;
> use mental images to remember and understand words and concepts rather than word associations;

> watch and then do rather than employ trial and error;
> value conciseness of speech, slightly varied intonation, and limited vocal range (pp. 490–491).

The authors hasten to add that culture is neither static nor deterministic. Specifically, while there is clear sense that culture, particularly ethnicity, is a powerful force that influences students' predispositions toward learning, cultural practices are also learned behaviors that can be unlearned and modified. Their literature review also finds that, although people in the same social class do exhibit some similar learning-style characteristics, there is evidence that the effects of ethnicity persist across social-class segments within an ethnic group. For instance, Stanton and Salazar (1997) pointed to cultural synchronization as a powerful intervention to poor achievement among students. In his view, "minority youngsters must learn to engage in the academic process communally, rather than individualistically." To accomplish this, they should learn how to "decode the system" and to "participate in power," understood as learning how to engage socially those agents and participants in mainstream worlds and social settings who control or manage critical resources (p. 33). As schools are currently designed, students tend to detach from the community and act "native within the mainstream social world." Most working-class minority youth will reject an assimilationist network-oriented model no matter how generous the institutional support that is offered" (p. 34).

An understanding of culturally defined learning styles does not provide an easily adaptable model for culturally responsive practice. Aside from the hazard of stereotyping youngsters and avoiding the more critical task of providing for individual differences, teachers may presume that students of certain backgrounds can only learn one way, thus depriving them of a broad repertoire of learning mechanisms. In this vein Irvine and York (1995) concluded their findings by noting three attributes of learning-styles theory: It emphasizes the cultural context of teaching and learning, which, arguably, is absent from the dialogue of teaching strategies; it documents the importance of affect in teaching culturally diverse students; and it rightly places the responsibility for student learning with teachers, instead of ascribing blame to students and their parents (p. 494).

While learning-style theory tends to monopolize much of the literature that responds to racial-ethnic and linguistic difference among students, there are other theories that emerge as important. A number of authors consider "critical pedagogy" the most useful and constructive approach to the disenfranchised (Freire & Macedo, 1995; Giroux, 1994; McLaren, 1994; Murrell, 1997). Emanating from Paulo Freire's classic work, the *Pedagogy of the Oppressed,* critical pedagogy has come to mean many things to many people. This work, narrowly defined was written with the prescription to reduce the high level of adult illiteracy of the poor in Brazil, captured worldwide attention. However, as Macedo and Freire (1998) wrote, "No longer can it be argued that Freire's pedagogy is appropriate only in Third World contexts." In their view, "North American inner cities more and more resemble the shantytowns of the Third World, with high levels of poverty, violence, illiteracy, human exploitation, homelessness, and human misery" (p. ix).

Simplistically, critical pedagogy focuses on the notion that

"The oppressed need to develop the necessary critical tools that will enable them to read their world so they can apprehend the globality of their reality and choose what world they want for themselves" (Freire & Macedo, 1995, p. 389). Freire's notions for educating the disenfranchised have been translated in varying forms by authors who see it as radical and progressive—appropriate and designed for the empowerment and liberation of oppressed peoples. Some will argue that this suggests that the teachers of youngsters from these groups ought to be prepared and to feel comfortable to articulate their political stances and beliefs, while others will find this an inappropriate imposition on the student's ability to construct knowledge. This rich dialogue is played out in a number of thoughtful articles, such as hooks (1993), whose interpretation suggested that "I enter the classroom with the assumption that we must build 'community' in order to create a climate of openness and intellectual rigor" (p. 94). Others, such as Murrell (1997), Ladson-Billings (1997), and Matzen (1996), have made close and vivid connections to children and schools and are fairly critical of Freirian thought in its absence or failure to attend to issues of race and ethnicity.[5] While others, including Tarule (1997) and hooks (1993), find Freirian thought less than fulfilling on issues of gender. In his last work, *Teachers as Cultural Workers* (1998), Freire clearly explained his temperament:

We have a strong tendency to affirm that what is different from us is inferior. We start from the belief that our way of being is not only good but better than that of others who are different from us. The dominant class, then, because it has the power to distinguish itself from the dominated class, first rejects the differences between them but, second, does not pretend to be equal to those who are different; third, it does not intend that those who are different shall be equal. (p. 71)

In explaining the educators' role as politician, he is clear in his convictions:

It is absolutely necessary that educators act in a way consistent with their choice—which is political—and furthermore that educators be ever more scientifically competent, which teaches them how important it is to know the concrete world in which their students live, the culture in which their students, language, syntax, semantics, and accent are found in action, in which certain habits, likes, beliefs, fears, desires are formed that are not necessarily easily accepted in the teachers' own worlds. (p. 72)

It is somewhat ironic that Freire, who has been criticized over-time for the complexity of words and ideas (Freire & Macedo, 1995), in his last book offers such a precise definition of what researchers in this decade convey as culturally responsive practice. He said,

Educators need to know what happens in the world of the children with whom they work. They need to know the universe of their dreams, the language with which they skillfully defend themselves from the aggressiveness of their world, what they know independently of the school, and how they know it. (p. 72)

Another popular approach to learning that is of significance to racial-ethnic and linguistic difference is the constructivism approach. Richardson (1997) posited that there is little consensus about constructivism as a concept. It is "a descriptive theory of learning . . . it is not a prescriptive theory of learning" (p 3). Yet, she allowed that there are two basic approaches: the Piagetian, psychological approach and the situated sociocultural-constructivist approach. There are, however, authors who argue that neither is sufficient and offer alternatives throughout the spectrum (Cobb, 1996; Vadeboncoeur, 1997). In regard to what we know of teaching and learning, especially in the venue of diverse learners, a theory that disassociates itself from the student's social context is of less value than one that embraces and is grounded in this conception. Although both constructivist approaches regard student prior knowledge as vital, the teachers' role in subscribing to it varies. The Piagetian concept sees. ". . . the meaning-making process as individualistic, with the purpose of constructivist teaching being to lead toward higher levels of understanding and analytic capabilities" (Richardson, 1997, p. 5), while "social constructivists view the social as instrumental, if not essential, in both the construction and appropriation of knowledge" (Richardson, 1997, p. 7). According to Von Glasersfeld (1996),

There are only two facets of the constructivist model, but they go a long way toward establishing the fundamental principle that learning is a constructive activity that the students themselves have to carry out. From this point of view, then, the task of the educator is not to dispense knowledge but to provide students with the opportunities and incentives to build it up. (p. 7)

Vadeboncoeur (1997) argued for a third form of constructivism, emancipatory—which is akin to sociocultural constructivism as propagated by Vygotsky. As she stated, "Recent support for the infusion of discussions of class, race, and gender within pedagogy and practice, as well as an exploration of relationships of power within society, necessitate the development of a constructivist epistemology with a method for exposing inequality" (p. 29). In her view, "Emancipatory constructivism permits students to deconstruct and reconstruct cultural assumptions that have been taken for granted, thereby allowing for the possibility of social transformation" (p. 34). "Pedagogies derived from Piagetian constructivism do not offer the liberatory power to expose or reduce the discourses that reproduce inequality within our society. . . . In order to be liberatory for all children, the underlying assumptions of constructivist theories—epistemology and derived pedagogical approaches—must be deconstructed and reframed with a social orientation" (p. 34). "Consistent with the theses of sociocultural constructivism, teachers will strive to develop students as critical thinkers able to . . . explore their own situatedness, as well as decon-

---

[5] Freire (1995) in recent times has responded to such criticisms by noting that at the time of writing *Pedagogy of the Oppressed* he was "extremely more preoccupied with the oppression of social class" (p. 397). He offered a thesis of unity in diversity so that the various oppressed groups can become more effective in their collective struggle against all forms of oppression (p. 398).

struct social factors that influence them" (p. 30). The responsibility of the teachers is to learn how to capably explore their own biases and model them. This allows for a learning environment wherein there is a fair exchange and distribution of student as well as teacher voices.

In Grossberg's (1994) view, there are three existing models of progressive pedagogical practice that attempt to accomplish much of what emancipatory teaching hopes to accomplish, but none are sufficient.

> The first, a hierarchical practice, assumes that the teacher already understands the truth to be imparted to the student. Of course, sometimes such a practice is quite appropriate and can truly contribute to emancipatory struggles. But the problems with such a practice become more apparent when the teacher assumes that he or she understands the real meanings of particular texts and practices, the real relations of power embodied within them, and the real interests of the different social groups brought together in the classroom or in a broader society. Then it is the teacher who draws the line between the good, the bad, and the ugly, between the politically correct and the politically incorrect.
>
> The second, a dialogue practice, aims to allow the silenced to speak; only when absolutely necessary does it claim to speak for them. But this assumes that they are not already speaking simply because we, the teachers, do not hear them, perhaps because they are not speaking the right languages or not saying what we would demand of them. Moreover, such a practice fails to see that there are often real material and social conditions that have disenabled people from speaking at particular places, in particular ways at particular moments.
>
> The third, a praxical pedagogy, attempts to offer people the skills that would enable them to understand and intervene into their own history. Hopefully, such skills would enable them to move beyond the realm of discursive struggles to challenge the institutional relations to power by connecting themselves up with "the broader struggles of communities to democratize and reconstruct the public sphere" (Fraser, 1994). The problem with this practice is not only that it assumes that people are not already trying to intervene into their own history but, more importantly, that it also assumes that the teacher already understands the right skills which would enable emancipatory and transformative action, as if such were themselves contextually determined. (pp. 16–17)

Grossberg (1994) offered a fourth model of articulation and risk that ". . . while refusing the traditional forms of intellectual authority, would not abandon claims to authority." In his view, "The task of politically engaged pedagogy is . . . to win an already positioned, already invested individual or group to a different set of places, a different organization of the space of possibilities" (p. 19).

The necessity for educators to incorporate cultural knowledge in their practice is consistent in the literature. Hoffman (1996) found that discourse, text, and practice in the multicultural domain are imbued with the unexamined assumptions concerning such basic concepts as culture, self, and individual identity" (p. 545). "It is critical for multicultural educators to become more aware of how the elements of that symbolic order are constituted or culturally embedded, so that we may move toward a more self-aware multiculturalism with greater potential to inform practice" (p. 546).

"Anthropologists have criticized the way the concept of culture has been simplified and reified to fit multiculturalist discourse that supports visions of personal, ethnic, or national cultural identity that are fixed, essentialed, stereotyped, and normalized." "Yet, it is important to recognize that, when culture becomes a means for the pursuit of group self-interests, or a way of getting textbooks adopted, or a tool for identity politics, it is no longer emancipatory; rather it serves to feed the established categories and relations of power that thrives on simplification, reductionism, and universalism" (p. 555).

Although advocates of various learning-style approaches are seemingly rigid in forms and prescription, there is a compelling requirement that culturally responsive teachers embrace those elements of each that will fit for their students and dismiss those elements that will not fit.

Teacher Backgrounds and Styles[6]

As research has found (Cochran-Smith, 1995; Rosenberg, 1998), there are a significant number of teacher candidates, practicing teachers, and college faculty members who are bright and well-meaning but who are unable or unwilling to grasp the concept of culturally responsive practice. They come with an academic understanding that "all children can learn" but are limited in their ability to act on this knowledge and are hampered by preconceived notions that are directly attributable to their family, community, and school experiences. Universally, teachers come to their practice with a sense of empowerment that they can help youngsters grow and develop (Dilworth, 1990). Given opportunity and informed experience and training, teachers of any background have the capacity to craft a teaching repertoire that will promote student learning. The challenge for today's teachers and to those who work to educate them and to improve their practice is to craft a safe haven in schools for such teaching and learning to occur. This sanctuary ought to reflect all that is good in the society at large and, at the same time, ought to give balanced attention and sense to issues, theories, and themes that seemingly counter them. This is more difficult than we might expect.

Research has revealed differences in the general disposition of teachers toward school and teaching practice (Dilworth, 1990; Farkas & Johnson, 1996). A survey conducted in 1995 specified a number of varying attitudes. For instance, teachers generally do not rate their local public schools as excellent. A total of 38% of White teachers rate their schools as excellent; 18% of African-American teachers and 17% of Hispanic teachers rate their schools the same way. Teachers of color indicate a greater concern than White teachers do about the threat of violence in their schools. Approximately 61% of African-American and 71% of Hispanic teachers, compared to 47% of White teachers, identify drugs and violence as problems in their

---

[6] An extended version of this discussion is offered in an Office of Educational Research and Improvement background paper, *Educators of Color,* by Linda Darling-Hammond, Mary E. Dilworth, and Marcy Bullmaster for the January 1996 invitational conference Recruiting, Preparing, and Retaining Persons of Color in the Teaching Profession.

schools. Conversely, teachers of color are consistent with White teachers on issues such as maintaining high academic standards for students and in being wary of teaching innovations (Farkas & Johnson, 1996).

The need for teachers who are consciously responsive to their students' cultural backgrounds and learning styles is considered crucial by many scholars in efforts to improve academic achievement (Delpit, 1988; Dilworth, 1990; Foster, 1995; Irvine, 1992; Ladson-Billings, 1994a; Nieto, 1994). They have pointed to numerous instances where understanding the culture precipitates a greater level of learning than had been developed under culturally insensitive conditions. Language; posture; relationships with teachers, parents, and peers; and communication styles are all factors that, when misunderstood, can prove to be detrimental to academic advancement. Educators who are attuned to these variations in ethos and mores are highly desirable and apparently are more effective.

The parochialism of preservice teachers and the tenacity of educators' preexisting attitudes and beliefs are recognized as conditions that inhibit a teachers' ability to know and understand students from cultures other than their own. Zimpher and Ashburn's (1992) portrayal of those pursuing a teaching career is instructive—she is "typically a White female from a small town or suburban community, who matriculates in a college less than 100 miles away from home and intends to return to small town America to teach middle-income children of average intelligence in traditionally organized schools" (p. 41). Consider as well that these prospective teachers also exhibit reluctance to teach students from cultures other than their own as well as students who are mentally and physically challenged (AACTE, 1990).

Research has corroborated these premises over and over again. Virtually all authors speak to the rigidity of neophyte teacher beliefs and attitudes. These premises include the inability or difficulty in unpacking prior understandings, conceptualizing new paradigms, and trusting that there is merit in diversity. While these insights are familiar to us, there is a broader variation on the same theme. Recent research has suggested (Agee, 1998; Rios, McDaniel, & Sowell, 1998) that these fixed notions appear universally among students as well as seasoned practitioners and are not restricted by age, race-ethnicity, language, or regionality. The notions provide a broader dimension to the research that thrives on the limitations of young White preservice students and omits significant attention to the perspectives of others (Dilworth, 1990; Ladson-Billings, 1996).

For instance, consider Jane Agee's (1998) story of Latasha, a neophyte African-American teacher in the Deep South as she was challenged by her own middle-class background, first in a majority White school setting and subsequently in a diverse school setting. As Agee described Latasha,

The conflict for Latasha was complex. She had a deep desire to help African-American students. "I would prefer teaching African-American students because I see that there is a need there." Yet, she worried that "people will think that if I'm thrown in a room, or I'm teaching in a county that is majority White . . . that I really won't care, because that's where my heart is." She countered this imaginary scenario quietly and firmly. "That's not the type of person I am." (p. 24)

And there is Greeson's (1997) report of one of his students, who was a native of a college town, but who reported that she wished to work in an urban area:

I want to help them people. . . . I can identify with them as a minority [she looks East Indian] but I wasn't raised in the city, so I don't know how to teach them. . . . [W]e've talked about them in a lot of classes. . . . One of my teachers said you can't teach them unless you grew up in the city, but I think I can . . . can't I? But I don't know how I am going to do it. (p. 345)

There is much to hear in the voice of the young Latina woman, in California, as described by Reyes et al. (1998), who, through her teacher education coursework, became more keenly aware of the differences in treatment between men and women in this society and felt compelled to challenged her male relatives in their comfort with stereotypical roles. Similar are the voices of Rosenberg's (1998) students in the Northeast, who grappled for meaning in multicultural issues that only became apparent to them in the form of startling incidents like Rodney King or in movies like *Boyz in the Hood.* Rosenberg (1998), Webb (1998), Walker and Tedick (1998), Rios et al. (1998), and Zeichner and Hoeft (1995) have suggested that this challenge also extends to the teachers of teachers—that is, the faculty in the academy and cooperating teachers in the schools. The consensus indicates that no one is exempt from continuing to explore their beliefs and labor for greater understanding of that which is different. We seem to be gradually moving beyond the notion that Whites have a more thorough grasp on "interrogating" their beliefs than others do.

At the same time, there is much to suggest that teachers with similar backgrounds to their students are able to leverage this knowledge in a greater way than those with dissimilar backgrounds. As Dilworth (1990) stated, "Given their culturally diverse backgrounds and the academic training defined by the White majority, Black, Hispanic, and other minority teachers possess a consummate understanding of the relationship between education and this society" (p. xi). Conversely, the number of educators of color are so limited that it is very difficult to establish culturally responsive learning communities and cohort formats that we understand contribute significantly to the learning process of teachers (Nelson-Barber & Mitchell, 1992).

Learning communities that include teachers with an understanding of these cultural nuances are essential to the development and delivery of culturally responsive pedagogy. Students, Ladson-Billings (1994a) argued on the basis of her in-depth classroom observations, develop commitments to such teachers—they will learn for these teachers as much as they will learn from them. In addition, these individuals provide direct instruction to students, but they are also available to guide and engage colleagues at the school site to broader contextual understanding (Dilworth, 1990).

The minimal supply of educators of color makes culturally diverse learning communities particularly difficult to establish. The proportion of African-American, Hispanic, Native-American and Asian- and Pacific-American teachers decreased precipitously for more than a decade. The current teaching force is approximately 13% of color, while roughly 32% of the nation's elementary and secondary school population belong to minority groups. Although teachers of color are much more likely to teach in central cities, in schools with a large population of students of color, very few teach in PK-12 classrooms with 10% or fewer students of color. In addition, Although African-American, Hispanic and Asian-American teacher representation is greatest in the central cities and urban fringe areas, their presence is dwarfed in relation to the proportion of students from their respective groups. Similarly, while diversity among school principals is even greater than among teachers, it is insufficient to meet the educational needs of the nation's highly diverse inner cities and corridors (AACTE, 1998). Thus, the goal of all youngsters learning from individuals representing a variety of cultures—perspectives—is far from actualization.

While it is somewhat heartening that there is a core of educators of color in urban and suburban areas, there are few educators of color in rural and small towns. These communities, too, are increasing in student racial-ethnic and linguistic diversity and are often less able to compete with larger school districts. Spears, Oliver, and Maes (1990) reported that, in rural communities west of the Mississippi River, all-Anglo communities have difficulty in locating and attracting non-White teachers. Racially and ethnically diverse communities have difficulty helping local citizens gain the proper credentials. Techniques for increasing student access to teachers of color range from joint appointments with local Native-American tribal governments to hiring an Asian-American resource teacher to rotate among school districts for a period of 2 weeks (pp. 45–46).

The need for teachers who are consciously responsive to their students' cultural backgrounds and learning styles is considered crucial by many scholars (Au, 1980; Calderon & Diaz, 1993; Carew & Lightfoot, 1979; Delpit, 1988; Foster, 1995; Garibaldi, 1992; Hale, 1991; Hale-Benson, 1986; Hilliard, 1992; Irvine, 1992; Kunjufu, 1984, 1989; Ladson-Billings, 1994; Nieto, 1994; Waters, 1989). They have pointed to numerous instances where understanding the culture precipitates a greater level of learning than had been developed under culturally insensitive conditions. For example, Au (1980) analyzed a reading lesson led by a Hawaiian teacher with four Hawaiian students in a school that was successful in raising achievement levels of urban Native-Hawaiian students of lower socioeconomic class. Within the lesson she studied, Au identified nine different "participation structures" that could be placed on a continuum ranging, from those most closely resembling the conventional classroom recitation situation to those more closely resembling the Hawaiian "talk story." Au concluded that the teacher's success in structuring the context of the reading comprehension lesson to more closely match the interaction patterns of the children's culture was a key factor in raising student achievement levels.

In a videocase of multicultural practice, Dilworth (1995) provided an example of how understanding culture can allow teachers to connect curriculum to students' lives. As New Mexican resource teachers discussed the importance of being familiar with the culture of their students, a seasoned educator, "Consuela," offered the following:

> It is an asset to be able to speak a child's language, because the teacher can get so much more participation from the student if she can relate to the language. For instance, a child can come and tell

the teacher, "Teacher, teacher, we killed a pig yesterday!" *Hubo una matanza.* And an Anglo teacher will just say, "Great, the kid has meat in the freezer now." But a bicultural person can make a whole hour [of learning] out of that comment and involve the whole class. Because slaughtering a pig is not meat in the freezer in the Mexican culture. It is a *fiesta,* when aunts, uncles, and others come together. (p. 14)

Donna Deyhle (1995) offered some examples of how educators' ignorance of Navajo culture stifles the academic achievements and aspirations of Native-American students in a high school that borders on the reservation. Consistent with Irvine and York (1995), she noted that Whites frequently distort Navajo values and view them as inadequate compared to their own cultural values. For instance, they presume that Navajo students work well with hands-on activities but do not capture theoretical or abstract ideas and notions. Thus, Navajo youngsters are tracked away from academic training that will prepare them for white-collar positions. She described instances of blaming the victim (student) for school failure, with very few causes attributed to questionable teacher support, lack of counseling, and nonrelevant curriculum. By comparison, she showed how awareness of Navajo students' cultural identity as well as a sympathetic connection between the community and the school academically advantages students who attend a high school located on the reservation. She also found that, where there are fewer White students and more Navajo teachers, racial conflict is minimized and students move through their school careers in a more secure and supportive community context.

Studies of exemplary African-American teachers have consistently indicated that they maintain and utilize their knowledge of culture to advance student learning. Foster (1993, 1995) studied 17 African-American teachers who had been recommended as exemplary teachers by members of the African-American community. Using life and career history interviews, Foster found that these teachers were vital members of their communities and expressed feelings of connection, affiliation, and solidarity with the pupils they taught. They were characterized by their cultural solidarity with the African-American community, their ability to link classroom content to students' experiences, their focus on the whole child, and their use of familiar cultural and communication patterns in their teaching.

Similarly, Henry (1992), in a study of African-Canadian women teachers, found that these teachers juggle activist roles in community work, school work, and parenting. The relationship between classroom teaching, family life, and community service was seen by Henry as a symbiotic one in which the "personal lives of these teachers inform their practice and their classroom experiences sharpen their understandings of African-American children's marginalization in schools" (p. 395). Their teaching, then, serves as a counterpractice to that marginalization of the students and is marked by standards of mutuality, cooperation, and flexibility.

Both Foster (1993) and Hollins (1982), noted deliberate attempts to incorporate forms from the African-American church into classrooms. These included encouraging the release of emotional tensions, providing strong adult leadership, validating interaction modes, such as call-and-response, and the use of familiar language patterns. They also included fostering a climate in which cooperation, acceptance, participation, and learning were stressed above competition. These teachers built relationships in their classrooms that were marked by social equality, egalitarianism, and mutuality stemming from a group, rather than an individual, ethos. Genuine concern for the children, high expectations, and consistent discipline characterized their work with students. Also, moral or personal messages were frequently identified from texts read in class.

Related to African-American teachers' community orientation, an accent on collective and personal responsibility (Henry, 1992) is another signature of the work of African-American teachers. Both King (1991) and Hollins (1982) reported that the teachers they studied teach students to be responsible for their own learning, emphasizing personal values like patience and friendship that embody the important qualities of being in respectful relationship with others and maintaining a steadfast commitment to their own development or self-determination.

Closely associated with the notions of community orientation and collective-personal responsibility is that of kinship or family as a metaphor for the classroom work of African-American teachers. These teachers often act as surrogate parents to the children they teach (Foster, 1993; Willis, 1995). Henry (1992) reiterated this theme when she wrote of her own respondents:

> In their school and classroom practice, these women continue to act as other mothers. In other words, they tend to envisage African-American children, whether in classrooms or in the community, as part of their "family." . . . In such a "family" climate, certain kinds of conversations and interactions are possible, and the affective domain becomes a place of departure to extirpate the cumulative weight of racial oppression. (p. 399)

Henry (1992) viewed these "other mother" relationships as a challenge to the Eurocentric patriarchal notion of the nuclear family and of children as private property. The teachers in her study reported being influenced by their own mothers' and grandmothers' examples of looking out after neighborhood children. Of one teacher, Henry wrote, "She recognizes that the kinds of antiracism work she has done within her family as a mother are the frames of reference that shaped her practice during her former years as a teacher working with poor African-American students" (p. 395).

Of the eight teachers she studied, Ladson-Billings (1994a) observed:

> There is a lot of "mothering" in these classes. The teachers are all perceived as "strict" or "stern." Yet they all indulge in a lot of touching. They put their arms around the children, they hug them, they hold their hands. They believe that they are responsible for what happens to the students at school and, consequently, they make almost no referrals to the principal or to other support staff. They are most often "rewarded" for their work by being given other teachers' "problem" children. They take them on and blend them into the fold without missing a beat. None of the teachers believes she is doing anything special. (p. 24)

Some researchers (Nieto & Rolon, 1997; Schuhmann, 1992) also suggested that Hispanic teachers are advantaged by understanding how the concept of family may be used as a motif for practice, where the teacher is perceived as a parent, mentor, or godmother. They understand the benefits of creating a sense of intimacy and trust with their students that translates to a comfortable learning environment. Equally instructive are researchers' understandings of the Asian-American community that typically perceive schooling as a very formal process where parents trust teachers and expect them to practice with authority (Chinn & Wong, 1992; Pang, 1997).

King (1991) concluded that the African-American teachers who participated in her research had adopted an emancipatory pedagogy to the extent that they were aligned with the interests of their pupils as opposed to the institutional concerns of their school systems. King found that their "struggle is about whether education is for social transformation or system maintenance" (p. 260), and that these teachers "say their rewards come from the students, not their colleagues or supervisors" (p. 261).

A very similar view was described by African-American women teachers interviewed by Casey (1993):

> Enlisted by their elders, and motivated by their own oppressive experiences, for these women, being a African-American teacher means "raising the race"; accepting personal responsibility for the well-being of one's people, and, especially, for the education of all African-American children. (p. 152)

This theme of African-American teachers' community orientation was echoed by King (1991) and Sims (1992), although with differing outlooks and inferences. Sims, who inquired into her own practice as an African-American teacher through keeping a journal, pondered over her sense that

> Sharing a similar background did not guarantee productive, fluid, or uncomplicated interactions with students nor did it reduce the pain I felt when I saw or learned about the conditions in which many of my students lived. . . . The complexities of families and their survival are critical issues that factor into the dynamic relationships between the school world and the real world. . . . How can I define my role as teacher/kin/mentor in children's development?. . . What is an appropriate balancing of the academic and the affective in schools and classrooms? (pp. 343–344)

Problems of practices do not vanish for committed teachers of color; they are framed and informed by a deep appreciation for the meaning of education and teacher-student relationships in the lives of the children they serve.

Unfortunately, because of the relatively small number of culturally relevant, successful teachers of African-American and other minority students spread over large school systems, the long-term effect of these effective teachers is minimized for many students, who may encounter only one or two such teachers in their school career (Ladson-Billings, 1990). Carew and Lightfoot (1979) noted that incorporating the knowledge and commitments of communities of color is a critical component of effective education:

> In order for schools to successfully teach Black children, they will have to incorporate the cultural wisdom and experience of Black families and meaningfully collaborate with parents and community. Black families and communities have been settings for cultural transmission, survival training, moral and religious instruction, role

modeling, mythmaking, and ideological and political indoctrination. (p. 129)

Accessing cultural knowledge is problematic in schools and in colleges of education. Delpit (1988) contended that African-American educators, rather than sustaining a central position in the dialogue about how to educate African-American children, have too often been silenced instead. This has happened because of the dominant "culture of power," its control of the education community, and the place of African-American teachers of urban students at the margins of that culture of power. Ladson-Billings (1990) agreed that the voice of these educators is critically needed to advance the profession's knowledge:

> [T]eacher education programs must recognize the importance of the teacher's voice (McLaren, 1989). There is a huge void in the literature concerning the experiences of Black teachers and others who have been successful educators of Black students. This void underscores the need for what Giroux (1986) identifies as the need for a "critical and affirming pedagogy (that) has to be constructed around the stories that people tell, the ways in which students and teachers author meaning, and the possibilities that underlie the experiences that shape their voices." (McLaren, 1989, p. 229). (pp. 241–242)

In his study of teacher education students, Murrell (1991) found that prospective teachers of color experienced frustration with their preparation program's theoretical content about teaching and learning, because it did not connect with their experiences:

> There is the concern that the lifelong knowledge these students accumulated about their communities does not count. Community-oriented characteristics of good teaching, affirmed in their decision to enter the profession, are not rewarded or reaffirmed in their university classroom experiences. African-American students report that the personal, experiential knowledge of how to foster development and learning among African-American children is not considered legitimate in the classroom. . . . A major theme in the discussions of the African-American education students who met as a support group was the profound sense of voicelessness—an inability to participate in academic discourse in their own words and to draw on their own experience. (p. 217)

Some research has suggested that the involvement of educators of color in decision making can have real value. In a study of 142 school districts, Meier and Stewart (1991) found that significant Hispanic representation on school boards and in the teaching force positively influences dropout and grade-retention rates and standardized test scores of Hispanic students. Further, Hispanic students are less likely to be assigned to special education classes and more likely to be identified as gifted in these districts. Rates of corporal punishment, out-of-school suspensions, and expulsions of Hispanic students are also lower than in districts with minimal Hispanic presence in the educational community. Unfortunately, representation on school boards of Hispanic as well as other groups of color are minimal.

In summary, the research suggests that teachers of color utilize a number of approaches to teaching learning that seem to emerge naturally from their prior and community experiences.

Universal among these approaches are the perceptions that learning and, thus, teaching are not segregated from students' day-to-day life but, rather, are integrally connected and ought be treated as such. This perception allows teachers to bring techniques to the classroom that are familiar to the youngsters that they teach but that are foreign to the traditional, mainstream culture of most schools. Issues of strict discipline, high expectations, and mothering are just a few of the things that find their place in the repertoire of effective teachers of youngsters placed at risk and are open to all educators for consideration as they craft and define their own practice.

Conclusions

The challenges and rewards of the teaching profession have never been greater. The range and type of information that students need to know far exceeds that of previous decades, and the academic expectations for all students are increasing in virtually every state and community. The nation's schools are more racially, ethnically, and linguistically diverse than at any other point in history, and there is much apprehension about how all students will meet the emerging subject-matter standards. Most school systems are seeking to transform their schools to respond to a host of issues, ranging from these increased student expectations to the conditions that students must confront in their communities.

The perceptions of the nation and local communities toward difference—that is, racial, ethnic and linguistic differences—greatly influence knowledge access and acquisition in schools. Societal ills of disenfranchisement—for example, racism, broad variations in socioeconomic status, and a general temperament of indifference toward groups other that ones own—control the level and type of information that is offered in schools, the models of instruction, and the resources available to support learning. All of these factors serve to compromise educators' ability to educate all youngsters to their potential.

The research provides a number of pedagogical and administrative approaches that help to advance learning in schools. These approaches help minimize the affect of external forces on the learning of youngsters who are most affected by them. Knowledge of cultural learning-style theory and culturally responsive pedagogy and an appreciation of the richness of diversity are necessary factors in the professional development of effective educators in this society. Educational systems that support high-level and engaging curriculum for all students and that incorporate elements of students' backgrounds and understandings into the day-to day educational process will do much to enhance the conditions of the disenfranchised and to leverage racial, ethnic, and linguistic diversity to a valued and meaningful station in this society.

REFERENCES

Agee, J. (1998). Confronting issues of race and power in the culture of schools: A case study of a preservice teacher. In M. E. Dilworth (Ed.), *Being responsive to cultural differences: How teachers learn* (pp. 21–38). Thousand Oaks, CA: Corwin Press.

Ahlquist, R. (1991). Manifestations of inequality: Overcoming resistance in a multicultural foundations course. In C. Grant (Ed.), *Research and multicultural education* (pp. 59–105). London: Falmer Press.

American Association of Colleges for Teacher Education. (1989). *Teaching teachers facts and figures.* Washington, DC: AACTE.

American Association of Colleges for Teacher Education. (1990a). *Teaching teachers facts and figures.* Washington, DC: AACTE.

American Association of Colleges for Teacher Education. (1990b). *Teacher education pipeline: Schools, colleges, and Department of Education enrollments by race, ethnicity.* Washington, DC: AACTE.

American Association of Colleges for Teacher Education. (1998). *Teacher education pipeline IV: SCDE enrollments by race, ethnicity, and gender.* Washington, DC: AACTE.

Anyon, J. (1995). Race, social class, and educational reform in an inner-city school. *Teachers College Record, 97*(1), 69–94.

Apple, M. W., & Oliver, A. (1996). Becoming right and the formation of conservative movements. *Teachers College Record V, 97*(3), 419–445.

Aronowitz, S. (1997). Between nationality and class. *Harvard Educational Review, 67*(2), 188–207.

Au, K. (1980). Participation structures in a reading lesson with Hawaiian children: Analysis of a culturally appropriate instructional event. *Anthropology and Education Quarterly, 1*(2), 91–115.

Ball, D. L., & Wilson, S. (1996). Integrity in teaching: Recognizing the fusion of the moral and intellectual. *American Educational Research Journal, 33*(1), 155–192.

Banks, J. A., & Banks, C. (1995). Multicultural education historical development, dimensions, and practice. In J. A. Banks (Ed.), *Handbook of research on multicultural education* (pp. 3–24). New York: Macmillan.

Bartolome, L. I., &. Macedo, D. P. (1997). Dancing with bigotry: The poisoning of racial and ethnic identities. *Harvard Educational Review, 67*(2), 222–246.

Beck, L. G., & Newman, R. L. (1996). Caring in one urban high school: Thoughts on interplay among race, class, and gender. In D. Eaker-Rich & J. Van Galen (Eds.), *Negotiating borders and barriers in schools* (pp. 1–22). Albany, NY: State University of New York Press.

Beckum, L. (1992). Diversifying assessment: A key factor in the reform equation. In M. E. Dilworth (Ed.), *Diversity in teacher education: New expectations* (pp. 215–22). San Francisco: Jossey-Bass.

Bell, D. (1992). *Faces at the bottom of the well: The Permanence of racism.* New York: Basic Books.

Blackwell, J. E. (1991). *The Black community: Diversity and unity.* New York: HarperCollins.

Boyer, P. (1997). *Native American colleges: Progress and prospects.* Princeton, NJ: Carnegie Foundation for the Advancement of Teaching.

Bradby, D. (1992). *Language characteristics and academic achievement: A look at Asian and Hispanic eighth graders in NELS: 88.* Washington, DC: National Center for Educational Statistics.

Brooks, R. L. (1990). *Rethinking the American race problem.* Berkeley, CA: University of California Press.

Brown, C. E. (1992). Restructuring for a new America. In M. E. Dilworth (Ed.), *Diversity in teacher education: New expectations* (pp. 1–22). San Francisco: Jossey-Bass.

Calderon, M., & Diaz, E. (1993). Retooling teacher preparation program to embrace Latino realities in schools. In R. E. Castro & Ingle (Eds.), *Reshaping teacher education in the Southwest: A response to the needs of Latino students and teachers* (pp. 1–70). Claremont, CA: Tomas Rivera Center.

Carew, J. V., & Lightfoot, S. L. (1979). *Beyond bias: Perspectives on the classroom.* Cambridge, MA: Harvard University Press.

Carey, N., & Farris, E. (1996). *Racial and ethnic classifications used by public schools.* Washington, DC: National Center for Educational Statistics.

Castenell, L., & Pinar, W. (1993). Introduction. In L. Castenell & W. Pinar (Eds.), *Understanding curriculum as racial text: Representations of identity and difference in education* (pp. 1–30). Albany, NY: State University of New York Press.

Chavez-Chavez, R. (1995). *Multicultural education in the everyday: A renaissance for the recommitted.* Washington, DC: AACTE.

Cheeseman Day, J. D. (1995). Population of the United States by age, sex, race and Hispanic origin 1993–2050. In U.S. Bureau of the Census, *National Population Projections* (Current Population Series, pp. 25–1104). Washington, DC: U.S. Bureau of the Census.

Chinn, P. C., & Yuen Wong, G. (1992). Recruiting and retaining Asian/Pacific-American teachers. In M. E. Dilworth (Ed.), *Diversity in teacher education: New expectations* (pp. 112–133). San Francisco: Jossey-Bass.

Cobb, P. (1996). Where is the mind? A coordination of sociocultural and cognitive constructivist perspectives. In C. T. Fosnot (Ed.), *Constructivism: Theory, perspectives, and practice* (pp. 34–54). New York: Teachers College Press.

Cochran-Smith, M. (1995). Uncertain allies: Understanding the boundaries of race and teaching. *Harvard Educational Review, 65*(4), 541–570.

Cochran-Smith, M. (1997). Knowledge, skills, and experiences for teaching culturally diverse learners: A perspective for practicing teachers. In J. J. Irvine (Ed.), *Critical knowledge for diverse teachers and learners* (pp. 27–88). Washington, DC: AACTE and ERIC Clearinghouse on Teaching and Teacher Education.

Collins, M., & Tamarkin, C. (1990). *Marva Collins' way.* Los Angeles: J. P. Tarcher.

Darling-Hammond, L. (1995). Inequality and access to knowledge. In J. A. Banks (Ed.), *Handbook of research on multicultural education* (pp. 465–479). New York: Macmillan.

Darling-Hammond, L. (1996). The right to learn and the advancement of teaching: Research, policy, and practice for democratic education. *Educational Researcher, 25*(6), 5–17.

Darling-Hammond, L., & Bullmaster, M. (in press). The changing social context of teaching in the United States. In T. Good (Ed.), *The international handbook on teachers and teaching* (pp. 1053–1077). New York: Macmillan.

Darling-Hammond, L., Dilworth, M. E., & Bullmaster, M. (1996). *Educators of color.* Commissioned paper for Phi Delta Kappa, National Alliance of Black School Educators, Office of Educational Research and Improvement, and Recruiting New Teachers.

Davidson, A. L. (1997). Marbella Sanchez: On marginalization and silencing. In M. Seller & L. Weis (Eds.), *Beyond Black and White: New faces and voices in the U.S. schools.* Albany, NY: State University of New York Press.

Delpit, L. D. (1987). Skills and other dilemmas of a progressive Black educator. *Equity and Choice, 3*(2), 9–14.

Delpit, L. D. (1988). The silenced dialogue: Power and pedagogy in educating other people's children. *Harvard Educational Review, 58*(3), 280–298.

Denbo, S. (1982). *Color our children carefully: A guide to equity and excellence in education.* Washington, DC: American University, Mid-Atlantic Center for Sex Equity.

Denbo, S. (1986). *Improving minority student achievement: Focus on the classroom.* Washington, DC: American University, Mid-Atlantic Center for Sex Equity.

Deyhle, D. (1995). Navajo youth and Anglo racism: Cultural integrity and resistance. *Harvard Educational Review, 65*(3), 403–444.

Dilworth, M. E. (1990). *Reading between the lines: Teachers and their racial/ethnic cultures.* Washington, DC: AACTE and ERIC Clearinghouse on Teacher Education.

Dilworth, M. E. (1995). Critical perspective: Deming, New Mexico. In R. McNergney & J. Herbert (Eds.), *Multicultural videocases* (pp. 15–25). Washington, DC: University of Virginia, AACTE, and ERIC Clearinghouse on Teaching and Teacher Education.

Dilworth, M. E. (1998). Old messages with new meanings. In M. E. Dilworth (Ed.), *Being responsive to cultural differences: How teachers learn* (pp. 197–201). Thousand Oaks, CA: Corwin Press.

Dilworth, M. E., & Robinson, S. (1995). K-12 and postsecondary education: Same issues, same consequences. *Educational Record, 76* (2–3), 82–89.

Dryfoos, J. (1995). *Full service schools: A revolution in health and social services for children, youth, and families.* San Francisco: Jossey-Bass.

D'Souza, D. (1991). *Illiberal education: The politics of race and sex on campus.* New York: The Free Press.

Du Bois, W. E. B. (1969). The talented tenth. In B. T. Washington (Ed.), *The Negro problem* (pp. 31–71). New York: Arno Press and the *New York Times.*

Dyson, A. H. (1996). Cultural constellations and childhood identities: On Greek gods, cartoon heroes, and the social lives of schoolchildren. *Harvard Educational Review, 66*(3), 471–495.

Edelman, M. (1992). *The measure of our success: A letter to my children and yours.* Washington, DC: Children's Defense Fund.

Edmonds, R. (1979). Effective schools for the urban poor. *Educational Leadership, 37*(1), 15–18, 20–24.

Education Trust. (1995). *A new change: Making the most of Title 1.* Washington, DC: Author.

Education Watch. (1996). *The education trust: Community data guide.* Washington, DC: Education Trust.

Edwards, L. (1995). *Immigration/migration and the CUNY student of the future.* New York: CUNY.

Epstein, T., & Elias, M. (1996). To reach for the stars: How social/affective education can foster truly inclusive environments. *Phi Delta Kappan, 78*(2), 157–162.

Essed, P. (1991). *Understanding everyday racism: An interdisciplinary theory.* Newbury Park, CA: Sage.

Etzioni, A. (1983). *An immodest agenda: Rebuilding America before the 21st century.* New York: McGraw-Hill.

Farkas, S., & Johnson, J. (1996). *Given the circumstances: Teachers talk about public education today.* New York: Public Agenda.

Farley, R., & Allen, W. (1987). *The color line and the quality of life in America.* Oxford, UK: Oxford University Press.

Feinberg, W. (1990). The moral responsibility of public schools. In J. I. Goodlad, R. Soder, & K. A. Sirotnik (Eds.), *The moral dimensions of teaching* (pp. 155–187). San Francisco: Jossey-Bass.

Ferguson, D. L. (1995). The real challenge of inclusion: Confessions of a rabid inclusionist. *Phi Delta Kappan, 77*(4), 281–287.

Fernandez, J. P. (1981). *Racism and sexism in corporate life: Changing values in American business.* Lexington, MA: Lexington Books.

Finlay, B. (Ed.). (1996). *The state of America's children yearbook: 1996.* Washington, DC: Children's Defense Fund.

Foster, M. (1993). Educating for competence in community and culture: Exploring the views of exemplary African-American teachers. *Urban Education, 27*(4), 370–394.

Foster, M. (1995). African-American teachers and culturally relevant pedagogy. In J. A. Banks (Ed.), *Handbook of research on multicultural education* (pp. 570–581). New York: Macmillan.

Fraser, N. (1994). Rethinking the public sphere: A contribution to the critiques of actually existing democracy. In H. A. Giroux & P. McLaren (Eds.), *Between borders: Pedagogy and the politics of cultural studies* (pp. 74–98). New York: Routledge.

Fraser, J. W. (1997). Preface. In J. J. Irvine (Ed.), *Critical knowledge for diverse teachers and learners* (pp. v–x). Washington, DC: AACTE and ERIC Clearinghouse on Teaching and Teacher Education.

Freire, P. (1973). *Pedagogy of the oppressed.* New York: Seabury Press.

Freire, P. (1998). *Teachers as cultural workers: Letters to those who dare to teach.* Boulder, CO: Westview Press.

Freire, P., & Macedo, D. P. (1995). A dialogue: Culture, language, and race. *Harvard Educational Review, 65*(3), 377–402.

Fuchs, L. H. (1995). The American civic culture and an inclusivist immigration policy. In J. A. Banks (Ed.), *Handbook of research on multicultural education* (pp. 293–309). New York: Macmillan.

Fuller, B., Eggers-Pie'rola, C., Holloway, S., Liang, X. E., & Rambaud, M. F. (1996). Rich culture, poor markets: Why do Latino parents forego preschooling? *Teachers College Record, 97*(3), 400–418.

Gadsden, V., & Smith, R. (1994). African-American males and fatherhood: Issues in research and practice. *Journal of Negro Education, 63*(4), 634–648.

Garbarino, J. (1997). Educating children in a socially toxic environment. *Educational Leadership, 54*(7), 12–16.

Garcia, E. (1993). Language, culture, and education. In L. Darling-Hammond (Ed.), *Review of research in education, 19* (pp. 51–98). Washington, DC: AERA.

Garcia, & McLaughlin. (1995). *Fostering second language development in young children: Principles and practices* (Education Practice Report 14). Santa Cruz.

Garibaldi, A. M. (1988). *Educating Black male youth: A moral and civic imperative.* New Orleans, LA: Orleans Parish School Board.

Garibaldi, A. M. (1992). Preparing teachers for culturally diverse classrooms. In M. E. Dilworth (Ed.), *Diversity in teacher education: New expectations* (pp. 23–39). San Francisco: Jossey-Bass.

Gibson, M., & Ogbu, J. (1991). *Minority status and schooling: A comparative study of immigrant and involuntary minorities.* New York: Garland.

Giroux, H. A. (1994). Living dangerously: Identity politics and the new cultural racism. In H. A. Giroux & P. McLaren (Eds.), *Between borders: Pedagogy and the politics of cultural studies* (pp. 29–55). New York: Routledge.

Gonzalez, R. D. (1993). *Language, race and the politics of educational failure: A case of advocacy.* Urbana, IL: National Council of Teachers of English.

Goodlad, J. I. (1990a). Common schools for the common weal: Reconciling self-interest with the common good. In J. I. Goodlad & P. Keating (Eds.), *Access to knowledge: An agenda for our nation's schools* (pp. 1–22). New York: College Entrance Examination Board.

Goodlad, J. I. (1990b). *Teachers for our nation's schools.* San Francisco: Jossey-Bass.

Goodlad, J. I., & Keating, P. (Eds.). (1990). *Access to knowledge: An agenda for our nation's schools.* New York: College Entrance Examination Board.

Gordon, B. M. (1993). Cultural knowledge and liberatory education: Dilemmas, problems, and potentials in postmodern American society. *Urban Education, 27*(4), 448–470.

Graff, H. J. (1995). *Conflicting paths: Growing up in America.* Cambridge, MA: Harvard University Press.

Grant, C. A., & Millar, S. (1992). Research and multicultural education: Barriers, needs, and boundaries. In C. A. Grant (Ed.), *Research and multicultural education: From the margins to the mainstream* (pp. 7–18). Bristol, PA: Falmer Press.

Greeley, K., & Mizell, L. (1993). One step among many: Affirming identity in antiracist schools. In T. Perry & J. W. Fraser (Eds.), *Freedom's plow: Teaching in the multicultural classroom* (pp. 215–230). New York: Routledge.

Gresson, A. D. (1997). Identity, class, and teacher education: The persistence of "class effects" in the classroom. *Review of Education/Pedagogy/Cultural Studies, 19*(4), 335–348.

Grossberg, L. (1994). Introduction: Bringin' it all back home-pedagogy and cultural studies. In H. A. Giroux and P. McLaren (Eds.), *Between borders: Pedagogy and the politics of cultural studies* (pp. 1–25). New York: Routledge.

Grossman, H. (1995). *Teaching in a diverse society.* Boston: Allyn & Bacon.

Hale, J. (1991). The transmission of cultural values to young African-American children. *Young Children, 46*(6), 7–15.

Hale-Benson, J. (1986). *Black children: Their roots, culture, and learning styles.* Baltimore: Johns Hopkins University Press.

Haney, W. (1993). Testing and minorities. In L. Weis & M. Fine (Eds.), *Beyond silenced voices* (pp. 45–73). New York: State University of New York Press.

Harry, B. (1992). *Cultural diversity, families, and special education system: Communication and empowerment.* New York: Teachers College Press.

Henry, A. (1992). African-Canadian women teachers' activism: Recreating communities of caring resistance. *Journal of Negro Education, 61*(3), 392–404.

Hilliard, A. G., III. (1995, November). *Teacher education from an African-American perspective.* Paper presented at an Invitational Conference on Defining the Knowledge Base for Urban Teacher Education, Atlanta, GA.

Hoffman, D. M. (1996). Culture and self in multicultural education: Reflections on discourse, text, and practice. *American Educational Research Journal, 33*(3), 545–569.

Hollins, E. R. (1982). The Marva Collins story revisited: Implications for regular classroom instruction. *Journal of Teacher Education, 33*(1), 37–40.

hooks, b. (1993). Transforming pedagogy and multiculturalism. In T. Perry & J. W. Fraser (Eds.), *Freedom's plow: Teaching in the multicultural classroom* (pp. 91–99). New York: Routledge.

Howe, K. R. (1995). Diversity in education: Some currents in conversation. *Educational Theory, 45*(4), 525–540.

Irvine, J. J. (1990). *Black students and school failure: Policies, practices, and prescriptions.* New York: Greenwood.

Irvine, J. J. (1992). Making teacher education culturally responsive. In M. E. Dilworth (Ed.), *Diversity in teacher education: New expectations* (pp. 79–92). San Francisco: Jossey-Bass.

Irvine, J. J., & York, D. E. (1995). Learning styles and culturally diverse students: A literature review. In J. A. Banks (Ed.), *Handbook of research on multicultural education* (pp. 484–497). New York: Macmillan.

Jones, L., & Newman, L. (1997). *Our America: Life and death on the south side of Chicago.* New York: Scribner.

Katz, M. (1971). *Class, bureaucracy, and schools.* New York: Praeger.

Kendall, F. E. (1983). *Diversity in the classroom: A multicultural approach to the education of young children.* New York: Teachers College Press.

Kids count data book: State profiles of child well-being. (1996). Baltimore: Annie E. Casey Foundation.

King, J. (1991). Dysconscious racism: Ideology, identity, and the miseducation of teachers. *Journal of Negro Education, 61*(3), 317–340.

Kitano, H. H. L. (1976). *Japanese Americans: The evolution of a subculture.* Englewood Cliffs, NJ: Prentice-Hall.

Knapp, M. S. (1995). The teaching challenge in high-poverty classrooms. In M. S. Knapp (Ed.), *Teaching for meaning in high-poverty classrooms.* Menlo Park, CA: SRI International.

Kozol, J. (1985). *Illiterate America.* New York: New American Library.

Kozol, J. (1991). *Savage inequalities.* New York: Crown Publishers.

Kunjufu, J. (1984a). *Countering the conspiracy to destroy Black boys.* Chicago: African American Images. Kunjufu, J. (1984b). *Developing positive self-images and discipline in Black children.* Chicago: African American Images.

Kunjufu, J. (1986). *Countering the conspiracy to destroy Black boys, Volume II.* Chicago: African American Images.

Kunjufu, J. (1989). *A talk with Jawanza.* Chicago: African American Images.

Kuykendall, C. (1992). *From rage to hope: Strategies for reclaiming Black and Hispanic students.* Bloomington, IN: National Education Service.

Ladson-Billings, G. (1990). Culturally relevant teaching: Effective instruction for Black students. *College Board Review, 155,* 20–25.

Ladson-Billings, G. (1994a). *The dreamkeepers: Successful teachers of African-American children.* San Francisco, CA: Jossey-Bass.

Ladson-Billings, G. (1994b). What can we learn from multicultural education research? *Educational Leadership, 51*(8), 2–26.

Ladson-Billings, G. (1994c). Watching a naked emperor: A critique of national standards efforts. *Educational Forum, 58*(4), 401–408.

Ladson-Billings, G. (1996). Silences as weapons: Challenges of a Black professor teaching White students. *Theory into Practice, 35*(2), 79–85.

Ladson-Billings, G. (1997). I know why this doesn't feel empowering: A critical race analysis of critical pedagogy. In P. Freire, J. W. Fraser, D. Macedo, T. McKinnon, & W. T. Stokes (Eds.), *Mentoring the mentor: A critical dialogue with Paulo Freire* (pp. 127–141). New York: Peter Lang.

LaFranchi, H., & Harbison, R. (1996, March 7). Test time for schooling across U.S.-Mexico line. *The Christian Science Monitor,* p. 1.

Lee, A. A. (Ed.). (1984). *Circle of unity.* Los Angeles: Kalimat Press.

Leitman, R., Binns, K., & Steinberg, A. (1996). *The Metropolitan Life survey of the American teacher: Student voices voice their opinions on: Learning about multiculturalism part IV.* New York: Louis Harris and Associates.

Lewis, A. C. (1993). *Changing the odds: Middle school reform in progress.* New York: Edna McConnell Clark Foundation.

Lezotte, L. W., & Bancroft, B. A. (1985). School improvement based on effective schools research: A promising approach for economically disadvantaged minority students. *Journal of Negro Education, 54*(3), 301–312.

Lightfoot, S. (1986). On goodness in schools: Themes of empowerment. *Peabody Journal of Education, 63*(3), 9–28.

Lincoln, C. E. (1989). Knowing the Black church: What it is and why. In J. Dewart (Ed.), *The state of Black America 1989.* New York: National Urban League.

Lipsky, D. K, & Gartner, A. (1996). Inclusion, school restructuring, and the remaking of American society. *Harvard Educational Review, 66*(4), 762–796.

Macedo, D., & Freire, A. M. (1998). Foreword. In P. Freire, *Teachers as cultural workers: Letters to those who dare to teach* (pp. ix-xx). Boulder, CO: Westview.

Madden, N., & Slavin, R. (1983, Winter). Mainstreaming students with mild handicaps: Academic and social outcomes. *Review of Educational Research, 53*(4), 519–569.

Marshall, K. (1996). No one ever said it would be easy. *Phi Delta Kappan, 78*(4), 307–308.

Matzen, R. N. (1996, March). Emancipatory education without enlightenment? Thais, Americans, and the pedagogy of the oppressed. Paper presented at the annual "Pedagogy of the Oppressed" conference, Omaha, NE.

McDonnell, L. M., & Hill, P. T. (1993). *Newcomers in American schools: Meeting the needs of immigrant youth.* Santa Monica, CA: Rand Corporation.

McLaren, P. (1994). Multicultural education and the postmodern critique: A pedagogy of resistance and transformation. In H. A. Giroux & P. McLaren (Eds.), *Between borders: Pedagogy and the politics of cultural studies* (pp. 192–222). New York: Routledge.

McLeskey, J., & Waldron, N. L. (1996). Responses to questions teachers and administrators frequently ask about inclusive school programs. *Phi Delta Kappan, 78*(2), 150–156.

McMannon, T. (1995). *Morality, efficiency, and reform: An interpretation of the history of American education work in progress, series 5.* Seattle, WA. Institute for Educational Inquiry.

McNergney, R., & Herbert, J. (Eds.). (1995). *The case of Columbus, New Mexico.* Washington, DC: AACTE and ERIC Clearinghouse on Teaching and Teacher Education.

Murrell, P. (1991). Cultural politics in teacher education: What's missing in the preparation of minority teachers? In M. Foster (Ed.), *Qualitative investigations into schools and schooling* (pp. 205–225). New York: AMS Press.

Murrell, P. (1993). Afrocentric immersion: Academic and personal development of African-American males in public schools. In T. Perry & J. W. Fraser (Eds.), *Freedom's plow: Teaching in the multicultural classroom* (pp. 231–260). London: Routledge.

Murrell, P. (1997). Digging again the family wells: A Freirian literacy framework as emancipatory pedagogy for African-American children. In P. Freire, J. W. Fraser, D. Macedo, T. McKinnon, & W. T. Stokes (Eds.), *Mentoring the mentor: A critical dialogue with Paulo Freire* (pp. 19–58). New York: Peter Lang.

National Center for Children in Poverty. (1996–97). One in four: America's youngest poor. *News and Issues, 6*(2), 1–2.

National Commission on Teaching and America's Future. (1996). *What matters most: Teaching for America's future.* New York: NCTAF.

Nelson-Barber, S., & Mitchell, J. (1992). Restructuring for diversity: Five regional portraits. In M. E. Dilworth (Ed.), *Diversity in teacher education: New expectations* (pp. 229–262). San Francisco: Jossey-Bass.

Newby, R. G. (Ed.). (1995). The bell curve: Laying bare the resurgence of scientific racism. *American Behavioral Scientist, 39*(1), 12–24.

Nieto, S. (1994). Lessons from students on creating a chance to dream. *Harvard Educational Review, 64*(4), 393–426.

Nieto, S. (1997). Ethnicity and education forum: What difference does difference make? *Harvard Educational Review, 67*(2), 169–187.

Nieto S., & Rolon, C. (1997). Preparation and professional development of teachers for culturally diverse schools: Perspectives from the standards movement. In J. J. Irvine (Ed.), *Critical knowledge for diverse teachers and learners* (pp. 89–124). Washington, DC: AACTE and ERIC Clearinghouse on Teaching and Teacher Education.

Noddings, N. (1986). Fidelity in teaching, teacher education, and research for teaching. *Harvard Educational Review, 56*(4), 496–510.

Noddings, N. (1995). Teaching themes of caring. *Phi Delta Kappan, 76*(9), 675–679.

Oakes, J. (1985). *Keeping track: How schools structure inequality.* New Haven, CT: Yale University Press.

Oakes, J., & Lipton, M. (1990). Tracking and ability grouping: A structural barrier to access and achievement. In J. I. Goodlad & P. Keating (Eds.), *Access to knowledge: An agenda for our nation's schools* (pp. 187–204). New York: College Entrance Examination Board.

Ogbu, J. U. (1974). *The next generation: An ethnography of education in an urban neighborhood.* New York: Academic Press.

Ogbu, J. U. (1987). Variability in minority school performance: A problem in search of a solution. *Anthropology and Education Quarterly, 8*(4), 312–334.

Ogbu, J. U. (1994). Racial stratification and education in the United States: Why inequality persists. *Teachers College Record, 96*(2), 265–298.

Olneck, M. R. (1995). *Immigrants and education.* In J. A. Banks (Ed.), *Handbook of research on multicultural education* (pp. 310–327). New York: Macmillan.

Orner, M. (1996). Teaching for the moment: Intervention projects as situated pedagogy. *Theory into Practice, 35*(2), 72–78.

Ouchi, W. G. (1981). *Theory Z: How American business can meet the Japanese challenge.* New York: Avon.

Pang, V. O. (1997). Caring for the whole child: Asian Pacific American students. In J. J. Irvine (Ed.), *Critical knowledge for diverse teachers and learners* (pp. 149–188). Washington, DC: AACTE and ERIC Clearinghouse on Teaching and Teacher Education.

Pang, V. O., & Sablan, V. (1998). Teacher efficacy: How do teachers feel about their ability to teach African-American students? In M. E. Dilworth (Ed.), *Being responsive to cultural differences: How teachers learn* (pp. ?). Thousand Oaks, CA: Corwin Press.

Parish, R., & Aquila, F. (1996). Cultural ways of working and believing in school: Preserving the way things are. *Phi Delta Kappan, 78*(4), 298–308.

Parker-Jenkins, M. (1995). *Children of Islam: A teacher's guide to meeting the needs of Muslim pupils.* Staffordshire, UK: Trentham Books.

Peck, M. S. (1986). *The different drum: Community making and peace.* New York: Simon and Schuster.

People for the American Way. (1992). *Democracy's next generation II.* Washington, DC: Author.

Perry, T., & Fraser, J. W. (Eds.). (1993). *Freedom's plow: Teaching in the multicultural classroom.* New York: Routledge.

Perry, T., & Fraser, J. W. (1993). Reconstructing schools as multiracial/multicultural democracies: Toward a theoretical perspective. In T. Perry & J. W. Fraser (Eds.), *Freedom's plow: Teaching in the multicultural classroom* (pp. 3–26). New York: Routledge.

Phelan, P., Davidson, & Yu. (1993). Students' multiple worlds: Navigating the borders of family, peer, and school cultures. In P. Phelan & A. L. Davidson (Eds.), *Renegotiating cultural diversity in American schools* (pp. 52–88). New York: Teachers College Press.

Phelan, P., & Davidson, A. L. (Eds.). (1993). *Renegotiating cultural diversity in American schools.* New York: Teachers College Press.

Pignatelli, F., & Pflaum, S. W. (1993). *Celebrating diverse voices: Progressive education and equity.* Newbury Park, CA: Corwin Press.

Pollard, D. S. (1996). Perspectives on gender and race. *Educational Leadership, 53*(8), 72–74.

Pollard, D. S., & Avery, M.-P. B. (1993). *Toward a pluralistic perspective on equity.* Newton, MA: Education Development Center.

Pressley, S. A. (1997, August 24). Law keeping many Mexican students from crossing border. *The Washington Post,* p. A4.

Reyes, S., Capella-Santana, N., & Khisty, L. (1998). Prospective teachers constructing their own knowledge in multicultural education. In M. E. Dilworth (Ed.), *Being responsive to cultural differences: How teachers learn* (pp. 110–125). Thousand Oaks CA: Corwin Press.

Richardson, V. (1997). Constructivist teaching and teacher education: Theory and practice. In V. Richardson (Ed.), *Constructivist teacher education: Building new understandings* (pp. 3–14). London: Falmer Press.

Rios, F., McDaniel, J., & Sowell, L. (1998). Pursuing the possibilities of passion: The affective domain of multicultural education. In M. E. Dilworth (Ed.), *Being responsive to cultural differences: How teachers learn* (pp. 160–181). Thousand Oaks, CA: Corwin Press.

Rosenberg, P. (1998). The presence of an absence: Issues in teacher education at a predominantly White campus. In M. E. Dilworth (Ed.), *Being responsive to cultural differences: How teachers learn* (pp. 2–20). Thousand Oaks, CA: Corwin Press.

Schaps, E., Lewis, C., & Watson, M. (1995). Schools as caring communities. In National Center for Restructuring Education, Schools, and Teaching, *Resources for restructuring* (pp. 1–6). New York: Author.

Schuhmann, A. M. (1992). Learning to teach Hispanic students. In M. E. Dilworth (Ed.), *Diversity in teacher education: New expectations* (pp. 93–111). San Francisco: Jossey-Bass.

Seller, M., & Weis, L. (1997). Introduction. In M. Seller & L. Weiss (Eds.), *Beyond Black and White: New faces and voices in U.S. schools* (pp. 1–11). New York: State University of New York Press.

Shields, P. (1995). Engaging children of diverse backgrounds. In M. S. Knapp (Ed.), *Teaching for meaning in high-poverty classrooms* (pp. 33–46). Menlo Park, CA: SRI International.

Smith, J. O. (1992). *The politics of ethnic and racial inequality.* Dubuque, IA: Kendeall Hunt Publishers.

Sowell, T. (1981). *Ethnic America: A history.* New York: Basic Books

Sowell, T. (1983). *The economics and politics of race: An international perspective.* New York: William Morrow.

Sowell, T. (1990, Spring). On the higher learning in America: Some comments. *Public Interest, 99,* 68–78.

Spears, J. D., Oliver, J. P., & Maes, S. C. (1990). *Accommodating change and diversity: Multicultural practices in rural schools: A report of the Ford Western Task Force.* Lawrence, KS: Kansas State University, Rural Clearinghouse for Lifelong Education and Development.

Stanton-Salazar, R. (1997). A social capital framework for understanding the socialization of racial minority children and youths. *Harvard Educational Review, 67*(1), 1–40.

Sumberg, A. D. (Ed.). (1991). *Education budget impact alert for fiscal year 1991: A compilation of federal education programs.* Washington, DC: Committee on Education Funding.

Suzuki, B. (1977). Education and the socialization of Asian Americans: A revisionist analysis of the "model minority" thesis. *Amerasia Journal, 4,* 2, 23–51, 77.

Takaki, R. (1993). *A different mirror: A history of multicultural America.* Boston: Little, Brown, and Co.

Takaki, R. (1997). Ethnicity and education forum: What difference does difference make? *Harvard Educational Review, 67*(2), 169–187.

Tarule, J. M. (1997). A letter to Paulo Freire. In P. Freire, J. W. Fraser, D. Macedo, T. McKinnon, & W. T. Stokes (Eds.), *Mentoring the mentor: A critical dialogue with Paulo Freire* (pp. 11–17). New York: Peter Lang.

Tettegah, S. (1996). The racial consciousness attitudes of White prospective teachers and their perceptions of the teachability of students from different racial/ethnic backgrounds: Findings from a California study. *Journal of Negro Education, 65*(2), 151–163.

U.S. Department of Commerce, Bureau of the Census. (1984). *1980 census of population, detailed population characteristics, United States.* Washington, D.C.: U.S. Government Printing Office.

U.S. Department of Commerce, Bureau of the Census. (1993). *1990 census of population, social and economic characteristics, United States.* Washington, DC: U.S. Government Printing Office.

U.S. Department of Commerce, Bureau of the Census. (1999, January 7). *Interracial married couples 1960-present, MS-3* [On-line]. Available: http://www.census.gov/population/www/socdemo/interrace.html.

Vadeboncoeur, J. A. (1997). Child development and the purpose of education: A historical context for constructivism in teacher education. In V. Richardson (Ed.), *Constructivist teacher education: Building new understandings* (pp. 15–37). London: Falmer Press.

Vavrus, M., & Ozcan, M. (1998). Multicultural content infusion by student teachers: Perceptions and belief of cooperative teachers. In M. E. Dilworth (Ed.), *Being responsive to cultural differences: How teachers learn* (pp. 94–101). Thousand Oaks, CA: Corwin Press.

Von Glasersfeld, E. (1996). Introduction: Aspects of constructivism. In C. T. Fosnot (Ed.), *Constructivism: Theory, perspectives, and practice* (pp. 3–7). New York: Teachers College Press.

Walker, C., & Tedick, D. (1998). Multicultural education in practice. In M. E. Dilworth (Ed.), *Being responsive to cultural differences: How teachers learn* (pp. 182–196). Thousand Oaks, CA: Corwin Press.

Washington, B. T. (1969). Industrial education for the Negro. In B. T. Washington (Ed.), *The Negro problem* (pp. 7–30). New York: Arno Press and the *New York Times.*

Waters, M. M. (1989). An agenda for educating Black teachers. *Educational Forum, 53*(3), 267–279.

Webb, M. (1998). Culture: A view toward the unexplored frontier. In M. E. Dilworth (Ed.), *Being responsive to cultural differences: How teachers learn* (pp. 61–77). Thousand Oaks, CA: Corwin Press.

Wells, A. S., & Serna, I. (1996). The politics of culture: Understanding local political resistance to detracking in racially mixed schools. *Harvard Educational Review, 66*(1), 93–118.

Welner, K. G., & Oakes, J. (1996). (Li)ability grouping: The new susceptibility of school tracking systems to legal challenges. *Harvard Educational Review, 66*(3), 451–470.

West, C. (1993). *Race matters.* Boston: Beacon.

Willis, M. G. (1995). *Creating success through family in an African-American public elementary school.* Paper presented at the annual meeting of AERA, San Francisco.

Wilson, W. J. (1987). *The truly disadvantaged: The inner city, the underclass, and public policy.* Chicago: University of Chicago Press.

Winfield, L. F., & Manning, J. B. (1992). Countering parochialism in teacher candidates. In M. E. Dilworth (Ed.), *Diversity in teacher education: New expectations* (pp. 181–214). San Francisco: Jossey-Bass.

Wong, K. K. (1994). Governance structure, resource allocation, and equity policy. In L. Darling-Hammond (Ed.), *Review of Research in Education, 20* (pp. 257–289). Washington, DC: AERA.

Zeichner, K. M., & Hoeft, K. (1995). Teacher socialization for cultural diversity. In J. A. Banks (Ed.), *Handbook of research on multicultural education* (pp. 525–547). New York: Macmillan.

Zimpher. N., & Ashburn, E. (1992). Countering parochialism in teacher candidates. In M. E. Dilworth (Ed.), *Diversity in teacher education: New expectations* (pp. 40–62). San Francisco: Jossey-Bass.

34.

The Learner: "Race," "Ethnicity," and Linguistic Difference

Carmen I. Mercado

Hunter College of City University of New York

Introduction

This chapter is about differences among learners attributed to "race," "ethnicity," and language, which means that it is about learners' differences that are social in origin. Understanding the sources of group-based differences among learners as a basis for responsive teaching and learning is necessary; however, it is also fraught with the potential for dangerous stereotyping. Much attention has been given to group-based differences in academic achievement that have been well documented over the history of educational research (Olneck & Lazerson, 1974). However, our understandings about the origin of these differences remain limited, at best, while differences pertaining to the developmental needs of children living in a socially stratified society remain invisible. During the past 2 decades, a growing number of scholars have reoriented the study of difference through complex, multilayered analyses of the social, historical, and economic forces that shape differences and that are implicit in the construction of differences in school and community contexts. These scholars have gone beyond the narrowly conceived cultural deficits-difference explanations that focus on culture as fixed (and maladaptive) traits and values and that have dominated the scholarship for the past century. One central theme emerging from this scholarship is that learner differences are shaped by the material resources of families, schools, and communities living in a socially stratified society. Another related theme is that learner differences are constructed through pedagogical processes that reflect beliefs and practices shaped by institutional and societal ideologies (referring both to a system of ideas and beliefs and to the connotations that texts and practices carry). A few of these scholars have collaborated with teachers (practitioner-scholars) to demonstrate that it is possible to create democratic learning environments that facilitate, rather than impede, healthy human development. Many of these efforts are challenging perceptions about the meaning and value of diversity, and, more importantly, questioning fundamental beliefs about traditional school practices and procedures that misinterpret and underestimate students' capabili-

ties. These efforts are shifting the negative valence commonly associated with group-based differences, creating new possibilities (or visions) for individuals who are preparing to enter the teaching profession and who may doubt in their capabilities to make a difference. The changing U.S. demographics and the enduring achievement gap among indigenous minorities demand that we pay close attention to this scholarship in the preparation of the nation's teachers, particularly if research on teaching is to be at the service of equity and social justice.

The study of learner differences at this historical juncture is important given the dramatic changes in the U.S. population that have resulted from the post 1965 immigration, which has increased the diversity found among school-age children and youth. Because the Census Bureau counts and describes the U.S. population using classification schemes that mark differences (or create social collectivities) in terms of "race" and "ethnicity," which imply culture and language differences, schools and educational researchers also mark differences among learners in this manner, despite the controversy that surrounds this practice (Torres & Ngin, 1996). A small number of social scientists have begun to study the character of recent immigration, documenting the complex and richly varied patterns of the immigrant experience and the impact of this experience on the school adaptation and achievement of children and youth. What these scholars are learning challenges conventional wisdom derived from the great Atlantic migration of the last century (Portes & Rumbaut, 1996; C. Suarez-Orozco & M. Suarez-Orozco, 1995; M. Suarez-Orozco, 1998).

"Race," "ethnicity," and linguistic differences among learners are also constructed through social processes in and out of the classroom. Although diversity is often represented as a problem in the educational literature, social scientists point out that human diversity is continually shaped through social processes of mutual influence and accommodation. These processes are evidence for human adaptability—the infinite potential that human beings have to adapt to people and circumstances in their environment, under the best and worst of circumstances. It is also through these processes that human diversity evolves and changes, despite the common perception that diversity is static and fixed. However, in a socially stratified society, the meaning and value attached to this evidence of a positive life force is also variable. We have known for some time now that for students from social groups on the lower end of the social hierarchy, variability from an imagined or real norm is treated as an impediment to learning. Historically, these groups include indigenous populations, that is, students of African, American Indian (and Alaskan), Hawaiian, Mexican, and Puerto Rican ancestry. Many scholars suggest that it is the treatment of difference (particularly differences associated with stigmatized forms of communication and interaction commonly attributed to culture) and not the diversity it represents that has serious consequences for learners and the communities with which they are identified. We can find well documented evidence that the treatment of learner differences in school results in educational advantage for some and educational disadvantage for others. Literacy, the principal gatekeeper in access to knowledge and opportunity to learn, continues to be differentially distributed among classes and ethnic groups in U.S. society (Snow, Burns, & Griffin, 1998).

As scholars explain, societal ideologies (for example, supporting the use of classification schemes that mark "racial" and "ethnic" distinctions) combine with institutional policies and practices (for example, using performance on standardized tests as the basis for sorting children, differentiating instruction, and designing promotional policies) to limit access to a rigorous academic preparation for those students who stand to benefit the most from this access. Locating the problem of differences in institutional policies and practices that appear natural and neutral suggests that we are all complicit in constructing educational disadvantage. Consequently, this theoretical perspective implies the need to reformulate social policy, transform schools, and alter the preparation of teachers. This is not a new perspective; variants of it are evident in the work of disciplinary scholars since the 1960s (see the work of Mehan, 1980, on student competence and McDermott, 1977, 1982, on the social construction of failure). Although this body of knowledge has important implications for teaching and the preparation of teachers, to date, it has had little influence on research, on teaching and teacher preparation.

The theorizing of scholars who study the social construction of difference provides us with powerful tools and a language to understand the range of social processes that shape human diversity. This emphasis is important given the global economic transformations that have occurred over the past two decades. A college or post- secondary education is now deemed essential for economic survival in light of the competitive demands of the new information and service economy (Reyes, 1994). Although Carnoy (1994) documents how government policies and programs have been able to lessen the social, economic, and educational disadvantages of groups on the lower end of the social hierarchy, the will of the people is required to sustain support for such policies on pragmatic grounds (in terms of its cost to society), if not on moral and ethical grounds. Presently, however, the treatment of differences among learners, resulting from federal intervention and through approaches such as multicultural education and bilingual education, is debated in the mass media (Bartolome & Macedo, 1997), which paints a particularly grim picture of American children and schools (Berliner & Biddle, 1995). In the current sociopolitical climate, the treatment of group-based differences that is directed at educational equity is being construed, by some, as unnecessary (given the perception that discrimination and racism are not serious problems in our society), and as discriminatory (for the white mainstream) (Bartolome & Macedo, 1997; Feinberg, 1998; McLaren, 1989).

Although poverty (Anyon, 1997; Pallas, Natriello, & McDill, 1989), "institutional racism" (Nieto, 1992), and political decisions affecting education (Anyon, 1997) are beyond the control of teachers, what "teachers know and can do is one of the most important influences on what students learn" (Darling-Hammond, 1998, p. 6). Scholarship reviewed by Darling Hammond (1998), including the findings of the National Commission on Teaching and America's Future, which she chaired, suggest that what teachers know or believe about learners (and differences among learners) structure pedagogical relationships and shape differences in the classroom (Attinasi, 1996; Gee, 1990). Some scholars argue that teachers are transformative intellectuals (Aronowitz & Giroux, 1985), that it is possible to undermine societal and institutional racism through the teaching-learning process, namely, through fair and equitable assessment, the organization of challenging learning environments, the selection and use of textual materials, grouping, homework, and disciplinary practices. It is assumed that understanding the origin and character of differences among learners, and the educational needs they may imply, will enable teachers to guide the teaching-learning process more effectively toward the attainment of valued educational and societal goals. However, as Shulman (1987) indicates, knowledge of learner characteristics (and their developmental needs) has not been deemed a legitimate part of the knowledge base on teaching, which has been decidedly biased toward the findings of research on effective teaching. He acknowledges its importance by pointing out that teachers' knowledge and understandings mediate their pedagogical reasoning and consequently their pedagogical actions.

The Study of Difference

Not surprisingly, anthropology has dominated the study of differences in the United States; the study of language and culture may be less problematic to address than are issues of "race." However, contemporary scholarship emerges from a broader range of disciplines and fields of study. Immigration studies, cultural and ethnic studies, critical education studies, and sociolinguistic research are rich sources of insights for teacher education and for research on teaching, particularly because learner differences that both shape and are shaped by teaching are represented quite differently within and across disciplines and fields of study. Much of this scholarship constitutes a counterdiscourse to early (1940s–1960s) mainstream social science, which has had an enduring influence on contemporary scholarship and on the social construction of "race" and "ethnicity." Some of the most celebrated and influential works of this past century, for example, Oscar Lewis's *La Vida* (1968), made visible how social and economic contexts affect children's lives, but they also contributed to the stigmatization of the poor in our society, in Lewis's case, through the introduction (or the validation) of the construct, "culture of poverty." The view that cultural values and attitudes facilitate or impede educational and economic progress, for groups as well as for countries (Harrison, 2000), is a variant of the culture of poverty thesis which has been invoked to explain group-based differences for the past 5 decades.

The impact of researcher ideology on the construction of knowledge in a socially stratified society continues to be a debated issue. Some argue that scholars need to be both rigorous and principled in the realities they seek to explain, precisely because those who are the objects of their research experience long-term social consequences (Banks, 1998). Typically, these are children and families who tend to be at the bottom of the social order. Others argue for a democratization of the research process itself, to be more inclusive of divergent views and voices, particularly educational research in marginalized communities (Torres-Guzmán, Mercado, Quintero, & Rivera Viera, 1994). Also growing is a recognition of the need for more detailed studies of mainstream groups to better understand the character of the unexamined comparison group, the dominant "ethniclass" by which nonmainstream groups are understood and ultimately judged (C. Suarez-Orozco & M. Suarez-Orozco, 1995).

In response to misrepresentations and false claims, which constitute an attack on public education, considered by many to be the principal vehicle for status mobility for America's working class, scholars who are concerned about societal inequalities are assuming a more active role as public intellectuals despite efforts to render powerless educational research that addresses issues of social justice (Aronowitz & Giroux, 1985; Berliner & Biddle, 1995; D. Taylor, 1998). As a result, the genres and avenues for making accessible to the public divergent theoretical viewpoints and empirical knowledge about differences have been broadened. With a wider representation of individuals and shifting terrains of power, the scholarly discourse on difference has become more representative, and, not surprisingly, more polyphonic. Within this politically charged context, teacher preparation and scholarship unfolds, shaping both practice and research on difference.

Chapter Overview

This chapter represents a first effort to render coherent and useful divergent, convergent, and complementary bodies of knowledge on immigrant and indigenous minorities emanating from a wide range of disciplinary scholars, discipline-based scholars in schools of education, and educationists. It builds on and extends the review of research on teaching diverse populations edited by Hollins, King, and Hayman (1994), which constitutes the first major effort to generate a knowledge base for teaching indigenous minorities, that is, African Americans, Appalachian, Native Alaskan, Native Americans, and Latino Americans, through a synthesis of available scholarship. Dominant in the scholarship represented here are previously absent or muted voices, many referred to as "minority scholars," who, through their presence in the academy, have introduced different questions, assumptions, and theoretical frameworks, and, conse-

quently, new explanations of the social construction of difference in schools and classrooms (Baugh, 1993; Delpit, 1995; Pedraza, 1987; Smitherman, 1997; Zentella, 1997). However, as Banks (1998) points out, great variation can be found among scholars of "difference," in general, and among "minority scholars," in particular. He offers a typology of crosscultural researchers that has guided the inclusion of scholarship in this chapter. Accordingly, the perspectives included in this chapter are those of "indigenous insiders" (researchers who endorse the unique values, perspectives, behaviors, beliefs, and knowledge of their primordial community and culture) and "indigenous outsiders" (researchers who have been socialized within nonmainstream communities but who have experienced high levels of desocialization or assimilation to the mainstream). The chapter also includes the views of "external outsiders" (researchers from mainstream communities) and "external insiders," (researchers socialized within a community different from the one in which they are doing research but who are knowledgeable about and sensitive to the values, perspectives, and knowledge of the community they are studying).

Consequently, the scholarship that is presented here has been selectively culled from a wide range of viewpoints and genres, including personal narratives, argumentative essays, theoretical discussions, basic and applied research, and teacher research. Because of the complexities, tensions, and costs associated with research on "race," "ethnicity," and linguistic differences, systematic investigations of these issues are limited, at best. Although much in the scholarly literature constitutes informal theorizing that is tentative and speculative, it is insightful when it reflects understandings about "race," "ethnicity," and linguistic difference derived from lived experiences, whether they are those of leading scholars or those of ordinary people (Cladinin & Connelly, 1996). As Ladson-Billings (1994, 1999) emphasizes, "people's narratives and stories are important in truly understanding their experiences and how those stories may represent confirmation or counter knowledge of the way that society works" (p. 219). Clearly, this chapter is not a research review in the traditional sense.

The chapter is organized into five major sections. The first presents sociodemographic data on the "new" diversity, which reveals the dramatic intragroup variation that is inherent in the "new" diversity and suggests the dangers of normative descriptions of social collectivities. The second examines the constructs of "race," "ethnicity," and linguistic difference through a broad range of views and perspectives, demonstrating how multilayered and complex these constructs are. New understandings on the adaptation to school and school achievement of racialized populations are examined in the third section, reflecting a shift in the scholarship from a focus on failure to a focus on success—a more useful emphasis for research on teaching. The fourth section reviews educational initiatives for adolescent students, a neglected population in much of the research on teaching but one that informs our understanding of learners at a time when the identity formation process is heightened. The chapter concludes with the implications of current scholarship for the preparation of all teachers. Because the terms "race" and "ethnicity" are generally considered to be social constructs rather than scientific concepts (Gimenez, 1996; Miles, 1989; Omi &

Winant, 1994), these terms will appear in quotes in this chapter as they do in some of the scholarly literature.

Difference Is Real

There are real differences among learners in terms of national origin or birthplace of primary caretakers, languages spoken in the home, and length of residence in the United States. Prior to 1965, the vast majority of new immigrants to the United States were of European (and Canadian) origin. After 1965, Afro-Caribbeans, Asians, and Latin Americans became the largest group of immigrants" (p. 32). These trends are evident in the "ethnic/racial" composition of the school-age population, which has changed more dramatically between 1980 and 1990 than at any time this century (Crawford, 1997; Pallas, Natriello, & McDill, 1989; M. Suarez-Orozco, 1998). During this decade, the number of school-age children classified as "Hispanic" rose by 1.25 million, or 57%, and the number of children classified as "Asian" grew by more than 600,000—an 87% increase.

When seen in relation to changes in the school-age population classified as "White," this change is even more pronounced. Rather than evidencing growth, the school-age population classified as "White" has declined by more than 4 million children, about 12%, from 74% to 66%. In contrast, the population of students classified as Blacks and American Indian or Alaskan Natives has remained fairly stable. Consequently, the segment of the population classified as "Hispanic" has grown far more than the reported increase from 9% of the child population in 1980 to 14% in 1996 (Federal Interagency Forum on Child and Family Statistics, 1997). Because of the youth and high fertility rates of the Latino population, demographers project that it will continue to grow even more than it has over the past five decades, as Table 34.1 illustrates.

Seen from this perspective, it is evident that "White" (non-Hispanics) will no longer be the overwhelming majority of the school-age population, as the groups we persist in representing as "minority"—Hispanics, Blacks, and "other groups"—combine to achieve numerical parity with the "White" population. In this country, as Omi and Winant (1994) argue, being "White" is synonymous with being American, hence all others are "minority" no matter how large a group it is. Yet, as striking as these changes are, Crawford (1997) and others argue that statistics "understate the nation's diversity, owing to an acknowledged undercount of minorities and other limitations in census data" (p. 9).

Sources of the "New" Diversity

Scholars of immigration indicate that a variety of factors have contributed to these dramatic demographic shifts. Differential birthrates and changing patterns in immigration that have resulted from the lifting of the national-origins quota, which favored Europeans in the Immigration Law of 1965, are largely responsible for these changes (Fuchs, 1990; Portes & Rumbaut, 1996; M. Suarez-Orozco, 1996, 1998). Current research on immigration reveals that the nature of this phenomenon is unlike and more complex than anything in our history. The "pull" of

Table 34.1. Changes in the School-Age Population by Race and Ethnicity

	White	Hispanic	Black
1945	87.0%	2.5%	10.0% (M. Suarez-Orozco, 1998)
1982	72.0%	9.3%	14.7% (Pallas et al., 1987)
1995	73.6%	10.2%	12.0% (M. Suarez-Orozco, 1998)
2050	52.8%	24.5%	13.6% (M. Suarez-Orozco, 1998)

educational and economic opportunities that immigrants expect to find continue to lure many to the United States (Portes & Rumbaut, 1996). However, some immigrants are actively recruited to meet labor demands in the new borderless economy, and, thus, they form part of a mass movement of people responding to powerful forces that are forging global economic and political transformations (M. Suarez-Orozco, 1996, 1998). Even so, as M. Suarez-Orozco (1998) emphasizes, "immigrants are not automatons exclusively driven by economic forces: Human agency, social relations, and cultural practices are powerfully implicated in the migration process" (p. 35). He explains that people tend to migrate "because others—especially kith and kin—migrated before them" (M. Suarez-Orozco, 1998, p. 34). Thus, as scholars emphasize, immigration today is qualitatively (not quantitatively) different from earlier patterns of immigration and assimilation.

Not surprisingly, given the circular migration that is common, immigrants are likely to participate in binational citizenship, remaining powerful protagonists in the economic, political, and cultural spheres back home. M. Suarez-Orozco (1991) and C. and M. Suarez-Orozco (1995) theorize that immigrants have a "dual frame of reference," remaining psychologically in their homeland while living in the host society. As these scholars describe it, this dual frame of reference is a form of psychological protection against violence, disparagement, and discrimination and also against the "stresses of acculturation" that historically have formed part of the immigrant experience. These stresses, which have a serious impact on the children of immigrants, are believed to be more acute today given the anti-immigrant hysteria evident in all postindustrial societies, including England, France, Germany, Spain, Italy, and Belgium, where immigration is common (C. Suarez-Orozco & M. Suarez-Orozco, 1995). C. and M. Suarez-Orozco (1995) explain that rapid and profound demographic changes are marked by an increase in social malaise, anxiety, or hysteria. Their analysis of public opinion polls indicates that Americans fear (or have been led to believe) that new immigrants and their children do not seem (or want) to assimilate into the institutions of mainstream society the way previous waves of immigrants are believed to have done. Thus, what some scholars regard as essential survival strategies in hostile environments, that is, the maintenance of immigrants' cultural traditions, languages, and other "habits of the heart" (C. Suarez-Orozco & M. Suarez-Orozco, 1995, p. 5), the less informed take as evidence of an anti-assimilationist, therefore anti-American, attitude. Immigration scholars have found that the successful adaptation of parents is significant as it has a favorable impact on the socioemotional well-being and academic success of their children (Ogbu & Matute-Bianchi, 1986; C. Suarez-Orozco & M. Suarez-Orozco, 1995; Trueba, 1998).

However, included in this diversity are U.S.-born citizens from long-established ethnic groups—some, original inhabitants of this nation—as are some African Americans, American Indians, Asian Americans, Hawaiians, Mexican Americans, and Puerto Ricans, for example. These U.S.-born "national-origin minority groups" are also referred to as "domestic migrants" (Portes & Rumbaut, 1996), "involuntary or caste minorities" (Ogbu, 1992), "language minority students," and "disadvantaged populations" (Pallas, Natriello, & McDill, 1989), terms that emphasize the hazards associated with membership in particular social groupings.

Although many national-origin minority groups share common origins with more recent immigrants, they are distinct. For example, Latinos form part of the "new" and the old diversity but have been treated as a monolithic category by the public, by the media, by scholars, and, not surprisingly, by teachers. However, because national-origin minority groups have had to endure a longer history of discrimination than more recent immigrants, some theorize that these different experiences have affected the forms of adaptation or sociocultural practices that have evolved among members of these groups in comparison to those of more recent immigrants (Ogbu & Matute-Bianchi, 1986; Portes & Rumbaut, 1996; M. Suarez-Orozco, 1991).

Further, most, but not all, members of national-origin minority groups are fluent speakers of English. Puerto Ricans are often perceived to be foreign-born immigrants because in Puerto Rico, where approximately one-half of the population resides, the national language is Spanish. Nonetheless, they are, and have been since 1917, U.S. citizens by birth, whether born in the United States or on the island of Puerto Rico. In the same way that citizenship was imposed without fulfilling the language requirement, English was imposed in schools in a society in which Spanish was, and continues to be, the lingua franca. Because of frequent back-and-forth migration, a pattern that also characterizes more recent immigrants from Latin America (M. Suarez-Orozco, 1998), the majority of those who reside in the United States and who are second, third, and fourth generation Americans are usually bilingual to some degree and speak different variations of English, Spanish, and a combination of the two (Zentella, 1997).

Despite some common characteristics, Latinos are a diverse demographic and sociocultural population, often, but not always, evident in the varieties of Spanish that many (not all) speak and in the range of proficiency they have developed in English. "Blacks" are similarly diverse demographically and socioculturally (which includes, among others, Afro-Caribbean, Jamaican, Cuban, and Dominicans who self-identify or are identified as Black) even though they are often referred to as a monolithic group. In general, the treatment of immigrant and nonimmigrant Americans suggests how racial and ethnic identities are constructed for individuals. Individuals and groups are treated differently on the basis of perceived or real physical and linguistic characteristics. The stereotyping of groups and the categorical treatment of students who have very different historical trajectories has serious consequences when it occurs in the classroom and dangerous implications when it is reinforced in the scholarship.

The Origin and Character of the "New" Diversity

The origin and character of the "new" immigration is distinct from previous immigrations. The current wave of immigrants are incredibly diverse, coming from 174 nations and colonies: 34 in Europe, 26 in North America and the Caribbean, 20 in Central and South America, 42 in Asia and the Middle East, and 52 in Africa (Fuchs, 1990). M. Suarez-Orozco (1998) reports that 80% of the new immigrants tend to be non-White, non-English-speaking, non-Europeans emigrating from developing countries in Latin America, the Caribbean, and Asia. In addition to differences in national origin, the new immigrants differ along language dimensions.

According to the 1990 U.S. Census, 9.9 million school-aged children (5–17 years) or about 20% of the total number of students in the U.S. population (more than one in five youth), live in a setting where a language other than English is spoken (Anstrom, 1996; Crawford, 1997). Of these language-minority students, some 14% had limited proficiency in English, which includes households or families of newly arrived immigrant children or "Limited English Proficient Students."

August and Hakuta (1997) report that in the fall of 1991, the number of recently arrived, school-age English Language Learners was estimated to be 2,314,079. The term, English Language Learners, was coined by LaCelle-Peterson and Rivera (1994) to refer, in a more neutral manner, to the broad range of language abilities among students who are just beginning to learn or who have developed considerable proficiency in English. Other estimates range from 2.3 to 3.3 million, a difference that reflects the estimation methods used but that has important consequences for how these differences are addressed. New immigrants are likely to speak a wide range of languages (see Table 34.2).

However, varieties of English spoken by newly arrived students from the Caribbean, India, and other English-speaking countries do not appear in this listing, even though phonological, lexical, and cultural differences associated with these may affect communication and understanding. Thus, important sociocultural and sociolinguistic variations among English-

Table 34.2. The Most Frequently Spoken Language among New Immigrants

Spanish	73.0%
Vietnamese	3.9%
Hmong	1.8%
Cantonese	1.7%
Cambodian	1.6%
Korean	1.6%
Laotian	1.3%
Navajo	1.3%
Tagalog	1.3%
Russian, French Creole, Arabic, Portuguese, Japanese, Armenian, Chinese (unspecified), Mandarin, Farsi, Hindi, and Polish	

Source: August & Hakuta (1997)

Table 34.3. The Ten Most Frequently Spoken Languages in the United States Not Including English

(out of a population of 230,466,777)	
Spanish	17,339,172
French	1,702,176
German	1,547,099
Italian	1,308,648
Chinese	1,249,213
Tagalog	843,251
Polish	723,483
Korean	626,478
Vietnamese	507,069
Portuguese	429,860

Source: Crawford (1997)

Table 34.4. Changes in the Mexican Origin Population

1960	1.7 million	(1.0% of the total U.S. population)
1970	4.5 million	(2.2%)
1980	8.7 million	(3.9%)
1990	13.3 million	(5.4%)
1995	17 million	(6.6%)
1996	18 million	(6.7%)

Source: Trueba (1998)

speaking immigrants are erased through the current classification process.

In an analysis of language diversity in the United States that did not limit itself to the language diversity introduced by recent immigrants, Crawford (1997) found that "more than 325 languages are now used at home by U.S. residents, including at least 137 Native American Languages" (p. 9). Of these, the ten most frequently spoken languages other than English are listed in Table 34.3.

These data illustrate that language diversity is a fact of life in the United States, even among assimilated groups, and suggests the need to better understand the English-speaking mainstream. In the same way that "Whiteness" is associated with American identity, so is the exclusive use of English. According to both sets of data, Spanish is by far the language spoken by most Americans, second only to English. Although the "new" immigration is 44% Latino and 37% Asian (C. Suarez-Orozco & M. Suarez-Orozco, 1995), this growth in Spanish within the United States is not surprising as Spanish is the oldest European language in this hemisphere.

Latinos are a diverse, socioeconomic, sociocultural population coming from different countries as well as educational and professional backgrounds. However, two thirds of all immigrants from Latin America are Mexicans. The 7-million-or-so Mexican immigrants residing in the United States today constitute roughly a third of the total foreign-born population of this nation, and this immigration is expected to continue over the next several decades (M. Suarez-Orozco, 1998). C. and M. Suarez-Orozco (1995) point out that Mexican-origin Latinos are themselves a highly heterogeneous population that includes new arrivals from various regions of Mexico. Trueba's (1998) synthesis of demographic data on the Mexican-origin population in the United States between 1960 and 1996 illustrates the dramatic increases that this population has experienced over a brief 30-year period (see Table 34.4).

Portes and Rumbaut (1996) indicate that among the new wave of immigrants, Mexicans have the lowest levels of schooling in comparison to Asians, who are the "best educated" group. They report that immigrants from India, Taiwan, Iran, Hong Kong, the Philippines, Japan, Korea, and China all rank above the United States average in educational attainment. To assert that the educational level of immigrants has been declin-

ing is simply not true emphasize Portes and Rumbaut (1996). The socioeconomic status of immigrants and migrants in the United States encompasses wide differences. Although these differences often go unrecognized, they may affect the school achievement (and treatment) of immigrant students and result in unfair comparisons among groups, with profound consequences for learners.

Poverty is a serious problem for many Americans, however, it is particularly acute for immigrant populations and national-origin minority groups. According to A. Taylor (1996), cross-national comparisons indicate that the United States ranks last among 18 industrialized nations in the number of children who live below the poverty level. "The U.S. child poverty rate was more than three times the rates for West Germany and France, and almost nine times that of the first-ranked country, Finland" (p. 10). Puerto Ricans have the highest poverty rate, lowest household incomes, and lowest labor force participation of all Latino groups in the United States (Cordero-Guzman, 1992–93). Mexican-origin Latinos have the highest unemployment rates of all subgroups (C. Suarez-Orozco & M. Suarez-Orozco, 1995). However, some scholars believe that the upward mobility of earlier arrivals has been obscured by the larger, ever increasing number of new immigrants (Trueba, 1998).

This discussion makes clear the tremendous diversity within a diversity that is often described in broad brush strokes. New immigrants are more socioculturally diverse than ever before, a diversity that is sustained by a massive back-and-forth migration that was virtually impossible for earlier waves of immigrants. They are at once the most educated and skilled and the least educated and skilled, overrepresented in the category of people with doctorates and overrepresented in the category of people without a high school diploma. Consequently, recent immigrants are more "bimodal" (M. Suarez-Orozco, 1998) or more dichotomous in their economic profile.

Settlement Patterns

Both concentration and diffusion characterize settlement patterns (Portes & Rumbaut, 1996). Although immigrants may be found in every state of the union, they are largely concentrated in a few states and metropolitan areas. Major urban centers such as New York, Los Angeles, Chicago, Miami, Houston, San Francisco, New Orleans, and Seattle have large concentrations of immigrant students and national-origin minority groups where established ethnic communities serve as magnets and sources of financial, social, and emotional support for newcomers. New York City, historically the destination for a large number of immigrants, has evidenced dramatic changes over the past decade, most notably in terms of the growth and diversification of its Latino presence, which now constitutes 25% of the total population (Flores, 1996). Although New York City has had the largest concentration of Puerto Ricans in the United States, where they have outnumbered all other Latino groups since the turn of the past century, the large influx of immigrants during the past decade from the Caribbean and Central America, overwhelmingly from Santo Domingo, and in large numbers from Colombia, Ecuador, and Mexico is changing the face of the city (Flores, 1996).

Similarly, in a state where Latinos represent 25% of the population, Los Angeles is said to be one of the largest cities of Spanish speakers in the world (M. Suarez-Orozco, 1996). The Latino population in Los Angeles, unlike the population in New York, is predominantly Mexican. As Trueba (1998) points out, changes in California have been particularly stark: "After 140 years of predominantly White enrollment, in 1990 , 50% of California public school students belong to ethnic/racial subgroups" (p. 254). In contrast, New York City public schools have been predominantly African American and Latino for more than 30 years.

Data on the distribution of the immigrant and migrant population indicates that different regions in the United States have distinctive ethnic influences. However, ethnic influences do not remain static; they are dynamic and in constant flux. These settlement patterns influence the social adaptation of immigrants on a number of different levels (Flores, 1996; C. Suarez-Orozco & M. Suarez-Orozco, 1995). Flores (1996) gives one sense of what happens when different ethnic groups have differential opportunity for contact with others living in geographical proximity. In his study of the popular culture of Puerto Rican youth in El Barrio, Flores indicates that

New York Puerto Ricans have been living at close quarters with Blacks, perhaps closer than any other national group in the history of this country. In addition to unprecedented cultural fusions, most social indicators point consistently to Puerto Ricans bearing greater similarities to Blacks than to other Latino groups. . . . Similarly, Puerto Ricans . . . bear closer historical ties to the Chicano population than do their ancestral kin from Central America. (pp. 183–184)

As social science research is beginning to illuminate, variations or hybridizations are being found in cultural practices, language, and resources that are revitalized, created, or transformed through this mutual influence and accommodation (see the work of Flores, 1993, 1996; Portes & Rumbaut, 1996; M. Suarez-Orozco, 1998; Zentella, 1997). Although these hybrid cultural practices have received little attention by educational researchers, Black and Latino scholars are finding these practices have important implications for the development of culturally relevant pedagogy (Ladson-Billings, 1994; Mercado, 1992, 1997; Sola & Bennett, 1991), as will be discussed further on.

However, more fundamental concerns have been raised about immigrant settlement patterns. These populations, many who live below the poverty level, are often concentrated in the poorer sections of large central cities, under less than adequate living conditions. According to Portes and Rumbaut (1996),

American central cities have largely become the repository of the children and grandchildren of earlier migrants and immigrants who were unable to move up the socioeconomic ladder. As sociologists emphasize, to assume that each new generation tends to do substantially better in school than the previous one, eventually reaching parity with the mainstream population is no longer true (Portes & Rumbaut, 1996; M. Suarez-Orozco, 1998). Inner-city communities have undergone profound social and economic transformations in the last two decades, which, in turn, affect schools and children in these contexts. However, indications are increasingly showing that some of these communities are experiencing economic revitalization precisely because of the influx of immigrant populations over the past decade, even though these changes may not, as yet, be affecting the quality of schooling in these communities.

In her review of educational research, Greene (1994) indicates that "there has been intensified concern on the part of educational researchers for the social and economic contexts that affect what is learned and taught" (p. 424) in these marginalized communities. As Snow, Barnes, Chandler, Goodman, and Hemphill (1991) explain in the Harvard study on home-school influences on literacy, low-income families and children are more subject to a wide variety of psychological stressors—for example, scarcity of financial resources, inadequate and crowded housing, dangerous neighborhoods, and unemployment—than are middle-income families. C. and M. Suarez-Orozco (1995) argue that the stresses of acculturation that immigrant families experience further aggravate these social and psychological stressors. Trueba (1998) expresses concern that immigrant children, in particular, face hostile conditions in these environments; many suffer from neglect and malnutrition because parents cannot afford to pay for child care and for health insurance. "Dysfunctional housing conditions increase the chances of health problems . . . and in some cases even the safety of children is jeopardized in dilapidated housing infested with drug addicts and vandals" (Trueba, 1998, p. 258). Although proponents of cultural explanations have focused on what families do, their cultural traits, or their aspirations for their children, Cordero-Guzman (in press) presents persuasive empirical evidence to support the view that material resources (that is, family income and other learning resources) that families have to promote youth development do affect children's academic attainment and achievement.

Orfield (1989) documents, as did Coleman and his colleagues in the now classic Coleman Report, that schools in these communities continue to be unequal in terms of facilities, educational offerings, and academic achievement, which suggests how schools contribute to the shaping of differences. Furthermore, racial and ethnic segregation between cities, suburbs, schools, and classrooms is growing worse. Trueba (1998) reports that three measures of state rankings in segregation (percentage of Latino students in majority White schools, percentage in minority schools, and percentage of "White" students in Latino schools) show clear trends of marked isolation of Latinos in school. Nieto (1995) explains that segregation limits access to English language development, college preparation, and advanced placement curricula. Cordero-Guzman emphasizes (once again) that the problem is basically that there are differences in the material resources schools have available and that these resources do influence the quality of experience provided to learners. "Schools are environments that under specific circumstances can accelerate or retard learning and individual development" (Cordero-Guzman, in press, p. 12).

Wells (1993) argues that even if instruction and the physical conditions of schooling are improved, these are not sufficient to offset the basic problem: Social mobility and the life chances of individuals are limited under segregated conditions. A number of social scientists believe that the phenomenon of ethnically segregated public schools has serious implications for the reproduction of inequality inasmuch as social status (which buys access to greater human and material resources to support schooling) is the key to academic success and not vice versa (Flores, Attinasi, & Pedraza, 1981). Of particular concern to some scholars is the long-term consequence of this situation (Fordham & Ogbu, 1986; Steele, 1997; Trueba, 1998) and its impact on children and youth—on their socioemotional development, their social and intellectual identities, their group affiliations, and their language use (Baugh, 1993; Labov, 1987; San Miguel, 1987; M. Suarez-Orozco, 1996, 1998; Trueba, 1998), with attendant consequences for social mobility through education.

These demographic changes have important consequences for teachers. M. Suarez-Orozco (1998) reports that public schools in the two largest U.S. cities, New York and Los Angeles, are already encountering an unprecedented range of sociocultural and linguistic variability in their classrooms. As Berliner and Biddle (1995) indicate, "public schools in one region or community may face problems that are far different from those encountered elsewhere in the country" (p. 227). Research is finding that "Underprepared teachers constitute more than 25% of those hired each year . . . and they are assigned disproportionately to schools and classrooms serving the most educationally vulnerable children" (Darling-Hammond, 1996, p. 6). However, even teachers with preparation feel inadequately prepared to teach in complex learning environments—for example, where there is a broad range of language abilities. Ashton (1996) reports that 30% of first-year teachers surveyed did not believe that the education they received prepared them to teach students from a variety of ethnic backgrounds, and, of these, 15% had abandoned the belief that they could make a difference. Although these findings need to be examined carefully, they are reason for concern in light of the growing number of English Language Learners (ELLs), whose opportunities to learn are impeded by teachers who lack the expertise to understand and respond to language and cultural differences (let alone to issues of poverty) in the classroom.

August and Hakuta (1997) report that only 55% of the teachers of English Language Learners have taken relevant college courses or have received recent in-service professional development relating to the range of human diversity introduced by immigration.

This section has presented recent scholarship on the "new" diversity, which includes not only children of recent immigrants but also long-term citizens or national-origin minorities. Although these two groups have significantly different historical trajectories and distinct sociocultural profiles, both groups are concentrated in poor, urban settings where children are likely to attend segregated, underfunded, and underachieving schools with underprepared teachers. The scholarship presented here highlights how differences in family, school, and community level material resources adversely affect students' academic attainment, even though an unbalanced emphasis continues to be placed on the cultural traits and aspirations of families. This limited focus may be misguided and deceptive as it does not constitute adequate preparation for teachers who need to understand how learner differences are also shaped within the context of families or households that reside in communities with limited access to human and material resources. That is, ecological differences affect the social, emotional, physical, communicative, and intellectual development of learners—in sum, human development. Addressing these needs effectively requires a clearer understanding of their origins.

Differences Are Socially Constructed

[R]ace is a concept that signifies and symbolizes social conflicts and interests by referring to different types of human bodies. Although the concept of race invokes "biologically based" human characteristics (so-called "phenotypes"), selection of these particular human features for purposes of racial signification is always and necessarily a social and historical process. . . . Indeed, the categories employed to differentiate among human groups along racial lines reveal themselves, upon serious examination, to be at best imprecise, and at worst completely arbitrary. (Omi & Winant, 1994, p. 55)

In their incisive analysis of racial formation in the United States, Omi and Winant (1994) document how "race" and "racial classification" are a legacy of slavery and bigotry that had their origins when European explorers first encountered the indigenous populations on this continent. Issues of "race" and racism are not Black-White issues, as they are typically framed; they involve all racialized populations. Omi and Winant (1994) argue that from "the very inception of the Republic to the present moment, race has been a profound determinant of one's political rights, one's location in the labor market, and indeed one's sense of identity" (p. 1). The fact that the federal government has used "race" as an analytical category to study and describe demographic changes in the U.S. population since the first decennial census in 1790 suggests this possibility (Federal Register, Standards for the Classification of Federal Data on Race and Ethnicity, August 26, 1995). Although they are assumed to have the semblance of rigor, census data are both imprecise and arbitrary. In addition to being a mixture of self-identification and the perceptions of observers, who may use their own understanding of what is salient to distinguish among populations, the classification schema has changed over time. Even so, census data are used to generate analyses and policies that affect the educational experiences and opportunities of "racial," "ethnic," and linguistic minorities (Omi & Winant, 1994).

Some scholars have called for a complete rejection of the use of the term "race" in academic and public discourse, arguing, for example, that to have long-term inhabitants of this nation, as are Americans of Mexican ancestry, included under the category of "Hispanic" along with more recent immigrants from Mexico is "racist" (Gimenez, 1996; Miles, 1989; Torres & Ngin, 1995). Gimenez (1996) believes that bombarding the population with statistics that constantly stress the differences among

Whites, Asians, Blacks, and "Hispanics" as well as the ethnic and racial politics and practices that put everyone who is not from Europe in the minority encourages the young, the uneducated, and the prejudiced to strengthen stereotypes and maintain an oversimplified view of the world.

One suggestion has been made to replace the word *race* with *ethnic group* (Miles, 1989). However, Omi and Winant (1994), Ladson-Billings (1994), Nieto (1992), among others contend that reducing race to ethnicity is also problematic. Omi and Winant (1994) argue that despite its uncertainties and contradictions, "the concept of race continues to play a fundamental role in structuring and representing the social world" (p. 55). The persistence of de facto segregation and inequities in the conditions and outcomes of schooling for low-status groups is cited as evidence for the enduring significance of "race" in our society. Further, recent studies of students' experiences of schooling indicate that children and youth are racially conscious and aware of the differential treatment they receive (for example, see the work of Nieto, 1992; C. Suarez-Orozco & M. Suarez-Orozco, 1995; Walsh, 1994).

While the use of "racial" and "ethnic" labels is generally regarded as problematic (Flores, Teft Cousin, & Diaz, 1991), these labels are also acknowledged to be a means of securing additional funding to meet the needs of youngsters who attend seriously underfunded schools and whose needs have not been met through traditional schooling experiences. Since the 1960s, data on race and ethnicity have been used in civil rights monitoring and enforcement covering areas such as employment, voting rights, housing and mortgage lending, health-care services, and educational opportunities. Omi (1996) emphasizes that racial classification is political, reflecting changes in racial consciousness and mobilization. For example, prior to the late 1960s, no "Asian American" label was used.

> The racialization of Asian Americans involved the muting of profound cultural and linguistic differences, and of significant historical antagonisms that existed among the distinct nationalities and ethnic groups of Asian origin. . . . Asian American activists found the political label a crucial rallying point for raising political consciousness about problems in Asian ethnic communities. . . . (p. 180)

According to Ladson-Billings (1994), educational research "has failed to examine adequately the special historical, social, economic, and political role that race plays in the United States" (p. 16). Darder (1991) and Stanton-Salazar (1997) agree that the mainstream scholarly community has given little attention to examining the developmental challenges faced by members of low-status groups who have to participate in multiple, often conflicting, and contradictory social systems and contexts. Darder (1991) refers to children and youth from these groups as "bicultural" learners to emphasize the sociocultural differences that have shaped their development:

> [Bicultural students have experienced] an enculturation process that is distinct from that of Anglo-American students. This distinction is derived from the fact that bicultural students, throughout their development, must content with: (1) two cultural systems whose values are very often in direct conflict; and (2) a set of sociopolitical and historical forces dissimilar to those of mainstream, Anglo-

American students and the educational institutions that bicultural students must attend. (p. xvi)

Claude Steele (1997) documents how stereotypes shape intellectual identity and performance, and imperil achievement among students who are considered to be academically successful. Steele (1997) theorizes that achievement may suffer when students perceive that they are being judged as members of stigmatized groups who are not considered to have the interests, skills, and abilities that are needed to prosper in particular academic domains. Although his concern is with student retention in postsecondary education, Steele's analysis has implications for learners across the developmental continuum. Using a sociocultural approach to research that examines how factors such as "race," "ethnicity," and nationality shape young people's perspectives on the past, Epstein (2000) found that students' racialized identities significantly influence their concepts of historical events, illustrating how students' racialized identities also shape their experience of the curriculum.

Ladson-Billings and Tate (1995) agree that "race" continues to be significant in explaining unequal educational outcomes in the United States. They agree with Omi and Winant (1994) that race, gender, and class "overlap, intersect, and fuse with one another"; that as "stand alone variables, class and gender do not explain all of the educational achievement differences apparent between whites and students of color" (p. 51). The problem, in their view, is that "race" has remained undertheorized:

> We are not suggesting that other scholars have not looked carefully at race as a powerful tool for explaining social inequity, but that the intellectual salience of this theorizing has not been systematically employed in the analysis of educational inequity. Thus, like Omi and Winant, we are attempting to uncover or decipher the sociostructural and cultural significance of race in education. (p. 50)

As Omi and Winant (1994) explain, race is a social construct that is shaped and transformed by the social structure, preeminently by politics as well as by culture through socialization, and plays a fundamental role in structuring relationships among people and influencing the way they experience the world. Consequently, it is both structural and cultural. Further, Omi and Winant clarify the meaning of racism, which they maintain has also changed over time. As they explain it, a project may be considered racist if it "creates or reproduces structures of domination based on essentialists categories of race" (p. 71). The term *essentialist* is used to refer to "true human essences existing outside or impervious to social and historical contexts" (p. 71).

These scholars, among others (Rodriguez-Morazzani, 1996; Torres & Ngin, 1995) build on the influential thinking of British sociologist Robert Miles (1989). Miles argues for the need to understand and explain the construction and reproduction of the idea of "race" given that races are not naturally occurring populations. While he acknowledges the political appeal to "race" as part of the discourse of resistance evident in the Black Power movement of the 1960s, he is critical of its use by social scientists who have employed it uncritically, "reified it and then attributed it with the status of a scientific concept" (p. 75).

Miles proposes changing the way we talk about race by introducing the notion of "racialization," particularly because the terms "race" and "racism" are frequently used interchangeably. As he explains it, "racialization" refers to "those instances where social relations between people have been structured by the signification of human biological characteristics in such a way as to define and construct differentiated social collectivities" (p. 75). The categorization process that results in the representation of an "Other" and that involves the attribution of signification to somatic features such as skin color and hair texture is a reflection of ideology. This is a dialectic process because the "Self" is always defined in relation to an "Other," usually by the opposite criterion. Miles makes this distinction to emphasize that the term "racism," which he views as an exclusionary practice, is a term that has been overused and is consequently losing its explanatory power.

Further, recent studies of students' experiences of schooling indicate that children and youth are racially conscious and aware of differential treatment they receive, which they construe as "racist" (for example, see the work of Epstein, 2000; Nieto, 1992; C. Suarez-Orozco & M. Suarez-Orozco, 1995; Walsh, 1991). Darder (1991) suggests that students need to "reflect together on their lived experiences and to explore critically how these experiences relate to their participation in the larger society and to their process of emancipation" (p. 60). However, as Osborne's (1996) synthesis of cross-national ethnographic research on culturally relevant pedagogy indicates, teacher education programs have not prepared teachers to address issues of race and racism in the classroom. Because "race" is a topic that generally provokes a great deal of discomfort among teachers, teacher educators, and researchers on teaching, it has remained suppressed. By providing a language to talk about "race," theories of racialization may facilitate these discussions. In addition, racialization theories provide a powerful lens for reorienting the study of how physical and linguistic characteristics of individuals shape pedagogical relationships within a racialized social order.

In our society, racialization and racism are, at once, structural and cultural. The ideology that perpetuates both is learned behavior. As scholars of Critical Race Theory argue, racism is "normal, not aberrant in American society" (Ladson-Billings, 1999). Stated differently, in our society racism is cultural (Carnoy, 1994). Consequently, teachers need to understand the subtle ways the racism is manifested in government policy, in society, and in public institutions such as schools. Similarly, scholars need to question the empirical and moral purposes for using "racial" labels in their research. Although research is sparse, empirical data suggest the use of racial labels affects students' perceptions of what they know, who they are, where they come from, and what they are capable of becoming. It also affects students' relationship with teachers, peers, and family, and their experience of the curriculum. Left unexamined are the perceptions of children and youth from the dominant ethniclass who are also affected by these distinctions.

Ethnicity and Differences among Learners

That ethnic groups have a unique cultural character can hardly be denied. The problem, however, is that culture does not exist in a vacuum; nor is it fixed and unchanging. . . . Without a doubt eth-

nicity informs consciousness and influences behavior. But what informs ethnicity and influences its character? (Steinberg, 1981, p. ix)

The term "ethnicity" has been used to refer to national origin, religion, ancestry, culture, and language (Steinberg, 1981); however, Omi and Winant (1994) indicate that the definition of the term is "muddy." They point out that the ethnicity-based paradigm that evolved after the abolition of slavery put into disfavor the biologistic paradigm, which attributed differences among social groups to genetic superiority or inferiority. Within the present sociopolitical context, theories of maladaptive cultural patterns are perceived as safe or neutral variants of biologistic views.

PROBLEMS AND DILEMMAS IN THE USE OF ETHNIC LABELS

Over the past decade, scholars have continued to interrogate the meaning and use of ethnic labels and how these contribute to the formation of ethnic stereotypes. In a study of first-generation adult immigrants, which sought to illuminate the difference between ethnic labels and ethnic lives, Oboler (1995) argues that ethnic labels homogenize differences and conceal more than they reveal. As she explains, the term "Hispanic," which first appeared in the 1980 census as a substitute for "Spanish-Origin," fails to recognize the extremely rich ethnic and racial diversity of Latin Americans,

for example, . . . Mexicans of Irish or Japanese ancestry; Cubans with Spanish, Lebanese, African or Chinese forebears; Peruvians of English, Russian-Jewish, or Inca lineage. . . . [T]here are many Latin Americans who are entirely or partly of African and American Indian ancestry with some of the above. . . . (Mora cited in Oboler, 1995, p. xv)

Further, the use of these labels contributes to ethnic stereotyping. Oboler (1995) argues that contrary to popular perception, not all Latinos in the United States are Spanish dominant. In fact, increasingly, a significant number among the second and later generations are English dominant, and some, although relatively few, do not speak Spanish at all. The assumption that if you are Latino, you speak Spanish has an equivalent in the perception that if you are "White" and mainstream, you are monolingual in English. As alluded to previously, more bilingualism among the "White" mainstream population may occur than is typically assumed. Omi and Winant (1994) explain that because of its privileged status, "White ethnics" have remained above scrutiny and, as a result, have gone largely unexamined in the scholarship. Mehan (1995) is critical of this omission when he argues that "social scientists are more likely to study the people who tend to reside in the lower portions of the status hierarchy or power structure, notably teachers and students in low-income or urban schools, than they are to study the powerful" (p. 243).

Moreover, as Flores's (1996) analysis of popular culture among Puerto Rican youth who reside in El Barrio in New York City and Heath and McLaughlin's study of community organizations for inner-city youth make clear, ethnicity is dynamic and in constant flux, even though labeling suggests that it is invariable and fixed. Flores (1996) and M. Suarez-Orozco

(1998) have found that prolonged contact, as occurs among groups living in close geographic proximity, typically results in a natural and dynamic process of mutual influence and change resulting in "cultural conversions and fusions." Portes and Rumbaut (1996) agree that cultural conversions and fusions are natural and inevitable processes but prefer to describe these as forms of assimilation and Americanization. That individuals adapt to the group(s) with whom they have greater physical contact seems inevitable unless a concerted effort is made to prevent it, as occurs with "autonomous language minority" groups (Ogbu & Matute-Bianchi, 1986), for example, the Amish in Pennsylvania and the Hasidic community of Williamsburg, New York, who isolate themselves for religious or cultural reasons. This also occurs with low-status groups whose isolation is imposed through de facto segregation. Ogbu and Matute-Bianchi (1986) explain that "autonomous minorities" are integrated into the economic or political domain and are not disparaged in the same way that low-status or "caste-like minorities" are, suggesting how societal ideology affects the process of mutual influence, and thereby, contributes to shaping group-based differences.

In their ethnographic study of community youth organizations organized on the basis of ethnicity, Heath and McLaughlin (1993) began to question just how central ethnic identity is to inner-city youth in the 1990s. According to these researchers, young people repeatedly told them "Ethnicity isn't what it's really all about."

> Many young people pointed out that at one time their communities may have been identified with a single ethnic group but that what they see today is different ethnic groups continually moving in and out of their housing projects and neighborhoods. They have learned to "hang with all kinds," "to be with locals," and "to survive." (p. 6)

Heath and McLaughlin conclude that the identities of inner-city youth are embedded in multiple and situationally diverse environments of community, neighborhood, family, peer groups, and local institutions such as churches or youth groups.

As scholars emphasize, the problem with the use of ethnic labels is that it does not recognize that human diversity is continually shaped through social processes of mutual accommodation and assimilation when diverse social collectivities come in contact. Culture, a central aspect of ethnicity, is shaped by these dynamics and is therefore dynamic and in constant flux, even though it is often represented as fixed and immutable.

ETHNIC IDENTITY FORMATION

While it is commonly believed that ethnic identity is an impediment to assimilation, scholars of the formation of ethnic identity suggest otherwise. Portes and Rumbaut (1996) theorize that ethnic identity grows out of the immigrant experience. Accordingly, a heightened sense of identification with those sharing a common ancestry or history is, in effect, a "reaction formation" on the part of second-generation immigrants to hostile societal treatment of the first generation. Thus, initial identification with national origin or nationality is transformed into an "ethnic" identity, which, in a sense, acts as a protective shield for surviving in hostile environments.

However, C. and M. Suarez-Orozco (1995) suggest that ethnic identity is more complex and that it may be experienced differently by immigrants and by children of immigrants.

> In our view, immigration is an open-ended process that affects the experiences of the generations (. . . the first generation, . . . the second generation). Hence we are critical of theories of immigration assimilation and acculturation that make "closed" statements (e.g., "by the second generation, X will be fully assimilated") about what is, in our estimation, a dynamic intergenerational process. (p. 52)

Gay (1987) calls attention to differences in the ethnic identity formation process between recent immigrants and historically disparaged groups in our society. For example, "for most Black Americans, pride in their ethnic identity does not happen automatically, nor does it happen to everyone. When it does happen, it is the result of individual developmental growth and learning, as well as a person's changing perceptions of, and interactions with, different ethnic referent groups. . . . [For African Americans, the] ethnic identity development process is a form of psychological liberation" (p. 70).

According to Darder (1991), bicultural students (the term she prefers when referring to Black, Latino, Native American, and Asian students) learn to function in or adapt to two distinct sociocultural environments: their primary culture and that of the dominant mainstream culture of the society in which they live, a process she refers to as biculturalism. Building on the empirical literature on biculturalism and biculturation, Darder (1991) proposes that there are four major response patterns related directly to the biculturation of members of subordinate cultures: alienation, dualism, separatism, and negotiation.

> Responses categorized under cultural alienation reflect those that suggest an internal identification with the dominant culture and a rejection of the primary culture . . . [such as] refusal to speak Spanish. . . . A cultural dualist . . . response pattern is informed by a perception of having two separate identities, one that is identified with the primary cultural community, and one that is related to acceptance of mainstream institutional values. . . . The cultural separatist response pattern identify those responses related to remaining strictly within the boundaries of the primary culture while rejecting adamantly the dominant culture. . . . The cultural negotiation response reflects attempts to mediate, reconcile, and integrate the reality of lived experiences in an effort to retain the primary cultural identity and orientation while functioning toward social transformation within the society at large. (pp. 55–56)

Darder emphasizes that educators need to have an understanding of the dynamics of biculturalism if they are to meet the needs of students of color. To date, little, if any, attention has been given to the dual socialization and biculturation processes of students from subordinate groups in our society as part of teacher preparation.

ETHNIC IDENTITY, SOCIAL STATUS, AND ACADEMIC ACHIEVEMENT

Although only a few scholars have focused on the ethnic identity formation process as it relates to academic achievement, scholars agree that this process is influenced by the position of particular groups in the "racial" and "ethnic" hierarchy (Groes-foguel & Georas, 1996; Portes & MacLeod, 1996). Specifically, Portes and MacLeod (1996) have found that a favorable governmental and societal reception to newly arrived immigrants leads to faster socioeconomic mobility, a more positive self-image, and better integrated immigrant communities. In the present sociopolitical climate, immigrants from communist countries continue to be accorded greater status than other immigrants. Portes and MacLeod (1996) theorize that this "contextual advantage" is a significant mediating influence on economic mobility and, consequently, on students' academic achievement. Specifically, parental socioeconomic status (SES), length of U.S. residence, and hours spent on homework significantly affect students' academic performance, with children of groups that were well received (in their study, Cuban and Vietnamese parents) performing better than children of groups that were not well received (in their case, Haitian and Mexican parents), regardless of their school context. In contrast, the identities of groups at the bottom of the "racial" and "ethnic" hierarchy, who have a low or negative symbolic capital, do not benefit from the contextual advantage accorded higher-status groups.

Scholars are finding that when social identities are tied to low-status groups, it has a profound negative impact on the psychosocial adjustment and school achievement of children and youth (Apple, 1996; Bartolome & Macedo, 1997; Steele, 1997; C. Suarez-Orozco & M. Suarez-Orozco, 1995). Walsh's (1991) poignant example is consistent with scholarship that indicates that even elementary school children are sensitive to status differences:

> Puerto Ricans are sad. Puerto Ricans are dirty. Puerto Ricans are lazy. Puerto Ricans *hace lo que le da la gana* (do whatever they feel like). . . .
> But I'm Puerto Rican, and I'm not sad, I'm not dirty or lazy, and I work real hard. . . . Maybe all Puerto Ricans are not like that, right? (a ten-year-old student, p. 47)

However, Takaki (1989) reminds us that this status is subject to change, illustrating not only how the social construction of identity changes over time but also that the positioning of different groups is subject to change. Presently, Asians are described as the "model minority" and set as a standard for others to emulate or as a standard to suggest that the failures of some groups are of their own doing. Nevertheless, Takaki (1989) explains that at the beginning of this century, Asians were viewed as undesirable and were excluded from entering the United States through racist immigration policy such as the Chinese Exclusion Act of 1882 and the National Origins Act of 1924.

This differential positioning of groups in the social hierarchy has led some scholars (Omi & Winant, 1994; Portes & Rumbaut, 1996; C. Suarez-Orozco & M. Suarez-Orozco, 1995) to question the value of using the European immigrant analogy to understand the relatively lower social positioning of populations who continue to be excluded or marginalized from the economic mainstream in our society. That racialized populations may be incorporated into American life in the same way that White ethnic groups had been (the European immigrant analogy) is, at best, a source of public confusion and a source of misconceptions about the assimilation and acculturation of

immigrant children and youth, and, at worst, the basis of societal racism or discrimination. Omi and Winant (1994) point out that the problem with the European analogy is that ethnicity is construed as a barrier to economic and political integration, which has not been the case for the majority of African Americans, American Indians, Chicanos, and Puerto Ricans for some time now.

Because conventional wisdom construes ethnic affiliations as barriers to assimilation, relatively little scholarly attention has been given to examining ethnicity as a source of strength among "national-origin minority groups" (Boykin, 1994; Gay, 1987) and among more recent immigrants (C. Suarez-Orozco & M. Suarez-Orozco, 1995). Yet contemporary scholarship by African American and Latino scholars suggests the importance of this approach. This scholarship suggests a positive (not negative) relationship between ethnicity and learning, a sharp contrast to the way this relationship has been studied by mainstream scholars.

In sum, the scholarship alluded to in this section highlights the tensions, conflicts, and contradictions associated with marking learner variablity through "ethnic" and "racial" labels. The danger is that these constructed identities structure pedagogical relationships and elicit and reinforce stereotypic perceptions that are held about particular groups of learners and, thereby, reproduce the same inequalities they presumably seek to redress.

However, "ethnicity" is also about the quest for community and belonging—whether by those who share a common historical bond (African-American youth) or by those who create other ties and affinities (social groups based on age, gender, profession). While attention to this dimension has been generally neglected in the literature and in teacher preparation, the scholarship reviewed in this section supports the view that ethnicity is an important source of identity and a marker of solidarity for children and youth. These group affiliations are essential for coping in emotionally (and physically) hostile environments (Portes & Rumbaut, 1996; C. Suarez-Orozco & M. Suarez-Orozco, 1995). Teachers need to have a more expansive view of the complex role that ethnicity and ethnic identification have in human development, both of which influence and are influenced by the teaching and learning process.

Linguistic Differences among Learners

> Ethnic identity is twin-skin to linguistic identity—I am my language. Until I take pride in my language, I cannot take pride in myself. (Anzaldua in Flores and Yudice, 1990, p. 73)
> To see language as a mere instrumental tool for communication is to miss its deep affective roots. Giving up Spanish to acquire English is a symbolic act of ethnic renunciation: it is giving up the mother tongue for the instrumental tongue of the dominant group. (C. Suarez-Orozco & M. Suarez-Orozco, 1995, p. 73)

As current scholarship emphasizes, language is a marker of ethnic affiliation, even though it is often treated as an independent, individual competence in the research literature. This section is about language differences among learners that are group-based. We can identify two broad contexts for understanding language variation and use in the United States today. One such context is the learning of English as a second, third (or more) language among recently arrived immigrant students. The other primarily involves the learning of English by national-origin minority groups, who are, in many cases, English monolinguals. For the sake of clarity, these will be treated separately in the narrative that follows.

Linguistic Differences among Immigrant Students

As previously described, demographic data suggest the wide variation across languages that exists in the United States today and that has become the norm, particularly in large, urban school districts. Recent scholarship also suggests the wide variation that exists among English Language Learners in the acquisition of English. Although learning the national language is perceived to be essential for assimilation and for success in school among immigrant populations, the belief is widespread that willful refusal to learn English occurs and, indeed, that languages other than English will be used to communicate in public institutions such as schools. Despite the prevalence of this perception, research findings suggest otherwise. In their sociologically oriented study of immigrant populations, Portes and Rumbaut (1996) found that (a) the larger the proportion of an ethnic group that is U.S. born, the stronger is the shift to English; and (b) minority children consistently prefer English to the mother tongue (p. 214).

Nevertheless, researchers have found group-based variations in this general pattern. Portes and Rumbaut (1996) indicate that Asian immigrants appear to be "more inclined to shed their native language" than those from Latin America, with Mexicans being "the most resilient Spanish speakers," even though among them language shift is unmistakable. However, recent sociolinguistic and sociological studies shed insight on the causes of these differences. Smith's (1996) study of the circular migration patterns among Mexicans reveals that circular migration is influenced by the economic needs of families in search of labor and livable wages. This situation, in turn, affects the language development of immigrants and migrants, and their children. Although this phenomenon has received little attention by educational researchers, evidence suggests a strong relationship between a groups' economic status and language use and development within particular communities.

Heath (1986) points out that differences within languages may be more important than differences across languages. "For all children, success depends less on the specific language they know than on the ways of using language they know" (p. 144). As studies on second language learning emphasize, this is a complex developmental process because there are differences between the demands of the social uses of language and those required for successful academic performance. Achievement in formal learning contexts such as schools requires the type of competency that takes at least seven years to develop (Collier, 1995; Cummins, 1989). However, within the present antibilingual education context, scientific evidence is often set aside in favor of the demands of the politically influential who insist, for example, that students in bilingual programs should be given, without exception, one year to develop competence in academic English.

Linguistic Differences and Racial and Ethnic Identity

Variation in the use of English among long-term inhabitants reflects the essential connection between language, race, ethnicity, and identity in the United States. Although Baugh (1993) insists that to understand this variation and its use in social contexts is important, Zentella (1997) argues for the need to understand the conditions that give rise to this variation—how it is influenced and shaped by the larger political, socioeconomic, and cultural forces (the social context), including the specific dialects in contact. However, both agree that understanding intralanguage variation requires a reconceptualization of language.

> [A] language is not a collection of vocabulary, sounds, and grammatical rules divorced from the geographical, ethnic, racial, gender, and class identities of its speakers. Membership in one or more speech communities is reflected in our dialect(s), that is, in the specific configuration of vowels, consonants, intonation patterns, grammatical constituents, lexical items, and sentence structure shared with other community members, as well as the rules for when, where, how to speak. (Zentella, 1997, p. 269)

Baugh (1993) claims that sociolinguistic studies over the past two decades—primarily by "minority scholar,"—"have collectively offered new insights into the complexity of sociolinguistic behavior," (p. 153) (a) on the character of this variation in the Black community (Baugh, 1993; Smitherman, 1977, 1997), (b) in the Latino communities in the Southwest among Chicanos and Mexican Americans, and (c) in the Northeast among Puerto Ricans (Pedraza, 1987; Zentella, 1997). Throughout the past three decades, especially since the Supreme Court decision in the case of *Martin Luther King Junior Elementary School v. Ann Arbor School District Board,* 1979, sociolinguists and psycholinguists have called attention to the importance of sociolinguistic knowledge in the preparation of teachers, even though little specific attention has been given to it in mainstream teacher preparation (Baugh, 1993; Wolfram, 1998; Zentella, 1997) and despite the knowledge base that has existed for the past three decades. However, as Cazden (1986) suggests, the lack of attention to language variation in research on teaching and teacher education may reflect concerns over deficit models of minority children's language that gained prominence in the sixties and that are still prevalent today.

U.S. EBONICS

Recently, the Oakland Unified School District (OUSD) stirred a great deal of controversy by declaring that students whose primary language is Black English or Ebonics qualified under California statute as "limited English proficient students" in order to secure special funds to address the needs of African-American students (Jackson, 1997). Although Smitherman (1997) and others believe that when the Oakland School Board tapped into the Ebonics framework, they were seeking an alternative pedagogical paradigm to redress the noneducation (or miseducation) of Black youth in underfunded schools, their actions brought this issue to public and academic scrutiny, once again, since the Ann Arbor case gave legal recognition to Black

English. Smitherman (1997) maintains that although research on U.S. style Ebonics can be traced back at least as far as 1884 when James A. Harrison published a 47-page description of "Negro English" in the journal *Anglia,* she believes that this research has been marginalized.

Smitherman (1997) explains that Ebonics is a superordinate term that covers all the African-European language mixtures developed in the various African-European language contact situations throughout the world and that encompasses the linguistic-cultural practices of slave descendants. The term *Ebonics,* coined by Black scholars in 1973, is also referred to in the literature as "Vernacular Black English" (VBE) and African-American Vernacular English" (AAVE). Ebonics includes Haitian Creole, a West African language mixture; the Dutch Creole spoken in Surinam; Jamaican Creole; West African Pidgin English; and a number of others, including the West African English mixture spoken in the United States. Accordingly, Ebonics symbolizes the linguistic unity of the Black world and locates Black American English and U.S. Ebonics (USEB) within a broader African linguistic-cultural context. USEB is a "new language forged in the crucible of enslavement," that reflects the transformation of ancient elements of African languages, intertwined with American-style English (Smitherman, 1997).

McWhorter (1997) disagrees about the extent of African influence on Black English. In his analysis, most nonstandard features in Black English are directly traceable to regional dialects spoken by the British settlers, the English to which African slaves in America were exposed. However, Jackson (1997) argues that

> vernacular varieties of Black English in the United States are an outgrowth of Caribbean slaves using "pidgin English" to communicate between and among themselves and their landowners, and "when their children were born, the pidgin gradually began to be used as the mother tongue, producing the first Black Creole speech in the region," which spread in new varieties among slaves. (Crystal, 1995, quoted in Jackson, 1997, pp. 21–22)

One specific concern raised by the discourse on U.S. Ebonics is the possibility for stereotyping that results when the speech styles are homogenized and characterized monolithically. McWhorter (1997) points out that Black English and standard English are generally spoken together, often mixed within the same sentence—an inevitable consequence of the intermingling of speech patterns that occurs on a daily basis. A similar pattern has been found by Zentella (1997) in her study of Puerto Rican English in New York City, which she characterizes as a "bilingual, multidialectal repertoire." Characterizing students as speakers of "Black English" and "Puerto Rican English" as if it were a monolithic entity is to misrepresent how students use language.

PUERTO RICAN ENGLISHES

Sociolinguists affiliated with El Centro de Estudios Puertorriquenos (The Center for Puerto Rican Studies) of the City University of New York, which has as its primary mission research on the Puerto Rican community in the United States, engaged during the 1970s and 1980s in research on the nature of language and language use among members of this community. Much of this research on language has been conducted in East Harlem or in El Barrio in New York City, which historically, and until recently, has been one of the largest of the Puerto Rican communities in the United States. What is most significant about this research is that it has been undertaken from an interdisciplinary perspective by anthropologists, sociologists, and sociolinguists, among others, including Centro historians and political economists, in analyses of different facets of community life, with implications for teaching and teacher education.

Pedraza (1987), one of the scholars who has been affiliated with El Centro since its inception in 1974, has conducted extensive sociolinguistic research on the use of Spanish and English in the community, most notably, language use in the public domain, where it is most visible. Pedraza's ethnographic analysis of language use in daily life within an area of East Harlem, estimated to have been, at that time, 90% Puerto Rican, reveals "the social diversity and linguistic complexity found even within such an ethnically homogeneous population" (p. 23). Even so, Pedraza concludes that the Puerto Rican community of East Harlem is clearly bilingual, despite the popular misconception that they are not developing skills in English. A majority of residents can utilize both languages to some extent, and those over 30 and born, raised, or both in New York City are particularly adept bilinguals.

Although many of the younger members of the community are bilingual and communicate with their parents and other adults in Spanish, a life-cycle phenomenon seems apparent in which youth appear to put Spanish aside in adolescence and resuscitate it in young adulthood. Social networks are used to explain the linguistic choices and changes that are evident over time. For example, youth use mainly Spanish with the older members of the community while using English with peers, a complex process that involves shifting styles among Black English, Puerto Rican English, and New York City English. According to Pedraza, the influence of Black vernacular speech on the English vernacular of Puerto Rican adolescent males has been well documented in the work of Labov and Wolfram during the 1960s and 1970s. However, its role today in a possible pan-Latino New York City English remains to be documented.

Studies of code-switching, a highly stigmatized feature of Puerto Rican English that has received a great deal of attention, have found that children attempt to speak the language that the hearer knows best, which often requires switching from one language to another (see Zentella, 1990). However, children also switch languages while speaking to the same person, which is taken as evidence of their linguistic adaptability. Zentella (1990, 1997) and Pedraza (1987) interpret the bilingual and multidialectal code-switching among members of this community to be an expression of their different identities and social roles (e.g., gender). Pedraza found that while a number of different factors trigger Spanish usage, the presence of monolingual English speakers from outside the community is of special significance. Spanish may be used as a device to screen out and distance outsiders, in the same way that African Americans used AAVE to communicate with one another in the presence of outsiders, or "Whites." Most important, Pedraza found that a person's migratory history turns out to be the most critical factor influencing language behavior, which, in turn, is explained by a person's positioning in the social networks of the community. Whether first, second, or third generation Puerto Rican, the migration experience of individuals is the one sociohistorical feature common to all community members, which explains more fully the language patterns of the community and which affects other related and important factors such as education and occupation.

Zentella (1997) took another approach in her sociolinguistic research in East Harlem, a two-prong study (intermittently between 1979 and 1993), first, of 20 households and, eventually, of 5 households that were headed by females (1993) who had been elementary school friends during the first phase of the study. Thus, Zentella (1997) was able to trace changes in language development over time in different contexts of use, most notably for these five girls (in 1979), later, women (in 1993), in the school as students and in the home as parents.

Zentella's study documents and examines the important role social networks have in socializing youth to language uses in the Puerto Rican community. Social networks, which go beyond kinship (blood relations) and fictive kinship (close friends who are like family) and include institutional relationships such as coworkers and the church, may play an important role in the socialization of children. Zentella's research reveals precisely how life on the block constitutes a bilingual acquisition experience for most children because of the wide range of speakers who have a role in their care and supervision.

This research also extends our understanding of Puerto Rican English, which Zentella says is also spoken by second generation Latinos in a variety of New York City working-class, Spanish-speaking communities. These consistent patterns reflect the interpenetrating influences of collectivities who have intensive and sustained contact through occupational and geographic proximity. However, the speech of Puerto Ricans is characterized by features such as code-switching, which reflect sociohistorical influences that are also evident in the varieties of English spoken by African Americans. As Baber (1987) explains: "Black communication does indeed reflect the lives and souls of Black folk. . . . Communication is a dynamic, transactional, personal, and symbolic process. Black communication has all these attributes and is a process that is culturally, historically, linguistically, philosophically, socially, and situationally relativistic" (p. 76).

El Centro researchers Pousada and Greenlee (1988) offer an insightful interpretive framework for understanding the use of language among marginalized and racialized communities, which has gained increased attention by contemporary scholars.

> [L]inguistic variation is a manifestation of the contradictions experienced by humans in their daily lives. The material circumstances or interests of individuals lead to differences in language patterns and these linguistic differences are then utilized to perpetuate social differences in a circular, mutually supportive chain. Any variation or change in language . . . stems ultimately from changes in the social activities and relations of people. . . . (p. 63)

Labov (1987) expresses concern that as African Americans and Latinos live increasingly in urban ghettoes and face isolation from the prosperous mainstream, it seems inevitable that their varieties of English will become the language of the poor and the disempowered in our society. "The issue is not simply that blacks should have exposure to whites but simply to children who speak other dialects closer to the standard English of the classroom" (p. 144). However, not all scholars agree. Baugh (1993) argues, and Gay (1987) agrees that "recent linguistic innovations by black youth are not the result merely of social and linguistic isolation from white Americans but a reaffirmation of pride in black culture, which is most visible through speaking style," and which is a reaction to their historical treatment in this society (p. 155). San Miguel (1987) similarly observes that the educational segregation that characterizes the Chicano community may contribute to the strengthening of Mexican-American culture and the Spanish language.

For close to three decades, a number of scholars have argued forcefully that the treatment of language differences in the classroom, not the language difference itself, is problematic for linguistically diverse learners. That is, the academic achievement of students may be threatened in situations where teachers have the mistaken notion that students' language is somehow inferior (Bloom, 1991; Goodman, 1965/1982, 1983; Zentella, 1997). Sociolinguistic studies have found that when children's use of linguistic codes varies from a perceived standard, it is viewed negatively in the classroom by bilingual teachers (Bloom 1991; Zentella, 1997) and by "White" teachers" (De Stefano, 1973; Williams & Whitehead, 1973). Flores and Yudice (1990) further argue that language has been accurately characterized as "an automatic signaling system, second only to race in identifying targets for possible privilege or discrimination" (p. 61).

The scholarship reviewed in this section suggests the importance of linguistic knowledge in the preparation of teachers, and this emphasis has been central to teacher education within specialized fields of study such as bilingual education and English as a Second Language for more than two decades. Little specific attention has been given to it within mainstream teacher education (Baugh, 1993; Goodman, 1965/1982; Wolfram, 1998; Zentella, 1997). Teachers need to understand important sources of variability in language use, in particular, the relationship between language differences and mental abilities and the relationship between language and identity (Baugh, 1993; Smitherman, 1997). Back in the 1960s, Goodman (1965/1982), a leading scholar in the study of dialect and reading in the then emerging field of psycholinguistics, documented that "speakers of low-status dialects of English have a much higher rate of reading failure than high-status dialect speakers" (1965/1982, p. 197). He reasoned that because there is a tendency to confuse linguistic difference with linguistic deficiency, "the solution lies in changing the attitudes of teachers and writers of instructional programs toward the language of learners" (Goodman, 1965/1982, p. 197). That this advice is still appropriate and novel is instructive.

Zentella (1997) acknowledges that questions and contradictions remain that require thoughtful discussion, study, and collective research. For example, How do teachers deal with language use in academic settings so they neither impede the life chances of students nor, at the same time, adversely affect the social identities that students construct for themselves through language? Valdes (1991) argues that we need to know more about how living in bilingual and multidialectal communities shapes the writing practices of school-age children and youth, as relatively less attention has been given to the study of written expression among incipient bilinguals (learners in bilingual and ESL programs), and among functional bilinguals (learners in mainstream, nonbilingual programs). This scholar found that even functional bilinguals evidence non-native qualities in their writings that distinguish them from monolingual peers. Similarly, Delpit raises concerns that students must be taught the codes needed to participate fully in the mainstream of American life, not by being forced to attend to hollow, inane, decontextualized subskills but, rather, by being encouraged to endeavor within the context of meaningful communication. Students must be allowed the resources of the teacher's expert knowledge while being helped to acknowledge their own expertness. Even while students are assisted in learning the culture of power, they must also be helped to learn about the arbitrariness of those codes and about the power relationships they represent. What is, perhaps, the biggest challenge for teachers is to understand that the social history of a collective is also reflected in that group's speech, and because the community is its forms of communication, the language is ineradicable. The view that "critical mastery of the standard dialect can never be achieved fully without the development of one's own voice, which is contained within the social dialect that shapes one's reality" (Freire in Freire & Macedo, 1987, p. 129) is guiding a small number of literacy initiatives (see Mercado, 1992, 1997; Sola & Bennett, 1991; Walsh, 1994). However, as D. Taylor's (1998) analysis also demonstrates, this type of thinking is not new. More than three decades ago, Ralph Ellison stated that

> The way to teach new forms or varieties or patterns of language is not to attempt to eliminate old forms but to build upon them while at the same time valuing them in a way that is consonant with the desire for dignity that lies in each of us. (Ellison in D. Taylor, 1998, p. 37)

THE CHILDREN OF IMMIGRANTS AND LONG-TERM MINORITIES

From our viewpoint, the problems facing Latinos in U.S. schools have less to do with the cultural background of Latinos per se than with the process of immigration, resettlement, and resulting minority status. (C. Suarez-Orozco & M. Suarez-Orozco, 1995, p. 58)

[P]arental status (SES) and the distinct characteristics of immigrant communities impinge on the educational attainment of the children of immigrants. (Portes & MacLeod, 1996)

[F]or all children and youths, healthy human development, general well-being, school success, and economic and social integration in society depend upon regular and unobstructed opportunities for constructing instrumental relationships with institutional agents across key spheres and institutional domains dispersed throughout society. . . . [F]or low status children and youth, the development of supportive relations with institutional agents . . . is systematically problematic. (Stanton-Salazar, 1997)

Over the past two decades, research has focused increasingly on examining how minority status shapes children and youth

from racialized groups. A marked shift has been made in the research from a focus on failure to a focus on the successful adaptation of immigrant children and youth. There is growing evidence that it is possible for students, teachers, parents, and community—"amidst their marginality—to construct successful educational experiences" (Ernst & Statner, 1994, p. 200). This change of emphasis is significant for two reasons. Delpit (1992) articulates one of them:

> Teacher education usually focuses on research that links personal failure and socioeconomic status, failure and cultural difference, and failure and single-parent households. It is hard to believe that these children can possibly be successful after their teachers have been so thoroughly exposed to so much negative indoctrination. (p. 241)

Scholars also point to the potential negative impact that scholarship oriented toward dysfunctionality may have on teachers' sense of efficacy and, consequently, on their interactions with learners. Because teaching is a reciprocal, interactive process, learners construct perceptions of themselves and of their capabilities (see the work of Bigler, 1996; Ladson-Billings, 1994; Mercado, 1992, 1997; Sola & Bennett, 1991; Torres, 1997; Walsh, 1991), as teachers construct their understanding of student competence, and each is an influence on the other.

In an important transnational psychosocial study, C. and M. Suarez-Orozco (1995) found that despite the harsh conditions that immigrant children and youth endure when they are transplanted to the United States, they evidence "phenomenal" school success in comparison to long-term Americans from both nondominant and dominant groups. These findings are compelling because they are derived from a methodologically rigorous study that sought

1. to employ cross-national comparisons to better understand the school achievement of recent immigrants, second-generation Mexicans, Mexicans, and the "white" U.S. mainstream, thereby distinguishing among diverse social collectivities that are often conflated in the scholarship;
2. to be interdisciplinary, combining cross-cultural psychology with psychological anthropology, also reflected in a methodology that employed ethnographic tools such as participant observation and interviews with projective and objective tests; and
3. to understand school achievement in terms of family values and peer affiliations.

The finding that new immigrants are extremely motivated to learn English and use the educational system to improve their lot whereas more acculturated Latinos drop out of schools at alarmingly high rates is both illuminating and disturbing. Equally illuminating is C. and M. Suarez-Orozco's finding that groups differ in their attitudes toward school and that "White" Americans and second-generation Mexican-American students are comparatively less preoccupied with hard work and success than Mexican immigrants and Mexican students. Moreover, for all Latino groups, but especially for Mexican and Mexican immigrants, the family is an important source of support for its members.

The finding that immigrant children's learning ability and social skills deteriorate the longer they are exposed to the alienating environment of American society, which undermines their overall school achievement and adaptation to this society, runs counter to the dominant ideology. This study warrants close attention as it has important implications for teachers and for research on teaching in general and for supporting the psychosocial development of children through home-school continuity. San Miguel (1987), a historian, is among those who argue for more comparative studies of varied language and racial minorities to increase our understanding of the differential experiences of all these groups. Contrastive case studies help us to better understand the diverse character of our American educational heritage.

The findings of the C. and M. Suarez-Orozco (1995) study provide a context for understanding Ogbu's theoretical framework, which has received a great deal of attention in the scholarly and popular literature this past decade. According to Ogbu (1992), involuntary minorities develop "secondary cultural differences" through prolonged contact with "Whites," which mediate their relationships with others. Secondary cultural differences identified by Ogbu include: (a) differences in style rather than in content, such as cognitive style, communication style, interaction style, and learning style; (b) "cultural inversion," or the tendency to regard certain forms of behavior, events, symbols, and meanings as inappropriate because they are associated with "Whites" while simultaneously valuing other behaviors, events, symbols that may be in opposition to those of "Whites." Specific examples cited by Ogbu are ingroup meanings of words; different notions and use of time; different emphasis on dialects and communication style; and, most importantly, the value associated with school learning and achievement.

Thus, according to Ogbu, involuntary minorities develop a new sense of social or collective identity that is in opposition to the social identity of the dominant group in response to their treatment by the dominant "White" ethniclass. This treatment includes deliberate exclusion from economic and political integration or forced superficial assimilation. This treatment explains why involuntary minorities have greater difficulty than voluntary minorities crossing cultural and language boundaries in school, which adversely affects the academic achievement of involuntary minorities. In contrast, voluntary minorities tend to adopt the strategy of "accommodation without assimilation," which Ogbu believes enables them to cross cultural boundaries and do relatively well in school.

Ogbu's theoretical formulations are derived from ethnographic studies of high school students in California, which studies from other settings support. Included among these examples of ethnographic research are Fordham's (1991) study of African-American students in Washington, D.C., and MacLeod's (1987) study of "hall hangers" in a northeastern city. Comer's research with Black children in segregated elementary schools in Connecticut also supports Ogbu's views. Comer notes that "the contrast between a child's experiences at home and those in school deeply affects the child's psychosocial development, and that this, in turn, shapes academic achievement. This contrast [is] particularly sharp for poor minority children

from families outside the mainstream" (p. 43). Unable to achieve in school, children begin to see academic success as unattainable, and so they protect themselves by deciding school is unimportant. Many seek a sense of adequacy, belonging, and self-affirmation in nonmainstream groups that do not value academic achievement; consequently, they are at risk of school dropout, teenage pregnancy, drug abuse, and crime. On the other hand, the decision to pursue academic achievement and to join the mainstream also exacts a heavy price: rejecting the culture of one's parents and social group.

San Miguel (1987) argues that individuals are active participants in shaping their own destinies; they are not passive victims. Sometimes this agency can result in resistance to learning, as Ogbu claims, but it also results in resilience and fuels a commitment to personal and social struggle that make possible positive educational outcomes. In case studies of low-income, African-American adolescents, which included analyzing their life stories, O'Connor (1997) found that students expressed optimism and high academic achievement in the midst of recognizing their subjugation. Moreover, their contact with individuals who had made it or were making it did not lead them to place any less stress on structural constraints on social opportunity and mobility (p. 623).

Stanton-Salazar (1997) explains, "children are seldom raised exclusively within the confines of their nuclear family; rather, they are embedded in social networks, which extend into various social worlds where a wide variety of socialization actors and spheres are found" (p. 7). Children from dominant groups are socialized before entering school to develop social ties or interpersonal relationships with informal mentors, gatekeepers, and other institutional agents to gain access to institutional support, that is, resources, opportunities, and privilege that make possible participation and mobility within school settings. Institutional agents make accessible key forms of institutional support that promote effective participation within mainstream institutional spheres. This support includes (a) socialization into institutionally acceptable ways of communicating and of how the bureaucracy works; (b) acting as a human bridge to social networks and opportunities; (c) advocacy or personalized intervention; (d) role modeling; (e) providing emotional and moral support; and (f) providing regular and personal evaluative feedback and advice.

However, establishing supportive, trusting, and committed relations with nonfamilial institutional agents is often problematic for youth from disenfranchised communities. As Stanton-Salazar (1997) explains, "social antagonisms and divisions existing in the wider society operate to problematize (if not undermine) minority children's access to opportunities and resources that are, by and large, taken-for-granted products of middle-class family, community, and school networks" (p. 3). Therefore, unlike their middle-class counterparts, minority youth experience structural constraints in gaining access to institutional privileges and resources. Some explanations are rooted in the institution, including differential opportunities for developing mainstream discourses and decoding skills and the conflicting roles of teachers as mentors and gatekeepers, etc.

Nevertheless, it is possible to create social networks within schools through strategic planning, which also requires attention to essential social skills for initiating and sustaining these networks. The challenge for minority children and youth is to learn to decode and negotiate the culture of power within mainstream institutions to attain individual mobility and success but also to democratize the system from within. Stanton-Salazar (1997) emphasizes the central role of individual and cultural agency in developing supportive ties or relations with various types of institutional agents, gatekeepers, and informal mentors. Empowering educational experiences can broaden young people's social frames of reference, "expand their access to larger number and variety of potential network members" and "develop the necessary skills for both initiating and maintaining network relations" (p. 4). According to Trueba (1998), the successes that have been reported about the educational achievement of recent immigrants have been socially "engineered" by concerned parents through the activation of binational social networks. They are not the results of individual or institutional effort, as commonly believed.

Adaptive Responses to Difference in the Classroom

That educators need to take into account the special circumstances of students' backgrounds—both the disadvantages that derive from conditions of poverty or discrimination and the strengths that come from cultural traditions and family experiences—is a dominant theme in the scholarship reviewed in the previous sections of this chapter. A number of scholars argue that traditional pedagogy fails to acknowledge the developmental needs of students who have experienced social and educational inequalities in the United States, and perpetuates the underachievement of children of color (Darder, 1991; Hollins, King, & Hayman, 1994; Ladson-Billings, 1994, 1995; Villegas, 1994). However, pedagogical responses to group-based differences are not likely to be successful unless these efforts are explicitly designed and implemented in ways that make equity a priority (Reardon, Scott, & Verre, 1994). Because the past is very much in the present, to understand the current climate for addressing group-based differences in the classroom, it is worth reviewing briefly the divergent reactions that addressing group-based differences elicit since the beginnings of the common school. According to Feinberg (1998) one of the historical purposes of American education was to develop a common American identity. However, this view has always been contested. At one extreme, those who subscribed to Kallen's notion of "cultural pluralism" argued for the acceptance of the different immigrant-based cultures of White ethnics (Omi & Winant, 1994). At the other extreme, those who believed that some groups were genetically inferior to others insisted they attend segregated schools or denied access to education altogether, as occurred with Mexican Americans in the Southwest and African Americans in the South, respectively (Omi & Winant, 1994; Spring, 1997).

In the 1950s, and corresponding with the beginning of the Cold War, the federal government was obligated to sponsor and monitor programs that addressed language and cultural differences in institutional settings that received public funds, in response to massive movements of nonmainstream communities pressuring for access to education as a civil right. These actions culminated in legal recognition of the need to protect the right to an equal educational opportunity through landmark Supreme Court decisions and Civil Rights legislation. Beginning in the late 1960s, funds were allocated to establish a federally sponsored research agenda to understand the influence of language and culture on teaching and learning and to develop culturally responsive education (Cazden, 1980) and multicultural education in teacher education. According to Banks (1992), one of the chief architects of the multicultural education movement in the United States, multicultural education is a broad interdisciplinary field that aims to restructure schools, colleges, and universities so that students from diverse racial, ethnic, and social-class groups will experience an equal opportunity to learn. Nieto (1992) conceptualizes multicultural education as a critical and liberating education that is in keeping with Freire's notion of critical pedagogy. Darder (1991) provides an extensive analysis of the concept of critical pedagogy that is in keeping with Freirian principles.

> Critical pedagogy refers to an educational approach rooted in critical theory. Critical educators perceive their primary function as emancipatory and their primary purpose as commitment to creating conditions for students to learn skills, knowledge, modes of inquiry that will allow them to examine critically the role that society has played in their self-formation. (p. xvii)

Multiculturalists view this pedagogical emphasis as essential preparation for responsive and informed participation in our democratic society. Critical pedagogy engages students in analyzing events and situations from different perspectives to understand how these perspectives position students in the world and to use this knowledge to reposition themselves and thereby act on the world (Nieto, 1992). As a pedagogical approach, multicultural education has been challenged by advocates of accountability models of school reform such as Success for All, that embed a standardized and highly scripted pedagogical approach as a means to guarantee results on achievement tests. Arguing that "student achievement cannot change unless America's teachers use more effective instructional methods" (Slavin, 1996), teachers in these programs are provided with standardized, highly scripted practices and the support needed to implement them. In effect, the approach to difference represented by such approaches is standardization or one-size-fits-all.

A recent doctoral study of critical pedagogy by Garcia-Gonzalez (1998) provides a rare glimpse of critical pedagogies (implying that variability is essential to respond to difference) as they are actually practiced by elementary school teachers from the studied viewpoint of a classroom teacher-researcher. This viewpoint is typically missing from research on teaching. Note that the five teachers that Garcia-Gonzalez studied did not identify themselves directly with multicultural education but with critical pedagogy that is associated with the work of Brazilian educator Paulo Freire. Some distinctive aspects of critical pedagogy that Garcia-Gonzalez found are illustrated in her use of Sylvester's case study as an example of the teacher's ideal vision of critical pedagogy. Sylvester is an African-American third-grade teacher, who creates a curriculum that engages students "as grown-ups in roles of power in a mythical town called *Sweet Cakes.*" The questions that guide this third-grade teacher's practices are insightful and informative:

> (1) How do we as teachers educate so that we do not replicate existing social inequalities and (2) How do we avoid the twin pitfalls of (a) stressing the obstacles of economic success, thereby encouraging defeatism and (b) stressing the possibilities for economic success and thereby encouraging the view that those who have not "made it" have only themselves to blame? (p. 40)

Garcia-Gonzalez (1998) summarizes salient features of critical pedagogy as practiced by Sylvester, which include (a) providing repeated and meaningful applications of academic skills; (b) enabling students to imagine themselves in new roles; (c) helping students divorce academic success from "acting White"; (d) allowing students to take proactive stances in relation to those in power; (e) creating curricula that treats reality as something to be questioned and analyzed; (f) helping students to develop strategies for overcoming barriers to economic success; and (g) offering students opportunities to experience social structures as impermanent and changeable. However, as this teacher researcher concludes, the implementation of philosophies such as critical pedagogies "is colored by the identity, alliances, and relationship to power of the practitioner in question." In other words, implementation of broad philosophical approaches is always filtered through the personal biographies of teachers. That approaches cannot be separated from the individuals who breathe life into them raises important issues that have implications for the recruitment and preparation of teachers.

Drawing upon a study of eight exemplary teachers of African-American students, Ladson-Billings (1995) proposes a grounded theory of culturally relevant pedagogy which is very similar to critical pedagogy. Accordingly, culturally relevant pedagogy develops students academically, nurtures and supports cultural competence, and develops a sociopolitical or critical consciousness. Thus, teachers build on students' cultural strengths to accomplish academic excellence while affirming and strengthening the identities of students, thereby enabling them to transcend the negative effects of the dominant culture. Ladson-Billings (1994) emphasizes, however, that "these cultural referents are not merely vehicles for bridging or explaining the dominant culture; they are aspects of the curriculum in their own right" (p. 18). Ladson-Billings emphasizes that exemplary teachers of African-American students (not all of whom are black) believe their students as capable of academic success and as having knowledge to be pulled out by teachers. They also perceive themselves as members of the community and teaching as a way to give back to the community. Further, teachers demonstrate a connection to all their students and encourage students to learn collaboratively and to be responsible for one another. Lastly, exemplary teachers of African-American students assume a critical perspective toward knowledge precisely because it is socially constructed; they have, as well, the responsibility to facilitate and monitor learning, by building bridges between the new and the known and by employing multiple forms of assessments.

In the section that follows, four initiatives are presented which illustrate variants of critical or culturally relevant pedagogy for middle and secondary schools.

A number of these initiatives are long-term efforts (5 or more years) and go beyond representing learning solely in terms of academic achievement. Most of these initiatives approach learning and learners more holistically, documenting and assessing changes in students' participation in the classroom, their belief systems, their sociolinguistic awareness, and their ability to navigate different social worlds.

Few, however, focus on the impact these experiences have on access to postsecondary education.

Students as Researchers Approach

Heath developed an inquiry-oriented approach to teaching and learning in which students are junior ethnographers, and this approach enables teachers to learn about students' homes and communities as students broaden their understandings and uses of language in their efforts to learn. Research has documented the value of this approach for accelerating the academic preparation of underachieving students in special education and English as a Second Language (ESL) classes (Heath, 1985). Socializing students into the literacy practices of educational ethnographers enables students to acquire valued cultural tools for directing their own learning and for increasing their awareness of how language works. Mercado (1992, 1997), a former teacher and now college-based teacher educator, and Torres (1997), a school-based practitioner, collaborated over a 5-year period to implement a similar approach with sixth graders in an underachieving middle school in New York City.

For one academic year, 1st- and 2nd-generation children of Spanish-speaking immigrants from countries such as the Dominican Republic, Ecuador, El Salvador, and Honduras, 2nd- and 3rd-generation Americans of Puerto Rican ancestry, Afro-Caribbean, and African-American students adapted the literacy practices of social scientists to locate and document local knowledge that responds to questions of concern to students but are not part of the required curriculum. As others have found, students' interests center on understanding health and social problems associated with poverty, for example, children's illnesses and homelessness. Locating the local knowledge embedded in their daily lives enables students to re-experience the ordinary, transforming routine activities such as going to a medical appointment or running an errand into opportunities to practice forms and functions of literacy associated with academic pursuits. Redefining students' social worlds as sources of knowledge, wisdom, and emotional support, rather than as obstacles to overcome, proves significant. Students do not have to stop being who they are (or put aside one identity to assume another) to enter this intellectual community.

Even so, the writing requirements of this special project (often referred to as "College Work") were intense. Students' written forms of language, often stigmatized because they evidence non-native features (Valdes, 1991), did not exclude them from participating in the knowledge construction process. All students were expected to collaborate in (a) preparing research plans and field notes, (b) summarizing information from divergent sources, including interviews of local authorities, and (c) preparing handouts and transparencies for "talks" at professional gatherings. These combined activities, which required students to weave back and forth between the worlds of the home, the school, and the university, influence their use of oral and written language to accomplish the academic goals they valued. They also elicit beliefs that students have about what they don't know (that they are "stupid") and what they may accomplish (they "cannot possibly do college work") that require sensitive mediation. Ongoing assessment guides students to organize and interpret indicators of their progress, including examining responses of familiar and unfamilar peers and adults. This type of assessment makes students conscious of how they are developing and inspires them to continue with their work.

Quantitative analysis indicates the impressive and statistically significant gains on standardized tests of reading and writing made by students. Qualitative changes using observations, interviews, case studies, portfolios, and recordings (primarily photographs and videotapes) indicate an increase in students' confidence to harness the power of literacy to take control of their own learning and development.

Specifically, students learn to value and use the knowledge that resides in their homes, and they relate to family members in qualitatively different ways. They also develop a serious interest in addressing problems of their community. Legitimizing students' sociocultural resources in school signals an unconditional acceptance of the person of the student, making them more receptive to experiment with and appropriate what they are learning. However, appropriating the discourse of research transforms them into intellectuals in the eyes of teachers and, over time, students reorient themselves to their communities, coming to see it and themselves in a new light. Although small in scale, this initiative demonstrates the importance of creating more fluid boundaries between the world of the home-community, the world of the school, and adult academic communities.

Language and Dialect Awareness

Wolfram (1998) proposes a program of study in language arts that introduces a curriculum of study on language variation that exposes basic prejudices and myths about language differences. Wolfram indicates that these efforts are already underway in other countries; in the United States, however, there has been no wide scale curriculum related to language awareness (Wolfram, 1998). Wolfram explains the focus of this program:

> A language awareness program may concentrate on a cognitive parameter in which the focus is on the patterns of language, an affective parameter in which the focus is on attitudes about language, or a social parameter in which the focus is on the role of language in effective communication and interaction. (p. 172)

Curricular units may emphasize: (a) the naturalness of dialect variation in American English; (b) that language patterns or rules have their reality in the minds of speakers; (c) that language patterning and language variation take place on several different levels simultaneously, including phonology, syntax, and semantics; and (d) the consequences of using varieties of language, including standard and vernacular dialects. In this approach, students engage in a wide range of activities, from completing relatively simple exercises in dialect patterning, to

more complex activities such as being introduced to the methods of dialectologists. Thus, students engage in dialect investigation as a scientific study, gathering, analyzing, and interpreting language data.

A five-unit dialect awareness curriculum was piloted in the Baltimore Public Schools. Fourth and fifth graders were introduced to fundamental concepts about language variation; the program has also been used experimentally with middle school students. This curriculum combines humanistic, scientific, and sociohistorical objectives.

> On a humanistic level, the object is to introduce students to the naturalness of language differences. . . . On a scientific level, the objective is to introduce students to the notion of systematic language patterning in dialects. . . . On a cultural-historical level, the objective is to have students gain a sense of appreciation for the historical development of a variety of English dialects. (Wolfram, 1998, p. 179)

The approach taken in this curriculum is largely inductive. It assumes a critical approach to language inquiry as students are asked to manipulate language, to formulate hypotheses about language patterning, and to reflect on some of the popular misconceptions about dialects. However, despite its emphasis on critical thinking and inquiry, Wolfram admits to the difficulty of embarking upon an approach that runs counter to dominant ideologies:

> [T]he sociolinguistic confrontation in education that has taken place over the last several decades, has [made it] necessary to guard against possible misinterpretation. The road leading to such a program has hardly been a smooth one. . . . Part of the difficulty comes from the ways in which the program is perceived by administrators, practitioners, and parents. (p. 181)

Advancement through Individual Determination (The AVID Program)

The AVID "detracking" program was developed by the San Diego School District in response to a court-ordered school desegregation plan (Mehan, Hubbard, & Villanueva, 1994). Initiated in 1980 in one high school, AVID was eventually expanded to other schools in San Diego County and to high schools outside of the county. High-potential, low-performing students are selected for the program in the eighth or ninth grades under the condition that parents agree to support their children's participation. The goals of the program are to "motivate and prepare underachieving students from underrepresented linguistic- and ethnic-minority groups to perform well in high school and to seek a college education." As described by Mehan et al. (1994), students from low-income ethnic- and linguistic-minority backgrounds are placed in college prep classes along with high-achieving peers and in an elective class that emphasizes collaborative instruction, writing, and problem solving.

Specifically, this class emphasizes (a) writing as a tool of learning, which includes techniques for taking detailed academic notes and essay writing; (b) inquiry as a pedagogical procedure in which trained tutors (from local colleges) assist students in answering questions derived from academic notes, and (c) collaboration and interdependence in learning among students through the organization of study teams in small groups.

Most important, students are guided through the intimidating college application process, which includes field trips to different college campuses. Thus, "AVID gives low-income students some of the cultural capital at a school that is similar to the cultural capital that more economically advantaged parents give to their children at home" (Mehan et al., 1994, p. 109).

The project has been documented, primarily, through interviews, classroom observations, and case studies of four participating high schools; the character and influence of this experience on the college enrollment record of the program's graduates; and on students' attainment ideologies. African Americans and Latinos who have participated in AVID for the full 3 years enroll in college at numbers that exceed local and national averages.

> Of the 144 students who graduated from AVID, 72 (50%) reported attending four-year colleges, 60 (42%) reported attending two-year or junior colleges, and the remaining 12 students (8%) said they are working or doing other things. The 50% four-year college enrollment rate for students who were "untracked" compares favorably with SDCS's average of 37% and the national average of 395. (Mehan et al., 1994, p. 99)

Mehan et al.'s (1994) report found social consequences of this untracking effort that they had not anticipated. As they describe it, African-American and Latino students in the AVID program

> developed an interesting set of beliefs about the relationship between school and success. They do not have a naive belief in the connection between academic performance and academic success. While they voice enthusiastic support for the power of their own agency, their statements also display a critical awareness of the structures of inequality and strategies for overcoming discrimination in society. (p. 101)

While students recognize that academic performance is necessary for occupational success, they also display a critical consciousness about the limits and possibilities of the actions they take and the limitations and constraints they face in life. Further, students in the AVID program develop "border crossing strategies" that enable them to negotiate their different social and cultural worlds. They are able to maintain "dual identities," one at school and one among friends who are not part of their academic world, and they engage in activities that bridge their different worlds. AVID participants also initiate nonacademic friends into academic settings by bringing them to classes with them. Mehan et al. (1994) did not find an oppositional ideology or a pattern of resistance among the AVID students. Rather, they found that students formed an academic identity and developed a reflective and critical ideology.

The AVID program has several elements in common with the Success for All Model at the high school level developed at Johns Hopkins University Center for Research on Effective Schooling for Disadvantaged Students (McPartland & Braddock, 1993). Both are comprehensive approaches that are designed to expand and support human development through carefully crafted experiences that support the work of teachers. The Comer Project represents another type of comprehensive approach.

The Comer Project

For more than 3 decades, psychiatrist James Comer has been involved in the development of a comprehensive approach to the schooling of children in inner-city schools that respond to the specific needs of this student population (Summary of School Development Program, 1991): The School Development Program (SDP) or Comer Project grew out of systematic observation of schooling practices "that failed to meet the psycho educational needs of children" (Haynes, in Summary of School Development Program, 1991). The School Development Program is a systems approach to school management using mental health principles of child development and relationships. It is also a process that uses the talents and interests of parents and school staff as collaborative decision makers to develop policies, procedures, and programs that affect the academic and social climate of schools.

Consequently, the School Development Program creates mechanisms within the school to address the "unique psycho educational and developmental needs" of children and youth from low-income families as these needs change over time. The School Planning and Management Team (SPMT) engages parents, teachers, administrators, and support staff in planning the social, academic, and staff development programs intended to make teaching and learning responsive to learner needs, as these needs change over time. The Mental Health Team (MHT), which includes psychologists, counselors, special education teachers, the school nurse, reading specialists, resource teachers, and social workers, meets weekly to discuss and respond to referrals from school staff and parents. The MHT also suggest changes in school policy and program via communication with the SPMT. The intent is to address students' developmental needs and potential problems before they develop into crises. These mechanisms are intended to support the instructional approach, which is grounded on six fundamental principles:

1. Children perform best when their basic physical needs are met.
2. Learning is best facilitated when children have a positive self-concept.
3. Children learn best when positive bonds are created within and between the home and school, and individuals who are best able to impart concepts and beliefs are those with whom learners identify.
4. Language differences should not be equated with intellectual differences.
5. All new learning should be connected to previous learning.
6. Schools and families must find a common ground for the moral development of children.

An array of formal and informal measures have examined the impact of the SDP on students' behavior, classroom and school climate, students' self-concept, and academic achievement, including teachers' and parents' perception of the school climate. As reported in the 1991 research summary, students in the SDP schools perform better in the areas of reading, mathematics, and language than peers In non-SDP schools. Further, an examination of the impact of parental participation suggests its positive "significant gains" on students' self-concept, behavior, and achievement. However, the SDP has not significantly influenced the attendance of students.

Comer's emphasis on the resocialization of children and families has been troublesome for some African-American scholars who view it as a reflection of a deficit-oriented ideology (see, for example, Hollins, King, & Hayman, 1994). However, Comer's approach has also been acknowledged for being among the first to address the very real social and emotional needs of students who bear the scars of living in a racialized and racist social order. It is an approach reflected in the multiservice schools that Stallings (1995) describes; multiservice schools address all of the issues associated with living under conditions of poverty.

The initiatives described in this section address some of the vulnerabilities that result from historical oppression and challenge institutional and classroom practices that contribute to educational disadvantages. Despite the successes of these special educational interventions, they focus exclusively on the educational disadvantages of U.S. ethnic minorities and make no fundamental changes to a system of public education that mirrors and sustains social, educational, and economic inequalities.

Implications for Teacher Education

Although a discussion about the transformation of teacher education is beyond the scope of this chapter, the body of knowledge it presents about "race," "ethnicity," and linguistic difference among learners makes clear the need to reconceptualize the content and process of teacher education. A number of scholars have been arguing for some time now for the "explicit, informed treatment of issues of race and ethnicity as part of the curriculum in the preparation of the nation's teachers" (Trent, 1990, p. 361), even though few programs of teacher education address these issues in an integrated manner (see Ladson-Billings, 1999, for a review of these programs). Part of the problem is that the experience of diversity of those preparing the nation's teaching force may be very different from that which their graduate and undergraduate students (will) encounter in the classroom. Although there is sparse research on the beliefs and practices of individuals who are primarily responsible for preparing the nation's teaching force, Ladson-Billings (1999) provides this demographic profile:

> there are 489,000 full-time regular instructional faculty in the nation's colleges and universities. Seven percent or 35,000 are in the field of education. Eighty-eight percent of the full-time education faculty is White. Eighty-one percent of this faculty is between the ages of 45 and 60 or older. Also, of all the fields offered in our colleges and universities, education has the highest percentage (11 %) of faculty members who are classified as having no rank. (pp. 225–226)

Ladson-Billings argues that this demographic profile does not prove that teacher educators are incapable of preparing teachers, simply that their own experiences of diversity are different from those their preservice and in-service teachers will encounter in the classroom. To paraphrase Banks (1998), the biographical journeys of teacher educators (and teachers) greatly influence their values, their approaches, and the knowledge they deem worth knowing. Consequently, the recruitment of faculty with the experience and willpower to address these issues remains a major concern (Nieto & Rolon, 1997).

Teaching requires expertise in areas not typically within the domain of mainstream teacher preparation such as knowledge about the school adjustment of immigrant students, and health and quality of life issues associated with poverty that affect learning. New perspectives on familiar topics (such as human development as dual socialization and language acquisition as language socialization; racial and ethnic identity formation; the relationship between language, culture, and identity; and culturally responsive pedagogy) are also required. Although the scholarship reviewed in this chapter gives little specific attention to the central role that nontraditional forms of assessment play in the adaptation and modification of instruction, and in monitoring and supporting student progress and growth, this type of ongoing assessment is both essential and demanding. Clearly, the assessment of learning and learner differences within the context of social and educational inequalities requires competencies and theoretical knowledge that go beyond what traditional teacher preparation programs have been able to provide.

Teachers need to be knowledgeable about the socio-historico-political realities beyond the school that constrain much of what happens in classrooms and that contribute to the educational disadvantages of some groups in society. In particular, teachers need to understand how minority status affects socialization and human development among bicultural students. Clearly, the scholarship and ideas discussed in this chapter suggest the importance of interdisciplinary collaboration in the preparation of teachers.

Scholarship on culturally relevant teaching, as evident in the work of Darder (1991), Ladson-Billings (1994, 1995), and Osborne (1994), provides useful starting points for reconceptualizing pedagogical processes and approaches to address the range of learner differences found in the classroom. However, as Shulman (1987) argues, clear descriptions of the application of these new conceptualizations to the teaching–learning process in the day-to-day experiences of teachers are needed. Descriptions that give careful attention to the management of ideas within classroom discourse are needed to guide the design of better education (for an excellent example, see Sola & Bennett, 1991).

Further, in view of the sensitive nature of the content which has been discussed, learning experiences and processes used to promote teacher development need to be crafted with great care. In effect, a reconceptualization of pedagogy to address the needs of different learners across the life span is required. Crafting powerful experiences that will mediate the learning of preservice and in-service teachers is perhaps the biggest challenge. Confronting the treatment of differences in the classroom may put into question teachers' sense of self, including fundamental ways of being in the world and beliefs about the unfamiliar "Other." Cochran-Smith (2000) states it clearly: "Part of our responsibility as teachers and teacher educators is to struggle along with others in order to unlearn racism" (p. 158). Although narratives about the experiences of teacher educators have been forthcoming in recent years (see the work of Cochran-Smith, 1995, 2000; Mercado, 1996), a broader range of stories is needed to understand the challenges that arise in the preparation of teachers in different social contexts, with different teaching populations.

Two distinctive approaches to teacher preparation and professional development that have evolved over the past decade provide one response to this concern. One involves efforts to work directly with teachers in the modification of social learning contexts so that they respond to variability among learners. Through these "ethnographic experiments," university researchers and teacher educators document these modifications and observe their consequences for particular groups of learners. This procedure was introduced by Hymes (1980) and applied to the study of bilingual and English as a second language classrooms in the early 1980s by scholars at the Laboratory on Human Cognition, in San Diego (see the work of Diaz, Moll, & Mehan, 1986).

A second, related approach, in large part attributable to the pioneer work of Heath (1983; 1985), also supports teachers in the transformation of practice within specific teaching-learning contexts. Heath (1983) was among the first to demonstrate how teacher preparation may be informed through ethnographic research in students' homes and communities. Her seminal 10-year study of "Trackton" in North Carolina enabled her to document differences in language development in students' homes, which she then used to help teachers achieve "mutual accommodation." One current transformation of this approach, the Study of Funds of Knowledge, engages teachers more directly in researching cultural resources for learning in students' households, a term that acknowledges that individuals other than family members form part of the family-home unit. Once identified, these resources are used as a basis for transforming the contexts of learning in school in ways that capitalize on the cultural riches students bring from home. The major difference is that teachers are involved in all phases of the process as social scientists.

The Study of Funds of Knowledge

For the past decade, Moll (Moll, Amanti, Neff, & Gonzalez, 1992) and his collaborators at the University of Arizona and the Tucson Unified School District have engaged teachers as research collaborators to identify intellectual, social, and emotional resources developed by modest income families to help them survive with dignity and respect. Bilingual and mainstream teachers collaborate with anthropologists, educational psychologists, and teacher educators to identify funds of knowledge for literacy in the homes of low-income students, the majority of whom are of Mexican ancestry. Through these guided home visits, teachers generate theoretical knowledge based on direct examination of culture as lived experience, rather than on narrow and normative models of culture that may result in dangerous stereotypes. Specifically, ethnographic procedures are used to understand the resources for learning in the family's migratory history, in work and recreational activities, in the use of language and literacy, and in the family's child-rearing practices and beliefs. This knowledge will be used to transform classroom learning contexts in ways that build on and extend the cultural resources for learning in students' homes and communities.

This multifaceted approach is especially powerful for teacher development, particularly, in large urban centers where even teachers with experience are challenged to address the constantly changing diversity of their student population. Direct participation in research can be an important influence on teachers' thinking, particularly with regard to their expectations for students. It is also a powerful pedagogical approach and demonstrates how teachers may generate knowledge about students' homes and communities through collaborative inquiry with students, not unlike the junior ethnographer approach developed by Heath (1985).

Similar work was conducted in New York City and on Long Island (Mercado & Moll, 1997), where 50% of the households visited are of 1st- and 2nd-generation Puerto Ricans. The teachers' research is yielding important new insights on the character of these households, which earlier studies tended to characterize as dysfunctional. Experienced teachers admit that they know little about students' lives outside of the classroom, especially the extent of the impoverished living conditions of many, not all, of them. Teacher researchers also learn that there is great diversity in the resources for learning within these households. Most important, observing children within the home often changes teachers' perceptions of the capabilities of children they have come to know within the limited context of the school.

The implications of the Funds of Knowledge research are far-reaching. Through their direct involvement in research, teachers also learn that responding to the diversity that is inherent in all classrooms requires building community across professional, social, and ideological boundaries. Currently, much of the emphasis in teacher education is on identifying or changing individual teacher competencies. Little, if any, attention is given to the development of collaborative skills or to building community as an essential professional competence. In effect, this approach requires skills in collaboration and new roles and new responsibilities for teachers, teacher educators, and researchers.

Conclusions

Current scholarship suggests that teachers need to be knowledgeable about the social lives of the children and the conditions of their lives outside of school. What teachers know about the lives of children outside of school affects their pedagogical practices. Inquiry needs to become a common pedagogical practice. In light of the diversity that is inherent in all classrooms, having the means to construct knowledge about differences among learners may be more important and less problematic than having information on learners in prepackaged forms.

Teachers need to be reflective practitioners. Erickson (1986) states it clearly: "The capacity to reflect critically on one's own practice and to articulate that reflection to oneself and to others can be thought of as an essential mastery. . . ." (p. 157). Working with learners whose experiences may be very different from their own requires teachers to confront unexamined beliefs and assumptions they have about students in relation to particular institutional practices and procedures that may serve as barriers to the equitable treatment of students. As students also have beliefs and assumptions about themselves and their capabilities, teachers need to help students make these transparent. To help students challenge their perceptions of self, teachers need to be sensitive to students' experiences of schooling and the curriculum, including classroom interactions with teachers and peers.

Teachers are also advocates. They need to respond to diversity in ways that protect the rights of learners to an equal educational opportunity within the context of institutional racism. Students from economically and politically marginalized communities are more dependent on schools to gain access to social capital and cultural resources that facilitate entry into academic communities than are their more privileged counterparts.

Further, teachers need to develop critical media literacy (Cortes, 1991) to make sense of educational issues that are represented or misrepresented in the mass media. Teaching is political. Consequently, efforts to address the needs of diverse learners may bring on tension, conflict, and contradiction, but ultimately, classroom decisions may have to be made on moral and ethical grounds, not simply on the basis of public and scholarly discourses on difference.

As Osborne (1996) states, "quality schooling for all is a necessary condition for an ongoing participatory democracy" (p. 286). As has been emphasized throughout this chapter, learning begins with the teacher. What teachers know and do is one of the most important influences on what students learn. However, education is also a shared responsibility in a participatory democracy. We need to harness our vast wealth of resources to support the work of teachers in accomplishing this social goal. The knowledge we have provides a framework for beginning.

REFERENCES

Anstrom, K. (1996, February). *Federal policy, legislation, and educational reform: The promise and the challenge for language minority students.* Washington, DC: The National Clearinghouse on Bilingual Education.

Anyon, J. (1997). *Ghetto schooling.* New York: Teachers College Press.

Apple, M. W. (1996). *Cultural politics and education.* New York: Teachers College Press.

Aronowitz, S., & Giroux, H. A. (1985). *Education under siege.* South Hadley, MA: Bergin & Garvey.

Ashton, P. T. (1996). Improving the preparation of teachers. *Educational Researcher, 25*(9), 21–22, 35.

Attinasi, J. J. (1996). Racism, language variety, and urban U.S. minorities: Issues in bilingualism and bidialectalism. In S. Gregory & R. Sanjek (Eds.), *Race* (pp. 319–347). New Brunswick, NJ: Rutgers University Press.

August, D., & Hakuta, K. (Eds.). (1997). *Improving schooling for language-minority students: A research agenda.* Washington, DC: National Academy Press.

Baber, R. C. (1987). The artistry and artifice of Black communication. In W. L. Baber & G. Gay (Eds.), *Expressively Black* (pp. 75–108). New York: Praeger.

Banks, J. A. (1992). African American scholarship and the evolution of multicultural education. *The Journal of Negro Education, 61*(3), 273–286.

Banks, J. A. (1998). The lives and values of researchers: Implications for educating citizens in a multicultural society. *Educational Researcher, 27*(7), 4–17.

Bartolome, L. I., & Macedo, D. P. (1997, Summer). Dancing with bigotry: The poisoning of racial and ethnic identities. *Harvard Educational Review, 67*(2), 222–246.

Baugh, J. (1993). Research trends for Black American English. In A. W. Glowka & D. M. Mace (Eds.), *Language variation in North American English: Research and teaching* (pp. 153–163). New York: The Modern Language Association.

Berliner, D.C., & Biddle, B. J. (1995). *The manufactured crisis: Myths, fraud, and the attack on America's public schools.* Reading, MA: Addison-Wesley.

Bigler, E. (1996). Telling stories: On ethnicity, exclusion, and education in upstate New York. *Anthropology & Education Quarterly, 27*(2), 186–203.

Bloom, G. M. (1991). *The effects of speech style and skin color on bilingual teaching candidates and bilingual teacher attitudes toward Mexican American pupils.* Unpublished doctoral dissertation, Stanford University, Stanford, CA.

Boykin, A. W. (1994). Afrocultural expression and its implications for schooling. In E. R. Hollins, J. E. King, & W. C. Hayman (Eds.), *Teaching diverse populations: Formulating a knowledge base* (pp. 243–273). Albany, NY: State University of New York Press.

Carnoy, M. (1994). *Faded dreams: The politics and economics of race in America.* Cambridge, UK: Cambridge University Press.

Cazden, C. B. (1980). Culturally responsive education: Recommendations for achieving Lau remedies. In H. T. Trueba, G. P. Guthrie, & K. H. Au (Eds.), *Culture and the bilingual classroom* (pp. 69–86). Rowley, MA: Newbury House Publishers.

Cazden, C. B. (1986). Classroom discourse. In M. C. Wittrock (Ed.), *Handbook of research on teaching* (3rd ed., pp. 432–463). New York: Macmillan.

Cazden, C. B., & Mehan, H. (1989). Principles from sociology and anthropology: Context, code, classroom, and culture. In M. C. Reynolds (Ed.), *A knowledge base for the beginning teacher* (pp. 45–57). Oxford: Pergamon Press.

Cladinin, D. J., & Connelly, F. M. (1996, April). Teachers' professional knowledge landscapes: Teacher stories—stories of teachers—school stories—stories of school. *Educational Researcher, 25*(3), 24–30.

Cochran-Smith, M. (1995). Uncertain allies: Understanding the boundaries of race and teaching. *Harvard Educational Review, 65*(4), 541–570.

Cochran-Smith, M. (2000). Blind vision: Unlearning racism in teacher education. *Harvard Educational Review, 70*(2), 157–190.

Collier, V. P. (1995). *Promoting academic success for ESL students: Understanding second language acquisition for school.* Elizabeth, NJ: New Jersey Teachers of English to Speakers of Other Languages-Bilingual Educators.

Comer, J. P. (1988). Educating poor minority children. *Scientific American, 259,* 28–42.

Cordero-Guzman, H. R. (1992–93, Winter). The structure of inequality and status of Puerto Rican youth. *CENTRO, Journal of the Center for Puerto Rican Studies, 5*(1), 100–115.

Cordero-Guzman, H. R. (in press). Cognitive skills, test scores, and social stratification: The role of family and school level resources on racial/ethnic differences in scores on standardized tests (AFQT). *Review of Black Political Economy.*

Cortes, C. (1991). Empowerment through media literacy: A multicultural approach. In C. E. Sleeter (Ed.), *Empowerment through multicultural education* (pp. 143–158). Albany, NY: State University of New York Press.

Crawford, J. (1997, March). *Best evidence: Research foundations of the bilingual education act.* Washington, DC: National Clearinghouse for Bilingual Education.

Cummins, J. (1989). *Empowering minority students.* Sacramento, CA: California Association for Bilingual Education.

Darder, A. (1991). *Culture and power in the classroom.* New York: Bergin & Garvey.

Darling-Hammond, L. (1996). The right to learn and the advancement of teaching: Research, policy, and practice for democratic education. *Educational Researcher, 25*(6), 5–17.

Darling-Hammond, L. (1998). Teachers and teaching: Testing policy hypotheses from a national commission report. *Educational Researcher, 27*(1), 5–15.

Delpit, L. (1992). Education in a multicultural society: Our future's greatest challenge. *The Journal of Negro Education, 61*(3), 237–249.

Delpit, L. (1995). *Other people's children: Cultural conflict in the classroom.* New York: The New Press.

De Stefano, J. S. (Ed.). (1973). *Language, society, and education: A profile of Black English.* Worthington, OH: Charles A. Jones Publishing Co.

Diaz, E., Moll, L. C., & Mehan, H. (1986). Sociocultural resources in instruction: A context-specific approach. In *Beyond language: Social and cultural factors in schooling language minority students* (pp. 187–230). Los Angeles: Evaluation, Dissemination, and Assessment Center, California State University, Los Angeles.

Epstein, T. (2000). Adolescents' perspectives on racial diversity in U.S. history: Case studies from urban classrooms. *American Educational Research Journal, 37*(1), 185–214.

Erickson, F. (1986). Qualitative methods of research on teaching. In M. C. Wittrock (Ed.), *Handbook of research on teaching* (3rd ed., pp. 119–161). New York: Macmillan.

Erickson, F. (1990, Spring). Culture, politics, and educational practice. *Educational Foundations, 4*(2), 21–46.

Ernst, G., & Statner, E. L. (1994, September). Alternative visions of schooling: An introduction. *Anthropology & Education Quarterly, 25*(3), 200–207.

Federal Register. (1995, August 26). Standards for the classification of federal data on race and ethnicity.

Feinberg, W. (1998). *Common schools/uncommon identities: National unity and cultural difference.* New Haven, CT: Yale University Press.

Flores, B., Teft Cousin, P., & Diaz, E. (1991, September). Transforming deficit myths about learning, language, and culture. *Language Arts, 68,* 369–379.

Flores, J. (1993). "Que assimilated, brother, yo soy asimilao": The structuring of Puerto Rican identity. In J. Flores (Ed.), *Divided borders: Essays on Puerto Rican identity* (pp. 182–198). Houston, TX: Arte Publico.

Flores, J. (1996). The pan-Latino/Trans-Latino: Puerto Ricans en Nueva York. *CENTRO, Journal of the Center for Puerto Rican Studies, 8*(1–2),170–186.

Flores, J., Attinasi, J., & Pedraza, P. (1981). La carreta made a u-turn: Puerto Rican language and culture in New York City. *Daedalus, 110,* 221–231.

Flores, J., & Yudice, G. (1990). Living borders/Buscando America. Languages of Latino self-formation. *Social Text, 8*(2), 57–84.

Fordham, S. (1991). Peer proofing academic competition among Black adolescents: "Acting White" Black American style. In C. E. Sleeter (Ed.), *Empowerment through multicultural education* (pp. 69–93). Albany, NY: State University of New York Press.

Fordham, S., & Ogbu, J. U. (1986). Black students' school success: Coping with the burden of "acting White." *Urban Review, 18*(3), 176–206.

Freire, P., & Macedo, D. (1987). *Literacy: Reading the word and reading the world.* South Hadley, MA: Bergin & Garvey.

Fuchs, L. H. (1990). *The American kaleidoscope: Race, ethnicity, and the civic culture.* Hanover, NH: University Press of New England.

Garcia-Gonzalez, R. (1998). *Teachers' biographies as an influence on beliefs and practices of critical pedagogy: A case study approach.* Unpublished doctoral dissertation, University of San Francisco, San Francisco, CA.

Gay, G. (1987). Ethnic identity development and Black expressiveness. In W. L. Baber & G. Gay (Eds.), *Expressively Black.* New York: Praeger.

Gee, J. (1990). *Social linguistics and literacies.* Bristol, PA: Falmer Press.

Gimenez, M. E. (1996). Latinos, Hispanics . . . What next! Some reflections on the politics of identity in the U.S. *Heresies,* 39–42.

Goodman, K. (1982). Dialect barriers to reading comprehension. In F. V. Gollasch (Ed.), *Language and literacy: The selected writings of Ken Goodman* (pp. 187–196). Boston: Routledge and Kegan Paul, Ltd. (Original work published 1965)

Greene, M. (1994). Epistemology and educational research: The influence of recent approaches to knowledge. In L. Darling-Hammond (Ed.), *Review of research in education* (pp. 423–464). Washington, DC: AERA.

Groesfoguel, R., & Georas, C. (1996). The racialization of Latino Caribbean migrants in the New York metropolitan area. *CENTRO, Journal of the Center for Puerto Rican Studies, 8*(1–2), 190–201.

Harrison, L. E. (2000). [Introduction] Why culture matters. In L. E. Harrison & S. P. Huntington (Eds.), *Culture matters: How values shape human progress.* New York: Basic Books.

Heath, S. B. (1983). *Ways with words: Language, life, and work in communities and classrooms.* New York: Cambridge University Press.

Heath, S. B. (1985). Literacy or literate skills? Considerations for ESL/EFL learners. In P. Larson, E. L. Judd, & L. S. Messerschmidt (Eds.), *On TESOL 84': Brave new world for TESOL* (pp. 15–28). Washington, DC: TESOL.

Heath, S. B. (1986). Sociocultural contexts of language development. In *Beyond language: Social and cultural factors in schooling language minority students* (pp. 143–186). Los Angeles: Evaluation, Dissemination and Assessment Center, California State University, Los Angeles.

Heath, S. B., & McLaughlin, M. (1993). Ethnicity and gender in theory and practice: The youth perspective. In S. B. Heath & M. McLaughlin (Eds.), *Identity and inner city youth* (pp. 13–35). New York: Teachers College Press.

Hollins, E. R., King, J. E., & Hayman, W. C. (Eds.). (1994). *Teaching diverse populations: Formulating a knowledge base.* Albany, NY: State University of New York Press.

Hymes, D. (1980). Ethnographic monitoring. In H. T. Trueba, G. P. Guthrie, & K. H. Au (Eds.), *Culture and the bilingual classroom* (pp. 56–68). Rowley, MA: Newbury House Publishers.

Jackson, J. J. (1997). On Oakland's ebonics: Some say gibberish, some say slang, some say dis-den-dat, me say dem dumb, it be mother tongue. *The Black Scholar, 27*(1), 18–25.

Labov, W. (1987). The community as educator. In J. Langer (Ed.), *Language, literacy, and culture: Issues of society and schooling* (pp. 128–146). Norwood, NJ: Ablex.

LaCelle-Peterson, M. W., & Rivera, C. (1994). Is it real for all kids? A framework for equitable assessment policies for English language learners. *Harvard Educational Review, 64*(1), 55–75.

Ladson-Billings, G. (1994). *Successful teachers of African American children.* San Francisco: Jossey-Bass.

Ladson-Billings, G. (1995). Toward a theory of culturally relevant pedagogy. *American Educational Research Journal, 32*(3), 465–491.

Ladson-Billings, G. (1999). Preparing teachers for diverse student populations. In A. Iran-Nejad & P. D. Pearson (Eds.), *Review of research in education* (vol. 24, pp. 211–247). Washington, DC: The American Educational Research Association.

Ladson-Billings, G., & Tate, W. F. (1995). Toward a critical race theory of education. *Teachers College Record, 97*(1), 47–68.

Lagemann, E. C. (1997). Contested terrain: A history of education research in the United States, 1890–1990. *Educational Researcher, 26*(9), 5–17.

Lewis, O. (1965). *La vida.* New York: Random House.

Macedo, D. (1995). *Literacies of power.* Boulder, CO: Westview Press.

Macias, J. (1996). Racial and ethnic exclusion: A problem for anthropology and education. *Anthropology & Education Quarterly, 27*(2), 141–150.

MacLeod, J. (1987). *Ain't no making it: Leveled aspirations in a low-income neighborhood.* Boulder, CO: Corwin Press.

Massey, D. S. & Denton, N. A. (1993). *American apartheid: Segregation and the making of the underclass.* Cambridge, MA: Harvard University Press.

McCarthy, T. L., Wallace, S., Hadley Lynch, R., & Benally, A. (1991). Classroom inquiry and Navajo learning styles: A call for reassessment. *Anthropology & Education Quarterly, 22,* 41–59.

McDermott, R. (1977). School relations as contexts for learning in school. *Harvard Educational Review, 47*(2), 298–313.

McDermott, R. (1980). Social contexts for ethnic borders and school failure. In H. T. Trueba, G. P. Guthrie, & K. H. Au (Eds.), *Culture and the bilingual classroom* (pp. 212–230). Rowley, MA: Newbury House Publishers.

McDiarmid, G. W. (1992). What to do about differences? A study of multicultural education for teacher trainees in the Los Angeles school district. *Journal of Teacher Education, 43*(2), 83–93.

McLaren, P. (1989). *Life in schools.* New York: Longman.

McPartland, J., & Braddock II, J. H. (1993). *A conceptual framework on learning environments and student motivation for language minority and other underserved populations.* Proceedings of the third national research symposium on limited English proficient student issues: Focus on middle and high school issues. Washington, DC: USDE, Office of Bilingual Education and Minority Language Affairs.

McWhorter, J. H. (1997). Wasting energy on an illusion. *The Black Scholar, 27*(1), 9–14.

Mehan, H. (1980). The competent student. *Anthropology & Education Quarterly, XI*(3), 131–152.

Mehan, H. (1995). Resisting the politics of despair. *Anthropology & Education Quarterly, 26*(3), 239–250.

Mehan, H., Hubbard, L., & Villanueva, I. (1994). Forming academic identities: Accommodation without assimilation among involuntary minorities. *Anthropology & Education Quarterly, 25*(2), 91–117.

Mercado, C. I. (1992). Researching research: A student, teacher-researcher collaborative. In A. N. Ambert & M. D. Alvarez (Eds.), *Puerto Rican children on the mainland: Interdisciplinary perspectives* (pp. 167–192). New York: Garland.

Mercado, C. I. (1997). When young people from marginalized communities enter the world of ethnographic research: Scribing, planning, reflecting and sharing. In A. Egan-Robertson & D. Bloome (Eds.), *Students as researchers of culture and language in their own communities* (pp. 69–92). Cresskill, NJ: Hampton Press.

Mercado, C. I. (in press). Reflections on the study of households in New York City and Long Island: A different route, a common destination. In N. Gonzalez, L. C. Moll, & C. Amanti (Eds.), *Theorizing practice: Funds of knowledge in households and classrooms.* Cresskill, NJ: Hampton Press.

Mercado, C. I., & Moll, L. C. (1997). The study of funds of knowledge: Collaborative research in Latino homes. *CENTRO, Journal of the Center for Puerto Rican Studies, IX*(9), 26–42.

Miles, R. (1989). *Racism.* London: Routledge.

Moll, L. C., Amanti, C., Neff, D., & Gonzalez, N. (1992). Funds of knowledge for teaching: Using a qualitative approach to connect homes and classrooms. *Theory into Practice, 31*(2), 132–141.

Nieto, S. (1992). *Affirming diversity: The sociopolitical context of multicultural education.* New York: Longman.

Nieto, S. (1995). A history of the education of Puerto Rican students in U.S. mainland schools: "Losers," "outsiders," or "leaders"? In J. Banks & C. McGee Banks (Eds.), *Handbook of research on multicultural education* (pp. 388–411). New York: Macmillan.

Nieto, S., & Rolon, C. (1997). Preparation and professional development of teachers: A perspective from two Latinas. In J. J. Irvine (Ed.), *Critical knowledge for diverse teachers and learners* (pp. 89–123). Washington, DC: AACTE.

Oboler, S. (1995). *Ethnic labels, Latino lives: Identity and the politics of re-presentation in the United States.* Minneapolis, MN: University of Minnesota Press.

O'Connor, C. (1997, Winter). Dispositions toward (collective) struggle and educational resilience in the inner city: A case study analysis of six African-American high school students. *American Education Research Journal, 34*(4), 593–629.

Ogbu, J. U. (1992). Understanding cultural diversity and learning. *Educational Researcher, 21*(8), 5–14.

Ogbu, J. U., & Matute-Bianchi, M. E. (1986). Understanding sociocultural factors: Knowledge, identity, and school adjustment. In *Beyond language: Social and cultural factors in schooling language minority students* (pp. 73–142). Los Angeles: Evaluation, Dissemination, and Assessment Center, California State University, Los Angeles.

Olneck, M.R., & Lazerson, M. F. (1974). The achievement of immigrant children: 1900–1930. *History of Education Quarterly, XIV*(4), 453–482.

Omi, M. (1996). Racialization in the post Civil-Rights era. In A. F. Gordon & C. Newfield (Eds.), *Mapping multiculturalism* (pp. 178–186). Minneapolis, MN: University of Minnesota Press.

Omi, M., & Winant, H. (1994). *Racial formation in the United States.* New York: Routledge.

Orfield, G. (1989). *The growth of segregation in American schools: Changing patterns of segregation and poverty since 1968.* Alexandria, VA: National School Boards Association.

Osborne, A. B. (1996). Practice into theory into practice: Culturally relevant pedagogy for students we have marginalized and normalized. *Anthropology & Education Quarterly, 27*(3), 285–314.

Pallas, A. M., Natriello, G., & McDill, E. L. (1989). The changing nature of the disadvantaged population: Current dimensions and future trends. *The Educational Researcher, 18*(5), 16–22.

Pedraza, P. (1987). *An ethnographic analysis of language use in the Puerto Rican community of East Harlem.* New York: Centro de Estudios Puertorriquenos, Hunter College of CUNY.

Portes, A., & MacLeod, D. (1996, October). Educational progress of children of immigrants: The roles of class, ethnicity, and school contexts. *Sociology of Education, 69,* 255–275.

Portes, A., & Rumbaut, R. G. (1996). *Immigrant America* (2nd ed.). Berkeley, CA: University of California Press.

Pousada, A., & Greenlee, M. (1988). Toward a social theory of language variability. In C. Alvarez, A. Bennett, M. Greenlee, P. Pedraza, & A. Pousada, *Speech and ways of speaking in a bilingual Puerto Rican community* (pp. 11–92). New York: Language Policy Task Force, Center for Puerto Rican Studies, Hunter College of CUNY. Research Foundation of the City of New York.

Reyes, L. (Chair) (1994, March). *Making the vision a reality: A Latino agenda for educational reform. Final report of the Latino commission on educational reform.* Brooklyn, NY: New York City Board of Education.

Rodriguez-Morazzani, R. P. (1996). Mapping the discourse on Puerto Ricans and "race." *CENTRO, Journal of the Center for Puerto Rican Studies, VII*(1–2), 128–149.

San Miguel, G. (1987, Winter). Historical research on Chicano education. *Review of Educational Research, 57*(4), 467–480.

Shulman, L. S. (1987). Knowledge and teaching: Foundations of the new reform. *Harvard Educational Review, 57*(1), 1–22.

Slavin, R. E. (1996). Reforming state and federal policies to support adoption of proven practices. *Educational Researcher, 25*(9), 4–5.

Smith, R. (1996). Mexicans in New York: Membership and incorporation in a new immigrant country. In G. Haslip-Viera & S. L. Baver (Eds.), *Latinos in New York* (pp. 57–103). Notre Dame, IN: University of Notre Dame Press.

Smitherman, G. (1977). *Talkin and testifyin: The language of Black America.* Detroit, MI: Wayne State University Press.

Smitherman, G. (1997). Black language and the education of Black children: One mo' time. *The Black Scholar, 27*(1), 28–35.

Snow, C. E., Barnes, W. S., Chandler, J., Goodman, I. F., & Hemphill, L. (1991). *Unfulfilled expectations: Home and school influences on literacy.* Cambridge, MA: Harvard University Press.

Snow, C. E. , Burns, M. C., & Griffin, P. (Eds.). (1998). *Preventing reading difficulties in young children.* Washington, DC: National Academy Press.

Sola, M., & Bennett, A. (1991). The struggle for voice: Narrative, literacy, and consciousness in East Harlem. In C. Mitchell & K. Weiler (Eds.), *Rewriting literacy: Culture and the discourse of the other* (pp. 35–55). New York: Bergin & Garvey.

Spring, J. (1994). *The American school,* 1642–1996. New York: McGraw-Hill.

Stallings, J. (1995). Ensuring teaching and learning in the 21st century. *Educational Researcher, 24*(6), 4–8.

Stanton-Salazar, R. D. (1997). A social capital framework for understanding the socialization of racial minority children and youths. *Harvard Educational Review, 67*(1), 1–40.

Steele, C. M. (1997, June). How stereotypes shape intellectual identity and performance. *American Psychologist, 52*(6), 613–629.

Steinberg, S. (1981). *The ethnic myth: Race, class, ethnicity in America.* Boston: Beacon Press.

Suarez-Orozco, C., & Suarez-Orozco, M. M. (1995). *Transformations: Immigration, family life, and achievement motivation among Latino adolescents.* Stanford, CA: Stanford University Press.

Suarez-Orozco, M. M. (1991). Migration, minority status, and education: European dilemmas and responses in the 1990's. *Anthropology & Education Quarterly, 22*(2), 99–120.

Suarez-Orozco, M. M. (1996). California dreaming: Proposition 187 and the cultural psychology of racial and ethnic exclusion. *Anthropology & Education Quarterly, 27*(2), 151–167.

Suarez-Orozco, M. M. (1998). [Introduction] Crossings: Mexican immigration in interdisciplinary perspectives. In M. M. Suarez-Orozco (Ed.), *Crossings* (pp. 3–53). Cambridge, MA: Harvard University Press.

Summary of School Development Program. (1991). New Haven, CT: The Child Development Program of Yale University.

Takaki, R. (1989). *Strangers from a different shore: A history of Asian Americans.* New York: Penguin Books.

Taylor, A. (1996). Conditions for America's children, youth, and families: Are we world class? *Educational Researcher, 25*(8), 10–12.

Taylor, D. (1998). *Beginning to read and the spin doctors of science.* Urbana, IL: National Council of Teachers of English.

Torres, M. (1997). Celebrations and letters home: Research as an ongoing conversation among students, parents, and teacher. In A. Egan-Robertson & D. Bloome (Eds.), *Students as researchers of culture and language in their own communities* (pp. 59–68). Cresskill, NJ: Hampton Press.

Torres, R. D., & Ngin, C. (1995). Racialized boundaries, class relations, and cultural politics: The Asian-American and Latino experience. In A. Darder (Ed.), *Culture and difference* (pp. 55–70). Westport, CT: Bergin & Garvey.

Torres-Guzmán, M. E., Mercado, C. I., Quintero, H. L., & Rivera Viera, D. (1994). Teaching and learning in Puerto Rican/Latino collaboratives: Implications for teacher education. In E. R. Hollins, J. E. King, & W. C. Hayman (Eds.), *Teaching diverse populations: Formulating a knowledge base* (pp. 105–127). Albany, NY: State University of New York Press.

Trent, W. (1990). Race and ethnicity in the teacher education curriculum. *Teachers College Record, 91*(3), 361–369.

Trueba, E. T. (1998). The education of Mexican immigrant children. In M. M. Suarez-Orozco (Ed.), *Crossings* (pp. 251–275). Cambridge, MA: Harvard University Press.

Valdes, G. (1991). *Bilingual minorities and language issues in writing: Toward profession-wide responses to a new challenge.* Technical Report No. 54. University of Berkeley, Berkeley, CA: Center for the Study of Writing.

Villegas, A. M. (1991). *Culturally responsive pedagogy for the 1990s and beyond* [Trends and Issues Paper No. 6]. Washington, DC: ERIC Clearinghouse on Teacher Education.

Walsh, C. E. (1991). *Pedagogy and the struggle for voice: Issues of language, power and schooling for Puerto Ricans.* New York: Bergin & Garvey.

Walsh, C. E. (1994). Engaging students in learning: Literacy, language, and knowledge production with Latino adolescents. In D. Spener (Ed.), *Adult biliteracy in the U.S.* (pp. 211–237). Washington, DC: Center for Applied Linguistics.

Wells, A. S. (1993). Reexamining social science research on school desegregation: Long-term versus short-term effects. *Teachers College Record, 96*(4), 691–706.

Wells, G. (1990). Changing the conditions to encourage literate thinking. *Educational Leadership, 47*(6), 13–17.

Williams, F., & Whitehead, J. L. (1973). Language in the classroom: Studies of the Pygmalion effect. In J. S. De Stefano (Ed.), *Language, society, and education: A profile of Black English* (pp. 169–176). Worthington, OH: Charles A. Jones Publishing Company.

Wolfram, W. (1998). Dialect awareness and the study of language. In A. E. Robertson & D. Bloome (Eds.), *Students as researchers of culture and language in their own communities* (pp. 167–190). Cresskill, NJ: Hampton Press.

Zentella, A. C. (1990). Returned migration, language, and identity: Puerto Rican bilinguals in dos mundos/two worlds. *International Journal of the Sociology of Language, 84,* 81–100.

Zentella, A. C. (1997). *Growing up bilingual: Puerto Rican children in New York.* Malden, MA: Blackwell.

35.

Contemporary Research on Special Education Teaching

Russell Gersten
University of Oregon, Eugene Research Institute

Scott Baker
University of Oregon, Eugene Research Institute

Marleen Pugach
University of Wisconsin at Milwaukee

with

David Scanlon
Boston College

David Chard
University of Oregon

Contemporary Teaching of Special Education

To convey the complexity of special education teaching, we begin this chapter with four vignettes that portray something of the range of issues confronting the field and, in particular, of those individuals whose job it is to teach students with disabilities.

Mark

The first concerns Mark, a middle school student with significant cognitive impairments, limited expressive language, and virtually no reading ability. Mark spends some of his school day in a special education some in a vocational and "life skills" class. Mark has a friend, Adrienne. When it was time for the school play, Adrienne felt that Mark should play a role. She figured out a role he could play despite the potential problems he might have following cues for moving on and off the stage.

Mark could play the Queen's guard, her constant escort. The queen could easily prompt him by nudging him when he needed to move around the stage.

Rehearsals and the play went fine. During the curtain calls, Mark went out on stage with the entire cast, which was applauded warmly. His mother noticed him crying, and, after the play, she asked him why. He said that no one had ever applauded for him at school before. Here was a boy who had spent nine years at school and had never received applause for his efforts. One is left to ponder the cumulative effect on students with disabilities who, after attending school for many years, never experience this relatively common and lasting type of recognition.

One is also left to ponder the role of the teacher (Ferguson & Ferguson, 1997; Woolfson, 1997) in helping to bring on this spontaneous recognition. In one sense, she did nothing; the actual suggestion came from a student. In another sense, the teacher did everything—by her actions, by her support of a stu-

The authors would like to acknowledge the valuable feedback on previous versions of the chapter from Carol Sue Englert, Sharon Vaughn, Sylvia Smith, Tom Keating, and Janet Otterstedt. An earlier version of the conceptual framework underlying the chapter was presented at the annual conference of AERA in Chicago, Illinois, in April 1997.

dent's idea, and by her taking the risk to let this opportunity evolve, she accomplished meaningful integration of a teenager with multiple disabilities into a school activity, supported a friendship, and provided Mark with an opportunity to experience the joy of being appreciated publicly by others.

Math Class

The second scenario involves a research study of an innovative approach to teaching key concepts and arithmetic operations that involve fractions to high school students with learning disabilities (Woodward & Gersten, 1992). The setting is an inner-city high school math class of 15 special education students, all from ethnic minority groups. These students are in "special education math"; topics include fractions, long division, decimals, and currency. Essentially, the course involves a smattering of the typical math curricula for grades 4 through 7. At the beginning of the year, the teacher in this special education class agreed to use a laser disc instructional program that was based on principles of direct and explicit instruction.

A major motivating factor for this teacher and her colleagues was that fractions were the most difficult unit in the curriculum for these students, and few of them succeeded with conventional textbooks. In fact, virtually the same material was covered in both middle school and high school special education math classes because so few students really learned the content.

Watching a typical lesson is interesting. For an adult, the laser disc instructional program moves at a glacial pace, yet clearly, something about the flow of the program, the clarity of the explanations, and the number of examples "clicks" with this difficult-to-teach group of students. The success of the program, documented by the increase over the six-week unit from an average score of 30% correct to 79% correct, provides evidence of the benefits of the technology to special education. The program's success also supports the application of the principles of direct instruction and instructional design, which have become a mainstay of special education practice. Yet, for observers in the classroom, another element was also essential. The way the teacher followed the procedures of the laser disc program, reviewed material when students experienced difficulty, and adjusted the pace of the lesson so that motivation remained high for all the students in the class also clearly played a key role in the success that the students experienced.

Social Studies

The third vignette involves a middle school student with learning disabilities in a social studies class where the teacher, using techniques from "situated cognition," bases much of the unit on a video that the class watches and analyzes. The unit is on the Holocaust, and the central "situation" in this case is a laser disc version of *Playing for Time*, a book by Arthur Miller, which includes vivid representation of life in concentration camps. As part of the unit, students also watch a documentary about the Nazis and write in their journals about what they learn. One boy with learning disabilities, recounting what he had learned that day, wrote that Adolph Hitler was Jewish. The shocking inaccuracy of this conclusion would be apparent to most middle school students without benefit of a unit on the Holocaust, let alone after having just viewed a documentary about the Nazis.

Yet, it also represents not only the severity of the gaps in background knowledge of many students with disabilities but also the difficulties they have in drawing inferences.

The teacher was experienced in teaching special education students and had a system in place where students frequently wrote their interpretations of important concepts that had been presented to them. The teacher was able to easily provide the correct information to students the next morning in such a way that this particular student was not humiliated and felt comfortable enough to continue to take chances in his writing about what he was learning in class.

English Language

The fourth vignette involves a student with learning disabilities who is also an English-language learner. Maria is in a fourth-grade language arts and reading class. The class has just finished reading an Australian story called "Wilfred Gordon McDonald Partridge," which is about a woman who is losing her memory.

At the conclusion of this brief story, a discussion of mood ensues. The teacher asks,

"What did you think about it?"

One student answers, "It was kind of sad."

The teacher responds, "How do you know?"

Maria says, "Because old people."

Though the language is primitive, it is considered acceptable, because the content is thoughtful. The student's response helps the group elucidate the mood and theme. This teacher told us that she always evaluates responses for content, not grammatical correctness, during literature instruction and, in this case, praises Maria for her insight. During these discussions, responses are never labeled right or wrong, but students are frequently asked to explain the rationale for their answers or opinions. Jorge, for example, explains that he "liked it because it was sad and it was happy," and proceeds to provide several examples of sad and happy instances.

Both Jorge's and Maria's responses are accepted and contribute to the group's analysis of the story. Maria, though limited in her reading ability and language proficiency, is an active participant in the lesson and is receiving instruction in grade-appropriate material, an increasingly important consideration for students with disabilities.

Purpose and Overview

As these vignettes illustrate, the field of special education seems to lurch forward on waves of humanistic impulses, legal initiatives, and impressive technical advances. The speed of these advances has been extraordinary.

In the mid-1970s, as a result of strong pressure from parents and advocacy groups and a series of pivotal court cases, federal legislation (PL 94–142) was enacted to provide "free appropriate public education" for students with disabilities. This law, now referred to as IDEA (the Individuals with Disabilities Education Act), has undergone several reauthorizations, most recently in 1997. Not only changes in the law but also research findings have helped shift the nature of special education practices.

Current special education legislation (U.S. Department of

Education, 1997) reflects the increasingly high standards for students with disabilities which requires that students' instruction be aligned to age-appropriate curriculum standards regardless of the nature and severity of the disability and that all students be included in statewide assessments (with appropriate modifications or adaptations). A major impetus for these changes is a small body of research demonstrating that, given appropriate support, many students with disabilities can participate in cognitively challenging activities well beyond what one would predict from their actual reading abilities. For example, when asked to write about complex ideas, students with learning disabilities often can write at a level that far exceeds what would be predicted by their performances, performances that demonstrate only lower-level skills such as capitalization, punctuation, and spelling (Graham & Harris, 1989b, 1994). In math and science, contemporary research describes the knowledge that many students with disabilities possess as "inert," indicating that students may possess this knowledge but either have little awareness of it or are uncertain about how and when to apply it (Goldman, Hasselbring, & the Cognition and Technology Group at Vanderbilt, 1996; Kolligian & Sternberg, 1987).

Unlike many other fields of research, we believe that too little energy has gone into reflecting on the nature of the advances, and not enough effort has been put into synthesizing research findings into coherent patterns that could improve practice. That synthesis is the goal of this chapter. To accomplish that goal, we traverse several philosophical orientations to uncover what we view as the major advances and the replicable findings of recent research in special education teaching.

To adequately survey these orientations, we needed to restrict the range of topics covered. Thus, we focus primarily on instructional issues (as opposed to social skills, transition planning, or life skills) and on research for students with high incidence disabilities (i.e., learning disabilities and behavior disorders). We also explicitly address some of the key issues connected to cultural and linguistic diversity as they relate to special education policy and practice.

The chapter is organized in the following fashion. First, we provide some background information on the legal and practical shifts that have occurred in special education over the years. Next, we focus on what we view as cornerstones of current instructional practice. In this section, we review the concept of procedural facilitators, namely, the application of findings from cognitive science to writing and reading instruction for students with disabilities.

We believe that a confluence of exciting findings has occurred in the areas of writing and reading instruction over the past 15 years and that this body of research increasingly is changing the nature of American classrooms. We intentionally link the research from diverse theoretical orientations because of the convergence in findings and the serious implications for practice. We do our best to disentangle the somewhat amorphous topics and numerous labels attached to various techniques that have guided some of the best special education research on teaching. Then we conclude this section with the empirical legacy of direct instruction, for years the hallmark of special education practice. We include a discussion of findings on the transfer and generalization of problem solving and teaching.

In the next section, we present problems that are connected with the research and teaching practices focusing on students with disabilities who are from culturally or linguistically diverse backgrounds. Because of the relatively few empirical studies on effective instructional practices for minority students with disabilities, our treatment of the topic focuses more on what we believe are critical concepts that must be addressed to improve the quality of research on effective teaching practices for these students.

We conclude the chapter with an attempt to integrate the material from the various sections. To frame this effort, we turn to an articulation of critical issues for researchers that was developed in late 1996 for the U.S. Department of Education by groups of parents, professional development experts, teachers, and researchers. This articulation serves to ground the research in real experiences that teachers and students confront on a daily basis.

Background on Special Education

The students described in the introductory vignettes represent students all over the United States who receive special education. special education has changed considerably in multiple ways over the past two decades. Some of the transformations that are germane to this chapter have redefined who receives instruction from special education teachers, what the range of instruction is that makes up special education, where this instruction is delivered, and how special education instruction is delivered in accordance with the law.

Shortly after initial special education legislation was enacted, efforts to bring children with disabilities into public schools shifted and became efforts to identify effective instructional interventions and programs (Schiller, Malouf, & Danielson, 1995). The 1980s were dominated by research on academic and behavioral interventions to help students with disabilities meet their academic and social goals.

The current version IDEA focuses on three issues. The first is to ensure access to "the general curriculum" for students with disabilities. In particular, federal policy now requires that each student be provided with special education, modifications of grade-appropriate curriculum, and other types of support so that she or he can progress in the general curriculum. A second major issue is to ensure that students are educated and participate in activities with other children with and without disabilities. The 1997 version of IDEA is more specific than its predecessors in stressing the inclusion of students with disabilities in regular classrooms to the maximum extent possible. The legislation also ensures that student with disabilities will receive access to grade-level content rather than different curricula that focus primarily on the remediation of skill deficits. Finally, the revised IDEA stresses that, beginning at age 14, to the maximum extent feasible, special education must address the issue of transition from school to the world of work and independent living. Outlined in the recent reauthorization, these issues dictate, at least in part, current thinking about the who, what, where, and how of special education.

Determining exactly who a special education student is remains a complex, unresolved, and potentially unresolvable issue. Under federal law, children who are identified as having one or more of 13 specific disabling conditions and who need special education are entitled to an individualized education plan (IEP), which includes specific goals and objectives that are formulated by a team of professionals and the student's parents.

Since the initial passage of Federal special education legislation 25 years ago, the number of students identified as eligible for special education has increased every year and currently includes about 12% of public school students (although there are large regional variations). In particular, the specific learning disability category has experienced the most growth and now includes approximately half of all children receiving special education (U.S. Department of Education, 1999).

Despite the fairly specific criteria for special education eligibility, special education teachers often provide services both to students who are not identified as having a disability and to many students who are incorrectly identified as having a disability.

What special education teachers consider to be the curriculum for the children they teach has drastically shifted over the past 20 years. During the 1960s and 1970s, a good deal of teaching addressed the presumed underlying cognitive processes that caused disabilities, such as sensory-motor integration, rather than the actual content of reading, writing, and mathematics. After a consistent lack of empirical support for this approach (Kavale & Mattson, 1983; Salvia & Ysseldyke, 1981) teachers shifted toward providing remedial academic instruction at each student's level of functioning. Currently, with recent changes in legislation, another shift is underway from an exclusive diet of remedial instruction toward a broader menu providing instruction in grade-level content (Gersten, 1997).

Growing diversity in student populations has created greater need for services that may not be available in the general education classroom. For example, many urban schools are faced with high percentages of students who are English-language learners or who otherwise have low levels of English language skills. It is difficult for these districts to distinguish between students who are experiencing troubling delays in language development from students who are going through the normal difficulties involved in learning a second language. As a consequence, special educators often provide services to students with a wide range of language needs. Similarly, many children enter school with emotional or behavioral difficulties. Although these difficulties mayor may not be disability related, the realities of schools are such that the special education teacher is likely to be called on to intervene, even in cases when students are not formally identified.

Another major focus of special education research in the past decade has been the development and validation of measures that more accurately predict which students are likely to experience academic or social problems in school. Advances have been significant, particularly in the area of early detection of potential reading disabilities (Felton, 1992). Although these measures are far from perfect, their precision is such that sensitive preventative programs in both the academic (Ball & Blachman, 1991; Griffin, 1998; O'Connor, Jenkins, Leicester, & Slocum, 1993) and social domains (Reid, 1993; Walker, 1998; Walker, Colvin, & Ramsey, 1995) are now feasible. A major area of research on teaching has focused on understanding the types of beginning reading, mathematics, and social skills instruction that can be implemented by teachers in the primary grades. In addition, a wide array of promising early intervention programs for students from infancy to preschool have been developed (Bagnato, Neisworth, & Munson, 1997; Bailey & Wolery, 1992; Bricker 1995).

At the same time, naive thinking that disabilities can be "cured" by effective remedial programs has eroded (Kornblet, 1997). In other words, increasingly, we conceptualize means to help students with disabilities learn academic material and become competent readers and writers, taking into account the problems they will experience throughout their lives that are related to memory, organization, comprehension of abstract material, and the application of strategies and skills that are taught.

The past few years also have seen renewed emphasis on placing students with disabilities in instructional settings with their nondisabled peers. Advocacy efforts have focused on the placement of students with disabilities in general education classrooms as much as possible so that students experience the world around them and develop relationships with age-mates in their local communities. Part of the rationale for these efforts is that to include students with disabilities in classrooms helps educate all children, insofar as awareness of diversity and relationships with individuals with disabilities is part of education. Another motivation behind these efforts is the longstanding belief that to relegate students with disabilities to special schools or to classrooms in the back of school buildings is an unjust and harmful practice.

The increasing practice of educating students with disabilities in general education settings led to descriptive research studies that examined the kinds of experiences these students have when they are instructed in general education classrooms (Baker & Zigmond, 1990; McIntosh, Vaughn, Schumm, Haager, & Okhee, 1994; Vaughn, Elbaum, & Schumm, 1996). Vaughn et al. found that, overall, students with learning disabilities were treated by their general education classroom teachers much like other students. Students with disabilities were accepted by the teacher; treated fairly and impartially by the teacher; were involved in the same seating arrangements as other students; and, particularly at the middle and high school level, worked on the same activities and used the same materials as other students in class.

The potentially troublesome side of this finding is that instruction in mainstream classes often was not differentiated to meet the needs of students with disabilities, and few adaptations were provided (Vaughn, Hughes, Schumm, & Klinger, 1997). Although students with learning disabilities were included in class activities, their actual participation rates were very low. They were not consistently or seriously engaged in the learning process, neither through their own initiation nor through the initiation by the teacher. Across all grade levels, when these students were compared with their classmates without disabilities, they infrequently asked the teacher for help or assistance, they seldom volunteered to answer questions, they participated at a lower rate in teacher-directed activities, and overall, they interacted with both the teacher and other students at a lower rate.

Even teachers who were identified by their peers, the principal, or themselves as being effective with students who had learning disabilities made few adaptations to meet their students' special learning needs. The findings by Vaughn et al. (1997) were similar to those of Baker and Zigmond (1990), who stated, "The overriding impression of observers in these classrooms was of undifferentiated, large-group instruction" (p. 525). The observational findings as a whole suggest that students with learning disabilities appear to be accepted by the teachers and cause few interruptions to other students, but their learning can be characterized as passive—students with learning disabilities ask questions infrequently and rarely volunteer to answer questions.

The picture painted by these studies may appear rather bleak. Also critical to realize is the fact that, in pullout special education settings, students rarely receive access to challenging, grade-level appropriate curricula or material. However, exploratory research by Zigmond, Wolery, Meng, Fulmer, and Bean (1994) demonstrated that students with disabilities did learn content in general education settings, although often in a somewhat fragmented or superficial fashion.

A series of major efforts have been made to improve the quality of instruction provided to students with disabilities in general education classrooms. Findings from this complex body of research have been mixed. Studies clearly indicate that the meaningful inclusion of students with disabilities in day-to-day classroom instruction requires a good deal of hard work and thoughtfulness on the part of teachers. The studies also elucidate promising practices and curricular approaches that can greatly assist in this process. These practices and approaches will be woven throughout this chapter. Our emphasis is on the quality of instruction rather than where instruction takes place.

The effort to include more children with disabilities in general education classrooms has caused a shift in the role of many special education teachers (Friend & Cook, 1990; Pugach & Johnson, 1989). In some schools, the special education teacher moves from classroom to classroom, assisting general education teachers to modify instruction so it will meet the needs of all the students in the classroom, including students with high- and low-incidence disabilities. In other schools, coteaching models have replaced traditional special education classrooms. At the same time, in other schools, special education teachers monitor the instruction of students with disabilities throughout the school while they supervise paraprofessionals who may actually provide the instruction and ongoing support. In almost all schools, regardless of the instructional model used, the special education teacher serves as a consultant on a myriad of issues including not only behavior, early reading acquisition, mathematics problem-solving strategies, and social skills but also a host of substantive and procedural issues pertinent to special education.

Increasingly, in fact, special education teachers find themselves spending as much time training adults how to work with special education students or collaborating with other educators (classroom teachers, instructional assistants, or other special service personnel) as they do directly teaching children (Gersten, Keating, Blake, & Morvant, 1994). Although more and more educators are emphasizing collegiality and collaboration throughout the teaching field, these efforts to work together are most prevalent and most intense in special education. As an illustration of this increased collaboration, we find that having special education teachers coteach classes with general educators is widely endorsed and increasingly implemented (Bauwens, Schumm, Vaughn, & Harris, 1997).

We now shift to the major section of this chapter—an exposition of the major advances in teaching students with disabilities that has occurred in the past two decades. The strategies and approaches discussed have broad relevance—regardless of setting. As will be seen in the concluding section, these advances have begun to seriously address concerns raised by parents about problems in current practice.

This review is far from comprehensive. The focus is on research that has immediate implications for students with high-incidence disabilities (learning disabilities, attention deficit disorders, behavior disorders). We review in-depth a small number of studies, each of which we feel is typical of a significant line of research.

The organizational framework used to encompass this broad range of instructional studies involves

- Procedural facilitators and cognitive strategies
- Content enhancement strategies in the general education classroom
- The legacy of direct instruction
- The merger of explicit instruction and situated cognition

Procedural Facilitators and Cognitive Strategies: Tools for Unraveling the Mysteries of Reading Comprehension and the Writing Process

In the early 1980s, instructional researchers realized that systematic, step-by-step, explicit instruction is inappropriate for cognitive activities like expressive writing, because flexibility is always important, revising and refining (i.e., self-monitoring) are critical, and no two people engage in the process the same way. All researchers were aware that algorithmic or lockstep strategies—effective in teaching many students with disabilities how to decode or compute—were not appropriate for complex, cognitive activities such as comprehension, expressive writing, and problem solving.

Somehow, flexibility needed to be taught. Instruction needed to include ways to decipher the meaning of paragraphs in which more than one main idea was conveyed, ways to identify and integrate the range of character clues that may support valid inferences about the reasons characters in novels take action, and ways to communicate to students that literature and historical events can be interpreted from multiple perspectives.

Thus, the dilemma was posed: How was it possible to teach something as mysterious as the process of writing (Graham & Harris, 1989a) or the process of discerning the theme of a short story (Williams, Brown, Silverstein, & deCani, 1994). The field of special education has made extraordinary progress in tackling this dilemma.

From the beginning, researchers were aware that teaching students when to use what they learned was often as important as teaching the strategy itself. Frequently, the term *metacognition* was used in early research to describe the reflective and self-monitoring nature of what was required on the part of students to learn effectively. Studies consistently indicated, for example, that students with learning disabilities fail to spontaneously organize unfamiliar material, tend to ask themselves fewer questions when they read, and have difficulties transferring approaches or strategies to novel situations (Brown, 1978; Kolligian & Sternberg, 1987; Miller, 1985; Swanson, 1987;

Torgesen, 1977; Wong, 1991). To address these difficulties, researchers have tried essentially to encapsulate the processes used by competent readers and writers and have used a variety of ingenious methods to teach them to students with disabilities. Much of the impetus for these approaches has come from cognitive psychology (Anderson, 1984; Beck & McKeown, 1989; Brown, 1978; Collins, Brown, & Newman, 1989).

These methods have been called a variety of names, including "procedural facilitators" (Bereiter & Scardamalia, 1987; Englert, Raphael, Anderson, Anthony, & Stevens, 1991; Graves & Montague, 1991), "cognitive strategies" (Harris & Pressley, 1991), "learning strategies" (Bulgren, Deshler, & Schumaker, 1997; Deshler, Ellis, & Lenz, 1996), "coached elaborations," or "scaffolds." Some rely heavily on graphic organizers (Englert et al., 1991; Idol, 1987). Most involve intensive modeling and monitoring by the teacher (Graham & Harris, 1989a; Wong, Butler, Ficzere, & Kuperis, 1997). Many rely heavily on peer interaction (Englert et al., 1991; Palincsar, David, Winn, & Stevens, 1991). All are multifaceted. In this section, we use the term *procedural facilitators* to refer to the whole set of instructional approaches described by these various terms. Although we see many common features among these various approaches, the researchers who developed them rarely stress those similarities. And as will be seen, some distinct differences can be found among them, particularly, differences in the concept of the teacher's role.

Procedural Facilitators to Guide Students Toward Expert Performance

Procedural facilitators are questions, prompts, or simple outlines of important structures that teachers use on a daily basis (a) to help students emulate the performance of more expert learners (Scardamalia & Bereiter, 1986) and (b) to provide a common language for discussing the cognitive task or activity. Despite the different terminologies, the goal is the same—to provide a plan of action and a system for providing ongoing feedback and support. This plan of action is derived from the learners' need for help with organization and structure (Kolligian & Sternberg, 1987), and their need for a road map or guide to move through the process. A rich empirical base has established the effectiveness of procedural facilitators to scaffold learning for students with disabilities.

Helping students effectively use a plan of action is accomplished by having competent adults or peers verbalize the processes they go through when they read or write. These procedural facilitators assist the teacher (or peer) in the unfamiliar task of verbalizing how they actually compose a piece of narrative writing, know when they need to reread a troubling portion of a textbook, glean the central concept from a page of text, or infer character motives. They typically help to provide a shared language between teachers and students, and to provide students with a permanent reminder of the steps and strategies used by highly proficient readers or writers.

As will be seen, although the earliest research stressed teacher modeling and thinking aloud, subsequent research suggests that how teachers—or proficient peers—respond to students' attempts to use the strategies or procedural facilitators is every bit as important. Concepts such as cognitive apprentice-

ship (Brown, Collins, & Duguid, 1989) have been used to describe this process.

For example, Englert, Raphael, Anderson, Anthony, and Stevens (1991) used procedural facilitators called "think sheets" to encourage students to organize their written products in which they compared a child and his dad, a child and her best friend, or a chimpanzee and a giraffe. Figure 35.1 displays such a think sheet.

Much of the research on procedural facilitators has been conducted in reading and writing. This approach has occasionally been studied in mathematics and science; however, work in this area for individuals with disabilities is in its infancy, and a rich body of research exists in writing and reading comprehension, so we will use examples from the waves of research in reading comprehension and expressive writing.

Story Grammar and Story Mapping as Tools to Enhance Reading Comprehension

One of the seminal studies on the use of procedural facilitators was conducted by Idol (1987), who used a story mapping technique to enhance the reading comprehension of students with and without learning disabilities. In particular, the study was important because Idol wanted to try out the technique in an inclusive setting with heterogeneous groups of students. Her earlier research had established the efficacy of the story mapping procedure with a small group of students with learning disabilities (Idol & Croll, 1987).

Idol's goal was to use a procedural facilitator that would "draw the readers' attention to the common elements among stories," which she hoped would enhance the "possibility of the reader searching his or her mind for possible information" related to the text, or activating background knowledge in contemporary terminology (p. 197). In other words, the story map was to serve as a framework for integrating story elements from the text with the reader's own experiences.

The procedural facilitator was a story map. This map had room for students to record information directly related to 9 or 10 story grammar questions. The map helped students record as they were reading—or after they finished reading—important elements of the story, including descriptions of the setting, the problem, the actions taken to solve problems, and final outcomes. Examples of the questions used throughout the intervention include the following:

- Where did the story take place?
- When did the story take place?
- How did [Main Character] try to solve the problem?
- Was it hard to solve the problem? (Explain in your own words.)

Numerous studies that followed Idol's confirmed that explicitly teaching text structures such as the story map enhances reading comprehension for students with learning disabilities (Dimino, Gersten, Carnine, & Blake, 1990; Gurney, Gersten, Dimino, & Carnine, 1990; Williams, Brown, Silverstein, & deCani, 1994).

The use of heterogeneous cooperative groups was also an important contribution of Idol's study. She hypothesized that inte-

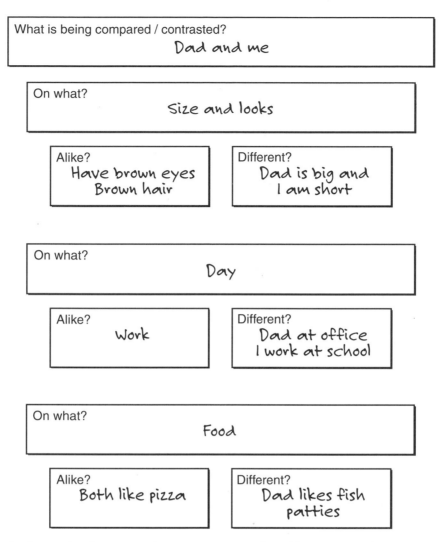

Figure 35.1. An example of a completed comparison/contrast organization form. [*Source:* Englert, C. S., Raphael, T. E., & Anderson, L. M. (1992). Socially mediated instruction: Improving students' knowledge and talk about writing. *Elementary School Journal, 92*(4), 412–447.]

grating students with and without disabilities would help students with disabilities engage in a "beneficial form of vicarious learning by viewing the desired responses of more skilled readers" (Idol, 1987, p. 197). Subsequent research has established the numerous benefits of cooperative groups, including enhancing learner understanding, increasing engaged time, and maximizing practice opportunities.

Results demonstrated that the three students with learning disabilities and the two low-achieving students clearly benefited from the story mapping instruction. This benefit occurred even though, during the activity, these five students were reading in materials that were written for grade levels one or more years beyond where those students' placement levels indicated. On the measure of listening comprehension, the results showed that both average- and low-achieving students made gains from pretest to posttest. However, the gains made by students with disabilities were far stronger than those made by the average-achieving group.

Of interest is that, when given the option, Idol found that students almost unanimously preferred to use the maps after reading a story rather than during their reading. The flexibility in how and when to use the procedural facilitator anticipated the wave of research in the 1990s attempting to understand the type of discourse that assists students with disabilities in their comprehension of text (Beck, McKeown, Sandora, Kucan, & Worthy, 1996; Englert & Mariage, 1996; Okolo & Ferretti, 1996).

Idol also found that, when the use of story maps was discontinued, the comprehension of students on average remained high (indicating deep processing and internalization). However, the comprehension of some students decreased significantly, indicating that, for them, the early removal of procedural facilitators, mentoring by teachers and peers, or both can lead to serious comprehension difficulties.

A third interesting finding by Idol (1987) was timely and unexpected. The intervention called for the classroom teacher to require that students keep a journal of the stories they wrote. Idol analyzed these stories for inclusion of story grammar elements in the students' writing before and after the intervention. Not surprisingly, she found that, prior to the intervention, students in the low-achieving group (i.e., the three students with learning disabilities and the two low-performing students) included fewer story grammar components in their journal entries than other students. After the intervention, students in the low-achieving group showed a significant increase in the number of elements they included in the stories they wrote. In fact, four of the five students in the low-achieving group wrote stories in their journals that usually included all of the story grammar elements they were taught. This finding showed generalization of the skills students learned during the interventions across tasks and subject areas.

Using Text Structures to Enhance the Quality of Students' Writing

Writing instruction has become a major thrust of instructional research and an area for which the use of procedural facilitators has clear benefits. Wong, Butler, Ficzere, and Kuperis (1997) enumerated several barriers to effective writing that had been documented by research from the past two decades. Specifically, they noted that students with learning disabilities experience difficulties both with mechanical aspects of writing (e.g., spelling, grammar) and with knowledge of—or comfort with—procedures used by skilled writers. Empirical findings over the decades have consistently shown that these barriers affect the writing done by students with disabilities so that it is very short, poorly organized, and lifeless (Isaacson, 1995).

A cornerstone of the approach to teaching writing, adopted by the researchers whose work we review, is that the technical demands of a cognitive task, such as accuracy of spelling and punctuation, may be temporarily de-emphasized so that teachers and students can focus their intellectual energy on the conceptual aspects of writing. This is a radically different way of teaching for many special educators. Much of special education instruction on writing has focused on the teaching of mechanical skills (Englert et al., 1991). This rigid focus is probably a function of (a) the traditional view in special education that students need to learn the basics before they can learn and understand more difficult concepts (Klenk & Palincsar, 1996) and (b) how the writing process seems so mysterious to describe and so difficult to teach.

Although certain writing conventions are specific to certain genres, no one can claim a "correct" way to construct text. In narrative writing, for example, some writers like to begin with the climax of a story and proceed outward; others like to develop their characters before developing the plot. The approach used to construct a narrative is not what makes the story more or less engaging.

Moreover, different types of writing are based on different inherent structures. For example, a persuasive argument contains elements (e.g., thesis with supporting points) that differ considerably from those found in narrative writing (e.g., characters and plot). This variability makes the explicit teaching of writing difficult if not impossible. Rather, good writing instruction involves teaching what Englert et al. (1991) call "overlap-

ping and recursive processes." These processes do not proceed in a particular order, and one process may inform another in such a way that the author returns to previous steps to update or revise on a regular basis. Teaching learners to write requires showing students how to develop and use "plans of action" or procedural facilitators that help them to organize what they want to say and guide them to get it down on paper.

Pioneering work in this area has come from Englert and her colleagues, who studied the development and use of procedural facilitators to teach writing to students with learning disabilities. The instructional approach that was developed by Englert et al. (1991) challenges students not only to use text structures to develop relevant details in their writing but also to revise their writing in relation to standard text structure conventions (Englert et al., 1991).

Englert et al. (1991) evaluated the effectiveness of an instructional approach called Cognitive Strategy Instruction in Writing, which focused on helping students learn strategies that were related to the writing process. Components of instruction included extensive teacher modeling of the inner dialogue that expert writers engage in during the writing process, extensive support to students during lessons and writing sessions, procedural facilitators to guide students in the process, and peer collaboration through writing conferences. The authors hypothesized that students who received this cognitive strategy instruction would perform better on writing and reading comprehension tests and on measures of metacognitive knowledge than comparison students.

The study was simultaneously conducted in both general and special education settings. In the experimental classrooms were 100 fifth-graders (33 with learning disabilities), and 74 students were in the comparison classrooms (22 with learning disabilities). Students in the cognitive strategy condition received five months of instruction that consisted of four phases: text analysis, modeling of the writing process, guided student practice in composition, and independent writing. Students in the comparison classrooms received their regular writing instruction that included opportunities to compose texts two to three times per week.

The primary procedural facilitator that was implemented in the experimental classrooms was a "think sheet" to assist students in planning, organizing, writing, editing, and revising their compositions. Figure 35.2 is an example of the think sheet that Englert et al. used to facilitate organization of explanatory writing.

The think sheets were used and referred to extensively during all four phases of the cognitive instructional approach. Interviews that were conducted to assess students' metacognition in writing revealed that students in the experimental group learned more about the writing process than did the comparison students. On a measure of writing ability, the overall effect favored students in the experimental group. This positive effect occurred across high- and low-achieving groups, as well as for students with learning disabilities. On a near transfer measure where students were asked to compose an expository text of their choice, results again revealed a significant overall effect that favored students in the experimental classrooms. On a far transfer measure of reading comprehension, students in the experimental group did significantly better on identifying the ma-

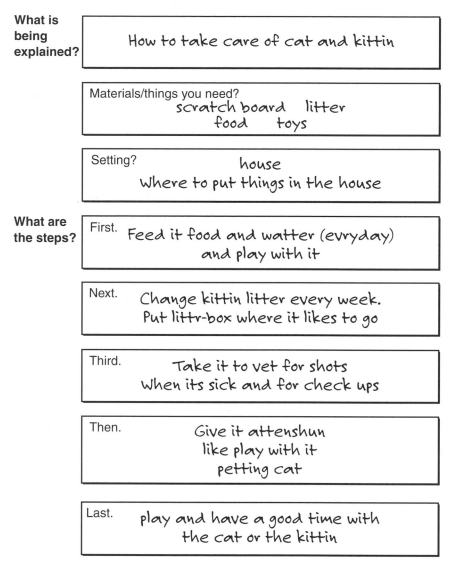

What is being explained?
How to take care of cat and kittin

Materials/things you need?
scratch board   litter
food   toys

Setting?
house
Where to put things in the house

What are the steps?

First. Feed it food and watter (evryday) and play with it

Next. Change kittin litter every week. Put littr-box where it likes to go

Third. Take it to vet for shots When its sick and for check ups

Then. Give it attenshun like play with it petting cat

Last. play and have a good time with the cat or the kittin

Figure 35.2. An example of a completed explanation organization form. [*Source:* Englert, C. S., Raphael, T. E., & Anderson, L. M. (1992). Socially mediated instruction: Improving students' knowledge and talk about writing. *Elementary School Journal, 92*(4), 412–447.]

jor parts of expository text structures and on the number of comparisons recalled. Primarily, the gains made by students with learning disabilities produced these treatment effects.

Another important finding in the Englert et al. (1991) study was that, despite huge differences at pretest favoring students without disabilities, no significant differences were found between students with and without learning disabilities on posttest writing performance. On comprehension, the only significant posttest difference was on the ability of students to recall the main idea of the text they read.

The study by Englert et al. was important because it illustrated the effects of teaching the writing process through procedural facilitators and discourse. The think sheets clearly played a central role in the writing gains made by students in the experimental group. However, an important point to emphasize is that the primary purpose of the think sheets was to provide a

concrete support for the extensive interactions about writing that took place between teachers and students and between students and students.

Another important point to note is that the task of writing expository text was not at all modified for the special education students. Modification came instead in the level of guidance and extended practice that was provided. The intervention was also noteworthy because consistent, positive effects were attained across achievement levels. This approach, using procedural facilitators combined with rich classroom discourse, suggests that most students can benefit from instruction that makes explicit the details of a complex process such as writing. In contrast, reading comprehension research by Wong (1979), Wong and Jones (1982), and Chan and Cole (1986) has shown that teaching explicit strategies to improve comprehension helped students with disabilities, but not average-achieving students.

A final note on Englert's findings, however, is that although students' writing had improved in its substance, it continued to lack style; few students had developed voices as writers. Even though more elements of conventional text were successfully included, student writing samples were often tedious to read and were rigidly constructed. For students to begin to develop a voice as writers, peer dialogue was necessary.

Developing a Personal Writing Style

An extensive line of research on procedural facilitators in writing by Graham and Harris (1989a; Graham, MacArthur, & Schwartz, 1995; Graham, Schwartz, & MacArthur, 1993) has tackled the problem of how to improve the quality of writing by students with learning disabilities. In their earlier studies, Graham and Harris (1989a) taught students a question-asking strategy that they could use to write better stories. This question-asking approach was quite similar to the story map questions used by Idol (1987). They demonstrated that procedural facilitators significantly improved the writing quality of students with learning disabilities. However, like Englert et al. (1991), they found that the writing, which was somewhat rigid and overly mechanical, was still considerably poorer than the writing of their grade-level peers.

In a recent study, Graham, MacArthur, and Schwartz (1995) directly addressed the problem of how to further improve the quality of writing by students with disabilities and make it more closely resemble the writing produced by their peers. They approached this challenge by targeting one of the crucial stages of the writing process, revision. Graham et al. (1995) targeted this area because they found that students in general "revise infrequently, or concentrate their revising efforts on proofreading . . . [on] mechanical and word-level changes, that have little or no effect on the quality of their writing" (p. 230). The authors of the study noted that this problem is particularly acute for students with learning disabilities, who "approach the revision of their compositions as a 'housecleaning task.' Most of their revisions are aimed at trying to tidy up the appearance of the paper, making it neater and correcting errors of mechanics and usage as best they can" (p. 237).

Graham et al. (1995) wanted to investigate the effects of procedural facilitators on the revising techniques and writing products of students with learning disabilities. Students in the comparison condition were requested to think about what they wanted to change or add to their first drafts to make their stories better, and they then rewrote their stories with the accompanying changes. In two experimental conditions, students were taught to use procedural facilitators to add at least three things to their stories to make them better. Some students in this condition were given a sheet that contained a series of prompts to help them in the revision process. The goal of these "planning sheets" was to help them organize the information they wanted to add to the final drafts of their papers.

The final drafts in the experimental and comparison conditions did not differ significantly in terms of length. However, students in the experimental conditions wrote final drafts that were judged higher in terms of overall quality than the drafts of students in the comparison condition. The analysis of the changes made in the revisions is particularly interesting. Stu-

dents in both the experimental and comparison conditions frequently revised their first drafts, averaging about 23 revisions per 100 words. This ratio of the number of revisions per words written was comparable to the number of revisions made by average-achieving students in a pilot study.

An important finding was that, although the number of revisions was not influenced by the instructional condition, the types of revisions were. Students in experimental conditions made more revisions that changed the meaning of the text than students in the comparison condition (47% to 16%). Also, most of the revisions that changed the meaning and were made by students in the experimental condition had a positive effect on the quality of the final draft. Three out of four revisions were rated as making the text better, and the quality of those revisions was rated significantly higher in the experimental condition. This fact, together with the finding that the overall quality of the final drafts was higher in the procedural facilitator conditions than in the comparison condition, supports the conclusion that students in the experimental conditions made more complex changes (i.e., meaning change versus mechanical change) and made changes that more often improved the quality of their writing and final papers than did comparison students. In other words, with the support of a procedural facilitator, students with disabilities were able to reflect on, critically analyze, and improve their own writing. Importantly, we must realize that this finding was achieved in the presence of a very low-cost and entirely feasible instructional approach.

Problematic findings include the fact that many changes, even ones that changed the meaning of the text, were at the individual word level only. It seems that the difficulties experienced during revision by students with learning disabilities encompass much more than just problems with self-monitoring and task persistence (Graham & Harris, 1994). Clearly, the procedural facilitators helped students get organized and direct their attention towards revising, but many of the revisions remained at the crude level only, despite the obvious need for many other more substantial revisions. For this process to occur, some sort of cognitive apprenticeship (Collins, Brown, & Newman, 1989), or ongoing dialogue and feedback from either a teacher or a proficient peer is necessary.

Graham et al. (1995) suggested that an optimal instructional strategy for students with learning disabilities, at least in writing, might be to pair self-monitoring techniques (such as specific goals during revising) with more substantive instructional methodologies such as teacher modeling, thinking aloud, and strategy instruction—a cognitive apprenticeship. This suggestion echoes the type of hybrid approach to instruction that is used in studies on situated cognition in math and science (Bottge & Hasselbring, 1993; Hollingsworth & Woodward, 1993; Woodward, Carnine, & Gersten, 1988) and in models for teaching writing that are used in the current research by Englert and her colleagues (1991).

New Directions in the Teaching of Writing and Comprehension

From the beginning, clearly, all a procedural facilitator or a cognitive strategy could do was support a student taking action, stimulate thinking, or promote organization. The classic research of Graham and Harris (1989a) intentionally juxtaposed formal questions related to story grammar elements (i.e., the text structure for narratives) such as "Who is my story about?" or "What is the problem that the character faces?" with more casual aesthetic steps such as "let your mind wander" in an attempt to actively encourage personal expression. Even researchers like Wong (1994), who initially had difficulty including whimsical steps in the procedural facilitators or strategies that were taught, have come to realize that elaborated dialogue between students and teachers or between students and their peers is likely a critical instructional factor in enhancing the quality of students' writing and, in fact, appears to be more important than the individual steps in the strategy.

This important role of dialogue represents a fundamental shift in reading and writing instruction, one highlighted in a recent review by Kucan and Beck (1997) and MacArthur, Schwartz, Graham, Molloy, and Harris, (1996).

Thinking Aloud and Together: Elaborated Dialogue as a Means of Teaching

Almost from the beginning, researchers seemed to be implicitly aware (a) that the only thing procedural facilitators or cognitive strategies could really accomplish was to encourage students to think aloud and (b) that, often, groups of peers were essential for promoting this process, because it easily becomes contrived between an adult and a child. The importance of peers working together to really learn to use procedural facilitators and cognitive strategies was apparent in the seminal research of Idol (1987).

Englert et al. (1991) found that when students used text structures such as compare and contrast, their essays were well organized but, sometimes, extraordinarily boring. Peer feedback was necessary to breathe life into the essays and support students in their development of writing style. Even the earliest research on story grammar (Idol, 1987) used heterogeneous groups to promote dialogue.

Researchers have begun to make more explicit the primarily supportive role that strategies and facilitators play in helping students develop not only interesting ideas to write about and to discuss with their peers but also ways to express those ideas effectively in their writing. MacArthur et al. (1996) suggested that the major goal of procedural facilitators and cognitive strategies was to help students bridge the gap they experienced between oral and written language—to encourage "elaborated dialogue." Kucan and Beck (1997) are explicit in noting "the shift from identifying and teaching discrete strategies to focusing on students' efforts to make sense of ideas or build their own understanding of them" (p. 285).

Kucan and Beck (1997) go on to describe a more fluid, interactive mode of teaching where (a) multiple strategies are introduced in a short time frame; (b) students are coached (rather than directly taught) at points when a given strategy might be appropriate; (c) student "personalization" of strategies is actively encouraged; and (d) comprehension instruction is, in the best possible way, tailored to students' current ways of making meaning of text.

Frequently, those who are researching procedural facilitators and learning strategies have drawn on the social nature of learn-

ing (Moll, 1990; Vygotsky, 1978) to help students arrive at greater degrees of independence and flexibility (Englert & Mariage, 1996; Palincsar & Brown, 1989; Scanlon, Deshler, & Schumaker, 1996; Wong et al., 1997). The vehicle most commonly used today for maximizing the social nature of learning is elaborated dialogue.

Elaborated dialogue is also known as "interactive dialogue," "think-alouds," and "collaborative processes." It is a verbal exchange among a teacher and students or among students with each other about a complex cognitive activity. The dialogue can include the explicit modeling of strategies, critical evaluation of verbal or written student responses, and questioning and elaborated responses. During these exchanges, students are apprenticed into higher, more detailed, and richer forms of expression and processes for higher order activities (Englert & Mariage, 1996; Wong et al., 1997).

This more complex and extended dialogue process represents yet one more fundamental shift in special education teaching. We see a movement to integrate procedural facilitators and learning strategies with elaborated dialogue, which is consonant with the movement to teach complex, multicomponent strategies in the context of sophisticated, cognitive activities in the regular classroom.

Also important to note is that, unlike the large body of research done on the use of procedural facilitators, currently, only a small body of research on the effectiveness of elaborated dialogue with students with disabilities can be found. One study in particular, however, does suggest its widespread potential.

Wong, Butler, Ficzere, and Kuperis (1997) designed a multiple component strategy to improve the quality of essay writing by students with learning disabilities in grades 9 and 10. They combined aspects of the Englert et al. (1991) compare-contrast think sheets as the basis for composing essays. The Capitalization, Organization, Punctuation, Spelling (COPS) learning strategy (Schumaker, Nolan, & Deshler, 1985) was used in a peer tutoring during the third, or revision, phase. Pairs of students took turns assuming the role of teacher-critic and checked each other's work for clarity, lack of ambiguity, and use of conventions. Wong et al. also included three phases of instruction, starting with extensive teacher modeling and thinking aloud, and moving toward collaborative planning with a partner and revisions that were based on feedback from the partner. Elaborated dialogue was a key feature of each phase.

This multicomponent intervention led to significant growth in the quality of writing. This growth was maintained over time. Students' metacognitive awareness of the writing process also showed significant growth. The differences in performance between prewriting and postwriting samples were significant, with strong effects found for clarity (effect size of 1.70), appropriateness of ideas (1.71), and organization (2.49). This study pinpoints directions for instruction that are aligned with the contemporary state standards specified in IDEA. It also further demonstrates the integration of explicit instruction and socially mediated instruction.

Elaborated dialogue in all phases of the intervention served the key function of helping students first to engage in the process of compare-contrast writing and then to improve their writing. For example, during the planning phase, elaborated dialogue helped two students establish clearer ideas and see information they had overlooked. One student said to the other, "we've got enough ideas for comparison . . . we need more for contrast" (Wong et al., 1997, p. 13). Wong and her colleagues hypothesized that elaborated dialogues, which lead students through multiple cycles of reflection, realization, and redress of problems, helped each student "see" her thoughts and write from another's perspective.

Elaborated dialogue was central among the teacher and peers in phases one and two, and among peers in phase three. Wong and her colleagues concluded that elaborated dialogue in the context of an ongoing recursive process of reflection helped the students see the inadequacies of their own writing and, in the process, develop a sense of audience. The "talk" appeared necessary for students with learning disabilities who had trouble "translating their verbalized ideas into words and sentences" (Wong et al., 1997, p. 7). In an earlier study designed to teach revision skills, Wong and colleagues (1994) found comparable results between two intervention conditions consisting of a planning strategy, coupled with either (a) elaborated dialogue between teachers and students, or (b) elaborated dialogue between students and students. Wong et al. concluded the comparability of effects suggested that elaborated dialogue, per se, may have been the pivotal factor in improved writing.

Thus, elaborated dialogues appear to play the role of a scaffold, taking students with learning disabilities from simple to more complex states of learning by building on the students' current levels of understanding, their abilities to articulate their ideas, and their abilities to develop ideas and the relationships between ideas. Several researchers suggest that dialogue helps bridge the gap between oral and written language (MacArthur et al., 1996; Wong et al., 1997). The implicit theory behind studies using elaborated dialogues is that students learn through verbal interactions with teachers and peers and that thinking aloud through dialogue leads to internalization of the procedures, processes, and ways of thinking. This internalization is assumed to cultivate a more independent learner who knows and can flexibly apply the "secrets" of the experts in a given complex, cognitive activity. Wong and colleagues (1997) noted the increasing empirical support for socially mediated learning with impressive gains in such areas as reading comprehension and writing (Bos, Anders, Fillip, & Jaffe, 1989; Palincsar & Brown, 1984; Wong et al., 1994).

Contemporary research recognizes the importance of elaborated dialogue between students and teachers as a means of teaching students reading comprehension and writing. Procedural facilitators are essentially tools that provide a common language between teachers and students to guide dialogue on these elusive topics. Because procedural facilitators (think sheets, story maps, etc.) are visible to the students with disabilities, they help demystify the process. In other words, to teach all steps in a strategy to a student seems to be less important than to use a strategy or procedural facilitator to initiate and focus dialogue that then leads to higher levels of performance. In these interactions, teachers model ways of thinking, and students display their current ways of thinking, either with the teacher or with their peers. Teachers and peers also respond to students' attempts at organization, originality, and unique interpretation. Then, as part of the dialogical process that revisits expert ways of thinking, questioning, answering, and elaborat-

ing dialogue, students construct and practice new ways of thinking.

Focused dialogue devoted to comprehending texts has been increasingly assimilated into classwide peer tutoring, a procedure that provides students with opportunities to work cooperatively while providing strategic feedback to each other (D. Fuchs, L. S. Fuchs, Mathes, Simmons, 1997; Greenwood et al., 1992; Simmons, D. Fuchs, L. S. Fuchs, Hodge, & Mathes, 1994). These studies begin to provide empirical support for the effect of elaborated dialogue on the ability of students with disabilities to comprehend written texts. Using both contemporary models of peer tutoring and contemporary approaches to teaching the process of writing and comprehending, feedback can be truly tailored to the unique abilities and perspectives of each student.

We believe this recurring theme, thoughtfully integrating a variety of instructional approaches and techniques, is critical if students with disabilities are going to be successful in today's classrooms. The emphasis on integration also speaks directly to what parents of these students see as one of the primary challenges facing those who teach their children: an expansion of teaching repertoires, a move away from exclusive reliance on single strategies and toward the use of complex, multiple approaches that promote the learner's independence and flexibility.

Content Enhancement: Evolution of a Paradigm

We now discuss a significant line of research in secondary special education teaching that has been conducted for nearly two decades. The purpose of this research, in part, was to prepare students with disabilities to succeed in general education classrooms. The model of instruction used in this research, however, is a marked departure from the format of lecture and large group discussion, which is the current predominant model of content instruction at the secondary level (Putnam, Deshler, & Schumaker, 1993) and the elementary level (Baker & Zigmond, 1990; McIntosh et al., 1994).

Beginning 20 years ago, Alley, Deshler, and their colleagues realized that teaching students how to learn was as important as continuing to build their specific academic skills. This discovery led to a quiet revolution in special education teaching at the high school and middle school level.

New teaching approaches were developed with two goals in mind: (a) to enhance students' learning of the material presented in social studies, math, and science classes, and (b) to develop students' abilities to learn from conventional classroom teaching. The initial learning strategies developed by Deshler and colleagues were different from the procedural facilitators discussed previously. They were based on the principles of behavior analysis and task analysis rather than on attempts to make the nature of expertise as discussed in cognitive psychology more relevant to classroom teaching. Also, with some notable exceptions, the strategies tended to rely less on visual organizers and more on mnemonics. The most significant contribution of these approaches for students with mild disabilities has been the Strategies Intervention Model. This model has eight stages of instruction that teachers follow to teach specific academic strategies to their students (Ellis, Deshler, Lenz,

Table 35.1 Eight Stages of the Strategies Intervention Model: Purpose Statements

1. Students make a commitment to learning strategies that can help them do better in content-area class
2. Present the new strategy to students so they can learn the processes involved in using it
3. Teachers model the strategy primarily by thinking aloud and working through the strategy
4. Students describe the learning strategy in their own words
5. Students apply the strategy in the context of carefully selected materials and situations
6. Students apply the strategy in the context of real classroom demands
7. Students learn how the strategy can be applied in other settings
8. Students apply and adapt the strategy in other settings

Schumaker, & Clark, 1991). The primary purpose of each of the eight stages is listed in Table 35.1.

Many of the studies on the learning strategies by Deshler, Schumaker, and their colleagues have addressed the importance of getting students to understand the purpose of the learning strategies and to articulate the steps involved in executing them successfully. One of the significant features of the eight stages of instruction is the transfer of responsibility for performance from the teacher to the student. As the student improves in use of the strategies, the teacher moves from being a director of learning to being a facilitator or coach.

The success of this set of learning strategies (developed in the 1980s) at enhancing this type of transfer has been limited, despite the fact that the strategies were conceived as a way to prepare students to "attack situations not previously encountered" (Clark, Deshler, Schumaker, Alley, & Warner, 1984, p. 145). Typically, students with disabilities have been able to learn the necessary steps in executing the strategies and then use these strategies on tasks that are very similar to the teaching tasks, but they have not been able to apply them outside of the contexts in which they were learned.

The effects of content-free learning strategies may have been diminished because, until quite recently, a common pattern in special education at both of the elementary and secondary levels has been to separate the content taught in the classroom from strategies taught in the resource room. Strategies were often taught in a resource setting to prepare the student for general education classrooms. However, students with mild disabilities who "mastered" these compensatory strategies consistently failed to demonstrate their ability to use these strategies outside the resource room or other special education contexts where they were taught (Schumaker & Deshler, 1988; Wong, 1991, 1994).

Attempts to understand why students, regardless of educational disability, failed to transfer skills across classroom settings at the secondary level contributed to the insight that each academic discipline has its own unique ways of reasoning and its own structure. The transfer of knowledge and strategies across academic domains is often limited for students with and without disabilities (Alexander & Judy, 1988; Jones, Palincsar, Ogle, & Carr, 1987). For example, Palincsar, Anderson, and David (1993) quickly learned that the reciprocal teaching approach they had used so successfully to teach reading compre-

hension was fundamentally different from what was needed to teach the language of science—the nature of discourse in science and the methods of science. Thus, new approaches needed to be developed for learning science.

A recent study by Bulgren, Hock, Schumaker, and Deshler (1995) addressed this troublesome issue of teaching students to successfully apply strategies in new learning situations. To accomplish these goals, Bulgren et al. incorporated the use of concept maps, a type of procedural facilitator. Twelve high school students with learning disabilities were taught a strategy for recalling information for test taking. Students were shown a method to identify and group important information using a concept map. Then they learned to create a mnemonic to help them recall the information in their concept maps. They were encouraged to practice the strategy and use it while taking tests.

Results of the study showed that students improved substantially at creating mnemonic procedures (Mastropieri & Scruggs, 1989) to recall information. More important, students also demonstrated the ability to construct different mnemonic devices that were based on the demands of the task. Thus students demonstrated the flexible thinking that Bulgren et al. (1995) were looking for. The most important finding was that, on content area tests, students demonstrated improved performance that was directly attributable to the learning strategies intervention.

The process of constructing concept maps with extensive support from the teacher appears to be a promising technique for helping students with disabilities truly to understand historical concepts. The routine to teach concept map construction also required extensive dialogue between teachers and students, a fact that also was likely to have contributed substantially to the strong effects of the process. We believe that, because the concept maps were visible to students (as were the think sheets and story maps), the process of thinking and learning was demystified.

Historically, in both elementary and secondary settings, early attempts to teach cognitive strategies focused on generic skills without giving sufficient attention to how those skills are executed in specific academic domains (Wong, 1994). We now know that many learning strategies are domain specific and that using those strategies to learn content in other academic domains is extremely difficult (Brown, Collins, & Duguid, 1989). When generic learning strategies are taught separately from the teaching of academic content in science or math or history, students tend not to apply these strategies when it really counts, in learning academic content or in daily living.

We believe that the shift to teaching strategies within a specific academic domain will increasingly become the norm. As coteaching and other collaborative teaching efforts evolve and as special education teachers increasingly respond to the new IDEA's specification that students with disabilities have access to the general curriculum, we predict that instruction in domain-specific strategies for learning mathematics, social studies, science, and other subject areas will Increase.

Other researchers have written about teaching in a way that conveys this domain-specific perspective. Jones, Palincsar, Ogle, and Carr (1987) and Cobb (1994) have called for a conception of teaching in which the classroom teacher's role is both to convey the content of a lesson and to teach students the processes of learning that are required for reasoning, analysis, and problem solving in a particular academic domain. The goal is that the two be truly integrated. As we mentioned, this approach of intergrating content with learnng processes is a significant shift from conceptions of strategy instruction that were developed in the 1980s.

Perhaps the most significant shift in the work of Deshler and colleagues is the move away from "changing the student"—providing students with strategies to learn the general curriculum in mainstream classrooms where traditional texts and assignments are used—to "changing the system"—providing general education teachers with guidance and training to organize and deliver instruction that benefits all students, including students with disabilities (Joint Committee on Teacher Planning for Students with Disabilities, 1995).

In fact, research on learning strategies is increasingly conducted with general education teachers in general education classrooms. For example, Scanlon, Deshler, and Schumaker (1996) conducted a study to determine the effects of training those secondary teachers who teach content areas to teach learning strategies in inclusive classrooms. All the learning strategies were taught in the context of the units that these teachers had planned to cover. The procedure included a series of steps for recognizing the text structure used in a textbook, identifying key information, and depicting how that information could be represented graphically. Results showed that students with learning disabilities made large gains in their knowledge of the strategy steps and in the quality of the graphic organizers they developed. Their posttest scores in these areas were similar to the students without disabilities.

Two features of the study are noteworthy. First, Scanlon et al. considered that critical to success was the quality of the dialogue students engaged in to describe or explain the graphic organizers they developed. This feature connects the study to other studies that incorporate the use of elaborated dialogue to internalize strategies that are being learned. Second, the study shows that students with learning disabilities can learn complex, flexible strategies in inclusive settings.

Significant changes have taken place in learning strategies research. Teachers are still encouraged to learn the stages of strategy instruction that have been empirically established, but they are now encouraged also to take greater responsibility for manipulating activities within those stages to make them compatible with the individual learner and the content being learned. In this content enhancement model, teachers think critically about the content they cover, determine what approaches to learning must be used for students to be successful, and then teach using routines and instructional devices that students can then apply as strategies and techniques to learn the content (Bulgren, Deshler, & Schumaker, 1997). The teacher, in effect, coaches content and process learning simultaneously.

We believe the emerging empirical findings do hold promise for the potential of learning strategies and other procedural facilitators to help students with learning disabilities receive instruction in complex, context-rich settings with their peers.

The Legacy of Direct Instruction

Whereas widespread use of cognitive strategies or procedural facilitators in special education is rare and only slowly increasing in recent years, direct instruction has been the traditional cornerstone of much special education teaching practice in many regions of the country. However, although this method has been used to teach special education students topics as complex as chemistry (Woodward & Noell, 1991), mathematics fractions (Kelly, Gersten, & Carnine, 1990), and American history (Carnine, Caros, Crawford, Hollenbeck, & Harniss, 1996), by far, its main use has been to teach essential academic skills to students with disabilities. In particular, it has been used to teach students how to read—using a highly systematic approach for teaching phonemic awareness and phonics skills (e.g., Lovett et al., 1994).

One of the most lucid definitions of direct instruction comes from a researcher who, until recently, has been one of direct instruction's staunchest critics, Courtney Cazden. Cazden (1992) noted that the key feature of direct instruction is "explicitness. . . . Direct instruction means being explicit about what needs to be done, or said, or written—rather than leaving it to learners to make inferences from experience" (p.111).

This structured approach to teaching, with a minimal emphasis on hands-on, inductive, experiential learning and relatively few opportunities for personalization of learning, was extremely controversial at its inception. It remains so to this day. Its use—or overuse in special education—has been steadily questioned (Heshusius, 1991; Palincsar et al., 1991; Pugach & Warger, 1993; Ruiz, 1989, 1995a, 1995b).

In this section, we hope to enhance understanding of direct instruction as one means of teaching students with disabilities (as opposed to the sole means). We also hope to clarify some misconceptions, explore relevant research findings, provide insights into the evolution of direct instruction, and discuss its legacy.

Defining Direct Instruction

During the 1980s, several researchers, including the senior author of this chapter, attempted to define direct instruction. These attempts at definition help clarify the difference between direct instruction and traditional teacher-led group instruction with which it is often confused.

Stein, Leinhardt, and Bickel (1989, p.164) stated that real learning does "not materialize from brief encounters" with new material but, rather, develops with the type of systematic guidance and structure provided by an approach such as direct instruction. Research by Zigmond et al. (1994) on the effect that traditional social studies instruction had on students with learning disabilities demonstrates this point. Observational data that was collected by Zigmond et al. in general education classrooms revealed that "students with learning disabilities in these . . . classes were selectively attentive, often focusing on an extraneous part of a lesson or explanation. [They were] easily confused and [overly] concrete in their understandings" (p. 14). Concepts that were discussed only incidentally were rarely even remembered.

Direct instruction strives to provide a structure or framework so that students can make sense of new concepts, relationships, and learning experiences. This approach provides students with: (a) explicit models of reasonable ways to solve problems, such as converting letter sounds in meaningful words; (b) ample support during the stages of the learning process; (c) frequent opportunities to respond; and (d) extensive practice and review (Gersten, Woodward, & Darch, 1986).

The opportunity for students to respond frequently, a core component of direct instruction, also gives teachers a chance to see one dimension of what students are learning or not learning during a lesson. For many teachers who work with students with disabilities, the frequent and easily observable progress their students are making in learning how to read is crucial. This observable means of assessing progress may well explain why Swanson and Hoskyn (1998) concluded in their meta-analysis that of all academic domains, the ability to read words was the area that direct instruction had the strongest, most consistent effect for students with learning disabilities.

An associated essential feature of direct instruction is the focus on high rates of student success. High rates of success are considered crucial to increase students' self-confidence, their willingness to take risks, and their persistence in academic problem-solving activities. With direct instruction, high rates of success are partly ensured by designing instruction so that students learn how to solve each step of a particular strategy or concept.

The overarching principle in direct instruction is deceptively simple: To ensure that all students learn, presentation of the curriculum must be clear and unambiguous. We once described this method of curriculum presentation as "the pursuit of clarity" (Gersten, Carnine, & White, 1984).

This pursuit of clarity entails analyzing the crucial, essential concepts in a given body of knowledge (be it chemistry or American history or basic arithmetic)—what Kameenui and Carnine (1998) call the "big ideas" in a given discipline—conveying these big ideas clearly along with numerous examples, and providing numerous opportunities for students to demonstrate their understandings.

A final step in this pursuit of clarity requires teachers to anticipate the types of problems that students are likely to experience and to provide clear support and guidance in advance.

This principle was illustrated in a study of teaching fractions to students with learning disabilities in high school (Kelly, Gersten, & Carnine, 1990).

What the Meta-Analyses Reveal About Direct and Explicit Instruction

A meta-analysis conducted by White (1988) of 25 studies involving students with disabilities found consistently strong effects (mean effect size of .82 standard deviation units) on academic outcomes for teaching approaches that used direct instruction. A decade later, Swanson and Hoskyn (1998) performed an extensive meta-analysis of the effect that various instructional models and approaches had on students with learning disabilities. After analyzing 180 studies, Swanson concluded that two approaches were effective to enhance learning. Both direct instruction and strategy instruction had consistent, moderately strong effects, with virtually identical magnitudes (.68 for direct instruction and .72 for strategy instruction). (The strategy approaches are essentially the approaches we discussed in the preceding section that involve procedural facilitators or cognitive strategies.) When the two were used in combination, the effect was even stronger (.84).

Interestingly, Swanson and Hoskyn (1998) concluded that commonly used terms such as direct instruction or strategy instruction may be increasingly problematic when classifying types of teaching. He noted a huge overlap between the two constructs. Ultimately, he concluded that an array of instructional techniques and strategies appears to frequently promote learning for special education students. These techniques and strategies derive from various philosophies of teaching. In the final analysis, the Swanson research synthesis is most helpful in its delineation of these specific teaching strategies and techniques. These instructional components are listed in Table 35.2.

Table 35.2 Effective Instructional Strategies and Techniques for Students with Learning Disabilities

Instructional Component	Definition and/or Example
Sequencing	Breaking down the task, fading prompts or cues, sequencing short activities, step-by-step prompts
Drill repetition and practice-review	Daily testing of skills (e.g., statements in the treatment description that were related to mastery criteria; distributed review and practice; use of redundant materials or text; repeated practice; sequenced review; daily feedback, weekly review, or both)
Segmentation	Breaking down targeted skill into smaller units and then synthesizing the parts into a whole (e.g., statements in the experimental condition included breaking down the task into short activities or step-by-step sequences, breaking down targeted skill into smaller units, breaking the text or problem into component parts, segmenting and then synthesizing components parts)
Directed questioning and responses	The teacher verbally asking "process-related" and "content related" questions of students (e.g., treatment may include dialectic questioning, questions by students (directed by teacher), dialogue engaged in by teacher and student, questions asked by teacher)
Controlled difficulty or processed demands of a task	Task sequenced from easy to difficult, and only necessary hints and probes are provided the child (e.g., statements in treatment reflect short activities with controlled difficulty level, assistance provided by teacher when necessary, simplified demonstration provided by teacher, task sequencing from easy to difficult, discussion of task analysis)
Modeling of problem solving steps by teacher	Teacher demonstrates processes or steps to solve problem or how to do a task (e.g., writing, comprehension, decoding words)
Group instruction	Instruction occurs in a small group; students and teacher interact within the group
Strategy cues	Reminders to use strategies or multisteps; problem solving or procedures to solve verbalized by teacher, instruction that makes use of "think-aloud" models, benefits of strategy use or procedures presented by teacher

Adapted from Swanson and Hoskyn (1998).

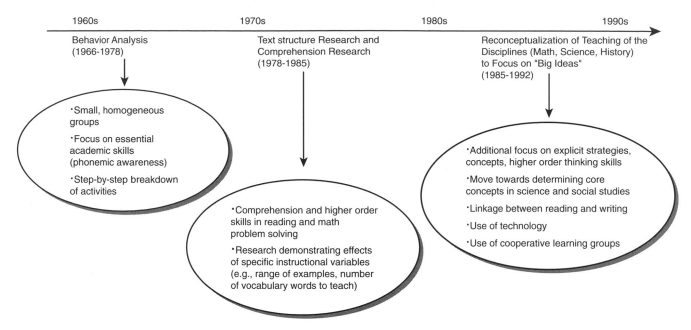

Figure 35.3. A graphic representation of the evolution of direct instruction.

Evolution of Direct Instruction

During the past 10 years, innovations from cognitive psychology also have played a large role in shaping the conceptualization of direct instruction curriculum design and research interventions. Some of these innovations evolved through the integration of technology with instruction. The move toward more integration of special education students into general education classrooms and curricula also has spurred change. Despite such developments and the diversity of curricula topics, however, the key underlying principles presented above continue to be central to direct instruction principles.

A graphic representation of the evolution of direct instruction is shown in Figure 35.3. Perhaps the primary shift is that the concept of explicitness is defined more broadly than it was in the 1960s, when step-by-step breakdowns of all learning activities and every strategy were deemed essential. Direct instruction research is focusing more on strategies, relationships, and concepts and less on rudimentary academic skills. It is also addressing topics such as literary classics (Dimino et al., 1990), history (Carnine, Steely, & Silbert, 1996), and chemistry (Woodward & Noell, 1991). However, an emphasis remains to develop students' phonological awareness (O'Connor, Notari-Syverson, & Vadasy, 1996; Torgesen & Davis, 1996).

Example of Contemporary Direct Instruction Research

Rosenshine (1995) suggested that the primary goal of education is to ensure that students develop knowledge structures in which "the parts are well organized, the pieces well connected, and the bonds between connections are strong" (p. 263). Newer conceptualizations of direct instruction have suggested that the ways to strengthen these connections among ideas and concepts

needs to be articulated clearly to students. These critical connections and how to make them are sometimes referred to as "big ideas."

An example of a contemporary research study using explicit or direct instruction to teach complex content to students with disabilities was recently completed by Carnine, Steely, and Silbert (1996). The focus was on teaching U.S. history to middle school students, using an approach that was compatible with ideas expressed by Leinhardt. According to Leinhardt (1994), history instruction needs to move away from the idea that "students . . . need to learn the facts first and then start to do the interesting 'good' stuff." Instruction, instead, should focus on "helping the student learn to reason about and with history" (p. 253). Investigating this approach was a major goal of this research by Carnine and colleagues. The entire U.S. history course was based on the problem-solution-effect text structure. In other words, the text consistently articulated problems for a group of people (e.g., colonists, American Indians, British), described attempts of the group to resolve the problem, and then described effects. Students were taught to see events from two different perspectives, how a solution for one group (e.g., the colonists) might be perceived as a major problem for another.

The problem-solution-effect text structure is very flexible in the way it can be applied to a wide array of situations (Harniss, Hollenbeck, Crawford, & Carnine, 1994; Kinder, Bursuck, & Epstein, 1992). The components of the framework, as it was used in Carnine, Steely, and Silbert (1996), are shown in Figure 35.4. In general, students are taught that historical events or problems can typically be organized according to whether they involve the rights of people, have an economic focus, or include aspects of both dimensions. The way people or groups respond to these problems can be organized according to five broad cat-

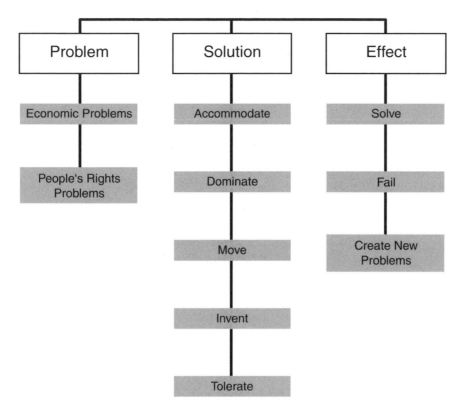

Figure 35.4. Carnine and colleagues' problem-solution-effect text structure. [Adapted from Carnine, D., Steely, D., Silbert, J. (1996). *Understanding U.S. history.* Eugene, OR: University of Oregon.]

egories of responses or solutions. In turn, these solutions have effects that can be tied to the original problem: the problem is solved, the problem continues, or a new problem is created.

For students with learning disabilities, this framework helps them understand historical events in a way that de-emphasizes the memorization of names, dates, and places while it emphasizes the meaning-based aspects of history. With the help of this framework, students could better understand the human dimension of history and grapple with the idea that multiple perspectives on key events do exist.

Carnine, Steely, and Silbert (1996) used a variety of graphic organizers and semantic maps within the direct instruction framework because these tools conveyed information with clarity, illustrated vivid contrasts that students could easily see, and contained key information that students who had difficulty reading could easily access.

Middle school students with learning disabilities and behavior disorders were taught using this approach, and their performance was contrasted with similar students who were taught using conventional texts, texts that did not rely on an underlying conceptual framework. The resultant effect size difference was .68 standard deviation units (Harniss, 1996). Similar results were reported by Kinder and Bursuck (1993) for students with emotional and behavioral disorders. This study helps elucidate

how principles and findings from cognitive psychology and curriculum reformers increasingly have been woven into the direct or explicit instruction research tradition. The findings also demonstrate a means of providing students with disabilities access to the general curriculum in a meaningful fashion, as current Federal policy requires.

In the remaining sections, we broach critical issues in the use of direct instruction, issues that have only infrequently been discussed. These include transfer, generalization, and personalization of knowledge.

Ambiguities and Paradoxes: Use Different Instructional Approaches for Different Effects?

Increasingly, researchers have raised the issue of whether explicit instruction[1] can and should be merged with more experiential or activity-based learning approaches to create instructional approaches that result in better patterns of achievement than would be realized if either instructional approach were used in isolation. Issues such as these have increased interest in whether and how different instructional approaches might be integrated and also in how such integration of approaches might effect learning outcomes.

A recent study by Losardo and Bricker (1994) shows that

---

[1] The terms *direct instruction* and *explicit instruction* are not synonymous, although they clearly overlap. See Swanson and Hoskyn (1998) for a detailed discussion.

pitting one instructional approach against another may be least effective and that, instead, different approaches may likely lead to different types of learning outcomes, and a combination of approaches may result in overall superior performance when compared to any instructional approach in isolation. The study's most important finding was that two fundamentally different approaches for teaching language to young children with disabilities led to very different types of outcomes, each of which is important in language acquisition.

The purpose of the study was to compare whether direct instruction intervention or activity-based intervention (using a variant on Dewey's approach to teaching) resulted in greater acquisition and generalization of 12 object names. The study involved four- and five-year-olds with expressive language delays assessed at between 11 and 31 months below average. Each child was taught 6 object names using an explicit instruction approach and 6 object names using an activity-based approach.

High-quality implementation of both approaches was carefully addressed. For example, the explicit instruction approach was based on empirically derived principles of instructional sequence for introducing noun concepts (Kameenui & Simmons, 1990). The range of examples was broad, including six positive examples that varied by features such as color, size, and actual or toy representation. Minimally different examples, similar in feature, name, or both, were used for discrimination practice. The activity-based condition was based on principles developed in years of research by Bricker and her colleagues in applications of Dewey to early childhood special education. For example, a billfold was included in the "shopping environment" in the activity-based intervention.

Important to note is that the activity-based instructional approach was quite structured and explicit, (much like the procedural facilitators used to teach writing and reading comprehension to older students). Teachers arranged the classroom settings so there were multiple opportunities for students to attend to the target objects. Teachers also intervened with carefully planned prompts and cues to help students direct their attention to the objects. In both conditions, 20 structured practice opportunities per student were provided for each session, and these were designed so that many nonstructured practice opportunities may have occurred while other students responded.

During instructional interactions, all six children produced more target vocabulary words in the explicit instruction condition than in the activity-based condition. In other words, in terms of efficiency and effectiveness of teaching, the explicit approach was invariably superior. Yet, on the generalization measures, results indicated superiority for activity-based learning. On a test of expressive language (use of the words taught), five of the six children performed consistently and clearly better on the words they learned in the activity-based condition compared to the words they learned in the direct instruction condition. On a test of receptive language, the two approaches were essentially equivalent.

The explicit instruction condition was much more efficient in eliciting verbal responses; the rate of responding was very low in the activity-based condition. Yet, the higher performance on the expressive language measure for activity based instruction indicates that, it too, produced demonstrable benefits. The authors conclude that teachers "may want to consider the use of more structured training procedures during initial acquisition phases complemented by using more naturalistic approaches to assure generalization and functional use of acquired lexicons" (Kameenui & Simmons, 1990, p. 764).

Recent research by Lovett, Borden, DeLuca, Lacerenza, Benson, and Brackstone (1994) with fourth-grade students with severe reading disabilities supports the use of a combined or integrated approach. As in Losardo and Bricker (1994), the results of Lovett et al. (1994) showed differential effects by condition. Students in an explicit, phonological-based intervention achieved greater gains in areas associated with the abstract phonological aspects of reading (such as fluency with sound-symbol recognition), whereas students in the metacognitive, strategy-based intervention achieved greater gains in the reading of real words. Lovett et al. encouraged researchers to investigate the effects of integrating these contrasting interventions: "A next step in these investigations will be the evaluation of how the strengths of both programs could be used in combination, allowing direct treatment of phonological deficits at the speech and print levels and specific metacognitive decoding training" (p. 820). We will explore this theme of integrated instruction in the next section.

Using a Combination of Situated Cognition and Explicit Instruction in Science and Mathematics Instruction[2]

Contemporary approaches to mathematics and science instruction attempt to create learning situations where students are forced to (a) think through several options before making a decision about how to proceed, (b) articulate rationales for their decisions, and (c) learn to evaluate the success or failure of the approach taken. The primary goal is to increase understanding of concepts rather than to focus strictly on step-by-step procedures.

Still unclear are the implications of using situated cognition approaches to create learning environments that enhance understanding for students with disabilities. One obstacle is that we do not know the extent or nature of the instructional supports these students need to participate in more ambiguous, open-ended problem solving, a cornerstone of situated cognition. Contemporary research describes the math and science knowledge that many students with disabilities possess as "inert," indicating that students with learning disabilities possibly possess this knowledge but either have little awareness of it or are uncertain about how and when to apply it (Goldman et al., 1996; Kolligian & Sternberg, 1987). For example, while learning to solve math word problems, many students learn to identify and use "key words" as a means to know when to add or subtract or divide, but shifts in how these key words are used can easily derail students with disabilities (Goldman et al., 1996).

The well-documented difficulties that many students with learning disabilities have in organizing information and in spon-

---

[2] This section is adapted in part from Gersten and Baker (1998).

taneously generating hypotheses about information contribute to this problem (Kolligian & Sternberg, 1987; Miller, 1985). Furthermore, these students often struggle with large gaps in relevant background knowledge (Goldman et al., 1996). These problems are exacerbated by the tendency of many students with learning disabilities to withdraw from cognitively demanding or ambiguous situations, in part, because many of them have experienced a history of failure throughout school (McKinney, Osborne, & Schulte, 1993).

Numerous compelling reasons support inclusion of students with learning disabilities in the activity-oriented exercises that are a critical element of both the contemporary mathematics and science reform movements. Mastropieri and Scruggs (1994) note that "Students with disabilities are likely to encounter far fewer difficulties with language and literacy demands when participating in activities-oriented approaches to science . . . than in the textbook-dominated type of science instruction that still remains prevalent in American schools" (p. 83). An equally important argument for including students with learning disabilities in activity-oriented science instruction is made by Woodward (1994): "Students can experience science as a subject for testing hypotheses and making predictions, enabling them to develop creative and critical thinking [abilities]" (p. 101). They can also learn to think like scientists (Anderson & Fetters, 1996).

How, then, do we capitalize on these advances from cognitive science and also on the natural interest in scientific phenomena and the desire to use mathematics to solve real world problems that these students have? In the past decade, this predicament has been addressed by a small number of important studies in special education that provide important direction for how special education students can be taught math and science. These studies combine situated cognition with explicit instruction.

The premise of situated cognition is that conceptual learning is "situated" in the activities with which students acquire knowledge of the concepts taught (Brown, Collins, & Duguid, 1989). Goldman et al. (1996), illustrate the intuitive appeal of situated cognition by suggesting that "if we want students to solve complex . . . problems that arise in day-to-day life, they need opportunities to learn in these contexts" (p. 202). A series of studies that combine direct or explicit instruction with real-world science and math problems has revealed an exciting trend in the research in science and mathematics instruction (Bottge & Hasselbring, 1993; Hollingsworth & Woodward, 1993; Mastropieri, Scruggs, & Chung, 1997; Woodward, Carnine, & Gersten, 1988).

To give the reader a flavor for this type of teaching, we briefly describe two related studies (Hollingsworth & Woodward, 1993; Woodward, Carnine, & Gersten, 1988) of middle and high school students with learning disabilities. Students were explicitly taught key concepts and biological principles related to health and lifestyle choices. Topics included the causes of heart disease, lung cancer, and diabetes.

Each simulation was built around a fictitious character who needed to make one or more changes in lifestyle to reduce major health risks and increase life expectancy. Students were presented with information about weight, exercise, nutrition, alcohol and tobacco consumption, and potential problems that were based on hereditary factors.

Students learned a series of procedural prompts to help them understand the information and their task. The prompts were presented in the form of a "decision tree," the key purpose of which was to help remind them of and guide their focus on the critical concepts they needed to consider as they made decisions. Students were prompted to address each area of priority by beginning at the top of the decision tree. Material was also available to help them decide about how to deal with stresses and maintain positive lifestyle changes.

Data from these two experimental studies indicate that significant positive effects resulted from the combination of explicit instruction and extended practice with the real-world health simulations. On tests of knowledge of relevant biological facts and concepts, students who used the simulation to reinforce the core conceptual material scored significantly higher than those students in the comparison group. These differences were maintained over a two-week period, indicating a strong degree of retention. Further, retention was strongest for those items (such as knowledge of the circulatory system) that students needed to use in the simulation.

Students' abilities to analyze and set priorities for problems were assessed on a series of performance measures. When students worked on the simulation with the procedural prompt (the decision tree), effect sizes were extremely high, approximately 2 standard deviation units. However, when students worked on the simulation without procedural prompts, the effect was cut in half (Hollingsworth & Woodward, 1993).

These studies and the mathematics research of Bottge and Hasselbring (1993) indicate that students with disabilities can engage in relatively sophisticated cognitive activities that require complex discriminations and reasoning. Taken as a whole, we believe studies in the area of situated cognition suggest that an emerging database is beginning to support a promising instructional approach for moving special education teaching beyond its current overreliance on skill development and toward the teaching of problem solving. This database highlights the importance of promoting understanding and providing environments in which students are not overly preoccupied with obtaining the right answer as they begin learning to think through problem-solving situations. One possible strategy is to develop instructional procedures that balance attempts to induce understanding with efforts to achieve proficiency.

For many problem-solving and experimental activities, the use of such procedural facilitators including flow charts (Woodward et al., 1988), graphic organizers (Bos & Anders, 1990; Darch & Carnine, 1986), and other mnemonic devices (Bulgren et al., 1997) are likely to dramatically increase involvement of students with learning disabilities and enhance learning. Without such procedural facilitators, students' ability to draw inferences on their own from abstract scientific material will often be limited (Mastropieri, Scruggs, & Butcher, 1997).

Important to note, however, is that students are unlikely to benefit from these activities unless they are also provided with explicit instruction in the key concepts that underlie the scientific or mathematical material. At times, this instructional approach may only entail explicit instruction (with adequate practice) in the key vocabulary words (Mastropieri, Scruggs, & Chung, 1997). Often, in the case of science—and invariably in mathematics—vocabulary instruction is merely one component. In addition, students need to be explicitly taught relevant facts and concepts (i.e., declarative knowledge) essential for meaningful involvement in problem-solving activities. This teaching should be done so that adequate practice is provided for students to become fluent with the essential factual and conceptual knowledge (Bottge & Hasselbring, 1993). When available, visual models seem to enhance this process (Darch & Carnine, 1986; Gersten et al., 1998; Woodward, 1994). The bottom line is that without the combination of explicit instruction and guided problem solving, guided dialogue, or other types of situated cognition activities, transfer and generalization is unlikely to occur.

Diversity, Disability, and Instructional Research in Special Education Teaching

As recently as 1994, Keogh stated that "issues of ethnicity and culture have a long and dismal history in special education practices" (1994, p. 68). As an example, a recent review of the empirical research on the effects of instructional approaches for English-language learners with disabilities (Gersten & Baker, 2000) found only two experimental studies conducted over the past decade. Similarly, for African-American students with disabilities, Franklin (1992) found a very small body of relevant instructional research.

In contrast, the general education community has begun to pay attention to the roles of culture, race and ethnicity, and language, and it wrestles publicly with the question of the relationship between instruction and these "diversity" variables (Delpit, 1995; Gay, 1995; Irvine, 1991; Reyes, 1992).

The one area in which special education research has focused explicitly on cultural and linguistic diversity is in the diagnosis and assessment of disability, beginning with Mercer's (1970) classic research. This longstanding interest in how to promote and ensure nonbiased assessment and how to reduce the chronic problem of inappropriately identifying students of color as disabled (Artiles & Trent, 1994; Dunn, 1968; Figueroa, 1989; Heller, Holtzman, & Messick, 1982; Mercer, 1970) has continued to predominate. Mercer's line of research set a direction for how the field would define its relationship to issues of diversity for the next two decades. Yet despite these years of attention to the issue of nonbiased assessment, in the last *Handbook of Research on Teaching* (1986), MacMillan, Keogh, and Jones (1986) noted the persistence of inequity in the special education assessment process.

Current data from the Office for Civil Rights document the continued disproportionate number of minority students in special education, especially African-American males in classes for emotional and behavior disorders (Harry & Anderson, 1994; Irvine, 1991; Russo & Talbert-Johnson, 1997). Elegant statistical analyses by Coutinho and Oswald (1998) reveal that, even when controlling for socioeconomic status (SES), level of parents' education, and other potential explanatory factors, African-American males continue to be overrepresented in behavior disorder categories. Further, Robertson, Kushner, Starks, and Drescher (1994) found that geographic location was a significant factor in identifying students with disabilities. The district itself, they argue, is a "major determinant" (p. 2) not only of culturally and linguistically diverse students being iden-

tified as having a disability but also of the specific disability category to which they are assigned.

In addition to the continuing problem with some students of color being overrepresented in special education, a related problem involves the extent to which others who may have real learning disabilities or other serious learning problems may be underrepresented. For example, Latino and Asian students are consistently underrepresented in the learning disability category given their percentages in the general school-aged population in virtually every large urban district surveyed by the Office of Civil Rights (Robertson et al., 1994). In these districts, however, because of a lack of services or of personnel knowledgeable in second-language issues, some teachers do not bother to refer students who may be in need of special services (Gersten & Woodward, 1994). In other cases, fear of legal action along with the realization that assessment procedures for these students are of weak validity contribute to the failure to provide support services (Baca & Cervantes, 1996).

Brantlinger (1997) suggests that the most cogent explanation for the continued disproportionate placement of students of color is that this disproportion signifies a much larger and more complex set of issues involving race and ethnicity, culture, language, and social class that have not been well addressed by special education researchers. Embedding issues of assessment within the larger context of the educational system echoes Messick's (1994) notion of consequential validity, the serious study of the consequences of actions that are taken on the basis of test information.

To understand and improve the school experiences of minority students—both for those who have been inappropriately placed in special education and for those who may have a genuine disability—these more extensive and fundamental issues regarding race and ethnicity, culture, language, and class will need to be incorporated explicitly into research on special education teaching. But this agenda is by no means simple. Several fundamental questions will need to be addressed including, What beliefs do special educators hold about the potential of minority students and the strengths, or "funds of knowledge" (Moll, Amanti, Neff, & Gonzalez, 1992), that families of minority students can bring to the educational process? How will the cultural gap between primarily European-American teachers and minority students be bridged (Delpit, 1995; Gersten, 1999; Reyes, 1992)? What is the relative role of culture in relation to individual difference?

In special education, the situation is complicated by the need to clarify the complex relationship among diversity, deficit, and disability (Artiles & Trent, 1994; Barrera, 1995; Pugach & Seidl, 1996; Ruiz, 1989, 1995a, 1995b). Obviously, these three concepts are not interchangeable.

Instructional Research and Diversity

As this chapter illustrates, the body of research on instruction in special education is large and spans a variety of approaches. To date, however, instructional research that explicitly studies minority children within disability categories is rare, as noted by Gersten and Baker (2000) in a recent review of research on instructional approaches with English-language learners.

The risks for students of color can be high, for example, when dynamics like the cultural mismatch between teachers and students or low expectations on the part of teachers affect classroom instruction. Consequently, a need exists for intentional inquiry into the role of language, class, and ethnicity as critical factors in understanding teaching and learning. When researchers document outcomes for students with disabilities, for instance, the situation is more complex if the students are also members of a minority group, are English-language learners, or both.

Another example of the increased risk when decisions are made regarding students of color is the way special education teachers sometimes interpret student behavior (Harry, 1992; McElroy-Johnson, 1993). This process is particularly important in understanding the overrepresentation of African-American males in classes for behavior disorders.

Elaborated dialogues and procedural facilitators that are used to promote comprehension (instructional approaches described earlier in this chapter) could also help to identify the potential cultural mismatch between teachers and students. What might the nature of the dialogue be between a white teacher and minority students? What are examples of culturally relevant dialogue that promotes comprehension (Jiménez, García, & Pearson 1995, 1996; Ladson-Billings, 1995)? If a student grows only a little as a result of using these instructional approaches, how would these problems be interpreted? As special education instruction begins to rely more not only on peer-mediated and socially mediated instruction but also on direct instruction, then considering the social context—inevitably affected by issues of culture, language, and class—in which these instructional strategies are practiced will be more and more important. The research of Echevarria (1995), Jiménez and his colleagues (1995, 1996), and Ruiz (1995b) begin to provide a foundation for this type of analysis.

Consistent with the focus of this chapter, special education research for Hilliard (1992) would focus less on systemic problems raised in the past decade by researchers like Rueda (1989) and more on identifying powerful pedagogies that significantly and reliably increase levels of achievement for culturally and linguistically diverse students. Hilliard (1992) explicitly states that what he considers to be pedagogically valid special education services *"also assumes that they are culturally sensitive and salient"* (p. 171, emphasis added). Hilliard posed a challenge to educational professionals: Merge concerns for the quality of instruction with concerns for the role of cultural sensitivity in establishing that quality. In so doing, Hilliard redrew the parameters for how good instruction was to be conceptualized.

The role of cultural relevance (Ladson-Billings, 1995) in pedagogical research differentiates Hilliard's concern (focusing special education research on instruction) from that of other special education researchers who also argue for an explicit focus on instructional research (e.g., Carnine, 1995; L. S. Fuchs, D. Fuchs, & Hamlett, 1994; Torgesen, 1998) but do not necessarily specify a cultural framework for it. Do more powerful, culturally sensitive instructional techniques help teachers to make better distinctions between students who truly require special assistance and those who have other educational needs that may be manifestations of systemic problems? For instructional research in special education to be maximized, it must

continue to address issues from a perspective that joins instruction and culturally sensitive teaching for students with disabilities.

The historical absence of attention to diversity increases the need for a set of future practices that can help special education researchers to craft an agenda for the conduct of instructional research. Such inquiry will require (a) building collaborative research teams that are themselves diverse to force conversations about race and ethnicity, language, and class as they relate to special education; (b) recognizing that differences do exist between diversity and disability and clarifying what these differences are; (c) continuing to use qualitative methods to study instructional issues related to disability; and (d) pursuing instructional research that will enable students with disabilities to achieve more successfully and that may simultaneously reduce the persistent overreliance on special education for certain ethnic groups. The challenge for those concerned with research on special education teaching is how best to bring together the agenda of special education, which is appropriately focused on the educational needs of children and youth with disabilities, and the larger social agenda.

Bringing Culture, Race and Ethnicity, Language, and Class into Special Education Research

A critical study that illustrates the importance of framing special education research around issues of diversity is Harry's 1992 ethnographic inquiry into the experiences of 12 Puerto Rican families who have children in special education. Using qualitative methods of interviewing family members over time, in-depth participant observation, and document analysis, Harry provides a multifaceted picture of both the families' interactions with and interpretations of the special education system.

Harry's study provides a naturalistic description of the day-to-day frustrations and difficulties that some parents endure when they are strangers to the special education system—in this case, both culturally and linguistically. Despite procedural safeguards, they feel they are without power. Harry depicts a world of power relationships that mayor may not always be apparent to special education professionals. Although concern for distinguishing between the simple presence and real participation of families has been longstanding in the special education literature, Harry's work offers a multicultural dimension that is essential if special educators, specifically those in early intervention programs, are to meet the expectation to provide a comprehensive view of the role family members can play in their children's education (Dunst et al., 1998; Harry, 1996; Lynch & Hanson, 1992).

Harry portrays the complex nature of immigrants adjusting to a new society and new expectations at the same time they are trying to negotiate school for their children who are also struggling to acculturate. Further, Harry offers a vital distinction between trust and deference in parents' attitude toward school. The vignettes she offers unmistakably connect the reader to the specific experiences these 12 families have as they attempt to understand and navigate the educational system in which their children are entangled. Harry concludes her analysis with important directions for restructuring the discourse between parents and professionals, and specific methods professionals can use to learn about cultural difference.

The field of special education has always been predicated on its sensitivity to set goals that were based on individual differences. The Harry study (1992) shifts the focus away from issues of individual difference alone and toward the relationship between individual educational needs and the manner in which educational institutions acknowledge the influence of culture and language in their practice (see also Dunst et al., 1998; Valdes, 1996). Harry's study reminds us that without considering cultural and systemic inequities, instructional decisions may not reflect the best educational efforts that can be offered to children and youth.

Grounding the Research Analysis in Concerns of End Users

In preparing this chapter, we relied heavily on information from a series of focus group interviews we conducted with family members of students with disabilities, teachers (special and general education), educators involved in teacher education and professional development, prominent educational researchers, and school psychologists. Many of the participants held leadership positions in major national advocacy or professional organizations, such as the Council for Exceptional Children, Learning Disabilities Association, American Federation of Families for Mental Health, and the research and development unit of the American Federation of Teachers. Not all participants were in leadership positions; some were rank and file members of the organization.

Using focus group methodology (Vaughn, Schumm, & Sinagub, 1996), participants were asked to identify the areas of research that would be most beneficial to synthesize and disseminate to teachers and other professionals (e.g., counselors, psychologists, and paraprofessionals) who work directly with students with disabilities (Gersten & McInerney, 1997). We attempted to probe below the surface for underlying themes and issues that cut across the different groups. Many of the themes and issues that emerged from these focus group interviews helped shape the focus for this chapter and helped us select issues to target and probe in our analysis of selected research studies. We conclude the chapter by trying to link our synthesis of the research and emerging trends with the concerns voiced by the participants in these groups.

Unsurprisingly, the major concerns of these groups related to academic instruction, which included quality instruction for culturally diverse students with disabilities. Such quality entails understanding why these students are disproportionately represented in many special education categories. Other themes that emerged include the teaching of social skills and schoolwide values, reduction in bullying of students with disabilities, transition from school to the challenges and tasks of adulthood, and school support of families. These topics are crucial for special education practice. However, we were struck by the consistent return to issues related to academic instruction, conceived in the broadest sense.

Although we highlighted the major advances in the field of academic instruction in the past decade or so, we tried to use the concerns of the end user groups as a lens to identify the most important, relevant advances in knowledge and to decide which individual findings to highlight.

Interestingly, discussions only occasionally compartmentalized academic learning into the conventional subareas of reading, mathematics, science, writing, etc. Most salient concerns included transfer of material that was learned in school to day-to-day tasks or, to paraphrase one parent, helping students use what they know.

Another parent talked specifically about how her son never really understood "how the pieces fit together and could be used." As we have seen, this topic has become a major focus of the past decade of special education research on teaching. For example, studies on the integration of direct instruction with more open-ended, problem-solving extension activities show promise in addressing the intransigent problem of helping students retain and transfer what they learn.

The Importance of Multiple Teaching Strategies to Achieve a Broad Array of Objectives

A fascinating issue was a consistent concern that many special education teachers will not use more than one teaching approach to reach an instructional goal, and, if the student does not benefit from that approach, they tend to blame the student for the failure. Parents, in particular, felt that teachers—both special education and general education—frequently used only one general approach to teach content. If the approach was not successful with a student or group of students, the tendency was to persevere with that approach and make other changes, such as lowering expectations or modifying tests. This observation parallels a consistent research finding by Fuchs, Fuchs, and their colleagues (e.g., Fuchs, Fuchs, & Hamlett, 1994), who showed that when teachers were presented with data indicating that a particular student was not progressing at a desired rate, the majority simply indicated they would try to spend more time with the student rather than seriously consider how the particular teaching approach might be contributing to the student's difficulty.

For special education teachers, the goal to become adept at a variety of instructional approaches is likely to be a challenge. Most are trained to use one basic approach and are taught that consistency and intensity of that approach are critical for special education students. Also, a reality of special education is that many special education teachers have large caseloads; consequently, much of the actual instruction is provided by instructional assistants. The extent to which instructional assistants can learn to provide the breadth and depth of instruction that special education students need is unclear. Instructional assistants are typically more comfortable providing the remedial, skills-oriented instruction that is the standard for so many special education students.

The predominant model of teaching students with disabilities in pullout or self-contained settings increases the detachment from other teachers and from the general education curriculum that many special education teachers feel. This isolation may also contribute to the tendency for many special education teachers to teach using the single best (and most familiar) method they know. However, as special education students become more common in general education classrooms, special education teachers will have much more contact with a variety of teaching approaches used in general education classrooms. We predict this contact will require general and special educators to increase instructional planning regarding when and how different teaching approaches may contribute to learning outcomes for students with disabilities.

A major achievement of special education research over the past two decades, which is demonstrated in this chapter, are findings that show how students with disabilities are capable not only of learning the basics but also of engaging in the organization and learning necessary to understand complex content. Research on the use of procedural facilitators and other organizational tools that help students develop and follow plans of action provides a concrete framework of ways students can be taught to link organizational strategies with the learning of complex concepts and principles. These strategies and facilitators provide some of the supports that students with disabilities need to be successful in general education classrooms.

Using more collaborative teaching models is also likely to increase the familiarity that general education teachers have with a variety of teaching methods. As this familiarity occurs, however, we will need to study the effect of training teachers to use multiple teaching approaches on overall teaching quality. In one of the few implementation studies of cognitive strategy instruction, Englert et al. (1991) found that the less effective teachers were those who taught the steps to the strategy in a very rigid fashion, usually those who were not overly familiar with the technique. Although these less effective teachers modeled the writing process and even gave students a glimpse of the inner dialogue that writers engage in during monitoring and revision, they provided few opportunities for students to contribute to the construction of the text.

The more effective teachers engaged the students in the writing process by bridging "the gap between their experiences and what they needed to know about writing" (Englert & Mariage, 1992, p. 131). The importance of this teaching quality was immediately apparent. In the more effective classrooms, once students knew how to use the action plan, the cognitive workload involved in writing was lessened so they could actually devote energy to articulating ideas and organizing their texts. This transfer of control is critical to students' effective strategy use but represents, perhaps, one of the most difficult aspects of teaching. For example, asking teachers to implement different approaches to writing instruction may risk decreasing the quality with which anyone approach is implemented.

However, this potential need to simplify the complexity of any individual approach to broaden the range of possible approaches was addressed by group members in our interviews. Clearly, participants were not talking about variety for the sake of variety but, rather, that serious professional development opportunities for teachers include which strategies were likely to assist them in reaching a particular instructional goal, which strategies might be helpful in the face of specific kinds of problems, and more general knowledge about which approaches tended to be effective for students with disabilities.

Throughout this chapter, we have stressed the importance of using multiple teaching approaches to reach the complex goals of special education and have attempted to delineate occasions where intentional use of multiple teaching strategies leads to greater learning and greater transfer.

Another related issue is the tendency of some teachers and some schools to give up too early on teaching children to read or become competent in mathematics. Focus group participants noted that although virtually all parents supported a life-skills curriculum, they also felt that, after elementary school, academic growth was too easily abandoned as a goal for many children with disabilities. Focus group participants noted the sparse research base on English-language learners with disabilities and urged more research in this area. Recent research by Benz and colleagues (1997) demonstrated that academic proficiency was a key predictor of vocational success for young adults with disabilities. Thus, research reinforces the wisdom of continuing some academic instruction for students through adolescence.

Organizational Strategies

One topic, rare during the official focus group discussions but a major focus of "small talk" during coffee breaks, was that so many students with disabilities lacked organizational strategies. By organizational strategies, we mean both instruction in the teaching of strategies for academic tasks, such as writing and mathematical problem solving, and for daily life tasks, such as remembering which books to bring home or what to buy at a supermarket. Parents highlighted how these well-documented inabilities hinder and embarrass students, especially as they grow older.

Parents stressed the need for schools to take on the task of assisting students in organization and teaching them organizational strategies. In many ways, the research on procedural facilitators is beginning to meet this need. This research provides concrete ways to help students get organized and develop plans of action for accomplishing academic tasks.

Task Persistence

The concept of task persistence must also continue to concern teachers who work with students with disabilities. Longitudinal research conducted by McKinney, Osborne, and Schulte (1993) demonstrated clearly that task persistence was a powerful predictor of achievement for students with learning disabilities. Students with learning disabilities who also have difficulty with task persistence complete less academic work and acquire less general knowledge than their peers (other students with learning disabilities who exert the energy and continue to think through problems and tasks presented to them). The findings by McKinney et al. show that difficulties with task persistence lead to achievement problems that steadily worsen over time.

If students have opportunities to develop task persistence on relatively easy tasks, the hope is they would learn to extend that persistence to more difficult tasks, such as comprehending context-area texts, where task persistence can be a significant challenge for even average students (DeWitz, 1997). This area is where the research on peer-mediated (Fuchs et al., 1997; Greenwood et al., 1992) and socially mediated (Palincsar & Klenk, 1992) instruction is truly relevant.

More than 10 years of research have demonstrated that peer-mediated instruction techniques provide a concrete way for teachers to increase the academically engaged time of all students in the general education classroom (Greenwood et al., 1992). Because the activities are clear and organized, students know precisely what to do from moment to moment, and teachers can easily circulate around the room and monitor involvement. The benefit of these extended learning opportunities for students with disabilities is the chance it gives them to develop fluency in accessing their knowledge in subjects like reading or math. In addition, students have a chance to verbalize their ideas on reading passages or math problems to a peer, a much less anxiety-invoking experience than doing so before the entire class.

A recurrent refrain from the parent and teacher focus groups was the necessity to better understand how to infuse the use of research-based strategies into current practice. As one researcher who participated noted, "There are gaps of 30 years on some topics between research and practice." Such gaps are of critical and immediate concern to the field. Researchers are experimenting with a vast array of models, using a range of alternative approaches and conceptual frameworks to begin to bridge the gap between research and practice. Using issues raised by parents and teachers as a point of departure for research studies has been a major focus in current writing (Billups, 1997; Carnine, 1997; Dunst et al., 1998; A. P. Turnbull & H. R. Turnbull III, 1990) and has been increasingly used in collaborative action research (Englert & Tarrant, 1995; D. Fuchs & L. S. Fuchs, 1998; Gersten, 1995; Malouf & Schiller, 1995) as a means to reduce the gap between research and practice (Beck et al., 1996; Carnine, 1997; Englert & Tarrant, 1995; Kline, Deshler, & Schumaker, 1992; Malouf & Schiller, 1995; Richardson, 1990; Schumm & Vaughn, 1995) and to create instructional approaches that are both empirically validated but also are feasible for classroom use and that resonate with concerns of the end users. This is an extraordinarily ambitious undertaking.

The dramatic increase in communication between researchers and teachers, and, in recent years, researchers and family members of those with disabilities is promising. That the concerns among researchers and parents, and researchers and teachers have so many commonalties is, in our view, an encouraging indicator that progress has been made and will continue to be made in special education.

REFERENCES

Alexander, P., & Judy, J. (1988). The interaction of domain-specific and strategic knowledge in academic performance. *Review of Educational Research, 58,* 375–404.

Anderson, C. W., & Fetters, M. K. (1996). Science education trends and special education. In M. C. Pugach & C. L. Warger (Eds.), *Curriculum trends, special education, and reform: Refocusing the conversation* (pp. 53–67). New York: Teachers College Press.

Anderson, R. C. (1984). Role of the reader's schema in comprehension, learning, and memory. In R. C. Anderson, J. Osborn, & R. J. Tierney (Eds.), *Leaning to read in American schools: Basal readers and content texts.* Hillsdale, NJ: Lawrence Erlbaum Associates.

Artiles, A. J., & Trent, S. C. (1994). Overrepresentation of minority students in special education: A continuing debate. *The Journal of Special Education, 27,* 410–437.

Baca, L. M., & Cervantes, H. T. (1996). *The bilingual special education interface* (2nd ed.). Columbus, OR: Merrill.

Bagnato, S., Neisworth, J., & Munson, S. (1997). *Linking assessment and early intervention. An authentic curriculum-based approach.* Baltimore, MD: Brookes.

Bailey, D., & Wolery, M. (1992). *Teaching infants and preschoolers with disabilities.* Engelwood Cliffs, NJ: Prentice-Hall, Inc.

Baker, J., & Zigmond, N. (1990). Are regular education classes equipped to accommodate students with learning disabilities? *Exceptional Children, 56,* 515–526.

Ball, E. W., & Blachman, B. A. (1991). Does phoneme awareness training in kindergarten make a difference in early word recognition and developmental spelling? *Reading Research Quarterly, 26*(1), 49–66.

Barrera, I. (1995). To refer or not to refer: Untangling the web of diversity, "deficit," and disability. *New York State Association for Bilingual Education Journal, 10,* 54–66.

Bauwens, J., Schumm, J. S., Vaughn, S., & Harris, J. (1997). Pyramid power for collaborative planning. *Teaching Exceptional Children, 29*(6), 62–66.

Beck, I. L., & McKeown, M. G. (1989). Expository text for young readers: The issue of coherence. In L. B. Resnick (Ed.), *Knowing, learning and instruction. Essays in honor of Robert Glaser* (pp. 47–65). Hillsdale, NJ: Lawrence Erlbaum Associates.

Beck, I. L., McKeown, M. G., Sandora, C., Kucan, L., & Worthy, J. (1996). Questioning the author: A yearlong classroom implementation to engage students with text. *The Elementary School Journal, 96*(4), 385–414.

Benz, M. R., Yovanoff, P., & Doren, B. (1997). School-to-work components that predict postschool success for students with and without disabilities. *Exceptional Children, 63,* 151–165.

Bereiter, C., & Scardamalia, M. (1987). *The psychology of written composition.* New York: Lawrence Erlbaum Associates.

Billups, L. H. (1997). Response to bridging the research-to-practice gap. *Exceptional Children, 63*(4), 525–527.

Bos, C. S., & Anders, P. L. (1990). Interactive teaching and learning: Instructional practices for teaching content and strategic knowledge. In T. E. Scruggs & B. Y. L. Wong (Eds.), *Intervention research in learning disabilities* (pp. 166–185). New York: Springer-Verlag.

Bos, C. S., Anders, P. L., Fillip, D., & Jaffe, L. E. (1989). The effects of an interactive instructional strategy for enhancing learning disabled students' reading comprehension and content area learning. *Journal of Learning Disabilities, 22,* 384–390.

Botlge, B., & Hasselbring, T. (1993). A comparison of two approaches for teaching complex, authentic mathematics problems to adolescents in remedial math classes. *Exceptional Children, 59*(6), 556–566.

Brantlinger, E. (1997). Using ideology: Cases of nonrecognition of the politics of research and practice in special education. *Review of Educational Research, 67,* 425–459.

Bricker, D. (1995). The challenge of inclusion. *Journal of Early Intervention, 19*(3), 179–194.

Brown, A. L. (1978). Knowing when, where, and how to remember: A problem of metacognition. In R. Glaser (Ed.), *Advances in instructional psychology* (Vol. 1, pp. 77–165).

Brown, J. S., Collins, A., & Duguid, P. (1989). Situated cognition and the culture of learning. *Educational Researcher, 18*(1), 32–41.

Bulgren, J. A., Deshler, D. D., & Schumaker, J. B. (1997). Use of a recall enhancement routine and strategies in inclusive secondary classes. *Learning Disabilities Research and Practice, 12*(4), 198–208.

Bulgren, J. A., Hock, M. F., Schumaker, J. B., & Deshler, D. D. (1995). The effects of instruction in a paired associate strategy on the information mastery performance of students with learning disabilities. *Learning Disabilities Research & Practice, 10*(1), 22–37.

Carnine, D. (1995). The professional context for collaboration and collaborative research. *Remedial and Special Education, 16,* 368–371.

Carnine, D. (1997). Bridging the research-to-practice gap. *Exceptional Children, 63*(4), 513–521.

Carnine, D., Caros, J., Crawford, D., Hollenbeck, K., & Harniss, M.

(1996). Designing effective United States history curricula for all students. In J. Brophy (Ed.), *Advances in research on teaching: Vol. 6. History teaching and learning* (pp. 207–256). Greenwich, CT: JAI Press.

Carnine, D., Steely, D., & Silbert, J. (1996). *Understanding U.S. history: Vol 2. Reconstruction to world leadership.* Eugene, OR: University of Oregon.

Cazden, C. B. (1992). *Whole language plus: Essays on literacy in the United States & New Zealand.* New York: Teachers College Press.

Chan, L. K. S., & Cole, P. G. (1986). The effects of comprehension monitoring training on the reading competence of learning disabled and regular class students. *Remedial and Special Education, 7,* 33–40.

Clark, F. L., Deshler, D. D., Schumaker, J. B., Alley, G. R., & Warner, M. M. (1984). Visual imagery and self-questioning: Strategies to improve comprehension of written material. *Journal of Learning Disabilities, 17*(3), 145–149.

Cobb, P. (1994) Where is the mind? Constructivist and sociocultural perspectives on mathematical development. *Educational Researcher, 23*(7), 13–20.

Collins, A., Brown, J. S., & Newman, S. E. (1989). Cognitive apprenticeship: Teaching the craft of reading, writing, and mathematics. In L. B. Resnick (Ed.), *Knowing, learning and instruction.: Essays in honor of Robert Glaser* (pp. 453–494). Hillsdale, NJ: Lawrence Erlbaum Associates.

Coutinho, M., & Oswald, D. (1998, February). *Can rigorous empirical studies inform controversial policy issues? Examples from three lines of research.* Paper presented at the Pacific Coast Research Conference, La Jolla, CA.

Darch, C., & Carnine, D. (1986). Teaching content area material to learning disabled students. *Exceptional Children, 53,* 240–246.

Delpit, L. (1995). *Other people's children.* New York: The New Press.

Deshler, D. D., Ellis, E. S., & Lenz, B. K. (1996). *Teaching adolescents with learning disabilities (2nd ed.): Strategies and methods.* Denver: Love Publishing.

DeWitz, P. (1997, March). *Comprehension instruction: A research agenda for the 21st century: Understanding expository texts.* Paper presented at the annual meeting of the American Educational Research Association, Chicago, IL.

Dimino, J., Gersten, R., Carnine, D., & Blake, G. (1990). Story grammar: An approach for promoting at-risk secondary students' comprehension of literature. *Elementary School Journal, 91*(1), 19–32.

Dunn, L. M. (1968). Special education for the mildly retarded: Is much of it justifiable? *Exceptional Children, 23,* 5–21.

Dunst, C., Ferguson, P. M., Singer, G. H. S., Bryan, T., Gersten, R., Irvin, L., & Keating, T. (1998). *The relationship between professional practices and family involvement: A review of research* (Contract # HS 92017001). Washington, DC: American Institutes for Research.

Echevarria, J. (1995). Interactive reading instruction: A comparison of proximal and distal effects of instructional conversations. *Exceptional Children, 61,* 536–552.

Ellis, E. S., Deshler, D. D., Lenz, B. K., Schumaker, J. B., & Clark, F. L. (1991). An instructional model for teaching learning strategies. *Focus on Exceptional Children, 22*(9), 1–16.

Englert, C. S., & Mariage, T. V. (1992). Shared understandings: Structuring the writing experience through dialogue. In D. Carnine & E. Kameenui (Eds.), *Higher order thinking* (pp. 107–136). Austin, TX: Pro-Ed.

Englert, C. S., & Mariage, T. V. (1996). A sociocultural perspective: Teaching ways-of-thinking and ways-of-talking in a literacy community. *Learning Disabilities Research and Practice, 11*(3), 157–167.

Englert, C. S., Raphael, T. E., & Anderson, L. M. (1992). Socially mediated instruction: Improving students' knowledge and talk about writing. *Elementary School Journal, 92*(4), 412–447.

Englert, C. S., Raphael, T. E., Anderson, L. M., Anthony, H. M., & Stevens, D. D. (1991). Making writing strategies and self-talk visible: Cognitive strategy instruction in regular and special education classrooms. *American Educational Research Journal, 28,* 337–372.

Englert, C. S., & Tarrant, K. L. (1995). Creating collaborative cultures for educational change. *Remedial and Special Education, 16,* 325–336.

Felton, R. H. (1992). Early identification of children at risk for reading disabilities. *Topics in Early Childhood Special Education, 12,* 212–229.

Ferguson, D. L. & Ferguson, P. M. (1997). Debating inclusion in Synecdoche, New York: A response to Gresham and MacMillan. *Review of Educational Research, 67,* 416–420.

Figueroa, R. (1989). Psychological testing of linguistic-minority students: Knowledge gaps and regulations. *Exceptional Children, 56,* 145–152.

Franklin, M. E. (1992). Culturally sensitive instructional practices for African-American learners with disabilities. *Exceptional Children, 59*(2), 115–122.

Friend, M., & Cook, L. (1990). Collaboration as a predictor for success in school reform. *Journal of Educational and Psychological Consultation, 1*(1), 69–86.

Fuchs, D., & Fuchs, L. S. (1998). Researchers and teachers working together to adapt instruction for diverse learners. *Learning Disabilities Research and Practice, 13*(3), 126–137.

Fuchs, D., Fuchs, L. S., Mathes, P. H., & Simmons, D.C. (1997). Peer-assisted strategies: Making classrooms more responsive to diversity. *American Educational Research Journal, 34*(1), 174–206.

Fuchs, L. S., Fuchs, D., & Hamlett, C. L. (1994). Strengthening the connection between assessment and instructional planning with expert systems. *Exceptional Children, 61*(2), 138–146.

Gay, G. (1995). Curriculum theory and multicultural education. In J. A. & C. A. Banks (Eds.), *Handbook of research on multicultural education* (pp. 25–43). New York: Macmillan.

Gersten, R. (1995). Collaborative research in special education. Introduction to the topical issue. *Remedial and Special Education, 16,* 323–324.

Gersten, R. (1997). Advances in teaching and instructional design. In *To assure the free appropriate public education of all children with disabilities.* U.S. Department of Education's nineteenth annual report to Congress on the implementation of the Individuals with Disabilities Education Act (pp. III57–III74).

Gersten, R. (1999). Lost opportunities: Challenges confronting four teachers of English-language learners. *Elementary School Journal, 100*(1), 37–56.

Gersten, R., & Baker, S. (1998). Real word use of scientific concepts: Integrating situated cognition with explicit instruction. *Exceptional Children, 65*(1), 23–35.

Gersten, R., & Baker, S. (2000). What we know about effective instructional practices for English-language learners. *Exceptional Children, 66*(4), 454–470.

Gersten, R., Keating, T., Blake, G., & Morvant, M., (1994, April). *Working in special education.* Experiences of urban special educators. Paper presented at the annual meeting of the American Educational Research Association, New Orleans, LA.

Gersten, R., & McInerney, M. (1997). *What parents, teachers and researchers view as critical issues in special education research* (Technical Report 97–1). Washington, DC: American Institutes for Research.

Gersten, R., Williams, I., Fuchs, L., Baker, S., Kopenhaver, D., Spadorcia, S., & Harrison, M. (1998). *Improving Reading Comprehension for Children with Disabilities.* A Review of Research (Final Report, U.S. Department of Education Contract HS 9217001). Washington, DC: American Institutes for Research.

Gersten, R., & Woodward, I. (1994). The language-minority student and special education: Issues, trends, and paradoxes. *Exceptional Children, 60,* 310–322.

Gersten, R., Woodward, I., & Darch, C. (1986). Direct instruction: A research-based approach for curriculum design and teaching. *Exceptional Children, 53*(1), 17–36.

Goldman, S. R., Hasselbring, T. S., & the Cognition and Technology Group at Vanderbilt. (1996). Achieving meaningful mathematics literacy for students with learning disabilities. *Journal of Learning Disabilities, 30*(2), 198–208.

Graham, S., & Harris, K. R. (1989a). Components analysis of cognitive strategy instruction: Effects on learning disabled students' compositions and self-efficacy. *Journal of Educational Psychology, 81,* 353–361.

Graham, S., & Harris, K. R. (1989b). Improving learning disabled students' skills at composing essays: Self-instructional strategy training. *Exceptional Children, 56*(3), 201–214.

Graham, S., & Harris, K. R. (1994). Implications of constructivism for teaching writing to students with special needs. *Journal of Special Education, 28*, 275–289.

Graham, S., MacArthur, C., & Schwartz, S. (1995). Effects of goal setting and procedural facilitation on the revising behavior and writing performance of students with writing and learning problems. *Journal of Educational Psychology, 87*(2), 230–240.

Graham, S., Schwartz, S., & MacArthur, C. (1993). Learning disabled and normally achieving students' knowledge of the writing and the composing process, attitude toward writing, and self-efficacy. *Journal of Learning Disabilities, 26*, 237–249.

Graves, A., & Montague, M. (1991). Using story grammar cueing to improve the writing of students with learning disabilities. *Learning Disabilities Research and Practice, 6*, 246–250.

Greenwood, C. R., Carta, I. I., Hart, B., Kamps, D., Terry, B., Arreaga-Mayer, C., Atwater, J., Walker, D., Risley, T., & Delaquadri, I. (1992). Out of the laboratory and into the community: Twenty-six years of applied behavior analysis at the Juniper Gardens Children's Project. *American Psychologist, 47*, 1464–1474.

Griffin, S., & Case, R. (1997). Re-thinking the primary school math curriculum: An approach based on cognitive science. *Issues in Education, 3*(1), 1–49.

Gurney, D., Gersten, R., Dimino, J., & Carnine, D. (1990). Story grammar: Effective literature instruction for high school students with learning disabilities. *Journal of Learning Disabilities, 23*, 335–342.

Harniss, M. K. (1996). *The instructional design of United States history texts. Student and teacher effect.* Unpublished doctoral dissertation, University of Oregon, Eugene.

Harniss, M. Hollenbeck, K. L., Crawford, D. B., & Carnine, D. (1994). Content organization and instructional design issues in the development of history texts. *Learning Disability Quarterly, 17*, 235–248.

Harris, K., & Pressley, M. (1991). The nature of cognitive strategy instruction: Interactive strategy construction. *Exceptional Children, 57*, 392–404.

Harry, B. (1992). *Cultural diversity, families, and the special education system: Communication and empowerment.* New York: Teachers College Press.

Harry, B. (1996). These families, those families: The impact of researcher identities on the research act. *Exceptional Children, 62*, 292–300.

Harry, B., & Anderson, M. G. (1994). The disproportionate placement of African American males in special education programs: A critique of the process. *Journal of Negro Education, 63*, 602–619.

Heller, K. A., Holtzman, W. H., & Messick, S. (Eds.). (1982). *Placing children in special education: A strategy for equity.* Washington, DC: National Academy Press.

Heshusius, L. (1991). Curriculum-based assessment and direct instruction: Critical reflections on fundamental assumptions. *Exceptional Children, 57*, 315–328.

Hilliard, A. G. (1992). The pitfalls and promises of special education practice. *Exceptional Children, 59*, 168–172.

Hollingsworth, M., & Woodward, J. (1993). Integrated learning: Explicit strategies and their role in problem-solving instruction for students with learning disabilities. *Exceptional Children, 59*(5), 444–455.

Idol, L. (1987). Group story mapping: A comprehension strategy for both skilled and unskilled readers. *Journal of Learning Disabilities, 20*, 196–205.

Idol, L. & Croll, V. J. (1987). Story-mapping training as a means of improving reading comprehension. *Learning Disability Quarterly, 10*, 214–229.

Irvine, J. J. (1991). *Black students and school failure.* New York: Praeger.

Isaacson, S. (1995, February). *A comparison of alternative procedures for evaluating written expression.* Paper presented at annual meeting of Pacific Coast Research Conference, Laguna Beach, CA.

Jiménez, R., García, G. E., & Pearson, P. D. (1995). Three children, two languages, and strategic reading: Case studies in bilingual/monolingual reading. *American Educational Research Journal, 32*(1), 67–98.

Jiménez, R., García, G. E., & Pearson, P. D. (1996). The reading strategies of bilingual Latina/o students who are successful English readers: Opportunities and obstacles. *Reading Research Quarterly, 31*(1), 2–25.

Joint Committee on Teacher Planning for Students with Disabilities. (1995). *Planning for academic diversity in America's classrooms. Windows on reality, research, change, and practice.* Lawrence: The University of Kansas Center for Research on Learning.

Jones, B. F., Palincsar, A. S., Ogle, D. S., & Carr, E. G. (1987). *Strategic teaching and learning. Cognitive instruction in the content areas.* Alexandria, VA: Association for Supervision and Curriculum Development.

Kameenui, E., & Carnine, D. (Eds.). (1998). *Effective teaching strategies that accommodate diverse learners.* Upper Saddle River, NJ: Prentice-Hall.

Kameenui, E. J., & Simmons, D. (1990). *Designing instructional strategies: The prevention of academic learning problems.* Columbus, OH: Merrill.

Kavale, K., & Mattson, P. D. (1983). "One Jumped Off the Balance Beam" Meta-Analysis of Perceptual-Motor Training. *Journal of Learning Disabilities, 16*(3), 165–173.

Kelly, B., Gersten, R., & Carnine, D. (1990). Student error patterns as a function of curriculum design. *Journal of Learning Disabilities, 23*(1), 23–32.

Keogh, B. K. (1994). What the special education research agenda should look like in the year 2000. *Learning Disabilities Research and Practice, 9*(2), 62–69.

Kinder, D., & Bursuck, W. (1993). History strategy instruction: Problem-solution-effect analysis, timeline, and vocabulary instruction. *Exceptional Children, 59*(4), 324–335.

Kinder, D., Bursuck, W., & Epstein, M. (1992). An evaluation of history textbooks. *The Journal of Special Education, 25*, 472–491.

Klenk, L., & Palincsar, A. S. (1996). Enacting responsible pedagogy with students in special education. In M. C. Pugach & C. L. Warger (Eds.), *Curriculum trends, special education, and reform: Refocusing the conversation. special education series.* New York: Teachers College Press.

Kline, F. M., Deshler, D. D., & Schumaker, J. B. (1992). Implementing learning strategy instruction in class settings: A research perspective. In M. Pressley, K. R. Harris, & J. T. Guthrie (Eds.), *Promoting academic competence and literacy in school* (pp. 361–406). San Diego: Academic Press.

Kolligian, J., & Sternberg, R. J. (1987). Intelligence, information processing, and specific learning disabilities: A triarchic synthesis. *Journal of Learning Disabilities, 20*(1), 8–17.

Kornblet, A. (1997). Response to bridging the research-to-practice gap. *Exceptional Children, 63*, 523–524.

Kucan, L, & Beck I. L. (1997). Thinking aloud and reading comprehension research: Inquiry, instruction, and social interaction. *Review of Educational Research, 67*, 271–299.

Ladson-Billings, G. (1995). Toward a theory of culturally relevant pedagogy. *American Educational Research Journal, 32*(3), 465–491.

Leinhardt, G. (1994). History: A time to be mindful. In G. Leinhardt, I. L. Beck, & C. Stainton (Eds.), *Teaching and learning in history* (pp. 206–255). Hillsdale, NJ: Lawrence Erlbaum Associates.

Losardo, A., & Bricker, D. (1994). A comparison study: Activity-based intervention and direct instruction. *American Journal on Mental Retardation, 98*(6), 744–765.

Lovett, M. H., Borden, S. H., DeLuca, T., Lacerenza, L., Benson, N.J., & Brackstone, D. (1994). Treating the core deficits of developmental dyslexia: Evidence of transfer of learning after phonologically and strategy based reading training programs. *Developmental Psychology, 30*, 805–822.

Lynch, E. W., & Hanson, M. J. (1992). *Developing cross-cultural competence.* Baltimore, MD: Brookes.

MacArthur, C., Schwartz, S., Graham, S., Molloy, D., & Harris, K. R. (1996). Integration of strategy instruction into a whole language classroom: A case study. *Learning Disabilities Research and Practice, 11*, 168–176.

MacMillan, D. L., Keogh, B. K., & Jones, R. L. (1986). Special education research on mildly handicapped learners. In M. C. Wittrock (Ed.), *Handbook of Research on Teaching* (3rd ed., pp. 686–724). New York: Macmillan.

Malouf, D. B., & Schiller, E. P. (1995). Practice and research in special education. *Exceptional Children, 61*(5), 414–424.

Mastropieri, M. A., & Scruggs, T. E. (1989). Mnemonic social studies instruction: Classroom applications. *Remedial and Special Education, 10,* 40–46.

Mastropieri, M. A. & Scruggs, T. E. (1994). Text versus hands-on science curriculum: Implications for students with disabilities. *Remedial and Special Education, 15*(2),72–85.

Mastropieri, M., Scruggs, T., & Butcher, K. (1997). How effective is inquiry learning for students with mild disabilities? *Journal of Special Education, 31*(2), 199–211.

Mastropieri, M. A., Scruggs, T. E., & Chung, S. (1997). *Qualitative and quantitative outcomes associated with inclusive science teaching.* Paper presented at the American Educational Research Association annual meeting, Chicago, IL.

McElroy-Johnson, B. (1993). Giving voice to the voiceless. *Harvard Educational Review, 63*(1), 85–104.

McIntosh, R., Vaughn, S., Schumm, J. S., Haager, D., & Okhee, L. (1994). Observations of students with learning disabilities in general education classrooms. *Exceptional Children, 60*(3), 249–261.

McKinney, J. D., Osborne, S. S. & Schulte, A. C. (1993). Academic consequences of learning disability: Longitudinal prediction of outcomes at 11 years of age. *Learning Disabilities Research and Practice, 8*(1), 19–27.

Mercer, J. (1970). *Labeling the mentally retarded.* Berkeley: The University of California Press.

Messick S. (1994). The interplay of evidence and consequences in the validation of performance assessments. *Educational Researcher, 23*(2), 13–23.

Miller, P. H. (1985). Metacognition and attention. In D. L. Forrest-Pressley, G. E. MacKinnon, & T. G. Waller (Eds.), *Metacognition, cognition, and human performance* (Vol. 2, pp. 181–218). New York: Academic Press.

Moll, L. C. (1990). *Instructional implications and applications of socio-historical psychology.* New York: Cambridge University Press.

Moll, L. C., Amanti, C., Neff, D., & Gonzalez, N. (1992). Funds of knowledge for teaching: Using a qualitative approach to connect homes and classrooms. *Theory into Practice, 31,* 132–141.

O'Connor, R. E., Jenkins, J., Leicester, N., & Slocum, T. (1993). Teaching phonological awareness to young children with learning disabilities. *Exceptional Children, 59,* 532–546.

O'Connor, R. E., Notari-Syverson, A., & Vadasy, P. F. (1996). Ladders to literacy: The effects of teacher-led phonological activities for kindergarten children with and without disabilities. *Exceptional Children, 63*(1), 117–130.

Okolo, C. M., & Ferretti, R. P. (1996). Knowledge acquisition and technology-supported projects in the social studies for students with learning disabilities. *Journal of Special Education Technology, 13*(2), 91–103.

Palincsar, A. S., Anderson, C., & David, Y. M. (1993). Pursuing scientific literacy in the middle grades through collaborative problem solving. *Elementary School Journal, 93,* 643–658.

Palincsar, A. S., & Brown, A. L. (1984). Reciprocal teaching of comprehension-fostering and comprehension-monitoring activities. *Cognition and Instruction, 1*(2), 117–175.

Palincsar, A. S., & Brown, A. L. (1989). Classroom dialogues to promote self-regulated comprehension. In J. Brophy (Ed.), *Advances in research on teaching* (pp. 35–72). Greenwich, CT: JAI Press.

Palincsar, A. S., David, Y. M., Winn, J. A., & Stevens, D. D. (1991). Examining the context of strategy instruction. *Remedial and Special Education, 12,* 43–53.

Palincsar, A. S., & Klenk, L. (1992). Fostering literacy learning in supportive contexts. *Journal of Learning Disabilities, 25*(4), 211–225, 229.

Pugach, M. C., & Johnson, L. (1989). The challenge of implementing collaboration between general and special education. *Exceptional Children, 56*(3), 232–235.

Pugach, M. C., & Seidl, B. L. (1996). Deconstructing the diversity-disability connection. *Contemporary Education, 68*(1), 5–8.

Pugach, M. C., & Warger, C. L. (1993). Curriculum considerations. In J. Goodland & T. Lovitt (Eds.), *Integrating general and special education* (pp. 125–148). New York: Merrill.

Putnam, L., Deshler, D., & Schumaker, J. (1993). The investigation of setting demands: A missing link in strategy instruction. In L. Meltzer (Ed.), *Strategy assessment and instruction for students with learning disabilities* (pp. 325–354). Austin: Pro-Ed.

Reid, J. (1993). Prevention of conduct disorder before and after school entry: Relating interventions to developmental findings. *Developmental and Psychopathology, 5,* 243–262.

Reyes, M. de la luz (1992). Challenging venerable assumptions: Literacy instruction for linguistically different students. *Harvard Educational Review, 62*(4), 427–446.

Richardson, V. (1990). Significant and worthwhile change in teaching practice. *Educational Researcher, 19*(7), 10–18.

Robertson, P., Kushner, M. I., Starks, J., & Drescher, C. (1994). An update of participation rates of culturally and linguistically diverse students in special education: The need for a research and policy agenda. *The Bilingual Special Education Perspective, 14*(1), 2–9.

Rosenshine, B. (1995). Advances in research on instruction. *Journal of Educational Research, 88*(5), 262–268.

Rueda, R. (1989). Defining mild disabilities with language minority students. *Exceptional Children, 56,* 121–128.

Ruiz, N. T. (1989). An optimal learning environment for Rosemary. *Exceptional Children, 56,* 130–144.

Ruiz, N. T. (1995a). The social construction of ability and disability: I. Profile types of Latino children identified as language learning disabled. *Journal of Learning Disabilities, 28*(8), 476–490.

Ruiz, N. T. (1995b). The social construction of ability and disability: II. Optimal and at-risk lessons in a bilingual special education classroom. *Journal of Learning Disabilities, 28*(8), 491–502.

Russo, C. J., & Talbert-Johnson, C. (1997). The overrepresentation of African American children in special education: The resegregation of educational programming? *Education and Urban Society, 29*(2), 136–148.

Salvia, J., & Ysseldyke, J. E. (1981). *Assessment in special and remedial education.* Boston: Houghton-Mifflin.

Scanlon, D. J., Deshler, D. D., & Schumaker, J. B. (1996). Can a strategy be taught and learned in secondary inclusive classrooms? *Learning Disabilities Research & Practice, 11,* 41–57.

Scanlon, D. J., Schumaker, J. B. & Deshler, D. D. (1994). Collaborative dialogues between teachers and researchers to create educational interventions: A case study. *Journal of Educational and Psychological Consultation, 5,* 69–76.

Scardamalia, M., & Bereiter, C. (1986). Written composition. In M. Wittrock (Ed.), *Handbook on research on teaching* (3rd ed., pp. 778–803). New York: Macmillan.

Schiller, E., Malouf, D., & Danielson, L. (1995). Research utilization: A federal perspective. *Remedial and Special Education, 16*(6), 372–375.

Schumaker, J. B. & Deshler, D. D. (1988). Implementing the regular education initiative in secondary schools: A different ball game. *Journal of Learning Disabilities, 21*(1), 36–42.

Schumaker, J. B., Nolan, S. M., & Deshler, D. D. (1985). *The Error-Monitoring Strategy.* Lawrence: University of Kansas.

Schumm, J. S., & Vaughn, S. (1995). Meaningful professional development in accommodating students with disabilities: Lessons learned. *Remedial and Special Education, 16,* 344–353.

Simmons, D.C., Fuchs, D., Fuchs, L. S., Hodge, J. P., & Mathes, P. G. (1994). Importance of instructional complexity and role reciprocity to classwide peer tutoring. *Learning Disabilities Research and Practice, 9,* 203–212.

Stein, M. K., Leinhardt, G., & Bickel, W. (1989). Instructional issues for teaching students at risk. In R. E. Slavin, N. L. Karweit, & N. A. Madden (Eds.), *Effective Programs for Students at Risk* (pp. 145–194). Boston: Allyn & Bacon.

Swanson, H. L. (1987). Information-processing theory and learning disabilities: An overview. *Journal of Learning Disabilities, 20,* 3–7.

Swanson, H. L., & Hoskyn, M. (1998). Experimental intervention research on students with learning disabilities: A meta-analysis of treatment outcomes. *Review of Educational Research, 68,* 277–321.

Torgesen, J. (1977). The role of nonspecific factors in the task performance of learning disabled children: A theoretical assessment. *Journal of Learning Disabilities, 10*(1), 33–39.

Torgesen, J. (1998, February). *Individual differences in response to reading intervention.* Paper presented at the Pacific Coast Research Conference, La Jolla, CA.

Torgesen, J. K., & Davis, C. (1996). Individual differences variables that respond to training in phonological awareness. *Journal of Experimental Child Psychology, 63,* 1–21.

Trent, S. C., Pernell, E., Mungai, A., & Chimeda, R. (1998). Using concept maps to measure conceptual change in preservice teachers enrolled in a multicultural education/special education course. *Remedial and Special Education, 19*(1), 16–31.

Turnbull, A. P. & Turnbull, H. R., ill (1990). *Families, professionals, and exceptionalities: A special partnership.* Columbus, OH: Charles E. Merrill.

U.S. Department of Education. (1997). IDEA Proposed Regulations, 42 Fed. Reg. 55026, 55115, to be codified at 34 C.F.R. § § 300.660–662.

U.S. Department of Education. (1999). Twenty-first annual report to Congress on the implementation of the Individuals with Disabilities Education Act. Washington, DC: Author.

Valdes, G. (1996). *Con respecto: Bridging the distances between culturally diverse families and schools.* New York: Teachers College Press.

Vaughn, S., Elbaum, B., & Schumm, J. S. (1996). The effects of inclusion on the social functioning of students with learning disabilities. *Journal of Learning Disabilities, 29*(6), 582–588.

Vaughn, S., Hughes, M., Schumm, J. S., & Klinger, J. K. (1997). Implementation of instructional practices for students with learning disabilities in general education classrooms. *Learning Disabilities Quarterly, 7,* 41–45.

Vaughn, S., Elbaum, B., & Schumm, J. S. (1996). The effects of inclusion on the social functioning of students with learning disabilities. *Journal of Learning Disabilities, 29*(6), 582–588.

Vaughn, S., Schumm, J. S., & Sinagub, J. M. (1996). *The focus group interview. Use and application in educational and psychological research.* Newbury Park, CA: Sage.

Vygotsky, L. (1978). *Mind in society.* Cambridge, MA: Harvard University Press.

Walker, H. M. (1993). Antisocial behavior in school. *Journal of Emotional and Behavioral Problems, 2*(1), 20–24.

Walker, H. M., Colvin, G., & Ramsey, E. (1995). *Antisocial behavior in school.* Pacific Grove, CA: Brooks/Cole Publishing Co.

White, W. A. T. (1988). A meta-analysis of the effects of direct instruction in special education. *Education and Treatment of Children, 11,* 364–374.

Williams, J. P., Brown, L. G., Silverstein, A. K., & deCani, J. S. (1994). An instructional program in comprehension of narrative themes for adolescents with learning disabilities. *Learning Disability Quarterly, 17,* 205–221.

Wong, B. Y. L. (1979). Increasing retention of main ideas through questioning strategies. *Learning Disability Quarterly, 2,* 42–47.

Wong, B. Y. L. (1991). The relevance of meta cognition to learning disabilities. In B. Y. L. Wong (Ed.), *Learning About Learning Disabilities* (pp. 232–258). San Diego, CA: Academic Press.

Wong, B. Y. L. (1994). Instructional parameters promoting transfer of learned strategies in students with learning disabilities. *Learning Disability Quarterly, 17,* 110–120.

Wong, B. Y. L., Butler, D. L., Ficzere, S. A., & Kuperis, S. (1997). Teaching adolescents with learning disabilities and low achievers to plan, write, and revise compare-contrast essays. *Learning Disabilities Research and Practice, 12*(1), 2–15.

Wong, B. Y. L., Butler, D. L., Ficzere, S. A., Kuperis, S., Corden, M., & Zelmer, J. (1994). Teaching problem learners revision skills and sensitivity to audience through two instructional modes: Student-teacher versus student-student elaborated dialogues. *Learning Disability Research and Practice, 9,* 78–90.

Wong, B. Y. L., & Jones, W. (1982). Increasing metacomprehension in learning disabled and normally achieving students through self-questioning training. *Learning Disability Quarterly, 5*(2), 228–238.

Woodward, J. (1994). The role of models in secondary science instruction. *Remedial and Special Education, 15*(2), 94–104.

Woodward, J., Carnine, D., & Gersten, R. (1988). Teacher problem solving through computer simulations. *American Educational Research Journal, 25*(1), 7–28.

Woodward, J., & Gersten, R. (1992). Innovative technology for secondary learning disabled students: A multi-faceted study of implementation. *Exceptional Children, 58*(5), 407–421.

Woodward, J., & Noell, J. (1991). Science instruction at the secondary level: Implications for students with learning disabilities. *Journal of Learning Disabilities, 24*(5), 277–284.

Woolfson, N. E. (1997). *Integration in Lake Wobegone—when not all our children are above average. A qualitative study.* Unpublished doctoral dissertation, University of Oregon, Eugene.

Zigmond, N., Wolery, R., Meng, Y., Fulmer, D., & Bean, R. (1994, April). *Students with learning disabilities in elementary-level mainstream history classes: What gets taught? What gets learned?* Paper presented at the American Educational Research Association annual meeting, New Orleans, LA.

36.

Feminist Perspectives on Gender in Classrooms

Sari Knopp Biklen
Syracuse University

Diane Pollard
University of Wisconsin–Milwaukee

Feminist research on gender and education has expanded enormously since feminists pointed to the significance of gender inequity almost 30 years ago. This research has developed theoretically (so that it is framed by wider, deeper, and more provocative ideas than gender inequity, the original focus of much research), substantively (so that the topics investigated are broader than how girls do in school), and politically (with increased attention to questions of power and to the ways that such markers as race, class, sexuality, and disability intersect with gender). The authors' research careers reflect this shift. One author used to think of herself as having two areas of research: African-American children and gender issues. That dualism has collapsed because when she studies an initiative like African-centered schooling, she approaches the problem thinking about gender. And when she studies a problem that she first sees connected to gender, she goes to the site thinking about race. The other author has written about how her overly narrow conceptions of race in a research project caused her to miss significant data in interviews about gender (Biklen, 1995). These issues are methodological as well as substantive.

Researchers have come to some consensus on particular issues and approach others with quite different and sometimes opposing perspectives. The amount of research, policy initiatives, curriculum practices, and interventions is so broad, currently, that this review is necessarily limited, highlighting a few significant issues to provide an overview of current approaches, conflicts, and innovations (Biklen & Pollard, 1993). Our goal in this chapter is similar to that of Yates (1993b) in her review of the research on the education of girls in Australia, when she wrote that she wanted to "give the reader a way of making sense of the body of work that has been produced" (p. 2). Before we take up this body of work, we explore the construction of gender itself.

Several trends in the research suggest how much more complicated the task of understanding gender in educational fields is recognized to be. These complications are reflected first in the increased use of qualitative methods to study gender and education, methods that insist on studying meaning made in context, and, second, in the breadth of issues connected to particular problems. For example, what affects the learning of mathematics, researchers have come to suggest, is much more than the intersection of biology and social expectations. In this chapter, the subsection on gender and mathematics will point to the range of topics that researchers have begun investigating. Thus, the more we learn about how gender works in schools, the less isolated the marker of gender appears.

The language of gender also points to the complexities. When we examine the language that has emerged around feminism and gender in education, metaphors of presence are significant. Often framed as binaries, the vocabulary of visibility or invisibility, voice or silence, access or denial, center or margin, and so on occur in texts that both directly take up these issues and those that critique these formulations. What spaces are allotted to gendered students? How and where do students take up these spaces? When gender was a code for girls, these metaphors might have been simpler to map. But when gender refers to girls who are not unitary subjects, who are differentiated from each other as well as from boys because of race, class, and sexuality, and when it also refers to one's sexual identity, to transgendering, and to masculinity, the vocabulary of absence or presence is both difficult to map onto actual bodies and inadequate to capture what young people do in school classrooms.

Gender has been a significant marker in the social construction of identity, humanity, and subjectivity. As a marker, gender is a kind of minefield. While the term is important to use, we must also watch problems associated with its use so that its flu-

723

idity, its complexity, and its fluctuating significance (by context) remain visible.

In this chapter, we address the research on gender and education with the hopes of providing assistance for readers who want to make their way through this rapidly expanding and complicated body of literature. In addition to specific points we make in relation to individual literatures in specific subfields, like gender and mathematics, or feminist curriculum theory, we point to tensions that arise in the relationship between identifying a problem and developing strategies to address it.

First, problems are identified because they both affect a group of people, and public notice occurs. Discrimination against girls in school; unequal treatment according to gender, race, and class; and the production of particular forms of masculinity are different kinds of problems. How gender issues get named relates both to the field the researchers are in and to the kind of feminist theory the authors hold. The conceptualization of the problem, in other words, is linked to ways that particular disciplines, like psychology, or specific theories, like postmodern feminism, frame the terrain.

Second, policy initiatives that are developed to address or redress these concerns do not necessarily have the effects that are intended. Certainly, we can say that policies are always tricky in these ways, but, additionally, it appears that global issues like gender discrimination play themselves out in particular ways in different communities. Regions in Australia, the American Midwest, and Britain confront specific differences that make it difficult for change efforts to be transported whole. Therefore, when feminists discuss avenues for change, their implementation is contextually dependent. The section on reform and policy initiatives addresses this concern.

A significant issue in the study of gender in classrooms relates to how young people are represented and theoretically conceptualized (Steedman, 1982; Walkerdine, 1990). If they are seen as adults in the making and a socialization model is used, then the complexities of gender identity are sometimes ignored. If young people are represented as having a view of the world that is particular to them and in which they are seen as making choices, responding to institutions, and interacting with others because they evaluate their situations and come to some conclusions about them, then the complexities of gender identity and reform get taken up more directly. Different ways of conceptualizing young people help to make us aware of the problems associated with particular aspects of gender identity formation. Davies (1989) looked at how gender was discursively constructed among preschool children in Australia, Anyon (1984) examined how young people both accommodated and resisted gender lessons in school, and Thorne (1993) described the value of seeing children "not as the next generation's adults, but as social actors in a range of institutions" (p. 3). West and Zimmerman (1987) described "doing gender" and Young (1997) did a phenomenological analysis of girls and boys playing ball to examine how they practiced gendered actions and encoded gender. These researchers all rejected sex-role socialization conceptualizations because of their inability, despite some efforts, to avoid a one-way model of more powerful active agents socializing passive children (see also Britzman, 1993, p.35, for an additional critique of the model). Connell (1996) also showed that

socialization theories ignore issues of power and fail "to grasp the diversity of race and class" (p. 212).

Researchers tend to address separately markers of sexuality, gender identity, and race as if they were distinct and separate. This action creates a false appearance that identities can be artificially distinguished from each other for the purposes of research. It is the intersections of these identities that are real in people's everyday lives. Researchers, however, tend to study these markers as if they were separate. In the Woods and Hammersley (1993) collection of ethnographic accounts, *Gender and Ethnicity in Schools,* Part I of the book is devoted to gender while Part II takes up ethnicity. While recently more attention has been given to markers like whiteness that were previously taken as the norm (Fine, Weis, Powell, & Wong, 1997; Frankenberg, 1993), most of the work on intersectionality has been theoretical rather than empirical (Guillaumin, 1995). Razack (1998) does take up the intersectional analysis of gender, race, ability, and culture when she reads legal texts and documents as data. The most complete work in intersectionality still seems to take place in autobiographical accounts. Some collections contain articles which address gender, race, and class (e.g., Biklen & Pollard, 1993; Leadbetter & Way, 1996; Weis & Fine, 1993).

What Are Representations of Gender?

In this chapter of the handbook, we represent gender as a system of relations that organizes masculinity in relation to femininity in a way that usually privileges masculinity. People make meaning of their sex and of the other sex. In addition, these meanings are also institutionalized, a process that gives them more power. A structural as well as interpersonal relationship, gender is discursively constructed. That is, being a man or woman, boy or girl is situated within a set of written and unwritten rules or regulations produced in language that become normative either in particular settings or across settings.

Gender is a complex relationship. On one level, we continually have to accomplish gender every day. We adorn our bodies, manage our language, and structure our interactions to do gender, that is, to influence others to read our gender identities in particular ways. At the same time, we have to read and interpret other people's gender work. Gender is so pervasive, we have to reduce it to a series of codes to manage it. Because it is signaled around a series of codes, we need to learn to become sophisticated at reading these codes. (See Finders, 1997, for a portrait of a teacher's and students' daily reading of gender codes.) Classrooms are one important place to learn these codes and to come to negotiate them. It is not as if the teacher directly teaches or radiates gender codes that the student picks up unquestioningly. Rather, everyone radiates and negotiates gender in classrooms. A problem to consider is that even though everyone is doing it, young people need to have the tools to know how it works. Many of the codes with currency in classrooms are not gender neutral because they privilege White, heterosexual, male students. This more recent representation of gender has a history, even if it is not a linear one, a history we suggest in the following pages.

Following the introduction, this chapter is organized into

three major sections, plus a conclusion. The first section titled "What Are Representations of Gender?" explores and analyzes the social construction of gender. Questions that this first section takes up include how gender is represented by those who research it, how the discipline of psychology, as an example of a powerful discipline in education, frames questions of gender, and what the term gender references.

The second section titled "What Gender Issues Get Taken Up in Classroom Research?" both examines some of the substantive issues that the research explores and questions some approaches that are used in the research process. This section considers institutional policies on gender, the research on gender in teacher–student and student–student interactions, achievement, pedagogy, and curricular concerns.

The third section titled "What Are the Effects of Policy and Reform?" addresses policy and reform issues, examining three kinds of interventions, equity issues in schools and classrooms, targeted schools, and sexual harassment, including flirting and bullying.

In the following subsection, we discuss some issues that are critical to understanding what it means in research and scholarship to be gendered. These areas include the binary between sex differences and the social construction of gender, the reference of gender to males and females, and the significance of sexuality as well as sex.

Sex Differences Versus the Social Construction of Gender

This subsection considers two orientations to research on gender in education that account for gender in contrasting ways. The first orientation concerns a large body of research in which the focus is on describing and explaining sex differences. Girls and boys are seen as different from each other in particular ways. The second orientation represents gender from a social constructionist perspective. This perspective gives attention to how gender is read in particular contexts.

SEX DIFFERENCES PERSPECTIVES

To a large extent, research on gender and education has been represented as research on sex differences in achievement, attitudes, and school-related behavior. Much of this emphasis is derived from the individual differences model used by psychologists. The individual differences model envisions a single human being as composed of a set of stable, internal, or internalized traits, aptitudes, and abilities (Riger, 1997). For some researchers, these characteristics are seen as biologically, cognitively, or emotionally based (Epstein, 1997). For others, the differences result from powerful and pervasive socialization practices that teach gender roles and stereotypes to children beginning when they are very young. Regardless of the hypothesized source of these differences, research that is aligned with this model asks to what extent some of the traits, aptitudes, and abilities girls have differ in important ways from the ones possessed by boys. Included in this subsection are some examples of research embodying the sex-differences approach. The studies discussed here were published within the past decade and are intended to be illustrative rather than exhaustive examples of the large amount of literature in this area.

Some researchers seem to assume that differences between boys and girls are innate. For example, Mills, Ablard, and Stumpf (1993) studied differences in the mathematical reasoning abilities of a very large sample of students who were categorized as academically talented. The 2,586 students studied were between 7 and 11 years of age. The researchers stated that most were European American or Asian. Using the School and College Ability Test (SCAT), a nationally normed standardized test, the researchers reported finding consistent gender differences across age levels. Furthermore, these researchers stated that the sex differences could not be explained by differences in test-taking styles of attitudes. As James (1997) noted, a shortcoming of research such as this is that it only documents differences and does not explain them or indicate how they might be lessened.

Other work also documented gender differences but suggested that those differences may not be fixed. For example, in another study of mathematics problem solving, Zambo and Hess (1996) began by stating that gender differences exist: girls perform better on "lower level computational algorithmic, activities . . ." and boys do better on "arithmetic reasoning, application, and problem solving" (p. 362). They noted that several studies have demonstrated that these differences increase with age. Although these authors did not attempt to explain the source of these differences, they indicated that they can be ameliorated. They described a procedure for presenting an explicit step-by-step problem-solving plan that was used with sixth-grade students. They found that girls benefited from this plan under certain conditions and suggested this plan could be used to help improve the girls' math performance.

Several researchers have suggested that gender differences in school-related behavior and attitudes are not necessarily inherent but rather are the result of socialization practices that teach young children societally preferred gender roles and stereotypes, beginning at an early age in families and intensifying as children move into school and are exposed to the larger society. For example, Eccles, Wigfield, Harold, and Blumenfeld (1993) were interested in the development of children's perceptions about their competencies in various school subjects and their values of those tasks in these subjects. After analyzing questionnaires given to first-, second-, and fourth-grade students from 10 elementary schools, these researchers found that boys held higher views of their competence in math, general sports, and throwing and that girls had higher views of their competencies in instrumental music and tumbling. Furthermore, they found that boys were more consistent than girls in their views. Eccles et al. attributed these differences to gender-role socialization that begins early and leads girls and boys to absorb stereotypic sex-role beliefs. They also argued that boys are pressured to accept these beliefs more strongly than girls are.

A number of other studies implicitly or explicitly espoused the idea that gender differences in school performance are socialized throughout childhood. For example, D'Amico, Baron, and Sissons (1995), observing fifth and sixth graders in schools in Montreal, Canada, studied gender differences in attributions about success or failure in learning about microcomputers.

These researchers concluded that girls' attributions were characterized by a learned helplessness orientation and that boys' attributions were characterized by a mastery orientation. They argued that these differences could be related to the limited experiences girls had with computers along with sex-role stereotyping. However, they also indicated that other factors, such as characteristics of the task and setting, mediated these differences in attributions.

Rech (1994) studied the mathematics attitudes of African-American boys and girls, speculating that differences in attitudes might underlie achievement differences. This researcher found that boys reported higher self-concepts and greater enjoyment of math than girls. Rech implied these differences may be because of socialization experiences by arguing that African-American girls needed to be supported and encouraged to engage in math to a greater extent. Pottorff, Phelps-Zientarski, and Skovera (1996) studied gender perceptions of elementary and middle school students about literacy. These researchers began by noting evidence of gender differences favoring girls in reading performance and critiquing biologically based explanations for these differences. Using questionnaires, they asked 730 second, fourth, sixth, and eighth graders from rural, urban, and suburban schools whether girls or boys are better readers and asking them which of their parents was a more frequent reader. They found that girls were perceived to be better readers and that mothers were perceived to read more in general and to read more to children than fathers. While these researchers did not explicitly discuss socialization, this study is similar to other sex-difference research with this orientation.

Research focusing on sex differences has been criticized on a number of accounts. For example, some have argued that the singular focus on sex differences fails to consider similarities in the behaviors of boys and girls (Epstein, 1997; James, 1997). However, some researchers have attempted to confront this particular criticism. For example, Meece and Jones (1996a) studied gender differences in motivation and the types of strategies learners use in classrooms. By using a sample of 213 fifth and sixth graders, these researchers found that girls reported less confidence in their abilities even in those situations in which there were no differences between them and boys in grades or standardized test scores. However, these researchers found no differences between boys and girls in motivational goals or in their use of learning strategies. They concluded that the factors underlying gender differences in school-related behaviors and attitudes are more complex than previous studies have suggested.

In addition, researchers have criticized research focusing on sex differences for failing to consider the effect of race, class, and sexuality (Halpern, 1995; Meece & Jones, 1996b). Halpern (1995) wrote that much of the research on sex differences is based on predominantly White samples and does not consider diversity. In particular, Halpern questioned the salience of sex differences in cognition across diverse populations and suggested that considerations of the effect of poverty on school performance should be included in these studies.

Similarly, Catsambis (1995) criticized research on sex differences for ignoring race and ethnicity. She used the National Educational Longitudinal Study of 1988 (NELS-88) to assess the science achievement, interests, and attitudes of African-American and European-American eighth-grade students. Among European-American students, she found girls had more negative attitudes toward science and were less likely to participate in science extracurricular activities and to choose science as a career even when they exhibited high achievement scores in science. However, she found a different pattern among African-American students. These students, especially African-American boys, reported positive attitudes toward science despite low achievement scores. Catsambis concluded that barriers to participation in science were a function of attitudes among Europeans and achievement among African Americans.

SOCIAL CONSTRUCTIONIST PERSPECTIVES

An alternative to the sex-differences approach to gender is a social-constructionist approach. Those who take a social-constructionist approach to gender argue that conceptualizations of gender are neither inherent nor cemented by socialization practices in early childhood. Rather, definitions of gender as well as most of the behaviors of boys and girls, women and men are produced through interactions in cultural, political, and social contexts. These contexts reflect the inequitable positions of men and women in societies. Feminist researchers often take a social-constructionist perspective in attempting to understand how gender is conceptualized and transmitted in school. In classrooms, for example, social constructionists are interested in understanding how art and reading come to be seen as feminine whereas gym and science are seen as masculine and how behaviors such as shouting out answers are seen as masculine whereas raising one's hand is seen as feminine. Bryson and de Castell (1995) took a social constructionist approach in their work on gender and educational technology. Other examples buttress concerns about girls' needs and performance.

Meece and Jones (1996b) took a social-constructivist perspective in their analysis of the performance of girls in math and science. These researchers noted that efforts to increase girls' access to math and science have only been moderately successful. Although the gender gap in performance in these areas shows declines in some national studies, such as the National Assessment of Educational Progress (NAEP), it remains evident in the mathematics portion of the Scholastic Aptitude Test (SAT-M). In addition, girls still lag far behind boys in participation in science and math activities, and high-ability girls score below high-ability boys in these subjects. In general, according to these researchers, girls continue to report lower confidence in their abilities in these subjects, and evidence of the unfair treatment of girls in classrooms abounds. After reviewing these data, Meece and Jones concluded that increased access is not what is needed to support girls in math and science. Instead, what is needed is a change in the interactions that are produced within classrooms. They suggested that constructivist teaching could offer a feminist perspective to classroom dynamics.

In a similar vein, Wheary and Ennis (1995) offered a social-constructionist perspective to explain how critical thinking in classrooms is shaped by gender. They argued that most conceptions of critical thinking have an implicit male bias. This bias is manifested in three ways. First, women who write about critical thinking are not recognized or presented in texts. Girls are discouraged from participating in class discussions thus denying them access to opportunities to engage in critical thinking in the classroom. Second, research on critical thinking tends to be dominated by men. Third, critical thinking as portrayed in classrooms tends to privilege characteristics associated with masculinity, such as rationality and an impersonal and objective orientation, while ignoring or devaluing characteristics associated with femininity, such as emotion and attention to context, the links between self and object, and personal voice.

In summary, a vast amount of the research on gender in education has taken a dichotomous perspective, focusing on differences between girls' and boys' school-related behavior. Much of this research assumed these differences are rooted in either inherent, enduring characteristics or in early socialization practices that are difficult to overcome. Although this research has highlighted some of the gender inequities that exist in schools and classrooms, some researchers have criticized the sex-differences perspective, arguing that not enough attention has been given to similarities between boys' and girls' behavior and to how factors other than sex mediate the differences that are documented.

A quite different perspective is presented by researchers who argue for a social-constructionist perspective of gender. This perspective situates gender within particular social, cultural, historical, and political circumstances that are dynamic. This view has important implications for research in education. Riger (1997) argued that continuing research on sex differences would be unproductive. Rather, she called for investigations of the ways in which society is gendered and creates unequal opportunities and expectations for women and other dominated groups. In addition, she argued for research on how women counter these inequalities. This perspective could help explain how these processes occur in contemporary classrooms.

Gender of Males as Well as of Females

Early feminist efforts in educational research and practice emphasized the experiences of girls as students and cultural consumers, as well as of women as teachers and female adults. The invisibility of girls and women in all the research literature were problems that needed immediate address. Attention focused on bringing the voices of girls and women into the literature by discovering the situation of women, critiquing what kept and made women the "other," and developing and integrating new knowledge into a gendered view of social life. To center girls, this agenda was oriented toward putting girls and women at the center of any educational research agenda. This approach required reference to a group whose needs could be described and for whom policy change could benefit. A study of the research sponsored by the American Association of University Women represented this situation:

> The tactic of constructing girls as a unified category rather than as a loose conglomerate enabled the researchers [of *How Schools Shortchange Girls*] to categorize how our educational system consistently put the concerns of girls on the back burner. . . . It was not only that the concerns of girls were not part of the discussion on educational reform, and hence marginalized, but that fem-

inists themselves were marginalized in this conversation. (Biklen, Luschen, & Bogad, 1996)

Girls could be problematized as a unified group, and differences of race, class, sexual orientation, disability, and geography could be explored because girls had been shown to exist and to be a group that faced discrimination.

When feminists shifted their references to gender as a marker, they referred to gender as a social relationship, but they continued to focus most of their research on girls and women. This research practice compensated for the invisibility of girls' perspectives and deconstructed practices that masked the specificity of gender. The category, gender, signified resistance because it proclaimed that researchers could not study boys and generalize to children, certainly a practice common in earlier studies. As feminist strategies to decenter boys as "the norm" gained acceptance, interest grew in looking at how masculinity, as well as femininity, was socially constructed.

Coming to the study of boys and masculinity differs from feminist studies of girls because of this history of connecting gender with resistance. Yates (1997) has suggested that some of the recent attention to boys needs discussion in terms of how gender is to be "reconstructed" (p. 338). She argued that to construct the story as one where the "'disadvantage' of girls was discovered, attended to, at least partially fixed up and then replaced by some of the same processes in relation to boys" (p. 339) covers up assumptions around how inequalities are assessed. Evaluating how girls and boys perform in schools by using examination results, she suggested,

> gives undue emphasis to what is happening to a small group at the top and re-frames the agenda for schooling away from a consideration of the *form* of girls' inequality, but it also deals poorly with masculinity and with how gender contributes to some patterns of failure for boys and to the restrictions in 'pay-off' for high-ability girls. (pp. 341–342)

Any approach that assumes a zero-sum game in relation to serving the needs of boys *or* girls will develop models of evaluation that attend to neither adequately.

Work on masculinity, Connell (1995) argued, comes from clinical knowledge, social psychological knowledge, focusing particularly on sex roles, and the new social science. Masculinity, like femininity, is not a unitary phenomenon but is disrupted by race, class, and sexuality. Connell (1995, 1996), who described masculinities rather than masculinity, argued that it is inadequate to recognize that masculinity takes diverse forms. Rather, he insisted, "we must recognize the relations between the different kinds of masculinity: relations of alliance, dominance and subordination. These relationships are constructed through practices that exclude and include, that intimidate, exploit, and so on. There is a gender politics within masculinity" (Connell, 1995, p. 37). Boys who reject sports prowess, for example, have to develop alternative statuses for recognition (Walker, 1988).

Social institutions like schools both support particular sorts of masculine identities through activities, discipline, and sports, as well as respond to gender strategies of families (Heward, 1988). For example, Skelton (1996) did an ethnographic case study to explore "how primary age boys learn through various discourses to position girls and women negatively" (p. 185). He argued that the particular form of masculinity supported by the school was connected to the kind of masculinity exalted in the community surrounding the school. This community upheld an aggressive masculinity that depended on physical violence, and the school also armed itself to defend against threats of physical aggression. All students, girls as well as boys, ended up being controlled by the teachers' masculine authority that perpetuated stereotypical images of good girls and naughty boys.

Humor is another institutional practice that regulates and controls masculinity. Kehily and Nayak (1997) conducted an ethnographic study of humor among boys in school. Results from 100 interviews with teachers and students in two working-class British high schools in the early 1990s suggested that humor promoted conformity among boys. The boys ridiculed and insulted each other and had to show they could take it to maintain their coolness. Humor "consolidated male peer group culture" (p. 69).

This consolidation of groups of particular boys was also taken up by Jordan (1995) who was interested in how little boys developed definitions of masculinity that always opposed girls. She argued that researchers should study boys rather than girls to learn more about inequality in schools. Gender identity is central to children, is constructed by forces beyond the control of the teacher, and is brought into schools where it is performed and re-inscribed daily. "Teachers are . . . faced with the fact that most children are thinking in terms of gender, that being male or female is important to them, and that they are actively looking for guidance on what is gender-appropriate behavior" (p. 73). It is "impractical" for teachers in the early grades to work toward transcending male–female binaries, but rather gender equity goals should reflect expanding the gender definitions that kids see as possible.

In his research with older students, Mac an Ghaill (1994) examined students' participation in the construction of their gender identities. He explored the kind of masculinity that Connell (1996) has called hegemonic, that is, the "form of masculinity that is culturally dominant in a given setting" (p. 209). Mac an Ghaill showed how boys' talk about sex and girls publicly "validated their masculinity to their male friends" (p. 92). This issue of a public representation of masculine identity that distanced peers, teachers, and even the researcher was central to how codes of masculinity were constructed.

Issues of public representation of masculinity were also prevalent in a study of power, gender, and identity in a primary classroom. Gallas (1998) looked at how boys publicly represent themselves, but her population was 6-, 7- and 8-year-olds. In her study, boys in her classroom caricatured themselves as "bad boys." This caricature increased their classroom power but, when read as a performance, could be seen to conceal "many layers of social awareness, creative activity, and ambivalence toward powerful others . . ." (p. 33). The students' interests could not be read as resistance to inadequate or unfair teaching practice. Bad boys, she argued, however, "do not care about power only in relation to established authority figures like teachers or principals; they desire more of an encompassing social control, rather than political control" (p. 34). Gallas' boys showed how hegemonic masculinity is enforced in classrooms, using examples of boys' use of storytelling to maintain power and to isolate particular children.

Perhaps the most compelling example of hegemonic masculinity and its relation to sports prowess at the secondary level can be found in Lefkowitz's (1997) study of what has come to be know as the Glen Ridge rape case. This case involved the 1989 rape and sexual abuse of a teenage girl with intellectual disabilities by a group of the star athletes and most popular boys in the senior class. The author showed how "their status as youth athlete celebrities in Glen Ridge influenced their treatment of girls and women, particularly those of their own age" (p. 6). Like Skelton's (1996) study of community production of particular masculinities, Lefkowitz's work showed the community support (defined through a marginalizing of the young woman with disabilities and a rewriting of the experience as the girl's enticement) for activities that included raping a young woman with intellectual disabilities with a bat and broom, "voyeuring" in which one of the youth had sex with a young woman with other pals hiding in the closet or nearby, self-fondling to erection in class, and other such actions. Lefkowitz did not read these behaviors as disconnected with the community in which the boys lived (Biklen & Bogad, 1998): "the Jocks didn't invent the idea of mistreating young women. The ruling clique of teenagers adhered to a code of behavior that mimicked, distorted, and exaggerated the values of the adult world around them . . ." (p. 424).

Studies that construct the experiences of boys and girls as separate cultures fail, as Thorne (1993) pointed out, to notice children who are on the margins. Generalizations are often made from the experiences of the most rather than the least popular kids, as if that group represented all students. Her ethnography portrayed Mexican immigrant boys who hung out with a mixed-gender group of Spanish-speaking students and played dodge ball. Thorne argued that their "mixed-gender experiences" are rendered invisible in studies that are framed around the model of girls and boys each having separate cultures (p. 98).

Gender and Sexuality

Gender refers not only to gender identity but also to sexual identity as well, because the performance of femininity or masculinity in day-to-day interactions is structured by heterosexuality. Femininity carries social meaning, in other words, because it is constructed around its relationship to masculinity. Masculinity has also traditionally been performed in opposition to femininity. Same-sex relationships shift both the meanings of femininity and masculinity and the purposes of their performance. Hence, sexuality has come to be seen as central to gender. Traditionally, the research on gender did not address sexuality. More recent research, however, has addressed this issue. Mac an Ghaill (1991, 1994), as we discussed earlier, showed how central sexuality was to the construction of heterosexual masculine identities among boys. Gay and lesbian activism around questions of difference also provided an impetus for research connecting gender and sexuality (Epstein, 1994). An example of the increased interest in research emanating from this activism is found in the special issue of the *Harvard Educational Review* on "Lesbian, Gay, Bisexual, and Transgender

People and Education" (Braatz et. al., 1996). Additionally, as with other identities, sexuality is not seen as stable or coherent. For example, although Thompson's (1995) study of adolescent girls' narratives of sex, romance, and pregnancy emphasized the heterosexual experience, she remarked that had she followed the girls through adulthood, some of them who had represented themselves as heterosexuals would come to define their sexuality differently.

Writing on gender and sexuality takes several forms. One of the most prevalent is personal testimonies about experiences as gay or lesbian students, as gay or lesbian teachers, or as coming out stories. Some of these narratives stand alone, and others are included in texts that also examine historical, theoretical, or policy issues (Epstein, 1994; Harbeck, 1992; Khayatt, 1992; Rensenbrink, 1996; Thompson, 1995; Tolman, 1994; Unks, 1995). The books may be devoted solely to issues connected with queerness or be part of works that also address heterosexuality. Another significant area of research and scholarship can be categorized as part of curriculum studies, although the work addresses a wider arena than the school curriculum through its attention to questions of theory and the regulation of sexuality (Sears, 1992a, 1992b). These texts address issues such as why and how gay, lesbian, or transgender sexuality is absent from sex education curricula in schools (Fine, 1988), critiques of sexuality education in public schools (Carlson, 1992), culturally appropriate curricula (Ward & Taylor, 1992), arguments about the relationship between lesbian and heterosexual women because of the shared interests they have in redefining sexual identities (Holly, 1989), the dangers of essentialism in relation to sexuality (Irvine, 1995), and the struggles gay and lesbian youth have to negotiate the ideologies of different sexual cultures and subcultures (Carlson, 1997; Raymond, 1994). A much smaller literature addresses policy questions of many sorts, including the utility and significance of schools for gay and lesbian youth (Friend, 1993; Rofes, 1989; Snider, 1996).

Disciplinary Constructions of Gender: Psychology

Another way in which gender is represented is through the lens of disciplines and their discursive constructions of a field of study. Because psychology has been so significant in education, we take it up as an example of how to trace the representations of gender. The discipline of psychology has had a profound effect on research and practice in K–12 education in general and on conceptualizations about gender in particular. In general, conventional psychology has positioned the child as a developing learner. Although some theorists argue that the child develops through clearly defined, universal stages, others reject this perspective. Similarly, debates within the field about the nature of learning focus most often on the degree to which the child is viewed as a passive receiver or an active constructor of knowledge. Despite these debates, conventional psychologists tend to agree on a perspective that claims to be an "objective science, capable of consistent, complete explanation and prediction. Psychology takes subjectivity, unique individual consciousness as its object" (Squire, 1989, p. 9). Furthermore, this discipline purports to attain these objectives through the use of the experimental method, which studies behavior in controlled, artificial settings and attempts to screen out the historical, situational, social, and cultural contexts within which behavior normally occurs.

This perspective has guided psychologists' research on gender and education in two important ways. On one hand, the discipline has positioned itself as "gender neutral," and, on the other hand, how research questions are asked, answered, and explained suggests that widely held cultural assumptions about gender are accepted with little or no question (Howard & Hollander, 1997). One example of this somewhat paradoxical position can be seen in conventional psychology's perspectives on gender. Gender, in many cases, is reduced to a categorical variable synonymous with biological sex that is seen as an innate and stable trait. Women and girls, therefore, are portrayed like men and boys except in those areas in which they are their opposites. Given this perspective, then, it was possible for psychological research related to education to either ignore gender and generalize theories from boys to girls as Kohlberg (1981, 1984) did in his work on moral development or to conceptualize gender almost entirely in terms of sex differences (Howard & Hollander, 1997; Squire, 1989). Conventional psychologists' concern with differences between boys and girls in verbal and mathematical abilities is an example of this latter conceptualization of gender as sex differences.

An alternative to the perspective of gender as biological sex comes from those psychologists who focus on the development of gender identity or, what is often referred to as, sex-role development, particularly in childhood. From this standpoint, gender is socialized by the environment: first families and then later schools, peers, and the mass media. This socialization process begins at birth, and gender identity is established early in childhood. Once established, these gender identities are relatively impervious to change. Girls and boys learn the prevailing sex-role norms of their society, and "normal" development involves conforming to these roles and norms (Howard & Hollander, 1997). Although this view may appear, on the surface, to offer a more flexible conceptualization, gender is still seen as static and, once established, relatively permanent. Furthermore, this particular developmental perspective accepts socially defined gender roles as given and ignores issues of inequality, oppression, and multiple statuses. In this conception, schools function as agents of socialization, perpetuating that which was begun by families and ensuring that the larger social order will be maintained.

Despite the claims of neutrality with respect to research on gender and education, much psychological research on gender and education is permeated with cultural assumptions, and expectations about girls and boys and the women and men they will grow up to become. For example, in an essay on how masculinity and femininity are represented in childhood, Burman (1995) noted that traditional developmental psychology privileges behavioral characteristics associated with masculinity. Therefore, "normal" development requires moving from attachment to separation, from concrete to abstract thinking, and from dependence to independence. These aspects of development tend to be supported and reinforced in conventional schools and classrooms. Furthermore, often White, middle-class, heterosexual males are presented as the norm against which development or maturity is measured. As masculinity is privileged, femininity is often devalued and marginalized in psychology. For example, Lovering (1995) interviewed young adolescent boys and girls and demonstrated that sex education classes in school brought forth the problem of girls' development in this period by focusing on female sexual development, especially menstruation, as embarrassing and shameful and as a source of ridicule for boys. Lovering attributed this attitude, in part, to psychological conceptualizations of development for girls versus boys in adolescence.

Finally, the reductionist orientation of conventional psychology leads to a study of gender as a variable separate from race, social class, sexuality, and so forth. Thus, considerable research in schools investigates *either* gender *or* race *or* class. In those situations in which more than one status is studied, often psychologists end up asking whether one status is more important or significant than another. This type of question is often far removed from the real world in which individuals simultaneously occupy several status positions that interact in various ways in particular situations. Two other problems emanate from this perspective. First, the focus on gender to the exclusion of race, class, and sexuality often results in a focus on the behaviors of White, middle-class, heterosexual girls in school. Reid, Haritos, Kelly, and Holland (1995) have raised critical questions about the tendency to generalize findings from this group to all girls. Second, these authors have noted that few methodologies in conventional psychology allow for the study of the multiple statuses girls and boys hold.

In summary, conventional psychology, with its perspectives on the developing learner, has created several scenarios of girls in school. In the first scenario, girls are ignored. They are simply extensions of the generalized child. However, this generalized child is imbued with normatively masculine characteristics against which all children are judged. In the second scenario, girls are important only to the extent that they are different from boys. Most often these differences are assessed in the areas of academic abilities, such as math, science, and verbal proficiencies, or in behaviors considered problematic in the classroom, such as aggression. In the third situation, girls are viewed as the problem. In some cases, for example, in studies of classroom interactions, they are presented as passive, vulnerable victims of unfair treatment by boys and teachers. In others, for example, in studies of adolescent sexuality and motherhood, they are referenced as irresponsible, ignorant, and immoral. The first two scenarios tend to treat girls as a single category, ignoring differences in race, social class, and sexuality. By contrast, when girls are viewed as the problem, as in the third, the focus often shifts to poor girls and girls of color.

In recent years, various groups of feminists have challenged many of the tenets of conventional psychology. These challenges have come from within as well as outside the discipline. We will focus here on challenges from within the field. Carol Gilligan's early studies on moral development raised significant questions and objections to conventional assumptions in psychology. In this work, Gilligan (1982) questioned Kohlberg's (1984) stage theory of moral development, a theory based on all-boy samples, with respect to its relevance to girls. Her work led to an alternative configuration of morality that foregrounded relationships and care as well as justice. This work provided a significant departure from conventional psychology's perspective on gender and education because it contested a theory that had been based on studies of boys, studies in which women were relegated to inferior positions. According to Squire (1989), feminist work such as Gilligan's early studies attempted to combine conventional psychological methods with feminist perspectives. Gilligan focused on gender as a discrete and unitary category and ignored race, class, and sexuality. Thus, she generalized work on a sample of White, middle-class girls to girls in general. Over the years, however, Gilligan and her colleagues took this criticism into account and expanded their research program to include girls of different classes and cultures (Brown & Gilligan, 1992; Taylor, Gilligan, & Sullivan, 1995).

Other feminist researchers in psychology have critiqued the basic assumptions of psychology's positivist orientation, especially with respect to its claims to being value free, its assertions that context can be ignored, and its espousal of experimental methods as ideal (Nicholson, 1995; Squire, 1989). These researchers argued that studies of behavior must consider the cultural and political contexts in which they occur, the meanings attributed to behavior and contexts by participants in the studies, as well as the role, values, and behaviors of the psychologist as an active and, often powerful, participant in the research. Furthermore, they argued that knowledge produced through such interactions is not static but dynamic and dependent on changes in time, situations, and participants. These researchers call for the use of qualitative methodologies and more cross-disciplinary interactions (Nicholson, 1995; Squire, 1989). Michelle Fine's (1991) analysis of the production of dropouts from a New York high school is one example of research emanating from this perspective of feminist psychology. Although this type of research is still often considered marginal, it is receiving increased attention within education and psychology. It is expected that research of this type will continue to expand our understanding of the interactive dynamics of schools and classrooms.

Although psychology has had a powerful effect on the study of gender and education, particularly at the precollege level, other disciplinary contributions have been substantial. Scholarship defining the relationship of gender and cultural capital are rooted in sociological theory (Bourdieu, 1986) and have been usefully applied to the study of gender in family–school relationships (Lareau, 1987). Historical work has analyzed, for example, coeducation (Tyack & Hansot, 1990), women and the superintendency (Blount, 1998), and women's careers in teaching, using both historical records (Clifford, 1989) and life history interviews (Munro, 1998).

Interdisciplinary Constructions of Gender

In addition to how more traditional disciplines have approached and represented gender have been the significant contributions that define gender from a transdisciplinary location. This research draws from cultural studies, poststructuralism, and critical theory both when it takes the form of empirical work and when it "does theory." It cannot be neatly categorized by any single disciplinary focus, and it tends to explore questions that traditional disciplinary approaches have ignored for a number of reasons: the issues might be too much on the margins, considered insignificant, or have unclear policy implications.

The work of McRobbie (1991) and other feminists, who drew from the cultural studies approach popularized by the Centre for Contemporary Cultural Studies in Birmingham (United Kingdom) but critiqued and reworked it because of its consideration of gender as a secondary phenomenon (Roman, 1988), has been influential in a number of ways. First, it provided a way for researchers to seriously examine topics that most educational researchers did not see as a significant line of exploration. Roman's (1988) work on the punk slam dance, Christian-Smith's (1988, 1993) studies of girls' encounters with adolescent romance novels, and Lesko's (1988) study of "the curriculum of the body" all examined topics most researchers would previously not have taken seriously, using a methodological approach that read places, bodies, institutions, and activities as texts. These "sites" were approached as critical avenues for understanding the social construction of power and gender. More recent work continues this emphasis through study of high school proms (Best, 2000) and cheerleaders (Swaminathan, 1997). Discourse analysis has even been applied to the study of physical education (Wright, 1996).

Poststructural work has challenged the idea that identities, programs, or concepts are unified, emphasizing these sites as fragmentary and contradictory. And it has argued that empirical work on any topic, including gender, always takes place within theoretical understandings of power, reflects struggles over meaning, and needs to be careful not to replace one regime of truth with another. Taken together, this theoretical frame is made visible in works on such topics as pedagogy (Kenway & Modra, 1992; Lather, 1991; Luke & Gore, 1992), teacher education (McWilliam, 1994), and sexuality (Fine & McPherson, 1993).

Feminist research that is interdisciplinary and draws on critical theory shares with poststructural work an emphasis on the discursive construction of meanings and their relationships to power, difference, and privilege (Biklen, 1995). This emphasis fuels studies of race and identity in a private school that serves upper middle-class girls (Proweller, 1998), of sex education for girls in high school (Fine, 1988), and of masculinity (Connell, 1995, 1996).

If the above paragraphs imply that the characteristics of each of these types of interdisciplinary feminist work on gender are individual and separate, that must be corrected. These approaches, because they are interdisciplinary, do not rigidly define boundaries around their approaches. Poststructuralism is visible in much current research in addition to the studies cited here. The movement away from only doing empirical work (i.e., also doing readings of texts), the interest in including multiple kinds of approaches in research, including analysis of fictional texts in conjunction with, say, ethnographic data, means that there is a greater fluidity in these interdisciplinary texts. Also, because much of the theory these works engage is discussed outside education in philosophy, literary theory, and cultural studies, an intellectual border crossing is promoted.

What Gender Issues Get Taken Up in Classroom Research?

The previous subsections of this chapter explored some of the ways gender is represented and framed in various contexts. It is evident that conceptualizations of gender have become increasingly complex as researchers have moved from studies that simply documented differences between girls and boys, women and men to attempts to understand the various meanings of gender in contemporary society. In the remaining portions of this chapter, we will focus on research that investigates how gender is played out in elementary and secondary schools and classroom settings.

The range in methodological approaches to exploring how gender works in K–12 classrooms includes differences not only in procedures but also in the focus of investigations. The research in classrooms that has identified and examined sexism and other gender-based inequities is considerable. Perhaps best known of this genre is the work of Sadker and Sadker (1994). Beginning in the 1970s, the Sadkers have conducted more than 25 years of research on sex bias in schools and classrooms. By relying primarily on classroom observations and the analyses of videotapes of classes at a variety of grade levels, the Sadkers focused their attention on teacher–student interaction and found that teachers' gender biases were powerful and pervasive. In addition, the Sadkers reported that many teachers indicated they were unaware that much of their interactions with students consistently privileged boys at the expense of girls. The Sadkers went on to illustrate the consequences of this differential treatment for girls and, later, for some boys. For girls, this biased teacher interaction was associated with declines in both self-esteem and achievement as they moved through school. In addition, these writers argued that boys, especially those who were low achievers, were also miseducated as they did not "fit" the teachers' perceptions of what boys behavior "ought" to be (Sadker & Sadker, 1994). Another focus on gender in classrooms examined students' constructions of gender. For example, Alton-Lee, Nuthall, and Patrick (1993) studied the public and private speech of sixth-and seventh-grade children in an introductory social studies lesson in New Zealand. These researchers were interested in understanding how these children used private speech to construct knowledge gleaned from the curriculum and to deal with the judgments that teachers and other students made of them. Four students, two girls and two boys, wore microphones that recorded their talk. In addition, the class was videotaped. Analyses of the students' talk as well as the teacher's behavior illustrated the power boys held in the classroom. This power was reinforced by the teacher who constructed the curriculum around White males as the normative reference point from which knowledge emanated. Not only did boys talk more, but also they made more public sexist and racist comments directed toward the girls and toward the one Maori student in the class. The authors concluded that, for these students, understanding the curriculum meant viewing the world as sexist and racist in which both girls and people of color were devalued.

Gilbert and Taylor (1991) analyzed language learning in the classroom with emphasis on how the increasing use of popular culture in this subject area often reinforces gender stereotypes that privilege boys and devalue girls. These authors described a project that attempted to implement a cultural-studies approach with adolescent girls in an inner city girls' school in Australia. When the girls were invited to incorporate interviews with and pictures of their families into their work, they found that, in some cases, the girls were unwilling or unable to reflect on the work critically because they did not consider this work important. Although these girls had learned stereotypical images of femininity, much from popular culture, these authors noted that these images were not static. They argued that popular culture could be rewritten and re-taught in ways that could help girls become more critically aware of how images of femininity are constructed and how they can be changed. The researchers concluded that equity could only be achieved with changes in both structural arrangements in schools and in the cultural sphere.

Other writers have cautioned against treating gender relations in classrooms as if these were isolated from out-of-classroom experiences and from other statuses students hold. For example, Purcell-Gates (1993) argued that gender is constructed within the family sphere before the child even comes to the classroom. Furthermore, this author pointed out that gender constructions are related to constructions of social class and race that the child learns before coming to school. Children come to school with complex views of self, including ideas about race, class, as well as gender. They must then negotiate these perceptions with classroom teachers who have their own perceptions and assumptions about relationships between gender (and race and class, etc.) and learning.

Institutional and Discursive Practices That Construct Students' Knowledge About Gender

It could be argued that students learn and do gender continually in classrooms. Similarly, they learn and do race, ethnicity, sexual orientation, and social class. These statuses, and assumptions about them, are embedded in the schools' institutional policies, in teacher–student and student–student interaction, in curricular material, in pedagogical practices, and in assessment procedures. Most often, however, this learning and doing is unstated and unacknowledged. Furthermore, it is often shrouded by myths and assumptions that are taken for granted as realities.

The following subsections discuss policies and practices that teach students about gender relations in school and in society. We focus on the interactive aspects of the classroom. A later subsection will discuss curricular materials and specific pedagogical practices.

INSTITUTIONAL POLICIES

Morgan (1996) described three myths that underlie assumptions about gender equity or inequity in schooling. Each of these myths underscores institutional practices that provide White males power to dominate all others. According to Morgan, "power in education is operationalized by creating, defining, encoding, transmitting and evaluating claims to knowledge" (1996, p. 108). The first myth, called by Morgan the "universality myth," assumes that the learning and knowledge of White males is all that is worth knowing and learning. The second myth, the "coeducational myth," asserts that girls and boys get the *same* education because they have the same access to schools and classrooms in the public schools. The third myth is called the "educational equality of opportunity" myth. This

myth assumes that girls and boys have access to equal opportunities in responses, privileges, and rewards in public schools. As each of these myths pervade classrooms, they inform students about the relative privileges available to boys and girls in school and in society.

In *How Schools Shortchange Girls* (AAUW, 1992), evidence of institutional policies that encourage girls and boys to take up institutional gender roles is plentiful. For example, this report documented that policies promoting different types of vocational courses for girls and boys tend to support gender stereotypes about appropriate work roles each should fulfill. As a result, the report says girls are often relegated to low-paying clerical jobs whereas boys are channeled into higher-paying skilled work. Similarly the AAUW report argued that, although boys and girls tend to participate in school extracurricular activities at similar levels of frequency, the activities in which boys predominate tend to offer more opportunities for students to take on leadership roles and to engage in teamwork. Both of these activities would stand students in good stead in the world of work.

TEACHER–STUDENT INTERACTION

In addition to the work of Myra and David Sadker discussed previously, many other researchers have documented teachers' differential interactions with boys and girls in classrooms. Most of this work supports the Sadkers' findings. Furthermore, studies indicate that differential teacher behavior toward girls and boys seems to be quite pervasive. Loudet-Verdier and Mosconi (1995), for example, observed four 1-hour math classes, three elementary and one secondary, in France. Two of the classes were taught by women and two by men. By recording the number of times the teachers called students' names, the number of exchanges between students and teachers, and the amount of time teachers gave to students, these researchers found that all the teachers interacted more with boys than with girls. Interestingly, they also reported that the women teachers gave more attention to boys than did the men. The researchers hypothesized that the women teachers perceived the boys as presenting more disciplinary problems.

Hamilton, Blumenfeld, Akoh, and Miura (1991) obtained similar results in a study of teacher attention to boys and girls in 9 fifth-grade classrooms in Ann Arbor, Michigan, and 10 fifth-grade classrooms in Chiba City, Japan. All the classrooms were described as working or middle class and as relatively racially homogeneous. Communication patterns between teachers and students were observed in each of these classrooms for 5 hours. The researchers reported that both Japanese and American teachers attended to boys more often than to girls. However, they also found that Japanese teachers tended to give boys more negative feedback. Their analysis of observed students' behavior in both countries found that Japanese boys and American boys and girls were similar with respect to off-task behavior, while Japanese girls exhibited this type of activity less.

A third study supporting this pattern of differential teacher interaction with boys and girls was conducted by Nairn (1991) who observed 25 geography teachers in 37 secondary classes in New Zealand. Nairn studied only "successful" teacher interactions, which were defined as those that were initiated by a teacher and responded to by a student or initiated by a student and responded to by a teacher. This researcher compared the number of successful teacher–student interactions involving girls in proportion to the number of girls in the class. As in the other studies, Nairn found that in a majority of the classes the teachers' attention favored boys; although girls were 56% of the total student population studied, in 57% of the classes observed, the interaction favored boys. In 13% of the classes, the interaction favored girls, and in 30% of the classes the interaction was similar for girls and boys. In addition, although 80% of the teachers were men, Nairn found no differences in interaction patterns between men and women teachers.

Finally, Lee, Marks, and Byrd (1994) asked whether there were differences in the level of sexism in single-sex or coeducational classrooms. They studied three single-sex and coeducational private high school senior-level classes. Their procedures included classroom observations, interviews with students and teachers, and reviews of school records. Eighty-six classrooms were observed. The authors found evidence of sexism in both single-sex and coeducational classrooms. Incidents involving sexism appeared in 54% of the coeducational classrooms, in 37% of the all-boys classes, and in 45% of the all-girls classes. Almost all the sexist incidents were initiated by teachers, and male teachers initiated them more frequently.

All these studies used quantitative methodologies and consistently documented differential behaviors by teachers toward boys and girls. However, only two of the studies attempted to ascertain why these differential behaviors existed. Both Loudet-Verdier and Mosconi and Hamilton et al. linked them to the more disruptive behaviors of boys. Of these two, only Hamilton et al. actually tallied off-task behavior for boys and girls in the Japanese and American classrooms; their findings tended to support this hypothesis. However, other possibilities to explain this behavior may also be considered. For example, Shepardson and Pizzini (1992) suggested that the differential treatment by teachers of boys and girls in science classes could be because of teachers' perceptions of the students' abilities in the subject. To test this hypothesis, 42 elementary teachers in Iowa were asked to list the scientific skills of their students. Teachers reported that boys had more scientific skills than girls. According to the authors, the teachers indicated that girls had more social skills than scientific skills. In addition, although girls were perceived to have cognitive process skills, that is, "skills related to physically completing a task," boys were perceived to have cognitive intellectual skills, those "requiring mental or abstract operations" (Shepardson & Pizzini, 1992, p. 149). The researchers pointed out, although this was not studied, that the different perceptions held by these teachers could lead to differential behaviors toward boys and girls in class. However, it could be argued that these teachers who held such beliefs could easily transmit stereotypical notions about the relative roles boys and girls should take with respect to interests, achievement, and aspirations in science.

STUDENT–STUDENT INTERACTION

Teachers are not the only purveyors of knowledge in classrooms. Students learn a great deal from their peers both implicitly and explicitly. Considerable evidence exists that students also teach each other about gender equity and gender relations. Much of this teaching and learning occurs through discursive practices taken up by boys and girls. Furthermore, there is some evidence that this informal pedagogy begins at quite a young age. Henkin (1995) described a year-long participant observation study of a first-grade writing workshop. Most of the students observed were middle class and White. Henkin found that boys refused to work with girls and described girls as inadequate partners. Although girls seemed to be puzzled by this rejection, they did not resist this representation. Henkin also reported that when girls attempted to make sense of the boys' behavior, they were denigrated by the boys.

A study of slightly older students reinforced Henkin's findings. Evans (1996) looked at a fifth-grade literature discussion group in a multicultural, socioeconomically heterogeneous elementary school. She focused on five students, three boys and two girls, for 6 days during a 2-week period. Evans argued that people establish discursive positions in relation to each other. She found that the boys tended to position themselves in such a way as to marginalize the girls and that the girls were unsuccessful in their attempts to resist this positioning.

Kistner, Metzler, Gatlin, and Risi (1993) investigated how students' interactions with their peers were related to both gender and race. They obtained sociometric data from third-, fourth-, and fifth-grade students in seven elementary schools. The students were asked to identify three students with whom they liked to play and three with whom they preferred not to play. The students were also asked to name peers who best fit 36 behavioral characteristics. Finally, the racial and gender composition of the classrooms was observed. The researchers found that both African-American and European-American children received fewer positive nominations when their group was in the minority in a class. They also found that, overall, girls received more negative nominations than boys when they were in the minority in their classes and that African-American girls received more negative nominations than the other groups. The authors speculated about the implications of these findings for placing girls in classrooms with few or no same-raced and same-sexed peers.

In this subsection, we have reviewed a number of different studies that indicated students learn about gender through a variety of institutional and classroom activities and practices. These studies indicated that schools continue to be places where children learn stereotypical gender roles, where male privilege is preserved through policies as well as classroom interaction, and, conversely, where girls are devalued and denigrated.

Achievement

By almost any accounting, the bottom line for educational policy and practice is academic achievement. Despite a considerable lack of consensus about what actually constitutes achievement and how it should be measured, globally, academic achievement is the most commonly used marker of individual and school progress. As a result, it is not surprising that research on gender and education would eventually focus on gender and academic achievement. Much of this work has focused on sex differences, concentrating on achievement outcomes in subject areas such as math and science in which boys were purported to perform better than girls. Findings from this research have been quite inconsistent. Studies conducted in the 1970s and early 1980s seemed to support this conclusion. However, work in the latter part of the 1980s and in the 1990s has not found consistent differences in achievement favoring boys, thus calling this conclusion into question (Adelman, 1991; Linn & Petersen, 1985; Ma, 1995).

Rather than focus on outcomes, more recently, researchers concerned with gender differences in achievement have attempted to understand the processes constituting achievement. Some research has attempted to analyze gender differences in the cognitive strategies underlying achievement outcomes. A recent example of this approach is evident in the work of Fenema and her colleagues (1998) concerning math performances of boys and girls. These researchers found dramatic differences in the problem-solving strategies used by girls and boys as early as first through third grade. It should be noted that the sample used for this study consisted primarily of White, middle-class children.

A review of research on gender and achievement in Scotland found variations in performance associated with gender (Powney, 1996). Overall, Powney found similar patterns of achievement for girls and boys "at standard" grade in Scotland. In some areas, such as language, girls performed better than boys, and in others, such as math, boys showed higher attainment than girls. Powney argued that the gender difference in math performance could reflect girls' more tentative approach to problem solving and guessing. Sounding a cautionary note, however, Powney argued school achievement is affected by a variety of factors including race, ethnicity, and the school experiences children have.

Many researchers, especially feminist researchers, locate the roots of sex differences in achievement in the social environment in which girls and boys operate. For example, Fennema and her colleagues (1998) invited a panel of researchers who were experts on gender issues to comment on their findings. The panelists identified girls' personal preferences (Sowder, 1998), teacher–student interaction (Hyde & Jaffee, 1998), and societal values that give more worth to men's interests than women's interests (Noddings, 1998) as mediators of achievement.

These arguments all suggest that academic achievement may not be seen as a viable gender role for girls or by girls. However, evidence concerning this conclusion is not always consistent. For instance, Shroyer, Smith, Borchers, and Wright (1994) conducted a case study of girls' and boys' performance in science and mathematics in one Midwestern school district. They found that boys performed better than girls on standardized tests while girls got higher grades. Furthermore, these researchers found boys were more likely to pursue math and science careers than girls. Data gathered from adults in this community indicated support for very traditional and stereotypical gender roles that was reinforced by the schools. The researchers concluded that the differences in performance were linked to very different educational experiences girls and boys received in school. However, a study by Suitor and Reavis (1995) suggested that achievement could be part of the gender roles that girls took on at the high school level although it could be construed differently for boys and girls. Suitor and Reavis asked two cohorts of college students to describe how boys and girls could gain prestige in the high schools they attended. One cohort had graduated from high school between 1978 and 1982; the other graduated in 1988 and 1989. Both cohorts identified achievement as one means both girls and boys could gain prestige; however, for girls, achievement was combined with physical attractiveness and sociability, whereas for boys it was combined with sports abilities.

Few studies have focused on situations in which girls have outperformed boys academically. However, Bulcock, Whitt, and Beebe (1991) asked why girls' school achievement was higher than boys in almost all subjects in Newfoundland high schools. They suggested that when relative incomes are high, men are more likely to invest in schooling and to marry younger. These two activities tend to keep girls out of school. When relative incomes are low, men are less likely to invest in schooling and they delay marriage, thus allowing women more access to educational experiences. These researchers argued that, at the time of their study, the demographic characteristics of Newfoundland favored girls, thus they were more likely to remain in high school and to perform better. They also reported that the girls in their study were more satisfied with their school experiences than the boys were. The findings from this study suggested that issues around gender and achievement may have less to do with girls' attitudes and interests and more with basic power relationships in society that are mirrored in schools (Weiner, 1994).

Almost all the researchers cited here who have studied gender and achievement have been somewhat cautionary about their findings and have indicated a need for further research in this area. In addition, many have pointed out that academic achievement is the result of complex interactions of a number of factors in addition to gender. Recent research such as that of Yates (1997) as well as Bulcock et. al. (1991), discussed above, suggested that relationships between gender and achievement vary with time and place. Schools in a number of countries, for example, have recently documented evidence that girls are beginning to outperform boys because of gender-oriented school reforms in Australia and the United Kingdom. A further caution on this research is that much of the work on gender and achievement has focused primarily on White girls and boys and has not taken sufficient account of the intersections of gender and race and how these intersections may have an effect on achievement among girls and boys of different racial and ethnic groups (Pollard, 1998). In addition, issues of social class and sexuality in relation to achievement are often discussed apart from gender.

Deconstruction of the Typical Student

How have some learners moved from being marginalized, invisible objects of others' research to being central, visible subjects of their own studies? Research on gender and education has often been characterized by a perspective of gender as a single, all-encompassing variable of study that was stable and consistent across all differences. A preponderance of writing published on feminist issues in education was by White feminists whose research focused mainly on White, middle-class, heterosexual girls. As a result, girls of color, poor girls, lesbians, and others who did not fit the alleged "mainstream" position were marginalized and made invisible. However, researchers and students in these groups did not necessarily accept their positions at the edges of feminist work. Students representing these groups kept appearing in schools and classrooms, although often, initially, as troublesome presences.

More important, researchers—often women representing these same marginalized groups—were calling attention to these students' presence and considering them as legitimate subjects for study and analysis. As a result, these groups began to move from the faint edges of feminist scholarship toward center stage. Although this move is far from complete and although resistance to it continues, these groups' demands for inclusion within feminist research has forced the consideration of diversity in feminist theory and practice in education.

In this subsection, research on African-American girls in school is examined as an illustration of the move from marginalized invisibility toward a more centered visibility. We demonstrate how research on African-American girls has shifted over the past decade or so and discuss how these shifts have influenced perspectives on these particular students. In addition, we discuss the implications of this shift for current and future feminist research on gender and education.

As Hull, Scott, and Smith proclaimed in 1982, "All the women were White and all the blacks were men . . ." in most writings about gender, race, and equity at the time. African-American girls simply were not present. Lightfoot (1976) pointed out this anomaly in a review of research published more than 20 years ago. When African-American females were considered in research, usually in adulthood, stereotypical images and simplistic conceptions prevailed. For example, researchers who even mentioned Black girls and women focused on the "double whammy" perspective, thus limiting their identity to the effect of victimization as a result of additive effects of racism and sexism (Lightfoot, 1976). As Lightfoot and others have argued, such perspectives are simplistic. They artificially dichotomize race and gender, thus portraying African-American girls and women as passive objects caught in the tensions between two seemingly contradictory forces. Girls and women thus conceived were easily relegated to marginality.

Other researchers, some using feminist perspectives and others not, have rendered a less marginal conception of African-American girls in schools by studying their school-related behavior and perceptions in comparison to other students. In some cases, African-American girls are compared with African-American boys as well as European-American girls and boys (e.g., Grant, 1984; Irvine, 1986). The importance of studies such as these lies in their recognition not only of African-American girls' existence but also of their unique positions in classrooms. For example, Irvine found that African-American girls in upper-elementary grades had fewer chances for interaction with teachers than those in lower-elementary grades. Grant's study of six first-grade classrooms that varied widely in racial composition also found differential interactions of teachers toward African-American girls. In addition, unlike other raced-sexed groups, African-American girls were encouraged to develop social rather than academic skills. Grant further reported that, unable to get responses to their attempts to initiate interactions with their teachers, African-American girls often turned to peers and became mediators between groups

of students in the classroom. Although Grant's study portrays African-American girls as victimized by their teachers who ignore their academic persona and limit interactions with them, it also provides an alternative perspective by demonstrating how these girls claim a place for themselves in the classroom setting.

Another body of comparative research focuses exclusively on African-American girls and boys. Sometimes, this research may not be explicitly feminist. It often takes a cultural approach to the study of African-American girls in school, arguing that gender must be understood within cultural contexts. For example, Dawkins (1980) and Reid et al. (1995) argued that differences between African-American girls and boys could be attributed to family socialization practices in the African-American community. Specifically, Dawkins drew connections between these differential socialization patterns and African-American adolescents' educational and occupational goals. Reid et al. (1995) called attention to the importance of culture in understanding African-American girls' school behavior. She noted that, although teachers may hold low expectations for these girls' academic achievement, families often have high expectations for them in this area. Studies such as these center gender within the contexts of race and culture and, as such, provide an alternative to the hegemonic position of European-American culture as the standpoint for observing and interpreting behavior. However, their emphasis on comparisons of African-American girls with others can be seen as constraining.

In contrast to the comparative studies, a body of literature is emerging in which African-American girls are the central subjects of study, and their experiences are conveyed as legitimate in their own right. In so doing, this research often challenges stereotypes and assumptions that have been incorporated into research on African-American women and girls in education. For example, Simms (1988) studied the kinds of choices African-American adolescents and young women between the ages of 16 and 21 make with regard to schooling, training, work, marriage, and childbearing. She finds that, contrary to often-expressed popular opinion, these choices are not seen as mutually exclusive choices, thus challenging two popular and opposing stereotypes of African-American women: the superwoman and the poor welfare mother.

As part of her ethnographic study of Capitol High, an urban public school, Fordham (1993, 1996) focused on African-American girls specifically. She discussed various ways that society, schools, and teachers attempt to silence African-American girls or force them to "gender pass," that is, take on White and male images to achieve academic success. However, Fordham also demonstrated that some African-American girls vigorously resist these oppressions and construct their own visible identities. Fordham also argued that, for some African-American girls, silence represents defiance rather than acquisition to oppression and can lead to a rejection of low expectations of others. In this study, academic achievement among African-American adolescent girls was analyzed and interpreted from the central perspective of the girls themselves. In addition, they construct their identities in a manner that is informed not only by the norms and expectations of the school but also by the teachings and learnings they bring to school from their own communities.

The establishment of a specific standpoint for observing, analyzing, and interpreting work on African-American girls and women is articulated in the theoretical conceptualizations of African-American feminists that argue for the importance of studying the histories of African-American girls and women in education (Burgess, 1994; Fordham, 1993; Perkins, 1983). African-American feminist perspectives also consider the intersections between race, sex, and class, as well as other defining attributes of African-American women, and assert the importance of African-American women's culture (Collins, 1991). Some writers have argued that an Afrocentric perspective is particularly informative to African-American feminist thought (Burgess, 1994; King, 1991–1992). Currently, relatively little empirical research focusing on African-American girls in K–12 classrooms incorporates this perspective. However, it is expected that this perspective will guide continuing research in this area.

In this subsection, we have illustrated, with examples of research on African-American girls, how some groups can move from the margins toward the center of feminist research on gender and education. The examples presented indicate that, in the course of that move, several changes in the perceptions of the group can occur. First, we have seen the position of African-American girls move from anonymity to victim to independent assertive actor in classroom settings. Second, in the course of the move, commonly held assumptions and stereotypes are confronted and challenged, and the limitations of research focusing on African-American girls as objects of others scrutiny are revealed. Finally, as African-American girls move from marginal to more central positions in research, the complexities of their experiences are revealed. Simple additive analyses of race, class, and gender are inadequate explanations of their lives; rather, analysis must include not only the various statuses they hold but also their own interpretations of the meanings these statuses hold at various times and situations.

When research shifts some learners from the margins, what happens to the center? As the earlier subsections on masculinity and sexuality demonstrate, others who occupied the privileged and normative center as if they were generic students have become gendered, raced, and classed. Feminists have taken the markers of White, middle-classed, heterosexual boys seriously, examining how each works in the construction of masculinity. There is no undifferentiated and normative youth.

Feminist Pedagogy

How adults contribute to the production of gender knowledge in classrooms is most obvious in the interpretive and interpersonal work they do. In this subsection, we discuss questions of feminist pedagogy. At the same time all this work must be contextualized. Multiple contexts include the economic and social dimensions of the communities in which the schools are located, the culture of the particular school, and the school as a workplace for adults. How teachers come to understand the workplace contributes to what students learn about gender. The broader institutional arrangements of education, for example, the association of preschools and elementary school with women, and administration and leadership with men are not invisible to students.

Early studies of pedagogical practice related to gender looked at how teachers treated boys and girls differently. Boys got more of the teachers' attention and took up space when they acted out, and that treatment was seen as significant for why boys did better in high school. Even though they might be getting reproached, they still received more direct attention from the teacher. Girls' quietness, their choosing to act as "good girls," meant that they did not take up enough space and were more invisible in the classroom. One response to this critique was for teachers to act as if differences of gender, race, and class were not there and to treat boys and girls similarly. This method could be characterized as the gender equity approach. Another approach was to emphasize girls' particular ways of knowing, learning, and interacting and to develop pedagogical practices that supported these girls (Belenky, Clinchy, Goldberger, & Tarule, 1986; Brown & Gilligan, 1992).

Feminist pedagogy linked the idea of feminist practices with teaching. Central issues included the division of power and authority in the classroom, the idea that girls are multiply constituted, and the struggle to make the classroom a feminist space (Middleton, 1993; Weiler, 1988). The vocabulary of voice and silence were both central and troubling to these effects (Luke & Gore, 1992; McLeod, Yates, & Halasa, 1994). Weiler (1988) showed in her ethnographic data that some teachers struggled to engage gender and race simultaneously. One of the teachers she studied made room for White girls in the classroom but in the process silenced Black boys. Discussions of the danger of reading silence as powerlessness (Gallas, 1998; Orner, 1992) and substituting one regime of truth for another in feminist pedagogy are significant (Gore, 1993) because they suggest that meanings that both students and teachers make are continually shifting.

Feminist pedagogy takes up questions of how power and authority are differently defined in various cultural groups so that what some White feminists may construe as changing the power or authority structure in the classroom may be read by some African-American students as limiting their access to knowledge needed for empowerment. If all students do not have access to the language of power, as Delpit (1988) argued, then putting power aside, or setting it up as male dominated, may have differential effects on students who have already been marginalized. These illustrations point to the importance of feminist pedagogies being multicultural (Hooks, 1993; Maher & Tetreault, 1994).

Curriculum Practices

Teachers are central to any discussion of the curriculum because whether or not they choose it, they interpret it and guide students through it. Until the early 1980s, the literature representing the perspectives of women teachers was sparse. Women who taught school were seen as failed men or as individuals who did not take their work seriously enough. Feminist influences on what got studied changed that, however, beginning with Weiler (1988), who studied the perspectives of women who tried to change practice for girls in secondary schools. The connections between women teachers and feminism have been important, not only historically, but also in contemporary work on the everyday lives of women teachers in the United States (Biklen, 1995; Foster, 1993; Munro, 1998) and in New Zealand (Middleton, 1993), in questions about the role of women teachers in relations to girls (Dorney, 1995), and in the struggles first-year women teachers have with sexism (Coulter, 1995). In addition to the expansion of literature on teachers' experiences with work, which can be construed as connected with curricular maters, there has been research on particular aspects of the school curriculum. Some subject areas in the curriculum have been studied to different degrees in relationship to gender. Science has received significant attention (e.g., Matthews, 1996; McLaren & Gaskell, 1995; Rosser, 1995), while technology lagged until recently (Bryson & de Castell, 1995; Sanders, 1995). This discussion examines a few of these areas, including social studies, English, and mathematics, looking at the significant issues in each domain.

GENDER AND SOCIAL STUDIES

Research on gender in the field of social studies research and education has been slow to develop a rich body of knowledge that we could draw on for this review. Bernard-Powers (1996) found, however, that this field does reflect the larger debates in feminism about the immutability of gender identity; about the intersection of race, class, and gender; and about the significance of feminist scholarship for transforming the curriculum. Knowledge in fields that social studies draws from (e.g., anthropology, sociology, economics, political science, history) has expanded because of feminist theory and scholarship, and these fields look different. Bernard-Powers questioned whether social studies also reflected these changes. Feminism has made its way into social studies education in ways that Bernard-Powers said are "narrowly defined" (p. 4). Can a revised social studies education be transformative (Singer, 1995)?

K–12 social studies has resisted including difference in significant ways. One difficulty in transforming the curriculum is the "somewhat loose organization of the field" (Bernard-Powers 1995, p.192). Social studies is particularly prominent in attacks by American conservatives concerned about cultural literacy and political correctness. Like the field of English, social studies has been centered around the concept of a canon; that is, that there are specific things young American students need to know to be literate in American history (Osler, 1994). So feminists anxious to change the social studies curriculum to reflect the experiences of a wider range of ethnic, racial, class, and gender groups continually come up against this particular rigidity. Whose experiences and what events are central to this curriculum and, in the larger sense, to our past?

Bernard-Powers reviewed a number of studies that had been done on the representation of gender in social studies textbooks. These studies suggested the range of struggles feminists face to work for a more inclusive curriculum, including the representation of more than White, middle-class women, having women represented in the text as well as in the pictures, and doing history from a perspective that does not center only the views of privileged peoples. The effect of social studies education on ideas that young men and women hold is significant, so how and what gets taught needs attentive revision. Bernard-Powers reported a study that indicated that over 50% of young White and Black males did not think that women were as qualified as men to be leaders of a country.

Gender reforms that have been implemented in social studies curricula have been studied with mixed results. Hahn (1996) studied two ninth-grade civics classes around gender issues. She found no gender differences in a number of issues including interest in politics. In interviews, however, she found that females had more views on policy issues than boys did and were more supportive of women holding political office. This research also emphasized the relationship of social studies classes to civic understanding, suggesting that social studies is related to ideas men and women have about American politics. She also found that boys and girls who share high interest in politics share common characteristics.

In 1990 and 1991, the Netherlands included women's history as a compulsory subject in its national examination for secondary school students. Ten Dam and Rijkschroeff (1996) identified three aspects of women's history that were included on the exam: women in traditionally male roles, women in traditionally female roles, and "gender as a historical construct" (p. 71). The research project worked with 16 teachers and 22 classes, 11 of which taught women's history and 11 of which taught traditional history. In total, 497 students, 291 girls and 206 boys, between the ages of 14 and 16 participated in the project. After studying their curriculum for a few weeks, students were asked to complete sentences about what they had learned or discovered during the lessons that was important to them. The researchers found that 65% of the girls responded very favorably to the women's history classes and only 38% of the boys did. But more girls than boys also responded positively to the traditional history lessons. The most important parts of the material for the girls, the learners' reports suggested, concerned oppression and resistance.

Commeyras and Alvermann (1996) were interested in how the content of textbooks is political, and how change around gender or multicultural issues raises political critique from the right. They examined world history texts, published in 1991 and 1992, at three high schools for how "gender messages are subtly conveyed through content and language that perpetuate particular ways of thinking about women" (p. 35) because they were interested in how gendered constructions are textually inscribed. They did a macroanalysis and microanalysis. The macroanalysis looked at content, and the microanalysis looked at language. They found that, although women were constructed with more agency and with more attention given to their status and rights, the language used suggested that the word "women" had no meaning in the texts except through contrasts to other groups, usually men, and that causes of women's devaluation and discrimination in societies was often obscured by general language that ignored power relations.

GENDER AND ENGLISH

The literature on gender and English looks at both English as a curricular area and the curriculum materials that are used. White (1996) summarized research that demonstrated significant evidence around girls' enjoyment of and pleasure in English as a subject area. From the time they enter school until their examinations at the end of their final year in high school, girls as a group do better than boys do in English. Whether or not boys and girls read for the same reasons (White, 1996) or whether their success has particular meanings, the research in this area compares boys to girls.

The literature on what young people read looks at how students negotiate texts, whether these are romance novels for young adults (Christian-Smith, 1988, 1993) or multicultural literature for young adults (Clark & Kulkin, 1996). Clark and Kulkin (1996) studied characters from what they called nontraditional backgrounds who were represented in 16 award-winning books. The books were studies of "non-White, non-American, or nonheterosexual main characters" (p. 293). Their approach differed from the predominant approach. The theoretical perspectives of feminist social scientists who have studied the representation of gender in children's books have been significant. The dominant perspective has been liberal feminist even though feminist theory has moved more toward a global perspective. Liberal feminist views have propelled investigation toward examination of whether the representation of girls and women has been equal to that of boys and men.

Two kinds of researchers have benefited from this theoretical approach: (a) what Clark and Kulkin (1996) called the "experimentalists," who look at what happens to children from their exposure to literature in which there is gender inequality, and (b) the "content analyzers," who document the unequal representation of male and female characters in children's books (p. 292). The study argued that one of the dangers of these approaches, despite some enhanced understanding of inequality of representation and its effects on girl readers, is that there is always an ideal standard that the authors have in mind to which they compare what they study. An emphasis on multiculturalism would shift this outside standard to which the characters are compared and against which equality is measured to a more interpretive approach that centers oppression and resistance. A multicultural approach centers on how the characters and authors construct both oppression and resistance, highlighting the problematic ideas of justice; hence, it is more expansive. The researchers found a preponderance of the works depend on first-person narratives. Oppression and resistance were represented in many variations and with subtlety.

GENDER AND MATHEMATICS

In the attention given to gender and education, few areas have been as significant for researchers and reformers alike as girls' performance in mathematics. The problem is framed as whether or not girls do as well as boys in mathematics given the long-standing outperformance of boys as compared to girls on standardized tests. In recent years, studies have shown that gender differences in mathematics may be decreasing, although they still exist at the more advanced levels, that how teachers structure their classrooms is influential to girls' (and boys) results, and that when some interventions are attempted, they sometimes successfully lower the gender differences in mathematics (Boaler, 1997; Fennema, 1996; Powney, 1996). What causes the differences? Researchers seem to lean toward biological differences at some times and toward differential treatment at others. Many of the researchers who come down on different sides of this issue call themselves feminist researchers, so it is not easy to differentiate them by their general approach, although they do not all call on similar feminist perspectives.

Some researchers have taken up this question of conceptualizing the problem. Volman and Van Eck (1995) argued that too much of the research on girls and mathematics conceptualizes the issue as either the problem girls have with mathematics or

that the problem is girls, themselves. When the question is viewed as a problem in this way, girls' biology or socialization experiences or lack of motivation are blamed rather than posing a structural issue.

Boaler's (1997) study articulated this perspective clearly. She suggested in her study of British girls that the problem of girls' lack of achievement and lower participation rates in mathematics improperly conceptualized girls as the problem and that this formulation penalizes girls. These approaches have traditionally looked at problems in, for example, girls' motivation. Boaler argued that from her comparative 3-year longitudinal study of two mathematics classrooms, one in a school that was hierarchical and constructed mathematics as rule-based, teacher-directed, and textbook-based and the other in a school that was more democratic and promoted a project-oriented curriculum that depended on deep degrees of student initiation, that it is the conceptualization of mathematics that failed the girls, not the girls who failed mathematics. The girls were much more involved and invested in the project classroom in her study because they always understood why they were doing what they were doing. The girls emphasized understanding, and so they were much less willing just to follow the rules and play what the author called "the mathematics game." The boys were less enthusiastic about the project classroom and were willing to work in mathematics even though they understood no more than the girls in the traditional classroom because they could emphasize competition. Both schools served White, working-class youth. This study also showed how approaches not intentionally focused on gender affect gender relations.

Boaler argued that the back-to-basics approach that one of her schools took up emphasized a form of mathematics teaching that alienated girls. Other theorists might argue that the back-to-basics approach is not a neutral approach that does not serve girls well but an approach that is invisibly masculinist. This research suggested that reforms not specifically addressing gender may have, as we have suggested earlier in this subsection, particular outcomes for gendered relationships and attainment.

Other research has specifically addressed particular aspects of mathematics instruction and mathematics classrooms like issues of confidence and criticism (Willis, 1995), gender stereotyping (Wellesley Center for Research on Women, 1995), and teachers' relationships with students (Fennema, Peterson, Carpenter, & Lubinski, 1990). In this latter study, the teachers knew more about which boys were successful than about which girls were successful. The teachers claimed at the same time that they thought successful boys and girls in math were similar. The teachers attributed boys' success to ability and girls' success to effort. Another study (Weisbeck, 1992) reported that teachers said that during their instruction time they thought more about boys than about girls. Fennema (1996) suggested that teachers appear to be very aware of whether their students are boys or girls. At the same time, though, teachers say that they do not think there are important differences between girls and boys that teachers need to be aware of when they make instructional decisions. "Boys are apparently just more salient in the teachers' minds. Teachers appear to react to pressure from students, and they get more pressure from boys" (p. 76).

Clearly, issues around gender and mathematics are complex

to figure out and difficult to address. But the debate still lingers. Fennema and her associates published an article in 1998 in the *Educational Researcher* on their findings from a longitudinal study that even at a young age boys do better on more complicated or advanced math problems than do girls, showing more inventive strategies for solving problems. Girls performed as well as boys on all the straightforward addition and subtraction problems, but they did not show that they could develop inventive logarithms to approach new problems. The researchers argued that their findings were true even at first through third grades, the years of schooling they studied. They then asked researchers from different fields—social psychology, math education, and feminist philosophy—to respond to their analysis.

The debates about mathematics within feminism are reflected over the course of Fennema's work as well as within these pieces. The sex-differences approach that Fennema and her colleagues use appears to be a traditional one that isolates issues about mathematics instruction from the larger social and educational contexts within which children get educated. The research attempted to specify which parts of mathematics learning girls did less well on because, they suggested, it will help us to find out how to improve girls' performance in mathematics in high school and in higher education. Their approach decontextualizes mathematics learning partly because of the research methods that they relied on which depend on this strategy. The responses questioned different aspects of the approach, but none of them addressed the problem with gender difference studies themselves.

Some researchers contextualize gender and mathematics. Burton (1996), for example, argued that learning mathematics is connected to learning social behavior. The devaluing of girls as learners of mathematics contributes to how they learn math. Also, the pressure on girls to follow the rules, to work hard, and to be good girls is about gender more generally but connects to specific conditions with mathematics learning. Breaking rules, as inventive logarithms demands, becomes a gendered issue of pedagogy and success at mathematics. Figuring out how gender works in relation to math is complex. But girls' success at math is an issue of gender relations, as the AAUW report, *How Schools Shortchange Girls,* argued many years ago, not a question of math genes. Both boys and girls become increasingly negative about mathematics and science as they progress through high school. Many children share this dislike, as girls and boys who both use inventive logarithms share similar approaches to mathematics.

What Are the Effects of Policy and Reform?

As we said in our introduction, the literature describes the difficulty reformers have faced, on both larger and smaller levels, when they enact gender reform. Sometimes, programs that directly address gender inequities find little success. Sometimes, reforms that engage all students turn out to be particularly effective with gender injustices. The difference between naming the problem, in other words, and redressing it is substantial. Much research reflects this concern (see Yates, 1993a, for a discussion of the larger questions).

In the Netherlands, for example, a major government initiative, as in the United States, Britain, and Australia, addressed gender issues in education around the focus of girls in science and mathematics. One "girl-friendly" program attempting to contextualize the learning of mathematics around interests and concerns of girls, as researchers established these interests and concerns, ended up increasing rather than decreasing the exclusion of girls from tracks that would lead them to science and technology fields in higher education (Volman, Van Eck, & Ten Dam, 1995).

Research on middle school girls in the United States sponsored by the AAUW (Research for Action, 1996) specifically studied schools that had initiated gender reforms. Their study examined how successful girls in these schools, as well as parents, teachers, and staff, negotiated gender and the reforms in their daily lives. The report argued that the strategies girls use to negotiate gender are all regulated by and sometimes resistant to cultural definitions of femininity. These strategies frame girls' participation in school around the three themes of "speaking out" in which girls take up space as either "maverick leaders" or "troublemakers," "doing school" in which girls outwardly conform to more traditional expectations of girls as either "schoolgirls" or "play schoolgirls," and "crossing borders" in which girls traverse different cultures and sets of expectations as "schoolgirls/coolgirls," who gain status because of their comprehension and competencies in multiple codes of talking and behaving, or as "translators," leaders who assist others to move and communicate across borders.

Geography, culture, and ethnicity were significant in the different ways that schools addressed equity and in their effects. Suburban schools, for example, saw equity problems as challenges that they could meet through policy and reform initiatives. A policy that a suburban school in the Midwest designed and put in place to decrease sexual harassment of girls had the effect of alienating girls from the concept of sexual harassment and increased their defense of boys' bad behavior. One could argue that the problem here was due not to the initiative but to problems with its implementation, but still the effects were opposite to the intentions. Rural schools engaged gender through the back door, sometimes purposefully, but occasionally unintentionally. They were sites that were more conflicted about the relationship between traditional femininity and the importance of preparing girls for economic independence. Urban schools needed to address girls as multiply situated, as gendered, raced, and classed, to have any influence on gender (Biklen et al., 1996).

In Australia, Kenway and Willis and their associates conducted a major study of gender reform in schools using both qualitative and quantitative data. They conducted six major case studies over a 2- to 3-year period, and eight smaller studies in multicultural schools. They interviewed and did participant observation with school administrators, gender reformers, students, and others. They analyzed policy documents and did surveys of 100 schools in two Australian states. Gender reform included such initiatives as single-sex classes for math, girls' self-defense classes, classes on girls and careers, courses that were supposed to raise girls' self-esteem and enhance personal development, programs directed to boys that worked to shift their attitudes, projects on girls and technology, staff development programs on gender, and programs that encouraged girls into science and technology projects. In many of these cases, there was a significant gap between intention and effect. The schools that were more successful understood power differently from those whose programs lacked strong effects. These latter schools defined power in more traditionally male and hierarchical ways (Kenway & Willis, 1998).

Other scholars have argued that the definitions institutions use are significant for the reforms (Blackmore, 1996). What happens when institutions put in place policy initiatives that appear to be progressive, particularly policies that promote gender equity in education? Bryson and de Castell (1997) worry that initiatives like these may "risk consolidating and reifying those very problems which they are officially sanctioned to champion . . ." (p. 85) by sometimes giving more substance to categories that are not clearly distinguished in practice (e.g., equity) and by failing to clarify unequal power relations that are central to any injustice. Again definitions of power are central to efforts.

In an earlier study of gender reform, Kenway, Blackmore, Willis, and Rennie (1996) studied Australian teachers who worked toward gender reform using specific strategies: seeking to change girls' choices ("their subject choices and postschool ambitions"), to change girls themselves (enhancing self-esteem, encouraging students to value their femaleness, putting positive spin on their difference), to change the curriculum (developing gender-inclusive curriculum), to change the learning environment ("the development of school and classroom policies and the appointment of committees and personnel to change the gendered culture of the school" [p. 242]). Again, they found that success was "fragile" and intermittent, partly because it depended on the energy of a committed but small group.

Reay (1990) also studied a gender reform effort in classrooms and found that teachers as well as students contested the change. Her work discussed an initiative for gender equality that brought together girls in an all-girls group one afternoon a week. She found that boys take up too much space in primary school classrooms and playgrounds, that girls get less attention from the teacher, and that they lack confidence in science, math, and technology (time, attention, and space). The program was dropped after 1 year for a number of reasons, including the boys disliking their activities and developing resentment. Also, teachers felt ambivalence toward the girls' developing sense of power and strength.

> There were massive contradictions in providing for girls something we had never felt entitled to ourselves. As feminists we genuinely wanted to tackle gender inequality and help the girls discover new skills, confidence, and above all, a voice strong enough to be heard, but on a subconscious level I am sure we all increasingly felt they should be grateful for what they had been given, and not demand more. (p. 44)

She argued that any efforts at change must consider "pupil culture" and how it operates in classrooms.

This issue of the culture of classrooms has been significant in a number of studies. Clarricoates (1980) showed that teachers used girls to get the classroom to run more smoothly. This finding connects with other studies about how girls use their energies in classrooms. Reay (1990) was interested in what happens when girls are together with boys or separated from them. Grant (1992) was interested in differences between Black girls'

and White girls' behavior toward peers and teachers and teachers' ways of talking about and approaching these girls. In her study, African-American girls could be said to facilitate the smooth running of classrooms around the issue of race. Do these actions serve the interests of girls? Certainly this is both a key research question and a reform problem that still needs to be addressed.

So far reform efforts suggest that gender cannot be addressed outside of specific contexts; that gender is intimately tied to race, class, and other markers; that context is significant; and that the school's definition of power is prominent. Good intentions do not bring significant change.

Interventions I: The Approach to Equity in Schools and Classrooms

Other studies have demonstrated the difficulty of identifying interventions that are effective in leading to changes in girls' attitudes and behaviors. Aebischer and Valabreque (1995) described two pilot experiments that were designed to encourage girls in early adolescence to think of careers in science and technology for themselves. One experiment, conducted in France, focused on changing girls' attitudes toward the idea of working in nontraditional areas by using role-playing and discussions with women in nontraditional fields. The second experiment, conducted in Ireland, aimed at changing the girls' behavior by teaching them skills in the use of tools and technical equipment. Neither intervention was successful in changing the girls' negative orientation toward nontraditional careers, although the authors reported that both experiments increased the girls' awareness of occupational inequalities in these fields. Similar results were reported in a study by Desmet-Goethals (1995) of a project aimed at encouraging girls to enroll in technical courses in Belgium. Desmet-Goethals argued that programs such as this cannot be effective themselves. Instead, structural barriers to equity in the educational system and supports for discrimination in the labor market must be removed.

Campbell (1989) critiqued intervention programs aimed at increasing gender equity in education on several issues. She noted that these programs have not had much effect and suggested that this is, in part, because they often operate in isolation from other activities in schools and from each other. In addition, she argued that some of these interventions may not make use of some practices that have been shown to be effective in general. For instance, she reviewed research on girls and mathematics and noted effective teachers are those who involve students as active learners, identify and correct deficiencies, and make learning enjoyable. These strategies, she argued, should be included in any intervention program aimed at improving mathematics performance. Finally, Campbell cautioned against identifying interventions for gender without considering the issues of race, class, and disability because these attempts can be misleading. As an example, she argued that, although research indicates that teachers tend to have higher expectations for boys with respect to math, in some urban schools, they may demand more from African-American girls than African-American boys.

Recently, the U.S. Department of Education's Office of Educational Research and Improvement (OERI) launched an ambitious initiative aimed at identifying programs across the country that have been shown to be effective in promoting gender equity (S. Klein, personal communication, October 26, 1997). The Gender Equity Expert Panel, established in 1994, attempts to identify these projects with the idea of serving as a kind of clearinghouse through which the projects can be shared with educational practitioners and researchers on a wide scale. Researchers and practitioners who have implemented activities aimed at promoting gender equity are invited to submit them for review by the panel. Although this group has begun its work, it is too early to determine how great its effect will be.

Some researchers have advocated intervention approaches that are aimed at changing the whole culture of schools rather than focusing on specific programs for equity. Four philosophers of education, Diller, Houston, Morgan, and Ayim, took this perspective in their book, *The Gender Question in Education: Theory, Pedagogy and Politics.* These writers addressed as a central question: "What do we discover when we pay careful, systematic, sensitive attention to the difference that gender makes in educational thought and practice?" (Diller, 1996, p. 2). In the first section of the book, the authors discussed different viewpoints about how gender should be treated in public education. They addressed and rejected arguments for treating gender in traditional and stereotypic ways as this reinforces gender inequities and sexism in classrooms and schools. They also rejected the idea that schools can be gender free, arguing that it is neither possible nor useful to ignore gender. Indeed, they suggested that the gender-free stance, by ostensibly ignoring gender, supports the status quo (Houston, 1996). Finally, they rejected androgyny as a viable approach, arguing that it is conceptually unclear and socially undesirable in that it establishes a single norm to which everyone should conform (Morgan, 1996). Instead they offered a gender-sensitive perspective that involves "monitoring gender interactions closely and intervening to equalize opportunities" (Houston, 1996, p. 60) and focusing on developing a "critical awareness of the meanings and evaluations attached to gender" (Diller, 1996, p. 5). Although this perspective is interesting, conceptually, its application, particularly in public education, would very likely be quite problematic. The writers did not devote much discussion to the widespread resistance such attempts at cultural change might engender.

Interventions II: Targeted Versus Nontargeted Schools

Are K–12 schools able and willing to organize and structure themselves to provide equitable educational experiences to the diverse students for whom they are responsible? Can American education ever become truly pluralist in meeting the needs and desires of students from different genders, ethnic groups, socioeconomic statuses, sexualities, (dis)abilities? Or, will schools continue to define and center education on those children who represent powerful political, cultural, and social interests in this society, marginalizing all others? Can groups who are marginalized ever have a voice in schools dominated by those in power or must they establish their "own" schools to educate their children effectively? Questions such as these have existed for many years in this society; for example, women and African Americans have long histories of establishing schools for specific pop-

ulations, most often White girls and African-American youth, respectively. Conversations around these questions have been reinvigorated recently around the efficacy of single-sex and Afrocentric schools. Embedded in these conversations are questions around equity. In this subsection, we address the issue of the degree to which schools targeted toward specific groups, that is, girls; African Americans; and gay, lesbian, bisexual, and transsexual youth, effect equity.

Research on school practices and outcomes indicates that gender inequity continues to be persistent and pervasive. Although there is some evidence of a narrowing of the gender gap in academic achievement (Campbell & Wahl, 1998) in areas such as math and science, differences in academic outcomes for girls and boys in school are still evident. In addition, studies of curriculum have demonstrated that support for male-dominant perspectives in various disciplines continues to pervade the content of the curriculum that both girls and boys are expected to engage in school (Gaskell & Willinsky, 1995). Similarly, classroom studies suggested that pedagogical practices as well as classroom interactions and other aspects of classroom climate remain gendered in ways that have a negative effect on girls (AAUW, 1992).

Recently, an increased interest has been in single-sex schooling at the K–12 level. In part, this interest may reflect a reaction to frustrations created by the awareness that girls continue to be subordinated in coeducational classrooms and schools. In addition, however, this interest has been heightened by recent legal cases that have challenged *all boys* single-sex education at the Citadel and the Virginia Military Institute. Some might argue that the co-existence of interests in these two, seemingly disparate, situations is a paradox—how could one simultaneously advocate *for* single-sex schools for girls and *against* single-sex schools for boys? Moreover, it could also be argued that such a standpoint, far from being paradoxical, reflects the view of the society in which power resides in a patriarchy that privileges male education over female education, thus reserving resources to support all-boys schools in the public sector while continuing to maintain male-dominant models in coeducational schools in practice (Plateau, 1995).

Although the rhetoric concerning single-sex schooling has been lively, the research on these schools suggests that considerable caution is necessary in coming to conclusions about their efficacy and outcomes. A recent report sponsored by the American Association of University Women's (AAUW) Educational Foundation indicated that there is little clear-cut evidence that single-sex schools are unequivocally favorable for girls (AAUW, 1998). This finding can be attributed to a number of factors. The question is often posed in simplistic terms; for example, are single-sex schools and classrooms "better" or "worse" for girls than coeducational ones (Haag, 1998). Single-sex schools are often assessed in narrow terms, focusing only on academic achievement and, to a lesser extent, on attitudinal variables as outcomes (Haag, 1998). In addition, studies of single-sex schools and classrooms often do not seem to recognize that these schools may be established by different groups with quite different aims, goals, and intended outcomes (Haag, 1998; Pollard, 1998). Furthermore, studies in this area have focused on macro-level variables, such as school or class composition, and have overlooked micro-level issues, such as school organization and climate, classroom dynamics, and processes by which students come to participate in them (Lee, 1998; Riordan, 1998). Research in this area has also accepted certain questionable assumptions such as the ideas that girls and boys are opposites and that negative behaviors by boys toward girls cannot be changed (Campbell & Wahl, 1998). Finally, much of this research not only has focused on girls (Campbell & Wahl, 1998), but also has assumed that *girls* are a fixed, stable, and coherent category (Britzman, 1997). This assumption ignores the intersections for girls between markers of identity such as gender and race, class, and sexuality.

Given these research issues, the inconsistencies in findings regarding single-sex versus coeducational schools are not surprising. For example, Lee (1998; see also Lee & Bryk, 1986; Lee et al., 1994) found outcomes favoring girls in single-sex versus coeducational, secondary-level Catholic schools but not in single-sex versus coeducational independent schools; yet Le Pore and Warren (1997), in another study, found no differences for girls in single-sex versus coeducational Catholic secondary schools. Riordan (1998) found that single-sex education is more effective for girls of color and lower socioeconomic status that for White, middle-class girls.

A number of researchers have begun to question whether single sex or coeducation is even the most important issue to raise with respect to improving gender equity in schools. For example, Lee (1998) argued that factors, such as school size, academic orientation, authentic instruction, and personal relationships among staff members and between staff members and students, may be key to equity and achievement. She speculated, however, that these factors may be more prevalent in single-sex schools. Riordan (1998) suggested that a key factor in assessing outcomes from these schools is that the student and her parents have made a "pro-academic choice" (p. 56) to attend single-sex schools. In her review of literature, Haag (1998) noted that peer influences may mediate achievement outcomes in single-sex and coeducational schools. She further cautioned that, even when differences are found between single-sex and coeducational schools, the reasons for these differences often remain unknown.

It is clear that there is a need to reframe research questions regarding single-sex versus coeducational education with respect to judging the outcomes of effectiveness of such school and classroom types (Campbell & Wahl, 1998). In addition, the research methods of studying these schools must be expanded to include more qualitative studies that can provide richer, more in-depth perspectives of the perceptions and actions of the various participants in them. Finally, gender is not the only perspective from which to consider equity; gender equity can often intersect with other equity issues in the consideration of targeted schooling.

One area in which this intersection is particularly clear concerns African-centered or Afrocentric schools. African-centered education in the United States is not a new phenomenon; such schools have existed as independent schools for 200 years (Ratteray, 1994). However, interest in Afrocentric education increased when some educators advocated it for African-American boys. Recognizing that African-American boys have been severely marginalized in contemporary public schools and that African-American boys and men have been demonized in

the society at large, particularly in urban settings, several educators promoted Afrocentric school models as vehicles to help them establish positive identities, to learn in environments that were culturally relevant to them, and to negotiate the broader society. One of the first such schools was established for young African-American males in Baltimore, Maryland (Narine, 1992), and other schools were proposed for Milwaukee, Wisconsin, and Detroit, Michigan. While some of these schools were implemented, others emerged as coeducational schools, in part, because of legal challenges to the single-sex aspect in the public school setting (Pollard & Ajirotutu, 1994) and, in part, because some writers reminded educators that equity issues involved African-American girls as well as boys (King, 1991–1992). As African-American schools were implemented in public school settings, however, it became clear that they could not be gender neutral. Rather, they encountered issues related to gender roles and gender equity. In some cases, however, these issues arose and were interpreted within cultural frameworks (Pollard, 1998). Although considerable media attention was given to these schools when they were first proposed for public school settings, little research has been done, documenting their effect on student outcomes. Currently, one longitudinal study of two Afrocentric public schools in a large urban community is being completed (Pollard & Ajirotutu, 1994, 1997).

Schools targeted toward gay, lesbian, bisexual, and transgender youth have also emerged within the past decade or so. Like the Afrocentric schools, these schools developed, partly, in response to the failure of traditional schools to meet the needs or, in this case, even to recognize the existence of these particular groups of young people. Ill served or not served by most public and independent schools, alternatives were established for them. Often, however, these alternatives were temporary stopgaps for gay, lesbian, bisexual, and transgender youth to give them a safe place from homophobic schools. By recognizing the toll homophobia takes on gay, lesbian, bisexual, and transgender youth, in terms of dropping out of school, homelessness, suicide, substance abuse, and increased risk of HIV infections, schools targeted toward them often include support and counseling services (Snider, 1996).

Although schools for gay, lesbian, bisexual, and transgender youth have been applauded, they have also been criticized. Snider (1996) studied a school program, the Triangle Program, established by the Toronto Board of Education. She argued that, like the public schools, the Triangle Program did not pay sufficient attention to the intersections of sexuality with other statuses. Indeed, she argued that this school did not serve females or youth of color adequately because it ignored the effect of sexism and racism on them, assuming that homophobia, alone, was the defining issue for all gay, lesbian, bisexual, and transgender young people. In addition, Snider argued that this program was marginalized by the Toronto Board of Education that defined its participants as "disadvantaged" and "maladjusted" rather than oppressed.

It is evident from the research reviewed that the question of whether targeted or nontargeted schools are more effective in achieving gender equity is much too simplistic. Rather, one must consider who these schools are targeted for, what their purposes are, how they are constructed and implemented, and how they are construed both by the various participants in them and by those who sponsor them. Furthermore, these schools, in particular those targeted at statuses other than gender, throw into sharp relief the need to consider gender in relation to race, sexuality, class, and other markers of identity girls and boys bring to the setting. Much more research is needed to obtain a better understanding of how gender works in these different school settings.

Interventions III: Sexual Harassment, Flirting, and Bullying

When does an intervention begin? In this subsection, we argue that interventions begin even as early as when a problem is named and when legal remedies are sought. We describe interventions that begin with the recognition of sexual harassment as a problem, with legal remedies introduced into the courts, with surveys to determine the extent and nature of the problems, and with school and curricular interventions.

DEFINING AND DETERMINING THE EXTENT OF THE PROBLEM

Stein (1999) defined sexual harassment as "unwanted and unwelcome behavior of a sexual nature that interferes with the right to receive an equal educational opportunity" (p. 3). The definition of this problem is related to federal civil rights law, including Title IX, but the problem was identified when girls told others that students and adults in schools were making them uncomfortable because of inappropriate touching or comments to them. It is not just girls who are harassed, however. Girls, boys, and gay and lesbian students all face harassment, a situation that shows how hegemonic masculinity (Connell, 1995, 1996) and how marginalization of particular groups works. The most significant aspect of sexual harassment is that it occurs in public, in hallways, and in classrooms, often in front of teachers who do not intervene (Stein, 1999; Stein, Marshall, & Tropp, 1993). One response to the survey *Seventeen* magazine did of its teenage readers on sexual harassment reflected both the public nature of the activity and the failure of adult response:

> Of the times I was sexually harassed at school, one of them made me feel really bad. I was in class and the teacher was looking right at me when this guy grabbed my butt. The teacher saw it happen. I slapped the guy and told him not to do that. My teacher didn't say anything and looked away and went on with the lesson like nothing out of the ordinary had happened. It really confused me because I knew guys weren't supposed to do that, but the teacher didn't do anything. . . . (Stein, 1995, p. 146)

The courts and the government recognize two forms of sexual harassment. *Quid pro quo* harassment (literally, "this for that") when conditions or favors are promised or offered in exchange for certain sexual behaviors. Hostile climate harassment takes place when a student's ability to participate or benefit from an educational program is limited by unwanted sexual language or conduct or when other students' ability to participate is affected by the sexual harassment of a third party. These guidelines have emerged from law cases in which students brought charges against teachers and other students.

A number of surveys to determine the issues related to sexual harassment have produced data on how widespread the problem is, on the types of behaviors students report, and on the language young people use to describe their harassment. Stein (1999) characterized the level of substantiation with each of the surveys, and how attentive each is to questions of race and class. In addition to the *Seventeen* survey, these surveys have been conducted by the Harris pollsters and sponsored by AAUW (*Hostile Hallways,* 1993) and by various states, including Connecticut, Massachusetts, New Jersey, and North Dakota. The results from these different studies showed that anywhere from 67% to 85% of respondents reported harassment, and that gendered violence had extremely negative effects on those who were harassed, including making them less willing to go to school, to talk in class, and to think that they could graduate from high school. Sexual harassment lowered self-confidence, caused students who were harassed to withdraw, and, in the case of gay and lesbian students, raised the numbers of physical attacks they experienced (Stein, 1999). Shakeshaft (1997) showed through her studies of 1,000 junior high students that girls are harassed for their looks and boys for their actions. The surveys agreed that sexual harassment is a severe problem in public schools.

SCHOOL AND CURRICULAR INTERVENTIONS

Stein, with the support of the Wellesley Center for Research on Women, has done the most significant work on school interventions. Several points connect the interventions. First, it is important to identify sexual harassment as public activity. Because it occurs in public, remedies also must be public. These remedies can take the form of "school-wide efforts to normalize the conversation about sexual harassment and other forms of gendered violence" (Stein, 1995, p. 159). Punitive reactions that respond to sexual harassment only through discipline without talk do not work. As part of the defining of public space, Stein (1995) argued, talk about sexual harassment needs to be connected to other analyses of the curriculum. When harassment is related to different forms of inequity and injustice in schools, students are more likely to be able to name and to respond to this particular form. Second, it is important to have the words of the students who have been harassed receive attention. Students' writing and talk about sexual harassment, said Stein (1995), creates a "common classroom vocabulary" (p. 160), makes it more difficult for adults to sit on the sidelines, and attends to the troubles that sexual harassment causes even for those who are observers of the harassment. Third, Stein (1999) recommended that public schools develop partnerships or collaborations with domestic violence or sexual assault organizations. The expertise of these groups is useful for adults in schools who need to intervene. Katz's (1995) description of an intervention project that address violence prevention and masculinity is a case study which raises useful questions for practitioners.

All these recommendations, taken together, suggest that addressing sexual harassment must be part of a larger agenda, because the context as well as the behavior must be considered (Brandenburg, 1997). Sexual harassment can flourish when students are not encouraged to see how others may experience the same events differently from them and when adults do not play a strong role in defining and acting on behalf of students who have been harassed. It is important for students as well as teachers to be informed so that sexual harassment can be distinguished from flirting and teasing.

Curricula have addressed this issue of distinguishing behaviors in both elementary and secondary classrooms. *Bullyproof* (Sjostrom & Stein, 1996) is a curriculum on bullying, teasing, and harassing for fourth- and fifth-grade students. It helps students distinguish between teasing and bullying, teaches students how to observe, provides examples of role plays for practicing intervention, teaches the law around sexual harassment and bullying, and provides guidelines for students on how to write a letter to a bully or harasser to stop the behavior. All of the curricular ideas suggest that alternatives to litigious actions are preferable. *Flirting or Hurting* (Stein & Sjostrom, 1994) addresses sexual harassment between students in Grades 6 through 12. This curriculum manual emphasizes the importance of teaching style, including emphasizing the significance of respect, and attending to issues of diversity. It also underscores the consequences of the language teachers use in discussion, advising, for example, against the use of the word "victim" in the discussions. The curriculum also suggests that teachers should help students become school ethnographers, that students can do surveys about sexual harassment in their school, that students need to think about harassment in terms of rights and to develop activities to assert their rights, and to connect harassment to other forms of social injustice.

Too few states have sophisticated policies in place, have state laws against the harassment of gay and lesbian students (Linn, Stein, Young, & Davis, 1992), and have significant training programs that are sponsored by the state education departments. Interventions against sexual harassment need to take place at all levels, be school and community specific, and connect issues in harassment to larger concerns about the well-being of all students. Sexual harassment interventions take up questions of difference.

Conclusion

This discussion of gender and classroom research is partial. The literature is so enormous that to discuss any issues in-depth requires a selectivity that ignores significant concerns. Important issues of economics, methodology, and disability, for example, have been ignored. We have tried to make several points, however, that are important for the understanding of gender research in education. First, gender differences within groups are significant and should not be ignored or minimized even while groups like White, Black, or Asian-American girls; gay and lesbian students; or boys who have been labeled as wimps or sissies may interest the researchers. Second, as the above sentence suggests, gender does not stand alone, but rather it is always connected to raced, classed, and sexualized subjectivities. The work on intersectionality is much stronger on the theoretical level than in empirical efforts. We need to see more research that does not falsely separate, for example, race and gender. Third, feminist perspectives on gender and schools differ from each other, and, in their differences, they recognize, emphasize, and articulate conflicting understandings of gendered subjectivity. Fourth, we need more research that addresses ideas of difference. Research like *The Bell Curve* illustrated the dangers of assuming that questions of difference are in the person rather than in the social context. When applied to gender and mathematics, this weak understanding of difference leads to blaming girls for their problems in math and emphasizing the situation of the elite rather than the rest.

The study of gender means that while attending to difference we must also study relationships between girls and boys, gay and straight youth, traditionally gendered and transgender people. We need approaches that observe connections as well as distinctions and that promote dialogue without privileging those that educational institutions decide have the most cultural capital.

REFERENCES

Adelman, C. (1991). *Women at thirty-something: Paradoxes of attainment.* Washington, DC: U.S. Department of Education, Office of Educational Research and Improvement.

Aebischer, V., & Valabreque, C. (1995). The difficulty of changing social behavior. In R. Clair (Ed.), *The scientific education of girls: Education beyond reproach?* (pp. 151–162). London: Jessica Kingsley/ UNESCO Publishing.

Alton-Lee, A., Nuthall, G., & Patrick, J. (1993). Reframing classroom research: A lesson from the private world of children. *Harvard Educational Review, 63*(1), 50–84.

American Association of University Women (AAUW). (1992). *How schools shortchange girls.* Washington, DC: American Association of University Women Educational Foundation.

AAUW. (1998). *Separated by sex: A critical look at single-sex education for girls.* Washington, DC: American Association of University Women Educational Foundation.

Anyon, J. (1984). Intersections of gender and class: Accommodation and resistance by working class and affluent females to contradictory sex-role ideologies. *Journal of Education, 166,* 25–48.

Belenky, M. F., Clinchy, B. M., Goldberger, N. R., & Tarule, J. M. (1986). *Women's ways of knowing.* New York: Basic Books.

Bernard-Powers, J. (1995). Out of the cameos and into the conversation: Gender, social studies, and curriculum transformation. In J. Gaskell & J. Willinsky (Eds.), *Gender in/forms curriculum* (pp. 191–208). New York: Teachers College Press.

Bernard-Powers, J. (1996). Engendering social studies: Perspectives, texts, and teaching. *Theory and Research in Social Education, 24,* 2–7.

Best, A. (2000). *Prom night: Youth, schooling and popular culture.* New York: Routledge.

Biklen, S. (1995). *School work: Gender and the cultural construction of teaching.* New York: Teachers College Press.

Biklen, S. & Bogad, L. (1998, April). Generational imperatives: Consuming representations of youth in ethnography, memoir and fiction. Paper presented at the annual meetings of the American Educational Research Association, San Diego.

Biklen, S., Luschen, K., & Bogad, L. (1996, April). Feminism and the lives of girls in schools: Scholarship, method and change. Paper presented at the annual meeting of the American Educational Research Association, New York.

Biklen, S., & Pollard, D. (Eds.). (1993). *Gender and education. National Society for the Study of Education yearbook.* Chicago: University of Chicago Press.

Blackmore, J. (1996). Feminist dilemmas: An Australian case study of a whole-school policy approach to gender reform. *Journal of Curriculum Studies, 28,* 253–279.

Blount, J. (1998). *Destined to rule the schools: Women and the superintendency, 1873–1995.* Albany, NY: State University of New York Press.

Boaler, J. (1997). Reclaiming school mathematics: The girls fight back. *Gender and Education, 9*(3), 285–305.

Bourdieu, P. (1986). The forms of capital. In J. Richardson (Ed.), *Handbook of theory and research for the sociology of education* (pp. 241–258). Westport, CT: Greenwood Press.

Braatz, J., et al. (1966). Lesbian, gay, bisexual, and transgender people and education [Special issue]. *Harvard Educational Review, 66*(2).

Brandenburg, J. B. (1997). *Confronting sexual harassment: What schools and colleges can do.* New York: Teachers College Press.

Britzman, D. (1993). Beyond rolling models: Gender and multicultural education. In S. Biklen & D. Pollard (Eds.), *Gender and education. National Society for the Study of Education yearbook* (pp. 25–42). Chicago: University of Chicago Press.

Britzman, D. P. (1997). What is this thing called love? New discourses for understanding gay and lesbian youth. In S. de Castell & M. Bryson (Eds.), *Radical interventions* (pp. 183–107). Albany, NY: State University of New York Press.

Brown, L. M., & Gilligan, C. (1992). *Meeting at the crossroads: Women's psychology and girls' development.* Cambridge, MA: Harvard University Press.

Bryson, M., & de Castell, S. (1995). So we've got a chip on our shoulder! Sexing the texts of "educational technology." In J. Gaskell & J. Willinsky (Eds.), *Gender in/forms curriculum* (pp. 21–42). New York: Teachers College Press.

Bryson, M., & de Castell, S. (1997). En/gendering equity: Paradoxical consequences of institutionalized equity policies. In S. de Castell & M. Bryson (Eds.), *Radical interventions: Identity, politics, and differencels in educational praxis* (pp. 85–103). Albany, NY: State University of New York Press.

Bulcock, J. W., Whitt, M. E., & Beebe, M. J. (1991). Gender differences, student well-being and high school achievement. *The Alberta Journal of Educational Research, 37*(3), 209–224.

Burgess, N.J. (1994). Gender roles revisited: The development of the "women's place" among African American women in the United States. *Journal of Black Studies, 24*(4), 391–401.

Burman, E. (1995). What is it? Masculinity and femininity in cultural representations of childhood. In S. Wilkinson & C. Kitzinger (Eds.), *Feminism and discourse: Psychological perspectives* (pp. 49–67). London: Sage.

Burton, L. (1996). A socially just pedagogy for the teaching of mathematics. In P. Murphy & C. Gipps (Eds.), *Equity in the classroom* (pp. 136–145). London: Falmer Press.

Campbell, P. B. (1989). So what do we do with the poor, non-White female? Issues of gender, race and social class in mathematics and equity. *Peabody Journal of Education, 66*(2), 95–112.

Campbell, P. B., & Wahl, E. (1998). What's sex got to do with it? Simplistic questions, complex answers. In *Separated by sex: A critical look at single-sex education for girls* (pp. 63–73). Washington, DC: American Association of University Women Educational Foundation.

Carlson, D. (1992). Ideological conflict and change in the sexuality curriculum. In J. T. Sears (Ed.), *Sexuality and the curriculum: The politics and practices of sexuality education.* New Haven, CT.: Yale University Press.

Carlson, D. (1997). Gayness, multicultural education and community. In M. Seller & L. Weis (Eds.), *Beyond black and white* (pp. 233–256). Albany, NY: State University of New York Press.

Catsambis, S. (1995). Gender, race, ethnicity and science education in the middle grades. *Journal of Research in Science Teaching, 32*(2), 243–257.

Christian-Smith, L. (1988). Romancing the girl: Adolescent romance novels and the construction of femininity. In L. Roman, L. Christian-Smith, & E. Ellsworth (Eds.), *Becoming feminine: The politics of popular culture* (pp. 76–101). London: Falmer Press.

Christian-Smith, L. (1993). Voices of resistance: Young women readers of romance fiction. In L. Weiss & M. Fine (Eds.), *Beyond silenced voices: class, race, and gender in United States schools* (pp. 169–190). Albany, NY: State University of New York Press.

Clark, R., & Kulkin, H. (1996). Toward a multicultural feminist perspective on fiction for young adults. *Youth & Society, 27,* 291–312.

Clarricoates, K. (1980). The importance of being Ernest . . . Emma . . . Tom . . . Jane . . . The perception and categorization of gender conformity and gender deviation in primary schools. In R. Deem (Ed.), *Schooling for women's work* (pp. 26–41). London: Routledge and Kegan Paul.

Clifford, G. J. (1989). Man/woman/teacher: Gender, family, and career in American educational history. In D. Warren (Ed.), *American teachers: Histories of a profession at work.* New York: Macmillan.

Collins, P. H. (1991). *Black feminist thought: Knowledge, consciousness and the politics of empowerment.* Boston: Unwin Hyman.

Commeyras, M., & Alvermann, D. E. (1996). Reading about women in world history textbooks from one feminist perspective. *Gender and Education, 8*(1), 31–48.

Connell, R. W. (1995). *Masculinities.* Berkeley, CA: University of California Press.

Connell, R. W. (1996). Teaching the boys: New research on masculinity and gender strategies for schools. *Teachers College Record, 98,* 207–235.

Coulter, R. P. (1995). Struggling with sexism: Experiences of feminist first-year teachers. *Gender and Education, 7*(1), 33–51.

D'Amico, M., Baron, L. J., & Sissons, M. E. (1995). Gender differences in attributions about microcomputer learning in elementary school. *Sex Roles, 33*(5–6), 353–384.

Davies, B. (1989). Education for sexism: A theoretical analysis of the sex/gender bias in education. *Educational Philosophy and Theory, 21*(1), 1–19.

Dawkins, M. (1980). Educational and occupational goals: Male versus female Black high school seniors. *Urban Education, 15*(2), 231–242.

Delpit, L. (1988). The silenced dialogue: Power and pedagogy in educating other people's children. *Harvard Educational Review, 58,* 280–298.

Desmet-Goethals, J. (1995). Proposed diversification for choosing a stream in secondary technical and vocational schools. In R. Clair (Ed.), *The scientific education of girls: Education beyond reproach?* (pp. 180–188). London: Jessica Kingsley/UNESCO Publishing.

Diller, A. (1996). Introduction. In A. Diller, B. Houston, K. P. Morgan, & M. Ayim (Eds.), *The gender question in education: Theory, pedagogy and politics* (pp. 1–6). Boulder, CO: Westview Press.

Dorney, J. (1995). Educating toward resistance: A task for women teaching girls. *Youth & Society, 27,* 55–72.

Eccles, J., Wigfield, A, Harold, R. D., & Blumenfeld, P. (1993). Age and gender differences in children's self- and task perceptions during elementary school. *Child Development, 64,* 830–847.

Epstein, C. F. (1997). The multiple realities of sameness and difference: Ideology and practice. *Journal of Social Issues, 53*(2), 259–278.

Epstein, D. (Ed.). (1994). *Challenging lesbian and gay inequalities in education.* Buckingham, UK: Open University Press.

Evans, K. S. (1996). Creating spaces for equity? The role of positioning in peer-led literature discussions. *Language Arts, 73,* 194–202.

Fennema, E. (1996). Scholarship, gender and mathematics. In P. Murphy & C. Gipps (Eds.), *Equity in the classroom* (pp. 73–80). London: Falmer Press.

Fennema, E., Carpenter, T., Jacobs, V. R., Franke, M. L., & Levi, L. W. (1998). A longitudinal study of gender differences in young children's mathematical thinking. *Educational Researcher, 27*(5), 6–11.

Fennema, E., Peterson, P., Carpenter, T. P., & Lubinski, C. A. (1990). Teachers' attributions and beliefs about girls, boys and mathematics. *Educational Studies in Mathematics, 21*(1), 55–65.

Finders, M. J. (1997). *Just girls.* New York: Teachers College Press.

Fine, M. (1988). Sexuality, schooling and adolescent females: The missing discourse of desire. *Harvard Educational Review, 58,* 29–53.

Fine, M. (1991). *Framing dropouts: Notes on the politics of an urban high school.* Albany, NY: State University of New York Press.

Fine, M., & McPherson, P. (1993). Over dinner: Feminism and adolescent female bodies. In S. Biklen & D. Pollard (Eds.), *Gender and education. National Society for the Study of Education yearbook* (pp. 126–154). Chicago: University of Chicago Press.

Fine, M., Weis, L., Powell, L., & Wong, L. M. (Eds.). (1997). *Off white.* New York: Routledge.

Fordham, S. N. (1993). Those loud Black girls: (Black) women, silence and gender "passing" in the academy. *Anthropology and Education Quarterly, 24*(1), 3–32.

Fordham, S. N. (1996). *Blacked out: Dilemmas of race, identity, and success at Capital High.* Chicago: University of Chicago Press.

Foster, M. (1993). Resisting racism: Personal testimonies of African-American teachers. In L. Weiss & M. Fine (Eds.), *Beyond silenced voices: Class, race and gender in United States schools* (pp. 273–288). Albany, NY: State University of New York Press.

Frankenberg, R. (1993). *White women, race matters: The social construction of whiteness.* Minneapolis, MN: University of Minnesota Press.

Friend, R. (1993). Choices, not closets: Heterosexism and homophobia in schools. In L. Weiss & M. Fine (Eds.), *Beyond silenced voices: Class, race, and gender in United States schools* (pp. 190–208). Albany, NY: State University of New York Press.

Gallas, K. (1998). *Sometimes I can be anything: Power, gender and identity in a primary classroom.* New York: Teachers College Press.

Gaskell, J., & Willinsky, J. (Eds.). (1995). *Gender in/forms curriculum.* New York: Teachers College Press.

Gilbert, P., & Taylor, S. (1991). *Fashioning the feminine: Girls, popular culture and schooling.* Sydney, Australia: Allen & Unwin.

Gilligan, C. (1982). *In a different voice: Psychological theory and women's development.* Cambridge, MA: Harvard University Press.

Gore, J. (1993). *The struggle for pedagogies: Critical and feminist discourses as regimes of truth.* New York: Routledge.

Grant, L. (1984). Black females' "place" in desegregated classrooms. *Sociology of Education, 59,* 98–111.

Grant, L. (1992). Race and the schooling of young girls. In J. Wrigley (Ed.), *Education and gender equality* (pp. 91–113). London: Falmer Press.

Guillaumin, C. (1995). *Racism, sexism, power and ideology.* London: Routledge.

Haag, P. (1998). Single-sex education in grades K–12: What does the research tell us? In *Separated by sex: A critical look at single-sex education for girls* (pp. 13–38). Washington, DC: American Association of University Women Educational Foundation.

Hahn, C. (1996). Gender and political learning. *Theory and Research in Social Education, 24,* 8–35.

Halpern, D. F. (1995). Cognitive gender differences: Why diversity is a critical research issue. In H. Landrine (Ed.), *Bringing cultural diversity to feminist psychology: Theory, research and practice* (pp. 77–92). Washington, DC: American Psychological Association.

Hamilton, V. L., Blumenfeld, P., Akoh, H., & Miura, K. (1991). Group and gender in Japanese and American elementary classrooms. *Journal of Cross Cultural Psychology, 22*(3), 317–346.

Harbeck, K. M. (Ed.). (1992). *Coming out of the classroom closet. Gay and lesbian students, teachers, and curricula.* New York: Haworth Press.

Henkin, R. (1995). Insiders and outsiders in first grade writing workshops: Gender and equity issues. *Language Arts, 72,* 429–434.

Heward, C. (1988). *Making a man of him.* London: Routledge.

Holly, L. (Ed.). (1989). *Girls and sexuality: Teaching and learning.* Philadelphia: Open University Press.

Hooks, B. (1993). Transformative pedagogy and multiculturalism. In T. Perry & J. Fraser (Eds.), *Freedom's plow: Teaching in the multicultural classroom* (pp. 91–98). New York: Routledge.

Hostile hallways: The AAUW survey on sexual harassment in America's schools. (1993). Washington, DC: American Association of University Women Educational Foundation.

Houston, B. (1996). Gender freedom and the subtleties of sexist education. In A. Diller, B. Houston, K. P. Morgan, & M. Ayim (Eds.), *The gender question in education: Theory, pedagogy and politics* (pp. 50–63). Boulder, CO: Westview Press.

Howard, J. A., & Hollander, J. A. (1997). *Gendered situations, gendered selves: A gender lens on social psychology.* Thousand Oaks, CA: Sage.

Hull, G. T., Scott, P. B., & Smith, B. (1982). *All the women are white, all the blacks are men, but some of us are brave: Black women's studies.* Old Westbury, NY: Feminist Press.

Hyde, J. S., & Jaffee, S. (1998). Perspectives from social and feminist psychology. *Educational Researcher, 27*(5), 14–16.

Irvine, J. (1995). *Sexuality education across cultures: Working with differences.* San Francisco: Jossey Bass.

Irvine, J. J. (1986). Teacher-student interactions: Effects of student race, sex, and grade level. *Journal of Educational Psychology, 78*(1), 14–21.

James, J. B. (1997). What are the social issues involved in focusing on *difference* in the study of gender? *Journal of Social Issues, 53*(2), 213–232.

Jordan, E. (1995). Fighting boys and fantasy play: The construction of masculinity in the early years of school. *Gender and Education, 7*(1), 69–85.

Katz, J. (1995). Reconstructing masculinity in the locker room: The mentors in violence prevention project. *Harvard Educational Review, 65,* 163–174.

Kehily, M. J., & Nayak, A. (1997). "Lads and laughter": Humor and the production of heterosexual hierarchies. *Gender and Education, 9*(1), 69–87.

Kenway, J., Blackmore, J., Willis, S., & Rennie, L. (1996). The emotional dimension of feminist pedagogy in schools. In P. Murphy & C. Gipps (Eds.), *Equity in the classroom* (pp. 242–259). London: Falmer Press.

Kenway, J., & Modra, H. (1992). Feminist pedagogy and emancipatory possibilities. In C. Luke & J. Gore (Eds.), *Feminisms and critical pedagogy* (pp. 138–166). New York: Routledge.

Kenway, J., & Willis, S. (1998). *Answering back: Girls, boys and feminism in schools.* London: Routledge.

Khayatt, M. D. (1992). *Lesbian teachers: An invisible presence.* Albany, NY: State University of New York Press.

King, D. K. (1991–92). Unraveling the fabric, missing the beat: Class and gender in Afro American social issues. *The Black Scholar, 22*(3), 36–44.

Kistner, J., Metzler, A., Gatlin, D., & Risi, S. (1993). Classroom racial proportions and children's peer relations: Race and gender effects. *Journal of Educational Psychology, 85*(3), 446–452.

Lareau, A. (1987). Social class differences in family–school relationships: The importance of cultural capital. *Sociology of Education, 60,* 73–85.

Larkin, J. (1994). *Sexual harassment: High school girls speak out.* Toronto, ON: Second Story Press.

Lather, P. (1991). *Getting smart: Feminist research and pedagogy with/in the postmodern.* New York: Routledge.

Le Pore, P. C., & Warren, J. P. (1997). A comparison of single-sex and coeducational Catholic secondary schooling: Evidence from the National Educational Longitudinal Study of 1988. *American Educational Research Journal, 34*(3), 485–511.

Leadbeater, B., & Way, N. (Eds.). (1996). *Urban girls.* New York: New York University Press.

Lee, V. E. (1998). Is single-sex secondary schooling a solution to the problem of gender inequity? In *Separated by sex: A critical look at single-sex education for girls* (pp. 41–52). Washington, DC: American Association of University Women Educational Foundation.

Lee, V. E., & Bryk, A. S. (1986). Effects of single-sex secondary schools on student achievement and attitudes. *Journal of Educational Psychology, 78*(5), 381–395.

Lee, V. E., Marks, H. M., & Byrd, T. (1994). Sexism in single-sex and coeducational independent secondary school classrooms. *Sociology of Education, 67,* 92–120.

Lefkowitz, B. (1997). *Our guys: The Glen Ridge rape and the secret life of the perfect suburb.* Berkeley, CA: University of California Press.

Lesko, N. (1988). The curriculum of the body: Lessons from a Catholic high school. In L. Roman, L. Christian-Smith, & E. Ellsworth (Eds.), *Becoming feminine: The politics of popular culture* (pp. 123–142). London: Falmer Press.

Lightfoot, S. L. (1976). Socialization and education of young black girls in school. *Teachers College Record, 78*(2), 239–262.

Linn, E., Stein, D. N., Young, J., & Davis, S. (1992). Bitter lessons for all: Sexual harassment in schools. In J. T. Sears (Ed.), *Sexuality and the curriculum: The politics and practices of sexuality education* (pp. 106–123). New York: Teachers College Press.

Linn, M. C., & Petersen, A. C. (1985). Facts and assumptions about the nature of sex difference. In S. S. Klein (Ed.), *Handbook for achieving sex equity through education* (pp. 53–77). Baltimore: Johns Hopkins Press.

Loudet-Verdier, J., & Mosconi, N. (1995). Interaction between teachers and students (girls or boys) in mathematics classes. In R. Clair (Ed.), *The scientific education of girls: Education beyond reproach?* (pp. 139–148). London: Jessica Kingsley Publishers/UNESCO Publishing.

Lovering, K. M. (1995). The bleeding body: Adolescents talk about menstruation. In S. Wilkinson & C. Kitzinger (Eds.), *Feminism and discourse: Psychological perspectives* (pp. 10–31). London: Sage.

Luke, C., & Gore, J. (Eds.). (1992). *Feminisms and critical pedagogy.* New York: Routledge.

Ma, X. (1995). Gender differences in mathematics achievement between Canadian and Asian educational systems. *Journal of Educational Research, 89*(2), 118–127.

Mac an Ghaill, M. (1991). Schooling, sexuality and male power: Towards an emancipatory curriculum. *Gender and Education, 3,* 291–309.

Mac an Ghaill, M. (1994). *The making of men: Masculinities, sexualities and schooling.* Milton Keynes, UK: Open University Press.

Maher, F., & Tetreault, M. K. (1994). *The feminist classroom.* New York: Basic Books.

Matthews, B. (1996). Drawing scientists. *Gender and Education, 8*(2), 231–243.

McLaren, A., & Gaskell, J. (1995). Now you see it, now you don't: Gender as an issue in school science. In J. Gaskell & J. Willinsky (Eds.), *Gender in/forms curriculum* (pp. 136–156). New York: Teachers College Press.

McLeod, J., Yates, L., & Halasa, K. (1994). Voice, difference and feminist pedagogy. *Curriculum Studies, 2,* 189–202.

McRobbie, A. (1991). *Feminism and youth culture.* Boston: Unwin Hyman.

McWilliam, E. (1994). *In broken images: Feminist tales for a different teacher education.* New York: Teachers College Press.

Meece, J. L., & Jones, M. G. (1996a). Gender differences in motivation and strategy use in science: Are girls rote learners? *Journal of Research in Science Teaching, 33*(4), 393–406.

Meece, J. L., & Jones, M. G. (1996b). Girls in mathematics and science: Constructivism as a feminist perspective. *The High School Journal, 79*(3), 242–248.

Middleton, S. (1993). *Educating feminists: Life histories and pedagogy.* New York: Teachers College Press.

Mills, C. J., Ablard, K. E., & Stumpf, H. (1993). Gender differences in academically talented young students' mathematical reasoning: Patterns across age and subskills. *Journal of Educational Psychology, 85*(2), 340–346.

Morgan, D. (1996). Learning to be a man: Dilemmas and contradictions of masculine experience. In C. Luke (Ed.), *Feminisms and pedagogies of everyday life* (pp. 103–115). Albany, NY: State University of New York Press.

Morgan, K. P. (1996). Describing the emperor's new clothes: Three myths of educational (in-)equity. In A. Diller, B. Houston, K. P. Morgan, & M. Ayim (Eds.), *The gender question in education: Theory, pedagogy and politics* (pp. 105–122). Boulder, CO: Westview Press.

Munro, P. (1998). *Subject to fiction: Women teachers' life history narratives and the cultural politics of resistance.* Buckingham, UK: Open University Press.

Nairn, K. (1991). Geography and gender in the secondary school classroom. *New Zealand Journal of Geography, 91,* 14–15.

Narine, M. L. (1992). *Single-sex, single-race public schools: A solution to the problems plaguing the black community.* Washington, DC: U.S. Department of Education, Office of Educational Research and Improvement. (ERIC Document ED 348 423)

Nicholson, P. (1995). Feminism and psychology. In J. A. Smith, P. Harre, & L. V. Langenhove (Eds.), *Rethinking psychology* (pp. 122–142). London: Sage.

Noddings, N. (1998). Perspectives from feminist philosophy. *Educational Researcher, 27*(5), 17–21.

Orner, M. (1992). Interrupting the calls for student voice in "liberatory" education: A feminist poststructuralist perspective. In C. Luke & J. Gore (Eds.) *Feminisms and critical pedagogy* (pp. 74–89). New York: Routledge.

Osler, A. (1994). Still hidden from history?: The representation of women in recently published history textbooks. *Oxford Review of Education, 20,* 219–235.

Perkins, L. (1983). The impact of the "Cult of True Womanhood" on the education of black women. *Journal of Social Issues, 39*(3), 17–28.

Plateau, N. (1995). Coeducational classrooms: An unfinished process. In R. Clair (Ed.), *The scientific education of girls: Education beyond reproach?* (pp. 51–64). London: Jessica Kingsley Publishers/UNESCO Publishing.

Pollard, D. S. (1998). The contexts of single-sex classes. In *Separated by sex: A critical look at single-sex education for girls* (pp. 75–78). Washington, DC: American Association of University Women Educational Foundation.

Pollard, D. S., & Ajirotutu, C. S. (1994). *Documenting the African American immersion schools: A work in progress.* Unpublished manuscript, University of Wisconsin-Milwaukee, the African American Immersion Schools Evaluation Project.

Pollard, D. S., & Ajirotutu, C. S. (1997). *Five-year report: Dr. Martin Luther King Elementary School: The African American Immersion School Evaluation Project.* Milwaukee, WI: University of Wisconsin-Milwaukee.

Pottorff, D. D., Phelps-Zientarski, D., & Skovera, M. (1996). Gender perceptions of elementary and middle school students about literacy at school and home. *Journal of Research and Development in Education, 29*(4), 203–211.

Powney, J. (1996). *Gender and attainment: A review* (SCRE Research Report No. 81). Edinburgh, Scotland: Scottish Council for Research in Education.

Proweller, A. (1998). *Constructing female identities: Meaning making in an upper middle class youth culture.* Albany, NY: State University of New York Press.

Purcell-Gates, V. (1993). Focus on research: Complexity and gender. *Language Arts, 70*(2), 124–127.

Ratteray, J. D. (1994). The search for access and content in the education of African Americans. In M. J. Shujaa (Ed.), *Too much schooling, too little education: A paradox of black life in white societies* (pp. 123–141). Trenton, NJ: Africa World Press.

Raymond, D. (1994). Homophobia, identity, and the meaning of desire. In J. Irvine (Ed.), *Sexual cultures and the construction of adolescent identities* (pp. 115–150). Philadelphia: Temple University Press.

Razack, S. (1998). *Looking white people in the eye: Gender, race, and culture in courtrooms and classrooms.* Toronto, ON: University of Toronto Press.

Reay, D. (1990). Girls' groups as a component of anti-sexist practice— One primary school's experience. *Gender and Education, 2*(1), 37–49.

Rech, J. F. (1994). A comparison of the mathematics attitudes of black students according to grade level, gender, and academic achievement. *Journal of Negro Education, 63*(2), 212–220.

Reid, P. T., Haritos, C., Kelly, E., & Holland, N. E. (1995). Socialization of girls: Issues of ethnicity in gender development. In H. Landrine (Ed.), *Bringing culture diversity to feminist psychology: Theory, research and practice* (pp. 93–111). Washington, DC: American Psychological Association.

Rensenbrink, C. (1996). What difference does it make? The story of a lesbian teacher. *Harvard Educational Review, 66,* 257–270.

Research for Action, Inc. (1996). *Girls in the middle.* Washington, DC: American Association for University Women.

Riger, S. (1997). From snapshots to videotape: New directions in research on gender differences. *Journal of Social Issues, 53*(2), 395–408.

Riordan, C. (1998). The future of single-sex schools. In *Separated by sex: A critical look at single-sex education for girls* (pp. 53–62). Washington, DC: American Association of University Women Educational Foundation.

Rofes, E. (1989). Opening up the classroom closet: Responding to the educational needs of gay and lesbian youth. *Harvard Educational Review, 59,* 444–452.

Roman, L. (1988). Intimacy, labor, and class: Ideologies of feminine sexuality in the punk slam dance. In L. Roman, L. Christian-Smith, & E. Ellsworth (Eds.), *Becoming feminine: The politics of popular culture* (pp. 143–184). London: Falmer Press.

Rosser, S. V. (Ed.). (1995). *Teaching the majority: Breaking the gender barrier in science, mathematics, and engineering.* New York: Teachers College Press.

Sadker, M., & Sadker, D. (1994). *Failing at fairness: How America's schools cheat girls.* New York: Charles Scribner & Sons.

Sanders, J. (1995). Girls and technology: Villain wanted. In S. V. Rosser (Ed.), *Teaching the majority: Breaking the gender barrier in science, mathematics, and engineering* (pp. 147–159). New York: Teachers College Press.

Sears, J. T. (1992a). The impact of culture and ideology on the construction of gender and sexual identities: Developing a critically based sexuality curriculum. In J. T. Sears (Ed.), *Sexuality and the curriculum: The politics and practices of sexuality education* (pp. 139–156). New York: Teachers College Press.

Sears, J. T. (Ed.). (1992b). *Sexuality and the curriculum: The politics and practices of sexuality education.* New York: Teachers College Press.

Shakeshaft, C. (1997, April). Peer harassment and the culture of schooling. Paper presented at the annual meetings of the American Educational Research Association, Chicago.

Shepardson, D. P., & Pizzini, E. L. (1992). Gender bias in female elementary teachers' perceptions of the scientific ability of students. *Science Education, 76*(2), 147–153.

Shoop, R. J., & Edwards, D. L. (1994). *How to stop sexual harassment in our schools: A handbook and curriculum guide for administrators and teachers.* Boston: Allyn and Bacon.

Shroyer, M. G., Smith, N.J., Borchers, C. A., & Wright, E. L. (1994). Science and mathematics equity issues at a local school district level. *School Science and Mathematics, 94*(2), 65–77.

Simms, M. C. (1988). *The choices that young black women make: Education, employment and family formation* (Working Paper No. 190). Wellesley, MA: Wellesley College Center for Research on Women.

Singer, A. (1995). Challenging gender bias through a transformative high school social studies curriculum. *Theory and Research in Social Education, 23,* 234–259.

Sjostrom, L., & Stein, N. (1996). *Bullyproof.* Wellesley, MA: Wellesley Center for Research on Women.

Skelton, C. (1996). Learning to be "tough": The fostering of maleness in one primary school. *Gender and Education, 8*(2), 185–197.

Snider, K. (1996). Race and sexual orientation: The (im)possibility of these intersections in educational policy. *Harvard Educational Review, 66*(2), 294–302.

Sowder, J. T. (1998). Perspectives from mathematics education. *Educational Researcher, 27*(5), 12–13.

Squire, C. (1989). *Significant differences: Feminism in psychology.* London: Routledge.

Steedman, C. (1982). *The tidy house.* London: Virago Press.

Stein, N. (1995). Sexual harassment in school: The public performance of gendered violence. *Harvard Educational Review, 65*(2), 145–162.

Stein, N. (1999). *Between the lines: Sexual harassment in K–12 schools.* New York: Teachers College Press.

Stein, N., Marshall, N., & Tropp, L. (1993). *Secrets in public: Sexual harassment in our schools.* Wellesley, MA: Wellesley Center for Research on Women.

Stein, N., & Sjostrom, L. (1994). *Flirting or hurting?* Washington, DC: National Education Association.

Suitor, J. J., & Reavis, R. (1995). Football, fast cars, and cheerleading. Adolescent gender norms, 1978–1989. *Adolescence, 30*(118), 165–272.

Swaminathan, R. (1997). *"The charming sideshow": Cheerleading, girls' culture, and schooling.* Unpublished doctoral dissertation, Syracuse University, Syracuse, NY.

Taylor, J., Gilligan, C., & Sullivan, A. (1995). *Between voice and silence: Women and girls, race and relationship.* Cambridge, MA: Harvard University Press.

Ten Dam, G., & Rijkschroeff, R. (1996). Teaching women's history in secondary education: Constructing gender identity. *Theory and Research in Social Education, 24,* 71–89.

Thompson, S. (1995). *Going all the way: Teenage girls' tales of sex, romance & pregnancy.* New York: Hill and Wang.

Thorne, B. (1993). *Gender play.* New Brunswick, NJ: Rutgers University Press.

Tolman, D. (1994). Doing desire: Adolescent girls' struggles for/with sexuality. *Gender and Society, 8,* 324–342.

Tyack, D., & Hansot, E. (1990). *Learning together.* New Haven, CT: Yale University Press.

Volman, M., Van Eck, D., & Ten Dam, G. (1995). Girls in science and technology: The development of a discourse. *Gender and Education, 7*(3), 283–293.

Walker, J. (1988). *Louts and legends.* Sydney, Australia: Allen & Unwin.

Walkerdine, V. (1990). *Schoolgirl fictions.* London: Verso.

Ward, J. V., & Taylor, J. M. (1992). Sexuality education for immigrant and minority students: Developing a culturally appropriate curriculum. In J. T. Sears (Ed.), *Sexuality and the curriculum: The politics and practices of sexuality education* (pp. 183–202). New York: Teachers College Press.

Weiler, K. (1988). *Women teaching for change.* South Hadley, MA: Bergin & Garvey.

Weiner, G. (1994). *Feminism in education: An introduction.* Buckingham, UK: Open University Press.

Weis, L., & Fine, M. (Eds.). (1993). *Beyond silenced voices: Class, race and gender in United States schools.* Albany, NY: State University of New York.

Weisbeck, L. (1992). *Teachers' thoughts about children during mathematics instruction.* Unpublished doctoral dissertation, University of Wisconsin, Madison.

Wellesley Center for Research on Women. (1995). *How schools shortchange girls: The AAUW report.* New York: Marlowe.

West, C., & Zimmerman, D. (1987). Doing gender. *Gender & Society, 1,* 125–151.

Wheary, J., & Ennis, R. H. (1995). Gender bias in critical thinking: Continuing the dialogue. *Educational Theory, 45*(2), 213–224.

White, J. (1996). Research on English and the teaching of girls. In P. Murphy & C. Gipps (Eds.), *Equity in the classroom* (pp. 97–110). London: Falmer Press.

Willis, S. (1995). Mathematics: From constructing privilege to deconstructing myths. In J. Gaskell & J. Willinsky (Eds.), *Gender in/forms curriculum* (pp. 262–264). New York: Teachers College Press.

Woods, P., & Hammersley, M. (Eds.) (1993). *Gender and ethnicity in schools: Ethnographic accounts.* London: Routledge.

Wright, J. (1996). Mapping the discourses of physical education: Articulating a female tradition. *Journal of Curriculum Studies, 28,* 331–351.

Yates, L. (1993a). Feminism and Australian state policy: Some questions for the 1990s. In M. A. Arnot & K. Weiler (Eds.), *Feminism and social justice in education* (pp. 167–185). London: Falmer Press.

Yates, L. (1993b). *The education of girls.* Melbourne, Australia: Australian Council for Educational Research.

Yates, L. (1997). Gender equity and the boys debate: What sort of challenge is it? *British Journal of Sociology of Education, 18,* 337–347.

Yates, L., & Leder, G. (1996). *Student pathways: A review and overview of national databases on gender equity.* A report for the Gender Equity Taskforce of the Ministerial Council on Education, Employment, Training and Youth Affairs. Australian Capital Territory: Commonwealth of Australia.

Young, I. M. (1997). *Intersecting voices: Dilemmas of gender, political philosophy, and policy.* Princeton, NJ: Princeton University Press.

Zambo, R., & Hess, R. K. (1996). The gender differential effects of a procedural plan for solving mathematic work problems. *School Science and Mathematics, 96*(7), 362–370.

Part 5
Policy

37.

Standard Setting in Teaching: Changes in Licensing, Certification, and Assessment

Linda Darling-Hammond
Stanford University

Now is an important time to review the status of standards for teaching. As the 21st century arrives, it is increasingly clear that the capacities teachers need to succeed at teaching much more challenging content to a much more diverse group of learners can only be widely acquired throughout the teaching force by greater investments in teacher preparation and development. Such reforms, many policymakers and practitioners believe, will in turn require comprehensive restructuring of the systems by which states and school districts license, hire, induct, support, and provide for the continual learning of teachers (Carnegie Forum on Education and the Economy [Carnegie Forum], 1986; Holmes Group, 1986, 1996; National Commission on Teaching and America's Future [NCTAF], 1996).

New standards for teacher education accreditation and for teacher licensing, certification, and ongoing evaluation have become a prominent lever for promoting systemwide change in teaching (Darling-Hammond, Wise, and Klein, 1995). The National Commission on Teaching and America's Future (1996) argued as follows:

> Standards for teaching are the linchpin for transforming current systems of preparation, licensing, certification, and ongoing development so that they better support student learning. (Such standards) can bring clarity and focus to a set of activities that are currently poorly connected and often badly organized. . . . Clearly, if students are to achieve high standards, we can expect no less from their teachers and from other educators. Of greatest priority is reaching agreement on what teachers should know and be able to do to teach to high standards. (p. 67)

The effort to define what teachers should know and be able to do to be successful—and the use of assessments of such knowledge and skills to make decisions about entry and continuation in teaching—has gained momentum with the advent of new standards for student learning promulgated by both national associations and state governments (Darling-Hammond, 1997b; O'Day & Smith, 1993). These standards change the nature of teaching work and knowledge, positing a more active, integrated, and intellectually challenging curriculum for all students, not just the most academically able. Thus, they also require more diagnostic teaching with multiple pathways to learning so that students who encounter difficulty get the help they need to succeed. Because restructured schools are creating ambitious performance standards while increasingly using "push-in" rather than "pull-out" methods for children with special needs, teachers need to know more about both subjects and wide-ranging needs of students than they have in the past.

Current education reforms also create a broader range of roles for teachers in developing curriculum and assessing student performance, coaching and mentoring other teachers, and working more closely with families and community agencies. For their success, school-based management and shared decision-making initiatives rely on the capacity of education practitioners to make knowledgeable judgments about curriculum and assessment, school organization, and program evaluation. This increased responsibility means that teachers need to be prepared to make such decisions responsibly.

With the recognition that teacher preparation should reflect the demands of teachers' evolving roles, state policymakers are beginning to link their efforts to raise standards for students to initiatives that would also raise standards for teachers. As a consequence, substantial changes are taking place in teacher preparation programs across the United States; approaches to

This chapter was completed while the author was a Fellow at the Center for Advanced Study in the Behavioral Sciences. The author is grateful for support provided by the Spencer Foundation (Grant #199400132).

accreditation, licensing, induction, and ongoing professional development are being reconsidered; and a new National Board for Professional Teaching Standards (National Board) has begun to offer advanced certification for highly accomplished teachers.

In this chapter, I review these changes, their rationales, and their implications for teaching as a practice and as an aspiring profession. I describe the history of standard setting in teaching in the United States, the content and character of the new standards, and the policies that are being adopted to encourage their use. I discuss some of the controversies and questions that surround various standard-setting initiatives and policy strategies, evaluating their implications for the pursuit of both educational quality and equity for students. I conclude by suggesting areas of continued research and policy analysis that may inform the development of approaches that support teacher learning for the challenges of the 21st century.

The History of Standard Setting in Teaching

Professions generally set and enforce standards in three ways: (a) through professional accreditation of preparation programs; (b) through state licensing, which grants permission to practice; and (c) through certification, which is a professional recognition of high levels of competence (Darling-Hammond et al., 1999).[1] In virtually all professions other than teaching, candidates must graduate from an accredited professional school to sit for state licensing examinations that test their knowledge and skill. The accreditation process is meant to ensure that all preparation programs provide a reasonably common body of knowledge and structured training experiences that are comprehensive and up to date. Licensing examinations are meant to ensure that candidates have acquired the knowledge they need to practice responsibly. The tests generally include both surveys of specialized information and performance components that examine aspects of applied practice in the field: Lawyers must analyze cases and, in some states, must develop briefs or memoranda of law to address specific issues; doctors must diagnose patients through case histories and must describe the treatments they would prescribe; engineers must demonstrate that they can apply certain principles to particular design situations. Members of the professions develop these examinations through state professional standards boards.

In addition, many professions offer additional examinations that provide recognition for advanced levels of skill, such as certification for public accountants, board certification for doctors, and registration for architects. This recognition generally takes extra years of study and practice, often in a supervised internship or residency, and is based on performance tests that measure greater levels of specialized knowledge and skill. Those who have met these standards are then allowed to do certain kinds of work that other practitioners cannot. The certi-

fication standards inform the other sets of standards governing accreditation, licensing, and relicensing: They are used to ensure that professional schools incorporate new knowledge into their courses, and they guide professional development and evaluation throughout the career. Thus, these advanced standards may be viewed as an engine that propels the knowledge base of the profession. Together, standards for accreditation, licensing, and certification compose a "three-legged stool" (NCTAF, 1996) that supports quality assurance in the mature professions.

Teacher Licensing, Certification, and Accreditation

This three-legged stool is quite wobbly in teaching, a profession in which each of the quality-assurance functions is still underdeveloped. Until recently, no national body existed to establish a system of professional certification. Meanwhile, states have managed licensing and the approval of teacher education programs with the use of widely varying standards and generally weak enforcement tools.

State licensing of teachers began with the use of examinations during the late 19th century; however, this strategy changed in the early 20th century when licensing was centralized in state departments of education. Since the 1920s, most states have licensed teachers primarily on the basis of their graduation from a state-approved teacher education program. Thus, a critical check on quality that exists in other professions—a system for individual candidate assessment against some common standards of knowledge and skill—was missing for many decades in teaching. The program-approval process, generally coordinated by the state's department of education, typically assesses course offerings rather than what students actually learn in these programs and what they can do as a result.

Admitting individuals into practice on the basis of their graduation from a state-approved program was a wholesale approach to licensing. It assumed that program quality could be well defined and monitored by states, that programs would be equally effective with all of their students, and that completion of the courses or experiences mandated by the state would be sufficient to produce competent practitioners. The state approval system also assumed that markets for teachers were local: that virtually all teachers for the schools in a given state would be produced by colleges within that state, a presumption that has become increasingly untrue over time.

Because states relied until recently on graduation from teacher education programs instead of examination of candidates to grant a license, and because no independent professional certification standards existed, the nature of the approval system for teacher education programs was the critical point for quality control. Here, too, states have eschewed professional mechanisms of quality assurance for teaching. As of 2001, only four states required all of their schools of education to be pro-

---

[1] In education, the term "certification" has often been used to describe states' decisions regarding admission to practice, commonly termed licensing in other professions. Until recently, teaching has had no vehicle for advanced professional certification. Now, advanced certification for accomplished veteran teachers is granted by a National Board for Professional Teaching Standards (NBPTS; hereafter the National Board). To avoid confusion between the actions of this professional board and those of states, I use the terms licensing and certification as they are commonly used by professions: "licensing" is the term used to describe state decisions about admission to practice and "certification" is the term used to describe the actions of the National Board in certifying accomplished practice.

fessionally accredited,[2] and only about 600 of the nation's nearly 1,300 education programs had been certified as meeting the standards of the NCATE, the national accrediting body.[3] (These programs, however, produce more than two thirds of the nation's teachers.) Because accreditation is voluntary in most states, some programs that are unaccredited would likely have little difficulty meeting the NCATE standards but have had no incentive for pursuing accreditation. Many others would not meet the standards because the content, coherence, and resources of their programs are inadequate. Studies indicating that negative NCATE reviews have led to substantial changes and investments in weak education programs (e.g., Altenbaugh & Underwood, 1990) also highlight the fact that professional accreditation can be at odds with universities' desires to use education schools as revenue sources for other parts of the university.

As one indication of the gap between program practices and professional standards, the initial failure rate for programs seeking accreditation in the 3 years after NCATE strengthened its standards in 1987 was 27%. During the first 3 years of implementation, almost half of the schools reviewed could not pass the new "knowledge base" standard, which specified that schools must be able to describe the knowledge base on which their programs rested. Most of these schools have made major changes in their programs since that time, such as garnering new resources, making personnel changes, and revamping curriculum, and were successful in their second attempt at accreditation. However, NCATE upgraded its standards again in 1995 to incorporate the Interstate New Teacher Support and Assessment Consortium (INTASC) and National Board standards, and the Council introduced more ambitious plans for performance-based accreditation in the year 2000 (discussed later). This upgrade in standards means that many programs that want to secure or maintain professional accreditation will need to increase their efforts further. Unresolved financial, political, and substantive issues will determine how many programs undertake these efforts.

Most states, meanwhile, routinely approve virtually all of their teacher education programs, despite the fact that these programs offer dramatically different kinds and qualities of preparation, guaranteeing little in the way of a common knowledge base for practice (Goodlad, Soder, & Sirotnik, 1990; NCTAF, 1996; Tom, 1997). One problem with state approval of teacher education, according to some critics, is that the standards in many states have been out of touch with advances in knowledge about teaching and learning (Darling-Hammond, Wise, & Klein, 1999).

A second problem is that many state education agencies have inadequate budgetary resources and personpower to conduct the intensive program reviews that would support enforcement of high standards (Campbell, Sroufe, & Layton, 1967; David, 1994; Lusi, 1997). In state departments with few resources, reviews of programs are infrequent and perfunctory, revealing

little about the quality of experience provided by the institutions. For example, teacher education programs in some states have been approved for more than 15 years without any active external review.

A third problem is that, even when state agencies find weak programs, political forces within states make it difficult to close them down. Teacher education programs bring substantial revenue to universities and local communities, and the availability of large numbers of teaching candidates, no matter how poorly prepared, keeps salaries relatively low. As Dennison (1992) noted, "the generally minimal state-prescribed criteria remain subject to local and state political influences, economic conditions within the state, and historical conditions which make change difficult" (p. A40).

Over time, each state has developed its own set of standards for every type of program. Thus, there are literally hundreds of sets of standards for teacher preparation—some high, some low; some enforced, some not. Teachers and policymakers have criticized the standards that many states have developed as poor reflections of important teaching knowledge and skill (Conant, 1963; Feistritzer, 1994; Tom, 1997). The conventional wisdom among many veteran practitioners is that the teacher education courses they experienced were too often unhelpful to them in their practice (Kagan, 1992; Leslie & Lewis, 1990). Many teachers remember irrelevant courses taught by marginally qualified instructors. They recall that important areas of knowledge were never made available to them and that they had to learn real teaching skills in their own classroom, on their own, through trial and error (Zeichner, 1988).

Most members of the public continue to think of professional training requirements for teachers as weaker than those of other professions such as medicine, and they support much more rigorous requirements (NCATE, 1993). Meanwhile, many policymakers' suspicions have led them to create special routes into teaching that avoid teacher education and standard licensing requirements either because they believe these are unnecessary or ineffective (Darling-Hammond, 1990) or because they want to fill vacancies cheaply (Goodlad, 1990). For various reasons, then, the traditional system of teacher licensing that is based on completing specified courses in state-approved programs of study has left most practitioners, members of the public, and policymakers unconvinced that licensing standards separate out those who can teach responsibly from those who cannot.

With recent reforms of teacher education, these perceptions appear to be changing in some places. Since 1990, surveys of beginning teachers who experienced teacher education (Gray et al., 1993; Howey & Zimpher, 1993; Kentucky Institute for Education Research, 1997) have found that the majority—more than 80%—felt that they were well prepared for nearly all of the challenges of their work. Somewhat smaller proportions (60%–70%) felt prepared to deal with the needs of special education students and those with limited English proficiency (Gray et al., 1993; Howey & Zimpher, 1993). Studies report that

---

[2] Only Arkansas, New York, North Carolina, and West Virginia require all of their schools of education to be professionally accredited. Fifteen other states use national accreditation standards issued by NCATE as the basis for approving all programs.

[3] The fact that there are contested counts of how many schools, colleges, and departments of education there are is one indication of how unstable the definition of professional education program is in teaching.

veteran teachers and principals who work with teacher preparation programs, particularly 5-year programs that feature professional development schools, also perceive their young colleagues as much better prepared than they were some years earlier (Andrew & Schwab, 1995; Baker, 1993; Darling-Hammond, 1994; NCES, 1996, tables 73 and 75).

Whereas public confidence in teacher education and licensing has generally been low, a large number of studies that have compared the relative effectiveness of teachers who are fully prepared and licensed with those who are not find that teachers with greater professional education in their field and with full "certification," as it is generally called, are generally more effective in fields ranging from elementary reading to secondary mathematics, science, and even vocational education (Ashton & Crocker, 1986, 1987; Begle, 1979; Begle & Geeslin, 1972; Bledsoe, Cox, & Burnham, 1967; Darling-Hammond, 1990; Druva & Anderson, 1983; Erekson & Barr, 1985; Evertson, Hawley, & Zlotnick, 1985; Gomez & Grobe, 1990; Greenberg, 1983; Grossman, 1989; Guyton & Farokhi, 1987; Haberman, 1984; Hawk, Coble, & Swanson, 1985; Hice, 1970; LuPone, 1961; Olsen, 1985; Perkes, 1967–1968).

As weak as some preparation programs and licensing systems have been, they appear to have been better than none at all. However, demands for effectiveness in teaching are growing as are concerns about the effects of widely varying standards for teachers in different communities, states, and fields. Understanding the nature of these concerns requires a foray into the cluttered landscape of state and local teaching policies, a journey that I undertake briefly below.

A Morass of Teaching Standards

Over the past several decades, the teacher policy environment has grown extremely complex. I have discussed standards for teaching as though they were an easily definable entity, if in need of revision. For the most part, however, teacher education, accreditation, licensing, induction, on-the-job evaluation, and ongoing professional development have operated in splendid isolation from one another, using different implicit criteria for judging good teaching and different explicit procedures from one district or state to the next. Even within states, enormous variability often exists in the requirements associated with the many types of licenses, endorsements, and certifications that are issued. A wide variety of loopholes and exceptions can be found for any requirement, and all kinds of additions and changes to requirements and practices are made by a wide variety of actors. These actors include state legislatures, state departments of education, separate state boards for higher education and K–12 education, local boards of education, local school district officials, accrediting bodies for schools and colleges, and a wide variety of private commercial enterprises involved in the provision of professional development and the development of texts, curriculum materials, and tests for teachers. These parties introduce into the teaching arena implicit and explicit standards that are frequently contradictory or inconsistent with one another. It would be an oxymoron to call the

highly fragmented U.S. teacher education enterprise a "system." At least three major sources of incoherence can be found.

1. VARIABILITY IN STANDARDS FOR CANDIDATES

There is extremely wide variation in the standards to which entering teachers are held. Licensing standards are noticeably different from state to state. Some high-standards states require a college major in the subject to be taught plus intensive preparation for teaching, including well-defined studies of learning and teaching, and 15 or more weeks of student teaching. Some low-standards states require no coherent program of studies in the field to be taught, only a handful of education courses, and a few weeks of student teaching.

In Wisconsin or Minnesota, for example, a prospective high school teacher must complete a bachelor's degree that includes a full major in the subject area to be taught plus coursework covering learning theory, child and adolescent development, subject-matter teaching methods, curriculum, effective teaching strategies, uses of technology, classroom management, behavior and motivation, human relations, and the education of students with special needs. In the course of this work, the prospective teacher must complete at least 18 weeks of student teaching in Wisconsin (at least a college semester in Minnesota) under the supervision of a cooperating teacher who meets minimum standards. In Minnesota, this experience must include work in a multicultural setting and with special needs students. If a teacher were asked to teach outside the field of his or her major for part of the day, he or she must already be licensed with at least a minor in that field and could receive a temporary license in the new field only briefly while completing a major.

By contrast, in Louisiana, a prospective high school teacher could be licensed without even a minor in the field he or she plans to teach. The state does not require the teacher to have studied curriculum, teaching strategies, classroom management, uses of technology, or the needs of special education students, and only 6 weeks of student teaching are required (Darling-Hammond, 1997a; NASDTEC, 1997).

In addition to differences in the standards themselves, there are great differences in the extent to which they are enforced. Whereas some states refuse to allow districts to hire unqualified teachers, other states routinely allow the hiring of candidates who have not met their standards, even when qualified teachers are available. In Wisconsin and 11 other states, for example, no new elementary or secondary teachers were hired without a license in their field in 1994. By contrast, in Louisiana, 31% of new entrants were unlicensed and another 15% were hired on substandard licenses. At least six other states allowed 20% or more of new public school teachers to be hired without a license in their field (Darling-Hammond, 1997a, Appendix A). Because of these differences in licensing standards and enforcement, more than 80% of high school teachers of academic courses in Wisconsin and Minnesota have fully met state licensing requirements and have at least a college major in the field they teach.[4] The comparable proportion in Louisiana is only 64%. Not surprisingly, perhaps, students in Minnesota and

---

[4] Because veteran teachers are "grandfathered" in when licensing standards change, there are some older teachers who are fully licensed but were not required to have a major in their field at the time they entered the field.

Wisconsin achieve at the top of the distribution on national assessments, whereas those in Louisiana score at the bottom (Darling-Hammond, 1997a).

More than 30 states allow teachers to be hired on temporary or emergency licenses without having completed preparation or having met other licensing requirements. During the late 1980s and early 1990s, at least 50,000 emergency or substandard licenses were issued annually by states (NCTAF, 1996; NCES, 1997). Nationally, in 1994, 27% of those who were new entrants into public school teaching held no license or a substandard license in their main teaching field (Darling-Hammond, 1997a). Even the rigor of these restricted licenses varies. States like Minnesota will issue a restricted license only to a teacher who has already been fully prepared in a teaching field but who needs to complete additional coursework to enter from out of state or switch to a new field or teaching level. Such a license is good for 1 year only. Other states, like Louisiana and Texas, will issue an emergency license to a person who does not even hold a bachelor's degree and will allow the emergency license to be renewed for several years while the candidate makes little progress toward becoming licensed.

Finally, standards for teaching candidates vary with the wide range of licensing examinations enacted in 46 states during the 1980s and early 1990s. These licensing examinations, too, set very different standards of knowledge and skill in terms of content and levels of performance. Whereas a few states require examinations of subject-matter knowledge, teaching knowledge, and teaching skill and use relatively high standards for evaluating those assessments, other states require only basic skills or general knowledge tests that do not seek to measure teaching knowledge or performance. In 1999, 38 states required basic skills tests for admission to teacher education or for an initial license, 31 required tests of subject-matter knowledge, 28 required tests of pedagogical knowledge, and only 5 required assessments of applied teaching skills (NASDTEC, 2000). About half of the states involved in testing use national examinations constructed by the Educational Testing Service. Others have constructed their own or use vendors such as the National Evaluation Systems.

The nature, content, and quality of tests constructed and selected across the states vary greatly, as do their cutoff scores (Haney, Madaus, & Kreitzer, 1987; NCTAF, 1996; Strauss, 1997). Whereas other professions control the content of their licensing and certification tests, teaching tests have been largely developed by commercial testing companies or state agencies without the benefit of a formal professional body charged with determining the nature and content of the examinations. Professional input has been limited to survey respondents and advisory panels that review test categories and items. The most widely used tests have been subject to extensive criticism by researchers and practitioners for oversimplifying teaching, for paying inadequate attention to teaching content and contexts, and for displaying low validity (Andrews, Blackmon, & Mackey, 1980; Ayers & Qualls, 1979; Darling-Hammond et al., 1995; Quirk, Witten, & Weinberg, 1973). Haertel (1991) summarized the many concerns as follows:

> The teacher tests now in common use have been strenuously and justifiably criticized for their content, their format, and their impacts, as well as the virtual absence of criterion-related validity

evidence supporting their use. . . . These tests have been criticized for treating pedagogy as generic rather than subject-matter specific, for showing poor criterion-related validity or failing to address criterion-related validity altogether, for failing to measure many critical teaching skills, and for their adverse impact on minority representation in the teaching profession. (pp. 3–4)

2. VARIABILITY IN STANDARDS FOR PROGRAMS

The regulation of teacher education institutions has been subject to similar criticisms. As noted earlier, teaching, unlike other professions, does not require professional accreditation for education schools, and many state procedures for approving programs are inadequate to ensure quality. Although some states, like Minnesota, have devoted serious attention to setting and enforcing standards for teacher education programs (Darling-Hammond et al., 1999), most states have, until recently, invested few resources in the development of meaningful standards and their enforcement. It can be argued that, until quite recently, professional accreditation procedures also allowed enormous differences in quality and content across programs (Goodlad, 1990). Changes in these procedures and their outcomes are discussed further below.

Most states have relied on an input strategy for approving programs: They have specified the kinds of courses approved programs must offer, the topic areas they must address, or the amount of time they must allocate for certain activities, such as student teaching. (In rare cases, such as the ceilings on undergraduate education coursework enacted by New Jersey, Texas, and Virginia, states have also limited the amount of time that can be spent on certain things.) Because state program approval has been the primary basis for candidate licensing, some of the differences among state standards for programs were illustrated in the previous section regarding standards for candidates. Although virtually all states require programs to offer at least some courses in subject matter and in teaching methods, there is substantial variation in the number of courses or credit hours required and whether they include such areas as learning theory, child and adolescent development, curriculum development, assessment, or knowledge about special learning needs, such as the teaching of children with disabilities or of second-language learners. Clinical requirements also vary widely; in 1999, state requirements for student teaching ranged from 6 weeks in Louisiana to 18 weeks in Wisconsin (Darling-Hammond, 1997a, Appendix B; NASDTEC, 2000). The range has grown since. By 2000, at least two states required a full year of clinical experience while at least one specified no student teaching requirement at all. Clearly, a program of studies that could be easily approved in one state would fail to meet the standards in another. It should be noted, however, that in any given state, many programs far exceed the minimal requirements imposed by their state agencies, whereas others barely meet them.

Newly enacted "alternate routes," introduced in more than 40 states during the 1980s, also operate under widely divergent standards. Some are year-long postbaccalaureate models, including 5th-year master's degree programs, that have integrated theory and skills development more productively than some traditional programs. They are alternatives to the undergraduate program model that many states have required as the basis for program approval, but they meet or exceed normal licensing standards. By linking key coursework to intensively supervised student teaching internships, they provide a high-quality preparation to midcareer recruits who want to enter teaching.

Other alternate routes, however, are alternatives to the notion of licensure itself in that they dramatically lower expectations for candidates' content and pedagogical knowledge and, in many cases, shift the decision about candidate competence to the employing school districts. These models generally offer only a few weeks of training that do not include such fundamentals as learning theory, child development, and content pedagogy, and they place recruits in classrooms without a period of supervised practice (Darling-Hammond, 1992).

The amount of professional education beyond a liberal arts degree required of alternate route candidates can vary from only 9 hours in Virginia to the 45 credit hours required for a full master's degree or its equivalent in Alabama or Maryland (Darling-Hammond, 1992; Feistritzer, 1990). Even among programs that require alternate route candidates to complete all regular certification requirements, there is a stark difference between the rigorous 12-month preparation program required *before* entry in Maryland (Maryland State Department of Education, 1990) and the Texas requirement that apparently allows candidates to enter without professional preparation while earning credits toward certification at the leisurely rate of 6 hours every 5 years (Cornett, 1990). At that rate, a teacher could spend many years in the classroom before meeting the licensing requirements still on the books in most states. Proponents of these routes have rarely raised the question of what kind of teaching is made available to students during the years between entry and completion of study.

To make matters more confusing, alternate route candidates in high-standards states, such as Maryland or Connecticut, have had to meet higher selection standards and undertake a more rigorous professional preparation than either regular or alternative certification candidates in low-standards states such as New Jersey or Texas. In 1992, alternate route candidates in Connecticut and Maryland, for example, had to have a bachelor's degree with a major in the field they wish to teach and an undergraduate grade point average (GPA) of at least 3.0; they must have passed all of the same subject area, basic skills, and pedagogical tests as regular candidates; and they must have completed at least 45 hours of graduate-level coursework in education before receiving a professional certificate.[5]

By contrast, regular candidates in New Jersey and Texas often completed only 18 credit hours of professional coursework because of the legislated ceiling on undergraduate education courses, and alternative candidates completed even less study. In New Jersey, alternate route candidates took 200 contact hours of instruction. Studies found that the on-the-job supervision they are supposed to receive during their first year of teaching rarely materialized (Gray & Lynn, 1988; Smith, 1990a, 1990b, n.d.). With no grade requirement, the average GPA for

alternate route candidates fell below 3.0 in 1990 (Natriello, Zumwalt, Hansen, & Frisch, 1990). Texas requires a GPA of only 2.5 for its alternate route program, and it does not specify coursework requirements. Because candidates were initially not required to study teaching and learning, the Texas law specified that alternate route candidates could *not* be asked to pass the Texas test of pedagogical knowledge (Cornett, 1990).

Not only does the amount of preparation vary across the programs but also the nature of teaching knowledge sought (Zumwalt, 1990). For example, whereas Connecticut's alternate route program incorporates subject-matter pedagogy into its curriculum, alternatives in New Jersey, California, and Texas, like most other truncated routes, rely on generic conceptions of teaching and offer only a few days of training in methods. This training is typically organized around formulaic strategies for lesson delivery that preclude consideration of content, students, or teaching context and are not designed to support inquiry-based learning. Whereas Connecticut's alternate route incorporates educational theory and research into its training program, courses in the Los Angeles Teacher Trainee Program do not (Stoddart, 1990). Instead, the Los Angeles program explicitly emphasizes district-sanctioned procedures and teaching models—including some methods that have been criticized elsewhere as ineffective or counterproductive. Although a state evaluation found this problematic (Wright, McKibbon, & Walton, 1987), the program director saw it as a strength: "(O)ne of the side benefits (for the interns) is that they have an initial learning: one way—the way things are done in the district" (Stoddart, 1990). The delegation of the state licensing responsibility to local districts and the tolerance of practices that do not meet profession-wide standards suggests how weak the licensing structure is in teaching.

State standards for schools of education have also used very different conceptions of good teaching to guide program design and approval decisions. Compare, for example, the teaching competencies articulated in two states that sought to transform the usual input requirements into outcome-based standards for programs during the 1980s. Minnesota's standards, grounded in a view that teachers should be thoughtful decision makers, describe *knowledge* about specific disciplines to be taught, people and social organizations, cultures, human growth and development, epistemology, communication and language, scientific inquiry, and research on effective teaching and learning; *skills* associated with assessment, planning, instruction, evaluation, and social behavior management that are used to diagnose student needs and create teaching strategies appropriate to different contexts and goals; and *dispositions* toward self, toward the learner, toward teaching, and toward the profession that support continual self-evaluation, learning, and change (Minnesota Board of Teaching, 1986).

Minnesota's criteria for evaluating program outcomes are expressed in statements about what teachers should know and should be able to do, such as the following: "Teachers must be able to analyze and interpret both objective and subjective in-

---

[5] In Maryland, the professional education coursework is all completed before beginning to teach. In Connecticut, candidates complete 8 weeks of intensive training before entry (the equivalent of at least 6 credits), plus 15 hours of inservice training and intensive mentoring over the next year and a half, and they must complete 30 more credits beyond the bachelor's degree before they receive a professional certificate.

formation about students' learning characteristics, attitudes, and backgrounds, (including) levels of readiness in student learning and development, student learning style, strengths, and needs, levels and sources of student motivation. . . ." (Darling-Hammond et al., 1995, p. 172).

Instead of emphasizing teachers' abilities to make diagnostic judgments, Georgia's standards, summarized in its teacher education program evaluation standards and operationalized in the Georgia Teacher Performance Instrument, required that teachers exhibit a uniform set of teaching behaviors. Rather than consider the different goals of instruction, demands of subject matter, or needs of students, Georgia teachers were trained to implement an externally prescribed curriculum and were evaluated on their ability to do such things as "start class on time," "keep a brisk pace of instruction," "manage routines," and "write behavioral objectives."

One study found that two of the instrument's behaviors—the teacher's abilities to attend to routine tasks and to specify and select learner objectives for lessons—were significantly and negatively related to student progress in mathematics (Ellett, Capie, & Johnson, 1981). These findings, along with more general research on effective teacher planning, suggest that the competencies were based on views of teaching as too divorced from considerations of content and context to allow effective performance in the nonstandardized world of classrooms. Although the Georgia Teacher Performance Appraisal Instrument was eventually declared "arbitrary and capricious" by the courts and is no longer required, the competencies it embodied continued to be used for the approval of teacher educating institutions (Darling-Hammond et al., 1999).

Aside from the formal requirements of programs, the extent to which standards are actually applied also varies. Whereas a few states have been able to maintain resources for program reviews, many states saw great decreases in funding of their state education departments during the 1980s and 1990s, with the staffing allocated to such functions as teacher education program approval cut so sharply that onsite program reviews by panels of experts almost never occur. In some of these states, colleges have felt free to reduce their own standards for and investments in teacher education. Whatever the ostensible standards are, they are meaningless if not enforced.

3. VARIABILITY IN TEACHER EDUCATION CURRICULUM AND FACULTY

For all of the reasons described above, what teachers encounter when they try to prepare for their future profession is quite idiosyncratic to the state, college, and program in which they enroll and to the teachers with whom they study. Aside from the differences associated with varying state requirements, there are many opportunities for differences and disjunctures in the courses of study available to most future teachers. Prospective teachers take courses in the arts and sciences and in schools of education, and they spend time in schools. What they study and who teaches it vary widely. Unlike other professions in which the professional curriculum is reasonably common across institutions and has some substantive coherence, the curriculum of teacher education is often idiosyncratic to the professors who teach whatever courses are required, which are different from

place to place. These courses are distributed widely, rarely with any effort at coordination (Darling-Hammond & Ball, 1997).

Many of those who teach teachers—faculty in English or mathematics, for example—do not think of themselves as "teacher educators," and most have little preparation for the task of educating teachers. They teach their courses as they would to any college student, leaving it to the prospective teachers to integrate subject matter and pedagogical studies. Many faculty in schools of education do not think of themselves as teacher educators, either. Instead, they are specialists in subjects like sociology, psychology, or reading. They do not always feel a mandate to figure out how what they know should apply to teaching or to coordinate their work with that of other faculty who work with prospective teachers. Those who do have direct responsibility for the operation of teacher education programs often hold the lowest status and are among the least well-paid faculty on the college campus (NCES, 1997). They often have insufficient clout to effect much coordination or consideration of change in the content or methods of these widely distributed courses.

In the past decade, important structural changes have been made in some programs. In large part because of the reform efforts of groups like the Holmes Group of education deans and the National Network for Education Renewal, growing numbers of teachers are now prepared in 5- or 6-year programs of study that include a disciplinary degree at the undergraduate level, graduate level education coursework, and intensive year-long internships, often in professional development schools that seek to model state-of-the-art practice. In 1994, about 20% of newly entering teachers already possessed a master's degree, most because they graduated from such new model programs (Darling-Hammond, 1997a). Recent studies have indicated that graduates of these extended teacher education programs are rated by principals and teaching colleagues as better prepared than graduates of 4-year programs, and they are as confident and effective in their teaching as more senior colleagues. They are also significantly more likely to enter teaching and remain in the profession after several years (Andrew & Schwab, 1995; Baker, 1993; Denton & Peters, 1988; NCTAF, 1996; Shin, 1994).

Nonetheless, most prospective teachers are still prepared in 4-year programs that must juggle the competing demands of core requirements, disciplinary preparation, and pedagogical preparation within a tightly constrained period of time. Most teacher preparation programs are funded at lower levels than other departments and schools in the university (Howard, Hitz, & Baker, 1997), producing greater revenues for the education of future businessmen, lawyers, and accountants than they spend on the education of the future teachers they serve. This financial situation can join with other structural conditions to impede change. As Strauss (1997) noted:

(H)igher education faces its own financial incentives, and also has its own rigidities towards change. Colleges and universities with sizable education faculties find it difficult to alter the activities of their own highly tenured education faculties, some also unionized, to . . . ensure that those trained are able to help students achieve high learning standards. Another aspect of higher education's struggle with its schools of education involves the cross-subsidization which education schools provide for other parts of their campus. While education schools are often the intellectual orphan of a college campus, they are also often the cash-cow. . . . (p. 3)

Finally, states differ in whether they require or fund the kinds of internships routinely provided for new entrants in other professions, such as architecture, psychology, nursing, medicine, and engineering. In 1997, only nine states had induction programs that provided a structured program of mentoring for beginning teachers, including trained, state-funded mentors (Darling-Hammond, 1997a, Appendix A). These state induction programs are often tied to state assessments that provide the basis for a continuing professional license. The most highly developed statewide mentoring and assessment program, described later in this chapter, exists in Connecticut. Some local districts, such as Cincinnati, Ohio, Columbus, Ohio, Toledo, Ohio, Rochester, New York, and Seattle, Washington, have also created well-developed internship programs that continue the preparation of beginning teachers into their first year of teaching, under the guidance of master teachers (NCTAF, 1996). Altogether, about 55% of teachers with less than 5 years of experience reported in 1994 that they had received some kind of formal induction during their first year of teaching (Darling-Hammond, 1997a).

Once again, the nature and content of this early training is very different from place to place, producing very distinct conceptions of adequate teaching and teacher knowledge. Furthermore, some state approaches widely adopted in the 1980s represent views of teaching directly at odds with new standards developed by the National Board. One such approach is the Florida Performance Measurement System (FPMS) that was the basis for similar systems used to evaluate beginning teachers for licensing in Kentucky, South Carolina, North Carolina, Texas, Mississippi, Tennessee, and Virginia during the 1980s and into the 1990s (French, Hodzkom, & Kuligowski, 1990; Hazi, 1989). To reduce judgments about teaching, the FPMS relied on an observation-based behavioral tally: Observers record the frequencies of specific behaviors in two columns, one for "effective" behaviors and the other for "ineffective" behaviors. The observer does not record any other behaviors, any information about contextual factors, or any information about the behaviors of students or others in the classroom but does write any interpretive narrative.

The instrument evaluates only a limited set of generic teaching behaviors and excludes consideration of the teacher's content knowledge and treatment of subject matter; the relationship between teacher practices and student responses or outcomes; and the teacher's performance outside of the observation context, including curriculum planning, the types of assignments and feedback given to students, the quality and variety of materials used, diagnostic efforts on behalf of pupils having difficulty, the depth and breadth of content covered, the coherence among lessons or units over time, and interactions with parents and colleagues (French et al., 1990).

Furthermore, the FPMS presumes that all instruction involves teacher presentations of material in whole class situations using tightly prescribed teacher-directed routines that do not reflect recent research on learning. For example, despite research that suggests the importance of linking classroom work

to students' prior knowledge and personal experiences, the FPMS codes as "ineffective" any teacher questions that "call for personal opinion or that are answered from personal experience." The coding manual notes that "these questions may sometimes serve useful or even necessary purposes; however, they should be tallied here [in the "ineffective" column] since they do not move the class work along academically" (Florida Department of Education, 1989, p. 5b).

The FPMS instrument includes many similar statements, suggesting that beginning teachers should be trained to ignore the backgrounds of the students they teach and the implications of much research on teaching. Perhaps the most dramatic evidence of the problems of this approach is the fact that Michael Reynolds, Florida's 1986 Teacher of the Year (and a runner-up in the National Aeronautics and Space Administration's Teacher in Space program) did not pass the FPMS assessment when he was evaluated for a merit pay award. His principal and vice-principal could not find enough of the required behaviors during the laboratory lesson they observed to qualify him for merit pay. Furthermore, they had to mark him down for answering a question with a question, a practice forbidden by the FPMS, although popular with Socrates and many other fine teachers (Darling-Hammond & Sclan, 1992). Floden and Klinzing (1990) noted the outcomes of this system:

Training teachers to follow a fixed set of prescriptions discourages teachers from adapting their instruction to the particular subjects and students they are teaching. Hence, the instructional effectiveness of teachers given such training is unlikely to be at a high level. (pp. 16–17)

These examples suggest how much distance there has been between the notion of a shared set of standards that guides preparation and practice in most professions and the activities that have governed teaching.

CONSEQUENCES OF THE CURRENT NONSYSTEM

The effect of all of this variability is that teachers in the United States, unlike members of other professions, have not had access to similar preparation or to a common knowledge base about teaching and learning and have not met common standards before they are admitted to practice.

An additional effect is that the lack of a floor under the standards for candidates and programs has contributed to serious inequities in children's opportunities to learn. Stark differentials in the allocation of qualified teachers to low-income and minority students have been pronounced. Recent evidence indicates not only that student achievement is substantially determined by teachers' qualifications (for reviews, see Darling-Hammond, 1997a; NCTAF, 1996) but also that unqualified and underprepared teachers are significantly more likely to be assigned to schools serving minority and low-income students than those who are more affluent. Several studies have found that much of the differential in achievement between Black and White students, for example, is a function of the differences in the qualifications and expertise of the teachers to whom they have been assigned (Dreeben, 1987; Ferguson, 1991; Ferguson & Ladd, 1996; Sanders & Rivers, 1996).

Difficulties in Setting Standards for Teaching

Why has the occupation of teaching had such difficulty defining and enforcing standards? One reason may be that teaching has not, until recently, had a base of research evidence sufficiently well developed and widely shared to inform practice. A second reason is that, in contrast to other professions that have developed throughout the 20th century, teaching has been governed through lay political channels and government agencies—state legislatures, school boards, and departments of education—rather than professional bodies charged with articulating and enforcing standards. A third reason related to the first two, has been the political inefficacy of professional standards-setting initiatives, which have been largely ignored by those engaged in regulating teaching. This problem is, in turn, related to the dynamics of supply and demand, the sociological structure of teaching as an occupation, and widely held presumptions about the nature of teaching.

KNOWLEDGE ABOUT TEACHING

Most sociologists define professions as occupations that meet at least three conditions: (a) They possess and continually develop a body of knowledge and skill that is to be mastered by all who would call themselves members of the profession; (b) they assume responsibility for defining, transmitting, and enforcing standards of practice; and (c) they are committed to making decisions in the best interests of clients on the basis of this shared knowledge and standards of practice (Boreham, 1983; Flores & Johnston, 1983). This moral commitment, reflected in such precepts as the Hippocratic oath in medicine, is the principle that motivates a profession in its continual quest for knowledge to guide more effective practice.

At least two difficulties have been associated with the development of a common knowledge base for teaching. First, the development of useful and usable knowledge about teaching has been a long, slow process of assembling and connecting insights across many fields. These areas include, among others, the understanding of human development and learning, generally, as well as learning and development in specific domains, in cultural contexts, community circumstances, and for unique individual conditions; the nature of intelligence and performance; the effects of curricular approaches and teaching strategies for particular purposes under particular circumstances; and the possibilities for assessments that provide insights about learning and the effects of teaching.

Much has been learned in all of these areas over the past 30 years, especially as the critical importance of different contexts for learning has been acknowledged. To become useful, knowledge has had to traverse the long distance from the findings of experimental studies conducted with small numbers of subjects under controlled conditions to the real world of classrooms in which huge numbers of variables interact in unpredictable ways at all times. Codifying the "wisdom of practice" (Shulman, 1986), that is, the understanding of teaching developed by expert practitioners, has also been critical to the development of knowledge useful for practice. Tremendous strides have occurred as research from psychology, sociology, and anthropology has been combined with research on teaching, classroom

work, and school organizations to produce a greater consensus about how educators can contribute to the development of human learning and performance (Brown, 1994; Darling-Hammond, 1996; Resnick, 1987; Shulman, 1987). This growing base of knowledge is reflected in volumes of work, such as the handbooks of research on teaching (Richardson, this volume; Richardson-Koehler, 1987; Wittrock, 1986), on curriculum (Jackson, 1992), and on teacher education (Houston, Haberman, & Sikula, 1990; Reynolds, 1989; Sikula, 1996) that outline some parameters of shared knowledge for teaching.

Another problem, however, is that of knowledge diffusion. Although researchers may now have greater understanding of teaching and learning than they once did, few reliable vehicles exist for transmitting this knowledge to the field. In the United States, education knowledge has been disseminated largely through research journals and monographs read by other researchers rather than clinical journals widely read by practitioners. Practitioner journals tend to feature thin descriptions of programs and practices that provide neither research-based analyses nor sufficient detail to aid adoption or use. This shortcoming is partly because the conception of knowledge use for teaching for most of this century has been one in which research was supposed to develop generalizable principles that could be used by administrators, policymakers, textbook publishers, and test makers to *control* teaching rather than by teachers to *inform* teaching decisions and develop practices that could be responsive to the diverse students and various situations in which they worked (Darling-Hammond, 1996).

Furthermore, because education has not had common standards or well-developed, universal vehicles for accrediting professional education programs and licensing candidates, it has lacked the primary means other professions use to incorporate knowledge advances into the training of each generation of practitioners. The way in which medicine, for example, ensures that new research knowledge actually gets used is by including it on medical licensing examinations and specialty board examinations and in accreditation guidelines to which professional schools and hospitals must respond.

In education, however, teacher examinations have reflected little of what might be called a knowledge base for teaching (Darling-Hammond, 1986; Shulman, 1987). Furthermore, professional accreditation was not based on specific knowledge-related standards until 1995. Although NCATE introduced a standard in 1988 requiring that programs be able to present and defend the knowledge base underlying their efforts, the standard did not require attention to specific kinds of knowledge and skill until NCATE incorporated the INTASC standards for beginning teacher licensing into its criteria in 1995. Few programs have yet been accredited using these more rigorous expectations. Thus, although there are areas of consensus among "experts" in the field who read the same journals and attend the same conferences, this knowledge is not widely shared among practitioners.

Finally, in part because of the great disjuncts between knowledge production and use, long-standing differences in the field have existed about the nature of teaching knowledge and the goals of practice. These disputes, often tacit, are guided by different presumptions about how students learn and what effective teachers should know and do. On the one hand, the bureaucratic management of teaching has involved a quest for instructional tools and systems that can be prescribed for teacher use. Such a quest rests on the assumption that students are sufficiently standardized that they will respond in routine and predictable ways to a common stimulus and that teaching tasks are sufficiently routine that they can be proceduralized. On the other hand, a more professional conception starts from the assumption that, because students learn in different ways and at different rates, teaching must be responsive to their needs if it is to be effective. As a consequence, teachers must make decisions in nonroutine situations, using a multifaceted knowledge base applied through highly developed judgment and skill.

In the bureaucratic conception of teaching work, little rationale exists for substantial teacher education or ongoing opportunities for learning: If teaching can be routinized, teachers need only the modest training required to apply the procedures indicated by a textbook, curriculum guide, or management technique. The professional conception, however, emphasizes the *appropriateness* of teaching decisions to the goals and contexts of instruction and the needs of students. It envisions evaluation not as a discrete annual event staged to determine whether teachers adequately administer the expected procedures but as a constant feature of organizational and classroom life. It assumes that practitioners inquire continually into the usefulness of their actions and revise their plans in light of these inquiries. In this view, teachers construct knowledge about their students, classrooms, and subject matter in the course of practice, just as they use knowledge that has been developed by researchers and other teachers.

A great many decisions by actors outside the classroom determine what conceptions of teaching knowledge govern teachers' opportunities to learn both before they enter teaching and throughout their careers. These decisions are reflected in the content and character of teacher education and professional development programs that seek either to educate teachers to use wide-ranging knowledge or to train them to implement set routines; in the standards that govern licensing, teacher evaluation, and professional development; in the daily schedules that either isolate teachers or allow them to engage in collective learning and problem solving; and in the organizational structures that determine who will decide about all of the above.

THE PROBLEMS OF POLITICAL GOVERNANCE

Whereas professions typically assume responsibility for defining, transmitting, and enforcing standards of practice, teachers have historically had little or no control over most of the mechanisms that determine professional standards. In professions like medicine, nursing, architecture, accounting, and law, professional standards boards composed of expert members of the profession establish standards for education and entry. Until recently, though, such boards have been absent in teaching. Instead, in most states, authority for determining the nature of teacher preparation, the types and content of tests used for licensure, and the regulations that govern practice has resided in governmental bodies (legislatures and school boards) and in administrative agencies (state departments of education and

central offices). These authority relations have tended to produce bureaucratic rather than professional controls over teaching—controls aimed at standardizing procedures rather than at building knowledge that can be applied differentially depending on the demands of a particular subject, the social context in a specific community, or the needs of a given child.

In addition, legislatures and state agencies experience some conflict of interest in enforcing rigorous standards for entry to teaching, because they must ensure a warm body in every classroom—and often prefer to do so without boosting wages—even when they are charged with defining the minimum preparation needed to teach. As Goodlad (1990) has noted:

> The states . . . [have] found themselves with a set of internally conflicting demands: Improve quality, but guarantee a body in every public classroom. . . . Temporary and emergency certificates ease the shortage in times of undersupply; while in times of oversupply, a glut of teachers removes any rising interest in providing incentives for the improvement of quality. The call for higher salaries is muted when many of those teaching have done little to be temporarily certified, just as it is muted when there are dozens of applicants for each vacancy. (pp. 94–95)

Teacher salaries have continually lagged behind the salaries of other professions requiring similar educational qualifications (NCTAF, 1996). Consequently, "despite brief periods of surplus, there has always been a shortage of willing and qualified teachers" (Sedlak & Schlossman, 1986, p. vii). Thus, there has been a constant tension between raising standards of practice and keeping pace with the need for teachers.

Pressures to keep salaries low, to allow patronage hiring, and to preserve schools of education as "cash cows" for their universities all influence the politics of standard setting and create incentives for the status quo. In addition, lack of knowledge about what *would* make a difference for teaching has allowed the continuation of licensing, hiring, and selection systems that often miss the point. For all of these reasons, many states that rely on legislatively directed state agencies to administer their own standards have proved incapable of closing down shoddy schools of education, creating and enforcing meaningful standards of entry, or inspiring substantial changes in practice.

Educators have not yet been able to establish widely the kinds of peer review and other accountability mechanisms that would ensure that only those who meet acceptable standards of practice are admitted, graduated, licensed, hired, and retained in the profession. Because regulation of entry to practice has not been rigorous, regulation of practice itself has been extensive in many places. An extraordinary array of rules governing curriculum and testing as well as course requirements and procedures for tracking and promoting students, for organizing instruction and schooling, and for specific educational programs are promulgated by legislatures, state agencies, and lay boards of education at the federal, state, and local levels (Wise, 1979).

This micromanagement of teaching work can be predicted by the laissez-faire approach to admitting individuals to teaching. In fact, the states that have invested least in the quality of teacher preparation and have allowed the greatest unevenness in the quality of the teaching force are those that regulate practice most intensively (Darling-Hammond, 1997a, 1997b). Because the public has had no real guarantee about what teachers can be expected to know and be able to do, the felt need to regulate practice against the prospect of incompetence has created in some states and communities a highly regulated occupation that has sometimes discouraged highly talented candidates from entering and remaining (Darling-Hammond, 1984). As Sykes (1983) noted:

> Administratively mandated systems of instruction not only hinder teachers' responsiveness to students but over time discourage teachers from learning to be responsive, from developing sensitivity to individual differences, and from broadening their repertoire of approaches. Ultimately such systems become self-fulfilling prophecies: routinized instruction, and the attendant loss of autonomy, makes teaching unpalatable for bright, independent-minded college graduates and fails to stimulate the pursuit of excellence among those who do enter. Over the long run, then, the routinization of instruction tends to deprofessionalize teaching and to further discourage capable people from entering the field. (p. 120)

PRESUMPTIONS ABOUT TEACHING

The view of teaching as relatively simple, straightforward work, easily controlled by prescriptions for practice, is reinforced by the "apprenticeship of experience" adults have lived through during their years as students in schools. When some of these adults are later charged with making decisions about the regulation of teaching, they often view questions of required knowledge and skill through the lens of a former pupil rather than the lens of a trained practitioner. Just as an untrained member of a symphony orchestra's audience may see the conductor's job as merely waving a stick in time to the music, the lay observer of teaching may see the teacher's job as simply giving information and making assignments. The view that little knowledge is needed to teach contributes both to policymakers' ambivalence about standard setting in teaching and to the simplistic nature of the standards that are often established.

Furthermore, teaching's status as a feminized occupation has made reform more difficult. Apple (1987) suggested that "we have built whatever excellence we have in schools on the backs of the low-paid labor of a largely women's work force" (p. 73). In a society that continues to measure status according to compensation, teaching as a meagerly paid, predominantly female occupation has had low prestige. Until the 1960s, teaching was viewed as an "in and out" career (Lortie, 1975), with women continually entering and leaving the profession for child-rearing purposes and with many men and women staying only a short time before leaving for other pursuits. For these reasons and many others—including the public's ambivalence about education generally—investments in building, codifying, and transmitting a knowledge base for teaching have historically been small (Lortie, 1975; Sedlak & Schlossman, 1986).

As a consequence of the historical regulation of teaching, the process of codifying knowledge and establishing standards is just beginning. Of course, there is a chicken-and-egg problem that makes this enterprise problematic. Because low standards for entry into teaching have been commonplace, the resulting unevenness in the capacities of teachers has led many to perceive, accurately, that a substantial number of teachers seem unable to make sound judgments about curriculum and teaching methods on their own. As a result, prescribed teaching behaviors appear to some to be necessary and warranted. And if the prescribed structures for teaching make it appear mechanical and thoughtless, unexciting and low-skilled in nature, then any need for greater knowledge and skill may seem to have been obviated by the routinized nature of the job. Prospective entrants looking for more intellectually challenging work will be dissuaded from seeking it in the teaching profession. Whereas teaching requires a great deal of discretion and flexibility if it is to be effective, the structure of teaching jobs in bureaucratized schools presses for routine implementation of standardized procedures. This contradiction frequently places teachers in the nonprofessional position of having to treat diverse students uniformly and ineffectively. The standardized practice required for bureaucratic accountability is often malpractice if evaluated by the standards of professional accountability (Wise, 1979). Unless these conditions are changed, it will be difficult to raise standards for teaching and maintain a large pool of talented recruits.

Although the interaction of low standards and deskilled roles for teachers has slowed progress toward standard setting, the heightened demands of schools as education has ever greater influence on individual and social progress are changing both the expectations for teachers and the requirements for teacher preparation. As school reformers have stressed the need for more students to be better prepared for critical thinking and advanced disciplinary inquiry, they have also emphasized the need for teachers who themselves have these characteristics and who can do more than march students through textbooks, who can educate students for inquiry and invention and can reach students traditionally left behind. Greater knowledge about the complexities of teaching and learning confirms that there is no simple set of easily prescribed teaching behaviors that invariably add up to teaching effectiveness. "Effective" teaching behaviors vary for different subject areas and grade levels, for students at different developmental stages and with different cognitive and psychological characteristics, and for different learning outcomes. Strategies useful for provoking recall of facts and development of simple skills are different from those effective in promoting more complex learning (Darling-Hammond, Wise, & Pease, 1983; Good & Brophy, 1986). As the goals of education change from the acquisition of basic skills and facts to the development of higher order thinking and performance skills, society's conceptions of what teachers need to know and be able to do is changing as well.

Reforms of Licensing, Certification, and Accreditation

Growing concerns for school improvement and unhappiness with the results of the nonsystem described above have stimulated major changes in state licensing provisions over the past decade or so. As policymakers, practitioners, and the public have sought greater assurance that teachers are prepared for their work, states have promulgated new requirements for teacher education, licensure, and certification with substantial zeal (Darling-Hammond, 1997a; Darling-Hammond & Berry,

1988). These requirements include new course expectations, examinations, and organizational structures as well as new approaches to the content and delivery of professional development.

First-Generation Reforms

During the 1980s, state legislatures, boards of education, and departments of education became increasingly active in mandating admissions and graduation requirements for schools of education, testing requirements, and even specific course requirements. Between 1980 and 1990, at least 22 states enacted some form of testing for entry into teacher education and 15 states set minimum GPAs for entry. Fifteen states required both testing and minimum GPAs. On their own initiative or as a result of state mandate, at least 70% of teacher education programs established minimum grade requirements that must be met before a student is admitted. More than half also required that students pass a proficiency test before completing the program. During this decade, more than 40 states introduced tests for initial licensure (Darling-Hammond & Berry, 1988; Howey & Zimpher, 1993).

Although most of the tests enacted in this decade relied on fairly simplistic views of teaching, the reforms of admission standards, coupled with salary increases during the late 1980s, appear to have made a difference in the characteristics of the teaching force. In the early 1980s, following a decade of declining salaries and demand, education was one of the fields least selected by those students scoring highest on aptitude and achievement tests. College students pursuing teaching had Scholastic Aptitude Test scores and grades below the average for college students, and fewer than half had completed college preparatory coursework while in high school (Carnegie Forum, 1986; Lanier & Little, 1986; SREB, 1985; Vance & Schlechty, 1982). The defection of highly able students from teaching was most pronounced for women and minority college students (Astin, 1992; Darling-Hammond, 1984). By 1990, however, most teachers in training had completed college preparatory courses of study and scored at or above the average on college admissions tests. The college GPAs of newly qualified teachers in 1991 and 1994 were actually higher than those of other bachelor's degree recipients, with 50% earning a GPA of 3.25 or better as compared with 40% of all graduates (Gray, et al., 1993; NCES, 1997).

The new requirements, however, were not sufficiently credible or easily met to prevent many policymakers from simultaneously enacting loopholes to their states' newly enacted standards. Members of the profession, who frequently had not been involved in creating the standards, were also unpersuaded that they captured the important aspects of teaching. Many teachers felt the tests measured things that were peripheral rather than central to their core knowledge and skill. By the early 1990s, there was a growing sense that additional efforts were required to create licensing standards and systems that would be defensible and meaningful, acceptable to the profession and the public, and useful to the improvement of teaching practice. States and professional associations began to examine a variety of new approaches to licensing and program approval, including performance-based approaches that would rely more heavily on assessments of teacher knowledge and skill conducted during and after teacher education and induction.

Second-Generation Reforms

Some policymakers and educators believe that one of the most important policy strategies for improving teaching and learning is the recent development of standards by teachers themselves. In recent years, several major reports calling for the professionalization of teaching have argued that teachers must take hold of professional standard setting if teaching is to make good on the promise of competence that professions make to the public (Carnegie Forum, 1986; Holmes Group, 1986). Teacher education leaders have suggested that teachers and teacher educators ". . . must take greater control over their own destiny. A powerful place where this can be done is in standards-setting. . . . Professionals must define high standards, set rigorous expectations, and then hold peers to these standards and expectations" (Imig, 1992).

The National Commission on Teaching (1996) concluded that newly created standards for teacher education accreditation, initial licensing, and advanced certification of teachers "could become a powerful lever for change" (p. 30). The report noted:

> Of greatest priority is reaching agreement on what teachers should know and be able to do in order to teach to high standards. This standard-setting task was left unaddressed for many decades, but it has recently been accomplished by the efforts of three professional bodies that have closely aligned their work to produce standards outlining a continuum of teacher development derived directly from the expectations posed by new student standards (pp. 67–68).

Efforts currently under way to develop and implement more meaningful standards for teaching include the move toward performance-based standards for teacher licensing (INTASC, 1992); the companion efforts to develop more sophisticated and authentic assessments for teachers; and the development and integration of national standards for teacher education, licensing, and certification (Darling-Hammond et al., 1995). These national efforts are being led by the new National Board, an independent organization established in 1987 as the first professional body—comprising a majority of classroom teachers—to set standards for the advanced certification of highly accomplished teachers; by INTASC, a consortium of states working together on "National Board-compatible" licensing standards and assessments; and by NCATE, which has been strengthening standards for teacher education programs, recently incorporating the performance standards developed by INTASC.

The standards developed by the National Board, INTASC, and NCATE are linked to one another and to the new student standards developed by professional associations, such as the National Council of Teachers of Mathematics (NCTM). These initiatives incorporate knowledge about teaching and learning that supports a view of teaching as complex, contingent on students' needs and instructional goals, and reciprocal, that is, continually shaped and reshaped by students' responses to learning events. The new standards and assessments take into explicit account the teaching challenges posed by a student body that is multicultural and multilingual, that possesses multiple intelligences, and that includes diverse approaches to learning. By reflecting new subject-matter standards for students and the demands of learner diversity as well as the expectation that teachers must collaborate with colleagues and parents to succeed, the standards define teaching as a collegial, professional activity that responds to considerations of subjects and students. By examining teaching in the light of learning, they put considerations of effectiveness at the center of practice. This view contrasts with that of the recent "technicist" era of teacher training and evaluation in which teaching was seen as the implementation of set routines and formulas for behavior, unresponsive to the distinctive attributes of either clients or curriculum goals.

Another important attribute of the new standards is that they are *performance-based,* that is, they describe what teachers should know, be like, and be able to do rather than listing courses that teachers should take to be awarded a license. This shift toward performance-based standard setting is in line with the approach to licensing taken in other professions and with the changes already occurring in a number of states. This approach aims to clarify what the criteria are for a determination of competence, placing more emphasis on the abilities teachers develop than the hours they spend taking classes. Ultimately, performance-based licensing standards could enable states to permit greater innovation and diversity in how teacher education programs operate by assessing their outcomes rather than merely regulating their inputs or procedures. Well-developed assessments of candidates, if they actually measured the important attributes of teaching knowledge and skill, could open up a variety of pathways and types of preparation for entering teaching without lowering standards as current emergency licensure provisions and many alternative certification programs now do.

Performance-based licensing might also enable states to deregulate the content and structure of "traditional" teacher education programs. Many believe that transforming teacher education will require reshaping both education courses and the structure of teacher education programs. The Holmes Group, for example, urged the creation of professional development schools, school–university partnerships in which expert teachers join with university faculty to provide carefully structured practicum and internship experiences for prospective teachers (Holmes Group, 1990). Several hundred such partnerships have been launched in recent years (Darling-Hammond, 1994). These initiatives have been constrained, however, by the traditional approach to teacher licensing, which relies heavily on state prescriptions of course offerings and regulation of undergraduate teacher education programs (Goodlad, 1990).

Input regulations are unlikely to facilitate major changes in teacher education. One proposal for deregulation is for states to stipulate only the broad outlines of teacher education programs, such as the inclusion of certain areas of study (e.g., child development, methods of teaching) and program components (e.g., student teaching), without prescribing the particular courses and credit hours required in each area (Zeichner, 1993).

The possibilities for pursuing this approach are strengthened by the creation of a program for state partnerships for performance-based licensing and accreditation through NCATE that

has developed several strategies by which states can work with the Council to review and approve programs. NCATE's standards revision in 1987 aimed to ensure that teacher education programs were grounded in knowledge about teaching and learning; another revision in 1994 incorporated the model INTASC standards for what beginning teachers should know and be able to do; an initiative launched in 1997, "NCATE 2000," aims to create a performance-based system that takes into account graduates' performance in the accreditation decision. While continuing to examine what programs do in the course of preparing teachers, the system will also use performance measures ranging from education schools' internal assessments of students, including portfolios, videotapes, and performance events of various kinds, to scores on performance-based state licensing examinations that are compatible with NCATE's standards (Bradley, 1997). In addition to incorporating the INTASC standards for preservice teacher education programs, the standards for advanced programs are expected to reflect those for accomplished teaching established by the National Board.

As a result of these combined initiatives, systems of licensing and certification that directly assess what teachers know and can do are gradually replacing the traditional methods of requiring graduation from an approved program or tallying specific courses as the basis for granting program approval, a license, or credit for professional growth. Furthermore, because the three sets of standards described above are substantively connected and form a continuum of development along the career path of the teacher, they conceptualize the main dimensions along which teachers can work to improve their practice. By providing vivid descriptions of high-quality teaching in specific teaching areas, "they clarify what the profession expects its members to get better at. . . . Profession-defined standards provide the basis on which the profession can lay down its agenda and expectations for professional development and accountability" (Ingvarson, 1997, p. 1).

New Standards and Assessments

The assessments developed by the National Board and INTASC stand in contrast to first-generation approaches to teacher testing that relied primarily on multiple choice tests of basic skills and subject-matter knowledge or generic observations of teaching performance. They seek to assess teaching knowledge and skill through portfolios and performances that include authentic, complex teaching tasks as well as systematic analyses of on-the-job performance that take content and context into account. Proponents argue that such strategies may not only improve the validity of teacher assessment but also support the development of teacher education programs organized more explicitly around the attainment of important teaching abilities.

An analogue to the bodies that offer board certification in medicine, architecture, and accounting, the mission of the National Board is to "establish high and rigorous standards for what accomplished teachers should know and be able to do, and to develop and operate a national, voluntary system to assess and certify teachers who meet these standards" (NBPTS, 1989, p. 1). The National Board has organized its standards development around five major propositions, which are more fully elaborated in the standards for each of 30 areas defined by subject-matter discipline and developmental level. In brief, they are these:

1. **Teachers are committed to students and their learning.** National Board-certified teachers are dedicated to making knowledge accessible to all students. They treat students equitably, recognizing individual differences. They adjust their practice according to their observation and knowledge of their students' interests, abilities, skills, knowledge, family circumstances, and peer relationships. They understand how students develop and learn. They are aware of the influence of context and culture on behavior. They develop students' cognitive capacity and their respect for learning. Equally important, they foster students' self-esteem, motivation, character, civic responsibility and their respect for individual, cultural, religious and racial differences.

2. **Teachers know the subjects they teach and how to teach those subjects to students.** National Board-certified teachers have a rich understanding of the subject(s) they teach and appreciate how knowledge in their subject is created, organized, linked to other disciplines and applied to real-world settings. Accomplished teachers command specialized knowledge of how to convey and reveal subject matter to students. They are aware of the preconceptions and background knowledge that students typically bring to each subject and of strategies and instructional materials that can be of assistance. Their instructional repertoire allows them to create multiple paths to knowledge, and they are adept at teaching students how to pose and solve their own problems.

3. **Teachers are responsible for managing and monitoring student learning.** National Board-certified teachers create instructional settings to capture and sustain the interest of their students and to make the most effective use of time. Accomplished teachers command a range of instructional techniques, know when each is appropriate, and can implement them as needed. They know how to motivate and engage groups of students to ensure a purposeful learning environment, and how to organize instruction to allow the schools' goals for students to be met. They understand how to motivate students to learn and how to maintain their interest even in the face of temporary failure. Board-certified teachers regularly assess the progress of individual students as well as that of the class as a whole. They employ multiple methods for measuring student growth and understanding and can clearly explain student performance to parents.

4. **Teachers think systematically about their practice and learn from experience.** National Board-certified teachers exemplify the virtues they seek to inspire in students—curiosity, tolerance, honesty, fairness, respect for diversity and appreciation of cultural differences—and the capacities that are prerequisites for intellectual growth: the ability to reason and take multiple perspectives, to be creative and take risks, and to adopt an experimental and problem-solving orientation. Striving to strengthen their teaching, Board-certified teachers critically examine their practice, seek the advice of others, and draw on educational research and scholarship to expand their repertoire, deepen their knowledge, sharpen their judgment and adapt their teaching to new findings, ideas and theories.

5. **Teachers are members of learning communities.** National Board-certified teachers contribute to the effectiveness of the school by working collaboratively with other professionals on instructional policy, curriculum development and staff development. They can evaluate school progress and the allocation of school resources in light of their understanding of state and local educational objectives. They are knowledgeable about specialized school and community resources that can be engaged for their students' benefit, and are skilled at using such resources as needed. Accomplished teachers find ways to work collaboratively and creatively with parents, engaging them productively in the work of the school. (NBPTS, n.d.)

The National Board has nearly completed standards development within each of the more than 30 certification fields it has defined by developmental levels of students (early childhood, middle childhood, early adolescence, and late adolescence or young adulthood) and by subject areas to be taught (e.g., mathematics, science, English and language arts, generalist, etc.). Of significance in the National Board's propositions—and in its standards and assessments—is the extent to which the highly accomplished teachers who compose the National Board have clearly rejected previous conceptions of teaching as resting on the implementation of a few basic behaviors rather than the acquisition of a broad base of knowledge to be used strategically. In articulating standards that anticipate the appropriate use of knowledge and techniques in a variety of ways on behalf of diverse student needs, the National Board has begun to capture the complex, contingent nature of teaching. It now confronts the challenge of appropriately assessing such knowledge and skills.

This example from the standards for early adolescence English and language arts teachers provides an illustration of how the National Board articulates what highly accomplished teachers need to know and be able to do. This statement integrates understandings of learners and learning, educational goals, teaching, pedagogy, and context. Part of the discussion of "Standard I: Knowledge of Students" states:

Accomplished middle-grades English teachers create classrooms centered around students; in these classrooms all students take pride in their growing language facility and in their increasingly adventurous explorations of literature and other texts . . . While they believe all students can learn, accomplished teachers are keenly aware that not all students learn in the same way. . . . Because language acquisition builds on prior achievements and experiences, accomplished English language arts teachers make it a point to find out early in the school year who their students are as individual learners—and use this knowledge to help shape decisions in the classroom.

Practically everything about the young adolescent learner is grist for the middle grades English teacher's mill, including an awareness and appreciation of the student's cultural, linguistic and ethnic heritage, family setting, prior learning experiences, personal interests, needs and goals. In particular, knowing their students entails gaining a sense of each student's capacity to read, write, speak and listen in English and/or other languages. . . . The accomplished middle-grades English teacher complements his or her knowledge of individual students with a broad perspective on patterns of adolescent development and language acquisition. Such teachers know that children mature according to their own internal biological clocks and that a wide variation in students' developmental stages and life experiences within the same classroom is to be expected and accommodated. (NBPTS, 1993)

These discussions are further elaborated with vignettes that provide vivid descriptions of teachers enacting the standards. The vignettes illustrate how teachers draw on many kinds of knowledge—knowledge of content, of pedagogy, of curriculum goals, and of their students—when they are making decisions. Such vignettes, along with actual samples of teachers' reflections, analyses, and performances on the examinations, are used as benchmarks in the scoring process and as feedback to candidates when they receive their scores. The standards and vignettes closely resemble richly described cases that incorporate context and illuminate the teacher's capacity to transform knowledge into decisions in distinctive situations. As Shulman (1992) has argued, cases are particularly suited to teaching, because both are instances of transformation:

> [T]eaching is a form of transformation in which teachers create representations of complex ideas that connect with the constructions of their students. Case methods are a particular strategy of pedagogical transformation—a strategy for transforming more propositional forms of knowledge into narratives that motivate and educate. If, however, the knowledge base and reasoning processes of teaching (or law, medicine, or other practical domain) are themselves case-based, then the use of case methods does not require a very elaborate transformation. . . . The field is itself a body of cases linked loosely by working principles, and case methods are the most valid way of representing that structure in teaching. (p. 17)

The standards provide the working principles that reflect the knowledge base and reasoning processes used by accomplished teachers. The National Board's assessments provide a means for teachers to demonstrate not only what they do but also how they reasoned their way to each decision while using their knowledge about teaching, learning, and learners. The examinations for certifying accomplished practice use a portfolio assessment completed over several months of classroom work augmented by performance tasks completed in an assessment center. Teachers demonstrate their practices through videotapes and other evidence of their teaching, accompanied by discussions of their goals and intentions and samples of student work over time. In the portfolio and the assessment center exercises, they evaluate textbooks and teaching materials, analyze teaching events, assess student learning and needs, and defend teaching decisions on the basis of their knowledge of curriculum, students, and pedagogy.

The National Board's approach has several advantages over early attempts to look at on-the-job teaching. First, it takes a long view of the course of instruction, documenting how teaching and learning evolve over a number of weeks and attending to how the events occurring at a given moment in time (captured in videotapes, lesson plans, assignments, and samples of student work) relate to what has gone on in the weeks previous and to the particular needs of students in the class. Second, it provides a variety of ways to examine teaching in the context of students and subjects and to examine whether teachers can recognize and address important contextual considerations. These strategies for tying commentary to specific, contextualized teaching events provide examiners with information regarding the rationale for curricular and pedagogical decisions. Third, the portfolio, through the samples of individual student work over time, enables an examination of how student learning is influenced by teaching, how teachers' analyses of student work and progress influence teaching decisions and practices, and how these in turn support, or fail to support, student progress. Because teachers are asked to select the students with di-

verse approaches to learning and to display their work over time in relation to teaching actions, the teacher's ability to recognize and support different learning styles and needs is also tapped.

Teachers' abilities to assess student learning and to evaluate the effects of their own efforts also appear to be enhanced by a portfolio process that asks them to analyze their own and students' work in light of standards (Athanases, 1994). Evidence suggests that the assessments may expand not only what is *measured* about teaching but also what is *learned*. In an early pilot of portfolios in the Stanford Teacher Assessment Project, which led to the National Board's work, 89% of teachers who participated felt that the portfolio process had had some effect on their teaching. Teachers reported that they improved their practice as they pushed themselves to meet specific standards that had previously had little place in their teaching. Most frequently mentioned were teachers' approaches to the assessment of their students.

As the portfolio process continually demanded evidence of how teachers planned and adapted their instruction on the basis of individual as well as collective student needs, teachers expanded the variety of informal as well as formal assessments they used to keep track of learning, paying more attention to how individual students were doing. A corollary was the observation that teachers found themselves adjusting their instruction more frequently in response to these assessments. The processes of analysis teachers undertook often expanded their overall understanding of student learning in ways that had more far-reaching implications for their teaching. For example, one teacher described how she began to better understand students' writing development in ways that strengthened her ability to support them:

> Putting together a portfolio forced me to spend a great deal of time looking over student work (student portfolios). I was able to develop an understanding of patterns in the growth of third graders in written response to literature. This knowledge has been valuable to me this year as my students work in their literature response journals. The Assessment of Students entry had given me the opportunity to look at the responses to literature of five diverse students. This year when I began literature response journals I was more quickly aware of where the students were and how I could help them to develop their responses and thereby increase their understanding of and appreciation of literature. (Athanases, 1994, p. 431)

Teachers also noted that they continued to use practices they had developed to meet the portfolio requirements, that they now better understand how various aspects of children's development and learning interact, that they are able to integrate skills more effectively in their planning, that they are now more aware of their actions and think harder about the rationales for all of their decisions, that they are more deliberate and self-confident in approaching their teaching decisions, and that they have gained colleagues with whom to brainstorm and solve problems.

Another study of teachers' perceptions of their teaching abilities before and after completing portfolios for the National Board found that teachers reported statistically significant increases in their performance in each area assessed (planning, designing, and delivering instruction; managing the classroom;

diagnosing and evaluating student learning; using subject-matter knowledge; and participating in a learning community) (Tracz, Sienty, & Mata, 1994; Tracz et al., 1995). The teachers in this study often commented that videotaping their teaching and analyzing student work made them more aware of how to organize teaching and learning tasks more thoughtfully, how to analyze whether and how students were learning, and how to intervene and change course when necessary. Teachers repeatedly reported that they learned as much or more about teaching from their participation in the assessments as they learned from any other previous professional development experience (see also Haynes, 1995).

Typical is the account offered by Rick Wormeli, an English teacher at Herndon Middle School in Virginia, who credits the National Board certification process with changing his teaching. During the course of the assessment, his close scrutiny of his work in light of the standards caused him to integrate other subjects into his lessons, rethink how he organized reading discussion groups, and scrap the vocabulary book that taught words out of context in favor of using words from the students' work. Even after he had finished the assessment, he continued to experiment with the changes he had begun. "I can't turn it off," he noted. Shirley Bzdewka, a teacher in Dayton, New Jersey, agreed. In addition to creating a group of colleagues with whom she continues to share ideas and solve problems, she believes the assessment process deepened her approach to teaching:

> I know I was a good teacher. But . . . I am a much more deliberate teacher now. I can never, ever do anything again with my kids and not ask myself, "Why? Why am I doing this? What are the effects on my kids? What are the benefits to my kids?" It's not that I didn't care about those things before, but it's on such a conscious level now. (Bradley, 1994)

These same effects on practice are reported by beginning teachers who have experienced the National Board-compatible assessments created by the INTASC consortium (Bliss & Mazur, 1997; Pecheone & Stansbury, 1996). The INTASC standards articulate what entering teachers should know, be like, and be able to do to practice responsibly as well as to develop the kinds of deeper expertise that will eventually enable highly accomplished practice. The introduction to these model standards states:

> The National Board and INTASC are united in their view that the complex art of teaching requires performance-based standards and assessment strategies that are capable of capturing teachers' reasoned judgments and that evaluate what they can actually do in authentic teaching situations. (INTASC, 1992, p. 1)

The INTASC task force decided to begin its work by articulating standards for a common core of teaching knowledge that should be acquired by all new teachers, to be followed by additional specific standards for disciplinary areas and levels of schooling. Like the first tier of assessment for licensing in medicine, engineering, and many other professions, this "common core" is intended to outline the common principles and foundations of practice that cut across specialty areas—the knowledge of student learning and development, curriculum and teaching,

contexts and purposes that creates a set of professional understandings, abilities, and commitments that all teachers share.

Recognizing that applications of these common understandings and commitments are manifested in specific contexts—defined by students, subjects, and school levels, among others—the task force emphasized that common core standards are not analogous to "generic" or context-free teaching behaviors. The assessment of specific teaching decisions and actions must occur in varied contexts that will require differential responses. In some cases, these are grounded in the discipline being taught: Thus, subject-specific pedagogical decisions are evaluated in the context of subject-specific standards developed by INTASC committees in English language arts, mathematics, science, social studies, elementary education, special education, and the arts, with others to follow. In other cases, contextual considerations must be made part of the assessment structure and response possibilities.

Whereas INTASC used a deductive strategy for developing the overarching principles that would then guide subject-matter standards, the National Board used an inductive strategy, looking for common elements that emerged as standards in each of the specific fields were developed by committees of expert teachers. Once standards had been written in several fields, the common elements became clear; now certain shared principles are woven into the standards for each subject area. These standards closely match the core principles developed by INTASC.

The INTASC task force developed its standards by building on the work of student standards committees, the National Board, new licensing standards in a number of states (including California, Minnesota, New York, and Texas), and efforts of performance-oriented teacher education programs such as Alverno College. The resulting standards are articulated in the form of 10 principles, each of which is further elaborated in terms of the knowledge, dispositions, and performances it implies. These principles, in turn, are the basis for subject-specific standards. In summary form, the 10 principles are:

- Principle #1: The teacher understands the central concepts, tools of inquiry, and structures of the discipline(s) he or she teaches and can create learning experiences that make these aspects of subject matter meaningful for students.
- Principle #2: The teacher understands how children learn and develop and can provide learning opportunities that support their intellectual, social, and personal development.
- Principle #3: The teacher understands how students differ in their approaches to learning and creates instructional opportunities that are adapted to diverse learners.
- Principle #4: The teacher understands and uses a variety of instructional strategies to encourage students' development of critical thinking, problem solving, and performance skills.
- Principle #5: The teacher uses an understanding of individual and group motivation and behavior to create a learning environment that encourages positive social interaction, active engagement in learning, and self-motivation.
- Principle #6: The teacher uses knowledge of effective verbal, nonverbal, and media communication techniques to foster active inquiry, collaboration, and supportive interaction in the classroom.

- Principle #7: The teacher plans instruction based upon knowledge of subject matter, students, the community, and curriculum goals.
- Principle #8: The teacher understands and uses formal and informal assessment strategies to evaluate and ensure the continuous intellectual and social development of the learner.
- Principle #9: The teacher is a reflective practitioner who continually evaluates the effects of his/her choices and actions on others (students, parents, and other professionals in the learning community) and who actively seeks out opportunities to grow professionally.
- Principle #10: The teacher fosters relationships with school colleagues, parents, and agencies in the larger community to support students' learning and well-being. (INTASC, 1992)

As is true of the National Board standards, the INTASC standards explicitly acknowledge that teachers' actions or performances depend on many kinds of knowledge and on dispositions to use that knowledge and to work with others to support the learning and success of all students. The definition of each of the principles is elaborated in terms of the knowledge and dispositions upon which teachers should be prepared to make decisions and the performances that result. These principles provide the basis for evaluating evidence about the achievement of the standard, thus providing guidance for both preparation and assessment.

For example, principle #2 indicates, in part, that teachers understand how learning occurs—how students construct knowledge, acquire skills, and develop habits of mind—and can use that knowledge, along with knowledge about physical, social, emotional, moral, and cognitive development, in structuring learning opportunities. On the basis of those understandings, the teacher accesses students' thinking, prior knowledge, and experiences through discussion, observation, written reflections, and other means. He or she links new ideas to already familiar ideas and makes connections to students' experiences, providing opportunities for active engagement, manipulation, and testing of ideas and materials. The particular learning opportunities constructed and the particular actions of the teacher will vary depending on curriculum goals and on what is learned about students' experiences, prior knowledge, development, strengths, and needs. The anticipation that teaching behaviors will be contingent on these factors stands in direct contrast to older instruments for evaluating teachers that posited one unvarying set of formulaic teaching behaviors.

In addition, the standards explicitly deal with normative concerns of teaching, laying a foundation for ethical considerations in teaching. This particular standard indicates that among the dispositions that allow teachers to act on what they know about learning and development in the interests of students are an appreciation for individual variation, a respect for the diverse talents of all learners, a disposition to use student strengths as a basis for growth and errors as an opportunity for learning, and a commitment to help them develop self-confidence and competence. These dispositions are grounded both in knowledge about what motivates learners and aids skills development (e.g., building on areas of learning strength enables more effective acquisition of new skills) and in values about how children

should be treated. Such understandings derive from a knowledge base, but they extend beyond its technical boundaries into a domain concerned with the ethical use of knowledge in a process that has far-reaching consequences for students.

Zeichner (1993) noted that, while focusing on outcomes, the INTASC and National Board standards differ in important ways from earlier attempts to institute competency-based teacher education in the 1970s. Whereas the earlier efforts sought to break down teacher behaviors into tiny discrete skill bits, articulating literally hundreds of desired competencies to be individually assessed, these recent efforts are defined at a broader level, communicating a vision about what teachers should know and be able to do, and resting on expert judgments to evaluate the ways in which they demonstrate their capacity to do it. Ingvarson (1997) noted as well that these kinds of standards "go far deeper into the nature of what it means to teach well than the lists of criteria and competencies typical of most managerial models for teacher appraisal and evaluation" (p. 1).

The view of teaching articulated in the new performance-based standards demands, as the INTASC report (1992) suggested, "that teachers integrate their knowledge of subjects, students, the community and curriculum to create a bridge between learning goals and learner's lives" (p. 8). Thus, rather than fragmenting and trivializing teacher knowledge and performances, these efforts use research about practice to define the *kinds* of knowledge and understandings teachers should be able to use in an integrated fashion, not the specific minute behaviors they should exhibit on demand.

The INTASC standards call for a staged set of examinations that evaluate subject-matter knowledge and knowledge about teaching and learning in paper-and-pencil tests at the end of preservice education, and then assess applied teaching skills when the candidate is practicing under supervision during an internship or induction year through a portfolio assessment much like that of the National Board. Most states have opted to use the new Praxis examinations of subject-matter knowledge developed by the Educational Testing Service to satisfy the first of this trio of assessments. More than 15 INTASC states have banded together to construct a new Test of Teaching Knowledge to be offered as the basis for an initial teaching license before practice. The prototypes for this test include constructed response items in response to scenarios of teaching, samples of student work, and videotapes of classroom events that seek to evaluate whether prospective teachers understand the fundamentals of child development, motivation and behavior, learning theory, the identification of common learning difficulties, principles of classroom management, and strategies for assessment. For example, a candidate might watch a videotape of a classroom and be asked to evaluate specific presentation techniques or aspects of the teacher's classroom management strategies for individual, small group, or whole class work. The candidate might receive a portfolio of a child's work and, with extensive background information about the child, be asked to comment on strengths and concerns and to formulate additional questions for the parents or other teachers. The candidate might be asked to write a letter to parents explaining his or her plans for organizing the classroom work in light of curriculum goals and considerations of child or adolescent development.

During the first year or two of teaching, states are encouraged to create an internship program in which additional assessments of performance can be embedded alongside mentoring for beginners. Ten states have been working since 1995 to develop and pilot portfolio assessments that new teachers can undertake during a mentored first year of practice that will then be scored by state-trained assessors as the basis for determining whether a continuing, professional license will be issued. Tightly linked to subject-area standards, the portfolio assessment emphasizes content pedagogy along with the capacity to attend to student needs. Assessments were initially developed and piloted for middle and high school teachers in English language arts and mathematics. In 1997, development of standards and assessments in secondary school science and elementary education were launched. The portfolio assessments examine how teachers plan and guide instruction around new standards for student learning, evaluate student learning and adapt teaching accordingly, use a variety of curriculum materials, and handle problems of practice. For example, in mathematics, one assessment task requires teachers to plan an instructional unit structured around the NCTM standards of mathematical problem solving, reasoning, communication, and connections; show how they use curriculum tools including manipulatives and technology; and reflect on and revise the instruction in practice. Other tasks require teachers to analyze student work and assess learning for purposes of planning, diagnosis, feedback, and grading.

Tony Romano, a seventh-grade math teacher in Stamford, Connecticut, who was part of the pilot group for the new INTASC-based portfolio development, found this assessment process much more helpful to the development of his teaching than the generic classroom observations that were part of Connecticut's earlier induction program. Romano recalls that, after he recorded each lesson every day for 6 weeks, "I would have to reflect on what I had done and how I would change the lesson to make it better, and (answer) basic questions like: How did I meet the needs of every student?" This process posed a very different set of questions for him than a process that asked him to demonstrate specific behaviors that focused his attention on his own performance rather than the learning of the students:

> Although I was the reflective type anyway, it made me go a step further. I would have to say, okay, this is how I'm going to do it differently. I think it made more of an impact on my teaching and was more beneficial to me than just one lesson in which you state what you're going to do. . . . The process makes you think about your teaching and reflect on your teaching. And I think that's necessary to become an effective teacher.

Uses and Effects of the New Standards

In a short time, the new teaching standards have achieved a noteworthy consensus among policymakers and members of the profession: By 1997, 34 states belonged to INTASC and at least 24 had formally adopted or adapted the INTASC standards for beginning teacher licensing. Nearly 20 states were involved in developing or piloting INTASC assessments for either the preservice Test of Teaching Knowledge or the portfolio for beginning teachers. Twenty-six states and more than 70 school districts had established incentives for teachers to pursue National Board certification, including fee supports, professional devel-

opment offerings, and stipends or advancement opportunities for those achieving certification. Seventeen states had agreed to accept National Board certification as the basis for granting a license to out-of-state entrants or as the basis for granting "recertification" to experienced teachers. Eight had agreed to offer higher salaries, sometimes significantly so, to teachers successful in achieving certification. School districts like Cincinnati, Ohio, and Rochester, New York, had incorporated the National Board standards into teacher evaluation criteria, using it as one basis for recognition as a "lead teacher" who mentors others and as a basis for salary increments in a performance-based compensation schedule.

In addition, by 2000, 47 states had established partnerships with NCATE—more than double the number engaged in such partnerships 5 years earlier. These partnerships include various approaches to the use of national professional standards, ranging from the possibility of joint institutional reviews by state and NCATE teams to permission for teacher education programs to become state-approved by meeting NCATE accreditation standards. Fifteen states were using NCATE standards to approve all of their teacher education institutions, a fivefold increase over the previous 3 years. And several states were making plans to participate in NCATE's new performance-based accreditation plan that will approve institutions using data about the performance of their graduates on assessments like those developed by INTASC.

Finally, by 2000, at least 15 states had established fully independent or quasi-independent professional standards boards for teaching like those that exist in other professions. Most of these boards were created after 1990. In these states, teachers, other educators, and public members who sit on the standards board have assumed responsibility for setting standards for program approval of teacher education and for licensing. These actions lay the initial foundations for professional teaching standards that could ultimately influence practice. New boards like those in Indiana, Georgia, Kentucky, and North Carolina have adopted the continuum of teaching standards represented by NCATE, INTASC, and the National Board as a foundation for redesigning the preparation, licensing, induction, and ongoing professional development of teachers.

These actions, collectively, lay the groundwork for what Ingvarson (1997) called a standards-guided model of professional development, which would include

1. Profession-defined *teaching standards* that provide direction and milestones for professional development over the long term of a career in teaching;
2. An *infrastructure for professional learning* whose primary purpose is to enable teachers to gain the knowledge and skill embodied in the teaching standards;
3. Staged career structures and pay systems that provide *incentives and recognition* for attaining these teaching standards; and
4. A credible system of *professional certification* that is based on valid assessments of whether teachers have attained the levels of performance defined by the standards.

Although some of these components have begun to be put in place, the real effect of standards—widespread use for professional development and for making decisions about which institutions are allowed to prepare teachers, which individuals are allowed to enter teaching, and how advancement in the field will be acknowledged—has yet to occur.

Thus far, only Connecticut has a nearly fully functioning system of INTASC-based performance assessments, although several other states are moving ahead rapidly with pilots. As of October 1997, just 900 teachers had been certified by the National Board, although 6% of public school teachers (about 160,000) had participated in professional development to prepare for certification (Darling-Hammond, 1997a). Federal funds were appropriated late in 1997 to support candidate fees for the National Board, with an intention to underwrite the costs of 100,000 candidacies for National Board-certification by the year 2005. The National Board's plans for scale-up anticipate more than 100,000 National Board-certified teachers within the next decade. By 2000, more than 5,000 teachers had achieved National Board Certification.

There are reasons to believe that the new standards, as they are being implemented, could exert greater leverage on practice than program approval and licensing systems have in the past. For one thing, the standards offer a conception of teaching that is linked to student learning, and they use performance-based modes of assessment. These two features together engage teachers in activities that help them evaluate their effects on students and actively refine their practice, a much different outcome than that associated with the completion of multiple choice tests. The standards envision licensing, certification, and accreditation systems that are structured to *develop* more thoughtful teaching rather than merely to *select* candidates into or out of teaching. They do this by engaging teachers in the individual and collective analysis of teaching and its effects and in professional decision making. They offer new roles for teachers that involve them more deeply in the processes of assessment. For example, in addition to being assessed themselves, teachers

- sit on boards and committees in charge of developing and reviewing the standards and assessments;
- participate in the writing, piloting, and refinement of assessment tasks;
- analyze the practice of exemplary teachers to develop standards, tasks, benchmarks, and professional development materials aimed at helping other teachers meet the standards;
- serve as assessors for the assessments;
- act as mentors for teachers who are developing their portfolios. (Darling-Hammond et al., 1995; Delandshire, 1996)

Because these activities center around authentic tasks of teaching that are examined from the perspective of standards within the contexts of subject matter and students, they create a setting in which serious discourse about teaching can occur. Because evidence of the effects of teaching on student learning is at the core of the exercises, candidates and assessors are continually examining the nexus between teachers' actions and students' responses. Focusing on the outcomes of practice while making teaching public in this way creates the basis for developing shared norms of practice (Shulman, 1996).

Connecticut's process of implementing INTASC-based portfolios for beginning teacher licensing illuminates how these changes in teachers' roles and the role of assessment can occur.

Connecticut's licensing system is designed as much as a professional development system as a measurement activity, and educators are involved in every aspect of its development and implementation, so that these opportunities are widespread. Each assessment is developed with the assistance of a teacher in residence in the department of education; advisory committees of teachers, teacher educators, and administrators guide the development of standards and assessments; hundreds of educators have been convened to provide feedback on drafts of the standards; and many more educators have been involved in the assessments themselves, as cooperating teachers and school-based mentors who work with beginning teachers on developing their practice, as assessors who are trained to score the portfolios, and as expert teachers who convene regional support seminars to help candidates learn about the standards and the portfolio development process. Individuals involved in each of these roles are engaged in preparation that is organized around the examination of cases and the development of evidence connected to the standards.

System developers Pecheone and Stansbury (1996) explained how the standards are used in professional development settings for beginning and veteran teachers.

> The state support and assessment system must be centered around standards that apply across contexts and that embrace a variety of teaching practices. Teaching is highly contextual, however, varying with the strengths and needs of students, strengths of the teacher, and the availability of resources. The support program needs to help beginning teachers see how to apply general principles in their particular teaching contexts. The design currently being implemented in the Connecticut secondary projects begins support sessions by modeling selected principles, then having teachers discuss work they have brought (e.g., a student assignment, a videotape illustrating discourse, student work samples) in light of the principles presented.
>
> For experienced teachers who will become the assessors and support providers the reverse is true. They typically understand contextual teaching practices well. Although they are acquainted with the general principles at some level because they keep abreast of developments in their teaching specialty, they do not generally have extensive experience in either articulating the principles to others or in seeing their application across multiple contexts. An intensive training program for both assessors and mentors ensures similar understandings among individuals and gives them opportunities to articulate how these principles are applied in classrooms. (pp. 172–173)

These kinds of assessments can have far-reaching effects. By one estimate, more than 40% of Connecticut's teachers have been prepared and have served as assessors, mentors, or cooperating teachers under either the earlier beginning teacher performance assessment or the new portfolio assessments. By the year 2010, 80% of elementary teachers, and nearly as many secondary teachers, will have participated in the new assessment system as candidates, support providers, or assessors (Pecheone & Stansbury, 1996).

Creating licensing and certification systems that are deliberately constructed so as to support actively the development of teaching knowledge, skills, and dispositions is a new undertaking. This effort places greater attention on both the validity of the assessments—the extent to which they represent authentic and important tasks of teaching—and on the relationship between assessment and teacher learning. For the most part, previous testing programs were designed primarily to screen out candidates rather than to encourage better training or to induce good practice. In these new systems, decisions about what is tested and how it is tested are made as much on the basis of whether test content and methods encourage useful teacher learning and teaching practice as on the ability of tasks to rank or sort candidates. This concern for consequential and systemic validity has implications for the nature of the assessments developed and for the ways in which they are used.

Delandshire (1996), for example, argues that, to be valuable for teacher learning, assessments must be dynamic and principled rather than static and prescribed; that is, they must allow for the construction of knowledge and for diverse practices that are the result of principled action in different contexts, rather than presuming one set of unvarying behaviors. Further, she suggests that "In order for an assessment to have a continuous effect on teaching and learning, teachers must play an important role in defining and discussing their own knowledge during the assessment process" (p. 110).

The process of defining and discussing knowledge as it applies to an instance of teaching also occurs when standards are used in the study of cases, a strategy increasingly used by preservice teacher educators and teacher networks or study groups to help teachers think about and develop their practice. Cases and narratives about teaching illuminate the concerns and dilemmas of teaching. Yet to be educative, they need to be linked to broad principles of knowledge (Bliss & Mazur, 1997). Standards can provide the structure for making meaning of cases, while cases can provide the vitality that makes standards come alive. Together they can nurture the reflective dialogue, collective focus on student learning, de-privatization of practice, and shared norms and values that characterize professional communities (Ingvarson, 1997).

Bliss and Mazur (1997) found that using the INTASC standards as a basis for analyzing cases allowed preservice teachers gradually to integrate standards, theory, and actual classroom practice. With repeated opportunities to reflect on cases in this way, they moved from simple awareness of standards or critiques of teaching actions to an appreciation of principled decision making and an ability to plan approaches to or changes in their own teaching. Other researchers who have used curriculum standards in mathematics and science as a basis for case-based professional development have found that they stimulate professional dialogue and actually contribute to professional knowledge building as well as to collaborative curriculum reform (Barnett & Ramirez, 1996; Ingvarson & Marrett, 1997; Schifter & Fosnot, 1993).

Assessment systems like those of the National Board and INTASC support this kind of knowledge building as they allow teachers to construct and discuss their understandings while they continually reflect on, critique, and defend their practice. Although this approach to assessment appears to lead to a powerful kind of learning, it creates a tension between the tests' "concerns for standardization, comparability, fairness, and efficiency, on the one hand, and for engaging teachers in meaningful activities and evaluating their performances in ways that inform their practice . . ., on the other" (Delandshire, 1996, p. 111). This issue is just one of many raised by these new approaches to licensing and certification.

Challenges and Issues Associated with Standards

Although there is currently substantial political and professional support for new teacher standards, there are many knotty issues that must be resolved as these new systems are created. These issues range from technical measurement concerns and practical implementation problems to social and political issues associated with changes in the balance of power and authority in government agencies and the profession. A full treatment of these issues is beyond the scope of this chapter, but some of the more pressing concerns are identified here, along with associated areas of research.

GETTING THE STANDARDS AND ASSESSMENTS "RIGHT"

One set of issues concerns how to further develop and refine the cutting-edge technologies represented in the new standards and assessments: how to balance concerns for validity and reliability, how to develop and evaluate assessment strategies to ensure that they capture good teaching in a variety of settings and contexts, and how to refine scoring approaches to avoid biases about both individuals and pedagogies.

A key question for those concerned with the use of standards and assessments as a lever for reform is whether developers have gotten the standards and assessments "right," recognizing that there are multiple possible definitions of quality, that these may be contextually determined, and that there is always room for improvement. Despite great enthusiasm for the new assessments among teachers and others, there is as yet insufficient research to ascertain whether the assessments of INTASC and the National Board, for example, actually identify as successful those teachers who are more successful with students; whether the practices of teachers who are successful in different contexts are sufficiently similar to be equally well captured by the standards and assessments; and whether judgments made on the basis of these standards and assessments will be fair and unbiased, not creating adverse effects on the diversity of the teaching force on the basis of scoring presumptions that are unrelated to teacher effectiveness. Similarly, widely used tests like PRAXIS have been unexamined for the extent to which they will represent the conceptions of teaching embedded in new student standards and related teaching standards, such as those developed by the NCTM. Thus, in all of these cases, states are making decisions about the use of assessments for which they yet have little empirical evidence about validity and effects. Much more research on these matters is needed to continue to improve the standards and assessments so that they are as valid as possible across candidates, content areas, and contexts.

These issues, however they are resolved for the moment, must be the subject of an ongoing discussion and debate that continually reevaluates what good teaching is and revises assessment tools accordingly. For example, should teaching knowledge and skills be conceived as those understandings and abilities needed to teach in most current schools, where teachers' roles are limited largely to classroom instructional activities? Or should they be conceived as the kinds of understandings that will be needed for teachers to assume the broader roles many reform plans envision—roles as curriculum developers, peer coaches, and school-level decision makers? Should notions of "good teaching" reflected in the teacher assessments rest on traditional practices which are widespread but do not reflect state-of-the-art understandings of learning and teaching? Or should emerging notions of good teaching—such as those reflected in the standards issued by the NCTM—be favored? Should ideas about new pedagogies be accepted as the current gospel, or should a more eclectic stance prevail? Can assessments that measure "good teaching" in affluent White communities equally capture the features of "good teaching" in a variety of other communities representing different cultural, economic, and social contexts? As Sykes (1990) noted in his discussion of how one justifies knowledge claims in teaching, "There is no simple and completely fair answer to the question, 'Why should a teacher know *that*?' Tough choices must be made followed by wide consultation and sensitive implementation" (p. 19).

PREPARING TEACHERS TO MEET THE STANDARDS

There are also serious questions about how to prepare teachers for the more sophisticated practice the new standards represent. There is presently very limited knowledge of what learning opportunities—in preservice settings, induction contexts, later professional development activities, and school-based work—are associated with success in meeting the new teaching standards. As Wilson and Ball (1996) noted:

> New teacher assessments are for teacher educators what the new student assessments are for teachers. They represent the standards toward which teacher educators must aim. . . . Reformers hope that changing the process by which new teachers are licensed will in turn effect changes in how they are prepared. Less well understood, however, are the challenges this presents for teacher educators, who must devise ways of preparing beginning teachers to succeed on these performance-based assessments. (p. 122)

This challenge is made greater by the fact that reforms of schooling expand the gap "between where prospective teachers start and where they are to end up" (Wilson & Ball, 1996, p. 124). That is, what beginners know from their own schooling experience is even more likely than in the past to be dissimilar from reform visions of education and, hence, to require greater learning and unlearning on their parts. In addition, the kind of teaching for critical thinking and deep understanding envisioned by the new standards is more difficult to develop because it is more indeterminate and less susceptible to prescription. When children actually think, there is no way to predict precisely what they will uncover and what paths they will pursue.

Knowledge is just beginning to accrue regarding effective strategies for preparing beginning teachers for the kind of practice that takes account of student thinking in the pursuit of challenging subject-matter goals. There is much to learn about the efficacy and trade-offs of various tactics for building thoughtful, multidimensional practice. Wilson and Ball (1996) suggested that these tactics may include the creation and use of new images of practice through school-based work with teachers who engage in such practice; through curriculum materials like written cases, videotapes of practice, and computerized databases of linked artifacts of teaching that allow inquiries into lessons, units, teacher thinking, and student work; and through modeling the pedagogy anticipated by new standards in the teacher education program itself.

Various lines of research suggest that such strategies may be useful. Part of their value is that they capture the interactive nature of teaching, the fact that "teaching is what teachers do, say, and think *with students, concerning knowledge,* in a particular social organization of instruction" (Ball, this volume). Teaching cannot be well understood without taking all of these interactions into account, simultaneously, in practice. Thus, professional development tools are needed that allow for the study of teaching in light of these factors, not in the abstract or piece by piece.

Whereas evidence of the power of these tools for engendering more thoughtful practice is hopeful, we still do not know what combinations of teacher development opportunities and school conditions are most likely to result in high-quality teaching of the sort anticipated by the standards and, in turn, in high levels of student learning. Nor do we know which combinations of conditions will be cost effective or whether these vary according to the context, stage of teaching career, and so forth. These questions must be studied in the context of teacher development efforts that seek to create such learning opportunities and then to evaluate their effects. Finally, although there is substantial testimony to the fact that teachers learn a great deal by participating in these assessments, we do not know exactly what kind of learning takes place, under what circumstances, and how it can be harnessed to the cause of sustained professional development and widespread improvements in teaching.

It will be equally important to examine the extent to which the new standard-setting efforts are having their desired effects; that is, changing practices and enhancing knowledge across the profession. Whereas enthusiasm and apparent consensus among educational organizations are promising indicators, there is little concrete information yet collected or analyzed to demonstrate whether and how schools of education, school districts, schools, and states are changing the ways in which they educate teachers, develop and use knowledge, and pursue change. To gauge the utility of various efforts, changes in policies and programs must be monitored over time.

As the profession engages the tough work of developing more rigorous and meaningful methods of assessing teachers and preparing teachers to succeed at them, it must also confront a set of problematic social realities.

THE RECURRING DILEMMAS OF SUPPLY, STANDARDS, AND INEQUALITY

While these challenges and changes are being tackled, teaching is posed with the perennial problem it has experienced for decades: Disparities in salaries and working conditions have recreated teacher shortages in central cities and poor rural areas. And, for a variety of reasons, many state and local governments continue to lower or eliminate standards for entry rather than to create incentives that will attract an adequate supply of teachers. As a consequence, this era is developing an even more sharply bimodal teaching force than ever before. Whereas some children are gaining access to teachers who are more qualified and well prepared than in years past, a growing number of poor and minority children are being taught by teachers who are sorely unprepared for the task they face. The underpreparation of so many students/teachers poses the risk that the nation may undergo heightened inequality in opportunities to learn and in outcomes of schooling—with all of the social dangers that implies—at the very time it is crucial to prepare all students more effectively for the greater challenges they face.

A legitimate question can be raised as to whether improving standards will create or exacerbate teacher shortages and whether standards will limit access to historically underrepresented groups, as the professionalization of medicine did many years ago. Interestingly, the reverse has historically been true in teaching. As Sedlak and Schlossman (1986) found in their historical study:

> It has proved possible, time and again, to raise standards during periods of protracted shortage. Not only has the raising of standards not exacerbated teacher shortages, it may even—at least where accompanied by significant increases in teachers' salaries—have helped to alleviate them and, at the same time, enhanced popular respect for teaching as a profession. (p. 39)

During these periods of raised standards and salaries, representation of women and minorities remained stable or increased. Declines in the entrance of minority candidates to teaching occurred during the 1970s and 1980s, primarily because, as other professions previously closed to such students opened up and teaching salaries declined, able students defected from teaching in large numbers (Darling-Hammond, Pittman, & Ottinger, 1988). Disparate pass rates on teacher licensing tests were in part the result of the defection of the more academically able minority students into better-paying fields. As teaching salaries increased once again in the late 1980s and early 1990s, the numbers of minority entrants to teaching have also increased, although not to levels that mirror the growing share of children of color in the nation's schools (Darling-Hammond, 1997a).

Today, there is no absolute shortage of teachers but a shortage in particular fields and locations. In fact, the United States prepares many more teachers each year than actually enter teaching. Spot shortages occur because of inequalities in salaries and working conditions: inattention to planning and recruitment, inadequate national and regional information about vacancies, lack of reciprocity in licensing across states, and inadequate incentives for recruiting teachers to the fields and locations where they are most needed (NCTAF, 1996). In addition, with nearly 30% of new teachers leaving within 5 years of entry, especially in the most disadvantaged districts that offer fewest supports, a revolving door of candidates leads to continual pressure for hiring. States and communities that have reversed these trends have equalized resources for schools and salaries and have created proactive recruitment and induction systems with appropriate incentives and supports for teaching in high-need areas (NCTAF, 1996). A key question is whether other states and communities are willing to invest in these kinds of strategies in lieu of lowering standards for the teachers of the most vulnerable and least powerful students.

Perhaps the most critical concern regarding standards is that they represent meaningful goals for candidates and colleges to prepare for. The goal in standard setting should not be to increase the failure rates of candidates but to improve the caliber of their preparation for the real tasks of teaching. One of the most important aspects of the new standards for teaching is that, like those of other professions, they bring clarity to the pursuit of teaching skills by focusing on performance of critical teaching tasks rather than listing courses to be taken or testing arcane knowledge in forms far distant from its actual use. The fact that candidates consistently report that they learn from the new standards and that the assessments actually help them develop and refine their skills suggests that these efforts may advance the overall capacity of the profession to do its work, rather than merely rationing slots in a more constrained labor market.

POLITICS, POLICY, AND GOVERNANCE

An additional barrier to the widespread use of standards and to the solution of teacher supply problems is the decentralized, crazy-quilt nature of educational governance in the United States. The major players who would need to monitor and manage teacher supply and agree about the use of standards for accreditation, licensing, and advanced certification are balkanized. Different government agencies (legislative and executive, at least) at different levels of government (federal, state, and local) are involved in standard-setting, preparation, and employment decisions, along with a range of professional organizations (teacher associations and professional boards) and unorganized professionals. Anything that can be done in one part of the system can be easily undone in another. This situation poses major challenges to those who would undertake a consensus-building process.

Standards that really count can be uncomfortable, because they highlight shortcomings in current practice, and meeting them requires change. Thus, it is often the case that as standards are raised, loopholes are created. This situation has occurred in a number of states as they have raised licensing standards: The higher standards simultaneously gave rise to temporary or alternative routes that allowed many candidates to avoid meeting the new standards. In virtually every case, the less-prepared candidates are hired to teach the least advantaged students, thus denying them the benefits of the intended reforms. Conversely, some states have simultaneously enacted incentives and created development opportunities while raising standards, thus enhancing the quality of practice and equality of opportunity across the board (NCTAF, 1996). Similar differences in responses to the discomforts of change associated with higher standards have occurred with regard to teacher education accreditation. As NCATE has raised its standards, alternative accreditation proposals have been put forward to allow schools to continue to practice with the imprimatur of accreditation without having to meet external scrutiny against rigorous, profession-wide standards. Whereas some colleges have argued they should be able to define their own accreditation standards in terms of their current practice, others have upgraded their curriculum, faculty, and teaching to meet national professional standards where states have insisted they do so.

Reallocations of roles and resources may also create resistance to a standard-based model for inservice education (Ingvarson, 1997), because

> an attempt to build an in-service education system around professional standards would represent a fundamental shift in the balance

of authority and control over teachers' work and its evaluation. It would also change the traditional methods for allocating and distributing resources for professional development. (p. 6)

Ingvarson hypothesized that employers and universities, who have historically controlled most professional development dollars and decisions, will initially be reluctant to entrust these decisions to the profession. State agencies might also be added to the list of those who could resist allocating greater authority to the profession. For example, the Council of Chief State School Officers issued a statement in 1997 indicating the organization's lack of support for state professional standards boards that would authorize the profession to assume responsibilities for standard setting currently managed by state education departments in most states.

Some evidence suggests that such shifts are, nonetheless, beginning to occur. In addition to the creation of more state standards boards in recent years, teacher survey data show that teachers' engagement in decision making about practice and professional development has increased (Darling-Hammond, 1997a). Interestingly, teacher participation in courses offered by universities dipped sharply between 1994 and 1996, whereas participation in professional development aimed at National Board certification increased noticeably (NEA, 1997). At the same time, new kinds of professional development partnerships are being forged among universities, school districts, and professional associations that may be harbingers of a more productive, synergistic future for teachers' learning opportunities.

A final barrier is the set of political and programmatic realities that exist and hold current practice in place. These realities include a geological dig of policies that shape curriculum and teaching as well as those that influence what standards teaching programs, aspiring candidates, and veteran teachers are called upon to meet. As new policies and programs are added, few are ever discarded. These conflicting forces must be identified before they can be addressed, and then substantial organized work by many parties would be needed to challenge the inertia that maintains the status quo.

Conclusion

Recently developed professional standards for teaching hold promise for mobilizing reforms of the teaching career and helping to structure learning opportunities that reflect the complex, reciprocal nature of teaching work. Their potential value lies partly in their authenticity—their ability to capture the important interactions between teachers and students, content and contexts that influence learning. In addition, the participatory nature of the accompanying assessment systems supports knowledge development widely throughout the profession, enhancing the establishment of shared norms by making teaching public and collegial. Finally, the connection of a continuum of teaching standards to one another and to new student standards could bring some focus and coherence to a fragmented, chaotic system that currently leaves teacher learning largely to chance.

Teaching standards are not a magic bullet. They cannot by themselves solve the problems of dysfunctional school organizations, outmoded curricula, inequitable allocations of re-

sources, or lack of social supports for children and youth. Standards, too, like all other reforms, hold their own dangers. Standard setting in all professions must be vigilant against the possibility that practice could become constrained by the codification of knowledge that does not sufficiently acknowledge legitimate diversity of approaches or advances in the field, that access to practice could become overly restricted on grounds not directly related to competence, or that adequate learning opportunities for candidates to meet the standards may not emerge on an equitable basis. Although there are many dilemmas to be resolved and barriers to be overcome, the efforts thus far of educators and policymakers to confront and address these concerns leave much hope that new standards for teaching can make an important contribution to the education of educators who are prepared for the challenges of the 21st century.

REFERENCES

Altenbaugh, R. J., & Underwood, K. (1990). The evolution of normal schools. In J. L. Goodlad, R. Soder, & K. Sirotnik (Eds.), *Places where teachers are taught* (pp. 136–186). San Francisco: Jossey-Bass.

Andrew, M., & Schwab, R. L. (1995). Has reform in teacher education influenced teacher performance? An outcome assessment of graduates of eleven teacher education programs. *Action in Teacher Education 17*, 43–53.

Andrews, J. W., Blackmon, C. R., & Mackey, A. (1980). Preservice performance and the National Teacher Examinations. *Phi Delta Kappan, 6*(5), 358–359.

Apple, M. W. (1987). The De-skilling of teaching. In F. S. Bolin & J. M. Falk (Eds.), *Teacher Renewal* (pp. 59–75). New York: Teachers College Press.

Ashton, P., & Crocker, L. (1986). Does teacher certification make a difference? *Florida Journal of Teacher Education, 3,* 73–83.

Ashton, P., & Crocker, L. (1987, May–June). Systematic study of planned variations: The essential focus of teacher education reform. *Journal of Teacher Education,* 2–8.

Astin, A. W. (1992). *What matters in college? Four critical years revisited.* San Francisco: Jossey-Bass.

Athanases, S. Z. (1994). Teachers' reports of the effects of preparing portfolios of literacy instruction. *Elementary School Journal, 94*(4), 421–439.

Ayers, J. B., & Qualls, G. S. (1979). Concurrent and predictive validity of the National Teacher Examinations. *Journal of Educational Research, 73*(2), 86–92.

Baker, T. (1993). A survey of four-year and five-year program graduates and their principals. *Southeastern Regional Association of Teacher Educators Journal, 2*(2), 28–33.

Barnett, C., & Ramirez, A. (1996). Fostering critical analysis and reflection through mathematics case discussions. In J. A. Colbert, P. Desberg, & K. Trimble (Eds.), *The case for education: Contemporary approaches for using case methods* (pp. 1–13). Boston: Allyn & Bacon.

Begle, E. G. (1979). *Critical variables in mathematics education.* Washington, DC: Mathematical Association of American and National Council of Teachers of Mathematics.

Begle, E. G., & Geeslin, W. (1972). *Teacher effectiveness in mathematics instruction* (National Longitudinal Study of Mathematical Abilities Reports No. 28). Washington, DC: Mathematical Association of America and National Council of Teachers of Mathematics.

Bledsoe, J. C., Cox, J. V., & Burnham, R. (1967). *Comparison between selected characteristics and performance of provisionally and professionally certified beginning teachers in Georgia.* Washington, DC: U.S. Department of Health, Education, and Welfare.

Bliss, T., & Mazur, J. (1997, February). *How INTASC standards come alive through case studies.* Paper presented at the annual meeting of the American Association of Colleges for Teacher Education, Phoenix, AZ.

Boreham, P. (1983). Indetermination: Professional knowledge, organization, and control. *Sociological Review, 32,* 693–718.

Bradley, A. (1994, April 20). Pioneers in professionalism. *Education Week, 13,* 18–21.

Bradley, A. (1997, October 29). Accreditors shift toward performance: NCATE to stress candidate evaluation. *Education Week, 17,* 1–2.

Brown, A. L. (1994). The advancement of learning. *Educational Researcher, 23*(8), 4–12.

Campbell, R. F., Sroufe, G. E., & Layton, D. H. (1967). *Strengthening state departments of education.* Chicago: Midwestern Administration Center, The University of Chicago.

Carnegie Forum on Education and the Economy (1986). *A nation prepared: Teachers for the 21st century.* Washington, DC: Carnegie Forum on Education and the Economy, Task Force on Teaching as a Profession.

Conant, J. B. (1963). *The education of American teachers.* New York: McGraw-Hill.

Cornett, L. M. (1990). Alternate certification: State policies in the SREB states. *Peabody Journal of Education, 67*(3), 55–83.

Darling-Hammond, L. (1984). *Beyond the commission reports: The coming crisis in teaching.* Santa Monica, CA: The RAND Corporation.

Darling-Hammond, L. (1986). Teaching knowledge: How do we test it? *American Educator, 18,* 46.

Darling-Hammond, L. (1992). Teaching and knowledge: Policy issues posed by alternative certification for teachers. *Peabody Journal of Education, 67*(3), 123–154.

Darling-Hammond, L. (1994). *Professional development schools: Schools for developing a profession.* New York: Teachers College Press.

Darling-Hammond, L. (1996). The right to learn and the advancement of teaching: Research, policy, and practice for democratic education. *Educational Researcher, 25*(6), 5–17.

Darling-Hammond, L. (1997a). *Doing what matters most: Investing in quality teaching.* New York: National Commission on Teaching and America's Future.

Darling-Hammond, L. (1997b). *The right to learn.* San Francisco: Jossey-Bass.

Darling-Hammond, L. & Ball, D. L. (1997). *Teaching for high standards: What policymakers need to know and be able to do.* Paper prepared for the National Education Goals Panel, Washington, DC

Darling-Hammond, L., & Berry, B. (1988). *The evolution of teacher policy.* Santa Monica, CA: The RAND Corporation.

Darling-Hammond, L., Pittman, K. J., & Ottinger, C. (1988*). Career choices for minorities: Who will teach?* Paper prepared for the National Education Association/Chief State School Officers Task Force on Minorities in Teaching, 1988.

Darling-Hammond, L., & Sclan, E. (1992). Policy and supervision. In C. Glickman (Ed.), *Supervision in transition.* Alexandria, VA: Association for Supervision and Curriculum Development.

Darling-Hammond, L., Wise, A. E., & Klein, S. (1999). *A license to teach: Building a profession for 21st century schools.* San Francisco: Jossey-Bass.

Darling-Hammond, L., Wise, A. E., & Pease, S. (1983). Teacher evaluation in the organizational context: A review of the literature. *Review of Educational Research, 53*(3), 285–328.

David, J. L. (1994). *Transforming state agencies to support education reform.* Washington, DC: National Governors' Association.

Delandshire, G. (1996). From static and prescribed to dynamic and principled assessment of teaching. *The Elementary School Journal, 97*(2), 105–120.

Dennison, G. M. (1992) National standards in teacher preparation: A commitment to quality. *The Chronicle of Higher Education,* A40.

Denton, J. J., & Peters, W. H. (1988). *Program assessment report: Curriculum evaluation of a non-traditional program for certifying teachers.* College Station, TX: Texas A & M University.

Dreeben, R. (1987, Winter). Closing the divide: What teachers and administrators can do to help black students reach their reading potential. *American Educator, 11*(4), 28–35.

Druva, C. A., & Anderson, R. D. (1983). Science teacher characteristics by teacher behavior and by student outcome: A meta-analysis of research. *Journal of Research in Science Teaching, 20*(5), 467–479.

Ellett, C. D., Capie, W., & Johnson, C. E. (1981). *Teacher performance and elementary pupil achievement on the Georgia Criterion Referenced tests.* Athens, GA: Teacher Assessment Project, University of Georgia.

Erekson, T. L., & Barr, L. (1985). Alternative credentialing: Lessons from vocational education. *Journal of Teacher Education, 36*(3), 16–19.

Evertson, C., Hawley, W., & Zlotnick, M. (1985). Making a difference in educational quality through teacher education. *Journal of Teacher Education, 36*(3), 2–12.

Feistritzer, C. E. (1990). *Alternative teacher certification: A state-by-state analysis.* Washington, DC: National Center for Education Information.

Feistritzer, C. E. (1994). The evolution of alternative teacher certification. *Educational Forum 58,* 132–138.

Ferguson, R. F. (1991, Summer). Paying for public education: New evidence on how and why money matters. *Harvard Journal on Legislation, 28*(2), 465–498.

Ferguson, R. F., & Ladd, H. F. (1996). How and why money matters: An analysis of Alabama schools. In H. Ladd (Ed.), *Holding schools accountable* (pp. 265–298). Washington, DC: Brookings Institution.

Floden, R. E., & Klinzing, H. G. (1990). What can research on teacher thinking contribute to teacher preparation? A second opinion. *Educational Researcher, 19*(5), 15–20.

Flores, A., & Johnston, D. G. (1983). Collective responsibility and professional roles. *Ethics, 93,* 537–545.

Florida Department of Education. (1989). *Manual for coding teacher performance on the screening/summative observation instrument: Florida Performance Measurement System.* Tallahassee, FL: Author.

French, R. L., Hodzkom, D., & Kuligowski, B. (1990, April). *Teacher evaluation in SREB states. Stage I: Analysis and comparison of evaluation systems.* Paper presented at the annual meeting of the American Educational Research Association, Boston, MA.

Friedson, E. (1973). Professionalization and the organization of middle class labour in postindustrial society. In P. Halmas (Ed.), *Professionalization and social change* (Sociological Review Monograph 20). Keele, UK: University of Keele.

Gomez, D. L., & Grobe, R. P. (1990, April). *Three years of alternative certification in Dallas: Where are we?* Paper presented at the annual meeting of the American Educational Research Association, Boston, MA.

Good, T. S., & Brophy, J. E. (1986). *Educational psychology* (3rd ed.). White Plains, NY: Longman.

Goodlad, J. I. (1990). *Teachers for our nation's schools.* San Francisco: Jossey-Bass.

Goodlad, J. I, Soder, R., & Sirotnik, K. A. (1990). *Places where teachers are taught.* San Francisco: Jossey-Bass.

Gray, L., Cahalan, M., Hein, S., Litman, C., Severynse, J., Warren, S., Wisan, G., & Stowe, P. (1993). *New teachers in the job market, 1991 update.* Washington, DC: U.S. Department of Education, OERI.

Gray, D., & Lynn, D. H. (1988). *New teachers, better teachers: A report on two initiatives in New Jersey.* Washington, DC: Council for Basic Education.

Greenberg, J. D. (1983). The case for teacher education: Open and shut. *Journal of Teacher Education, 34*(4), 2–5.

Grossman, P. L. (1989). Learning to teach without teacher education. *Teachers College Record, 91*(2), 191–208.

Guyton, E., & Farokhi, E. (1987, September–October). Relationships among academic performance, basic skills, subject matter knowledge and teaching skills of teacher education graduates. *Journal of Teacher Education, 37*–42.

Haberman, M. (1984, September). *An evaluation of the rationale for required teacher education: Beginning teachers with or without teacher preparation.* Prepared for the National Commission on Excellence in Teacher Education, University of Wisconsin–Milwaukee.

Haertel, E. H. (1991). New forms of teacher assessment. In G. Grant (Ed.), *Review of research in education* (Vol. 17, pp. 3–29). Washington, DC: American Educational Research Association.

Haney, W., Madaus, G., & Kreitzer, A. (1987). Charms talismanic: Testing teachers for the improvement of American education. *Review of Research in Education, 14,* 169–238.

Hawk, P., Coble, C. R., & Swanson, M. (1985). Certification: It does matter. *Journal of Teacher Education, 36*(3), 13–15.

Haynes, D. (1995). One teacher's experience with national board assessment. *Educational Leadership, 52*(8), 58–60.

Hazi, H. M. (1989). Measurement versus supervisory judgment: The case of *Seeney v. Turlington. Journal of Curriculum and Supervision, 4*(3), 211–229.

Hice, J. E. L. (1970). The relationship between teacher characteristics and first-grade achievement. *Dissertation Abstracts International, 25*(1), 190.

Holmes Group. (1986). *Tomorrow's teachers: A report of the Holmes Group.* East Lansing, MI: Author.

Holmes Group. (1990). *Tomorrow's schools: Principles for the design of professional development schools.* East Lansing, MI: Author.

Holmes Group. (1996). *Tomorrow's schools of education.* East Lansing, MI: Author.

Houston, R., Haberman, M., & Sikula, J. (1990). *Handbook of research on teacher education.* New York: Macmillan.

Howard, R., Hitz, R., & Baker, L. (1997). *Comparative study of expenditures per student credit hour of education programs to programs of other disciplines and professions.* Missoula, MT: University of Montana.

Howey, K. R., & Zimpher, N. L. (1993). *Patterns in prospective teachers: Guides for designing preservice programs.* Columbus, OH: The Ohio State University.

Imig, D. G. (1992) *The professionalization of teaching: Relying on a professional knowledge base.* St. Louis, MO: AACTE Knowledge-Base Seminar.

Ingvarson, L. (1997). *Teaching standards: Foundations for professional development reform.* Clayton, Victoria, Australia: Monash University.

Ingvarson, L., & Marrett, M. (1997). Building professional community and supporting teachers as learners: The potential of case methods. In L. Logan & J. Sachs (Eds.), *Meeting the challenge of primary schooling for the 1990s.* London: Routledge.

Interstate New Teacher Support and Assessment Consortium (INTASC). (1992). *Model standards for beginning teacher licensing and development: A resource for state dialogue.* Washington, DC: Council for Chief State School Officers.

Jackson, P. (1992). *Handbook of research on curriculum.* New York: Macmillan.

Kagan, D. M. (1992). Professional growth among preservice and beginning teachers. *Review of Educational Research, 62*(2), 129–169.

Kentucky Institute for Education Research. (1997). *The preparation of teachers for Kentucky schools: A survey of new teachers.* Frankfort, KY: Author.

Lanier, J. E., & Little, J. W. (1986). Research on teacher education. In M. C. Wittrock (Ed.), *Handbook of research on teaching* (3rd ed., pp. 527–569). New York: Macmillan.

Leslie, C., & Lewis, S. (1990, October 1). The failure of teacher ed. *Newsweek,* 58–60.

Lortie, D. (1975). *Schoolteacher: A sociological study.* Chicago: University of Chicago Press.

LuPone, L. J. (1961). A comparison of provisionally certified and permanently certified elementary school teachers in selected school districts in New York State. *Journal of Educational Research, 55,* 53–63.

Lusi, S. F. (1997). *The role of state departments of education in complex school reform.* New York: Teachers College Press.

Maryland State Department of Education (MSDE). (1990). *Maryland's alternative programs for teacher preparation.* Baltimore: Author.

Minnesota Board of Teaching (MBOT). (1986). *Minnesota's vision for teacher education: stronger standards, new partnerships.* St. Paul, MN: Task Force on Teacher Education, Minnesota Higher Education Coordinating Board.

National Association of State Directors of Teacher Education and Certification (NASDTEC). (1996). *Manual on certification and preparation of educational personnel in the United States and Canada, 1996–97.* Dubuque, IA: Kendall-Hunt Publishing.

National Association of State Directors of Teacher Education and Certification (NASDTEC). (1997). *Manual on certification and preparation of educational personnel in the United States and Canada, 1997–98.* Dubuque, IA: Kendall-Hunt Publishing.

National Association of State Directors of Teacher Education and Certification (NASDTEC). (2000). *Manual of certification and preparation of educational personnel in the United States and Canada, 1999–2000.* Dubuque, IA: Kendall-Hunt Publishing.

National Board for Professional Teaching Standards (NBPTS). (1989). *Toward high and rigorous standards for the teaching profession.* Detroit: Author.

National Board for Professional Teaching Standards (NBPTS). (1993, April). *Early adolescence/English language arts standards.* Washington, DC: Author.

National Board for Professional Teaching Standards (NBPTS). (n.d.). *What teachers should know and be able to do.* Detroit, MI: Author.

National Center for Education Statistics (NCES). (1996). *The digest of education statistics, 1996.* Washington, DC: U.S. Department of Education.

National Center for Education Statistics (NCES). (1997). *America's teachers: Profile of a profession.* Washington, DC: U.S. Department of Education.

National Commission on Teaching and America's Future (NCTAF). (1996). *What matters most: Teaching for America's future.* New York: National Commission on Teaching and America's Future, Teachers College, Columbia University.

National Council for Accreditation of Teacher Education (NCATE). (1993). *NCATE public opinion poll.* Washington, DC: Author.

National Education Association (NEA). (1997). *Status of the American public school teacher, 1995–96.* Washington, DC: Author.

Natriello, G., Zumwalt, K., Hansen, A., & Frisch, A. (1990). *Characteristics of entering teachers in New Jersey.* Revised version of a paper presented at the 1988 annual meeting of the American Educational Research Association.

O'Day, J. A., & Smith, M. S. (1993). Systemic reform and educational opportunity. In S. H. Fuhrman (Ed.), *Coherent policy: Improving the system* (pp. 250–312). San Francisco: Jossey-Bass.

Olsen, D. G. (1985). The quality of prospective teachers: Education vs. noneducation graduates. *Journal of Teacher Education, 36*(5), 56–59.

Pecheone, R., & Stansbury, K. (1996). Connecting teacher assessment and school reform. *Elementary School Journal, 97,* 163–177.

Perkes, V. A. (1967–1968). Junior high school science teacher preparation, teaching behavior, and student achievement. *Journal of Research in Science Teaching, 6*(4), 121–126.

Quirk, T. J., Witten, B. J., & Weinberg, S. F. (1973). Review of studies of the concurrent and predictive validity of the National Teacher Examinations. *Review of Educational Research, 43,* 89–114.

Resnick, L. (1987). *Education and learning to think.* Washington, DC: National Academy Press.

Reynolds, M. (1989). *Knowledge base for the beginning teacher.* Washington, DC: American Association of Colleges for Teacher Education.

Richardson-Koehler, V. (1987). *Educator's handbook: A research perspective.* New York: Longman.

Sanders, W. L., & Rivers, J. C. (1996). *Cumulative and residual effects of teachers on future student academic achievement.* Knoxville, TN: University of Tennessee Value-Added Research and Assessment Center.

Schifter, D., & Fosnot, C. T. (1993). *Reconstructing mathematics education: Stories of teachers meeting the challenge of reform.* New York: Teachers College Press.

Sedlak, M., & Schlossman, S. (1986, November). *Who will teach? Historical perspectives on the changing appeal of teaching as a profession* (R-3472). Santa Monica, CA: The RAND Corporation.

Shin, H. S. (1994, April). *Estimating future teacher supply: An application of survival analysis.* Paper presented at the annual meeting of the American Educational Research Association, New Orleans, LA.

Shulman, L. S. (1986). Those who understand: Knowledge growth in teaching. *Educational Researcher, 15*(2), 4–14.

Shulman, L. (1987). Knowledge and teaching: Foundations of the new reform. *Harvard Educational Review, 57*(1), 1–22.

Shulman, L. (1992). Toward a pedagogy of cases. In J. Shulman (Eds.), *Case methods in teacher education* (pp. 1–29). New York: Teachers College Press.

Shulman, L. (1996). Just in case: Reflections on learning from experience. In J. Colbert, K. Trimble, & P. Desberg (Eds.), *The case for education: Contempoary approaches for using case methods* (pp. 197–217). Boston: Allyn & Bacon.

Sikula, J. (1996). *Handbook of research on teacher education.* New York: Macmillan.

Smith, J. M. (1990a, February). *School districts as teacher training institutions in the New Jersey alternate route program.* Paper presented at the annual meeting of the Eastern Educational Research Association, Clearwater, FL.

Smith, J. M. (1990b, April). *A comparative study of the state regulations for and the operation of the New Jersey provisional teacher certification program.* Paper presented at the annual meeting of the American Educational Research Association, Boston, MA.

Smith, J. M. (n.d.). *Supervision, mentoring and the "alternate route."* Mimeograph.

Southern Regional Education Board (SREB). (1985). *Access to quality undergraduate education.* Atlanta, GA: Author.

Stoddart, T. (1990). Los Angeles Unified School District intern program: Recruiting and preparing teachers for an urban context. *Peabody Journal of Education, 67*(3), 84–122.

Strauss, R. (1997). *Teacher preparation and selection in Pennsylvania* (Background paper). Harrisburg, PA: Pennsylvania State Board of Education.

Sykes, G. (1983). Public policy and the problem of teacher quality. In L. S. Shulman & G. Sykes (Ed.), *Handbook of teaching and policy* (pp. 97–125). New York: Longman.

Sykes, G. (1990). Sources of justification for knowledge claims in teaching. *The assessment of teaching: Selected topics* (pp. 11–29). Amherst, MA: National Evaluation Systems.

Tom, A. R. (1997). *Redesigning teacher education.* Albany, NY: State University of New York Press.

Tracz, S. M., Sienty, S., & Mata, S. (1994, February). *The self-reflection of teachers compiling portfolios for national certification: Work in progress.* Paper presented at the annual meeting of the American Association of Colleges for Teacher Education, Chicago.

Tracz, S. M., Sienty, S., Todorov, K., Snyder, J., Takashima, B., Pensabene, R., Olsen, B., Pauls, L., & Sork, J. (1995, April). *Improvement in teaching skills: Perspectives from National Board for Professional Teaching Standards field test network candidates.* Paper presented at the annual meeting of the American Educational Research Association, San Francisco.

Vance, V. S., & Schlechty, P. C. (1982). The distribution of academic ability in the teaching force: Policy implications. *Phi Delta Kappan, 64*(1), 22–27.

Wilson, S. M., & Ball, D. L. (1996). Helping teachers meet the standards: New challenges for teacher educators. *The Elementary School Journal, 97*(2), 121–138.

Wise, A. E. (1979). *Legislated learning.* Berkeley, CA: University of California Press.

Wittrock, M. C. (1986). *Handbook of research on teaching* (3rd ed.). New York: Macmillan.

Wright, D. P., McKibbon, M., & Walton, P. (1987). *The effectiveness of the teacher trainee program: An alternate route into teaching in California.* Sacramento: California Commission on Teacher Credentialing.

Zeichner, K. M. (1988, April) *Understanding the character and quality of the academic and professional components of teacher education.* Paper presented to the annual meeting of the American Educational Research Association, New Orleans.

Zeichner, K. M. (1993). *Reflections on the career-long preparation of teachers in Wisconsin.* Madison, WI: University of Wisconsin.

Zumwalt, K. (1991). Alternate routes to teaching: Three alternative approaches. *Journal of Teacher Education, 42*(2), 83–92.

38.

International Experiences of Teaching Reform

James Calderhead
University of Bath

Introduction

Over the past decade, the educational systems and practices within many countries have encountered an unprecedented level of reform. The curriculum, the management of schools, teacher training, teachers' conditions of work, teachers' career structures, inservice support, and the relationships of teachers and schools to the communities they serve have all come under intense scrutiny in efforts to change and to improve the quality of education. A deluge of sometimes quite radical reforms, often instigated as a part of national or state policy, has had a variety of intended and unintended effects, influencing, for example, the character of teachers' work, its status, its knowledge and skill base, and the level of satisfaction of those within the profession adapting to the rapidly changing demands made on them.

The focus and pace of these reforms have frequently been accounted for in terms of two distinct sets of social and economic pressures. On the one hand, there is dissatisfaction with the products of existing educational systems. In the West particularly, alarm has been expressed at high levels of illiteracy and innumeracy among the young, for instance, and schools have commonly been implicated in a variety of current social issues, such as unemployment, disaffection, juvenile crime, and teenage pregnancy.

Hopmann and Künzli (1997), reflecting on schooling in Sweden, but conscious of its similarities to many other Western countries, exclaimed that common social problems that are difficult to resolve have come to be blamed on schools with little thought about what it is appropriate or realistic to expect of schools, or the purposes for which schools are actually resourced:

Problems in society tend to become a focus for criticism of school. School is expected to defuse, integrate, prevent, compensate, in short to make good when problems remain unsolved elsewhere. . . . School is being sucked into a vortex of endless demands and re-

duced to a problem-solving institution at whose door the ills of society are laid. (Hopmann & Künzli, 1997, pp. 259–260)

Schools have come to be popularly viewed as ineffective and inefficient in their purposes of educating the young and preparing them to take up responsible roles within society, and reform has been seen as an essential part of social development.

On the other hand, education has also been linked, perhaps more closely than ever before, to notions of future national prosperity. International comparisons of educational attainment, for instance, in the areas of mathematics and science (e.g., IEA, 1997) have tended to emphasize the high educational achievement of Far Eastern countries, particularly the Tiger Economies, and the comparatively poor performance of many Western ones. Consequently, reforms of the educational system are viewed in some contexts as necessary to provide the skilled workforce of the future and to ensure economic development and national competitiveness. As Hargreaves (1994) noted,

With so many traditional Western economic strongholds looking increasingly precarious in the context of an expanding global marketplace, school systems and their teachers are being charged with onerous tasks of economic regeneration. They are being pushed to place more emphasis on mathematics, science and technology, to improve performance in basic skills, and to restore traditional academic standards on a par with or superior to those of competing economies. (p. 5)

Whether these concerns are real or contrived is itself a matter of debate, as is the alleged relationship between education and national prosperity or social reform. Some commentators have argued that the current obsession with educational standards in many Western countries has developed at least in part as a result of the government's loss of national economic control because of the expansion of a global economy and the consequent search by politicians for other areas in which to exert influence (Henig, 1994). Furthermore, the collapse of the Tiger

Economies in 1998, contrasted with the relative prosperity of the United States, has further thrown into question the relationship between education and economic performance. Some have also pointed to the lack of evidence for anything other than a weak relationship between educational performance standards and economic productivity (Levin, 1998) and to the complex social and economic interactions involved in attempts to solve social problems such as unemployment (Brown & Lauder, 1996).

Nevertheless, education has indisputably taken a prominent place on the political agenda, and, in many countries, educational reform has become characterized by a top-down approach, an extensive reform agenda, and a rapid implementation schedule. In the United States, a turning point was the Nation at Risk report (National Commission on Excellence in Education, 1983) that concluded that America's education system was "mediocre" and that students' performance, when compared to that in other countries, was unacceptably low. This report was followed by further reports, including the National Education Commission on Time and Learning's (1994), Prisoners of Time, and the National Education Summit (1996) of the Nation's Governors and Corporate Leaders, which have had substantial effect in promoting public awareness of alleged weaknesses in the education system. Calls for improvements in education have been a significant feature of the Clinton administration, culminating in the Goals 2000: Educate America Act, setting national targets for schools and asserting the importance of education as an investment in America's future, leading to greater individual and national prosperity. Similarly, during the 1997 general election in the United Kingdom, "Education, education, education . . . " became a popular election slogan for the Labour Party, and their first White Paper, titled *Excellence in Schools* (Department for Education and Employment [DfEE], 1997), asserted: "Education will be at the heart of government" (p. 5), and "Education is the key to creating a society which is dynamic and productive, offering opportunity and fairness to all" (p. 9).

In contrast, however, to widespread views about the nature of educational difficulties, to the common linking of educational reform to future prosperity, and to the pervasive political call to act, reform efforts themselves have frequently been ill-coordinated and often focus on simple answers to complex problems. Good (1996), commenting on educational reforms in the United States, pointed out that there seems to be little disagreement about the need for reform, but the purpose and direction of reform, and any articulation of its rational basis or the relationship of the reform to the contexts in which action has to be taken, are much less clear. He suggested that

> Simple answers are often popular because they involve less thought and thoughtful expenditures of money than do more complex alternatives. In the rush for immediate action, policymakers often overlook subtle but vital issues of context. A program that might be a partial solution in one context may turn out to be a disaster in another. (Good, 1996, p. 6)

Recent educational reform efforts have been characterized by considerable diversity, and this diversity can be categorized in numerous ways. For example, the impetus for reform has originated from different sources (government bodies, political parties, employer groups, and groups within the field of education); the focus of reform has been at different levels (national, regional, schools, or teachers); the object of reform has varied across such areas as educational management, teacher education, pedagogy, classroom organization, and curriculum; the rationales and justifications for reform have differed; the processes of reform have ranged from gradual and consultative to radical and imposed; and, not surprisingly, reform efforts have also varied substantially in terms of their effects.

An international review of recent reforms could clearly be an extremely ambitious task. Within this review, the emphasis has been placed on major reforms that aim to redefine the nature of teachers' work or the means by which they are prepared and supported. Many reform efforts, however, indirectly impinge on teachers' work through their influence on the contexts of teaching. Such reforms may affect the ways that teachers think about themselves and about teaching, may frame the practical situations and constraints within which they operate, or may affect the ways in which others look on teaching or aim to interact with, or influence, those in the profession. Teachers' practices and perspectives have been affected by a wide range of reforms. The fact that these reforms may be contradictory or place competing demands on teachers may also be responsible for confusion, stress, and disorientation in how teachers view their roles and responsibilities. For the purposes of this review, therefore, a relatively broad definition of teaching reform has necessarily been adopted.

In considering reports of recent educational reforms in a number of different countries, and in drawing on available research studies and evaluations, the focus of this chapter is on

- identifying international patterns and variations in recent major educational reform efforts,
- considering the processes involved in generating educational reforms,
- identifying the extent to which the effect of reforms on teaching has been evaluated and the role of evaluation in the processes of reform,
- raising issues about how we conceptualize the role of teachers and researchers in the reform process, and
- considering changes in the roles and responsibilities of teachers as a result of recent reforms.

Scope of Chapter

The remainder of this chapter falls into two sections. The first section provides an account of recent reforms in each of 10 different countries. These accounts identify the nature of the reforms, describe how they have been devised and implemented, and cite evidence on their effects if available. The accounts focus on major reforms that relate to the compulsory phase of schooling (usually between about the ages of 5 and 16) and that concern organizational, curricular, or professional matters that are likely to have intended or unintended effects on teachers or teaching. Although other areas of substantial reform have taken place in many countries, particularly in higher education with the rapid development of a mass higher education system, such areas are themselves substantial and would warrant a review in their own right, and, for reasons of space, they have been omitted from this review. The information was compiled by correspondents within each country, who were asked to complete a questionnaire aimed at identifying significant reforms, which have influenced teachers and their work, occurring within their educational system. These reforms included

- the governance and management of schools,
- the curriculum and assessment,
- the school or classroom organization,
- the initial training of teachers, and
- the continuing professional development of teachers.

For each area of reform, correspondents were asked to provide details of the reform, how it was being implemented and monitored, the effects of the reform on teachers and their practice, and any other significant contextual information. These responses were used to construct an overview for each country, and they were supplemented by a review of related literature concerning reform efforts over the past decade and their effects. Inevitably, it is possible to construct a fuller account for some countries than others, either because educational reform has been more prominent on the national agenda, or because the nature of the reforms and their effects have been more fully documented. Given that many of the reforms have been quite recent, it is not surprising that research on their effects tends to be quite sparse or still in progress, although that which is available frequently challenges some of the assumptions on which the reforms themselves are based. It is also the case that, in some countries, reforms have been strongly ideologically driven, and there seems to have been such unquestioning confidence in their efficacy that little research or evaluation has been commissioned.

The countries were chosen to represent a wide range of different approaches to innovation and reform, but they are not internationally representative in any way and do not include any third-world countries where priorities in reform and approaches to innovation may be of quite a different order altogether.

The second section of the review looks across the different country accounts, identifies common patterns and unique variations in the reforms themselves, considers the reform process and its effects on teachers and teaching, and identifies issues concerning the role of teachers together with trends in the ways in which teachers' future roles and practices are being shaped.

Accounts of Reform in Different Countries

England and Wales

The past decade has witnessed a period of extensive educational reform and rapid change for teachers. Reform has occurred at a number of levels throughout the educational system. Many of these reform efforts have been characterized by a devolution of decision making concerning resources and staffing to individual schools, coupled with increasing centralized control of the curriculum and teacher training; by an increase in the level of accountability demanded of local education authorities,

schools, teacher training institutions, and teachers themselves; and by an increase in the involvement of parents as consumers.

Educational reform has gradually accelerated in pace since the late 1970s, but a recent landmark was the Education Reform Act of 1988. Before 1988, all state schools were in many respects managed by local education authorities (LEAs) that had responsibility for such aspects as buildings maintenance, the recruitment of teachers, and the resourcing of schools, to the inservice training of teachers and the provision of support services. The 1988 Act, however, greatly weakened the role of the LEAs, because it was required that funds be devolved to schools on a formula basis, with schools being placed in control of "buying back" central services from the LEAs as required.

Schools were also encouraged to opt out of LEA control altogether to become grant-maintained schools and to be funded directly from central government at a higher rate to compensate for the loss of LEA services; they would then be free to contract from whatever source they please. Some grant-maintained schools have been awarded additional grants to develop particular specializations such as modern languages or technology. Several city technology colleges have also been established, jointly funded by central government and some industrial sponsorship, catering to 11- to 18-year-olds, with a special emphasis on science and technology.

In all cases, however, schools have come to be required to manage their own financial affairs. This requirement has involved changes in the roles of headteachers, emphasizing their responsibilities as chief executive rather than as academic and professional leader. The introduction of local decision making on school finances has also resulted in several staffing changes—more short-term contracts for teaching positions, an increase in student-staff ratios, and, in primary schools, an increasing use of support staff to undertake teaching and teaching-related duties—as schools act to protect their financial interests (Bullock & Thomas, 1997).

The responsibility for both the financial and academic control of schools does not legally rest, however, with the headteacher. The Act requires schools to be managed by governing bodies, consisting mostly of representatives from the local community. In effect, this requirement often means that headteachers manage the school, consulting the governing body on major matters of policy and keeping them informed of day-to-day management matters. This situation is not always the case, however, and there are examples of governing bodies taking on a more directive role in the management of schools. It has also been argued that schools can be advantaged or disadvantaged by the pool of people available within a community from whom the school can seek support (Bullock & Thomas, 1997; Earley, 1994). Some areas, for instance, may have a preponderance of supportive parents who can contribute managerial and financial expertise to their governing role or who possess sufficient knowledge and confidence in school affairs that they can offer various means of support in the local community; in other areas, such expertise may be nonexistent.

The level of accountability demanded of schools has increased substantially and has taken three main forms. The first level concerns information and entitlements. Schools are required to publish an annual prospectus, providing information to prospective parents about the school, its curricular provision, and the performances of its students in public examinations in the past year. Central government also publishes a Parent's Charter that specifies what parents and their children can expect from local schools and courses of action open to them if they are dissatisfied.

The second level of accountability concerns the inspection of schools. Approximately every 4 years, a school is subject to scrutiny by a team of external inspectors who visit the school; observe lessons; talk to staff members, children, and parents; and produce a report on the quality of teaching and management within the school. This report is publicly accessible and is available as a published report and through the Internet. Recently, the framework for school inspections was adapted to include the identification of teachers judged by inspectors to be either poorly performing or to be exceptionally good; inspectors being required to report these performances to the headteacher. Inspectors are also required to judge the quality of teaching of newly qualified teachers, using a standard rating scale, and to note the institutions in which they trained. This latter measure is to be used as an indicator of the effectiveness of teacher training institutions.

The third level of accountability concerns testing and the publication of test results as school performance indicators. In secondary schools, public examinations taken at the ages of 16 and 18 years are published annually in the national press in the form of school performance tables. In addition, standard assessment tests are given to all children across the core curriculum at the ages of 7, 11, and 14, and the information on 11-year-olds and 14-year-olds is again published as school performance tables. This publication of information on schools' performance together with schools' own prospectuses is intended to enable parents and children to exercise choice in their selection of schools. Because funding is allocated to schools largely on the basis of student numbers, this process has inevitably increased competition and has led to some "sink schools" where shrinking numbers and consequent reductions in finances have resulted in the school heading into an inescapable spiral of decline.

More directly, and perhaps more profoundly affecting the work of teachers, have been the reforms concerning the curriculum, school organization, and teacher education. The 1988 Education Reform Act established a national curriculum covering three core subjects (English, mathematics, and science) and six foundation subjects (history, geography, design technology, art, music, and physical education) to be studied during the years of compulsory schooling. The national curriculum in its original form was highly prescriptive in terms of detailed content and was found by teachers to be virtually unmanageable within the time and resource constraints normally operating. An extensive review of this curriculum in 1993 led to a slimming down of the mandatory content, especially in science and the foundation subjects in the primary-age range (Dearing, 1993). The effects of the introduction of the national curriculum were probably felt more strongly in primary schools. The strong subject focus of the curriculum and its initial breadth and comprehensiveness meant that teachers had to spend large amounts of time planning and assessing within the different subject areas. Interestingly, recent studies of primary schools have attributed an increase in collaborative work among teachers, particularly

the sharing of subject expertise, to the effect of the national curriculum (Pollard, Broadfoot, Croll, Osborn, & Abbott, 1994).

A further organizational change developing at the same time, which strongly affected teachers, was the mainstreaming of children with special educational needs. Rather than being segregated in special schools or units, a policy of admitting children with special needs to ordinary schools was introduced (DES, 1981). Additional financial resources were allocated to schools to support this change, and these resources were often used to provide either specialist teacher support or teacher assistants. The funding provided, however, has frequently been reported by schools to be inadequate, resulting in additional pressures on teachers (Bines, 1995; Lee, 1992). A code of practice introduced in 1994 placed much of the responsibility for the assessment of special needs and the arrangement of appropriate educational provision on the teacher, supported as necessary by the school's special educational needs coordinator (Department for Education [DfE], 1994), usually a teacher with a particular interest in special needs who has undertaken some inservice training in the field and who may be allocated some time within the school day to work with other teachers.

While teachers have generally been left to decide on the teaching methods appropriate for the children and context in which they work, there have been exceptions in which prescriptions are made from central agencies. A government-sponsored inquiry into teaching methods in primary schools (Alexander, Rose, & Woodhead, 1992), for example, was critical of the quality of teaching and learning in project work and recommended the inclusion of more whole-class teaching in teachers' everyday instructional repertoire. The report, initially intended as a discussion document, became popularly interpreted as a rebuke for progressive primary teachers who, it was argued, had been too easily persuaded by the child-centered rhetoric of the 1960s (Alexander, 1997). More recently, there has been a trend for government agencies to claim that it is well known which teaching approaches and strategies "work" and to make clear prescriptions for teachers' practice, particularly in the areas of literacy and numeracy.

Accompanying the reforms of school management and the curriculum have been radical changes to the nature of teacher education. In 1992, the Department for Education introduced regulations that required all existing teacher training to be delivered by a partnership between teacher training institutions and schools, and it also became a requirement that the former fund schools for their contribution to the new courses. In addition, alternative routes to obtaining qualified teacher status were introduced to enable mature students with at least 2 years of higher education experience to train on the job; their training program is tailored to their own specific needs and is coordinated and assessed by their employer.

The school-centered, initial teacher training (SCITT) scheme was introduced in 1993 to encourage schools or consortia of schools to provide their own courses of initial training, drawing support from LEAs or higher education institutions where appropriate. SCITTs are funded directly from the Teacher Training Agency (TTA) that was established by central government in 1993 to deal with the funding of all teacher training. A national curriculum for teacher training has also been established by the TTA with a clear list of competencies to be attained by successful students (TTA, 1997), and a career entry profile has been introduced that identifies and records individual student teachers' strengths and weaknesses with the intention that this information will help the new teacher's first employer to provide appropriate support in their first year of teaching.

The adherence to TTA curriculum and assessment requirements is monitored by the Office for Standards in Education (OFSTED) that regularly inspects all teacher training provision. The TTA and OFSTED together exercise a powerful control over teacher education in that noncompliance with TTA requirements can result in the withdrawal of funding from an institution. Not surprisingly, a school-based approach to teacher training has led to additional demands being placed on teachers, who are required to offer much higher levels of support to student teachers than previously and to contribute to other aspects of course planning, teaching, and assessment. It has frequently been argued that the level of resourcing provided to schools (and to initial teacher training overall) is inadequate, and the successful functioning of school-based courses depends highly on the goodwill and dedication of the teachers involved (Whitehead, Menter, & Stainton, 1996).

Continuing professional development has undergone substantial reform. Whereas funds for the inservice education of teachers were in the past mostly directed to LEAs and higher education institutions, with the local management of schools, these funds became increasingly allocated to schools themselves, which then had the option of purchasing inservice education wherever appropriate. This market-led approach to the continuing professional development of teachers places the onus on schools to identify the inservice needs of their teachers and to plan ways of meeting them. It has been argued that whereas some schools carry out such procedures very effectively, integrating inservice training with the development of individual teachers and the school, many schools are merely reactive to external provision or have cut back on external sources of inservice training, assigning it less prominence among the other competing demands for time and resources (Harland, Kinder, & Keys, 1993; Wright & Bottery, 1996).

The TTA has recently introduced accreditation for a number of inservice courses for teachers, focusing on preparation for headship and subject leadership. It has also been proposed to introduce a grade of Advanced Skills Teacher, recognizing and rewarding those teachers possessing high-level competencies in teaching, and also to introduce a standardized training for special educational needs coordinators. The TTA proposals aim to introduce more of a career structure to the teaching profession with clearly defined competencies that mark out different levels and roles. The fact that there is low morale within the profession and there is a looming crisis in recruitment has focused attention not only on how the quality of teaching and teacher training might be improved but also on how teaching can be made more appealing to attract and retain well-qualified staff. Financial incentives have been introduced to attract more science and mathematics graduates into secondary teaching. A national advertising campaign, aimed at the late teens and early 20s age group, has attempted to promote the image of teaching by including well-known media personalities recalling their good teachers and acknowledging the influence they had on their lives.

Concerns for the image of teaching are evident in the new Labour government's first white paper that focuses on further reform in education. The paper aims to improve the status of teaching by stressing its social significance and highlighting the need for greater public recognition. The main focus of the paper, however, is to improve standards in schools, particularly those of literacy and numeracy at the primary level, with proposals to adopt a zero tolerance of underperforming schools. When schools are consistently underperforming, it is suggested that they should be closed and reestablished with new management and possibly new staff. A more recent proposal has been to establish educational action zones, where businesses will be invited to take over the management of groups of underperforming schools, either replacing or working in partnership with local education authorities, providing a range of new expertise that, it is claimed, will lead to improved school management and higher standards.

Linked to staff development has been the introduction of teacher appraisal. School teacher appraisal was introduced as part of the 1986 Education Act. It was initially piloted in a few local education authorities. Procedures were later formalized (DES, 1991), and all teachers and headteachers were to be appraised between 1992 and 1994, the process being repeated on a 2-year cycle. The purposes of appraisal were stated to be twofold: "to assist (a) school teachers in their professional development and career planning; and (b) those responsible for taking decisions about the management of school teachers" (DES, 1991, p. 1). Local education authorities were responsible for training staff to undertake the process. It was intended that appraisal would be linked to the objectives of the school and that schools would develop their own procedures to link appraisal, staff development, and school development planning. For teachers, the process includes self-appraisal, classroom observation, the collection of other relevant data, an appraisal interview, target setting for future development, and a follow-up review.

Evaluations of the appraisal process (Barber, Evans, & Johnson, 1995; Wragg, Wikeley, Wragg, & Haynes, 1996) suggested that, although many teachers were initially suspicious of it, the majority became broadly positive about the benefits of appraisal after they had experienced it. Both appraisers and appraisees reported that they learned about classroom practice as a result of the process and that it enhanced their sense of professionalism. Classroom observation was reported to be particularly valuable if it was focused and analytical and discussed in a sensitive manner. Barber et al. (1995) found, in a survey of 18 schools, that appraisal outcomes would often be used to inform school decisions on the use of inservice training funds, but it was rare for schools to take a more integrated view of appraisal, staff development, and school improvement. The main constraints on the process concerned the large investment of time and energy needed to ensure that appraisal was rigorous and productive.

Scotland

Scotland has a system of education separate from England and Wales. It is distinguished by the fact that it consists of a relatively small number of schools, under 4,000, serving a total population of slightly more than 5 million. In consequence, relationships among teachers, local authorities, and the central administration are generally much closer. Furthermore, it is frequently claimed that education has traditionally been valued more highly in Scotland than in England. One manifestation of this claim is the fact that teachers in Scotland have their own professional association, the General Teaching Council, established in 1965, that deals with the probation and registration of teachers, with the accreditation of initial teacher training courses, and with advising and commenting on matters of policy that concern education, including teacher supply. Another manifestation is its maintenance of a professional, independent inspectorate, HMI, with the Senior Chief Inspector being the principal adviser to the Secretary of State for Scotland on standards and quality in schools.

Although Scotland has been involved in several reforms similar to those in England, they tend to occur over a longer period of time, involve greater consultation, and are accompanied by systematic evaluation. As a consequence, many of the recent reforms have taken a different emphasis from those in England and have been implemented with greater sensitivity to the needs of teachers and children. For example, devolved school management, equivalent to England's local management of schools, delegates responsibility for school management to the headteacher, or principal, rather than the school board, or governors, thereby avoiding the possible undermining of the headteacher's authority. Furthermore, the formula on which budgets are delegated includes school's actual salary costs, and, in consequence, there is no pressure on schools to reduce staffing or to replace experienced teachers with less costly, newly qualified ones (see Raab et al., 1997). As in England and Wales, schools were encouraged to opt out of local authority control but only two have done so, both small schools in unusual circumstances.

Scotland has, in effect, always had a national curriculum in the secondary school because external examinations taken at the ages of 16 and 17 years are controlled by one examination board. A 5–14 Curriculum, however, was formally introduced shortly after the national curriculum in England. Unlike the English variant, the 5–14 Curriculum consists of guidelines for teachers and has no statutory support, although in practice, schools do follow the guidelines. Also, unlike England, all guidelines on curriculum, assessment, and reporting are devised after wide consultation, and they tend to be trialed and revised before being confirmed. The 5–14 Curriculum also had a national evaluation of its implementation built in from the start. A distinguishing feature of curriculum and assessment reforms in Scotland has been its generally consensual nature and the involvement of teachers at all stages of the process (see Croxford, 1994; Munn, 1995).

Although schools are required to publish information about themselves including their examination results, proposals to introduce a program of national testing, equivalent to England's standard assessment tests, were rejected by teacher and parent groups as not being in the interests of the children, and this aspect of the English reforms was not pursued further. The Scottish Office Education and Industry Department (SOEID), however, has developed performance tables, which are published in the press, and school inspectors and headteachers have been encouraged to use performance indicators as a means of assessing school quality. The SOEID publication, *How Good Is Our School?* (SOEID, 1996), recommended a set of 33 indicators for schools to use in self-evaluation and that are also used by HMI and local authorities.

Since 1978, an increasing trend has been to educate children with learning difficulties in mainstream schools with specialist teachers working alongside other teachers in mainstream classes (HMI, 1978). More recently, encouragement from HMI has been to move away from mixed-ability classes toward ability grouping (HMI, 1997) in the belief that this more easily managed system of teaching is associated with greater learning gains for the children.

From 1995, considerable emphasis has been on early intervention strategies, particularly in the area of reading, in which additional financial and staff support is provided to schools in deprived areas. Preschool provision for all 4-year-olds has also become a government priority. Mandated changes, however, have tended to focus on organizational and administrative features rather than on teaching and learning processes that have been regarded as matters of teachers' own professional responsibility.

In the field of initial teacher training, a pilot scheme for school-based teacher training was introduced and evaluated (Cameron-Jones & O'Hara, 1993; Powney, Edward, Holroyd, & Martin, 1993), but concerns about quality and adequate levels of funding, together with teacher opposition, led to its abandonment. All courses of initial teacher training are required to conform to broad curriculum guidelines and to assess student teachers on an agreed set of competencies. All teacher education institutions in Scotland use the same broad assessment criteria for judging teaching competencies. There are no school-centered initial training schemes, and the TTA's remit does not extend to Scotland. The quality of provision is inspected through a UK peer-review system of teaching quality assessment, through the accreditation process of the General Teaching Council, and through the quality assurance systems of the higher education institutions themselves.

School-based continuing professional development appears to suffer the same disadvantages as in England, although local authorities in Scotland have been able to hold back part of the staff development budget to provide authority-wide training on local priorities (see Clark & Munn, 1997). School teacher appraisal was introduced in Scotland in 1991 (Scottish Office Education Department [SOED], 1991). Guidelines were devised on how the process might operate, and documentation produced on supporting the development of appraisal skills among staff in schools and also on the incorporation of appraisal into school development planning. Another distinctive feature of reform in a Scottish context is the initiation and use by the SOEID of research and evaluation. It has its own research and intelligence unit that is responsible for commissioning research and evaluation projects. An audit unit, headed by a chief inspector, gathers information on the performance of the Scottish education system relative to others and supports school self-evaluation.

Sweden

The past decade has been a turbulent time in Swedish education, being influenced by substantial changes in political control. The election of a Conservative government in 1991, at a time of economic recession, initiated the gradual dismantling of the welfare state. In education, the political belief in the importance of choice and competition stimulated the introduction of educational markets, the encouragement of private education, and increased accountability of schools for educational outcomes. In the devolution of educational governance and accountability, teachers changed from being civil servants to employees of local municipalities or of individual schools. Dissatisfaction with schools for being insensitive to the need for change and being unresponsive to parent demands added to the incentive for reform (Lindblad, 1996). In 1992, a voucher system was introduced that covered 85% of municipal funding, aimed to encourage both the development of private schools and competition between schools. Such moves had marginal effect, however. Given the geography of Sweden, with a widely dispersed population and generally long distances between schools, only in larger cities could parents and students realistically exercise their new power of choice. The notion of choice in education was also a particularly difficult concept to introduce into the Swedish culture, because parents were used to thinking of all schools offering similar qualities of educational experience, a view that is to some extent supported statistically in the low variance among schools in academic performance (Organisation for Economic Cooperation and Development [OECD], 1995).

These reforms were only partly underway when the Social Democrats took office in 1994. Although they shared the previous government's enthusiasm for restructuring and deregulating the school system, their ideal was the development of the community-focused comprehensive school. The value of the school voucher was reduced to 75% in 1994, and legislation was later introduced making schools much more accountable to their local communities, being governed by school boards comprising parents, teachers, representatives of the local community, and students themselves.

Sweden has for many years had a national curriculum undergoing periodic revision. In 1994, a radical change in the curriculum was made, moving away from prescription for curriculum content and teaching approaches to prescriptions for learning goals to be achieved with children at particular ages. Schools are held accountable for achieving these goals, and their effectiveness is assessed by municipal inspectors, who visit schools and carry out opinion surveys of parents, teachers, and children. Although officially teachers have considerable autonomy in deciding how the curriculum is delivered, national curriculum documents encourage teachers to adopt individualized, child-centered approaches to instruction. Longitudinal studies of classroom processes, however, are ambivalent on whether teachers' instructional styles have actually become any more interactive or less focused on information delivery (Ekholm & Kull, 1996; Lindblad, 1997).

The 1994 national curriculum involved a departure from previously established procedures for dealing with educational and social reform in Sweden. Whereas Sweden has had a long tradition of establishing government committees with wide representation, which would consult different interest groups before making recommendations for change, the 1994 National Curriculum Committee was a small group of educationists and civil servants who were given a clear brief for the work of their committee, representing a move toward much more centralized control (see Carlgren, 1995).

Since the 1970s, all teacher training has occurred within the university system, and initial differences between primary and secondary teachers in terms of length and nature of training and in terms of status have now largely been eroded. Education in Sweden is comparatively well resourced, with a higher proportion of gross domestic product being spent on education than in almost any other European country (OECD, 1996). Teachers' salaries are relatively high, it is generally seen as an attractive profession to enter, and there are no difficulties in teacher recruitment. All teachers are expected to be educated to the master's level. The teacher training curriculum is overseen by a national accreditation body that, since 1993, has set specific training targets and monitors the extent to which these targets are being achieved.

Funding for the inservice training of teachers has been devolved to schools and local education authorities that are now able to buy inservice support where they feel it is needed. A widespread belief that teacher training, both preservice and inservice, has in the past been too dominated by universities' conceptions of useful knowledge has led to a number of experimental schemes of inservice development, some of them involving teacher unions in the organization and provision of professional development activities.

Spain

A period of substantial educational reform began in Spain in 1970 with the introduction of the General Education Act. This act marked a change in the structure and management of education, with a move from centralization to devolution in the curriculum, with a move from elitism to equal opportunities, and with a greater reliance on consultation and research in curriculum development. The General Education Act viewed education as central to the future economic and social development of Spain and signaled the beginning of a period of new thinking in education that has been sustained to the present day.

Two further acts were also greatly influential. The 1985 *Ley Orgánica del Derecho a la Educación* (LODE) established a system of governance for schools in which school staff and the local community are jointly involved in the management of schools. The 1990 *Ley Orgánica de ordenación General del Sistema Educativo* (LOGSE) laid down the general purposes of education and an outline of the basic school curriculum, to be elaborated and implemented by the Autonomous Regions. The curriculum is detailed but flexible and was designed with a modern, democratic, and pluralist society in mind. Guidelines were established for different levels: infant education (up to 6 years of age), primary education (6–12 years of age), compulsory secondary education (12–16 years of age) and the *bachillerato* (16–18 years of age). This act also proposed the establishment of teachers' centers, emphasized the importance of teachers' continuing professional development, and affirmed the contribution of universities in teacher education. A later act (LOPEG, *Ley Orgánica de la Participación, la Evaluación Gobierno de los centros docentes,* 1995) further elaborated the role of the Board of Governors and procedures for the election of headteachers and provided greater freedom to individual institutions to devise and pursue their own educational programs.

This legislative framework enabled schools to develop their own curriculum and teaching methods within a set of national guidelines and within a framework of accountability to their local communities. While the importance of preservice and in-service training and support is recognized and has resulted in the establishment of many Teachers' Centers that provide resources and support, it is claimed that financial constraints have prevented the ambitious reform objectives from being fully attained (see Boyd-Barrett, 1995).

The demand for education, both for children in schools and among adults, has increased greatly over the past 2 decades. Education is popularly seen as a major means to the improvement of the Spanish economy and the advancement of Spanish society, and this improvement has greatly added to the momentum of reform. Another result appears to have been that the prestige of teachers has increased and so, comparatively, have their salaries.

Community involvement in the management of schools has maintained a level of local accountability but has also led to heavy demands on headteachers who find themselves having to satisfy many competing requirements. As a result, in many parts of Spain it is difficult to find staff members willing to take up these appointments. In addition, teachers have found themselves under pressure as a result of the reforms. Although curriculum guidelines are provided at the national level and are further elaborated at the level of the Autonomous Region, much curriculum development and planning is left to individual schools and teachers. This situation has led to some collaborative work among teachers in schools, though they are often working with few resources and little external support.

Although teachers' centers were established with the intention that they would facilitate the processes of reform, their effect has commonly been regarded as disappointing. Morgenstern de Finkel (1995) suggested that this disappointment can be attributed to two main factors. First, the staff within the teachers' centers were themselves inadequately selected and prepared for the tasks they were required to undertake. They were not trained or prepared to facilitate innovation and were sometimes teachers who might themselves be poor role models for new practice. Second, the efforts of the teachers' centers were directed to individual teachers rather than whole schools, and it is arguable whether the individual teacher has much potential to produce any substantial change unless the whole school is adequately prepared to support it.

Children with special needs are generally integrated into normal schools, and additional support and specialist teachers are provided to facilitate this integration. While the differentiation of tasks to cater for children's different abilities is widely reported to have improved in recent years, integration remains an area of great difficulty for teachers, who argue for more support and better curriculum materials.

Preservice teacher education for primary school teachers has now become based within universities and typically takes 3 years. Classes, however, tend to be large and rely heavily on lecture modes of delivery, with insufficient staff time available for small-group work or practicum supervision. Secondary school teachers receive only a few weeks of basic preservice training and virtually enter teaching on the strength of their university degree in a teaching subject. This situation is nationally recognized as in need of improvement. The motivation and training of teachers has been identified as a major issue in the further development of the Spanish educational system (see Doz Orrit, 1995).

Evaluations of schools are carried out by inspectors, appointed within the Autonomous Regions. They are usually charged with the task of providing advice and support to schools, but limitations on time and resources have tended to result in their fulfilling a largely bureaucratic role with little obvious effect on school management or classroom practice. An awareness of the need to evaluate the educational system at various levels—whole system, school, curriculum, teachers, and students—led to the establishment of the *Instituto Nacional de Calidad y Evaluacion* (INCE) in 1994, that has been allocated responsibility for providing regular information on Spain's educational performance, including data for international comparisons (see Chico Blas, 1995).

Slovenia

Slovenia is one of the new European states that came into existence in 1991 with the partitioning of the former Yugoslavia. It is a small country, half the size of Switzerland, with a population of about 2 million. Its transition from a state within a communist country to an independent parliamentary democracy has required some radical rethinking of its educational system. Such a transition, however, has been particularly difficult when a central policy of encouraging diversity in school provision and the encouragement of private enterprise in education is matched with a popular adherence to conservative attitudes that value traditional education and view private schools as elitist (see Piciga, 1995).

The 1995 White Paper on Education proposed some wide-ranging reforms in the curriculum and the management of schools. The same structure of schooling was maintained in which primary schools offer 8 years of compulsory education from the age of 6 years, followed by 2 to 5 years of secondary education that in the later years takes place in a specialist school, providing either a vocational, professional, or academic emphasis, the latter leading on to higher education.

A national curriculum specifies the subjects, goals, and content to be covered in schools. Teaching approaches tend to be highly didactic and transmission oriented, although encouragement throughout the 1990s has been for primary schools to engage in experimental curriculum projects, involving the development of more child-centered teaching methods (Marentic-Pozarnik, 1994). Collaborative curriculum development projects with other European countries, encouraged through European Union funding, have also led to the encouragement of particular teaching styles, such as a constructivist approach in science teaching, which was previously unknown in Slovenia, and modern language teaching techniques that have been introduced into primary schools. Adherence to national regulations on education is maintained through a regular system of inspection by the Board of Education and Sport.

Assessment and examination has in the past been decentralized so that schools were responsible for making their own assessments of the children. In 1991, a common examination was introduced for those entering secondary education, and, in 1994, the Matura was introduced, a national examination for those intending to enter universities. It has been suggested that these external examinations have tended to reinforce traditional transmission-oriented approaches to teaching (Piciga, in press), with teachers teaching for the test.

The Ministry of Education and Sport attaches a high priority to involvement in international projects concerning the monitoring or improvement of educational achievement. Comparisons with other countries have been used to identify particular problems or difficulties in Slovenian schools—the high dropout rate and children's low achievement in mathematical and scientific problem solving—and have been used to guide educational policy decisions. The ministry also looks to other countries for ideas and collaboration in curriculum development projects (see Piciga, 1994).

Increasing attention has recently been given to preservice, induction, and inservice training for teachers. Initial teacher training courses last 4 years and include academic, practical, and professional preparation. The emphasis within teacher training courses, however, tends to be on learning the appropriate subject-matter knowledge (particularly in the case of secondary teachers), with relatively little time spent on pedagogy or classroom practice (Marentic-Pozarnik & Bizjak, in press). Attention has recently been given, however, to the induction of new teachers in schools. New teachers are given a substantially reduced teaching load, are assigned a mentor to help develop their classroom practice, and are required to pass an assessment of their practice before their teaching appointments are confirmed. Inservice provision has developed substantially since 1990. Numerous providers (including university faculties, schools, and private agencies) bid for central funds to support inservice training. Costs are covered 100% in areas in which the ministry attaches a high priority, inservice courses that are regarded as less essential are funded at lower rates (Zlahtic, 1996). Although inservice training remains voluntary, teachers are encouraged to take advantage of this provision, and successful completion of inservice courses has become a significant factor in the consideration of promotions.

The training of headteachers has been identified as an important feature in promoting school effectiveness. A national "School for Headteachers" was established in 1994, and, from 1996, training and appropriate certification have become mandatory for all existing headteachers in Slovenian schools and will be an essential prerequisite for all applicants for headships from the year 2000. The curriculum for the headship training program was derived after examining headship training in other European countries, and it focuses on such matters as managing conflict, staff development, planning and resource management, leadership and team building, and the management of change.

Russia

Over the past decade, the Russian education system has been dramatically influenced by two major factors. The first factor has been the democratization of Russia with the removal of Marxist-Leninist ideology from the curriculum, the local financing of schools, a relaxation of constraints on schools resulting in greater diversity that includes the development of private schools, and the introduction of parental choice. Many of the "new" ideas on school organization and the curriculum are not imported from other countries but come from an earlier phase of Russian reform in education. During the early 1920s, considerable diversity and experimentation was prevalent in education, creativity was encouraged, and schools were controlled by local school councils. These exemplars from the past are providing many of the guides for current practice.

The second major factor influencing reform has been finance. During the 1950s, expenditure on education in the Soviet Union was 10% of the gross domestic product. Between 1994 and 1996 in Russia, it was less than 4%. Furthermore, the dissolution of the Soviet Union has accompanied a serious slump in the Russian economy. As a result, schools are inadequately financed, with generally poor quality buildings and few resources. Nikandrov (1997) reported that teachers' salaries are about half of what they used to be in the Soviet Union and are often paid 2 to 5 months in arrears. However, because schools are locally financed, there is a wide variation in provision, with schools in wealthier districts being much more favorably resourced and staffed than those in areas facing high unemployment and poverty.

Most state schools are overcrowded and operate a shift system, with two or three shifts per day, to cope with the numbers of children (Jones, 1994). Within this climate, private schools in wealthier areas have flourished, providing an attractive option for those parents in a position to afford them. Private schools have also become associated with innovative teaching approaches, which are seen as attractive by many parents, and some of these "progressive" schools have indirectly influenced the practices of nearby state schools (Westbrook, 1994).

In return for local sponsorship from industry, some state schools have become "profile schools," specializing in areas that help to serve local employment needs. In rural areas, children are often expected to be part of the workforce, inevitably leading to some obstruction in the continuity of their education. Ivanov (1992) estimated that in rural Russia, poor resourcing of schools and other social demands on young people present a serious problem, resulting in the loss or underdevelopment of a large amount of human talent.

The picture painted by researchers and evaluators following the state of Russian education is one of a system with many ideas for change and new procedures for control, seriously hampered by a lack of resourcing and coordination and also by the poverty of the families the school system exists to serve. Hunger, child mortality, teenage pregnancies, child prostitution, youth crime, drug abuse, and poor health are growing problems and present serious obstacles to social, economic, and educational development (see OECD, 1997).

Although education has traditionally ranked high in the Russian public consciousness, Nikandrov (1997) pointed out "there are still more pressing problems in almost each family like food, clothing, housing, personal security, environment, health, etc., so in public opinion polls education usually takes tenth-eleventh place" (p. 9). Faced with these constraints, schools have to some extent became isolated, and morale among teachers is low. As Jones (1994) commented, "the central authorities are weak, the path ahead ill-defined, and the finances necessary for the task unavailable. Today, the schools are expected to find their own solutions to educational problems . . . " (p. xiii).

Teacher education has traditionally been the responsibility of specialized institutions—pedagogical institutes for secondary school teachers, and pedagogical schools for primary and kindergarten teachers. Preservice training has lasted 5 years for secondary teachers and 2 years for primary teachers. In addition, all teachers have had one semester's secondment for inservice training every 5 years. In recent times, however, a number of factors have led to the diversification of teacher education. Pedagogical institutes and schools have generally been poorly resourced, and some of the larger institutes have converted to being pedagogical universities, undertaking preservice and inservice education and educational research, aiming to be funded at the more generous level of universities. Previously tight controls over the preservice education curriculum have also been relaxed, resulting in much greater diversification. Teacher dissatisfaction with the quality of both preservice and inservice education has been very high for many years, and the decentralization of control in teacher education has been welcomed as an opportunity to increase the relevance of teachers' professional training (Webber & Webber, 1994). Difficulties in the recruitment and retention of teachers, however, have also led to the development of a number of short postgraduate courses and retraining courses, for example, to prepare officers being discharged from the military, to take up vacant teaching posts in schools.

Australia

In Australia, constitutional responsibility for education rests with individual state governments. However, over the past 2 decades, the central commonwealth government has become increasingly involved in national reform efforts. Through its control of central funds, the commonwealth government has come to exert considerable influence on education, although its suggested reforms have frequently been interpreted differently in different states. The following account identifies central policies and general trends.

In common with many Western countries, education has been perceived as both the problem and the solution of the country's economic ills. Poor education is perceived as a threat to the nation's international competitiveness, and future prosperity is viewed as necessitating tighter controls on the functioning and accountability of the educational system (see Dawkins, 1988).

Most states have established quality assurance offices that collect data on student performance from state-mandated tests, particularly of numeracy and literacy, together with data on truancy, student satisfaction, and school enrollment levels. This information is used for management and planning purposes and is generally not publicly available. Most states have also introduced a form of school-based management in which school principals are responsible for school finances and staffing. This management has been accompanied by a dramatic increase in short-term contract posts for teachers as opposed to permanent positions. Teachers are more likely to be employed on a needs basis for short periods of time. In some states, schools are encouraged to contract out work, such as staff development, that would normally have been undertaken by state ministries of education.

School councils have also been introduced that enable parents and others within the community to have a stronger voice in the management of schools. The school principal in such cases becomes the executive officer of the council, which is responsible for policy development and implementation, but the principal also remains accountable to the state education department that is his or her employer. This dual accountability can result in school principals having to manage many contradictory pressures on them.

Competition among schools has increased, particularly between the private schools (which receive funds directly from the commonwealth government as well as fees from parents) and the state schools (which are funded through state governments). The commonwealth government's increases in the level of funding allocated to private schools have led to concerns in state schools about defections from the state system and have inevitably heightened the awareness of senior managers in state schools of the importance of the presentation and marketing of their school within their local community. Some state ministries of education have also introduced benchmark testing to try to demonstrate that learning outcomes from state schools are not inferior to those of the private school sector.

The commonwealth government, with varying levels of cooperation with state governments, has been largely instrumental in developing a national curriculum framework and a set of key competencies that is suggested all students should have developed through schooling. Teacher professional development programs have also been devised, focusing on the teaching of these competencies. The commonwealth government has developed its own commercial organization, The Curriculum Corporation, to market support materials. A number of curriculum priorities have also been emphasized by the commonwealth government and taken up by state governments, including the development of intensive numeracy and literacy programs, Asian languages, information technology, as well as the broadening of late secondary education to encompass a vocational strand, including apprentice training programs.

Curriculum developments have not been uniform across Australia, however. Allegiances between commonwealth and state governments have been patchy and have led to various levels of development with respect to different reform initiatives in different parts of the country. Piper (1997) suggested that one of the reasons for this varying level of development is the highly variable quality and level of detail within the curriculum documentation itself, enabling a wide variety of interpretations.

In several states, a trend has started in closing down special schools and educating children with special needs in mainstream schools. However, much of the material associated with the national curriculum was developed with mainstream students in mind, and teachers frequently report its inappropriateness for children with special needs and the inadequacy of the assessment schedules associated with it.

In 1990, the National Board for Employment, Education, and Training published *Australia's Teachers: An Agenda for the Next Decade* (NBEET, 1990) that recognized teachers' work had become more complex in recent decades and that it was now appropriate to review and clarify teachers' roles and their conditions of employment and to consider structural changes that might improve efficiency in teaching and learning. In a few states, there has been a reevaluation of the overall structure of schools and the responsibilities of teachers, leading to some experimentation. In some cases, new schools have been created, catering, for instance, for children from preschool to Year 12. Such experiments have emerged from discussions about the traditional boundaries of schooling sectors and how school structure might better match the developmental stages of children and maintain curriculum continuity (NBEET, 1993).

In initial teacher education, the curriculum has come to be driven by a set of competencies for beginning teachers. Of particular influence has been the National Competency Framework for Beginning Teaching that identifies five broad areas of competence—using and developing professional knowledge and values; communicating, interacting, and working with students and others; planning and managing the teaching and learning process; monitoring and assessing student progress and learning outcomes; and reflecting, evaluating, and planning for continuous improvement (National Project on the Quality of Teaching and Learning, 1996).

School-based teacher training courses have become well established, with periods of time in schools and the responsibilities of schools and higher education institutions varying from state to state. A 2-year postgraduate master of teaching degree has been created in some universities, replacing the 1-year postgraduate route into teaching. New joint first degrees (BSc/BEd or BA/BEd) have also developed in which a full 2 years are spent in professional education. Because the same level of funding is being allocated to teacher education, the effect of this extension of professional training has been to reduce teacher supply, substantially curbing the oversupply of teachers that occurred in the early 1990s.

Induction arrangements for new teachers vary from state to state. In the Northern Territories, for instance, where there are particular difficulties of retaining teaching staff, substantial support for teachers comes from outside the region. Induction programs focus on the acculturation and orientation of new teachers to life and work in remote and often isolated communities and on working with Aboriginal groups in which the language, values, and mores may differ from those to which teachers are more commonly accustomed (Moskowitz & Whitmore, 1997).

In the field of continuing professional development, there has been a diversification of providers, with the commonwealth government encouraging teachers' associations concerned with specific subject areas to become more involved. Associations for mathematics, science, and language teachers have been particularly active in providing inservice courses. Changes in the career structures of teaching, with the introduction of several specialist roles, such as finance manager, counselor, or advanced teacher, have also been accompanied by specific training courses, closely tied to teachers' work in schools. Some of these courses have incorporated new technology and are delivered nationally with the use of interactive satellite television or through the Internet.

Considerable effort has been expended within the state departments of education in establishing appropriate competencies for both teachers and school principals. In Victoria, the state government established the Professional Recognition Program in 1995, thereby moving away from the traditional salary structure for teachers in which annual salary increments were automatically provided to teachers appointed on specific salary scales. Instead, the state government made salary increments dependent on a performance review in which teachers' practice was assessed against external standards. Three different levels of teaching were defined. Each of the three levels involves a full teaching load but with progressively increasing schoolwide and leadership responsibilities. School principal roles have also come to be more explicitly defined. Salary increments now depend on a successful annual review for both principals and teachers. Furthermore, bonus schemes have frequently been negotiated for Level 2 and Level 3 teachers and school principals, in which further monetary rewards are provided conditional on the attainment of certain targets. Studies of teachers' reactions to these developments suggest a generally positive response, although there is an awareness that the workload of Level 2 and Level 3 teachers has become substantial in many cases (Odden & Odden, 1996). There was some initial antagonism from teacher unions, but now widespread support appears to be growing for the scheme that establishes a system of reward based on merit and expertise rather than on length of service. Many teachers appear to view these developments in terms of improving their career structure and of increasing the professional standing of teaching by making teachers more accountable for maintaining high standards of expertise. In Queensland, a Center for Leadership Excellence has been established that has the task of overseeing the recruitment and training of school principals. The center has created a competence framework that is to be used in the appointment of principals and to identify needs for their future professional development. Similarly, a Center for Teaching Excellence is working on the development of a competence framework for teachers.

Australia has also been involved in a number of educational reforms that are peculiar to its own cultural or geographical situation. The delivery of language tuition using satellite television, for instance, is not uncommon in regions where there is a shortage or absence of specialist teachers. Many states have been engaged in reforms that recognize the specific needs of Aboriginal or Torres Strait Islander students or those from non-English speaking backgrounds.

The relationship between general education and vocational education is a further issue that is receiving considerable attention within the country. Policy in this area attained considerable momentum following the Finn Committee (1991) and the Mayer Committee (1992). Currently, an initiative that enables students to begin apprenticeship training while completing academic studies in secondary school is underway in several states. This initiative, however, has been found to create considerable role ambiguity for teachers, whose traditional definitions of their role have come to be challenged by these developments, resulting in reportedly high levels of stress (Pierce & Molloy, 1990).

New Zealand

Many of the recent reforms in New Zealand have originated from the Picot Taskforce that was appointed in 1987 to review the administration of education in New Zealand and reported the following year (Picot, 1988). Not all its recommendations were accepted, but many of them became incorporated into government policy, outlined in a government publication, *Tomorrow's Schools* (Lange, 1988). These reforms were compulsory, with a brief time frame for implementation, and teachers were generally left out of implementation and review groups.

Principal among the reforms has been a move toward self-managing schools. The former regional education boards were abolished and operational finances became managed by individual schools governed by boards of trustees, consisting of parents and local business people. This move was aimed at allowing schools to be more responsive to the quasi-market conditions that were being created at the same time by the removal of controls on enrollment. Responsibility for salary funding has generally been retained by the national ministry of education rather than devolved to schools, except in bulk-funded schools (currently only 10% of schools) in which actual salary costs are provided on a given teacher-student ratio, rather than average salary costs as in the English system. Several studies have been conducted on schools' adaptation to self-management. Although principals seem to welcome the control that it offers (Gordon, 1994), the nature of their role has been found to change with much more time being spent on administration. According to Wylie (1997), this increase in administrative work is "sapping principals' energy and attention for educational matters at the very time when educational leadership has become the pivot of their work" (p. 13). More time has also been found to be spent on school presentation (Wylie, 1995), and several studies (Hughes, Lauder, Watson, Hamlin, & Simiyu, 1996; Waslander & Thrupp, 1995) have reported the strong social polarization effects of introducing educational markets. As Gordon (1994) pointed out, on the basis of a study of schools in Canterbury, "schools in poor areas are getting poorer, while schools in wealthy areas are able to maintain, if not improve, their funding position" (p. 113).

A national curriculum, titled the New Zealand Curriculum Framework, was introduced by the ministry of education in 1993. The framework provides an overview of principles for teaching and learning, specifies seven essential learning areas, and identifies essential skills to be developed by all students, also acknowledging the place of attitudes and values in the school curriculum. Guidance is provided to teachers on the required knowledge, understandings, skills, and attitudes in each learning area. Levels of attainment in each area are specified and form the basis for regular assessment and the construction of children's learning profiles. Guidelines on teaching, however, are much less detailed and prescriptive than in the national curriculum in England and also take account of Maori interests. In fact, concerns with Maori interests are quite prominent in the reforms and include provision of immersion schools in which the curriculum is oriented toward the Maori culture and the language of instruction is Maori, in an attempt to address the relative underachievement of this indigenous group.

Assessment reforms have also been introduced by the New Zealand Qualifications Authority that is attempting to establish a single comprehensive and integrated qualifications structure, including school, industrial, vocational, further, and higher education. This structure is skills-oriented, involving competence assessment. The assessment demands of this development have contributed substantially to teachers' workload, with reports of it contributing to teacher burnout (Chamberlain, 1995).

School adherence to reforms is monitored by the Educa-tion Review Office (ERO) that makes periodic inspections of schools, reports from which are made available to principals, trustees, and the ministry of education. The local media are also informed of inspection outcomes. It has been argued, however, that ERO reports take little account of the social context of schools with the result that schools in deprived areas are frequently labeled as underachieving (Thrupp, 1997).

In terms of school organization, encouragement has been to educate children with special needs in the mainstream, although schools have also moved more toward streaming and accelerated classes. In the educational marketplace, the latter seem to be used as a means of attracting good students, whereas children with special needs have come to be viewed as a drain on school resources and as a negative contribution to a school's performance ratings. Mitchell (1994) suggested that "failing" schools have a disproportionate effect on children with special needs, because they are more prevalent among families with low socioeconomic status. He also suggested that budgetary constraints result in many schools not fully meeting the educational needs of these children. A new policy on special education, Special Education 2000 (Ministry of Education, 1996), aims to clarify the expectations of schools with respect to special needs and to clarify the basis on which schools are funded to meet these needs.

Initial teacher training has been relatively unaffected by reforms, though the number of training providers has greatly increased. In an overview of teacher education in New Zealand, Ramsay (1997) identified an increase in the diversity of courses, both in terms of length and content since its deregulation and also a greater level of experimentation, involving, for instance, the Internet, telephone conferencing, and electronic mail. Current difficulties with teacher supply have led to a growth in the recruitment of teachers from overseas and the encouragement of accelerated courses of teacher training (Sarney, 1996). The ministry of education has also launched a 3-year program, titled "Teach NZ," to persuade more people to take up teaching and to offer incentives to trained teachers overseas, encouraging emigration to New Zealand.

With respect to inservice training, schools are largely expected to make their own arrangements and to finance this training through their operational grant. At present, the government continues to fund some local advisory services, although the possibility of devolving this funding to schools to allow them a choice of "providers" including private agencies has also been recently raised. Newly qualified teachers are expected to follow a 2-year advice and guidance program, constructed by their schools and involving a structured program of support and advice from colleagues together with observation and feedback on performance. In 1989, teacher appraisal for all teachers became the responsibility of individual schools' boards of trustees, but little progress seems to have been made in this area. In 1995, the ERO commented that few schools were implementing appraisal systems (ERO, 1995).

The rapid imposition of reform with minimal consultation with teachers and with increased accountability of teachers to school boards is reported to have had an alienating effect on teachers, lowering morale and decreasing their sense of professionalism. As Sullivan (1994) pointed out, the relationship between teachers and parents has changed: Whereas teachers used to enjoy the respect of parents, many now look on them as employees accountable to the community for their actions.

Hong Kong

Several major educational reforms have occurred in Hong Kong in the 1990s. Probably most significant among these reforms is the establishment of the target-oriented curriculum (TOC), a set of learning targets sequenced throughout the period of compulsory schooling in the three core areas of Chinese, English, and mathematics. TOC was introduced into the first year of primary schools in 1995 and is gradually being phased in after a process of trialing, evaluation, and review. The curriculum was derived from the English national curriculum but adapted with a view to the particular social and economic needs of Hong Kong in the 21st century (Clark, Scarino, & Brownell, 1994).

The development and implementation of TOC was a government initiative, which was accompanied by highly prescriptive documentation on teaching methods and materials. As well as specifying the learning outcomes that teachers should be working toward, TOC aimed to change the aims of education, styles of teaching, and the types of assessment practices used. Teaching in schools in Hong Kong has generally been dominated by highly didactic styles of instruction with an emphasis on rote learning and a narrow "academic" curriculum, assessed through regular formal tests focusing on the mastery of subject matter. The TOC was intended to introduce a more learner-centered approach to teaching, structuring the curriculum around learning activities and the application of knowledge. The TOC emphasized five different types of learning activity—communicating, conceptualizing, inquiring, problem solving, and reasoning (Education Department, 1994). Criterion-referenced formative and summative assessment practices relating to these different ways of learning were also advocated in place of regular norm-referenced testing that focused on recall of subject matter.

TOC was initially met with considerable teacher resistance, partly because it was government mandated with virtually no teacher consultation, and, second, because it was implemented with little teacher preparation for the reform and with few appropriate teaching materials available. Morris and his colleagues at the University of Hong Kong conducted an evaluation of the first phase of TOC implementation and found that the effect of the reforms on classroom practice was highly variable among schools. Teaching styles and assessment practices were often slow to change, and, in some cases, teachers tried to fit their existing practices to the new curriculum demands with little adjustment. However, as the availability of suitable materials has increased and inservice training together with demonstrations of the TOC in action have come to be more widespread, resistance among teachers has declined. Some increase in student involvement in teaching-learning processes has been noted, although most of the effect of TOC still seems to be at the school organization level rather than in the classroom (Morris, 1996a, 1996b).

A further reform of importance in Hong Kong is the require-

ment placed on schools to develop their own clear policy on the language of instruction. While the majority of primary schools use Chinese, secondary schools have tended to use a combination of English and Chinese. This combination of languages is thought to have resulted in some ineffective teaching because of students', and also teachers', inadequate mastery of the language of instruction. Schools are now required to make judgments about the language abilities of their teachers and to formulate a school policy on the language to be used. Over three quarters of secondary schools have opted for Chinese as the sole language of instruction, and some of the remainder have retained Chinese as the language for the lower part of the school, using English as the medium of instruction in the senior section. Despite the recent political changes accompanying the transition to Chinese control, some incentive to become fluent in English is still apparent, because it is quite widely used in the university sector and in the business community.

Concerns with language proficiency have also led to the development of a series of benchmarking tests that all teachers of English, Chinese, and Putonghua will shortly be required to take. The intention is that language teachers will have to demonstrate their own competence in the language and will be given 5 years to ensure that they reach benchmark levels. Not surprisingly, this proposal has met with resistance from teacher unions, but the government has pronounced a strong commitment to proceeding with this reform and ultimately to introducing language proficiency tests for all teachers.

Following similar reforms in the United States, Australia, and the United Kingdom, Hong Kong has introduced the school management initiative (SMI). This initiative aims to define clearly the roles of those involved in school management; to develop greater participation of teachers, parents, and former students; and to devolve resource management to the level of the individual school. The scheme is voluntary, the first cohort joining in 1991. By 1995–96, only a quarter of schools had opted into the scheme. Dimmock and Walker (1997), in a survey of school principals, found many feeling uncertain about possible future changes, particularly with regard to a potential, large influx of Chinese families and uncertainties about the curriculum, and, consequently, the school principals were uneasy about accepting greater levels of responsibility for school management at this time.

Teacher education is also going through a period of reform. Concern about the adequacy of initial teacher education has led to the development of a number of criterion competencies that all teachers are expected to achieve. The Advisory Committee on Teacher Education and Qualifications has come to take a more active role in shaping the teacher education curriculum by defining criterion competencies and prescribing means for their assessment and in monitoring the quality of initial teacher education through developing means for the assessment of new teachers after they have been appointed to schools.

China

In 1985, the Central Committee of the Chinese Communist Party introduced the first major structural reform of the education system since 1949. These reforms involved the decentralization of both funding and administration, as well as a loose structuring of the curriculum for the 9 years of compulsory schooling. As a consequence, schools have become heavily reliant on parental and community support. As Cheng (1994) pointed out, this reform is resource driven rather than motivated by political ideology.

The demand for education has simply far exceeded the government's ability or willingness to finance it. Kwong (1997) estimated that now more than 60,000 private schools are in China, known as "society-run" or "people-run" schools. This estimate, however, includes training institutions that may have a very narrow, vocationally oriented curriculum but provide education and training to meet local needs.

The increasing dependence of schools on local financial support, however, has led to wide variations in the resourcing of schools across the country. In 1989, the China Youth Development Foundation was established to raise funds to support the education of children in poor areas, to improve educational facilities, and to encourage school dropouts to return to education. Project Hope, administered by the foundation, has raised funds both within China and from overseas to sponsor educational development in the poorest regions. Such efforts have helped to increase the enrollment rate in both primary and junior secondary schools that for 1996 are reported in the Chinese government's official publication, *China: Facts and Figures,* as 98.8% and 82.4%, respectively. A target of the Chinese government is to attain full enrollment in the 9-year compulsory education system and to eliminate illiteracy among young people by the year 2000.

A national curriculum is laid down by the state education commission with two versions of the 6-year primary school curriculum, one for urban schools and one for rural schools. These recommended curricula include Chinese, mathematics, and moral education; but whereas urban schools are expected to include sports activities, the rural school curriculum includes agricultural studies. English has come to be introduced as an optional subject from the late primary phase, and science subjects are introduced at the beginning of secondary education. However, given huge regional socioeconomic disparities, understandable variations exist within the implementation of the curriculum with many adaptations to local needs and conditions (Teng, 1994).

The salaries of teachers are 10% higher than for those in other public services, and the academic qualifications of those entering teaching tend to be comparatively high. Teacher training has not been tightly regulated in the past, although state control over the professional training of teachers has begun to increase (Teng, 1994) with the intention of improving the quality of both preservice and inservice provision.

Summary

The above accounts outline the major reforms that have affected teachers and their work in 10 different countries over the past decade. As these descriptions illustrate, the boundaries and foci of reform efforts have varied substantially. In some countries, educational reform has been extensive and radical, and the changes have placed sizable demands on teachers. In other countries, reform has been more focused and gradual. Some common features, however, exist both in terms of the nature of the reforms and in the ways in which they have been implemented. This commonality may be partly attributable to the fact that countries are often facing similar problems. In particular, expectations on schools are becoming more exacting, and all countries face the need to develop a mass education system that delivers high-quality education for all. The costs of such a system are high, and education is competing for public funds along with other expanding areas such as health and welfare. This situation presents a number of common dilemmas that, together with the prevalence of an ideology that has come to view public services as business operations, have led to similar solutions being found at the policy level. A further explanation for the commonality of reforms may lie in the increasing internationalization of education, in which government education departments are progressively using national performance indicators as a means of judging the comparative effectiveness of their educational systems and looking to other countries to import ideas and policies that might lead to further improvement. Educational ideas and innovations appear to be increasingly transferred across national boundaries with the expectation that what "works" in one national context will also "work" in another.

Most of the reforms noted above fall into four main categories. The first category consists of reforms relating to the marketization of schools. The devolution of financial control to individual schools and the opening up of an educational market in which schools compete with each other for students and, therefore, funding has been widely perceived as a means of offering efficiency and improvement in the quality of education and has found favor in countries as politically diverse as New Zealand, Sweden, and China. Market principles have not always been interpreted or implemented in the same way, however. Whitty (1997), for example, in a comparison of local school management in the United States, England, and New Zealand, emphasized that ". . . the reforms are being implemented in significantly different social and cultural contexts. Education systems have particular structures and embody particular assumptions that are deeply embedded in their time and place" (p. 5). Although he noted the overall effect of market principles in education has been to introduce greater selectivity into the system, the severity of this effect has varied substantially from country to country, with varying opportunities for professional or democratic input into school management.

An interesting alternative explanation for the widespread popularity of market principles has been offered by Gewirtz, Ball, and Bowe (1995) who suggested that this strategy enables politicians to abdicate responsibility for more detailed educational policy: "the market provides politicians with all the benefits of being seen to act decisively and very few of the problems of being blamed when things go wrong . . . " (p. 1). In their study of three London local education authorities, in which they interviewed LEA representatives, parents, and staff members in schools to evaluate how market principles were operating, they found that local school management operated differently in each case. The social class and ethnic mix of schools' catchment areas were found to be particularly influential in how the market functioned. Parents of different social class were found to have access to different types of information and to interpret this information in different ways. In consequence, Gewirtz, Ball, and Bowe argued that no one general education market operates within a country or education system: "Education markets are localized and need to be analyzed and understood in terms of a set of complex dynamics which mediate and contextualise the impact and effects of the Government's policy" (p. 3). Similar conclusions have emerged from other studies of local school management in New Zealand (Waslander & Thrupp, 1995) and Hong Kong (Dimmock & Walker, 1997).

Overviews of the ways in which education markets function suggest that rather than leading to enhanced parental choice they frequently lead to stratification of schools in which the successful schools are the ones that have the power of choice over their student intake (OECD, 1994). It has also been argued that such trends also have an effect on the demography of the teaching profession. Darling-Hammond and Sclan (1996) suggested that in the United States, on the whole, better schools with better facilities and more amenable children are able to recruit the more successful teachers, whereas schools in inner cities and poor rural areas are more reliant on recruiting unqualified, less experienced or less successful staff.

The second area in which reform efforts have focused is the school curriculum, and in this area the direction of reform has been more variable. In Spain, for instance, the national curriculum was abandoned in favor of a more devolved system of curriculum management; in Sweden the structure of the national curriculum was changed from a detailed list of content to be covered to a much briefer list of learning objectives to be attained; in England and Wales a move has been made from a devolved system to quite a highly structured, national curriculum. A popular trend, however, has been toward increasing the demands on teachers for greater curricular coverage and toward establishing targets or levels of attainment for children of particular ages, and the achievement of these targets is frequently being used as a measure of teacher or school effectiveness. The emphasis within national curriculum policies has commonly moved from content to the outcomes of education and the setting of learning goals to be achieved.

A third common area of reform in recent years concerns accountability. Many countries have now established some form of national monitoring system that provides performance indicators at the school level, as well as indicating educational achievements at the regional and national level, perhaps even with international comparisons. OECD (1995) described the variety of school inspection systems developing in several countries, which are becoming more reliant on objective and quantitative data. The use of national tests given to particular age groups within a country is also increasing in popularity, often being incorporated into league tables or a system of accountability to the local community whereby the examination performance of children can be compared between schools and used as a basis for choice. Means of maintaining individual teacher accountability, however, are not widespread. Appraisal schemes have been introduced in some countries principally as a mode of fostering professional development, and, although concerns

with identifying underperforming teachers are evident in several countries and are frequently expressed, systems for addressing poor teaching performance have not been widely established.

A fourth area in which reform has been commonly introduced is teacher education. These reform efforts seem to have been motivated by two typical concerns. The first concern is with the quality of existing training that has frequently been criticized for being overacademic and remote from the practicalities of teaching. The other is the widespread recognition that the quality of education ultimately rests on the quality of the teaching profession and how well prepared it is to meet the educational challenges of the future. Although the need for reform in teacher education seems to be widely recognized, the directions of reform are not. Reform efforts themselves are directed to various and, sometimes contrary, objectives—involving universities more (Slovenia, Spain) or less (England and Wales), increasing the length of initial training (Australia), centralizing control over the curriculum (Hong Kong), or diversifying the provision of teacher education by devolving control to individual providers (New Zealand). At the level of policy, there seems to be little agreement internationally about the most appropriate approach to managing teacher education, and implicit within the reform policies lies a diverse range of conceptions of what teaching is and of how prospective teachers are best inducted into the profession.

The national accounts of reform also reveal many differences in the approach to reform—the extent to which teachers and researchers, for instance, are consulted or involved in the process, the extent to which reforms are evaluated and monitored, the time scale of reform, and the extent to which preparation is made for its implementation. These issues and others are discussed further below.

International Issues in Teaching Reform

Educational Reform and the Nature of Teachers' Work

VIEWS OF TEACHING

How teaching is viewed, both within and outside the profession, varies among countries and cultures. The relative emphasis that is placed on the pastoral and academic aspects of teachers' work, for instance, the teaching approaches that are thought to be appropriate, or the esteem in which the profession is held differ widely. The actual tasks that teachers undertake or the emphasis placed on different aspects of the curriculum also vary as indicated in several comparative studies (Broadfoot, Osborn, Gilly, & Bucher, 1994; Laffitte, 1993).

In addition, the roles and responsibilities of teachers, both actual and perceived, change over time in response to a variety of social and economic pressures. Sikula (1996) for instance argued that a loss of parental support for teachers has occurred in recent years, with the result that teachers are faced with more serious behavioral difficulties in class. He suggested that this loss of support is at least in part attributable, in some sections of society, to a widening rift in the values that are held as important within the home and the school. Similarly, Hargreaves (1994), in a study of teachers in Ontario, documented how the role of the teacher has changed in recent times; substantial additional administrative, pastoral, and pedagogic demands have been made of teachers, often under the guise of increasing teachers' professionalism, resulting in several changes to the teacher's working life.

National policies for the reform of teaching frequently present two visions of teachers' work, although these visions are rarely explicitly articulated. The first vision is of teaching at the present time, including perceived problems and difficulties, the second vision is of how teaching ought to be or how it is expected to be in the future. Neither of these visions, it seems, may necessarily be accurate or well supported by evidence or reason, and frequently little consideration has been given to the practicalities of how one moves from one vision to another. The visions are also embedded within a particular cultural and ideological context, attaching importance to particular values or practices and identifying others as problematic. In Hong Kong, for instance, the concern in recent policy initiatives has been with reducing the amount of rote learning within the curriculum and with encouraging teaching styles that are more likely to support children's creativity and their learning of higher-order skills of analysis and critical thinking. In Sweden, reform efforts have maintained an awareness of the social benefits of schooling and the importance of the preparation of children for citizenship. In contrast, many recent reforms in England have been geared toward controlling both what teachers teach and how they teach it, focusing especially on a basic skills curriculum.

UNINTENTIONAL EFFECTS

Although reform efforts may be attempting to realize a particular vision of how teaching ought to be, they also have a number of unintentional effects. Educational systems are complex and the effects of particular policies or actions are not entirely predictable. In addition, the very act of initiating reform and exercising control over teachers' work can itself affect the ways in which teachers and others view teaching, the motivation that teachers extract from their work, and the energy they invest in it, as well as their sense of professional responsibility and feelings of general worth.

One common side effect of some centralizing reforms, for instance, has been to foster among teachers a more instrumental view of their own work. Commenting on curriculum development in the United States, Novick (1996) suggested that

> teachers are often viewed as technicians, purveyors of a "canned curriculum" provided by a very powerful knowledge industry . . . the classroom has been frequently portrayed as a factory and children regarded as products to be produced as efficiently and systematically as possible. (p. 3)

Such a view among curriculum reformers, she argued, leads teachers to lose a sense of ownership of the curriculum and to view their task as one of knowledge delivery. Indeed, several studies from around the world offer support to such claims. A number of case studies of schools and teachers in England sug-

gest that the introduction of the national curriculum, particularly within primary schools, has led teachers to change the way they view themselves. Instead of thinking of their role as one of controller of the curriculum, they have come to see themselves as the implementor of other people's plans and to adopt a more restricted, subject-focused view of the curriculum (Menter, Muschamp, Nicholls, Ozga, & Pollard, 1997; Woods, 1995). In New Zealand, Wylie (1997) similarly reported that recent reforms have led to a narrowing of teachers' roles and a focusing of the actual curriculum on that which is tested. The effects of large scale changes, however, are rarely uniform. In contrast, Cooper and McIntyre (1996), in a series of case studies of English secondary school teachers, found that, although the imposition of the national curriculum was often strongly resented by teachers, some at least viewed it as a challenge and a spur to creativity and appreciated that it indirectly promoted greater levels of collaborative work among teachers.

Another area in which unintended effects have commonly been noted is in the increasing levels of accountability within schools. The development of local school management, the introduction of school inspection systems, the introduction of national assessment schemes, and the use of league tables have collectively instigated some profound effects on the roles of teachers and headteachers and on the relationships within schools and between teachers and parents. For example, Menter et al. (1997), in a study of primary schools in one town in England, reported that teachers attributed feelings of loss of autonomy and a lessening of their job satisfaction to imposed reforms, and their accounts of reform frequently expressed anger and frustration at the demands being placed on them. Several studies (Pollard, 1992; Sullivan, 1994) have also suggested that the overprescribing of the teacher's role and the consequent reduction in teachers' autonomy has resulted in reduced levels of commitment and enthusiasm.

Bowe, Ball, and Gold (1992) claimed that recent reforms in England have resulted in several changes in staff relationships within schools, with professional and collegial relations being replaced by financial and managerial ones. Sullivan (1994) similarly suggested that educational reforms in New Zealand have moved schools from a high-trust collegial system to a low-trust managerial one. He observed that one of the consequences of introducing a hierarchical management structure in which school principals adopt the role of business manager rather than academic leader is that they become isolated from their staff with the effect that teachers are often less likely to provide him or her with support. Menter et al. (1997) have also documented the change of the English primary headteacher's role from professional leader to chief executive, resulting in less time being available for classroom teaching and for talking with staff, leading to a more isolated role within the school.

Sullivan (1994) suggested that the enhanced power of parents on school governing bodies has also changed the relationships between parents and teachers. Parents are more likely to perceive themselves as having a significant role in determining decisions within the school and to perceive teachers as employees with a responsibility to implement the results of those decisions. Sullivan claimed that this change in power relations has resulted in a loss of status and authority for teachers as well as a reduction in their self-esteem.

INTENSIFICATION OF TEACHERS' WORK

It has been widely documented that both the intended and unintended effects of recent reforms have contributed to an overall intensification of teachers' work. As Hargreaves (1994) pointed out, teachers have generally been expected to do more and more, often with less and less support. The devolution of financial management to schools, for example, has been found to result in the same or increased amounts of work being performed by fewer teachers (Bullock & Thomas, 1997) and in greater proportions of teachers' time being spent on administration, school marketing, and presentation (Wylie, 1997), whereas demands for their effectiveness in terms of promoting children's learning have increased.

Curricular reforms have brought additional demands on teachers in terms of preparation and of planning and developing new ways of teaching (Pollard et al., 1994), and assessment reforms have also added to teachers' administrative load (Chamberlain, 1995). Teachers are generally being asked to deliver a fuller curriculum and, in some cases, to children of much wider ability ranges. In the inner-city areas of some countries, the proportion of children with emotional and behavioral disorders in ordinary schools has increased substantially (Rutter & Smith, 1995), and the policy to integrate children with special needs into ordinary classrooms has meant that "a whole new set of demands on the teachers' time, skills, and commitments are 'added on' to their existing classroom tasks" (Bowe et al., 1992, p. 174). Such demands, which have also to be met within certain budgetary and curricular constraints, inevitably make the task of teaching more time-consuming, onerous, and stressful.

Accompanying reform efforts, there have been many reports of the personal effects on teachers of large-scale change. Most of these reports have suggested that reforms have led to a substantial increase in the amount of stress experienced by teachers, which in turn has resulted in increasing levels of illness, burnout, and early departures from the profession (Travers & Cooper, 1996).

The levels of stress attributed to reform have been accounted for in several ways. Not surprisingly, the intensification of teachers' work, including the increased burdens on teachers and the rapid pace of change, has been identified as a major contributor to teachers' experiences of stress (Hargreaves, 1994). Another source, however, has been the role ambiguity experienced by teachers. Reform efforts have frequently required teachers to adapt their role, becoming, for example, more of an entrepreneur or a vocational trainer, or to adopt a different teaching style, becoming, for instance, more focused on basic skills, or pursuing a more constructivist teaching approach. Such demands, particularly when teachers are left to grapple with them on their own, create uncertainty and anxiety. Teachers can no longer turn to their normal indicators of performance to reassure themselves that they are doing a good job, and this lack of identity, sense of purpose, and personal effectiveness can be anxiety provoking and demotivating (Pierce & Molloy, 1990).

A third source of stress lies in teachers' loss of self-esteem. Many recent reforms have resulted in a reduction in teacher autonomy, greater levels of accountability for individual teachers, and, even in some cases, the blame for poor educational standards being attributed to teachers. The effect of some re-

forms has been to devalue the status of teaching with a resulting loss of self-worth on the part of teachers (Woods, 1995). A fourth source of stress identified in several studies of innovation and change in education is poor management. Often senior personnel in schools have been given the task of managing institutional change without appropriate training in the planning and managerial skills needed to carry out the task. As a result, unnecessary confusion and conflict have been generated, contributing to the stress experienced within the school (Travers & Cooper, 1996).

The added pressures on teachers, the demanding roles they are expected to fulfill, and, in some countries, the shortage of appropriately qualified people willing to embark on a teaching career are leading to reappraisals of the structure of the teaching profession and of the ways in which teachers are prepared to undertake their work. Hargreaves (1997), for example, argued that Western countries are facing an ethical and economic dilemma. On the one hand, they are striving for an ideal of a high-quality, mass education system that enables access to quality education for all. On the other hand, the education system is being managed within inevitable budgetary constraints that make the delivery of high quality impossible. He argued that this dilemma must result in a reappraisal of the purposes of education in the 21st century and of the roles of teachers. He suggested, as does Darling-Hammond and Sclan (1996), that one of the consequences may be a much more differentiated teaching profession in which some teachers follow the route of career teachers, taking on the full range of teaching tasks and responsibilities and being rewarded appropriately for it, whereas others work as assistant teachers, accepting only some minor or supporting roles—the majority of the latter would not embark on such posts as a career route to teaching and may well see teaching as a temporary source of employment before moving into other fields. Such speculations appear to offer a solution to the economic and educational dilemma that governments commonly face, though, if implemented, it could well result in a dramatic change in the culture of schools. Some advocates of the importance of collegial relations within the teaching profession have warned that such a hierarchical structuring of teaching would do little to promote the dissemination, sharing, and debate of good practice within the profession that may be an essential feature of quality education (Fenstermacher, 1990).

Teacher Education Plus Career Development, Recruitment, and Retention

Although many factors beyond the school affect educational outcomes, such as support within the family and among peers, the principal in-school factor influencing children's learning is, not surprisingly, the teacher (Scheerens, 1992; Rutter, Maughan, Mortimore, & Oston, 1979). Furthermore, ethnographies of schooling would suggest that teachers can be highly significant people in the lives of children, often acting as role models, moral exemplars, sources of inspiration, confidantes, and friends (Jackson, 1968; Pollard, 1991). One might expect, therefore, that in efforts to improve the quality of education, matters concerning the training and support of teachers would take high priority. Although there are instances of this prioritizing, for example in Spain and Slovenia, it often seems to occur in countries where teacher education has a relatively recent history and where it has only previously developed to a fairly minimal level. In most Western countries, it has rarely been the case that teacher education and the ongoing professional development of teachers have been viewed as keys to educational improvement. In fact, in several countries, rather than being supported, teachers and teacher educators are perceived as part of the problem. In England and Wales, Australia, and New Zealand, in particular, government policy is aimed at taking control out of the hands of teachers and teacher educators, and training and support are being replaced by prescription and regulation.

Reforms in teacher education have in the past been informed by a variety of views of the teacher and the purposes of teacher education (Feiman-Nemser, 1990; Zeichner, 1983). Recent reform efforts, however, seem to be particularly reliant on notions of teaching as a set of behavioral skills, and they often aim to define effective teacher education purely in terms of a set of outcomes or performance criteria to be attained. A trend in several countries has been to specify a set of basic teaching competencies that all beginning teachers should achieve, and this set of competencies has often been accompanied by some encouragement to the growth of diversity in the actual provision of initial teacher training. In England and Wales, for instance, higher education institutions are no longer the sole provider of preservice education, and, further, education colleges, LEAs, and schools themselves have become involved. In some cases, qualified teacher status is awarded to individuals on the basis of minimal training while in post. Such practices are well established in parts of the United States and can also be found in several European countries, New Zealand, and Australia.

The downgrading of professional education and support can be seen in part as the influence of a market ideology and the "commodification" of education in which education is viewed as a commodity to be produced and delivered at the best price. With an increasingly global economy in which industry and commerce are more and more able to locate and relocate their bases around the world where economic and labor conditions present the best advantage, an educated workforce is seen as a national asset able to attract industry and subsequent economic growth. National policies on education are in consequence becoming more prescribed, more demanding, and more determined by economic factors. Policymakers are also becoming more conscious of international comparisons. In several Western countries, education and teacher education are seen as providing poor value for money. In international comparisons of educational attainment, the Tiger Economies can be seen to realize higher levels of attainment for children, based on much lower levels of investment in education (see OECD, 1995). Such comparisons, of course, are simplistic and misleading because the balance of the curriculum, the teaching methods, and the expectations on schools and teachers vary widely among countries. Even leaving aside the methodological difficulties of making international comparisons of educational attainment, the substantial differences in culture between Western countries and the Tiger Economies, in which families and peer groups offer different levels of support and in which the expectations of schools are quite differently defined, render comparisons of costs and achievement scores quite meaningless. Such compari-

sons nevertheless seem to have accompanied a view of education and of teacher education that examines costs and outcomes with little attention to the underlying processes.

The ongoing professional development of teachers and the career structure of the profession have also tended to receive scant attention within reform efforts, and, in some cases, educational reforms have in effect undermined their growth. For example, research and evaluation within teacher education has frequently identified induction as a phase of a teacher's career that is particularly in need of support (Huling-Austin, 1990; Tickle, 1994). Some researchers have also identified a number of career stages in the development of teachers that can be viewed in terms of requiring different types of training and assistance (Huberman, 1989). However, the popular trend to devolve financial management to schools has been found in some cases to result in inservice funds being targeted on short courses of immediate instrumental significance to the school at the expense of long-term support and professional development for teachers. There are even some cases in which funds for inservice training have been diverted to other basic necessities for schools instead (Harland et al., 1993; Wright & Bottery, 1996).

The move toward decentralized, market-led education systems has also been found to have some deleterious effects, in some countries, on the career structure of teachers. As schools have become more cost conscious, teaching assistants and younger, less experienced teachers have become more attractive appointments than experienced ones (Bullock & Thomas, 1997). Financial rewards for taking on positions of responsibility have also become less common. Although there have been attempts to protect the career structure of teachers by, for instance, defining positions of responsibility and gearing training programs toward them, the overall effect of some reforms seems to have been to obscure and to depress the career structure of teachers and to make it more difficult for teachers to enhance their expertise and to be rewarded through progression through a particular career route.

The intensification of teachers' work, its weakened career structure, and, in some countries, its loss of esteem in the eyes of the public have made it a much less attractive profession for young people to enter. Both England and Wales and New Zealand are facing severe shortages of teachers, and both the recruitment and retention of teachers have become matters of national concern. Advertising campaigns and overseas recruitment are short-term measures and make little effect when a profession is demoralized and is viewed as unsupported and unrewarded.

Surprisingly, in the formulation of reforms, little attention has been given to understanding the processes of teaching and learning as they occur in classrooms and to the factors that influence and support the quality and effectiveness of those experiences. Reform efforts have often been based on quite simple and probably quite inappropriate notions of how teaching and learning interact and of how schools and teachers produce the effects that they do. It could well be argued that there is a need for policymakers to appreciate much more fully the complexity of teachers' work, the contribution of appropriate training and support, and the importance of maintaining a work environment that elicits and fosters teachers' enthusiasm, energy, commitment, and expertise.

The School as Education Provider

One of the common trends across countries, intensified by the promulgation of a market ideology, the demands for accountability, and the striving for higher levels of educational attainment, is that schools have come increasingly to be viewed as the responsible agent for educational provision. They are seen as the main agency for the maintenance of educational standards and as the location where significant decisions are made that influence the quality of teaching and learning. In some countries, this primary responsibility of schools in the educational process is so taken for granted that it would seem strange even to question it. In others, such as Sweden, this relatively recent view of the school has challenged deep-seated assumptions about education and the equality of opportunity that is offered to the young: Notions that all schools offer a similar provision and that a child's educational attainment is marginally, if at all, affected by which school he or she attends are becoming no longer tenable.

The identification of schools as the responsible agent for educational provision can itself of course become a self-fulfilling prophecy. As public attention is focused on the variability of performance of individual schools, the exercise of choice by parents and students is likely to exacerbate that variability, increasing the likelihood that schools themselves will be seen as the prime causes of children's educational success or failure. The fact that some schools inevitably fail and necessitate the instigation of recovery and support procedures does not seem to have challenged the dominant view of schools competing within an education marketplace but has instead been used as supportive evidence for the school as the appropriate responsible agent for educational provision.

While hard evidence on the effects of this trend is scant, one could speculate on a number of potential consequences, particularly for teachers, their attitudes to their work, and their views of the profession, on the ways in which schools themselves operate and on how we typically view educational matters and the influence on the strategies that are adopted at a national level to solve educational problems.

Competition among schools has in several cases been reported to lead to a greater isolation and to less willingness to collaborate or share resources (Whitty, Power, & Halpin, 1998). In turn, such structural changes might well lead teachers to change the ways in which they look on teaching. Rather than being part of a profession with common values, goals, and concerns, teachers may be encouraged to think of themselves more as employees of the school. The problems that concern them may become more focused on their immediate situation and particular school, and the solutions that are sought or offered may be seen as controlled within the resources and decision-making structures of the school. The independence of schools and the introduction of more managerialist systems may well weaken the professional culture for which teachers in some countries have been striving.

When schools are viewed as the unit of educational provision, we can also see substantial changes in the way in which they structure and manage themselves. Functions such as marketing become important, selection of children takes on a new significance, and financial criteria become prominent in the making of many school decisions. Even the language that comes to be used to describe schools and their functions has sometimes changed to reflect the new managerialist culture. Schools become "education providers," and principals and their deputies become "resource managers." The overall purposes of schools and how they work to achieve them have clearly been influenced to a substantial extent by recent changes in the ways schools are viewed.

Finally, attaching greater significance to the role of schools changes the ways in which educational problems are viewed, the ways in which responsibility and blame are attributed, and the ways in which the solutions to these problems are sought. If schools are the main agent for educational provision, the causes for success or failure are much more readily attributed to matters within their control. Yet, arguably, some of the strongest influences on children's academic achievement lie within the home and the community (Brown, Duffield, & Riddell, 1995). Furthermore, many of the social ills that attend the lives of young people and that are highly influential in determining academic achievement—poverty, insecurity, violence, drug addiction—require much more coordinated social reform efforts if they are to be effectively tackled at the root level. If the educational achievement of children in inner-city areas is to be raised, for example, this reform cannot be meaningfully viewed as a task for individual schools on their own. A much more comprehensive view of the problem, of its causes, and of potential solutions needs to be sought.

In fact, one of the consequences of viewing schools as relatively independent education providers may be that education comes no longer to be regarded as part of the social processes by which young people learn, are inducted into society, and prepared to play a responsible role within it. The responsibilities of schools become more distinct and perhaps oversimplified, even though, at the same time, they are frequently attributed blame for problems that are well beyond their control.

The Role of Teachers and Researchers in the Reform Process

The process of educational reform has attracted much attention from researchers and educationalists, many of whom have pointed to the centrality of the teacher in managing educational change. Stenhouse (1975), analyzing his experiences of curriculum development, recognized that efforts devoted to the generation of new materials or innovative curriculum packages intended to promote particular classroom practices were in vain unless the teachers who were expected to use them were engaged in rethinking their ideas about teaching and their own practice. Fullan (1991) similarly highlighted the importance of the teacher both in the creation and implementation of educational innovations. Furthermore, Goodlad (1984), commenting on reform in the United States, has pointed to the complexity of the process and emphasized the importance of schools working within the context of community support:

> Schools will improve slowly, if at all, if reforms are thrust upon them. Rather, the approach having most promise, in my judgment, is one that will seek to cultivate the capacity of schools to deal with their own problems, to become largely self-renewing. Schools will

have great difficulty, however, in becoming self-renewing without support from their surrounding constituencies. (Goodlad, 1984, pp. 31–32)

Within the research literature, a number of functions and roles have been assigned to teachers in the processes of reform. In particular, investigations of educational change have highlighted that teachers possess extensive knowledge concerning practice—about children, about teaching strategies, about ways of structuring the curriculum, and about the constraints on school and classroom life (Calderhead, 1996; Fullan & Hargreaves, 1992). Such knowledge can usefully contribute to the development of new curricula or teaching approaches, indicating what is possible and desirable, and how it might practically be achieved. Consequently, an important role for teachers is in the design and formulation of educational reforms. This knowledge also enables new ideas to be translated into workable classroom strategies, and it has been suggested that teachers have a very significant role in the interpretation of new ideas and their incorporation onto meaningful classroom routines (Cooper & McIntyre, 1996; Doyle & Ponder, 1977).

However, the expertise of teachers, their potential to contribute to reform, and their possession of a body of "expert knowledge" related to the processes of education are rarely acknowledged. Within the rapid educational reforms that have occurred over the past decade, the processes involved have not generally mirrored the textbook ideals. More typically, teachers have been viewed as production workers, mechanically implementing the plans of others. Or, where they are involved in the development and management of reform, their involvement has been viewed as either a motivational strategy, winning teachers round to the new ideas, or as a perfunctory acknowledgment or token act of respect for the profession that carries the responsibility for making the new ideas work in practice (Carlgren, 1995).

The models of educational change processes that are implicit within reform efforts in reality reflect a diversity of approaches and are often the result of a complex interplay of social, political, and practice factors that manifest themselves differently in different contexts. In Scotland, for instance, reform has by and large followed a rational consultative approach in which teachers have played a significant role. Several factors have clearly contributed to this process. The educational community in Scotland is relatively small and close knit. School inspectors, headteachers, researchers, and policymakers frequently meet in a variety of professional fora and relationships are well established. Teaching itself is well regarded within the Scottish culture in which education is seen as an important means of personal advancement. The political climate in Scotland also has a long socialist history with a strong community orientation. In such circumstances, it is perhaps not surprising that educational reform is approached in a relatively collegial and consultative manner. In New Zealand, however, which has many similarities to Scotland in terms of geography, population, and education system, reform has been approached in a much more autocratic manner, following a strong political agenda, with teachers being excluded from policy decisions. In Sweden, which has a history of rational, consultative approaches to educational change, a gradual move appears to be toward more centralized control, reflecting political and social changes within the country.

Comparisons of reform in the United States and in England and Wales have led some commentators to identify policymakers' alternative views of teachers and their role in the reform process. Maguire and Ball (1994), Lawn (1995), and Whitty (1997) suggested that, in the United States, reform efforts are seen much more in terms of supporting teachers and enhancing their professional status, with policymakers using a discourse suggestive of working with teachers and researchers. Whereas in the United Kingdom, teachers are viewed as the recipients of reform, and policymakers' discourse seems quite antagonistic to what is regarded as "the educational establishment." Such observations have not always been shared, however, by commentators within the United States (see Good, 1996).

Research studies on educational change have also identified a number of roles for research within the reform process. Typically, the research function within reform programs is viewed in terms simply of gathering prespecified data on performance, and, in many cases, the need even for this data gathering has gone unrecognized. Reports on several national reform programs have suggested that educational reform is frequently motivated by ideological factors, with little concern for any thorough and systematic evaluation of the evidence or of any systematic monitoring of the effects of reforms (Whitty et al., 1998). Yet research can occupy a much more fundamental and productive role in both the development and management of reform. First, educational research offers a wide spectrum of evidence and perspectives on education that could potentially inform consideration of the need for reform and of the areas in which change is desirable. Second, research can contribute to the ways in which we think about managing educational change, offering models of the reform process and of the involvement of different interested parties. Third, research can provide appropriate evaluation models and suggest the kinds of data that need to be collected and the methods of collection necessary to monitor the development of desired change.

Relationships between research, policy, and practice are not straightforward, however. Several writers have pointed to the frequent mismatches of intentions and expectations when researchers, policymakers, and practitioners work together and to the need for the different interest groups to appreciate more fully the contribution of each party to the processes of educational change and improvement (Bonnet, 1997; Husén & Kogan, 1984). It is argued that such efforts are essential to engage in meaningful, sustained, and effective educational development.

Thoughtful, planned systematic change in education, however, appears to be quite a rarity. The broader picture of education, how it can be changed, and where it is going is frequently not considered. Reform, in actuality, is often piecemeal, ill coordinated, and sometimes contradictory. Reforms of the curriculum, school management, assessment, preservice teacher education, and inservice training frequently occur almost independently and, not surprisingly, result in conflict in the educational system and stress for those working within it.

If educational reform is to be systematically and effectively managed, the roles of teachers and researchers need to be more fully recognized and incorporated into reform processes. National and local administrative authorities involved in developing policies for reform need to develop much closer working relationships with other interest groups and to construct systems for managing change that are more sensitive to the various sources of knowledge, information, and feedback that these groups can provide.

Conclusion

For many countries, the past decade has been a period that has witnessed the rapid development and implementation of much educational reform. In some cases, these reforms have been especially extensive, involving changes in the curriculum, in the management of schools, in teacher education, and in the structure of the teaching profession itself. Most have directly or indirectly had an effect on the working lives of teachers and have influenced, to varying extents, their practice in the classroom. In several countries, the number and magnitude of the reforms have so changed the role of teachers that it has contributed to a gross intensification of their work, to problems of stress and burnout, and to difficulties of recruitment and retention within the profession.

Looking across the accounts of reform in different countries, it seems that, commonly, educational innovation has not been well planned or well resourced. The actions taken by policymakers, though generally claiming to be in the interests of the quality of teaching and learning, have not been conceptually linked to the processes that are transacted in the classroom and, in fact, often seem to be based on extremely simple notions of how learning is enhanced. There are, therefore, many unintended consequences of reform in which the effects on teachers and students turn out to be different from those intended or in which attempts to improve the quality of education have resulted in increased levels of work but little evidence of any worthwhile effect on learning.

In making comparisons across countries, clearly care needs to be taken to recognize the different social and political contexts in which reforms are being proposed, the different stages of development of educational systems, and the diverse histories that have preceded them. The same educational reform can have different meanings and effects in different countries, cultures, and contexts.

Nevertheless, one of the features that is emphasized in looking across the reform programs of different countries is the generally unrecognized role of teachers and researchers in the development and implementation of educational change. Policymakers frequently view teachers merely as the implementors of other people's ideas without recognizing that they have developed considerable knowledge and expertise of teaching and learning and of the ways that classrooms and schools can and do operate. Teachers may not have fully articulated this knowledge and may not be used to working in collaborative contexts in which their expertise is used, but working with teachers in the processes of reform seems far more likely to tap into this expertise and use it to advantage than isolating them from the development of reform programs altogether. Similarly, a widespread trend for policymakers is to use the products of research when it supports their own ideas and to ignore the other contributions that research might make, such as in the systematic evaluation of educational change or in considering the theoretical and conceptual frameworks that might underpin the reform and the implementation process.

These difficulties have been recognized for a long time. Policy, practice, and research have frequently been separate in discussions of educational matters, and, although greater collaboration among the three groups has regularly been proposed, it seems difficult in fact to establish. There are relatively few attempts to tackle educational innovation in a way that capitalizes on the knowledge and expertise of those who work closely in promoting teaching and learning. On occasions, this knowledge and expertise may not only lie with teachers and researchers but also with social workers, child care workers, or others who work closely with the ideas and practices of child development and education. If reform is to build on available expertise, the contribution of practitioners and researchers needs to be more fully acknowledged, and ways need to be devised of including them in the reform development as well as its implementation.

Without efforts to capitalize on the available expertise, without an attempt to develop a broader view of how education functions within society and of how teachers and students work within schools, we are left with an inefficient, slow, and costly means of promoting educational change: Waves of innovation sweep across national boundaries, substantial effort is expended, and only some way further ahead do we discover the problems that have been created. Without building and sharing the expertise that we have and developing systems for managing change that respect the diverse knowledge bases of those involved, educational reformers seem destined to continue proposing simple solutions to complex problems, with little appreciation of their real effect on the lives and learning of the teachers and students in our schools.

REFERENCES

Alexander, R. (1997). *Policy and practice in primary education* (2nd ed.). London: Routledge.

Alexander, R., Rose, J., & Woodhead, C. (1992). *Curriculum organisation and classroom practice in primary schools: A discussion paper.* London: HMSO.

Barber, M., Evans, A., & Johnson, M. (1995). *An evaluation of the national scheme of school teachers.* London: Department for Education.

Bines, H. (1995). Special educational needs in the market place. *Journal of Education Policy, 10*(2), 157–171.

Bonnet, G. (1997). Policy making in evaluation at the European level. *European Educational Research Association Bulletin, 2*(3), 16–19.

Bowe, R., Ball, S. J., & Gold, A. (1992). *Reforming education and changing schools: Case studies in policy sociology.* London: Routledge.

Boyd-Barrett, O. (1995). Structural change and curriculum reform in democratic Spain. In O. Boyd-Barrett & P. O'Malley (Eds.), *Education reform in democratic Spain* (pp. 6–24). London: Routledge.

Broadfoot, P., Osborn, M., Gilly, M., & Bucher, A. (1994). *Perceptions of teaching: Primary school teachers in England and France.* London: Cassell.

Brown, P., & Lauder, H. (1996). Education, globalization and economic development. *Journal of Education Policy, 11,* 1–24.

Brown, S., Duffield, J., & Riddell, S. (1995). School effectiveness research: The policy-makers' tool for school improvement? *European Educational Research Association Bulletin, 1*(1), 6–15.

Bullock, A., & Thomas, H. (1997). *Schools at the centre?* London: Routledge.

Calderhead, J. (1996). Teachers: Beliefs and knowledge. In D.C. Berliner & R. C. Calfee (Eds.), *Handbook of educational psychology* (pp. 709–725). New York: Macmillan.

Cameron-Jones, M., & O'Hara, P. (1993). *The Scottish pilot PGCE (secondary) course 1992–1993.* Unpublished report, Moray House Institute, Edinburgh, Scotland.

Carlgren, I. (1995). National curriculum as social compromise or discursive politics? Some reflections on a curriculum-making process. *Journal of Curriculum Studies, 27*(4), 411–430.

Chamberlain, J. (1995, February). Who'd be a teacher? *North and South,* pp. 48–59.

Cheng, K. M. (1994). Issues in decentralizing education: What the reform in China tells. *International Journal of Educational Research, 21,* 799–808.

Chico Blas, A. (1995). The place of evaluation in educational reform. In O. Boyd-Barrett & P. O'Malley (Eds.), *Education reform in democratic Spain* (pp. 140–152). London: Routledge.

Clark, J. L., Scarino, A., & Brownell, J. A. (1994). *Improving the quality of learning: A framework for target-oriented curriculum renewal.* Hong Kong: Institute of Language in Education.

Clark, M. M., & Munn, P. (1997). *Education in Scotland: Policy and practice from pre-school to secondary.* London: Routledge.

Cooper, P., & McIntyre, D. (1996). *Effective teaching and learning: Teachers' and students' perspectives.* Buckingham, UK: Open University Press.

Croxford, L. (1994). Equal opportunities in the secondary school curriculum in Scotland 1977–91. *British Educational Research Journal, 20*(4), 371–390.

Darling-Hammond, L., & Sclan, E. M. (1996). Who teaches and why: Dilemmas of building a profession for twenty-first century schools. In J. Sikula (Ed.), *Handbook of research on teacher education* (2nd ed., pp. 67–101). New York: Macmillan.

Dawkins, J. (1988). *Strengthening Australia's schools: A consideration of the focus and content of schooling.* Canberra, Australia: Australian Government Publishing Service.

Dearing, R. (1993). *The national curriculum and its assessment: Final report.* London: School Curriculum and Assessment Authority.

DES. (1981). *Education for all.* London: HMSO.

DES. (1991). *The education (school teacher appraisal) regulations 1991.* London: HMSO.

Department for Education. (1994). *Code of practice on the identification and assessment of special educational needs.* London: Department for Education.

Department for Education and Employment. (1997). *Excellence in schools.* London: Department for Education and Employment.

Dimmock, C., & Walker, A. (1997). Hong Kong's change of sovereignty: School leader perceptions of the effects on educational policy and school administration. *Comparative Education, 33*(2), 277–302.

Doyle, W., & Ponder, G. A. (1977). The practicality ethic and teacher decision-making. *Interchange, 8,* 1–12.

Doz Orrit, J. (1995). Problems of implementation in Spanish educational reform. In O. Boyd-Barrett & P. O'Malley (Eds.), *Education reform in democratic Spain* (pp. 79–93). London: Routledge.

Earley, P. (1994). *School governing bodies: Making progress?* Slough, UK: NFER.

Education Department. (1994). *The report of the advisory committee on implementation of TOC.* Hong Kong: Government Printer.

Ekholm, M., & Kull, M. (1996). School climate and educational change: Stability and change in nine Swedish schools. *European Educational Research Association Bulletin, 2*(2), 3–11.

Education Review Office. (1995). *Managing staff performance in schools, report no. 4.* Wellington, New Zealand: Education Review Office.

Feiman-Nemser, S. (1990). Teacher preparation: Structural and conceptual alternatives. In W. R. Houston (Ed.), *Handbook of research on teacher education* (pp. 212–233). New York: Macmillan.

Fenstermacher, G. D. (1990). Some moral considerations on teaching as a profession. In J. I. Goodlad, R. Soder, & K. A. Sirotnik (Eds.), *The moral dimension of teaching* (pp. 130–151). San Francisco: Jossey-Bass.

Finn Committee. (1991). *Young people's participation in post-compulsory education and training: Finn report.* Canberra, Australia: Australian Government Publishing Service.

Fullan, M. (1991). *The new meaning of educational change.* London: Cassell.

Fullan, M., & Hargreaves, A. (Eds.). (1992). *Teacher development and educational change.* London: Falmer Press.

Gewirtz, S., Ball, S., & Bowe, R. (1995). *Markets, choice and equity in education.* Buckingham, UK: Open University Press.

Good, T. L. (1996). Educational researchers comment on the Education Summit and other policy proclamations from 1983–1996. *Educational Researcher, 25*(8), 4–6.

Goodlad, J. I. (1984). *A place called school: Prospect for the future.* New York: McGraw-Hill.

Gordon, L. (1994). "Rich" and "poor" schools in Aotearoa. *New Zealand Journal of Educational Studies, 29*(2), 113–125.

Hargreaves, A. (1994). *Changing teachers, changing times.* London: Cassell.

Hargreaves, D. H. (1997). A road to the Learning Society. *School Leadership and Management, 17*(10), 9–21.

Harland, J., Kinder, K., & Keys, W. (1993). *Restructuring inset.* Slough, UK: NFER.

Henig, J. R. (1994). *Rethinking school choice.* Princeton, NJ: Princeton University Press.

HMI. (1978). *Children with learning difficulties.* Edinburgh, Scotland: Scottish Office Education Department.

HMI. (1997). *Achievement for all.* Edinburgh, Scotland: Scottish Office Education and Industry Department.

Hopmann, S., & Künzli, R. (1997). Close our schools! Against trends in policy-making, educational theory and curriculum studies. *Journal of Curriculum Studies, 29*(3), 259–266.

Huberman, M. (1989). The professional life cycle of teachers. *Teachers College Record, 91*(1), 31–57.

Hughes, D., Lauder, H., Watson, S., Hamlin, J., & Simiyu, I. (1996). *Markets in education: Testing the polarisation thesis. Fourth report to the Ministry of Education, November 1996.* Wellington, New Zealand: Ministry of Education.

Huling-Austin, L. (1990). Teacher induction programs and internships. In W. R. Houston (Ed.), *Handbook of research on teacher education* (pp. 535–548). New York: Macmillan.

Husén, T., & Kogan, M. (1984). Educational research and policy: How do they relate? Oxford, UK: Pergamon.

IEA. (1997). Performance assessment in IEA's third international mathematics and science study [Online]. Available: http://www.csteep.bc.edu/TIMSS1/PAreport.html. (Accessed 3 September 1998).

Ivanov, A. F. (1992). The rural school: Current state and prospective development. *Russian Education and Society, 34*(3), 56–71.

Jackson, P. W. (1968). *Life in classrooms.* New York: Holt, Rinehart & Winston.

Jones, A. (1994). The educational legacy of the Soviet period. In A. Jones (Ed.), *Education and society in the new Russia* (pp. 3–23). Armonk, NY: M. E. Sharpe.

Kwong, J. (1997). The re-emergence of private schools in socialist China. *Comparative Education Review, 41*(3), 244–259.

Laffitte, R. (1993). Teachers' professional responsibility and development. In C. Day, J. Calderhead, & P. Denicolo (Eds.), *Research on teacher thinking: Understanding professional development* (pp. 75–86). London: Falmer Press.

Lange, D. (1988). *Tomorrow's schools.* Wellington, New Zealand: Government Printer.

Lawn, M. (1995). Restructuring teaching in the USA and England: Moving towards the differentiated, flexible teacher. *Journal of Education Policy, 10*(4), 347–360.

Lee, T. (1992). Local management of schools and special educational needs. In W. Swann (Ed.), *Learning for all* (pp. 50–62). Milton Keynes, UK: Open University Press.

Levin, H. M. (1998). Educational performance standards and the economy. *Educational Researcher, 27*(4), 4–10.

Lindblad, S. (1996, October). *Loyalty, exit or voice? Transitions of governance of education in Sweden.* Paper presented at the conference of the Human Sciences and Education, Moscow.

Lindblad, S. (1997, May). *Learning about late modernity.* Paper presented at the conference of the Professional Actions and Cultures of Teaching (PACT), Oslo, Norway.

Maguire, M., & Ball, S. J. (1994). Discourses of educational reform in the United Kingdom and the USA and the work of teachers. *British Journal of Inservice Education, 20*(1), 5–16.

Marentic-Pozarnik, B. (1994). Slovenia: System of education. In T. Husén (Ed.), *International encyclopaedia of education* (2nd ed., pp. 5490–5497). Oxford, UK: Pergamon Press.

Marentic-Pozarnik, B., & Bizjak, N. (in press). To train the mentors for a new role or to redefine the role? *European Journal of Teacher Education.*

Mayer Committee. (1992). *Employment-related key competencies: A proposal for consultation.* Melbourne, Australia: Mayer Committee.

Menter, I., Muschamp, Y., Nicholls, P., Ozga, J., & Pollard, A. (1977). Work and identity in the primary school: A post-fordist analysis. Buckingham, UK: Open University Press.

Ministry of Education. (1996). *Special education 2000.* Wellington, New Zealand: Ministry of Education.

Mitchell, D. R. (1994). *The rules keep changing: Special education in a reforming education system.* Keynote address to the 18th National Conference of the Australian Association of Special Education, Adelaide, Australia.

Morgenstern de Finkel, S. (1995). The teachers' centres. In O. Boyd-Barrett & P. O'Malley (Eds.), *Education reform in democratic Spain* (pp. 178–187). London: Routledge.

Morris, P. (1996a). *The Hong Kong school curriculum: Development, issues and policies.* Hong Kong: Hong Kong University Press.

Morris, P. (1996b). *Target oriented curriculum evaluation project: Interim report.* Hong Kong: Faculty of Education, University of Hong Kong.

Moskowitz, J., & Whitmore, W. (1997). Strangers in their own country: Teachers in the Northern Territories of Australia. In *From students of teaching to teachers of students: Teacher induction around the pacific rim* [Online]. Asia Pacific Economic Cooperation. Available: http://www.ed.gov/pubs/APEC/. (Accessed 5 March 1998).

Munn, P. (1995). Teacher involvement in curriculum policy in Scotland. *Educational Review, 47*(2), 209–217.

National Board for Employment, Education, and Training. (1990). *Australia's teachers: An agenda for the next decade.* Canberra, Australia: Australian Government Publishing Service.

National Board for Employment, Education, and Training. (1993). *In the middle: Schooling for young adolescents.* Canberra, Australia: Australian Government Publishing Service.

National Commission on Excellence in Education. (1983). *A nation at risk.* Washington, DC: U.S. Government Printing Office.

National Education Commission on Time and Learning. (1994). *Prisoners of time.* Washington, DC: U.S. Department of Education, National Commission for Excellence in Education.

National Education Summit. (1996). [Online]. Available: http://www.summit96.ibm.com. (Accessed 3 February 1998).

National Project on the Quality of Teaching and Learning. (1996). *National competency framework for beginning teaching.* Melbourne, Australia: The Australian Teaching Council.

Nikandrov, N. D. (1997). *Educational developments in Russia since 1991.* Unpublished report, Russian Academy of Education, Moscow.

Novick, R. (1996). *Actual schools, possible practices: New directions in professional development* [Online]. Educational Policy Analysis Archives, 4(14). Available http://seamonkey.ed.asu.edu/epaa. (Accessed 3 February 1998).

Odden, A., & Odden, E. (1996). *The Victoria, Australia, approach to standards-based reform and full school-site management.* Unpublished paper, The Consortium for Policy Research in Education, University of Wisconsin, Madison.

Organisation for Economic Cooperation and Development. (1994). *A matter of choice.* Paris: OECD.

Organisation for Economic Cooperation and Development. (1995). *Schools under scrutiny.* Paris: OECD.

Organisation for Economic Cooperation and Development. (1996). *Education at a glance—OECD indicators.* Paris: OECD.

Organisation for Economic Cooperation and Development. (1997). *Re-views of national policies for education—the Russian federation: Examiners' report.* Paris: OECD.

Piciga, D. (1994). Introduction: Tempus project—Primary science development. *The School Field, 5*(3/4), 5–9.

Piciga, D. (1995). *Secondary education in Slovenia.* Strasbourg, France: Council of Europe Press.

Piciga, D. (in press). The current curriculum policy in Slovenia in a broader context. *The School Field.*

Picot, B. (1988). *Administering for excellence.* Wellington, New Zealand: Government Printer.

Pierce, M., & Molloy, N. (1990). Relations between school type, occupational stress, role perceptions and social support. *Australian Journal of Education, 34*(3), 330–338.

Piper, K. (1997). *Riders in the chariot: Curriculum reform and the national interest, 1965–95.* Melbourne, Australia: Australian Council for Educational Research.

Pollard, A. (1991). *Learning in primary schools.* London: Cassell.

Pollard, A. (1992). Teachers' responses to the reshaping of primary education. In M. Arnot & L. Barton (Eds.), *Voicing concerns* (pp. 104–124). London: Triangle Books.

Pollard, A., Broadfoot, P., Croll, P., Osborn, M., & Abbott, D. (1994). *Changing English primary schools: The impact of the education reform act at key stage one.* London: Cassell.

Powney, J., Edward, S., Holroyd, C., & Martin, S. (1993). *Monitoring of the pilot programme of Moray House PGCE (secondary)* (Research Report). Edinburgh, Scotland: Scottish Council for Research in Education.

Raab, C. D., Munn, P., McAvoy, L., Bailey, L., Arnott, M., & Adler, M. (1997). Devolving the management of schools in Britain. *Education Administration Quarterly, 33*(2), 140–157.

Ramsay, P. D. K. (1997). *The provision of preservice primary and secondary education in New Zealand. A report to the Ministry of Education.* Wellington, New Zealand: Ministry of Education.

Rutter, M., Maughan, B., Mortimore, P., & Oston, J. (1979). *Fifteen thousand hours: Secondary schools and their effects on children.* London: Open Books.

Rutter, M., & Smith, D. (1995). *Psychosocial disorders in young people: time trends and their causes.* London: Wiley.

Sarney, E. (1996, February 3). Education in crisis. *Listener,* pp. 16–19.

Scheerens, J. (1992). *Effective schooling research, theory and practice.* London: Cassell.

Sikula, J. (1996). Introduction. In J. Sikula (Ed.), *Handbook of research on teacher education* (2nd ed., pp. xv–xxiii). New York: Macmillan.

Scottish Office Education Department. (1991). *Guidelines for staff development and appraisal in schools.* Edinburgh, Scotland: SOED.

Scottish Office Education and Industry Department. (1996). *How good is our school?* Edinburgh, Scotland: SOEID.

Stenhouse, L. (1975). *An introduction to curriculum research and development.* London: Heineman.

Sullivan, K. (1994). The impact of educational reform on teachers' professional ideologies. *New Zealand Journal of Educational Studies, 29*(1), 3–20.

Teng, T. (1994). China, People's Republic of: System of Education. In T. Husén & T. N. Postlethwaite (Eds.), *The international encyclopaedia of education* (2nd ed., pp. 750–755). Oxford, UK: Pergamon.

Thrupp, M. (1997). Shaping a crisis: The Education Review Office and South Auckland schools. In M. Olssen & K. Morris Matthews (Eds.), *New Zealand education policy in the 1990s* (pp. 145–161). Palmerston North, New Zealand: Dunmore Press.

Tickle, L. (1994). *The induction of new teachers: Reflective professional practice.* London: Cassell.

Travers, C. J., & Cooper, C. L. (1996). *Teachers under pressure: Stress in the teaching profession.* London: Routledge.

Teacher Training Agency. (1997). *Training curriculum and standards for new teachers.* London: TTA.

Waslander, S., & Thrupp, M. (1995). Choice, competition and segregation: An empirical analysis of a New Zealand secondary school market 1990–1993. *Journal of Education Policy, 10,* 1–26.

Webber, S., & Webber, T. (1994). Issues in teacher education. In

A. Jones (Ed.), *Education and society in the new Russia* (pp. 231–259). Armonk, NY: M. E. Sharpe.

Westbrook, M. A. (1994). The independent schools of St. Petersburg. In A. Jones (Ed.), *Education and society in the new Russia* (pp. 103–117). Armonk, NY: M. E. Sharpe.

Whitehead, J., Menter, I., & Stainton, R. (1996). The reform of initial teacher training: The fragility of the new school-based approach and questions of quality. *Research Papers in Education, 11*(3), 307–321.

Whitty, G. (1997). Creating quasi-markets in education: A review of recent research on parental choice and school autonomy in three countries. *Review of Research in Education, 22,* 1–83.

Whitty, G., Power, S., & Halpin, D. (1998). *Devolution and choice in education: The school, the state and the market.* Buckingham, UK: Open University Press.

Woods, P. (1995). *Creative teachers in primary schools.* Buckingham, UK: Open University Press.

Wragg, E. C., Wikeley, F. J., Wragg, C. M., & Haynes, G. S. (1996). *Teacher appraisal observed.* London: Routledge.

Wright, N., & Bottery, M. (1996). Choice of INSET in the LEA, GM and independent sectors: Is a market at work? *British Journal of Inservice Education, 22*(2), 151–173.

Wylie, C. (1995). Contrary currents: The application of the public sector reform framework in education. *New Zealand Journal of Educational Studies, 30*(2), 149–164.

Wylie, C. (1997, March). *Do new bottles alter the taste of the wine? Long-term trends in systemic school reform in New Zealand.* Paper presented at the annual meeting of the American Educational Research Association, Chicago, IL.

Zeichner, K. M. (1983). Alternative paradigms of teacher education. *Journal of Teacher Education, 34*(3), 3–9.

Zlahtic, J. (1996). *Information on INSET in Slovenia.* Paper prepared for the Association of Teacher Education in Europe. Ljubljana, Slovenia: Centre for Education and Inset.

Part 6
Teachers and Teaching

39.
Teachers' Work in Historical and Social Context

Dee Ann Spencer
Arizona State University

This chapter examines teaching as an occupation. Its focus is on teachers as workers in the labor market; on the social, demographic, economic, and political forces that have influenced teachers' work and working conditions in schools; and on the public's and teachers' perceptions of teaching as an occupation. It weaves statistical and demographic data on teachers with historical and contemporary descriptions and accounts. The intention is not only to document the past and current status of teachers and teaching but also to illustrate the remarkable similarities in teaching as an occupation over time, despite the equally remarkable transformation of the educational system in the United States.

An historical overview of teachers' work is possible because of the incredibly extensive literature on teachers and their work from multiple sources: governmental agencies, professional teachers' organizations and associations, scholarly works, texts for teachers, and most recently, historiographical collections of teachers' accounts of their work. The last source is the most recent and has made significant contributions to our understanding of teachers' perceptions of their work. Prentice and Theobald (1991) pointed particularly to the development of the historiography of women teachers as important to filling the striking absence of women's voices in the history of teaching. These works have offered views of the teaching world from the personal perspectives of those who taught and have provided a more realistic view of teaching than the idealized images in the media or the dispassionate discussions in research reports and in texts (e.g., Cuban, 1984; Hoffman, 1981; Kaufman, 1984; Myres, 1982; Rothschild & Hronek, 1992; Warren, 1985, 1989). Overviews of these personal perspectives are found in Hoffman

(1981), Kaufman (1984), and Altenbaugh (1992), each of whom examined women's personal accounts of their teaching in the United States at the turn of the century as did Spencer (1986) in her accounts of contemporary women teachers. Teachers' accounts in other countries are found in Goodson's (1992) volume of life histories (including accounts from New Zealand, Canada, the United States, and the United Kingdom); in the work of Prentice and Theobald (1991), who focused on women teachers in England, Australia, Canada, and the United States; and in the work of DeLyon and Migniuolo (1989) and Acker (1989), who looked at British teachers. These historiographical studies have made a significant contribution to a better understanding of women's roles in the history of teaching.

These works fill in a void of many decades in which classical works were seen as the only representation of teaching as an occupation. The most prominent of these was written by Willard Waller (1932) and was the singular sociological statement about the work of teachers until Lortie's *Schoolteacher* (1975). In historical retrospect, however, Waller's work was not the most kindly toward teachers. In an analysis of Waller's work, Hansot (1989) concluded that Waller described a depressing picture of "unrelieved pessimism" toward teachers and viewed them as "seriously flawed human beings." She found that Waller's writing was similar to that of a Greek tragedy through his creation of a bleak moral landscape with teachers as victims of communities. Waller's pessimism about teachers is seen in the following:

Concerning the low social standing of teachers much has been written. The teacher in our culture has always been among the persons

The author wishes to thank Mark L. Wardell, Pennsylvania State University, and Larry Saha, Australian National University, for the meticulous care they took in reviewing this chapter. Their sociological perspectives and their comments and suggestions were of inestimable help, particularly Wardell's attention to issues related to teachers' participation in the broader workforce and Saha's attention to issues related to teachers' work in schools.

Some sections of this chapter appeared in a chapter entitled "Teaching as Women's Work," in B. J. Biddle, T. L. Good, and I. F. Goodson (Eds.), *International Handbook of Teachers and Teaching,* pp. 153–198, published in Dordrecht, The Netherlands, by Kluwer in 1997. It was used with the kind permission of the publishers.

of little importance, and his place has not changed for the better the last few decades. Fifty years or more ago it used to be argued that teachers had no standing in the community because they whipped little children, and this was undoubtedly an argument that contained some elements of truth. But flogging, and all the grosser forms of corporal punishment, have largely disappeared from the modern school, and as yet there is little indication that the social standing of the profession has been elevated. (Waller, 1932, p. 58)

This bleak picture aside, the lack of other analyses of teachers' work until more recent times left a gap in the continuity of discussion about teaching as an occupation. This chapter brings various sources together to bridge some of the gaps in this discussion. The discussion begins with an overview of the historical and social context in which teaching developed as an occupation.

The Feminization of Teaching

To write about the history of teaching would be impossible without discussing its transition to a female-dominated occupation nearly 150 years ago. Examining the social, political, and economic forces in the United States that led to the feminization of teaching and to the continuing influence on the teaching workforce is important. Until recent times, however, the fact that most teachers are women has not been included in research or scholarly work as a factor influencing the nature of teaching. Although Waller (1932) mentioned gender as a factor in understanding teachers, he also reflected near contempt toward women teachers, and throughout his work his judgments were particularly severe in regard to single women (Hansot, 1989).

> The life history of the unmarried teacher seems to follow a pretty definite pattern. There are a number of years in which the hope of finding a mate is not relinquished. There is a critical period when that hope dies. An informant has suggested that hope has died when a woman buys a diamond for herself. The critical period is an incubation period during which spinsterhood ripens. During this critical period many desperate and pathetic things occur. The woman going through this period falls in love very easily, and may come to make the most open advances upon slight or no provocation.... Perhaps this hope of finding a mate always dies hard and slowly, and requires little stimulant to keep it alive after its time. (Waller, 1932, pp. 408–409)

Although Casey and Apple (1989) referred to Dreeben (1970) and Lortie (1975) as classic works on teaching as a profession, they also pointed out that these seminal works regarded women teachers as deficient and uncommitted to their work because of family obligations.

In the following sections, the history of teaching in the United States is discussed in relationship to political, economic, and social factors that affected the labor market for teachers. These factors are organized by general time periods associated with industrialization and are crosscut by gender issues and attitudes toward women's roles in the paid labor force.

The Preindustrial Period: A Family-Based Economy

During the periods of the family-based economy (the 17th and 18th centuries), there were no sharp distinctions between eco-

nomic and domestic life (Anderson, 1983; Parelius and Parelius, 1987). The work of family members was interdependent, with all family members contributing to household labor. Men, women, and children worked together in the production of goods. Teaching, as a choice of labor outside the home, was taken as temporary work to supplement men's income (Parelius & Parelius, 1987). The view of teaching as temporary work led to the lasting perception of teaching as an "episodic" occupation (Clifford, 1989).

Although teaching rarely required specific qualifications in the United States during this period, the New England states established more rigorous standards where teachers taught in either town schools or Latin grammar schools. In town schools, teachers were not as well-educated and earned about half as much as the Latin grammar school teachers. Teachers in the latter had college degrees and were held in high regard in their communities. All teachers in grammar schools were males who had to be sanctioned by the church.

High rates of teacher shortages in this period were common. Beale (1941), in an overview of schooling in colonial America, cited many examples in colonial records showing that no suitable teachers could be obtained in communities. At times, because of teacher shortages, colonists purchased indentured servants as teachers, or they were willing to hire who they could get even if they were redemptioners or convicts. Another factor contributing to the inadequacies of teachers in this period was linked to the fact that schoolmasters were often ministers who supplemented their salaries by teaching. Although training in the early colonial period was exceptional because ministers were well educated in England, by the 2nd and 3rd generations of colonists, ministers were locally trained. As a result, they were less well educated. In an attempt to improve the quality of teachers, an act was passed in Massachusetts in 1701, which required a full-time teacher in schools. This stipulation disallowed ministers who could not devote full-time work to teaching. Beale thought this legal ruling resulted in keeping the best educated people from teaching.

Elsbree (1939) wrote that the main reason teachers were mostly men during the colonial period was that they were the most highly educated. A woman's place was thought to be in the home, not in the classroom. He added that there were other reasons for reliance on men: Boys had to be kept under control by being beaten, and the general belief maintained that women could not be expected to carry out some of the other roles teachers were expected to perform such as sexton or gravedigger.

Although most teachers were men in this period, to say that women played no part in schools during this time is not accurate. In addition to being hired to teach in the summers, women taught small children (similar to primary schools today) by conducting dame schools from their own homes. Beale (1941) claimed that with some exceptions, women who taught in dame schools were mostly incompetent because the schools developed in an era when women were restricted in how much education they could receive. As a result, teachers often knew just a little more than their students. Dame schools had the lowest standards for teachers, and the pay was very low.

Women were also employed in Quaker schools in Pennsylvania as early as 1699, presumably because the Friends' philosophy was not as discriminatory against women as were other religions or society in general. Elsbree (1939) also provided an example from the 1700s in the South where wives of planters taught in "old field schools," which were private neighborhood schools established in fields not being used for crops. But he noted, all in all, women played a minor role in teaching through the colonial period and for 5 or 6 decades after the American Revolutionary War.

Although some women worked as teachers during the pre-industrial period, most women worked in their homes and were central to the family-based economy. Women's work roles changed, however, as the result of significant changes in the broader social and economic context and the effects of rapid industrialization.

The Early Industrial Period: A Family-Wage Economy

The shift in women's work roles was possible because of the transition from a family-based economy to the family-wage economy. Rooted in complex and extensive demographic growth and shifts in economic, social, and cultural patterns that occurred in the late-19th and early-20th century, the center of labor moved out of the household and into the factory system. The transformation of society from an agricultural to an industrial base also created changes in the educational system.

Occurring in parallel to rapid population growth was the decentralization of public school education and the requirement that children in all regions of the country have access to schools. Schools were created where the children were located, and teachers moved to these schools or were hired from among available applicants in the area. Teachers typically taught only a few months a year, however, so salary, prestige of teaching, and job security were seriously diminished. Teaching was seen as something anyone could do. The shift to local control of schools meant districts were often short of funds, which forced them to look for less expensive teachers. The need was fulfilled by women. The structure of industrial work, then, significantly changed the structures of families by providing avenues for women to work outside the home. The acceptance of women as wage earners and, at the same time, the dependence of families on women's wages outside their homes made teaching appealing work—especially when compared to the horrendous working conditions found in factories.

In an historical overview of the history of teaching in the United States in the 19th century, Finkelstein (1989) wrote that not only was teaching seen as respectable work for women, but it also provided them with financial and social independence and, at the same time, provided local school districts with cost-effective moral stewards of popular primary schools. These women were perceived by reformers of the time period to be instrumental in the transformation from an agrarian to an industrialized society—a society based on contractual relationships, on impersonal forms of association, and on training for an industrial, rather than agricultural, work force. The focus was to be on civic obligations, patriotism, a sense of community, and commitment to the work ethic. "They were to become creators of the self-governed, self-controlled, self-disciplined, and virtuous citizens who would embody in their behavior and disposition a fusion of public and private good" (1989, p. 18).

Elsbree (1939) also noted that sentiments among educational leaders published in the mid-1800s supported hiring women teachers based on characteristics assumed to be common to women. Among these characteristics were women's mild and gentle manners; their "natural" parental impulses; their lack of interest in winning honors, making money, or seeing the world; and their morals, which were purer than those of men.

Richardson and Hatcher's (1983) work traced the changing roles for women's work through women's increasing entrance into the workforce outside the home in the 1830–80 preindustrial period. Richardson and Hatcher focused on the cultural constraints that emanated from religious values. These values permeated the time and served as a resistant force to the economic independence of women. Through their research, Richardson and Hatcher were able to demonstrate how the establishment of state school systems and compulsory school attendance created a demand for more teachers and, therefore, greater costs to schools districts. Although school districts found it more cost efficient to hire women, these districts were constrained by the prevailing critical and alarmist reactions to the "peril" of hiring women. As a result of the competing forces of economic realities and cultural constraints, school districts across states responded unevenly to hiring women.

These moral standards were a subtext to the fact that a serious teacher shortage existed as the result of the beginning of the American Civil War. Taking away thousands of males to join the armies created the final catalyst for the transition to a predominance of women in teaching (Elsbree, 1939). After the Civil War when men returned to join the workforce, they were attracted to jobs more lucrative than teaching and, at the same time, were deterred from teaching, because by then, women predominated in schools, especially at the elementary levels (Clifford, 1989).

Musgrave (1968) described teachers in Britain through the turn of this century as similar to those of the United States; they were basically untrained or "sweated labour." In both countries, variations to this pattern ranged from teachers in rural areas, who had the lowest levels of training and lowest pay, to those in urban areas, who had the highest levels of training and highest pay. More men were teachers in secondary schools, in part, because of the persistent belief that they could control older boys better than women teachers. This belief was discrepant from Clifford's (1989) analysis of school district reports, letters from parents, teachers' diaries, and other primary sources, which showed that women were able to successfully control large, older boys. Change was also slow for women in teaching, because they were prohibited for so long from entering institutions of higher education and from obtaining the credentials they needed to teach in secondary schools (Elsbree, 1939). In brief, male teachers earned more than female teachers, because they qualified for higher paying secondary school teaching jobs.

The Mature Industrial Period: A Family-Consumer Economy

Beginning in the early decades of the 20th century, the family-consumer economic period was characterized by rapid technological change, increased productivity, and the mass production of goods. Households became centers of reproduction and consumption with many family activities relegated to other institutions such as schools, social services, and fast food industries (Anderson, 1983). Women's economic productivity became greater than ever because of these combined factors: the dependency of the family on her wages outside the home, her continued unpaid labor in the home, and her role as the primary consumer of goods.

Changes in the labor market for women were transformed by the need for a huge army of labor created by rapid industrialization. Tremendous needs developed to fill clerical and administrative positions in business and industry, nursing positions in the growing public health movement, and teaching positions in the rapidly expanding system of public education. All these jobs were linked to ideologies that expounded the advantages of hiring women for certain kinds of jobs; they were ideal as typists because their small fingers made them more dexterous, and they were ideal nurses and teachers because of their innate caring and nurturing abilities.

The growth of mass public education, which in turn created a critical shortage of trained teachers, led to the development of normal schools as teacher training institutions. [The first discussion of normal schools began in the 1830s. The first public city normal school was opened in 1852 in Boston. By the 1870s, normal schools were created on a widespread basis at universities across the country (Herbst, 1989b).] Normal schools have served, in most countries in the world, to fulfill the need for a certified labor force in schools (Herbst, 1989a). Previous to this development, requirements for teachers were nonexistent or quite minimal. As a result, a person could begin teaching at the age of 14 or 15 with no credentials (Clifford, 1978).

The typical course of study for teachers in normal schools required only 1 or 2 years. By 1900, raising standards for teacher certification was under the domain of individual states. Although teacher training increased, and teachers had acquired an increased body of knowledge and expertise that had been taught in normal schools, their pay remained low, and chronic teacher shortages continued. In fact, teachers were seen as expendable, they had no benefits, and they were subject to close monitoring of their private lives.

By the early-20th century, the high mobility rates of teachers and shortages of qualified teachers continued to be a serious problem (Rury, 1989). For men who stayed in teaching, most went on to administrative positions, and turnover rates for women teachers were extremely high, because sanctions forbid them to continue teaching once married. These drains on teaching staff were magnified because school districts were controlled by local communities that often fell short of funds. As a result, school districts, especially in rural areas, looked for less expensive teachers.

As the job market opened for males, men left teaching, and because most job markets were closed to females, women entered teaching and worked for the lower wages paid in school districts. This is not to say that school districts only hired women because they were cheaper or that women willingly accepted low wages. Instead, cash-poor school districts hired women because they were an available labor source; women accepted low wages, because their options in the work force were seriously limited, and because teachers' wages were higher than other work for women with an education (Strober & Lanford 1986; Warren, 1985). Women stayed in teaching because they did not have other options. These economic realities were combined with cultural norms that fostered the belief that women, as the natural caretakers of children, should be teachers.

Rury (1991) examined the motivations for women to continue their secondary education and participate in the job market in the United States between 1870 and 1930. Rury found that the reasons girls went to high school and went into teaching in the United States differed in two distinct time periods. In the first period from 1870 to 1900, after the American Civil War, few middle-class women worked outside the home in the United States. Although males and females attended secondary school in equal numbers, the reasons for girls' attendance were not related to entering the work force. Instead, girls stayed in school because they liked school and valued education. Rury speculated that girls focused on learning all they could before taking on the responsibilities of motherhood, as compared to boys, who focused on getting jobs. Diaries written by girls of that period supported Rury's notion that girls did not think of schooling in vocational terms but stayed in school because they enjoyed it.

Rury then demonstrated that the increasing demands of the rapidly expanding workforce intersected with women's increased willingness to work outside the home and with their interest to attend high school as a vehicle for getting a better job. [As stated on the previous page, the rationale for women joining the workforce, as well as for staying in school, differed for the period of 1870–1900 and 1900–1930.] These factors led to the second period of growth of the American high school, from 1900 to 1930, during which time more women entered the workforce. For those who entered teaching, although they earned less than males, they earned more than other working women, generally worked under better conditions, and had more prestige. We might project from Rury's analysis that women teachers, like educated girls, stayed in school because they enjoyed it.

In summary, over the periods of history discussed here, the work of teaching shifted from a piecemeal job filled by educated male clergy to a full-time job filled by educated, certified female teachers. The social, economic, and political forces of industrialization, which changed the composition of the teaching workforce, were considered in relation to the concomitant changes in demographic growth and composition of the United States and its educational system. The focus of the next section will be on the work of teachers and their roles in the workforce in recent decades.

Social Characteristics of Teachers

Occupational prestige, social approval accorded to an occupation, or societal judgments of teachers have been relatively low (Spencer, 1994; 1997a). For example, a rating system of occupational prestige, developed in the United States in 1947 by the National Opinion Research Center (NORC), has shown that for the past 45 years, teachers rank below professions such as medicine and law and above other public service semiprofessions.

While society's judgments of teaching have been lower than of other professions, expectations for teachers' behaviors have been held to higher, more restrictive standards than other occupations. These restrictions were based, in part, on the fact that most teachers have been women for the past century and a half. Traditional values and patriarchal ideologies shaped definitions of women teachers as paragons of virtue, whose purity and high morals should serve as models to children and be subject to close public scrutiny. An historical review offered here of rules and regulations imposed by communities and school districts shows the extent of these restrictions (Spencer, 1997b).

Teachers' Social Status in Historical Context

Because a woman teacher typically boarded with a family in a school's community during the last decades of the 19th century and the early decades of the 20th century, her personal behaviors could be closely observed (Almack and Lang, 1925). As boarding houses, teachers' clubs, and teacherages developed to provide alternative living arrangements for women teachers, school or school district rules and regulations allowed that their behaviors could be carefully monitored. Male teachers' social behaviors were also constrained by these rules; however, rules for males were less restrictive than those for females, although rules varied considerably by region of the country and by the size of community. Restrictions before World War I included those that banned both male and female teachers from movie theaters and frowned on teachers who played cards, danced, gambled, and swore (Beale, 1936). Smoking was not permitted, especially for women. Although there were even stricter bans on teachers' drinking alcohol, Beale (1936) noted that in some communities, drinking with a school board member or the superintendent would help a male teacher gain or keep his job.

In the 1920s and 1930s, women teachers were forbidden to cut their hair short or to use cosmetics (Beale, 1936) and were cautioned not to dress in too dowdy or too showy a fashion but, rather, to use businesswomen as their models of how to dress (Almack and Lang, 1925). Waller (1932) agreed that both men and women should dress conservatively but carried his cautions even further by advising women teachers to dress in such a way as to obscure their femininity. He also commented on the body types of teachers and thought their size had an impact on students. For example, he asserted that a small man would fail as a disciplinarian because he would be overly timid and unassertive, although he added that a "homunculus" teacher could be equally "absurd" (1932, p. 218). He thought a small woman teacher might have difficulty controlling students and that a "fat" woman was more "absurd" than a fat man. The ideal woman teacher, in Waller's opinion, was one with "a rather large dash of the masculine" (p. 220). In addition to body size, Waller also expounded on the appropriate nonverbal behaviors of teachers—their voices, mannerisms, and facial expressions. For example, he advised that a male teacher's voice should not be effeminate, emotional, or strained.

Perhaps the most constrictive rules about teachers' behaviors were about their sexual, marital, and family activities. Both male and female teachers' sexual behaviors were carefully scrutinized, and instances of promiscuity or any impropriety were not only taboo but were also grounds for dismissal (Beale, 1936). However, only the marital status of women teachers was restricted. The reasons for forbidding women teachers to marry were based on stereotypes about the proper roles for women, including that a married woman might neglect her school duties or that she might focus too much on her school duties and neglect her obligations at home. If married, it was assumed that a woman had a man to support her and, therefore, didn't need the money or that she would soon be pregnant if married and would leave teaching. Although societal attitudes toward divorce were negative, Beale (1936) wrote that it would be to a woman's advantage in getting hired if she appeared as the injured party in a divorce, although not as advantageous as getting her husband to die.

Two studies provided strong evidence of the fallacy in thinking by school districts that refused to employ married women. One study, conducted in 1928 by Elsbree, looked at the effects of marriage on leaving rates for women teachers. He found that, contrary to common beliefs, the turnover rates for men and women teachers were about the same and that marriage accounted for only 21% of women's exits from teaching (Elsbree, 1928). A few years later, Peters (1934) studied the hiring patterns of married women teachers and whether being married affected their effectiveness in the classroom. His study revealed a collective prejudice in school districts against hiring married women. However, this was not true of the large commercial and industrial organizations he included in his study. Peters' data also lead to his conclusion that being married did not negatively affect teaching effectiveness.

Despite the findings of these two studies, the ban on hiring married women continued until major shifts took place in the labor market as the result of the world wars. Just as the Civil War was the turning point in the development of teaching as a female-dominated occupation in the United States, subsequent wars drew men out of the labor force and also forced school districts not only to hire women but also to lift their restrictions on hiring married women. The postwar baby boom put the issue of women teachers' marital status to rest because of the severe shortages of teachers in schools.

These examples are but a few that demonstrate the extent to which teachers' behaviors were monitored and controlled. Such restrictions continued through the mid-20th century and, in some areas of the country, still persist. In the next section, the demographic characteristics of contemporary teachers are reviewed to examine what continuities and discontinuities have occurred with regard to the composition and social status of the teaching workforce.

Demographic Characteristics of Teachers

The teaching force composes a significant proportion of the labor force throughout the world (Organization for Economic Cooperation and Development, 1990). In the United States, teachers made up 2.1% of the total labor force by 1992 (Henke et al., 1997). In 1990–91, there were 2,559,000 teachers in public schools and 356,000 in private schools (Choy, Henke, Alt, & Medrich, 1993). By 1996–97, the number of teachers had reached an all-time high of 3.1 million, with most (2.7 million) in public schools and the remainder in private schools (392,000) (Snyder, 1996).

In 1991, the typical American teacher was a 42-year-old, white, married woman with two children, who held a graduate

Table 39.1 Selected Characteristics of Public School Teachers, 1961–91

Characteristics	Date			
	1961	1971	1981	1991
Percentage women	68.7	65.7	66.9	72.1
Percentage white	—	88.3	91.6	86.8
Percentage married	68.0	71.9	73.0	75.7
Percentage Master's or specialist degree	23.1	27.1	49.3	52.6
Average years of experience	11.0	8.0	12.0	15.0
Average age	41.0	35.0	37.0	42.0

Snyder, 1996, p. 79.

Table 39.2 Proportion of Women in Teaching in the United States, 1905–88

Level	Date					
	1905	1928	1950	1972–73	1982–83	1993–94[a]
Elementary	97.9	89.2	91.0	84.0	83.0	88.3
Secondary	64.2	63.7	56.2	46.0	48.9	56.1

Adapted from Shakeshaft, 1987, p. 20.

[a]Henke et al., 1997, p. A–9.

degree and had taught about 15 years (Snyder, 1996). Over the past 30 years, the only changes seen in this typical picture were for degrees held and years of teaching experience (see Table 39.1). Today's teacher is more highly educated and has more teaching experience than in the past.

Looking more closely at the demographic characteristics of teachers, three factors have been used to describe the composition of the teaching workforce: gender, race, and age. Each are discussed in some detail in this section.

GENDER

As described in this chapter, the most distinctive social characteristic of school teachers is that they have been predominantly female since the early stages of the transition to an industrially based economy. By 1991, women made up 72.1% of the teaching workforce, a proportion that was only slightly higher than that of 1961 (see Table 39.1). Considerable differences in gender distribution were apparent, however, when comparing teachers at the elementary and secondary levels (see Table 39.2). Women have been dominant at the elementary level, but their representation at the secondary level has varied over time. From 1905 to 1928, 64% of secondary teachers were women, but by 1972–73 this proportion was 46% of teachers. By 1993–94, this figure had increased to 56.1%—about the same as that of 1950 (52.2%).

An important question in regard to the disproportionately low number of men in teaching is whether male teachers experience their work and working conditions in similar ways as women. Research on gender composition in the workforce has focused on women in male-dominated professions and the discrimination they face in those professions. It has been argued (Kanter, 1977) that in an organization, anyone in a minority or token group—whether male or female—will experience the same kinds of problems. Williams (1992; 1993; 1995) was the first to study the question of whether men in female-dominated professions also faced discrimination. She interviewed men in four female-dominated professions: nursing, librarianship, elementary school teaching and social work. Men represent a very small minority in all four occupations. In 1990, only 5.5% of nurses, 14.8% of teachers, 16.7% of librarians, and 31.8% of social workers were men.

Williams found that although the men didn't experience dis-

crimination in hiring or promotion practices, once at work, they were "tracked" into areas of their profession that were considered more legitimate for men. This tracking worked to their advantage and directed the men toward the more prestigious and better paying positions, for example, toward administrative or supervisory positions. This type of tracking was quite different than what women experienced. They reported encountering a "glass ceiling" when trying to move up in organizational hierarchies. Instead, Williams found that the men she interviewed experienced a "glass escalator," or invisible pressures to move up in their profession, "as if on a moving escalator, they must work to stay in place" (1992, p. 256).

Williams also examined the extent to which men in female-dominated professions experienced the same subtle forms of discrimination through being excluded from informal networks as did women in male-dominated professions. While having a male supervisor can work to a woman's disadvantage, it worked to these men's advantage. Many men described a close mentoring relationship and close social ties with their supervisors, which served to promote their careers. In other subtle ways, men's work environments were enhanced; they were cast into leadership roles by female colleagues, which in turn enhanced their authority and control in the workplace and promoted the "glass escalator" phenomenon.

Williams also found that while being male was advantageous within the workplace, men reported that the public had negative perceptions of them for being in a low-status, female-dominated occupation. In fact, she noted that male elementary teachers even had to deal with the added public suspicion that they were pedophiles. She concluded that in addition to the low pay, the cultural stigma attached to men in elementary teaching deterred them from entering the profession. She speculated, however, that even if the pay were better, the cultural barriers would still persist toward men entering elementary teaching and, at the same time, would push male teachers onto the "glass escalator" and up to more lucrative, "manly" positions such as principal. She concludes that, "Men take their gender privilege with them when they enter predominantly female occupations; this translates into an advantage in spite of the numerical rarity" (Williams, 1992, p. 263).

In another study of male elementary teachers, Allan (1993) explored several contradictions that men experienced based on the encouragement they received to move ahead in their profession versus their low status as tokens in a female-dominated profession. On the one hand, they formed gender alliances with their women coworkers, but on the other hand, if too closely allied, they were seen as unreliable or threatening. They also felt that to be a good teacher they had to exhibit certain "feminine" qualities, yet they had to prove they were "real men" to avoid assumptions about their character. In other words, they felt they had to "negotiate the meaning of masculinity every day" (Allan, 1993, p. 114).

Allan found that men reported preferential treatment in hiring because of affirmative action and the attempt to bring more men into the classroom to provide different role models for children. Another explanation for preferential hiring was that male principals wanted other men with whom they could form gender alliances, especially around interests in sports. Indeed, male teachers reported that they frequently talked about sports with their male principals in informal settings. At the same time, some reported being judged by female colleagues as having been hired for those reasons rather than for their qualifications as a teacher. However, this was not always true. A few male teachers reported that they were viewed as threats to the principal because of their "masculine" qualities, as compared to women teachers who were seen as more "docile and tractable" (Allan, 1993, p. 120).

Allan found that male elementary teachers were in a double bind as to how they should act. The paradox for them was that "The man who is too 'masculine' would be suspected of being an incompetent and insensitive teacher, while the man who is nurturing and empathic would be stereotyped as feminine and 'unnatural'" (Allan, 1993, p. 126).

Historically, gender stratification has characterized teaching—particularly the gender composition of elementary and secondary schoolteachers—and, as to be discussed later, the management of schools. As was seen in this section, teachers experience their work in schools differently depending on their gender, which concomitantly affects their mobility in the profession.

RACE

In addition to differences in employment of United States teachers based on gender, differences in employment for these teachers also occurs based on racial factors. For example, Perkins (1989) traced the growth of a dual system for educating African Americans and Whites in the South and found that there was serious discrimination against African-American teachers, not only in hiring them but also in paying them pitifully low salaries and limiting training so that they scored lower on tests, which justified claims that they shouldn't be paid as much as White teachers. A rural-urban split occurred, with most African-American teachers working in urban areas because urban school districts were able to offer higher pay. As a result, it was nearly impossible to find African-American teachers for rural schools. Most African-American teachers in both rural and urban areas were women because other jobs were closed to them. By 1900, about 5% of the teaching force was African American, but because African-American teachers were restricted to teaching African-American children and because they were prohibited from entering White colleges, the numbers of African Americans in teaching were further limited.

After World War I, as other jobs opened, fewer and fewer African Americans chose teaching, and those who did enter teaching left for higher paying jobs. By 1950, after the feminization of teaching had become an accepted fact, sharp regional differences had disappeared and the teaching force was female and White—except for African-American teachers, who lived mostly in the South. By 1950, an increased number of African-American teachers were women, a transformation that had been occurring since 1900. Administrators, however, remained overwhelmingly male. After 1954, when African-American schools were closed, White schools often didn't hire African-American teachers. Therefore, although school desegregation began, it worked to the detriment of African-American teachers. As other job opportunities expanded for African Americans, teaching was not a top career choice (Perkins, 1989).

By 1993–94, 7.4% of the public school teaching force and 10% of the principals in the United States were African-American, only a slight increase since 1900. There were even fewer African-American teachers in private schools (3.1%) (Henke et al., 1996). Minority teachers were more likely to teach in schools with higher proportions (more than 50%) of minority students (Henke et al., 1996). Although minority students constituted the majority of enrollments in 23 of the 25 largest city school systems in the country, most of their teachers, 87% of females and 90% of males, were white, non-Hispanic. While 29.6% of all students in urban schools were African American and 51.8% were of minorities, only 3%, of all teachers in urban schools were African American and only 9% were of minorities. Minority teachers were not only underrepresented in urban schools, but were seriously underrepresented in suburban and rural or small city school districts. The low representation of minority teachers in schools composed primarily of minority students and the extremely low proportions of minority teachers in suburban and rural or small city schools has perpetuated a problem mentioned by educational researchers: Children should have teachers not only who may better motivate and work with minority students but also who will serve as role models of successful professionals for both minority and nonminority students (Carnegie Task Force on Teaching as a Profession, 1986; Henke et al., 1997).

Rury (1989) explained that although African Americans have been underrepresented among teachers, they are still more highly represented in teaching than any other profession. Historically, the addition of African Americans and immigrants to the teaching force also reduced teachers' status because of racist attitudes in American society. Perkins (1989) predicted that the problem of underrepresentation of African Americans would continue to increase in the future as fewer African Americans enter teaching. She added that to not choose teaching is a liberating choice for many African Americans.

AGE

The age of teachers has changed drastically over the past century. The tremendous shortage of teachers and the lack of training available in normal schools during the early decades of the 20th century meant that teachers, usually girls, often entered teaching at 15 or 16 years of age. As requirements for training increased, the age of entrance to teaching also increased. School district policies that forced married women out of teaching and the eventual changes in these policies, which were dictated by severe teacher shortages, resulted in what Rury (1989) described as a bimodal age distribution of teachers. That is, women entered teaching at a young age and later reentered after having married and raised their children to school age.

Although some sources have taken recent figures on teachers' ages to indicate that the teaching force is aging, Table 1 shows that their average age of 42 years in 1991 was actually the same as that in 1961—41 years (Snyder, 1996; Henke et al., 1997). For women, the teaching force was younger in 1991 with an average age of 42 years than it was in 1961 with an average age of 46 years (Snyder, 1996).

In 1993–94, the average age of teachers was nearly the same for elementary and secondary levels, for public and private sectors, and for all ethnicities. The highest proportion of teachers were 40–49 years old (41%), followed by 50 years or older (24.6%), 30–39 years old (22.7%), and less than 30 years old (11.8%) (Henke et al., 1997).

The Economic Status of Teachers

Salaries

As mentioned earlier, teaching has not been regarded as an occupation with high prestige. A major factor in ranking teachers' occupational prestige is their salaries. During the early decades of the 20th century, when subsistence level pay was the norm, tremendous population growth occurred in the United States. This resulted in huge teacher shortages. The lack of teachers needed to provide basic education to the growing population reached what some believed to be an "alarming" level (Evenden, 1919). The alarm centered on high dropout rates, high illiteracy rates, physically "inefficient" children, children who did not speak English, the lack of teachers' training or professional preparation, and the press by industry for children to leave school to more directly "serve their country" in the industrial workforce. Although the concern today with dropouts, illiteracy, children's health, English language usage, and the school-to-work transition are still of concern to the public and to educators, in 1919, 5 out of 6 children dropped out of school, less than 10% finished high school, only 1 out of 100 graduated from college, and 1 out of every 20 people over the age of 10 years could neither read nor write.

This alarm resulted in the creation of a special commission by the National Education Association (NEA) in 1919 to address the "National Emergency in Education." The commission came to this conclusion: All of these problems were related to the fact that low teachers' salaries did not attract people into teaching (Evenden, 1919). Especially the poorer, rural communities that were faced with serious teacher shortages couldn't attract teachers. After World War I, demobilization camps were canvassed for possible teacher recruits, but few people were located who had the necessary preparation, and of those eligible, few wanted to enter teaching because of the growing belief that teaching and the low pay teachers received was not a "man's task." As a result, people were hired who were described as "inexperienced, untrained, immature, or 'erstwhile' teachers who had been introduced into the schools in a valiant, tho [sic] often misguided effort to open the schools" (Evenden, 1919, p. 3).

Normal schools were criticized for their inadequate preparation of teachers, although this problem was linked to the low pay that normal school faculty made.

Low pay also lead to an extraordinary exodus of teachers into more lucrative fields such as stenography, bookkeeping and other clerical work, nursing, reconstruction work, and other jobs associated with the end of World War I. The impetus for the creation of the commission was to attack the central problem of low salaries and make a "frantic appeal" to schools to act on the problem. The commission claimed that teachers' salaries had not kept up with the cost of living between 1906 and 1918. They found that 80% of teachers in the country at that time made at or below that period's minimal standards of living, despite the fact that more and more was expected of teachers in terms of their training and work. They concluded that the acceptance of low salaries was a relic of the past when money was "rather a means for the stay-at-home girl to make a little 'ready money' and have in addition the 'peace of mind' which is the reward of the missionary and the social worker" (Evenden, 1919, p. 99).

In the same report, comparisons of teaching to other professions showed that teachers earned far less than other professionals and less than skilled laborers such as bricklayers, bakers, blacksmiths, and carpenters. They also reported that in New York City, teachers were paid the same as butchers, chauffeurs, clerks, machinists, tailors, and waiters.

Low teachers' salaries, in comparison to other occupations, particularly those requiring a college degree, continues to be a problem. For example, over half a century since the NEA report described above, Ornstein (1980) looked at teachers' salaries during the decade between 1969–70 and 1979–80 and found that, even when taking into account an average increase in the consumer price index, teachers experienced decreased purchasing power. When projecting average annual salaries of classroom teachers, he estimated that in 1985 their salaries would "amount to less than two thirds of the family budget needed for an intermediate standard of living (a family of four), and by 1990 it would approach a mere half" (p. 679).

In other recent research, Salmon (1987) found that during the ten-year period in the United States between 1976–77 and 1986–87, not only were teachers' salaries lower than other professions, but their salaries also decreased in relation to inflation rates. Anthony (1987) took this fact a step further and found that not only were teachers' salaries less than other professions requiring a four-year college education, but teachers were also no better off than those in occupations that did not require a college degree.

Not surprisingly, low teacher pay is linked to teacher dissatisfaction and also to the number of new entrants who are attracted into teaching (Henke et al., 1997). On the 1993–94 Schools and Staffing Survey (SASS) only 45% of teachers agreed or strongly agreed with the statement, "I am satisfied with my teaching salary." Although less than half were satisfied, the number of those who strongly agreed had increased since 1987–88. In 1987–88, 8% of public school teachers strongly agreed that they were satisfied with their salaries; by 1993–94 this proportion had increased to 12%.

In 1993–94, 53% of all public and 40% of private school teachers earned some type of supplemental income related to their teaching jobs (Henke et al., 1997). Teachers earned money from jobs outside school through summer employment or a second job (moonlighting) during the school year. Of public school teachers, 25% earned incomes from outside sources, while 31% of private school teachers did so. Speculations suggest that the differences may be explained either by the fact that private school teachers earned lower salaries than public school teachers and, therefore, needed the extra income or that private schools may have provided fewer opportunities for school-related supplemental income (Henke et al., 1997). For both public and private school teachers, earning supplemental income—whether school-related or not—was more common among secondary, less-experienced, younger, and single teachers.

VARIATIONS IN TEACHERS' SALARIES

Teachers' salaries vary considerably depending on teachers' genders, races, teaching levels, school sectors, and the geographic regions in which they teach. These salaries are further varied because each school district in the country relies on different salary schedules—each based on experience and education to determine teachers' pay. In some school districts, the use of merit pay and career ladders adds to the complexity of understanding variations in teachers' pay.

Salary schedules were adopted in school districts in response to pressures by teacher organizations to equalize the pay of elementary and secondary teachers, male and female teachers, and White and African-American teachers (Newman, 1994). Newman (1994) pointed out that salary schedules varied widely between school districts in terms of their beginning salaries, the spread between beginning salaries and those of the most experienced and highly educated teachers, and the amount of money afforded for the steps between the two. Salary schedules that have had low increments and relatively little difference between their first and last steps have given teachers little incentive to stay in teaching. More attractive salary schedules that offer rewards for teachers who stay in teaching and gain more education are more likely to encourage teachers to stay in the occupation.

Newman (1994) also explained that the subject of merit pay has been controversial over the past century. Although increasing salaries for better teachers has been regarded, in principle, as a sound idea, determining what characterizes "better" teachers has become a problem. The use of teacher tests, students' test scores, and classroom evaluation forms have been the subject of controversy until the present time, and no clear solutions have been found.

The career ladder concept emerged in the 1980s as a strategy that would provide incentives for teachers to stay in the occupation by recognizing a more complex set of stages to signify progress in their work as compared to the previously automatic movement from one step to the next on a salary schedule (Newman, 1994). The qualifications for climbing the rungs on a career ladder vary considerably by state and local plans. In addition, a nationwide career ladder has also been proposed (Newman, 1994). The effects and outcomes of this proposal are not clear at this point.

Gender. Teachers have always been paid low wages, often barely at subsistence levels, and females have been paid even less than males. Brenton (1970) noted that in 1847, male teachers in Massachusetts (considered the most progressive state in education) earned $24.51 per month, whereas females earned $8.07. In Connecticut during the same year, males earned $16 a month, whereas females earned $6.50. In New York, males earned $14.96 a month, and females earned $6.69.

> By contrast, shoemakers, harness-makers, carpenters, blacksmiths, painters, and other skilled workers often made twice the wage male teachers did. Seamstresses, factory workers, and even some servant girls earned more than female teachers did. The *Forty-sixth Annual Report,* issued by Philadelphia in 1864, noted that "a large proportion of the [women] teachers receive each less than the janitress who sweeps the School-House." (Good, 1970, p. 70)

In recent times, Lawton (1987) estimated it would require a 25% increase in pay for United States teachers to place them at international norms for the position of teachers in the overall global occupational structure. However, teachers' salaries have been high for women when compared to other women workers, while low for men when compared to men's salaries in other occupations (OECD, 1990). Low pay is a factor clearly associated with the predominance of women in teaching. As suggested earlier in this chapter, the link between the two factors is a reflection of the low status assigned to jobs in the United States that are predominantly performed by females.

A precursor to these attitudes was the perception that women who taught did so as an activity to fill their time until marriage. Unfortunately, this perception was firmly entrenched in the minds of the public as was the cultural stereotype that teaching appealed to emotion (a feminine trait) rather than to intellect (a masculine trait) (Feiman-Nemser & Floden, 1986). Dealing with children was seen as something that came naturally to women and something that parents did with no training. Therefore, teachers were not considered as deserving of the high wages that those in more "scientific," male-dominated occupations received.

These perceptions have been disputed by numerous research studies, including Prentice and Theobald (1991), who reviewed studies in Australia, the United States, and England that showed women taught because they needed the income. Clifford (1978) examined hundreds of letters and diaries written by 19th-century teachers and found that although teachers' salaries were not considered equally important in the lives of women as of men, the women did not wish to be "a financial burden nor otherwise indebted to anyone" (p. 10). Even though low, the salaries of women teachers gave them economic independence and were important contributions to their families.

Today large differences exist between the salaries of men and women in schools, because principals, who earn far more than teachers, are mostly males (see Table 39.6 later in this chapter). As shown in Table 39.3, the differences in salaries of teachers and principals in 1990–91 were significant across all school districts, regardless of the district's size (Choy et al., 1993). The gender gap, therefore, has created and perpetuated a parallel wage gap within schools.

In 1996, national data were available for the first time to ana-

Table 39.3 Basic Salary for Full-time Teachers and Principals in Public Schools, United States, 1990–91

Location	Salary by Position	
	Teachers	Principals
Central city	$32,202	$53,253
Urban fringe/large town	34,935	56,304
Rural/small town	27,748	44,272

Choy et al., 1993, p. 68.

lyze variations in patterns of teachers' salaries (Chambers & Bobbitt, 1996). Based on the 1990–91 SASS data from 40,000 public and 5,000 private school teachers, patterns of compensation by teachers' background characteristics, their qualifications, and their working conditions were identified.

The NCES report found that despite the closing gap between male and female teachers' salaries, male teachers' salaries were higher than those of females—from 10 to 13% higher in public schools (Chambers & Bobbitt, 1996). In private schools the differential was even higher with males earning 16–18% more than females. They asked how this was possible when formal salary schedules are used in most school districts (94% of public and 63% of private schools). Their research, which allowed them to control for far more school characteristics than are reflected in salary scales, revealed the answer. The analysis revealed that gaps between the salaries of male and female public school teachers were accounted for by differences in their qualifications and their working conditions, by how females were treated and perceived compared to males, and by how teachers responded to differences in employment opportunities in the larger teacher labor market. They also found that there were differential effects of teachers' marital status. Married females earned lower salaries than unmarried females, while there were no differences in males' salaries related to their marital status. The authors noted that the general structural differences in the labor market by gender have indicated that women may be willing to accept lower wages to move when their spouse takes a different job or to support conditions that allow them to care for their children (Chambers & Bobbitt, 1996).

Anthony (1987) also compared the incomes of male and female married teachers and found that the annual salary of a classroom teacher was $32,000, while the total combined income of a married teacher whose spouse worked was over $55,000. While 84% of the male teachers and 72% of females were married, only 54% of the males had spouses who worked full time, so their teaching salaries were the primary income; in 20% of the cases, the male spouse was the sole support for the family. For female teachers, however, 91% had working spouses.

Teachers' gender is a continuing factor in the differentiation of teachers' work and pay. Although the gap between men and women's salaries has closed tremendously over time, a gap still exists, particularly when considering the disproportionate number of males who hold higher paying administrative positions in schools and school districts. This gap is likely to continue if the work discussed earlier of Williams (1992, 1993) and Allan (1993) confirms that interaction in informal networks in schools served to promote men's careers and guide them toward administrative positions.

Race. The NCES report showed that the only differences in the salaries of teachers of various races or ethnicities were among public schools teachers where White and Hispanic males earned higher salaries than White females (Chambers & Bobbitt, 1996).

Teaching Level. The NCES report found that both male and female secondary teachers earned more than elementary teachers (Chambers & Bobbitt, 1996). This differential was even greater in public schools than in private schools. The SASS survey also included data from teachers employed in special education, vocational or technical, and alternative schools. Comparisons of teacher's salaries in these schools and of those in public schools showed little difference. Teachers in special education private schools earned 36% more than teachers in private elementary, secondary, and Montessori schools. Further analysis showed that these differences could be attributed to the fact that a greater proportion of private special education teachers held state teacher certification than did other private school teachers.

Public and Private Sectors. Again, looking at the NCES report, findings showed that the salaries of public school teachers far exceeded those of private school teachers (Chambers & Bobbitt, 1996). In fact, public school teachers earned from 25% to 119% more than private school teachers, depending on the type of private school. Much of this gap was explained by the differences in teachers' characteristics: Public school teachers had higher qualifications. However, other factors related to the characteristics of their work environments in public and private schools could have explained differences in teachers' salaries. Controlling for differences in both teacher and school characteristics in public and private schools, residual differences were hypothesized to relate either to unobservable characteristics that made private schools such attractive workplaces to teachers that they would accept lower wages or to factors such as certification requirements, which influenced the movement of teachers between the sectors. In both public and private schools, teachers with higher degrees earned higher salaries, as did teachers in public schools with undergraduate majors in mathematics, business, and vocational education. Teachers who worked in school beyond normal school hours also earned higher salaries. The authors acknowledged that definitive answers about these differences, however, were not possible from the existing data.

Geographic Region. Extreme differences in teachers' salaries have existed consistently depending on the geographic region in which teachers work. For example, in 1920, Almack and Lang found great variability in teachers' salaries in different states and cities and even within school districts in the United States: "In one city the lowest salary paid to elementary-school teachers is $500 a year; the highest is $2,000. In another city the median salaries for men in the elementary schools are $2083; for women, $1255" (1925, p. 238).

Ornstein (1980) compared teachers' salaries among states and regions of the country. The Far West region ranked as the top paying region, the Southeast as the lowest, and the Great Lakes region as the national average. In another report, data from 1990–91 showed extreme differences when comparing salaries between states (Choy et al., 1993). Teachers salaries were highest in Connecticut ($43,326) and the lowest in South Dakota ($20,354), and in 1994–95, these states were still the highest and lowest paying—Connecticut ($51,495) and South Dakota ($26,747). For principals, salaries were highest in Connecticut ($66,685) and lowest in North Dakota ($32,273). These figures showed that in the highest paying states, salaries were over twice those of the lowest paying states for both teachers and principals (Choy et al., 1993). Regardless of the location, principals (mostly males) were paid at least 50% more than teachers. Ornstein (1980) found that the greatest differences in teachers' salaries, however, were within states, a fact concealed when looking only at state averages. For example, teachers in large cities made far more than those in rural or small city areas.

The reason for this discrepancy in teachers' salaries is found in the fact that tremendous inequities in school funding exist between and within states. Biddle (1997) found that these inequities in funding and rates of child poverty were strongly correlated to differences in math and science achievement scores of students. In brief, students in poorer districts do less well than students in affluent school districts. Following Biddle's findings, these inequities in funding would also account for differences in teachers' salaries and in their working conditions. That is, poorer school districts cannot offer salaries nor provide working conditions that would adequately compensate teachers for the problems they face in these schools—a factor ultimately leading to the detriment of student learning.

Social Mobility of Teachers

For many sociologists, occupational mobility is considered the most important measure of social mobility. Social mobility, or the movement from one social-class position or status to another in a social system, is typically examined in terms of intragenerational mobility (movement within a person's career) and intergenerational mobility (movement in social class between generations).

In the United States, teachers' social-class backgrounds have shifted since the turn of the century from farm and blue-collar backgrounds to middle- and upper-middle-class backgrounds. Havighurst and Levine (1979) found that by 1939, teachers were mostly from more heterogeneous backgrounds. Between 1961 and 1986, the percent of teachers reporting that their fathers were farmers decreased from 26.5% to 13.3%. There was an increase of teachers who reported that their fathers were professionals or semiprofessionals from 14.5% to 21.9%. By 1986, teachers' fathers' occupations were as follows: farmers, 13.1%; unskilled workers, 8.7%; skilled or semiskilled workers, 29.9%; clerical or sales workers, 5.0%; managerial or self-employed, 21.5%; and professional or semiprofessionals, 21.9% (National Education Association, 1987). As teachers' backgrounds have become more similar to that of their parents, it has reduced the extent to which they show intergenerational mobility.

In brief, teachers have suffered from low pay and low prestige in most societies throughout the history of teaching (Herbst, 1989a). As the overall level of education in American society increased, and as teachers came from higher social classes, both the intergenerational and intragenerational mobility became

more limited. Within teaching, social mobility, particularly for women, continued to be mostly horizontal or lateral movement from one similar teaching position to another.

Supply and Demand

As school enrollments increased during the late-19th and early-20th centuries in the United States, the number of teachers increased at nearly the same the rate (Henke et al., 1997). Beginning in 1946, high birthrates continued for twenty years into the mid-1960s. From the mid-1960s to the mid-1970s, the number of births fell. This pattern paralleled the increase in teacher demand through the years when children of the baby boom were in school and the drop in teacher demand through the years until 1984. However, in 1976, when baby-boom children became of childbearing age, the number of births rose as did enrollments in schools when the children reached school age. The demand for teachers will continue into the 21st century (Newman, 1994).

Newman (1994) calls teacher supply a "complex guessing game" influenced by the number of college students who may choose to major in education and enter teaching, the ability of school districts to attract teachers from other districts or states, the return of former teachers to teaching, or the number of people who enter teaching through nontraditional routes such as alternative certification or post baccalaureate teacher education programs.

Although predictions stated that teacher shortages would occur in the mid- to late-1980s, this did not happen, neither generally nor for specific subject areas (Henke et al., 1996). A SASS data report for 1993–94 looked at factors affecting whether school districts filled vacancies in specific teaching fields: the type of financial incentives they offered, the difficulty they had in filling a vacancy, and whether the district provided free training to teach in the field where shortages existed (Henke et al., 1996). The report found that few districts offered financial incentives to fill positions where there were shortages; that although 87% of public and private schools reported at least one vacancy, only 3% of elementary schools found it difficult to fill the vacancies; and that about 20% of public and 25% of private schools provided free teacher training. The report concluded that no school districts in 1993–94 were experiencing teacher shortages with any severity. Of greatest concern in regard to teacher supply and demand was that school districts serving low-income students had excessive difficulty finding teachers. The SASS data showed that these schools were more likely to hire teachers who were not fully qualified in their fields and to fill vacancies with long-term substitute teachers (Henke et al., 1997).

Although the 1993–94 SASS data indicated no national shortage of teachers in the 1990s, this will not be true by the year 2006. With the exception of schools serving larger proportions of low-income students, projections to 2006 show that there will be a 10% increase in enrollments, which will concomitantly require an increase of 325,000 to 600,000 teachers. Although the supply and demand relation for teachers is dependent on a variety of economic and demographic fluctuations, the demand would be affected particularly by the potential retirement of teachers from the baby-boom generation.

Attraction to Teaching

The single most powerful recruiter of teachers are schools themselves. People who have had positive experiences in school can prolong that experience by becoming teachers. Observing teachers for many years from a student perspective serves as a basis for making a career decision to teach and as a model for a future teacher's own behaviors in the classroom.

That people are attracted to teaching for its intrinsic rewards is not surprising in view of teachers' low salaries. In fact, annual surveys administered to teachers over the past several decades reflect teachers' altruism as one of the most common reasons given for entering teaching (Lortie, 1975). The results of a poll administered in the 1980s also reflected some of these specific attractions to teaching: a desire to work with young people (65.6%), belief in the value of education in society (37.2%), and interest in a particular subject (37.1%) (NEA, 1987). The adherence to altruistic ideals and intrinsic rewards among teachers, especially given the historical limitations on the range of jobs open to women, has served to somewhat offset the lack of extrinsic rewards in teaching.

The Teacher Follow-up Survey administered in 1993–94 (SASS), showed that teachers were satisfied with their jobs (Henke et al., 1997). For example, 82% of all teachers indicated they were satisfied overall with their jobs and about 79% were satisfied with their working conditions. Ranked lowest were both their satisfaction with the prestige of teaching (58%) and with their salaries (58%). Teachers who left teaching and entered new occupations were far more favorable about the prestige of their new jobs (81 to 83%).

Although teachers do leave teaching because of their dissatisfaction with their low pay, the Teacher Follow-up Survey (Henke et al., 1997) showed that teachers who left teaching to enter another occupation did not earn more in the first year of their new job. In fact, overall they earned about the same, or even less, as when teaching. Some of the lack of differences in teaching and nonteaching salaries may be accounted for by the fact that, in 1993–94, the salaries of these former teachers may have been based on having taught a number of years, while the 1994–95 salary in a new job represented earnings for the first year in a new occupation. Increases in income when leaving teaching were seen, however, for those who took nonteaching jobs in schools, usually an administrative position. (See Table 3 for differences in teachers' and principals' salaries.)

Teachers may stay in teaching for a variety of reasons, whether they are satisfied with teaching or not. In fact, in 1985, 51% of all public school teachers had thought about leaving teaching (Snyder, 1996). Although this proportion dropped by 1995, still 41% of teachers had, at some time, seriously considered leaving teaching. Because 97% of teachers for both time periods also indicated that they loved to teach (Snyder, 1996), we might conclude that their thoughts of leaving teaching were related to working conditions in their schools, financial problems, or circumstances in their personal lives.

Carter (1989) attempted to determine how school districts have been able to attract good teachers despite the low salaries they pay. Her answer was that the teaching force has included people who have experienced discrimination in other work, and therefore teaching salaries may not have seemed so low to them (e.g., women, people of color, new immigrants). Historically, teaching was more accessible to women than other occupations, and for African Americans, access to teaching had few additional barriers when compared to other occupations.

While interpersonal and service themes have been prevalent over time, other factors that have influenced recruitment to teaching have been crosscut by gender issues. The past restriction of occupational choices for women in the work force has served as an attraction to teaching, and the flexibility of teachers' work schedules allowed women greater compatibility with family life. However, changing roles for women have altered this pattern. For example, of the teachers who returned to teaching after an absence in 1993–94, only 22% were absent to spend time in homemaking or child-care activities (Henke et al., 1997). The other 80% left to take other jobs, to go back to school, to become substitute teachers, to teach at another level, to enter the military, or were unemployed. However, when looking at how "breaks in service" influence salaries, teachers experienced a loss of salary each time they returned to teaching after a break.

A measure of teachers' satisfaction is whether they would enter teaching if they could start over (Henke et al., 1997; Snyder, 1996). Responses to this question for several decades showed some fluctuation. Teachers' satisfaction was high in 1961 and in 1971, with over three-fourths of teachers indicating they would enter teaching if starting over. This proportion dropped to less than one half of teachers in 1981 but increased in 1991 and again in 1993–94 to about two thirds of teachers. This pattern matches that of teachers' salaries, which diminished sharply in the 1970s, compared to other professionals (Henke et al., 1997). In other words, teachers' degree of satisfaction with teaching appeared to have been correlated with changes in their salaries.

Teachers' Working Conditions

Teachers' perceptions of their work are influenced by many factors, particularly by the working conditions in their own schools. The National Center for Education Statistics has described schools as workplaces using the following characteristics: sector (public or private school), school location (central city, urban fringe or large town, or rural or small town), level of the school (elementary, secondary, or combined), and school size. These characteristics provide a wide range of possible working conditions for teachers, especially as influenced by differences in the social, political, and economic factors within schools and school districts. Some of these factors are discussed in the following sections.

School Types

In 1993–94, as seen in Table 39.4, private schools were more common in central cities, while public schools were more concentrated in rural areas or small towns; the number of elementary schools was three times greater than secondary when both sectors were combined; private elementary schools were far more common than private secondary schools; and private schools were smaller than public school at all levels and were more likely to combine elementary and secondary than were public schools (Henke et al., 1997).

Table 39.4 Percentage Distributions of Schools According to Sector, Community Type, and Level, and Average Size by Level, 1993–94

	Percentage of Schools			Average Size		
	Total	Public	Private	Total	Public	Private
Community Type						
Central city	27.0	23.8	37.2			
Urban fringe/large town	28.5	27.1	29.9			
Rural/small town	44.4	49.1	29.9			
School Level						
Elementary	68.8	71.9	59.5	404	463	180
Secondary	20.8	24.3	9.8	656	700	318
Combined	10.4	3.8	30.7	211	318	169

Henke et al., 1997, p. 13.

Class Size

As school enrollments increased during the late-19th and early-20th centuries in the United States, the number of teachers increased at nearly the same rate. Until the mid-1920s, the pupil to teacher ratio ranged from 34 to 37 pupils for every one teacher (Snyder, 1993). After that time, the ratio showed a slow decline until the 1960s, when it fell more rapidly from 27 to 23 pupils per teacher. In the 1970s, enrollments declined, but the number of teachers remained steady, and the pupil to teacher ratio dropped to 18 by 1984–85. By 1993–94, the pupil to teacher ratio had risen to 23.5 for public schools, and to 20.4 for private schools (Henke et al., 1997).

Workload

A number of factors can be taken into account when calculating teachers' workloads such as the number of hours in teaching, the hours spent on teaching-related activities (preparing lessons, grading students' work, and other activities of a nonstudent nature), the size and number of classes taught, and the number of students with whom teachers have contact. Between 1961 and 1993–94, as seen in Table 39.5, the average number of hours per week that public school teachers spent on all teaching activities stayed about the same—46 to 47 hours per week—while their class sizes became smaller—from 28 students in 1961 to 24 students in 1993–94 (Henke et al., 1997; Smith et al., 1997).

Availability of Resources

The extent to which teachers reported having adequate teaching materials varied by school sector, size of school, and the income level of students (Henke et al., 1997). More teachers in private schools (86%) than in public schools (73%), more public school teachers in smaller districts and schools, and those in schools with students of higher income levels reported having adequate materials. Or, larger schools and those with more low-income students reported less access to adequate materials.

Student Characteristics

Of all schools participating in the National School Lunch Program in 1993–94, 40% of elementary students and 28% of sec-

Table 39.5 Average Hours per Week on All Teaching Duties and Average Class Size for Public School Teachers from 1961 to 1993–94

	Date				
	1961	1971	1981	1991	1993–94
Average hours worked on all teaching duties	47	47	46	47	45.5
Class size					
Elementary	29	27	25	24	23.2
Secondary	28	27	23	26	23.7

Henke et al., 1997; Smith et al., 1997.

ondary students qualified for free or reduced-price lunches. Of these students, more were enrolled in central-city schools, in schools of more than 50% minority enrollments, and schools with 10% or more Language Minority (LM) students (Henke et al., 1997).

In 1993–94, most teachers (90%) taught in schools that had at least some minority students, although the proportion of minority students was greater in public than in private schools and greater in central-city schools than in other community types (Henke et al., 1997). Nearly 40% of all teachers also reported having LM students in their classes (Henke et al., 1997). Although the estimated average number of LM students per teacher was only two, only 19% of the teachers with fewer than 10% LM students had the training necessary to teach them. In contrast, 87% of those teachers with more than 50% LM students in their classes had special training. More teachers in schools with higher proportions of LM students (in central cities) thought that students' problems with the English language were a "serious" problem, than those with lower proportions of LM students (in urban fringe or large towns and rural areas or small towns).

School Climate

The 1993–94 SASS survey of teachers asked if they felt safe in their schools (Henke et al., 1997). Of the responding teachers, 23% reported being threatened by a student, and 9.6% reported being attacked. The greatest proportion of public school teachers who reported that safety was of concern were in central-city schools, secondary schools, and schools with the highest percentage of students on free and reduced-price lunches. The same pattern was true of the teachers' responses to questions about how much student misbehavior interfered with teaching and learning. Far fewer private school teachers reported these problems as a serious disruption in their classrooms.

When teachers were asked to indicate what students' problems they thought were most serious in their schools, the two most common were that students came to school unprepared to learn (25.6%) and that they were apathetic (21.2%) (Henke et al., 1997). Again, few private school teachers reported these problems.

Collegial Relationships

Most teachers (85%) felt their colleagues shared the beliefs and mission of the school, and about 80% agreed that their staff worked cooperatively. Less than two thirds (63.7%) thought teachers in their school consistently enforced rules. The differences in responses to these items were not surprising if we consider that teachers typically establish statements of school mission and goals as a cooperative whole and that mission and goal statements are often global and sometimes vague in nature, for example, "We will build a community of learners." The enforcement of rules, however, is subject to multiple interpretations within each teacher's classroom and, therefore, subject to the interpretation that rules are inconsistently enforced.

Parental Involvement

Although the assumption is made that strong parental support is conducive to creating more desirable working conditions for teachers and more effective learning conditions for students, in 1993–94 only 12% of public school teachers reported they had strong support from parents (Henke et al., 1997). In contrast, far more private school teachers, 42%, indicated they had strong parental support. Accordingly, 28% of public school teachers indicated that the lack of parental support was a serious problem in their schools, while only 4% of private school teachers found this to be a serious problem.

The NCES report provided important data for understanding the complex conditions under which teachers work and the differential effects of these conditions. Other factors, however, also shape teachers' perceptions of their work. Perhaps the most important of these is the influence of teachers' and students' social class and how it affects interaction within the school culture.

Social Class and School Culture

Some researchers have explored the ways in which working conditions are experienced, mediated, and shaped by teachers' interaction within school cultures. This research assumes that teachers come into schools with sets of beliefs, attitudes, and values linked to their family social-class backgrounds and to their own social-class positions within their work and personal worlds. Their perspectives not only serve as lenses through which they perceive and experience their work in schools but they also serve as the basis for making judgments about students and colleagues within the school setting.

The culture of teaching was the focus of a groundbreaking chapter in the last volume of the *Handbook of Research on Teaching* (Wittrock, 1986). The chapter, "The Cultures of Teaching," by Feiman-Nemser and Floden (1986), explored the growing literature on how teachers define their work, with particular focus on the roles of women in the formation of the cultures of teaching. The authors defined a teaching culture as "embodied in the work-related beliefs and knowledge teachers share—beliefs about appropriate ways of acting on the job and rewarding aspects of teaching, and knowledge that enables teachers to do their work" (p. 508). Similarly, in the words of Louis and Smith, school culture is a "collective understanding about 'how this school got to be the way it is'" (1990, p. 41). Since the appearance of Feiman-Nemser and Floden's chapter, the literature on understanding school cultures and teachers' work by listening to teachers' experiences and opinions has grown considerably (Carter, 1993; Goodson & Walker, 1991; Hargreaves, 1996).

The ways that teachers' cultures and social class have influenced their teaching practices has been approached in different ways. For example, these issues have been a theme in the vast literature on teachers' expectations as they influence treatment of students and student learning (see extensive review in Brophy & Good, 1986). While this literature is not the subject of this chapter, what is of interest are those studies that have described the influence of teachers' social class and that of their students on teachers' perceptions of their work. Schools then, are viewed as contexts for understanding the interactive effects of teachers' and students' social-class positions. Cicourel and Kitsuse (1963), in an early study of this phenomenon, were interested in the ways that school counselors categorized high school students and placed them in either college- or noncollege-bound tracks. They found that although counselors used teachers' opinions, test scores, and grades to place students, those placements were not consistent. That is, some students had low scores, low grade point averages (GPAs), or both but were in the college-bound track, while others had high scores, high grades, or both but were placed in the noncollege-bound track. Cicourel and Kitsuse gained additional information about what had been passed along from the students' past counselors and teachers and what had been collected about parents' socioeconomic status (SES). They found the highest correlation between parents' SES and whether the students were placed in a college-bound track. For example, if a student from a high SES background was placed in the noncollege-bound track, and parents insisted they be moved, then those students were transferred to the college-bound track. Conversely, because parents of lower SES didn't actively seek the transfer of their children, no action was taken.

In 1967, Rist conducted a longitudinal qualitative study of African-American children in an inner-city school (1986). He was interested in exploring the concept of teachers' expectations as self-fulfilling prophecies and in describing how the phenomenon occurred over time. He began observing children in a kindergarten class and found that the teacher had made permanent seating arrangements based on information gained from registration forms, from a list provided by the school's social worker about children receiving ADC (Aid to Dependent Children), from an interview with the children's mothers, and from information based on the teacher's own or other teachers' experiences with older siblings. Rist identified the characteristics of children based on where they were seated in relationship to the teacher. He found that students sitting closest to the teacher were dressed better, emerged as leaders, were more at ease in interaction with the teacher, and more frequently used standard American English than children seated farthest away from the teacher. Furthermore, teachers spoke of the children as "fast learners" and "slow learners" despite the fact that they had no formal tests of their academic potential. Rist concluded that teachers based these conclusions on notions or beliefs about what constituted a successful student, and these notions were basically representative of teachers' middle-class values.

By the end of the kindergarten year, students farthest away from the teacher had more difficulty seeing the chalkboard, had less interaction with the teacher, were less involved in class activities, and had less instruction. Students at the closer table began belittling students farther away. Rist followed this same group of children though the second grade and found that the same pattern occurred. He described the repeated arrangement as a caste system that provided no upward mobility. Over time, the students seated in the back of the room did indeed perform less well than those in the front. Thus, the teachers' expectations, based on their beliefs about social-class characteristics, served as self-fulfilling prophecies for the children.

More recently, Metz (1986, 1990) studied magnet schools and the social-class influences that affected teachers' work—both the social class of teachers and that of the school and community where they worked. She interviewed teachers and other key staff members and conducted observations in classrooms in three schools representing low, middle, and high income levels. Metz found that differences in the SES level of the three communities were revealed through the different priorities established both in the schools' goals and for the daily practices within teachers' classrooms. Parents from middle and high SES had more power in the schools to influence policy and practices, while those parents of low SES had more limited access to decision making, in part, because of the larger size and more complicated bureaucracy of the large cities in which the schools were located.

Metz (1986, 1990) found that teachers experienced the effects of students' different SES directly in their everyday classroom interactions and, particularly, in the attitudes and behaviors of their students. Students in the high SES school showed greater engagement in school, while students in the middle- to working-class school showed greater detachment, and students in the poor school showed even greater detachment. At the same time, the SES backgrounds of teachers and consequent differences from their students in attitudes, lifestyles, and social networks not only defined their work but also influenced their responses to students. This relationship between teachers and students was complicated by factors such as their similarity to or difference from students' backgrounds, which made them potentially more understanding of their students if their beliefs corresponded or less understanding if they didn't. If there was no foundation for shared or, at least, accepted differences in their beliefs, tensions or barriers in communication grew. Metz found

that these beliefs were incorporated into the collective views embedded in the school culture and passed on to new teachers through the socialization process.

Page (1987) also studied teachers' perceptions of students in two tracks but found differences even between teachers who were in two very similar midwestern high schools of middle-class White students. Because she found "dramatic differences" in the ways that students behaved in the two schools, it suggested to her that tracking alone was not the determining factor in creating these differences. Instead, she found that differences in classroom climates between the two schools affected students' behaviors and that the differences in classroom climates were linked to the "ethos" or culture of each school. That is, a different set of beliefs, values, and assumptions were shared by teachers of each school. In one school, for example, the shared ethos consisted of high expectations for students that were exhibited through positive statements about students and their potential for success, a high value in academic excellence, pride in teachers' expertise, and high levels of perceived professionalism.

In the other school, the ethos was described by Page as one of "pedestrian competence, rather than academic preeminence" (1987, p. 87). Teachers dominated students, discipline was stressed, and expectations were lower than in the first school. Teaching was regarded as a job with duties to be performed in a bureaucratic mode rather than a professional mode.

Within the context of the school ethos, teachers' perceptions of students' social-class characteristics permeated both schools. Yet the situation was even more complicated by the differentiation of the tracked classes and the assignment of students to the tracks.

In short, the culture of a school both shapes teachers' understanding of their mode of operation and of their students and is grounded in faculty members' shared definitions. The culture is linked to the larger social order by staff members; shared perceptions of the social class of the school's typical student and of the educational demands of the community. At the same time, the culture is reflected and re-created in classrooms as teachers provide the school's version of a curriculum appropriate for students of a particular social class. Thus, curriculum differentiation translates principles of social differentiation. Faculty members enact a school's stereotype of class differences, producing an educational norm of self-confident engagement with academics for students perceived to be from "upper middle-class, largely professional families" or punctilious coverage of skills for "your typical blue-collar kids." (1987, p. 90)

In a study of high school teachers in schools of varying social-class composition, Hemmings and Metz (1990) examined how teachers defined their work as "Real Teaching." Teachers' definitions included their understanding of how societal expectations for schooling and the sociocultural characteristics of local school communities were translated into their views of effective teaching. They found that it was easier for teachers in schools that served well-educated, middle-class students to integrate their definitions of real teaching than it was for teachers in working-class and lower-class schools. They linked their work to calls for reform, which do not take into account the differences in social class that affect how well programs will be accepted by other than middle-class parents. They advised

Table 39.6 Percentage of Women in Administrative Positions, United States, 1905–85

Position	Date					
	1905	1928	1950	1972–73	1982–83	1984–85
Elementary principals	61.7	55.0	38.0	19.6	23.0	16.9
Secondary principals	5.7	7.9	6.0	1.4	3.2	3.5
Superintendents	Unknown	1.6	2.1	0.1	1.8	3.0

Adapted from Shakeshaft, 1987, p. 20.

policymakers to view teachers as "cultural brokers," or as "individuals who negotiate productive settlements between societal, community and student understandings about what and how knowledge should be taught in schools" (p. 110).

Authority Structures in Schools

The question of autonomy and control in schools has been addressed in terms of the extent of autonomy and the extent and locus of control. Within the walls of their classrooms, teachers have felt a great deal of control over such matters as instructional practices, classroom organization, and their relationships with students (Henke et al., 1997). However, as Lortie (1975) pointed out, this autonomy, or egg-crate segmentation between teachers' classrooms, also has isolated teachers from other teachers and has limited how much they could share their knowledge and expertise or seek help with problems.

Asked about issues related to autonomy and control on the 1993–94 SASS teacher questionnaire, teachers, as in the past, felt they had a great deal of control over what happened in their classrooms (Henke et al., 1997). However, less than 40% of teachers felt they had a great deal of control over disciplinary policy, curriculum design, or the content of in-service programs, and less than 10% felt they had control over spending the budget, hiring new teachers, or evaluating teachers. Although 60% of teachers reported that they had input into decision making, apparently teachers felt this input had little effect on the creation and adoption of policies in key areas of school organization and governance.

Power and control within schools has been by segmented along gender lines, because administrators have been mostly male, and teachers have been mostly female. In fact, since the turn of the century in the United States, the proportion of female administrators at the secondary level has never been significant. However, the proportion of female elementary principals has shown a steady decline from nearly two thirds (61.7%) of the principals in 1905 to less than 20% in 1984–85 (see Table 39.6) (Shakeshaft, 1987). Schmuck (1987) found that this decrease was attributable to an increase in males who entered elementary teaching after World War II; the consolidation of schools, which eliminated administrative positions in rural schools and put men in charge of the newly created larger schools; a change in requirements for administrators, which necessitated earning graduate degrees; and the sex-role stereotyping that occurred and that was based on the attitude that managing a school was men's work. This reflects the fact that, as Benn (1989) pointed out, two distinct gender-specific functions have always been present in schools—one for women, linked to mothering, and one for men, linked to power and authority. The

research that Williams (1992, 1993) and Allan (1993) conducted regarding male teachers would support this assertion. As mentioned earlier, men get support from male administrators who guide them toward administrative positions as though they were on a "glass escalator."

The sex-segregated power structure of school districts, which emerged over the decades of the past 2 centuries, continues to this day. Clearly, male domination in administrative positions in schools has also created a hierarchical arrangement in which decisions are made by males and carried out by females. Although they have considerable autonomy in the classroom, teachers often lack control over organizational decisions that have an impact on their work in classrooms. This is not to say that teachers are not positive toward their own administrator's leadership and support. Based on the results of the 1993–94 SASS survey and the Teacher Follow-up Survey of 1994–95, overall, teachers in both public and private schools, at elementary and secondary levels, and across income levels of student populations were extremely positive about their principal's performance (Henke et al., 1997). Over 80% thought their principal communicated his or her expectations, enforced school rules, and demonstrated supportive and encouraging behavior. About 70% of teachers felt their principal recognized staff members for jobs well done. Less than one half (45.5%), however, reported that their principal talked to them about instruction. Elementary school teachers ranked their principals higher across these items than secondary teachers, and teachers in private schools ranked their principals higher than did public school teachers.

Spencer (1986, 1988) found that inequitable power relationships between teachers and principals affected the nature and frequency of their interaction. Her case study research revealed that women teachers felt constrained when interacting and negotiating with male principals. Contacts with principals were often limited to formal settings such as faculty meetings or infrequent classroom visitation by principals for the purpose of teacher evaluation. In these settings, the principal was in a position of power and controlled the situation. In addition, her work, completed in the early 1980s before some schools—particularly rural schools—had dealt with affirmative action rulings, showed that some women teachers encountered overt sexist remarks or sexual harassment (e.g., kissing or pinching) from their male principals. One example is found in a diary excerpt written by a secondary teacher in a rural school where the lack of information about and legal recourse for sexual harassment placed the woman in a particularly powerless position.

When I got into the carpool this morning, everyone was laughing. Mr. [the superintendent] had commented that I looked like Dolly

[Parton] as I walked to the car. I asked if it was my long blonde hair. There was no comment (since my hair is short and brown). That comment didn't set well with me and my whole day seemed off to a poor start. There was nothing to do but laugh it off, but I kept thinking what I could have done to give him the impression that I would even appreciate a comment like that. I took it as a lack of respect for women. I would certainly not comment on the size of his testicles. (Spencer, 1986, p. 117)

Even where principals had more collegial relationships with women teachers, Spencer's case studies provided examples of a subtle undercurrent in which male principals sometimes referred to teachers as "the girls" or expected them to cook for school gatherings.

While these examples were particularly blatant and would not occur (we would hope) at this time, the fact that most administrators are male and, therefore, are in positions of power and authority over their mostly female faculties perpetuates a gender-based division of labor and inequitable power relationships in schools. Although, as described in the work of Williams (1992, 1993) and Allan (1993), male teachers, too, have special problems in negotiating their careers through the gender-based social networks in schools.

The Professional Status of Teaching

The professional status of teachers and their commitment to teaching has been approached from two perspectives. One approach is gender neutral while the other has been gender specific by placing the fact that teaching is a female-dominated profession at the center of analyses. The first approach entails identifying the characteristics of teaching and the elements considered conducive to teachers' commitment to their work. Some have compared these characteristics to other professions. These characteristics have included utilizing a specialized body of knowledge that is based on systematic theories and transmitted through a formalized educational process; a clearly defined code of ethics, which serves as the basis for self-monitoring by others in the profession; an orientation to serving the public; authority over clients; and autonomy and control over the work environment. When compared to these standards, teaching has not conformed, because no specialized body of knowledge has been used, teachers have had less training than the traditional professions, and teachers have worked in isolated environments with little autonomy over working conditions. Because teaching did not fit this model, it was considered a "semiprofession," along with other female-dominated occupations such as social work, library science, and nursing (Etzioni, 1969).

Commitment to a career was the focus of Geer's (1968) sociological analysis of teaching. She concluded that women teachers lacked commitment to their work, because, when compared to other professions, they were transmitters rather than creators of knowledge; because they taught involuntary clients (students) who could not give teachers "useful and prestigious relationships;" because they worked in isolated classrooms disconnected from colleagues; because they were not monetarily rewarded for their work; and because their moonlighting activities interfered with their teaching.

Spencer (1986, 1988) found Geer's claim that teachers were not committed to their work as quite discrepant from her re-

search on women teachers, who often demonstrated their commitment to teaching to the point of exhaustion and illness. And as highly educated and committed teachers, they defined themselves as professionals. In addition, Spencer also took exception to Etzioni's constricted model of a profession in which teaching and other female-dominated occupations were deemed only partly professional (semiprofessional). Spencer then asked, if teachers are committed, highly educated professionals, why does society not afford teachers higher status? In her research on the daily lives of women teachers she identified factors that helped to answer this question. These factors—low pay, the lack of control over decisions affecting school policy and school organizational matters, and membership in a female-dominated profession—had significant effects on teachers' working conditions, their lives, and their lifestyles. Spencer saw the enduring and powerful effects of these interrelated factors as characteristic of a "quasi-profession," that is, work that almost resembles a profession but not quite, because our society continues to afford low status to lower paying jobs and women's work. She concluded: Rather than teachers aspiring to become professionals by following some externally contrived checklist, society should grant them higher status by paying them more.

In other recent research, the concept of teacher commitment has taken on a much less constrictive definition from both sociological and educational research positions. This work has served as the basis for a multidimensional rather than unidimensional view of the factors that affect teachers' commitment to their work and to their workplace. For example, Rosenholtz (1989) examined teachers' workplace commitment within the social organization of schools. Her work was based on the assumption that more highly motivated teachers would be more effective and would experience more commitment to their work. Therefore, she concluded that the more school organizations acknowledge teachers' efforts the more often school success will occur. Conversely, schools that do not have the conditions for teachers to nurture high internal motivation suffer negative consequences.

Rosenholtz also identified the key conditions necessary to teachers' professional fulfillment: (a) teacher autonomy or feelings that their actions could lead to positive change, (b) psychic rewards that outweigh frustrations with work, and (c) ample opportunities for professional development. These three factors accounted for 76% of teachers' commitment to their workplace. Where they existed, teachers felt optimistic, empowered, challenged, and committed. Where they were absent, they felt unappreciated, alienated, and terminally bored. Teaching and learning suffered as a result (1991).

In the same gender-neutral vein, Louis and Smith (1990) examined two perspectives on teachers' working conditions. The first—the drive toward greater professionalization—has dominated the second—the attention to improving the quality of teachers' work lives. In their view, the attention that policymakers have focused on professionalization has ignored the variety of sources from which teachers derive satisfaction from their work. The drive toward professionalization, in fact, has "lead to a conclusion that the increasingly bureaucratic and regulated conditions of schools make unabridged professionalism virtually impossible" (p. 24). The work of teachers has become deskilled through relegating teaching into a set of highly specified tasks within prescribed units of curriculum and instruction.

Furthermore, teacher autonomy has become more restricted to decisions within their classrooms. This restrictive system for teachers, however, does not fit with the realities of today's school or its students.

Louis and Smith (1990) argue that two models have dominated discussions of teacher professionalism, both of which create problems in the practical realities of implementation. The first, "The Expert-Centered Image" is based on the belief that teachers should have better and more extensive education and training, gain more expert knowledge, pass more rigorous tests for credentialing, undergo more stringent hiring practices in school districts, and continue professional development through, for example, career ladders. Such expert teachers, proponents of this model presume, would have greater autonomy and control over their classrooms and greater decision making roles within their schools. The problem with this model, the authors found, is that while some aspects may be applied, others are not feasible or are impossible because of the political, bureaucratic, and organizational constraints and realities teachers face. It also does not explain why or how teacher professionalism should necessarily lead to better teaching.

A second model discussed by Louis and Smith (1990) is the "Empathy-Centered Image." This perspective focuses on the importance of teachers' interpersonal relationships with other teachers and with students as a way of understanding their professionalism and status of their work. These two models represent opposite ends of a continuum with an expert-centered focus at one end and an ego-centered focus at the other.

Louis and Smith offered a third model, based on social psychological studies of organizations and their Quality of Work Life (QWL). This model looks at the effects of the "micro-organizational environments of schools" (p. 34), or job characteristics that affect teachers' work, rather than at the issue of whether or not teachers are professionals. This model directly targets the effects of working conditions on teachers' job satisfaction and the effects of promoting greater teaching effectiveness. They asked, "What kinds of school reform might promote working conditions that tangibly contribute to the establishment of a more professional work life and career for teachers?" (p. 35). They then linked the conditions of QWL to the ways the conditions can be reached to "balance the opportunities for individuals to learn and exercise new skills, and the need to achieve some value consensus and congruence with regard to the essential tasks of the school" (p. 43).

In a special report prepared by the NCES entitled "Teacher Professionalization and Teacher Commitment: A Multilevel Analysis," the 1990–91 SASS was used to assess the relationship between measures of teacher professionalism and commitment and various background characteristics of teachers and schools (Ingersoll & Alsalom, 1997). The central question of the study was, which characteristics were related to greater teacher commitment? Since the mid-1980s, professionalization, sometimes regarded as "upgrading" of the teaching occupation, has been seen by educational reformers, researchers, and policymakers as the key to improving schools. Experts assume that by improving teachers' working conditions, salaries, other resources, and support and recognition for their work, teachers' commitment to teaching would improve. No consensus has been reached, however, about the definitions and criteria for what identifies "professional," "professionalism," or "professionalization" nor about to what extent those terms currently exist or have been influenced by various reform movements. This special report, in combination with other projects on teachers and teaching supported by the NCES, focused specifically on the characteristics of teacher professionalization and teachers' commitment to their teaching careers. Commitment was defined as "the degree of positive, affective bond between the teacher and the school" that reflected "the degree of internal motivation, enthusiasm, and job satisfaction teachers derive from teaching and the degree of efficacy and effectiveness they achieve in their jobs" (p. 2). The report was based on the assumption of some voices within the teacher reform movement that teacher professionalization leads to increased teacher commitment, which, in turn, positively affects teacher performance and, ultimately, has positive effects on student learning.

The NCES report looked at the ways sociologists have distinguished between professionalization and professionalism and concluded that the focus would be on five characteristics: (a) teachers' credentials—skills, intellectual functioning, and knowledge combined with the degree or certification credentials that ensure their expert status, (b) teachers' formal and informal induction or follow-up to preservices training to help inductees adjust to the everyday realities of school life and to dealing with students, (c) teachers' professional development or the expectation of ongoing, in-service training to update skills and knowledge, (d) the degree of teachers' authority over their workplace, and (e) teachers' compensation or to what extent they are well-paid for their knowledge and skills.

The results of the study showed differences in teachers' commitment across all the demographic characteristics examined. Females showed somewhat higher levels of commitment than males, and White teachers showed somewhat more commitment than minority teachers. Teachers with less experience and education showed slightly higher levels of commitment. Neither the racial composition of the school nor the school's size, however, had any effect on teachers' commitment. However, rural teachers showed slightly higher levels of commitment than teachers in urban and suburban schools, and secondary teachers reported less commitment than elementary and combined schools. The strongest school demographic effect was that of sector: Private school teachers reported more commitment than public school teachers.

Schools providing all types of teacher professionalization were positively associated with teacher commitment including those schools with higher end-of-career salaries, schools where teachers had influence in decision making over policy and in their own classrooms, and schools where effective assistance for new teachers was provided.

In summary, the report generated mixed results—some professionalization factors were associated with teacher commitment and some were not. One implication for research and policy considerations, for example, suggests that schools should have formal mentoring programs for new teachers, but that the mere existence of these programs doesn't insure their effectiveness. Also, traditional forms of professional development, such as continuing education or seminars sponsored by professional organizations and associations, did not have a positive effect on teacher commitment. The report recommended that future research questions concern the characteristics of effective and ineffective programs.

With regard to issues of teachers' power and authority over decision making, the report showed that the concept of site-based management was vague and unclear in terms of the degree of centralization that was necessary or extant. In other words, it was unclear who should have power, how much, and why.

The other approach to the study of teachers' professionalism and commitment to their workplaces focuses on the fact that most teachers are women. The claims that teaching is a semi-profession have had a lasting negative impact on public impressions and on research related to women teachers by creating a negative perception of teaching as less than a real profession. The question of whether or not teaching is a profession has been suggested as having use only to sociologists who want to compare teaching to other kinds of work. Such exercises have been considered by some to be of "limited practical value" (Griffin, 1992).

Others have pointed to a need to discard the traditional male model of what constituted a real profession and to reconceptualize career trajectories to reflect women's work patterns. As stated by Feiman-Nemser and Floden, "Generally women don't have the luxury of concentrating on their careers in a single-minded way" (1986, p. 519). Because women's work histories typically have not followed a linear path, their work should be considered in relation to changing labor markets for women—as being in a state of constant change and adaptation to new situations and organizational contexts (Goodson & Walker, 1991). Therefore, either women's careers should be described as points along a continuum rather than viewed as a dichotomous categorization, (Darling-Hammond & Wise, 1992) or they should be described using a more fluid model that better reflects the lives of women teachers (compare Casey & Apple, 1989; Tozer, Violas, & Senese, 1993). The term "open professionalism" has also been suggested to indicate blurred distinctions in categorization (OECD, 1990).

In a study of women elementary teachers, Biklen (1986) also called for a reconceptionalization of teachers' professionalism and visions of their careers. She found that traditional definitions of careers were based on males' work patterns. Biklen added that because men have been free from housework and child care they have been able to devote themselves—be committed—to careers. By this definition, women who have had to put work in a secondary position in relation to their families are not committed to a career. But in interviews with women teachers, Biklen found that they regarded themselves as committed to teaching whether or not they had taken off to have children or only worked part time. They thought of themselves as teachers and planned to continue working. Biklen called for a reconceptionalization of the concept of career commitment to reflect women's perspectives.

Acker (1989) also reexamined sociologists' use of the term career in regard to teachers. She found that the research had been polarized: Some sociologists looked at the concept from the individual's perspectives, including examination of patterns throughout a person's work history, whereas other sociologists explained career patterns in terms of the structural facilitators or impediments that occurred within social contexts. More re-

cent research using feminist frameworks and qualitative methodological approaches has defined careers as complex patterns of choices and constraints. Acker's work looked more in-depth at how individual career choices were influenced by internal labor markets for teachers. She recommended that careers be regarded as "a series of experiences in coming to terms with situations and making choices subject to constraints" (Acker, 1989, p. 9). In later work, Acker (1992) concluded that teachers had to believe they had the power to "shape their own destinies" or else schools would have been filled with demoralized teachers. She added that teachers shaped their own destinies by redefining the meaning of careers and commitment through their experiences in the workplace and in their family situations. As a result, their careers reflected the ongoing change in their lives and were "provisional, kaleidoscopic constructions" (1992, p. 161).

Clearly, the definitions of "professionalism" among teachers has changed greatly over the past 30 years toward a more realistic and fluid reflection of teachers' work and their commitment to teaching. The merger of these gender-neutral analyses with those that place teaching as women's work at the forefront of their analyses would create a more realistic and meaningful view of teachers' work.

The Relationship Between Teachers' Personal and Work Lives

Our knowledge of teachers' lives outside their classrooms is extremely well documented when compared to other occupations, both in historical and contemporary work. As described earlier in this chapter, historiographical accounts from teachers and about teachers are extensive. The personal narratives of teachers allows us a glimpse of the balance of teachers' work and personal lives in historical context. In fact, balancing work and family were not always a problem for teachers. For example, Nelson (1992) interviewed female school teachers in Vermont who taught between 1915 and 1950. These women brought their children to school when other baby-sitting arrangements were unsatisfactory. Teachers' family networks, their mothers or their daughters, acted as substitute teachers when teachers were sick or pregnant. The close relationships between these teachers' work and family life had the benefit of less time away from their work at school; and at home, teachers reported they got more help with housework from their families.

Widdowson (1983) also reported that teachers in 19th-century England lived next to the schoolhouse and were able to take care of their children and also teach. This situation ended, as it did for Nelson's teachers, when larger, age-graded schools were built, which employed many teachers. It was no longer possible to live next to the school nor to bring one's children to the school.

Although not an option for most teachers because of low salaries, examples have been found of teachers hiring servants to care for their children. In 1928, Collier studied 100 employed married women, all of whom had 1 or more children (Peters, 1934). The largest group of working women were teachers. Of the sample, 49 had one servant, 31 had two servants, and 11 had three or more servants. Sixty years later, Spencer (1992, 1993) interviewed 40 teachers in El Paso, Texas, most of whom reported that they hired women from Mexico to clean their houses and take care of their children. The *mexicanas* lived with the teachers through the work week and returned to their homes in Ciudad Juárez, Mexico, on the weekends. This situation was possible because labor was cheap and because El Paso was close to Ciudad Juárez.

Collier's and Spencer's findings are not typical, however, because most teachers are not able to afford full-time housekeepers, child-caregivers, or both. Studies in the past 10 years show that, more typically, women teachers take on full responsibility for housework and child care in addition to their work as teachers (Acker, 1992; Blase & Pajak, 1986; Claesson & Brice, 1989; Pajak & Blase, 1989; Spencer, 1986, 1988). In case studies she documented, Spencer (1986, 1988) found this to be true among the 8 United States teachers whom she followed for 2 years to observe them in their schools and in their homes. She found differences between the women depending on whether they taught in elementary or secondary schools; whether they worked in rural, urban, or suburban school districts; whether they were married, single or divorced; and whether they had children. Her study showed that the women went beyond the description of a "double-day" of work, typical of working women, and, instead, worked a "triple-day" of work. The day included teaching all day, coming home to all the housework and care of their children, then grading papers or doing other school-related work. An attraction to teaching as an occupation was that the work schedule fit with their own children's schedules, especially in the summer months. This factor made the juggling act manageable.

In her study of women teachers in two primary schools in England, Acker (1992) found that women had a "triple-shift" of work, which consisted of teaching, housework, and child care. A "quadruple-shift" was mentioned by some teachers in reference to university course work they took at night, which added to their other work and home roles. Acker aptly commented that "school followed teachers everywhere."

Acker's (1992) interviews revealed that teachers thought about school when at home, but few said they thought about home when at school. This was not true of teachers in Spencer's (1986) study. She found that only one woman out of her 8 case study teachers was able to separate her home and work lives—the others found it impossible. Teachers whose own children were ill had a particularly difficult time. When they were home, they felt guilty for not being at school, and when at school, they felt guilty for not being with their children. Again, her findings were more similar to Colliers' research on working women conducted 60 years earlier (Peters, 1934). In his sample of 124 women, 75 thought that the value of their work outside their homes was enhanced by their marriage and 49 said that they drew upon their experiences as wives and mothers for part of its "contents."

Blase and Pajak (1986) also found that when work tended to spill over, it had a negative effect on teachers' personal lives. When teachers' work and their personal lives conflicted, they usually resolved it in favor of their work demands. Despite this, experiences in their personal lives that may have appeared as burdensome were transformed into positive factors for their work roles—for example, they felt stronger, more caring, more compassionate, and more understanding. Similar to Acker's

(1992) findings mentioned earlier, the teachers were able to adapt to ongoing change and integrate their roles.

Role integration was also examined by Claesson and Brice (1989) who conducted in-depth interviews with kindergarten through third-grade teachers who were also the mothers of young children. They found that the dual roles of teacher and mother were complementary and that role interaction was mostly beneficial. Although dual role expectations were sometimes ambiguous and unrealistically high, Spencer (1986, 1988) found that teachers learned effective coping strategies as the result of having both roles. In the words of a first-grade teacher and mother of 2 preschool-aged children,

> I started working on grades and also on trying to get some house-cleaning done and sometimes I feel like I neglect my home and I spend too much time preparing for school. I don't want my kids to have to suffer because of it and I try not to. Therefore, I spend more time with them and just forget the house—as I have to decide what priorities are going to rule my life and what priorities aren't. (1986, p. 107)

Studies of the relationships between teachers' home and work lives are unique documentations, which are not common in studies of other occupations and are important to understanding how work in a particular occupation affects and is affected by personal situations and relationships. Expanding the study of teachers to include these personal factors can also broaden an understanding of teachers' perceptions of their work and working conditions and, ultimately, an understanding about what happens in their classrooms. In the words of Goodson,

> . . . in the accounts they give about life in schools, teachers constantly refer to personal and biographical factors. From their point of view, it would seem that professional practices are embedded in wider life concerns. We need to listen closely to their views on the relationship between "school life" and "whole life" for in that dialectic crucial tales about careers and commitments will be told. It remains true that the balance of commitments between teaching and life may be precariously affected by educational cuts and changes in public esteem. Studying teachers' lives helps us monitor this most crucial of all equations. (1992, p. 16)

Teachers' Work: Prospects for the Future

This chapter began with the promise that it would provide a review of the history of teachers as workers and, in that process, would illustrate the continuities and discontinuities that have occurred. One of the most striking recurring problems for teachers has been the issue of their low salaries in comparison to salaries of other occupations and professions that require college degrees. The fact that half of all public school teachers take on other jobs to supplement their incomes is a remarkable statement about their low pay, especially given that the typical teacher has earned a graduate degree.

One of the most interesting historical documents in this chapter related to the issue of teachers' low pay was reported by the National Education Association's commission, which was created to deal with the "Nation Emergency in Education" in 1919. The alarm that the organization felt stemmed from issues parallel to those of concern today both for students and for teachers. The report of 1919 concluded that the real problem was low pay, which did not attract people into teaching and drove others to leave teaching for higher paying jobs. Like many calls for action, the report urged that drastic steps be taken by school districts to change this situation.

Decades later, in the 1980s, reports such as "Tomorrow's Teachers: A Report of the Holmes Group" (Holmes Group, 1986) and "A Nation Prepared: Teachers for the Twenty-first Century" (Carnegie Task Force on Teaching as a Profession, 1986) and, again in the 1990s, reports such as "What Matters Most: Teaching for America's Future" (National Commission on Teaching and America's Future, 1996) have called for more highly credentialed teachers based on the assumption that credentialing teachers would also "professionalize" them. The reports have also included recommendations to raise teachers' salaries. However, in the 80 years since the NEA report, teachers have gone from having very little training to holding graduate degrees, while their salaries have not risen significantly in relationship to this high level of training and education. Recent reports also have not had an impact on teachers' pay. The fact that teachers' pay is controlled by independent school districts across the country does not hold promise for this situation to change in the future. Such change might occur, however, if state and federal policymakers placed the same importance on teacher's pay as they do with pressing teachers to gain more credentials. If this does not happen, the same situation that occurred in the early part of this century will repeat itself in the early part of the 21st century when teacher shortages are predicted; teachers will not be attracted to teaching and those who are teachers may be attracted to other fields for the higher pay.

The tremendous inequities in funding for schools within and between states is related to inequities in teachers' pay, of course, and schools with inadequate funds also have the least desirable working conditions for teachers. More research on the effects that these inequitable conditions have on teachers' perceptions of their work, their students, and the communities in which they teach is needed. Research in the tradition of Metz (1986, 1990) and Page (1987), for example, would provide more powerful evidence of the wide disparity in teachers' experiences based on their social-class backgrounds and the social-class designations of their students. Understanding the role that these disparities play in affecting teachers' expectations for their students is crucial to assuring that all students are regarded in ways that are most conducive to optimal learning.

Another area that warrants exploration is related to the movement toward site-based or school-based management. At a superficial glance, the shift to giving schools control over important issues appears reasonable and democratic from the standpoint of teachers. However, as reported in the chapter, many teachers have expressed that even though they do have input into decision making in their schools, they believe that this input has little effect on actual policies. This belief has significant implications for schools that claim to be working toward new forms of school management that give teachers and all other stakeholders a true voice. When teachers give input that is not considered, they can become disenchanted and may begin to wonder whether their voices are truly heard and, if heard, whether their voices really have the power to influence policy. Furthermore, when teachers' input takes the form of participation on committees, which, in turn, make recommendations to administrators or schools boards, who, in turn, ultimately disregard recommendations because of more pressing political and financial concerns, then teachers' uncompensated time outside the classroom has been wasted and their input purely token rather than politically important in school governance. What the role of a teacher is and should be needs to be reconceptualized if schools truly wish to operate on a site-based or shared decision-making model.

This chapter has looked in-depth at factors that have shaped the teaching workforce, particularly as a female-dominated profession. Little has been known, however, until the groundbreaking work of Williams (1992, 1993, 1995) and Allan (1993), about differences in the perceptions and experiences of male and female elementary teachers. Future research should be expanded to include secondary teachers and teachers in different-sized school districts in different parts of the country. These studies should also examine the relationship between male teachers' work and home lives. While several studies have been done of this relationship for female teachers who take responsibility for housework and child care when they are at home, do male teachers take on the same responsibilities, or do they follow a more typical male model of leaving these matters to their wives or significant others? This line of research will expand our knowledge of the complexities of teachers' lives.

REFERENCES

Acker, S. (Ed.). (1989). *Teachers, gender and careers.* London: Falmer Press.

Acker, S. (1992). Creating careers: Women teachers at work. *Curriculum Inquiry, 22*(2): 141–163.

Allan, J. (1993). Male elementary teachers: Experiences and perspectives. In C. L. Williams (Ed.), *Doing "women's work"* (pp. 113–127). Newbury Park, CA: Sage.

Almack, J. C., & Lang, A. R. (1925). *Problems of the teaching profession.* Boston: Houghton Mifflin.

Altenbaugh, R. J. (Ed.). (1992). *The teacher's voice: A social history of teaching in twentieth-century America.* London: Falmer Press.

Anderson, M. L. (1983). *Thinking about women: Sociological and feminist perspectives.* New York: Macmillan.

Anthony, P. (1987). Teachers in the economic system. In K. Alexander & D. Monk (Eds.), *Attracting and compensating America's teachers* (pp. 1–20). Cambridge, MA: Ballinger.

Beale, H. K. (1936). *Are American teachers free?* New York: Scribner.

Beale, H. K. (1941). *A history of freedom of teaching in American schools.* New York: Scribner.

Benn, C. (1989). Preface. In H. DeLyon & F. W. Migniuolo (Eds.), *Women Teachers: Issues and experiences* (pp. xviii–xxvi). Buckingham, UK: Open University Press.

Biddle, B. J. (1997). Foolishness, dangerous nonsense, and real correlates of state differences in achievement. *Phi Delta Kappan, 79*(1), 8–13.

Biklen, S. K. (1986, March). "I have always worked": Elementary schoolteaching as a career. *Phi Delta Kappan, 67,* 504–508.

Blase, J. J., & Pajak, E. F. (1986). The impact of teachers' work life on personal life: A qualitative analysis. *The Alberta Journal of Educational Research, 32*(4), 307–322.

Brenton, M. (1970). *What's happened to teacher?* New York: Coward-McCann, Inc.

Brophy, J., & Good, T. (1986). Teacher behavior and student achievement. In M. C. Wittrock (Ed.), *Handbook of research on teaching* (3rd ed., pp. 328–375). New York: Macmillan.

Carnegie Task Force on Teaching as a Profession. (1986). *A nation prepared: Teachers for the 21st century.* New York: Carnegie Foundation.

Carter, K. (1993). The place of story in the study of teaching and teacher education. *Educational Researcher, 22*(1), 5–12.

Carter, S. B. (1989). Incentives and rewards to teaching. In D. Warren (Ed.), *American teachers: Histories of a profession at work* (pp. 49–62). New York: Macmillan.

Casey K., & Apple M. W. (1989). Gender and the conditions of teachers' work: The development of understanding in America. In S. Acker (Ed.), *Teachers, gender and careers.* Falmer Press, New York.

Chambers, J., & Bobbitt, S. A. (1996). *The patterns of teacher compensation* (U.S. Department of Education, Office of Educational Research and Improvement, National Center for Education Statistics NCES 95–829). Washington, DC: U.S. Government Printing Office.

Choy, S. P., Henke, R. R., Alt, M. N., & Medrich, E. A. (1993). *Schools and staffing in the United States: A statistical profile, 1990–91* (U.S. Department of Education, National Center for Education Statistics NCES 93–146). Washington, DC: U.S. Government Printing Office.

Cicourel, A. V., & Kitsuse, J. (1963). *The Educational decision-makers.* Indianapolis: Bobbs-Merrill.

Claesson, M. A., & Brice, R. A. (1989). Teacher/mothers: Effects of a dual role. *American Educational Research Journal, 26*(1), 1–23.

Clifford, G. J. (1978). Home and school in 19th century America: Some personal history reports from the United States. *History of Education Quarterly, 18*(3), 3–34.

Clifford, G. J. (1989). Man/woman/teacher: Gender, family, and career in American educational history. In D. Warren (Ed.), *American teachers: Histories of a profession at work* (pp. 293–343). New York: Macmillan.

Cuban, L. (1984). *How teachers taught: Constancy and change in American classrooms, 1890–1980.* New York: Longman.

Darling-Hammond, L., & Wise, A. E. (1992). Teacher professionalism. In M. C. Akin (Ed.), *Encyclopedia of educational research* (6th ed., pp. 1359–1366). New York: Macmillan.

DeLyon, H., & Migniuolo, F. W. (Eds.). (1989). *Women teachers: Issues and experiences.* Buckingham, UK: Open University Press.

Dreeben, R. (1970). *The nature of teaching.* Glenview, IL: Scott, Foresman.

Elsbree, W. S. (1928). Teacher turnover in the cities and villages of New York state. New York: Teachers College Press.

Elsbree, W. S. (1939). *The American teacher: Evolution of a profession in a democracy.* Westport, CT: Greenwood Press.

Etzioni, A. (1969). *The semi-professions and their organization: Teachers, nurses, social workers.* New York: The Free Press.

Evenden, E. S. (1919). *Teachers' salaries and salary schedules in the United States, 1918–19.* Washington, DC: The National Education Association.

Feiman-Nemser, S., & Floden, R. E. (1986). The cultures of teaching. In M. C. Wittrock (Ed.), *Handbook of research on teaching* (3rd ed., pp. 505–526). New York: Macmillan.

Finkelstein, B. (1989). *Governing the young: Teacher behavior in popular primary schools in nineteenth-century United States.* New York: Falmer Press.

Geer, B. (1968). Occupational commitment and the teaching profession. In H. S. Becker, B. Geer, D. Riesman, & R. S. Weiss (Eds.), *Institutions and the person* (pp. 221–234). Chicago: Aldine.

Good, H. G. (1970). A history of American education. In M. Brenton, *What's happened to teacher?* (p. 70). New York: Coward-McCann, Inc.

Goodson, I. F. (Ed.). (1992). *Studying teachers' lives.* New York: Teachers College Press.

Goodson, I. F., & Walker, R. (Eds.). (1991). *Biography, identity and schooling: Episodes in educational research.* London: Falmer Press.

Griffin, G. (1992). Teacher education. In M. C. Akin (Ed.), *Encyclopedia of educational research* (6th ed., pp. 1333–1345). New York: Macmillan.

Hansot, E. (1989). Waller on what teaching does to the teacher. In D. J. Willower & W. L. Boyd (Eds.), *Willard Waller on education and schools: A critical appraisal* (pp. 125–133). Berkeley, CA: McCutchan.

Hargreaves, A. (1996). Revisiting voice. *Educational Researcher 25* (1), 12–19.

Havighurst, R. J., & Levine, D. U. (1979). *Society and education.* Boston: Allyn & Bacon.

Hemmings, A., & Metz, M. H. (1990). Real teaching: How high school teachers negotiate societal, local community, and student pressures when they define their work. In R. Page & L. Valli (Eds.), *Curriculum differentiation: Interpretive studies in U.S. secondary schools* (pp. 91–111). Albany, NY: State University of New York Press.

Henke, R. R., Choy, S. P., Chen, X., Geis, S., Alt, M. N., & Broughman, S. P. (1997). *America's teachers: Profile of a profession, 1993–94* (U.S. Department of Education, National Center for Education Statistics NCES 97–460). Washington, DC: U.S. Government Printing Office.

Henke, R. R., Choy, S. P., & Geis, S. (1996). *Schools and staffing in the United States: A statistical profile, 1993–94* (U.S. Department of Education, National Center for Education Statistics NCES 96–124). Washington, DC: U.S. Government Printing Office.

Herbst, J. (1989a). *And sadly teach: Teacher education and professionalization in American culture.* Madison, WI: University of Wisconsin Press.

Herbst, J. (1989b). Teacher preparation in the nineteenth century: Institutions and purposes. In D. Warren (Ed.), *American teachers: Histories of a profession at work.* New York: Macmillan.

Hoffman, N. (1981). *Woman's "true" profession: Voices from the history of teaching.* Old Westbury, NY: The Feminist Press.

Holmes Group. (1986). *Tomorrow's teachers: A report of the Holmes group.* East Lansing: Michigan State University.

Ingersoll, R. M., & Alsalam, N. (1997). *Teacher professionalization and teacher commitment: A multilevel analysis* (U.S. Department of Education, National Center for Education Statistics NCES 97–069). Washington, DC: U.S. Government Printing Office.

Kanter, R. (1977). *Men and women of the corporation.* New York: Basic Books.

Kaufman, P. W. (1984). *Women teachers on the frontier.* New Haven, CT: Yale University Press.

Lawton, S. (1987). Teachers' salaries: An international perspective. In K. Alexander & D. Monk (Eds.), *Attracting and compensating America's teachers* (pp. 69–89). Cambridge, MA: Ballinger.

Louis, K. S., & Smith, B. (1990). Teacher working conditions. In P. Reyes (Ed.), *Teachers and their workplace: Commitment, performance, and productivity* (pp. 23–47). Newbury Park, CA: Sage.

Lortie, D.C. (1975). *Schoolteacher: A sociological study.* University of Chicago Press, Chicago.

Metz, M. H. (1986). *Different by design: The context and character of three magnet schools.* New York: Routledge.

Metz, M. H. (1990). How social class differences shape teachers' work. In M. McLaughlin, J. Talbert, & N. Basia (Eds.), *The contexts of teaching in secondary schools: Teachers realities.* New York: Teachers College Press.

Myres, S. L. (1982). *Westering women and the frontier experience, 1800–1915.* Albuquerque, NM: University of New Mexico Press.

Musgrave, P. W. (1968). *Society and education in England since 1800.* London: Methuen & Co.

National Commission on Teaching and America's Future. (1996). *What matters most: Teaching for America's future.* New York: Carnegie Corporation.

National Education Association. (1987). *Status of the American public school teacher, 1985–86.* Westhaven, CT: National Education Association.

Nelson, M. K. (1992). Using oral case histories to reconstruct the experiences of women teachers in Vermont, 1900–50. In I. F. Goodson (Ed.), *Studying teachers' lives* (pp. 167–186). New York: Teachers College Press.

Newman, J. W. (1994). *America's teachers: An introduction to education* (2nd ed.). New York: Longman.

Organization for Economic Cooperation and Development. (1990). *The teacher today: Tasks, conditions, policies.* Paris: Organization for Economic Cooperation and Development.

Ornstein, A. C. (1980). Teacher salaries: Past, present, future. *Phi Delta Kappan, 61*(10), 677–679.

Page, R. (1987). Teachers' perceptions of students: A link between classrooms, school cultures, and the social order. *Anthropology and Education Quarterly, 18,* 77–99.

Pajak, E., & Blase, J. J. (1989). The impact of teachers' personal lives on professional role enactment: A qualitative analysis. *American Education Research Journal, 26*(2), 283–310.

Parelius, R. J., & Parelius, A. P. (1987). *The sociology of education.* Englewood Cliffs, NJ: Prentice-Hall.

Perkins, L. M. (1989). The history of Blacks in teaching: Growth and decline within the profession. In D. Warren (Ed.), *American teachers: Histories of a profession at work* (pp. 344–369). New York: Macmillan.

Peters, D. W. (1934). *The status of the married woman teacher.* New York: Teachers College Press.

Prentice, A., & Theobald, M. R. (Eds.). (1991). *Women who taught: Perspectives on the history of women and teaching.* Toronto, Ontario: University of Toronto Press.

Richardson, J. G., & Hatcher, B. W. (1983). The feminization of public school teaching, 1870–1920. *Work and Occupations, 10*(1), 81–99.

Rist, R. C. (1986). Student social class and teacher expectations: The self-fulfilling prophecy in ghetto education. In M. Hammersley (Ed.), *Case studies in classroom research.* Philadelphia: Open University Press.

Rosenholtz, S. J. (1989). *Teachers' workplace: The social organization of schools.* New York: Longman.

Rothschild, M. L., & Hronek, P. C. (1992). *Doing what the day brought: An oral history of Arizona women.* Tucson, AZ: University of Arizona Press.

Rury, J. L. (1989). Who became teachers? The social characteristics of teachers in American history. In D. Warren (Ed.), *American teachers: Histories of a profession at work* (pp. 9–48). New York: Macmillan.

Rury, J. L. (1991). *Education and women's work: Female schooling and the division of labor in urban America, 1870–1930.* Albany, NY: State University of New York Press.

Salmon, R. G. (1987). Teacher salaries: Progress over the decade. In K. Alexander & D. Monk (Eds.), *Attracting and compensating America's teachers* (pp. 249–261). Cambridge, MA: Ballinger.

Schmuck, P. A. (1987). Women school employees in the United States. In P. A. Schmuck (Ed.), *Women educators: Employees of school in western countries* (pp. 75–97). New York: State University of New York Press.

Shakeshaft, C. (1987). *Women in educational administration.* Newbury, CA: Sage.

Smith, T. M., Young, B. A., Bae, Y., Choy, S. P., & Alsalam, N. (1997). *The condition of education 1997* (U.S. Department of Education, National Center for Education Statistics NCES 97–388). Washington, DC: U.S. Government Printing Office.

Snyder, T. D. (1993). *120 years of American education: A statistical portrait* (U.S. Department of Education, National Center for Education Statistics). Washington, DC: U.S. Government Printing Office.

Snyder, T. D. (1996). *Digest of education statistics 1996* (U.S. Department of Education, National Center for Education Statistics NCES 96–133). Washington, DC: U.S. Government Printing Office.

Spencer, D. A. (1986). *Contemporary women teachers: Balancing school and home.* New York: Longman.

Spencer, D. A. (1988). Public schoolteaching: A suitable job for a woman? In A. Statham, E. M. Miller, & H. O. Mauksch (Eds.), *The worth of women's work: A qualitative synthesis* (pp. 167–186). New York: State University of New York Press.

Spencer, D. A. (1992). *Border classrooms: A comparison of U.S. and Mexican teachers.* Paper presented at the meeting of the Midwest Sociological Society, Kansas City, MO.

Spencer, D. A. (1993). *Teachers-maestras: U.S. and Mexican teachers in historical context.* Paper presented at the meeting of the Midwest Sociological Society, Chicago, IL.

Spencer, D. A. (1994). The sociology of teaching. In T. Husén & T. N. Postlethwaite (Eds.), *The international encyclopedia of education* (2nd ed., pp. 5607–5614). Oxford: Pergamon Press.

Spencer, D. A. (1997a). The sociology of teaching. In L. J. Saha (Ed.). *International encyclopedia of the sociology of education* (pp. 206–212). Oxford: Pergamon Press.

Spencer, D. A. (1997b). Teaching as women's work. In B. J. Biddle, T. L. Good, & I. Goodson (Eds.), *International handbook of teachers and teaching.* The Netherlands: Kluwer Academic Publishers.

Strober, M., & Lanford, A. G. (1986). The feminization of public school teaching: Cross-sectional analysis, 1850–1880. *Signs, 11*(2), 212–235.

Tozer, S. E., Violas, P. C., & Senese, G. B. (1993). *School & society: Educational practice as social expression.* New York: McGraw-Hill.

Waller, W. (1932). *The sociology of teaching.* New York: Wiley.

Warren, D. (1985). Learning from experience: History and teacher education. *Educational Researcher, 14,* 5–12.

Warren, D. (Ed.). (1989). *American teachers: Histories of a profession at work.* New York: Macmillan.

Widdowson, F. (1983). *Going up into the next class: Women and elementary teacher training, 1840–1914.* London: Hutchinson.

Williams, C. L. (1992). The glass escalator: Hidden advantages for men in the "female" professions. *Social Problems, 39*(3), 253–267.

Williams, C. L. (Ed.). (1993). *Doing "women's work."* Newbury Park, CA: Sage.

Williams, C. L. (1995). *Still a man's world.* Berkeley: University of California Press.

Wittrock, M. C. (Ed.). (1986). *Handbook of research on teaching* (3rd ed.). New York: Macmillan.

40.
Teaching as a Moral Activity

David T. Hansen
University of Illinois at Chicago

Introduction

The idea that teaching is a moral endeavor is at least as old as recorded knowledge of the practice. Plato, Confucius, Lao Tzu, Aristotle, the Buddha, the Bhagavad Gita—to name only a few of the more well-known sources—all provide arguments and testimonials about the moral significance of teaching. Moreover, from the moment these pioneering accounts first appeared, people have sought to bring to life the ideas contained in them. In so doing, they have fashioned an almost unbroken conversation about the moral aspects of teaching, a conversation that continues through the present day. The notion that teaching is a moral practice constitutes one of the world's most enduring understandings of the work.

What do we learn about teaching when we conceive it as a moral activity? What does it mean to call teaching a moral practice in the first place? And why might it be important for researchers and practitioners to think of teaching as a moral endeavor? In this chapter, I will reply to these questions by reviewing recent philosophical and field-based research on the moral dimensions of teaching The literature points to several conclusions, which I summarize here and then address in detail in the pages to come:

1. Studies suggest that teaching is inherently a moral endeavor. Moral matters do not have to be imported into the classroom as if teaching were itself devoid of moral significance. According to the literature, it is not the introduction of an externally defined set of conditions, issues, or actions that determines whether teaching is or is not moral in meaning. Rather, the activity of teaching is itself saturated with moral significance, and it is so in ways that illuminate both the beneficial and the harmful influence teachers can have on students.

2. Extending the first point, the literature suggests that teaching is at one and the same time an intellectual and a moral endeavor. Whether working with preschool children or with graduate students, teaching embodies both intellectual and moral dimensions. It distorts teachers' work to suggest that intellectual and moral matters operate independently of each other. According to the literature, it is also mistaken to assume that teachers' intellectual and moral influence on students materialize independently of each other.

3. Any action a teacher undertakes in the classroom is capable of expressing moral meaning that, in turn, can influence students. How and where teachers stand while talking with students, what their tones of voice are, who they pay attention to, what curricular content they focus on—these and many other familiar, often routine aspects of teachers' work can all harbor moral meaning. Moreover, they can do so without teachers being aware of that fact.

4. Moral perception, moral judgment, moral knowledge, and other related terms that I will elucidate play a dynamic role in the work of teaching. The literature suggests that educators may want to reconceive more well-known and widely applied terms such as teachers' decision making, teachers' thinking, and teachers' ways of knowing. Up to the present time, those terms have sometimes been associated with intellectual or cognitive processes divorced from moral considerations. As the previous points attest, the intellectual and the moral dimensions of teaching can be separated only for heuristic purposes.

These understandings and others that I will examine spark questions that call for further research. In that spirit I will conclude the chapter with some suggestions for future study. One reason for doing so is that, in comparison with research on such issues as effective instructional methods and the teaching of specific subjects, school- and classroom-based inquiry into the

The author thanks reviewers Robert Boostrom (University of Southern Indiana) and Roger Soder (University of Washington). Michelle Piercyzn-ski-Ward provided thoughtful editorial assistance. The preparation of this chapter was made possible in part by a grant from The Spencer Foundation. The views expressed in the chapter are those of the author.

moral aspects of teaching has just begun. Its emergence reflects, in part, changing conceptions of research in the social sciences. Those changes embody new, philosophically reconstructed perspectives on the nature and place of knowledge, of meaning, and of interpretation in human life (Bernstein, 1983; Geertz, 1973, 1983; Haan, Bellah, Rabinow, & Sullivan, 1983; Rabinow & Sullivan, 1979). This sea change has worked its way into educational research on teaching. It has resulted, for example, in an enormous proliferation of field-based studies. It has altered the field's conception of the purposes of research and of the kinds of knowledge needed from it (Jackson, 1990). Lampert captures the aim of many inquirers today when she writes that they seek "not to determine whether general propositions about learning or teaching are true or false but to further our understanding of the character of these particular kinds of human activity" (1990, p. 37). As part of this evolving state of affairs, the moral dimensions of teaching have become a more researchable and, in a sense, a more accessible topic of investigation than earlier generations of educational researchers perceived.

Before beginning the discussion, I want to clarify several points that might otherwise trigger confusion about the intent of the present chapter or about the idea of teaching as a moral endeavor.

I will not be discussing what is called "moral education," understood as a formal aspect of educational practice, nor will I discuss the research on moral development that informs the current conversation on moral education, much of it triggered by scholars such as Carol Gilligan and Lawrence Kohlberg. Moral education can include the deliberate teaching of particular values, attitudes, dispositions, and beliefs. It can describe efforts to assist students in learning how to think and talk about values and beliefs. It can encompass programs to help students learn how to judge situations wisely and to act ethically. Furthermore, it can comprise efforts to teach students how to care for people and their differing hopes and aspirations and how to care for the natural world. A separate chapter on the topic of moral education can be found in this handbook (also see Oser, 1986; Sockett, 1992). Of related interest is a separate chapter in this handbook on Noddings' (1984) idea of caring as a moral orientation that can inform educators' beliefs, values, and conduct.

It is fitting to have separate treatments of moral education and of teaching as a moral endeavor because the two are not the same. As we will see, philosophical and field-based research shows that moral considerations do not have to be imported from without, but rather permeate the work of teaching. Moreover, in contrast with moral education, many of the moral meanings inherent in teaching are unwilled and unintentional. Some are built into the terms of the work and consequently await teachers even before they set foot through the classroom door. Others—many others—are unforeseen aspects and consequences of what teachers say and do. It is worthwhile to keep these ideas distinct. If we are to judge from some of the prescriptive literature in education, the tendency is to reduce the idea of teaching as a moral endeavor to the idea of formal moral education. This mistake echoes the equally mistaken tendency to restrict the concept of the moral to differing value positions, or to specific prohibitions or strictures, or to possible stances on controversial social issues rather than to see the place of the moral in countless forms of human interaction including those in classrooms.

If teaching as a moral activity differs from moral education, what is meant by the concept "moral" as it pertains to teaching? I will show how research on many aspects of teaching suggests that the practice will be poorly conceived if it is divided a priori into components that have moral significance and others that do not. The literature suggests that teaching as an *activity* or *endeavor* is inherently moral, and it shows that any specific teaching *act* is capable of conveying moral meaning. This view of the moral also differs from the aforementioned concept of caring. As Noddings (1984) conceives it, caring takes its character from a distinctively feminine orientation to ethics, one that, in her view, has applicability to all walks of human life rather than just teaching. Put differently, the roots of the concept of care reside outside the practice of teaching. The viewpoint on the moral in this chapter has family resemblances with caring, especially with its emphasis on the particularities of how individuals regard and treat one another. However, the moral, as it is used here, is not a feminine- or masculine-based idea. It pertains to teachers and their work at all levels of the educational system.

The chapter takes a pedagogical-or practice-centered view of the moral: The latter's meaning derives more from what characterizes teaching as a distinctive activity than it does from a particular moral philosophy. Finally, the perspective developed here differs from how the term *moral* is sometimes used in anthropology and sociology. Scholars in those disciplines often equate the term with "mores," which are customary ways of regarding roles and the people who occupy them. In their research, the moral sometimes boils down to a culturally or socially defined category. That is not the perspective that emerges from the literature reviewed in this chapter.

The following propositions can serve as a preliminary guide to thinking about the moral in teaching:

1. Making use of the term, *the moral,* may be preferable to the term *morality* in thinking about teaching. The latter word often conjures up images of a particular set of values embraced by a particular group, community, or society. However, the idea of teaching as a moral endeavor points as much to an orientation toward practice—to a way of perceiving the work and its significance—as it does to a specific family of values.

2. It may be unwise to insist on a single, airtight definition of the moral as it pertains to teaching. Over the millenia, inquiry into the moral has generated different theories and viewpoints of what the concept means. (For extended discussion see MacIntyre, 1984, and Taylor, 1989; Audi, 1995, provides synopses that are helpful starting points.) For example, *emotivism* assumes that the moral can be reduced to personal preference. The moral is whatever we want it to be; it is a name we give to things we happen to prize. You have your values, I have mine, and that is just the way it is. However, many scholars in education, like many people everywhere, find this strong version of relativism uninhabitable, not to mention untrue. Instead, they may take a *deontological* view, in which the moral is primarily

a duty- or obligation-based concept. Or, they may take a *consequentialist* view, in which the moral is associated not with people' intentions, aims, and purposes—which figure heavily in talk about duty—but rather with the outcomes of actions. For consequentialists, what is moral is that which yields the greatest good to the greatest number of people. In contrast with both deontological and consequentialist views, some scholars associate the moral with virtue and personal character. People and their moral qualities are central here, rather than the consequences of action or notions of impartial, rational procedure for determining one's duty (i.e., what the moral thing to do is). As we will see, none of these specific views of the moral, when considered individually, can capture the moral dimensions of teaching.

3. Rather than define the moral in this chapter, I will try to characterize it as it sheds light on the work of teaching. Teaching as an activity can be described as moral, because, in very general terms, it presupposes notions of better and worse, of good and bad. As typically understood, teaching reflects the intentional effort to influence another human being for the good rather than for the bad. Teaching presumes that it is good, rather than bad, for students to learn and for teachers to teach. It presumes that students' lives will be better as a result of teaching. These claims, perhaps deceptively commonsensical, emphasize the inherently moral nature of the practice.

4. Teaching comprises infinitely varied acts that are bound up with familiar and desirable qualities of human relation: being patient with others, attentive to them, respectful of them, open-minded to their views, and so forth. Teachers enact these and other virtues (or fail to) in strikingly diverse ways. In this light, the claim that teaching is a moral activity calls attention to teachers' conduct, character, perception, judgment, understanding, and more.

These propositions, to which more will be added, provide, I hope, an appealing introduction to what is to come.

Finally, I want to mention the principles of selection I have adopted in determining what literature to review. Identifying those principles has been something of a task in itself, as has been sorting out what kinds of publications fall within their purview. This situation reflects, in part, the simple fact that this is the first chapter on teaching as a moral activity to appear in this series of handbooks. Moreover, I am not aware of any previous attempt to review work on teaching as a moral endeavor in the wide-ranging fashion I shall do here. (See Oser, 1994, for a review of research that addresses the importance of what he calls "procedural morality" in teaching.) In addition, many studies of teaching that do not consider moral matters take for granted moral assumptions about the nature of people and about the educational process. But no single chapter, perhaps not even a whole handbook, can analyze all such studies for their moral assumptions about teaching.

I have made use of the following four criteria of selection for this chapter:

1. The literature must focus on teachers and teaching. This criterion rules out studies that center on educational policies, on schools as institutions, and so forth. Consequently, I will not be examining research on topics such as moral climates in schools or ethical codes that might govern teachers' practice. Important as these and related issues may be, they remain distinct from what is meant by teaching as a moral endeavor.

2. The research must address the moral dimensions of teaching in an explicit way. From one point of view, countless studies of teaching undertaken in the history of educational research—whether they examine high school instruction, nursery school play, or a medical school seminar—reveal the ways in which moral considerations are woven into the everyday fabric of educational practice. However, it is impossible to examine in a single chapter the light shed on the moral aspects of teaching by studies focused on topics other than the moral.

3. I have limited myself to studies published in English. This third criterion of selection results from my own limited language skills, but it also reflects the judgment that much (though clearly not all) of the terminology and influence of work on teaching as a moral endeavor published in other languages has found its way into recent work in English (compare Barcena, Gil, & Jover, 1993; Oser, Dick, & Patry, 1992; van Manen 1991b).

4. I will include conceptual work on teaching as a moral endeavor that is philosophically informed and that contains an argument. This criterion will rule out a substantial body of educational writing that is largely ungrounded or hortatory. With respect to field-based studies, I will review work that is based on what Malen, Ogawa, and Kranz (1990, p. 294) call "systematic investigations" (see Smylie 1994, p. 130). As Smylie puts it, "these studies identify the conceptual perspectives and specific questions that guide the research, specify methodology, address issues of validity and reliability, and present interpretations of findings" (1994, p. 130). These sound remarks do not imply that studies of the moral dimensions of teaching must frame matters in identical ways, nor that they must use the same research vocabulary and methodology. For example, researchers can adequately address validity without so much as mentioning that term. They can satisfactorily address reliability by criticizing that very concept as it applies to a particular project. For the purposes of this chapter, an essential criterion requires that field-based research be systematic and reflect an in-depth engagement with the moral dimensions of teaching.

I have separated insights and conclusions from scholarship and divided them into several broad themes that follow below. The themes are not exhaustive, but are intended to capture what we have learned about teaching as a moral activity. I describe individual studies under the heading of one or more of the themes, but readers should understand that this tactic is often equally for organizational as for substantive reasons. Many of the studies touch in one way or another on all of the themes I examine, attesting thereby to the complexity of teaching, but space limitations make it impossible to draw all the connections here.

Teaching Is Inherently a Moral Activity

This section focuses on the relationship between means and ends and between the intellectual and the moral in the practice of teaching. The purpose is to show why many scholars have argued that teaching is inherently a moral activity.

Means and Ends in Teaching

As mentioned previously, the idea that teaching is a moral endeavor is one of the oldest and most enduring conceptions of the work. But it is not the most widely espoused or discussed view of teaching today. Rather, what drives much of today's educational research, policy, and practice is the view that teaching is a means to an end. For many educators and the public at large, that end or aim boils down to outcomes such as academic learning, socialization, or preparation for work. For other educators and members of the public, the end or aim of teaching is seen as political (e.g., promoting democratic life), as cultural (e.g., promoting cultural awareness), or as religious (e.g., advancing a particular set of religious values). A strong case could be made that each of these ends is grounded in moral assumptions. For example, the idea that teaching is a means to students' academic learning presumes a moral commitment: namely, that academic learning is good rather than bad for people. It is good, so the argument might go, to know how to read, to write, and to numerate. It is good to know about subjects such as history, geography, and science. Such knowledge, advocates of this view might add, expands rather than contracts the range of possible experiences in which young people can engage. It invites students to become broad as contrasted with narrow in their outlook on life, with all the consequences that a broadened viewpoint can have for how persons regard and treat other people and their respective strivings. If by "moral assumption" we mean a conception of who and what people ought to become, or of what it is good for human beings to do and to be, then all of the ends popularly ascribed to teaching harbor moral meaning.

The point is that teaching is widely assumed today to be an instrumental activity. "Teaching is a means to an end," argues White (1992) in a recent collection of essays treating moral and academic aspects of the work. "[I]t is responsible and effective only when it leads to a valued and morally defensible change in students" (p. 50). According to this commonly held viewpoint, teaching is a set of activities intended to bring about desirable changes in students. This view holds regardless of whether one thinks of teaching as passing on knowledge to the young or whether one thinks of teaching as releasing students' own interests and desires. Advocates of both approaches, however much they might disagree with one another, hope to see desirable change in students. This view of teaching as a means to an end is so commonsensical that it might seem strange to question it. How could teaching be anything other than a means to an end? Surely teaching should not be valued by either educators or the public for its own sake. Perhaps some teachers might do so—those, for example, who derive deep fulfillment from the work—but teaching is a social endeavor intended to bring about positive changes in young people.

However, scholars have pointed out problems in means and ends thinking that make it difficult to understand teaching, especially its moral significance. The source of their criticism and the languages in which it is couched can be traced back to a number of influential figures. I shall touch briefly on three of them: Socrates, Kant, and Dewey.

Although Socrates never calls himself a teacher in so many words, his entire life centered around systematic conversation with others. He pursued basic questions such as what is virtue or goodness, and what is knowledge. He engaged anyone willing to talk with him: the rich and the poor, the young and the old, the thoughtful and the impatient. Regardless of the topic or the interlocutor, he appeared to pursue truth in an honest, courageous, and (in a certain sense) humble fashion—moral qualities, incidentally, which many would ascribe to good teaching at any level of the system. Truth was key; Socrates takes pains to distinguish truth from falsehood, from ignorance, and from mere opinion. Honesty, courage, and humility are crucial virtues, because, according to Socrates, truth is among the hardest things to uncover and to bring to life in human affairs. People must be honest with one another and say what they believe rather than what they feel others expect from them. They must be courageous because pursuing truth is risky, frustrating, perhaps even unsettling. Far easier, Socrates implies, to remain cocooned uncritically within the beliefs and values one has inherited. People must also be humble, willing to take seriously the perspectives of others rather than just their own, and willing to drop their views if they do not hold up to scrutiny. In dialogues such as the *Protagoras, Meno, Apology, Phaedo,* and *Republic,* Plato renders vivid these and other aspects of Socrates' practice.

I want to draw two conclusions from this abbreviated interpretation. First, Socrates' pursuit of goodness and truth led him well beyond means and ends thinking. Posed differently, it dissolved any hard and fast distinction between the two. At first glance, one could argue that the ends Socrates sought and the means he pursued do stand alone, and consequently could be advanced separately from one another. Socrates sought the true and the good, and conversation was the means to get nearer to them. The upshot, evidently, is that one could study Socrates at work and then create a manual for how to lead a good conversation that is independent of the ends or aims of the conversation. But this description fails to do justice to Socrates' actual conduct. Conversation was not a means to discovering truth. Rather, it was the enactment of getting as close to the truth as human beings are capable. Nor was conversation a means to discovering virtue and the good. Rather, it was the enactment of some of the very best moral qualities human beings are capable of actualizing in life: honesty, courage, and humility (the capacity for friendship is another such quality—compare the *Lysis*—as is love itself—compare the *Symposium*). It appears that for Socrates, the means embody the ends, and the ends are realized in the means. We can examine the means and the ends separately, but it would distort them to believe that in actual practice the one is essentially distinct from and leads to the other.

The second conclusion I draw from Socrates' historically influential example follows from the first and should now be evident: For Socrates, teaching is inherently a moral endeavor. Teaching has to do with who and what we are becoming as people, with the "we" encompassing teachers and students alike (for discussion see, e.g., Gadamer 1980; Vlastos, 1991).

I will devote a bit more space to several of Immanuel Kant's ideas. Kant has had an incalculable influence on both moral and political thought ever since the publication of his work in the 18th and early 19th centuries. Few writers have captured more compellingly the idea of human dignity. Kant's viewpoint casts helpful light on the ambiguity and limitations of some forms of means and ends thinking as they apply to the practice of teaching.

Kant was a rigorous critic of what would later come to be called utilitarianism, which today is considered an example of consequentialism in moral theory. Utilitarianism presumes that the criterion for judging moral worth or moral action—such as in teaching—is consequences, not intentions, principles, beliefs, or values. What actually happens, utilitarians ask? More specifically, have the actions undertaken yielded the greatest amount of good to the greatest number of people? (The good, or "happiness," is grounded for some writers in this tradition in the presence of pleasure and the absence of pain.) Utilitarian thinking has been immensely influential in our era. Much of the work undertaken today in educational thought, policy, and practice, in which teaching is perceived almost exclusively as a means to an end, is undergirded by an often unarticulated utilitarian calculus. Desirable outcomes (or "consequences") such as higher scores on standardized tests, deeper democratic thinking, improved graduation rates, enhanced cultural understanding, better economic returns, and so forth are regarded as representing the present and future welfare (i.e., "happiness") of society writ large. Personal intentions, beliefs, and aspirations are rarely part of this picture of teaching, except insofar as what teachers think translates into action to bring about such ends. Teaching becomes a moral endeavor solely with respect to its consequences.

Kant would describe this perspective as instrumental in the negative sense of that term. For Kant, utilitarianism tends to reduce fundamental qualities of human being and of human practice into means, or tools, or techniques, whose moral merit resides in whether they bring about ends defined apart from those qualities. This viewpoint threatens to drain human qualities and practices of inherent meaning and value. Pushed to the extreme, it converts a parent's love for a child into an effective technique of upbringing, rather than perceiving it as that which constitutes the parent as a human being, as a loving person. Pushed to the extreme, it reduces a teacher's agency, autonomy, and character as an educator to a set of techniques to be judged by criteria divorced from that agency, autonomy, and character. From this point of view, teaching comes to take on what Kant calls a "price," or purely instrumental value, calculated by the extent to which it serves one or another externally defined end.

However, Kant argues (1785/1990, 1795/1960), human beings and their formation as human beings have no price. "In the realm of ends," he writes, "everything has either a *price* or a *dignity*. Whatever has a price can be replaced by something else as its equivalent; on the other hand, whatever is above all price and therefore admits of no equivalent, has dignity. . . . [T]hat which constitutes the condition under which alone something can be an end in itself does not have mere relative worth (price) but an intrinsic worth (dignity)" (1785/1990, pp. 51–52).

According to Kant, human beings have intrinsic worth, or dignity, because they are capable of acting morally (for discussion see, for example, Herman, 1993; Korsgaard, 1996). They are capable both of conceiving and of doing the right thing with respect to dwelling with other people. They are capable of valuing goodness more than personal inclination. Put differently, they are capable of acting on the basis of more than sheer instinct, the desire for power or pleasure, or the fear of pain. And they can do more than merely react or passively await things to come upon them. Kant argues that because of their moral capacity, human beings must be seen as ends in themselves, rather than as means to others' ends. As moral beings capable of living in a moral world of their own making, human beings have a basic dignity and are not subject to a "price." Moreover, it matters what kind of life people try to build, and the moral life, which for Kant is one in which all people are recognized and treated as ends, has no "equivalent." Kant condemns utilitarian thinking for treating human desires in the forms in which they presently appear as fixed, or at any rate as the exclusive guides for current practice. He urges, instead, a focus on what human beings can become because of their capacity to conceive and realize moral conduct.

The upshot of this all-too-brief interpretation is that means and ends educational thinking, as frequently undertaken, fails to capture the significance of teaching. Of course, Kant would grant, the practice of teaching is intended to bring about learning in students. But according to his perspective, the "bringing about" and the "learning" cannot be meaningfully separated. To do so would be to relegate teachers to the realm of "price," that is, to deny that the people they are and the things they do have inherent value (thereby implying, among other things, that machines or other technology could just as easily perform the work). Such an approach renders teachers and teaching entirely subservient to some external end, one that, moreover, might merely have its own price rather than being valuable in itself. For Kant, that which is valuable in and of itself—above all, human beings and how they realize their humanity—does not change. Proper human growth, for Kant, is in part a process of realizing moral capability—of treating others and being treated as an end—and that process has no equivalent. It is the enactment of dignity itself. From this point of view, teaching is more than solely a means, because it is a moral practice that partakes in the idea of dignity (rather than price). We will see in due course how recent research has helped flesh out these abstract terms by showing that the work of teaching embodies moral meaning.

John Dewey's educational philosophy, as it bears on means and ends thinking, extends what I have said thus far about Socrates and Kant. According to Dewey, teaching is a form of service to the society in which it is embedded. Teachers are moral agents, people who can and often do have a positive influence on students. However, Dewey argues that the terms of the service teachers provide cohere with society's best possibilities, not necessarily with its current practices. Teachers stand on the side of truth rather than of falsehood, of justice rather than of harm, and of the value of growth and development for each person rather than for the idea of preordaining individuals to set places in life (Dewey 1897/1974a, 1909/1975, 1916/1997). Moreover, Dewey emphasizes, what teachers stand for should not be seen as ends that are external to the work of teaching. Teaching is not, in other words, merely a means to some prespecified end. The act of teaching embodies ends. Teaching is a moral endeavor because its constituent acts have moral meaning in their own right; they do not take their meaning solely from what they supposedly lead to (compare the utilitarian viewpoint).

Dewey argues that neither education nor teaching, which facilitates education, should be seen as preparatory endeavors. Of course, Dewey grants, society supports them because they do, in a certain way, "prepare" people for a broader life. But the moment they are not conceived as important in their own right is the moment we begin to drain significance, energy, and purpose from them. They become merely a means, and (echoing Kant) Dewey shows how unfulfilling if not dispiriting something that is merely a means to an end can be. According to Dewey, only the substantive, not the instrumental (as I am using the term), is educative and meaningful. We will be prevented from learning adequately in the present moment—the only moment in which we can learn, Dewey reminds us—if what we are learning is treated as having value only for some future moment.

Dewey diagnoses in an unparalleled way the harm to students, to teachers, and to society that results from instrumentalizing educational practice—from reducing its meaning to some external end regardless of how esteemed that end may be. He developed an original conception of experience (Dewey, 1916/1997, 1925/1958, 1938/1963) in order to spotlight what it means to take the present moment with the utmost educational seriousness. To do so requires reconstructing the meaning of terms such as means and ends. In Dewey's analysis, ends sometimes become means and vice versa, but always in the spirit of an almost sacramental attention to seizing the possibilities in the present. He argues repeatedly that this focus does not mean ignoring the future. Rather, it is the only way to truly bring into being a future in which, to recall Kant's terms, all partake of dignity. If we attend properly to the present, Dewey argues, the future will take care of itself; that is, the present will lead naturally into the future (1916/1997, p. 56). Teaching is a moral endeavor because it influences directly the quality of the present educational moment, a moment in which, Dewey reminds us, the persons we are becoming hang in the balance.

Socrates, Kant, and Dewey, each in his own way, illuminate the moral nature of teaching. There are many other historical figures whose work sheds light on the topic: Confucius' *Analects*, Aristotle's *Nicomachean Ethics*, and Rousseau's *Emile* come quickly to mind. But I hope this brief commentary provides a flavor of the richness and the vitality in the educational thought that has been handed down to us, in which moral rather than instrumental considerations are paramount.

Contemporary scholars have continued the historical critique of narrow means and ends thinking as it bears on education and teaching. For example, Peters (see, e.g., 1964) calls into question the often sharp disjunction between educational ends and means. In an explicit criticism of the idea that educators must have an "aim," he writes:

> Given that "education" implies, first, some commendable state of mind and, secondly, some experience that is thought to lead up to or to contribute to it, and given also that people are usually deliberately put in the way of such experiences, it is only too easy to think of the whole business in terms of models like those of building a

bridge or going on a journey. The commendable state of mind is thought of as an end to be aimed at, and the experiences which lead up to it are regarded as means to its attainment. For this model of adopting means to premeditated ends is one that haunts all our thinking about the promotion of what is valuable. In the educational sphere we therefore tend to look round for the equivalent of bridges to be built or ports to be steered to. (1963/1968, p. 90)

The consequence, Peters argues—in terms that recall Kant's distinction between having a price or having dignity—is that people "thus think that education must be for the sake of something extrinsic that is worth while, whereas the truth is that being worthwhile is part of what is meant by calling it 'education'" (1964, p. 18). Peters suggests that morally significant ends such as knowledge, self-realization, citizenship, and so forth are not discrete entities or objects to be attained through particular means, namely, teaching. Rather, they are "high-sounding ways of talking about doing some things rather than others and doing them in a certain manner" (p. 91). The so-called "ends," according to Peters, are in fact ways of living and interacting with other human beings. Knowing things, realizing one's self, becoming a good citizen are all processes, not products or ends. For Peters, knowing things or being a good citizen are lifeless and inert if treated as ends per se. "[G]oing to school is not a *means* to these in the way in which getting on a bus is a means of getting to work; and they are not made or produced out of the material of the mind in the way in which a penny is produced out of copper" (p. 91). According to Peters, ends are preeminently ways of being and living. Teachers need not have an "aim," but they must have an orientation—what might be called a vision of the moral life that guides their work in the classroom.

Carr (1992) fuels this line of criticism in his analysis of instrumental thinking in education:

> [T]he means to moral ends—such as the effective discipline of children—are related *internally* or constitutively; moral means contribute qualitatively to the very character—in this case of human discipline—of the goals which they produce. . . . [I]n the case of a moral practice like education our aims and goals are not logically separable or distinct from the procedures we adopt for their achievement. (p. 249)

Stengel and Tom (1995) substantiate this point in their argument for building a morally defensible teacher education program. Doing so, they emphasize, requires that teacher educators spend time together, share resources, and craft common agendas. However, the authors argue, these are not means to the realization of good practice, rather they are constitutive of sound teacher education practice (p. 162). In an extended critique of the idea of formal moral education, Philips (1979) argues that teaching an academic subject such as history embodies moral aspects in its own right. Consequently, in Philips' view, teaching history should not be understood as a means to promote certain moral ends such as tolerance or cultural understanding. To do so wrenches the subject apart from its own internal meanings. It can lead to a scenario in which students do not learn history and its associated values—such as respect for humanity, a sense of humility, and a feel for why people come to esteem certain things—but rather learn that they are supposed to draw moral lessons from history. Philips writes:

Do we need to refer to anything other than the study of history in order to see how it can free one from parochialism? But this matter must be stated carefully. It will not do to say that we study history *in order* to avoid parochialism, or *in order* to appreciate the lives and times of our own and other people. On the contrary, parochialism may be avoided and times other than our own appreciated *in* the study of history. (p. 53)

Mounce (1973) adds that teaching history has moral meaning because it provides human beings with a sense of what is important to attend to in human affairs. It enables people to look beyond immediate circumstance with its own localized definition of what is and what is not noteworthy. However, Mounce argues, it would be a mistake to approach the study of history for "lessons" about what is important. In his view, such an orientation cannot help but be clouded if not compromised by parochial criteria of what matters, precisely because those very criteria typically define the kind of desired "lessons" sought for (moreover, they are criteria that people may not be mindful of). According to Mounce, "we derive a sense of what is important from becoming absorbed in the study of the subject" (p. 20), a process in which we put immediate needs and concerns temporarily aside—in order to return to them enriched with new perspectives. According to Philips (1979), instead of treating the teaching of subjects like history as a means to moral development, we should emphasize "the [inherent] demands made by the pursuit of the subject in question" (p. 53). I return to this theme below in discussing why some scholars regard teaching as both an intellectual and a moral endeavor.

Boostrom (1991, 1994) shows how narrow means and ends thinking undermines educators' attempts to have a positive moral influence on their students' development. Based on extensive fieldwork in elementary schools, he focuses upon the nature and functions of classroom rules. At first glance, he argues, nothing could be more easily conceived as a means to an end than classroom rules: They are intended to bring about and maintain order, pure and simple. From this widely shared viewpoint, rules have no inherent significance. Rather, they are seen as "strictly instrumental and their content largely irrelevant. All that really matters is that students toe *some* mark" (Boostrom, 1991, p. 196). However, based on a detailed analysis of how rules actually operate in classroom life, Boostrom emerges with a viewpoint that sees rules as constitutive rather than as merely instrumental. In actual practice, rules can become not tools of management but "structures of meaning used by teachers and students to make sense of the world" (p. 193). Rules "express a way of seeing the world" (p. 194). They help define what counts as "events," and they help place events within an evolving system of beliefs and practices. According to Boostrom, rules help create a "way of life" or, put differently, a community. "The rule is a thread in the fabric of classroom life," he writes; "pull out the thread and the fabric falls apart" (p. 200). Throughout the analysis, Boostrom urges educators to reconceive their view of means and ends in classroom practice.

A vision of rules that separates them, as mere means, from ends separates them also from meaning. . . . The belief that a rule, for example, "Write your name on your paper," is only a tool for making things run smoothly blinds teachers and students to the significance

of saying, by the name at the top of the paper, "This is my work; this is a part of me." (pp. 193, 212)

Such beliefs, Boostrom argues, divorce means from ends "rather than clarifying their relationship" (p. 212). Boostrom concludes that "[t]o view rules only as instruments for establishing and maintaining discipline and deportment undercuts reflection and, ultimately, the teacher's conviction by denying the meaningfulness of everyday life" (p. 214).

The arguments reviewed in this section caution educators to be wary of uncritical means and ends thinking. Such thinking can inadvertently block from view moral dimensions of educational practice. The arguments also point to a second lens through which to appreciate why many scholars claim that teaching is inherently, rather than conditionally, a moral endeavor. The first lens has had to do with means and ends thinking or, more precisely, some of its limitations. The second helps us appreciate that teaching academic subjects engages moral much as it does intellectual matters.

The Intellectual and the Moral in Teaching

Teaching as a practice is always directed toward student learning, and such learning always involves, in one way or another, the use of the mind. The intellectual meaning of teaching comes to the fore in such claims as teachers assist students in learning how to reason about mathematical, scientific, historical, social, and other issues; how to do things like read, write, numerate, paint, and hit a baseball; how to articulate their interests and views; and much more. All of these activities involve intellectual activity. A nursery school teacher is engaged in it as is a teacher in an advanced law school seminar, even if the content and sophistication of the respective endeavors differ. In short, teaching is always an intellectual activity, or it could hardly be called teaching.

There is a growing body of work, however, that focuses on how and why teaching academic subjects is at one and the same time an intellectual and a moral endeavor. As we have seen with the topic of means and ends, this line of inquiry has roots in the historical conversation on education. Founding figures in the history of teaching such as Socrates and Confucius saw intellectual and moral learning as intimately related, so much so that they worried about the consequences of people acquiring knowledge divorced from considerations of the effect that knowledge has on the persons we become. They distinguished the "clever" from the "wise." Both sets of people can know a great deal, but the one group might use knowledge for harmful ends, perhaps without being aware of doing so, while the other group keeps in view its social dimensions. Socrates suggests on many occasions that the search for knowledge and truth should be understood as a moral quest, as an attempt to make ourselves into better people.

In the *Meno,* for example, he responds to skeptical questions about the human ability to learn by asserting:

[O]ne thing I am ready to fight for as long as I can, in word and act—that is, that we shall be better, braver, and more active men if we believe it right to look for what we don't know than if we believe there is no point in looking because what we don't know we can never discover. (in Hamilton and Cairns, 1961, p. 371)

Socrates believes that open-minded inquiry holds the promise of making us "better, braver, and more active" human beings. It can lead both to knowledge—which might mean knowledge of our ignorance, such that we lower our pretentions—and to moral improvement. Such inquiry makes men and women better than they would otherwise be: more courageous in facing doubts, fears, and obstacles and more active, more willing to try to understand and improve matters than to resign themselves to them. In the passage quoted above, Socrates takes care to introduce these claims by saying he will defend them in both "word and act," again attesting to the view that intellectual development and learning to act in moral relation with other people can be understood as coterminous rather than as separate processes.

Dewey has been an articulate 20th-century exponent of this viewpoint. In many of his works, Dewey argues that genuine intellectual development always implies moral development, and vice versa. According to Dewey, to learn to think independently and critically in a classroom context means learning to think feelingly. It means developing a sense of regard if not passion for the things of the world, which include one's own and others' ideas and hopes. For Dewey, genuine thought and reflection always imply a "concern with the issue—a certain sympathetic identification of our own destiny, if only dramatic, with the outcome of the course of events" (1916/1997, p. 147). Reflection means learning to think respectfully, to be mindful that one exists in relation with other human beings, and that one's own thought always both presumes human community and may have an effect on subsequent human community. Moreover, the qualities of mind Dewey associates with intellectual growth are "all of them," he concludes, "intrinsically moral qualities. Open-mindedness, single-mindedness, sincerity, breadth of outlook, thoroughness, assumption of responsibility for developing the consequences of ideas which are accepted are moral traits" (1916/1997, pp. 356–357; see also pp. 173–179 passim; also Dewey, 1933, pp. 30–34 passim).

In sum, Socrates, Dewey, and many other pioneering thinkers in education associate intellectual growth with moral growth. They conceive learning as extending well beyond adding fact upon fact or skill upon skill, important as that process may be in various contexts. Learning encompasses the intellectual and the moral; it describes the emergence and formation of human being. To be a learned person, in the best sense of that term, means more than having a lot of information at one's fingertips. It means being thoughtful about what one has learned, aware of how what one has learned is significant and fits into human life, and sensitive to the limitations and gaps in what one has learned. It means understanding that knowledge emerges from human interaction and can, in turn, effect subsequent human interaction. Such moral comprehension can be adequately learned only in community with other people who are also focused on learning. Recent research suggests that classrooms remain one of the best places in society for building this kind of learning community.

Tom's (1984) analysis of teaching as a "moral craft," for example, underscores the inherently moral and intellectual nature of the work. According to Tom, "teaching involves a subtle moral relationship between teacher and student" (p. 11). That relationship takes its point of departure, in part, from "the dominant power positions of the teacher" (p. 78; see also pp. 80–88). In addition, teaching is a moral endeavor because it represents "an attempt to bring important content to the awareness of a student" (p. 11). While some scholars focus on the inherent moral aspects of subject matter, Tom emphasizes that "teaching is moral in the sense that a curriculum plan *selects* [italics added] certain objectives or pieces of content instead of others; this selective process either explicitly or implicitly reflects a conception of desirable ends" (p. 78; see also pp. 88–95). According to Tom, if the moral is taken to encompass the idea of "desirable ends," then questions of curriculum take on immediate moral meaning.

In addition to teacher-student relationships and curricular selection, Tom regards teaching as moral because it entails "the ability to analyze situations and to use instructional skills appropriate to these situations" (p. 11). For Tom, this ability has moral overtones, because it bears directly on the kind of influence a teacher might have on students. A hypothetical example sheds light on how this conception might appear in classroom practice. Tom asks us to consider a teacher weighing the use of behavior modification with certain students. Considering effectiveness—a term that foreshadows the work of Oser et al. (1992), reviewed below—behavioral modification might succeed quite well. However, considering responsibility to students' overall growth—again, to use a term central for Oser et al. (1992)—this action might produce an authoritarian atmosphere in the classroom. Writes Tom,

> In such a case, the teacher would have to weigh carefully the advantages of a workable classroom management system against the importance he attaches to a certain type of student-teacher relationship. Several possibilities might occur to him. Perhaps the behavior modification approach should be abandoned. Or maybe this approach can be altered . . . [or] perhaps the problem with discipline is so serious that for the time being the teacher will tolerate a student-teacher relationship not to his liking. In the end the teacher must either decide to live with the tension underlying this situation or take action to reduce it. This hypothetical example is but one instance of what might happen when a teacher considers the moral craft metaphor in his work. (pp. 126–127)

Green (1984) suggests that becoming aware of both the significance and the obligations built into one's craft constitutes an important step in cultivating a professional and moral self. He calls this awareness "the consciousness of craft," and regards it as particularly crucial in contemporary times when any number of institutional and other pressures threaten to break apart the integrity of craft.

Jackson (1986) raises the question whether good teaching always features aspects of what he calls the "mimetic" and the "transformative," terms he gives to two historical traditions in teaching. The mimetic approach pivots around the transmission of knowledge: The teacher endeavors to transfer or transmit a body of knowledge to students using lecture, recitation, exercises based on repetition, and so forth. Such knowledge is objective in that it has a status independent of both teacher and students. The teacher's office boils down to ensuring that students come to possess that knowledge. In contrast, Jackson explains, the transformative approach centers upon both moral and intellectual change in learners (and possibly in teachers, too). It addresses not just whether students have learned how to read, but whether they have learned to like reading; not just whether they have learned mathematical formulae, but whether they appreciate the power and significance of such formulae; not just whether they can accurately present an historical timeline, but whether their vision and sympathy with humanity has broadened and deepened. In short, the transformative approach calls attention to moral dispositions and attitudes that can accompany learning academic subject matter. The approach focuses upon qualitative rather than quantitative change; it means more than just adding on facts or skills but, rather, emphasizes changes in the person. Jackson's argument implies that good practice entails aspects of both traditions. Teaching any subject involves attention to fact and skill, but it also involves consideration of what is happening to students as people.

Jackson's two traditions—whose origins, he argues, go back very far in the history of the practice—highlight differences between teaching, on the one hand, and socialization and indoctrination on the other. Socialization implies a process of passing on cultural and social knowledge, perhaps although not necessarily in an uncritical spirit. Indoctrination connotes a deliberate attempt to avoid engaging students' reasoning powers while seeking to convert them into certain kinds of people. According to Hirst (1973), the latter can result in what we might call learning, but what the young learn may not be morally defensible or worthy. Hirst writes,

> [The] end achievements of learning are new states of the person and . . . these differ radically from each other. We seem to be under a perpetual temptation to think that all learning results in knowledge. Clearly this is false. Along with this too goes the temptation to think that what we learn . . . is necessarily a truth or fact of some kind. Clearly this is also false. (1973, pp. 170–171)

In these remarks, Hirst underscores the view that teaching means engaging the mind of student and teacher as fully as possible. This view is predicated on a moral vision: People can become better rather than worse or, more prosaically, they can become more thoughtful and knowledgeable rather than less so, and they can become more open-minded and sympathetic rather than less so. What Hirst calls "new states of the person" mirrors Jackson's idea of the transformative. Their choices of terms spotlight the moral significance of teaching.

Oser et al. (1992) analyze what they regard as the effective and responsible dimensions of good teaching. The concept *effective* pertains to sound, research-based instructional method and curricular substance, linked also to state-of-the-art forms of assessment. According to the authors, the concept encompasses more than technical issues, which is how it is sometimes treated in the educational literature. Rather, the idea of effectiveness emphasizes the intellectual nature of all good teaching and the extent to which it should embody, according to the authors, reflection, imagination, self-criticism, knowledge of subject matter and of the tools of best practice, and so forth. Here, the concept merges with the idea of being responsible, which

the authors associate directly with the moral. Responsible teaching takes into consideration students' capacities and interests, rather than perceiving them as empty vessels into which knowledge must be poured (a pure version of the mimetic approach). Responsible teaching obliges teachers to reflect upon and anticipate the consequences of their actions on students' academic and moral development. Teachers must understand that teaching an academic subject effectively always involves addressing responsibly (i.e., morally) the countless social aspects of learning in classrooms and schools.

"[T]eachers and their students are moral philosophers," Oser writes elsewhere, "confronted every day with difficult moral problems involving honesty, truth, and the keeping of promises" (1986, p. 919). Responsible teaching is predicated on the idea that learning includes moral growth—learning to reason well and justly in one's dealings with other people. From the perspective captured in the idea of effective and responsible teaching, teaching is at once an intellectual and a moral endeavor. According to Oser (1994), teachers are or must become people "who know how to accompany students into the process of questioning, justifying, deciding, and realizing the moral point of view in any decision and in any learning behavior" (p. 66).

Using extended classroom observation and interviews with four high school teachers, Gudmundsdóttir (1990) shows that along with teaching a subject, practitioners are also teaching a set of subject-based values. Those values strongly influence the teachers' curricular choices, instructional methods, and approaches to evaluation. For example, a history teacher Gudmundsdóttir observed seeks not just to "pass on" knowledge but "to make [students] participants in, rather than spectators of, the democratic process" (p. 44). That value commitment leads this teacher to engage in considerable interpretive discussion with students around thorny historical and contemporary issues. An English teacher believes that literature "has answers" to some of her students' most pressing personal and social problems. To make those answers accessible to students, the teacher uses a "circling" instructional approach (p. 47), in which students probe the reading, then apply their understanding to their lives, then study the text further, then examine their lives, and so forth. In short, for all four teachers, the subjects they teach and the ways in which they teach them embody moral values and assumptions. Gudmundsdóttir traces the origins of those values back to teachers' education and formal preparation. "When future teachers study the subject matter they will later teach to high school students," she argues, "they are not just learning facts; they are acquiring a world view imbued with values. When teachers have forgotten many of the facts they learned in college, they will still remember value-laden impressions" (p. 47). According to Gudmundsdóttir, those value-laden impressions frame teachers' personal curriculum, which she contends is "the most hidden and least studied of all school curricula, yet it is the slice of secondary education that is most likely to remain with the student" (p. 47).

Court (1989) and Stutz (1995) also suggest that values influence how teachers think about their subjects and how they teach them in the classroom. Court suggests that much of the research on teacher thinking neglects to consider what she calls the "moral condition" of teaching, which encompasses the ways in which teachers' values shape their classroom conduct. Court argues that teachers can gain insight into their moral values in order to analyze their influence on how and what they teach. Stutz studied the ways in which five English teachers conceive and teach literature. According to her research, all five believe that the study of literature can promote moral awareness in students and can assist them in developing an ethical orientation toward life.

Lampert (1990) illuminates the intellectual and moral aspects of teaching mathematics in school. She does so while showing that math can be taught in a way that resembles what it means to study and to know mathematics in the discipline itself. Her example is from a fifth-grade classroom (her own) in which she had conducted systematic research for several years. The classroom features considerable intellectual give-and-take between teacher and student and among students themselves. The class learns to strive for more than the "answers." Instead, the students come to grips with what it means to undertake mathematical inquiry. According to Lampert's analysis, the class leaves behind what she calls "conventional" attitudes all too often associated with school math: passivity, uncritical obedience to the teacher's or text's word, mistrust of one's own imagination and reactions, and belief in a single way of doing things. In their place, Lampert reports, the class realized in its own rough-and-ready fashion what the mathematician Polya calls "the moral qualities" embedded in serious-minded mathematical study. These qualities include (a) intellectual courage—"we should be ready to revise any one of our beliefs," (b) intellectual honesty—"we should change a belief when there is good reason to change it," and (c) wise restraint—"we should not change a belief wantonly, without some good reason, without serious examination" (1990, p. 31). To this list Lampert adds, building on the work of another mathematician, the moral virtue of modesty in one's claims and presumptions. She also demonstrates the indispensability of trust between classroom participants. Genuine inquiry, she shows, entails considerable vulnerability and uncertainty on the part of both students and teachers and, consequently, demands a moral orientation from all. Applebaum (1995) sheds helpful light on this theme in a study of the idea of trust in teaching.

Lampert's study echoes Socrates' approach to teaching and it recalls Aristotle's trenchant discussion of what he calls the moral and the intellectual virtues. Moral virtues include self-control, compassion, generosity, and more. Intellectual virtues include theoretical insight—implying, in part, the ability to stand back from a situation to take in more than one perspective—and what might be called a commitment to understanding people and things in the world. In its highest forms, Aristotle argues, intellectual virtue becomes wisdom (see especially his *Nicomachean Ethics*).

Lampert's study reveals the place of intellectual virtue in teaching and learning. Hansen (1992) highlights the place of moral virtue in those processes. His study is based on several years of extended observation in a sixth-grade social studies classroom; the study also makes use of recorded interviews with the teacher, Kathy Smythe. Hansen shows how a moral community, or "shared morality," emerged in the classroom over the course of a schoolyear. He argues that a shared morality embodies four related characteristics. First, it is a shared good in the sense that it is constitutive of a community, such as the kind that can exist in a classroom. It does not imply that teacher and students must hold common values (religious, political, and so forth); rather, it captures the idea of membership in a purposeful endeavor.

Second, a shared morality is an enabling good. Over time, a teacher and that teacher's students accept and take on certain responsibilities and obligations—for example, listening to rather than shouting at one another—which enable them to focus on learning.

Third, a shared morality is an emerging good. It cannot be legislated into being by an outside authority nor can it be established by fiat, for example, by announcing a set of procedural rules the first day of class and leaving it at that. "[A] shared outlook on conduct in the classroom," Hansen argues, "emerges and continually evolves over time" (1992, p. 347).

Finally, a shared morality is a fragile good, subject to shocks from within or from outside the classroom (sudden switches in school policy, students who transfer in or out, etc.). Making use of this framework, Hansen describes the evolutionary nature of a classroom's ethos. He calls particular attention to the role played in this process of moral virtues such as patience, persistence, attentiveness to others, and a posture of respect for peers and for ideas that differ from what one finds customary. Hansen concludes that "it is impossible to teach a subject in a classroom without also teaching, or at least inviting, dispositions toward that subject and toward one's fellow human beings" (p. 355). He also concludes that teachers may have to help students learn moral virtue, just as, according to Lampert, teachers may have to help students learn intellectual virtue. Both authors suggest, however, that such teaching is built into the process of intellectual work in the public circumstances of the classroom.

Sockett (1988) examines the virtues in an argument based on the idea that teachers might conduct themselves as "guides" through intellectual and moral difficulty. He suggests that teaching always implies helping students to develop what he calls "personal capability," a concept that embodies aspects of both moral and intellectual virtue. Kozolanka and Olson (1994) found that some teachers are actively concerned with their students' emerging moral and intellectual capability. Their interview-based study centers on the views of three secondary school technology teachers (who teach subjects such as woodworking) and three secondary school science teachers. Kozolanka and Olson sought to understand how the teachers view their respective subjects' worth in helping students learn to manage in life. To their surprise, they report, the teachers focused not just on the value of their subjects but even more on their personal role, as teachers, in helping students learn how to work successfully (e.g., being punctual, organized, systematic) and in how to relate civilly to their peers (e.g., learning self-control and how to reason with rather than just react mindlessly to others). "The teachers were concerned about the students' own unformed social and intellectual habits. They wanted to develop these habits in productive ways. . . . They were concerned that their students become good people" (p. 224). In the authors' analysis, the intellectual and the moral merge as the teachers describe their strong desire to be a force for good in students' lives. "These shops and laboratories," Kozolanka and Olson conclude, "are places where students learn not to become expert workers but to exercise certain virtues having to do with civility and responsibility and ultimately with character. . . . We see that the practical capability the teachers want their students to have transcends the instrumental to become moral" (p. 224). Sockett (1988) and Kozolanka and Olson (1994) spotlight the fact that teachers are not working with disembodied minds. They are working with individual (and usually young) human beings involved in the complicated process of becoming people of one kind or another.

Ball and Wilson (1996) extend the argument that teaching is both intellectual and moral in nature by delving into another mathematics classroom (in this case Ball's own) and also into a social studies classroom (Wilson's). The authors describe events in the classrooms that shed light on what they call the "recognition" on the teacher's part that the work embodies both moral and intellectual dimensions. Good teaching, the authors suggest, entails respecting both students and the discipline itself. It involves steering a middle course between a kind of abstract aloofness from students, on the one hand, and a sentimental attachment to them, on the other hand. To chart that course, the authors suggest, teachers need to cultivate intellectual honesty with students and fair, sensitive forms of social interaction in the classroom. They also need to recognize the moral commitments embodied in the study of a discipline. "Teachers are responsible for helping students gain access to the world of ideas. Disciplines are part of the world of ideas, and teachers need to respect the values and the mores of the subject matters they teach" (p. 178). The authors draw upon Kerr's (1987) argument that teaching, among other things, involves assisting students in becoming "moral agents." According to Kerr—who echoes here the earlier discussion of Socrates—"to act as a moral agent is to assume for oneself the role of critical inquirer. Hence, the teacher is responsible not only for introducing students to the forms of critical inquiry but also for inviting and encouraging students to demand such disciplined thought of themselves" (1987, pp. 35–36). Ball and Wilson's classroom-based analyses show how this viewpoint appears in actual classroom practice.

These studies recall Philip's (1979) criticism of unwarranted means and ends thinking. For Philips, teaching is a moral endeavor, not because it can lead to moral development in students (or teachers), but because the moral is inherent in the work of teaching any subject matter. Consequently, the purpose of teaching is not to teach morals per se; it is not, in his view, to teach anything we would name moral. Rather, according to Philips, moral growth materializes, in part, through coming to grips with the ideas, the facts, and the intellectual orientations embodied in subject matter. Philips urges teachers to turn toward, rather than away from, the values in the subjects to which they are committed (p. 55). Many of the teachers in the studies reviewed here appear to have taken that "turn" toward their subjects. Philips questions some moral education programs for what he regards as their tendency to promote the opposite course of action. "Is moral education possible?" Philips asks. "Its possibility," he replies, "resides in the necessary involvement of values in educational enquiry" (p. 55).

Philips' criticism also applies to watered-down curricula, to simplistic back-to-basics programs, and, of pertinence here, to how educators think about pedagogical method. For example,

in a study mentioned previously, Jackson (1986) suggests that a straightforward mimetic approach seems to be used disproportionately with poor and minority students, as if the transformative approach was for some reason inappropriate for such students. Philips' argument illuminates moral dimensions of Jackson's concern. "[T]he values which have a place in educational activities," Philips argues, "should be derived, not from the social backgrounds of the individuals who participate in them, but from those activities themselves" (p. 44). This argument does not imply ignoring the social backgrounds of students—far from it. Rather, as the studies just reviewed document, it means not prejudging students in such a way that teaching itself and the treatment of subject matter become truncated. It means recognizing intellectual and moral virtues that are inherent in approaches to teaching and in the study of subjects such as mathematics, social studies, and science. This posture also implies avoiding positions that presume that teaching is essentially either a moral or an intellectual endeavor (compare Barrow, 1992). Barcena et al. (1993) illuminate the problems in presuming that either the moral or the intellectual (or technical, as they put it) can serve, in and of itself, as a "global concept for explaining the meaning of education" (p. 242). They criticize some educational writing for confusing the technical dimensions of teaching with a technicist orientation, according to which teaching is a purely instrumental activity or delivery system of knowledge from point A (teacher and textbook) to point B (student). They advance a viewpoint reflected in the literature reviewed in this section, that using sound or effective technique goes hand-in-hand with a moral outlook on the work of teaching.

The Pervasiveness of the Moral in Teaching

In an inquiry titled "Learning and Teaching," Oakeshott recalls how he first became aware "that there was something else in learning than the acquisition of information" (1965/1989, p. 62). This awareness began to happen, he suggests, when he sensed that the ways in which people thought was often more important than what they said. It happened in "concrete situations" such as when historical facts were "suspended in an historian's argument," or when, while reading a passage of literature, he recognized "the reflection of a mind at work in a language" (p. 62). In pondering these matters, Oakeshott suggests that learning encompasses both intellectual and moral growth. He describes how his teachers helped form his very character as a person. "[I]f you were to ask me," he writes,

the circumstances in which patience, accuracy, economy, elegance and style first dawned upon me, I would have to say that I did not come to recognize them in literature, in argument or in geometrical proof until I had first recognized them elsewhere; and that I owed this recognition to a Sergeant gymnastics instructor who lived long before the days of "physical education" and for whom gymnastics was an intellectual art—and I owed it to him, not on account of anything he ever said, but because he was a man of patience, accuracy, economy, elegance and style. (p. 62)

Oakeshott's remarks introduce the theme of this section. The research I reviewed previously indicates that values and moral assumptions are embedded in the act of teaching, and consequently do not have to be imported from without. However, scholars such as Oakeshott, while concurring with this point of view, have suggested that what makes teaching a moral practice is not just what inheres in subject matter or in particular acts of teaching. In addition, what renders it moral is that teaching is the work of individual human beings, each with a distinctive voice and perspective on students and on learning. That individuality cannot help but break into the role—for better or for worse. The role itself does not teach students, rather, individual adults do. Who teachers are as people is often decisive for what students learn, or fail to learn, in the classroom.

In this section, I focus on what scholars have called the teacher's "manner," "style," or "tact." Each of these concepts illuminates the moral significance of the person who occupies the role of teacher. The concepts do so, in part, by pinpointing how much of a teacher's influence on students proceeds indirectly rather than through deliberate, preplanned activities. In this respect, the work reviewed here can be seen as a response to an argument made by Broudy (1963) in the first edition of this handbook. "It often happens," Broudy wrote, ". . . that we can imitate the teaching procedures of the master teacher quite faithfully and yet not achieve [the master's] results. The spirit of the method seems to be a vital ingredient in it, and yet it seems detachable from the techniques and devices through which it is expressed" (p. 40). Broudy concluded: "Educational schemes that profess to produce scientific attitudes, a sense of responsibility, aesthetic sensitivity and creativity may require aspects of teaching method that are indirect and without which the direct procedures are not sufficient to achieve the desired results. The temptation not to aim research at these indirect aspects of method is understandable, but what may be needed are ways of making such aspects of methods 'researchable'" (p. 40). Work on the teacher's manner, style, and tact suggests that what Broudy calls "indirect aspects of method" are very much an expression of who the teacher is as a person.

Manner

Oakeshott's remarks on the personal character of his gymnastics instructor highlight a way of thinking about the teacher's manner. According to Oakeshott, the teacher's manner can play a vital role in students' intellectual and moral development. For example, it can shape how and whether students learn such things as judgment. Oakeshott describes judgment as a process of discernment, thought, and appreciation, by which I take him to mean discerning what is at stake or what is significant in a situation, thinking the matter through with persistence and care, and appreciating contrasting viewpoints and their consequences. That process "cannot be *taught* separately," he writes; "it can have no place of its own in a timetable or a curriculum. It cannot be taught overtly by precept, because it comprises what is required to animate precept; but it may be taught in everything that is taught. It is implanted unobtrusively in the manner in which information is conveyed, in a tone of voice, in the gesture which accompanies instruction, in asides and oblique utterances, and by example" (1965/1989, p. 61). This kind of moral learning, Oakeshott suggests, is potentially happening all the time in educational settings. Oakeshott emphasizes that such moral learning "is not a separable part of educa-

tion. One may set apart an hour in which to learn mathematics and devote another to the Catechism, but it is impossible to engage in any activity whatever without contributing to this kind of moral education, and it is impossible to enjoy this kind of moral education in an hour set aside for its study" (1962/1991, p. 469). Such moral learning takes place, or fails to as the case may be, in everyday interaction between teacher and student.

Peters (1964, 1963/1968) builds on Oakeshott's view of the teacher's manner and argues that it is important because of the nature of education itself. "To be educated," Peters writes, "is not to have arrived at a destination; it is to travel with a different view. What is required is not feverish preparation for something that lies ahead, but to work with precision, passion and taste at worth-while things that lie to hand" (1964, p. 47). I interpret Peters to be saying that precision involves working attentively and persistently to get things right; its opposite is sloppiness, carelessness, laziness. Passion involves caring for what one is doing—solving a problem, writing a poem, working collaboratively with peers—and caring so much that, in the moment of doing it, nothing else seems more important. Taste implies aesthetic and instrumental judgment; not just getting the job done, but doing it well and doing it artfully. The terms recall what Oakeshott says he learned from his gymnastics instructor: patience, accuracy, economy, elegance, and style. For Oakeshott and Peters, these are moral qualities because they accompany what Oakeshott describes as the process of making oneself "at home in the natural and civilized worlds" (1962/1991, p. 469). Oakeshott's poetic terms dramatize the fact that, in his view, people cannot realize their potential moral relation with others without taking on the kind of moral traits he examines. Peters (1963/1968) suggests that teachers help convey or pass along such moral qualities, not through precept but through their everyday manner of working. In terms that recall Oakeshott's distinction between ways of thinking and what is thought, Peters contends that "it is surely the *manner* in which any course is presented rather than its matter which is crucial in developing a liberal attitude of mind" (1963/1968, p. 93). However, research reviewed previously reveals that subject "matter" remains crucial to that process, too.

Scheffler (1960/1968) argues that the practice of teaching embodies a "restriction of manner" on how teachers can conduct themselves. "To teach," Scheffler argues, ". . . is at some points at least to submit oneself to the understanding and independent judgment of the pupil, to his demand for reasons, to his sense of what constitutes an adequate explanation. . . . Teaching . . . requires us to reveal our reasons to the student and, by so doing, to submit them to his evaluation and criticism" (1960/1968, p. 17). Scheffler cautions that the demand for reasons is not appropriate at each and every step of teaching, otherwise the work might be brought to a standstill. However, according to Scheffler, the teacher must not prevent students from asking questions such as How? Why? and On what grounds? (p. 27). Teaching entails the moral requirement to be open-minded—to be willing to consider students' questions and input—or else it reverts, Scheffler argues, into mere training or even indoctrination. The teacher's manner of working must reflect this requirement of open-mindedness. Green (1971) argues that what he calls the "manners" of teaching are "the manners of argu-

ment. They are the manners of civility, deliberation, and inquiry. . . ." They are "the manners of civility expressed in the
institutions of free speech, due process, and freedom of dissent"
that, according to Green, should unfold in both the classroom
and society (pp. 218, 220). Greene (1986) echoes these briefs on
behalf of students. "The student as free agent, as a center of
consciousness," she writes, "must be respected. Manipulation
of the other, conditioning of the other, submission of the other
to some rule of 'necessity' (whether psychological or social or
political) are not activities selected out by the concept of teaching" (p. 486).

Fenstermacher (1990, 1992) ascribes a self-conscious, deliberative component to the concept of manner. He does so because he regards teachers' manner as decisive for the quality
and effect on students of their work. "Nearly everything a
teacher does while in contact with students carries moral
weight," Fenstermacher writes. "Every response to a question,
every assignment handed out, every discussion on issues, every
resolution of a dispute, every grade given to a student carries
with it the moral character of the teacher. This moral character
can be thought of as the *manner* of the teacher" (1990, p. 134).
Elsewhere Fenstermacher writes, echoing Oakeshott and
Peters,

> Manner is the term that I apply to human action that exhibits the
> particular traits or dispositions of a person. It refers to such charac-
> teristics as compassion, selfishness, caring, mean-spiritedness, in-
> dustriousness, narrow-mindedness, tolerance, and so forth. When
> we say that a person is thoughtful or snobbish, we are referring to
> the manner of that person. (1992, p. 97)

Fenstermacher argues that teachers should become mindful of
their manner and its possible influence on students. "Teachers
who understand their impact as moral educators," he contends,
"take their manner quite seriously. They understand that they
cannot expect honesty without being honest" (1990, p. 135).
His argument recalls Scheffler's view that teaching embodies a
"restriction of manner." For Fenstermacher, the restriction centers on the teacher's obligation to reason and judge well regarding specific classroom situations. He grants that reason alone is
insufficient. "Practical reasoning does not tell us what virtues
to embrace" in the classroom (1994b, p. 218). Rather, Fenstermacher argues, practical reasoning is "a means of determining
how to act virtuously in this or that situation. In other words,
the problem is seldom whether or not to be compassionate or
courageous, but what it means to act courageously or compas-
sionately in this or that particular situation. These are the deliberations in daily life that take place around the possession and
exercise of virtue, and as such require a finely developed capacity to reason and judge" (1994b, p. 218). In Fenstermacher's
view, teachers become that much more effective and responsible
(Oser et al., 1992) to the extent that they build practical reasoning into their manner.

Style

Jackson, Boostrom, and Hansen (1993) make use of the concept
of style to capture the moral importance of the teacher's everyday ways of interacting with students. In their research, the
term *style* is rooted in art. People speak of a painter's style and,
in so doing, merge the artist's vision with his or her technique.
For example, Vermeer's precise, measured, and balanced technique embodies his vision both of human grace and virtue and
of their fragility. Analogously, to identify teachers' influence on
students as it materializes in the classroom, one can focus on
their styles of teaching. The concept underscores the dynamic
relation between teachers' visions of what education is about
and their actual doings in the classroom. It helps bring into
view the complex, often ambiguous interplay between teachers'
intentions on the one hand and their actual conduct on the
other.

Jackson et al. (1993) illuminate these claims in their detailed
analyses of everyday classroom life. The book is based on a 3-
year-long study called The Moral Life of Schools Project. The
authors observed hundreds of hours of teaching in elementary
and secondary schools, all located in diverse urban settings.
They also conversed at great length, both formally and informally, with the 18 teachers who participated in the project
(Boostrom, Hansen, & Jackson, 1993). The authors construct a
taxonomy of the moral influences at work in schools and classrooms. These influences range from explicit attempts to educate
students morally, which the authors describe as categories of
moral instruction (pp. 3–11), to the often unwilled, unplanned,
and implicit moral dimensions of daily practice, which they
place in categories called moral practice (pp. 11–42). They suggest that the latter are more important and more enduring in
their formative effect on students than are explicit attempts to
shape students' character. The authors depict teachers leading
discussions, interacting individually with students, adjudicating
disputes, lecturing, handing out grades, organizing activities,
giving students permission to leave the room, making use of the
blackboard, and much more. They scrutinize each event for its
possible moral significance, illuminating how the smallest gesture, the most fleeting word can all leave a mark on students'
emerging intellectual and moral sensibilities.

The teacher's style of working figures prominently in the
analysis. Style calls attention to "personal qualities of teachers
that—sometimes unintentionally—embody a moral outlook or
stance" (p. 11). Style encompasses "patterns of action" whose
shape and contour, the authors argue, can only be discerned
through long-term observation (p. 36). Over time, however, one
can get a sense of how a teacher usually responds to students
and to classroom events, how he or she initiates activities, and
so forth. "This consistency of manner, reaction, poise . . . we
tend to call style. Style refers to the teacher's typical ways of
handling the demands of the job" (p. 37). Style is noteworthy,
the authors argue, because it "embodies attributes that we normally think of as moral. . . . A teacher's style can be reserved
and aloof or warm and intimate. It can express kindness or cruelty" (p. 37). In short, style is expressive of moral qualities, all
of which can potentially influence students for good or for ill.

According to Jackson and his coauthors, the teacher's everyday style can have greater moral potency than the occasional
explicit moral lesson that teacher might offer, precisely because
style is ongoing and permanent, even if evolving. Teachers cannot turn off their styles nor control all the moral messages they
emit. The authors illustrate the expressive complexity and
moral significance of style by examining many classroom hap-
penings, from the first-grade teacher, who habitually asks questions to help students understand how to conduct themselves,

to the high school English teacher, whose dramatic and effusive style injects meaning into even the most mundane features of subject matter, to the third-grade teacher, who uses humor in ways that undermine instruction as often as it cultivates cordial relations. They show how a style can express contradictory messages, and how it can illuminate the larger philosophy of life that a teacher brings to everyday work. Style becomes a central vehicle for thinking about the positive and negative influence teachers have on students.

Using data gathered during the same project, Hansen (1993b) sheds additional light on the moral importance of the teacher's style. He draws his framework on style from sociological analysis of everyday social interaction. Style denotes "a set of habits that includes gestures, body movements, facial expressions and tones of voice. The term encompasses a teacher's customary ways of attending to students, for example how he or she typically responds to what they say and do" (p. 397). Hansen suggests that style reflects more than personality or conventional behavior. Rather, it "can be seen to reveal the interest, the involvement, the expectations that guide the teacher's efforts. Through a close look at style, one can perceive how a teacher provides students over the course of a school year with an ongoing model of conduct" (p. 398). The analysis contrasts the idea of a teacher's style of working with the more familiar notion of *teaching styles,* a generic concept that has been used in previous research on teaching. Hansen examines in detail the everyday styles of three high school teachers. Their styles contrast vividly—from the dramatic to the low-key, from the intimate to the more distant—but they all reveal how a teacher's moral influence on students appears in actual classroom practice. The teachers' styles, Hansen concludes, "constitute a medium through which their values and aspirations, some of which they may not be fully aware of themselves, infuse the ethos of their classrooms" (p. 419).

Schwartz, Merten, and Bursik (1987) further document how a teacher's everyday conduct sends moral signals to students. Their analysis focuses on three generic teaching styles that they dub the "impersonal," the "nonpersonal," and the "personal." They constructed these ideal types (in the sociological sense of that term) based, in part, on interviews they conducted with junior high school teachers. The authors use the concepts to show how teachers negotiate the tensions between the performance expectations of school and the individual needs of early adolescents. As with the previous studies reviewed here, Schwartz et al. show that a teacher's style can send harmful, not just beneficial, messages to students. For example, the authors discuss what they call the "symbolic denigration" of students (p. 366), in which teachers signal through their gestures, their postures, their tones of voice, and so forth that they regard students as incapable, if not also untrustworthy, as persons. The study by Schwartz et al. (1987) complements previous work on manner and style in urging teachers to bring such matters into awareness.

In addition to addressing issues of manner, Oakeshott (1965/1989) develops a notion of style. For Oakeshott, style connotes a thoughtful person's characteristic ways of thinking and acting. In other words, he associates the term with desirable or positive traits, unlike other scholars who suggest a style can be positive or negative in its nature and effect on others. Oakeshott argues that style has to do with the ability to judge wisely, to discrimi-

nate the better from the worse, and to discern the good in human affairs. Not to detect a person's style, he argues, is to have missed "three-quarters of the meaning" of the person's actions and utterances; "and not to have acquired a style is to have shut oneself off from the ability to convey any but the crudest meanings" (1965/1989, p. 56). In a discussion of Oakeshott's educational philosophy, Peters adds that "most difficult of all for the pupil to acquire is the ability to detect the individual intelligence at work in every utterance and act, the style which each individual brings to his thought and action" (1981, p. 97). In this perspective, style comes close to merging with personal character in all its moral and intellectual complexity.

Van Manen (1991b) associates style with a similarly comprehensive meaning. "Style is the outward embodiment of the person," he writes. ". . . Hav[ing] a style is being yourself, being who you really are. When someone says, 'That is not my style,' he or she is really saying, 'That is not the way I am. That's not me'" (p. 121). According to van Manen, style reveals the extent and depth to which a teacher has embraced the subject to be taught:

> A science teacher is more than just a person who happens to teach science. A real science teacher is a person who thinks science, who wonders about the nature of science and the science of nature—a real science teacher is a person who embodies science, who lives science, who in a strong sense is science. And so we can often tell whether a person is a real teacher by the way this person "stylizes" what he or she teaches." (1991b, p. 121)

These studies of manner and style reveal that much of what makes teaching a moral endeavor is unintentional and unwilled on the part of teachers. Certainly, as Fenstermacher (1992) and Oser et al. (1992) argue, teachers can become more deliberate in their reasoning and in their day-by-day classroom conduct. Moreover, as the chapters on moral education and on caring in this handbook show, teachers can engage in deliberate attempts to influence students morally. However, the research reviewed here attests to the truth in an observation drawn a century and a half ago by Ralph Waldo Emerson. "Character teaches above our wills," Emerson wrote (1841/1983). People "imagine that they communicate their virtue or vice only by overt actions, and do not see that virtue or vice emit a breath every moment" (p. 266).

Concepts such as manner and style highlight the fact that teachers are always sending more moral messages than they can possibly keep track of or control. "[M]any of the unintended influences" that operate in classrooms, Jackson et al. (1993) show, do so *all or most of the time,* whereas the intended ones are more episodic and self-contained. The rules that structure the classroom, assumptions that undergird the curriculum, and the teacher's style or character are almost always present" (p. 44). What Jackson (1992) calls "untaught" moral lessons—but lessons nonetheless—appear to be an ubiquitous outcome of teachers' work.

Tact

Van Manen's (1991a, 1991b, 1994) focus on the concept of tact further illuminates the moral relevance of who the person is who occupies the role of teacher. Van Manen's point of departure is an argument made by the 19th-century educator Herbart: "The real question as to whether someone is a good or bad educator is simply this: has this person developed a sense of tact?" (quoted in van Manen, 1991b, p. 128). Tact is "the immediate ruler of practice," having to do with making "instant judgments" and being "attuned to the uniqueness of the situation." It is "first of all dependent on *Gefuhl* [feeling or sensitivity] and only more remotely on convictions" (1991a, p. 523). "Tactful action," adds van Manen, "is an immediate involvement in situations where I must instantaneously respond, as a whole person, to unexpected and unpredictable situations" (p. 519).

Van Manen suggests that tact is related phenomenologically to "pedagogical moments" (1991b, pp. 37–64). These are moments that arise time and again in educational settings: a student is stuck, or asks a question, or quarrels with a peer, or, perhaps, sits silently in response to a query. The teacher's tact is called out by such moments; it is pressed into action by them. The process is so immediate that the very term process is somewhat distorting, as is, according to van Manen, the language of decision making. "[T]he pedagogical moment requires the teacher to act instantly," he writes. "With the hindsight of rational observation, this instant action may look like a kind of decision-making-on-the-spot, but it is not really decision making in the usual problem-solving and deliberative sense" (1991a, p. 515). Rather, tact is a kind of "mindfulness" (p. 523) that enables the teacher to act thoughtfully and sensitively with students. It materializes in gesture, much as in word, and it may mean holding back rather than acting in some way. Above all, according to van Manen, tact means being responsive to the particularity of the situation. "To exercise tact," he argues, "means to *see* a situation calling for sensitivity, to *understand* the meaning of what is seen, to *sense the significance* of this situation, to *know how and what to do,* and to actually *do* something right. To act tactfully may imply all these and yet tactful action is instantaneous" (1991b, p. 146).

Van Manen uses a wide variety of classroom events, many of which he observed firsthand, to elucidate these elements and phases of tact. For example, tact "expresses itself" in being open and attuned to students and in having an improvisational gift to take advantage of moments to connect with students (1991b, pp. 126–160). Van Manen argues that tact protects the student's vulnerability, prevents hurt, strengthens and builds upon what is good in the student, and enhances what is unique to him or her (pp. 160–172). Finally, tact is mediated through the teacher's talk, silences, eyes, and gestures and through the classroom atmosphere or ethos that emerges over time (pp. 172–186). In van Manen's analysis, tact becomes a lens through which to highlight the moral meaning in teaching.

Comments on Manner, Style, and Tact

According to the research reviewed here, manner, style, and tact are concepts that illuminate how pervasive moral concerns are in the daily work of teaching. The concepts reveal the complexity and the immediacy of classroom teaching, and they spotlight how thoroughly intertwined are academic and moral matters in the interaction between teachers and students. Researchers who make use of the concepts agree that the person who occupies

the role of teacher can strongly influence what is learned in the classroom. The teacher's character as a person infuses the curriculum and instructional approach in such a way that that character may prove as influential in the long run on students as subject matter and its associated values. This conclusion appears to hold even for teachers who remain aloof from the classroom, or who keep their distance, metaphorically speaking, from the role (compare Schwartz et al., 1987). Such teachers can emit moral messages—perhaps, in this case, of a negative kind—just as powerfully as more engaged practitioners. The next section examines additional research-based perspectives on the moral importance of the person who occupies the role of teacher.

Researchers differ on what might be called the rational dimensions of concepts such as manner, style, and tact. Style and tact have more to do with the teacher's personal character or virtue than with his or her reasoning powers per se (compare Bator, 1997). They reveal what teachers are disposed to do as human beings, which can include the willingness to think through complicated classroom situations in the first place. While not divorced from rational considerations, style and tact spotlight that which is, in a sense, prior to reasoning, namely moral disposition, sensibility, perception, and so forth. In contrast, scholars who have made use of the idea of manner focus as much or more on the rational foundations of good practice. They might agree that character and virtue have a certain primacy in determining, for example, whether a teacher is willing in the first place to try to do the right thing in the classroom. However, they argue that manner encompasses a crucial deliberative dimension that assists the teacher in deciding how to do the right thing. From this point of view, one can grant that teaching is an intimate and heartfelt endeavor and that it does call repeatedly upon the kind of person the teacher has become. However, the practice also obliges teachers to achieve at important points a certain detachment from the scene, and here, according to the argument, practical reasoning and rational judgment are indispensable. This claim recalls Scheffler's notion of the "restriction of manner" that he suggests governs teachers' conduct.

To an extent, the difference outlined here has to do with the focus of research. To scholars who are concerned with such issues as how teachers adjudicate disputes, how they resolve thorny disagreements in the classroom, and how they help students learn to reason their way through intellectual and moral difficulties, the rational dimensions of practice are paramount (Oser, 1986; Oser et al., 1992; and Oser, 1994). Thus, concepts such as manner and "effective and responsible teaching" become useful analytically when they are understood as embodying the quality of the teacher's reasoning in the midst of the busy world of the classroom. Other scholars are struck by the immediacy of much that occurs in the activity of teaching. That immediacy makes it impossible for teachers to weigh in a detached fashion each and every word and act. Time and again, they must act in the here and now. Because of that fact, who teachers are as persons comes to the fore. Whether they are patient, attentive, thoughtful, and respectful persons, or the opposite, becomes decisive. And the persons they are find expression in what can be called their styles or in what can be called their tact.

This difference in research focus attests to at least two distinct conceptions of the moral that are at work in the studies reviewed thus far. The first conception of the moral centers on rational justification and criticism, the other on the constitution and expression of personal character. The former gives rise to a procedural morality (Oser, 1994, pp. 80, 83, 103, 117) and renders secondary, although not unimportant, issues of personal character and virtue. What matters here is whether teachers and students learn to reason their way through things in a just, fair-minded, intellectually sound manner. Those who advance this view draw on work by Rawls (1971) among others.

The second conception is a morality of character, of virtue, of dispositions and orientations and sensibilities. Its focus is not on impartial procedure but on what it means to engage with the particularities of contexts and people. Investigators who take this perspective draw on work by Blum (1994), Murdoch (1970/ 1985), and Nussbaum (1990), among others. Where the former conception urges persons to think well, this second urges them to perceive well—to develop their character such that they are willing and able to pay attention to others and to the unique features of the contexts in which they dwell with them.

Both conceptions have a bearing on why teaching is a moral endeavor. To judge from the literature reviewed here, it would be a mistake to think that either impartial procedure or virtue alone is sufficient for good practice. Some would dispute whether the two can be meaningfully separated (see especially Dewey, 1932/1989). In a series of essays, Buchmann and Floden (1993) elucidate an inclusive perspective in arguing that teaching involves both detachment—drawing back from the context at certain moments—and concern—throwing oneself selflessly and wholeheartedly into the work.

One difficulty teachers face is developing a sense of when to draw close and when to stand back from the scene. Dewey poses the issue as knowing when to raise to awareness the moral dimensions of what is taking place (1932/1989, p. 170). According to Dewey, "[t]he business of the educator—whether parent or teacher—is to see to it that the greatest possible number of ideas acquired by children and youth are acquired in such a vital way that they become *moving* ideas, motive-forces in the guidance of conduct. This demand and this opportunity make the moral purpose universal and dominant in all instruction—whatsoever the topic" (1909/1975, p. 2). However, Dewey goes on to suggest that it would be counterproductive to focus exclusively on the moral. "[T]he direct and immediate attention of teachers and pupils," he argues, "must be, for the greater part of the time, upon intellectual matters. It is out of the question to keep direct moral considerations constantly uppermost" (1909/ 1975, p. 2). Dewey warns that to focus unduly upon the moral could give rise to a "mania of doubt" (1932/1989, p. 170) on the part of the teacher that might bring teaching to a standstill.

As we have seen, teachers must often act in the immediate moment; attempting to analyze each and every step as one is taking it will surely lead to a fall. Research on the teacher's manner, style, and tact renders the issue all the more complicated. All three concepts underscore the point that much of what teachers do is non-self-conscious—indeed, it must be non-self-conscious, or teachers are not doing their proper job of attending closely to students. While in the act of teaching, teachers must focus on students' performance, not solely on their own. This condition creates a permanent blind spot in teaching, since practitioners cannot "watch" their manner, their style, their tactfulness, while in the act of working. However, they can reflect upon such matters before and after the fact and, in so doing, can strengthen their own character—for example, make themselves more patient, more attentive, and more thoughtful. From what research has shown, this reflective process can be crucial because personal character is closely bound up with the teacher's manner, style, and tact.

Scholars who have used these concepts would perhaps agree with Dewey's still timely claim: "It is not too much to say that the most important thing for the teacher to consider, as regards his present relations to his pupils, is the attitudes and habits which his own modes of being, saying, and doing are fostering or discouraging in them" (1904/1974b, p. 326). They would perhaps agree that to understand the moral significance of the person who occupies the role of teacher, researchers need to take a broad look at classroom affairs. The moral dimensions of teaching materialize in more than how teachers discipline students, or how they adjudicate disputes and disagreements, or how they discuss controversial issues. These are moral matters, to be sure, but they do not exhaust the moral meanings discernible in the practice, partly because the bulk of classroom teaching, in most settings, does not involve resolving disputes or dealing with global moral issues. Concepts such as the teacher's manner, style, and tact can bear considerable analytic weight because they spotlight the moral importance of ordinary, everyday classroom activities, the kind that most easily escape scholarly notice precisely because of their ubiquity and apparent casualness.

The philosopher Ludwig Wittgenstein poses the matter this way: "The aspects of things that are most important for us," he writes, "are hidden because of their simplicity and familiarity. (One is unable to notice something—because it is always before one's eyes.) . . . And this means: we fail to be struck by what, once seen, is most striking and most powerful" (1953, p. 50e). Research has disclosed that the moral is pervasive in teaching, but it has also shown that the moral is not always easy to identify and to keep in view.

Moral Practice and Moral Activity in Teaching

As we have seen, some scholars have argued that teaching is inherently a moral endeavor. In their view, teaching is not merely a means to distant ends, in part because education itself is not an end state divorced from the means of bringing it into being. Moreover, teaching is not solely an intellectual or academic affair. According to the literature, the intellectual and moral aspects of learning are thoroughly intertwined. Finally, teaching is more than mere instruction or training, aspects of which could in principle be left to computers or other technology. Teaching is undertaken by persons, each bringing to bear a particular understanding of what education, students, and learning are all about and each bringing into the classroom an individual character as a human being. Concepts such as manner, style, and tact illuminate the moral importance of the person who occupies the role of teacher.

That importance stands out even more as a result of studies of teachers' moral perception and moral and ethical judgment.

To set the stage for addressing these concepts, I want in this section to examine two related issues, which have emerged from the literature and which throw light upon teaching as a moral activity: (a) why teaching can be viewed as a "practice" and (b) why teaching involves action or intentional activity rather than merely behavior.

Teaching as a Practice

Some scholars who have studied the moral dimensions of education have suggested that we think of teaching as a practice (e.g., Arnold, 1997; Buchmann, 1989; Hansen, 1995; Jackson, 1986; Olson, 1992; Sockett, 1993). They have made use of MacIntyre's (1984) pioneering argument, according to which a practice is distinct from the institutions in which it is carried out. Practicing medicine, for example, is not identical with working in a hospital. Practicing law is not synonymous with being employed by a law firm. Teaching is not the same thing as working in schools, despite the fact that the bulk of it takes place in those institutions. The practice of teaching is much older than any particular school—just as the practice of medicine is older than any contemporary hospital—and will presumably outlast any school or system of schooling in existence today. The idea of a practice calls attention to what it means to be a doctor or teacher as contrasted with being, for example, a cab driver, an astrologer, a politician, or a sculptor.

Practices differ from one another. For example, helping young people is not identical with teaching. An adult can be helpful as a parent, a minister, a nurse, a counselor, and so forth. But parenting, ministering, nursing, counseling, and other practices do not place both intellectual and moral development at their centers in the formal and public ways that teaching does. In the usual course of events, parents, ministers, nurses, and counselors are not formally responsible for educating other peoples' children. Teachers are. Moreover, because a person may have achieved success in an endeavor like parenting or social work does not imply that the person will be a successful teacher, any more than becoming an accomplished golfer means that one will automatically achieve success at tennis. In brief, teaching has its own characteristic set of responsibilities and obligations.

In the course of meeting those requirements, teachers often find that the work gives rise to its own distinctive "internal goods" (MacIntyre, 1984, pp.187–191). These are constitutive goods that render teaching into more than just a job—or, as MacIntyre would put it, into more than solely a means for securing "external goods" such as a salary or recognition (which in principle could just as easily be obtained through other kinds of work). Although MacIntyre does not address teaching directly, his analysis suggests that the constitutive goods of the practice include coming to know the mind and spirit of young people in ways not otherwise possible, influencing in a positive way the intellectual and moral growth of students, coming to understand more richly and comprehensively the subject one teaches, and feeling oneself part of a tradition of service whose roots lie deep in the human past. According to MacIntyre's argument, these goods are realized by teachers only if they commit themselves to fulfilling the terms of the work. They tend to elude those who keep their distance from the role, or who treat

teaching as merely a stepping stone to something else, or who simply dislike what the work calls on them to do. These persons may never even know that such constitutive, or internal, goods exist.

The basic terms of the practice of teaching are familiar: assisting others in learning things they do not know or do not know how to do, and inviting them to take on enabling attitudes toward learning, toward themselves, and toward other people. As contrasted with harming, corrupting, or shortchanging students, teaching means developing students' knowledge. Teaching means promoting positive attitudes, orientations, and understandings—the kind that allow students to progress rather than regress as human beings, to grow in both intellectual and moral terms. In short, from the perspective of MacIntyre's analysis, teaching as a practice is steeped in presuppositions about moral goodness and about what it means to live a flourishing life. The practice calls on teachers to conduct themselves in particular ways. Teachers do not invent these obligations out of whole cloth. Rather, they accompany the practice itself; they are part of any serious-minded and genuine attempt to teach.

Some scholars have argued that to fulfill such obligations, teachers need to develop certain moral qualities, or virtues. Some investigators build on MacIntyre's (1984) argument that realizing a practice—committing oneself to it, to recall the terms above—entails the enactment of virtues such as courage, honesty, and fairness. These virtues, Olson argues, "allow teaching as a practice to exist" (1992, p. xi), and as such are the "central basis" (p. 92) of teachers' work. "Excellence [in teaching] is dependent on virtue foremostly," Olson concludes, and "only on technique in a subsidiary way" (p. 95).

Duval (1990) conducted a study of the views and work of teachers recognized as outstanding. Using his analysis of these data, he suggests that virtues of dedication and commitment to students undergird teaching excellence. Garrison (1997) argues that the "most important thing practitioners can do to improve the quality of their practice is to improve themselves. That involves developing the habits, abilities, thoughts, ideals, technical mastery, and virtues of the practice" (p. 73). Sockett (1993) centers a conception of teacher professionalism around five "primary" although not necessarily sufficient virtues: "Teachers trade in *truth,* so they must avoid deceit; learning is difficult and demands *courage;* teachers are responsible for the development of people, a process demanding infinite *care; fairness* is necessary to the operation of rules in democratic institutions; and *practical wisdom* is essential to the complex process teaching is" (p. xi). Practical wisdom, Sockett explains, "requires qualities of reflectiveness and judgment interwoven with the four other virtues" (p. 85; also see pp. 62–63, 86–88; and see Garrison, 1997, pp. 80–84).

In a collection of commentaries on the moral dimensions of teaching, edited by Goodlad, Soder, and Sirotnik, (1990), Soder criticizes some of the rhetoric surrounding the idea of teaching as a profession by recalling certain fundamental aspects of the practice:

Children by nature are defenseless. Children by tradition are taught to distrust strangers. But parents, in complying with compulsory schooling laws, turn their defenseless children over to virtual strangers. (Consider the amount of information most parents seek in selecting a baby-sitter versus the amount of information those same parents have about public school educators.) The surrendering of children to the state's schools thus represents a considerable act of trust. The state claims that surrender is for the general good; the parent accepts the claim but demands in return a guarantee that the child will be kept free from physical and mental harm. Those responsible for the physical and mental health of children in schools have a moral obligation to ensure that children are kept from harm. (1990, p. 73)

Soder adds that "it is precisely *because* children are compelled and children are defenseless and have low status that teaching has moral obligations and thus moral praiseworthiness" (p. 74). Clark, in the same collection, emphasizes "overarching principles" that apply to the practice of teaching such as "honesty, fairness, protection of the weak, and respect for all people. The real work of teaching, morally speaking, is carried out when a teacher rigorously struggles to decide how best to act in relation to these general principles" (1990, p. 252). Strike's chapter (1990) in the same book examines basic requirements of the work—some touched on previously in this chapter—such as reasoning with students, being fair and just in working with them and in evaluating their work, respecting the values inherent in subject matter, and more. Strike argues that these are responsibilities embodied in teaching, and teachers must be people willing to embrace them.

Cox (1982) captures what many have argued in writing that "the fact that a person is engaged in education implies that he has accepted certain moral values. Inherent in education are such things as a liberal respect for differing opinions honestly held, accuracy in thought and expression, logical thinking, genuine feeling, and a sense of truth to be sought for and eventually found. To these things an educator is committed by the very fact of being an educator. His stance must include them if he is to be credible" (pp. 79–80).

These arguments imply that in an important moral sense, the practice of teaching, rather than individual occupants of the role, set the terms of the work. The practice calls on all who occupy the role to fulfill to the best of their ability its requirements and responsibilities. For example, the moral requirement to treat students as ends in themselves (to recall Kant's terms)—to see them as embodying a certain dignity not subject to manipulation and coercion—greets every teacher upon walking through the classroom door. Because a teacher "helps to shape what a person becomes," argues Sockett, "so the moral good of every learner is of fundamental importance in every teaching situation" (1993, p. 13). Teachers are there to serve and to support their students' learning; they are not there to have students serve them or to fulfill some need or agenda of their own (Banner & Cannon, 1997). As Rosenholtz (1989) argues, teachers are obliged to do more than seek "to enhance their own self-esteem by selecting only those goals that suit them best" (p. 15). According to the literature reviewed here, the intellectual and moral dimensions of teaching touched upon throughout this chapter make up the very fabric of the practice.

The Moral Activity of Teaching

The concept of a practice highlights what is distinctive about teaching. It emphasizes personal and professional qualities practitioners will want to develop to fulfill the terms of the work and to realize the internal goods that emerge from that engagement. The notion of a practice also sheds light on two additional features of the activity of teaching that help account for its moral significance: (a) The activity differs from mere behavior, and (b) it includes reflection and private thought rather than solely what is visible to others. The analysis of these features will provide a bridge to discussing work on moral perception and judgment in teaching.

Teaching is at heart a public activity. Teachers undertake their work face-to-face with students, and sometimes also in the presence of other adults. Teachers lecture or lead discussions with students, they comment on students' work and conduct in full hearing of the class, and they guide and direct students in how to carry out various activities. Moreover, public doings that at first glance have no relation to teaching often turn out to be part of the endeavor. Opening a window to let in fresh air, sharpening pencils, erasing the blackboard—these and countless other mundane affairs become pedagogically relevant when seen as helping to make learning possible (see Hirst, 1973, for a discussion of the "enterprise" of teaching as contrasted with specific "teaching activities"). It is through this remarkably broad array of public acts, large and small, that the practice of teaching comes to life.

However, research has documented that the moral significance of teaching resides in more than observable behavior alone. For example, Boostrom (1991, 1994), in studies mentioned earlier, shows how morally complex and ambiguous classroom rules can be. At first glance, nothing is more obvious than the familiar lists of do's and don'ts teachers everywhere are known to share with students. Such lists have definite moral overtones; they all imply that certain forms of conduct are better than others. However, Boostrom shows that such rules are often the surface manifestations of deeply held moral convictions on the part of teachers, convictions that have to do with their perceptions of their role and their views of education. Boostrom examines in fine-grained detail how several teachers actually present and implement classroom rules. Just as we should not judge a book by its cover, he shows that we should not judge a teacher's possible moral influence on students solely by their explicit statements of rule and precept.

Hansen (1989, 1993a) suggests that there is a moral layeredness to teaching. Teachers' "behavior," or that which everyone can see immediately, is not always a clear-cut clue to teachers' underlying intentions or aims, much less hopes and aspirations. Hansen (1989) examines classroom "beginnings," the moments during which students (and sometimes teachers if the room is not theirs) enter the classroom, take their seats, exchange greetings, and otherwise ready themselves for instruction. Through a close analysis of the details of these beginnings, Hansen argues that they are often more than instrumental or functional in meaning. Rather, they manifest moral assumptions shared by teacher and students regarding their purposes for being in the classroom in the first place. Those assumptions center around notions of responsibility, respect for roles and their occupants, and a seriousness of purpose (or, as the case may be, their opposites). Beneath the otherwise routine and humdrum process of getting down to business reside intentions and assumptions imbued with moral overtones.

In a related study (1993a), Hansen focuses on the moral dimensions of turn taking, another ubiquitous feature of classrooms everywhere. On the surface, turn taking appears to be a socially constructed mechanism for regulating talk and behavior in the classroom. At this level, its moral meaning is captured by the notion of *mores,* or customary, often nonreflective ways of regarding roles and their occupants. The teacher's power and authority figure prominently here, because the teacher is typically the arbiter and enforcer of turn-taking practices. Indeed, the teacher's prerogative to initiate and monitor turn taking heightens that already predominant position in the classroom. However, according to Hansen's analysis, "holding the reins of institutionalized power intensifies the challenge each teacher faces of employing that power responsibly" (p. 657). Here, issues of personal character and virtue come to the fore. Through examining a variety of episodes drawn from high school classrooms, Hansen illuminates how morally intricate turn taking can be. It discloses issues of personal dignity, self-worth, sensitivity to others, sentiments of rights and obligations that reside below the surface of behavior—or, put differently, that reside below the layer of mores or customary patterns of behavior. Turn taking reveals "the ways in which qualities of fairness, respectfulness, and attentiveness (or their opposites) constitute threads woven into the fabric of everyday classroom interaction" (p. 660). However, those threads are not always obvious or easy to detect.

Uhrmacher (1993b) sheds additional light on the importance of looking beneath the surface of behavior in order to discern the moral significance of teaching. His work is drawn from a larger study of Waldorf education (compare Uhrmacher, 1993a), in the course of which he observed four elementary school teachers for several hundred hours. He also conducted extensive interviews with them and with other members of the school community. Uhrmacher describes and analyzes what he calls "focal conditions," which are "those times when teachers establish, confirm, or discontinue contact between themselves and students. Focal signifies a moment of attention" (1993b, p. 437). These moments are sometimes fleeting—a look in the eye, a smile, a touch on the shoulder—but they can also be enduring. Examples of the latter include teachers who deliberately shake hands with students in welcoming them each day, or who engage students in singing as an initial classroom activity (one teacher makes taking attendance into a singing affair), and so forth.

Uhrmacher emphasizes that focal conditions differ from mere "transitions," which are an ubiquitous part of classroom life—changing from reading groups to doing individual deskwork to engaging in writing activities, etc. According to Uhrmacher, focal conditions have meaning in and of themselves. Put differently, they help establish meaningfulness. They are morally significant dimensions of teaching because they create a certain quality of relationship and interaction between teacher and students. Uhrmacher argues that such conditions are important for influencing, in a positive way, the ethos that will emerge in a classroom. In focal conditions, he contends, each student receives personal attention, not a trivial matter in the often bureaucratic environment of schools; the teacher can quickly gauge student moods and emotions (and act accordingly, for example, by not calling on a student early in a lesson);

and such acts provide students a sense of security and predictability.

These studies of the moral aspects of teaching highlight the difference between "behavior" and "action," with the latter understood as doings that presuppose human intentions and concerns (for discussion see, e.g., Taylor, 1985). In a broad sense, all the scholarship reviewed in this chapter attests to the fact that the activity of teaching is more than a matter of that which is immediately observable. Teaching embodies what are variously called intentions, hopes, aspirations, beliefs, biases, inclinations, dispositions, virtues, and more. According to the literature, the activity in which teachers engage—what they actually do—is often deeply influenced by the persons they are. The persons they are encompasses all of the terms listed above, to which we can add their knowledge of people, their understanding of subject matter, their confidence or lack of such, and so forth. Moreover, the things teachers do reflect their response both to external constraints—limited time, for example, or a lack of other resources—and to others' interests—those of administrators, peers, parents, and students. In short, to understand teachers' actions requires more than just tallying up the observable things they do. As research has shown, from a moral point of view behavior in itself may signify nothing. Or it may signal radically different meanings depending upon the person engaging in the behavior. Two teachers might perform the identical acts, for example, standing by the door at the beginning of each period and closing it officiously at the bell. But if placed in the larger context of the teachers' views and their other classroom doings, these gatekeeping behaviors can send contrasting meanings. For a teacher dedicated to the practice, they may symbolize the importance of taking advantage of the limited time school offers for instruction. For a teacher with little real interest in the work, those very same behaviors may express a desire for power and control.

One consequence of this argument is that the activity of teaching should not be divorced from the preparing, thinking, deliberating, wondering, worrying, hoping, and so forth that teachers engage in between the periods of actual teaching. In his pioneering study of classroom life, Jackson (1968) called this "preactive" teaching to distinguish it from actual classroom work; nonetheless, he argues that it is a vital part of practice. It is a kind of "ancillary business," to use a term from Murdoch (1970/1985), and it is not typically made public. For example, most teachers prepare lessons and think about their students when they are alone, although many certainly do discuss such matters with peers or other adults and sometimes with their students. But although not usually made public, it would seem odd to conclude that a teacher's solitary reflections and preparations have no meaning, moral or otherwise. Who would claim that a teacher's pensive ruminations on how to help a struggling student are not part of teaching, and, indeed, not part of the moral activity of teaching?

A utilitarian might make such a claim. As mentioned previously, with respect to the moral, utilitarians presume that the outcomes or results of action that affect others are what matter. Do the teacher's actions have a clear, observable, and positive effect on students? If so, those actions might be described as morally significant. If not, they are at the very least ambiguous. They would be immoral if they resulted in harm to students, intellectual or otherwise. For example, one can argue that it is immoral to teach students falsehoods, because they may base their future choices and conduct on such falsehoods. According to the utilitarian viewpoint, a teacher's internal thoughts, concerns, and feelings are relevant to the practice of teaching only if they issue in direct, public, and positive change in students.

However, it is one thing to say that teaching is a public act but another to conclude that all activity, to qualify as activity, must be undertaken publicly. The teacher, thinking alone in the classroom, office, or home about how to assist a struggling student, is engaged in a quite recognizable form of activity. We call it reflecting, considering, contemplating, worrying, weighing, musing, and deliberating. Such activity may not entail talking with other people nor altering something in the world—in one's conduct, for example—but it remains a form of activity all the same. Moreover, it can be morally significant even if it results in no outward change in conduct on the part of the teacher.

Suppose that after considerable pondering and perhaps also after consulting with a colleague or two, the teacher decides not to alter his or her conduct regarding a struggling student. The teacher decides that the student just needs time, that sustaining engagement with the student along with the rest of the class stands an equally good chance as any other strategy to help that student succeed. Or the teacher decides to change nothing, because the teacher believes this approach is the best way to respect the student as an individual. After surveying all that the teacher knows about this student, including what the student has had to say, the teacher decides that the student is genuinely performing at the best level currently possible and will benefit from the experience of making it on self-set terms. The teacher makes a note to be prepared, when and if the student can make a breakthrough, to provide extra, individualized instruction that can help clinch success. The teacher is also cautious, perhaps while walking into the classroom one morning, not to wait too long but to be ready to intervene actively if, in fact, the student continues to struggle.

The point of this example is that, at least at first, nothing has changed in the classroom world. Not the student in question, not the rest of the class; nor could outside observers detect any change in the teacher's treatment of the student. The utilitarian framework, attached as it is to observable change, makes it difficult to take this example seriously from a moral point of view. But anyone who has ever reflected on his or her relations with another person can recognize what this teacher has done and, moreover, can recognize it as morally significant. Murdoch (1970/1985) would carry this argument a step further (although she does not talk about teachers per se). "Action tends to confirm, for better or worse," she writes, "the background of attachment from which it issues" (p. 71). This "background of attachment" reflects what the teacher thinks about, cares about, worries about, is concerned about. It shapes the teacher's perceptions: what he or she is disposed to notice, to pay attention to, to take seriously in the classroom context. In this view, what occupies the teacher's mind in between the actual moments of teaching is in some respects more morally significant than those moments themselves. What becomes a moment in the first place depends, in part, on the teacher's fundamental disposition or on what Murdoch would call "capacity to attend." A teacher who thinks about students' individual growth positions him- or

herself to notice the student who all of a sudden is making use of new terms or concepts. In acknowledging such growth or supporting it in some way, the teacher and the student have created a classroom moment. A teacher who does not ponder such matters in between classes may not notice the new depth in the student's comment, and so nothing will happen.

This argument highlights the perhaps counterintuitive fact that the teacher's internal activity of pondering and thinking can be more significant, from a moral point of view, than subsequent changes in any external activity. The moral significance of teaching, in other words, does not necessarily reside at what Murdoch calls the actual "point of action" (1970/1985, p. 16). It resides as much in the complex, often unpredictable process of thought, doubt, wonder, concern, and more, which constitutes the fabric of pedagogical intentionality and which figures prominently in what teachers perceive in the first place in their classrooms. Murdoch describes this perspective as a fundamental shift in how we think about the moral. Moral conduct becomes more than a matter of implementing certain principles or following a prespecified rational procedure. Rather, according to Murdoch, it depends crucially on perception or on what she calls "moral vision." "[O]ur ability to act well 'when the time comes' depends partly, perhaps largely, upon the quality of our habitual objects of attention" (p. 56). "We act rightly," she goes on to say, "'when the time comes' not out of strength of will but out of the quality of our usual attachments and with the kind of energy and discernment which we have available" (p. 92). As illustrated previously, what teachers habitually take note of and think about can greatly influence their conduct—in other words, what they do "when the time comes," to use Murdoch's dramatic terms. From this point of view, teachers' internal thoughts and ruminations—what they are mentally and emotionally "paying attention" to, as Murdoch would put it—become that much more morally relevant. The moral meaning in teaching becomes more than just whether teachers do the right thing when the time comes. For practitioners, teaching as a moral activity "is something that goes on continually, not something that is switched off in between the occurrence of explicit moral choices. What happens in between such choices is indeed what is crucial" (Murdoch, 1970/1985, p. 37).

Buchmann (1989) applies this point of view in a sustained critique of certain conceptions of teachers' thinking. She argues for a shift in organizing ideas about teaching from a rationalistic language of decision making to a more contextualized language centered on perception and contemplation. Making use of Murdoch's emphasis on what goes on in between moments of public action, Buchmann highlights the practical place and value of contemplation. She describes the latter as an ongoing process of "careful attention and wonderstruck beholding" that is brought to bear on both students and on subject matter (p. 35). She shows why the process should be understood as an integral dimension of teachers' thinking. In so doing, she suggests that "scholars have—in equating teacher thinking with making particular and solitary decisions—only partially comprehended, if not misunderstood, the human activity of thinking in teaching" (p. 56). That activity, Buchmann contends, is deeply implicated by what teachers habitually ponder, what they remember, what they imagine, and what they hope for when not actually engaged in instruction. This kind of thinking, she goes on to argue, can have a strong influence on teachers' perceptions and, consequently, on what they do in the classroom. It is therefore worth examining on the part of both practitioners and researchers. "The moral force of the requirement for looking," Buchmann concludes, "stems from the fact that people are almost compelled by what they *can* see: virtue depends on vision" (p. 57).

Moral Perception, Moral Judgment, and Moral Knowledge in Teaching

Moral Perception

The emphasis in the previous section on paying attention and looking gives rise to the idea that teaching involves moral perception. Simpson and Garrison (1995) describe moral perception as "the capacity to comprehend the unique needs and aspirations of individual people and the best possibilities of equally unique social contexts. . . . Moral perception is about recognizing and responding thoughtfully to the needs, interests, beliefs, values, and behavior of others" (p. 252). The authors focus on the case of an eleven-year-old student who, up the point when he ended up in Simpson's classroom, had spent little time in formal educational settings (the boy traveled with a carnival). The authors highlight difficulties in determining ways to assess his progress in the classroom. In the course of their analysis, the challenge of assessment becomes their vehicle for identifying the constituents of moral perception in teaching. They emphasize thinking about students' possibilities rather than focusing on their deficiencies and failures. "What we *should* always do morally," they write, "is to perceive our students in terms of their best possibilities. But assessing students in [this way] is difficult and often requires a great deal of imagination" (p. 253). The authors explicate the process (also see Garrison, 1997) by drawing upon Aristotle's discussion of practical reasoning and upon ideas from Dewey such as the latter's analysis of aesthetic perception. "Moral perception is an indispensable part of practical reasoning," argues Garrison (1997), "because such perception is necessary for grasping the uniqueness of a practical context and the particularity of those participating in it" (p. 171). He suggests that there is an aesthetic dimension to moral perception, taking his point of departure from Dewey's argument that

> . . . [n]othing can make up for the absence of immediate sensitiveness. . . . Unless there is a direct, mainly unreflective appreciation of people and deeds, the data for subsequent thought will be lacking or distorted. A person must *feel* the qualities of acts as one feels with the hands the qualities of roughness and smoothness of objects, before he has an inducement to deliberate or material with which to deliberate. (Dewey, 1932/1989, pp. 268–269, quoted in Garrison, 1997, p. 33)

According to Simpson and Garrison (1995) and Garrison (1997), moral perception constitutes a process of careful looking and attending to concrete details, juxtaposed with and informed by careful thinking about context and circumstance.

Pendlebury (1990) and Bricker (1993) also make use of Aristotle's analysis of practical reasoning, in which perception and

thought are both necessary to right action. The authors illuminate what they regard as the importance of "situational appreciation" in good teaching, a concept closely related to the idea of moral perception. Pendlebury zeros in on difficult, nonroutine cases in the classroom when a teacher must engage in practical reasoning to determine what to do. She emphasizes that such reasoning, as Aristotle underscored, must be seen as "moral reasoning: it is concerned with what we ought to do in particular situations, given our commitment to the Good Life or to the demands of our professions or to the roles we have undertaken" (1990, p. 175). In terms that recall the discussion above of teaching as a practice, Pendlebury suggests that teachers must be committed to developing "a rich understanding of the goods of the practice and a realistic, clear-sighted perception of what is possible under different circumstances" (p. 178). However, Pendlebury argues, when it comes to resolving difficult teaching dilemmas, even the best reasoning, considered in itself, is inadequate. A teacher must also develop the capacity to see what is relevant or "salient" in the situation in the first place. That capacity is "situational appreciation." According to Pendlebury, situational appreciation "is crucial to sound practical reasoning, because if a practitioner is wrong in her identification of the salient features of a case, the result will be inappropriate or misguided action, regardless of the internal coherence of the argument she may give in support of her actions" (p. 176).

According to Bricker (1993), situational appreciation is "like aesthetic appreciation; that is, it is a matter of letting the most striking feature of a situation catch one's eye much as we let the aesthetically prominent features of a painting capture our attention when we perceive beauty. A visual ability is at work here, not an ability to reason" (p. 14). Like Pendlebury, Bricker argues that situational appreciation presupposes the intent to do good or, put differently, to live up to the ideals embodied in a moral practice like teaching. He contends that this is not, however, an issue of means and ends in which people use nonmoral means to achieve moral ends. "The challenge that people face," Bricker argues, "is not to identify actions that might be causally efficacious toward some future goal; rather, the challenge is, situation after situation, to be true to an overarching ideal by examining the situation in order to see what would qualify as a suitable, achievable instantiation of the ideal at that moment" (p. 17). Instead of treating the moral as a means to an end, Bricker implies that teachers might conceive the work as itself pregnant with moral meaning and possibility. For Bricker, teaching becomes not a matter of fulfilling distant goals but of living up to certain ideals of sound moral practice in the here and now. Situational appreciation is a central element in that process.

The process appears to require both moral perception and practical reasoning. However, for purposes of future research, moral perception can be distinguished from situational appreciation. In describing and illustrating situational appreciation, Pendlebury and Bricker focus on dilemmas or unusual difficulties. Simpson and Garrison also focus on a difficult, demanding predicament. However, moral perception does not necessarily come into play only when things have become problematic—quite the contrary. According to Buchmann (1989), Buchmann and Floden (1993), and others, the concept has to do with the quality of everyday, routine affairs, as well as with more dramatic matters. Whether a teacher does or does not notice a student's frown in the course of doing a science experiment, does or does not notice a student's ounce more of effort in completing a thought, does or does not notice a student picking up something off the floor for a peer with whom friction had occurred previously—all of these apparently mundane phenomena take on moral meaning, from the point of view of teaching, if a teacher sees them and acts upon them (which, as argued previously, need not mean doing something publicly). Other research endeavors reviewed previously—for example, Jackson et al. (1993), and van Manen (1991b)—treat the place of perception in teaching in this broad, not strictly dilemma-oriented way.

Moral Judgment in Teaching

Research reviewed thus far on the moral dimensions of teaching suggests that practitioners at all levels of the system need to be independent and moral thinkers. They must cultivate qualities of moral perception, learn to read situations appreciatively, and make decisions and appraisals that affect their students' intellectual and moral growth. Moreover, they must be active and imaginative when engaged in such processes. In short, according to the literature, it appears that teachers must be willing and able to render continuous moral judgments.

At first glance, this claim may strike some educators as presumptuous if not pernicious. They might object that teachers have no business morally judging their students. Who has granted teachers that authority, critics might ask? On what grounds would teachers base their moral judgments? Such questions raise the disturbing image of a teacher condemning out of hand a student's ideas, beliefs, or values simply because the teacher disagrees with them. That image conflicts with arguments reviewed previously that suggest that teaching involves reasoning with students, not converting or indoctrinating them.

However, according to Midgley (1991), "moral judgment" differs from what she calls "judgmentalism." (See the chapter on moral education in this handbook for perspectives on moral judgment that are rooted in psychological research on moral development in children and adults.) For Midgley, moral judgment differs from being dogmatic or authoritarian in one's thinking about other people and their claims and interests. Rather, moral judgment entails taking a reasoned approach in which the best interests of others—in this case, of students—are front and center. Moral judgment draws on a person's knowledge, experience, and character. It is "not simply accepting one of two ready-made alternatives as the right one," writes Midgley. "It cannot be done by tossing up [a coin]" (p. 25). Instead, she argues, moral judgment "is seeing reason to think and act in a particular way. It is a comprehensive function, involving our whole nature, by which we direct ourselves and find our way through a whole forest of possibilities. No science rules here; there is no given system of facts which will map our whole route for us. We are always moving into new territory" (p. 25).

The "new territory" into which teachers venture is their students' learning. In entering that world, teachers quickly discover that students differ from one another, sometimes in striking ways, in terms of personality, character, background, and

readiness and interest in learning. This familiar observation constitutes a major reason why teaching continually demands that teachers make moral judgments. As Midgley implies, to render such judgments takes teachers well beyond the confines of instructional manuals or other handbooks of do's and don'ts. Rather, teachers are constantly impelled to say things such as "this activity, or this exercise, or this homework, or this project, is what my student will most benefit from now, given my best sense of what the student seems to know and not to know, what the student can do and apparently not do, what the student's confidence and interests are—" and more, often much more. Perhaps the student argued with the teacher the day before. To reach the student today, the teacher has to take that additional fact into consideration and make use of it to best work with the child.

This teacher is engaged in making moral judgments. According to Midgley's analysis, that term is broader and richer than "decision making" as the latter is often used (for criticism of such uses when applied to teaching, see Buchmann, 1989; Buchmann & Floden, 1993; Court, 1989; and Oser, 1994). Auto mechanics, pilots, and baseball pitchers are constantly making decisions. But teachers are engaged in doing things, when in the presence of their students, that can directly influence the people their students will ultimately become. For this reason, the decisions about individual students that teachers make involve what Midgley would call their whole nature, encompassing their general knowledge of instruction and the curriculum, their particular knowledge of particular young human beings, and their character itself, which would include whether they are the kind of people disposed in the first place to reflect on their students' intellectual and moral well-being. Moral judgment is a more comprehensive activity than decision making and it better captures the stakes involved in teachers' everyday work.

Moral judgment is a complex, unpredictable affair. Recalling an earlier discussion in this chapter, it often entails not doing publicly visible things. It can mean holding back, keeping mum, letting a student find his or her own way, at least for a time. In this context, teachers' seeming inaction represents an active judgment on their parts. At other times, a teacher enacts a moral judgment by doing public things such as speaking to a student—"Please give R the respect you would like when you have the floor of discussion"—or by taking concrete action like photocopying an article that a student will surely appreciate and placing it on that person's desk before class, or by standing between two quarreling students, seeking to restore peace and resume the lesson. These doings all reflect moral judgment, and they have the potential to influence, however modestly at the moment, students' emerging knowledge and attitudes.

The enactment of moral judgment does not require the use of a formal moral vocabulary. Posed differently, while the language of the moral is indispensable for understanding the practice of teaching, it may not be required in order to teach in the moral spirit articulated by some of the work reviewed here. Murdoch (1970/1985) helps us appreciate that, in making moral judgments, teachers need not use terms with their students such as "It's the moral thing to do," or "That's good; that's bad," or "This is right; that is wrong." She draws a helpful distinction between formal and what she calls "secondary" moral terms (1970/1985, pp. 22–23). The latter are terms that reflect moral judgment but that do so in a more implicit than explicit way. They are gentler, humbler, and more responsive terms in their tone and meaning than the more dramatic (and perhaps even draconian) language of "moral student" or "immoral student." A teacher might reason through a situation as follows: "N is kind of a cautious student, careful, reserved, but sometimes N really becomes involved in things, and I like to say something special when that happens. Maybe I should do so now when N is a bit upset with me and how the class is coming along." This teacher's reasoning has not required a single Big Moral Word. We do not hear the teacher thinking or saying, "It's Moral and Good and Just to attend to N." Rather, the teacher sees what N is doing, and this seeing is a moral seeing reflected in the secondary moral terms—cautious, careful, reserved, upset—that describe N as a person at that moment in time and in that learning setting. Attending to this student and acting accordingly, the teacher reveals that moral judgment is better conceived as a process than as an outcome or product. This teacher is not "judging" N as we might typically use that term. To judge wisely about the appropriate course of action, the teacher, in fact, refrains from judgment. The teacher does not *pass* judgment on N but rather *reaches* a judgment through the kind of attentiveness to context that Midgley (1991) and Murdoch (1970/1985) associate with moral judgment.

Schultz (1997) provides numerous examples and fine-grained analysis of teachers' moral judgments in his study of the educational philosophies and practices of four elementary school teachers. According to Schultz, the process of moral judgment is complicated, ambiguous, and unpredictable, even for experienced, successful teachers. It is an inescapable feature of teaching.

Ethical Judgment in Teaching

Moral judgment in teaching is not necessarily the same thing as ethical judgment. Moral judgment is the enactment of what the teacher sees as right and appropriate, guided by a sense or vision of the goods of the practice. It depends equally on moral perception and on reasoning with, if anything, an emphasis on the former. This understanding coheres with the focus in the previous section on particularity and context rather than on principles or codes of conduct. It also reflects the emphasis on process rather than on outcome that some scholars associate with moral judgment. Stott (1988) captures the moral depth of this kind of judgment: "[I]t is certainly true that if I have been moved by the beauty of a river, I cannot throw trash into it; moved by the presence of a person, I cannot deceive him or her. It is not a matter at all that I ought not, it is that I *must* not; it is not a matter of obedience to a general principle, but rather a specific feel of the right and good" (p. 63).

Moral judgment can also be understood as an ongoing aspect of practices like teaching. In contrast, ethical judgment comes into play when addressing serious and pressing dilemmas and difficulties. In such circumstances, people must be able to stand back from their own values and commitments and think about how to decide what is right and wrong—indeed, to think about whether their own value systems are coherent, justified, and comprehensive enough to form the basis for judgments of right and wrong. Ethical judgment as those terms are often understood embodies a detached, reasoned examination of alternative possibilities. This examination includes considering the larger ethical and political perspectives that might underlie each alternative.

A number of recent studies illuminate the place of ethical judgment in teaching. Strike and Soltis (1985), for example, discuss various conceptions of ethics and then apply them to a series of classroom- and school-based cases. They demonstrate that ethics is not a relativistic or merely subjective affair. Rather, they argue, "questions of ethics can be objectively discussed and morally justified courses of action undertaken" (p. 6). "[T]eachers have a special obligation," they suggest, "to help their students see and share the potential objectivity and rationality of ethical thinking so that we can all lead morally responsible lives together" (p. 7). Strike and Ternasky (1993) present essays on ethical matters from a number of scholars and also include perspectives from the same writers on common problems and dilemmas. As with Strike and Soltis (1985), their studies take their point of departure from the idea that ethical problems are difficult and sometimes unresolvable. On some occasions, the best one can do is to reach a temporary, dissatisfying compromise. Consequently, making ethical judgments in the classroom should not be conceived as a means of avoiding problems or obstacles to learning—quite on the contrary. Philips (1979) criticizes the notion that the desired outcome of moral thinking is "being happy and socially responsible" (p. 54). "[I]s morality a way of avoiding obstacles to living happy and useful lives?" he asks. "And how serious a concern with moral issues could speak of facing moral issues with confidence? Is there no recognition of the fact that moral beliefs often create obstacles; that without regard for them often there would be no problems? Is there no recognition of the fact that if moral ideals may direct one's aspirations they may also show one the limits of one's aspirations?" (p. 54).

The cases and analyses provided by Strike and Soltis (1985) and by Strike and Ternasky (1993) amply document why ethical judgment is often a thorny process, in part because of the very facts Philips dramatizes. Teaching is a morally complex activity because it embodies convictions about better and worse, about what is good and what is bad for people, and so forth—all of which can create tensions and dilemmas for teachers and students. Campbell (1992) interviewed twenty teachers and ten principals to identify their ethical principles and how or to what extent they harmonize them with school-based practice. Their collective testimony shows how difficult it can sometimes be to translate principle into action. According to Campbell's analysis, school cultures often necessitate ethical compromise. Colnerud (1997) buttresses this viewpoint in a study of teachers' perceptions of ethical conflicts in teaching. Many of those conflicts, Colnerud suggests, "can be seen as the result of the collision of structural conditions and personal preferences" in teaching (p. 633). Based on teachers' self-reports, she sketches what she calls a "map" of the ethical challenges she regards as inherent in the practice.

Hostetler (1997) also presents a series of classroom- and school-based situations that call for ethical judgment. His book includes contributions from various scholars on how educators might confront such situations. The format of the book enacts its message: Ethical judgment in teaching is an exploratory, back and forth, often messy, and uneven process that is quite distinct from slapping down a rule or precept and mechanically following it. Hostetler distinguishes ethical from moral judgment, preferring the former term because, according to some conceptions of the moral, when faced with moral problems people need only implement a particular principle or code of conduct. For Hostetler, those conceptions of the moral effectively vitiate the need for judgment because all that people have to do is follow the principle or code. (Such views of the moral embody a much more attenuated sense of the term than that taken by almost all the work reviewed in this chapter.) Hostetler and his collaborators agree that ethical judgment often involves choosing between goods. That is, educators frequently find themselves torn in what to do because each option that comes to mind can be morally justified, yet each option also means sacrificing or at least shelving for the time being things people value. A teacher might wonder: "Should I abandon my curriculum because my students would rather discuss certain difficulties in their lives? I may be able to assist students in crafting a response to those difficulties, and doing so can be understood as a moral good. But I may sacrifice another moral good, namely, the knowledge, the insight, even the access to wisdom that may be embedded in my curriculum. Moreover, perhaps my students will never again be exposed to such a curriculum. Their immediate lives might be better for my having shelved it now, but their future lives may be less rich for not having had the curriculum." Both of these courses of action embody values and goods, and the teacher's predicament, according to Hostetler, is not a matter of routinely following some abstract principle. In a sense, the latter course effectively denies the existence of the predicament. For Hostetler, what matters for teachers is "to keep open the question of what we ought to do in any particular situation. . . . Broadly speaking, the 'ethical' is our answer(s) to the question of 'How should people live?' But part of our task in ethical judgment is to decide just how that question should be answered in any particular situation" (p. 17).

Moral Knowledge in Teaching

The literature reviewed in this chapter suggests that educators should be cautious about assuming that teachers can develop expertise in their moral or ethical judgment. This warning is not because teachers are somehow incapable of doing so but, rather, because the language of expertise is simply the wrong idiom for capturing the moral dimensions of the practice. In explicit or implicit ways, many scholars distinguish expertise from practical wisdom. Aristotle's account of practical wisdom, especially in his *Nicomachean Ethics,* remains singularly useful here. For Aristotle, practical wisdom encompasses much of what previous sections in the chapter have called moral perception and moral and ethical judgment. It describes a seasoned ability to size up a situation, to consider participants' points of view and concerns, to weigh alternative options, and to act in a fair-minded way that also increases the likelihood of a better rather than worse future for all involved. Practical wisdom is necessarily fallible, in part because human beings are imperfect and, in part, because each social context brings unique and often unpredictable demands and challenges. But practical wisdom is morally potent precisely because it recognizes the reality

of fallibility while also recognizing the possibility of human improvement and growth.

From this perspective, practical wisdom, in contrast with notions of expertise, is an orientation more in keeping with the contingent nature of pedagogical work and with the always evolving moral character of both teachers and students. According to the literature, the notion of the teacher as a moral or ethical expert ill-suits the practice of teaching—unlike, perhaps, talk of a legal expert on certain matters of law, or of an expert surgeon for an operation, or of an expert guide for hiking through a rain forest. Expertise, rather than moral insight, is what clients want from such people. However, Welker (1992) asks educators to consider "whether teachers can or should be considered full professionals in the exclusive and technical sense of the term—people whose vocation is more formed by their competence than their character, more dependent on legal jurisdiction than human relation" (p. 10). Wise teachers are not necessarily expert teachers. They may not know, for example, the same amount about instructional methodology or computer technology as their peers in classrooms down the hall. But they may have broader moral knowledge. That is, they may understand students better and know how to connect them more meaningfully with subject matter than people possessed of even the best technical skills (Sockett, 1993; van Manen, 1991b). Competence and wisdom are not antithetical. Moral knowledge in teaching becomes ineffectual without technical skill. But technical skill and expertise may be damaging or even dangerous without a moral vision informing their use.

According to some scholars, understanding teaching as a moral activity can give value and direction to teachers' technical knowledge. Stott (1988) suggests that such understanding can remind educators that "[e]xpertise in teaching a subject is not enough; the medium of a teacher's classroom teaches more, and more deeply, than the message" (p. 4). Stott's remarks recall the adage that much of what people learn both intellectually and morally is "caught, not taught." That familiar distinction brings to mind Dewey's (1916/1997) argument that educators "never educate directly"—as if they could literally reach into the minds of children—"but indirectly by means of the environment" (p. 19). That environment is infused with the teacher's commitments, values, and beliefs, which as we have seen are brought to life through their manner, style, tact, perception, judgment, and more. Wisdom in teaching seems to imply recognizing, in practice, the morally contextualized nature of curricular and instructional matters.

The notion of expertise in teaching spotlights what teachers know with respect to a particular domain of knowledge and application. The idea of moral knowledge points neither to a specific body of facts and theories nor to a predefined content of any kind. Rather, it signifies an appreciation of how difficult it is to know something well, of how little most of us in fact know, and of how much we will always want and need to know to live flourishing lives and contribute the best way we can to others. If assuredness is a hallmark of expertise, humility is an aspect of moral knowledge. Murdoch (1970/1985) describes humility as "a rare virtue and an unfashionable one and one which is often hard to discern. Only rarely does one meet somebody in whom it positively shines, in whom one apprehends with amazement the absence of the anxious avaricious tentacles of the self" (p. 103). Murdoch's dramatic terms perhaps underplay the fact that, with respect to teaching, humility is an active rather than passive virtue. It does not imply self-abnegation but rather a serious-minded attempt to attend closely to students' intellectual and moral development. It can be discerned in the familiar claims by experienced teachers that even after many years in the field they still have not "gotten it right," have still not learned how to teach as successfully as they believe they can and should. But these teachers have grasped what is meant by describing the practice as a moral activity. The activity is such that nobody anywhere ever gets it fully right. Teaching is a field with boundless opportunities for betterment, in part, because there always exist new ideas to incorporate into subject matter and instruction and, in part, because such opportunities emerge right in front of one's nose if one sharpens perception and awakens a spirit of questioning.

Dewey (1909/1975) suggests that moral knowledge is a difficult quality to put into words. However, he writes,

> We all know the difference between the character which is hard and formal, and one which is sympathetic, flexible, and open. In the abstract the former may be as sincerely devoted to moral ideas as is the latter, but as a practical matter we prefer to live with the latter. We count upon it to accomplish more by tact, by instinctive recognition of the claims of others, by skill in adjusting, than the former can accomplish by mere attachment to rules. (pp. 52–53)

Dewey's remarks suggest that the source of moral knowledge is responsiveness to human beings and their circumstances. In this light, moral knowledge has clear associations with the previous analysis of the processes of moral perception and moral judgment (and there are echoes here of the earlier discussion of manner, style, and tact). What the concept magnifies is the notion of something retained; moral knowledge describes something a teacher can retain. With its repeated enactment in dealing with students, it can help constitute the teacher's character. Thus moral knowledge contrasts with other forms of knowledge more easily forgotten: a foreign language we no longer use, mathematical and scientific formulae we no longer apply, a piece of music we used to play, how to get from one place to another in a city, how to prepare a particular dish, and much more. But moral knowledge can endure and enlighten a practitioner's work with students over a lifetime. Aristotle's *Nicomachean Ethics* remains a helpful source for thinking about the distinction between moral knowledge and others forms of knowledge.

More research is needed to assess adequately the value of the idea of moral knowledge in teaching. However, Lyons (1990) sheds light on the development of teachers' moral knowledge in a project focused on the interplay of ethical and epistemological considerations in teaching. Of particular moment here is her field-based study of three teachers who, confronted with difficult classroom dilemmas, found themselves reorienting, but also reconfirming, their sense of what teaching obliges them to do. The teachers struggled with several issues: how to balance high expectations of students with the reality of students who slip and stumble in their performance, how to avoid preaching at students regarding controversial topics while also not downplaying their own stance, and how to support students in thinking for themselves rather than either accepting opinions uncritically or relying on external authorities—including teachers (pp. 163–167). These dilemmas challenged the teachers to think that much more deeply about their students as people and about their possible influence on them. Lyons reports that the teachers emerged from the challenge with a broader view of students' individuality and circumstances yet also with a deeper confidence in the role they can and, indeed, must play in supporting students' intellectual and moral growth. For example, the teacher who worried about the effect of his own opinions on students' thinking learned to be more circumspect in his remarks. However, at the same time he also learned to be much more forceful in pushing students to develop arguments and reasoning powers rather than settling for the bland and easier course of "It's only an opinion" (pp. 170–171). This teacher's pedagogical connectedness with students became intellectually and morally deeper. He was developing his moral knowledge: his nuanced appreciation both for his students' individuality and for the requirement that, as teacher, he enact a commitment to educational values.

Teachers as (Moral) Role Models

The idea that teachers are moral role models may be as old as formal education itself. According to numerous commentators, figures such as Confucius, Socrates, the Buddha, and Christ—all of whom helped give rise to the practice of teaching—embodied or "modeled" what they stood for (Jaspers, 1957/1962). For example, in the *The Analects* Confucius urges his students to develop what he calls "humaneness," a virtue at once both intellectual and moral and one difficult to attain, yet not inaccessible. Confucius' own conduct exemplifies the meaning of humaneness. He is patient, self-critical, frank, reflective, and keenly observant in his dealings with other people. Time and again he speaks of what it takes to treat people humanely: "One does not worry about the fact that other people do not appreciate one. One worries about not appreciating other people" (I:16); "Firmness, resoluteness, simplicity, and reticence are close to humaneness" (XIII:27); "Putting the job first and what you get out of it last—is this not exalting virtue? Attacking one's own bad qualities and avoiding attacks on other people's bad qualities—is not this the way to reform wickedness?" (XII:21). In seeking to harmonize his words and deeds in the spirit of humaneness, Confucius models his own message.

Many educators today continue to give the idea of being a role model an explicit, normative meaning. Teachers need not be able to walk on water, they suggest, but they should model excellence both in their academic work and in their personal decorum. They should do so because, like it or not, students look to them for models of how to regard education and how to treat other people. From this perspective, being a role model—or, at any rate, being perceived as one—comes with the territory. Teachers cannot prevent themselves from being perceived in this way, any more than they can prevent themselves from expressing moral messages through what they say and do. In short, even as a descriptive term the idea of a role model carries moral weight. Teachers can be good or bad role models, but what they cannot do, it appears, is sidestep the reality of modeling something.

Recent research suggests that some teachers unhesitantly regard themselves as role models, even if they may be reluctant or unaccustomed to using that particular term. They also make use of moral language in describing what they seek to model, although the term "moral" appears less often than what Murdoch (1970/1985) calls secondary moral terms (see above).

For example, the experienced teachers with whom Jackson et al. (1993) worked were uncomfortable calling themselves role models because, in their view, what they model are not "heroic" virtues like courage and wisdom but "humbler" qualities such as showing respect for people, demonstrating intellectual engagement in a task, paying close attention to what is being said, and so forth (pp. 284–287). Nonetheless, the teachers do accept the mantle of role model, and they feel it is crucial to acknowledge themselves as such. As a high school math teacher posed the matter: "I have to be a role model; I have to be. Because I am one of the persons who affect the lives of the people that I teach" (Hansen, Boostrom, & Jackson, 1994, p. 26). These men and women see themselves as teachers of subject matter. At the same time, however, they also believe that they are teaching a broader outlook on life. A high school English teacher, Mr. Turner, suggested that in addition to literature he is also teaching "Turner 101" (Jackson et al., 1993, p. 284). He did not mean that he preaches or cajoles students into accepting his own values and beliefs. Rather, he meant that he cannot help but bring his vision of life and his very character as a person into the classroom. Over the long nine or ten months of the schoolyear, the person he is will find expression in his work with students. The other teachers agreed that they are modeling such things "all the time" (p. 285), even when unaware of doing so.

Several of the teachers couched their remarks about role modeling in the context of their perceptions of students, whom they appear to regard highly but whom they also often see as in dire need of guidance, direction, and support (Hansen et al., 1994). The teachers feel compelled to enact qualities that they believe their students both want and need to see in them: confidence, poise, fairness, commitment, hopefulness, consistency, being knowledgeable, and being organized. A high school Special Education teacher, Mr. James, who works with students whom other adults often treat as impossible and as "losers," is emphatic about the importance of his modeling good conduct. He seeks to bring what he calls order, peace, and clarity to his students' lives. He does so through enacting a calm, poised demeanor, most especially when his students are behaving poorly. In a consistent, almost habitual way, he seeks to model what respectful conduct might mean, in the hope that over time he can assist his students in perceiving themselves through a more enabling social and personal lens (Hansen, 1995, pp. 68, 84, 87). Mr. James and other dedicated colleagues believe it crucial to model conduct they expect to see in their students. As practitioners who have come to appreciate their possible moral effect on students, they "understand that they cannot expect [for example] honesty without being honest" (Fenstermacher, 1990, p. 135). Needless to say, these self-expectations place a burden on the teachers to be at their best when in the presence of students.

Joseph and Efron (1993) found that such self-expectations can lead teachers into moral dilemmas if not into actual conflicts with students, colleagues, administrators, and parents. The authors temper the call that teachers conduct themselves as role models by reminding us that teachers "experience the same quandaries and emotional responses as other human beings as they identify and grapple with value issues or encounter others who violate their deeply felt beliefs" (p. 202). Joseph and Efron surveyed 180 teachers to learn about their perceptions of the moral aspects of teaching. They also conducted follow-up interviews with 26 of the teachers. Almost all of the teachers believe that they should act as role models, for example, by consistently demonstrating high moral standards in their work with students. A high school teacher reflects the sense of the group when he says: "I realize that when I go into the classroom, I teach honesty and hard work. I teach fairness and I do that on a daily basis. Strictly by walking in the door as a role model I am teaching things . . . the way I dress, the way I treat kids" (p. 209). He adds that teachers "teach values more than I ever thought possible. It's the nature of having to be with those students every day, of having to run the classroom in a way that you are comfortable. When I say, 'The way you are comfortable,' that means you are going to teach your values. I can't be comfortable in that setting with values that I am not comfortable with" (p. 209). The act of modeling honesty, hard work, and fairness—all values to which this teacher is committed—leads him into conflicts with students who for one reason or another do not work hard or who treat classmates badly. Joseph and Efron argue that such moral choices and conflicts accompany the work of teaching.

Aurin and Maurer (1993) surveyed and, in some cases, interviewed 124 secondary school teachers on their views and understandings of professional ethics. Like Joseph and Efron, they found that many teachers are both aware of and articulate about the moral dimensions of their work, including the importance of their conducting themselves ethically when under the watchful eyes of students. McEwan (1994) echoes these findings. In her interview-based inquiry, centered primarily on the perspectives and practices of three teachers, she found that teachers can and will talk at length about the moral aspects of their work if given the opportunity. According to her analysis, the teachers are quite aware of the effect they can have on students' intellectual and moral growth. Using numerous examples, the teachers illustrate how caring acts on their part affect and impress students. They talk repeatedly about the importance of their modeling for students values such as fairness and respect in dealing with other peoples' ideas and aspirations.

According to Higgins (1995), "[b]eing a role model is one of the expectations of teaching that defines the job as a moral one for all teachers" (p. 151). In an interview-based study, Higgins sought to discern how American and Russian teachers might compare in their conceptions of their work and in what they endeavor to model for students. She found that some of the American teachers focused on "shaping" certain kinds of experiences in the classroom so that students can learn (p. 149). Other teachers in both groups mentioned students' moral growth and placed moral considerations at the center of their practice—"not only when discussing their philosophies," Higgins points out, "but also when describing their personal daily goals" (p. 148). The Russian teachers were most outspoken regarding this point. Higgins suggests that they take a more deontological view of the moral than do American teachers. That is, they appear more allied to broad notions of ethical principle—what can technically be called formal principle—and less patient with prima facie principles, those that can be shelved or, perhaps, even broken depending upon context and circumstance. American teachers, according to Higgins, articulate a somewhat more individualized, or particularized, view of the moral. Nonetheless, teachers from both societies appear to believe that they can and should model a moral stance for their students.

As part of a larger inquiry into the development of professional perspectives and behavior in prospective teachers, Bergem (1990) interviewed 65 candidates about their perceptions of teachers as role models. His point of departure is the idea that "[s]ince teachers are given the responsibility to take care of and nurture other peoples' development we believe that teaching can to a very large extent be conceived as a *moral enterprise*" (p. 89). He found that two thirds of the candidates associated the idea of role model with being a "paragon of virtue," meaning a person who consistently does the right thing and who does so both in- and outside the school. About half of the candidates believed that teachers should consciously act as role models. Teachers, they suggested, should be aware of how large an effect their actions can have on the young. The candidates offered extensive testimony about the positive influence they believe teachers can have if they set the right "example," which is another term for role model. "The example the teacher sets is part of his teaching," said one candidate (p. 97). Another pointed out that, as students, "[t]hose [teachers] we didn't respect lacked commitment, lacked basic human sympathy and understanding, and lacked insight into the nature of students and the way they think" (p. 96). Bergem summarizes his own views through lines taken from Henrik Ibsen's play, *Brand:* "Not even a thousand words/Make such an impression as an action does" (quoted on p. 99).

Future Inquiry on Teaching as a Moral Activity

According to the literature reviewed in this chapter, teaching is inherently a moral endeavor. Individual practitioners vary enormously in how they fulfill the terms of the work, but those terms embody moral dimensions and obligations that distinguish teaching from other practices and activities. Moreover, like education itself, teaching is not merely a means to an end. According to the literature, an uncritical view of means and ends in education can produce a truncated vision of the practice. In addition, research has illuminated why teaching is at one and the same time an intellectual and a moral endeavor. Those two aspects can be examined separately for heuristic purposes, but in actual practice they take form simultaneously. This process is not always easy to identify, a fact that gives rise to another central lesson from the literature: Moral considerations permeate the practice of teaching. Teaching is morally layered work. On the surface are teachers' words and acts, many with obvious moral overtones. But underneath the behavior reside teachers' values, beliefs, perceptions, judgments, and more. Those underlying values and convictions help produce the infinite variety of moral messages teachers emit to their students, many of them unintended and unwilled and many of them beyond teachers' own awareness.

Teaching calls on practitioners' personal characters and on their capacities to reason reflectively and morally. Research has shown that these demands of the practice do not occur according to a schedule. They are ubiquitous and unpredictable in classroom work. Moreover, they cannot be rigidly segregated from judgments about curriculum, instructional method, evaluation, and more. Research also suggests that both character and moral thinking play a more influential role in what teachers do than previous research on the practice indicates.

More study is needed to clarify the nature and place of character and of moral thinking in teaching. Research is also needed to clarify the relation between the two. Concepts such as manner, style, and tact help point the way to issues of character, as do concepts such as moral perception, situational appreciation, and moral judgment. With respect to moral thinking in teaching, researchers can draw on concepts such as effective and responsible teaching, ethical judgment, practical reasoning, and others touched on throughout the chapter. A potentially useful line of research also lies ahead, which connects in an explicit and systematic fashion these moral dimensions of the work both with forms of knowledge in teaching—what some call, for example, craft knowledge (compare the review by Grimmett & MacKinnon, 1992) or practical knowledge (compare the review by Fenstermacher, 1994b)—and with current conceptions of teaching such as its being a "reflective" practice. Valli (1990), for example, reviews several approaches to thinking about the moral aspects of "reflective" teaching.

Waller (1932) wrote that teaching's most "pronounced effect" (p. 375) is on teachers themselves. That claim calls to mind another potential area of research: the moral influence of teaching on teachers themselves. At first glance such a topic may seem tangential to the theory and practice of teaching. Surely what matters, a critic might point out, is the influence teachers have on students. What happens to teachers is part of their personal biographies but has little to do with students or the public at large. However, the literature on teaching suggests that performing the work day after day does have a moral influence on teachers' beliefs, values, perceptions, and judgments. Because those beliefs and perceptions influence, in turn, teachers' classroom actions—powerfully so, according to both researchers and practitioners—then it seems sensible, even essential, to investigate the moral influence teaching has on its practitioners. Posed differently, if teachers' actions have a bearing on student learning—as they are universally acknowledged to do—then research on what may morally influence those actions merits attention.

Waller (1932) argued in his pioneering study that teaching often appears to wear down its practitioners' moral sensitivity and perspective. The demands of the work, in his view, harden teachers' temperaments, narrow their thinking, and reduce their expectations. Ultimately, those demands drive many teachers from the field. Other studies show that some teachers thrive the longer they remain in the practice. They come to realize the "internal goods" inherent in the work (see above). They find that teaching broadens and deepens their human sympathies, their imaginations, and their desire to learn (Ben-Peretz, 1995; Cohen, 1991; Grimmett & MacKinnon, 1992; Hansen, 1995; Lyons, 1990). Some teachers argue that the work has made them better people. For example, the majority of the 180 teachers Joseph and Efron (1993) surveyed "believe that since they have become teachers, they have become more caring and altruistic" (p. 205). Jackson et al. (1993) report that the veteran teachers with whom they worked believe it vital to put up not just "a front" but a morally good front when actually teaching. They deliberately place their best foot forward, morally speaking, when in the presence of their students. According to their testimony, they "usually exhibit . . . a better self than the one they actually possess . . . or at least better than the one they customarily credit . . . themselves as possessing" (1993, p. 288). The teachers explained that in so doing—in acting as what they euphemistically came to call "upward hypocrites" (pp. 288–290)—they slowly become better people themselves. In their view, the moral qualities they seek to model hold the promise of eventually becoming an integral part of their own character. They added that the negative qualities they seek to correct in students are often qualities they hope to exorcise in themselves.

Loukes (1976) suggests that the "picture" we have of a good teacher—especially one of the very young—encompasses a sense of curiosity, outgoing warmth, the desire and the ability to nurture growth, and a philosophy of life. These "are qualities that teaching itself develops," argues Loukes. "Those who live sensitively among the young cannot but learn them. These children work on us, to bring out the personal, to make us laugh at ourselves and puzzle about life and its meaning. They teach us to care" (quoted in Cox, 1982, p. 81). "Teachers are rewarded for their efforts to improve," adds Olson (1992), "not only by seeing students better able to think well, but by being a teacher—by being engaged deeply in a morally worthwhile life" (p. 93). "In carefully attending to learners, subject matter, and the ends of their work," argues Buchmann (1989), "teachers maintain and perfect their craft and themselves, and enlighten and perfect others" (p. 57). In a broad sense, according to Oakeshott (1927/1993), becoming a better person and teacher is "an endless, practical endeavor resulting in momentary personal failures and achievements and in a gradual change of moral ideas and ideals, a change that is perhaps more than mere change, a progress toward a finer sensibility for social life and a deeper knowledge of its necessities" (p. 44).

Future research can shed light on the nature of this kind of moral odyssey as it unfolds in teaching. All serious-minded teachers surely hope that through the vicissitudes of a career, they will learn to act better rather than worse when they are working with students. However, they also might be the first to admit that such moral progress is uneven and unpredictable. Teachers might grow in patience with certain students but become less so with others. They might learn to take students' views more seriously but come to ignore those of parents or colleagues. They might help students learn how to focus and concentrate but neglect their own short- and long-term lesson planning, with negative consequences for student learning. In short, the idea of straightforward, unbroken moral progress in teaching seems problematic. Moreover, the very meaning of qualities such as being patient with or attentive to students can change depending on context, on where the teacher is in his or her career, and other factors. These and related questions invite further study.

Students' views of their teachers' moral influence might also

be investigated, an idea in keeping with Sockett's (1992) recommendation that research examine the moral effect on students of teachers' work. (The chapter on moral education in this handbook reports on research on young peoples' conceptions of ethical and moral matters including how they pertain to educational practice.) Readers of this handbook can doubtless recall teachers who had a moral effect on them. These teachers did more than add to their stores of knowledge, for example, of botany or of the events of the French Revolution. Rather, they transformed their lives, often in ways not immediately apparent, by quickening their love of learning, by fueling their self-understanding and their understanding of other people, or by enhancing their ability to perform disciplined work. Future research can shed light on students' awareness and conceptions of their teachers' moral influence upon them. Cutforth (1994) demonstrates how this research might be accomplished (also see Hayes, Ryan, & Zseller, 1994). Cutforth spent hundreds of hours over the course of four consecutive years in an urban elementary school. He cotaught with the school's physical education teacher, engaged in participant observation in her gymnasium, and conducted systematic research that included recorded interviews with students, both individually and in small groups. Their collective testimony gives rise to a multifaceted portrait of the physical education teacher's moral influence. In the eyes of the children, the teacher influences them through her daily manner or style and through her handling of problematic events, both within and outside the school.

Preparing for Research

What kind of background is useful for studying teaching as a moral activity? Two suggestions come to mind. The first is that reading moral philosophy constitutes both an invaluable preparation for and companion of research. There exist remarkable traditions of thought on the moral, some of them mentioned in this chapter, which researchers can tap for insight and guidance. Numerous helpful works seek to synthesize and criticize these traditions. I have found it most helpful to study moral philosophy in the company of others—and to take a generous amount of time in doing so. Reading excellent literature can also be of value. George Eliot's novel, *Middlemarch,* for instance, is as provocative a source for reflection on the moral life as any work of philosophy that comes to mind. A piece of advice Shulman (1988) offers to new educational researchers holds here. Shulman suggests that entrants should all learn both a qualitative and a quantitative approach to inquiry. I would reframe that sound advice as follows: Investigators interested in teaching as a moral activity might read and study at least two orientations to the moral—for example, an obligation-based perspective (Kant comes to mind, along with commentators on his work such as Barbara Herman, 1993, and Christine Korsgaard, 1996), a care-based viewpoint (a good place to start is Nodding's chapter in this handbook), or a virtues-based perspective (with Aristotle as a prime exemplar, along with commentators such as Martha Nussbaum, 1986, and Nancy Sherman, 1997). It would also be helpful to read in depth a thinker like Dewey who resists classification but who, rather, raises questions about the sufficiency of any particular conception of the moral.

A second suggestion to researchers new to this field is to appreciate some of the factors that account for why attention to the moral dimensions of teaching is a relatively recent phenomenon in the research community. This suggestion seems sensible if only because some of those factors are likely to persist for some time to come..For example, the very term "moral" continues to call to mind, in many public quarters, the image of a particular set of values held by a particular group of people and often in explicit opposition to values held by other groups. To the extent that researchers are influenced by the public ethos in which they live, it has doubtless appeared natural (or even necessary) to steer clear of talk of the "moral" dimensions of teaching. Public school teachers, for instance, are obliged to teach subject matter to all students regardless of their own religious, cultural, social, or political values. Talk of teaching as a moral endeavor—if "moral" is construed in this narrow way—seems to imply acknowledging only a particular set of values, namely those of the teacher or, more typically, those of some particular social group. This chapter has illustrated how off-course such a perspective is. The idea of teaching as a moral practice raises not the question "Whose morals?" but, rather, many questions about the nature and effect of teaching itself.

"It is obvious if we look for it," writes Elbaz (1992), "that moral concern pervades all of teachers' work and the knowledge that grows out of that work" (p. 421). Elbaz bases her claim on the research literature on teachers' thinking and on a specific analysis she undertook of students' views in a foundations of curriculum course she taught. A major problem, she concludes, is that the educational community simply does not look for "it"—for the moral meanings in practice. Instead, the community, in her view, all too often acts on the assumption that teaching is essentially a technical delivery system for transferring knowledge. According to Carr (1992), the idea of education "as a more or less straightforward and value-free technical exercise is quite widely subscribed to in an explicit or implicit theoretical or pretheoretical way both inside and beyond professional educational circles" (p. 245). Researchers interested in teaching as a moral endeavor will want to be mindful that the larger themes highlighted in this chapter—for example, that teaching is both an intellectual and a moral activity and that it is more than merely a means to an end—are not received opinion or, at any rate, are not well understood in some educational quarters today.

The fact that there are different conceptions of the moral, from virtue-based to consequentialist, has doubtless contributed to a scientist bias that still haunts the research community. According to one strand of this bias, most of the various scholarly positions on the moral reflected in this chapter are simply wrong or confused. The moral can be boiled down once and for all, or so it is claimed, to an airtight definition. According to another strand, the sheer fact that there are numerous conceptions demonstrates that the moral is a fundamentally subjective dimension of human experience, which lacks the ontological status of a researchable object—in other words, an object in the natural or observable or objective world. If the moral is assumed to lack such status, researchers may not feel inclined to study it. Court (1989) suggests that some researchers may also have assumed that moral values are tacitly held and are therefore inarticulable, which would mean they are inaccessible to research. However, she argues that tacit knowing (compare Polanyi, 1962) can become articulate, either through self-

examination or through being interviewed by others. As we have seen, long-term observational work can also be enlightening on this score.

The development in recent decades of interpretive social science (Rabinow & Sullivan, 1979), juxtaposed (not by accident) with a renewed interest in both ancient and modern conceptions of the moral (MacIntyre, 1984; Taylor, 1989), has helped educational researchers challenge or at least sidestep emotivist and subjectivist views of the moral, which often appear to go hand-in-hand with scientific views of reality (Greene, 1986; Strike, 1991). The research reviewed in this chapter makes plain that we can see a teacher's patience with the same certainty with which we can see the wooden desks where students sit. The teacher's patience is no more "in the eye of the beholder" than is the rising sun—which is not to say that everyone awake at that hour notices the rising sun, any more than all classroom occupants notice the teacher's patience (whether students have to be aware of the teacher's patience for it to have a moral influence on them is another intriguing question).

In the discussion of means and ends thinking that opened this chapter, we saw that numerous scholars have highlighted the dangers of thinking of teaching as purely a means to fulfill ends defined apart from the practice. Those same scholars emphasize how difficult it is to remember these dangers in an achievement-oriented ethos that esteems results rather than processes. It seems to me that this ethos bears down especially hard on conceptual and field-based research on teaching as a moral endeavor. "Is it practical?" is the question likely to be hurled at educators interested in thinking systematically about this complex topic. The literature reviewed here suggests that this ubiquitous question is itself both impractical and potentially anti-intellectual. The question overlooks the fact that thinking well remains one of the most practical things a human being can do (Buchmann, 1989). The question is misguided, because it ignores the fact that, as teachers and parents could quickly attest, sometimes doing nothing publicly or, perhaps, doing fewer things is the better part of wisdom (van Manen, 1991b). Dewey argues that "the fundamental trouble" in fields such as education "is lack of conversation. We do so much and say so little. Or our saying is so much of it just a little more doing rather than a conversation. Perhaps we need just one more foundation or reform society—one to encourage sitting down and talking things over, and to discourage other organizations from doing any more things which only add to the infinite heap of things which already oppress us" (1929, p. 126). Higgins (1995) echoes Dewey's point in urging educators to "spread ideas rather than programmes" (p. 157).

The inextinguishable question, Is it practical?, not only produces an endless, often overwhelming flurry of activity, but it may also be morally damaging because it can intimidate the natural desire many educators feel to reflect on the nature of their work rather than just on its measurable outcomes. Moreover, the question makes demands on others and on what they think and do rather than inviting the questioner to reflect personally and ask, What does "practical" mean? Should we think of a teacherly virtue like patience as something practical? What about being attentive? considerate? diligent? serious-minded? thoughtful? humble? respectful of students? Are such qualities practical, or are they, perhaps, better understood as constitutive of both persons and the ways they might relate with one another? And what if we cannot prove that patient teachers help produce patient students? Does that imply teachers can dispense with being patient? Or is being patient with students less a means to an end than the enactment of a fundamental, graceful human quality, which enriches all the lives touched by it and which is not diminished in significance if it cannot be measured? Research on the moral dimensions of teaching can perform the helpful service of muting the impractical and often harmful demand for "practicality," especially when the latter reflects a narrow, instrumental way of conceiving means and ends. Research can illuminate the fact that teachers do not make things happen in the manner of a builder or manufacturer (Olson, 1992). They cannot produce quick and dramatic results in the ways in which business people, sports stars, and others in the public limelight do. Teachers help bring into being environments in which intellectual and moral growth can occur, but, as the literature has established, that process is painstaking, unpredictable, and emergent only over time. There remains much to learn about this process as it unfolds at all levels of the educational system.

Research and Moral Memory

Dewey's sobering words about the pace of events perhaps ring truer today than when he wrote them years ago. They suggest another potential value of research on the moral dimensions of teaching: to assist the educational community in remembering what it knows but too often loses sight of in the rush of events. Surely even the most hard-nosed efficiency expert knows that the moral is real and that it points to our deepest human needs for meaning and for purpose. But that expert may have lost sight of such facts and may have forgotten languages in which to keep them articulate and in view. This oversight underscores the importance in educational life of reanimating what may have become stilled.

Murdoch describes moral philosophy as a "movement of return." It must, she writes, "keep trying to return to the beginning: a thing which it is not at all easy to do" (1970/1985, p. 1). Murdoch does not mean an historical beginning, rather she means that the process obliges us to engage our most fundamental understandings and assumptions about the moral. Similarly, research on teaching as a moral endeavor can also be understood as a return: an attempt to discern and to better understand what resides at the heart of the practice. Such a return appears to have become progressively more difficult in our era. Educators everywhere at all levels of the system seem to feel the press of countless and immediate concerns. These seem to pile up like people and vehicles at an enormous traffic jam in which nobody can any longer see the road or the direction to take. Perhaps there has never been a greater need for research that seeks to spotlight enduring aspects of educational work, those that constitute the very reasons for performing such work in the first place. As we have seen, the idea of teaching as a moral activity captures many of these aspects. Keeping the idea in view in a sharp and lucid manner remains an important task of both research and practice. It is a potentially vast undertaking having more to do with recovery, recollection, and remembrance than with the discovery of brand-new knowledge. However, what is recovered or remembered are not moral protocols or blueprints from days of yore but, rather, moral understandings—such as the fact that there are no such blueprints for a teacher to rely upon. Each day, each class, and each student presents a distinctive challenge and set of demands on the teacher's intellectual and moral sensibility. The literature reviewed in this chapter suggests that as long as educators care about teaching, they will have reason to study, to ponder, and to bring to life its moral meaning.

REFERENCES

Applebaum, B. (1995). Creating a trusting atmosphere in the classroom. *Educational Theory, 45*(4), 443–452.

Aristotle. *Nicomachean ethics* (M. Ostwald, Trans.). New York: Library of Liberal Arts. 1962.

Arnold, P. J. (1997). *Sport, ethics and education.* London: Cassell.

Audi, R. (Ed.). (1995). *The Cambridge dictionary of philosophy.* Cambridge, UK: Cambridge University Press.

Aurin, K., & Maurer, M. (1993). Forms and dimensions of teachers' professional ethics—Case studies in secondary schools. *Journal of Moral Education, 22*(3), 277–296.

Ball, D. L., & Wilson, S. M. (1996). Integrity in teaching: Recognizing the fusion of the moral and intellectual. *American Educational Research Journal, 33*(1), 155–192.

Banner, Jr., J. M., & Cannon, H. C. (1997). *The elements of teaching.* New Haven, CT: Yale University Press.

Barcena, F., Gil, F., & Jover, G. (1993). The ethical dimension of teaching: A review and a proposal. *Journal of Moral Education, 22*(3), 241–252.

Barrow, R. (1992). Is teaching an essentially moral enterprise? *Teaching and Teacher Education, 8*(1), 105–108.

Bator, M. G. (1997). *Identifying the good in teaching.* Unpublished doctoral dissertation, University of Illinois at Chicago.

Ben-Peretz, M. (1995). *Learning from experience: Memory and the teacher's account of teaching.* Albany, NY: State University of New York Press.

Bergem, T. (1990). The teacher as moral agent. *Journal of Moral Education, 19*(2), 88–100.

Bernstein, R. J. (1983). *Beyond objectivism and relativism.* Philadelphia: University of Pennsylvania Press.

Blum, L. A. (1994). *Moral perception and particularity.* Cambridge, UK: Cambridge University Press.

Boostrom, R. (1991). The nature and functions of classroom rules. *Curriculum Inquiry, 21*(2), 193–216.

Boostrom, R. (1994). Learning to pay attention. *Qualitative Studies in Education, 7*(1), 51–64.

Boostrom, R., Hansen, D. T., & Jackson, P. W. (1993). Coming together and staying apart: How a group of teachers and researchers sought to bridge the "research-practice gap." *Teachers College Record, 95*(1), 35–44.

Bricker, D.C. (1993). Character and moral reasoning: An Aristotelian perspective. In K. A. Strike & P. L. Ternasky (Eds.), *Ethics for professionals in education* (pp. 13–26). New York: Teachers College Press.

Broudy, H. S. (1963). Historic exemplars of teaching method. In N. L. Gage (Ed.), *Handbook of research on teaching* (pp. 1–43). Chicago: Rand McNally.

Buchmann, M. (1989). The careful vision: How practical is contemplation in teaching? *American Journal of Education, 98,* 35–61.

Buchmann, M., & Floden, R. E. (1993). *Detachment and concern: Conversations in the philosophy of teaching and teacher education.* New York: Teachers College Press.

Campbell, E. C. (1992). *Personal morals and organizational ethics: How teachers and principals cope with conflicting values in the context of school cultures.* Unpublished doctoral dissertation, University of Toronto.

Carr, D. (1992). Practical enquiry, values and the problem of educational theory. *Oxford Review of Education, 18*(3), 241–251.

Clark, C. (1990). The teacher and the taught: Moral transactions in the classroom. In J. I. Goodlad, R. Soder, & K. A. Sirotnik (Eds.), *The moral dimensions of teaching* (pp. 251–265). San Francisco: Jossey-Bass.

Cohen, R. M. (1991). *A lifetime of teaching: Portraits of five veteran high school teachers.* New York: Teachers College Press.

Colnerud, G. (1997). Ethical conflicts in teaching. *Teaching and Teacher Education, 13*(6), 627–635.

Court, D. J. (1989). *Questions of value: An inquiry into the nature of research on teacher thinking.* Unpublished doctoral dissertation, University of British Columbia.

Cox, E. (1982). The moral stance of the teacher. *Journal of Moral Education, 11*(2), 75–81.

Cutforth, N. (1994). *The place of physical education in schooling: An ethnographic study of an urban elementary school.* Unpublished doctoral dissertation, University of Illinois at Chicago.

Dewey, J. (1929). Events and meanings. In *Characters and events* (Vol. 1, pp. 125–129). New York: Henry Holt and Company.

Dewey, J. (1933). *How we think.* Lexington, MA: D.C. Heath & Company.

Dewey. J. (1958). *Experience and nature.* New York: Dover. (Original work published 1925)

Dewey, J. (1963). *Experience and education.* New York: Macmillan. (Original work published 1938)

Dewey, J. (1974a). My pedagogic creed. In R. D. Archambault (Ed.), *John Dewey on education* (pp. 427–439). Chicago: University of Chicago Press. (Original work published 1897)

Dewey, J. (1974b). The relation of theory to practice in education. In R. D. Archambault (Ed.), *John Dewey on education* (pp. 313–338). Chicago: University of Chicago Press. (Original work published 1904)

Dewey, J. (1975). *Moral principles in education.* Carbondale, IL: Southern Illinois University Press. (Original work published 1909)

Dewey, J. (1989). Theory of the moral life. In J. A. Boydston (Ed.), *John Dewey: The later works, 1925–1953* (Vol. 7, pp. 159–310). Carbondale, IL: Southern Illinois University Press. (Original work published 1932)

Dewey, J. (1997). *Democracy and education.* New York: The Free Press. (Original work published 1916)

Duval, J. H. (1990). *Dedication/commitment: A study of their relationship to teaching excellence.* Unpublished doctoral dissertation, University of Vermont.

Elbaz, F. (1992). Hope, attentiveness, and caring for difference: The moral voice in teaching. *Teaching and Teacher Education, 8*(5/6), 421–432.

Emerson, R. W. (1983). Self-reliance. In *Essays and lectures* (pp. 257–282). New York: Library of America. (Original work published 1841)

Fenstermacher, G. D. (1990). Some moral considerations on teaching as a profession. In J. I. Goodlad, R. Soder, & K. A. Sirotnik (Eds.), *The moral dimensions of teaching* (pp. 130–154). San Francisco: Jossey-Bass.

Fenstermacher, G. D. (1992). The concepts of method and manner in teaching. In F. K. Oser, A. Dick, & J.-L. Patry (Eds.), *Effective and responsible teaching: The new synthesis* (pp. 95–108). San Francisco: Jossey-Bass.

Fenstermacher, G. D. (1994a). The knower and the known: The nature of knowledge in research on teaching. In L. Darling-Hammond (Ed.), *Review of Research in Education, 20,* 3–56.

Fenstermacher, G. D. (1994b). On the virtues of van Manen's argument: A response to "Pedagogy, virtue, and narrative identity in teaching." *Curriculum Inquiry, 24*(2), 215–220.

Gadamer, H.-G. (1980). *Dialogue and dialectic: Eight hermeneutical studies on Plato* (P. C. Smith, Trans.). New Haven, CT: Yale University Press.

Garrison, J. (1997). *Dewey and eros: Wisdom and desire in the art of teaching.* New York: Teachers College Press.

Geertz, C. (1973). *The interpretation of cultures.* New York: Basic Books.

Geertz, C. (1983). *Local knowledge.* New York: Basic Books.

Goodlad, J. I., Soder, R., & Sirotnik, K. A. (Eds.). (1990). *The moral dimensions of teaching.* San Francisco: Jossey-Bass.

Green, T. F. (1971). *The activities of teaching.* New York: McGraw-Hill.

Green, T. F. (1984). The formation of conscience in an age of technology. *American Journal of Education, 94*(1), 1–33.

Greene, M. (1986). Philosophy and teaching. In M. C. Wittrock, *Hand-*

book of research on teaching (3rd ed., pp. 479–501). New York: Macmillan.

Grimmett, P. P., & MacKinnon, A. M. (1992). Craft knowledge and the education of teachers. In G. Grant (Ed.), *Review of Research in Education, 18,* 385–456.

Gudmundsdóttir, S. (1990). Values in pedagogical content knowledge. *Journal of Teacher Education, 41*(3), 44–52.

Haan, N., Bellah, R. N., Rabinow, P., & Sullivan, W. M. (Eds.). (1983). *Social science as moral inquiry.* New York: Columbia University Press.

Hamilton, E., & Cairns, H. (Eds.). (1961). *The collected dialogues of Plato.* Princeton: Princeton University Press.

Hansen, D. T. (1989). Getting down to business: The moral significance of classroom beginnings. *Anthropology and Education Quarterly, 20*(4), 259–274.

Hansen, D. T. (1992). The emergence of a shared morality in a classroom. *Curriculum Inquiry, 22*(4), 345–361.

Hansen, D. T. (1993a). From role to person: The moral layeredness of classroom teaching. *American Educational Research Journal, 30*(4), 651–674.

Hansen, D. T. (1993b). The moral importance of the teacher's style. *Journal of Curriculum Studies, 25*(5), 397–421.

Hansen, D. T. (1995). *The call to teach.* New York: Teachers College Press.

Hansen, D. T., Boostrom, R. E., & Jackson, P. W. (1994). The teacher as moral model. *Kappa Delta Pi Record, 31*(1), 24–29.

Hayes, C. B., Ryan, A., & Zseller, E. B. (1994). The middle school child's perceptions of caring teachers. *American Journal of Education, 103*(1), 1–19.

Herman, B. (1993). *The practice of moral judgment.* Cambridge, MA: Harvard University Press.

Higgins, A. (1995). Teaching as a moral activity: Listening to teachers in Russia and the United States. *Journal of Moral Education, 24*(2), 143–158.

Hirst, P. H. (1973). What is teaching? In R. S. Peters (Ed.), *The philosophy of education* (pp. 163–177). Oxford, UK: Oxford University Press.

Hostetler, K. D. (1997). *Ethical judgment in teaching.* Boston: Allyn & Bacon.

Jackson, P. W. (1968). *Life in classrooms.* New York: Holt, Rinehart, & Winston.

Jackson, P. W. (1986). *The practice of teaching.* New York: Teachers College Press.

Jackson, P. W. (1990). The functions of educational research. *Educational Researcher, 19*(7), 3–9.

Jackson, P. W. (1992). *Untaught lessons.* New York: Teachers College Press.

Jackson, P. W., Boostrom, R. E., & Hansen, D. T. (1993). *The moral life of schools.* San Francisco: Jossey-Bass.

Jaspers, K. (1962). *Socrates, Buddha, Confucius, Jesus* (R. Mannheim, Trans.). New York: Harcourt Brace. (Original work published 1957)

Joseph, P. B., & Efron, S. (1993). Moral choices/moral conflicts: Teachers' self-perceptions. *Journal of Moral Education, 22*(3), 201–220.

Kant, I. (1960). *Education* (A. Churton, Trans.). Ann Arbor, MI: University of Michigan Press. (Original work presented as a lecture in 1795).

Kant, I. (1990). *Foundations of the metaphysics of morals* (L. W. Beck, Trans.). Englewood Cliffs, NJ: Prentice Hall. (Original work published 1785)

Kerr, D. (1987). Authority and responsibility in public schooling. In J. Goodlad (Ed.), *The ecology of school renewal* (86th Yearbook of the National Society for the Study of Education, pp. 20–40). Chicago: University of Chicago Press.

Korsgaard, C. M. (1996). *Creating the kingdom of ends.* Cambridge, UK: Cambridge University Press.

Kozolanka, K., & Olson, J. (1994). Life after school: How science and technology teachers construe capability. *International Journal of Technology and Design Education, 4*(3), 209–226.

Lampert, M. (1990). When the problem is not the question and the solution is not the answer: Mathematical knowing and teaching. *American Educational Research Journal, 27*(1), 29–63.

Loukes, H. (1976). Morality and the education of the teacher. *Oxford Review of Education, 2*(2), 139–147.

Lyons, N. (1990). Dilemmas of knowing: Ethical and epistemological dimensions of teachers' work and development. *Harvard Educational Review, 60*(2), 159–180.

MacIntyre, A. (1984). *After virtue* (2nd ed.). Notre Dame, IN: University of Notre Dame Press.

Malen, B., Ogawa, R. T., & Kranz, J. (1990). What do we know about school-based management? A case study of the literature—A call for research. In W. H. Clune & J. F. Witte (Eds.), *Choice and control in American education* (Vol. 2, pp. 289–342). New York: Falmer Press.

McEwan, A. E. (1994). *The moral possibilities in teaching: Teachers' voices.* Unpublished doctoral dissertation, Florida State University.

Midgley, M. (1991). *Can't we make moral judgements?* New York: St. Martin's.

Mounce, H. O. (1973). Philosophy and education. *The Human World, 13,* 11–20.

Murdoch, I. (1985). *The sovereignty of good.* London: Ark. (Original work published 1970)

Noddings, N. (1984). *Caring: A feminine approach to ethics and moral education.* Berkeley, CA: University of California Press.

Nussbaum, M. C. (1986). *The fragility of goodness.* Cambridge, UK: Cambridge University Press.

Nussbaum, M. C. (1990). *Love's knowledge.* Oxford, UK: Oxford University Press.

Oakeshott, M. (1989). Learning and teaching. In T. Fuller (Ed.), *The voice of liberal learning: Michael Oakeshott on education* (pp. 43–62). New Haven, CT: Yale University Press. (Original work published 1965)

Oakeshott, M. (1991). The tower of Babel. In M. Oakeshott, *Rationalism in politics and other essays* (expanded ed., pp. 465–487). Indianapolis: LibertyPress. (Original work published 1962)

Oakeshott, M. (1993). Religion and the moral life. In T. Fuller (Ed.), *Michael Oakeshott: Religion, politics and the moral life* (pp. 39–45). New Haven, CT: Yale University Press. (Original work published 1927)

Olson, J. (1992). *Understanding teaching: Beyond expertise.* Milton Keynes, England: Open University Press.

Oser, F. K. (1986). Moral education and values education: The discourse perspective. In M. C. Wittrock (Ed.), *Handbook of research on teaching* (3rd ed., pp. 917–941). New York: Macmillan.

Oser, F. K. (1994). Moral perspectives on teaching. In L. Darling-Hammond (Ed.), *Review of Research in Education, 20,* 57–127.

Oser, F. K, Dick, A., & Patry, J.-L. (Eds.). (1992). *Effective and responsible teaching: The new synthesis.* San Francisco: Jossey-Bass.

Pendlebury, S. (1990). Practical arguments and situational appreciation in teaching. *Educational Theory, 40*(2),171–179.

Peters, R. S. (1964). *Education as initiation.* London: Evans Brothers.

Peters, R. S. (1968). Must an educator have an aim? In C. J. B. Macmillan and T. W. Nelson (Eds.), *Concepts of teaching: Philosophical essays* (pp. 89–98). Chicago: Rand McNally. (Original work published 1963)

Peters, R. S. (1981). *Essays on educators.* London: Allen & Unwin.

Philips, D. Z. (1979). Is moral education really necessary? *British Journal of Educational Studies, 27*(1), 42–56.

Polanyi, M. (1962). *Personal knowledge.* Chicago: University of Chicago Press.

Rabinow, P., & Sullivan, W. M. (1979). *Interpretive social science: A reader.* Berkeley, CA: University of California Press.

Rawls, J. (1971). *A theory of justice.* Cambridge, MA: Harvard University Press.

Rosenholtz, S. J. (1989). *Teachers' workplace: The social organization of schools.* New York: Longman.

Scheffler, I. (1968). The concept of teaching. In C. J. B. Macmillan and T. W. Nelson (Eds.), *Concepts of teaching: Philosophical essays* (pp. 17–27). Chicago: Rand McNally. (Original work published in 1960).

Schultz, D. R. (1997). *Toward wisdom in practice: A study of teachers' pedagogic judgments.* Unpublished doctoral dissertation, University of Illinois at Chicago.

Schwartz, G., Merten, D., and Bursik, R. J., Jr. (1987). Teaching styles and performance values in junior high school: The impersonal, nonpersonal, and personal. *American Journal of Education, 95*(2), 346–370.

Sherman, N. (1997). *Making a necessity of virtue: Aristotle and Kant on virtue.* Cambridge, UK: Cambridge University Press.

Shulman, L. S. (1988). Disciplines of inquiry in education: An overview. In R. J. Jaeger (Ed.), *Complementary methods for research in education* (pp. 3–20). Washington, DC: American Educational Research Association.

Simpson, P. J., & Garrison, J. (1995). Teaching and moral perception. *Teachers College Record, 97*(2), 252–278.

Smylie, M. A. (1994). Redesigning teachers' work: Connections in the classroom. In L. Darling-Hammond (Ed.), *Review of Research in Education, 20,* 129–177.

Sockett, H. (1988). Education and will: Aspects of personal capability. *American Journal of Education, 96*(2), 195–214.

Sockett, H. (1992) The moral aspects of the curriculum. In P. W. Jackson (Ed.), *Handbook of research on curriculum* (pp. 543–569). New York: Macmillan.

Sockett, H. (1993). *The moral base for teacher professionalism.* New York: Teachers College Press.

Soder, R. (1990). The rhetoric of teacher professionalization. In J. I. Goodlad, R. Soder, & K. A. Sirotnik (Eds.), *The moral dimensions of teaching* (pp. 35–86). San Francisco: Jossey-Bass.

Stengel, B. S., & Tom, A. R. (1995). Taking the moral nature of teaching seriously. *The Educational Forum, 59*(2), 154–163.

Stott, L. J. (1988). *Essays in philosophy and education.* Lanham, MD: University Press of America..

Strike, K. A. (1990). The legal and moral responsibility of teachers. In J. I. Goodlad, R. Soder, & K. A. Sirotnik (Eds.), *The moral dimensions of teaching* (pp. 188–223). San Francisco: Jossey-Bass.

Strike, K. A. (1991). The moral role of schooling in a liberal democratic society. In G. Grant (Ed.), *Review of Research in Education, 17,* 413–483.

Strike, K. A., & Soltis, J. F. (1985). *The ethics of teaching.* New York: Teachers College Press.

Strike, K. A., & Ternasky, P. L. (Eds.). (1993). *Ethics for professionals in education.* New York: Teachers College Press.

Stutz, C. K. (1995). *"The soul of life": Literature, moral awareness, and teaching.* Unpublished doctoral dissertation, Boston University.

Taylor, C. (1985). *Philosophical papers, II: Philosophy and the human sciences.* Cambridge, England: Cambridge University Press.

Taylor, C. (1989). *Sources of the self: The making of the modern identity.* Cambridge, MA: Harvard University Press.

Tom, A. (1984). *Teaching as a moral craft.* New York: Longman.

Uhrmacher, P. B. (1993a). "Coming to know the world through Waldorf education." *Journal of Curriculum and Supervision, 9,* 87–104.

Uhrmacher, P. B. (1993b). Making contact: An exploration of focused attention between teacher and students. *Curriculum Inquiry, 23*(4), 433–444.

Valli, L. (1990). Moral approaches to reflective practice. In R. T. Clift, W. R. Houston, & M. C. Pugach (Eds.), *Encouraging reflective practice in education* (pp. 39–56). New York: Teachers College Press.

Van Manen, M. (1991a). Reflectivity and the pedagogical moment: The normativity of pedagogical thinking and acting. *Journal of Curriculum Studies, 23*(6), 507–536.

Van Manen, M. (1991b). *The tact of teaching: The meaning of pedagogical thoughtfulness.* Albany, NY: State University of New York Press.

Van Manen, M. (1994). Pedagogy, virtue, and narrative identity in teaching. *Curriculum Inquiry, 24*(2), 135–170.

Vlastos, G. (1991). *Socrates: Ironist and moral philosopher.* Ithaca, NY: Cornell University Press.

Waller, W. (1932). *The sociology of teaching.* New York: Wiley.

Welker, R. (1992). *The teacher as expert: A theoretical and philosophical examination.* Albany, NY: State University of New York Press.

White, R. T. (1992). "Raising the quality of learning: Principles from long-term action research." In F. K. Oser, A. Dick, & J.-L. Patry (Eds.), *Effective and responsible teaching: The new synthesis* (pp. 50–65). San Francisco: Jossey-Bass.

Wittgenstein, L. (1953). *Philosophical investigations* (3rd ed., G.E.M. Anscombe, Trans.). New York: Macmillan.

41.

The Power of Collective Action: A Century of Teachers Organizing for Education

Susan Moore Johnson and Katherine C. Boles
Harvard Graduate School of Education

Educational researchers disagree about many things, but they concur that teachers' work is isolated and isolating (Lortie, 1975; Rosenholtz, 1989; Fullan, 1991; Johnson, 1990; Wasley, 1991; Huberman, 1993). The egg-crate structure of the school, large classes and heavy teaching loads, a daily schedule that includes little noninstructional time, and norms that discourage collegial interaction all combine to separate teachers from their peers. Notable by contrast, therefore, are the instances in which teachers work collectively and purposefully, reaching beyond their individual classrooms to address issues of professional policy and practice.

The best-known examples of teachers' collective action are teachers' unions, those professional organizations, such as the American Federation of Teachers (AFT) and the National Education Association (NEA), that represent teachers' interests in state legislatures and at local bargaining tables. Recently, other groups promoting teachers' collective action—teacher networks, teacher research groups, and professional development schools—have gained the attention of teachers, the public, and researchers. Many observers of education regard these emerging groups as totally different from, and sometimes in contention with, teachers' unions. However, they are not as unrelated as they seem. Many similarities in the issues and themes emerge when teachers act together. It is informative, therefore, to review the research on teachers' collective action within a broad historical context, one that reaches back to teachers' experiences before the beginning of the 20th century and that looks forward to consider where teachers' collective action might head as educators enter the 21st century.

Whatever methods researchers use—whether they study historical documents, administer surveys, analyze large data sets, or conduct field studies—similar sets of tensions emerge in the conception and implementation of such teacher initiatives. First, there is the tension that exists between teachers organizing to advance their own self-interest and teachers organizing on behalf of children. Are these purposes different and incompatible, or, as many activists argue, are these purposes one and the same? Is what's good for teachers really good for kids? Second, there is a tension between teachers allying to address narrowly defined issues of curriculum and pedagogy or allying to address broader issues of educational governance and social change. Do teachers' collective responsibilities range widely or should they be confined to the classroom and school? Third, there is tension between the image of the unionized teacher affiliated with laborers' concerns and the image of the professional teacher, whose identity rests with independent professionals, such as lawyers and doctors.

There is a fourth tension apparent in the literature that is linked to the demographics of public education and that poses the concerns of women teachers in opposition to the interests of educational authorities, who, historically, have been men. And, finally, there is a tension between the conservative culture of schools (Sarason, 1971)—which discourages teacher-teacher and administrator-teacher collaboration, denigrates self-declared teacher leaders, and reinforces the isolation of teachers in their classrooms—and the political and organizational demands that teachers act assertively to build relationships beyond teaching, demands that inevitably emerge when teachers work together to improve education.

This review traces research about teachers' collective action from the early days of teacher activists such as Maggie Haley and the school councils she and her peers introduced in the

---

The authors wish to thank research assistants, Joanne Marshall and Jessica Evans, Harvard University, and reviewers, Sharon Feiman-Nemser, Michigan State University, and Patricia Wasley, University of Washington.

early 1900s, through the development of collective bargaining in the 1960s and 1970s, on to the organized professional reform movement in the late 1980s, and finally to the teacher networks and professional development schools developing today. Throughout this review, we consider how the tensions identified above as being inherent in teachers' collective action have shaped both practice and research about practice.[1]

Early Activists

Early teacher activists were simultaneously classroom teachers, feminists, and union leaders who believed that aggressively advancing the interests of teachers, most of whom were women, would inevitably improve the lot of children. These reformers saw no conflict between union goals and educational purposes and, in fact, believed that progress on one front required simultaneous progress on the other. Examining the writings of these key women organizers in *Women's "True" Profession* (1981), Nancy Hoffman observed that, although nearly 82% of urban teachers were women in 1900, "they had almost no power over working conditions, school governance, or program" (p. 212). The challenge for reformers, therefore, was great.

Unquestionably, the most influential teacher organizer early in the century was Maggie Haley, an experienced classroom teacher of 20 years and leader of the Chicago Federation of Teachers (CFT), founded in 1897. Haley did not distinguish between improving the lot of teachers and improving the education of children as she entreated teachers to "take up the knapsack of service" (Reid, 1982, p. x) while striving to improve teachers' salaries and working conditions. Haley allied with Catherine Goggin, president of the CFT, and

> forced the state supreme court to wrest unpaid taxes from five public utility companies—money, they argued, that should have gone for teachers' raises. Subsequently, they took the Board of Education to court and won, after it earmarked the back taxes for school maintenance, not salaries. Haley also won a tenure law, a pension plan, and a system of teachers' councils with some powers over curriculum and discipline." (Hoffman, 1981, p. 215)

David Tyack (1974) noted that in cities such as Chicago only about 2% of the elementary teachers were men at the turn of the century (p. 61). Reid reported that "significantly higher percentages of men were found in the high school classrooms and the administrative ranks. The result of this pattern of staffing was that a disproportionate number of men held the jobs that provided both higher pay and higher status. Women in the schools were expected to play a subordinate role, similar to that found in the society at large outside the schools" (Reid, 1982, p. xxii).

Notably, Haley's CFT excluded administrators and limited its membership to elementary school teachers, making it almost exclusively a women's organization. Thus, she sought to advance the causes of women teachers and public education si-

multaneously. Reid noted that "the federation was a purposive organization which recognized the material needs of its members. A secure pension system, tenure, and improved salaries were the necessary conditions to meet the organization's primary objective: to raise the standard of the teaching profession" (Reid, 1982, p. x).

Not everyone thought these teacher leaders' goals and tactics were appropriate for women or professionals; Kerchner and Mitchell (1988) described the "widespread popular belief" that it was illegitimate for teachers to organize on behalf of causes that would benefit them, such as higher wages or better working conditions (p. 56). In 1916, when the Chicago Board of Education denied the CFT the right to affiliate with a trade union and fired 68 teachers, including all the officers of the CFT, "the board majority portrayed Haley and her associates as 'lady labor sluggers,' and in so doing conveyed the image that these foes of entrenched privilege themselves served a 'special interest' detrimental to the public good" (Reid, 1982, p. xvii).

Later in 1916, seven other teacher groups that emerged in Chicago, including the comparatively small Chicago Federation of Men Teachers, allied to form "the American Federation of Teachers, with the Chicago Federation of Teachers being chartered as Local Number One" (Reid, 1982, p. xxvii). In contrast to AFT ideology, which coupled concerns about teacher welfare and educational improvement, Wesley (1980) reported that the National Teachers Association, precursor of the NEA, was formed in Philadelphia 1857 "to elevate the character and advance the interests of the profession of teaching, and to promote the cause of professional education in the United States" (pp. 22–23). For NEA leaders, building the profession took precedence over addressing teachers' personal and professional problems. They believed, according to Wesley, that once the profession was established, "teachers would naturally achieve status, security, and dignity" (p. 23).

Ella Flagg Young, district superintendent of Chicago and an advocate of teachers' rights, served as NEA president in 1910. Although this might suggest that women had substantial influence in the NEA, Kerchner and Mitchell (1988) reported that the NEA presidency "was substantially honorific in character during those years. The real power was held by the 'natural aristocracy' of college deans, presidents, and professors—a group which was predominately male and intensely conservative in its view" (p. 56). Murphy (1990) painted a similar picture of male dominance in the NEA but went on to describe how women challenged this order:

> The women proposed their own vision of education that was based on experience in the classroom as opposed to university credit; they thought that knowing the community was more important than satisfying the top administrative personnel. In the beginning, the women did not regard their battle as being particularly feminist; instead they modeled their cry for human dignity on the example set by the trade unions. Eventually, however, as the educational stage became more contested, they responded more self-consciously as

---

[1] Although there is much to be learned from considering this story of U.S. teachers' collective action in a broader international context, that analysis is beyond the scope of this paper. Notably, however, although many of the same themes emerge in the literature of other countries, the unique context of public education in the United States (its decentralized governance and funding resulting from traditions of local control) make this a unique story.

working women and identified the inherent sexism in the educational establishment. (p. 53)

Therefore, from the perspective of teachers, particularly women teachers, the NEA remained an organization apart during the early 1900s, paying little attention to their professional concerns and aspirations.

Teachers' Councils

Reid observed that little attention was given nationwide to the role of teachers during the early years of the 20th century. In part, this was because the efficiency movement focused attention on administrative practice and dismissed the notion that teachers could take a role in improving the profession. In Chicago, however, "educators such as Francis W. Parker of the Cook County Normal School and John Dewey at the University of Chicago made this issue [of the teacher's role] a topic of concern" and recommended that Chicago establish a "system of representation through teachers' councils from building to district to central system" (1982, p. xvii).

Teachers' councils, established from 1895 to 1935 in "at least 157 school systems in such cities as New York, Atlanta, San Francisco, Boston, and Washington, D.C.," were designed to give teachers a say in decisions about policy and practice (Tegnell, 1994, p. 1). Tegnell wrote that "these organizations met on a regular basis, sometimes over decades, to consider issues of teacher concern such as tenure, curriculum development, and school construction programs" (p. 1). To many, the promise of these councils was great: "Indeed, many advocates of the stature of Charles W. Eliot and John Dewey believed that the teachers' council movement would transform American school decision making by institutionalizing teacher collaboration in educational administration" (p. 1).

However, much of the potential of teacher councils rested in the control of the men who administered school districts and headed local school boards. Historian Wayne Urban (1982) contended that, in the midst of the influence of administrative reformers who sought to centralize school governance, these councils had little power. Albert Bushnell Hart, a Harvard historian and member of the NEA's Committee of Ten, proposed a teachers' association and council in Cambridge, Massachusetts, in 1894, but it was ignored by the school committee of which he was a member, and the proposal died (Urban, pp. 35–36).

In Chicago, however, similar proposals in 1913 for councils took a different turn, largely because of "allegiance to District Superintendent Ella Flagg Young, who had introduced councils in her district" (Urban, 1982, p. 42). Notably, Young had been one of Dewey's doctoral students and then had become the "leading theorist" in the CFT's efforts to oppose the efficiency movement and to establish teachers' councils throughout the district (Reid, 1982, p. xxvi). Having risen through the ranks of teachers and administrators to become superintendent of Chicago's schools, Young instituted a two-tiered system of councils in 1920 that diminished the influence of principals and brought teacher representatives of subgroups of schools to meet directly with the superintendent (Tegnell, 1994, p. 52). Tegnell reported that the elementary Teachers General Council, which took on many of the issues championed by Haley and the CFT, "made

resolutions upgrading the entry requirements into teaching, protesting employment of unqualified substitute teachers, arguing for equal pay for equal training, requesting more access to teacher education opportunities, and attempting to take more control over curriculum development (p. 57). The Chicago councils enjoyed broad-based support and continued through the 1920s, with the last teachers' council, the Teachers' Section of the Superintendent's Advisory Council in Chicago, meeting from 1929 to 1933 (pp. 3–4).

In Atlanta, the school board established four "advisory faculties" in 1897 "using an argument that echoed the views of teachers' council advocates like A. B. Hart and Ella Flagg Young" (Urban, 1982, p. 48). But the Atlanta superintendent opposed them, and Urban reported that the advisory faculties had no impact. He observed, however, that, although councils were initially opposed by superintendents who feared the challenge they posed to their authority, after World War I, the NEA, which was controlled by administrators, "looked favorably at the idea of councils" in its "drive to keep teachers out of unions," and "local superintendents also moved to establish councils during and after the war" (p. 159).

Urban was skeptical about the impact of teachers' councils, noting that, even when superintendents established councils, the administrators did not intend to use them to empower teachers. He reported that Minneapolis's Frank G. Spaulding "astutely used the council to siphon off discontent, respond with a flourish to those issues which he could handle, and thwart the development of independent initiatives by teachers" (1982, p. 160). By contrast, Tegnell assessed the councils' records positively, seeing in these efforts more evidence of teachers' collective action than administrators' control. He argued that the Teachers' Section in Chicago "was not a fundamentally top-down entity" (1994, p. 12) but that it "did indeed respond to grassroots teacher concerns, consider important school issues, and foster teacher development in organizational, policymaking and leadership skills" (p. 4). Tegnell concluded that "the 1919–1924 councils were not a bureaucratic co-optation of teachers, as Urban alleged, but rather a political concession to teachers," teachers influenced by the leadership of Maggie Haley (p. 52).

Expansion of Teacher Organizations

The CFT provided the inspiration and design for teacher organizations throughout the country. The success of the CFT, Reid noted, "inspired other groups. Women grade teachers in urban areas throughout the country, from Boston to Los Angeles and St. Paul to Atlanta, modeled their organizations along its lines, but without labor affiliation. As an invited speaker and by correspondence, Haley helped to bring the story of the CFT to the women teachers of the nation" (1982, p. xxv).

In New York City, Kate Hogan, a seventh-grade teacher, organized the Interborough Association of Women Teachers (IAWT), which was then led by District Superintendent Grace Strachan, head of its executive committee. Like the CFT, the IAWT focused on the salaries of elementary school teachers, the lowest paid women in the system—and fought for equal pay for equal work (Hoffman, 1981, p. 215). Subsequently, as district superintendent, Strachan angered the local board of education when she took her case to the state legislature in Albany, but her efforts led to a law that granted women equal pay.

Throughout these early years of teacher organizing, teacher leaders in predominantly female teacher federations saw no conflict between union membership and the purest of educational purposes. Collective action on behalf of children and union action on behalf of teachers were seen to be fully compatible. By contrast, within the NEA, efforts to improve teachers' welfare and public education were treated as separate and not necessarily mutually reinforcing. Members self-consciously emphasized that they were professional members of an education association, rather than members of a teachers' union. And as Eaton (1975) observed in his study of the NEA, "the role of the classroom teacher, and more specifically the woman, was limited to listening" (p. 10).

Growth of Teacher Unionism

Between 1920 and 1962, when the first major collective bargaining agreement was negotiated in New York City (Cresswell & Murphy, 1980, p. 52), the NEA grew rapidly, "spurred by an effective membership campaign" (Reid, 1982, p. xxx), which Urban dubbed "an open anti-AFT offensive" (1982, p. 606). "Membership expanded from about 8,500 in 1917 to more than 141,000 in 1927 and 200,000 by 1940" (Kerchner & Mitchell, 1988, p. 59). "The AFT," Reid reported, "also experienced a strong burst of union activity after World War I before going into precipitous decline during the 1920s" (p. xxx). Kerchner and Mitchell reported that by 1920 "the total [AFT] membership was 10,000" (p. 57).

Kerchner and Mitchell judged the NEA to have been "among the primary instruments for defining teaching from the 1920s to the 1950s" (1988, p. 59). The organization of the NEA, which mirrored school districts in its hierarchical structure, "included everybody in public education: teachers, superintendents, and the university educationists. The teachers, of course, represented the vast majority of the members. . . . But control over the organization, and thus over the profession, was placed in the hands of male superintendents" (p. 59).

By the mid-1960s, however, attention in the NEA had shifted to the concerns of teachers, and collective bargaining had gained credibility as a legitimate lever of influence. West (1975), who documented this "dramatic change in the NEA," attributed that development to a variety of factors, including: "changes in the teaching staff, changes in the school districts, the failure of local and state governments to respond to school needs, the impact of the civil rights revolution, President Kennedy's Executive Order 10988 [authorizing collective bargaining for federal employees], the urban crisis, the New York collective-bargaining election, and new public expectations of the public schools." (p. 28) By contrast, Eaton (1975) argued that "the new spirit of activism" in the 1960s favored the AFT and was

divisive for the NEA. A growing discontent among classroom teachers within the NEA surfaced. The result was internal feuding, political manipulation, and general confusion. . . . This new spirit of activism was ready-made for the AFT. The time was ripe for new organizational efforts. The times had finally caught up with the philosophy of the teachers' union. By 1972, the AFT had nearly 250,000 teachers as members. This represented about 12% of the 2,063,000 teachers in America, and the membership was growing. (p. 194)

Historical analyses such as these document how the AFT and NEA influenced each other's priorities and approaches. The AFT had successfully convinced teachers that the union could focus simultaneously on concerns of teacher welfare and educational improvement. In response to AFT expansion and success at the bargaining table in New York City, the NEA dropped its opposition to collective bargaining and adopted a more militant, proteacher stance (Johnson, 1986, p. 606). The NEA changed, West concluded, "as a matter of survival" (1975, p. 38).

Why Did Teachers Unionize?

While historians have studied the origins and development of teachers' unions, sociologists and political scientists have examined why teachers unionized and which teachers have supported militant activities. Notably, however, these patterns of militancy during the 1960s and 1970s, in which male high school teachers took the lead, contrast with those of 1900–1920, when men's voices were rarely heard and women elementary teachers boldly confronted authorities on behalf of teaching and teachers. Murphy observed that "the most dramatic structural change in the teaching industry between 1954 and 1964 was the 94% growth of the number of male schoolteachers compared with the 38% growth of female teachers in the same period." She reported that "in 1951 men were only 21.3% of classroom teachers, whereas in 1964 they were 31.4%" (1990, p. 220). Murphy noted that most of these young, male teachers entered the high schools, where they joined the union, demanded higher wages, and withheld support for elementary teachers' pursuit of a single-salary scale.

Rosenthal (1969) studied patterns of union membership in Boston and New York during the mid-1960s and found that, although male teachers were more likely than female teachers to join unions, all teachers were more likely to join unions in predominantly male schools than in predominantly female schools. Winick (1963) studied New York City teachers' support for the 1963 strike and found it to be greatest among males, younger teachers, and teachers with advanced academic degrees. Similarly, Hellriegal, French and Peterson (1976) found that males and younger teachers were more likely to support strikes, and Cole (1969) concluded that teachers in New York and New Jersey were more likely to support a strike if they were male, under 40, Jewish, Democratic, and from working-class families. Alutto and Belasco, who in 1976 compared teachers' and nurses' attitudes toward strikes, unions, and collective bargaining, concluded that support for militant teachers' organizations was greater among male, younger, and secondary school teachers than among female, older, and elementary teachers (pp. 82–83). Fox and Wince (1976) also found sex and age the most significant variables affecting teacher militancy in their 1976 study of a Midwest city. As Johnson (1987) observed in an earlier review of this research:

These findings are consistent with common wisdom about teacher militancy. Young teachers are expected to endorse confrontation with authorities. The aggression associated with militancy is more consistent with male norms of behavior than female, and until recently, male teachers could be expected to be sole supporters in purposeful pursuit of higher wages and better benefits. Also, because male teachers are more likely to teach in secondary than elementary schools, militancy might be expected to be greater there. (p. 607)

Other researchers have studied the issues that compel teachers to ally and take action. Corwin (1970) contended that organizational conflict and teacher militancy result, not from dissatisfactions with the school or district, but from broad social and political features, including a bureaucratized society, professionalized work, and complex organizations. Having studied 2,000 teachers and administrators in 23 Ohio public high schools, Corwin concluded that, although men generally were more inclined toward militant action, women were more influenced by dissatisfaction over professional issues. Jessup (1978) studied why teachers supported unions in New York City during the 1960s and concluded that a "major motivating factor was teachers' frustration with their powerlessness in educational decision making" (p. 44). Bacharach, Mitchell, and Malanowski (1985) studied New York teachers in 42 elementary and 45 secondary schools and found that age and gender were unrelated to militancy and that seniority predicted militancy only at the high school level. Although age and gender were not found to be correlated with union membership and militant attitudes, "decisional deprivation" at both the elementary and secondary levels was found to correlate. Elementary teachers sought greater professional prerogative and secondary teachers were willing to trade off involvement in decision making for higher pay (p. 21).

Currently, approximately 90% of U.S. teachers are members of teachers' unions—1.8 million in the NEA and 600,000 in the AFT (Berube, 1988, p. 1)—and evidence suggests that, in their views and decisions about union membership and militancy, teachers are likely to be influenced as much by organizational forces as by personal concerns. Interviews with almost 200 unionized teachers in six districts of a national sample (Johnson, 1984) revealed that teachers are often ambivalent about union membership and that they endorse union actions selectively, usually in response to local conditions and events. Studying three small school districts in New York, Jessup (1985) also concluded that, in contrast to interpretations by other scholars who have "suggested teachers' dissatisfaction with salaries and prestige as the major motivations underlying teacher unionization, this research suggests that teacher frustrations over larger, administrative issues were of equal, if not greater, importance" (p. 189). Similarly, Duplantis, Chandler, and Geske (1995), who studied teachers' union activity in 106 large school districts in 11 states having no collective bargaining legislation, found evidence of dissatisfaction with both salary and working conditions. Superintendents who were surveyed in these districts "reported that three issues prompted teachers to join the union in their districts—wages, job security, and a desire for a voice in administrative decisions" (p. 171).

Recently, Bascia (1994) completed case studies of three California high schools, where she found considerable variety, even within a school or department, among teachers' views about the union. Her work underscores the importance of studying personal choices in an organizational context:

Teachers' conceptions of themselves as professionals, their relationships with colleagues and others, their perceptions of who supported and who impeded their work, and the values they shared form a logical fit. Teachers viewed local union strategies in relation to this fit because the union was, after all, one of the many dimensions of teachers' work lives. (p. 63)

Moreover, Bascia found that for the teachers she studied "the meaning of 'union' is primarily pragmatic rather than ideational, and is rooted in teachers' encounters with particular conditions of their work rather than in abstract notions of professional control or class conflict" (1994, p. 85). Therefore, research indicates that, over time, teachers have looked to unions to address matters of teacher welfare—protecting jobs, winning good wages, and ensuring satisfactory working conditions—and to secure opportunities for influence over policy and practice in their classrooms and beyond.

Virtually all research about teachers' unions focuses on their activities within school districts rather than on their activities beyond districts as legislative lobbyists or participants in political elections. There is no doubt, however, that teachers' unions have pursued and achieved many of their goals outside school districts by influencing legislators and executives at both the state and national levels. Certainly, their most significant activity has been winning mandatory bargaining rights in all but 16 states. Murphy (1990) observed that, although the AFT actively and intensively pursued collective bargaining rights for many years, the NEA experienced its "deepest concern" (p. 226) about collective bargaining:

The NEA thought collective bargaining would destroy professionalism; leaders in the NEA warned that if teachers behaved like trade unionists they would lose all respect and status in the community. In contrast, the AFT pointed out that teachers would gain respect because at last their salaries would be commensurate with their preparation. (p. 210)

Eventually, both unions embraced the new policy and competed vigorously to represent local teachers organizations.

Berube (1988) concluded that the unions' impact on politics and policies has been tremendous: "[T]eachers' unions have become the most powerful political constituency in education" (p. 1). He further observed that teachers did not always endorse political action by their unions: "[T]he transformation from political naïf to political sophisticate was not made without a struggle" (p. 17). However, the "change in political attitudes has been dramatic" (p. 18). Only a fourth of NEA members polled in 1956 said that members should participate in politics. Nearly 20 years later, at a meeting of the 1975 Representative Assembly, ". . . 92.6% of the delegates favored the NEA's endorsement of a presidential candidate. Even though this latter group was composed of the most active NEA members, it signaled a major shift in attitude" (p. 18).

The Practice of Collective Bargaining

State laws permitting or requiring school boards to negotiate with teachers over the terms and conditions of their work have shaped the dominant form of teachers' collective action since 1960. Currently, 34 states require negotiation with teachers, and 10 others provide legal frameworks to make it possible (Duplantis et al., 1995). Not only do these laws empower teachers to negotiate, but also they regulate other elements of labor relations, including organizing activities and representation procedures, unfair labor practices, union security provisions (agency shop, union shop), scope of bargaining, strikes, and impasse procedures that may include mediation, fact finding, and binding arbitration. Because state labor relations statutes are modeled largely on the National Labor Relations Act, which regulates bargaining in the public sector, practices and agreements have been substantially influenced by labor traditions in noneducational sectors. Research about the legal context of collective bargaining—including the variety of state laws and their effects on bargaining practices; the impact of various impasse procedures, such as mediation or last-best-offer arbitration; and the effect of legalizing strikes among teachers—is reviewed elsewhere by Johnson (1986) and will not be discussed here, primarily because this line of research virtually ended as bargaining for public school teachers in the United States became nearly universal. However, one related issue—the legal scope of bargaining—has received considerable research attention since 1980 and continues to have important implications for current efforts by organized teachers to reform schools.

The scope of bargaining, which is defined by labor statutes, typically limits negotiations to wages, hours, and working conditions. Thus, by law, teachers in most states are entitled to bargain about matters of teacher welfare such as pay, class size, layoff procedures, or the length of the school day, while broader professional concerns about such issues as curriculum, governance, and budget lie beyond the legal limits of negotiation. Kerchner and Mitchell (1988) explained that the formal definition of scope has great symbolic meaning:

> For management and most all state legislatures, limitations on the scope of bargaining became the substitute for the doctrine of sovereignty, a way of asserting that collective bargaining had not contaminated the policymaking process. A legal line is drawn between contract and policy. Virtually every state declares that it distinguishes between those issues which are bargainable and those which related to educational policy. (p. 139)

In fact, however, researchers have found less than complete correspondence between law and practice. Doherty (1981) compared New York contracts with those from other states and concluded that "although it would appear that there are substantial differences among the states as to what issues constitute appropriate subject matter, there is considerable similarity in the actual scope of collective bargaining contracts" (pp. 529–530). By contrast, McDonnell and Pascal (1979) concluded that in both 1970 and 1975 "state law mandating or permitting bargaining on a specific provision was a comparatively strong predictor of whether that provision was included in a given contract" (p. 28). However, in subsequent field work, McDonnell and Pascal discovered that negotiators often are not aware of the legal scope of bargaining and that they negotiate with little conscious attention to the prevailing statute. Kerchner's (1978) analysis of the issue led him to observe that the scope of bargaining expands over time,

> this despite general concurrence that there should be a limitation, and despite the many attempts to limit scope by statute and by court

decision. The scope expands because what appears firmly fixed in the law is eroded by *legal interpretations* as conditions change and it is further eroded by the actions of *labor and management themselves* [emphasis in original]." (p. 67)

Similarly, Goldschmidt, Bowers, Riley, and Stuart (1984) analyzed 80 contracts from 37 states and found that almost half set curriculum policies, including the grouping and placement of students, decisions that lie beyond the legally defined scope of bargaining.

Case studies and informal evidence also suggest that the scope of bargaining has expanded considerably since the late 1980s, largely as a result of the deliberate and collaborative efforts by both labor and management to empower teachers and to engage them in the school reform movement. This is intriguing, since unionism and collective bargaining are often blamed for obstructing reform, and opponents of unionism frequently criticize those teachers who seek to expand the scope of bargaining for infringing on the rights of management. Kerchner and Mitchell (1988) observed:

> Contract analyses show repeatedly that the scope of items covered in labor contracts expands over time. But most frequently the implication drawn is that teachers have breached the barrier between collective bargaining and policy, thereby intruding on managerial or civic prerogatives. But the question of whether the policies are good ones or not is seldom asked. (p. 29)

If teachers seek to exercise greater professional responsibility through collective bargaining, the scope of bargaining must necessarily expand beyond the conventional boundaries of wages, hours, and working conditions. Kerchner and Mitchell suggest that those who assail collective bargaining as a roadblock to reform should not assume that the union deliberately expands the scope of bargaining to limit the prerogatives of management:

> The scope of bargaining does expand, and bargaining affects policy. However, where bargaining affects the curriculum or the technology of teaching, it almost always does so by indirection, and the policy impacts of contract come as spillovers, unforeseen consequences of fairly ordinary industrial union decisions about pay, hours, job classification, working conditions, and duties associated with each job. (1988, p. 140)

Those who have studied the scope of bargaining usually conduct their work at some distance from the negotiating table, analyzing the contract provisions that result from deliberations, rather than studying the deliberations themselves. Although there is far less analysis of the process of negotiation than is warranted given its importance, effort has been made to study who participates in negotiations. McDonnell and Pascal (1979) reported that a "typical set of bargaining participants includes a teacher organization team headed by its leadership and a district team led by a full-time professional negotiator, typically the director of personnel" (p. 51). In 1970, Perry and Wildman observed a trend toward the use of professional negotiators, a practice that McDonnell and Pascal concluded had become "almost universal" by 1979 (p. 45). Ironically, as teachers' collective efforts increasingly are played out in the arena of labor negotiations, teachers themselves once again stand at the periphery, looking on at the "experts." As professional negotiators vie to protect interests, lay strategies about settlements, and warily guard precedent, bargaining becomes ritualized and adversarial and there is less focused attention on educational concerns.

Recent experiments with collaborative or "principled" negotiations (Fisher & Ury, 1981), which are discussed below, have been designed to achieve sound settlements while preserving both educational standards and civil labor-management relationships. Some of these experiences in districts such as Cincinnati and Dade County, Florida, are documented in case studies (Rosow & Zager, 1989; Kerchner & Koppich, 1993), but no researchers have carefully compared either the practices or the outcomes of these collaborative approaches with those achieved through conventional bargaining.

Although the process of negotiation has not been studied carefully, researchers have sought to understand the impact of collective bargaining by examining its direct effects on wages, hours, and working conditions as well as its indirect effects on educational governance, teaching practice, student performance, and organizational culture.

Wages and Fringe Benefits

Efforts to understand the effect of collective bargaining on teachers' wages have generated more research and more methodological dispute than any other topic considered here. Lipsky (1983) and Johnson (1986) provided comprehensive reviews of the bulk of these wages studies. Lipsky explained the methodological challenge of isolating the impact of a contract in unionized districts. Because bargaining is likely to affect indirectly the wages of unorganized teachers ("the spillover effect") and because "it is difficult to match organized and unorganized groups that are identical except for the fact that one group bargains and the other does not," researchers have not definitively identified the effect of collective bargaining on teachers' wages. Despite such challenges, across many studies the effects of bargaining have been found to be modestly—approximately 3% to 9% (Duplantis et al., 1995, p. 169)—lower, Lipsky observed, than critics believe and "substantially below estimates of the effects of private-sector bargaining on wages" (p. 35), which are usually thought to be between 15% and 20%. Baugh and Stone (1982) alone reported a large effect, as much as 21%.

Two recent studies underscored the generalization that wage gains have been moderately affected by collective bargaining. Duplantis et al. (1995) studied large school districts in the 11 states without collective bargaining legislation and concluded that the average teacher's salary in districts with negotiated agreements was 9.5% higher than in districts without them. Hoxby (1996) examined the issue, compiling nationwide data on union activity and contract settlements since 1970, and concluded that teachers' salaries increased 5% as a result of unionized bargaining. Research on future salary settlements is unlikely to be productive, since collective bargaining is now the common practice both in states that require and those that only permit collective bargaining; therefore, it is now virtually impossible to design comparative studies that control for the spillover effect.

Fringe benefits, such as health insurance and retirement contributions, have increased in size and importance to teachers and now must be considered along with wages in any effort to estimate the financial value to teachers of a contract settlement. Gallagher (1977) studied school budgets in 133 Illinois school districts and concluded that unions have increased nonsalary benefits, although districts seldom report these gains as wage increases. Given increasing attention to the importance of fringe benefits in contract negotiations, this topic warrants further research.

Hours and Working Conditions

While much research attention has been devoted to the effect of collective bargaining on salaries, far fewer studies have centered on working conditions, such as class size, length of school year, and layoff procedures. Like wage studies, this research is complicated by "spillover effects" in that nonbargaining districts seek to avoid labor organizing by granting teachers benefits that are similar to those of bargaining districts. Thus, the indirect effect of collective bargaining on working conditions in nonunion districts is probably sizable, but it is impossible to determine precisely.

Studies of unionized districts conclude that collective bargaining has provided teachers with more say about when and how they work. Sometimes management's concessions about working conditions are made in trade for low salary settlements. McDonnell and Pascal (1979) explained that

> organized teachers continue to gain influence over what happens in their classrooms, their schools, and their school systems. In the classroom, teachers have increased control over class size, curriculum, disciplinary matters, and use of aides. In the school and district, teachers more and more contribute to decisions over who is employed and where, who administers, who evaluates, and the duration and composition of the teaching day. (p. 34)

However, on the basis of contract analysis and site visits, Johnson, Nelson, and Potter (1985) concluded that, although collective bargaining agreements may have become more comprehensive over time, their added provisions do not uniformly favor the union. Rather, many contract provisions strengthen the position and priorities of management.

Hours

In an early study of nine districts, Perry and Wildman (1970) found that "collective bargaining had resulted in a shortening of the effective school year or day in a few systems," (p. 12). By 1979, however, Perry (1979) found that the length of the school day and school year still were addressed by only five of these nine contracts, including those of the three largest districts. He attributed the "discernible reduction in hours" in those five districts to collective bargaining (Perry, 1979, p. 13). By contrast, Johnson (1984) found in her study of six districts that, while the number and length of instructional days had remained constant since the 1950s, teachers' formal work days (which extend beyond the instructional school day) had been specified and reduced.

The regulation of teachers' time while at work is of great concern to teachers, but it has received little research attention even though issues such as the provision of preparation time are major elements in many districts' collective negotiations.

Class Size

There is evidence of expansion over time in the number of districts negotiating about class size. McDonnell and Pascal (1979) found that 20% of the districts they studied had class-size provisions in 1970, while 34% had them by 1975 (p. 12). This is consistent with McDonnell and Pascal's broader finding that there is "convergence of collective bargaining outcomes over time. As more and more school systems follow the lead of flagship districts, there is less variation among individual contracts" (p. 31). However, the fact that a provision is bargained does not mean that it necessarily advances teachers' self-interest. Perry (1979) concluded that, although all nine systems he studied negotiated about class size, the unions had "made relatively little concrete progress in achieving definite, enforceable limits on class size or in reducing those limits where they exist" (p. 13.). Johnson (1984) found fixed class size limits in only two of six districts studied (pp. 208–210). Finch and Nagel (1984) reviewed the research on class size and found that "it offers evidence of both decreased and increased pupil loads resulting from collective bargaining. When effects are found, however, they are small" (p. 1624).

The issue of class size provides a good example of how concerns about teacher welfare are entwined with the unions' pursuit of better educational conditions. Teachers widely believe that they can serve students better in classes with fewer than 25 students (Johnson, 1990); there is also no doubt that, for many teachers, large classes make their work discouraging and less attractive. During the 1980s, negotiators often tied issues of class size to those of job security, since unions could control the number of layoffs if they could receive assurances that class size limits would be maintained. However, with rapidly increasing enrollments in the late 1990s, teachers' arguments for reducing class size have taken on a more professional slant as they worry about the effects of large class size on student welfare and instruction.

Seniority

Seniority and its use in determining promotions, involuntary transfers, and layoffs has long been a standard feature of labor contracts because of the objectivity it introduces into job decisions. Its use is controversial in education, however, particularly when it leads to stagnancy or disrupts staffing in innovative programs. In the view of those who oppose seniority-based practices, seniority is included in negotiations simply to protect older teachers who control the union's agenda. Proponents, though, regard seniority as an evenhanded standard guarding all teachers from administrative abuse. Many teachers would prefer job decisions to be merit based, but they doubt that fair comparative judgments about performance can or will be made (Johnson, 1990).

The impact of seniority on school practice must be understood within the context of particular schools and programs, for all seniority provisions are not alike. Moreover, the same contract language can have dramatically different effects in different contexts. Using seniority to determine layoffs within narrow categories, such as primary education or biology, affects practice much differently than using it to assign, lay off, and bump teachers within broad categories, such as elementary education or science. Research, however, has centered on the existence of seniority language in written contracts rather than on the details of that language or its effects on actual practice.

Perry (1979) found that six of the nine districts he studied used seniority as the sole criterion in determining layoffs. Johnson (1984) found that seniority within classifications (grade levels and subject areas) was used to determine layoffs in four of six districts and that, unlike many contract provisions, seniority-based layoff and transfer provisions were fully enforced by teachers. Eberts and Stone (1984), too, found that the presence of seniority language in a contract makes it likely that layoffs will be based on years of experience in the district rather than other factors. Notably, seniority is also widely used to determine layoffs in nonunion districts, and it is difficult to discern whether that practice is the indirect result of settlements in unionized districts or whether management actually finds seniority-based decisions easier to administer than performance-based decisions.

Organizational Impact of Collective Bargaining

Managerial Authority

Once a collective bargaining agreement is signed, its implementation introduces complex demands on schools and school personnel. This phase of labor relations has received little research attention, although it determines much about the impact of collective bargaining on schooling. Generally, researchers studying contract administration have found that demands for standardizing practice centralize administration and promote conformity. Mitchell, Kerchner, Erck, and Pryor (1980) noted "that bargaining has produced a trend toward more homogeneous and consistent interpretation and application of work rules among all the schools within any given district" (p. 20). McDonnell and Pascal (1979) also concluded that contract implementation had become "highly routinized. The administration usually works with school principals, briefing them on any new provisions, and preparing them to implement the contract at the building level" (p. 76). Johnson (1984), too, documented a "trend toward centralized administration of the contract" in the six districts of her sample, but noted that "no district had achieved anything resembling lockstep conformity in labor practices" (p. 82). Despite considerable evidence of standardization, researchers have also documented variation in contract management in the schools, finding, for example, that in some districts school-site committees "co-administer the building," while in others they "have no influence" (McDonnell & Pascal, 1979, pp. 77–78).

Whatever teachers' collective efforts to negotiate a contract, the principal has proven to be key in determining the effect of that contract at the school. McDonnell and Pascal (1979) concluded that "the principal plays a central role in determining whether collective bargaining works in the school building. Truly effective principals usually accept collective bargaining and use the contract both to manage their building more systematically and to increase teacher participation in school decision making. Less effective principals may view the contract as an obstacle to a well-run school and then use it as an excuse for poor management" (p. 81). Similarly, Johnson (1984) found that teachers were often willing to abridge the terms of their contracts in such matters as class size or supervisory assignments if they believed their principal needed these concessions to make the school work well: "Few contract provisions are implemented fully throughout the schools of any district, most being subject to interpretation, amendment, or informal renegotiation at the school site" (p. 165).

The grievance procedures, often called the "heart of the contract" by union leaders (McDonnell & Pascal, 1979), are included in contracts to ensure compliance. Researchers have found that participants seek to resolve contract grievances at the lowest level possible and that the number of formal grievances filed is actually quite small. Overall, teachers seek to avoid adversarial and hostile relationships with administrators. However, it is also clear that the possibility of a formal grievance encourages contract compliance by administrators. Johnson (1984) wrote that "casual comments, complaints, reminders, warnings, and threats" by teachers all have the potential to become grievances (p. 47). Mitchell et al. (1980), who call grievances "communications mechanisms," explained that "grievance threats force management to give attention to situations they might have preferred to ignore" (section 6, p. 25).

It is very difficult to assess the extent to which collective bargaining has compromised managerial authority, although conventional wisdom and some analysts (Lieberman, 1993) have held that it has done so extensively. Although there is no question that school administrators are constrained by negotiated rules and procedures, it is not clear just how these rules and procedures have changed their administrative practice. Kerchner and Mitchell (1988) argued:

> Managers often find that the new rules work in their favor and proceed to use them aggressively. In some respects, management authority increases: At least the attention given to explicitly managing schools increases, as does the recognition of school administrators as 'managerial.' At the same time, management itself becomes rule based. (p. 190)

Shedd and Bacharach (1991) observed that "the evidence on collective bargaining's effects is confusing," with some researchers concluding that school management is more rigid and school managers are more constrained as a result of unionism, while others note the important ways in which teachers "now have new leverage to insist that they be included in school and district decision making" (p. 166). Shedd and Bacharach reconciled these seemingly contradictory reports by noting that

> the evidence that collective bargaining has produced rigidity, centralization, diminished supervisory authority, and a "laboring" conception of the teacher's role may be drawn from settings where a traditional (industrial) model of collective bargaining continues to predominate. (p. 167)

They went on to say that

> the evidence that bargaining has produced increased flexibility, responsiveness to public concerns, respect for the leadership role of building principals, and teacher involvement in professional decision making may reflect labor-management relationships in settings where the parties have made the transition to a newer form of collective decision making. (p. 167)

Changes in Decision Making

Kerchner and Mitchell (1988) found that collective bargaining had altered the patterns of decision making in the school districts they studied. They documented "changes in the *agenda* (the list of decisions to be made), the *arena* (the forums in which decisions are made), and the *actors* (those who participate in decisions)" (p. 167). Ironically, although teachers were more involved in decisions about policy and practice, the process of decision making was more centralized and hierarchical, by virtue of being formalized. "Decisions become increasingly hierarchically linked with one another in long chains. Such changes give teachers a voice in decisions but decrease the organization's ability to make quick affirmative decisions" (p. 189). Notably, the research of Kerchner and Mitchell was conducted before unions' efforts to establish school-based management through collective bargaining, a change that likely has introduced more decentralized decision making in many districts.

Union Roles for Teachers

The teachers formally responsible for enforcing the contract are the building representatives or stewards, the official union delegates in the schools. Although Glassman and Belasco (1976) found building representatives to be central in regulating union activities in schools, Mitchell et al. (1980) found that only 50% of the districts they studied had building representatives at each school and that "these persons were not particularly well trained or active" (section 6, p. 36). Researchers have offered few explanations for the fact that election of teachers to formal union roles, such as building representative, grievance chairperson, or member of the negotiating team, are frequently uncontested and that the positions often go unfilled. Although teachers collectively support contract negotiation and, as Jessup (1985) reported, "felt far more protected, by their unions, against arbitrary, administrative actions" than before they were formally represented (p. 205), they also seem to find the routine responsibilities of contract administration unattractive or uninteresting. In her 1994 study of teachers in three unionized schools, Bascia offered a partial explanation, noting that teachers' responses to their unions vary from person to person and from school to school: "[T]he union was, after all, one of the many dimensions of teachers' work lives" (p. 63).

The Impact of Collective Bargaining on Teachers' Work

It is far easier to study contract language, or even alternative approaches to contract management, than it is to track the indirect effects of bargaining on teachers' work. Eberts (1984) approached the challenge by combining an analysis of data from the Sustaining Effects Survey of 6,000 teachers with the contents of teachers' diaries, which offer detailed accounts of how teachers use their time. Comparing data from teachers who worked under collective bargaining agreements and those who did not, Eberts concluded that collective bargaining decreased instructional time by 3%, increased preparation time by 4%, increased administrative-clerical duty time by 13%, and increased parental meeting time by 8% (p. 352). Unfortunately, it is difficult to interpret these findings, since the consequences of such changes in time allocation are not readily apparent.

Kerchner and Mitchell (1988) took a very different approach to considering the effects of collective bargaining on the work of teachers. On the basis of survey and field-based data, they concluded that collective bargaining rationalizes teaching and formalizes administrators' supervisory practices, making teaching more like labor and less like professional work. However, they acknowledge that it is difficult to attribute such effects exclusively to collective bargaining when state and local policies demand teachers' compliance with regulations that also standardize and rationalize instructional practice.

Impact on Student Performance

Of all the methodological challenges undertaken by researchers, tracing the links between bargaining gains and student performance is the most difficult and hazardous. Doherty (1981) cautioned: "We sometimes attribute to bargaining certain changes in educational performance on the sole ground that one preceded the other. As Samuel Johnson once observed of physicians, they tended to 'mistake subsequence for consequence'" (p. 64). In his work, Doherty could find neither "substantial improvement in student achievement" nor responsibility for declining performance that was attributable to collective bargaining (p. 75). Eberts and Stone (1984) found the net difference in gains in student achievement between union and nonunion schools to be "negligible" (p. 166). However, their 1987 analysis of individual student data from the Sustaining Effects Survey led them to conclude that "the impact of collective bargaining appears to vary for different students" (p. 361), being more productive for average students and less productive for students who are significantly above or below average. The authors speculated that, because unions standardize teaching practice, average students benefit. Kleiner and Petree (1988) used state-level data from 1972 to 1982 to estimate the impact of teacher unionism on student performance by regressing "the average level of the SAT [Scholastic Aptitude Test] and ACT [American College Testing] standardized test scores and the proportion of students who graduate [from] high school on the percentage of teachers who are union members and the percentage of teachers who are covered by collective bargaining and various control variables" (p. 312). Their analysis "suggests that greater teacher unionism is associated with better performance of students across states, consistent with the analysis of individual students by Eberts and Stone" (p. 317). They concluded that, "at a minimum," their work "rejects any claim that unionization contributed to the decline in student achievement scores during the 1970s and early 1980s" (p. 317). In responding to this work, Eberts and Stone (1988) noted how their findings differed from those of Kleiner and Petree:

We find that teachers covered by collective bargaining faced smaller classes; they find the opposite. We find that teachers represented by unions are more experienced; they find that these teachers are less experienced, although their estimates are statistically insignificant. We find that resources are diverted away from school activities not related to teacher salaries, presumably to finance higher salaries; they find that nonwage expenditures per student go up. Finally, we both find a significant union productivity gain. However, we may also disagree here as well because of the difference in test score measures. (p. 320)

Eberts and Stone concluded that these findings were contradictory not only because they "use different data sets and look at students in different grades" (p. 321), but also because Kleiner and Petree pooled time-series and cross-section data and introduced selection bias by using SAT and ACT scores as measures of achievement. Eberts and Stone observed, "It is very difficult to find data that meet all the needs of a project of this magnitude" (p. 321).

In a related study, Grimes and Register (1991) sought to understand the relationship between teacher unionism and Black students' scores on the SAT and ACT. Using data from the National Assessment of Economic Education survey and applying a standard educational production function regression model to samples of White and Black high school students, they found that "students in unionized schools score higher on the SAT than like students in nonunion schools, *ceteris paribus*" (p. 492). Further, Black students attending unionized schools scored "13.11% above the Black SAT mean" (p. 492). Grimes and Register observed that labor unions "tend to standardize the working environment through formal work rules and procedures. Thus, in a unionized environment a teacher will have less autonomy, in and out of the classroom, than in a nonunionized environment." They hypothesize that "union work rules may reduce the possibility of discriminatory practices by the school staff" and that the mix of "capital and labor inputs in unionized districts may be more suited to the learning styles of minority students" (p. 499).

Zigarelli (1994) revisited Eberts and Stone's conclusions using High School and Beyond data and interpreted them somewhat differently:

Management fear of forfeiting control of the education process to teachers and to their union may prompt greater administrative intervention into the classroom and greater demands for teacher accountability for the performance of their classes. Teachers are expected to react to this heightened scrutiny by targeting the average student in an effort to maximize classroom, rather than individual, achievement. Thus, tighter coupling between administrators and classroom practices generates a change in instructional strategy that may underlie the effects first observed by Eberts and Stone. (pp. i–ii)

Though plausible, Zigarelli's conjecture about the lines of influence between collective bargaining and student performance would be very difficult to confirm empirically. Recently, Hoxby (1996) concluded that collective bargaining has negative effects on student achievement. However, her measure of student achievement—"the percentage of 16- to 19-year-olds who are not enrolled and do not have high school degrees" (p. 686)—was drawn from census data rather than school records. Critics could suggest other explanations than collective bargaining for the concentration of dropouts in districts where teachers are unionized.

School Reform

A new line of research about teachers' collective action developed during the late 1980s in response to the so-called "second wave" of school reform. This new set of approaches to change, which treated teachers as agents rather than the targets of reform, was spurred early on by Albert Shanker, president of the AFT, who encouraged local union leaders to experiment with new approaches to change, which they did enthusiastically.

Until that time, studies of unionism and its effects on schooling had been primarily based on large sets of quantitative data or contract contents that were analyzed at some distance from local schools. In the late 1980s, researchers studying school reform more frequently adopted qualitative methodologies and produced detailed case studies about reforming districts. Whereas earlier studies about the effects of teacher unionism estimated bargaining's impact on wages, class size, or student performance, this group of studies explored the background of change in a district, the process of local reform bargaining, and the varieties of programs these new approaches yielded. To the extent that these studies addressed outcomes, they were the new alliances, contract language, and programs, all of which were examined and described within local contexts.

Two major research projects sponsored many of these case studies. Rosow and Zager (1989) initially did not intend to study teacher unionism, but rather to find schools and school systems, especially in urban areas, where teachers and school managers had allied successfully to effect educational change. Searching for such reforming sites brought teachers' unions to their attention and convinced them of "the urgent need to adapt the industrial model of labor-management to urban public schools" (p. xix). The cases conducted by scholars affiliated with this project convinced the sponsors of the study that labor-management alliances are essential for reform, that teachers and their unions do not block reform, and that many creative approaches to schooling have emerged from collaborative efforts.

In a subsequent project, Kerchner and Koppich (1993) sponsored a set of studies in 12 school districts, some of which had been included in Rosow and Zager's project (Cincinnati, Ohio; Jefferson County, Kentucky; Pittsburgh, Pennsylvania; Miami-Dade County, Florida; and Los Angeles, California). From the start, Kerchner and Koppich's study focused directly on teachers' unions and the way in which the process of collective bargaining was being adapted to promote and support school reform in selected exemplary districts. The schools and school systems they studied were "testing the proposition that it is possible to make systemic change gradually" (p. 6). Since this research focused on deliberate efforts to reform educational practice through the labor-management collaboration, these studies are quite different from earlier research designed to identify the indirect effects of collective bargaining on school organization and instruction.

Kerchner and Koppich (1993) dubbed the change that they observed "professional unionism," which is "anchored in three mutually reinforcing tenets: joint custody of reform, union-

management collaboration, and concern for the public interest. Each of these principles of the emergent unionism breaks with tradition" (p. 194). Not only do labor and management both assume responsibility for improving education, but also the

> "we-they" mentality that commonly characterized industrial-style labor relations gives way to working, collegial union-management teams. Negotiations become a continuous set of ongoing problem-solving sessions in which union leaders and administrators are able to lay their organizational cards on the table and work toward resolution of mutually identified education issues. (p. 194)

Moreover, under these principles, the union explicitly addresses issues of educational quality. Kerchner and Koppich (1993) were encouraged by the effort and programs they discovered, but they noted that reform was more apparent in the pursuit of change than in its outcomes:

> These schools have not changed their form and function so much as they have established processes for continual improvement. . . . Teachers have also expanded their conception of their work, taking responsibility for school improvement. Of equal importance is the administration's recognition that joint custody of reforms is a legitimate role for teachers. (p. 7)

Researchers in Kerchner and Koppich's (1993) study documented collaborative approaches to negotiation, innovative contract language, new roles for teachers as mentors and quasi administrators, waivers of contract provisions, and joint labor-management oversight of ongoing programs. The introduction of peer review programs in which experienced teachers formally assessed their colleagues, school-site councils that made policy and budgeted funds, and career ladders with financial incentives for experienced teachers all challenged established notions about the interests and principles of teacher unionism. For example, Kerchner and Koppich wrote of the peer review programs enacted in Toledo, Cincinnati, Rochester, and Miami:

> Peer review changes both the substance and the symbolism of teacher evaluation and assessment. The concept of teachers making substantive judgments about the quality of teaching places them in a new social and intellectual position. For such an idea to emerge from labor relations suggests a vastly different viewpoint about the function of unions. Traditionally, unions are built on internal cohesion: solidarity. Placing a union member in a position of judgment over another violates the existing norms of solidarity, and many unionists believe that it will wreck the organization. But peer review has not wrecked the unions that practice it, because teachers have a deep understanding of the dualism of their professional and personal interests. (pp. 20–21)

The details of local stories differ, but evidence of labor-management collaboration and of teachers' willingness to exercise professional responsibility run throughout these accounts. When Shedd and Bacharach (1991) saw in such accounts movement by teachers and managers toward establishing joint responsibility, they understood the needs of public education in new ways:

> The problems now besetting America's systems of public education require more discretion *and* more control, more flexibility *and* more

direction, more room for professional judgment *and* more ways of ensuring accountability. . . . Teachers are realizing that what is needed is real involvement in the decisions that affect them collectively, not just autonomy within their individual classrooms." (p. 5)

Not all who have considered these reforms see teachers' unions championing genuine educational reform. Some have found evidence of union leaders obstructing reform and their contracts impeding change. For example, Pitner and Goldschmidt (1987), who analyzed bargaining agreements and documents from California's Teacher Mentor Program in the 11 largest districts, found that the program had been "shaped through bargaining to reflect more closely the teacher union goals of deference to seniority" (p. 5) and that collective bargaining agreements still included policies that are "contrary to the reform movement" (p. 41). These charges of union obstruction, which have great public currency, have been more often asserted by unions' detractors than they have been demonstrated empirically. A great deal more research is needed about whether and how teachers' unions and contracts promote or obstruct school reform.

Clearly, the evidence is mixed and informed analysts differ about whether teachers' unions have been proponents or opponents of school reform. It does seem likely that researchers have reached different conclusions about these reforms, in part, because the reforms themselves vary and the attitudes and purposes of teachers and their unions vary from site to site as well. But assessments are inevitably subjective, and approaches to data collection and analysis are shaped by researchers' differing levels of optimism about the promise of professional unionism and the prospects of effecting true reform from within the union.

Such varied judgments exist among teachers themselves. Bascia (1994) found that, in three unionized high schools where reform was under way, teachers' assessments of their initiatives varied greatly from site to site and from person to person:

> Personnel in each district could identify school faculties that were inspired by the collaboratively sponsored programs to engage more fully and successfully with curriculum, colleagues, and students and with other schools where teachers ignored or rejected the innovations. Some teachers found the new nonadversarial dynamic between union and district administration consonant with their own conceptions of professional community, while others did not find the logic of collaboration persuasive. In some contexts, the new projects had an obvious practical utility, filling a perceived gap in service or support, providing intellectual grist for teachers' professional growth, and creating valued new roles and activities. At other schools, the need for programmatic change was not obvious, and for some teachers the whole enterprise was threatening and debilitating. (p. 92)

Nonetheless, in exploring the tension between unions' "traditional protection and representation functions" and their concern for professional issues, Bascia (1994) found that teachers "persisted in expecting a vigilant union role with respect to matters of job protection, economic issues, and representation—the same general sorts of issues that teachers have expected unions to promote since the inception of these organizations" (p. 76).

In addition to offering differing assessments of reform initia-

tives, scholars differ about whether these cases are anomalies that will progress no further or early stages of an evolutionary change that will firmly establish teachers' unions as collaborative and professional organizations in which teachers' interests and students' interests coincide. Kerchner and Mitchell (1988) first made the case for evolutionary change, identifying 3 "generations" of labor relations—the meet-and-confer generation, the good-faith-bargaining generation, and the negotiated-policy generation (p. 4). During the 3rd generation—negotiated policy—which is characterized by the kinds of reforms discussed above, they found "an explicit attempt to shape school district policy through the contract and the union rather than attempting to manage 'around the contract' or through informal accommodation with the union," as occurred during the good-faith-bargaining generation (p. 8). Drawing on the qualitative and quantitative analyses of survey and interview data collected in California and Illinois, Kerchner and Mitchell concluded that an evolutionary pattern does exist and that unionized districts eventually do enter the era of negotiated policy. Urban (1991) rejected this analysis, which he said subordinates teachers' welfare concerns to the more "professional" concerns of school reformers, an act he called "sophisticated antiunionism" (p. 334). He concluded:

> Thus, the jury is still out on whether or not the second wave of decentralizing efforts will take place and, if they do take place, if they will actually empower teachers. Until definitive results are offered, there is substantial reason to remain skeptical. (p. 336)

There are as yet no "definitive results." Informal accounts suggest that some reforms negotiated during the 1980s endure and expand, while other ventures have stalled or faded from the scene. Economic changes and public demands for fiscal constraints often temporarily shift unions' priorities and derail reformers' efforts, reducing teachers' support for subsequent collaborative ventures. Bascia (1994) cautioned that the new understandings of reform are fragile and easily disrupted:

> Even to the extent that local administrators are willing to share authority, the hierarchical nature of school systems is reinforced by larger systemic forces. A new superintendent, a powerful state policy that requires traditional authority relationships for compliance, and any number of other events could threaten the collaborative nature of relationships. . . . (p. 96)

The priorities of organized teachers and the fate of negotiated school reform deserve close research attention in the years ahead. It is important to study whose interests—teachers' interests, students' interests, or both—guide change over time; which policies and practices endure in the face of shifting economic conditions; how collective bargaining figures into the process of change; whether changes in leadership, both in the school administration and union, redirect, halt or accelerate initiatives; whether school governance is really different as a result of new approaches to decision making; whether and how teachers' roles change over time; and, most important, whether instruction and student learning improve in response to these reforms.

Drawing on the difficulties that they had seen as districts seek to reform, Kerchner, Koppich, and Weeres (1997) proposed a set of policies and practices that would enable unionism to adapt to the new "knowledge society." They suggested that unions should be organized around individual schools rather than around school districts, that high standards for teaching should be maintained by strong professional development and peer review systems, and that pensions and benefits should become "portable" so that teachers can move easily from position to position across district lines. Each of these reforms would require that teachers' unions assume even greater responsibility for the quality of schooling. If instituted, such changes warrant close study as well.

Non-Union Collective Action

While teachers' unions focused increasingly on issues of governance and working conditions during the 20th century, other groups of teachers embarked on activities intended exclusively to improve curriculum and pedagogy and to increase teachers' understanding of schools and children. These groups have included participants in the Child Study Movement, teacher centers, and various teacher networks and teacher research groups, as well as professional development schools. Whereas union leaders contended that students' needs would be addressed by attending to teachers' needs for a supportive and rewarding workplace, these nonunion groups set aside matters of self-interest and concentrated directly on students and pedagogy. They did not seek to reform society, but rather, their own practice, and they took what some might call a more "professional" stance than their counterparts leading the labor movement. As with the NEA, it was administrators and university professors, rather than teachers themselves, who took the lead in these initiatives, especially during their early stages of development. The course of their efforts also has been shaped by the conservative culture of teaching with its powerful norm of "noninterference," which limits "the possibilities for stimulation, growth, and collegial control" (Feiman-Nemser & Floden, 1986, p. 506). Although these groups have been influential over the course of the century, that influence has been quiet, apolitical, and noncoercive.

The Child Study Movement

The Child Study Movement, initiated at the University of Chicago in the late 1930s, focused primarily on understanding children's thinking and psychology. Promoted by Daniel Prescott at the University of Maryland, the Child Study Movement was not initiated by teachers themselves but attracted a large following of teachers and grew in size and influence through the middle of the century. Brandt (1976) reported that, at its peak, the Child Study Movement "operated in a dozen states and had more than 3,000 teachers participating" (p. 10). Over the course of 3 decades, Brandt reported that "more than 70,000 teachers and administrators received at least a year of child study training" (p. 10).

The Child Study model provided a structured approach that participants used to write case records of children and to analyze those records with their peers' help. Teachers studied the analytic method for at least a year, meeting biweekly in small groups of 6 to 15. They read textbooks, took tests, and completed written assignments using a prescribed method to summarize and interpret the case studies (Brandt, 1976, p. 1). One member, who had been formally trained in the process, served as leader, and the meetings were conducted four-fifths of the time "in the absence of an external authority" (p. 48). Although the groups were often initiated by university faculty members or by school district administrators, teachers determined the content and structure of their meetings, and the work of groups varied greatly. Brandt concluded that, when teachers collected and considered their own data, this process "force[d] them to recognize the complex network of interacting forces that gives rise to behavior. It help[ed] one to see how general knowledge about children and youth is applicable in specific ways to particular children" (p. 46).

Brandt attributed the decline of interest in child study during the 1960s to a number of factors, including (a) increased competition from other in-service programs, (b) decreased uniqueness of the program, (c) school districts' preoccupation with broader social and political issues, (d) rapid turnover of school administrators and child study coordinators, and (e) increased mobility of teachers. It also "increased resistance of teachers to work outside of regular school hours without extra reward and firm contractual agreements" (p. 44).

The Teacher Center Movement

The Teacher Center Movement, which emerged in the mid-1960s and which continued to grow through the early 1980s, had two main strands. One conception of a teacher center emerged from the U.S. Office of Education in response to a recommendation in the National Defense Education Act that the National Institute of Education establish a national network of teacher-training complexes to be jointly sponsored by universities, state education agencies, and local education agencies. Thus the National Teacher Center Project, created in 1971, gave planning grants to four sites to develop teacher centers that would improve preservice and in-service teacher education (Feiman, 1978).

The second strand of teacher centers originated in Great Britain and reached the United States in the late 1960s (Feiman, 1977). These centers, with large numbers of practicing teachers on their governing boards, were places where in-service teachers could meet and develop curriculum and teaching materials for their own classrooms (Devaney, 1977). This second approach, which rapidly attracted participants, was particularly appealing to elementary teachers with an interest in open education. Teacher centers were frequently founded by groups of teachers or by collaborating groups of school and university personnel (Devaney & Thorn, 1976). Devaney (1977) reported that the experiences of the centers were "so varied that it cannot be said to constitute a full-fledged model for a new form of in-service" (p. 6). Teacher centers variously offered assistance and instruction that enabled teachers to enrich the learning experience of children; provided a work environment where teachers could develop projects for their classrooms, receive instruction, and provide encouragement for each other; advised and assisted teachers in their schools, beginning with the teacher's designated needs; and encouraged teachers to take increasing responsibility for their own curriculum and instruction decisions, as well as to participate in the design of district wide professional programs. (Lance & Kreitzman, 1977, p. xviii).

Schmieder and Yarger (1974) estimated that, by 1974, about 4,500 teacher centers had been established. The Teachers' Center Exchange, supported by the National Institute of Education, was established in 1975 to maintain communication among a core group of 100 teacher centers in order to

investigate interactive networking as a means of disseminating education innovations to find out whether an informal network can be stimulated, strengthened, and stretched, all the while retaining its qualities of voluntarism, mutuality, trust, and easy access to the dispersed centers of action. (Devaney & Thorn, 1976, p. 15)

Teacher centers became further formalized in 1976, when federal legislation (PL94-482) authorized

as much as $68 million a year for 3 years . . . which they defined as local school district-sponsored "sites," where working teachers could pursue professional improvement directly related to their own classrooms, and where the improvement program would be overseen by a "policy board" composed of teachers in the majority, with a little help from administrators, professors, and the school board. (Devaney, 1977)

The first projects were funded late in 1976. In his historical review of teacher centers, Yarger (1990) maintained that this program affected the professional lives of thousands of teachers at approximately 90 sites in the country. The AFT and NEA endorsed the concept of teacher centers and urged affiliates to seek district funding and to insist on teachers' control of center programs. Simultaneously, the American Association of Colleges of Teacher Education (AACTE) advocated a strong role for colleges and universities in these centers. (Feiman, 1977). By regulation, teacher centers were to be governed by policy boards consisting of 20 to 22 members, the majority of whom were to be teachers. In their 1981 comprehensive evaluation of 37 federally funded teacher centers, Mertens and Yarger (1981) reported that the average teacher center policy board—the "centerpiece" of the new institution—had 20.9 members; that teachers predominated on these boards, with a mean membership of 13.6; that there tended to be more elementary teacher members than either secondary or special area teachers and more central office administrators than building principals on these boards; and that the board involvement of higher education institutions was less than that of either teachers or administrators. The chairperson of the policy board was almost always a classroom teacher, and the policy board met once a month.

Teacher centers provided various events for their clients, including workshops, seminars, symposia, or courses. Yarger (1990) reported that the average teacher center sponsored about 60 events per year, each serving about 25 teachers in specific content areas, and that over three-fourths of teacher center activities focused on the instruction of children. Teachers learned about pedagogical techniques, curriculum development, specific types of children who might be in their classroom, and the special needs of these children (p. 110).

According to Yarger (1990), the typical teacher center, which

was funded for between $100,000 and $200,000 per year, rarely had more than one or two staff members, and it typically served one school district, although a few represented consortiums of two or more districts. On the average, about 1,000 teachers in the service area were eligible to take advantage of the teacher center, although Edelfelt (1982) noted that, on average, fewer that 30% of teachers in a district took part in teacher center activities.

Teacher centers made staff development credible for many teachers and, according to Yarger (1990), "contributed a new breed of education professionals to the field. These professionals accept as a given that teachers define the need and suggest solutions, while their job is to translate that need and develop a program that is viewed by the client to be helpful" (p. 114). Yarger also saw in the policy board a lever for "teacher empowerment. For the first time, the administrator had to work with teachers in a political structure in which teachers were the dominant force" (p. 114).

In another study, Zigarmi and Zigarmi (1979) documented the development of administrative support for 12 teacher centers, noting that most teacher center staffs and administrators focused their work on individual teachers, and few addressed whole school staffs or systemwide change. Administrators were not considered to be clients, nor were they actively involved in the changes that teacher centers promoted. Zigarmi and Zigarmi found that few central office administrators, principals or curriculum specialists "saw teacher centers as important vehicles for addressing or implementing district goals and priorities" (p. 266).

Funding presented serious problems for many centers, and members had little experience seeking grants; when federal funding ended in 1981, many centers closed or reduced their services. Some externally funded centers, such as those with state support in New York, have managed to survive (Towbin, 1994, p. 2).

The Emergence and Development of Teacher Networks

During the 1970s, small study and support groups for teachers grew up around the country. Typically, participants in these groups, who came from different schools and who crossed subject areas and grade levels, explored common interests and pursued questions about teaching and schools. Although such groups have not been studied formally, members of a few have written about their work.

For example, the North Dakota Study Group on Evaluation, which included many teacher center activists, as well as other individuals from schools and universities, studied the common problem of the "inappropriateness of standardized achievement instruments for measuring learning of children in open classrooms" (Devaney & Thorn, 1976, p. 4). The group has published a series of position papers and continues to meet yearly (Patton, 1975; Hein, 1975; Albert et al., 1981).

Teachers who have been associated with Patricia Carini, founder of the Prospect School in Vermont, and the North Dakota Study Group have established groups in their local schools that are committed to progressive education and that are based on the work of the Prospect community. One such group, the Philadelphia Teachers Learning Cooperative, established in

1978, meets weekly to use the processes developed at the Prospect School to examine their work. The Prospect community takes a "phenomenological view of knowledge and learning wherein teachers grapple with children's meanings as expressed in their projects and with the varied meanings that their colleagues find in children's work" (Cochran-Smith & Lytle, 1993, p. 56). According to Rhoda Drucker Kanevsky, founding member of the Philadelphia group, the teachers have become "a community of learners" that uses "reflective processes, procedures that are both open-ended and systematic . . . to have productive conversations week after week" (p. 151).

The Secondary Study Group, organized by two teachers in 1982 following a 3-day conference on cross-school collegiality sponsored by the Education Collaborative for Greater Boston, gave members "the chance to talk with one another about our teaching" (McDonald, 1992, p. 43). The group was founded to host discussion; the members read books and articles about education and then talked about what they had read. One member described the group's aims as both political and psychological,

> to transform the teacher's passive role from that of passive recipient of policy made to active participant in policymaking. Nor did we think of our political voice as something to be given to us, but rather something to be taken. (McDonald, 1992, p. 44)

Another study group, The Boston Women's Teachers Group, functioned as a teacher support group for 3 years in the late 1970s. (Freedman, Jackson, & Boles, 1982). Much like the Secondary Study Group, these teachers from elementary and secondary schools met weekly to discuss their pedagogy and to "discuss teaching from a political perspective, trying to see our work against the larger fabric of economics, history, and schools as institutions of society" (p. 2). Over 2 years, the group studied the work lives of 25 Boston-area teachers and subsequently published their work (Freedman, Jackson, & Boles, 1983). Like members of the North Dakota Study Group and the Secondary Study Group, these teachers raised questions that reached beyond the boundaries of their individual classrooms. They "sought to analyze the relationship between teachers' work experiences over the course of their careers within specific institutional structures and their perceptions of the meanings of these work experiences to their self-esteem, sense of job satisfaction, and sense of efficacy" (Freedman et al., 1982, p. 4).

Over time, these informal study and support groups have multiplied, become better established, and engaged larger numbers of teachers in a variety of settings. Still, they remain rather loose organizations, extending across school and school district boundaries. They are intended explicitly for long-term, in-depth teacher professional development, much of it complementing the current agenda for school reform.

Current-day networks provide the opportunity for self-chosen professional development. Unlike teacher centers, which prided themselves on being eclectic institutions that met the varied curricular and instructional needs of a diverse population, each network is organized around a specific subject matter, teaching approach, or school reform. They range from the National Writing Project—a network based in Berkeley, California, that serves some 160,000 teachers at 158 project sites in 43

states—to smaller organizations, such as the regional networks run by the Foxfire National Programs and the Breadloaf Network in rural Vermont. Some networks have been initiated by foundations or educational organizations, others by states or local groups. Some networks now employ full-time staff, hold annual meetings, publish newsletters and journals, produce research on practice, and link members through electronic bulletin boards.

No figures exist on how many teacher networks exist, although their numbers are said to be in the hundreds (Richardson, 1996, p. 27). Most are not visible beyond their own membership circles (Kaplan & Usdan, 1992, p. 666). Small numbers of teachers in individual schools take part in any one network, and, thus, the influence of these organizations occurs in many places but does not run deeply in individual schools or school districts, thereby limiting their systemwide impact.

Much like teacher centers and the teacher discussion groups that were their precursors, teacher networks value teachers' expertise and encourage teachers to pool their knowledge and build new understandings of their craft. Some networks, such as Foxfire, founded by high school teacher Eliot Wigginton, have been initiated by teachers, while others, such as the Urban Math Collaborative (Firestone, 1993), Project CHART, and IMPACT II, are organized by other educators, but then draw a large following among teachers (Richardson, 1996).

There are only a few systematic studies of teacher networks. In one, Useem, Buchanan, Meyers, and Maule-Schmidt (1995) examined the impact of four teacher networks in the School District of Philadelphia, documenting their effects on teachers' "individual professional growth, their classroom practices, and broader reform efforts in teaching and learning in school" (p. 1). According to Useem and her colleagues, when participants were asked to name "the most important thing" they had gotten out of their network experiences, teachers most often wrote about "collegiality, networking, and community building" (p. 8). They also noted the intellectual stimulation of such networks (p. 11). Participants perceived the broader effect that their groups had on academic or social policies affecting students (p. 20). Though valuable, Useem found these networks to be vulnerable, because, when they were "dependent on 'soft money,' based outside of school districts in organizations which themselves experience vicissitudes of funding, caught up in the inevitable struggles over turf in politically charged urban districts, and often lacking a stable governance structure, networks can easily fall by the wayside" (p. 22). Since participants constituted only about 5% of the district's teaching force, they had limited influence on broader school reform efforts. Still, Useem et al. observed, "their impact in some schools appears to be felt way beyond their numbers, particularly when they have the support of building-level administrators" (p. 24).

Similarly, Firestone and Pennell (1996) studied state-sponsored teacher networks and concluded that they contributed primarily to individuals—teacher learning, motivation, and empowerment—rather than to the larger educational system (p. 1). Useem et al. (1995) suggested that the organizational structures of networks, which range beyond school and school district boundaries, may not be stable. Yet, according to Lieberman (1995) networks do have advantages: "Important opportunities for teacher development exist more readily in environments that provide a level of flexibility and collaborative work not usually possible in existing organizations" (p. 595).

Lieberman and McLaughlin (1992) reviewed a variety of networks and found that successful networks: (a) shared a focus on specific activities related to their "common interests and objectives" (p. 674); (b) provided a variety of "opportunities for colleagueship and professional growth by engaging members in varied activities, such as curriculum workshops, leadership institutes, internships, conferences, and work on reform politics" (p. 674); (c) created discourse communities among teachers that enabled teachers to share their work and validate their knowledge of students and their schools (p. 674); and (d) expanded the pool of teachers who were able to provide leadership in curriculum and teaching practices (p. 674).

Lieberman and McLaughlin (1992) also identified a number of problems that might threaten the efficacy and longevity of these networks, including a lack of monitoring of the networks; their possible overextension; the possibility that teachers would lose their loyalty to their school or be treated badly by peers in their schools; the potential instability of the network's membership; and the lack of clarity about how the network is evaluated and who controls the network's agenda (p. 676). Similarly, Firestone (1993) cautioned that networks "run the risk of isolating teachers from their in-school colleagues and increasing the marginalization that already happens to some teachers who use more challenging approaches to instruction" (p. 10). Lieberman and McLaughlin suggested that networks should be viewed "through an occupational rather than organizational lens" (p. 677) to encourage teachers to make significant changes in their work rather than to reorganize school systems.

Teacher Research Groups

Teacher research, defined by Lytle and Cochran-Smith (1990) as the "systematic and intentional inquiry carried out by teachers" (p. 2) in their own schools and school districts, is usually loosely organized. These authors noted that, "unlike the academic community, which is organized to provide formal and informal structures to support research on teaching, the community of teacher researchers is disparate, and there are few structures that support that work" (p. 5). Huberman (1996) compared the work of teacher research groups with the earlier efforts of teacher centers, noting that

> . . . the Teachers' Center movement had many of the same objectives and practices, but its main purpose was to foster individual awareness and to practice change. Creating and exchanging ideas and materials, reflecting on current practices, providing technical and social support to innovators and risk takers, setting up networks and the like were the priorities. Gradually, however, the Centers saw that institutional arrangements were getting in the way and that they were often marginalized." (p. 136)

By contrast, Huberman saw teacher research as having "a research agenda that is tied (for some) to a political mission" and gives teachers a "mutual education forum" that could lead to "collective action" (p. 136).

Although the potential benefits of teacher research are many, and teachers regularly describe what they have gained from their research work, Cochran-Smith and Lytle (1993) warned that this movement will require "the building and sustaining of intellectual communities of teacher-researchers or networks of individuals who enter with other teachers into 'a common search' for meaning in their work lives (Westerhoff, 1987) and who regard their research as part of larger efforts to transform teaching, learning, and schooling" (p. 86). Cochran-Smith and Lytle saw obstacles to teacher research "deeply embedded in the cultures of school and university organizations, in pervasive assumptions about the nature of teaching and learning, and in the traditions involved in the generation of new knowledge" (p. 86). These obstacles, which include teacher isolation and the conservative socialization of teachers, are akin to those that limited the expansion and influence of other initiatives.

Dana's 1995 study of her own teacher research group confirmed the effects of the conservative culture of teaching, noting that "As teachers in our action research group voiced and acted upon their visions for change, their voices were silenced not by traditional outsiders but by their teaching peers and their principal" (p. 61). "In essence," she reported, "the more empowered the teachers in our research group became, the more criticism they received from other teachers" (p. 68).

Professional Development Schools

Professional Development Schools (PDS), promoted by school reformers since 1986, when the Holmes Group published *Tomorrow's Schools* (1990), are school-university collaboratives designed to simultaneously improve preservice teacher education and in-service professional development opportunities for veteran teachers. Ultimately, they are intended to significantly improve the education of children. As designed, these schools enable teachers and university faculty members to engage jointly "in research and rethinking of practice, thus creating an opportunity for the profession to expand its knowledge base by putting research into practice—and practice into research" (Darling-Hammond, 1994, p. 1).

Since 1986, hundreds of professional development schools have been established in the United States. Funded by foundations, universities, colleges, and school districts, professional development schools have also been supported in their work by organizations such as the Holmes Group, the National Network for Educational Renewal, AACTE, the NEA, and the AFT. Clusters of professional development schools are sponsored by the Michigan Partnership; the Gheens Professional Development Academy in Louisville, Kentucky; and the Puget Sound Educational Consortium at the University of Washington in Seattle (Darling-Hammond, 1994, p. 2).

Most professional development schools seek to involve teachers in significant ways in the reform of teaching and teacher education. Teachers serve on their policy boards, act as adjunct faculty at the collaborating college or university, and mentor student teachers at the school site (Darling-Hammond, 1994). While most have been initiated by professors or administrators, the Learning/Teaching Collaborative in Boston and Brookline, Massachusetts, was initiated by teachers and is now governed collaboratively by the teachers, school district central office personnel, and college faculty (Boles, 1992). Currently functioning in six Brookline and one Boston elementary school, the collaborative supports teachers in moving between their school and the college (Boles & Troen, 1997).

Although much has been written about the principles and programs of professional development schools, little systematic research is available about their effects, particularly with regard to teachers' roles in them. For example, Button, Ponticell, and Johnson's 3-year case study of a West Texas PDS project (1996) focused primarily on the organizational aspects of this reform, documenting that school and college faculties learned to interact in new ways. According to these researchers, university faculty liaisons were a "familiar and comfortable presence," the isolation between schools and districts was broken down through visits, in-house support was provided for research, study and focus groups at each site were formed to address site-specific question, and graduate courses "provided teachers ways to participate in a larger research community" (pp. 17–19).

Troen, Boles, and Larkin, in their 1995 study of "boundary spanners" (p. 4) in three professional development school partnerships, found that teachers who assumed roles as college instructors, supervisors, and mentor teachers in professional development schools "increase[d] their influence and power" (p. 16) at the college as they taught courses and proposed curriculum changes. In addition, the PDS, governed jointly by teachers and college faculty, "provided a structure for teaming" (p. 15), which enabled the principal at one school to implement a change he had been trying to introduce for many years. Thus, teachers were able to serve as "catalyst[s] for change" (p. 14) at both the school and the college.

Darling-Hammond, Bullmaster, and Cobb's 1995 study of seven professional development schools concluded that such schools tend to elicit teacher commitment. They found that 70% of teachers in their study reported that they had changed the way they reflected on practice, 61% reported a change in their conception of collegial work, and 55% reported having changed the way they teach (p. 96). These researchers also reported that teachers' new roles in professional development schools violate the strong egalitarian ethic among public school teachers and, thus, have a less extensive effect on practice than they otherwise might (p. 91). Thus, in these schools, the conservative culture of teaching prevails, often moderating the broader political and organizational intentions of teacher leaders seeking to promote collective action.

The National Board for Professional Teaching Standards

While teacher centers, teacher networks, teacher research groups, and even professional development schools encounter ongoing challenges to their expansion and survival as a result of their loose organization, precarious funding, and explicitly nonpolitical purposes, the National Board for Professional Teaching Standards (NBPTS), which also focuses on improving the practice of teaching, is strategically organized and well funded. The NBPTS, which assesses the practice of experienced teachers and awards board certification, seeks to change both the practice and the profession of teaching (Barringer, 1993). Ultimately, it is intended to change public education broadly. Championed by a strong alliance of educational organizations,

including teachers' unions and subject matter organizations such as the National Council of Teachers of English, teachers have held a majority of seats on the board since its inception.

No systematic studies of teachers' roles on the board or the impact of board certification on educational policy and practice have been completed at this time, but they are certainly warranted. The board's potentially powerful position at the intersection of teachers' unions and teacher professional organizations could give it an unprecedented opportunity to promote teachers' collective action as the profession enters the 21st century.

Conclusion

U.S. teachers have embarked on collective action during the 20th century in two broad movements. One, led primarily by unionized teachers, sought to achieve simultaneous benefits for students and teachers by organizing politically and acting aggressively to secure better working and teaching conditions. Researchers studying teachers' unions and their impact offer mixed assessments, with some concluding that teacher unionism and collective bargaining have improved public education, and others finding that the effects have been largely negative. Union critics contend that students' interests must be distinguished from teachers' interests and, therefore, they urge that teachers pursue less political and more "professional" approaches to change, such as those typified by the Child Study Movement, teacher centers, teacher study groups and networks, teacher research groups, and professional development schools. Available research suggests, however, that these nonunion initiatives, while valuable for the individual, are limited in duration and have an effect largely because of the conservative culture and decentralized organization of schools. There is evidence in recent ventures, however, that the collective action of unionized teachers need not be focused solely on professional self-interest, address issues of educational governance to the exclusion of classroom practice, feature the practices of organized labor, or spurn collaborative opportunities with nonteachers, including university faculty members or government officials. Nor must teachers who join with others to improve pedagogy and school practice in groups such as teacher centers, networks, or teacher research groups, resist formal organization, eschew political activity, or defer to "expert" administrators or academics. Increasingly, there is evidence that collective action by teachers can be a hybrid effort, organized to support both the individual and the group, to improve practice at both the classroom and system levels, and to address educational concerns from teaching and learning to policy and social change.

REFERENCES

Albert, B., Neujahr, J., & Weber, L. (1981). *Use and setting: Development in a teachers' center.* Grand Forks, ND: North Dakota Study Group on Evaluation.

Alutto, J. A., & Belasco, J. A. (1976). Determinants of attitudinal militancy among teachers and nurses. In A. M. Cresswell & M. J. Murphy (Eds.), *Education and collective bargaining* (pp. 78–94). Berkeley, CA: McCutchan.

Bacharach, S. B., Mitchell, S. M., & Malanowski, R. (1985). Strategic choice and collective action: Organizational determinants of teachers' militancy. In D. B. Lipsky (Ed.), *Advances in industrial and labor relations. Vol. 2* (pp. 197–222). Greenwich, CT: JAI.

Barringer, M. D. (1993). How the national board builds professionalism. *Educational Leadership, 50*(6), 18–22.

Bascia, N. (1994). *Unions in teachers' professional lives: Social, intellectual, and practical concerns.* New York: Teachers College Press.

Baugh, W. H., & Stone, J. A. (1982). Teachers, unions, and wages in the 1970s: Unionism now pays. *Industrial and Labor Relations Review, 35,* 410–417.

Berube, M. R. (1988). *Teacher politics: The influence of unions.* New York: Greenwood Press.

Boles, K. (1992). School restructuring: A case study in teacher empowerment. *The Journal of Applied Behavioral Science, 28*(2), 173–203.

Boles, K. & Troen, V. (1996). Teachers as leaders and the problems of power: Achieving school reform from the classroom. In M. Katzenmeyer & G. Moller (Eds.), *New directions for school leadership: Every teacher a leader* (pp. 41–61). San Francisco: Jossey-Bass.

Boles, K., & Troen, V. (1997). How the emergence of teacher leadership helped build a professional development school. In M. Levine & R. Trachtman (Eds.), *Making professional development schools work: Politics, practice, and policy* (pp. 52–75). New York: Teachers College Press.

Brandt, R. (1976). The child study movement. In R. Brandt, R. Mesa, M. Nelson, D. March, L. Rubin, M. Ashworth, E. Brizzi, H. Whiteman, B. Joyce, K. Howey, J. Boyer, & B. Vance, *Cultural pluralism and social change: A collection of position papers.* (ISTE—In-Service Teacher Education Concepts Project—Report V. National Center for Education Statistics). Washington, DC: Office of Education, Washington DC Teacher Corps.

Button, K., Ponticell, J., & Johnson, M. J. (1996). Enabling school-university collaborative research: Lessons learned in professional development schools. *Journal of Teacher Education, 47*(1), 16–20.

Cochran-Smith, M., & Lytle, S. L. (1990). Research on teaching and teacher research: The issues that divide. *Educational Researcher, 19*(2), 2–11.

Cochran-Smith, M., & Lytle, S. L. (1993). *Inside/outside: Teacher research and knowledge.* New York: Teachers College Press.

Cole, S. (1969). Teachers' strike: A study of the conversion of predisposition into action. *American Journal of Sociology, 74,* 506–520.

Corwin, R. G. (1970). *Militant professionalism. A study of organizational conflict in high schools.* New York: Appleton-Century-Crofts.

Cresswell, A. M., & Murphy, M. J. (1980). *Teachers, unions, and collective bargaining in public education.* Berkeley, CA: McCutchan Publishing Corporation.

Dana, N. F. (1995). Action research, school change, and the silencing of teacher voice. *Action in Teacher Education, 16*(4), 59–60.

Darling-Hammond, L. (1994). Developing professional development schools: Early lessons, challenge, and promise. In L. Darling-Hammond (Ed.), *Professional development schools: Schools for developing a profession* (pp. 1–27). New York: Teachers College Press.

Darling-Hammond, L., Bullmaster, M., & Cobb, V. (1995). Rethinking teacher leadership through professional development schools. *The Elementary School Journal, 96*(1), 87–106.

Devaney, K.(1977). *Surveying teachers' centers.* Washington, DC: The National Institute of Education.

Devaney, K., & Thorn, L. (1976). *Exploring teachers' centers.* San Francisco: Far West Laboratory for Educational Research and Development.

Doherty, R. E. (1981). Does teacher bargaining affect student achievement? In G. W. Angell (Ed.), *Faculty and teacher bargaining* (pp. 63–85). Lexington, MA: Lexington.

Duplantis, M., Chandler, T., & Geske, T. (1995). The growth and impact of teachers' unions in states without collective bargaining legislation. *Economics of Education Review, 14*(8), 167–178.

Eaton, W. E. (1975). *The American Federation of Teachers, 1916–1961: A history of the movement.* Carbondale, IL: Southern Illinois University Press.

Eberts, R. W. (1984). Union effects on teacher productivity. *Industrial and Labor Relations Review, 37*(3), 346–358.

Eberts, R. W., & Stone, J. A. (1984). *Unions and the public schools: The effect of collective bargaining on American education.* Lexington, MA: Lexington.

Eberts, R. W., & Stone, J. A. (1987). Teacher unions and the productivity of public schools. *Industrial and Labor Relations Review, 40*(3), 354–363.

Eberts, R. W., & Stone, J. A. (1988). Comment. In R. B. Freeman & C. Ichniowski (Eds.), *When public sector workers unionize* (pp. 305–319). Chicago: University of Chicago Press.

Edelfelt, R. A. (1982). Critical issues in developing teacher centers. *Phi Delta Kappan, 63*(6), 390–393.

Feiman, S. (1977). Evaluating teacher centers. *School Review, 85,* 3.

Feiman, S. (1978). *Teacher centers: What place in education?* Chicago: Center for Policy Study, the University of Chicago.

Feiman-Nemser, S., & Floden, R. E. (1986). The cultures of teaching. In M. C. Wittrock (Ed.), *Handbook of research on teaching* (3rd ed., pp. 505–526). New York: Macmillan.

Finch, M., & Nagel, T. W. (1984). Collective bargaining and the public schools: Reassessing labor policy in an era of reform. *Wisconsin Law Review, 1984*(6), 1580–1670.

Firestone, W. A. (1993). Why "professionalizing" teaching is not enough. *Educational Leadership, 50,* 6–9.

Firestone, W. A., & Pennell, J. R. (1996). *Designing state-sponsored teacher networks: A comparison of two cases.* New Brunswick, NJ: Consortium for Policy Research in Education.

Fisher, R., & Ury, W. (1981). *Getting to yes: Reaching agreement without giving in.* Boston: Houghton-Mifflin.

Fox, W. S., & Wince, M. H. (1976). The structure and determinants of occupational militancy among public school teachers. *Industrial and Labor Relations Review, 30,* 47–58.

Freedman, S., Jackson, J., & Boles, K. (1982). *The effects of the institutional structure of schools on teachers. Final report* (NIE Grant No. NIE-G-81-0031). Washington, DC: Department of Education.

Freedman, S., Jackson, J., & Boles, K. (1983). Teaching: An imperiled "profession." In L. Shulman & G. Sykes (Eds.), *Handbook of teaching and policy* (pp. 261–299). New York: Longman.

Freeman R., & Ichniowski, C. (Eds.). (1988). *When public sector workers unionize.* Chicago: University of Chicago Press.

Fullan, M. G. (1991). *The new meaning of educational change.* New York: Teachers College Press.

Gallagher. D. G., (1977). Teacher bargaining and school district expenditures. *Industrial Relations, 17,* 231–237.

Glassman, A. M., & Belasco, J. A. (1976). The chapter chairman and school grievances. In A. M. Cresswell & M. J. Murphy (Eds.), *Education and collective bargaining* (pp. 400–410). Berkeley, CA: McCutchan.

Goldschmidt, S., Bowers, B., Riley, M., & Stuart, L. (1984). *The extent and nature of educational policy bargaining.* Eugene, OR: Center for Educational Policy and Management, University of Oregon.

Goldschmidt, S. M., Riley, M. R., & Pitner, N.J. (1988). School characteristics and contrary educational policies. *Educational Research Quarterly, 12*(3), 2–8.

Grimes, P. W., & Register, C. A. (1991). Teacher unions and Black students' scores on college entrance exams. *Industrial Relations, 30*(3), 492–500.

Hein, G. (1975). *An open education perspective on evaluation.* Grand Forks, ND: North Dakota Study Group on Evaluation, University of North Dakota.

Hellriegal, D., French, W., & Peterson, P. (1976). Collective negotiations and teachers: A behavioral analysis. In A. M. Cresswell & M. J. Murphy (Eds.), *Education and collective bargaining* (pp. 214–239). Berkeley, CA: McCutchan.

Hoffman, N. (1981). *Woman's "true" profession.* Old Westbury, NY: Feminist Press.

The Holmes Group. (1986). *Tomorrow's teachers.* East Lansing, MI: Author.

The Holmes Group. (1990). *Tomorrow's schools.* East Lansing, MI: Author.

Hoxby, C. M. (1996, August). How teachers' unions affect education production. *The Quarterly Journal of Economics,* 671–718.

Huberman, M. (1993). The model of the independent artisan in teachers' professional relations. In J. W. Little & M. W. McLaughlin

(Eds.), *Teachers' work: Individuals, colleagues, and contexts* (pp. 11–50). New York: Teachers College Press.

Huberman, M. (1996, February). Focus on research moving mainstream: Taking a closer look at teacher research. *Language Arts, 73,* 124–140.

Jessup, D. K. (1978, January). Teacher unionization: A reassessment of rank and file motivations. *Sociology of Education, 51,* 44–55.

Jessup, D. K. (1985). *Teachers, unions, and change: A comparative study.* New York: Praeger Publishers.

Johnson, S. M. (1984). *Teacher unions in schools.* Philadelphia: Temple University Press.

Johnson, S. M. (1987). Unionism and collective bargaining in the public schools. In N. Boyan (Ed.), *The handbook of research on educational administration* (pp. 603–622). New York: Longman Press.

Johnson, S. M. (1990). *Teachers at work: Achieving excellence in our schools.* New York: Basic Books.

Johnson, S. M., Nelson, N., & Potter, J. (1985). *Teacher unions, school staffing, and reform.* Cambridge, MA: Harvard University.

Kaplan, G. R., & Usdan, M. D. (1992). The changing look of education's policy networks. *Phi Delta Kappan, 73*(9), 664–672.

Kerchner, C. T. (1978, Winter). From Scopes to scope: The genetic mutation of the school control issue. *Educational Administration Quarterly, 14*(1), 64–79.

Kerchner, C. T., & Koppich, J. E. (1993). *A union of professionals: Labor relations and educational reform.* New York: Teachers College Press.

Kerchner, C. T., Koppich, J. E., & Weeres, J. G. (1997). *United mind workers: Representing teaching in the knowledge society.* San Francisco: Jossey-Bass.

Kerchner, C. T., & Mitchell, D. E. (1988). *The changing idea of a teachers' union.* New York: Falmer Press.

Kleiner, M. M., & Petree, D. L. (1988). Unionism and licensing of public school teachers. In R. B. Freeman & C. Ichniowski (Eds.), *When public sector workers unionize* (pp. 305–319). Chicago: University of Chicago Press.

Lance, J., & Kreitzman, R. (1977). *Teachers' centers exchange directory.* San Francisco: Far West Laboratory for Educational Research and Development.

Lieberman, A., & McLaughlin, M. W. (1992). Networks for educational change: Powerful and problematic. *Phi Delta Kappan, 73*(9), 673–677.

Lieberman, M. (1993). *Public education: An autopsy.* Cambridge, MA: Harvard University Press.

Lieberman, A. (1995). Practices that support teacher development. *Phi Delta Kappan, 76,* 591–596.

Lipsky, D. B. (1983). The effect of collective bargaining on teacher pay: A review of the evidence. *Educational Administration Quarterly, 18,* 14–42.

Lortie, Dan. (1975). *Schoolteacher: A sociological study.* Chicago: University of Chicago Press.

Lytle, S., & Cochran-Smith, M. (1990). Research on teaching and teacher research: The issues that divide. *Educational Researcher, 19*(2), 2–11.

Mertens, S. K., & Yarger, S. (1981). *Teacher centers in action: A comprehensive study of program activities, staff services, resources, and policy board operations in 37 federally funded teacher centers.* Syracuse, NY: Syracuse Area Teacher Center.

McDonald, J. P. (1992). *Teaching: Making sense of an uncertain craft.* New York: Teachers College Press.

McDonnell, L., & Pascal, A. (1979). *Organized teachers in American schools.* Santa Monica, CA: Rand.

Mitchell, D. E., Kerchner, C. T., Erck, W., & Pryor, G. (1980). *The impact of collective bargaining on school management and policy.* Claremont, CA: Claremont Graduate School.

Murphy, M. (1990). *Blackboard unions: The AFT and the NEA, 1900–1980.* Ithaca, NY: Cornell University Press.

Patton, M. Q. (1975). *Alternative evaluation research paradigms.* Grand

Forks, ND: North Dakota Study Group on Evaluation, University of North Dakota.

Perry, C. R. (1979). Teacher bargaining: The experience in nine systems. *Industrial and Labor Relations Review, 33,* 3–17.

Perry, C. R., & Wildman, W. A. (1970). *The impact of negotiations in public education: The evidence from the schools.* Worthington, OH: Charles A. Jones.

Pitner, N., & Goldschmidt, S. (1987, April). *Bargaining over school reform: California's teacher mentor program.* Paper presented at the annual meeting of the American Educational Research Association, Washington, DC.

Reid, R. L. (Ed.). (1982). *Battleground: The autobiography of Margaret A. Haley.* Urbana, IL: University of Illinois Press.

Richardson, J. (1996). Teacher to teacher. *Education Week, 25*(30), Supplement: Inquiring Minds, 25–35.

Rosenholtz, S. J. (1989). *Teachers' workplace: The social organization of schools.* New York: Longman.

Rosenthal, A. (1969). *Pedagogues and power.* Syracuse, NY: Syracuse University Press.

Rosow, J. M., & Zager, R. (1989). *Allies in educational reform: How teachers, unions, and administrators can join forces for better schools.* San Francisco: Jossey-Bass.

Sarason, S. B. (1971). *The culture of the school and the problem of change.* Boston: Allyn & Bacon.

Schmieder, A., & Yarger, S. (1974). Teacher/teacher centering in America. *Journal of Teacher Education, 25,* 5–12.

Shedd, J. B., & Bacharach S. B. (1991). *Tangled hierarchies: Teachers as professionals and the management of schools.* San Francisco: Jossey-Bass.

Tegnell, G. (1994). *The teachers' section: A teachers council case study.* Unpublished qualifying paper, Harvard Graduate School of Education, Cambridge, MA.

Towbin, J. (1994). *Lessons and examples for CES centers projects.* Unpublished manuscript, Coalition of Essential Schools, Brown University, Providence, RI.

Troen, V., Boles, K., & Larkin, E. (1995, April). *Boundary spanners in professional development schools.* Paper presented at the 1995 annual meeting of the American Educational Research Association, San Francisco.

Tyack, D. (1974). *The one best system: A history of American urban education.* Cambridge, MA: Harvard University Press.

Urban, W. J. (1982). *Why teachers organized.* Detroit, MI: Wayne State University Press.

Urban, W. J. (1991). Is there a new teacher unionism? *Educational Theory, 41*(3), 331–339.

Useem, E., Buchanan, J., Meyers, E., & Maule-Schmidt, J. (1995, April). *Urban teacher curriculum networks and systemic change.* Paper presented at the 1995 annual meeting of the American Educational Research Association, San Francisco.

Wasley, P. (1991). *Teachers who lead: The rhetoric of reform and the realities of practice.* New York: Teachers College Press.

West, A. M. (1975). *The National Education Association: The power base for education.* New York: The Free Press.

Winick, C. (1963). When teachers strike. *Teachers College Record, 64,* 593–604.

Yarger, S. J. (1990). The legacy of the teacher center. In B. Joyce (Ed.), *Changing school culture through staff development. The 1990 ASCD handbook* (pp. 104–116). Alexandria, VA: The Association for Supervision and Curriculum Development.

Zigarmi, P., & Zigarmi, D. (1979). Developing administrative support. In K. Devaney (Ed.), *Building a teacher center* (pp. 241–268). New York: Teachers College Press.

Zigarelli, M. A. (1994). The linkages between teachers' unions and student achievement. Unpublished dissertation, Rutgers University, New Brunswick, NJ.

42.

Teachers' Knowledge and How It Develops

Hugh Munby
Queen's University, Kingston, Ontario

Tom Russell
Queen's University, Kingston, Ontario

Andrea K. Martin
Queen's University, Kingston, Ontario

> *The Answer to the Great Question . . . Of Life, the Universe and Everything . . . Is . . . Forty-two.*
>
> (Douglas Adams, *The Hitch Hiker's Guide to the Galaxy*)

Despite the "infinite majesty and calm" with which Deep Thought uttered the number 42, the approach taken in this chapter does not result in answers to the great question or to any great question for that matter. The research material available to a chapter titled "Teachers' Knowledge and How It Develops" is considerable; indeed, the growth of research interest in the area of teachers' knowledge has been of sufficient scope to warrant several reviews in recent years. Our approach, then, is to steer away from an exhaustive account and, instead, to provide a guide—a hitchhiker's guide perhaps. The guide is to chart the course of research in the area since the appearance of the previous edition of the *Handbook;* in addition, the chapter considers differences in conceptualizations of teachers' knowledge and thus in research approaches. To complete its task, the guide considers the relationship between conceptualizations of teachers' knowledge and teacher education, and it ends with an account of enduring issues like validity and values.

It is difficult to imagine the title "Teachers' Knowledge and How It Develops" appearing in the first edition of the *Handbook of Research on Teaching* (Gage, 1963). The category "teachers' knowledge" is new in the last 20 years, and the nature and development of that knowledge is only beginning to be understood by the present generation of researchers in teaching and teacher education. Bruner (1985) outlined two fundamental modes of thought—"narrative" and "paradigmatic"—and we assume that teachers' knowledge and its development can be understood more fully and completely by relying on both. Much about teachers' knowledge can be expressed in propositions that say what they mean and mean what they say—two characteristics associated with paradigmatic thinking. People talk freely of the "knowledge base" for teaching, and such knowledge includes both maxims and findings from classroom research. Yet a teacher's knowledge is also heavily dependent on the unique context of a particular classroom, and teachers often express and exchange their knowledge in the narrative mode of anecdotes and stories. Narrative thinking comes

This chapter is prepared as part of the 1996–99 research project, "Mapping the authority of experience in learning to teach," (Hugh Munby and Tom Russell, principal investigators), funded by the Social Sciences and Humanities Research Council of Canada. Our thanks to James Calderhead, University of Lancaster, for his thoughtful suggestions to improve this chapter.

naturally to teachers, perhaps more naturally than paradigmatic thinking. Hardly coincidental, paradigmatic thought parallels what Schön (1983) terms the "high ground"—where researchers may feel more comfortable—while narrative thought is readily associated with the "swampy lowlands" of day-to-day practice that so many teachers know so well:

> There are those who choose the swampy lowlands. They deliberately involve themselves in messy but crucially important problems and, when asked to describe their methods of inquiry, they speak of experience, trial and error, intuition, and muddling through. Other professionals opt for the high ground. Hungry for technical rigor, devoted to an image of solid professional competence, or fearful of entering a world in which they feel they do not know what they are doing, they choose to confine themselves to a narrowly technical practice. (Schön, 1983, p. 43)

The bias in favor of the swampy lowlands is obvious in Schön's choice of words, and the implicit downgrading of the high ground and paradigmatic thought may help to explain the complex array of responses by educational researchers and teacher educators to Schön's initial presentation of his epistemology of practice. A hitchhiker in this territory will find that moving freely and comfortably between paradigmatic and narrative modes of thought—between the high ground of theory and the swampy lowland of practice—is neither familiar nor easy.

The work of the chapter falls into four parts. The first part attempts to answer the question, "What do we understand teachers' knowledge to be?" The second part addresses the question, "How do we understand teachers' knowledge to develop?" The third part, titled "Teachers' Knowledge through the Eyes of Teacher Education," shows how the close relationship between conceptions of teachers' knowledge and teacher education has shaped our understanding of how teacher knowledge develops. The final part of the chapter considers issues of validity in work on teachers' knowledge and revisits the inevitable tensions between work *on* teaching and the work *of* teaching that are revealed in research on teachers' knowledge.

A fundamental tension in the area of teachers' knowledge also permeates the discussion of this chapter. The root tension lies in the different views of what counts as professional knowledge and even in how to conceptualize knowledge. The root tension is manifested differently in different domains of educational practice.

1. Within the academy, there is a tension among conflicting approaches to depicting teachers' knowledge, and these conflicting approaches do not share the same turf. For example, researchers in teacher education and educational psychology often seem to be working at cross purposes: Helping teachers to acquire knowledge and generating psychological accounts of how teachers acquire knowledge are not necessarily miscible.
2. There is a tension between the academy of research and the professional field of teaching, especially when these two solitudes are as tenuously linked as they are in both preservice and inservice teacher education.
3. There is a tension in the teaching profession between

teachers' development, understanding and use of practical knowledge, and the generally acceptable understanding that knowledge is propositional. For example, teachers know that there is much more to their knowledge than knowing the subject matter to be taught.

These tensions hinder a hitchhiker's progress. But they are not the only hazards to be encountered in mapping this area of educational research. The hitchhiker may find it difficult to get a bearing on any feature of the terrain when each person seems to have a unique perspective on that feature, when each person appears to be expert about that feature, when each person seems to have a piece, and when each person believes his or her piece is more important than anyone else's.

What Do We Understand Teachers' Knowledge to Be? Selected Propositional Accounts

The first part of this chapter concerns the nature of teachers' knowledge. As we worked through the extensive literature on this topic and tried to be mindful of how teachers' knowledge is acquired, we encountered major challenges. These challenges stem from the legion of interpretations not just of teachers' knowledge but also, importantly, of knowledge itself. Grimmett and MacKinnon (1992), for example, describe the major perspectives in the field in terms of historical traditions: conservative, progressive, and radical (critical theory and feminism). Quite different perspectives on knowledge stem from philosophers of education such as Dewey, Green, Phillips, and Fenstermacher, who offer different takes on concepts like the knower and the known, experience, and the activity of teaching, and who persistently challenge the community with questions like, What is knowledge? What is teaching? What is learning? Other readings in the territory of teachers' knowledge and knowledge itself give us a confusing list of schools of thought: positivism, behaviorism, constructivism, social constructivism, cognitive psychology, and so on. And then we encounter Bruner's modes of thought (narrative and paradigmatic) and Shulman's multiplicity of types of knowledge. Quite clearly, it becomes impossible to account for all these viewpoints. Instead, we notice that the literature seems characterized by a root tension: Different views have developed about what counts as professional knowledge and even how to conceptualize knowledge.

Two major threads are clear in this portion of the chapter. (Later we attend to how teachers' knowledge develops.) The first thread concerns the work that seems to have influenced our understandings of teacher knowledge from a theoretical, even propositional stance. The second thread moves us toward a more practice-oriented conception of knowledge as we describe important milestones in our developing understanding of the epistemology of practice. Some philosophers such as Fenstermacher have become more comfortable with the concept of the epistemology of practice even though serious questions still remain. Interestingly, this gradual move toward a reconciliation of propositional and practical knowledge reinforces our view of the complexity involved in rendering the field into neat and exclusive categories.

Teachers' Knowledge from Propositional Perspectives

The thrust of this section is to reveal clearly how complex the area of teachers' knowledge is. We achieve this by providing recent accounts of reviews by scholars who have rather different perspectives on the field. Taken together, this material presents serious questions for anyone who would understand the area. While traversing this ground, the hitchhiker is bound to hear the voices of philosophers like John Dewey and Thomas Green who have been concerned, as Fenstermacher is today, with issues relating to professional knowledge. Maxine Greene (1986) has a clear sense of the significance of philosophy to journeys like this. She argues that philosophic perspectives do not provide guidelines for situation-specific practice. But they can provoke far-reaching questions and more examination of preconceptions and assumptions, opening possibilities for further inquiry and clarification of concepts and terms.

> If the "doing" of philosophy moves researchers and teachers to do more thinking about their own thinking, it is justified. If it intensifies the wonder with regard to teaching, enhances awareness of what remains unsolved, philosophers may have accomplished what they have set out to do. (p. 499)

Calderhead (1996) describes the charting of a human knowledge base in any area of professional activity as a challenging and potentially endless task. Given the "vast and somewhat idiosyncratic knowledge base that may be continuously changing and restructuring" (p. 710), the task is necessarily complicated and intricate. Shulman (1987a) says: "Begin a discussion on the knowledge base of teaching, and several related questions immediately arise: What knowledge base? Is enough known about teaching to support a knowledge base? Isn't teaching little more than personal style, artful communication, knowing some subject matter, and applying the results of recent research on teaching effectiveness?" (pp. 5–6). Only the last question is accorded legitimacy as part of the knowledge base. Therefore, what may initially (albeit naively) have been perceived as a straightforward discussion, instead, opens up a field of questions.

Jackson (1986) opens his chapter "On Knowing How to Teach" by asking, "What must teachers know about teaching?" and, as did Shulman, generates a plethora of related questions:

> What knowledge is essential to their work? Is there a lot to learn or just a little? Is it easy or difficult? How is such knowledge generated and confirmed? Indeed, dare we even call it knowledge in the strict sense of the term? Is not much of what guides the actions of teachers nothing more than opinion, not to say out-and-out guesswork? But even if that were so, what of the remainder? If any of what teachers claim to know about teaching qualifies as knowledge (and who dares deny that some does?), what can be said of its adequacy? How complete is it? Does much remain to be discovered or do the best of today's teachers already know most of what there is to learn? And whether the bulk of it is fully known or yet to be discovered, what, if anything, must be added to such knowledge to ready the teacher for his or her work? In other words, is there more to teaching than the skilled application of something called know-how? If so, what might that be? (p. 1)

Teasing out the frameworks that these questions represent and understanding the arguments surrounding the conceptualiza-

tion of possible answers moves us closer to the epistemic puzzles that underlie the knowledge of teachers. To understand teachers' knowledge requires embracing the tensions that underlie the epistemology without falling prey to the dichotomies that characterize them. The essential dichotomy is the divide between theory and practice. Building on this dichotomy, the tensions that reside in the realm of teachers' knowledge lead directly to the epistemological issues noted earlier. In their review, Borko and Putnam (1996) describe an additional pitfall that awaits those who pursue psychological representations of knowledge.

> A potential danger inherent in any description of categories of knowledge is that people may come to see the categories as representing an actual storage system in the human mind rather than a heuristic device for helping us think about teacher knowledge. That is, we may find ourselves thinking that teachers' knowledge is organized into abstract, isolated, discrete categories whereas, in fact, what teachers know and believe is completely intertwined, both among domains and within actions and context. (p. 677)

In a sense, Borko and Putnam underestimate the danger, because a larger threat lurks in the unwarranted rejection of particular viewpoints or theoretical perspectives. Phillips (1996) appears to address this threat when he describes the purpose of his chapter in the Handbook of Educational Psychology:

> The aim is to sensitize readers to the important role played by the underlying models or analogies, and to argue for flexibility, tolerance, and caution in dismissing (in the name of science) models that rival one's own, especially when those models and metaphors embody different major assumptions about the nature of human phenomena. (p. 1017)

His caution against the balkanization of knowledge is echoed by a recent commentary on the breakup of the epistemological monopoly created by the logico-scientific approach:

> The old criteria for "knowledge" are kaput, while there are yet no new criteria to take the place of the old. A difficult spot. The question is whether this difficulty is temporary. Will we eventually gain a new, more generous and robust set of criteria for using the concept of knowledge, or are the post-modernists going to prevail with their claims that there are multiple sets of criteria, depending on one's culture and discourse? (G. Fenstermacher, personal communication, October, 1996)

CARTER ON TEACHERS' KNOWLEDGE AND LEARNING TO TEACH

We have selected Carter's (1990) chapter from the first edition of the *Handbook of Research on Teacher Education* to be part of the hitchhiker's guide not just because it is an early and major review chapter of the area but also because it shows the beginning of a transition from propositional to practical accounts of teachers' knowledge. Later, when we discuss how teachers' knowledge develops, we return to some of Carter's insights.

Carter (1990) reframes what "learning to teach" means by grounding the process in terms of knowledge acquisition that is directly linked to classroom practice. She contends that although the phrase "learning to teach" rolls easily off the tongue, a number of conceptual problems arise from inconsistent use where the meaning may relate to the entire enterprise of teacher education, substitute for constructs such as teacher development or teacher socialization, or subsume and mask assumptions about outcomes, effects, and learning. Carter suggests that the focus needs to change from a global to an explicit level that attends to what is learned and how that knowledge is acquired. She selectively surveys research that relates to the learning-to-teach question, arguing that few conclusions can be drawn, apart from broad-stroke generalizations about complexity and multiple interactions.

Shifting to research on teachers' knowledge, Carter identifies three approaches and accompanying research programs that influence the meaning of learning to teach: information processing, practical knowledge, and pedagogical content knowledge. The differing approaches, although overlapping, highlight the varying assumptions, emphases, theoretical frameworks, and methodological commitments that underscore the epistemological complexity of teachers' knowledge.

Information-Processing Studies. Information-processing studies have a psychological framework and focus on the cognitive processes that teachers use in thinking about teaching. Research in the 1970s looked at teacher planning and decision making. More recent studies (e.g., Borko, Lalik, & Tomchin, 1987; Borko, Livingston, McCaleb, & Mauro, 1988) looked more closely at the context of teaching and planning and concluded that stronger student teachers engaged in more complex planning activities than weaker novices, which lead Rohrkemper (1989) to suggest that teachers with richer understandings about teaching were able to learn well from lessons that were less than successful. In the 1980s, expert-novice studies emerged, built on cognitive psychology's pursuit of expert-novice differences, and focused on unraveling the knowledge structures and respective schema of each group. Carter provides a useful critique of this category of research and acknowledges its value as a framework for examinations of teachers' knowledge and as the path to expertise, but she cautions that better conceptions are needed of what experts know, not simply what distinguishes them from novices.

Teachers' Practical Knowledge. Pursuing conceptions of knowledge, Carter reviews research on teachers' practical knowledge. This knowledge relates to practices within and navigation of classroom settings and highlights the complexities of interactive teaching and thinking-in-action. This knowledge is anchored in classroom situations and includes the practical dilemmas teachers encounter in carrying out purposeful action. Therefore, it includes both personal, practical knowledge that is based on the personal understandings that teachers have of the practical circumstances in which they work and classroom knowledge that is situated in classroom events.

Carter highlights major research programs tied to personal, practical knowledge. These include the work of Elbaz (1983), who explored, through a case study of a high-school English teacher, five broad domains of practical knowledge: self, the milieu of teaching, subject matter, curriculum development,

and instruction. Added to this was a three-tiered framework for organizing practical knowledge that consisted of rules of practice, practical principles, and images, all of which move from the particular to the general. Lampert's (1985) case analyses of two elementary teachers and of her own teaching provide a perspective on the choices teachers make in classrooms and the personal meanings attached. Munby and Russell (e.g., Munby, 1986, 1987; Russell, Munby, Spafford, & Johnston, 1988), grounding their work on Schön's epistemology of practice, explore the metaphors used in teachers' accounts of their experience to uncover how teachers frame and solve classroom dilemmas. Working with a sample of preservice, beginning, and experienced teachers, they suggest that metaphors may unlock the levels and types of professional knowledge held by different teachers. Connelly and Clandinin's (1985, 1986) work is the most personal, concentrating on specific teaching episodes and the images attached to a teacher's knowing of the classroom situation. Using narrative methodology, they emphasize the image as a type of knowledge that interconnects past, present, and future. Clandinin and Connelly reject a general conceptual understanding of teaching and use, instead, an experiential understanding that does not separate knowledge from the knower.

Overall, Carter suggests that the research in the area of teachers' personal knowledge does not provide generalized conceptions of what teachers know but, rather, provides a theory of how teachers learn by teaching and how they use their knowledge. Because the research is closely tied to the particulars of practice, a richly textured picture emerges of the effects of teachers' experience within the fluid and complex world of the classroom.

Also linked to practical knowledge is research that has focused on classroom knowledge. Built on the frameworks of ecological and schema-theoretic approaches, this type of knowledge becomes situated and grounded in the experience of classroom events. The central construct of classroom knowledge is "task" (Doyle, 1983), focusing on classroom order and curriculum progress—what Doyle (1988) has labeled "curriculum enactment." Studies of teachers' comprehension processes (Carter & Gonzalez, 1993; Pinnegar, 1988), tied to the ecological tradition, attend to the processes by which teachers use their knowledge to interpret tasks and events. Carter is optimistic about the points of convergence between the personal and ecological views that can embrace idiosyncratic variations that are close to the action of teaching and to patterns and themes across situations. She contends that resolving the learning-to-teach question requires tying knowledge to situations. Therefore, the tasks of teacher education require closer examination, interpretation by those who are accomplishing them, and evaluation as a result of task accomplishment.

Pedagogical Content Knowledge. For Carter, pedagogical content knowledge involves both what teachers know about their subject matter and how that knowledge is translated into classroom curricular events. It is domain specific and includes a teacher's knowledge of students' interest and motivation to learn particular topics within a discipline and understandings about students' preconceptions that can interrupt or derail their learning (Shulman & Sykes, 1986; Tamir, 1988). Noting that research inquiries into this form of knowledge have been highly active since 1985, Carter reviews representative research in the disciplines of mathematics, social studies, and English. However, she cautions that general statements about teachers' content knowledge and its transformation into accessible forms for their students would be premature. (Later, we return to pedagogical content knowledge because it has a significant place in research on novice and expert teachers. The hitchhiker may note that the place of pedagogical content knowledge here and elsewhere is further testimony to our claim that the area of teachers' knowledge is complex and interwoven. That this complexity multiplies when we turn to accounts of teacher education will be no surprise.)

Carter draws a useful distinction between practical knowledge and pedagogical content knowledge, with the former more tied to personal and situational forms of knowledge and the latter more formal and built on the profession's collective wisdom. Accordingly, the learning-to-teach problem becomes one of translating knowledge from one form into another, from propositional to procedural, rather than a problem of disentangling the meaning of complex experiences. For the teacher who is learning to teach, pedagogical content knowledge and classroom knowledge may not be very different. Carter concludes by reconceptualizing teacher education with a greater focus on the substance of teacher knowledge—what teachers know and need to know and how that knowledge is organized. She suggests that case methodology be used to tap these knowledge sources and ways of thinking about learning to teach. Although expensive and labor intensive, case methodology may prove promising for richer understandings of knowledge construction and pedagogical learnings.

SUBJECT MATTER KNOWLEDGE

Shulman's name is often associated with research on teachers' subject matter knowledge, and his seven categories of teachers' knowledge are often linked to the development of a knowledge base for teaching. Shulman's (1987a) categories are: (a) content knowledge, (b) general pedagogical knowledge, (c) curriculum knowledge, (d) pedagogical content knowledge, (e) knowledge of learners and their characteristics, (f) knowledge of educational contexts, and (g) knowledge of educational ends, purposes, and values. Pedagogical content knowledge, "that special amalgam of content and pedagogy that is uniquely the province of the teacher, their own special form of professional understanding" (p. 8), has given rise to a program of research led by Shulman. "The central feature of this research program was the argument that excellent teachers transform their own content knowledge into pedagogical representations that connect with the prior knowledge and dispositions of the learner" (Shulman & Quinlan, 1996, p. 409).

Shulman and Quinlan on the "Comparative Psychology of School Subjects." Shulman and Quinlan's (1996) chapter in the *Handbook of Educational Psychology* (Berliner & Calfee, 1996) is built around the question, "What does it mean to know a school subject?" The chapter opens with accounts of the works of Dewey, Thorndike, Judd, and Brownell and then moves to consider how the psychological view of subject matter has influenced research on teaching. Specific attention is given to the

research programs of four researchers. Leinhardt's (e.g., 1989) studies of mathematics teaching clearly establish the significance of the subject matter in determining teaching approaches. Wineburg (1991, 1996) contrasted students' learning of history with historians doing history and so emphasized the significance of an understanding of the subject to its teaching. Similarly, Lampert (1990) and Ball (1993), whose work represents early examples of the self-study of professional practice, used their classrooms to show the specific relationships between subject matter knowledge in mathematics and the teaching of mathematics. When combined with the work of Grossman (1990) and the work of others, this line of work is compelling evidence for the role of pedagogical content knowledge "in the process of subject matter teaching" (Shulman & Quinlan, 1996, p. 409).

Subject-Specific Reviews of Subject Matter Knowledge. The hitchhiker may wish to extend the approach in the Shulman and Quinlan chapter with subject-specific reviews such as Wineburg's (1996) review in the *Handbook of Educational Psychology* and Cochran and Jones' (1998) review of the subject matter knowledge of preservice science teachers. Cochran and Jones ascribe the term "subject matter knowledge" to Schwab (1978) and identify four components of the concept:

- Content knowledge (the facts and concepts of the subject matter)
- Substantive knowledge (the explanatory structures or paradigms of the field)
- Syntactic knowledge (the methods and processes by which new knowledge in the field is generated)
- Beliefs about the subject matter (learners' and teachers' feelings about various aspects of the subject matter)

An important contribution of the Cochran and Jones (1998) review is the discussion of the relationships between preservice teachers' subject matter knowledge and preservice program characteristics. A consistent finding, report Cochran and Jones, "is that the process of teaching itself increases teachers' subject matter knowledge . . . although we have very little information on how this occurs." The concept of pedagogical content knowledge (Shulman, 1986) promoted research on the relationship between subject matter knowledge and pedagogical knowledge. This concept was originally construed as a form of content knowledge composed of subject matter transformed for the purposes of teaching. In this view, teachers reflect on the subject matter and find ways to adapt it, represent it, and tailor it to the needs of learners. Cochran, DeRuiter, and King (1993) argue for a revised concept of pedagogical content knowledge that integrates content knowledge and pedagogical knowledge in a fashion consistent with constructivist teaching and learning. In general, Cochran and Jones (1998) find that experienced teachers have more complete pedagogical content knowledge than inexperienced teachers. Also, they report that "the connections between content knowledge and pedagogical knowledge become much more clear, sophisticated, and complex with teaching experience." In the area of science teaching, at least, the sense is that teaching experience makes a substantial contribution to the richness and interconnectedness of teachers' knowledge. This approach merits extension to all subjects in the school curriculum.

Murray's (1996) *Teacher Educators' Handbook* contains chapters that consider subject matter knowledge, but the material is varied, which adds more weight to the message that the area of teachers' knowledge is complex. For example, Copes (1996) describes what mathematicians do, and the chapter authored by the National Academy of Science (1996) deals with creationism. In contrast, the two chapters on reading (Ehri & Williams, 1996; Graves, Pauls, & Salinger, 1996) deal more directly with strategies. Subject matter knowledge, as represented in the *Teacher Educators' Handbook,* is a mix of content knowledge, curriculum knowledge, and pedagogical content knowledge.

Teachers' Knowledge and Professionalism. Grossman (1995) links the renewed interest in teachers' knowledge to the professionalization of teaching, taking evidence of a specialized knowledge base as one hallmark of a profession. She considers the domains of teacher knowledge, the forms that knowledge takes, and its relation to classroom practice. Drawing on Shulman's categories, she presents six domains for a typology of teacher knowledge: (a) knowledge of content, (b) knowledge of learners and learning, (c) knowledge of general pedagogy, (d) knowledge of curriculum, (e) knowledge of context, and (f) knowledge of self. Because more research has focused on the domains of content, general pedagogy, and self-knowledge, Grossman focuses on these. What emerges is the complexity of this knowledge and the intersection and integration of the domains as teachers draw on them. For example, content knowledge includes the subdomains of subject knowledge and pedagogical content knowledge, each of which affects general pedagogy and instructional delivery.

Grossman highlights self-knowledge as differing from the other domains by virtue of its personal and idiosyncratic nature. Knowledge of self affects the process of learning to teach (Britzman, 1986), the negotiation of classroom dilemmas and reflection upon practice (Lampert, 1985), and the metaphors that teachers use to understand their practice (Munby, 1986). Grossman presents self-knowledge as a filter through which abstract or theoretical knowledge is sifted and suggests that this perspective has stimulated the use of narrative inquiry and biography to explore teacher knowledge (Clandinin & Connelly, 1987). She applies Bruner's (1985) paradigmatic and narrative ways of knowing to forms of teacher knowledge and its relation to classroom practice, and she suggests that each should inform practice. "Practitioners within these ill-structured domains must integrate multiple knowledge domains in constantly shifting circumstances" (Grossman, 1995, p. 23). Future research should include investigation into all domains of teacher knowledge, examination of the connections among teacher knowledge, school context, student learning, and pursuit of the nature of knowledge and cognition.

THE PERSPECTIVE FROM EDUCATIONAL PSYCHOLOGY

Berliner and Calfee's "Introduction" to the Handbook of Educational Psychology. Berliner and Calfee's (1996) "Introduction"

marks out the territory of interest to educational psychologists in ways that underscore the tensions identified for the hitchhiker in this chapter. The central message of their introduction is illustrated with a fictional teacher's story, a story about "Andrea" (not to be confused with one of the present chapter's authors). Not surprisingly, Andrea is depicted as someone whose teaching might be informed by the propositional or theoretical products of educational psychology: "While teaching history, Andrea wondered what students would remember and be able to apply from her lesson, and by doing so she connected to two topics that are central to scientific psychology: learning and transfer" (p. 3). Later we read, "The body of knowledge that informs Andrea as she addresses her students' developmental needs is treated in two *Handbook* chapters" (p. 3)— the two chapters on developmental psychology. This is quite appropriate so far as describing the discipline is concerned, yet the implicit message is that Andrea would do well to acquire some of this disciplined knowledge. This message comes particularly close to the surface when we listen carefully to the suggestions for how Andrea might improve her mathematics teaching:

> Mathematics was not Andrea's strong suit, and she knew it. She had done all right in her math courses because she worked hard on assignments. But she lacked the pedagogical knowledge to be confident in teaching mathematics. Her task was all the more difficult because her students were struggling and discouraged by failure. Her mathematics methods class was helping her to understand how children think about different kinds of math problems, how they construct their math knowledge, and how these constructions differ for various mathematical tasks. . . . (p. 4)

Importantly, the understanding Andrea appears to need is said to lie in educational psychology and not in her own thinking about her teaching experience. While pedagogical knowledge can be acquired from listening to professors, it may also be acquired from experience. Given the quotation's obvious interest in how learners construct knowledge, it is surprising that the advantages of having Andrea construct her own understandings from her experience are set aside in deference to the authority of her methods class.

None of this is meant to signal to the hitchhiker that some fundamental flaw exists within the discipline of educational psychology. Instead, it is to say something about the underlying conception of how psychological knowledge is conveyed to teachers and also to say something about the underlying conception of what knowledge is and what knowledge counts. Berliner and Calfee see two features characterizing educational psychology, "(a) the renewed engagement in issues of practice, and (b) the emergence of cognition as the prevailing theoretical framework" (p. 10). We suggest that educational psychology as a discipline will be limited in its role if the "renewed engagement in issues of practice" fails to address the relationships among educational psychology, teacher education, and the character of teachers' knowledge. To assume that teacher education and educational psychology meet only in on-campus courses is insufficient. Munby and Hutchinson (1998) demonstrate how knowledge of teaching for inclusion of students with special needs can be acquired through school-based courses within a teacher education program directed at learning in and from experience. And this approach needs to be contrasted with the approach to teachers' knowledge taken by Borko and Putnam (1996) in the *Handbook of Educational Psychology*.

Borko and Putnam's Review of Learning to Teach. Early in their review, Borko and Putnam (1996) state, "Numerous researchers have posed alternative constructs to capture the rich contextualised nature of teachers' knowledge" (p. 677) and they refer the reader to Calderhead's (1996) chapter in the same handbook. The authors continue:

> Some of these ideas grow out of the movement in cognitive science toward thinking of knowledge as situated in physical and social contexts (Brown, Collins, & Duguid, 1989) or out of the movement toward acknowledging narrative forms of knowing (Bruner, 1986). This search for alternative conceptions of knowledge has led educational researchers to write about *situated knowledge* (Leinhardt, 1988), *event-structured knowledge* (Carter & Doyle, 1987) *personal practical knowledge* (Connelly & Clandinin, 1985; Elbaz, 1983), *images* (Calderhead, 1988), and *knowledge in action* (Schön, 1983). All of these constructs are attempts to depict teachers' knowledge about teaching in ways that preserve its close connection to the practice from which it arose and in which it is used.
>
> Although the organizational structure of the chapter does not reflect these alternative representations of knowledge, we incorporate relevant research based on these constructs into our discussions of the various domains of teacher knowledge. By doing so, we assume a certain compatibility among the different ways of representing knowledge—that it makes sense in all of them to talk about various domains or categories of teachers' knowledge and beliefs. (p. 677)

Within these limitations, Borko and Putnam provide an extensive review of the field under three major categories. Under the first of these, "General Pedagogical Knowledge," they describe research into conceptions of self and teaching (e.g., Bullough & Knowles, 1991), of learners and learning (e.g., Feiman-Nemser, 1990), and of classroom management (e.g., Calderhead, 1988). Sometimes the cited studies seem closely aligned to the implicit theme of the review that this knowledge is propositional but, at other times, the alignment is not so close—Calderhead's study is about what teacher candidates report they have learned from teaching experience, for instance. A second major category, "Knowledge and Beliefs about Subject Matter," contains a description of the Knowledge Growth in a Profession project (Grossman, Wilson, & Shulman, 1989), and concludes that teachers enter the profession with widely varying understandings of the subjects they are to teach, and that this variance is found among practicing teachers. The third category, "Pedagogical Content Knowledge and Beliefs," considers overarching conceptions of what it means to teach a subject, knowledge of instructional strategies and representations, and teaching pedagogical content knowledge to novice teachers. The concluding section deals more directly with learning to teach, and cites several alternatives to the more traditional teacher education. All the while, the importance of experience is acknowledged, for example, "Teachers must have the opportunity to learn and reflect about new instructional strategies and ideas in the context of their own practice" (Borko & Putnam, 1996, p. 603). Yet without a treatment of the epistemology of experience and of

experiential knowledge, the review implies that the having of an experience is enough for the development of the knowledge of teaching. When the title, "Learning to Teach," is juxtaposed with the considerable emphasis on propositional knowledge and belief, the hitchhiker is afforded a picture of two unproblematic transfers: an unproblematic transfer of experience to propositional knowledge, and an unproblematic transfer of propositional knowledge to teaching actions.

NARRATIVE AND STORY AS CONCEPTIONS

Connelly and Clandinin (1990) are widely recognized for their development of the field of "narrative inquiry" as an approach to the study of teachers' experiences of teaching: "The central value of narrative inquiry is its quality as subject matter. Narrative and life go together and so the principal attraction of narrative as method is its capacity to render life experience, both personal and social, in relevant and meaningful ways" (p. 10). In the 1980s, they directed the hitchhiker's attention to experience in the following conclusion:

> Educators need to focus on experience, in particular, teacher and student narrative unities. In drawing up, developing, remaking and introducing narratives, the richness of past experience may be brought forward and credited as teachers' and students' personal knowledge of their teaching and learning situations. Teaching and learning situations need continually to "give back" a learner's narrative experience so that it may be reflected upon, valued, and enriched. We want knowing to come alive in classrooms as the multifaceted, embodied, biographical, and historical experience that it is. (Connelly & Clandinin, 1985, p. 197)

Almost a decade later, Connelly and Clandinin contrasted "injection" and "reconstruction" as alternative metaphors for thinking about the curriculum of teacher education. Acknowledging a debt to Dewey's (1938) view of "education as the reconstruction of experience," they argue for a reconstruction view in contrast to the traditional "injection" view. Their focus is not just on telling and writing stories but also on the "retelling and rewriting of teachers' and students' stories [that can] lead to awakenings and to transformations, to changes in our practices as teachers" (Connelly & Clandinin, 1994, p. 158).

To summarize the many publications arising from narrative inquiry as developed by Clandinin and Connelly is difficult. They have extended our vocabulary in interesting ways, with terms such as "teachers' professional knowledge landscapes" and "sacred theory-practice story" (Clandinin & Connelly, 1995). The telling and retelling of professional stories are clearly intended to contribute to teachers' professional development, and the hitchhiker may recognize the power of narrative modes of knowing, as did Bruner.

Carter and Doyle on Narrative and Life History. Carter and Doyle's (1996) chapter offers a further widening of the territory and thus challenges the hitchhiker to consider again what might count as teachers' knowledge. Their approach is to focus on programs involving attention to biography, and they deliberately exclude knowledge from their review, noting that it has become increasingly problematic, and prefer, instead, to use the terms *interpretation* and *understanding*

. . . as vehicles for capturing what personal narrative and life history inquiries are all about. A narrative or life story is an interpretation of experiences or events that reflects, perhaps, a more general understanding of similar experiences and events. Presumably, individuals draw their interpretations from a variety of remembered experiences, bits of information, beliefs, knowledge, dispositions, commitments, cultural forms, as well as the tasks at hand. (p. 121)

Carter and Doyle's (1996) review reveals the rich and varied information that narrative and biographical studies yield. They trace the development of the field from early studies of apprenticeship (e.g., Fuller & Bown, 1975) and teacher cognitions, and they show the more recent and marked influence of feminist approaches, of the concept of story, and of scholars like Clandinin and Connelly (1987). This history acknowledges the place of the concept *currere,* developed by Pinar (1975), and the importance of narrative method and narrative unity (Connelly & Clandinin, 1990). Carter and Doyle examine these approaches within the areas of learning to teach and of teachers' lives, showing clearly the contributions that this research has made. This makes it more puzzling that the reviewers are reluctant to situate this research within teachers' knowledge. To some extent, their concluding cautions may explain the reluctance: They ask if biographical research is truly biographical and if teachers' voices are muffled just as gender and class may be. They ask if biographical approaches are too personal, too intrusive, and thus too exclusive in focus. And they ask what a finding in biographical and personal narrative approaches might be. Here they raise the issue of validity and this tends to draw the hitchhiker back to the question, "Why is this not to be counted as knowledge?" Carter and Doyle conclude by arguing that becoming a teacher means "(a) transforming an identity, (b) adapting personal understandings and ideals to institutional realities, and (c) deciding how to express oneself in classroom activity" (p. 139), all of which they contrast with obtaining credentials and acquiring skills. To show how different autobiographical understandings of knowledge are from the version of knowledge that seems to underlie credentialing in parts of the United States is of more than passing interest and is apparent in the following section.

A KNOWLEDGE BASE FOR TEACHING?

As explained in Christensen (1996), research on the knowledge base for teaching has become a major tool in the United States for the formal accreditation of teacher education programs. Christensen's chapter analyzes the reports from 42 institutions submitting programs for accreditation and for which campus visits were completed in spring 1993. According to Christensen, Shulman is the scholar most frequently cited in these reports, and he repeats the elements of Shulman's model stating that, "It also identified the following sources for the teaching knowledge base: (1) scholarship in the content disciplines, (2) educational materials and structures, (3) formal educational scholarship, and (4) the wisdom of experience" (p. 49). Munby and Russell (1989) have argued that "the wisdom of practice" is too terse a description of how experience and knowing are related.

The idea of a knowledge base for teaching seems to have drawn strength from the Shulman (1987a) paper "Knowledge and Teaching: Foundations of the New Reform." Shulman's seven categories of knowledge and the relatively new pedagogical content knowledge may well be responsible for the large number of citations the hitchhiker might find to this source. Thus the hitchhiker may be interested that Sockett's (1987) critique and Shulman's (1987b) rejoinder met with a much smaller press. Sockett found the knowledge base to be driven by assessment, to lack an adequate description of the moral framework of teaching, and to give insufficient attention to the relationship between reason and action. The hitchhiker will also find Cochran-Smith and Lytle's (1990) critique helpful; their concern is with the lack of teachers' voice in research leading to the knowledge base.

The full title of *The Teacher Educator's Handbook: Building a Knowledge Base for the Preparation of Teachers* (Murray, 1996) explains why Donmoyer (1996) opens his chapter with the observation that the book's publication is either routine or audacious:

. . . routine because since the beginning of this century scholars have attempted to articulate knowledge that could provide the basis for professional rather than political control of education; audacious because, to put the matter simply, knowledge today is not what it used to be. (p. 92)

For Donmoyer, the enterprise of building a knowledge base is naive because it overlooks the political character of knowledge, so he reviews arguments linking knowledge and politics and then offers four rebuttals. The rebuttal of significance to the hitchhiker and the one that Donmoyer believes to have potential for establishing professional control over teaching is the response from practical reasoning. He makes the case that the distinctiveness of teaching as a profession, the claim to a distinctive expertise, "is rooted in an ability to reason in a particular way" (p. 112) and that this mode, after Aristotle, Schön, Schwab, and others, involves careful consideration of means, ends, alternatives, relevant information, and deliberate choosing. Donmoyer's knowledge base, the hitchhiker might imagine, would be as rich with argument as it would be with propositions.

Tom and Valli on Professional Knowledge. The review by Tom and Valli (1990) of professional knowledge for teachers testifies to the dilemma of relating knowledge and practice and to the challenges faced by the university in dealing with craft knowledge. Tom and Valli move with relative comfort through discussions of positivism, interpretivism, and critically-oriented views of professional knowledge, but when they arrive at craft knowledge, they offer a startling conclusion: "A fourth orientation is outside recognized epistemological traditions yet is generally acknowledged to be the dominant orientation among both classroom teachers and teacher educators" (p. 377). They suggest that those in universities are unable to interpret craft knowledge, and they comment that "there is in reality little consensus on what is meant by craft knowledge" (p. 377). In addition, they report that the "great confusion over how craft knowledge ought to be construed" (p. 378) leads them to omit craft knowledge from their subsequent discussions of knowledge and practice in terms of "linkages and purposes" and "warrants and status."

The hitchhiker might be momentarily stunned by this comment on how those in the academy have come to use the term "knowledge" to embrace "knowing that" at the expense of "knowing how." Recovering, the hitchhiker should see Tom and Valli's review as support for Schön's position that the academy has undervalued and neglected processes of learning from experience, including its own learning. One of Tom and Valli's final comments merits inclusion here to drive home the point:

> Classroom practitioners and some teacher educators continue to rely upon a craft conception of professional knowledge; they seem to find little of generative or effective value in knowledge derived from the standard epistemological traditions. The reasons for their rejection of knowledge from the conventional traditions are unclear. . . . (p. 390)

Tom and Valli conclude with a call for greater attention to craft knowledge "as a systematic way of knowing" (p. 390). More recent reviews, such as Grimmett and MacKinnon (1992), discussed below, have contributed to that process. At this point, the hitchhiker may believe that many bridges remain to be built in both directions between practice and knowledge as we seek to understand the nature of teachers' knowledge and its development.

Teachers' Attitudes, Beliefs, and Knowledge

RICHARDSON ON ATTITUDES AND BELIEFS

The second edition of the *Handbook of Research on Teacher Education* (Sikula, Buttery, & Guyton, 1996) contains several chapters that, together, offer the reader a variety of perspectives on teachers' knowledge and its development. Richardson's (1996) chapter is important to the present review because she offers a secure view of the concepts *attitude, belief,* and *knowledge* and because she casts the review widely. Richardson moves rather quickly away from attitudes, finding that the increased interest in cognition has deflected attention from a concept that, in some cases, was defined as a belief and that, in other cases, did not yield significant information in empirical studies. She distinguishes beliefs from knowledge by relying on the standard "truth condition" found in the philosophical literature: beliefs, as propositions, do not have to satisfy a truth condition, but knowledge claims do. Richardson recalls Feiman-Nemser and Floden's (1986) observation, "It does not follow that everything a teacher believes or is willing to act on merits the label 'knowledge'" (p. 515). But, as she notes, the research literature does not always adhere to this convention; thus research on teacher's knowledge can be as much about teachers' beliefs as teachers' knowledge. Kagan (1990), for example, uses the terms synonymously. Richardson argues that, "There is also considerable similarity between the terms *knowledge* and *beliefs* in the concept of personal practical knowledge" (p. 104), introduced by Elbaz (1983) and then elaborated by Clandinin and Connelly (1987). In introducing her review, Richardson relies on Green's

(1971) view that belief "describes a proposition that is accepted as true by the individual holding the belief" (p. 104). She explains, however, that the review includes studies involving such terms as *attitudes, conceptions, theories, understandings, practical knowledge,* and *values.*

Richardson's conclusions are sobering, suggesting that the beliefs of preservice teachers are so strong that they may be impervious to change within teacher education programs. She also questions if change in beliefs represents improvement and asks that researchers become "more explicit about normative considerations if the research is to become truly educative" (1996, p. 114). Her review ends with a call for studies that examine relationships between beliefs and actions of teachers and of teacher educators, especially studies that employ designs commensurate with constructivist approaches, as suggested by Richardson and Anders (1994).

Block and Hazelip (1995) underscore Richardson's (1996), Pajares' (1992) and Kagan's (1992) disquieting conclusions that belief systems, once established, are highly resistant to change. Distinguishing among descriptive, inferential, and informational beliefs, Block and Hazelip suggest that descriptive beliefs, based on personal observation, are central in shaping teachers' images and are the most difficult to modify. They caution that for research to have an impact on teachers, researchers must create a voice for talking with practitioners, and they criticize researchers for failing to share "knowledge with teachers in ways that they can understand and appreciate" (Block & Hazelip, 1995, p. 27).

CALDERHEAD'S "TEACHERS: BELIEFS AND KNOWLEDGE"

Calderhead's (1996) review, "Teachers: Beliefs and Knowledge," is more catholic than Borko and Putnam's (1996) review in the *Handbook of Educational Psychology.* Its opening is helpful for its references to less well-known reviews such as Morine-Dershimer's (1991) and to the work of those associated with the International Study Association of Teacher Thinking, which has had a considerable impact on Australian, Canadian, and European research and practice (e.g., Lowyck & Clark, 1989; Day, Pope, & Denicolo, 1990). Calderhead's review is also helpful for its historical introduction in which the emergence of interest in teachers' cognitions is laid at the feet of the growing respectability of ethnographic studies, of cognitive psychology, and of teacher education. Noting that observation alone is of little value to understanding teacher cognition, Calderhead (1996) explains that increased interest in the area resulted in the emergence of a range of research methods and data gathering approaches. His account of research methods such as concept mapping, metaphors, narratives, and repertory grids illustrates the scope of his review. And the wide appeal is evident in how his review embraces positivist, interpretivist, and critical traditions of research:

> Research on teacher cognitions has occurred within each of these traditions, and consequently has been carried out with various purposes in mind, complying with different methodological conventions. This plurality must be borne in mind in any comparisons or synthesis of research findings. (p. 713)

This stance allows Calderhead to explore the territory widely. Under the banner, he reviews teachers' preactive and postactive thinking, teachers' subject knowledge, teachers' craft knowledge, teachers' personal practical knowledge, teachers' case knowledge, teachers' theoretical knowledge, and teachers' metaphors and images. A similar array of topics is reviewed under teachers' beliefs. And the concluding discussion echoes Calderhead's pluralism:

> Because of the complexity of the area, diverse methodologies are needed, each contributing its own evidence and perspective to an overall understanding of teaching. Such an eclectic approach may enhance our appreciation of teachers' work and contribute to a fuller recognition of what it means to teach and to learn, and how the quality of such processes might be improved. (p. 722)

By broaching theoretical distinctions between knowledge and belief, Calderhead's (1996) review is more adventuresome than Borko and Putnam's. In acknowledging that the dominant view of knowledge is propositional, Calderhead points out that "Research, however, has identified a variety of content and forms that teachers' knowledge and beliefs can take" (p. 715). Calderhead relies on Pajares' (1992) account of beliefs, noting that such terms as values, predispositions, attitudes, opinions, perceptions, and personal ideologies are all used and seem to have overlapping meanings.

Practical Reasoning and Argument: A Bridge to Practice?

The hitchhiker might well wonder how propositional versions of teachers' knowledge become connected to the sphere of practical knowledge. Bridging the gap between theory and practice and between the fields of research and teaching is a perilous activity, given the tensions between competing views of knowledge, the presentation of that knowledge, varying research approaches, and teachers' understandings of what they do. Introducing the concepts of practical reasoning and practical argument may prove helpful in negotiating the epistemic issues of practice, in part, because the arguments surrounding the concept represent differing views and highlight some of the puzzles of practice. Eraut (1994) contends that practical reasoning has been sorely neglected and questions whether this is due to problems in definition, problems in conceptual accommodation, or confusion over allegiance to the theoretical or practical component of professional preparation. Orton (1993) indicates that practical reasoning has been more particularly the province of philosophical literature (e.g., Audi, 1989; Bratman, 1987; Davidson, 1980; MacIntyre, 1984; Walsh, 1974), focusing on questions of reasons as causes of actions and differences between moral and prudential judgments.

Fenstermacher (1994a), using an Aristotelian framework, presented phronesis or practical reasoning as justification of practical knowledge. Without considerations of justification or warrant, "practical knowledge is without epistemic merit; it merely serves as a kind of grouping concept or appropriates the 'purr' word knowledge as a means of making legitimate the labor of practitioners" (p. 48). Pursuing justification and troubled by the question of whether a systematic way to establish warrants that would lead "to a codified body of accepted practical knowledge" (p. 48) exists or could exist, he advanced practical reasoning to access the moral aspects of action and the moral core of teaching. Additionally, practical reasoning could tap the tacit knowings of the teacher to open the possibility for reflective consideration: "Once aware of it, the teacher can deliberate or reflect on it and, if it is found meritorious in that teacher's conception of his or her work, advance it as a reason to justify acting as he or she did" (p. 46).

Linking reasons to action and building on Green's (1971) analysis of the premises of practical argument, Fenstermacher (1986) used practical argument to explain how teachers make use of knowledge, how they think through the findings from research on teaching, and how they subsequently use them. Arguing for methodological pluralism between quantitative and qualitative research, he drew the distinction between the production of knowledge and the use or application of knowledge and argued that the "relevance of research for teaching practice can be understood as a matter of how directly the research relates to the practical arguments in the minds of teachers" (p. 44). Russell (1987) has criticized Fenstermacher for separating thought from action and singularly focusing on teacher thoughts that only relate to practical arguments. In contrast to Fenstermacher's position, Russell offered Schön's (1983) analysis of knowing-in-action (practical knowledge) and reflection-in-action (the process used by a professional to develop and test knowing-in-action) where thought and action are united and a new perspective on the relationship between research and practice advanced. Munby (1987) critiqued Fenstermacher's conceptualization of practical argument on three counts: the conceptualization assumes that teachers need such arguments; the reconstructed logic upon which practical arguments are based is linear, and cognitive processes need not and often do not progress linearly; and practical arguments assume that teachers' thinking is singularly propositional.

Pursuing practical argument, Fenstermacher and Richardson (1993) developed and elaborated its utility to practical knowledge, considered the interest shown in the concept (Buchmann, 1987; Fenstermacher, 1987; Morine-Dershimer, 1987; Munby, 1987; Russell, 1987), and provided an example of its application in Richardson and Anders' (1990) study of teachers' beliefs and practices in the area of reading comprehension, where practical argument sessions with the teacher and two researchers were part of the research design. They highlighted the distinction between practical reasoning—the more general and inclusive activities of thinking—that forms intentions and acts and practical argument—the elaboration of practical reasoning where reasons are connected to action.

To aid the process of developing practical argument, Fenstermacher and Richardson introduced the notion of an "other" as an element in eliciting and reconstructing practical arguments. The other acts as a critical friend (Kroath, 1990) who can engage the teacher in a dialogical relationship that enables a careful scrutiny of the practical reasoning that underpins practical argument. The critical friend both confirms and supports a teacher's classroom reality and challenges and destabilizes taken-for-granted assumptions about one's teaching practice (Kroath, 1990). Fenstermacher and Richardson initially asked How does a teacher use research or practice reflectively? Are there ways to enhance one's capacity or skill at using research or practicing reflectively and, if so, what are they? The notion of "the other" is particularly helpful in answering those questions about knowledge use and acquisition, while practical argument opens up the inquiry into some of the epistemological and moral questions that are attached.

Taken together, practical reasoning and practical argument become a bridge to practice by establishing warrants to practical knowledge and a means to tap the tacit knowings and understandings of teachers. Fenstermacher (1994a) argues that "There is much merit in believing that teachers know a great deal and in seeking to learn what they know, but that merit is corrupted and demeaned when it is implied that this knowledge is not subject to justification or cannot or should not be justified" (p. 51). He contends that the critical challenge for teacher knowledge research is to show not "that teachers think, believe, or have opinions but that they know. And, even more important, that they know that they know" (p. 51).

How Do We Understand Teachers' Knowledge to Develop?: Nonpropositional Accounts

We have already forewarned the hitchhiker of the overlaps and competitions among the perspectives and approaches to work on teachers' knowledge. These difficulties become more awkward as we move into accounts that take a position on the epistemology of practice. As shown below, these accounts draw the hitchhiker into considerations about how teachers' knowledge is acquired and developed. The treatment of work based on an epistemology of practice is followed by the third major part of this chapter, on teacher education. As we explain in that section, the teacher education literature provides the hitchhiker with a fruitful perspective on how those in faculties and colleges of education believe that prospective teachers acquire the knowledge they need to teach.

The language used to describe the wedding of theory and practice is not semantic scrabbling, but it underscores the tensions. Leinhardt, Young, and Merriman (1995) argue convincingly that true integration of declarative professional knowledge, learned at the academy, and procedural professional knowledge, acquired in practice,

> . . . involves examination of the knowledge associated with one location while using the ways of thinking associated with the other location by asking learners to particularize abstract theories and to abstract principles from particulars. The task before us, then, is to enable learners to make universal, formal, and explicit knowledge that often remains situational, intuitive, and tacit; and to transform universal, formal, explicit knowledge for use in situ. (p. 403)

They continue, using Greeno's (1991, 1994) metaphor that configures knowledge integration as producing a "landscape of professional knowledge filled with intellectual affordances that serve as signposts and landmarks within and between the sources and types of knowledge involved in complex practice" (p. 403). Greeno's environmental metaphor invokes Schön's (1983) topography of the hard, high ground of well-formed theoretical problems that are solved by scientific methodology and the swamp with its messy problems of practice, requiring particular, bridging lines of action.

Bromme and Tillema (1995) move beyond integration to advance the fusion of experience and theory. They suggest that becoming a professional requires fusion, not substitution of theory for experience. Sketching the academic and skills traditions that have represented approaches to the equilibrium between theory and practice, they add a problem-solving orientation where action and reflection may bridge the gap between theoretical knowledge and practical action. They then describe professional activity as occurring within a field of tension between the poles of knowledge and action.

Carter (1990) argues for a reconceptualization of teacher knowledge, building on the evidence that teachers' "knowledge is not highly abstract and propositional. Nor can it be formalized into a set of specific skills or preset answers to specific problems. Rather it is experiential, procedural, situational, and particularistic" (p. 307). Therefore, what is required is "to develop forms of representation that capture these essential features of what teachers know with a high degree of situation and task validity" (p. 307).

An epistemology of practice requires attending to the nature of experiential knowledge and how it is acquired (Munby & Russell, 1998). Anchoring this epistemology, however, demands unpacking experiential knowledge and the experiences that lead to its acquisition. Borko and Putnam (1996) caution against conceptualizing teachers' knowledge as being organized into abstract, isolated, discrete categories; rather, it is richly contextualized and embedded in the practice "from which it arose and in which it is used" (p. 677). They highlight several of the constructs that have been advanced to get at the representation of this experiential knowledge. These constructs include situated knowledge (Leinhardt, 1988), event-structured knowledge (Carter & Doyle, 1987), personal practical knowledge (Connelly & Clandinin, 1985; Elbaz, 1983), images (Calderhead, 1988; Clandinin, 1986), and knowing-in-action (Schön, 1983). To these may be added metaphors (Munby, 1986), voice (Richert, 1992), and craft knowledge (Grimmett & MacKinnon, 1992).

The process of acquiring experiential knowledge likewise has a variety of constructs attached. These include tacit understandings (Polanyi, 1962), reflection (Schön, 1983, 1987), authority of experience (Munby & Russell, 1992, 1994), nested knowing (Lyons, 1990), and reframing (Munby & Russell, 1992). Many of the studies that draw distinctions between the novice and the expert teacher (Berliner, 1986; Bullough, Knowles, & Crow, 1991; Kagan & Tippins, 1992; Peterson & Comeaux, 1987; Shulman, 1987a) or that examine the professional knowledge of preservice, neophyte, and experienced teachers (Munby & Russell, 1994; Russell et al., 1988) have been presented as a means to capture aspects of the acquisition of experiential knowledge and its differential presentations. These studies are helpful in the contrasts they reveal, yet they are also confounding in the questions that they raise. As argued later, good teaching tends to reinforce the view that teaching is effortless because the knowledge and experience supporting it are invisible to those taught. Good teaching looks like the ordering and deployment of skills, so learning to teach looks like acquiring the skills. This mechanistic view of teaching accounts, in part, for the prescriptive demands of some preservice students to acquire particular, prerequisite skills, while dismissing theory and research.

The complexity and unpredictability of teaching preclude "the replication of a blueprint or the application of a simple set of principles to provide a sufficient foundation for good practice" (Eraut, 1994, p. 27).

Craft Knowledge

Grimmett and MacKinnon's (1992) important contribution to the teacher knowledge literature is their handling of the concept of craft knowledge in a review that will strike the hitchhiker as ambitious and comprehensive. It differs from other reviews in its transparent political and moral stance, as shown below. Early in their argument, the authors amend Shulman's seven categories by "devising pedagogical learner knowledge," an amalgam of pedagogical content knowledge and general pedagogical knowledge, which allows them to characterize craft knowledge in terms of knowledge derived in response to experience: "Craft knowledge represents teachers' judgment in apprehending the events of practice from their own perspectives as students of teaching and learning, much as a 'glue' that brings all of the knowledge bases to bear on the act of teaching" (p. 387). In this, teaching as craft embodies a teaching sensibility rather than a knowledge of propositions, and craft knowledge is defined as a "construction of situated, learner-focused, procedural and content-related pedagogical knowledge" (p. 393).

Grimmett and MacKinnon trace connections between their conceptions of craft knowledge and other work on teachers' knowledge. They show its relation to Resnick's (1991) theory of situated practice and to an "action-based situated knowledge of teaching" (Leinhardt, 1990, p. 23). They note that sensibility and reflectivity are essential features of teaching as craft. They draw on Schön (1983) and Ryle (1949) in their discussion of the validity of craft knowledge and on Gutman (1987) for an account of the moral appropriateness of craft teaching's intelligent and sensible actions. The authors consider sources of craft knowledge, distinguishing between the first-order abstractions of pedagogical content and learner knowledge (in research and writing by practicing teachers in action settings) and the second-order abstractions of university researchers. The sources they consider include research on pedagogical content knowledge, on reflective practice—giving attention to the research of Bullough et al. (1991), Russell and Munby (1991), and Yinger (1990)—on narrative (e.g., Connelly & Clandinin, 1990), on teachers' lives (e.g., Butt & Raymond, 1989) and on teacher research (e.g., McNiff, 1988).

The work of three educators is used to bring life to the concept of craft knowledge: Kohl's (1988) *36 Children,* Paley's (1981) *Wally's Stories,* and Wigginton's (1991) *Foxfire: 25 Years.* These works share pedagogies that are nonprescriptive, that have academic integrity, and that are responsive to student and community needs. Grimmett and MacKinnon use this body of narrative to show that craft knowledge represents "accumulated wisdom derived from teachers' and practice-oriented researchers' understandings of the meanings ascribed to the many dilemmas inherent in teaching" (Grimmett & MacKinnon, 1992, p. 428). Craft knowledge emphasizes judgment and empathy, and it is infused with morality and contextual understanding. Further, craft teaching may be understood in terms of its immediate intentions for learners, for instance: to foster an insatiable desire for learning, to make learning memorable, and to transform schools into places where "all students become celebrated learners controlling their own inquiries" (p. 429). Grimmett and MacKinnon's prescription for teacher education reflects these ideas. Explorations of the dilemmas of practice, action research, and forms of reflective and critical writing are envisaged for a school-based approach to preparing for craft teaching.

In summarizing their review, Grimmett and MacKinnon (1992) highlight the relationship between experience and learning the craft:

> Craft knowledge is vastly different from the packaged and glossy maxims that govern the "science of education"—at the very least, the expectation that rules and findings can drive practice. Craft knowledge has a different sort of rigor, one that places more confidence in the judgment of teachers, their feel for their work, their love for students and learning, and so on, almost on aesthetic grounds. Ryle and Schön reminded us that there were good reasons for distinguishing between "knowing that" and "knowing how," suggesting that craft is something that is acquired "at the elbows" rather than in books. In that sense, our review of craft knowledge is a bit of an oxymoron. (p. 437)

The hitchhiker will doubtless recognize the inherent awkwardness of writing about the nonpropositional, and will forgive the oxymoron in light of the refreshing moral openness in this account of craft.

Knowledge Use and Knowledge Acquisition

Many of the tensions attached to teacher knowledge are exhibited when one pursues the relationship between how professional knowledge is used and how it is acquired. Eraut (1994) is helpful in describing the interweaving of knowledge use and knowledge acquisition. He argues that to assume the customary position, given the appropriate circumstances, that knowledge is acquired first and then used is a false assumption. Treating professional knowledge broadly as the whole domain within which clusters of meaning reside, he proposes that knowledge cannot be characterized independently from how it is learned and how it is used. The learning that is tied to any change in practice occurs within the context of use. In other words, learning may be associated with knowledge acquisition, with new use, or as a result of contemplation of use. Further, knowledge use in one context is no guarantee for the transfer of learning into another context. He considers learning associated with knowledge use in three contexts: academic, school, and classroom. Each context has its own learnings attached and each requires different forms of knowledge use. This contextual feature of knowledge is also considered by Yinger and Hendricks-Lee (1993), who suggest that knowledge lies within the interaction of particular contexts and situations. Thus teachers' working knowledge depends both on their school environment and on the individuals within that environment.

Constructivist perspectives are likewise helpful in drawing attention to the connectedness in knowledge acquisition and use (Prawat, 1992). Advancing the Tinkertoy model of knowledge organization, Prawat describes the constructivist conceptualization of a system that consists of "nodes" (elements of knowledge) and "connectors" (associative links) (Clancey, 1988). The nodes may include procedural nodes, built on skills and processes; conceptual nodes; representational nodes, which include pictures, analogies, and metaphors; and informal or intuitive nodes that are an idiosyncratic type of knowledge, personalized and cut out of whole cloth (Prawat, 1992). Some elements may be regarded as more meaningful than others, allowing for richer sets of connections within the structure (Prawat, 1989).

Similarly, Eraut (1994) explains change in knowledge as transformation into situationally appropriate forms that modify knowledge by virtue of use; it is not the same knowledge as it was prior to being used. This contextual dependency can, at first glance, appear to fragment knowledge further, particularly with regard to theory-practice issues. To unravel this, Eraut introduces the framework of modes of knowledge use, based on a four-fold typology of replication, application, interpretation, and association (Broudy, Smith, & Burnett, 1964), to assist in understanding the contexts of knowledge acquisition and use. Using replicated knowledge does not require reorganization by the user. Replicating practical knowledge consists of doing routine, repetitive tasks. But neither using replicated knowledge nor replicating practical knowledge is sufficient to capture the professional practice of teaching, which is complicated and variable. Application involves working with rules or procedures—the prescriptive features of practice whereby knowledge is translated into action in particular situations where such action is considered as right or wrong. The interpretive mode gets at the interplay between theory and practice while raising questions about the grounds used for theoretical interpretation and practical application. Eraut explains the associative use of theory with the example of teachers acquiring and using information about their students in a highly contextualized form, never based on a single incident or performance. The associative use of practical knowledge, on the other hand, works from practical problems and situations. These may generate ideas that subsequently have theoretical value. Because this associative use of knowledge is semiconscious and intuitive, it often has metaphors or images attached.

By adding modes of knowledge use to the cauldron of professional knowledge, Eraut suggests that professional education can move beyond paradigm domination and open up opportunities for theory-in-action. Professional judgment can devolve from the interpretive mode, where judgment involves practical wisdom, and the acquisition of judgment depends on an abundance of professional experience. The associative mode enables a reconceptualization of practice through the use of metaphors that, while serving as carriers of theoretical knowledge, are derived from practical experience.

Novice-Expert

We view the research on novice-expert teachers as a subset of knowledge use and acquisition. The hitchhiker may find, yet again, that reviewing this area underscores epistemological complexities and highlights tensions. Knowledge that is particular to practice has various rubrics; for example, craft knowledge (Grimmett & MacKinnon, 1992), professional knowledge (Bromme & Tillema, 1995), pedagogical content knowledge (Shulman, 1986), knowledge-in-action (Schön, 1983), and the

wisdom of practice (Schwab, 1971; Shulman, 1987a). Grossman (1995) identifies the interest in the practices of experienced teachers when she explains: "While teachers can acquire knowledge from a wide variety of sources, they also create new knowledge within the crucible of the classroom. Because teaching has lacked a method for capturing and recording such knowledge, both researchers and practitioners have turned their attention to documenting the wisdom of practice of experienced teachers" (Grossman, 1995, p. 22).

Leinhardt (1990), approaching craft knowledge from the perspective of teacher assessments for certification purposes, neatly identifies two critical problems in the explication of craft knowledge: (1) the problem of determining what composes craft knowledge and whose craft knowledge should be tapped, and (2) the problem of how to access that knowledge and transform it into an assessment that is sufficiently general to have utility for a broad clientele without being overly general and losing meaning. Parallel concerns include the often murky contexts of craft knowledge and the identification and selection aspects of craft knowledge that are appropriate for assessment purposes.

Studies of the contrasts between novices and experts (for example, Berliner, 1988; Borko, Bellamy, & Sanders, 1992; Kagan & Tippins, 1992; Peterson & Comeaux, 1987) have been a means to get at the context-specific nature of craft knowledge. These studies, in turn, drew on information-processing and on what Bromme and Tillema (1995) called the "expert approach" in cognitive psychology (see Bereiter & Scardamalia, 1993; Chi, Glaser, & Farr, 1988; Ericsson & Smith, 1991) that focused on teachers' thinking processes, problem solving, and structures or schemata of knowledge.

Neatly summarizing the implications of this research for teachers' knowledge, Carter (1990) identified the highly domain-specific knowledge of expert teachers, the organization of that knowledge, and its tacit nature. Expert teachers possess richly elaborated knowledge about curriculum, classroom routines, and students that allows them to apply with dispatch what they know to particular cases. Where novices may focus on surface features or particular objects, experts draw on a store of knowledge that is organized around interpretative concepts or propositions that are tied to the teaching environment. Because the knowledge is tacit, it does not translate easily into direct instruction or formalization. This may help to account for the difficulty that teachers have in articulating the pieces that comprise their performance and knowledge base (Leinhardt, 1990). Similarly, McIntyre and Hagger (1993) have argued that teachers' expertise is embedded in their practice and not necessarily readily articulated, which accounts for teachers' talk that fails to measure up to the complexity and subtlety of the craft knowledge that they employ in their practice. Likewise, Ericsson and Simon (1984) contend that engaging in an act skillfully and interpreting it accurately is inherently problematic.

This line of research is not without its critics, however. Taking a global perspective, Britzman (1991) contends that the construct of teacher as expert produces an image of the teacher as autonomous, unitary, and the source of knowledge. In effect, the construct is "a normalizing fiction that serves to protect the status quo, heighten the power of knowledge to normalize, and deny the more significant problems of how we come to know, how we learn, and how we are taught. The understanding that all knowledge is a construct and can thus be deconstructed and transformed by the knower is also disregarded" (Britzman, 1991, p. 230). The problem of tracing the path from novice to expert and detailing how expert knowledge is acquired from experience is seen as a serious omission by Carter (1990), Clift (1989), and Munby and Russell (1994). As in any studies that are comparative, the risk is real that distinctions will become categorical, which may minimize the complexity of what the expert appears to do with little effort. Further, the danger exists that generalizing from a few, seemingly representative cases can translate into a reversion to process-product formulations where certain characteristics of experts' thinking become criteria for judging teaching effectiveness (Carter, 1990; Kagan, 1990). Desforges (1995) raises validity issues surrounding the relationship between elaborate talk and classroom practice, where one may belie the other without sufficient corroboration based on students' learning or other possible effects of teachers' cognition.

Leinhardt's (1993) caution is well advised: "Knowing how experts tend to behave does not help in getting someone to that point, and more importantly, simply copying expertise alone is likely to result in an inappropriate conservatism and lack of innovation" (p. 44). Arguing for the integration of professional knowledge, Leinhardt et al. (1995) explain that "examples of expertise can remain relatively opaque to the novice if not mediated with both pragmatic and theoretical annotations that lead to knowledge integration" (p. 405). Recognizing that skilled practitioners have a "wealth of teaching information . . . [a] deep, sensitive . . . contextualized knowledge" (Leinhardt, 1990, pp. 18–19) derived from the "wisdom of practice," opens the door to epistemological understandings while underscoring their complexities. Grossman (1990), working from the perspective of teacher educators, pursues the linkages between pedagogical content knowledge and subject-specific pedagogical coursework. Following Gage's (1978) description of the well-crafted case that instantiates the possible, she amends that case studies can suggest an image of the possible rather than a portrait of the probable. The hitchhiker may find this to be a helpful metaphor while traveling the lowlands of practice.

Teachers' Knowledge Through the Eyes of Teacher Education

An account of teachers' knowledge and how it develops is incomplete without attention to the teacher education literature. Our review shows that elements of this literature reflect implicit views about the character of teachers' knowledge and its acquisition, and these are clearly important to the hitchhiker. Interestingly, while evidence exists that understandings of teacher education shaped early views of teacher knowledge, there is less evidence that the reverse is true. As we have warned the hitchhiker before, the territory is still not easy to chart, and the perspectives used to address questions about teachers' knowledge stand in conflict with one another and frequently share part of the same space. In addition, views about teacher education are complex and tend to reflect varying metaphors that describe who teachers themselves are. Anderson (1995) suggests that these metaphors shape teachers' thinking about themselves and

have an impact on researchers' and the public's perceptions. Four of these metaphors are relevant here because they speak directly and differently to teachers' knowledge.

Delamont (1995), for example, considers the "teacher as artist" metaphor and contends that it is helpful in understanding the tensions of teaching, particularly the tension between the technical and the creative. To see teaching as a practical art requires the recognition of intuition, creativity, improvisation, and expressiveness (Gage, 1978). Delamont cautions that to lose sight of the indeterminate aspects of teaching, which are more difficult to capture than the technical, condemns researchers to failure. Calderhead's (1995) description of "teachers as clinicians" opens with the conceptualization of teaching as a form of problem solving and decision making that has several properties that are shared with the work of physicians. The perspective of teachers as clinicians has generated research that investigates the decision making of teachers, focusing particularly on how teachers use information about students to tailor instruction to meet individual needs. This research has added to knowledge of teachers' planning and interactive thinking.

Calderhead (1995) sets the historical context that led to the development of the metaphor of teaching as clinical decision making, considers the research focus and methodology, and highlights major findings. Overall, these point to the complexity of teachers' cognitions, to the problem solving attached to their planning, and to the deeply contextualized nature of their teaching. In turn, these have led to newer models for understanding teachers' knowledge such as Putnam's (1987) curriculum script and agenda and Clark and Yinger's (1987) design process metaphor that incorporates Schön's notion of reflection-in-action. The informed decision making of experienced teachers highlights the complexity of their knowledge and has implications for teacher education and further research in making that knowledge accessible to the novice.

Hoyle (1995) suggests that the "teacher as professional" is a potent metaphor, one that raises substantive issues extending well beyond semantics, while also providing a frame for the knowledge and skill base that underpins professional practice. Of particular note is his depicting the knowledge base of "teaching as a profession" as contentious. The dilemma is threefold: criticisms of theory as irrelevant to practice downgrade the importance of the acquisition of professional knowledge; distinctions among types of professional knowledge (e.g., pedagogical, curricular, and socioeducational theory) are not always drawn nor are they clear; and the theory-practice debate often proceeds "on the assumption that pre-existing, systematic, codified knowledge is somehow applied to pupils" (p. 13).

Last, Hollingsworth (1995) describes the "teacher as researcher" metaphor (pp. 16–19), identifying three interrelated areas as foci for teacher researchers: (a) curriculum improvement, which builds on action research and which extends into collaborative research models that include teachers and academics; (b) professional and structural critiques that include teacher preparation and professionalism; and (c) societal reform that encompasses epistemological critique and the problem of gender. The hitchhiker might compare these metaphors with earlier ones: For instance, almost four decades ago, Sarason, Davidson, and Blatt (1962) introduced the image of the teacher as a psychological observer-diagnostician-tactician.

Implicit in their image is a sense that teachers' knowledge involves not only strategies but also content and that how teachers' knowledge develops and the extent to which teachers understand the development of their own knowledge make all the difference to children's learning. These metaphors for teachers lurk just beneath the surface of the accounts of teachers' knowledge that are available to the hitchhiker in the handbooks and other reviews that treat teacher education.

Teachers' Knowledge as Portrayed in the Early Handbooks of Educational Research[1]

The early handbooks of research on aspects of teaching tend to depict teacher education, implicitly or explicitly, as an unproblematic matter of passing along the findings from logical positivist research, which, in turn, is assumed to be a significant source of teacher knowledge. For the hitchhiker, the importance of Gage's (1963) *Handbook of Research on Teaching,* after more than 30 years, resides in its portraying how logical positivism influenced early research on teaching. In retrospect, the chapter by Getzels and Jackson (1963) marks the close of work on teacher personality, while that by Medley and Mitzel (1963) heralds the era of classroom observation research—the forerunner of the process-product research of the 1970s. Interestingly, no chapter devoted to teacher education or to how teachers acquire knowledge of teaching was included.

Not surprisingly, Travers' (1973) *Second Handbook of Research on Teaching* reflects the growth in classroom observation research and the continued allegiance of educational research to logical positivism. Yet three specific chapters show that the field was beginning to recognize alternative approaches, each of which begins to give insight into teachers' knowledge: Light's (1973) chapter on issues in analysis of qualitative data, Dreeben's (1973) chapter on the school as workplace, and Lortie's (1973) chapter on teaching as work. Also, for the first time, research on teacher education merits a chapter of its own. Peck and Tucker (1973) open their chapter with reference to classroom interaction studies (e.g., Amidon & Hough, 1967; Flanders, 1970). Section headings indicate clearly the research approach and the skills and training expected to emerge from this strategy: virtues of the systems approach, programmed instruction, effects of performance feedback, interaction analysis as a training device, microteaching, and the training of teachers in behavior modification techniques. A later section acknowledges the importance of "active involvement of preservice teachers in the teaching act as early as possible in their professional training" (Peck & Tucker, 1973, p. 955). Yet the knowledge to be derived from these approaches is undifferentiated.

Teacher educators of the 1990s might be misled by the title of the 1973 *Handbook* section, "Promoting Self-directed Learning," because while the teaching approaches that are advocated would promote this learning in students in school, contributors make no mention of doing the same for teacher education students. The chapter describes the Personalized Teacher Educa-

tion program at the Research and Development Center of the University of Texas, with outcome measures in terms of classroom interaction variables. Then, somewhat incongruously, the authors report that "there is ample and impressive testimony that student teaching tends to be the most practical and useful part of preservice education in the minds of prospective teachers" (p. 967). Peck and Tucker conclude optimistically and prophetically:

> Teacher education can no longer remain in a happily ignorant and ineffectual state consisting of romanticizing lectures, on the one hand, and fuzzy or unplanned "practical" experience on the other. We are genuinely in sight of the theoretical principles, the operational measures, and even the developmental technology for moving on to a performance-based method of appraising teaching. (p. 971)

In 1973, researchers seemed committed to an easy transition from the world of research knowledge to the world of experience. Teacher education's contribution to the development of teachers' knowledge was implicitly portrayed as training in the acquisition of specific and identifiable skills. Although the Shulman and Tamir (1973) chapter in the 1973 *Handbook* makes no mention of teacher education, one might note with more than passing interest that work on learning by discovery is featured along with research involving Ausubel's (1963) theory of meaningful learning. The contradiction between the training and skills approach to teacher education, evident in Peck and Tucker's chapter, and the discovery learning approach, described by Shulman and Tamir, is one of many tensions that beset teacher education research. In this light, the 1973 *Handbook* illustrates clearly the different assumptions for the education of preservice teachers, on the one hand, and the education of the students they are to teach, on the other.

Teachers' Knowledge in the Third (1986) Edition

The contents of the third edition of the *Handbook of Research on Teaching* (Wittrock, 1986) reveal the beginning of substantial interest in studying how teachers think about their work (e.g., Clark & Peterson, 1986) and in qualitative research methods. The growth of qualitative approaches to research on teaching since the publication of the second edition is reflected in a major chapter on qualitative methods (Erickson, 1986). The swift growth in work that takes seriously the minds of teachers and accords them a place in research accounts is evident in Feiman-Nemser and Floden's (1986) chapter:

> Consideration of teachers' tacit knowledge suggests a shift in the balance between teacher education and teacher training. The success of behaviorally oriented research on teaching encourages a technical skills approach in teacher preparation and renewal. Though technical skills are valuable, research on the cultures of teaching suggests that much of what teachers know does not fit the means-ends statements that summarize process-product research on teaching. Teacher education must build on or rebuild what teachers-to-be already believe about their work. (p. 523)

---

[1] This portion of the review follows closely our account of research in teacher education, which appears in H. Munby and T. Russell (1998), "Epistemology and Context in Research on Learning to Teach Science," in *International Handbook of Science Education,* B. Fraser and K. Tobin, Eds., Dordrecht, The Netherlands: Kluwer.

This useful articulation of the tension between research knowledge and the experience of teacher education is matched only by the chapter on research on teaching. In direct contrast to the behaviorist orientation reflected in the 1973 edition, Lanier and Little (1986) offer sobering sociological commentary, still germane a decade later, on the dilemmas of university-based teacher education.

Lanier and Little (1986) begin their chapter by charging that, although the problems of teacher education have been well known since the beginning of the century and remain virtually unchanged, "few people concerned with such matters seem to recognize the enduring nature of the problems" (p. 527). In their view, "the study of teacher education is apt to be advanced least by adherence to the classical natural science modes of inquiry" (p. 528). They therefore reject reviewing studies with pre- and postinstructional measures of knowledge, predictably finding that "prospective and practicing teachers can indeed 'learn new tricks' and master all sorts of subject matter knowledge and skills of the trade" (p. 528). By attending to how teacher educators view themselves, Lanier and Little (1986) find that professors of methods courses identify with the school subjects of their expertise and "tend to consider themselves science educators, or mathematics educators or reading educators, and point to those who coordinate or supervise student teachers as the real teacher educators" (pp. 528–529). Lanier and Little continue by commenting on the low regard in which professors of education are held, suggesting that low esteem and low research productivity are explicable in terms of social class and values and the move of normal schools in North America into the university community. "The reciprocal effects of personality and job conditions for those most closely associated with teacher education may have affected selective recruitment, selective retention, and, subsequently, formation of intellectual propensities and working norms that conflict with the traditional values of higher education" (p. 533).

The suggestion here is that openness to new ideas, cognitive complexity, and self-direction were typically lacking among teacher education faculty of two decades ago. For example, Zeichner and Tabachnik (1982) and Stones (1984) found that supervisors were unlikely to have given thought to the theory and practice of supervision. Lanier and Little (1986) are not concerned with epistemological questions about the status of knowledge of teaching or what teachers and teacher educators know. Yet the sociological account sharpens questions about the faculty who teach methods courses. This bleak picture of teacher education continues with an account of its students: "The overall group norm for teacher education students falls below the average for all college students [in the United States] due to the larger number of learners scoring in the lowest ranks on such measures [of academic ability]" (Lanier & Little, 1986, p. 540). When this is joined to the work on low student expectations and general dissatisfaction, Lanier and Little's conclusion that the work environment of teacher education generally lacks intellectual stimulation is not surprising.

Neither does the teacher education curriculum (rich in assumptions about teachers' knowledge as propositional) escape criticism: "Little is known about what prospective teachers typically encounter or learn from academic studies in [general studies and subject matter concentrations]" (p. 546). Lanier and

Little remind us of the lack of agreement about the university curriculum, and they report that foundations, methods, and practice teaching are common elements that vary considerably in time given to each component. They criticize both the demands of teacher education programs and their failure to offer anything that would educate prospective teachers "to consider their own personalities and to take them into account when working with people" (p. 549). Because student teachers face large classes, beginning teaching tends to focus on management, and "beginning with these initial experiences, teachers learn to think that the way to learn more about teaching is through trial and error, not through careful thought and scholarship" (p. 551). "The tension between the practical apprenticeship and the more intellectual pedagogy has continued to be resolved in favor of the technical, a management approach suited for the non-career teacher" (p. 551). And this, for Lanier and Little, restricts views on the possibilities, ultimately giving little change to the overall practice of the profession.

The background of methods faculty, the low standards and expectations of education students, the teacher education curriculum itself, and the class sizes in the student teaching experience together conspire to make teacher education both unsatisfactory and vulnerable. In this condition, teacher education seems especially prone to adopt not only the results of research directed at determining teaching skills and competencies but also the accompanying assumptions about what teachers need to know.

> The absence of a firm knowledge base for teacher education has led to a long-standing and wide-ranging search for the sort of expertise that would be helpful to the practitioner and at the same time raise the status of teacher education in the academic community. (p. 552)

For Lanier and Little, the search for helpful, status-raising expertise gave rise to identifying "strategic clusters of teaching behaviors" and led to classroom intervention studies (e.g., Good & Grouws, 1979). But aside from successes in skill interventions, "the research as a whole has not seemed to cumulate into a more coherent understanding of teaching and teacher education" (p. 552). Ultimately, Lanier and Little ascribe the teacher education curriculum's resistance to change to the rapid expansion of the teaching cadre and to a lengthy adherence to a dominant research paradigm in education (p. 554). That paradigm takes little account of what teachers, teacher educators, and teacher education students know. In summary, Lanier and Little paint a dismal picture of teacher education—education that is conducted more by trial and error than by thought and scholarship. The absence of an overall guiding image of teachers' knowledge could not be more obvious.

Teachers' Knowledge in the Handbooks of the 1990s

The appearance of Houston's (1990) *Handbook of Research on Teacher Education* gave some credence to teacher education as an area of professional study and action. Doyle's (1990b) opening chapter, for example, argues that one can find codifiable knowledge in teaching practices, content, and classroom enactment that is substantially richer than anything derived from process-product research. His clear case for interpretive and procedural accounts of practical knowledge, rather than prescriptive ones, signaled the need for teacher education to be grounded in something more than the results of research in the logical positivist tradition.

A distinctive feature of the Houston *Handbook* is the space given to professional knowledge, construed in various ways. Carter (1990) identifies three major categories of research in this area: pedagogical content knowledge (e.g., Shulman, 1987a), practical knowledge (Connelly & Clandinin, 1986; Russell et al., 1988), and information processing and novice-expert studies (e.g., Peterson & Comeaux, 1987). While cautioning that the research insufficiently emphasizes a theory of learning to teach, Carter's review demonstrates that "the range and complexity of what are learned in teacher education are enormous" (p. 307). Tom and Valli's (1990) chapter on professional knowledge complements Carter's treatment by raising concerns about the warrants and epistemological status of claims about professional knowledge.

The growth of attention to epistemological issues in teacher education is accompanied by work that focuses on predicaments within the circumstances of teacher education. Feiman-Nemser's (1990) account of the traditional models and arrangements of teacher education and their history is balanced by Ginsburg and Clift's (1990) more sociological account, which revisits some of the themes of the earlier review by Lanier and Little (1986). Teacher educators are found to honor the maxim, "Do as I say and not as I do," and the delivery of teacher education is cast as course-work intensive, with inadequate time for reflection and with an emphasis on the teacher as technician and consumer of propositional knowledge rather than as reflective practitioner. Guyton and McIntyre's (1990) review of student teaching describes the large variance in time devoted to school experience within teacher education programs. Not surprisingly, they found research on teaching practice to be largely atheoretical, commenting that "the atheoretical nature of field experience that has existed for many years can be attributed partly to the imposition of a scientific research paradigm on situations that are not compatible with the methods, purposes, philosophy, epistemology, or assumptions of the paradigm" (p. 529). As with Doyle (1990b), Guyton and McIntyre argue for the appropriateness of interpretive methodologies for the study of school experience components within teacher education programs.

Anderson and Mitchener's (1994) discussion of the teacher education curriculum in a specific subject (science) moves from subject matter preparation into a review of the changing nature of professional knowledge. They find a transition from the image of the teacher as a technical expert to one of reflective practitioner, citing the work of Schön (1983, 1987), Russell (1989), and Doyle (1990a), among others, and acknowledging Schön's contribution to viewing teaching as a problematic enterprise. "These changes in professional education, however, are still in the deliberation and early research stages, and have not had a significant impact in the realities of actual practice" (p. 16). Significantly, Anderson and Mitchener find that this changing conception of the teacher has failed to influence the traditional learning-to-teach elements of foundations, methods, and field experiences. For instance, while they acknowledge that Shulman's work on pedagogical content knowledge has altered

views on methods courses, they also note the difficulties that continue to attend this concept. Their review does not make it clear that the full impact of changes in the conception of teaching is totally embraced. Their account of a dilemma with respect to the role that student teaching plays in learning to teach is illustrative:

> The dilemma science teacher educators face here is whether or not the experiences in the field have the focus they desire. Is it a setting in which prospective teachers can practice the new approaches they are learning in their teacher education programs, or is it a setting in which they become socialized to entrenched ineffective practices? (p. 18)

The first horn of the dilemma portrays teacher education as a matter of applying new approaches within field experience, while the second horn suggests that little of value could be learned from being in a classroom. Framing the dilemma in this way misses entirely the import of learning through experience, which is highlighted by Schön's view of knowledge-in-action. A "knowledge-in-action" perspective suggests that student teaching can be a setting where prospective teachers identify what they already know (in action) and what they need to learn (in action) in a program of teacher education.

Anderson and Mitchener's account of the challenge facing teacher educators is not comforting: "How will you address in a coherent, comprehensive manner such emerging issues as new views of content knowledge, constructivist approaches to teaching and learning, and a reflective disposition to educating teachers?" (p. 19). Importantly, this challenge seems to relegate reflection to the realm of "technique" and fails to indicate that constructivism might provide a useful way to consider how teacher candidates themselves develop practical or craft knowledge. Issues such as this arise frequently in the teacher education literature, indicating that these are indeed times of rapid change in assumptions and beliefs about what teachers know and how teachers learn.

Anderson and Mitchener themselves suggest that new approaches (e.g., Baird, 1992; Roberts & Chastko, 1990) have resulted in substantial changes to how we think of teacher development, the teaching and learning process, and teacher education:

> We are still a long way, however, from research that addresses such issues in the context of total teacher education programs grounded in a theoretical framework. Furthermore, there is a need to address the question of what theoretical frameworks for a teacher education program are consistent with what research is telling us about teacher thinking and how teachers come to have an outlook and competencies that are consistent with emerging understandings of student learning. (p. 31)

Two features here are worthy of note: first, the authors do not specify what sort of research might address these issues, and, second, the students in "student learning" seem to be school students rather than teacher education students. The hitchhiker may share our gratitude to Anderson and Mitchener for citing Griffin's (1989) conclusion about the importance of the earliest years of teaching:

Despite our growing acknowledgment of the complexity of teaching, there still exists the notion that somehow, if teachers just mastered teaching methods in their college or university preparation programs, many of the barriers to delivering quality instruction would be removed. What is ignored in this view is the power of the first years of actual teaching experience to influence a teaching career. . . . (p. 397)

The significance of teaching experience to the development of teachers' knowledge, especially within teacher preparation programs, has been overlooked consistently in this and the other reviews mentioned above. The hitchhiker will have wondered why craft knowledge or practical knowledge is accorded barely a glance. Also overlooked is the opportunity to connect ideas about youngsters' learning, for example, constructivism, with the learning of preservice teacher education candidates. Notably, teaching teachers is rarely portrayed as helping teachers to construct a constructivist view of their own teaching.

Here Borko and Putnam's (1996) "Learning to Teach" is again relevant to the hitchhiker. They argue for the significance of teachers' knowledge and beliefs when learning is construed as a constructive process within physical and cultural contexts. They show that practical knowledge studies reveal how the conceptions that novice teachers have of themselves as teachers influence how they teach. Although beliefs about teaching and learning can change, clearly, existing knowledge and beliefs influence the knowledge preservice teachers actually acquire about learners, with initial images frequently drawn from their personal experiences as school children. These beliefs often seem "resistant" to teacher education experiences: Studies show that the most growth among preservice teachers is found in those who see learners as multifaceted. Not surprisingly, experienced teachers are found to be more expert than beginning teachers, with some studies identifying the general pedagogical skills that novices need to acquire.

Borko and Putnam suggest that it may be important to find ways to help experienced teachers change routines and the knowledge and beliefs underlying them. On the whole, they conclude, the research literature offers mixed evidence regarding the success of strategies designed to influence teachers to change their beliefs and knowledge about teaching. Knowledge and beliefs about subject matter seem more readily changed; for instance, Smith and Neale (1989) show how teachers with little understanding of science concepts improved their understanding. The rising interest in the concept of pedagogical content knowledge is reflected in Borko and Putnam's (1996) review, though the doubts about this concept, which were raised by Anderson and Mitchener (1994), are not aired. Particularly intriguing is Borko and Putnam's account of impediments to learning to teach, because the psychological orientation of their review appears to predispose them to see these impediments as features of teacher education candidates: their beliefs about teaching and learning and their subject matter knowledge, for example. To be sure, "contextual factors" are noted: the quality of discipline-based courses, the lack of opportunity to reflect in teacher education courses, the sometime unsupportive environments in which student teaching is conducted, and the dominant beliefs about teaching and learning that pervade these environments. In the closing pages of their review, they list

features "that contribute to successful learning opportunities for teachers," which follow:

1. Addressing teachers' [existing] knowledge and beliefs about teaching, learners, learning, and subject matter;
2. Providing teachers with sustained opportunities to deepen and expand their knowledge of subject matter;
3. Treating teachers as learners in a manner consistent with the program's vision of how teachers should treat students as learners;
4. Grounding teachers' learning and reflection in classroom practice; and
5. Offering ample time and support for reflection, collaboration and continued learning. (pp. 700–701)

The underlying issues of the epistemology and context of teacher education may not be sufficiently understood for the hitchhiker to share the optimism that Borko and Putnam hold for these approaches. In a recent review of perspectives on learning to teach, Feiman-Nemser and Remillard (1996) provide a similar account, which describes the difficulties of understanding the development of teachers' knowledge: "The phrase learning to teach rolls easily off the tongue, giving the impression that this is a straightforward, easily understood process. In fact, we do not have well-developed theories of learning to teach and the phrase itself covers many conceptual complexities" (p. 63). They comment that "knowing what good teachers do, how they think, or what they know is not the same as knowing how teachers learn to think and act in particular ways and what contributes to their learning" (p. 63), recalling for the hitchhiker the tensions introduced much earlier.

Feiman-Nemser and Remillard also share our view of the inadequacies of prevalent assumptions about learning to teach, whether they be "lay theories" that trust to trial and error or the "conventional" position that teachers first acquire knowledge and then use it in practice settings (p. 79). A significant contribution of their review comes in their directing attention to the conceptual change and situated cognition literatures (pp. 79–85) and in their pointing out that these perspectives apply both to learning in school classrooms (practice teaching) and to learning in university classrooms (teacher education courses and undergraduate education generally). The obvious implication is that how teachers learn in university classrooms does make a difference in terms of teachers' knowledge and their understanding of that knowledge. Until learning experiences in university settings evolve to match our understanding of situated cognition, the development of teachers' knowledge will continue to be problematic.

The Issue of Context in Teacher Education

The hitchhiker might be wary of expressions of optimism for teacher education when some of the conditions over which teacher educators have little or no control are not given the attention they deserve. Context is clearly important and, as the setting for teaching practice, schools will always play a major role in the preparation of teacher education candidates. Also significant is the observation by Griffin (1989) and others that all there is to teaching is not learned during initial or preservice teacher preparation. Any teacher will attest to the significance of the first two years of professional experience, and many will acknowledge how their continuing classroom work persistently informs and improves their practice. Yet there will be variability in the quality of teaching and, rather than lay the blame for this on teachers themselves, the hitchhiker may prefer to inquire into the extent to which school settings are conducive to the learning of those who teach in them. As Borko and Putnam (1996) point out,

> Many of the beliefs about teaching, learning, learners, and subject matter that may serve as personal impediments to change pervade the culture of schools. Such views are widely held by other teachers, school administrators, students, and parents. They underlie many existing school practices and policies such as grading of students, evaluation of teachers, and commitments to standardized testing. Teachers struggling to adopt a view of students as active learners and to think through and try out the implications of this view in their classrooms may bump up against countervailing beliefs held by students, their parents, and other teachers, making it that much more difficult for teachers to change their beliefs and practices. (p. 90)

While beliefs and practices are clearly constituents of school culture, there are other elements that, together, may conspire against productive learning by school staffs. These include inadequate facilities and resources, large classes of students requiring varied amounts of individual attention, insufficient time to prepare instruction and to respond in detail to student work, and, in some settings, responsibilities for controlling aggression and even violence. Yet engaging in the serious reflection, study, and renewal associated with constructing professional knowledge is not so much an issue of time and energy as it is an issue of perspective on the nature of professional development and, more broadly, a frame of mind. If the culture of schools (Sarason, 1996) does not encourage, support, and reward reflection and experimentation by teachers and by students, then we have little hope of overcoming the challenges that school contexts present to the development of professional knowledge within teacher education. The hitchhiker may note with interest that Sarason (1971) seems to have been one of the first to draw close parallels between conditions in schools for student learning and for teachers' professional learning.

> The research literature, as well as more informal observation, is replete with examples of the self-defeating consequences of (a) the lack of spontaneous question asking and (b) the overlearned tendency to absolve the asker of responsibility by unreflectively and quickly providing the asker with answers.
>
> What I am saying here I said in the book but, I have since concluded, I did not sufficiently emphasize how bedrock the asker-answerer relationship is for school change. *Any effort at systemic reform that does not give top priority to altering that relationship will not improve educational outcomes.* (Sarason, 1996, p. 367)

Sarason quickly makes the link to conditions for teachers' learning by adding, "*Teachers cannot create and sustain contexts for productive learning unless those conditions exist for them*" (p. 367). The hitchhiker will find progress being made in developments like the Project for Enhancing Effective Learning (PEEL) in Australia (Baird & Mitchell, 1986; Baird & Northfield, 1992).

In many ways, the institution of school seems to fall short of the expectations one might hold of an institution of learning. Nor are colleges, faculties, and schools of education within the university environment immune from similar critical inspection, as Lanier and Little (1986) demonstrate in their review. They are not alone in calling attention to the inherent contradiction of lecturing about learning by discovery. Not surprisingly, teacher educators have little control over the contexts of school, nor should they have. What teacher educators and researchers plainly need is a clear understanding of how school contexts feature in teacher education. Without attention to context, calls for more research with coherent theoretical frameworks are rendered vapid. And without attention to context, teacher educators will not be challenged to reframe their own practices to rejoin experiences of teaching with the knowledge of teaching. A significant part of this reframing can come from confronting an important reality in teacher education programs: School experience remains a constant in these programs, and teacher education candidates continue to aver that this experience is the most influential and significant feature of their professional preparation. Here knowledge and experience seem to go together, but the fact that the knowledge is not propositional leads us to consider the epistemological tensions in teacher education.

The Tensions of Epistemology in Teacher Education

One need have little more than a rudimentary grasp of the difference between the concepts of behavior and action to understand the appeal of school experience to teacher education candidates. As many have noted, intending teachers' prior experience of teaching is severely restricted. Although they have observed thousands of hours of teaching behavior, they have not been privy to the profound and extensive knowledge and thinking that underlies this behavior. As with any good performance, good teaching looks easy. When we witness a near-perfect performance in, say, the long program of a figure-skating competition, we recognize the many hours of intensive work that lie behind the apparent ease of execution under demanding circumstances. But we typically do not do this of teaching. Indeed, teaching is so commonplace that successful, proficient, even artful teaching can be its own undoing. Because those of voting age have experienced its apparent effortlessness, teaching seems in no need of political champions. Good teaching in the eyes of those taught unwittingly reinforces this view of teaching, and its manifestations suggest strongly that, if some of its students should wish to become teachers, all they need do is attend a teacher education program, acquire the skills, and then practice them. Certification and good teaching will follow. The hitchhiker may have heard, as we have, teacher education candidates reject in-college courses and commit themselves to the view that nothing in books can have any bearing on how they might conduct themselves professionally. This view is entirely consistent with the final chapter of Kagan's (1993) study, which argues that educational theory and the research on which it is based are irrelevant to classroom teaching and learning.

For teacher education and teacher education research, the irony of teaching is at first epistemological. To the uninitiated, teaching unfolds as sets of skills but, to the initiated, teaching depends on, is grounded in, and constitutes knowledge. The character of this knowledge poses the irony for teacher education: The knowledge is, in part, practical, and that part can only be learned in practice, the very setting over which teacher educators have little direct control. Unaccountably, some teacher education research verges on duplicity in this irony: Calls for instructors to have their students teach in a fashion consistent with constructivist accounts of learning are not typically accompanied by clear calls for these instructors to acknowledge anything about how their students will construct their own views of teaching. Constructivism in teacher education seems to apply only to school-age learners and not to the preparation of their teachers.

Despite the tight grip that quantitative research approaches held prior to the 1980s, qualitative research on teaching seems to have established a place for itself in the field of teacher education. Quantitative traditions appear to underlie such concepts as "a knowledge base for teaching," with its implicit orientation to propositional knowledge and skills. The substantial review of the knowledge base by Wang, Haertel, and Walberg (1993) covers 91 meta-analyses, 179 chapters and other reviews, and the views of 61 experts. But the concept of a knowledge base is not without its detractors. Kliebard's (1993) critique of the review by Wang et al. argues:

> The failure of that kind of research to affect practice is not a matter of obstinacy, ignorance, or malfeasance on the part of teachers, or for that matter a failure on the part of researchers to employ sophisticated research techniques, or to amass large enough data bases. It is a failure on the part of the research establishment generally to take seriously enough the conditions of teaching as well as the perspective of teaching professionals. (p. 301)

This underscores for the hitchhiker the importance of the knowledge and understandings of teachers and, of course, preservice teacher education students.

Conceivably, qualitative research's most significant contribution to teacher education has been its inclination to listen to teachers and students of teaching. As a consequence of this move toward phenomenological accounts, we have witnessed considerable growth in our understanding of the knowledge teachers possess, and in our understanding of how this knowledge is acquired, modified, and elaborated through experience. In some instances, research has invented quite novel ways to speak of these. For instance, the work on narrative, initiated and promulgated by the continuing research of Connelly and Clandinin (1986), has, in large measure, laid the foundation for the adoption in teacher education courses of narrative methods such as journal writing. Narrative method employs an epistemology of practice that, at root, asserts that teachers' knowledge is storied. By building on the work of Schön (1983, 1987), Munby and Russell (1992, 1994) have developed an epistemology of professional knowledge rooted in action itself. While these and other approaches are incomplete and not without problems of their own (Fenstermacher, 1994a), they plainly signal a marked change in how the knowledge of teaching can be conceived and, to some extent, developed. Despite advances in conceptualizing the knowledge of teachers, teacher education

retains its predilection for injecting research findings into methods courses and programs without attending to wide variances in epistemology. "Reflection," for example, has become an organizing theme in some teacher education programs, as if Schön intended the term "reflection-in-action" to refer to a set of skills (Munby & Russell, 1993).

Teacher Education's Response to the Challenge to Reinterpret Teachers' Knowledge

The hitchhiker might reasonably ask how the field of teacher education is responding to the calls to view teaching as a practical endeavor undergirded by an epistemology quite different from that of propositional knowledge, so long the mainstay of quantitative research on teaching. In the preceding discussion, we are critical of conclusions in *Handbook* chapters that contain the somewhat traditional call for "more research" such as the conclusions of Anderson and Mitchener (1994). A parallel call for "more time" can be found in teacher education research itself. For example, Gallagher's (1991) study of the beliefs held by prospective and practicing science teachers about science contains a proposal that teacher education be expanded to five years so that students have an adequate knowledge of history and philosophy of science. Calls for more research and more time are usefully contrasted with some of the findings of Pajares' (1992) review on teachers' beliefs, findings that should occasion pause for teacher educators:

- Beliefs about teaching are well established by the time a student gets to college.
- The earlier a belief is incorporated into the belief structure, the more difficult it is to alter.
- Individuals develop a belief system that houses all beliefs acquired through the process of cultural transmission.
- Belief change during adulthood is a relatively rare phenomenon, the most common cause being a conversion from one authority to another or a gestalt shift. (pp. 325–326)

The authority of additional courses is not clearly sufficient to the task of changing the beliefs of prospective teachers. Typically, prospective teachers have been accustomed to the two traditional forms of authority: the authority of position and the authority of argument (reason and evidence). Part of the significance of an epistemology of practice is the implicit credence it affords to experience itself, a feature of student teaching that underlies its significance to students in teacher education. This switch to a different authority, the authority of experience (Munby & Russell, 1994), may well represent the power needed for changes in beliefs. Certainly, there is evidence that the authority and place of experience are being taken seriously within teacher education courses. Case-study approaches and narrative writing appear to be gaining ground, as Carter and Anders (1996) demonstrate. These styles move in the direction of having teacher education students give voice to their experiences in the schools and, so, honor them and their connection with in-college courses. Neither is rigor sacrificed for relevance in these approaches (Munby & Russell, 1995). The significance of the authority of experience is especially clear in programs (e.g.,

Russell, 1995) in which prospective teachers receive between 10 and 16 weeks of classroom experience before they attend courses in teacher education. And further evidence of the difference that experience can make is evident in those inservice teacher education programs that take the needs of their students at face value. As teacher educators, we seem to express what Whitehead (1995) calls a living contradiction: By requiring our students to have field experience, we espouse its significance, but we have tended to give more time, emphasis, priority, and status to on-campus courses within programs of preservice teacher education.

When the concept of the authority of experience is joined to recent work by Fenstermacher (1994b), it becomes more obvious that teacher education needs to reconsider the place of student teaching and the balance, chronologically and epistemologically, between this teaching experience and in-college courses. In his address, Fenstermacher distinguishes between the systemic functions and the educational purposes of school. Systemic functions, he suggests, are the functions that keep the system working: classroom management, testing, grading, attendance, and so forth. The essence of his argument is that the schools should be given the major responsibility for introducing prospective teachers to systemic functions and that the universities should be responsible for the remainder of teacher education. This argument is appealing for several reasons.

1. It exposes what teacher educators have known for some time about the immediate concerns of prospective teachers: their principal concerns center around their being able to manage the systemic functions of school. No amount of in-college classes can accomplish this; it is attained only through the experience of working in schools.
2. Related to the first, the dominance of these concerns can detract prospective students' attention from the substance of teacher education classes that schools cannot supply. Schools, as Fenstermacher suggests, are not suited to undertaking research nor to bringing a critical eye to education. Universities, however, have this social obligation. Once prospective teachers have assured themselves that they can indeed practice systemic functions, they are likely to be able to attend to the understandings and issues of education that are generated in the universities.
3. The overwhelming evidence of a decade of research on teacher knowledge is that knowledge of teaching is acquired and developed by the personal experience of teaching.

Traditionally, we have assumed that no one should be permitted to teach until he or she has been told how to perform. This view is founded on arrogance so deeply rooted that it has given rise to the very description of the field experience as "practice teaching," as though all that our students need do to develop professional knowledge is to practice what teacher educators have preached. Perhaps the hitchhiker will decide that now is the time to expose this assumption and to turn teacher education programs around so that the work of the universities may build productively upon what can be and must be learned in schools.

This discussion has documented the substantial growth in research in teacher education, mirroring the growth in research on teachers' knowledge over the last decade. Teacher educators have reason to be pleased with this substantial growth. Yet in a context where student teaching appears to be relegated by teacher educators —but not by those learning to teach—to a status lower than other components of teacher education programs, there is a clear danger that educational research activities and their products may become increasingly distant from the student teaching experience of our students. This can be especially true of the more traditional social-scientific research in education. The more recent emergence of a focus on reflective approaches in teacher education (e.g., Knowles & Cole, 1994), with its implicit connections to qualitative research, clearly encourages our students to join their practice to systematic thinking. And a similar joining of research results to practice is evident in the work of Fenstermacher and Richardson (1993). Notably, both approaches demand that student teaching precede reflection and attention to practical arguments. The evident success of these approaches should allay any concern that prospective teachers cannot profit immeasurably from early teaching experience without our initial intervention: Knowledge of experience is acquired in experience, as the hitchhiker knows only too well.

Validity, Research, and the 21st Century

The final part of this chapter is designed to take the hitchhiker into the 21st century, which is achieved by first considering issues of validity. This leads into the terrain of research, with particular attention to the moral dimensions of research and to the moral dimensions of teacher knowledge. As in the earlier portions of this chapter, the hitchhiker is not to be burdened with detailed descriptions of studies but is presented with more pages of the guide. Here particularly, the guide explains the difficulties confronting this area of educational research, and it returns the hitchhiker to the tensions introduced at the outset of our journey.

Conventional and Technical Accounts of Validity

The hitchhiker will have noticed that this guide has avoided direct discussion about issues of truth and validity to this point. It is appropriate to explore the territory of this discussion here because, as shown below, the issue of truth is as relevant to research on teachers' knowledge as it is to teachers' knowledge itself.

In quantitative research, the notion of truth is replaced at one level by constructions about chance and sampling error. But the statistical portion of this research is just a small part of the overall argument, and assessing the epistemic merit of research conclusions is a matter of establishing the validity of the entire argument. In this respect, quantitative and qualitative research are similar. Despite the surface similarity, the relative youth of qualitative research in education, especially that of such modes as narrative, has engendered a suspicion that Roberts (1996) portrays succinctly with a view to argument and its point:

Whether qualitative research is recognized as research at all, as opposed say to parochial storytelling or incestuous opinion swapping or unproductive navel gazing, is a complicated issue that has at least two intertwined parts: (a) the *quality* of an individual piece of such research, which is very much a function of (b) the *argumentative structure* of the research report itself. (p. 244)

The following look at conventional accounts of validity and how they unfold in narrative research shows the hitchhiker that research in teachers' knowledge has tended to neglect moral dimensions. Indeed, it could be argued that issues of validity are closely associated with moral arguments about educational practice.

McMillan and Schumacher (1997) and similar texts present validity in a technical way, suggesting to us such familiar statements as: "Internal reliability in a qualitative design addresses whether (or not), within a single study, multiple observers agree." "Could other researchers use the same data to generate the same explanations or constructs?" "Is there good use of verbatim accounts of participant conversations, descriptions phrased as concretely and precisely as possible from field notes or recordings of observations, and direct quotations?" "Are there multiple researchers?" and "Are tape recorders, photographs, or videotapes used for data collection?" But these questions cannot be viewed as checklists with check marks to be treated like interval data. Ultimately, the technical or conventional accounts are found wanting because something normative is left unstated in one way or another.

Some attempts at modifying conventional approaches involve abandoning validity and embracing trustworthiness, although it seems to make little difference when it comes to making judgments. Eisenhart and Howe's account (1992) tackles validity on broader criteria. Their "five general standards for validity" of which the first three are "rules of thumb for systemic consideration of research studies qua arguments" (p. 657) consist of the following:

- The fit between research questions, data collection procedures, and analysis techniques
- The effective application of specific data collection and analysis techniques
- Alertness to and coherence of prior knowledge
- Value constraints
- Comprehensiveness.

Within the fourth item of their list, "value constraints," Eisenhart and Howe discuss both internal and external value arguments. Internal arguments concern the ethics of research. External arguments concern "whether (or not) the research is valuable for informing and improving educational practice" (p. 660) and urge that "valid studies must be worthwhile" (p. 660). The charge that validity depends, in part, on the value of the research is problematic. Because educational practice is normative, either the warrant or the conclusion must be normative, so the significance of a study must be grounded in an argued value position. Eisenhart and Howe (1992) appear to be acknowledging this when they state "judgments of the worth of research projects are difficult to make. They have the potential to be exceedingly biased" (p. 660). Eisenhart and Howe's external value

constraint clearly signals that moral arguments about practice belong in considerations about research validity.

Arguments about the Validity of Narrative Study

The appearance of narrative research challenged the usefulness of conventional accounts of validity. Although narrative method, as developed by Connelly and Clandinin (e.g., Connelly & Clandinin, 1990), was primarily a route to conceptualizing the character of teachers' professional knowledge as storied, narrative method has assumed a life of its own. Cizek (1995) complains about the incursion of aspects of narrative research into quantitative research reports, and he asks:

If research doesn't relate to anything we currently know (i.e., theory-driven), if it doesn't address a question of interest posed by the researcher (i.e., hypothesis testing) or produce knowledge that others can use and is *bound* to a particular setting (i.e., not generalizable) then how can it even be called research? (p. 27)

He suggests, "Qualitative researchers are often not so much practitioners as believers. It's almost a religious thing" (p. 27). And in calling for assistance from philosophers, he wonders what happened to the concept of falsifiability, asking, "Is qualitative research falsifiable?" (p. 27). Cizek's piece captures the difficulties of assuming that narrative research has a similar function to quantitative forms of research and should be bound by similar principles such as falsifiability.

O'Dea's (1994) "Pursuing Truth in Narrative Research" addresses philosophical critiques of validity in narrative research, such as Phillips' (1994) paper, which is written from an epistemological and analytical perspective. (Fenstermacher and Richardson, 1994, have suggested that Phillips confounds narrative itself, narrative inquiry, and narrative use.) O'Dea's approach is from literary criticism, and she tends to set aside other positions: Connelly and Clandinin's view that narrative research goes beyond reliability, validity, and generalizability and that time, place, plot, and scene are intended to work together to create the experiential quality of the narrative; van Manen's (1990) focus on features like animating and evocative description; and Barone's (1992) attachment to features like accessibility, compellingness, and moral persuasion. O'Dea takes up the challenge in terms of artistic truth, building on Doris Lessing's "a writer must above all else speak the truth" and Margaret Murdoch's "Good art speaks truth, indeed 'is' truth, perhaps the only truth." For O'Dea, artistic truth is grounded in authenticity, in being true to oneself. Not only does this involve taking account of what actually occurred, it also involves "existential freedom," the duty to question one's adherence to norms, roles, and attitudes perpetuated by external society. While authenticity may satisfy concerns for validity, O'Dea's view of the place of narrative may be perplexing:

The point of the process, however, is not for researchers and practitioners to entertain each other with provocative, compelling stories from classroom practice. Rather it is to encourage practitioners to reflect deeply and discerningly on their teaching practice, to see it from a variety of perspectives, to uncover and bring to conscious awareness the multiple levels of presuppositions that inform their perceptions and that determine (often unconsciously) their interpretations of particular situations. (p. 167)

If narrative is meant to be educational, then it has an obligation to its readership beyond the obligations of literature: The truths need to be true, as Phillips (1994) suggests. O'Dea's literary truth does not appear to help here for all she seems to have done is to replace the idea of truth with calls for authenticity, as in literature. For some literary theorists, literature itself does offer up truths. We as readers understand that the features of plot, character and setting function to deliver the truth and that, in fulfilling this function, they do not themselves have to be accurate accounts of anything real, whatever that might mean, because literature is fiction. And narrative inquirers' interest in the validity of a narrative's features may represent an appropriation of the language of the academy's disciplines (science and logic) to gain legitimacy (Fenstermacher, personal communication, February, 1995).

O'Dea's concluding paragraph takes the hitchhiker into a circle:

> And now finally one may begin to understand Phillips' concern that essentially inaccurate stories may be used to further students' "knowledge" of the exigencies of classroom practice. For if teachers' stories are indeed to be used as texts to guide the uninitiated, then they must be more than accessible, compelling and morally persuasive, they must offer more than animating, evocative descriptions of classroom events. In short, above all else, they must be true and reliable, they must render faithfully and precisely the realities of classroom practice, and "compellingness," "animation," and so on, must serve only as a means toward that end. (p. 170)

When narrative inquiry is used to educate prospective teachers, then the criterion of authenticity is to be supplemented with characteristics that sound much like the conventional requirements for the validity of empirical claims, all of which are presumably to be faithful and precise representations of a reality. The hitchhiker's perplexity is excusable: The appeal to literary criticism has not resolved questions about assessing validity in narrative. But it has opened the issue of the function of research on teachers' knowledge.

THE CRITIQUE FROM POSTSTRUCTURALISM

Tochon's (1994) trenchant critique, which draws substantially upon narratology and semiotics, usefully cautions about the abuse of narrative research. His argument illustrates the use of semiotic tools (the semiotic square, actantial analysis, and focal analysis) as deconstructivist devices to ensure validity and establishes the gravity of the risks attending a deep penetration into the field of personal analysis, of personal deconstruction. Among these risks are:

> . . . psychologizing and psycho-analyzing [one's] development, becoming dependent, uncritically adopting implicit ideological norms, submitting oneself to a conformity network, pathologizing professional problems, developing verbal rather than true identity, developing egotism and/or delusory experiences,. . . taking the narrative tools for the life goals, . . . justifying gossip as a sort of criterial evaluation on its own, justifying salaries and social parasitism. (p. 238)

Tochon's concern is, "Narrative inquiry, as it is usually known in teacher education, focuses on individual psychology, and may become narrative therapy" (p. 237). Tochon is doubtful that narrative inquirers are prepared or warranted to engage in such personal analysis, and he is concerned that without proper preparation, "the specificity of pedagogical intervention may be lost and replaced by a grand orientation keeping the real problem of the teacher's self-sufficiency out of sight" (p. 239).

The previous discussion of conventional validity, with mention of rules of thumb and value constraints, plainly shows that moral arguments have a place in discussions about the validity of teacher knowledge research. Our consideration of work by O'Dea and by Tochon obliges us to recognize different functions served by research on teachers' knowledge independent of the research style. It may no longer be enough for research to be directed at creating explanations for "making practice more intelligible" (Roberts, 1996, p. 246). Discussions of function are closely tied to value positions, so it becomes increasingly plain that research validity has a weighty moral dimension.

The Moral Dimension within Teachers' Knowledge

Moral dimensions enter discussions of research and validity, but they ought also to enter discussions of teachers' knowledge itself. If we assume that the essence of professionalism is professional action, then teaching actions should be based on the best available knowledge and should be in the best interests of clients. One important consequence of making knowledge a central feature of professionalism is that it allows one to characterize teaching as appropriate or inappropriate according to the epistemic merit of the claims upon which it is based. For Green (1971), the concept of teachers' knowledge is clearly a stronger concept than teachers' beliefs, and traditional accounts of knowledge suggest that it involves justification, validity, or truth. We may go further and say that the concept of teachers' knowledge, distinct from teachers' beliefs, is stronger on moral grounds also. Interestingly, there seems to have been little empirical research into the moral appropriateness of the content of teachers' knowledge and beliefs.

The moral dimension in teachers' knowledge becomes more complex when we recognize that teachers' knowledge is not just propositional but is also practical. In describing these two types of knowledge, Fenstermacher and Richardson (1994) distinguish between an educational psychology oriented toward the discourse of the discipline of psychology and an educational psychology oriented toward the discourse community of educators. For Fenstermacher and Richardson, an essential feature of this difference is that the discourse community of educators is about practice and so has moral dimensions. But the discourse of practice is not a clear discourse with a well-understood vocabulary and syntax. Although Fenstermacher (1994a) urges that "Performance knowledge, particularly when it falls within the domain of expert, specialist, or professional practice, must meet evidentiary standards if it is to have epistemic merit" (p. 38), the matter is far from simple. The epistemic merit he seeks is bound tightly with moral considerations as well as purely epistemological ones, and deciding on good warrants and good reasons is not straightforward. Green (1971) clarifies this with respect to judgment as a feature of teaching.

The complexity that ensues will not surprise the hitchhiker who has heeded Schön's warning about the swampy lowlands of practice.

Teachers' Knowledge and a Salve for Complexity

The moral dimensions of validity and of teachers' knowledge itself and the epistemological uncertainties (Phillips, 1997) of research on teachers' knowledge should be enough to discourage the hitchhiker from further travel in this area of educational inquiry. On the face of it, it looks relatively easy to depict teachers' knowledge as invented or acquired, and as acquired from others or from one's experiences, but this guide has shown otherwise. What is at first disarmingly simple turns out to be endlessly complex with many conceptions, many researchers, many viewpoints, and many epistemological and moral issues each vying for our attention. These competing interests constitute the root tension and its manifestations, as identified for the hitchhiker much earlier: There is a tension in the different views of what counts as professional knowledge and even of how to conceptualize knowledge.

Within the academy, there is a tension among conflicting approaches to depicting teachers' knowledge, and these conflicting approaches do not share the same turf. For example, researchers in teacher education and educational psychology often seem to be working at cross purposes: Helping teachers to acquire knowledge and generating psychological accounts of how teachers acquire knowledge are not necessarily miscible. There is a tension between the academy of research and the professional field of teaching, especially when these two solitudes are as tenuously linked as they are in both preservice and inservice teacher education. There is a tension in the teaching profession between teachers' development, understanding and use of practical knowledge, and the generally acceptable understanding that knowledge is propositional. For example, teachers know that there is much more to their knowledge than knowing the subject matter to be taught.

Given these tensions, the hitchhiker would not be blamed for thinking that the area of teachers' knowledge exemplifies the "Goldilocks Principle," as recalled by Kagan (1990) when she reviewed measures of teachers' cognitions:

> The more tools and procedures I discovered, the more ambiguous became the notion of teacher cognition, prompting me to recall an observation made by Katz and Raths (1985) regarding the apparent relationship between the "size" of ideas in education and their utility. According to Katz and Raths' Goldilocks Principle, some concepts appear to be too small (specific) for reasonable application, whereas others seem to be too large (vague, general or ambiguous) to be translated into concrete terms. (p. 419)

Although the field of teachers' knowledge is too large for mundane consideration, the evidence is that we in teacher education still proceed as if it were simple: "We tell our students and they go out and teach," seems to sum it aptly. But the field of teachers' knowledge has developed immeasurably since the publication of the third edition of the *Handbook of Research on Teaching* (Wittrock, 1986), and understandings of epistemology, especially about the epistemology of practice, have also matured. The hitchhiker will have noticed that research on teach-

ers' knowledge and teacher education does not always keep pace with these developments. Indeed, the academy still seems to be experiencing difficulties in assimilating an adequate understanding of craft or practical knowledge. The hitchhiker might be tempted to ascribe the tensions we have identified to this resistance.

The guide's final advice prepares the hitchhiker for a detailed exploration of the field of teachers' knowledge. In the context of the tensions, the advice is that the hitchhiker take heed of the complexity of the field and keep philosophical thinking at hand as a constant traveling companion. This advice matches Maxine Greene's (1986, p. 499) outlook for those in the academy and in the professional field: "If the 'doing' of philosophy moves researchers and teachers to do more thinking about their own thinking, it is justified."

REFERENCES

Amidon, E., & Hough, J. (Eds.). (1967). *Interaction analysis: Theory, research, and application.* Reading, MA: Addison-Wesley.

Anderson, L. W. (1995). The nature and characteristics of teachers. In L. W. Anderson (Ed.), *International encyclopedia of teaching and teacher education* (2nd ed., pp. 3–5). Kidlington, Oxford, UK: Elsevier Science Ltd.

Anderson, R. D., & Mitchener, C. P. (1994). Research on science teacher education. In D. Gabel (Ed.), *Handbook of research on science teaching and learning* (pp. 3–44). New York: Macmillan.

Audi, R. (1989). *Practical reasoning.* London: Routledge.

Ausubel, D. (1963). *The psychology of meaningful verbal learning: An introduction to school learning.* New York: Grune & Stratton.

Baird, J. R. (1992). Collaborative reflection, systematic inquiry, better teaching. In T. Russell & H. Munby (Eds.), *Teachers and teaching: From classroom to reflection* (pp. 33–48). London: Falmer Press.

Baird, J. R., & Mitchell, I. J. (Eds.). (1986). *Improving the quality of teaching and learning: An Australian case study—the PEEL project.* Melbourne: Monash University Printery.

Baird, J. R., & Northfield, J. R. (Eds.). (1992). *Learning from the PEEL experience.* Melbourne: Monash University Printery.

Ball, D. (1993). With an eye on the mathematical horizon: Dilemmas of teaching elementary school mathematics. *Elementary School Journal, 93,* 373–397.

Barone, T. (1992). A narrative of enhanced professionalism: Educational researchers and popular storybooks about school people. *Educational Researcher, 21*(8), 15–24.

Bereiter, C., & Scardamalia, M. (1993). *Surpassing ourselves: An inquiry into the nature and implications of expertise.* Chicago: Open Court.

Berliner, D.C. (1986). In pursuit of the expert pedagogue. *Educational Researcher, 15*(7), 5–13.

Berliner, D.C. (1988). Implications of studies on expertise in pedagogy for teacher education and evaluation. In *New directions for teacher assessment* [Proceedings of the 1988 ETS Invitational Congress] (pp. 39–68). Princeton, NJ: Educational Testing Service.

Berliner, D.C., & Calfee, R. C. (Eds.). (1996). *Handbook of educational psychology.* New York: Macmillan.

Block, J. H., & Hazelip, K. (1995). Teachers' beliefs and belief systems. In L. W. Anderson (Ed.), *International encyclopedia of teaching and teacher education* (2nd ed., pp. 25–28). Kidlington, Oxford, UK: Elsevier Science Ltd.

Borko, H., Bellamy, M. L., & Sanders, L. (1992). A cognitive analysis of patterns in science instruction by expert and novice teachers. In T. Russell & H. Munby (Eds.), *Teachers and teaching: From classroom to reflection* (pp. 49–70). London: Falmer Press.

Borko, H., Lalik, R., & Tomchin, E. (1987). Student teachers' understandings of successful teaching. *Teaching and Teacher Education, 3,* 77–90.

Borko, H., Livingston, C., McCaleb, J., & Mauro, L. (1988). Student teachers' planning and post-lesson reflections: Patterns and implications for teacher preparation. In J. Calderhead (Ed.), *Teachers' professional learning* (pp. 55–83). London: Falmer Press.

Borko, H., & Putnam, R. (1996). Learning to teach. In D.C. Berliner & R. C. Calfee (Eds.), *Handbook of educational psychology* (pp. 673–708). New York: Macmillan.

Bratman, M. (1987). *Intention, plans, and practical reason.* Cambridge, MA: Harvard University Press.

Britzman, D. P. (1986). Cultural myths in the making of a teacher: Biography and social structure in teacher education. *Harvard Educational Review, 56,* 442–456.

Britzman, D. P. (1991). *Practice makes practice: A critical study of learning to teach.* Albany, NY: State University of New York Press.

Bromme, R., & Tillema, H. (1995). Fusing experience and theory: The structure of professional knowledge. *Learning and Instruction, 5,* 261–267.

Broudy, H. S., Smith, B. O., & Burnett, J. (1964). *Democracy and excellence in American secondary education.* Chicago: Rand McNally.

Brown, J. S., Collins, A., & Duguid, P. (1989). Situated cognition and the culture of learning. *Educational Researcher, 18*(1), 32–42.

Bruner, J. (1985). Narrative and paradigmatic modes of thought. In E. Eisner (Ed.), *Learning and teaching the ways of knowing* (84th Yearbook of the National Society for the Study of Education, Part II, pp. 97–115). Chicago: University of Chicago Press.

Bruner, J. (1986). *Actual minds, possible worlds.* Cambridge, MA: Harvard University Press.

Buchmann, M. (1987). Impractical philosophizing about teachers' arguments. *Educational Theory, 37,* 409–412.

Bullough, R. V., Jr., & Knowles, J. G. (1991). Teaching and nurturing: Changing conceptions of self as teacher in a case study of becoming a teacher. *Qualitative Studies in Education, 2,* 121–140.

Bullough, R. V., Jr., Knowles, J. G., & Crow, N. A. (1991). *Emerging as a teacher.* London: Routledge.

Butt, R. L., & Raymond, D. (1989). Studying the nature and development of teachers' knowledge using collaborative autobiography. *International Journal of Educational Research, 13,* 403–419.

Calderhead, J. (1988). The development of knowledge structures in learning to teach. In J. Calderhead (Ed.), *Teachers' professional learning* (pp. 51–64). London: Falmer Press.

Calderhead, J. (1995). Teachers as clinicians. In L. W. Anderson (Ed.), *International encyclopedia of teaching and teacher education* (2nd ed., pp. 9–11). Kidlington, Oxford, UK: Elsevier Science Ltd.

Calderhead, J. (1996). Teachers: Beliefs and knowledge. In D.C. Berliner & R. C. Calfee (Eds.), *Handbook of educational psychology* (pp. 709–725). New York: Simon & Schuster Macmillan.

Carter, K. (1990). Teachers' knowledge and learning to teach. In W. R. Houston (Ed.), *Handbook of research on teacher education* (pp. 291–310). New York: Macmillan.

Carter, K., & Anders, D. (1996). Program pedagogy. In F. B. Murray (Ed.), *The teacher educator's handbook: Building a knowledge base for the preparation of teachers* (pp. 526–557). San Francisco: Jossey-Bass.

Carter, K., & Doyle, W. (1987). Teachers' knowledge structures and comprehension processes. In J. Calderhead (Ed.), *Exploring teachers' thinking* (pp. 147–160). London: Cassell.

Carter, K., & Doyle, W. (1996). Personal narrative and life history in learning to teach. In J. Sikula, T. J. Buttery, & E. Guyton (Eds.), *Handbook of research on teacher education* (2nd ed., pp. 120–142). New York: Simon & Schuster Macmillan.

Carter, K., & Gonzalez, L. (1993). Beginning teachers' knowledge of classroom events. *Journal of Teacher Education, 44,* 223–232.

Chi, M., Glaser, R., & Farr, M. (Eds.). (1988). *The nature of expertise.* Hillsdale, NJ: Lawrence Erlbaum Associates.

Christensen, D. (1996). The professional knowledge-research base for teacher education. In J. Sikula, T. J. Buttery, & E. Guyton (Eds.), *Handbook of research on teacher education* (2nd ed., pp. 38–52). New York: Simon & Schuster Macmillan.

Cizek, G. (1995). Crunchy granola and the hegemony of the narrative. *Educational Researcher, 24*(2), 26–28.

Clancey, W. J. (1988). Acquiring, representing, and evaluating a competence model of diagnostic strategy. In M. Chi, R. Glaser, & M. Farr (Eds.), *The nature of expertise* (pp. 343–418). Hillsdale, NJ: Lawrence Erlbaum Associates.

Clandinin, D. J. (1986). *Classroom practice: Teacher images in action.* London: Falmer Press.

Clandinin, D. J., & Connelly, F. M. (1987). Teachers' personal knowledge: What counts as "personal" in studies of the personal? *Journal of Curriculum Studies, 19,* 487–500.

Clandinin, D. J., & Connelly, F. M. (1995). *Teachers' professional knowledge landscapes.* New York: Teachers College Press.

Clark, C. M., & Peterson, P. L. (1986). Teachers' thought processes. In M. C. Wittrock (Ed.), *Handbook of research on teaching* (3rd ed., pp. 255–296). New York: Macmillan.

Clark, C. M., & Yinger, R. J. (1987). Teacher planning. In J. Calderhead (Ed.), *Exploring teachers' thinking* (pp. 84–103). London: Cassell.

Clift, R. (1989). Unanswered questions in graduate teacher preparation. In A. E. Woolfolk (Ed.), *Research perspectives on the graduate preparation of teachers* (pp. 179–193). Englewood Cliffs, NJ: Prentice-Hall.

Cochran, K. F., DeRuiter, J. A., & King, R. A. (1993). Pedagogical content knowing: An integrative model for teacher preparation. *Journal of Teacher Education, 44,* 263–272.

Cochran, K. F., & Jones, L. L. (1998). The subject matter knowledge of preservice science teachers. In B. Fraser & K. Tobin (Eds.), *International handbook of science education* (pp. 707–718). Dordrecht, The Netherlands: Kluwer.

Cochran-Smith, M., & Lytle, S. (1990). Research on teaching and teacher research: The issues that divide. *Educational Researcher, 19*(2), 2–11.

Connelly, F. M., & Clandinin, D. J. (1985). Personal practical knowledge and the modes of knowing: Relevance for teaching and learning. In E. Eisner (Ed.), *Learning and teaching the ways of knowing* (84th Yearbook of the National Society for the Study of Education, Part II, pp. 174–198). Chicago: University of Chicago Press.

Connelly, F. M., & Clandinin, D. J. (1986). On narrative method, personal philosophy, and narrative unities in the story of teaching. *Journal of Research in Science Teaching, 23,* 283–310.

Connelly, F. M., & Clandinin, D. J. (1990, June-July). Stories of experience and narrative inquiry. *Educational Researcher, 19*(4), 2–14.

Connelly, F. M., & Clandinin, D. J. (1994, Winter). Telling teaching stories. *Teacher Education Quarterly, 21*(1), 145–158.

Copes, L. (1996). Teaching what mathematicians do. In F. B. Murray (Ed.), *The teacher educator's handbook: Building a knowledge base for the preparation of teachers* (pp. 261–276). San Francisco: Jossey-Bass.

Davidson, D. (1980). *Essays on actions and events.* Oxford: Clarendon Press.

Day, C., Pope, M., & Denicolo, P. (Eds.). (1990). *Insights into teachers' thinking and practice.* London: Falmer Press.

Delamont, S. (1995). Teachers as artists. In L. W. Anderson (Ed.), *International encyclopedia of teaching and teacher education* (2nd ed., pp. 6–8). Kidlington, Oxford, UK: Elsevier Science Ltd.

Desforges, C. (1995). How does experience affect theoretical knowledge for teaching? *Learning and Instruction, 5,* 385–400.

Dewey, J. (1938). *Experience and education.* New York: Collier Books.

Donmoyer, R. (1996). The concept of a knowledge base. In F. B. Murray (Ed.), *The teacher educator's handbook: Building a knowledge base for the preparation of teachers* (pp. 92–119). San Francisco: Jossey-Bass.

Doyle, W. (1983). Academic work. *Review of Educational Research, 53,* 159–199.

Doyle, W. (1988, April). *Curriculum in teacher education.* Paper presented at the meeting of the American Educational Research Association, New Orleans, LA.

Doyle, W. (1990a). Classroom knowledge as a foundation for teaching. *Teachers College Record, 91,* 347–360.

Doyle, W. (1990b). Themes in teacher education research. In W. R. Houston (Ed.), *Handbook of research on teacher education* (pp. 3–24). New York: Macmillan.

Dreeben, R. (1973). The school as a workplace. In R. Travers (Ed.), *Second handbook of research on teaching* (pp. 450–473). Chicago: Rand McNally.

Ehri, L. C., & Williams, J. P. (1996). Learning to read and learning to teach reading. In F. B. Murray (Ed.), *The teacher educator's handbook: Building a knowledge base for the preparation of teachers* (pp. 231–244). San Francisco: Jossey-Bass.

Eisenhart, M., & Howe, K. (1992). Validity in education research. In M. LeCompte, W. Millroy, & J. Preissle (Eds.), *Handbook of qualita-*

tive research in education (pp. 643–680). San Diego, CA: Academic Press.

Elbaz, F. (1983). *Teacher thinking: A study of practical knowledge.* London: Croom Helm.

Eraut, M. (1994). *Developing professional knowledge and competence.* London: Falmer Press.

Erickson, F. (1986). Qualitative methods in research on teaching. In M. C. Wittrock (Ed.), *Handbook of research on teaching* (3rd ed., pp. 119–161). New York: Macmillan.

Ericsson, K. A., & Simon, H. A. (1984). *Protocol analysis: Verbal reports as data.* Cambridge, MA: MIT Press.

Ericsson, K. A., & Smith, J. (Eds.). (1991). *Toward a general theory of expertise. Prospects and limits.* Cambridge, UK: Cambridge University Press.

Feiman-Nemser, S. (1990). Teacher preparation: Structural and conceptual alternatives. In W. R. Houston (Ed.), *Handbook of research on teacher education* (pp. 212–233). New York: Macmillan.

Feiman-Nemser, S., & Floden, R. E. (1986). The cultures of teaching. In M. C. Wittrock (Ed.), *Handbook of research on teaching* (3rd. ed., pp. 505–526). New York: Macmillan.

Feiman-Nemser, S., & Remillard, J. (1996). Perspectives on learning to teach. In F. B. Murray (Ed.), *The teacher educator's handbook: Building a knowledge base for the preparation of teachers* (pp. 63–91). San Francisco: Jossey-Bass.

Fenstermacher, G. D. (1986). Philosophy of research on teaching: Three aspects. In M. C. Wittrock (Ed.), *Handbook of research on teaching* (3rd ed., pp. 37–49). New York: Macmillan.

Fenstermacher, G. D. (1987). Prologue to my critics, and a reply to my critics. *Educational Theory, 37,* 413–422.

Fenstermacher, G. D. (1994a). The knower and the known: The nature of knowledge in research on teaching. *Review of Research in Education, 20,* 3–56.

Fenstermacher, G. D. (1994b, February). *Where are we going? Who will lead us there?* Presidential address to the meeting of the American Association of Colleges of Teacher Education, San Antonio, TX.

Fenstermacher, G. D., & Richardson, V. (1993). The elicitation and reconstruction of practical arguments in teaching. *Journal of Curriculum Studies, 25,* 101–114.

Fenstermacher, G. D., & Richardson, V. (1994). Promoting confusion in educational psychology: How is it done? *Educational Psychologist, 29,* 49–55.

Flanders, N. (1970). *Analyzing teaching behavior.* Reading, MA: Addison-Wesley.

Fuller, F. F., & Bown, O. H. (1975). Becoming a teacher. In K. Ryan (Ed.), *Teacher education* (74th Yearbook of the National Society for the Study of Education, Part II, pp. 25–52). Chicago: University of Chicago Press.

Gage, N. L. (Ed.). (1963). *Handbook of research on teaching.* Chicago: Rand McNally.

Gage, N. L. (1978). *The scientific basis of the art of teaching.* New York: Teachers College Press.

Gallagher, J. (1991). Prospective and practicing secondary school science teachers' knowledge and beliefs about the philosophy of science. *Science Education, 75,* 121–133.

Getzels, J., & Jackson, P. (1963). The teacher's personality and characteristics. In N. L. Gage (Ed.), *Handbook of research on teaching* (pp. 506–582). Chicago: Rand McNally.

Ginsburg, M., & Clift, R. (1990). The hidden curriculum of teacher education. In W. Houston (Ed.), *Handbook of research on teacher education* (pp. 450–465). New York: Macmillan.

Good, T., & Grouws, D. (1979). The Missouri Mathematics Effectiveness Project: An experimental study in fourth-grade classrooms. *Journal of Educational Psychology, 71,* 355–362.

Graves, M. F., Pauls, L. W., & Salinger, T. (1996). Reading curriculum and instruction. In F. B. Murray (Ed.), *The teacher educator's handbook: Building a knowledge base for the preparation of teachers* (pp. 217–230). San Francisco: Jossey-Bass.

Green, T. F. (1971). *The activities of teaching.* New York: McGraw-Hill.

Greene, M. (1986). Philosophy and teaching. In M. C. Wittrock (Ed.), *Handbook of research on teaching* (3rd ed., pp. 479–501). New York: Macmillan.

Greeno, J. (1991). Number sense as situated knowing in a conceptual domain. *Journal for Research in Mathematics Education, 22,* 170–218.

Greeno, J. (1994). Some further observations of the environment/model metaphor. *Journal for Research in Mathematics Education, 25,* 94–99.

Griffin, G. (1989). A state program for the initial years of teaching. *Elementary School Journal, 89,* 395–403.

Grimmett, P. P., & MacKinnon, A. M. (1992). Craft knowledge and the education of teachers. *Review of Research in Education, 18,* 385–456.

Grossman, P. L. (1990). *The making of a teacher: Teacher knowledge and teacher education.* New York: Teachers College Press.

Grossman, P. L. (1995). Teachers' knowledge. In L. W. Anderson (Ed.), *International encyclopedia of teaching and teacher education* (2nd ed., pp. 20–24). Kidlington, Oxford, UK: Elsevier Science Ltd.

Grossman, P. L., Wilson, W. M., & Shulman, L. S. (1989). Teachers of substance: Subject matter knowledge for teaching. In M. Reynolds (Ed.), *Knowledge base for the beginning teacher* (pp. 23–36). New York: Pergammon Press.

Gutman, A. (1987). *Democratic education.* Princeton, NJ: Princeton University Press.

Guyton, E., & McIntyre, D. J. (1990). Student teaching and school experiences. In W. R. Houston (Ed.), *Handbook of research on teacher education* (pp. 514–534). New York: Macmillan.

Hollingsworth, S. (1995). Teachers as researchers. In L. W. Anderson (Ed.), *International encyclopedia of teaching and teacher education* (2nd ed., pp. 16–19). Kidlington, Oxford, UK: Elsevier Science Ltd.

Houston, W. R. (Ed.). (1990). *Handbook of research on teacher education.* New York: Macmillan.

Hoyle, E. (1995). Teachers as professionals. In L. W. Anderson (Ed.), *International encyclopedia of teaching and teacher education* (2nd ed., pp. 11–15). Kidlington, Oxford, UK: Elsevier Science Ltd.

Jackson, P. W. (1986). *The practice of teaching.* New York: Teachers College Press.

Kagan, D. M. (1990). Ways of evaluating teacher cognition: Inferences concerning the Goldilocks principle. *Review of Educational Research, 60,* 419–469.

Kagan, D. M. (1992). Professional growth among preservice and beginning teachers. *Review of Educational Research, 62,* 129–169.

Kagan, D. M. (1993). *Laura and Jim and what they taught me about the gap between educational theory and practice.* Albany, NY: State University of New York Press.

Kagan, D. M., & Tippins, D. J. (1992). How US teachers "read" classroom performances. *Journal of Education for Teaching, 18,* 149–158.

Katz, L. G., & Raths, J. D. (1985). A framework for research on teacher education programs. *Journal of Teacher Education, 36*(6), 9–15.

Kliebard, H. M. (1993). What is a knowledge base and who would want to use it if we had one? *Review of Educational Research, 63,* 295–303.

Knowles, J. G., & Cole, A. L. (1994). *Through preservice teachers' eyes: Exploring field experiences through narrative and inquiry.* New York: Merrill.

Kohl, H. R. (1988). *36 children.* New York: New American Library.

Kroath, F. (1990, September). *The role of the critical friend in the development of teacher expertise.* Paper presented at the International Symposium on Research on Effective and Responsible Teaching. Université de Fribourg Suisse, Fribourg, Switzerland.

Lampert, M. (1985). How do teachers manage to teach? Perspectives on problems in practice. *Harvard Educational Review, 55,* 178–194.

Lampert, M. (1990). When the problem is not the question and the solution is not the answer. *American Education Research Journal, 27,* 29–63.

Lanier, J. E., & Little, J. W. (1986). Research on teacher education. In M. C. Wittrock (Ed.), *Handbook of research on teaching* (3rd ed., pp. 527–569). New York: Macmillan.

Leinhardt, G. (1988). Situated knowledge and expertise in teaching. In J. Calderhead (Ed.), *Teachers' professional learning* (pp. 146–168). London: Falmer Press.

Leinhardt, G. (1989). Math lessons: A contrast of novice and expert competence. *Journal for Research in Mathematics Education, 20,* 52–75.

Leinhardt, G. (1990). Capturing craft knowledge in teaching. *Educational Researcher, 19*(2), 18–25.

Leinhardt, G. (1993). On teaching. In R. Glaser (Ed.), *Advances in instructional psychology, Vol. 4* (pp. 1–54). Hillsdale, NJ: Lawrence Erlbaum Associates.

Leinhardt, G., Young, K. M., & Merriman, J. (1995). Integrating professional knowledge: The theory of practice and the practice of theory. *Learning and Instruction, 5,* 401–408.

Light, R. (1973). Issues in the analysis of qualitative data. In R. Travers (Ed.), *Second handbook of research on teaching* (pp. 318–381). Chicago: Rand McNally.

Lortie, D. (1973). Observations on teaching as work. In R. Travers (Ed.), *Second handbook of research on teaching* (pp. 474–498). Chicago: Rand McNally.

Lowyck, J., & Clark, C. M. (1989). *Teaching thinking and professional action.* Leuven, Belgium: Leuven University Press.

Lyons, N. (1990). Dilemmas of knowing: Ethical and epistemological dimensions of teachers' work and development. *Harvard Educational Review, 60,* 159–180.

MacIntyre, A. (1984). *After virtue.* Oxford, UK: Basil Blackwell.

McIntyre, D., & Hagger, H. (1993). Teachers' expertise and models of mentoring. In H. H. D. McIntyre & M. Wilkin (Ed.), *Mentoring: Perspectives on school-based teacher education* (pp. 86–102). London: Kogan Page.

McMillan, J. H., & Schumacher, S. (1997). *Research in education: A conceptual introduction* (4th ed.). New York: Longman.

McNiff, J. (1988). *Action research: Principles and practice.* London: Macmillan Education.

Medley, D., & Mitzel, H. (1963). Measuring classroom behavior by systematic observation. In N. L. Gage (Ed.), *Handbook of research on teaching* (pp. 247–328). Chicago: Rand McNally.

Morine-Dershimer, G. (1987). Practical examples of the practical argument: A case in point. *Educational Theory, 37,* 395–408.

Morine-Dershimer, G. (1991). Learning to think like a teacher. *Teaching and Teacher Education, 7,* 159–168.

Munby, H. (1986). Metaphor in the thinking of teachers: An exploratory study. *Journal of Curriculum Studies, 18,* 197–209.

Munby, H. (1987). The dubious place of practical arguments and scientific knowledge in the thinking of teachers. *Educational Theory, 37,* 361–368.

Munby, H., & Hutchinson, N. (1998). Using experience to prepare teachers for inclusive classrooms: Teacher education and the epistemology of practice. *Teacher Education and Special Education, 21*(2), 75–82.

Munby, H., & Russell, T. (1989). Educating the reflective teacher: An essay review of two books by Donald Schön. *Journal of Curriculum Studies, 21,* 71–80.

Munby, H., & Russell, T. (1992). Transforming chemistry research into teaching: The complexities of adopting new frames for experience. In T. Russell & H. Munby (Eds.), *Teachers and teaching: From classroom to reflection* (pp. 90–108). London: Falmer Press.

Munby, H., & Russell, T. (1993). Reflective teacher education: Technique or epistemology? *Teaching and Teacher Education, 9,* 431–438.

Munby, H., & Russell, T. (1994). The authority of experience in learning to teach: Messages from a physics methods class. *Journal of Teacher Education, 45,* 86–95.

Munby, H., & Russell, T. (1995). Towards rigour with relevance: How can teachers and teacher educators claim to know? In T. Russell & F. Korthagen (Eds.), *Teachers who teach teachers: Reflections on teacher education* (pp. 172–184). London: Falmer Press.

Munby, H., & Russell, T. (1998). Epistemology and context in research on learning to teach science. In B. Fraser & K. Tobin (Eds.), *International handbook of science education* (pp. 643–665). Dordrecht, The Netherlands: Kluwer.

Murray, F. B. (Ed.). (1996). *The teacher educator's handbook: Building a knowledge base for the preparation of teachers.* San Francisco: Jossey-Bass.

National Academy of Science. (1996). Science and creationism: A case study in biology. In F. B. Murray (Ed.), *The teacher educator's handbook: Building a knowledge base for the preparation of teachers* (pp. 277–294). San Francisco: Jossey-Bass.

Orton, R. E. (1993, April). *How can teacher reasoning be practical? (Toward a normative theory of teacher reasoning).* Paper presented at the meeting of the American Educational Research Association, Atlanta, GA.

O'Dea, J. (1994). Pursuing truth in narrative research. *Journal of Philosophy of Education, 28,* 161–171.

Pajares, M. (1992). Teachers' beliefs and educational research: Cleaning up a messy construct. *Review of Educational Research, 62,* 307–332.

Paley, V. G. (1981). *Wally's stories.* Cambridge, MA: Harvard University Press.

Peck, R., & Tucker, J. (1973). Research on teacher education. In R. Travers (Ed.), *Second handbook of research on teaching* (pp. 940–978). Chicago: Rand McNally.

Peterson, P., & Comeaux, M. (1987). Teachers' schemata for classroom events: The mental scaffolding of teachers' thinking during classroom instruction. *Teaching and Teacher Education, 3,* 319–331.

Phillips, D.C. (1994). Telling it straight: Issues in assessing narrative research. *Educational Psychologist, 29,* 49–55.

Phillips, D.C. (1996). Philosophical perspectives. In D.C. Berliner & R. C. Calfee (Eds.), *Handbook of educational psychology* (pp. 1005–1019). New York: Simon & Schuster Macmillan.

Phillips, D.C. (1997, March). *On being rigorous about interpretations.* Paper presented at the meeting of the American Educational Research Association, Chicago.

Pinar, W. F. (1975, April). *The method of "currere."* Paper presented at the meeting of the American Educational Research Association, Washington, DC.

Pinnegar, S. (1988, April). *Throwing a hard ball into a stack of cotton: An examination of the term "with me."* Paper presented at the meeting of the American Educational Research Association, New Orleans, LA.

Polanyi, M. (1962). *Personal knowledge.* Chicago: University of Chicago Press.

Prawat, R. S. (1989). Promoting access to knowledge, strategy, and disposition in students: A research synthesis. *Review of Educational Research, 59,* 1–412.

Prawat, R. S. (1992). Teachers' beliefs about teaching and learning: A constructivist perspective. *American Journal of Education, 100,* 354–395.

Putnam, R. T. (1987). Structuring and adjusting content for students: A study of live and simulated tutoring of addition. *American Education Research Journal, 24,* 13–48.

Resnick, L. (1991, April). *Situations for learning and thinking.* Recipient's address for the award for distinguished contributions to educational research, 1990, at the meeting of the American Educational Research Association, Chicago.

Richardson, V. (1996). The role of attitudes and beliefs in learning to teach. In J. Sikula, T. J. Buttery, & E. Guyton (Eds.), *Handbook of research on teacher education* (2nd ed., pp. 102–119). New York: Simon & Schuster Macmillan.

Richardson, V., & Anders, P. (1990). *Final report of the Reading Instruction Study. Report to OERI, US Department of Education.* Tucson, AZ: College of Education, University of Arizona. (ERIC Document Reproduction Service No. ED 324 655)

Richardson, V., & Anders, P. (1994). The study of teacher change. In V. Richardson (Ed.), *Teacher change and the staff development process: A case of reading instruction* (pp. 159–180). New York: Teachers College Press.

Richert, A. E. (1992). The content of student teachers' reflections within different structures for facilitating the reflective process. In T. Russell & H. Munby (Eds.), *Teachers and teaching: From classroom to reflection* (pp. 171–191). London: Falmer Press.

Roberts, D. A. (1996). What counts as quality in educational research? *Science Education, 80,* 243–248.

Roberts, D. A., & Chastko, A. M. (1990). Absorption, refraction, reflection: An exploration of beginning science teacher thinking. *Science Education, 74,* 197–224.

Rohrkemper, M. M. (1989). Self-regulated learning and academic achievement: A Vygotskian view. In D. H. Schunk & B. J. Zimmerman (Eds.), *Self-regulated learning in academic achievement: Theory, research and practice* (pp. 143–167). New York: Springer-Verlag.

Russell, T. (1987). Research, practical knowledge, and the conduct of teacher education. *Educational Theory, 37,* 369–375.

Russell, T. (1989). Defective, effective, reflective: Can we improve science teacher education programs by attending to our images of teachers at work? In J. P. Barufaldi (Ed.), *Improving preservice/inservice science teacher education: Future perspectives* (pp. 161–168). Columbus, OH: Association of Educators of Teachers of Science.

Russell, T. (1995). Reconstructing educational theory from the authority of personal experience: How can I best help people learning to teach. *Studies in Continuing Education, 17,* 6–17.

Russell, T., & Munby, H. (1991). Reframing: The role of experience in developing teachers' professional knowledge. In D. A. Schön (Ed.), *The reflective turn: Case studies in and on educational practice.* New York: Teachers College Press.

Russell, T., Munby, H., Spafford, C., & Johnston, P. (1988). Learning the professional knowledge of teaching: Metaphors, puzzles, and the theory-practice relationship. In P. P. Grimmett & G. L. Erickson (Eds.), *Reflection in teacher education* (pp. 67–90). New York: Teachers College Press.

Ryle, G. (1949). *The concept of mind.* New York: Barnes & Noble.

Sarason, S. B. (1971). *The culture of the school and the problem of change.* Boston: Allyn & Bacon.

Sarason, S. B. (1996). *Revisiting "The culture of the school and the problem of change".* New York: Teachers College Press.

Sarason, S. B., Davidson, K. S., & Blatt, B. (1962). *The preparation of teachers: An unstudied problem in education.* New York: Wiley.

Schön, D. A. (1983). *The reflective practitioner: How professionals think in action.* New York: Basic Books.

Schön, D. A. (1987). *Educating the reflective practitioner.* San Francisco: Jossey-Bass.

Schwab, J. J. (1971). The practical: Arts of the eclectic. *School Review, 79,* 493–542.

Schwab, J. J. (1978). Education and the structure of the disciplines. In I. Westbury & N.J. Wilkof (Eds.), *Science, curriculum and liberal education* (pp. 229–272). Chicago: University of Chicago Press.

Shulman, L. S. (1986). Those who understand: Knowledge growth in teaching. *Educational Researcher, 15*(2), 4–14.

Shulman, L. S. (1987a). Knowledge and teaching: Foundations of the new reform. *Harvard Educational Review, 57,* 1–22.

Shulman, L. S. (1987b). Sounding an alarm: A reply to Sockett. *Harvard Educational Review, 57,* 473–483.

Shulman, L. S., & Quinlan, K. M. (1996). The comparative psychology of school subjects. In D.C. Berliner & R. C. Calfee (Eds.), *Handbook of educational psychology* (pp. 399–422). New York: Simon & Schuster Macmillan.

Shulman, L. S., & Sykes, G. (1986). *A national board for teaching? In search of a bold standard: A report for the task force on teaching as a profession.* New York: Carnegie Corporation.

Shulman, L. S., & Tamir, P. (1973). Research on teaching in the natural sciences. In R. Travers (Ed.), *Second handbook of research on teaching* (pp. 1098–1148). Chicago: Rand McNally.

Sikula, J., Buttery, T. J., & Guyton, E. (Eds.). (1996). *Handbook of research on teacher education* (2nd ed.). New York: Macmillan.

Smith, D., & Neale, D.C. (1989). The construction of subject matter knowledge in primary science teaching. *Teaching and Teacher Education, 5,* 1–20.

Sockett, H. T. (1987). Has Shulman got the strategy right? *Harvard Educational Review, 57,* 209–219.

Stones, E. (1984). *Supervision in teacher education: A counseling and pedagogical approach.* London: Methuen.

Tamir, P. (1988). Subject matter and related pedagogical knowledge in teacher education. *Teaching and Teacher Education, 4,* 99–110.

Tochon, F. (1994). Presence beyond the narrative: Semiotic tools for deconstructing the personal story. *Curriculum Studies, 2,* 221–247.

Tom, A. R., & Valli, L. (1990). Professional knowledge for teaching. In W. Houston (Ed.), *Handbook of research on teacher education* (pp. 373–392). New York: Macmillan.

Travers, R. (Ed.). (1973). *Second handbook of research on teaching.* Chicago: Rand McNally.

van Manen, M. (1990). *Researching lived experience.* London, Ontario: Althouse Press.

Walsh, W. H. (1974). Kant's concept of practical reason. In S. Koerner (Ed.), *Practical reason* (pp. 189–211). Oxford, UK: Basil Blackwell.

Wang, M. C., Haertel, G. D., & Walberg, H. J. (1993). Toward a knowledge base for school learning. *Review of Educational Research, 63,* 249–294.

Whitehead, J. (1995). Educative relationships with the writing of others. In T. Russell & F. Korthagen (Eds.), *Teachers who teach teachers: Reflections on teacher education* (pp. 113–129). London: Falmer Press.

Wigginton, E. (1991). *Foxfire: 25 years.* Garden City, NY: Doubleday.

Wineburg, S. S. (1991). Historical problem solving: A study of the cognitive processes used in the evaluation of documentary and pictorial evidence. *Journal of Educational Psychology, 83,* 73–87.

Wineburg, S. S. (1996). The psychology of learning and teaching history. In D.C. Berliner & R. C. Calfee (Eds.), *Handbook of educational psychology* (pp. 423–437). New York: Simon & Schuster Macmillan.

Wittrock, M. C. (Ed.). (1986). *Handbook of research on teaching* (3rd ed.). New York: Macmillan.

Yinger, R. (1990). The conversation of practice. In R. Clift, R. Houston, & M. Pugach (Eds.), *Encouraging reflective practice in education: An analysis of issues and programs* (pp. 73–94). New York: Teachers College Press.

Yinger, R., & Hendricks-Lee, M. (1993). Working knowledge in teaching. In C. Day, J. Calderhead, & P. Denicolo (Eds.), *Research on teacher thinking: Understanding professional development* (pp. 100–123). London: Falmer Press.

Zeichner, K. M., & Tabachnik, B. R. (1982). The belief systems of university supervisors in the elementary student teaching program. *Journal of Education for Teaching, 8,* 34–54.

43.
Teacher Change

Virginia Richardson
University of Michigan

Peggy Placier
University of Missouri

Introduction

This chapter is about change in teachers and teaching. The topic is complex, because radically different approaches to the concept of change have been used in its scholarship. These approaches vary in terms of the types of change being undertaken, studied, and advocated; understandings of the ownership of change processes and how they should be initiated; and purposes of scholarly study of change in teachers and teaching.

Teacher change is described in terms of learning, development, socialization, growth, improvement, implementation of something new or different, cognitive and affective change, and self-study. The focus of this field of study extends from preservice teacher education students as they learn about and enter the teaching profession through to the teacher who is getting ready for retirement or exiting from the profession. Change is often assumed to lead to better teaching or teachers and, although the relationship is often not drawn, to a better education for students. However, some research examines change that is thought to be negative (e.g., Fox, 1995), although that type of negative change is often attributed to the organizational context or leadership (e.g., Blase, 1990). The topic of teacher change is, consequently, extremely broad, encompassing a number of solid research traditions and often competing views of how change is to occur and whether change is a good thing.

In this chapter, we have made a concerted effort to bring together two views of change that occupy primarily separate literatures. The first position examines individual or small group cognitive, affective, and behavioral change processes. The second is an organizational view of change that links structural, cultural, and political aspects of the school organization to changes in teachers and teaching. While one literature often informs the other, each has its place within different disciplinary boundaries—individual change literature within behavioral, cognitive, and social psychology and the organizational literature within sociology, anthropology, political science, and organization theory. The research and practice approaches of these two views are quite different as are the purposes for conducting the research.

Approaches to Change and Teacher Change

In 1969, Chin and Benne described three types of planned change strategies: empirical-rational, normative-reeducative, and power-coercive. The empirical-rational approach uses the development of models for change that is based on utopian goals and a rational approach to achieving them. In this approach, research and dissemination are treated as a linear process: The research is conducted by academics or professional researchers, and change agents give the research results to those who, we would presume, will use the research. The system is approached as something to analyze and change, and the utopian vision is thought to be obtainable through the diffusion of research on effectiveness. Normative-reeducative techniques of change are naturalistic in that they focus on providing autonomy for and cultivating growth in the people who make up the system and on increasing the problem-solving capabilities of the system. Power-coercive approaches attempt to affect change through the type of collective action strategies advocated by Mahatma Ghandi and Martin Luther King, Jr. These forms involve nonviolence, use of political institutions to achieve change, and the recomposition and manipulation of power elites.

The approach to change in the education system and change as it relates to teachers was located, until quite recently, within Chin and Benne's (1969) first strategy, the empirical-rational

The authors would like to thank Karl Jordell, University of Oslo, for his helpful comments and Patricia Watson and Jacqueline Kelly for their help with the literature review.

strategy. Within this approach, the general perception of teachers among change agents, policymakers, and educators was that teachers are the recipients and consumers of research and practice. In this archetype, a linear process of change originates outside the classroom with a new behavior, way of thinking, or instructional program that is usually based on research, theory, or both. Teachers are told about the change topic, it is demonstrated to them, and, as rational human beings, they are expected to implement it in their classrooms. In this conception, change is seen as extremely difficult and painful. Someone outside the classroom holds the power over change, and teachers are often characterized as recalcitrant and resistant when they do not implement the suggested change (e.g., Duffy & Roehler, 1986; Fullan, 1985). This view is not too surprising, suggests Klein (1969), who concludes that the research conducted within this approach to change is biased in the direction of the change agent:

> Though it is generally acknowledged that human beings have a predilection both to seek change and to reject it, much of the literature has isolated the latter tendency for special emphasis. In fact studies of change appear to be taken from the perspective of those who are the change agents seeking to bring about change rather than of the clients they are seeking to influence. (pp. 498–499)

Quite recently, the literature has shifted in the direction of Chin and Benne's (1969) second strategy, the normative-reeducative strategy. While this type of change approach has been in use for some time,[1] it has only recently been acknowledged as an important avenue for significant and worthwhile change. This acknowledgment has been helped, in part, by the sense that the empirical-rational strategies have not been particularly successful in educational projects (Chin & Benne, 1969). This change strategy is also, however, part of a larger movement toward the phenomenological and hermeneutic study of how individuals make sense of and contribute to the situations in which they live and work (Erickson, 1986). Within this normative-reeducative change approach, the assumption is made that change is enhanced through deep reflection on beliefs and practices. Because the change process entails understanding one's beliefs and knowledge and determining whether or not to change them, dialogue has been used as a critical element of this process. The dialogue could take place with other teachers or with an "other" or critical friend.[2] Gallagher, Goudvis, and Pearson (1988) call the approach "mutual adaptation," which, they suggest, is the best form for dramatic change such as shifts in orientations and beliefs.

A major difference between the normative-reeducative conception of change and that of the empirical-rational approach relates to the direction for change. In the empirical-rational approach, the state toward which the change process is directed and the process itself are determined by individuals outside the classrooms—administrators, school board members, or policy-makers at the local, state, or national levels. In the normative-reeducative approach, the direction for change comes from the individuals involved in the process—in this case, from the teachers themselves in collaboration with the "other."

The third strategy for change, the power-coercive strategy, is seldom viewed or written about within the teacher change literature. Examples within education, most notably, the recent school choice movement, can be found. However, the focus has not yet been placed on teacher change, other than to make the assumption that teachers will do something different in a situation in which parents provide the direction for schooling. The teacher organization and labor movement is also one example of such a strategy, but, again, the focus has only recently shifted from conditions of and rewards for teaching and political roles (see chapter 41 in this *Handbook*) to an examination of teacher change in classroom instruction (e.g., Bascia, 1994; Kerchner & Koppich, 1993; McClure, 1991).

We, therefore, attempt to take a broad view of conceptions of change in this chapter, focusing primarily on studies that examine teacher change within the first two of Chin and Benne's strategies but also on studies that consider several examples of the third strategy. This framework, built around Chin and Benne's strategies, has helped us organize a number of the summaries of the research that are included in the following two sections.

The Literature

The literature on teacher change is vast and scattered. Some pieces of scholarship focus directly on teacher change, and others focus on new or different factors or programs such as an experimental curriculum or a schoolwide structural reform within which teacher change is one of the intended outcomes. The literary genres that are used to describe change processes and teacher change include wisdom or theory pieces—albeit often with an empirical grounding (Fullan, 1991; Lieberman, 1995); reviews of research (e.g., Borko & Putnam, 1996; Carter, 1990; Kagan, 1990); reports of empirical studies (e.g., Marx et al., 1994; Peterson, Fennema, Carpenter, & Loef, 1989; Richardson, 1994b); narratives (e.g., Anyon, 1994; Beattie, 1995; Ladson-Billings, 1994; Wasley, 1994); and other newer genres such as written readers theater (Clark et al., 1996).[3] Because the literature that examines teacher change is extensive, we will provide analyses of each of the particular areas with selected examples of the empirical research. The wisdom and theory scholarship will be used in our overall analyses of categories, trends, and paradigms.

Given the extensive literature on this topic, our methods of review place three limitations on this summary. ERIC, one of our primary sources of citations, cites primarily studies of North American schools and classrooms. As Fuller, Snyder, Chapman,

---

[1] Examples include the teacher center movement (Devaney, 1977) and the Advisory Model of Professional Development (Katz, 1979; Rubin, 1978).

[2] In this chapter, we refer to the person who is outside the individual teacher's classroom and who helps the teacher work on change as the "other" (see Fenstermacher, 1994). "Others" can include staff developers, administrators, research or staff developers, change agents or consultants, and other teachers.

[3] A practitioner-oriented "how to" genre is also used in the field; however, we are not including it in this review. This genre consists largely of prescriptions for practice but without thorough discussions of the research base or theoretical frameworks.

and Hua (1994) point out, studies of U.S. schools and teachers cannot be generalized to nations with different political structures and cultures. We have included a number of non-North American studies, but these have not been accessed in a systematic manner. Second, teachers in many studies are often presented as a generic category and are not differentiated by grade level, discipline, ethnicity, gender, or social class. Third, we have concentrated on research published in the past 10–15 years, which limits our historical perspective.

Organizational Framework of the Chapter

The focus in this chapter is placed on teachers and teaching and on the processes of change. The next two sections will address the literature that considers the ways in which teacher change takes place. The first of these two sections focuses on research that is meant to elucidate individual and small-group change. The second section examines the research and theoretical literature that attempts to promote understanding of the structure and functions of the organization and the relationships among aspects of the organization, the context of schools, and teacher change. The two categories represented by these sections are not mutually exclusive. A number of writings combine both approaches, either because they are written by two or more researchers who represent the different areas, (e.g., Peterson, McCarthy, & Elmore, 1996; and the book edited by Richardson, 1994b and the chapter within it by Placier and Hamilton, 1994) or by individual researchers who are attempting to bridge the two approaches (e.g., Little, 1992b; McLaughlin, 1994; Smylie, 1988). The final section of the chapter attempts to bring together these two approaches to the study of teacher change in terms of common and not-so-common themes in methodology, findings, and underlying assumptions. We then arrive at some conclusions, including issues that need to be addressed.

Individual and Small Group Change

The questions of when, why, and how teachers change have become particularly significant during the current reform era. These questions, however, did not always accompany improvement efforts. Following the Sputnik scare, attempts to change instruction and help students become better able to compete with the Russians centered on the curriculum. Substantial amounts of federal money went into the development of curriculum packages in all subject matter areas. By and large, these were disappointing projects. For example, only an estimated 12–20% of schools implemented the most popular elements of the New Social Studies materials, developed during the 1970s (Shaver, 1987). One problem, it appeared, related to a curriculum package, developed with amazingly little attention to the teachers and the realities of the classrooms, being imposed on schools and classrooms. As Shaver (1987) pointed out, program developers and researchers

> . . . rarely treat the difficult problems of classroom management that teachers find pressing, questions of how to use content for management purposes (a use that university professors find difficult to accept as legitimate), or how to achieve the content learning goals, as well as school socialization goals, that teachers view as important. (p. 112)

In the next phase of implementation research, teachers became a somewhat stronger focus of attention (McLaughlin, 1987). However, the view of change that dominated this era was that someone outside the classroom makes decisions about what someone inside the classroom should do. The criterion for successful implementation related to the degree to which teachers' adoption of the new curriculum or method conformed to the original developer's view of what it should look like. Teachers who did not implement the changes (and for most of these programs, many teachers did not) were seen as recalcitrant (McLaughlin, 1987).

More recently, attention has moved in two directions: the first is toward a concentration on individual teachers and the factors that contribute to change, and the second is toward a concentration on organizational and structural changes that are thought to affect teacher change. This section reviews the literature on individual teachers, and the next section will move to the organizational change literature.

In this section, the mechanisms for affecting change in individual teachers have been categorized into three groups:

1. Voluntary and Naturalistic Changes. This group examines change that is related to biography, personhood and experience, and differences among teachers in their approaches to change.
2. Stages of Development. This group is a special case of naturalistic change but is significant enough within its own theoretical framework to warrant a separate category. It includes an analysis of developmental stages and descriptions of research on teachers' stages of development, stages of development within specific programs or contexts, and movement from one stage to another.
3. Formal programs for the preparation of teachers and the improvement of teaching. The programs that are examined include teacher education and staff development.

In all of this literature, the term *development* is prominent but is used in different ways. The term can refer to a more naturalistic concept of learning and movement toward becoming an experienced and, sometimes, expert teacher. This use of the term will be found in connection with naturalistic change. Studies using the term in connection with a notion of stages, phases, or level may be placed within the designation of stage theory, and these studies will be examined in the second group below. The term *development* is also increasingly being used to describe what used to be called "inservice education" or "training." Assumptions that are inherent in the use of the term *staff development* are borrowed from but are not synonymous with the way the concept is used in stage theoretical conceptions and will, therefore, be discussed in the section on staff development.

Voluntary and Naturalistic Change

Most of the education, school, and teacher change literature describes the direction and process of change phenomena that are determined by someone other than the teacher who is going through the change process. In these conceptions, the others are policymakers, administrators, researchers, staff developers, teacher educators, or teams of teachers who are involved in decisions concerning a school- or systemwide change. The changes proposed are often mandatory or at least strongly advised. Use of this concept of change often leads to the conclusion that change is difficult, that it hurts, and that teachers are recalcitrant, won't change, or both.

Another concept of change, however, that is only recently receiving attention suggests that most teachers change all the time. Some of the changes may be what (Cuban, 1988) described as first-order change—minor changes in the organization of the classroom, curriculum, etc.—or they may be second-order changes that entail different ways of thinking, teaching, and learning. These changes may be prompted, promoted, or supported by discussions with other teachers, an evaluation by an administrator, a workshop, experience with an often-tried activity that no longer works, an article in a practitioner or research journal, a new grade level or population of students, etc. These changes take place over the career of the teacher and are voluntary. This form of change has not been considered in conceptions of change in which the power over the change is perceived to be held outside the classroom nor has this form of change been examined much in the literature until recently.

Conducting research on naturalistic change is complex. It differs from research on and evaluations of specific change processes, because it asks different questions. In the traditional evaluations, the question often is: Did the teachers change in the intended direction? In the naturalistic change research, an assumption of change is present, and the questions are How do teachers change? In what direction? and Why and when do teachers change? Are there different approaches to change, and what affects those differences? These questions are designed to lead to theories of individual change.

Studies of naturalistic change often take place within a planned change process; but the form of the change process is usually voluntary and collaborative, and the focus of the studies is teacher change. Because these studies usually involve teachers in a formal change (e.g., Lester & Onore, 1990; Richardson, 1994b), they will be described in the section on normative-reeducative approaches to staff development. At this point, we describe studies of change within the contexts of biography and experience and on individual differences in responses to change.

CHANGE RELATED TO BIOGRAPHY, PERSONHOOD, AND EXPERIENCE

These studies focus on the relationship between biography, life and professional experience, and learning to teach or changing practice. For example, Butt, Raymond, McCue, and Yamagishi (1992) examine the relationship between teachers' biography and the development of personal practical knowledge. They worked with a number of teachers and present case studies of two teachers who have been interviewed and observed and have written the following: (a) a depiction of the context of their current working reality, (b) a description of their current pedagogy and curriculum-in-use, (c) an account of their reflections on their past personal and professional lives as they might relate to their present professional thoughts and actions, and (d) a projection of their personal and professional futures as related to a personal critical appraisal of the previous three accounts. The researchers conclude that evolution of the teachers' personal practical knowledge is affected by various forms of ex-

periences. Influences include experiences as children, peers, parents, and teachers; experiences within a particular cultural background; and personal and professional experiences—though each person is affected in unique ways.

Another biographical approach to teaching and teacher change is described by Bullough and Baughman (1997). This 8-year study followed Kerrie, a beginning teacher, from her 1st to her 8th year of teaching. Through the use of metaphor analysis, the authors found that the teacher began teaching by drawing on her experience as a mother. The authors document the evolution of this metaphor in Kerrie's beliefs and practices over the years.

> No specific event or factor produced the change, although evolving life circumstances and altered work conditions played important parts. Moreover, no staff developer could have designed a program with such outcomes in mind; rather, they happened in the course of living a life, aging, and selectively responding to dynamic and unpredictable situations at home and at work. That selves and professional identities change is certain, but teacher identity needs to be understood in relationship to living a life and forming and seeking to maintain a self within shifting contexts. (p. 95)

Some researchers have suggested that stable aspects of an individual teacher's approach can be determined. Louden (1991) concluded from a case study of a teacher that this teacher exhibited growth and change in her teaching but also maintained some traditions. These traditions, Louden suggests, may be thought of "as highly specific meanings and practices which exist within any particular setting. These sedimented meaning structures exert a powerful force on the limits of teachers' possible actions" (p. 189). Zahorik (1990) developed case studies of four teachers and found that each teacher had a stable, dominant style of teaching yet was flexible within the style, and that each teacher had a coherent teaching ideology that was consistent with his or her teaching style.

Tom Russell, Hugh Munby, and colleagues have conducted a research program since 1985 that examines teacher learning of professional knowledge that develops with experience (Munby & Russell 1992; Munby & Russell, 1994; Russell, 1988; Russell, 1995; Russell, Munby, Spafford, & Johnston, 1988). For example, Russell, Munby, Spafford, and Johnston (1988) looked at changes in metaphorical allusions and knowledge in novice and experienced teachers through extensive interviews and observations. They focused on how two of the teachers viewed the relationship between theory and practice.

The first-year teacher knew that practice and theory relate to each other, but was not clear about how. She felt that she learned routines first. Conversely, the experienced teacher "displays confidence in her professional knowledge and an acute awareness of how that knowledge developed over time and in relation to experience. . . . She presents a striking account of the importance of acquiring routines and mastering their use as a basis for moving on to consider theory and ask questions about one's practices" (p. 86). Russell (1988) suggests that experience shapes the meaning that teachers read into research, theory, and other recommendations for change in practice. From this work, Russell et al. began to question the nature of our teacher education programs that focus on theory, often prior to practice.

More recently, Russell moved into a self-study of knowledge growth by teaching a high school physics class for 2 years. Munby observed him teach as did preservice students. From this experience, Munby and Russell (1994) developed the concept of the authority of experience, which involves

> . . . listening to one's self in relation to students' experiences of one's own teaching. . . . It requires a willingness and an ability to listen to one's own experiences as one also listens to the wisdom of those with more experience and those who have explored educational issues analytically and empirically. (Russell, 1995, p. 100)

Experience is also an important factor in Au's (1990) work on the development of expertise in teaching. She views this development of expertise as the evolution of a teacher's concepts about instruction or practice knowledge. In her work, she uses Vygotsky's (1962) distinction between spontaneous or everyday concepts and scientific concepts and the notion that interaction between them leads to true concepts. She used extensive discourse analyses to follow a novice teachers' development of understandings of comprehension and sorted the discourse into Elbaz's (1983) categories of rules of practice, practical principal, and image. She found that the growth of practical knowledge began with the identification of a problem. Rules of practice evolved as solutions to problems—but not for all issues. Images then developed for only two of the issues (see also Markel, 1995, and S. Johnston, 1992, for additional studies of the growth of practical knowledge during student teaching).

DIFFERENCES AMONG TEACHERS

Inevitably, whether a change is mandated or voluntarily endorsed, teachers have a considerable amount of discretion as to whether they implement the change in their classrooms. This discretion has contributed to proposed changes not being implemented in many staff development programs. In attempts to explain why some teachers implement change and others do not, a number of studies have been conducted that examined or found differences among teachers in their reaction to change. Ball and Goodson (1985) suggest, for example, that teacher development is inevitably idiosyncratic and must be viewed in relationship to life history and the context in which development is taking place. Ashton (1984) found that teachers with a greater sense of self-efficacy were more willing to change practices than those with less. M. Johnston (1994) studied teachers' changes in thinking and practices as they moved through an M.A. program designed to increase teacher reflection and continued teaching following the M.A. for 2 years. Using interviews, observation, journals, course work, and, at the end, an assignment that asked them to write a metaphor to describe their experiences in the M.A. program, she developed case studies of 3 teachers. M. Johnston found some similarities and some differences in the teachers' reactions to change. Their thinking became more complex, but one of the teachers did not enjoy the complexity.

In their longitudinal study of preservice students moving into beginning teachers' acquisition of pedagogical knowledge, Munby and Russell (1992) found that some students are more predisposed than others to reframe the puzzles of practice.

They suggest that this reframing process (Schön, 1983) is essential in learning from experience. Thus, those students and teachers who do not reframe, for whatever reason, are not able to learn from experience.

Lindblad (1990) interviewed 19 teachers to determine how they were responding to a new mandated curriculum in Sweden. He found six different responses to the mandate. For example, "the alienated" sees oneself as a victim of external forces of change; "the spectator" feels that vested interests are inherent in the demand for change and that the change is imposed on the teachers; and "the loyal official" feels that the reasons for change are very reasonable and that to participate is one's duty.

Marks and Gersten (1998) examined levels of engagement of 17 classroom teachers for Grades 1–7. These teachers were involved in a collaborative and voluntary staff development program designed to help teachers work with special needs students. Marks and Gersten developed cross-case data display matrices (Miles & Huberman, 1994) to develop hypotheses about themes that may explain differences in teachers' engagement levels and their impact in terms of beliefs and behaviors in the classroom. They found four categories of teachers: high engagement and high impact, high engagement and moderate impact, moderate engagement and moderate impact, low engagement and low impact. They found that low engagement and low impact resulted when teachers' philosophies contradicted the assumptions underlying the practice being encouraged.

SUMMARY: NATURALISTIC CHANGE

The concept of naturalistic change is not deterministic. It assumes individual autonomy and choice. At the same time, the research on this form of change suggests that biography, experience, perhaps personality, and context play a role in the change choices that individuals make. Further, many of the changes that are studied, such as learning from experience, may not involve a completely conscious process. Learning from experience often leads to changes in tacit knowledge that becomes expressed only through reflection—a process that is enhanced through dialogue. The naturalistic frame provides a strong foundation for new forms of normative-reeducative staff development that will be described in the next section. This framework leads to ways of working with teachers undergoing change that enhance the naturalistic change process and that are particularly useful with teachers for whom autonomy and professional expertise are important aspects of their identity.

Stages of Development

Two approaches to developmental stage theory are found in the literature. The first is classic stage theory in which the individual moves through a series of stages in a relatively deterministic manner (e.g., Case, 1988; Piaget, 1970). The second is a much more flexible, contextual conception of stage theory that is neither completely deterministic nor completely sequential and invariant (Goldsmith & Schifter, 1994). Within all uses of the term, the focus is on an individual in the process of becoming. The state of being that is coming next is usually considered better, more complex, and desirable. But that is not always the case. The last stage of Huberman's (1989) career development, for example, is called "disengagement" and may be one of unhappiness and burnout. Further, several researchers stress that all stages of their developmental theories are important at one point or another in teaching and should not be thought of as consecutive or hierarchical. Griffiths and Tann (1992), for example, suggest that all five stages in their theory of reflection are needed at any point for a teacher to do an adequate job. We will now turn to the following two forms of developmental stages: developmental stage theories and stage theories within a particular change context.

DEVELOPMENTAL STAGE THEORIES

A number of stage theories have been proposed and studied to describe teachers' progress through their careers. The theories range in terms of the degree to which the stages are invariant and sequential. They also focus on different aspects of the teacher's learning, thinking, and action. For example, Fuller (1969; Fuller & Bown, 1975) focused on teachers' stages of concern, Huberman (1989) on career stages, Feiman-Nemser (1983) on learning to teach, Berliner (1994) on stages in the development of expertise, Sprinthall, Reiman, and Thies-Sprinthall (1996) on cognitive and moral development of teachers, Black and Ammon (1992) on pedagogical thinking, Griffiths and Tan (1992) on teacher reflection, and Knowles (1992) on the development of professional identity. The theories also vary in terms of the manner in which they were developed. Some were based primarily on literature review and experience (Feiman-Nemser, 1983; Sprinthall, Reiman, & Thies-Sprinthall, 1996); others emerged from studies that were designed specifically to examine the question of teacher development (Fuller, 1969; Huberman, 1989), differences between groups of teachers who vary in years of teaching experience (Berliner, 1994; Black & Ammon, 1992), or both. The studies described here are representative of theories of and research on teachers' stages of development, moving from quite unidimensional and linear theories to those that posit multiple and complex paths.

Of the stage theories described here, Francis Fuller's (1969; Fuller & Bown, 1975) is perhaps the most classic of stage theories in that it was meant to be relatively invariant, sequential, and hierarchical. Developed in the 1960s, this theory describes the stages that teachers go through as they become teachers. Drawing on extensive interviews of preservice students and experienced teachers, literature reviews, and checklists, Fuller and colleagues developed the Teacher Concerns Questionnaire, which was used to collect data in developing the description of stages of development. She suggested the following cluster of concerns that individuals at different stages of becoming a teacher express: preteaching concerns, concerns about survival, teaching situation concerns, and, finally, concerns about pupils.

Perhaps the best known adaptation of Fuller's theory is Hall and Loucks' (1977) work on teachers who are implementing an innovation. Hall and Loucks (1977) examined the nature of stages of teacher concern in relation to levels of use of an innovation. They found that the stages of concern do not just occur in beginning teachers but also occur when teachers make changes in a classroom by implementing an innovation. They

posited a way of determining whether a teacher is fully implementing an innovation that is based on measures of levels of use. While the stages of concern appeared quite sequential in their studies, levels of use did not correlate with years of experience with the innovation.

Following up on Hall and Loucks (1977) and others, Mevarech (1995) poses a five-stage professional development model in which an innovation is introduced to the teachers from someone outside the classroom. The stages of development are survival—experienced teachers become (temporary) novices; exploration and bridging; adaptation—from technical application to reflective implementation; and conceptual change. The empirical basis of this stage theory involved interviewing and observing two groups of teachers: computer teachers (50 teachers) and a group that had received training in and were implementing a computer-assisted training program (90 teachers).

Nias (1989) also demonstrates the influence of Fuller's work in the results of her interview study of 99 just-graduated primary teachers. Her results emphasized the importance of self—the way in which her sample of teachers thought of their roles and the development of their identities. Initially they did not think of themselves as teachers. Their self-conception changed with experience and developed in a manner similar to Fuller's stage theory: survival, task concerns, and impact concerns. Those who didn't view themselves as teachers eventually left the profession.

In a review of the learning-to-teach literature, Sharon Feiman-Nemser (1983) describes the characteristics of four phases in the process of learning to teach: the pretraining phase (early influences); preservice phase; induction phase; and inservice phase (on-the-job learning). This sequential stage theory is based on the level of experience in teaching. Her work emphasizes the life-long learning-to-teach process and brings sociology of education literature into the discussion of teacher learning. For example, she brings together the work on the "apprenticeship of observation" by Lortie (1975), student-teaching literature and learning-by-doing (e.g., Hoy, 1967), work on the shock of reality for beginning teachers by Waller (1961) and Lortie (1975), and the teacher center work by Devaney and Thorn (1975). She suggests that the different phases of knowing about and experience with teaching requires different approaches to inservice programs.

Van Manen's (1977) work focuses on levels of reflectivity in teaching and is based on criteria related to the interpretation of and deliberate decisions about an action. He identifies three levels of reflection: technical or instrumental action; practical or awareness of alternative principles; and critical or consideration of moral implications related to social conditions. While Van Manen's levels are quite invariant and sequential, Zeichner and Liston (1987) suggest that all levels are important and should be used at different points in time by the teacher. Griffiths and Tann (1992) agree with Zeichner and Liston and add two additional levels. Their five levels begin with two that they characterize as reflection-in-action: (a) rapid reaction (action react); and (b) repair (react-monitor/rework-plan-act). The next three are reflection-on-action and are likely to be interpersonal and collegial: (c) review (act-observe-analyze and evaluate-plan-act); (d) research (act-observe systematically-analyze rigorously-evaluate-plan-act); and (e) retheorize and reformulate (act-observe systematically-analyze rigorously-evaluate-retheorize plan-act). The last two lend themselves to engaging in public discussions of theory.

Schön (1983) also identified a cyclical process in reflection-in-action in which each cycle consists of three phases: problem identification, reframing, and resolution. MacKinnon (1987) identified a number of criteria for detecting the phases within the discourse that takes place between a student teacher and the supervising teacher. He found that such phases can, indeed, be identified, indicating that the student teacher is involved in reflection-in-action while still a preservice student teacher. Valdez (1992) used similar constructs in an analysis of the discourse of inservice teachers who were involved in a practical argument process (Fenstermacher, 1994b).

Black and Ammon (1992) posit a development stage theory of pedagogical thinking based on interviewing a cross section of beginning student teachers, graduating student teachers and experienced teachers. The stage theory suggests that teachers begin with associationist and behaviorist conceptions (levels 1 and 2) and move to constructivist conceptions that are, at first, quite global (level 3) but then become more differentiated and integrated (levels 4 and 5). They used this model to examine their own constructivist-oriented teacher education program at the University of California, Berkeley, and found that most of the entering preservice students were at levels 1 or 2 and that they exited the program at levels 3 or 4.

Sprinthall, Reiman, and Thies-Sprinthall (1996) summarize various stage theories related to adult development, including those developed by Hunt (1974), Kohlberg (1969), and Loevinger (1966) and suggest their appropriateness to the development of teachers. They examine stages of cognitive complexity, ego and self-development, and moral and ethical development. Their examination of the research literature on these theories leads them to conclude that such stages are useful in the consideration of the development of teachers and that there is a relationship between stages of cognitive complexity and the behavior of teachers: "In problem-solving situations requiring complex and human response, adults in general and teachers specifically who process experience at higher stages of development are more competent, effective, and efficient" (Sprinthall, Reiman, Thies-Sprinthall, 1993, p. 676). They also present a model for helping teachers attain high levels of cognitive development.

Berliner (1994) developed a stage theory of teachers' cognitive processes as they moved to become expert teachers. This theory was developed on the basis of his and his colleagues' extensive study of differences between novice and expert teachers' cognitive processes, (Carter, Cushing, Sabers, Stein, and Berliner, 1988) and other novice and expert studies such as Bullough's (1989) and Borko's (1992, April). Berliner describes five levels: novice, advanced beginner, competent, proficient, and expert. He suggests that teachers do not necessarily move through these stages on the basis of experience alone. Some teachers remain fixed at a particular level such as advanced beginner at which the teachers do not take responsibility for their

actions. At the expert level, Berliner (1994) suggests that teachers "are not consciously choosing what to attend to and what to do. They are acting effortlessly, fluidly, and in a sense, that is arational because it is not easily described as deductive or analytic behavior" (p. 167).

Knowles (1992) moved backward in the teacher's life to examine the ways in which student teachers develop teacher role identity. Using biographical case studies of 5 student teachers, he proposed a theory describing the phases of the biographical transformation model in the development of role identity. The following phases emerged: formative experiences, interpretation, schema, framework for action, and, finally, teacher role identity. He then indicated how role identity affects student teacher and beginning teacher practices.

Michael Huberman's (1989) career development study offers a complex set of stages and paths within stages.[4] This study was a (self-described) middle-scale study of 160 secondary teachers with varying levels of experience. Extensive interviews were conducted with open- and closed-ended questions. The resulting stage theory elaborates and provides different paths within six stages of development: survival and discovery; stabilization; experimentation and activism; taking stock—self-doubts, serenity, consternation; and disengagement. One of the more interesting, if not disconcerting, findings for those interested in reform programs was the following conclusion:

> Teachers who steered clear of reforms or other multiple-classroom innovations but who invested consistently in classroom-level experiments—what they called "tinkering" with new materials . . . were more likely to be satisfied later on in their careers than most others, and far more likely to be satisfied than their peers who had been heavily involved in school-wide or district-wide projects (p. 50).

Further, movement from one stage to the next, particularly toward the end of one's career, does not assume progress.

STAGES OF DEVELOPMENT WITHIN SPECIFIC PROGRAMS OR CONTEXTS

An often unstated assumption of the preceding stage theories is that these stages are meant to be generalized to teachers other than those involved in the studies, including teachers in quite different contexts. A number of studies also examine stage theory within a particular context such as a specific program of change, with the usually unstated assumption being that the findings are not necessarily generalizable to other contexts or programs of change. The following are representative of these studies.

Deborah Schifter (1995) describes four stages of conceptions of mathematics teaching that accompany teachers' attempts to become more constructivist in their teaching of mathematics. The data were derived from studies of teachers within professional development programs that were designed to help teachers move in this direction. The stages are

---

[4] See, also, Fessler (1995) for a description of his study that provided a differentiation among those teachers previously placed in the "mature" category.

. . . (1) an ad hoc accumulation of facts, definitions, and computational routines; (2) student-centered activity, but with little or no systematic inquiry into issues of mathematical structure and validity; (3) student-centered activity directed toward systematic inquiry into issues of mathematical structure and validity; (4) systematic mathematical inquiry organized around investigation of "big" mathematical ideas. (p. 18)

Peter John (1991) explored 5 student teachers' perspectives on planning and how they changed with experience in the classroom. He found differences in the stages in planning among the student teachers. For example, one student teacher exhibited three stages: idealism in planning, emergence of realism in planning, and consideration of new planning routines. Another only exhibited one stage. John found that the changes had generic outlines but varied depending on subject matter, the student teachers' own beliefs as they came into the program, and their specific school experiences.

Hoy (1967) found a pronounced shift in pupil control ideology from humanistic to custodial as preservice students move from the university classroom into their student teaching. Hoy and Woolfolk (1990) revisited this work by comparing education students with liberal arts majors and with educational psychology students at Rutgers University. The questionnaires related to efficacy, pupil control ideology, and social problem-solving orientation. The pupil control ideology became more custodial for the student teachers. Neither of the other two groups' philosophies became more custodial. Also, social problem-solving orientation became more controlling for student teachers. Educational psychology students became more oriented toward student autonomy. Hoy and Woolfolk suggest that the context of student teaching moves students from one state (humanistic) to another (custodial).

Sandra Hollingsworth (1989) studied the levels of knowledge about teaching reading that was acquired by two cohorts of preservice students in a 5th-year constructivist teacher education program. She found that certain types of knowledge were required before the student teachers could attend to other types of knowledge and that interrelated management and academic routines needed to be established before teachers could begin to focus on students' learning. In other words, classroom management routines had to be in place before students could attend to subject specific content and pedagogy. In turn, each new level of knowledge affected the student teachers' beliefs about learning and teaching that they had brought with them into the program. However, the context in which they were learning to teach and the degree to which the students could confront their own beliefs affected the level of knowledge growth they attained. The ultimate knowledge level observed in this study was "task awareness or understanding students' learning from text-related tasks" (p. 185).

Work by Wood, Cobb, and Yackel (1991) originally focused on creating a classroom environment in which children could make meaning of mathematics. They worked with a teacher to create a more constructivist environment and, in the process, made discoveries about teacher change. In questioning students about their conceptions, the teacher had found that the students were not learning what the teacher thought she was teaching them. Through interviews and observations, Wood et al. (1991)

found that the teacher went through three major reconceptualizations of the role of the teacher from (a) teacher presenting information to teacher as learner and encourager to (b) teacher not imposing ways of thinking but creating opportunities for students to develop meaning and resolve conflicts to (c) teacher not having to impose one's way of thinking on the students.

MOVEMENT FROM ONE STATE OR STAGE TO ANOTHER

Seldom do developmental theorists address the issue of what prompts natural movement from one stage or phase to another or how one moves along a developmental continuum. Many of the theorists and researchers mentioned above are interested in using an understanding of their theories to promote movement, because the stages are generally considered to be hierarchical. However, because much of the research on stages of development is cross-sectional, determining the factors, other than years of experience, that help to move a teacher from one stage to another is difficult.

Kelchtermans and Vandenberghe (1994), however, used a biographical perspective to determine how teachers themselves described factors that led to professional development. Using a critical incident approach, they developed three extensive interview schedules for 12 elementary schoolteachers in Belgium. They found that incidents leading to perceived professional development are identified as critical by the individual involved but may not be critical for others who experience the same incident. Further, they found that the teachers experienced their careers, by and large, as a gradual evolution; however, there were situations, experiences, and people that they spoke of in great detail. The authors, therefore, redefined critical incidents as situations, people, or both that are distinctive and have a "strong personal meaning" (p. 53).

SUMMARY: STAGES OF DEVELOPMENT

Over the past several years, we have seen a movement from relatively rigid, deterministic, hierarchical, and traditional stage theories in teaching to more flexible accounts of the developmental process. This more flexible approach suggests that a number of factors affect either the movement from one stage to another or the acquisition of another phase. These factors include biography, experience, context, personality (or stance), and beliefs. These flexible approaches are not deterministic models in which factors—including teachers' decisions—may be altered to add another stage or phase in the teacher's development. For some researchers (e.g., Griffiths & Tan 1992; Zeichner & Liston 1987), these stages or phases become more like sets of developing approaches, perspectives, or ways of thinking. Relating the usefulness of this research to educational practice, Goldsmith and Schifter (1994) suggest that research that identifies flexible stage or phase theories provides reformers with valuable information about the process of change: This research indicates an "'orderliness' in the transformation of pedagogical practice when viewed from the standpoint of the goals of the reform and a set of ongoing efforts to achieve the goals" (p. 5). Thus, these phases may be viewed as benchmarks in assessing a particular change process. At the same time, the use of a very flexible approach to stages or phases may have taken us so far from the original concept of a stage theory that the usefulness of the work must be rethought.

Formal Programs for Teacher Change: Teacher Education and Staff Development

This section examines research on the deliberate process of preparing teachers for teaching and helping teachers improve their practices. Because the teacher education and staff development research literature has grown extensively since the last *Handbook of Research On Teaching* (Wittrock, 1986), we cannot refer to it all. Further, a series of quite recent handbooks and handbook articles summarize the literature in teacher education and staff development. For example, three recent handbooks focus exclusively on teacher education and staff development (Houston, 1990; Murray, 1996; Sikula, 1996). Additionally, in all of the content-area handbooks, at least one chapter is devoted to teacher education, staff development, or both. We will, therefore, examine the literature from the frame of current themes that are shared by both the teacher education and staff development literatures and then explore the two literatures separately.

COMMON THEMES

The following themes are shared by both the current teacher education and staff development literatures.

An Emphasis on Cognition. Since the cognitive revolution began to affect the study of education a number of years ago, research that explores and describes outcomes and processes of education has shifted from considering behaviors to considering various forms of cognition. While some interest in teacher attitudes and their impact on practice was present during the 1960s (Richardson, 1996), one might suggest that the roots of the current cognitive movement in research on teaching may be found in the 1974 National Conference on Studies in Teaching. One of the 10 panels was called *Teaching as Clinical Information Processing* (National Institute of Education, 1975) and was chaired by Lee Shulman. The report of this panel proposed the application of cognitive psychology to the study of classrooms and teaching and became the basis of the request for proposals for a national center of research on teaching that was funded by the National Institute of Education. This center was funded at Michigan State University, and the research that was conducted there led the field in the examination of teachers' decision making and cognitive processes. For summaries of this initial work, see Shavelson and Stern (1981), Clark and Peterson (1986), and Borko and Niles (1987).

Since that point, and particularly during the latter half of the 1980s, the proportion of cognitive studies in relation to behavioral studies has grown dramatically. Many of the cognitive constructs are examined to determine their effect on the process of change, and others are studied to determine if and how they are acquired as desirable outcomes of interventions. For example, the following cognitive concepts are thought to affect the change process: predispositions to reframe puzzles of practice (Munby & Russell, 1992), perspectives (Zeichner, Tabachnick, & Densmore, 1987), and images of teaching and teachers (Britzman, 1985; Britzman, 1991; Calderhead & Robson,

1991; Clandinin, 1986; Clift, Meng, & Eggerding, 1994). Other concepts are examined in relation to their acquisition in teacher education, inservice teaching, or both. These concepts include practical knowledge (Elbaz, 1983); personal practical knowledge (Clandinin & Connelly, 1987); situational knowledge (Leinhardt, 1988); practice-generated theories (Jordell, 1987); pedagogical content knowledge (Grossman, 1990; Shulman, 1987); and content knowledge (Borko, Lalik, & Tomchin, 1987). Concepts such as beliefs (Richardson, 1996) and metaphors (Tobin, 1990) are referred to as affecting change in practice and, therefore, require attention in any change process and become the focal point of change efforts.

Two concepts that have received considerable attention are reflective practices and beliefs. The growth in research on reflective practice was advanced by the acceptance of Schön's (1983) conception of the reflective practitioner. While it appeared originally to be a descriptive concept in Schön's framework, the reflective practitioner became a normative conception that began to drive teacher education programs and affect staff development (Clift, Houston, & Pugach, 1990; Grimmett & Erickson, 1988). A challenge facing researchers in this area has been to develop ways of determining whether teachers and preservice students are reflective and ways to assess whether changes in reflection occur as a result of an intervention.

The second construct that has dominated the literature on change in teacher education and staff development over the past several years is beliefs (Richardson, 1996). Beliefs are examined as factors that interact with the change process and affect outcomes and are also examined as outcomes that are affected by change processes. For example, Smylie (1988) studied the relationships between organizational contexts of schools and changes in individual teacher practice (among other relationships). One of his conclusions was "[T]eachers' perceptions and beliefs are the most significant predictors of individual change" (p. 23). Beliefs are generally viewed as different from knowledge in that the latter has a requirement for some form of warrant (Fenstermacher, 1994a; Nespor, 1987; Pajares, 1992; Richardson, 1994a).

Constructivist Learning and Teaching. Constructivism refers to a learning or meaning-making theory that suggests that individuals create their own new understandings, which are based upon the interaction of what they already know and believe and the ideas with which they come into contact. Recent and somewhat competing roots of the movement toward constructivism may be found in Piaget (1970) and Vygotsky (1962). (See Vadeboncoeur, 1997, for a historical discussion of these theories in relation to teacher education.) Constructivism has become a significant element of the educational policy and practice scene. Constructivist approaches are reflected in national- and state-level policy documents, such as the national standards documents, that are designed to influence the curriculum and pedagogy in American classrooms. As a descriptive theory of learning, however, constructivism does not translate directly into teaching practices. Further, most teachers in the schools today and many preservice teacher education students have not experienced constructivist classrooms in their own education. Thus, to change teacher-centered, traditional classrooms to more constructivist environments, experienced teachers and teachers-in-training require the acquisition of a new set of beliefs and practices. A considerable amount of the teacher education and staff development literature recently has focused on the development of these beliefs and practices.

The constructivist literature may be divided into two types: studies that describe attempts to help teachers create constructivist classrooms and those that focus directly on the constructivist nature of the staff development and teacher education process itself. In the staff development literature, attempts at helping teachers cultivate constructivist classrooms may be found in the various content area literatures, particularly those of mathematics (Civil, 1995; Peterson et al., 1989; Schifter & Simon, 1992) and science (e.g., Blumenfeld, Kracjik, Marx, & Soloway, 1994; Krajcik, Layman, Starr, & Magnusson, 1991, April; Smith & Neale, 1989). This work is often directly tied to the implementation of national standards that call for constructivist approaches to teaching these subjects. A number of these studies indicate the relationship between a teacher's development of an effective constructivist environment in the classroom and that teacher's high levels of content knowledge. For example, Heaton (1992) and Putnam (1992) describe the classrooms of elementary teachers who are trying to situate math instruction in real-world tasks and are moving away from the straightforward content of textbook math. These studies indicate limitations in teachers' knowledge of mathematics—a problem that may be more apparent in constructivist teaching than traditional approaches. MacKinnon and Scarff-Seatter (1997) provide real-life examples of this issue, drawn from a case of a student teacher who is teaching science.

A number of studies focus more directly on the constructivist nature of the process of change in teachers in such areas as beliefs about science (Lampert, 1997), the teaching of reading and writing (Lester & Onore 1990; Richardson, 1994b), and high expectations for students (Weinstein, Madison, & Kuklinski, 1995). Work on constructivist teacher education somewhat lagged behind the constructivist staff development research but is now a more popular consideration (Richardson 1997).

Complexity of Teaching and the Importance of the Context. The movement away from an emphasis on behavior was accompanied by an understanding of the nature of teaching as a complex endeavor, the effectiveness of which depends, in part, on the context in which one teaches. Doyle (1979) wrote about the characteristics of classrooms that affect the complexity of teaching. These include multidimensionality, simultaneity, immediacy, unpredictability, publicness, and history. Context began to be seen as important toward the end of period of domination by behaviorist approaches. For example, Brophy (1976) suggested that a publication similar to the *Merck Manual* used by physicians could be developed that would describe elements of the context and then would suggest effective behaviors for that context. In this case, context included such factors as grade level, achievement levels of students and subject matter. However, context blossomed in full at the beginning of the cognitive era with the widespread realization that while teachers could be

trained in behavior, training them to make decisions about the appropriateness of a particular behavior within a specific context was much more difficult.

The complexity of teaching and the variability of the context work together to help justify the view of the teacher as a thinking, decision-making, reflective, and autonomous professional. Because teaching is complex, and contexts vary, teachers themselves need to make decisions and reflect on their situations and teaching in order to act appropriately in their classrooms. Training in particular practices is no longer the dominant approach to teacher education and staff development; training has given way to education, and the focus is on developing ways of thinking and exposing teachers to many different strategies.

Quantitative to Qualitative Methodological Approaches. Along with a move away from behaviorism, researchers turned to qualitative methodologies for inquiry into teacher education and staff development. Qualitative approaches allow researchers to move more deeply and hermeneutically into the thinking processes of preservice and inservice teachers, and account more fully for context. The initial move away from quantitative research led to great debates and some consternation in the field (e.g., Rist, 1977). In research on teaching, the development of qualitative approaches appeared to be, in part, a reaction against process-product research (e.g., Doyle, 1977; Fenstermacher, 1979). However, qualitative approaches soon became recognized in their own right. Although qualitative research was often defined as ethnography (Erickson, 1986), the field opened up to include many different approaches to qualitative research. Mary Lee Smith's (1987) treatment of the topic was particularly helpful in describing four approaches to qualitative research: interpretive, artistic, systematic, and theory-driven.

At this point, small sample and case studies dominate the research work in teacher education and staff development. These allow for in-depth examinations of process, context, content, and change. Case studies and small sample research also facilitate research within the movement known as teacher research for teachers in K–12 settings (see Cochran-Smith & Lytle, 1990; Sockett & Hollingsworth, 1994) and as self-study for teacher educators (see Loughran & Russell, 1997; Russell & Korthagen 1995).[5] Qualitative studies have not completely overtaken quantitative studies, however, and many examples of the latter may be found in the literature, such as the studies by Corporaal (1991), Veenman, Leenders, Meyer, and Sanders (1993), and Marso and Pigge (1989). In addition, a number of research projects such as Fennema, Carpenter, Franke, and Carey (1992) use both qualitative and quantitative methodologies.

We now turn to the individual literatures of teacher education and staff development.

TEACHER EDUCATION

In their 1986 chapter on teacher education in the *Handbook of Research on Teaching,* Judith Lanier with Judith Warren Little (Lanier, 1986) pointed out that changing teachers' behaviors

---

[5] Interestingly, two different terms are used to describe the same form of study. To a certain degree, one can look at the formation of the American Educational Research Association's Self-Study Special Interest Group to understand how the term "Self-Study" was developed separately from teacher research.

and thoughts is always possible: "we already know that teachers, like other normal human beings, are capable of learning new thoughts and behaviors in ways that conform to a set of generally accepted principles of human learning" (p. 528). In their chapter, they, therefore, did not describe the myriad studies that provide evidence to show that affecting short-term changes in teacher education students' learning of behaviors is possible. We agree that to move students to the point of indicating on a short-answer or multiple-choice test that they have acquired academic knowledge about teaching and learning is possible. Also, to train students to perform a particular method of teaching or pedagogical strategy such as wait time is possible. However, much of the current research investigates changes in teachers' deep cognitions and reflective orientations that are intended to be long term and, eventually, to affect teaching practice at the appropriate point in a local context.

What we see expressed in these current studies of teacher education is the difficulty in changing the type of tacit beliefs and understandings that lie buried in a person's being. These cognitions and beliefs drive everyday classroom practice within local contexts. Thus, a critical question that emerges from this work asks, "To what degree do teacher education programs affect deep and meaningful cognitive changes in preservice students?"

A number of studies indicate the difficulty in changing beliefs in preservice students. For example, before and after student teaching experiences, Zeichner, Tabachnick, and Densmore (1987) asked novices to solve 18 classroom dilemmas, explaining and justifying their solutions. They referred to Becker, Geer, Hughes, and Strauss's (1961) definition of perspective as a coordinated set of ideas and actions a person uses in dealing with some problematic situation. The solutions to the dilemmas, along with interview and observational data, were then used by the researchers to infer for each novice a characteristic style of resolving classroom problems. Analysis of before and after solutions indicated that the novices' perspectives tended to solidify rather than to change over the course of the student teaching experiences.

Olson (1993) also found that students did not change their beliefs and assumptions about good teaching during the course of their teacher education programs. More recently, Tillema and Knol (1997) compared student teachers who were engaged in a conceptual change process and those in a direct instruction program. They found that the conceptual change students outperformed the direct instruction students in such teaching behaviors as "representation;" however, they did not change beliefs. The authors suggest that without changes in beliefs, the changes in performance will be superficial. Weber and Mitchell (1996) compared drawings of teachers by elementary classroom students and those by elementary education preservice teachers. They found that the overwhelming image was one of a pleasant, traditional, female teacher who points out and explains. The researchers suggest that this image probably cannot be overcome in preservice teacher education and that perhaps teacher educators should acknowledge and work within the image.

While perspectives and beliefs did not appear to change in the preceding studies, Winitzky (1992) and Winitzky and Kauchak (1997) did find considerable cognitive growth in their teacher education students. They worked with the cognitive maps of 19 elementary teacher candidates. Classroom management terms were selected and subjects grouped the terms four successive times. A computer program was then used to symbolically represent how the 20 items were chunked or grouped by each individual. A person with a highly organized tree tends to remember the same item in the same order over a series of trials. The students also were presented with a reflective interview that allowed the researchers to place the students in one of seven levels of reflection. Over the course of the class, students' cognitive structures were increasingly organized; and a trend toward a direct relationship between reflection and structure was identified.

Jones and Vesilind (1996) also used concept maps (in addition to interviews) in their exploration of changes in the organization of 23 preservice teachers' knowledge during their senior year. They found the students' schemas to be quite fluid as they moved from the academic program to student teaching. In addition, cognitive reorganization during student teaching was evident in the students' revised definitions of flexibility and planning. Jones and Vesilind concluded that the impetus for the cognitive reorganization was the researchers' interactions with students.

Korthagen (1988), however, concluded from his study of students in his reflective teacher education program that students who come into the program without reflective orientations do not gain very much from teacher education courses that emphasize reflection. The students were studied in terms of their learning orientations. Korthagen and his colleagues found that some students learn by internal direction or orientation (reflective), and others learn by an external orientation. The researchers then examined the longitudinal development of students with different learning orientations. The teacher educators who were reflective themselves understood only the learning orientations of reflective students. Many of the nonreflective students dropped out after the first year; others changed their learning orientations. Korthagen suggests that in such a situation, students may drop out or "simulate learning behaviour (*quasi-adaption* to the conceptions of learning of the educators)" (p. 48). He suggests that externally oriented students should be allowed to learn the art of reflection gradually.

Munro (1993) also faced discouraging results with his teacher education program that attempted to develop reflective teachers, and Tickle (1991) concluded that novice teachers do not develop skills in reflective practice until they start teaching. Bolin (1990) found through his case study of a student teacher that not all students gain from a reflective teacher education program; the student teacher in his study appeared to resist becoming reflective rather than develop reflective capacities.

Harrington and Hathaway (1994) examined whether a computer conference during a preservice teacher education class helped students become more aware of their taken-for-granted assumptions, which the researchers felt might be a necessary condition for critical reflection. They defined critical reflection as "(1) recognizing limitations in sociocultural, epistemic, and psychological assumptions, (2) acknowledging and including multiple perspectives, (3) considering the moral and ethical consequences of choices, and (4) clarifying reasoning processes when making and evaluating decisions" (p. 2). Using transcripts of "The Dialogical Community Exercise" that were generated completely by students with no interference from the instructor, they examined sociocultural, epistemic, and psychological assumptions. They identified several students who represented complex levels of professional development (questioned assumptions, etc.). These students seemed to disrupt equilibrium for the less complex students. Harrington and Hathaway concluded that the conferencing activity provided a rich source of assumptions but that most students did not recognize them as such. As the semester progressed, however, participants raised more questions regarding assumptions.

Civil (1996) examined epistemological change as preservice teachers went through an elementary methods class that focused on constructivist mathematical teaching. The study involved examining beliefs about and understandings of mathematics. Interviews and class-associated tasks were used to document the process of introducing the preservice teachers to a different conception of mathematics and teaching mathematics. The process was difficult, and the preservice teachers complained that they had not learned mathematics this way. But they began to accept the nature of the tasks and even use them with their own students.

Like the teacher education program at Wisconsin, the various programs at Michigan State University (MSU) have also conducted considerable investigation to identify cognitive changes in their students. For example, Feiman-Nemser, McDiarmid, Melnick, and Parker (1989) looked at conceptual change in 91 students who were enrolled in an introductory course at MSU that was designed to help students examine their preconceptions about teaching and learning. The researchers found four themes concerning change in the students' work: (a) the nature of teaching—"students began to realize that teaching may be other than—and more than—what they assumed it to be" (p. 4); (b) the relationship between teaching and learning—they had never thought about it before—now they did; (c) the contexts of teaching—students became more aware of issues at the school and classroom level rather than at the broader level; and (d) teacher knowledge—of 91 students, 47 commented on teacher knowledge, suggesting that their preconceptions about what teachers need to know had changed.

While the study by Feiman-Nemser et al. indicates some conceptual change, the authors suggest that it often does not take place. Feiman-Nemser and Buchmann (1989) present a case study of a student who "combined past experience with ideas she encountered in formal preparation in a way that reinforced earlier beliefs and reversed the intended message of her assigned readings on the inequitable distribution of school knowledge" (p. 371).

Wilcox, Schram, Lappan, and Lanier (1991) described their Michigan State University program that was designed to change prospective elementary teachers' knowledge and beliefs about mathematics education. The intervention consisted of a sequence of mathematics courses, a methods course, and a curriculum seminar in which establishing a community of learners was a central feature. Research on the process indicated that the program made significant contributions toward empowering prospective elementary teachers to learn mathematics, to sustain beliefs about themselves as learners of mathematics, and to understand what it means to know mathematics and how mathematics is learned; however, the students did not change their beliefs about how the elementary math curriculum should be presented. Case studies of 2 teachers in their first year indicated how complex the process was to connect their own experiences as learners of mathematics to new visions of classrooms they might construct for children.

McDiarmid (1992) examined changes in teacher trainees' beliefs following a series of presentations in multicultural education. Few changes were noted, and McDiarmid suggests that the content of the course confused the students. McDiarmid (1990) also studied changes in conceptions of preservice students in a class that was designed to change students' misconceptions. Although he found some changes in conceptions, he stated that he remains skeptical about these changes. Preservice students' beliefs, he feels, are very difficult to change.

Pedagogical content knowledge is another area that has been explored in preservice students. Phillip, Armstrong, and Bezuk (1993) provided students with knowledge about how students learn and develop strategies in a specific content area within a math methods course for elementary students. They were interested in the way knowledge was eventually used in student teaching by one student teacher. They found that the pedagogical content knowledge influenced practice but not all the time. Markel (1995) examined the growth of practical knowledge in 5 student teachers and found that several of these novice teachers did begin to develop practical knowledge in those areas in which they had opportunities for experience and self-conscious, reflective awareness.

Those areas used to examine the development of practical knowledge were drawn from Elbaz (1983), who articulated five domains of practical knowledge: (a) self, (b) the milieu of teaching, (c) subject matter, (d) curriculum development, and (e) instruction. Evidence of the growth of practical knowledge was collected through classroom observations of teaching and conversations about practice. Dialogues within a seminar setting were analyzed for self-conscious, reflective awareness and decision making and the development of teaching. Not all student teachers experienced growth in practical knowledge over the period of student teaching.

These studies indicate the difficulty in affecting cognitive change, particularly change in deep-seated beliefs, in preservice teacher education programs. This problem, some suggest, relates to the preservice students' lack of teaching experience and therefore of practical knowledge (Richardson, 1996). This hypothesis is bolstered by evidence of changes that took place during student teaching when preservice teachers began to experience the overwhelming tasks associated with full-time teaching.

Several approaches to increasing experience and practical knowledge in preservice teachers have been suggested. One is to concentrate more on bringing the academic together with the practical during preservice teaching, for example, with the use of cases (Merseth, 1996) and with experiences within professional development schools. As Mayer-Smith and Mitchell (1997) suggest

> . . . it is not possible for a teacher education course to achieve changes in preservice teachers' beliefs about teaching and learning without influencing attitudes and promoting behaviours consistent with such beliefs. However, as we regard conceptual change as grad-

ual and evolutionary, it would be illogical to suggest that change begins and ends with a single methods course. If conceptual change is to continue we contend that the practicum experience must provide a supportive environment and multiple opportunities for preservice teachers to explore and experiment with the ideas and procedures presented in methods courses. (p. 149)

Another suggested approach is to make structural changes, in particular, to change the timing of preservice teacher education in relation to the development of practical knowledge through experience. Fenstermacher (1993) has suggested that colleges of education are best suited to helping teachers with the educative functions of schooling—those functions related to assisting students in becoming autonomous, enlightened, and virtuous human beings. He proposes that these aspects should be developed after the teacher has acquired an understanding of the systemics of schooling, that is, after they develop some practical knowledge about classroom management, assessment, the curriculum in this school, etc. He suggests that these first elements should be taught through internships within professional practice schools and that after receiving several years of a mentoring type of apprenticeship approach, they go to the University for certification. At that point, topics in foundations, psychology, pedagogical content knowledge, etc. may be successfully explored with the teachers. Tom (1995) has also made a strong case for this approach to teacher education.

After reviewing much of the research on the learning-to-teach process, particularly the acquisition of practical knowledge through experience (Carter, 1990), the structure proposed by Fenstermacher makes sense. Russell (1995) provides some empirical backing for this suggestion. He examined the differences between 2 groups of students' approaches to their science methods courses. One was a typical 5th-year group and the other was a group that had begun their teacher education program with 9 weeks of student teaching. The differences between these 2 groups that were related to beliefs, approaches, and understandings were profound. Those who had been in the classroom for 9 weeks had more need to know than those who had not experienced classroom teaching.

We now turn to the research that examines programs that involve inservice teachers in change processes—research demonstrating that helping inservice teachers to develop new understandings, beliefs, and perceptions is more often successful than working with preservice students.

STAFF DEVELOPMENT

The distinctions made by Chin and Benne (1969) between empirical-rational and normative-reeducative approaches to change that were described in the first section of this chapter are particularly useful in examining the staff development literature. To summarize, the empirical-rational approach assumes that individuals, if shown by others that a new practice is good, will act in their rational self-interest and make the appropriate changes. The changes that take place are in knowledge, information, intellectual premises, and behaviors. The normative-

reeducative approach suggests that individuals act on the basis of sociocultural norms to which they are committed. A necessary condition for change is that individuals alter their normative orientations and develop new ones. Reports of research on staff development practices fit quite neatly into these two categories, in regard to both the type of staff development being examined and the research approach used in the inquiry.

Empirical-Rational. The more traditional form of staff development begins with someone outside the school determining that a process, method, or system should be implemented in classrooms. The conception of teacher education represented in this form is that of the training model, which has at its core a clearly stated set of objectives and learner outcomes. Initially, these objectives were teaching skills (Cruickshank & Metcalf, 1990). Showers, Joyce, and Bennett (1987) added thinking processes to the list of outcomes. Sparks and Loucks-Horsley (1990) identified a number of important assumptions inherent in the training model of which the following are two:

- that behaviors and techniques are worthy of replication by teachers in the classroom
- that teacher education students and teachers can learn or change their behaviors to replicate behaviors in their classrooms (p. 241)

Many of the staff development programs in this category are relatively short term, involving teachers in several hours or days of workshops, with limited follow-up activities (Goldenberg & Gallimore, 1991; Sparks, 1983; Ward, 1985). Such programs have only a chance of succeeding with those teachers whose beliefs match the assumptions inherent in the innovation, and, even still, these teachers might not try the new innovation. In fact, Joyce (1981, cited in Meyer, 1988) estimated that such practices garner an implementation level of 15%. Hargreaves (1995) described such practices in this manner:

[T]he dominant paradigms of teacher development research and practice tend to be rational, calculative, managerial, and somewhat masculine in nature. The professional values of rational debate and analysis in the seminar room are imposed upon the pedagogical practice of intuition and improvisation in the classroom. (p. 23)

More recently, however, an understanding of the qualities needed in staff development processes have entered the consciousness of staff developers and school district officials. These qualities, extracted from research on staff development, have been summarized by many, including Fullan (1990), Griffin (1986), Loucks-Horsley et al. (1987), McLaughlin (1991), and Ward (1985). They include the following:[6]

- The program should be schoolwide and context-specific.
- School principals should be supportive of the process and encouraging of change.
- The program should be long-term with adequate support and follow-up.

---

[6] The question of whether or not the teachers have a choice of attending the staff development is included as an important quality by some but not by others.

- The process should encourage collegiality.
- The program content should incorporate current knowledge obtained through well-designed research.
- The program should include adequate funds for materials, outside speakers, and substitute teachers so that teachers can observe each other.

Recent empirical-rational staff development processes focus on ways of thinking and teacher action rather than on behaviors. They use as many of the qualities mentioned above as possible. Gallagher, Goudvis, and Pearson (1988) call this form of staff development "directed development," and Meyer (1988) provides a strong argument for such an approach to staff development.

For example, Krajcik, Layman, Starr, and Magnusson (1991, April) conducted and studied an intensive 3-week summer program with middle school teachers on using microcomputer-based laboratory equipment to teach temperature and heat energy concepts to middle school students. The goals were to increase knowledge about heat and energy and pedagogical content knowledge. They used pre- and postsemistructured interviews and formed each teacher's responses into propositions and concept maps to represent change in teacher's understandings over time. They found that the teachers held partial or alternative conceptions of temperature and heat. At the end of the program, most teachers could distinguish between temperature and heat energy, but they did not develop richer understandings of the more difficult heat energy concept.

In Sparks's (1988) study, three groups of junior high teachers ($N = 19$) attended five workshops on effective teaching. Pre- and posttraining observations, questionnaires, and interviews were used to assess behavior changes and attitudes. She found that teachers who came to view the practice promoted in the staff development as important implemented the practice in their classrooms more than those who did not. The improving teachers indicated that the training gave them a heightened sense of control over their teaching environments. They seemed to have a higher sense of self-efficacy. They had been dissatisfied but had not known what to do.

Stallings (1989, March) summarized the various process-product studies that have been conducted around her Reflective Use of Time (RUOT) staff development process. The particular form of study and approach to staff development allowed her to compare three different structures of staff development and determine whether they made a difference in terms of secondary student achievement in reading. She compared situations in which only reading teachers were trained, all language arts teachers and reading teachers received the training, and all teachers in a district were trained. She found the greatest gain occurred for the group in which all teachers in the district underwent the staff development. The next lower gain was for all reading and language arts teachers, and the lowest gain was for the reading teachers. She concluded that "when a staff development program is generic, it is most effective to have all teachers involved so that students meet the same type of expectations and procedures" (p. 9).

Even if the project is successful, as determined by the percentage of teacher participants who immediately implement the process in their classrooms, the longer term effects are questionable. For example, in a 4-year study of a Madeleine Hunter staff development process, Stallings and Krasavage (1986) found that in the 3rd year, teachers implemented the desired behaviors much less often than they had in the first two years. Further, the opposite effects may be created—that is, a situation in which teachers cling to a way of teaching they learned in a staff development program that is no longer deemed appropriate (see also McLaughlin, 1991).

One hypothesis used to explain the disappointing long-term effects of the Madeleine Hunter model is appropriate here. Stallings and Krasavage (1986) suggest that the model could not sustain teachers' interest:

> We believe that the innovative practices teachers learn will not be maintained unless teachers and students remain interested and excited about their own learning. . . . A good staff development program will create an excitement about learning to learn. The question is how to keep the momentum, not merely maintain previously learned behaviors. (p. 137)

We now move to research on staff development programs that operate within the second approach toward change, the normative-reeducative approach.

Normative-Reeducative. This approach is based on concepts of personal growth and development and on collaboration within the organization that leads to collective change. Many of the staff development programs in this category are designed to help teachers develop a constructivist orientation toward teaching a particular subject matter, to attempt to develop and study the nature of constructivist teacher education processes, or both. Many of those projects that help teachers develop a constuctivist orientation may be found in the content areas of mathematics and science.

In mathematics, a major project that received considerable research attention was Cognitively Guided Instruction (CGI), which was developed at the University of Wisconsin. The focus of the project was on helping teachers learn to study students' learning of mathematics. During Phase 1 of the CGI study, the teacher participants were interviewed with structured questions about their knowledge of and beliefs about the teaching of mathematics. Twenty of the teachers were then randomly assigned to participate in a staff development program (Peterson, Fennema, Carpenter, & Loef, 1989). The remaining 20 teachers participated in a workshop on problem solving. Observations, interviews, and questionnaires were used to assess pedagogical content knowledge. Also, student achievement was assessed with standardized tests of computation and problem solving, interviews, and experimenter-constructed measures.

CGI teachers taught problem solving significantly more and taught number facts significantly less than control teachers. They were more constructivist. Experimental students scored higher than control students in knowledge of number facts and on some tests of problem solving. They were also more confident (Carpenter, Fennema, Peterson, Chiang, & Loef, 1989). During the following year, a type of coaching took place in addition to group meetings. One key characteristic of successful CGI classrooms was that teachers listened to their students and built on what they already knew. Case studies of these CGI teachers were presented in Fennema, Carpenter, Franke, and Carey (1992).

Civil (1995) also studied an inservice training that was designed to develop constructivist approaches in classrooms. Teachers were asked to interview two of their students on mathematics tasks. Case studies of two teachers undergoing the staff development effort indicated that the teachers were extremely surprised with the students' answers to their questions and found that they learned a great deal from interviewing their students.

D. Ball (1990) and D. Cohen (1990) examined teachers' change processes while involved in a staff development designed to help teachers become more constructivist in the teaching of mathematics. They were struck by the need for one particular teacher's beliefs to match the assumptions underlying a particular approach to teaching. They found that while this teacher made some changes in behavior and, perhaps, in beliefs, the teacher did not undergo the fundamental change in beliefs necessary to make changes in a classroom approach. While the teacher believed that she had changed—dramatically, in fact—the changes came about within a traditional form of teaching.

Barnett and Sather (1992) used cases of teaching and learning to help 20 teachers involved in a staff development program to improve their abilities to teach rational numbers. Many teachers began to question their conceptions, and several teachers were changing their orientation toward teaching at a more fundamental level—toward a more constructivist orientation. Schifter and Simon (1992) and Wood, Cobb, and Yackel (1991) also examined their staff development programs that were designed to develop a constructivist orientation in teachers' instruction of mathematics.

An example of the study of a staff development process designed to help teachers teach for conceptual change in science is found in Smith and Neale (1989). They trained teachers to implement a teaching strategy that incorporates a Piagetian view of constructivism and found that this training required the teachers to restructure their cognitions. The process involved videotaping and interviewing teachers, having teachers read about students' misconceptions, having students interview their teachers, etc. Hoban (1995) also examined the development of constructivist beliefs and practices in teachers. He worked with three teachers and asked them to interview their students about the nature of science. Performing the interviews and sharing their results with others helped the teachers reframe their practices.

Blumenfeld, Kracjik, Marx, and Soloway (1994) designed and implemented a collaborative staff development process to help middle school teachers develop and implement project-based instruction in science. They studied teacher change through extensive interviews, observations, and discourse analysis of the conversations the teachers had with other teachers and with the university researchers. During the course of the project, teachers' concerns moved from attempts to enact the approach with accuracy to strategies for dealing with problems they were confronting to explorations of the theory underlying the practice. The researchers suggest a model for supporting teachers that focuses on a dynamic interplay of cycles of collaboration with other teachers, collaboration with university personnel and experts in the field, enactment of new approaches, and reflection about the new approaches and new information.

Weinstein, Madison, and Kuklinski (1995) examined the process and outcomes of developing a constructivist staff development program. A collaborative team of researchers, administrators, and teachers in an inner-city high school met over a 2-year period to attempt to raise teacher expectations for at-risk students. Teachers' initial spoken beliefs placed the blame for poor achievement on a number of external factors, such as deficits in students and lack of support for collaboration and mixed-ability teaching. Over time, teachers took responsibility, challenged their initial beliefs, and made changes in policies and practices. They concluded that "preventive action must move beyond the teacher-student dyad to include an understanding of the context in which expectations for students, teachers and schooling are embedded" (p. 121). The Weinstein et al. study was a case of what Cole and Knowles (1993) called "partnership research."

Studying the nature of teacher change often becomes an important element of a study originally designed to test the effects of a change process such as a particular staff development topic. For example, Lester and Onore (1990) closely examined an inservice program that they designed and that involved 45 teachers to inquire into how language is used to enhance learning across the curriculum. The staff developers, who had developed the inservice program, also had an interest in democratic schooling. The staff developers began to collect extensive field notes, interviews, learning logs, etc. While the study continued to focus on the particular staff development process, the researchers also became interested in the relationship between the research and the staff development practice and between the staff developers' own change processes and those of the teachers.

The Reading Instruction Study (Richardson, 1994b) was designed to examine the use of research in the teaching of reading comprehension. The researchers worked with 39 Grade 4, 5, and 6 teachers in 5 schools in the Southwest. Embedded within the study was a staff development process that was based on the importance of beliefs in the staff development process and the use of practical arguments (Fenstermacher, 1986; Fenstermacher, 1994b; Richardson and Hamilton, 1994). However, in the course of conducting the study, the development of a theory of the naturalistic teacher change process became a significant focus of the study, the results of which were described in Richardson (1990) and other places. During the study, the researchers were able to pursue studies of teacher change and studies of the process and effects of a collaborative staff development process.

For example, a major question in the teacher change literature revolves around whether changes in beliefs precede or follow changes in practices. Richardson (1994b) and her colleagues were able to investigate this question in their study. Before the staff development process began, extensive belief interviews and observations were conducted in the spring. The staff development process began the next fall, and videotapes of teaching were gathered at the beginning of the process.

In a case study of a teacher whose stated beliefs about teaching reading comprehension in the spring did not match her classroom practices, Richardson, Anders, Tidwell, and Lloyd (1991) found that she was undergoing a second-order change in her teaching, moving from the use of a traditional program that relied on basal readers to the use of literature in the teaching of reading. She had made changes in her beliefs prior to changes in her practices. However, by the fall, she had made significant changes in her teaching. She ascribed the changes to hearing about them at a workshop and from other teachers.

Of interest in the findings for these researchers was that changes in beliefs were preceding changes in practice, contradicting a number of other researchers who suggest that changes in belief follow those changes in practices that lead to success (Guskey, 1986; Mevarech, 1995; Prawat, 1992; Sparks, 1988). These other researchers conducted their research within the more traditional conception of change and evaluation design in which the teachers are asked (or told) by others to change their practices. However, in the naturalistic change process, changes in beliefs appear often to precede changes in practices (e.g., Bullough & Knowles, 1991) or that the process of changing beliefs and practices is interactive or synergistic (Goffman, 1973; Peterman, 1993; Richardson & Anders, 1994).

The authors of this chapter and colleagues (see Anders & Richardson, 1991; Placier & Hamilton, 1994; Richardson & Hamilton, 1994), developed and studied the Practical Argument Staff Development (PASD) process. This voluntary and collaborative process was designed to help teachers inquire, both in groups and individually, into their beliefs and practices regarding current research on reading and practices described by other teachers and to support their attempts at change.[7] This PASD process is similar to one described by Tierney, Tucker, Gallagher, Crismore, and Pearson (1988) as the Metcalf Project.

We and our colleagues found that over a 3-year period, the teachers changed their beliefs and practices in directions that related to dialogues about practices in the teaching of reading, including those in the individual practical argument sessions and the group discussions. Bos and Anders (1994) conducted a substudy and found that the students of the teachers who participated in the staff development process achieved more in certain aspects of reading comprehension than did the students in a contrast school.

In a follow-up 2 years later, the authors of this chapter and their colleagues found that the teachers had continued to change (Valdez, 1992). The teachers appear to have developed a change orientation that led them to reflect continually on their teaching and classrooms and to experiment thoughtfully with new practices. The teachers became confident in their decision-making abilities and took responsibility for what was happening in their classrooms. Thus, they had developed a strong sense of individual autonomy and felt empowered to make deliberate and thoughtful changes in their classrooms.

Freeman (1993) followed four high school French and Spanish teachers during and after their participation in an M.A. degree program. He was interested in how they made the tacit explicit and in whether and how they changed their practices. As the teachers learned to express their tacitly held ideas about teaching through shared professional discourse, they gained greater control over their classroom practice. Using Gee's (1990) concept of local language or their primary "identity

kits" as the expression of their tacit and unanalyzed understandings of practice, Freeman found that "the teacher's local language can create a barrier to reconceptualizing their teaching and changing their classroom practices" (1993, p. 489). Articulation occurs when they begin to combine their local and professional knowledge to reflect on and critique their practice. Thus, articulation transforms local language and leads to reconceptualization and change in practice.

McDonald (1986) followed a group of teachers who were involved in a voluntary inquiry process in which the teachers set the agenda. He was particularly interested in the nature of the process and also in the content of their deliberations. He described three phases in the evolution of these teachers' voices: talking to break the silence, taking a voice in policy, and creating power through knowledge. Theory began to enter their voices in the third phase, even though it was originally seen by the group as unimportant.

An important element of these projects appears to be community dialogue. For example, Palincsar, Magnusson, Marano, Ford, and Brown (1998) developed a long-term "learning community" (Lave & Wenger, 1991) of 18 elementary teachers who were interested in improving their instruction of science. The anchor concept used was an instructional heuristic called "guided inquiry supporting multiple literacies," which is social constructivist in nature (engage, investigate, describe relationship, construct/revise explanation, and engage again). To date, changes have occurred in the teachers' interactions with each other—conversation has increased among them about practices. Further, the teachers' notions of expertise have changed from seeing the university researchers as the experts to seeing everyone in the group as experts. Moll (1992) also discussed the importance of the long-term collaboration between teachers and university researchers. In his "funds of knowledge" project, teachers were trained as ethnographers and gathered information on their Latino students' communities. Moll documents how this collaboration leads to culturally relevant pedagogy.

Community was found to be important in change—perhaps the most important ingredient in a 3-year field study of change in secondary school settings (McLaughlin, 1994). McLaughlin concluded that "enabling professional growth is, at root, about enabling professional community" (p. 31). Also, McLaughlin and Talbert (1993a) suggest that professional communities of teachers in which teacher satisfaction is high appear to work well on behalf of students. McLaughlin and her colleagues (McLaughlin, Talbert, & Phelan, 1990) also found by teachers' reports, that today's students create the most problematic context for teaching (see also Metz, 1993; Nias, 1989). This concern shows up in relation to teacher efficacy (Ashton & Webb, 1986; Smylie, 1988). A survey of secondary teachers indicated three adaptations to today's students: maintain and enforce traditional standards, change (lower) expectations, and change practices. Teachers who have made an effort to change their practices, however, also report fatigue, low morale, and professional

---

[7] Practical reasoning has been described by Fenstermacher (1979) as reasoning that leads to an action. Practical arguments are constructed and reconstructed on the basis of the reasoning used in an action. In practice, practical reasoning involves the use of videotapes of teachers in their classrooms that are viewed and discussed by each teacher and the staff developer. See Fenstermacher (1994) for a thorough description of the process.

isolation. But another smaller group, within the group who are changing practices, report feeling efficacious and energized by responding to the challenges of diverse students in their classrooms. The teachers in this smaller group were diverse in their ages, experience levels, subject matter knowledge, and conceptions of pedagogy. However, they all singled out their professional discourse community—their source of professional motivation and support, and the reason they did not burn out—as the key element of their success in adapting to today's students. Professional communities have been fostered at the department, school, and school district levels.

Gitlin (1990) was able to take advantage of the importance of community dialogue in the development of a process called "educative research." He chronicles the effects of the process in which "teachers start out by collaboratively analyzing the relationship between their teaching intentions and their practices in ways that point to living contradictions" (p. 451). In his work, he documents how such dialogue may lead to collective action.

To conclude, a number of aspects of the normative-educative staff development processes work together to enhance learning and change. Beginning with the individual, participants must begin to understand their own often tacit beliefs and understandings. This process is enhanced through dialogue, particularly dialogue with those who understand practice and the particular context in which one is working. A strong trust level is important within the community since it is important for the participants to discuss with others their practices that don't seem to work, and to accept responsibility for their own practices. Thus, the development of a discourse community is productive in beginning this process of change. Also helpful in the next stage, participants may begin to question their beliefs and practices and consider change. During this stage, an outside person, other, or critical friend who can provide a language for tacit understandings and bring into the conversation potentially alternative ways of thinking and acting can be helpful.

SUMMARY: TEACHER EDUCATION AND STAFF DEVELOPMENT

By and large, recent research that focuses on preservice teacher education documents the difficulties of making deep and lasting impacts on the students' beliefs and conceptions. However, while some studies suggest disappointing results in staff development (e.g., Hargreaves & Grey, 1983 Stevenson, 1991), the long-term, collaborative, and inquiry-oriented programs with inservice teachers appear to be quite successful in changing beliefs, conceptions, and practices, although not all teachers respond well to such approaches. Some teachers would seem to prefer to be presented with practices that they may immediately try out in their classrooms rather than to reflect on their own practices and develop possible alternatives (Borko et al., 1992; Richardson, 1992).

The inquiry-oriented, conceptual staff development process operates within a view that teaching consists of a set of ill-defined tasks and, therefore, calls for a long-term conceptual approach to the change process. However, not all teachers agree that the tasks of teaching are uncertain. Rowan (1995, April) suggested four different approaches to thinking about the task of teaching that are based on the following two dimensions: task variety (low and high) and task uncertainty (low and high).

These four approaches are (a) routine (low variety, low uncertainty); (b) nonroutine (high variety, high uncertainty); (c) expert (high variety, low uncertainty); and (d) amateur (low variety, high uncertainty).

Using data from teachers in 16 diverse high schools, Rowan found that 47% of the teachers felt that teaching is routine, 35% felt that it is an expert task, 14% felt that it was a nonroutine task, and 3% felt that it was an amateur task. He also found that those teachers who indicated behaviorist beliefs reported lower levels of task variety and task uncertainty than those who demonstrated constructivist beliefs. Rowan's (1995, April) findings may help to explain the popularity of the Teacher Center movement that offered highly focused, brief inservices around needs identified by teachers (Yarger, 1990). Helsby and McCulloch (1996) concluded from their studies of the recent reform process in England that a small group of teachers will always be actively supportive of and involved in the change process, even if the change is mandated from the top down.

These findings suggest that different teachers will respond quite differently to the particular approaches taken in the staff development. Staff developers themselves should be aware whether their support of a particular approach to staff development—be it long-term, collaborative, conceptual and inquiry-oriented, or short-term—is, in part, a function of the staff developers' own orientations to change (implied by Korthagen, 1988, for preservice programs). In the long run, combinations of approaches to teacher education and staff development may be the better way of approaching the change process.

We now turn to a very different way of approaching the teacher change process; one that focuses on the structure and function of the organization in affecting teacher change.

Organizational Influences on Teacher Change

In the late 1980s, the authors of this chapter were researchers on a study of the effects that a practical argument staff development process had on elementary teachers' practices in reading comprehension (Richardson, 1994b), the results of which were described in the previous section of this chapter. We knew that other researchers had found that the school context could have profound effects on staff development. In fact, Little (1981) argued that the school is not the "context" of staff development but the "heart of the matter" (p. 4). Accordingly, we developed case studies of participating schools, collecting data on school factors that researchers had identified as those influencing teacher change.

While neither of the two focus schools were ideal contexts for staff development according to Little's work (1982), we believed that one school had a clear edge. However, school factors did not predict the outcomes. Resistant at first, teachers at the school with a negative climate for teacher change became receptive, shedding their isolation and conservatism for a new-found collegiality and innovativeness. In contrast, the seemingly more progressive and receptive teachers at the school with a positive climate were less willing to dialogue about their practices because of a deep culture of privatism and avoidance of philosophical differences (Placier & Hamilton, 1994). At one school, the project disrupted a culture of isolation and produced mostly positive consequences; at the other, it disrupted a culture of surface sociability and produced mixed consequences (Hamilton & Richardson, 1995).

Of course, two cases do not refute the relationships between school organizations and teacher change that are based on studies of large numbers of schools and teachers, but our findings suggested that in particular schools, those relationships would be complex and unpredictable. Since our study was completed, research and theoretical work on the relationship between school organizations and teacher change has mushroomed. In this section, we attempt to synthesize and organize these studies into a meaningful patchwork, which, today, is much more complete.

Theoretical Frameworks for Research in This Area

A shared assumption among researchers who examine school organizations and teacher change is that teacher change is not entirely an individually determined, psychological phenomenon. However, researchers differ in their relative emphasis on teachers versus schools. Some researchers are primarily interested in teachers and consider the school as a social context that nurtures or constrains teachers' growth. Other researchers are primarily interested in planned teacher change through adoption of new practices and consider the school as an influence on this process. Still, other researchers are primarily interested in schools and school change and consider teachers as key participants. Researchers also use at least five different theoretical perspectives to understand school organizations.

FUNCTIONALISM

Schools have social functions that people with rôles within them are supposed to fulfill. New teachers change as they are socialized to fit their roles, according to societal norms and the norms of their particular schools. The conservative function of schools is to transmit values and knowledge to maintain social stability; however, to remain functional, schools are also supposed to adapt to societal change. Schools and teacher practices may become dysfunctional and may fail to achieve these purposes. If this disfunction happens, leaders should diagnose the problem and develop a systematic plan to solve it. This rational-empirical process of planned change (Chin & Benne 1969) entails externally prescribed changes in schools, teachers, or both.

CONFLICT THEORY

Schools are the way they are, not because they are functional but because they are controlled by dominant political interests. Teachers have limited power compared with other groups in the school hierarchy. As those groups respond to political pressure, they in turn pressure teachers to change, and teachers in turn comply or resist. Teachers have formed organizations or unions to protect their interests. This approach is consistent with Chin and Benne's (1969) power-coercive category. Conflict theorists see teachers as targets of top-down policies that make them scapegoats for deeply rooted social and economic problems. But conflict theorists can also be critical of teachers' power over students and may advocate teacher change (albeit not externally coerced) to better serve students' interests.

SYMBOLIC INTERACTIONISM

Schools in a given society share certain cultural patterns, but each school culture is somewhat unique, because, over time, people in a school develop shared patterns of interaction and meaning construction. One's role or position in the power hierarchy is important but not deterministic. Teachers may influence principals, and students may influence teachers. Planned changes in schools and teachers, therefore, are always somewhat unpredictable, as the best-laid plans can lead to unintended local consequences. From this perspective, school and teacher changes are long-term, interdependent, microlevel processes that entail changes in beliefs and interactions, as in Chin and Benne's (1969) normative-reeducative category.

MICROPOLITICAL THEORY

A recent synthesis of conflict and symbolic interactionist theories produced a micropolitical theory that brings macrolevel conflicts down to the microlevel of a school in which power relationships are not static or unidirectional. Actors, individually or collectively, mobilize power in the school arena to achieve their goals, but their exercise of power may be more indirect, symbolic, or covert than in a power-coercive model. Astute leaders use norms and beliefs in lieu of direct authoritarian control to motivate school or teacher change. Those who are less astute find their efforts blocked by overt or subtle resistance.

CRITICAL THEORY

This perspective incorporates elements of the other theories but also entails a critique of them. Schools reproduce society and serve conservative ends, teachers have limited power, and the microsocial context is the site for constructing this, but other possibilities can occur. If teachers were more empowered and were more critical of the status quo, and if schools were more democratic organizations, then schools could become sites for reconstructing society. School and teacher change should be driven by values of democracy and social justice. The paradox is that democracy and empowerment cannot be mandated from the top down—thus maintaining the power hierarchy. The change process must be consistent with the values that drive it.

We searched for and found studies in which teacher change was influenced by the organizational context rather than solely by individual development or decision making. We coded each study on the basis of claims about the relationship between the school and teacher change. These codes were then collapsed into three major categories:

1. *How Teaching in Schools Changes Teachers.* Studies in this category are studies of teachers that claim that school contexts significantly influence the teachers' beliefs, behaviors, or both. Two subcategories can be found here and are based on (a) the socialization process and (b) the associations between school characteristics and teacher characteristics. Studies of the socialization process and the effects on a teacher of working in a school over time and of changing in response to the school context claim that certain aspects of the school context (structure, supervision, peers,

students) actually cause teachers to change in particular ways. The strong inference is that only changing schools will change teacher socialization. Studies of the associations between school characteristics and teacher characteristics cannot really make claims about causation but can claim only that association between school and teacher characteristics are based on one-time observations or measures. However, the researchers often assume a directional relationship, that schools cause teachers to be the way they are and that changing the schools, therefore, would change the teachers. Several important studies in this category that were based on this assumption contributed to the knowledge base for intentional school reform efforts.

2. *How School and District Contexts Influence Planned Efforts to Change Teachers.* In this category, researchers studied planned efforts intended to change individual teachers' practices in particular ways. That is, teachers were the focus, but the organizational context intervened to influence (positively or negatively) the change process. Again, a common inference is that efforts to change teachers will only succeed in certain school contexts and that school reform must precede teacher change.

3. *How Planned Efforts to Change Schools Change Teachers.* This category includes studies in which the school is the focus of planned change (e.g., restructuring) and studies that show how the change in the school context changed teachers as key participants. These studies address the claims made in the other categories—that changes in schools will change teachers' beliefs, practices of planned change in schools involving teachers as key participants, or both.

We found from our review of these studies that the relationship between school contexts and teacher change is complex and ambiguous. To develop a model that can depict all the ways in which teacher change and the organizational context are interrelated is difficult, if not impossible. In some cases, individual teachers change despite their unsupportive social context, and, in other cases, they do not change, despite changes in the organization that would support it.

How Teaching in Schools Changes Teachers

TEACHER SOCIALIZATION

Although teacher socialization begins much earlier, we will consider only studies of teacher socialization for teachers used in schools. First published in 1932, Waller's *The Sociology of Teaching* introduced themes still prevalent in research on this topic (Waller, 1961). He applied functionalist social theory and psychological theories to the question "What does teaching do to teachers?" (1961, p. 375). Waller notes that even if teachers self-select because they think they will fit, and even if they complete teacher education courses, most have great difficulty adjusting to their role. The organization molds them to produce traits such as inflexibility, formality, inhibition, and patience "because these traits have survival value in the schools of today. If one does not have them when he joins the faculty, he must develop them or die an academic death" (p. 382).

Students are the most important agents of socialization, because a fundamental conflict exists between the moral code of adult society and the youth culture. Good teachers learn to maintain control while letting students know they are real human beings. Unfortunately, many teachers lose this human touch, and many also lose any creativity or intellectual curiosity they had at the start. Because they face constant threats to control, dignity, and job security, teachers must also learn to maintain a lonely distance from students, colleagues, administrators, and community.

Another classic, Lortie's *School Teacher* (1975), bears reviewing as a foundation for many subsequent studies. His findings were based on interviews with Boston area teachers and on survey data from Dade County, Florida, schools. One of his premises is "Occupations shape people" (p. 55). Another is that the organization in which an occupation is practiced—in this case, the school—shapes the practitioner. Lortie found that after an "apprenticeship of observation" in which they internalize their own teachers' practices, a weak formal preparation, and a miniapprenticeship that reinforces traditional ways of teaching, new teachers are cast into classrooms to sink or swim with the same responsibilities as veterans. In the egg-crate school structure, they are isolated with students most of the day. This isolationism leads to high anxiety when inevitable but unanticipated problems arise. Because of a norm of individualism, teachers are not supposed to ask for help or intervene in others' classrooms. If teachers receive advice from other teachers, they filter this advice through their own personalities, styles, or intuitions. A common technical culture and consensus about "what should be done in these cases" do not exist as they do in other professions.

Administrators are formally responsible for teacher supervision, but their limited guidance is given even less heed than that of peers. Teachers come to be motivated by intrinsic psychic rewards that accrue when students respond positively rather than by external recognition or evaluation. "From this perspective," Lortie concludes, "socialization into teaching is largely self-socialization" (1975, p. 79). Such autonomy might entail wide variations in practice, but teachers "self-socialize" to reproduce similar ways of teaching. Lortie attributes this socialization to the apprenticeship of observation, the history of teaching as an occupation that attracts conservative people, and the structure and culture of the school.

From this functionalist perspective that has prevailed in teacher socialization studies, schools change teachers more than teachers change schools. Teacher socialization entails learning to fit an existing occupational and organizational role. Since Lortie's study, teacher socialization research has become too extensive to review in its entirety here. Fortunately, two recent reviews of research on this topic have been conducted. In the first, Zeichner and Gore (1990) divide research on teacher socialization into three paradigms—functional, interpretive, and critical theories. They review research from each paradigm but favor the critical approach, because the others do not "challenge the status quo" (p. 331). Functionalists depict teachers as determined by their biographies or their school contexts. Interpretive studies are less deterministic but neglect structure and collectivity. The other reviewers, Staton and Hunt (1992), also reject functionalism but claim that research supports an interpretivist model in which a teacher experiences affective, behavioral, and cognitive changes through interactions with agents of socialization over time, with the teacher's biography acting as a filter. Despite their theoretical differences, the two reviews come to similar conclusions about organizational influences on teacher socialization, which are described as follows.

Teacher Agency. Both reviews question the functionalist view of the organization's power over the teacher. According to Zeichner and Gore (1990), teachers actively respond to their social context and are not passively molded to fit. There is a need for more research on the "reciprocal nature of the agency-structure relationship" (p. 341) and on how teachers change schools. Staton and Hunt (1992) emphasize the teacher's active role in social interactions.

Agents of Socialization. The reviewers agree with Waller and Lortie that the most important agents of socialization are students, because a teacher's greatest difficulty is coping with student complexity and diversity. Teachers and students engage in a process of mutual socialization that changes the teachers' approaches, language use, expectations, and instructional methods. Colleagues are next in importance, primarily, because of the support they provide, although they can be unsupportive in some schools. Mentors may be significant for novice teachers (Staton & Hunt, 1992). The influence of supervisors is highly variable (Zeichner & Gore, 1990). They influence teacher socialization, not through direct control but through control of the school context (Staton & Hunt, 1992). Finally, parents influence teachers, directly or indirectly, depending on the socioeconomic and cultural context of the community (e.g., Metz, 1990).

Organizational Context. Research evidence exists for the effects of classroom characteristics (class size, organization, scheduling, resources) and school characteristics (teaching assignments, scheduling, role demands) on teacher socialization. The following section reviews recent research on teacher socialization and organizations not included in the two reviews above and tends to support the conclusions in this section.

Cross-Sectional Studies. From a synthesis of four grounded theory studies of teacher socialization from preservice education through the 1st year of teaching, Hall, Johnson, and Bowman (1995) constructed a longitudinal model that reiterates themes from Waller (1961) and Lortie (1975). Three findings on first-year teachers refer to the school context. First, new teachers recognized the organizational realities of their work: isolation, nonteaching duties, working despite physical illness, and negotiating teacher contracts. Second, they had confidence in themselves to the degree that others treated them according to their image of a teacher. Third, they discovered the difficulty of working with students with variable attitudes and abilities. Beginning teachers in this study were already showing symptoms of stress and burnout.

Joseph Blase (1987) has expanded our understanding of the principal's role in socialization. In two symbolic interactionist studies, he examines principals as negative influences. Teachers in one urban, U.S. high school described ineffective principals with whom they had worked as inaccessible, lacking in expertise, closed to teacher input, stingy with praise, authoritarian,

prone to favoritism, unsupportive, and unwilling to delegate (Blase, 1987). The teachers said that such behaviors reduced their self-esteem, involvement, commitment, and improvement and contributed to a survival orientation. Responding to a qualitative survey (Blase, 1990), a broader cross-section of teachers identified strategies of "political" principals as manipulative, unilateral, top-down, and nonnegotiable. Principals also used "protection" strategies such as responding to external audiences in the community rather than to teachers. Most teachers said that principals' control strategies negatively affected classroom instruction, involvement, morale, and collegial relationships—and made them angry. On another questionnaire (Blase, 1993), teachers rated principals as closed or open, ineffective or effective, and authoritarian or participative and described their leadership strategies. Although few described empowering or democratic leaders, the majority of teachers responding to this questionnaire described open, effective, participative principals who practiced "normative-instrumental" leadership, which is control that is based on symbolic rewards for conformity with shared norms. Teachers said that, in response, they experienced positive affective, cognitive, and behavioral changes. In contrast, they judged formal authority and contrived requests for advice as less effective. In another report of this study (Blase & Roberts, 1994), three principal strategies—visibility, giving suggestions, and involving teachers in decisions—were associated with greater teacher reflection and complex thinking.

Interviews with teachers and principals in U.S. elementary schools that were categorized as effective or ineffective suggested that general school-level differences in teacher socialization exist, with principals and peers as key agents (Crone & Teddlie, 1995). Teachers in effective schools were more likely to learn about school policies and procedures from other teachers, to be assigned mentors or to receive informal help from other teachers, to report that their school had schoolwide rules for students, and to have frequent, supportive contacts with principals. Teachers in ineffective schools had to figure out school and classroom rules for themselves, with less collegial and principal support. A confounding factor was that principals in effective schools were more thoughtful about hiring teachers who were creative, flexible, and caring; therefore, the sets of teachers may have differed before they were hired into the schools.

Case Studies. Teacher socialization in cross-sectional studies involves teachers learning to fit broad occupational and organizational cultures. In case studies, teacher socialization also involves teachers learning to adapt to the microculture of a particular school. Bullough (1989) makes a strong argument for the individual case study as a way of learning about socialization. From a cohort of beginning teachers identified as "empowered," Kuzmic (1994) selected Kara for a study that is a good example of this genre. Kara knew how she wanted to teach and chose a district in which she thought she could do so. She chose kindergarten because she believed that was where an "excellent" teacher could make the most difference. However, she was not "organizationally literate" enough to know when and how to change her practices to adapt to the realities of the school and classroom. When she encountered problems, she blamed herself for failing rather than look for the sources of problems in the organizational context. By year's end, she learned that she had to adapt to the organization to achieve her own goals.

Palonsky's (1986) *900 Shows a Year* is a critical ethnographic study of his experience as a new high school social studies teacher. As an academic who was both practicing and studying a job he had left years before, he was not a typical novice. Nevertheless, he could not overcome the organizational pressures: too much work, too many students, and too little time and support. Many of his colleagues felt vulnerable, isolated, disrespected, and burned out. Because the school had no unifying academic purpose, teachers defined their work individually and, at most, identified with other teachers in their departments. Department heads and administrators had weak roles in socialization. Palonsky concludes that "the behaviors of teachers, both desirable and undesirable, are developed as a rational set of responses to the demands of the job. . . . Good teachers, in the context of public secondary schools, may be examples of social deviance: They survive in the face of all the forces that work against them" (p. 187).

Case studies can make visible the aspects of teacher identity such as gender, race, class, and generation that can be neglected in cross-sectional studies of generic teachers and that can show how these aspects interact with aspects of schools (Goodson, 1992). For example, Middleton (1989) used life-history interviews with four feminist teachers in New Zealand, three white and one Maori, to identify themes in their socialization. The teachers reported that they were marginalized in their schools and even openly criticized by colleagues and students because of their student-centered teaching and feminist perspectives. However, rather than conform, they became more radical, more determined to succeed and change the system. Beginning with the "flower power" 1960s, (Harris, 1993) examines journals chronicling her tumultuous life as an English teacher in South Philadelphia High School. She recognized that during the 1960s, organizational factors such as class size, limited resources, low teacher morale, strikes, demographic changes, and school reconfigurations had profound effects on her practice that she recognized from her first day. Yet, she says, she kept her focus on students and their academic growth rather than on organizational politics.

In some case studies, the case is the school rather than the teacher, and different agents of socialization in the school come into play. Consistent with previous studies, two high school studies found that students are the primary teacher socializers. In a micropolitical study of an urban high school, Blase (1991) found that teachers had developed two orientations toward students. Influence or proactive strategies included staying in touch with students' needs and being open, friendly, and diplomatic, while also inspiring respect. Protection or reactive strategies included compromising, avoiding conflict, and being cautious with discipline. For beginning teachers, adopting these strategies meant manufacturing a role model image, but veterans had internalized conventional school and community norms.

From a set of high school case studies, Metz (1993) similarly found that teachers depended on student cooperation to derive intrinsic rewards from their work, but they had limited means to gain this cooperation: grades (which do not matter to some students), coercion (which is limited by law and used sparingly),

and negotiation (which limits demands in return for good behavior). The last strategy was most obvious in working-class schools, where demanding teachers could be very unpopular with students. Still, Metz found variation among teachers in any school; socialization that is based on student social class was not deterministic.

Peer socialization is another important theme. A case study of a Belgian primary school (Staessens & Vandenberghe, 1994) suggests that teachers in "high vision" schools, schools with high consensus on goals and values, intentionally socialize new teachers to share the vision. In low vision schools, no intentional socialization occurs, and teachers are left to their own devices. This lack of socialization results in individualistic, isolated teachers who are invested in their classrooms but not in the school community. In a study of peer socialization of beginning teachers in an Ontario elementary school, Cole (1991) describes positive, collegial leadership, teacher teamwork, and school spirit. Beginning teachers here had the same needs and concerns as those in other schools, but their socialization was less traumatic, because they had a sense of belonging, security, and support for taking risks and learning.

In two urban, U.S. high schools in Weiler's (1988) critical feminist study, feminist teachers and administrators worked together over time, albeit with tensions and struggle, to construct communities, each with a collective vision in which they were able to act on their beliefs. They supported each other to challenge resistance from male teachers. In another feminist study, Cunnison (1989) studied "gender joking" in a British comprehensive secondary school. Often initiated by male teachers, gender joking reinforced stereotypes of women as stay-at-home wives or examples of sexual attractiveness. Cunnison connects such joking to competition for promotions, because some men's jokes conveyed a message that women should not pursue positions traditionally held by men. Women responded to joking most often with silence but also by playing along, counterjoking, or challenging stereotypes.

Case studies illustrate the mutual socialization of principals and teachers in specific social contexts. Critical theorist Kanpol's (1988) study of an urban, unionized middle school shows that teachers acquired habits of both resisting administrators' ineptness and accommodating to it by taking on more responsibility rather than engaging in a more profound critique of the culture of schooling. The principal in Greenfield's (1991) micropolitical study of a working-class elementary school used "professional leadership" that is based on moral influence, motivating teachers to change through their ethical commitments to students. Because her efforts were limited by the union contract, time, district norms, and veteran teacher resistance, she adopted an indirect, incremental approach, building the groundwork for change and downplaying her political power.

In an affluent suburban district, Anderson (1991) describes cognitive or ideological administrative control over teachers that is also indirect but less benign. The teachers here were well paid, hard-working, and seemed content despite having little power. District leaders expected principals to create a cooperative, balanced school "climate." Principals buffered teachers from parent complaints in exchange for school harmony. In one elementary school, the principal tried to use school loyalty to motivate teacher effort toward her goal of doing well on a state evaluation. Teachers complained about the pressure but were socialized to believe that open conflict would be "inappropriate." According to a cross-sectional teacher survey (Blase, 1990), this response is common among U.S. teachers.

Summary: Organizational Effects on Teacher Socialization. The studies that have been described illustrate two aspects of teacher socialization: socialization into occupational and organizational norms that cut across local contexts and socialization into local norms that are highly variable. However, findings in both sets of studies are often disturbing; teacher socialization can mean giving up power, ideals, or expectations to adapt to occupational or organizational realities. These two strands of research seem to lead toward different strands of planned change, according to Chin and Benne's (1969) typology. If the culture of teaching is a barrier to reform, we need to change the occupation. In fact, Lortie (1975) predicted that social pressures would force such change, and many legislative reforms of teaching that he anticipated have been attempted. But these rational-empirical strategies have faltered as they have confronted either the unexpectedly powerful norms of teaching or the differences in local contexts. The negative portrayal of principals' socialization practices in some studies might suggest a need for more teacher control or empowerment, a power-coercive or political change strategy that is also in evidence in recent reforms. If teacher socialization is locally variable, change efforts must be responsive to the local context, calling for a normative-reeducative strategy that is evident in the school restructuring movement. We will discuss these teacher change strategies later in the chapter.

SCHOOL EFFECTS ON TEACHERS

A related set of studies identify, on a number of dimensions, the aspects of schools associated with teacher variability. One cannot infer cause-effect relationships from these associations. If teachers in certain kinds of schools share certain characteristics, it may not mean that they acquired those characteristics after they entered the schools. Teachers may select a school or be selected for a school because they fit school norms. The teachers may even have changed the schools. Nevertheless, most studies end with recommendations for changing schools in order to change teachers, and used the basis of a cause-effect assumption. Although we cannot review this research at length, we have summarized major findings, which are organized by teacher variables. Three large studies that include multiple variables are cited throughout. In *A Place Called School: Prospects for the Future,* Goodlad (1984) reports teacher survey and interview findings from 38 schools at all levels in 13 diverse U.S. communities. *Teachers' Workplace: The Social Organization of Schools* (Rosenholtz, 1989; see also Rosenholtz, Bassler, & Hoover-Dempsey, 1986) is a symbolic interactionist study that is based on quantitative questionnaires and interviews with Tennessee elementary teachers. Johnson's (1990) *Teachers at Work: Achieving Success in Our Schools* is that is based on interviews with systematically selected "good" teachers at private and public Massachusetts schools.

Teacher Learning. The variable most directly linked to this chapter's theme is teacher learning. Rosenholtz, Bassler, and Hoover-Dempsey (1986) analyzed teacher questionnaires to identify organizational factors associated with skill acquisition. Five factors combined to explain most of the variance: principal collegiality, recruitment and socialization of teachers, goal setting in regard to instruction, managing student behavior, and evaluation practices. The authors conclude that a tightly coupled "collaborative normative climate" is associated with teacher learning, while a climate of individualistic teacher isolation is not. Rosenholtz (1989) reports that no school demographic or teacher background variables were associated with skill acquisition; therefore, conditions associated with teacher learning can be controlled within the school. In this analysis, four factors explained most of the variance: goal-setting activities, effective evaluation practices, shared instructional goals, and collaboration.

Rosenholtz's (1989) interview data revealed two school types: learning enriched and learning impoverished. In learning-enriched schools, teachers had the sustained view that teacher learning would continue as students and contexts changed. Their work was not routine but was situational, responsive, and focused on academics and student motivation. Teachers and principals tried to help colleagues and took an interest in their progress, drawing on a belief that all teachers can learn. In learning-impoverished schools, teachers expressed a terminal view of learning: New teachers can "figure teaching out" quickly by conforming to school routines and using assigned textbooks. The curriculum for them was uniform, not adaptable, and teaching accomplishments were individual, not collective. Teachers in learning-impoverished schools also believed that teaching is a gift and that it cannot be taught. Thus, they did not take an interest in peers' learning. Troubled teachers were the principal's problem—the subject of gossip, perhaps, but not of collegial concern.

Learning-impoverished public schools may be the norm. Johnson (1990) found that public schools did not invest in teacher learning, and, as a result, most teachers took charge of their own learning. They looked first to classroom experience as a source of learning and rarely turned to peers. They viewed the few formal learning opportunities in their schools such as inservice workshops as very ineffective. Few believed that college courses leading to salary increments led to better teaching. Because of financial constraints, teachers in some schools had to bear the costs of their learning. Evaluations in most schools were not learning-oriented but were summative processes based on minimal criteria that were designed to identify poor teachers. In some schools, teachers could set their own goals, but their fear of revealing weaknesses to others undermined this option. Conversely, private schools (with some exceptions) were more likely to invest in teacher learning, to offer sabbaticals, to have formative evaluations, and to foster collegial learning experiences.

Orientations Toward Teaching and Learning. Teachers' openness to change may depend on their attitudes toward teaching and learning. Rosenholtz (1989) found that high-consensus elementary schools had high clarity and solidarity around goals for student learning, while low-consensus schools had norms of self-reliance and individual goal setting. Four studies examine the greater complexity of teacher goals in secondary schools.

In high schools with student tracking, teacher goals vary with their teaching assignments. Oakes' (1985) cross-sectional data from U.S. high schools show that teachers in high-track classes provided students with greater opportunities to learn, exemplified more qualities of effective teaching, and engaged students more actively than teachers in low-track classes. School structure, the segregation of students by "ability," created cultural norms that constrained both teachers and students. Tracking is one aspect of the historical bureaucratization of high schools.

In a critical ethnographic study of social studies teaching in four U.S. high schools, McNeil (1986) found that teachers lowered expectations for themselves and their students because of administrative control that reinforced bureaucratic rather than educational purposes of schools. Even knowledgeable teachers who expressed excitement about their content areas in interviews used defensive teaching strategies that limited discussion, minimized controversy and complexity, and reduced academic demands on students. Not surprisingly, students were uninspired and convinced that their teachers did not know very much. In only one school did the administration lend strong support to educational purposes.

In a study using teacher survey data from a national sample of U.S. high schools, Newmann, Rutter, and Smith (1989) attempted to identify which school characteristics were most closely related to teacher efficacy, sense of community, and expectations. When school background variables were considered alone, efficacy and expectations were associated with student ability, race, and urban or suburban location, and community was associated with school size—all conditions beyond teachers' control. But when internal school factors were added, the strongest associations were with students' behavior, encouragement for innovation, knowledge of other teachers' courses, administrator responsiveness, and teachers helping one another— conditions that can be changed. Finally, McLaughlin's (1993) survey and fieldwork study found that secondary teachers' goals depended on their perceptions of students—perceptions influenced by the school culture. Of five types of U.S. secondary schools, only those with "missions," such as alternative or elite academic schools, had high goal consensus. When a school or department, acting as a professional community, encouraged responding to student differences, solving problems, and supporting teachers through collegiality and professional growth, teachers more often expressed positive goals for students. When these conditions were missing, teachers were likely to persist in ineffective traditional practices or to lower their expectations.

According to Lortie (1975), teachers feel very uncertain about their practices and about the effects those practices have on students. Rosenholtz (1989) found more uncertainty in schools with "routine technical cultures," where teachers did not make use of colleagues' expertise. These schools had low parent involvement, more punitive relationships with students, more attribution of problems to homes, and greater belief that students' learning potential is fixed. All of these variables relieved teachers of responsibility for student learning. In "nonroutine technical cultures," teachers perceived students as capable and themselves as capable of making a difference. In Johnson's (1990) study, elementary teachers expressed more certainty about their accomplishments than middle school and high school teachers, and private school teachers seemed more certain of success than public school teachers. Public school teachers more often qualified the belief that "all students can learn" with concerns about poor working conditions and differences in students' academic deficits.

Synthesizing the results of four large teacher surveys on working conditions along with factors identified in effective schools research, Corcoran (1990) developed a gestalt of interrelated conditions for effective teaching. In interview data from teachers in five districts, a similar set of variables was associated with teacher attitudes and behaviors. The critical factors were adequate physical conditions, levels of teacher influence and collegiality, teacher recognition, student behavior, and positive leadership. Corcoran claims that "the entire gestalt must be present to produce the desired effects on teachers" (p. 155). Unfortunately, this comprehensive approach seems to be rare.

Commitment to Teaching as a Career or Profession. It seems logical that teachers' willingness to invest in change might be related to their long-term commitment to teaching. Lortie (1975) found that few teachers had a sense of teaching as a long-term career, but McLaughlin and Yee (1988) argue that this finding is true if one conventionally defines "career" as vertical movement that is based on other people's decisions. Teachers' model of career is individual, subjective, and related to two organizational conditions: opportunity (the chance to learn and develop, especially for novices) and capacity (the ability to exercise power and influence to control resources, especially for veterans). In their qualitative study, California teachers' sense of career was related to these school factors: adequate resources, common goals, collegiality, problem-solving orientation, and investment-centered reward structures.

Rosenholtz (1989) found that "moving" teachers had plans and goals for their teaching, while "stuck" ones did not. Three organizational conditions mattered: task autonomy and discretion, psychic rewards, and learning opportunities. However, per pupil expenditures may have confounded the findings, because stuck teachers more often worked in stuck districts, with low resources allocated to teaching. Of the teachers in Johnson's (1990) study, 13% said they had decided to leave teaching, others were undecided, and many had struggled with the idea of leaving and had decided to stay because of the intrinsic rewards. Johnson argues that salaries are also important to teachers, because low salaries serve as a disincentive to commitment. Yet, private (especially Catholic) schoolteachers often had lower salaries but greater intrinsic rewards because of enthusiastic students, stability, shared values, parent support, and greater respect for their expertise. When asked if their goals for teaching had been fulfilled, most public school teachers answered with a very qualified Yes. Most qualifications regarding teaching fulfillment derived from dissatisfaction with school conditions. A large majority of public school teachers were dissatisfied with low rewards or respect, limited learning opportunities, heavy workloads, poor physical conditions, limited resources, or distractions such as discipline and bureaucratic demands.

In *A Place Called School,* Goodlad (1984) reports that frustration and dissatisfaction were the most common reasons teachers gave for considering leaving their jobs; salaries were second. Schools with problems seemingly beyond their control, such as school size, limited resources, low parent interest, poor administration, and excess bureaucracy, were the most frustrating for teachers. Disturbingly, many less satisfying schools had high proportions of minority students. Teacher satisfaction with schools was associated with principal leadership, control of their work, staff cohesiveness, and problem-solving and decision-making climates.

Conley, Bacharach, and Bauer (1989) surveyed teachers in New York on school factors associated with career dissatisfaction and found that both role ambiguity and routinization, either too little or too much control over teachers' work, were significant. Positive supervisory behaviors were associated with low career dissatisfaction. In a critical life-history study of progressive women who left teaching (Casey, 1992), most blamed the system for their defection. "Administrative repression" caused their most severe dissatisfaction (p. 199). Students, in contrast, were their primary reason to stay because of an ethos of care.

Goodlad (1984) also reports that teachers are less satisfied in secondary than in elementary schools. Studies seem to link this difference to organizational factors peculiar to the secondary level. In case studies of urban high schools with low-income, diverse student populations, Firestone (1991a) found that teachers have multiple commitments: to the school, to students, to their discipline, and to academic versus social roles. He found four major influences on commitment: quality of teachers' social relations with each other and with the administration, administrative support, clear expectations and goals, and influence or control over daily activities. But the crux of low teacher commitment in the case-study schools, he claims, was the structure and curriculum of the high school, which is not the best environment for teaching low achieving students.

Through high school case studies, Louis (1992) identified "quality of work life" variables associated with teachers' commitment to and excitement about their work. The schools differed widely, but some findings cut across the cases. Important variables were respect, significant opportunity to use skills and learn new ones, collaboration (though rare and ad hoc), principal leadership, and caring as a school theme. Although resources among the schools differed widely, resources (with the exception of time) were relatively unimportant, perhaps, because they were at least adequate in all cases. A surprise was the low importance teachers placed on empowerment gotten through participation in decisions. They saw other conditions, however, that enhanced their work and made it empowering.

Talbert and McLaughlin (1994) surveyed and interviewed secondary teachers and asserted from their symbolic interactionist position that "teacher professionalism" may not be a static concept but may be locally constructed and contextual. They examined three dimensions of professionalism: technical culture, service ethic (caring for students and expectations for achievement), and professional commitment. Findings showed that the department was the most important context for technical culture, expectations for achievement, and professional commitment. However, the "professional commitment" was to the discipline of teaching, not to students. The secondary school department as a professional community may uphold standards of the disciplines but fail students by not upholding a service ethic.

Collaboration. Like Lortie (1975), Goodlad (1984) found little teacher collaboration and a high reliance on personal judgment or student responses as the basis of teacher decisions. According to Rosenholtz (1989), isolation negatively affects teacher learning and development in elementary schools, because isolated teachers become territorial and do not want to admit their failings. In collaborative schools, teachers share and solve problems and thereby become more certain about their practice. Johnson (1990) found that both school organizations and teacher norms work against teacher collaboration. Teachers recognized that collaboration could meet personal and organizational needs and said that they valued collegial interactions, but such interactions were often limited to a few colleagues and did not often extend to collaboration on instruction. The exceptions were small, private, or alternative schools that had been built on different principles. Teachers said the following factors encouraged interaction: teachers who are open and generous, organizational norms that encourage collaboration, reference groups such as departments and teams, sufficient time, and administrators who design faculty meetings around teacher concerns.

Hargreaves'(1994) case studies of two high schools suggest that in balkanized schools, collaboration in small, stable, impermeable, competitive groups such as departments really divides teachers. In a traditional academic high school with veteran teachers and an elite image, teacher relationships were valued and supportive, yet the school was very balkanized. Teachers attended well only to high achieving students, identified with their disciplines, and did not perceive a need to change as long as they prepared students well for college. The other school was established on the basis on principles that seemed to preclude balkanization, yet it reappeared. The school had a cohort-based structure with cross-curricular themes, but some teachers opted out of the themes and returned to subject-based instruction. Department power overrode the power of cohort teams (Talbert & McLaughlin, 1994).

Empowerment. Most teachers have a degree of classroom autonomy, and autonomy is logically a necessary condition for teacher change (Placier & Hamilton, 1994), but empowerment goes beyond this. Lightfoot (1986) defines empowerment as "the opportunities a person has for autonomy, responsibility, choice and authority" (p. 9). In qualitative portraits of six high schools that were identified as "good" by their communities, administrators worked against "paternalistic authority" (p. 19) and redistributed power to teachers and students. Teachers felt supported, respected, nurtured in their development, able to be creative, and able to be individuals while also being committed to the community. Teachers enjoyed students and understood them but had clear patterns of discipline and authority. Pendlebury (1990) describes this kind of teacher autonomy as "liberty as independence" within a "community of practice" (p. 272), which differs from liberty as "license" to do whatever one chooses in the classroom.

In contrast, public school teachers in Johnson's (1990) study did not participate in school decisions in any systematic way and were not convinced that their participation mattered. Many had become cynical, because they might be consulted for their opinions, but policy was always set by someone higher in the system. Principals often undemocratically controlled meeting agendas and outcomes, and teacher power depended on the principal's "leadership style." In private schools, small school size made teacher participation more possible, but some parochial school teachers had even less power than public school teachers. At other private schools, for example, a Quaker school with consensus-based decisions, teachers had a great deal of influence.

SUMMARY: TEACHING IN SCHOOLS

One can see a bridge between this line of research and the school restructuring movement, which presumes that changes in school structure and culture are preconditions for meaningful changes in teaching. Across the studies, learning opportunities, common goals, control, administrative support, and a shared, complex view of teaching reoccur as significant organizational conditions related to teacher learning, commitment, collaboration, and empowerment. Such conditions appear in few U.S. public schools. Studies also suggest important differences between elementary and secondary schools. Lieberman and Miller (1992) detail these differences and their implications for teacher and school improvement. In the next sections we examine planned efforts to change these patterns.

How Organizational Contexts Influence Planned Efforts to Change Teachers

Teachers often experience changes in their work (Mager, Myers, Maresca, Rupp, & Armstrong, 1986), but some reformers believe that most teachers are "stuck" and that intervention is needed to unstick them. Rosenholtz (1987) notes that reforms of teaching entail dilemmas of "standardization and autonomy, management by hierarchical control or facilitation of professionalism and mandatory versus voluntary change" (p. 535). Top-down reforms attempt to motivate teachers to change through incentives or require them to change through controls. As Darling-Hammond (1995) puts it, "The tendency of educational policymakers over recent decades has been to assume little knowledge, capacity or ethical commitment on the part of school faculties, and to prescribe practices accordingly" (p. 160).

In this section, we have divided research into two categories: (a) professionalism, attempts to change teachers by changing their occupational roles, and (b) classroom practice, direct attempts to change teachers' classroom practices.

PROFESSIONALISM

Teacher professionalism motivated a number of recent reforms, the outcomes of which are disputable because different versions of the supposedly same reform and multiple, conflicting definitions of "professionalism" as an outcome conflict. Firestone and Bader (1991) argue that many professionalizing reforms do not deserve the label, because professionalism would enhance teacher authority and autonomy, while the reforms enhance bureaucratic control over teachers. In fact, teacher changes reported in these studies are often something unintended such as dissatisfaction or resistance. Many reforms entail some form of differentiation among teachers that runs counter to teachers' occupational norms. Mixed findings also suggest that the same

reform may be differently interpreted and implemented in different local contexts.

Rosenholtz (1987) interviewed Tennessee elementary teachers on whether the state career ladder program (CLP) enhanced their commitment to teaching. The CLP was intended to give talented teachers new duties in exchange for higher salaries and status, but teachers challenged the fairness and validity of processes for moving up the ladder. The implication is that little positive change occurred in most districts. Two district studies (Freiberg & Knight, 1991; Smylie & Smart, 1990) indicate local variation in teacher attitudes toward career ladders in other states but leave effects of the programs on teaching practices in doubt. Conley, Bas-Isaac, and Scull (1995) examined effects of a state career ladder in a district that required teachers to serve as mentors or as peer coaches to move up. Critics could construe this practice as "contrived collegiality" (Hargreaves, 1991), but on a qualitative teacher survey, most teachers said that their mentoring and coaching practices were genuinely collaborative. Still, the study begs the question of whether the reform changed teachers' classroom practices.

In two district case studies (Firestone, 1991b), teachers did report changes in their teaching and feelings about their work as a result of reforms, but changes occurred in opposite directions. The contrast was due both to the reforms and to organizational contexts. One district implemented a plan with two permanent promotions tied to merit pay, with a state-mandated, prescriptive teacher evaluation as the basis for promotion. State legislation limited the district's flexibility in this case, but district administrators were also inflexible. Although a large percentage of teachers qualified for promotions, they were dissatisfied with the stressful, standardized evaluation process. The other, more flexible district was located in a state with a more flexible policy. Teachers participated in adapting a merit pay plan into a "career enhancement" plan with three temporary leadership or specialist positions and with access determined by evaluations and peer review. Because promotions were temporary, many teachers could participate, and they liked having more time for professional growth and interaction. In both districts, teachers said they "did it for the money," but in the second district, money was linked to time for doing intrinsically rewarding work.

A qualitative study of a suburban district's implementation of a state career ladder program reports school-level variation but no positive effects on teaching (Henson & Hall, 1993). The career ladder was linked to performance-based teacher evaluation (PBTE). This linkage, especially as interpreted by some principals, transformed the intent and effects of both programs. At first, administrators presented the career ladder as a kind of entitlement—"more money for what you're already doing." But linking the career ladder to PBTE meant that teachers needed high ratings on summative evaluations to move up the ladder, and development-oriented, formative evaluations were de-emphasized. Policy also limited the number of high ratings principals could give, introducing more competitiveness. "Traditionalist" principals took a low-key approach, using the career ladder to keep their teachers happy and their schools harmonious. "Reformist" principals believed that school reform required a tough stance and that the career ladder should reward only exceptional teachers. Teachers predictably reported different reactions to these administrative strategies but no meaningful changes in their teaching.

Several studies examine "teacher leader" roles, again, with mixed findings in different contexts. Both differentiation among teachers and intervention in other teachers' classrooms challenge teacher norms. For example, Reading Recovery trains elementary teachers in intensive techniques for teaching reading to first graders. Teacher leaders receive additional preparation that qualifies them to train other teachers. Rinehart and Short (1991) sent a questionnaire to teacher leaders in the United States and Canada and found positive relationships between leadership and empowerment, work redesign, and knowledge of teaching and learning. Other teachers respected the teacher leaders' expertise. However, some organizational constraints existed. Some administrators provided neither for a teacher leader role nor for teacher leaders to have more time or resources. School policies on, for example, schedules, grouping, and testing constrained classroom teachers and did not support the program's goals.

A qualitative study of two elementary schools in an affluent suburban district recounts how a district committee of administrators and university representatives recommended a teacher leader role as part of a package of school reforms (Noblit, Berry, & Dempsey, 1991). Seven schools volunteered to pilot the reforms, and the two case-study schools were contrasting outliers in this group. Despite their different cultures, teacher leaders in both schools defined themselves as faculty "representatives" and used their roles to contest administrative power. Faced with this, one principal backed out of the program. District administrators defined "professionalism" as a tightly coupled bureaucracy guided by administrative rationality and a technical definition of good teaching. The plan had the unintended result of increasing teacher power, to the administrators' chagrin. Yet teacher leaders did act as professionals by taking control of reform.

Using a teacher questionnaire, Smylie (1992b) studied a small metropolitan school district in which teacher leaders were appointed after an application and review process. Somewhat contradictory rationales for the plan were to provide upward mobility for some teachers and to enhance collaboration. Smylie asked nonleader teachers how they perceived the program, including "school context" as a variable. He found that they reacted negatively to the program when it violated their norms of equality, autonomy, and privacy. An unexpected finding was that school context was not important. Whether the school culture was collegial or isolated, some teachers still rejected interactions with teacher leaders.

Using a micropolitical approach, Smylie and Brownlee-Conyers (1992) interviewed the teacher leaders and their principals and found that the new role was structurally and culturally ambiguous. Both parties tried to resolve the ambiguity, relying on their own expectations and interests. Three types of relationships between principal and teacher leader emerged in different schools—collaborative, controlled and confrontational—each with different consequences for the teacher leader's effectiveness.

Three case studies also show that interpretation of the teacher leader role depends on the school context (Wasley, 1991a; Wasley, 1995). A high school teacher became a national expert, creating a leadership role that took him outside the school to run a grant-funded center and teach university classes. In interviews, his colleagues expressed great respect for him and his class, but did not change their practices as a result. In the other two cases, administrators created teacher leader roles without consulting other teachers, and this decision had consequences for interpretations of the two teachers' "leadership." One teacher leader was a specialist who observed and consulted with elementary teachers on the adoption of a prescribed model of instruction. The other was a lead teacher in a middle school classroom that was used as a demonstration site for visiting teachers and student teachers. Colleagues of these teacher leaders had mixed reactions. While positive about them as individuals, some resented their "privileged" positions or questioned administrator decisions to promote them to leadership roles. Such resentment limited the teacher leaders' influence on their colleagues.

Teacher evaluation is a problematic aspect of some of these reforms, especially if evaluation means more bureaucratic control. Several studies show that in some districts and schools, teachers are gaining more control over evaluation in exchange for greater accountability and are using professional norms. McLaughlin and Pfeifer (1988) conducted case studies of teacher evaluation in four districts, to see if differences in policymaker and teacher meanings of "evaluation" could be reconciled. For policymakers, evaluation means accountability, while teachers emphasize improvement. All the districts had overcome teacher resistance to evaluation, but the researchers gave one district the highest ratings for perceptions of fairness, involvement, openness, and a combination of pressure and support. In this context, evaluation served both accountability and improvement. Teachers shared a professional norm of enhancing student achievement and development, and when evaluation was tied to this norm, they supported it.

This normative approach to evaluation is also evident in case studies of Canadian teachers in clinical supervision processes with their principals (Grimmett & Crehan, 1992). The researchers developed a typology of school cultures as social contexts for evaluation that was based on tight versus loose coupling around norms and structure. A "tight-loose" or "strong" school culture is "framed around tightly structured professionally oriented beliefs and values" within a loose structure (p. 64). In one case of administratively imposed clinical supervision, the researchers show that the principal emphasized external motivation, control, and suppression of conflict. The teacher shut down, defended her practice, and did not change. In two cases of "organizationally induced" but not forced clinical supervision, principal-teacher relationships were voluntary and open to negotiation. Teachers in these schools were open to change because of the tight-loose school culture.

The next step in teacher control of evaluation may be peer review, which contradicts the traditional role relationships of teachers and principals. Teacher unions have also opposed peer review as contradicting the norms of labor-management relations, but two case studies show unions participating in peer review plans (Gallagher, Lanier, & Kerchner, 1993). In one district, after a long, contentious process, the union and district agreed on peer evaluation or mentoring for new teachers and on evaluations and individual plans developed by a peer "consulting teacher" for tenured teachers in trouble. The latter was a major union shift from defending colleagues toward collective, professional accountability. Opposition from administrators, who lost power over evaluation, was strong. In the other case, a similar plan that was written into an agreement outside the contract created a governing board to hear consulting teachers' recommendations on tenure for new teachers. These meetings opened productive discussions of the district's definition of "good teaching." Administrators were beginning to trust teacher judgments, while teachers were willing to pressure their colleagues to improve.

Finally, some districts are experimenting with self-evaluation. In a case study of a rural New York school district, Poole (1995) used a symbolic interactionist approach to understand how people in different roles constructed the meanings of evaluation. The superintendent, who believed teachers should be responsible for their professional growth, appointed a committee that devised a Supportive Supervision Model with three levels: (a) directive, for untenured teachers; (b) intensive, for teachers in danger of termination; and (c) self-directed, for most tenured teachers. The last level was controversial, because it changed principal-teacher relationships. Principals had to recognize teachers' competence and trust them to self-evaluate. Teachers had to trust other teachers to be honest. Old meanings of "evaluation" undermined this trust, but once evaluation was open for discussion, the construction of meaning became multidirectional and administrators lost control.

Many public school teachers have little time for the planning and preparation that would mark their work as "professional." Hargreaves (1991, 1992) studied the consequences of an Ontario school board policy that provided teachers with additional preparation time, as demanded by the teachers' organization. The micropolitics of the organization led to conflicting interpretations of the policy that was based on different priorities and definitions of "professionalism." Hargreaves (1991) reports that administrators wanted teachers to use the time for collaboration between regular and special education teachers and for peer coaching. Teachers wanted to use the time flexibly and to collaborate as needed. This desire for flexibility illustrates a contrast between contrived collegiality and a collaborative culture in which collaboration is spontaneous. Hargreaves (1992) uses the same case to contrast intensification (external demands for productivity) and professionalization (teacher control). He found that teachers' work did intensify after the prep-time policy but largely because teachers drove themselves to meet higher standards. Their use of prep time was based on their professional commitments, but it did not lead to more collaboration, as administrators intended. It was "my time" for "my students."

Other reforms expand teachers' decision-making roles. In the metropolitan K–8 school district mentioned earlier, Smylie (1992a) administered questionnaires on creating councils that would be established to decentralize school management. Teachers reported that they were more likely to participate in curriculum and instruction decisions than in administrative decisions. Principal-teacher relationships in a school were also significant; if teachers perceived principals as open, collaborative, facilitative, and supportive, they were more willing to become involved. Smylie, Lazarus, and Brownlee-Conyers (1996)

created a model with teacher changes as intervening variables between teacher participation and student outcomes. Findings showed large declines in teacher perceptions of autonomy, but increases in perceived accountability. Organizational learning opportunities, perceived instructional improvement, and teacher-reported student outcomes were highly correlated with participation.

Two school patterns were identified. In highly participative schools, teacher participation was regular, frequent, and inclusive; decision making was collaborative and consensual; and leadership was shared. In low participative schools, teacher participation was limited, decisions were based on majority rule, and the principal held onto leadership. Both studies show that the policy's intent was mediated by school context, which led to different effects on teachers, but the findings on student outcomes were inconclusive.

In a longitudinal, qualitative study of 12 high schools, Weiss (1993) compared schools with and without shared decision making (SDM) to test two claims: SDM focuses attention on student performance, and SDM leads to more innovative and progressive decisions. Her data did not substantiate either claim. Teaching and student learning were barely mentioned in either set of schools as topics for decision making. However, when curricular innovations were introduced, teachers in SDM schools were more likely to support them, suggesting a benefit of teacher "buy-in." SDM schools also implemented more innovations, although Weiss attributes these innovations to reformist administrators. In all but one school, teachers steered a fairly conservative course through SDM unless administrators supported change or perhaps co-opted teachers to lend a democratic aura to change. Weiss concludes that SDM may improve professionalism, morale, and commitment, but unless it focuses on student learning, it is a "process without a direction" (p. 87).

CLASSROOM PRACTICE

Studies in this category report organizational effects on planned changes that are aimed more directly at the technical core of teaching in two subcategories. In the first subcategory, the district or school context is important in understanding the effects of top-down curriculum reforms on teachers. In the second subcategory, the organizational context helps to explain teacher responses to staff development.

Top-Down Curriculum Reforms. Several studies examine U.S. "excellence" reforms of the 1980s, which were attempts to centralize the control of curriculum and instruction according to statewide standards and testing. Rosenholtz (1987) interviewed teachers about state Minimal Competency Testing (MCT) in Tennessee. Most teachers were dissatisfied with MCT, because alignment of the curriculum to the test routinized their work and undermined their autonomy and professional judgment. The exceptions were teachers in schools with more resources and student homogeneity, where most students performed well. Teachers could move those students to deeper levels of knowing, while using low scores to identify the small number with learning difficulties. A case study of implementation of state science curriculum reform in a Mississippi junior high school (Wood, 1988) found that teachers shifted from teaching for understanding to emphasizing memorization of facts on criterion-referenced tests used to evaluate school districts. As a result, they were less satisfied with their work. Wood attributes these changes to the policy, but the findings also suggest school effects. The principal, who considered test scores to be an indicator of his performance, rigidly interpreted the policy and required teachers to follow lockstep curriculum and testing procedures. We do not know if the policy was similarly interpreted in other schools.

In an ethnographic study, McNeil (1988) was encouraged to find teachers in secondary urban magnet schools who were engaging students in experiences that would lead to deep and critical understandings of content. Despite limited resources and facilities, the teachers saw themselves as empowered professionals who were making a difference with their students. McNeil was preparing to report these findings when the state and district implemented back-to-basics reforms. Principals were to monitor teachers' lessons for a match with proficiencies on a test of basic skills and to monitor teachers for behaviors specified by the state career ladder plan. The magnet school teachers tried to juggle their own and the district's agendas but felt that the administration's attempt to bring all teachers up to a minimum standard constrained them from doing their best.

In case studies of two urban, secondary schools, Carlson (1992) interprets teacher resistance to the state's back-to-basics reforms as part of a "vicious cycle" set off by centralized attempts to control teaching. In the first school, teachers expressed their resistance through the union grievance process, which Carlson interprets as a form of goal displacement. Rather than deciding school and classroom goals, teachers became caught up in exercising their "largely reactive and defensive" power in relation to administrators (p. 182). In the second case, replacement of authoritarian "discipline" with impersonal, depoliticized "classroom management" in a middle school was not working, and administrators and teachers blamed each other. Some teacher resistance was based on White teachers' law-and-order attitude toward minority students, rather than on the creation of caring, democratic relationships. Teachers in these schools were so demoralized that they could not pose positive alternatives to top-down reforms.

While some researchers argue that conservative reforms stifle progressive teachers, Cuban (1995) argues that school and teacher norms can stifle progressive reforms. Darling-Hammond (1990) characterizes the California Mathematical Framework as an attempt to implement progressive, top-down reform (based on teaching for understanding) that failed because policymakers did not understand conditions at the local level. Case studies showed that in some districts, teachers simply received new textbooks that were based on new theories, with no explanation of the broader framework. With little information and guidance, they constructed their own understandings of the policy. Policy accretion was a problem, as older policies contradictory to the new one remained in place and teachers had to mediate these conflicting demands. Therefore, teachers did change as a result of the policy but not in the intended direction.

As Fuller, Snyder, Chapman, and Hua (1994) explain, school variation in response to top-down curriculum policies may be more common in a decentralized, loosely coupled system than

in nationalized systems with more uniform, prescriptive policies. However, Olorundare's (1990) qualitative study of teachers' implementation of a national science curriculum in Nigerian schools found wide discrepancies between the prescribed and actual curriculum in most schools. He attributes this, in part, to governmental actions, in part, to teacher preparation and attitudes, in part, to socioeconomic and cultural factors in communities, but also, in part, to school factors such as a principal's lack of reinforcement for implementation or limited school resources devoted to science.

Darling-Hammond (1990) concludes that policymakers have little understanding of teachers and are unwilling to invest in the teacher learning at the school level that would be required to implement complex reforms. A local example of this conclusion is Apple and Junck's (1992) case study of a reform of teaching in a middle school. The administration wanted to implement a new computer literacy curriculum but did not give teachers the necessary time or resources to do it well. Male teachers with more computer knowledge developed a canned computer unit that "any teacher" could teach, whether or not they could use a computer. Time and resources were inadequate to give students hands-on computer experience, and the teachers, for the most part, told them about computer use. Female teachers, with no time outside of work or at work to develop computer skills, became deskilled deliverers of the unit. Both student learning and genuine teacher development were sacrificed in favor of efficiency.

In response to critics of centralized curriculum policies, Archbald and Porter (1994) tested the hypothesis that high school teachers in schools with high control over curriculum feel less autonomous and empowered because of prescriptive state and district policies. They surveyed teachers in six urban high schools in three states, two each from low-, medium- and high-control categories. Teachers in all schools reported that they controlled their practice, regardless of centralized policies, although teachers in low-control schools did report more power over curriculum content. Yet teachers in high-control districts did not feel measurably less empowered or less satisfied. The authors' interpretation is that teachers define power from a classroom-centric perspective and work around or even ignore external constraints in a loosely coupled system. However, they also note that higher test scores in high-control districts suggest that policy controls do influence teachers.

It seems likely that state curriculum reform efforts will continue but, one would hope, with more attention to the conditions of local implementation. One of the most mentioned conditions is the need for more professional development for teachers. Staff development can be a top-down or a bottom-up strategy for teacher change and should be based on state or district priorities or teacher decisions.

Staff Development. Using interviews with staff developers, principals, and teachers, and on teacher surveys, Little (1992a) shows how top-down district and school decisions about staff development affect teachers' learning opportunities. Four policy priorities emerged:

1. Expenditures on formal professional development, decided at the district level, were the top priority. Most funds went

to staff developers and prepackaged programs, with teachers then choosing from a menu of listings. This choice was the extent of their active involvement; in most programs, they were a passive audience who were involved, at best, in hands-on activities.

2. Opportunity cost for allocation of teacher time for professional development was a lower priority in most settings. School leaders viewed pupil-free time for teachers as too costly, both in money and in pupil instruction time, but schools where teachers were most positive about professional development had such time.

3. Salary increments or incentives in most districts, such as career ladders, were most meaningful to new teachers but not to veterans who needed renewal. Districts also encouraged a choice of "easy" or district-provided credits.

4. Policies did not account for how much teachers voluntarily invest in their development, although for them this investment may be the most meaningful commitment.

Like Placier and Hamilton (1994) and Hamilton and Richardson (1995), other researchers have attempted to identify school effects on staff development. In a study of staff development called an Effective Use of Time, Smylie (1988) observed and interviewed teachers before and after the process and surveyed them on classroom interaction, certainty, and efficacy. He posited three antecedents of teacher change: individual psychological traits, the immediate task environment, and the interactive contexts of schools. Individual efficacy was significantly related to change, but, in this case, school context variables, with the exception of interactions with colleagues, were not.

Smylie and Conyers (1991) suggest that the relevant organizational variable is the prevalent model of teaching. In their case study, a district that promoted a model of teaching as "complex, dynamic, interactive, intellectual activity" (p. 13) transformed staff development. A district committee set staff development priorities, but teacher learning was decentralized to the school. The outcomes of the staff development were increases in teacher involvement in planning, participation in school activities, informal learning, collaboration, interest in learning, and commitment to work. Similarly, Levine and Sherk's (1989) case study of a low-income, urban middle school concludes that the school provided an effective context for staff development because of its shared emphasis on active and higher order learning, support for students and teachers, coordination of instruction, and positive leadership.

In a qualitative and quantitative study, Hopkins (1990) followed teachers in South Wales after their participation in a year-long staff development project to identify which individual or context factors accounted for their implementation decisions. Few teachers had an adequate grasp of the content of the staff development, but variation was present. To understand why comprehension of the content varied, Hopkins created school profiles and categorized teachers on Maslow's hierarchy. Low Maslow scores, poor school climate, and low implementation grouped together. Teacher personality seemed to have a stronger effect than school context, but the two were not independent. Data suggested that the role of the school head and consensus on school goals were key school variables. The question remained whether good schools attract more developed

teachers or whether those teachers create a positive climate for change.

A voluntary 2-year multicultural education staff development project in two midwestern U.S. districts had discouraging results (Sleeter, 1992a, 1992b). Teachers were released to attend 14 all-day sessions, yet, according to observations and interviews, they made few classroom changes. One report of the study (Sleeter, 1992a) emphasizes teacher ideology as a barrier to change, but Sleeter (1992b) centers on teacher comments about their schools: lack of time for curriculum work, large class sizes, required textbook-based curricula, differentiated program structures, disjuncture between school and community, and lack of power in the bureaucracy. She argues that multicultural education will fail without school restructuring, because even if individual teachers change, their schools do not support curriculum transformation.

Anyon (1994) found teacher change to be particularly difficult to accomplish in a poor, urban context. She vividly describes an urban school in which she was attempting to work with teachers to develop cooperative learning techniques. She watched a parent whip a student in the face with a belt in the school hallway and then listened to the teachers' frustrated stories of the day and to their negative descriptions of students. Anyon reported that she wondered what she was doing in the school and why anyone thought cooperative learning would help. A number of the teachers did begin to use cooperative learning; however, Anyon concluded that the social, economic, and political context outside the school and classroom would have to be changed to significantly help this school (see also Berliner & Biddle, 1995).

Two case studies report on staff development entailing organizational and teacher change in which staff development meets restructuring (Joyce & Murphy, 1990). In Clift, Veal, Holland, Johnson, and McCarthy's (1995) action science study of schools that participated in a university-school partnership on teacher reflection, staff development was open-ended, with constant renegotiation among the parties. Teachers examined their assumptions and collected data to confirm or disconfirm them. Then faculty developed individual action plans for improvement that were based on their priorities, and researchers provided feedback through school data profiles.

One important finding was that reflection can extend beyond the classroom to school-level decisions. In Wallace, LeMahieu, and Bickel's (1990) district case study, a Pittsburgh high school became a professional development center. Teachers were released to attend sessions at the center under the guidance of Clinical Resident Teachers, who then observed teachers in their classrooms and provided feedback. High school achievement had begun to improve, but some schools still did not support teacher change. The focus shifted from individual teachers to school renewal. Each school created a center for school improvement, and each faculty was encouraged to develop a staff development plan.

SUMMARY: ORGANIZATIONAL CONTEXTS

No simple conclusions can be drawn from these studies, but they do suggest that school and district contexts mediate the effects of planned efforts to change teachers, with positive or negative results. Certain reforms, such as merit pay, run so counter to the norms of teaching that they may fail even in effective schools. A general problem with external incentives is that teachers tend to be intrinsically motivated; a specific problem is that different teachers are attracted to different intrinsic rewards (Mitchell, Ortiz, & Mitchell, 1987). The intentions of other policies were transformed as they moved to the school and teacher levels, resulting in unintended consequences (Hall & McGinty, 1997; Rosenholtz, 1987). The relationship between individual teacher characteristics and school characteristics in staff development processes is still at issue. Some studies also evidence a turning away from narrowly defined teacher change or from staff development efforts toward school restructuring that have a broad agenda of "creating learner-centered schools with teacher involvement in schoolwide decision-making and program development" (Lieberman, 1992b, p. 5). Studies of these efforts are the focus of our next section.

How Planned Efforts to Change Schools Change Teachers

Many studies of schools and teachers end with recommendations for changing schools, with the authors making the assumption that changing schools will change teachers or that teacher change efforts will fail if the school does not support new ways of teaching. "Teacher development is thus tantamount to transforming educational institutions" (Fullan & Hargreaves, 1992, p. 6). This section reports on studies of school "restructuring," an ambiguous buzzword that connotes something beyond piecemeal or incremental change (Newmann, 1996). It can be defined "literally as changes in the structure of schools—for example, changes in the way students are grouped for purposes of learning, the way teachers relate to groups of students and to each other, and the way content or subject matter is allocated time during the school day" (Elmore, Peterson, & McCarthy, 1996, p. 2). A recurring issue in these studies is the relative importance of the process versus content of change. Darling-Hammond (1995) argues that people must know why they are engaged in change. Analyzing case studies of restructuring schools, she concluded that teachers who started with learners and learning and questioned their practices in relation to student benefits made more serious changes. A related theme is the need for both structural and cultural change (Newmann & Wehlage, 1996).

Restructuring falls into Chin and Benne's (1969) normative-reeducative category. Some leaders have abandoned "bureaucratic accountability mechanisms" (Darling-Hammond, 1995, p. 157), recognizing that bureaucracy itself may be the problem and that local educators have expertise and ethical commitments and do not need "prescriptions" for change. Most of the following studies are qualitative accounts of restructuring in these local contexts, making it impossible to isolate school "variables" that influence teacher change and difficult to draw generalizations. Many of the studies are written by participants in the process, providing not only a close, insider perspective but also ambiguity concerning the roles of researcher and project advocate.

Wideen's (1992) longitudinal study of a British Columbia elementary school shows how restructuring evolved as a nonlinear "moving target." Despite uncertainty and ambiguity, restructuring succeeded in improving teaching and student achievement for several reasons. The principal stressed norms of teaching as intellectual, professional, democratic, and value-driven and channeled district support to the school. The teacher group established expectations for change and empowerment. Most important, Wideen argues, was the content of restructuring: a change in language arts that challenged teachers' deepest assumptions. Constraints on change were identified as the drain on teacher energy, staff turnover, and ministry and district policies.

A major structural change occurred in Wasley's (1992) study of a southwestern U.S. elementary school—the teachers ended up running the school. The school was involved in several reforms, and the successive loss of two principals raised teacher concerns about protecting innovations from leadership turnover. The teachers proposed that a teacher team run the school, and, after negotiations, the superintendent and school board agreed. Benefits of a teacher-run school were identified as more outside contact as the school attracted outside attention and more helping relationships. Teachers welcomed more pressure if it meant more control, and they were learning a great deal but had to admit that the structure was a strain. While enthusiastic about the concept, Wasley questions if school governance and the many innovations these teachers adopted improved teaching or distracted attention from it. Most teachers had not changed their practices.

Three researchers (Elmore, Peterson, & McCarthy, 1996; Peterson, McCarthy, & Elmore, 1996) examine the relationship between restructuring and teacher change in three elementary schools. All the schools had created a new vision, all had strong leaders, and all teachers believed they had changed their practices. However, at two schools, only a few teachers had reconceptualized their teaching to create learning environments that enhanced students' understanding. The third school, an open-classroom school for almost 20 years, had been involved in improvement efforts much longer. In that time, it had become a collegial community in which teachers were expected to grow intellectually. While the most conventional in structure, it was the only school in which most teachers were teaching for understanding, largely because they were more knowledgeable.

Elmore, Peterson, and McCarthy (1996) identify another difference between this school and the others, and they use the basis of the process versus content of restructuring. The school's identity was forged as part of a district choice plan in which schools developed distinct purposes, not different structures. The other two schools had not paid as much attention to teacher skill and knowledge development. The researchers conclude that changing teachers is a "problem of learning, not a problem of organization" and that "school structure follows from good practice not vice versa" (Peterson, McCarthy, & Elmore, 1996, pp. 148–149).

In a study including both elementary and high schools, Short, Greer, and Melvin (1994) compare and contrast cases of nine schools in the Empowered Schools Project, which entailed developing and implementing empowerment processes suited to each context, with outside support and autonomy from district control. After 3 years, the schools fell evenly into three categories. "Opportunity" schools evidenced both "process" changes (high enthusiasm, school-community bridges, good communication, problem-solving strategies, trust, respect, and facilitative principals) and "content" changes (a shared focus on student success, common conceptions of empowerment, a commitment to tackling significant problems). "Shifter" schools had initial difficulties, largely because of controlling principals. Teachers took the initiative, with lead teachers facilitating communication with the principals, who gradually relinquished control. The content of decisions was limited to immediate, practical problems, but success at this level built support for the project. "No-go" schools evidenced little change, essentially because of the absence of all the factors present in the "opportunity" schools.

Informed by Sarason (1982), Maehr and Midgley's (1996) study of an elementary and a middle school emphasizes the priority of cultural change over structural change. Structural changes that occurred during the 2 years the researchers were involved with the schools were driven by changes in thinking and beliefs about teaching, learning, and student motivation. From the researchers' perspective, the most important cultural change was from "ability goals," which draw attention to individual competition and to learning as a means to an end, to "task goals," which draw attention to learning for its own sake. They collected teacher survey data at the two demonstration schools and two matched-comparison schools and found that teachers who were most involved in the process were changing from ability goals to task goals. However, teachers who avoided or overtly rejected involvement had not changed.

The School Restructuring Study included case studies of 24 significantly restructured public schools at all levels (Newmann, 1996). Assuming that the purpose of restructuring is to improve teaching and learning, the researchers developed standards for authentic pedagogy. Applying the standards to classroom observations, they found wide variation among the schools. The success of restructuring depended on whether the process was aimed at "advancing the intellectual quality of student learning" and "nurturing professional community" (p. 14). Louis, Kruse, and Marks (1996) use the cases to show how professional community among teachers supported pedagogical change. The cultural aspects of professional community were shared norms and values, a focus on student learning, reflective dialogue, deprivatization of practice, and collaboration— counter to traditional norms of teaching (Lortie, 1975). King, Louis, Marks, and Peterson (1996) connect authentic pedagogy and teacher decision-making power. They identified four kinds of power relations in the cases: consolidated (a small group held power), balkanized (power was dispersed among autonomous groups), laissez-faire (individualistic autonomy), and shared power. Shared power in decision making was most strongly related to authentic pedagogy, but the process was not sufficient unless the content of decisions was pedagogical change. Supportive, participative principals and freedom from external control were also key factors.

High school studies emphasize the difficult changes required of secondary teachers who have been socialized to fit the high school structure. For example, in response to critics of tracking such as Oakes (1985), some high schools have attempted to "detrack." Two micropolitical studies reveal the dynamics of this process. According to S. J. Ball (1987), restructuring that challenges traditional divisions in high schools and that is based

on discipline, department, student ability groups, and gender is bound to be threatening. The change to mixed ability classes in one British comprehensive high school threatened the interests, careers, and status of teachers identified with the top students and brought forth opposing ideologies and tensions among teachers along age and gender lines. The head teacher was a crucial figure in mediating or exacerbating these teacher conflicts.

Behar and George (1994) studied a rural southeastern U.S. high school in which the administration decided to detrack not because of equity but because of the cost of small honors classes. Teachers were to design different curricula for regular and honors students in the same classes, but the teachers were inadequately prepared. Most persisted in teacher-centered, didactic instruction that did not account for student differences. Many felt the change was imposed without their assent and refused to make any special effort. Even teachers who had planned to change their practices did not, in part, because they felt the administration did not support them. All the conditions that might make detracking work were missing in this case.

McNeil (1986) observed a similar situation of administratively imposed detracking with little teacher participation or preparation in one high school in her study. Interestingly, Mintrop and Weiler (1994) observed a reverse process of attempted "retracking" in secondary schools in the former East Germany after reunification.

A study of three U.S. high schools that were creating alternatives to the academic-vocational dichotomy (Little, 1995) addresses the question: What opportunities for teacher development occur in these settings? Southgate had a history as an academic school, but its student population was diversifying. The school created a career academy that combined academics and career preparation and that attracted additional resources and external involvement, but teachers were exhausted by the demands and pace of change. Prairie was a new school with alternative programs based on academic and vocational curriculum integration. Teachers liked the new structure, but, again, were exhausted by change, had difficulty reconciling different roles and disciplines, and were constrained by state curriculum guidelines. Rindge, a well-known technical school, merged with Cambridge Latin, an elite high school. A design team formed to create a new curriculum, and this process entailed a great deal of professional development. For restructuring and teacher development to converge, Little concludes, a school needs structures of support (teaming, space, time, resources) and a culture of support (exploring beliefs and creating norms of collegiality and experimentation). Rindge came closest to this ideal.

In *Horace's Compromise* (Sizer, 1984), a veteran U.S. English teacher is confronted with high school conditions that work against teacher change and quash idealism: too many students, too little time, too much emphasis on curriculum coverage, and too little teacher control. Based on nine principles (including detracking) that emerged from this analysis, Sizer initiated the Coalition of Essential Schools (CES). CES faculties agree to engage in serious negotiation about what the principles mean in their school contexts. Wasley (1991b, 1994) documented teacher change in five very different CES schools to identify common themes. Once again, change ran counter to high school norms and posed problems for teachers. Teacher teams cut across departmental boundaries, with implications for collegiality, curriculum integration, scheduling, and budgets. Insider-outsider dynamics were a problem in large schools where CES was a school-within-a-school and seemingly gave some teachers more privileges. On the positive side, teachers were questioning academic disciplinary divisions and the race to cover material, redefining their roles from teacher- to student-centered, and attempting to move from assessment of recall to assessment of performance or application. Most were developing a more constructivist conception of learning and teaching, and most reported substantial growth.

In a book of charter school cases from the Philadelphia Schools Collaborative, Fine (1994) presents a cross-case analysis that is based on qualitative and quantitative data, including findings on teacher change. Some teachers initially wanted to maintain their autonomy, despite their lack of power and efficacy. They had to overcome fears of collaboration, peer pressure, and closer involvement with students. Some believed firmly in tracking and special education segregation. Some were well adapted to the school bureaucracy but were involved in external networks they found rewarding. Others were cynical about yet another reform. The process was a struggle, but once it caught on, teachers, students, and parents demanded more control and freedom from bureaucracy. Data also showed improved achievement in charter schools. Two cases in Fine's volume (J. Cohen, 1994; Vanderslice & Farmer, 1994) especially highlight teacher change.

The professional development school (PDS) involves joint restructuring of schools and colleges of education. Darling-Hammond (1994) argues that new demands on schools require more skilled, professional teachers, which requires both reforming teacher education and retooling practicing teachers. The PDS interrupts three patterns in teacher socialization: "figure it out for yourself," "do it all yourself," and "keep it to yourself" (p. 8). In a synthesis of PDS case studies, Darling-Hammond identifies two teacher change themes: (a) new frames for teacher learning—as teachers become teacher educators, not recipients of expert knowledge, intern teachers learn more because of the context of reflection and collaboration, and both draw parallels between their learning and student learning; and (b) new ways of knowing and building knowledge—negotiation between research-based knowledge and teachers' context-based knowledge honors both and privileges neither. The problem with the PDS, Darling-Hammond argues, is the disincentive for change in both settings. Teacher development is a low priority in school districts, and the low status of teacher education does not warrant more university investment.

A case from Darling-Hammond's volume that highlights teacher change is Snyder's (1994) study of one elementary and one middle school PDS involving Teachers College, New York Public Schools, and the United Federation of Teachers (UFT). In Fine's charter school volume, Vogel and Abrahams-Goldberg (1994) describe teacher change in a PDS involving Millard Fillmore High School and Temple University. A case study by Hardy (1993) chronicles the first year of a collaboration involving an elementary school in Akron, Ohio, the National Education Association (NEA), and Kent State University.

School restructuring studies often mention teacher unions as participants, and a brief discussion of the teacher change entailed by this observation is warranted. Unions have been accused of resisting school and teacher change efforts, but a new "professional unionism" means that unions and administrators collaborate in school reform, even when it means rethinking old power-coercive relationships. For example, McClure (1991) describes the Mastery In Learning project, founded when NEA leaders realized they must participate in reform or be left out. Teachers in 26 schools voted to reconstruct their schools to better serve students, with the support of project staff. Collegiality in the project centered on learning and teaching (content), not "sociability" (process); in fact, sociability was sometimes strained by the difficulty of change. Teachers' initial self-descriptions showed them to be traditional, textbook-bound, and risk-averse; change reportedly occurred on all counts.

A book of district case studies by Kerchner and Koppich (1993) emphasizes interdependency of workers and managers and protection of teaching, not teachers. Bargaining techniques changed to allow agreements beyond wages and working conditions that built in flexibility and accountability. Union members saw themselves as collaborating with management for common, public ends. Some structural changes such as site-based management moved unionism to the school and led to some resistance from principals who did not want to share leadership. Kerchner's (1993) case study of the Louisville school district in Kerchner and Koppich's volume emphasizes teacher development. Finally, Bascia's (1994) high school case studies also demonstrate this change in union strategies but raise some cautions. Unions collaborated with administrators around restructuring and professionalism (teachers being responsible for other teachers), changing from an adversarial to a mutual relationship. Where new policies complemented teacher norms, such policies were well received; where they did not, results were more uncertain. School management teams, for example, might actually include fewer teachers in decisions and be perceived as less egalitarian than union meetings. Moreover, because collaboration does not change the official school power structure, teachers must still be concerned about job security.

Some researchers ask teachers how restructuring changes their work, and findings suggest that teachers have mixed reactions. Noting that restructuring rhetoric often excludes teaching and learning in favor of structure, Murphy, Evertson, and Radnofsky (1991) interviewed 14 Tennessee teachers on their conceptions of restructuring. The teachers were enthusiastic and recognized the need for change, but tempered this response with realism about the possibility of changing an entrenched system. They envisioned change in these areas: interdisciplinary curricula, school climate, teacher work structures to provide time for collaboration, positive interpersonal dynamics, better management of student behavior, a supportive structure with ample resources, and student outcomes (but not testing). The authors conclude that teachers pay more attention to the "content" issues of teaching and learning but pay less attention to parent involvement than restructuring advocates.

Two studies asked teachers about changing decision-making roles. On a qualitative questionnaire, Blase and Blase (1994) asked teachers in shared governance schools about how principals contributed to their empowerment. Teachers noted several positive changes in principal behaviors that enhanced their self-esteem and satisfaction. They in turn were ready to give up norms of isolation to accept responsibility and power. Professional development was now teacher-initiated, which was also very well-received. They said they were highly motivated to improve their performance. In a large district known for restructuring, Taylor and Bogotch (1994) asked teachers if participation was associated with satisfaction and if they had sufficient decision-making power. They sampled schools from two matched groups, those that began restructuring as pilot schools and those that began later. They administered a teacher questionnaire to ascertain the dimensions and extent of participation and, based on these findings, divided the schools into high- and low-participation categories.

Pilot schools were much more likely to be in the high-participation category. However, teachers in both school categories still reported decision-making deprivation. They were most involved in decisions about how and what to teach—the "core technology" of teaching—but this kind of participation correlated less strongly with satisfaction than participation in areas beyond the core. There was a significant correlation between participation and student attendance but not between achievement and participation. A context factor that may have affected the findings was that the district had recently withdrawn support for school-level decision making, a reminder that restructuring can be fragile and temporary.

Three studies suggest that restructuring advocates should listen closely to teachers, especially minority teachers. Dandridge (1993) interviewed teachers at three urban high schools in Massachusetts. Findings show that external factors (neighborhood crises, students' lives outside of school, resources) and school micropolitics (competing demands on teacher time, layoffs, lack of respect and recognition) affected teacher attitudes toward change. Teachers were also skeptical of participation or managerial roles.

Foster (1993) interviewed exemplary African-American teachers, most of them veterans who had seen reform come and go and most of whom worked in schools with many students of color but few African-American teachers. Three categories emerged. Cynical dissenters did not participate, because they were alienated from the school. Their ideas about teaching were either not considered progressive enough or threatened others' assumptions. Coincidental cooperators did participate, either because reforms matched their own commitments or because they had no choice. One committed advocate emerged from the interview data, but she also reported racial tension among teachers. In general, Foster says that African-American teacher participation in restructuring is limited by teaching philosophy, strained relationships with colleagues, alienation from White teachers' negativity, skepticism about reform, and differing conceptions of leadership, parents, and students. Decision-making structures that are based on majority rule are likely to exclude these perspectives.

If a goal of restructuring is culturally responsive teaching, efforts may fall short according to Lipman's (1996) ethnographic study of two junior high schools. Both schools had significant percentages of African-American students, too often categorized as low achievers, and a small number of African-American teachers, among them three exemplary teachers known for their success with African-American students. White teachers, believing these students had deficits, often expressed this perspective toward these students and were not concerned about developing a culturally relevant pedagogy or curriculum. When restructuring arrived, the African-American teachers at first were enthused, but this feeling waned as they realized that their contributions would not be valued on collaborative teams. White teachers were not interested in learning from them but, instead, attributed their success with African-American students to natural talents. Restructuring may change structures but leave teacher beliefs associated with low student achievement unexamined.

SUMMARY: EFFECTS OF RESTRUCTURING ON TEACHERS

In a synthesis of findings from case studies of restructuring schools in five states, Lieberman (1995) identifies themes related to teacher change that seem to cut across the above studies and to include both process and content and structure and culture: (a) learning from experience and turning problems into possibilities for change rather than falling back on old patterns; (b) shaping new relationships as partnerships, with teachers in the foreground and principals in the background; (c) building shared meaning through joint action, reflection, communication, and the breaking down of teacher isolation; (d) tension and conflict, whether between district and school control or among teachers because of different perspectives on teaching; (e) using and making new structures such as teacher development academies, teams, retreats, or planning groups; (f) student work and engagement as the agenda for teacher work and teacher change; and (g) creating a professional community. We would add the theme of complexity and ambiguity of restructuring involving colleges of education, national networks such as CES, teacher unions, and cultural differences among teachers. Because restructuring is a long-term and multilayered process, studies showing definitive effects of restructuring on teachers' work lives and practices are slow in emerging, but the number of conference presentations and ERIC documents on this topic indicate a great deal of research activity.

One uncertainty is how long restructuring will last. Elmore, Peterson, and McCarthy (1996) note that leaders pursue restructuring for political, symbolic, or economic reasons that are unrelated to student learning. They also may be too impatient for "results" (improved test scores) to wait out this long process. Restructuring is politically and financially vulnerable and, often, dependent on temporary, external support. The intensity and pace of change in restructuring schools is also daunting for teachers. Of the thousands of U.S. schools, how many are likely to undertake such changes? How many teachers will be genuinely affected? Lieberman (1992b) argues that given the extent of social, economic, and political change in society and higher expectations for school and teacher performance, school and teacher change are inevitable.

Conclusion

One of the most interesting findings from our work on this chapter is the degree to which both the individual and organizational change literatures stand on their own—almost entirely uninformed by the other. As we explained in the introduction, these literatures seem independent of each other, because they emerge from different disciplinary frameworks. This review has led us to the conclusion that both approaches to considerations of teacher change are viable, and perhaps both are necessary in a systematic teacher change process. However, three questions remain. Are there linkages between the two bodies of research? Is it feasible to develop a model that includes individual change and the organizational context? What questions remain that could be addressed through research?

Viewed separately, the individual and organizational change literatures leave significant gaps in our understanding of change processes and our abilities to facilitate change. The individual approach to change, suggest Hargreaves and Fullan (1992), can be "self-indulgent, not replicable, slow, time-consuming, costly, and unpredictable" (pp. 12–13). This approach, they state, over-emphasizes the personal and ignores context. However, the organizational approach has led to bureaucratic solutions and structural changes that ignore the core of teaching (Fullan, 1993). Hargreaves and Fullan (1992) also suggest that such approaches have a tendency to be overtly political.

While the individual and organizational change literatures have remained quite separate, we have found considerable agreement on the processes of change, the methodologies used to elucidate change processes, and conclusions concerning the complexity, difficulty, and promises of change in schooling and teaching. One assumption that pulls these two areas together is that major and sustainable changes in education probably require a normative-reeducative approach to change. Many of the reforms being called for today, for example, constructivist teaching and teaching for understanding, require deep changes in content and pedagogical knowledge and in understandings about schooling, teaching, and learning. These instructional changes require belief changes and, therefore, cultural change, a concept of interest in both the organizational and individual change literatures.

Fullan (1992) suggests that teacher development and school development must go together. His thinking concludes that because school change requires culture change, a consideration of both school structure and teacher development is necessary. Nelson and Hammerman (1996) also suggest that changes in individual teachers' mathematics instruction require the development of a school culture that fosters "intellectual curiosity" (p.11).

Lieberman (1996) suggests that a school-level "culture of inquiry" (p. 189) will facilitate teacher learning and change. Cultural change involves changes in beliefs and understandings at all levels of schooling. And much of the literature within the individual change literature focuses on changes in beliefs. Thus, both the organizational and individual literatures help us understand both the content and processes of these changes. Further, we have moved away from the "one solution" conception of change that accompanied the empirical-rational approach and away from the use of top-down mandates that ignore local contexts and threaten educators' sense of autonomy. Thus, current research in both literatures acknowledges that deep and lasting change requires consideration of a multitude of aspects and interests and should be viewed as an ongoing and local process.

While these two literatures and the ways of bringing them

together—for example, through culture change (described above)—share commonalities, they also generate tensions and disagreements. These tensions may be exacerbated by the nature of the change process that is being proposed. For example, McLaughlin and Talbert (1993b) suggest that we do not know whether a direct role for policy in a change process leading toward "teaching for understanding" can be found, and if a role can be found, we do not know what the administrators and policymakers can do to facilitate such teaching. Further, Rowan (1995) does not necessarily agree that the normative-reeducative approach is essential in change process. He describes two forms of change: management-mechanistic (corresponding, somewhat, with rational-empirical) and organic (normative-reeducative). In a review of the literature on both forms, he concludes that the first form of management, consistently and carefully applied, has positive effects on teacher morale, efficacy, and cohesiveness.

One way of understanding the tensions between individual and organizational change is to look at issues of autonomy and accountability. The individual change literature identifies the need for teachers to have a sense of autonomy that is tied to ownership of change (Ayers, 1992; Barksdale-Ladd & Thomas, 1996; Fagan, 1989). Rudduck (1988) states: "I see it [ownership of change] as bringing about a motivation towards change that is personally founded, and I see it as being about meaning that is explored in relation to the self as well as in relation to the professional situation." (p. 213). And yet, what does it mean for each individual teacher to feel autonomous in the classroom? For teachers to experience autonomy and empowerment does not guarantee that teachers will make the most appropriate decisions. Deardon (1975) points out that we cannot avoid risk and error. A conscious choice that an autonomous teacher makes may be ineffective or worse for students and may be in conflict with other teachers' choices in the same school.

Richardson (1998) relates what may happen within an individualistic teacher change approach through a description of an elementary school in which teachers' sense of autonomy and their change orientations are strong but in which the teachers use highly individualistic approaches for the teaching of reading. The teachers in this school were deeply divided between those who used the whole language approach and those who used approaches that are more structured. Students in this school could start out in a whole language classroom in kindergarten, move to a highly structured, semiphonics program in Grade 1, experience a workbook approach to reading instruction in Grade 2, and shift into a literature-based whole language program in Grade 3. The teachers felt a great sense of autonomy and were willing to change within the contexts of their individual classrooms and their own philosophies of the reading process. However, from year to year, the students experienced a dramatic lack of coherence that could be particularly detrimental for the low-achieving students.

What is lacking in this school is a sense of autonomy and responsibility that goes beyond the individual classroom and moves to the school and community levels. Little (1992a) describes this broader sense of autonomy as civic responsibilities, but cautions against "formally orchestrated" collaboration that becomes bureaucratic and contrived. Little suggests that a solution to the individual autonomy-civic responsibility tension is the development of "joint work" that brings teachers together and creates interdependence among them. Pendlebury (1990) suggests that we need a different conception of autonomy, one that does not imply individual "liberty as license"—a conception that can be detrimental to students and to the profession. She suggests that the concept of autonomy as independence is important in that members of a community are granted equal respect and concern. However, this new image of autonomy requires that there is an agreed upon conception of the good life within this community. Thus, the consideration of autonomy should be thought of within a community of practice in which one finds "ongoing critical discussions of the good, standards and procedures which is necessary for a thriving practice" (Pendlebury, 1990, p. 274).[8]

The Individual Teacher in the Professional Community of Practice

One way of bringing together teachers in a school (or larger unit) in a nonbureaucratic and unforced way is to focus our attention on what happens to a student over the course of the schooling process. Our current approach to testing and assessment is school-based but is cross-sectional and based on grade level. This approach tends to focus administrators' and teachers' attention on the individual classroom rather than on the nature of the entity. If we focus on what happens to a student over the course of the schooling process—across grade levels—the focus for teachers might shift from the students in their classrooms to a consideration of students within their schools and school districts as students move through their schools and transition into others. This change shifts the responsibility, in part, to the collective and requires consideration of both individual and organizational change. Teacher autonomy and accountability would, therefore, not be considered as an individual right or responsibility but would be earned and assumed within a community of practice.

Further Research

The following three areas of research would provide important knowledge in our quest for a better understanding of teacher change.

1. *Effects of Teacher Change on Students.* Few studies of teacher change in either the individual or organizational literature move toward examining what happens to student learning when teachers change their practices. Within a community, student learning should be assessed longitudinally to determine the effects of teacher change on student learning over a number of years. Conceptual and methodological issues would have to be worked out related to student mobility. For example, in some schools with high student mobility, only a small percentage of the students could be followed longitudinally.

2. *The Interface Between Individual Teachers and Their Schools.* Zeichner and Gore (1990) suggest that this interface between individual teachers and their schools reveals a critical gap in our understanding of change. Are there differences among individual teachers in response to the same organizational conditions? How do changes in the organizational context affect different individual teachers? How do teachers, working individually and collaboratively, affect the school context? These effects may be obvious, as when teachers act as change agents in restructuring processes, but they also may be subtle. Much attention has gone into studies of the effect of the principal on school contexts, but more attention needs to be paid to teachers, because they may be more likely to stay in a school longer and have more to do with shaping the norms into which new teachers are socialized.

3. *Communities of Practice.* This construct should be developed further. For example, is the community located within an individual school, a cluster of schools that includes a high school and the feeder schools, or a wider network of teachers with common interests? What is the best way of working out accountability within a community of practice?

For all three of these sets of questions, it will be important to draw upon both the individual and organization literatures in teacher change. In so doing, we will hope to approach the change process in ways that preserve individual and group teacher autonomy yet provide, over the long term, a coherent and effective education for our students.

REFERENCES

Anders, P., & Richardson, V. (1991). Research directions: Staff development that empowers teachers' reflection and enhances instruction. *Language Arts, 68*(4), 316–321.

Anderson, G. L. (1991). Cognitive politics of principals and teachers: Ideological control in an elementary school. In J. Blase (Ed.), *The politics of life in schools: Power, conflict and cooperation* (pp. 120–138). Newbury Park, CA: Sage.

Anyon, J. (1994). Teacher development and reform in an inner-city school. *Teachers College Record, 96*(1), 14–31.

Apple, M. W., & Junck, S. (1992). You don't have to be a teacher to teach this unit: Teaching, technology and control in the classroom. In A. Hargreaves & M. G. Fullan (Eds.), *Understanding teacher development* (pp. 20–42). New York: Teachers College Press.

Archbald, D. A., & Porter, A. C. (1994). Curriculum control and teachers' perceptions of autonomy and satisfaction. *Educational Evaluation and Policy Analysis, 16*(1), 21–39.

Ashton, P. (1984). Teacher efficacy: A motivational paradigm for effective teacher education. *Journal of Teacher Education, 35*(5), 28–32.

Ashton, P., & Webb, R. (1986). *Making a difference: Teachers' sense of efficacy and student achievement.* New York: Longman.

Au, K. (1990). Changes in teacher's views of interactive comprehension instruction. In L. C. Moll (Ed.), *Vygotsky and education* (pp. 271–286). New York: Cambridge University Press.

Ayers, W. (1992). Work that is real: Why teachers should be empowered. In G. Hess, Jr. (Ed.), *Empowering teachers and parents. School restructuring through the eyes of anthropologists* (pp. 13–28). Westport, CT: Bergin and Garvey.

Ball, D. (1990). Reflections and deflections of policy: The case of Carol Turner. *Educational Evaluation and Policy Analysis, 12,* 241–245.

---

[8] This view of community of practice is derived from MacIntyre's (1981) view of practice that is communitarian in concept. However, Noddings (1996) cautions us that building such communities in schools and elsewhere, where the type of coercion that comes about without violence could be included, can cause potential problems.

Ball, S. J. (1987). *The micro-politics of the school: Towards a theory of school organization*. London: Methuen.

Ball, S. J., & Goodson, I. (1985). Understanding teachers: Concepts and contexts. In S. J. Ball & I. F. Goodson (Eds.), *Teachers' lives and careers* (pp. 1–26). London: Falmer Press.

Barksdale-Ladd, M. A., & Thomas, K. F. (1996). The development of empowerment in reading instruction in eight elementary teachers. *Teaching and Teacher Education, 12*(2), 161–178.

Barnett, C., & Sather, S. (1992, April). *Using case discussions to promote change in beliefs among mathematics teachers*. Paper presented at the annual meeting of the American Educational Research Association, San Francisco, CA.

Bascia, N. (1994). *Unions in teachers' professional lives: Social, intellectual and practical concerns*. New York: Teachers College Press.

Beattie, M. (1995). *Constructing professional knowledge in teaching*. New York: Teachers College Press.

Becker, H., Geer, B., Hughes, E., & Strauss, A. (1961). *Boys in white*. Chicago, IL: University of Chicago Press.

Behar, L. S., & George, P. S. (1994). Teachers' use of curriculum knowledge. *Peabody Journal of Education, 69*(3), 48–69.

Berliner, D. (1994). Expertise: The wonder of exemplary performances. In J. N. Mangiere & C. C. Block (Eds.), *Creating powerful thinking in teachers and students: Diverse perspectives* (pp. 161–186). Fort Worth, TX: Harcourt Brace College.

Berliner, D., & Biddle, B. (1995). *The manufactured crisis*. New York: Addison Wesley.

Black, A., & Ammon, P. (1992). A developmental-constructivist approach to teacher education. *Journal of Teacher Education, 43*(5), 323–335.

Blase, J. J. (1987). The dimensions of ineffective school leadership: The teacher's perspective. *Journal of Educational Administration, 25*(2), 193–213.

Blase, J. J. (1990). Some negative effects of principals' control-oriented and protective political behavior. *American Educational Research Journal, 27*(4), 727–753.

Blase, J. (1991). Everyday political perspectives of teachers toward students: The dynamics of diplomacy. In J. Blase (Ed.), *The politics of life in schools: Power, conflict and cooperation* (pp. 185–206). Newbury Park, CA: Sage.

Blase, J. (1993). The micropolitics of effective school-based leadership: Teachers' perspectives. *Educational Administration Quarterly, 19*(2), 142–163.

Blase, J., & Blase, J. R. (1994). *Empowering teachers: What successful principals do*. Thousand Oaks, CA: Corwin Press.

Blase, J., & Roberts, J. (1994). The micropolitics of teacher work involvement: Effective principals' impacts on teachers. *Alberta Journal of Educational Research, 40*(1), 67–94.

Blumenfeld, P. C., Kracjik, J. S., Marx, R. W., & Soloway, E. (1994). Lessons learned: How collaboration helped middle-grade science teachers learn project-based instruction. *Elementary School Journal, 94*(5), 539–551.

Bolin, F. (1990). Helping student teachers think about teaching: Another look at Lou. *Journal of Teacher Education, 41*(1), 10–19.

Borko, H. (1992, April). *Patterns across the profiles: A critical look at theories of learning to teach*. Paper presented at the annual meeting of the American Educational Research Association, New Orleans, LA.

Borko, H., Eisenhart, M., Brown, C. A., Underhill, D., Jones, D., & Agard, P. (1992). Learning to teach mathematics: Do novice teachers and their instructors give up too easily? *Journal of Research in Mathematics, 23*, 8–40.

Borko, H., Lalik, R., & Tomchin, E. (1987). Student teachers' understandings of successful teaching. *Teaching and Teacher Education, 3*, 77–90.

Borko, H., & Niles, J. (1987). Descriptions of teacher planning: Ideas for teachers and research. In V. Richardson-Koehler (Ed.), *Educators' Handbook: A research perspective* (pp. 167–187). New York: Longman.

Borko, H., & Putnam, R. (1996). Learning to teach. In R. C. Calfee & D. C. Berliner (Eds.), *Handbook of educational psychology*. New York: Macmillan.

Bos, C., & Anders, P. (1994). The study of student change. In V. Richardson (Ed.), *Teacher change and the staff development process* (pp. 181–198). New York: Teachers College Press.

Britzman, D. (1985). Reality and ritual: An ethnographic study of student teachers. (University Microfilms International. No. 8517084)

Britzman, D. (1991). *Practice makes perfect: A critical study of learning to teach*. Albany, NY: State University of New York Press.

Brophy, J. (1976). Reflections on research in elementary schools. *Journal of Teacher Education, 27*, 31–34.

Bullough, R. V. (1989). *First-year teacher: A case study*. New York: Teachers College Press.

Bullough, R. V., & Baughman, K. (1997). *"First year teacher" eight years later: An inquiry into teacher development*. New York: Teachers College Press.

Bullough, R. V., & Knowles, J. G. (1991). Teaching and nurturing: Changing conceptions of self as teacher in a case study of becoming a teacher. *Qualitative Studies in Education, 4*, 121–140.

Butt, R., Raymond, D., McCue, G., & Yamagishi, L. (1992). Collaborative autobiography and the teacher's voice. In I. Goodson (Ed.), *Studying teachers' lives* (pp. 51–98). New York: Teachers College Press.

Calderhead, J., & Robson, M. (1991). Images of teaching: Student teachers' early conceptions of classroom practice. *Teaching and Teacher Education, 7*, 1–8.

Carlson, D. (1992). *Teachers and crisis: Urban school reform and teachers' work culture*. New York: Routledge.

Carpenter, T., Fennema, E., Peterson, P. L., Chiang, C., & Loef, L. (1989). Using knowledge of children's mathematics thinking in classroom teaching. *American Educational Research Journal, 26*, 499–532.

Carter, K. (1990). Teachers' knowledge and learning to teach. In W. R. Houston (Ed.), *Handbook of research on teacher education* (pp. 291–310). New York: Macmillan.

Carter, K., Cushing, K., Sabers, D., Stein, P., & Berliner, D. (1988). Expert-novice differences in perceiving and processing visual classroom information. *Journal of Teacher Education, 39*, 25–31.

Case, R. (1988). *Intellectual development: Birth to adulthood*. New York: Academic Press.

Casey, K. (1992). Why do progressive women activists leave teaching? Theory, methodology and politics in life history research. In I. F. Goodson (Ed.), *Studying teachers' lives* (pp. 187–208). New York: Teachers College Press.

Chin, R., & Benne, K. (1969). General strategies for effecting changes in human systems. In W. Bennis, K. Benne, & R. Chin (Eds.), *The planning of change* (2nd ed., pp. 32–59). New York: Holt, Rinehart & Winston.

Civil, M. (1995). Listening to students' ideas: Teachers interviewing in mathematics. In L. Meira & D. Caraher (Eds.), *Proceedings of the 19th Psychology of Mathematics Education conference* (Vol. 2, pp. 154–161). Brazil: Universidade Federal do Pernambuco.

Civil, M. (1996). Thinking about mathematics and its teaching: An experience with preservice teachers. In J. Gimenez, S. Llinares, & V. Sanchez (Eds.), *Becoming a primary teacher: Issues from mathematics education* (pp. 137–154). Spain: Autores.

Clandinin, D. J. (1986). *Classroom practice: Teacher images in action*. London: Falmer Press.

Clandinin, D. J., & Connelly, F. M. (1987). Teachers' personal knowledge: What counts as personal in studies of the personal. *Journal of Curriculum Studies, 19*(6), 487–500.

Clark, C., Moss, P., Goering, S., Herter, R., Lamar, B., Leonard, D. Robbins, S., Russell, M., Templin, M., & Wascha, K. (1996). Collaboration as dialogue: Teachers and researchers engaged in conversation and professional development. *American Educational Research Journal, 33*(1), 193–231.

Clark, C., & Peterson, P. L. (1986). Teachers' thought processes. In M. C. Wittrock (Ed.), *Handbook of research on teaching* (3rd ed., pp. 255–296). New York: Macmillan.

Clift, R. T., Houston, W. R., & Pugach, M. (Eds.). (1990). *Encouraging reflective practice in education*. New York: Teachers College Press.

Clift, R. T., Meng, L., & Eggerding, S. (1994). Mixed messages in learning to teach English. *Teaching and Teacher Education, 19*(3), 265–279.

Clift, R. T., Veal, M. L., Holland, P., Johnson, M., & McCarthy, J.

(1995). *Collaborative leadership and shared decision making: Teachers, principals and university professors.* New York: Teachers College Press.

Cochran-Smith, M., & Lytle, S. (1990). Research on teaching and teacher research: The issues that divide. *Educational Researcher, 19*(2), 2–10.

Cohen, D. (1990). A revolution in one classroom: The case of Mrs. Oublier. *Educational Evaluation and Policy Analysis, 12*(3), 311–344.

Cohen, J. (1994). "Now everybody want to dance": Making change in an urban charter. In M. Fine (Ed.), *Chartering urban school reform: Reflections on public high schools in the midst of change* (pp. 98–111). New York: Teachers College Press.

Cole, A. L. (1991). Relationships in the workplace: Doing what comes naturally? *Teaching and Teacher Education, 7*(5/6), 415–426.

Cole, A. L., & Knowles, G. (1993). Teacher development partnership research: A focus on methods and issues. *American Educational Research Journal, 30,* 473–495.

Conley, S. C., Bacharach, S. B., & Bauer, S. (1989). The school work environment and teacher career dissatisfaction. *Educational Administration Quarterly, 25*(11), 58–81.

Conley, S. C., Bas-Isaac, E., & Scull, R. (1995). Teacher mentoring and peer coaching: A micropolitical interpretation. *Journal of Personnel Evaluation in Education, 9*(1), 7–19.

Corcoran, T. B. (1990). Schoolwork: Perspectives on workplace reform in public schools. In M. W. McLaughlin, J. E. Talbert, & N. Bascia (Eds.), *The contexts of teaching in secondary schools: Teachers' realities* (pp. 142–166). New York: Teachers College Press.

Corporaal, A. (1991). Repertory grid research into cognitions of prospective primary school teachers. *Teaching and Teacher Education, 7*(4), 315–329.

Crone, L. J., & Teddlie, C. (1995). Further examination of teacher behavior in differentially effective schools: Selection and socialization process. *Journal of Classroom Interaction, 30*(1), 1–9.

Cruickshank, D., & Metcalf, K. K. (1990). Training within teacher preparation. In W. R. Houston (Ed.), *Handbook of research on teacher education* (pp. 469–497). New York: Macmillan.

Cuban, L. (1988). Constancy and change in schools (1880s to the present). In P. Jackson (Ed.), *Contribution to educational change: Perspectives on research and practice* (pp. 85–106). Berkeley, CA: McCutcheon.

Cuban, L. (1995). The hidden variable: How organizations influence teacher responses to secondary science curriculum reform. *Theory into Practice, 34*(1), 4–11.

Cunnison, S. (1989). Gender joking in the staff room. In S. Acker (Ed.), *Teachers, gender and careers* (pp. 151–167). London: Falmer Press.

Dandridge, W. (1993). Conditions of school reform: The views of urban high school teachers. *Equity and Excellence in Education, 26*(3), 6–15.

Darling-Hammond, L. (1990). Instructional policy into practice: "The power of the bottom over the top." *Educational Evaluation and Policy Analysis 12*(7), 339–347.

Darling-Hammond, L. (1994). Developing professional development schools: Early lessons, challenge and promise. In L. Darling-Hammond (Ed.), *Professional development schools: Schools for developing a profession* (pp. 1–27). New York: Teachers College Press.

Darling-Hammond, L. (1995). Policy for restructuring. In A. Lieberman (Ed.), *The work of restructuring schools: Building from the ground up* (pp. 157–175). New York: Teachers College Press.

Deardon, R. (1975). Autonomy and education. In R. Deardon, P. Hirst, & R. Peters (Eds.), *Education and reason* (pp. 58–75). London: Routledge & Kegan Paul.

Devaney, K. (1977). *Essays on teachers' centers.* San Francisco: Far West Laboratory for Educational Research and Development.

Devaney, K., & Thorn, L. (1975). *Exploring teachers' centers.* San Francisco: Far West Laboratory for Educational Research and Development.

Doyle, W. (1977). Paradigms for research on teacher effectiveness. In L. Shulman (Ed.), *Review of research in education* (Vol. 5, pp. 3–16). Itasca, IL: Peacock.

Doyle, W. (1979). Classroom tasks and students' abilities. In P. L. Peterson & H. Walberg (Eds.), *Research on teaching: Concepts, findings and implications.* Berkeley, CA: McCutchan.

Duffy, G., & Roehler, L. (1986). Constraints on teacher change. *Journal of Teacher Education, 35,* 55–58.

Elbaz, F. L. (1983). *Teacher thinking: A study of practical knowledge.* London: Croom Helm.

Elmore, R. F., Peterson, P. L., & McCarthy, S. J. (1996). *Restructuring in the classroom: Teaching, learning and school organization.* San Francisco: Jossey-Bass.

Erickson, F. (1986). Qualitative methods in research on teaching. In M. C. Wittrock (Ed.), *Handbook of research on teaching* (3rd ed., pp. 119–161). New York: Macmillan.

Fagan, W. (1989). Empowered students: Empowered teachers. *The Reading Teacher, 42,* 572–578.

Feiman-Nemser, S. (1983). Learning to teach. In L. S. Shulman & G. Sykes (Eds.), *Handbook of teaching and policy* (pp. 150–171). New York: Longman.

Feiman-Nemser, S., & Buchmann, M. (1989). Describing teacher education: A framework and illustrative findings from a longitudinal study of six students. *The Elementary School Journal, 89*(3), 365–377.

Feiman-Nemser, S., McDiarmid, G. W., Melnick, S. L., & Parker, M. (1989). *Changing beginning teachers' conceptions: A description of an introductory teacher education course* (Research Report 89–1). East Lansing, MI: National Center for Research on Teacher Education, College of Education, Michigan State University.

Fennema, E., Carpenter, T. P., Franke, M., & Carey, D. (1992). Learning to use children's mathematical thinking: A case study. In R. Davis & C. Maher (Eds.), *Schools, mathematics and the world of reality* (pp. 93–117). Needham Heights, MA: Allyn & Bacon.

Fenstermacher, G. D. (1979). A philosophical consideration of recent research on teacher effectiveness. In L. S. Shulman (Ed.), *Review of research in education* (Vol. 6, pp. 157–185). Itasca, IL: Peacock.

Fenstermacher, G. D. (1986). Philosophy of research on teaching: Three aspects. In M. Wittrock (Ed.), *Handbook of research on teaching* (3rd ed., pp. 37–49). New York: Macmillan.

Fenstermacher, G. D. (1993). *Where are we going? Who will lead us there?* Washington, DC: American Association of Colleges of Teacher Education.

Fenstermacher, G. D. (1994a). The knower and the known: The nature of knowledge in research on teaching. In L. Darling-Hammond (Ed.), *Review of research in education* (Vol. 20, pp. 1–54). Washington, DC: American Educational Research Association.

Fenstermacher, G. D (1994b). The place of practical arguments in the education of teachers. In V. Richardson (Ed.), *Teacher change and the staff development process* (pp. 23–42). New York: Teachers College Press.

Fessler, R. (1995). Dynamics of teacher career stages. In T. R. Guskey & M. Huberman (Eds.), *Professional development in education: New paradigms and practices* (pp. 171–192). New York: Teachers College Press.

Fine, M. (1994). Chartering urban school reform. In M. Fine (Ed.), *Chartering urban school reform: Reflections on public high schools in the midst of change* (pp. 5–30). New York: Teachers College Press.

Firestone, W. A. (1991a). Increasing teacher commitment in urban high schools: Incremental and restructuring options. In S. C. Conley & B. S. Cooper (Eds.), *The school as a work environment: Implications for reform* (pp. 142–168). Boston: Allyn & Bacon.

Firestone, W. A. (1991b). Merit pay and job enlargement as reforms: Incentives, implementation and teacher response. *Educational Evaluation and Policy Analysis, 13*(3), 269–288.

Firestone, W. A., & Bader, B. D. (1991). Professionalism or bureaucracy? Redesigning teaching. *Educational Evaluation and Policy Analysis, 13*(1), 67–86.

Foster, M. (1993). Urban African American teachers' views of organizational change: Speculations on the experiences of exemplary teachers. *Equity and Excellence in Education, 26*(3), 16–24.

Fox, D. (1995). From English major to English teacher: Two case studies. *English Journal, 84*(2), 17–25.

Freeman, D. (1993). Renaming experience/reconstructing practice: Developing new understandings of teaching. *Teaching and Teacher Education, 9*(5/6), 485–497.

Freiberg, H. J., & Knight, S. L. (1991). Career ladder programs as incentives for teachers. In S. C. Conley & B. S. Cooper (Eds.), *The school as a work environment: Implications for reform* (pp. 204–220). Boston: Allyn & Bacon.

Fullan, M. (1985). Change process and strategies at the local level. *The Elementary School Journal, 84,* 391–420.

Fullan, M. (1990). Staff development, innovation and institutional development. In B. Joyce (Ed.), *Changing school culture through staff development* (pp. 3–25). Alexandria, VA: Association for Supervision and Curriculum Development.

Fullan, M. (1992). *Successful school improvement: The implementation perspective and beyond.* Philadelphia: Open University Press.

Fullan, M. (1993). *Change forces: Probing the depths of educational reform.* London: Falmer Press.

Fullan, M. G. (1991). *The new meaning of educational change.* New York: Teachers College Press.

Fullan, M., & Hargreaves, A. (1992). Teacher development and educational change. In M. Fullan & A. Hargreaves (Eds.), *Teacher development and educational change* (pp. 1–9). London: Falmer Press.

Fuller, B., Snyder, C. W., Chapman, D., & Hua, H. (1994). Explaining variation in teaching practices: Effects of state policy, teacher background and curricula in southern Africa. *Teaching and Teacher Education, 10*(2), 141–156.

Fuller, F. (1969). Concerns of teachers: A developmental conceptualization. *American Educational Research Journal, 6*(4), 207–226.

Fuller, F., & Bown, O. (1975). Becoming a teacher. In K. Ryan (Ed.), *Teacher education* [74th Yearbook of the National Society for the Study of Education, Part 2] (pp. 25–52). Chicago: University of Chicago Press.

Gallagher, J. J., Lanier, P., & Kerchner, C. T. (1993). Toledo and Poway: Practicing peer review. In C. T. Kerchner & J. E. Koppich (Eds.), *A union of professionals: Labor relations and educational reform* (pp. 158–176). New York: Teachers College Press.

Gallagher, M., Goudvis, A., & Pearson, P. D. (1988). Principles of organizational change. In J. Samuels, & P. D. Pearson (Eds.), *Changing school reading programs* (pp. 11–39). Newark, DE: International Reading Association.

Gee, J. (1990). *Social linguistics and literacy: Ideology in discourses.* Philadelphia: Falmer Press.

Gitlin, A. (1990). Educative research, voice, and school change. *Harvard Educational Review, 60*(4), 443–465.

Goffman, E. (1973). *The presentation of self in everyday life.* Woodstock, NY: Overlook Press.

Goldenberg, C., & Gallimore, R. (1991). Changing teaching takes more than a one-shot workshop. *Educational Leadership, 49*(3), 69–72.

Goldsmith, L. T., & Schifter, D. (1994). *Characteristics of a model for the development of mathematics teaching* [Center for the Development of Teaching Paper Series]. Newton, MA: Center for the Development of Teaching, Education Development Center, Inc.

Goodlad, J. I. (1984). *A place called school: Prospects for the future.* New York: McGraw-Hill.

Goodson, I. (1992). Studying teachers' lives: An emergent field of inquiry. In I. Goodson (Ed.), *Studying teachers' lives* (pp. 1–17). New York: Teachers College Press.

Greenfield, W. D. J. (1991). The micropolitics of leadership in an urban elementary school. In J. Blase (Ed.), *The politics of life in schools: Power, conflict and cooperation* (pp. 161–184). Newbury Park, CA: Sage.

Griffin, G. (1986). Clinical teacher education. In J. Hoffman & S. Edwards (Eds.), *Reality and reform in clinical teacher education* (pp. 1–24). New York: Random House.

Griffiths, S., & Tann, S. (1992). Using reflective practice to link personal and public theories. *Journal of Education for Teaching, 18*(1), 69–84.

Grimmett, P. P., & Crehan, E. P. (1992). The nature of collegiality in teacher development: The case of clinical supervision. In M. Fullan & A. Hargreaves (Eds.), *Teacher development and educational change* (pp. 56–85). London: Falmer Press.

Grimmett, P. P., & Erickson, G. L. (Eds.). (1988). *Reflection in teacher education.* New York: Teachers College Press.

Grossman, P. L. (1990). *The making of a teacher: Teacher knowledge and teacher education.* New York: Teachers College Press.

Guskey, T. R. (1986). Staff development and the process of teacher change. *Educational Researcher, 15,* 5–12.

Hall, G. E., & Loucks, S. (1977). A developmental model for determin-

ing whether the treatment is actually implemented. *American Educational Research Journal, 14*(3), 263–276.

Hall, J. L., Johnson, B., & Bowman, A. C. (1995). Teacher socialization: A spiral process. *The Teacher Educator, 30*(4), 25–36.

Hall, P. M., & McGinty, P. J. (1997). Policy as the transformation of intentions: Producing program from statute. *Sociological Quarterly, 38*(3), 439–467.

Hamilton, M. L., & Richardson, V. (1995). Effects of the culture of two schools on the process and outcomes of staff development. *The Elementary School Journal, 95*(4), 367–385.

Hardy, J. T. (1993). The effects of a school-university collaborative change project on teacher behaviors: A case study. *Mid-Western Educational Researcher, 6*(3), 8–13.

Hargreaves, A. (1991). Contrived collegiality: The micropolitics of teacher collaboration. In J. Blase (Ed.), *The politics of life in schools* (pp. 46–72). Newbury Park, CA: Corwin Press.

Hargreaves, A. (1992). Time and teachers' work: An analysis of the intensification thesis. *Teachers College Record, 94*(1), 87–108.

Hargreaves, A. (1994). *Changing teachers, changing times: Teachers' work and culture in the postmodern age.* New York: Teachers College Press.

Hargreaves, A. (1995). Development and desire: A postmodern perspective. In T. R. Guskey & M. Huberman (Eds.), *Professional development in education: New paradigms and practices* (pp. 9–34). New York: Teachers College Press.

Hargreaves, A., & Fullan, M. (1992). Introduction. Hargreaves & M. Fullan (Eds.), (pp. 1–19). New York: Teachers College Press.

Hargreaves, J., & Grey, S. (1983). Changing teachers' practice: Innovation and ideology in a part-time B.ED. course. *Journal of Education for Teaching, 9*(2), 161–183.

Harrington, H., & Hathaway, R. (1994). Computer conferencing, critical reflection, and teacher development. *Teaching and Teacher Education, 10*(2).

Harris, M. (1993). Looking back: 20 years of a teacher's journal. In M. Cochran-Smith & S. L. Lytle (Eds.), *Inside/outside: Teacher research and knowledge* (pp. 130–140). New York: Teachers College Press.

Heaton, R. (1992). Who is minding the mathematics content: A case study of a fifth-grade teacher. *Elementary School Journal, 93,* 153–162.

Helsby, G., & McCulloch, G. (1996). Teacher professionalism and curriculum control. In I. Goodson & A. Hargreaves (Eds.), *Teachers' professional lives* (pp. 56–74). London: Falmer Press.

Henson, B. E., & Hall, P. M. (1993). Linking performance evaluation and career ladder programs: Reactions of teachers and principals in one district. *Elementary School Journal, 93*(4), 323–353.

Hoban, G. (1995). *Reflection on what? Assisting teachers to frame and reframe their practice.* Paper presented at the annual meeting of the American Educational Research Association, San Francisco, CA.

Hollingsworth, S. (1989). Prior beliefs and cognitive change in learning to teach. *American Educational Research Journal, 26*(2), 160–189.

Hopkins, D. (1990). Integrating staff development and school improvement: A study of teacher personality and school climate. In B. Joyce (Ed.), *Changing school culture through staff development, 1990 Yearbook of Association for Supervision and Curriculum Development* (pp. 41–68). Alexandria, VA: Association for Supervision and Curriculum Development.

Houston, W. R. (Ed.). (1990). *Handbook of Research on Teacher Education.* New York: Macmillan.

Hoy, W. (1967). Organizational socialization: The student teacher and pupil control ideology. *The Journal of Educational Research, 61,* 153–259.

Hoy, W., & Woolfolk, A. (1990). Socialization of student teachers. *American Educational Research Journal, 27*(2), 279–300.

Huberman, M. (1989). The professional life cycle of teachers. *Teachers College Record, 91*(1), 31–58.

Hunt, D. E. (1974). *Matching models in education.* Ontario, Canada: Ontario Institute for Studies in Education.

John, P. D. (1991). A qualitative study of British student teachers' lesson planning perspectives. *Journal of Education for Teaching, 17*(3), 310–320.

Johnson, S. M. (1990). *Teachers at work: Achieving success in our schools.* New York: Basic Books.

Johnston, M. (1994). Contrasts and similarities in case studies of teacher reflection and change. *Curriculum Inquiry, 24*(1), 9–26.

Johnston, S. (1992). Images: A way of understanding the practical knowledge of student teachers. *Teaching and Teacher Education, 8,* 123–136.

Jones, G. M., & Vesilind, E. (1996). Putting practice into theory: Changes in the organization of preservice teachers' pedagogical knowledge. *American Educational Research Journal, 33*(1), 91–117.

Jordell, K. (1987). Structural and personal influence in the socialization of beginning teachers. *Teaching and Teacher Education, 3,* 165–177.

Joyce, B. (1981). *Guaranteeing carryover from workshops to classrooms* Invited address presented at University of Oregon, Eugene, OR.

Joyce, B., & Murphy, C. (1990). Epilogue: The curious complexities of cultural change. In B. Joyce (Ed.), *Changing school culture through staff development, 1990 Yearbook of Association for Supervision and Curriculum Development* (pp. 243–250). Alexandria, VA: Association for Supervision and Curriculum Development.

Kagan, D. (1990). Ways of evaluating teacher cognition: Inferences concerning the Goldilocks principle. *Review of Educational Research, 60*(3), 419–469.

Kanpol, B. (1988). Teacher work tasks as forms of resistance and accommodation to structural factors of schooling. *Urban Education, 23*(2), 173–187.

Katz, L. (1979). *Helping others learn to teach: Some principles and techniques for inservice educators.* Urbana, IL: ERIC Clearinghouse on Early Childhood Education.

Kelchtermans, G., & Vandenberghe, R. (1994). Teachers' professional development: A biographical perspective. *Journal of Curriculum Studies, 26*(1), 45–62.

Kerchner, C. T. (1993). Louisville: Professional development drives a decade of school reform. In C. T. Kerchner & J. E. Koppich (Eds.), *A union of professionals: Labor relations and educational reform* (pp. 25–41). New York: Teachers College Press.

Kerchner, C. T., & Koppich, J. E. (1993). *A union of professionals: Labor relations and educational reform.* New York: Teachers College Press.

King, M. B., Louis, K. S., Marks, H. M., & Peterson, K. D. (1996). Participatory decision making. In F. M. Newmann (Ed.), *Authentic achievement: Restructuring schools for intellectual quality* (pp. 245–263). San Francisco: Jossey-Bass.

Klein, D. (1969). Some notes on the dynamics of resistance to change: The defender role. In W. Bennis, K. Benne, & R. Chin (Eds.), *The planning of change* (pp. 498–507). New York: Holt, Rinehart & Winston.

Knowles, J. G. (1992). Models for teachers' biographies. In I. Goodson (Ed.), *Studying teachers' lives* (pp. 99–152). New York: Teachers College Press.

Kohlberg, L. (1969). Stage and sequence: The cognitive-developmental approach to socialization. In D. Goslin (Ed.), *Handbook of socialization theory and research* (pp. 347–480). New York: Rand McNally.

Korthagen, F. A. J. (1988). The influence of learning orientations on the development of reflective teaching. In J. Calderhead (Ed.), *Teachers' professional learning* (pp. 35–50). Philadelphia: Falmer Press.

Krajcik, J., Layman, J., Starr, M., & Magnusson, S. (1991, April). *The development of middle school teachers' content knowledge and pedagogical content knowledge of heat energy and temperature.* Paper presented at the annual meeting of the American Educational Research Association, Chicago, IL.

Kuzmic, J. (1994). A beginning teacher's search for meaning: Teacher socialization, organizational literacy, and empowerment. *Teaching and Teacher Education, 10*(1), 15–27.

Ladson-Billings, G. (1994). *The Dreamkeepers.* San Francisco: Jossey-Bass.

Lampert, M. (1997). Teaching about thinking and thinking about teaching, revisited. In V. Richardson (Ed.), *Constructivist teacher education: Building new understandings* (pp. 84–107). London: Falmer Press.

Lanier, J., with Little, J. W. (1986). Research on teacher education. In M. Wittrock (Ed.), *Handbook of research on teaching* (3rd ed., pp. 527–569). New York: Macmillan.

Lave, J., & Wenger, E. (1991). *Situated learning: Legitimate peripheral participation.* Cambridge, UK: Cambridge University Press.

Leinhardt, G. (1988). Situated knowledge and expertise in teaching. In J. Calderhead (Ed.), *Teachers' professional learning* (pp. 146–168). London: Falmer Press.

Lester, N., & Onore, C. (1990). *Learning change.* Portsmouth, NH: Boynton/Cook.

Levine, D. U., & Sherk, J. K. (1989). Implementation of reforms to improve comprehension skills at an unusually effective inner city intermediate school. *Peabody Journal of Education, 66*(4), 87–106.

Lieberman, A. (1992). Introduction: The changing contexts of teaching. In A. Lieberman (Ed.), *The changing contexts of teaching, Ninety-first yearbook of the National Society for the Study of Education* (pp. 1–10). Chicago: University of Chicago Press.

Lieberman, A. (1992a). The meaning of scholarly activity and the building of community. *Educational Researcher, 21*(6), 5–12.

Lieberman, A. (1995). Restructuring schools: The dynamics of changing practice, structure, and culture. In A. Lieberman (Ed.), *The work of restructuring schools: Building from the ground up* (pp. 1–17). New York: Teachers College Press.

Lieberman, A. (1996). Practices that support teacher development: Transforming conceptions of professional learning. In M. W. McLaughlin & I. Oberman (Eds.), *Teacher learning: New policies, new practices* (pp. 185–201). New York: Teachers College Press.

Lieberman, A., & Miller, L. (1992). *Teachers—Their world and their work: Implications for school improvement.* New York: Teachers College Press.

Lightfoot, S. L. (1986). On goodness in schools: Themes of empowerment. *Peabody Journal of Education, 63*(1), 9–28.

Lindblad, S. (1990). From technology to craft: On teachers' experimental adoption of technology as a new subject in the Swedish primary school. *Journal of Curriculum Studies, 22*(2), 165–175.

Lipman, P. (1996). The missing voice of culturally relevant teachers in school restructuring. *The Urban Review, 28*(1), 41–62.

Little, J. W. (1981). *The power of organizational setting: School norms and staff development.* Paper presented at the annual meeting of the American Educational Research Association, Los Angeles, CA. (ERIC Document Reproduction Service No. ED 221 918)

Little, J. W. (1982). Norms of collegiality and experimentation: Workplace conditions of school success. *American Educational Research Journal, 19,* 325–340.

Little, J. W. (1992a). The black box of professional community. In A. Lieberman (Ed.), *The changing contexts of teaching: Ninety-first yearbook of the National Society for the Study of Education, Part 1* (pp. 157–178). Chicago: University of Chicago Press.

Little, J. W. (1992b). Teacher development and educational policy. In M. Fullan & A. Hargreaves (Eds.), *Teacher development and educational change* (pp. 170–193). London: Falmer Press.

Little, J. W. (1995). What teachers learn in high school: Professional development and the redesign of vocational education. *Education and Urban Society, 27*(3), 274–293.

Loevinger, J. (1966). The meaning and measurement of ego development. *American Psychologist, 21*(3), 195–206.

Lortie, D.C. (1975). *Schoolteacher: A sociological study.* Chicago: University of Chicago Press.

Loucks-Horsley, S., Harding, C., Arbuckle, M., Murray, L., Dubea, C., & Williams, M. (1987). *Continuing to learn: A guidebook for teacher development.* Andover, Maine: Regional Laboratory for Educational Improvement of the Northeast and Islands/National Staff Development Council.

Louden, W. (1991). *Understanding teaching: Continuity and change in teachers' knowledge.* New York: Teachers College Press.

Loughran, J., & Russell, T. (Eds.). (1997). *Teaching about teaching: Purpose, passion and pedagogy in teacher education.* London: Falmer Press.

Louis, K. S. (1992). Restructuring and the problem of teachers' work. In A. Lieberman (Ed.), *The changing contexts of teaching: Ninety-first yearbook of the National Society for the Study of Education* (pp. 138–155). Chicago: University of Chicago Press.

Louis, K. S., Kruse, S. D., & Marks, H. M. (1996). Schoolwide professional community. In F. M. Newmann (Ed.), *Authentic achievement: Restructuring schools for intellectual quality* (pp. 179–204). San Francisco: Jossey-Bass.

MacIntyre, A. (1981). *After virtue. A study in moral theory.* London: Gerald Duckworth & Co.

MacKinnon, A. (1987). Detecting reflection-in-action among preservice elementary science teachers. *Teaching and Teacher Education, 3*, 135–145.

MacKinnon, A., & Scarff-Seatter, C. (1997). Constructivism: Contradictions and confusions in teacher education. In V. Richardson (Ed.), *Constructivist teacher education: Building new understandings* (pp. 38–56). London: Falmer Press.

Maehr, M. L., & Midgley, C. (1996). *Transforming school cultures.* Boulder, CO: Westview Press.

Mager, G. M., Myers, B., Maresca, N., Rupp, L., & Armstrong, L. (1986). Changes in teachers' work lives. *Elementary School Journal, 86*(3), 345–357.

Markel, S. (1995). *Acquiring practical knowledge: A study of development through observations of student teaching practice and dialogues of community.* Unpublished dissertation, University of Arizona, Tucson.

Marks, S. U., & Gersten, R. (1998). Engagement and disengagement between special and general educators: An application of Miles and Huberman's cross-case analysis. *Learning Disabilities Quarterly, 21*, 34–56.

Marso, R., & Pigge, F. (1989). The influence of preservice training and teaching experience upon attitude and concerns about teaching. *Teaching and Teacher Education, 5*(1), 33–41.

Marx, R., Blumenfeld, P., Krajcik, J., Blunk, M., Crawford, K., Kelly, B., & Meyer, K. (1994). Enacting project-based science: Experiences of four middle-grade teachers. *Elementary School Journal, 94*(5), 498–517.

Mayer-Smith, J., & Mitchell, I. J. (1997). Teaching about constructivism using approaches informed by constructivism. In V. Richardson (Ed.), *Constructivist teacher education: Building new understandings* (pp. 129–153). London: Falmer Press.

McClure, R. M. (1991). Individual growth and institutional renewal. In A. Lieberman & L. Miller (Eds.), *Staff development for education in the '90s: New demands, new realities, new perspectives* (pp. 221–241). New York: Teachers College Press.

McDiarmid, G. W. (1990). Tilting at webs: Early field experiences as an occasion for breaking with experience. *Journal of Teacher Education, 41*(3), 12–20.

McDiarmid, G. W. (1992). What to do about differences? A study of multicultural education for teacher trainees in the Los Angeles Unified School District. *Journal of Teacher Education, 43*(2), 83–93.

McDonald, J. P. (1986). Raising the teacher's voice and the ironic role of theory. *Harvard Educational Review, 56*(4), 355–378.

McLaughlin, M. W. (1987). Learning from experience: Lessons from policy implementation. *Educational Evaluation and Policy Analysis, 9*, 171–178.

McLaughlin, M. W. (1991). Enabling professional development: What have we learned. In A. Lieberman & L. Miller (Eds.), *Staff development for education in the 90's* (pp. 61–82). New York: Teachers College Press.

McLaughlin, M. W. (1993). What matters most in teachers' workplace context? In J. W. Little & M. W. McLaughlin (Eds.), *Teachers' work: Individuals, colleagues and contexts* (pp. 79–103). New York: Teachers College Press.

McLaughlin, M. W. (1994). Strategic sites for teachers' professional development. In P. Grimmett & J. Neufeld (Eds.), *Teacher development and the struggle for authenticity* (pp. 31–51). New York: Teachers College Press.

McLaughlin, M. W., & Pfeifer, R. S. (1988). *Teacher evaluation: Improvement, accountability, and effective learning.* New York: Teachers College Press.

McLaughlin, M. W., & Talbert, J. E. (1993a). *Contexts that matter.* Stanford, CA: Center for Research on the Context of Secondary Teaching.

McLaughlin, M. W. & Talbert, J. E. (1993b). Introduction: New visions of teaching. In D. K. Cohen, M. W. McLaughlin & J. E. Talbert (Eds.), *Teaching for understanding: Challenges for policy and practice* (pp. 1–12). San Francisco: Jossey-Bass.

McLaughlin, M. W., Talbert, J., E., & Phelan, P. (1990). *CRC Report to the field sites.* Stanford, CA: Stanford University, Center for Research on the Context of Secondary School Teaching.

McLaughlin, M. W., & Yee, S. M.-L. (1988). School as a place to have a career. In A. Lieberman (Ed.), *Building a professional culture in schools* (pp. 23–44). New York: Teachers College Press.

McNeil, L. M. (1986). *Contradictions of control: School structure and school knowledge.* New York: Methuen/Routledge & Kegan Paul.

McNeil, L. M. (1988). *Contradictions of control: School structure and school knowledge.* New York: Routledge.

Merseth, K. (1996). Cases and case methods in education. In J. Sikula (Ed.), *Handbook of research on teacher education* (2nd ed., pp. 722–744). New York: Macmillan.

Metz, M. H. (1990). How social class differences shape teachers' work. In M. W. McLaughlin, J. E. Talbert, & N. Bascia (Eds.), *The contexts of teaching in secondary schools: Teachers' realities* (pp. 40–107). New York: Teachers College Press.

Metz, M. H. (1993). Teachers' ultimate dependence on their students. In J. W. Little & M. W. McLaughlin (Eds.), *Teachers' work: Individuals, colleagues and contexts* (pp. 104–190). New York: Teachers College Press.

Mevarech, Z. (1995). Teachers' paths on the way to and from the professional development forum. In T. R. Guskey & M. Huberman (Eds.), *Professional development in education: New paradigms and practices* (pp. 151–170). New York: Teachers College Press.

Meyer, L. (1988). Research on implementation: What seems to work. In S. J. Samuels & P. D. Pearson (Eds.), *Changing school reading programs* (pp. 41–57). Newark, DE: International Reading Association.

Middleton, S. (1989). Educating feminists: A life-history study. In S. Acker (Ed.), *Teachers, gender and careers* (pp. 53–67). London: Falmer Press.

Miles, M., & Huberman, M. (1994). *Qualitative data analysis* (2nd ed.). Thousand Oaks, CA: Sage.

Mintrop, H., & Weiler, H. N. (1994). The relationship between educational policy and practice: The reconstitution of the college-preparatory gymnasium in East Germany. *Harvard Educational Review, 64*(3), 247–277.

Mitchell, D. E., Ortiz, F. I., & Mitchell, T. K. (1987). *Work orientation and job performance: The cultural basis of teaching rewards and incentives.* Albany, NY: State University of New York Press.

Moll, L. (1992). Literacy research in community and classrooms: A sociocultural context approach. In R. Beach, J. Green, M. Kamil, & T. Shanalas (Eds.), *Multidisciplinary perspectives on literacy research* (pp. 211–244). Urbana, IL: National Council of Teachers of English.

Munby, H., & Russell, T. (1992). Transforming chemistry research into chemistry teaching: The complexities of adopting new frames for experience. In T. Russell & H. Munby (Eds.), *Teachers and teaching: From classroom to reflection* (pp. 90–123). London: Falmer Press.

Munby, H., & Russell, T. (1994). The authority of experience in learning to teach: Messages from a physics methods class. *Journal of Teacher Education, 45*(2), 86–95.

Munro, R. (1993). A case study of school-based training systems in New Zealand secondary schools. In J. Elliott (Ed.), *Reconstructing teacher education* (pp. 95–109). London: Falmer Press.

Murphy, J., Evertson, C. M., & Radnofsky, M. L. (1991). Restructuring schools: Fourteen elementary and secondary teachers' perspectives on reform. *The Elementary School Journal, 92*(2), 135–148.

Murray, F. (Ed.). (1996). *Teacher educators' handbook: Building a knowledge base for the preparation of teachers.* San Francisco: Jossey-Bass.

National Institute of Education. (1975). *Teaching as clinical information processing* (Report of Panel 6, National Conference on Studies in Teaching). Washington, DC: Author.

Nelson, B., & Hammerman, J. (1996). Reconceptualizing teaching: Moving toward the creation of intellectual communities of students, teachers and teacher education. In M. McLaughlin & I. Oberman (Eds.), *Teacher learning: New policies, new practices* (pp. 3–21). New York: Teachers College Press.

Nespor, J. (1987). The role of beliefs in the practice of teaching. *Journal of Curriculum Studies, 19*(4), 317–328.

Newmann, F. M. (1996). Introduction: The school restructuring study. In F. M. Newmann (Ed.), *Authentic achievement: Restructuring schools for intellectual quality* (pp. 1–16). San Francisco: Jossey-Bass.

Newmann, F. M., Rutter, R. A., & Smith, M. S. (1989). Organizational factors that affect school sense of efficacy, community and expectations. *Sociology of Education, 62*(4), 221–238.

Newmann, F. M., & Wehlage, G. G. (1996). Conclusion: Restructuring for authentic student achievement. In F. M. Newmann (Ed.), *Authentic achievement: Restructuring schools for intellectual quality* (pp. 286–301). San Francisco: Jossey-Bass.

Nias, J. (1989). Teaching and the self. In M. Holly & C. McLoughlin (Eds.), *Perspectives on teacher professional development* (pp. 155–172). London: Falmer Press.

Noblit, G., Berry, B., & Dempsey, V. (1991). Political responses to reform: A comparative case study. *Education and Urban Society, 23*(4), 379–395.

Noddings, N. (1996). On community. *Educational Theory, 46*(3), 245–267.

Oakes, J. (1985). *Keeping track: How schools structure inequality.* New Haven: Yale University Press.

Olorundare, S. (1990). Discrepancies between official science curriculum and actual classroom practice: The Nigerian experience. *Journal of Education Policy, 5*(1), 1–19.

Olson, M. R. (1993). *Knowing what counts in teacher education.* Paper presented at the Canadian Association of Teacher Educators, Canadian Society of Studies in Education, Ottawa, Ontario, Canada.

Pajares, M. F. (1992). Teachers' beliefs and educational research: Cleaning up a messy construct. *Review of Educational Research, 62*(3), 307–332.

Palincsar, A., Magnusson, S., Marano, N., Ford, D., & Brown, N. (1998). Design principles informing and emerging from the GisML Community: A community of practice concerned with guided inquiry science teaching. *Teaching and Teacher Education, 14*(1), 5–19.

Palonsky, S. B. (1986). *900 shows a year: A look at teaching from a teacher's side of the desk.* New York: McGraw-Hill.

Pendlebury, S. (1990). Community, liberty and the practice of teaching. *Studies in Philosophy and Education, 10,* 263–279.

Peterman, F. (1993). Staff development and the process of changing: A teacher's emerging constructivist beliefs about learning and teaching. In K. Tobin (Ed.), *The practice of constructivism in science education* (pp. 226–245). Washington, DC: AAAS Press.

Peterson, P. L., Fennema, E., Carpenter, T. P., & Loef, M. (1989). Teachers' pedagogical content beliefs in mathematics. *Cognition and Instruction, 6*(1), 1–40.

Peterson, P. L., McCarthy, S. J., & Elmore, R. F. (1996). Learning from school restructuring. *American Educational Research Journal, 33*(1), 119–153.

Phillip, R., Armstrong, B., & Bezuk, N. (1993). A preservice teacher learning to teach mathematics in a cognitively guided manner. In J. Becker & B. Pence (Eds.), *Proceedings of the fifteenth annual meeting of the PME-NA* (Vol. 2, pp. 159–165). Pacific Grove, CA: San Jose State University.

Piaget, J. (1970). Piaget's theory. In P. Mussen (Ed.), *Charmichael's handbook of child psychology.* New York: Wiley.

Placier, P., & Hamilton, M. L. (1994). Schools as contexts: A complex relationship. In V. Richardson (Ed.), *Teacher change and the staff development process: A case in reading instruction* (pp. 135–159). New York: Teachers College Press.

Poole, W. (1995). Reconstructing the teacher-administrator relationship to achieve systemic change. *Journal of School Leadership, 5*(4), 565–596.

Prawat, R. (1992). Are changes in views about mathematics teaching sufficient? The case of a fifth-grade teacher. *The Elementary School Journal, 93*(2), 195–211.

Putnam, R. T. (1992). Teaching the "hows" of mathematics for everyday life: A case study. *Elementary School Journal, 93,* 163–177.

Richardson, V. (1990). Significant and worthwhile change in teaching practice. *Educational Researcher, 19*(7), 10–18.

Richardson, V. (1992). The agenda-setting dilemma in a constructivist staff development process. *Teaching and Teacher Education, 8*(3), 287–300.

Richardson, V. (1994a). The consideration of beliefs in staff development. In V. Richardson (Ed.), *Teacher change and the staff development process: A case in reading instruction* (pp. 90–108). New York: Teachers College Press.

Richardson, V. (Ed.). (1994b). *Teacher change and the staff development process: A case in reading instruction.* New York: Teachers College Press.

Richardson, V. (1996). The role of attitudes and beliefs in learning to teach. In J. Sikula (Ed.), *Handbook of research on teacher education* (2nd ed., pp. 102–119). New York: Macmillan.

Richardson, V. (Ed.) (1997). *Constructivist teacher education: Building new understandings.* London: Falmer Press.

Richardson, V. (1998). Professional development in the instruction of reading. In J. Osborn & F. Lehr (Eds.), *Literacy for all: Issues for teaching and learning* (pp. 303–318). Chicago: Guilford Press.

Richardson, V., & Anders, P. (1994). A theory of change. In V. Richardson (Ed.), *Teacher change and the staff development process: A case of reading instruction* (pp. 199–216). New York: Teachers College Press.

Richardson, V., Anders, P., Tidwell, D., & Lloyd, C. (1991). The relationship between teachers' beliefs and practices in reading comprehension instruction. *American Educational Research Journal, 28*(3), 559–586.

Richardson, V., & Hamilton, M. L. (1994). The practical argument staff development process. In V. Richardson (Ed.), *Teacher change and the staff development process: A case in reading instruction* (pp. 109–134). New York: Teachers College Press.

Rinehart, J. S., & Short, P. M. (1991). Viewing Reading Recovery as a restructuring phenomenon. *Journal of School Leadership, 1*(4), 379–399.

Rist, R. (1977). On the relations among educational research paradigms: From disdain to detente. *Anthropology and Education Quarterly, 8*(2), 42–49.

Rosenholtz, S. J. (1987). Education reform strategies: Will they increase teacher commitment? *American Journal of Education, 95*(4), 534–562.

Rosenholtz, S. J. (1989). *Teachers' workplace: The social organization of schools.* New York: Longman.

Rosenholtz, S. J., Bassler, O., & Hoover-Dempsey, K. (1986). Organizational conditions of teacher learning. *Teaching and Teacher Education, 2*(2), 91–104.

Rowan, B. (1995). The organizational design of schools. In S. Bacharach & B. Mundell (Eds.), *Images of Schools* (pp. 11–42). Thousand Oaks, CA: Corwin Press, Inc.

Rowan, B. (1995, April). *Teachers' instructional work: Conceptual models and directions for future research.* Paper presented at the annual meeting of the American Educational Research Association, San Francisco, CA.

Rubin, L. (1978). *Inservice education of teachers: Trends, processes, and prescriptions.* Boston: Allyn & Bacon.

Rudduck, J. (1988). The ownership of change as a basis for teachers' professional learning. In J. Calderhead (Ed.), *Teachers' professional learning* (pp. 205–222). London: Falmer Press.

Russell, T. (1988). From pre-service teacher education to the first year of teaching: A study of theory into practice. In J. Calderhead (Ed.), *Teachers' professional learning* (pp. 13–34). London: Falmer Press.

Russell, T. (1995). Returning to the physics classroom to re-think how one learns to teach physics. In T. Russell & F. Korthagen (Eds.), *Teachers who teach teachers* (pp. 95–112). London: Falmer Press

Russell, T. & Korthagen, F. (Eds.). (1995). *Teachers who teach teachers.* London: Falmer Press.

Russell, T., Munby, H., Spafford, C., Johnson, P. (1988). Learning the professional knowledge of teaching. In P. Grimmett & G. Erickson (Eds.), *Reflection in teacher education* (pp. 67–90). New York: Teachers College Press.

Sarason, S. B. (1982). *The culture of the school and the problem of change.* Boston: Allyn & Bacon.

Schifter, D. (1995). Teachers' changing conceptions of the nature of mathematics: Enactment in the classroom. In B. S. Nelson (Ed.), *Inquiry and the development of teaching: Issues in the transformation of mathematics teaching.* [Center for the Development of Teaching Paper Series]. Newton, MA: Center for the Development of Teaching, Education Development Center, Inc.

Schifter, D., & Simon, M. (1992). Assessing teachers' development of a constructivist view of mathematics learning. *Teaching and Teacher Education, 8,* 187–197.

Schön, D. A. (1983). *The reflective practitioner.* New York: Basic Books.

Shavelson, R., & Stern, P. (1981). Research on teachers' pedagogical thoughts, decisions, and behavior. *Review of Educational Research, 51,* 455–498.

Shaver, J. (1987). Implications from research: What should be taught in Social Studies. In V. Richardson-Koehler (Ed.), *Educators' handbook: A research perspective.* New York: Longman.

Short, P. M., Greer, J. T., & Melvin, W. M. (1994). Creating empowered schools: Lessons in change. *Journal of Educational Administration, 32*(4), 38–52.

Showers, B., Joyce, B., & Bennett, B. (1987). Synthesis of research on staff development: A framework for future study and state-of-art analysis. *Educational Leadership, 45*(3), 77–87.

Shulman, L. S. (1987). Knowledge and teaching: Foundations of the new reform. *Harvard Educational Review, 57*(1), 1–22.

Sikula, J. (Ed.). (1996). *Handbook of Research on Teacher Education* (2nd ed.). New York: Macmillan.

Sizer, T. R. (1984). *Horace's compromise: The dilemma of the American high school.* Boston: Houghton Mifflin.

Sleeter, C. E. (1992a). *Keepers of the American dream.* London: Falmer Press.

Sleeter, C. E. (1992b). Restructuring schools for multicultural education. *Journal of Teacher Education, 43*(2), 141–148.

Smith, D., & Neale, D. (1989). The construction of subject matter knowledge in primary science teaching. *Teaching and Teacher Education, 5*(1), 1–20.

Smith, M. L. (1987). Publishing qualitative research. *American Educational Research Journal, 24,* 173–183.

Smylie, M. A. (1988). The enhancement function of staff development: Organizational and psychological antecedents to individual teacher change. *American Educational Research Journal, 25*(1), 1–30.

Smylie, M. A. (1992a). Teacher participation in school decision making: Assessing willingness to participate. *Educational Evaluation and Policy Analysis, 14*(1), 53–67.

Smylie, M. A. (1992b). Teachers' reports of their interactions with teacher leaders concerning classroom instruction. *The Elementary School Journal, 93*(1), 85–98.

Smylie, M. A., & Brownlee-Conyers, J. (1992). Teacher leaders and their principals: Exploring the development of new working relationships. *Educational Administration Quarterly, 28*(2), 150–184.

Smylie, M. A., & Conyers, J. G. (1991). Changing conceptions of teaching influence the future of staff development. *Journal of Staff Development, 12*(1), 12–16.

Smylie, M. A., Lazarus, V., & Brownlee-Conyers, J. (1996). Instructional outcomes of school-based participative decision making. *Educational Evaluation and Policy Analysis 18*(3), 181–198.

Smylie, M. A., & Smart, J. C. (1990). Teacher support for career enhancement initiatives: Program characteristics and effects on work. *Educational Evaluation and Policy Analysis, 12*(2), 139–155.

Snyder, J. (1994). Perils and potentials: A tale of two professional development schools. In L. Darling-Hammond (Ed.), *Professional development schools: Schools for developing a profession* (pp. 98–125). New York: Teachers College Press.

Sockett, H., & Hollingsworth, S. (Eds.). (1994). *Teacher research and educational reform: Ninety-third yearbook of the National Society for the Study of Education.* Chicago: University of Chicago Press.

Sparks, D., & Loucks-Horsley, S. (1990). Models of staff development. In W. R. Houston (Ed.), *Handbook of research on teacher education* (pp. 234–250). New York: Macmillan.

Sparks, G. M. (1983). Synthesis of research on staff development. *Educational Leadership, 41*(3), 65–72.

Sparks, G. M. (1988). Teachers' attitudes toward change and subsequent improvements in classroom teaching. *Journal of Educational Psychology, 80*(1), 111–117.

Sprinthall, N. A., Reiman, A. J., & Thies-Sprinthall, L. (1993). Role taking and reflection: Promoting the conceptual and moral development of teachers. *Learning and individual differences.*

Sprinthall, N. A., Reiman, A. J., & Thies-Sprinthall, L. (1996). Teacher professional development. In J. Sikula (Ed.), *Handbook of research on teacher education* (2nd ed., pp. 666–703). New York: Macmillan.

Staessens, K., & Vandenberghe, R. (1994). Vision as a core component in school culture. *Journal of Curriculum Studies, 26*(2), 187–200.

Stallings, J. (1989, March). *School achievement effects and staff development: What are some critical factors?* Paper presented at the annual meeting of the American Educational Research Association, San Francisco, CA.

Stallings, J., & Krasavage, E. (1986). Program implementation and student achievement in a four-year Madeleine Hunter Follow-Through project. *Elementary School Journal, 87*(2), 117–138.

Staton, A. Q., & Hunt, S. L. (1992). Teacher socialization: Review and conceptualization. *Communication Education, 41*(2), 109–137.

Stevenson, R. B. (1991). Action research as professional development: A U.S. case study of inquiry-oriented inservice education. *Journal of Education for Teaching, 17*(3), 277–292.

Talbert, J. E., & McLaughlin, M. W. (1994). Teacher professionalism in local school contexts. *American Journal of Education, 102*(2), 123–153.

Taylor, D. L., & Bogotch, I. E. (1994). School-level effects of teachers' participation in decision making. *Educational Evaluation and Policy Analysis, 16*(3), 302–319.

Tickle, L. (1991). New teachers and the emotions of learning teaching. *Cambridge Journal of Education, 21*(3), 319–329.

Tierney, R., Tucker, D., Gallagher, M., Crismore, A., Pearson, P. D. (1988). The Metcalf Project: A teacher-researcher collaboration. In S. Samuels, and P. D. Pearson (Eds.), *Changing school reading programs* (pp. 207–226). Newark, DE: International Reading Association.

Tillema, H., & Knol, W. (1997). Promoting student teacher learning through conceptual change or direct instruction. *Teaching and Teacher Education, 13*(6), 579–595.

Tobin, K. L. (1990). Changing metaphors and beliefs: A master switch for teaching? *Theory into Practice, 29*(2), 122–127.

Tom, A. (1995). Stirring the embers: Reconsidering the structure of teacher education programs. In M. Wideen & P. Grimmett (Eds.), *Changing times in teacher education* (pp. 117–132). London: Falmer Press.

Vadeboncoeur, J. (1997). Child development and the purpose of education: A historical context for constructivism in teacher education. In V. Richardson (Ed.), *Constructivist teacher education: Building new understandings* (pp. 15–37). London: Falmer Press.

Valdez, A. (1992). *Changes in teachers' beliefs, understandings, and practices concerning reading comprehension through the use of practical arguments: A follow-up study* Unpublished doctoral dissertation, College of Education, University of Arizona, Tucson.

Vanderslice, V., & Farmer, S. (1994). Transforming ourselves: Becoming an inquiring community. In M. Fine (Ed.), *Chartering urban school reform: Reflections on public high schools in the midst of change* (pp. 85–97). New York: Teachers College Press.

Van Manen, M. (1977). Linking ways of knowing with ways of being practical. *Curriculum Inquiry, 6,* 205–228.

Veenman, S., Leenders, Y., Meyer, P., & Sanders, M. (1993). Effects of a pre-service teacher preparation programme on effective instruction. *Educational Studies, 19*(1), 3–18.

Vogel, M. J., & Abrahams-Goldberg, E. (1994). The professional development school as a strategy for school restructuring: The Millard Fillmore High School-Temple University connection. In M. Fine (Ed.), *Chartering urban school reform: Reflections on public high schools in the midst of change* (pp. 47–62). New York: Teachers College Press.

Vygotsky, L. (1962). *Thought and language.* Cambridge, MA: MIT Press.

Wallace, R. C., LeMahieu, P. G., & Bickel, W. E. (1990). The Pittsburgh experience: Achieving commitment to comprehensive staff development. In B. Joyce (Ed.), *Changing school culture through staff development, 1990 Yearbook of Association for Supervision and Curriculum Development* (pp. 185–202). Alexandria, VA: Association for Supervision and Curriculum Development.

Waller, W. (1961). *The sociology of teaching.* New York: Russell & Russell.

Ward, B. (1985). Teacher development: The challenge of the future. In S. Hord, S. O' Neal & M. Smith (Eds.), *Beyond the looking glass* (pp. 283–312). Austin, TS: The Research and Development Center for Teacher Education, The University of Texas.

Wasley, P. A. (1991a). Stirring the chalkdust: Changing practices in essential schools. *Teachers College Record, 93*(1), 28–58.

Wasley, P. A. (1991b). *Teachers who lead: The rhetoric of reform and the realities of practice.* New York: Teachers College Press.

Wasley, P. A. (1992). Teacher leadership in a teacher-run school. In

A. Lieberman (Ed.), *The changing contexts of teaching, Ninety-first yearbook of the National Society for the Study of Education* (pp. 212–235). Chicago: University of Chicago Press.

Wasley, P. A. (1994). *Stirring the chalkdust: Tales of teachers changing classroom practices.* New York: Teachers College Press.

Wasley, P. A. (1995). The practical work of teacher leaders: Assumptions, attitudes and acrophobia. In A. Lieberman & L. Miller (Eds.), *Staff development for the 90s: New demands, new realities, new perspectives* (pp. 158–183). New York: Teachers College Press.

Weber, S., & Mitchell, C. (1996). Using drawings to interrogate professional identity and the popular culture of teaching. In I. Goodson & A. Hargreaves (Eds.), *Teachers' professional lives* (pp. 109–126). London: Falmer Press.

Weiler, K. (1988). *Women teaching for change: Gender, class and power.* New York: Bergin and Garvey.

Weinstein, R., Madison, S., & Kuklinski, M. (1995). Raising expectations in schooling: Obstacles and opportunities for change. *American Educational Research Journal, 32*(1), 121–159.

Weiss, C. H. (1993). Shared decision making about what? A comparison of schools with and without teacher participation. *Teachers College Record, 95*(1), 69–92.

Wideen, M. F. (1992). School-based teacher development. In M. Fullan & A. Hargreaves (Eds.), *Teacher development and educational change* (pp. 123–149). London: Falmer Press.

Wilcox, S., Schram, P., Lappan, G., & Lanier, P. (1991). *The role of a learning community in changing preservice teachers' knowledge.* East Lansing: National Center for Research on Teacher Learning, College of Education, Michigan State University.

Winitzky, N. (1992). Structure and process in thinking about classroom management: An exploratory study of prospective teachers. *Teaching and Teacher Education, 8*(1), 1–14.

Winitzky, N., & Kauchak, D. (1997). Constructivism in teacher education: Applying cognitive theory to teacher learning. In V. Richardson (Ed.), *Constructivist teacher education: Building new understandings* (pp. 59–83). London: Falmer Press.

Wittrock, M. (Ed.). (1986). *Handbook of Research on Teaching* (3rd ed.). New York: Macmillan.

Wood, T. (1988). State-mandated accountability as a constraint on teaching and learning science. *Journal of Research in Science Teaching, 25*(8), 631–641.

Wood, T., Cobb, P., & Yackel, E. (1991). Change in teaching mathematics: A case study. *American Educational Research Journal, 28*(3), 587–616.

Yarger, S. (1990). The legacy of the teacher center. In B. Joyce (Ed.), *Changing school culture through staff development* (pp. 104–116). Alexandria, VA: Association for Supervision and Curriculum Development.

Zahorik, J. (1990). Stability and flexibility in teaching. *Teaching and Teacher Education, 6*(1), 69–80.

Zeichner, K. M., & Gore, J. (1990). Teacher socialization. In W. R. Houston (Ed.), *Handbook of research on teacher education* (pp. 329–348). New York: Macmillan.

Zeichner, K. M., & Liston, D. P. (1987). Teaching student teachers to reflect. *Harvard Educational Review, 57*(1), 3–9.

Zeichner, K. M., Tabachnick, R., & Densmore, K. (1987). Individual, institutional, and cultural influences on the development of teachers' craft knowledge. In J. Calderhead (Ed.), *Exploring teachers' thinking* (pp. 21–59). London: Cassell.

Part 7
Social and Cultural Contexts and the Role of the Teacher

44.

Classroom Cultures and Cultures in the Classroom

Margaret A. Gallego, Michael Cole, and The Laboratory of Comparative Human Cognition
University of California, San Diego

Classroom Cultures: Introduction

The adage that "those who cannot remember the past are condemned to repeat it" (Santayana, 1906) has special relevance to the issue of classroom cultures. Current discussions of classroom cultures depend heavily on debates about the most effective forms of classroom organization that occupied the originators of psychology. These discussions also parallel arguments about the nature of culture, which preoccupied the originators of anthropology, of sociology, and of the nascent social sciences in general (Bruner, 1996; Erickson, 1986). Because of its obvious importance, we have attempted, insofar as our scholarly reach allows, to locate current discussions about classroom cultures in a long tradition of research on the role of the culture in the organization of classroom life.

A good deal of what follows can be found distributed in various previously published sources, which we acknowledge in the course of this review. Our task is to bring this material together in a productive way with newer information that is appropriate to contemporary problems of teaching.

As we surveyed this vast territory and attempted to focus our efforts, we have relied heavily on the way in which the editors of this *Handbook* specified our charge. We were told to write about the following:

- The structural, social, cultural organization of classrooms (for example, groups in classrooms)
- The symbols and rituals of classrooms
- The ways that various classroom groups work together to create a dynamic that is consequential
- The ways that inclusion can be a classroom cultural issue
- The issues of culturally congruent teaching

Drawing on the research summarized by Cazden, Doyle, Erickson, and Feiman-Nemser and by Floden in the previous edition of this *Handbook* (Wittrock, 1986) and on the research reviewed in many similar publications (e.g., Cazden & Mehan, 1989) has sensitized us to the fact that the term *culture* (or *cultures*) is used to refer to quite different orders of phenomena. This disquieting circumstance is evident in the specification of our task. Culture is variously described as a group dynamic that is "consequential" and that involves symbols and rituals, as well as issues of inclusion, that require special attention in order to create conditions called "culturally congruent teaching." That description would present too much weight for one concept to carry, even if the meaning of the term *culture* were not disputed (which it is) among anthropologists when it is being used in what is presumed to be a common fashion!

First, as the opening phrase of our task description indicates, the field widely agrees that every continuing social group develops a culture and a body of social relations that are peculiar and common to its members (Hollingshead, 1949). Hence, without delving into exactly what we mean by culture, we can expect that every classroom will develop its own variant. Fine (1987) refers to these variants as "idiocultures," which result from shared activity in a shared space.

Second, at the opposite pole and despite idiosyncrasies, a particular pattern appears to emerge from the variety of individual forms of classroom life that can fairly be called "the culture of the classroom." This normative form, often referred to

Special thanks to Honorine Nocon and Katherine Brown, to the participants of the LCHC meetings of Winter 1996, and to the students of the Classroom, Culture, and Communication Graduate Seminar, Fall 1996.

as "the recitation script," was evident in the first formal classrooms that emerged in different parts of the ancient world (Lucas, 1972). That form dominates schooling in many parts of the world today (Gallimore & Goldenberg, 1993; Hoetker & Ahlbrand, 1969; Mehan, 1997). According to Tharp (1993),

> Its basic operation is to assign a text for students to learn on their own and then assess the students to see if they learned it. It consists of a series of unrelated teacher questions that require convergent factual answers and student display of (presumably) known information, acquired almost entirely from an assigned textbook. It includes up to 20% "yes/no" questions. Only rarely during recitation are teacher questions responsive to student productions. Only rarely are questions used to assist students to develop more complete or elaborated ideas. (pp. 270–271)

This form of activity, as we will make clear below, has many of the aspects of a ritual, although it is only one of several rituals that are a common part of schooling. This uniformity of classroom life was expressed when the dean of a prestigious college of education remarked that what totally boggled his mind when he went into a tiny, isolated Inuit village in northern Alaska was that the classroom looked just like the many he had seen countless times before in his travels around the lower 48 states.

Our assignment orients us to additional ways in which the term *culture* is applied in discussions of classroom dynamics. Identifying inclusion as an issue for understanding classroom culture reminds us that participants differ from each other in many ways that influence and are influenced by the cultures of their classrooms. Historically, references to inclusion have been associated primarily with the mainstreaming of children with special needs. Those special needs often are defined in terms of either physical or intellectual handicaps or challenges (Putnam, 1993; Speece & Keogh, 1996). For such children, the ways in which the culture of the classroom is modified to enable effective instruction is a central issue. But categories such as "exceptional" and "normal" are not given characteristics of children; they are themselves culturally constructed and are influenced by teachers' prior expectations and preferences. One teacher may not tolerate a child talking out of turn and may deem the child "abnormal," whereas another may accept the same behavior as viable and normal classroom interaction. McDermott and Varenne (1995) and Mehan, Hertweck, and Meihls (1986) among others have shown that classroom cultures routinely include features that mark children as deviant, even in the absence of any visible handicap.

Contemporary discussions of classroom cultures generally contrast the normative classroom cultural configuration, as described by Gallimore (1996), with the group dynamics (cultural configurations) that characterize the other settings in which children and teachers live, particularly what is referred to as "the home" (Corno, 1989; Shultz, Florio, & Erickson, 1982; Volk, 1997). Later, we will return to this and other attempts to characterize classroom cultures with respect to other settings that children and teachers inhabit. For the moment, it is sufficient to suggest that classrooms—even in the most ethnically homogenous population centers—exhibit patterns of contrasting features that distinguish their sociocultural organization from that of other community settings. All children are "at risk"

for exhibiting inappropriate behaviors imported from their home cultures.

The request that we deal with culturally congruent teaching indexes a concern that goes beyond the organization of individual classrooms and beyond a generic contrast between schools and homes. The request orients us to the fact that, in a great many and growing number of cases, teachers and school administrators who implement normative classroom cultures come from one home or community cultural background, whereas students and their families come from another. In these cases, "culture" refers to demographic variations that apply to large populations with long common histories, distinctive languages or dialects, and distinctive ways of life. The prototype that is likely to come to mind when we think about culture and classrooms in this light is a contrast between the teachers and administrators who are middle class, Anglo, monolingual speakers of English and the students who are working class, members of a socially recognized minority group, and speakers of either a different dialect of English or one of many other languages.

At the time of the previous *Handbook,* recognition of the need to address the home-culture-versus-school-culture issue had generated several interesting research projects that sought to design what was termed "culturally congruent teaching." That term referred to efforts to modify the normative forms of classroom cultures so they would incorporate cultural features of the home. The concept was based on the assumption that such efforts would make mastering the school curriculum easier for children. This work responded to the temper and problems of a time when, because of the Civil Rights movement, the need to address social problems that were associated with cultural diversity and economic inequality became a national priority. Although we will return to consider this line of research later, we can mention the classic work of Au and Jordan (1981), Erickson and Mohatt (1982), Heath (1983), and Philips (1983) as exemplary cases. Each of these investigators dealt with what we might refer to (oversimplifying somewhat) as the "two culture" case. In each study, classroom cultures, including the teacher's cultural background, were analyzed, and classroom procedures were deliberately changed to be more congruent with patterns of adult–child interaction that were prevalent in local community cultural practices. Such changes required new roles and responsibilities for both teacher and student, mediated by different participation structures and implemented through different interaction routines. We judge this work to have been successful in demonstrating the utility of paying close attention to the way that classroom cultures can productively interarticulate with a contrasting home culture to promote academic achievement.

What makes the current historical moment so interesting and difficult is that diversity enters the process of North American education in a way that it did not for the earlier *Handbook* writers. Current discussions of "culturally congruent teaching" can no longer restrict themselves to cases where children come predominantly from a single cultural group and the teacher comes from another. Rather, teachers are more routinely facing three, five, and seven culturally distinct demographic groups and languages in their classrooms. Efforts to include children who vary in a number of physical, psychological, and social ways increase the complexity of classroom cultures and require that we create effective means to deal with the resulting diversity.

Our assignment to consider inclusion and culturally congruent teaching in relation to the question of classroom cultures sets the stage for the sections to follow. We begin by considering more carefully the concepts of "classroom" and "culture," both individually and in relation to each other, and closely allied concepts of "context" and "activity." We argue that classroom cultures are most effectively studied in terms of the activities that constitute them and in relation to the institutional contexts that they, in turn, constitute. After reviewing research on classroom versus home culture issues, we turn to research on modifying classroom cultures to take account of the home–school disjunction, particularly in cases where the cultural backgrounds of the school personnel and the home–community participants are different. We then arrive at the multicultural case and discover that, in important senses, every classroom is multicultural. The challenge is to make this knowledge useful in the organization of teaching and learning. Finally, we discuss the relevance that the activity-centered approach may have for the inclusion of students identified as learning disabled and for the increasing use of computer-assisted instruction.

One note of caution: whether one is speaking of the generic home–school contrast or cases in which different "home cultures" of children and teachers are the focus of concern, we are mistaken to think about classrooms and communities as "pure" types, disjoint from each other. This point was made by Akinasso (1991), who suggested that one should view the home, the classroom, and the social communities that children participate in as a continuum where oral (speaking) and literate (written) traditions blend and reinforce each other. Akinasso was writing primarily in terms of West African conditions, but the same applies in the United States. Many recent studies suggest that a complex web of discontinuities and continuities characterize the relationship between classrooms, communities, and homes (Morine-Dershimer, 1985). McDermott and Varenne (1995) express this complicity by arguing that home and school are two points within a wider system for analyzing differences among people along race and class lines.

Basic Issues of Definition and Theorizing

Roy D'Andrade (1984) argued that competing definitions of terms like *culture* are not, technically speaking, definitions (e.g., "a paraphrase that maintains the truth or falsity of statements in a theory when substituted for the word defined" [pp. 114–115]). Rather, they are more like theories in that they seek to make substantive propositions about an aspect of the world to which they refer. The definitions one offers depend on what kinds of propositions about what aspects of the world one is interested in. In this chapter, we are interested in (a) what definitions and theories can be used to understand how the dynamics of group life in classrooms are related to the consequences of the instructional interactions that occur there and (b) how to deal with the complexities that result from the presence of socially and culturally diverse participants in such settings. Most obviously, we need to agree on what we mean by *classrooms*

and what we mean by *culture(s)*, and we need to explore the implications of their conjunction in the phrase, "classroom cultures."

Classrooms

Because our focus is on processes that occur in places called classrooms, to start the definitional exercise by examining what we mean by this term seems best. *The New Lexicon Webster's Dictionary* (1988) makes the matter seem clear-cut; a classroom is "a room in a school or college in which classes are taught." These words are fair enough, but not very informative. And how does this dictionary define a class? "A group of students taught together according to standing, subject, etc." When we put these two definitions together, we get an explanation that classrooms are places in schools where deliberate instruction is arranged for students who are grouped by age and other criteria.

The restriction of classrooms to settings that are a part of social institutions called schools may prove somewhat constraining when we begin to examine ways in which classrooms might be modified to make their cultural constitution more supportive of teaching and learning, but the more restricted commonsense notion of classroom is a good starting place. Matters are more complicated with respect to culture.

Culture

Two decades ago, Raymond Williams (1976) commented that "Culture is one of the two or three most complicated words in the English language" (p. 76). Among other resources, he could refer to the classic monograph, *Culture: A Critical Review of Concepts and Definitions,* by Alfred Kroeber and Clyde Kluckhohn (1952/1963) that offered more than 250 different definitions of culture.

In its most general sense, the term *culture* is used to refer to the socially inherited body of past human accomplishments that serves as the resource for the current life of a social group, ordinarily thought of as the inhabitants of a country or region (D'Andrade, 1996). The classic expression of this view was provided by E. B. Tylor in one of anthropology's founding documents. In Tylor's view (1871/1903, p. 1), culture is ". . . that complex whole which includes knowledge, belief, art, morals, law, custom, and any other capabilities and habits acquired by man as a member of society."

Following their encyclopedic review of differing ideas about culture, Kroeber and Kluckhohn (1952/1963, p. 181) offered their own omnibus definition, which includes features that we will find useful in later discussions:

Culture consists of patterns, explicit and implicit, of and for behavior acquired and transmitted by symbols, constituting the distinctive achievements of human groups, including their embodiment in artifacts; the essential core of culture consists of traditional (i.e., historically derived and selected) ideas and especially their attached values; cultural systems may on the one hand be considered as products of action, on the other as conditioning elements of further action.

Finally, Dahlke (1958), who was explicitly concerned about culture with respect to classrooms, writes that culture has three aspects:

> A culture is instrumental: from it people select the techniques of doing things, the means to reach an objective. A culture is regulative: the actions of persons and the use of the instruments are subject to rules and regulations, the dos and don'ts of living. They specify what should be done or must be done. A culture is directive: from it individuals derive their ultimate as well as immediate values, their interpretation of life, the goals for which they strive. Cultural behavior is action based upon a complex of evaluations, i.e., as to what is good or bad, proper or improper, efficient or inefficient, adequate or inadequate, beautiful or trivial, valuable or valueless, free or compulsory. Cultural reality is thus a value reality. (p. 5)

Culture as a social inheritance, as should be clear even from this limited sample, encompasses a broad range of phenomena. Of necessity, scholars draw selectively on this range in their discussions, inviting disagreement and confusion.

KULTUR AND CULTURES, MORE OR LESS

One of the major areas of confusion concerning discussions of culture, whether in classrooms or in society as a whole, centers around a cluster of dichotomies that produce two opposed interpretations of the "culture-as-inherited-goods" conception. These different interpretive frames have served as the justifications for different ways of thinking about classroom cultures. Despite the simplifications entailed by any general dichotomy, we will follow Stocking (1966) and will refer to these contrasting views as the "anthropological" and the "humanist-evolutionary" approaches (see also Erickson, 1986; Goodenough, 1981; and Harris, 1968, for extensive accounts of this history from different perspectives within anthropology).

Table 44.1 contains Stocking's (1966) series of contrasts between these two views. On the left-hand side of the table is the humanist-evolutionary view. As interpreted within this tradition, culture is something that people have more or less of. As Stocking (1966, p. 870) puts it, culture was associated with the "progressive accumulation of the characteristic manifestations of creativity: art, science, knowledge, refinement, things that freed man from control by nature, by environment, by tradition, by instinct, or by custom." This view implies some absolute criteria for determining "which way is up." To the Northern Europeans, whose technological successes had provided them the power to dominate those people whom their anthropologists studied, their own societies provided the measure against which cultural progress was measured. According to this view, societies do not have discrete cultures. Rather, they possess, to lesser or greater extent, the general culture created by humankind up to the present time. As a consequence, societies can be compared quantitatively to assess their rank on the ladder of cultural progress. Following Goodenough (1981), we refer to this notion of culture as Kultur, because it is so well embodied in German historical theorizing of the 19th century.

Important to the humanist-evolutionary point of view, creating and using culture is a conscious process, which is something that people set out to do. Culture is deliberately created using the highest of human characteristics: reason. Consequently, the fact that one group of people has a higher level of culture than

another indicates that those people also use a higher (more powerful) level of intellect. The fact that cultural products are created through conscious action implies that those products are there for anyone to see; they are objective consequences of the process of human creativity. They can be studied by standard quantitative and experimental methods.

The final characteristic attributed to the humanist-evolutionary view by Stocking (1966) may appear out of place: the claim that levels of culture are racially determined. However, as Harris (1968) documents in some detail, in the late 19th century, it was common practice to ascribe differences in Kultural levels to racial differences.

The notion of race occupies a contentious place in contemporary social science that we do not propose to review here (see Hirschfeld, 1997, for a recent discussion). Drawing on experimental evidence, Hirschfeld claims that, in the United States, even 3-year-olds treat race as "not simply a function of outward appearance and that, instead, it represents an essential aspect of a person's identity, it is something that does not change over the course of one's lifetime, and it is something that parents pass on to their children" (p. 193). That is, American children and adults treat race as an essential human feature, whether or not it is one. In the study of educational achievement, 19th-century beliefs that inherited, immutable differences in intellectual potential limit the attainable levels of culture continue to have their champions, especially among psychologists who focus on individual differences (e.g., Herrnstein & Murray, 1994).

In the literature on classroom cultures, the term *ethnicity*, which mixes the notions of race (differences arising from phylogenetic history) with the notion of culture (in which differences arise from historical experience following the origin of any variations in genetic constitution) is most likely to be used (Portes, 1996). For example, Gumilev (1990, p. 171) defines an ethnic group as "a system comprising not only individuals who vary both genetically and functionally, but also the products of their activity over many generations (technique, anthropological terrain, cultural tradition)." Aside from emphasizing the co-evolution of human beings' genetic and cultural characteristics, resorting to the term *ethnicity* does nothing to reduce the belief that racial differences are part of differences in cultural levels.

THE ANTHROPOLOGICAL VIEW

The "anthropological" view, summarized in Table 44.1, can be traced back at least to the writings of Johannes Herder (1966),

Table 44.1. Humanist–Evolutionary vs. Anthropological Views of Culture

Humanist–Evolutionary View	Anthropological View
Culture Varies by Degree	Culture Varies by Quality
Progressive	Homeostatic
Absolute Criteria of Value	Relative Criteria of Value
Singular	Plural
Quantitative Comparisons	Qualitative Comparisons
Culture Used Consciously	Culture Used Unconsciously
Objective	Subjective
Racially Determined	Culturally Determined

Note: Adapted from "Franz Boas and the Culture Concept in Historical Perspective," by G. W. Stocking, Jr., 1966, *American Anthropologist, 68,* pp. 867–882.

whose ideas about culture gained prominence in anthropology through the writings of Franz Boas (1911). Contrary to the humanist–evolutionary view of a single Kultur, which varies in degree, Boas posited the existence of many different cultures, which vary qualitatively from each other. Each culture, he held, is a historically unique configuration of the residue of collective problem-solving activities among a social group in its efforts to survive and prosper within its environment(s). In contrast to the progressivism and certainty about absolute values of the Kultural view, the Boasian cultural view was decidedly relativistic—relative to historically contingent circumstances. From this pluralistic perspective, all human groups are equally cultured. They make sense to their participants, and they have proven successful in perpetuating the group, even if not in circumstances of their choosing.

In line with his emphasis on the qualitative uniqueness of cultures, Boas noted facts contrary to the humanist–evolutionary perspective's emphasis on the uniformities that distinguish higher and lower cultures. Thus, it was possible to find domains of practice in presumably lower, primitive societies that were distinctly higher, according to the progressivist view, than corresponding achievements in the same domain in various European societies. The abstract art of the otherwise "primitive" Kwakiutl of the northwest coast of North America provides a good example of this phenomenon. Qualitative uniqueness was also supported by evidence indicating a society's culture is not homogenous. It varies internally, depending on the particular patterns of life that the group has evolved together. Consequently, levels of development cannot be measured in terms of a general level of cultural or mental achievement. Levels of development have to be specified in terms of the aspect of culture in question as well as of the framework for judging.

Several additional important features of the anthropological view that is summarized by Stocking (1966) are important to keep in mind. First, this view assumes that, although it is learned, a great deal of cultural knowledge is tacitly acquired and not easily accessible to conscious reflection. The anthropological view does not imply that cultural knowledge is rational in any formal sense; rather, it must be adequate to its everyday problem-solving environments. Second, the dominant versions of the anthropological view tend to restrict the domain of culture to the learned ideational and symbolic systems of the social heritage. This view is most closely associated with the work of Ward Goodenough (1994, p. 265), for whom culture consists of "what one needs to know to participate acceptably as a member in a society's affairs."

> Material objects people create are not in and of themselves things they learn. . . . What they learn are the necessary precepts, concepts, recipes, and skill—the things they need to know in order to make things that will meet the standards of their fellows. (p. 50)

From this perspective, in contrast to the humanist–evolutionary perspective, culture is in people's minds—the mental products of the social heritage.

The symbolic systems view of culture has dominated the study of classroom cultures, and we have great sympathy for it. But we will take issue with the tendency of the culture-as-acquired-knowledge view to reduce the role of culture to purely mental doings inside the head or to skills, which are those routinized forms of action that occur automatically and beneath consciousness. A more congenial perspective is offered by Geertz (1973), who balanced a view of culture as subjective knowledge with a view of culture as material practices. In an oft-quoted passage, he wrote that his view of culture begins with the assumption that

> human thought is basically both social and public—that its natural habitat is the house yard, the market place, and the town square. Thinking consists not of "happenings in the head" (though happenings there and elsewhere are necessary for it to occur) but of trafficking in . . . significant symbols—words for the most part but also gestures, drawings, musical sounds, mechanical devices like clocks. (1973, p. 45)

Our task would be simplified greatly if we could report that a consensus has been reached within the field of anthropology regarding the correct way to think about culture so that the application of this concept to classrooms would be straightforward. As even a cursory analysis of discussions in the *Anthropological Newsletter* will quickly reveal, no such consensus exists. Naturally enough, what is true of the field as a whole regarding consensus is true of those anthropologists who specialize in trying to understand the nature of education in general and the processes of teaching and learning that occur in classrooms in particular.

For purposes of this chapter, we will seek to turn these terminological uncertainties-cum-theoretical disagreements into a virtue, because, by our analysis, classrooms are, by their very nature, places where at least some aspects of both the anthropological and humanist–evolutionary approaches are relevant.

The Historical Origins of Western Schooling

The earliest known classrooms appeared in what is now referred to as the Middle East in approximately 3000 B.C. (Bowen, 1972; Lucas, 1972). Their appearance coincides with a veritable explosion in the complexity of life associated with the origins of the first relatively large cities and the new social configurations they produced. Crucial to these changes were (a) improved methods for making tools that enabled the building of canals to control the availability of water, thus, changing the nature of agricultural production; (b) weapons for conquering neighboring people; and (c) writing, which was essential for keeping records of the storage, exchange, and redistribution of goods that the new economic potentials and social structures made necessary. These changes were associated with the emergence of a complex class structure that was dominated by an aristocracy of kings and by priests who headed temples. The first schools arose to train a class of scribes who could serve the administrative and economic needs of newly complex societies. These schools were located in either the palace or the temple, which were, in any event, closely connected. According to Bowen (1972), becoming literate appears not to have been blocked initially by any particular social barriers, but, over time, scribes came to be drawn from the more influential social classes.

Schooling was divided into two basic levels, basic literacy and numeracy, followed by specialization in a branch of the bureaucracy such as religion, law, medicine, the army, or teaching. Pupils were given clay tablet workbooks onto which they copied their lessons. They sat in rows facing a teacher, often assisted by a monitor, ominously referred to as "the man in charge of the whip." The summary of one schoolboy's day, recounted by Lucas (1972) on the basis of a text from about 2500 B.C., has an eerily contemporary flavor:

> He fears being late to school "lest his teacher cane him." His mother prepares a lunch hurriedly. Evidently the young scholar has a bad time of it. He misbehaves and is punished for standing up and talking out of turn. He writes in his tablet, gives a recitation, eats his lunch, prepares a new tablet, writes his lesson upon it, is assigned some oral work, and in the afternoon is given another written assignment. Catastrophe strikes when the teacher severely reprimands the student for careless copywork. (p. 24)

Surveying the characteristics of early education in a number of ancient societies,

Lucas (1972) identifies the following commonalties:

- Formal, differentiated schools first arose when the complexity of culture outstripped the capacity of its society to arrange for its reproduction by informal means.
- Formal instruction was possible only when a society achieved a level of complexity that required role specialization, accompanied by an economic base sufficient to free a class of people from direct involvement in production.
- Formal schooling relied on the invention of writing.
- Formal schooling was confined to a small minority of the population, and the knowledge associated with literacy was accorded high value.
- Basic literacy and numeracy were the gateway to esoteric knowledge that was opaque to the ordinary classes of people.

Without belaboring the point, many of these characteristics of the earliest schools were in full evidence when mass schooling was introduced into industrializing societies in the middle of the 19th century. Lucas, who pursues these parallels in some detail, notes that, in 1910, Woodrow Wilson declared that "we want one class of persons to have a liberal education and we want another class of persons, a very much larger class, to forgo the privilege of a liberal education and fit themselves to perform specific difficult manual tasks" (quoted in Lucas, 1972, p. 42).

From his comparative analysis, Lucas (1972) draws two conclusions that are worth keeping in mind as we survey research on classroom cultures, insofar as one's goal of research on this topic is to assist in the process of improving schooling for the broad masses of the public:

1. Institutionalized education never directly initiates social change.
2. The school inevitably treats students as means to social ends.

CLASSROOMS AND THE KULTURAL PERSPECTIVE

Central to classrooms from the beginning has been a focus on the transmission of certain "basic" skills associated with liter-

acy and numeracy, which serve as the medium for the preservation, elaboration, and control of highly valued knowledge and skills. From these same beginnings, we find evidence that individuals were considered to differ in their access to the requisite skills, differences that have their origins in class privilege on the one hand, and what, in today's parlance, is termed "academic abilities" on the other hand.

Looked at from the Kultural anthropological tradition, classroom cultures can be compared in terms of the quality of the products that they produce. These products are, of course, student knowledge as indexed by grades and test results. They are the visible, objective evidence of the level of the local classroom culture. These products are assumed to be the result of conscious action on the part of participants, both teachers and students. The focus is on the explicit curriculum and its associated norms and values. Through conscious application of rational thinking and self-control, pupils achieve mastery of the cultural corpus.

Put in somewhat different terms, schooling provides the path to enlightenment and the application of reason to human activities. It is not just a socializing institution; it is a civilizing institution. The products of the highest layers of the social order associated with schooling are taken as the criterion against which the quality of the culture of all those "below" is measured by the social system. This perspective underlies the writings of Hirsch (1987), Bloom (1987), and others who urge the need to maintain the canon of Western civilization and to hold all students, regardless of their cultural background, responsible for knowledge of that canon and acceptance of its underlying values. Alternative criteria have difficulty gaining a hearing, which makes multiculturalism an awkward notion to think about approvingly. Rather, culturally different is, more or less by definition, culturally inferior.

THE ANTHROPOLOGICAL VIEW OF CLASSROOM CULTURE

The historical fit of the evolutionary–humanist perspective to classroom cultures might, at first glance, seem to render irrelevant the anthropological perspective with its emphasis on relativism, plurality, and the unconscious nature of culture. But as several decades of work on classrooms cited at the beginning of this article have demonstrated, the anthropological approach to culture has played a central role in research on the dynamics of classroom interactions and their consequences for children's educational achievement.

Ethnographic research on schools has long shown that to describe classroom cultures as if they varied on only a single, quantitative dimension is inadequate. Rather, from at least the early 1930s, research has shown that schools (and classrooms within them) are institutionalized settings with their own qualitatively distinctive cultures. For instance, Waller (1932/1965) described schools as distinct social units set apart by well-defined characteristics:

1. They are composed of a definite population.
2. They have a clearly defined political structure.
3. They are the "nexus of a compact network of social relations."

4. They are "pervaded by a we-feeling."
5. They have a culture definitely their own.

Waller (1932/1965) emphasized that "the" culture of the school is really made up of a number of different subcultures, which are in conflict with each other as a consequence of the contradictions inherent in the institution.[1] Working mostly from secondary sources, Waller details the ways in which school cultures work. He places a strong emphasis on the rituals, folkways, mores, and moral codes that develop within schools. Especially valuable is his awareness that school cultures, although they have a certain exteriority with respect to individual children, do not automatically determine behavior. Behavior is mediated by what Waller calls, following W. I. Thomas (1923), "the definition of the situation."

> When we take an abstracting attitude toward these group products we may think of them as folkways, mores, taboos, collective representations, group attitudes, laws, etc. But all of these things affect the individual only as they are incorporated into the situations of his life. (Waller, 1932/1965, p. 292)

This process of incorporation is not a one-way street; rather, it involves a "dynamic reorganization of the parts of the situation into a pattern" (p. 294). Although this reorganization is effected through the explicit communication of norms and values, a great deal of the process is affected by implicit understandings that constitute the "invisible curriculum" of the classroom.

Paramount in his analysis is the fact that teachers represent the culture of the wider social group, whereas students are "impregnated" with the culture of the local community and with what Waller refers to as the special culture of the young that arises in their peer interactions, which take place in settings where adults are not in control. From this perspective, schools are really multicultural social settings where several different cultures converge (even in cases where the population from which students and teachers come is the same):

> The culture of the school is a curious mélange of the work of young artisans making culture for themselves and old artisans making culture for the young; it is also mingled with such bits of the greater culture [of the society as a whole] as children have been able to appropriate. (Waller, 1932/1965, p. 107)

Waller cautioned that serious conflicts emerge when the teacher, as representative of the larger society and the culture of adults, attempts to impose adult culture on the indigenous culture of the students. Thus, the teacher's responsibility is to facilitate this imposition by offering students "a finely graded and continuously evolving culture, organized into ever more complex configurations, which simultaneously reduce the tension between the generations" (p. 107).[2]

THE HYBRID NATURE OF CLASSROOM CULTURES

Even this brief account should be sufficient to urge on us the relevant and necessary view that classrooms are social settings in which we must consider simultaneously classroom cultures both as processes that vary by degrees—for which we find progressivist criteria of valuation, the contents of which are acquired consciously—and as a mediums or processes that vary qualitatively—where what is valued depends much on local aspects of social inheritance, the contents of which are acquired both explicitly and implicitly.

Despite our view that classroom cultures are most usefully viewed in this double-sided way, in terms of general social evaluation of classroom cultures, an asymmetrical means–end relationship exists between the two sides of the classroom–culture coin. Schools have historically served as the means of social sorting and preservation of the social position of more powerful segments of society. Classrooms that do not produce students who master the Kultur of the society in the classroom will be negatively evaluated, whatever the variety of their internal cultural forms and however well they may function from the perspective of those who participate in them. That is, related to classrooms, Kultur sets the criteria for evaluations of cultures, and diversity is, de facto, reduced to a matter of greater and lesser value. At the same time, we cannot understand how schools function without adopting the anthropological viewpoint and its methodology, which focuses on the internal dynamics of classrooms and the relationships of these dynamics to the social context of the school, the community, and the society as a whole.

Activities

To agree on a proper unit of analysis that allows for comparisons across levels of social aggregation is a key issue for studying classroom cultures as a hybrid of the local and the social–historical levels of analysis. Two distinct academic traditions, one from anthropology and one from psychology, converge on the idea that activities are focal units for the acquisition, use, and reproduction of culture that can serve this purpose.

GOODENOUGH'S "WORKING THEORY OF CULTURE"

In a recent article titled "Toward a Working Theory of Culture," Goodenough (1994) provides a way to meld the different cultural traditions that go into every classroom. Goodenough argues explicitly that culture should not be considered uniform across a society. Rather, culture is rooted in human activities and culture pertains to groups "insofar as they consist of people who engage with one another in the context of those activities" (p. 266). In words that echo Waller's statements about classrooms, Goodenough wrote that

---

[1] Although the earliest known suggestion that activities should be considered the locus of culture came from sociologist Waller (1932/1965), usually, we are taught by cultural anthropologists to analyze the activities of human beings who are living in a certain culture and organize them into cultural patterns. In particular, sociologists and anthropologists who work from an ethnographic tradition have been very useful to understanding classroom life (e.g., Thomas, 1923).

[2] Partially formalized structures of behavior known as "activities" serve as excellent examples of cultural patterns existing in the school. Unfortunately, Waller excluded classrooms from his analysis, focusing instead on clubs, sports, and other extra curricular activities.

the cultural makeup of a society should not be seen as a monolithic entity determining the behavior of its members, but as a mélange of understandings and expectations regarding a variety of activities that serve as guides to their conduct and interpretation. (p. 267)

Activities are the proper unit of analysis for cultures, simple or complex, because, in Goodenough's (1994) words,

People who interact with one another regularly in a given kind of activity need to share sufficient understanding of how to do it and communicate with one another in doing it so that they can work together to their satisfaction. All they need to share, in fact, is whatever will enable them to do that. (p. 266)

He goes on to argue,

There is a different culture of the activity for each set of role performers. These differences form part of the cultural makeup of the group of people who perform the activity, but there is no one culture of that activity for the group as a whole, one that all its members share. (Goodenough, 1994, p. 266)[3]

Both parts of the way in which Goodenough links culture to material practice are important. First, one must create sufficient understanding to get the task accomplished. Second, one must differentiate cultural tool kits, depending on the social roles one plays so that (as Waller argued 30 years earlier) the culture associated with an activity is made up of different subcultures.

Applying this line of reasoning to classroom culture sensitizes one to the fact that children and teachers, by virtue of their varying roles, possess different classroom cultures in important ways. This conclusion seems natural enough given that classrooms are explicitly organized for purposes of having adults organize instruction for children. However, it also implies that what transpires in classrooms is likely to involve a fair amount of misunderstanding and to be closely tied to the contexts of acquisition. Although the failure of school-based knowledge to be used outside of the contexts of acquisition is certainly a widespread and widely decried phenomenon (which goes under the rubric of "lack of transfer" in the educational psychology literature), Goodenough's view does not lead to a radical particularism. As he notes, the features he identifies as cultural imply a quasi-organized patterning of knowledge in networks of interdigitized activities. Hence, one can expect shared characteristics across activities (and hence, groups) within a society, to the extent that activities entail each other in networks that structure social life. However, general transfer is not to be expected. As Goodenough (1994, p. 267) puts it, "What is understood about the conduct of an activity may apply to the conduct of many others, but is unlikely to apply to all."

PSYCHOLOGICAL APPROACHES TO LEARNING-IN-ACTIVITY

Despite his views about culture being learned during face-to-face interaction in activities, Goodenough did not, himself, un-

dertake the task of analyzing how cultural knowledge is acquired. And despite repeated discussions of the issue among anthropologists over the past several decades (see, e.g., exemplary materials in Spindler, 1987, 1997), the process of culture acquisition, which presumably classroom instruction is to ensure, has not been the focus of anthropological research. Rather, anthropologists have, by and large, adopted a disciplinary division of labor according to which (a) psychologists are accorded responsibility for understanding the process of acquiring culture and (b) anthropologists focus on cultural content (note that the background to this division is discussed by Wolcott, 1987).

Until 10 to 15 years ago, the result of this division of labor was more or less a total divorce between anthropological and psychological approaches to thinking about culture and thought, either in societies as a whole or with respect to classrooms and the processes of teaching and learning that go on there. A major reason for this disconnectedness was that dominant psychological theories of knowledge acquisition (learning) assumed that culture is irrelevant to the process of knowledge acquisition. One branch of educational psychology, under the influence of the major learning theories of the day, emphasized learning as a process that is guided by reinforcement through which the proper associations, habits, and skills are formed. Even when this view was supplanted by theories that emphasized the learner as an information processor, the outside-to-inside view of knowledge acquisition remained a dominant view. The role of the teacher from this perspective was to organize classroom lessons in such a manner as to transmit information from the outside to the inside in the most efficient manner.

A second branch of educational psychology, influenced by Piaget's ideas concerning knowledge as a constructive process, viewed the teacher's role as one of arranging the conditions for children to construct knowledge through active engagement with curricular materials but did not view such arrangements or the process of knowledge acquisition as cultural processes (see for example the chapters in section 5 of the previous volume of this Handbook [Wittrock, 1986] for applications of these viewpoints). Despite their differences concerning the role of teacher and child in the educational process, neither psychologists nor anthropologists assigned to culture an explicit role as an intrinsic part in the learning and construction of knowledge and skills. Consequently, educationalists were confronted with a cultural anthropology that lacked a theory of learning and a psychology of learning that lacked a theory of the role of culture and activity in the process!

Since the early 1980s, interest has markedly increased in approaches to education that view learning and teaching as two sides of a single, culturally mediated process that occurs in socially organized activities (Bruner, 1996; Chaiklin & Lave, 1993; Cole, 1996; Forman, Minick, & Stone, 1993; Moll, 1990; Tharp & Gallimore, 1988). Consequently, in the past decade, a new opportunity has arisen to bring together within a single

---

[3] Goodenough's view that cultural knowledge is, at best, partially shared has been widely substantiated by others (Schwartz, 1978; Wallace, 1961; Wolcott, 1991).

academic enterprise the two sides of the culture–learning nexus that is so central to classrooms.

For contemporary psychological approaches that emphasize the role of culture in the development of thought, a major inspiration was Lev Vygotsky (1978, 1987), a Russian scholar who founded what he referred to as a cultural–historical psychology that was based on the premise that human psychological functions develop through participation in culturally organized activities. He formulated what he described as a "general law of cultural development" that serves as the starting point for thinking about the role of classroom cultures in the process of education. According to Vygotsky (1981, p.163),

> Any function in children's cultural development appears twice, or on two planes. First it appears on the social plane and then on the psychological plane. First it appears between people as an interpsychological category and then within the individual child as an intrapsychological category . . . but it goes without saying that internalization transforms the process itself and changes its structure and function. Social relations or relations among people genetically underlie all higher functions and their relationships.

According to psychologists who adopt a focus on activities as units of analysis, "Through participation in cultural activities that require cognitive and communicative functions, children are drawn into the use of these functions in ways that nurture and develop them" (Gallimore & Goldenberg, 1993, p. 315). As a heuristic device for making the study of learning-in-activity the object of empirical research, Gallimore and Goldenberg (1993) suggest five activity–setting variables: (a) the personnel present during an activity, (b) the salient cultural values, (c) the operations and task demands of the activity itself, (d) the scripts for conduct that govern the participants' actions, and (e) the purposes or motives of the activity (p. 316).

Barbara Rogoff (1993), who also draws on Vygotsky, directs our attention to close affinities between his thinking and the educational philosophy developed by John Dewey. For example, in a passage that resonates strongly with Gallimore and Goldenberg's application of Vygotsky's ideas, Dewey (1916, p. 26, cited in Rogoff, 1993, p. 141) wrote:

> The social environment . . . is truly educative in its effects in the degree in which an individual shares or participates in some conjoint activity. By doing his share in the associated activity, the individual appropriates the purpose which actuates it, becomes familiar with its methods and subject matters, acquires needed skill, and is saturated with its emotional spirit.

In her research, Rogoff (1994) applies these ideas to a school organized around her conception of communities of learners. In her discussion of the community-of-learners model, she examines what she refers to as the pendulum swing between adult-run and child-run models of educational activity. She makes clear that the community-of-learners model "is not a balance or 'optimal blend' of the two one-sided approaches, but is instead a distinct instructional model" (p. 214). In the community-of-learners model, children are involved in ways that connect authentically to the object of the activity and that

provide them with genuine motives for their actions instead of ways that require them to carry out preset pieces of an activity. For example, students' decisions on curricular projects are based on students' interests and on the potential effect of such projects on local settings and global circumstances (i.e., research on pollution versus memorization of weather terms). Working together in changing participation structures that are appropriate to the goals at hand, participants (including the adults present) serve as resources to the community of learners. The resulting educational activity is a blend that does not replicate either side of the dichotomy between adult-run and child-run instructional approaches.

Context

Whether individual lessons or the ensemble of lessons that occur over the course of a classroom day, classroom-based activities serve as the center of the process of teaching and learning. Psychologists and anthropologists who are concerned with culture and learning in the classroom are acutely aware that to focus only on such activities without attending to their contemporaries, which are historical and sociocultural-ecological contexts, is insufficient. Whether inspired by cultural anthropologists or psychologists who adhere to activity-based approaches to learning and development, theorists of classroom cultures and learning often evoke the idea of context along with or in place of the concept of activity as a routine part of their attempts to understand classroom processes (see Cole, 1996, for a comparative analysis of different formulations of these general ideas).

CONTEXT AS THAT WHICH SURROUNDS

As noted by Cole, Griffin, and LCHC (1987), context—no less than culture—is an extremely complex and polysemous concept. Dictionary-derived definitions define context as "the whole situation, background, or environment relevant to a particular event," whereas environment is defined as "something that surrounds." The notion of context as "that which surrounds" is often represented as a set of concentric circles representing different "levels of context" (see Figure 44.1).

Roughly speaking, the different rings of context correspond to disciplinary boundaries used by those interested in educational processes. Psychologists, microsociologists, and ethnographers are most likely to focus on the activity or unit in the middle, which is some kind of face-to-face instructional interaction between the teacher and a student (or small group of students). The level of the classroom as a whole is most likely to be investigated by sociologists and anthropologists with interests in the activities at that particular level. The same is true of the community of which the school is a part; when the focus is the activities that take place at this level, sociologists, economists, and political scientists are likely to be conducting the research. To the extent that scholars do not work together across those borders, the dynamics among levels that are intrinsic to the contextual approach to thinking about teaching and learning are obscured. The result is a strong proclivity to see larger contexts as determining smaller, embedded ones, thereby over-

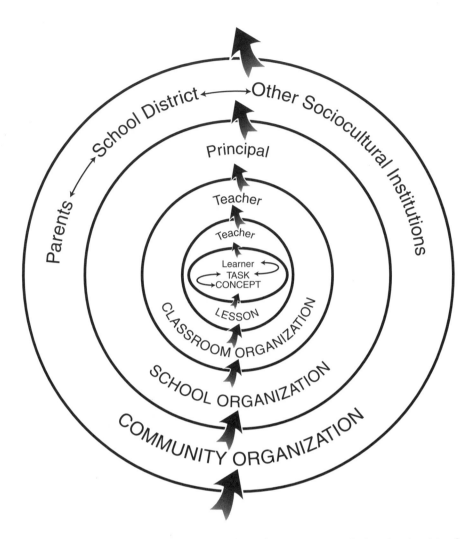

Figure 44.1. An application of the notion of context to thinking about the organization of educational activity. *Source:* From *Contextual Factors in Education* (p. 7), by Cole, Griffin, and the Laboratory of Comparative Human Cognition, 1987, Madison, WI: Center for Education Research.

looking the interactive coconstruction of the different levels of context.

This same concern motivates ecological–psychological approaches to study behavior with respect to classrooms in their social–ecological context, the tradition that has been closely associated with such figures as Roger Barker (1968), Irwin Altman and Joachim F. Wohlwill (1978), and many of their colleagues and students (e.g., Gump, 1978; Schoggen, 1963, 1979). Their use of the term *ecological* orients us to the interdependence of each component in a system. With respect to the concentric circles representation of context in Figure 44.1, a sociocological approach underlines the fact that every activity is embedded in a set of reciprocally linked relationships.

As useful as it has proven itself to be in ecopsychological work and despite the constant warnings of microsociologists, ethnographers, and ecological psychologists, the notion of context as "that which surrounds" is typically used in a linear way, from "top to bottom"—from the macrosociocultural context to

the local, face-to-face context. This tendency is especially strong in discussions of education (the quality of a lesson depends on the quality of the classroom, which depends on the quality of the school, etc.). Used in this fashion, the notion of context is reduced to the notion of an independent variable, which makes it convenient as a tool of analysis within a Kultural framework.

CONTEXT AS THAT WHICH WEAVES TOGETHER

Critics who favor "levels of context" as being actively woven together in interaction, point out that context as that which surrounds implies that environmental events come before, during, and after behavior. Consequently, context cannot function as an independent variable (for representative discussions, see Bateson, 1972; Lave, 1993; McDermott, 1993). This tradition draws on the Latin root of the term *context—contexere*—which refers to the process of weaving together. Ethnography figures large in adherents of this approach, because to observe the process of weaving is necessary; it cannot be discerned from the pattern it produces. From this latter perspective, we are not surprised that good lessons can occur in dingy classrooms and bad schools can occur in what would ordinarily be construed as good neighborhoods (Kozol, 1991; Rutter, Maughan, Mortimore, & Ouston, 1979).[4]

CONTEXT AS ACTIVITY

At present, we are witnessing a coming together of the research traditions associated with those for whom context or activity served as the core organizing category. Engeström (1987, p. 67) provides one model of a synthetic approach when he declares "From an activity theory perspective, contexts are activity systems." This central premise is foundational to Engeström's (1987, 1990) applications of activity theory. Engeström also rejects a choice between context as that which surrounds and that which weaves together. He identifies human activity as a system comprising the subjects (agents, viewpoints, or subjectivities); the tools (skills, equipment, ideas); the object (which provides motive); the desired outcomes (objects transformed into some end); the rules (formal and informal, explicit or tacit ways of working with the object); a community (which shares the object with the subject, even if for different desired outcomes); and a division of labor (how actions are divided up in an activity). (See Figure 44.2.)

All of these aspects of human activity are drawn together around the object—the problem or topic that compels the subject into engagement. The object is only partially understood; it continually evades the subject's efforts to define and transform it into some outcome. We can apply this heuristic device to a hypothetical discussion of a class lesson as an activity. Let us position the teacher as the active subject. The teacher confronts a student or the students as the object of her work to effect a particular change in the children, the object. The tools used might include a lesson plan, chalk, a blackboard, and past experiences. The students engage with the teacher and with one another. As the teacher acts toward the students (object), she or he plus others in the community who share the object (other students, others involved in the lesson plan, potentially including administrators who concerned with what goes on in the classroom or parents who hear about the child's day) are drawn together around the object but hold variable orientations to it. Each party to the work directed toward the object seeks to transform its own conception of the object into a desired outcome or result (for example, normatively, a successful lesson, a quiet student, a good speller, an efficient test taker, and so forth).

Engeström's notion of an activity system is similar in important respects to the ideas of Gallimore and Goldenberg (1993) mentioned above. Engeström's framework provides a set of useful heuristics for analyzing the organization of educational activity and, therefore, the process of change. The activity system

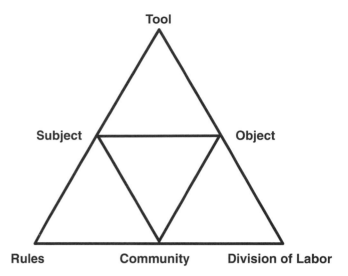

Figure 44.2. Human activity depicted as a system. *Source:* Adapted from *Learning by Expanding: An Activity–Theoretical Approach to Developmental Research* (p. 78), Y. Engeström, 1987, Helsinki: Orinta-Konsultit Oy.

as a unit of analysis also provides for including an expanded social–ecological world indicated in the concentric circles model (Cole, Griffin, & LCHC, 1987).

ACTIVITIES AND PARTICIPATION STRUCTURES

We need to consider one additional conceptual tool that is widely used by those who adopt an activity-centered approach to classroom culture, the concept of *participation structures.* Courtney Cazden (1986, p. 437) defined participation structures as "the rights and obligations of participants with respect to who can say what, when, and to whom." Cazden was drawing on the work of Susan Philips (1983), who identified four participation structures that were characteristic of the classrooms she studied: (a) the teacher interacting with the whole class at once, (b) the teacher and students interacting in small groups, (c) the one-to-one interaction between a teacher and a single student, and (d) the student's having no interaction with the teacher or peers (seat work). In addition to identifying distinctive participation structure types, Philips found that their frequency and duration differed both within classrooms and across grade levels. She makes a point that will reoccur throughout the rest of this chapter: Each participation structure has distinct advantages and disadvantages for providing students with access to curriculum content, thus limiting the extent to which any single arrangement comes to be used to the exclusion of the others.

As one seeks to evaluate the relationship between the activities and participation structures and the people who use the vocabulary of activity systems, it is helpful to note that both

---

[4] As Kenneth Burke (1945, p. 23) remarked several decades ago, consideration of action and context lead easily into paradox because the very notion of substance (sub-stance) must include a referent to the thing's context "since that which supports or underlies a thing would be a part of the thing's context. And a thing's context, being outside or beyond the thing, would be something the thing is not."

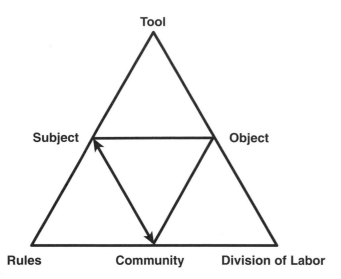

Figure 44.3. The relationship of participation structures to activity showing the absence of an object. *Source:* Adapted from *Learning by Expanding: An Activity-Theoretical Approach to Developmental Research* (p. 78), by Y. Engeström, 1987, Helsinki: Orinta-Konsultit Oy.

Philips (1983) and Doyle (1986) are mute with respect to the object(ive) of the activity that students and teachers engage in when they come together in the classroom. That is, a focus on participation structures is a necessary part of the analysis of any activity, but it undertheorizes the object of the activity. This difference is illustrated by comparing Doyle's "natural segments of classroom life," which include the following:

- Patterns for arranging participants
- Roles and responsibilities for carrying out actions
- Rules of appropriateness
- Props and resources used

In Figure 44.3, we see the relation of participation structures to activity by noting that Doyle includes four features, all of which map onto Engeström's model of activity, but the object is absent. The significance of including the object of activity in one's analysis is illustrated by the way in which differential objects and corresponding motives may occur with the same participant structure. This analysis indicates that activities cannot be reduced to participation, but must address the intentionality of these participants. That is, arranging the physical classroom environment to support variable interaction patterns does not address the distinct and sometimes competing understanding in the purpose of the task (i.e., object) among participants.

The Road Ahead

Using our brief treatment of basic conceptual and definitional issues as a foundation, we now move to consider recent research

on classroom cultures with respect to the teaching and learning processes that go on there. We begin with what might be considered a monocultural view of classrooms, which gives rise to the whole-group recitation as the dominant cultural form. We highlight the similarities in those normative classroom arrangements across a multitude of specific instances, and we examine evidence on both how this kind of classroom culture is constructed and how it is learned by children in the early school years. The monocultural, recitation-based approach to classroom cultures, despite its prevalence, also generates problems and forms of resistance. After viewing the manifest difficulties with the monocultural approach, we turn to its alter ego, which is activity-based educational programs in which the overall culture of the classroom emerges from lessons that are organized in small groups with a more distributed system of power and responsibility among participants.

These additional materials set up the conditions for approaching a main concern in this review, namely, how to conceive of the sources of educational inequalities and how to think productively about teaching in classrooms peopled by increasingly diverse students. We seek to make clear (a) how current evidence argues for full recognition of the multicultural nature of all classrooms, (b) the need for teaching strategies that use well-integrated sets of appropriately organized activities, and (c) what the policies are that break down barriers between schools and local communities.

The **Culture of the Classroom**

As we noted above, research has shown that all classrooms are heterogeneous with respect to the participation and activity structures that constitute the school day and the objectives of instruction that are implemented with children according to many criteria. This variability in participation structures and activities is made explicit in Doyle's (1986) excellent review of classroom activities in the previous edition of this *Handbook*. Summarizing his own work as well as that of Gump (1974, 1975), Silverstein (1979), and others, Doyle views classroom organization as an organized system of participant structure and activities. He notes that although all classrooms are characterized by particular distributions of segments defined in these terms, even a classroom that might be characterized a la Philips as "teacher acting with the whole class at once" does not use this participation structure 100% of the time. Rather, although certain kinds of segments may dominate daily classroom life, all classrooms are organized into classrooms segments. For instance, Doyle summarizes research conducted across two decades that consistently categorized classroom organization into three dominate segments: approximately 65% seat work, 35% whole-class presentation or recitation, and 15% transitions and other housekeeping events (Adams & Biddle, 1970; Gump, 1967, 1982; Sanford & Evertson, 1981, quoted in Doyle, 1986, p. 398). That is, individual seat work plus recitation accounts for the overwhelming time spent in a significant number of classrooms.[5]

Different schools and classrooms are characterized by differ-

---

[5] These activity structures sum to more than 100% because, at times, seatwork and whole-class instruction overlap.

ences in the number of segments identified (from 11 to more than 50), depending on researchers' definitions. So, for example, Berliner (1983) identified 11 such segments in K–6 classrooms: reading circle, seat work, one-way presentation, two-way presentation, mediated presentation, silent reading, construction, games, play, transitions, and housekeeping. Yinger (1977, 1979) moved outside the classroom to include a range of educational events that members of a classroom might encounter. He reports 53 activities including book reports, library, reading group, reading aloud, silent reading, math games, math units, creative writing, newspaper, spelling bee, weekly reader, science unit, art in room, assembly, cooking, field trips, and the like. Consequently, in discussing *the* culture of the classroom, we must keep in mind that local cultures are woven together from variable numbers of local activities and their constituent participation structures.

The Canonical Pattern: The Case Study of Westhaven

Although the precise number and structure of activities differ somewhat from study to study, almost all American elementary school classrooms are dominated by the cultural pattern identified with the recitation model, which Philips refers to as the participation structure in which the teacher acts with the whole class at once.

An excellent example of the overall process that creates this dominant pattern is provided by Norris Brock Johnson's (1985) study of a school he calls Westhaven. Johnson's study is unusual in the concrete detail with which he reveals the interconnections among different levels of context that constitute classrooms. He pays close attention to the architecture of the school and the ideology of the local community. His study provides an unusually full picture that illustrates the emergence of the dominant pattern over the course of the age-graded curriculum from kindergarten to sixth grade. At the same time, he places the developmental pattern in its broader institutional, community, and ideological context.

Johnson (1985, p. 15) clearly states the basic contextual–ecological perspective that activity-centered approaches are a part of the following:

> The school buildings children are required to frequent and the special areas with which and in which they interact are much more than passive wrappings for classroom life. The buildings, spaces, and associated artifacts that make up public school environments of traditional design (Gump & Good, 1976) physically manifest and replicate core themes in American society and culture. Sociocultural information is presented to children in public school both consciously and unconsciously through physical and spatial school environments as well as through teachers in classrooms.

This starting point makes it clear that the relationship between people and the environments they construct is reciprocal (Sarason, 1971, 1996). Buildings and architectural spaces are products of human social and cultural activity that simultaneously shape the processes that produce them. Johnson (1985) describes how the physical arrangement of classrooms and school buildings not only facilitates explicit practical functions (e.g., the separation between classroom areas and playground

areas) but also reveals the implicit assumptions of the participants (e.g., that schoolwork and play do not mix). He goes beyond this general level of analysis to show that deep, unstated assumptions pervade the physical construction of the school and the activities that occur there. For example, although it is generally believed that play and work cannot be appropriately mixed for sixth graders, the same is not true for kindergartners. When viewed through a contextual–ecological lens, we can see how assumptions about age-related developmental differences are built into the overall architecture of the school as well as the physical properties of each classroom and the way that activities are organized there (see Figures 44.4–44.6).

At Westhaven Elementary School, approximately 30 students are assigned to each classroom. In the earlier grades, the children are small and their furniture is small. In the older grades, the same number of children are present in a classroom, but because their desks are larger to accommodate their growing bodies, they are relatively more crowded. Mobility is restricted according to age-grade level. In the preschool classroom, children sit at desks pushed together or at a large table. The classroom contains a set of toy stoves, a toy kitchen, a large rug, and ample space for storing books and toys. Johnson (1985, p. 33) writes that these arrangements orient children toward behaviors and types of interaction that reinforce classroom norms and values of cooperation and interdependence.

> The free play, mobility, and comparatively unstructured activities associated with this grade are congruent with the physical and spatial characteristics of the classroom. Throughout the school year, preschool children are conditioned to adhere to predominant classroom cultural and social themes through their interactions with specific furniture shapes and furniture social arrangements.

These convergences extend, of course, to the social relations that characterize the preschool classroom. The relations are designed to initiate children into the culture of classroom life. In this sense, the preschool classroom (as its name implies) is deliberately designed to be transitional. The children learn to accept the authority of the teacher, but this authority is exercised in a parentlike way that Johnson refers to as "in locus parentis behaviors," characterized by nurturing and accommodation. (He notes that all teachers in the lower grades are women; the only men are in the upper-grade classrooms). A great many of the activities that occur in this preschool classroom focus on routines of learning, self-maintenance and control, and the ability to follow the sequences of activities in a timely and orderly manner.

As Johnson traces the spatial arrangements and activities to higher and higher grades, a regular, converging change is seen in the physical layout of the room, the forms of activity that occur within the room, and the relationship of the room to both the building it is in and the school campus as a whole. In kindergarten, the toy stoves and sink are gone. Children still sit together at tables in groups, but the tables are separated to form five distinctive groupings. By second grade, the rug area has disappeared, and by fifth grade, students are no longer grouped at tables but sit in their own chairs, bolted to the floor in neat rows, with all desks facing the front of the classroom where the teacher sits at a desk facing them. Now no play is sanctioned

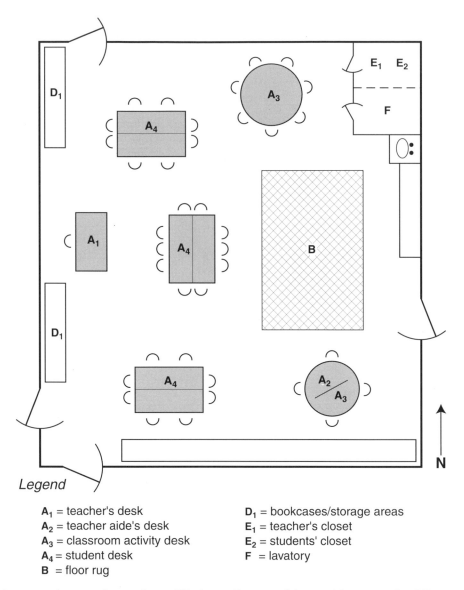

Legend

A₁ = teacher's desk   D₁ = bookcases/storage areas
A₂ = teacher aide's desk   E₁ = teacher's closet
A₃ = classroom activity desk E₂ = students' closet
A₄ = student desk   F = lavatory
B = floor rug

Figure 44.4. A kindergarten classroom layout. *Source: Westhaven: Classroom Culture and Society in a Rural Elementary School* (p. 58), by N. Johnson, 1985, Chapel Hill, NC: University of North Carolina Press.

in the classroom; play occurs out on the playground. The range of classroom activities is greatly reduced and the recitation script is fully implemented as the normative cultural order of the classroom.

The blend of functionality and value expressed at the classroom level is also illustrated in the physical arrangement of the school building. That is, the building layout and equipment are points of reference for action. They become elements in action and organize the normative and functional order. (See Figure 44.7.)

The sociocultural themes of separation and specialization of domestic tasks are represented in the architectural forms associated with rank and stratification. For example, the elementary school building is organized for dividing labor into specialized tasks. Learning areas are separated and isolated from the office and support areas (lunchroom, supply rooms, maintenance,

and so on). The administration area is located strategically near the school's main entrance so personnel can monitor behavior and can restrict access of parents or other visitors. This order is illustrated by the prominent posting at the front of the building that instructs all visitors to sign in at the main office.

These modes of surveillance that are represented in the architectural organization of the school grounds are consistent with larger societal trends. For example, Foucault (1979) observed that the traditional school classroom's physical arrangement—students in rows facing forward and the teacher on a raised platform at the front of the room, enabling the teacher to maintain surveillance of students—was developed in the same time period (roughly 1820–1840) as the development of prison architecture that enabled surveillance of all inmates from a central observation tower (the metaphorical Panopticon). The resemblance of schools and prisons does not escape notice. It is evi-

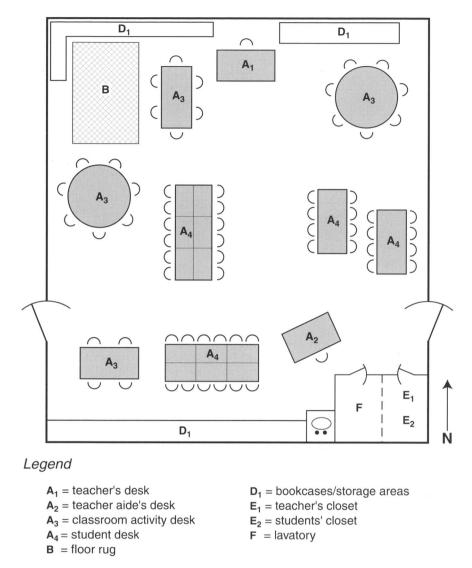

Legend

A₁ = teacher's desk
A₂ = teacher aide's desk
A₃ = classroom activity desk
A₄ = student desk
B = floor rug

D₁ = bookcases/storage areas
E₁ = teacher's closet
E₂ = students' closet
F = lavatory

Figure 44.5. A first-grade classroom layout. *Source: Westhaven: Classroom Culture and Society in a Rural Elementary School* (p. 95), by N. Johnson, 1985, Chapel Hill, NC: University of North Carolina Press.

dent in students' complaints that school is like a jail and that they are treated like criminals, as well as in teachers' comments that they feel "locked in" (Johnson, 1985, p. 243).

The segregation of the students is purposeful and deliberate. Johnson focuses great attention on the distinction between elementary, middle, and secondary school in regard to the differential rank, status, and prestige. A student's passage through the elementary building to the middle school mobile trailers to the high school building involves crossing several sociocultural boundaries. (See Figure 44.8.) Segregation of the children is strictly enforced; for example, carrying messages back and forth requires special passes.

Johnson (1985) reports that becoming a student is a process of cultural conditioning in which children are pressed to adopt the way of life of the classroom (the classroom culture) as their own. For instance, many features found in the Westhaven preschool were associated with modifying the values and behaviors

that children bring to school. "The social system of classroom expects norms for behavior not merely to be obeyed by children but to be internalized by them as well" (Johnson, 1985, p. 51). A distinction is made between those children who have internalized customary classroom norms (for example, good students) and those who have not (for example, problem students). To some degree, the ability to adhere to norms of decorum is also used as the basis for academic sorting.

At Westhaven, the sorting of children within age groups happens early. Preschool students are ranked, divided, and then placed in different kindergarten rooms. The schooling of children ranked into high and low groups occurs in different classroom spaces that are designated as high and low classrooms. The spatial separation between the ranked subgroups is important and makes the status and rank of each more distinct. Johnson (1985) noted that "as the grade level increases, high and low sessions between grade levels grow more similar than high

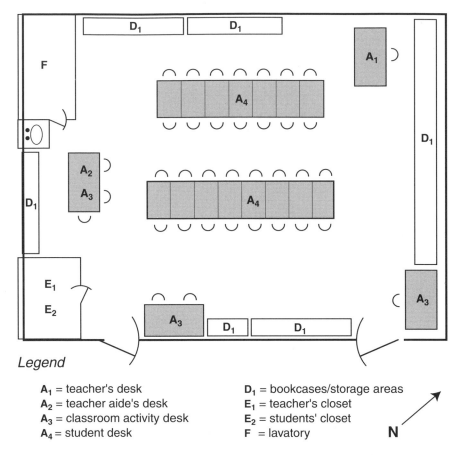

Legend

A₁ = teacher's desk
A₂ = teacher aide's desk
A₃ = classroom activity desk
A₄ = student desk

D₁ = bookcases/storage areas
E₁ = teacher's closet
E₂ = students' closet
F = lavatory

N

Figure 44.6. A fourth-grade classroom layout, typical of middle and upper elementary grades. *Source: Westhaven: Classroom Culture and Society in a Rural Elementary School* (p. 185), by N. Johnson, 1985, Chapel Hill, NC: University of North Carolina Press.

and low sessions within each grade level" (p. 243). Low-group instruction introduces more public ridicule and monitoring of students by the teacher but less literacy instruction than in the high sessions. As Mehan and his colleagues have shown, this kind of tracking is almost impossible to undo without explicit and deliberate institutional efforts (Mehan, Villanueva, Hubbard, & Lintz, 1996).

Johnson documents differential treatment according to gender throughout the children's schooling experience. These patterned, gendered roles apply to both students and teachers. The association with a motherlike figure in the preschool is consistent with the themes of nurturing and tolerance encouraged in the early grades. However, as expectations for children change (to perform academic tasks and produce products), so too do the desirable attributes of the teacher. In the upper grades, male teachers are associated with more instrumental, task-oriented activities. Different bodies of knowledge and subject areas are associated with males (e.g., wood shop) and females (e.g., art and music). In addition, classroom bias regarding females was strongly expressed in the upper grades. For example, girls were routinely delegated to carry out classroom housekeeping chores. Johnson noted a ". . . harem-like quality to the classroom as the male teacher crowded out younger males (students) and was surrounded by prepubescent females" (p. 242).

Johnson's analysis of Westhaven richly supports the ecologi-

cal view that the physical environment is a set of "symbols representing ideas and practices in the social realm" (Rappaport, 1976, quoted in Johnson, 1985, p. 15) that store social and cultural information. They make concrete the dominant sociocultural themes, make visible the conceptual order of the sociocultural system, and serve as "material manifestations of metaphysical ideas" (Leach, 1976, p. 36).

Learning the Culture of the Classroom

The foregoing should make clear that the average classroom is likely to present real challenges to children encountering it for the first time. Several analyses of children participating in elementary school classrooms support this basic expectation. The following examples illustrate how a single participation structure (in this case the structure of "one teacher to whole classroom") take different forms depending on the object of the lesson.

LEARNING THE RECITATION SCRIPT

Mehan (1979) studied a mixed, first-through-third-grade classroom in San Diego, California. He focused on a discourse pattern referred to as an initiate-respond-evaluate (I-R-E) sequence. This pattern embodies the basic recitation script in

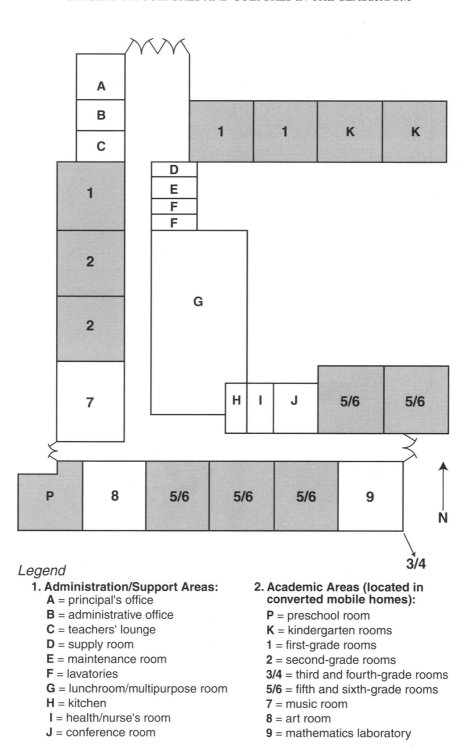

Legend

1. Administration/Support Areas:
  A = principal's office
  B = administrative office
  C = teachers' lounge
  D = supply room
  E = maintenance room
  F = lavatories
  G = lunchroom/multipurpose room
  H = kitchen
  I = health/nurse's room
  J = conference room

2. Academic Areas (located in converted mobile homes):
  P = preschool room
  K = kindergarten rooms
  1 = first-grade rooms
  2 = second-grade rooms
  3/4 = third and fourth-grade rooms
  5/6 = fifth and sixth-grade rooms
  7 = music room
  8 = art room
  9 = mathematics laboratory

Figure 44.7. The Westhaven Elementary School building layout. *Source: Westhaven: Classroom Culture and Society in a Rural Elementary School* (p. 23), by N. Johnson, 1985, Chapel Hill, NC: University of North Carolina Press.

which the teacher initiates the interaction, the students supply a response, and the teacher evaluates this response. For example,

Teacher: What does this word say?
Beth: One.
Teacher: Very good.

In line with the idea that patterns of discourse are socioculturally organized so classroom cultures can be learned, Mehan (1979) reports that, over the course of the school year, these kinds of interaction sequences run more and more smoothly; students learned when was appropriate for them to talk and what was appropriate for them to say. For example, at the start

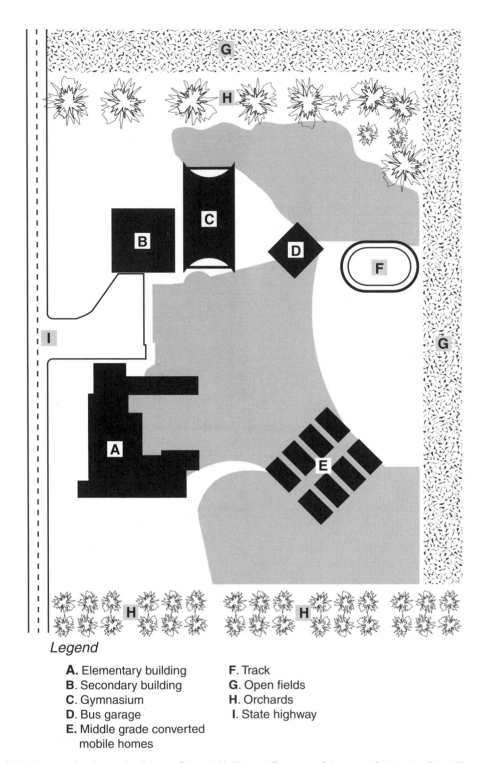

Figure 44.8. The Westhaven school complex layout. *Source: Westhaven: Classroom Culture and Society in a Rural Elementary School* (p. 14), by N. Johnson, 1985, Chapel Hill, NC: University of North Carolina Press.

of the school year, when students offered information, it was appropriate to the ongoing interactions and was responded to by the teacher and other students only 30% of the time. By the middle of the year, students were making appropriate contributions that were followed up on 80% of the time. Students not only contributed more appropriately, but also contributed more actively. In September, only 10% of the instructional sequences that Mehan observed were initiated by students. By January, students were initiating more than 30% of the sequences, manifesting their knowledge of and participation in the normative cultural order of classroom lessons. In this simple form, much of the teaching of the I-R-E discourse pattern happens implicitly because it is modeled within the interaction.

TAKING ATTENDANCE IN BRITISH FIRST SCHOOLS

Mary Willes (1983) documented the work required of children and teacher in learning a particular version of the I-R-E sequence. She conducted her study in British first schools during the earliest months of children's participation in formal schooling. Because the children are so unfamiliar with the requirements of life in classrooms, a good deal of rather explicit culture teaching is directly observable. For example, in the classroom she observed, the teacher made an explicit routine of calling the register. She noted that many teachers simply mark children present when they arrive, but in this classroom, the teacher said that registration was a requirement the children would meet frequently in the future, so it was worth taking up lesson time for. Willes describes one session in which the teacher assembled the children and reminded them of what was to happen and what they were to do: "Teacher: Now, are you ready to answer to your names? (murmur of assent). Yes. Good. And we only answer to our own names, don't we? We don't say 'yes' to anybody else's" (Willes, 1983, p. 69).

With these very young, novice, school-goers, formulation of the rules was insufficient. The children had to learn to behave appropriately. A few minutes after giving the instructions, a young boy responded "yes" when the teacher called the name of a girl named Catherine. The teacher responded by jokingly suggesting to the little boy who answered to Catherine that she should call him Catherine for the rest of the day. Willes comments, "The teacher's response was good humored, but it left nobody in doubt that a mistake has been made, and that it was regarded as foolish" (p. 70).

FIRST CIRCLE IN A U.S. SCHOOL

In kindergarten and the early elementary school grades, a common practice is for teachers and children to begin the school day by gathering as a group in a special part of the classroom that is designed for informal interaction (Bremme & Erickson, 1977; Dorr-Bremme, 1990; Michaels, 1981). In the classroom studied by Bremme and his colleagues, this activity was referred to as "first circle." During first circle, a group of 25 or so children engage in a variety of tasks: "They organize for activities to go on later that morning, fill in a calendar, and determine who is absent; they share personal experiences and engage in brief teaching–learning experiences" (Bremme & Erickson, 1977, p. 153). Dorr-Bremme (1990) has noted that the conduct of first circle seems a simple matter, something that the teacher and children just do. But close analysis of videotaped sessions of first circle over the course of 2 years revealed that it was composed of seven distinctive kinds of activities, each with its own internal structure and norms of appropriate behavior. (See Table 44.2.)

Two additional kinds of events were also observed: "time out," when someone from outside the classroom came to talk to the teacher and students looked on while murmuring quietly among themselves, and "breakdowns," when none of the con-

stituent events of first circle was in evidence and order was reestablished through negotiation between children and teacher. Looking closely at the patterning of interactions among teachers and children during each potential first circle segment revealed that each was characterized by certain rules that constrained the meaning and appropriateness of participants' behaviors. The hidden complexity in the simple arrangement is illustrated here:

1. Teacher: It should be a good day today, as a
2. matter of fact.
3. Lisa: It's cold out.
4. Teacher: It's cold out so Lisa ⌈wants to keep
5. Wannetta: ⌊Me and
6. Teacher: Lisa wants to keep her jacket on.
7. Wannetta: Me and Jimmy went ⌈over to, me and
8. Teacher: ⌊Ah, ah, ah! Wait a
9. minute. Wa⌈it a minute!
10. Richard: ⌊Yeah, wait a minute!

During segment-types 1–6 (see Table 44.2), the children sit facing the teacher in a semicircle, and the teacher invariably initiates the topics for discussion. The appropriateness of student responses depends on which segment is in effect. During segment 7, children initiate topics by making "bids" for a turn to speak, either by calling out or raising their hand. Children orient toward the speaker, not the teacher. In contrast with segments 1–6, during segments 7–9 children never mention school topics, and what the teacher says supports and reinforces the student's topic.

Bremme and Erickson (1977) note that when they first started their research, they were aware of neither the segments of first circle nor the patterning of behavior that characterized each segment. They learned about the appropriate cultural patterns through detailed observations, which they verified with the teacher. If these adults needed time to learn the appropriate cultural order, so did the children. At the beginning of the school year, the teacher discussed first circle routines with the children. But the children also learned through experience by participating in the activity. Evidence for the processes by which learning occurred came from cases where the children behaved inappropriately (from the perspective of the local cul-

Table 44.2. Potential Segments of First Circle

1. Greeting and noticing (about the weather, about clothing, etc.)
2. Reviewing morning activities, in particular, "work time" (which follows first circle and during which instruction takes place in small groups)
3. Distributing students to work-time activities
4. Doing the calendar (which allows the teacher to involve individual children in filling in the date and to engage all children in orienting to units of time, etc.)
5. Taking attendance (which provides multiple opportunities to count and to scan the group for missing members, etc.)
6. Teaching specific matters relevant to morning activities (e.g., how to paste, being measured by a visiting nurse, etc.)
7. Sharing personal things (e.g., recounting personal events that occurred outside the classroom such as a birthday party or an unusual trip)

Note: Adapted from "Contextualization Cues in the Classroom: Discourse Regulation and Social Control Functions," by D. W. Dorr-Bremme, 1990, *Language in Society, 19,* 379–492.

tural norms) because their breaches called forth corrections from the teacher.

To understand how children came to learn the behaviors appropriate to the different segments of first circle, the researchers noted that the teacher engaged in various behaviors that marked the end of one segment and the beginning of another. Following the work of Gumperz (1982), they referred to these behaviors as "contextualization cues" or "context markers." The most obvious such cues were formulations, which are more or less explicit statements about what was currently supposed to be happening in first circle. "Let's see who is not here today" is a cue that attendance is now the relevant context. Paralinguistic cues that mark a shift in context (or an effort to maintain an ongoing context), such as increases or decreases in the rate or loudness of the teacher's speech and the use of framing words (such as "All right" or "OK") followed by a brief pause, were recurrent markers that a new context was about to occur. Nonlinguistic cues, such as where the teacher was looking or how she oriented her body with respect to the group, also played the role of contextualization cues.

The importance of contextualization cues for creating and maintaining the normative classroom culture is highlighted by the fact that when such cues were present, the relevant context was always established or maintained. But when the teacher failed to provide contextualization cues, the cultural order came unglued or, in the researchers' terms, was "unestablished." Then the teacher and children engaged in somewhat chaotic interactions until an appropriate segment of first circle was reestablished.

An important fact about the processes observed by Bremme and his colleagues is that contextualization cues appeared to be deployed and responded to without ever being the explicit topic of conversation. This finding highlights a central characteristic of the anthropological approach to culture in general, including classroom cultures: Although some cultural knowledge is acquired through explicit instruction, a great deal is acquired implicitly and often occurs outside of participants' conscious awareness. Whether cultural knowledge is conscious or not, the data are clear: Children learn to behave in terms of their local classroom cultures.

Difficulties Engendered by the Dominant Patterns

Despite its dominance, the widespread and persistent treatment of the recitation script in classrooms is associated with well-recognized problems. We will take up two prominent problematic areas: tracking and resistance.

Differential Instruction (Tracking) in Classrooms and Schools

Numerous studies have demonstrated a pattern, which has been shown to vary with ethnicity and class, of differential instruction within classrooms according to ability level (Cazden &

Mehan, 1989; Eder, 1983; Rist, 1970). Others have examined differences across classrooms (Henry, 1963; McDermott, 1993; Mehan, Hertweck, & Meihls, 1986; Oakes, 1985) and between entire schools and school districts (Anyon, 1980; Oakes, Gamoran, & Page, 1992).[6]

Focusing on within-classroom practices, many researchers have recorded systematic instructional differences during teacher and student interactions in the participation structure that is often referred to as "small group reading" (Allington, 1980; J. Collins, 1986; Eder, 1981; McDermott, Godspodinoff, & Aron, 1978). As a means of providing appropriate and necessary instruction to children of variable reading abilities, reading groups have the advantage of supporting more intimate discussions between children and teachers than is afforded by a whole-group approach. However, they can also be used as a means of providing systematically different kinds of educational activity, despite a superficially similar participation structure.

For instance, Eder's (1981) analysis of the teacher–student interactions across the groups revealed different objectives of the instruction. Participants in the high reading group were engaged in attempting to comprehend the text, whereas the instruction for those in the low reading group was primarily concerned with the objective of decoding text. These instructional differences were reinforced by the teachers' presumptions concerning students' content knowledge. That is, teachers assumed children in the high group had read the entire text before their participation in reading group. Therefore, the teacher discussed the main themes of the text with the children. The open discussion format provided opportunities for children to apply the story's content to their own lives.

When the same teacher interacted with the children assigned to the low reading group, she assumed that the children had not read the text and, therefore, the task for the reading group was "getting through" the story. Each child was directed to read a designated portion of the text aloud (round-robin). This approach resulted in children tuning out until their turn to read. As students struggled to read aloud, others lost patience, and the teacher interrupted the flow of the story to help the child sound out the word in an effort to move the action along. These children did not gain experience understanding text and, in turn, required more help, which resulted in more interruptions. These factors work to ensure that the low group children remain the low group children.

Differential treatment also occurs across classrooms within a single school according to the type of course, for example, advanced, regular, remedial. In addition to gaining differential access to curriculum and instruction, students in different tracks get different kinds of teachers. Some schools allow teachers to choose their teaching assignments according to seniority, whereas other schools rotate the teaching of low- and high-ability classes among teachers. Whether teachers choose classes or schools assign teachers to classes, students in low-income and minority neighborhoods are more likely to get less-

---

[6] In addition, a growing body of research has documented differential treatment of students according to gender. See, for instance, Paley, 1986; Sadker & Sadker, 1994; Thorne, 1993; Walkerdine, 1989; Weis, 1988.

experienced teachers than students in more affluent neighborhoods (Oakes, Gamoran, & Page, 1992). Thus, students who have the greatest need for the best teachers are apt to get the least qualified.

Even in the face of apparent instructional differences, many schools would deny curricular tracking. Oakes (1985) documented that tracking is widespread but is often described as selective career tracks. Yet research has documented that the distribution of students to general or academic tracks seems to be related to ethnicity and socioeconomic status rather than simple preference or selection of career aspirations. Oakes, Gamoran, & Page (1992) found that students from low-income or one-parent households, or from families with an unemployed worker, or from linguistic and ethnic minority groups are more likely to be assigned to a low-ability group or track. Those researchers concluded that the relationship is both simple and direct (for example, the greater the percentage of minorities, the larger the low-track program; the poorer the students, the less rigorous the college prep program). Mehan and his colleagues (Mehan, Villanueva, Hubbard, & Lintz, 1996) not only have documented the practice of tracking but also have challenged it through creating special classes designed to untrack students.

Allan Luke (1991, pp. 133–135) described the tracking phenomenon as reflective of selective traditions.

The literature we select, the methods and strategies we use to teach and assess, and the knowledges and competencies we disburse selectively to different groups of students are selections from the plurality of cultures extant in the modern Western nation state. Perhaps more importantly, these selections are not random, but selections which serve particular economic interests and political ends. . . . From this perspective no approach [to literacy] is neutral. All are utterly implicated in distributing to and perhaps depriving children and adults power, knowledge, and competence to particular economic and political ends.

Resistance to Official and Unofficial Discourse

At the same time, one can identify a dominant cultural pattern in any classroom or school. To demonstrate that this cultural pattern is acquired and performed by participants, one can also identify various countercultures that exist in contrast to the official classroom order. Clearly, teachers' and students' official and unofficial verbal exchanges influence each other. During official discourse, the teacher controls classroom interactions. Using the basic recitation script, teachers can initiate, regulate, and terminate all interaction and can manage the allocation of student turns.

In addition to the official classroom discourse, students learn how to negotiate an unofficial system of communication among peers. The classic study conducted by Opie and Opie (1959) revealed the extensive and creative use of language in children's interaction with each other both inside and outside the classroom and school. But the unofficial script is often ignored or is used as an example to other classroom members of what not to do. Although much of the unofficial talk is off-task (i.e., not directly relevant to the teacher's definition of the instructional task at hand), current research has documented that, in some

cases, the unofficial discourse represents the students' attempts to work out a connection between the two discourses. For example, Gutierrez, Rymes, and Larson (1995) identified points in an ongoing classroom discussion when students seemed to be having a separate conversation, but closer examination indicated that the discussion was not a counterscript but earnest attempts by students to make sense of the classroom content.

Unofficial discourse is often interpreted as resistance to adult authority and the prescribed classroom culture. D'Amato (1987, p. 359) claims that resistance is inherent in the nature of the school, "and all children need some rationale for justifying to themselves the act of participating in it." Drawing on the work of Ogbu (1978, 1983) and Erickson (1984), he argues that children develop the rationale for participating in school from the beliefs held by their parents and the people in their communities about the value of school. Such beliefs are based on their experiences with matters of family history, racial or ethnic history, and class structure, as well as from the meaning of school events "for ongoing identities and relationships, particularly within children's peer groups" (D'Amato, 1987, p. 359).

When children are persuaded by the structural "implications of school for settings outside the school," such as the potential rewards of school achievement and the harms of school failure, they apply themselves to the work of education with little more than token resistance (D'Amato, 1987, p. 360). In this case, D'Amato (p. 360) argues, "Teachers hold the cards of power, and children are willing to organize their peer affairs in terms of teacher standards and of social processes managed and evaluated by teachers."

When the structural implications of school are not compelling to children, however, they confront school politics directly and openly. Thus they exhibit more hostile, disruptive opposition to school (D'Amato, 1987, p. 360). Paul Willis (1977) describes working-class, male high school students who are destined for futures as laborers and who resisted both the meritocratic model for success espoused by their teachers and the work values used to disqualify their resistance to the status quo. When such opposition is present, D'Amato argues, youths are more likely (a) to organize peer relationships around peer standards and processes that are managed and evaluated by peers and (b) to judge the acceptability of teachers and lessons in terms of their peer culture. D'Amato's concern for the factors influencing the contexts in which students comply with or resist educational activities could be extended to emphasize things such as student perceptions of the meaningfulness of the activity and rapport with the teacher.

Many applications of resistance theory (Erickson, 1987; Giroux, 1983) highlight how student's attitudes and behaviors, influenced by history and the social context, influence their educational careers. Resistance theory provides a way to introduce human agency into overly deterministic models of school's influence on the economic, social, and cultural reproduction of the social order. Such models often leave little room for the "moments of self-creation, mediation, and resistance," which active human agents experience (Giroux, 1983, p. 259). Resistance theory provides an additional element in our understanding of and explanation of (a) how school experiences vary, even within similar social groups, and (b) how microcultures that develop in different contexts (i.e., classroom cultures) support or interfere with school success.[7]

Although the oppositional behavior of working-class youths makes sense as a form of resistance to an institution that cannot deliver on its promise of upward mobility for all students, Mehan (1997) cautions us not to romanticize student's nonconformity. Not every instance of student misbehavior is a case of resistance (Erickson, 1984; Mehan, Villanueva, Hubbard, & Lintz, 1996; Ogbu, 1992). Mehan (1997) suggests that acts of resistance be examined through careful analysis of the social situations. For instance, ditching school, smoking in the hallway, and crumbling homework may not stem from an articulate critique of relations of domination from the point of view of the student. Because researchers in the critical ethnography tradition associate conflict and resistance with relations of teachers to children from historically subordinated groups, the fact that resistance is not limited to interaction between children from low-status families and teachers from higher-status groups is important to note. Linking resistance only to subordinated groups is dangerous, because it can stigmatize their actions as abnormal or pathological (Panofsky, 1995).[8]

Disputing the Dominant Pattern: Activity-Based Classroom Cultures

Although the whole-group-lesson recitation paradigm dominates classrooms in the United States and other industrialized countries, attempts have long been made to implement alternative participation and activity structures. In these attempts, classrooms are physically arranged to change the normative social relationships, and efforts are made to ensure that content is of interest to children. Cuban (1984) reviews the history of efforts to replace what he refers to as teacher-centered instruction with child- or activity-centered instruction, which we will treat as more or less synonymous with what Dewey (1938) referred to as progressive education. Cuban discusses in some detail two major attempts to implement child-centered instruction.

The New York City Activity Program

The Progressive movement in America was the foundation for the Activity Program, a 6-year experiment beginning in 1934. Eventually involving 75,000 students and 2,200 teachers in 69 schools, it became the largest demonstration of progressive practices in the nation. Although the program's goals shifted throughout a 6-year period, major concepts in the Activity Program were (a) children as well as teachers participate in selecting subject matter and in planning activities; (b) the program centers on the needs and interests of individuals and groups; (c) time schedules are flexible, except for certain activities that may have fixed periods; (d) learning is largely experimental and inquiry-based; (e) formal recitation is supplemented by confer-

ences, excursions, research, dramatization, construction and sharing, interpreting, and evaluating; (f) discipline is based on self-control rather than on imposed control; (g) teachers are encouraged to exercise initiative and to assume responsibility for what transpires in their classrooms; (h) the teacher enjoys considerable freedom in connection with the course of study, time schedules, and procedure; and (I) emphasis is placed on instruction and creative expression in the arts and crafts.

During the Activity Program experiment, teachers participated in staff development and in the design of elaborate syllabi and classroom suggestions. Listings of community resources were compiled and distributed to teachers interested in the Activity Program. Teachers filled out questionnaires and surveys. Students took tests. Classrooms were observed regularly to record teacher and student behaviors.

Physical environments were sought that were conducive to the proposed learning and teaching activities and styles. Referring to the trend in education toward an activity program, project-based method, William Caudill (1941, quoted in Dahlke, 1958) stated: "The architect should interpret the curriculum in terms of architecture. That is, the architecture must meet the educational demands." Caudill suggested that because courses of study were not regarded as finished products but were always revised, classroom structure should be flexible, using movable furniture and partitions. This flexibility in course structure would also allow for cooperative work in different-sized groups.

The focus on aiding children to develop their interests and abilities called for nooks or corners in classrooms for individual instruction. Conference rooms should be provided for parents. Meeting rooms for PTA and neighborhood culture programs would help to integrate home, church, community, and school as well as provide educational opportunities for adults. Flower gardens, vegetable gardens, and schoolground landscape could facilitate taking mathematical problems from the experiences and environment of the children. Small health clinics were essential for most schools to support the health and the physical and mental development of the child.

The Activity Program experiment ended in 1941 with mixed results. A major evaluation of the project revealed that few teachers put the Activity Program into practice for the entire school day. The regular classes spent 93% of their time in teacher-led whole groups, whereas the activity classes spent 84% in the same manner. The researchers declared that this difference was "not as large as one might expect in view of the fact that the programs presumably are quite different." Observations in experimental and control classrooms revealed that the amount of time spent on formal subjects such as arithmetic, reading, spelling, and social studies was "nearly the same in activity and control classes." In short, findings showed a notable, though not revolutionary, shift in the dominant participation structures, but the content of instruction was materially unchanged.

Members of the evaluation team did find that the average

---

[7] To describe and fully critique "resistance theory" as it is used by different theorists is beyond the scope of this paper. Giroux (1983) and Lave, Duguid, Fernandez, & Axel (1992) offer critiques of work that falls under the general category of resistance theory.

[8] Moreover, emphasis on racial stratification in explaining minority school failure may underemphasize the role that class, or socioeconomic status, plays in making possible or in constraining school success. See Fine (1987), Foley (1991), and Willis (1977) for examples of this issue.

activity class differed from the average control class in various ways. They found an outward appearance of pupil self-direction in activity classes. Activity classes allowed more diversity and a larger range of tasks during certain periods of the day. The Activity Program included more projects of the sort that correlate various enterprises and skills as distinguished from projects that study isolated subject matter. Also, activity classes provided for greater public display of the products of the pupil's work.

The study concluded that the Activity Program had been most successful (a) at getting students to participate and cooperate in group; (b) at encouraging student movement in classrooms; (c) at developing positive student attitudes toward school, teacher, and peers; and (d) at teaching purposeful, orderly, and courteous behavior. Teachers were less successful at developing flexible use of classroom furniture, workbenches, and tools and at reporting regularly to parents. The study also revealed that elements of the Activity Program had spread to regular schools, some of which had nearly as much of the Activity Program components as those selected for the intensive study. In short, the Activity Program proved to be as effective as conventional methods at teaching knowledge and skills and was superior to conventional methods for educating children to think and for improving pupils' attitudes and social behavior.

The Activity Program was extended throughout the school system gradually and on a voluntary basis, but this expansion was launched during a time of severe economic retrenchment. It received no additional funds for furniture, materials, or training. At the same time, cutbacks in the number of teachers resulted in class size increases. A decade after the program began, it was estimated that 25% of all city elementary schools were implementing the activity method to some degree. Precise accounts were not possible because funds were not available to visit teachers or their classrooms.

Some schools had remained untouched by the ideology of the Progressive movement and the Activity Program. Significantly, in light of current interest in activity-centered pedagogy, many teachers were opposed to the program because of the extra work required of them. The researchers found that 36% of teachers in the activity schools preferred the regular program. In regular schools, an unsurprising 93% favored classroom activities that involved whole-group instruction, little student movement, and a recitation script format. Despite the supposed benefits of the Activity Program, most teachers were convinced of the workability (if not effectiveness) of conventional instruction.

Open Schools

The mid-1960s and early 1970s brought another wave of Progressive reform to many large districts in the nation—the open classroom. Charles Silberman's (1970) *Crisis in the Classroom* proposed the open classroom as the keystone in the arch of educational reform. The concept of open-space schools was seen as a way of revolutionizing the curriculum, the instruction, and the customary role of a teacher at both the elementary and secondary levels. An open-space environment was said to encourage teaming among teachers, varied groupings of children, nongraded arrangements, and diverse uses of space.

In New York City, the extent to which the elements of open classrooms were implemented is similar to the extent to which progressive practices (e.g., the Activity Program) were implemented two generations earlier. Definitions of openness varied, teachers were selective in what they introduced, and the pattern of adoption was uneven both within and across schools. By the last training cycle held in 1974, 28% of the 200 participants reported they had opened up their classrooms. Of course, not all teachers in open-space rooms used open-classroom pedagogy. Outcomes were difficult to document because no large-scale formal assessment of open schooling was conducted. By 1975, interest in open education had fallen. Federal funds for the training center had run out. The city had produced large deficits and drafted long lists of budget cuts that led to cuts of aides, staff development, and other services that had nurtured open education.

In Washington, D.C., a similar pattern emerged. Initially, teachers who volunteered to work in open-space classrooms were provided in-service workshops. A study of Washington, D.C., classrooms revealed that student-centered open classrooms were strongest with regard to furniture arrangement, learning centers, and students moving around the room without asking the teachers' permission. Teacher-centered patterns still registered strongly; almost half of the open classrooms were taught through whole-group instruction; students engaged in listening, working at desks, and responding to teacher questions. In more than half of the classes, one could find little student movement; in nearly two of every three of those classrooms, teachers dominated verbal exchanges. A study that compared reading achievement and other student outcomes in 372 open-space and self-contained classrooms found that "the self-contained classroom provided a better learning environment than . . . the open-space classroom" (District of Columbia Board of Education, 1922, pp. 96, 97, 104, cited in Cuban, 1984, p. 83).

The concentration to improve basic skills was growing. Teachers were charged to provide specific and direct instruction in skills students had to know, whether or not students had performed at the appropriate level on a given day. Testing to monitor progress expanded. Standards for semiannual promotions of students were tightened and enforced. Children were retained; remedial programs were expanded. The stress on academic skills signaled the reduction of tangible support for open classrooms. Teachers created self-contained rooms by building walls of portable blackboards and bookcases. Learning centers gradually disappeared.

The 1960s Activity-Centered Curricula

The implementation of activity-centered instruction was a common characteristic of the most innovative curricula in mathematics, science, and technology education that was introduced during the 1960s, such as the Elementary Science Study Curriculum, the Science Curriculum Improvement Study, and the Active Learning Approach to Mathematics Curriculum (Briggs & MacLean, 1969). These curricula were generally child and activity centered. They called for breaking large classes into small working groups, and they required flexible support activities by teachers. The programs attempted to make explicit the principles that teachers might use to implement such curricula (for example, they provided a wide range of do-it-yourself hints for using readily available materials). But these lists had serious omissions. They did not provide explicit principles in practice for coordinating classroom activities over an entire school day or a large segment of the curriculum. They did not discuss how to maintain discipline. They also failed to describe how to fit the diverse entering skills of students into the diversity called for by the curriculum. Nonetheless, the overall picture was positive. In a meta-analysis of evaluation of the new science curricula of the 1960s, Kyle (1984, p. 21) concluded:

> Recent research syntheses demonstrate the effectiveness of the hands-on, inquiry-oriented science curricula developed during the 1960s and early 1970s. Evidence shows that students in such courses had enhanced attitudes toward science and scientists; enhanced high-level intellectual skills such as critical thinking, analytical thinking, problem solving, creativity, and process skills, as well as a better understanding of scientific concepts. Inquiry-oriented science courses also enhance student performance in language arts, mathematics, social studies skills and communication skills.

Despite this conclusion, science classes experienced little uptake of an inquiry-oriented curriculum since Kyle's (1984) study. Rather,

1. Nearly all science teachers (90%) emphasized goals for school science that were directed only toward preparing students for the next academic level (for future formal study of science).
2. Over 90% of all science teachers used a textbook 95% of the time; hence the textbook became the course outline, the framework, the parameters for students' experience, testing, and the world view of science.
3. There was virtually no evidence of science being learned by direct experience.
4. Nearly all science teachers presented science via lectures and/or question-and-answer techniques; the lectures and question-and-answer periods were based on the information that existed in textbooks used.
5. Over 90% of the science teachers viewed their goals for teaching in connection with specific content; further, these goals were static, i.e., seldom changing, givens. (p. 7)

Overall, results seem to clearly show that activity-centered innovations demonstrated their effectiveness for enhancing students' education (Doyle, 1986). Yet each failed. Why? Several reasons are given (Cuban, 1984):

- Teachers lacked support—indicated by their assessment that preparation for these arrangements were too difficult and required too much time.
- The extra continual effort required to combat the recitation script interaction pattern was sustained by only a few teachers and supported by only a few communities.
- Support for continued staff development and in-service workshops was not enduring enough to allow teachers to develop strategies for "doing it alone."
- No systemic commitment existed to sustain change.
- Funds were insufficient to evaluate the outcomes of the ac-

tivity. Traditional outcome measures were used to assess the effect of new innovations.
- The innovations failed because they lacked external as well as internal support for change throughout the institution.
- The new way of doing things required extra resources of teaching time and preparation time and presented difficulties in obtaining the proper logistic resources on-site.
- By and large, the required changes were too much trouble.

The Culture of the Classroom Versus *The* Culture of the Home

As we noted in our introduction and despite the heterogeneity in the kinds of classroom cultures that characterize U.S. schools (as a class of institutionalized forms of activity), they all differ in significant ways from the forms that characterize children's lives in their homes and communities. Hence, while keeping in mind Akinasso's (1991) warning against treating classroom cultures as pure types (our earlier review fully warrants that warning), one can find some important discontinuities between the range of cultural forms that characterize classrooms as a category and the range of forms that characterize children in their homes and other community settings.

Terms of Contrast

Waller (1932/1965), whose arguments for a marked discontinuity between home and school were discussed previously, traces the distinctive culture of the school to its focus on instructional interactions as the giving and receiving of information. Like many before and since, Waller notes that instruction is dominated by the transmission of facts and skills for which, as he delicately puts it, "the spontaneous interests of students do not usually furnish a sufficient motivation" (p. 8). Yet teachers are responsible to the community to motivate their students to acquire those very skills and facts.

According to Waller, the result of the conflicting interests and obligations of students and teachers is a political organization that is, by and large, autocratic, so autocratic in fact that he is led to remark: "The generalization that the schools have a despotic political structure seems to hold true for nearly all types of schools, and for all about equally, without much difference in fact to correspond to radical differences in theory" (p. 9).

More recently, Lynn Corno (1989) contrasted the culture of the home and the culture of the school in terms of differences in linguistic features, normative interactions, and value orientations (see Table 44.3). Among the several features listed by Corno, the difference in adult–child ratio appears to be especially influential. It poses the special problem of how to create participant structures that both allow for effective communication and maintain classroom order, as Doyle (1986) and others have emphasized.

We can see this contrast and the importance of adult–child ratio clearly at work in research by Shultz, Florio, and Erickson (1982), who compared the participant structures in a first-grade math lesson with the dinner table conversation in one of the student's homes. They found that chiming in was acceptable and occurred at all phases of dinnertime at home but that the

Table 44.3. Contrasting the Culture of the Home with the Culture of the School

Culture of the Home	Culture of the School
Oral Language Tradition	Written Language Tradition
Context-Bound	Decontextualized
Natural	Unfamiliar
Casual	Formal
Paralinguistic	Linguistically Complex
Continuous Deployment	Discontinuous Deployment
Low Child–Adult Ratio	High Child–Adult Ratio
Emphasis on Quality of Life and Quality of Products or Results	Emphasis on Quantity and Experience or Process
Adults as Transmitters or Nurturers	Adults as Leaders or Managers

Note: Adapted from "What It Means to Be Literate about Classrooms," by L. Corno in *Classrooms and Literacy* (pp. 29–52), by D. Bloom, 1989, Norwood, NJ: Ablex.

same conversation strategy occurred only during the instructional climax of lessons in the classroom. That is, during the early part of a math lesson, the teacher stops all efforts at overlapping talk among the children, or chiming in, and only later in the lesson relaxes the rules to allow children to focus mainly on the academic task rather than on monitoring their use of the appropriate interaction pattern. During dinner conversation, participants often overlap speech and interpret such interruptions as evidence of interest in the topic. In this way, multiple simultaneous speakers and multiple ways of listening could be found among dinnertime participants, which resulted in multiple conversational floors that speakers could address. In the classroom, however, holding the floor, defending it from interruptions, and allocating it at appropriate times to students are significant concerns for the teacher. Nonetheless, at other times in the lessons, the teacher's concerns for control were less visible, and talking while others were talking seemed to be an acceptable way of listening and interacting.

Wells (1986) investigated the language experience of 5-year-old children at home and at school. He examined samples of naturally occurring conversations between the children and whoever interacted with them over a period of 6 weeks in both the school and the home. The data indicate that children talk significantly less in the classroom than at home. By contrast, the amount of talk addressed to the children by adults does not differ significantly from one setting to the other. The figure for adult talk in the classroom, however, includes both utterances that are addressed to the child as a member of a group and utterances that are addressed to the child in one-to-one interaction. Wells also found that in terms of syntactic complexity, the child is less frequently exploiting her or his full linguistic resources when talking to the teacher than when talking to parents. This research finding is underlined by the fact that talk with peers in the classroom is significantly more complex than talk with adults, although this language complexity is present in the home. Wells suggests that two factors influence the amount and type of speech that occurs: (a) the contexts and activities children choose to be engaged in or are required to engage in and (b) the number of available adults.

In a similar vein, Carolyn Panofsky (1994) concludes that so-

cially assembled situations at home are likely to differ significantly from the socially assembled situations typical at schools:

> At home the purposes and goals of an activity are usually continuous with the child's ongoing experiences and valued by others in her intimate social network. The child's active participation will be a pivotal factor in the home situation, where the choice to withhold participation or to participate on one's own terms or in one's own way exerts a definitive role. By contrast, at school the purposes and goals of an activity may be difficult for a child to understand and a child's lack of participation can go unnoticed and unnoted. At home, the child's participation is the sine qua non: if the parent, for example, wants book reading with the child to occur, a way must be found to engage the child's active involvement. (p. 225)

As these examples make clear, the peculiar circumstances of activity settings where 30-or-so children and one adult are together, along with the special purposes for which adults have arranged for children to be there, make it almost inevitable that cultural discontinuities will occur between schools and homes. In addition, sources of intergenerational cultural conflict are inherent in this discontinuity.

Complicating the Dichotomy

In evaluating such proposals for dealing with how to create curriculum that takes into account the home–school contrast, we need to keep in mind that both classroom and school cultures vary greatly among themselves. As with any dichotomy, the social reality they represent is more complex. Binary classifications hide internal variety. Panofsky (2000) contrasts the normative order and participation structures in the home and in the classroom during child–adult, book-reading episodes. She provides evidence that the same event (parents reading to children) differs markedly among homes within what appears to be a single (class) population. She draws on Heath (1982), who found that when adults looked at books with very young children, they engaged in point-and-naming games, or ritual naming (Ninio & Bruner, 1978). However, Heath documented that once children's vocabulary needs diminished, some parents demanded an end to verbal interaction during book reading—children were expected to be quiet and listen—whereas other parents allowed the verbal interaction to remain a part of the activity. Therefore, differences in reading interactions were not clear and exclusive markers of working-class or middle-class interaction norms.

Cultural match or mismatch between home and school is further complicated by the variability across school settings. In a set of recent studies, Harry Daniels (1989, 1995) and colleagues (Daniels, Holst, Lunt, & Johansen, 1996) have applied Bernstein's concept of cultural transmission. Studying the researcher's collected visual displays (e.g., photographs of wall displays from different schools, such as art displays), they found that students were able to identify those displays that would be favored and found in their own schools. Students' communicative competence at school, their understanding of the implicit and explicit curriculum guiding their manner of talk, and their criteria for their success in classrooms and schools vary within communities too. In one case, researchers documented the existence of communicative competence in different schools by studying one student who switched schools during the experiment. The student eventually unlearned the previous school's criteria for communicative competence and learned the new criteria for competence in his new school.

Confronting Educational Inequalities

In earlier sections, we established a number of reasons to use the concept of classroom cultures to understand why learning and instruction are patterned the way they are. We have seen a dominant pattern that is emblematic of a basic educational philosophy: the transmission of cultural information under controlled conditions. This pattern is periodically challenged by a mélange of views focused around the idea of activity-based instruction that permits students to be active participants in the process of their own education, but this alternative is rarely sustained.

In this section, we will seek to understand the role played by the cultural divide between dominant forms of classroom culture and home cultures in producing the relatively poor achievement of major demographically defined groups. This concern is motivated by three factors: (a) the variable school achievement among our diverse student population (Erickson, 1987; Mehan, 1997; Mehan, Lintz, Okamoto, & Wills, 1995; Ogbu, 1991, 1992); (b) the growing demographic disparity between the background experiences of teachers and those of their students (Grant & Secada, 1990); and (c) the overall increase of American citizens of non-European backgrounds.

Bredo, Henry, and McDermott (1990) point out that how one frames the problem of variable student achievement greatly influences how one explains it and, therefore, the strategy used to deal with it. The dominant assimilationist frame is formulated in terms of the need to hasten the assimilation of the culturally different into the traditional culture of the school, an approach that draws directly on the humanist–evolutionary view. From this perspective, deviation from the culture of the school and the predominantly Anglo-Saxon, Christian heritage on which it was founded bespeaks a cultural deficit. Within this framework, school failure is a reflection of inadequately preparing children to measure up to the traditional forms of knowledge transmission and acquisition because of the inadequacies of their culture.

The alternative, the accommodationist framework, argues for the equal value of different cultural traditions, thus following in the anthropological tradition for understanding cultures. Its advocates seek to ameliorate the relatively poor performance of nonmainstream children by creating some form of accommodation between the culture of the school and the culture of the home, although their strategies differ in significant ways. One group seeks to reduce the discontinuities between home and school cultures by changing the organization of classroom activities to incorporate home cultural patterns. A second group seeks to make the (largely implicit) culture of the school explicit and to teach children how to be competent members of that culture. In effect, the second position seeks accommodation by deliberately making children both bicultural and bilingual.

The Assimilationist View: Cultural Difference Equals Cultural Deficit

The cultural deficit view has a long history. Cuban (1984) reminds us that, at the turn of the century, public schools were so overwhelmed with the number of immigrant children entering them that education's primary goal was to transform immigrant children into Americans. Superintendents, principals, and teachers—who reflected the larger society's dominant attitudes—induced children to discard their (deficient) ethnic cultures in order to embrace American ideals and habits. New curricula incorporating manual arts and vocational courses were developed. Special classrooms for teaching English to newcomers were common. Such classes were large, 60 or more, especially in the lower grades, because non-English-speaking children were placed in the first grade, regardless of age.

From the beginning, two explanations were offered to account for the perceived cultural deficits: one attributed them to historical experience; the other, to flawed genetic endowment (Gould, 1981). More contemporary versions of the environmental and inherited-flaw explanations came to prominence in the 1960s. Arthur Jensen (1969) concluded that biology limited the development of African Americans' human potential. He argued that large-scale interventions such as Head Start would not close the achievement gap between Blacks and Whites because of the limited learning capacities of African Americans. At about the same time, Bereiter and Englemann (1966), who adopted an environmentalist interpretation of putative deficits, declared that "the speech of lower-class people . . . is inadequate for expressing personal or original opinions, for analysis and careful reasoning, for dealing with anything hypothetical or beyond the present, and for explaining anything very complex" (p. 32), which, in turn, led to their poor academic performance. These two positions rationalize educational underachievement of the culturally different or culturally poor in terms of different causes, but both, in effect, view children's families as the agents of their shortcomings.

The pedagogical strategy that has generally accompanied the assimilationist model is one that places a premium on (a) mastery of the basics as a prerequisite to engagement in higher levels of the curriculum, (b) classroom management processes that ensure discipline and adherence to the teacher's instructions, and (c) efforts to maximize the amount of time children spend on a task. The teacher-centered transmission approach is the choice for those who frame the problem of educational inequality within an assimilationist framework.

The goal for assimilationists is to replace the native (deficient) culture with American cultural knowledge. Assimilationists in the United States have lamented a variety of deficiencies. Too many students do not have a grasp of fundamental information and basic historical facts about their own country. Too many have trouble reading the newspaper. Too many cannot complete functional mathematical tasks. Too many do not know how to spell (Bloom, 1987; Hirsch, 1987; Postman, 1995; Schlesinger, 1992). One of the most visible responses to students' underachievement is the notion of cultural literacy, that is, the explicit teaching (transmission) of the American culture advocated by some assimilationists. Hirsch (1987) states that "cultural literacy constitutes the only sure avenue of opportunity for disadvantaged children, the only reliable way of combating the social determinism that now condemns them to remain in the same social and educational condition as their parents" (p. xiii).

Hirsch (1987) argues that to be culturally literate is to posses the basic information needed to thrive in the modern world. It is not confined to one social class nor is it confined to an acquaintance with the arts. Hirsch (1987, p. xiv) further claims, "Although the greatest benefactors from gaining cultural literacy are 'disadvantaged' children, it will also enhance the literacy of children from middle-class homes. The educational goal is mature literacy for *all* our citizens" (italics in original). The means to this goal offered by Hirsch is a cultural literacy master list consisting of all the must-know information. This list is found as an appendix at the end of Hirsch's book and has been further elaborated in other publications such as *The Dictionary of Cultural Literacy* (Hirsch, Kett, & Trefil, 1988), written in more accessible language for use by parents at home (because one cannot trust the schools to teach the really important stuff).

Hirsch and others (Bloom, 1987; Schlesinger, 1992) blame faulty educational theories that guide teachers' instructional practices in schools for the decline in students' basic and cultural knowledge. Hirsch does not, however, engage in the great debate (Chall, 1983) about instructional methods and practices. Rather, he contends that literacy is much more than a skill to be mastered, and he requires a great deal of specific information. The basic goal of education is the transmission to children of the specific information shared by the adults of the group. Like any other aspect of acculturation, literacy requires the early and continued transmission of specific information.

Hirsch agrees that Americans should press reforms that advocate for greater representation of women, minorities, and non-Western cultures. They should also insist, he adds, that literate culture keep up with historical and technical change. He claims that 80% of the items from his list have been in use for more than 100 years. What is not clear is who has been using them and for what purposes.

Assimilationists believe that a common set of understandings is necessary for building both communities and nations and, therefore, that cultural conservatism is essential for purposes of national communication.

> It enables grandparents to communicate with grandchildren, southerners with midwesterners, Whites with Blacks, Asians with Hispanics, and Republicans with Democrats—no matter where they were educated. If each local school system imparts the traditional reference points of literate culture, then everybody will be able to communicate with strangers. In the modern age, effective communication with strangers is altogether essential to promote the general welfare and to ensure domestic tranquillity. The inherent conservatism of literacy leads to a subtle but unavoidable paradox: The goals of political liberalism require educational conservatism. We make social and economic progress only by teaching myths and facts that are predominantly traditional. (Hirsch, 1987, p. xii)

For assimilationists, the solution to confronting educational inequities is the direct transmission from teacher to student of cultural literacy, which is based on classic material. The delivery and the content of the lessons are traditional. This perspective also acknowledges that the classics themselves are self-defined by their traditional history in use. Not on Hirsch's cultural literacy list are terms that we have found necessary in our discussion of classroom cultures and cultures in the classroom. For instance, the term *bilingualism* is absent (but *bile* is present); neither *biculturalism* nor *multiculturalism* is mentioned.

Accommodationist View: Cultural Difference Equals Cultural Difference

Researchers following the "cultural difference" approach (Jacob & Jordan, 1987), also referred to as the communication process explanation by (Erickson, 1987), examine how communicative differences between home and school cultures "can lead to interpersonal conflicts that interfere with minority children's abilities to perform well in school" (Jacob & Jordan, 1987, p. 259). United in their opposition to assimilationism and in their emphasis on the "different but equal" position, those who adopt a cultural differences perspective vary in how best to deal with the problem of unequal educational achievements across ethnic groups.

THE CULTURALLY CONGRUENT TEACHING SOLUTION

According to this group of cultural difference theorists, the existence of marked, cultural differences requires deliberate modification of the school and classroom culture. To reduce the cultural mismatch, researchers use as a point of continuity those cultural practices from the home culture of minority students. The purpose of such matching is to use what the children already know, along with associated cultural practices, as resources for understanding in the classroom (Dewey, 1938; Moll & Greenberg, 1990).

Cuban (1984) reports on efforts earlier in this century to use this accommodation strategy. In 1935, only a brief generation after the era in which assimilating immigrants to become Americans was the leading strategy, the goals of schooling shifted to encompass preserving the cultural heritage of particular groups while bringing different cultures together in a harmonious whole. Schools preserved children's languages and introduced intercultural curricula. Multicultural assemblies provided students with opportunities to watch artists perform and to hear leaders from different cultures speak. Homeroom periods in secondary schools were used for lessons about the contributions and unique character of particular ethnic groups. Teachers participated in in-service education about different cultures. Significantly, this effort coincided with the large-scale New York City Activity Program discussed earlier.

The cultural difference movement of the 1930s did not survive the conservative societal climate accompanying the cold war, which accentuated efforts toward national unity, conformity, and the assimilation of newcomers into the melting pot. Cultural differences were once again viewed as deficiencies, and efforts at recognizing and building on cultural diversity fell dormant.

When the anthropology of education became a distinct field

in the 1960s, the cultural deficit model dominated the thinking of professional educators. But by the late 1960s, sociolinguistically oriented anthropologists identified cultural differences that were in the communication style between teachers and their students and that played an important role in the underachievement of minority students (Erickson, 1987).

The main argument of cultural mismatch theorists is that students and teachers of different cultural backgrounds develop culturally distinctive ways of speaking and act on different assumptions about how to communicate things such as "irony, sincerity, approval and positive concern, rapt attention, disinterest, disapproval, and the like" (Erickson, 1987, p., 337). When cultural differences in ways of speaking and listening exist between child and teacher, systematic and recurrent miscommunication can occur in the classroom with damaging consequences for students' educational achievement. The literature on attempts to modify classroom practices to accommodate cultural patterns from the home culture has been reviewed several times, so we will treat it relatively briefly here (for valuable summaries, see Cazden, 1986; Cole, Griffin, & LCHC, 1987; Mehan, Lintz, Okamoto, & Wills, 1995).

In her important comparison of the language socialization practices of low- and middle-income families with those of the classroom, Shirley Brice Heath's (1983) ethnography of a small, southeastern U.S. town illustrated the kinds of cultural mismatches that can occur. She found that in school, teachers practiced forms of language associated with the recitation script: asking children known-information questions, using utterances that were interrogative in form but directive in function, and using questions that asked for information in books. Those language practices paralleled the ways that the middle-income teachers talked to their own children at home but were quite different from those practices prevalent in the homes of low-income students, either Anglo or African-American. In the latter homes, adults rarely addressed questions to their children, favoring imperatives and statements instead. Differences also occurred according to ethnicity among the working-class families, so that children from each kind of home experienced a different kind of mismatch when attending school. But in both cases, youths from low-income homes were not prepared for language uses that were characteristic of the classroom.

The study by Philips (1983) of the interaction patterns of Native American children on a reservation in Oregon is perhaps the first study to highlight differences between backgrounds of teachers and students and to contribute to the discussion about incongruity of discourse. In her description of the classroom verbal interaction, she compared the participant structures of the recitation script with those of the local community. She found that the normative culture in the classroom violated Native American children's ideas of appropriate behavior. Her observations were followed by changes, which were made in the participation structures and which provided Native American children with the culturally congruent means of interacting with peers and the teacher. Those changes afforded the students access to more information and opportunities for fuller classroom participation and allowed them to achieve greater academic success.

In a similar study, Erickson & Mohatt (1982) videotaped a Native American teacher in a village school in northern On-

tario and found that the teacher consistently avoided round-robin reading discussions typical of classrooms. Rather than use the recitation script, she taught reading either by having whole-class discussions in which she allowed choral answers to content questions or by walking around the room among the students' desks. Individual students (who were reading silently at their seats) summoned her with a glance or some other subtle nonverbal sign. She would then lean over to meet the child, to engage in quiet conversation, and, by that means, to evaluate the child's performance and provide feedback.

Au and Jordan (1981) and Au and Mason (1981) based the work they did among Polynesian students in Hawaii on the Philips (1983) and Erickson and Mohatt (1982) studies. Specific reading group routines were modified to include the speech style of the local community. A "talk-story discourse pattern," common in Hawaiian homes, encourages "interruptions" that add supplements from the audience to the main story line. By introducing "talk-story" procedures into classrooms, the children—that is, the audience in this case—were able to participate in story reading in a more culturally congruent manner. The Kamehameha Early Education Program (KEEP), created by Au and her colleagues, was a language arts program that lasted several years (Au & Mason 1981; Vogt, Jordan, & Tharp 1987). The initial 3 years of the program emphasized classroom management strategies instead of cultural congruence with the home culture. In 4th year, the class received a full year of instruction with the new, culturally congruent, "talk-story" reading program. This program included changes in instructional practice, classroom organization, and motivational management that were thought to be more culturally congruent with Hawaiian culture (Vogt, Jordan, & Tharp, 1987). Although earlier techniques had included high praise for on-task behavior, the new approach attempted to balance warmth and toughness in ways effective for Hawaiian children. An emphasis on working together allowed students to draw on familiar home-culture patterns of giving and seeking help from peers and siblings, a natural tendency that had made previous efforts to get children to "do their own work" hard to enforce.

During the first 3 years, KEEP was unsuccessful at teaching its students how to read, and the reading scores of their classes were not significantly different from those of control group children drawn from nearby public schools. The 4th year, which involved the culturally congruent program, produced a dramatic increase in reading achievement to a mean score above grade level (Au & Jordan, 1981). Student enthusiasm and engagement for the activities also improved.

Later, some of the researchers and teachers from KEEP worked with Navajo members of the Rough Rock community to implement the KEEP language arts program and to find out if it was as effective with children from another culture (Vogt, Jordan, & Tharp, 1987). Many changes were necessary to make the program work well. The "tough-nice" technique of motivation management did not work well with Navajo children. Praise worked better when handled more subtly, and misbehavior was controlled better when ignored or addressed in a short lecture to the whole group. Whereas, for Hawaiian children, four to five students of mixed sex and ability produced the best peer interaction and assistance in groups at learning centers, this grouping did not work at all for Navajo children who were used to a strict separation of the sexes. For them, smaller groups of the same sex worked best. Finally, the KEEP team found differences in the ways that the comprehension lesson developed, namely that students preferred to read and discuss the stories as complete units rather than in an event-by-event, linear way.

Moll, Diaz, Estrada, and Lopes (1992) illustrated the importance of cultural congruence in a different way among Mexicano students in Southern California. All children were assessed as capable of communicating in both English and Spanish. The researchers documented that children who received native language (Spanish) reading instruction in one classroom were assessed as "high-group" readers. Yet, many of the same children were assessed as "low-group" readers in English.

The researchers intervened in the English reading lessons. Instead of reading aloud, the children were asked to read the English text silently and then were encouraged to discuss the text using either their Spanish- or English-language skills. The children's Spanish description of the English text illustrated that the children understood much more of the text than they could articulate in properly pronounced English. Conversely, the monolingual English-speaking teacher relied on children's ability to pronounce the English words correctly as evidence of decoding skills, which she believed to be required for reading comprehension. The Spanish-speaking teacher assessed children's comprehension of text material, knowing that the children could decode the text. Because teachers taught full days and because daily responsibilities restricted them from observing the other's teaching and classroom, the teachers were unaware of each other's teaching practices and of their variable expectations and assessments of the literacy ability of the same children.

Sarah Michaels's (1981) account of "sharing time" activities in an ethnically mixed, first-grade classroom provides another example of the type of interaction difficulties that can result from a mismatch between the language of the home and that of the school. During sharing time, students would talk about an object or a past event. The teacher, through questions and comments, would help students "focus and structure their discourse and put all their meaning into words, rather than relying on contextual cues or shared background knowledge" (p. 425). This activity amounted to an oral preparation for literacy, because in order to make the transition to literacy, children would need to acquire discourse strategies for making explicit relevant background knowledge. Yet children in the class that Michaels observed were differentially prepared for this activity and were treated differently along ethnic group lines. The African-American children usually received interactions of a lesser quality, leading Michaels to hypothesize that "such differential treatment may ultimately affect the children's progress in the acquisition of literacy skills" (p. 40). As with our previous description of Bremme and Erickson's (1977) investigation of a similar classroom event (first circle), participating in "sharing time" in an appropriate manner is clearly a learned skill that is previewed as foundational to literacy acquisition, a highly valued activity in the classroom context. Her case, Michaels asserts, suggests that what begins as miscommunication may end in differential treatment, in differential practice in literate-style speech, and, potentially, in educational failure.

In an attempt to disrupt the perceived off-task interaction

by African-American children, Michaels allowed the children more time to develop their stories without interruption (guidance toward the normative "sharing time" discourse pattern). She found that, when given sufficient time and the opportunity to develop their stories, African-American children provided all the elements of "good" sharing. She also noted that "waiting on" the children was difficult because other students were ready to redirect the child's story (i.e., evidence that they had learned the appropriate format for story time) and that the constraints of time and number of children worked against providing children adequate time to relay their stories.

Overall, these examples make it clear that a strategy of local accommodations of school culture to home culture can be educationally productive.

MAKING THE IMPLICIT CLASSROOM CULTURE EXPLICIT

Several cultural mismatch proponents agree that change in the classroom culture to incorporate and better match children's home cultures is desirable, and yet those proponents are not willing to "wait on" change, which is likely to be slow (Ladson-Billings, 1992, 1995). Rather, those scholars advocate that teachers should be explicit about the "standards" (e.g., culture) that are presently in place. The explicit transmission of this knowledge is said to be a teacher's moral responsibility because it is necessary to prepare children for their participation in the classroom community and their role in the broader society (Corno, 1989; Reyes, 1992; Delpit; 1995; Ladson-Billings, 1992, 1995).

Lisa Delpit (1988, 1995) has been a major spokesperson for this position. In her critique of contemporary methods of reading and writing instruction, she contrasts the explicit teaching of isolated reading skills and the specific mechanics of writing with a "holistic process" approach to literacy. In the classrooms Delpit refers to as "holistic," skills are not explicitly taught. According to Delpit, this situation puts working-class, African-American children at risk of school failure. Contemporary teachers who favor holistic methods avoid providing students with education facts because doing that is too directive and teacher centered. The children are left to rely on their own literacy and cultural backgrounds, without explicit and direct instruction regarding the skills necessary for full participation in the classroom (and in society). By contrast, working-class parents view traditional instruction based on the recitation-script format and associated practices as being basic education.

This difference in "approved standards" exposes class differences between (middle-class) teachers and (working-class and poor) students and parents. Parents who lack a clear rationale for pedagogical shifts toward child-centered approaches are suspicious, especially when the method is espoused by teachers who are middle class and often Caucasian. The shift may be understood by working-class, African-American parents as attempts to change social relationships they value—in particular, authority relationships between adult and child—that are seen by teachers as violations of "proper behavior." At best, the teachers' child-centered instructional methods are perceived as laissez-faire, and, at worst, they are seen as an academic conspiracy that is aimed at keeping African-American children in their "place" (school failures).

The work of Bernstein is widely evoked by those who advocate direct and explicit instructions of the culture in classrooms. In particular, they note his emphasis on discoordinations that occur when children and parents from working-class families interact with teachers and schools. He argues that such families encounter additional symbolic discontinuities between the home and school when dealing with the invisible pedagogy (e.g., the unspoken assumptions that guide participation and communication in school). Especially influential was Bernstein's (1973) argument that a progressive pedagogy reflects the culture of the middle class and acts implicitly to exclude the culture of the working class in a way that the "up-frontness," or explicitly stated rules, of traditional pedagogy does not.

The work of Marva Collins (M. Collins & Tamarkin, 1982) illustrates how one energetic teacher explicitly taught the knowledge and modes of learning expected according to the standards set by the mainstream and dominant culture. Collins noted that she did not favor the idea of the "africanization" of curriculum. She argued that she had never met a Black child who didn't know he or she was Black, so her duty was to provide the opportunities for them to move beyond their neighborhood cultures to participate in larger society.

For Corno (1989), identifying the distinctive qualities of interaction in both the home and school setting provides the basis from which to organize and develop a "blended" environment in the classroom. For example, more recent attempts at curricular modification in schools in Native American communities have documented that when a teaching style exclusively uses interaction patterns that resemble home discourse, the approach may not provide students optimal engagement and practice with a range of learning approaches, including those that are not found in the community. Specifically, McCarty, Wallace, Lynch, & Benally (1991) state that exclusive use of culturally relevant pedagogy may have unfortunate ramifications (e.g., Indian students who have not been taught higher-order questioning and inquiry methods). They found Navajo students in the Red Rock community to be enthusiastic participants in inquiry-based classrooms (which required students to be active and vocal) when the curriculum drew on students' background knowledge and directed them toward solving new problems, namely, a "blended" approach.

Corno (1989) offers her set of home-school contrasts (see Table 44.3, p. 39) to enable teachers to identify the hidden curriculum of the favored cultural forms. Corno argues for exposing the hidden curriculum and advises teachers not only to be (self-) conscious of their teaching methods and motives but also to explain the implicit curricular agenda to children along with its role in their acculturation. The resulting form of knowledge should be metaconscious awareness.

Primary and Secondary Cultural Discontinuity: Accommodation without Assimilation

The results of cultural congruence studies illustrate the significance of cultural difference in the educational underachievement of children whose cultural backgrounds differ from the culture of the classroom. However, cultural miscommunication (mismatch) alone is not adequate to explain of the variable school achievement of some minority students. As Erickson (1987) has noted, some students of minority cultures have not required culturally congruent pedagogy. Thus, some groups have done very well in the school setting in spite of significant cultural differences associated with their home culture. For example, Margaret Gibson (1988) documents students' abilities to participate in academic communities while maintaining their cultural traditions, what she refers to as "accommodation without assimilation." Specifically, she found that patterns of community attitudes and student attitudes toward school and eventual achievement in school were similar among both the children of well-educated Asian-Indian professionals and those of Punjabi Indian agricultural laborers, factory workers, and small-scale orchard farmers. This congruence in attitudes toward schooling coincides with ethnic pride and strong community support for education.

For more than two decades, John Ogbu has investigated why differences between home and school cultures pose more serious obstacles to school success for some groups of minority students than for others, that is, why different minorities adjust and perform differently in school in spite of cultural and language differences, along with why and how the problems created by cultural and language differences seem to persist among some minority groups but not among others (Ogbu, 1974, 1978, 1983, 1987; Ogbu & Simons, 1998).

Ogbu's analysis has focused on two types of forces that influence student achievement in school. The first is the nature of a minority group's history, including the initial terms by which that group was incorporated into the society in which it now exists. The second is the nature of the adaptive response, both instrumental and expressive, that the group has made to the subsequent treatment it has experienced (Gibson, 1997).

Ogbu's typology characterizes minorities as experiencing either primary cultural differences or secondary cultural differences, according to their historical positions in relation to the dominant group in society. Voluntary minorities have primary cultural differences, that is, differences that existed before the two populations came in contact. Involuntary minorities (also referred to as "subordinate" or "caste-like"), in contrast, have both primary and secondary cultural differences. Those differences have arisen after contact, often involving the domination of one group by another. Voluntary minorities are individuals who came to the United States more or less voluntarily because they believed their immigration would lead to greater economic opportunities, greater political freedom, or both. Involuntary minorities are those groups who were originally involuntarily brought or incorporated into the United States through slavery, conquest, or colonization and who, thereafter, were relegated to menial positions and denied true assimilation into mainstream society (Ogbu, 1978, 1987, 1996).

Voluntary minorities tend to accept the dominant culture's folk theory, believing that hard work, school success, and individual ability will lead to occupational and economic success. Their experiences with discrimination are tempered by the fact that they perceive the opportunities of the new environment to be better than those in their country of origin, and they do not perceive mistreatment as institutionalized or permanent. In sum, their attitudes toward the public schools are positive, and they actively ensure that their children study hard and follow school rules of behavior. Gibson's (1988) study of the Sikhs provides one example.

Involuntary minorities also believe a good education is necessary, but they might not really believe that they have a chance equal to that of White Americans to get ahead through education. Historical experiences with racism, unequal opportunities, and discrimination have led them to question how far one can get with an education, so they develop alternative strategies for "making it" without a formal education. Involuntary minorities distrust institutions and suspect those institutions of organizing their failure (see our previous discussion of differential treatment and tracking). These factors, Ogbu believes, have

> . . . led involuntary minority parents and communities to be less likely to be directly involved in their children's schooling and may unconsciously teach children ambivalent attitudes about education and success, providing a weak socialization of children to develop good academic work habits and perseverance at academic tasks. (Ogbu, 1987, p. 104)

These attitudes have strong implications for the identity formation of minority children. According to Ogbu, voluntary minorities perceive their social identity as at least equal to, if not superior to, the social identity of White Americans. They reveal these attitudes in both a family and community emphasis to value education, follow school rules, and develop good academic work habits. Voluntary minority students are often highly motivated to do well in school, are encouraged and supported in the home to pursue academic opportunities, and eventually achieve after they overcome initial difficulties related to their cultural differences.

Involuntary minorities, in contrast, develop a social identity that historically arises in opposition to the dominant group. For instance, Ogbu argues that the standard language and behavior practices required at school are equated with the dominant group's language and culture, "a practice which results in conscious or unconscious opposition or ambivalence toward school learning." Therefore, language differences in home and school are viewed as markers of identity to be maintained rather than as barriers to be overcome. Furthermore, adopting attitudes conducive to school success is often felt as threatening to their language, culture, and identity. These differences produce an oppositional cultural frame of reference and an identity for involuntary minorities that makes the task to overcome their cultural and linguistic differences with the school culture more difficult. Encouraged by peers, family, and community (explicitly or implicitly) to express hostility or ambivalence toward the school culture and its rules, involuntary minorities often become active accomplices in their own school failure.

Thus, Ogbu argues that the academic success of immigrant minority groups in the United States (e.g., Asian, Indian, Central, and South American) and the widespread academic failure of other nonimmigrant minorities (e.g., African Americans, Native Americans, Native Hawaiians, Mexican Americans, and Puerto Ricans on the U.S. mainland) correspond to whether the minorities are members of voluntary or involuntary minority groups. In this way, "school performance is not due only to

what is done to or for the minorities; it is also due to the fact that the nature of the minorities' interpretations and responses to instruction differ" (1996), namely, folk theories about how one gets ahead in the United States. Although Ogbu (1991) has noted that classrooms should be sites of mutual accommodation where the school, classroom, children, and communities accommodate one another, he does not clarify which aspects of school or classroom culture are negotiable. As a result, Ogbu's view fails to draw direct pedagogical implications or suggestions for classroom practice.

Complicating the Typology

Although Ogbu's typology incorporates societal forces that influence academic success and, therefore, supplements the cultural difference perspective, it fails as a dichotomous typology to account for hybridity and variation among participants and local conditions. As Gibson (1997) notes, empirical reality proves to be far more complex than what can be explained through dichotomous typologies of accommodation and resistance, success and failure, or voluntary or involuntary minorities. For this reason, Ogbu's opponents view the distinction of minorities that is based on collective historical relations with the dominant culture as being overly deterministic in its attempt to explain minority students' current and predicted future academic performance.

For example, Jeannette Abi-Nader (1990) describes a 3-year program for Hispanic high school students designed and implemented by one teacher in an inner-city public school. The program, Programa: Latinos Adelantarán de Nuevo (Program: Latins Shall Rise Again) (PLAN), is a college-prep program that is designed both to address psychosocial conditions that predict minority student failure and to motivate students to create a vision of the future that will redefine their images of self and will build a supportive community. The program provides sequences of courses in reading (for sophomores), writing (for juniors), and public speaking (for seniors). During the year-long study, 23 sophomores, 19 juniors, and 16 seniors were enrolled in the program. They met in their respective groups for 45 minutes each morning and spent the rest of the school day in bilingual education classes or in the traditional English monolingual program. The most commonly used term to describe PLAN was "family." Students looked upon the teacher as father, brother, and friend.

Similarly, Mehan, Hubbard, and Villanueva (1994) report on academically successful Latino and African-American high school students who participated in an "untracking" program, Achievement Via Individual Determination (AVID). Those students developed strategies for managing an academic identity at school and a neighborhood identity among friends at home and formed academically oriented peer groups. The researchers report that from these new voluntary associations, new ideologies developed. The students' belief statements displayed a healthy disrespect for the romantic tenets of achievement ideology and an affirmation of cultural identities while they acknowledged the necessity of academic achievement for occupational success. This example resonates with Gibson's (1988) idea of "accommodation without assimilation." Mehan and his colleagues found Latino and African-American (involuntary minorities) groups to be capable of accommodation without assimilation—an ideology presumed to be restricted to voluntary minorities (Cummins, 1986; Gibson & Ogbu, 1991; Suarez-Orozco, 1989).

Ogbu's typology continues to be challenged and refined. A recent issue of *Anthropology and Education Quarterly* (September 1997) was dedicated to testing the usefulness of Ogbu's typology for international applicability. Collectively, five case studies reported mixed results. Three European studies of minority populations within each country were conducted in the Netherlands, France, and Britain. In each country, the overall patterns of school achievement did not tidily fit Ogbu's framework. In studies from Israel and Canada (countries where immigrants and their descendants have come to form the dominant cultural groups), data did support Ogbu's model; involuntary minorities fared, on average, far less well in school than the children of immigrants. Thus, the typology works better in what might be characterized as "new nations," traditional immigrant-receiving countries where a colonizing population from Europe conquered or displaced an indigenous group and subsequently has accepted and encouraged the immigration of other groups. Countries of this type include Canada, Israel, the United States, Australia, and New Zealand.

Therefore, the quantitative data that has been collected in countries where both types of minorities reside do indicate that, in the aggregate, voluntary minorities are more successful in school than involuntary minorities. In addition, voluntary minorities may have an adaptive advantage over those who have been incorporated involuntarily into the society in which they now reside, as Ogbu has suggested (Ogbu, 1978, 1991). However, Gibson (1997) points out that his analysis has centered on one particular type of voluntary minority, namely, those who have migrated voluntarily to a new country to enhance their economic opportunities and who have entered the new country with full rights of permanent residence. She also notes that Ogbu has paid too little attention to other types of voluntary minorities (e.g., refugees, undocumented aliens, and temporary workers). This unequal focus on various types of voluntary minorities represents one factor illustrating "within group" differences.[9]

Thus, to focus on whether a particular group should be categorized as voluntary or involuntary is not necessarily the appropriate question and is probably not one that can be answered for many groups. A more productive approach is to take stock of what the comparative research on minorities reveals about the factors that serve either to promote or to impede success in school and that then determine how this knowledge can be used in our efforts to improve educational practice. Ultimately, Gibson (1997) concludes that minority youths do better in school when they feel strongly anchored in the identities of their families, communities, and peers and when they feel supported in pursuing a strategy of selective or additive acculturation. What is needed are learning environments that support additive or empowering forms of acculturation and teacher–student relations based on collaboration rather than on coercion. Navarro (1997) concludes that to construct such collaborative power relations is transformative not only for the educator but also for the students.

Dodging Dichotomies: Dealing with Diversity

So far, the studies we have reviewed have dealt with situations in which only one community culture is represented by the students in the classroom and only a single culture is assumed to exist within the classroom. The reality of many classrooms in the United States and around the world is that the classroom is a setting in which many cultures come together to create a unique set of circumstances. Therefore, even the most homogeneous populations will encounter multiple cultures in the classroom. Although we previously may have given these multiple cultures insufficient attention, the simultaneous existence of popular cultures, teacher cultures, ethnic group cultures, and social-class-related cultures now must be taken as a reality of classroom cultural production and social reproduction. How best to deal with that reality remains the question. Cazden (2000) recently posed the question in this manner, "How do we ensure that differences of culture are not barriers to educational success? More positively, how should we take cultural differences into account when designing programs and pedagogies?" (p. 249).

Up to this point in our discussion, we have repeatedly encountered two seemingly dichotomous views for dealing with diversity. The first advances a "one right way" that features back to basics, including high discipline, tradition, and an emphasis on recitation participation structures. It implements a Kultural view of school that seeks to reduce diversity by minimizing the recognition of cultural difference and by maximizing the role of individual effort in "doing it our way." Clearly, this view has many advocates in American society. This approach, however, stratifies the existing diversity into higher and lower sectors where many minorities and the "different" along

---

[9] In response to what Ogbu (Ogbu & Simons, 1998) has referred to as a misinterpretation of this work, namely, that minority school performance is caused only by sociocultural adaptation, his most recent explanation of minority school performance uses cultural ecological theory.

This theory considers the broad societal and school factors *as well as* the dynamics within the minority communities. In this case ecology is the "setting," "environment," or "world" of people (minorities), and "cultural" broadly refers to the way people (in this case the minorities) see their world and behave in it. The theory has two major parts. One part is about the way the minorities are treated or mistreated in education in terms of educational policies, pedagogy and the returns for their investment or school credentials. Ogbu calls this the *system.* The second part is about the way the minorities perceive and respond to schooling as a consequence of their treatment. Minority reposes are also affected by how and why a group became a minority. This second set of factors is designated as *community forces.* (italics in the original, Ogbu & Simons, 1998, p. 158).

He further states that he is attempting only to describe the general pattern within a group; his analyses cannot be applicable to each and every individual that composes a group of people (in this case, minorities).

many dimensions fare poorly. A second approach to dealing with diversity is to emphasize meaning-oriented, language-mediated activities in which students talk and participate as active subjects in the classroom. This approach minimizes stratification while it promotes diversity. It requires more complex methods to implement because of the diversity it spawns and because the qualities of its achievements are controversial.

Principle reasons can be found to reject either alternative to the exclusion of the other. We noted at the outset and throughout the chapter that all classrooms are actually hybrids of activities that combine features characteristic to notions of both Kultur and cultures. In this section, we explicitly argue for a mixed model in which the overall ethos of classroom culture satisfies the goals of diversity and student agency while it recognizes that self-discipline, excellence, and tradition play essential roles. The desired mix is attempted by distributing the power, goals, and activities throughout different participation structures that constitute the learning–teaching experience in an effort to change, rather than perpetuate, educational inequities among students along ethnically, economically, or medically defined lines.

Many before us have argued for a change in the organization of classrooms to deal effectively with the diversity of classroom cultures (in all senses). The challenge is to provide an alternative form of classroom that is sustainable on a widespread scale. If this alternative is not provided, classrooms revert to what Cazden and Mehan (1989) have referred to as the "default" interaction pattern—the recitation script.

Framing and Classification

To address this problem, Cazden (2000) has highlighted Basil Bernstein's idea that classroom cultures can be categorized along two dimensions: *classification* and framing. By *classification,* Bernstein means the degree to which social practices are kept separate, whereas *framing* refers to the degree to which control is rigidly maintained in the practices. Bernstein (1990) has suggested that to weaken the relationship between social class and educational achievement, one must weaken the classification and framing of classroom practices. These modifications apply to both the interaction among participants within the classroom and to the flow of communication between the school classroom and the community(ies) that the school draws on.

Several researchers have recently followed Bernstein in advocating the change (weakening) of classroom frames and classifications; they have offered general suggestions for how this change should be implemented. For instance, Lisa Delpit (1988, 1995) has argued that teachers should validate students' home language without using it to limit students' potential. Therefore, providing educational opportunities for students' positive feel-

ings by itself does not result in student achievement (Au & Carroll, 1997). According to Delpit, teachers must also acknowledge the unfair "discourse-stacking" that our society engages in and must recognize the conflict between students' home cultures and the culture of the school. She argues, consistent with the evidence on student resistance, for what teachers need to understand: Students who appear to be unable to learn are, in many instances, choosing to "not-learn" to maintain their sense of identity in the face of a painful choice between allegiance to "them" or "us." Teachers can reduce this sense of conflict by transforming classroom discourse so that it contains within it a place for the students' selves.

Delpit disagrees with James Gee (1989), who has argued that the dominant discourse of classroom culture cannot be explicitly taught.[10] She urges teachers to be explicit about the dominant culture of the classroom and to teach children how to succeed there. To do so, they must saturate the dominant discourse with new meanings and must wrest from it a place for their students and their students' cultural heritage.

Gloria Ladson-Billings (1995) does not refer to Bernstein directly. However, she has identified teaching practices that help to create classroom cultures where children can "succeed academically while retaining their cultural identities" and can become aware of the "political underpinnings of [their] community and social world" (p. 477)—what she refers to as "culturally relevant" pedagogy. Those practices can be expected to weaken the typical classroom frames and classifications in the manner suggested by Bernstein. Ladson-Billings identified three key characteristics of culturally relevant teaching, two of which implicate framing and classification. First, as members of the community, the teachers developed relationships with their students and their communities that were fluid, equitable, and reciprocal. Second, those teachers viewed knowledge as dynamic, shared, recycled, and constructed. Teaching and learning for such teachers was about "doing," and they organized the classroom to encourage students to be responsible for one another and to learn collaboratively.

Generalizing to other dimensions of student variation under the general rubric of "inclusion," Erickson (1996) explicitly suggests that teachers make classroom frames more elastic. For him, loosening the frames (which is not to create chaos but to allow for flexibility) achieves inclusion in its most general sense. Erickson reviews the findings of the studies he collectively refers to as culturally relevant pedagogies (many of which have been reviewed here) for insights about modifying classrooms to accommodate the inclusion of children with learning disabilities. Specifically, he recommends that teachers should modify both their lesson pacing and the time they allot for completion of written tasks, and they should make use of cooperative learning groups.

As important as such suggestions are, their widespread adop-

---

[10] Gee (1989) maintains that there are primary discourses, which are learned in the home, and secondary discourses, which are attached to institutions or groups one might later encounter. He emphasizes that all discourses are not equal in status, that some are socially dominant—carrying with them social power and access to economic success—and that some are subordinate. The status of individuals born into a particular discourse tends to be maintained because primary discourses are related to secondary discourse of similar status in our society (e.g., the middle-class home discourse to school discourse, or the working-class African-American home discourse to the black church discourse). Status is also maintained because dominant groups in a society apply frequent tests of fluency in the dominant discourses, which are often focused on its most superficial aspects—grammar, style, mechanics—to exclude from full participation those who are not born to positions of power.

tion is very much an issue. Telling people to change their habits is not a simple matter nor is change a matter of individual will (Vaughn & Schumm, 1996; Wells, 1986). Indeed, some otherwise sound advice may become counterproductive if it makes teachers self-conscious about their practices but does little to assist them.

Wells (1986) focuses on classification practices that organize the children's relations to the specific activity. For instance, asking children to generate an ending to their own unfinished story is likely to generate a very different set of power relations than the quizzes about names, attributes, and main events of a typical reading instruction story. Wells argues that one must attend to the ways in which the participants themselves construe the task.

Wells identifies two major impediments to developing quality interactions with children that we believe illustrate issues of classroom classification and framing, respectively. One impediment is the teacher's unfamiliarity with individual children's interests and abilities (e.g., background knowledge). Consequently, teachers find themselves seeking to classify individuals in terms of preexisting stereotypes of what children of a given age or group should be like. The second impediment identified by Wells occurs when teachers become so concerned with teaching what they believe children should learn that they allow very little opportunity for the children to take responsibility for their own learning. As a result of those problems, teachers are likely to underestimate children's true capabilities. In sum, Wells argues that teachers need to start with recognizing that children are already active, self-directed learners. On this basis, teachers should seek to find out more about the particular interests and abilities of individual pupils by listening to what they have to say and by encouraging them to ask the questions they want to ask. Then teachers can develop a style of collaboration and negotiation in the planning of learning activities to which both teacher and pupil contribute and for which both take responsibility, thus weakening both framing and classification as viewed from a traditional perspective.

In a similar vein, Bowers and Flinders (1990) suggest that teachers use "responsive teaching techniques" to become aware of and to reframe cross-cultural interactions and to take into account the balance of power and solidarity in their classrooms. Bruner (1996) notes that this approach to teaching emphasizes "consciousness, reflection, breadth of dialogue, and negotiation" (p. 42). Clearly, these are recommendations for the weakening of classroom classification and framing.

Whatever the terms used to describe the recommended pedagogical approach, the resulting suggestions remain largely abstract for teachers at the level of implementation. Unsurprisingly, Au and Carroll (1997) have documented teachers' dissatisfaction with generalities and teachers' requests for guidelines that are specific enough to guide practice.

Combining Bernstein and Activity-Based Approaches

By considering framing and classification at the level of activity and by considering classroom cultures as emergent hybrids of differently organized activity systems, we obtain an adaptable model for designing activities that support local goals and ob-

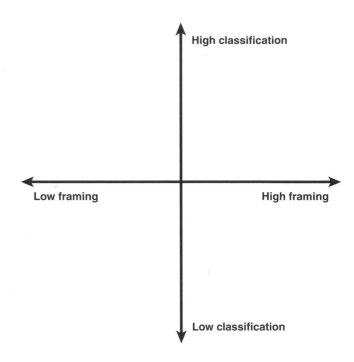

Mixed model of framing and classification

Figure 44.9. Mixed model of framing and classification.

jectives and that produce favorable outcomes. The key features of a "mixed model" are as follows:

1. Activity as the unit of analysis
2. A dual object (e.g., excellence with diversity)
3. Fluid and deliberate movement within and between systems
4. Achievement of balance (center) according to object
5. Many "centers"

The merits of activity as a unit of analysis have been described in previous sections of this chapter. To consider the level of activity as the unit of analysis and, therefore, the unit of change helps to organize environments that meet and support particular objects. In our case, the object is to produce a mixed model that disrupts underachievement patterns for nonmajority students and ensures that they acquire standard school knowledge. We believe a mixed model is best achieved through a combination of activities that lower framing and control of the classroom by encouraging student responsibility and active participation and that lower the classification of the classroom by integrating students' out-of-school knowledge in ways that guarantee students' full participation in school, community, and society.

From this view, the overall classroom culture emerges from the particular hybrid of framing and classification configurations that organize the individual activities. (See Figure 44.9.) The variety of hybrids can be illustrated by the location of any given activity relative to other activities within the quadrants across the two continua. In this way, throughout a day and across the year, many centers exist among activities according to the relative high and low framing (control) and classification (separation of social practices) of the activity. Deliberate movement up and down (high-low) along the framing and classification continua is motivated by an object relative to a local context.

Beyond the Best Practices Classroom

We have argued that the activity-based instructional approaches described here can be effective instruction for all classrooms regardless of the cultural variation of their members. Yet, Au (1998) cautions that simply adopting an active and participatory approach, or what she refers to as a constructivist approach, will not confront and change the underachievement of minority students. Au (1998; see also Au & Carroll, 1997) draws on the experience of KEEP to suggest that activity-based instructional approaches may improve student achievement but only when fully implemented. Full implementation requires that attention be given to (a) the culture (diversity) in the classroom (membership, ethnic, linguistic, cultural) and (b) the diversity of classrooms (cultures).

To address the de facto multicultural nature of classroom culture, Au (1998) calls for a diverse constructivist orientation. She views the difference between mainstream and diverse constructivism as a matter of emphasis and degree rather than kind. In her opinion, the mainstream constructivist orientation does not take adequate account of differences (ethnicity, primary language, and social class) that may affect school success. A diverse orientation attempts to look at how schools devalue and could revalue the cultural capital of students of diverse backgrounds. For instance, the mainstream constructivist orientation recognizes that students' knowledge claims must be considered valid within students' own cultural contexts. A diverse constructivist orientation inquires into the ways that knowledge claims are related to cultural identity and are shaped by ethnicity, primary language, and social class. A mainstream constructivist orientation may assume that students need primarily to acquire the proficiency in literacy needed for self-expression and for success in the larger society, but the diverse constructivist orientation suggests that a concern for proficiency should not be allowed to override a concern for the transformative possibilities of literacy for both the individual and the society. Au and Carroll (1997) underscore the support required from resources outside the classroom (e.g., extensive staff development, time for planning, school restructuring) if one seeks to fully implement an activity-based instructional approach. Teachers can get beyond generalizations and can arrive at specific visions of local classrooms.

In similar fashion, Brown and Campione (1994) distinguish between two types of change (implementation): immanent change that is created within the social system and contact change that is created outside the social system in question. Selective contact occurs when people learn about a new idea and choose to implement it, and directed contact occurs when outsiders force the innovation to be adopted. Brown and Campi-

one's dissemination effort has been one of selective contact and immanent change, with teachers free to select new ideas and innovations according to their needs—as long as they adhere to the first principles of learning on which the program is based. The notion of "implementation as evolution" (Majone & Wildavsky, 1978), which is constrained by those first principles, provides a way to for adaptation and modification to be organic parts of the implementation process. Ironically, specificity (e.g., addressing the special classroom culture) is the key to generalizing the activity-based approach to teaching and learning.

Activity-Based Learning: Concrete Examples

In this section, we focus on four significant and current instantiations of activity-based approaches that can serve as concrete models for thinking about diversity-oriented classroom cultures. The examples also illustrate the manipulation of framing and classification within activities, and they support the flow of communication between schools and communities. We describe each example in sufficient detail to illustrate a range of useful activity combinations.

First, we describe the case of sheltered English instruction, which highlights the instructional modifications for the instruction of second-language learners. Second, we describe the Fostering a Community of Learners project, which explicitly designs classroom activities to take advantage of classroom diversity and to enhance student responsibility and control. Third, we describe efforts to expand the classroom social practices to include local funds of knowledge and to change the social relationship between schools and their surrounding communities. Finally, we describe a combination or mixed model, which uses activity approaches to address Bernstein's concerns with framing and classification.

SHELTERED ENGLISH INSTRUCTION

For many children who enter public schools unable to speak English, the classroom is an alien place with unfamiliar language and social practices. The task of providing instruction to the increasing number of nonnative speakers is a huge challenge (Nieto, 1992). The enormity of this task is illustrated by the following description of the situation facing many schools and teachers today.

> School started the day after Labor Day. Our enrollment suddenly included 150 Hmong who had recently immigrated to our school district. We had neither classrooms nor teachers to accommodate such a large influx, and no one was qualified to deliver instruction in Hmong. By October, it was obvious that our policy of placing these students in regular content classes was not working. The students were frustrated by their inability to communicate and keep up with classwork, and teachers felt overwhelmed and inadequate to meet the needs of students who were barely literate and did not know English. (high school teacher journal entry, quoted in Diaz-Rico & Weed, 1995, p. 114)

Unlike English as a Second Language instruction that provides focused language instruction by pulling children out of classrooms so they receive segregated instruction with other non-English-proficient children, "sheltered English" deliberately modifies content area instruction to accommodate the diversity in the student population. Rather than expect students who are new to English to participate independently in content classes designed for native English speakers, students are given additional language and academic support in situ.

The approach of Specially Designed Academic Instruction in English (SDAIE) to sheltered English instruction combines second language acquisition principles with those elements of quality teaching that make a lesson understandable to students (Sobul, 1984, 1994). SDAIE has four goals for students: learn English, learn content, practice higher-level thinking skills, and advance individual literacy skills (Law & Eckes, 1990). Diaz-Rico and Weed (1995) build on Hudleson's (1989) suggestions and provide five principles to guide the design of SDAIE classrooms:

- Active participation: Students learn both content and language through active engagement in academic tasks that are directly related to a specific content.
- Social interaction: students learn both content and language by interacting with others as they carry out activities.
- Integrated oral and written language: Students become more able language learners when language processes are integrated in a variety of ways and for a variety of purposes.
- Real books and real tasks: Students learn to read authentic texts and to write for useful purposes.
- Background knowledge: Student's prior knowledge of a topic may be activated through classroom activities that are drawn from a variety of language resources.

Teachers in SDAIE classrooms use language to further knowledge acquisition rather than to focus on language itself. Classroom activities are designed to promote students' concurrent learning of English and academic content (Diaz-Rico & Weed, 1995). Lesson modifications include changes from "teacher-fronted" classrooms in which teacher talk dominates and directs the flow of information (i.e., the recitation script) toward classrooms that support cooperative work among students. Teachers in collaborative classrooms focused on assisting students with the learning task rather than on providing (language) error correction, gave fewer commands, and imposed less-disciplinary control. In addition, teachers consciously altered the pace of lessons and used cues both to support the language of the classroom and to provide their students with "comprehensible input" (Krashen, 1980). Cueing devices included the use of charts, diagrams, maps, and other visual displays to orient the students to the important aspects of the lesson content.

Teachers who use the SDAIE approach also modify the classroom organization with the dual purpose of language and content instruction in mind. Teachers attend to language-based objectives and subject matter objectives in ways that do not overburden the student. Clearly, the selection, modification, and organization of instructional materials is an essential aspect of a successful lesson. Materials must be selected according to their utility to provide the students with "comprehensible input." This approach means selecting a variety of materials including video and various texts (magazines, articles, books) with good graphics and little jargon. Some material re-

quires simplification of language, elaboration of concepts, or direct definitions (and may require using the students' native language). While providing instruction, teachers seek to integrate students' experiences or background knowledge through techniques such as brainstorming. Displaying this information using multiple graphic organizers such as semantic webs, maps, grids, and matrices supports students' understanding of the verbal discussion. Such understanding is also facilitated by using a wide range of presentation styles including lecturing (cueing students by including terms such as first, second, etc.); demonstrating with hands-on and show-and-tell explanations; working with text (outlining; overview of main headings, subheadings, etc.); and providing variable interaction patterns (individual practice, small group, dyads, whole group), thereby allowing students to test their language skills and content knowledge.

Evaluation of students is made consistent with the methods of instruction. For example, to expect a student to indicate his or her understanding by making a formal oral presentation to the entire class would be unfair. SDAIE teachers provide a range of ways for students to demonstrate their understandings, including those with which they are not completely comfortable. Finally, a crucial step is the follow-up lesson. Because each lesson has a dual purpose (language and content understanding), the follow-up provides an additional opportunity for students to test their understandings and to express their concerns and questions.

FOSTERING A COMMUNITY OF LEARNERS

The Fostering a Community of Learners (FCL) project is a system of interactive activities that are designed to produce a self-consciously active and reflective learning environment. The role of the teacher is key to organizing this type of classroom. Brown and Campione (1994, 1996) avoid the dichotomy between discovery learning and didactic instruction by arguing in favor of a Deweyesque middle ground that they refer to as "guided discovery." In guided discovery, the teacher acts as a facilitator, guiding the students' learning. Brown and Campione (1994) willingly admit that guided discovery is difficult to orchestrate and requires a teacher's sensitive clinical judgment of when to intervene and when to leave well enough alone.

FCL teachers promote guided discovery by drawing on the expertise among the students (reducing classification and enhancing recognition of diversity) and the wider community beyond the classroom itself, again weakening framing and classification. At its simplest level, the FCL instructional approach has three key parts: research, share, and perform. Students engage in independent and group research on a selected aspect of a topic of inquiry, mastery of which is ultimately the responsibility of all members of the class. The division of labor requires that children share their expertise with their classmates. This sharing is further motivated by some consequential task or activity (e.g., a test or quiz or the design of a "biopark" for endangered species) that demands that all students have learned about all aspects of the joint topic. The cycles of research–share–perform are the backbone of FCL (Brown & Campione, 1996).

In addition to other instructional techniques (see Table 44.4), reciprocal teaching and a modified version of the jigsaw method of cooperative learning are used. Specifically, students are assigned curriculum themes (e.g., changing populations), each divided into approximately five subtopics (e.g., extinct, endangered, artificial, assisted, and urbanized populations). Students form separate research groups, each assigned responsibility for one of the five-or-so subtopics. These research groups prepare teaching materials using commercially available, stable computer technology. Then the students regroup into reciprocal teaching seminars in which each student is expert in one subtopic, holding one-fifth of the information. Each fifth needs to be combined with the remaining fifths to make a whole unit, hence "jigsaw." All children in a learning group are expert on one part of the material, teach it to others, and prepare questions for the test that all will take as part of the complete unit. Thus, the burden of teaching others and learning from others' expertise is a real one and is a mainstay of these classrooms (Brown & Campione, 1996). By having students regularly disseminate information to classmates who depend on each other to get data for their projects, as well as by having projects connect with real-world consequences, teachers can organize learning activities to connect students with each other and with the world beyond the classroom. The particular activity structures of FCL are chosen to motivate, enable, and support the central research–share–perform cycles. Several activities and their classroom organization are summarized in Table 44.4.

Brown and Campione (1994, 1996) have identified the following features that characterize the ideal FCL classroom:

- Individual responsibility is coupled with communal sharing, which results in increased diversity of experience, knowledge, and skills among the classroom members.
- The use of ritual and familiar participation structures and routines enable children to make the transition from one participation structure to another quickly and effortlessly. For example, as soon as students recognize a participation structure, they understand the role expected of them. These routines include (a) the organization of students into groups (composing on computers, conducting research through various media or interaction with the teacher, editing manuscripts, discussing progress); (b) jigsaw teaching activity; and (c) benchmark lessons in which the teacher or outside expert introduces new information for reflection.
- A community of discourse guides the development of normative discourse that operates during each type of participation structure. This discourse knowledge is essential for active and productive participation in the classroom routines.
- Multiple zones of proximal development among classroom members are organized in activities such as the jigsaw technique to capitalize on the range of expertise and diversity among the children and teacher, a process that circulates power in the classroom routinely.
- Strategies are used such as seeding, migration, and appropriation of ideas. The role of the teacher is to "seed" new ideas and concepts into the classroom and to allow those that work to be "taken up." Those ideas migrate and are appropriated differently among the children, thus cultivating and enhancing the diversity of expertise in the classroom.

Table 44.4. Elements of Fostering a Community of Learners

Research	Shared Information	Consequential Task
Reading/Studying (Reciprocal Teaching) (Research Seminar)	Jigsaw	Exhibitions
Guided Viewing	Cross-Talk	Tests, Quizzes
Guided Writing	Distributed Exercise	Design Tasks
Consulting Experts (face-to-face)	Majoring	Publishing
Consulting Experts (electronic mail)	Help-Seeking	Transparent Assessments
Peer- and Cross-Age Teaching/Research	Exhibitions	Authentic Assessments

Note: Adapted from "Psychological Theory and the Design of Innovative Learning Environments," A. Brown and J. C. Campione in *Innovations in Learning* (pp. 289–325), by L. Schauble and R. Glaser, 1996, Mahwah, NJ: Lawrence Erlbaum Associates.

Using a similar approach, also referred to as "community of learners," Rogoff (1994) extends the notion of transforming roles to include parents and the relationships between teachers and neighborhood representatives. According to a theory of participation and transformation of roles that leads toward greater responsibility and autonomy, each participant is viewed as key and active in guiding the decisions and instruction that occur in the school and classrooms. This approach to a community of learners provides opportunities for teachers and parents to inform each other regarding their respective knowledge bases and requires both to transform the traditional boundaries associated with their roles as teachers and parents (for more details see Matusov, Bell & Rogoff, 1994). This entire ensemble of changes materially affects the framing and classification practices in the classroom as a whole.

FUNDS OF KNOWLEDGE

The previous two examples have focused primarily on weakening the framing and classification of classroom culture within the classroom settings themselves while giving secondary attention to connections between classroom and community. The Funds of Knowledge project extends the changes in the classroom beyond its physical walls. Luis Moll and his colleagues (Moll, 1996; Moll, Amanti, Neff, & Gonzalez, 1992; Vélez-Ibáñez, Moll, Gonzalez, & Neff, 1991; Moll & Greenberg, 1990) have established what they refer to as "strategic connections" between household research and classroom practice through teachers' participation in "ethnographic experiments" (Moll, 1996). Ethnographic experiments lower the classification of classrooms by lessening the separation of social practices in and out of school, and they have facilitated the flow of communication between school and community that has been suggested by Bernstein (1990).

The Funds of Knowledge project consists of three main, interrelated activities: (a) an ethnographic analysis of the transmission of knowledge and skills among households, (b) creation of an after-school laboratory where researchers and teachers use community information to experiment with literacy instruction, and (c) classroom observations in which researchers and

Table 44.5. Examples of Household Funds of Knowledge

Agriculture and Mining	Material and Scientific Knowledge
Ranching and farming	Construction
Horse riding skills	Carpentry
Animal management	Roofing
Soil and irrigation systems	Masonry
Crop planting	Painting
Hunting, tracking, dressing	Design and architecture
Mining	Repair
Timbering	Airplane
Mineral	Automobile
Blasting	Tractor
Equipment operation and	House maintenance
maintenance	
Economics	Medicine
Business	Contemporary medicine
Market values	Drugs
Appraising	First aid procedures
Renting and selling	Anatomy
Loans	Midwifery
Labor laws	
Building codes	Folk medicine
Consumer knowledge	Herbal knowledge
Accounting	Folk cures
Sales	Folk veterinary cures
Household Management	Religion
Budgets	Catechism
Child care	Baptisms
Cooking	Bible study
Appliance repairs	Moral knowledge and ethics

Note: Adapted from "Funds of Knowledge for Teaching: Using a Qualitative Approach to Connect Homes and Classrooms," by L. C. Moll, C. Amanti, D. Neff, and N. Gonzalez, 1992, *Theory into Practice, XXXI,* pp. 132–141.

teachers examine existing methods of instruction and explore how to change instruction by applying what is learned at the after-school site (Moll & Greenberg, 1990).

The household analysis highlights the networks formed by the social sharing of knowledge that are part of the households' functioning. This sharing is referred to as the exchange of "funds of knowledge" (see Table 44.5) (Greenberg, 1989; Vélez-Ibáñez, 1988). The social networks serve as a buffer against uncertain and changing economic circumstances, promote labor markets by acting as a pipeline to formal and informal jobs, and serve important emotional functions that are most prominent in child care and rearing.

Moll (1996) stresses that funds of knowledge are not context-free possessions or traits of people in the family but characteristics of people brought to life in an activity. What is important about these activities is the process by which skills are acquired through productive activity and then exchanged through social relationships. These social relations provide a motive and context for applying and acquiring knowledge. Household observations suggest the importance of taking into account not only visible and apparent knowledge but also the more latent or hidden knowledge that is displayed in helping or teaching others. Unlike typical classroom arrangements, much of the teaching and learning within these activities is initiated by the children's interests and their questions. Children are active in creating their own activities or are active within the structure of the tasks created by the adults. In either case, knowledge is obtained by the children, not imposed by the adults.

Moll believes that, without a focus on social relationships and people in activity as the unit of analysis, outsiders (educators) can very easily underestimate the wealth of funds of knowledge available in working-class households; those funds of knowledge may not be patently obvious to teachers or students. This knowledge and all its forms represent a major, untapped resource for academic instruction because it rarely makes its way into classrooms in any substantive manner (Moll & Greenberg, 1990). Cazden (2000) refers to a similar notion as "transferable design resources" (i.e., the knowledge students have gained from their community interactions). Cazden states that a teachers' assumption that all students have such resources is the indispensable first step toward incorporating those resources into the classroom.

The ultimate purpose of the household analysis is to change classroom practice (Moll & Diaz, 1987). Specifically, teachers use the information gained in households to change the sorts of activities and routines available within classrooms. The goal is not to replicate the household in the classroom, but to recreate strategically those aspects of household life that may lead to productive academic activities within the classroom. To support those changes in the classroom culture and to develop appropriate instructional materials, teachers and researchers participate in "change labs," which are seminars held after school. In addition, teachers participate in study groups aimed at understanding the data collected in households, its "fit" and utility for changing classroom practices, and the changes that are likely to be worthwhile (i.e., make a difference for student learning). (See Figure 44.10.)

An example of a topic used in the after-school change lab is one focused on construction and building, one of the most prominent funds of knowledge found in the children's homes that Moll studied. The group started collaborating by showing the students slides of a group of men constructing a home in rural Mexico as a way of eliciting their comments on the building process. Children then developed models of buildings or houses constructed with wood, paper, and other materials. One teacher decided to extend the topic as a research project with her sixth-grade students. After discussing the topic with the students, the teacher instructed them to visit the library and start locating information on building or construction, including materials on the history of dwellings and on different ways of building structures. Together, the students and teacher collected information on architects and carpenters. During the first phase, students built model houses and wrote brief essays describing their research and explaining their constructions. In the second phase, they mobilized funds of knowledge by inviting parents as experts to provide information on specific aspects of construction. For example, a mason described his use of construction instruments and tools. He then explained how he estimated or measured the area or perimeter of the location in which he worked. What is important is that the teacher invited parents and others in the community to contribute substantively to the development of lessons in order to access their funds of knowledge for academic purposes (a total of 20 people visit the classroom during this lesson). The visits provided opportunities for extending the initial lesson.

In one visit, a student's brother, who was studying to be a draftsman, presented construction plans to the class. This visit

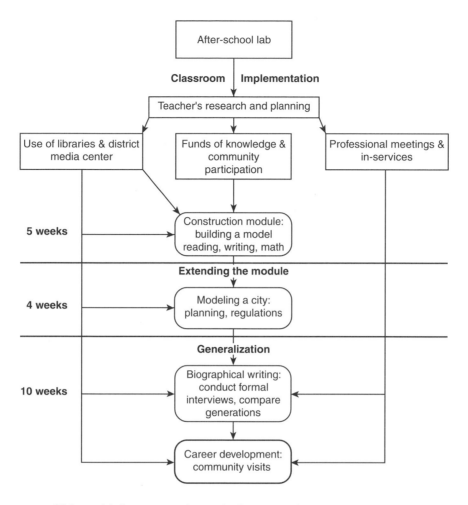

Figure 44.10. The process of "change labs" to support changes in classroom culture.

sparked the students to combine their individual structures to form a community. The students conducted subsequent research on what a town or city requires (e.g., water, electricity, etc.). Students supplemented their library research by conducting observations in their own communities to determine what other aspects of urban life they might need to incorporate into their model city. During this phase of classroom work, the teacher continued to participate in the change labs in which she received advice from researchers and other teacher colleagues.

During final phase, referred to as "generalization," the teacher extended the lesson without the direct assistance of the research team. This important phase illustrated how the teacher creates something to support new curricular goals that would address the needs of a specific classroom. Having attended an in-service on writing, the teacher incorporated developed materials into the lesson by giving students an assignment to write biographies about people from different generations. Key interview questions regarding the types of jobs that people had done were included. Visitors from different generations came to the class, and students asked them relevant questions. In addition, students were asked to interview two more people in their community from two different generations and to compare their interviews.

In recent efforts toward sustaining the project, teachers have become teacher–researchers, not only in the traditional sense of studying their own classrooms but also in conducting their own fieldwork in their students' communities (Moll, 1996; Moll, Amanti, Neff, & Gonzalez, 1992). The purpose of this policy is for teachers to develop both theory and method while they identify community cultural resources that could be used for teaching. Their aims necessarily engage families and family knowledge, thereby developing the "confianza," or mutual trust, needed to create new social relationships that are flexible and reciprocal between teachers and families (Moll, 1996). Parents and other people contributed to lessons because of the implicit assumption that the students would benefit academically. Clearly, such relationships could not be sustained if the parents, teachers, or students believed them to be educationally insignificant (Moll & Greenberg, 1990).

Computers, Activity, and Classroom Culture

Several general reviews of the effect that computers have on classroom processes have been done to which the interested reader can turn (Cognition and Technology Group, 1996; Crook, 1998; Kerr, 1996; Koschmann, 1996; Mandinach,

Cline, & Service, 1994; Papert, 1993; Riel, 1992; Riel & Fulton, 1998; Schofield, 1995; Scott, Cole, & Engel, 1992). Although the general tenor of this work has been one of optimism that computers and associated telecommunications facilities will provide clear benefits to education, others predict that computers are destined to follow typewriters and television into the dustbin of failed educational reforms (Cuban, 1986; Stoll, 1996).

Clearly, the way that computers are integrated into the classroom depends on the culture the teacher is seeking to promote there (Cuban, 1993). When computer use is blended into classrooms that depend heavily on the recitation script and on the educational philosophy it supports, teachers are likely to treat the computer as a tutor—a substitute human for individual instruction. When computers are blended into activity-centered classrooms, they are more likely to be conceived of as tools (Crook, 1998; Riel & Fulton, 1998). Some successes with respect to issues of educational achievement can be noted for those who adopt both metaphors.

Computer Use to Enhance Teacher-Centered Instruction

Two examples give the flavor of what can be accomplished within a more-or-less standard classroom using computers as tutors. Reinking and Rickman (1990) investigated whether the vocabulary learning and comprehension of readers in intermediate grades would be affected by displaying texts on a computer screen that provided the meanings of difficult words. Among sixth-grade subjects, 60 read two informational passages containing several target words that had been identified as difficult. The results indicated that subjects who read passages with computer assistance scored significantly higher on a vocabulary test that measured the subjects' knowledge of target words.

Such programs have the power to go well beyond basic skills in ways that are designed to create greater reflective awareness of literacy skills. For example, a program developed by Glynda Hull and her colleagues (Hull, Ball, Fox, Levin, & McCutchen, 1985) was designed to teach basic writing to university students. A taxonomy of writing errors, called a "bug library," is inserted into the memory of a computer, and writing errors are detected through a process of pattern matching. With this intelligent word processor, a student composes a text and then asks the machine to scan it to pick out standard bugs. When the computer detects one of these errors, it calls up the passage with the error in it and displays it on the screen with the erroneous sentence highlighted in boldface type. Instead of explicitly stating the correct writing rule, the computer prompts the student to search for and solve the problem independently. The machine thus requires such active engagement that the author starts to recognize typical errors and, by repeatedly correcting them, learns to avoid making them. Studies carried out in both laboratory and instructional settings confirm that novice writers do improve (Hull, 1989).

However, despite their apparent potential, no quantum leap in educational achievement can be associated broadly with the inclusion of computers as instructional media in standard classrooms. Most important, they have shown no special power in amplifying the learning rates of children from nonmainstream cultural backgrounds.

Reviews are unanimous that introducing computers with sophisticated software is no guarantee of a significant change in either student performance or classroom cultures. For example, the large and initially well-funded Apple Classrooms of Tomorrow (ACOT) failed to show significant increases in student's academic skills from the use of computers (Baker, Gearheart, & Herman, 1990). Instead, the need to reorganize classrooms to take advantage of and support heavy computer use is emphasized. Curriculum design, building organization, teacher preparation, and their histories (academic, personal, and cultural) all profoundly affect and are affected by the realization of the potential of the computer in the classroom (Riel & Fulton, 1998; Sandholtz, Ringstaff, & Dwyer, 1992).

Computer Use to Support Activity-Centered Instruction

Of particular interest in this chapter is computer hardware and software that is designed to change the standard instructional climate by creating an activity-centered curriculum (Cole, Griffin, & LCHC, 1987; Koschmann, 1996; Riel & Fulton, 1998). Many demonstration proofs have been conducted to show that, when combined with extensive use of telecommunications, the use of new information technologies can bring about significant changes in classroom cultures. The concept that computers can provide solid benefits to children's education that are multicultural and inclusive appears at least plausible. Diaz-Rico and Weed's (1995) summary of key features of specially designed academic instruction in English provides a good summary of the kinds of features to strive for.

The expectation for active participation, at most, biases the selection of computer programs against those that amplify the "drill and kill" potential of computers or, at least, motivates the careful inclusion of computers in a broader range of activities so that the basics are learned in the context of the higher-order activities they are designed to mediate.

Social interaction is oriented to the joint use of computers or to the use of computers as means of obtaining information about issues of interest. Use of e-mail discussions has a leveling effect on traditional hierarchies of classroom status, a shift that disproportionately aids those who are least likely to be active participants in a traditional classroom. Goldman & Newman (1992) examined the features of e-mail discourse among sixth-grade students and their teacher who communicated with each other within a single classroom. The similarities found between face-to-face and electronic communication included (a) frequent metacommunication through letters, notes, and memos and (b) mindfulness of the differences in status and hierarchy between teachers and students. Complex and interrelated differences were also found between classroom discourse and e-mail discourse.

The researchers used the initiate-respond-evaluate sequence from research on patterns of classroom interaction (Mehan, 1979) to analyze network discourse. They found that, in classroom discourse, teachers usually initiated interaction, but in network discourse, students and teachers both initiated interaction. The temporal sequence of the exchange was altered by the fact that a single sequence might extend over days or weeks. Invitations made electronically by the teacher might go unanswered or receive parallel responses on different days. Reply interactions made electronically involved more than three turns, with less competition for the reply slot. Students could take turns as they wished, each responding to more than one question at a time, and they experienced fewer restrictions on the numbers of possible replies. Evaluation of replies was much less common in electronic communication. Correct answers were sometimes provided by the teacher, but often they contained no mention of any incorrect responses. Private messages from the teacher to students sometimes contained evaluative statements. In this case, the network was used to complement rather than replace the interaction that routinely occurs in the classroom. More recently, the Cognition and Technology Group (1996), Harasim (1996), and Riel and Fulton (1998), among others, have argued that the attributes of "anytime, anyplace communication" that distinguishes network learning actually make group interaction and collaboration in this medium especially effective when implementing activity-centered curricula.

INTEGRATION OF ORAL AND WRITTEN LANGUAGE

The integration of oral and written language is a normal characteristic of activity-based classrooms that makes for a heavy use of computers as tools for communication within and between classrooms. In fact, the within–between distinction itself gets becomes problematic when children at different sites work collaboratively through networks with others who may or may not be nearby geographically. Cross-classroom collaboration (Riel, 1993, 1996; Riel & Fulton, 1998) can involve a portion of the curriculum that is conducted on-line and in which students in distant classrooms work together to conduct projects that are integrated with the total curriculum. This collaboration involves extensive and reciprocal interaction among classes. An example of cross-classroom collaboration is the Learning Circles, implemented on the AT&T learning network. Learning Circles was specifically designed as global education to promote multicultural sensitivities. It provided tangible opportunities for collaborative problem solving. Similar to "quality circles," which are common in the business field, six to nine classes form a learning circle. Students in these classes design and organize the curriculum using computer telecommunications. Students learn how to plan, organize, and complete projects with distant partners as they conduct research on societal or global issues. Multiple sources are used in research, including local community interviews and archival research. Each classroom group in a learning circle helps create the circle publication that summarizes the complete work at the end of the session. This publication process helps students review and evaluate the exchanges they had with others in distant locations. No one teacher controls a learning circle. It is a collective construction by the participants.

REAL TEXT AND REAL TASKS

Real text and real tasks can be enhanced through network access that provides a broader array of information and classroom members. For instance, Levin, Boruta and Vasconcellos (1983) showed more than a decade ago that elementary school children's writing improved when they used computer networks to communicate—not with computer tutors, but with other students. They speculated that using a computer to communicate with other writers from a distance may have a positive effect on writing performance because the students perceive the assignment as a real task and sense the presence of an authentic reader.

More recently, Neuwirth and Wojahn (1996) found that the use of PREP, a computer writing program, supported the cooperative writing process among university students. Students' original text drafts were shared for peer review coaching among students. The PREP program allowed multiple users to review and mark up the electronic document as if they were marking up a printed copy of the document (e.g., to add text, draw arrows, and so forth) without replacing the original text. Once a peer provided the author with suggestions and critique, the teacher could add suggestions for consideration. The program records the suggestions and organizes them to reveal the original draft in one column, a peer's suggestions for revision in the second column, and teacher's suggestions in a third column.

BACKGROUND KNOWLEDGE

Background knowledge is most clearly enhanced through computer networking and use of worldwide web (www) resources. The more-familiar association between computers and collaboration that involves interactions among a small group of learners working together at a computer can also furnish the settings for the construction of shared knowledge around computers, a benefit not derived in one-computer-to-one-child arrangements (Cole, Griffin, & LCHC, 1987; Crook, 1998. For instance, Pease-Alvarez and Vasquez (1990) found that the collaboration around computers not only provided computer knowledge but also enabled dominant Spanish speakers opportunities to use their native language as a support while learning subject matter content using the computer. In addition, students who participated in peer tutoring around computers used oral language in ways that differed markedly from interactions during typical classroom lessons. As student tutorial pairs learned more about using computers and their applications, they, in turn, became tutors and were then paired with younger and less-experienced students. In this way, the background knowledge of older students, both linguistically and academically, led to improved reading and writing performance in the younger students.

Despite the potential and promise of computers, commentators— even those such as Riel who advocate their use—continue to point out the downside of widespread use of computers and networks in classrooms at all levels of the curriculum (Noble, 1998; Riel, 1996; Stoll, 1996). Inequalities in access remain a severe problem. Even when access is achieved, the virtues of computers and telecommunications for reorganizing classroom cultures require ongoing support and attention. By all accounts, the technology will continue to change dramatically from year to year and will require an ongoing level of investment that is taken into account all too rarely by those who act on demonstrations of the possible without fully considering the costs to implement those possibilities. In sum, new information technologies enable new patterns of communication with people and resources located outside the classroom and provide important resources for building effective classroom cultures. But whether technology will fulfill this potential on a broad basis and fulfill it in a way that enhances the effectiveness of multicultural classrooms remains to be seen.

Concluding Remarks: Hybridity All the Way Down

Many years ago, John Dewey formulated the underlying tension that has suffused our discussion.

> [M]ankind likes to think in terms of extreme opposites. It is given to formulating its beliefs in terms of Either-Ors, between which it recognizes no intermediate possibilities. When forced to recognize that the extremes cannot be acted upon it is still inclined to hold that they are all right in theory but that when it comes to practical matters circumstances compel us to compromise. Educational philosophy is no exception. (Dewey, 1938, p. 17)

Clearly, the literature we have reviewed here has been replete with the "either-or" that characterized the debate between traditional and progressive approaches to education. Consistent with Dewey's call to overcome dualistic thinking, we have repeatedly referred to the hybrid nature of classrooms that builds on, rather than fights against, diversity.

In *Hybrid Cultures*, anthropologist Reynato Rosaldo (1995) differentiates two meanings of the term *hybridity*. Although his remarks are made with respect to the situation in Latin America, we believe they are well suited to our present discussion:

> On the one hand, hybridity can imply a space betwixt and between two zones of purity in a manner that follows biological usage that distinguishes two discreet species and the hybrid pseudo species that results from their combination. . . . On the other hand, hybridity can be understood as the ongoing condition of all human cultures, which contain no zones of purity because they undergo continuous processes of transculturation (two-way borrowing and lending between cultures). Instead of hybridity versus purity, this view suggests, it is hybridity all the way down. (1995, p. xv)

We believe classroom cultures provide strong examples of what Rosaldo referred to as "hybridity all the way down." Clearly, the local classroom culture is affected by the products (tangible in objects, less tangible in tradition) of the ongoing practice and process of schooling. Each element embodies the philosophies, values, and concrete realities of the communities in question. Those elements are present in the federal regulations, the state curriculum guides, the policies of the local school board, and the district and school administrations. The teacher and the students all have birth cultures that, by providing a base of prior experience, serve as the test beds for their understandings of the classroom and the world. The teacher and students also have experience in multiple local institutional cultures that are mediated by gender, ethnicity, and class. None of these is left at the doorway of the classroom.

In addition to the presence of home cultures, but only par-

tially represented in this chapter, one finds in the classroom the local school culture (Bernstein, 1975; Daniels, 1995; Hamilton & Richardson, 1995; Sarason, 1996; Seeger, Voigt, & Waschescio, 1998), the professional culture of teachers (Feiman-Nemser & Floden, 1986; Gitlin, 1983); the pop culture (Giroux & Simon, 1992); and the kid culture (Fine, 1987). We could add to this list. What is clear is that "the culture" of the classroom is always "the cultures" of the classroom.

In our search for relevant literature for the task of writing about classroom culture, we found a text written more than 20 years ago titled *Culture in the Classroom* (Reynolds & Skilbeck, 1976), which resonates with the current situation. The authors stated:

> [S]chools are entering a phase in which reaction against inadequately planned, overambitious curriculum innovations will be justifiably strong. But the need is for the better planning of curriculum reconstruction rather than less planning and curriculum inertia. (p. 126)

In final chapter of Reynolds and Skilbeck (1976), the complexity of classroom culture is reduced to four poignant choices:

1. Schools can swim with the tide, identifying basic trends and features of culture and go along with rather than resisting them,
2. Schools may identify particular values, beliefs and outlooks in the cultural heritage and seek to preserve them,
3. Schools may largely ignore current cultural trends and preserve some island existence, or
4. Schools may set out to analyze, assess, and think critically and creatively about their culture, looking for ways to contribute to its future development. (p. 126)

Reynolds and Skilbeck state that if the fourth alternative is chosen, clarity regarding what counts as "critical and creative contributions to the development of culture" is essential. These four decisions hinge on conceptions and valuations of culture so tacit that they are not easy to externalize, operationalize, or test. And they will always be contested.

We have chosen the fourth option. We have attempted to understand former successes and failures both through the historical context of their implementation and in the present school circumstances. Moore (1980) suggests that the only sustainable alternative may be to have it both ways by working for the transformation of schooling while also working within its reproduction.

At first impression, we were disconcerted to find that a 20-year-old reference to the culture in the classroom would offer alternatives that still ring true and appropriate. We now find solace in the hope that what we have written will be judged as an example of the fourth option offered by Reynolds and Skilbeck (1976)—as a critical and creative assessment that is based on current (and ever-changing) circumstances.

REFERENCES

Abi-Nader, J. (1990). "A house for my mother": Motivating Hispanic high school students. *Anthropology & Education Quarterly, 21*(1), 41–58.

Adams, R. S., & Biddle, B. J. (1970). *Realities of teaching: Exploration with videotape.* New York: Holt, Rinehart, & Winston.

Akinasso, F. N. (1991). Literacy and individual consciousness. In E. M. Jennings & A. C. Purves (Eds.), *Literate systems and individual lives: Perspectives on literacy and schooling* (pp. 73–94). Albany, NY: State University of New York Press.

Allington, R. L. (1980). Teacher interruption behaviors during primary grade oral reading. *Journal of Educational Society, 72*(3), 371–374.

Altman, I., & Wohlwill, J. F. (Eds.). (1978). *Human behavior and environment: Advances in theory and research* (Vol. 3). New York: Plenum Press.

Anthropology & Education Quarterly, 28(3), 1997.

Anyon, J. (1980). Social class and the hidden curriculum of work. *Journal of Education, 162*(1), 69–92.

Au, K. (1998). Social constructivism and the school literacy learning of students of diverse backgrounds. *Journal of Literacy Research, 30*(2), 297–319.

Au, K. H., & Carroll, J. H. (1997). Improving literacy achievement through a constructivist approach: The KEEP demonstration classroom project. *Elementary School Journal, 97*(3), 203–221.

Au, K. H., & Jordan, C. (1981). Teaching reading to Hawaiian children: Finding a culturally appropriate solution. In H. Trueba, G. P. Guthrie, & K. H. Au (Eds.), *Culture in the bilingual classroom* (pp. 139–152). Rowley, MA: Newbury House.

Au, K. H., & Mason, J. (1981). Social organizational factors in learning to read: The balance of rights hypothesis. *Reading Research Quarterly, 17*(1), 115–152.

Baker, E., Gearhart, M., & Herman, J. (1990). *Apple Classrooms of Tomorrow (ACOT) evaluation study: First and second year findings* (ACOT Report #7). Cupertino, CA: Apple Computers.

Barker, R. G. (1968). *Ecological psychology: Concepts and methods for studying the environment of human behavior.* Stanford, CA: Stanford University Press.

Bateson, G. (1972). The role of somatic change in evolution. In *Steps to an ecology of mind* (pp. 346–363). New York: Ballantine.

Bereiter, K., & Englemann, S. (1966). *Teaching the disadvantaged child in the preschool.* Englewood Cliffs, NJ: Prentice-Hall.

Berliner, D.C. (1983). Developing conceptions of classroom environments: Some light on the T in classroom studies of ATI. *Educational Psychologist, 18,* 1–13.

Bernstein, B. (1973). On the classification and framing of educational knowledge. In R. Brown (Ed.), *Knowledge, education, and cultural change* (pp. 363–392). London: Tavistock.

Bernstein, B. (1975). Class, codes and control. In B. Bernstein (Ed.), *Primary socialization, language and education* (Vol. 3, pp. 116–145). London: Routledge & Kegan Paul.

Bernstein, B. (1990). *Class, codes and control: Vol. 4. The structuring of pedagogical discourse.* London: Routledge.

Bloom, A. (1987). *The closing of the American mind.* New York: Simon & Schuster.

Boas, F. (1911). *The mind of primitive man.* New York: Macmillan.

Bowen, J. (1972). *A history of western education* (Vol. 1). London: Methuen & Co.

Bowers, S. A., & Flinders, D. J. (1990). *Responsive teaching.* New York: Teachers College Press.

Bredo, E., Henry, M., & McDermott, R. P. (1990). The cultural organization of teaching and learning. *Harvard Educational Review, 60*(2), 247–258.

Bremme, D. W., & Erickson, F. (1977). Relationships among verbal and nonverbal classroom behaviors. *Theory Into Practice, XVI*(3), 153–161.

Briggs, E. E., & MacLean, J. R. (1969). *Freedom to learn: An active learning approach to mathematics.* Canada: Addison-Wesley.

Brown, A. L., & Campione, J. C. (1994). Guided discovery in a community of learners. In K. McGilly (Ed.), *Classroom lessons* (pp. 229–270). Cambridge, MA: MIT Press.

Brown, A. L., & Campione, J. C. (1996). Psychological theory and the design of innovative learning environments: On procedures, principles, and systems. In L. Schauble & R. Glaser (Eds.), *Innovations in learning: New environments for education* (pp. 289–325). Mahwah, NJ: Lawrence Erlbaum Associates.

Bruner, J. (1996). *The culture of education.* Cambridge, MA: Harvard University Press.

Burke, K. (1945). *A grammar of motives.* New York: Prentice-Hall.

Caudill, W. (1941). Space for teaching. *Bulletin of the Agricultural and Mechanical College of Texas, 12*(9), 42–46.

Cazden, C. B. (1986). Classroom discourse. In M. C. Wittrock (Ed.), *Handbook of research on teaching* (3rd ed., pp. 432–463). New York: Macmillan.

Cazden, C. B. (2000). Taking cultural differences into account. In W. Cope & M. Kalantzis (Eds.), *Multiliteracies: Literacy learning and the designs of social futures* (pp. 249–266). London: Routledge.

Cazden, C. B., & Mehan, H. (1989). Principles from sociology and anthropology: Context, code, classroom, and culture. In M. C. Reynolds (Ed.), *Knowledge base for the beginning teacher* (pp. 47–58). Exeter, Great Britain: A. Wheaton & Co.

Chaiklin, S., & Lave, J. (Eds.). (1993). *Understanding practice: Perspectives on activity and context.* Cambridge, UK: Cambridge University Press.

Chall, J. (1983). *Learning to read: The great debate.* New York: McGraw-Hill.

Cognition and Technology Group at Vanderbilt. (1996). Looking at technology in context: A framework for understanding technology and education research. In D. Berliner & E. R. Calfee (Eds.), *Handbook of educational psychology* (pp. 807–840). New York: Wiley.

Cole, M. (1996). *Cultural psychology: A once and future discipline.* Cambridge, MA: Belknap Press of Harvard University Press.

Cole, M., Griffin, P., & Laboratory of Comparative Human Cognition. (1987). *Contextual factors in education.* Madison, WI: Wisconsin Center for Educational Research.

Collins, J. (1986). Differential instruction in reading groups. In J. Cook-Gumperz (Ed.), *The social construction of literacy* (pp. 117–137). Cambridge, UK: Cambridge University Press.

Collins, M., & Tamarkin, C. (1982). *Marva Collins' way.* Los Angeles: J. P. Tarcher, Inc.

Corno, L. (1989). What it means to be literate about classrooms. In D. Bloome (Ed.), *Classrooms and literacy* (pp. 29–52). Norwood, NJ: Ablex Publishing.

Crook, C. (1998). Computer networks in education. *Psychologist, 11*(8), 378–380.

Cuban, L. (1984). *How teachers taught: Constancy and change in American classrooms, 1890–1980.* New York: Longman.

Cuban, L. (1986). *Teachers and machines: The classroom use of technology since 1920.* New York: Teachers College Press.

Cuban, L. (1993). Computers meet classroom: Classroom wins. *Teachers' College Record, 95*(2), 185–210.

Cummins, J. (1986). Empowering minority students: A framework for intervention. *Harvard Educational Review, 56*(1), 18–36.

Dahlke, H. O. (1958). *Values in culture and classroom.* New York: Harper & Brothers.

D'Amato, J. (1987). The belly of the beast: On cultural differences, castelike status, and the politics of school. *Anthropology & Education Quarterly, 18*(4), 335–356.

D'Andrade, R. (1984). Cultural meaning systems. In R. A. Shweder & R. A. LeVine (Eds.), *Culture theory: Essays on mind, self, and emotion* (pp. 88–119). Cambridge, UK: Cambridge University Press.

D'Andrade, R. (1996). Culture. In *Social Science Encyclopedia* (2nd ed., pp. 161–163). New York: Routledge.

Daniels, H. (1989). Visual displays of tacit relays of the structure of pedagogic practice. *British Journal of Sociology of Education, 10*(2), 123–140.

Daniels, H. (1995). Pedagogic practices, tacit knowledge, and discursive discrimination: Bernstein and post-Vygotskian research. *British Journal of Sociology of Education, 6*(4), 517–532.

Daniels, H., Holst, J., Lunt, I., & Johansen, L. U. (1996). A comparative study of the relation between different models of pedagogic practice and constructs of deviance. *Oxford Review of Education, 22*(1), 63–77.

Delpit, L. (1988). The silenced dialogue: Power and pedagogy in educating other people's children. *Harvard Educational Review, 58,* 280–298.

Delpit, L. (1995). *Other people's children: Cultural conflict in the classroom.* New York: The New Press.

Dewey, J. (1916). *Democracy and education.* New York: Macmillan.

Dewey, J. (1938). *Experience and education.* New York: Collier Books.

Diaz-Rico, L. T., & Weed, K. Z. (1995). *The cross-cultural, language, and academic development handbook: A complete K–12 reference guide.* Boston: Allyn & Bacon.

District of Columbia Board of Education. (1922). *Report of Board of Education 1921–1922.* Washington, DC: Government Printing Office.

Dorr-Bremme, D. W. (1990). Contextualization cues in the classroom: Discourse regulation and social control functions. *Language in Society, 19,* 379–492.

Doyle, W. (1986). Classroom organization and management. In M. C. Wittrock (Ed.), *Handbook of research on teaching* (3rd ed.). New York: Macmillan.

Eder, D. (1981). Ability grouping as a self fulfilling prophecy. *Sociology of Education, 54,* 151–161.

Eder, D. (1983). Ability grouping and students' self-concepts: A case study. *Elementary School Journal, 84*(2), 149–161.

Engeström, Y. (1987). *Learning by expanding.* Helsinki: Orinta-Konsultit Oy.

Engeström, Y. (1990). *Learning, working and imagining: Twelve studies in activity theory.* Helsinki: Orinta-Konsultit.

Erickson, F. (1984). School literacy, reasoning and civility: An anthropologist's perspective. *Review of Educational Research, 54*(4), 525–546.

Erickson, F. (1986). Qualitative methods in research on teaching. In M. C. Wittrock (Ed.), *Handbook of research on teaching* (3rd ed., pp. 119–161). New York: Macmillan.

Erickson, F. (1987). Transformation and school success: The politics and culture of educational achievement. *Anthropology & Education Quarterly, 18,* 335–356.

Erickson, F. (1996). Inclusion into what?: Thoughts on the construction of learning, identity, and affiliation in the general education classroom. In D. L. Speece & B. K. Keogh (Eds.), *Research on classroom ecologies: Implications for inclusion of children with learning disabilities* (pp. 91–107). Mahwah, NJ: Lawrence Erlbaum Associates.

Erickson, F., & Mohatt, G. (1982). Cultural organization of participation structures in two classrooms of Indian students. In G. Spindler (Ed.), *Doing the ethnography of schooling: Educational anthropology in action* (pp. 132–175). Prospect Heights, IL: Waveland Press.

Feiman-Nemser, S., & Floden, R. E. (1986). The cultures of teaching. In M. C. Wittrock (Ed.), *Handbook of research on teaching* (3rd ed., pp. 505–526). New York: Macmillan.

Fine, G. A. (1987). *With the boys: Little League baseball and preadolescent culture.* Chicago: University of Chicago Press.

Foley, D. E. (1991). Reconsidering anthropological explanations of ethnic school failure. *Anthropology & Education Quarterly, 22*(1), 60–86.

Forman, E. A., Minick, N., & Stone, C. A. (1993). *Contexts for learning.* New York: Oxford University Press.

Foucault, M. (1979). *Discipline and punish.* New York: Vintage.

Gallimore, R. (1996). Classrooms are just another cultural activity. In D. L. Speece & B. K. Keogh (Eds.), *Research on classroom ecologies: Implications for inclusion of children with learning disabilities* (pp. 229–250). Mahwah, NJ: Lawrence Erlbaum Associates.

Gallimore, R., & Goldenberg, C. (1993). Activity setting of early literacy: Home and school factors in children's emergent literacy. In E. Forman, N. Minick, & C. A. Stone (Eds.), *Conflicts for learning: Sociocultural dynamics in children's development.* New York: Oxford University Press.

Gee, J. (1989). Literacy, discourse, and linguistics [Special issue]. *Journal of Education, 171*(1).

Geertz, C. (1973). *The interpretation of cultures.* New York: Basic Books.

Gibson, M. A. (1988). *Accommodation without assimilation: Sikh immigrants in an American high school.* Ithaca, NY: Cornell University Press.

Gibson, M. A. (1997). Exploring and explaining the variability: Cross-national perspectives on the school performance of minority students. *Anthropology & Education Quarterly, 28*(3), 318–329.

Gibson, M. A., & Ogbu, J. U. (Eds.). (1991). *Minority status and schooling: A comparative study of immigrant and involuntary minorities.* New York: Garland Publishing.

Giroux, H. A. (1983). Theories of reproduction and resistance in the new sociology of education: A critical analysis. *Harvard Educational Review, 53*(3), 257–293.

Giroux, H. A., & Simon, R. I. (1992). Schooling, popular culture, and a pedagogy of possibility. In K. Weiler & C. Mitchell (Eds.), *What schools can do: Critical pedagogy and practice* (pp. 217–236). New York: State University of New York.

Gitlin, A. (1983). School structure and teachers' work. In M. W. Apple & L. Weis (Eds.), *Ideology and practice in schooling* (pp. 193–212). Philadelphia: Temple University Press.

Goldman, S., & Newman, D. (1992). Electronic initials: How students and teachers organize schooling over the wires. *Interactive Learning Environments, 2*(1), 31–45.

Goodenough, W. H. (1981). Problems in the conception of culture. In *Culture, language, and society* (2nd ed., pp. 47–59). Menlo Park, CA: The Benjamin/Cummings Publishing Company.

Goodenough, W. H. (1994). Toward a working theory of culture. In R. Borotsky (Ed.), *Assessing cultural anthropology* (pp. 262–273). New York: McGraw-Hill.

Gould, S. J. (1981). *The mismeasure of man.* New York: W. W. Norton.

Grant, C., & Secada, W. (1990). Preparing teachers for diversity. In W. R. Houston (Ed.), *Handbook of research in teacher education.* New York: Macmillan.

Greenberg, J. B. (1989). *Funds of knowledge: Historical constitution, social distribution, and transmission.* Paper presented at the annual meeting of the Society for Applied Anthropology.

Gumilev, L. N. (1990). *Ethnogenesis and the biosphere* (L. Gumilev, Trans.). Moscow: Progress Publishers.

Gump, P. V. (1967). *The classroom behavior setting: Its nature and relation to student behavior* [Final report]. Washington, DC: U.S. Office of Education, Bureau of Research. (ERIC Document Reproduction Service No. ED 015 515)

Gump, P. V. (1974). Operating environments in schools of open and traditional design. *School Review, 82*(4), 575–593.

Gump, P. V. (1975). *Ecological psychology and children* (Vol. 82). Chicago: University of Chicago Press.

Gump, P. V. (1978). School environments. In I. Altman & J. F. Wohlwill (Eds.), *Human behavior and environment: Advances in theory and research* (Vol. 3, pp. 131–169). New York: Plenum Press.

Gump, P. V. (1982). School settings and their keeping. In D. L. Duke (Ed.), *Helping teachers manage classrooms* (pp. 98–114). Alexandria, VA: Association for Supervision and Curriculum Development.

Gump, P. V., & Good, L. R. (1976). Environments operating in open space and traditionally designed schools. *Journal of Architectural Research, 5,* 20–27.

Gumperz, J. J. (1982). *Discourse strategies.* Cambridge, UK: Cambridge University Press.

Gutierrez, K., Rymes, B., & Larson, J. (1995). Script, counterscript, and underlife in the classroom—Brown, James versus Brown v. Board of Education. *Harvard Educational Review, 65*(3), 445–471.

Hamilton, M., & Richardson, V. (1995). Effects of the culture in two schools on the process and outcomes of staff development. *Elementary School Journal, 9*(4), 367–385.

Harasim, L. (1996). Computer networking for education. In T. Husen & T. M. Postlethwaite (Eds.), *International encyclopedia of education* (2nd ed., pp. 977–982). Oxford, UK: Pergamon.

Harris, M. (1968). *The rise of anthropological theory.* New York: Crowell.

Heath, S. B. (1982). Questioning at home and at school: A comparative study. In G. Spindler (Ed.), *Doing the ethnography of schooling: Educational anthropology in action* (pp. 102–131). Prospect Heights, IL: Waveland Press.

Heath, S. B. (1983). *Ways with words: Language, life, and work in communities and classrooms.* Cambridge, UK: Cambridge University Press.

Henry, J. (1963). *Culture against man.* New York: Random House.

Herder, J. G. (1966). *Outlines of a philosophy of the history of man.* New York: Bergman Publishers.

Herrnstein, R. J., & Murray, C. (1994). *The bell curve: Intelligence and class structure in American life.* New York: The Free Press.

Hirsch, E. D. (1987). *Cultural literacy: What every American needs to know.* New York: Vintage Books.

Hirsch, E. D., Kett, J. F., & Trefil, J. (1988). *The dictionary of cultural literacy.* Boston: Houghton Mifflin.

Hirschfeld, L. A. (1997). Conceptual politics of race: Lessons from our children. *Ethos, 25,* 63–92.

Hoetker, J., & Ahlbrand, W. P. (1969). The persistence of the recitation. *American Educational Research Journal, 6,* 145–167.

Hollingshead, A. B. (1949). *Elmtown's youth: The impact of social classes on adolescents.* New York: Wiley.

Hudelson, S. (1989). Teaching English through content-area activities. In P. Rigg & V. Allen (Eds.), *When they don't all speak English* (pp. 139–151). Urbana, IL: National Council of Teachers of English.

Hull, G. (1989). *Rethinking remediation: Toward a social-cognitive understanding of problematic reading and writing* (Technical Report 19). Washington, DC: Office of Educational Research and Improvement.

Hull, G., Ball, C., Fox, J. L., Levin, L., & McCutchen, D. (1985). *Computer detection of errors in natural language texts: Some research on pattern-matching.* Paper presented at the annual meeting of the Educational Research Association, Chicago, IL.

Jacob, E., & Jordan, C. (1987). Moving to dialogue. *Anthropology & Education Quarterly, 18*(4), 259–261.

Jensen, A. R. (1969). How much can we boost IQ and scholastic achievement. *Harvard Educational Review, 39*(1), 1–123.

Johnson, N. B. (1985). *Westhaven: Classroom culture and society in a rural elementary school.* Chapel Hill, NC: University of North Carolina Press.

Kerr, S. T. (Ed.). (1996). *Technology and the future of schooling: Ninety-fifth yearbook of the National Society for the Study of Education.* Chicago: University of Chicago Press.

Koschmann, T. (1996). *CSCL: Theory and practice of an emerging paradigm.* Mahwah, NJ: Lawrence Erlbaum Associates.

Kozol, J. (1991). *Savage inequalities: Children in America's schools.* New York: Harper Perennial.

Krashen, S. (1980). The theoretical and practical relevance of simple codes in second language acquisition. In T. Scarcella & S. Krashen (Eds.), *Research in second language acquisition* (pp. 7–18). Rowley, MA: Newbury House.

Kroeber, A. L., & Kluckhohn, C. (1963). *Culture: A critical review of concepts and definitions.* New York: Vintage Books. (Original work published 1952)

Kyle, W. C., Jr. (1984). What became of the curriculum development projects of the 1960s? How effective were they? What did we learn from them that will help teachers in today's classrooms? In D. Holdzkom & P. B. Lutz (Eds.), *Research within reach: Science education.* Charleston, WV: Appalachia Educational Laboratory.

Ladson-Billings, G. (1992). Reading between the lines and beyond the pages: A culturally relevant approach to literacy teaching. *Theory Into Practice, XXXI*(4), 312–320.

Ladson-Billings, G. (1995). Toward a theory of culturally relevant pedagogy. *American Educational Research Journal, 32*(3), 465–491.

Lave, J. (1993). The practice of learning. In S. Chaiklin & J. Lave (Eds.), *Understanding practice: Perspectives on activity and context* (pp. 3–32). New York: Cambridge University Press.

Lave, J., Duguid, P., Fernandez, N., & Axel, E. (1992). Coming of age in Birmingham: Cultural studies and conceptions of subjectivity. *Annual Review of Anthropology, 21,* 257–282.

Law, B., & Eckes, M. (1990). *The more-than-just-surviving handbook.* Winnipeg, Canada: Peguis.

Leach, E. (1976). *Culture and communication: The logic by which symbols are connected.* Cambridge, UK: Cambridge University Press.

Levin, J., Boruta, M. J., & Vasconcellos, M. T. (1983). Microcomputer based environments for writing: A writer's assistant. In A. C. Wilkinson (Ed.), *Classroom computers and cognitive science* (pp. 219–232). New York: Academic Press.

Lucas, C. J. (1972). *Our western educational heritage.* New York: Macmillan.

Luke, A. (1991). Literacies as social practices. *English Education* (October), 131–147.

Majone, G., & Wildavsky, A. (1978). Implementation as evolution. In H. E. Freeman (Ed.), *Policy studies review annual 2* (pp. 103–117). Beverly Hills, CA: Sage.

Mandinach, E. B., Cline, H. F., & Service, E. T. (1994). *Classroom dynamics: Implementing a technology-based learning environment.* Hillsdale, NJ: Lawrence Erlbaum Associates.

Matusov, E., Bell, N., & Rogoff, B. (1994). *Collaboration and assistance in problem solving by children differing in cooperative schooling backgrounds.* Unpublished manuscript.

McCarty, T. L., Wallace, S., Lynch, R. H., & Benally, A. (1991). Classroom inquiry and Navajo learning styles: A call for reassessment. *Anthropology & Education Quarterly, 22*(1), 42–59.

McDermott, R. (1993). The acquisition of a child by a learning disability. In S. Chaiklin & J. Lave (Eds.), *Understanding practice: Focus on activity and context* (pp. 269–305). Cambridge, UK: Cambridge University Press.

McDermott, R., & Varenne, H. (1995). Culture as disability. *Anthropology & Education Quarterly, 26*(3), 324–348.

McDermott, R. P., Godspodinoff, K., & Aron, J. (1978). Criteria for an ethnographically adequate description of concerted activities and their contexts. *Semiotica, 24*(3–4), 245–275.

Mehan, H. (1979). *Learning lessons.* Cambridge, MA: Harvard University Press.

Mehan, H. (1997). *The study of social interaction in educational settings: Accomplishments and unresolved issues.* Unpublished manuscript, University of California San Diego, La Jolla.

Mehan, H., Hertweck, A. J., & Meihls, J. L. (1986). *Handicapping the handicapped: Decision making in students' careers.* Stanford, CA: Stanford University Press.

Mehan, H., Hubbard, L., & Villanueva, I. (1994). Forming academic identities: Accommodation without assimilation among involuntary minorities. *Anthropology & Education Quarterly, 25*(2), 91–117.

Mehan, H., Lintz, A., Okamoto, D., & Wills, H. (1995). Ethnographic studies of multicultural education in classrooms and schools. In J. A. Banks & C. A. M. Banks (Eds.), *Handbook of research on multicultural education* (pp. 129–144). New York: Macmillan.

Mehan, H., Villanueva, I., Hubbard, L., & Lintz, A. (1996). *Constructing school success: The consequences of untracking low achieving students.* Cambridge, UK: Cambridge University Press.

Michaels, S. (1981). "Sharing time": Children's narrative styles and differential access to literacy. *Language in Society, 10,* 423–442.

Moll, L. C. (1990). *Vygotsky and education: Instructional implications and application of sociohistorical psychology.* Cambridge, UK: Cambridge University Press.

Moll, L. C. (1996, February). *Inspired by Vygotsky: Ethnographic experiments in education.* Paper presented at the Vygotsky Centennial Conference: Vygotskian Perspectives on Literacy Research. Sponsored by the Research Assembly of the National Council of Teachers of English, Chicago, IL.

Moll, L. C., Amanti, C., Neff, D., & Gonzalez, N. (1992). Funds of knowledge for teaching: Using a qualitative approach to connect homes and classrooms. *Theory Into Practice, XXXI*(2), 132–141.

Moll, L. C., & Diaz, S. (1987). Change as the goal of educational research. *Anthropology & Education Quarterly, 18,* 300–311.

Moll, L. C., Diaz, S., Estrada, E., & Lopes, L. M. (1992). Making context: The social construction of lessons in two languages. In M. Saravia-Shore & S. F. Arvizu (Eds.), *Cross-cultural literacy: Ethnographies of communication in multiethnic classrooms* (pp. 339–363). New York: Garland.

Moll, L. C., & Greenberg, J. B. (1990). Creating zones of possibilities: Combining social contexts for instruction. In L. C. Moll (Ed.), *Vygotsky and education: Instructional implications and applications of sociohistorical psychology* (pp. 319–348). Cambridge, UK: Cambridge University Press.

Moore, D. T. (1980). Having it BOTH ways: The reproduction and transformation of schooling. *Anthropology & Education Quarterly, XI*(3), 153–172.

Morine-Dershimer, G. (1985). *Talking, listening, and learning in elementary classrooms.* New York: Longman.

Navarro, R. (1997). Commentary. *Anthropology & Education Quarterly, 28*(3), 455–462.

Neuwirth, C., & Wojahn, P. (1996). Learning to write: Computer support for a cooperative process. In T. Koschmann (Ed.), *CSCL: Theory and practice of an emerging paradigm* (pp. 147–170). Mahwah, NJ: Lawrence Erlbaum Associates.

New Lexicon Webster's Dictionary of the English Language (encyclopedic ed.). (1988). New York: Lexicon Publications.

Nieto, S. (1992). *Affirming diversity.* New York: Longman.

Ninio, A., & Bruner, J. (1978). The achievement and antecedents of labeling. *Journal of Child Development, 5,* 1–15.

Noble, D. (1998). The automation of higher education. *First Monday*

[On-line serial], *3*(1). Available: http://www.firstmonday.dk/issues/issue3_1/index.html (accessed September 1, 1998).

Oakes, J. (1985). *Keeping track: How schools structure inequality.* New Haven, CT: Yale University Press.

Oakes, J., Gamoran, A., & Page, R. N. (1992). Curriculum differentiation: Opportunities, outcomes, and meanings. In P. Jackson (Ed.), *Handbook of research on curriculum* (pp. 570–608). New York: Macmillan.

Ogbu, J. U. (1974). *The next generation: An ethnography of education in an urban neighborhood.* New York: Academic Press.

Ogbu, J. U. (1978). *Minority education and caste: The American system in cross-cultural perspective.* New York: Academic Press.

Ogbu, J. U. (1983). Minority status and schooling in plural societies. *Comparative Education Review, 27*(2), 168–190.

Ogbu, J. U. (1987). Opportunity structure, cultural boundaries, and literacy. In J. Langer (Ed.), *Language, literacy, and culture: Issues of society and schooling* (pp. 149–177). Norwood, NJ: Ablex.

Ogbu, J. U. (1991). Immigrant and involuntary minorities in comparative perspective. In M. Gibson & J. U. Ogbu (Eds.), *Minority status and schooling: A comparative study of immigrant and involuntary minorities* (pp. 3–36). New York: Garland Publishing.

Ogbu, J. U. (1992). Understanding cultural diversity and learning. *Educational Researcher, 21*(November), 5–15.

Ogbu, J. U. (1996). Frameworks—Variability in minority school performance: A problem in search of an explanation. In E. Jacob & C. Jordan (Eds.), *Minority education: Anthropological perspectives* (pp. 38–107). Norwood, NJ: Ablex.

Ogbu, J., & Simons, H. (1998). Voluntary and involuntary minorities: A cultural-ecological theory of school performance with some implications for education. *Anthropology & Education Quarterly, 29*(2), 155–188.

Opie, I., & Opie, P. (1959). *Lore and language of schoolchildren.* Oxford, UK: Oxford University Press.

Paley, V. G. (1986). *Mollie is three: Growing up in school.* Chicago: University of Chicago Press.

Panofsky, C. P. (1994). Developing the representational functions of language: The role of parent-child book-reading activity. In V. John-Steiner, C. P. Panofsky, & L. W. Smith (Eds.), *Sociocultural approaches to language and literacy: An interactionist perspective* (pp. 223–242). Cambridge, UK: Cambridge University Press.

Panofsky, C. P. (1995, May). *Struggles, visible and invisible: Conflict and identity in a sociocultural theory of learning.* Paper presented at the Conference on Discourse and Mind in Honor of Courtney Cazden, Clark University, Atlanta, GA.

Panofsky, C. P. (2000). Toward rewriting our narrative in early literacy research: The case of parent-child book reading activity. In M. A. Gallego & S. Hollingsworth (Eds.), *What counts as literacy: Challenging the school standard* (pp. 190–212). New York: Teachers College Press.

Papert, S. (1993). *The children's machine.* New York: Basic Books.

Pease-Alvarez, C., & Vasquez, O. (1990). Sharing language and technical expertise around the computer. In *Computers in schools* (Vol. 7, pp. 91–107). New York: Haworth.

Philips, S. U. (1983). *The invisible culture: Communication in classroom and community on the Warm Springs Indian Reservation.* Prospect Heights, IL: Waveland Press.

Portes, P. R. (1996). Ethnicity and culture in educational psychology. In D.C. Berliner & R. C. Calfee (Eds.), *Handbook of educational psychology* (pp. 331–357). New York: Macmillan Library Reference USA.

Postman, N. (1995). *The end of education: Redefining the value of school.* New York: Knopf.

Putnam, J. W. P. D. (Ed.). (1993). *Cooperative learning and strategies for inclusion: Celebrating diversity in the classroom.* Baltimore, MD: Paul H. Brookes Publishing.

Rappaport, A. (1976). Sociocultural aspects of man-environment studies. In A. Rappaport (Ed.), *The mutual interaction of people and their built environment: A cross-cultural perspective* (pp. 7–35). The Hague: Mouton.

Reinking, D., & Rickman, S. S. (1990). The effects of computer-mediated texts on the vocabulary learning and comprehension of intermediate-grade readers. *Journal of Reading Behavior, XXII*(4), 395–411.

Reyes, M. de la Luz. (1992). Challenging venerable assumptions: Literacy instructions for linguistically different students. *Harvard Educational Review, 62*(4), 427–446.

Reynolds, J., & Skilbeck, M. (1976). *Culture and the classroom.* London: Open Books.

Riel, M. (1992). Making connections from urban schools. *Education and Urban Society, 24*(4), 477–488.

Riel, M. (1993). Global education through learning circles. In L. Harasim (Ed.), *Global networks: Computers and international communication.* Cambridge, MA: MIT Press.

Riel, M. (1996). Cross-classroom collaboration: Communication and education. In T. Koschmann (Ed.), *CSCL: Theory and practice of an emerging paradigm* (pp. 187–207). Mahwah, NJ: Lawrence Erlbaum Associates.

Riel, M., & Fulton, K. (1998, April). *Technology in the classroom: Tools for doing things differently or doing different things.* Paper presented at the annual meeting of the American Educational Research Association, San Diego, CA.

Rist, R. C. (1970). Student social class and teacher expectations: The self-fulfilling prophecy in ghetto education. *Harvard Educational Review, 40*(3), 411–451.

Rogoff, B. (1993). Children's guided participation and participatory appropriation in sociocultural activity. In R. H. Wozniak & K. W. Fischer (Eds.), *Development in context: Acting and thinking in specific environments* (pp. 121–153). Hillsdale, NJ: Lawrence Erlbaum Associates.

Rogoff, B. (1994). Developing understanding of the idea of communities of learners. *Mind, Culture, and Activity, 1,* 209–229.

Rosaldo, R. (1995). Foreword. In L. Canclini (Ed.), *Hybrid cultures: Strategies for entering and leaving modernity* (pp. xi–xvii). Minneapolis, MN: University of Minnesota Press.

Rutter, M., Maughan, B., Mortimore, P., & Ouston, J. (1979). *Fifteen thousand hours: Secondary schools and their effects on children.* Cambridge, MA: Harvard University Press.

Sadker, M., & Sadker, D. (1994). *Failing at fairness: How America's schools cheat girls.* New York: Scribner.

Sandholtz, J. H., Ringstaff, C., & Dwyer, D. D. (1992). Teaching in high-tech environments: Classroom management revisited. *Journal of Educational Computing Research, 8*(4), 479–505.

Sanford, J. P., & Evertson, C. M. (1981). Classroom management in a low SES junior high: Three case studies. *Journal of Teacher Education, 76,* 140–147.

Santayana, G. (1906). *The life of reason: Or, the phases of progress* (Vol. 5). New York: Scribner.

Sarason, S. B. (1971). *The culture of the school and the problem of change.* Boston: Allyn & Bacon.

Sarason, S. B. (1996). *Revisiting "The culture of the school and the problem of change."* New York: Teachers College Press.

Schlesinger, A. M. (1992). *The disuniting of America: Reflections on a multicultural society.* New York: W. W. Norton.

Schofield, J. W. (1995). *Computer and classroom culture.* New York: Cambridge University Press.

Schoggen, P. (1963). Environmental forces in the everyday lives of children. In R. Barker (Ed.), *The stream of behavior* (pp. 42–69). New York: Appleton-Century-Crofts.

Schoggen, P. (1979). Environmental forces on physically disabled children. In R. G. Barker (Ed.), *Habits, environments, and human behavior* (pp. 125–145). San Francisco: Jossey-Bass.

Schwartz, T. (1978). The size and shape of culture. In F. Barth (Ed.), *Scale and social organization* (pp. 215–252). Oslo: Universitetsforlaget.

Scott, T., Cole, M., & Engel, M. (1992). Computers and education: A cultural constructivist perspective. In G. Grant (Ed.), *Review of research in education* (Vol. 18, pp. 191–251). Washington, DC: American Educational Research Association.

Seeger, F., Voigt, J., & Waschescio, U. (1998). *The culture of the mathematics classroom.* Cambridge, UK: Cambridge University Press.

Shultz, J. J., Florio, S., & Erickson, F. (1982). Where's the floor? Aspects of the cultural organization of social relationships in communication at home and in school. In P. Gilmore & A. A. Glatthorn (Eds.), *Children in and out of school* (pp. 88–123). Washington, DC: Center for Applied Linguistics.

Silberman, C. (1970). *Crisis in the classroom.* New York: Random House.

Silverstein, J. M. (1979). *Individual and environmental correlates of pupil problematic and nonproblematic classroom behavior.* Unpublished doctoral dissertation, New York University, New York.

Sobul, D. (1984). *Bilingual policy and practice: Loose coupling among curriculum levels.* Unpublished doctoral dissertation, University of California, Los Angeles, CA.

Sobul, D. (1994). *Strategies to meet the goals of SDAIE.* Paper presented at the California Association for Bilingual Education, San Jose, CA.

Speece, D. L., & Keogh, B. K. (Eds.). (1996). *Research on classroom ecologies: Implications for inclusion of children with learning disabilities.* Mahwah, NJ: Lawrence Erlbaum Associates.

Spindler, G. D. (Ed.). (1987). *Education and cultural process: Anthropological approaches* (2nd ed.). Prospect Heights, IL: Waveland Press.

Spindler, G. D. (Ed.). (1997). *Education and cultural process: Anthropological approaches* (3rd ed.). Prospect Heights, IL: Waveland Press.

Stocking, G. W., Jr. (1966). Franz Boas and the culture concept in historical perspective. *American Anthropologist, 68,* 867–882.

Stoll, C. (1996). *Silicon snake oil: Second thoughts on the information highway:* New York: Doubleday.

Suarez-Orozco, M. M. (1989). Immigrant adaptation and schooling: A Hispanic case. In M. A. Gibson & J. U. Ogbu (Eds.), *Minority status and schooling: A comparative study of immigrant and involuntary minorities* (pp. 37–62). New York: Garland Publishing.

Tharp, R. (1993). Institutional and social context of educational practice and reform. In E. A. Forman, N. Minick, & C. A. Stone (Eds.), *Contexts for learning: Sociocultural dynamics in children's development* (pp. 269–282). New York: Oxford University Press.

Tharp, R. G., & Gallimore, R. (1988). *Rousing minds to life: Teaching, learning, and schooling in social context.* Cambridge, England: Cambridge University Press.

Thomas, W. I. (1923). *The unadjusted girl.* Boston: Little Brown.

Thorne, B. (1993). *Gender play: Girls and boys in school.* New Brunswick, NJ: Rutgers University Press.

Tylor, E. B. (1903). *Primitive culture: Research into the development of mythology, philosophy, religion, art, and customs.* London: John Murray. (Original work published 1871)

Vaughn, S., & Schumm, J. S. (1996). Classroom ecologies: Classroom interactions and implications for inclusion of students with learning disabilities. In D. L. Speece & B. K. Keogh (Eds.), *Research on classroom ecologies: Implications for inclusion of children with learning disabilities* (pp. 107–134). Mahwah, NJ: Lawrence Erlbaum Associates.

Vélez-Ibáñez, C. G. (1988). Networks of exchange among Mexicans in the U.S. and Mexico: Local level mediating responses to national and international transformations. *Urban Anthropology, 17*(1), 27–51.

Vélez-Ibáñez, C., Moll, L. C., Gonzalez, N., & Neff, D. (1991). *Promoting learning and educational delivery and quality among "at-risk" U.S. Mexican and Native American elementary school children in Tucson, Arizona: A pilot project* [Final report to W. K. Kellogg Foundation]. Tucson, AZ: University of Arizona, Bureau of Applied Research in Anthropology.

Vogt, L. A., Jordan, C., & Tharp, R. G. (1987). Explaining school failure, producing school success: Two cases. *Anthropology & Education Quarterly, 18*(4), 276–286.

Volk, D. (1997). Questions in lessons: Activity settings in the homes and school of two Puerto Rican kindergartners. *Anthropology & Education Quarterly, 28*(1), 22–49.

Vygotsky, L. S. (1978). *Mind in society: The development of higher psychological processes.* Cambridge, MA: Harvard University Press.

Vygotsky, L. S. (1981). The genesis of higher mental functions. In J. V. Wertsch (Ed.), *The concept of activity in Soviet psychology* (pp. 144–188). Armonk, NY: M. E. Sharpe.

Vygotsky, L. S. (1987). *Thinking and speech.* New York: Plenum.

Waller, W. (1965). *The sociology of teaching.* New York: Wiley. (Original work published 1932)

Wallace, A. F. C. (1961). The psychic unity of human groups. In B. Kaplan (Ed.), *Studying personality cross-culturally* (pp. 129–163). Evanston, IL: Row, Peterson.

Walkerdine, V. (1989). *Counting girls out.* London: Virago.

Weis, L. (1988). *Class, race, and gender in American education.* Albany, NY: State University of New York Press.

Wells, G. (1986). *The meaning makers: Children learning language and using language to learn.* Portsmouth, NH: Heinemann.

Willes, M. J. (1983). *Children into pupils: A study of language in early schooling.* London: Routledge & Kegan Paul.

Williams, R. (1976). *A vocabulary of culture and society.* New York: Oxford University Press.

Willis, P. (1977). *Learning to labor: How working class kids get working class jobs.* New York: Columbia University Press.

Wittrock, M. C. (Ed.). (1986). *Handbook of research on teaching* (3rd ed.). New York: Macmillan.

Wolcott, H. F. (1987). The anthropology of learning. In G. D. Spindler (Ed.), *Education and cultural process: Anthropological approaches* (2nd ed., pp. 26–49). Prospect Heights, IL: Waveland Press.

Wolcott, H. (1991). Propriospect and the acquisition of culture. *Anthropology & Education Quarterly, 22*(3), 251–273.

Yinger, R. J. (1977). *A study of teacher planning: Description and theory development using ethnographic and information processing methods.* Unpublished doctoral dissertation, Michigan State University, East Lansing, MI.

Yinger, R. J. (1979). Routines in teacher planning. *Theory Into Practice, 18*(3), 163–169.

45.

School–Community Connections: Strengthening Opportunity to Learn and Opportunity to Teach

Meredith I. Honig
Stanford University

Joseph Kahne
Mills College, Oakland, California

Milbrey W. McLaughlin
Stanford University

Introduction: Why Consider School–Community Connections?

Schools today exist in very different social, economic, and political contexts than they did a century ago. Communities have changed, families have been reconfigured, and workplace demands are radically different from what they were when public schools were founded (Darling-Hammond, 1997; Graham, 1995; Heath & McLaughlin, 1987; Schorr, 1989). As a result, teaching and learning occur in fundamentally different social and economic contexts than in previous decades.

Despite these changes in social institutions and conditions, education reformers generally fail to examine and challenge old assumptions about institutional relationships and roles that have defined and supported teaching and learning in policy and practice. Specifically, education's century-old institutional frame casts the school as a social institution that is complementary to but separate from other institutions and agents of the community. For example, content and performance standards tend to focus on narrow academic measures. Much of the current standards debate—including discussions of rewards and sanctions for teachers, students, and schools—concerns what these academic standards should be; few have questioned the narrow academic scope of these standards and how students and teachers can achieve them (see, e.g., the discussion in Ravitch, 1995).

In particular, public discourse about opportunity to learn[1]—the resources, supports, and occasions students need to achieve at higher levels—has been especially school-centric and process-oriented. The same can be said about conversations regarding what we call "opportunity to teach"—the resources, supports, and occasions teachers need to teach so that students achieve at higher levels. Notions of opportunity to learn and opportunity to teach generally have been school-centric because they focus on programs, staff, and other resources that schools, school districts, and state educational agencies should provide if students are to meet challenging content and performance standards (McLaughlin & Shepard, 1995). This focus assumes that schools alone—teachers and students—can achieve these high standards. The conversations are process-oriented because they focus on the availability of resources, supports, and occasions rather than their use. For

---

A grant to Shirley Brice Heath and Milbrey W. McLaughlin from the Spencer Foundation contributed to the preparation of this chapter.

[1] The legislation introducing the federal Goals 2000 initiative acknowledged the importance of students' opportunity to learn and designated the idea as "school delivery standards." This name subsequently was changed to "opportunity to learn" in response to congressional concern that school delivery standards would mean federal involvement in the business of curricula and texts, and would signal a new era of federal control of the schools (Ravitch, 1995, p. 13).

example, they assume that the availability of new funding or technology will mean that teachers and students are able to use the funding and technology to enhance learning. This focus presupposes that the cursory exploration of the means for achieving high standards in the current policy debate is adequate.

On the contrary, many of the factors that shape students' opportunities to learn and teachers' opportunities to teach are beyond the purview of schools. For example, teachers comment that too many students come to school fatigued from family or job responsibilities and, figuratively, are not present for them to teach. Other students are not present in a more literal sense: Some teachers say student absenteeism is their single greatest teaching challenge (McLaughlin & Talbert, 1993). Also, for example, many of today's students say they see few community role models that attribute their success to formal education. Others say they have few incentives to work hard in school, because neither the workplace nor higher education seem to place premiums on taking challenging courses and doing well (Cohen, 1994; Dryfoos, 1990; McLaughlin, Irby, & Langman, 1994; Phelan, Davidson, & Yu, 1998).

In short, the current reform movement in education appears conceptually and strategically incomplete. It has triggered an avalanche of initiatives to reform how schools do business, but these initiatives, generally, reconsider neither the institutional assumptions nor the policy frameworks within which schools operate. If they did, they would recognize an important dilemma: Today's schools alone cannot provide the opportunities and support that America's students require to learn and achieve at the high levels that reformers expect and the public demands (Cahill, 1993; Pittman & Cahill, 1992). Patricia Graham advises, "The battleship, the school, cannot do this alone. The rest of the educational flotilla must assist: families, communities, government, higher education, and the business community. Only then will all of our children be able to achieve that which by birthright should be theirs: enthusiasm for and accomplishment in learning" (Graham, 1995, p. 22).

Students' opportunities to learn and, by extension, teachers' opportunities to teach in contemporary America require that schools and communities join in new ways—and in some old ways—to accomplish the objectives our society assigns to public education. To meet contemporary education goals, we must expand our notions of the resources, occasions, and supports for teaching and learning. We must also broaden our understanding of how students and teachers might make effective use of them.

The Importance of a Youth's and Teacher's View to Defining Opportunity to Learn and Opportunity to Teach

What definition of opportunity to learn and opportunity to teach should undergird policy, practice, and research agendas? We argue in this chapter that education reformers currently use the wrong analytic frame for a meaningful examination of stu-

dents' opportunities to learn and teachers' opportunities to teach. Policymakers, practitioners, and researchers tend to focus narrowly within the formal educational system on what schools can do to raise students' scores on measures of academic achievement (that is, academic means to academic ends). They identify generic students and teachers without considering the variety of resources, supports, and occasions available for both in particular contexts.

If we view resources, supports, and occasions for learning, not from the top of the policymaking system down, but from a student's-eye view, we can see that youth have many opportunities for learning in and out of school. These opportunities include occasions for exercising leadership, developing a range of skills to solve their own problems and concerns, and establishing relationships with peers and adults. They include a time and place to do homework, assistance with that homework, access to resources (such as computers and libraries), and occasions in their homes and neighborhoods to work independently and to practice, reinforce, and extend the skills and perspectives presented in and out of the classroom. An essential aspect of many out-of-school opportunities for learning is that they are not extensions of the academic day. Rather, they are often nonacademic occasions, resources, and supports that develop in youth a range of competencies (e.g., academic, social, emotional, vocational, civic, physical, per Pittman & Cahill, 1992) that are important to success in school.

If we consider where learning takes place from the perspective of a student, then, we can see that students have many teachers throughout their day in youth organizations, families, school classrooms, and other settings. It reminds us that young people are more than students; they are youth[2] with many affiliations in addition to their school. A youth perspective on opportunity to learn highlights that the availability of youth organizations, adult role models, and leadership experiences, for example, are not sufficient for improving learning. Beyond that, researchers, policymakers, and practitioners need to be concerned with the various barriers that prevent youth from taking advantage of these resources, supports, and occasions for learning. Keeping a youth perspective in mind, we must, for example, ask these questions: Are resources located in parts of the community that are accessible to youth? Do adults and peers whom the youth know and trust provide activities to youth?

Likewise, from a teacher's-eye view, opportunity to teach, in practical terms, means more than adequate texts, classroom space, and materials to support their work. If youths' experiences out of school are essential parts of their opportunities to learn, then teachers' opportunities to teach would be enhanced if they had the time and occasions to become familiar with their students' families and neighborhoods and with other contexts for learning out of school. Long-term relationships with other professionals who work with students—not only teachers but also youth workers, mentors, coaches, and social workers, among others—can help to expand teachers' own capacities for working with youth. By this statement, we do not mean only that teachers should be able to access social services and other

---

[2] Throughout this chapter we use the term "youth" to refer to all young people of school age.

nonacademic supports for students to remove barriers to learning. Beyond that expectation, youth workers and others who work with youth outside school may use strategies and what we might consider formal and informal curricula for teaching youth in ways that can inform classroom teaching. Likewise, classroom teachers can inform the work of youths' teachers outside school. Connections among youths' various teachers can enhance school performance by building on the strengths that are offered through these various learning opportunities, both in and out of school.

Opportunity to teach, then, refers to the occasions, resources, and supports that multiple teachers, both in and out of school, can use to enhance their own practices through consultation and other connections with one another. The opportunity to teach depends in part on whether the context in which they work—the school climate, the broader policy environment—provides the flexibility and support they need to enter into these relationships with professionals and students.

Opportunity to learn and opportunity to teach in their fullest senses, then, incorporate and depend upon more than the resources found in the school. They implicate a broad array of community-based resources and supports as well as youths' and teachers' abilities and willingness to use them.

To summarize, we argue that expanded notions of opportunity to learn and opportunity to teach mean more than improved academic means to improved academic outcomes. Opportunity to learn and opportunity to teach mean recognizing three important circumstances:

- What happens to youth outside school affects their performance in school in many positive ways. In particular, youth learn throughout their day—both in and out of school—and many of their nonacademic experiences in and out of school can be important to their academic success in school.
- Youth have multiple teachers in and out of school. These teachers include schoolteachers, youth workers, mentors, coaches, social workers, and parents.
- Youths' multiple teachers, both in and out of school, together can use these in-school and out-of-school resources, occasions and supports to strengthen teaching and learning in ways that exceed what schools or community agencies could accomplish alone.

Chapter Overview

This chapter outlines a framework for further research and discussion about how we can redefine opportunities to learn and teach, both conceptually and in practice, to improve youths' performance in school. We base our argument on the premise that the mission and work of schools and "communities"—agencies, organizations, individuals, resources, and occasions outside school—can and should be joined. The primary question we address at the heart of this chapter is as follows: How can we connect schools and communities to improve youths' performance in school?

At the end of the 20th century, few ongoing or well-developed examples of school–community partnerships around teaching and learning exist. (We identify exceptions to this general statement in section III.) Most previous work on this topic focuses on improving health or social outcomes for students and on removing barriers to learning. It has not focused on what school–community connections mean for teachers and how such links might benefit teachers' work and enable students' learning (Cahill, 1996; Lawson & Briar-Lawson, 1997). We highlight throughout the chapter that removing barriers to learning and enabling learning are two related but distinguishable sets of activities. Most of our analysis is concerned with how out-of-school settings and school–community collaboration might enable learning.

Thus, our review necessarily moves beyond the scope of a traditional research review to consider more broadly what we know from theory and practice about how school–community connections might best be used to enhance opportunities to learn and teach. Our research framework suggests how future research on teaching and learning can examine more specifically what school–community connections might look like in practice for opportunity to learn and teach.

In section I, we discuss how education reform policy, including plans that address opportunity to learn, has taken a narrow view of the occasions and resources that learning and teaching require. In particular, education policy and research generally ignore out-of-school factors that affect learning and teaching—both those that present barriers to learning and teaching and those that might enable it. In section II, we review four bodies of research —family, neighborhood, peers, and work— that are generally used to explain which out-of-school factors affect students' performance. Also in section II, not only do we identify *which* factors matter, but also we begin to suggest *why* they matter for youth and teachers.

In section III, we turn to the empirical literature on planned (as opposed to spontaneous or incidental) supports for teaching and learning outside school. Building on section II, we examine experience with and research on a range of programs, policies, and initiatives that are aimed at connecting schools and communities in diverse ways. We conclude this section with our research framework, school–community connections for opportunity to learn and opportunity to teach, that begins to specify how school–community connections might enhance opportunities to learn and, by extension, opportunities to teach. In section IV, we extend this review to consider the limits and barriers to linking schools and communities, and the implications of this review for policy, practice, and research.

I. The Problem for Practice and Policy

A Limited Target for Reform in Current Policy Initiatives

Although an elaborated view of students' opportunity to learn and teachers' opportunity to teach might seem sensible, at the start of the 21st century, most educational reforms underway in American schools are school reforms. These reforms tinker inside the box of traditional institutional roles and relationships within schools and assume that improved academic performance can result from extended and intensified academic instruction in school classrooms. From merit pay to technology, from new literacy curricula to new pedagogical forms for classroom interaction, and from site-based management to class-size reduction, reforms presuppose that the school alone can realize ambitious expectations for teaching and learning (see Tyack, 1995; Tyack & Cuban, 1995). These reforms tacitly assume that schooling can and should provide more or less the same experience for every student and that school-focused reform could work if reformers could only get it right. Such a school-centric frame assumes that schools are the primary influences for learning in the lives of children and youth rather than one part of students' broader developmental contexts.

Paradoxically, many of the reforms that do look outside school walls also take a limited view. Consider the example of parent involvement programs. Many so-called "parent involvement" efforts engage parents, not as partners with schools and teachers, but as adjuncts to the school's work (e.g., helping with homework, supporting extracurricular activities) rather than as primary teachers for youth. Most major public and private sources of funding for schools require or encourage these forms of parental involvement, particularly for schools with high concentrations of low-achieving or at-risk students. However, little evidence shows that such requirements lead to closer substantive ties between communities and schools or to enhanced learning for students either in or out of school (Knapp & Shields, 1991). Perhaps as a consequence, links between parents and schools have been erratic and uneven, and not much rethinking has taken place either of adult roles in schools and families (Blase, 1987; Lightfoot, 1978; Smrekar, 1996) or of the types of learning experiences (academic and nonacademic) that many parents already provide and that can be essential to academic success in school.

Exceptions to limited parental involvement occur in some charter schools where parents determine school goals and monitor progress toward them (Wohlstetter, 1997). However, experience suggests that the parent-school partnerships in many charter schools focus on school governance and broad curricular content within schools, not on questions of learning and teaching in and out of school. Likewise, some school-choice strategies engage parents as consumers, but typically not as partners or resources in teaching and learning (see, e.g., Schneider, Teske, Marschall, Mintrom, & Roch, 1997). Even reformers who have a broader agenda for parents and who assume that schools must change usually work within traditional institutional frames. For example, James Comer and Henry Levin see parent involvement as essential to meeting students' and teachers' goals, but, generally, they confine learning, teaching, and opportunities to learn and teach to students' academic experiences within the school walls.

The literature about extracurricular activities, project-based learning, and experiential education contains some examples of nonacademic activities designed deliberately to enhance students' performance in school. However, this literature provides examples of weak linkages between school and community around teaching and learning. That is, most researchers in these extracurricular activities, project-based learning, and experiential education agree that these three traditions are important ways to expand classrooms beyond their four walls and to ground curriculum in practical applications (Calabrese & Schumer, 1986; Conrad & Hedin, 1982; Hamilton & Fenzel, 1988; Larson, 1994; Westheimer, Kahne, & Gerstein, 1992; Wigginton, 1985; Wood, 1992). However, these approaches in research and practice tend to focus on what classroom teachers can do to use the community as a setting for learning. In this way, they do not always consider how teachers and schools can engage educators who already work with youth outside the formal educational system (e.g., youth workers, mentors, religious leaders, and coaches of athletic teams) as partners to enhance the educational experiences of youth in and out of school. Nor do they consider how these teachers, in and out of school, might enhance their respective practices through observation of and deliberate planning with one another.

Other exceptions to academic, school-centric reforms include certain efforts to link schools with social services (e.g., Gomby & Larson, 1992). These reformers base their arguments on the changed social conditions of students and their concerns that the "excellence movement" overlooks many social purposes of schooling (Sedlak, 1995).[3] They treat conditions outside school as sources of risk that must be ameliorated before students can learn. Many posit that if we locate social resources in the "universal institution," the public school, we will be in a better position to mediate the effects of these poor conditions outside school. However, like many of the parent involvement initiatives, these strategies generally link their efforts to otherwise unchanged schools.

Recent research suggests that unless schools restructure—that is, unless schools rethink roles and relationships around teaching and learning—additional social services will have only a limited effect on learning outcomes (Wehlage, Smith, & Lipman, 1992). Put another way, this research suggests that the focus of many efforts to create school-linked services has been to fix students (Pittman & Cahill, 1992) so teachers can really teach and to remove barriers to learning, rather than to rethink the learning and teaching that occurs for students—all day, in and out of school—and to rethink the conditions, resources, and supports that enable it.

Finally, an emerging strand of education reform focuses on after-school programs (e.g., 21st Century Learning Centers) and the use of schools as community centers after hours. Many of these initiatives respond not primarily to concerns about teaching and learning but, rather, to recent statistics that most crimes and violence involving youth (either as perpetrators or as victims) occur in the hours immediately after school. Accordingly, an unfortunate focus of many of these initiatives is on keeping youth busy during these hours or on providing more academic instruction after school. Few of these programs and initiatives seek to expand or connect with the out-of-school re-

---

[3] Sedlak observes that many who issue this call to action are ignorant of the long history of the integration of school and social services: "Health services advocates Ernest Hoag and Lewis Terman drew one of the most expansive visions for the social services movement when they claimed that 'the public school has not fulfilled its duty when the child alone is educated within its walls. The school must be the educational center, the social center, and the hygiene center of the community in which it is located—a hub from which will radiate influences for social betterment in many lives'" (Sedlak, 1995, p. 60).

sources, occasions, and supports for learning that already exist in many communities through youth organizations, mentoring programs, and others—many of which are not primarily academic but, again, can strengthen the performance of youth in school (Carnegie Council on Adolescent Development, 1994; Dryfoos, 1998; Schorr, 1997).

The Persistent Limitations of Policy in Connecting Communities and Schools

Our arguments about the limits of a school-centric view of learning and teaching are not new. For example, the earliest theories of adolescent development recognized the importance of the community and its resources to child development and, less often, to children's learning. Between the turn of the century and World War II, educators and social activists responded with a vision of "the school as social center" (Dewey, 1902/1976). Many worked in explicit and powerful ways to connect learning in school with resources, occasions, and supports for learning out of school. Jane Addams's Hull House, for example, provided health care, health education, job training, courses in English, and a variety of artistic, vocational, athletic, and intellectual opportunities for youth and adults. In part, through her partnership with John Dewey, she envisioned settlement houses as essential formal and informal settings for academic and non-academic learning and for the expansion and deepening of youths' relationships with each other and adults.

In the early part of the 20th century, Leonard Cavello, a New York City teacher, principal, and community activist, developed community advisory committees for schools and curricular components linked to students' cultural heritage. He worked with students, teachers, parents, and the community to reform housing and community services, in part, to create a neighborhood deliberately structured to support child development and learning. In short, he transformed the institution of his school into a center of community life that included recreation, academic pursuits, and collective social action—a jumping off point for lifelong learning (Tyack & Hansot, 1982).

In the 1930s, Elsie Ripley Clapp made her rural West Virginia school a "center for the entire community" to learn and develop. To help parents enrich the learning that occurred at home and on the farm, the school provided health care, technical support for farmers, and classes on nutrition for mothers. The school encouraged older students to support the education of younger students both during and after school hours. Participation in and study of Appalachian folk traditions provided one strategic link between in-school and out-of-school learning (Clapp, 1939; Perlstein, 1996).

These early reformers were committed to school-community links to support teaching and learning.[4] Perhaps as a consequence of this explicit focus on learning in these examples, "school-community" connections meant connections that linked already existing teaching and learning resources for youth and their many teachers (both in and out of school) in ways that could reinforce both teaching and learning.

However, current discourse about educational reform suggests a general inattention to how opportunity to learn or opportunity to teach could incorporate broader conceptions of what teaching and learning are and where they take place. Educators and reformers who are concerned with community occasions, resources, and supports for learning often proceed without a theoretical basis or a clear definition of what it means to connect community and school, specifically around teaching and learning. Most current efforts to connect communities and schools in the ways that concern us in this chapter (like the examples described above) are efforts of single schools or a few schools acting alone, often outside or in spite of the resources, occasions, and supports provided by broader education policy.

The current status of school-community ties may reflect deeper pitfalls in education policy. The many targets of education policy—budgets, curricula, teachers, standards, teacher education, parent involvement, and so on—have not reformed schools in any consistent, predictable, or sustained fashion (National Research Council, 1993). Teachers and youth are not surprised by this absence of meaningful change. Education reformers generally have not considered the changed conditions for schools and the social realities of youth when they fire their salvos.

Thus, those responsible for policy and practice face two challenges when creating the school-community links that contemporary students and teachers require to support their work. Conceptually, we must first define out-of-school resources for teaching and learning. Then, strategically, we must find ways to join schools and communities to strengthen the resources, occasions, and supports for learning in and out of school. The latter point requires not that opportunities for learning simply be available in and out of school but that people have the resources and supports necessary to take advantage of them.

II. The Effect of Out-of-School Factors on School Performance: What Matters About Family, Neighborhood, Peers, and Work

The importance of the time youth spend out of school is obvious: Development and learning do not stop at the end of the school day. Moreover, out-of-school experiences and conditions affect participation in school (Carnegie Council on Adolescent Development, 1994; Grubb & Lazerson, 1982). However, the haphazard track record that documents efforts to forge effective school-community links suggests that we need a clearer rationale for why community occasions, resources, and supports are important to teaching and learning. The record also suggests that we need more systematic knowledge of how communities and schools can work together to enhance teaching and learn-

---

[4] To a greater degree than is currently the case, these reformers also emphasized a democratic rationale for their efforts. These reformers agreed with Dewey when he wrote in *School and Society* that participation in activities that mirror community life provided excellent opportunities for developing "a spirit of social cooperation and community life" (Dewey, 1902/1956, p. 16) needed to inform democratic civic life. These reformers worked to add common and productive activity to the content of schooling because, as Dewey put it, "We have lost a good deal of our faith in the efficacy of purely intellectual instruction" (Dewey, 1902/1956, p. 84).

ing. In this section, we take up the first issue: What do we know about how out-of-school contexts affect youths' opportunities to learn? What aspects of community should be marshaled in a partnership with schools to expand teachers' opportunities to teach?

Traditionally, research on out-of-school contexts for youth has focused on the effects that community conditions and influences have on development and learning. These factors include, in a broad sense, the primary institutions and avenues for associations among youth and adults—families, neighborhoods, peers, and work. Similarly, in this section, we review the extensive research on the effects that these factors have on youth's development and learning, emphasizing trends and the most recent empirical work.

Though the effects are often intertwined, research in this area can be divided into these four broad categories: families, neighborhoods, peers, and work. Our interest in reviewing this broad and diverse set of literature is to understand how each of these nonschool elements create, support, or frustrate young people's opportunity to learn and so, too, their teachers' opportunity to teach. In other words, we are interested not only in *which* out-of-school resources, occasions, and supports matter for youth development and learning but also in *how* they matter.

We find that virtually all of this research highlights the ways that nonschool influences in students' lives affect their attitudes about themselves as learners, their motivation and ability to engage in school work, and their expectations for adulthood. In this way, this literature provides a rationale for considering that community is important to learning and teaching, and it begins to provide a rationale for linking school and community. However, we find that it provides few clues about how youth and their teachers might connect day to day to these out-of-school resources, occasions, and supports to enhance learning and teaching.

How Families Affect Youth's School-Related Attitudes and Outcomes

Much of the literature on the relationship between family and developmental and educational outcomes for youth stems from James Coleman's 1966 study of racial and ethnic segregation, inequality, student and family characteristics, and student achievement (Coleman et al., 1966). Using surveys of superintendents, principals, teachers, and approximately 645,000 students in more than 3,000 schools nationwide, Coleman found that such family factors as household composition, socioeconomic status, and parents' education are stronger predictors of educational progress than are school-related factors.

The publication of *Equality of Educational Opportunity Report* (Coleman et al., 1966) triggered more than three decades

of quantitative studies on so-called "family effects." Some studies involved reanalyses of Coleman's data (e.g., Bowles & Levin, 1968) or attempts to test explicitly Coleman's theory and conclusions (e.g., Summers & Wolfe, 1977). Other data-intensive efforts evaluated the association between various family-related characteristics (e.g., family poverty, length of time in poverty, socioeconomic status) and education-related outcomes (e.g., academic achievement, graduation, and attendance). The studies generally agreed that parents in poor, low-income families are more likely to have both low levels of formal education and children who do not perform optimally in school than are families with higher socioeconomic status (see, e.g., Jencks et al., 1972).[5]

Studies of such family effects on school performance were particularly prominent in the 1980s, partly in response to demographic data on the perceived increase of children born in single-parent, Black families between 1970 and 1980 (Milne, Myers, Rosenthal, & Ginsburg, 1986; Thompson, Alexander, & Entwisle, 1988).[6] Accordingly, many such studies in the 1980s and early 1990s focused on family structure in relation to such outcomes as drop-out rates (Coleman, 1987), social and emotional adjustment, standardized test scores (Entwisle & Alexander, 1995), and school behavior and discipline (Featherstone, Cundick, & Jensen, 1992; Heiss, 1996; Steinberg, Lamborn, Darling, Mounts, & Dornbusch, 1994). Generally, these studies found that the children in two-parent families fare better than those from families otherwise structured. These analyses concluded that youth growing up in single-parent families generally were at greater risk of dropping out of school, achieving at lower levels in school, and not attending college.

However, concern for opportunity to learn and opportunity to teach directs us to look beyond the coincidence of family status variables and educational variables and ask more specifically, What day-to-day experiences of youth in families lead to the observed outcomes? What features of family relationships are essential to youth development and learning, and may explain the conditions under which certain factors enable or inhibit teaching and learning? For example, the fact that two-parent families are correlated with higher educational outcomes in the aggregate neither tells us whether two parents are actually present day-to-day in the individual households nor what transpires day-to-day between parents and children that may contribute to particular learning or developmental outcomes. A nuclear family may provide a nourishing environment where children are cherished, a "haven in a heartless world," or it may be the place of hidden abuse and neglect (Larson, 1994). Similarly, most correlational studies do not address what happens in single-parent families with high-achieving children that enables them to buck the trends. In fact, looking across studies of family effects, we learn that family both can ameliorate risk

---

[5] This continued analytical focus on the effects of family poverty, in part, reflects the emphasis of Great Society programs on low-income children and families. Many of the federal initiatives of the Great Society period were responses to early research on associations between poverty, family characteristics, and school achievement. This analytical focus also reflects the availability, for the first time, of large data sets (e.g., High School and Beyond, National Educational Longitudinal Survey) that enabled broad-scale analyses of such self-reported family factors as parents' education and income (Buehler et al., 1997).

[6] Some studies note that the total number of children born to Black households did not increase during this period. Rather, the percentage of children born to two-parent, White households decreased, raising the percentage of Black children in the overall population. This change in percentage contributed to the perception that we were witnessing a greater total number of children born to single Black households (Jarrett, 1997).

(Garbarino, 1992; Harnish, Dodge, & Valente, 1995; Hashima & Amato, 1994; McLanahan & Sandefur, 1994) and exacerbate it (McLeod, 1990; Sampson & Laub, 1994).

In response to such apparently contradictory findings, quantitative researchers have probed variables that may mediate other variables to expand developmental and educational opportunities for youth. For example, McLanahan & Sandefur (1994) used data from four national surveys to investigate more specifically why single parenting in the aggregate generally correlates with poor outcomes for youth. They found that youth tend to do well, regardless of family structure, when their parents regularly provide significant supervision of homework and out-of-school time. Youth tend to achieve in school not only when their parents say they have high levels of aspirations for academic and future achievement but also when parents translate these aspirations into enriching opportunities for learning from day to day—independent of family structure.

In addition, higher achievement across different family structures is associated with parents who have strong roots in their neighborhoods—roots that can provide additional support and supervision for youth and networks for personal and professional advancement (Entwisle & Alexander, 1995, 1996; Heiss, 1996; McLanahan & Sandefur, 1994) Bianchi and Robinson also found that, in terms of youth's day-to-day experiences, family structure may not be as consequential as studies that are less nuanced suggest. They argue that the most powerful influence on how children spend their time is not simply their parents' education, but the expectations that parents communicate and the opportunities they are able to extend in part because of their own higher levels of education (Bianchi & Robinson, 1997).[7] Csikszentmihalyi, Rathunde, & Wahlen (1993) found that parents tend to foster talent, academic success, and creativity in their children when they prod them to do their best and give them unconditional support in their efforts to succeed in challenging situations.[8]

Ethnographers and other qualitative researchers have long focused on the experience of many youth and families who succeed despite the odds. Many of these studies enrich our understanding of how, on a day-to-day basis, families matter to the improved educational performance of youth. For example, Robin Jarrett (1995) reviewed qualitative studies that explore an array of family strategies that buffer the effects of poverty, as summarized in the work of such scholars as Carol Stack (1974), Elijah Anderson (1989, 1990), and Reginald Clark (1983). Jarrett concludes that families expand developmental and educational opportunities for youth regardless of income by using some type of "community-bridging" strategy to link their youth with mainstream institutions and opportunities. Jarrett's synthesis describes five family activities that are associated with community bridging:

- Development and maintenance of a supportive adult network structure that enables parents to provide broader opportunities for youth
- Restricted family-community relations that establish a limited scope of relationships within the local neighborhood and "defend" the family
- Strict parental monitoring strategies that keep track of the time, friendships, and activities of adolescents
- Involvement with "mobility-enhancing" institutions such as churches that offer youth social and academic activities, and link them to broader social networks
- Adult-sponsored opportunities for youth to develop adult roles and responsibilities such as fund-raising for a sport team or club project

Families who engage in these activities use their broader community to find opportunities for their young people to develop the skills, attitudes, and experiences that would help them move successfully into mainstream roles and institutions (Jarrett, 1995; see also Anderson, 1978; Clark, 1983; Stack, 1974).

In summary, research demonstrates that the interest and support parents provide to their children can expand opportunities to learn and teach—regardless of family structure and status. Of particular importance is the supervision and structure that parents and guardians give children outside school and the connections families or adult caregivers make to broader opportunities and occasions for development. Families that engage in these activities protect and focus youths' out-of-school time not only around the concrete responsibilities of school but also around the social and other activities essential to their development as learners. When the family functions as an advocate, inspiration, teacher, and coach, it can motivate youths' interest to do well in school, support a positive vision of the future, and otherwise extend and reinforce teachers' classroom efforts.

Our review also suggests that other factors influence the challenges families face as they engage in these activities and relationships. In particular, various conditions within their neighborhoods clearly are formidable direct influences on such activities and relationships. Accordingly, we turn now to a brief examination of selections from the literature on how neighborhoods affect school attitudes, learning outcomes, and possibilities for development—hence, how neighborhoods boost or constrain opportunity to learn and to teach.

How Neighborhoods Affect Youth's School-Related Attitudes and Outcomes

The significance of neighborhoods for youth development and learning is not news to psychologists and educators. Systematic studies of the effects of neighborhoods on youth and families

---

[7] Several other parenting studies are based on typologies of parenting styles, use surveys, and large sets of data about students' school success to identify relations between "ideal types" of parenting (e.g., authoritative, permissive) and various educational and developmental outcomes (Dornbusch, Ritter, Roberts, & Fraleigh, 1987; Steinberg et al., 1994; Steinberg, Lamborn, Dornbusch, & Darling, 1992). Although these studies are somewhat limited in their depiction of the day-to-day relationships between youth and their parents (the conditions under which various parenting styles may be beneficial or detrimental is not always clear), these studies do find positive relationships between parents who set clear goals and guidelines for their children and who consistently enforce rules for the family and for children's school performance.

[8] Clearly, certain conditions impede the ability of families to provide such expanded opportunities to learn. For example, a common theme in studies of the relationship among parenting styles, family environment, and school performance is the struggle that many low-income parents have to provide safe, educationally rich environments for youth and many of the day-to-day resources youth need to succeed in school.

were particularly prominent during the Great Society period in the 1960s when political and research-related resources focused on identifying neighborhoods in poverty for targeted public assistance and evaluations of such efforts. This research included rich ethnographic studies of youth and their neighborhoods (Liebow, 1996; Stack, 1974; Whyte, 1955) and a significant body of empirical work that was based on large data sets (e.g., Banfield, 1970). Both strands of research were central to debates during the 1960s and 1970s about causes and consequences of neighborhood poverty as related to school performance (Newman, 1997).

William Julius Wilson's *The Truly Disadvantaged* (1987) shifted the discussion of neighborhood effects on youth and families from the discussion of neighborhood cultures and demographics to the discussion of neighborhood economic conditions as significant factors in youth's attitudes, activities, and achievements. Wilson argued that changes in the American economy (e.g., deindustrialization, transition to a service economy) led to the flight of white middle- and working-class families out of central cities and the concentration of poor, often African-American families within them. These ghetto neighborhoods became increasingly isolated from the kinds of social networks necessary for adults' success or children's healthy development, a point also illustrated in the family effects literature (Wilson, 1987).[9]

A number of theoretical models elaborate how neighborhood characteristics do or could influence youth's relationships with school and concepts of themselves as students.[10] Although these research traditions use different analytical lenses, together, they reveal some remarkable similarities and limitations.[11] First, of critical importance for youth and families is the availability of social networks within and between neighborhoods that can provide a web of support to parents and other adults (see, e.g., Anderson, 1978; Bronfenbrenner, 1986; Bronfenbrenner, Moen, & Garbarino, 1984; Caplan & Killilea, 1976; Garbarino, 1992; Sorin, 1990). High levels of social support mean opportunities for youth development, even in hostile circumstances (McLaughlin et al., 1994).

Second, social coherence and neighborhood stability (Sampson, 1991) seem strongly correlated with positive developmental and learning outcomes for youth. Researchers find that social disorganization (litter, boarded buildings, disorderly behavior) that persists over time, regardless of the turnover of individual residents, predicts such negative outcomes as high crime rates and, by extension, other poor developmental conditions for youth (see, e.g., Coulton, Korbin, & Su, 1996; Garbarino, 1992; Murphy & Moriarty, 1976).[12] However, Bernard and other researchers investigating sources of resilience in children and youth found that a socially coherent community with strong relationships among adults and between adults and children can do much to overcome the otherwise debilitating effects of poverty (Bernard, 1990; Werner, 1992).[13]

---

[9] One significant synthesis of major research on the effects of concentrated poverty in neighborhoods is the recently published *Neighborhood Poverty,* edited by Jeanne Brooks-Gunn, Greg J. Duncan, and J. Lawrence Aber. This two-volume set of studies is the product of the Working Group on Communities and Neighborhoods that was appointed by the Social Science Research Council in 1989 (Brooks-Gunn, Duncan, & Aber, 1998a, 1998b). See Volume 1, *Context and Consequences for Children* (Brooks-Gunn et al., 1998a), for a comprehensive review of literature on the effects of neighborhood poverty on children and families and for additional data on the concentration of poverty from the 1950s to the present. Our review also considers this research.

[10] For example, studies in the Wilson tradition that are based, in part, on an epidemiological model (Granovetter, 1978; Schelling, 1971) argue that neighborhood residents are "carriers" of behaviors that can "infect" others depending on their degree of susceptibility (Crane, 1996). Residential crowding in low-income neighborhoods thus becomes a source of risk (Ensminger, Lamkin, & Jacobson, 1996). Similarly, others use the presence of affluent neighbors as a proxy for a wide range of factors, such as higher prevalence of role models, social influence on parenting style, social isolation, and institutional strengths and resources of the neighborhood itself (e.g., Brooks-Gunn, Duncan, Klebanov, & Sealand, 1993). Other studies are largely centered on neighborhood-related causes of crime and delinquency, and often identify structural factors—ethnic heterogeneity, residential mobility, high unemployment, high proportion of female-headed households, high proportion of households on welfare—that disrupt the social organization of local communities (Gottfredson, McNeill III, & Gottfredson, 1991; Sampson, 1993).

[11] Many researchers of social disorganization are engaged in a debate about how to account for factors that mediate opportunity and risk and how to link youth with mainstream opportunities and institutions (Jarrett, 1995). The number of qualitative studies of success stories has reached a critical mass, and a more systematic synthesis of these individual studies may now be possible (Jarrett, 1995). However, the focus of this research is not always of primary interest to educators (e.g., crime and delinquency rates among primarily adult neighborhood residents in Sampson & Laub, 1994).

[12] We found certain studies more helpful than others for informing opportunity to learn and teach. As we explained with regard to the family effects literature, large data sets may not define other variables in ways that are meaningful to youth and families in actual neighborhoods. For example, studies of social disorganization that rely on large surveys generally define disorganization by concentrated characteristics of individual families and other neighborhood residents (e.g., socioeconomic status, number, and percentage of female-headed households). By contrast, an ethnomethodological study found that residents of a given neighborhood define disorganization by such factors as litter, boarded buildings, unkempt yards or homes, and loitering or disorderly behavior (Coulton et al., 1996). Such studies are significant because they are based on residents' conceptions of actions or behaviors that they experience from day to day rather than on researchers' categories of individual characteristics. Significantly, the definition offered by residents indicates actions or behaviors that can be discouraged or deterred rather than individual characteristics that are impossible or not easy to manipulate. In this sense, "local knowledge" may be more useful to policymakers, practitioners, and others interested in how to improve community and school conditions for expanded opportunities to learn and teach.

[13] Despite this unanimity about the importance of social coherence and neighborhood stability, implications of this research are limited for our purposes. For example, across disciplines, researchers rely on data sets that identify these social networks as "neighborhoods," defined by census tracts and other geographical and jurisdictional boundaries. These boundaries, generally developed for researchers' analytic purposes, often do not correspond with the relevant social unit for youth, families, or teachers. Certain recent ethnomethodological studies attempt to remedy this problem by using the social units and labels constructed by neighborhood residents themselves to define "neighborhood." However, to construct large samples, many researchers use this information to guide their choices of various predefined neighborhood categories; these categories may be closer to but are not entirely contiguous with "neighborhood" as defined by residents (Coulton et al., 1996). Nor are these categories necessarily meaningful to teachers who are interested in the specific conditions faced by the children and youth in their classrooms and schools and in the resources that might be available to expand opportunities for teaching and learning. Also, for example, adopting the poverty line as a measure of neighborhood

In addition, research on resiliency is part of a broader trend in studies of neighborhoods and youth. Instead of dwelling on neighborhood deficits and their debilitating consequences for youth, research on resiliency highlights local assets and supports for development (e.g., Blyth & Leffert, 1995; Kretzman & McKnight, 1993).[14] In particular, resiliency research expands notions of opportunity to learn and opportunity to teach because it emphasizes not what conditions simply should be avoided (many are beyond the control of teachers and even youth and families, anyway) but what supports should be cultivated intentionally to expand teaching and learning.

These researchers stress that every community has assets and strengths upon which to build opportunities and resources for youth. Chief among these, according to many studies, are strong community ties and intergenerational networks (such as those found in ethnic-based community organizations) that provide youth with resources, strong behavior norms, and connections to broader employment and other opportunities (Anderson, 1978; Bronfenbrenner, 1979; Sorin, 1990).[15] In these studies, the neighborhood extends the classroom. It also extends the family in the values, supports, and expectations that youth encounter there.

This analysis also suggests that neighborhoods are important settings for interactions among youth that also affect opportunities to learn and teach. More specifically, how do various peer groups operate as essential influences and resources for teaching and learning?

Peer Influences on Engagement with School and Achievement

Researchers have examined peer influences from at least two different perspectives. One line of research addresses the importance of peer relationships—that is, friends—in adolescent development. Erik Erikson, for example, found that peer affiliations are essential to healthy identity development in adolescents, partly, because they provide opportunities for youth to explore new interests, relationships, and ideologies (Erikson, 1968; Swanson, Spencer, & Petersen, 1998).

A second line of research examines how peer groups help youth frame goals, values, and commitments. Early research in this area was somewhat narrow in its conception of peer groups. For example, James Coleman's influential 1961 classic, *Adolescent Society,* depicted peer groups and youth culture as uniform and largely oppositional to adult society. According to Coleman, youth assert their culture to reject connections with parents and other adults. Such studies recognize that asserting a youth culture can be one means for achieving autonomy but that, if this assertion of their culture constitutes full rejection of parental values, then deviant behavior generally results (Coleman, 1961; Parsons, 1942).[16]

However, others have not concurred with this portrait of adolescent society. Some researchers who also have based their work on direct observation and participation find that youth culture is varied rather than uniform and that membership in one or another group has important influence on a youth's choices and sense of identity. Qualitative researchers such as Penelope Eckert identified distinctive youth cultures in the high schools. Eckert studied social categories she named "jocks" and "burnouts" (Eckert, 1989). Black youth in Fordham and Ogbu's study avoided the "brainiacs" in the belief that inclusion would signal "selling out" their ethnic identity and that academic achievement represents "acting White" (Fordham & Ogbu, 1986). Eckert's jocks and burnouts likewise were contemptuous of high-achieving youth.

Researchers find that youth select a particular peer group for a variety of reasons. For some, one important consideration is the "social address"—the groups' cultural, economic, and achievement characteristics with which youth may want to be associated (e.g., Elder, 1985). Many youth choose a group on the basis of ethnicity (Phelan et al., 1998). Other youth are not so much pulled by features of a youth group as they are pushed by other aspects of their lives. Researchers investigating gangs, for example, claim that youth are driven to gangs by stress at home, ineffective parenting practices, and search for the care, safety, and support missing at home (Hagedorn, 1988; Padilla, 1992).[17] Some studies suggest that youth, particularly urban youth of various ages, develop strong peer cultures in gangs that foster destructive values and behaviors (MacLeod, 1987). However, reconsiderations of the role of gangs suggests that gangs fill social, economic, and psychological needs for youth that, given certain supports, do not necessarily lead to negative behavior (Padilla, 1992; Vigil, 1993).

Whatever the path to a peer group and whatever the charac-

---

conditions ignores variations in households, resources, and types of poverty that may be particularly relevant to designers of educational policies and programs (Schram, 1995).

[14] This line of research echoes and extends the work of researchers such as Anderson (1978), Lefkowitz (1987), Stack (1974), Werner (1992), Williams and Kornblum (1985), and others who have sought to explain the success of young people from poor neighborhoods. However, this research is largely decontextualized. That is, it provides little information on the conditions under which resiliency factors matter to improved outcomes for youth—specifically, which of them matter under which circumstances for which youth. Therefore, we provide only a brief mention of this literature here.

[15] In a sense, these studies are the bright side of Wilson's 1987 study of employment, which found that the absence of jobs limits youth's motivation to stay in school or to imagine a future of meaningful employment. In part, Wilson said youth are discouraged because they cannot find role models of success nor relationships among people in "ghetto" neighborhoods that lead to broader opportunities.

[16] Later theoretical arguments suggest that peer culture may "coexist with continued commitment to parents and their adult-related values" (Fasick, 1984). However, generally, studies that consider the effects of peers and families on youth are concerned with whether families ameliorate the deleterious effects of peer pressure. For example, Steinberg examined the relationship between family structure and susceptibility to peer pressure and found a correlation between single-parent families and youth engagement in deviant behavior that could be attributed to peer pressure (Steinberg, 1987).

[17] Related to this point, Youniss & Smollar (1989) found that peer relationships are particularly powerful when youth's experiences do not bear out parental teachings.

ter of peer culture, researchers find that the values, expectations, and activities associated with a particular group sway a youth's school attitudes, behaviors, and achievement. Erikson, for instance, recognized that peer "crowds" can vary substantially in terms of their normative attitudes, interests, behaviors, and consequences (Erikson, 1968). Comparing peer groups in nine Midwestern and West Coast high schools, one study found that the average grade point average varied by nearly two full letter grades between groups (Brown, Lamborn, Mounts, & Steinberg, 1993). A meta-analysis of 110 correlations taken from 10 studies conducted between 1966 and 1978 confirmed that peer influence is a small but consistent correlate of educational outcomes (standardized achievement tests, course grades, educational aspirations, and occupational aspirations) (Ide, Parkerson, Haertel, & Walberg, 1981).

Other studies find that having high-achieving peers boosts adolescents' educational expectations, report card grades, standardized achievement scores, and satisfaction with school (Epstein, 1983). In a longitudinal study of 500 ninth to eleventh graders between 1987 and 1990, researchers predicted grade point average and drug use by friends' grades and drug use (Mounts & Steinberg, 1995).[18] Bernard (1990) suggests that peer relations provide such benefits as support, opportunities, and models for prosocial development (e.g., sharing, help, comfort, and empathy). She also argues that these groups teach critical social skills (e.g., impulse control, communication, creative and critical thinking, and relationship or friendship skills). These effects may be strongest when opportunities for peer interaction are structured through extracurricular activities or other planned opportunities for positive, stable engagement with peers and adults (Spady, 1970). Further, stable friendships have been directly correlated with good conduct and self-esteem (Keefe & Berndt, 1996).

In summary, research identifies how peer groups function as a powerful influence on youth development and academic engagement. First, friends can provide youth with safety nets for intellectual, creative, and emotional risk taking that can be essential to healthy development and learning. Second, such friendship groups and other associations can reinforce values, habits, activities, or goals that can lead youth toward healthy development and fundamentally shape their identities as learners. In these ways, peers form an important context that affects how youth respond to their teachers' efforts and expectations. Third, deliberate efforts to structure opportunities for youth to engage in peer groups can enhance outcomes. For example, after-school jobs often provide the location and occasion for peer interactions. Beyond that, work itself can be a significant out-of-school influence on learning. We turn now to an exploration of how work specifically effects learning outcomes.

How Work Affects Youth's Attitudes, Behaviors, and Capacities

Youth's experiences during employment have received little attention from researchers. Only a few studies examine the effects of work on school-related attitudes and performance, despite the significant and growing participation of youth in the labor market. In 1940, only 4% of 16-year-old boys and 1% of 16-year-old girls in school held jobs. By 1970, these rates of employment had increased to 20% and 16%, respectfully (Greenberger, Steinberg, Vaux, & McAuliffe, 1980). This trend continues. By some estimates, 76% of adolescents have begun working by the age of 16 (Mihalic & Elliott, 1997). In one study, 41% of youth in one study worked an average of 18 hours per week while also attending school (Larson, 1994).

Researchers differ in how they assess the value of work for youth development and school success. On the one hand, employment supports personal responsibility and behaviors expected in the workplace, such as punctuality (Steinberg, Greenberger, Garduque, Ruggiero, & Vaux, 1982). Work experience also appears to promote autonomy, especially for girls. On the other hand, some studies are less sanguine about the effects of employment on school-age youth. For example, one study found that working promotes cynical attitudes, comfort with unethical work practices, and increased cigarette and marijuana use. Greenberger et al. speculate that this last effect may be linked to increased stress brought on by working (Greenberger, Steinberg, & Ruggiero, 1981; Greenberger, Steinberg, & Vaux, 1981).

How much time youth spend in jobs outside of school also matters. Working more than 20 hours a week for certain youth appears to lessen the likelihood of dropping out of school—but working more than 20 hours may increase dropout rates for some (D'Amico, 1984; National Research Council, 1993). Working in high school may lower some boys' grade point averages, educational and occupational aspirations, and educational attainments (Mortimer & Finch, 1996). It also may lead to less time on homework and, consequently, lower grades (Lillydahl, 1990; Steinberg & Dornbusch, 1991) and lower academic aspirations (Mihalic & Elliott, 1997). In contrast, work has positive effects in other cases. For example, Marsh finds that employment improves grades, but only for students who are saving for college (Marsh, 1991). Adolescents, especially Whites, may be more involved in school activities when they work (Mihalic & Elliott, 1997). Youth who work tend to socialize with others who work, and these relationships are more positive in terms of school-related outcomes than those with nonworking peers (Newman, 1996).

How do we reconcile these apparently contradictory findings about the value of work for school-related attitudes and outcomes? First, these findings, at a minimum, suggest that youth do work and will continue to work out of either necessity or interest. Second, work experiences do influence youth's academic, personal, and social development, for better or worse. Third, when youth view a work experience as meaningful—when it builds the skills they, their schools, and their employers value—then it tends to promote healthy development, confidence, and academic engagement (Hess, Petersen, & Mortimer, 1994).

Thus, researchers need to distinguish among the quality of

---

[18] These findings were tempered by parents: The effect of high-achieving friends was stronger if parents were more authoritative; the effect of having drug-using friends was greater if parents were less authoritative.

different types of work and work settings. Researchers tend to lump various types of work together under one variable, such as "holding a job" (Greenberger, Steinberg, & Ruggiero, 1982) and thereby treat employment as a generic experience.[19] Some jobs provide few opportunities for growth; others offer youth opportunities to help others, make decisions, establish relationships, build trust, develop various competencies, and exercise leadership (Stern, Stone, Hopkins, & McLillon, 1990). For this reason, we distinguish between having a job and having meaningful work. Our interest is in work that engages and connects youth with various valuable opportunities for academic, social, and personal development.

Defined this way, work can benefit youth in a variety of ways (Schulenberg & Bachman, 1993). In some circumstances, it creates a track record for future employment and a structured, focused culture that is supportive of continued involvement in education. Through work, youth can become connected to social networks and otherwise develop the social capital that can be essential to future employment. As a result, teenage workers may adopt an identity as a worker, which they see as superior to their unemployed peers. All are important bases for an "honored sense of self," which may be unavailable at school but which is critical to success in it (Newman & Lennon, 1995; Newman, 1996).

In short, a job can provide youth with important relationships, experience, and exposure to the attitudes and behaviors that are necessary to succeed in school and in the workforce. In many instances, employed youth form a peer community that affects attitudes about school, self, and the future—for better or worse. When employment involves youth in meaningful and challenging tasks and when it builds skills valued both by youth and the public, out-of-school jobs can make a critical and particular contribution to a young person's self-esteem, confidence, motivation, and aspirations for academic success. In such instances, it contributes to opportunities for learning and teaching consistent with the goals society sets for schools.

Considering School–Community Connections: Shared Directions and Limitations of the Literature on Out-of-School Effects

Within a chapter that examines school–community connections, we present this abridged review of the literature on various out-of-school effects for two primary reasons. First, researchers have long known that out-of-school conditions in families, neighborhoods, peer groups, and on the job affect students' opportunities to learn and that many of these effects, under certain conditions, can be positive. The rationale for focusing on out-of-school contexts as resources, occasions, and supports for learning seems clear and uncontestable.

Second, the bodies of literature presented here explain how out-of-school conditions affect learning outcomes in strikingly similar ways. Specifically, families, neighborhoods, peers, and work seem to improve opportunity to learn through strong relationships among peers and adults; connections to personal,

professional, and other networks throughout and beyond the youths' neighborhoods; strong peer and adult role models; clear identity structures; a focus on youth and neighborhood strengths; and values that acknowledge youths' success in multiple arenas.

At the same time, these bodies of literature provide a limited guide for developing a research and policy agenda around opportunities to learn and teach, because they do not elaborate on how we can think strategically about organizing families, neighborhoods, peers, and workplaces in support of learning. Specifically, they do not suggest how out-of-school contexts for learning might be structured and marshaled in partnerships with schools to expand opportunities for learning and teaching.

This limitation arises, in part, because these lines of research are generally variable based. In variable-based studies, researchers reduce community contexts to factors such as "poverty rates," "incidence of violence," and "number of community-based organizations." Then they correlate these factors with various indicators of youth development and learning. This approach poses five fundamental problems for our inquiry. First, the "risk factors" that are of interest in these studies tend to be individual attributes or are otherwise beyond the influence of teachers, schools, and other youth-serving organizations. Second, researchers usually determine these factors and indicators a priori and, thus, may miss other factors that are important to youths' learning from day to day.

Third, variable-based studies focus on the correlation of resources and relationships to outcomes, not on what enables youth to take advantage of the presence of these resources and relationships in ways that may lead to favorable outcomes. In other words, the presence of resources, supports, and occasions does not itself mean they will be used. Most of this research focuses on avoiding risks and other deficits rather than on developing strengths. Research on family, neighborhoods, peers, and work provides strong evidence of a consistent relationship between a variety of out-of-school factors and poor school performance, but it tells us little about factors that promote successful learning and teaching among children and youth who are disadvantaged, as assessed by conventional categories.

Fourth, these lines of research tend to focus on point-in-time correlations and not on the developmental progress of particular youth over time. This focus on point-in-time correlations means that these data deal on a level of abstraction that does not illuminate day-to-day design features of neighborhoods that have strong school–community connections. Fifth, even when researchers use longitudinal data, they rarely consider changing contextual factors such as a changed youth labor market to explain trends over time, rendering the studies essentially ahistorical and the findings generally incomplete.

In summary, this research on out-of-school factors that influence youth's school performance—families, neighborhood, peers, and work—suggests that for us to understand how to strengthen school–community connections around opportunity to learn and opportunity to teach, we need a framework for policy and practice that does the following:

---

[19] For many youth, working is an economic necessity. For many of these youth, concern with the quality of the job as a learning experience is a luxury that should not lead to the devaluation of these jobs (Rist, 1981).

- Focuses on relationships, social networks, and other factors that are meaningful to or valued by youth and adults
- Emphasizes the developmental nature of learning including building on youths' strengths
- Recognizes the diversity of contexts in which youth learn that can correlate positively with youths' performance in school

Beyond expanding youths' opportunities to learn—one part of the context of teaching for classroom teachers—the research is less clear about how out-of-school contexts matter for teachers' opportunities to teach.

As the program initiatives and projects that are reviewed in the next section show, school–community efforts that contribute to opportunities to learn and to teach are distinguished by many of the features identified in the literature on effects. An examination of these deliberate attempts to structure out-of-school environments and, in some cases, link them with schools helps us begin to specify the design features of such initiatives that matter for opportunities to learn and teach. We turn now to that review.

III. Prospects for Connecting Schools and Communities for Teaching and Learning: Learning from Experience

We see in the literature on effects that youth's attitudes about school and their performance in school can be and are affected by a variety of contexts and experiences both in and out of school. We also see that, by extension, teachers' efforts could be and are supported and strengthened by actors and opportunities out of school—even when those efforts are not directly connected. Furthermore, from the literature on effects, we can derive qualities of community that can enhance learning. Our questions then become, Why should we connect in-school and out-of-school resources, occasions, and supports for learning? How can we forge such school–community connections to enhance and extend educational and developmental opportunities in and out of school?

Deliberate attempts to connect in-school and out-of-school resources, supports, and occasions for learning are few and far between in the late 1990s. Evidence about them and related efforts is found in a largely fugitive literature that consists mostly of scattered studies of single programs in limited geographic areas, studies that are difficult to find through mainstream sources of educational research. We find relevant evidence of deliberate school–community connections for opportunity to learn from research on five types of programs or initiatives. The first four that we consider are

- Initiatives for school-linked services that provide health and human services and supports at or near schools
- Community service or service–learning programs that engage youth in various community agencies and activities

- School-to-work initiatives that involve local businesses in providing educational experiences for youth
- Community-based organizations that take a developmental perspective on their work with youth and strategically build youths' "social capital"

The fifth group that we consider includes programs that strategically combine certain elements of each of the above groups and link them with schools. We find that the programs and initiatives in this latter group—what we call school–community connections for opportunity to learn and teach—provide an important rationale for connecting in-school and out-of-school resources to enhance learning. They demonstrate that, when these connections are forged in certain ways, teaching and learning are enhanced to levels that seem to exceed what would be possible with either in-school or out-of-school resources alone. An examination of these efforts with a focus on learning suggests that these school–community connections improve opportunities to learn and teach when they

- Improve conditions both in and out of school that may impede learning
- Provide opportunities both in and out of school for youth to succeed and develop academic and other competencies that are essential for learning
- Link teachers and other school professionals with expanded networks for professional support and development that inform the professional practice of youths' various teachers in and out of school
- Continually identify and connect the formal and informal curriculum and pedagogy of youth's in-school and out-of-school learning in ways that allow each to reinforce and inform the other

Finally, we conclude this section with a definition of school–community connections for opportunity to learn and to teach that draws on lessons learned to date from the experiences described below.

School-Linked Services Initiatives

Initiatives for school-linked services have grown more prominent in the past 15 years in both the public and private sectors. These initiatives generally attempt to (a) connect family support services with schools to increase access to health and human services and to recreation for youth and families; (b) provide health and human services more efficiently, effectively, and comprehensively;[20] and (c) improve the status of youth along a range of indicators from health to citizenship to academics. Various nonacademic services, from the hygiene classes of the Progressive era to drug prevention programs in recent decades, have been an important part of schools since the common school movement (Tyack, 1992). Initiatives for school-linked services mark a distinct development: Whereas many Progres-

---

[20] Definitions of "comprehensive" vary from those that include a broad range of predetermined services (Dryfoos, 1994) to those that provide such services that meet the needs and build on the strengths of target children and families (e.g., California's Healthy Start School-linked Services Initiative).

sive era reforms expanded the services that schools provide, initiatives for school-linked services generally involve partnerships with community agencies that already provide these services and, thus, enhance the performance of both schools and community agencies. In this way, initiatives for school-linked services provide an important source of evidence about the school–community connections of interest here.

Many initiatives for school-linked services are based on the explicit assumption that connections between family support services and schools will improve opportunities to learn and teach in a number of respects. First, if services are located at or near school, youth will be more likely to use them, their health and mental health status will improve, they will become better able to meet their basic needs, and their families will become stronger. Because their nonacademic needs have been met, youth will come to school better prepared to learn. Second, the presence of social workers, health care providers, counselors, parents and others on school campuses will mean that teachers will have the support of other service providers in addressing the nonacademic needs of their students. Consequently, teachers will be able to focus more of their time and resources on teaching and learning in a potentially less stressful classroom environment and will otherwise be free to "really teach."

Initiatives for school-linked services range from single school efforts (Philliber Research Associates, 1994) to statewide efforts to integrate services and connect them with schools (e.g., see Illback, 1997, on Kentucky; SRI International, 1996, on California). For example, a city-level partnership of health and human services and educational agencies in San Diego launched New Beginnings in the late 1980s at Hamilton Elementary School. Through New Beginnings, this city partnership provided additional discretionary funding to Hamilton Elementary and other agencies serving youth in its neighborhood to create an interagency partnership that would deliver a range of health and human services on the school campus including mental health counseling, health services, adult basic education, and recreation.

In Kentucky and California, state educational agencies provide funding for schools and other neighborhood-based agencies to deliver health, social, recreational, employment, educational, and other services in more collaborative and comprehensive ways. In Kentucky, the Kentucky Education Reform Act of 1991 requires all schools where at least 20% of the students are eligible for free and reduced-price lunches to establish family resource or youth services centers at or near school campuses to offer a range of family support and employment services. California's statewide Healthy Start initiative provides discretionary funding to school-level interagency partnerships on a competitive basis. These partnerships implement school-linked services that best meet the needs and build on the strengths of youth and families in that neighborhood. Healthy Start collaboratives across California (from kindergarten through Grade 12) currently implement family resource centers, child-care and recreation programs, school-based health clinics, itinerant case management teams, and other services.

In addition to their broader scope, these initiatives differ from the traditional efforts to provide nonacademic services at schools in two significant ways. First, the initiatives are generally governed at the school level by interagency partnerships or collaboratives whose members each contribute various funding and services to the effort. Thus, the school is not the sole provider, funder, or decision maker in the school-linked services initiative. This approach is generally based on the belief that no one agency serving youth can meet its goals alone and that services would be provided more efficiently and effectively if they were delivered collaboratively. Such collaboration is generally believed to require shared governance and funding. Second, these initiatives are usually part of a deliberate strategy to effect broader changes in systems of health and human services. For example, the New Beginnings program at Hamilton Elementary School in San Diego was designed as a demonstration site for a broader effort to redesign the county's social services system (Philliber Research Associates, 1994).

School-linked services initiatives such as these demonstrate results in a number of areas. Early evaluations suggest that these initiatives are meeting families' previously unmet needs for health and human services and are improving access to comprehensive services. Customer satisfaction is generally high (Philliber Research Associates, 1994; SRI International, 1996). Some of the longer-standing initiatives are showing improved school retention, reduced absenteeism, and improvements in grade point averages (Rossman & Morley, 1995). Other studies indicate that gains are greatest in the first six months (SRI International, 1996) and for youth that are worst off at the start (Rossman & Morley, 1995). This finding suggests that connecting health and human services and educational supports may lead to improvements in school performance, at least in the short term, in such areas as school attendance and school climate (e.g., incidence of graffiti, classroom behavior).

However, initial evaluations also suggest that the disconnections between the in-school and out-of-school components of most initiatives for school-linked services limit the capacity of these initiatives to significantly expand opportunity to learn, because many of them involve adding services to otherwise unchanged in-school programs. They suggest that, for school-linked services to contribute to more significant gains in school performance, schools must somehow restructure as part of these initiatives if we expect academic achievement to improve significantly. For example, the Communities in Schools (CIS) initiative has provided discretionary funding and technical assistance to schools to provide a range of largely formal health and human services at or near school campuses. A recent evaluation of CIS found that students who were enrolled in schools that had formed academies—schools within schools or alternative schools—as the primary vehicle for delivering school-linked services through the CIS program showed greater improvements in school achievement than students in CIS at typical schools—schools that had not been restructured or otherwise integrated with the out-of-school supports and occasions for learning (Rossman & Morley, 1995).

The Annie E. Casey foundation launched a multimillion dollar, multicity effort in the late 1980s to stimulate the development of city-level interagency partnerships that would reform the citywide delivery of health and human services in ways that were more closely connected with schools. The evaluation of Annie E. Casey's New Futures initiative found that, in part, because schools failed to restructure when additional services were added on, prospects for gain in academic achievement were constrained (Wehlage et al., 1992; see also Smylie & Crowson, 1996). These findings suggest that, if the school-linked services were more than merely linked but were integrated into the core of schools for students, perhaps greater gains in academic achievement and other school outcomes would result. Early policy documents on school-linked services emphasize that linking services with schools is important because teachers are then freed from addressing social problems and can focus on teaching. However, these initiatives do not always engage schools similarly in reforming their interactions with youth (Wehlage et al., 1992).

Many initiatives are trying to create stronger connections between the integrated services and the regular school program. However, many noneducational agencies may face significant difficulties in partnering with schools. Some find school staff members averse to collaboration because of bureaucratic barriers such as rigid scheduling and lack of experience (Chaskin & Richman, 1993; McLaughlin et al., 1994). A 5-year study of such school–community integration in 36 states revealed that little integration was in practice at this stage in the development of school-linked services initiatives (Lawson & Briar-Lawson, 1997).

In summary, experience to date with school-linked services suggests a number of lessons that are relevant to the question of joining school and community around opportunity to learn and teach. For one, school-linked services, as presently implemented, may be a necessary precondition for enhancing teaching and learning, especially in high-poverty settings where students and their families may tend to lack access to basic resources. However, these initiatives may not sustain improvements in learning short of fundamentally strengthening the connections between community and school.

School-linked services also can provide opportunities for parents and other adults in the lives of youth to gain important knowledge and develop the kinds of networks that are identified as essential in section II. For example, a number of researchers note that the presence of family support services on school campuses increases the opportunities adults and youth have to establish relationships with professionals connected to schools (Smrekar, 1994; Smrekar, 1996). This increased social capital (Coleman, 1988; Putnam, 1995) can mean improved parental involvement with the school and in their children's education. Nonetheless, most initiatives for school-linked services adopt a school-centric view of where teaching and learning occur. Even though many initiatives are designed expressly to achieve educational goals, few view out-of-school learning environments as settings for learning rather than as barriers to learning. These initiatives focus on removing barriers to learning rather than on

identifying where learning takes place in their neighborhoods and linking that learning with schools.

Community Service and Service Learning

For more than a decade, foundation leaders, educational reformers, and policymakers including Presidents George Bush and Bill Clinton have promoted community service and service learning as ways to foster personal growth, civic commitment, and academic competence and engagement (Boyer, 1983; Commission on Work, Family, and Citizenship, 1988; Council of Chief State School Officers, 1989; Harrison, 1987). School districts, schools, and individual teachers now have substantial new funding opportunities for community service and service learning from foundations, businesses, and government groups at the national, state, and local levels. In 1993–94, approximately 434,000 school-aged youth participated in Learn and Serve America programs.[21] In 1994–95, this number rose to 750,000 (Melchior, 1997). Additionally, many school districts, cities (including Chicago and Atlanta), and the entire state of Maryland now require students to take part in service activities as one prerequisite for high school graduation. A study of data from the National Education Longitudinal Survey (NELS) and from the 1992 follow-up survey indicated that, of 12th graders, nationally 44% had participated in some form of community service within the past 2 years in either their school or their community and 8% had worked in a school-based community service program within the past 2 years (Alt, 1997).

In research and in practice, a fundamental distinction is often made by many between community service and service learning. Generally, community service refers to activities designed primarily to meet community needs. Activities can include peer tutoring or mentoring; recycling; clearing trails and roads; organizing safety patrols; helping out at a hospital, museum, or senior center; and so forth. Service–learning activities often involve similar types of service work, but, in addition, they are deliberately designed to develop skills and deepen understanding of academic content. In other words, service learning, by definition, is a form of community service that connects schools and communities in a deliberate effort to construct learning opportunities for youth.[22]

The best and most consistent data regarding the effect of service learning on academic goals come from studies of cross-age and peer tutoring. Meta-analyses of studies indicate that tutors make modest academic gains when compared with more traditional instructional methods (Cohen, Kulik, & Kulik, 1982; Hedin, 1987). A more recent study that focused on 1,000 students who participated in "high quality" programs (fully implemented programs with links to course content) yielded statisti-

---

[21] Learn and Serve America is a program of the Corporation for National Service, a government entity that funds community service and service–learning programs. Learn and Serve America refers to service–learning programs, in particular, that are funded through schools, community-based organizations, and other agencies.

[22] The conceptual basis for this approach is most commonly associated with the work of John Dewey (Dewey, 1900/1956, 1916/1966, 1938/1963) and with reformers like William Heard Kilpatrick (Kilpatrick, 1918) and Paul Hanna (Hanna, 1936). The goal of these educators was to create opportunities for students to work together on matters of social value. By linking these efforts to student interests, community needs, and academic subject matter, proponents argued such curriculum could ground and deepen students' understanding of academic content, foster youth development, build capacities for the kinds of collective action needed in a democratic society, and promote students' commitment to civic participation. Overall, studies of these initiatives indicate that such outcomes are often attained, but are not guaranteed.

cally significant gains on measures of academic performance (Melchior, 1997). The Teen Outreach Program, offered in dozens of schools throughout the country, combines structured community service experiences with classroom discussions about life decisions that are related to careers and relationships. Studies using matched comparisons of students at 35 sites (Allen, Philliber, & Hoggson, 1990) and true experimental designs at 25 sites (Allen, Philliber, Hoggson, & Kuperminc, 1997) have found that the program dramatically diminishes rates of school suspension, school dropout, school failure, and teenage pregnancy. Indeed, Allen, Philliber, Herrling, and Kuperminc found that the program cut the risk of pregnancy, school failure, and school suspension in half (Allen et al., 1997). Moreover, Allen, Philliber, and Hoggson found that students at sites that made significant use of a volunteer service component had significantly better outcomes than did students at sites where volunteer service was not much used as a program component (Allen et al., 1990).

How do service–learning activities lead to these positive academic outcomes? First, when schoolteachers, youth workers, and others provide opportunities for learning through service, they expand the kinds of learning environments, resources, and supports available to youth beyond those that schools alone can provide. For example, some youth show greater academic gains when enabled to learn through applied work-related settings such as those available through service–learning activities (e.g., hospitals, child care centers, construction sites). The experiential nature of a service–learning curriculum may increase motivation and deepen understanding.[23] Unlike some of the experiential education programs described in section I, many service–learning programs expand the settings for learning, the variety of adults that serve as youths' teachers and mentors, and the opportunities for success in school beyond those that have been traditionally legitimated by schools. Participation in these programs also means that youth have opportunities to establish meaningful relationships with adults apart from school who can link them with additional occasions for learning and from whom they can learn. In fact, researchers have shown that service–learning experiences for youth tend to promote more positive attitudes toward adults (Conrad & Hedin, 1982).

Second, studies also suggest that service–learning activities may enhance academic achievement, in part, by developing nonacademic competencies—social, emotional, physical, civic, and vocational—which can be essential to academic achievement. Gains in self-confidence, self-esteem, and self-worth are noted in some studies (Conrad & Hedin, 1982; Hamilton & Fenzel, 1988; Newmann & Rutter, 1983), though these effects vary by certain factors (see Wade & Saxe, 1996, for a review). Other studies show that service learning can decrease alienation and discipline problems among junior high school students with behavioral difficulties (Calabrese & Schumer, 1986) and can foster gains in moral development (Cognetta & Sprinthall, 1978).

A number of studies also have examined the effect of service–learning experiences on self-report measures of personal and social responsibility. Measures ask students, for example, if they think that having everyone recycle is important or if they try to help others in need. Most of these studies report modest gains in one or more measures (Conrad & Hedin, 1981; Hamilton & Fenzel, 1988; Melchior & Orr, 1995; Newmann & Rutter, 1983). In terms of civic commitments, studies uniformly find that youth who participate in high school government or community service projects are more likely to vote and join community organizations when they are adults than those who did not participate during high school (see Youniss & Yates, 1997, for a review). Yates and Youniss (1996) and Youniss and Yates (1997) have found that service–learning experiences can have a significant effect on political and moral identity development.[24] These studies, like the work with journals done by Conrad and Hedin (1987), and studies by many qualitative researchers highlight the diverse, subtle, and often profound ways service experiences provide opportunities for forms of reflection and growth that are rarely achieved through traditional pedagogy. Students frequently reexamine stereotypes, confront fears, learn about new environments, and recognize personal capacities.

What does research to date tell us about the features of service–learning activities that build in youth these nonacademic competencies that are essential to expanded opportunities to learn? First, high-quality, service–learning activities provide ongoing (at least weekly) structured time for reflection and analysis of the content and process of the service–learning experience. Conrad and Hedin's (1982) national study of 27 experiential education programs, many of which were service–learning programs, found that this design feature was the strongest predictor of positive student change—particularly in measures of social and intellectual development. Similarly, longer and more intensive programs were also associated with meaningful opportunities for reflection (Conrad & Hedin, 1982).[25]

Second, the qualities of programs related to student growth were those that reflected opportunities for personal agency (e.g., students felt "free to develop and use own ideas" or "free to pursue my own interests") and those that reflected collegial relationships with adults (e.g., students "discussed experiences with teachers"). Although some overlap occurred, the characteristics of programs most associated with personal agency were the ones most strongly related to increased self-esteem. Program participants felt that the characteristics most associated with collegial adult relationships were the ones most strongly related to improved prosocial attitudes and reasoning skills.

---

[23] Consistent with this assessment, service–learning activities in schools are generally rated positively by participating students (see, e.g., Melchior, 1997).

[24] Yates and Youniss's theoretical frame draws on work by Erikson (1968) that emphasizes the sociohistorical components of identity and work by Luckmann (1991) on transcendent identification. Rather than aim directly at measures of personal or social responsibility, Youniss and Yates examine students' writing and the statements that students make during discussions and demonstrate that service provides opportunities for stimulating identity development regarding the ways students think about social, moral, and political issues.

[25] In this study, reflection was unrelated to measures of personal growth such as self-esteem. Conrad and Hedin did not find any significant differences regarding the type of service in which the students were involved.

Third, similar to findings related to school-linked services, some studies of service learning suggest that links to the in-school curriculum are essential to the effect of service learning whether it is provided as part of the school day or after school. The closer the service–learning experiences are to the academic curriculum, the greater the gains (Dewsbury-White, 1993; Hamilton & Zeldin, 1987; Levinson, 1986; Melchior, 1997).

School-to-Work and School-to-Career Initiatives

In connecting work and school in ways that enhance opportunity to learn, schools have a long history on which they might build. Though such efforts have largely focused on preparing youth who are not college bound for work through vocational (nonacademic) programs during the school day, current policies mark a significant shift in orientation, and their emphasis is now on preparing students for high skills jobs (National Center on Education and the Economy & Commission on the Skills of the American Workforce, 1990; U.S. Department of Labor, 1991). The School-to-Work Opportunities Act of 1994 (e.g., the most recent reauthorization of the largest federal education program for vocational education) is theoretically consistent with our concern for school–community connections and the lessons identified in section II. It emphasizes creating a school-to-work transition program that is (a) valued (i.e., a viable option for all students including the college-bound student); (b) work-based and school-based with high-quality, well-planned connecting activities that link in-school and out-of-school learning for youth; and (c) highly structured (i.e., youth have clear expectations and relationships with adults and peers who support their success by providing career counseling and guidance, job shadowing, and mentoring).

Many of the more innovative efforts to connect schools and workplaces around teaching and learning have been developed by Jobs for the Future (JFF), a Boston-based group that designs and supports school-to-career initiatives in both school and community settings. In 1995, JFF launched a 5-year project, the Benchmarks Communities Initiative (BCI), to demonstrate that a comprehensive work-and-learning initiative "could and should be central to a community's core educational strategy" (Martinez, Goldberger, & Alongi, 1996). The BCI is a partnership in five communities: Boston, Massachusetts; Jefferson County, Kentucky; Milwaukee, Wisconsin; North Clakamas, Oregon; and Philadelphia, Pennsylvania. BCI engages a significant number of employers in work and learning partnerships as part of their strategy to restructure the K–16 education system. BCI's program involves school-based learning, work-based learning, and connecting activities to make learning more active and relevant to students and to provide the kinds of learning experiences appropriate to the contemporary job market.

In contrast to some school-to-work programs that target youth who are either not enrolled in or not succeeding in academic tracks, BCI involves all youth to integrate work-based learning as an integral part of all students' core curriculum. For example, in Milwaukee, teachers and employers collaborated to integrate science courses with hospital apprenticeships. In Boston, schools and employers joined together in the ProTech initiative to offer work-site learning that was integrated with a strong academic curriculum across several industries. ProTech students who are interested in working in area hospitals must first learn about basic operations within hospital units such as the cardiology unit, the pharmacy, the radiology unit, and the medical library. Once there, ProTech students then take on meaningful responsibilities in the hospital departments (Zeldin & Charner, 1996). BCI establishes school–community partnerships through a formal "Compact"—an agreement that specifies goals and responsibilities and that describes strategies for ensuring that any youth's experiences at both the school and the worksite is of high-quality (Martinez et al., 1996).

Preliminary evaluation and anecdotal evidence about the consequences of BCI for school outcomes are promising. Students report excitement about their work-based learning and, as a result, high levels of engagement with school. The documented experience of the most established JFF program, Boston Compact's ProTech program, shows that students' grades and attendance improved, as did graduation rates (Martinez et al., 1996).

Career Academies have proliferated in urban districts since the 1970s and provide another promising example of school–community connections around school and work (Stern et al., 1990). Career Academies began as a strategy to motivate underachieving students and connect their high school experience directly to the workplace (and to respond to employers' complaints that high school graduates are poorly prepared). Career Academies are schools within schools that simultaneously aspire to train students for an occupational field and prepare them for college. Career Academies thus are designed to bring both increased relevance and rigor to the high school experience of youth who have been traditionally turned off or tuned out and who, too often, have been slogging through dreary "low track" classes. Connections with the community are key to the operation and success of Career Academies. These community connections mean students are engaged in real-life work settings while they learn. Business managers, medical professionals, and other adults outside schools serve as primary teachers, mentors, and bridges to other networks and opportunities for development and learning.

Evaluations of Career Academies regarding their effective function as an opportunity for learning and teaching are encouraging. For example, California's Peninsula Academies for tenth through twelfth graders prepare youth for careers in electronics, finance, health, and other fields by providing an integrated vocational and academic curriculum, mentoring, summer internships, and a family-like structure that personalizes the environment. Although programmatic effect varied significantly, with some schools showing no effect, one evaluation found that academy students overall had half the dropout rate of a comparison group as well as better attendance and grades (Stern et al., 1990). Connections to meaningful work and caring adults in and out of school were key sources of motivation and engagement for Academy students. By their own reports, also important to their success was the peer group created in the Academy, one that transformed peer norms from those that opposed academic achievement to those that essentially supported it (see, e.g., Pauly, Kopp, & Haimson, 1995).

Taken together, the experiences of JFF and Career Academies offer some common evidence about why and how such examples of school–community connections expand opportunities to learn. First, high-quality school-to-work programs— those that achieve the positive outcomes indicated above—help youth develop the skills to identify and take advantage of opportunities to learn in their work experience. Similar to high-quality service–learning programs, these programs engage youth in reflecting on their work experience, challenge them to identify challenging situations or analyze the skills they will need to address those challenges, and develop strategies for enhancing those skills. Research shows that when youth are so engaged, they show evidence of greater commitment to quality performance in school and on the job, expanded capacity for coping with difficult situations that require new knowledge, and less cynicism about the world of work and their future in it (Kopp & Kazis, 1995; Stern et al., 1990).[26]

Second, high-quality school-to-career programs engage youth in the types of work they are likely to find meaningful and the types of work that offer avenues for future advancement. Although many youth have opportunities to hold jobs, the connections between employment opportunities and schools may be essential to ensure that their employment is meaningful work. Youth who work outside school (and also attend school) generally work in the secondary labor market—in nonunion jobs with low skill requirements, high turnover, and few opportunities for advancement. Most of these jobs are service sector positions such as restaurant, retail, clerical, and janitorial work. Youth who participate in school-to-work transition programs or other work situations that are enabled by school–community collaborations such as those found in BCI and Career Academy initiatives typically are engaged in such industries as health care, electronics, hotel management, construction, and other high-skills work settings. Although the actual qualities of these programs vary, overall, evaluators have found that the work opportunities students find through these initiatives are of higher quality than those they find on their own.

"Higher quality" includes links to youth's expressed career interests, significant time for learning and practicing skills, and structured opportunities for training and ongoing development (Hershey, Hudis, Silverberg, & Haimson, 1997). These opportunities and orientations include connections to broader networks within and across specific industries and the development of transferable skills. Accumulating evidence finds that young people who have opportunities to work at more complex jobs not only have higher wages but also have lower levels of unemployment 3 years later (Stern et al., 1990; see also Goldberger & Kazis, 1996).

The school-to-work or school-to-career programs that connect schools with community employers around learning and active engagement also are distinguished from earlier vocational education or career education efforts in that they expressly move beyond a limited list of job-focused youth out-comes to consider motivation, self-esteem, cognitive complexity, and sense of responsibility and belonging (Zeldin & Charner, 1996). Likewise, the program elements identified as essential to these broader successful youth outcomes implicate more than narrow factors of curriculum, job placements, and the like. They consider school-to-work programs in terms of opportunities: active and self-directed learning, new roles and responsibilities, ongoing emotional support from adults and peers, high standards, and ongoing access to supportive social networks (Zeldin & Charner, 1996).

Third, high-quality school-to-career programs connect learning in school and on the job. This connection between in-school and out-of-school learning means that the skills developed in the classroom are directly applied on the job. Experiences on the job are seen as an extension of the classroom, and success on the job is validated as a part of school success. In this process, teachers and employers engage in ongoing dialog and strategizing about how to apply their respective expertise to enhance youth's experiences in school and on the job.[27]

Fourth, when schools and work are connected in ways that can enhance opportunities to learn and teach, teachers, employers, and other adults have expanded opportunities to develop as professionals and, accordingly, to teach. The Benchmark Community Initiative, for example, provided important professional development opportunities for teachers. Professional learning communities came together in ways that, as teachers reported, provided effective ways for them to rethink their practices, assumptions they had made about the youth with whom they worked, and enhanced opportunities to teach in very real terms. BCI also provided job shadowing and internships for teachers in local industry—experiences that gave teachers direct experience with the kinds of skills and competencies their students would need to succeed in the workplace (Martinez et al., 1996). Jobs for the Future has seen that successful apprenticeship programs can provide important education for employers, too. Employer's positive experiences with JFF programs amended the stereotypes they held about youth and contributed to more trusting and positive relationships on both sides (Kazis, 1993). Evaluations of both JFF and Career Academy programs also comment on the important learning about the abilities and promise of youth that occurs for employers as a result of their participation (Kazis, 1993; Pauly et al., 1995; Stern et al., 1990).

Youth Development Programs and Youth Organizations

Approximately 4,000 national youth service organizations operate in this country including Boys and Girls Clubs, 4-H programs, YMCAs, neighborhood drop-in centers, after-school clubs, Departments and Offices of Parks and Recreation, churches, and others. More than 17,000 U.S. nonprofit organizations classify themselves as "youth development organiza-

---

[26] Grubb (1995) remarks on the promise of such school-to-career initiatives to turn the city itself into a learning place for youth.

[27] Kazis and Kopp (1997) observe that these positive outcomes appear to contradict findings from many school-to-work demonstration programs such as the Youth Incentive Entitlement Pilot Project and other vocational education or jobs programs, which show either uneven academic or career benefit to participants, or sustained involvement with the program. The difference, in their view, lies in the quality of the work experience and in the extent to which community employers and schools integrate and support youth's experiences.

tions," and 70% of eighth graders in a recent large-scale study report that they participate in the activities of such organizations (Pittman & Wright, 1991).[28]

Youth organizations embrace multiple purposes and goals. Central among these goals are those of providing safe, positive recreational opportunities for young people. Youth organizations also vary in the type and quality of programs they offer. For example, some youth organizations such as Little League focus solely on sports; others such as Boys and Girls Clubs or Girls, Inc. are club programs that offer a range of activities in the arts, sports, citizenship, service, and education. Some YMCAs are primarily "gym and swim,"—providing supervised recreation—whereas others offer an array of structured, explicitly developmental opportunities for young people. Some neighborhood-based organizations, or local affiliates of national organizations such as the YMCA, operate primarily as drop-in centers, with the purpose of providing a safe place for various youth to come after school. Others are "24–7"—open 7 days a week for extended hours—to serve as a haven for a core group of neighborhood youth and to engage them in a variety of activities and long-term relationships with peers and adults (see, e.g., Carnegie Council on Adolescent Development, 1994; McLaughlin et al., 1994).

Many of these youth organizations provide a broad range of formal and informal academic and nonacademic supports for learning and growth. These supports include the expectations they raise and hold for their young members, the role models they offer, the nurturing environments they provide, and the structures they provide for youth to explore their own interests. Evaluation and anecdotal evidence show that youth organizations that take this broad developmental approach have important effects on young people's achievement and school performance (e.g., Kahne & Bailey, 1999; Posner & Vandell, 1994; Villarruel & Lerner, 1994).

Important social and developmental outcomes for youth including improved behavior in school, raised academic expectations, better social skills and improved self-confidence also are associated with many of these programs (McLaughlin et al., 1994; Villarruel & Lerner, 1994). For example, youth responses to items from the National Educational Longitudinal Survey 1988 (NELS: 88) showed that, when compared to the "typical" American youth, low-income, urban youth who were participating regularly in youth organizations were more likely to receive recognition for good grades in high school, plan to go to college, feel good about themselves, feel like they could make plans and achieve them, and express commitment to work in the community (McLaughlin, 2000). Participation in a community-based youth organization, in other words, appeared to mediate the detrimental aspects of other aspects of their environment—most especially, struggling neighborhoods, inadequate institutional supports, and, often, poor schools.

Much of the available data on the effects of youth organizations come from studies of mentoring relationships that are usually part of a broader set of programs at a youth organization. In one study, participants in the mentoring program of a youth organization were three times more likely than a comparison group to attend college. They had higher grade point averages in the tenth and eleventh grades (Johnson, 1996). In a large-scale comparative study of 959 10- to 16-year-olds who applied for Big Brother and Big Sister programs in 1992 and 1993, participants in the programs, when compared to a control group, were 46% less likely to start using drugs, 27% less likely to start using alcohol, and more than 30% less likely to hit someone. Participating youth showed improvements in school attendance, school performance, and attitudes toward completing schoolwork. These gains were strongest among minority Little Sisters (Tierney, Grossman, & Resch, 1995).

Yet all youth organizations do not have the same effect on opportunities to learn and teach. Some youth organizations affect opportunities to learn directly by providing additional academic supports (e.g., homework assistance, after-school classes, tutoring). However, evidence suggests that, beyond the provision of direct academic supports, the high-quality youth organizations also engage youth in a less formal curriculum that builds their multiple competencies—including social, emotional, vocational, civic, and physical competencies—that can be essential to academic success (Pittman & Cahill, 1992; Pittman & Wright, 1991). These high-quality youth organizations engage youth in varied activities that build on their strengths and provide them with strong relationships with peers and adults.

The curricula within high-quality youth organizations include identity structures such as rituals, systems of loyalty, and identity markers such as uniforms (Fine & Mechling, 1993). These curricula allow youth choice in whether to participate and in how to participate. Such curricula appeal to an array of interests and abilities, are readily usable and accessible, engage the young person in an active learning stance, and challenge participants to stretch their skills and build new competencies (Martin & Ascher, 1994; McLaughlin et al., 1994; U.S. Department of Education & U.S. Department of Justice, 1998).

Relationship structures also facilitate a high rate of personal interaction between youth and adults. The mere encouragement of relationships is not enough to ensure positive outcomes. Rather, high-quality youth organizations deliberately structure these relationships by stringently screening volunteers, requiring intensive training for and supervision of adults to ensure they are strong role models, and continually monitoring and re-

---

[28] The 1998 review of after-school programs, prepared jointly by the U.S. Departments of Education and Justice (U.S. Department of Education & U.S. Department of Justice, 1998), contains many diverse examples of projects run by youth development organizations around the country that enhance students' interest in school, achievement, and engagement in academic work. For example, more than one-half of the students participating in The 3:00 Project, a statewide network of after-school programs in Georgia, improved their grades in at least one subject; students participating in Los Angeles' BEST program made academic gains far beyond those in a comparison group; students in Louisiana's Church-Based After-School Tutorial Network increased their grade point averages in math and language arts by 1.5 to 3 points, depending on the number of years they participated. One-half of the teachers of students participating in the Los Angeles 4-H after-school program rated the students' homework completion as improved or much improved. Coca-Cola's Valued Youth program, a cross-age tutoring program, finds not only that tutored students' grades and school attitudes improve but also that participation in the program has reduced school drop-out rates for the older student tutors.

evaluating progress by staff and youth (Fine & Mechling, 1993; Furano, Roaf, Styles, & Branch, 1993; Johnson, 1996; Tierney et al., 1995). Long-term relationships are particularly important to positive outcomes. The average length of matches for one successful mentoring program is 1.5 years (Furano et al., 1993); in another it is 5 years (Johnson, 1996).

Many evaluations and reports stress the importance of providing mentors and facilitating other relationships either within the context of a program that involves broader supports and a robust peer culture (Fine & Mechling, 1993) or through relationships with a community of participants (Hanks & Eckland, 1978). Program supports beyond the scholarships and mentoring were the class coordinator, academic support coordinator, summer enrichment program, and cultural events (Johnson, 1996).

Evaluations also indicate that for relationships in these organizations to facilitate opportunities to learn and teach, they should be developmental rather than prescriptive. In a review of 82 mentoring matches by eight Big Brother and Big Sister organizations, two-thirds of all relationships were found to be developmental rather than prescriptive (Tierney & Grossman, 1995). Developmental relationships were defined as follows: Adult volunteers "held expectations that changed over time in relation to their perceptions of the needs of the youth; focused on building trusting relationships" (Tierney & Grossman, 1995); and involved youth in decision making processes. Prescriptive relationships were defined as ones in which adults set the goals, focused shared time on achieving those goals, and required youth to share responsibility for maintaining relationships. In general, prescriptive relationships tended to set expectations too high and were, therefore, not developmentally appropriate. They also did not build on the strengths of youth (Gambone & Arbreton, 1997).

Organizations that engage youth on a consistent basis share common features. Although they are "place neutral"—that is, their effectiveness does not depend on their location—the environment created for youth within them is key. Effective youth organizations all had (a) consistent, caring adults who involved themselves in many aspects of youth's lives; (b) clear rules for membership and safety; (c) a "whole" youth approach; and (d) activities that were valued and assessed by youth and community—real responsibilities, real work (McLaughlin et al., 1994; U.S. Department of Education & U.S. Department of Justice, 1998; Villarruel & Lerner, 1994).

In conclusion, cumulating evidence identifies curricular and organizational features of youth organizations that do and do not promote youths' opportunities to learn. For example, centers that function as little more than drop-in locations do little more than provide a place off the streets. Older youth typically shun these programs in favor of the streets, where they can find engaging activity and a consistent peer group (McLaughlin et al., 1994). Older youth, given the chance to do so, also reject out-of-school educational opportunities that are too much like school. Youth and children alike dislike program settings that are designed to "fix" them—programs to which they are assigned to remedy problem behaviors. Such programs, too often, only reinforce youth's view that something is wrong with them, that they are somehow deficient, and that they are a problem (McLaughlin, 1993, p. 59).

Although many community-based youth programs and organizations function as powerful supports for youth development and success in school, they, with few exceptions, provide this support for learning (and, by extension, support for teaching) effectively in isolation from schools. In Heath and McLaughlin's 10 years of field research in community-based programs and organizations that were judged effective by youth, not one had any formal affiliation with local schools (e.g., McLaughlin, 2000). When links did exist, they existed between individuals (e.g., between the middle school teacher who e-mailed students' homework assignments down the hill to the neighborhood Boys and Girls Club and her friend who worked there after school) not organizations. However, a growing number of exceptions to this separation between youth organizations and schools are demonstrating how such connections can powerfully expand opportunities to learn and teach. These strong examples of connections between youth organizations and schools usually also involve relationships with other community organizations—providing youth development activities in and out of school as part of a broader web of supports for youth and families, teachers, and youth workers. We discuss these school–community efforts to support learning and teaching at the end of this section.

Crosscutting Lessons for Opportunity to Learn

In summary, schools and communities that are connected in the various ways described here—through school-linked services, service learning, school-to-work initiatives, and community-based organizations—reinforce and extend youth's opportunity to learn in a number of important ways. For example, they provide the following supports.

Improved health and social support. Enhanced social services enable young people to come to school with the energy and health that is essential to engage in classroom activities and goals as learners.

Places and spaces to learn. Many youth lack places to do homework and resources to support their learning. In neighborhood youth-organizations, youth may find quiet spaces to work, helpful tutors, technology, and other resources to support their work.

Involved, caring adults. The literature on out-of-school influences consistently highlights the importance of a caring adult to mentor, support, guide, and motivate young people in consistent and ongoing ways. Community-based youth organizations, school-to-work initiatives, and service–learning projects can provide these adult resources and role models to young people who may lack them in their home environments. These adults expand youths' horizons and expectations and help young people find the connections and resources they will need to achieve their goals.

Positive peer groups. Peers who define productive goals for themselves and value education and learning depict a most fundamental sort of opportunity to learn, because they influence other youth's choices about how to spend time and ideas about possible futures. Organizations and activities such as service–learning efforts, community organizations, and school-to-work programs provide structures and activities for the development of positive peer environments.

Expanded occasions for learning and success. Community-based organizations, school-to-work initiatives, and many service–learning efforts extend learning in a number of important ways. For one, they focus on many of the nonacademic skills that young people need to succeed in school and as adults—among them, leadership, persistence, entrepreneurship, and civic responsibility. They also equip youth with the soft but essential skills of eye contact, a firm handshake, habits of punctuality, and even table manners. These out-of-school contexts offer opportunities for youth to practice the skills, roles, and relationships that are essential to their success as students and adults. They provide engagement in real-world enterprises such as business or community work. These community classrooms are often more meaningful and motivating than those found in school, and the engagement with learning that is generated in community classrooms often carries back to school.

Crosscutting Lessons for Opportunity to Teach

The literature on the programs described here in this section, like the effects literature in section II, is generally silent on the value of these initiatives for classroom teachers. However, our analysis suggests a number of ways that these deliberately structured out-of-school contexts can enhance teachers' opportunities to teach, particularly when they are linked with schools.

Improved in-school climate for teaching. Teaching and learning are two sides of a single coin. Expanded opportunities for youth to learn can mean expanded opportunities for teachers to teach, in part, because youth may come to class better prepared, eager to learn, and motivated to do well. Youth might come to school with a stronger base of social supports and assistance to cope with the myriad factors that compete with teachers for energy, attention, and time.

Extended space and time for teaching. Connections between schools and community-based organizations that are organized around learning can extend teachers' space and time for teaching by providing opportunities for youth to continue their school projects or expand them into new activities. The work of a youth newspaper group, for example, can provide important practice in literacy skills and concrete rewards for good writing and analysis. A basketball team's calculations about their nutritional needs lend relevance to the work of math teachers. Boys and Girls clubs, YMCAs and YWCAs, and local churches have critical assets of space and adult support to provide places for studying, assistance with homework, and access to important learning tools such as computers and books. Through connections with such community-based organizations, teachers can extend their teaching into youth's nonschool time in ways that compliment and reinforce instructional goals.

Access to funds of knowledge about their students. Insufficient knowledge about the circumstances, neighborhoods, and supports of their students hampers teachers' effectiveness with many students, most particularly, with students who come from backgrounds different from the teacher's. Many teachers say they "just don't know how to relate to students today" (McLaughlin & Talbert, 1993, 2001). School–community connections give teachers access to new knowledge about youth's learning and effective settings for it. That is, parents, youth workers, athletic coaches, and youth's other teachers each have knowledge about youth's learning that is generally unavailable to classroom teachers unless they have opportunities to collaborate and build trusting relationships and social networks. Thus, closer connections between teachers and their students' communities can provide important information that teachers need to make their practices substantively student-centered. For example, through school-to-work initiatives, teachers have learned about the kinds of employment opportunities for which their students will compete.

Teachers' collaborations with community social service workers can also provide valuable information about family conditions that teachers should consider. For example, on learning from a school-site social worker that several students in her classroom had no place to do homework, a California teacher revised her classroom activities to be sure that the most important "home" work was done in school. In the same vein, a project in Arizona's Mexican communities shows that when teacher-researchers visit households as learners, establish connections with parents, and base instruction on these observations, the subsequent teaching that is based in these local "funds of knowledge" enhances the school performance of nonmainstream students (Moll, 1992). Collaboration between schools, community organizations, and caring adults in the neighborhood can provide a bridge between school and community, between youth and mainstream institutions.

Partners in teaching. The community contains many teachers—from "old heads," to adults wise about life and the community, to parents, to staff members of the various community-based organizations. If these adults could meet at intervals throughout the year with teachers of local youth, they could work jointly toward achieving the learning activities and goals of particular students or groups of students. A YMCA- or YWCA-based drama group, for example, could build upon the English curriculum; a "Weed and Seed" effort sponsored by a church or youth organization could collaborate with science teachers to generate ways youths could develop particular skills in their science classes that would enhance their work in the community. In addition, schools and community organizations that work together have more opportunities to match adults' teaching styles with youths' learning styles in ways that can build on the strengths both of youth and of their multiple teachers in and out of school.

Expanded professional networks and supports. When schools and communities are connected in ways that realize improved opportunities to learn, the scope of school extends beyond the resources available on campus to those throughout the neighborhoods of which the school is a part. For teachers, this extension beyond school can mean expanded access to professional networks and supports that include other classroom teachers, youth workers, social workers, parents, and others.

These interdisciplinary professional networks can expand the types of professional practice with youth that teachers have available to them. For example, as part of an after-school arts program, teachers may work alongside visiting artists and have opportunities to observe these adults working with their students in ways that may inform their classroom teaching.[29] One finding from the literature on program effects suggests that, unless adults see the benefit of enriching youth's learning out of school and somehow link it with youths' experiences in their classrooms, the effect of these "community" efforts on academic achievement is not likely to be significant, at least, in the short term (Morrow & Styles, 1995; Wehlage et al., 1992). Professional networks and supports may provide the necessary opportunities for teachers and other adults to consider what these linkages between communities and classrooms might look like for themselves and for their youth.

School–Community Connections for Opportunity to Learn and Opportunity to Teach

As indicated above, these crosscutting lessons for opportunity to learn and teach collect design features of school–community partnerships from across the four types examined above—school-linked services, service learning, school-to-work programs, and community-based youth organizations. In practice, we find that these lessons are embodied in a fifth type of school–community initiative—efforts that fit neatly neither into any one of the categories used above nor in the program effects literature. For example, these efforts might provide social services linked to schools that include opportunities for work and service learning and a strong role for youth organizations. We consider initiatives of this fifth group to be best examples of school–community connections for opportunity to learn and opportunity to teach because, either explicitly or implicitly, they embody the lessons regarding features most essential to opportunities for learning and teaching that we derive from the effects literature presented in section II and from the program evaluations in section III. Accordingly, we call them "school–community connections for opportunity to learn and opportunity to teach." Two examples follow.

EL PUENTE ACADEMY FOR PEACE AND JUSTICE

In the heart of the Williamsburg section of Brooklyn, El Puente Academy for Peace and Justice links in-school and out-of-school learning through projects, themes, and skill building that extend throughout the youths' day. For example, as part of their math and science classes, students spent afternoons and weekends turning vacant lots into community gardens—planning, budgeting, choosing suitable plants and equipment, and so forth—and designing ads opposing pollution and cigarettes. Also, the youth-written newspaper at El Puente is a primary vehicle for the development of writing skills. These are not simply examples of project-based learning—extensions of traditional classrooms. Rather, the El Puente Academy and the El Puente community organization (whose directors founded the Academy for Peace and Justice that shares the same church building) work in close partnership to infuse all activities of both organizations with opportunities for youth to contribute to their community and build their leadership skills. For example, students assessed community needs and decided to organize an immunization drive for young children. With support from their classroom teachers and youth workers, they designed and implemented this project. During a recent summer, building on skills developed in the classroom, students researched their neighborhood and developed a walking tour of the south side of Williamsburg including an historic, economic, and environmental analysis of the neighborhood. As part of this research, youth surveyed 500 residents.

At El Puente, where the youth organization ends and school begins is difficult to determine. School teachers and staff members of the youth organization work collaboratively with one another and with youth both during and after traditional school hours. Students build skills in class that they apply to their projects after formal school hours; their shared projects after school provide important contexts for lessons in civics, English, math, and other classes. In the first graduating class (1997) of 33 seniors, 92% attended college.[30]

El Puente Academy for Peace and Justice was founded in 1993 by the El Puente community organization with assistance from New York City's New Visions initiative. An explicit goal of El Puente is to build social capital. As expressed by Luis Garden Acosta, founder of El Puente, "What is needed in schools are human relations. People must realize that these are our children. We're all one family and that transcends our homes, the street, and the public institutions. When we bond with each other and build the realization that nurtures our humanity, that is when education happens" (Gonzalez, 1997). El Puente clearly makes the child's-eye view essential to its work. "We must respond to the unique challenges every child, every school provides and not think of them as abstractions that do not fit into an assessment, a budget, a union contract" (Rose, 1995, pp. 225–226; see also Burg, 1998; de Pommereau, 1996; Gonzalez, 1995; Gonzalez, 1997).

ST. JOHN'S EDUCATIONAL THRESHOLDS CENTER: THE BUILDING OF A BEACON

In the summer of 1993, school-age youth participating in St. Johns Educational Thresholds Center decided that they wanted to feel safer in their neighborhood—the North Mission in San Francisco, California. First, they surveyed 12 street corners and found that 10 of the 12 were "dangerous." Then they mapped their neighborhood, indicating the dangerous and safe places for youth, and presented their maps to the San Francisco Board of Supervisors. They enlisted the help of local shop and restau-

---

[29] The potential strength of these interdisciplinary professional networks is suggested not only by the research presented here but also by related research that suggests professional networks improve school climate by improving teachers' perceptions of the school as a workplace (SRI International, 1996).

[30] This percentage is well above the city and state averages. Of seniors at other New Visions schools, 81% were accepted to college during that year.

rant owners and launched Quick Calls. Today, if you walk down 16th Street in the North Mission, you will see signs for Quick Calls in many storefront windows. These signs signal to youth that they can use the phone in any participating business to call home if they feel unsafe. St. Johns works with elementary school-age youth to maintain the signs and otherwise continue and expand their relationship with business owners in their school neighborhoods. In these ways, Quick Calls not only provides resources to youth at a time of need but also works to change the relationship between youth and adults in this densely populated commercial neighborhood.

Quick Calls is one example of several programs and activities developed by St. Johns Educational Thresholds Center (a community-based youth organization) and neighboring schools. For example, St. Johns, Everett Middle School, and Sanchez Elementary School were primary partners in a school-linked services program (funded through California's Healthy Start School-linked Services Initiative) that brought together 25 agencies at each school site to provide a range of formal and informal services and supports for youth. These collaborations laid the basis for Everett becoming the first Beacon School in San Francisco. Although the idea for Beacon Schools originated in New York City, San Francisco has become one of several cities across the country providing grants to community-based organizations to partner with schools and transform schools into community centers. Drawing on the resources of their various partners, the Community Bridges Beacon resource center (CBB) at Everett offers after-school tutoring and case management. Neighborhood youth of all ages participate in after-school clubs and service learning at Everett and at St. Johns. CBB is also the home of BOSS—Beacon Office Student Servers. Through BOSS, students receive credit for their extra-curricular activity requirement, a paycheck, and training in job skills as they answer phones, greet visitors, prepare materials for meetings, and perform other office jobs. Recently, BOSS has evolved into a school-to-career awareness initiative in all classes at Everett that includes a week-long speaker series organized by youth who participate in BOSS.

The work of St. Johns literally bridges the gap between in-school and out-of-school learning. In math class at Everett Middle School, students learned how to design and tally surveys to be used in the community assessment for their Healthy Start grant application. In language arts class, they wrote and practiced speeches that they delivered to the San Francisco school district about conditions in their community and their school. In Kid Power, a weekly elective for Everett students and the youth advisory board to the Healthy Start site and CBB, students wrote and practiced their speeches for the San Francisco Youth Summit. Also through Kid Power, they designed and practiced a 2-hour lesson that they provide to Stanford University students on how to construct community maps and use them to assess the quality of neighborhoods for youth. The Urban Institute, a project of St. Johns, partners with the San Francisco Unified School District to run a summer school for neighborhood students in Grades 5–9. The Urban Institute facilitates conversations among summer school teachers about how to provide a varied and integrated educational experience for youth in the summer around a theme that is based on students' concerns and interests. For example,

through the language arts component, students might write poems that they will use in art class as the basis for illustrations and other projects.

Through these links with classroom teachers and its other activities, St. Johns essentially facilitates and otherwise participates in formal and informal interdisciplinary professional networks for various teachers both in and out of the classroom. At St. Johns and through its various partnerships with schools and other organizations, youth are not clients; they are active participants in constructing solutions to their own concerns (Honig & Fiore, 1997; Wagner, 1996).

The Community Bridges Beacon at St. Johns, the El Puente programs, and others do not identify their mission by the categories of services they provide (see Cahill, 1996). Rather, their mission is to provide the resources and supports that their particular youth need to have expanded developmental and educational opportunities. Although resource constraints may mean these organizations make choices about when and how to work with their youth, they recognize that all youth need supports for learning. They engage youth in activities that build on their strengths—often engaging the youth in leadership roles and other activities to generate solutions to problems. Importantly, they identify where youth already look for support and education, and seek to engage those places and people in collaborative efforts to improve youth's experiences in their neighborhoods. In this way, they are developmental or strengths-based and youth-centered. They view all the resources in a youth's neighborhood from a youth's-eye view to determine what boundaries delineate "school" and "community" for the youth with which they work and what connections can be made between the two that are meaningful for those particular youth.

A FRAMEWORK FOR RESEARCH AND PRACTICE

From the categories of school–community connections explored above, we have identified major design features of school–community connections that enhance opportunities to learn and opportunities to teach. School–community initiatives that have these features generally provide the resources, occasions, and supports that youth need to achieve at high levels and that teachers need to help students reach those high levels. Table 45.1 outlines these design features. As indicated, we find that when schools and communities are connected in ways that enhance opportunities to learn and opportunities to teach, they can be described as (a) focused on whole youth; (b) focused on all youth; (c) strengths-based, prosocial, and developmental; (d) responsive to specific youth and neighborhoods; (e) youth-centered; (f) with expanded funds of knowledge available to youths' multiple teachers in and out of school.

Not all examples of effective school–community connections can be described as high impact all the time. Creating connections is a difficult, developmental process and partnerships will grow at different rates along various dimensions over time. The nature of the daily challenge to connect communities and schools is that school and community partners must continually devise strategies to engage changing neighborhoods and youth. Therefore, we define school–community connections that support opportunity to learn and opportunity to teach as a series of continua to reflect their developmental nature. These continua deliberately outline largely conceptual dimensions. With this approach, we intend to emphasize that we are still learning what school–community connections look like when they expand opportunities to learn and teach. Accordingly, we are just beginning to specify, in general terms, what these connections mean for teachers and students. Thus, Table 45.1 is intended as a broad research framework that requires further specification of its elements through additional examination of practice and policy. We turn to specific recommendations for practice, policy, and research in the subsequent section.

IV. Limitations and Barriers to Joining Schools and Communities in Support of Teaching and Learning: Implications for Policy, Practice, and Research

> A traditional school asks teachers to think about what happens to their students in the classroom; a school linked to a social service delivery system asks teachers and administrators to go further, to think about what happens to their students when they go home. Linking schools with social services demands a reorientation for both families and schools, which exceeds the tenuous, negotiated parameters that demarcate professional and private spheres. (Smrekar, 1994)

The arguments for the importance of school–community connections for opportunity to learn and opportunity to teach seem obvious. Schools, social service agencies, youth organizations, families, or any other single institution alone cannot ensure that youth and teachers have the opportunities necessary for youth to achieve at the high levels that reformers and the public increasingly demand and expect. The evidence from and experience with various efforts to join schools and communities around support for teaching and learning offer promising support and direction for education reform.

However, schools and their community partners face numerous barriers when creating school–community connections, particularly, connections focused on teaching and learning. School–community connections for opportunity to learn and opportunity to teach call for a fundamental rethinking of the roles and relationships between schools and communities, a reframing of educational policy so it incorporates more than school reform, and a reconsideration of education policy from the eye-view of students and teachers. In this concluding section, we explore some of these challenges and suggest several overall implications of this chapter for future research on teaching practice and policy.

The Challenge of School–Community Connections in Practice and Policy

ORGANIZATIONAL BARRIERS: THE PROBLEM OF TURF

Many researchers who study various types of school–community connections generally characterize the problem of connecting communities and schools as an organizational challenge: how to facilitate interagency collaboration. Barriers to interagency collaboration include concerns with turf. That is,

schools and their collaborative partners have difficulty sharing responsibility, funding, and resources, in part, because they do not want to lose control, power, or prestige (e.g., Crowson & Boyd, 1993). Some researchers characterize this protection of turf as a typical reaction to change.

Others recognize that organizations and schools serving youth may be reluctant to collaborate with agencies if collaboration, at least in the short term, may lead to interruption of services or supports for youth and families. One director of a youth organization recalls a time he arranged for students at his organization to swim once a week at another youth organization: "'We'd come over there and they [would have] just fired this guy or he didn't show up or the pool was locked. Here I was, I made this commitment to these kids that they'd go swimming. If I said we're gonna do something, we're gonna do it. It was like, now what I the hell do I do? I became so frustrated and angry being dependent upon another institution'" (McLaughlin et al., 1994, p. 195).

Schools may present special barriers to collaboration. Schools are places where many parents feel isolated. They are places where many youth do not succeed. Schools are sources of red tape. In fact, one often-cited benefit of community organizations as sites for development and learning is that they have the organizational, financial, and institutional flexibility to respond to the needs of youth in ways that schools do not always have. Community partners, thus, may be concerned that, if they are connected with schools, particularly, with schools that are not the most trusted organizations in a given neighborhood, they may compromise their ability to serve their youth. These organizations see certain benefits in maintaining clear separations between in-school and out-of-school opportunities for youth (Carnegie Council on Adolescent Development, 1994; Pittman & Wright, 1991).

Schools themselves may also protect their turf in an effort to better serve youth and families. At one school-linked service site, principals felt threatened by the presence of family advocates at a school-based family resource center. Concerned that the family advocates were collecting information about families that was important to the work of the school, the principals generally attempted to assume authority over the advocates to ensure that families were well served. This response by the principals created a paradox for the family advocates. On the one hand, the presence of the resource centers on school campuses made services more accessible to youth and their families and gave them new opportunities to participate in school. On the other hand, family advocates found that, at times, they needed to set themselves apart from schools to maintain their accessibility and effectiveness in the community (Smrekar, 1996; Smylie & Crowson, 1996; Smylie, Crowson, Chou, & Levin, 1994).

INSTITUTIONAL BARRIERS

Organizational barriers may be symptoms of more profound barriers to reconceptualizing the roles, norms, and beliefs that underlie our current systems of support for teaching and learning. Significant segments of the cited literature suggest that, by connecting communities in their various forms with schools, schools will be transformed, and teachers will have expanded opportunities to teach. However, a number of researchers have

Table 45.1 School-Community Connections for Opportunity to Learn and Opportunity to Teach: A Framework for Research and Practice

LOW IMPACT	←→	HIGH IMPACT
Focused on discrete needs • Specific services are provided based on the particular needs of youth (e.g., youth with poor mental health receive counseling services)	←→	**Focused on whole youth** Youth need academic and nonacademic supports to reach high academic standards. Youth learn throughout their day—on their athletic teams, in their community service projects, and in less formal interactions with adults and peers—in ways that can and do improve youths' performance in school. Accordingly collaborations: • Provide youth with an array of supports to succeed and multiple ways to access learning resources and develop new competences • Strengthen the quality of nonacademic supports as primary vehicles to strengthen students' school performance
Targeted for youth "at risk" or "in need" • Services and supports are provided to certain youth considered in need of additional academic and nonacademic supports to participate successfully in school • Programs tend to be added on to otherwise unchanged regular school programs	←→	**Targeted to all youth** All youth need appropriate supports for learning. Accordingly collaborations: • Provide supports to all participating youth, even if youth appear "high achieving" by various standards • Move beyond add-on approaches for certain youth and strengthen core aspects of schools and community agencies for all students
Deficit-oriented • Partners fix problems, meet needs, and avoid risk as a precondition to learning • Youth are clients and recipients of services	←→	**Strengths-based/Prosocial and developmental** All youth, schools and communities have strengths. Accordingly collaborations: • Meet youth's need by building on their strengths • Engage youth as co-constructors of solutions to their own problems and concerns
Generic standardized programming • Programs and/or program models developed by national headquarters or another outside source; carried out without consultation with or reference to the youth they are to benefit	←→	**Responsive to specific youth and neighborhoods** Youths become more engaged in activities when activities stem from their particular needs and interests. Accordingly collaborations: • Use programs—whether brought in from the outside or developed locally—that are designed with the specific interests and needs of local youth in mind • Implement programming changes as the needs and interests of participating youth change
Organization-centered/Adult-centered • "School-community connections" means integration or a linking of organizations • Efforts focus on meeting the needs of adults (including parents) as a primary strategy to improve student outcomes	←→	**Youth-centered** "School-community connections" means the experiences of youth in and out of school are connected and used to strengthen the other. "Connection" occurs at the level of the youth. Accordingly collaborations: • Feature social networks among adults and peers within and beyond the school as essential aspects of the partnership
Expands access to information for various professionals who work with youth • Efforts provide opportunities for teachers, youth workers, and others to learn about youths' experience in their school and their various communities • Partners tend to focus on expanding the information available to classroom teachers about why their students may not be achieving	←→	**Expands funds of knowledge for youths' multiple teachers in and out of school** Youth have multiple teachers throughout their day, each of whom brings essential and different knowledge, experiences, and expertise to bear in their relationships with youth. Accordingly collaborations: • Build trust and shared values • Move beyond the provision of services at or near a school campus and strengthens the day-to-day interaction among youth and the various adults at a school-community site • Provide multiple opportunities for these teachers to learn from one another's practice and to enhance and expand their own professional practice

suggested that these expanded opportunities are not always used by schools. That is, schools do not always reform roles for teachers, students, and school administrators that might enable expanded opportunities to learn and teach (Jehl & Kirst, 1992; Mawhinney & Smrekar, 1996; Smylie & Crowson, 1996; Smylie et al., 1994; Wehlage et al., 1992).

In several respects, it is not surprising that roles are not always reshaped or recast. First, practitioners who try to forge school–community connections have few guides. What, for example, is the role of a school principal or a classroom teacher in a school that is connected with its community in the ways described in section III? In most studies of leaders at school–community sites, the leaders tend not to be members of the school staff. When school staff personnel are considered, they are generally depicted as barriers to school–community connections (Chaskin & Richman, 1993; Kahne et al., 2000; McLaughlin, et al., 1994; Smrekar, 1996).

Second, we do not find significant reconsideration of roles for school staff members, in part, because school–community partnerships tend to occur at the margins of school systems. Discretionary grant programs, waivers, or other regulatory relief provide the support for most of the examples of school–community connections cited above. Many of the schools are chosen to participate because of their one-of-a-kind leaders and staff members. Such conditions set these examples apart from typical schools. Although these special schools provide examples of what school–community connections might look like, they offer few guides to typical schools about how to overcome constraints and redefine activities and roles, because they operate in different institutional contexts (Honig, 1998). Even within schools, the community partnerships are often on the periphery, focused primarily on youth who are in need or at risk. During these times of limited resources, such targeting may be a wise use of resources in the short term. However, if we are interested in effecting the institutional shifts that may make school–community connections for opportunity to learn and teach more than extraordinary events, then such marginal changes reflect, at best, early progress.

Viewing the problem of school–community connections with an institutional lens, we can see that schools and community organizations may face certain challenges as they redefine their roles in partnership with one another, in part, because they operate in different institutional contexts that may constrain such changes (Chaskin & Richman, 1993; Pittman & Wright, 1991). Community-based organizations, for example, tend to have broader missions than schools and may view learning opportunities for youth as situated in a youth development perspective from the outset. These organizations tend to (a) be backed by strong traditions and philosophies that undergird this approach to supporting youth, (b) have more diversified funding sources than schools, and (c) operate under fewer constraints. Schools, in contrast, have persisted as strictly hierarchical organizations. Most funding for public schools comes from public sources, and little of that funding is discretionary. These different institutional contexts may afford community-based organizations the flexibility necessary to work responsively with youth in the ways suggested by the research reviewed in this chapter, whereas schools may face greater challenges.

THE PROBLEM OF POLICY

Public policy concerning schools largely assumes a narrow frame, focusing on issues of finance, administration, curriculum, and pedagogy within schools. However, meaningful opportunity to learn and opportunity to teach as described here require education policy that operates on a community level and, thus, engages the multiple resources and supports available in a school's neighborhood.

Policymakers have few guides for this kind of cross-sector policy. First, the scope of educational policy itself has become increasingly narrow. As discussed in section I, debates about standards focus almost entirely on academic content, with little consideration for the range of competencies that youth will need to develop in order to achieve these high standards. Second, the model on which public policy is designed at various levels remains largely unchanged from that used during the Great Society period when categorical mandates dominated the political agenda. Today, we see more examples of local government (e.g., school district, city, county) being allowed greater discretion in return for increased local accountability for improving the status of youth. However, these accountability systems remain largely prescriptive and may more accurately be considered a variation on the familiar top-down mandates that focus on particular students and needs strictly within the formal educational system. Thus, they tend not to take a student's- or teacher's-eye view of the relevant supports necessary for improving teaching and learning.

One benefit of the current policy context for school–community connections is that we have several examples of successful school–community connections for opportunity to learn and opportunity to teach. However, many of these initiatives operate at single schools as isolated projects, not as part of comprehensive strategies (Fine & Mechling, 1993; Gomby & Larson, 1992). In state-initiated efforts, local coordination is encouraged often without parallel development among the state agencies and policymakers themselves (Crowson & Boyd, 1993, p. 148). The irony is that modest projects may be more successful than larger-scale initiatives. However, unless we figure out how to take these initiatives to scale, they will continue to operate on the margins of the educational system and will not engage educators throughout the system in redefining their roles (Mawhinney & Smrekar, 1996).

Various literatures on school–community connections suggest that we have enough examples of successful school–community practice; the policy challenge now is to cull and disseminate this knowledge (Schorr, 1989, 1997). Sometimes this line of debate leads researchers to list characteristics of schools that are linked with communities or to identify models of school–community connections that can be replicated. However, creating meaningful connections is not merely a matter of listing what a "full-service school" contains or of sharing information among community agencies and schools. School–community connections require a deliberate effort to profoundly restructure roles and expectations throughout the formal and informal education systems. We must reconsider the role of schools in communities, and, specifically, we must reconsider the roles of teachers and other educational leaders as people who operate not only in a school but also in a community (neighborhood). This new perspective may require corresponding shifts in the roles of policymakers at various levels that allow them to build policy that enables school–community connections for opportunity to learn and teach.

Policy to support such shifts in roles for schools and community agencies may lag behind practice. Although education policy continues to tinker inside schools, the day-to-day demands on principals and teachers may mean that they do, in fact, operate on a community level. Some have argued that the new context for school principals is a school–community context in which school principals are increasingly engaged in issues of neighborhood renewal and change and community members are increasingly enlisted in school governance (Fullan, 1996). Without policy to support these shifting demands on schools, the success of school–community connections may continue to rest on the backs of extraordinary leaders who are able to succeed despite otherwise constraining conditions (Elmore, 1996; Honig, 1998).

Toward a Research Agenda on School–Community Connections for Opportunity to Learn and Opportunity to Teach

The implications of this chapter for research on teaching primarily relate to the frame within which we have traditionally viewed problems of teaching and learning. Specifically, researchers who focus on teaching and learning generally do not examine and have not examined contexts for teaching and learning that extend beyond the work of classroom teachers and the purview of schools. Education research, like education policy, tends to be school-centric in its consideration of opportunities for learning and teaching.

An expanded understanding of opportunity to learn and opportunity to teach, as suggested in this chapter, asks researchers to redefine their terms and rethink their research tools. To help enable effective school–community connections, education researchers and policymakers would do well to enact the following five strategies.

1. *Develop a broader conception of what learning is and where it takes place.* One clear implication of this research review is that out-of-school resources, occasions, and supports— academic and nonacademic, formal and informal—affect youths' performance in school. One challenge for research is to identify these out-of-school contexts and explore in more detail how they affect learning—both when they are and when they are not connected with schools. The research framework suggested here, school–community connections for opportunity to learn and opportunity to teach, suggests certain categories that may provide a useful first guide for this research. Specifically, this framework can be used to identify promising school–community efforts, describe them in terms of teaching and learning, and analyze them along common dimensions. The latter will be particularly important for comparisons across school–community efforts. A promising line of inquiry would focus directly on the elements of this framework to explore specifically what

these elements look like for youth and their multiple teachers in day-to-day practice.

2. *Focus on what enables school–community connections for opportunities to learn and teach.* As we have indicated throughout this chapter, resources, occasions, and supports for teaching and learning not only must exist but also must be used. We know significantly more about barriers to collaboration than we know about the factors and conditions that enable school–community connections. Further research on the implementation challenges of school–community connections for opportunities to learn and teach should focus not only on constraining conditions but also on enabling conditions. This line of research will require that we not simply describe efforts that seem to embody principles of best practice (Schorr, 1997) but that we consider the contexts in which these models might be successful day-to-day for particular teachers and students. This line of research may also require that we focus on typical schools that are attempting various forms of school–community collaboration, not on only those flagship schools that often boast significant discretionary funding and extraordinary leadership.

3. *Examine specifically the roles of classroom teachers and principals at schools engaged in school–community collaborations.* What is the role of a classroom teacher and a principal in a school that is connected with community in the ways suggested in our research framework? What do curriculum and pedagogy look like—and what can they look like—when classroom teachers are connected to networks of youths' formal and informal teachers in and out of school? Under what conditions within schools are teachers enabled to use lessons in their own classrooms that are learned from youths' teachers out of school? Although available research on these issues is limited, various studies that used institutional theory to examine factors that constrain changes in the roles of teachers and principals suggest promising directions (e.g., Mawhinney & Smrekar, 1996; Smrekar, 1994; Smrekar, 1996; Smylie & Crowson, 1996; Smylie et al., 1994).

4. *Recast the frame for research on education policy.* The research agenda proposed in this chapter suggests that education policymakers, too, must expand the types of information and sources of knowledge that are considered relevant to policy analysis in education. This expansion includes information about the limitations of schools and teachers attempting, alone, to meet high academic standards. In addition, this approach includes, for "low achieving" schools, the ways that certain remedies—such as those that require extensions of the academic day—may strain relationships between schools and community agencies and otherwise paradoxically limit the ability of schools to marshal the resources, occasions, and supports necessary to improve their performance.

5. *Reconsider traditional relationships between researchers and practitioners to expand knowledge about opportunity to learn and opportunity to teach.* This new research agenda suggests that we need to rethink traditional relationships between researchers and school–community partnerships.

The line of research suggested here puts a premium on local knowledge and on sharing it in ways that support local action. Local partners can help researchers identify which school–community connections and which results may be meaningful in their particular communities. Overall, schools and communities must be engaged meaningfully in investigations of school–community connections.

REFERENCES

Allen, J. P., Philliber, S., & Hoggson, N. (1990). School-based prevention of teenage pregnancy and school dropout: Process evaluation of the national replication of the Teen Outreach Program. *American Journal of Community Psychology, 18*(4), 505–524.

Allen, J. P., Philliber, S., Herrling, S., & Kuperminc, G. P. (1997). Preventing teen pregnancy and academic failure: Experimental evaluation of a developmentally based approach. *Child Development, 64*(4), 729–742.

Alt, M. (1997). How effective an educational tool is student community service? *NASSP Bulletin, 81*(591), 8–16.

Anderson, E. (1978). *A place on the corner.* Chicago: University of Chicago Press.

Anderson, E. (1989). Sex codes and family life among inner-city youths. *Annals of the American Academy of Political and Social Science, 501,* 59–78.

Anderson, E. (1990). *Streetwise: Race, class, and change in an urban community.* Chicago: University of Chicago Press.

Banfield, E. C. (1970). *The unheavenly city: The nature and future of our urban crisis.* Boston: Little Brown.

Bernard, B. (1990). *The case for peers.* Portland, OR: Northwest Regional Educational Laboratory.

Bianchi, S., & Robinson, J. (1997). What did you do today? Children's use of time, family composition, and the acquisition of social capital. *Journal of Marriage and the Family, 59,* 332–344.

Blase, J. J. (1987). The politics of teaching: The teacher-parent relationship and the dynamics of diplomacy. *Journal of Teacher Education, 38*(2), 53–60.

Blyth, D. A., & Leffert, N. (1995). Communities as contexts for adolescent development: An empirical analysis. *The Journal of Adolescent Research, 10*(1), 64–87.

Bowles, S., & Levin, H. M. (1968). The determinants of scholastic achievements—An appraisal of some recent evidence. *The Journal of Human Resources, 3*(1), 1–24.

Boyer, E. (1983). *High school: A report on secondary education in America.* New York: Harper & Row.

Bronfenbrenner, U. (1979). *The ecology of human development: Experiments by nature and design.* Cambridge, MA: Harvard University Press.

Bronfenbrenner, U. (1986). Ecology of the family as a context for human development: Research perspectives. *Developmental Psychology, 22*(6), 723–742.

Bronfenbrenner, U., Moen, P., & Garbarino, J. (1984). Families and communities. In R. Parke (Ed.), *Review of child development research* (Vol. 7). Chicago: University of Chicago Press.

Brooks-Gunn, J., Duncan, G. J., & Aber, J. L. (Eds.). (1998a). *Neighborhood poverty: Vol. 1. Context and consequences for children.* New York: Sage.

Brooks-Gunn, J., Duncan, G. J., & Aber, J. L. (Eds.). (1998b). *Neighborhood poverty: Vol. 2. Policy implications in studying neighborhoods.* New York: Sage.

Brooks-Gunn, J., Duncan, G. J., Klebanov, P., & Sealand, N. (1993). Do neighborhoods influence child and adolescent development. *American Journal of Sociology, 99*(2), 353–395.

Brown, B. B., Lamborn, S. L., Mounts, N. S., & Steinberg, L. (1993). Parenting practices and peer group affiliation in adolescence. *Child Development, 64,* 467–482.

Buehler, C., Anthony, C., Krishnakumar, A., Stone, G., Gerard, J., & Pemberton, S. (1997). Interparental conflict and youth problem behaviors: A meta-analysis. *Journal of Child & Family Studies, 6*(2), 6, 2, 223–247.

Burg, S. (1998). El Puente: The real deal. *New Designs for Youth Development, 14*(1), 10–16.

Cahill, M. (1993). *A documentation report on the New York City Beacons Initiative.* New York: The Youth Development Institute, Fund for the City of New York.

Cahill, M. (1996). *Schools and community partnerships: Reforming schools, revitalizing communities.* Chicago: Cross City Campaign for Urban School Reform.

Calabrese, R. L., & Schumer, H. (1986). The effects of service activities on adolescent alienation. *Adolescence, 21,* 675–687.

Caplan, G., & Killilea, M. (Eds.). (1976). *Support systems and mutual help: Multidisciplinary explorations.* New York: Grune & Stratton.

Carnegie Council on Adolescent Development. (1994). A matter of time: Risk and opportunity in the out-of-school hours. New York: Carnegie Corporation of New York.

Chaskin, R. J., & Richman, H. A. (1993). Concerns about school-linked services: Institution-based versus community-based models. *Education and Urban Society, 25*(2), 201–211.

Clapp, E. R. (1939). *Community schools in action.* New York: Viking.

Clark, R. M. (1983). *Family life and school achievement: Why poor black children succeed or fail.* Chicago: University of Chicago Press.

Cognetta, P. V., & Sprinthall, N. A. (1978). Students as teachers: Role taking as a means of promoting psychological and ethical development during adolescence. In N. A. Sprinthall & R. L. Mosher (Eds.), *Value development as the aim of education.* Schenectady, NY: Character Research Press.

Cohen, D. L. (1994). Working in harmony: A community school supports the whole family. *Education Week,* 28–29.

Cohen, P. A., Kulik, J. A., & Kulik, C.-L. C. (1982). Educational outcomes of tutoring: A meta-analysis of findings. *American Educational Research Journal,* 237–248.

Coleman, J. S. (1961). *The adolescent society.* New York: The Free Press.

Coleman, J. S. (1987). Families and schools. *Educational Researcher* (August-September), 32–38.

Coleman, J. S. (1988). Social capital in the creation of human capital. *American Journal of Sociology, 94*(Suppl.), S95–S120.

Coleman, J. S., Campbell, E., Hobson, J., McPartland, J., Mood, A., Weinfeld, F., & York, R. (1966). *Equality of educational opportunity report.* Washington, DC: U.S. Office of Education.

Commission on Work, Family, and Citizenship. (1988). *The forgotten half: Pathways to success for America's youth and young families.* Washington, DC: William T. Grant Foundation.

Conrad, D., & Hedin, D. (1981). *Assessment of experimental education: A final report.* St. Paul, MN: University of Minnesota, Center for Youth Development and Research.

Conrad, D., & Hedin, D. (1982). The impact of experiential education on adolescent development. *Child and Youth Services, 3,* 57–76.

Coulton, C. J., Korbin, J. E., & Su, M. (1996). Measuring neighborhood context for young children in an urban area. *American Journal of Community Psychology, 24*(1), 5–32.

Council of Chief State School Officers. (1989). *Community Service: Learning by doing.* Washington, DC: Author.

Crane, J. (1996). The epidemic theory of ghettos and neighborhood effects on dropping out and teenage childbearing. *American Journal of Sociology, 96*(5), 1226–1259.

Crowson, R. L., & Boyd, W. L. (1993). Coordinated services for children: Designing arks for storms and seas unknown. *American Journal of Education, 101*(2), 140–179.

Csikszentmihalyi, M., Rathunde, K., & Wahlen, S. (1993). *Talented teenagers: The roots of success and failure.* New York: Cambridge University Press.

D'Amico, R. (1984). Does employment during high school impair academic progress? *Sociology of Education, 57*(3), 152–164.

Darling-Hammond, L. (1997). *The right to learn.* San Francisco: Jossey-Bass.

de Pommereau, I. (1996, April 24). It takes the community to educate the child at this urban school. *The Christian Science Monitor,* 15.

Dewey, J. (Ed.). (1956). *The child and the curriculum and the school and society.* Chicago: University of Chicago Press. (Original work published 1900)

Dewey, J. (1976). The school as social center. In J. A. Boydston (Ed.),

John Dewey: The middle works (Vol. 2, pp. 80–93). Carbondale, IL: Southern Illinois University Press. (Original work published 1902)

Dewey, J. (1966). *Democracy and education.* New York: The Free Press. (Original work published 1916)

Dewey, J. (1963). *Experience and education.* New York: Collier Macmillan. (Original work published 1938)

Dewsbury-White, K. E. (1993). *The relationship of service–learning project models to the subject-matter achievement of middle school students.* East Lansing, MI: Michigan State University.

Dornbusch, S. M., Ritter, P. L., Roberts, D. F., & Fraleigh, M. J. (1987). The relation of parenting style to adolescent school performance. *Child Development, 58*(5), 1244–1257.

Dryfoos, J. G. (1990). *Adolescents at risk: Prevalence and prevention.* New York: Oxford University Press.

Dryfoos, J. G. (1994). *Full-Service schools.* San Francisco: Jossey-Bass.

Dryfoos, J. G. (1998). *Safe passage.* New York: Oxford University Press.

Eckert, P. (1989). *Jocks and burnouts: Social categories and identity in the high school.* New York: Teachers College Press.

Elder, G. H., Jr. (Ed.). (1985). *Life course dynamics: Trajectories and transitions, 1968–1980.* Ithaca, NY: Cornell University Press.

Elmore, R. (1996). Getting to scale with good educational practice. *Harvard Educational Review, 66*(1), 1–26.

Ensminger, M. E., Lamkin, R. P., & Jacobson, N. (1996). School leaving: A longitudinal perspective including neighborhood effects. *Child Development, 67*(5), 2400–2416.

Entwisle, D. R., & Alexander, K. L. (1995). Family type and children's growth in reading and math over the primary grades. *Journal of Marriage and the Family, 58*(2), 341–355.

Entwisle, D. R., & Alexander, K. L. (1996). A parent's economic shadow: Family structure versus family resources as influences on early school achievement. *Journal of Marriage and the Family, 57*(2), 399–409.

Epstein, J. L. (1983). The influence of friends on achievement and affective outcomes. In J. L. Epstein & N. Karweit (Eds.), *Friends in school* (pp. 177–200). New York: Academic Press.

Erikson, E. (1968). *Identity, youth and crisis.* New York: Norton.

Fasick, F. A. (1984). Parents, peers, youth culture and autonomy in adolescence. *Adolescence, 19*(73), 143–157.

Featherstone, D. R., Cundick, B. P., & Jensen, L. C. (1992). Differences in school behavior and achievement between children from intact, reconstituted, and single-parent families. *Adolescence, 27*(105), 1–12.

Fine, G. A., & Mechling, J. (1993). Child saving and children's cultures at century's end. In S. B. Heath & M. W. McLaughlin (Eds.), *Identity and inner city youth* (pp. 120–143). New York: Teachers College Press.

Fordham, S., & Ogbu, J. (1986). Black students' school success: Coping with the "Burden of 'Acting White.'" *Urban Review, 18,* 176–206.

Fullan, M. (1996). Leadership for change. In K. Leithwood (Ed.), *International handbook of educational leadership and administration* (pp. 701–722). The Netherlands: Kluwer Academic Press.

Furano, K., Roaf, P. A., Styles, M. B., & Branch, A. Y. (1993). *Big Brothers/Big Sisters: A study of program practices.* Philadelphia: Public/Private Ventures.

Gambone, M. A., & Arbreton, A. J. A. (1997). *Safe havens: The contributions of youth organizations to healthy adolescent development.* Philadelphia: Public/Private Ventures.

Garbarino, J. (1992). The meaning of poverty in the world of children. *American Behavioral Scientist, 35,* 220–237.

Goldberger, S., & Kazis, R. (1996). Revitalizing high schools: What the school-to-career movement can contribute. *Phi Delta Kappan, 77*(8), 547–554.

Gomby, D. S., & Larson, C. S. (1992). Evaluation of school-linked services. *The Future of Children, 2*(1), 68–84.

Gonzalez, D. (1995, May 23). A bridge from hope to social action. *The New York Times,* A1, B4.

Gonzalez, D. (1997, June 28). Going ahead, grounded in reality. *The New York Times.*

Gottfredson, D.C., McNeill III, R. J., & Gottfredson, G. D. (1991). Social area influences on delinquency: A multilevel analysis. *Journal of Research in Crime and Delinquency, 28*(2), 197–226.

Graham, P. A. (1995). Assimilation, adjustment, and access: An antiquarian view of American education. In D. Ravitch & M. Vinovskis (Eds.), *Learning from the past* (pp. 3–24). Baltimore: Johns Hopkins Press.

Granovetter, M. (1978). Threshold models of collective behavior. *American Journal of Sociology, 83*(6), 1420–1443.

Greenberger, E., Steinberg, L. D., & Ruggiero, M. (1981). The workplace as a context for the socialization of youth. *Journal of Youth and Adolescence, 10*(3), 185–210.

Greenberger, E., Steinberg, L. D., & Ruggiero, M. (1982). A job is a job is a job . . . or is it? Behavioral observations in the adolescent workplace. *Work and Occupations, 9*(1), 79–96.

Greenberger, E., Steinberg, L. D., & Vaux, A. (1981). Adolescents who work: Health and behavioral consequences of job stress. *Developmental Psychology, 17*(6), 691–703.

Greenberger, E., Steinberg, L. D., Vaux, A., & McAuliffe, S. (1980). Adolescents who work: Effects of part-time employment on family and peer relations. *Journal of Youth and Adolescence, 9*(3), 189–202.

Grubb, W. N. (1995). Reconstructing urban schools with work-centered education. *Education and Urban Society, 27*(3), 244–59.

Grubb, W. N., & Lazerson, M. (1982). *Broken promises.* New York: Basic Books.

Hagedorn, J. (1988). People and folks: Gangs crime, and the underclass in a rustbelt city. Chicago: Lake View Press.

Hamilton, S. F., & Fenzel, L. M. (1988). The impact of volunteer experience on adolescent social development: Evidence from program effects. *Journal of Adolescent Research, 3*(1), 65–80.

Hamilton, S. F., & Zeldin, S. R. (1987). Learning civics in the community. *Curriculum Inquiry, 17*(4), 407–420.

Hanks, M., & Eckland, B. K. (1978). Adult voluntary associations and adolescent socialization. *The Sociological Quarterly, 19*(Summer), 481–490.

Hanna, P. (1936). *Youth serves the community.* New York: Appleton Century.

Harnish, J. D., Dodge, K. A., & Valente, E. (1995). Mother-child interaction quality as a partial mediator of the roles of maternal depressive symptomatology and socioeconomic status in the development of child behavior problems. *Child Development, 66,* 739–753.

Harrison, C. (1987). Student service: The new Carnegie unit. Princton, NJ: The Carnegie Foundation for the Advancement of Teaching.

Hashima, P. Y., & Amato, P. R. (1994). Poverty, social support, and parental beliefs. *Child Development, 65,* 394–403.

Heath, S. B., & McLaughlin, M. W. (1987). A child resource policy: Moving beyond dependence on school and family. *Phi Delta Kappan, 68*(8), 576–580.

Hedin, D. (1987). Students as teachers: A tool for improving school climate. *Social Policy, 17*(3), 42–47.

Heiss, J. (1996). Effects on African American family structure on school attitudes and performance. *Social Problems, 43*(3), 246–267.

Hershey, A., Hudis, P., Silverberg, M., & Haimson, J. (1997). *Partners in progress: Early steps in creating school-to-work systems.* Princeton, NJ: Mathematica Policy Research.

Hess, L. E., Petersen, A. C., & Mortimer, J. T. (1994). Youth, unemployment, and marginality: The problem and the solution. In A. C. Petersen & J. T. Mortimer (Eds.), *Youth unemployment and society* (pp. 3–33). New York: Cambridge University Press.

Honig, M., & Fiore, K. (1997). *Working with young people as partners.* Davis, CA: Healthy Start Field Office.

Honig, M. I. (1998, April 17). *Opportunities to lead for school–community connections.* Paper presented at the American Educational Research Association, San Diego, CA.

Ide, J. K., Parkerson, J., Haertel, G. D., & Walberg, H. J. (1981). Peer group influence on educational outcomes: A quantitative synthesis. *Journal of Educational Psychology, 73*(4), 472–484.

Illback, R. (1997). *Bridges over barriers: Kentucky's family resource and youth services centers: A summary of education-related evaluation findings.* Louisville, KY: R.E.A.C.H. of Louisville

Jarrett, R. L. (1995). Growing up poor: The family experiences of socially mobile youth in low-income African-American neighborhoods. *Journal of Adolescent Research, 10*(1), 111–135.

Jarrett, R. L. (1997). African American family and parenting strategies in impoverished neighborhoods. *Qualitative Sociology, 20*(2), 275–288.

Jehl, J., & Kirst, M. (1992). Getting ready to provide school-linked services: What schools must do. *The Future of Children, 2*(1), 95–106.

Jencks, C., Smith, M., Acland, H., Bane, M., Cohen, D., Gintis, H., Heyns, B., & Michelson, S. (1972). *Inequality: A reassessment of the effects of family and schooling in America.* New York: Basic Books.

Johnson, A. (1996). *An evaluation of the impacts of the Sponsor-A-Scholar program on student performance: Final report to the Commonwealth Fund.* Philadelphia: Institute for Research on Higher Education, University of Pennsylvania.

Kahne, J., & Bailey, K. (1999). The role of special capital in youth development: The case of "I Have a Dream." *Educational Evaluation & Policy Analysis, 21*(3), 321–343.

Kahne, J., Nagaoka, J., Brown, A., O'Brien, J., Quinn, T., & Thiede, K. (2000). School and after-school programs as contexts for youth development: Qualitative and quantitative assessment. In M. Wang & W. Boyd (Eds.), *Improving results for children and families by connecting collaborative services with school reform efforts.* Greenwich, CT: Information Age Publishing Inc.

Kazis, R. (1993). *Improving the transition from school to work in the United States.* Washington, DC: American Youth Policy Forum.

Kazis, R., & Kopp, H. (1997). *Both sides now: New directions in promoting work and learning for disadvantaged youth.* Boston: Jobs for the Future.

Keefe, K., & Berndt, T. (1996). Relations of friendship quality to self-esteem in early adolescence. *Journal of Early Adolescence, 16*(1), 110–129.

Kilpatrick, W. H. (1918). The project method. *Teachers College Record, 19*(4), 319–335.

Knapp, M. S., & Shields, P. M. (1991). Better schooling for children of poverty. Berkeley, CA: McCutchan.

Kopp, H., & Kazis, R. (1995). *Promising practices: A study of ten school-to-career programs.* Boston: Jobs for the Future.

Kretzman, J. P., & McKnight, J. L. (1993). *Building communities from the inside out: A path toward finding and mobilizing a community's assets.* Evanston, IL: Center for Urban Affairs and Policy Research.

Larson, R. (1984). Youth organizations, hobbies, and sports as developmental contexts. In R. Silbereisen & E. Todt (Eds.), *The interplay of family, schools, peers, and work in adjustment* (pp. 46–65). New York: Springer-Verlag.

Lawson, H., & Briar-Lawson, K. (1997). *Connecting the dots: Progress toward the integration of school reform, school-linked services, parent involvement, and community schools.* Oxford, OH: The Danforth Foundation and the Institute for Educational Renewal at Miami University.

Lefkowitz, B. (1987). *Tough change: Growing up on your own in America.* New York: The Free Press.

Levinson, L. (1986). *Community service programs in independent schools.* Boston: National Association of Independent Schools.

Liebow, E. (1996). *Tally's corner.* Boston: Little, Brown.

Lightfoot, S. L. (1978). *Worlds apart.* New York: Basic Books.

Lillydahl, J. (1990). Academic achievement and part-time employment of high school students. *Journal of Economic Education*(Summer), 307–316.

Luckmann, T. (1991). The new and old religion. In P. Bourdiev & J. S. Coleman (Eds.), *Social theory for a changing society* (pp. 167–188). Boulder, CO: Westview Press.

MacLeod, J. (1987). *Ain't No Makin' It.* Boulder, CO: Westview.

Marsh, H. (1991). Employment during high school: Character building or a subversion of academic goals. *Sociology of Education, 64,* 172–189.

Martin, L., & Ascher, C. (1994). Developing math and science materials for school-age child care programs. In F. A. Villarruel & R. M. Lerner (Eds.), *Promoting community-based programs for socialization and learning* (pp. 11–24). San Francisco: Jossey-Bass.

Martinez, M., Goldberger, S., & Alongi, A. (1996). *A year of progress in school-to-career system building.* Boston, MA: Jobs for the Future.

Mawhinney, H. B., & Smrekar, C. (1996). Institutional constraints to advocacy in collaborative services. *Educational Policy, 10*(4), 480–501.

McLanahan, S., & Sandefur, G. (1994). *Growing up with a single parent.* Cambridge, MA: Harvard University Press.

McLaughlin, M. W. (1993). Embedded identities: Enabling balance in urban contexts. In S. B. Heath & M. W. McLaughlin (Eds.), *Identity and inner-city youth* (pp. 36–67). New York: Teachers College Press.

McLaughlin, M. W. (2000). *Community counts.* Washington, DC: Public Education Network.

McLaughlin, M. W., Irby, M. A., & Langman, J. (1994). *Urban sanctuaries.* San Francisco: Jossey-Bass.

McLaughlin, M. W., & Shepard, L. A. (1995). *Improving education through standards-based reform.* Stanford, CA: National Academy of Education.

McLaughlin, M. W., & Talbert, J. E. (1993). *Contexts that matter for teaching and learning: Strategic opportunities for meeting the nation's educational goals.* Washington, DC: U.S. Department of Education, Office of Educational Research and Improvement.

McLaughlin, M. W. & Talbert, J. E. (2001). *Communities of practice and the work of high school teaching.* Chicago: University of Chicago Press.

McLeod, V. C. (1990). The impact of economic hardship on black families and children: Psychological distress, parenting, and economic development. *Child Development, 61,* 311–340.

Melchior, A. (1997). *National evaluation of Learn and Serve America school and community-based programs.* Waltham, MA: Center for Human Resources, Brandeis University.

Melchior, A., & Orr, L. (1995). *Overview: National evaluation of Learn and Serve America.* Cambridge, MA: Abt Associates and Brandeis University Center for Human Resources.

Mihalic, S. W., & Elliott, D. (1997). Short and long-term consequences of adolescent work. *Youth and Society, 28*(4), 464–498.

Milne, A. M., Myers, D. E., Rosenthal, A. S., & Ginsburg, A. (1986). Single parents, working mothers, and the educational achievement of school children. *Sociology of Education, 59*(July), 125–139.

Moll, L. C. (1992). Funds of knowledge for teaching: Using a qualitative approach to connect homes and classrooms. *Theory into Practice, 31*(1), 132–141.

Morrow, K. V., & Styles, M. (1995). *Building relationships with youth in program settings.* Philadelphia: Public/Private Ventures.

Mortimer, J. T., & Finch, M. D. (1996). Work, family, and adolescent development. In J. T. Mortimer & M. D. Finch (Eds.), *Adolescents, work, and family: An intergenerational developmental analysis* (pp. 1–24). Newbury Park, CA: Sage Publications.

Mounts, N. S., & Steinberg, L. (1995). An ecological analysis of peer influence on adolescent grade point average and drug use. *Developmental Psychology, 31*(6), 915–922.

Murphy, L. B., & Moriarty, A. E. (1976). *Vulnerability, coping, and growth: From infancy to adolescence.* New Haven, CT: Yale University Press.

National Center on Education and the Economy, & Commission on the Skills of the American Workforce. (1990). *America's choice: High skills or low wages!* Washington, DC: National Center on Education and the Economy.

National Research Council. (1993). *Losing generations: Adolescents in high-risk settings.* Washington, DC: National Academy Press.

Newman, K. (1999). No shame my game: The working poor in the inner city. New York: Knopf/Sage.

Newman, K. S. (1996). Working poor: Low-wage employment in the lives of Harlem youth. In J. A. Graber, J. Brooks-Gunn, & A. C. Petersen (Eds.), *Transitions through adolescence: Interpersonal domains and context* (pp. 323–343). Mahwah, NJ: Lawrence Erlbaum Associates.

Newman, K. S. (1997). Culture and structure in the truly disadvantaged. *City and Society,* 3–25.

Newmann, F. M., & Rutter, R. A. (1983). *The effects of high school community service programs on students' social development.* Madison, WI: Wisconsin Center for Educational Research, University of Wisconsin.

Padilla, F. M. (1992). *The gang as an American enterprise.* New Brunswick, NJ: Rutgers University Press.

Parsons, T. (1942). Age and sex in the social structure of the United States. *American Sociological Review, 7,* 604–616.

Pauly, E., Kopp, H., & Haimson, J. (1995). *Homegrown lessons: Innovative programs linking school and work.* San Francisco: Jossey-Bass.

Perlstein, D. (1996). Community and democracy in American schools: Arthurdale and the fate of progressive education. *Teachers College Record, 97*(4), 625–650.

Phelan, P., Davidson, A. L., & Yu, H. C. (1998). *Adolescents' worlds: Negotiating family, peers, and school.* New York: Teachers College Press.

Philliber Research Associates. (1994). *An evaluation of the Caring Communities program at Walbridge Elementary School.* Accord, NY: Author.

Pittman, K., & Cahill, M. (1992). Pushing the boundaries of education: The implications of a youth development approach to education policies, structures, and collaborations. In Council of Chief State School Officers (Ed.), *Ensuring student success through collaboration: Summer Institute papers and recommendations of the Council of Chief State School Officers.* Washington, DC: Council of Chief State School Officers.

Pittman, K. J., & Wright, M. (1991). *Bridging the gap: A rationale for enhancing the role of community organizations in promoting youth.* Washington, DC: Carnegie Council on Adolescent Development.

Posner, J. K., & Vandell, D. L. (1994). Low-income children's after-school care: Are there beneficial effects of after-school programs? *Child Development, 65*(2), 440–456.

Putnam, R. (1995). Bowling alone: America's declining social capital. *Journal of Democracy, 6*(1), 65–78.

Ravitch, D. (1995). *National standards in American education.* Washington, DC: Brookings Institution.

Rist, R. C. (1981). Walking through a house of mirrors: Youth education and employment training. *Education and Urban Society, 14*(1), 3–14.

Rose, M. (1995). *Possible lives.* New York: Penguin Books.

Rossman, S. B., & Morley, E. (1995). *The national evaluation of Cities in Schools.* Washington, DC: The Urban Institute.

Sampson, R. J. (1991). Linking the micro- and macrolevel dimensions of community social organization. *Social Forces, 70*(1), 43–64.

Sampson, R. J. (1993). Family management and child development: Insights from social disorganization theory. In J. McCord (Ed.), *Facts, frameworks, and forecasts: Advances in criminological theory* (Vol. 3, pp. 63–93). New Brunswick, NJ: Transaction Publishers.

Sampson, R. J., & Laub, J. H. (1994). Urban poverty and family context of delinquency: A new look at structure and process in a classic study. *Child Development, 65*(2), 523–540.

Schelling, T. C. (1971). Dynamic models of segregation. *Journal of Mathematical Sociology, 1,* 143–186.

Schneider, M., Teske, P., Marschall, M., Mintrom, M., & Roch, C. (1997). Institutional arrangements and the creation of social capital: The effects of public school choice. *American Political Science Review, 91*(1), 82–93.

Schorr, L. B. (1989). *Within our reach: Breaking the cycle of disadvantage.* New York: Anchor Books.

Schorr, L. B. (1997). *Common purpose: Strengthening families and neighborhoods to rebuild America.* New York: Doubleday.

Schram, S. (1995). *Words of welfare.* Minneapolis, MN: University of Minneapolis Press.

Schulenberg, J., & Bachman, J. G. (1993, April). *Long hours on the job? Not so bad for some adolescents in some types of jobs: The quality of work and substance use, affect, and stress.* Paper presented at the Society for Research on Child Development, New Orleans, LA.

Sedlak, M. W. (1995). Attitudes, choices, and behavior: School delivery of health and social services. In D. Ravitch & M. Vinovskis (Eds.), *Learning from the past* (pp. 57–96). Baltimore: Johns Hopkins Press.

Smrekar, C. (1994). The missing link in school-linked social service programs. *Educational Evaluation and Policy Analysis, 16*(4), 422–433.

Smrekar, C. (1996). The Kentucky Family Resource Centers: The challenges of remaking family-school interactions. In J. G. Cibulka & W. J. Kritek (Eds.), *Coordination among schools, families, and communities* (pp. 3–26). Albany, NY: State University of New York Press.

Smylie, M. A., & Crowson, R. L. (1996). Working within the scripts: Building institutional infrastructure for children's service coordination in schools. *Educational Policy, 10*(1), 3–21.

Smylie, M. A., Crowson, R. L., Chou, V., & Levin, R. A. (1994). The principal and community-school connections in Chicago's radical reform. *Educational Administration Quarterly, 30*(3), 342–364.

Sorin, G. (1990). *The nurturing neighborhood: The Brownsville Boys Club and Jewish community in urban America.* New York: New York University Press.

Spady, W. G. (1970). Lament for the letterman: Effects of peer status and extracurricular activities. *American Journal of Sociology, 75*(January), 680–702.

SRI International. (1996). *California's Healthy Start school-linked services initiative: Results for children and families.* Menlo Park, CA: Author.

Stack, C. (1974). *All our kin: Strategies for survival in a black community.* New York: Harper & Row.

Steinberg, L. (1987). Single parents, stepparents, and the susceptibility of adolescents to antisocial peer pressure. *Child Development, 58,* 269–75.

Steinberg, L., & Dornbusch, S. M. (1991). Negative correlates of part-time employment during adolescence: Replication and elaboration. *Developmental Psychology, 27*(2), 304–313.

Steinberg, L., Greenberger, E., Garduque, L., Ruggiero, M., & Vaux, A. (1982). Effects of working on adolescent development. *Developmental Psychology, 18*(3), 385–395.

Steinberg, L., Lamborn, S. D., Darling, M., Mounts, N. S., & Dornbusch, S. M. (1994). Over-time changes in adjustment and competence among adolescents from authoritative, authoritarian, indulgent, and neglectful families. *Child Development, 63*(3), 754–770.

Steinberg, L., Lamborn, S. D., Dornbusch, S. M., & Darling, N. (1992). Impact of parenting practices on adolescent achievement: Authoritative parenting, school involvement, and encouragement to succeed. *Child Development, 63*(5), 1266–1281.

Stern, D., Stone, J. R., Hopkins, C., & McLillon, M. (1990). Quality of students' work experience and orientation toward work. *Youth and Society, 22*(2), 263–282.

Summers, A. A., & Wolfe, B. L. (1977). Do schools make a difference? *The American Economic Review, 67*(4), 639–652.

Swanson, D. P., Spencer, M. B., & Petersen, A. (1998). Identity formation in adolescence. In K. Borman & B. Schneider (Eds.), *The adolescent years: Social influences and educational challenges. Nineteen-seventy yearbook of the National Society for the Study of Education* (pp. 18–41). Chicago: National Society for the Study of Education.

Thompson, M. S., Alexander, K. L., & Entwisle, D. R. (1988). Household composition, parental expectations, and social achievement. *Social Forces, 67*(2), 424–451.

Tierney, J. P., Grossman, J. B., & Resch, N. L. (1995). *Making a difference: An impact study of Big Brothers/Big Sisters.* Philadelphia: Public/Private Ventures.

Tyack, D. (1992). Health and social services in public schools: Historical perspectives. *The Future of Children, 2*(1), 19–31.

Tyack, D. (1995). Reinventing schools. In D. Ravitch & M. Vinovskis (Eds.), *Learning from the past* (pp. 191–216). Baltimore: Johns Hopkins Press.

Tyack, D. B., & Cuban, L. (1995). *Tinkering toward utopia: A century of public school reform.* Cambridge, MA: Harvard University Press.

Tyack, D., & Hansot, E. (1982). *Managers of virtue: Public school leadership in America, 1820–1980.* New York: Basic Books.

U.S. Department of Education, & U.S. Department of Justice. (1998). *Safe and smart: Making after-school hours work for kids.* Washington, DC: Authors.

U.S. Department of Labor. (1991). *What work requires of schools: A SCANS report for America 2000.* Washington, DC: Author.

Vigil, J. D. (1993). Gangs, social control, and ethnicity: Ways to redirect. In S. B. Heath & M. W. McLaughlin (Eds.), *Identity and inner-city youth* (pp. 94–119). New York: Teachers College Press.

Villarruel, F. A., & Lerner, R. M. (Eds.). (1994). *Promoting community-based programs for socialization and learning.* San Francisco: Jossey-Bass.

Wade, R. C., & Saxe, D. W. (1996). Community service–learning in the social studies: Historical roots, empirical evidence, critical issues. *Theory and Research in Social Education, 24*(4), 331–359.

Wagner, V. (1996, April 21). Shining a beacon on community needs. *San Francisco Examiner,* B-1, B-5.

Wehlage, G., Smith, G., & Lipman, P. (1992). Restructuring urban schools: The new futures experience. *American Educational Research Journal, 29*(1), 51–93.

Werner, E. E. (1992). Overcoming the odds: High risk children from birth to adulthood. Ithaca, NY: Cornell University Press.

Westheimer, J., Kahne, J., & Gerstein, A. (1992). School reform in the nineties: Opportunities and obstacles for experiential educators. *Journal of Experiential Education, 15*(2), 44–49.

Whyte, W. F. (1955). *Street corner society* (3rd ed.). Chicago: University of Chicago Press.

Wigginton, E. (1985). *Sometimes a sharing moment: Twenty years at Foxfire.* Garden City, NY: Anchor Press/Doubleday.

Williams, T., & Kornblum, W. (1985). *Growing up poor.* Lexington, MA: D.C. Heath.

Wilson, W. J. (1987). *The truly disadvantaged.* Chicago: University of Chicago Press.

Wohlstetter, P. (1997). *First lessons: Charter schools as learning communities.* Philadelphia: Graduate School of Education, University of Pennsylvania.

Wood, G. (1992). *Schools that work: America's most innovative public education programs.* New York: Dutton.

Yates, M., & Youniss, J. (1996). Community service and political-moral identity in adolescents. *Journal of Research on Adolescence, 6*(3), 271–284.

Youniss, J., & Smollar, J. (1985). *Adolescent relations with mothers, fathers, and friends.* Chicago: University of Chicago Press.

Youniss, J., & Smollar, J. (1989). The role of peer groups in adolescents' adjustment to secondary school. In T. J. Berendt & G. W. Ladd (Eds.), *Peer relationships in child development.* New York: Wiley.

Youniss, J., & Yates, M. (1997). *Community service and social responsibility in youth.* Chicago: University of Chicago Press.

Zeldin, S., & Charner, I. (1996). *School-to-work opportunities through the lens of youth development.* Washington, DC: Academy for Educational Development.

Part 8
Instruction

46.

Choreographies of Teaching: Bridging Instruction to Learning

Fritz K. Oser and Franz J. Baeriswyl
University of Fribourg, Switzerland

Fundaments of the Teaching–Learning Process

The Engineering of Billions of Lessons

Every teacher has in mind some fuzzy idea of what a real or ideal instructional process is. During their careers, teachers produce approximately 900 lessons a year that are based on these fuzzy models. For each lesson, they construct and produce a learning world that serves as a "life island" for young learners. The architecture of such worlds requires that chains of activities in which each element is connected to the next according to a certain logic must be embedded in meaningful situations. To create these learning worlds successfully, teachers must possess professional knowledge about the stimulation and the coordination of learning-based, multiform activities.

As we consider how these worlds are constructed, the following questions are obvious. What kind of research leads to a better understanding of how such worlds are constructed? Are cognitive psychological concepts involved in this chaining during learning situations, and what do we know about the respective cognitive planning structures in the minds of teachers? How are mind-activity chunks organized, guided, and evaluated? What can we say about the real relationship between the activities of teachers and the operations of learners in a classroom with a high complexity of contexts? Do we know how teachers set priorities for learning and for chaining conditions when they try to tailor lessons so that children can build up knowledge that is not inert but insightful? Is it possible to elicit more than normative demands? Can we synthesize more than the individual experiences of one teacher or one instructional designer at a time? What is the difference between "legitimate peripheral participation" (Lave & Wenger, 1991) and a normal daily instructional setting?

These questions touch on the idea of the situated embeddedness of learning sequences and how such sequences lead to new learning. Johann Friedrich Herbart first postulated a cyclical sequence of learning steps in 1883. Herbart was the successor to Kant. He was interested primarily in epistemological growth. He believed that, in learning, one element of knowledge follows the other through a process of association and that teachers are forced to prepare these elements in a way that the new ones can be connected with what is already achieved (preknowledge). Hence, each process of learning consists of formal stages that must be completed then to acquire new understanding.

For the chaining of the formal stages, Herbart introduced the notion of articulation. He believed that such articulation clarifies instruction and simplifies the acquisition of knowledge. Since its introduction 120 years ago, this concept has been subject to various interpretations. In the beginning, it was viewed by its followers as a fundamentalist formalism, which consisted of the correct step sequence that should be used by every teacher. John Dewey's famous problem-solving steps (which are based on his belief that all learning is problem solving) are a similar type of orthodoxy.

Before World War II, the articulation of instruction became so formal that any teaching or learning process had to be structured in the same way. However, in the 1950s, pedagogical reformers in Europe changed this articulation by creating the so-called "functional rhythm" of the formal stages of the teaching process. Each phase of a lesson had to be subdivided into three activating steps—reception, processing, and evaluation—that were based on an input–output system. No matter how many phases a lesson had and no matter what form it had, dividing it into three steps was compulsory. Teachers were asked to switch phases as often as they thought proper.

The research in the Choreographies of Teaching was sponsored by the Swiss National Science Foundation. Co-workers on the project were Jean-Luc Patry, Traugott Elsaesser, Susanne Sarasin, and Birgit Wagner. Thanks for help in translating and correcting this chapter to Susan Rose and Wolfgang Althof.

Later, during the 1960s and 1970s, especially in Europe, experts and educational philosophers replaced formal phase teaching with intuitive instruction (Gage, 1978). Phases, or obligatory articulations, were viewed as inhibitory to spontaneous teaching and as a corruptive influence on teaching style. The latest approach toward teaching is based on research in perception, memory, cognition, and the resulting recognition of cognitive psychological nomothetic knowledge (e.g., conceptual change or concept building). At the same time, constructivism has led to concepts of situated learning, anchored instruction, and shared knowledge, in which each lesson is seen as a unique specimen. Concepts of learning environments are used to structure the lesson.

A major objective of this latest approach is to demonstrate that an instructional model must be designed at different levels, in different contexts, and with different forms of learning, different kinds of contents, and different types of controls (see Achtenhagen & Grubb, chapter 32, this volume). Distinctions should be made especially between (a) creating conditions for concrete activities of students, which we call the visible or sight structure of a lesson, and (b) creating conditions for inner, nonvisible constructive activities, namely, the learning process itself or the mental operations that refer to the deep structure of learning (basis–model). The combination of these two aspects of the teaching–learning activities and students' learning process are the core of this chapter, namely, the choreography of teaching and learning.

A choreography of teaching, therefore, is composed of the planning and processing of teaching (sight structure) and of the planning and processing of the learning process (basis–model) in the classroom. Planning is defined as organizing in advance a structured form of action (instructional plans) in which the mental models of the steps can stimulate cognitive operations in learners. In general, we admit that any planning sequence is guided by tasks, situational aspects, cultural ethos, and, of course, motivational and cognitive elements.

For our work, we have elaborated on four principal assumptions that form the basis for lesson preparation and for the corresponding selection of a choreography of teaching. These four assumptions help us to understand what occurs simultaneously in the teaching and the learning processes. They describe the most important elements that are needed for the learner to make sense out of the learning and to understand his or her own learning processes.

The first of these assumptions refers to constructivism. It claims that teachers always positively design blueprints for activating learning that has school-based constraints, developmental constraints, children's prior knowledge, and motivational styles in mind.

The second assumption refers to the belief that teachers can hypothesize the kind of inner acts or mental operations students use when they learn. This belief is based on the Piagetian tradition of learning as an inner activity of the individual.

The third assumption has to do with measurement: The success of choreographed instructional scripts or plans (chained steps of instruction) is measurable by the end performance as well as by the ease and security of understanding that are exhibited in each step along the way, in other words, as hands-on performance during the instruction. Obviously, good teaching influences students to become intrinsically motivated to learn and instinctively able to apply an appropriate learning style that stimulates knowledge building, problem solving, and similar types of mental operations. However, good lessons do not lead automatically to good performance. Students must rehearse, do their homework, and possess a high level of responsibility and self-understanding related to their own learning.

The fourth assumption refers to the distinction between optimal teaching (expert teaching)—which is a scaffolding that sets conditions for children to act effectively—and inexpert teaching—which does not take into account that children can lose track, become sidetracked by their own interests, or be unable to build real knowledge within a reasonable time.

These four assumptions that refer to the teaching–learning relationship are mostly compatible with each other and are examined in greater depth further on. To learn how teachers worldwide construct billions of lessons and how they imply a consideration of these four assumptions, we must distinguish between sufficient and insufficient instructional planning and acting. Sufficient practical planning and instructional acting, at the least, does not inhibit learning. Insufficient planning and acting actually inhibits not only learning but also the knowledge-building process with respect to a choreographed teaching–learning optimum.

Emergency Room Classroom: The Disturbing Effects of Lack of Didactical Flexibility

In a certain sense, a teacher can be compared to an expert in an emergency room: He or she must react constantly to the immediate events in the classroom despite having a basic plan or model of instruction that determines the most important components of the lesson. The emergency interventions include the individual needs of the students, the organization of the material, the special controls and aides for slow or weak learners, etc. In other words, the teacher needs a long-range, step-by-step model of instruction to depend on and, yet, must react immediately to the many short-term events that occur in a classroom. A lesson period can be seen as a learning episode in which a teacher sends the learners off to execute a specific chain of operations according to certain rules. During this episode, innumerable helping, piloting, and controlling activities are simultaneously required. Most teachers see only the latter: They organize what is visible (the sight–structure of learning) and neglect to consider the more important question of what is happening in the mind of the student (the basis–model). Why is this shortsightedness so?

A first clue may be the fact that learning has become a mass product that highly values things that concern all of the students and not just the inner activity of one individual. Aptitude–Treatment–Interaction studies (Snow, 1992), time-on-task studies (Fisher et al., 1980), and studies on mastery learning (Bloom, 1968; Slavin, 1987) are good examples of attempts to combine both the general learning path and activities for individual aptitudes.

A second reason is that it is simpler to define the conditions for learning than it is to define learning itself. The earlier belief that learning can, in fact, be initiated outside the learner has gradually weakened as teachers focus more on creating a positive learning climate, on enhancing communication, and on stimulating cooperation. Teachers often even shy away from pushing students to learn and are sometimes even inhibited in giving minimal directions just to keep the learning in motion (e.g., open the book to page 10; try to draw the distance from X to Y with a pair of compasses).

A similar class of reactions refers to the "therapy-i-zation" of the classroom setting, which also inhibits learning. Instead of taking both the process activity and the interaction dynamic into account, only social cohesion or experiences of autonomy and similar dynamic variables are considered. These conditions are important, of course, to consider, but they must be connected to the learning of content. (In one of our interviews, a boy said, "You know, our teacher is so good-hearted, and we love each other so much, but we do not learn anything.") The exaggeration of the person-centered, nondirective, and therapy-oriented concept of teaching often leads to "noble motives and pedagogical kitsch" (Reichenbach & Oser, 1995, reacting to the second edition of Rogers & Freiberg, *Freedom to Learn*).

A third possibility for the lack of emphasis on internal learning in Europe is that teacher trainers reinforce in student teachers the belief that the classroom is a "field of burden." Overly concerned with issues of burnout, the pressures of the curriculum, the multiplicity of educational requirements, the complexity of the multicultural demands from parents, etc., they fail to teach student teachers how to master the "emergency room" reality of the classroom—this previously mentioned necessity for both a structural learning frame and many thousands of small reactions to the children. Instruction, in this sense, means (a) to have a chain of learning steps in mind and (b) to have actions that can be simultaneously activated: hearing, helping, ordering, commanding, controlling, connecting, adjusting, explaining, demanding, advising, and so on. If a novice teacher believes all of this is too difficult and too stressful, he or she will behave with a learned helplessness, thus, creating a self-fulfilling prophecy.

A fourth reason why teachers take a myopic approach to teaching relates to the lack of a culture of mistakes. Student teachers do not have enough opportunities to build up so-called "negative professional knowledge." The sources of building such processes lie in the possibilities to repeat each small teaching behavior and, thus, to accumulate experiences of avoiding certain problematic classroom acting, of ignoring the inner learning, and of being bored with the children as a result of following the tenets of this teaching–learning mode.

A final reason for the separation between instructional models and the actual process of learning is that, for generations of teachers, the deeply held belief that teaching is basically the transmission of knowledge continues to be passed down. Teaching is viewed as the art of presentation, and learning, as the duty to repeat what was presented (Gage, 1978). The idea that teaching should stimulate a certain kind of thinking and action is very old—but is consistently forgotten in new ways.

The concept of a choreography of instruction is one new attempt to overcome the five problematic features described above. We will try to demonstrate how teaching and learning can and should come together with this concept.

The Relationship between Learning and Teaching

We have found, until now, that the relationship between instruction and children's learning arises whenever models of the teaching–learning process are discussed or whenever problems of learning occur. Now, we would like to take a closer look at this relationship from a point of view of recent research movements that, on the one hand, clearly try to resolve this tension and, yet, on the other hand, never properly disentangle it. Generations of researchers have failed when faced with the complexity of this relationship. Reigeluth (1983) stated: "Instructional design theory is concerned with what teachers do, whereas learning theory is concerned with what happens to the learner. Like instructional theory, learning theory may be descriptive or prescriptive. But prescriptive learning theory is *not* instructional theory" (p 23).

This statement is typical of the problem mentioned; in our opinion, it fails to connect both fields. Gagné (1965), for example, emphasizes the activity of the learner in applying types of intellectual skills and the respective performance they produce; he then strictly but differentially assigns "instructional events."

Reigeluth and Stein (1983), in contrast, limit themselves to a description of what a teacher does in their elaboration of a theory of instruction. Tennyson and Breuer (1997) take a different tack. In their approach, cognitive subsystems, learning objectives, and instructional prescriptions are shown in reference to declarative, procedural, and contextual knowledge. The connection is freely drawn and is lacking in dimensions. How-to-do books, such as the book from Cangelosi (1992) titled *Systematic Teaching Strategies,* also miss this connection. The chapter "Design Lessons" (p. 67 ff.) is completely separate from the one on "Engaging Students in Learning Activities" (p. 167). Even some of the newest concepts, such as "A System Dynamics Approach to Instructional Systems Development" from Tennyson (1997), do no more than tell what the instructor has to do (foundation, maintenance, design, production, evaluation, implementation, etc., with some overlapping) and almost completely ignores the inner activity of the learner.

Dijkstra and Van Merriënboer (1997) put the problem succinctly when they say that traditional instructional design models are not capable of sufficiently defining the relationship between instructional actions, learning process, and content structure. They suggest bridging this hiatus with a "theory of no problem," but their suggestion is not convincing. Their assertion that "instructional strategies should concentrate on original problem-solving activities and theory building based on exploration and experimentation" (p. 39) is subject to the same tendency to search for a unifying model of instructional design theory without distinguishing between instruction and learning.

Schott and Driscoll (1997), suggest a "universal constructive instructional theory" that similarly attempts to cover as many characteristics of a learner, different learning environments, and subject matters as possible. This theory leads to a sequence that is interesting on a macrolevel (Stage 1: instructional goal; Stage 2: state of the learner; Stage 3: instruction; Stage 4: diagnosis of success) but loses sight of the relationship between instruction and learning at the microlevel.

Authors who are rooted either in educational research or in the psychology of knowledge are more modest in terms of the relationships they propose. Theories that fall under constructivism, for instance, Mandl and Reinmann-Rothmeier (1995), attempt to describe only the conditions for possible learning for teachers, no more. In describing only conditions for possible learning, they must give priority to construction rather than instruction. The learner is active while the teacher is faced with the task of simply being available for consoling on problem situations and for providing the necessary tools. In this conception, knowledge is no image of reality but, rather, the construction of a situation and the mastering of that situation, and thus, the learner side is stressed. In this sense, Shulman (1986) gave an excellent overview of the problems of the process–product research, showing that the question of what is effective is also a question of how instruction fits learning.

According to our opinion, teacher cognition has also been researched too little, leading to a program that lacks an examination of the most varied types of professional knowledge (didactic knowledge, subject matter knowledge, pedagogical knowledge, developmental knowledge, etc.—the professional knowledge base of teachers). Both methods would have been possible: (a) the three steps from the description to the correlation and to the assumption of causality through the experiment (Gage, 1978; Medley, 1987) or (b) the three steps reversed, from the correlational and experimental studies to the classroom ethnographies (Erickson, 1986). But even Shulman (1986) does not go into enough depth in describing how the relationship of the inner activity of the learner (the operations) must be structured with the external teaching conditions.

The model of teaching choreographies that we are suggesting is based on the assumption that teachers build hypotheses about how their actions effect the inner activity of pupils at almost every step that the pupils attempt. Basically, the teachers follow, not an instructional psychology, but, rather, a teaching–learning psychology that produces the assumptions about which actions of the teacher will lead to which constructive activity on the part of the students. This model is maybe something like an anticipation–process I–process II–product paradigm.

Thus, our model is based on the assumption that while teaching, teachers are constantly generating hypotheses about the anticipation–process relationship, the process–process relationship, and the process–product relationship. They develop relational thinking within the framework of a teaching–learning situation and decide on actions that can generate constructive learning processes in the students. Our four-leveled anticipation–process, process–product scheme is as follows.

At the first level, *anticipation,* the teacher anticipates the desired learning result for the learner and initiates appropriate learning activities. Usually, the teacher is very focused on the content of what is to be taught in this phase (Bromme, 1992). The content is structured and simplified to identify a clear step-by-step learning strategy. Lesson anticipation, in this case, touches on mental process models that vary depending on the level of the teacher's expertise. The mental models of expert teachers are more complex and explicit than those of novice teachers (Dick, 1994). Experts reflect in advance on both teaching and learning. They have a large variety of teaching, learning, and instructional action possibilities at their command.

According to Burns (1996), "Models of learning focus on the salient instructional conditions influencing school learning. Because of their content, models of learning can have direct implications for the design of school curriculum and instruction, and some of them have generated specific instructional models for

implementations in school" (p. 327). Psychological theories of learning, (behavioral, constructivist, social–constructivist) interact in this phase with teaching models (direct-teaching, cooperative teaching, etc.). We expect, however, not only a learning theory type of anticipation but also an anthropological type in this phase.

At the second level, the visible *process* (process I) of the teacher's actions is the focus. The outflow of these actions have a certain structure that correlate only partially with the inner representation mentioned in level one because they often come under scrutiny when the hard limitations of teaching—such as motivations problems, discipline questions, size of classes, and other, often unexpected events—are reached (see paragraph 2 of "The Engineering of Billion of Lessons" in this chapter). In an ideal case, every one of these a teacher's actions contains a hypothesis about an assumed effect on the cognitive operation and inner events of the students that will result from the teacher's actions. Those who teach believe (at least now and then) that they make learning possible through their teaching. In the choreography of teaching, we can show this belief clearly by differentiating what is visible in teaching (the visible structure) and what is invisible (the basis–model). Thus, the second element in our teaching–learning model refers to the visible, the actual planning structure of the teacher.

The third level focuses on the mental operations or *processes* (process II) of the learner, namely, the so-called basis–model itself. The act of learning is at the center of the teacher's planning behavior. Here, along with Lompscher (1996, p. 348), we make the distinction between learning through activity and learning as a special activity. Learning as a special activity refers to planning specific activities that lead to learning. For example, when learners relate one element to another, make comparisons, go on searches, find solutions, etc., the inner mental activity is what makes the actual learning process unfold.

The instructional designs for action that fall under level two and the intended learning activities that fall under level three are in an interdetermining relationship with each other. Teaching should be only for the purpose of causing mental operations and making constructive work possible. Intended and anticipated mental operations, in turn, demand specific instructional conditions. In other words, a conditioning question-and-answer lesson, for instance, promotes narrow, directed thinking by the students, not independent, critical thinking.

At the fourth level, the *product,* we are concerned with two things: the mastery of knowledge and the practice of skills. Factual knowledge can be shown diagrammatically by a scale that goes from reconstructed recall to automatic recall. The added processes relate to the problem of doing, namely, the skills. Additional products, such as the development of a self-efficacy belief, and emotional learning products, such as self-confidence and motivation, can be anticipated in addition to the learning products that are often determined by the curriculum.

Models Matter: Recent History of American Movements

After distinguishing visible structure from basis–models of instruction at the beginning of this section, we now question the different notions of "models of instruction." When is a model a model? Is a teaching style a model of instruction? Is a method or an articulation schema a model? Is an instructional design a model?

Instructional models, in our view, fill the following four conditions: (a) they must have a behavioral or acting base that mediates learning (teachers behave in a way that students can learn); (b) they must be—as seen in the different basis–models—applicable to different types of learning and goals (e.g., stimulating a social attitude or building and changing a mathematical concept are two very different matters); (c) they must be contextual pivots that can be clearly defined (e.g., the necessity to cope with computer programs within a technical framework); and (d) they must be connected to views of the man as personality (Menschenbild) and to the development of humans (i.e., man as machine or man as the constructor of his personal identity).

The four determinants of an instructional model—(a) a chain of stimulating acts for the purpose of learning, (b) types of goals, (c) influence of contexts, and (d) the "Menschenbild"—must be an interconnected web of elements, each contributing to the model. To illustrate, the following is an example of a definition that lacks some of these elements:

> A model of teaching consists of guidelines for designing educational activities and environments. It specifies ways of teaching and learning that are intended to achieve certain goals. A model includes a rationale, a theory that justifies it and describes what it is good for and why; the rationale may be accompanied by empirical evidence that it "works." (Weil & Joyce, 1978, p. 2)

This example fulfills items (a) and (b), but it does not fulfill item (c), which determines the contextual connectedness, or item (d), an a priori view of human potential.

To take another example, the chapter of Wallen and Travers (1963) on "Analyses and Investigation of Teaching Methods" in the first *Handbook of Research on Teaching* describes different roles and patterns of teaching behavior, gives an overview on teaching methods, and relates teaching methods to principles of learning within a completely behaviorist framework. The notion of a model in that chapter is found in only the one unique basic model of learning that underlies all the teaching methods and related research. The dependent variables in this model are the number of test points, the observed behavior, the changes in attitude, etc. Independent variables consist of situational characteristics, motivation, reinforcement, mediated actions, etc. Here we find, for the first time, research on instruction that is based on a psychological learning model. But this notion of a model lacks item (b), different types of learning, and (d), an open, formulated view of humanity. Of course, this model depicts a restricted point of view because the authors believe that there is only one psychological model of learning for many methods of teaching.

In the mid-1970s, Gagné and Briggs (1974) began referring to multiple models of learning for the first time. These models are distinguished by a hierarchy of competence that begins with motor skills, attitudes, cognitive strategies, and verbal information and that ends with intellectual skills. The two authors interpretively combine each of these learning types with so-called instructional events that form a kind of process sequence—(a) gaining attention, (b) informing the learner of the objectives, (c) stimulating recall of prerequisite learning, (d) presenting

stimulus material, (e) providing learning guidance, (f) eliciting the performance, (g) providing feedback about performance correctness, (h) assessing the performance, and (i) enhancing retention and transfer.

How does this well-known and well-cited theory of instruction compare to our model conditions? Gagné and Briggs neither provide a framework for understanding the kind of structure underlying the teaching process nor sufficiently relate their concept to the real-life, two-element process: the complex and sequential process of classroom learning. In real teaching, it is not possible to distinguish complexities of learning types; rather, they unfold and overlap in turns, appearing simultaneously and quickly transforming each other. For this reason, it was difficult for Gagné to apply his types of learning to concrete content. Nevertheless, he is the first author who distinguishes different, complex types of learning in his theory and who, consequently, offers a model that has a general, heuristic value.

During the mid-1980s, the problem of sequencing the process of teaching, although not dealt with in the 1986 edition of the *Handbook of Research on Teaching,* was given a lot of attention in Reigeluth's (1983) *Instructional-Design Theories and Models: An Overview of Their Current Status.* The *Handbook* represents rather huge visions of how the whole of the teaching process can be taken into consideration (see Shulman, 1986). Reigeluth, however, is, to some degree, the only one who distinguishes between (a) instructional design that prescribes methods for instructional development or that prescribes procedures for either instructural implementation or management and (b) instructional design that identifies weaknesses with respect to instructional evaluations. He uses the word *model* precisely for these five forms of treating instruction, namely, design, development, implementation, management, and evaluation. And most important, he distinguishes strongly—like we mentioned before—between "a theory of instructional design and a theory of learning." Whereas the former focuses on methods of instruction, the latter stresses the learning process (p. 23).

Two other approaches in the same volume that are worth mentioning are those of Scandura (1983) and those of Merrill (1983). Scandura stresses (a) the analysis of the rules to be learned with respect to the concrete subject matter knowledge and (b) the respective prescriptions for teachers. Merrill presents a "Component Display Theory," which "is a set of prescriptive relationships that can be used to guide the design and development of learning activities" (p. 283).

What is noticeable in all of these models is that although they pose the question of strategies for sequencing and synthesizing instruction in a profound way, they neither make the distinction between teaching and learning precise nor differentiate enough between types of learning and types of goals, which are presented very abstractly (even context free). Finally, they do not offer a real concept for the basic anthropological idea about the role that learning plays in human development. In the *Review of Educational Research,* Van Patten, Chao, and Reigeluth (1986) presented an overview of such sequencing possibilities on microlevels and macrolevels, as well as an overview of the respective scramble studies that theoretically procure the "logic" of the connection of sequences.

The 1990s have seen new and more comprehensive models of instruction, most of them fulfilling the four conditions of a complete model. These models are based on the constructivist movement, which proposes that the student shall be active within a frame of experience and autonomy (see Piaget, 1970; von Glasersfeld, 1989, 1995). Within this movement, several directions can be distinguished.

The first direction is the so-called "situated cognition movement." Situated cognition supposes that, in different variants, the thinking and acting of a learner can be understood only in his or her unique context and that the knowledge of a society is always shared knowledge (Resnick, 1991). The limits of this approach concern the fixed borders of a context and the lack of abstraction and generalization (Anderson, Reder, & Simon, 1996; see also Greeno 1989; Lave 1991; Resnick 1987; Rogoff 1990). However, the model (a) has an action base, (b) refers to different learning forms, (c) includes contextual constraints, and (d) preaches the constructivist basics.

In the anchored instruction method (Cognition and Technology Group at Vanderbilt, 1992, 1993, 1997), the idea of context is mostly meaningful in a narrative sense. These narrative approaches include contrasting means and processes of abstraction as well as making connections to already acquired knowledge. Adventures and fairy tales, for instance, can become means for constructing and transporting knowledge. The cognitive flexibility theory, a similar child of the constructivist family, refers to case studies and the technique of crisscrossing landscapes, a form of knowledge transfer into different contexts (Jacobson & Spiro, 1992; Spiro & Jehng, 1990). This model is most often applied to higher-order learning.

The last model we mention is the cognitive apprenticeship learning model (Collins, Brown, & Newman, 1989) in which learners are introduced into a world of practical and social expertise through reflective imitation (modeling, coaching, scaffolding, facing, articulation, reflection, exploration). Mandl & Reinmann-Rothmeier (1995) postulate a combination of all of these models and develop the following basic ideas: (a) learning must be situated and must take place through authentic problems; (b) learning is connected with multiple situations; (c) learning takes place with multiple perspectives; (d) learning takes place in different social contexts (Greeno, 1995, 1998).

No matter how convincing each of these models or a combination of them appears to be, they all share a fundamental weakness. They postulate different kinds of learning that, in the end, all have the same goal: to avoid inert knowledge. But learning is different not only with respect to the context and the social field but also with respect to different types of learning and goals (our basis–models). To reach a higher developmental stage, for example, has nothing to do with the knowledge-building process. Generally, in our view, these models tend to reflect a philosophy of epistemic activity rather than to reflect the teaching–learning process.

From Didactics to Instruction: A Summary of the European Tradition

The Origins

Before we consider the basis–models in a deeper way, let us look more closely at the European movements and the development there of what we call instructional models. History can help to reframe the genesis of what we call "bridging instruction to learning." For this, we particularly refer to Kron (1993) and Heidemann (1981), who give excellent overviews of this process. We refer in each case to the four previously mentioned model criteria:

1. have a behavioral or acting base mediating learning
2. be applicable to different types of learning or goals
3. be contextual pivots that can be clearly defined
4. be connected to views of the man as personality to the development of humans (Menschenbild)

To define didactics as a scientific discipline is difficult (Kron, 1993). Not long ago, at the beginning of a conference, the second author was embarrassed when an American colleague sitting next to him asked what didactics were. "The science of teaching" was his immediate response. Whether didactics is a scientific discipline by itself is, indeed, an often discussed issue. A "hmm . . ." was the answer of the unknown neighbor, who seemed satisfied with the first attempt at an explanation. The lecture had a promising title; however, it was badly presented. The topic had no recognizable structure and the content was confusingly grouped. Part of the content was omitted because time was limited. After a lengthy development, the key word was not explained. Several slides were projected upside down, and many of them did not correspond to the issue presented. The speaker was very nervous. After 45 minutes, the second author turned to his neighbor and commented, "What we are experiencing here lacks didactics!" She smiled and responded, "Now I know what you mean by didactics!"

Etymologically, the original Greek word *didactic* has several meanings: (a) the act of teaching; (b) the instructor who is qualified to teach; (c) one who is qualified to teach, who chooses appropriate contents and explains his choice; (d) the teaching manuals as a method and media of teaching; (e) the school as a definite place, where students and classes are taught; and (f) the learning process, which is the central activity of the learner (cf. Kron, 1993, p. 40; much of the following information is informed by this article).

The first explicit work on didactics, the *Didactica Magna* (Comenius, 1657/1957), which systematically includes the above-cited meanings, was written by Johannes Amos Comenius (1592–1670). It is a collection of basic principles on how to select contents, how to lead a class, the anthropology of the child as a learner, and above all, the methods of teaching. Comenius drew a curriculum, which included the scientific standards of that time. He required universality in the sense that all scientific branches should be presented and taught in the mother tongue and that every child should have the right to learn in his natural language (his mother tongue). This requirement was not self-evident. Latin was the language of science in the monastic and convent schools. Comenius worked out a "curricular cosmos" in which the elements followed an inner order, namely, the order "from God to man, from man to God." Comenius's new curriculum became a directive for the teaching schools of the following century. His methodological "recipes" were to give, through the teaching and learning process, optimal results for completing the educational cycle "from God, to

God." Comenius's greatest hope was to bring a general education to all people.

His anthropology has its roots in the complex religious tradition of the Catholic church. His postulated methods of teaching and learning are simple, secure, and well-structured; good examples and clear rules are given. Comenius's didactics describe the objectives, the means, and the rules of instruction—an instruction with the aim of effective learning. The semantic field of the concept of "didactics" is comprehensive, multifaceted, and has long-term and extensive aims, contents, and media of instruction.

If we compare Comenius's *Didactica Magna* with the four criteria of our model, we can say that Comenius clearly reflects a consideration of criterion 4, that of a "Menschenbild." Criteria 1 (the action) and 2 (the differentiation of the goal) are somehow mentioned, but the relationship between teaching and learning is discussed only in an indirect way through the developmental aspects. His didactics consider mainly the developmental level of the student, which is a general pedagogical requirement.

The Difference between Didactics and Methodology

Herbart (1776–1841) was a former home teacher before he took over the chair of philosophy (as we mentioned previously) from Kant at the University of Königsberg. He is of interest because his theory is rooted in Aristotle's three-step learning rhythm: perception, deepening and reflection, and application. In his theory of pedagogy, he relied on the principle that man is a rational being who can recognize and shape the world with the power of his mind (first perception theory). Children and young adults act through experience and cognition. The child draws conclusions, establishes relationships, recognizes structures, and makes generalizations that are based on single cases. The motivation for development lies simply in the nature of the child. Higher judgments are attained through reasoning.

The job of the teacher is to lead students to literacy, to surpass the limits of naive, everyday experience, and to become engaged in an ongoing, intellectual striving. Young people already think, systematize, and interpret activities in their everyday life in a scientific way. Students are interested in the world, and the thinking they do, the "thinking circle," brings an inner order in their minds, thus, creating an ethical fundament. The ability to gain new knowledge through experience relies, therefore, in the nature of human beings. Presumably, learning has the task of diversifying interests and enhancing the ability to systematically perceive, interpret, and recognize. This assumption led Herbart to the question of how such inner activities can occur at school.

Herbart created the concept of what he called the "articulation of instruction." As mentioned in the beginning of this paper, this articulation schema consists of (a) creating cognitive clarity of the old knowledge, (b) stimulating new knowledge elements that are connected to the old knowledge through association, (c) systematizing these associations, and (d) applying this newly systematized knowledge. This articulation of instruction is what Herbart means with methods, and these four steps are called "formal stages." "Educational teaching" is given, if the formal stages are applied in every instruction. Herbart believed that promoting intellectuality also fosters morality. When compared to our model's conditions, Herbart's methods stress the first criterion (the activity of the student) and the fourth criterion (the human as an autonomous learner). He does not fulfill the requirements of the second criterion (the differentiation of goals) and the third criterion (contextuality). In his conception—and here is the absolute novelty of it—he accentuates the thinking and reasoning process of the learner. In his view, didactics is only a means of learning.

The educators in the teaching seminaries, founded in the 19th century, accentuated the articulation scheme of Herbart's pedagogy and actually overused it as a methodology of instruction. The power of his scheme remained in place up until modern times because it was emphasized as the basic idea of instructional processing to many generations of teachers (Heidemann, 1981).

The application of Herbart's systematic "articulation of instruction" led teacher education to distance itself from a philosophical background and from a focus on child thought processes. It was interpreted only as an instructional and functional method. From this point on, the notion of didactics was scientifically truncated to refer simply to aspects of "methods of teaching." Questions about curriculum, contents, and justifications in instruction were disregarded. This absoluteness has, meanwhile, been broken down by the constructivism of our period. However, the imprint of Herbart's' articulation of instruction remains. It advances the systematic construction of knowledge and was a long-time base for complex instructional orchestration.

The articulation scheme of Herbart's was changed by Kerschensteiner (1854–1932), a famous pedagogue and founder of the vocational schools in Germany. Kerschensteiner transferred it into the following four levels of logical thinking: (a) discovery and selection of the problem-solving method (in which a problem has to be found, searched, and formulated); (b) search for hypotheses about solutions; (c) discussion and analyses of hypotheses; and (d) the verification of the solution.

Gaudig (1860–1923), a contemporary of Kerschensteiner, formulated a similar articulation scheme. Gaudig proposed five levels of instruction preparation: (a) registration of a working goal; (b) selection of the means of work; (c) drawing a plan for the way of working; (d) defining individual working steps and determining how they are joined together as a whole; and, finally, (e) registration, testing, assessment, and evaluation of the working results (Heidemann, 1981, p. 259).

Kerschensteiner and Gaudig are the founders of the so-called "Arbeitsschule" (working school). Their concern was, on the one hand, to prepare children and young adults in school for the work world and, on the other hand, to relate the work place to the classroom. In the working school, authentic work situations where created in which children learned through examples that prepared them for a real situation. An uncritical adoption of the ideas of the working school, however, led many educators to an uncritical application that simply tried to produce good workers.

On the other hand, from a purely psychological point of view, articulation now became more and more positively valued through a "pedagogical working process" where students can positively experience the complexity of an authentic working process. Most important, learning here is goal oriented, and applicable work skills are learned. Today, the principle of "situated learning" parallels the idea of the working school. The working school idea is highly related to the third criterion of our model, namely, contextual learning. In this working school model, teaching and learning are tightly and holistically connected.

An influential continuation of Aristotle's three steps of learning and Herbart's formal level models formal stages methods was Heinrich Roth's (1906–1983) psychological model of teaching (Roth, 1957). Roth's starting point is the consideration on how the learning process functions and how lessons are to be planned (Heidemann, 1981, p. 261). Roth differentiates three types of learning and six steps in the process of learning. The three types of learning are (a) indirect learning, (b) direct learning, and (c) school learning. Indirect learning results from the specific requirement of an act. For example, if a bicycle has a flat tire, a youngster learns how to repair this defect because the bicycle is needed. The youngster could carry out this repair in several ways: Maybe he or she has observed how one dismantles tires, how one searches for the hole and patches it; maybe the child knows a good friend who does it well and asks that friend to help; or maybe the youngster takes the bicycle to a workshop. The child always learns something new—either new strategies or new facts—from each situation. In direct learning, the person pursues a precise aim. For example, a youngster goes through a first aid training course or gets a motorcycle class driving license. For school learning, the instructor prepares the contents of the lesson and motivates the students to work on it. Learning content is a book-based procedure.

For each of the three types of learning, one must go through six levels before the learning process can be considered complete. Motivation is the first level. It is the kickoff for the learning process and the inherent aim of both direct and indirect learning. In school, motivation to learn has to be initiated by the instructor. The second level is that of perceived difficulties. Here, the learner experiences that, in most cases, the aim is not easily attained. The complexity of a problem needs to be perceived. At the third level, a solution must be found. The process of finding a solution must be followed through (and must be repeatable in case of emergency). In school learning, the problem that must be recognized and solved is often presented by the instructor. At the fourth level is implementation. This implementation must be done with respect to the content and goal-oriented activity, which is highly required. The self-determination of the student is emphasized. The fifth level is that of drilling, or practice and rehearsing. The learning material must be built up and automated through a variety of exercises. The final level is the transference and integration of what has been learned. Roth emphasizes the transference of learning to situations in real life.

Roth's articulation scheme has left its mark on instruction in the German-speaking world. It is often used in a very formal way and, according to Roth, connects itself exclusively to school learning. This very schematic use leads to clever techniques at the individual level. Many motivation techniques lead to an opera-like opening of the lesson with an awkwardness that far exceeds the awkwardness of American speakers' opening jokes at meetings or conferences.

It is mainly due to Roth that learning is treated as an inner psychological process and that his model did not refer to American behaviorism. His reference to the European tradition of problem solving (Köhler, 1917/1963; Wertheimer, 1945), which was the basic scheme of school learning, however, had some shortcomings. Although he bases his pedagogical psychology on a detailed anthropology of learning, the schematic use of the six levels are based on experience.

With respect to the four criteria required in a model, the Roth model is close to fulfilling all of them. There is (a) an activity frame, (b) a goal differentiation, (c) contextuality, and (d) a constructivist view of the world. The problem with Roth's model is that he accentuates only the psychological aspects of school learning and neglects the instructional theory.

Klafki's Perspective Schema for Instructional Design

Wolfgang Klafki is a well-known philosophical didactitian who teaches at the University of Marburg. Klafki's work (Klafki, 1959, 1968, 1974) follows the tradition of "categorical instruction" within the classical educational theory espoused by Humboldt (1767–1835). Humboldt saw education as the development and strengthening of the "primary mental powers." With this view, he supported the ideal of general education without consideration of later employability (Roth, 1991, p. 470). He was the first to distinguish between functional education in which children learn what is necessary for the professional, social, and political life and general education with its moral, cultural, and human goals.

Klafki relativized the idealistically humanistic educational theory by setting the knowledge of formal education in relation with that of material education, or education that is based on real life. Education was to be seen as a unity of the two. Cultural processes of transmission were to be goal oriented and justifiable. Thus, in addition to the intellectual powers (the formal educational aspect), the transmission of society's culture must take place (the material education). Klafki's resulting concept, categorical education (Klafki, 1974), emphasized that the goal of the lesson content must be so chosen and presented that the learner arrives at some kind of general insight and fundamental (educative) experience. Klafki later integrated the dimension of emancipation and postulated the idea of "education as a capacity for rational self-determination" (Klafki, 1991, p. 19). He was referring to elements such as freedom, emancipation, autonomy, maturity, reasonability, and self-motivation. Education should develop values that apply to all humanity—the maintenance of the world, health, ecological balance, and peace (key problems). Within this topic, Klafki refers to a multidimensionality, multiperspectivity in the educational process, which must "be brought forth in the subject himself, and which alone can possibly structure modern education, thus leading to the responsibility which is the goal of a subject-oriented society" (Kron, 1993, p. 131). This multiperspectivity must consider teachers, schools, and educational policies. What exactly constitutes multiperspectivity?

- A thorough analysis of the starting conditions of the learners, the teacher, and the institution as well as the preconditions that are directly relevant to the instruction
- Primacy of goal orientation—reflection on the hierarchical norms of sensibility and the societal relationships by every

decision-making person, independent of the level at which they decide; objects of learning and the themes chosen in view of the goals

- A choice of themes that must be justifiably related to each other—relations worked out between the contemporary reference, the future reference, and the exemplary relevance of the object of learning; justification for the instruction of the content derived from the three-dimensional analysis
- Analysis of the thematic structure that leads to the concrete intermediate and final learning goals
- An approach and possibilities for presenting a theme that provide the basis for media choices
- An analysis that requires a methodological structuring of the teaching and learning process

At this point, forms of instructional organization and social interaction should be determined. Klafki's multiperspective scheme for instructional design is an analysis schema that is founded on educational and pedagogical theory. His theory is also didactically exemplary and well suited for teacher education. By his employing the analysis schema, the sense of responsibility for the instruction is strengthened, and the complexities of lesson planning and the corresponding social meaning become apparent. In his own words, the theory of categorical education, first and foremost, has formal educational value. For this theory to be useful in daily teaching, it must become a mental model that can be applied as an implicit grid over the concrete activities that guide lesson planning. With respect to our four-point conceptual model, Klafki does not have an articulation scheme. Instead, he gives a catalogue of criteria that should be taken into consideration during lesson preparation. Klafki's theory is built on a clear "Menschenbild" with an anthropological broad theory. Klafki's six-point didactic theory, rare in its philosophical basis, views the learning process itself as having no intrinsic interest. In the last view, Klafki has a philosophy rather than a psychology of teaching: The application of his criteria to a lesson preparation lacks any empirical control.

The Berlin/Hamburg Model

Paul Heimann (1901–1967) was an experienced teacher and, later, a professor who founded a scientific and experientially based theory of didactic analysis and instructional design. The actual motive for the development of his learning-theory approach toward teaching was the request by the Berlin Congressional House of 1958 to develop a longer practicum (in-service teaching) for the core teacher training program. Beginning from such pragmatic involvement, Heimann tried to scientifically reveal teaching practices, thereby placing the focus of his interest on the situation of the teacher and the interrelationship between the conditions and the forms of teaching. Teachers analyze and plan their lessons simultaneously and, in this way, act simultaneously as teacher and researcher. To reveal such complex factors, Heimann applied structure analysis and factor analysis. He combined empirical research with teaching experiments and observations, whereby the interrelationship between individual, social, and societal factors is as important as the task of isolating instructionally determined factors such as methods, media, and goals. Although he based his work on factor analysis, he attempted, above all, to find a fundamental

structure that underlies all teaching processes, even when the processes appear to be different. The structuration consists of two fields:

1. The field of conditions, including the anthropological conditions of the learner and his social, situative, and cultural conditions
2. The four fields of decision making: intention, content, methods, and media

The second field is directly chosen and controlled by the teacher. The field of conditions is an area where teachers can have only indirect influence. With factor analysis, Heimann is referring to the application of findings in developmental and learning psychology as well as in sociology to reflect on instruction. This reflection is neutral and objective in that it takes existing social norms and ideologies into critical consideration while, likewise, critically examining the scientific theories and existing models of instruction and methods.

The primary goal of every teaching act is to initiate learning. Learning is such a fundamental process that Heimann does not consider it a structural element. The structural elements are aids for initiating learning (Heimann, 1970). A student of Heimann (later, a professor in Hamburg) expanded Heimann's Berlin model by adding the dimensions of critical learning theory (Schulz, 1980). Schulz's "critical turn" of didactics were based, above all, on the critical theory that was developed by Habermas. In bringing attention to Habermas's theory of communicative action, Schulz highlighted the dilemma of using instruction as a means toward functionalization and emancipation (Schulz, 1976).

Schulz critically observed the intertwining spheres of interest: spheres of functionalization and emancipation as well as spheres of individual and social actions. From these observations, he developed three central aims of education: competence, autonomy, and solidarity. Every goal is at the same level as the experience of objects, emotions, and social interactions. Schulz developed eight criteria for planning instruction: (a) real-life orientation, (b) scientific or subject-matter orientation, (c) action orientation, (d) method orientation, (e) orientation to the learner, (f) media orientation, (g) orientation toward forms of instructional organization, and (h) orientation toward the evaluation of success. Schulz does not mention learning itself. Planning refers only to teaching, which always implies learning. Processes of learning do not require specification because the planning criteria possesses general applicability. At the same time, he emphasizes the concrete acts that make up the didactic acts—the analysis, planning, realizing, advising, and evaluating as well as the administering and cooperative action.

The Hamburg model of instructional design and analysis is unique because it includes the dimension of social criticism in lesson planning. Schulz approaches Klafki's design but abandons the empirical and scientific basis of teaching theory postulated by Heimann.

The models for instructional design that were created by Klafki, Heimann, and Schulz have had the most durable influence on the newest teacher-training approaches in the German-speaking countries of Europe. At the same time, we should note that these three models have remained more as showpieces in educational theory than have become impulses for actual action. They remain interesting models that spur discussion on teaching even though none of the three approaches took the psychology of learning and its procedural character into consideration. They give scant attention to the teacher and offer little guidance for the mastery of teaching in real life.

Hans Aebli, the Transformer of Piaget's Learning Theory

Before we discuss the transformation of Piaget's theory of development by Hans Aebli, we should look at the special role that Piaget played in the development of learning research in Europe. To clarify his role, we need an exact description—if not the definition—of instruction according to Piaget. Piaget was interested neither in instruction as the mediation of knowledge nor in teaching as an institutionalized form of knowledge mediation. He was also not interested in methods of teaching that accelerated the levels of cognitive development. But he did emphasize the interaction of the individual with the environment, the active act of experiencing, and the role of language as a deciding factor in the development of intelligence (in the sense of recognition and understanding) (Piaget, 1947/1980). In this sense, we see Piaget as a cofounder of constructivism. Even the development of language as a medium for understanding symbols and social values was seen as an act of accommodation and assimilation that could not be intentionally or instructionally guided (Piaget, 1947/1980, German translation, 1980, p. 178).

For Piaget, inner activity (constructivism) forms the basis of mental development in children. This activity is composed of three elements: (a) the organization of development, (b) experience and training, and (c) social interaction and transmission (Piaget & Inhelder, 1977).

Hans Aebli, in his postdoctoral work (Aebli, 1951), expanded the second element of experience and training into a didactic model. He developed a concrete model for the active, experiential approach to the teaching of mathematics and social studies. His goal was to systematically construct learning processes from the experiential interaction with objects through the didactically reinforced internalized operation. As he constructed these learning processes, he was less concerned with the transmission of content than with the placing of students into situations in which they had to create and recognize relationships between objects and problems. According to Aebli, the recognition behind an operation is a necessary requirement for learning with understanding.

Aebli (1983) operationalized his operative didactics and described 12 basic forms, or models, of instruction. These forms coincide only in some regards with our basis–models of teaching. The number of 12 basic forms and 12 basis–models is incidentally the same. Aebli (1983) sometimes describes more visible structures and sometimes operations, sometimes only parts of an operational chain, yet without the chaining aspect emphasized in our basis–models. His models are titled as follows:

1. Telling and referring
2. Presenting
3. Watching and observing
4. Reading with students
5. Writing texts
6. Working out plans of action
7. Constructing an operation
8. Constructing a concept
9. Constructing solutions
10. Working through
11. Practicing and repeating
12. Using

Aebli's didactical models have two noticeable characteristics: He establishes a constructivist approach to learning that is focused on the quality of learning and, simultaneously, is psychologically based. The approach is constructivist in that the learner is seen as someone who constructs the world through his or her actions. This constructivist approach is a didactic that is focused on the construction of knowledge. Knowledge is acquired only when the learner or person operates with objects from the real world, thereby creating relationships. The teacher is seen as a guidance person who creates the learning situation in such a way that this knowledge acquisition is possible. The teacher steers and structures the school knowledge process. This teaching is rooted at the interactional level between teacher and learner while learning is concentrated on the cognitive content. Students do assimilate (without changing their cognitive basis schema) or accommodate (with changing the basis schema).

The second characteristic of Aebli's didactical model is that it is limited by the values and the ethical–moral aspects of the instructional content, which are not constructed with regard for the 12 basic forms of instruction. Aebli also bypasses the aspect of social interaction in school learning by not taking student interaction into consideration (Aebli, 1983).

The social–constructivist viewpoint of classroom learning has not yet found a didactic model. Only particular aspects of instructional organizational forms have been developed, and these try to enhance project-based teaching, group work, and the concept of open-ended teaching. The basis–models of teaching are an attempt to include more content, cognitive, emotional–affective, ethical, social–societal, and creative aspects into a didactic model. Learning processes and teaching processes are viewed as mutually determining within the basis–models.

Nevertheless, Aebli's theory (and also Piaget's theory) provides a fundamental basis for bringing instruction and learning together. Aebli looks at these two sides in a visionary way—and the type of model that we have formulated is also applicable—children can be innerly active only when teachers create the conditions for such activity. Aebli's theory fell short of our model in that he was too occupied with the construction of knowledge and knowledge transfer. He did not see the distinction between learning processes and inner activity. Nevertheless, he is the first person to obligate the combination of education and psychology.

A New Theory: Underpinnings of Teaching Choreographies. Basis–Models and Sight Structures

Teaching and Learning

To the dismay of teachers, children's cognitive sequences often do not follow the path indicated during the course of teaching.

In fact, they often go in completely different directions. This divergence occurs because sequences for learning are not the same as those for teaching. In this chapter we have presented already the notion of a "visible structure of teaching." With that, we mean the events initiated by teachers. We also speak of basis–models, and with that term, we mean the internal learning sequences, or operations, that children follow to appropriate knowledge, develop socially, solve problems, acquire skills, etc. The visible structure is highly situated or situation related; the basis–model is highly linear and generalizable.

Immediately, the questions on the first page of this chapter again become apparent. How do these visible teaching structures influence children's operation sequences? How are the sequences (these basis–models) created in general and in particular? What do teachers believe about their students' subjective processing in relation to the visible structures that they themselves continually produce? How do teachers order student's operation elements when they are presented in an unconnected way? Which types of basis–models are stimulated most frequently? Again, it is assumed that learning consists of outer activities that stimulate mental (i.e., inner) activity. The tension between the two kinds of activity is the bridging problem found between teaching and learning in general.

Teaching can prepare only the conditions for possible learning and can only guide, support, and evaluate those conditions. The mental actions, or operations, that are stimulated by these teaching activities are not clearly perceptible. In the tradition of Piaget and Aebli, who construct learning as the transformation of cognitive schemata that occur by way of diverse inner activities (assimilation, accommodation), we are focused on the mental activity of learners in connection with intention and with the respective hypotheses that teachers have. Searle (1996) writes about the ability of consciousness to perceive aspects: "To see an object from a certain standpoint means, for example, to see it under certain aspects and not others" (p. 153). All forms of intentionality are representations that take place under such aspects, and learning is such an aspect. Mental actions are those that serve to remember a thing, to change a value system, to acquire a skill, to understand a cult figure, and so forth. From such a standpoint, the kind of learning that is represented here can occur only as different mental activities by the learner.

Teaching, thus, is interesting only because it represents the somewhat gentler constraint on the execution of a group of these mental activities. Even university teaching is a modest form of setting mental activity in motion.

Perhaps the study of education, flanked as it is by troves of practical know-how, has neglected to make the mental activity of learners the center of observation and analysis. Whether learners do something (who does what and how it is done) or whether the teacher is successful are, as mentioned, two different things. These antipodes create a complicated but not always oppositional tension. Good speakers, for instance, can make audience members lazy in their thinking by telling them what they already know. Bad speakers can often stimulate the audience to reflect on, contradict, or create a disequilibrium in preexisting mental structures. The pedagogical viewpoint needs turning around; it needs to emphasize the activation of learners' mental activity and not the teaching methods, social forms, or content structure. Viewed from this aspect, the usual brilliance

of teaching can be perverted into its opposite, namely, the inactivity of the learners. Thus, we judge teaching in this project primarily from the aspect of the hypothesized mental activity of students—the amount, quality, and effectiveness of their operations.

Such a focus on the autonomy of students' learning leads to certain kinds of insecurity on the part of not only the teachers but also the teacher trainers. These teacher trainers must advocate activities for prospective teachers who will need to promote or make possible the mental actions or many inner operations of their eventual students. The emphasis on student activity and mental operations is only indirectly ascertainable through language and symbolic interaction. Teachers can hinder learners when, instead of making mental interaction and activity possible, they represent the factual as something objective. Children who believe that the mental world is something objective are misled.

The Path Metaphor

The connection between teaching and learning can be viewed as a path with intersections and nodes. The nodes are groups of operation (operation units); the intersections are processes of relational activities. Each unit is followed by the next operation unit. The units are connected in a chain so that every link has a relational function. The time used and the quality of the learning context are influenced by the intensity of those processes.

If we accept that a teaching lesson, or more generally, a learning event has always been divided into operational units, then we imply also that this division has been done in such a way that content followed content with alternated different methods and different social forms. The concept of "method orchestration" (see Gage & Berliner, 1991) fits quite well into this image. This process is controlled by an inner plan of a learner. We illustrate this with the following analogy: On Saturday morning, one first goes to the department store where a list of items needs to be found; then one has an appointment with someone in the Café Gotthard where the election of a new colleague needs to be negotiated; the next stop is the newspaper stand where newspapers must be sought and bought, etc. These groups of activities have apparently little to do with one another, but they are connected to each other within the context of "Saturday morning" activities. The Saturday morning is the background for a form of occupation that we can refer to as "the time period for expediting a list." The hidden plan in it is quieted by different needs and priorities.

If we would view learning as nothing more than a content-content sequence or an alternation between method and social form, this view would, precisely, not be enough. We are looking to the hidden plan underlying the intentionality. This intentionality is determined by the way in which learning occurs. For that reason, we call it a "basis–model" of learning. Each activity—executing a list, building a friendship, acquiring knowledge, moving to a higher level of development, experiencing and storing an episode, etc.—is a different form of learning and requires a different chain of operations.

Learning paths vary as the intentionality and contextuality influence the basis–models. To drive on the freeway, climb a mountain, or step into a cathedral are very different activities.

Each of them has its own intentionality and contextuality that determine the type of movement.

We can also use the metaphor of a street or path to express the success or failure of learning processes. In this sense, learning can be seen as a voyage and teaching as the means to create a world in which children or other learners can be operational, follow this path, and make up their own stories that lead to permanent enrichment or loss. But why are the phases and paths of a process so seldom identified and described in depth? Why is success or failure seldom diagnosed in terms of process, so that the tracks can be switched early, the obstacles avoided, or the route changed?

We must especially keep the stations, or the large interchanges in a learning process, in view. No one can understand sequences without understanding the linkage of the large nodes. We must look for the expressive–constructivist representation of scenes that are successively and meaningfully illuminated and brought alive by teachers and learners together and that are experienced as life. And what, then, appears?

Schemata related to how teachers repeatedly reconstruct lessons are sequences that, in the end, become crystallized. They can be described as cognitive professional plans that form generations of children in their impressions and motivational inclinations or disinclinations to learn. These plans are necessary but must be flexible and adjusted to fit different clusters of operational chains, contents, contexts, and goals. Their flexibility has to last, so that they can be influenced and even directed by the thinking and perceptions of the children, or they can be directed entirely by the obligation of the teachers toward the content or by something else. From a normative point of view, the demands to "properly" create the sequences are appropriate because splintered sequences without correction leave a world of splintered knowledge behind. Our children are full of this splintered knowledge. They spend a lot of time on dysfunctional self-correction and too little time on the functional correction of mistakes. Some even drop out and do not follow the path any longer. Others become depressed because they cannot experience success. We would like to state that without a minimal path structure, learning is chaotic and leads to self-deception instead of self-efficacy. But which form does this minimal structure have?

The Critical Point in a Conflict: Freedom of Method versus the Law of the Learning Sequence

A new monument resides in the didactic hall of fame: the freedom of method concept. Basically, it is the belief that teachers should have the freedom to choose the method, the social form, the media, and the situation or content determinants that, in their opinion, lead to an intended goal. A professional–political criterion, thus, has been established with potentially disastrous consequences. One consequence is that the theoretical models for teaching methodology all have become fuzzy theories with no action-driving character. Klafki's model of didactic analysis, for example, has, as mentioned, five dimensions: (a) current meaning of content; (b) future meaning of content; (c) fundamental structure of content; (d) illustrative meaning; and (e) accessibility, or, respectively, typical phenomena or cases (Klafki, 1963). Because his model cannot ensure that an empirical crite-

rion can be given to fulfill its normative requirements. Professionals will never be unanimous about what is most exemplary about a given historical epoch, and the spirit alone will not be satisfied by key questions (Klafki, 1991). Something similar can be said for the structure-grid model from the Berliner School (Heimann, 1962; Heimann, Otto, & Schulz, 1965). The famous topology of Heimann and his colleagues of the Berliner School consisting of two fields of conditions (anthropogenic and social–cultural prerequisites), four fields of decision making (intention, theme, method, and media), and two fields of effects (individual and social), contributes nothing to empirical quality assurance. It merely says something about the rationality of decision making and the phenomenology of a flexible system. What evolves receives no intentional qualitative character.

Professional postulates for the freedom of teaching not only refuse these normative models but also lead further to the refusal to accept nomothetical assumptions about learning processes. Becker (1984), for instance, in his book *Planung von Unterricht* (Teaching Preparation), says that the assumption that teaching can occur following a schema is a false one (p. 171). According to his logic, the diversity of existing articulation schemata already suggests the questionable nature of this assumption. He states: "It is to be shown that there is no schema and should not be a schema that can be made obligatory" (p. 17). Instead, depending on the learning requirements, the amount of time available, and the content, teaching sequences should be conceived of individually.

Not accepting nomothetical assumptions about the learning processes leads to an additional effect, namely, the rejection of traditional expert knowledge without a proposed alternative. The professional knowledge that is gathered by teachers through experience is not worthless; rather, it must be observed and analyzed under a scientific aspect. Because every teaching–learning situation is, in fact, unique, the exaggerated professional constructivism postulated here should not be allowed simply to wash away time-tested systems without proposing alternatives.

But the actual core point of the conflict follows: Unnoticed by these freely available didactic models, educational psychology that has always been able to describe learning processes much more exactly—even when based on older learning theories—is completely neglected, and—at least partially—teaching–learning–processes are being analyzed in terms of a nomothetic viewpoint. By using cognitive experimental prerequisites and operational sequences that are based on Piaget's work, we could easily look at the mental activities of the learner in a new way. Developmental psychology has made important contributions to the understanding of mental processes in learning through the work that has been done in the areas of cognition, morals, language, emotions, the psychology of memory using storage models, communication theories (as far as they have an empirical basis), theories of thinking that are based on computer simulations, the expectations-values theories, and others. In fact, from the point of view of these empirically based theories, learning cannot be left to the discretion of teachers in the name of professional freedom. When looking at the mental processes of children, flexible rules of the mental construction process should be kept. One cannot, for example, construct concepts in hundreds of ways because only a limited number of these constructions promise success.

At first sight, then, an immense drama seems to be developing: The teacher has the right, on one side, to structure his or her lesson however he or she wants, and, on the other side, he or she must stay within the limits of rule-based learning. How can this hiatus be overcome? Is one or the other to be emphasized? Is teaching free, or is it constrained? We would like to try to formulate answers to these questions through our theory of the choreographies of teaching.

The Core Theory: Choreographies of Teaching–Learning Processes

Our hypothesis is that every sequence of (school) learning is based on a choreography that binds, on the one side, freedom of method, choice of social form, and situated improvisation with, on the other side, the relative rigor of the steps that are absolutely necessary in inner learning activity. Such a hypothesis requires a double operationalization: (a) from the viewpoint of the relationship between the basis–models and the visible structure and (b) from the viewpoint of, on the one hand, the rule-bound character already referred to and, on the other hand, the freedom to stimulate.

To undertake this operationalization, one needs to first explain the concept of choreography. A choreography is a series of dance steps that simultaneously fulfills two sorts of demands. On the one hand, the dancer can freely create within the space available to him or her and expressively show a whole palette of artistry. On the other hand, the dancer is constrained by the structures of the rhythm, the metric structure, and the deep form of the musical sequence. The same is valid for the choreographer. The dancer must be able to connect freedom and constraints to achieve the expression that he or she wishes. Both are implied in the lovely title of Nathaniel Gage's (1978) book, *Teaching—Art or Science?*

A similar choreography can be found in significant learning processes, for example, when a mother shows her 2-year-old daughter how to tie a shoe, when a teacher demonstrates a chemical experiment to a group, when a master gardener shows an apprentice the proper way to set a walnut tree, or when the leader of an adult education group stimulates the participants to reflect on their own practice. In each of these situations, a visible row of actions can be identified (the visible structure that we mentioned above). At the same time, we must assume that all of these visible sequences are underpinned by a rule-based concatenation, or a linkage of learning steps or learning elements (the basis–models). In the above-mentioned situations, the learners must first imagine a sequence of acts irrespective of the visible structure of the teaching (discussing, telling, offering, demonstrating, etc.) and then ascertain the appropriateness of their sequences in hindsight. Such sequences—preconceiving actions, subsequently evaluating them, and then repeatedly practicing them—are the types of operations to be defined. They are not visible and can be implied based on only the visible structure, but they can be described as mental movements.

To recapitulate, the visible structure is the free part of the choreography—the flexible, the exchangeable, the part that is continually newly adapted by and for learners. It includes meth-ods, social forms, context, representations, teaching styles, learning styles, function rhythms, media, control forms, and so forth. The visible structure represents the free and freely structurable moment in learning.

In contrast, the basis–model consists of those concatenations of operations or operation groups that are somehow necessary for every learner and that cannot be replaced by anything else. The complete character of these chains is determined (a) through rules from the psychology of learning, on the one hand, and (b) through the type of goal, on the other hand—both belonging together. If we look at a unit of teaching, we can easily describe how students, for example, first look at a picture, then process the characteristics of an object in groups, then make notes about a short lecture, and finally, discuss a short text in pairs. This structure is the visible or sight structure of a lesson and can be done by any teacher.

The basis structure, conversely, is not visible at first look. It must be hypothetically inferred or requested from the learner. Probably, in this case, it has to do with concept building and, thus, with a relatively commonly used basis–model that has the following linking elements:

1. Direct or indirect consciousness of an already acquired knowledge structure
2. Elaboration of a prototypical example
3. Representation of one or more new criteria that are not in the old knowledge structure but that appear in the prototype (propositional elements)
4. Incorporation of the new elements through activities such as comparing, relating, including, separating, etc.
5. Creation of an optimal coordination within the new knowledge structure by using the new knowledge in another context (testing for the efficacy or transfer, analyzing and synthesizing similar knowledge structures, etc.

The visible structure of this simple learning process is easier to describe than the basis-model and, at the same time, is dependent on many situative, personal, social, or content variables. The basis structure—which will be described as knowledge construction in more detail below—that underpins the visible structure, however, is much more abstract and, at the same time, has a more definitive and unchangeable form. It is constructed in such a way that, in general, no single element can be left out. Its origin or appropriate concatenation is quasi-nomothetically anchored. Figure 46.1 shows the relationship between two visible structures and one and the same basis–model. The visible structure presented by the first teacher is completely different from that of the second. The first teacher begins with an elaboration, moves on to a presentation, and then stimulates individual work, at which point the cycle repeats itself: elaboration and individual work. The second teacher begins with group work, splitting the class into two sections whereby half of the class does pair work and the other half works with her in a group discussion, and then proceeds with lesson development, selection, individual work, and, finally, lesson development again. Both teachers proceed completely differently, have different conditions, but implicitly follow the same basis–model of learning, namely, "knowledge construction."

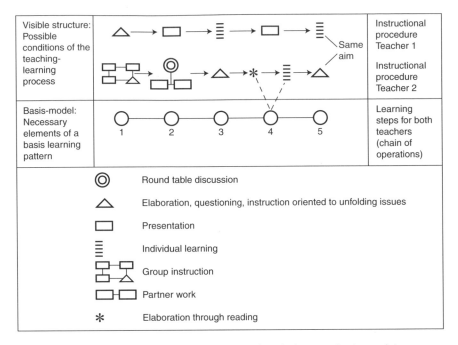

Figure 46.1. Visible structure of two teachers (teaching–learning process) with the same basis–model.

Diverse approaches, thus, can lead to the same linkage of operations, operations groups, or both. In fact, from the view point of a constructivist learning psychology, they must lead to the same operations linkage. Conversely, the elements of a basis–model function as an undercover steering mechanism for teaching. Visible structures should be examined to ensure that they lead to the students' carrying out of certain operations. Now it is easier to understand why we said that the view must always be directed toward the child. This statement is not a romantic statement; rather, it is a demand, a challenge, to verify that teaching actions have a form that stimulates the mental operations appropriate for a learning goal. Teaching, thus, becomes a condition for the possibility of necessary, rule-bound mental activity on the part of a student. Without such mental activity, thought is not possible. The ways that students assimilate and accommodate are not determined simply by assignments to be completed; rather, they have a process–character that corresponds to a certain form of learning or basis–model.

The complementary relationship between visible structure and basis–model has been neither accepted nor researched in the literature up to the present. For instance, recent literature on instructional designs presents arranged summaries of possible articulation schemata (e.g., Mandl & Reinmann-Rothmeier, 1995; Mayer, 1988) or synthesis of learning strategies and visible structures (e.g., Gunter, Estes, & Hasbrouck Schwab, 1990; Nold & Schnaitmann, 1995). One also finds all types of learning strategies researched in terms of their effect (e.g., Friedrich, 1995; Krapp, 1993; Weinstein & Mayer, 1986). But it is exactly this complementary relationship that guarantees the professional freedom to structure teaching and learning as well as the constraints made by the construction of inner cognitive structures. On the one hand, we have the possibility of setting conditions that present an immeasurable diversity; on the other

hand, we make assumptions about how thought could possibly be an "ordered activity" (Aebli, 1980, 1981) so that, exactly through these conditions, the rule-bound quality becomes visible.

The Basis–Model as a Learning Script: Determining Criteria

The linking of mental actions (operations) leads to the question of their guiding principle. To talk about concatenations of operations in abstract is not enough. Patterns of constructions need to be found. Such patterns are special learning scripts. Basis–models, thus, are learning scripts with a more or less high degree of familiarity, which indicates that the linkage is not simply invented but, rather, follows a pedagogical and psychological tradition. Learning scripts as concatenations of operations can be viewed in two ways. They can be described as phenomena (e.g., when children construct a concept, and they proceed in a particular way), or one can ask how teachers and children subjectively imagine such scripts. Both approaches complement each other.

To determine a basis–model and to describe a theoretical concept, we must consider five criteria. We list them here:

1. One or more fundamental theories in psychology need to be assumed for a basis–model. For example
   - Development as an aim of education—Discontinuity approach
   - Concept building—Schema theory
   - Hypertext—Informational network theory
   - Problem solving—Problem-solving theories

- Routine learning—Theories of memory
- Experiential learning—Theories of episodic memory or situated learning theory
- Negotiation as learning—The "Gulliver" theory

2. A transformation model is needed. It must be possible to theoretically explain how changes take place. This explanation might seem easy at first in the case of concept building and knowledge construction, but it is more complicated, for example, in the case of a developmental model or a motility model (see below).

3. The possibility of illustration must follow. It must be possible and plausible to give examples of concrete teaching events and to describe them in a simple way. These examples have prototypical character.

4. It must be possible to formulate an operative order so that a microanalysis of teaching is unnecessary but, at the same time, a generalization to all basis–models is impossible. This middle-level formulation is determined by the visible structure, namely, by the chosen and determined divisions of the lesson.

5. The operative order must be empirically proven. This requirement is necessary but not sufficient by itself for what determines a basis–model.

THE LIMITED NUMBER OF POSSIBLE BASIS–MODELS

Various basis–models differ in their learning goals, the types of elements in the chain, and the way in which those elements are linked (see Table 46.1). As a learning script, every basis–model is a sort of "mother structure" (compare Piaget, 1970). In other words, as a type, it cannot—without reasons—be mixed with another type and cannot refer to another type. The creation of these basis–models is not unequivocal. In psychology, they grew out of experimental givens (e.g., research in motivation). In contrast, the tradition of didactics retains more intuitive ideas about process or expert recommendations, such as the problem-solving model from John Dewey. Certain basic assumptions hold for all basis–models independently of the individual concatenations of central elements. These are (a) the inner activity of the learner; (b) the disequilibrium process as a necessary requirement for learning (motivational, social atmospheric, and emotional conditions belong here); and (c) the subject's achievement in linking the elements. All three basic assumptions are included a priori in every basis–model and are conditions for the realization of a learning script.

Table 46.1 shows an overview of the basis–models with the respective learning goal, an especially outstanding characteristic, and an indication of the visible structure associated for each. The models are described in more detail and with examples later on. The order of the presentation in Table 46.1 has no meaning. A possible affinity between one or another basis–model is given here and there (i.e., possible grouping) but they have not been further examined.

Table 46.1 also makes clear that different basis–models aim for different types of goals. Someone who is capable of solving a mathematical problem or someone who follows through with a change in attitude by developing toward a higher stage change in structure (e.g., judges from a higher level of moral development) do not represent the same abilities, the same kind of process, the same type of goal, or the same kind of content necessity. Knowing how to get along with my friend or arranging information in a network of knowledge units are fundamentally different activities whose completion demands different basis–models and, with that, different chains of operational groups.

Instead of speaking in terms of learning paths, we can also speak of visualizations of processes in which concatenations of elements are represented and in which each element has a clear determinant. In other words, the procedural knowledge of teaching grows out of the teaching subject's act of decomposing the elements of a serial operating system. This view leans somewhat toward the subjective theories of teaching procedures and not so much toward the traditions of learning psychology. It can help teachers sharpen their knowledge about learning scripts. At the same time, expert teachers can contribute immensely to deepening our current knowledge about learning scripts.

This section of the chapter has limited itself to a consideration of basis–models. It should, however, be asked, on the one hand, whether this representation is complete and, on the other hand, whether the scripts presented here are, in fact, orthogonally separated from one another. Both questions are to be empirically tested continually. Until now, the proposition has not been disproved that the number of basis–models is limited and that the orthogonality can be proved through certain characteristics.

WHAT HOLDS THE CHAIN OF THE BASIS–MODEL TOGETHER OR WHY INDIVIDUAL ELEMENTS OF OPERATION CHUNKS CANNOT BE EXCHANGED

The basis–model system is held together by (a) the reference of successive elements to their predecessor, (b) the temporal focus on a single element (instantiation), and (c) the teleological determination of the type of goal. Although only local variables are important for a single realization, these variables are actually directed by global variables, or at least, that is our hypothesis. A more or less complete inner picture of a learning sequence can be made only insofar as the basis–model can be recognized by an expert and carried over into a visible structure. Inner images have the power to initiate, remain viable, and direct processes.

The chain of absolutely necessary steps in a basis–model consist of the sequenced elements that cannot be bypassed. The strength of the linkage between elements must be empirically determined for each individual model. It is possible that the position of an element in the chain is less clear, but an element cannot be left out. It is also possible that the sequence of a basis–model (e.g., knowledge construction) can be temporarily combined with another sequence. Similarly, many learning processes with deep structures are hypothetically difficult to determine because the visible structure is confusing. Even if this is the case, the connection of elements is bound to the logic of the concatenation of operation groups (the elements) in a basis–model. This logic is determined by the teleology of the goal type. For example, how to automate a complex formula (Basis–Model 7) cannot be learned through problem solving (Basis–Model 3), or one cannot play a guided tour in a hypertext system (Basis–Model 11) by using experiential learning in a field

Table 46.1 Overview of Teaching Basis–Models

Basis–Model	Type of Learning Goal	Special Characteristic	Example of Visible Structure
1a. Learning through personal experience	Appropriating experiential knowledge	Direct relationship to everyday life	Work in a social or production environment
1b. Discovery learning	Appropriation through reality search processes; generative learning	Authentic situatedness	"Re-"discovery of a light bulb; "re-" discovery of a mathematical proof
2. Development as an aim of education	Deep structure transformation (e.g., moral judgment)	Disequilibration process	Controversial issue discussion; dilemma discussion
3. Problem solving	Trial and error learning	Hypothesis testing	Tower of Hanoi problem
4a. Knowledge building (learning of word meaning)	Explaining an object; understanding the meaning of a word	Criteria describing a notion or a fact; combination or hierarchy of such criteria	Foreign-language course; presentation of new facts; questioning with processing phases
4b. Concept building	Constructing a knowledge network	Analysis and synthesis of complex theories	Development of critical–historical thinking by working with the concept of Democracy; understanding a mathematical function
5. Contemplative learning	Reflexive abstraction	Contemplation of ontological, fatalistic, religious, or other realities	Relaxation exercises, suggestopedy, neurolinguistic behavior, meditation; development of metaphoric and symbolic language
6. Use of learning strategies	Learning to learn (meta-learning)	Use of a formally fixed scaffold to make learning easier; reflection on own learning	Strategies for working with texts, for rehearsal, for memorization, for time management
7. Development of routines and skills	Automatization	High frequency of practice and repetition; process of freeing the mind for other complex operations	Learning to drive, to recite the multiplication table, to play a piece of music by memory
8. Learning through motility	Transformation of affective states into creative production	Creative work from personal experiences; musical expressivity	Drawing; playing a musical instrument; writing poetry; dancing, etc.
9a. Social learning	Development of the ability to relate to someone through social behavior, social exchange	Prosocial actions, group experiences, discourse behavior, etc.	Cooperative learning; partner learning; helping; development of friendship
9b. Learning through realistic discourses	Conflict resolution, need balance	Round tables: elaboration of consensus or live dissension	Community approval
10. Construction of values and value identity	Value clarification, value development, critical value analysis	Value hierarchy; shared values; community identity; school culture	Value analysis and comparison of students in the class; active participation in school life
11. Hypertext learning	Reordering and revaluing of information bits	Random surfing on Internet or CD-ROMs; "guided tours"	Reading on-line newspapers; analyzing a piece of music on a CD-ROM
12. Learning to negotiate	Producing consensus in various situations	Negotiation as the coordination of needs or as a technique for producing agreement	Economical and legal negotiation exercises; negotiation of collective or shared norms

trip (Basis–Model 1). The teleology of the goal type corresponds to the logic of a sequence of steps that stimulates the shortest and most efficient operation.

The succession of elements can be compared to the famous restaurant script (Schank & Abelson, 1977). The four steps of the restaurant schema are (a) arrival (going to the restaurant, deciding where to sit, etc.); (b) ordering (reading the menu, ordering wine, etc.); (c) eating (being served, eating, talking, etc.); and (d) departure (paying the bill, leaving a tip, leaving the restaurant, etc.). No one orders after they have eaten, few people pay before they have eaten unless in a self-service restaurant (in which case a different script is in play), and no one leaves a restaurant before they have arrived.

The research of Bower, Black, and Turner (1979) showed that experimental subjects frequently arranged the actions of going to the restaurant in the same way. But the comparison here is not perfect because the restaurant script represents a visible structure sequence. Nevertheless, basis–models, which we have called learning scripts, function in a similar way. Their inner logic is a sequence in which one element is a prerequisite for understanding the following element, which, in turn, provides the basis for understanding the next element. But this connection is only a simplified formulation of a very complicated relationship. The logic of the concatenation of the elements of a basis–model is structured differently for every type of learning. It is different for the concept "development as an aim of education" (Basis–Model 2) and different for "knowledge construction" (Basis–Model 4) and, again, different for "problem solving" (Basis–Model 3). In the first instance, an a priori principle has priority; in the second, an additive principle is at work; and in the third, a concatenation principle (in which the fulfillment of one element consequently leads to the next) is needed. Basis–models have a history and a history of their effects. As traditional ways of dealing with diverse learning, they are accumulated experience that require different kinds of tests.

REFERENCE AND BASIS–MODELS

Teachers have ideas concerning the way teaching–learning processes proceed that they usually carry with them in an unarticulated form. If they are confronted with a segment of their own teaching and asked to say something about it, they talk about intentions that are implicitly present but not usually announced or noted. Depending on the amount of reflection that the teacher does about inner activity and the corresponding interlinking of these activities by the learner, this reference approaches the basis–model. For example, a teacher organizes work groups to solve a geometry problem together. When the sequence is replayed for the teacher, the teacher is asked to make reflective recall. Responses are

1. I wanted to let the students do group work there.
2. I wanted to let the students do group work there for a change of pace.
3. I wanted to let the students do group work so that students could learn socially.
4. I wanted the students to cooperatively (i.e., reflectively) practice something that I had demonstrated to them and to correct each other. The task was this: Two straight lines . . .

The statements have been ordered so that they gradually reflect an operation as it would be presented in the element of a basis–model. Statements 1 and 2 are at the level of the visible structure. Statement 3 is a hybrid between visible structure and basis–model. Statement 4 is an incomplete statement at the level of the basis–model; it is incomplete because the linkage is not mentioned.

It should be clear from what has been said that the reference is variously specific and variously strong in intention[1] depending on how the teacher attempts to understand what is going through the mind of the child, on the one hand, and attempts to create the optimal conditions (sight structure) for certain operations to take place in the child's mind, on the other hand. Both specification and intentionality are viewed in pedagogical terms here; the former is in the sense of professional constructive attention, the latter in the sense of the intention to understand that certain processes take place.

Similarly, a professional hierarchy of values is implicit in the above statements. The more the mental operations of children are thought about, hypothesized, and discussed, the better the

possibility to produce actually optimal conditions for learning processes. The visible structures, thus, carry an increased mediating function. They are used because their contextual givens, which are established out of experience, guarantee the probability that this form of operation occurs in the child. Some of our analysis of teaching processes must also be understood in the same way.

What happens, however, when one is knowledgeable about basis–models and then analyzes one's own teaching step by step? Here we discover a unique phenomenon: Teachers cannot let go of the linked elements in the basis–model, and any reference to these elements is specific only in that it seeks to approach an ideal model (basis–model). In a first interview excerpt, two teachers who had been initiated into the basis–model and could articulate a higher awareness of learning steps said critically,

Teacher A (57)
Yeah, I've benefited to the extent that I, when I became aware of the basis–models in intervention training, very often leave out or skip certain parts of a lesson that I assumed were correct according to the basis–model (at the moment I won't question them) because of time constraints and that perhaps I got fewer of the desired results than I could have if I would have used the basis–model for the students. Then I ignore certain of the students' behaviors for whatever reasons. And maybe that I structure more consciously.

Teacher B (58)
Yeah, me too. I'm a lot more conscious of certain things now that have to do with teaching procedures. And, it would also be important that students make comparisons, that perhaps links are made to the present, the connection to reality or the link to the familiar.

I'm a lot more conscious of that now when I work according to the basis–models. And I have wondered what students think when I do this or that. Somehow I'm more aware that I've thought about my teaching. That's helped me quite a bit. And above all, the comparison now with my lesson, the second lesson. In the second lesson I even dared to try to create an even closer connection to reality, make a bridge, from one historical theme to something that is happening here or now.

A third teacher (96) also speaks of the security that the basis–model has given her. She says, in regard to a lesson,

And there I noticed, for example, that the students were insecure last Friday. They came and said, yeah, what do you want. And I imagined that there would be quite a bit to achieve. So when, for example, a student would automatically think about why he just got something or whether something fits? When he would automatically do that, then the student awareness during the lesson would surely be much more active. And sometimes I have the feeling that these young teachers go and simply let things take their course, they do that for some reason that I don't understand.

Basis–models are the backbone of freely structured activities at the level of the visible structure. They are what make the purpose of an activity relevant to actions and learning. Reference,

---

[1] These two determinants are used by Norman and Rumelhart (1975, p. 78 ff.) more in the sense of understanding language. *Specific reference* means that the speaker has a particular word in mind. *Intentionality,* however, refers to when a general statement is made.

thus, means a legitimization of all kinds of arrangements of optimally thought-out student learning processes.

Teachers have varying referential awareness. They can do many things without making a clear connection to the mental operations that their actions will cause in the students. School can be entertaining when a high level of stimulation is coupled with a low level of effort; then, an operation can float in completely uncontrolled. What is represented in the statements of the teachers above has another reference, namely, that an awareness of the effect of a visible structure on the inner activity of students is present. Reference means that student reflection is stimulated through the visible structure.

In general, the task of the visible structure does not receive enough attention and is generally achieved only by expert teachers. In fact, when teachers are asked, for example, what a high ethos means, they often answer, "when I take responsibility," "when I'm very involved," "when I respect children," etc. The answer is seldom "when I can inspire my students to take responsibility," "when I can inspire them to be very involved, to respect others," etc. This last statement implies a much more difficult task than the first because it demands close reflection of the conditions needed for concrete learning activities to take place in children. Research by Janssen (1987, p. 14) has shown a similar phenomenon: Novice teachers spend approximately 50% of their time thinking about the content, 45% on their own behavior and image, and only 5% thinking about the students and their learning processes.

BE AWARE OF VISIBLE STRUCTURES!

Visible structures are dependent on current tastes and vary depending on the teaching experience and the teacher's personality. A creative ordering of visible structures without guaranteeing the possibility of basis–model sequences is like didactic theater. Learning and learning sequences are not the focus, instruction is. The choice and the effect of visible structures can be measured or tested only by the hypothesized student operations and how they are linked. It can happen that the variability of the visible structure and the orchestration of the methods are minimal because the teacher is not oriented to the methodology, and yet, important learning processes take place. Instead, the teacher is concentrating on the learning sequences and the self-efficacy confidence of the learner that occurs when these sequences can take place. Such a teacher shows a high degree of reference.

Educational researchers who observe and analyze school classes in countries where schools are lacking are astonished to find that, with a small degree of variability in visible structures and a high level of motivation, the central learning sequences of various basis–models can be applied. While visiting a village in Calabria, Italy, the first author visited a class with 40–50 students. I was sitting at the back of the classroom, observing the lesson. The teacher presented a student to the class who then posed biology questions to her classmates for an hour. The classmates in return questioned the student. I was shocked. How can one allow a student to be exposed in this way? During the second class period the same activity went on, only this time, I sat at the front of the classroom. And there I realized in astonishment that the students were eagerly participating in this question-and-answer activity with great concentration. During the third period, I realized that the basis–model "creating a routine" underpinned the schema that the teacher was using. First, a theme was presented, then repetitive answers were given, and finally, an overview of the whole theme was given by quizzing the steps of the pattern. There are simple, serious visible structure processes that make it possible to link learning sequences and, thereby, to experience successful learning. Contrarily, there are didactographic methods that do not always allow learning and can become almost a sort of pedagogical kitsch: narrative teaching, learning as playing, programmed teaching, communicative didactics, iconographic didactics, etc.

The idea of multidimensional teaching–learning arrangements has been popular recently (Achtenhagen, 1994; Achtenhagen & John, 1992). These arrangements refer to relationships between outer stimulation and inner processes of change. They can be complex, and they can overlap. But it is exactly the process of change in the learner that receives the least attention, especially, as the split between didactics and educational psychology increasingly widens (Treiber & Weinert, 1982, p. 10).

Visible structures can, in fact, create didactic confusion when they do not refer to the basis–model. When things are done because they are more attractive and not because they stimulate a relatively invariable element of the concatenation in a basis–model, students end up doing a lot of activity that is superficial and inconsequential for their own mental life. In an extreme case, even attractive content can erode the basis–model and leave only a trace of true learning processes.

The theory of the basis–model appears to be fruitful also because it makes it possible—and this possibility has been shown by a number of case studies—to direct teacher attention from themselves toward the inner processes of the learners, namely, the basis–model. This concept has been expressed by Fuller and Brown (1975) as "concern for the child" versus "concern for the content," or concern for the teacher. The basis–model theory provides a concrete, pedagogical psychological form for the first time: *The basis–models are hypotheses about the learning processes of children that we stimulate or encourage with visible structures.*

WHEN THE BASIS–MODEL DETERMINES THE VISIBLE STRUCTURE (BRIDGING INSTRUCTION TO LEARNING)

People who are engaged in teacher education continually make us believe that they have more faith in the visible structure than in the basis–models. It is the visible and, thus, provable that teachers feel they can directly show and perceive. This visible structure is where the decisions that are made and the actions that are taken can be perceived, corrected, and evaluated. In addition, it is often doubtful that the elements of the basis–model can even be shown, that they—as previously mentioned—can be only hypothetically discovered or inferred on the basis of the students' behavior.

But how, from an upside-down standpoint, does the basis–model influence the visible structure? Our assumption is that, in an ideal case, the elements of the basis–model influence the visible structure and not the converse. The visible structure is formed, interpreted, and connected by the basis structure elements. For example, teachers can reason that, by showing this or that film, they present students with a prototype for analyzing new elements of a concept. The question of the relationship between the basis–model and the visible structure is, thus, not just a question of high referentiality. The visible structure does not simply serve the child's operations; rather, the basis–model offers an answer to the question, Why is a certain visible structure phase useful for an instance of learning? The answer is because this or that element of a basis–model or, respectively, this or that operation is made possible. We can sharpen this fact: From the viewpoint of the visible structure, it is impossible to justify a certain form of work (e.g., individual learning, underlining certain words in a text, or discussing a conflict at a level above the classroom) that is purely based on the teaching–learning aspect. The basis–model is the first to tell us why, from a pragmatic point of view, these stimulated actions are useful. The basis–models are called into service by the visible structures from the perspective of the richness and exchangeability of the actions that take place at the level of the visible structure. The expert's thinking originates a priori from the basis–model, not from the visible structure.

This phenomenon can have an unexpected result. Teachers, when they have been introduced to the basis–model theory, begin to direct their teaching more intensively than before. For example, a participant in our pilot study said, "With me, I feel like I'm more directive in my teaching now, and I don't really want that. It actually should be that you have the time to individually help students. But that didn't work in my lesson." This statement shows that the basis–model elements can give direction, but they can also have too strong of an effect on or even inhibit the visible structure. Naturally, this inhibition should be avoided. But the statement also shows that the basis–model elements can start a certain organizational order, that they can force a change in the visible structure and steer it in the direction of the required and hypothesized operations.

In this connection, we see clearly that some basis–models, depending on their character and concatenation, are accompanied by other social conditions. One could call this their microsocial character. For example, it is not necessary to have any extraordinary respect for individual students when a prototype is presented and followed by analytical work with the elements in the knowledge structure to be constructed. The normal, daily presupposition of respect and consideration are enough. However, the situation is completely different when personal problems are discussed at a round table discussion or when a Japanese poem is expressively read. Here, rules regarding protection and the intimacy of individual phases must hold. It must be made clear that very delicate things break when the artistic expression of a student is ridiculed. Every basis–model demands the framework for this type of social climate. For that reason, intervention is meaningful only in field conditions. Simply to recall individual elements of a basis–model chain would be an insufficient guarantee for their real-life application.

Here is also the place to make clear that basis–models are embedded in situatedness. A narrative or an interactive stimulation or a productive reality outside the school gives life to the instructional flow, and is, of course, motivational for processing the respective basis–models. An authentic and highly motivational situatedness is the best guarantee for the effectiveness of the basis–model. But here again, different situations refer to

different basis–models and vice versa. And again, the linearity of the learning process concerns neither the situatedness nor the visible structure but only the basis–model. Situatedness deepens the validity of the learning content.

The Combination of Basis–Models

If it is true that basis–models are professional scripts for increasing and assuring student activity, then the question of how they can be related to one another—in other words, intercalating, merging, connecting—is important. Such combinations can influence the effect of basis–models, in either a positive or negative sense, and can endanger or benefit the clarity of their structure. As soon as teachers achieve a certain confidence with the basis–models, they automatically want to use them in multiple or interrelated ways. The question is whether there are plausible reasons to allow certain combinations of basis–models to appear. Such reasons would prevent accidental combinations. The fruit of basis–model combinations, applied to an object, must show at least an increase in complexity or an explanation and reconstruction according to several types of goals. This last point is important because it establishes the legitimacy of the combination. One can easily imagine, for instance, that during a thorough treatment of the theme "European Democracy after World War 2" a teacher could engage several basis–models, such as concept development, hypertext learning, problem solving, and so on. The theme "Pythagorean hypothesis" could engage personal experience, concept building, and routine learning. In fact, an object can be connected to various types of goals, and various things can be learned in various ways from or through the activity. Curricula are often, in this sense, poor aids because they normally do not include information about learning procedures.

If we want to do more than string basis–models together, what are the possibilities? The most important is intercalating, the best reason for it being the ease of learning. By intercalating, we mean the following. Let us assume that the fourth element, working through and applying new schemata, is at work during concept building. A desirable goal would be to automate the functional determinants of the newly acquired concept. In this case, Basis–Model 7, establishing a routine, would be inserted after the fourth element of the work in Basis–Model 4b. The result is a sort of capsule implant (see Figure 46.2) where the first element of Basis–Model 7 occurs at the point in Basis–Model 4b where this step is already achieved by the fourth element. The necessity of inserting Basis–Model 7 into the structure of Basis–Model 4b is not the same as a union. It is the need to automate a concept to reduce mental effort. Formulas such as figuring the surface of a triangle, square, rectangle, or circle,

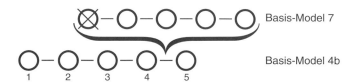

Figure 46.2. Insertion of one basis–model into the structure of another.

for example, have to be automated so that the mind is free to concentrate on carrying out other complex calculations without difficulty. Thus, the ways in which basis–models are intercalated is determined by convention and external criteria. The models are formulas for required achievement that are established by subject or culture specifics.

The reasons for the combinations are to be found, on the one hand, in these formulas and, on the other hand, in purposeful consideration of which basis–models to choose. The course of every basis–model remains intact for the most part. In our example, element five of Basis–Model 4b is made possible as soon as the establishment of a routine through Basis–Model 7 has been completed. The fact that the sequence of a basis–model cannot be broken when another model is inserted is important because it prevents the learner from becoming disoriented and makes it possible to return to the original concept after the automating procedure has occurred. Furthermore, element five makes it possible to integrate routine into a broader relationship with the knowledge structure.

We would like to present a second example of basis–model insertion. Let us assume that a teacher has formulated a very simple kind of problem that requires a square root calculation, a calculation with which the teacher knows the students are unfamiliar. For this reason, the students attempt to solve the problem with trial and error, hypothesis building, and testing but still do not solve it. Now the teacher introduces the concept of square root according to Basis–Model 4b. This action has the effect that the students have the prerequisites to search for a solution themselves (see Figure 46.3). Element five (or possibly further elements) of concept building is naturally no longer necessary because it has been covered by the whole problem-solving model.

Such insertions are meaningful because they are the conditions for enabling a solution of a given problem to be found, especially in this example. Through such an intercalation, a teacher becomes aware that the conditions must first be created and that he or she gives each child an equal opportunity to discover a solution for themselves by doing so.

Some further examples follow: (a) inserting Basis–Model 4b (concept building) into Basis–Model 7 (establishing routines) after element one; (b) building Basis–Model 2 (development as a aim of education) into Basis–Model 10 (value and identity construction) after element one; and (c) in the hypertext model (Basis–Model 11), building in the basis–model for problem solving after element four. All of these intercalations must take place for functional and goal-oriented reasons or to further understanding. They do not destroy the original model; rather, they require it in its complete form for the purpose of preparing, broadening, or deepening the learning process—the operation—in progress.

We have been examining the combination of basis–models and their intercalations. What about the possibility of exchanging the individual elements in a basis–model? If this exchange were possible, it would destroy the theory of the concatenation of necessary elements and, with that, the idea of a retrospective binding of the elemental steps in well-accepted models in the constructivistic psychology of learning. Bauch-Schremmer (1993) examined 52 teaching samples from all of the available teaching journals from the year 1992. She found that she could

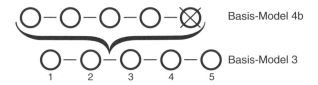

Figure 46.3. Insertion of Basis–Model 4b, "Concept Building," into Basis–Model 3, "Problem Solving."

easily deduce the underlying basis–models from the teaching designs. In addition to finding complete basis–models, she also found incomplete basis–models and many examples of individual elements from other basis–models in a primary basis–model. Clearly, besides an intercalating of complete basis–models, an individual element can benefit another basis–model by being left out or even multiplied. This finding, however, does not say anything about the validity of the theory of basis–models; it says only that the creators of the teaching designs did not have basis–models available to them. Often, they proceeded intuitively, thereby running the risk of endangering the very learning processes they were trying to stimulate. To make things more confusing, different basis–models can have individual elements that appear to be similar in their function. For instance, it is completely impossible to clone the element "first attempt" (element three) for Basis–Model 3 (problem solving) onto Basis–Model 2 (development as an aim of education) because that model has a completely different function. To do make that graft would create a sort of distorted body of common sense in terms of learning.

Now is the moment to look at such distortions. They are generally ascertainable when elements are connected to one another in such a way that the learning process is hindered or negatively influenced in reaching the learning goal. Hindering can take the form of interference when the previous element proactively or, in the case of the following element, retroactively disturbs its neighboring element. The vulnerability of individual basis–model elements depends on the validity of the concatenation and the level of logical necessity of individual elements within the chain. Dempster (1995) mentions that many irregularities in the results reached by developmental psychology research have to do with interference (p. 12 ff.). Also important, Dempster states that the neurosciences contribute to the detection of these irregularities (p. 18 ff.).

Recently, three theories have been developed to explain such interference: (a) the inefficient inhibition theory (Bjorklund & Harnishfeger, 1995) wherein the subject represses external stimuli that do not contribute to the thing in question; (b) the fuzzy trace theory (Reyna, 1995), which has to do with the differential meaning in the stating of propositions or ambiguous results; and (c) the resistance to interference theory (Dempster, 1990, 1992, 1995), which is based on the subject's inner resistance to a lack of logic when in working on a math problem, for instance, irregularities occur. These three theoretical approaches can be used with our basis–models only in an analogous way. One can easily imagine, for example, that students' mental stimulation drops quickly when a question–answer period (visible structure) or a study exercise at the basis structure level occurs following the buildup of tension in a motility model (Basis–Model 8) where restructuring and creative transformation should have occurred instead. Such an event destroys the tension.

Teachers have told us how they held student attention with a narrative event but then lost it because they did not dare to take the next step (analogous to the inefficient inhibition theory). The same thing happens when students are required to look up in a textbook what a certain disease means and how it progresses just when they are in the middle of taking care of a patient (analogous to the fuzzy trace theory). A third example is when students who can establish routines and memorize with no problem suddenly have to work on a new prototype (Basis–Model 4b, element two). They get lost because they have not concluded the old material and the new information is too dense. The result is that the repetitive process of memorization becomes difficult (analogous to the resistance to interference theory).

We now present the basis–models in a relatively dense form and short manner without giving all the necessary details. This presentation is, thus, a first attempt to structure the twelve chaining types of basis–models, always using a similar pathway: first, defining the form of learning and the respective transformation; second, adding the basis elements; and finally, giving some hints with respect to limits in the application of the model.

BASIS–MODELS 1A AND 1B: LEARNING THROUGH EXPERIENCE AND LEARNING THROUGH DISCOVERY

Experiential knowledge is bound to a specific context: Students take part in an archeological excavation, conduct a chemical experiment, reflect on the meaning of a Jewish memorial site, etc. Such experiences demand more than transferring well-structured knowledge. European reform pedagogy has stressed this aspect over a hundred years. To give an example, Wagenschein (1970), who emphasized experiential learning in the 1950s, had students recreate an experiment that a famous researcher had carried out (something like Edison's incandescent bulb, Chomsky's LAD-theory, or Caesar's bridge at Biberakte) repeatedly during the course of their school years. Chapter 11 of Dewey's *Democracy and Education* (1916/1944) develops the notion of the bodily presence of students in different contexts of learning. Bruner (1966) speaks of "enactive representations." In the situated cognition movement, such experiential knowledge refers to experiences in manifold contexts and in different interactional social settings (see, e.g., Greeno, 1989; Lave, 1991; Resnick, 1991; Rogoff, 1990). Lave (1991)used the notion of "legitimate peripheral participation," which means really being part of a life situation.

Such a variety of approaches makes it understandable that no uniform theory of learning through experience has been generated. Only pragmatic and existential philosophies have tried to establish a theory of learning through experience. What we know from these movements is, of course, the following:

1. Self-experienced knowledge is limited by context and, therefore, is not generalizable. In educational terms, the generalization of such knowledge is a special task that relates to textbooks, structured content, and the experiences of other people.

2. Experiential knowledge is unstructured and is not systematic.
3. Experiential knowledge is meaningful, stays longer, and is more active in the episodic long-term memory.
4. Experiential knowledge can almost only be reconstructed narratively, and because it is episodic, it strongly defines the personality of a learner.

A transformational model for this first learning concept involves mastering changed conditions in new situations by concrete action. For instance, when we do something, we learn more than only the specific act that we intended to learn. When we visit an ill person, we speak with him or her, we give comfort, we arrange the room, etc. As a result, we have both a holistic and episodic situated script of illness.

We spoke about choreographies of teaching earlier. Now we must think about the operational steps—the chain of related actions—that guide teaching when we involve students experientially. Remember that the teaching act has to be submitted to hypotheses about the learning phases we called basis–models. The elements in this case that must be absolutely ensured are the following:

1. Anticipation and planning of possible actions (to produce, to manipulate, to help, to transform, to collect, etc.); inner representations of such acts under the conditions of possible difficulties and constraints
2. Performance of such possible actions in respective contexts
3. Construction of meaning for the activity, first, through communicative interchange (i.e., the learner beginning to tell the story of his experience)
4. Generalization of the experience through analysis of common elements among various individual perceptions of events
5. Reflection of similar experiences found in the stories of others, in literature, in textbooks, etc.

This chain of actions constitutes Basis–Model 1, one first fundamental basis–model of possible choreographies. Each learner must face all of these five chunks of operations if he or she wants to learn through experience. The model has a moderate level of abstraction; no microactions or macroconceptions are required. Note that according to research, especially elements four and five are often left out by teachers. In element four, the detachment of experience from immediate emotions takes place. The generalization, thus, means the distancing of oneself from the particularity of an event. Element five is the entry into the systematic part of the learning process. When we abstract from our experience, we include knowledge from culture or science.

Basis–model 1a refers to goal-oriented learning in context. Note again that the instruction here refers to setting conditions so that students can follow the chain of operational nodes. One special form of experiential learning refers to the general human search on new ground, namely learning through discovery (Bruner, 1966/1971; Neber, 1973). We speak about Basis–Model 1b because here we also learn through high situatedness and unstructured surprising episodes. Wagenschein (1970), an important reform pedagogue and physics teacher, stated that every child should experience once in his or her life the difficulties of the rediscovery of a new theory, a new object, or a new functioning of some thing. This is, of course, only possible if a child experiences all the constraints, the hopeless errors, and the demotivating consequences of a false hypothesis. The basis–model elements in 1b are the same as in 1a, with the difference being that (a) the goal of a discovery process is clear from the beginning on; (b) there are many repetitions of the elements 1, 2, and 3; and (c) teachers found many similarities with Basis–Model 3, problem solving which makes sense only insofar as problem solving takes place in a real professional or societal field.

BASIS–MODEL 2: DEVELOPMENT AS THE AIM OF EDUCATION

The theory behind Basis–Model 2 is anchored in developmental psychology. It presupposes that the higher the level of development (i.e., of moral development, according to Kohlberg, 1981, 1984), the more autonomous, integrated, equilibrated, reversible, and complex a person's judgment will be. The theory requires (a) a discontinuity concept of development and (b) intervention studies that prove the possibility that stimulation through certain instructional techniques can move students to a higher stage of development. With reference in particular to findings in the fields of social development (Damon, 1977; Selman, 1980), moral development (Leming, 1981; Lockwood, 1978; Oser & Althof, 1992; Rest, 1979; Rest & Narvaez, 1994), religious development (Fowler, 1974; Oser & Gmünder, 1991), esthetic development (Parsons, 1987), and the development of cognitive abilities (e.g., Case, 1985), the aim of education is defined as helping students grow developmentally and, hence, improving their ability to construct their life phases according to societal expectations.

The following assumptions underpin this goal-oriented education:

1. A well equilibrated, cognitive structure in one area becomes disequilibrated because of problems, dilemmas, or tasks that the person cannot solve immediately.
2. Through this disequilibration, the old structure dissolves, and new elements of a yet unknown structure become visible.
3. The new elements appear to be of high importance; they lead to a transformation or a dismantling of the old structure or the old elements, respectively.
4. The new elements are integrated into a new structure; all the old elements are reevaluated and reintegrated into the new structure, thereby receiving a new function.

Figure 46.4 Illustrates this transformational process. The question is how the process can be initiated and subsequently realized.

Here again, Basis–Model 2 helps us understand the hidden learning process in such a possible transformation. The elements are:

1. Confronting a conflict among social, political, moral, religious, etc., issues through dilemma presentation

2. Confronting the previous structure with controversial different positions within the dilemma
3. Being presented with and, subsequently, confronting arguments from the next higher stage (or 1/2 stage) through group work, dialogues, discussions, etc.
4. Analyzing different student arguments with respect to reversibility, role taking, differential, complexity, etc.
5. Reflecting on opinion change, value change, conceptional change, stage change, etc.

Basis–model 2 is different from all other basis–models. It is presented more precisely elsewhere (see Berkowitz, 1981; Kohlberg, 1984; Lickona, 1983). We believe that the chain of operational chunks is, again, absolutely necessary. None of the elements can be left out. Additionally, the type of goal here refers to the transformation of a basis cognitive stage structure, not to knowledge, episodic experience, or problem-solving capacity. This basis–model is also suitable for explaining the difference between teaching and learning or between the sight structure and the cognitive operational oriented basis–model: Each teacher frames the five elements outlined above completely differently on the level of sight structure. They use different dilemmas, different sorts of group work, different media, different forms of controversies, different analytical forms. But they always keep in mind that these settings and these methods need to be able to stimulate the respective chunk of operations. Our research shows that teachers often forget elements four and five and, thus, run the risk of an incomplete learning process.

BASIS MODEL 3: PROBLEM SOLVING

Traditionally, the operational steps of a problem-solving process are investigated in manifold ways (Mayer, 1992). Nevertheless, the difference between concept building and problem solving, experiential learning and problem solving, developmental transformation and problem solving was never clearly developed. Many researchers believe that problem solving is a kind of knowledge building, but in fact, this belief is false. In a problem-solving situation, we mostly know the solution, but we do not know how to reach it. Our mind is not yet flexible enough, and we need strategies and heuristics to reach what we can conceive.

The story of problem-solving pedagogy and problem-solving psychology is a long one and may be best represented by John Dewey's problem-solving phases that were developed in 1910 (Dewey, 1910). The notion of "trial and error" is one of its important elements. The "Gestaltpsychologists" investigated the holistic and associative aspects of problem solving; Wolfgang Köhler investigated the "insight" in problem form (Köhler, 1917/1963).

Recently, cognitive psychologists have occupied themselves intensively with theories of problem solving. Concerned with questions of algorithm and heuristics (Lüer, 1973; Newell & Simon, 1972; Polya, 1945; Simon & Reed, 1976; Steiner, 1966), they looked at questions such as (a) how novices and experts solve problems (Mayer, 1983; Tuma & Reif, 1980); (b) which previous knowledge of transformation of the problem is used to help means–aim analysis (Greeno, 1978); or (c) how one pro-

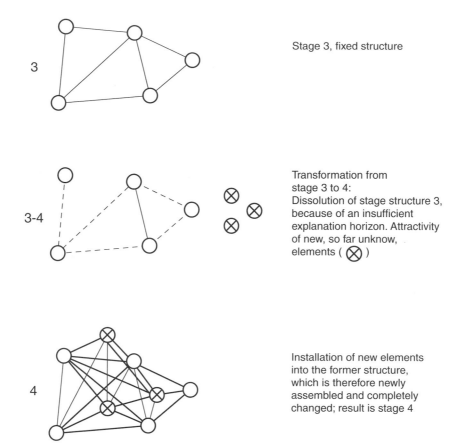

Stage 3, fixed structure

Transformation from stage 3 to 4: Dissolution of stage structure 3, because of an insufficient explanation horizon. Attractivity of new, so far unknow, elements (⊗)

Installation of new elements into the former structure, which is therefore newly assembled and completely changed; result is stage 4

Figure 46.4. Structural transformation of cognitive judgment structures.

ceeds depending on whether problems are structured poorly or well (Frederiksen, 1984; Simon, 1979). Equally, Dörner and his colleagues have studied how one sets priorities among complex political, ecological, or economical problems and have found that the solution process—directed here through stimulated tasks—often leads to catastrophic consequences (Dörner, 1989).

Finally, computer simulation studies (Wessells, 1984) have allowed exact testing of theories about subject's reactions in problem-solving situations. These studies lead to the question of how metacognitive consciousness contributes to the easing of hypotheses construction in problem-solving processes (King, 1995; Swanson, 1990). An example of practical problem solving is offered in the book *The Ideal Problem Solver* by Bransford, Stein, Delclos, and Littlefield (1986). They suggest an effective model to improve critical thinking, memory ability, and creativity in connection with problem solving. Such steps can also be found in Hayes (1984), Newell & Simon (1972), Polya (1945), Rubenstein (1975). The most extensive review of problem-solving knowledge is in Dorothy L. Gabel's *Handbook of Research on Science Teaching and Learning* (1994), which has six extensive chapters on the subject. These chapters make clear that problem solving on all levels and in whatever discipline—natural science, genetics, chemistry, physics—is always content-bound and specific.

Problem solving is an area that abounds with suggestions for

stepwise successions and algorithms within the framework of means–aim analysis in terms of problem area (ill-structured versus well-structured), problem types, and the involved activity (compare, e.g., Bransford et al., 1986; Dewey, 1910; Fenton, 1977; Lippitt, Fox, & Schaible, 1962; Polya, 1945).

From all these approaches, we tried to deduce a chain of absolutely necessary operational elements compared to other basis–models here. Surprisingly enough, teachers and, especially, expert teachers generally accepted the difference between sight structure and the problem-solving basis–model. They immediately felt that the sight structure could be changed but not the elements or sequence of operational activities. Thus, we developed the following elements:

1. Students perceive and understand the problem (problem presentation, the discovery of a problem, reformulation of the problem task).
2. Students develop hypotheses about possible ways to find a solution (heuristics, strategies).
3. Students test the hypotheses (gather indicators, gather data, search for direct or indirect solutions, test by trial and error).
4. Students evaluate and apply the solutions found (eventually redesigning element 2); they relate the solution to a broader understanding of learning.

This forward step succession is located, again, at a medium abstraction level of descriptive operations. We believe that these four elements are absolutely necessary, independent of whether the problem is well- or ill-structured, independent of which area of mathematics or natural science it corresponds to, independent also of whether the problem is simple or complex. The psychological basis of this "problem solving" scheme always includes an imbalance that leads to the creation of a problem area. These bases lead to applying other types of problems, perhaps, with the end point gone but, always, with a limited number of operations. Problem indetermination varies: indetermination of complexity, of goals, of possibilities, of solution, etc.

Interestingly, in the classroom, genuine problem-solving solutions seldom are applied. Solving a task simply by using a given rule is not a genuine problem-solving process, especially if it is only a repetitive exercise. Sternberg and Davidson (1982) discovered that experts are not necessarily better problem solvers than novices. Experts may try crystallized procedures that do not allow any procedural openness. By repeating tasks often, they become habitual and less open to alternative options. Learning independent of old patterns is, therefore, more difficult than learning something completely new because given structures must be dismantled to make room for new abilities.

Teachers find it difficult to accept that problem solving helps mobilize already acquired structures but does not automatically bring new concepts or new knowledge. When we know how to do something, we can use more effective hypothesis testing. But our content knowledge is not necessarily greater than before.

BASIS–MODELS 4A AND 4B: KNOWLEDGE BUILDING (LEARNING OF WORD MEANINGS) AND CONCEPT BUILDING

Most instructional activity is done to transfer knowledge, to build concepts (conceptual change) and to introduce learners to new word meanings. In one of our first pieces of research, we analyzed 180 lessons that were given by 90 teachers and found that approximately 71% of them served a knowledge-building goal. No textbook on educational psychology (e.g., Gage & Berliner, 1991; Sternberg, 1994) or general didactics (e.g., Aebli, 1983; Dubs, 1985) is without a chapter on this issue. The description and diagnosis of cognitive knowledge structures are central to what processes teachers have to prepare and what processes they use to stimulate learning.

In the 1980s, research was done on knowledge representation on the basis of propositional analysis, on schema–theoretical processes, and on production-oriented concepts. Propositional knowledge refers to how humans connect one argument with the other (e.g., Collins & Quillian, 1969; Kintsch, 1974, 1998; Norman & Rumelhart, 1975). Schema–theoretical analysis was interested in partial networks of knowledge that are hierarchically structured or that are based on frames or scripts (e.g., Anderson, 1976; Minsky, 1975; Schank & Abelson, 1977). The production-oriented models of knowledge representation were interested in how a person applies heuristics and strategies to build and recall knowledge chunks on a procedural basis (e.g., Anderson, 1983; Newell & Simon, 1972). In addition to this research, investigations in the field of language development give insight on how children develop meanings of words (see e.g., Clark, 1973).

This body of research has an astonishing normative significance for the instructional field. Teachers, indeed, need to have a clear concept of (a) how learners represent knowledge, (b) which form the preknowledge has, (c) how pupils build up and memorize knowledge, (d) which trajectories of knowledge acquisition are necessary, (e) how the architecture of the mind relates to the structure of scientific information, and (f) how situatedness influences knowledge representation.

By studying knowledge and concept building theories, we have developed a simple basis–model that includes two levels of complexity: The acquisition of simple word meanings falls under Basis–Model 4a, and complex concept building falls under Basis–Model 4b. Model 4a has the following form:

1. Direct or indirect stimulation of what the learners already know concerning the meaning of the new notion (preknowledge)
2. Introduction of the new meaning in connection with an example
3. Development of the characteristics that (a) describe and (b) contrast the new notion or word and its meaning
4. Active application of the new notion or word and its meaning
5. Application of the new notion or word and its meaning in other contexts (analysis and synthesis of similar words and their meanings)

The trajectory of the more complex concept building process is similar. We propose the following elements for Basis–Model 4b:

1. Direct or indirect stimulation of the awareness of what the learner already knows regarding the new concept
2. Introduction of and the working through of a prototype as a valid example of the new concept
3. Analysis of essential categories and principles that define the new concept (positive and negative distinctions)
4. Active dealing with the new concept (application, synthesis, and analysis)
5. Application of the new concept in different contexts (incorporation of different but similar concepts into a more complex knowledge system)

Each of these elements has—as in all the other basis–models—its own history of research. The first element, for instance, was already postulated by Ausubel, Novak, and Hanesian (1968), who spoke about positive effects of learning when the preknowledge is actualized (advance organizers). Element two, the effect of using prototypes, is especially postulated by Rosch (1975) and also by Smith and Medin (1981) with respect to language development, etc. Finally, in an effort to make the elements of this basis–model more comprehensible, an often used example may help.

Let us assume that a teacher must teach the concept "democracy." In element one, the teacher will gather what pupils know about democracy. In element two, the Greek example "Solon's legislation of 593 B.C." will be analyzed as a prototype. In element three, the connection to the prototype will be made by analyzing the criteria of what belongs to Solon's democracy and what does not. In element four, modern democracies will be investigated, and in element five, other forms of government (oligarchy, partial democracy, representative versus direct democracies) are—on the basis of philosophical and historical tests—illustrated and discussed.

As with all the basis–models, a teacher can use different methods, textbooks, social forms of learning, etc. as long as they are at the appropriate level; at the basis level, the teacher must adhere to all five basis nodes of operations. Our research shows, for example, that when teachers miss stimulating elements four and five, learners feel less secure (according to their own estimation) about the knowledge they learned than when teachers included the two elements.

In our attempt to bring conceptual coherence to the current state of the choreographies of teaching, we now, for the following eight basis–models, will shorten the presentation to (a) a brief introduction to the idea, (b) the basis elements, and (c) some remarks on educational consequences.

BASIS–MODEL 5: CONTEMPLATIVE LEARNING

Contemplative learning means inner, active participation in things such as cultural beauty or secrets of nature. This inner participation leads to the creation of meaning through social, aesthetic, ontological, or religious symbolization. To speak about contemplation is to ask, What is the goal of such an endeavor? Existential philosophers like Karl Jaspers talk about thinking as an existential enlightening that is reached by following an inner path and by reflecting on transitional situations such as death, life, love, or belief. At the sight structure, there are no limits to the form that meditation can have for contemplation to occur. The basis–model we propose here has the following operational elements:

1. Deconstruction (making oneself empty)
2. Description (touching, listening) of the immediate phenomenon (an art piece, an object in nature, etc.)
3. First interpretation (what is the meaning of this situation or experience for me?)
4. Second interpretation (what kind of symbol can this situation or experience become for mankind?)
5. Reflecting this trajectory in relationship to one's deep existence and contingency experiences

This model is a unique, operative basis–model because it has, as suggested, a certain special influence. In Europe, these meditation techniques are often used to motivate students, to make them receptive to learning, to calm down aggression, etc. In this sense, Howald (1989) states that more than 1,000 studies show the influence of such techniques with respect to states of consciousness such as arousal reduction (Shapiro, 1987) or blood pressure reduction (Wallace, Silver, Mills, Dillbeck, & Wagoner, 1983).

We mention this basis–model because (a) it contains a unique form of learning, and (b) there are many different techniques—such as suggestopedy (Lozanov, 1978; Schiffler, 1989), psycholinguistic programming (Bachmann, 1991; Bandler & Grinder, 1984), etc.—at the surface level.

BASIS–MODEL 6: LEARNING STRATEGIES

Strategies are a clear step-by-step procedure for learning. They guide the sequence of learning acts from a relatively abstract

net of orders. SQ3R (Robinson, 1970) is a well-known strategy to work through textbook chapters. Two central psychological aspects go along with the acquisition of a strategy, namely, (a) independent, autonomous learning, and (b) guided metacognition. Independent learning is the goal and the consequence of an acquired strategy: Whoever uses it has at his or her disposition a hidden compass that provides direction. The task of guided metacognition is to use judgment regarding the correct use of a certain strategy and to guide and correct it. There are "investigative strategies," "organizational strategies," "monitoring strategies," "mnemonic strategies" (Bjorklund, Schneider, Cassel, & Ashley, 1994; Wood, Willoughby, & Woloshyn, 1995), "guided self-questioning and guided peer-questioning strategies" (King, 1995), "strategies for reading comprehension" (Symons, Richards, & Greene, 1995), heuristic strategies (Schoenfeld, 1979), and others. Strategies are especially meaningful for the resource management of effort and effect (task on time). According to Weinstein and Mayer (1986), strategies can have different functions such as selection, elaboration, construction, and integration. We propose the following basis–model:

1. Exposure to a new, short learning procedure; reflection on how different students learned differently with respect to their spontaneous strategies
2. Perception of a new strategy (elements, chaining, functioning)
3. Conscious application of that strategy with the help of teacher guidance
4. Evaluation and generalization after applying this strategy in different situations with different content

In practice, schools do not emphasize much the learning and use of strategies. Research, however, until now, has stressed the kind of strategies students use under "natural" or guided conditions and how teachers can help students successfully use strategies. Although Sweller (1988) doubts the success of trained strategies, Chinnappan and Lawson (1996) demonstrate success, especially with problem-solving strategies (executive strategy planning). Sarasin (1995) carried out research that precisely applied the steps of Basis–Model 6. Her results show that most children (but not all) changed their reading and writing behavior significantly when they applied complex reading strategies that were modeled according to the elements in Basis–Model 6. Metzger (1996) also showed that using strategies changes the self-motivation of students, the effectiveness of the management of learning time, etc. (for outstanding work on strategies, see also Baumert, 1993; Entwistle 1988; Weinstein & Mayer, 1986). To sum up, we found that (a) mostly, students are not introduced to meaningful strategy use, but (b) if they are, they gain on both the metacognitive reflection and the learning effect.

BASIS–MODEL 7: ROUTINES

The goal of this model is to build up motoric or mental routines through repetition and rote learning. Routines and subroutines are automated competencies. In using them, the learner can use his or her attention capacity for something else, precisely, because the routine is working correctly. A car driver can, while driving, use his or her mind for different things: to discuss or listen to music, etc. An actor who has memorized a text can concentrate on expression and gesture. The question is not whether routines should be built up but how they can be learned. In general we can assume that two-thirds of all human activities have the form of routines. Baddeley (1982) is convinced that the storage of routines is based on different repetition techniques. The elements we propose for the basis–model "learning routines" are as follows:

1. Try out (a) a chain of actions, (b) a chain of text, or (c) an application of a set of rules.
2. Develop of an inner representation of that action chain, text, or rules application through
   • advance organized deconstruction of the whole
   • anticipated determination of limits of each part
   • understanding of the rules for the connections of each part
   • definition of each component
3. Realize parts (a), (b) or (c) with controlled feedback.
4. Evaluate repetitive realizations of (a), (b) or (c).
5. Repeat parts (a), (b), or (c) until automatization occurs.

Schools, in general, do not train students enough in the use of automatization skills. Research shows that students (or workers or specialists) with highly automatized skills are better learners of new material. Plausibly, whoever can do something without needing to focus attention on it has resources available for new activities and thoughts (see Steiner, 1988). It must be mentioned also that strategies (Basis–Model 6) can help to foster automatization.

BASIS–MODEL 8: THE "MOTILITY" MODEL

"Motility" is an expression used by Freud to explain how the inner forces of the libido are transformed. We use this expression to refer to the transformation of emotions in children that are antecedent to creative expression such as gesture, music, dance, language, and painting. The basic idea is that students should be stimulated into an affective state through stories, films, or interactive affecting experiences. Motility means that this state is then used to engage in expressive acts of creativity, thus, transforming the inner emotional forces into art. This process has to be subtly controlled by how the teacher stimulates the students and how they are able to constructively reflect on what is happening. The concept is similar to Gardner's (1983) "aesthetic intelligence" or Eisner's (1985) "expressive educational objectives." Accepting this kind of special and extraordinary procedural model of learning, the elements of the Basis–Model 8 are the following:

1. Sensitivity that is promoted through advance organizers (a required anticipatory understanding of all notions as well as a preparation of the materials and other necessities so the later creative process is not disturbed)
2. Buildup of emotional tension through presentation of a text, narrative, story, or a film
3. Slight cognitive structuring; a framing of the accumulated energy by stressing the core feature of the narrative (can be structured through a mind map of the most important elements of the story)

4. Transformation of the energy into a creative expression (can be drawing, pantomime, music, story, social drama, etc.)
5. Presentation and reflection of similar but recognized works of art (a form of indirect reinforcement of the creative products of the students)

This model has a psychodynamic fundament that consists of transforming accumulated energy into expression. Research shows that ordering the elements of the basis–model differently yields artistic products of less quality (according to experts) than maintaining the original order (Haenni, 1996). Our own research shows that this model is seldom applied, presumably, because it refers to aesthetic education, which is generally less valued than purely cognitive work. Nevertheless, motility is one form of human learning and human representation.

BASIS–MODELS 9A AND 9B: SOCIAL LEARNING AND LEARNING THROUGH REALISTIC DISCOURSES

Our culture expects each individual to help in situations of distress, to support peers, to show impartiality in settling differences, to engage in immediate action in case of accidents, to respect agreed-upon rules, to express loyalty toward friends, etc. But how do we learn all these competencies? Which situations help to generalize these social capacities so they can be referred to as secure social and moral capital?

We refer to two forms of a learning process, namely, (a) a set of social-action skills that are generated through situated learning and (b) a conflict-resolution capacity that often presupposes the direct social action. Both are necessary to the social life in classrooms.

One of the first authors to convincingly describe the genesis of social competencies from a constructive point of view is Youniss (1978, 1981, 1987). He rejects any behavioristic position that simply reinforces the "right" social act and denies the theory of minimal social arousal, which presupposes the triggering of endogenous developmental processing (Krappmann, 1994; Krappmann & Oswald, 1985, 1995). Instead, he stresses the process of constructing a social world directly and interactively through engagement in social acts and social reflections. The task is not only to build up a social competence but also to differentiate it twofold: (a) as an inner schema or attitude of role taking and (b) as an outer social action capacity that can be realized in new or habitual situations.

Both must be acquired: the ability to act and the ability to make a social judgment, which—in contrast to Basis–Model 2—stresses the shaping of a dynamic relationship between individuals (Blanc, Michel, & Villard, 1994). A dynamic relationship is the by-product of an acquired ability to share values with others, solve problems, have controversies, etc. and an ability to frame all these interactions. Framing is done through an ordering process and by creating interactive scripts that generate security in interactive actions. The ordering and the security frame are expressed through the application of rules of conduct. Only by repeatedly using rules of conduct in repetitive situations can children learn how to act in such a way that social and prosocial competencies are tried out and applied with others. The social exchange and the framing of that exchange through role taking helps to generate prosocial competencies.

Whether in close friendships or in loose discussions with peers, whether socially guided and controlled or loosely improvised, the social exchange is always about the arrangement of the activities that are complexly interwoven so that social competence is generated in reference to judgment and action. Teachers seldom intentionally develop such capacities.

One of the few research and school development projects to investigate social competence on the level of the whole system school was developed by Watson, Battistich, and Solomon (1999). The project contained goals such as those presented in basis–models 9a and 9b. The difference between basis–models 9a and 9b is that, in one case (9a), the social activity is immediately stimulated through situational necessities and, in the other (9b), the flow of teaching is interrupted by the so-called "round table," a place in which moral or prosocial acts are generated through a democratic decision-making process. The elements of Basis–Model 9a are as follows:

1. Consensus for a necessary prosocial or moral act demanded by a situation (teachers tell, students claim)
2. Perception of possible appropriate prosocial or moral acts in a holistic way through narrative examples, propositions, requests, etc.
3. Creation of conditions in which these prosocial or moral acts can be tried out and evaluated with regard to success
4. Reflection and critical legitimization of such prosocial or moral acts that are based on role taking and general discussion
5. Application of the same social or moral acts in new situations and justification of its efficacy

Examples of these learning elements are helping others in distress, helping in academic work, building up friendships, taking turns for a responsibility in the school setting, settling conflicts in general, making peace, sharing a gift, apologizing after hurting another, forgiving after someone has lied, etc.

Basis–model 9b is similar to 9a, but now decisions are made in a democratic and interactive way (Oser, 1998). The elements follow:

1. On the basis of an occurrence in which someone is hurt, treated unjustly, unfairly pressed, etc., the "round table" is created, and all people concerned are gently forced or convinced to participate.
2. A controversial exchange takes place in which the validity claims of every concerned person are brought to the table and propositions for a solution are made.
3. By taking the role of the other, participants of the round table learn to listen to each other, to coordinate the validity claims, and to trust in advance that each one on the table tries to be truthful, caring, and just (asymmetrical or realistic discourse).
4. A common decision is made with respect to some act that helps to solve the problem or to a new rule that will solve the problem in the long run.
5. The decision will be carried out and reflectively tried out in different contexts. The realization of the prosocial or moral act is evaluated on the basis of the trust that this new act or rule is the best for the moment.

One of the most fruitful schooling approaches, the "Just and Caring School Committee," refers explicitly to this social learning basis–model. In addition to the participation of students in the planning and shaping of their school life and moral development, the schools that use this approach foster social understanding, prosocial values (sharing, helping, comforting others, etc.), active readiness to overcome antisocial behavior like recklessness and violence, and the opportunity to take partial responsibility for school life (Althof, 1998; Dalton & Watson, 1997; Power, Higgins, & Kohlberg, 1989; Solomon, Watson, & Battistich, this volume). Data show that students of schools using this approach (in comparison to students in schools without this program) develop more and better qualified prosocial behavior, less antisocial acts, and significantly more developmental discipline (see also Walker, Colvin, & Ramsey, 1995).

BASIS–MODEL 10: CONSTRUCTION OF A LIVED VALUE SYSTEM

According to a new inquiry on values by the magazine *Life and Education* (1999), German parents rated the values of self-confidence and joy along with independence, truthfulness, responsibility, and tolerance as most important. Values such as diligence and discipline, which were important for the parents' generation and also for previous generations, were rated to be of medium importance. At the end of the value hierarchy were values such as religious bonding, parsimony, modesty, and discretion. Etiquette, such as table manners and polite greetings, were rated as being only relatively important. Interestingly, those parents who responded to the questionnaire also agreed that achievement and discipline will become more important again in the future.

To deal with values—to change negative values into positive ones, to develop social, moral, political, and aesthetic values—we again need a basis–model that helps build good and meaningful lives. Criteria for such values are universal impartiality, tolerance, reversibility, and high acceptance within a reflective society. Such values must be constructed in interactions within families and schools, peer groups, and work places. At the same time, existing values must be reconstructed, evaluated, and incorporated into the moral, social, or political self. A fundamental problem in education is that teachers and parents see less necessity to deal with (a) the internal value hierarchy and (b) the external value structure of the societal context. The consequences are conflicts between generations, animistic behavior, and, sometimes, even extremist or fundamentalist racist spirit.

In general, sociologists analyze the central values of generations and compare them with the values of other contemporaries. Classical examples are Rokeach (1960) for values in modern society, Giddens (1990, 1991) for values in a postmodern society, and Jackson, Boostrom, and Hansen (1993) for moral values in the classroom. Our basis–models are less concerned with a description of what exists and more concerned with the transformation of the value system through intervention. For such changes, we must know what kind of goal is acceptable; not everybody accepts a value change that is initiated by teachers.

The goals for transforming the value systems of the moral, social, or political self can be trifold: (a) teachers would like to sensitize students to the range of power and actuality that potential values have (Bennett, 1986; Narvaez ,1998), (b) teachers would like to raise a person's awareness of his or her own values (Simon, Howe, & Kirschenbaum, 1972), and (c) teachers would like to alter the value hierarchy of a person (Leming, 1997; Regenbogen, 1998).

For these three goals, we propose the following basis–model:

1. Values are taken into consideration through exercises of value clarification (e.g., Where was a situation in which I hurt someone intentionally? What are my most important values? What are the values in such texts?).
2. Options for value changes are developed in such a way that each important value is questioned with respect to tolerance, reversibility, and universality (e.g., What would happen if I had much more time? How can I change my value hierarchy? What are the real opponents of my own values? Have I more spiritual or materialistic values?).
3. Value changes are experienced and evaluated (How important are "new" values to me? Why do I stick to my own values without questioning them?); new values are merged with old ones (value comparison, value justification).
4. New value systems are applied to stories, narratives in films, life events, etc.

It is again surprising how seldom this model is applied. We believe, however, that change in values is fundamental to educational change. Only if we give students the occasion to co-construct and reconstruct their values does our work yield each student having a value identity. We can develop a higher sensitivity to values only if tolerance, universality, and reversibility are shareholders of it. During adolescence, an especially important fundamental developmental task is to develop a value identity that refers to such principles. Values are social capitals of a nation.

BASIS–MODEL 11: HYPERTEXT LEARNING

No time before ours has had to process such amounts of information as we do today. A new form of doing this processing is to search and combine pieces of information through manipulations of computer-based hypertexts. In contrast to concept building, manipulations of information chunks through hypertext (focusing, adding, including, binding, deducting, centering, etc.) demand no prerequisites. Anybody at any time can use whatever he or she wants. A rich literature is developing on this subject. Computer information as software units can be used in any other basis–model in a service-oriented way. But the ease of playing with chunks of information in hypertext has led to a new and special style of learning that has different scaffolding procedures and different steps of progression.

The word *hypertext* originates, according to Meyerhof (1994, p. 11), from Ted Nelson, who created it to illustrate bodies of written or iconically illustrated material that are connected through computer programs in a highly complex way. No normal text could be connected in such a differentiated way. This corpus contains overviews and reviews, maps, footnotes by celebrities, summaries, tables, graphics, biographical insertions, illustrations, sounds, films, extracts of narratives, poems, confessions, laws, mathematical rules, etc. Computer specialists are convinced of the full meaning of the high amount of free choice

involved in the ordering device of such possibilities. At the same time, they also see the necessity of guided tours, which are a better guarantee of learning success, thereby generating a higher level of motivation and increased pleasure in learning.

The depth of processing as determined by the learner is the most important characteristic of work with hypertext. Today the general term for this processing is "Individualized Electronic Newspaper." This idea can be used in two different ways. First, a newspaper reader offers a good prototype for the browsing type of learning that people do every day. Each chunk of information has little or no connection to the other, and still, a kind of hidden interaction takes place—a somewhat superficial way of getting information. The pleasure lies precisely in jumping from one piece to the next. Second, hypertext can also be used to penetrate a large field of knowledge (e.g., sports) in the search for a specific topic. A reader can get information not only from one newspaper but also from many simultaneously.

Hypertext makes it possible to work with information in quite a deep way of processing. For example, a researcher can use this method first to get a profound overview of a special subject area and then to build a meaningful review. He or she can discover connections with different combinations of old chunks of information and with different arrangements of new information such as scientific theories or research programs. When processing information in this way, hypertext systems are epistemic worlds that contain a high potential for future visual worlds. The key to such constructed, possible worlds is the manifestation of active learning.

Although the basic learning steps in hypertext "playing" have not yet been empirically established, we hypothesize the following plausible steps:

1. A topic is searched and chosen; it should be processed in a nonintentional but complex way.
2. An overview is sought and control is intended. The subject tries to create a frame for the information flow (index, titles, synopsis, etc.) using back and forward browsing. The development of expectations relative to learning possibilities occurs.
3. The desired results of the work are decided upon—a product, a game without any further function, a discovery by chance, etc.
4. A free or controlled ("guided tour") way of learning is chosen.
5. A free or guided path is realized. For both possibilities, deviations are always possible.
6. Relevant parts are stored; unimportant parts are eliminated. Valid arrangements are expressed and, thus, results are presented.

Most research in the area of hypertext stresses context, nodes, and networking (e.g., Eigler, 1997; McKnight, Dillon, & Richardson, 1990a, 1990b; Nielsen, 1995; Tergan, 1993; Winter, 1998). Although we do not yet understand enough to explain precisely the process of free path taking in hypertext, we have found that new arrangements of already shared information take place more often than concept learning. Investigations in the coming years will make the process more cognitively transparent.

BASIS–MODEL 12: NEGOTIATING

When children's interactions with each other in the classroom are discreetly observed, it has been found that most of the interactions have the form of classical negotiation (see Krappmann, 1996). The underlying principle follows: You do that action, and in response, I will do this action; you give that thing away, and in response, I will keep my mouth shut; you give me the possibility to do that activity, and in response, I will give you this object as a present, etc. On the one hand, the negotiations are a daily enterprise. On the other hand, they must be done in such a way that they lead not only to positive results but also to good relationships. The basic schema of negotiation is similar in many cases: A need that concerns two partners arises; the need is expressed and the question of what each party shall contribute, pay, control, inhibit, or renounce to reach an agreement is proposed.

Children generally believe that the outcome of a negotiation process is—at least for themselves—positive. They do not see that a negotiation process can be disrupted. But if disruption occurs, they feel excluded, negatively treated, or hurt. Children also express additional criteria, especially if the situation is unclear or lacks transparency: that both parties mutually accept the needs of the other, that both create a balance between objective discrepancies, and that both want to reach a goal. The formula for results is somewhat arbitrary: the subjective value that someone is willing to contribute minus the share of the other person, which nobody knows in advance. Deficit solutions will be taken into consideration only if they meet a certain minimum, namely, the best offer from someone else. This idea of a deficit solution refers to the principle of the Best Alternative to a Negotiated Agreement (BATNA) (see Fisher & Ury, 1981).

The most impressive research in the field of the development of negotiation competence has been conducted by Selman (1980). He has developed stages of "Interpersonal Negotiation Strategies" (INS) that, on a descriptive level, reconstruct the cognitive interpersonal negotiation orientation throughout the life span (Level 0: egocentric impulsive; Level 1: subjective, unilateral; Level 2: self-reflective, reciprocal; Level 3: mutual). Other examples of excellent literature on the subject can be found in Gulliver (1979). He describes a phase series that can serve as a background for our basis–model. Here again, we think in terms of intentional stimulation of educationally desirable goals. The elements follow:

0. Disagreement and crisis in ongoing social life
1. A search for an arena and agenda definition
2. Exploration of the field, emphasis of differences
3. A narrowing of the differences (emphasis on tolerable agreement)
4. Preliminary efforts to final bargaining and final bargaining
5. Ritualization of the outcome
6. Execution of outcome (adapted from Gulliver, 1979, p. 122)

Because Gulliver is not a learning specialist but an ethnologist, his focus is on the competitive or cooperative aspects of each phase. However, the steps, or elements, he developed are precise and are crystallized from a long inductive procedure. Each step describes the main feature of what happens in that part of the process. Later research yields to a normative interpretation of this sequence: Skipping an element or omitting a phase is expected to deliver poor negotiation results of the negotiation process (see Laupper, 1999).

At first, it seems as if this sequence is a description of the sight structure of the teaching choreographies. However, this assumption is not the case because Gulliver was referring to the operations of people who negotiate. He arranged each element to be either more competitive or more cooperative. Our basis–model is useful in learning fruitful negotiation skills if it is adapted normatively for teaching and learning. It then can become a script for action-oriented learning.

With respect to children, Krappmann (1994) found that negotiations could fail and, thus, could become stressful endeavors when they were forced through coercion or when they became too egotistical. Because children function at a lower stage of INS, they must, naturally, learn to negotiate peacefully.

Each of these 12 basis–models—as we stressed before—can be connected with different sight structures to yield different choreographies of teaching. In addition, each of these models expresses (a) an action base (the students' operations are stressed); (b) a different type of goal (according to the learning form); (c) a contextual base (methodological, situated, context specific, or media specific); and (d) an anthropological background (*Menschenbild*), which is in each of them related to constructivism. These four criteria are used to select a basis–model and to define what we call a choreography of teaching and its long-term effectiveness.

Research on the Choreographies of Teaching

In this last section of our chapter, we would like to report some of our findings and summarize our work.

One major question we had concerned the degree to which teachers generally applied the basis–models presented here. We randomly analyzed videotaped lessons that were given by 90 teachers from two different cantons in Switzerland (a total of 3,682 minutes of instruction) and found the following results: Basis–Model 4a (knowledge building) and Basis–Model 4b (concept building) were used in 71% of the lessons (4a = 61%; 4b = 10%); Basis–Model 1 (learning through experience) was used in 6% of the lessons; Basis–Model 7 (routines) was also used in 6%; Basis–Model 10 (influencing the value system of students) was used in 4%; and all the other basis–models were used in less than 3% (e.g., Basis–Model 3—problem solving— was used in less than 1% of the lessons). These results are an awakening for all who believe that school strives for more than knowledge reconstruction and knowledge building. At the same time, it is evident that instruction deals a lot with content and additive learning, both of which are necessary goals of instruction.

Looking at the distribution of time used within Basis–Model 4, the results show that element 1 = 12.5%; element 2 = 14%; element 3 = 32.5%; element 4 = 32.5%; element 5 = 5%. From this distribution, we can deduce the following: Teachers use most of their time to analyze essential characteristics or categories and to actively deal with and work through new concepts.

(This distribution may explain why Switzerland shows such good results concerning the TIMMS-Study (see Baumert et al., 1997; Moser, Ramseier, Keller, & Huber, 1997; Ramseier, Keller, & Moser, 1999).

For Basis–Model 1 (learning through experience), the distribution of time was the following: element 1 = 31%; element 2 = 41%, element 3 = 27%; element 4 = 1%; element 5 = 0%. As with element 5 in Basis–Model 4, we found that the last two elements are mostly left out by teachers. This finding means that the generalizations and reflections on similar experiences of others are omitted, thus, weakening the completeness of the learning procedure.

We were also interested in how students reflected on their own learning during each element of a basis–model. We asked them to report their thinking directly after each lesson and, especially, to remember the most important part of that lesson. The results were again astonishing: 78.6% of all student statements did not include any metacognitive reflections; 18.4% included some metacognitive reflections, but without justifications; and only 3% included metacognitive reflections with justifications. Emotions were reported by approximately only 3.5% of the students. And, interestingly, the looser the structure of the lesson, the more students reported social or physical distractions (high structure = 5.4% distractions; middle structure = 8.1%; low structure = 18.1%).

We also looked at the extent to which teachers reflect on their students' learning and on the operations that their students use, especially in regard to sequencing the elements in the basis–models. This research refers to the role of teachers' beliefs about their teaching process (see Richardson, 1996). We hypothesized that, in general, teachers would know how they would connect operational elements because, over their teaching biography, they would have developed a chaining belief system that refers to sequencing content. The technique we used was taken from a repertory grid design of research. We gave cards with the elements of the basis–models to a group (total n = 44) of student teachers and experienced teachers and asked them to order the cards according to the sequence of the respective basis–model (without knowing it, of course). The elements (each card for one element) were formulated on different levels of abstraction: (a) high abstractness and (b) high concreteness. An example of high abstractness is "confronting the moral judgment structure with controversial different positions within the dilemma" (Basis–Model 2, element 2). An example of high concreteness is "students listen to the biblical story of the creation of the world and compare it with a text on the Big Bang" (Basis–Model 4b, element 2).

The results showed that the more abstractly the basis–model was formulated, the more teachers' rating corresponded highly with our theory (with moderate fit of basis–models 3 and 7). Basis–model elements differed much more from our theory when cards with concrete formulations were used. With concrete formulations, the mean correspondence of Basis–Model 1 is 63.85%; of Basis–Model 2, 94.6%; of Basis–Model 3, 97.7%; of Basis–Model 4b, 52.95%; of Basis–Model 6, 94.7%; and of Basis–Model 7, 71.65%. (All these results are corrected for misunderstandings of these teachers concerning the formulation on the cards.)

We interpreted this information to mean that teachers in-

tuitively show—after misunderstandings of instructions were clarified—a high correspondence with the theoretical frames of basis–models 2, 3, and 6 and a medium correspondence with basis–models 1, 4, and 7. We concluded that teachers must intuitively grasp elements in learning or elements of operational chunks but that they do not have the ability to reflect on this understanding theoretically and analytically. However, one possibility may be that the insertion of a chain of elements into a situated learning context dissolved the clarity of the basis–model.

Another group of studies concerned the relationship between the sight structures of teaching and the basis–models (namely, the relationship between teaching and learning). We found that (a) for a few elements, like element two in Basis–Model 2, student-centeredness is given through the description of the basis–model itself; (b) for most other elements, the manner and method of teaching depends completely on the desire of the teacher to plan his or her lessons within the broad range provided by the sight structure. This finding corresponds with our theory on the choreographies of teaching. In addition, we can conclude that the more the teaching is teacher-centered (presentation of material, lecturing, presentation of films, etc.), the less the teachers reflect on what happens in the mind of their students (and the less effective the basis–models are).

A final group of studies investigated the effects of teacher training programs on the level to which teachers respect students' cognitive operations. In general, all intervention studies had the following form. First, we presented the theory of choreographies of teaching, stressing the aspect of cognitive activity of students. Second, we prepared lessons with the teachers in which they structured the sight structure of their teaching according to the basis–models. Third, teachers tried to teach according to their new preparations, discussed the effects and their results, and then developed new lessons with more emphasis on student thinking in accordance with their hypotheses.

Our results showed that, first, teachers accepted the theory of the choreographies of teaching positively, but they did not want to be guided too much by the basis–models. Second, in the beginning, teachers felt very limited if they thought in terms of the basis–model but, at the same time, felt more secure in terms of each step of their teaching. Third, when teachers used the basis–models, students had a higher awareness of the steps in their own learning during a lesson than when teachers did not teach according to basis–models. Fourth, when teachers stimulated the thought processes of students by way of the basis–models, approximately only two-thirds of the students profited from it. Fifth, students in the experimental group showed significantly higher performances in all subject matter than students in the control group. Sixth, no differences between both groups emerged with respect to the social climate in the classroom. Seventh, students (not teachers) did not experience more learning security when the teachers taught according to the basis–models; this result was probably caused by the shortness (about six weeks) of most of our intervention studies (see Wagner, 1999).

Teachers found it difficult to remember the basis–model elements when the content was challenging and the learning was based on what we described, for example, in Basis–Model 1. Another intervention study we did found that student teachers, when informed about the basis–models (experimental group), indeed, felt more at ease and secure in preparing their lessons than the student teachers in the control group.

In summary, these results lead us to hope that we have made the first steps in training young teachers to increasingly bridge instruction to learning. Young teachers who are willing to use the concept of choreographies of teaching will be more able to teach according to a sound psychology of learning. In our view, European teacher training (curricula and methods) is being transformed from focusing on good teaching to focusing on good classroom learning. In this process, situated sight structures, which had too much influence for a long time, will give way to situated cognition.

Piaget's statement—that teachers who convey only knowledge without considering the operations of students inhibit student learning—must be taken more seriously. Teachers who think about the cognitive work and emotional responsiveness of students teach different from those teachers who stress their own expressiveness. Teachers who stress content alone do not see that the content is fruitful only if the students use and model it. The relationship of teaching and learning is a hypothetical one, of course. But hypotheses about what is going on in students' minds can be tested only once they exist. We must train teachers to pose and to test hypotheses about what students are doing cognitively and emotionally when teaching is going on. We must use the sight structure of teaching as a means for learning.

REFERENCES

Achtenhagen, F. (1994). Komplexe Lehr-/Lernarrangements und Lernumgebungen: Didaktische Differenzierung und curriculare Verknüpfung als zentrale Themen der Berufsbildungsforschung. In F. Buttler, R. Czycholl, & H. Pütz (Eds.), *Modernisierung beruflicher Bildung vor den Ansprüchen von Vereinheitlichung und Differenzierung* (Beiträge zur Berufsbildungsforschung der Arbeitsgemeinschaft Berufsbildungsforschung, No. 1, pp. 207–238). Nürnberg: Institut für Arbeitsmarkt und Berufsforschung der Bundesanstalt für Arbeit.

Achtenhagen, F., & John, E. G. (1992). *Mehrdimensionale Lehr-Lern-Arrangements. Innovationen in der kaufmännischen Aus- und Weiterbildung.* Wiesbaden: Gabler.

Aebli, H. (1951). *Didactique psychologique.* Neuchâtel: Delaux et Niestlé.

Aebli, H. (1980). *Denken: Das Ordnen des Tuns: Band 1. Kognitive Aspekte der Handlungstheorie.* Stuttgart: Klett-Cotta.

Aebli, H. (1981). *Denken: Das Ordnen des Tuns: Band II. Denkprozesse.* Stuttgart: Klett-Cotta.

Aebli, H. (1983). *Zwölf Grundformen des Lehrens.* Stuttgart: Klett-Cotta.

Ajzen, I., & Fishbein, M. (1980). *Understanding attitudes and predicting social behavior.* New York: Prentice-Hall.

Althof, W. (1998). *Transforming schools into just and caring communities: Conception and outcomes.* Paper presented at the annual meeting of the American Educational Research Association, San Diego.

Anderson, J. R. (1976). *Language, memory, and thought.* Hillsdale, NJ: Lawrence Erlbaum Associates.

Anderson, J. R. (1983). *The architecture of cognition.* Cambridge, MA: Harvard University Press.

Anderson, J. R., Reder, L. M., & Simon, H. A. (1996). Situated learning and education. *Educational Researcher, 25*(4), 5–11.

Ausubel, D. P., Novak, J. D., & Hanesian, H. (1968). *Educational psychology: A cognitive view.* New York: Holt, Rinehart & Winston.

Bachmann, W. (1991). *Das neue Lernen. Eine systematische Einführung in das Konzept des NLP.* Paderborn: Junfermann.

Baddeley, A. (1982). *Your memory.* London: Multimedia Publications.

Bandler, R., & Grinder, J. (1984). *Metasprache und Psychotherapie. Die Struktur der Magie I.* Paderborn: Junfermann.

Bauch-Schremmer, C. (1993). *Untersuchungen zu den Choreographien des unterrichtlichen Lernens bei Oser—Über die Kombinierbarkeit der Basismodelle.* Ludwigsburg: Pädagogische Hochschule.

Baumert, J. (1993). Lernstrategien, motivationale Orientierung und Selbstwirksamkeitsüberzeugungen im Kontext schulischen Lernens. *Unterrichtswissenschaft, Zeitschrift für Lernforschung, 21*(4), 327–354.

Baumert, J., Lehmann, R., Lehrke, M., Schmitz, B., Clausen, M., Hosenfeld, I., Köller, O., & Neubrand, J. (1997). *TIMSS Mathematisch-Naturwissenschaftlicher Unterricht im internationalen Vergleich.* Berlin: MPI für Bildungsforschung.

Becker, G. E. (1984). *Planung von Unterricht. Handlungsorientierte Didaktik, Teil I.* Weinheim: Beltz Verlag.

Bennett, W. J. (1986). *What works. Research about teaching and learning.* Washington: Department of Education.

Berkowitz, M. W. (1981). A critical appraisal of the "plus-one" convention and moral education. *Phi Delta Kappan, 62,* 488–489.

Bjorklund, D. F., & Harnishfeger, K. K. (1995). The evolution of inhibition mechanisms and their role in human cognition and behavior. In F. N. Dempster & C. J. Brainerd (Eds.), *Interference and inhibition in cognition* (pp. 141–173). San Diego, CA: Academic Press.

Bjorklund, D. F., Schneider, W., Cassel, W. S., & Ashley, E. (1994). Training and extension of a memory strategy: Evidence for utilization deficiencies in the acquisition of an organizational strategy in high- and low-IQ children. *Child Development, 65,* 951–965.

Blanc, Ch., Michel, D., & Villard, I. (1994). *Interactions sociales et transmission des savoirs techniques. Document de recherche dur projet "Apprendre un métier technique aujourd' hui"* (No. 1). Neuchâtel: Université de Neuchâtel, Séminaire de psychologie.

Bloom, B. S. (1968). Learning for mastery. *Evaluation Comment, 1*(2).

Bower, G. H., Black, J. B., & Turner, T. J. (1979). Scripts in memory for text. *Cognitive Psychology, 11,* 177–190.

Bransford, J. D., Stein, B. S., Delclos, V., & Littlefield, J. (1986). Computers and problem solving. In C. Kinzer, R. Sherwood, & J. Bransford (Eds.), *Computer strategies for education: Foundations and content-area applications* (pp. 147–180). Columbus, OH: Merrill.

Bromme, R. (1992). *Der Lehrer als Experte. Zur Psychologie des professionellen Wissens.* Bern: Hans Huber.

Bruner, J. S. (1966). *Studies in cognitive growth.* New York: Wiley. [In German: *Studien zur Kognitiven Entwicklung.* Stuttgart: Klett, 1971]

Bruner, J. S. (1970). *The process of education.* Cambridge, MA: Harvard University Press.

Burns, R. B. (1996). Models of learning. In E. de Corte & F. E. Weinert (Eds.), *International encyclopedia of developmental and instructional psychology.* Oxford: Pergamon.

Cangelosi, J. S. (1992). *Systematic teaching strategies.* New York: Longman.

Case, R. (1985). *Intellectual development. Birth to adulthood.* New York: Academic Press.

Chinnappan, M., & Lawson, M. J. (1996). The effects of training in the use of executive strategies in geometry problem solving. *Journal of the European Association for Research on Learning and Instruction, 26*(1), 1–18.

Clark, E. V. (1973). What's in a world? On the child's acquisition of semantics in his first language. In T. E. Moore (Ed.), *Cognitive development and the acquisition of language.* New York: Academic Press.

Cognition and Technology Group at Vanderbilt. (1992). The Jasper series as an example of anchored instruction: Theory, program, description, and assessment data. *Educational Psychologist, 27,* 291–315.

Cognition and Technology Group at Vanderbilt. (1993). Anchored instruction and situated cognition revisited. *Educational Technology, 33*(3), 52–70.

Cognition and Technology Group at Vanderbilt. (1997). *The Jasper project: Lessons in curriculum, instruction, assessment, and professional development.* Mahwah, NJ: Lawrence Erlbaum Associates.

Collins, A., Brown, J. S., & Newman, S. E. (1989). Cognitive apprenticeship: Teaching the crafts of reading, writing and mathematics.

In L. B. Resnick (Ed.), *Knowing, learning and instruction. Essays in the honour of Robert Glaser* (pp. 453–494). Hillsdale, NJ: Lawrence Erlbaum Associates.

Collins, A. M., & Quillian, M. R. (1969). Retrieval time from semantic memory. *Journal of Verbal Learning and Verbal Behavior, 8,* 240–247.

Comenius, J. A. (1957). Grosse Didaktik (2nd ed.). Düsseldorf: Schwann. (Original work published 1657)

Dalton, J., & Watson, M. (1997). *Among friends.* Oakland, CA: Developmental Studies Center.

Damon, W. (1977). *The social world of the child.* San Francisco: Jossey-Bass.

Dempster, F. N. (1990). *Resistance to interference: A neglected dimension of cognition.* Paper presented at the annual meeting of the Psychonomic Society, New Orleans, LA.

Dempster, F. N. (1992). The rise and fall of the inhibitory mechanism: Toward a unified theory of cognitive development and aging. *Developmental Review, 12,* 45–75.

Dempster, F. N. (1995). Interference and inhibition in cognition: An historical perspective. In F. N. Dempster & C. J. Brainerd (Eds.), *Interference and inhibition in cognition* (pp. 3–26). San Diego, CA: Academic Press.

Dewey, J. (1910). *How we think.* Boston: Heath.

Dewey, J. (1944). *Democracy and education.* New York: Macmillan. (Original work published in 1916)

Dick, A. (1994). *Vom unterrichtlichen Wissen zur Praxisreflexion.* Bad Heilbrunn: Julius Klinkhardt.

Dijkstra, S., & Van Merriënboer, J. J. G. (1997). Plans, procedures, and theories to solve instructional design problems. In R. D. Tennyson, F. Schott, N. M. Seel, & S. Dijkstra (Eds.), *Instructional design: International perspectives* (Vol. 2, pp. 23–43). Mahwah, NJ: Lawrence Erlbaum Associates.

Dörner, D. (1989). *Die Logik des Misslingens. Strategisches Denken in komplexen Situationen.* Reinbeck: Rowohlt.

Dubs, R. (1985). *Kleine Unterrichtslehre für den Lernbereich Wirtschaft, Recht, Staat und Gesellschaft.* Aarau: Verlag Sauerländer.

Eigler, G. (1997). Zur Einführung: Lernen im Medienverbund in der betrieblichen Weiterbildung. In H. F. Friedrich, G. Eigler, H. Mandl, W. Schnotz, F. Schott, & N. M. Seel (Eds.), *Multimediale Lernumgebungen in der betrieblichen Weiterbildung. Gestaltung, Lernstrategien und Qualitätssicherung* (pp. 1–18). Neuwied: Luchterhand Verlag.

Eisner, E. W. (1985). *The art of educational evaluation. A personal view.* London: Falmer Press.

Entwistle, N. (1988). Motivational factors in students' approaches to learning. In R. R. Schmeck (Ed.), *Learning strategies and learning styles* (pp. 21–51). New York: Plenum Press.

Erickson, F. (1986). Qualitative methods in research on teaching. In M. C. Wittrock (Ed.), *Handbook of research on teaching* (3rd ed., pp. 119–161). New York: Macmillan.

Fenton, E. (1977). The cognitive–development approach to moral education. A response to Jack R. Fraenkel. *Social Education, 41,* 56–61.

Fisher, C. W., Berliner, D.C., Filby, N. N., Marliave, R., Cahen, L. S., & Dishaw, M. M. (1980). Reaching behaviors, academic learning time, and student achievement: An overview. In C. Denham & A. Lieberman (Eds.), *Time to learn.* Washington, DC: National Institute of Education.

Fisher, W. T., & Ury, M. C. (1981). *Getting to yes.* Boston: Houghton Mifflin.

Fowler, J. W. (1974). Stages in faith. The structural–developmental approach. In Th. Hennessey (Ed.), *Values and moral development* (pp. 173–211). New York: Paulist Press.

Frederiksen, N. (1984). Implications of cognitive theory for instruction in problem solving. *Review of Educational Research, 54,* 363–407.

Friedrich, H. F. (1995). Analyse und Förderung kognitiver Lernstrategien. *Empirische Pädagogik, Zeitschrift zu Theorie und Praxis erziehungswissenschaftlicher Forschung, 9*(2), 115–153.

Fuller, F. F., & Brown, O. H. (1975). Becoming a teacher. In K. Ryan (Ed.), *Teacher education* (75th yearbook of the NSSE, pp. 25–52). Chicago: NSSE

Gabel, D. L. (1994). *Handbook of research on science teaching and learning.* New York: Macmillan.

Gage, N. L. (1978). *The scientific basis of the art of teaching.* New York: Teachers College Press.

Gage, N. L., & Berliner, D.C. (1991). *Educational psychology.* Boston: Houghton Mifflin.

Gagné, R. M. (1965). *The conditions of learning.* New York: Holt, Rinehart & Winston.

Gagné, R. M., & Briggs, L. J. (1974). *Principles of instructional design.* New York: Holt, Rinehart & Winston.

Gardner, H. (1983). *Frames of mind. The theory of multiple intelligences.* New York: Basic Books.

Giddens, A. (1990). *The consequences of modernity.* Oxford: Polity Press.

Giddens, A. (1991). *Modernity and self-identity.* Stanford: Stanford University Press.

Greeno, J. G. (1978). A study of problem solving. In R. Glaser (Ed.), *Advances in instructional psychology* (Vol. 1). Hillsdale, NJ: Lawrence Erlbaum Associates.

Greeno, J. G. (1989). Situations, mental models, and generative knowledge. In D. Klahr & K. Kotovsky (Eds.), *Compels information processing: The impact of Herbert A. Simon* (pp. 285–318). Hillsdale, NJ: Lawrence Erlbaum Associates.

Greeno, J. G. (1995). Understanding concepts in activity. In C. A. Weaver, III, S. Mannes, & C. R. Fletcher (Eds.), *Discourse comprehension: Essays in honor of Walter Kintsch* (pp. 65–96). Hillsdale, NJ: Lawrence Erlbaum Associates.

Greeno, J. G. (1998). The situativity of knowing, learning, and research [Paper presented at the International Association of Applied Psychology, San Francisco]. *American Psychologist, 58,*(1), 5–26.

Gulliver, P. H. (1979). *Disputes and negotiations. A cross-cultural perspective.* New York: Academic Press.

Gunter, M. A., Estes, T. H., & Hasbrouck Schwab, J. (1990). *Instruction. A models approach.* Boston: Allyn & Bacon.

Haenni, St. (1996). Das Motilitätsmodell Eine empirische Studie zum Kunstunterricht der Maturitätsschulen. Unpublished doctoral dissertation, Philosophische Fakultät Freiburg i.Ue, Freiburg.

Hayes, J. R. (1984). *Problem solving techniques.* Philadelphia: Franklin Institute Press.

Heidemann, R. (1981). Artikulationsmodelle und Planungsbeispiele. In H. Frommer (Ed.), *Handbuch Praxis des Vorbereitungsdienstes.* Düsseldorf: Schwann.

Heimann, P. (1962). Didaktik als Theorie der Lehre. *Die Deutsche Schule, 54,* 407–427.

Heimann, P. (1970). *Unterricht. Analyse und Planung.* Hannover: Schroedel.

Heimann, P., Otto, G., & Schulz, W. (1965). *Unterricht—Analyse und Planung.* Hannover: Schroedel.

Howald, W. (1989). Meditationsforschung—Einführung und Überblick. *In Gruppendynamik, 20*(4), 345–367.

Jackson, P. W., Boostrom, R. E., & Hansen, D. T. (1993). *The moral life of schools.* San Francisco: Jossey-Bass.

Jacobson, M. J., & Spiro, R. J. (1992). Hypertext learning environments and cognitive flexibility: Characteristics promoting the transfer of compels knowledge. In L. Birnbaum (Ed.), *The international conference on the learning sciences* (1991 conference proceedings, pp. 240–248). Charlottesville, VA: Association for the Advancement of Computing in Education.

Janssen, S. (1987). *What are beginning teachers concerned about?* Paper presented at the AEPF conference, Düsseldorf.

King, A. (1995). Cognitive strategies for learning from direct teaching. In E. Wood, T. Willoughby, & V. Woloshyn (Eds.), *Cognitive strategy instruction for middle and high schools* (pp. 18–65). Cambridge, MA: Brookline Books.

Kintsch, W. (1974). The representation of meaning in memory. Hillsdale, NJ: Lawrence Erlbaum Associates.

Kintsch, W. (1998). *Comprehension. A paradigm for cognition.* Cambridge: Cambridge University Press.

Klafki, W. (1959). *Das pädagogische Problem des Elementaren und die Theorie der kategorialen Bildung.* Weinheim: Beltz.

Klafki, W. (1963). *Studien zur Bildungstheorie und Didaktik.* Weinheim: Beltz.

Klafki, W. (1968). Die didaktischen Prinzipien des Elementaren, Fundamentalen und Exemplarischen. In H. Heiland (Ed.), *Didaktik* (pp. 64–83). Bad Heilbrunn: Klinkhardf.

Klafki, W. (1974). Studien zur Bildungstheorie und Didaktik. Weinheim: Beltz.

Klafki, W. (1991). *Neue Studien zur Bildungstheorie und Didaktik. Zeitgemässe Allgemeinbildung und kritisch-konstruktive Didaktik* (2nd ed.). Weinheim: Beltz.

Kohlberg, L. (1981). *Essays on moral development: Vol. 1. The philosophy of moral development. Moral stages and the idea of justice.* San Francisco: Harper & Row.

Kohlberg, L. (1984). *Essays on moral development: Vol. 2. The psychology of moral development. The nature and validity of moral stages.* San Francisco: Harper & Row.

Köhler, W. (1963). *Intelligenzprüfungen an Menschenaffen.* (2nd ed.). Berlin: Springer. (Original work published 1917)

Krapp, A. (1993). Lernstrategien: Konzepte, Methoden und Befunde. *Unterrichtswissenschaft, Zeitschrift für Lernforschung, 21,*(4), 291–311.

Krappmann, L. (1994). Misslingende Aushandlungen—Gewalt und andere Rücksichtslosigkeiten unter Kindern im Grundschulalter. *Zeitschrift für Sozialisationsforschung und Erziehungssoziologie, 14,* 102–117.

Krappmann, L. (1996). Streit, Aushandlungen und Freundschaften unter Kindern. In M.-S. Hnig, H. R. Leu, & U. Nissen (Eds.), *Kinder und Kindheit. Soziokulturelle Muster, sozialisationstheorie Perspektiven* (S. 99.116). Weinheim: Juventa.

Krappmann, L., & Oswald, H. (1985). Schulisches Lernen in Interaktionen mit Gleichaltrigen. *Zeitschrift für Pädagogik, 31*(3), 321–337.

Krappmann, L., & Oswald, H. (1995). *Alltag der Schulkinder. Beobachtungen und Analysen von Interaktionen und Sozialbeziehungen.* München: Juventa.

Kron, F. W. (1993). *Grundwissen Didaktik.* München: E. Reinhardt.

Laupper, M. (1999). *Voraussetzungen für erfolgreiches Verhandeln. Analyse von videographierten Verhandlungsverläufen nach normativen und deskriptiven Verhandlungsmodellen.* Lizentiatsarbeit, Philosophische Fakultät der Universität Freiburg i.Ue, Freiburg.

Lave, J. (1991). Situating learning in communities of practice. In L. B. Resnick, J. M. Levine, & S. D. Teasley (Eds.), *Perspectives on socially shared cognition* (pp. 63–82). Washington, DC: American Psychological Association.

Lave, J., & Wenger, E. (1991). *Situated learning. Legitimate peripheral participation.* Cambridge: Cambridge University Press.

Leming, J. S. (1981). Curricular effectiveness in moral/values education: A review of research. *Journal of Moral Education, 10,* 147–164.

Leming, J. S. (1997). Research and practice in character education: A historical perspective. In A. Molnar (Ed.), *The construction of children's character.* Chicago: University of Chicago Press.

Lickona, Th. (1983). *Raising good children.* Toronto: Bantam Books.

Lippitt, R., Fox, R., & Schaible, L. (1962). *Social science laboratory units.* Chicago: Science Research Associates.

Lockwood, A. (1978). The effects of values clarification and moral development curricula on school-age subjects: A critical review of recent research. *Review of Educational Research, 48,* 325–364.

Lompscher, J. (1996). Aufsteigen vom Abstrakten zum Konkreten—Lernen und Lehren in Zonen der nächsten Entwicklung. Lern- und Lehr-Forschung (Bericht No. 16, pp. 98–118). Universität Potsdam: Interdisziplinäres Zentrum.

Lozanov, G. (1978). *Suggestology and outlines of suggestopedia.* New York: Gordon and Breach.

Lüer, G. (1973). Gesetzmässige Denkabläufe beim Problemlösen. Weinheim: Beltz.

Mandl, H., & Reinmann-Rothmeier, G. (1995). *Unterrichten und Lernumgebungen gestalten* (Forschungsbericht No. 60). München: Ludwig-Maximilians-Universität, Institut für Pädagogische Psychologie und Empirische Pädagogik, Lehrstuhl für Empirische Pädagogik und Pädagogische Psychologie.

Mayer, R. E. (1983). *Thinking, problem solving, cognition.* New York: Freeman.

Mayer, R. E. (1988). Learning strategies: An overview. In C. E. Weinstein, E. T. Goetz, & P. A. Alexander (Eds.), *Learning and study strategies. Issues in assessment, instruction, and evaluation* (pp. 11–22). San Diego, CA: Academic Press.

Mayer, R. E. (1992). *Thinking, problem solving, cognition* (2nd ed.). New York: Freeman.

McKnight, C., Dillon, A., & Richardson, J. (1990a). A comparison of linear and hypertext formats in information retrieval. In R. McAleese & C. Green (Eds.), *Hypertext: State of the art* (pp. 10–19). Oxford: Intellect.

McKnight, C., Dillon, A., & Richardson, J. (1990b). *Hypertext in context.* Cambridge: Cambridge University Press.

Medley, D. M. (1987). Evolution of research on teaching. In M. J. Dunkin (Ed.), *The international encyclopedia of teaching and teacher education* (pp. 105–113). New York: Pergamon Press.

Merrill, D. M. (1983). Component display theory. In C. M. Reigeluth (Ed.), *Instructional-Design theories and models: An overview of their current status* (pp. 335–382). Hillsdale, NJ: Lawrence Erlbaum Associates.

Metzger, Ch. (1996). *Lern- und Arbeitsstrategien.* Aarau: Sauerländer Verlag.

Meyerhoff, D. B. (1993). Hypertext und tutorielle Lernumgebungen: Ein Ansatz zur Integration. GMD-Bericht No. 322. München-Wien: Oldenbourg.

Minsky, M. (1975). A theoretical framework for representing knowledge. In P. Winston (Ed.), *The psychology of computer vision.* New York: McGraw-Hill.

Moser, U., Ramseier, E., Keller, C., & Huber, M. (1997). *Schule auf dem Prüfstand. Eine Evaluation der Sekundarstufe I auf der Grundlage der "Third International Mathematics and Science Study."* Chur: Verlag Rüegger.

Narvaez, D. (1998). The influence of moral schemas on the reconstruction of moral narratives in eighth graders and college students. *Journal of Educational Psychology, 90,* 13–24.

Neber, H. (1973). *Entdeckendes Lernen.* Weinheim and Basel: Beltz.

Newell, A., & Simon, H. A. (1972). *Human problem solving.* Engelwood Cliffs, NJ: Prentice-Hall.

Nielsen, J. (1995). *Multimedia and hypertext—The Internet and beyond.* New York: Academic Press.

Nold, G., & Schnaitmann, G. W. (1995). Lernbedingungen und Lernstrategien in verschiedenen Tätigkeitsbereichen des Fremdsprachenunterrichts. *Empirische Pädagogik, Zeitschrift zu Theorie und Praxis Erziehungswissenschaftlicher Forschung, 9,*(2), 239–261.

Norman, D. A., & Rumelhart, D. E. (1975). *Explorations in cognition.* San Francisco: Freeman.

Oser, F. (1998). *Ethos-die Vermenschlichung des Erfolgs. Zur Psychologie der Berufsmoral von Lehrpersonen.* Opladen: Leske & Budrich.

Oser, F., & Althof, W. (1992). *Moralische Selbstbestimmung. Modelle der Entwicklung und Erziehung im Wertebereich.* Stuttgart: Klett-Cotta.

Oser, F., & Gmünder, P. (1991). *Religious judgement. A developmental approach.* Birmingham: Religious Education Press.

Parsons, M. J. (1987). *How we understand art: A cognitive developmental account of aesthetic experience.* Cambridge: Cambridge University Press.

Piaget, J. (1947/1980). *La psychologie de l'intelligence.* Paris: Colin. *(German: Psychologie der Intelligenz. Stuttgart: Klett-Cotta, 1980)*

Piaget, J. (1970). *Genetic epistemology.* New York: The Norton Company

Piaget, J., & Inhelder, B. (1977). *Die Psychologie des Kindes.* Frankfurt am Main: Fischer Taschenbuch.

Polya, G. (1945). *How to solve it.* Garden City, NJ: Doubleday.

Power, C., Higgins, A., & Kohlberg, L. (1989). *Lawrence Kohlberg's approach to moral education.* New York: Columbia University Press.

Ramseier, E., Keller, C., & Moser, U. (1999). *Bilanz Bildung. Eine Evaluation der Sekundarstufe I auf der Grundlage der "Third International Mathematics and Science Study."* Chur: Verlag Rüegger.

Regenbogen, A. (1998). *Sozialisation in den 90er Jahren. Lebensziele, Wertmassstäbe und politische Ideale bei Jugendlichen.* Opladen: Leske & Budrich.

Reichenbach, R., & Oser, F. (1995). On noble motives and pedagogical kitsch. *Teaching and Teacher Education, 11*(2), 189–193.

Reigeluth, C. M. (Ed.). (1983a). *Instructional-design theories and models: An overview of their current status.* Hillsdale, NJ: Lawrence Erlbaum Associates.

Reigeluth, C. M. (1983b). Instructional design: What is it and why is it? In C. M. Reigeluth (Ed.), *Instructional-design theories and models: An overview of their current status* (pp. 3–36). Hillsdale, NJ: Lawrence Erlbaum Associates.

Reigeluth, C. M., & Stein, F. S. (1983). The elaboration theory of instruction. In C. M. Reigeluth (Ed.), *Instructional-design theories and models: An overview of their current status* (pp. 335–382). Hillsdale, NJ: Lawrence Erlbaum Associates.

Resnick, L. B. (1987). Learning in school and out. *Educational Researcher, 16,* 13–20.

Resnick, L. B. (1991). Shared cognition: Thinking as social practice. In L. B. Resnick, J. M. Levin, & S. D. Teasley (Eds.), *Perspectives on socially shared cognition* (pp. 1–20). Washington, DC: American Psychological Association.

Rest, J. R. (1979). *Development in judging moral issues.* Minneapolis: University of Minnesota Press.

Rest, J. R., & Narvaez, D. (1994). *Moral development in the professions: Psychology and applied ethics.* Hillsdale, NJ: Lawrence Erlbaum Associates.

Reyna, V. F. (1995). Interference effects in memory and reasoning: A fuzzy-trace theory analysis. In F. N. Dempster & C. J. Brainerd (Eds.), *Interference and inhibition in cognition* (pp. 29–59). San Diego, CA: Academic Press.

Richardson, V. (1996). The role of attitudes and beliefs in learning to teach. In J. Sikula (Ed.), *Handbook of research on teacher education* (2nd ed., pp. 102–119). New York: Macmillan.

Robinson, F. P. (1970). *Effective study.* New York: Harper & Row.

Rogers, C., & Freiberg, H. J. (1994). *Freedom to learn.* New York: Macmillan.

Rogoff, B. (1990). *Apprenticeship in thinking: Cognitive development in social context.* New York: Oxford University Press.

Rokeach, M. (1960). *The open and the closed mind.* New York: Basic Books.

Rosch, E. (1975). Cognitive representations of semantic categories. *Journal of Experimental Psychology, 104,* 192–233.

Roth, H. (1962). *Pädagogische Psychologie des Lehrens und Lernens* (6th ed.). Berlin: Schroedel. (Original work published 1957)

Roth, L. (1991). Allgemeine und berufliche Bildung. In L. Roth (Ed.), *Pädagogik* (pp. 469–481). München: Ehrenwirth.

Rubenstein, M. F. (1975). *Patterns of problem solving.* Engelwood Cliffs, NJ: Prentice Hall.

Sarasin, S. (1995). *Das Lehren und Lernen von Lernstrategien. Theoretische Hintergründe und eine empirische Untersuchung zur Theorie "Choreographien unterrichtlichen Lernens."* Hamburg: Verlag Dr. Kovac.

Scandura, J. M. M. (1983). Instructional strategies based on the structural learning theory. In C. M. Reigeluth (Ed.), *Instructional-Design theories and models: An overview of their current status* (pp. 335–382). Hillsdale, NJ: Lawrence Erlbaum Associates.

Schank, R. C., & Abelson, R. P. (1977). *Scripts, plans, goals, and understanding.* Hillsdale, NJ: Lawrence Erlbaum Associates.

Schiffler, L. (1989). *Suggestopädie und Superlearning—empirisch geprüft.* Frankfurt: Diesterweg.

Schoenfeld, A. H. (1979). Explicit heuristic training as a variable in problem-solving performance. *Journal for Research in Mathematics Education, 10,* 173–187.

Schott, F., & Driscoll, M. P. (1997). On the architectonics of instructional theory. In R. D. Tennyson, F. Schott, N. M. Seel, & S. Dijkstra (Eds.), *Instructional design: International perspectives* (Vol. 1, pp. 135–173). Mahwah, NJ: Lawrence Erlbaum Associates.

Schulz, W. (1976). Unterricht zwischen Funktionalisierung und Emanzipationshilfe. In H. Ruprecht (Ed.), *Modelle grundlegender didaktischer Theorien* (3rd ed., pp. 155–184). Hannover: Schroedel.

Schulz, W. (1980). *Unterrichtsplanung.* München: Urban & Schwarzenberg.

Searle, J. R. (1996). *Die Wiederentdeckung des Geistes.* Frankfurt: Suhrkamp.

Selman, R. L. (1980). *The growth of interpersonal understanding. Developmental and clinical analyses.* New York: Academic Press.

Shapiro, D. A. (1987). Implications of psychotherapy research for the study of meditation. In M. A. West (Ed.), *The psychology of meditation* (pp. 173–188). Oxford, MA: Clarendon.

Shulman, L. S. (1986). Those who understand. Knowledge growth in teaching. *Educational Researcher, 15*(2), 4–14, 21.

Simon, A. B., Howe, L. W., & Kirschenbaum, L. (1972). *Value clarification. A handbook of practical strategies for teachers and students.* New York: Hart.

Simon, H. A. (1979). Information-processing theory of human problem solving. In W. K. Estes (Ed.), *Handbook of learning and cognitive processes: Vol. 5. Human information processing).* Hillsdale, NJ: Lawrence Erlbaum Associates.

Simon, H. A., & Reed, S. K. (1976). Modeling strategy shifts in a problem-solving task. *Cognitive Psychology, 8,* 86–97.

Slavin, R. E. (1987). Mastery learning reconsidered. *Review of Educational Research, 57,* 175–213.

Smith, E. E., & Medin, D. L. (1981). *Categories and concepts.* Cambridge, MA.: Harvard University Press.

Snow, R. E. (1992). Aptitude theory: Yesterday, today, and tomorrow. *Educational Psychologist, 27,* 5–32.

Spiro, R. J., & Jehng, J. C. (1990). Cognitive flexibility and hypertext: Theory and technology for the nonlinear and multidimensional traversal of complex subject matter. In D. Nix & R. J. Spiro (Eds.), *Cognition, education, and multimedia: Exploring ideas in high technology* (pp. 163–205). Hillsdale, NJ: Lawrence Erlbaum Associates.

Steiner, G. (1988). *Lernen. Zwanzig Szenarien aus dem Alltag.* Bern: Hans Huber.

Steiner, I. D. (1966). Models for inferring relationships between group size and potential group productivity. *Behavior Science, 11,* 273–283.

Sternberg, R. (1994). *In search of the human mind.* Orlando, FL: Harcourt Brace.

Sternberg, R., & Davidson, J. (1982). The mind of the puzzler. *Psychology Today, 16,* 37–44.

Swanson, H. L. (1990). Influence of metacognitive knowledge and aptitude on problem solving. *Journal of Educational Psychology, 82,* 306–314.

Sweller, J. (1988). Cognitive load during problem solving: Effects on learning. *Cognition, 8*(5), 463–474.

Symons, S., Richards, C., & Greene, C. (1995). Cognitive strategies for reading comprehension. In E. Wood, T. Willoughby, & V. Woloshyn (Eds.), *Cognitive strategy instruction for middle and high schools* (pp. 66–87). Cambridge, MA: Brookline Books.

Tennyson, R. D. (1997). A system dynamics approach to instructional systems development. In R. D. Tennyson, F. Schott, N. M. Seel, & S. Dijkstra (Eds.), *Instructional design: International perspectives* (Vol. 1, pp. 413–426). Mahwah, NJ: Lawrence Erlbaum Associates.

Tennyson, R. D., & Breuer, K. (1997). Psychological foundations for instructional design theory. In R. D. Tennyson, F. Schott, N. M. Seel, & S. Dijkstra (Eds.), *Instructional design: International perspectives* (Vol. 1, pp. 113–134). Mahwah, NJ: Lawrence Erlbaum Associates.

Tergan, S. O. (1993). Zum Aufbau von Wissensstrukturen mit Texten und Hypertexten. *Nachrichten für Dokumentation, 44,* 15–22.

Treiber, B., & Weinert, F. E. (1982). *Lehr-Lern-Forschung. Ein Überblick in Einzeldarstellungen.* München: Urban & Schwarzenberg.

Tuma, D. T., & Reif, F. (1980). *Problem solving and education.* Hillsdale, NJ: Lawrence Erlbaum Associates.

von Glasersfeld, E. von (1989). Constructivism in education. In T. Husen & T. N. Postlethwaite (Eds.), *The international encyclopedia of education* (Suppl. 1, pp. 162–163). Oxford, UK: Pergamon.

von Glasersfeld, E. (1995). *Radical constructivism. A way of knowing and learning.* London: Falmer Press.

Van Patten, J., Chao, Ch.-I., & Reigeluth, C. M. (1986). A review of strategies for sequencing and synthesizing instruction. *Review of Educational Research 56*(4), 437–471.

Wagenschein, M. (1970). *Verstehen lehren* (3rd ed.). Weinheim: Beltz.

Wagner, B. (1999). *Lernen aus der Sicht der Lernenden.* Frankfurt am Main: Peter Lang.

Walker, H. M., Colvin, G., & Ramsey, E. (1995). *Antisocial behavior in school: strategies and best practices.* Pacific Grove, CA:Brooks/Cole.

Wallace, R. K., Silver, J., Mills, P. J., Dillbeck, M. S., & Wagoner, D. E. (1983). Systolic blood pressure and long-term practice of the Transcendental Meditation and TM-Sidhi Programme. *Psychosomatic Medicine, 45,* 41–46.

Wallen, N. E., & Travers, R. M. W. (1963). Analysis and investigation of teaching methods. In N. L. Gage (Ed.), *Handbook of research on teaching.* Chicago: Rand McNally.

Watson, M. S., Battistich, V. A., & Solomon, D. (1998). Enhancing students' social and ethical development in schools: An intervention program and its effects. *International Journal of Educational Research, 27,* 571–586.

Weil, M., & Joyce, B. (1978). *Social models of teaching. Expanding your teaching repertoire.* Englewood, NJ: Prentice-Hall.

Weinstein, C. F., & Mayer, R. E. (1986). The teaching of learning strategies. In M. C. Wittrock (Ed.), *Handbook of research on teaching* (3rd ed., pp. 315–327). New York: Macmillan.

Wertheimer, M. (1945). *Productive thinking.* New York: Harper.

Wessells, M. G. (1984). *Kognitive Psychologie.* New York: Harper & Row.

Winter, A. (1998). Arbeiten an und mit Hypertexten. *Unterrichtswissenschaft Zeitschrift für Lernforschung, 26*(1), 32–50.

Wood, E., Willoughby, T., & Woloshyn, V. (1995). An introduction to cognitive strategies in the secondary school. In E. Wood, T. Willoughby, & V. Woloshyn (Eds.), *Cognitive strategy instruction for middle and high schools* (pp. 1–4). Cambridge, MA: Brookline Books.

Youniss, J. (1978). The nature of social development: A conceptual discussion of cognition. In H. McGurk (Ed.), *Social development* (pp. 203–227). London: Methuen.

Youniss, J. (1981). Moral development through a theory of social construction: An analysis. *Merrill-Palmer Quarterly, 27,* 385–403.

Youniss, J. (1987). Social construction and moral development: Update and expansion. In W. Kurtines & J. Gewirtz (Eds.), *Social interaction and sociomoral development* (pp. 131–148). New York: Wiley.

47.

The Role of Classroom Assessment in Teaching and Learning

Lorrie A. Shepard
University of Colorado at Boulder

Historically, because of their technical requirements, educational tests of any importance were seen as the province of statisticians and not as that of teachers or subject matter specialists. Researchers who conceptualized effective teaching did not assign a significant role to assessment as part of the learning process. The past three volumes of the *Handbook of Research on Teaching,* for example, did not include a chapter on classroom assessment or even its traditional counterpart, tests and measurement. Achievement tests were addressed in previous handbooks but only as outcome measures in studies of teaching behaviors. In traditional educational measurement courses, preservice teachers learned about domain specifications, item formats, and methods for estimating reliability and validity. Few connections were made in subject matter methods courses to suggest ways that testing might be used instructionally. Subsequent surveys of teaching practice showed that teachers had little use for statistical procedures and mostly devised end-of-unit tests aimed at measuring declarative knowledge of terms, facts, rules, and principles (Fleming & Chambers, 1983).

The purpose of this chapter is to develop a framework for understanding a reformed view of assessment, where assessment plays an integral role in teaching and learning. If assessment is to be used in classrooms to help students learn, it must be transformed in two fundamental ways. First, the content and character of assessments must be significantly improved. Second, the gathering and use of assessment information and insights must become a part of the ongoing learning process. The model I propose is consistent with current assessment reforms being advanced across many disciplines (e.g., International Reading Association & National Council of Teachers of En-

glish Joint Task Force on Assessment, 1994; National Council for the Social Studies, 1991; National Council of Teachers of Mathematics, 1995; National Research Council, 1996). This model is also consistent with the general argument that assessment content and formats should more directly embody thinking and reasoning abilities that are the ultimate goals of learning (Frederiksen & Collins, 1989; Resnick & Resnick, 1992). Unlike much of the discussion, however, my emphasis is not on external accountability assessments as indirect mechanisms for reforming instructional practice. Instead, I consider directly how classroom assessment practices should be transformed to illuminate and enhance the learning process. I acknowledge, though, that for changes to occur at the classroom level, they must be supported and not impeded by external assessments.

The changes being proposed for assessment are profound. They are part of a larger set of changes in curriculum and in theories of teaching and learning, which many have characterized as a paradigm change. Constructivist learning theory, which is invoked throughout this volume, is at the center of these important changes and has the most direct implications for changes in teaching and assessment. How learning occurs, in the minds and through the social experience of students, however, is not the only change at stake. Equally important are epistemological changes that affect both methods of inquiry and conceptions of what it means to know in each of the disciplines. Finally, a fundamental change must be reckoned with regarding the diverse membership of the scholarly community that is developing this emergent paradigm. This community includes psychologists; curriculum theorists; philosophers; ex-

The author thanks Margaret Eisenhart, Kenneth Howe, Gaea Leinhardt, Richard Shavelson, and Mark Wilson for their thoughtful comments on drafts of this chapter.

The work reported herein was supported in part by grants from the Office of Educational Research and Improvement; the U.S. Department of Education to the Center for Research on Evaluation, Standards, and Student Testing (CRESST) (Award No. R305B60002); and to the Center for Research on Evaluation, Diversity, and Excellence (CREDE) (Award No. R306A60001). The findings and opinions expressed in this chapter do not reflect the positions or policies of the Office of Educational Research and Improvement or the U.S. Department of Education.

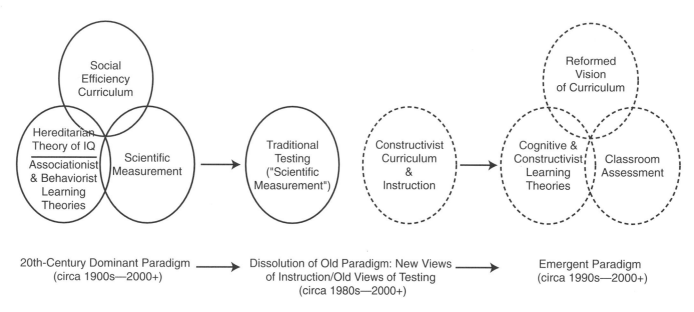

Figure 47.1. An historical overview illustrating how changing conceptions of curriculum, learning theory, and measurement explain the current incompatibility between new views of instruction and traditional views of testing.

perts in mathematics, science, social studies, and literacy education; researchers on teaching and learning to teach; anthropologists; and measurement specialists. How the perspectives of these scholarly community members come together to produce a new view of assessment is a key theme throughout this chapter.

The chapter is organized in the following way. First, three background sections describe underlying curriculum and psychological theories that have shaped methods of instruction, conceptions of subject matter, and methods of testing for most of the 20th century. Second, a conceptual framework is proposed based on new theories and new relationships among curriculum, learning theory, and assessment. Third, the connections between classroom uses of assessment and external accountability systems are described. In the fourth and fifth sections, I elaborate on a model for classroom assessment based on social-constructivist principles as I argue respectively for the substantive reform of assessment and for its use in classrooms to support learning. In the concluding section, I outline the kinds of research studies that will be needed to help realize a reformed vision of classroom assessment.

Historical Perspectives: Curriculum, Psychology, and Measurement

Assessment reformers today emphasize the need for a closer substantive connection between assessment and meaningful instruction. They are reacting against documented distortions in recent decades where teachers, in the contexts of high-stakes accountability testing, have reshaped instructional activities to conform to both the content and format of external standardized tests. By reshaping instruction in this way, teachers have lowered the complexity and demands of the curriculum and, at the same time, have reduced the credibility of test scores. In

describing present-day practice, for example, Graue (1993) suggests that assessment and instruction are "conceived as curiously separate," a separation that Graue attributes to technical measurement concerns. Considering a longer-term span of history, however, helps us to see that those measurement perspectives, now felt to be incompatible with instruction, came from an earlier, highly consistent theoretical framework in which conceptions of "scientific measurement" were closely aligned with curricula underpinned by behaviorist learning theory and directed at social efficiency.

Figure 47.1 was devised to show, in broad strokes, the shift from the dominant 20th-century paradigm (on the left) to an emergent, constructivist paradigm (on the right) in which teachers' close assessment of students' understandings, feedback from peers, and student self-assessment are a part of the social processes that mediate the development of intellectual abilities, construction of knowledge, and formation of students' identities. The middle portion of the figure, intended to represent present-day teaching practices, adapts a similar figure from Graue (1993) that shows a sphere for instruction entirely separate from the sphere for assessment. According to Graue's model, instruction and assessment are guided by different philosophies and are separated in time and place. Even classroom assessments, nominally under the control of teachers, may be more closely aligned with external tests than with day-to-day instructional activities. Although ample evidence indicates that the middle part of the figure describes current practice, this model has no theoretical adherents. The best way to understand this mismatch is to see that instructional practices (at least in their ideal form) are guided by the new paradigm, while traditional testing practices are held over from the old.

It is important to know where traditional views of testing came from and to appreciate how tightly entwined they are with past models of curriculum and instruction, because new theo-

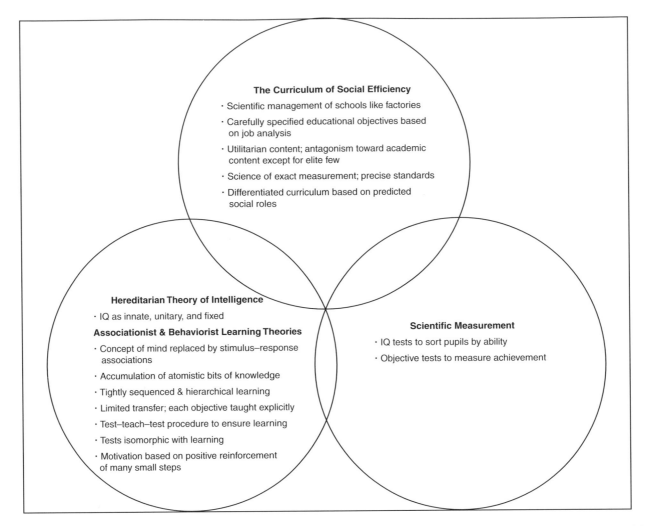

Figure 47.2. Interlocking tenets of curriculum theory, psychological theories, and measurement theory characterize the dominant 20th-century paradigm.

ries are defined and understood in contrast to prior theories. More important, however, dominant theories of the past continue to operate as the default framework, which affects current practices and perspectives. Belief systems of teachers, parents, and policymakers are not exact reproductions of formal theories. They are developed through personal experience and from popular cultural beliefs. Nonetheless, formal theories often influence implicit theories that are held and acted upon by these various groups.

Because it is difficult to articulate or confront formal theories once they have become a part of the popular culture, their influence may be potent but invisible long after they are abandoned by theorists. For example, individuals who have been influenced by behaviorist theories (even if the individuals are not identified as such) may believe that learning in an academic subject is like building a brick wall, layer by layer. They may

resist reforms intended to show connections between multiplication and addition or between patterns and functions because they disrupt the traditional sequencing of topics. Most important, adherence to behaviorist assumptions leads to the postponement of instruction that is aimed at thinking and reasoning until after basic skills have been mastered.

A more elaborated version of the 20th-century dominant paradigm is presented in Figure 47.2. The central ideas of social efficiency and scientific management were closely linked, in the first case, to hereditarian theories of individual differences and, in the second case, to associationist and behaviorist learning theories,[1] which saw learning as the accumulation of stimulus-response associations. These respective psychological theories were, in turn, served by scientific measurement of ability and achievement. The interlocking components of this historic and extant paradigm are summarized in the following sections, with

---

[1] Considering these ideas in parallel is not meant to suggest that hereditarian and behaviorist theories were compatible with each other. Behaviorists strongly favored environmental over genetic explanations for human ability. However, these psychological theories coexisted throughout the 20th century, and both exerted great influence over educational and testing practices.

particular attention given to the legacy of these ideas for classroom assessment practices.

The Curriculum of Social Efficiency

In the early 1900s, public concerns about education were shaped by industrialization, fears of the loss of community, and the need to absorb and Americanize large numbers of immigrants (Callahan, 1962; Kliebard, 1995; Tyack, 1974). The social efficiency movement grew out of the belief that science could be used to solve these problems. The movement was led by sociologists and psychologists but was equally embraced by business leaders and politicians.

According to this theory, modern principles of scientific management, intended to maximize the efficiency of factories, could be applied with equal success to schools. Acting on this theory meant taking Taylor's example of a detailed analysis of the movements performed by expert bricklayers and applying similar analyses to every vocation for which students were being prepared (Kliebard, 1995). Then, given the new associationist or connectionist psychology, with its emphasis on fundamental building blocks, every step would have to be taught specifically. Precise standards of measurement were required to ensure that each skill was mastered at the desired level. And because it was not possible to teach every student the skills of every vocation, scientific measures of ability were also needed to predict one's future role in life and thereby determine who was best suited for each endeavor. For John Franklin Bobbitt, a leader in the social efficiency movement, a primary goal of curriculum design was the elimination of waste (1912); and it was wasteful to teach people things they would never use. Bobbitt's most telling principle was that each individual should be educated "according to his capabilities." These views led to a highly differentiated curriculum and a largely utilitarian one that disdained academic subjects for any but college preparatory students.

Thus, scientific management and social efficiency launched two powerful ideas: (a) the need for detailed specifications of objectives and (b) the tracking of students by ability. Although social efficiency began to lose popularity among sociologists and psychologists after the 1930s, these ideas continued to profoundly influence educational practice because they were absorbed in eclectic versions of curricula, such as life adjustment education and work-oriented curriculum, which had strong appeal with school administrators (Kliebard, 1995). These ideas contributed to and were buttressed by concomitant developments in psychology and measurement.

Hereditarian Theory and IQ Testing

When intelligence tests were brought to the United States in the early 1900s, their interpretation and use were strongly influenced by the eugenics movement and prevalent racist beliefs. Binet, who had developed the first IQ tests in France, believed in "the educability of the intelligence" and deplored the "brutal pessimism" of those who thought it to be a fixed quantity. His program of "mental orthopedics" was intended to improve the use of mental resources and, thus, help the student become more intelligent than before. In contrast, American psychologists such as Terman, Goddard, and Yerkes promoted IQ test

results as a scientifically exact measure of a fixed trait that conformed to the laws of Mendelian genetics.

In a climate of fear about degeneration of the race and the threat of immigration from southern and eastern Europe (Cronbach, 1975; Gould, 1981), most American psychologists emphasized the biological nature of IQ. Goddard (1920, p. 1) referred to intelligence as a "unitary mental process," which is "inborn" and "determined by the kind of chromosomes that come together with the union of the germ cells." Terman (1906, p. 68) asserted without evidence his belief in "the relatively greater importance of endowment over training as a determinant of an individual's intellectual rank among his fellows" (as cited in Gould, 1981, p. 175). Both men also pursued the exact ordering of individuals on the scale of IQ, which they believed accounted for moral behavior and cognitive performance. Goddard fine-tuned distinctions among the feebleminded, creating the categories of idiot, imbecile, and moron. Terman (1916) saw a precise deterministic relationship between IQ score and lot in life. He stated, "An IQ below 70 rarely permits anything better than unskilled labor . . . the range of 70–80 is preeminently that of semiskilled labor; from 80–100 that of ordinary clerical labor" (p. 27), and so forth.

Because measured differences were taken to be innate (and because society would not agree to a program of sterilization), the only way to cope with inexorable differences in capacity was a highly differentiated curriculum. For example, having attributed the higher rate of "borderline deficiency" scores among "Indians, Mexicans, and Negroes" to inherited differences that were most likely racial, Terman (1916) urged that, "Children of this group should be segregated in special classes and be given instruction which is concrete and practical. They cannot master abstractions, but they can often be made efficient workers, able to look out for themselves" (pp. 91–92).

These beliefs and policies were advocated almost 100 years ago, yet they continue to have a profound effect on school practices and public understandings about education. Streaming, or tracking by ability, began in the 1920s and has continued with only slight diminution in recent decades. As Cronbach (1975) explained, the most extreme nativist claims had received widespread attention in the popular press. In contrast, for half a century, more temperate scholarly debates about the fallibility of measures, contributions of environment, and the self-fulfilling consequences of test-based sorting were conducted out of the public eye—until Jensen's (1969) work rekindled the controversy. Not until relatively late in the century did scholars or public officials give attention to the potential harm of labeling children (Hobbs, 1975), the inaccuracy of classifications that are based on single tests (Education for All Handicapped Children Act, 1974), and the possible ineffectiveness of special placements (Heller, Holtzman, & Messick, 1982).

Now at the end of the 20th century, superficially at least, the tide has changed. Most scientists and educated citizens assign a much more limited role to heredity, recognize the multidimensional nature of ability, and are aware of the large effect of past learning opportunities on both test performance and future learning. Herrnstein and Murray's (1994) argument—that inherited cognitive differences between races account for apparent differences in life chances—is an obvious attempt to carry forward earlier ideas, but the argument no longer has support in the current scientific community. Such a summary, however, ignores the persistence of underlying assumptions in popular opinion and cultural norms.

As Wolf and Reardon (1996) point out, enduring beliefs about the fixed nature of ability and the need to segregate elite students explain why we see such a conflict in American education between excellence and equity. Although group IQ tests are no longer routinely used to determine children's capabilities, many teachers, policymakers, and other people implicitly use family background and cultural difference as equally fixed characteristics that account for school failure (Valencia, 1997). The use of readiness measures and achievement tests to categorize students' learning capacities still has the same negative effects as IQ-based tracking had, because implicit in these assessments is the assumption that students in the lower strata should receive a simplified curriculum.

More subtly perhaps, the sorting and classification model of ability testing for purposes of curriculum differentiation has left a legacy that also affects the conception of assessment within classrooms. Even when aptitude measures are replaced by achievement tests, educators still tend to assign students to gross instructional categories, based on test results, rather than to have the test tell something particular about what a student knows or how that student is thinking about a problem. This tendency suggests that achievement is seen as a unidimensional continuum and that tests are "locator" devices. In this regard, the tradition of ranking by ability became curiously entwined with lockstep assumptions about learning sequences that are discussed in the next section.

Associationist and Behaviorist Learning Theories

Edward Thorndike's (1922) associationism and the behaviorism of Hull (1943), Skinner (1938, 1954), and Gagne (1965) were the dominant learning theories for the greater part of the 20th century. Their views of how learning occurs focused on the most elemental building blocks of knowledge. Thorndike was looking for constituent bonds or connections that would produce desired responses for each situation. Similarly, behaviorists studied the contingencies of reinforcement that would strengthen or weaken stimulus-response associations. The following quotation from Skinner is illustrative:

> The whole process of becoming competent in any field must be divided into a very large number of very small steps, and reinforcement must be contingent upon the accomplishment of each step. This solution to the problem of creating a complex repertoire of behavior also solves the problem of maintaining the behavior in strength. . . . By making each successive step as small as possible, the frequency of reinforcement can be raised to a maximum, while the possibly aversive consequences of being wrong are reduced to a minimum. (Skinner, 1954, p. 94)

Although this chapter cannot give a full account of associationist and behaviorist theories, several key assumptions of the behavioristic model had consequences for ensuing conceptualizations of teaching and testing: (a) Learning occurs by accumulating atomized bits of knowledge; (b) learning is sequential and hierarchical; (c) transfer is limited to situations with a high

degree of similarity; (d) tests should be used frequently to ensure mastery before proceeding to the next objective; (e) tests are the direct instantiation of learning goals; and (f) motivation is externally determined and should be as positive as possible (Greeno, Collins, & Resnick, 1996; Shepard, 1991b; Shulman & Quinlan, 1996).

Behaviorist beliefs fostered a reductionistic view of curriculum. To gain control over each learning step, instructional objectives had to be tightly specified, just as the efficiency expert tracked each motion of the brick layer. As Gagne (1965) explains,

> To "know," to "understand," to "appreciate" are perfectly good words, but they do not yield agreement on the exemplification of tasks. On the other hand, if suitably defined, words such as to "write," to "identify," to "list," do lead to reliable descriptions. (p. 43)

Thus, behaviorally stated objectives became the required elements of both instructional sequences and closely related mastery tests. Although behaviorists shared the intention that learners would eventually get to more complex levels of thinking—as evidenced by the analysis, synthesis, and evaluation levels of Bloom's (1956) taxonomy—their emphasis on stating objectives in behavioral terms tended to constrain the goals of instruction.

The rigid sequencing of learning elements also tended to focus instruction on low-level skills, especially for low-achieving students and children in the early grades. Complex learnings were seen as the sum of simpler behaviors. It would be useless and inefficient to go on to ABC problems without first having firmly mastered A and AB objectives (Bloom, 1956). For decades, these beliefs—that learning should be broken down into constituent elements and taught according to strict hiearchies—undergirded every educational innovation. Such innovations included programmed instruction, mastery learning, objectives-based curricula, remedial reading programs, criterion-referenced testing, minimum competency testing, and special education interventions. Only later did researchers begin to document the diminished learning opportunities of children who were assigned to drill-and-practice curricula in various remedial settings (Allington, 1991; Shepard, 1991a).

For all learning theories, the idea of transfer involves generalization of learning to new situations. Yet because behaviorism was based on the building up of associations in response to a particular stimulus, there was no basis for generalization unless the new situation was very similar to the original one. Therefore, expectations for transfer were limited; if a response were desired in a new situation, it would have to be taught as an additional learning goal. Cohen (1987), for example, praised the effectiveness of closely aligning tests with instruction citing a study by Koczor (1984) in which students did remarkably better if they were taught to convert from Roman to Arabic numerals and then were tested in that same order. If groups were given "misaligned" tests, however, asking that they translate in reverse order from Arabic to Roman numerals, the drop-off in performance was startling, with effect sizes from 1.10 to 2.74 in different samples. Consistent with the behaviorist perspective, Cohen and Koczor considered Roman-to-Arabic and Arabic-to-Roman conversions to be two separate learning objectives. They were not troubled by lack of transfer from one to the other, nor did they wonder what this lack of transfer implied about students' understanding.

Testing played a central role in behaviorist instructional systems. To avoid learning failures caused by incomplete mastery of prerequisites, testing was needed at the end of each lesson, and reteaching was to continue until a high level of proficiency was achieved. To serve this diagnostic and prescriptive purpose, test content had to be exactly matched to instructional content by means of the behavioral objective. Because learning components were tightly specified, very limited inference or generalization was required to make a connection between test items and learning objectives. Behaviorists worked hard to create a low-inference measurement system so that if students could answer the questions asked, their correct answers proved that they had fully mastered the learning objective.

The belief that tests could be made perfectly congruent with the goals of learning had pervasive effects in the measurement community despite resistance from some. For decades, many measurement specialists believed that achievement tests only required content validity evidence, and they did not see the need for empirical confirmation that a test measured what was intended. Behavioristic assumptions also explain why, in recent years, advocates of measurement-driven instruction were willing to use test scores themselves to prove that teaching to the test improved learning (Popham, Cruse, Rankin, Sandifer, & Williams, 1985), although critics insisted on independent measures to verify whether learning gains were real (Koretz, Linn, Dunbar, & Shepard, 1991).

Behaviorist viewpoints also have implications for assessment in classrooms. For example, when teachers check on learning by using problems and formats identical to those used for initial instruction, they are operating from the low-inference and limited transfer assumptions of behaviorism. For most teachers, however, these beliefs are not explicit, and unlike Koczor and Cohen in the example above, most teachers have not had the opportunity to consider directly whether a student "really knows it" if he or she can solve problems only when posed in a familiar format.

Behaviorism also makes important assumptions about motivation to learn. It assumes that individuals are externally motivated by the pursuit of rewards and avoidance of punishments. In particular, Skinner's (1954) interpretation of how reinforcement should be used to structure learning environments had far-reaching effects on education. As expressed in the earlier quotation, Skinner's idea was that to keep the learner motivated, instruction should be staged to ensure as much success as possible with little or no negative feedback. It was this motivational purpose, as much as the componential analysis of tasks, that led to the idea of little steps. In Individually Prescribed Instruction (Education U.S.A., 1968), for example, lessons were designed around skills that the average student could master in a single class period.

"Scientific Measurement" and Objective Examinations

It is no coincidence that Edward Thorndike was both the originator of associationist learning theory and the father of "scientific measurement"[2] in education (Ayers, 1918). Thorndike and his students fostered the development and dominance of the objective test, which has been the single most striking feature of achievement testing in the United States from the beginning of the 20th century to the present day. Recognizing the common paternity of the behaviorist learning theory and objective testing helps us to understand the continued intellectual kinship between one-skill-at-a-time test items and instructional practices that are aimed at mastery of constituent elements.

Borrowing the psychometric technology of IQ tests, measurement experts pursued objective measures of achievement with the goal of making the study of education more scientific. According to Ralph Tyler (1938), "The achievement-testing movement provided a new tool by which educational problems could be studied systematically in terms of more objective evidence regarding the effects produced in pupils" (p. 349). Objective tests were also promoted for classroom use as a remedy for embarrassing inconsistencies in teachers' grading practices that had been documented by dozens of research studies. In one classic study, for example, the same geometry paper was distributed to 116 high school mathematics teachers and received grades ranging from 28% to 92% (Starch & Elliott, 1913). Many of the arguments made in favor of teacher-developed objective tests suggest issues that are still relevant today. For example, in addition to solving the problem of grader subjectivity, discrete item types also allowed "extensive sampling" (better content coverage) and "high reliability per unit of working time" (Ruch, 1929, p. 112). The emphasis on reliability, defined as the consistency with which individuals are ranked, followed naturally from the application to achievement tests of reliability and validity coefficients that were developed in the context of intelligence testing.

Examples from some of the earliest "standard" tests and objective-type classroom tests are shown in Figure 47.3. Looking at any collection of tests from early in the 20th century, one is immediately struck by how much the questions emphasize rote recall. To be fair, this emphasis was not a distortion of subject matter that was caused by the adoption of objective-item formats. Rather, the various recall, completion, matching, and multiple-choice test types fit closely with what was deemed important to learn in the first part of the 20th century. Nonetheless, once knowledge of curriculum became encapsulated and represented by these types of items, we can reasonably say that these formats locked in and perpetuated a particular conception of subject matter.

Also shown in Figure 47.3 is an example of the kind of essay question asked alongside objective questions in a 1928 American history test. Little data exist to tell us how often the two types of examinations were used or to document their relative quality. For example, Ruch (1929) defended his new-type objec-

---

[2] Note that "scientific measurement" was the term used historically, but it is based on the conception of science and scientific inquiry that was held at the turn of the previous century. The honorific label does not imply that early achievement tests were scientific according to present-day standards for scientific inquiry.

New Stone Reasoning Tests in Arithmetic (1908)

1. James had 5 cents. He earned 13 cents more and then bought a top for 10 cents. how much money did he have left?   *Answer:* _____

2. How many oranges can I buy for 35 cents when oranges cost 7 cents each?   *Answer:* _____

Sones-Harry High School Achievement Test, Part II (1929)

1. What instrument was designed to draw a circle? ....(_____)1
2. Write "25% of" as "a decimal times." ....(_____)2
3. Write in figures: one thousand seven and four hundredths...(_____)3

The Modern School Achievement Tests, Language Usage

1. I borrowed a pen
       a. off
       b. off of   my brother.   _____
       c. from

2. Every student must do
       a. your
       b. his   best.   _____
       c. their

3. He
       a. has got
       b. has   his violin with him.   _____
       c. has gotten

The Barrett-Ryan Literature Test: Silas Marner

1. ( ) An episode that advances the plot is the—a. murdering of a man. b. kidnapping of a child. c. stealing of money. d. fighting of a duel.

2. ( ) Dolly Winthrop is—a. an ambitious society woman. b. a frivolous girl. c. a haughty lady. d. a kind, helpful neighbor.

3. ( ) A chief characteristic of the novel is—a. humorous passages. b. portrayal of character. c. historical facts. d. fairy element.

Examples of True-False Objective Test (Ruch, 1929)

1. Tetanus (lockjaw) germs usually enter the body through open wounds.   *True False*

2. Pneumonia causes more deaths in the United States than tuberculosis.   *True False*

3. White blood corpuscles are more numerous than are the red ones.   *True False*

Examples of Best-Answer Objective Test (Ruch, 1929)

1. Leguminous plants play an important role in nature because: Bacteria associated with their roots return nitrogen to the soil. They will grow on soil too poor to support other crops. The economic value of the hay crop is very large.

2. The best of these definitions of photosynthesis is: The action of sunlight on plants. The process of food manufacture in green plants. The process by which plants give off oxygen.

American History Examination, East High School
Sam Everett and Effey Riley, 1928

I. Below is a list of statements. Indicate by a cross (X) after it, each statement that expresses a social heritage of the present-day American nation.
Place a (0) after each statement that is not a present-day social heritage of the American nation.
1. Americans believe in the ideal of religious toleration.   _____
2. Property in land should be inherited by a man's eldest son.   _____
3. Citizens should have the right to say what taxes should be put upon them.   _____

II. To test your ability to see how an intelligent knowledge of past events help us to understand present-day situations and tendencies.
(Note: Write your answer in essay form on a separate sheet of paper.)
Someone has said that we study the past relationships in American life in order to be able to understand the present in our civilization and that we need to understand the present so as to influence American national development toward finer things.

State your reasons for every position assumed.

4. Take some *economic* fact or group of facts in American history about which we have studied and briefly show what seems to you to be the actual significance of this fact in the past, present, and future of America.
5. Show this same *three-fold relationship* using some *political* fact or facts.
6. Show this same *three-fold relationship* using a *religious* fact or facts.

III. 7. The rise of manufacturing in New England was greatly aided by the fact that their physical environment furnished: (a) cold temperature, (b) all kinds of raw materials, (c) many navigable rivers, (d) easy communication with the West, (e) water power.
8. The wealth of colonial South Carolina came chiefly from: (a) rice, (b) tobacco, (c) cotton, (d) furs, (e) wheat.

IV. 9. The Constitution represents a series of compromises rather than a document considered perfect by its signers.   R ? W
10. Since a great number of the colonists had come to America for political freedom and to found governments on democratic ideals, full manhood suffrage was granted in every colony from the first.   R ? W
11. The major reason why slavery did not flourish in the New England colonies was because it was not a good financial proposition.   R ? W

V. 12. As part of your education, you have been studying in American history about the Constitutional Convention. Has the study of that historical event meant to you simply memorizing a list of the facts or events,—or has it given you (a) insight into the significance of certain decisions made by the men of the Constitutional Convention; (b) ability to evaluate certain clauses of our Constitution; (c) ability to decide whether our forefathers intended to give us a democracy or not?

If you have gained any of these three things, will you try to show that you have acquired them through use of practical illustrations in each of the three cases?

Figure 47.3. Examples from some of the earliest 20th-century "standard" tests and objective-type classroom tests.

tive examination against the complaint that it only measured memory by saying that "teachers and educators pay lip service to the thought question and then proceed merrily to ask pupils to 'Name the principal products of New England' or to 'List the main causes of the Revolutionary War'" (p. 121).

Present-day calls for assessment reform are intended to counteract the distorting effects of high-stakes accountability tests. Under pressure to improve scores, teachers not only have abandoned untested content but also have reshaped their classroom instruction to imitate the format of standardized tests (Darling-Hammond & Wise, 1985; Madaus, West, Harmon, Lomax, & Viator, 1992; Shepard & Dougherty, 1991; Smith, 1989). By hearkening to a day before standardized achievement measures had such serious consequences, reformers seem to imply that there was once a golden era when teachers used more comprehensive and challenging examinations to evaluate student knowledge. A longer-term historical view suggests, however, that the current propensity to focus on low-level skills is merely an exaggeration of practices that have continued without interruption throughout the 20th century.

The long-term, abiding tendency has been to think of subject matter in a way that is perfectly compatible with recall-oriented test questions. The 1946 National Society for the Study of Education (NSSE) yearbook (Brownell, 1946), for example, was devoted to "The Measurement of Understanding." In introducing the volume, William Brownell explained that techniques for measuring factual knowledge and skills were well worked out and used in evaluation and in teaching while "understanding," "meaningful learning," and "the higher mental processes" were neglected (Brownell, 1946, p. 2). In a 1967 national survey, Goslin reported that 67% of public secondary teachers and 76% of elementary teachers reported using objective items "frequently," "most of the time," or "always" (Goslin, 1967). Many teachers used both types of questions, but objective questions were used more often than essays. In recent decades, analysts have documented the reciprocal influence of textbooks on standardized tests and standardized tests on textbooks (Tyson-Bernstein, 1988), which has also carried forward a conception of subject matter that is mostly vocabulary, facts, and decontextualized skills.

The dominance of objective tests in classroom practice has affected more than the form of subject matter knowledge. It has also shaped beliefs about the nature of evidence and principles of fairness. In a recent assessment project (Shepard, 1995), for example, where teachers were nominally seeking alternatives to standardized tests, teachers nonetheless worked from a set of beliefs that were consistent with traditional principles of scientific measurement. As documented by Bliem and Davinroy (1997), assessment was seen as an official event. To ensure fairness, teachers believed that assessments had to be uniformly administered; therefore, teachers were reluctant to conduct more intensive individualized assessments with only below-grade-level readers. Because of the belief that assessments had to be targeted to a specific instructional goal, teachers felt more comfortable using two separate assessments for separate goals: (a) a notation system known as "running records" to assess fluency and (b) written summaries to assess comprehension. Teachers kept these assessments separate instead of, for example, asking students to retell the gist of a story in conjunction with running records. Most significantly, teachers wanted their assessments

to be "objective," they worried often about the subjectivity involved in making more holistic evaluations of student work, and they preferred formula-based methods such as counting miscues because these techniques were more "impartial."

Any attempt to change the form and purpose of classroom assessment to make it more fundamentally a part of the learning process must acknowledge the power of enduring and hidden beliefs. I have suggested that the present dissonance between instruction and assessment arises because of the misfit between old views of testing and a transformed vision of teaching. However, even reformed versions of instruction have only begun to be implemented. As many studies of teacher change and attempted curriculum reform have documented, all three parts of the old paradigm—social efficiency, behaviorism, and scientific measurement—continue to provide a mutually reinforcing set of ideas that shapes current thinking and practice.

Conceptual Framework: New Theories of Curriculum, Learning, and Assessment

To develop a model of classroom assessment that supports teaching and learning according to a constructivist perspective, we must understand how a reconceptualization of assessment follows from changes in learning theory and from concomitant changes in epistemology and what it means to know in the disciplines. Figure 47.4 summarizes key ideas in an emergent, constructivist paradigm. According to constructivist theory, knowledge is neither passively received nor mechanically reinforced. Instead, learning occurs by an active process of sense making. The three-part figure was developed parallel to the three-part dominant paradigm to highlight respectively changes in curriculum, learning theory, and assessment. In some cases, principles in the new paradigm are direct antitheses of principles in the old paradigm. The interlocking circles again are intended to show the coherence and interrelatedness of these ideas taken together.

The new paradigm is characterized as emergent because it is not fully developed theoretically and, surely, not adopted in practice. Although one can find some shared understandings among cognitivists and constructivists about how learning principles should lead to reform of curriculum and instruction, one also finds competing versions of these theories and ideas. In choosing among the different versions, I summarize key ideas that are widely shared and that, for the most part, are compatible with my own view. In the case of constructivist learning theory, for example, I focus on sociocultural theory and a Vygotskian version of constructivism rather than on either Piagetian or radical constructivism (von Glasersfeld, 1995). In the case of standards-based curriculum reform, however, I consider the importance of the standards movement in refuting the principles of tracked curricula despite my personal misgivings about the likely harm that standards-based assessments impose as part of an external accountability system.

Cognitive and Social-Constructivist Learning Theories

I began the description of the old paradigm with the tenets of the social efficiency curriculum because zeal for scientific efficiency had led to both the popularity of an atomistic psychology and enthusiasm for objective measurement formats. Here,

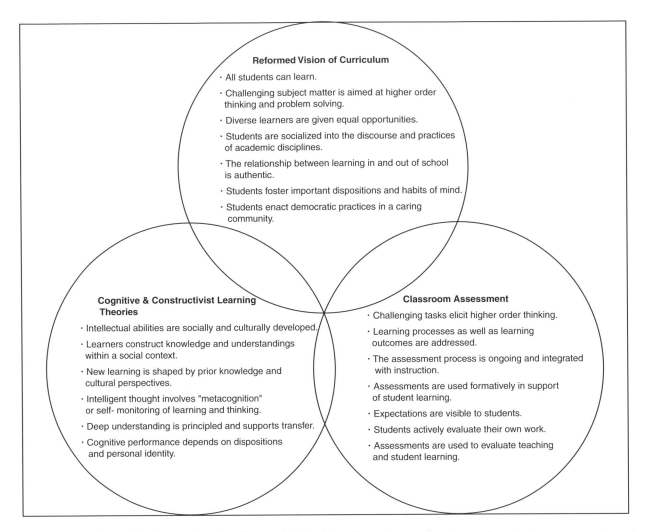

Figure 47.4. Shared principles of curriculum theories, psychological theories, and assessment theory characterize an emergent, constructivist paradigm.

I treat changes in learning theory as primary and then consider their implications for changes in curriculum and assessment. My summary of new learning theories borrows from similar analyses by Greeno, Collins, and Resnick (1996) and by Eisenhart, Finkel, and Marion (1996). However, unlike Greeno et al. (1996), who separate contemporary views into the cognitive and situative perspectives, I list a combined set of propositions that might come to be a shared set of assumptions about learning. Although some of those ideas clearly come from the cognitive tradition, emphasizing mainly what goes on in the mind, and others focus on social interactions and cultural meanings in the tradition of anthropology, the most important feature of this new paradigm is that it brings together two perspectives that account for cognitive development in terms of social experience.

The constructivist paradigm takes its name from the fundamental notion that all human knowledge is constructed. As noted by D.C. Phillips (1995), this statement applies to the construction of public knowledge and modes of inquiry in the disciplines as well as to the development of cognitive structures in the minds of individual learners. According to this paradigm,

then, scientists build their theories and understandings rather than merely discovering laws of nature. Similarly, individuals create their own interpretations, or ways of organizing information, and their own approaches to problems rather than merely accepting preexisting knowledge structures. For purposes of this framework, I am concerned more with constructivist learning theory than with epistemology. However, an important aspect of individual learning is developing experience with and being inducted into the ways of thinking and working in a discipline or community of practice. Both the building of science and individual learning are social processes. Although the individual must do some private work to internalize what is supported and practiced in the social plane, learning cannot be understood apart from its social context and content.

INTELLECTUAL ABILITIES ARE SOCIALLY AND CULTURALLY DEVELOPED

Hereditarian theories of intelligence have been replaced by interactionist theories. We now understand that cognitive abilities are "developed" through socially mediated learning opportunities (Feuerstein, 1969) as parents or other significant adults interpret and guide children in their interactions with the environment. Interestingly, Vygotsky's model of supported learning, which has such importance in this volume for the teaching and learning of mathematics, social studies, and so forth, initially was conceived to describe the development of intellectual competence more generally—namely, how one learns to think. Indeed, efforts to study mental processes and how they are developed have blurred the distinctions between learning to think, learning how to solve problems within specific domains and contexts, and developing intelligence. Earlier work in this vein demonstrated the modifiability or instructability of intelligence by working with extreme populations such as educably mentally retarded children (Budoff, 1974) and low-functioning adolescents (Feuerstein, 1980). More complex, present-day intervention programs by Denny Wolf, Ann Brown, and others can be seen as extensions of this same idea, although improving intelligence per se is no longer the aim. Wolf and Reardon (1996), for example, talk about "developing achievement" by devising a staged curriculum that allows students supported practice with all of the enabling competencies (writing an essay, piecing together historical evidence, or conducting an experiment) that ensure proficient performance of the final, challenging goals. Wolf and Reardon also note that teachers who struggle to create such a curriculum must confront "the fundamental difference between raw aptitude and hard-earned achievement" (p. 11).

LEARNERS CONSTRUCT KNOWLEDGE AND UNDERSTANDINGS WITHIN A SOCIAL CONTEXT

To learn something new, the learner must actively teach herself or himself what new information means. How does it fit with what I already know? Does it make sense? If it contradicts what I thought before, how am I going to reconcile the differences? If I substitute this new idea for an old one, do I have to rethink other closely related ideas?

Although earlier, Piagetian versions of constructivism focused on individual developmental stages or processes (Eisenhart et al., 1996), over time, cognitive psychologists have increasingly acknowledged the influence of social processes. The rediscovery of Vygotsky provided a theoretical model for understanding how social interactions between adult and child could supply both a model of expertise and the opportunity for guided practice so that the child could eventually internalize desired skills and perform them independently. According to Vygotsky, the zone of proximal development (what an individual can learn) "is the distance between the actual developmental level as determined by independent problem solving and the level of potential development as determined through problem solving under adult guidance or in collaboration with more capable peers" (1978, p. 86). Bruner's notion of "scaffolding" elaborated on the kinds of social support that would assist a child in performing a task that would otherwise be out of reach; these supports include engaging interest, simplifying the problem, maintaining direction, marking critical features, reducing frustration, and demonstrating (Wood, Bruner, & Ross, 1976).

Other contemporary perspectives (also borrowing from Vygotsky) go further, suggesting that historical and cultural factors do not merely influence learning but constitute or form identity, images of possible selves, and the repertoire of knowledge and skills that are needed to participate in a community of practice (Eisenhart et al., 1996; Lave & Wenger, 1991). This line of thinking—emphasizing socially negotiated meaning—has complicated the models of effective learning. In contrast to the decontextualization and decomposition fostered by associationism, now no aspect of learning can be understood separate from the whole or separate from its social and cultural context. For example, in describing the "thinking curriculum," Resnick and Klopfer (1989) emphasized that thinking skills could not be developed independent of content nor could cognitive skills be separated from motivation. Apprenticeship models are a natural extension of this reasoning because they provide for role development and support for novice performances as well as the contextualization of skill and knowledge development in a particular community of practice.

NEW LEARNING IS SHAPED BY PRIOR KNOWLEDGE AND CULTURAL PERSPECTIVES

For those eager to throw off the shackles of the old paradigm, the role of content knowledge has posed an interesting dilemma. Because mastery of subject matter knowledge has traditionally implied at least some rote memorization, curriculum reformers have sometimes swung to the other extreme, emphasizing processes over content. Yet, a fundamental finding of cognitive research is that knowledge enables new learning (Resnick & Klopfer, 1989). Those with existing knowledge stores can reason more profoundly, elaborate as they study, and thereby learn more effectively in that knowledge domain (Glaser, 1984). Knowledge in a domain includes facts, vocabulary, principles, fundamental relationships, familiar analogies and models, rules of thumb, problem-solving approaches, and schemas for knowing when to use what. Not only does effective teaching (and assessment) begin by eliciting students' prior knowledge and intuitions, but also it develops a community of practice where it is customary for students to review and question what they already believe.

Ironically, the validity of efforts to assess prior knowledge are themselves affected by a student's knowledge base and by cultural practices. Often, prior knowledge is measured using skills checklists or a pretest version of the intended end-of-unit test. Such procedures are likely to underestimate the relevant knowledge of all but the most sophisticated members of the class because most will not be able to make the translation between pretest vocabulary and their own intuitive knowledge gained in other contexts. Open discussions or conversations are more likely to elicit a more coherent version of students' initial conceptual understandings and the reasoning behind their explanations (Minstrell, 1989; Yackel, Cobb, & Wood, 1991). Teachers must also become familiar with relevant experiences and discourse patterns in diverse communities so that children who are entering schools will be able to demonstrate their competence rather than appear deficient because they are unfamiliar with the teacher's mode of questioning (Heath, 1983).

INTELLIGENT THOUGHT INVOLVES "METACOGNITION" OR SELF-MONITORING OF LEARNING AND THINKING

Adept learners are able to take charge of their own learning using a variety of self-monitoring processes (Brown, 1994). This concept of metacognition, or thinking about thinking, is a key contribution of the cognitive revolution. Being able to solve problems within each domain of practice involves what Sternberg (1992) called "executive processes" such as (a) recognizing the existence of a problem, (b) deciding on the nature of the problem, (c) selecting a set of lower-order processes to solve the problem, (d) developing a strategy to combine these components, (e) selecting a mental representation of the problem, (f) allocating one's mental resources, (g) monitoring one's problem solving as it is happening, and (h) evaluating problem solving after it is done.

Metacognitive abilities can be learned through socially mediated processes in the same way that first-order cognitive abilities are learned. For example, Brown, Bransford, Ferrara, and Campione (1983) conducted studies in which children's comprehension of texts could be improved by teaching them specific strategies such as questioning, clarifying, and summarizing—the kinds of strategies that proficient readers use without explicit training. These ideas were then extended to a full-blown reading comprehension intervention called "reciprocal teaching" (Palincsar & Brown, 1984), which blends the ideas of strategies training and cognitive apprenticeship. Although not a scripted lesson, the routines of reciprocal teaching dialogues give students socially supported practice with four metacognitive strategies—predicting, question generating, summarizing, and clarifying—so that students develop a shared understanding of the text. Reciprocal teaching has been used primarily with learning disabled children and students in remedial reading programs and has shown a median gain of .88 standard deviations for students receiving the intervention compared to controls (Rosenshine & Meister, 1994).

DEEP UNDERSTANDING IS PRINCIPLED AND SUPPORTS TRANSFER

A close relationship exists between truly understanding a concept and being able to transfer knowledge and use it in new situations. In contrast to memorization and in contrast to the earlier behaviorist example where students mastered Arabic to Roman numeral translations but couldn't do them in reverse, true understanding is flexible, connected, and generalizable. Not surprisingly, research studies demonstrate that learning is more likely to transfer if students have the opportunity to practice with a variety of applications while learning (Bransford, 1979) and if they are encouraged to attend to general themes or features of problems that imply use of a particular solution strategy (Brown & Kane, 1988). Learning the rules of transfer is, of course, an example of a metacognitive skill that can be supported instructionally.

In working with preservice teachers, I have suggested that a goal of teaching should be to help students develop "robust" understandings (Shepard, 1997). The term was prompted by Marilyn Burns's (1993) reference to children's understandings as being "fragile"—that is, children appear to know a concept in one context but appear not to know it when asked in another way or in another setting. Sometimes this fragility occurs because students are still in the process of learning. All too often, however, mastery appears pat and certain but does not transfer because the student has mastered classroom routines and not

the underlying concepts. To support generalization and ensure transfer, that is, to support robust understandings, "good teaching constantly asks about old understandings in new ways, calls for new applications, and draws new connections" (Shepard, 1997, p. 27).

From the situative perspective, or the perspective of activity theory (Greeno, Smith, & Moore, 1993; Lave & Wenger, 1991; Rogoff, 1990), the example of children not being able to use their knowledge in new settings might be attributed to their being removed from the original community of practice that provided both meaning and support for knowledge use—perhaps. However, a more probable explanation, given the pervasiveness of rote teaching practices, is that children do not really understand even in the initial setting. Although cognitivists and situativists appear to disagree regarding knowledge generalization (Anderson, Reder, & Simon, 1996), in fact, both groups of researchers acknowledge the importance of transfer. Cognitivists focus more on cognitive structures, abstract representations, and generalized principles that enable knowledge use in new situations, while "in situativity, generality depends on learning to participate in interactions in ways that succeed over a broad range of situations" (Greeno, 1996, p. 3). Given Vygotsky's explanation that learning occurs on two planes, first on the social plane between people and then within the individual child, a successful program of research will likely need to consider both.

COGNITIVE PERFORMANCE DEPENDS ON DISPOSITIONS AND PERSONAL IDENTITY

Historically, research on motivation was undertaken by social psychologists separately from the work of learning researchers (Resnick & Klopfer, 1989). Only when cognitive researchers began to study metacognition did they come to realize that students might not use the strategies they know unless they are motivated to do so.

Larger societal norms and traditional classroom practices, especially testing practices, have created environments in which students may not be motivated to take risks, to try hard, or to demonstrate their intellectual competence. For example, in controlled psychological studies, students are less likely to persist in working on difficult tasks if they know their performance will be evaluated (Hughes, Sullivan, and Mosley, 1985; Maehr & Stallings, 1972). According to motivational researchers, students who believe that academic achievement is determined by fixed ability are more likely to work toward "performance goals," that is, for grades, to please the teacher, and to appear competent.

Lave and Wenger (1991) harshly see this "commoditization of learning" to be a pervasive feature of school settings, where the exchange value of learning outcomes is emphasized over the use value of learning. According to this stark portrayal, performance-oriented students tend to pick easy tasks and are less likely to persist once they encounter difficulty (Stipek, 1996). Unfortunately, girls are overrepresented in this category (Dweck, 1986). Students who attribute academic success to their own efforts are more likely to adopt "learning goals," which means they are motivated by an increasing sense of mastery and by the desire to become competent. Not surprisingly, students with a learning orientation are more engaged in school work, use more self-regulation and metacognitive strategies, and develop deeper understanding of subject matter (Wittrock, 1986).

Social psychological research on achievement motivation has produced a list of evaluation practices that are more likely to foster learning goals and intrinsic motivation. For example, motivation is enhanced if errors and mistakes are treated as a normal part of learning and if substantive, mastery-based feedback is used rather than normative evaluation (Stipek, 1996). Although most of these laboratory-based recommendations make sense and would contribute to a classroom environment where learning and the development of competence are valued, a few points are worrisome. For example, research on intrinsic motivation urges teachers to "de-emphasize external evaluation, especially for challenging tasks" (Stipek, 1996, p. 102), despite the finding elsewhere (Dweck, 1986) that students with a learning orientation "see their teacher as a resource or guide in the learning process, rather than as an evaluator" (Stipek, 1993, p. 15). Moreover, this variable manipulation approach still leaves the teacher responsible for acting on the student in a way that will induce learning.

In my view, these findings about the negative effects of evaluation on motivation to learn are the product of the beliefs and practices of the old paradigm that, following Skinner's formulation, provided extrinsic rewards for success on easy tasks. In such an environment, it is not surprising to find that so many students have developed a performance orientation instead of a learning orientation. It does not follow, however, that evaluation would always stifle motivation if the culture of the classroom were fundamentally altered. In addition, to conclude on the basis of past studies that somehow students need to be protected from critical feedback is dangerous. Evaluative feedback is essential to learning and, presumably, can be of the greatest benefit when students are tackling problems that are beyond their level of independent mastery. Thus, the idea of withholding evaluation for challenging tasks is contrary to the idea of supporting students' efforts in the zone of proximal development.

Activity theory and Lave and Wenger's (1991) concept of legitimate peripheral participation provide a wholly different view of what might "motivate" students to devote their hearts and minds to learning. According to this theory, learning and development of an identity of mastery occur together as a newcomer becomes increasingly adept at participating in a community of practice. If one's identity is tied to group membership, then one naturally works to become a more competent and fullfledged member of the group. Such ideas come from studying learning in the world outside of school.

How is it that children learn their native language from parents and community members without the benefit of formal lessons or memorized rules? How do novices learn how to be tailors or Xerox repair technicians or members of Alcoholic's Anonymous (Lave & Wenger, 1991)? They are not told explicitly how to participate; instead, they are provided with opportunities in the context of practice to see, imitate, and try out increasingly complex skills under the guidance of experts and, at the same time, practice the role of community member. Again, Vygotsky's notion of socially supported learning is applied at once to the development of knowledge, cognitive abilities, and identity. Significantly, the beginner is also contributing to and

affecting the nature of practice shared with old-timers, which also adds to the worth and meaning of effort. Cognitive apprenticeship programs (Collins, Brown, & Newman, 1989) and Brown and Campione's (1994) community of learners are examples of projects in schools that are aimed at developing communities of practice where students' identities as capable learners are constructed as they participate in active inquiry and discussion of challenging problems.

Reformed Vision of Curriculum

The elements of a reformed vision of curriculum, summarized in Figure 47.4, set the direction for the kinds of changes that contemporary educational reformers are trying to make in classrooms. Some of these principles are part of the wider public discourse familiar to policymakers and journalists as well as educators and researchers. Others are articulated by a smaller circle of education reformers.

At the political level, present day educational reform is motivated by the poor performance of U.S. students in international comparisons and by anxiety about economic competitiveness. In this light, many politicians have accepted the argument from researchers that current problems are, in part, due to past reforms aimed at minimum competencies and low-level tests. As a result, standards and assessments have been given a central role in reforming public education. The mantra of standards-based reform, "high standards for *all* students," promises the pursuit of both excellence and equity, goals that were held at odds by prior belief systems. The first set of reform principles—all students can learn, challenging standards should be aimed at higher order thinking and problem solving, and equal opportunity should be provided for diverse learners—are widely shared and recur in legislation, various state and national policy reports, and in standards documents for each of the disciplines.

The remaining elements of the agenda are not so familiar in public arenas but are essential to accomplishing the first set. Given that it has never been done before, we cannot expect all students to master challenging subject matter and preform to high standards, unless we have new means whereby students can be engaged in learning in fundamentally different ways. Socialization into the discourse and practices of academic disciplines, authenticity in the relationship between learning in and out of school, the fostering of important dispositions and habits of mind, and the enactment of democratic values and practices in a community of learners are elements of the reform agenda that follow from the research on cognition and motivation described previously and from the basic empirical work that has documented the dreariness and meaninglessness of traditional practice. Taken together, they portray the curriculum and classroom environment that would be needed to support student learning at a much higher level.

While not diminishing the significance of these research-based "discoveries," we should acknowledge that many of the tenets of reform are not new but bear a remarkable resemblance to ideas advanced by John Dewey 100 years ago. Dewey envisioned a school curriculum that would develop intelligence by engaging students' experience, skills, and interests as the necessary first step in teaching more traditional subject matter. He recognized the social nature of learning and the desirability of creating a miniature community to initiate the child into effective social membership (Kliebard, 1995). In light of the ambitious claims of the current reforms, it is sobering to recognize how many attempts have been made to implement the ideals of progressive education since Dewey first advanced them. Successes have been short-lived because, as suggested by Cremin (1961), the complexity of such reforms required "infinitely skilled teachers."

A further caveat is also warranted. The framework in Figure 47.4 is intended to address how learning theory and curriculum reform come together at the level of the classroom to reshape instruction and assessment. One would be mistaken, however, to imagine that significant changes could occur in classrooms without corresponding changes in the community and at other levels of the educational and political system. McLaughlin and Talbert (1993), for example, identified the multiple, embedded contexts of teachers and classrooms that may constrain or facilitate educational change. These include subject matter cultures, state and local mandates, the parent community and social class culture, the expectations of teachers in the next higher level of schooling, and professional contexts including teachers' associations and university teacher education programs. In later sections of the chapter, I address two connections to contexts beyond the classroom: the relationship between assessments at classroom and system levels as well as the implications of assessment reform for professional development needs of teachers. Still, the chapter is limited by not being able to treat the concomitant changes that would be needed in these several other contexts to support change in the classroom.

ALL STUDENTS CAN LEARN

The slogan that "all students can learn" is intended to promulgate what the Malcolm Report (Malcolm, 1993) called "a new way of thinking." It is a direct refutation of the long-standing belief that innate ability determines life chances. Although such affirmations by themselves will not be sufficient to provide the necessary learning opportunities, the slogan is important because it serves to disrupt the self-fulfilling practices of the old paradigm whereby only certain students were smart enough to master difficult content and, therefore, only an elite group of students was given access to challenging subject matter.

CHALLENGING STANDARDS ARE AIMED AT HIGHER ORDER THINKING AND PROBLEM SOLVING

That the common curriculum should address challenging standards aimed at higher-order thinking and problem solving is likewise a rejection of past practices and theory. The transmission model of learning that was based on rote memorization of isolated facts removed learning from contexts that could provide both meaning and application. By watering down curricula and emphasizing minimum competencies, schools have lowered expectations and limited opportunities to learn. By contrast, if children are presented with more challenging and complex problems and given the support to solve them, they will develop deeper understandings and, at the same time, become more ad-

ept at the modes of inquiry and ways of reasoning that will help them solve new problems in the future.

EQUAL OPPORTUNITIES ARE PROVIDED FOR DIVERSE LEARNERS

The commitment to equity as part of standards-based reform implies changing both expectations and resources. Inequality of opportunity pervades the U.S. educational system. Not only do children from poor and minority communities receive less rigorous curricula (a problem that standards are intended to address), but also they are taught by teachers with less academic preparation and experience, have access to fewer books and computers, and often attend schools that are unsafe or where it is "uncool" to take schoolwork seriously (Fordham & Ogbu, 1986; Kozol, 1991; Oakes, 1985, 1990). Standards advocates, such as the National Council on Education Standards and Testing (1992), believe that public accountability based on standards and assessment will help ensure the availability of adequate resources.

Equal access to high quality instruction implies more than evenhanded allocation of fiscal and human resources, however. It also requires a more thoughtful and deeper understanding of the tension between treating everyone the same versus respecting and responding to differences. If prior knowledge enables new learning, then children from diverse backgrounds must have the opportunity to demonstrate what they "know" about a topic, and they should also be able to participate in the classroom in ways that are consistent with the language and interaction patterns of home and community (Au & Jordan, 1981; Heath, 1983; Tharp & Gallimore, 1988). Brown (1994) talks about providing multiple "ways in" to school learning but also insists on "conformity on the basics," everyone must read, write, think, reason, and so forth. Dewey was often misunderstood as being child-centered at the expense of subject matter. His rejection of this false dualism is equally applicable here. One begins with the experience of the child, but the purpose of the course of study was to bring that child into the logically organized and disciplined experience of the mature adult (Dewey, 1902).

STUDENTS ARE SOCIALIZED INTO THE DISCOURSE AND PRACTICES OF ACADEMIC DISCIPLINES

If psychological studies have demonstrated that both intelligence and expert reasoning in specific knowledge domains are developed through socially mediated cognitive activity, then the practical question still remains of how to ensure that these kinds of interactions take place in classrooms. And if, as Brown (1994) has suggested, higher thought processes are in part an "internalized dialogue" (p. 10), then how teachers and students talk to each other is of paramount concern. Borrowing from learning in informal settings, sociocultural theorists note that development of competencies normally occurs when experts and novices have the opportunity to converse as they work together on a common goal or product (Rogoff, 1991; Tharp & Gallimore, 1988).

The point of "instructional conversations" in school is not

just to provide information but also to develop shared meanings between teacher and students, to connect schooled concepts to everyday concepts, and to allow students to gain experience with the ways of reasoning and thinking in a field (Tharp, 1997). For example, if during classroom exchanges students are routinely asked to explain their thinking or to clarify terms, then eventually, these habits are internalized and become not only a part of their thinking process but also a social norm in the classroom (Hogan & Pressley, 1997). In mathematics, Schoenfeld (1989) discussed the kinds of classroom practices that would foster a "culture of sense making," where "figuring it out" was how students learned to approach mathematical content. The popular writers' workshop (Atwell, 1987; Graves 1983) satisfies the elements of activity theory in its efforts to support the development of young writers. It provides a model of mature practice, engages students in elements of the process (brainstorming ideas, drafting, exchanging critiques, revising, editing) in the context of the whole, and provides the opportunity to try on the role of author.

AUTHENTIC RELATIONSHIPS ARE CREATED BETWEEN LEARNING IN AND OUT OF SCHOOL

Whereas the previous principle borrows from models of informal learning in families and communities to change how students learn, this principle suggests that the content of subject matter should also change to provide better connections with the real context of knowledge use. School learning has traditionally been quite distinct from learning outside of school. In-school learning is formal and abstract and removed from the use of tools or contexts that would supply meaning (Resnick, 1987). This decontextualization and meaninglessness explain why, for example, students often lose track of the problem they are trying to solve or give silly answers such as 3 buses with remainder 3 are needed to take the class to the zoo. However, school learning is also more reflective, disciplined, and general. It thereby provides more adaptability to new problem situations than context-specific learning that is acquired on the job or in the streets. The intention of reformers like Resnick (1987) and Newmann and Associates (1996) is to make the boundaries between school and the world more porous by bringing authentic contexts into classrooms and, at the same time, by developing habits of inquiry in school that will make students good thinkers and problem solvers in the world.

Once again, these ideas were anticipated by Dewey. Dewey did not eschew subject matter or discipline-based study but suggested that students could be inducted into more and more formal knowledge by gaining experience with the practical problems that the disciplines had been developed to solve. His intention in "psychologizing" bodies of knowledge—forestalling treatment of them as polished, organized systems—was to connect with children's own understandings and interests and, at the same time, to reveal the human purposes underlying the disciplines. Today, Newmann et al. (1996) similarly use authenticity as a key principle of curriculum reform. For Newmann, authentic achievement involves tasks that are significant and meaningful, like those undertaken by scientists, musicians, business owners, craftspeople, and so forth. Authentic peda-

gogy is "more likely to motivate and sustain students in the hard work that learning requires" (Newmann et al., 1996, p. 27) because their intellectual work has meaning and purpose.

IMPORTANT DISPOSITIONS AND HABITS OF MIND ARE FOSTERED

Several of these reform principles, all aimed at changing the nature of classroom interactions and curriculum content, are closely interconnected. The goal of fostering important dispositions and habits of minds is largely redundant in the context of the foregoing principles, except that it is worth calling attention to the importance of motivational goals per se. For example, classroom discourse practices that help students develop "a habit of inquiry" (Newmann et al., 1996; Wiggins, 1993) improve academic achievement in the present and, in addition, increase the likelihood that students will be motivated to adapt and use their knowledge and skills in new situations. Not only will they know how to tackle problems, to ask and persist in trying to answer the right questions (Wiggins, 1993), to use prior knowledge, to strive for in-depth understanding, and to express their ideas and findings through elaborated communication (Newmann et al., 1996), but also these ways of thinking will have become habits from long practice in a social setting. As suggested earlier under the learning principle that links motivation and cognitive performance, the goal here is not just to motivate students to work hard on challenging problems, but also to ensure that they develop identities as capable learners.

DEMOCRATIC PRACTICES ARE ENACTED IN A CARING COMMUNITY

Preparation for democratic citizenship requires more than teaching literacy skills or knowledge about government; it requires providing students from diverse backgrounds the opportunity to learn to live and work together in the world. A number of curriculum theorists and educational reformers have called for a more personalized educational system (Darling-Hammond, 1996; Martin, 1992; Sizer, 1984). Smaller schools, longer-term relationships between teachers and students, and more nurturing roles can clearly be shown to enhance academic learning, but enhancing academic learning is not the only purpose behind these actions. Joint productive activity around meaningful tasks also develops common understandings and habits of cooperation and mutual respect.

Dewey's concept of democracy was based on community, and his intent was to create a miniature society in the school. His interest in bringing practical occupations into schools was not only to connect with students' understandings but also to "cultivate the social spirit" and to "supply the child with motives for working in ways positively useful to the community of which he is a member" (Dewey, 1897, p. 72). Similarly, Jane Roland Martin (1992) argues for a more inclusive curriculum that emphasizes caring, concern, and connection as well as academic knowledge. By engaging students in "integrative activities of living," such as publishing a school newspaper, producing a play, farming, or building an historical museum, students could connect thought to action and gain experience as contributing members of society.

Classroom Assessment

The third circle in the emergent, constructivist framework addresses principles of classroom assessment. What kinds of assessment practices are compatible with and necessary in classrooms that are guided by social-constructivist views of supported learning? How does assessment fit or intrude when students are engaged in collaborative conversations and tackle extended, real-world problems? If we think of Vygotsky's zone of proximal development, how might assessment insights help extend a student's current level of learning?

The several principles identified in Figure 47.4 fall into two main categories having to do with transformation of both the substance of assessments and how they are used. Because these principles are elaborated in the subsequent sections of the chapter, I present them here only briefly. First, the substance of classroom assessments must be congruent with important learning goals. In contrast to the reductionistic and decontextualized view of subject matter knowledge produced by the scientific measurement paradigm, this requirement means that the content of assessments must match challenging subject matter standards and be connected to contexts of application. As part of this, assessments must mirror important thinking and learning processes, especially modes of inquiry and discourse, as they are valued and practiced in the classroom.

The purpose of assessment in classrooms must also be changed fundamentally so it is used to help students learn and to improve instruction, not just to rank students or to certify the end products of learning. The nearly exclusive use of normative tests in the United States to compare students to one another and to determine life chances is the key factor behind the development of classroom cultures that are dominated by an exchange value of learning, where students perform to please the teacher or to get good grades rather than to pursue a compelling purpose. By contrast, in classrooms where participation in learning is motivated by its use value, students and teachers would have a shared understanding that finding out what makes sense and what does not is a joint and worthwhile project, one that is essential to taking the next steps in learning. To serve this end, more specific principles of classroom assessment require that expectations and intermediate steps for improvement be made visible to students and that students be actively involved in evaluating their own work.

Clearly, such a view of assessment is an ideal that is rarely observed in practice. In fact, efforts to pursue this vision of assessment practice must contend with the powerful belief system associated with scientific measurement and the dominant paradigm. To be sure, all of the changes called for by the reform agenda and constructivist theory require new knowledge and profound changes in teaching practices. However, I would argue that changing assessment practices is the most difficult because of the continued influence of external standardized tests and because most teachers have limited training —beyond writing objectives and familiarity with traditional item formats — to prepare them to assess their students' understandings (Ellwein & Graue, 1995).

Relationship of Classroom Assessment to External Assessments

Although this chapter focuses on classroom assessment, we must also consider how teacher-initiated assessments and the external assessments that are required by district, state, or national mandates should relate if both kinds of assessment were reformed in keeping with the constructivist paradigm. Often, assessment reform is promoted without distinguishing among several different assessment purposes, yet it is well known that validity depends on how a test is used. A test designed for one purpose may not be valid if used for a different purpose. Should a statewide literacy test administered to third-graders every April for purposes of school accountability and grade-to-grade promotion also be used instructionally? Gipps (1996), speaking from the context of the British educational system, affirms that "assessment for selection, monitoring and accountability can be assessment to support learning" (p. 261). Although something about one's own teaching and students' strengths and weaknesses can be learned from every assessment, I argue that the uniform nature of external assessments and their infrequency means that they will rarely ask the right questions at the right time to be an effective part of the ongoing learning process.

The distinction between external and classroom assessment is closely related to the familiar distinction between formative and summative evaluation. Scriven (1967) distinguished between the formative role of evaluation feedback when used internally to improve a program or product and the summative role of evaluation data that is used by outsiders to make final decisions about funding or adopting a program. Typically, external assessments serve summative purposes such as large-scale monitoring of achievement trends, school accountability, school funding, and certification of student proficiency levels. Sometimes external assessments are used formatively at the level of programs, for example, when curriculum revisions are made on the basis of assessment results; however, large-scale assessments are rarely used to refocus and improve instruction for individual students.

In contrast, as I argue in later sections of the chapter, classroom assessment should be primarily formative in nature, aimed more at helping students take the next steps in learning than at judging the end points of achievement. Still, I also argue that summative evaluation is a natural part of the learning process and should be established as part of classroom routines, especially for older students. Just as students learn the difference between first draft and final versions of their writing, they should also gain experience with making final presentations and reviewing a body of work to reflect on what has been learned. Summative information is also important for reporting to parents, and if done well, classroom assessments can provide more valuable information about student progress than external measures.

External assessments typically dictate uniformity of content and standardization of procedures, even if they have been reformed to include more open-ended tasks and group problem solving. Large-scale assessments need to be standardized to ensure that numbers mean the same thing in different contexts. Standardization is necessary, not because some lingering positivist assumption of pure objectivity requires it but because it involves a basic matter of fairness. For example, if a state assessment is going to be used for school accountability, then content and administration procedures must be standardized to ensure comparability of school results. Everyone takes the same grade-level test at the same specified time of year. Aside from other issues of validity, an unfair situation would occur if some schools were tested in March and others in May or if some groups had unlimited time to complete the test. Teachers should not give help during the assessment or restate the questions unless it is part of the standard administration.

In contrast, for teaching and learning purposes, the timing of assessments makes the most sense if they occur on an ongoing basis as particular skills and content are being learned. Similarly, the level of the test should be focused closely on the student's current level of functioning, even if meeting this requirement means using assessment material that is well above or well below a child's nominal grade level. For example, it is well known that the National Assessment of Educational Progress Grade 4 Reading Test, designed for external purposes, could not be used to measure progress for below-grade-level readers because improvement from reading second-grade texts to third-grade texts is off the scale of the fourth-grade test. In the classroom context, teachers may well provide help while assessing to take advantage of the learning opportunity, to gain insight into a child's thinking, and to see what kinds of help make it possible to take the next steps (Shepard, Kagan, & Wurtz, 1998).

Although they are offered as an alternative to standardized procedures, current calls for more interpretive forms of assessment (Gipps, 1999; Moss, 1994, 1996) do not obviate the need for external assessments to be consistent and generalizable across sites. Moss (1996) contrasted traditional psychometric emphases on nomological or generalizable explanation with the goal of the interpretive tradition, which is to understand meaning in context. The interpretive model she proposes, in the context of a teacher licensure assessment, eschews independent ratings of various portfolio components and, instead, engages pairs of judges in weighing evidence from multiple sources to arrive at a defensible interpretation.

This more comprehensive and contextualized look at candidates' performance increases the likelihood of valid assessment results because judges have access to more information. Indeed, they have access, as part of the assessment, to the kinds of corroborating evidence that would normally be gathered as part of traditional validity investigations. Although judges interpret evidence from various sources rather than use a standard algorithm to combine scores, Moss is nonetheless concerned about whether different pairs of judges will produce consistent results. For example, to ensure adherence to common standards, she finds it necessary to build in review by a "criterion" reader to verify the evidentiary warrant of interpretive summaries and to resolve disagreements between judges.

The degree of consistency required of external assessments will depend on how they are used and whether they rely on precise meanings of scores or less formal assurances of comparability. Linn (1993) identifies five different levels of precision

in "linking" large-scale assessments, ranging from statistical "equating" to more judgmentally based "social moderation." For example, a report that National Assessment Reading scores improved by 5 points requires strict equivalence of the assessments from year to year. Professional judgment models that result in accreditation of institutions or passing of degree candidates can rely on less precise correspondence between judgments and standards, but fairness and validity still require that results not depend on the idiosyncrasies of individual judges.

Shepard, Kagan, and Wurtz (1998) showed how assessment systems could be designed to serve both external and classroom purposes. However, such multipurpose assessments are costly because the technical and content requirements for each purpose must be satisfied. Although advocates of interpretivist forms of assessment would like to see context and local meanings preserved in what is aggregated for state and national purposes, it is more likely that combining external and classroom purposes will impose standardization in classrooms. In Kentucky, for example, all fifth-grade teachers had to use the same mathematics tasks as portfolio entries so that school comparisons could be made. Using instructionally based assessments for accountability purposes also requires standardization of scoring and external checks, called moderation, to make sure that data being aggregated across classrooms are comparable. The BEAR[3] Assessment System (Wilson & Sloane, 2000) is a rare example of a curriculum-embedded, issues-oriented science assessment that was developed to support classroom level assessment but that also satisfies requirements for comparability across classrooms through scoring moderation and a system of link tests.

A single articulated system usually cannot be devised because budgets are limited or, more likely, because curriculum is locally controlled. Considering these constraints, the model I propose is one that provides substantive compatibility between two separate assessment systems. Large-scale assessments should be substantively consistent with high-quality classroom assessments though procedurally separate; that is, they should be guided by the same curriculum standards, engage students in the same kinds of inquiry and demonstrations of proficiency, and be evaluated in terms of shared criteria for judging high quality work.

Given the extensive evidence that external, high-stakes assessments drive instruction, it is essential that external tests reflect more ambitious conceptions of subject matter knowledge than found in traditional tests. External assessments should also elicit thinking and problem-solving skills. Therefore, the kinds of content reforms that are proposed in the next section, involving more extended and open-ended tasks, are relevant to both large-scale formal assessments and day-to-day classroom assessments. Although I believe that using assessments, even good ones, to drive instructional reform makes the mistake of continuing to de-skill and disempower teachers, I also admit that grassroots, professionally initiated reforms are unlikely to be successful if teachers continue to feel pressured to drill students

---

[3] This assessment system was developed at the Berkeley Evaluation and Assessment Research (BEAR) Center at the University of California at Berkeley.

in preparation for traditional basic skills tests. So ideally, top-down and bottom-up reforms would be made in concert, with plenty of support for professional development in the middle.

As indicated above, the recommendation that classroom assessments should operate independently from large-scale, external assessments is based on the needs implied by the two types of assessment for quite different types of information: immediate and contextualized data on the one hand and rigorously comparable results on the other hand. In addition, the two types of assessments differ sharply in the stringency of technical standards they must meet. External tests must demonstrate higher reliability because they are limited, one-time assessments and are often used to make critically important decisions. In contrast, day-to-day evaluations that are made in the context of classroom lessons do not have such high-stakes consequences for students. If a teacher makes an invalid inference on a given day about a student's understanding, that error can be corrected by new information in subsequent days.

The purpose of classroom assessment is not primarily to certify student proficiency levels at a fixed point with precision but rather to generate hypotheses and guide intervention. Although single-teacher assessments may be significantly less reliable than formal, external tests, teachers can, nonetheless, operate in systematic ways over time to develop highly accurate assessments of student learning.[4]

Improvement in the Content and Form of Assessments

Assessment reform is part of a larger effort to raise standards and improve the quality of education. Standards-based reform envisions a more challenging curriculum for all students that is focused on higher-order thinking skills and depth of understanding. This kind of reform involves a thoroughgoing reconceptualization of what it means to know in each of the disciplines, and it involves fundamental changes in teaching and learning that are consistent with constructivist theory. The transformation of assessment is seen as an essential part of curriculum reform because of widespread beliefs and evidence documenting the distorting effects of high-stakes basic skills tests on teaching and learning (Madaus, West, Harmon, Lomax, & Viator, 1992; Resnick & Resnick, 1992; Romberg, Zarinnia, & Williams, 1989). This belief, that the content of assessments had to be changed to effect other changes, was captured in the slogan "WYTIWYG," or "What You Test Is What You Get."

In organizing this section and the next, I follow the logic of assessment reform rhetoric. I consider first the transformation of assessment content, then its form, and finally, its use as part of the teaching and learning process. In this section, I review the development of content standards and efforts to redefine important learning goals in each of the disciplines. Sample problems and assessment tasks instantiate the meaning of new curricular goals and, at the same time, help to illustrate how the form of assessments must change to better represent students'

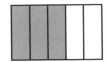

a)   Can you see 3/5 of something?
b)   Can you see 5/3 of something?
c)   Can you see 5/3 of 3/5?
d)   Can you see 2/3 of 3/5?
e)   Can you see 1 ÷ 3/5?
f)   Can you see 5/4 ÷ 3/4?

Figure 47.5. From Thompson (1995, p. 203)

thinking and problem-solving abilities. In the subsequent section, I consider how classroom norms, attitudes, and practices might be changed so that assessment can be used to check on prior knowledge, provide feedback, engage students in self-evaluation, and so forth. Although this sequential arrangement is useful for describing each aspect of assessment reform, in practice, these changes are all entwined. Changing the content and form of assessment is essential in changing assessment's use as part of instruction and, in some cases, helping it to become indistinguishable from instruction.

Reconceptualizing Learning and Achievement in Subject Areas

Expressly with the intention of changing what it means to know and do mathematics, the National Council of Teachers of Mathematics developed *Curriculum and Evaluation Standards for School Mathematics* (1989). *Standards for School Mathematics* departs from traditional mathematics instruction, which has a focus on computation and rote activities, and instead, emphasizes sense making in a much broader range of content area topics. In Grades K–4, for example, the topics include number sense and numeration, concepts of whole number operations, whole number computation, geometry and spatial sense, measurement, statistics and probability, fractions and decimals, patterns and relationships. In each of the content areas, the emphasis is on understanding and on students' ability to investigate and represent relationships. In addition, the *Standards for School Mathematics* includes what might be termed process goals that emphasize problem solving, communication, mathematical reasoning, and mathematical connections.

Documents accompanying the standards and scores of other mathematics reform projects provide sample problems both to illustrate and to enact the reform. For example, Patrick Thompson (1995) provided the set of questions in Figure 47.5 to illustrate how nonalgorithmic problems can help students "see" a mathematical idea. A traditional fraction question that is based on the same picture would have asked students only to supply

---

[4] The vision of assessment that is proposed in this chapter—how classroom assessment should relate to external assessments and how it should be reformed to reflect social-constructivist learning principles and reformed curriculum standards—is an idealization. No claim is made that teachers will automatically be effective in using assessment in these new ways without training in assessment techniques and help to develop extensive subject matter knowledge as well as expertise in constructivist pedagogy.

or pick the answer 3/5. In contrast, ongoing experience with a more extended set of questions, like those in Figure 47.5, helps students develop their understanding of part-whole relationships and multiplicative reasoning applied to fractions. Thus, students can begin to see fractions greater than one and are able to conceptualize a fraction of a fraction as well as a fraction of a whole number.

Additional open-ended tasks for fourth and twelfth graders respectively are shown in Figure 47.6. The fourth-grade problem set, for example, asks that children recognize and then generalize a pattern, which is an important precursor to understanding functions. Several features are worth noting. Each mathematics task engages students in thinking and reasoning about important content. Each task could be used interchangeably as an instructional activity, as an assessment, or both. The tasks are complicated and rich enough to involve students in talking about problem solutions so they can gain experience with explaining and evaluating their own thinking. If students were provided an organized diet of these kinds of activities and more extended projects in the same spirit, there would be no divergence of purposes between the content of assessments and important learning goals.

Similarly in science, several reform documents, especially *Benchmarks for Science Literacy* produced by the American Association for the Advancement of Science's Project 2061 (1993) and the *National Science Education Standards* developed by the National Research Council (NRC) (1996), have articulated a vision of how curricula should be revitalized to ensure that all students become scientifically literate. The NRC *National Science Education Standards* identify fundamental concepts and principles, the "big ideas," in each area of science as well as inquiry skills that are needed to conduct investigations and evaluate scientific findings. For example, in Grades K–4, students should know (a) that plants need air, water, nutrients, and light; (b) that many characteristics of organisms are inherited from their parents but that other characteristics result from interaction with the environment; and (c) that the sun provides light and heat necessary to maintain the temperature of the earth.

More important, however, the NRC standards emphasize that students should have the opportunity to learn fundamental concepts in depth, to develop subject matter knowledge in the context of inquiry, and to become adept at using scientific knowledge to address societal issues and make personal decisions. Inquiry skills that should be manifest in both instructional activities and assessment tasks include being able to formulate questions, to design and conduct scientific investigations, to use tools for data collection, to formulate and defend a scientific argument, to evaluate alternative explanations on the basis of evidence, and to communicate the results of scientific studies.

Assessment reform has played a key role in giving flesh to the intended science reform, just as it has done for mathematics reform. Examples are provided in Figure 47.6 to illustrate the alignment of assessment with important content and inquiry skills, the use of extended tasks to elicit student reasoning, and the expectation that students be able to communicate their ideas. The character of these tasks and problems is in marked contrast to earlier item types that emphasized knowledge of scientific facts and terminology.

In English language arts and literacy, the same needs for curricular and instructional reforms are felt as in every other field. If anything, the hostility toward traditional standardized measures has been even greater in this subject area than in others because of the serious ways that tests have misrepresented children's skill development. For example, in their review of formal early literacy tests, Stallman and Pearson (1990) document that most measures are based on outmoded theories of early reading development. In fact, readiness tests and first-grade reading tests look very similar to those designed by Gates and Bond (1936) in the 1930s. Moreover, such tests engage young children in a set of activities that are anathema to high quality reading instruction. Skills are tested out of context, items require that students recognize answers instead of produce an oral or written response, and the activity is dominated by test-taking behavior such as keeping the right place and filling in answer bubbles rather than reading for meaning. The complaints against tests of writing skills are even more severe. Typically, writing tests measure grammar, spelling, and punctuation skills but not the ability to write. When writing tests include an essay component, they still lack the properties of authentic writing situations. The reason for writing is artificial and often unmotivating, the assigned topic may be unfamiliar, the absence of resources such as books and peers is inauthentic, timing constraints are unlike the usual time allotted to develop a piece of writing, and the lack of opportunity to revise and edit is inconsistent with good writing practice.

Perhaps it is because existing measures were so at odds with the substance of good instruction that literacy experts have gone to the greatest lengths to revise both the form of assessment and its content. For example, over the past two decades, research in emergent literacy has produced increasingly rich descriptions of the typical progressions (and variations) in children's reading and writing development (Sulzby, 1990). This knowledge base could then be used to establish the idea of benchmarking (Au, 1994), not only to document students' progress but also to increase teachers' knowledge about the next steps forward.

The writing samples in Figure 47.7, excerpted from the North Carolina Grades 1 and 2 assessment materials, illustrate the normal progression in children's increasing writing proficiency. Although there is considerable variation in how children gain command over different conventions of writing and how those conventions are used in different contexts to convey meaning, North Carolina could construct, nonetheless, the following rough "control of writing" continuum to be used as a framework in analyzing children's writing samples.

- Uses invented spelling to convey meaning
  - random letters
  - letter names
  - phonetic spelling
- Spells frequently used words correctly
- Uses lower and uppercase letters appropriately
- Spaces words
- Writes complete thoughts and ideas
- Ties one thought to another
- Sequences events and ideas
- Uses details

Grade 4 Mathematics Problem Set
(Mathematical Sciences Education Board, 1993)

All of the bridges in this part are built with yellow rods for spans and red rods for supports, like the one shown here. This is a 2-span bridge like the one you just built. Note that the yellow rods are 5 cm long.

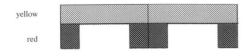

1. Now, build a 3-span bridge.
   a. How many yellow rods did you use? _____
   b. How long is your bridge? _____
   c. How many red rods did you use? _____
   d. How many rods did you use altogether? _____

2. Try to answer these questions without building a 5-span bridge. If you want, build a 5-span bridge to check your answers.
   a. How many yellow rods would you need for a 5-span bridge? _____
   b. How long would your bridge be? _____
   c. How many red rods would you need? _____
   d. How many rods would you need altogether? _____

3. Without building a 12 span-bridge, answer the following questions.
   a. How many yellow rods would you need for a 12-span bridge? _____
   b. How long would your bridge be? _____
   c. How many red rods would you need? _____
   d. How many rods would you need altogether? _____

4. How many yellow rods and red rods would you need to build a 28-span bridge? _____ yellow rods and _____ red rods. Explain your answer.

5. Write a rule for figuring out the total number of rods you would need to build a bridge if you knew how many spans the bridge had.

6. How many yellow rods and red rods would you need to build a bridge that is 185 cm long? _____ yellow rods and _____ red rods. Explain your answer.

Grade 12 Open-Ended Mathematics Questions
(California Assessment Program, 1989)

1. Look at these plane figures, some of which are not drawn to scale. Investigate what might be wrong (if anything) with the given information. Briefly write your findings and justify your ideas on the basis of geometric principles.

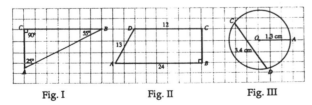

Fig. I   Fig. II   Fig. III

2. James knows that half of the students from his school are accepted at the public university nearby. Also, half are accepted at the local private college. James thinks that this adds up to 100 percent, so he will surely be accepted at one or the other institution. Explain why James may be wrong. If possible, use a diagram in your explanation.

Grade 5 Science Tasks
(California Learning Assessment System, 1994)

Fossils
You are a paleontologist (a scientist who studies past life forms). You were digging and just discovered a large group of fossils.
Directions:
Open BAG A and spread the fossils on the table.
Use the hand lens to carefully observe each fossil.
Sort your fossils into groups. You may make as many groups as you like.
Write answers to these questions in your journal.
1. Draw your groups. Circle and number each group.
2. How many groups do you have?
3. List the number of each group and tell why you sorted your fossils into these groups.

_____

BAG B has a fossil that was found in the area near where you were digging.
Directions:
Open BAG B.
Take out the new fossil and compare it with the other fossils on the table.
4. Does this new fossil fit into one of your groups? If YES, how are they alike?
5. If the new fossil does not fit into any of your groups, describe a new group in which this fossil would fit.
6. Choose one of the fossils and draw a picture of it.
7. In what kind of habitat (environment) do you think this fossil might have once lived? Why?

Grade 8 Illinois Hands-on Tests for Science
(Pendulum Performance Assessment Task, R.J. Dagenais, circa 1992)

1. *Hypothesis:* Write a hypothesis in your journal on how different lengths of string affect the number of swings of the pendulum in 15 seconds.

   Set up materials according to the diagram below:

   A. Vertical Position   B. Horizontal Position

2. Work with a partner on the pendulum task. Procedure:
   a. Hold the string in one hand with the washer hanging at the other end of the string in the vertical position shown in Diagram A above. The length of the string from the top of the washer to your hand should measure 100 cm.
   b. With your other hand raise the washer up until the string is now parallel to the floor in the horizontal position shown in Diagram B above.
   c. Release the washer and let it swing back and forth. Do not move your hand. A swing is counted every time the washer makes one complete trip back and forth.
   d. Count how many swings the washer makes in 15 seconds and record this information in your journal. If the final swing is not completed at the end of 15 seconds, count it as one swing.

3. Use the same procedure (steps a–d) to compare how many swings the string and washer make for various lengths of string. Measure the length of each string between the top of the washer and your hand in cm and record this length in a data table in your journal.

4. Graph the data from your investigation in your journal.

5. Use your data and graph to help you answer this question. If the string was longer than 100 cm, what do you predict would happen to the number of swings? Explain your prediction.

Figure 47.6. Examples of open-ended assessment tasks intended to engage students in thinking and reasoning about important content.

Figure 47.7. Samples of student work illustrating progress on an emergent writing continuum (North Carolina Grades 1 and 2 Assessment).

- Moves from a beginning, develops the idea, and concludes
- Uses conventional punctuation
- Uses conventional spelling

A shared feature of various literacy assessment practices is that they began in the context of instruction and then made explicit both the process and products indicative of children's increasing proficiency. In the next section, I discuss further how alternative forms of assessments such as running records and portfolios do a better job of capturing what is important to measure and, at the same time, work more smoothly to blend assessment with ongoing instruction.

Rounding out the reforms, curriculum standards have also been developed in history (National Center for History in the Schools, 1996), civics and government (Center for Civic Education, 1994), geography (Geography Education Standards Project, 1994), and social studies (National Council for the Social Studies, 1994). Following the same general outline as the science standards, these documents emphasize the development of inquiry skills and conceptual understanding of core ideas. For example, in geography, students should know and understand the patterns and networks of economic interdependence on earth's surface. Interestingly, however, these documents of standards are largely silent about the need for assessment reform. Perhaps because these subject areas were less frequently tested in external accountability programs and because many history and social studies teachers have held onto essay questions and

term projects as means of evaluation, assessment was not seen as the driving force for curricular change. Nonetheless, content standards in each area are accompanied by "performance standards" that clearly imply the need for in-depth assessment methods (not short-answer questions) to tap important skills. For example, the Historical Research Standard for Grades 5–12 is elaborated by six statements about what "the student is able to do," three of which read as follows:

1. Formulate historical questions from encounters with historical documents, eyewitness accounts, letters, diaries, artifacts, photos, historical sites, art, architecture, and other records from the past.
2. Interrogate historical data by uncovering the social, political, and economic context in which it was created; testing the data source for its credibility, authority, authenticity, internal consistency, and completeness; and detecting and evaluating bias, distortion, and propaganda by omission, suppression, or invention of facts.
3. Employ quantitative analysis in order to explore such topics as changes in family size and composition, migration patterns, wealth distribution, and changes in the economy. (National Center for History in the Schools, 1996, p. 68)

To develop these abilities, students clearly need support as they practice undertaking the very sorts of tasks, like those mentioned in the quote above, that will, in turn, be used to assess mastery at the end of a course of study or in application contexts. Again, no distinction has been made between desirable instructional activities and authentic assessment tasks.

Tools and Forms of Assessment

A broader range of assessment tools is needed to capture important learning goals and to more directly connect assessment to ongoing instruction. As illustrated above, the most obvious reform has been to devise more open-ended performance tasks to ensure that students are able to reason critically, to solve complex problems, and to apply their knowledge in real-world contexts. In addition, if instructional goals include developing students' metacognitive abilities, fostering important dispositions, and socializing students into the discourse and practices of academic disciplines, then it is essential that classroom routines and accompanying assessments reflect these goals as well. Furthermore, if assessment insights are to be used to move learning along rather than merely tally how much learning has occurred so far, then assessment has to occur in the middle of instruction, not just at end points, and must focus on processes of learning—what strategies are children using—not just outcomes. In response to these needs, the armamentarium for data gathering has been expanded to include observations, clinical interviews, reflective journals, oral presentations, work samples, projects, and portfolios. Here I review several of the more prominent alternative forms of assessment. Performance assessments are not considered as a separate category because performance tasks are expected to be a part of ongoing instructional activities. Therefore, performance tasks are included in observation-based assessments, are among the entries in a portfolio assessment system, and are used as well in on-demand, formal tests.

External assessments are necessarily structured and formal to ensure comparability across school settings. Within classrooms, however, both formal and informal assessments can be used, although the balance in their use will shift depending on students' ages. For very young children, assessments should be almost entirely informal. For example, parents and teachers use observations and work samples (children's drawings) to know when scribbling has progressed enough and letter recognition is in place so that demonstration of specific letter shapes would be appropriate. As children grow, not only can they participate in more formal events that are designated for assessment purposes, but doing so is desirable if such events are authentic and consistent with the goal of inducting students into the practices of the discipline. For example, middle school students might make presentations to report findings from a field project or take a performance-based examination to see if they can use inquiry skills to help conceptualize the class's next project.

Observation-based assessment tools used in early literacy classrooms (Hiebert & Raphael, 1998) illustrate how data about learning can be collected systematically alongside normal instructional activities. For example, "running records" developed by Marie Clay (1985) are a notation system used during oral reading to keep track of a child's omissions, substitutions, and self-corrected miscues. By close attention to the nature of student errors—called "miscues" (Goodman, 1973) to emphasize that students are responding to cues even when mistaken—teachers can identify students' word recognition skills and their ability to make sense of the text. To assess comprehension, teachers might also use story retellings or ask specific questions

about the text. Used routinely as a follow-up to reading activity, such assessments provide valuable information, but they also convey to students the importance of thinking and talking about what they read. Brief assessments during reading time can be used to make immediate instructional decisions, such as focusing on compound words, emphasizing sense making, or changing text level, but informal assessment techniques can also be structured to document children's growth over time, especially if running records and story retells are recorded in relation to graded texts or reading passages of increasing difficulty (Hiebert & Raphael, 1998). Consistent with the idea of socializing students into the discourse and practices of a literacy community, Mervar and Hiebert (1989) documented that children's abilities to choose books can be developed as a goal of instruction, and these abilities, correspondingly, are amenable to systematic observation. For example, they noted that students without previous modeling by adults might pick a book without opening it, whereas children in a literature-based classroom were more likely to sample a number of books by reading segments aloud or by looking for specific topics before finally choosing a book.

Clinical interviews or think-alouds are research techniques that can also be used in classrooms to gain insights about students' learning. One-on-one interactions provide a more extended opportunity to hear and observe students' strategies and to have students explain their reasoning. Individual interviews also make it possible to conduct "dynamic assessments" that test (and thereby extend) what a student can do with adult support. In these interactions, a teacher-clinician is not merely collecting data but also is gathering information and acting on it at the same time, thus, completely blurring the boundaries between assessment and instruction. Clinical interviews, like good teaching, require that teachers be knowledgeable about underlying developmental continua.

In an analysis of a video transcript of Marilyn Burns (1993) conducting an individual assessment (Shepard, 1997), I note that when a student cannot answer a question about place value, Burns poses a new problem that is more meaningful to the child by backing up along an implied developmental progression. She also knows clearly (at a slightly easier point on the imagined continuum) when the child is ready to learn something just out of reach, and she provides a hint. Indeed, the child answers correctly. In other instances, Burns does not attempt to resolve errors that are too far beyond where the child is functioning. Although researchers can provide support for teachers' learning by developing benchmarks, teachers cannot likely develop the kind of detailed knowledge evidenced by Burns except by accumulating extensive experience working with children of a specific age and subject-specific curricula. Fortunately, conducting such interviews, possibly with only a few students at any given time, is one way for teachers to develop this knowledge base regarding typical progressions and common errors.

Portfolios are another, highly popularized, new form of assessment. Borrowing from the arts and from professions such as architecture and advertising where individuals collect samples of their best work to demonstrate their talents and skills, the intention of assessment reformers is to use portfolios of student work to provide more authentic documentation of achievement. When considered from the perspective of external, accountability assessments, portfolio-based assessments face a number of serious obstacles including reliability of scoring and fairness questions such as Whose work is it, really? However, when used solely for teaching and learning purposes in classrooms, portfolios can provide an organizing structure for teacher-student critiques and student self-reflections, thereby fostering metacognitive goals that might not be attended to if the various assignments in the portfolio were undertaken separately. Within classrooms, the relevant comparison is not whether portfolio assessments can be made as reliable and rigorously comparable as standardized measures but whether a portfolio structure can help teachers and students become more systematic in analyzing and learning from student work than would ordinarily occur as a part of instructional activities.

A number of researchers have written about the unique features of portfolios as a teaching tool. Yancey (1996), for example, argues that reflection is the defining characteristic of the writing portfolio. Through construction of portfolios, students set goals for learning, review their work and develop criteria for selecting particular pieces over others, learn to evaluate the strengths and weaknesses of their own work, and gain experience in communicating their purposes and judgments to others. Work by Camp (1992) and Hilgers (1986) among others illustrates that students can develop the ability to articulate and apply critical criteria if they are given practice and experience doing so. Klimenkov and LaPick (1996), teachers at Orion Elementary School, combined the use of portfolios with student-led conferences. Their goals included empowering students and helping them understand what steps they needed to take to move ahead. Evaluation of the Orion project found that students indeed took greater responsibility for their own learning, but the drop-off in effort after the midyear conference suggested that the device still relied on external motivation to a large extent. Duschl and Gitomer (1997) sought to create what they call a portfolio culture in classrooms by using portfolio assignments and negotiated criteria to engage in "assessment conversations." Through such conversations, teachers find out what students know; students gain experience with processes of scientific explanation, argument, and presentation; and students learn to apply standards of scientific plausibility. Portfolios are the vehicle for conceptualizing and structuring these classroom interactions.

Whether portfolios can be used for both classroom and external purposes is highly controversial. As suggested previously, large-scale assessment purposes bring with them the need for uniform assignments and scoring criteria. Not only will such constraints make it less likely that instructional activities will fit the learning needs of individual students, but also the high-stakes, evaluative context may defeat efforts to engage students in taking responsibility for their own learning. Although acknowledging the tension, Au and Valencia (1997) argued that the benefit teachers derived from learning to score portfolios and the improvement in students' writing proficiency, even from a mandated portfolio system, were sufficient to warrant their use. Myers (1996) suggested that establishing a conscious interaction (or articulation) might be possible between portfolios constructed for formative purposes and those created for summative purposes, rather than expecting that a single portfolio could reasonably serve both purposes. Although I think it will be impractical to implement two full-blown portfolio systems

in the same subject area throughout the school year, classroom portfolios could feasibly include evidence from other forms of external assessments, such as on-demand performance tasks or standardized tests, and could address explicitly the relationship of these assessments to classroom-based evidence.

As a general rule, teachers should use a variety of assessment tools, choosing, in each case, the mode of data collection that best captures intended knowledge and skills in their context of use. Sometimes the appropriate assessment tool will be a more traditional-looking quiz or examination. As is the case for all assessment modes, an explicit rationale for using conventional assessment techniques should be given with respect to both the format of test questions and the "on-demand" character of test events. Essay questions, for example, may still be the best means for students to demonstrate their ability to use either historical or scientific evidence to support an argument. Traditional fill-in-the-blank, short-answer, or multiple-choice questions may also be useful to check for certain kinds of procedural knowledge, so long as these skills are represented in proportion to their substantive importance in the curriculum and not simply because they are the easiest to measure.

Learning goals should also determine whether and in what proportion assessments should be administered on demand. In my personal experience, this point is often in contention both within teacher education circles and among doctoral students. They may ask, If you believe in assessment reform, why give tests or doctoral comprehensive examinations? The answer should be that classroom participation, extended projects, research papers, and tests each support and reflect different kinds of learning and, therefore, provide different kinds of evaluation data. If content has been reformed in the ways described previously, then tests demonstrate "walking around knowledge" (i.e., the conceptual schemes and big ideas that should be established in one's head so that looking them up in a book or asking a colleague is not necessary). Formal examinations for prospective teachers, then, should tap the kinds of knowledge required on demand in authentic applications. For example, prospective teachers should be able to respond appropriately when asked for one's teaching philosophy in a job interview, when making an instructional decision on the fly, when arguing for one choice over another in a district curriculum committee meeting, or when explaining student work and assessment data to a parent.

Similarly, for doctoral students, tests can be an authentic measure of professional knowledge if those tests draw on the expertise one needs to answer questions from school board members, to review manuscripts submitted to journals, to brainstorm about study designs, to respond off the cuff in a professional debate, and so forth. In a later section on the culture of the classroom, this issue of authentic but formal examinations is taken a step further, emphasizing that students should be made aware of the pedagogical rationale for the balance of assessments chosen—how they, as a set, represent the learning goals for the class.

Multiple Modes of Assessment to Ensure Fairness and Transfer

Variety in assessment techniques is a virtue not just because different learning goals are amenable to assessment by different devices but also because the mode of assessment interacts in complex ways with the very nature of what is being assessed. For example, the ability to retell a story after reading it might be fundamentally a different learning construct than being able to answer comprehension questions about the story; both might be important instructionally. Therefore, even for the same learning objective, we can find compelling reasons to assess in more than one way both to ensure sound measurement and to support development of flexible and robust understandings.

In the measurement literature, it is well known that assessment formats can have significant effects on performance levels. For example, one of the best-known and pervasive effects is the relative advantage that women have over men on essay examinations compared to the relative performance of the two groups on multiple-choice measures of the same content domain (Mazzeo, Schmitt, & Bleistein, 1993). In science, Shavelson, Baxter, and Pine (1992) found that students did not score equivalently on paper-and-pencil, computer simulation, or hands-on versions of the same electric circuit problems. In the Orion portfolio project described previously, teachers worried that students who were shy or suffering from stage fright were at a disadvantage when demonstrating their knowledge in student-led conferences (Klimenkov & LaPick, 1996). When different results occur from different assessment formats, then the question whether one result should be treated as more valid than the others will depend on the situation. Validity studies of male-female differences on Advanced Placement history exams, for example, suggest that multiple-choice and essay exams are actually measuring different constructs that roughly correspond to historical knowledge and historical argument. Instead of concluding that one format is biased, the evidence suggests that both formats are needed to adequately represent the content domain.

By contrast, in the accommodations literature, certain test formats would be deemed biased if irrelevant features of the assessment prevent students from demonstrating their true levels of competence. This bias occurs, for example, when English language proficiency is confounded with assessment of mathematics or when learning disabled students are unable to demonstrate their knowledge because of excessive writing demands or lengthy examination periods. In the case of nonconstant results for tasks that are believed to be equivalent, when one has no basis for choosing between bias or multiple-construct interpretations, as in the Shavelson example above, the best strategy is to use multiple data sources for purposes of triangulation without presuming that one assessment mode is more accurate than others.

From the perspective of assessment fairness in classrooms, students should be allowed to demonstrate their competence using the particular conditions that show them to best advantage (at least, as one of the ways they are assessed). Using this approach, the student might give an oral presentation rather than take a written exam, write about a topic that is familiar, have access to translated versions of the task, and so forth. From a teaching perspective, however, students should not always rely on the format that is most comfortable. Good instruction focuses on both areas of weakness and strength and ensures that students' knowledge becomes increasingly flexible and robust (i.e., transfers) across contexts of application. To

make these kinds of instructional decisions, teachers must be aware of how the variation in assessment or instructional task features affects performance.

For many students, teachers will not be able to see reliable patterns of difference across assessment modes, but when consistent patterns emerge, those patterns should prompt targeted interventions. For example, English-language learners should have the opportunity to demonstrate their mathematical knowledge without the confounding effects of language proficiency. At the same time, those learners should be supported in working to improve mathematical communication. Similarly, in the Orion portfolio example, teachers worked with students who had difficulty presenting at conferences to set goals for developing public speaking skills and strong public voices.

Using a variety of tasks for both instruction and assessment is also important in teaching for understanding and transfer. Teaching-the-test research reminds us that repeated practice with identical instructional and test formats leads to an inflated picture of student achievement (Shepard, 1997), because students can appear to have mastered instructional routines without understanding underlying concepts. Students are more likely to develop understanding and the ability to apply knowledge in new situations if they are presented with a variety of problems and encouraged to draw connections. For example, a 6-year-old may not be troubled if after adding 4 + 6 on paper, he gets 11 and then counts 4 beans and 6 beans and gets 10 beans altogether. (Developmentally, the 6-year-old does not see a discrepancy; one is numbers and the other is beans.) Obviously, the goal of early numeracy instruction is to help children develop the correspondence between numbers and objects. Similarly in third grade, students who are helped to draw the connections between area problems (4 × 7) and number line problems (counting by sevens) will thereby develop more robust understandings of how multiplication works. The principle of multiple assessment modes does not suggest that we use one set of formats for teaching and another for testing but rather that we use a range of activities for both and make awareness of task features an explicit part of classroom discourse (How is this problem the same as problems we've done before? How is it different?).

Qualitative Methods of Evaluation and Data Synthesis

Evaluating open-ended tasks and drawing valid inferences from both formal and informal data sources requires new methods of data analysis and interpretation. Discerning a student's progress can no longer be calculated as the percentage of problems answered correctly. Using all of the assessment methods described in the previous sections creates a profoundly greater need for teacher judgment and qualitative methods of inquiry.

The most visible new technique for evaluating open-ended tasks and complex performances is scoring "rubrics." Rubrics provide a set of ordered categories and accompanying criteria for judging the relative quality of assessment products. However, rubrics and formal scoring schemes are inappropriate for many moment-to-moment uses of instructional assessments and, more generally, in classrooms with young children. Furthermore, serious questions have been raised about whether assigning a quantitative score and ordering performance on a continuum are compatible with sociocultural and constructivist perspectives.

Lave and Wenger's (1991) complaint, for example, that testing contributes to the commoditization of learning is likely to apply to new forms of assessment as well unless those new forms have a very different role in the cultural practices of the classroom. Wile and Tierney (1996) argue against "positivistic" or objectified analytic schemes because such schemes "assume relationships between elements which may not be accurate" (p. 212) and "risk excluding or discounting experiences that do not coincide with curriculum guides or checklist descriptors" (p. 213).

My own view is that good assessment practice should include a combination of both locally negotiated scoring routines and clinical, or interpretivist, approaches to data synthesis. Explicit scoring criteria, or qualitative descriptors, are essential for giving feedback to students and, as I discuss in the next section, for engaging students in self-assessment. Formal criteria for evaluating student work can become the locus of important negotiations and dialogue among teachers and students as they develop a shared understanding of what it means to do excellent work. Although it may be nice for the teacher occasionally to write "good idea" in the margin of a history paper, feedback is much more useful if on every paper the teacher or peer critic addresses familiar categories such as "quality of ideas," "use of evidence," "historical content," and "clarity of communication" and if, over time, students have ample opportunity to connect the meaning of these criteria to examples in their own work. I agree with Wile and Tierney (1996) that keeping these descriptive categories separate is more useful than subsuming them arbitrarily under one holistic score. For older students, however, whose grades will be extracted by some alchemy from numerous sources of evidence, students deserve to know how various elements are being sifted and weighed if not strictly added up, because this aggregation process, whether quantitative or qualitative, also embodies and communicates what is important to know. Teachers need not share their scoring rules with very young children but might comment, "Oh, that's great Ramona, I see you're making spaces between your words."

But what about all of the other learning occasions and classroom interactions that do not result in a product that is amenable to scoring? Given multiple sources of evidence, how should a teacher make sense of the whole (not for purposes of a composite grade but to make instructional decisions)? Like a number of other authors, I see the need for an interpretivist approach to data analysis and synthesis (Gipps, 1999; Graue, 1993; Moss, 1996). In my own case, I see a strong connection between the use of qualitative research methods and my training as a clinician when I use observations to form a tentative hypothesis, gather additional information to confirm or revise, plan an intervention (itself a test of the working hypothesis),

and so forth. Indeed, some time ago, Geertz (1973) drew an analogy between clinical inference as used in medicine and the way in which cultural theorists "diagnose" the underlying meaning of social discourse, meaning that they use theory to generate cogent interpretations, or generalizations, that have explanatory power beyond thick descriptions.

In classrooms, to make sense of observational and work-sample data means to look for patterns, check for contradictions, and compare the emerging description against models of developing competence. Thus, teachers need to be adept at methods of data sifting and triangulation and, at the same time, must have a good command of theory (about subject matter learning) to use when interpreting evidence. Cambourne and Turbill (1990) have observed that when teachers attempt to make sense of information collected from a variety of classroom literacy activities, they proceed in the same way as classical field anthropologists would, by reading through the information and attempting to categorize it. Cambourne and Turbill go on to suggest that the kinds of strategies promoted by Lincoln and Guba (1986) to ensure the dependability and confirmability of naturalistic data (i.e., triangulation, purposive sampling, and audit trails) apply also to classroom-based interpretations of student performance.[5]

Although many would endorse the use of qualitative methods as more philosophically compatible with constructivist approaches to teaching than traditional grading, not everyone would subscribe to the eclectic use of qualitative and quantitative methods that I propose or even to more systematic qualitative schemes. Wile and Tierney (1996), for example, object to the use of benchmarking and categorical descriptions as merely the reimposition of positivistic requirements for experimental control and objectivity. Theirs is a relatively extreme position that is more consistent with radical constructivism, which allows learners to invent their own reality, and with a particular version of qualitative research known as grounded theory (Glaser & Strauss, 1967), which resists the imposition of prior theory on data shifting and interpretation.

From Wile and Tierney's (1996) viewpoint, assessment is either positivistic or highly personal and unique, standardized or divergent, simplistic or complex, deductive or inductive, colonial or empowering. I would argue, however, that the use of benchmarks does not have to mean that categories are rigidly imposed, nor does having an eye on shared curricular goals mean that children's individuality must be stifled. Although I agree that creating regularized scoring rules for the purposes of external assessments will necessarily compromise the flexibility and responsiveness of assessments for classroom purposes, the question here has to do with the role of discipline-based and developmentally based expectations when the assessment is entirely under the control of the classroom teacher.

Both social constructivism and Deweyan philosophy suggest

---

[5] Admittedly, to expect teachers to identify consistent and inconsistent patterns of student performance across different types of assessments and to act as amateur anthropologists is a tall order. Although many good teachers have these skills, much more training would be needed for these techniques to be consistently and appropriately used as a normal part of teaching practice. Note, however, that professional development activities that help teachers cultivate a deeper understanding about how competence develops in a discipline, about criteria for judging student work, and about the process for making judgments using multiple sources of evidence need not be separate training activities but can be closely linked with efforts to develop teachers' pedagogical content knowledge (of which assessment strategies are a part) and to enhance teachers' subject matter knowledge.

that teaching should begin with the child but should move toward the organized and disciplined knowledge of mature practice. Correspondingly, more deductive forms of qualitative research balance what emerges from the data with insights provided by theory. Phillips (1996), for example, takes the position that "a person whose mind is a blank slate cannot do research. A researcher notices things that are of interest or that are pertinent—and interest and pertinence depend on, or are relative to, the prior beliefs or assumptions or expectations that are held by the researcher" (p. 1008). By the same reasoning, how could a teacher as researcher form an opinion about student growth without a mental model of effective literacy participation? Indeed, Cambourne and Turbill (1990) found that when teachers tried to make sense of assessment data, "the categories they subsequently devised were inevitably related to their values and beliefs about language and language development" (p. 344). If theory drives data interpretation (whether implicit or explicit), why not make it explicit and amenable to critique? In fact, interrogating the adequacy of one's curricular or instructional theory can be an important aspect of using assessment to improve instruction.

Use of Assessment in the Process of Learning

Improving the content of assessments is important but is not sufficient to ensure that assessment will be used to enhance learning. In this section, I consider the changes in classroom practices that are also needed to allow assessment to be used as part of the learning process. How should the culture of the classroom be changed so that students and teachers look to assessment as a source of insight and help rather than as the occasion for meting out rewards and punishments? In particular, how is learning helped by assessing prior knowledge and providing feedback as part of instruction? How might assessment-based classroom routines, such as reviewing evaluation criteria and engaging students in self-assessment, be used to develop metacognitive skills and students' responsibility for their own learning? How might these endeavors become so seamlessly a part of classroom discourse that students develop a learning orientation that is motivated by the desire to increase their competence instead of the need to perform to get good grades or to please the teacher? As part of this collaborative bargain, how might teachers explicitly use assessment to revise and adapt instruction?

Changes in the Role of Assessment in the Classroom Culture

In a recent review, Gipps (1999) summarized several of the shifts in assessment at the classroom level that follow from sociocultural and interpretive perspectives. I suggest that these can be seen as changes in the cultural practices of the classroom. First, according to Vygotsky's zone of proximal development, assessment should be interactive and dynamic (Lunt, 1993). By providing assistance as part of assessment, the teacher can gain valuable insights about learning strategies and how understandings might be extended. My own view goes further than information gathering. I suggest that, except when there is a formal requirement to record assisted versus independent performance, dynamic assessment can be used as the occasion to teach, especially to scaffold next steps. Second, assessments should be conducted in the social setting of the group. Closely tied to the view of learning as enculturation, students are socialized into the discourse of the disciplines and become accustomed to explaining their reasoning and receiving feedback about their developing competence as part of a social group. Third, the traditional relationship between teacher and student should be opened up to recognize the learner's perspective. For teachers to develop more open relationships with students does not mean that teachers give up responsibility—they have expert knowledge—but rather that the process becomes more collaborative. Finally, students are given an understanding of the assessment process and evaluation criteria as a means to develop their capacity as self-monitoring learners.

These cultural changes will, of course, prompt resistance. As Sadler (1998) points out, "the long-term exposure of students to defective patterns of formative assessment and the socialization of students into having to accept a wide variety of practices and teacher dispositions (many of which may appear incoherent or inconsistent), promote accommodating survival habits among students" (p. 77). Consistent with my earlier summary of the motivational literature in which some students are found to have a learning orientation and others a performance orientation, Perrenoud (1991) notes that we can always find certain students in a class who are willing to work harder to learn more and, therefore, go along with formative assessment. But other children and adolescents are "imprisoned in the identity of a bad pupil and an opponent" (p. 92). Perrenoud's description of students whose aim is to get through the day and school year without any major disaster is reminiscent of Holt's (1965) earlier observation that children hide their lack of understanding and use dysfunctional strategies—like guessing or mumbling so the teacher will answer his own question—because of their fears and their need to please grownups. According to Perrenoud, therefore, "every teacher who wants to practice formative assessment must reconstruct the teaching contract so as to counteract the habits acquired by his pupils" (p. 92).

Changing cultural practices will be especially difficult because it requires that teachers change their own habits as well. Tobin and Ulerick (1989) described the changes that occurred when a teacher, whose assessment practices had been built on the metaphor of being a "fair judge," adopted instead the metaphor of "a window into students' minds." The result was greater sharing of responsibility between teacher and students. In particular, students had to decide how to represent what they knew and had to schedule time to meet with the teacher to demonstrate their learning. Efforts to transform assessment routines should not be undertaken, however, as if they were separated from curricular goals. Instead, particular assessment processes should be selected to model the habits of inquiry, problem-solving approaches, brainstorming, modes of debate and critique, and other discourse practices associated with each discipline.

For example, a study by Cobb, Yackel, Wood, Wheatley, and Merkel (1988) was meant to help teachers develop a problem-solving atmosphere, but several of its strategies would foster collaborative assessment as well. In the study, students had to listen to and make sense of explanations given by other children and had to evaluate and resolve conflicting solutions when they occurred. At the same time, teachers had to learn to communicate to children that they were genuinely interested in the children's thinking and that one can learn from errors. Duschl and Gitomer (1997) explicitly promote the blending of instructional and assessment goals through the creation of a "portfolio culture" and "assessment conversations." For them, central practices include (a) acknowledging student conceptions through assessment strategies; (b) jointly evaluating knowledge claims by applying scientifically legitimate criteria; (c) emphasizing explanations, models, and experimentation as critical forms of scientific reasoning; and (d) making communication a requisite skill in all science activities.

Assessment of Prior Knowledge

Consistent with the principle that new learning is shaped by prior knowledge and cultural perspectives, classroom practices should include assessment of students' relevant knowledge and experience not only to inform teaching but also to draw students into the habit of reflecting on their own knowledge resources. The number of studies documenting the effect of prior knowledge on new learning is quite large (e.g., see the special issue of *Educational Psychologist,* Spring 1996, edited by Patricia Alexander), but unfortunately, many of these studies involve contrived examples in nonclassroom settings. Most studies are merely predictive, indicating that subjects who start out knowing more end up with greater knowledge. A much smaller number of studies demonstrate how background knowledge might be elicited as a means to adapt, focus, or connect instruction. For example, in Au and Jordan's (1981) study, Hawaiian children were encouraged to tell about experiences in their own lives that related to the stories they were learning about in school. Importantly, Au and Jordan's strategy elicited relevant information and invited children to apply it directly without the need for a separate assessment step. Similarly, Pressley, Wood, Woloshyn, Martin, King, and Menke (1992) reviewed studies that used questioning to help students activate prior knowledge and make connections to new content.

Again, the purpose of the questioning was not so much for the teacher to gain information about students' knowledge but to engage students in explaining their own understandings as a step in learning.

Although relevant background knowledge is usually a help in learning, researchers, especially in science education, have documented how students' intuitive and often naive beliefs about scientific phenomena may impede development of scientific understanding. For example, students may hold everyday conceptions of heat and temperature that do not match scientific terminology, they may believe that heavy objects fall faster than light ones, or they may be confused about how atoms act together (having only seen textbook pictures of single atoms). Similarly, in learning the subject of history, students may have quite fanciful beliefs about historical events or expect the past to be a timeless extension of present-day culture (Wineburg, 1996). Although earlier cognitive studies tried confrontation as a means for overturning students' misconceptions, contemporary approaches are more collaborative and provide students with multiple supports, including investigations and opportunities to hear ideas from other students to help them reformulate

their own ideas (Smith, diSessa, & Roschelle, 1993/1994).

In my own experience working in schools, I note two divergent sets of teaching practices that address students' prior knowledge. First, many teachers rely on a traditional, pretest-posttest design to document student progress. The premeasures are often formal, commercially purchased tests and may bear little resemblance to instructional materials. Pretest results are used to establish each student's achievement level or location but are typically not used to gain insight into the nature of student's understanding. For example, when a problem is missed, the teacher does not know what partial knowledge or competing conception is at work. Detailed objective-referenced measures may tell that a student "can do 2-digit subtraction" but cannot "subtract across zeros," but formal survey measures of this type are often filed away as baseline data with using the information for specific interventions. At the same time, a significant number of teachers, especially in reading and language arts, use prior knowledge activation techniques as a part of teaching but without necessarily attending to the assessment information provided. For example, K-W-L is an instructional strategy suggested by Ogle (1986) in which students first brainstorm about what they "Know" about a new topic, then try to make predictions about "What" they want to learn from the text or activity, and finally review what they have "Learned." As typically used, K-W-L discussions heighten student interest and focus attention, but assessment insights from the knowledge step are not so routinely used to adjust for what students already know or to supply missing background information.

Better prior-knowledge assessments possibly could be devised along the same lines as the content reforms of outcome assessments that are described in the previous section. However, as classroom discourse patterns are changed to help students draw connections and reflect on their own understandings, one can argue that assessing background knowledge should disappear as a separate pretest step and should, instead, become a part of scaffolding and ongoing checks for understanding. Nonetheless, as part of our efforts to change the culture of the classroom, I would suggest that prior knowledge activation techniques should be marked and acknowledged as "assessments."

After all, what safer time to admit what you do not know than at the start of an instructional activity? What better way to demonstrate to students that assessment (knowing what you know and what you do not know) helps learning? Moreover, to develop students' metacognitive knowledge about what helps in their own learning, explicit discussions of both the facilitating and inhibiting effects of background knowledge might be initiated. The present research literature does not provide clear guidance on the effectiveness of prior knowledge assessments that are used not only as an engagement and reflective activity for students but also as an information source for teachers. But this kind of question will be important in a program of research aimed at changing the role of assessment in instruction.

Effect of Feedback on Learning

The idea of feedback comes from electronics where the output of a system is reintroduced as input to moderate the strength of a signal. Correspondingly, both behaviorist and constructivist learning theories take for granted that providing information to the learner about performance will lead to self-correction and improvement. Extensive reviews of the effects of feedback on learning are provided by Black and Wiliam (1998) and Kluger and DeNisi (1996). Although, on average, feedback does improve learning outcomes, Kluger and DeNisi found that one-third of 607 effect sizes were negative. The authors were able to explain some of the variation in study findings using a theoretical hierarchy that was linked to the motivation literature. This hierarchy distinguished between task-oriented feedback, which tended to enhance learning, and self-oriented evaluation, which was more likely to be ineffective or debilitating.

The self-versus-task distinction may well be worth attention as educators try to develop a learning-oriented classroom culture. For the most part, however, meta-analyses of the feedback literature are of limited value in reconceptualizing assessment from a constructivist perspective, because the great majority of existing studies are based on behaviorist assumptions. The outcome measures used in typical feedback studies may be narrowly defined indicators of academic achievement, feedback may consist of simple reporting of right and wrong answers, and the end-of-study test may differ only slightly from the prior measure and from instructional materials. For example, a meta-analysis by Bangert-Drowns, Kulik, Kulik, and Morgan (1991) of 40 studies on feedback reveals that (a) half of the studies were based on programmed instruction, (b) nearly all of the studies involved interventions of only one-week duration, (c) feedback consisted mostly of telling students the right answer to the items they had gotten wrong, and (d) both formative and instructional materials were described as "test-like events" by the authors.

Although the content of feedback is different from that in behavioristic models, giving feedback is nonetheless an essential feature of scaffolding. As summarized by Hogan and Pressley (1997),

> A key role of the scaffolder is to summarize the progress that has been made and point out behaviors that led to the successes, expecting that eventually students will learn to monitor their own progress. One type of feedback is pointing out the distinction between the child's performance and the ideal. Another important type of feedback is attributing success to effort in order to encourage academically supportive attributions. Explicitly restating the concept that has been learned is another helpful form of feedback. (p. 83)

This portrayal derives mostly from research leading to Wood, Bruner, and Ross's (1976) original conception of scaffolding, from Vygotskian theory, and from naturalistic studies of effective tutoring that are described next. Relatively few studies have been undertaken in which explicit feedback interventions have been tried in the context of constructivist instructional settings.

In one study by Elawar and Corno (1985), teachers were trained, using a cognitive perspective, to provide written feedback on mathematics homework. For example, comments were focused on specific errors and on poor strategy, gave suggestions about how to improve, and emphasized understanding rather than superficial knowledge. Not only did written feedback improve achievement significantly, but it also reduced the initial superiority of boys over girls and improved attitudes toward mathematics.

A slightly different view of the role of feedback emerges, however, from Lepper, Drake, and O'Donnell-Johnson's (1997) study of selected, highly successful tutors. The most effective tutors do not appear to directly correct student errors routinely. Instead, they ignore errors when they are inconsequential to the solution process and forestall errors that the student has made systematically before by offering hints or asking leading questions. Only when the forestalling tactic fails do expert tutors intervene with a direct question that is intended to force the student to self-correct. The tutor also may engage in debugging, using a series of increasingly direct questions to guide the student through the solution process. According to the analysis of Lepper et al., the tendency of expert tutors to use indirect forms of feedback when possible was influenced by their desire to maintain student motivation and self-confidence while not ignoring student errors.

These two studies highlight a tension in the literature on constructivist teaching practices about the role of formative assessment and feedback. Some might argue that discourse practices in inquiry-based classrooms would allow students to revise their thinking without the need for explicit, corrective feedback because the evidence gathered in the course of an investigation would naturally challenge their misconceptions. My own view is that, yes, formative assessments should be embedded in ongoing instructional activities. Sometimes, conducting these formative assessments will mean that students will receive feedback from the teacher, classmates, or self-reflections without the interactions being marked explicitly as assessments. At other times, however, as I suggest in the next sections, students should consciously participate in assessment so they can develop an understanding of the criteria that define good work and take responsibility for monitoring their own learning. As was the case with prior knowledge assessment, the question of whether to use indirect means versus explicit feedback to help students reexamine their ideas will be an important part of a research agenda on constructivist assessment practices.

Explicit Criteria and Self-Assessment

Frederiksen and Collins (1989) used the term *transparency* to express the idea that students must have a clear understanding of the criteria by which their work will be assessed. In fact, the features of excellent performance should be so transparent that students can learn to evaluate their own work in the same way that their teachers would. According to Frederiksen and Collins (1989),

> The assessment system [should] provide a basis for developing a metacognitive awareness of what are important characteristics of good problem solving, good writing, good experimentation, good historical analysis, and so on. Moreover, such an assessment can address not only the product one is trying to achieve, but also the process of achieving it, that is, the habits of mind that contribute to successful writing, painting, and problem solving (Wiggins, 1989). (pp. 29–30)

For example, in a more recent study, Frederiksen and White (1997) developed assessment criteria to address the most important attributes that they wanted students to develop and exhibit while conducting investigations in science. The list included content-oriented criteria (Understanding the Science, Understanding the Processes of Inquiry, and Making Connections), process-oriented criteria (Being Inventive, Being Systematic, Using the Tools of Science, and Reasoning Carefully), and socially oriented criteria (Communicating Well and Teamwork). Although access to evaluation criteria satisfies a basic fairness criterion (we should know the rules for how our work will be judged), the more important reasons for helping students develop an understanding of standards in each of the disciplines are to directly improve learning and to develop metacognitive knowledge for monitoring one's own efforts. These cognitive and metacognitive purposes for teaching students explicitly about criteria then speak to a different sense of fairness than merely being even-handed in evaluating students; that is, these two purposes provide students with the opportunity to get good at what it is that the standards require.

Wolf and Reardon (1996) have this same sense of fairness and equity in mind when they talk about "making thinking visible," and "making excellence attainable." The specific classroom strategies they describe from Project PACE (Performance Assessment Collaboratives for Education) blend the modeling of important processes—for example, showing students what it means "to have a theory" and "support it with evidence" (p. 12)—and explicit discussion by teacher and students of the evaluative criteria they will use in peer editing. Consistent with learning principles in the conceptual framework, these strategies that involve instruction and assessment together are examples of socially mediated learning opportunities that help to develop cognitive abilities.

As Wolf and Reardon (1996) anticipate, there is a tension regarding the prescriptive nature of scoring rubrics. Claxton (1995) cautions that students could learn to apply prespecified criteria and thereby raise their achievement but may not improve learning acumen if they become dependent on others for clarification and correction. He argues that "quality" in a particular domain is "*in principle* incapable of complete explication".... "Self-evaluation, the ability to recognize good work as such and to correct one's performance so that better work is produced, grows in the doing as much as in the reflecting, and is irreducibly intuitive" (Claxton, 1995, p. 341). In other words, the ability to self-evaluate is developed in the same way as— and, indeed, is indistinguishable from—intelligence and discipline-related cognitive abilities. Although Wolf and Reardon (1996) describe a context in which evaluation criteria were negotiated and made a part of the learning process, Claxton's point is well taken. The mere provision of explicit criteria will not enable learning in all the ways desired if they are imposed autocratically and are mechanically applied. For the intended benefits to occur, self-assessment has to be a part of more pervasive cultural shifts in the classroom. Students have to have the opportunity to learn what criteria mean (surely not memorize them as a list), be able to apply them to their own work, and even be able to challenge the rules when they chafe.

In its ideal form, self-assessment serves social and motivational purposes and also improves cognitive performance. Engaging students in reflecting on their own work and in debates about standards can increase student responsibility for their own learning and redistribute power, making the relationship between teacher and students more collaborative. As stated previously, the teacher does not give over responsibility, but by

sharing it gains greater student ownership, less distrust, and more appreciation that standards are not capricious or arbitrary. In case studies of student self-evaluation practices in two Australian and English sites, Klenowski (1995) found that students who participated in self-evaluation became more interested in the criteria and substantive feedback than in their grade per se. Students also reported that they had to be more honest about their own work as well as being fair with other students, and they had to be prepared to defend their opinions in terms of the evidence. Klenowski's (1995) data support Wiggins's (1992) earlier assertion that involving students in analyzing their own work builds ownership of the evaluation process and "makes it possible to hold students to higher standards because the criteria are clear and reasonable" (p. 30).

Although claims about the expected benefits of explicit criteria and self-assessment follow logically from the research literature on motivation and cognitive and metacognitive development, only a few studies directly examine the effects of these practices on student learning. The Frederiksen and White (1997) study that was described previously provided criteria and also engaged students in a set of activities to foster "reflective assessment." At several stages in the Inquiry Cycle curriculum, students evaluated their own work in terms of the criteria. Each time, they not only applied the criteria but also wrote a brief rationale pointing to the features of their work that supported their rating. In addition, students in the reflective assessment classrooms used the criteria to give feedback to classmates when projects were presented orally in class. Compared to control classrooms where students evaluated the curriculum rather than their own learning, students who participated in reflective-assessment processes produced projects that were much more highly rated by their teachers. Importantly, these positive gains were greatest for low-achieving students. On a follow-up test of conceptual understanding in physics that was less directly tied to the inquiry criteria, no difference was found between the high-achieving students in reflective assessment and those in control classrooms. However, heretofore low-achieving students showed dramatic gains in conceptual understanding as a result of reflective self-assessment.

Evaluation and Improvement of Teaching

In addition to using assessment to monitor and promote individual students' learning, classroom assessment should also be used to examine and improve teaching practices. Although a number of authoritative sources (National Council of Teachers of Mathematics (NCTM), 1995; National Forum on Assessment, 1995; National Research Council, 1996; Shepard, Kagan, & Wurtz, 1998) have acknowledged the importance of using assessment data as a tool for systematic reflection and teacher learning, much less empirical research or formal theorizing has been done regarding this collateral use of student assessment. How is assessment used to learn about one's own pedagogy different from the use of assessment data to promote individual student growth? Is one just the aggregation of data from the other (e.g., the whole class is struggling with a concept versus three students need extra help)? Although reform rhetoric implies that a shared understanding exists about what it means to use assessment data to improve instruction, examples offered suggest considerable ambiguity. On the one hand, "using assessment to improve instruction" might mean using assessment data to select the best technique from one's repertoire to address an observed problem; on the other hand, it could imply much more critical inquiry and a transformative purpose.

The authors of the NCTM (1995) *Assessment Standards for School Mathematics* offer a conception of classroom assessment that depends on the close intertwining of student growth and instructional improvement purposes. "Although evidence of progress originates with individual students, as indicated in the 'Purpose: Monitoring Students' Progress' section, teachers also sample and collect such evidence to provide information about the progress of the groups of students they teach" (p. 45). Evidence about what students are understanding leads to instructional decisions about both individuals and groups. The NCTM *Assessment Standards* go on to elaborate three types of instructional decisions that are informed by assessment data: moment-by-moment decisions, short-term planning, and long-term planning. During instruction, informal observation and questioning help teachers know when to clarify directions, when to redirect instruction to address misconceptions, when to capitalize on student insights to extend a lesson, and so forth. As part of planning for the next day, to ensure the close integration of instruction and assessment, teachers should not only review goals but also consider what questions or samplings of student work will be used to check on understanding. This process is recursive because insights from one day's questioning help in shaping the direction of subsequent lessons. Longer-term planning requires that teachers consider not only what broader set of learning goals are be addressed but also how students' learning will be assessed across various modes and contexts and in a way that is responsive to students' cultural experiences.

The National Research Council's (NRC) *National Science Education Standards* (NRC, 1996) go further than the NCTM *Assessment Standards* in laying out a continuum of teaching-oriented assessment uses that range from instructional decision making to critical analysis of teaching effectiveness. At one end of the continuum, the NRC *Science Standards,* like the NCTM *Assessment Standards,* propose that ongoing assessment of students' understanding be used to adjust lessons and teaching plans. At a midpoint on the continuum, assessment data are also used to plan curricula, especially, by helping to evaluate "the developmental appropriateness of the science content, student interest in the content, the effectiveness of activities in producing the desired learning outcomes, the effectiveness of the selected examples, and the understandings and abilities students must have to benefit from the selected activities and examples" (p. 87). Finally, at the other end of the continuum, the NRC *Science Standards* suggest how assessment might be used in "researching" teaching practices. "Engaging in classroom research means that teachers develop assessment plans that involve collecting data about students' opportunities to learn as well as their achievement" (p. 89).

Although teachers follow procedures of systematic inquiry for each of these purposes, the "instructional adjustment" end of the continuum is much less critical and seeks to make the best decisions (efficiently within the flow of instruction) without seeking root causes. In contrast, the "teacher as researcher" or "critical inquiry" end of the continuum requires more formal problem identification, involves more systematic data collec-

tion, and seeks better understanding and explanation about why certain teaching strategies work better. The critical end of the continuum is more consistent with seminal theories of action research (e.g., Corey, 1953; Lewin, 1948).

The NCTM and NRC visions are idealizations that are based on beliefs about constructivist pedagogy and reflective practice. Although both are supported by examples of individual teachers who use assessment to improve their teaching, little is known about what kinds of support would be required (a) to help large numbers of teachers develop these strategies or (b) to ensure that teacher education programs prepared teachers to use assessment in these ways. Research is needed to address these basic implementation questions, but serious theoretical questions challenge us as well:

- To what extent are models of action research applicable to the systematic use of assessment data to improve teaching? A number of different definitions can be applied to action research, some of which emphasize formal reporting of results to give teachers voice outside the classroom. Even those that focus within the classroom require more formal procedures than could be applied to all areas of instruction all of the time. To be feasible then, how do master teachers learn to balance the ongoing uses of assessment to revise instruction with the action research studies that are reserved for deeper and more systematic investigation of specific instructional practices?

- To what extent and in what ways should teachers make their investigations of teaching visible to students? This question seems to me to be fundamentally important to the issue of transforming the culture of the classroom. If we want the cultural practices in the classroom to support development of students' identities as learners—where students naturally seek feedback and critique their own work as part of learning—then it is reasonable that teachers would model this same commitment to using data systematically as it applies to their own role in the teaching and learning process.

- How are idealizations about reflective practices affected when external assessment mandates are used to leverage instructional changes? Although aggregate classroom assessment data may indeed be useful when teachers are attempting to make major changes in their instruction, assessment-driven reform may distort the intended curriculum (Koretz & Barron, 1998) and undermine the role of teacher as researcher.

Conclusions

In this chapter, I considered how classroom assessment practices might be reconceptualized to be more effective in moving forward the teaching and learning process. To develop a "social-constructivist" conceptual framework, I borrowed from cognitive, constructivist, and sociocultural theories. (To be sure, these camps are warring with each other, but I predict that it will be something like this merged, middle-ground theory that will eventually be accepted as common wisdom and carried into practice.) Key ideas are recapitulated briefly here to emphasize the close interconnections among new theories of learning, reformed curricula, and new ideas about assessment. Then, in closing, I turn to the implications of this vision of classroom assessment for future research.

Summary of Concepts

The cognitive revolution reintroduced the concept of the mind. In contrast to past, mechanistic theories of knowledge acquisition, we now understand that learning is an active process of mental construction and sense making. From cognitive theory, we have also learned that existing knowledge structures and beliefs enable or impede new learning, that intelligent thought involves self-monitoring and awareness about when and how to use skills, and that expertise in a field of study develops as a principled and coherent way of thinking and representing problems—not just as an accumulation of information. At the same time, rediscovery of Vygotsky and the work of other Soviet psychologists led to the realization that what is taken into the mind is socially and culturally determined. Fixed, largely hereditarian theories of intelligence have been replaced with a new understanding that cognitive abilities are developed through socially supported interactions. Although Vygotsky was initially interested in how children learn to think, over time, the ideas of social mediation have been applied equally to the development of intelligence, the development of expertise in academic disciplines, the development of metacognitive skills, and the formation of identity. Indeed, a singularly important idea in this new paradigm is that development and learning are primarily social processes.

These insights from learning theory then lead to a set of principles for curriculum reform. The slogan that "all students can learn" is intended to refute past beliefs that only an elite group of students could master challenging subject matter. A commitment to equal opportunity for diverse learners means providing genuine opportunities for high-quality instruction and "ways into" academic curricula that are consistent with language and interaction patterns of home and community (Au & Jordan, 1981; Heath, 1983; Tharp & Gallimore, 1988).

Classroom routines and the ways that teachers and students talk with each other should help students gain experience with the ways of thinking and speaking in academic disciplines. School learning should be authentic and connected to the world outside of school not only to make learning more interesting and motivating to students but also to develop the ability to use knowledge in real world settings. In addition to the development of cognitive abilities, classroom expectations and social norms should foster the development of important dispositions, such as students' willingness to persist in trying to solve difficult problems, and their identities as capable learners.

To be compatible with and to support this social-constructivist model of teaching and learning, classroom assessment must change in two fundamentally important ways. First, the form and content of classroom assessments must be changed to better represent important thinking and problem-solving skills in each of the disciplines. These changes include assessing learning that is based on observations, oral questioning, significant tasks, projects, demonstrations, collections of student work, and students' self-evaluations. Such changes also require that teachers engage in systematic analysis of the available evidence. Second, the way that assessment is used in

classrooms and how it is regarded by teachers and students must change.

This change to the purpose of assessment literally calls for a change in the culture of classrooms so that students no longer try to feign competence or work to perform well on the test—as an end separate from real learning. Instead, students and teachers should collaborate to assess prior knowledge, probe apparent misconceptions, and resolve areas of confusion because it is agreed that such assessments will help students understand better. Students should engage in self-assessment not only to take responsibility for their own learning but also to develop metacognitive skills by learning to apply to their own work the standards that define quality work in a field. Similarly, teachers should demonstrate their own willingness to learn by explicitly using assessment data to evaluate and improve instruction.

Implications for Research

This social-constructivist view of classroom assessment is an idealization. The new ideas and perspectives underlying it have a basis in theory and empirical studies, but how they will work in practice and on a larger scale is not known. The chapter's framework is offered as a conceptual framework for the ambitious program of research and development that will be needed to make the idealization real. In the following paragraphs, I suggest important questions to be addressed from this perspective in three broad areas of investigation: (a) the reliability and validity of classroom assessments, (b) the effects of social-constructivist uses of assessment on learning and motivation, and (c) the professional development of teachers.

RELIABILITY AND VALIDITY OF CLASSROOM ASSESSMENTS

I argued previously that classroom assessments do not have to meet the same standard of reliability as external accountability assessments primarily because no one classroom assessment has as much importance as a one-time accountability test and because erroneous decisions can be corrected in the classroom context. Still, some level of consistency should be established in classroom assessments to ensure both the accuracy of information and fairness. None of the aforementioned benefits will accrue if students perceive assessment to be erratic or unfair.

Teachers are generally accurate in ranking students in their class though not with the same precision as standardized tests. For example, in a recent study, teachers' standards-based ratings of students' mathematics achievement showed a strong correlation with test results ($r = .58$) (Shepard, Taylor, & Betebenner, 1998). This degree of agreement is impressive given that the rating scale had only four categories and teachers received no special training. However, we also know that teacher-based evaluations are prone to certain biases such as the use of idiosyncratic criteria, halo effects, and the tendency to persist with initial judgments of ability rather than to adjust in response to evidence (Shavelson & Stern, 1981).

We know also that specific training improves the consistency of teachers' judgments; that is, evaluations can become more self-consistent and also congruent with shared criteria and exemplar papers. Important practical questions, then, will be

When does such specialized training makes sense for classroom uses of assessment? To what extent might common training in the development and use of criteria for classroom assessment scoring lead to greater teacher understanding of curriculum reform as well as enhanced reliability of assessments? In contexts where external assessments are aligned with curriculum reform, what connections should be drawn between criteria for evaluating classroom work and external performance standards? For classroom purposes only, what kind of training do teachers need to effectively develop and evaluate hypotheses about students' understandings that will allow them then to gain insights from assessment and not just produce a reliable score?

Validity has ostensibly received the most attention in the assessment reform literature to date because of the emphasis on representing more meaningful content and processes in assessment tasks. Questions still remain, however, as to whether new forms of assessment are measuring as intended. Are students developing and using advanced thinking and problem-solving abilities? Are students able to show what they know, or do artifacts of assessment format interfere with their abilities to demonstrate proficiency? In particular, how should emphases on communication skills and shared academic discourse patterns be mediated for special needs and language-minority students without implicitly setting lower standards for these groups? Are open-ended forms of assessment vulnerable to the same sorts of teaching-to-the-test corruption as traditional closed forms of assessment? Can students "pretend to know" by repeating formulaic routines? Returning to the points raised earlier about the close correspondence between validity across modes of assessment and teaching for transfer, what kinds of studies can be undertaken to address this relationship explicitly? If students can appear to be proficient when asked to perform in one way (e.g., paper-and-pencil electric circuit problems) but not when asked to perform in another way (e.g., hands-on versions of the same electric circuit problems) (Shavelson, Baxter, & Pine, 1992), then is this inconsistency a measurement problem or a learning problem? How might teachers use multiple modes of assessment to support development of flexible and robust understandings?

EFFECTS OF SOCIAL-CONSTRUCTIVIST USES OF ASSESSMENT ON LEARNING AND MOTIVATION

Contemporary validity theory asks not only, "Does the test measure what it purports to measure?" But also it asks, "Does its use produce effects as intended?" This concept is sometimes referred to as "consequential validity" (Messick, 1989). If formative use of assessments in classrooms is claimed to improve student learning, is this claim warranted? To find out how things work while using constructivist perspectives, we must conduct studies in classrooms where instruction and assessment strategies are consonant with this model. In many cases, conducting these new studies will mean starting over again and not assuming that findings from previous research studies can be generalized across paradigms.

Reconceptualizing and restarting a program of research will be especially important, for example, when conducting studies on topics such as feedback and motivation. The concept of feedback derives from the behaviorist model of learning and, as suggested previously, the great majority of studies available on feedback conform to behaviorist assumptions: instruction is of short duration; posttests closely resemble pretests and instructional materials; feedback is in the form of being told the correct answers; and so forth. New studies will be needed to evaluate the effect of feedback when it has been provided in ways that reflect constructivist principles, for example, as part of instructional scaffolding, assessment conversations, and other interactive means of helping students self-correct and improve.

Similarly, the research literature on motivation makes sweeping claims about the risks of evaluating students, especially when they are tackling difficult problems. Yet, these findings are based on students' experiences with traditional, inauthentic, and normative forms of assessment where students took little responsibility for their own learning and criteria remained mysterious. If the classroom culture were to be shifted dramatically, consistent with social-constructivist learning perspectives, then the effects of assessing students on difficult problems will have to be reexamined. The same is also true for many other research areas. Likewise, when conducting comprehensive reviews or meta-analyses it will be important to consider the perspective represented and not aggregate studies across paradigms.

Although I have worked to merge cognitive and sociocultural perspectives (and, taken together, distinguish them from behaviorally oriented studies), there are, nonetheless, some important questions and controversies separating these two perspectives that should be addressed by a serious program of research. In this chapter, for example, I have taken the position that teachers should act as clinicians, using interpretive forms of data analysis as well as formal assessments, and I emphasized social, motivational, and identity-producing aspects of self-assessment, classroom discourse practices, and so forth.

By contrast, more cognitively oriented approaches to assessment tend to emphasize the use of computer modeling to help diagnose student thinking (Pellegrino, Baxter, & Glaser, 1999). Although these two approaches hold most theoretical principles in common, as outlined in the conceptual framework, they disagree about the extent to which most of student learning in various domains can be formalized, that is, modeled by computer algorithms so that feedback from the machine could be equal to interacting with the teacher. Even if certain domains can be adequately specified to account for most student developmental pathways, I would argue that too many domains are present in the teaching day to be captured by the sum of a set of models. These are, of course, points of debate that should be addressed empirically.

To what extent are computer-delivered curricula effective in helping students learn challenging subject matter and develop habits of inquiry? What are the positive and negative side effects of using technology-based curricula? Do boys and girls participate equally (or more or less equally) than they do with hands-on, nontechnology curricula? Do students with less technology sophistication engage in the same science or history learning as students who are adept at using technology? Do students generalize inquiry skills and discourse practices, such as self-assessment and principled peer critique, to nontechnology parts of the school day? Importantly, what are the effects of such embedded assessment projects on teacher learning? Do teachers develop richer understandings of student development because of the benchmarking that is provided by computerized assessments, or do teachers learn less about students' understandings because the machine is doing the thinking? Are teachers marginalized as nonexperts if branches of computer and Internet resources go beyond their own knowledge? What support do teachers need to model the role of learner in contexts where they are not expert?

Of course, parallel questions should be asked regarding more clinical approaches to assessment, as I suggest below. My own view is that complex, new, cognitive and psychometric models are unlikely to be successful in creating an entire diagnostic and prescriptive system independent of teacher judgment. Nonetheless, projects such as those described by Minstrell (1999) and the Cognition and Technology Group at Vanderbilt (1998) could serve as powerful professional development aids to help teachers become more insightful about techniques that provide access to students' thinking.

PROFESSIONAL DEVELOPMENT OF TEACHERS

Clearly, the abilities needed to implement a reformed vision of curriculum and classroom assessment are daunting—reminiscent of Cremin's (1961) earlier observation that progressive education required "infinitely skilled teachers." Being able to ask the right questions at the right time, anticipate conceptual pitfalls, and have at the ready a repertoire of tasks that will help student take the next steps requires deep knowledge of subject matter. Teachers will also need help in learning to use assessment in new ways. They will need a theory of motivation and a sense of how to develop a classroom culture with learning at its center. Given that new ideas about the role of assessment are likely to be at odds with prevailing beliefs, teachers will need assistance to reflect on their own beliefs and those of students, colleagues, parents, and school administrators. Because teachers' beliefs, knowledge, and skills are pivotal in bringing about change in assessment practices, teachers' knowledge and beliefs should be a primary site for research.

In studies such as Frederiksen and White's (1997), where students have clearly benefited from inquiry-based curricula and reflective assessment practices, what have been the corollary effects on teachers' beliefs and practices? What supports have led to enactment of the vision, what impediments have subverted change? In Wilson and Sloane's (2000) study of the BEAR Assessment System, for example, benefits from curricular change and teacher professional development led to improvements in students' learning, like those found by Frederiksen and White (1997). In addition, as a result of using the BEAR assessments and participating in scoring moderation sessions, teachers exhibited greater collegiality and used openended questions more than teachers in a reform-oriented comparison group, "which retained their rosy perceptions of alternative assessment strategies, but never really used them" (Roberts, Wilson, & Draney, 1997). Although in theory all aspects of the reform are conceptually interrelated, practically speaking, how can teachers try out manageable segments of the reform (one subject area or one instructional unit) to gain experience with these ideas in the context of their own practice? Although incremental change seems the most practical, what happens when conceptually incompatible systems are overlaid, as might occur when self-assessment is used alongside traditional grading practices?

This chapter began with a portrayal of ideas from the past—those about inherited ability, tracked curricula, atomistic conceptions of knowledge, and "scientific" measurement—that continue to shape educational practice and popular beliefs. Against this backdrop, a reformed vision for classroom assessment was offered consistent with social constructivist principles. This vision may seem overly idealistic and optimistic given the demands it makes on teachers' knowledge and insight. Nonetheless, this vision should be pursued because it holds the most promise for using assessment to improve teaching and learning. To do otherwise means that day-to-day classroom practices will continue to reinforce and reproduce the status quo.

Each time that teachers hold conferences with students, grade papers, ask students to explain their answers, or use results from a quiz to reorganize instruction, they are either following in the rut of existing practices and beliefs or participating in transforming the culture of the classroom. The task of implementing new assessment practices can be made easier if specific innovations are chosen to support and complement concomitant changes in curriculum and instruction. Indeed, attempts to improve instruction without corresponding changes in assessment are likely to be thwarted by powerful assumptions underlying assessment practices.

REFERENCES

Alexander, P. A. (Ed.). (1996). The role of knowledge in learning and instruction [Special issue]. *Educational Psychologist, 31*(2), 89–145.

Allington, R. L. (1991). Children who find learning to read difficult: School responses to diversity. In E. H. Hiebert (Ed.), *Literacy for a diverse society: Perspectives, practices, and policies* (pp. 237–252). New York: Teachers College Press.

American Association for the Advancement of Science. (1993). *Benchmarks for science literacy.* New York: Oxford University Press.

Anderson, J. R., Reder, L. M., Simon, H. A. (1996). Situated learning and education. *Educational Researcher, 25,* 5–11.

Atwell, N. (1987). *In the middle: Writing, reading, and learning with adolescents.* Portsmouth, NH: Heineman.

Au, K. H. (1994). Portfolio assessment: Experiences at the Kamehameha Elementary Education Program. In S. W. Valencia, E. H. Hiebert, & P. Afflerbach (Eds.), *Authentic reading assessment: Practices and possibilities* (pp. 103–126). Newark, DE: International Reading Association.

Au, K. H., & Jordan, C. (1981). Teaching reading to Hawaiian children: Finding a culturally appropriate solution. In H. Trueba, G. P. Guthrie, & K. H. Au (Eds.), *Culture in the bilingual classroom: Studies in classroom ethnography* (pp. 139–152). Rowley, MA: Newbury House.

Au, K. H., & Valencia, S. W. (1997). The complexities of portfolio assessment. In N. C. Burbules & D. T. Hansen (Eds.), *Teaching and its predicaments* (pp. 123–144). Boulder: Westview Press.

Ayers, L. P. (1918). History and present status of educational measurements. *Seventeenth yearbook of the National Society for the Study of Education: Part II* (pp. 9–15). Bloomington, IL: Public School Publishing Company.

Bangert-Drowns, R. L., Kulik, C. C., Kulik, J. A., & Morgan, M. T.

(1991). The instructional effect of feedback in test-like events. *Review of Educational Research, 61*(2), 213–238.

Black, P., & Wiliam, D. (1998). Assessment and classroom learning. *Assessment in Education: Principles, Policy, and Practice, 5*(1), 7–74.

Bliem, C. L., & Davinroy, K. H. (1997). *Teachers' beliefs about assessment and instruction in literacy.* Unpublished manuscript, University of Colorado at Boulder.

Bloom, B. S. (Ed.). (1956). *Taxonomy of educational objectives: The classification of educational goals.* New York: David McKay Company.

Bobbitt, F. (1912). The elimination of waste in education. *The Elementary School Teacher, 12,* 259–271.

Bransford, J. D. (1979). *Human cognition: Learning, understanding, and remembering.* Belmont, CA: Wadsworth.

Brown, A. L. (1994). The advancement of learning. *Educational Researcher, 23,* 4–12.

Brown, A. L., Bransford, J. D., Ferrara, R. A., & Campione, J. C. (1983). Learning, remembering, and understanding. In J. H. Flavell & E. M. Markman (Eds.), *Handbook of child psychology: Vol. 3. Child development* (4th ed., pp. 77–166). New York: Wiley.

Brown, A. L., & Campione, J. C. (1994). Guided discovery in a community of learners. In K. McGilly (Ed.), *Classroom lessons: Integrating cognitive theory and classroom practice* (pp. 229–270). Cambridge, MA: Bradford Books, MIT Press.

Brown, A. L., & Kane, M. J. (1988). Preschool children can learn to transfer: Learning to learn and learning from example. *Cognitive Psychology, 20,* 493–523.

Brownell, W. A. (1946). Introduction: Purpose and scope of the yearbook. *The forty-fifth yearbook of the National Society for the Study of Education: Part I. The measurement of understanding.* Chicago: University of Chicago Press.

Budoff, M. (1974). Learning potential and educability among the educable mentally retarded. (Final Report Project No. 312312). Cambridge, MA: Research Institute for Educational Problems, Cambridge Mental Health Association.

Burns, M. (1993). *Mathematics: Assessing understanding.* White Plains, NY: Cuisenaire Company of America.

California Assessment Program. (1989). *A question of thinking: A first look at students' performance on open-ended questions in mathematics.* Sacramento: California Department of Education.

California Learning Assessment System. (1994). *A sampler of science assessment—elementary.* Sacramento: California Department of Education.

Callahan, R. E. (1962). *Education and the cult of efficiency: A study of the social forces that have shaped the administration of the public schools.* Chicago: University of Chicago Press.

Cambourne, B., & Turbill, J. (1990). Assessment in whole-language classrooms: Theory into practice. *The Elementary School Journal, 90,* 337–349.

Camp, R. (1992). Portfolio reflections in middle and secondary school classrooms. In K. B. Yancey (Ed.), *Portfolios in the writing classroom* (pp. 61–79). Urbana, IL: National Council of Teachers of English.

Center for Civic Education. (1994). *National standards for civics and government.* Calabasas, CA: Author.

Claxton, G. (1995). What kind of learning does self-assessment drive? Developing a "nose" for quality: Comments on Klenowski. *Assessment in Education, 2*(3), 339–343.

Clay, M. M. (1985). *The early detection of reading difficulties* (3rd ed.). Auckland, New Zealand: Heinemann.

Cobb, P., Yackel, E., Wood, T., Wheatley, G., & Merkel, G. (1988). Research into practice: Creating a problem-solving atmosphere. *Arithmetic Teacher, 36,* 46–47.

Cognition and Technology Group at Vanderbilt. (1998). Designing environments to reveal, support, and expand our children's potentials. In S. A. Soraci & W. McIlvane (Eds.), *Perspectives on fundamental processes in intellectual functioning* (Vol. 1, pp. 313–350). Greenwich, CT: Ablex.

Cohen, S. A. (1987). Instructional alignment: Searching for a magic bullet. *Educational Researcher, 16,* 16–20.

Collins, A., Brown, J. S., & Newman, S. E. (1989). Cognitive apprenticeship: Teaching the crafts of reading, writing, and mathematics.

In L. B. Resnick (Ed.), *Knowing, learning, and instruction: Essays in honor of Robert Glaser* (pp. 453–494). Hillsdale, NJ: Lawrence Erlbaum Associates.

Corey, S. M. (1953). *Action research to improve school practices.* New York: Teachers College Bureau of Publications, Columbia University.

Cremin, L. (1961). *The transformation of the school: Progressivism in American education, 1876–1957.* New York: Vintage Books.

Cronbach, L. J. (1975). Five decades of public controversy over mental testing. *American Psychologist, 30,* 1–14.

Darling-Hammond, L. (1996). The right to learn and the advancement of teaching: Research, policy, and practice for democratic education. *Educational Researcher, 25,* 5–17.

Darling-Hammond, L., & Wise, A. E. (1985). Beyond standardization: State standards and school improvement. *The Elementary School Journal, 85,* 315–336.

Dewey, J. (1897). The university elementary school: History and character. *University Record, 2,* 72–75.

Dewey, J. (1902). *The child and the curriculum.* Chicago: University of Chicago Press.

Duschl, R. A., & Gitomer, D. H. (1997). Strategies and challenges to changing the focus of assessment and instruction in science classrooms. *Educational Assessment, 4*(1), 37–73.

Dweck, C. (1986). Motivational processes affecting learning. *American Psychologist, 41,* 1040–1048.

Education for All Handicapped Children Act of 1975, Pub. L. No. 94–142, 20 U.S.C. §1401 *et seq.* (1974).

Education U. S. A. (1968). *Individually prescribed instruction.* Washington, DC: Author.

Eisenhart, M., Finkel, E., & Marion, S. F. (1996). Creating the conditions for scientific literacy: A re-examination. *American Educational Research Journal, 33,* 261–295.

Elawar, M. C., & Corno, L. (1985). A factorial experiment in teachers' written feedback on student homework: Changing teacher behavior a little rather than a lot. *Journal of Educational Psychology, 77,* 162–173.

Ellwein, M. C., & Graue, M. E. (1995). Assessment as a way of knowing children. In C. A. Grant & M. L. Gomez (Eds.), *Making schooling multicultural: Campus and classroom* (pp. 77–109). Englewood Cliffs, NJ: Merrill.

Feuerstein, R. (1969). *The instrumental enrichment method: An outline of theory and technique.* Jerusalem: Hadassah-Wizo-Canada Research Institute.

Feuerstein, R. (1980). *Instrumental enrichment: An intervention program for cognitive modifiability.* Baltimore: University Park Press.

Fleming, M., & Chambers, B. (1983). Teacher-made tests: Windows on the classroom. In W. E. Hathaway (Ed.), *Testing in the schools. New directions for testing and measurement,* no. 19 (pp. 29–38). San Francisco: Jossey-Bass.

Fordham, S., & Ogbu, J. U. (1986). Black students' school success: Coping with the burden of acting white. *Urban Review, 18,* 176–206.

Frederiksen, J. R., & Collins, A. (1989). A systems approach to educational testing. *Educational Researcher, 18,* 27–32.

Frederiksen, J. R., & White, B. Y. (1997, March). *Reflective assessment of students' research within an inquiry-based middle school science curriculum.* Paper presented at the annual meeting of the American Educational Research Association, Chicago.

Gagne, R. M. (1965). *The conditions of learning.* New York: Holt, Rinehart & Winston.

Gates, A. I., & Bond, G. L. (1936). Reading readiness: A study of factors determining success and failure in beginning reading. *Teachers College Record, 37,* 679–685.

Geertz, C. (1973). *The interpretation of cultures.* New York: Basic Books.

Geography Education Standards Project. (1994). *Geography for life: National geography standards 1994.* Washington, DC: National Geographic Research and Exploration.

Gipps, C. V. (1996). Assessment for learning. In A. Little & A. Wolf (Eds.), *Assessment in transition: Learning, monitoring and selection in international perspective* (pp. 251–262). Oxford, UK: Pergamon Press.

Gipps, C. V. (1999). *Socio-cultural aspects of assessment.* In A. Iran-Nejad & P. D. Pearson (Eds.), *Review of Research in Education,* Vol. 24 (pp. 355–392). Washington, DC: American Education Research Association.

Glaser, B. G., & Strauss, A. L. (1967). *The discovery of grounded theory: Strategies for qualitative research.* New York: Aldine de Gruyter.

Glaser, R. (1984). Education and thinking: The role of knowledge. *American Psychologist, 39,* 93–104.

Goddard, H. H. (1920). *Human efficiency and levels of intelligence.* Princeton: Princeton University Press.

Goodman, K. S. (1973). Miscues: Windows on the reading process. In K. Goodman (Ed.), *Miscue analysis: Applications to reading instruction* (pp. 3–14). Urbana, IL: National Council of Teachers of English.

Goslin, D. A. (1967). *Teachers and testing.* New York: Sage.

Gould, S. J. (1981). *The mismeasure of man.* New York: W. W. Norton.

Graue, M. E. (1993). Integrating theory and practice through instructional assessment. *Educational Assessment, 1,* 293–309.

Graves, D. (1983). *Writing: Teachers and children at work.* Portsmouth, NH: Heineman.

Greeno, J. G. (1996). *On claims that answer the wrong questions.* Stanford, CA: Institute for Research on Learning.

Greeno, J. G., Collins, A. M., & Resnick, L. B. (1996). Cognition and learning. In D.C. Berliner & R. C. Calfee (Eds.), *Handbook of educational psychology* (pp. 15–46). New York: Simon & Schuster Macmillan.

Greeno, J. G., Smith, D. R., & Moore, J. L. (1993). Transfer of situated learning. In D. K. Detterman & R. J. Sternberg (Eds.), *Transfer of trial: Intelligence, cognition, and instruction* (pp. 99–167). Norwood, NJ: Ablex.

Heath, S. B. (1983). *Ways with words: Language, life, and work in communities and classrooms.* Cambridge: Cambridge University Press.

Heller, K. A., Holtzman, W. H., & Messick, S. (Eds.). (1982). *Placing children in special education: A strategy for equity.* Washington, DC: National Academy Press.

Herrnstein, R. J., & Murray, C. (1994). *The bell curve: Intelligence and class structure in American life.* New York: The Free Press.

Hiebert, E. H., & Raphael, T. E. (1998). *Early literacy instruction.* Fort Worth, TX: Harcourt Brace College Publishers.

Hilgers, T. (1986). How children change as critical evaluators of writing: Four three-year case studies. *Research in the Teaching of English, 20,* 36–55.

Hobbs, N. (Ed.). (1975). *Issues in the classification of children* (Volume I). San Francisco: Jossey-Bass.

Hogan, K., & Pressley, M. (1997). Scaffolding scientific competencies within classroom communities of inquiry. In K. Hogan & M. Pressley (Eds.), *Scaffolding student learning: Instructional approaches and issues* (pp. 74–107). Cambridge, MA: Brookline Books.

Holt, J. (1965). *How children fail.* New York: Pitman.

Hughes, B., Sullivan, H., & Mosley, M. (1985). External evaluation, task difficulty, and continuing motivation. *Journal of Educational Research, 78,* 210–215.

Hull, C. L. (1943). *Principles of behavior: An introduction to behavior theory.* New York: Appleton-Century.

International Reading Association & National Council of Teachers of English Joint Task Force on Assessment. (1994). *Standards for the assessment of reading and writing.* Urbana, IL: National Council of Teachers of English.

Jensen, A. R. (1969). How much can we boost IQ and scholastic achievement? *Harvard Educational Review, 39,* 1–123.

Klenowski, V. (1995). Student self-evaluation process in student-centered teaching and learning contexts of Australia and England. *Assessment in Education, 2,* 145–163.

Kliebard, H. M. (1995). *The struggle for the American curriculum: 1893–1958* (2nd ed.). New York: Routledge.

Klimenkov, M., & LaPick, N. (1996). Promoting student self-assessment through portfolios, student-facilitated conferences, and cross-age interaction. In R. Calfee & P. Perfumo (Eds.), *Writing portfolios in the classroom: Policy and practice, promise and peril* (pp. 239–259). Mahwah, NJ: Lawrence Erlbaum Associates.

Kluger, A. N., & DeNisi, A. (1996). The effects of feedback interventions on performance: A historical review, a meta-analysis, and a preliminary feedback intervention theory. *Psychological Bulletin, 119(2),* 254–284.

Koczor, M. L. (1984). *Effects of varying degrees of instructional alignment in posttreatment tests on mastery learning tasks of fourth grade children.* Unpublished doctoral dissertation, University of San Francisco.

Koretz, D. M., & Barron, S. I. (1998). The validity of gains in scores on the Kentucky Instructional Results Information System (KIRIS). Washington, DC: RAND.

Koretz, D. M., Linn, R. L., Dunbar, S. B., & Shepard, L. A. (1991, April). *The effects of high-stakes testing on achievement: Preliminary findings about generalization across tests.* Paper presented at the annual meeting of the American Educational Research Association, Chicago, IL.

Kozol, J. (1991). *Savage inequalities: Children in America's schools.* New York: Crown.

Lave, J., & Wenger, E. (1991). *Situated learning: Legitimate peripheral participation.* Cambridge, UK: Cambridge University Press.

Lepper, M. R., Drake, M. F., O'Donnell-Johnson, T. (1997). Scaffolding techniques of expert human tutors. In K. Hogan & M. Pressley (Eds.), *Scaffolding student learning: Instructional approaches and issues* (pp. 108–144). Cambridge, MA: Brookline Books.

Lewin, K. (1948). *Resolving social conflicts.* New York: Harper and Brothers.

Lincoln, Y., & Guba, E. (1986). *Naturalistic inquiry.* Beverly Hills, CA: Sage.

Linn, R. L. (1993). Linking results of distinct assessments. *Applied Measurement in Education, 6(1),* 83–102.

Lunt, I. (1993). The practice of assessment. In H. Daniels (Ed.), *Charting the agenda: Educational activity after Vygotsky* (pp. 145–170). New York: Routledge.

Madaus, G. F., West, M. M., Harmon, M. C., Lomax, R. G., & Viator, K. A. (1992). The influence of testing on teaching math and science in grades 4–12. Chestnut Hill, MA: Center of Study of Testing, Evaluation, and Educational Policy, Boston College.

Maehr, M., & Stallings, W. (1972). Freedom from external evaluation. *Child Development, 43,* 117–185.

Malcolm, S. M. (Chair) (1993). *Promises to keep: Creating high standards for American students.* Washington, DC: National Education Goals Panel.

Martin, J. R. (1992). *The schoolhome.* Cambridge, MA: Harvard University Press.

Mathematical Sciences Education Board. (1993). *Measuring up: Prototypes for mathematics assessment.* Washington, DC: National Academy Press.

Mazzeo, J., Schmitt, A. P., & Bleistein, C. A. (1993). *Sex-related performance differences on constructed-response and multiple-choice sections of Advanced Placement examinations* (CB Rep. No. 92–7; ETS RR-93-5). New York: College Entrance Examination Board.

McLaughlin, M., & Talbert, J. E. (1993). *Contexts that matter for teaching and learning: Strategic opportunities for meeting the nation's education goals.* Stanford, CA: Stanford University, Center for Research on the Context of Secondary School Teaching.

Mervar, K., & Hiebert, E. H. (1989). Literature-selection strategies and amount of reading in two literacy approaches. In S. McCormick & J. Zutell (Eds.), *Cognitive and social perspectives for literacy research and instruction, 38th yearbook of the National Reading Conference* (pp. 529–535). Chicago, IL: National Reading Conference.

Messick, S. (1989). Validity. In R. L. Linn (Ed.), *Educational measurement,* (3rd ed., pp. 13–103). New York: American Council on Education and Macmillan.

Minstrell, J. (1989). Teaching science for understanding. In L. B. Resnick & L. E. Klopfer (Eds.), *Toward the thinking curriculum: Current cognitive research* (pp. 129–149). Alexandria, VA: Association for Supervision and Curriculum Development.

Minstrell, J. (1999). Student thinking and related assessment: Creating a facet-based learning environment. In N. S. Raju, J. W. Pellegrino, M. W. Berteythal, K. J. Mitchell, & L. R. Jones (Eds.), *Grading the nation's report card: Research from the evaluation of NAEP* (pp. 44–73). Washington, DC: National Academy Press.

Moss, P. A. (1994). Can there be validity without reliability? *Educational Researcher, 23,* 5–12.

Moss, P. A. (1996). Enlarging the dialogue in educational measurement: Voices from interpretive research traditions. *Educational Researcher, 25,* 20–28, 43.

Myers, M. (1996). Sailing ships: A framework for portfolios in formative and summative systems. In R. Calfee & P. Perfumo (Eds.), *Writing portfolios in the classroom: Policy and practice, promise and peril* (pp. 149–178). Mahwah, NJ: Lawrence Erlbaum Associates.

National Center for History in the Schools. (1996). *National standards for history.* Los Angeles: Author.

National Council for the Social Studies. (1991). Testing and evaluation of social studies students. *Social Education, 55,* 284–286.

National Council for the Social Studies. (1994). *Curriculum standards for social studies.* Washington, DC: Author.

National Council of Teachers of Mathematics. (1989). *Curriculum and evaluation standards for school mathematics.* Reston, VA: Author.

National Council of Teachers of Mathematics. (1995). *Assessment standards for school mathematics.* Reston, VA: Author.

National Council on Education Standards and Testing. (1992, January). *Raising standards for American education.* Washington, DC: Author.

National Forum on Assessment. (1995). *Principles and indicators for student assessment systems.* Cambridge, MA: National Center for Fair and Open Testing.

National Research Council. (1996). *National science education standards.* Washington, DC: National Academy of Sciences.

Newmann, F. M., & Associates. (1996). *Authentic achievement: Restructuring schools for intellectual quality.* San Francisco: Jossey-Bass.

Oakes, J. (1985). *Keeping track: How schools structure inequality.* New Haven, CT: Yale University Press.

Oakes, J. (1990). Multiplying inequalities: The effects of race, social class, and tracking on opportunities to learn math and science. Santa Monica, CA: RAND.

Ogle, D. M. (1986). K-W-L: A teaching model that develops active reading of expository test. *The Reading Teacher, 39*(6), 564–570.

Palincsar, A. S., & Brown, A. L. (1984). Reciprocal teaching of comprehension-fostering and comprehension-monitoring activities. *Cognition and Instruction, 1,* 117–175.

Pellegrino, J. W., Baxter, G. P., Glaser, R. (1999). Addressing the "two disciplines" problem: Linking theories of cognition and learning with assessment and instructional practice. In A. Iran-Nejad & P. D. Pearson (Eds.), *Review of research in education,* Vol. 24 (pp. 307–353). Washington, DC: American Educational Research Association.

Perrenoud, P. (1991). Towards a pragmatic approach to formative evaluation. In P. Weston (Ed.), *Assessment of pupils' achievement: Motivation and school success* (pp. 77–101). Amsterdam: Swets and Zeitlinger.

Phillips, D.C. (1995). The good, the bad, and the ugly: The many faces of constructivism. *Educational Researcher, 24,* 5–12.

Phillips, D.C. (1996). Philosophical perspectives. In D.C. Berliner & R. C. Calfee (Eds.), *Handbook of educational psychology* (pp. 1005–1019). New York: Simon & Schuster Macmillan.

Popham, W. J., Cruse, K. L., Rankin, S. C., Sandifer, P. D., & Williams, P. L. (1985). Measurement-driven instruction: It's on the road. *Phi Delta Kappan, 66,* 628–634.

Pressley, M., Wood, E., Woloshyn, V. E., Martin, V., King, A., & Menke, D. (1992). Encouraging mindful use of prior knowledge: Attempting to construct explanatory answers facilitates learning. *Educational Psychologist, 27*(1), 91–109.

Resnick, L. B. (1987). Learning in school and out. *Educational Researcher, 16,* 13–20.

Resnick, L. B., & Klopfer, L. E. (Eds.). (1989). Toward the thinking curriculum: An overview. In L. B. Resnick & L. E. Klopfer (Eds.), *Toward the thinking curriculum: Current cognitive research* (pp. 1–18). Alexandria, VA: Association for Supervision and Curriculum Development.

Resnick, L. B., & Resnick, D. P. (1992). Assessing the thinking curriculum: New tools for educational reform. In B. R. Gifford & M. C. O'Connor (Eds.), *Changing assessments: Alternative views of aptitude, achievement, and instruction* (pp. 37–75). Boston: Kluwer Academic.

Roberts, L., Wilson, M., & Draney, K. (1997). *The SEPUP Assessment System: An overview* (BEAR Report Series SA-97-1). Berkeley: Berkeley Evaluation and Assessment Research Center, University of California.

Rogoff, B. (1990). *Apprenticeship in thinking: Cognitive development in social context.* New York: Oxford University Press.

Rogoff, B. (1991). Social interaction as apprenticeship in thinking: Guidance and participation in spatial planning. In L. B. Resnick, J. M. Levine, & S. Teasley (Eds.), *Perspectives on socially shared cognition* (pp. 349–364). Washington, DC: American Psychological Association Press.

Romberg, T. A., Zarinnia, E. A., & Williams, S. (1989). *The influence of mandated testing on mathematics instruction: Grade 8 teachers' perceptions.* Madison, WI: National Center for Research in Mathematical Science Education, University of Wisconsin-Madison.

Rosenshine, B., & Meister, C. (1994). Reciprocal teaching: A review of the research. *Review of Educational Research, 64,* 479–530.

Ruch, G. M. (1929). *The objective or new-type examination: An introduction to educational measurement.* Chicago: Scott Foresman.

Sadler, D. R. (1998). Formative assessment: Revisiting the territory. *Assessment in Education: Principles, Policy and Practice, 5,* 77–84.

Schoenfield, A. H. (1989). Problem solving in context(s). In R. I. Charles & E. A. Silver (Eds.), *The teaching and assessing of mathematical problem solving,* Vol. 3 (pp. 82–92). Reston, VA: The National Council of Teachers of Mathematics and Lawrence Erlbaum Associates.

Scriven, M. (1967). The methodology of evaluation. In R. W. Tyler, R. M. Gagne, & M. Scriven, *Perspectives of curriculum evaluation.* Chicago: Rand McNally.

Shavelson, R. J., Baxter, G. P., & Pine, J. (1992). Performance assessments: Political rhetoric and measurement reality. *Educational Researcher, 21,* 22–27.

Shavelson, R. J., & Stern, P. (1981). Research on teachers' pedagogical thoughts, judgments, decisions, and behavior, *Review of Educational Research, 51*(4), 455–498.

Shepard, L. A. (1991a). Negative policies for dealing with diversity: When does assessment and diagnosis turn into sorting and segregation? In E. H. Hiebert (Ed.), *Literacy for a diverse society: Perspectives, practices, and policies* (pp. 279–298). New York: Teachers College Press.

Shepard, L. A. (1991b). Psychometricians' beliefs about learning. *Educational Researcher, 20,* 2–16.

Shepard, L. A. (1995). Using assessment to improve learning. *Educational Leadership, 52,* 38–43.

Shepard, L. A. (1997). *Measuring achievement: What does it mean to test for robust understanding?* Princeton, NJ: Policy Information Center, Educational Testing Service.

Shepard, L. A., & Dougherty, K. (1991, April). *Effects of high-stakes testing on instruction.* Paper presented at the annual meeting of the American Educational Research Association, Chicago.

Shepard, L. A., Kagan, S. L., & Wurtz, E. (Eds.). (1998*). Principles and recommendations for early childhood assessments.* Washington, DC: National Education Goals Panel.

Shepard, L., Taylor, G., & Betebenner, D. (1998). *Inclusion of limited-English-proficient students in Rhode Island's grade 4 Mathematics Performance Assessment* (CSE Technical Report 486). Los Angeles: National Center for Research on Evaluation, Standards, and Student Testing.

Shulman, L. S., & Quinlan, K. M. (1996). The comparative psychology of school subjects. In D.C. Berliner & R. C. Calfee (Eds.), *Handbook of educational psychology* (pp. 399–422). New York: Simon & Schuster Macmillan.

Sizer, T. R. (1984). *Horace's compromise: The dilemma of the American high school.* Boston: Houghton Mifflin.

Skinner, B. F. (1938). *The behavior of organisms: An experimental analysis.* New York: Appleton-Century-Crofts.

Skinner, B. F. (1954). The science of learning and the art of teaching. *Harvard Educational Review, 24,* 86–97.

Smith, J. P., diSessa, A. A., & Roschelle, J. (1994). Misconceptions reconceived: A constructivist analysis of knowledge in transition.

Journal of the Learning Sciences, 3, 115–163. (Original work published 1993)

Smith, M. L. (1989). *The role of external testing in elementary schools.* Los Angeles: Center for Research on Evaluation, Standards, and Student Testing, University of California.

Stallman, A. C., & Pearson, P. D. (1990). Formal measures of early literacy. In L. M. Morrow & J. K. Smith (Eds.), *Assessment for instruction in early literacy* (pp. 7–44). Englewood Cliffs, NJ: Prentice Hall.

Starch, D., & Elliott, E. C. (1913). The reliability of grading high-school work in mathematics. *School Review, 21,* 254–259.

Sternberg, R. J. (1992). CAT: A program of Comprehensive Abilities Testing. In B. R. Gifford & M. C. O'Connor (Eds.), *Changing assessments: Alternative views of aptitude, achievement, and instruction* (pp. 213–274). Boston: Kluwer Academic.

Stipek, D. J. (1993). *Motivation to learn: From theory to practice* (2nd ed.). Boston: Allyn & Bacon.

Stipek, D. J. (1996). Motivation and instruction. In D.C. Berliner & R. C. Calfee (Eds.), *Handbook of Educational Psychology* (pp. 85–113). New York: Simon & Schuster Macmillan.

Sulzby, E. (1990). Assessment of emergent writing and children's language while writing. In L. M. Morrow & J. K. Smith (Eds.), *Assessment for instruction in early literacy* (pp. 83–109). Englewood Cliffs, NJ: Prentice Hall.

Terman, L. M. (1906). Genius and stupidity. A study of some of the intellectual processes of seven "bright" and seven "stupid" boys. *Pedagogical Seminary, 13,* 307–373.

Terman, L. M. (1916). *The measurement of intelligence.* Boston: Houghton Mifflin.

Tharp, R. G. (1997). *From at-risk to excellence: Research, theory, and principles for practice.* Santa Cruz, CA: Center for Research on Education, Diversity and Excellence.

Tharp, R. G., & Gallimore, R. (1988). *Rousing minds to life: Teaching, learning, and schooling in social context.* New York: Cambridge University Press.

Thompson, P. W. (1995). Notation, convention, and quantity in elementary mathematics. In J. T. Sowder & B. P. Schappelle (Eds.), *Providing a foundation for teaching mathematics in the middle grades* (pp. 199–221). New York: State University of New York Press.

Thorndike, E. L. (1922). *The psychology of arithmetic.* New York: Macmillan.

Tobin, K., & Ulerick, S. (1989, March). *An interpretation of high school science teaching based on metaphors and beliefs for specific roles.* Paper presented at the annual meeting of the American Educational Research Association, San Francisco.

Tyack, D. (1974). *The one best system: A history of American urban education.* Cambridge, MA: Harvard University Press.

Tyler, R. (1938). *Thirty-seventh yearbook of the National Society for the Study of Education: Part II.* Bloomington, IL: Public School Publishing.

Tyson-Bernstein, H. (1988). A conspiracy of good intentions: The textbook fiasco. *American Educator, 12,* 20, 23–27, 39.

Valencia, R. R. (1997). The evolution of deficit thinking: Educational thought and practice. London: Falmer Press.

von Glasersfeld, E. (1995). *Radical constructivism: A way of knowing and learning.* London: Falmer Press.

Vygotsky, L. S. (1978). Mind in society: The development of higher psychological processes. Cambridge: Harvard University Press.

Wiggins, G. (1989). A true test: Toward more authentic and equitable assessment. *Phi Delta Kappan, 70,* 703–713.

Wiggins, G. (1992). Creating tests worth taking. *Educational Leadership, 49,* 26–33.

Wiggins, G. (1993). Assessment: Authenticity, context, and validity. *Phi Delta Kappan, 74,* 200–214.

Wile, J. M., & Tierney, R. J. (1996). Tensions in assessment: The battle over portfolios, curriculum, and control. In R. Calfee & P. Perfumo (Eds.), *Writing portfolios in the classroom: Policy and practice, promise and peril* (pp. 203–215). Mahwah, NJ: Lawrence Erlbaum Associates.

Wilson, M., & Sloane, K. (2000). From principles to practice: An embedded assessment system. *Applied Measurement in Education, 13,* 181–208.

Wineburg, S. S. (1996). The psychology of learning and teaching history. In D.C. Berliner & R. C. Calfee (Eds.), *Handbook of educational psychology* (pp. 423–437). New York: Simon & Schuster Macmillan.

Wittrock, M. (1986). Students' thought processes. In M. Wittrock (Ed.), *Handbook of research on teaching* (pp. 297–327). New York: Macmillan.

Wolf, D. P., & Reardon, S. F. (1996). Access to excellence through new forms of student assessment. In J. B. Baron & D. P. Wolf (Eds.), *Performance-based student assessment: Challenges and possibilities* (pp. 1–31). Chicago: University of Chicago Press.

Wood, D., Bruner, J., & Ross, G. (1976). The role of tutoring in problem solving. *Journal of Child Psychology and Psychiatry, 17,* 89–100.

Yackel, E., Cobb, P., & Wood, T. (1991). Small-group interactions as a source of learning opportunities in second-grade mathematics. *Journal for Research in Mathematics Education, 22,* 390–408.

Yancey, K. B. (1996). Dialogue, interplay, and discovery: Mapping the role and the rhetoric of reflection in portfolio assessment. In R. Calfee & P. Perfumo (Eds.), *Writing portfolios in the classroom: Policy and practice, promise and peril* (pp. 83–102). Mahwah, NJ: Lawrence Erlbaum Associates.

48.

Theory and Research on Teaching as Dialogue

Nicholas C. Burbules and Bertram C. Bruce
University of Illinois, Urbana/Champaign

Introduction

The Prescriptive Tradition

The concept of dialogue has held a central place in Western views of education ever since the teachings of Socrates. The back-and-forth form of question and answer, challenge and response, has been viewed as the external communicative representation of a dialectical process of thinking based on conjecture, criticism, and reconstruction of ideas. Some of these views of dialogue have stressed the role of the teacher as a facilitator of a student's discovery of certain insights on his or her own; in some cases, it is in pursuit of an answer the teacher has in mind already, in others, of an answer neither participant could have anticipated. Other views have stressed the role of vigorous debate and argument as a basis for hewing defensible conclusions out of the raw material of opinion and speculation. Still other views have stressed the role of the teacher as a partner in inquiry, learning with the student as both explore a problem together through reciprocal questions and answers. Other, quite different, traditions of thought such as Zen Buddhism also have a view of dialogue, but denigrate the value of express communication as a way of sharing knowledge or insight, relying instead upon the indirect effect of riddles, paradoxical statements, and questions (*koans*) that precisely *cannot* be answered.

Such brief genealogical reflections should make clear that the contemporary vision of dialogue as a pedagogy that is egalitarian, open-ended, politically empowering, and based on the co-construction of knowledge, reflects only certain strands of its history. Contrasting accounts see dialogue as a way of leading others to preformed conclusions, or as a way for a master teacher to guide the explorations of a novice, or as a set of ground rules and procedures for debating the merits of alternative views, or as a way to frustrate, problematize, and deconstruct conventional understandings. Dialogue is not simply a multiform approach to pedagogy; its different forms express deeper assumptions about the nature of knowledge, the nature of inquiry, the nature of communication, the roles of teacher and learner, and the mutual ethical obligations thereof.

A special challenge for this chapter, therefore, is to carve out a useful terrain between two unproductive extremes. One extreme considers any verbal interaction between teacher and student or among students to be a dialogue, which simply equates dialogue with communication. Building on Dewey's (1916, p. 5) famous formulation that "Not only is social life identical with communication, but all communication (and hence all genuine social life) is educative," it would elide any distinctions among dialogue, pedagogy, and communication. The other unproductive extreme prescriptively narrows the multiple forms of dialogue to a single form as true dialogue, which neglects its historical genealogy (but, even more importantly, is pedagogically counterproductive). One of our central claims will be that there are forms of dialogue, and that their usefulness in educational settings will depend on the relation among forms of communicative interaction and (a) the contexts of such interaction, (b) other activities and relations among participants, (c) the subject matter under discussion, and (d) the varied differences among those participants themselves. Conceptions of dialogue need to be rethought within the changing institutional and demographic circumstances of teaching and learning, and within the changing educational needs and aims of society.

The authors wish to thank reviewers Richard Beach of the University of Minnesota and Annemarie Palinscar of the University of Michigan for their comments. The authors also wish to acknowledge the very helpful comments and criticisms of Virginia Richardson and Joyce Atkinson. Finally, the authors appreciate the research assistance and substantive contributions of Kevin Leander.

The Discursive Tradition

This rethinking of dialogue is informed by another tradition of theorizing that regards all communicative and representational acts as forms of social practice (Bruce, 1994; Cazden et al., 1996; Fairclough, 1989; Foucault, 1972, 1980; Gee, 1990; Luke, 1995). This tradition explores discourses as forms of sociohistorically constituted relations among people, activities, texts, and situations. Participating in a discourse then means assuming a role within a community of practice (Wenger, 1993), rather than simply producing a pattern of decontextualized utterances. The discursive perspective implies that the various types of dialogue do not carve out distinct natural kinds; dialogical forms generally are not discontinuous with discursive patterns. For particular analytical purposes, it may be helpful to set criteria for what will be counted as a kind of dialogue and what is not—but this decision in itself becomes a discursive move, not a search for the true essence of dialogue.

Yet it is fruitful to ask why traditions do count certain types of communicative interaction as dialogue and do not count others, why dialogue has had particular appeal for some as a model of teaching and inquiry, and what is at stake in appropriating the term "dialogue" for one approach to teaching rather than another.

Because the major prescriptions in favor of dialogue as an approach to pedagogy have generally come from philosophical sources, these accounts have tended to emphasize either the epistemological advantages of dialogue as a way to pursue knowledge and understanding (see, for example, Socrates or Plato: Hamilton, 1961) or the moral and political reasons for favoring dialogue, because it is egalitarian, mutually respectful, and so forth (see, for example, Buber, 1970; Freire, 1968, 1985; Levinas, 1981). Both kinds of arguments have tended to arise from a priori assumptions that may or may not have been tested against studies of pedagogical practice. As a result, the prescriptive tradition has often neglected the ways in which idealized forms of interaction either may not be feasible in certain circumstances, or may have effects contrary to their intent.

It may seem ironic that a quintessentially communicative activity such as dialogue has often been discussed in ways that ignore research on discourse generally. But the philosophical origins of this concept, its prescriptive intent, and its idealized characterizations have all tended to promote an antiempirical approach toward elaborating what dialogues look like and how they work—or fail to work—educationally. While some accounts of dialogue have drawn from personal experiences in communicative engagement, in general there has been a desire to insulate the prescriptive model of dialogue from the conflicted rough-and-tumble of discourse. (However, see Carlson, 1983.)

In this essay we favor a model of discourse that stresses a tripartite set of relations among discursive practices, other practices and activities, and mediating objects and texts (see Figure 48.1).

Discursive practices are related to other practices and activities within a setting. What people say and how they are heard is wrapped up with other kinds of relations and interactions among them, which might range from very specific practices

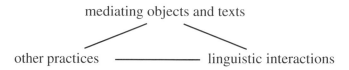

Figure 48.1. The tripartite model.

(how close together people stand or sit while talking, for example) to very general institutional norms or structures (such as requirements in school to raise one's hand before speaking, or the physical arrangements of classrooms). At the same time, despite the oral connotations of *discourse, speaking,* and so forth, spoken language is obviously not the only form that discourse takes: It is manifested through a range of kinds of texts and other mediating objects (for example, notes passed between students, bulletin boards, or dress codes). Finally, those texts and objects are also artifacts within a setting of practices (for example, the differences in content, but also the differences in forms of production, sales, and patterns of use, between daily newspapers and weekly newsmagazines). Various research studies have emphasized these connections among linguistic interactions, mediating objects or texts, and other practices (for example, Anderson, Holland, & Palincsar, 1997; Cazden et al., 1996; Engestrom, 1990, 1991; Hicks, 1996; Lave & Wenger, 1991; Law, 1991; Moll, 1990; Raphael et al., 1992; Rogoff, 1990; Rogoff & Lave, 1984; Scribner & Cole, 1981; Tharp & Gallimore, 1989).

These relations among discursive practices, other practices and activities, and mediating objects and texts are not simply interactions among discrete social factors; they are dialectical relations among elements that mutually constitute one another. A letter to a relative is not only a discursive practice, but also a text, and also a practice with nondiscursive significance (such as buying or perhaps collecting stamps). A Web page on a computer screen is not only a mediating object or text, but also a practice (it was made by someone in a particular situation), and it is a practice with nondiscursive significance such as using electricity (which is available to only a fraction of the world's population). A variety of new representational forms are blurring traditional distinctions between written and oral text, or between what we have ordinarily thought of as texts (such as books) and what we have not thought of as texts (such as modes of dress). In the recent film *The Pillow Book,* for example, lovers actually write on one another's bodies. Does this make the body into a text, or merely highlight the ways in which the body (through gestures, and so on) has always been a text of sorts?

Within this model, then, any particular pattern of speech acts—such as dialogue—must be seen as situated in a complex net of interactions that govern how those speech acts are expressed, heard, interpreted, and responded to. In such a net of interactions, the full meaning and effects of discourse will be impossible to read off the surface meanings of the words themselves. The nature of the relations fostered by particular forms of verbal interaction may be utterly unpredictable from the actual intentions and purposes of the agents concerned.

Conversely, as scholars have investigated broader social activities and processes, they continually return to discourse as the glue that holds these interactions together. For example, current works on inquiry models for learning have shown how teachers and students shape learning contexts through dialogues (Bruce & Davidson, 1994; Easley, 1987; Hansen, Newkirk, & Graves, 1985; Harste, Short, & Burke, 1988; Raphael et al., 1992; Wells, 1986) in which participants highlight, identify, and negotiate which aspects of the institutional—even physical—arrangements of the classroom are most salient for their interests and needs. Such dialogues frame modes of interaction and directions of inquiry; furthermore, as learners pursue a line of inquiry, their questions are developed not only by the evidence or experiences themselves, but also in part through the social structure of teacher-student and student-student verbal interactions. Similarly, activity theory (Engestrom, 1990, 1991; Leont'ev, 1981; Moll, 1990; Rogoff & Toma, 1997; Smagorinsky & Fly, 1993; Vygotsky, 1978, 1986; Wertsch, 1980, 1991), which has grown out of the work of Vygotsky, Luria, Leont'ev, and other Soviet psychologists, has expanded into a substantial discipline of study. A distinctive feature of activity theory is the sociocultural formation of mind. In contrast to other traditions in psychology such as behaviorism, this approach conceives learning and mental development as a process mediated by social relations; dialogue comes to be seen not only as a means of transmitting information or an overlay on cognition, but also as a constitutive dimension of the activity systems that construct and display thinking. Work on inquiry and activity systems and related work has pointed to the idea of shared thinking, or distributed intelligence, as a basic metaphor for how knowledge is formed, which suggests a fundamental shift in how we conceive education. Learning aims are seen in terms of group dynamics and meaning making, and not only as individual achievements among the participants. Once again, dialogue plays a central role because it is a medium through which participants are able to share their conceptions, verify or test their understandings, and identify areas of common knowledge or of difference. This is particularly true when dialogue is understood to include a range of communicative acts, gestures, or facial expressions and is not limited to spoken words.

The difficulty of such an inclusive, relational model is that it threatens to count everything as discourse (even things); every social relation or practice becomes a discursive practice. It is clear that any particular study or account of discourse in the classroom will have to set some boundaries, however provisional, for the factors that will be included as most significant. There may be a discursive component to nearly all human activities and artifacts, but it is analytically useless to conclude then that everything is discourse. This choice to set boundaries is necessary, we maintain, but it is a choice—and a choice that can be argued or reframed differently. What one will not know in advance is where the most fruitful boundaries are or what will be gained (or lost) by approaching the situation with preexisting distinctions or categories (such as discrete teacher and student roles) that one tries to overlay onto the continuities of actual roles and performances. This gain or loss is something to be interrogated, we believe, within the framework of the study itself—and this is something we will be trying to do ourselves here. Considering dialogue through the prescriptive and the discursive lenses means a process of both proposing and contesting such boundaries and distinctions.

Pedagogy and Discourse Theory

Pedagogical Communicative Relations

We want to begin by demarcating a range of interactions that could be termed pedagogical communicative relations. Dialogue in its various forms represents one family of such communicative relations, but there are many others (lecturing, for example). When we refer to "dialogue," as it is typically used, we mean a definition grounded in the number of participants and in patterns of verbal interaction that are ostensibly distinguishable from monological models—although such simple distinctions are difficult to maintain as absolute categories.

According to some theories such as Bakhtin's, for instance, all language has an underlying dialogic nature, meaning that every word participates in a history of rich intertextual relations in which it is related to all other utterances (Bakhtin, 1981). People do not simply use language; it comes already used and has a history that surpasses particular uses, so that each use becomes an intersection point of multiple historically constituted discourses. On this account, there is a dialogical element in every utterance and even in internal thoughts (this view informs and underlies the work of much activity theory, discussed above).

At the same time, there are communicative relations that are not explicitly pedagogical (ordering dinner in a restaurant, for example), and there are classroom utterances that may have pedagogical effects, even though they are not intended to. One cannot limit *pedagogical* solely to the things teachers say when they think they are teaching. The involvement of a teacher is not necessary for communicative relations to be pedagogically significant, nor is overt and intentional speech always the form that such communicative relations might take. Here, too, a particular analytical category that helps to delimit a scope of discussion still must be situated generally within the continuities of discourse. But every theory of teaching and learning incorporates, at least implicitly, a set of prescriptions about pedagogical communicative relations, and depending on how these are framed, teachers see certain activities as within their purview and responsibility and others as not. An emphasis on particular pedagogical communicative relations constitutes a basis for teacher reflection, for defining a set of research questions, and for establishing a basis for the evaluation or assessment of teaching performance. It is not merely a descriptive endeavor.

In considering dialogue as a form of pedagogical communicative relation, then, certain simple distinctions and categories interfere with deeper understandings of the issues at stake. Certain accounts of dialogue, notably those of Paulo Freire (1968, 1985) and, to an extent, those of Socrates as we encounter him in some of Plato's dialogues, have suggested that there are basically only two alternative choices for pedagogy. The first is variously termed lecturing, recitation, monologue, "banking education," or even "jug and mug"—all views holding that knowledge, possessed by the teacher, is poured, fed, or otherwise transmitted more or less directly to a passive, receptive student. In this dichotomous characterization, the alternative to this approach is dialogue, a relation in which the student is more of an active partner in the teaching-learning process.

This dichotomy oversimplifies important issues on each side of the relation, obscures multiple forms that both lecture and dialogue might take, and places a range of important issues along a single either/or dividing line. On the one side, lecturing or more monological approaches can actually take a range of forms. Some lectures do indeed ask only to be heard and remembered (although even doing this with some success at gaining understanding requires a much more active response by the student than simply hearing and recording the data). Other lectures invite a high degree of thoughtfulness, skepticism, and imaginative response by the audience; some could even be considered dialogical in the sense that the speaker frames issues and questions in a way that invites an active reinterpretation of meaning from multiple standpoints among the listeners. Still other lectures contain a dialectical moment within them (the teaching style of Wittgenstein, reputedly, had this quality): By visibly working through various sides of an issue in a public way, a teacher expresses not a body of information or conclusions, but models a method of investigation or diagnosis that students can observe and adapt for their own purposes. It may even be that in certain areas of "tacit knowledge," as Polanyi (1962) calls it, the only way that novices can learn is by observing or listening to experts who are engaged in a complex practice and reflect openly about their processes of thought and deliberation. In all of these ways, the simple image of monological or directive modes of teaching needs to be understood in the context of relations among the characteristics of a field of inquiry, the nature of complex human practices, and the multiple needs of learners at different stages of experience and sophistication.

On the other side of this putative divide, dialogue can also take many forms. As noted in our opening, not all of these necessarily imply egalitarian, open-ended modes of inquiry. Dialogue can have a highly didactic, directed quality, as it often does in the Platonic dialogues (such as the exchange with the slave in the *Meno*); Socrates sometimes says that all the teacher is doing is drawing out a set of conclusions that a learner already knows unconsciously. In other kinds of dialogue, the students are led to a set of conclusions that the teacher intends them to reach; the interaction might be one of question and answer, but the conclusion is foregone. It is certainly debatable, in some of these cases, whether a straightforward lecture might not be in fact a more efficient (and less manipulative) way of getting the same ideas across—students often rightfully resent the can-you-guess-what-I'm-thinking type of teacher question. This transcript comes from a classroom discussion about *Antigone:*

TEACHER: So is it a feminist or antifeminist play?
STUDENTS: Anti!
TEACHER: Anti?
STUDENT 1: Anti.
TEACHER: Huh?
STUDENT 2: Do you want us to say feminist?
TEACHER: Huh?
STUDENT 2: Because every time we say anti, you say—
TEACHER: (Interrupting) Okay. No, I want—I want examples. I

want something to support your opinion. (Alvermann & Hayes, 1989, p. 321)

Socrates also distinguishes what he calls "disputatious" and "friendly" forms of dialogue: one kind characterized more by aggressive questioning and critique; the other more by tolerant acceptance (at least provisionally) of alternative points of view and by attempting to build upon the understandings of others rather than to defeat them. Elbow (1986) calls these the "doubting" and "believing" games; some feminist theorists call these ways of "separate" and "connected" knowing (Belenky, Clinchy, Goldberger, & Tarule, 1986). Forms of dialogue could also be distinguished on the basis of how active the learner is in the pedagogical relation; of the extent to which the process is truly one of coinvestigation, as opposed to a method (even if a more humane method) of drawing others to one's own conclusions or point of view. Such concerns have led some to ask of ostensibly emancipatory dialogical pedagogies, "Why doesn't this feel empowering?" (Ellsworth, 1989).

Similarly, even when a single dialogue is taking place among different participants, they may not all regard the experience of participation in the same way; to some participants, an open dialogue may feel like a kind of imposition. Pratt (1987) has argued that conventional characterizations of dialogue have ignored some of the most significant aspects of linguistic interactions, namely, the way in which dialogue patterns are localized within particular social groups. Pratt goes beyond pointing out that dialogues are cultural constructions, showing that at the point of contact among different forms of talking, the effects upon dialogue participants are strongest. Classrooms, even those that appear to manifest dialogical interactions, often manifest hidden tensions and conflicts that this analysis of contact zones would reveal. Pratt calls for a "linguistics of contact" that explicitly examines these dialogical boundaries. By implication, educators might consider that the surface features of dialogue obscure the meanings of these zones for the diverse participants in classroom discussion. Gutierrez, Rymes, and Larson (1995) have termed this sort of focal point the "third space," where teacher discourses and student discourses engage, conflict with, or speak past one another:

Thus, for example, when the teacher begins asking students about *Brown v. Board of Education*, one student quickly rekeys the line of questioning by making the association with a "Brown" [James Brown] with which he is more familiar. (Gutierrez et al., 1995, p. 461)

According to this model, it is here that meaningful dialogical engagements might occur, but now within a discursive space that is itself open to question and negotiation: "The potential for intersubjectivity exists when the teacher and student depart from their rigidly scripted and exclusive social spaces. The disruptive nature of the third space allows for the commingling of various social and cultural perspectives, the existence of multiple scripts, and the potential to contest the transcendent script" (Gutierrez et al., 1995, p. 467–8).

As a result of such considerations, any useful theoretical frame will need to move beyond the simple, dichotomous monologue-dialogue distinction to, at the very least, a spectrum along which various pedagogical communicative relations can be classified from the relatively univocal and directive to the relatively reciprocal and open-ended. From this perspective, some things that look like lectures might be in fact quite dialogical; while things that look like dialogues might be highly directive and narrow. Here, again, we need to move beyond speech act analyses (who speaks, how much they speak, etc.) to look at discursive content and how it is heard and responded to by others. Despite the etymologies of monologue and dialogue, the idea that all we have to do is count how many people are speaking in order to settle the pedagogical question appears quite crude and unhelpful:

> Discourse is dialogic not because speakers take turns, but because it is continually structured by tension, even conflict, between the conversants, between self and other, as one voice "refracts" the other. (Nystrand, Gamoran, Kachur, & Prendergast, 1997, p. 8)

In *Dialogue in Teaching,* Burbules (1993) recommends the interaction of at least two distinct spectrums to characterize different forms of dialogue: the degree to which an interchange is *critical* or *inclusive* (a revision of the disputatious-friendly distinction noted above), and the degree to which the investigation is intended to be *convergent* (upon a single answer) or *divergent* (allowing for multiple conclusions). This two-by-two grid generates four different types of dialogue, discussed later. But a number of other considerations might be usefully added to these: (a) the age of the persons who are engaged; (b) the extent to which their participation is active (given various meanings of what might constitute active engagement); (c) the range of affective and cognitive considerations that are considered germane to the subject at hand; (d) the degree to which one participant is steering or directing the discussion, as opposed to an open-ended, nonteleological investigation; and (e) the degree of opportunity within a dialogue for questioning its presuppositions and scope—all might count as criteria marking off different types of dialogue.

Such considerations highlight the multiple considerations of form and purpose that can be raised about different pedagogical communicative relations, and how to demarcate some of these as dialogical in spirit. Clearly, situating any particular set of interactions along these dimensions will require judgments about a number of matters that cannot be read off a transcript of the interaction; moreover, such judgments will themselves involve assumptions about cultural norms and practices that are going to vary across the different groups or individuals who may be party to such interactions. (For a study of forms of dialogue across different cultures, see Maranhão, 1990.) When something is to be called a dialogue, and by whom, now comes to be seen as a social and political problem that runs to deeper assumptions about communication and social relations.

The T/S Model

Within the context of current educational practice in the United States, most discussions of dialogue are influenced by a predominant pedagogical communicative relation that we will term the *Teacher/Student* (or *T/S*) model. This model represents both a form of teaching practice, and also a paradigm of how teaching has been conceptualized for research purposes. In certain forms, the T/S model is antagonistic to dialogical possibilities; in other forms, it restricts dialogue to a very narrow range of communicative interactions. The problem, in our view, is not that this model is never appropriate; but that it often tends to colonize pedagogy, driving out alternative perspectives on teaching and learning and making its own assumptions seem natural or inevitable—and hence less visible and harder to question.

The T/S model assumes, first, that the performative roles of teacher and student are given, distinct, and relatively stable. If one walks into a classroom, in any part of the country and at virtually any grade level, who the teachers and students are should be readily apparent by their different communicative roles and by other aspects of their behavior and interactions. The particular characteristics of persons—their gender, race, and so forth—are regarded, within this framework, as unimportant to these specific roles or their enactment of them: A teacher teaches and a student learns. Thus, the T/S model is part of a larger set of norms and assumptions about what classrooms are and what teachers and students are. These roles and patterns of performance are reinforced by adults' memories of their own school experiences, images in the popular media, and implicit, shared scripts by which these roles ought to be performed. Teachers stand in front of the class, initiate topics, question students, discipline misbehavior, write on blackboards, and so on; similarly, students raise hands, answer questions, pass notes, whisper to each other, and watch the clock pass time in slow-motion.

The T/S model assumes, second, that discourse in the classroom is primarily a medium for expressing information, for directing behavior, and for offering praise or other forms of evaluation. This model assumes, in turn, that what the teacher says is what is most important, because the activities of expressing information, directing behavior, and evaluating performance are regarded as primarily, if not exclusively, teacherly prerogatives (Cazden, 1986).

The T/S model assumes, third, that teaching is centrally a matter of intentionally communicating content knowledge either directly, in the form of didactic instruction, or indirectly, through guided readings of curriculum materials, supervised work on problems and assignments, or the review and rehearsal of what has been learned through structured question and answer. (This latter activity is sometimes regarded as a kind of teaching through dialogue.)

The T/S model assumes, fourth, that education is an activity of instrumental practices directed intentionally toward specific ends, and that it can, therefore, be evaluated along a scale of effectiveness in meeting those ends.

The limiting case of the T/S model—its ideal type—is the form of pedagogical communicative relation commonly known as *IRE,* or *Initiation-Response-Evaluation* (Alvermann & Hayes, 1989; Cazden, 1986, 1988; Gutierrez, 1993; Mehan, 1979; Nystrand et al., 1997). The teacher questions, the student replies, the teacher praises or corrects the response:

> Despite an emerging consensus about the sociocultural foundations and character of discourse, we discovered that most schooling continues to be based on a transmission and recitation model of communication. (Nystrand et al., 1997, p. xiv)

This basic pattern is so predominant in educational practices and institutions, so ingrained in the experiences of teachers (or the memories of students) that it constitutes an unreflective habitual pattern that teachers fall into even when they imagine that their teaching is dialogical in nature (Alvermann & Hayes, 1989; Alvermann, O'Brien, & Dillon, 1990). On this model, all responses are filtered back through the teacher for recognition and approval. The teaching moment is unitary, constituted in the completion of one IRE cycle, to be followed by another unitary teaching moment.

The IRE cycle has its uses. There are many contexts in which the review and rehearsal of information is beneficial to learning, and a skillful use of questioning, even within this model, can go beyond merely the review and rehearsal of information. Moreover, for certain students, a successful response to a direct question, followed by explicit teacher approval, can constitute a significant source of motivation and morale—which, in turn, can carry over into greater confidence to pursue other, more independent learning goals (so long, we would stress, as the IRE pattern organized around teacher questioning and approval is not the sole basis for opportunities to learn in the classroom). Sometimes, an apparent IRE pattern can actually mask a more dynamic teaching-learning encounter (Forman, 1989). As with the monological-dialogical distinction, we want to move beyond sharp dichotomies or simple value judgments here. But as a general model of dialogue, IRE is inadequate, and the danger is evident when the T/S model comes to dominate common conceptions of what teaching is. As the research of Alvermann shows, once entrenched as a habitual pattern, IRE colonizes more and more how a teacher conceives and enacts teaching. Forman's work reinforces this insight, suggesting that analyses of teaching tend to see IRE everywhere, whether critically or favorably, even when something more complex is actually going on.

As an approach to teaching and understanding teaching, IRE and other forms of the T/S model are confronting numerous contemporary challenges. The roles of teacher and student in classroom discourse, for example, can no longer be regarded as distinct, stable, or cultureless (Cazden et al., 1996). On the side of teaching, educators have become increasingly aware of the fuzzy boundaries of discrete teaching moments. An awareness of the hidden curriculum and the unintended teaching effects of offhand or inadvertent practices and habits along with the burden of responsibility on teachers to carry out other social interventions that are related to, but distinct from, instruction per se makes it frequently impossible to identify only particular activities as teaching. Moreover, within this framework of understanding, the particular characteristics of a teacher— sex, age, racial or ethnic proximity to (or distance from) students—become inseparable from the effects a teacher has in influencing, inspiring, intimidating, or inuring students to the benefits of education. From such a perspective, it is deeply problematic to assume merely that a teacher teaches and a student learns: In classrooms of radical diversity, for example, the teacher should be actively involved in learning about the interests, needs, and learning styles of a range of different students, including mainstreamed students with special learning difficulties (Commeyras, 1992).

From the side of students, the teacher's role and authority has undergone a kind of decentering. For many students, learning opportunities in the classroom are supplemented and sometimes overshadowed by opportunities outside of the classroom: other peer interactions; learning in their neighborhoods or other institutional settings; and information gleaned from books, television, other media of popular culture, or the Internet, for example. It is hardly news that interactions with peers in schools are much more important to many students, especially at certain ages, than their interactions with the teacher. Especially when this incongruity of interests and priorities is reinforced by gulfs of racial, ethnic, or class difference between student and teacher, the engagements of students merely as students in many classrooms is intermittent and their learning opportunities are not delimited solely, or even primarily, in terms of relations with their teacher (Gutierrez et al., 1995).

This problem of disengagement from the teacher is complicated still further by current understandings of diverse speech communities and learning. Contexts of diversity vastly complicate the preference for any particular pattern of pedagogical communicative relation. The benefits or effects of any single form of interaction cannot be expected to hold constant for all types of students; in certain cases, indeed, the effects may be directly contrary to the pedagogical purposes desired. Effects can be not only unintended but also multiple, and can extend beyond what can possibly be anticipated. In addition, changes in the relative influence of new information and communication technologies and of other media are requiring teachers to find new ways to engage, challenge, and motivate students. The idea that a teacher can individually hold sway in the classroom, directing the interests of students along pathways that he or she can control, is increasingly outmoded, especially as students grow into middle or high school years.

Such challenges to the T/S model of teaching are largely social and institutional in nature. At the same time, however, the very conceptions underlying the T/S model and the way in which it has functioned as a research paradigm have fallen under criticism from more theoretical sources derived from contemporary theories of discourse. When these underlying conceptions are made explicit, it is easier to see how the assumptions of the T/S orientation to teaching have tended to shape interpretations even of alternative approaches to pedagogy, including dialogue: The forms classroom dialogue can take are often constrained by the T/S model's assumptions about classroom roles and interactions, about language, about learning, and about the relation between means and ends in education.

Toward New Questions About Teaching

The Discursive Perspective on Language

The notion that language is more than a vehicle for the transparent conveyance of information has an ancient tradition. In Western philosophy, the sophists' focus on language as power placed rhetoric, the art that matches expression with idea, in the center of philosophy. Later writers such as Aristotle, Cicero, and Quintillian continued to consider rhetoric as a topic of enormous practical and theoretical significance. Throughout the Middle Ages, various writers such as Augustine continued the tradition of seeking to understand the relations between language and idea, form and content.

The search to understand these relations advanced in one of its most significant steps through the philosophy of Kant, who argued that our understanding of the world is both enabled and constrained by our capabilities for mental representation. It is our capacity to represent time, space, and causality, he claimed, that enables us to make sense of the otherwise restless confusion of the world in the way we do. Kant's emphasis on representation stimulated a vast field of 19th- and 20th-century thought, a thread running through Hegel, Marx, Schopenhauer, and later thinkers.

But it was the linking of British work in logic (such as Russell and Whitehead) with the Viennese thought of Wittgenstein and others that laid the foundation for a flourishing emphasis on language in the 20th century. From the positivist insistence on operational definitions to the hermeneutic account of texts as imperfect links across cultures, major threads of 20th-century thought have acknowledged that language does far more than simply convey information, and that whatever it does with meaning cannot be described as transparent expression.

Despite this long tradition in the West, an intellectual historian working chronologically might be ill prepared for the rupture in recent years brought about by the shift of theoretical focus onto certain taken-for-granted relations between language and thought. One can label this broad shift of focus as *discourse theory,* or the turn to discursive analysis. The ideas in this movement have grown out of diverse traditions of scholarly and empirical studies, including:

- *reader-response criticism* (see Beach, 1993; Freund, 1987; Suleiman & Crosman, 1980; Tompkins, 1980), itself a large and diverse field, which has restored the reader to a central place in literary studies;
- *hermeneutics* (see Palmer, 1969), which includes ideas such as Gadamer's (1976) "fusing of horizons";
- the *new rhetoric* (see Nelson, Megill, & McCloskey, 1987), which has examined rhetorical practices in diverse disciplines such as mathematics, history, economics, science, theology, and anthropology (Gross, 1990; Myers, 1990; Nelson et al., 1987);
- *critical social theory* (Foucault, 1972, 1980; Habermas, 1984; McCarthy, 1978);
- *language studies* (see Bakhtin, 1981, 1986; Gee, 1990), which have explored the social, historical, cultural, and ideological dimensions of language use;
- *feminist studies* (see Commeyras, Orellana, Bruce, & Neilsen, 1996; Lather, 1991; Luke & Gore, 1992; Walkerdine, 1992);
- *cultural studies* (see Grossberg, Nelson, & Treichler, 1992; Hall, 1996);
- *semiotics* (see Barthes, 1974, 1985; Eco, 1976; Umiker-Sebeok, 1991);
- *composition studies* (see North, 1987);
- *deconstruction* (see Derrida, 1976); and
- *social constructionism* (see Rorty, 1979, 1989), which has

questioned the epistemological foundations of Western philosophy.

What ties these eclectic traditions together is that they have all come to use, in one way or another, textual or discourse analysis as a fundamental methodological tool (Graesser & Gernsbacher, 1997). In so doing, they speak of "understanding the discourse participants engage in" or "new ways of reading." They are concerned with issues of race, class, and gender as these are played out in talk and text. They examine different roles people take in social interaction, consider how meaning is constructed, and regard interpretation as central to the processes of representing and understanding in communication.

Discourse theory says that every word we utter draws its meaning from the social practices of which it is a part or, recursively, from the sediment of prior practices. Thus, as we noted, all language is deeply intertextual for Bakhtin, each word invoking the history of its previous uses in diverse circumstances. Ultimately, these uses relate to the material reality of talk at any other time and place.

This conception of the material grounding of discourse has received added impetus from work on the sociology of science and technology (Bijker & Law, 1992; Bijker, Hughes, & Pinch, 1987; Latour, 1986, 1993; Star, 1988; Wenger 1993). Science seems to be the paragon of formalized methods of investigation and verification, objective knowledge, and operationalized language and description. Theories about science practices and scientific methods had once been limited to such idealized models and addressed only reluctantly the exigencies of ordinary scientific work. An important lack was any account of how the material components of science practice relate to the formulation of theories, data gathering, and hypothesis testing. Thus, with the exception of biographies (which were viewed as nonanalytical), earlier descriptions often failed to acknowledge any role for notebooks, gauges, conference rooms, laboratory benches, microscopes, word processors, computer networks, and all the other artifacts that give structure to science practice (Latour & Woolgar, 1986; Law, 1991; Star, 1989). But such artifacts are not incidental to practice. Close and extended examination of scientists' actual work has shown that their discursive practices are constituted out of human participation with these artifacts and other practices and social interactions. Abstract theories develop in the context of and through artifacts. This perspective has tended to demythologize the cleanness and objectivity of scientific discourse and to highlight the social, practical, and institutional dimension of all discourse; if it is true of science, where conscious effort is made to minimize such influences, how much more must it be true of more ill-structured contexts?

Discursive analysis has also highlighted the ways in which communicative practices and traditions are embedded in diverse communities. Cultural difference is expressed not only in strictly distinct languages or dialects but also in the ways in which the same language is used differently and the ways in which differences in other practices affect how language is expressed and understood (Heath, 1983; Pratt, 1987, 1996). One important difference in discourse communities is sexual difference, and a good deal of research has revealed pervasive patterns in how men and women speak, listen, and pursue different aims in communication (Belenky et al., 1986; Gilligan, 1982; Lakoff, 1975; Tannen, 1989, 1990, 1994). The importance of this research is obviously crucial in considering the nature of discourse in the classroom, where most teachers (and half the students) are female. But studies of the effects of linguistic differences arising from class, race, and ethnicity have had equally sweeping significance in highlighting the ways in which inequities in school treatments affect students along multiple dimensions of identity (see, for example, Bernstein, 1972; Bourdieu, 1977, 1990, 1991; Bourdieu & Passeron, 1990).

Another kind of discourse community is a discipline or subject area, and here too discursive analysis has reinscribed, in its own language, nearly every field of humanistic and social science inquiry (Cazden, 1986; Luke, 1995). For example, today one cannot talk about history, that is, engage in historical discourse, without some cognizance of how historical theorizing has been transformed by attendance to discourse and how language not only reflects but also shapes the constructed rhetoric and reality of that field (Nelson et al., 1987). The situation is similar in many areas including economics (McCloskey, 1985), anthropology (Clifford & Marcus, 1986), sociology (Strauss, 1986), biology (Myers, 1990), medical science (Foucault, 1980), psychology (Bazerman, 1988), technology studies (Ellul, 1980), statistics (Gigerenzer & Murray, 1987), literary theory (Scholes, 1985), and theology (Klemm, 1987).

Discourse theories, then, have both changed the ways in which we think about language (and what constitutes the boundaries of linguistic practices as opposed to other social practices) and revealed the fundamentally discursive character of other fields of inquiry. Discourse is the realm of *parole,* language in use, not language as a formalized object of study (*langue*). In this realm, language is materially grounded in texts, artifacts, gestures, actions, relations, situations; it has consequences and effects beyond expressions of meaning. The philosopher John Austin (1962) explored "how we do things with words" (promising, questioning, flattering, and so forth) as actions; similarly, Wittgenstein (1958) argued that the meaning of language is its use. Discourse analysis interrogates language in its sociohistorical situatedness and materiality. From such a standpoint, practices of expression and interpretation are specific enactments, carried out by agents in particular circumstances. Every utterance is susceptible to multiple interpretations and can have multiple effects. In trying to account for such diversity, easy distinctions of form and content, intention and effect, or linguistic meaning and social consequence are all fundamentally put to question.

In educational research, discursive analysis, as discussed earlier, has been joined with studies of inquiry, meaning making, shared thinking, and classroom activity in general (see Heap, 1985; Lankshear, 1997; Van Dijk, 1997), to illuminate and inform theories about, for example, reading (see Raphael et al., 1992), science learning (see Burbules & Linn, 1991; Lemke, 1990; Michaels & Bruce, 1989; Rosebery, Warren, & Conant, 1992), and mathematics (see Forman, 1989). Belying, to some extent, the stereotype of science and math education as the most content-driven and technocratic areas of teaching, much of the research and theory that has pushed the envelope of ideas

about inquiry, group thinking, and hands-on learning has come from investigators in these areas.

Discursive Critiques of Decontextualized Pedagogy

The issues just raised pose distinct challenges to the relatively decontextualized models of teaching proposed by the T/S perspective on pedagogy or, alternatively, certain dialogical pedagogies. These challenges include the following:

- *Who is speaking.* Forms of acceptable or conventional discourse are socially and culturally constituted. How individuals and groups prefer to speak, the practices and gestures that enact speech, the implications and inferences people make in interpreting the speech of others, and so on, differ substantially by the ways in which discourse is formed among social and cultural groups. Such considerations can mean widespread differences in the meanings and effects of speech acts, apart from whatever the words themselves might mean. For example, linguistic or gestural forms of politeness or respect may be understood at cross-purposes in culturally different settings.
- *When people speak.* Discursive engagements are historically situated, in the sense that language has a history, speech actors have a history, and the circumstances in which they come together (such as the form and purposes of curricula) have a history. These histories often inform and shape the ways in which discourse takes place, and can impose significant limits on certain discursive possibilities. For example, conventions of correct and incorrect usage in language are not only culturally but historically specific; they are neither natural nor inevitable.
- *Where people speak.* Discourse has a materiality: It takes place in physical settings and circumstances that are situated in space and time. Discourse is an activity interwoven and occurring simultaneously with other activities. It matters, for example, whether speakers are standing or sitting; smiling or winking; speaking face-to-face, on the phone, or through a computer link (which may make facial expressions moot or require iconic representations such as emoticons to replace them).
- *How people speak.* Discourse theory has also greatly expanded the forms of representation that can be fruitfully understood as discursive in nature. Humans use a variety of ways, consciously and unconsciously, to express meaning and intent. Moreover, the mode of discursive analysis can revealingly analyze elements that are not thought of as primarily representational (for example, the design of classroom furniture) to suggest meaning and effects no one might have intended.

From this discursive perspective, both T/S and dialogical models of teaching often suffer from limited attention to the who, when, where, and how of classroom interactions. Situating them in the context of discursive theory is a first step toward reconceptualizing these pedagogical communicative relations as something more than patterns of speech acts. A reconstructed conception of dialogue—our main focus here—will need to be responsive to the same pragmatic, theoretical, and research challenges we are posing against the T/S model.

A fruitful mode of analysis must therefore go beyond simple, sweeping assessments such as T/S is bad or dialogue is good. *Both* of these forms have often reflected decontextualized, abstract conceptions of discourse. Among other issues, we need to ask why the dialogical form (in certain incarnations at least) has been regarded as the paragon of education. What have been the educational consequences of promoting the idealized norms of egalitarian, open-ended, reciprocal communicative interaction? Is there anything about the dialogical form itself that protects dialogue from having discriminatory, damaging, and educationally counterproductive effects? What are the circumstances and audiences for which the ideal of dialogue may be not only unobtainable but even a harmful aspiration? Can the idealized image of dialogue as one of reciprocal engagement make it, ironically, more susceptible to manipulation or ulterior purposes? As Ellsworth (1989, 1997) asks, when might dialogue itself become oppressive?

The discursive perspective alerts us, then, to the larger social and institutional dynamics within which dialogue occurs. Sometimes these contexts introduce or reinforce real tensions that inhibit the possibilities of dialogical teaching and learning. For example, Eckert (1989) shows how the primary activity for students in schools is identity construction; Goldman (1991) similarly shows the strong interpersonal interactions that shape learning possibilities in the classroom. Studies such as Taylor and Cox (1997) or Anderson et al. (1997) analyze in detail how social processes can work against group sense making and the negotiation of meaning:

> Classroom conditions are often assumed to be the ideal place for all forms of learning. In our view they are, in fact, highly problematic. There is undoubtedly ongoing practice in the classroom, and there is learning. But the gap between these and the didactic goals of education is often severe. (Brown & Duguid, 1993, p. 14)

The preceding sections of this essay have raised central questions that should guide a rethinking of dialogue as an approach to teaching. First, we need to go beyond the idea that dialogue can be simply characterized as a particular pattern of question and answer among two or more people. Many instances of pedagogical communicative relations that might have this external form are not dialogical in spirit or involvement, while interactions that may not have this particular form can be dialogical:

> Pedagogical communication is not reducible to the formally defined relations of communication (sender-receiver), much less to the explicit content of the message. For in addition to whatever conscious symbolic mastery is conveyed, the educational process also communicates an implicit pedagogy, transmitting a kind of "total" knowledge of a cultural code or style. (Ulmer, 1985, p. 171; see also Bernstein, 1990; Bourdieu, 1991)

Second, we need to attend to the complex genealogy of dialogue as both a philosophical ideal and a pedagogical method. Dialogue is not unitary but multiple, and while particular conceptions of dialogue (for example, the Socratic method or Freirean critical pedagogy) hold currency for certain audiences,

it must be pointed out that even those paradigms (the teaching styles of Socrates or those of Freire) were actually multiple, not homogeneous. No single approach holds the patent on dialogue and it is even undialogical to think that it can (Burbules, 1993). In all of these ways, then, we ought to find a way of explaining dialogue in teaching that goes beyond the two-people-talking stereotype. The remainder of this chapter is devoted to spelling out what such a reconception might look like.

Rethinking Dialogue

From T/S to Dialogue

The first step in this reconception is to detail the ways in which the who, when, where, and how of discourse have forced a rethinking of classroom interactions.

Who. The first theoretical shift reflects in part a demographic shift discussed earlier: the growing diversity of classrooms and an increasing awareness of the margins or borders of common school culture as it interacts with the very different values and orientations that students bring to the classroom. The conditions of globalization and mobility have promoted both direct forms of migration across national-cultural categories and (especially with the rise of new communication and information technologies) an increasing proximity and interpenetration of multiple lines of national-cultural influence. In this context, the central assumptions of common schooling—of a canon of texts, of a shared historical tradition, of a common language—are thrown into question, because even where a common aim or reference point might be retained, its value and significance are going to be regarded differently from different positions as teachers and students. In some cases they will be directly challenged. From this standpoint, the linear, goal-directed dimensions of the T/S model are incompatible with a context of multiple purposes and intentions, not all of which move in parallel lines. But a shift to a dialogical approach, in itself, may not remedy these limitations.

A dialogue is not an engagement of two (or more) abstract persons, but of people with characteristics, styles, values, and assumptions that shape the particular ways in which they engage in discourse. Any prescriptive conception of dialogue must confront the challenge of acknowledging persons who do not engage in communication through those forms, and who might in fact be excluded or disadvantaged by them. Conversely, an account of dialogue that acknowledges the enormous multiplicity of forms in which people from different cultures do enact pedagogical communicative relations (let alone communicative relations generally) needs to address the question of why some versions are counted as dialogue and others not.

The discursive perspective raises questions with the *who* engaging in dialogue, which is often regarded as if it were a fixed, given condition. Work such as Hicks (1996) explores the ways in which participants construct and change identities through the processes of dialogue. In many contexts, indeed, the formation and negotiation of identity may constitute the primary purpose in mind for some participants in a dialogical relation, supplanting more overt teaching-learning goals.

Furthermore, such dynamics may be only partly intended or conscious (and hence only partly susceptible to reflection or change). Participation in dialogue, even at the microlevel of apparent personal choice, is not simply a matter of choice. The utterances that constitute an ongoing dialogue are already made (or not made) in the context of an awareness of the reactions—real, anticipated, or imagined—of other participants. The more that one pushes this sort of analysis, the more the achievement, or suppression, of dialogical possibilities comes to be seen as an expression of a group interdynamic, and not something achievable simply by changing the choices and actions of individuals.

When. The second theme from contemporary discourse theory challenges the utilitarian idea of language: We do not just use language; language uses us. As Bakhtin (1981) argued, the nature of discourse is that the language we encounter already has a history; the words that we speak have been spoken by others before us. (He calls this "the internal dialogism of the word.") As a result, what we speak always means more than we mean to say; the language that we use carries with it implications, connotations, and consequences that we can only partly intend. The words that others hear from us, how they understand them, and what they say in response is beyond our unilateral control. This relation of speaker, hearer, and language is reflected not only in spoken communication but with authors, readers, and texts of a variety of types. The multivalence of discourse situates specific speech acts or relations in a web of potential significations that is indeterminate, nonlinear, and highly susceptible to the effects of context and cultural difference. From this standpoint, the roles of teacher and student and other features of schools and classrooms that underlie the T/S model must be viewed as historical artifacts, discursively constructed and institutionalized, not as inherent concepts that define the educational endeavor.

Yet the same point can be raised with many dialogical pedagogies. A dialogue is not simply a momentary engagement between two or more people; it is a discursive relation situated against the background of previous relations involving them and the relation of what they are speaking today to the history of those words spoken before them. These background conditions are also not simply matters of choice, and they impinge upon the dialogical relation in ways that may shape or limit the possibilities of communication and understanding. Often these relations are expressed as forms of power or privilege that shape the purposes and limits of discourse because of the relative positions of people that place asymmetrical constraints on who can speak, who can be heard, and who has a stake in maintaining a particular dialogue or in challenging it (Robinson, 1995). The form of philosophical dialogues, often entirely or partly imagined (even those that ostensibly report the dialogues of Socrates), has reinforced a view of dialogue as a finite and bounded engagement, often described with little or no context, and with scant consideration given to what might have transpired before or after the dialogue at hand. This view has tended to support the idea of a dialogue as a unitary, goal-oriented conversation with a discrete purpose, and a beginning, middle, and end, not as a slice of an ongoing communicative relation (as it usually is in educational settings).

Where. The third shift has involved a greater emphasis on the social construction of knowledge and understanding. As we discussed earlier, interest in recent years has grown within research on teaching and learning in such problems as situated cognition, group learning, the relation of expert and novice understandings, real-world problem solving, distributed intelligence, and a whole range of similar notions that address in different ways the actual means by which the learning of individuals occurs in the contexts of existing social relations and practices (Cazden, 1988; Cole, Hood, & McDermott, 1978; Lave & Wenger, 1991; Moll, 1994). One can identify in these trends a kind of neoprogressivist approach to teaching and learning, based not solely on a set of social and political values and assumptions, but on contemporary research on culture, cognition, and learning. This trend emphasizes two important principles that work against the T/S model. The first is an emphasis on process over outcome: that learning how to learn, developing a degree of metacognitive reflectivity, and acquiring a flexible set of strategies for inquiry and problem solving are more important in the long run than learning any particular fact or idea. The second is an awareness that every teaching-learning moment has multiple outcomes, which are not limited to deriving the specific answer requested: Some outcomes have to do with a sense of social participation and solidarity; others have to do with involvement in specific social practices and traditions.

Similar concerns apply to dialogue. The situatedness of dialogue, considered as a discursive practice, means that the dialogical relation depends not only on what people are saying to each other, but also on the context in which they come together (the classroom or the gymnasium, for example), where they are positioned in relation to each other (standing, sitting, or communicating on-line), and what other gestures or activities work with or against the grain of the interaction. If dialogue has a materiality, then we must pay attention to both facilitating and inhibitive characteristics in the circumstances under which it takes place (Harste et al., 1988).

Not only simply the present context at hand but also other contexts—including anticipated future contexts of need or use—shape the understanding of purposes that guide or direct a discursive production. For example, interactions at home, on the playground, in the lunchroom, or on the street before or after school may constitute contexts of teaching and learning that are at least as important for certain participants as the interaction in the classroom. Relative importance aside, they certainly impinge on the thoughts, feelings, and motivations that participants bring to the classroom.

How. Another aspect of this situatedness, or materiality, is that the texts and objects of representation that mediate classroom discourse can have distinctive effects on what can be said and how it can be understood. Where interaction takes place in an immediate, face-to-face circumstance, these texts include not only the words themselves, but also facial expressions, gestures, and similar representational forms. The T/S model tends to conceive text too narrowly and instrumentally, as simply the means for achieving explicit instructional purposes.

Yet dialogue often takes place in clearly mediated forms such as a dialogue between a book's reader and its author, a dialogue between correspondents writing to one another, a dialogue over a telephone or audiovisual link, a dialogue over electronic mail, and so on. The tendency of previous accounts of dialogue has been to ignore such factors or, if they are considered at all, to relegate them to trivial significance compared to what the words themselves express. Discourse theory has highlighted the ways in which the circumstances of form and medium are not trivial, but can influence what is said and how it is understood and the ways in which these media are representational elements themselves (Lankshear, 1997). For example, a computer's user interface constitutes a discursive field with distinct, non-neutral properties. To examine a typical feature of computers today, it is significant (i.e., it signifies) that the computer screen is based on a desktop metaphor and is organized around files, folders, trash cans, and so forth—artifacts of a particular sort of work environment (as opposed to a kitchen countertop, or a carpenter's workbench, etc.), and artifacts that shape assumptions about who will be working there and what those people will be trying to do. Such interfaces mediate and influence the dialogue one has with a computer (or with others who are using the computer), how one uses it to create or articulate ideas, what one learns from it, and how one is changed by this non-neutral mediating text (Selfe & Selfe, 1994).

We want to stress here the growing impact of new information and communication technologies on educational aims and practices and on the teacher and student roles (Bruce, 1987, 1991, 1997; Burbules & Callister, 2000; Spender, 1995; Turkle, 1984, 1997). It is not a matter of new technologies replacing teachers, but a matter of radically changing our views about what the teaching role entails. As vast amounts of information, opportunities for exploration and discovery, and media for communication become readily available in classrooms, teachers will need to see themselves more as guides and interpreters, not as sources of authority. In some cases, the significance of a distinct teaching role recedes into the background. On the side of students (many of whom often end up teaching the teacher about how these technologies work and what can be found with them), their roles and identities are shifting in the digital context of direct communication (e-mail or chat rooms) and indirect communication mediated by web pages, avatars, MUD (Multi-User Domain) personae, and other representations of a virtual identity. Here too is an increasingly important context with which school and classroom priorities relate or (possibly) conflict.

In these ways, then, the traditional understanding of classroom discourse has been impeded by the formal, idealized models in which it has been described: impeded because these models have often not taken account of the situated, relational, material circumstances in which such discursive practices actually take place (see Dascal, 1985). As a result, such models have not always worked pedagogically to good effect in particular circumstances; often, indeed, they have ended up having effects quite contrary to the pedagogical purposes desired. The problem here is not the T/S model itself, limited as it might be. It is not as simple as transforming all teaching to a dialogical model (as if this were simple itself!). Attending to the social dynamics and contexts of classroom discourse heightens the awareness of the complexities and difficulties of changing specific elements within larger communities of practice. These communities may be the primary shapers of learning processes, but not always in

ways that serve intended or ideal educational objectives. Other purposes, such as identity formation or negotiating interpersonal relations, may predominate. The power of social processes may restrict lines of inquiry, distort discursive interactions, and silence perspectives in ways that conflict with the explicit purposes of schools.

At a different level of analysis, there has also been a change in the tools of research themselves. As researchers have come to think about classroom discourse in different ways, the means of recording and studying those phenomena have changed also. Where at one time it was thought sufficient to record verbal interactions and to base conclusions on the analysis of transcripts, looking for particular speech patterns (such as IRE), there is a greater awareness today of the ways in which discursive practices occur in complex relations with one another and with other, nonverbal phenomena. As a result, new research methods incorporate video recordings, more complex and detailed systems for coding, and more explicit analyses of artifacts. Continued work in the ethnography of communication and sociolinguistics (Cazden, 1988; Gumperz & Hymes, 1972; Hymes, 1995; Schieffelin & Ochs, 1986; Sudnow, 1972) has emphasized the connections between language use and social norms and relations. Earlier research that tended to use formal models and relatively narrow conceptions of social context has been extended to address more macrolevel aspects of social and institutional relations.

Rethinking dialogue as a discursive practice holds promise for developing theoretical accounts of dialogue that are richer, more complex, and better attuned to the circumstances of pedagogical practice. Dialogue, from this standpoint, cannot be viewed simply as a form of question and answer, but as a relation constituted in a web of relations among multiple forms of communication, human practices, and mediating objects or texts (Roschelle, 1996; Soloway & Prior, 1996). The T/S model, from this standpoint, becomes understood as one possible pedagogical communicative relation, not the fundamental ontology of the classroom. It has its uses, but it becomes constrictive and counterproductive when it defines the assumptions of what teaching is in general—yet here again it must be said that the same criticism could be leveled at many particular views of dialogue. It does remain useful to retain the prescriptive element of articulating which sorts of discursive interaction will be considered as dialogue, and to offer a normative account of why some teaching ought to be pursued in those forms rather than in others. Yet, it must be said: This prescriptive account is itself a discursive endeavor, which entails its own questions of relations, circumstances, and effects; accordingly, the questions of who, when, where, and how can also be posed against it. To this topic we now turn.

Dialogue as Relation, Not Speech Act

Counting a pedagogical communicative relation as dialogical cannot be based simply on a momentary slice-of-time observation. It cannot be based simply on counting the number of people involved. It cannot be based on finding a particular pattern of questions and answers. A dialogue is a pedagogical relation characterized by an ongoing discursive involvement of participants, constituted in a relation of reciprocity and reflexivity.

Here *ongoing* means that the form of verbal interaction at any single moment may not appear dialogical; the question is not a matter of who is speaking and who is listening but whether over time the participants are engaged intersubjectively in addressing the issue or problem at hand. A *relation of involvement among participants* means that active efforts at interpretation, questioning, and rethinking the issue or problem at hand are continually open possibilities. A certain capacity for *reflexivity,* including comment on the discursive dynamic itself, must be a characteristic of dialogical engagement. (See Ellsworth's 1997 account of "analytic dialogue.") A *reciprocal relation* means that the prerogatives of questioning, answering, commenting, or offering reflective observations on the dynamic are open to all participants. Impediments to these capabilities for interaction undermine the quality of the dialogical relation.

Dialogue and Teacher and Student Roles

As should be clear from this discussion, then, the very demarcation of distinct teacher and student identities is only a feature of certain kinds of dialogue: In many cases of coinvestigation or open-ended exploration, such roles might be actually counterproductive. Nor are these roles clearly distinct, stable, or cultureless.

Moreover, even when those roles do have a certain applicability, dialogue tends to promote a situation in which any participant can raise certain types of questions—including questions about the necessity or benefits of these roles—as part of the engagement itself. A major element of the T/S model is that these roles are taken as givens and that many tacit assumptions about the appropriate ways of enacting those roles are shared by most of the participants. In dialogical relations, these roles are neither distinct nor stable: The activities of teaching and learning are open to all participants at different moments, and in many contexts cannot even be separated—which is what learning with others entails. Instead of a Teacher/Student model, we might think about a *Teaching-Learning* relation, with the slant and hyphen themselves connoting different type of relation (one of separateness, the other of interdependence), and the change in verb forms a shift from roles to activities. Learning within this relation is seen as intrinsically intersubjective, situated, and problem based.

Beyond this point, the framework of dialogue presented here challenges the cultureless, decontextualized quality of the teacher and student roles. The attitude of responsiveness with which one formulates questions or comments in a dialogical relation (With whom am I speaking? How will they hear this? What are their possible responses?) requires actors to be aware of the particularity of other participants. Especially, though not exclusively, in forms of dialogue aimed toward intersubjective understanding or toward the possibility of agreement or consensus (though, as will be discussed in a moment, this is not necessarily a feature of all forms of dialogue), attention must be granted to the culture, experiences, and situations of others and to the horizons of one's own culture, experience, and situation as a position from which to try to apprehend them and vice versa.

This concern leads to the issues posed by what Gutierrez et al. (1995) called the "third space": the construction of a zone of potential communication that is explicitly not the discourse of the teacher nor of the students but a zone of potential meaning and representation constituted by how those discourses relate. Their study provides a particularly striking illustration of how certain models of dialogue do not address the complex communicative and noncommunicative issues involved with creating and negotiating such a third space. The discursive model places such questions and all their communicative difficulty and messiness at the center of analysis.

We also want to highlight a tension, or paradox, in this analysis. On the one hand, there is a difficulty in maintaining the conditions of dialogue and free participation when the teacher is the one framing the scope and context of discussion. As Ellsworth and others point out, this framing may inadvertently restrict the possibilities and direction of dialogue, especially for certain participants. On the other hand, it is less than clear that any one participant in a complex context can actually manage things that strongly. Elements of this context and of contexts outside this context may be beyond the awareness and control of any participant, multiple participants may have conflicting understanding and purposes, and actions toward intended results may actually impede those outcomes. This lack of control may be especially true in the case of discursive interactions such as dialogue, where the negotiation of purpose and direction is often an element within the exchange. What analyses such as the third space (Gutierrez et al., 1995) suggest is a deep indeterminacy in shaping dialogue toward any particular teleological end.

Dialogue as Situated

Classical models of dialogue and, even more generally, standard models of talk coming out of classical linguistics, suggest an idealized, disembodied picture of verbal interchange. We can ignore how the participants stand or sit, what they wear, what their physical attributes are, what the timbre of their voices might be, what the ambient noise level is, what the room decorations and furniture are, and whether they are inside or outside. None of these things are thought to matter. These models of pedagogical communication have tended to support the ideal that anyone can aspire to intellectual heights regardless of their circumstances of age, gender, race, culture, class, or physical conditions. What such views gain in inspirational potential they lose, unfortunately, in their engagement with the tensions and limitations of real school settings.

Every act of dialogue is, in fact, embodied and situated. We could say that each act participates in a material reality as much as it does in a mental realm or, to avoid that duality, we could say that the logical development of a dialogue is inseparable from its material grounding (compare Haas, 1995; Luke, 1992).

As we have seen, the argument that all dialogue is grounded in this way grows out of a long line of theorizing about discourse in which discourses are conceived as sociohistorically constituted. It has become difficult even to imagine a wholly decontextualized dialogue among abstract, unspecified participants. Thus, when we revisit *Meno,* we now want to ask new questions: What representational tools were available to the participants—a stick and sand, paper, hand gestures? How would the dialogue proceed differently with different tools for manipulating symbols? How did the participants position themselves physically? How did that relate to their understanding of each other's intellectual positions? How did their social status—slave, master, philosopher—affect their construction of meaning in the dialogue? Had the participants had prior dialogical interactions? How did those experiences shape their interpretations of the dialogue?

Dialogue as Multiple, Not Singular

Within these broad characteristics, as noted previously, dialogue can take a number of forms in the actual pattern of communicative performances and in the purposes to which it might be directed. Elsewhere, Burbules (1993) has discussed the forms of inquiry, conversation, instruction, and debate as a variety of types of dialogical engagement. *Inquiry* involves a coinvestigation of a question, the resolution of a disagreement, the formulation of a compromise, all as ways of addressing a specific problem to be solved or answered. *Conversation* involves a more open-ended discussion in which the aim of intersubjective understanding, rather than the answering of any specific question or problem, is foremost. *Instruction* involves an intentional process in which a teacher leads a student, through questioning and guidance, to formulating certain answers or understandings (this approach is often seen as the paradigm of the Socratic method). *Debate* involves an exchange less about reaching agreement or finding common answers than about testing positions through an agonistic engagement for and against other positions; it may include a process of problematizing even the terms of discussion themselves. The aim is that alternative points of view can each be clarified and strengthened through such an engagement. Burbules argues that any of these forms can serve educational purposes, and that each can have deleterious and antieducational effects also—success or benefit is not built into any procedures of communicative engagement. Other forms of dialogue may be possible besides these four, and there are certainly hybrid cases; moreover, any ongoing dialogical engagement will pass through several of these forms in the course of interactions. The key point is that the actual form and tone of utterances in such interactions may vary widely: some are more critical, others more inclusive; some tend toward convergent answers, others toward a divergent multiplicity of conclusions. Yet all can be dialogical in spirit, and many examples for each type can be found in the philosophical and pedagogical literature on dialogue.

Our purpose in reviewing these four forms here is not to provide an exhaustive typology of all types of dialogue; as noted earlier, other analyses with other points of emphasis may establish different criteria of distinction. But these four forms illustrate that dialogue, in the sense of "a pedagogical relation characterized by an ongoing discursive involvement of participants, constituted in a relation of reciprocity and reflexivity," can take different forms and be directed toward different goals. A skillful teacher will have a repertoire of dialogical strategies from which to draw, and will be creative and flexible in shifting from approach to approach with different students, different circumstances, and different subject matter.

Yet this analysis can be pushed even further. The forms of dialogue may not always even involve active speaking back and

forth. In certain cases silence—that is, the choice not to engage in dialogue—can express rejection, intimidation, boredom, irrelevance, and so forth (Delpit, 1988; Fine, 1987; Lewis, 1990). It can be a "dialogue move" itself (Burbules, 1993). If not engaging in dialogue becomes a way of communicating, then we have the clearest possible case of where the communicative form itself cannot delimit what is and is not part of the dialogue. Similar points might be raised with nonverbal communication (gestures, etc.), with texts that speak for others, with artifacts that are also forms of representation, and so on.

Still another problem with thinking of dialogue only in terms of what is said is Emmanuel Levinas's (1981) exploration of what *cannot* be said, what remains incommunicable in any relation, what remains unknowable about the "Other"—and the way that this poses a sharp contrast to views, such as Gadamer's (1976) fusion of horizons and Habermas's (1984) uncoerced consensus, which assume the possibility and the value of more or less complete understanding or agreement in dialogue. In all of these cases the prescriptive model of dialogue leads to some potentially dangerous presumptions.

Dialogue with Texts

Classical models of dialogue were developed when textual interaction, that is, discursive interactions mediated by written symbols, were far from the norm. Few people could read and write, and those who could looked with suspicion upon symbolic representations of the assumed-to-be primal form of meaning making through the spoken word. Plato's famous critique of writing in the *Phaedrus,* even when given an ironic reading, manifests not only a distrust of writing, but also a view that this form of communication is qualitatively different from oral discourse.

Despite the fact that Plato's position on the oral-written divide has had a distinguished history in Western thought (Ong, 1982), recent work in communication theory says that any simple divide is difficult to maintain. Moreover, technological developments suggest that at the very least, the modality, such as audio versus written text, may be one of the least significant aspects of communication. How does a rapid-fire conversation over a synchronous network in a classroom differ from face-to-face oral exchange? There are indeed many differences, but either can be dialogical, even though the former is constituted by the exchange of written texts, not spoken words. Conversely, an audiotape stores spoken words, but Plato's accusation that writing is mute (i.e., static and unchanging) must apply equally to the tape. Where do we classify electronic mail, video conferencing, hypertexts, lectures, note passing in class, broadcast television, subtitled movies, text produced by speech recognition software, talk radio, or stored audio on a web site? What is clear is that dimensions of interactivity, temporal or spatial commonality, direct address, and so on often matter much more than oral or written modality per se.

This raises the question: Can one have a dialogue with a text? For some, the answer has long been no. Indeed, dialogue might be defined as a form of communication contrasted with the noninteractive text. For others, the answer has been yes. Hutchins (1952) argues that the defining characteristic of the West is dialogue; the Western ideal is the Great Conversation as embodied primarily in the Great Books. Thus, dialogue is not opposed to reading, but rather, finds its highest expression through reading (Pearce, 1994; Rosenblatt, 1978). Hutchins's position finds support in the major threads of 20th-century literacy theory, especially through various varieties of reader-response theory. This is not the place for an overall account of reader-response theories. Nevertheless, it is important to show, at least cursorily, how such theories enlarge our conception of dialogue.

A capsule account of the reader-response move and why it is significant follows that of Freund (1987). She starts with Abrams's model of the situation of a work of art in which the work of art, the artifact itself, is at the center. Those aspects of nature or life that it represents are signified by the "Universe." The other nodes are the "Artist" who creates the "Work" and the "Audience" to whom it is addressed. Abrams argues that a comprehensive critical approach would need to address all four elements and the relations among them.

At first thought, a focus on reader-response would seem to highlight the Audience in Abrams' model, or perhaps the Audience-Work relation. In fact, Rosenblatt's (1978) classic work talks of turning the spotlight on the heretofore "invisible reader." But as Freund and others have pointed out, opening up the reader's perspective does more than shift the spotlight. It is not just a matter of exposing a different piece of the geography but more like a tectonic shift that challenges the privileged position of the Work.

This perspective puts the Audience at the center, not the Work itself. The whole structure destabilizes as we give serious consideration to the Audience's construction of the Artist, the Work, and the World to which it refers. New questions emerge, such as what stance the Audience takes with respect to the Work, or, more accurately, to the Audience's conception of what counts as the Work (Beach, 1997; Hartman, 1990; Rosenblatt, 1978; Umiker-Sebeok, 1991). Stance implies an active role for the reader in dialogue with a text. If anything, reader-response accounts, both conceptual and empirical (Beach, 1993; Bruce, 1981), have tended to show active, often idiosyncratic readers who construct meaning in divergent ways with little regard for conventional depictions of the Artist, the Work, or the Universe—much less for received critical analyses of how these elements should be interpreted or understood. Such constructions of meaning shift our models of reading or interpretation away from trying to guess what something *really* means, or what an author *really* intended, to interpretations of the reader's situation and outlook. The nature of the relation between text and reader is more interactive, and hence more indeterminate, than an acquisition of received meanings.

Models of reading that may have served reasonably well in the past have thus been challenged. Literacy research is now reaching beyond its familiar boundaries to consider alternative conceptions of reading, writing, and sense making. In particular, the field of literary studies and its concern with issues such as how understanding across horizons is possible, how readers adopt different stances toward a text, and how the meanings of authors, readers, and communities interrelate, leads inexorably to new conceptions of literacy (see Cazden et al., 1996). From this standpoint, it is helpful to reconceive the relation of reader to text as a kind of dialogue.

The radical reconfiguration entailed by the reader-response movement has further consequences for Abrams's model. His choice of the inclusive term "Work" and the nonspecific "Audience" to allow for a wide range of artistic productions is obviated by current conceptions of text. Because the Audience constructs the relation, text is no longer restricted to the literary Work, nor even to some broader category of published documents. Instead, the term is increasingly applied today to any and all representational forms, that is, to any object that the Audience can construct as bearing meaning. Thus, texts can include menus, street signs, electronic mail, World Wide Web pages, or cloud writing. Beyond alphabetic or ideographic representations, maps (Monmonier, 1991; Star, 1989), photographs, paintings, instrument gauges, even room keys in a hotel (Latour, 1991) can be texts. Texts can be dynamic, as on television or film. They can even include practices, such as dress or rules of etiquette (Barthes, 1974, 1985).

Among the practices that can be read as text are interactions through speech, including dialogical interactions under any of various definitions. Thus, the constructivist account of reading comes full circle to encompass the earlier conception of dialogue. Rather than saying that dialogue with or through texts shares some of the characteristics of standard oral dialogue, or that it is almost like oral dialogue, this view leads us to the position that dialogical interactions through speech are simply one of the many ways in which people can interact dialogically. Each of these ways enables a diverse set of readings by participants or observers.

This expansion of the term "text" may at first seem to threaten a dilution of meaning. But it has proven to be a useful analytic step, because while eliding differences across media, it brings to the fore the relation of discourse to other social practices, the construction of meaning by participants, and the possibility of textual analysis as a unifying construct across disciplines. Scholes (1985) argues that when students learn textual analysis in this broader sense, they develop a rigorous and general practice far more valuable than understandings of any particular readings. As Beach (1997) notes, once we consider these multiple reader stances and reader identities, we recognize how the meaning of individual texts emerges out of a relation to multiple other discourses in which both text and reader participate. This means that reading involves not only a relation to a text in front of us (oral or written), but also a reading of these larger intertextual relations.

Dialogue and Difference

Dialogue, understood within the discursive context, engages the issue of difference at various levels. First, consider the fact of diversity as a condition of all learning: It is precisely where people differ in outlook, background, belief, experience, and so forth that dialogue creates an opportunity for some to learn from and with others. Such diversity, however, does not merely create a set of possibilities and opportunities; it also constitutes a potential barrier—for these very same differences can lead to misunderstandings, disagreements, or speaking at cross purposes. Dialogue exists at the points of tension and difficulty between these possibilities.

At a second level, differences speak to positions in broader contexts that go beyond the identities of the persons engaged in dialogue. In many cases, these differences are invested with elements of power and privilege in relation to one another; these elements can be highlighted or exacerbated even further when they overlap with elements of power and privilege invested in institutionalized roles (including teacher and student). The discursive view of dialogue presented here means always situating the particular dialogical relation within the web of other relations that exist between and among participants.

At a third level, the issue of multiple effects, broached earlier, complicates the picture still further. No social act ever causes only what it intends. The perspective of difference adds to this complexity. Multiplying the dimensions along which we see ourselves and others as related or different makes it impossible to focus on unidirectional effects, on straightforward intentions, on clear demarcations of purpose and responsibility. As we have seen, even who the agents are is a shifting determination and so is the language with which they speak. The complex dynamics between teacher and student have multiple effects (and effects that are different for different types of students), not all of which can be subsumed under intentional teaching acts. While problematizing the sense of predictability and responsibility in any dialogical relation, this view of difference also introduces another imperative for dialogue: Where persons cannot know all that they intend, cannot know all that what they say signifies for different hearers, or cannot see all the effects that their acts produce, it becomes all the more important to keep open a process in which others can call to attention, question, or challenge the nature of the dialogue itself and the consequences it might have for them. This openness also implies that the boundaries of who is part of a dialogue, or who has a stake in it, can themselves be contested.

At a fourth level, difference raises question with the very aims of understanding, agreement, consensus, and community that are typical objectives of dialogue. In some cases, differences may be so great that incommensurabilities simply frustrate the process of dialogue from going very far. In other cases, the history and context of differences put some persons and groups in asymmetrical positions relative to goals like consensus or community: to be *with* means to be *like;* but to be *like* means to be alienated from qualities of self or relations to others. The risks and temptations of this sort of dynamic can be very subtle, infused with all sorts of mixed intentions (including those of sincerely trying to help people). Dialogue, because it derives from humanistic traditions, because it explicitly eschews methods of overt domination or coercion, and because it expresses values such as reciprocity and respect for all participants, is (ironically) all the more susceptible to the trap of good intentions.

Instead, the perspective argued for in this chapter means situating judgments about particular pedagogical communicative relations in the tripartite context of the elements of discursive practice, the multiple relations and activities that engage persons around those discursive practices, and the nature of the objects and texts that mediate those relations. Differences—differences of identity and position relative to one another, differences in the meanings that language has for different people, differences in the stakes that persons have in the varied activities and practices at hand and in their consequences, differences in the ways that people engage and experience the

mediating objects and texts that represent discursive elements—all run through this context and problematize the effort to analyze it in simple cause and effect terms or to delineate certain effects as pedagogically relevant and others not.

Beyond the Prescriptive Model of Dialogue

The considerations about dialogue raised in this section yield a significant shift in thinking about dialogue as a pedagogical communicative relation. Instead of traditional models of dialogue, which have tended to prescribe a particular form of communicative interaction, and which have been generated out of a priori assumptions about the ways that language should work, the view developed here is articulated specifically with the perspective of discursive analysis in mind. This account yields a more multivalent account of dialogue: that it can take very different verbal (and nonverbal forms); that it can arise in very different sorts of circumstances; that it can be mediated by very different sorts of textual or representational practices; that it can be directed toward quite different purposes, and can have still further effects apart from how it may be intended; and that these different forms will have different degrees of familiarity or utility for different sorts of people and different degrees of suitability for different subject matters.

In our view, the significance of this approach to understanding dialogue is not that it abrogates the value of prescriptive norms. Rather, it identifies these norms as themselves discursively constituted, not as givens. Moreover, it interrogates the consequences in practice of invoking certain models of dialogue and their norms in discursive contexts where the potentialities in principle of dialogue run up against contexts of situated roles, of institutionalized power and privilege, of multiple forms and styles of discourse, of cultural and other kinds of difference, and so on.

At the same time, however, we also want to emphasize the prescriptive elements inherent in any discursive model. As Habermas (1984), Apel (1987), and others have argued, the success of any communicative process depends on a set of shared, if often tacit and unspoken, norms about the acceptable forms and purposes of communication. As is often the case with such norms, they are typically invisible in the ordinary course of events and become salient only when they are breached or when one or another participant wants to question them. Difficulties emerge, of course, when these implicit norms vary, as they do, between or across different communities of discourse, although we believe there are strong reasons to conclude that they cannot differ entirely, and that some norms appear to be inherent to the communicative process itself. As a result, one important educational aim is to identify these norms and to seek ways to foster respect for them so that learners can engage in successful communication and diagnose what is happening when communication goes awry.

This shift in viewpoint has enormous implications, both for our views about how education should proceed and what aims it should serve. First, it reveals the fundamental tension between ground-level assumptions about the teacher as authority, as director of classroom dynamics, as provider of information, and as evaluator of student responses, and an awareness of classroom discourse as an arena of intersubjective meaning making in which multiple voices have a share. Second, it makes educators aware of the nonneutral features of dominant discourses, both in the sense of formal languages and in the dynamics of language in use, as factors in shaping, limiting, and in some cases excluding discursive possibilities for certain participants. Where these dynamics are linked with identity-formation and interactions with contexts outside the classroom, the issues go far beyond the questions often associated with public debates over ESL (English as a Second Language) and bilingual education (for example, whether learning one language or another is helpful on the job market). A deeper issue is when and how engagements with different patterns of discourse can create the conditions for developing multiple literacies that do not require simple choices or priorities among primary and secondary languages; the conditions of dialogue involve accommodation along two-way paths, and not simply reorienting those who are different along dominant patterns and norms. Third, then, this means a reflection on our larger educational aims, beyond the dichotomy of unquestioned goals of assimilation with dominant norms and beliefs on the one hand versus a rejection of what is common and the desire to preserve discrete cultural elements and traditions at all costs on the other hand. We believe that educators need to think beyond these options to an awareness of how a respect and tolerance for difference is necessary, even when one is trying to pursue common learning goals and, conversely, how the melding and transformation of culture and language is inevitable in moments of discursive engagement. As a result, the sensitive problem becomes a matter of educators appreciating the potential for creating conflict, suffering, or resistance even when the explicit purpose is one of transmitting information or teaching valuable skills while, at the same time, being prepared to question assumptions about the neutrality or value of dominant forms of discursive engagement (simply because they happen to be dominant).

For example, the assumptions of the (apparently neutral) school stance of dispassioned objectivity and distance toward texts (often termed the "essayist" stance; see Scollon, 1994; Scollon & Scollon, 1981) seem to highlight some potentially valuable educational goals: analyzing what the "text itself" means, holding personal judgment and response in abeyance, being able to articulate and defend views one may not personally hold, and so on. Researchers have shown, however, that this essayist stance comes into conflict with the ways that certain readers define their identities in relation to a text or conversational exchange (see Gee, 1990; Keller-Cohen, 1994; Michaels, 1981). The more dialogical analysis of difference suggests that there are multiple ways of approaching texts, and that movement from one discourse pattern to another can involve not only a simple matter of learning new skills or linguistic conventions but also can create deeper crises in the negotiation of identity in the classroom, especially for students from nondominant cultural groups.

Dialogue and New Research Questions

It is not within the scope of this chapter to attempt to stipulate a set of future research issues surrounding dialogue and teaching, nor is it consistent with the exploratory, pluralist approach

we have tried to emphasize here. However, we do want to acknowledge a set of questions that have arisen for us in the course of surveying this literature and trying to reframe some of the theoretical issues at stake. Perhaps some of these issues will be salient for others also.

The first and perhaps the most difficult question is to apply the discursive perspective to our own activity here. When we refer to dialogue as "a pedagogical relation characterized by an ongoing discursive involvement of participants, constituted in a relation of reciprocity and reflexivity," what is at stake in offering such a definition? Given the concerns expressed throughout this essay with the prescriptive approach, it cannot simply be a matter of saying that this definition fits the literature better, or carves out the right issues, or constitutes a generalizable educational ideal. We need to ask what work such a definition does, what effects it might have; we need to ask whose definition it is, and whose perspectives may not be represented by it; we need to consider the range of contexts in which pedagogical communication occurs, and explore how the definition may work differently in different contexts. We think this definition is recommendable because it is generated from within a discursive perspective itself. As we have characterized it here, the definition is grounded in ideas of situatedness, multiplicity, and difference and so explicitly acknowledges a range of forms of communicative interaction that can constitute dialogue. Moreover, the element of reflexivity puts within the concept of dialogue the possibility of renegotiating, as part of an ongoing dialogical engagement, questions of inclusiveness, linguistic difference, bias, domination, and so forth. None of this guarantees the success of such attempts to identify, critique, and renegotiate those limits, but one need not necessarily step outside of the dialogical relation in order to challenge them. This conception even acknowledges that silence and withdrawal from dialogue are possible moves within it—"within it" in the sense that such moves may constitute necessary steps for eventual dialogue (even critical dialogue) to be possible. For others, silence and withdrawal are not a choice, because a dialogue has excluded them entirely, and this too needs to be questioned.

Other questions arise from the multiple forms that dialogue can take, and their relation to specific subject areas and particular students. For example, when can debate work as a teaching-learning relation, and when not (and for whom)? More specifically, how do different discursive practices, such as treating information as problematic, relate to students' abilities to make conceptual changes? A wide variety of research on knowledge building, mediating objects and texts, and discourse is beginning to show a more fine-grained connection between dialogue and particular learning goals.

Other questions arise from the changing technological environment in which pedagogical communication and information sharing are taking place. Some questions, for example, have to do with how conversation on-line changes the ways people engage in dialogue, and how different participants experience the advantages and disadvantages of indirect conversation rather than face-to-face (Bruce, Peyton, & Batson, 1993).

Other questions concern the "communicative competencies" (Habermas's phrase) that enable students to engage in certain kinds of dialogue effectively. For example, what role do questions play in various forms of dialogue (Benyon, 1987; Dillon,

1983, 1987, 1988; Gall 1970, 1984; Hintikka, 1982; Macmillan & Garrison, 1983, 1988; Morgan & Saxton, 1991; Wilen 1984)? When do certain utterances operate pragmatically as questions? When is a question likely to elicit an educationally fruitful answer? How do students learn to ask questions? Similar questions relate to other communicative competencies that teachers must master to be successful: How does a teacher's background knowledge of content prepare him or her for being able to ask fruitful investigative questions, and in what ways does this constitute a special area of "pedagogical content knowledge" that teachers need to learn (Shulman, 1987)? Is learning to foster dialogue a general pedagogical skill, or a subject-specific one?

What are the contextual circumstances, practices, and relations that encourage students to engage in certain kinds of dialogue effectively? Which students do? Which students don't? What features of schools and classrooms promote dialogue, and which features inhibit it (see Burbules, 1993)?

Once one regards the Teaching-Learning relation as such, and not as an enactment of discrete Teacher/Student roles, questions arise about the reversibility and interdependence of that relation. Palincsar and Brown's (1984; see also Palincsar, 1986) approach to reciprocal teaching, for example, asks what happens when the roles of teacher and student are reversed; similarly, what happens when they are challenged and contested? What possibilities do such challenges create in specific settings, and which do they tend to close off?

We find rich issues raised by Gutierrez et al. (1995) in their idea of a "third space" constituting the zone in which dialogue can take place. What happens when specific discourses engage one another? How different or conflicted can they be before no practical engagement is possible or worthwhile?

Addressing the question of aims, how necessary are specific learning outcomes for pursuing various kinds of dialogue? When can specific teleological goals interfere with inquiry and discovery, or true reciprocity and open-endedness? What happens to a dialogue when no one is steering?

We are interested in the ways in which dialogue, as a constructivist pedagogy, can foster general capabilities to pursue inquiry on one's own, or with new partners. To what extent, if at all, is dialogue an intrinsically critical mode of discourse, as Freire and others suggest (Bridges, 1988; McPeck, 1990; Paul, 1987; Young, 1990, 1992)? What are the multiple meanings of "critical" in such contexts (Burbules & Berk, 1999)? What is it about dialogue that tends to promote this aim or are there tendencies in certain kinds of dialogue that can work against it?

Finally, and in a way that combines many of these other issues, what are the implications of strong views of difference and diversity for dialogue? What happens when one tries to reconcile prescriptive approaches to pedagogy with the reality of diverse linguistic forms, attitudes, values, and experiences? Is dialogue inherently normalizing, or can it be adapted to broader horizons of inclusiveness? Yet (perversely), when it does succeed at being more inclusive, is this at the cost of requiring participants to give up or compromise elements of their differences? Can a theory of dialogue that accommodates radical difference—we ask by way of closing—still be a theory of dialogue?

REFERENCES

Alvermann, D. E., & Hayes, D. A. (1989). Classroom discussion of content area reading assignments: An intervention study. *Reading Research Quarterly, 24,* 305–335.

Alvermann, D. E., O'Brien, D. G., & Dillon, D. R. (1990). What teachers do when they say they are having discussions of content reading assignments: A qualitative analysis. *Reading Research Quarterly, 25,* 296–322.

Anderson C. A., Holland, D., & Palincsar, A. S. (1997). Canonical and sociocultural approaches to research and reform in science education: The story of Juan and his group. *Elementary School Journal, 97,* 357–381.

Apel, K.-O. (1987). The problem of philosophical foundations in light of a transcendental pragmatics of language. In K. Baynes, J. Bohman, & T. McCarthy (Eds.), *After philosophy: End or transformation?* (pp. 250–290). Cambridge, MA: MIT Press.

Austin, J. L. (1962). *How to do things with words.* Cambridge, MA: Harvard University Press.

Bakhtin, M. M. (1981). *The dialogic imagination* (M. Holquist, Ed.). Austin, TX: University of Texas Press.

Bakhtin, M. M. (1986). *Speech genres.* Austin, TX: University of Texas Press.

Barthes, R. (1974). *S/Z* (R. Miller, Trans.). New York: Hill & Wang. (Original work published 1970).

Barthes, R. (1985). *From speech to writing. The grain of the voice.* New York: Hill and Wang.

Bazerman, C. (1988). *Shaping written knowledge: The genre and activity of the experimental article in science.* Madison, WI: University of Wisconsin Press.

Beach, R. (1993). *A teacher's introduction to reader-response theories.* Urbana, IL: National Council of Teachers of English.

Beach, R. (1997). Critical discourse theory and reader response: How discourses constitute reader stances and social contexts. *Reader, 37,* 1–26.

Belenky, M. F., Clinchy, B. M., Goldberger, N. R., & Tarule, J. M. (1986). *Women's ways of knowing: The development of self, voice, and mind.* New York: Basic Books.

Benyon, J. (1987). An ethnography of questioning practices. *Questioning Exchange, 1,* 39–42.

Bernstein, B. (1972). A critique of the concept of compensatory education. In C. B. Cazden, V. John, & D. Hymes (Eds.), *Functions of language in the classroom* (pp. 135–151). New York: Teachers College Press.

Bernstein, B. (1990). *The structuring of pedagogic discourse: Class, codes, and control* (Vol. IV). New York: Routledge.

Bijker, W. E., Hughes, T. P., & Pinch, T. (1987). *The social construction of technological systems.* Cambridge, MA: MIT Press.

Bijker, W. E., & Law, J. (Eds.). (1992). *Shaping technology/Building society: Studies in sociotechnical change.* Cambridge, MA: MIT Press.

Bourdieu, P. (1977). *Outline of a theory of practice.* New York: Cambridge University Press.

Bourdieu, P. (1990). *The logic of practice* (R. Nice, Trans.). Stanford, CA: Stanford University Press.

Bourdieu, P. (1991). *Language and symbolic power.* Cambridge, MA: Harvard University Press.

Bourdieu, P., & Passeron, J.-C. (1990). *Reproduction in education, society, and culture* (R. Nice, Trans.). Newbury Park, CA: Sage.

Bridges, D. (1988). *Education, democracy and discussion.* New York: University Press of America.

Brown, J. S., & Duguid, P. (1993, March). Stolen knowledge. *Educational Technology,* pp. 10–15.

Bruce, B. C. (1981). A social interaction model of reading. *Discourse Processes, 4,* 273–311.

Bruce, B. C. (1987). An examination of the role of computers in teaching language and literature. In J. Squire (Ed.), *The dynamics of language learning: Research in reading and English* (pp. 277–293). Urbana, IL: National Conference on Research in English and ERIC Clearinghouse on Reading and Communication Skills.

Bruce, B. C. (1991). Roles for computers in teaching the English language arts. In J. Jensen, J. Flood, D. Lapp, & J. Squire (Eds.), *Hand-*

book of research on teaching the English language arts (pp. 536–541). New York: Macmillan.

Bruce, B. C. (1994). The discourses of inquiry: Pedagogical challenges and responses. In D. Keller-Cohen (Ed.), *Literacy: Interdisciplinary conversations* (pp. 289–316). Cresskill, NJ: Hampton.

Bruce, B. C. (1997). Literacy technologies: What stance should we take? *Journal of Literacy Research, 29*(2), 289–309.

Bruce, B. C., & Davidson, J. (1994). An inquiry model for literacy across the curriculum. *Journal of Curriculum Studies, 28*(3), 281–300.

Bruce, B. C., Peyton, J. K., & Batson, T. W. (Eds.). (1993). *Network-based classrooms: Promises and realities.* New York: Cambridge University Press.

Buber, M. (1970). *I and thou* (W. Kaufmann, Trans.). New York: Charles Scribner's Sons. (Original work published 1923).

Burbules, N. C. (1993). *Dialogue in teaching: Theory and practice.* New York: Teachers College Press.

Burbules, N. C., & Berk, R. (1999). Critical thinking and critical pedagogy: Relations, differences, and limits. In T. S. Popkewitz & L. Fendler (Eds.), *Critical theories in education: Changing terrains of knowledge and politics* (pp. 45–65). New York: Routledge.

Burbules, N. C., & Callister, T. A., Jr. (2000). *Watch IT: The risks and promises of information technology for education.* Boulder, CO: Westview Press.

Burbules, N. C., & Linn, M. C. (1991). Science education and philosophy of science: Congruence or contradiction? *International Journal of Science Education, 13,* 227–241.

Carlson, L. (1983). *Dialogue games: An essay in formal semantics.* Boston: Reidel.

Cazden, C. B. (1986). Classroom discourse. In M. C. Wittrock (Ed.), *Handbook of research on teaching* (3rd ed., pp. 436–442). New York: Macmillan.

Cazden, C. B. (1988). *Classroom discourse: The language of teaching and learning.* Portsmouth, NH: Heinemann.

Cazden, C., Cope, B., Fairclough, N., Gee, J., Kalantzis, M., Kress, G., Luke, A., Luke, C., Michaels, S., & Nakata, M. (1996). A pedagogy of multiliteracies: Designing social futures. *Harvard Educational Review, 66,* 60–92.

Clifford, J., & Marcus, G. E. (Eds.). (1986). *Writing culture: The poetics and politics of ethnography.* Berkeley: University of California Press.

Cole, M., Hood, L., & McDermott, R. P. (1978). *Ecological niche-picking: Ecological validity as an axiom of experimental cognitive psychology* (Monograph). New York: Rockefeller University, Laboratory of Comparative Human Cognition.

Commeyras, M. (1992). *Dialogical-thinking reading lessons: Promoting critical thinking among 'learning-disabled' students.* (Technical Report No. 553). Champaign, IL: Center for the Study of Reading.

Commeyras, M., Orellana, M. F., Bruce, B. C., & Neilsen, L. (1996). What do feminist theories have to offer to literacy, education, and research? *Reading Research Quarterly, 31*(4), 458–468.

Dascal, M. (Ed.). (1985). *Dialogue: An interdisciplinary approach.* Philadelphia: Benjamin's.

Delpit, L. (1988). The silenced dialogue. *Harvard Educational Review, 58,* 280–298.

Derrida, J. (1976). *Of grammatology* (G. C. Spivak, Trans.). Baltimore: Johns Hopkins University Press.

Dewey, J. (1916). *Democracy and education.* New York: Macmillan.

Dillon, J. T. (1983). *Teaching and the art of questioning.* Bloomington, IN : Phi Delta Kappa.

Dillon, J. T. (1987). Question-answer practices in a dozen fields. *Questioning Exchange, 1,* 87–100.

Dillon, J. T. (Ed.). (1988). *Questioning and discussion: An interdisciplinary study.* Norwood, NJ: Ablex.

Easley, J. (1987). A teacher educator's perspective on students' and teachers' schemes. *Thinking: The Second International Conference.* Hillsdale, NJ: Lawrence Erlbaum Associates.

Eckert, P. (1989). *Jocks and burnouts.* New York: Teachers College Press.

Eco, U. (1976). *A theory of semiotics.* Bloomington, IN: Indiana University Press.

Elbow, P. (1986). *Embracing contraries: Explorations in learning and teaching.* New York: Oxford University Press.

Ellsworth, E. (1989). Why doesn't this feel empowering? Working through the repressive myths of critical pedagogy. *Harvard Educational Review, 59,* 297–324.

Ellsworth, E. (1997). *Teaching positions: Difference, pedagogy, and the power of address.* New York: Teachers College Press.

Ellul, J. (1980). *The technological system* (J. Neugroschel, Trans.). New York: Continuum. (Original work published in French 1977).

Engestrom, Y. (1990). *Learning, working, and imagining: Twelve studies in activity theory.* Helsinki: Orienta-Konsultit Oy.

Engestrom, Y. (1991). Non scholae sed vitae discimus: Toward overcoming the encapsulation of school learning. *Learning and Instruction, 1,* 243–259.

Fairclough, N. (1989). *Language and power.* London: Longman.

Fine, M. (1987). Silencing in the public schools. *Language Arts, 64,* 157–174.

Forman, E. A. (1989). The role of peer interaction in the social construction of mathematical knowledge. *International Journal of Educational Research, 13,* 55–70.

Foucault, M. (1972). *The archaeology of knowledge and the discourse on language* (A. M. Sheridan Smith, Trans.). New York: Pantheon Books.

Foucault, M. (1980). *Power/knowledge: Selected interviews and other writings 1972–1977.* New York: Pantheon Books.

Freire, P. (1968). *The pedagogy of the oppressed* (M. B. Ramos, Trans.). New York: Seabury.

Freire, P. (1985). *The politics of education.* South Hadley, MA: Bergin & Garvey.

Freund, E. (1987). *The return of the reader: Reader-response criticism.* New York: Penguin.

Gadamer, H.-G. (1976). *Philosophical hermeneutics* (D. E. Linge, Ed. and Trans.). Berkeley, CA: University of California Press.

Gall, M. D. (1970). The use of questions in teaching. *Review of Educational Research, 40,* 707–721.

Gall, M. D. (1984). Synthesis of research on teachers' questioning. *Educational Leadership, 42,* 40–47.

Gee, J. P. (1990). *Social linguistics and literacies: Ideology in discourses.* London: Falmer.

Gigerenzer, G., & Murray, D. J. (1987). *Cognition as intuitive statistics.* Hillsdale, NJ: Lawrence Erlbaum Associates.

Gilligan, C. (1982). *In a different voice: Psychological theory and women's development.* Cambridge, MA: Harvard University Press.

Goldman, S. (1991). Computer resources for supporting student conversations about science concepts. *Sigcue Outlook, 21*(3), 4–7.

Graesser, A. C., & Gernsbacher, M. A. (1997). Special Issue: *Discourse Processes* after two decades. *Discourse Processes, 23*(3), 223–598.

Gross, A. G. (1990). *The rhetoric of science.* Cambridge, MA: Harvard University Press.

Grossberg, L., Nelson, C., & Treichler, P. (Eds.) (1992) *Cultural studies.* New York: Routledge.

Gumperz, J. J., & Hymes, D. (Eds.). (1972). *Directions in sociolinguistics: The ethnography of communication.* New York: Holt, Rinehart, & Winston.

Gutierrez, K. (1993, April). *Scripts, counterscripts, and multiple scripts.* Paper presented at the Annual Meeting of the American Educational Research Association, Atlanta, GA.

Gutierrez, K., Rymes, B., & Larson, J. (1995) Script, counterscripts, and underlife in the classroom: James Brown vs. Brown v. Board of Education. *Harvard Educational Review, 65,* 445–471.

Haas, C. (1995). *Writing technology: Studies on the materiality of literacy.* Hillsdale, NJ: Lawrence Erlbaum Associates.

Habermas, J. (1984). *The theory of communicative action.* Boston: Beacon.

Hall, S. (1996). *Stuart Hall: Critical dialogues in cultural studies* (D. Morley & K. H. Chen, Eds.). New York: Routledge.

Hamilton, E. (Ed.). (1961). *Plato: The collected dialogues.* New York: Pantheon.

Hansen, J., Newkirk, T., & Graves, D. (Eds.). (1985). *Breaking ground: Teachers relate reading and writing in the elementary school.* Portsmouth, NH: Heinemann.

Harste, J., Short, K. & Burke, C. (1988). *Creating classrooms for authors: The reading-writing connection.* Portsmouth, NH: Heinemann.

Hartman, D. (1990). *Eight readers reading: The intertextual links of able readers using multiple passages.* Unpublished doctoral dissertation, University of Illinois at Urbana-Champaign.

Heap, J. L. (1985). Discourse in the production of classroom knowledge: Reading lessons. *Curriculum Inquiry, 15*(3), 245–279.

Heath, S. (1983). *Ways with words.* New York: Cambridge University Press.

Hicks, D. (Ed.). (1996). *Discourse, learning, and schooling.* New York: Cambridge University Press.

Hintikka, J. (1982). A dialogical model of teaching. *Synthese, 51,* 39–59.

Hutchins, R. M. (1952). The great conversation: The substance of a liberal education. Chicago: Encyclopedia Britannica.

Hymes, D. (1995). *Education, linguistics, narrative inequality.* London: Taylor & Francis.

Keller-Cohen, D. (Ed.). (1994). *Literacy: Interdisciplinary conversations.* Cresskill, NJ: Hampton.

Klemm, D. E. (1987). The rhetoric of theological argument. In J. S. Nelson, A. Megill, & D. N. McCloskey, (Eds.), *The rhetoric of the human sciences: Language and argument in scholarship and public affairs* (pp. 276–297). Madison, WI: University of Wisconsin Press.

Lakoff, R. (1975). *Language and woman's place.* New York: Harper & Row.

Lankshear, C. (1997). *Changing literacies.* New York: Open University Press.

Lather, P. (1991). *Getting smart: Feminist research and pedagogy within the postmodern.* New York: Routledge & Kegan Paul.

Latour, B. (1986). Visualization and cognition: Thinking with eyes and hands. In *Knowledge and society: Studies in the sociology of culture, past and present, 6* (pp. 1–40). Greenwich, CT: JAI Press.

Latour, B. (1991). Technology is society made durable. In J. Law (Ed.), *A sociology of monsters: Essays on power, technology, and domination.* New York: Routledge.

Latour, B. (1993). *We have never been modern* (C. Porter, Trans.). Cambridge, MA: Harvard University Press.

Latour, B., & Woolgar, S. (1986). *Laboratory life: The construction of scientific facts* (Rev. ed.). Princeton, NJ: Princeton University Press.

Lave, J., & Wenger, E. (1991). *Situated learning: Legitimate peripheral participation.* Cambridge, UK: Cambridge University Press.

Law, J. (Ed.). (1991). *A sociology of monsters: Essays on power, technology and domination.* New York: Routledge.

Lemke, J. L. (1990). *Talking science: Language, learning, and values.* Norwood, NJ: Ablex.

Leont'ev, A. N. (1981). *Problems of the development of mind.* Moscow: Progress.

Levinas, E. (1981). *Otherwise than being, or beyond essence* (Alphonso Lingis, Trans.). The Hague: Martinus Nijhoff.

Lewis, M. (1990, April). *Framing, women, and silence: Disrupting the hierarchy of discursive practices.* Paper presented at the Annual Meeting of the American Educational Research Association, Boston, MA.

Luke, A. (1992). The body literate: Discourse and inscription in early literacy training. *Linguistics and Education, 4,* 107–129.

Luke, A. (1995). Text and discourse in education: An introduction to critical discourse analysis. In M. Apple (Ed.), *Review of research in education, 21* (pp. 3–48). Washington, DC: American Educational Research Association.

Luke, C., & Gore, J. (1992). *Feminisms and critical pedagogy.* New York: Routledge & Kegan Paul.

Macmillan, C. J. B., & Garrison, J. W. (1983). An erotetic concept of teaching. *Educational Theory, 33,* 156–166.

Macmillan, C. J. B., & Garrison, J. W. (1988). *A logical theory of teaching: Erotetics and intentionality.* Boston: Kluwer.

Maranhão, T. (Ed.). (1990). *The interpretation of dialogue.* Chicago: University of Chicago Press.

McCarthy, T. (1978). *The critical theory of Jürgen Habermas.* Cambridge, MA: MIT Press.

McCloskey, D. N. (1985). *The rhetoric of economics.* Madison, WI: University of Wisconsin Press.

McPeck, J. E. (1990). *Teaching critical thinking: Dialogue and dialectic.* New York: Routledge.

Mehan, H. (1979). *Learning lessons: Social organization in the classroom.* Cambridge, MA: Harvard University Press.

Michaels, S. (1981). "Sharing time": Children's narrative styles and differential access to literacy. *Language in Society, 10,* 423–442.

Michaels, S., & Bruce, B. (1989, April). *Discourses on the seasons.* Paper presented at the Annual Meeting of the American Educational Research Association, San Francisco, CA.

Moll, L. C. (Ed.). (1990). *Vygotsky and education: Instructional implications and applications of sociohistorical psychology.* New York: Cambridge University Press.

Moll, L. C. (1994). Mediating knowledge between homes and classrooms. In D. Keller-Cohen (Ed.), *Literacy: Interdisciplinary conversations* (pp. 385–410). Cresskill, NJ: Hampton.

Monmonier, M. (1991). *How to lie with maps.* Chicago: University of Chicago Press.

Morgan, N., & Saxton, J. (1991). *Teaching questioning and learning.* New York: Routledge.

Myers, G. (1990). *Writing biology: Texts in the social construction of scientific knowledge.* Madison, WI: University of Wisconsin Press.

Nelson, J. S., Megill, A., & McCloskey, D. N. (Eds.). (1987). *The rhetoric of the human sciences: Language and argument in scholarship and public affairs.* Madison, WI: University of Wisconsin Press.

North, S. M. (1987). *The making of knowledge in composition: Portrait of an emerging field.* Portsmouth, NH: Heinemann.

Nystrand, M., Gamoran, A., Kachur, R., & Prendergast, C. (1997). *Opening dialogue: Understanding the dynamics of language and learning in the English classroom.* New York: Teachers College Press.

Ong, W. (1982). *Orality and literacy: The technologizing of the word.* London: Routledge.

Palincsar, A. S. (1986). The role of dialogue in providing scaffolding instruction. *Educational Psychologist, 21,* 73–98.

Palincsar, A. S., & Brown, A. L. (1984). Reciprocal teaching of comprehension-fostering and comprehension-monitoring activities. *Cognition and Instruction, 1*(2), 117–75.

Palmer, R. E. (1969). *Hermeneutics: Interpretation theory in Schleirmacher, Dilthey, Heidegger, and Gadamer.* Evanston, IL: Northwestern University Press.

Paul, R. (1987). Dialogical thinking: Critical thought essential to the acquisition of rational knowledge and passions. In J. Baron & R. Sternberg, (Eds.), *Teaching thinking skills: Theory and practice* (pp. 127–148). New York: W. H. Freeman.

Pearce, L. (1994). *Reading dialogics (interrogating texts).* London: Edward Arnold.

Polanyi, M. (1962). *Personal knowledge: Toward a post-critical philosophy.* Chicago: University of Chicago Press.

Pratt, M. L. (1987). Linguistic utopias. In N. Fabb, D. Attridge, A. Durant, & C. MacCabe (Eds.), *The linguistics of writing: Arguments between language and literature* (pp. 48–66). New York: Methuen.

Pratt, M. L. (1996). Arts of the contact zone. In D. Bartholomae & A. Petrosky (Eds.), *Ways of reading: An anthology for writers* (pp. 528–546). Boston: St. Martin's Press.

Raphael, T. E., McMahon, S. I., Goatley, V. J., Bentley, J. L., Boyd, F. B., Pardo, L. S., & Woodman, D. A. (1992). Research directions: Literature and discussion in the reading program. *Language Arts, 69,* 55–61.

Robinson, V. (1995). The identification and evaluation of power in discourse. In D. Corson (Ed.), *Discourse and power in educational organizations* (pp. 111–130). Cresskill, NJ: Hampton.

Rogoff, B. (1990). *Apprenticeship in thinking: Cognitive development in social context.* New York: Oxford University Press.

Rogoff, B., & Lave, J. (Eds.). (1984). *Everyday cognition: Its development in social context.* Cambridge, MA: Harvard University Press.

Rogoff, B., & Toma, C. (1997). Shared thinking: Community and institutional variations. *Discourse Processes, 23,* 471–497.

Rorty, R. (1979). *Philosophy and the mirror of nature.* Princeton, NJ: Princeton University Press.

Rorty, R. (1989). *Contingency, irony and solidarity.* New York: Cambridge University Press.

Roschelle J. (1992). Learning by collaborating: Convergent conceptual change. *Journal of Learning Sciences, 2,* 235–276.

Rosebery, A. S., Warren, B., & Conant, F. R. (1992). Appropriating scientific discourse: Findings from language minority classrooms. *The Journal of the Learning Sciences, 2*(1), 61–94.

Rosenblatt, L. M. (1978). *The reader, the text, the poem: The transac-*

tional theory of the literary work. Carbondale, IL: Southern Illinois University Press.

Schieffelin, B. B., & Ochs, E. (Eds.). (1986). *Language socialization across cultures.* Cambridge, UK: Cambridge University Press.

Scholes, R. (1985). *Textual power: Literary theory and the teaching of English.* New Haven, CT: Yale University Press.

Scollon, R. (1994). Cultural aspects of constructing the author. In D. Keller-Cohen (Ed.), *Literacy: Interdisciplinary conversations* (pp. 213–228). Cresskill, NJ: Hampton.

Scollon, R., & Scollon, S. B. K. (1981). *Narrative, literacy, and face in interethnic communication.* Norwood, NJ: Ablex.

Scribner, S., & Cole, M. (1981). *The psychology of literacy.* Cambridge, MA: Harvard University Press.

Selfe, C., & Selfe, R. J. (1994). The politics of the interface. *College Composition and Communication, 45,* 480–504.

Shulman, L. S. (1987). Knowledge and teaching: Foundations of a new reform. *Harvard Educational Review, 57,* 1–22.

Smagorinsky, P., & Fly, P. K. (1993, April). The social environment of the classroom: A Vygotskian perspective on small group process. *Communication Education, 42,* 159–170.

Soloway, E., & Pryor, A. (1996). Using computational media to facilitate learning. *Communications of the ACM, 39,* 83–109 (Special issue).

Spender, D. (1995). *Nattering on the net.* North Melbourne, Australia: Spinifex.

Star, L. S. (1988). Introduction: Special issue on sociology of science and technology. *Social Problems, 35*(3), 197–205.

Star, L. S. (1989). Institutional ecology, 'translations,' and boundary objects: Amateurs and professionals in Berkeley's Museum of Vertebrate Zoology, 1907–39. *Social Studies of Science, 19,* 387–420.

Strauss, A. (1986). *Qualitative analysis.* New York: Cambridge University Press.

Sudnow, D. (Ed.). (1972). *Studies in social interaction.* New York: Macmillan.

Suleiman, S. R., & Crosman, I. (1980). *The reader in the text: Essays on audience and interpretation.* Princeton, NJ: Princeton University Press.

Tannen, D. (1989). *Talking voices: Repetition, dialogue, and imagery in conversational discourse.* New York: Cambridge University Press.

Tannen, D. (1990). *You just don't understand: Women and men in conversation.* New York: William Morrow.

Tannen D. (1994). *Gender and discourse.* New York: Oxford University Press.

Taylor, J., & Cox, B. D. (1997). Microgenetic analysis of group-based solution of complex two-step mathematical word problems by fourth graders. *Journal of Learning Sciences, 6,* 183–226.

Tharp, R., & Gallimore, R. (1989). *Rousing minds to life: Teaching, learning and schooling in social context.* New York: Cambridge University Press.

Tompkins, J. P. (Ed.). (1980). *Reader-response from formalism to post-structuralist criticism.* Baltimore: Johns Hopkins University Press.

Turkle, S. (1984). *The second self: Computers and the human spirit.* New York: Simon & Schuster.

Turkle, S. (1997). *Life on the screen: Identity in the age of the Internet.* New York: Touchstone.

Ulmer, G. (1985). *Applied grammatology: Post(e)-pedagogy from Jacques Derrida to Joseph Beuys.* Baltimore: Johns Hopkins University Press.

Umiker-Sebeok, J. (1991, October). *Meaning construction in a cultural gallery: A sociosemiotic study of consumption experiences in a museum.* Paper presented at the meeting of the Association for Consumer Research, Chicago.

Van Dijk, T. A. (1997). *Discourse as social interaction.* London: Sage.

Vygotsky, L. S. (1978). *Mind in society: The development of higher psychological processes* (M. Cole, V. John-Steiner, S. Scribner, & E. Souberman, Eds.). Cambridge, MA: Harvard University Press.

Vygotsky, L. S. (1986). *Thought and language* (A. Kozulin, Ed.). Cambridge, MA: MIT Press.

Walkerdine, V. (1992). Progressive pedagogy and political struggle. In C. Luke & J. Gore (Eds.), *Feminisms and critical pedagogy* (pp. 15–24). New York: Routledge.

Wells, G. (1986). *The meaning makers: Children learning language and using language to learn.* Portsmouth, NH: Heinemann.

Wenger, E. (1993). *Communities of practice.* Cambridge, UK: Cambridge University Press.

Wertsch, J. V. (1980). The significance of dialogue in Vygotsky's account of social, egocentric, and inner speech. *Contemporary Educational Psychology, 3,* 150–162.

Wertsch, J. V. (1991). *Voices of the mind: A sociocultural approach to mediated action.* Cambridge, MA: Harvard University Press.

Wilen, W. W. (1984). Implications of research on questioning for the teacher educator. *Journal of Research and Development in Education, 17,* 31–35.

Wittgenstein, L. (1958). *Philosophical investigations.* New York: Macmillan.

Young, R. (1990). *A critical theory of education.* New York: Teachers College Press.

Young, R. (1992). *Critical theory and classroom talk.* Philadelphia: Multilingual Matters, Ltd.

49.

Teaching in Higher Education

Robert J. Menges[†]
Northwestern University

Ann E. Austin
Michigan State University

Research on teaching at the postsecondary level has expanded rapidly. Although the quality of this body of literature sometimes fails to match its quantity, we believe that it has considerable potential for improving practice and for generating more sophisticated theoretical and conceptual frameworks. Our review focuses on work from about 1985, when the third edition of the *Handbook* was being prepared. By highlighting findings that are especially important, noteworthy, or consistent, we give a broad overview from which readers can consider and read the literature on teaching in higher education. Overall, we have taken an inductive approach. We looked at the literature subject to certain criteria—for example, date and quality of research—and decided about topics for the review based on what has been published.

A separate chapter on teaching in higher education is justified, in our view, because of the distinctive characteristics of postsecondary education: (a) higher education has different purposes than does K–12 education, including the nature of its professional training and career-related activities; (b) professors are oriented toward disciplines rather than primarily toward the profession of teaching; (c) professors are typically trained not as teachers but, rather, as disciplinary specialists; (d) somewhat different roles and missions in society are assigned to higher education institutions than to schools; (e) differing roles and responsibilities prevail for professors in higher education than for teachers in K–12; (f) higher education enrolls learners of very different age, experience, and development than do K–12 schools. An interesting area for future analysis is comparing research on teaching between K–12 and higher education literatures, but such a comparison is not the purpose of this chapter.

We first consider issues and trends pertinent to the context of teaching in higher education. We then look at research about faculty as teachers, about students as learners, and about the content of instruction. A major section of the chapter is devoted to research about creating and sustaining effective teaching–learning environments in higher education. We close by discussing future directions for the field. This organizing framework, depicted in Figure 49.1, draws attention to areas where those topics overlap. We believe that the most important area—the one from which research will be most revealing and will have the greatest effect—is the area of overlap in the center of the figure. This juncture is where explicit attention is given simultaneously to learners, to teachers, and to content.

For purposes of this chapter, we define teaching as "the intentional arrangement of situations in which appropriate learning will occur" (Menges, 1981, p. 556). Characterizing teaching in this way reminds us that studies of teaching are incomplete without due attention to learning and that we oversimplify whenever we consider one without the other. As Shuell (1993) points out, teaching and learning are dynamic and reciprocal processes, and research should attempt to account for the complex and simultaneous effects of developmental, affective, and motivational influences, as well as cognitive factors.

Outlets for research and commentary about postsecondary teaching have increased dramatically in recent years, and many of them are explicitly international in scope. They include not only the books and journals that are our primary sources for this review but also newsletters, professional organizations, conferences, and their associated web sites. Some of these resources focus on practice; others are devoted to research and to translations of research into implications for practice. During the past decade, *Teaching in Higher Education* (established in

We are grateful for constructive comments from Janet Donald and Raymond Perry, reviewers for this chapter, and from Sarah Dinham and Kenneth Feldman.

[†] Robert J. Menges was a Professor in the Center for Teaching Professions at Northwestern University. Sadly, he passed away in 1998, while he was engaged in writing this manuscript. He is greatly missed.

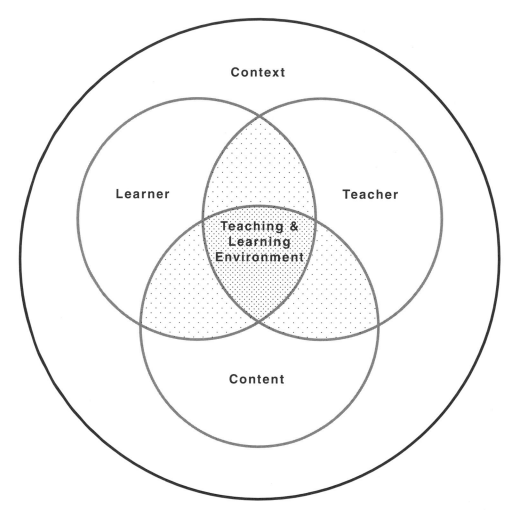

Figure 49.1. Framework for research.

1996) and the *International Journal for Academic Development* (est. 1996) joined *New Directions for Teaching and Learning* (est. 1980) and *Instructional Evaluation and Faculty Development* (est. 1980) as outlets dedicated to research-based discussions of teaching and faculty development in postsecondary education.

Numerous serials that focus broadly on higher education carry occasional articles or chapters about teaching: *Assessment and Evaluation in Higher Education, Canadian Journal of Higher Education, Higher Education, Higher Education Research and Development, Higher Education: Handbook of Theory and Research, Journal of Higher Education, Quality in Higher Education, Research in Higher Education,* and *Review of Higher Education.* Other resources focus generally on teaching, with occasional articles about postsecondary teaching, for example, *American Educational Research Journal* and *Teaching and Teacher Education.* Still other publications are limited either to a particular segment of the higher education teaching force, notably several volumes about training teaching assistants (e.g., Nyquist, Abbott, Wulff, & Sprague, 1991) and the *Journal of Teaching Assistant Development* or to particular types of institutions, such as *Community College Journal of Research and Practice.*

Special issues of research journals have been dedicated to postsecondary teaching (e.g., *Journal of Educational Psychology* in June 1990) as have individual monographs (e.g., items in the *ASHE/ERIC Higher Education Reports* series). In Great Britain, the Society for Research into Higher Education publishes noteworthy monographs and serials. Numerous professional societies publish journals about college teaching in their disciplines; these professional disciplines have been discussed by Weimer (1993). Anthologies have also appeared, notably the collection edited by Feldman and Paulsen (1998) and the volume combining original contributions with selected chapters from *Higher Education: Handbook of Theory and Research* (Perry & Smart, 1997). A perspective on earlier work is given by Menges and Mathis (1988), who described and reviewed key resources on teaching, learning, curriculum, and faculty development in higher education.

The Context for Teaching in Higher Education

During the past decade, social and political trends have altered the environment for higher education in the United States in ways that have profound implications for teaching. Although it is not this chapter's purpose to review these trends in detail, we state them briefly as background. Drawing on such sources as Altbach (1995), Graubard (1997), ASHE-ERIC Higher Education Reports, and the almanacs produced annually by the *Chronicle of Higher Education* and the National Education Association, we offer the following list of significant issues and trends.

- Financial support of higher education at the federal and state levels has declined, including state subsidies to institutions and funds to underwrite research. Support for students has moved away from grants and toward loans.
- In their quest to contain the costs of higher education, states have begun to assess the management of postsecondary institutions, to participate in setting institutional priorities, and to base allocations, at least in part, on performance. Performance-based funding typically relies on data such as faculty workload and student graduation rates.
- Undergraduate enrollments are predicted to increase significantly as children of baby boomers reach college age and as the employment sector responds to the need to train and retrain workers.
- Admission policies and procedures are complicated by several trends: a more ethnically diverse applicant pool, the politics of affirmative action, controversies over standardized tests, and public attention to ratings of colleges and universities.
- Roles of regional and professional accrediting associations are being reformulated. Accreditation guidelines are under revision.
- Discussions about faculty tenure have yielded suggestions for reforming and even eliminating traditional tenure. Post-tenure reviews have been implemented at the institutional, system, and state levels.
- Scholarly work is coming to be seen as broader and more differentiated than the traditional emphasis on the scholarship of discovery.
- Student ratings of instruction are accepted as a necessary source of information about teaching effectiveness, but they are also viewed as significantly limited and incomplete when used as the primary basis of faculty evaluation.
- Many policymakers believe that technologically mediated instruction can contain costs and increase access to higher education. Those beliefs are commonly resisted by faculty members.
- The national goals for education give some attention to higher education, specifically with regard to critical thinking and literacy.
- Finally, paradigms that underlie scholarly work on curriculum and instruction are shifting and are reflecting movement from modernist to postmodernist views (Bloland, 1995; Tierney & Rhoads, 1993), from objectivist ways of knowing to communal ways of knowing (Palmer, 1997), and from preoccupation with teaching to emphasis on learning (Barr & Tagg, 1995).

Faculty as Teachers

Teaching in higher education is influenced by the characteristics of members of the higher education teaching force, by the nature of the work they do as teachers, and by how they are prepared for that work.

Who Are the Teachers in Postsecondary Education?

Today is not a time of comfort and certainty for faculty members, and the future is not likely to bring greater stability. Altbach (1995) noted a decline in the number of full-time academic jobs, a loss of a sense of community in the profession, an erosion of the economic status of professors, an institutional retrenchment that affects faculty (including faculty with tenure), and a leveling of the growth of unions. Although predicting the future of the profession is difficult, a good deal is known about the present teaching force. Next we consider research about faculty demographics, attitudes, assumptions and expectations, personal theories, and stress.

DEMOGRAPHIC CHARACTERISTICS

Faculty members at colleges and universities in the United States totaled 931,706 in the fall of 1995 (U.S. Department of Education, 1998). Most were male (65%), and 85% were White. Numbers since 1970 have increased much more dramatically at 2-year institutions (210%) than at 4-year institutions (69%); in 1995, about one in three faculty worked at a 2-year institution. Nearly half of faculty members at 2-year institutions held part-time positions; at 4-year institutions, the proportion of part-timers was 28%. Overall, the proportion of part-timers nearly doubled from 1970 to 1995.

Of tenured, full-time faculty members in 1995, 59% were male. Among new full-time faculty members, 31,000 were newly hired in 1995 (the smallest number since the mid-1970s), and 51% of them were not on the tenure track.

Gappa and Leslie (1993) offered a four-category typology of part-time faculty members that can be useful in guiding further investigations: career-enders (those who are semi-retired); specialists (those who have a full-time career elsewhere); aspiring academics (those who seek status equivalent to full time, including those who have completed all doctoral work but dissertations and those with teaching jobs at several institutions); and freelancers (whose current career is the sum of part-time jobs, one of which is college teaching). Faculty diversity, including issues of gender, ethnicity, and sexual identity, is examined in a monograph by Tack and Patitu (1992), and in volumes edited by Gainen and Boice (1993) and by Harvey and Valadez (1994), the latter of which concerned community colleges.

To discern how the profession is changing, Finkelstein, Seal, and Schuster (1998) examined two cohorts of full-time academics who responded to the 1992–93 National Survey of Postsecondary Faculty. They compared "new entrants" (the cohort with seven or fewer years of experience) with other respondents (the "senior cohort"). The new entrants cohort is large (fully one-third of full-time faculty members), and 45% of them were hired at research and doctoral institutions. Only 43% of the new entrants are native-born White males (compared to 59% in the senior cohort). Finkelstein, Seal, & Schuster (1998) emphasized that the "new academic generation" is more diverse in gender, ethnicity, and place of birth. They went on to observe that the total core of academics (that is, the full-time tenured or tenure-track faculty) is shrinking.

ATTITUDES

For information about faculty attitudes related to teaching, we draw on surveys by the Carnegie Foundation for the Advancement of Teaching, particularly a 1991–92 survey comparing the faculties in 14 countries (Altbach, 1996). A robust finding is strong loyalty among faculty members to their disciplines; in every country, loyalty to the discipline rated higher than loyalty to the department, which was higher than loyalty to the institution. In most countries, faculty members reported that their classes are increasing in size and that their current students were less well prepared for college work. Most United States respondents (63%) agreed that their primary interests were in teaching or were leaning toward teaching (only Mexico, Chile, and Russia were higher). Most (75%) also agreed that to achieve tenure without publishing is difficult (only Germany and Israel were higher). In general, those who reported having produced more publications also reported feeling less pressure and the most satisfaction with their work.

In the 1995–96 survey by the Higher Education Research Institute (Sax, Astin, Arredondo, & Korn 1996), virtually all faculty members (more than 99%) endorsed "being a good teacher" as an essential or important goal. About two-thirds said their teaching load is satisfactory or very satisfactory (the highest agreement was at universities), but fewer than half said the same about student quality (agreement was highest at private universities). Only 12.5% said that faculty members are rewarded for good teaching (highest agreement is at private 4-year colleges).

UNDERLYING ASSUMPTIONS AND EXPECTATIONS

Researchers have studied the assumptions and beliefs held by teachers about their goals and their instructional approaches. In a survey of faculty members at 15 community colleges and 17 4-year colleges, Cross (1991) found, while examining faculty goals for teaching, that goal preferences were strongly related to discipline. Helping students develop thinking skills characterized humanities and social science teachers, whereas science teachers emphasized teaching facts and principles of their subject. Discipline is also related to the expectations that professors hold about their students' thinking abilities. In an interview study of 36 professors in selected disciplines, Donald (1988) found that social science professors held the highest expectations for students' thinking abilities, followed by natural science professors, whereas humanities professors appeared to emphasize abilities other than logical thought. Other studies have identified differences among disciplines in teachers' goals for undergraduate education (Smart & Ethington, 1995) and in students' perceptions of their learning and of their teachers (Cashin & Downey, 1995).

Discipline and institutional contexts also shape what faculty members believe are appropriate instructional practices—that is, their norms for teaching. Braxton, Eimers, and Bayer (1996) found general endorsement for the importance of "feedback on student performance," but support varied by discipline or by type of institution for "egalitarian classroom climate" and "systematic programs of advisement." Only weak normative support was found for "faculty–student interaction," for "learning about students," and for concern about the "improvement of teaching." Differences among disciplines are reflected in classroom teaching behaviors (H. G. Murray & Renaud, 1995). Elsewhere, Braxton (1995) contended that disciplines exhibiting "hard paradigmatic development" (e.g., chemistry, physics, and biology) are likely to be less receptive to teaching improvement initiatives than are disciplines exhibiting soft paradigmatic development (e.g., political science, sociology, and English).

Faculty knowledge about teaching is beginning to receive research attention, drawing on Shulman's (1986) distinctions between pedagogical knowledge and pedagogical content knowledge. Dinham (1996) discussed what college teachers need to know, and Irby (1994) discussed what clinical teachers in medicine need to know. Lenze and Dinham (1999) studied knowledge about student difficulties of 11 faculty members with minimal teaching experience. In general, those faculty members had limited repertoires for dealing with student difficulties. Most strategies were teacher-centered and often did not distinguish between difficulties caused by content and difficulties caused by process. Faculty members also make faulty estimates about what students are learning, typically overestimating student performance (P. W. Fox & LeCount, 1991).

PERSONAL THEORIES ABOUT TEACHING AND LEARNING

Numerous studies have explored faculty members' "personal" theories about teaching and learning. Those theories range from thinking about teaching as transmission of knowledge and information to thinking about teaching as a support for student learning (e.g., Samuelowicz & Bain, 1992).

Hughes (1992) looked for gender differences in the personal theories of 69 community college faculty members. Overall, more than half of them espoused "content theories," 24% espoused "motivation theories," and 20% espoused "process" theories. When diagnosing classroom problems, men tended to be more likely than women to rely on assumptions whereas women were more likely than men to seek new information. Regardless of gender, most said that to deal with the problem they would again review the content or go on to lecture about the next topic (the "default" strategy). Rando and Menges (1991) found similar theories in interviews with 20 graduate teaching assistants who divided equally across content theories, motivation theories, and process theories. The authors distinguished among those personal theories of teaching and formal theories presented in the literature, and they discussed how each kind of theory might affect practice.

First-year science teachers who endorsed an intention to transmit information (associated with surface learning) were more likely to report teacher-focused strategies, and those endorsing an intention to induce conceptual change (associated with deep learning) were more likely to report student-focused strategies (Trigwell & Prosser, 1996).

Faculty conceptions of teaching and of teaching excellence were studied by comparing novice and award-winning teachers in Australia (Dunkin, 1995). Awardees had more complex concepts of teaching and articulated a wider range of teaching strategies. They were also more confident of their teaching skills and more open to evaluation. However, consequences of an award for teaching are not necessarily positive. Schwartz (1992) found that for faculty members at the University of California, Berkeley, teaching awards were not associated with a subsequent salary increase.

More information is needed about the extent to which faculty members actually implement their theories and goals, particularly goals such as critical thinking and problem solving. California faculty members from postsecondary institutions throughout the state in arts and sciences and in education claimed overwhelmingly (89%) that critical thinking was a primary goal of instruction. However, only 19% gave a clear explanation of what critical thinking is, and only 9% included critical thinking procedures when describing a typical day in class (R. W. Paul, Elder, & Bartell, 1997). Medical faculty members indicated their preferred goals and preferred practices for teaching and then completed a written simulation (Hartman & Nelson, 1992). Most showed discrepancies between their preferences and their choices in the simulated teaching exercise (e.g., they indicated a preference for less-competitive testing but chose competitive test situations in their simulation).

TEACHING AS A SOURCE OF STRESS

Numerous researchers have studied the structure of faculty stress and the relationships between teaching and stress. Dey (1994) found teaching load to be one of the top three sources of stress (after time pressures and lack of personal time), especially for women. In another study, African-American faculty members reported significantly higher stress from service and research, but not from teaching (Smith & Witt, 1993). Comparing data from two Higher Education Research Institute surveys, Sax et al. (1996) found that students as a source of stress showed the largest increase from 1989 to 1995.

Gmelch, Wilke, and Lovrich (1986) identified five dimensions of stress. None was explicitly named for the act of teaching itself, but items about teaching contributed to each dimension: (a) "reward and recognition" includes receiving inadequate recognition for teaching, (b) "time constraints" includes inadequate time to prepare for teaching, (c) "department influence" includes not knowing how performance is evaluated by the chair, (d) "student interaction" includes class presentations and evaluation both by students and of students, and (e) "professional identity" includes excessively high self-expectations of which expectations about teaching are no doubt part. Untenured faculty members reported greater stress across all dimensions. In another study (Gmelch & Wilke, 1991), excessively high self-expectations were found to be the strongest source of stress for residential faculty members at the institution studied.

The New Faculty Project followed new hires at five institutions for their first 3 years (Menges & Associates, 1999). Stress tended to increase at all institutions from year 1 to year 3, but it was lowest at the community college district—the institution with the most clearly enunciated teaching mission. Stress from teaching was expected to decline over time (Boice, 1992; Olsen & Sorcinelli, 1992), but such was not the case. Stress about review and evaluation (of which teaching is a large component) typically increases and persists after tenure. Stress from

teaching load begins to decline during ages 45–54, although time stresses do not (Sax et al., 1996).

What is not clear from those studies are the dynamics by which time operates in relation to stress. Much depends on individual perceptions. Dinham (1999) pointed out that rather than regarding the stressor to be something uncontrollable, such as time, focusing on what is potentially more controllable is useful. Some parts of work and nonwork life are highly time sensitive (e.g., returning student tests, submitting a grant proposal, attending family events), whereas others are less so (e.g., uncertainty about what is expected, interpersonal conflicts, loneliness).

What Faculty Members Do as Teachers

In this section, we discuss how faculty members spend their time, what the relationships are between teaching and scholarly productivity, and what some important areas are for further research about faculty work.

HOW FACULTY MEMBERS SPEND THEIR TIME

Faculty workload is a topic of long-standing interest among researchers—for instance, Yuker (1984) cited a workload study published in 1919—perhaps because of the high degree of autonomy that faculty members possess and the solitary nature of faculty work in many fields. Bowen and Schuster (1986) affirmed that faculty members, on the whole, spend most of their time in teaching, even at research universities, and that most faculty members consider instruction to be their primary responsibility.

Faculty members reported typical work weeks ranging from 47 hours at 2-year institutions to 57 hours at research universities (reported by Layzell, 1996, from the 1988 National Survey of Postsecondary Faculty). Across institutions, the proportion of time spent teaching averaged 56%. Again, there were expected institutional differences. Contact hours per week averaged 9.8 overall, ranging from 6.6 hours at research universities to 15.2 hours at 2-year colleges. Milem, Berger, and Dey (1997) looked at faculty effort over time. Comparing data from a national survey in 1972 and combined data collected from national surveys in 1998 and 1992, they found that time devoted to research increased significantly for all categories of 4-year institutions. The proportional changes were greatest at comprehensive universities (20%) and doctoral universities (15%). Time on teaching (including both class preparation time and scheduled teaching time) also increased significantly at liberal arts colleges (12%), comprehensive universities (8%), and doctoral universities (6%) but was not significant at research universities (2%). Those increases came at the cost of decreasing the already small amount of time spent advising students, which decreased significantly except at doctoral universities. Looking at data from 1989 to 1995, Sax et al. (1996) found no changes regarding time on teaching and a slight decline in time on research.

The length of the work week may have increased somewhat from prior decades, but more interesting are institutional differences. Fairweather (1996) noted that faculty in doctoral-granting institutions spend less time on teaching and more on research than their colleagues in comprehensive institutions.

However, those teaching in comprehensive colleges and universities spent less time teaching and more time on research than colleagues in liberal arts colleges.

Reporting a study of more than 2,000 faculty members in 10 professional fields, Stark, Lowther, and Hagerty (1986) reported that the time faculty members spend on their different roles—teaching, research, independent professional practice, consulting, and administrative activities—varied to some extent across fields. Erdle and Murray (1986) found differences in teaching behaviors related to discipline, with arts and humanities faculty members more frequently using an interpersonal approach, with science faculty members more dominantly using a task orientation, and with social science faculty members using approaches that fall between the two other groups. Studying more than 2,000 teachers at 2- and 4-year colleges, Cross (1991) found variations across fields in teaching roles and goals.

Finkelstein, Seal, and Schuster (1998) found that faculty members with 7 or fewer years of experience reported a slightly lower proportion of time spent on teaching (51%) than their senior colleagues (55%). New entrants would prefer to reduce that time to an average of 45% and to increase research time from 25 to 30%. Senior colleagues' responses were very similar. The direction of the preferred shift (toward more time on research) is consistent across types of institutions, but substantial gender differences occur among new entrants. Women reported spending significantly more of their time teaching (58% for women compared to 46% for men) and much less time doing research (16% compared to 27%). Women preferred to allocate about 10% more time to teaching than did men. This pattern holds when only tenured or tenurable faculty members are considered, but it is less prominent for tenured or tenurable women at research universities.

In the United Kingdom, the academic work week appears to be similar to that in the United States. Time diaries kept during 1993–94 by about 2,600 academics at the "old" universities in Britain showed the average work week during the academic term to be 54.8 hours (Court, 1996), with about one-third of that time devoted to teaching. A surprising finding was the amount of time devoted to administrative tasks (an average of 18 hours per week), apparently one consequence of the extensive assessments of research and educational quality that are required at British universities.

Researchers of the Faculty at Work Project (Blackburn & Lawrence, 1995) interviewed 111 faculty members at four institutions. Faculty members at regional comprehensive universities reported 38% of their time going to teaching; liberal arts faculty members reported 60%, community college faculty members reported 67%, and faculty members at historically black comprehensive universities reported 73% (a 58% average across institutions). In the New Faculty Project (Menges & Associates, 1999), teaching accounted for about two-thirds of work time in year 1. This figure was highest at the community college district (70%); at the research university, time on teaching was nearly equal to time on research. By year 3, most work time still went to teaching. In fact, faculty members typically indicated that they were devoting more time to teaching than they thought their institution expected (a result different from the 1995 findings of Blackburn & Lawrence concerning the Faculty at Work Project). The greater this discrepancy, the more

stress those new hires reported.

In studies of junior faculty members at two comprehensive universities, R. Boice (1992) interviewed faculty members and examined their time diaries. At both institutions, one of which had higher expectations for scholarly productivity than the other, teaching dominated work life. Despite intentions to devote more time to writing, faculty members reported in their second semester on the job that about 15 hours were given to teaching for each hour devoted to writing. This proportion changed little by the fourth semester.

The intensity of faculty work life is vividly portrayed by quotations from 300 interviews of faculty members and administrators at 12 colleges and universities reported by Tierney and Bensimon (1996). "I always leave the office by 6:00 so I can have dinner with my family, but once the kids get to sleep, I probably work another 2 hours. I have to. I have no choice" (p. 60). About teaching, a sense of conflict almost always prevails: "I'm not good at giving tests, and, yes, I know there is an instructional development center on campus. After tenure, I'll probably go there. I don't have time now" (p. 62). The most realistic view about teaching seems to be: "If you excel at teaching, someone will undoubtedly think you're putting too much into your teaching and you should be doing research. So my advice is to be good, but not great" (p. 64).

Regarding teaching methods, surveys from 1989 and 1995 showed that most faculty members reported using class discussion and lecturing in all or most of their classes (Sax et al., 1996). Over time, lecturing declined slightly, whereas cooperative learning, group projects, and computer- and machine-aided instruction increased. The latter activities were more characteristic of younger faculty members, a finding that apparently contradicts the results of Finkelstein, Seal, and Schuster (1998) in which 7 in 10 of the new entrants reported that lecturing was their primary instructional method, virtually the same percentage was the senior cohort. This proportion who used lecturing as their primary instructional method (Finkelstein, Seal, & Schuster, 1998) was consistent across types of institutions, and it was higher for men than for women, who were more likely to use participatory teaching techniques. For both cohorts, discussion was most frequent at liberal arts colleges, and seminars were most frequent at doctoral-granting universities. Disciplinary differences can be expected; discussion, for example, was most common in the humanities.

TEACHING AND RESEARCH

The relationship between the teaching activities of faculty members and their research and scholarly activities is of interest to leaders in higher education, to state legislators, and to the public. Most often, the problem is defined as too little time. For example, a statement about the future of higher education was prepared by a prestigious group of people who had received Presidential Young Investigators Awards in engineering, mathematics, and the sciences (Lohmann & Stacey, 1992). Their summary report to the National Science Foundation began with this observation about faculty rewards: "The lack of support, indeed, occasional outright discouragement, of faculty achievements in teaching, instructional scholarship, and public service is among the most pressing problems in higher education" (p. 2).

Three approaches characterize research about the relationship of teaching to research: (a) how the relationship is perceived by faculty members, (b) how activities in the two areas are related to each other, and (c) how productivity in each area is related to faculty compensation. (In this discussion, we use *research* to refer to the full range of faculty investigative and creative activities.)

Perceptions of the Relationship Between Research and Teaching. Faculty members and administrators at 47 research universities were surveyed in 1990–91 about the balance between undergraduate teaching and research at their own institutions. Most said they prefer an equal balance, but the majority of both faculty members and administrators felt their institution actually favored research over teaching. Interestingly, each group (faculty, chairs, deans, and academic affairs officers) thought that the latter view applied less to themselves than to others in the organization. Furthermore, across institutions, all groups felt that their own institution was moving toward research more than they would prefer (Gray, Froh, & Diamond, 1991, 1992). A follow-up survey in 1996 of several of the same universities found movement toward a balance between research and teaching in 8 of the 11 institutions studied. The shift was especially pronounced in responses from deans (Diamond & Adam, 1997). Comparing attitudes of faculty members and administrators at six regional universities in Tennessee, Tang and Chamberlain (1997) found that administrators, but not professors, believed that teaching effectiveness is rewarded at their institutions.

Distinctions between emphasis on research and on teaching emerge when institutional climate is considered. Astin and Chang (1995) devised measures of institutional climate by which institutions could be characterized either as oriented toward students or as oriented toward research, characterizations that were based on survey responses of their faculty members. There was a strong negative correlation (−.69) across the 212 colleges and universities. However, none of the institutions in the top 10% for being oriented toward students was in the top 10% for being oriented toward research. The same issue might be examined at the department level and researchers might pursue differences among disciplines in the kind and amount of expected research.

Relationships Between Productivity in Teaching and Productivity in Research. Studies of this relationship have produced two meta-analyses. The first, Feldman (1987), identified 43 studies, 29 of which were used in his calculations. The average correlation between research accomplishments and teaching effectiveness across studies was slightly positive, but very low (.12). He separately examined 19 dimensions of teaching. The four dimensions with the strongest relationship to research productivity were knowledge of subject matter, intellectual expansiveness, course preparation and organization, and clarity of objectives and requirements. Factors such as age, rank, and personality characteristics were not common correlates of both research productivity and teaching effectiveness.

In the second, Hattie and Marsh (1996) introduced their meta-analysis and outlined arguments that have been advanced

to support a negative, a positive, or a zero relationship between those domains of faculty work. The relationship might be negative, for example, because time invested in one activity takes time away from the other activity. It might be positive, for example, because "everyone knows" that those activities are mutually supporting and enriching. It might be zero, for example, because the activities require very different and unrelated dispositions and personality characteristics. For their meta-analysis, Hattie and Marsh (1996) identified 58 studies of the relationship between teaching and research, including studies analyzed by Feldman (1987). All studies used measures of both instructional effectiveness (usually student evaluations and peer evaluations) and of research productivity (often a weighted index of publications) and were published between 1949 and 1992. The median number of academics participating was 136. One-third of the effect sizes were from liberal arts colleges and two-thirds were from universities.

On the basis of 498 correlations from the 58 studies, the average correlation between the quality of teaching and the quality of research was .06, which was in a positive direction but accounted for less than 1% of the total variability. Only 20% of the nearly 500 correlations were statistically significant. The strongest relationship occurred for the social sciences; for the humanities, the relationship was virtually zero. The relationship was stronger for the presentation aspect of teaching than for aspects of rapport and course management. Time on research was negatively related to time on teaching, but that relationship was complex: Those who spent more time on research have higher research productivity, but those who spent more time on teaching do not necessarily show greater teaching effectiveness. The authors observed,

> It would be folly to conclude that teaching at universities should not be based on research, but this does not mean that only those who partake in research can be effective communicators of this research. . . . At minimum, it is just not defensible to claim that only good researchers are the most effective teachers, or that good teaching follows from more research. Some of our best university teachers do not undertake research. (Hattie & Marsh, 1996, p. 533)

In their discussion of needed research, Hattie and Marsh suggested looking at teaching effectiveness in terms of the orientations that faculty members bring to teaching and learning (such as their personal theories of teaching discussed above) and of whether student evaluations allow for roles other than the common teacher-directed role.

Attempts have been made to reconcile the activities of research and teaching. Brew and Boud (1995) suggested reconciling those activities by emphasizing what is common to both teaching and research: Each is related to learning. Others proposed cultivating the scholarship of teaching, along with other indicators of quality in teaching, so that quality of teaching can be evaluated in ways that parallel how quality in research is assessed (Gibbs, 1995). Barnett (1992) pointed out that in a given department, not everyone must be productive in both areas. Rather, he argued, "Teachers corporately have a responsibility to assist in keeping alive the research tradition" (p. 629), but not all individual teachers must be researchers.

Faculty Compensation and Teaching. Using data from the National Survey of Postsecondary Faculty, Fairweather (1997) examined the basic salary reported by faculty members at 4-year public and independent colleges and universities in relation to teaching-related activities and workload on the one hand, and in relation to research or scholarly activities and productivity on the other. Almost without exception across institutions, there were positive correlations between salary and scholarly productivity, and there were null or negative relationships between salary and teaching productivity. Findings were virtually the same for the 1987–88 and 1992–93 surveys, despite widespread discussion during those periods about the need for greater balance between teaching and research. Such discussion was stimulated in part by the distinctions that Boyer (1990) made among types of scholarship. Thus, Fairweather concluded:

> In any case, regardless of type of institution or program area, faculty members who spent less time on teaching and more time on research, who published more, and who taught graduate students were more likely to receive higher salaries than their colleagues who devoted more of their time and their effort to undergraduate teaching. (p. 57)

Researchers who used data from the 1989 Carnegie survey (Carnegie Foundation, 1991) found similar results for salaries and for attitudes about teaching just as they found similar results for attitudes about teaching when they used a 1986–87 national survey of social science faculty members (M. F. Fox, 1992).

Far from supporting the commonly held belief that teaching effectiveness and research productivity are positively associated, this research failed to find such a relationship in studies of faculty members and of administrators' perceptions, in measures of teaching and research output, or in studies of compensation and productivity. We agree that, as Hattie and Marsh (1996) suggested, now is the time for research into why, even in the face of contrary evidence, the belief persists that research—as shown by publications—strengthens or is necessary for teaching effectiveness. So long as that myth persists, it forces many academics to work against the teaching mission of their institutions. If given limited discretionary time, faculty members, even at liberal arts colleges, prefer to direct that time toward research and writing (Austin & Neal, 1988; Massy & Zemsky, 1994). Is that because of perceived rewards, or is it because faculty members find research and writing to be more controllable and intrinsically satisfying activities?

ISSUES FOR RESEARCH

Although research over the past decade or so has done much to expand knowledge of what faculty members do as teachers, we highlight significant questions that invite further study, and we argue for the use of a greater array of research methods to explore those questions.

What counts as research importantly affects faculty rewards. The analysis of scholarship developed by Boyer (1990) and Rice (1996) argues that recognition and reward should not be limited to the discovery of knowledge but should include the activities of integrating knowledge, applying knowledge, and teaching. Glassick, Huber, and Maeroff (1997) advanced the argument by presenting six standards that are pertinent to assessing faculty work. They contended that the following six standards are commonly used to evaluate research but are rarely applied to teaching: (a) clear goals, (b) adequate preparation, (c) appropriate methods, (d) significant results, (e) effective presentation, and (f) reflective critique. Although the recent book is not a detailed guide to evaluation, it can help academics to think more clearly about faculty work and to document the activities of faculty members more fully. This analysis of scholarship has prompted much discussion in professional organizations and individual institutions, but little is known about specific changes in evaluation practice, which is a significant area for research.

Much of our discussion about faculty members and what they do rests upon survey data. Surveys are inadequate for gaining deep understanding about the complex work lives of faculty members. First, surveys typically depend on self-reports, which are not easily validated. Second, survey data about teaching are often limited to enrollment numbers and classroom contact hours, thereby failing to consider time that is devoted to planning for teaching, evaluating student work, and performing other noncontact tasks. Third, survey data rarely permit inferences about the quality of faculty work. Perhaps most important, survey questions yield information that refers almost exclusively to inputs and outputs; more relevant would be information about the processes of teaching and learning, that is, about the processes that transform inputs into outputs (Menges & Reyes, 1997). Recent discussions about "learning productivity" (*Learning Productivity News,* 1997) are promising. However, attempts to measure learning introduce their own problems, such as the formidable ones of measurement and of the fact that outcome assessments are more relevant to program evaluation than to evaluation of contributions by individual faculty members to student learning.

Blackburn et al. (1986) observed that few investigations are conducted from the perspective of the faculty member; that is, most research reveals what faculty members do but provides little insight about why they do it. Since that 1986 review, the predominant method continues to be survey research. Some surveys are national in scope, and some use sophisticated data analyses, but they necessarily focus more on what faculty members do than on why they do it.

Survey analyses typically take account of only a very few variables at a time and, thus, obscure distinctions that are critical for understanding the life of any particular teacher. An individual's identity is the product of interactions among (a) demographic variables, including age, gender, ethnicity, and socioeconomic background; (b) characteristics of the workplace, including discipline, institution, and department; and (c) personal characteristics, including attitudes, beliefs, knowledge, and values. Bensimon (1996) cautioned against seeking the essential identity of faculty members apart from considering the interactions between individual characteristics and contextual characteristics. "I propose," she said, "that the identities of faculty as teachers or researchers are individually constructed and contextually imposed and that we must address the question of faculty identity and faculty work contextually" (p. 38).

Other methods for fruitful research about faculty members include case studies, interviews, stimulated recall, and shadowing. A few studies have used multiple methods. Case studies that also use interviews lead investigators to consider both variability and commonality. Interviews with 170 faculty members at 16 colleges and universities led B. R. Clark (1987, 1989) to characterize the academic life as "small worlds, different worlds" because of the profound influences of discipline and type of institution. Comprehensive universities, which assume multiple missions, he described as having "inchoate institutional character. . . . Compared to the research universities, the overall institutional culture is weaker and less satisfying for many faculty members, at the same time that disciplinary identifications are weakened as heavy teaching loads suppress research and its rewards" (1989, p. 6). Clark also found variability to be so great that he had difficulty identifying common values across institutions. Academic freedom, for example, means the right to research and publish as one pleases in one sector of academe while in another sector, it means the right to give a failing grade to students. When Tierney and Bensimon (1996) conducted their interviews and case studies, they, too, were alert to variability. Their postmodern orientation led them to "hear divergent representations of reality as neither mistaken nor misguided, but as plausible interpretations of organizational life" (p. 17).

Time diaries, used, for example, by Court (1996) and Boice (1992), are appropriate for quantitative analysis but, depending on the level of detail, those diaries can also point to different ways of defining and approaching teaching tasks. They are excellent starting points for interviews and focus group discussions. In a study of lecturing, Pollio and Humphreys (1996) interviewed 10 award-winning professors whose classes had been recorded. Using the tapes, the researchers could replay specific examples as they asked the professor to "think about the lecture you just gave and tell me what you were aware of when you were teaching that class" (p. 122). Such research might be expanded by also asking students to report their thoughts (cued by an audiotape) at particular points of the class, as was done by Calderhead (1981).

To examine how disciplinary and organizational contexts affect the work of faculty members, Colbeck (1995) shadowed professors as they worked (5 consecutive work days for each of 12 faculty members at two types of universities). Her observations, supplemented with interviews, revealed that many of their activities fulfilled more than one of the purposes that are typically discrete categories on surveys. Her design revealed more integration in faculty work (e.g., between research and undergraduate education) than would otherwise be apparent.

More useful than any of these methods individually would be their use in appropriate combinations. Lenze (1995) based her conclusions about faculty pedagogical knowledge on multiple-year interviews along with surveys and class observations. For his studies of new faculty members, R. Boice (1992) interviewed faculty members, observed their classes, reviewed their time diaries and student evaluations, and interacted with some of them in faculty development programs.

The power of research can be strengthened even more if studies are generated from a coherent theoretical model. Blackburn and Lawrence (1995) turned to the larger social science literature to develop and test a model for predicting aspects of faculty work, including teaching. Their findings were less robust than they had hoped, in part because of limitations in the available data about teaching. Fairweather and Rhoads (1995), though limited to the 1987–88 National Survey of Postsecondary Faculty, fruitfully explored a model that included four policy perspectives related to teaching. They found that rewards and that institutional fit are more important than graduate school socialization in predicting commitment to teaching. The array of motivation theories discussed by contributors to Bess (1997) offer rich possibilities for theory-based research about motivation to teach.

How Faculty Members Develop as Teachers

Faculty development has been addressed in the higher education literature for about 25 years, with attention growing in the past decade. Several aspects of the literature on faculty development are relevant to this review: (a) how teachers learn and improve in their practice, (b) ways in which faculty development is conceptualized, (c) strategies or interventions that assist faculty members to improve their teaching, and (d) challenges and needs of specific groups of teachers who are targeted for professional development support.

HOW TEACHERS IN HIGHER EDUCATION LEARN

Within higher education, theory concerning how teachers learn and improve is not yet fully developed and tested. In an interview study with a small group of faculty members, Austin, Brocato, and LaFleur (1993) concluded that faculty members construct the role of teacher especially through the socialization offered by their observations of other teachers and through feedback from their students and teaching assistants. In summarizing the relevant literature on how teachers develop, Amundsen, Gryspeerdt, and Moxness (1993) cited the finding by Elrick (1990) that changes in teaching occur as a very personal process and evolve out of one's previous practice. They also cited a four-step developmental process for improving teaching, a process that involves moving a teacher from simply presenting information, the first stage, to the interaction of student, teacher, and content at the fourth stage (Sherman et al., 1987).

Another four-stage model was offered by Kugel (1993): (a) initially focusing on the teachers' classroom role, (b) paying attention to the subject matter, (c) having an interest in helping students to learn actively what is taught, and (d) viewing students as able to engage in independent learning.

APPROACHES TO FACULTY DEVELOPMENT

Faculty development has been conceptualized in a variety of ways. Centra (1989) identified four focuses that have emerged since approximately 1970: (a) instructional development, which primarily concerns course design and development, and, more recently, includes considerations of instructional technology; (b) personal development, which focuses on interpersonal skills, career development, and life planning issues; (c) organizational development, which concerns ways to improve the institutional environment to better support teaching; and (d) professional development, which emphasizes that faculty members must fulfill and be supported in their multiple roles of teaching, research, and service. Because faculty development may also involve four different developmental processes (improvement, remediation, retraining, and rejuvenation), the combination of different approaches and the possible emphases on different developmental processes can result in much ambiguity about the purposes of faculty development (Riegle, 1987).

Menges and Brinko (1990) offered a three-dimensional model for planning and assessing faculty development, one that takes into account the faculty role dimension (instructional role, scholarly and creative role, service role, and personal role); the temporal dimension (the extent of career experience); and the organizational dimension (the location of the faculty member's work within the organization). Despite the variety of those conceptions, the term *faculty development* most frequently refers to efforts to improve teaching.

Faculty development efforts that are specifically focused on improving teaching have been widely discussed in the literature. Webb (1996) examined theoretical frames through which faculty and staff development can be viewed, including hermeneutics, postmodernism, and phenomenography. Zuber-Skerritt (1992a, 1992b) emphasized action research as a vehicle for building a theoretical base for professional development. Angelo (1994) critiqued faculty development programs for focusing only on teaching and for ignoring student learning. Angelo called for a shift away from conceptualizing faculty development as an effort to improve teaching to a conceptualization that emphasizes student learning outcomes.

In their extensive discussion of strategies for improving instruction, Paulsen and Feldman (1995) proposed a model that involves processes of unfreezing, changing, and refreezing attitudes and practices. They suggested that teachers can develop as "reflective practitioners" not only through self-reflection but also through feedback from students, department chairs, colleagues, and consultants. Furthermore, they recommended that faculty development efforts be conceptualized and embedded in "a supportive teaching culture." Characteristics of this institutional culture include (a) senior administrators' clear support for teaching, (b) faculty involvement in and ownership of teaching improvement programs, (c) faculty collaboration regarding teaching issues, (d) a faculty development or institutional teaching center, (e) an expanded view of scholarship, (f) a teaching evaluation that is included in tenure and promotion reviews, and (g) a demonstration of teaching ability that is required in the hiring process.

Noting that faculty development can be conceptualized from the perspective of the organization, the faculty development program, or the faculty members themselves, Menges (1997) emphasized the importance of motivation in the design, delivery, and evaluation of faculty development approaches. Programs that are most likely to foster motivation to teach, Menges asserted, (a) encourage collaboration among administrators, faculty members, and faculty development leaders; (b) present consistent priorities concerning the place of teaching in faculty work; (c) encourage faculty involvement in designing programs; and (d) offer individualized activities and a variety of events.

STRATEGIES TO HELP TEACHERS DEVELOP

Literature of the past decade includes several kinds of work pertaining to strategies for teaching improvement. These works can be organized into three categories, which are described next and include relevant research sources.

Book-Length Works That Summarize and Recommend Various Strategies. Examples include Adams (1992) on promoting diversity in the classroom; R. Boice (1996) on basic principles to improve teaching; Brew (1995) on staff development; Brookfield (1995) on becoming a critically reflective teacher; Donald (1997) on improving the environment for learning; Seldin and Associates (1995) on a variety of approaches for improving college teaching; Svinicki and Menges (1996) on honoring exemplary teaching; Travis (1995) on models for improvements in teaching, models that were selected for "their relative novelty for faculty"; Weimer (1990) on strategies to improve instruction; and Wright and Associates (1995) on practices for teaching improvement.

Serials That Regularly Offer Articles on Strategies to Improve Teaching. Examples include *To Improve the Academy* and the *Journal on Excellence in College Teaching,* along with special issues of other journals such as the *Journal of Counseling and Development* (May/June, 1994).

Articles, Chapters, and Books That Describe or Evaluate Specific Strategies to Help Teachers Improve. Examples include Amundsen, Gryspeerdt, and Moxness (1993) on practice-centered inquiry; Angelo (1991) and Angelo and Cross (1993) on classroom research; Austin (1992) on the Lilly Teaching Fellows Program; R. Boice (1987) on the effectiveness of release time as part of faculty development programs; Boice (1995) on "writerly rules" for teachers; Brinko (1990) on instructional consultation with feedback; Brookfield (1990) on being a skillful teacher; Castle, Drake, and Boak (1995) on collaborative reflection as professional development; Katz and Henry (1988) on using faculty partners as part of faculty development; Menges, Mathis, Halliburton, Marincovich, and Svinicki (1988) on approaches to strengthening professional development; Pollio and Eskra (1993) on mentoring relationships; Seldin (1997) on the teaching portfolio; and Taylor (1994) on self-evaluation by teachers.

Strategies to help teachers develop have been categorized in several ways. According to their review of the literature concerning faculty development between 1965 and 1988, Bland and Schmitz (1988) categorized strategies or recommendations using a focus on the individual, departmental, or institutional levels. They concluded that individual-level strategies were most often included in the literature. Strategies mentioned most often were workshops, sabbaticals and leaves, evaluation of faculty members, and growth or professional development plans. After reviewing the literature since the mid-1980s, Weimer and Lenze (1997) organized their discussion of strategies around the five interventions most frequently mentioned in the literature: workshops, consultations, instructional grants, distribution of research material, and colleagues' efforts to help each other improve instruction. Weimer and Lenze concluded that workshops are used most frequently and that efforts of colleagues to help each other to improve their teaching are increasing in frequency.

We note that the literature of the past decade can also be categorized according to the participants: strategies used by teachers individually; strategies involving students; strategies involving colleagues; strategies coordinated by institutional leaders, such as faculty development or teaching improvement offices; and strategies promoted by scholarly and professional associations. Strategies that teachers can use on their own include developing critical reflection skills, preparing teaching portfolios, keeping autobiographical journals, and conducting classroom research. Strategies that involve students include regularly obtaining student feedback, such as through quality circles. Strategies that involve colleagues include orientation programs; teaching fellows programs that enable groups of faculty members to work on teaching-related projects and to discuss teaching issues; workshops, seminars, and retreats; and awards and certificates. The American Sociological Association's Project on Teaching Undergraduate Sociology is an example of a discipline-promoted strategy (Mauksch & Howery, 1986).

NEEDS OF SPECIFIC FACULTY GROUPS

Interest in the particular needs of faculty members at various career stages has increased in recent years (S. M. Clark & Lewis, 1988), resulting in literature that describes and recommends strategies especially appropriate for these specific target groups. Three groups, particularly, are the focus of interest: (a) graduate students serving as teaching assistants (Kirk & Todd-Mancillas, 1991; Nyquist, Abbott, & Wulff, 1989; Nyquist et al., 1991; Nyquist & Wulff, 1992; Saroyan & Amundsen, 1995); (b) new and early career faculty members (Austin, 1992; R. Boice, 1992; Eisen, 1989; Menges & Associates, 1999; Sorcinelli, 1988; Sorcinelli & Austin, 1992); and (c) senior faculty members (Bland & Bergquist, 1997; Finkelstein & LaCelle-Peterson, 1993; Menges, 1985).

ISSUES FOR RESEARCH

Although the literature on strategies to help teachers improve and develop is extensive, most of it is descriptive and rarely offers a theoretical base or research base for choosing and developing programs or for analyzing the effect of programs. Evaluations tend to be single-institution studies and often examine the effect of strategies only on teachers' beliefs and attitudes. As pointed out by Centra (1989) and Weimer and Lenze (1997), the literature less frequently addresses changes in the subsequent behavior of teachers and in the learning of students whose teachers have participated. In a thoughtful reflection about the research–practice divide in faculty development, B. Boice (1997) found that people in the field "however unintentionally, do things to discourage research–practitioners who conduct measurably effective interventions" (1997, p. 372). Additionally, he argued that an unspoken taboo prohibits dealing directly with the problems of procrastination and efficiency. He listed common myths about research in faculty development that perpetuate the research–practice divide and suggested some ways they might change.

Students as Learners

Because learners are the focal participants in the teaching–learning process, understanding students as learners is central to the work of teachers in higher education. The literature about students is much too extensive to review completely in this chapter. Instead, we highlight research about learning: what learning-related characteristics students have, what the processes of learning are, how students develop as learners, which other factors affect student learning, and how students perceive the variables that affect their learning.

For an overview of the extensive research on college students, we recommend chapters within Stage, Anaya, Bean, Hossler, and Kuh (1996) that summarize the field of traditional research on college students, discuss populations that only recently are gaining attention in the college student research, critique the research to date, and provide suggestions for new directions in research about the college student. An earlier volume in that series, *ASHE Reader on College Students* (Kuh, Bean, Hossler, & Stage, 1989), also compiles useful articles, though a number of them were first published before 1985. Pascarella and Terenzini (1991) comprehensively synthesized 20 years of research concerning how college affects students. The volume by Menges, Weimer, and Associates (1996) includes chapters on the characteristics of today's college students, the transition to college, and student motivation; from a student services perspective, similar topics are covered by chapters in Komives, Woodard, and Associates (1996). Voorhees (1997) discusses student learning and cognitive development in community colleges.

Characteristics of Students as Learners

Researchers and teachers in American higher education have benefited from annual surveys of college students that have been conducted since 1966 by the Cooperative Institutional Research Program. Those surveys are administered by the Higher Education Research Institute at the University of California, Los Angeles, with sponsorship from the American Council on Education. The Annual Freshman Survey collects data on demographic, experiential, and attitudinal issues among entering college freshmen, and it produces both individual campus profiles and national normative data. The 1996 report, for example, was based on more than 250,000 questionnaires from students at approximately 500 2- and 4-year colleges and universities in the United States. Highlights are available each January in the *Chronicle of Higher Education*.

A summary of trends concerning American freshmen from 1966 through 1985 was produced in 1987 from those surveys (Astin, Green, & Korn, 1987). Over the 20-year period, the balance of men and women reversed, with women making up the majority of the freshman class in 1985. Additionally, the number of minority students entering classes greatly increased by 1985. Although the age of first-time, full-time entering students remained constant from 1968 to 1985, the overall age of undergraduates increased considerably, particularly in community colleges and institutions with high numbers of commuters. Academic skills declined. On the one hand, high school grades had increased "dramatically" overall, which the researchers interpreted as evidence of grade inflation; on the other hand, a greater proportion of students in 1985 as compared to 1971 said they would need tutoring help.

Significant shifts also occurred in intended majors and careers between 1965 and 1985. Majors in business, computer science, and engineering became more popular, whereas education and the traditional liberal arts, including the humanities, the fine and performing arts, the social sciences, and the natural sciences, declined in popularity. Careers as educators, as research scientists, and as clergy lost appeal during those years, whereas careers in areas such as business, which does not require postbaccalaureate work and is relatively high paying, grew in popularity. Of particular note between 1965 and 1985, students became more interested in materialistic goals, such as "being very well-off financially," and were less committed to altruism and social concern, such as "developing a meaningful philosophy of life."

A more recent analysis (Astin, Parrott, Korn, & Sax, 1997) summarized trends during the 30 years from 1966 to 1996. During the late 1980s, the long-standing trends toward more emphasis on material goals and less emphasis on social issues and problems were reversed; students began to show a growing orientation toward social activism and an interest in protecting the environment. Comparing a 1980 survey of students with a more recent study of students in five colleges and universities, Levine and Hirsch (1991) also found evidence of less selfishness, more involvement in social action, and more volunteerism (along with increased optimism in volunteers). The 1996 freshman survey found that precollege involvement in volunteer work was at a record high level.

The 1996 data revealed that grade inflation is continuing, with 31.5% of entering freshmen reporting A averages in high school; the low was 12.5% in 1969. At the same time, more than one-third of the 1996 entering freshmen reported being frequently "bored in class," compared with a low in 1985 of about one quarter. Additionally, 35.7% of the 1996 entering freshmen indicated that they studied 6 or more hours per week, whereas 43.7% studied for a comparable time in 1987. Nevertheless, students reported more self-confidence and more optimism than they had in previous years about aspects of their academic future such as the likelihood of achieving a B average or better, of earning a bachelor's degree, and of graduating with honors.

Financial concerns are on the minds of students. More than one-third of entering freshmen in 1996 indicated that financial assistance was a "very important" reason for selecting a college to attend, a figure much higher than the low of 13.6% who answered similarly in 1976. Furthermore, 41.1% of the entering freshmen in 1996 indicated that they expected to get jobs to contribute to their college expenses, compared with a low of 34.7% having that expectation in 1989. Research now tells us little about how changes in available resources such as student loans affect enrollment, learning, and subsequent employment.

HOW STUDENTS LEARN

Literature about human learning has expanded greatly over the past quarter century. As P. M. King (1996) explained in introducing a comprehensive and carefully crafted analysis of the literature on student cognition and learning, "A dizzying array of approaches to student learning exists in the professional literature" with "a common theme of these approaches being . . . that the key to understanding student learning is understanding student differences" (p. 220). Reviewing this literature, P. M. King (1996) concluded that three factors affect student learning. First, cognitive factors (how individuals recognize, process, and evaluate information) affect learning. Cognitive factors can involve (a) learning styles and strategies (how students reason) and (b) learning and epistemology (why students reason as they do) (pp. 220–221). Second, motivational factors affect learning. And third, social factors in the learning context influence learning.

Writing about cognitive factors that relate to learning, P. M. King (1996) discussed research on learning styles and strategies, research on surface and deep approaches to learning, research on brain functioning that helps to explain thinking and reasoning processes (such as left-brain and right-brain functioning), research on field dependence or field independence in cognitive style, research on psychological type as expressed in perceiving and judging, research on multiple intelligences, and research on scientific reasoning. We refer readers to King's thorough overview and synthesis, and, here, we offer selected examples of the past decade's research.

A major theme about students' learning concerns (a) learning strategies, which are defined as "a sequence of procedures for accomplishing learning" (Schmeck, 1988, p. 5, cited in King, 1996, p. 221) and (b) learning styles, which are defined as "a predisposition to adopt a particular learning strategy" (Das, 1988, p. 101, cited in King, 1996, p. 221). Claxton and Murrell (1987) produced a comprehensive review on learning styles and their implications for improving educational practices. The reviewers organized the various approaches to their study of learning styles around four models: instructional preference, social interaction, information processing, and personality. In addition to explaining how knowledge of learning styles can be helpful to students, teachers, advisers, and administrators, Claxton and Murrell (1987) suggested three areas in which research should be advanced: (a) by examining how teaching methods that are incongruent with students' learning styles will affect learning; (b) by examining the research on relationships among learning styles, disciplinary perspectives, epistemology, and age; and (c) by examining research to develop instruments that measure cultural differences across learning styles.

Some researchers have found wide variation among students in terms of preferred learning styles. By studying students at a regular university and a distance university, Vermunt (1996) found that students demonstrated four different learning styles: undirected, reproduction directed, meaning directed, and application directed. Each style involves different cognitive strategies, mental models of learning, learning goals, and views of the effectiveness of instructional strategies. Schroeder (1993) summarized research showing that new, nontraditional students differ from traditional students in their preferred learning styles. He reported that approximately half of college students prefer a concrete–active learning style, and only 10% prefer an abstract–reflective pattern, but faculty preferences are roughly the opposite, favoring an abstract–reflective style.

Faculty members tend to teach in the ways by which they learn best; however, when encountering teaching styles at odds with their preferred ways of learning, students feel frustrated. An increased use of strategies that encourage experiential learning, such as discussions, simulations, service learning, and debates, is recommended. Other research that concerns learning styles includes: (a) Long and Walsh (1993) on self-directed learning at community colleges, which describes self-directed learning in situations when teaching and learning styles differ; (b) Severiens and Ten-Dam (1994) on gender differences in learning styles; (c) Lonka and Lindblom-Ylanne (1996) on epistemologies, conceptions of learning, and study practices of 1st- and 5th-year psychology and medical students in a Finnish university; and (d) Vermunt and Van Rijswijk (1988) on relationships between self-regulated learning and students' learning styles.

According to Pintrich (1995), self-regulated learning involves three aspects of academic learning: (a) actively controlling available resources, such as time and place of study; (b) controlling and changing motivational beliefs, such as beliefs about efficacy and anxiety; and (c) controlling cognitive learning strategies, such as using deep processing. Contributors to Pintrich's volume discussed research and practice about self-regulated learning in various fields and disciplines. Research about self-regulation can be informed by investigations of self-management in organizations. Rousseau (1997) placed emphasis on research that links goal setting with self-management, the latter focusing "on the learning and orchestration of cognitive processes for acquiring skills, self-monitoring progress, and providing self-reinforcement" (p. 527). The synthesis of research on self-directed learning by Candy (1991) resulted in a profile of the autonomous learner.

Research of particular interest to teachers (also highlighted in P. M. King, 1996) concerns the extent to which students use surface strategies (meeting requirements at a minimal level, usually through rote learning); deep strategies (working to develop competence and interest in the subject, such as trying to relate new knowledge to previous knowledge); or achieving strategies (striving to receive high grades, even if the subject is not of interest, by performing the activities typical of good students). In a tertiary institution in Hong Kong, Kember and Gow (1990) studied the usefulness of two instruments for examining those strategies: Biggs' Study Process Questionnaire and Ramsden's Approaches to Studying Inventory. Research on studying and involvement has been conducted with students in several countries, including, for example, Hong Kong (Kember & Gow, 1990), New Zealand (Willis, 1993), and the United Kingdom (Hayes & Richardson, 1995). Richardson (1994, 1995) contributed to research on cultural specificity of instruments to study students' approaches to studying. Hayes and Richardson (1995) furthered knowledge about how approaches to studying relate to gender, subject, and institutional context.

Other researchers have investigated the relationships between study approaches and academic involvement (Willis, 1993), as well as study approaches as they relate to study time and academic performance (Kember, Jamieson, Pomfret, & Wong, 1995). Kember and Gow (1994) found that deep learning was more likely in departments where teaching encouraged the development of critical thinking, independent reading, and problem-solving skills rather than in departments where teaching emphasized knowledge transmission through presenting information to students.

How Students Develop as Learners

Like the research on how students gather and process information, the literature on how students develop has been extensive, including both cognitive and psychosocial theories. We will highlight a few theories about developmental changes in assumptions about knowledge, because those findings have implications for the teaching–learning process. Belenky, Clinchy, Goldberger, and Tarule (1986) explored women's ways of knowing as they built on earlier work by W. G. Perry (1970), who examined ethical and intellectual development of male students. Belenky et al. conducted interviews with women in numerous educational circumstances and posited a stage theory of distinctive ways in which women develop self, voice, and mind, thus leading to the highest level that they called "connected knowing."

The reflective–judgment model of intellectual development (P. M. King & Kitchener, 1994; Kitchener & King, 1981, 1990) concerns one's assumptions about knowledge and one's ability to make reasonable judgments. This model includes seven stages organized into three levels: prereflective thinking, quasi-reflective thinking, and reflective thinking. The model has been developed from extensive research on traditional-age college students, some research on nontraditional-age freshmen and seniors, one study on African-American students, and some studies of gender differences. An overall conclusion from such research is that involvement in higher education helps students learn to make better and more reasonable judgments regarding complex problems (P. M. King & Kitchener, 1993).

A 5-year study by Baxter Magolda (1992) followed 101 students as they progressed from their freshman year through their first postgraduate year. She described four different ways of knowing, each supported by a particular set of epistemological assumptions. The four ways of knowing are absolute knowing ("receiving and mastering knowledge," p. 37); transitional knowing ("accepting that some knowledge is uncertain," p. 47); independent knowing ("assuming that knowledge is mostly uncertain," p. 55); and contextual knowing ("integrating one's own and others' ideas," p. 168). Baxter Magolda's research also revealed gender-related patterns and resulted in recommendations to support student learning: "validating the student as a knower, situating learning in the students' [sic] own experience, and defining learning as jointly constructing meaning" (p. 270). Those suggestions also appear in her more recent work (Baxter Magolda, 1994, 1996).

Each approach to the development of learners presents an epistemological model, a view of how people come to know. Hofer and Pintrich (1997) critically examined several of the models we have described and the associated research programs. As one area for future research, they identified four dimensions that are common to most models and that they believe form the core structure of an individual's epistemological theory. Two dimensions deal with the nature of knowledge, namely, certainty of knowledge and simplicity of knowledge, and two deal with the process of knowing, namely, source knowledge and justification for knowing.

Other Factors Affecting Student Learning

Research on student learning processes tends to be embedded in an understanding that both characteristics of students and factors in the educational environment are important. Stating that "we can never assume that the effect of teaching on student learning is what we expect it to be," Ramsden (1992) explained that "students' thoughts and actions are profoundly affected by the educational context or environment in which they learn" (p. 6).

Although both characteristics of students and instructional quality affect student success in important ways, as R. P. Perry (1997) pointed out, "Surprisingly little systematic inquiry has been undertaken to explore their combined effects" (p. 11). His comprehensive review explored the links between selected student attributes and the quality of instruction. It paid particular attention to lecturing, the most frequently used teaching strategy, and to perceived control, individuals' perceptions of their "capacity to influence and to predict events in the environment" (p. 2). He showed that a sense of loss of control can interfere with effective instruction and thus put a student at risk. Although "effective teaching enhances achievement when students perceive having some control over past test performances, . . . lack of control results in poor performance in the presence of effective instruction" (R. P. Perry, 1997, p. 46). Certain cognitive schema seem to function as "buffers" and protect students in the face of negative results when loss of control is experienced. In a later article, R. P. Perry, Schonwetter, Magnusson, and Struthers (1994) studied the relationship between explanatory schemas and the quality of college instruction, and they discussed the buffer qualities provided by students' explanatory schemas.

Attributional retraining seeks to alter how students think about their successes and failures and, thus, to affect students' motivation and achievement. R. P. Perry, Hechter, Menec, and Weinberg (1993) reviewed studies that have been reported since 1985 about attributional retraining. They concluded that this approach has considerable potential, along with other effective teaching efforts, especially in addressing problems associated with loss of control. Menec et al. (1994) reported experimental research and concluded that those who develop attributional retraining programs should consider both classroom contextual factors, including quality of instruction, and students' individual differences.

In addition to extensive and theoretically grounded research on the relationship between student characteristics and the quality of instruction, a variety of more modest studies have highlighted factors that teachers should keep in mind as they work with students. A. King (1992a, 1992b) found that students gain from reviewing notes about material and from summarizing material from a lecture, but that long-term retention is most likely to benefit from question-generating exercises. A study reported in *Teaching Sociology* (Wyatt, 1992) revealed that variables associated with skipping class include disliking the class, devoting little time to studying, and being female. McCabe and Trevino (1996) summarized trends over time related to a longstanding concern of teachers: cheating. Although cheating overall has increased only modestly, the increase for women is significant, and both men and women students report using a wider array of cheating behaviors on tests and examinations.

Studies focusing on student characteristics are complemented by research about the kinds of environments that support student learning and development. For example, Gardiner (1994) identified an array of problems in undergraduate education, including curricula with limited breadth, depth, and coherence; courses that fail to challenge students' misconceptions; insufficient expectations for hard work on the part of students; testing that emphasizes memory over understanding; lack of extensive student–faculty interaction; and minimal attention to the quality of advising. Arguing for a "redesign" of higher education in response to those problems, he recommended that institutional administrators and faculty members define institutional missions clearly, articulate outcomes, hold students to high expectations, encourage students to be involved actively in their learning, provide comprehensive assessment of outcomes, and develop climates more supportive of student learning and development. Drawing on both research and interviews with faculty members and administrators, Donald (1997) also identified strategies and policies that create optimal environments for student learning and development.

Supplemental instruction gives support both to students in high-risk courses and to high-risk students (Arendale, 1994). Although much of the writing about supplemental instruction is anecdotal, a large-scale study at one institution (82 sections from a variety of courses) found benefits from supplemental instruction for participating students over nonparticipants, especially in social science courses (Kochenour et al., 1997).

More is known about how students develop as learners than about what they actually learn. Perhaps the largest national assessment of college students' achievement (in general education) was based on the College Basic Academic Subject Examination (Osterlind, 1997). More than 75,500 undergraduates from 56 colleges and universities were tested from 1988 to 1993 to assess both factual knowledge and reasoning skills. Scores in English were generally lower than those in math, science, and social studies. Significant and interesting differences were related to race and gender. Those and other results (e.g., Pascarella, Edison, Hagadorn, Nora, & Terenzini, 1996) suggest the value of more ambitious national projects that would systematically sample achievement of college and university students.

Students' Perceptions of Variables Affecting Their Learning

Research on students' perceptions of teaching and learning can be useful to teachers. Analyzing 31 studies of students' and teachers' perceptions of important instructional characteristics, Feldman (1988) found high similarity (average correlation .71) between the views of teachers and of students. Using 18 of the studies, Feldman reported that students rated more highly than faculty members the importance of a teacher's stimulation of interest, elocutionary skills, availability and helpfulness, and concerns and respect for students. In a study of 116 undergraduates across majors at a small state university, Nance and Nance (1990) found that students perceived that most professors lectured and offered little class discussion, and that students thought their job was to sit and take notes in order to take the examination.

Pollio (1992) reported a study in which undergraduates indicated their preference for learning-oriented instructors and instructors indicated preference for learning-oriented students, but both thought students and faculty members tended to be grade oriented. Studying the use of seven teaching practices that have been widely publicized as effective, including attention to student–faculty contact, encouragement of cooperation between students, active learning, prompt feedback, encouragement of time on task, high expectations, and respect for diverse talents and ways of learning, Negron-Morales, Vasquez-Rodriguez, and De Leon-Lozada (1996) found that, whereas teachers reported that they often or very often used those practices, students reported that teachers only rarely or sometimes used the practices.

Some researchers have explored strategies that students perceive as helpful to their learning. Students in Australia were asked about teachers' behaviors that help their learning, as well as behaviors that hinder it. The five behaviors most often mentioned as helping learning were use of practical application and experiential learning, clear presentations and explanations, teachers asking questions of the class, and class discussion of the material (J. A. Clarke, 1995).

Those findings about how students learn and develop have important implications. First, teachers must recognize the diversity of students: students bring to their studies different approaches to learning and different epistemological assumptions about knowledge. Even though teachers recognize the differences and realize that students have varying strengths, teachers can encourage students to expand their learning strategies, to challenge their assumptions, and to develop expanded thinking and reasoning skills. Although the research about learning is vast, many questions remain about how people learn. For example, further research on relationships between such variables as students' cultural background or race and preferred learning strategies and learning styles would be helpful in higher education, as would further research about how teachers can best support and challenge students as learners.

Content: What Is Taught and Learned

Literature on content—what is often more broadly termed *the curriculum*—is challenging to review, because it is wide ranging in its nature and focus. As Stark and Lattuca (1997) pointed out, we see a proliferation of books and articles on special topics concerning the curriculum, but we find little work that synthesizes the thinking on curriculum or content. They noted useful pieces addressing particular topics related to curriculum issues. The topics included "Research on Academic Programs: An Inquiry into an Emerging Field" (Conrad & Pratt, 1986);

Designing and Improving Courses and Curricula in Higher Education (Diamond, 1989); *Meeting the Mandate: Renewing the College Departmental Curriculum* (Toombs & Tierney, 1991); and *New Life for the College Curriculum* (Gaff, 1991).

In their book *Shaping the College Curriculum: Academic Plans in Action,* Stark and Lattuca (1997) offered a synthesis of the literature on curriculum and content in higher education that was more thorough than anything previously available. They have synthesized earlier literature and discussed topics such as calls for reform, recurring debates about the curriculum, course and program planning, and the influence of academic fields on content and curriculum. One of their most useful contributions was conceptualizing the curriculum as the "academic plan," which includes "purposes, activities, and ways of measuring success" (p. 9). They asserted that an academic plan, or curriculum, always involves eight important elements, even if teachers or planners do not explicitly explain them: purpose (the goals for knowledge, skills, and attitudes to be learned); content (the subject matter); sequence (the arrangement of the subject matter); learners (the characteristics of and information about learners); instructional processes (the activities through which learning takes place); instructional resources (the materials and settings that support learning), evaluation (the strategies to determine if learning results in behavioral change); and adjustment (the changes in the academic plan that result from experience and evaluation).

Stark and Lattuca (1997) also indicated that the academic plan is influenced by external factors (e.g., society, disciplinary associations, the marketplace); organizational factors (e.g., resources or the government); and internal factors (e.g., faculty members, students, the mission of a program). In their work, Stark and Lattuca (a) provided conceptual guidance for those involved in planning, implementing, and evaluating teaching and learning experiences at the course, program, and institutional levels; (b) showed that academic planning involves more than mere consideration of content; (c) offered a conceptual framework for understanding and connecting various issues that relate to organization of the teaching and learning process; and (d) summarized and synthesized much research related to content and other aspects of the academic plan.

Another theme about content and curriculum concerns what content is worthy to be taught and how the content should be taught. The authors of three noteworthy collections of articles and chapters explored and illustrated the debates. Conrad and Haworth (1990) produced an edited volume titled *Curriculum in Transition: Perspectives on the Undergraduate Experience* in which they (Haworth & Conrad, 1990) argued that a reexamination and transformation of the American undergraduate curriculum was occurring in the 1980s, a time when various "stakeholders" took positions on the purpose, content, and appropriate approaches to pedagogy and inquiry. Four forces, they asserted, contributed to the discussions: (a) changing demographics; (b) a "traditionalist educational policy agenda" at the national level, which called for renewed attention to basic skills, the humanities, and accountability; (c) a more pluralistic environment; and (d) the emergence of new perspectives such as multiculturalism, feminism, critical theory, and interpretivism. Debates around the curriculum, according to Conrad and

Haworth, were framed primarily by "traditionalists," on the one hand, who claimed certain truths existed that should be taught, and "emerging voices," on the other hand, who saw knowledge as being socially constructed and, therefore, as representing decisions about what should be taught and learned as contestable territory.

In another volume published 5 years later in the same series, Haworth and Conrad (1995) emphasized that the "culture wars"—as the debates that have occurred in the 1980s and 1990s concerning curriculum issues are frequently called—have revolved around what knowledge is worth having, how knowledge should be organized and taught, and who should make decisions about what is worthy to be taught. Articles in both of those extensive volumes illuminate debates about knowledge, content, and pedagogy.

In addition to debates in scholarly publications and popular discourse about what the curriculum should include, the literature includes descriptions of specific efforts to revise what is taught and how it is taught through adding or integrating new areas into institutions' offerings. Chapters in the *Handbook of the Undergraduate Curriculum* by Gaff, Ratcliff, and Associates (1996), as well as chapters in the two volumes discussed above, highlight a number of those new developments, including interdisciplinary studies, teaching across the curriculum, multiculturalism, learning communities, and integration of technology as a new vehicle for educational delivery. *Revitalizing General Education in a Time of Scarcity* (Kanter, Gamson, & London, 1997) is timely in discussing general education, a topic of both long-standing and current interest in American undergraduate education. Their book includes case examples of institutions of many types that have grappled with the meanings and forms that general education can take.

Another theme pertaining to content and curriculum is the importance of the discipline in affecting both how teachers teach and how students learn. A substantive body of research and theoretical literature concerns the particularities of disciplines and disciplinary influences on teaching and learning. Donald (1986) examined and described disciplinary differences in the aims of learning and the criteria for defining learning, with attention to differences in the kinds of concepts emphasized, the logical structures in place, the truth criteria used, and the methods typically used. In related works, Donald examined disciplinary differences in content and curricular structures (1987); in thinking processes, including conceptualizing, analyzing, and reasoning (1992a, 1992b, 1993); in approaches to validating knowledge in the field (1995); and as an influence on the quality of learning (1997, Ch. 2).

Lattuca and Stark (1995) reported that their analyses of task force reports concerning improvements in undergraduate majors showed that a discipline's methodology, pedagogy, and curricular innovation were affected strongly by its characteristic epistemologies. Overviewing a number of studies, Pollio (1996) concluded that the university consists of two cultures—the sciences and the humanities—that differ on many dimensions, including methodology, teaching practices, grading habits, and students' preferred teaching behaviors. Teaching is affected not only by the inherent characteristics of disciplines but also by the external factors that are particular to disciplines and that

lead to variations in teaching and learning situations. Those factors are illustrated, for example, by the changes occurring in the accounting field (Wyer, 1993) in response to specific changes in licensing requirements.

Pedagogical strategies, curricular purposes, and goals for learning cannot be understood, studied, or selected without considering the disciplinary context. Stated more broadly, the literature on content and curriculum is diverse in its scope; nevertheless, any examination of teaching in higher education would be incomplete without emphasizing the relevance of content, disciplinary context, and societal debates about what is worth knowing. Those issues constitute the context in which teachers do their work.

The Teaching and Learning Environment

The late 1980s and 1990s brought many books for faculty members, administrators, and researchers about teaching and learning. Some of them were new (e.g., Brown & Atkins, 1988; B. G. Davis, 1993; J. R. Davis, 1993; Donald, 1997; Erickson & Strommer, 1991; Katz & Henry, 1988; Weimer, 1990). Others were new editions of respected works (e.g., Eble, 1988; Lowman, 1995; McKeachie, 1994). Edited collections also appeared, but are too many to list in this chapter. Some authors critiqued prevailing assumptions and instructional procedures. Ropers-Huilman (1998), for example, argued that feminism challenges traditional teaching and learning in higher education in three areas (the role and nature of knowledge, the meaning and role of difference and equality, and the functions of power relations) and went on to discuss how those areas can be reconceptualized through feminist perspectives.

Research confirmed that students consider the classroom experience to be extremely important (e.g., Volkwein, 1997) and that student–faculty contact outside the classroom has positive influences on students (Pascarella & Terenzini, 1991). Research accumulated about the limitations of lectures for most of the important goals of instruction (Pascarella & Terenzini, 1991); nevertheless, lecturing continued to be the dominant instructional method (Gardiner, 1994). Techniques that increase student engagement were advocated as effective for enhancing learning and satisfaction. Examples include active learning (Sutherland & Bonwell, 1996); collaborative learning (Bosworth & Hamilton, 1994); and problem-based learning (Wilkerson & Gijselaers, 1996). The "seven principles for good practice in undergraduate education" (Chickering & Garrison, 1991) were widely disseminated, and more specialized sets of principles emerged from other reviews of research, such as principles for teaching high-risk students (Stahl, Simpson, & Hayes, 1992). Electronic technologies were incorporated into instruction with the promise of virtual campuses and improved learning environments (Van Dusen, 1997).

In this section, we discuss research relevant to the creation of teaching and learning environments. Consistent with our definition of teaching as "the intentional arrangement of situations in which appropriate learning will occur," we have organized our discussion according to three phases of instruction: planning, implementing, and evaluating. During the planning phase, the teacher is involved primarily with the content of instruction. That is, in light of curricular requirements, available resources, and learner characteristics, the teacher plans appropriate procedures for instruction and evaluation. During the implementation phase, those plans are realized when learners interact with teaching materials and when the teacher interacts with learners. During the evaluation phase, the teacher reflects on the events of instruction, reviews evidence about student learning, grades student work, and considers modifications and revisions. In practice, these three phases are, of course, less discrete than described here. We separate them only for the convenience of this review.

Planning for Teaching and Learning

Geis (1996) enumerated eight key decisions about the process of developing new courses or revising existing ones. Some of those decisions are influenced by internal factors (department, discipline, students, and so on) and some by external factors (market forces, accrediting and licensing agencies, and so on). Using surveys and interviews of faculty members, Lowther and Stark (1990) found that the teachers' discipline was the major influence in course planning. Discipline constrains beliefs about what should be taught and about student strengths and weaknesses (Cashin & Downey, 1995). Faculty members have little detailed knowledge about a student's difficulties and how to respond to them (Lenze, 1995); faculty members also sometimes seem uncomfortable discussing matters of student motivation and learning styles (Stark & Lattuca, 1997). Instructional methods are chosen more often according to personal preferences or trial and error rather than through systematic attention to "the nature of the expected learning, the nature of the student group or audience, and many varied practical constraints, such as the size of the class" (Stark & Lattuca, 1997, p. 288). Weston and Cranton (1986) and Stark and Lattuca (1997) offered frameworks to aid faculty members in making decisions about instructional methods.

Both student cognition and student motivation should be considered when planning courses (Pintrich, 1989). In their proposed model, McKeachie, Pintrich, Lin, Smith, and Sharma, (1990) asserted that "the effects of instruction are mediated by students' cognitive and motivational characteristics" (p. 3). Thus, teachers should be concerned with outcomes such as motivation for continued learning and attitudes about oneself as a learner. Hagan and Weinstein (1995) discussed how goals can be related to motivation-based outcomes, including self-regulation and self-efficacy. They distinguished between mastery goals (that focus on learning course content) and performance goals (that focus on outcomes such as grades), and they discussed which instructional methods and evaluation tasks correspond to those goals.

Instructional designers have long stressed the need to align instructional methods and evaluative techniques with instructional goals (S. A. Cohen, 1987). Against the background of constructivist learning theory, Biggs (1996) applied the alignment principle to higher order learning goals. The usual teaching methods (lecture and discussion) and the usual assessment techniques (papers and examinations) are not in alignment with the kind of learning called for when students are asked to "make meaning." For those goals, Biggs asserted that learning

activities should be controlled less by the teacher and more by peers and by students and that a greater variety of assessment tasks should be used. The tasks that students are expected to complete affect their approaches to studying and, consequently, how well they learn (Crooks, 1988), but the qualitative studies needed to explore such issues are less common in North American research than in research abroad (Entwistle, 1995).

Maps of the major concepts for a course can inform decisions about selecting and sequencing content. Donald (1983) illustrated course knowledge structures. See also the work on knowledge maps by Dansereau (1995) in, for example, psychology courses (Czuchry & Dansereau, 1996). Angelo and Cross (1993) suggested exercises for mapping concepts in class. Naveh-Benjamin and Lin (1988) found that such exercises facilitated student learning.

Implementing Teaching and Learning Plans

The implementation phase of teaching brings students into interaction with their teachers and with materials and exercises provided by teachers. Research relevant to this phase usually investigates particular teaching methods or media. We discuss research about instructional climate in general, about particular teaching methods, and about electronic technologies as mediators of teaching and learning.

To guide our analysis, we refer to Laurillard's (1993) analytic framework, a framework reflecting European research that we believe deserves wider attention in North America. Laurillard distinguished between learning in everyday life and "academic" learning. "Everyday knowledge is located in our experience of the world. Academic knowledge is located in our experience of our experience of the world" (1993, p. 26). Academic learning is second-order experience, which has been abstracted from direct experience and which is usually represented in exposition and argument. "Thus teaching is a rhetorical activity: it is mediated learning, allowing students to acquire knowledge of someone else's way of experiencing the world" (1993, p. 29).

Laurillard found phenomenographic studies of learning to be most informative for a principled teaching strategy, and she pointed out shortcomings of other bases for research on teaching, namely instructional design, intelligent tutoring systems, and instructional psychology. The strength of the phenomenographic approach (Marton & Booth, 1997, especially chapter 6; Marton & Ramsden, 1988) lies in its basis in empirical studies of learning, that is, studies of real teachers working with real students. Phenomenographic research has indicated that learning is most successful with a democratic and cooperative style in the form of dialogue between students and teacher.

Phenomenographic research indicates, according to Laurillard (1993), that effective teaching has four characteristics. First, effective teaching is *discursive*—a description, usually by the teacher, of the topic at hand with sufficient teacher–student dialogue to ensure that teacher and student hold similar conceptions of the topic and that they agree on the goals and tasks of learning. Second, effective teaching is *adaptive;* that is, the teacher makes adjustments according to what students are doing. Third, effective teaching is *interactive.* Students must be actively engaged with the material being learned and must get feedback on their activities. Finally, effective teaching is *reflec-*

tive, as shown by the products of learning by which students demonstrate to teachers what they have learned.

These four characteristics are easy to endorse in principle, but their implementation is subject to severe constraints. This approach requires that students be actively involved in finding knowledge, in testing hypotheses, and in interpreting results (Ramsden, 1992), but those activities may seem incompatible with situations where classes are large and where teacher and student behaviors fit the transmission metaphor of instruction better than the conversation metaphor (Tiberius, 1986). We shall see that some methods and media fare better than others under this analytic framework.

INSTRUCTIONAL CLIMATE

Instruments for examining the psychosocial climate of instruction include the College Classroom Environment Scale (Winston, Vahala, Nichols, Gillis, Wintrow, & Rome, 1994), which yields scores on six scales (cathectic learning climate, professorial concern, inimical audience, academic rigor, affiliation, and structure) and can be used for appraising teaching and for evaluating instructional innovations. Fraser and collaborators developed the College and University Classroom Environment Inventory (Fraser & Treagust, 1986) for small seminar classes and the Science Laboratory Environment Inventory (Fraser, Giddings, & McRobbie, 1992) for laboratory settings. By varying instructions that are given to people who complete those instruments, researchers can compare actual and preferred environments, as well as perceptions of teachers and of students. Fraser and Tobin (1991) described a "personal form" that parallels such class inventories. Studies pertinent to instructional climate have dealt with on-task behaviors, taking notes, interpersonal interactions, and questioning.

On-Task Behaviors. For meaningful learning to occur, students must be attentive to their learning tasks. It is no easy matter for instructors to ensure that students are on task, although being on task is essential in many "active learning" techniques. W. C. Williams (1985) differentiated three levels of cognitive processing and gave examples of teacher and student verbal behaviors that match each level. At the highest level, for example, students show that they discriminate among subtle stimuli, associate the stimuli with previous learning, and exhibit insight that reveals broader-based meaning.

Lower levels of cognitive processing and attention are much more common in college classrooms than are higher levels. Pollio (1984) found that grade-oriented students (compared with those who were learning oriented) were more likely to be seen as on task by observers but were off task in terms of the thoughts they reported. Self-reports showed grade-oriented students to be on task only 48% of the time (compared with 69% for learning-oriented students), leading the author to note that "the student stream of consciousness is a highly variable and fickle process" (p. 15) and to recommend gathering student reports of their thoughts as "useful and non-threatening feedback to the caring lecturer" (p. 16). In a later study, Pollio (1994) asked students in six classes to identify three events that "stand out for you" in the course and to describe one of them in detail. Of the detailed descriptions, 25% were classified into off-target

categories (e.g., about other people). Engagement likely varies with such variables as class size and teaching method. In a problem-based class, Geerligs (1994) found that thoughts reported by students were related to the learning task 74% of the time.

If we return to Laurillard's (1993) framework, we see that none of the characteristics of effective teaching can be present when students are off task, which according to this research is not infrequent for many students. Typical teaching methods in typical classrooms do not effectively promote the kind of on-task cognitions that are essential for learning.

Taking Notes. The most evident student behavior in class, apart from verbal behavior, is note taking. In reviewing studies of the relationship between note taking and measures of learning, Kiewra (1985a) concluded that only 31 of 56 studies clearly supported the efficacy of taking notes. Students who reviewed the instructor's notes generally performed better than those who reviewed only their own notes (Kiewra, 1985b), and students using the teacher's notes did as well on higher order examination questions but less well on factual questions than students who took their own notes (Kiewra & Benton, 1987). Later work by Kiewra (1988, 1991) explored cognitive variables (e.g., control processes and learning strategies) that might affect note taking. He recommended instructional aids, such as a matrix, that are intended to engage those cognitive variables, and he proposed a model to guide research on autonomous note taking.

A theory of note taking derived from students' perceptions about note taking was presented by Van Meter, Yokoi, and Pressley (1994). Their ethnographic interview procedure revealed aspects of note taking that are not apparent from other research, such as how notetaking strategies change with increased college experience, how verbatim note taking (contrary to what might be expected) can be compatible with deep processing, and how note taking interacts with other studying strategies.

In terms of Laurillard's (1993) framework, if note taking lacks dialogue, teachers cannot adapt to students' level of understanding. Teachers would have to respond to notes if dialogue were to occur.

Interpersonal Interaction. Professors differ by disciplines in their propensity for interactive classroom behaviors. In an observational study of 124 professors, Erdle and Murray (1986) found that interpersonal behaviors were more characteristic of professors in the arts and humanities, whereas science teachers were more likely to follow a task approach. Students and professors differed in the interactions they found appropriate. Amsel and Fichten (1990) found that, despite agreement between students and teachers in many areas, professors were more welcoming of students' requests than students expected; however, students thought that grade-related requests were more acceptable than professors did.

In a questionnaire study, Fassinger (1995) found that men rated themselves as more confident and involved in class interactions, and that women rated themselves as better prepared and more interested in the subject matter and the comments of others in the class. Women professors were seen as more approachable and supportive, and women students in classes taught by women professors saw themselves as having more confidence and participating more.

Krupnick's (1985) videotape analysis showed that in classes with male instructors and a majority of male students, male students talked 2.5 times longer than females did, whereas female students talked 3.0 times longer with female than with male instructors. Canada and Pringle (1995) examined interactions by gender over time in 103 classes at a college to which men were admitted for the first time in 1987. As the proportion of men in a class increased, male students initiated many more follow-ups than did females. With male professors, interactions initiated by women dropped precipitously with increases in class size, but that drop did not occur with female professors.

At an urban midwestern university, 167 faculty members were interviewed and observed (roughly equal numbers of male and female teachers in both male-dominated and female-dominated departments), and information was collected from their students (Statham, Richardson, & Cook, 1991). Most class time was devoted to presenting material (63% for females and 70% for males). When interactions occurred, women instructors were more likely to check students' understanding, but there was no gender difference in answering and clarifying students' questions. Women more often solicited student input, and total student input was greater in classes taught by women. In interviews, men talked about learning in terms of themselves as the source of knowledge, whereas women were more likely to see the locus of learning in the student and to value students' contributions as ends in themselves. Findings were interpreted according to symbolic interactionist and feminist theories.

Physical touching was the independent variable in a study in which 171 community college students in three classes with different instructors were randomly assigned to be touched or not touched by the instructor during a postexam conference (Steward & Lupfer, 1987). No effects for student or teacher gender were found, but students who were touched rated the conference more positively and scored higher on the postconference examination.

Questioning. Students commented in interviews about classes in which they participated most and least (Auster & MacRone, 1994). For classes of greater participation, professors were described as showing that student questions, ideas, and knowledge were important (regardless of student gender). Students perceived their teachers to be supportive of questioning in a series of studies reported by Karabenick and Sharma (1994), although the incidence of questions was low (average of six student questions per class). Perceived support of questioning was positively related to reported motivation and learning activity. At a community college, students who expected to be questioned orally at random reported better preparation and scored better on a quiz than students without that expectation (McDougall & Cordeiro, 1993).

To study teacher questions, Pollio (1989) analyzed tapes of 550 lecture hours from 10 different courses in various fields. The number of teacher questions in a 50-minute period ranged from 0 to 50, with a mean of 21.3. More than one third of the questions required yes or no answers, and almost 70% of all questions were not answered by students. The length of postquestion pauses ranged from .77 seconds to almost 3.0 seconds (mean of

1.55), and the teachers who waited longest generally got the largest percentage of answers. Such results are quite similar to those from earlier studies (Dunkin & Barnes, 1986). Other studies of wait time, however, both naturalistic (Duell, Lynch, Ellsworth, & Moore, 1992) and experimental (Duell, 1994), have not always confirmed the effectiveness of longer pauses.

Questions can be a means of getting students to elaborate on material, and the questions are hypothesized to be more effective when they are self-generated than when provided by the teacher. A. King (1992a, 1992b) found that students trained in guided self-questioning and guided peer-questioning showed greater learning. When compared with a notetaking–review condition, students trained in self-questioning performed better on several measures and included a greater number of important idea units in their notes. King offered a model of the guided question-generating strategy, emphasizing that the student's perceived personal autonomy is an important factor for the success of this approach.

If classroom interaction and questioning are to have the characteristics described by Laurillard's (1993) framework, greater participation by greater numbers of students than is typical (or perhaps even possible in medium- to large-size classes) is required. Close research attention should be given to how student-teacher interactions are affected by (a) perceptions of teacher support and disclosure, (b) the gender and race of students, (c) the type and level of questions, and (d) wait time. Models for training students in generating questions may help to counter the scarcity of dialogue and feedback in the classroom.

SMALL GROUP LEARNING

Small instructional groups go by many names—discussion group, seminar, tutorial, quiz section, collaborative/cooperative group, learning community, and so on—and numerous resources are available about research and practice in small group teaching (Brown & Atkins, 1988; Jaques, 1992; Michaelsen, Fink, & Knight, 1997; Tiberius, 1989).

Dansereau and colleagues (see Hythecker, Dansereau, & Rocklin, 1988) extensively studied the smallest group, the dyad. They investigated what they called the structured dyadic learning environment, and they described each step in the dyadic process while offering evidence of its positive effects on learning. Research on peer teaching and tutoring, as reviewed by Whitman (1988) and by Topping (1996), is sufficiently positive to recommend wider adoption of those approaches. Topping's 10-dimension typology of peer tutoring is particularly helpful for guiding further research.

Learning in small cooperative or collaborative groups has increased in popularity more than any other college teaching innovation. In a multi-institution study by Kuh, Pace, and Vesper (1997), the greatest gains in self-rated learning were associated with participating in cooperative learning and active learning (compared with other experiences reported by students). Cooperative and collaborative approaches are not always clearly differentiated in the literature. Bruffee (1995) noted several distinctive characteristics of the collaborative approach: it shifts authority toward students, and it shifts beliefs about knowledge from the recognition that knowledge is certain toward the recognition that knowledge is communal. Conversely, student accountability is less prominent in collaborative than in cooperative learning. Bruffee (1993) concluded that research largely supports the effectiveness of collaborative learning. He developed a view of higher education as conversation, and he stated implications of that view for all curricular fields.

Applications of collaborative and cooperative learning, along with reports of supportive research, appear in Bosworth and Hamilton (1994), and D. W. Johnson, R. T. Johnson, and Smith (1991). Gabelnick, MacGregor, Matthews, and Smith (1990) and Tinto (1997) discussed research and practice with regard to learning communities, an approach in which collaboration and cooperation are often prominent. Academic conflict, when used to promote learning (D. W. Johnson, R. T. Johnson, & Smith, 1996), also requires that students engage in cooperative interactions.

Higher education research about learning in cooperative or collaborative groups lags behind K–12 research in both quality and quantity. For K–12, cooperative learning is generally accepted as having positive effects on most low-level learning outcomes and on some high-level outcomes (e.g., see Qin, D. W. Johnson, & R. T. Johnson, 1995, regarding problem-solving outcomes). Higher education research is beginning to generate reviews and meta-analyses. Springer, Stanne, and Donovan (1997) identified 39 studies in which undergraduates in science, mathematics, engineering, and technology participated in small group work. That work was defined as cooperative or collaborative activities among 2 to 10 students either inside or outside the classroom. Achievement was higher for students in cooperative or collaborative conditions than for others (a conclusion that was based on 49 independent samples from 37 studies), and persistence and attitudes also favored those students. Achievement results were particularly robust and applied across several measures: course examinations, course grades, and standardized tests. The effect size for achievement (0.51) is unusually high for a classroom innovation and on a standardized test would move a student from the 50th percentile to the 70th percentile.

Future research, according to Springer, Stanne, and Donovan (1997) should be based more closely on theory, should expand the variety of disciplines studied, and should explore the processes that occur in various kinds of small groups under various conditions. Given the demonstrated value of such group-based learning, research is also needed about circumstances that facilitate or inhibit implementing such learning. Small group learning has great potential, but careful process studies are needed to reveal the conditions under which teaching and learning are discursive, adaptive, interactive, and reflective (Laurillard, 1993).

ELECTRONIC TECHNOLOGIES

Electronically mediated teaching and learning are irrevocably changing the character of higher education. Electronic technologies are opening new avenues for learners to access opportunities and information, new forms of interactions among teachers and students, and new possibilities for collaborations across institutions.

Claims for Technology. Several forces are responsible for the momentum of technology in teaching. These forces include the experiences and expectations of students, the needs of students for convenient access to courses (Brey & Gigsby, 1988), presumed cost-effectiveness (Twigg, 1996), and expected gains in learning. Uses of such technologies will no doubt continue to accelerate, but the research base to inform practice is alarmingly small and there are few theoretical frameworks to guide research. Costs are rarely reported in detail, but the impression is that capital expenses increase without corresponding reductions in labor costs. Green and Gilbert (1995) were unable to identify instances where instructional productivity increased as a result of information technologies. Furthermore, professors, who are the source of "labor" in those cases, are typically unsympathetic to technologically driven changes in instructional practices (Massy & Zemsky, 1995).

As for enhancing learning, the claim is often stated modestly that there is "no significant difference" in learning between, say, distance learning and conventional classes. (See the compilation of 248 research reports by Russell, 1997, and the review by Moore & Kearsky, 1996). Some technologies merely add convenience or dazzle to what professors otherwise do in classes. Changes in typical patterns of communication necessarily occur when conferencing software is adopted. Van Dusen (1997) enumerated eight variations with such software, including two-way audiovisual classrooms, desktop groupware conferencing, and asynchronous/CD ROM hybrids. Little research has been conducted about teaching and learning environments such as those, where student–teacher communication can be more flexible but where communication is not face to face and not necessarily in real time.

In a review of research on computer-assisted instruction from 1987 through 1996, Emerson and Mosteller (1998a) identified 130 articles, reports, and chapters, some of which were reviews of research. Although Emerson and Mosteller state that "computers have delivered no great breakthroughs in college instruction" (p. 43), the authors' conclusions are more optimistic than the "no significant difference" studies. The authors found that computer-assisted instruction does lead to valuable achievement gains (especially for higher order and more complex intellectual tasks), is associated with positive student attitudes, and may shorten instructional time. Benefits appear to be greater when software requires higher levels of interaction, incorporates multiple senses of the learner, and involves collaboration among learners. A second report (Emerson & Mosteller, 1998b) focused on six controlled studies in science published from 1990 through 1996. After pointing out that the evidence "does not demonstrate that computer software is a viable replacement for creative and dedicated teachers" (p. 74), they concluded that learning gains and increased efficiency have been shown "in some settings for parts of some college courses" (p. 75).

Technology also has a place in the curriculum as a subject for study. Shapiro and Hughes (1996) see technology as a new liberal art that is essential for citizens in the information age, and the authors explicated seven dimensions for an "information literacy" curriculum.

Needed Research. We believe that research is most urgent regarding (a) the nature of electronically mediated learning, (b) the role of faculty members in technology-rich environments, and (c) issues of implementation. Are people who have grown up in the information age different as learners? Do they process information differently, perhaps in a more nonlinear fashion? Do they find that discovery and participative approaches to learning are more congenial? Are they able to function in virtual worlds as effectively as in the real world? Owston (1997) notes that the world wide web appeals to students partly because of its convenience and availability. For web-based courses, the in-person contact between teachers and students is often greatly reduced, even for courses offered on campus. We know little about how students use the resulting opportunities for self-direction. Are motivation and engagement (which serve as enablers of learning) greater in such environments? If so, which kinds of students experience the greatest effects?

Some scholars have argued that media have no influence on learning under any conditions. Media are merely conduits of content, they say, and it is the larger instructional design that influences learning (R. E. Clark, 1983; 1994). Kozma (1994) countered by reframing the question of media effects to consider the capabilities of media as they interact with the processes (cognitive and social) of knowledge construction. He contended that researchers should focus not on experimental studies that seek to demonstrate effects from particular causes, as in Clark's argument, but on examination of the mechanisms (the processes) that lead to effects. Ethnographic methodologies can reveal interactions between uses of a particular medium in interrelationship with cognitive, social, and psychological variables over time. An adequate approach to instructional design must "address complex interrelationships among media, method, and situation" (Kozma, 1994, p. 17). Those investigations require far more complex designs than the "no significant difference" studies that evaluate the presence or absence of one particular feature. Indeed, the latter designs have been called into question since the first *Handbook* chapter (McKeachie, 1963).

With regard to research on the role of faculty members, Guskin (1994) asserted that the faculty role should be structured "to maximize essential faculty–student interaction, integrate new technologies fully into the student learning process, and enhance student learning through peer interaction" (p. 19). Researchable questions emerge from this description of the faculty role. We might investigate what learnings are best gained through direct faculty–student interaction, what learnings are best gained through electronic technologies, and what learnings are best gained through peer interactions or through students working independently. Guskin suggests that we can approach answers to these questions based on existing research. We also suggest that new research should be undertaken concerning the kinds of faculty–student interactions that are most valuable within electronically mediated environments.

The primary roles for the information-age teacher, according to MacFarlane (1995) are (a) to structure knowledge to make it interactively accessible, (b) to facilitate the process of learning, and (c) to manage interactions among learners and between learners and knowledge. His analysis implies that the role of presenter, currently a major activity of professors, will become quite minor and that other roles will become more prominent. It may be that those new roles are best fulfilled by a team rather

than through an individual (Bess, 1998), making individual "ownership" of courses less common. Students have become more collaborative as learners, and faculty members have become more collaborative as scholars. Professors, willingly or not, will inevitably become more collaborative as teachers.

For research about technologically mediated learning to be useful, it must meet several criteria. It should focus on institutionalized as well as experimental courses (Mowrer, 1996), use both quantitative and qualitative techniques (Jones et al., 1996), and attend to contextual features of the teaching–learning environment (Neal, 1997). It must also be timely, because technologies under investigation may be superseded by speedier and more powerful technologies even before research findings can be used. Laurillard (1993) provided a checklist by which 17 media are compared across 12 categories related to her framework (p. 177). She saw most promise in tutorial simulations and tutorial systems, but she cautioned that the teacher–student dialogue necessary for effective teaching and learning "is undeniably labor intensive" (p. 178).

Research is also needed about implementation because electronic technologies are vulnerable to most of the same forces that have impeded adoption of other promising instructional innovations. Mastery learning (sometimes termed the personalized system of instruction), for example, is known to be an effective instructional approach. In their meta-analysis, C. C. Kulik, J. A. Kulik, and Bangert-Drowns (1990) reported a large effect size (0.52 based on 103 studies) for student examination performance under mastery conditions. Despite evidence of its effectiveness, this (nonelectronic) technology is not widely used. Menges (1994) speculated about the barriers that have prevented its further adoption: (a) planning mastery courses requires extensive time and energy; (b) a new role is expected of teachers, a role more like a coach or a tutor than the traditional role of information provider; (c) special demands are made on the institution, including space requirements and more flexible registration arrangements; and (d) the very effectiveness of mastery learning may work against its adoption because students, having learned more, receive higher grades, which the institution may resist as grade inflation. Electronically based technologies make many of the same demands on individuals and organizations. Their adoption and effectiveness are likely to be diluted by the same factors that inhibited institutionalization of mastery learning.

Assessing and Improving Teaching and Learning

In this section, we distinguish between two senses of evaluation. One is summative evaluation, in which judgments are tendered by administrators or colleagues about teaching and learning by using a variety of information including information from the teacher. Summative evaluation informs those who make decisions about salary, retention, promotion, and so on. Formative evaluation, by contrast, is the process in which teaching and learning are examined by experts, including the teacher, for developmental purposes. Those processes are sometimes combined in practice and are often confused (Blackburn & Pitney, 1988). Critical differences in their purposes require that they be pursued in different ways.

Summative Evaluation of Teaching

Decisions about performance effectiveness are inevitable for people who are employed by organizations. For academics, performance review often raises conflicts between competing values—for example, professional autonomy on the one hand and organizational participation on the other.

Blackburn and Pitney (1988) summarized research about performance evaluation systems. They emphasized the importance of having an employee participate in designing and implementing such systems and of separating the feedback for individual development from the feedback for personnel review. They noted that it is useful to individualize rewards because not all members of an organization are motivated by the same things, and they identified several unintended and undesirable consequences of performance review systems, including rewarding individual rather than collective performance, emphasizing short-term rather than long-term results, using extrinsic rather than intrinsic rewards, and relying on "quantity of activity rather than quality of the outcome" (p. 22).

In this section, we discuss two topics: student evaluations of teaching, in which considerable research has been done, and teaching portfolios, on which additional research is needed.

STUDENT EVALUATION OF TEACHING

Academics have contributed literally thousands of studies about student evaluations of teachers and teaching (the "student ratings" literature, as it is often called). Interest in this topic has been strongest in North America, although some research has been done in Europe (Husbands & Fosh, 1993) and elsewhere, including cross-culturally (Watkins, 1994).

By the late 1980s, many separate studies and several comprehensive reviews had appeared (notably, Cashin, 1988; Marsh, 1984, 1987; Scriven, 1988). We will review recent literature about dimensions of teaching, factors that may bias student evaluations, and the validity of student ratings.

Dimensionality. Teaching is undoubtedly a complex activity, and determining its component parts or underlying dimensions is challenging. Feldman (1997) derived 28 dimensions of teaching effectiveness from a logical analysis of items used on evaluation forms. Using a review of pertinent research, he ranked the dimensions in terms of importance and found relatively similar rankings whether importance was defined by the dimension's relationship with student achievement or its relationship with overall evaluations.

A review by Marsh and Dunkin (1997) put the number of dimensions at nine if the number was based on research with Students' Evaluation of Educational Quality. That instrument is derived from research and theory about adult learning and has been subjected to numerous and varied studies, including more than 30 published factor analyses drawing on an archive of 50,000 classes. The nine dimensions listed here are a useful framework for performance reviews, as well as for diagnosing and resolving teaching problems: leaning or value, instructor enthusiasm, organization or clarity, group interaction, individual rapport, breadth of coverage, examinations or grading, assignments or readings, and workload or difficulty. Referring to

work by Marsh (1991a, 1991b), who attempted to reduce the number of dimensions using hierarchical confirmatory factor analysis, Marsh and Dunkin (1997) concluded that, although the nine first-order factors could be confirmed and four second-order factors could be identified, too much variance was left unexplained by the four-factor solution.

Dimensions of teaching effectiveness were differently described by Abrami and his colleagues (see, e.g., Abrami, d'Apollonia, & Rosenfield, 1997). They have argued for a single underlying trait for teaching effectiveness (analogous to a general factor for intelligence), a position they believed was practical for summarizing information in personnel reviews. In their analysis, "an overall skill factor" accounted for 63 % of the variance. Other components were intercorrelated, but were considerably less important than the first. Those components corresponded roughly to viewing the teacher as instructor (things such as clarity, preparation, stimulation of interest, and relevance); as person (including general attitudes, respect for others, enthusiasm for subject); and as regulator (evaluation and feedback). Thus, d'Apollonia and Abrami (1997) asserted that general instructional skill is a composite of three subskills: delivering instruction, facilitating interaction, and evaluating student learning.

Scores for multiple factors can be helpful in faculty evaluation. Using only one or two overall scores per course may obscure important complexities of teaching. For example, because the purposes of instruction differ from course to course and from instructor to instructor, reviewers may need to consider separate ratings for factors such as clarity, group interaction, and workload.

Evaluation forms should include items relevant to all the objectives of the instructor. Forms are typically instructor centered and may neglect student-centered approaches such as students' responsibility for their own learning and students' responsibility for supporting the learning of others (Wilson, 1988). Balance should be sought between a research-based questionnaire required of everyone, and individualized forms that better reflect the situations of particular teachers and courses. Some institutions compromise by including a core of items (with a known factor structure) for everyone, along with optional items selected by individual instructors.

Research should explore how results of student evaluations are best summarized and reported: as separate scores for each empirically derived factor, as a single score weighted across factors, as one or two overall scores (e.g., summed across items or single ratings such as "instructor overall" and "teacher overall"), or in some other way. Another approach, favored by McKeachie (1997), is for students to rate their progress or their attainments in the course, as is called for in the IDEA system of evaluation (Cashin, 1995). Except for simulation studies by McKeachie and his colleagues (e.g., Lin, McKeachie, & Tucker, 1984), little is known about how such information is considered by the decision makers or how it is treated when review committees discuss particular cases (Franklin & Theall, 1990).

Bias from Extraneous Variables. If student evaluations of teaching are truly to reflect what a teacher does, they must be minimally influenced (biased) by circumstances over which the teacher has little or no control, such as class size and prescribed course content. For bias to be established, it is necessary to demonstrate that the variable in question (e.g., class size) is uncorrelated with teaching effectiveness (Feldman, 1998). Better teaching may well occur in smaller classes; if so, different ratings (e.g., between teachers of large and small classes) are not attributable to bias. As McKeachie (1997) points out, the error is not in student evaluations, but in comparing things that should not be directly compared—in this case, large and small classes. As another example, humanities courses typically receive more positive ratings than do natural science courses, but one cannot easily determine whether the difference is due to the discipline and content or to the true quality of instruction (Cashin & Downey, 1995). At one time, instructor expressiveness was seen as a biasing characteristic; later researchers found that more expressive instructors act in ways that positively influence learning (H. G. Murray, Rushton, & Paunonen, 1990).

Some researchers have advised using statistical adjustments to correct for demonstrated bias. Statistical adjustments may be appropriate when large data sets are available and when a large number of faculty members from diverse fields are being reviewed simultaneously. Typically, however, assessments are made about relatively few cases at any one time. Faculty members are then more appropriately judged in light of their own goals and their progress over time

Several sources of possible bias deserve further research, including student motivation to take a course (Hoyt, 1997); grading leniency (Greenwald & Gillmore, 1997); gender of students and teachers (Basow, 1995; Feldman 1992, 1993); workload, where the counterintuitive finding is that courses with heavier workloads are rated more favorably (Marsh & Roche, 1997); and approaches that students use when they study (Entwistle & Tait, 1995).

Validity. Student evaluations that are relatively bias free and that have established dimensionality still require validation to demonstrate that they measure what they are intended to measure, namely, teaching effectiveness or, strictly speaking, student satisfaction with teaching. As Marsh and Dunkin (1997) pointed out, teaching effectiveness is a "hypothetical construct for which there is no single indicator" (p. 282). Thus, the construct as represented by items and factors on student surveys must be validated against criteria with which we reasonably expect it to correlate. Consistently positive relationships have been found between student evaluations and each of the following: student learning (most notably in multisection courses); ratings by former students; and faculty self-evaluations of teaching, although faculty members tend to rate themselves more positively than students do (Marsh & Dunkin, 1997). Abrami, d'Apollonia, and Rosenfield (1997) offered a constructive critique of the three research designs used in validity studies: multisection studies, which they especially recommend; laboratory studies; and multitrait, multimethod studies.

Student evaluations have also been validated against the instructor's classroom behaviors. H. G. Murray (1997a, 1997b) summarized studies in which trained observers rated teachers' "low-inference" classroom behaviors (e.g., "talks with students before or after class" and "signals the transition from one topic and the next"). More positive student evaluations and more learning were associated with behaviors contributing to clarity,

expressiveness, and interaction. Those results suggest that when students complete evaluation forms, they are responding to what teachers do rather than to something extraneous and general, such as "popularity." Related studies showed that instructors can increase such behaviors, and consequently their ratings, through appropriate feedback and training programs.

Measurement imprecision and conceptual complications will always constrain the magnitude of such statistical relationships. Examinations, for instance, cannot fairly sample all the learning that instructors (or students) might consider important in a course. Nevertheless, the correlations are sufficiently strong to support the validity of student evaluations.

Student evaluations are essential as one component of an assessment of faculty work not only because students have a special perspective on teaching and learning, but also because the body of research supporting student evaluations is far more substantial than for any other component of faculty evaluation, including methods used to assess research productivity. Often, people are skeptical about student evaluations (a) because they fail to understand or acknowledge the worth of that research (e.g., Haskell, 1996; W. M. Williams & Ceci, 1997); (b) because users overinterpret quantitative data (assuming that there are meaningful distinctions in small statistical differences); (c) because the importance of student evaluations is inflated (considering evaluations from students as a proxy for other measures of teaching effectiveness); or (d) because the importance of context is underestimated (neglecting matters such as the teacher's previous performance and present goals, expectations that are held by the department, and other contextual conditions under which student evaluations are gathered and interpreted; see Feldman, 1998). Schmelkin, Spencer, and Gellman (1997) found greater acceptance and use of student ratings than might be inferred from anecdotal reports. A code of practice about how student evaluations can contribute to summative evaluation of teaching, published by the Association of University Staff of New Zealand (Hall & Fitzgerald, 1995), addresses practical implications of much of this research.

The body of research about student evaluations is vast, and we find strong conclusions about their reliability, validity, and potential utility. Researchers should now turn to new areas, such as investigations about how this evaluative information is used; about how students, colleagues, and administrators can be prepared for their evaluative roles (compare J. A. Clarke, 1995); and about the mechanisms by which teacher behaviors affect student learning (H. G. Murray, 1997a).

TEACHING PORTFOLIOS

Successful assessment of faculty work requires a portrait of teaching that is accurate and reasonably complete. The teaching portfolio is a mechanism designed to provide such a portrait for summative as well as formative purposes, and Blackburn and Pitney (1988) have advocated the portfolio process as appropriate for teachers in higher education. Portfolios typically contain a statement of one's beliefs, goals, and development as a teacher; sample teaching materials; examples of student work evaluated by the teacher; and evaluations of the teaching and learning experience by students, colleagues, and others. The portfolio should be prepared according to guidelines developed by the department or institution and judged according to collaboratively derived criteria.

The literature on portfolios typically includes more advocacy than empirical research (Edgerton, Hutchings, & Quinlan, 1991; J. P. Murray, 1995; Seldin, 1993). Research is needed about many issues: about the desirable contents and size of portfolios, about how to prepare faculty members to design portfolios, about training for those who review portfolios, and about how information from teaching portfolios is weighed relative to information about other aspects of faculty work. The role of collegial review needs clarification. Because classroom observations are likely to be expensive and unreliable (Braskamp & Ory, 1994; Root, 1987), peer review can more productively focus on teaching materials. Conflicts should be anticipated between uses of peer review for formative and for summative purposes (Cavanagh, 1996; Bernstein, 1996). See also the British work on teaching profiles (Gregory, 1996).

Several resources have treated broad issues of faculty evaluation, including evaluation of teaching (notably Arreola, 1995; Braskamp & Ory, 1994; Centra, 1993; Diamond, 1995; and Richlin & Manning, 1995). Each evaluation has given attention to the full range of faculty work and has included examples of checklists, rating forms, and other evaluative resources. The "reconceptualization" of evaluation proposed by Pratt (1997) is parallel to our views of teaching and learning environments in that he urged evaluation of planning, of implementation, and of results. Although student evaluations continue to be the most active research topic related to assessment of faculty performance, the most urgent area for further work concerns the uses and effectiveness of teaching portfolios.

Formative Evaluation of Teaching

Although faculty members can be evaluated for reasons of personnel decisions, they are also appraised as teachers for formative purposes—that is, for the improvement of teaching effectiveness. Several volumes offer extensive overviews of strategies that are useful in assisting faculty members to improve their teaching. Theall and Franklin's (1991) edited work includes articles on faculty views about sources of evaluation, ways to collect and use data to improve teaching (including student ratings), and factors that help faculty members accept and use feedback on their teaching. Centra (1993) examined reflective faculty evaluation as a way to improve teaching and discussed appraisal strategies such as student evaluations, teacher self-reports and portfolios, and evaluations by colleagues and chairs of departments.

Rather than offering specific strategies for appraisal of teaching effectiveness, Weston, McAlpine, and Bordonaro (1995) explained that formative evaluation (a) ensures that teaching goals are being addressed and (b) improves instruction by identifying problems and pointing the way to solutions or alternative approaches. Building on this definition, they developed a model to guide formative evaluation of teachers in higher education.

The literature on formative evaluation of teachers is most extensive concerning the use and effects of feedback from student ratings. Focusing on studies since 1980, L'Hommedieu,

Menges, and Brinko (1990) conducted a meta-analysis of "the quantitative research on feedback college teachers get from student ratings." Noting that the effects of feedback are modest, they recommended that future research analyze how student-ratings feedback is operationalized, develop reliable and valid rating instruments that can be used across disciplines while also providing detailed information, and rely on frequently used instruments such as Marsh's (1987) Students' Evaluations of Educational Quality or the Course/Instructor Evaluation Questionnaire (Aleamoni, 1978; Stevens & Aleamoni, 1985).

A second article, (L'Hommedieu & Menges, 1992) discussed threats to validity in these studies. Validity is threatened by use of midterm rating, which contaminate studies of end-of-term feedback; by use of different forms of feedback, ranging from simple statistical summaries to full consultations provided to faculty members; and by use of different rating systems across studies. Another problem is that student ratings feedback as a treatment is inconsistently implemented. Future research should examine effects of student ratings feedback through large scale classical experimental designs as well as smaller experiments with attention to controlling and matching moderator and environmental variables.

What is most clear from this research is that—although student ratings feedback has a small effect on subsequent ratings—adding personal consultation or other feedback (such as notes provided to the instructor from student discussion groups) to written reports of student ratings is associated with stronger positive effects on subsequent ratings (L'Hommedieu et al., 1990; L'Hommedieu & Menges, 1992; Menges & Brinko, 1986). This finding is consistent across an array of studies conducted over the past 10 years with faculty members in various fields, such as health sciences (P. A. Cohen, 1988; Tiberius, Sackin, Slingerland, Jubas, Bell, & Matlow, 1989) and dentistry (P. A. Cohen, 1991), and in various countries, such as Australia (Marsh & Roche, 1993) and the United States (Wilson, 1986). However, De Neve's (1991) work with a small group of university teachers in first-year classes indicated that, even with consultation, instructors' subjective theories about teaching are the most important factor affecting how they used student evaluations and what aspects of their teaching they were willing to consider changing.

Despite evidence that consultation adds to the effectiveness of student ratings feedback, further research should clarify how such feedback can be used most effectively. In particular, it is not clear whether the effect is "additive, interactive, or completely independent of feedback" (L'Hommedieu & Menges, 1992, p. 18). Because effective teaching is high on the agenda of most universities and colleges, further research on what interventions and strategies can be most productively paired with student ratings feedback will be useful additions to the literature on the formative evaluation of teachers.

Grading Student Learning

Just as teachers' performance is evaluated both for summative purposes and for formative, developmental purposes, so also are students evaluated as learners. Some form of learning assessment is typically part of college courses. Thus, the national movement calling for accountability, assessment, and evidence of student learning outcomes has prompted consideration of various approaches to assessment. The American Association for Higher Education has made this topic the focus of annual conferences for several years. McMillan (1988) edited a useful sourcebook that is about assessing students' learning and that highlights issues of interest: (a) strategies to assess specific skills such as critical writing and thinking, (b) strategies appropriate for use in the major, and (c) research on grading.

Within courses, tests and term papers remain the most traditional and typical ways of assessing learning. Some research focuses on the details of constructing valid and reliable tests; it has produced, for example, the counterintuitive result that multiple-choice tests with three alternatives to each question are more effective than tests with two, four, or five alternatives (Owen & Froman, 1987; J. Paul, 1994; Trevisan, Sax, & Michael, 1991). Other studies challenge long-held testing practices. For example, in a book-length examination of the work of external examiners in the United Kingdom, Piper (1994) concluded that various rationales exist for external examining, but little evidence shows that external examiners ensure educational quality. Researchers are interested in uses of quizzes or tests to influence student achievement. For example, Beaulieu and Utecht (1987) concluded that students scored better on final examinations in sections using weekly learning quizzes that did not contribute to the formal grade than did a comparison group that did not use the quizzes. They noted, however, that quizzes would attract more attention from students if they were linked to course grades. Term papers deserve research as vehicles for promoting higher order learning: analysis, synthesis, and evaluation of course content.

In a monograph-length work, Pollio (1985) evaluated research on grades and grading practices, then concluded that grades depend on human judgment in particular contexts. From this conclusion, he offered several recommendations for educators: (a) clarify the purpose for which grades are to be used; (b) use less-differentiated systems such as certify, not certify, and honors; (c) discontinue use of the grade point average (GPA); and (d) do not count on the precision that is implied by numerical grades.

Several studies examined the relationship between grading practices and student behaviors (Milton, Pollio, & Eison, 1986; Tuckman, 1992). Milton et al. studied attitudes toward grades of faculty members and students at 23 colleagues and universities, as well as the relationships between learning and grade orientation, plus various academic behaviors. They found that students with a high orientation to learning coupled with a low orientation to grades were likely to have more effective study habits. In contrast, cheating was more likely to occur among students who had a low orientation to learning and a high orientation to grades. Further, they reported that grade-oriented students focused more on how they impressed the teacher than on course content.

Appraising Learning for Improvement

In addition to interest in the summative assessment of student learning, the literature reveals growing attention to strategies for appraising learning in formative ways that help students develop as learners. Somervell (1993) discussed several approaches—self-evaluation, peer evaluation, and collaborative assessment —as alternatives to traditional evaluation methods. The literature holds both (a) essays on various issues connected with self-evaluation and (b) studies of methods and outcomes of self-evaluation. Research concerning self-evaluation includes communicating standards to students (Sadler, 1989), student-generated marks as compared to grades generated by teachers (Boud & Falchikov, 1989), and students' attitudes toward self and peer assessment (Williams, 1992).

Another approach to improving learning is through feedback from teachers or from student peers. The literature on feedback is diverse in its focus. For example, J. A. Kulik and C. C. Kulik (1988) conducted a meta-analysis on the relationship between feedback timing and verbal learning. Zellermayer (1989) reviewed the literature on feedback about students' compositions, including discussion of students' perceptions of teacher feedback. Coleman, Jussim, and Isaac (1991) analyzed black students' reactions to feedback conveyed by white and black teachers. Butler and Winne (1995) examined how feedback affects students' cognitive engagement and how engagement with tasks is related to achievement. In a study of the effects of different strategies to enhance students' behavior, Schemoglu and Fogelman (1995) reported positive results associated with a feedback-corrective procedure.

Classroom assessment is a formative appraisal approach that has gained many followers among college and university teachers nationwide since the early 1990s. As presented in two books (Angelo & Cross, 1993; Cross & Steadman, 1996), classroom assessment helps teachers clarify their goals for each course and ask questions about how students are learning. It also helps students to reflect on their learning processes. The literature includes descriptions of classroom assessment techniques and applications of those techniques in various class settings. Research on the influence of those techniques on student learning and teacher improvement would be an important contribution to the literature concerning such creative strategies.

Another development in appraisal practices involves using computers to help students monitor and improve their learning. Brohn (1986), for example, discussed how computers offer interesting possibilities for formative evaluation of learning.

Our inductive approach to this review led us to organize research about teaching and learning environments by clustering it under three headings: planning, implementing, and assessing and improving teaching and learning. A more prescriptive approach would have led to quite different headings. We might have categorized environments according to their dominant dimensions (e.g., cognitive, social, affective, behavioral, and physical). Or we might have adopted a taxonomy from the literature. For instance, Collins, Greeno, and Resnick (1994) proposed six types of learning environments: communication environments, information-transmission environments, problem-solving environments, training environments, evaluative-performance environments, and recitation and testing environments. They suggested that environments containing all of these types are likely to be most effective. We suggest using such taxonomies for studying the courses, course sequences, and other instructional environments in higher education.

Recommendations for Future Research

As shown earlier in Figure 49.1, we organized this review conceptually around the key elements of faculty members as teachers, students as learners, and subject matter content— all situated within the broader context in which teaching and learning occur. Research addressing each area is certainly important; we believe, however, that research falling in overlaps between those elements is likely to hold the greatest implications for teaching in higher education. In particular, the section on environments for teaching and learning—a major part of this review—reveals interesting research questions and fruitful findings when investigators simultaneously consider teachers, learners, content, and context, as well as the relationships among those elements.

This review documents much that can inform instruction in higher education. If applied to teaching and learning practices, the research could immediately increase efficiency and effectiveness. Particularly strong are findings about small group learning, students' contributions to evaluating teaching, and the academic reward structure as it relates to teaching. Analysis of the research on teaching in higher education also revealed some areas in which further research, as well as theory development, would be especially useful. We highlight the seven areas that follow:

Faculty Behaviors and Intentions

We know a good deal about what faculty members do as teachers; we know much less about how their behaviors and intentions are related. Research and theory are needed concerning *why* faculty members teach as they do. How are intentions derived, goals formulated, and personal theories about teaching and learning developed? Under what conditions do faculty members act on those personal theories? Under what circumstances do they not act on them? How do faculty members assess their attainments in terms of intentions, and with what consequences? What roles in this process, if any, are played by research findings and formal theories?

Faculty Learning and Development

More research is needed about how teachers learn and develop over time. Such research and theory could guide planning, implementation, and assessment of faculty development programs intended to contribute to improvement of teaching and learning. In particular, how can faculty members be encouraged to adopt and implement new findings about student learning, especially when they do not perceive teaching to be highly rewarded? Faculty members are asked to increase their orientation toward students and toward learning and to do more teaching-related work with fewer resources (in part through technologically-mediated instruction), yet rewards for faculty members typically depend largely upon their investigative and creative work and its dissemination. Researchers should systematically address the circumstances that contribute to alignment between expectations for faculty work and rewards for faculty performance, plus the consequences for morale, productivity, and student learning.

Interactions among Teacher, Learner, and Method Variables

Research has established that certain teacher behaviors are associated with student learning and satisfaction, and that certain instructional approaches are associated with enhanced learning. Research should explore further the variables and mechanisms that underlie these associations so that findings can contribute to theory construction and more fully inform teaching practice. Specifically, how do learner attributes, and learning processes interact with teacher characteristics and instructional approaches to affect learning outcomes? Furthermore, how do these interactions vary in the context of specific disciplines?

Technology-Mediated Instruction

Interactive, multimedia instructional technologies hold great promise, which research is beginning to document. As the student population becomes more diverse and as electronic technologies facilitate various distance-learning possibilities, the nature of student–faculty interactions must be better understood. How does the use of various media affect those interactions and, more broadly, affect learning processes and learning outcomes? How do learners, instructional situation and method, area of study, and learning goals interact? What instructional situations (e.g., face-to-face instruction or distance and media-facilitated instruction), along with what other instructional methods, are most appropriate for which learners—and in what disciplines or fields—to attain which learning outcomes?

Effective Evaluative Decisions

Research tells a great deal about information that is potentially useful for decisions about assessing and improving teaching and learning. Little is known, however, about how decisions using that information are made, including decisions that students make when evaluating their courses and their teachers or when implementing study practices. Little is known about how administrators and colleagues use evaluation information when assessing faculty performance. And little is known about how teachers themselves use evaluation information in planning, implementing, and appraising their own teaching.

Influence of the Discipline

We noted the frequency with which studies have indicated the importance of discipline and document differences according to discipline. The influence of the discipline (and of its organizational counterpart, the department) is pervasive, thereby predicting faculty commitment and loyalty, teaching goals and practices, norms for teaching, course and curriculum planning, and student perceptions of their courses and teachers. Researchers should examine more extensively the ways in which disciplinary context affects the development of teachers during graduate training and in the early career period.

Context-Specific Research

Research we have reviewed from the past decade was predominantly quantitative in method and was conducted largely by people trained in positivist traditions of psychology and sociology. Recent work has begun to reflect the paradigmatic shifts mentioned at the beginning of this chapter, as researchers recognize the importance of context-specific investigations and include the perspectives of a range of participants in teaching and learning. To take account of the complexities of the personal, organizational, and political contexts of teaching and learning, researchers must move data gathering beyond surveys (or any other single method), and they must vary data sources (including information from teachers and learners, and information about the content being learned and the context in which teaching and learning take place). Furthermore, the content of data should reflect participants' internal perceptions, as well as external behaviors. Such approaches, we believe, can comprehend the intersections and interactions of teacher, learner, content, and context, which we have argued constitute the most productive approach to research on teaching in higher education.

Although we urge new research and theory development that will extend knowledge, particularly in the areas outlined above, we also note that there is at hand much research ready for immediate application, more than could be claimed in previous editions of the *Handbook*. We urge researchers to be leaders in its verification, dissemination, and implementation.

REFERENCES

Abrami, P. C., d'Apollonia, S., & Rosenfield, S. (1997). The dimensionality of student ratings of instruction: What we know and what we do not. In R. P. Perry & J. C. Smart (Eds.), *Effective teaching in higher education: Research and practice* (pp. 321–367). New York: Agathon Press. (Original work published 1996)

Adams, M. (Ed.). (1992). *Promoting diversity in college classrooms: Innovative responses for the curriculum, faculty, and institutions.* New Directions for Teaching and Learning, No. 52. San Francisco: Jossey–Bass.

Aleamoni, L. M. (1978). The usefulness of student evaluations in improving college teaching. *Instructional Science, 7,* 95–105.

Altbach, P. G. (1995). Problems and possibilities: The U.S. academic profession. *Studies in Higher Education, 20,* 27–44.

Altbach, P. G. (Ed.). (1996). *The international academic profession: Portraits of fourteen countries.* Princeton, NJ: Carnegie Foundation for the Advancement of Teaching.

Amsel, R., & Fichten, C. S. (1990). Interaction between college students and their professors: A comparison of students' and professors' views. *College Student Journal, 24,* 196–208.

Amundsen, C., Gryspeerdt, D., & Moxness, K. (1993). Practice-centered inquiry: Developing more effective teaching. *Review of Higher Education, 16,* 329–353.

Angelo, T. A. (Ed.). (1991). *Classroom research: Early lessons from success.* New Directions for Teaching and Learning, No. 46. San Francisco: Jossey-Bass.

Angelo, T. A. (1994, June). From faculty development to academic development. *AAHE Bulletin, 46,* 3–7.

Angelo, T. A., & Cross, K. P. (1993). *Classroom assessment techniques: A handbook for college teachers* (2nd ed.). San Francisco: Jossey-Bass.

Arendale, D. R. (1994). *Understanding the supplemental and instructional model.* New Directions for Teaching and Learning, No. 60, (pp. 11–21). San Francisco: Jossey-Bass.

Arreola, R. A. (1995). *Developing a comprehensive faculty evaluation system: A handbook for college faculty and administrators on design-ing and operating a comprehensive faculty evaluation system.* Bolton, MA: Anker Publishing.

Astin, A. W., & Chang, M. J. (1995). Colleges that emphasize research and teaching: Can you have your cake and eat it too? *Change, 27*(5), 45–49.

Astin, A. W., Green, K. C., Korn, W. S. (1987). *The American freshman: Twenty year trends, 1966–1985.* Los Angeles: University of California at Los Angeles, Higher Education Research Institute.

Astin, A. W., Parrott, S. A., Korn, W. S., & Sax, L. J. (1997). *The American freshman: Thirty year trends.* Los Angeles: University of California at Los Angeles, Higher Education Research Institute.

Auster, C. J., & MacRone, M. (1994). The classroom as a negotiated social setting: An empirical study of the effects of faculty members' behavior on students' participation. *Teaching Sociology, 22,* 289–300.

Austin, A. E. (1992). Supporting the professor as teacher: The Lilly teaching fellows program. *Review of Higher Education, 16,* 85–106.

Austin, A. E., Brocato, J. J., & LaFleur, M. (1993, April). *Learning to teach: The socialization of university teachers.* Paper presented at the American Educational Research Association, Atlanta, GA.

Austin, A. E., & Neal, J. (1988, April). *Distinctions among liberal arts college faculty related to time use priorities.* Paper presented at the American Educational Research Association, New Orleans.

Barnett, R. (1992). Linking teaching and research: A critical inquiry. *Journal of Higher Education, 63,* 619–636.

Barr, R. B., & Tagg, J. (1995). From teaching to learning: A new paradigm for undergraduate education. *Change, 27*(6), 13–25.

Basow, S. A. (1995). Student evaluations of college professors: When gender matters. *Journal of Educational Psychology, 87,* 656–665.

Baxter Magolda, M. B. (1992). *Knowing and reasoning in college: Gender-related patterns in students' intellectual development.* San Francisco: Jossey-Bass.

Baxter Magolda, M. B. (1994). Post-college experience and epistemology. *Review of Higher Education, 18,* 25–44.

Beaulieu, R. P., & Utecht, K. M. (1987). Frequently administered formative tests and student achievement. *Journal of Instructional Psychology, 14,* 195–200.

Belenky, M. F., Clinchy, B., Goldberger, J. R., & Tarule, J. M. (1986). *Women's ways of knowing: The development of self, voice, and mind.* New York: Basic Books.

Bensimon, E. M. (1996). Faculty identity: Essential, imposed, or constructed. In National Center for Educational Statistics, *Integrating research on faculty: Seeking new ways to communicate about the academic life of faculty* (Report 96–849, pp. 37–50). Washington, DC: Office of Educational Research and Improvement, U.S. Department of Education.

Bernstein, D. J. (1996). A departmental system for balancing the development and evaluation of college teaching: A commentary on Cavanagh. *Innovative Higher Education, 20,* 241–248.

Bess, J. L. (Ed.). (1997). *Teaching well and liking it: Motivating faculty to teach effectively.* Baltimore: Johns Hopkins University Press.

Bess, J. L. (1998). Teaching well: Do you have to be schizophrenic? *The Review of Higher Education, 22*(1), 1–15.

Biggs, J. (1996). Enhancing teaching through constructive alignment. *Higher Education, 32,* 347–367.

Blackburn, R. T., & Lawrence, J. H. (1995). *Faculty at work: Motivation, expectation, satisfaction.* Baltimore: Johns Hopkins University Press.

Blackburn, R. T., Lawrence, J. H., Ross, S., Okoloko, V. P., Bieber, J. P., Meiland, R., & Street, T. (1986). *Faculty as a key resource: A review of the research literature.* (Technical Report No. 86–D–001.1). Ann Arbor: University of Michigan, National Center for Research to Improve Postsecondary Teaching and Learning.

Blackburn, R. T., & Pitney, J. A. (1988). *Performance appraisal for faculty: Implications for higher education.* (Technical Report No. 88–D–002.0). Ann Arbor: University of Michigan, National Center for Research to Improve Postsecondary Teaching and Learning.

Bland, C. J., & Bergquist, W. H. (1997). *The vitality of senior faculty members: Snow on the roof—fire in the furnace.* (ASHE–ERIC Higher Education Research Report, Vol. 25, No. 7). Washington, DC: The George Washington University, Graduate School of Education and Human Development.

Bland, C. J., & Schmitz, C. C. (1988). *Faculty vitality on review: Retrospect and prospect. Journal of Higher Education, 59,* 190–224.

Bloland, H. G. (1995). Postmodernism and higher education. *Journal of Higher Education, 66,* 521–559.

Boice, B. (1997). What discourages research-practitioners in faculty development. *Higher Education: Handbook of Theory and Research, 12,* 371–434.

Boice, R. (1987). Is released-time an effective component of faculty development programs? *Research in Higher Education, 26,* 311–326.

Boice, R. (1992). *The new faculty member: Supporting and fostering professional development.* San Francisco: Jossey-Bass.

Boice, R. (1996). *First-order principles for college teachers: Ten basic ways to improve the teaching process.* Bolton, MA: Anker Publishing.

Bosworth, K., & Hamilton, S. J. (Eds.). (1994). *Collaborative learning: Underlying processes and effective techniques.* New Directions for Teaching and Learning, No. 59. San Francisco: Jossey-Bass.

Boud, D., & Falchikov, H. (1989). Quantitative studies of student self-assessment in higher education: A critical analysis of findings. *Higher Education, 18,* 529–549.

Bowen, H. R., & Schuster, J. H. (1986). *American professors: A national resource imperiled.* New York: Oxford.

Boyer, E. L. (1990). *Scholarship reconsidered: Priorities of the professoriate.* Princeton, NJ: Carnegie Foundation for the Advancement of Teaching.

Braskamp, L. A., & Ory, J. C. (1994). *Assessing faculty work: Enhancing individual and institutional performance.* San Francisco: Jossey-Bass.

Braxton, J. M. (1995). Disciplines with an affinity for the improvement of undergraduate education. In N. Hativa & M. Marincovi (Eds.), *Disciplinary differences in teaching and learning: Implications for practice.* New Directions for Teaching and Learning, No. 64 (pp. 59–64). San Francisco: Jossey-Bass.

Braxton, J. M., Eimers, M. T., & Bayer, A. E. (1996). The implications of teaching norms for the improvement of undergraduate education. *Journal of Higher Education, 67,* 603–625.

Brew, A. (Ed.). (1995). *Directions in staff development.* Buckingham, UK: Society for Research into Higher Education and Open University Press.

Brew, A., & Boud, D. (1995). Teaching and research: Establishing the vital link with learning. *Higher Education, 29,* 261–273.

Brey, R., & Gigsby, C. (1988). *A study of telecourse students.* Washington, DC: Corporation for Public Broadcasting/Annenberg Project.

Brinko, K. T. (1990). Instructional consultation with feedback in higher education. *Journal of Higher Education, 61,* 65–83.

Brohn, D. M. (1986). The use of computers in assessment in higher education. *Assessment and Evaluation in Higher Education, 11,* 231–239.

Brookfield, S. D. (1990). *The skillful teacher: On technique, trust, and responsiveness in the classroom.* San Francisco: Jossey-Bass.

Brookfield, S. D. (1995). *Becoming a critically reflective teacher.* San Francisco: Jossey–Bass.

Brown, G., & Atkins, M. (1988). *Effective teaching in higher education.* New York: Methuen.

Bruffee, K. A. (1993). *Collaborative learning: Higher Education. interdependence, and the authority of knowledge.* Baltimore: Johns Hopkins University Press.

Bruffee, K. A. (1995). Sharing our toys: Cooperative learning versus collaborative learning. *Change, 27*(1), 12–18.

Butler, D. L., & Winne, P. H. (1995). Feedback and self-regulated learning: A theoretical synthesis. *Review of Educational Research, 65,* 245–281.

Calderhead, J. (1981). Stimulated recall: A method for research on teaching. *British Journal of Educational Psychology, 51,* 211–217.

Canada, K., & Pringle, R. (1995). The role of gender in college classroom interactions: A social context approach. *Sociology of Education, 68,* 161–186.

Candy, P. C. (1991). *Self-direction for lifelong learning: A comprehensive guide to theory and practice.* San Francisco: Jossey-Bass.

Carnegie Foundation for the Advancement of Teaching. (1991). The payoff for publication leaders. *Change, 23*(2), 27–30.

Cashin, W. E. (1988). *Student ratings of teaching: A summary of the research.* (IDEA Paper No. 20). Manhattan: Kansas State University, Center for Faculty Evaluation & Development.

Cashin, W. E. (1995). *Student ratings of teaching: The research revisited.*

(IDEA Paper No. 32). Manhattan: Kansas State University, Center for Faculty Evaluation & Development.

Cashin, W. E., & Downey, R. G. (1995). *Disciplinary differences in what is taught and in students' perceptions of what they learn and of how they are taught.* New Directions for Teaching and Learning, No. 64 (pp. 81–92). San Francisco: Jossey-Bass.

Castle, J. B., Drake, S. M., & Boak, T. (1995). Collaborative reflection as professional development. *Review of Higher Education, 18,* 243–263.

Cavanagh, R. R. (1996). Formative and summative evaluation in the faculty peer review of teaching. *Innovative Higher Education, 20,* 235–240.

Centra, J. A. (1989). Faculty evaluation and faculty development in higher education. In J. C. Smart (Ed.), *Higher Education: Handbook of Theory and Research* (pp. 155–179). New York: Agathon Press.

Centra, J. A. (1993). *Reflective faculty evaluation: Enhancing teaching and determining faculty effectiveness.* San Francisco: Jossey-Bass.

Chickering, A. W., & Gamson, Z. F. (Eds.). (1991). *Applying the seven principles for good practice in undergraduate education.* New Directions for Teaching and Learning, No. 47. San Francisco: Jossey-Bass.

Clark, B. R. (1987). *The academic life: Small worlds, different worlds.* Princeton, NJ: Carnegie Foundation for the Advancement of Teaching.

Clark, B. R. (1989). The academic life: Small worlds, different worlds. *Educational Researcher, 18*(5), 4–8.

Clark, R. E. (1983). Reconsidering research on learning from media. *Review of Educational Research, 53*(4), 445–459.

Clark, R. E. (1994). Media will never influence learning. *Educational Technology Research and Development, 42*(2), 21–29.

Clark, S. M., & Lewis, D. R. (1988). Faculty vitality: Context, concerns, and prospects. In J. C. Smart (Ed.), Higher education: Handbook of theory and research (pp. 282–318). New York: Agathon Press.

Clarke, J. A. (1995). Tertiary students' perceptions of their learning environments: A new procedure and some outcomes. *Higher Education Research and Development, 14,* 1–12.

Claxton, C. S. , & Murrell, P. H. (1987). *Learning styles: Implications for improving educational practices* (ASHE-ERIC Higher Education Research Report No. 4). Washington, DC: Association for the Study of Higher Education.

Cohen, P. A. (1988, April). *Student-rating feedback as a means of improving college instruction.* Paper presented at the American Educational Research Association–Division J, New Orleans.

Cohen, P. A. (1991). Effectiveness of student ratings feedback and consultation for improving instruction in dental school. *Journal of Dental Education, 55,* 145–150.

Cohen, S. A. (1987). Instructional alignment: Searching for a magic bullet. *Educational Researcher, 19*(3), 2–7.

Colbeck, C. L. (1995, April). *Organizational and disciplinary influences on the integration of faculty work.* Paper presented at the annual meeting of the American Educational Research Association, San Francisco.

Coleman, L. M., Jussim, L., & Isaac, J. L. (1991). Black students' reactions to feedback conveyed by white and black teachers. *Journal of Applied Social Psychology, 21,* 460–481.

Collins, A., Greeno, J. G., & Resnick, L. B. (1994). Learning environments. In T. Huden & N. Postlethwaite (Eds.), *International encyclopedia of education.* Oxford, UK: Pergamon.

Conrad, C. F., & Haworth, J. G. (Eds.). (1990). *Curriculum in transition: Perspectives on the undergraduate experience.* Needham Heights, MA: Ginn Press.

Conrad, C. F., & Pratt, A. M. (1986). Research on academic programs: An inquiry into an emerging field. In J. C. Smart (Ed.), *Higher education: Handbook of theory and research* (pp. 235–273). New York: Agathon Press.

Court, S. (1996, December). *Coping with overload: The use of time by academic and related staff in universities in the UK and USA.* Paper presented at the meeting of the Society for Research into Higher Education, Cardiff, Wales.

Crooks, T. J. (1988). The impact of classroom evaluation practices on students. *Review of Educational Research, 58,* 438–481.

Cross, K. P. (1991). College teaching: What do we know about it? *Innovative Higher Education, 16*(3), 7–25.

Cross, K. P., & Steadman, M. H. (1996). *Classroom research: Implementing the scholarship of teaching.* San Francisco: Jossey-Bass.

Czuchry, M., & Dansereau, D. F. (1996). Node-link mapping as an alternative to traditional writing assignments in undergraduate psychology courses. *Teaching of Psychology, 23,* 91–96.

Dansereau, D. F. (1995). Derived structural schemas and the transfer of knowledge. In A. McKeough, J. Lupart, & A. Marini (Eds.), *Teaching for transfer: Fostering generalization in learning* (pp. 93–121). Hillsdale, NJ: Lawrence Erlbaum Associates.

d'Apollonia, S., & Abrami, P. C. (1997). Navigating student ratings of instruction. *American Psychologist, 52,* 1198–1208.

Das, J. P. (1988). Simultaneous–successive processing and planning: Implications for student learning. In R. R. Schmeck (Ed.), *Learning strategies and learning styles* (pp. 101–129). New York: Plenum Press.

Davis, B. G. (1993). *Tools for teaching.* San Francisco: Jossey-Bass.

Davis, J. R. (1993). *Better teaching, more learning: Strategies for success in postsecondary settings.* Phoenix, AZ: Oryx.

De Neve, H. M. F. (1991). University teachers' thinking about lecturing: Student evaluation of lecturing as an improvement perspective for the lecturer. *Higher Education, 22,* 63–91.

Dey, E. L. (1994). Dimensions of faculty stress: A recent survey. *Review of Higher Education, 17,* 305–322.

Diamond, R. M. (1989). *Designing and improving courses and curricula in higher education.* San Francisco: Jossey-Bass.

Diamond, R. M. (1995). *Preparing for promotion and tenure review: A faculty guide.* Bolton, MA: Anker Publishing.

Diamond, R. M., & Adam, B. E. (1997). *Changing priorities at research universities: 1991–1996.* Syracuse, NY: Syracuse University, Center for Instructional Development.

Dinham, S. M. (1996). What college teachers need to know. In R. J. Menges, M. Weimer, & Associates, *Teaching on solid ground: Using scholarship to improve practice* (pp. 297–313). San Francisco: Jossey-Bass.

Dinham, S. M. (1999). New faculty talk about stress. In R. J. Menges & Associates, *Faculty in new jobs: A guide to settling in, becoming established. and building institutional support.* San Francisco: Jossey-Bass.

Donald, J. G. (1983). Knowledge structures: Methods for exploring course content. *Journal of Higher Education, 54,* 31–41.

Donald, J. G. (1986). Knowledge and the university curriculum. *Higher Education, 15,* 267–282.

Donald, J. G. (1987). Learning schemata: Methods of representing cognitive, content and curriculum structures in higher education. *Instructional Science, 16*(2), 187–211.

Donald, J. G. (1988). Professors' expectations of students' ability to think. *Higher Education Research and Development, 7,* 19–35.

Donald, J. G. (1992a). The development of thinking processes in post-secondary education: Application of a working model. *Higher Education, 24*(4), 13–30.

Donald, J. G. (1992b). Professors' and students' conceptualizations of the learning task in engineering courses. *European Journal of Engineering Education, 17,* 229–245.

Donald, J. G. (1993). Professors' and students' conceptualizations of the learning task in introductory physics courses. *Journal of Research in Science Teaching, 30*(8), 905–918.

Donald, J. G. (1995). Disciplinary differences in knowledge validation. In N. Hativa & M. Marincovich (Eds.), *Disciplinary differences in teaching and learning: Implications for practice.* New Directions for Teaching and Learning, No. 64 (pp. 7–17). San Francisco: Jossey-Bass.

Donald, J. G. (1997). *Improving the environment for learning: Academic leaders talk about what works.* San Francisco: Jossey-Bass.

Duell, O. K. (1994). Extended wait time and university student achievement. *American Educational Research Journal, 31,* 397–414.

Duell, O. K., Lynch, D. J., Ellsworth, R., & Moore, R. C. (1992). Wait-time in college classes taken by education majors. *Research in Higher Education, 33,* 483–495.

Dunkin, M. J. (1995). Concepts of teaching and teaching excellence in higher education. *Higher Education Research and Development, 14,* 21–33.

Dunkin, M. J., & Barnes, J. (1986). Research on teaching in higher education. In M. C. Wittrock (Ed.), *Handbook of research on teaching* (3rd ed., pp. 754–777). New York: Macmillan.

Eble, K. E. (1988). *The craft of teaching: A guide to mastering the professor's art.* San Francisco: Jossey-Bass.

Edgerton, R., Hutchings, P., & Quinlan, K. (1991). *The teaching portfolio: Capturing the scholarship of teaching.* Washington, DC: American Association for Higher Education.

Eisen, J. A. (1989). Mandatory teaching effectiveness workshops for new faculty: What a difference three years make. *Journal of Staff, Program, and Organizational Development, 7*(2), 59–66.

Elrick, M. F. (1990). Improving instruction in universities: A case study of the Ontario universities program for instructional development. *Canadian Journal of Higher Education, 20*(2), 61–79.

Emerson, J. D., & Mosteller, F. (1998a). Interactive multimedia in college teaching. Part I: A ten-year review of reviews. *Educational Media and Technology Yearbook, 23,* 43–58.

Emerson, J. D., & Mosteller, F. (1998b). Interactive multimedia in college teaching. Part II: Lessons from research in the sciences. *Educational Media and Technology Yearbook, 23,* 59–75.

Entwistle, N. (Ed.). (1995). Influences of instructional settings on learning and cognitive development: Findings from European research programs. (Special issue). *Educational Psychologist, 30*(1).

Entwistle, N., & Tait, H. (1995). Approaches to studying and perceptions of the learning environment across disciplines. *New Directions for Teaching and Learning,* No. 64 (pp. 93–103). San Francisco: Jossey-Bass.

Erdle, S., & Murray, H. G. (1986). Interfaculty differences in classroom teaching behaviors and their relationship to student instructional ratings. *Research in Higher Education, 24,* 115–127.

Erickson, B. L., & Strommer, D. W. (1991). *Teaching college freshmen.* San Francisco: Jossey-Bass.

Fairweather, J. S. (1996). *Faculty work and public trust: Restoring the value of teaching and public service in American academic life.* Boston: Allyn & Bacon.

Fairweather, J. S. (1997). The relative value of teaching and research. *NEA 1997 Almanac of Higher Education,* pp. 43–62.

Fairweather, J. S., & Rhoads, R. A. (1995). Teaching and the faculty role: Enhancing the commitment to instruction in American colleges and universities. *Educational Evaluation and Policy Analysis, 17,* 179–194.

Fassinger, P. A. (1995). Understanding classroom interaction: Students' and professors' contributions to students' silence. *Journal of Higher Education, 66,* 82–96.

Feldman, K. A. (1987). Research productivity and scholarly accomplishment of college teachers as related to their instructional effectiveness: A review and exploration. *Research in Higher Education, 26,* 226–298.

Feldman, K. A. (1988). Effective college teaching from the students' and faculty's view: Matched or mismatched priorities? *Research in Higher Education, 28,* 291–344.

Feldman, K. A. (1992). College students' views of male and female college teachers: Part I—Evidence from the social laboratory and experiments. *Research in Higher Education, 33,* 317–375.

Feldman, K. A. (1993). College students' views of male and female college teachers: Part II—Evidence from students' evaluations of their classroom teachers. *Research in Higher Education, 34,* 151–211.

Feldman, K. A. (1997). Identifying exemplary teachers and teaching: Evidence from student ratings. In R. P. Perry & J. C. Smart (Eds.), *Effective teaching in higher education: Research and practice* (pp. 368–395). New York: Agathon Press.

Feldman, K. A. (1998). Reflections on the study of effective college teaching and student ratings: One continuing quest and two unresolved issues. *Higher Education: Handbook of Theory and Research, 13,* 35–74.

Feldman, K. A., & Paulsen, M. B. (Eds.). (1998). *Teaching and learning in the college classroom* (2nd ed.). Needham Heights, MA: Simon & Schuster.

Finkelstein, M. J., & LaCelle-Peterson, M. W. (Eds.). (1993). *Developing senior faculty as teachers.* New Directions for Teaching and Learning, No. 55. San Francisco: Jossey-Bass.

Finkelstein, M. J., Seal, R. K., & Schuster, J. H. (1998). *The new aca-*

demic generation: A profession in transition. Baltimore: Johns Hopkins University Press.

Fox, M. F. (1992). Research, teaching, and publication productivity: Mutuality versus competition in academia. *Sociology of Education, 65,* 293–305.

Fox, P. W., & LeCount, J. (1991, April). *When more is less: Faculty misestimation of students' learning.* Paper presented at the American Educational Research Association, Chicago.

Franklin, J., & Theall, M. (1990). *Communicating student ratings to decision makers: Design for good practice.* New Directions for Teaching and Learning, No. 43 (pp. 75–93). San Francisco: Jossey-Bass.

Fraser, B. J., Giddings, G. J., & McRobbie, C. J. (1992). Assessment of the psychosocial environment of university science laboratory classrooms: A cross-national study. *Higher Education, 24,* 431–451.

Fraser, B. J., & Tobin, K. (1991). Combining qualitative and quantitative methods in classroom environment research. In B. J. Fraser & H. J. Walberg (Eds.), *Educational .environments: Evaluation, antecedents. and consequences.* Oxford, England: Pergamon.

Fraser, B. J., & Treagust, D. F. (1986). Validity and use of an instrument for assessing classroom psychosocial environment in higher education. *Higher Education, 15,* 37–57.

Gabelnick, F., MacGregor, J., Matthews, R. S., & Smith, B. L. (Eds.). (1990). *Learning communities: Creating connections among students, faculty, and disciplines.* New Directions for Teaching and Learning, No. 41. San Francisco: Jossey-Bass.

Gaff, J. G. (1991). *New life for the college curriculum: Assessing achievements and further progress in the reform of general education.* San Francisco: Jossey-Bass.

Gaff, J. G., Ratcliff, J. L., & Associates. (1996). *Handbook of the undergraduate curriculum: A comprehensive guide to purposes, structures, practices, and change.* San Francisco: Jossey-Bass.

Gainen, J., & Boice, R. (Eds.). (1993). Building a diverse faculty. *New Directions for Teaching and Learning,* No. 53. San Francisco: Jossey-Bass.

Gappa, J., & Leslie, D. (1993). *The invisible faculty: Improving the status of part-timers in higher education.* San Francisco: Jossey-Bass.

Gardiner, L. F. (1994). *Redesigning higher education: Producing dramatic gains in student learning* (Report No. 7). Washington, DC: The George Washington University, Graduate School of Education and Human Development.

Geerligs, T. (1994). Students' thoughts during problem-based small-group discussions. *Instructional Science, 22,* 269–278.

Geis, G. L. (1996). Planning and developing effective courses. In R. J. Menges, M. Weimer, & Associates, *Teaching on solid ground: Using scholarship to improve practice* (pp. 179–202). San Francisco: Jossey-Bass.

Gibbs, G. (1995). The relationship between quality in research and quality in teaching. *Quality in Higher Education, 1,* 147–157.

Glassick, C. E., Huber, M. T., & Maeroff, G. 1. (1997). *Scholarship assessed: Evaluation of the professoriate.* San Francisco: Jossey-Bass.

Gmelch, W. H., & Wilke, P. K. (1991). The stresses of faculty and administrators in higher education. *Journal for Higher Education Management, 6,* 23–33.

Gmelch, W. H., Wilke, P. K., & Lovrich, N. P. (1996). Dimensions of stress among university faculty: Factor-analytic results from a national study. *Research in Higher Education, 24,* 266–286.

Graubard, S. R. (Ed.). (1997, Fall). The American academic profession. *Daedalus: Journal of the American Academy of Arts and Sciences, 126*(4), v–x.

Gray, P. J., Froh, R. C., & Diamond, R. M. (1991). Myths & realities. *AAHE Bulletin, 44*(12), 4–5.

Gray, P. J., Froh, R. C., & Diamond, R. M. (1992). *A national study of research universities on the balance between research and undergraduate teaching.* Syracuse, NY: Syracuse University, Center for Instructional Development.

Green, K. C., & Gilbert, S. W. (1995). Great expectations: Content, communications, productivity, and the role of information technology in higher education. *Change, 27*(2), 8–18.

Greenwald, A. G., & Gillmore, G. M. (1997). Grading leniency is a removable contaminant of student ratings. *American Psychologist, 52,* 1209–1217.

Gregory, K. (1996). A construct for teaching profiles. In R. Aylett &

K. Gregory (Eds.), *Evaluating teacher quality in higher education* (pp. 101–116). Washington, DC: Falmer Press.

Guskin, A. E. (1994). Restructuring the role of faculty. *Change, 26*(5), 16–25.

Hagan, A. S., & Weinstein, C. E. (1995). Achievement goals, self-regulated learning, and the role of classroom context. In P. R. Pintrich (Ed.), *Understanding self-regulated learning.* New Directions for Teaching and Learning, No. 63 (pp. 43–55). San Francisco: Jossey-Bass.

Hall, C., & Fitzgerald, C. (1995). Student summative evaluation of teaching: Code of practice. *Assessment & Evaluation in Higher Education, 20,* 307–311.

Hartman, S. L., & Nelson, M. S. (1992). What we say and what we do: Self-reported teaching behavior versus performances in written simulations among medical school faculty. *Academic Medicine, 67,* 522–527.

Harvey, W. B., & Valadez, J. (Eds.). (1994). *Creating and maintaining a diverse faculty.* New Directions for Community Colleges, No. 87. San Francisco: Jossey-Bass.

Haskell, R. (1996). Academic freedom, tenure, and student evaluation of faculty: Galloping polls in the 21st century. *Education Policy Analysis Archives* [On-line serial], 5. <http:olam.ed.asu.edu/epaa/.>

Hattie, J., & Marsh, H. W. (1996). The relationship between research and teaching: A meta-analysis. *Review of Educational Research, 66,* 507–542.

Haworth, J. G., & Conrad, C. F. (1990). Curricular transformations: Traditional and emerging voices in the academy. In C. F. Conrad & J. G. Haworth (Eds.), *Curriculum in transition: Perspectives on the undergraduate experience.* Needham Heights, MA: Ginn Press.

Haworth, J. G., & Conrad, C. F. (Eds.). (1995). *Revisioning curriculum in higher education.* Needham Heights, MA: Simon & Schuster.

Hayes, K., & Richardson, J. T. E. (1995). Gender, subject, and context as determinants of approaches to studying in higher education. *Studies in Higher Education, 20,* 215–221.

Hofer, B. K., & Pintrich, P. R. (1997). The development of epistemological theories: Beliefs about knowledge and knowing and their relation to learning. *Review of Education Research, 67,* 88–140.

Hoyt, D. P. (1997, September). Studies of the impact of extraneous variables. *Exchange,* unpaginated. Manhattan: Kansas State University, IDEA Center.

Hughes, J. A. (1992). Gender differences in personal theories of teaching. *Journal of Staff, Program, & Organization Development, 10,* 87–94.

Husbands, C. T., & Fosh, P. (1993). Students' evaluation of teaching in higher education: Experiences from four European countries and some implications of the practice. *Assessment & Evaluation in Higher Education, 18,* 95–114.

Hythecker, V. I., Dansereau, D. F., & Rocklin, T. R. (1988). An analysis of the processes influencing the structured dyadic learning environment. *Educational Psychologist, 23,* 23–37.

Irby, D. M. (1994). What clinical teachers in medicine need to know. *Academic Medicine, 69,* 333–342.

Jaques, D. (1992). *Learning in groups* (2nd ed.). Houston, TX: Gulf.

Johnson, D. W., Johnson, R. T., & Smith, K. A. (1991). *Cooperative learning: Increasing college faculty instructional productivity.* (ASHE–ERIC Higher Education Research Report No. 4). Washington, DC: The George Washington University, Graduate School of Education and Human Development.

Johnson, D. W., Johnson, R. T., & Smith, K. A. (1996). *Academic controversy: Enriching college instruction through intellectual conflict* (ASHE–ERIC Higher Education Research Report, Vol. 25, No. 3). Washington, DC: The George Washington University, Graduate School of Education and Human Development.

Jones, A., Scanlon, E., Tosunoglu, C., Ross, S., Butcher, P., Murphy, P., & Greenberg, J. (1996). Evaluating CAL at the open university: 15 years on. *Computers & Education, 26,* 515.

Kanter, S. L., Gamson, Z. F., & London, H. B. (1997). *Revitalizing general education in a time of scarcity: A navigational chart for administrators and faculty.* Boston: Allyn and Bacon.

Karabenick, S. A., & Sharma, R. (1994). Perceived teacher support of student questioning in the college classroom: Its relation to student characteristics and role in the classroom questioning process. *Journal of Educational Psychology, 86,* 90–103.

Katz, J., & Henry, M. (1988). *Turning professors into teachers: A new approach to faculty development and student learning.* New York: American Council on Education/Macmiillan.

Kember, D., & Gow, L. (1990). Cultural specificity of approaches to study. *British Journal of Educational Psychology, 60,* 356–363.

Kember, D., & Gow, L. (1994). Orientations to teaching and their effect on the quality of student learning. *Journal of Higher Education, 65,* 58–74.

Kember, D., Jamieson, Q. W., Pomfret, M., & Wong, E. T. T. (1995). Learning approaches, study time, and academic performance. *Higher Education, 29,* 329–343.

Kiewra, K. A. (1985a). Investigating notetaking and review: A depth of processing alternative. *Educational Psychologist, 20,* 23–32.

Kiewra, K. A. (1985b). Providing the instructor's notes: An effective addition to student notetaking. *Educational Psychologist, 20,* 33–39.

Kiewra, K. A. (1988). Cognitive aspects of autonomous notetaking: Control processes, learning strategies, and prior knowledge. *Educational Psychologist, 23,* 39–56.

Kiewra, K. A. (1991). Aids to lecture learning. *Educational Psychologist, 26,* 37–53.

Kiewra, K. A., & Benton, S. L. (1987). Effects of notetaking, the instructor's notes, and higher-order practice questions on factual and higher-order learning. *Journal of Instructional Psychology, 14,* 186–194.

King, A. (1992a). Comparison of self-questioning, summarizing, and notetaking-review as strategies for learning from lectures. *American Educational Research Journal, 22,* 303–323.

King, A. (1992b). Facilitating elaborative learning through guided student-generated questioning. *Educational Psychologist, 27,* 111–126.

King, P. M. (1996). Student cognition and learning. In Komives, S. R., Woodard, D. B., Jr., & Associates (Eds.), *Student services: A handbook for the profession* (3rd ed., pp. 218–243). San Francisco: Jossey-Bass.

King, P. M., & Kitchener, K. S. (Eds.). (1993). *The development of reflective thinking in the college years: The mixed results.* New Directions for Higher Education, No. 84. San Francisco: Jossey-Bass.

King, P. M., & Kitchener, K. S. (1994). *Developing reflective judgment: Understanding and promoting intellectual growth and critical thinking in adolescents and adults.* San Francisco: Jossey-Bass.

Kirk, D., & Todd-Mancillas, W. R. (1991). Turning points in graduate student socialization: Implications for faculty. *Review of Higher Education, 14,* 407–422.

Kitchener, K. S., & King, P. M. (1981). Reflective judgment: Concepts of justification and their relationship to age and education. *Journal of Applied Developmental Psychology, 2,* 89–116.

Kochenour, E. O., Jolley, D. S., Kaup, J. G., Patrick, D. L., Roach, K. D., & Wenzler, L. A. (1997). Supplemental instruction: An effective component of student affairs programming. *Journal of College Student Development, 38,* 577–585.

Komives, S. R., Woodard, D. J., Jr., & Associates (Eds.). (1996). *Student services: A handbook for the profession.* San Francisco: Jossey-Bass.

Kozma, R. B. (1994). Will media influence learning? Reframing the debate. *Educational Technology Research and Development, 42*(2), 7–19.

Krupnick, C. G. (1985, May). Women and men in the classroom: Inequality and its remedies. *On Teaching and Learning, 1,* 18–25.

Kugel, P. (1993). How professors develop as teachers. *Studies in Higher Education, 18,* 315–328.

Kuh, G. D., Bean, J. P., Hossler, D., & Stage, F. K. (Eds.). (1989). *ASHE reader on college students.* Needham Heights, MA: Ginn Press.

Kuh, G. D., Pace, C. R., & Vesper, N. (1997). The development of process indicators to estimate student gains associated with good practices in undergraduate education. *Research in Higher Education, 38,* 435–454.

Kulik, C. C., Kulik, J. A., & Bangert-Drowns, R. L. (1990). Effectiveness of mastery learning programs: A meta-analysis. *Review of Educational Research, 60,* 265–299.

Kulik, J. A., & Kulik, C. C. (1988). Timing of feedback and verbal learning. *Review of Educational Research, 58,* 79–97.

Lattuca, L. R., & Stark, J. S. (1995). Modifying the major: Discretion-

ary thoughts from ten disciplines. *Review of Higher Education, 18,* 315–344.

Laurillard, D. (1993). *Rethinking university teaching: A framework for the effective use of educational technology.* New York: Routledge.

Layzell, D. T. (1996). Faculty workload and productivity: Recurrent issues with new imperatives. *Review of Higher Education, 19,* 267–281.

Learning Productivity News. (1997, Spring). Learning productivity: Studies under way in calendar year 1997. *Learning Productivity News, 1*(3), 1.

Lenze, L. F. (1995). Discipline-specific pedagogic knowledge in linguistics and Spanish. In N. Hativa & M. Marincovich (Eds.), *Disciplinary differences in teaching and learning: Implications for practice.* New Directions for Teaching and Learning, No. 64 (pp. 65–70). San Francisco: Jossey-Bass.

Lenze, L. F., & Dinham, S. M. (1999). Learning what students understand. In R. J. Menges and Associates, *Faculty in new jobs: Mastering academic work* (pp. 147–165). San Francisco: Jossey-Bass.

Levine, A., & Hirsch, D. (1991). Undergraduates in transition: A new wave of activism on college campus. *Higher Education, 22,* 119–128.

L'Hommedieu, R., & Menges, R. J. (1992). Toward more conclusive studies of student ratings feedback. *Instructional Evaluation, 12,* 17–23.

L'Hommedieu, R., Menges, R. J., & Brinko, K. T. (1990). Methodological explanations for the modest effects of feedback from student ratings. *Journal of Educational Psychology, 82,* 232–241.

Lin, Y.-G., McKeachie, W. J., & Tucker, D. G. (1984). The use of student ratings in promotion decisions. *Journal of Higher Education, 55,* 583–589.

Lohmann, J. R:, & Stacey, A. M. (1992). *America's academic future: A report of the Presidential Young Investigator Colloquium on U.S. engineering, mathematics, and science education for the year 2000.* Washington, DC: National Science Foundation, Directorate for Education and Human Resources.

Long, H. B., & Walsh, S. M. (1993). Self-directed learning research in the community/junior college: Description conclusions, and recommendations. *Community College Journal of Research and Practice, 17,* 153–166.

Lonka, K., & Lindblom-Ylanne, S. (1996). Epistemologies, conceptions of learning, and study practices in medicine and psychology. *Higher Education, 31,* 5–24.

Lowman, J. (1995). *Mastering the techniques of teaching.* San Francisco: Jossey-Bass.

Lowther, M. A., & Stark, J. S. (1990, April). *Course planning patterns of college teachers.* Paper presented at the American Educational Research Association, Boston.

MacFarlane, A. G. J. (1995). Future patterns of teaching and learning. In T. Schuller (Ed.), *The changing university?* Bristol, PA: Open University Press.

Marsh, H. W. (1984). Students' evaluations of university teaching: Dimensionality, reliability, validity, potential biases, and utility. *Journal of Educational Psychology, 75,* 707–754.

Marsh, H. W. (1987). Students' evaluations of university teaching: Research findings, methodological issues, and directions for future research. *International Journal of Educational Research, 11,* 253–388.

Marsh, H. W. (1991a). Multidimensional students' evaluations of teaching effectiveness: A test of alternative higher-order structures. *Journal of Educational Psychology, 83,* 285–296.

Marsh, H. W. (1991b). A multidimensional perspective on students' evaluations of teaching effectiveness: A reply to Abrami and d'Apollonia. (1991). *Journal of Educational Psychology, 83,* 416–421.

Marsh, H. W., & Dunkin, M. J. (1997). Students' evaluations of university teaching: A multidimensional perspective. In R. P. Perry & J. C. Smart (Eds.), *Effective teaching in higher education: Research and practice* (pp. 241–320). New York: Agathon Press. (Original work published 1992)

Marsh, H. W., & Roche, L. (1993). The use of students' evaluations and an individually structured intervention to enhance university teaching effectiveness. *American Educational Research Journal, 30,* 217–251.

Marsh, H. W., & Roche, L. A. (1997). Making students' evaluations of teaching effectiveness effective: The critical issues of validity, bias, and utility. *American Psychologist, 52,* 1187–1197.

Marton, F., & Booth, S. (1997). *Learning and awareness.* Mahwah, NJ: Lawrence Erlbaum Assocates.

Marton, F., & Ramsden, P. (1988). What does it take to improve learning? In P. Ramsden (Ed.), *Improving learning: New perspectives.* London: Kogan Page.

Massy, W. F., & Zemsky, R. (1994). Faculty discretionary time: Departments and the "academic ratchet." *Journal of Higher Education, 65,* 122.

Massy, W. F., & Zemsky, R. (1995, June). Using information to enhance academic productivity [Online]. Washington, DC: Educom. <http://www.educom.edu/>.

Mauksch, H. W., & Howery, C. B. (1986). Social change for teaching: The case of one disciplinary association. *Teaching Sociology, 14,* 67–72.

McCabe, D. L., & Trevino, L. K. (1996). What we know about cheating in college: Longitudinal trends and recent developments. *Change, 28*(1), 28–33.

McDougall, D., & Cordeiro, P. (1993). Effects of random-questioning expectations on community college students' preparedness for lecture and discussion. *Community College Journal of Research and Practice, 17,* 39–49.

McKeachie, W. J. (1963). Research on teaching at the college and university level. In N. L. Gage (Ed.), *Handbook of research on teaching* (pp. 1118–1172). Chicago: Rand McNally.

McKeachie, W. J. (1994). *Teaching tips: Strategies, research, and theory for college and university teachers* (9th ed.). Lexington, MA: D.C. Heath.

McKeachie, W. J. (1997). Student ratings: The validity of use. *American Psychologist 52,* 1218–1225.

McKeachie, W. J., Pintrich, P. R., Lin, Y.-G., Smith, D. A. F., & Sharma, R. (1990). *Teaching and learning in the college classroom: A review of the research literature* (2nd ed.). (Technical Report No. 90–B–003–1). Ann Arbor: University of Michigan, National Center for Research to Improve Postsecondary Teaching and Learning.

McMillan, J. H. (Ed.). (1988). *Assessing students' learning.* New Directions for Teaching and Learning, No. 34. San Francisco: Jossey-Bass.

Menec, V. H., Perry, R. P., Struthers, C. W., Schonwetter, D. J., Hechter, F. J., & Eichholz, B. L. (1994). Assisting at-risk college students with attributional retraining and effective teaching. *Journal of Applied Social Psychology, 24,* 675–701.

Menges, R. J. (1981). Instructional methods. In A. W. Chickering & Associates, *The modem American college* (pp. 556–581). San Francisco: Jossey-Bass.

Menges, R. J. (1985). Career-span faculty development. *College Teaching , 33,* 181–184.

Menges, R. J. (1994). Improving your teaching. In W. J. McKeachie (ed.), *Teaching tips: Strategies, research, and theory for college and university teachers* (9th ed.). Lexington, MA: D.C. Heath.

Menges, R. J. (1997). Fostering faculty motivation to teach: Approaches to faculty development. In J. L. Bess (Ed.), *Teaching well and liking it: Motivating faculty to teach effectively* (pp. 407–423). Baltimore: Johns Hopkins University Press.

Menges, R. J., & Associates. (1999). *Faculty in new jobs: A guide to settling in, becoming established, and building institutional supports.* San Francisco: Jossey-Bass.

Menges, R. J., & Brinko, K. T. (1986, April). *Effects of student evaluation feedback: A meta-analysis of higher education research.* Paper presented at the American Educational Research Association, San Francisco.

Menges, R. J., & Brinko, K. T. (1990). A three-dimensional model for planning and assessing faculty development efforts. *Journal of Staff, Program, and Organization Development, 8,* 133–142.

Menges, R. J., & Mathis, B. C. (1988). *Key resources on teaching. learning, curriculum, and faculty development.* San Francisco: Jossey-Bass.

Menges, R. J., & Reyes, E. A. (1997). *Teaching–learning productivity in higher education.* Evanston, IL: Northwestern University, Center for the Teaching Professions.

Menges, R. J., Weimer, M., & Associates (1996). *Teaching on solid ground: Using scholarship to improve practice.* San Francisco: Jossey-Bass.

Michaelsen, L. K., Fink, L. D., & Knight, A. (1997). Designing effective group activities: Lessons for classroom teaching and faculty development. *To Improve the Academy, 16,* 373–398.

Milem, J. F., Berger, J. B., & Dey, E. L. (1997, November). *Faculty time allocation: A longitudinal study of change.* Paper presented at the Association for the Study of Higher Education, Albuquerque, NM.

Milton, 0., Pollio, H. R., & Eison, J. A. (1986). *Making sense of college grades.* San Francisco: Jossey-Bass.

Moore, M., & Kearsky, G. (1996). *Distance education: A systems view.* Belmont, CA: Wadsworth Publishing.

Mowrer, D. E. (1996). A content analysis of student/instructor communication via computer conferencing. *Higher Education, 32,* 217–241.

Murray, H. G. (1997a, March). *Classroom teaching behaviors and student instructional ratings: How do good teachers teach?* Paper presented at the American Educational Research Association, Chicago.

Murray, H. G. (1997b). Effective teaching behaviors in the college classroom. In R. P. Perry & J. C. Smart (Eds.), *Effective teaching in higher education: Research and practice* (pp. 171–204). New York: Agathon Press. (Original work published 1991)

Murray, H. G., & Renaud, R. D. (1995). Disciplinary differences in classroom teaching behaviors. In N. Hativa & M. Marincovich (Eds.), *Disciplinary differences in teaching and learning: Implications for practice.* New Directions for Teaching and Learning, No. 64 (pp. 31–39). San Francisco: Jossey-Bass.

Murray, H. G., Rushton, J. P., & Paunonen, S. V. (1990). Teacher personality traits and student instructional ratings in six types of university courses. *Journal of Educational Psychology, 82,* 250–261.

Murray, J. P. (1995). *Successful faculty development and evaluation: The complete teaching portfolio.* (ASHE–ERIC Higher Education Research Report No. 8). Washington, DC: The George Washington University, Graduate School of Education and Human Development.

Nance, J. L., & Nance, C. E. (1990). Does learning occur in the classroom? *College Student Journal, 24,* 338–340.

Naveh-Benjamin, M., & Lin, Y.-G. (1988, August). *The effects of explicitly teaching an instructor's knowledge structure on students' cognitive structures.* Paper presented at the American Psychological Association Convention, Atlanta, GA.

Neal, E. (1997). Evaluation: The social context of educational leadership. In J. L. Morrison (Ed.), [CD ROM]. Redmond, WA: Microsoft Corporation.

Negron-Morales, P., Vasquez-Rodriguez, I., & De Leon-Lozada, A. (1996, May). *Good practices in undergraduate education from the students' and faculty's view: Consequences or disagreement.* Paper presented at the Association for Institutional Research, Albuquerque, NM.

Nyquist, J. D., Abbott, R. D., & Wulff, D. H. (Eds.). (1989). *Teaching assistant training in the 1990s.* New Directions for Teaching and Learning, No. 39. San Francisco: Jossey-Bass.

Nyquist, J. D., Abbott, R. D., Wulff, D. H., & Sprague, J. (Eds.). (1991). *Preparing the professoriate of tomorrow to teach: Selected readings in TA training.* Dubuque, IA: Kendall/Hunt.

Nyquist, J. D., & Wulff, D. H. (1992). *Preparing teaching assistants for instructional roles: Supervising TAs in communication.* Annandale, VA: Speech Communication Association.

Olsen, D., & Sorcinelli, M. D. (1992). The pretenure years: A longitudinal perspective. In M. D. Sorcinelli & A. E. Austin (Eds.), *Developing new and junior faculty.* New Directions for Teaching and Learning, No. 50 (pp. 15–25). San Francisco: Jossey-Bass.

Osterlind, S. J. (1997). *A national review of scholastic achievement in general education: How are we doing and why should we care?* (ASHE-ERIC Higher Education Research Report, Vol. 25, No. 8). Washington, DC: The George Washington University, School of Education and Human Development.

Owen, S. V., & Froman, R. D. (1987). What's wrong with three-option multiple choice items? *Educational and Psychological Measurement, 47,* 513–522.

Owston, R. D. (1997). The world wide web: A technology to enhance teaching and learning? *Educational Researcher, 26*(2), 27–33.

Palmer, P. J. (1997). *The courage to teach: Exploring the inner landscape of a teacher's life.* San Francisco: Jossey-Bass.

Pascarella, E. T., Edison, M., Hagadorn, L., Nora, A., & Terenzini, P. (1996). Cognitive effects of two-year and four-year colleges: New evidence. *Educational Evaluation and Policy Analysis, 17,* 83–96.

Pascarella, E. T., & Terenzini, P. T. (1991). *How college affects students: Findings and insights from twenty years of research.* San Francisco: Jossey-Bass.

Paul, J. (1994). Improving education through computer-based alternative assessment methods. In S. W. Cockton, S. W. Draper, & G. R. S. Weir (Eds.), *People and computers.* New York: Cambridge University Press.

Paul, R. W., Elder, L., & Bartell, T. (1997). *California teacher preparation for instruction in critical thinking: Research findings and policy recommendations.* Sacramento: California Commission on Teacher Credentialing.

Paulsen, M. B., & Feldman, K. A. (1995). *Taking Teaching Seriously: Meeting the challenge of instructional improvement.* (ASHE–ERIC Higher Education Research Report, Vol. 25, No. 2). Washington, DC: The George Washington University, Graduate School of Education and Human Development.

Perry, R. P. (1997). Perceived control in college students: Implications for instruction in higher education. In R. P. Perry & J. C. Smart (Eds.), *Effective teaching in higher education: Research and practice* (pp. 11–60). New York: Agathon Press. (Original work published 1991)

Perry, R. P., Hechter, F. J., Menec, V. H., & Weinberg, L. E. (1993). Enhancing achievement motivation and performance in college students: An attributional retraining perspective. *Research in Higher Education, 34,* 687–723.

Perry, R. P., Schonwetter, D. J., Magnusson, J.-L., & Struthers, C. W. (1994). Students' explanatory schemas and the quality of college instruction: Some evidence for buffer and compensation effects. *Research in Higher Education, 35,* 349–371.

Perry, R. P., & Smart, J. C. (Eds.). (1997). *Effective teaching in higher education: Research and practice.* New York: Agathon Press.

Perry, W. G., Jr. (1970). *Forms of intellectual and ethical development in the college years: A scheme.* New York: Holt, Rinehart & Winston.

Pintrich, P. R. (1989). The dynamic interplay of student motivation and cognition in the college classroom. In M. L. Maehr & C. Ames (Eds.), *Motivation Enhancing Environments, 6,* 117–160.

Pintrich, P. R. (Ed.). (1995). *Understanding self-regulated learning.* New Directions for Teaching and Learning, No. 63. San Francisco: Jossey-Bass.

Piper, D. W. (1994). *Are professors professional? The organisation of university examinations.* London: Jessica Kingsley Publishers.

Pollio, H. R. (1984). What students think about and do in college lecture classes. *Teaching–Learning Issues,* No. 53. Knoxville: University of Tennessee.

Pollio, H. R. (1985). A tiger examines his stripes. *Teaching–Learning Issues,* No. 55. Knoxville: University of Tennessee.

Pollio, H. R. (1989). Any questions, please? *Teaching–Learning Issues,* No. 66. Knoxville: University of Tennessee.

Pollio, H. R. (1992). Learning new material is fun—yes, but will it be on the test? *Teaching–Learning Issues,* No. 72. Knoxville: University of Tennessee.

Pollio, H. R. (1994). Ginger and the man: What stands out (and gets remembered) in college classrooms. *Teaching–Learning Issues,* No. 74. Knoxville: University of Tennessee.

Pollio, H. R. (1996). The two cultures of pedagogy: Teaching and learning in the natural sciences and humanities. *Teaching–Learning Issues,* No. 75. Knoxville: University of Tennessee.

Pollio, H. R., & Eskra, D. (1993). Respect, help, status, and relationship: Themes in faculty descriptions of being mentored. *Teaching–Learning Issues,* No. 73. Knoxville: University of Tennessee.

Pollio, H. R., & Humphreys, W. L. (1996). What award-winning lecturers say about their teaching: It's all about connection. *College Teaching, 44*(3), 101–106.

Pratt, D. D. (1997). Reconceptualizing the evaluation of teaching in higher education. *Higher Education, 34,* 23–44.

Qin, Z., Johnson, D. W., & Johnson, R. T. (1995). Cooperative versus competitive efforts and problem solving. *Review of Educational Research, 65,* 129–143.

Ramsden, P. (1992). *Learning to teach in higher education.* London: Routledge.

Rando, W. C., & Menges, R. J. (1991). How practice is shaped by personal theories. In R. J. Menges & M. D. Svinicki (Eds.), *College teaching: From theory to practice.* New Directions for Teaching and Learning, No. 45 (pp. 7–14). San Francisco: Jossey Bass.

Rice, R. E. (1996). *Making a place for the new American scholar.* (Report No. FROIWP). Washington, DC: American Association for Higher Education.

Richardson, J. T. E. (1994). Cultural specificity of approaches to studying in higher education: A literature survey. *Higher Education, 27,* 449–468.

Richardson, J. T. E. (1995). Cultural specificity of approaches to studying in higher education: A comparative investigation using the approaches to studying inventory. *Educational and Psychological Measurement, 55,* 300–308.

Richlin, L., & Manning, B. (1995). *Improving a college/university teaching evaluation system: A comprehensive, developmental curriculum for faculty and administrators.* Pittsburgh, PA: Alliance.

Riegle, R. P. (1987). Conceptions of faculty development. *Educational Theory, 37,* 53–59.

Root, L. S. (1987), Faculty evaluation: Reliability of peer assessment of research, teaching, and service. *Research in Higher Education, 26,* 71–84.

Ropers-Huilman, B. (1998). Feminist teaching is higher education. *Higher Education: Handbook of Theory and Research, 13,* 274–303.

Rousseau, D. M. (1997). Organizational behavior in the new organizational era. *Annual Review of Psychology, 48,* 515–546.

Russell, T. L. (1997). The "no significant difference" phenomenon. New Brunswick, Canada: Home Page of NB TeleEducation. <http://temb.mta,ca>.

Sadler, D. R. (1989). Formative assessment and the design of instructional systems. *Instructional Science, 18,* 119–144.

Samuelowicz, K., & Bain, J. D. (1992). Conceptions of teaching held by academic teachers. *Higher Education, 24,* 93–111.

Saroyan, A., & Amundsen, C. (1995). The systematic design and implementation of a training program for teaching assistants. *Canadian Journal of Higher Education, 25,* 1–18.

Sax, L. J., Astin, A. W., Arredondo, M., & Korn, W. S. (1996). *The American college teacher: National norms for the 1995–96 HERI faculty survey.* Los Angeles: University of California at Los Angeles, Higher Education Research Institute.

Schemoglu, N., & Fogelman, K. (1995). Effects of enhancing behavior of students and use of feedback-corrective procedures. *Journal of Educational Research, 89,* 59–63.

Schmeck, R. R. (1988). An introduction to strategies and styles of learning. In R. R. Schmeck (Ed.), *Learning strategies and learning styles* (pp. 3–19). New York: Plenum Press.

Schmelkin, L. P., Spencer, K. J., & Gellman, E. S. (1997). Faculty perspectives on course and teacher evaluations. *Research in Higher Education, 38,* 575–592.

Schroeder, C. C. (1993). New students–New learning styles. *Change, 25*(5), 21–26.

Schwartz, C. (1992). Is good teaching rewarded at Berkeley? *College Teaching, 40*(4), 33–36.

Scriven, M. (1988). The validity of student ratings. *Instructional Evaluation, 9*(2), 5–18.

Seldin, P. (1993). *Successful use of teaching portfolios.* Bolton, MA: Anker Publishing.

Seldin, P. (1997). *The teaching portfolio: A practical guide to improved performance and promotion/tenure decisions* (2nd ed.). Bolton, MA: Anker Publishing.

Seldin, P., & Associates. (1995). *Improving college teaching.* Bolton, MA: Anker Publishing.

Severiens, S. E., & Ten-Dam, G. T. N. (1994). Gender differences in learning styles: A narrative review and quantitative meta-analysis. *Higher Education, 27,* 487–501.

Shapiro, J. J., & Hughes, S. K. (1996). Information technology as a liberal art. *Educom Review, 31*(2), 31–35.

Sherman, T. M., Armistead, L. P., Fowler, F., Barksdale, M. A., & Reif, G. (1987). The quest for excellence in university teaching. *Journal of Higher Education, 58,* 66–84.

Shuell, T. J. (1993). Toward an integrated theory of teaching and learning. *Educational Psychologist, 28,* 291–311.

Shulman, L. S. (1986). Those who understand: Knowledge growth in teaching. *Educational Researcher, 15*(2), 4–14.

Smart, J. C., & Ethington, C. A. (1995). Disciplinary and institutional differences in undergraduate educational goals. In N. Hativa & M. Marincovich (Eds.), *Disciplinary differences in teaching and learning: Implications for practice.* New Directions for Teaching and Learning, No. 64 (pp. 49–57). San Francisco: Jossey-Bass.

Smith, E., & Witt, S. L. (1993). A comparative study of occupational stress among African American and white university faculty: A research note. *Research in Higher Education, 34,* 229–241.

Somervell, H. (1993). Issues in assessment, enterprise, and higher education: The case for self, peer, and collaborative assessment. *Assessment and Evaluation in Higher Education, 18,* 221–233.

Sorcinelli, M. D. (1988). Satisfactions and concerns of new university teachers. *To Improve the Academy, 7,* 121–131.

Sorcinelli, M. D., & Austin, A. E. (Eds.). (1992). *Developing new and junior faculty.* New Directions for Teaching and Learning. No. 50. San Francisco: Jossey-Bass.

Springer, L., Stanne, M. E., & Donovan, S. (1997, November). *Effects of cooperative learning on undergraduates in science, mathematics, engineering, and technology: A meta-analysis.* Paper presented at the Annual Meeting of the Association for the Study of Higher Education, Albuquerque, NM.

Stage, F. K., Anaya, G. L., Bean, J. P., Hossler, D., & Kuh, G. D. (Eds.). (1996). *College students: The evolving nature of research.* Needham Heights, MA: Simon & Schuster.

Stahl, N. A., Simpson, M. L., & Hayes, C. G. (1992). Ten recommendations from research for teaching high-risk college students. *Journal of Developmental Education, 16,* 2–10.

Stark, J. S., & Lattuca, L. R. (1997). *Shaping the college curriculum: Academic plans in action.* Boston: Allyn & Bacon.

Stark, J. S., Lowther, M. A., & Hagerty, B. M. K. (1986). Faculty roles and role preferences in ten fields of professional study. *Research in Higher Education, 25,* 3–30.

Statham A., Richardson, L., & Cook, J. A. (1991). *Gender and university teaching: A negotiated difference.* Albany, NY: State University of New York Press.

Steward, A. L., & Lupfer, M. (1987). Touching as teaching: The effect of touch on students' perceptions and performance. *Journal of Applied Social Psychology, 17,* 800–809.

Sutherland, T. E., & Bonwell, C. C. (Eds.). (1996). *Using active learning in college classes: A range of options for faculty.* New Directions for Teaching and Learning, No. 67. San Francisco: Jossey-Bass.

Svinicki, M. D., & Menges, R. J. (Eds.). (1996). *Honoring exemplary teaching.* New Directions for Teaching and Learning, No. 65. San Francisco: Jossey-Bass.

Tack, M. W., & Patitu, C. L. (1992). *Faculty job satisfaction: Women and minorities in peril.* (ASHE–ERIC Higher Education Report, No. 4). Washington, DC: The George Washington University, School of Education and Human Development.

Tang, T. L.-P., & Chamberlain, M. (1997). Attitudes toward research and teaching. *Journal of Higher Education, 68,* 212–227.

Taylor, L. (1994). Reflecting on teaching: The benefits of self-evaluation. *Assessment & Evaluation in Higher Education, 19,* 109–122.

Theall, M., & Franklin, J. (Eds.). (1991). *Effective practices for improving teaching.* New Directions for Teaching and Learning. No. 48. San Francisco: Jossey-Bass.

Tiberius, R. G. (1986). Metaphors underlying the improvement of teaching and learning. *British Journal of Educational Technology, 17,* 144–156.

Tiberius, R. G. (1989). *Small group teaching: A troubleshooting guide.* Toronto: Ontario Institute for Studies in Education Press.

Tiberius, R. G., Sackin, H., Slingerland, J. M., Jubas, K., Bell, M., & Matlow, A. (1989). The influence of student evaluative feedback on the improvement of clinical teaching. *Journal of Higher Education, 60,* 665–681.

Tierney, W. G., & Bensimon, E. M. (1996). *Promotion and tenure: Community and socialization in academe.* Albany, NY: State University of New York Press.

Tierney, W. G., & Rhoads, R. A. (1993). Postmodernism and critical theory in higher education: Implications for research and practice. *Higher Education: Handbook of Theory and Research, 9,* 308–343.

Tinto, V. (1997). Classrooms as communities: Exploring the educational character of student persistence. *Journal of Higher Education, 68,* 599–623.

Toombs, W., & Tierney, W. G. (1991). *Meeting the mandate: Renewing the college and departmental curriculum.* ASHE–ERIC Higher Education Report, No. 6. Washington, DC: The George Washington University, School of Education and Human Development.

Topping, K. J. (1996). The effectiveness of peer tutoring in further and higher education: A typology and review of the literature. *Higher Education, 32,* 321–345.

Travis, J. E. (1995). *Models for improving college teaching: A faculty resource.* ASHE–ERIC Higher Education Report, No. 6. Washington, DC: The George Washington University, Graduate School of Education and Human Development.

Trevisan, M. S., Sax, G., & Michael, W. B. (1991). The effects of the number of options per item and student ability on test validity and reliability. *Educational and Psychological Measurement, 51,* 829–837.

Trigwell, K., & Prosser, A (1996). Congruence between intention and strategy in university science teachers' approaches to teaching. *Higher Education, 32,* 77–87.

Tuckman, B. W. (1992). Does the length of assignment or the nature of grading practices influence the amount of homework students are motivated to produce? *Journal of General Education, 41,* 190–199.

Twigg, C. (1996). Academic productivity: The case for instructional software. Washington, DC: Educom, National Learning Infrastructure Initiative. <http://www.educom.edu/>.

Van Dusen, G. C. (1997). *The virtual campus: Technology and reform in higher education.* ASHE–ERIC Higher Education Research Report, Vol. 25, No. 5. Washington, DC: The George Washington University, Graduate School of Education and Human Development.

Van Meter, P., Yokoi, L., & Pressley, M. (1994). College students' theory of notetaking derived from their perceptions of notetaking. *Journal of Educational Psychology, 86,* 323–338.

Vermunt, J. D. (1996, January). Metacognitive, cognitive, and affective aspects of learning styles and strategies: A phenomenographic analysis. *Higher Education, 31,* 25–50.

Vermunt, J. D., & Van Rijswijk, F. A. (1988). Analysis and development of students' skill in self-regulated learning. *Higher Education, 17,* 647–682.

Volkwein, J. F. (1997, November). *The undergraduate classroom experience: Factors associated with its vitality.* Paper presented at the Association for the Study of Higher Education, Albuquerque, NM.

Voorhees, R. A. (1997). Student learning and development in the community college. *Higher Education: Handbook of Theory and Research, 13,* 313–370.

Watkins, D. (1994). Student evaluations of university teaching: A cross-cultural perspective. *Research in Higher Education, 35,* 251–266.

Webb, G. (1996). *Understanding staff development.* Buckingham, UK: Open University Press.

Weimer, M. (1990). *Improving college teaching.* San Francisco: Jossey-Bass.

Weimer, M. (1993). The discipline journals on pedagogy. *Change, 25*(6), 44–51.

Weimer, M., & Lenze, L. F. (1997). Instructional interventions: A review of the literature on efforts to improve instruction. In R. P. Perry & J. C. Smart (Eds.), *Effective teaching in higher education: Research and practice* (pp. 205–240). New York: Agathon Press. (Original work published 1991)

Weston, C., & Cranton, P. A. (1986). Selecting instructional strategies. *Journal of Higher Education, 57,* 259–288.

Weston, C., McAlpine, L., & Bordonaro, T. (1995). A model for understanding formative evaluation in instructional design. *Educational Technology Research and Development, 43*(3), 29–48.

Whitman, N. A. (1988). *Peer teaching: To teach is to learn twice.* (ASHE–ERIC Higher Education Research Report, No. 4). Washington, DC: Association for the Study of Higher Education.

Wilkerson, L., & Gijselaers, W. H. (Eds.). (1996). *Bringing problem-based learning to higher education: Theory and practice.* New Directions for Teaching and Learning, No. 68. San Francisco: Jossey-Bass.

Williams, E. (1992). Student attitudes towards approaches to learning and assessment. *Assessment and Evaluation in Higher Education, 17,* 45–58.

Williams, W. C. (1985). Effective teaching: Gauging learning while teaching. *Journal of Higher Education, 56,* 320–337.

Williams, W. M., & Ceci, S. J. (1997). How'm I doing? Problems with student ratings of instructors and courses. *Change, 29*(5), 13–23.

Willis, D. (1993). Academic involvement at university. *Higher Education, 25,* 133–150.

Wilson, R. C. (1986). Improving faculty teaching: Effective use of student evaluations and consultants. *Journal of Higher Education, 57,* 196–211.

Wilson, T. C. (1988). Student evaluation of teaching forms: A critical perspective. *Review of Higher Education, 12*(1), 79–95.

Winston, R. B., Jr., Vahala, M. E., Nichols, E. C., Gillis, M. E., Wintrow, M., & Rome K. D. (1994, January). A measure of college classroom climate: The college classroom environment scales. *Journal of College Student Development, 35,* 11–18.

Wright, W. A., & Associates. (1995). *Teaching improvement practices: Successful strategies for higher education.* Bolton, MA: Anker Publishing.

Wyatt, G. (1992). Skipping class: An analysis of absenteeism among first-year college students. *Teaching-Sociology, 20,* 201–207.

Wyer, J. C. (1993). Change where you might least expect it: Accounting education. *Change, 25*(1), 12–17.

Yuker, H. E. (1984). *Faculty workload: Research, theory, and interpretation.* (ASHE–ERIC Higher Education Research Report, No. 10. Washington, DC: Association for the Study of Higher Education.

Zellermayer, M. (1989). The study of teachers' written feedback to students' writing: Changes in theoretical considerations and the expansion of research contexts. *Instructional Science, 18,* 145–165.

Zuber-Skerritt, D. (1992a). *Action research in higher education: Examples and reflections.* London: Kogan Page.

Zuber-Skerritt, D. (1992b). *Professional development in higher education: A theoretical framework for action research.* London: Kogan Page.

50.
Teaching in Middle Schools

James A. Beane
National-Louis University

Barbara L. Brodhagen
Madison, Wisconsin, Metropolitan School District

Teaching cannot be separated from the social and institutional context within which it takes place, and that context cannot be fully understood without some historical grounding. Thus, it is important to begin a review of research on teaching at a particular level with a statement of the origins and evolution of education at that level. This approach is especially the case with regard to middle schools, for it is in the early years of the junior high school movement that we find the roots of the expectations of what that institution is intended to do. And to the extent that separate inquiry at this level is warranted at all, it is warranted only on the basis of those particular intentions and expectations. Moreover, it is in the evolution of middle-level schools that we find the multiple tensions and contradictions that so largely influence middle-level teachers and their teaching in relation to those expectations.

In retrospect, the scenario that unfolded in the first decade of the 20th century seems fairly clear. The last 2 years of the elementary school—Grades 7 and 8—had become a problem. Nearly 70% of those who finished sixth grade dropped out by the end of the eighth grade, not only exacerbating the growing issue of child labor, but also flooding the market with unskilled workers. The elementary schools were generally overcrowded with the large influx of immigrants and also, in the two upper grades, with increasing numbers of students who were held back for academic failure in grade.

It is true that developmentalists, following the work of G. Stanley Hall (1908), had been arguing for several years that early adolescents were neither children nor fully mature adolescents and therefore should be segregated to accommodate their uniqueness. Moreover, doing so would prevent their being negatively influenced by older adolescents, and, in turn, negatively influencing younger children. These arguments, focused as they were on young people themselves, were hardly sufficient to warrant institutional change (Toepfer & Marani, 1980). But in combination with other interests they would gain more power.

Charles Eliot and the rest of the Committee of Ten, as well as the Committee of Fifteen, had already concluded in the early 1890s that the average age of students entering college (18) ought to be lower, and one way of expediting earlier entrance was to introduce college preparatory courses earlier than high school (National Education Association, 1883, 1885). That idea fit well with concerns of social efficiency advocates who were more generally concerned with early tracking of students toward either academic or vocational training. An obvious way of simultaneously satisfying these interests presented itself: remove Grades 7 and 8 from the elementary school, simultaneously relieving overcrowding and opening the door for reconsidering the kind of education provided in those two grades. This case of converging interests of classical humanists and social efficiency advocates, bolstered by the stage-related arguments of the developmentalists, would change for good the educational experiences of young adolescents. For out of this moment, around 1910, came the establishment of a new institution: the junior high school.

Created out of multiple interests, the junior high school and its program were, not surprisingly, intended to serve several purposes (Briggs, 1920; Pringle, 1937). One was to provide vocational "guidance" to help young people decide whether they would pursue a path toward college or toward work. Following this, another purpose was to introduce to the college-bound initial college preparatory courses previously offered in the first years of the high school. Alternatively, vocational preparation courses were to be offered to those who would enter the workforce, along with a smattering of survey-level academic courses

---

The authors wish to thank reviewers Joanne Ahar (Kent State University), Richard Lipka (Pittsburg State University), Lori Martin (Verona, Wisconsin, Middle School), and Richard Powell (Texas Tech University).

as a basic introduction to intellectual culture. Still another purpose was to relieve the problem of general failure-in-grade through promotion by subject in a differentiated curriculum. And all of this was presumably to be delivered with an eye to the developmental level of young adolescents, who, while not altogether ready for the full high school program, were nonetheless too "mature" for the childhood-based program of the elementary school.

For the most part, this description of the junior high school and its program has persisted over time. The one serious departure occurred over the 3 decades beginning in the 1930s, as proposals were made to shift at least part of the program toward a problem-centered "core" or general education curriculum ostensibly more suitable than the pure subject approach for promoting democratic personal and social integration. By the 1950s, several surveys of junior high schools indicated roughly half had some kind of block-time program and 10% to 15% had a problem-centered type (Wright, 1950, 1958). Like other curriculum reforms associated with the progressive movement, general education "core" programs dwindled rapidly amid the conservative rumblings of the 1950s and the emphasis on disciplinary structures in the 1960s (Beane, 1997). However, even this relatively brief ascendance left a lingering controversy over whether the junior high school should offer a general or specialized curriculum and whether that curriculum ought to be based in differentiated subjects or personal and social problems of living.

Ironically, just as some of the more progressive aspects of the junior high school were eroding, a new movement started in relation to middle-level education that would eventually have major implications for the work of teachers (Alexander, 1965). As the children of the postwar "baby boom" stretched the capacity of the elementary schools in the late 1950s, many junior high school leaders began to argue for a new configuration of grades that would relieve overcrowding and, presumably, offer other important benefits. Their proposal was to remove Grade 6 from the elementary school and Grade 9 from the junior high school and, by combining Grades 6 through 8, create a new school: the "middle school." Moreover, if desired, Grade 5 could also be moved into the middle school, especially in urban areas, where ending elementary school earlier might help assuage the continuing effects of de facto neighborhood racial segregation on schools. To make room for these former elementary students, ninth graders would be moved to the high school, supposedly a more appropriate place anyway, given that the average age of achieving puberty had declined by roughly 1 year since the founding of the junior high school (Drasch, 1976; Tanner, 1961).

Meanwhile, advocates for the new middle schools also argued for rethinking aspects of the junior high school that contributed to a lack of alignment between the developmental characteristics of young adolescents and the organization and program of the school. Among many examples of that misalignment was the continued presence of high school-like scheduling and grouping structures that tended to make the school an impersonal and alienating place for young adolescents. In other words, advocates argued that it was finally time to change the middle-level school from a "junior" version of the high school to one that would be more appropriate for what they described

as the needs and interests of young adolescents. Their case was almost sure to resonate with many outside the profession, for as Charles Silberman would report after touring schools in the late 1960s, "[T]he junior high school, by almost unanimous agreement, is the wasteland—one is tempted to say cesspool—of American education" (1970. p. 324).

Repeating history then, the middle-level of schooling was once again opened to the possibility of change by a convergence of interests, in this case those of administrative efficiency coupled with those of developmentalism. Faced with the unattractive alternative of building more and more new elementary schools and the intransigence of segregation in neighborhood schools, and buoyed by the arguments of middle-level reformers, many school officials found the prospect of middle schools attractive enough that what is now called the middle school movement was soon under way. But no matter its multiple meanings and contradictions, the century-long, continuous movement, first for junior high schools and then for middle schools, must be taken seriously, for they constitute a most remarkable case: a reform that has persisted (Cuban, 1992).

Studying Teaching at the Middle Level

Three major tensions have complicated the middle school context and thus the lives and work of middle school teachers. One concerns whether the middle school ought to be more like the elementary school, with its presumed emphasis on adapting to the characteristics of the child, or more like the high school, with its presumed emphasis on external expectations and disciplinary rigor. While these stereotypes of the elementary and high schools are not necessarily accurate, their place in educational lore is more than sufficient to help form the debate over how the middle level ought to be framed (Hargreaves, 1986). A second tension, related to the first, concerns whether the middle school ought to emphasize a common, general education curriculum for all students or one that is differentiated along lines of students' ability, presumed postschool destiny, or some other factor. The third tension, which may perhaps be considered before the other two, concerns the question of whether or not the characteristics of young adolescents and their subsequent educational "needs" are sufficiently different from those of children and mature adolescents to warrant claims that the middle school should be treated as a unique level of schooling.

The fact that these tensions are part of a continuing debate over the purpose and form of the middle school places middle school teachers in an ambiguous position. Are they to be the child-centered advocates that their elementary colleagues are supposedly expected to be? Are they to be "professors" of academic subjects as their high school colleagues are supposedly expected to be? Or are they to be some unique kind of teacher, unlike either elementary or high school teachers? And, if so, is that unique kind of teacher a mix of the elementary and high school prototypes or someone different altogether? In short, are middle school teachers faced with the choice of "fish *or* fowl" or are they to be "fish *and* fowl" (Toepfer, 1965)?

These tensions also complicate a research review regarding teaching in middle schools, since the way in which one responds to the questions just raised influences choices among various curriculum approaches and instructional modes. Thus, there is no one approach or mode that can be said to be "the" middle school approach. Moreover, research around middle schools is not always as helpful as it might be for understanding middle school teaching, since the middle school is often a site of convenience or default for studying some arrangement rather than a site chosen intentionally for examining various arrangements as they function in the middle-level context. Again, there is the question of whether the findings of any research in relation to middle schools are unique to that level or whether they would just as well apply to other levels, and, conversely, whether findings gleaned at other levels might just as well apply to middle schools.

Amid the ambiguity and complexity involved in middle-level education, we have chosen to organize this review around one of the most promising lines of work, not only for research at the middle-level, but for middle-level education itself. That line of work regards the expectations of middle school teachers that have emerged from recommended teaching and learning reforms within the so-called middle school "movement." While there are many sources from which these expectations may be gleaned, the two most prominent, and the ones we use here, are the middle-level reform platforms from the Carnegie Council on Adolescent Development's *Turning Points: Preparing American Youth for the 21st Century* (1989) and the National Middle School Association's *This We Believe* (1995). While both offer many recommendations for improving middle-level education, such as increased heterogeneous grouping and better community connections, five common expectations for middle-level teachers emerge from these documents:

1. Teachers should have a thorough understanding of the young adolescents with whom they work.
2. Teachers should participate in collegial teaming arrangements.
3. Teachers should act as affective mentors for young adolescents.
4. Teachers should use varied teaching and learning activities.
5. Teachers should use curriculum approaches beyond the traditional separate subject approach.

Within each of these expectations, we examine four general issues: (a) the grounds upon which teachers are asked to agree to the expectation, (b) whether the expectation claims for students and teachers are warranted by available evidence, (c) what that evidence implies for teachers and teaching at the middle level, and (d) what kinds of questions ought to receive attention in continuing research around the expectation. For example, within the common expectation that middle school teachers participate in team-teaching arrangements, we look at examples of the rhetoric behind the expectation, what research says about the impact of teacher team arrangements on students and teachers, what that research suggests for teachers as they work in teams, and what questions about teaming seem to be in pressing need of further research.

In this review, we pay particular attention to research that is aimed at middle schools as a particular context and draw less thoroughly on research in which the middle school is merely a site of convenience or default. Likewise, we do not draw heavily from general areas, such as group processes and sociology of knowledge, that are in need of more attention in ongoing research within particular middle-level reform topics but that are beyond the scope of our purpose here.

The studies we do consider here range from other reviews of research through large sample investigations into middle school practices to case studies of single schools, programs, and teaching teams. While some use comparative methods, the majority, mirroring the general pool of middle school research, involve self-reporting by those within schools. Moreover, those self-reports are frequently made by administrators, a situation that in itself does not mean the reports are inaccurate but leaves open the question of whether teachers and students might have different perceptions of what is happening in particular schools.

Finally, while we consider evidence within the context of the aforementioned teacher expectation categories, several large-scale studies are cited repeatedly since they work across those categories. These include, for example, the Epstein and McPartland (1988) survey of 1,753 schools, the George and Shewey (1994) survey of 108 recommended middle schools, the Lee and Smith (1993) analysis of data from 377 schools, the McEwin, Dickinson, and Jenkins (1996) survey of 1,798 schools, the series of shadow studies conducted by Lounsbury and colleagues (Lounsbury & Johnston 1985; Lounsbury & Johnston, 1988; Lounsbury & Marani, 1964; Lounsbury, Marani, & Compton, 1980), and the cross-sectional, longitudinal, comparative study of 31 high-, medium-, and low-implementation middle schools by Felner, Jackson, Kasak, Mulhall, Brand, and Flowers (1997). While categories such as the five treated below may be temporarily considered distinct for analytical purposes, the studies just mentioned consistently point out that it is difficult to establish particular effects for any one taken alone; the strongest evidence in relation to middle schools is that which considers the various aspects of the middle-level reform platform as an integrated program for improving middle-level education.

Knowing About Young Adolescence

There is no more frequently raised expectation of middle school teachers than that they know about and be sensitive to the characteristics of the young adolescents with whom they spend their days. According to the National Middle School Association, for example, teachers "understand the developmental uniqueness of young adolescents and are as knowledgeable about their students as they are about the subject matter they teach" (1995, p. 13). This assignment is certainly not new for middle-level teachers. After all, one of the chief arguments for establishing junior high schools was that young adolescents were presumed be at a unique stage in human development, imbued with characteristics that were in need of special attention and instructional adaptation (Briggs, 1920).

For those teachers who take this expectation seriously, there is certainly no lack of information about young adolescence. Beginning with the work of G. Stanley Hall, research and commentary on the physical, psychosocial, and cognitive development characteristics of young adolescents has continued steadily throughout the century (e.g., Blair & Burton, 1951; Blos, 1941, Gruenberg, 1934; Redl, 1944). Today, research and commentary appear in general sources, such as publications of the

National Middle School Association and specialized research journals such as *The Journal of Early Adolescence.*

Importantly, while the developmental framing of that research has continued, the view of young adolescents has changed dramatically over the years. Most research today attempts to understand the perceptions and experiences of young adolescents rather than characterizing them as rebellious, antisocial, delinquent, and generally deviant with regard to adult social norms. Long defined as caught in a period of "storm and stress," contemporary research suggests instead that the overwhelming majority of young adolescents do not experience this as an unduly stressful period (Scales, 1991) nor should they be described in terms of a deficit model, a view that even the Carnegie reform report tended to continue (Lesko, 1994).

Research on the characteristics of young adolescents was crucial to the argument for shifting from junior high schools to middle schools. With regard to grade-level organization, for example, evidence from the medical studies of J. M. Tanner (1961) in England was especially crucial. Tanner's data showing a steady, historic decline in the average age of menarche that amounted to approximately 4 months per decade was frequently used as justification for starting the middle school with Grade 6 rather than 7 and for moving Grade 9 to the high school. Moreover, comprehensive reports of research on physical developments in young adolescents were used as data to encourage teachers to "understand" the dramatic physical changes through which their students were going (e.g., Drasch, 1976; Forbes, 1968).

With regard to cognitive development, the middle school movement has generally used a Piagetian frame of reference with emphasis on the idea that most young adolescents are at the concrete or formal operational stages, or in transition between the two (Eichhorn, 1996; Van Hoose & Strahan, 1988; Waverling, 1995). Some research has attempted to tie such functioning to brain growth periodization (e.g., Epstein, 1978), with the suggestion that young adolescents are in a plateau period that inhibits access to new and novel ideas, although the data used to support this theory have been strongly challenged (Gould, 1981). Not surprisingly, the middle school movement has also been influenced by more general topics in relation to cognitive development, such as multiple intelligences and moral development theories (Waverling, 1995). As we shall see below, however, the persistent issue in this area has not been within the research arena itself, but the probable misunderstanding of cognitive development that teachers are likely to construct as they observe young adolescents' lack of motivation in relation to disengaging school activities and tasks.

Meanwhile, research on psychosocial development (e.g., Kagan & Coles, 1971; Lipsitz, 1980a; Scales, 1991; and Thornburg, 1974) not only has shed increased light on the behavior and experiences of young adolescents, but also has served as a basis for promoting more responsive institutional structures and programs. Such sources range from the classic *Growing Up Forgotten,* in which Lipsitz (1980b) explored the general disrespect and disregard for young adolescents across a range of social institutions, to sources focusing on the middle-level school itself, beginning with early works of Eichhorn (1966), Alexander and his colleagues (Alexander, Williams, Compton, Hines, & Prescott, 1968), and James (1972), and continuing through many others such as those by Beane and Lipka (1987) and Stevenson (1986, 1992). Almost without exception, these works indict the traditional "junior high school" form of middle-level education as inappropriate for young adolescents, calling instead for major changes in the schools that involve teachers directly or by implication through their involvement in a range of school structures, procedures, and norms.

Evidence that the middle-level school as a potentially problematic environment for young adolescents has focused on a number of issue. For example, many young adolescents, especially early maturing females, evidence a loss of self-esteem as they make the transition from elementary school to the middle level (Beane & Lipka, 1986; Simmons & Blyth, 1987; Wigfield & Eccles, 1994; Wigfield, Eccles, Mac Iver, Reuman, & Midgley, 1991). While many young adolescents experience problems with academic achievement at the middle level (Crockett, Petersen, Graber, Schulenberg, & Ebata, 1989; Petersen & Crockett, 1985), declines appear to be more pronounced among African-American students (Simmons, Black, & Zhou, 1991). Moreover, many middle school students demonstrate a general sense of boredom (Larson & Richards, 1991) and a lack of motivation (Eccles & Midgley, 1989; Maehr & Anderman, 1993). That young adolescents find the middle-level school more than a little stressful is indicated by a survey of 3,382 middle school students conducted by Strubbe (1989), who reported that the prospect of failing one or more subjects was rated as a greater concern than the death of a parent or grandparent and concern about speaking in front of the class more so than the death of a brother or sister or even the respondents' own death.

Using the "stage-environment fit" concept, Eccles and Midgley (1989) and Eccles, Midgley, Wigfield, Miller, Buchanan, Reuman, Flanagan, and Mac Iver (1993) conclude that the typical middle-level school is, in several ways, a poor fit for the developmental stage of early adolescence. On the one hand, they point out that early adolescence is a stage when young people are seeking more autonomy and independence, are engaging in more self-assessment based on social comparison, are becoming more capable of using higher level cognitive strategies, are increasingly concerned about peer relationships, and are in need of close adult relationships outside the home. On the other hand, based on their own and others' research, they draw a picture of schools in which there is a high level of teacher control, few opportunities for student participation in decision making, an emphasis on whole-group instruction, frequent comparison of student ability and achievement, and relatively low teacher efficacy. This poor "fit," they claim, helps to explain young adolescents' loss of motivation, decline in self-esteem as learner, and other identified trends at this age.

Expectations for teachers stemming from this area of research generally focus on desired changes in curriculum and teaching, as we shall see in other sections of this paper. However, there are also implications for the personal behavior and perceptions of teachers. In interviews and surveys of young adolescents, Beane and Lipka (1986, 1987) found that they express a desire for teachers who are "nice," a generic term that is clarified in terms of personalness, understanding, concern, and willingness to help. Similar characteristics surfaced in a survey of 400 students conducted by Buckner and Bickel (1991), although Hayes, Ryan, and Zseller (1994) also pointed out that there are gender and race differences in how the characteristics of a "caring" teacher are defined by students.

The idea that middle-level teachers should evidence "nice" and "caring" attitudes and behaviors toward young adolescents poses a potential problem for implementation of the middle-level reform platform. As already noted, research about young adolescents has shifted from a historical use of delinquency and antisocial references to an attempt to understand the nature of experiences and developments in environmental and cultural contexts. Unfortunately, mainstream discussions of young adolescents are still often laced with demeaning metaphors of this age group such as "hormones with feet" (Arnold, 1980; Eccles et al., 1993). Furthermore, while some research has focused on cultural and class variations in young adolescence (e.g., Ford, 1992; Simmons, Black, & Zhou, 1991), mainstream work around middle-level education tends to ignore the possibility of such differences (Everhart, 1983; Gay, 1994). In this light, the expectation that middle-level teachers be sensitive to the characteristics of young adolescents appears problematic, since the characterizations of this group that many teachers often encounter tend to be inaccurate, incomplete, and stereotypically demeaning. And, unfortunately, that view is reinforced by misinformation or lack of knowledge regarding cognitive development in young adolescence and, as likely, mistaking the lack of motivation stemming from poor environmental fit for lack of cognitive capacity.

Furthermore, many middle-level teachers are situated at that level by circumstances other than choice and have not been prepared to work with young adolescents (Carnegie Council on Adolescent Development, 1989; Scales, 1992; Scales & McEwin, 1994). The latter issue is at least partly the function of the limited state of teacher education focused on middle-level education; only 33 states have specialized certification or licensure for middle-level teaching. In the survey conducted by Valentine et al. (1993), only about one-third of responding principals indicated that teachers in their buildings had special preparation for middle grades teaching, while in the survey by McEwin et al. (1996), nearly two-thirds reported that fewer than 25% of teachers had such preparation.

Conversely, Scales and McEwin (1994) reported more encouraging data from over 2,000 teachers in five states that had over half of the nation's middle grades teacher education programs. In this case, 49% of respondents held a middle-level teaching certificate and another 28% held elementary-middle or middle-secondary combination certificates. Of these, only a very small percentage indicated a desire to leave the middle grades level of teaching. To understand and be sensitive to the young adolescents they teach, teachers must presumably first know something about them. The Scales and McEwin findings suggest not only that possibilities for doing so may be increasing, but that being prepared with that knowledge may make teaching in the middle grades a more amenable setting for teachers.

Teaching as Part of a Team

Perhaps no other school feature has been associated more with the middle school movement than the organization of teachers into teams. As part of its platform, the National Middle School Association states that "large schools are subdivided into 'houses' or 'schools-within-a-school' . . . [that] may be further divided into interdisciplinary teams that build a sense of community and promote curriculum integration" (1995, pp. 28–29). Such arrangements are meant to make it possible for teachers to coordinate activities, schedules, grouping, skills, and content across subjects for a group of students whom they have in common.

The Carnegie Council saw additional benefits for teaming in suggesting that it would "provide a much-needed support group for teachers, eliminating the isolation teachers can experience in departmentalized settings" (1989, p. 40). In fact, the Council was so optimistic about the possibilities of teaming that they recommended that "teams of students and teachers would preferably remain together for students' entire middle grades experience" (p. 40).

Like other features of the middle-level reform platform, teaming is not an entirely new idea (Wraga, 1997). Reports of team teaching in junior high schools can be found at least as far back as the early 1930s (e.g., Sweeney, Barry, & Schoelkopf, 1932), although in some ways, important aspects of the organization have changed over time. For example, early team arrangements most often involved two teachers, usually language arts and social studies, in block-time programs such as "core" and "unified studies." As part of the middle school movement, however, teaming arrangements are almost always meant to involve teachers from the subject areas of language arts, social studies, mathematics, and science (Beane, 1990b).

Though the arrangement of teachers into teams is often described simply as a structural feature of middle schools, it has serious implications for teaching and learning as well as for the professional lives of teachers. What are the proposed benefits to team teaching? Are claims for team arrangements warranted by research? How do teachers perceive team arrangements?

As mentioned in the platform statements, team teaching arrangements are meant to benefit both students and teachers. In the case of students, team arrangements are meant to assuage the impersonality of large schools by creating smaller, decentralized communities. In addition, the possibilities of teacher-coordinated curriculum plans presumably offer benefits with regard to coherence in the curriculum, common skill and concept instruction across areas, and more personalized attention from teachers. In the case of teachers, team arrangements are purported to offer the possibility of small, collegial working groups that have some degree of autonomy with regard to curriculum planning, scheduling, grouping, and other types of decision making.

The use of team teaching arrangements appears to be reasonably widespread and increasing (Arhar & Irvin, 1995; McEwin, Dickinson, & Jenkins, 1996). From late 1980s surveys, Alexander and McEwin (1989) and Mac Iver (1990) reported respectively that 33% and 37% of middle schools claimed to use teaming arrangements, while Valentine, Clark, Irvin, Keefe, and Melton (1993) reported a level of 53% only a few years later. Moreover, those percentages increase when only Grade 6 through 8 middle schools are considered. Further evidence of this growth is indicated by comparing Alexander's 1968 report that 5–8% of language arts, social studies, science, and mathematics courses were included within teams to more recent data that place those figures at 22–37% (Alexander & McEwin, 1989) and 42–59% (McEwin, Dickinson, & Jenkins, 1996).

This general move toward teaming arrangements in middle schools is not ill-advised. In addition to the comprehensive reform data from Illinois (Felner et al., 1997), research reviews by Lee and Smith (1993) and Arhar and Irvin (1995) indicate that students in schools that have team organization tend to evidence higher academic achievement than those in schools that use a traditional departmentalized organization. In addition, Lee and Smith also found that the achievement effects appeared to equalize social class differences within schools that use interdisciplinary teaming arrangements.

Academic achievement is not the only benefit for students. In a survey of 5,000 middle school students, Arhar (1990) found that those from teamed middle schools reported higher levels of social bonding, bonding to teachers, and bonding to schools than those in nonteamed middle schools, though in a follow-up study (Arhar & Kromrey, 1995), these effects were found to be significant in urban but not suburban middle schools. Similarly, students who had been part of a 2-year team reported feeling less anxious and isolated while more cared for by teachers and supported by peers (Powell, 1993).

But what about teachers? Does teaming also offer benefits for them? Several studies, involving surveys and interviews, and one review would suggest so. Like students, teachers participating on teams report less isolation and a greater sense of community (Arhar, Johnston, & Markle, 1988; Ashton & Webb, 1986; George, Spruel, & Moorefield, 1987; Mills, Powell, & Pollak, 1992). At the same time, they report an increased sense of professional efficacy and self-esteem (Arhar et al., 1988; Gatewood, Cline, Green, & Harris, 1992). Despite these benefits, however, at least two studies (Gatewood et al., 1992; Mills et al., 1992) found that teachers reported no reduction in stress levels as a result of working on teams.

Participation in team teaching arrangements also appears to involve some changes in teachers' working conditions. Surveying 1,798 middle-level schools, McEwin et al. found that, while 32% of all schools had at least one planning period for teachers, those Grade 6 through 8 schools with teaming had two periods for most or all teachers. Moreover, seventh grade team teachers from 99 schools surveyed by Steffes and Valentine (1996) reported that they have considerable autonomy and decision-making opportunities in relation to their teams' operation. As part of their team planning and decision making, teachers use a variety of strategies and leadership forms to make decisions and become more flexible and confident in doing so (Hart, Pate, Mizelle, & Reeves, 1992; Polite, 1994). In a case study of teaming, Powell and Mills (1994) found that the teachers involved not only moved away from narrow views of teaching, but offered each other mentoring on collaboration, clerical logistics, professionalism, content, and social relations. Pushing collegiality even further, McLaughlin, Earle, Hall, Miller, and Wheeler (1995) described one team's success at using its opportunity for collaboration to carry out a team action research project around mutually defined questions.

While those findings are certainly encouraging for those seeking more teacher autonomy and collegiality, other researchers have offered some cautions. Mills et al. (1992) found that, while personal isolation diminished for members within teams, con-

cerns were expressed regarding their isolation from teachers from other teams and grade levels. Moreover teachers tend to spend most of their time in planning meetings discussing administrative issues and problems with students (Arhar et al., 1988; Shaw, 1993; Wehlage, Smith, & Lipman, 1992). While Shaw cautioned that such discussions could be positive if, for example, discussions about students involved "caring" for them, these studies indicate that anticipated instructional collaboration, including that across subjects, may not necessarily follow simply from the formation of teams. In fact, it may be that such instructional collaboration might not even be expected to take place given that 80% of the team teachers in the survey by Steffes and Valentine (1996) reported they had little or no in-service preparation for teaming while such preparation is, in turn, the best predictor of interdisciplinary instruction.

On the whole, given these various studies, it is not surprising that in their survey of middle schools in operation for an average of 14 years and recommended by professors and state education officials, George and Shewey (1994) found that 85% reported that an interdisciplinary team organization has contributed to the long-term effectiveness of their school program. That benefits accrue to teachers and students alike is also not surprising given the finding by McPartland (1987) that departmentalized arrangements (as theoretically opposed to teaming) have negative effects on teacher-student relations in general, and more so for low-income students.

Where the positive benefits of teaming are realized, they are not done so by accident. As the comprehensive study by Felner et al. (1997) indicates, such benefits are not to be had without commitment to careful and thoughtful implementation over time. Nor are they had without rethinking the relative roles of school personnel and resource investment. In their survey of team teachers, Steffes and Valentine (1996) studied teacher outcomes (creativity and empowerment), student-related outcomes (addressing individual problems and providing interdisciplinary learning), and environmental outcomes (parent involvement and communications). Teacher autonomy and decision-making opportunities turned out to be the best predictor of every student, teacher, and environmental benefit tested. With regard to the need for resource investment, the best predictors of teacher outcomes, after autonomy, were flexible scheduling and availability of adjacent rooms for the team. In the case of student benefits and school environment, common planning time, the extent of teaming across the school, and in-service education augmented autonomy.

The structural arrangement of team teaching is a centerpiece in the platform of the middle-level school reform movement. It calls on middle school teachers to join their colleagues as members of teams and thus helps to form the definition of what it means to be a teacher at this level. The evidence to date suggests that this call to teachers involves benefits for them: reduced isolation, more collegiality, peer mentoring, relative autonomy, decision-making opportunities, professional efficacy, and more. In addition, teaming also offers benefits to students with regard to academic and affective dimensions of learning that, in turn, contribute to teacher satisfaction and efficacy. In this sense, participation in team teaching has positive potential for enhancing teaching in middle schools.

However, the evidence also suggests that teachers should move into team teaching with their eyes open. It is not likely that the stress or workload of teaching will diminish with teaming. Furthermore, the level of benefits may well depend upon the availability of planning time, adjacent teaching spaces, and, most importantly, in-service preparation for working as a team. And the sense of support and collegiality felt within the team may come at the expense of persistent contact with teachers from other teams, grade levels, and subjects.

If current trends continue, team teaching arrangements will continue to become more widespread in middle-level schools. In addition to continuing the kind of research done to date, additional research is needed to more fully understand the promises and potential pitfalls of teaming for teachers. For example, teaming almost always involves only teachers of mathematics, science, social studies, and language arts—the "big four" of the traditional curriculum (Beane, 1993). What are the perceptions of teachers from "other" areas (e.g., art, music, and family and consumer science) regarding teaming? What do they perceive to be the benefits of teaming? And what might be learned about and from teams of different size and subject composition about variables like efficacy, autonomy, isolation, and other dimensions of teachers lives in schools? Pursuing such questions, through both ethnographic and experimental methods can only add to our understanding of what it means to teach in a middle school and, perhaps, what it might mean under more favorable conditions than many teachers experience today.

The Teacher as Affective Mentor

One of the primary purposes of the early junior high school was the provision of "guidance" for young adolescents. In keeping with the social efficiency function of the junior high school, the form often discussed was vocational guidance for those young people who would drop out before entering high school. Other forms were also provided, however, including personal-social guidance in relation to the typical normative rules of schooling (Bennett, 1919; Heironimus, 1917) and character education associated with efforts to "Americanize" immigrants (Beane, 1990a). As high school attendance became mandatory over the next several decades, the role of vocational guidance diminished. Conversely, increased emphasis on psychosocial development pushed the idea of personal-social guidance to the foreground, a trend that would become one of the hallmarks of the middle school movement. And given the intensity of the concern for psychosocial development, the responsibility for the general guidance function has shifted from understaffed guidance departments to those who see young adolescents on a daily basis: middle-level teachers.

The general notion of middle-level teachers as affective mentors for young adolescents is implied within the expectation that middle school teachers know about and will be sensitive to the developmental characteristics and concerns of young adolescents. But more than this, the middle school reform platform has included efforts to designate that role as a specific expectation of teachers and to formalize it through programmatic arrangements. According to the Carnegie Council, for example:

> Every student should be well known by at least one adult. . . . Students should be able to rely on that adult to help learn from their experiences, comprehend physical changes and changing relations

with family and peers, act on their behalf to marshal every school and community resource needed for the student to succeed, and help to fashion a promising vision for the future. (p. 40)

To accomplish this function, the National Middle School Association suggests that middle-level schools "use a variety of organizational arrangements such as advisory programs, home-base groups, and team-based mentorships . . . augmented by comprehensive guidance and support services" (p. 17). In other words, according to the Carnegie Council, the adviser "would not engage in formal counseling, which would be left to a mental health professional" (p. 40) but rather lead advisory-type programs intended to offer experiences to enhance self-esteem, values, character, and other affective dimensions of development and learning (James, 1986; Cole, 1994).

In their survey of middle schools, Alexander and McEwin (1989) found that 39% of respondents reported they had some kind of advisory program in their schools. Of those middle schools responding to the 1990 Epstein and Mac Iver survey, 28% reported they had strong advisory programs, while 25% reported having no advisory or homeroom program at all. More recently, McEwin, Dickinson, and Jenkins (1996) reported that 47% of the middle schools in their survey had advisory programs, though the frequency of everyday meetings had declined 15% since 1988. This modest growth of advisory programs across middle schools and their curtailment within particular schools correctly suggest that this aspect of the middle school reform platform is more than a little contentious. In fact, in their survey of long-standing, recommended middle schools, George and Shewey (1995) found that only 54% reported that advisory programs had contributed to their long-term effectiveness.

While advisory programs receive implied support from studies that deal with the middle school platform as an integrated set of reform arrangements, evidence specifically in support of advisory program arrangements comes almost entirely from self-report surveys. These range from surveys done as part of single program case studies to national-type surveys, and include responses from teachers, parents, and students. Across these studies, advisory type programs have been credited with successfully meeting counseling needs of young adolescents, lowering the dropout rate, helping overall school climate, providing teachers and students opportunities to know each other on a one-to-one basis, helping student self-esteem and citizenship attitudes, and generally improving other affective aspects of school life and student development (Connors, 1992; Epstein & Mac Iver, 1992; Espe, 1993; Putbrese, 1989; Totten & Nielson, 1994; Ziegler & Mulhall, 1994).

Despite these reports, the advisory program notion has been met with considerable apprehension and resistance. Valentine et al. (1993) found that, while principals gave high importance to advisory programs, they predicted a low-level of implementation for such arrangements. Ayers (1994), Cole (1994), and Watson (1992) reported similar findings from large surveys of teachers. Though many teachers had positive attitudes regarding their participation in advisory programs, there was relatively widespread lack of enthusiasm and commitment due to concerns over lack of time to prepare for advisory groups, time detracted from academic programs, lack of professional preparation for the advisory role, and other logistical concerns.

The apprehension of many teachers toward participation in advisory programs, as reported generally in studies of teachers roles as affective advisers, is not surprising. Aside from questions about support, successfully carrying out the role itself is a somewhat daunting prospect. On the one hand, for example, Bushnell and George (1993) found in surveys and interviews of teachers and students that effective advisers care about students in their advisory groups, were able to relate to individual differences among advisees, were available and accessible, felt positive toward the advisory concept, and had well-developed personal, individual advisory styles. To achieve such characteristics would, as previously noted, require considerable support and preparation, about neither of which teachers feel particularly confident. While lack of professional preparation might be taken simply as negativity toward a new type of program, Scales and McEwin (1994) found that 73% of recent graduates of teacher education programs specifically designed for the middle-level rated their preparation for the advisory role to be less than adequate. It is little wonder that Ziegler and Mulhall (1994) found that many teachers desired curriculum guidebooks for use with their advisory groups.

If, as the middle school reform platform suggests, teachers are to serve as affective mentors to young adolescents, at least partly through advisory programs, then it would appear that the advisory aspect of the reform platform will need both further study and consideration. Although the self-reports from schools with advisory programs are encouraging, many teachers remain wary of both the role expectation and the programs themselves. Especially where programs are intended to change the attitudes, values, or behavior, such suspicions are warranted by a lack of evidence, other than self-report surveys, regarding potential effects. Until evidence is forthcoming, both advocates and foes of the advisory concept must be concerned about related historical evidence that raises serious questions as to whether such programs have meaningful effects on student values, self-esteem, and behavior (Hartshorne & May, 1928, 1929, 1930; Lockwood, 1978; Strein, 1988).

Should needed research fail to show some evidence of effects, some other strategy for the programmatic aspect of affective mentorship might well need to be explored. One possibility, as described in some of the reports previously cited, would be to shift expectations for advisory arrangements from changing attitudes and behaviors to simply providing an opportunity for teachers and students to know one another in small, nonacademic groups. Another that has arisen in proposals for changing the middle-level curriculum, might involve embedding the teacher advisory role and desired program outcomes inside a curriculum that addresses personal and social concerns of students (Beane, 1990b; James, 1993). In any event, however, the expectation that teachers serve as affective mentors for young adolescents is almost certain to remain problematic in relation to teachers' uncertainty about the educational desirability of the role and their capacity to carry it out successfully.

Teaching Through Varied and Appropriate Strategies

According to the National Middle School Association, "the distinctive developmental and learning characteristics of young adolescents provide the foundation for selecting teaching strate-

gies" (1995, p. 24). Most prominently, those strategies are to involve activities that "provide hands-on experiences," "opportunities for peer interaction," varying forms of group work," and "student choice" (p. 25). The Carnegie Council especially recommends opportunities for group learning. "Learning," they reason, "often takes place best when students have opportunities to discuss, analyze, express opinions, and receive feedback from peers. Peer involvement is especially critical during early adolescence, when the influence of peers increases and becomes more important to the young person" (1989, p. 43). They add, " . . . Teachers must view themselves as facilitators through which young people construct knowledge themselves" (p. 43).

Both groups point to a need to alter patterns of assessment of learning outcomes. The National Middle School Association recommends "culminating experiences that call for "sharing, demonstrating, publishing, displaying, or creating behavioral evidence that augments that obtained through more conventional testing" (1995, pp. 25–26). Echoing that theme, the Carnegie Council suggests that "in the transformed middle grade school, tests will more closely resemble real learning tasks" (1989, p. 48). These "tests" might include long-term writing assignments, individual and group projects, and problem-centered demonstration of thinking skills.

With regard to positive effects on student achievement, there is certainly substantial evidence to support the expectation that teachers use such varied and appropriate strategies generally (e.g., Cawelti, 1995; Epstein & Mac Iver, 1992; Russell, 1997) as well as specific types such as cooperative learning (e.g., Johnson & Johnson, 1989), a hands-on project approach (e.g., Blumenfeld, Soloway, & Marx, 1991), and authentic instruction and assessment (Newman & Associates, 1996). The fact that research on these strategies cuts across grade levels, however, suggests that the argument that they are developmentally appropriate for young adolescents seems less important than one made on the general merits of the strategies. In this sense, arguments for particular strategies based on such studies in terms of developmental appropriateness may lack influence. While the arguments start with the purported importance of development itself in instructional decisions. middle school teachers report that their use of new strategies is based instead on observing student benefits in their own classrooms (Greengross, 1995).

Though research supports the use of these strategies in both general and grade-specific contexts, their use in middle-level schools is hardly widespread. Exploring life in middle schools, Lounsbury and colleagues conducted a series of brief "shadow" studies on four separate dates across 3 decades (Lounsbury & Marani, 1964; Lounsbury, Marani, & Compton, 1980; Lounsbury & Johnston, 1985; Lounsbury & Johnston, 1988). While they found some evidence of varied teaching and learning strategies, the preponderance of classroom time was devoted to passive, teacher-dominated, and intellectually nonstimulating activity. Similar findings surface in other studies of schools in general (e.g., Goodlad, 1984) and at the middle level (e.g., Center for Research on Elementary and Middle Schools, 1987; McEwin, Dickinson, & Jenkins, 1996). In the McEwin, Dickinson, and Jenkins study, regular use of direct instruction was reported by 90% of respondents, while cooperative learning was said to be used regularly by about half, inquiry teaching by slightly over a third, and independent study by about one-fifth.

That general lack of varied teaching and learning strategies in middle schools, as part of the overall reform agenda, is compounded by the widespread emphasis on ability rather than goal and task orientation, which reportedly inhibits motivation, engagement, and learning (Maehr & Anderman, 1993).

Any explanation for the gap between this part of the middle school reform platform and its implementation would be extremely complicated, since so many political, personal, and contextual factors are tied up in school reform work (e.g., Mitman & Lambert, 1993). Even explaining the extent to which teachers themselves are involved in that gap is hindered by a shortage of research on the beliefs of middle school teachers about varied teaching and learning strategies (Sparks, 1988). If middle school teachers, more so than high school counterparts, see motivating students as a part of their job rather than as a responsibility of students themselves (Huberman, Grounauer, & Marti, 1993), then we might well expect to see more frequent use of varied and appropriate teaching and learning strategies. Yet as noted above, quite the opposite seems to be the case in middle schools. What research is available to shed light on this gap in implementation of the reform platform begins to suggest a multifactor, rather than single-factor, explanation that recognizes the complexities involved in expecting teachers to change the way they teach.

First, to the extent that the recommended teaching and learning strategies are appropriate for middle-level instruction, only a relatively small number of middle school teachers have specific preparation for this level (McEwin, Dickinson, & Jenkins, 1996; Valentine et al., 1993). Second, even those who are graduates of programs in which these strategies are presumably promoted do not necessarily feel confident in their preparation (Scales, 1992; Scales & McEwin, 1994). Third, just because teachers feel they have high levels of knowledge about particular strategies does not necessarily mean they give them high levels of support (Watson, 1992).

Fourth, even when teachers find particular strategies useful, the strategies themselves do not come without a price. In that regard, Greengross (1995) found in a study of four middle schools that early implementation of such strategies is stressful, even among those who are committed to their use. Likewise, Tyrell (1990) found that, while many middle school teachers supported cooperative learning and found it useful for their students, they also found that it took a great deal of time and energy and required additional teaching of social skills. That finding is echoed in many action research studies wherein teacher-researchers consistently balance descriptions of the benefits of particular practices with accounts of the challenges faced in implementing them (e.g., Brodhagen, 1994; Buckmaster, 1994; Scott, 1994).

Finally, and ironically, even when teachers find these strategies useful, they may not receive especially positive feedback from students (Williams, Meyer, & Harootunian, 1992). As Theobald (1995) found in a survey of 155 seventh graders in two schools, games and simulations received high support while comparatively less support was offered for strategies that are more often mentioned in the middle school platform, like discussion, questioning, and problem solving.

The idea of using varied and appropriate teaching strategies is clearly a crucial part of the middle school reform platform.

Warranted by both general and level-specific research, the use of such strategies would substantively alter the kinds of day-to-day experiences that young adolescents are reportedly having in most middle-level classrooms. The crucial issue in this area of the reform proposal revolves around the contradiction between the support it receives in research and the lack of its implementation in schools. In this regard three questions are important for further study. What do teachers really believe about the varied teaching strategies called for in the reform platform? What level of personal, professional, and political preparation and support do teachers need to move ahead with the use of these strategies? Are there unique aspects of the middle school context, real or imagined, that must be accounted for in research on such strategies in order to propose and defend their use to middle school teachers?

However, even if these questions were answered to a level of practical sufficiency, there would remain the problem of the historic rejection of these strategies by some teachers (and other educators, as well as parents), in general and at the middle level, on the mistaken grounds that they are inappropriate for the academic purposes of the schools. It is here that the real challenge with regard to this aspect of the middle school reform platform lies and thus why the matter of teacher beliefs in this area needs much more attention than it has received.

Teaching Beyond the Separate Subject Approach

The curriculum of the middle-level school, like its original high school model, has traditionally been organized around separate subjects, The Carnegie Council suggests that this arrangement makes it difficult for students "to see connections between ideas in different disciplines" (1989, p. 47). Instead, they propose that the "core middle grade curriculum can be organized around integrating themes that young people find relevant to their own lives" in ways that "capitalize on young adolescents' concerns and curiosity about their own physical and emotional development and their place within the family, peer group, and larger society" (p. 48).

Similarly imagining a curriculum that addresses "students' own questions" (1995, p. 21) and is "focused on issues significant to both students and adults" (p. 23), the National Middle School Association suggests that important outcomes might follow:

Intellectual, communication, social, physical, and technological skills are learned and applied in context. Critical thinking, decision making, and creativity are enhanced when students examine appropriate problems and take steps to solve them. In such cases, they produce or construct knowledge rather than simply act as consumers of knowledge. (p. 23)

Like other components of the middle school reform platform, the idea of moving beyond the separate subjects in curriculum organization has its origins in the earlier junior high school movement (Beane, 1993; Lounsbury, 1984, 1992; Vars, 1991; Wraga, 1992). As early as the 1920s, proposals were made to center the middle-level curriculum on a "core" curriculum in which subject distinctions are broken down and emphasis is placed on personal and social aspects of life (Cox, 1929, p. 11).

Though the separate subject approach retained its prominent position, a variety of curriculum patterns surfaced over the next 3 decades. These ranged from mild content and skill correlations in multisubject approaches to full-blown attempts at curriculum integration that dissolved subject area identities and, in their stead, used personal and social issues to organize the curriculum (Hopkins, 1937). The latter was particularly evident in the emergence of problem-centered core programs taught in blocks of time by single teachers and teams (e.g., Bossing & Cramer, 1965; Faunce & Bossing, 1951; Noar, 1948; Van Til, Vars, & Lounsbury, 1961). From surveys conducted over several years, Wright (1950, 1958) found that about 30% of junior high schools reported having block-time classes, 80% of which involved various degrees of correlation among subjects and 12% involved problem-centered integration.

Though interdisciplinary instruction has been a part of the middle school reform agenda since its beginnings in the 1960s (e.g., Lounsbury & Vars, 1978), new emphasis has been placed on non-subject-area curriculum designs in the 1990s, including some that move beyond subject correlations to problem-centered curriculum integration (e.g., Beane, 1990b, 1993; Dickinson, 1993; Vars, 1987, 1993). Nevertheless, as Lipsitz (1984) pointed out in her study of four successful middle schools, the matter of moving the curriculum part of the middle school reform platform from philosophy to practice is perhaps the most difficult part of middle-level reform efforts. While moving beyond the separate subject curriculum partly involves the kind of structural changes that many middle schools have accomplished, it eventually requires that teachers make changes that also involve the more complex issues of self-identity, collegial relationships, and content loyalty.

Studies regarding the effects of non-subject-area curriculum designs on student learning have a history nearly as long as the designs themselves. Since the early 1940s several reviews of research have been developed in this area (Alberty, 1960; Informal Committee of the Progressive Education Association, 1941; Hanna & Lang, 1950; Jenkins, 1947; Mickelson, 1957; Vars, 1996; Wright, 1963). As these research reviews have indicated, young people tend to do at least as well, and often better, on traditional measures of academic achievement and adjustment to further education as the curriculum moves beyond the separate subject approach in the direction of other forms, such as interdisciplinary and integration. Moreover, with regard to other kinds of achievement, especially interpersonal understanding and relations, the separate subject approach appears to be significantly less successful than these other arrangements.

A few recent studies have raised questions about the possibility of some differential effects for various groups of students. Hough and St. Clair (1995) found that, after six teams in four schools taught the same interdisciplinary unit to 628 students, most of the students showed gains in problem-solving ability, but those gains were more prominent for students at the formal level of reasoning than for those at the concrete level. In reviewing content-specific test scores in a school attempting an integrative curriculum, Pearson, Pilcher, and Weeks (1996) reported that increases and decreases in those for particular subjects differed somewhat for majority and minority students over the first 3 years of implementation.

Despite the well-documented difficulties associated with curriculum change, survey evidence and school case studies suggest that there has been movement toward curriculum arrangements that involve multidisciplinary correlations and integration. In the national survey of recommended, long-standing middle schools that was conducted by George and Shewey (1994), 63% of the respondents reported that interdisciplinary curriculum and instruction involving teachers from diverse disciplines had contributed to the effectiveness of their middle school program. In a survey of Missouri middle schools, Arredondo and Rucinski (1995) found that about one-third reported some level of curriculum work beyond the separate subjects, though the largest number of these were large suburban and urban schools rather than poor, rural schools. Additional evidence of the increasing use of curriculum arrangements beyond the separate subject approach is indicated by the sheer number of books and papers involving case reports out of schools and classrooms (e.g., Brazee, 1995; Brodhagen, 1994, 1995; Pace, 1995; Pate, Homestead, & McGinnis, 1994, 1996; Powell & Skoog, 1995; Powell, Skoog, Troutman, & Jones, 1996; Stevenson & Carr, 1993).

The expectation that teachers will teach beyond the separate subject approach is fraught with complexity. In a survey of teachers anticipating a move toward the middle school reform platform, Newman (1993) found a positive correlation between attitudes toward the platform and attitudes toward non-subject-area curriculum arrangements. However, even where support for the latter was evident, it declined as potential arrangements moved from multidisciplinary to integration. Such attitudes are very important, since, unlike schoolwide structural and climate changes, curriculum decisions appear likely to involve more individual autonomy and preference. Arredondo and Rucinski (1995) found that the decision to use multidisciplinary and integrated curriculum approaches was usually initiated by teachers alone or in cooperation with a principal. Not surprisingly, then, in a study of teams in three schools, Burnaford (1993) found that, when such decisions are initiated by others, teacher support depended partly on respect for their autonomy and individuality. Moreover, Kain (1993) found that even at the single-team level, involvement in an interdisciplinary curriculum still involved individual, personal decisions by teachers regarding whether the planned curriculum was relevant to both external curriculum requirements and perceptions of the intent of their home subject areas.

Besides loyalty to home subject and respect for autonomy, other factors enter into teachers' decisions to use multidisciplinary and integrated curriculum arrangements. Burnaford (1993) and Whinery and Faircloth (1994) found that such decisions are affected by opportunities to understand curriculum change before moving in a particular direction, whether teachers came to view themselves as learners along with their students (as new curriculum forms were tried), and the availability of planning time, resources, and positive leadership. McDaniel and Romerdahl (1993), in their study of three schools, also found that the kind and degree of support are crucial.

These and other insights are most deeply explored in a series of studies by Powell and his colleagues (Powell & Skoog, 1995; Powell, Skoog, & Troutman, 1996; Powell, Skoog, Troutman, & Jones, 1996) in a school attempting schoolwide movement toward an integrative curriculum. While teachers and students report positive attitudes toward the school in general, and in such areas as transformed personal relationships and personal ownership of knowledge in particular, interviews have turned up a number of issues involved in sustaining their work. In the midst of conventional programs in surrounding schools, the integrative curriculum was problematic for both teachers and students with regard to feeling that they might be behind in content coverage, lacking confidence in the amount of learning, and dealing with high school teachers' perceptions of how well middle school students are prepared. (McDaniel and Romerdahl, 1993, found similar problematics where a few teachers using a multidisciplinary approach in a school were surrounded by colleagues using a traditional separate subject approach.) While they concluded that implementation of an integrative curriculum on a schoolwide basis is possible, Powell and his colleagues cautioned that sustaining such a curriculum involved difficulties with teachers reshaping relationships with students and colleagues, using autonomy in curriculum decision making, changing self-perceptions as a teacher, and dealing with internal and external threats of curriculum regression (e.g., excessive criticism of new methods and pressure to return to more subject-centered methods).

Looking across studies on curriculum organization as an aspect of the middle school reform platform, it is apparent that the matter of widespread implementation of new forms is not necessarily dependent on the existence of persuasive evidence of the effects of multidisciplinary and integrative curriculum arrangements on student learning. Such evidence does exist in comparative studies, case studies, and action research reports. Given the reported autonomy of teachers in curriculum decision, or at least their expectation of it, implementation of these approaches is likely more dependent upon teachers' perceptions of that evidence and the support (or lack of it) they believe they might receive were they to move away from the separate subject curriculum. For middle school teachers, these are important matters, since such moves clearly involve a variety of risks both within and outside the school (Beane, 1997).

Teachers might also feel more confident were more research available about what happens as efforts are made in the direction of creating more integrative curriculum arrangements. True, there is always a need for more evidence of the effects of these arrangements on student learning, but as Burnaford (1993) points out, there is also a need for more qualitative studies about what it means to be a teacher under these circumstances. Powell, Skoog, and Troutman (1996) suggest several compelling areas for future research on integrative curriculum contexts: political and epistemological dimensions, student and teacher metacognition, phenomenological accounts of teachers' and students lives, and metaphorical analyses of thinking about integrative curriculum. It is this kind of research, they suggest, that will help us more fully understand what it means for teachers to teach beyond the separate subject approach.

Summary and Implications

From its very beginnings, the middle-level education movement, first for the junior high school and later for the middle school, has been plagued by multiple and often contradictory expectations, including those for teachers and their work at this level. In recent years, however, a fairly consistent comprehensive reform platform has emerged in recommendations made by organizations and agencies at the national and state levels (Mac Iver & Epstein, 1993). Though that agenda is not above continuing contention, there is a growing body of evidence that suggests it has merit with regard to the education of young adolescents. Moreover, while the middle-level school has often been a site of convenience, rather than interest, for research, more and more efforts are focused on the middle school as a level of study in itself. That focus, along with an increased propensity to account for theoretical and research framings outside the middle-level field itself, has enhanced the depth and quality of middle-level research.

The strongest evidence for the middle school reform platform emerges from those larger studies that treat the reform platform as an integrated set of recommendations among which the systemic effects appear to be quite positive. This evidence is especially so when results from those studies are compared to the discouraging effects evident from schools that offer poor environmental fits for young adolescents. Given the concept of systemic effects, it is not surprising that studies attempting to examine particular aspects of the reform agenda independent of the others are somewhat less convincing, although they are generally in a positive direction.

The reform agenda itself appears to have powerful potential when local schools make a serious and systemic commitment to it over time. When undertaken with low-level commitment, in piecemeal fashion, or with the expectation of immediate results, the potential effects of the agenda seem to diminish rapidly. Our main interest here, however, has been on what the reform agenda means for the lives and work of middle-level teachers. As might be expected, our review of research on that topic raises at least as many questions as it answers, partly because of a lack of research on teacher perceptions of the middle-level reform agenda and partly because so many studies involve large-scale surveys that are completed by almost everyone but teachers.

Nevertheless, evidence available to date suggests that the reform agenda, if taken seriously, has much to offer teachers with regard to autonomy, collegiality, and efficacy. At the same time, the evidence involves the need for substantive departures from traditionally dominant middle-level practices and for a good deal of hard work. Those departures and that work can be informed by research, while, in turn, further research can and should be shaped in important ways by questions teachers raise about the reform agenda. Using that idea as a rule, we will now summarize our sense of research regarding the five major expectations of teachers that emerge from the middle-level reform agenda.

Knowing About Young Adolescents

The expectation that middle school teachers know about and understand the young adolescents they work with is an important one. Obviously, it is not that knowledge alone that would improve middle-level schools, but the ways in which such knowledge suggests the need to overcome the poor fit between young adolescents and the traditional models used in too many of their classrooms and schools. The sheer quantity of research regarding the characteristics, perceptions, and experiences of young adolescents is quite large and continues to grow. However, if middle-level teachers are expected to know as fully as possible about their students, several areas are in need of attention.

One area in need of attention derives from our observation that studies about young adolescents published in mainstream journals and other popular sources frequently involve large surveys that conclude with general information that does not necessarily explore crucial variations across cultural diversities and class, though there has been an increase in examination of gender differences. Conversely, research that appears in more specialized research sources often does involve explorations of cultural and class differences. However, the findings are not used often enough to revise more general and widely used descriptions of young adolescents that do not account for such diversities. Given this dichotomy, there clearly is a need for syntheses of research that reconsider widely held descriptions of young adolescents by integrating information from more specialized sources, as well as that gathered from most recent studies reflecting the changing conditions under which young people live today.

With regard to both mainstream and specialized sources, there is also a need for more research that involves thick, qualitative description of young adolescents' lives, both in and out of school, to supplement quantitative data that help teachers to "know about" these young people but that do not necessarily lead toward really "knowing" them. Among other topics, such research should examine differences across factors that have been noted but not explored deeply enough such as early and later stages of young adolescence, cultural and class diversity, and rural-urban-suburban environments.

Given these research directions, the gap between what middle-level teachers and other middle-level educators know about young adolescents might certainly be reduced. In turn, progress might also be made toward overcoming stereotypes about young adolescents as, for example universally mired in a period of "storm and stress" or little more than "hormones with feet." Informed more thoroughly about young adolescents and rid of demeaning stereotypes about them, middle-level teachers will perhaps be more likely to make the school a better environmental fit for young adolescents, thus contributing to their own and their students' sense of efficacy.

Teaching as Part of a Team

Of the various teacher expectations indicated by the middle school reform platform, the area of teaming appears to have received the most attention by researchers (e.g., Dickinson & Erb, 1997). Clearly, teaming has been the most visible and successful aspect of the platform and, consequently, the one area that has changed the working conditions of many teachers. Moreover, middle school reform advocates have held high hopes that multisubject teaming would eventually lead toward other reforms such as multidisciplinary and integrative curriculum forms. Given the evidence to date, the press for team approaches to middle school teaching appears to be warranted in terms of both student outcomes and the possibilities for teacher autonomy and collaboration.

As much as the area of teaming has received a disproportionate share of research attention, there are still aspects of it that need serious investigation. One aspect has to do with the effects of different size teams, especially as many middle schools have begun to experiment with two- and three-teacher teams in place of the typical four- and five-teacher arrangements. As team size varies, what variations in teachers' sense of autonomy, efficacy, and workload stress emerge? In what ways does the size of teams influence teacher-student relationships, curriculum flexibility, and use of varied teaching and learning strategies?

Another aspect of teaming in need of attention is the matter of team membership. Middle school teams almost always involve teachers of mathematics, language arts, social studies, and science, or some combination thereof. What happens with regard to curriculum and teaching when combinations within that set are used to form teams or, as importantly, when combinations are made that include teachers of areas such as music, art, technology, family, and consumer science, physical education, or others? How do such combinations seem to affect curriculum organization, uses of knowledge, teacher collegiality, and use of varied teaching and learning strategies?

Finally, there is a continuing need for research having to do with personal and professional dynamics within teams. While case studies have begun to address this aspect, important questions remain. How does the size of the team influence the team members' sense of collegiality? What happens when teams stay together over a long period of time, such as 15 or 20 years? Why do teams break up or become dysfunctional? Obviously questions like these call for continued use of systematic and longitudinal ethnographic, case study, and action research methods because the answers likely lie deep within a team's everyday interactions as those actions unfold over time rather than in short-answer survey responses. Yet, it is here that we are potentially most likely to learn what it really means to be part of a teaching team and thus to understand the deeper implications of teaming for middle school teachers' work.

The Teacher as Affective Mentor

The expectation that middle school teachers serve as affective mentors for young adolescents is a reasonable one but will almost inevitably remain problematic. Given the combination of developmental issues that virtually all young adolescents face and the serious environmental problems many of them confront, adult affective guidance would clearly be helpful to most young adolescents and crucial for some. Yet middle-level teachers are caught in an ambiguous position with regard to both kinds of issues. In the case of general developmental issues, teachers do not feel well prepared to serve as affective mentors nor confident of the support they believe they need to carry out that role. With regard to more serious and complicated issues, teachers cannot be expected to be well prepared for mentorship roles that call for specialized services. And in either case, middle school teachers are, by the nature of the institution itself, caught in the lack of clarity and consensus regarding the schools' role in affective issues.

The area of affective mentorship is also in need of far more research attention than it has been given to date. Very little is known about the effects of affective advisory programs except from self-reports and brief case studies. The positive tone of those studies contradicts historical evidence that affective programs do not necessarily have strong or lasting effects on the attitudes or behaviors of young people. More needs to be known about role and program variations in relation to various kinds of affective outcomes. For example, if there are positive affective outcomes in relation to teacher mentoring, are they a function of program-type experiences or simply closer teacher-student relationships? How do such outcomes emerge if the affective components are variously part of a separate program or included in the general education curriculum? What levels of teacher efficacy or perceptions of young adolescents are necessary to effectively carry out a mentorship role? What kinds of preparation and support would make the advisory role more attractive to larger numbers of teachers? Responses to questions like these are important not only for clarifying this function of middle-level education but also for clarifying the expectation that teachers participate in it.

Teaching Through Varied and Appropriate Strategies

The expectation that teachers use varied and appropriate teaching and learning strategies makes a good deal of sense given the volume of research in this area generally and at the middle level. Despite that research, however, it appears that the use of varied strategies is relatively low at the middle level and that classrooms are still dominated by direct instruction, low-level skill routines, and passive activity. What is unclear, and thus in need of research attention, is the reason for this gap. There is some indication that middle-level reformers have relied too much on developmental arguments in their call for varied teaching and learning strategies and too little on the effects evidence that teachers say they look for in making instructional decisions. Such a misplaced rationale is not surprising since the middle school movement has often seemed to elevate human development to the status of an ideology. Yet given the widespread reports of success generally with strategies such as hands-on projects, collaborative learning, and authentic instruction, it seems likely that other issues may be involved in the absence of such strategies in middle school classrooms.

Thus, with regard to the call for the use of varied and appropriate teaching and learning strategies, several questions are in need of study. What do teachers really think about these strategies? Are they unlikely to use them even if supporting evidence is offered or is it that such evidence, such as it is now, is simply not known? What contextual inhibitors exist that prevent teachers from using varied and appropriate strategies? If perceived institutional barriers to such strategies, such as scheduling or resource availability, were removed, would teachers be any more likely to use varied appropriate strategies? How do the stresses of implementing new practices interact with other agendas in teachers' lives, or with the career phase factors, or with both?

Two additional topics are in need of attention within this area. One involves questions about whether there is anything unique about use of the kind of varied teaching and learning strategies mentioned above with young adolescents. After all, such strategies are often associated with more student activity and autonomy, an association that could give rise to apprehen-

sion among middle school teachers who stereotypically view young adolescents as "hormones with feet." Whether there is some degree of uniqueness for such strategies at the middle level or if particular adaptations are needed may be important questions for teachers who are unsure of how to use them.

Beyond those two topics, there is also the issue of what the varied and appropriate teaching and learning strategies are supposed to be "about." Is this part of the reform platform simply a matter of motivation and engagement of young adolescents or are other issues involved? At one level, this question has implications for the question of whether teachers see the use of varied strategies as appropriate or not for a particular subject area. At a second level, it may be tied to concerns over whether strategies such as collaborative learning and hands-on projects are really aimed at certain outcomes that are not considered "basic" by some teachers and, therefore, not valued. At a third level, the question may also be tied to the expectation that curriculum approaches beyond the separate subject one be used.

Taken together, those three levels of concern begin to raise the more general question of whether teachers might look unfavorably on the use of such strategies because they finally represent, at the classroom level, the complicated and difficult agenda of change that the middle school reform platform involves. Whatever the case, however, this aspect of the reform platform, along with the next, are in need of serious attention from researchers, since, unless change is made with regard to curriculum and teaching, the reform platform as a whole may come to little in the end.

Teaching Beyond the Separate Subjects

Of all the reform platform expectations for middle school teachers, none has been more complicated historically than the call for use of curriculum approaches beyond the separate subject organization. This area of curriculum reform most explicitly involves the purpose of the middle-level school and is, therefore, most caught up in the ambiguities and contradictions associated with the middle level since early in the century. If there is lack of clarity about the school's mission, then there must inevitably be lack of clarity about what teachers are supposed to be teaching toward. Conversely, there is substantial evidence that multidisciplinary and integrative approaches to curriculum are comparatively more effective with regard to affective outcomes and at least, if not more, effective with regard to academic achievement outcomes. Given the possibility that curriculum approaches beyond the separate subject approach can meet multiple purposes, the expectation that teachers use them appears to be a reasonable one.

However, since this is a contentious topic, several kinds of research are needed to both inform and support teachers' participation within it. One needs to explore more fully what happens to teachers' thinking and work as they engage in curriculum approaches that involve philosophies of curriculum, learning, and knowledge organization that are fundamentally different from the separate subject approach. How does the teacher role change? How do teacher-student relationships change? How do relationships with colleagues change? What kind of professional support and development do teachers require as they work through new curriculum approaches? What is it like for a few teachers to undertake these changes in schools where they are surrounded by a large majority of colleagues using a traditional subject-centered approach? What conditions are needed for teachers to sustain this kind of work in that kind of isolation? Or is it necessary to be joined by a critical mass of colleagues in order to sustain curriculum change on this scale?

Since teachers are held accountable for results of standardized testing, however, there is also a need for continuing research that explores student outcome effects in relation to non-subject-area curriculum organizations. While typical basic skill areas should be included in this research, efforts must be made to assess more sophisticated skills in areas like problem solving and critical thinking, as well as affective outcomes such as interpersonal skills. At the same time, more research also needs to be done to investigate how students fare upon leaving integrative curriculum organizations and entering into (or reentering) separate subject organizations. Importantly, such research might investigate how the academic and affective outcomes that proponents of integrative approaches claim students have upon leaving will hold up in the context of separate subject approaches.

Finally, research in the area of curriculum organization and its effects on students and teachers must be made more clear with regard to the type of nonseparate subject approach being investigated. Mainstream work on curriculum reform uses terms such as multidisciplinary and integration interchangeably when, in fact, they are quite different approaches to curriculum organization and evolve as very different kinds of contexts for teaching and learning. As a consequence, results of research are often confusing and thus add little to the understanding of curriculum approaches beyond the separate subject one. This lack of clarity, in turn, threatens the quality of information that might inform teachers about curriculum organization as they face the expectation that they teach beyond the separate subjects.

Conclusion

The reform platform for middle-level education proposed by leading national and state associations and agencies involves a range of climate, structural, curriculum, and teaching ideas that depart substantially from the forms that have dominated education and schooling at this level throughout the century. From the platform, a particular portrait regarding teachers emerges: teachers who know about and understand the young adolescents with whom they work, who collaborate in team arrangements with other teachers, who provide affective mentorship for their students, and who use varied and appropriate teaching strategies in the context of curriculum approaches beyond the separate subject organization. Admittedly, this set of expectations amounts to a redefinition of the dominant tradition of middle-level teaching, but, as we have seen, such an agenda, especially when undertaken in an integrated fashion, holds promise for both students and teachers in a number of ways.

However, the potential benefits of this reform agenda will not be realized without changes in many institutional features of the school organization (Oakes, Hunter Quartz, Gong, Guiton, & Lipton, 1993). It is simply unlikely, to say nothing of unfair, to expect that teachers can or will undertake the work necessary to meet these expectations without support for their efforts and recognition of the difficulties involved. Such support includes, but is not limited to, adequate planning time, appropriate scheduling, money to locate or develop resources, and appropriate physical space and equipment. Recognition needs include respect for teacher autonomy, substantive roles for teachers in various levels of decision making, adequate guarantees of professional security, protection from unfair criticism, sufficient professional development to carry out new strategies and approaches, and reasonable expectations with regard to workloads. And, at a more general level, teachers will need, and should expect, adequate guarantees that school officials are committed to carrying out the reform agenda over an extended period of time, through well-organized professional dialogue, and in a comprehensive, integrated, and systemic fashion.

To the extent that research might contribute to clarifying and advancing the middle-level reform agenda, changes are also needed in ways of thinking about school-based research. First, just as the reform agenda depends on long-term, longitudinal commitments, so must the research agenda move beyond short-term and superficial studies of implementation issues. Second, where external researchers are involved in reform agenda studies, there is a need for closer and more collegial relationships with teachers that build upon the notion that teaching has more to do with intervention effects than with main effects (Lipka, in press). Third, more effort needs to be made to support and encourage teachers in carrying out action research studies so that they might reflect more fully on their own practice in relation to middle-level reform efforts (Burnaford, Brodhagen, & Beane, 1994). In short, the middle-level reform agenda is in need of more careful and systematic research that digs more deeply into the ongoing lives and work of teachers and young adolescents as they unfold over the longer term.

It would be inaccurate to suggest that the middle level of education has yet escaped from its historic role as a "junior" version of the high school and the low status for teachers that accompanies that. Moreover, it is still the case that many middle-level educators themselves cling to that definition of their school, especially with regard to curriculum organization and teacher-student role relationships (Polite, 1995). However, an increasing number of middle-level schools are pursuing the reform agenda outlined here, and, as we have seen, some have done so to the degree that they have demonstrated the possibilities for teachers and students suggested in the research reviewed here.

The work of middle-level reform advocates continues to present many challenges, including more widely disseminating a clear account of their proposals, seeking more research on the strategies and forms they recommend, and adequately arguing their case. At the same time, researchers, both inside and outside classrooms, who focus on the middle-level reform agenda must continue to explore what makes the middle level of education unique and how such uniqueness frames the roles and work of middle-level teachers. If current trends continue, we may expect a continuing shift in the direction of that reform agenda and, in that case, a substantial redefinition in what it means to be a middle school teacher.

REFERENCES

Alberty, H. (1960). Core programs. In *Encyclopedia of educational research* (3rd ed., pp. 337–341). New York: Macmillan.
Alexander, W. M. (1965). The junior high school: A changing view. In

G. Hass & K. Wiles, *Readings in curriculum.* Boston: Allyn & Bacon.

Alexander, W. M. (1968). *A survey of organizational patterns of reorganized middle schools.* Washington, DC: United States Department of Health, Education, and Welfare.

Alexander, W. M., & McEwin, C. K. (1989). *Schools in the middle: Status and progress.* Columbus, OH: National Middle School Association.

Alexander, W. M., Williams, E. L., Compton, M., Hines, V. A., & Prescott, D. (1968). *The emergent middle school.* New York: Holt, Rinehart, & Winston.

Arhar, J. M. (1990). Interdisciplinary teaming as a school intervention to increase the social bonding of middle-level students. In *Research in middle-level education, selected studies* (pp. 1–10). Columbus, OH: National Middle School Association.

Arhar, J. M., & Irvin, J. L. (1995). Interdisciplinary team organization: A growing research base. *Middle School Journal, 26*(5), 65–67.

Arhar, J. M., Johnston, J. H., & Markle, G. C. (1988). The effect of teaming and other collaborative arrangements. *Middle School Journal, 19*(4), 22–25.

Arhar, J. M., & Kromrey, J. D. (1995). Interdisciplinary teaming and the demographics of membership: A comparison of student belonging in high SES and low SES middle-level schools. *Research in Middle-Level Education, 18*(2), 71–86.

Arnold, J. (1980). Needed: A realistic perception of the early adolescent learner. *Clearinghouse, 54,* 4.

Arredondo, D. E., & Rucinski, T. T. (1995). The use of integrated curriculum in Missouri middle schools. *Review of Research in Middle-Level Education Quarterly, 19*(1) 27–42.

Ashton, P. T., & Webb, R. B. (1986). *Making a difference: Teacher's sense of efficacy and student achievement.* New York: Longman.

Ayers, L. R. (1994). Middle school advisory programs: Findings from the field. *Middle School Journal, 25*(3), 8–14.

Beane, J. A. (1990a). *Affect in the curriculum: Toward democracy, dignity, and diversity.* New York: Teachers College Press.

Beane, J. A. (1990b). *A middle school curriculum: From rhetoric to reality.* Columbus, OH: National Middle School Association.

Beane, J. A. (1993). *A middle school curriculum: From rhetoric to reality* (Rev. ed.). Columbus, OH: National Middle School Association.

Beane, J. A. (1997). *Curriculum integration: Designing the core of a democratic education.* New York: Teachers College Press.

Beane, J. A., & Lipka, R. P. (1986). *Self-concept, self-esteem, and the curriculum.* New York: Teachers College Press.

Beane, J. A., & Lipka, R. P. (1987). *When the kids come first: Enhancing self-esteem in the middle school.* Columbus, OH: National Middle School Association.

Bennett, G. V. (1919). *The junior high school.* Baltimore: Warwick and York.

Blair, A. W., & Burton, W. H. (1951). *Growth and development of the preadolescent.* New York: Appleton-Century-Crofts.

Blos, P. (1941). *The adolescent personality.* New York: Appleton-Century-Crofts.

Blumenfeld, P. C., Soloway, E., & Marx, R. W. (1991). Motivating project-based learning: Sustaining the doing, supporting the learning. *Educational Psychologist, 26,* 369–398.

Bossing, N. L., & Cramer, R. V. (1965). *The junior high school.* Boston: Houghton Mifflin.

Brazee, E., & Capelluti, J. (1995). *Dissolving Boundaries: Toward an integrative middle school curriculum.* Columbus, OH: National Middle School Association.

Briggs, T. H. (1920). *The junior high school.* Boston: Houghton Mifflin.

Brodhagen, B. L. (1994). Assessing and reporting student progress in an integrative curriculum. *Teaching and Change, 1,* 238–254.

Brodhagen, B. L. (1995). The situation made us special. In M. W. Apple & J. A. Beane (Eds.), *Democratic Schools* (pp. 83–100). Alexandria, VA: Association for Supervision and Curriculum Development.

Buckmaster, L. (1994). Effects of activities that promote cooperation among seventh graders in a future problem solving classroom. *Elementary School Journal, 1,* 49–62.

Buckner, J. H., & Bickel, F. (1991). If you want to know about effective teaching, why not ask your middle school kids? *Middle School Journal, 22*(3), 26–29.

Burnaford, G. (1993). Beginning curriculum integration: Three middle-level case studies in professional development. *Research in Middle-Level Education, 16*(2), 43–64.

Burnaford, G., Brodhagen, B., & Beane, J. (1994). Teacher action research: Inside and integrative curriculum. *Middle School Journal, 26*(2), 5–13.

Bushnell, D., & George, P. S. (1993). Five crucial characteristics: Middle school teachers as effective advisors. *Schools in the Middle, 3*(1), 10–16.

Carnegie Council on Adolescent Development. (1989). *Turning points: Preparing American youth for the 21st century.* New York: Carnegie Corporation.

Cawelti, G. (Ed.). (1995). *Handbook of research on improving student achievement.* Arlington, VA: Educational Research Service.

Center for Research on Elementary and Middle Schools. (1987). *Special report on middle school.* Baltimore: Johns Hopkins University Center for Research on Elementary and Middle Schools.

Cole, C. G. (1994). Teachers' attitudes before beginning a teacher advisory program. *Middle School Journal, 25*(5), 3–7.

Connors, N. A. (1992). Teacher advisory: The fourth r. In J. L. Irvin (Ed.), *Transforming middle-level education: Perspectives and possibilities* (pp. 162–178). Boston: Allyn & Bacon.

Cox, P. W. (1929). *The junior high school and its curriculum.* New York: Charles Scribner's Sons.

Crockett, L. J., Petersen, A .C., Graber, J. A., Schulenberg, J. E., & Ebata, A. (1989). School transitions and adjustment during early adolescence. *Journal of Early Adolescence, 9,* 181–210.

Cuban, L. (1992). What happens to reforms that last: The case of the junior high school. *American Educational Research Journal, 29,* 227–251.

Dickinson, T. (Ed.). (1993). *Readings in middle-level curriculum: A continuing conversation.* Columbus, OH: National Middle School Association.

Dickinson, T. S., & Erb, T. O. (Eds.). (1997). *We gain more than we give: Teaming in middle schools.* Columbus, OH: National Middle School Association.

Drasch, A. (1976). Variations in pubertal development and the school system: A problem and a challenge. *Transescence, 4,* 14–26.

Eccles, J. S., & Midgley, C. (1989). Stage/environment fit: Developmentally appropriate classrooms for early adolescents. In R. E. Ames & C. Ames (Eds.), *Research on motivation in education* (Vol. 3, pp. 139–186). New York: Academic Press.

Eccles, J. S., Midgley, C., Wigfield, A., Miller C., Buchanan, C., Reuman, D., Flanagan, C., & Mac Iver, D. (1993). Development during adolescence: The impact of stage-environment fit on young adolescents' experiences in schools and in families. *American Psychologist, 48*(2), 90–101.

Eichhorn, D. H. (1966). *The middle school.* New York: Center for Applied Research in Education.

Elliott, G. C. (1982, Winter). Self-esteem and self-presentation among young adolescents as a function of age and gender. *Journal of Youth and Adolescence, 11,* 135–53.

Epstein, H. T. (1978). Growth spurts during brain development: Implications for educational policy. In J. S. Chall, *Education and the brain,* 77th Yearbook of the National Society for the Study of Education (pp. 343–370). Chicago: University of Chicago Press.

Epstein, J. L., & Mac Iver, D. J. (1992). *Opportunities to learn: Effects on eighth graders of curriculum offerings and instructional approaches.* Baltimore: Johns Hopkins University Center for Research on Effective Schooling for Disadvantaged Students.

Epstein, J. L., & McPartland, J. M. (1988). *Education in the middle grades: A national survey of practices and trends.* Baltimore: Johns Hopkins University Center for Research on Elementary and Middle Schools.

Espe, L. (1993). The effectiveness of teacher advisories in a junior high school. *The Canadian School Executive, 12*(7), 15–19.

Everhart, R. B. (1983). *Reading, writing and resistance: Adolescence and labor in a junior high school.* Boston: Routledge and Kegan Paul.

Faunce, R. C., & Bossing, N. L. (1951). *Developing the core curriculum.* New York: Prentice-Hall.

Felner, R. D., Jackson, A. W., Kasak, D., Mulhall, P., Brand, S., & Flowers, N. (1997). The impact of school reform for the middle years. *Phi Delta Kappan, 78*(7), 528–550.

Forbes, G. B. (1968). Physical aspects of early adolescence. In T. E. Curtis (Ed.), *The middle school.* Albany, NY: State University of New York Press.

Ford, D. Y. (1992). Self-perceptions of underachievement and support for the achievement ideology among early adolescent African Americans. *Journal of Early Adolescence, 12,* 228–252.

Gatewood, T. E., Cline, G., Green, G., & Harris, S. E. (1992). Middle school interdisciplinary team organization and its relationship to teacher stress. *Research in Middle-Level Education, 15*(2), 27–40.

Gay, G. (1994). Coming of age ethnically: Teaching young adolescents of color. *Theory Into Practice, 33*(3), 149–55.

George, P .S., Spruel, M., & Moorefield, J. (1987). *Long-term teacher student relationships: A middle school case study.* Columbus, OH: National Middle School Association.

George, P., & Shewey, K. (1994). *New evidence for the middle school.* Columbus, OH: National Middle School Association.

Goodlad, J. (1984). *A place called school: Prospects for the future.* New York: McGraw-Hill.

Gould, S. J. (1981). *The mismeasure of man.* New York: W. W. Norton.

Greengross, S. A. (1995). *Middle-level education: Instructional strategies and teacher change.* Unpublished doctoral dissertation, Boston University, Boston, MA.

Gruenberg, S. (1934). Half-way up the stairs. *Child Study, 12*(1), 3–6.

Hall, G. S. (1908). *Adolescence,* (Vols 1–2). New York: D. Appleton.

Hanna, P. R., & Lang, A. D. (1950). Integration. In W. S. Monroe (Ed.), *The encyclopedia of educational research* (pp. 592–600). New York: Macmillan.

Hargreaves, A. (1986). *Two cultures of schooling: The case of middle schools.* London: Falmer.

Hart, L. E., Pate, P. E., Mizelle, N. B., & Reeves, J. L. (1992). Interdisciplinary team development in the middle school: A study of the delta project. *Research in Middle-Level Education, 16*(1), 79–98.

Hartshorne, H., & May, M. A. (1928). *Studies in the nature of character, Volume 1: Studies in deceit.* New York: Macmillan.

Hartshorne, H., May, M. A., & Shuttleworth, F. K. (1929). *Studies in the nature of character, Volume 2: Studies in service and self control.* New York: Macmillan.

Hartshorne, H., & May, M. A. (1930), *Studies in service and self control, Volume 3: Studies in the organization of character.* New York: Macmillan.

Hays, C. B., Ryan, A., & Zseller, E. B. (1994). The middle school child's perceptions of caring teachers. *American Journal of Education, 103,* 1–19.

Heironimus, N. C. (1917). The teacher-adviser in the junior high school. *Educational Administration and Supervision, 3*(2), 91–94.

Hopkins, L. T., & Others. (1937). *Integration: Its meaning and application.* New York: Appleton-Century.

Hough, D. L., & St. Clair, B. (1995). The effects of integrated curricula on young adolescent problem-solving. *Research in Middle-Level Education Quarterly, 19*(1), 1–25.

Huberman, M., with Grounauer, M.-M., & Marti, J. (1993). *The lives of teachers* (J. Neufeld, Trans.). New York: Teachers College Press.

Informal Committee of the Progressive Education Association on Evaluation of Newer Practices in Education. (1941). *New methods vs. old in American education.* New York: Bureau of Publications, Teachers College, Columbia University.

James, C. (1972). *Young lives at stake.* New York: Agathon.

James, M. A. (1986). *Advisor-advisee programs: Why, what, and how.* Columbus, OH: National Middle School Association.

James, M. A. (1993). Reforming advisories, thematically. *Middle School Journal, 25*(1), 44–45.

Jenkins, F. C. (1947). *The southern study: Cooperative study for the improvement of education.* Durham, NC: Duke University Press.

Johnson, D. W., & Johnson, R. (1989). *Cooperation and competition: Theory and research.* Edina, MN: Interaction.

Kain, D. (1993). Deciding to integrate curricula: Judgments about holding and stretching. *Research in Middle-Level Education, 16*(2), 25–42.

Kagan, J., & Coles, R. (1971). *12 to 16, early adolescence.* New York: W. W. Norton.

Larson, R. W., & Richards, M. H. (1991). Boredom in the middle schools years: Blaming schools versus blaming students. *American Journal of Education, 99,* 418–443.

Lee, V., & Smith, J. (1993). Effects of school restructuring on the achievement and engagement of middle grades students. *Sociology of Education, 66,* 164–87.

Lesko, N. (1994). Back to the future: Middle schools and the *Turning Points* report. *Theory Into Practice, 33*(3), 143–148.

Lipka, R. P. (in press). Epilogue. In R. P. Lipka & T. M. Brinthaupt, *The role of self in teacher development.* Albany, NY: SUNY Press.

Lipsitz, J. (1980a). *Growing up forgotten: A review of research and programs concerning early adolescence.* Lexington, MA: D.C. Heath.

Lipsitz, J. (1980b). The age group. In M. Johnson (Ed.), *Toward adolescence: The middle school years,* 79th Yearbook of the National Society for the Study of Education (pp. 7–31). Chicago: The Association.

Lipsitz, J. (1984). *Successful schools for young adolescents.* East Brunswick, NJ: Transaction.

Lockwood, A. L. (1978). The effects of values clarification and moral development curricula on school-age subjects: A critical review of research. *Review of Educational Research, 48,* 325–364.

Lounsbury, J. H. (Ed.). (1984). *Perspectives: Middle school education, 1964–84.* Columbus, OH: National Middle School Association.

Lounsbury, J. H. (Ed.). (1992). *Connecting the curriculum through interdisciplinary instruction.* Columbus, OH: National Middle School Association.

Lounsbury, J. H., & Johnston, J. H. (1985). *How fares the ninth grade?* Reston, VA: National Association of Secondary School Principals.

Lounsbury, J. H., & Johnston, J. H. (1988). *Life in the three 6th grades.* Reston, VA: National Association of Secondary School Principals.

Lounsbury, J. H. & Marani, J. (1964). *The junior high school we saw: One day in the eighth grade.* Washington, DC: Association for Supervision and Curriculum Development.

Lounsbury, J. H., Marani, J., & Compton, M. (1980). *The middle school in profile: A day in the seventh grade.* Columbus, OH: National Middle School Association.

Lounsbury, J. H., & Vars, G. F. (1978). *A curriculum for the middle school years.* New York: Harper.

Mac Iver, D. J. (1990). Meeting the needs of young adolescents: Advisory groups, interdisciplinary teaching teams, and school transition programs. *Phi Delta Kappan, 71*(6), 458–64.

Mac Iver, D. J., & Epstein, J. L. (1993, May). Middle grades research: Not yet mature, but no longer a child. *The Elementary School Journal, 93,* 519–34.

Maehr, M. L., & Anderman, E. M. (1993). Reinventing schools for early adolescents: Emphasizing task goals. *The Elementary School Journal, 93*(5), 593–610.

McDaniel, J. E., & Romerdahl, N. S. (1993). A multiple-case study of middle grades teachers' interdisciplinary curriculum work. *Research in Middle-level Education, 16*(2), 65–86.

McEwin, C. K., Dickinson, T. S., & Jenkins, D. M. (1996). *America's middle schools: Practices and progress, a 25 year perspective.* Columbus, OH: National Middle School Association.

McLaughlin, H. J., Earle, K., Hall, M., Miller, V., & Wheeler, M. (1995). Hearing from our students: Team action research in a middle school. *Middle School Journal, 26*(3), 7–12.

McPartland, J. M. (1987). *Balancing high quality subject matter instruction with positive teacher-student relations in the middle grades.* Baltimore: Johns Hopkins University Center for Research on Elementary and Middle Schools.

Mickelson, J. M. (1957). What does research say about the effectiveness of the core curriculum? *School Review, 65,* 144–60.

Mills, R. A., Powell, R. R., & Pollak, J. P. (1992). The influence of middle-level interdisciplinary teaming on teacher isolation: A case study. *Research in Middle-Level Education, 15*(2), 9–26.

Mitman, A. L., & Lambert, V. (1993). Implementing instructional reform at the middle grades: Case studies of seventeen California schools. *The Elementary School Journal, 93*(5), 495–518.

National Education Association. (1893). *Report of the committee on secondary school studies.* Washington, DC: U.S. Government Printing Office.

National Education Association. (1895). *Report of the committee of fifteen on elementary education, with the reports of the sub-committees: On the training of teachers; On the correlation of studies in elementary education; On the organization of city school systems.* New York: American Book.

National Middle School Association. (1995). *This we believe: Developmentally responsive middle schools.* Columbus, OH: The Association.

Newman, F. M., & Associates. (1996). *Authentic achievement: Restructuring schools for intellectual quality.* San Francisco: Jossey-Bass.

Newman, R. (1993). Development of a curriculum integration perception survey: Two future middle schools' staffs readiness for change. *Research in Middle-Level Education, 16*(2), 7–24.

Noar, G. (1948). *Freedom to live and learn.* Philadelphia: Franklin Publishing.

Oakes, J., Hunter Quartz, K., Gong, J., Guiton, G., & Lipton, M. (1993). Creating middle schools: Technical, normative, and political considerations. *The Elementary School Journal, 93*(5), 461–481.

Pace, G. (Ed.). (1995). *Whole learning in the middle school.* Norwood, MA: Christopher-Gordon.

Pate, E., Homestead, E., & McGinnis, K. (1994). Middle school students' perceptions of integrated curriculum. *Middle School Journal, 26*(2), 21–23.

Pate, E., Homestead, E., & McGinnis, K. (1996). *Making integrated curriculum work: Teachers, students, and the quest for a coherent curriculum.* New York: Teachers College Press.

Pearson, L. C., Pilcher, J. K., & Weeks, L .A. (1996). The effects of a magnet middle school's thematic curriculum on minority and majority student achievement and retention. *Current Issues in Middle-Level Education, 5*(1), 4–15.

Petersen, A. C., & Crockett, L. (1985). Pubertal timing and grade effect on adjustment. *Journal of Youth and Adolescence, 14,* 191–206.

Polite, M. M. (1994). Team negotiation and decision-making: Linking leadership to curricular and instructional evaluation. *Research in Middle-Level Education, 18*(2), 65–81.

Polite, M. M. (1995). Two cases of change: Understanding middle school reformation and transformation. *Middle School Journal, 26*(3), 3–6.

Powell, R. R. (1993). Seventh grader's perspectives of their interdisciplinary team. *Middle School Journal, 24*(3), 49–57.

Powell, R. R., & Mills, R. (1994). Five types of mentoring build knowledge on interdisciplinary teams. *Middle School Journal, 26*(2), 24–29.

Powell, R. R., & Skoog, G. (1995). Students' perspectives of integrative curricula: The case of Brown Barge Middle School. *Research in Middle-Level Education Quarterly, 19*(1), 85–114.

Powell, R. R., Skoog, G., & Troutman, P. (1996). On streams and odysseys: Reflections on reform and research in middle-level integrative learning environments. *Research in Middle-Level Education Quarterly, 19*(4), 1–30.

Powell, R. R., Skoog, G., Troutman, P., & Jones, C. (1996). Standing on the edge of middle-level curriculum reform: Factors influencing the sustainability of a non-linear integrative learning environment. Paper presented at the annual meeting of the American Educational Research Association, New York, NY.

Pringle, R. W. (1937). *The junior high school: A psychological approach.* New York: McGraw.

Putbrese, L. (1989). Advisory programs at the middle-level—The students' response. *NASSP Bulletin, 61,* 81–83.

Redl, F. (1944). Preadolescents: What makes them tick? *Child Study, 12*(1), 44–48.

Russell, J. F. (1997). Relationships between the implementation of middle-level program concepts and student achievement. *Journal of Curriculum and Supervision, 12,* 152–168.

Scales, P. C. (1991). *A portrait of young adolescents in the 1990s: Implications for promoting healthy growth and development.* Minneapolis, MN: Search Institute and Center for Early Adolescence.

Scales, P. C. (1992). *Windows of opportunity: Improving middle grades teacher preparation.* Minneapolis, MN: Search Institute.

Scales, P. C., & McEwin, C. K. (1994). *Growing pains: The making of America's middle school teachers.* Columbus, OH: National Middle School Association.

Scott, C. A. (1994). Project-based science: Reflections of a middle school teacher. *Elementary School Journal, 1,* 75–94.

Silberman, C. E. (1970). *Crisis in the classroom.* New York: Random House.

Shaw, C. C. (1993). A content analysis of teacher talk during middle school team meetings. *Research in Middle-Level Education, 17*(1), 27–45.

Simmon, R .G., Black, A., & Zhou, Y. (1991). African American versus white children and the transition into junior high school. *American Journal of Education, 99,* 481–520.

Simmons, R., & Blyth, D. (1987). *Moving into adolescence: The impact of pubertal change and school context.* Hawthorne, NY: Aldine de Gruyter.

Sparks, G. M. (1988). Teachers' attitudes toward change and subsequent improvements in classroom teaching. *Journal of Educational Psychology, 80,* 111–117.

Steffes, B., & Valentine, J. (1996). The relationship between organizational characteristics and expected benefits in interdisciplinary teams. *Research in Middle-Level Education Quarterly, 19*(4), 83–106.

Stevenson, C. (1986). *Teachers as inquirers: Strategies for learning with and about early adolescents.* Columbus, OH: National Middle School Association.

Stevenson, C. (1992). *Teaching ten to fourteen year olds.* New York: Longman.

Stevenson, C., & Carr, J. F. (Eds.) (1993). *Integrative studies in the middle grades: Dancing through walls.* New York: Teachers College Press.

Strein, W. (1988). Classroom-based elementary school affective education programs: A critical review. *Psychology in the Schools, 25,* 285–296.

Strubbe, M. A. (1989). An assessment of early adolescent stress factors. *Research Annual, Selected Studies* (pp. 47–59). Columbus, OH: National Middle School Association.

Sweeney, F. E., Barry, E. F., & Schoelkopf, A. E. (1932). *Western youth meets eastern culture: A study in the integration of social studies, English, and art in the junior high school.* New York: Teachers College Press.

Tanner, J. M. (1961). *Education and physical growth.* London: University of London.

Theobald, M. A. (1995). What students say about common teaching practices. *Middle School Journal, 26*(4), 18–22.

Thornburg, H. D. (1974). *Preadolescent development.* Tucson, AZ: University of Arizona Press.

Toepfer, C. F. Jr. (1965). Who should teach in the junior high school? *The Clearing House, 40*(2), 74–76.

Toepfer, C. F. Jr., & Marani, J. V. (1980). School-based research. In M. Johnson (Ed.), *Toward adolescence: The middle school years,* 79th Yearbook of the National Society for the Study of Education (pp. 269–281). Chicago: The Association.

Totten, S., & Nielson, W. (1994). Middle-level students' perceptions of their advisor/advisee program: A preliminary study. *Current Issues in Middle-Level Education, 3*(2), 8–33.

Tyrrell, R. (1990). What teachers say about cooperative learning. *Middle School Journal, 21*(3), 16–19.

Valentine, J. W., Clark, D.C., Irvin, J .C., Keefe, J. W., & Melton, G. (1993). *Leadership in middle-level education, Volume 1: A national survey of middle-level leaders and schools.* Reston, VA: National Association of Secondary School Principals.

Valentine, J. W., & Mogar, D. (1992). Middle-level certification: An encouraging revolution. *Middle School Journal, 24*(2), 36–43.

Van Hoose, J., & Strahan, D. (1988). *Young adolescent development and school practices: Promoting harmony.* Columbus, OH: National Middle School Association.

Van Til, W., Vars, G. F., & Lounsbury, J. H. (1961). *Modern education for the junior high school years.* Indianapolis, IN: Bobbs-Merrill.

Vars, G. F. (1987). *Interdisciplinary teaching: Why and how.* Columbus, OH: National Middle School Association.

Vars, G. F. (1991). Integrated curriculum in historical perspective. *Educational Leadership, 49*(1), 14–15.

Vars, G. F. (1993). *Interdisciplinary teaching: Why & how* (2nd ed.). Columbus, OH: National Middle School Association.

Vars, G. F. (1996). The effects of interdisciplinary curriculum and instruction. In P. S. Hlebowitsh & W. G. Wraga (Eds.), *Annual review of research for school leaders, Part II: Transcending traditional subject matter lines: Interdisciplinary curriculum and instruction* (pp. 147–164). Reston, VA: National Association of Secondary School Principals and New York: Scholastic Press.

Watson, C. (1992). *Attitudes of middle school teachers toward practices recommended for middle schools.* Unpublished doctoral dissertation, East Carolina University, Greenville, NC.

Waverling, M. J. (1995). Cognitive development of young adolescents. In M. J. Waverling, *Educating young adolescents: Life in the middle* (pp. 111–130). New York: Garland.

Wehlage, G., Smith, G., & Lipman, P. (1992). Restructuring urban schools: The new futures experience. *American Education Research Journal, 29*(1), 51–93.

Whinery, B., & Faircloth, C. V. (1994). The change process and interdisciplinary teaching. *Middle School Journal, 26*(2), 31–34.

Wigfield, A., & Eccles, J. S. (1994). Children's competence beliefs, achievement values, and general self-esteem: Change across elementary and middle school. *Journal of Early Adolescence, 14,* 107–138.

Wigfield, A., Eccles, J. S., Mac Iver, D., Reuman, D. A., & Midgley, C. (1991). Transitions during early adolescence: Changes in children's domain specific self-perceptions and general self-esteem across the transition to junior high school. *Developmental Psychology, 27,* 552–565.

Williams, D. R., Meyer, L. H., & Harootunian, B. (1992). Introduction and implementation of cooperative learning in the heterogeneous classroom: Middle school teachers' perspectives. *Research in Middle-Level Education, 16*(1), 115–30.

Wraga, W. G. (1992). The core curriculum in the middle school: Retrospect and prospect. *Middle School Journal, 23*(3), 19–23.

Wraga, W. G. (1997). Interdisciplinary team teaching: Sampling the literature. In T. S. Dickinson & T. O. Erb (Eds.), *We gain more than we give: Teaming in middle schools* (pp. 325–343). Columbus, OH: National Middle School Association.

Wright, G. S. (1950). *Core curriculum in public high schools: An inquiry into practices, 1949.* Bulletin 1950, No. 5, Office of Education. Washington, DC: U.S. Government Printing Office.

Wright, G. S. (1958). *Block-time classes and the core program in the junior high school.* Bulletin 1958, No. 6, Office of Education. Washington, DC: U.S. Government Printing Office.

Wright, G. S. (1963). *The core program: Unpublished research, 1956–1962.* Washington, DC: U.S. Government Printing Office.

Ziegler, S., & Mulhall, L. (1994). Establishing and evaluating a successful advisory program in a middle school. *Middle School Journal, 25*(4), 42–46.

51.

Teaching in Early Childhood Education: Understanding Practices Through Research and Theory

Celia Genishi
Teachers College, Columbia University

Sharon Ryan
Rutgers University

Mindy Ochsner
Rhode Island College

with

Mary Malter Yarnall
Teachers College, Columbia University

Contextualizing Teaching in Early Childhood Education

The following are descriptions of teaching in early childhood education settings:

Scene 1: Twelve children, ages 4 and 5 years old, sit on a rug in a circle with a woman. She holds a picture book and alternates between reading the text in the book and asking questions about it. Various children respond, and the adult attends primarily to those who have raised their hands before speaking. Three children are not responding to the teacher but occasionally speak to each other in Spanish.

Scene 2: Twenty-five second-grade children, ages 7 and 8 years old, sit at child-sized desks in front of a woman who is facing them. She holds a sturdy notebook-like textbook and points to letter combinations on a page, asking, "What sound does this make?" She refers occasionally to the textbook, which matches what she says perfectly. A close look at the book shows that various possible child responses are also printed there.

Scene 3: Three girls between the ages of 3 and 5 years talk in the housekeeping corner. Their conversation proceeds in this way:

Lee: I'm the mother.
Tessa: I'm the mother.
Lee: Un unh, I'm the mother! I'm the mother. She said I'm the mother.
Teacher: You can have two mothers.
Lee: No, we have to have one mother.
Tessa: Two.
Lee: One.
Tessa: Two.
Teacher: Lee, in our house we can have two mothers.

The authors have appreciated the reviews of Barbara Bowman, Erikson Institute, and M. Elizabeth Graue, University of Wisconsin-Madison, who provided numerous concrete suggestions and, as importantly, helped us to think more clearly about the content of this chapter. Their reviews were a gift. The authors also thank Virginia Richardson, who showed more editorial grace and patience than anyone deserves.

Tessa: I can be the grandmother.

Lee: No, we don't need a grandmother.

Tessa: Ye-e-es. You and me can be a sister, you and me can be sisters, and Lee's the mother, OK? (to Jennifer, another child). (Genishi & Di Paolo, 1982, pp. 59–60)

Scene 4: In a room with six infants between the ages of 3 and 12 months, one woman is changing a child's diaper. She moves quickly like one used to this task. At the same time, she is talking to the 7-month-old child as if he were able to understand her questions, "Is that a dirty diaper? Is that a dirty diaper?" She answers her own questions, "Yeah, it is! Unh huh, unh huh—it is!" while the boy smiles and watches his caregiver.

Each of these four scenes presents a sketch of classroom life and a representation of an aspect of teaching in the age range that is commonly referred to as *early childhood (EC)*. The purpose of this chapter is to present a comprehensive review of literature that is related to these and other aspects of teaching in early childhood education (ECE) and to examine enduring issues in the field that are either illustrated or implicit in the four scenes. These include issues of defining appropriate practices for young children, the nature of teaching in care and education, the role of cultural diversity, and representations of teachers and teaching across studies. We will also examine the theoretical perspectives that cast light on these issues.

The content of the chapter is descriptive and provides a historical context and a summary of recent research and theory, which is presented objectively in an attempt not to distort the intent or content of studies that are representative of varied theoretical perspectives. Our presentation is also ultimately interpretive. Despite our intention to be objective, we acknowledge that our own ideological commitments influence the selections and ideas that we include and the points that we make. As four individuals, we coauthors have varied ideologies—or firmly held beliefs and ideas that underlie our choices—although our individual training was grounded in child development. We also share a commitment to improving learning and teaching for individuals within the social and political complexities of global cultures. From our viewpoint, individuals and cultures are best understood through a critical lens. Two of us, Ochsner and Ryan, are committed to poststructuralisms and to the critiques they imply (described below). Genishi and Yarnall recognize that those critiques have the power to disturb the status quo, and, at the same time, they are committed to a hybrid form of constructivism—grounded in intersubjectivities—that combines sociocultural and psychological views of human relationships. Our overall aim is also prospective as we focus on issues and trends reflective of paradigm shifts in theory, research, and practice that will continue to influence the field in the 21st century.

We include work done primarily since the publication of the last *Handbook of Research on Teaching* (Wittrock, 1986) except when our focus is historical or when we address a topic such as teacher research that has not been previously reviewed in ECE. The chapter consists of these sections: contextualizing teaching in early childhood education (defining ECE); setting a historical context; research on teaching in ECE (process-product research, teacher cognition, ecological studies, teacher research);

critical voices (EC reconceptualists' theoretical frameworks); synthesizing diversity; and visions of future research on teaching in ECE.

Defining Early Childhood Education

We define *early childhood* as the age range from birth to about 8 years. This definition corresponds with that of major professional organizations such as the National Association for the Education of Young Children (NAEYC) and the Association for Childhood Education International (ACEI). Although the age range is broad, combining in one chapter studies from the prekindergarten years with those from the primary grades allows for a fuller discussion of current issues and dilemmas. These are sometimes unique to ECE and at other times overlap with issues and dilemmas in kindergarten through grade 12 (K–12) education.

The term *education* is broadly defined in order to be relevant to the specified age range and refers to group-oriented activities, usually in out-of-home settings that are intended to nurture, socialize, and educate young children. Those actions or arrangements that educate are "deliberately intended to affect the learning and development of children" (Almy, 1975, p. 2) in positive ways. Thus, they include the kind of infant-caregiver conversation presented above and didactic interactions in primary-grade classrooms. We acknowledge that education also occurs in homes between parents and children, but our review will be limited to programmatic efforts to affect learning and development.

Defining what is educative or appropriate for young children is a greater challenge than defining the parameters of early childhood. The ongoing debate about defining "developmentally appropriate practice" (DAP) (Bredekamp, 1987; Bredekamp & Copple, 1997; Kessler & Swadener, 1992; Mallory & New, 1994) is one of the persistent issues reflected in the four introductory scenes. Who should decide what is appropriate for both the children and the profession? For the profession, what is the appropriate knowledge base—what do early childhood (EC) educators need to know in order to deliberately affect learning and development (Stott & Bowman, 1996)? We do not present definitive answers to these questions. Instead, we offer a range of possible answers and suggestions about how the research and theory that we review might aid decision making about appropriateness.

Setting a Historical Context

Historically in the field of ECE, researchers have focused relatively little on teachers, teaching, or its effects. In fact, the formal education of young children is a relatively recent phenomenon, and the history of the field may be captured better through a review of representations of children than through a review of formal educational practices. Representing children is intimately linked to the ways in which adults conceptualize or construct theories about them. These theories are influenced by the particular social, economic, and political circumstances of an era. In this section we present a brief and selective review of what adults have constructed—their representations of children—and associated theories that underlie current research on teaching in ECE.

According to Ariès (1962), over time adults have constructed not only theories, but also the social and cultural phenomenon of childhood. Ariès has documented its social history, asserting that childhood is a modern invention. During the Middle Ages, once the young were weaned, cultural transmission occurred through the immersion of the young in everyday life, not through formal instruction. Children were educated through apprenticeships within a system of immediate social, often family, relationships. Ariès claims that the distinct category of *childhood* was not recognized until the 18th century when middle-class boys in Europe were segregated from adult society to be educated in schools. This educational landmark, which Ariès accurately points out was relevant only to males, coincided with the period of the Enlightenment, a period placing faith in reason rather than religious authority.

The views of two philosophers who are considered to be part of the Enlightenment—Locke, who wrote during the 17th century, and Rousseau, who wrote during the 18th—are still cited as influential in shaping views of childhood as a unique life phase. Locke is associated with the view of the child as a *tabula rasa,* or "blank slate" or white paper, as he called it, ready to be shaped by the environment and, chiefly, by experience. Locke advocated a sensitivity to the disposition of the learner and advised against harsh instructional methods that might destroy a child's desire to learn. However, he did emphasize, as did the behaviorists 3 centuries later, the environment's power to shape the behavior and character of children. In the United States, this view has dominated educators' efforts to understand children and affect their learning, particularly in K–12 settings.

In contrast, Rousseau advocated a romantic view of childhood and an education by nature. He viewed society as a corrupting influence that separated man from his pure and noble nature. His rejection of early schooling, with its imposition of an adult pedagogy onto children who are "innocents," emerged again 2 centuries later in the psychoanalytic writings of Anna Freud; in Neill's (1960) free school, Summerhill; and, recently, in contemporary, child-centered philosophies of education (Cleverley & Phillips, 1986).

Some current representations of young children as "experiencers" and "players" in educational contexts can be seen in the views of Pestalozzi in Switzerland and Froebel in Germany, who both spanned the 18th and 19th centuries (Weber, 1984). Pestalozzi took a highly experiential approach to educating neglected and orphaned children, teaching map reading (e.g., by having children chart the topography of their own geographic surroundings). He also saw teaching as highly relational and intuitive.

Pestalozzi's student, Froebel, carried on some of his mentor's ideas and incorporated his own spiritual vision of experience as unified and developed from children's play. He is credited with the creation of the kindergarten in Germany in 1837. The first kindergarten in the United States was opened in 1855 in Wisconsin by Margaretta Schurz. Many would cite this event as the beginning of formal ECE in the United States, although it was not until Susan Blow initiated a kindergarten in 1873 in Saint Louis, Missouri, that it was incorporated into a public school.

For the remainder of the 19th century, public school systems expanded, and childhood became increasingly institutionalized. By the end of the century, the kindergarten was recognized as a potential source of social regeneration and was carried into impoverished communities of many U.S. cities. (As early as the beginning of the 19th century, social reformers argued that poor children required improved cultural and educational experiences.) Movements similar to Robert Owen's infant school for mill workers' children in England; kindergartens in the 1860s; settlement house child-care centers in the 1900s; publicly funded day care and preschools in the 1930s and 1940s; and Head Start, established in 1964, continued the still-vital social reformist tradition in ECE. Within this tradition, childhood is constructed as a period of vulnerability to social crises and poor environmental conditions, which might be ameliorated by enhancing the care and education of children, who were represented as "victims."

Equally significant for contemporary constructs of childhood and even more significant for theoretical conceptions of children was the late-19th and early-20th century fascination with scientific studies of child growth and development. Weber (1984, p. 103) sees the diverse, theoretical roots entwined in this way:

> If we look back at all the theoretical formulations gaining momentum around the turn of the century: objective child study [Hall, 1895], a connectionist theory of learning [Thorndike, 1906], a democratic conception of education [Dewey, 1916], they have one common link—their evolutionary base.

From this perspective, Darwin's *The Origin of Species* (1859/1936) underpinned 20th-century science's acceptance of the inductive method, the gradual accumulation of observational, objective data to understand human growth and development. Thus, children within this view came to be represented as "subjects."

The view influenced ECE pioneers like Hill (Hill et al., 1923) at Teachers College, Columbia University, where she helped found a laboratory nursery school. A strong advocate of progressive education in the kindergarten, Hill and her teacher colleagues developed the conduct curriculum, which was based on the ideas of Thorndike and Dewey and was thus an intriguing combination of principles of behaviorist habit formation and of democratic social organization.

Also rooted in the 19th century and evolution was Freud's psychoanalytic theory (1920/1953), which portrayed children as "sexual beings" whose unconscious states figure importantly in individuals' development over the life span. The implications of Freud's theory for ECE were foregrounded by individuals like Frank (1938), Johnson (1928), and Mitchell (1934/1991)—the latter two at the Bureau of Educational Experiments (later the Bank Street College of Education) in the United States—and the McMillans (1919) and Isaacs (1932/1968) in England. These people's ideas influenced the development of the nursery school since the 1920s as a context where children's individual expression during play is both emphasized and valued. Thus, children in this scenario are "creative expressers."

Also psychoanalytic in orientation, Erikson (1950) depicted the life span as a series of conflicts that occur within societal contexts, not only within the sexual self. The ways that particular conflicts are resolved (e.g., between a sense of autonomy and a sense of shame in the first two years of life) have an impact on the entire course of individual development. Thus, the individual may be viewed as a "solver of conflict." Because of his focus on the relationship between the developing self and society, Erikson's psychodynamic theory has had clear implications for practice, and theorists such as Biber and Franklin (1962) who are interested in practice have grounded EC curriculum in Erikson's ideas.

The representation of children as "thinkers" was not foregrounded until the 1960s when Piagetian theory (Piaget & Inhelder, 1969) was incorporated into ECE (Almy, Chittenden, & Miller, 1966). According to this cognitive-developmental view, children are active thinkers and hypothesizers. Because of limitations that are inherent in the early phases of human development (grounded again in an evolutionary framework), children are incapable of mature ("formal") thinking until experiences with objects and people enable the development of adult-like cognitive structures. Although many have emphasized children's limitations within Piaget's stages of cognitive development, others have highlighted Piaget's focus on the distinctiveness, not the deficiency, of children's thinking.

Our view of contemporary ECE is that the representations of children and childhood just reviewed are still widely accepted (but see James & Prout, 1997; Jenks, 1982; and Richards, 1974 for sociological alternatives and critiques of this view). A tension between those who view children as "blank slates" and those who view them as "innocents" whose qualities unfold over time still exists, as does the social-reformist view of children as "victims." Less reductionist, theoretical portraits have been drawn by Jersild (1946), who elaborated a child development view of ECE using the assumption that curriculum should draw its authority from studies of children themselves. Decades later, Shapiro and Biber (1972) described a developmental-interactionist perspective that highlights the need for attention to cognition and emotion. Their views build on multiple theories of practice and development, including those referred to earlier of Dewey, Freud, Erikson, Piaget, Mitchell, and Johnson. Two primary educational goals for children are competence and autonomy. Teachers working toward those goals "should respond and relate to the children as individuals" (Shapiro & Biber, 1972, p. 69). This still-prevalent view of ECE that is focused on individuals and rooted in child development (Katz, 1996) has become a focus of controversy in the past decade and is challenged below in the section on "Critical Voices."

Locating Teaching: 20th Century Trends in ECE

Over time, representations of children and childhood have intersected with prevailing theories of development and beliefs about teaching young children. Not until the mid-20th century did the child as "thinker" become central. Thus, we should not be surprised that ECE has historically revolved around settings that enable children's development rather than the teaching of particular content. Even the highly specific activities for poor children that were designed by Montessori (1909/1964) in the early part of the century did not depend on explicit teaching. Indeed, the Froebelian kindergarten (nursery school with a child development focus) and the Montessori method represent children as learners who need explicit teaching less than they need teachers who observe carefully and provide multiple opportunities for children to experience the world. In short, prior

to the 1960s, the teacher as instructor was hard to locate in the literature of EC practice and research.

The 1960s, in contrast, highlighted some competing views of children. The most influential of these has been the representation of the young child as "responder" or "behaver" (Baer, Wolf, & Risley, 1968; Bereiter & Engelmann, 1966; Skinner, 1953). In this view, adults fashion education as a series of lessons with specified behavioral objectives (e.g., the learning of alphabet letter names, sound-symbol correspondences, or numbers). Some behaviorists reinforce children's learning with concrete objects or rewards ("tokens").

Since the 1960s, a number of program developers and researchers have constructed a representation of economically poor children not only as responders, but also as "disadvantaged" or "deficient learners" (Bereiter & Engelmann, 1966; Deutsch, 1967; Jensen, 1969). These representations have persisted despite changes in terminology. For example, in the 1980s and 1990s the "at risk" label has permeated the vocabulary of educational institutions, particularly those serving children traditionally disenfranchised by such factors as racism and inadequate school resources. The representation of children "at risk" appears in many cases to convey the same meanings as the terminology of "cultural deficit" of the 1960s (Fennimore, 2000). Children continue to be cast as "problems to be fixed" through participation in EC programs.

The professional literature, particularly of the NAEYC (e.g., Bredekamp & Copple, 1997) has traditionally rejected representations of children as responders or deficient learners and instead has supported child-centered and nonbehavioristic views of teaching, which stem largely from the historic dominance of developmental theories and of representations of the developing child. The fact that practitioner-oriented, professional journals for organizations, which consist largely of primary or elementary teachers, are called *The Arithmetic Teacher* (National Council of Teachers of Mathematics) or *The Reading Teacher* (International Reading Association), whereas the major journals for EC practitioners are called *Young Children* and *Childhood Education* reveals these different approaches. In the EC field, children and childhood are focal, not teachers or teaching.

Moreover, a look at earlier reviews of literature provides evidence for the distinctiveness of ECE. For example, of the 33 chapter titles in Spodek's *Handbook of Research on the Education of Young Children* (1993), only two contain the word *teacher* or *teaching*. In contrast, seven chapter titles contain the word *development* or *developmental,* reflecting a greater focus on those processes of human growth or change that we have traditionally thought of as relatively unaffected by direct teaching or instruction. In his chapter in Spodek's *Handbook,* Peters (1993), the only one to review recent research on teaching, reiterates and illustrates the point that the role of the teacher has not been featured in ECE research.

Reviews of research in earlier editions of the *Handbook of Research on Teaching* similarly demonstrate a dearth of research in ECE on teaching itself. In the first edition, Sears and Dowley (1963) cite mainly experimental studies of specific aspects of teaching in nursery school. Studies most closely related to teachers and teaching were correlational studies of personality variables and success as preschool teachers.

In the second edition of the *Handbook,* Beller (1973) reviews research on organized programs, whereas Gordon and Jester (1973) review observational methods for studying teaching in ECE. Both chapters contrast dramatically with Sears and Dowley's, primarily because of what Pines (1966) calls a "revolution in learning" or what EC educators might call a rediscovery of ECE, contemporaneous with U.S. President Lyndon Johnson's "war on poverty" and with the establishment of the Head Start program for economically disadvantaged 4-year-old preschoolers (Greenberg, 1990). The 1960s and 1970s were not only a period of social ferment in the United States but also one of optimism that earlier starts in school-like settings would improve children's educational achievement and reduce poverty and its long-term effects. In addition, research activity in ECE was at a high level and focused on programs for children from low-income families.

In the *Handbook's* third edition, Stallings and Stipek (1986) review a number of EC programs, originally Head Start or Follow Through models, exploring to what extent these compensatory programs have had long-term, positive effects. By describing the results of five long-term studies and three innovations of the 1970s—Mastery Learning, Cooperative Learning, and Madeline Hunter's Instructional Skills program—Stallings and Stipek conclude that the Head Start and Follow Through models were unable to sustain improved achievement on standardized measures. However, other indices of improved "life chances" were positive (e.g., graduates of some model programs were less often retained in a grade and less often placed in special education classes). Because the focus of the chapter is on programs, however, little is said about effects of teaching or teachers.

The same can be said for Karweit's review (1993) of effective preschool and kindergarten programs for children at risk. These programs include Head Start models, such as the Gray Early Learning Project and the Perry Preschool; specific curricular approaches; and kindergartens, both half-day and full-day. Karweit, whose review is based on only three studies, points out the lack of experimental studies that contrast EC programs providing combinations of educational and social services for young children and families. The author states that such comprehensive programs and studies that evaluate them are urgently needed.

Although growing numbers of children (more than half of all 4-year-olds) are enrolled in preschool, a large number remain unenrolled at a time when public school involvement in prekindergarten education is growing and when the significance of early education for later academic success is widely acknowledged. Thus, programs and the need for them retain primacy, and the impact of teachers and teaching remains embedded in "program effects." In our present chapter, then, we consider program effects in recent studies but with an eye toward identifying and discussing the influence of teaching in the complex arena of ECE. We delineate this task in the next section.

What Is Research on Teaching in ECE?

For most of this century, research concerning the learning and development of young children—not the practices of teachers—has been taken as the starting point for framing EC methods and programs. Therefore, to find that the body of work that has come to be known as research on teaching usually refers to the large and diverse group of inquiries that explore teaching in the elementary years and beyond is not surprising. While each of the *Handbooks of Research on Teaching* include at least one chapter on early education, teaching is usually defined as "an activity involving teachers and students working jointly" (Shulman, 1986, p. 7) in classrooms and formal school contexts. This definition does not span the diverse range of contexts suggested by the vignettes that opened our chapter. In many ways, research on teaching and research in ECE have existed as two parallel, seldom overlapping fields of inquiry. EC researcher Goffin (1989) is one of the few scholars who has begun to explore the intersections between these fields of research, arguing for a new research agenda that shifts its focus from a distinctive emphasis on program effects to the complexities of teaching and the importance of the role of the teacher. We attempt to take on Goffin's challenge in this fourth edition of the *Handbook.*

To achieve this aim, we draw on the research orientations outlined by Shulman (1986) in his introduction to the third edition of the *Handbook of Research on Teaching.* According to Shulman, four major programs or orientations for inquiry define the field of research on teaching: process-product research, mediating process research, classroom ecology, and teacher cognition and decision making. (We use the word orientation in place of program here because the word *program* is frequently used in ECE to refer to program models, as in various Head Start programs.) Reflecting the current trend toward teachers conducting their own research, we add a fifth orientation titled "teacher research." These five orientations guided our initial search of the EC literature. From the start, we were confronted by the ways in which research on teaching young children differs from its more mainstream counterparts as we found virtually no studies in which the research orientation could be considered as mediating process.

In this section, we explore research on teaching in ECE within the remaining four orientations, defining each of these approaches to inquiry. We also explore the research methods used and the kinds of research issues addressed. We recognize that any categorization of research is arbitrary, so we have considered the theoretical and methodological lenses used by the researchers to determine the orientation in which their research on teaching might best be located. In those cases where the authors address concerns that cut across several research orientations (what Shulman terms "hybrid studies"), we have used the major aims and purposes of the researcher to inform our sorting procedure. Our intent here is not to fit studies into a predetermined system of categorization but to illustrate the distinctiveness of studies of teaching when they are conducted in EC settings. We aim to both acknowledge the contributions of each research orientation and raise the possibility of reconceptualizing research within an ECE framework.

Process-Product Research

This orientation to research on teaching aims to "define the relationships between what teachers do in the classroom (the processes of teaching) and what happens to their students (the products of learning)" (Anderson, Evertson, & Brophy, 1979,

p. 193). Also referred to as teacher effectiveness studies, the aim of this research approach to the study of teaching is to identify generalizable teaching behaviors that result in improved student learning and achievement. To achieve this aim, most process-product researchers use correlational or experimental designs and a range of quantitative procedures to measure and determine the causality of different teaching behaviors on student learning. Teaching actions are presumed to occur under objective conditions (i.e., devoid of context) and are usually carefully defined and counted using some form of observational measure while teacher effects on student learning, particularly in the case of academic skills, are usually determined from standardized test scores.

In agreement with the authors of previous *Handbook* chapters on ECE, we have found that literature pertinent to teacher effects in ECE is still lacking. The work that has been done focuses primarily on the correlation between particular views of teaching that are embodied within program models and student achievement. This work has its roots in the evaluation studies of various curriculum models that have been funded and administered through projects Head Start and Follow-Through, which began in the 1960s and continue in some form today (Goffin, 1994). Drawing on different theories of learning and development, curriculum models hold ideal visions of children's learning that imply a particular role for the teacher. By comparing different models, such studies are in fact comparing different teacher effects by measuring students' academic achievement or other outcomes before and after they enter formal schooling.

A recent example of this kind of research is the High/Scope preschool curriculum comparison study conducted by Schweinhart and Weikart (1997). This longitudinal study has been examining the effects of three different curriculum models—High/Scope, direct instruction, and nursery school—on the development of 68 children, between the ages of 3 and 5 years, from poor backgrounds who were randomly assigned to one of these treatments almost 23 years ago. The study reported here compares the effects of each of these curriculum models on the social success of participants at age 23. Weikart and his colleagues hypothesized that those children who experienced the constructivist pedagogy of the High/Scope teachers or the child-centered approach of the nursery school teachers would be more socially competent and would demonstrate greater personal responsibility as adults than those who attended the direct instruction program. Significant differences were found among curriculum groups when 52 of the original participants were interviewed and their public documents (school, social service, police) were reviewed.

Compared to the direct instruction group, members of the High/Scope group were more likely to be married, vote in the Presidential election, or have done volunteer work. In contrast to the High/Scope and nursery school groups, adults who had experienced direct instruction in preschool were more likely to have been arrested for felonies or suspended from work, and a greater proportion of these individuals had experienced special education for emotional disturbance in their later school years. This longitudinal study, Schweinhart and Weikart argue, demonstrates the preventive value and positive long-term effects of child-centered early education programs. In their view, direct instruction is not in the best interests of children as it focuses on teaching academic skills rather than on educating children to be socially competent.

The Abecedarian Project (Campbell & Ramey, 1995) is another well-known, well-documented EC program whose effects have been studied longitudinally. Since its inception in 1972, the program provided preschool intervention services to 111 children, from infancy through age 5, and their families. Families were at "high risk" due to a combination of factors, such as low income, absence of fathers from the home, lack of social support for the mother, and so on. Children were randomly assigned to four treatment conditions: (1) preschool intervention plus school-age intervention, (2) preschool intervention but no school-age intervention, (3) school-age intervention but no preschool intervention, and (4) neither preschool nor school-age intervention. In contrast to the High/Scope study (Schweinhart & Weikart, 1997), which did not show significant cognitive benefits, an evaluation of educational effects of the Abecedarian Project on participants through age 15 showed positive effects. These effects were measured by such cognitive and academic achievement measures as the Stanford-Binet IQ and California Achievement Tests (Campbell & Ramey, 1995). The researchers attributed the effects primarily to the 5-year preschool intervention. Also in contrast to High/Scope, the Abecedarian Project (compared with five other programs) did not appear to prevent participants from engaging in delinquent or criminal behaviors (Clarke & Campbell, 1998). Because the Abecedarian Project had no provision for staff to make home visits during the preschool years, Clarke and Campbell speculated that the lack of a home-visit component, which is a feature of High/Scope, may account for the contrast in findings. Although the researchers' speculation may be correct, many explanations could be formulated to account for differences between programs as comprehensive as these two.

In recent years, process-product studies that examine the multiple and complex effects of programs like High/Scope or the Abecedarian Project have been supplemented by investigations that focus more exclusively on specific teaching behaviors and student outcomes. These student outcomes are defined differentially for students in the elementary school (K–3) and in preschool settings. Studies of teaching in the elementary grades, for the most part, reflect the process-product tradition by focusing on how specific teaching behaviors affect student achievement as measured by standardized test scores. In contrast, studies of child-care or prekindergarten settings are often based on the assumption that young children's social competence and emotional well-being are central to their later success in formal schooling. Because these developmental outcomes cannot be measured by standardized tests, researchers in ECE have created their own observational methods that are based on such tools as Likert scales to measure, for example, attachment behavior or children's reactions to emotions. The process-product studies we reviewed in ECE focus on a range of teaching strategies that we have grouped under the headings of staff development programs, the teaching of subject matter, and teaching for social competence.

STAFF DEVELOPMENT PROGRAMS

Staff development programs that aim to train teachers in specific strategies make up one group of studies that examine the effects of teaching strategies on student achievement. In these studies, both the effects of the staff development program and the teachers' instructional strategies are evaluated in terms of student performance. For example, Mandeville (1992) compared the basic skills achievement of second- and third-grade students after their teachers (n = 48) had participated in the Program for Effective Teaching (PET), which was based on Madeline Hunter's Instructional Skills program, with a control group of students whose teachers (n = 34) had not participated in the staff development program (NOPET). To test the hypothesis that 2 years of practice using PET had a positive correlation with student achievement, Mandeville followed students' test scores over a period of 4 years. He found no evidence to suggest that teachers who practiced these teaching strategies were more effective in improving student test scores than those teachers who had not received the training.

Kohler, McCullough, and Buchan (1995) examined how four preschool teachers, working within integrated settings, improved their practice through peer coaching by correlating the effects of this staff development with measures of children's participation in specific activities. Asking each of the teachers to select an activity (storytelling, board games) as a focus for improving their practice, the investigators observed these teachers in three different conditions: first, as they independently taught the activity; second, as these teaching tasks were implemented during a coaching phase; and third, during a maintenance period of individual enactment of these same activities. Children's participation was measured according to the kind of instructional strategies and activity each individual classroom teacher was attempting to refine. For example, one teacher, Angie, focused on board games, so the number of social interactions between children were coded as they participated in board games. A consistent and positive relationship was found between teachers' changes in practices and student behaviors.

TEACHING OF SUBJECT MATTER

Another group of studies investigates effective teaching strategies that improve student achievement in academic subjects. Most of this research is concerned with effective literacy instruction with low-achieving students. Duffy (1993), for example, explored the use of authentic literacy tasks to teach low achievers problem-solving strategies. Duffy conducted bimonthly observations of four teachers (two second-grade teachers and two third-grade teachers) as they taught reading to their low reading groups over a school year. Following each lesson, he interviewed randomly selected students about the strategies they had learned, when they would use these strategies, and why. Comparing measures of teachers' instructional actions (lesson transcripts) with measures of students' understandings (interview transcripts), Duffy found that in the early part of the school year, most students could not identify the strategies they had been taught. While each of the students progressed over the year, they did not express an increased understanding of strategy use. Duffy concludes that this result reflects teachers' assumptions that strategy instruction for low achievers should follow a skills-based model.

Morris, Blanton, Blanton, Nowacek, and Perney (1995) tested low-achieving third-grade spellers. After identifying 48 low-achieving spellers in seven third-grade classrooms, two

groups were formed. Half of the low-achieving third graders were taught from a second-grade spelling book, while the other group was taught from a third-grade spelling book. Those students who were taught from the second grade spelling book scored higher than the group being taught from a third-grade spelling book. This finding supports the use of materials and methods that are at the instructional level of the student.

At a time when the debate over the most effective method for teaching reading in the early primary grades is heated, Au (1998) reviews recent research related to literacy teaching, much of it supporting constructivist approaches to the teaching of reading to children of diverse backgrounds (in the case of Au's studies, these children are of Hawaiian background). For her, constructivist approaches incorporate student ownership of the literacy-learning process, comprehension, writing process, and language conventions. Phonics instruction (typically the explicit teaching of sound-to-symbol correspondences) is incorporated into these broader aspects of becoming literate. Of special interest in this article is the author's emphasis on the politics of reading instruction and her insistence that researchers inform policymakers of sound research findings with clear instructional implications. (For further discussion of controversies related to instruction and policymaking, see Allington & Woodside-Jiron, 1999, and McGill-Franzen, 1993.)

Two process-product studies are concerned with the teaching of mathematics to young children. Kohler, Ezell, Hoel, and Strain (1994) conducted a study of the effects of two kinds of math instruction on one teacher's behavior and on a group of low-achieving first graders' acquisition of math knowledge. Using an experimental reversal design to compare (a) teacher-directed math activities with a second condition of (b) teacher-directed activities supplemented by peer practice, the authors observed teacher instruction and student response during math lessons and tested before and after each math lesson. Teaching behavior, student response, and student achievement varied according to instructional conditions. Thus, in the teacher-led math lessons, the teacher spent most of her time standing in front of the class, providing some form of instruction with her attention usually directed to students who responded to her questions. Consequently, the five low-achieving students showed little academic response (i.e., writing, reading, etc.) to these lessons but showed a high proportion of task management behavior (attending, raising hand, etc.).

In contrast, during peer-practice activities, the teacher was more engaged with students, circulating around the room, monitoring and interacting with students as necessary to facilitate their understanding of math. In peer practice sessions, the five low achievers were observed to increase their active responses to the task of learning mathematics. These students were found to complete their tasks with higher accuracy and greater independence. Coinciding with this finding, the researchers also found that the five low achievers demonstrated superior gains in their math knowledge during peer practice.

In a two-part, quasi-experimental study, Billington (1994) investigated test-taking strategies and student retention in four third-grade mathematics classes in one school. For a period of 2 years, Billington had students in two classes take tests individually, while students in the other two classes were allowed to work together to complete the test. Students were retested 1 week after the initial test to determine what knowledge from the lesson they had retained. This procedure was followed in both years, although the lessons on which the tests were based differed according to the curriculum. In the 1st year of the study, Billington found that students who completed the test in collaborative groups retained more knowledge than their peers who completed the test individually. While the results of the 2nd year were not as clear, Billington concludes that differences in teachers' mode of instruction produced variable results in students' retention in both treatment conditions.

TEACHING FOR SOCIAL COMPETENCE

A number of process-product studies turn their attention to specific interactional styles of teachers and to the subsequent effects these styles have on children's social competence. Several of these studies are concerned with teachers' sensitivity and attachment to young children in the years before formal schooling. EC educators and researchers assume that healthy development in young children requires that they develop a strong affectional tie or attachment to special people in their lives, such as caregivers or teachers (Berk, 1991). Without such an attachment, the presumption is that children will be less likely to interact appropriately in their social worlds.

Because children are spending more time in out-of-home settings, EC researchers have become concerned as to whether children develop healthy attachment relationships with caregivers and, by implication, whether caregiver interactions promote optimal development. Howes and Hamilton (1993) examined the effects of teacher turnover and the consequent changes on children's abilities to interact with their peers. Following children through several years of child care, they found that those children who experienced teacher changes during their toddler years (between 18 and 24 months) were more aggressive as 4-year-olds, whereas older children (average ages 30, 36, and 42 months) who experienced such changes were influenced by their relationship with the new teacher. If a staffing change resulted in older children experiencing a less positive teacher-child relationship, those children tended to be more aggressive with their peers. The researchers conclude that children do depend on their teachers for emotional support and that such relationships are not easily interchangeable.

Building on this study, Howes (1997) explored the sensitivity of caregivers working in licensed family day care (FDC) and child care and what influence caregivers had on children's attachment and play with peers. Conducting a longitudinal study, Howes observed children's development before they entered FDC and then followed their development as they attended FDC over a number of years. After measuring the social behavior of individual children, the researcher rated both caregiver sensitivity and each child's interactions with the caregiver. Howes concludes that caregiving behaviors have an indirect influence on the complexity of observed children's play but a direct relation with children's attachment security.

In another study that examines the relationship between the quality of children's attachments and their social competence, Mitchell-Copeland, Denham, and DeMulder (1997) measured 62 children's attachment relationships in preschools and day care centers. Social competence was measured by observing focal children's reactions to peers and to emotions, in conjunction with teacher ratings of children's social competence. Attachment behavior was determined by observing mother-child and teacher-child interactions. Children who were observed to be insecurely attached to their mothers but securely attached to their teacher were found to be more prosocial and emotionally positive than children who were insecurely attached to mother and teacher.

The effects of FDC provider interactions on children's free play is examined by Hogan, Ispa, and Thornburg (1991) through the lens of parent-caregiver relations. Using questionnaires to supplement observations of caregiver-child interactions, individual children's behavior during free play, and the interactions between the mothers of these children and their caregiver during afternoon departures, the authors found differences in caregiver interaction styles with parents and children. Those children whose mothers had more interaction with the caregiver demonstrated more positive affect when interacting with their peers than children whose mothers had less interaction with their caregivers. Overall, however, few differences were found in children's social behavior and in the amount of mother-provider interaction.

Departing markedly from this focus on teachers, children, and children's social competence is a study of the influence that preschool teachers' participation in activities and program structure has on the play preferences of preschoolers. In this study, Swiecicka and Russell (1991) combined ecological factors (high-structured or teacher-directed versus low-structured or child-centered preschools) with teacher processes (participation) and student outcomes (play preferences). Testing the hypothesis that girls would prefer activities in which teachers participated and that the differences between girls and boys would be greater in low-structured preschools, the researchers observed in 26 preschools (13 high-structured, 13 low-structured) during activity or choice time. Swiecicka and Russell found that while gender differences occurred in the play preferences of boys and girls (e.g., boys chose blocks; girls were more likely to choose teacher-organized art), these preferences were not strongly correlated with the level of teacher participation or the structure of the preschool.

In summary, these ECE studies build upon previous process-product research in several key ways. First, rather than concentrate solely on the context of traditional classrooms (e.g., Stallings & Stipek, 1986), these researchers explore the range of programs encompassed in ECE. In addition to the kindergarten classroom, studies are situated within the homes of FDC providers, among the wide range of child-care programs available, and within the early elementary grades.

Second, perhaps because of the broad scope of the field known as ECE, the focus of some of these studies is not exclusively on the relationships between teacher and student but is also on relations with parents and the community and how these relations also influence student learning. The teacher in these cases is a liaison or mediator.

Third, and finally, in exploring the effects of teacher practices, these studies highlight the field's particular concerns with child development rather than student achievement. Thus, researchers have found that teachers in these studies are more concerned with affective than cognitive aspects of the teaching-learning relationship. The teacher is often represented as facilitator of development or nurturer rather than as instructor. Moreover, because process-oriented constructs like attachment are sometimes identified as outcomes, some EC studies are more accurately termed "process-process," rather than "process-product".

Despite these differences, a common theme in this section has been that of teaching as a set of observable behaviors that are consistent across contexts and specified groups of teachers. Teaching has been portrayed as a technical and value-free set of actions with little consideration given to the knowledge and understandings that teachers bring to their work. In fact, the teacher as a thinking individual with a biography, including characteristics of race, class, and gender, is not visible. The next orientation toward research on teaching begins to cast light on teachers' knowledge and thinking.

Teacher Cognition

Teacher cognition research is concerned with what teachers think, know, and believe about their teaching and why teachers behave as they do. Rather than view teachers as technicians and document what they do, researchers within this orientation assume that teachers are purposeful, reflective thinkers and actors who work in a complex environment. By studying the psychological context of teaching, researchers seek to gain insight into how teacher planning, thinking, and decision making influence the actions that teachers take in the classroom (Clark & Peterson, 1986).

In the third *Handbook of Research on Teaching,* Clark and Peterson (1986) outline a model for conceptualizing teacher cognition research. In this model, the thought processes of teachers are categorized as teacher planning or preactive decision making before entering the classroom; interactive thoughts or teacher decision making during classroom instruction; teacher beliefs; and teacher theories. Because we have found few studies that foreground the interactive decision making of teachers, we have organized our review of EC teacher cognition research by using Clark and Peterson's categories of teacher planning, teacher beliefs, and teacher theories.

TEACHER PLANNING

Teacher planning has been studied both as a psychological construct in which teachers visualize particular goals and develop frameworks for their implementation and as what teachers do when they say they are planning (Clark & Peterson, 1986). In the first instance, the emphasis is on planning as a cognitive skill, whereas in the second, planning is treated more descriptively. In both cases, researchers usually use think-aloud methods and ask teachers to talk out loud as they plan so they can record and later transcribe the content and function of teachers' preactive decision making (Clark & Peterson, 1986). In some studies, think-aloud techniques are used in conjunction with classroom observations to explore the links between teacher planning and action. While a number of studies of teacher planning in the elementary and secondary school years already exist (e.g., Clark and Peterson cite 22 studies), we have found only one recent study that looks at planning in an EC classroom.

In this study, Roskos and Neuman (1993) used a descrip-

tive approach to study teacher planning both as a preactive and interactive cognitive process. Using ethnographic techniques, they describe how two beginning kindergarten teachers planned and enacted integrated literacy instruction over the course of a school year. Each teacher was asked to plan out loud in the presence of the researchers. Teacher instruction was also videotaped and later shown to stimulate each teacher's recollection of the instructional scene to help them with future planning. The teachers were found to engage in six kinds of planning activities (metaplanning; planning by topic, content, activity, and environment; and planning for revision) and four strategies or problem-solving processes (considering the whole situation and outlining actions, searching for and selecting procedures, making and checking predictions, and defining and organizing the problem) when making their integrated literacy instructional plans. Reflecting on the multiple and complex cognitive demands that were required by these novice teachers in order for them to plan and implement integrated curriculum and instruction, Roskos and Neuman argue that teachers who are new to this integrated form of instruction will need professional development opportunities to develop these planning skills.

The dearth of research that examines the planning of EC teachers raises concern because of the folk belief that EC teachers do not engage in the professional work of teaching but are simply babysitters. Without a research base that demonstrates the range and complexity of EC teachers' thoughts and actions, demonstrating the challenges of teaching young children to professionals working with older learners and to the public is difficult. According to the research that has been done to date, EC researchers have been more interested in teachers' beliefs and theories than in their planning.

TEACHER BELIEFS

A large proportion of teacher cognition research in ECE is concerned with teachers' beliefs, perceptions, attributions, and attitudes about various aspects of their work. Teacher cognition researchers assume that beliefs are powerful cognitive constructs through which teachers filter meanings about teaching and learning and because of which teachers take certain actions in the classroom (K. E. Smith, 1997). These beliefs are usually gathered through surveys, interviews, or both. Often these methods are structured around a series of hypothetical incidents that stimulate teachers to express their perceptions of the issue under study. For example, Snider and Fu (1990) assessed teachers' knowledge of DAP by using 12 audiotaped vignettes representing a variety of teacher-preschool child interactions. Then 73 child-care workers responded by rating each of the vignettes as either developmentally appropriate or inappropriate.

While such methods permit large numbers of teachers to be sampled, they provide only a general sense of the beliefs held by teachers on particular issues. Therefore, some teacher cognition researchers have supplemented survey and interview methods with video and audiotaped observations of teachers at work in their own classrooms to gain deeper insight into how particular beliefs that are held by teachers influence their practices. For example Neale, Smith, and Johnson (1990) looked at how 10 teachers from kindergarten through third grade classes changed their pedagogical and conceptual knowledge of teaching science after participating in a staff development program. Using videotapes of lessons taught by the teachers before and after the program, interviews, and written self-evaluations that were produced by the participating teachers, the researchers documented how teachers' knowledge and practices changed over the school year.

As teaching is usually partnered with learning, not surprisingly, the majority of teacher belief studies are concerned with student learning and development. For example, Hyson and Lee (1996) used a Likert scale to sample 175 Korean and 279 American EC teachers across 10 domains of beliefs about children's emotional development. The majority of American EC teachers believed that children need warm, physically affectionate bonds with their adult caregivers and that teachers have a responsibility to scaffold children's emotional expression. In contrast, Korean teachers were more likely to believe that teachers should avoid endorsing children's emotional self-expression, developing emotional closeness with children, and demonstrating emotional displays of affection to children. However, both American and Korean EC educators believed in the importance of encouraging affectionate emotional bonds, talking about feelings with children, helping children to display and control emotions, and providing instruction and modeling of emotional expression and control.

Expression and control of emotions are foregrounded in a number of teacher belief studies that explore expectations and attributions about problem behavior exhibited by students. Teacher cognition researchers assume that these attributions influence the ways in which teachers interact with their students and, therefore, have a direct impact on students' social and academic success. Scott-Little and Holloway (1992) carried out one such study by exploring the relationship between caregivers' attributions to children's misbehavior and their classroom control strategies. They observed 40 teachers working in metropolitan child-care centers and recorded two incidents in which each teacher responded either to aggressive behavior or to a child's failure to comply with teacher directions. These recorded observations were then used to stimulate participating teachers' recollections of the incidents so researchers could elicit their reasoning as to why they thought the child in question misbehaved and teachers could provide some explanation of the actions they took in response to this misbehavior. The researchers found that caregiver attributions explained the amount of power or authority caregivers used to respond to children. Caregivers who attributed children's misbehavior to the individual child were more likely to respond to misbehavior in punitive ways.

In a similar study Kuhns, Holloway, and Scott-Little (1992) used a questionnaire with a series of hypothetical incidents pertaining to students' misbehavior in which they elicited responses from both mothers and caregivers. Mothers tended to believe that children could control their misbehavior, whereas caregivers assumed that children's individual personality traits interplayed with their behavior. Because of these differences in beliefs about children's behavior, mothers indicated that they tended to become more angry and assertive in response to children's misbehavior than did the caregivers.

In an in-depth study the concerns teachers had about teaching problem students, Brophy and McCaslin (1992) interviewed 98 experienced elementary school teachers using hypothetical vignettes of student "problem" behavior. General responses to these vignettes were supplemented by observations and a second round of interviews. All teachers reported that they believed they could effectively help students with problem behaviors. Strategies that were most frequently emphasized by teachers differed according to the kind of student within the vignette. For example, in response to shy and low-achieving students, teachers emphasized help-oriented strategies, whereas punitive responses were the most frequently identified strategies for disruptive and defiant students. Most of the teachers attributed problem behavior to the students rather than hold themselves responsible. Responses of primary grade teachers (K–3) were compared to the beliefs of teachers in the upper grades (4–6). Upper-grade teachers were found to be more verbal, demanding, and threatening, whereas EC teachers were more sympathetic and supportive of problem students. Despite this variability, Brophy and McCaslin conclude that elementary school teachers work from generally similar ideas about chronic behavior problems and effective strategies for dealing with them.

Labeling children as problematic has led some researchers to consider how various social factors (ability, ethnicity, culture, gender, etc.) interact with the attributions and beliefs about student behavior that are held by teachers. Conway (1989) addresses this issue by examining six teachers' attributions about children with special needs. Rather than survey these primary (early elementary) teachers, Conway conducted a content analysis of the written evaluations they had completed on their students with learning difficulties. To corroborate her analysis of the teachers' evaluations of their students, the researcher also interviewed teachers about their reports and the child in each report. The teachers attributed students' poor academic progress to characteristics within the child, specifically problems with motivation, intellectual ability, persistence, and self-control. In some cases, teachers also attributed children's problems in school to issues within their family and home life, although home background was cited far less often than children's inherent characteristics. What is of concern to Conway is that none of these teachers identified their pedagogy, curriculum, or other school context factors as instrumental in facilitating student success or failure in school.

Interested in the education of young children with disabilities, File (1994) explored how 36 teachers' beliefs about children's social development played out in their interactions with students in integrated EC classrooms. To tap teachers' beliefs about social development, each teacher was asked to complete a peer relations scale in which they had to rate the social skills of particular children in their care. Teachers' beliefs about their roles as mediators of children's peer interactions were elicited through their interview responses to six hypothetical vignettes that depicted different social interactions between children (e.g., conflicts, play initiation). In addition, researchers observed the teachers as they interacted with students with and without disabilities. In their ratings of children's social skills, most of the teachers reported that they believed children with disabilities needed more social support and that teachers had a role in influencing the development of this support. However, in practice, File found that these teachers were more directive in facilitating the cognitive play of all children and were less likely to support children's social skills.

Dare (1992) was interested in how the physical appearance of students influences teachers' expectations of their school behavior when the effects of appearance are mediated by school uniforms. Working with 16 first-grade teachers in Nigeria, Dare (1992) selected 10 children in each classroom, using their names in questionnaire statements to elicit the teachers' responses to statements pertaining to student behavior and physical appearance. A correlation was found between teachers' expectations of particular children and their perceptions of children's appearance. The teachers expected attractive children to be more intelligent, more well behaved, more interested in school, and more popular. Although teachers had known their students for at least 3 months, enough time to make realistic assessments of their academic, personality, and social attributes, most of these teachers continued to use appearance as an indicator of student ability and success.

Focusing on expectations that teachers hold about ethnic minority students when they are working in multicultural nursery schools, Ogilvy, Boath, Cheyne, Jahoda, and Schaffer (1990) interviewed and observed 26 teachers in eight nursery schools in Scotland. Teachers were asked about their views of multicultural education and their perceptions of two focal children of different ethnicities (one Scottish, one Asian). These focal children were also assessed individually on several British ability scales (e.g., visual recognition and early numbers) for the purposes of comparison with teacher judgments of their ability. The majority of teachers reported experiencing some difficulties with ethnic minority children, attributing some discipline issues to problems in communicating with children for whom English was not a first language. All of the teachers except for one compared ethnic minority children unfavorably with Scottish children. Asian children were perceived as having more behavior, motivation, and social problems in the classroom. As there was little evidence to support these views, the authors conclude that the teachers held superficial perceptions of ethnic minority children in their care and that few of these teachers showed insight into the learning and developmental needs of these children.

Also interested in how social factors interact with teachers' expectations of pupils who are perceived as different, Brucker and Hall (1991) explored the issue of AIDS in the classroom. Replicating an earlier survey on teacher attitudes toward AIDS (Brucker, Martin, & Shreeve, 1989), Brucker and Hall surveyed 400 educators (K–12). Teacher attitudes toward working with students or colleagues with AIDS were found to be more positive than they were 3 years earlier. Teachers in the K–7 grades were more open to allowing children with AIDS to participate in school activities and expressed beliefs that teachers should be required to teach students with AIDS. They were also more positive about colleagues with AIDS—expressing beliefs that certification should be open to colleagues testing positive for the AIDS virus—than their counterparts in the higher grades.

Another group of studies sample teacher beliefs and perceptions in relation to a wide array of curriculum issues. With the field's endorsement of DAP (Bredekamp & Copple, 1997) as its consensus definition of child-centered education, a number

of studies examine teachers' knowledge of what it means to be developmentally appropriate and how such beliefs interplay with the aims and methods that teachers enact in practice (e.g., see Charlesworth et al., 1993; Haupt, Larsen, Robinson, & Hart, 1995).

In a study by Oakes and Caruso (1990), the focus is on teacher attitudes about authority and their relationship to the use of DAP. The researchers observed and rated the practices of 25 kindergarten teachers as either developmentally appropriate or inappropriate. These observations were supplemented with questionnaire data in which teachers responded to eight vignettes of problem situations in the classroom, rating their attitudes to these vignettes along a continuum from "highly controlling" to "highly sharing" of authority. They found that kindergarten teachers who rated themselves as more likely to share authority with students were also more likely to use developmentally appropriate teaching strategies.

The DAP document (Bredekamp & Copple, 1997) recommends that EC teachers combine professional knowledge about children's learning and development with their understanding of individual children and the social and cultural contexts in which those children live and learn. Consequently, many EC teacher education programs offer a range of courses in child development and in developmentally appropriate methods and practices. However, the beliefs that students take from their teacher education programs are often subject to change when students work with cooperating teachers who may hold alternative beliefs about ECE. K. E. Smith (1997) was interested in the stability of beliefs about DAP that were held by two different cohorts of student teachers, one majoring in ECE, the other in elementary education, as they participated in their culminating practicum experiences. Relying on pre- and post-self-report measures in which the 60 students completed a scale measuring locus of control and questionnaires about their own and their cooperating teachers' beliefs about DAP, K. E. Smith found that the EC student teachers showed a higher level of endorsement of DAP than their counterparts with elementary preparation only. These patterns of beliefs remained stable throughout the practicum experience, even where the cooperating teachers were perceived to hold a different belief system. In other words, the influence of the cooperating teacher was found to be less than that of the students' teacher education program.

Stipek and Byler (1997) also compared the beliefs of different groups of EC teachers (60 preschool, kindergarten, and first grade teachers), regarding their orientations toward DAP. The researchers explored the relationships between child-centered or skills-based orientations to ECE, teachers' views of policies related to school entry, testing, and retention, and how all these beliefs operated in the teachers' practices. The teachers were observed in their classrooms on one occasion, and their practices were rated according to different aspects of practice (e.g., work and play, teacher acceptance).

Teacher beliefs were assessed through a questionnaire that examined their beliefs about appropriate education for young children. Preschool and kindergarten teachers tended to have strong associations among their beliefs, goals, practices, and the positions they took on policy issues, identifying themselves as either child centered or skills based. First-grade teachers, in contrast, were more ambivalent and less inclined to commit to one particular orientation. In general, teachers who identified themselves as skills based were more likely to delay entry to school for academic reasons and believed that standardized tests had some value. Teachers' beliefs and practices were found to be correlated neither with teachers' ethnicity nor with the socioeconomic status of the families they served. However, many of the teachers were not satisfied with the program they implemented, citing parental pressure to be more structured, particularly from families of children from low socioeconomic backgrounds.

Different philosophies about children's learning and development that underpin teachers' beliefs about DAP have also been found to influence teachers' practices (Hatch & Freeman, 1988; Pound, 1989; Wing, 1989), particularly their positions on readiness and retention (Smith & Shepard, 1988). Tomchin and Impara (1992), for example, examined teachers' beliefs about the practice of retaining students from kindergarten through Grade 7 through the use of a retention questionnaire, simulation exercise, and teacher interviews. All of the teachers agreed that retention was a valid and nonharmful strategy for students in the early elementary grades who were showing signs of being at risk academically and socially.

Less agreement existed about retaining children in the upper grades. Most of the upper grade teachers (Grades 4 through 7) identified themselves as remediationists, believing that retention should be avoided unless the teacher knew the child would not succeed in the next grade, and unless the teacher felt that he or she could help that child mature and develop. Interview data from the EC teachers indicated that they assumed that retention helps children to develop the basic skills required for later school success and that their decisions were influenced not only by their knowledge of individual children but also by the school context. Teachers reported that they were often judged by the kinds of students they sent on to the next grade; therefore, they were more likely to retain those students who needed the extra time to develop skills.

Many of the nonpromoted students who were interviewed by Byrnes (1989) in her study of retention would agree with the upper-grade teachers who were interviewed by Tomchin and Impara (1992). Byrnes surveyed principals, teachers, and parents on their beliefs about retention and then interviewed both students who had been retained and their teachers. Although retention has not been found to be an effective strategy for improving student achievement, the majority of parents, teachers, and principals supported retention for children who did not meet the requirements of the grade. In contrast, most of the students who were interviewed (Grades 1 through 6) reported that they felt punished and were anxious about the reactions of peers and family to their inability to succeed at school.

Transition classes or extra-year programs are one form of retention in which children who are believed to be unready for the next grade are grouped for developmentally appropriate instruction. Horm-Wingerd, Carella, and Warford (1993) surveyed 78 first-grade teachers about their experiences with and perceptions of children who had participated in transition classes. As in the survey responses that were collected by Byrnes (1989) and Tomchin and Impara (1992) and despite the lack of documented evidence to support retention strategies, the teachers in this study responded overwhelmingly in support of transition classes. Explanations given for this support included the perception that transition classes enhanced students' social, emotional, and cognitive development, and helped them cultivate a positive attitude toward school.

This ongoing concern with young children's readiness to succeed socially and academically in school has led some researchers to examine teachers' and parents' expectations at different levels of the EC system. Underpinning these inquiries is the question of whether differential expectations might contribute to some children's difficulties when they move from one EC program like preschool or child care to the more formal setting of schools. By making the expectations of different teachers and parents explicit, researchers assume that the differences and similarities that are revealed might contribute to changes in teachers' practices and might make transitions easier for children.

For example, in a study by Hains, Fowler, Schwartz, Kottwitz, and Rosenkoetter (1989), 21 preschool teachers and 28 kindergarten teachers' expectations about young children's readiness for school were compared. In a skill-expectation survey, teachers were asked to rate the importance of students' abilities to accomplish skills in nine categories (from academics to self-care). In general, both kindergarten and preschool teachers rated the same five categories as important for kindergarten readiness: conduct, instruction following, self-care, social interaction, and communication. However, preschool teachers tended to list more skill categories as important for entry than did kindergarten teachers.

Hadley, Wilcox, and Rice (1994) also compared kindergarten and preschool teacher expectations, although their emphasis was on children's verbal interaction. Researchers surveyed 140 teachers to investigate the occurrence of classroom talk during certain activities and teachers' responses to student behavior. Teachers were most likely to encourage talk during arrival, center times, and during those activities that were not teacher directed. However, preschool teachers encouraged more talk during teacher-directed activities than kindergarten teachers who exercised more control over the amount of talk. Not surprisingly, teachers who encouraged more talking were more tolerant of student misbehavior. Because of these differences, Hadley et al. (1994) call for preschool and kindergarten teachers to facilitate children's awareness of teacher expectations in order to make their transition between preschool and the primary grades smoother.

Knudsen-Lindauer and Harris (1989) were interested in examining both teachers' and parents' beliefs about what needed to be the priorities of kindergarten curricula. They surveyed both kindergarten teachers and parents about the skills and developmental areas that should constitute the curriculum of kindergarten. Mothers and fathers emphasized the importance of academic skills while teachers were more concerned about children being curious and independent. At the same time, parents and teachers believed that learning to listen and developing self-confidence were two of the most important achievements in the children's 1st year of formal schooling.

With increasing numbers of single-parent families and immigrant families and with the need for most parents to work, EC educators are being urged to expand the services and programs they offer to provide more family support. Burton (1992) combines a teacher-belief study with consideration of different EC contexts to investigate and compare the beliefs held by teachers about family-centered education. Surveying 280 EC educators (78 child-care, 48 Head Start, and 154 prekindergarten and kindergarten teachers), Burton found a variation in responses that depended on the program the teachers were working in. Public school teachers reported less-positive beliefs about both parents' child-rearing abilities and their own competence in relating to families than the other teachers. Yet, both public school and child-care teachers were less supportive of services to families than Head Start teachers. Burton hypothesizes that Head Start and child-care teachers may be more open to family-centered education because they already work in settings where opportunities for communication with parents are provided. The professional contexts in which teachers work need to be considered when examining why teachers think and act in particular ways, particularly if reform is being attempted.

Teacher cognition researchers are also interested in teachers' perceptions about different aspects of their work, such as family communication and job satisfaction, and about what teachers believe is important in the provision of high quality care for young children. Atkinson (1991), for instance, interviewed 48 family day care providers as to why they thought families chose their service, how well they thought their services met parental and children's needs, and what their curriculum goals were. Individualized and personal care offered to a small group of children was cited by all the providers as a key reason why parents chose their services. Most of these teachers thought they provided a high level of care and described their roles as those of child-care professionals. The most important curriculum goals were providing physical care for children, stimulating children's curiosity by providing a variety of experiences, and enhancing their social development.

Building on the work that examines ecological factors in the workplace that contribute to teacher turnover in child care, Kaiser, Rogers, and Kasper (1993) surveyed 235 teachers to collect their perceptions of well-being when working in various child-care-activities. For the purposes of the study, *well-being* was defined along two scales, one of happiness and the other of relaxation, with high ratings on both scales indicating a high level of well-being. Teachers were asked to outline their education and years of experience and to rate their feelings of happiness and relaxation according to 10 different child-care activities (e.g., toileting, indoor activity). Teachers with different amounts of child-care experience perceived their well-being differently when performing certain child-care tasks. Teachers with more than 6 years of experience were more relaxed and enjoyed group, indoor, outdoor, and lunch activities the most. They felt comfortable about managing children's behavior. The least experienced caregivers reported the most enjoyment when nurturing children and working with parents and staff members. These teachers experienced less enjoyment when engaged in routine activities like naptime and toileting. The authors conclude that by identifying these differences in well-being, more responsive training programs for child-care teachers can be developed.

In summary, these teacher belief studies incorporate significant topics such as student behavior, teacher authority, DAP, retention, continuity between programs, and quality of care in addition to a wide range of methods from large-scale surveys to in-depth interviews. Together, these studies provide important insights about the beliefs that teachers hold about diverse aspects of their work. Across a range of settings—child care, family day care, preschool, kindergarten, and elementary school—these complex beliefs are often mediated by years of work experience and the particular educational contexts in which teachers work. Interestingly, some of these studies highlight the incongruity between what teachers believe and what research has demonstrated. For example, research about readiness and retention has clearly illustrated that retention does not have a positive impact on students who are not achieving; yet in all of the studies reviewed, the majority of EC teachers believe retention is a useful and appropriate strategy. Similarly, while a growing body of research looks at the way in which knowledge is socially constructed and varies across context and culture, most teachers do not seem to believe that problems in student behavior are mediated by the curriculum, the school context, or their own behavior.

However, we should note that many of these studies look at teacher thinking out of context. Often conclusions are drawn from what teachers say about hypothetical scenarios rather than about their beliefs about teaching and learning in their own settings. To be sure, several researchers do observe teachers and interview or survey them, but for the most part, such observations are limited. Thus, even when the practices of teachers are observed in relation to their beliefs, getting a sense of the ways teachers develop, maintain, and alter their beliefs, why they hold such beliefs, and how these beliefs interplay with their interactions with young children and their families is difficult. To gain more in-depth understandings of the complexity of teacher thought, a growing number of researchers have begun to look at the theories teachers hold about their work.

TEACHER THEORIES

In many cases, the beliefs held by teachers are not independent cognitive constructs about teaching and learning, but their beliefs form an implicit system or theory of practice that shapes the way they go about their work. Implicit theories are "coherent sets of beliefs, [principles, and values] held by individuals which are theory-like because they have core ideas which resist disproof and peripheral ideas which modify readily in the face of evidence or experience" (Seifert, 1991, p. 3). These theories are tacit forms of knowledge that are embedded in the experiences of teachers and of others, which guide teachers' decision making and actions.

Research on implicit theories held by teachers attempts to move beyond documenting what teachers believe to making "explicit and visible the frames of reference teachers use to perceive and process information" (Clark & Peterson, 1986, p. 287). Because the emphasis is on assisting teachers to articulate and explain their deeply held assumptions, values, and beliefs about teaching and learning, many of these studies are descriptive, following small numbers of teachers over a period of time. The predominant research methods are clinical interviews, stimulated recall, participant observation, repertory grid techniques, and, in a few cases, in-depth observation.

Spodek (1987) conducted one of the earliest studies of the

relationships among four preschool teachers' theories-in-use and their classroom behavior. The teachers were observed on four different occasions, and these observations formed the focus of a series of interviews in which teachers were asked to explain particular interactions and why they behaved in certain ways. Analysis revealed that each teacher held a theory of practice that consisted of scientific concepts (what they believed to be true) and value concepts (what was thought to be right). However, each teachers' theory was unique and was characterized by different patterns of beliefs and values. Regardless of this diversity, the teachers most often articulated beliefs about classroom management, instructional processes, and organization. Play, children's development, and learning—concepts considered essential to an EC knowledge base—were minimally discussed by teachers as ideas that governed their actions in the classroom. A follow-up study that asks similar questions of teachers would be of interest now, given the publication of the DAP guidelines (Bredekamp & Copple, 1997).

As theories of child development have been assumed to be essential for teaching young children, Seifert (1991) interviewed three EC preservice teachers, three in-service teachers, and three parents about their understandings of children's development. He found that each group differed ontologically in their theories according to their personal experiences with children. The preservice students described their theories in more abstract terms; the in-service teachers' theories were embedded in their daily interactions with children; and parents described development in terms of biography and long-term change. Seifert posits that the differential experiences of individuals may account for the difficulties that preservice student teachers have in understanding academic theories of children's growth and learning.

Focusing on children's emotional development, Delaney (1995) examined how four very experienced teachers thought about the emotions of young children, and he compared their theories to academic and folk theories of emotion. In addition to conducting open-ended interviews and observations, Delaney used a Q sort (grid) to elicit teachers' constructs about emotional development. All of the teachers held similar personal theories of emotion; they believed that emotional development is a process of interaction. However, the teachers differed in their views as to the purposes of emotional development, the felt aspect of emotions, and the importance of separation in young children's emotional development. When compared with folk and scientific theories of emotion, Delaney found that the teachers' implicit theories were predominantly concerned with the emotional nature of the child while folk and scientific theories tended to emphasize the growth of specific emotions. She therefore argues that teachers' implicit theories are a separate knowledge system that must be considered in their own right.

M. L. Smith (1989) argues that the practical knowledge of teachers is in some ways superior to the propositional knowledge of psychological theorists because of the experiential base that teachers have. Interested in exploring the intersections between teachers' theories of school readiness and retention, M. L. Smith conducted clinical interviews with the kindergarten teachers in one school district. Interviews were structured around concrete episodes and teachers' personal experiences with children. Interviews were supplemented with classroom observations, district data on retention rates, and interviews with parents of children who had been retained by these teachers. M. L. Smith found that "teachers have beliefs and implicit theories that are explicable, internally consistent, and can be seen to reflect extant propositional theories in psychology" (p. 147). The theories of the teachers differed according to whether they believed readiness was a biological characteristic of children (nativists), amenable to environmental influences (remediationists, diagnostic prescriptive teachers), or involved an interaction between nature and nurture (interactionists). Although there was variation in teachers' beliefs, all of the teachers, including those who rarely retained students, believed that retention was an effective educational strategy. Several teachers acknowledged, however, that the success of retaining a child depends on both the support of the parents and the characteristics of the child.

While each of these studies go some way toward providing a context for the content and rationale of teachers' thinking, two final studies examine the thought processes of teachers in much more depth. Yonemura (1986), for example, drew on phenomenological perspectives to document the complexity of one exemplary teacher's thinking over the course of a school year. Working with the teacher as a co-researcher, Yonemura observed Jean as she interacted with parents, children, and her student teacher. These observations often then became a starting point for their taped conversations about Jean's theory of teaching. Yonemura describes Jean's theory and practice as holistic in orientation; she did not break down the curriculum or children's learning into smaller categories. Best practice for Jean was about connectedness, and cognition was never viewed separate from emotion.

The second study conducted by McLean (1991) also views teaching as a rich human encounter. Working with four experienced Australian preschool teachers over several months, McLean used a range of observation and interview techniques to document the teachers' theories and practices of teaching in relation to their involvement in children's peer interactions. For each of these teachers, McLean highlights how teachers' beliefs and values cannot be separated from their biographies or from the social and institutional contexts in which they live and work. Her case studies document the complexities and ambiguities of teaching young children and of trying to create a social world in which all children can learn even when certain ideals are less easy to attain.

To summarize, EC researchers have focused on the theories of teachers as they relate to children's development and to a range of curricular issues. A common focus in a number of these studies is the relationship between the propositional knowledge held by teachers and the psychological and educational theories that teachers have encountered in their professional preparation. Taken together, these studies highlight how the content of teacher theories are rooted in personal and experiential knowledge, much as they are informed by professional theories of curriculum and child development. Whereas teacher-belief studies tend to group teachers according to the similarities of their belief systems, studies of teachers' theories illustrate unique patterns of thinking. Moreover, the phenomenological and interpretive inquiries conducted by McLean

(1991) and Yonemura (1986) detail more closely the ways in which beliefs and values develop and change as teachers interact in the social world of the classroom, the school, and in life. While these two studies show the interaction between teacher thought and action and the environment in which teachers work, most studies of teacher cognition do not foreground the ecology of the classroom and its influence on teaching and learning. In the next section, we review studies of teaching in which physical, social, political, and intellectual contexts of teaching are investigated.

Classroom Ecology Research

In his description of research with an ecological orientation, Shulman (1986) places classroom ecology research outside of the positivist tradition of process-product research and most studies of teacher cognition and mediation. For Shulman, the methods of data collection and analysis characteristic of classroom ecology research, such as naturalistic observations, field notes, archival material, student work, video- and audiotaping, and interviews, are more closely associated with the interpretive tradition of cultural anthropology than with the experimental and quantitative methods derived from psychology. However, our survey of research on teaching in ECE shows that ecological research is more varied and includes both qualitative and quantitative studies, which range from those that describe one phenomenon or type of behavior in a classroom's ecology to complex ethnographies that describe and interpret many aspects of an EC setting. Thus, we present studies in two sections: first, studies that are behaviorally and environmentally focused and, second, ethnographic and interpretive studies, usually focusing on teachers.

BEHAVIORAL AND ENVIRONMENTAL FOCUS

Ecological researchers with a behavioral focus often investigate the frequency and nature of various behaviors in a given classroom condition. For example, at the time when this orientation was being instituted, Kounin and Gump (1974) studied teachers' "signal systems" in lesson formats that affected the rate of preschoolers' on-task behavior. Tizard, Cooperman, Joseph, and Tizard (1972) studied 2- to 5-year-olds' language development in residential nurseries in England and found that the way the nurseries were organized affected the quality of language used by staff members and children. Children with higher scores on measures of language comprehension and production attended nurseries in which staff members had greater autonomy in terms of administrative and instructional decisions and in which one adult, rather than two, attended to small groups of children. (Two adults tended to talk with each other, rather than with the children.)

In a more recent study, Saracho (1989) compares and contrasts the uses of physical space, materials, and teacher behaviors in two EC classrooms. She observed a prekindergarten and kindergarten in which the learning environments differed. One was "open" (with opportunities for choice and exploration of materials), whereas the other was "closed" (with activities that offered few options or leeway for errors). Saracho concluded that space and materials predicted little about the quality of

teachers' interactions with children. The teacher with the "closed" environment, for example, showed a higher degree of interaction with children than the one with the "open" environment.

Rosenthal (1991) takes a more comprehensive look at teacher behaviors in her analysis of multiple factors in the ecology of family day care in Israel. Using Bronfenbrenner's ecological framework (1979) as a foundation, the researcher studied two dimensions of teacher-caregiver behavior: (a) the quality of interaction between caregiver and child and (b) the quality of the educational program that the caregiver provided. These two dimensions were then correlated with caregivers' beliefs about development. According to this observational and interview study of 41 caregivers, quality of interaction was related to caregivers' conceptions of their roles. Those who believed they had a great influence on the child's social development interacted more positively with children. In contrast, the quality of the educational program was related to factors in the immediate environment, such as the socioeconomic status (SES) and age of children. Caregivers who cared for older children and children of higher SES parents provided higher quality programs. Caregivers' beliefs, however, were not related to their background or to factors of the work environment. In fact, their beliefs appeared to match those of "professional educators" (e.g., in their valuing of an authoritative rather than authoritarian approach to control).

Smith, McMillan, Kennedy, and Ratcliff (1992), also grounding their work in Bronfenbrenner's (1979) ecological orientation, focused on EC teachers' roles and relationships. They discovered variations in the degree to which 12 teachers in four New Zealand kindergartens (preschools in the United States) developed goal consensus and shared power. Clear definitions of roles and reciprocal relationships existed in the most successful kindergartens.

Sociomoral atmosphere in three kinds of kindergarten classrooms was the focus of an unusual study by DeVries, Haney, and Zan (1991). The researchers studied the intersections among curriculum models (DISTAR, constructivist, and eclectic), teachers' interpersonal understanding of teacher and child interactions, and consequent sociomoral atmosphere in the classroom. In these three classrooms, the DISTAR classroom focused on academic content, and the teacher exercised a high level of control; the constructivist classroom was characterized by a high degree of reciprocity and intimacy; and the eclectic classroom had both an academic and child-centered emphasis, though it was closer to the atmosphere of the DISTAR than the constructivist classroom.

The study of DeVries, Haney, and Zan (1991) links a pedagogical aspect of classroom ecology with psychological aspects. Other studies extend beyond the classroom to incorporate multiple ecological factors. For example, Bryant, Clifford, and Peisner (1991) examined the degree to which kindergarten classrooms reflect DAP, as defined by NAEYC. Using classroom observations and questionnaires completed by teachers and administrators, the authors found that only 20% of 103 randomly selected kindergarten classrooms across one state met the NAEYC criteria for developmental appropriateness. The most significant finding was that among the ecological variables examined (geographical location, school size, per pupil expenditure, and teacher or principal education or experience) none was related to the developmental appropriateness of instruction in these classrooms. The authors identified only one reliable predictor of developmentally appropriate instruction: the influence (i.e., either the understanding of or belief in DAP) of the teacher, the principal, or both.

The use of tracking or ability grouping in ECE has been a long-standing and controversial issue. Using systematic observations along with teachers' responses to questionnaires, Ross, Smith, Lohr, and McNelis (1994) compared 20 remedial and 20 regular first-grade classrooms with respect to classroom conditions, resources, and teaching methods. Despite slightly smaller remedial classes (17.9 in remedial classes as compared to 20.5 in regular classes), findings revealed few differences between the two groupings in terms of teaching methods, classroom structure, and use of instructional time. Adaptive teaching methods were rarely observed, regardless of class type. However, the observed teachers' responses to a 61-item survey revealed that teachers of remedial classes tended to perceive students less positively, rating them as more aggressive, as having short attention spans, and having poor abilities in the areas of test taking, impulse control, and classroom attendance. The authors suggest that the low expectations in low-ability classes may make it more difficult for teachers to recognize student improvement when it occurs. The use of tracking for low-ability students was not supported, especially considering that the disadvantages of isolation of low achievers from higher achievers, reduced student self-esteem, and less cognitive stimulation are more likely in remedial classes.

An example of research that focuses on only one aspect of child-care ecology is Endsley and Minish's (1991) study of parent-staff communication. This study was conducted in 16 proprietary day care centers. Systematic observations that included recording the frequency and content of communication and the context in which it occurred were made of the interactions between caregivers and parents during morning and afternoon transitions. The researchers found that communication was variable from center to center, suggesting that staff organization influenced the degree to which communication with parents was encouraged. Several patterns emerged that were explored for underlying meanings and purposes. The authors suggested that communication has different meanings for caregivers and parents depending on the time of day and the age of the child. Parents and caregivers of infants and toddlers were the most inclined to interact. This communication was most commonly sought at the end of the day and tended to have the greatest amount of substantive content. This communication, surprisingly, was more frequently initiated by staff members than parents, suggesting a need on the part of caregivers of infants and toddlers to engage parents in conversations about their children.

CAPTURING COMPLEXITY THROUGH ETHNOGRAPHIC AND INTERPRETIVE STUDIES

Unlike ecological researchers who identify and analyze individual aspects of the environment (e.g., communication or tracking), ethnographers attempt to relate such aspects to each other. They also attempt to uncover the meanings that are constructed by the participants as they interact within and between environments. Both a description of the surface structure—the physical and observable elements—and an analysis of the deeper structure of meanings are the focus of this type of "ecological" research. Because research oriented toward critical and poststructural concerns often addresses the relationships among larger political, social, and discourse patterns within classroom ecologies and cultures, it is often ethnographic. Research of this type, however, will be described more fully in the section of this chapter called "Critical Voices."

In the area of day care, Eheart and Leavitt (1989) looked at how family day care providers' perceptions of practice were enacted. First, they interviewed family day care providers about what they believed to be their main responsibilities to children in their care and the kinds of experiences they provided. The researchers then observed several of these family day care providers to determine whether their perceptions converged with their practices. Interviews revealed that most caregivers aim to provide a loving, attentive, and play-based environment for children in their care. However, after observing 6 of the 31 caregivers at work in their homes, Eheart and Leavitt found that these beliefs did not consistently occur in practice.

Also using an ethnographic approach, Wien (1995) conducted five comprehensive case studies of child-care teachers and their classroom practices. Using observations, interviews, and review of videotapes with teachers, Wien sought to understand how teachers enacted their articulated commitments to DAP. Wien identified personal, institutional, and cultural factors that constrained practice and limited teachers' capacities to provide children with the type of care these teachers valued as developmentally appropriate. Although institutional factors such as scheduling, child to staff member ratio, resources and materials, and physical space were implicated in limiting such practice, Wien found that teachers also held taken-for-granted expectations that reflected a more traditional teacher-dominated model, one that was in contradiction to the DAP model that these teachers aspired to enact. In addition to describing the observable surface structure of practice, Wien, through the use of ongoing interviews and feedback from teachers, explored the deeper structure of meanings, beliefs, and theories that underpinned these teachers' practices.

Writing from an economic and political viewpoint, Nelson (1990) combined quantitative and qualitative methods to investigate experiences of day care providers and those associated with family day care. She interviewed 31 registered family day care providers, 19 mothers of children in family day care, 18 center-based workers, 7 spouses of family day care providers, and others such as state licensing workers (in Vermont). Although Nelson was studying family day care as an ecological system, her primary interest was in the relationships that day care providers had with children and their mothers. Yet her respondents offered stories that reflected dilemmas of EC teachers in general. For example, one caregiver said:

> I'm doing this because it's a calling in life, it's something I thought about a lot and decided to do. This is a career choice for me. But not many people think of it as a career. And I find it demeaning to

work so hard, to have so much knowledge and so many skills and to get so little support. I did not want to just do child care. But I can't buy the materials I need to run a good program. Sometimes I can't even take care of my own survival. (p. 194)

This study provides striking examples of multiple viewpoints on a complex social, economic, and political phenomenon. Efforts at performing skilled and caring work with children were often overshadowed by other factors, such as conflict with children's mothers. Working with children in one's own home added to the struggle to be respected as a professional.

In the contrasting setting of schools, when major educational changes are initiated, ethnographic research can provide information regarding the change process and its influence on teacher practices and relationships. The recent trend toward including young children with disabilities in preschool programs is one such initiative that has resulted in a variety of innovative programs and practices. Lieber, Beckman, Hanson, and Janko (1997) examined the changing roles of program staff members in a variety of inclusive settings and identified themes and factors that influence the success of these efforts. The authors relied on data from interviews with teachers, administrators, and service providers; participant observations; and archival documents and identified key areas of concern that followed the inclusion of special needs children into preschool settings.

Some ethnographic research attempts to provide an internally consistent picture of educational programs and their underlying deep structure, a structure based on teacher theories, philosophies, or beliefs. For example, Pease-Alvarez, Garcia, and Espinosa (1991) describe the classroom of two effective bilingual team-teachers. Teacher effectiveness was not determined by external standards of student success but was based on standards intrinsic to the values, goals, and philosophy of their school. Through archival, interview, and observational data, the authors described the larger school context in general terms and then described how the bilingual, bicultural, and culturally integrative program of two primary-grade teachers was constructed internally and in interaction with the larger school and home communities.

The last group of studies in this section grew out of interests in particular issues in ECE or in a particular subject area such as literacy. For example, Roskos and Neuman (1993) used observations, interview responses, and teachers' journal entries to examine teachers' literacy-assisting behaviors during the spontaneous play of 3- and 4-year-olds in three literacy-based classroom settings. Through an analytic inductive process, the authors developed heuristic categories, conceptualizing teacher roles to describe how teachers responded to children's emergent literacy efforts. The authors found that in facilitating and supporting children's literacy-based play activities, teachers were intuitively aware of the learning readiness of the children and sensitively shifted between the roles of spectator, player, and leader.

Most studies of teachers and teaching that are related to subject matter are done in the primary grades. Ciupryk, Fraser, Malone, and Tobin (1989), for example, carried out a case study of a first-grade teacher in Australia who was exemplary at teaching math. Using ethnographic methods, they observed the

teacher for a period of 8 weeks and identified those qualities that appeared to make her a successful teacher generally and in the area of math specifically. Among other qualities, she had the ability to capitalize on situations with potential for mathematical learning at various points in the day.

Pace (1992) explored the reform of literacy instruction (changing from traditional to whole language instruction) in nine classrooms (one kindergarten, five first-grade, two fourth-grade, one sixth-grade) over a period of 6 years. This study was as much about the challenges of school change as about literacy instruction, thus illustrating the kinds of tensions that develop related to the culture of schools and to the abilities to withstand pressure or hostility from peers who are not engaged in change.

Culture and teacher values in one Head Start classroom were studied by O'Brien (1993).

The classroom culture seemed to be defined by the curriculum that was used (High/Scope) and by the need to be "developmentally appropriate." Thus, the researcher observed conflicts revolving around how to balance child choice with the requirements of the curriculum. The staff's view that the program was "compensatory" or remedial also led to tension between teacher and parents.

Issues of risk and curriculum implementation are also at the heart of an interpretive study by Walsh, Smith, Alexander, and Ellwein (1993). They investigated teachers' efforts to implement a curriculum for 4-year-olds, which the researchers describe as "an exemplar of the untidy compromise between developmental and social efficiency" approaches to curriculum (p. 320). Using observations of 13 public school classrooms, Walsh, Smith, et al. concluded that the curriculum was both a guide and a constraint. Since it was imposed on the teachers, they felt obligated to implement it. At the same time, they were not sure of whether they knew how to do that.

Issues of power and control also emerge in an interpretive study of readiness involving teachers and parents (Graue, 1992). After being a participant observer in three school communities for 12 months, Graue found that each community had different interpretations of readiness and that the communities' meanings were closely intertwined with the power held by participants in each setting. In the kindergarten classroom serving a predominantly working-class community, parents had minimal control over decisions about their child's readiness for first grade, whereas in the school serving a middle-class community, parents played a greater role in making such decisions. Graue's focus on power and how it might be related to each community's definition of the construct of readiness makes it an exemplar of a "sociological constructivist" study, which prompts questions about whether significant decisions about young children are always made in their best interests.

Relationships between parents and teachers in ethnoculturally diverse child-care settings are the focus of a study by Bernhard, Lefebvre, Kilbride, Chud, and Lange (1998). Using quantitative and qualitative methods, the researchers describe differences between groups of child-care teachers and supervisors and groups of minority (non-Caucasian) parents in three Canadian cities with large immigrant populations. Points of disagreement included the definition of proper child-rearing methods, choice of goals for ECE, and reasons for lack of involvement of minority parents. Bernhard et al. found "troubled relationships" that were characterized by frequent misunderstandings and dramatic differences between teachers' and parents' perceptions of even minor events. The researchers' attention to participants' perspectives within particular sociopolitical contexts makes this an interpretive study that addresses issues of power related to race, class, and forms of communication. The researchers conclude that the traditional model of EC educator as "expert" in school-family relationships needs to be reconsidered in favor of a collaborative model in which decision-making power is shared.

In this section, we have incorporated studies that differ in scope and theoretical orientation. They focus on specified aspects of classroom ecology that were operationally defined by the researchers, such as teaching approach, communication, quality of care, tracking, sociomoral atmosphere, and ethnographic studies that are focused on participants' experiences and perspectives. In the latter studies, researchers examine processes rather than correlations among predefined factors and often seek the participants' interpretation of phenomena such as inclusion, literacy, bilingual education, readiness, and educational goals. The studies reflect the contrast among psychological, anthropological, or sociological definitions of "ecological research" and the recent shift in ECE toward research methods that give voice to participants and the meanings they attach to experiences in classrooms and communities. In the next section, we review research in which EC teachers voice their ideas on the basis of a study of their own practices.

Teacher Research

The fifth approach to research on teaching is the most recent to gain visibility and is, perhaps, the hardest to define. *Teacher research* usually refers to research done by teachers in their own classrooms or settings. It is intended to contrast with and, in some cases, to challenge traditional approaches to research on teaching in which "experts" from universities or research institutions investigate questions that may be of little or no interest to teachers themselves. This category of research validates the expertise of those closest to learners in the classroom. Methods tend to be qualitative, and data sources include teachers' journals, oral histories, children's products, and in-depth classroom observations.

Cochran-Smith and Lytle (1993) provide a comprehensive analysis and demonstration of teacher research as "ways of knowing." They articulate the view that teacher research is not simply a way for an individual teacher to know more about her or his classroom and students but, as importantly, is a way for teacher researchers to add to a cumulative knowledge base about teaching. The ways in which teachers make public their experience and knowledge differ from traditional (academic) research, and Cochran-Smith and Lytle offer a framework or typology of different kinds of teacher research, ranging from oral examinations of experiences to formalized classroom studies. Teacher research, according to these authors, may be based on data, but it may also be related to teachers' conceptual or theoretical analyses, which take the form of essays. Thus, a fluid range of work may be termed teacher research, just as a range exists for types of ecological studies.

Our criteria for selection in this section were that (a) studies needed to be published or accessible, (b) at least one of the authors or researchers needed to be an EC classroom teacher, and (c) the motive for the research and writing appeared to be direct improvement of practice in the sense that a teacher researcher who studied or reflected upon her or his practices is also the principal agent of change. The task of selection was complicated by the fact that many teachers who systematically study their practices do not publish their work. For purposes of this chapter, however, we decided that studies to be included should be readily accessible to readers. Because the number of published teacher researchers has increased notably in the past 5 years, this section is not exhaustive; rather, we have tried to represent a range of available work and of varied ways of knowing. Finally, because of the researchers' identification with critical theory, some illustrations of teacher research are included later in the section of this chapter called "Critical Voices."

TEACHERS COLLABORATING WITH OTHERS

We have organized this section according to authorship; that is, we begin with teacher research in which teachers collaborate with college or institutional researchers, but the teacher is not an author of the published report of findings. We then present collaborations that are reflected in the multiple authorship: teachers and college or institutional researchers are all included. Finally, we present a section in which authors are teachers writing for themselves. Note that many of these studies have a kinship with ethnographic and interpretive work done by other researchers: Detailed observations and reflection are often integral to the teachers' studies. Thus, a straightforward presentation of findings does not capture the complexity of individual and collaborative learning that stems from the research. In the third section in which teachers are writing for themselves, some of this complexity is conveyed through their own words.

RESEARCHERS REPORTING TEACHER RESEARCH

McIntyre (1995) collaborated with teachers who were particularly interested in literacy instruction (three primary-grade teachers in multiaged settings for 5- through 8-year-olds). Their study was cast within the framework of DAP, and findings showed that appropriate practices for these three teachers were eclectic, incorporating holistic and skill-oriented instruction. Data were typical of many collaborative studies: audiotapes of researchers' discussions and field notes based on observations of classroom instruction and interaction. Saunders and Goldenberg (1996) similarly worked with four primary-grade teachers who were seeking to improve their language arts instruction. These researchers also found that insisting on a single approach (e.g., direct instruction) did not lead to improved practice. "Instructional conversation" (Tharp & Gallimore, 1988) in combination with direct instruction appeared to be productive.

Bussis, Chittenden, Amarel, and Klausner (1985) coordinated an unusually extensive collaborative study of children learning to read. The research team included EC teachers from six geographic areas in the United States and researchers from the Educational Testing Service. For 6 years, the collaborators focused on individual children and their ways of learning to read. An ethnographic and interpretive study, it illustrates how "research on teaching" or collaborative "teacher research" often results in research on children. Their book carefully documents two broad styles of learning to read (one leaning toward accuracy and the other toward anticipation of what is to come—toward momentum driven by the meaning of text). Data from primary-grade classrooms with children of diverse socioeconomic backgrounds included anecdotal observations, children's art and writing, and children's talk. This example of teacher research could not have been done without funding and without long-term collaboration. It may also be an example of how the theory of reading that emerges may be shaped by prevailing theories or by academic researchers more than by the teachers' own ways of articulating theory.

Halliwell (1992) provides both an overview about the complexities of teacher research and theory in ECE and a summary of collaborative research. She delineates characteristics of many practitioners (discomfort with analytic academic discourse, a preference for less analytic, perhaps visual, ways of showing relationships, and so on) as she supports the need for expanded ways of doing and reporting classroom research. Halliwell also describes her work with two teachers in Australia, Kate and Wendy, who created their own curricula but who were confronted with the challenges of negotiating it. Wendy needed to negotiate changes with children; Kate needed to negotiate with her teaching partner, who was new to the changes that Kate was suggesting.

TEACHERS AND ACADEMICS COLLABORATING

Collaborative teacher research sometimes focuses on questions related to particular grade levels and particular content. Archer (Archer, Coffee, & Genishi, 1985), for example, did a brief observational and interview study to see how she could promote kindergartners' language and language skills. She observed an experienced kindergarten teacher (Coffee) and discussed her findings with her university instructor (Genishi). The resulting report built upon Archer's observations and insights and Coffee's reflections on her own practices as she was interviewed by Genishi. A discovery of particular interest was that Archer and Genishi noted as major strengths Coffee's remarkable abilities to listen and respond to children, whereas Coffee talked about her strengths first in terms of being organized.

A longer term study by Walsh, Baturka, Smith, and Colter (1991) was a collaborative study of one first-grade teacher. For one school year, the teacher's (Colter's) collaborators observed her classroom two or three times per week, did formal interviews, often talked informally with Colter, and had contact with her outside of school. It is a story about how the teacher experienced change as she moved from "traditional" to "developmental" teaching. Reminiscent of Archer et al. (1985), Colter's view of herself contrasted with her collaborators' observations. Even if her room and activities looked notably different, she believed that she was essentially the same—her identity was still that of a teacher.

A number of examples of collaboration in which university researchers act as editors or scribes when they collaborate with EC teachers on a topic of mutual interest can be found. Lens-mire (1995), for example, carried out an unusual collaborative study in which he took the teacher-researcher role in the classroom of a third-grade teacher collaborator. The teacher allowed him to teach language arts, which incorporated a writing process approach in which students wrote in journals, conversed with each other, and discussed each others' writing in the whole group. Taking a critical perspective toward an approach that many teachers have adopted, and drawing on the writings of Calkins (1986) and Graves (1983), Lensmire described the kinds of conflicts that may occur among children. In his setting, children's conflicts appeared to grow out of social class differences, a topic that is seldom addressed directly in case studies of teaching.

Dyson (1997a), using a contrasting approach, collaborated with 12 primary-grade teachers in the San Francisco Bay Area as they discussed issues related to "difference," including social class and cultural and ethnic differences. The study continued for a year, during which teachers did case studies of selected children in their own classrooms. Dyson and two graduate students also observed the classrooms. Weekly conversations of the entire group grounded classroom events, observations, and ideas about difference, which took printed form in a report of the project. The report is woven together with the teachers' own words and ideas as the core. They raise issues for reflection that are critical to a discussion of race, class, and individual differences in learning and teaching.

Pairs or teams of EC teachers and academics wrote the core chapters of an edited collection on alternative (teacher-based, not standardized) assessment (Genishi, 1992). Each team described its own classroom or classrooms and described its ways of thinking about and doing everyday assessments of children's learning. Foote, Stafford, and Cuffaro (1992), for example, described their preschool (Foote) and kindergarten (Stafford) curricula and their ways of assessing children according to principles learned at Bank Street College (where Cuffaro advised them). Several teachers and an academic, who focused on two languages as resources for learning and teaching, described a second-grade bilingual program in Arizona as they introduced Spanish-speaking children to literacy (Fournier, Lansdowne, Pastenes, Steen, & Hudelson, 1992). Like Dyson and her collaborators (1997a) and Walsh et al. (1991), these collaborators constructed meaningful stories of practice through observation, action, reflection, and extended conversation.

TEACHERS WRITING FOR THEMSELVES

In writing for themselves, some teacher researchers in this section were also asked to address the topic of a book—in one instance, alternative assessment. Savitch and Serling (1997) describe their experiences as a team, creating alternative experiences and assessments for third graders, most of whom were Chinese American and some of whom had been identified as "gifted." The team describes their decision to split one class of "gifted" students in half and then to complete the class roster for both groups with "regular" students, thus, detracking the gifted class and creating two enrichment classes. In the course of planning a theme-based curriculum, Savitch and Serling also developed alternatives to individual seatwork and weekly tests. "Portfolio Night" for parents and their children was a highlight of the year that illustrated the teachers' and children's successful change process.

For a volume on *Theory and Practice in Early Childhood Teaching* (Chafel & Reifel, 1996), teacher researchers were asked to write about "teachable moments" and their connections with practice and theory. Cox (1996) reflects on how theories of development (e.g., Piaget's or Vygotsky's) underlie and interact with her practice—with her beliefs about how children learn and how she learns about their learning. The experiences and insights of other educators also offer ways of thinking about what is and can be taught. In the same volume, Kennedy (1996) describes the ways she learns about her 3-year-olds' understandings about literacy and emphasizes the "dialogue" she carries on with earlier researchers whose work she has read and studied as a graduate student. Lepine (1996) chooses the complexity of children's developing concept of "structure" (as in block constructions), and Scales (1996) focuses on videotaped preschool interactions that illustrate the "hidden curriculum," or ways in which the classroom ecology shapes interaction and either confirms or challenges existing theory. A detailed analysis of many interactions provided a bridge for Scales between practice and theory.

Martin (1990), also a kindergarten teacher, writes about social studies in the kindergarten curriculum by presenting the natural history of a club, originated by one child in the class, Dorrie. The club membership was determined by Dorrie at first and became a point of disagreement for children and some parents. Martin waited to see what would happen as Dorrie, a child who had taken on the role of "caretaker" and was formerly on the margins of children's activities, found herself in the center of controversy. Eventually, the club became a more open, outdoor activity, and Martin believed that the children had participated in a child-initiated social studies curriculum, one in which social issues of power, inclusion, and exclusion could be addressed on the children's own terms.

In contrast, Rennebohm-Franz (1996) studies a curriculum that is part of an international network called I*EARN, a multicultural peace education program in which children communicate with peers in other sites. For example, the researcher's class communicated with children in Kobe, Japan, following a severe earthquake, sending artwork and messages of encouragement. Within a programmatic framework, children learned about the everyday lives of peers in another culture, directing their own learning through questions that reflected their interests and experiences. This study, in which the children's electronic mail messages were treated as data, is an exemplar of databased classroom research, which becomes the basis for sharing aspects of an available "social studies" program aimed at developing young children's social consciousness. Martin, instead, illustrates the enactment of an emergent social studies curriculum, which is unlikely to be adopted by others, at least in its specifics. Both teachers used classroom data of different kinds but are on different points on the continuum of EC teacher research.

Ballenger (1992, 1996, 1999) is a preschool teacher who has also explored the challenges of cultural and racial differences, primarily within the contexts of classroom language use and early literacy learning. She writes with candor about how a classroom of Haitian preschoolers, speakers of Haitian Creole and English, caused her to examine her ways of talking as these reflect her ways of disciplining or controlling children (Ballenger, 1992). As a teacher researcher, she learned from her Haitian teacher peers about their discourse, their ways of structuring talk with children. Ballenger's research led her to alter her discourse so that it approximated that of her peers and of the children's parents. Controlling her class depended on her flexibility and her abilities to perceive and analyze cultural and linguistic differences.

In a subsequent study, Ballenger (1996) tells the story of what and how she learned about Haitian preschoolers who were learning about literacy. Because she knew that literacy is a significant part of the EC curriculum, she provided a writing table where children began to learn about letters and what they represented. What they represented, however, was not always congruent with adult notions of concepts of print. The children matched and copied letters and learned to write their names, but they also invested print with personal meanings; they "were exploring the uses of text in the creation of community" (p. 317). They were learning about and interpreting print to represent important relationships in their lives. This finding is not unique (see, e.g., Dyson, 1989, 1993) but is one that Ballenger came to know in her own situation; the exploring and knowing for oneself was key. She took as given the differences that exist between adults' and children's ways of knowing:

> It seems to me that teaching in multicultural classrooms, and in mainstream classrooms as well, is a matter of regularly and repeatedly researching the particular ways in which the school and teacher's intentions, on the one hand, and the children's intentions, on the other, both differ and coincide. (Ballenger, 1996, p. 322)

Stires, working with children in the primary and upper-elementary grades, has written on a range of topics related to language and literacy, a content area that has become increasingly central for teacher researchers, including some prekindergarten teachers. Stires writes largely about individual learners who have worked with her in special education resource rooms and in "regular" classrooms. For example, she writes "the story of Marcy's stories" (Stires, 1994), which she learned about as a resource teacher in Marcy's first-grade classroom in Maine. Stires' stories about children who are typically labeled "at risk" focus notably on what child learners are able to do despite being classified as "learning disabled." Moreover, the curriculum that was developed for children like Marcy and Gregory (Stires, 1990) was "regular," that is, it incorporated writing process, drawing, talking, and conferencing—elements of language arts programs for "regular" students. Indeed, the children with whom Stires worked learned some things more slowly than other children, but the "disabled" children did learn when they were included in a regular classroom. The practical theories that Stires developed as she taught and reflected on literacy learning are incorporated in her case study descriptions of the children in the articles cited, in books (e.g., Stires, 1991), and in journals such as *Primary Voices,* a publication of the National Council of Teachers of English that features articles by elementary-grade teachers.

Another prolific teacher-researcher in ECE is Paley, who, since the publication of *White Teacher* in 1979, has demonstrated teacher reflection and action in nine books and a number of articles. Thus, she could not claim to be a typical EC teacher. Yet her themes are the enduring and typical ones of many EC educators: the role of fantasy play, the importance of story, the significance and challenge of racial differences, the tension between individual and group needs, and the role of the teacher. These themes are artfully woven into her own stories, not as "variables" to be analyzed or correlated with products or learning outcomes, but as critical aspects of life in EC classrooms, the core of which is always children—what they think, know, and believe—and which is often captured in what they say. For example, Paley (1997) has written about Reeny, her most recent title character in *The Girl with the Brown Crayon:*

> When Reeny first comes upon Frederick she is wide-eyed with wonder. "That brown mouse seem to be just like me!" she announces, staring at the cover of *Frederick,* a Leo Lionni book that Nisha [Paley's coteacher] has just read to the class. "Because I'm always usually thinking 'bout colors and words the same like him." (p. 5)

Reeny's fascination with Frederick leads to a year-long "author study" of Leo Lionni, and although Paley is never prescriptive about her classroom practices, she offers to her readers a possibility for curriculum that is both literature-based and child-initiated. Similarly, in earlier books (e.g., 1981, 1984, 1995), she illustrates her ways of encouraging prekindergarten and kindergarten children to tell and dramatize their own stories. The author's overall goal seems to be a greater understanding of children as a basis for improved teaching in her own and, potentially, her readers' settings.

To enhance her understanding of children, Paley has focused on difficult issues such as race in *White Teacher* (1979) and *Kwanzaa and Me: A Teacher's Story* (1995), in which she struggles with questions like, Is racial integration desirable? The answers to her questions are multiple, complex, and, in addition, surprising and sometimes disturbing. A former student of the teacher-researcher, now an adult, tells Paley, "I'd have done better in a black school. I'd have been more confident. I was an outsider here" (Paley, 1995, p. 6). The African-American father of a current kindergartner at the same private school with a majority of White students says, "We're still pretty ambivalent. My wife especially. She'd like Jeremy to remain in an African American school until he's older" (p. 20). These ambiguities and feelings are what an intense listener-researcher attends to and reflects on. Paley's research is a continual search for questions of consequence and for possible, not definitive, answers. Her ways of knowing depend upon children's ways of experiencing the classroom, in part, through drama and stories—their own and their teacher's.

Gallas (1994, 1995, 1998) is another teacher researcher who has looked carefully at how children learn through language, print, science, and the arts. Like Paley and other teacher researchers, she uses audiotapes of classroom talk as the basis for analyses of what she calls the "languages of learning." In *Talking Their Way Into Science* (Gallas 1995), children's questions are the beginning point for their growing theories about science:

> How do your bones stay together?
> What is blood for?

> How does a baby grow inside?
> How do we grow?
> How do our dreams get into our head? (p.70)

Informal curricula developed from these beginnings as Gallas played the roles of both model and coach. Like other researchers who teach children, Gallas typifies certain perspectives on the classroom: She sees particulars, often in the context of individual children's learning and development. In other words, she appears to work like a child-study expert, able to construct case studies that are richly textured and unique. Thus, her observational skills are strong like the academic researcher seeking statistical connections between classroom processes and test scores.

Yet the connections Gallas seeks most intently are grounded in the people and events in her classroom.

Gallas is aware that she and her researcher peers are viewed as unusual phenomena in the world of educational research, and she is eloquent on the distinctiveness of both teacher as research "subject" and of teachers' ways of "teaching" and knowing:

> Any teacher who has attended national research conferences on education cannot help but come away with the feeling that she or he is an aboriginal. Every aspect of life in the community of the classroom is highlighted for study and discussion; and in those discussions, the person of the teacher is truly disembodied as a research subject. Even the stories teachers tell are studied as a curious sort of folklore that somehow represents a mythology about teaching.
>
> As a first grade teacher, perhaps I do represent some of the traits of an aboriginal. I speak of a child learning to read in magical terms. My colleagues do the same. While our methods, structure, and intent as teachers of reading imply a systematic approach, we know in our hearts that the event of reading is magical. When a child learns to read, we are awestruck—not knowing absolutely that any one thing we did so systematically caused that outcome. We know that the measurement of variables, coefficients, and reliability will not help us as teachers of reading. We know that one cannot measure or generalize about in absolute terms how the epiphany of reading happens for each child. Yet we all have important things to say to one another in our stories about what we have learned from the children, and those things can improve our teaching of reading. (Gallas, 1994, p. 3)

A believer, with many others, in the power and usefulness of stories, Gallas demonstrates how stories or narratives about classrooms are important elements of research on teaching. Educational researchers whose aim is to measure all classroom processes numerically might reject her position, but those who have looked closely at classrooms find it hard to ignore the wisdom of experience grounded in theory that teachers like Gallas offer.

In this section, we have focused on teacher research, which reflects a shift from teacher as "object of study" to teacher as agent of research. In contrast to process-product research, teacher researchers seldom specify statistical outcomes or correlations. Instead, these researchers seem to be deeply involved in child study and often write about individuals who have been especially challenging. Whether they are working collaboratively or alone, researchers in this group present themselves as people who learn from children, rather than s adults who "instruct." Some of these teachers have collaborated with academic researchers who have ultimately written about the collaboration (and have not included the teachers' names as authors), whereas others have shared authorship. The studies that offer teachers the most recognition and control and hence the most power are those in which teachers write for themselves, directly establishing who they and their children are and what they do and think.

In other words, teacher-researchers who are writing for themselves represent themselves and the children they work with; other researchers are neither representing nor speaking for them. In becoming researchers and writers, they have enacted Heilbrun's (1988) definition of *power:*

> Power is the ability to take one's place in whatever discourse is essential to action and the right to have one's part matter. This is true in the Pentagon, in marriage, in friendship, and in politics. (p. 18)

And, we add, in the highly political world of education. Teachers are beginning to participate in the public discourse about their work. Their degree of influence is hard to assess. An informal look at bibliographies related to research on teaching suggests that the writing of teachers is not yet in the consciousness of many academic researchers. In the next section we turn to alternative theories in which power and discourse are central themes. They provide new perspectives on the field of ECE.

Critical Voices: Theoretical Frames of the ECE Reconceptualists

Since the 1960s, a pivotal debate in the social sciences has centered on what the relationship between theory, research, and practice ought to be (Bernstein, 1976). Critiques of the adequacy of empirical theory to explain the "truth" about social phenomena have catalyzed a shift from modern to postmodern notions of thought and action. In response to this broader trend, researchers in ECE have moved from experimental and quasi-experimental (modern) designs to qualitative (sometimes postmodern) inquiries, characterized by a focus on culture and intersubjective interpretations of educational phenomena (Genishi, Dubetz, & Focarino, 1995; Walsh, Tobin, & Graue, 1993). While we have presented a number of studies that reflect this change in paradigms of inquiry, in this section, we introduce a group of studies labeled "reconceptualist" that aim to illuminate new visions of research, theory, and practice in ECE. We provide an overview of the reconceptualist movement; an explanation and review of research of alternative approaches to research on teaching—namely, critical theory, poststructuralism, and feminisms; and a brief overview of queer and postcolonial theories.

The EC Reconceptualists

To reconceptualize implies a questioning, a reconsidering of the traditions and assumptions that structure a field of endeavor with the aim of redefining that field in new and alternative ways (Lubeck, 1991). The term *reconceptualization* was first applied

to the field of education by Pinar (1975) to describe the work of a number of theorists who situated their inquiries within curriculum studies and the new sociology of education. These curriculum scholars challenged the dominance of the Tyler rationale for curriculum design by proposing that knowledge and the way it is presented in schools is not a technical, value-free enterprise but is, rather, a political endeavor. In recent years, this scholarship has inspired some EC educators to reexamine the psychological-developmental knowledge base that has informed much of the field's aims and programs.

Reflecting the wider debate in the social sciences, EC reconceptualists claim that the traditional psychological assumptions underlying the developmental knowledge base have been constructed over time and are neither neutral nor benign (Bloch, 1991; Burman, 1994; Cannella, 1997; Graue, 1992; Kessler & Swadener, 1992; Silin, 1995). Critiquing the positivistic and scientific methods that frame this research program, reconceptualists assert that the EC knowledge base is rooted in masculine, Western, middle-class (i. e., modern) assumptions about children and their optimal patterns of growth. Thus, while EC educators claim to subscribe to an objective knowledge base, in using this knowledge, they promote a narrowly normative view of young children's growth and learning (New & Mallory, 1994; Polakow, 1989; Silin, 1995). For reconceptualists, then, reliance on a knowledge base that is rooted in positivism and based on natural or evolutionary explanations of development leads to a biased view of both learning and teaching in ECE.

Recently, some reconceptualists have begun to extend their critique to the research program embodied in the interpretive paradigm of inquiry. An increase in qualitative studies in their view does not ensure that the social inequities embodied in a developmental knowledge base will be recognized and addressed in new visions of EC curriculum. While interpretive studies may provide thick and rich descriptions of teaching and learning in context, for the most part, such research fails to integrate theory with practice (Tobin, 1995). In other words, if a researcher captures the meaning of a classroom as a disinterested observer, she or he may enhance the knowledge base but does not necessarily ensure a critical questioning of the practices under study. As a consequence, according to Tobin, the knowledge generated by current research on EC teaching continues to perpetuate social inequalities, providing little insight into the inadequacies of contemporary EC practices or how they might be improved. Situating their inquiries in the EC curriculum and the relations between power, pedagogy, and learning, reconceptualists seek to re-envision ECE in theory, research, and practice.

As a group, reconceptualist researchers are characterized by their commitment to questioning the way power works in and through the practices of schooling (Popkewitz & Brennan, 1998). However, their work is extremely diverse, drawing on a wide range of theoretical perspectives. We have therefore chosen to organize this review around the key theoretical bases applied by reconceptualists to the study of early education: critical theory, poststructuralism, and feminisms. In addition, we briefly describe theories that are emerging as important influences on recent reconceptualist scholarship, queer theory, and postcolonialism. Although our framework belies the complexity of innovative studies in which, more often than not, multiple theoretical frameworks are used, we use the three major approaches as benchmarks from which to illuminate a range of studies labeled reconceptualist and to consider the potential of these perspectives to inform future research projects.

Critical Theory

Critical theory is a form of inquiry that seeks to question the patterns of knowledge and social conditions that maintain unequal social divisions (e.g., class, race, gender, sexuality), with the aim of orienting individuals toward actions that will lead to social change (Bernstein, 1976; Beyer & Bloch, 1996; Giroux, 1983; Habermas, 1971; Popkewitz, 1984). Critical theorists assume that all knowledge is socially constructed and distributed rather than given as an external objectified reality. What comes to be defined as knowledge is intimately tied to the producers of that knowledge, their interests, and the methods through which they legitimate and validate their conceptions of knowledge (Bernstein, 1976; Blum, 1971). Knowledge is political in nature, and just as ideologies that are embodied in social practices and institutions like schooling privilege certain groups over others, so knowledge can be used to redistribute power—hence, the central role of research in social change. By elucidating the taken-for-granted assumptions and practices that structure society and individual consciousness, the intellectual or researcher illuminates pathways for social action (Held, 1980; Lather, 1991).

Within this orientation to knowledge and inquiry, the modernist notion that reason and knowledge can lead to social progress is upheld (Popkewitz & Brennan, 1998). Human beings are self-conscious and responsible social agents and are a driving force in the shaping of social reality (Giroux, 1983). The individual is in a dialectical relationship with society. While society is socially constructed, the social context also shapes human freedom and potential. Research from a critical theoretical perspective seeks to explore the relationship between individual identity and the broader system of social relationships in which individuals are embedded to reveal how resources and opportunities are distributed and who benefits from such distributions. In highlighting the contradictions and barriers to human freedom in particular social contexts, the intellectual or researcher helps raise the consciousness of marginalized groups and offers directions for their liberation.

Using a range of methodologies (usually qualitative), reconceptualist researchers, who work from the viewpoint of critical theory, question the assumptions framing what appear to be innocent EC practices (e.g., DAP and readiness decisions) and examine the ways in which such practices produce inequalities that are mirrored in the broader society. These inequalities include unequal access to education (e.g., in neighborhoods in the United States with poorly funded public schools) or a minimal role in decision making (e.g., in schools or school districts that do not seek teacher, parent, or community input).

A common theme in many critical studies is the voice of teachers as both theory makers and co-researchers. (Most of the work featuring teachers' voices was included earlier in the section on teacher research because the authors did not identify or ally themselves with critical theory.) In a number of instances, university researchers have written about the work of teachers without collaborating on formalized research questions. Nonetheless, they sought teachers' expression and interpretation of their own experiences. Ayers (1989), for example, conducted multiple case studies of six practicing teachers that examined how their life histories contributed to their understandings of teaching. Applying a critical lens to a study of teachers' pedagogical authority, Silin (1982) found that teachers described themselves as objective professionals who provided protective control to vulnerable young children. Although most EC teachers believe they have close nurturing relationships with their students, Silin argues that by viewing themselves as apolitical carers of the young, EC educators distance themselves from the children in their care.

Other critical studies draw on earlier sociological research on school knowledge, such as Sharp and Green's (1975) investigation of child-centered pedagogy in British infant schools, to question whether common practices and programs achieve their desired outcomes for young children and their families. In one of the first cross-cultural ethnographies conducted of EC programs, Lubeck (1985) documented how the different child-rearing practices of Black educators in a working-class Head Start center and White teachers in a middle-class preschool socialized children differently. She postulates that poor Black children do not lack the stimulation to facilitate later academic success but that they are reared to value the collective over the individual, a value not embodied in the middle-class values underpinning school knowledge.

Drawing on the concept of cultural capital to investigate the relationships between school context, social class, and parent involvement, Lareau (1989) found class differences in home-school relationships. While parents in the White, middle-class school were expected to question school practices and sought a sense of interconnectedness between family and school life, the relationships between most working-class parents and their children's school was characterized by separation. Rather than highlight cultural differences, Polakow (1992), in a comparative ethnography of five child-care centers, critiques the regimentation of children's lives that takes place under the guise of best practice. In her words, "the institutional world that babies, toddlers, and the very young have increasingly come to inhabit and confront is a world in which they have become the objects, not the subjects of history" (p. 188). A multitheoretical study focused on the relations between power and emotion conducted by Leavitt (1994) resonates with Polakow's assertions. After spending 7 years observing 12 infant and toddler classrooms, Leavitt (1994) concludes that, for many children, early care is a somewhat sterile experience in which their emotions often go unrecognized and are not responded to in authentic ways.

From another angle, Wolf and Walsh (1998) write a report about everyday life in one day care center, Enchanted Gate. They present vignettes of events that occurred in a year's time between two teacher-caregivers (the authors' term) and their children and families. Although the focus is on a single center, the stories of the participants match those of others who care for, teach, and negotiate on behalf of young children. The privately owned center was selected for study because of its good reputation, but it was still a place where the teacher-caregivers had little power to make decisions or influence the state policies that regulated the center. Like the children in Polakow's study (1992), the teachers at Enchanted Gate seem to be "objects" and not subjects or agents. Wolf and Walsh urge readers to consider the sociopolitical realities of day care, an institution that will not change unless the EC community recognizes the need for change.

Studies of kindergarten classroom practices represent some of the earliest applications of critical theory to the study of EC teaching. Apple and King (1977) examined the hidden curriculum of one public school kindergarten classroom, finding that the organization of the kindergarten day and the curriculum enacted by the teacher socialized the children to dichotomize activities into work and play, preparing them for their role as workers in a capitalist society. Kessler (1992) conducted a more recent study of teaching in kindergarten. Like her predecessors, Kessler demonstrates how teachers' interactions in the classroom, including the form and content of the curriculum they enact, are embedded in and related to a number of sociocultural contexts that socialize children differently. For example, the kindergarten classroom located within a working-class community was more developmental in its approach to teaching and learning, while, in contrast, the kindergarten serving a middle-class community was more academic in orientation.

Reflecting a concern for the values embedded in the developmental knowledge base, a number of studies critique the guidelines for *Developmentally Appropriate Practice in Early Childhood Programs* (Bredekamp, 1987) as an ideology. Jipson (1991) examined the narratives and journal entries of 30 teachers related to DAP. In their statements, many of the teachers commented on the way the guidelines constrained their interactions with children from diverse cultural and linguistic backgrounds. Collaborating with these teachers in her university classroom, Jipson writes of their attempts to critique the cultural values implicit in DAP and of different actions they might take to address these social inequities within their classrooms. In this way, Jipson enacts a critical pedagogy using research as a tool for social change.

Examining the assertion that the guidelines represent the consensus definition of the field, Walsh (1991) interviewed teachers about their views of children's development. Finding a wide variation among the respondents (maturationists, vulgar-Piagetians, and Piagetians), Walsh demonstrates that the guidelines are not quite accurate in their claims to represent the field's agreement on what constitutes best practice.

A final group of critical studies concentrate on how teachers address social issues in the EC classroom (e.g., Carlsson-Paige & Levin, 1987). Interested in a curriculum that engaged students in experiences aimed at developing human freedom, social responsibility, and conflict resolution, Swadener and Pie-keilek (1992) conducted a collaborative ethnography of one Quaker school. Their research process did not end with written publication only; they also created a videotape that became an ongoing pedagogical tool for members of the school community. Marsh (1992) documents her own attempts to enact an "anti-bias" curriculum (Derman-Sparks, 1989) with her kindergarteners. Central to this curriculum is the aim of educating all students to appreciate diversity, including differences in gender, race, ability, culture, and class. As a teacher-researcher, Marsh used action research to inquire into the complexities of interacting with children about issues of diversity and difference.

While few in number, these critical studies highlight how educational practices cannot be considered separate from the wider social contexts in which they are embedded. They demonstrate how many taken-for-granted practices and beliefs about educating young children are not objective but value laden, often reflecting the values of the dominant social class. As happens with all frameworks, however, critical theory and its approaches to studying social relations have been critiqued on a number of grounds. Foremost are their conceptualizations of power and human agency and the way in which notions of race, class, and gender are presented as essential traits (Popkewitz & Brennan, 1998; Weiler, 1992). We elaborate on these points in the next section on poststructural social theories, which EC researchers have begun to explore in their own work (Tobin, 1995).

Poststructuralism

Like critical theory, poststructuralism does not refer to one theory but is an umbrella term used to define a diverse array of theoretical approaches that are concerned with how social power is organized, enacted, and contested. However, in contrast to structural analyses, poststructural inquiries are antifoundational and assume that language, meaning, and subjectivity are never fixed and, therefore, can never be fully revealed or understood by the research process (Anyon, 1994; Tobin, 1995).

Poststructuralists assume that language constitutes social reality. Language in the form of different discourses is the site where subjectivity, social organization, and various social meanings are constructed (Weedon, 1997). Discourses are socially organized frameworks of meaning embodying particular values and practices that stipulate rules and domains of what can be said and done, by whom, and when (Burman, 1994; Hicks, 1995). Discourses are never neutral, the differing social meanings they give to the world represent differing political interests. As such, poststructuralists conceive of reality as a semiotically produced social order in which various discourses compete and vie for status and power.

Poststructuralist theorists disagree with structuralists about the nature of language. Instead of assuming a direct relation between the signifier (word) and the signified (meaning), poststructuralists argue that meaning continually moves along a chain of signifiers or is constantly deferred. That is, meanings are never the same because the words (signifiers) that make up the text have no fixed or stable relationship to the things and concepts they are meant to signify (Tobin, 1995, p. 233). Meanings only exist in relation to other meanings, to their articulation in language, which is always socially and historically located in various discourses (Weedon, 1997, p. 40). As language is not transparent and meanings are not fixed as social facts, poststructuralists assert that there are no essential Truths, only truths.

Intertwined with a belief in the fluidity of language and meaning is the poststructuralist assumption that human subjectivity is symbolically produced by discourses (Anyon, 1994;

Wexler, 1987). Just as we can find no stable text, we can find no stable being or human consciousness (Sarup, 1993). Through institutionalized discursive practices supported by different forms of knowledge and power relations, human subjectivity is both formed and regulated (Wexler, 1987). Human beings in their everyday world are positioned or position themselves in a number of discourses, which, at one moment, render them powerful and, at another, powerless. Poststructuralists theorize subjectivity as conflicted and disunited, not as the authority and interpreter of meaning (Weedon, 1997). Therefore, change and control are not in the hands of all-knowing autonomous subjects but are located in the discursive practices that organize social life (Popkewitz, 1995).

As language, meaning, and subjectivity are never fixed, poststructuralists assume that power is not a commodity that some individuals or social groups possess to control others. Drawing on the work of Foucault, poststructuralists replace this sovereign notion of power with a strategic one in which power is conceptualized as circulating throughout social relations so that individuals both enact and undergo the effects of power (Sarup, 1993).

Poststructural investigations of ECE center on relations between language, power, and subjectivity as they are played out in the talk and action of specific classrooms. Teaching practices are read like texts for the multiple meanings and truths they convey (Lather, 1991). The intent of this scholarship is not to reveal a model of the teaching and learning process but to provide a partial view of the ambiguity and complexity of teaching and learning at the local level that facilitates social change (Anyon, 1994; Cherryholmes, 1988; Lather, 1991). For example, a study of the talk and action of circle time (usually a whole-group meeting) in a classroom may highlight how this practice can be both democratic and autocratic. It may not always facilitate children's self-expression and participation in the social life of the classroom, as is often presumed. Most EC researchers who use a poststructural framework base their analyses on a number of theoretical perspectives. We therefore review the few existing studies in our explorations of feminism, queer theory, and postcolonialism.

Feminisms

Feminism is not one theory that embodies a unified position. Instead, several feminist perspectives have evolved, each with its own priorities for the various aspects of women's struggles against oppressive forces and for the importance they give to the workings of patriarchy, or gender stratification (Weiner, 1994). Feminist scholarship in education has been rapidly expanding (Biklen, 1995; Gaskell & Willinsky, 1995; Gore, 1993; Lather, 1991; Luke & Gore, 1992; Middleton, 1993; Ropers-Huilman, 1998; Wrigley, 1992), and EC reconceptualists have shown a growing interest in feminist theories and their implications for curriculum and teaching (Beyer & Bloch, 1996; Hauser & Jipson, 1998; Kessler & Swadener, 1992; Ochsner, 1997; Ochsner & Ryan, 1997). Because approximately 97% of all preschool teachers are women, most poorly paid (National Center for the Early Childhood Workforce, 1993), an understanding of alternative theories such as feminisms should be paramount.

Four main feminist perspectives influence research in ECE. However, few studies, either with EC teachers or about EC teaching, have been conducted from these perspectives. These feminisms, although not exhaustive, are liberalism, radicalism, culturalism, and poststructuralism. The four orientations are located on a continuum, and all work toward improving the status of women by changing the ways in which social and political institutions promote and maintain women's inequality. Feminists also emphasize the need for a feminist consciousness, that is, the ability to understand the causes of women's oppression and subordination in order to confront and struggle against those forces (Donovan, 1992).

Inequality, oppression, and *subordination* are words that feminists often choose to express their circumstances in society. Although the terms are not mutually exclusive, each has unique implications for the problems and issues they describe (Phillips, 1987). For example, inequality refers to the unjust occasions when women are denied what is granted to men, such as (a) letting men vote when women could not, (b) giving men opportunities for higher-paid jobs while restricting women to low-status and low-income work, or (c) providing boys with more and better classroom instruction than girls receive (Sadker & Sadker, 1994). Instead of focusing on how women and girls have been excluded, oppression applies to prolonged coercion or injustices that women have endured, such as the lack of opportunity for women's expression in some Muslim cultures. Additionally, oppression refers to a complex set of ideological, political, and economic forces that combine to keep women "in their place." From this perspective, the lack of governmental subsidies for child care is an oppressive force that keeps some women out of the workforce. Subordination identifies agents in the process of oppression, for instance, teachers, administrators, law enforcement officials, and elected political officials who do not consider sexual harassment to be "violence" (Stein, 1995) and the U.S. government, which refuses to pass an equal rights amendment, are examples of agents (individual and institutional) who subordinate girls and women in society.

Liberal feminism, which asserts that women and men are equal, is often considered the most enduring and accepted of all feminisms. Drawing from the Enlightenment, liberal feminists are concerned with the individual, legal, and political rights of women and seek to include women in the public sphere (Echols, 1997). Drawing on reason and rationality, liberal feminists view education as a social institution that can facilitate progress and social reform (Donovan, 1992). Not surprisingly, liberal feminists focus on equal rights in education and advocate for equal educational opportunities for girls and boys. According to this view, providing equal education for both sexes creates environments in which everyone's individual potential is encouraged and developed.

Research on teaching conducted from a liberal perspective focuses on teaching strategies, teacher interactions, and teacher expectations—on how teachers do or do not promote equal educational opportunities for both girls and boys in their classrooms. Such studies were popular during the 1970s and continue during the 1990s; they are attempts to discover the nature of sexism within schools (Adelman, as cited in Delamont, 1990; King, 1978; Leinhardt, Seewald, & Engel, 1979; Sadker & Sadker, 1994).

During the Civil Rights and anti-Vietnam war movements, small groups of women in the United States became disenchanted with the male domination of political organizations and began to organize independent movements for women's liberation (Weiner, 1994). Radical feminist theory was developed by these women reformers in the late 1960s and early 1970s in reaction against the liberal feminist solution of integrating women into the public sphere (Echols, 1997) and the organizational structures of the male-dominated "New Left." Radical feminists assume that the oppression of women is universal and use the concept of patriarchy, or male domination, to analyze the power relationships that have served to create women as the oppressed class (Donovan, 1992). Although different feminisms produce different versions of how patriarchy is constituted, the radical perspective argues that patriarchal ideology is that of male supremacy, permeating every aspect of culture and touching every part of women's lives (Millet, 1971). By articulating the first critiques of the family, marriage, love, normative heterosexuality, and rape, radical feminists began to raise women's consciousness of how patriarchal ideologies are a part of everyday life (Echols, 1997).

Research conducted from a radical feminist perspective tends to focus on the patriarchal processes of schooling and male-dominated power relationships in which heterosexuality and hierarchy combine to construct dominant male and subordinate female power relations (Weiner, 1994). Not only is heterosexuality recognized as a man-made political institution that disempowers and oppresses women, but also it is viewed as compulsory and as a form of sexism that confines girls and women in their subordinate status as feminine (Rich, 1982; Weiner, 1994). Radical feminism critiques the compulsory heterosexuality found within schools and views it as a form of sexism that contributes to gender inequity.

Research on teaching in ECE from a radical feminist perspective is limited. The only study that is radical in orientation is a case study done by Epstein (1995). After providing a "girls only" time for playing blocks, Epstein analyzed a group of children's gendered and heterosexist behavior in the block area. Over time, the girls became more confident in their block building, and the boys' attitudes toward girls as builders changed. Although the girls' constructions were based on domestic narratives, Epstein argues that the enacting of domestic narratives in a masculine domain opened up possibilities for children to reconceptualize their identities as gendered subjects. In her words,

> My view was that allowing girls time on their own would help them to develop their confidence and would at the same time destabilize sexist stereotypes about what girls could and could not do. What I did not anticipate was that this would take place at the same time as the girls position themselves firmly within discourses of femininity which reinscribed conventional (hetero)sexist gendered relations. (p. 66)

For Epstein, (hetero)sexism is a form of sexism; therefore effective antisexist pedagogy must also be antiheterosexist. Furthermore, she argues the need for teachers to introduce alternative and oppositional discourses into the classroom so children can expand their understandings of what it means to be a boy or girl.

Evolving from radical feminism, the cultural feminist perspective is a countercultural movement aimed at reversing the cultural valuation of the male and the devaluation of the female (Echols, 1997). Cultural feminism moves beyond the rationalism of liberal theory toward a broader cultural transformation that emphasizes and values the role of the nonrational, intuitive, relational, and personal side of life (Donovan, 1992). Instead of concentrating on the similarities between women and men, cultural feminism focuses on gender differences in an effort to draw attention to the inequalities between the genders (e.g., Gilligan, 1982). Cultural feminists highly value feminine characteristics such as caring as well as women's experiences, perspectives, and ways of knowing. Additionally, according to this orientation, the ways in which women construct knowledge, solve problems, and interact with the world are distinctly different from the ways of men (Belenky, Clinchy, Goldberger, & Tarule, 1986). Like the liberal perspective, cultural feminism promotes equality in the classroom. However, instead of believing that boys and girls are similar and should be afforded equal educational opportunities, cultural feminists view girls as different so that teaching strategies and curricula that preserve or protect these differences are needed. From this feminist perspective, girls gain equality in the classroom by having their differences recognized and valued.

Cultural feminism seems to be the predominant feminist perspective influencing current EC research on teaching. Much of this research examines and describes the enactment of feminist pedagogy in teacher education and EC classrooms. Feminist pedagogy is attentive to women's ways of knowing. To enact it, teachers articulate "connected knowing," an idea borrowed from Belenky et al. (1986), which is based largely on females' experiential and relational modes of thought. These practices show how cultural feminism confronts gender inequity by concentrating on and valuing the differences between genders. Jipson (1991, 1992), for example, describes her own experiences in the university classroom as she attempted to work with her EC students in more relational and caring ways. In a similar vein, Miller (1992), a university professor collaborating with a group of classroom teachers, describes how they used autobiography to critique definitions of teaching as women's work. Interestingly, while both Jipson and Miller take cultural feminism as a starting point for their research, their inquiries are also critical. That is, both worked with their collaborators to critically examine the political contexts that continue to oppress women and children. In doing so, their research goes beyond description to action.

Hauser and Marrero (1998), a researcher and a first-grade teacher, collaborate to examine how Marrero defines, constructs, and maintains a classroom in which equity is central to its organization. Although each author uses different terms to explain the classroom, gender is present in both of their conceptualizations. Marrero sees her ideas and curriculum on the basis of equity, not gender, and does not relate her practice to feminist theory. At the same time, Hauser interprets Marrero's teaching and viewpoints to be consistent with feminist pedagogy. This collaborative study exemplifies the complexities and contradictions often found within feminism perspectives and research done from a feminist perspective.

Interested in feminist pedagogy for young children, Goldstein (1997) studies the experiences of two primary-grade teachers (Goldstein and a colleague) as they enact a feminist EC curriculum based on the notion of love. Grounded in an ethic of care (Noddings, 1984, 1992) and associated with women and women's ways of knowing (Belenky et al., 1986), this curriculum depends on teachers' mutually caring relationships with their students. Claiming that our educational decisions are made with love for children, Goldstein advocates for love to become a valued and respected source of the EC knowledge base, thus allowing teachers to center their practice and curriculum around love, care, and concern.

In the late 1980s, poststructural feminism emerged to challenge and critique both the women's movement and patriarchal relations that developed out of disillusionment with the dualistic and rationalizing assumptions of Enlightenment thinking (Weiner, 1994). What makes poststructural feminism distinctive is that it "rejects the logic of binary oppositions, the principles of humanism and the unified subject, the Enlightenment legacy, and meta-narratives predicated on unified groups of oppressors and oppressed, and revolutionary agents" (Kenway, Willis, Blackmore, & Rennie 1994, p. 200). Moving away from the universals of liberal and cultural feminisms, this antistructural feminism emphasizes new ways of seeing and knowing while continually seeking to analyze the workings of patriarchy in all its distinct and obscure forms (Weiner, 1994).

Recently a number of studies in ECE, done primarily in Australia and Great Britain, have framed their inquiries by combining a focus on gender with poststructural assumptions about power, knowledge, and subjectivity (Campbell, 1998; Danby, 1998; Danby & Baker, 1997; Davies, 1989; Grieshaber 1993, 1997; Robinson & Jones Diaz, 1996). Walkerdine (1990), for example, examines the construction of gender in a progressive EC classroom, arguing that the child-centered discourse of this pedagogy empowers boys to position girls and female teachers as powerless. Walkerdine argues that female teachers are unwilling to confront issues of sexism within the classroom, because a teacher who enacts child-centered pedagogy views development as a natural process of unfolding in which she or he must nurture and support children.

Using an action research design, MacNaughton (1995a) collaborated with 12 educators to explore how they might challenge traditional sex role stereotypes in their classrooms. Over an 18-month period, these teachers attempted to enact a gender equity curriculum in line with postmodern notions of identity and power relations. Many of these teachers reported struggling with conflicting conceptions of EC curriculum and the role of the teacher. In the framework of a developmentally appropriate, child-centered curriculum, the teachers found that they were expected to accept this curriculum as the truth; yet, in examining their own practices, they discovered that much of what they believed to be an appropriate and inclusive curriculum, in fact, maintained gender dualisms.

Recent Perspectives: Queer and Postcolonial Theories

Little work has been done that uses poststructural theory to frame research studies of EC teaching, and a smaller number of studies are based on poststructural concepts embedded in queer and postcolonial theories.

Queer theory implies the recognition and questioning of concepts of normalization and the privileges found within our heterosexual culture (Britzman, 1995; Warner, 1993). Tobin (1997) attempts to "queer up" ECE by bringing together authors who couple poststructural assumptions of meaning, power, and discourse with questions of subjectivity and desire to inquire into what are considered acceptable practices in ECE. Focusing on the discourse of desire and pleasure, Bailey (1998) explores how teachers and the EC curriculum regulate children's bodies. Interweaving a historical analysis of the body in discourses of rationality with an ethnography of one teacher's practice and her own reflections as a researcher, Bailey explores the tensions inherent in teaching young children when teaching is conceptualized as both objective and intimate.

Another example is the work of Boldt (1997). A classroom teacher concerned by her third graders' responses to a child in the class they perceived to be a "gender bender," Boldt uses queer theory as a tool for rethinking gender equity pedagogies. Johnson (1997), from a different perspective, documents his own experiences as a male teacher working with young children and the stories of other teachers who question "no touch" policies in ECE. His research illustrates how the public discourse of "moral panic" has altered the ways teachers conceptualize and enact their work, particularly the ways in which they touch children.

Postcolonial theory critically interrogates the master discourses of imperial Europe and America and the ongoing material effects of imperialism through the various experiences such as speaking and writing in which individuals participate in their social worlds (Ashcroft, Griffiths, & Tiffin, 1995). Operating across a variety of disciplines, postcolonial studies foreground "the interconnection of race, nation, empire, migration, and ethnicity with cultural production" (Moore-Gilbert, 1997, p. 6). Postcolonial theory has been used in ECE to examine the experiences of native Hawaiian teachers (Hewett, 1998), the colonial discourse pervading Hawaiian studies in the early elementary grades (Thirugnanam, 1998), representations of colonialism in films (Tobin, 1998), and how ethnography colonizes its subjects (Viruru & Cannella, 1998).

In this section, we have provided an overview of alternative approaches to social theory—theoretical approaches, not in the mainstream but at the margin. Because they are outside the mainstream, however, they offer powerful critiques of the usually conservative field of education. The theorists and researchers included here confront issues that often go unaddressed in polite conversation: relationships of power; subordination of less powerful groups such as women, racial minorities, or the colonized; sexism and heterosexism. Further confronting us are poststructuralist notions of fluid subjectivities, unstable meanings that may be interpreted indefinitely, and social relationships in which participants position and reposition themselves and others. These are subversive ideas, ideas that would subvert what poststructuralists would call the traditional EC project, which has been grounded for the past century in psychological theories of development.

Because these alternative theories are intended as critiques, we think that they too need critique. Thus we raise the question, In what ways do these subversive ideas actually influence the EC project? If we take a quantitative measure and count the total number of studies in which critical or poststructural theories are explicitly applied in EC settings, we would say there has been little influence to date. As the approaches are relatively new (compared to developmental theories), we might expect greater influence in the future, but we also recognize that these alternative theories are at the margin of EC discourses for particular reasons.

First, these alternative theorists and researchers intend to subvert or disrupt traditional theories and practices; disruption of the "establishment," including the EC establishment, is usually a long-term challenge. We would not expect to see short-term impact. Second, critical and poststructuralist theories are inaccessible to the vast majority of professionals in ECE. The theorists themselves often write in dense and inaccessible styles, although many of the research studies we reviewed are clear and accessible; with few exceptions, neither the theories nor research have been published in mainstream publications.

Third, EC educators familiar with these alternatives may be wary of a theoretical framework that proclaims its commitment to social action and change, especially when the theories within the framework are written in opaque ways. ECE is often characterized as being oriented more toward action and practice than theory; thus EC educators may claim that they have been engaged in social action since the field's inception. The framework in which they have acted is, of course, a contrast with the critical framework just presented so that recommended actions would differ in each framework. These points having been made—to critique the critiques—we think that the alternative framework must still be valued. For us coauthors the critical and poststructuralist framework offers a place to stand that enables us to question all assumptions and see alternative visions, which we propose in the last section of this chapter. In the next section, we attempt to synthesize the wide range of research and theory presented.

Synthesizing Diversity: Multiple Constructions of Teachers and Teaching

We have reviewed a wide-ranging, sometimes unwieldy, body of research and theory that illustrates the complexity characteristic of ECE. We took on a challenge to explore intersections between research on teaching in elementary education and in ECE and to lay the groundwork for a research agenda that focuses on the complexities of teaching and the importance of the teacher (Goffin, 1989). To anchor our synthesis, we return to the four scenes with which we began the chapter that portray different aspects of teaching young children. The first two involve literacy in contrasting contexts; the third, dramatic play; and the fourth, caregiver-infant interaction. We return as well to the overlapping issues that are illustrated or implicit in the scenes: defining appropriate practices, the nature of teaching in ECE, the role of cultural diversity, representations of teachers, and the relevance of theory.

Which scenes are appropriate? How is teaching represented? The topics, findings, and assumptions of the majority of studies reviewed suggest that direct instruction of skills in reading alone, as illustrated in scene 2, or highly structured curricula in general (Au, 1998; Schweinhart & Weikart, 1997) are inappropriate. But studies, particularly those by teachers, also support

both low-structured and skill-oriented approaches in the context of literacy instruction (Throne, 1994). The teacher as facilitator, intervening minimally when a disagreement arises in scene 3, and as conversational partner or model in scene 4 seem noncontroversial and thus may be inferred to be developmentally appropriate.

We do not know from research findings themselves how to define appropriate practices, especially if we consider the role of cultural diversity. Because our four scenes involve adults working with children who are not their own, the question of appropriateness is made complex. For which children and families are these contexts culturally appropriate? Do they take into account children's cultural and linguistic backgrounds? Are the conversations in scenes 3 and 4 appropriate across families and cultures? Can someone who has conversations with infants claim the status of teacher? Are the activities accessible—are Spanish-speaking children at a disadvantage in scene 1? Are boys excluded in scene 3? Or does the classroom environment strongly invite a girls-only context? We noted that little research on teaching in ECE addresses such difficult questions. Exceptions are some ethnographic (Pease-Alvarez, Garcia, & Espinosa, 1991; Wien, 1995) and teacher research (Ballenger, 1999; Paley, 1995) studies and, with respect to gender, studies done within the critical and poststructuralist framework (Epstein, 1995; MacNaughton, 1995a, 1995b).

As this chapter focuses on teachers and teaching, we continue to address persistent issues in ECE by centering on the representations of teachers encountered in the literature. (We use the term *representation* instead of *role* because the former has greater fluidity. Except in the case of teacher research, others are representing teachers in particular ways, which may or may not coincide with conventional teacher roles.) We refer to our previous categories of research and theory to organize a discussion of representations of teachers and the ways in which these intersect with some representations of children, introduced in the section on historical context. We glean no tidy conclusions, even within categories, although research, particularly related to the process-product and teacher cognition orientations, supports the traditional dichotomy between preschool/kindergarten and early elementary/primary teaching. Thus Britzman's (1986) portrayal of "teacher" is incompatible with that of much of the EC literature:

> Years of classroom experience allow students to have very specific expectations of how teachers should act in the classroom. Students, for example, expect the teacher to maintain classroom control, enforce rules, and present the curriculum. Students expect teachers to be certain in both their behavior and in their knowledge, and students articulate these expectations if the teacher in any way deviates from this traditional image. (p. 445)

In the studies we reviewed, representations of EC teachers as disciplinarians or presenters of curriculum or instructors are found only in some primary-grade classrooms. Disciplinarians are focal in some studies of staff development projects (Mandeville, 1992) or of teacher beliefs (Scott-Little & Holloway, 1992). Instructors emerge in studies that focus on particular subject matter such as spelling (Morris et al., 1995) or mathematics (Kohler et al., 1994). In primary-grade, process-product studies, the assumption seems to be that specific kinds of teacher "input," which sometimes included teacher and peer or student coaching, would be followed by specific student "output" or achievement. In contrast, studies of preschoolers link qualities of teacher-child relationships with outcomes such as strength of children's attachment (Mitchell-Copeland et al., 1997) or play preferences (Swiecicka & Russell, 1991). "Input" and "output" in these cases are much less specific constructs. Thus, we noted earlier that these latter studies are more aptly called "process-process" research.

We could conclude that studies related to subject matter in the primary grades and those related to preprimary learners are like the proverbial apples and oranges, except in one subject matter area—literacy. The appearance of literacy as a common topic suggests a significant intersection between previously separate bodies of research: preschool teachers doing research in their own classrooms as well as researchers in the process-product, teacher cognition, and ecological or ethnographic categories all meet at this intersection. The intersection is unsurprising in light of highly publicized debates involving educators and the general public about the most effective ways of teaching the skill of reading, a skill that has long been seen as the key to (K–12) school achievement. The prevalence of literacy as a topic, however, foregrounds the child as thinker and academic learner and teacher as instructor and, in skills-based classrooms, as technician. Thus, despite the supposed hegemony of DAP, which advocates holistic rather than skills-based approaches to literacy, EC teachers may be increasingly pressed to become instructors, and not mainly facilitators of development or nurturers.

Britzman's folk portrait of the teacher is most compatible with representations within the process-product orientation, which focuses on group findings. Teachers are represented as a group without individual biographies that include ideologies and characteristics such as race, class, gender, disability, or sexual orientation. In contrast, the three other orientations highlight factors other than the teacher (e.g., environmental features) or representations of teachers that are multifaceted. Teacher cognition studies show teachers represented as thinkers or reflectors who are also planners and theorists. They are also believers in ideologies who can often express the values that underlie their practices. No facile connection can be made between the thinking of particular teachers and the ways in which they represent the children they teach. Researchers' questions, instead, shape the facet of teachers' thinking that is explicit. For example, a study in which teachers are presented with hypothetical vignettes about student misbehavior (Kuhns, Holloway, & Scott-Little, 1992) casts the teacher in the role of disciplinarian, whereas a study of preschool teachers' theories of emotion is based on the assumption that teachers are theorists (Delaney, 1995). In the course of the study, teachers may represent themselves as facilitators of development or protectors of children who are, at times, vulnerable innocents.

The categories of research that revealed the most complex representations of teachers were ethnographic, teacher research, and critical and poststructuralist. Whether teachers were identified as researchers or not, their words often appear in these studies; and those words represent people who fit many of the representations already mentioned. In addition, they speak as child development experts, community liaisons, advocates, change agents, mediators of conflict, and collaborators. In short, they show multiplicity, complexity, and struggle; they often struggle with aspects of their work that they do not control (school district or state regulations, parent desires, budgetary shortages), such as in child-care settings where teachers often represent themselves as undervalued professionals (Nelson, 1990; Wolf & Walsh, 1998).

Teachers also struggle with their own beliefs (Paley, 1995; Stires, 1994). If, for instance, one has come to believe that appropriate ways of teaching young children have been developed but that some children in the classroom seem unresponsive to those ways, are one's beliefs faulty? Or are the children not "ready"? Or if one has always believed that ethnic and racial integration is universally good, how does one respond to parents who disagree? Teachers who write about their own practices address such questions. They focus on their experiences with children as they encounter further questions. Thus teacher researchers' audiences may represent them as insightful observer-assessors, writers, and researchers; teachers may represent themselves foremost as learners. They seldom show the certainty that Britzman (1986) attributes to students' representations of teachers. And teacher researchers avoid representations that reduce their children to "innocents" or "at-risk learners." Instead, their children seem to cover a wide and flexible band, in which a child may move from story resistor to story dramatist or behavior problem to problem solver or science expert.

The work reviewed here illustrates how representations of teachers and teaching are constructed more often by those studying teachers than by teachers themselves. At this time the process of "understanding practices" in our chapter title, then, refers primarily to understanding how particular researchers and theorists, with their own political and theoretical commitments, have constructed representations of teachers and teaching. The project that unites the multiple representations—and that teacher researchers share with academic researchers and theorists—is the improvement of practices for the benefit of young children. How this project can move forward in equitable ways is the topic of our final section, where we envision research on teaching in ECE in the years to come.

Visions of the Future: Research on Teaching in the 21st Century

In this section, we sketch a vision of future research that works toward the general goals of improving educational practices for young children and bridging practice, research, and theory. In the center of this vision are teachers and the multifaceted activities of teaching. EC practice, research, and theory merge at this center. As the vision comes to life, conversations are heard in a room with an indeterminate number of people articulating many ideas. From where we sit, we see a truly inclusive gathering. We recognize teachers, academics, policymakers, researchers, theorists, parents, and we hear support for divergent theories and practices: developmental-interactionist, social constructivist, behaviorist, critical and poststructuralist, among others.

A proponent-spokesperson for each theoretical position

summarizes a research agenda that demonstrates how her or his theory may be applied to a program of research that is clearly linked to particular practices. As the developmental-interactionist and social constructivist talk, a number of comments are voiced from other participants about how those theories may already have had too much influence. Still, what seems like a majority of the group speak in support of their agenda. The behaviorist speaks, stating that very few people do purely behavioral research now. Some in the audience respond about how it is time to abandon the simplistic principles of behaviorism and how its influence is still too great, specifically in the form of behaviorist tools such as standardized tests. The behaviorist points out that the behaviorist agenda is always clear and the findings leave no doubt about how teachers behaved and how children responded. Furthermore, the findings are statistically sound and generalizable.

When the poststructuralists take their turn, the discussion alternates between periods of intense argument and periods of silence. They have challenged the foundations of all the other theorists and are ready to articulate their agenda for the future. But several people in the group cut them off, asking how they can disagree with the position that EC educators should respond and relate to children as individuals, within the framework of child development theory. The poststructuralists reply that, within this framework, assumptions have been made about the appropriate ways to educate young children, namely, to become competent and autonomous individuals—a western, masculine ideal. These assumptions lead to a conception of ECE that may exclude the definitions of appropriateness of cultures that are not White and middle class. An argument follows in which one of the developmental-interactionists accuses poststructuralists of arrogance for suggesting that social change is only "worthy" change if it is defined within a poststructuralist framework. A poststructuralist retorts that the developmental-interactionist defines something as change only if it is compatible with Deweyan principles. Trying to return to the substance of recent research on teaching in ECE, a process-product researcher asks why, when researchers in every other orientation are deeply concerned with how children become literate, poststructuralists focus on disunited subjectivities and queer theory. A feminist poststructuralist has a quick response about the importance of seeing literacy instruction within a broader context, long constrained by western and masculine views of learning and literacy.

We step out of this vision, which could be neverending, to articulate our own agenda. It acknowledges the contributions of developmental theory and does not banish a perspective whose goals include the nurturance and education of competent and autonomous individuals, but it is also inclusive of goals other than competence and autonomy.

These are bold and general recommendations for an agenda for the future, based in part on the content of this chapter and in part on our values and commitments:

1. The research we have reviewed clearly shows that teachers doing research in EC classrooms address issues of relevance to the education of individuals and groups. They address them daily in their teaching and write about them in their published work. Thus, along with the findings of researchers in the other three orientations, teachers' research should be included in the knowledge base of ECE and EC teacher education. It should not be dismissed as curious examples of what Gallas (1994) terms aboriginal thinking, and it should also be subject to critique, just as the other orientations are. Incentives, such as free time during the school day, are needed so that the number of teachers studying their classrooms increases significantly.

2. Researchers in the areas of teacher cognition and ethnographic research seem to share methods and concerns with teacher researchers. Their projects in which participants' experiences and voices are foregrounded should continue. Many in this group are concerned with issues of power that arise in the contexts they study, such as family day care or classrooms where teachers and children come from different cultural or linguistic backgrounds. A shared question is, What are appropriate practices for those whom Delpit (1995) has called "other people's children"? With the poststructuralists, we urge the study of particular settings where social factors such as race, class, gender, disability, and sexual orientation are examined and power relationships are destabilized—that is, where teachers are experts alongside other researchers and family members, and administrators and policymakers share power with families and teachers. This destabilization may free us from the myth that educational practices alone (e.g., Head Start, "good" literacy instruction) can improve society.

3. We have avoided much use of the term *effective* because it is often defined narrowly in terms of standardized test scores or behavior management. Still, we support the efforts of researchers in the process-product orientation to discover what is effective in a broad sense—what kinds of teaching enhance children's learning. We are unconvinced that discoveries can be made within a research paradigm that assumes specified teacher behaviors cause specified learner behaviors. Instead, we think that it is necessary to describe learner outcomes (including those of judiciously-used standardized measures) within EC contexts that must also be described. In short, we recommend that "products" be contextualized so that we understand how they came to be constructed and what they mean for learners and teachers. Work such as that by Duffy (1993), related to problem-solving strategies in literacy tasks, moves us in this direction.

4. While exploring the range of research and theory included here, we began to think about how the term *research on teaching* needs to be reconceptualized. After completing our review, we have concluded that the conventional understandings of the term need to be permanently disrupted. Research on teaching should include multiple research perspectives, but have at its core the thoughts and actions of individual teachers (not primarily program effects). Its boundaries need to expand to encompass all the things teaching means when teachers are not mainly instructors in the style depicted by Britzman (1986). For example, in some EC settings children can initiate their own learning or are members of their own cultures (Dyson, 1997b; Gallas, 1998; Martin, 1990). We need more expansive ways of representing teachers in these settings. Moreover, the defi-

nition of research on teaching needs to become more complex in order to include child-care and family day care settings where teaching incorporates care of the very young and frequent communication with family members. Perhaps the next version of this chapter will be about reciprocal processes—about research on or by teachers and learners or about teaching as it is constructed across EC contexts.

5. Although we have focused primarily on research and EC practices in our other recommendations, we know a research agenda must exist in close relationship with theory—or theories. We recommend an attempt to be articulate about our own theoretical commitments, at the same time that we look beyond those commitments. This recommendation may be our most unrealistic, because one's theories determine the ways in which one looks at everything. To the extent possible, however, looking for points of intersection among theoretical perspectives and the research studies they frame may provide the richest possibilities for the improvement of practices—and for understanding how people from different perspectives together can construct practices that benefit young children and families across diverse and sometimes conflicting psychological, social, political, and cultural contexts.

Clearly, having many participants at the EC table will not banish dilemmas. In fact, dilemmas, debates, and conflicts are to be expected. Lubeck (1996, p. 163) notes

> The movement toward fostering "reflective practitioners" . . . and a situated knowledge base is significant, yet it is unlikely to lead us to new consensus. Writers have pointed to the fact that members of marginalized groups have been "silenced" in schools generally and in teacher preparation programs specifically. When everyone is able to speak, we may find that our differences are greater than we realized. . . . As the field of ECE enters the postmodern era, both challenges and possibilities confront us.

Indications of our differences have already surfaced. Different theoretical perspectives are often in conflict with each other, and academics often think that to hold strongly to one theory is a virtue. Significantly, EC teachers have less difficulty than academics in looking beyond single theoretical frameworks. In fact, they can be multitheoretical in their approaches to children (Genishi, Dubetz, & Focarino, 1995; Throne, 1994). Teachers' experiences and personal practical knowledge (Clandinin, 1985) underlie their own interpretations of theory, which are situated, relational, and derived from multiple sources (Richardson, 1994).

Through difficult conversations we can address the relative value of implicit versus academic theory and of research done by teachers versus that done by academics. We can also ask whether it is possible to achieve a delicate balance between participants "being themselves"—deeply committed to developmental or poststructuralist theory, holistic approaches to curriculum or behavioral objectives—and seeing beyond their own commitments to new possibilities. How, for example, are theoretical commitments enacted in research? If two teachers—one who calls herself a feminist and one who initially does not—

study their pedagogy within a feminist framework, should both identify themselves as feminists as a consequence of the study (Hauser & Marrero, 1998)? Can teachers and administrators change their beliefs about the value of retention in the face of research that finds it does not work (Byrnes, 1989)? In other words, is it necessary to disrupt everyone's practices and theories—where does consciousness-raising for educational change end and theoretical imperialism begin? And what are the consequences to young children if practices and theories are or are not disrupted?

We predict that in order to address questions like these, research during the next century on teaching in ECE will be not only challenging—with uncertainty and discomfort always lurking—but also truly exciting. Together, EC practitioners, researchers, and theorists can construct an agenda for thought and action. The challenge is huge, but the possibilities are limitless.

REFERENCES

Allington, R. L., & Woodside-Jiron, H. (1999). The politics of literacy teaching: How "research" shaped educational policy. *Educational Researcher, 28*(8), 4–13.

Almy, M. (1975). *The early childhood educator at work.* New York: McGraw-Hill.

Almy, M., Chittenden, E., & Miller, P. (1966). *Young children's thinking.* New York: Teachers College Press.

Anderson, L., Evertson, C., & Brophy, J. (1979). An experimental study of effective teaching in first-grade reading groups. *Elementary School Journal, 79*(4), 193–223.

Anyon, J. (1994). The retreat of Marxism and social feminism: Postmodern and post-structural theories in education. *Curriculum Inquiry, 24*(2), 115–133.

Apple, M. W., & King, N. R. (1977). What do schools teach? *Curriculum Inquiry, 6*(4), 341–358.

Archer, C., Coffee, M., & Genishi, C. (1985). Research currents: Responding to children. *Language Arts, 62,* 270–276.

Ariès P. (1962). *Centuries of childhood: A social history of family life.* New York: Knopf.

Ashcroft, B., Griffiths, G., & Tiffin, H. (Eds.). (1995). *The post-colonial studies reader.* London: Routledge.

Atkinson, A. M. (1991). Providers' evaluations of family day care services. *Early Childhood Development and Care, 68,* 113–123.

Au, K. H. (1998). Constructivist approaches, phonics, and the literacy learning of students of diverse backgrounds. In T. Shanahan & F. Rodriguez-Brown, *Forty-seventh yearbook of the National Reading Conference* (pp. 1–21). Chicago: National Reading Conference.

Ayers, W. (1989). *The good preschool teacher.* New York: Teachers College Press.

Baer, D., Wolf, M., & Risley, T. (1968). Some current dimensions of applied behavior analysis. *Journal of Applied Behavior Analysis, 1,* 91–97.

Bailey, C. (1998). *Excess, intimacy, and discipline: Curriculum of the body in the early childhood classroom.* Unpublished doctoral dissertation, University of Wisconsin, Madison.

Ballenger, C. (1992). Because you like us: The language of control. *Harvard Educational Review, 62,* 199–208.

Ballenger, C. (1996). Learning the ABC's in a Haitian preschool: A teacher's story. *Language Arts, 73,* 317–323.

Ballenger, C. (1999). *Teaching other people's children: Literacy and learning in a bilingual classroom.* New York: Teachers College Press.

Belenky, M. F., Clinchy, B. M., Goldberger, N. R., & Tarule, J. M. (1986). *Women's ways of knowing: The development of self, voice, and mind.* New York: Basic Books.

Beller, E. K. (1973). Research on organized programs of early education. In R. M. W. Travers (Ed.), *Second handbook of research on teaching* (pp. 530–600). Chicago: Rand McNally.

Bereiter, C., & Engelmann, S. (1966). *Teaching disadvantaged children in the preschool.* Englewood Cliffs, NJ: Prentice-Hall.

Berk, L. E. (1991). *Child development* (2nd ed.). Boston: Allyn & Bacon.

Bernhard, J. K., Lefebvre, M. L., Kilbride, K. N., Chud, G., & Lange, R. (1998). Troubled relationships in early childhood education: Parent-teacher interactions in ethnoculturally diverse child care settings. *Early Education and Development, 9,* 5–28.

Bernstein, R. J. (1976). *The restructuring of social and political theory.* New York: Harcourt Brace Jovanovich.

Beyer, L. E., & Bloch, M. (1996). Theory: An analysis (part 1). In S. Reifel & J. Chafel (Eds.), Advances in early education and day care (Vol. 8, pp. 3–39). Greenwich, CT: JAI Press.

Biber, B., & Franklin, M. B. (1962). The relevance of developmental and psychodynamic concepts to the education of the preschool child. *Journal of the American Academy of Child Psychiatry, 6,* 19.

Biklen, S. K. (1995). *School work: Gender and the cultural construction of teaching.* New York: Teachers College Press.

Billington, R. (1994). Effects of collaborative test taking on retention in eight third-grade mathematics classes. *Elementary School Journal, 95*(1), 23–32.

Bloch, M. (1991). Critical science and the history of child development's influence on early education research. *Early Education and Development, 2,* 95–108.

Blum, A. F. (1971). The corpus of knowledge as a normative order. In M. F. D. Young (Ed.), *Knowledge and control: New directions for the sociology of education* (pp. 117–132). London: Collier-Macmillan.

Boldt, G. (1997). Sexist and heterosexist responses to gender bending. In J. Tobin (Ed.), *Making a place for pleasure in early childhood education* (pp. 188–213). New Haven, CT: Yale University Press.

Bredekamp, S. (1987). *Developmentally appropriate practice in early childhood programs serving children from birth through age 8.* Washington, DC: National Association for the Education of Young Children.

Bredekamp, S., & Copple, C. (1997). *Developmentally appropriate practice in early childhood programs serving children from birth through age 8* (Rev. ed.). Washington, DC: National Association for the Education of Young Children.

Britzman, D. P. (1986). Cultural myths in the making of a teacher: Biography and social structure. *Harvard Educational Review, 56,* 442–456.

Britzman, D. P. (1995). Is there a queer pedagogy or, stop reading straight. *Educational Theory, 45*(2), 151–165.

Bronfenbrenner, U. (1979). *The ecology of human development: Experiments by nature and design.* Cambridge, MA: Harvard University Press.

Brophy, J., & McCaslin, M. (1992). Teachers' reports of how they perceive and cope with problem students. *Elementary School Journal, 93*(1), 2–68.

Brucker, B. W., & Hall, W. H. (1991). AIDS in the classroom: Are teacher attitudes changing. *Early Child Development and Care, 77,* 137–147.

Brucker, B. W., Martin, J. J., & Shreeve, W. C. (1989). AIDS in the classroom: A survey of teacher attitudes. *Early Child Development and Care, 43,* 61–64.

Bryant, D. M., Clifford, R. M., & Peisner, E. S. (1991). Best practices for beginners: Developmental appropriateness in kindergarten. *American Educational Research Journal, 28,* 783–803.

Burman, E. (1994). *Deconstructing developmental psychology.* London: Routledge.

Burton, C. B. (1992). Defining family-centered early education: Beliefs of public school, child care, and Head Start teachers. *Early Education and Development, 3*(1), 47–59.

Bussis, A. M., Chittenden, E. A., Amarel, M., & Klausner, E. (1985). *Inquiry into meaning: An investigation of learning to read.* Hillsdale, NJ: Erlbaum.

Byrnes, D. A. (1989). Attitudes of students, parents, and educators toward repeating a grade. In L. A. Shepard & M. L. Smith (Eds.), *Flunking grades: Research and policies on retention* (pp. 108–131). Philadelphia: Falmer Press.

Calkins, L. (1986). *The art of teaching writing.* Portsmouth, NH: Heinemann.

Campbell, F. A., & Ramey, C. T. (1995). Cognitive and school outcomes for high-risk African-American students at middle adolescence: Positive effects of early intervention. *American Educational Research Journal, 32,* 743–772.

Campbell, S. (1998,). *Multiple meanings—Social justice and equity is part of who I am.* Paper presented at the seventh Reconceptualizing Early Childhood Education in Research, Theory, and Practice Conference, Honolulu, HI.

Cannella, G. S. (1997). *Deconstructing early childhood education: Social justice and revolution.* New York: Peter Lang.

Carlsson-Paige, N., & Levin, D. E. (1987). *The war play dilemma.* New York: Teachers College Press.

Chafel, J., & Reifel, S. (1996). *Advances in early education and day care: Vol. 8. Theory and practice in early childhood teaching.* Greenwich, CT: JAI Press.

Charlesworth, R., Hart, C., Burts, D., Thomasson, R., Mosley, J., & Fleege, P. (1993). Measuring the developmental appropriateness of kindergarten teachers' beliefs and practices. *Early Childhood Research Quarterly, 8,* 255–276.

Cherryholmes, C. H. (1988). *Power and criticism: Post-structural investigations in education.* New York: Teachers College Press.

Ciupryk, F. A., Fraser, B. J., Malone, J. A., & Tobin, K. G. (1989). Exemplary grade 1 mathematics teaching: A case study. *Journal of Research in Childhood Education, 4*(1), 40–50.

Clandinin, D. J. (1985). Personal practical knowledge: A study of teachers' classroom images. *Curriculum Inquiry, 15,* 361–385.

Clark, C. M., & Peterson, P. P. (1986). Teachers' thought processes. In M. C. Wittrock (Ed.), *Handbook of research on teaching* (3rd ed., pp. 255–296). New York: Macmillan.

Clarke, S. H., & Campbell, F. A. (1998). Can intervention early prevent crime later? The Abecedarian Project compared with other programs. *Early Childhood Research Quarterly, 13,* 319–343.

Cleverley, J., & Phillips, D. (1986). *Visions of childhood.* Boston, MA: Allen & Unwin.

Cochran-Smith, M., & Lytle, S. L. (1993). *Inside/outside: Teacher research and knowledge.* New York: Teachers College Press.

Conway, A. (1989). Teachers' explanations for children with learning difficulties: An analysis of written reports. *Early Child Development and Care, 53,* 53–61.

Cox, T. (1996). Teachable moments: Socially constructed bridges. In J. Chafel & S. Reifel (Eds.), *Advances in early education and day care: Vol. 8. Theory and practice in early childhood teaching* (pp. 187–200). Greenwich, CT: JAI Press.

Danby, S. (1998). The serious and playful work of gender: Talk and social order in a preschool classroom. In N. Yelland (Ed.), *Gender in early childhood* (pp. 175–205). New York: Routledge.

Danby, S., & Baker, C. (1997). "What's the problem?" Restoring social order in the preschool classroom. In I. Hutchby & J. Moran-Ellis (Eds.), *Children and social competence: Arenas of action* (pp. 157–186). London: Falmer Press.

Dare, G. J. (1992). The effect of pupil appearance on teacher expectations. *Early Child Development and Care, 80,* 97–101.

Darwin, C. (1936). *The origin of species.* New York: Modern Library. (Original work published 1859)

Davies, B. (1989). *Frogs and snails and feminist tales: Preschool children and gender.* Sydney: Allen & Unwin.

Delamont, S. (1990). *Sex roles and the school* (2nd ed.). New York: Routledge.

Delaney, E. M. (1995). *The implicit theories of emotion of four experienced preschool teachers: A study in teacher thinking.* Unpublished doctoral dissertation, Teachers College, Columbia University, New York.

Delpit, L. (1995). *Other people's children: Cultural conflict in the classroom.* New York: Norton.

Derman-Sparks, L. (1989). *Anti-bias curriculum: Tools for empowering young children.* Washington, DC: National Association for the Education of Young Children.

Deutsch, M. (1967). *The disadvantaged child.* New York: Basic Books.

DeVries, R., Haney, J. P., & Zan, B. (1991). Sociomoral atmosphere in direct-instruction, eclectic, and constructivist kindergartens: A study of teacher enacted interpersonal understanding. *Early Childhood Research Quarterly, 6,* 449–471.

Dewey, J. (1916). *Democracy and education.* New York: Macmillan.

Donovan, J. (1992). *Feminist theory: The intellectual traditions of American feminism.* New York: Continuum.

Duffy, G. G. (1993). Rethinking strategy instruction: Four teachers' development and their low achievers' understandings. *Elementary School Journal, 93*(3), 231–247.

Dyson, A. H. (1989). *Multiple worlds of child writers: Friends learning to write.* New York: Teachers College Press.

Dyson, A. H. (1993). *Social worlds of children learning to write in an urban primary school.* New York: Teachers College Press.

Dyson, A. H. (1997a). *What difference does difference make? Teacher reflections on diversity, literacy, and the urban primary school.* Urbana, IL: National Council of Teachers of English.

Dyson, A. H. (1997b). *Writing superheroes: Contemporary childhood, popular culture, and classroom literacy.* New York: Teachers College Press.

Echols, A. (1997). *Daring to be bad: Radical feminism in America 1967–1975.* Minneapolis, MI: University of Minnesota Press.

Eheart, B. K., & Leavitt, R. L. (1989). Family day care: Discrepancies between intended and observed caregiving practices. *Early Childhood Research Quarterly, 4,* 145–162.

Endsley, R. C., & Minish, P. A. (1991). Parent-staff communication in day care centers during morning and afternoon transitions. *Early Childhood Research Quarterly, 6,* 119–135.

Epstein, D. (1995). Girls don't do bricks: Gender and sexuality in the primary classroom. In J. Siraj-Blatchford and I. Siraj-Blatchford (Eds.), *Educating the whole child: Cross-curricular skills, themes, and dimensions* (pp. 56–69). Bristol, PA: Open University Press.

Erikson, E. H. (1950). *Childhood and society.* New York: W. W. Norton.

Fennimore, B. S. (2000). *Talk matters: Refocusing the language of public schooling.* New York: Teachers College Press.

File, N. (1994). Children's play, teacher-child interactions, and teacher beliefs in integrated early childhood programs. *Early Childhood Research Quarterly, 9,* 223–240.

Foote, M., Stafford, P., & Cuffaro, H. K. (1992). Linking curriculum and assessment in preschool and kindergarten. In C. Genishi (Ed.), *Ways of assessing children and curriculum* (pp. 58–93). New York: Teachers College Press.

Fournier, J., Lansdowne, B., Pastenes, Z., Steen, P., & Hudelson, S. (1992). Learning with, about, and from children: Life in a bilingual second grade. In C. Genishi (Ed.), *Ways of assessing children and curriculum* (pp. 126–162). New York: Teachers College Press.

Frank, L. K. (1938). The fundamental needs of the child. *Mental Hygiene, 22,* 353–379.

Freud, S. (1953). *A general introduction to psychoanalysis* (J. Riviere, Trans.). New York: Pocket Books/Simon & Schuster. (Original work published 1920)

Gallas, K. (1994). *The languages of learning: How children talk, write, dance, draw, and sing their understanding of the world.* New York: Teachers College Press.

Gallas, K. (1995). *Talking their way into science.* New York: Teachers College Press.

Gallas, K. (1998). *Sometimes I can be anything: Gender, power, and identity in the classroom.* New York: Teachers College Press.

Gaskell, J., & Willinsky, J. (Eds.). (1995). *Gender in/forms curriculum: From enrichment to transformation.* New York: Teachers College Press.

Genishi, C. (Ed.). (1992). *Ways of assessing children and curriculum: Stories of early childhood practice.* New York: Teachers College Press.

Genishi, C., & Di Paolo, M. (1982). Learning from argument in a preschool. In L. C. Wilkinson (Ed.), *Communicating in the classroom.* New York: Academic Press.

Genishi, C., Dubetz, N., & Focarino, C. (1995). Reconceptualizing theory through practice: Insights from a first grade teacher and second language theorists. In S. Reifel (Ed.), *Advances in early education and day care* (Vol. 7, pp. 123–152). Greenwich, CT: JAI Press.

Gilligan, C. (1982). *In a different voice.* Cambridge, MA: Harvard University Press.

Giroux, H. (1983). *Critical theory and educational practice.* Victoria, Australia: Deakin University.

Goffin, S. G. (1989). Developing a research agenda for early childhood education: What can be learned from the research on teaching? *Early Childhood Research Quarterly, 4,* 187–204.

Goffin, S. G. (1994). *Curriculum models and early childhood education: Appraising the relationship.* New York: Merrill.

Goldstein, L. (1997). *Teaching with love: A feminist approach to early childhood education.* New York: Peter Lang.

Gordon, I. J., & Jester, R. E. (1973). Techniques of observing teaching in early childhood education and outcomes of particular procedures. In R. M. W. Travers (Ed.), *Second handbook of research on teaching* (pp. 184–217). Chicago: Rand McNally.

Gore, J. M. (1993). *The struggle for pedagogies: Critical and feminist discourses as regimes of truth.* New York: Routledge.

Graue, M. E. (1992). Meanings of readiness and the kindergarten experience. In S. Kessler & B. B. Swadener (Eds.), *Reconceptualizing the early childhood curriculum* (pp. 62–90). New York: Teachers College Press.

Graves, D. (1983). *Writing: Teachers and children at work.* Exeter, NH: Heinemann.

Greenberg, P. (1990). Head Start—Part of a multi-pronged anti-poverty effort for children and their families . . . Before the beginning: A participant's view. *Young Children, 4*(6), 40–52.

Grieshaber, S. (1993). *Parent and child conflict: A poststructuralist study of four families.* Unpublished doctoral dissertation, James Cook University, North Queensland, Australia.

Grieshaber, S. (1997). Mealtime rituals: Power and resistance in the construction of family mealtime rules. *British Journal of Sociology, 48,* 648–666.

Habermas, J. (1971). *Theory and practice.* Boston, MA: Beacon.

Hadley, P. A., Wilcox, K. A., & Rice, M. L. (1994). Talking at school: Teacher expectations in preschool and kindergarten. *Early Childhood Research Quarterly, 9,* 111–129.

Hains, A. H., Fowler, S. A., Schwartz, I. S., Kottwitz, E., & Rosenkoetter, S. (1989). A comparison of preschool and kindergarten teacher expectations for school readiness. *Early Childhood Research Quarterly, 4,* 75–88.

Hall, G. S. (1895). Child study as a basis for psychology and psychological teaching. In *Proceedings of the International Congress of Education of the World's Columbian Exposition* (2nd ed., pp. 717–718). New York: National Educational Association.

Halliwell, G. (1992). Practical curriculum theory: Describing, informing and improving early childhood practices. In B. Lambert (Ed.), *Changing faces: The early childhood profession in Australia.* Yass, N. S. W.: Australian Early Childhood Association.

Hatch, J. A., & Freeman, E. B. (1988). Kindergarten philosophies and practices: Perspectives of teachers, principals, and supervisors. *Early Childhood Research Quarterly, 3*(2), 151–166.

Haupt, J., Larsen, J., Robinson, C., & Hart, C. (1995). The impact of DAP inservice training on the beliefs and practices of kindergarten teachers. *Journal of Early Childhood Teacher Education, 16,* 12–18.

Hauser, M., & Jipson, J. (Eds.). (1998). *Intersections: Feminisms/Early childhoods.* New York: Peter Lang.

Hauser, M., & Marrero, E. (1998). Story #6 Challenging curricular conventions: Is it feminist pedagogy if you don't call it that? In M. Hauser & J. Jipson (Eds.), *Intersections: Feminisms/Early childhoods* (pp. 142–153). New York: Peter Lang.

Heilbrun, C. G. (1988). *Writing a woman's life.* New York: Ballantine.

Held, D. (1980). *Introduction to critical theory: Horkheimer to Habermas.* Berkeley, CA: University of California Press.

Hewett, K. (1998). *Can I be myself, be Hawaiian, and be a teacher?: The experiences of native Hawaiian student teachers in the DOE and COE.* Paper presented at the seventh Reconceptualizing Early Childhood Education in Research, Theory, and Practice Conference, Honolulu, HI.

Hicks, D. (1995–96). Discourse, learning, and teaching. In M. Apple (Ed.), *Review of research in education* (No. 21, pp. 49–95). Washington, DC: American Educational Research Association.

Hill, P. S., Burke, A., and others. (1923). *A conduct curriculum for the kindergarten and first grade.* New York: Scribner.

Hogan, E., Ispa, J. M., & Thornburg, K. R. (1991). Mother-provider interaction and the provider-child relationship in family child care homes. *Early Child Development and Care, 77,* 57–65.

Horm-Wingerd, D. M., Carella, P. C., & Warford, S. D. (1993). Teachers' perceptions of the effectiveness of transition classes. *Early Education and Development, 4*(2), 130–138.

Howes, C. (1997). Teacher sensitivity, children's attachment and play with peers. *Early Education and Development, 8*(1), 41–49.

Howes, C., & Hamilton, C. E. (1993). The changing experience of child care: Changes in teachers and in teacher-child relationships and children's social competence with peers. *Early Childhood Research Quarterly, 8,* 15–32.

Hyson, M. C., & Lee, K. (1996). Assessing early childhood teachers' beliefs about emotions: Content, contexts, and implications for practice. *Early Education and Development, 7*(1), 59–78.

Isaacs, S. (1968). *The nursery years.* New York: Schocken. (Original work published 1932)

James, A., & Prout, A. (Eds.). (1997). *Constructing and reconstructing childhood: Contemporary issues in the sociological study of childhood.* Washington, DC: Falmer Press.

Jenks, C. (Ed.). (1982). *The sociology of childhood: Essential readings.* London: Batsford.

Jensen, A. (1969). How much can we boost I Q. and scholastic achievement? *Harvard Educational Review, 39,* 1–123.

Jersild, A. T. (1946). *Child development and the curriculum.* New York: Bureau of Publications, Teachers College, Columbia University.

Jipson, J. (1991). Developmentally appropriate practice: Culture, curriculum, connections. *Early Education and Development, 2,* 120–136.

Jipson, J. (1992). The emergent curriculum: Contextualizing a feminist perspective. In S. Kessler & B. B. Swadener (Eds.), *Reconceptualizing the early childhood curriculum: Beginning the dialogue* (pp. 149–161). New York: Teachers College Press.

Johnson, H. M. (1928). *Children in the nursery school.* New York: John Day.

Johnson, R. (1997). The "no-touch" policy. In J. Tobin (Ed.), *Making a place for pleasure in early childhood education* (pp. 101–118). New Haven, CT: Yale University Press.

Kaiser, J., Rogers, C. S., & Kasper, A. (1993). Perceptions of well-being among child care teachers. *Early Child Development and Care, 87,* 15–28.

Karweit, N. (1993). Effective preschool and kindergarten programs for students at risk. In B. Spodek (Ed.), *Handbook of research on the education of young children* (pp. 385–411). New York: Macmillan.

Katz, L. G. (1996). Child development knowledge and teacher preparation: Confronting assumptions. *Early Childhood Research Quarterly, 11,* 135–146.

Kennedy, M. (1996). A teachable moment and the never-ending story. In J. Chafel, & S. Reifel (Eds.), *Advances in early education and day care: Vol. 8. Theory and practice in early childhood teaching* (pp. 201–216). Greenwich, CT: JAI Press.

Kenway, J., Willis, S., Blackmore, J., & Rennie, L. (1994). Making "hope practical" rather than "despair convincing": Feminist post-structuralism, gender reform, and educational change. *British Journal of Sociology of Education, 15*(2), 187–210.

Kessler, S. (1992). The social context of the early childhood curriculum. In S. Kessler & B. B. Swadener (Eds.), *Reconceptualizing the early childhood curriculum: Beginning the dialogue* (pp. 21–42). New York: Teachers College Press.

Kessler, S., & Swadener, B. (1992*). Reconceptualizing the early childhood curriculum: Beginning the dialogue.* New York: Teachers College Press.

King, R. (1978). *All things bright and beautiful?* Chichester: Wiley.

Knudsen-Lindauer, S. L., & Harris, K. (1989). Priorities for kindergarten curricula: Views of parents and teachers. *Journal of Research in Childhood Education, 4*(1), 51–61.

Kohler, F. W., Ezell, H. Hoel, K., & Strain, P. S. (1994). Supplemental peer practice in a first-grade math class: Effects on teacher behavior and five low achievers' responding and acquisition of content. *Elementary School Journal, 4,* 389–403.

Kohler, F. W., McCullough, K. M., & Buchan, K. A. (1995). Using peer coaching to enhance preschool teachers' development and refinement of classroom activities. *Early Education and Development, 6*(3), 215–239.

Kounin, J., & Gump, P. (1974). Signal systems of lesson settings and the task-related behavior of preschool children. *Journal of Educational Psychology, 66,* 554–562.

Kuhns, C. L., Holloway, S., & Scott-Little, M. C. (1992). Mothers' and childcare providers' cognitive, affective, and behavioral responses to children's misbehavior. *Early Education and Development, 3*(3), 232–243.

Lareau, A. (1989). *Home advantage: Social class and parental intervention in elementary education.* Philadelphia: Falmer Press.

Lather, P. (1991). *Getting smart: Feminist research and pedagogy with/in the postmodern.* New York: Routledge.

Leavitt, R. (1994). *Power and emotion in infant-toddler day care.* Albany, NY: State University of New York Press.

Leinhardt, G. M., Seewald, A., & Engel, M. (1979). Learning what's taught: Sex differences in instruction. *Journal of Educational Psychology, 71*(4), 432–439.

Lensmire, T. (1995). *When children write: Critical re-visions of the writing workshop.* New York: Teachers College Press.

Lepine, S. (1996). Children's notion of structure: Exploring thematic interdisciplinary instruction with pre-kindergarten students. In J. Chafel & S. Reifel (Eds.), *Advances in early education and day care: Theory and practice in early childhood teaching* (Vol. 8, pp. 217–236). Greenwich, CT: JAI Press.

Lieber, J., Beckman, P. J., Hanson, M., & Janko, S. (1997). The impact of changing roles on relationships between professionals in inclusive programs for young children. *Early Education and Development, 8,* 67–82.

Lubeck, S. (1985). *Sandbox society: Early education in black and white America.* London: Falmer Press.

Lubeck, S. (1991). Reconceptualizing early childhood education: A response. *Early Education and Development, 2*(2), 168–174.

Lubeck, S. (1996). Deconstructing "child development knowledge" and "teacher preparation." *Early Childhood Research Quarterly, 11,* 147–167.

Luke, C., & Gore, J. (1992). *Feminisms and critical pedagogy.* New York: Routledge.

MacNaughton, G. (1995a). *Transforming gendering in early childhood centers: An action research project.* Unpublished doctoral dissertation, Deakin University, Victoria, Australia.

MacNaughton, G. (1995b). Who's got the power? Rethinking gender equity strategies in early childhood. *International Journal of Early Years Education, 5* (1), 57–66.

Mallory, B. L., & New, R. S. (Eds.). (1994). *Diversity and developmentally appropriate practices: Challenges for early childhood education.* New York: Teachers College Press.

Mandeville, G. K. (1992). Does achievement increase over time? Another look at the South Carolina PET program. *Elementary School Journal, 93*(2), 117–129.

Marsh, M. (1992). Implementing anti-bias curriculum in the classroom. In S. Kessler & B. B. Swadener (Eds.), *Reconceptualizing the early childhood curriculum: Beginning the dialogue* (pp. 267–288). New York: Teachers College Press.

Martin, A. (1990). Social studies in kindergarten: A case study. *Elementary School Journal, 90,* 305–317.

McGill-Franzen, A. M. (1993). *Shaping the preschool agenda: Early literacy, public policy, and professional beliefs.* Albany, NY: State University of New York Press.

McIntyre, E. (1995). The struggle for developmentally appropriate literacy instruction. *Journal of Research in Childhood Education, 9,* 145–156.

McLean, S. V. (1991). *The human encounter: Teachers and children living together in preschools.* London: Falmer Press.

McMillan, M. (1919). *The nursery school.* New York: E. P. Dutton.

Middleton, S. (1993). *Educating feminists: Life histories and pedagogy.* New York: Teachers College Press.

Miller, J. L. (1992). Teachers, autobiography, and curriculum: Critical and feminist perspectives. In S. Kessler & B. B. Swadener (Eds.), *Reconceptualizing the early childhood curriculum: Beginning the dialogue* (pp. 103–121). New York: Teachers College Press.

Millet, K. (1971). *Sexual politics.* London: Hart Davis.

Mitchell, L. S. (1991). *Young geographers.* New York: Bank Street College of Education. (Original work published 1934)

Mitchell-Copeland, J., Denham, S. A., & DeMulder, E. K. (1997). Q-sort assessment of child teacher attachment relationships and social competence in the preschool. *Early Education and Development, 8*(1), 27–39.

Montessori, M. (1964). *The Montessori method.* New York: Schocken. (Original work published 1909).

Moore-Gilbert, B. (1997). *Postcolonial theory: Contexts, practices, politics.* London: Verso.

Morris, D., Blanton, L., Blanton, W. E., Nowacek, J., & Perney, J. (1995). Teaching low-achieving spellers at their "instructional level." *Elementary School Journal, 96*(2), 163–177.

National Center for the Early Childhood Workforce. (1993). *Who cares? Childcare, teachers, and the quality of care in America.* Washington, DC: Author.

Neale, D.C., Smith, D., & Johnson, V. G. (1990). Implementing conceptual change teaching in primary science. *Elementary School Journal, 91*(2), 109–131.

Neill, A. S. (1960). *Summerhill.* New York: Hart Publishing Co.

Nelson, M. K. (1990). *Negotiated care: The experience of family day care providers.* Philadelphia: Temple University Press.

New, R. S., & Mallory, B. L. (1994). Introduction: the ethic of inclusion. In B. L. Mallory & R. S. New (Eds.), *Diversity and developmentally appropriate practices: Challenges for early childhood education* (pp. 1–13). New York: Teachers College Press.

Noddings, N. (1984). *Caring.* Berkeley, CA: University of California Press.

Noddings, N. (1992). *The challenge to care in schools.* New York: Teachers College Press.

Oakes, P. B., & Caruso, D. A. (1990). Kindergarten teachers' use of developmentally appropriate practices and attitudes about authority. *Early Education and Development, 1*(6), 445–457.

O'Brien, L. (1993). Teacher values and classroom culture: Teaching and learning in a rural, Appalachian Head Start program. *Early Education and Development, 4*(1), 5–18.

Ochsner, M. (1997). *Feminist perspectives on gender differences and their implications for gender equity within the early childhood classroom.* Unpublished manuscript, Teachers College, Columbia University.

Ochsner, M., & Ryan, S. (1997). *Feminisms and teaching: The ambiguities of working in a female dominated profession.* Paper presented at the conference of Feminism and the Academy: Building Bridges to the World Outside, New York.

Ogilvy, C. M., Boath, E. H., Cheyne, W. M., Jahoda, G., & Schaffer, R. (1990). Staff attitudes and perceptions in multicultural nursery schools. *Early Child Development and Care, 64,* 1–13.

Pace, G. (1992). Stories of teacher-initiated change from traditional to whole-language literacy instruction. *Elementary School Journal, 92,* 451–465.

Paley, V. (1979). *White teacher.* Cambridge, MA: Harvard University Press.

Paley, V. (1981). *Wally's stories.* Cambridge, MA: Harvard University Press.

Paley, V. (1984). *Boys and girls: Superheroes in the doll corner.* Chicago: University of Chicago Press.

Paley, V. (1995). *Kwanzaa and me: A teacher's story.* Cambridge, MA: Harvard University Press.

Paley, V. (1997). *The girl with the brown crayon.* Cambridge, MA: Harvard University Press.

Pease-Alvarez, L., Garcia, E. E., & Espinosa, P. (1991). Effective instruction for language-minority students: An early childhood case study. *Early Childhood Research Quarterly, 6,* 347–363.

Peters, D. (1993). Trends in demographic and behavioral research on teaching in early childhood settings. In B. Spodek (Ed.), *Handbook of research on the education of young children* (pp. 493–505). New York: Macmillan.

Phillips, A. (1987). *Feminism and equality.* New York: New York University Press.

Piaget, J., & Inhelder, B. (1969). *The psychology of the child* (H. Weaver, Trans.). New York: Basic Books.

Pinar, W. (Ed.). (1975). *Curriculum theorizing: The reconceptualists.* California: McCutchan.

Pines, M. (1966). *Revolution in learning: The years from birth to six.* New York: Har/Row Books.

Polakow, V. (1989). Deconstructing development. *Journal of Education, 171*(2), 75–87.

Polakow, V. (1992). *The erosion of childhood.* Chicago: University of Chicago Press.

Popkewitz, T. S. (1984). *Paradigm and ideology in educational research: The social functions of the intellectual.* New York: Falmer Press.

Popkewitz, T. S. (1995). Foreword. In P. L. McLaren & J. M. Giarelli (Eds.), *Critical theory and educational research* (pp. xi–xxii). Albany, NY: State University of New York Press.

Popkewitz, T. S., & Brennan, M. (1998). Restructuring a social and political theory in education: Foucault and a social epistemology of school practices. In T. S. Popkewitz & M. Brennan (Eds.). *Foucault's challenge: Discourse, knowledge, and power in education* (pp. 3–35). New York: Teachers College Press.

Pound, L. (1989). You can always tell a good nursery by its ammunition box: Intentions underlying practice in nursery school and classes. *Early Child Development and Care, 49,* 75–90.

Rennebohm-Franz, K. (1996). Toward a critical social consciousness in children: Multicultural peace education in a first grade classroom. *Theory Into Practice, 35,* 264–270.

Rich, A. (1982). Compulsory heterosexuality and the lesbian existence. *Signs: Journal of Women in Culture and Society, 5,* 631–660.

Richards, M. P. M. (Ed.). (1974). *The integration of a child into a social world.* Cambridge, UK: Cambridge University Press.

Richardson, V. (1994). Conducting research on practice. *Educational Researcher, 23*(5), 5–10.

Robinson, K., & Jones Diaz, C. (1996). *Doing theory with early childhood educators: A feminist poststructuralist approach to difference and diversity in personal and professional contexts.* Paper presented at the sixth Reconceptualizing Early Childhood Education in Research, Theory, and Practice Conference, Madison, WI.

Ropers-Huilman, B. (1998). *Feminist teaching in theory and practice: Situating power and knowledge in poststructural classrooms.* New York: Teachers College Press.

Rosenthal, M. K. (1991). Behaviors and beliefs of caregivers in family day care: The effects of background and work environment. *Early Childhood Research Quarterly, 6,* 263–283.

Roskos, K., & Neuman, S. (1993). Two beginning kindergarten teachers' planning for integrated literacy instruction. *Elementary School Journal, 96*(2), 195–214.

Ross, S. M., Smith, L. J., Lohr, L., & McNelis, M. (1994). Math and reading instruction in tracked first-grade classes. *Elementary School Journal, 95,* 105–119.

Sadker, M., & Sadker, D. (1994). *Failing at fairness: How our schools cheat girls.* New York: Simon & Schuster.

Saracho, O. N. (1989). An analytic scheme to compare the early childhood teachers' classroom behaviors and environment. *Early Child Development and Care, 49,* 37–55.

Sarup, M. (1993). *An introductory guide to post-structuralism and postmodernism* (2nd ed.). Athens, GA: University of Georgia Press.

Saunders, W., & Goldenberg, C. (1996). Four primary teachers work to define constructivism and teacher–directed learning: Implications for teacher assessment. *Elementary School Journal, 97,* 139–161.

Savitch, J. H., & Serling, L. A. (1997). "I wouldn't know I was smart if I didn't come to this class." In A. L. Goodwin (Ed.), *Assessment for equity and inclusion: Embracing all our children* (pp. 141–161). New York: Routledge.

Scales, B. (1996). Researching the hidden curriculum. In J. Chafel & S. Reifel (Eds.), *Advances in early education and day care: Theory and practice in early childhood teaching* (Vol. 8, pp. 237–259). Greenwich, CT: JAI Press.

Schweinhart, L. J., & Weikart, D. P. (1997). The High/Scope preschool curriculum comparison study through age 23. *Early Childhood Research Quarterly, 12,* 117–143.

Scott-Little, M. C., & Holloway, S. D. (1992). Child care providers' reasoning about misbehaviors: Relation to classroom control strategies and professional training. *Early Childhood Research Quarterly, 7,* 595–606.

Sears, P. S., & Dowley, E. (1963). Research on teaching in the nursery school. In N. L. Gage (Ed.), *Handbook of research on teaching* (pp. 814–864). Chicago: Rand McNally.

Seifert, K. L. (1991). *What develops in informal theories of development.* (ERIC Document Reproduction Service, No. ED 342 489)

Shapiro, E., & Biber, B. (1972). The education of young children: A developmental-interaction approach. *Teachers College Record, 74,* 55–79.

Sharp, R., & Green, A. (1975). *Education and social control: A study in progressive primary education.* London: Routledge and Kegan Paul.

Shulman, L. (1986). Paradigms and research programs in the study of teaching: A contemporary perspective. In M. C. Wittrock (Ed.), *Handbook of research on teaching* (3rd ed., pp. 3–36). New York: Macmillan.

Silin, J. (1982). *Protection and control: Early childhood teachers talk about authority.* Unpublished doctoral dissertation, Teachers College, Columbia University, New York.

Silin, J. (1995). *Sex, death, and the education of children: Our passion for ignorance in the age of AIDS.* New York: Teachers College Press.

Skinner, B. F. (1953). *Science and human behavior.* New York: Macmillan.

Smith, A. B., McMillan, B. W., Kennedy, S., & Ratcliff, B. (1992). Early childhood teachers: Roles and relationships. *Early Child Development and Care, 83,* 33–44.

Smith, K. E. (1997). Student teachers' beliefs about developmentally appropriate practice: Pattern, stability, and the influence of locus of control. *Early Childhood Research Quarterly, 12,* 221–243.

Smith, M. L. (1989). Teachers' beliefs about retention. In L. A. Shepard & M. L. Smith (Eds.), *Flunking grades: Research and policies on retention* (pp. 132–150). London: Falmer Press.

Smith, M. L., & Shepard, L. A. (1988). Kindergarten readiness and retention: A qualitative study of teachers' beliefs and practices. *American Educational Research Journal, 25*(3), 307–333.

Snider, M. H., & Fu, V. R. (1990). The effects of specialized education and job experience on early childhood teachers' knowledge of developmentally appropriate practice. *Early Childhood Research Quarterly, 5,* 69–78.

Spodek, B. (1987). Thought processes underlying preschool teachers' classroom decisions. *Early Child Care and Development, 29,* 197–208.

Spodek, B. (Ed.). (1993). *Handbook of research on the education of young children.* New York: Macmillan.

Stallings, J. A., & Stipek, D. (1986). Research on early childhood and elementary school teaching programs. In M. C. Wittrock (Ed.), *Handbook of research on teaching* (3rd ed., pp. 727–753). New York: Macmillan.

Stein, N. (1995). Sexual harassment in school: The public performance of gendered violence. *Harvard Educational Review, 65*(2), 145–162.

Stipek, D. J., & Byler, P. (1997). Early childhood teachers: Do they practice what they preach. *Early Childhood Research Quarterly, 12,* 305–325.

Stires, S. (1990). Growing as a writer: L. D. and all. In Center for Teaching and Learning, *Insights* (pp. 6–12). Grand Forks, ND: Center for Teaching and Learning.

Stires, S. (1991). *With promise: Redefining reading and writing for "special" students.* Portsmouth, NH: Heinemann.

Stires, S. (1994). Lessons from Little Bear. In C. Dudley-Marling & D. Searle (Eds.), *Who owns learning?* (pp. 93–111). Portsmouth, NH: Heinemann.

Stott, F., & Bowman, B. (1996). Child development knowledge: A slippery base for practice. *Early Childhood Research Quarterly, 11,* 169–183.

Swadener, B. B., & Piekeilek, D. (1992). Beyond democracy to consensus: Reflections on a Friends school. In S. Kessler & B. B. Swadener (Eds.), *Reconceptualizing the early childhood curriculum: Beginning the dialogue* (pp. 227–255). New York: Teachers College Press.

Swiecicka, E. W., & Russell, A. (1991). The play preferences of preschool girls and boys: The effects of program structure and teacher participation. *Early Child Development and Care, 74,* 109–121.

Tharp, R. G., & Gallimore, R. (1988). *Rousing minds to life: Teaching, learning, and schooling in social context.* Cambridge, UK: Cambridge University Press.

Thirugnanam, J. (1998). *Colonialism and Hawaiian Studies in Hawaii's elementary schools: A post-structural critique.* Paper presented at the seventh Reconceptualizing Early Childhood Education in Research, Theory, and Practice Conference, Honolulu, HI.

Thorndike, E. L. (1906). What is "scientific method" in the study of education? In M. J. Holmes (Ed.), *On the teaching of English in elementary and high schools: Vol. 5. Yearbook of the National Society for the Study of Education* (part 1, pp. 81–82). Chicago: University of Chicago Press.

Throne, J. (1994). Living with the pendulum: The complex world of teaching. *Harvard Educational Review, 64,* 195–208.

Tizard, B., Cooperman, O., Joseph, A., & Tizard, J. (1972). Environmental effects on language development. *Child Development, 43,* 337–358.

Tobin, J. (1995). Post-structural research in early childhood education. In A. Hatch (Ed.), *Qualitative research in early childhood settings* (pp. 223–243). Westport, CT: Praeger.

Tobin, J. (Ed.). (1997). *Making a place for pleasure in early childhood education.* New Haven, CT: Yale University Press.

Tobin, J. (1998). *Young children's representations of colonialism in films.* Paper presented at the seventh Reconceptualizing Early Childhood Education in Research, Theory, and Practice Conference, Honolulu, HI.

Tomchin, E. M., & Impara, J. C. (1992). Unraveling teachers' beliefs about grade retention. *American Educational Research Journal, 29*(1), 199–223.

Viruru, R., & Cannella, G. S. (1998). *Postcolonial ethnography, young children, and voice.* Paper presented at the seventh Reconceptualizing Early Childhood Education in Research, Theory, and Practice Conference, Honolulu, HI.

Walkerdine, V. (1990). *Schoolgirl fictions.* London: Verso.

Walsh, D. J. (1991). Extending the discourse on developmental appropriateness: A developmental perspective. *Early Education and Development, 2*(2), 109–119.

Walsh, D. J., Baturka, N. L., Smith, M. E., & Colter, N. (1991). Changing one's mind—Maintaining one's identity: A first-grade teacher's story. *Teachers College Record, 93,* 73–86.

Walsh, D. J., Smith, M. E., Alexander, M., & Ellwein, M. C. (1993). The curriculum as mysterious and constraining: Teachers' negotiations of the first year of a pilot programme for at-risk 4-year-olds. *Journal of Curriculum Studies, 25*(4), 317–332.

Walsh, D. J., Tobin, J., & Graue, E. (1993). The interpretive voice: Qualitative research in early childhood education. In B. Spodek (Ed.), *Handbook of research on the education of young children* (pp. 464–476). New York: Macmillan.

Warner, M. (1993). *Fear of a queer planet: Queer politics and social theory.* Minneapolis, MI: University of Minnesota Press.

Weber, E. (1984). *Ideas influencing early childhood education: A theoretical analysis.* New York: Teachers College Press.

Weedon, C. (1997). *Feminist practice and poststructuralist theory* (2nd ed.) London: Blackwell Publishers.

Weiler, K. (1992). Introduction. In K. Weiler & C. Mitchell (Eds.), *What schools can do: Critical pedagogy and practice* (pp. 1–10). Albany, NY: State University of New York Press.

Weiner, G. (1994). *Feminisms in education: An introduction.* Philadelphia: Open University Press.

Wexler, P. (1987). *Social analysis of education: After the new sociology.* London: Methuen.

Wien, C. A. (1995). *Developmentally appropriate practice in "real life": Stories of teacher practical knowledge.* New York: Teachers College Press.

Wing, L. (1989). The influence of preschool teachers' beliefs on young children's conceptions of reading and writing. *Early Childhood Research Quarterly, 4*(1), 61–74.

Wittrock, M. C. (Ed.). (1986). *Handbook of research on teaching* (3rd ed.). New York: Macmillan.

Wolf, J. M., & Walsh, D. J. (1998). "If you haven't been there, you don't know what it's like": Doing day care. *Early Education and Development, 9,* 29–47.

Wrigley, J. (Ed.). (1992). *Education and gender equality.* Washington, DC: Falmer Press.

Yonemura, M. (1986). *A teacher at work: Professional development and the early childhood educator.* New York: Teachers College Press.

About the Contributors

Frank Achtenhagen is Professor for Economics and Business Education and Management Training, at Georg-August-University, Göttingen. He has won many national and international awards and is author of over 300 publications. He is Editor of *Unterrichtswissenschaft,* Advisory Editor of *LLinE* (Lifelong Learning in Europe), and former Editor of *Teaching and Teacher Education* and *Studies in Educational Evaluation.* His research interests include teaching and learning in the field of economics and business education and management training in schools and enterprises; long-term studies on teaching-learning processes; lifelong learning; curriculum development; performance assessment; and development of virtual environments and multimedia equipment.

Ann E. Austin is Associate Professor in the Higher, Adult, and Lifelong Education (HALE) Program at Michigan State University. Her research and publications concern faculty careers, roles, and professional development, teaching and learning issues in higher education, and organizational change and transformation in higher education. She was a Fulbright Fellow in South Africa in 1998, and serves as the 2000–2001 President of the Association for the Study of Higher Education (ASHE). In 1998, she was named one of the 40 "Young Leaders of the American Academy" by *Change: The Magazine of Higher Learning.*

Franz J. Baeriswyl is Honorary Professor of Didactics and Educational Psychology at the Department of Education, University of Fribourg, Switzerland. He is Director of the Section for College Teacher Education. He received his M.A. (1977) and his Ph.D. (1985) from the University of Fribourg. He spent one year of postgraduate research with Prof. W. Kintsch at the University of Colorado at Boulder. He is the Chief-Editor of *Schweizerische Zeitschrift far Bildungswissenschaften* (Swiss Journal of Educational Science) and Co-Editor of *Autonomie und Entwicklung* (Autonomy and Development) (1999). His research focuses on student assessment and learning concepts of adults.

Scott Baker received his Ph.D. in school psychology in 1993. Since then he has pursued a full-time research career at Eugene Research Institute and the University of Oregon. His research interests include the prevention of reading difficulties, learning disabilities, and the education of English-language learners. Baker is currently Principle Investigator on three research projects funded by Office of Special Education Programs.

Deborah Loewenberg Ball is Arthur F. Thurnau Professor of Mathematics Education and Teacher Education at the University of Michigan. An experienced elementary teacher, Ball conducts research on instruction and on the processes of learning to teach. She also investigates efforts to improve teaching through policy, curriculum, reform initiatives, and teacher education. Ball has received the American Educational Research Association's Cattell Early Career Award for Programmatic Research, and the Association of Colleges and Schools of Education in State Universities and Land Grant Colleges and Affiliated Private Universities Award for Outstanding Scholarship on Teacher Education. Ball's publications include articles on teacher learning and teacher education; the role of subject matter knowledge in teaching and learning to teach; endemic challenges of teaching; and the relations of policy and practice in instructional improvement.

Rebecca Barr is Professor of Education at National-Louis University. Her research and teaching focus on understanding the difficulties some children encounter as they learn to read and write and the challenges faced by classroom teachers as they develop experiences to support the reading and writing development of their students. She has written several books and many articles based on her clinical research and on her longitudinal studies of literacy development in classrooms.

Victor A. Battistich is Deputy Director of Research at the Developmental Studies Center (DSC), Oakland, California. He received a Ph.D. in Social Psychology from Michigan State University. Before coming to DSC, he was Assistant Professor of Psychology at Cleveland State University. His research interests and recent publications focus on the influence of social context, particularly schools, on children's social, ethical, and intellectual development. He has been conducting research on the Child Development Project since its inception in 1981.

James A. Beane is Professor in the National College of Education, National-Louis University. He has written extensively on curriculum design theory, curriculum integration, democratic schools, and affective dimensions of curriculum and teaching.

Sari Knopp Biklen is Laura and Douglas Meredith Professor at Syracuse University and Chair of Cultural Foundations of Education. She is the current recipient of the American Association of Women University Scholar Award for her research, *Vocabularies of Gender.* Her books include *School Work: Gender and the Cultural Construction of Teaching* (Teachers' College Press, 1995) and *Qualitative Research for Education, 3rd edition* (Allyn & Bacon, 1998) with Robert Bogdan, and *Gender and Education* (1993) with Diane Pollard. She directs the Institute on Popular Culture, Media, and Education at Syracuse University, where research projects focus on the intersection of youth, schooling, and popular culture. She is finishing a book on *The Qualitative Dissertation* (Teachers College Press).

Katherine C. Boles, Lecturer on Education at the Harvard Graduate School of Education, teaches about school reform and new forms of teacher leadership. Boles co-taught a fourth grade class at the Edward Devotion School, a public school in Brookline, Massachusetts, until 1999. She was a classroom teacher for over 25 years, and in that capacity co-founded the Learning/ Teaching Collaborative, a Professional Development School that links the public schools of Boston and Brookline with Wheelock College and Simmons College in Boston. Boles earned her doctorate in 1991 from Harvard and is the author of articles and chapters that focus on teacher leadership and school restructuring initiated by teachers. With co-author Vivian Troen, she is currently completing a book titled: *Who's Teaching Your Children? Why the Teacher Crisis Is Worse Than You Think and What Can Be Done About It.*

Barbara L. Brodhagen is a middle school teacher in the Madison Metropolitan Schools, Madison, Wisconsin. She has written and consulted widely on curriculum integration, democratic classrooms, and action research. She is a K–12 Carnegie Scholar and former Chair of the Curriculum Committee of the National Middle School Association. She received her doctorate from the University of Wisconsin–Madison.

Carlton E. Brown is the 11th President of Savannah State University. He received his B.A. in English with an emphasis in American studies from the University of Massachusetts at Amherst in 1971. After completing his undergraduate degree, he worked as a teacher and counselor in an inner-city alternative high school. He returned to the University of Massachusetts where he completed his doctoral studies in 1979, earning an Ed.D. in multicultural education with an emphasis in educational change and organizational development. Brown served on the faculty of the School of Education of Old Dominion University in Virginia from 1979 to 1987. In 1987, he joined the faculty of Hampton University in Virginia as Dean of the School of Education, and in 1996 he was appointed Vice-President for Planning and Dean of the Graduate College. He currently sits on the boards of the National Association for Equal Opportunity in Higher Education (NAFEO) and the Business, Education and Technology Alliance.

Bertram (Chip) C. Bruce is a Professor of Library & Information Science, Curriculum & Instruction, Bioengineering, and Writing Studies at the University of Illinois at Urbana/Champaign. His current research focuses on how communication and information technologies can support inquiry teaching and learning. He has written widely and developed software, including Quill, an integrated computer-based writing program; Statistics Workshop, an interactive system for learning statistical reasoning; and Discoveries, a series of CD/ROM-based multimedia environments for supporting students' interdisciplinary inquiry.

Nicholas C. Burbules is Professor of Educational Policy Studies at the University of Illinois, Urbana/Champaign. His research includes the areas of philosophy of education, technology and education, and critical social and political theory. His most recent books include *Watch IT: The Promises and Risks of Information Technologies for Education* (with Thomas A. Callister, Jr., Westview Press, 2000); *Postpositivism and Educational Research* (with D.C. Phillips, Rowman and Littlefield Publishers, 2000); and *Globalization and Education: Critical Perspectives* (edited with Carlos Torres, Routledge, 2000). He is the current Editor of *Educational Theory.*

James Calderhead is Professor of Education and Dean at the University of Bath in England. He has published widely in the field of teachers' expertise and teacher education, having authored eight books and over 50 chapters and articles. He is Past President of the European Educational Research Association, and has served on the Editorial Boards of six international education journals. His current research interests are forms of professional learning and the impact of professional education and training.

David Chard, Ph.D., is Assistant Professor at the University of Oregon and serves as Director of Graduate Studies for Special Education. Formerly, he was Assistant Director of the Texas Center for Reading and Language Arts at the University of Texas at Austin. His research and teaching interests are in the instruction and assessment of early literacy and mathematics skills for students at risk for school failure. Currently he is studying the professional development of teachers in the area of effective beginning reading instruction.

Cynthia Colbert is Chair of the Art Education Division, Professor of Art in the Department of Art at the University of South Carolina where she holds the Louis Fry Scudder Professorship of Liberal Arts. Her research and writing have focused on developmental issues of drawing, language development, memory, and aesthetic response with preschool and middle elementary children. Her research has been published in *Art Education, Studies in Art Education, Visual Arts Research, The Canadian Review of Art Education Research,* and *Childhood Education.* She is completing a 5-year study of the artistic development of children in an elementary art classroom.

Michael Cole received his Ph.D. from Indiana University in 1962. He is Professor of Communication and Psychology and Director of the Laboratory of Comparative Human Cognition at the University of California, San Diego. He has long conducted research on the problem of culture and human development with a special emphasis on influence of education as a sociocultural institution. At present, his research focuses on development in after-school educational institutions and the issue of how to sustain successful educational innovations.

David Coulter recently joined the Faculty of Education at The University of British Columbia after working 25 years in Canadian public schools. He has been a teacher in both elementary and secondary schools, a consultant, a principal, and a superintendent. His latest career change is motivated by curiosity about how educational practice might be better understood and improved. This has led him to investigate teacher research, hermeneutics and dialogue, and especially the work of Bakhtin and Habermas.

John Crawford is Assistant to the Superintendent for Planning, Evaluation, and Information Services, Millard Public Schools, Omaha, Nebraska. His doctorate degree is from the University of Texas at Austin. Book chapters, books, and journal articles have focused on research on teaching, evaluation of programs (especially programs for academically at-risk students), educational planning, school effects, and assessment. Publications have appeared in the *Journal of Educational Psychology, Journal of School Psychology, Elementary School Journal, Educational Planning,* and the *ERS Spectrum.*

Linda Darling-Hammond is Charles E. Ducommun Professor of Education at Stanford University's School of Education where she is faculty sponsor for the teacher education program. She is also Executive Director of the National Commission on Teaching and America's Future which produced the 1996 widely cited blueprint for education reform: *What Matters Most: Teaching for America's Future.* Darling-Hammond's research, teaching, and policy work focus on teaching and teacher education, school restructuring, and educational equity. She has been active in the development of standards for teaching, having served as a two-term member of the National Board for Professional Teaching Standards and as Chair of the Interstate New Teacher Assessment and Support Consortium (INTASC) committee that drafted model standards for licensing beginning teachers. She is author of *The Right To Learn, A License to Teach,* and *Professional Development Schools: Schools for Developing a Profession,* along with several other books and more than 200 book chapters, journal articles, and monographs on education.

Mary E. Dilworth is Vice-President for Research and Information Services for the American Association of Colleges for Teacher Education and also serves as Director of the ERIC Clearinghouse on Teaching and Teacher Education. She oversees the development of a number of research, equity, and technology projects and publications designed to enhance teacher education and professional development. She has written and edited numerous books, articles, and reports, most notably, *Teachers' Totter: A Report on Teacher Certification Issues, Reading Between the Lines: Teachers and Their Racial/Ethnic Cultures, Diversity in Teacher Education: New Expectations* (Jossey-Bass), and *Being Responsive to Cultural Differences: How Teachers Learn* (Corwin Press).

Robert Donmoyer has worked as an elementary school teacher, middle school principal and central office administrator, and university professor and administrator. Currently he is a faculty member and administrator at the University of San Diego. His research centers on issues of research and evaluation utilization in educational practice and policymaking. As part of this work, he has explored alternative methods of doing and reporting research. Most recently, with his wife, June Yennie-Donmoyer, a classroom teacher, he has experimented with and written about using drama as a mode of qualitative data display. He served as Editor of the AERA publication, *Educational Researcher* from 1996 through 1998.

Margaret Eisenhart is Professor of Educational Anthropology and Research Methodology, University of Colorado, Boulder. She received her Ph.D. in anthropology from the University of North Carolina at Chapel Hill and was a member of the College of Education Faculty at Virginia Tech for 7 years before moving to the University of Colorado. Her research and publications have focused on two topics: what students learn about race, gender, and academic content knowledge both inside and outside of U.S. schools, and applications of ethnographic methodology in educational research. She is co-author of *Educated in Romance: Women, Achievement and College Culture* (with D. Holland, University of Chicago Press, 1990), *Designing Classroom Research* (with H. Borko, Allyn & Bacon, 1993), and *Succeeding in Science: Women and Learning from the Margins of Practice* (with E. Finkel and others, University of Chicago Press, 1998).

Robert E. Floden is Director of the Institute for Research on Teaching and Learning and Professor of Teacher Education and Measurement & Quantitative Methods at Michigan State University. Floden has addressed educational issues in teaching, teacher education, philosophy, measurement, and policy. He has published in the *Handbook of Research on Teaching, 3rd edition,* the *Handbook of Research on Teacher Education,* and numerous journals and books. He is currently studying connections between policy and practice.

Sarah Warshauer Freedman is Professor of Education at the University of California, Berkeley and was Director of the National Center for the Study of Writing and Literacy from 1985 to 1996. She is the author of *Exchanging Writing, Exchanging Cultures: Lessons in School Reform from the United States and Great Britain,* published by Harvard University Press; *Response to Student Writing,* published by the National Council of Teachers of English; and *The Acquisition of Written Language,* published by Ablex. Her latest book, *Inside City Schools: Literacy Learning in Multicultural Classrooms* (1999, Teachers College Press), with Elizabeth Simons, Julie Kalnin, Alex Casareno, and the M-Class teams, highlights the results of a national action research project conducted by teachers in four urban cities. Freedman has also authored numerous journal articles and book chapters. She is a two-time winner of the National Council of Teachers of English (NCTE) Richard Meade Award for her writing in English education and a two-time winner of the Ed Fry Book Award from the National Reading Conference. She has been a Resident at the Rockefeller Foundation's Bellagio Study and Conference Center, and a Fellow at the Center for Advanced Studies in the Behavioral Sciences. She has chaired the Board of Trustees for the NCTE Research Foundation, served on the Board for the McDonnell Foundation's Cognitive Studies in Educational Practice program, assisted in planning and served on the Children Television Workshop's National Advisory Board, and regularly consults for national programs in the area of English language arts.

Ana Maria Araújo Freire holds a doctorate in education from the Pontificia Universidade Catolica de Sao Paulo. For the last three decades, her research has focused on the historical factors that produce illiteracy. During her marriage to Paulo Freire, she collaborated on several books with him by writing extensive notes that provided readers with the historical context to understand the work of Freire. She is also the author of several books, including *Nita e Paulo: Cronicas de Amor,* published by Olho d'Agua in Sao Paulo.

Margaret A. Gallego is Associate Professor at San Diego State University in the School of Teacher Education and is Project Scientist at the Laboratory of Comparative Human Cognition, University of California, San Diego. She has served as Chair of the American Educational Research Association's Committee on the Role and Status of Women in Research and Development (CRSWRD) and Chair of the Committee of Multicultural Issues for the National Reading Conference. She has also served on the Editorial Board of the *Journal of Literacy Research.* Her research has focused on the sociocultural influences within learning environments including schools and after-school clubs that support second language learners' English literacy development. She has also published in the areas of teacher staff development, heterogeneous classrooms, writing and learning disabilities, multiple literacies, and feminist and action research.

Jim Garrison is Professor of Philosophy of Education at Virginia Tech. His research interests focus on the philosophy of John Dewey. He has published over 50 papers on Dewey and his books include *The New Scholarship on Dewey* (Kluwer Academic Publishers, 1995) and *Dewey and Eros* (Teachers College Press, 1997). He wrote the chapter on Education for the companion volume to *The Collected Works of John Dewey* edited by Larry Hickman, Director of the Center for Dewey Studies. He was an invited participant at the World Congress of Philosophy in 1998 and a guest of the University of Calabria in Cosenza, Italy in 2000 for the inauguration of the European John Dewey Society. He is a Past President of the Philosophy of Education Society.

Celia Genishi, a former preschool and secondary Spanish teacher, is Professor of Education in the Department of Curriculum and Teaching, Teachers College, Columbia University. Previously she taught at the University of Texas at Austin and Ohio State University. She is currently at work on a book about children's language in contexts of difference and is Editor of *Ways of Assessing Children and Curriculum* and co-author (with Anne Haas Dyson) of *Language Assessment in the Early Years.* She is Co-Editor (with Dorothy S. Strickland) of the Language and Literacy book series published by Teachers College Press. Her publications and primary interests are related to young children's language use in the classroom, childhood bilingualism, and collaborative research with early childhood practitioners.

Russell Gersten is Professor in the College of Education at the University of Oregon and Director of the Eugene Research In-

stitute. His major research interests are education of English-language learners, studies of implementation and change in teaching, and instructional research on students with disabilities.

Kim C. Graber is Associate Professor with the Departments of Kinesiology and Curriculum/Instruction at the University of Illinois in Urbana/Champaign. Her research focuses on preservice teacher education, specifically the process by which undergraduate students learn to teach. Her interests include studying both prospective teachers and teacher educators, primarily from a naturalistic perspective. Her current research endeavors have included investigating the micropolitics of a teacher education faculty, examining the powerful socializing experiences that were designed by the faculty of an unusually successful undergraduate teacher education program, and examining the degree to which studentship would emerge if it was deliberately monitored and confronted by a teacher educator. She has served on numerous committees for scholarly and professional organizations, is a member of the Editorial Board of the *Journal of Teaching in Physical Education,* and has served as Chair of the Curriculum and Instruction Academy for the National Association for Sport and Physical Education.

Maxine Greene is Professor of Philosophy and Education (Emeritus) at Teachers College, Columbia University where she still teaches as an adjunct. Past President of AERA and the Philosophy of Education Society, she has written six books, the most recent being *The Dialectic of Freedom* and *Releasing Imagination.* She is Founder and Director of the Center for Social Imagination, under whose rubric she conducts "educational salons" at her home and a large national conference.

Jennifer C. Greene received her Ph.D. in educational psychology from Stanford University in 1976, a time when quantitative approaches to applied social research were dominant and unchallenged. Her early and continued immersion in field research and evaluation led her to join others in acquiring appreciation for qualitative and other alternative inquiry frameworks. From 1983 to 1999, she was on the faculty at Cornell University where she pursued her research interests and publications in qualitative, participatory, and mixed-method approaches to applied social inquiry. She now promotes these same interests at the University of Illinois at Urbana-Champaign. She has written widely on these issues, including a co-edited volume of *New Directions for Evaluation* (No. 74) on mixing methodologies for program evaluation.

Pamela L. Grossman is Professor of English Education in the School of Education at Stanford University. Her research interests include the content and processes of teacher education, the connection between professional knowledge and professional preparation in teaching, the teaching of English in secondary schools, and the role of subject matter in high school teaching. Her publications include: *The Making of a Teacher: Teacher Knowledge and Teacher Education,* a co-edited volume (with Sam Wineburg) entitled *Interdisciplinary Curriculum: Challenges to Implementation,* as well as articles in *Teachers College Record, American Educational Research Journal, Educational Researcher,*

Journal of Literacy Research, Teaching and Teacher Education, Review of Research in Education, among others. Her most recent research includes a 4-year longitudinal study of beginning language arts teacher and a study of the formation of professional community among teachers. She has recently served as Member-at-Large for the American Educational Research Association and on the Standing Committee on Research for the National Council of Teachers of English.

W. Norton Grubb is Professor and the David Gardner Chair in Higher Education at the School of Education, the University of California, Berkeley. He was Site Director of the former U.S. National Center for Research in Vocational Education at the University of California, Berkeley, between 1988 and 2000. He has published extensively on a variety of topics in the economics of education, public finance, education policy, community colleges, "second chance" programs including job training, adult education, and welfare to work, and social policy for children and youth. His book on teaching in community colleges, *Honored But Invisible: An Inside Look at Teaching in Community Colleges,* was published in March 1999 by Routledge. He is the author of *Learning to Work: The Case for Re-integrating Education and Job Training* (Russell Sage Foundation, 1996); *Working in the Middle: Strengthening the Education and Training of the Middle-Skilled Labor Force* (Jossey-Bass, 1996); and *Education for Occupations in American High Schools* (Teachers College Press, 1995), a two-volume edited work on the integration of academic and occupational education. He received his doctorate in economics from Harvard University.

Sigrún Gudmundsdóttir is Professor of Education in Didaktikk at the Department of Education at the Norwegian University of Science and Technology, in Trondheim, Norway. Her research interests include narrative inquiry, teacher development, classroom research, biography, and a sociocultural approach to mentoring. She is the former Associate Editor of *Teaching and Teacher Education.* In 1997 she edited a theme issue on Narrative Perspectives on Research on Teaching and Teacher Education for *Teaching and Teacher Education.* She has written books (with her students) on classroom research, and journal articles in Swedish, Norwegian, Spanish, and German. Her English language publications include *European Journal of Teacher Education, Curriculum Inquiry, Journal of Curriculum Studies,* and *Journal of Teacher Education.*

David Hamilton is Professor of Education at the University of Umeå, Sweden. Having taking his doctorate in the study of classroom life in secondary schools (University of Edinburgh, 1973), he has spent periods working at the University of Glasgow, the Scottish Council for Research in Education, and the Universities of East Anglia and Liverpool. His interest in classroom life has expanded across time and space to embrace research into different manifestations of schooling, and their association with key educational concepts such as curriculum, catechesis, class, pedagogy, and didactic. While expanding these ideas as they relate to the beginnings of modern schooling (1500–1700), he also examines the exigencies of contemporary classroom life to defend the thesis that education might still be validly regarded as a practical science.

Charles R. Hancock is Associate Dean for Curriculum & Programs and Professor of Foreign/Second Language Education at The Ohio State University, where he has also served as language coordinator. He has published in the major professional journals, including *Modern Language Journal, French Review,* and *Foreign Language Annals.* His research interests include teacher education, methods of foreign language learning, assessment and testing, and cultural factors in language learning. His previous professional service has included the presidencies of the American Council on the Teaching of Foreign Languages (ACTFL) at the national level and the Maryland and Ohio Foreign Language Associations at the state level. He has also worked as a member of the Board of Directors of both The Northeast Conference and the Central States Conference on Language Teaching. In 1994, he edited a volume of the Northeast Conference on the Teaching of Foreign Languages (NEC), entitled *Teaching, Testing, and Assessment: Making the Connection,* that has had wide acceptance.

David T. Hansen is Professor in the College of Education, University of Illinois at Chicago. He teaches in the doctoral program in Curriculum & Instruction and directs the College's Secondary Teacher Education Program. He received his B.A. and Ph.D. degrees from the University of Chicago and his M.A. from Stanford University. Hansen is the author of several books, including the recently published *Exploring the Moral Heart of Teaching,* and he has contributed numerous articles on the philosophy and practice of teaching. A former Reviews Editor for *The Journal of Curriculum Studies,* he now serves on the editorial board of several leading research journals. He is a past recipient of a National Academy of Education Spencer Post-Doctoral Fellowship, and was recently named a University Scholar by the University of Illinois for excellence in teaching and research.

Meredith I. Honig co-authored her chapter in the *Handbook* while a doctoral candidate in Administration and Policy Analysis at Stanford University's School of Education. Her areas of research, teaching, and practice include: policy implementation, organizational studies, urban education, social and child policy, and school–community collaboration.

Kenneth R. Howe is Professor in the School of Education, University of Colorado at Boulder, specializing in educational ethics and philosophy of education. He has published the *Ethics of Special Education* (with Ofelia Miramontes), *Understanding Equal Education: Social Justice, Democracy and School,* and *Values in Evaluation and Social Research* (with Ernest House). Professor Howe teaches courses in the teacher certification program and the graduate program in Educational Foundations, Policy, and Practice.

James C. Impara is the Director, Buros Institute of Assessment Consultation and Outreach, University of Nebraska-Lincoln. He is Editor/Co-Editor of several books and book series: *Licensure Testing, Multicultural Assessment;* The *Mental Measurements Yearbook* series, *Tests in Print* series, *Buros Desk Reference* series, and *The Buros/Nebraska Series on Testing and Measurement.* He is Co-Editor of *Applied Measurement in Ed-*

ucation. His major areas of research interest are applied measurement, standard setting, and test validation. Major publication outlets are *Journal of Educational Measurement* and *Educational Measurement: Issues and Practice.*

Susan Moore Johnson is Carl H. Phorzheimer, Jr. Professor at the Harvard Graduate School of Education, where she served as Academic Dean from 1993 to 1999. A former high school teacher and administrator, Johnson studies school organization and educational policy. She received her A.B. degree (1967) in English literature from Mount Holyoke College and her M.A.T. degree (1969) in English and her Ed.D degree (1982) in Administration, Planning, and Social Policy from the Harvard Graduate School of Education. Johnson is the author of many published articles and three books: *Teacher Unions in Schools* (1984), *Teachers at Work* (Basic Books, 1990), and *Leading to Change: The Challenge of the New Superintendency* (Jossey-Bass, 1996). She is currently heading up a multi-year research project, "The Next Generation of Teachers."

Joseph Kahne is Associate Professor and Director of the doctoral program in Educational Leadership at Mills College where he also directs the Institute for Civic Leadership. He writes on urban school reform, youth development programs, and the democratic purposes of schooling.

Patti Lather is Professor in the School of Educational Policy and Leadership at The Ohio State University where she teaches qualitative research in education and feminist pedagogy. Her work includes *Getting Smart: Feminist Research and Pedagogy with/in the Postmodern* (Routledge, 1991) and, with Chris Smithies, *Troubling the Angels: Women Living with HIV/AIDS* (Westview/Harper Collins, 1997). She has written articles for *Sociological Quarterly, Qualitative Inquiry, Harvard Educational Review,* and *Qualitative Studies in Education.* She received a 1989 Fulbright Lectureship in New Zealand, a 1995 sabbatical appointment as a Fellow at the Humanities Research Institute, University of California-Irvine, and a Spring 1997 visiting appointment at Goteborg University in Sweden.

Mary Leach is Associate Professor in the College of Education, The Ohio State University. She is in the School of Policy and Leadership in the section of Cultural Studies. Her areas of interest and scholarship are the foundations of education, particularly cultural, critical studies, and educational theory. She is active in the Philosophy of Education Society, American Educational Studies Association, American Educational Research Association, and The John Dewey Society. Her work has appeared in *Educational Theory, Harvard Educational Review, Philosophical Issues in Education,* and *Qualitative Studies in Education.*

Gaea Leinhardt, Senior Scientist, Learning Research and Development Center and Professor, School of Education, University of Pittsburgh, coordinates the Cognitive Studies in Education program and is Co-Principal Investigator for the Museum Learning Collaborative and the Teaching Causal Reasoning Online projects. Over the past 25 years she has conducted quantitative and qualitative research that addresses issues of effectiveness, teaching, and learning by examining classroom discourse, activities, and the specifics of subject-matter teaching. Her evaluation work has ranged from large-scale studies of federally funded programs to state and local programs. Her current research interests focus on how people learn in informal settings such as museums and in web-based environments. She has published over 100 articles in major educational research journals and she is the Co-Editor of three books (*Analysis of Arithmetic for Mathematics Teaching,* 1992; *Teaching and Learning in History,* 1994; and *Learning Conversations in Museum,* in press). She has been a Fellow at the Center for Advanced Study in the Behavioral Sciences and has won awards from the American Educational Research Association, the National Council on Geographic Education, and the American Federation of Teachers. She has been a member of several NRC panels on education.

Sarah Theule Lubienski is Assistant Professor of mathematics education in the Department of Curriculum and Instruction at Iowa State University. Combining qualitative and quantitative methods, Lubienski conducts research on equity in mathematics education, with attention to social class, race, gender, and their intersections. In this era of pedagogical and curricular reform, she is particularly interested in ways in which students' class/ethnic backgrounds influence their experiences with various instructional approaches.

Donaldo Macedo is Distinguished Professor of Liberal Arts and Education at the University of Massachusetts in Boston. His research interests are linguistics, literacy, and critical pedagogy. His publications include *Issues in Portuguese Bilingual Education* (1980), *Literacy: Reading the Word and the World* (with Paulo Freire, 1987), and *Literacies of Power: What Americans Are Not Allowed to Know* (1984). He also co-authored *Ideology Matters* with Paulo Freire.

Andrea K. Martin is Research Associate and Adjunct Professor in the Faculty of Education, Queen's University, Kingston, Ontario. Her research interests include teaching exceptional children and adolescents, literacy interventions, and the development of teachers' knowledge.

Milbrey W. McLaughlin is David Jacks Professor of Education and Public Policy, Director of the John Gardner Center for Youth and their Communities, and Co-Director of the Center for Research on the Contest of Teaching at Stanford University's School of Education. Her research focuses on community-based organizations for youth, policy implementation, and planned change in school, district, and community settings.

Erica McWilliam is Associate Professor in the School of Cultural and Language Studies, Faculty of Education, at the Queensland University of Technology, Australia. With a background in high school teaching, she completed her doctorate, an inquiry into the needs of preservice teachers, at the University of Queensland in 1992. Her current research interests cover a wide spectrum, as is evidenced in her publications, which range from pedagogy and erotics to postmodernism and research methodology. Her books *In Broken Images: Feminist Tales for Different*

Teacher Education (Teachers College Press, 1994), *Pedagogy, Technology and The Body* (with Peter G. Taylor, Peter Lang, 1996), and *Pedagogical Pleasures* (Peter Lang, 1999) map new modes of pedagogical work and inquiry within and outside the classroom.

Robert J. Menges was Professor and Program Director of the Center for the Teaching Professions at Northwestern University and Senior Researcher with the National Center on Postsecondary Teaching, Learning, and Assessment. He had a distinguished career as a scholar of higher education, publishing many books and articles on teaching, learning, curriculum, and faculty development, and serving as Editor-in-Chief of *New Directions for Teaching and Learning.* In 1991, he was honored by the American Educational Research Association with the W. K. McKeachie Achievement Award for significant and sustained contributions to the evaluation and development of faculty in postsecondary education. He died suddenly in 1998. The writing of this chapter with Ann Austin was almost complete at the time of his death. He is greatly missed.

Carmen I. Mercado is Associate Professor in the School of Education of Hunter College of the City University of New York. She received her Ph.D.in language and literacy from Fordham University in 1988. A native of Puerto Rico, she has extensive experience as a bilingual teacher and a teacher educator in New York City. Collaborative action research with teachers, students, and their families on sociocultural resources for learning in low-income communities has been her primary line of inquiry. Part of this work includes the study of biliteracy among Latino youth in bilingual and nonbilingual settings.

Denise Spangler Mewborn is Associate Professor of Mathematics Education at the University of Georgia. Her research addresses preservice elementary teachers' sense-making practices in the mathematics classroom and the role that teachers' mathematical content knowledge plays in the crafting of their instructional practices. Mewborn has published articles on the reflective thinking of elementary mathematics teachers, the design of field experiences in mathematics methods courses, and school–university partnerships in teacher education.

Luis C. Moll is Professor in the Department of Language, Reading and Culture, College of Education, University of Arizona. He has conducted educational research with language minority students for the past 22 years. Among other studies, he has analyzed the quality of classroom teaching, examined literacy instruction in English and Spanish, studied how literacy takes place in the broader social contexts of households and community life, and attempted to establish pedagogical relationships among these domains of study. He is presently conducting a longitudinal study of biliteracy development in children and the language ideologies that mediate that development. He was elected member of the National Academy of Education in 1998.

Greta Morine-Dershimer is Emeritus Professor at the University of Virginia's Curry School of Education, and Editor of the international journal, *Teaching and Teacher Education.* She completed her Ed.D. at Teachers College, Columbia University in

1965, and taught at Hofstra University, California State University at Hayward, and Syracuse University, as well as conducting research at the Far West Laboratory for Educational Research and Development. She was Vice President of AERA for Division K, Teaching and Teacher Education, from 1988 to 1990. Her research has focused on teacher and pupil cognitions.

Hugh Munby is Professor of Education, Queen's University, Kingston, Ontario, where he has taught in the graduate and preservice programs since 1971. In 1996, he received the Whitworth Award for Educational Research from the Canadian Education Association, recognizing his research contributions to fields such as science education and teachers' knowledge. His recent publications include *Teachers and Teaching: From Classroom to Reflection* (edited with Tom Russell) and *Finding a Voice While Learning to Teach* (edited with Derek Featherstone and Tom Russell).

Nel Noddings is Lee Jacks Professor of Education Emerita, Stanford University. She is the author of 12 books and more than 160 articles and chapters. Her latest books are *Starting at Home: Caring and Social Policy* (University of California Press) and *A Sympathetic Alternative to Character Education* (Teachers College Press).

Susan E. Noffke was a teacher of elementary and middle school-aged children for 10 years. She is currently Associate Professor of Curriculum & Instruction at the University of Illinois–Urbana/Champaign where she works with preservice and inservice teachers and with the graduate program in Curriculum and Teacher Education. Her writings address historical, conceptual, and field-based work with action research and the nature of collaborations between universities and schools. She has published numerous book chapters and articles, including "Professional, Personal and Political Dimensions of Action Research" which appeared in the *Review of Research in Education,* and is Co-Editor (with Robert Stevenson) of *Educational Action Research: Becoming Practically Critical.*

Mindy Ochsner, a former kindergarten and second grade teacher, is Assistant Professor in the Department of Elementary Education at Rhode Island College where she teaches undergraduate and graduate courses in early childhood education. Currently she is involved in a qualitative and field-based inquiry, supported by the Spencer Foundation, entitled "Locating, Sustaining, and Disrupting Gender Discourses: A Feminist Poststructuralist Study of Gender in Three Kindergarten Classrooms." Her primary research interests focus on feminisms and gender and their implications for researching, teaching, and learning in early childhood education.

Allan Odden is a Professor of Educational Administration at the University of Wisconsin–Madison. He is Director of the CPRE Education Finance Research Program and Principal Investigator for the CPRE Teacher Compensation project. He formerly was Professor of Educational Policy and Administration at the University of Southern California and Director of Policy Analysis for California Education (PACE), an educational policy studies consortium of USC, Stanford University, and the University of California, Berkeley. Odden has written widely, publishing over 70 journal articles, book chapters, and research reports and 20 books and monographs. He has consulted for the U.S. Congress, the U.S. Secretary of Education, governors, state legislators, chief state school officers, and many local school districts, national and local unions, the National Alliance for Business, the Business Roundtable, and New American Schools.

Fritz K. Oser is Professor of Education and Educational Psychology and Director of the Department of Education, University of Fribourg, Switzerland. He received his M.A. (1973) and Ph.D. (1975) from the University of Zurich. He was a Postdoctoral Fellow at the University of California at Los Angeles and at Harvard University, working with Richard Shavelson and Lawrence Kohlberg. In 1987, he received a doctor honoris causa of the University of Mainz, Germany. His research focuses, on the one hand, on standards of the teacher training process, on choreographies of teaching, and on working for the creation of Just Community Schools —involving teachers, administrators, and students—that foster justice, mutual respect, and caring classrooms. On the other hand, his research focuses on developmental issues like moral development, the ontogenetic course of the ethos of teachers, the development of the conceptions of future and of the so-called negative knowledge, which is generated through learning from mistakes. Publications include chapters in *Handbook of Research on Teaching, 3rd edition* (edited by W. Wittrock, Rand McNally, 1986), and *Review of Research in Education, Vol. 20* (edited by L. Darling-Hammond, 1994). He is the Co-Editor of *Moral Education: Theory and Application* (with M. W. Berkowitz, Lawrence Erlbaum Associates, 1984) and *Effective and Responsible Teaching: The New Synthesis* (with A. Dick & J. L. Patry, Jossey Bass, 1992).

Peggy Placier is Associate Professor in Educational Leadership and Policy Analysis at the University of Missouri in Columbia. A former early childhood teacher and administrator, she received her M.A. in anthropology and her Ph.D. in foundations of education from the University of Arizona. She teaches foundations of education at the undergraduate level, and educational policy and research methods at the graduate level. Her areas of research are the language and culture of educational policymaking and the effects of institutional cultures and structures on teaching practice. She is currently working on a National Science Foundation-funded project on socialization of preservice teachers in a restructured teacher education program.

Diane Pollard is Professor of Educational Psychology at the University of Wisconsin–Milwaukee. She has conducted research in two areas. One concerns the intersections of race and gender and their implications for teaching. The other focuses on psychological, social, and cultural factors underlying achievement in African-American children. She is Co-Editor of the books *Gender and Education* (1993) and *African Centered Schooling in Theory and Practice* (2000), has published numerous journal articles and book chapters, and has presented papers at national and international professional conferences. She has been an active member of AERA, was the 1996 recipient of the Willystine Goodsell Award, and consults for various community-

based organizations around issues of child and family empowerment. She is completing a book that focuses on children's perspectives of African-centered schooling.

Andrew C. Porter is a Professor of Educational Psychology and Director of the Wisconsin Center for Education Research at the University of Wisconsin–Madison (since 1989). From 1967 to 1988, he was on the faculty at Michigan State University, where he was also Associate Dean for Research and Graduate Study and Co-Director of the Institute for Research on Teaching. Porter co-directs the Institute for Science Education (funded by the National Science Foundation) and is Principal Investigator of the National Evaluation of the Eisenhower Program. He has published in the areas of research on teaching, education policy analysis, student and teacher assessment, and psychometrics, especially the problem of measuring change. In 1994, he was elected to the National Academy of Education. He is the current President of the American Educational Research Association.

Marleen Pugach is Professor in the Department of Curriculum and Instruction at the University of Wisconsin–Milwaukee, where she is director of the primary/middle level teacher preparation program. Her interests include: teacher preparation that links general and special education, the intersection of inclusion and school reform the recruitment of minority teachers for urban schools, school–university partnerships, building collaborative relationships between practicing special and general education teachers, and qualitative research methodology. She is co-author, with Lawrence Johnson, of *Collaborative Practitioners, Collaborative Schools;* and Co-Editor of *Encouraging Reflective Practice in Education; Changing the Practice of Teacher Education; Curriculum Trends, Special Education, and Reform: Refocusing the Conversation;* and *Teacher Education in Transition: Collaborative Programs to Prepare General and Special Educators.* She is Associate Editor of the journals *Exceptional Children* and *Teacher Education and Special Education.* In 1998, she received the Margaret Lindsey Award from the American Association of Colleges for Teacher Education for her contributions to research in teacher education.

Virginia Richardson is Chair of Educational Studies and Professor of Education in the School of Education, University of Michigan. She spent a number of years in Washington, D.C. directing federal expenditure on education research at the National Institute of Education before becoming an academic at the University of Arizona. Her research interests are teacher change, teacher education, and research methodology. She is Vice-President of Division K of the American Educational Research Association. She has written numerous chapters, articles, and books on the topic of teacher change, professional development, and teacher education.

Tom Russell is Professor of Education at Queen's University, Kingston, Ontario, where he has taught secondary science methods since 1977. His research on the development of teachers' professional knowledge has been supported since 1984 by a number of grants from the Social Sciences and Humanities Research Council of Canada, most in collaboration with his colleague Hugh Munby. His recent publications include *Teaching*

About Teaching: Purpose, Passion and Pedagogy in Teacher Education (edited with John Loughran) and *Finding a Voice While Learning to Teach* (edited with Derek Featherstone and Hugh Munby). Recent interests include action research and early extended experience as significant elements of preservice teacher education.

Sharon Ryan is Assistant Professor of Early Childhood Education in the Department of Learning and Teaching and Director of Qualitative Research in the Center for Early Education Research in the Graduate School of Education at Rutgers University. She has worked as a preschool and special education teacher and early childhood administrator in Australia and been a consultant and teacher educator in Australia and the United States. Her research interests include equity and social justice issues, the work of early childhood teachers, early childhood policy, and postmodem theories in early childhood education. She is currently conducting a qualitative study of the implementation of universal preschool in two school districts, focusing on how this statewide policy is enacted and experienced by administrators, teachers, and students.

David Scanlon, Ph.D., is Assistant Professor of Special Education at Boston College. He researches and teaches about content-area literacy learning with adolescent and adult learners and their teachers. He is formerly a Research Scientist at the University of Kansas Center for Research on Learning and is currently Chairperson of the Research Committee for the Council for Learning Disabilities.

Peter Seixas is Professor and Canada Research Chair in Education, Department of Curriculum Studies, Faculty of Education at the University of British Columbia, with responsibilities for social studies curriculum and instruction. He taught social studies in Vancouver over a period of 15 years while earning an M.A. in the history of education (U.B.C.), and a Ph.D. in history (UCLA). He has published articles and chapters on social studies curriculum, historical understanding, and school–university collaboration. He is Co-Editor, with Peter Stearns and Sam Wineburg, of *Knowing, Teaching and Learning History: National and International Perspectives* (New York University Press, 2000). He has been the recipient of the Exemplary Research Award from the National Council for the Social Studies (1994), a National Academy of Education Spencer Postdoctoral Fellowship (1994–96), a Killam Fellowship (1997–98), and the American Historical Association's William Gilbert Award (1999).

Lorrie A. Shepard is Professor and Program Chair of Research and Evaluation Methodology in the School of Education, University of Colorado at Boulder. She has served as President of the American Educational Research Association, President of the National Council on Measurement in Education, and Vice-President of the National Academy of Education. Dr. Shepard won the Distinguished Career Award from the National Council on Measurement in Education. Her research focuses on psychometrics and the use and misuse of tests in educational settings. Significant studies address standard setting, the influence of testing on instruction, teacher testing, identification of mild handicaps, and early childhood assessment. Her books include: *Flunking Grades: Research and Policies on Retention* (with M. L. Smith) and *Methods for Identifying Biased Test Items* (with G. Camilli). Her current interest is the use of classroom assessment to support teaching and learning.

Daniel Solomon is a consultant in social and educational research and evaluation. He was Director of Research at the Developmental Studies Center, Oakland, California, from 1980 through 1997. Prior to that, he conducted research at the U.S. Bureau of the Census, the Montgomery County (MD) Public Schools, the Institute for Juvenile Research (Chicago), and the Center for the Study of Liberal Education for Adults (Chicago). He received a Ph.D. in social psychology from the University of Michigan in 1960. He has published many research papers and monographs. His areas of research interest include classroom environments, teaching behavior, person–environment interaction, and children's social and moral development.

Dee Ann Spencer received her Ph.D. in sociology at the University of Missouri in 1976 and is currently Senior Research Specialist and Director of the Office of School Improvement in the College of Education at Arizona State University. She has conducted research in schools for nearly 30 years and has published articles and chapters in the fields of sociology and education. The focus of many of these has been on teaching as an occupation and on teaching as women's work, including a book, *Contemporary Women Teachers: Balancing School and Home* (1986). She has continued this focus by comparing teachers' lives in Mexico and the United States. Her recent research is focused on evaluation of school programs and reform efforts, including the translation into practice of literacy, mathematics, science and technology initiatives, and teacher training in bilingual education, and on teacher action research.

Melanie Sperling is Associate Professor of Education at the University of California, Riverside. She is interested in the teaching and learning of writing and the relationships between the discourse of learning contexts and literacy acquisition and development. She serves as Chair of the special interest group on writing and literacies of the American Educational Research Association and was the first recipient of that group's annual award for writing research. A member of various national committees on literacy education, her recent writings include "Uncovering the Role of Role in Writing and Learning to Write: One Day in an Inner-City Classroom," which appeared in the journal *Written Communication,* and "Teachers as Readers of Students' Writing," which appeared in the *97th Yearbook of the National Society for the Study of Education.*

Liane M. Summerfield is Professor at Marymount University in Arlington, Virginia. She teaches undergraduate and graduate courses in health, nutrition, and exercise physiology. Since 1989, she has been affiliated with the American Association of Colleges for Teacher Education (AACTE) as a subject area specialist in health, physical education, recreation, and dance for the ERIC Clearinghouse on Teaching and Teacher Education. Recently she was named Principal Investigator of an AACTE cooperative agreement with the Centers for Disease Control and Prevention (CDC) to infuse health and HIV education into teacher training programs. In addition to health education, her research and writing interests are in the areas of weight control and metabolism.

Martha Taunton is Area Coordinator of the Art Education program and is Associate Professor of Art Education in the Art Department at the University of Massachusetts, Amherst. Her research and writing have focused on the artistic development of young children and art curriculum development. She has published in *Art Education, Studies in Art Education,* the *Journal of Aesthetic Education,* and *Childhood Education.* She is co-author with Cynthia Colbert of *Adventures in Art Kindergarten and Developmentally Appropriate Practices for the Visual Arts Education of Young Children.* She is conducting research on art instruction by classroom teachers.

Marilyn S. Watson was formerly Program Director of the Child Development Project and the Director of Programs at the Developmental Studies Center, Oakland, California. She received her B.A. from Connecticut College in philosopny and her M.A. and Ph.D. degrees from the University of California, Berkeley, in education. Prior to the position at the center, she was Assistant Professor of Education and Director of the Children's School at Mills College, Oakland, California. Her research and writing have dealt with classroom discipline, teacher development, family socialization, and children's moral and social development.

Richard White has written journal articles and books, especially on learning science—*The Content of Science* (with Peter Fensham and Richard Gunstone) and *Probing Understanding* (with Richard Gunstone)—that address how teaching and assessment can be arranged to foster understanding. Sailing, cycling, painting, reading, computer games, and growing Australian plants help to keep his mind clear for work.

Suzanne M. Wilson is Professor in the Department of Teacher Education and Director of the Center for the Scholarship of Teaching at Michigan State University. She has been an elementary and high school history and mathematics teacher, and she currently teaches prospective and practicing social studies teachers, as well as educational researchers. She has published widely on teacher assessment, teacher knowledge, history and mathematics teaching, and educational policy. She is currently completing a history of mathematics education reform, *California Dreaming.*

Mary Malter Yarnall has been an early childhood teacher for 10 years and a school psychologist for 6 years. Currently she is a doctoral student in early childhood education at Teachers College, Columbia University. She has a long-standing interest in children's social and emotional development, as it relates to their learning in and out of school.

Peter Youngs is a doctoral student in the Department of Educational Policy Studies at the University of Wisconsin–Madison. He specializes in policy issues related to teacher education and professional development. He is currently a research associate for a study of professional development and school capacity (directed by Fred Newmann and funded by the U.S. Department of Education). For his Master's thesis, he examined the beliefs and practices of four beginning teachers who work with culturally diverse students. From 1996 to 1998, he served as one of the graduate student representatives for AERA Division K.

Kenneth M. Zeichner is the Hoefs-Bascom Professor of Teacher Education and Associate Dean for Teacher Education and Undergraduate Education, University of Wisconsin–Madison. He was Vice President of the Division of Teaching and Teacher Education of AERA, 1996–98; and member of the Board of Directors of the American Association of Colleges for Teacher Education, 1997–2000. His recent publications include *Reflective Teaching and Culture and Teaching* (with Dan Liston, Lawrence Erlbaum Associates), "Educational Action Research" in *Handbook of Action Research, Democratic Teacher Education Reform in Africa: The Case of Namibia* (with Lars Dahlstrom, Westview), and "The New Scholarship in Teacher Education" in *Educational Researcher.*

Subject Index

Page numbers followed by f and t refer to figures and tables, respectively.

Name Index

Pascal, A., 863, 864, 865, 866
Pascarella, E. T., 1132, 1135, 1137
Passeron, J. C., 28, 30, 31, 212, 1109
Passmore, J., 84, 85
Pastenes, Z., 1193
Patai, D., 243
Patberg, J. P., 398
Pate, E., 1166
Pate, P. E., 1162
Pate, R. R., 472, 506
Pate-Bain, H., 138
Pateman, B. C., 472, 473, 475, 480, 484
Pateman, N., 232, 233
Paterson, J. J., 398
Pati, J., 591
Patitu, C. L., 1124
Patrick, D. L., 1135
Patrick, J., 731
Patry, J. L., 828, 833, 834, 838, 840
Patterson, A., 35
Patterson, L., 405
Patton, M. Q., 175, 244, 253, 254, 871
Pätzold, G., 611, 612
Paul, J., 1146
Paul, R. W., 1118, 1126
Paulos, J. A., 434
Pauls, L. W., 766, 882
Paulsen, B., 613
Paulsen, M. B., 1123, 1131
Pauly, E., 1013, 1014
Paunonen, S. V., 1144
Paxton, R. J., 529
Pearce, L., 1115
Pearlman, M., 272, 273
Pearson, L. C., 1166
Pearson, P. D., 381, 395, 398, 715, 906, 918,
　　920, 1083
Pease, S., 761
Pease-Alvarez, C., 991
Pease-Alvarez, L., 1191, 1202
Pechacek, T., 473, 478, 484
Pecheone, R., 262, 279, 766, 769
Peck, M. S., 649
Peck, R. F., 566, 567, 568, 569, 595, 891
Peck, W., 381, 382, 384, 385
Pederson, P. V., 548, 554
Pedraza, P., 670, 675, 680, 681
Pedretti, E., 463
Pedro-Carroll, J. L., 590
Peebles, P., 463
Peirce, C. S., 73, 74, 76, 79
Peisner, E. S., 1189
Peled, I., 343, 347
Peleg, E. O., 475
Pelissier, C., 115
Pellegrini, A. D., 401
Pellegrino, J. W., 1096
Pellett, T. L., 498, 499, 501, 502, 506
Pelligrini, A. D., 393
Pemberton, S., 1003
Pendlebury, S., 234, 846, 928, 939
Pennell, J. R., 872
Pensabene, R., 766
Pentz, M. A., 476, 477, 484
Pepper, F. C., 574
Percy, W., 86
Perez, B., 397
Perez, R., 621
Perfetti, C. A., 342, 537
Perkes, V. A., 754
Perkins, D. N., 558, 606, 625
Perkins, L. M., 736, 809

Perl, S., 382
Perlmutter, J. C., 393
Perlwitz, M., 10, 13
Perney, J., 1181, 1202
Perrenoud, P., 1090
Perrin, E. C., 480, 481
Perrone, V., 303
Perry, A., 101
Perry, C. L., 473, 475, 476, 477, 478, 482, 483,
　　484
Perry, C. R., 863, 864, 865
Perry, D. G., 571
Perry, R. P., 1123, 1135
Perry, T., 646, 651, 653
Perry, W. G., Jr., 1134
Peshkin, A., 245
Peskin, J., 419
Peterman, C. L., 394
Peterman, F., 307, 920
Peters, D. W., 807, 821, 822, 1178
Peters, E. E., 398
Peters, R. S., 831, 837, 839
Peters, W. H., 426, 757
Petersen, A. C., 734, 1006, 1007, 1160
Petersen, O., 395
Peterson, K. D., 259, 262, 268, 935
Peterson, P., 51, 52, 57, 58, 174, 305, 313, 422,
　　428, 738, 861, 887, 889, 893
Peterson, P. L., 13, 53, 58, 59, 60, 64, 66, 346,
　　450, 891, 906, 907, 913, 914, 918, 934,
　　937
Peterson, P. P., 1183, 1187
Peterson, R., 463
Petrakis, E., 495
Petree, D. L., 867
Petrosky, A., 418
Pettit, G. S., 570
Peyton, J. K., 1117
Pfeifer, R. S., 930
Pfeiffer, E., 612
Pfister, O., 24
Pflaum, S. W., 653
Pfundt, H., 460
Phaik-Lah, K., 324
Phelan, A., 232, 233
Phelan, P., 649, 653, 920, 999, 1006
Phelps, S. F., 423
Phelps-Zientarski, D., 726
Philipp, R. A., 450
Philips, D. Z., 831, 832, 836, 848
Philips, S. U., 952, 961, 962, 978
Philliber, S., 1012
Phillip, R., 916
Phillips, A., 1199
Phillips, D., 49, 229, 230, 1177
Phillips, D. A., 498, 502
Phillips, D. C., 3, 6, 178, 181, 318, 319, 878,
　　879, 898, 899, 900, 1074, 1090
Phillips, G., 393
Piaget, J., 24, 392, 567, 569, 574, 579, 585,
　　594, 909, 913, 1036, 1040, 1041, 1045,
　　1061, 1178, 1194
Pica, T., 366
Piciga, D., 784, 785
Pickwell, A., 504
Picot, B., 787
Piekeilek, D., 1198
Pierce, M., 787, 793
Piéron, M., 499, 501, 503
Pieters, J. M., 612, 613
Pigg, R. M., Jr., 483
Pigge, F., 914

Pignatelli, F., 653
Pilcher, J. K., 1166
Pillsbury, J., 50
Pinar, W. F., 23, 31, 178, 192, 648, 884, 1196
Pinch, T., 1108
Pine, J., 141, 1096
Pines, M., 1179
Pink, W., 211
Pinkham, K. M., 492, 493, 494, 496, 498
Pinnegar, S., 880
Pintrich, P. R., 1134, 1138
Piper, D. W., 1146
Piper, K., 786
Pirie, P. L., 473, 476, 478, 484
Pissanos, B. W., 498
Pitcher, B., 261
Pitkanen-Pulkkinen, L., 567, 568, 569, 570
Pitman, K., 1015
Pitner, N., 869
Pitney, J. A., 1142, 1143, 1144
Pittman, K. J., 772, 999, 1001, 1015, 1020,
　　1022
Pizzini, E. L., 733
Placek, J. H., 492, 493, 494, 496, 499, 503, 508
Placier, P., 907, 920, 921, 928, 933
Plake, B. S., 150, 151
Plateau, N., 741
Plato, 826, 829, 1103, 1104, 1114
Platt, J. J., 590
Polakow, V., 1196, 1197, 1198
Polanyi, M., 448, 854, 887, 1105
Polite, M. M., 1162, 1170
Pollak, J. P., 1162
Pollard, A., 780, 792, 793
Pollard, D. S., 647, 723, 724, 734, 741, 742
Pollio, H. R., 1130, 1131, 1136, 1137, 1139,
　　1140, 1146
Pollock, M. L., 506
Pólya, G., 343, 349, 1052, 1053
Pomfret, M., 1134
Ponder, G. A., 796
Pontecorvo, C., 112, 113, 115, 342
Poole, W., 931
Pooley, J. C., 492
Pope, C. V., 497
Pope, M., 885
Popham, W. J., 159, 1071
Popkewitz, T. S., 178, 309, 551, 558, 1196,
　　1197, 1198, 1199
Popp, J., 616, 622, 623
Porter, A., 11, 183, 294, 932
Portes, A. C., 668, 671, 672, 673, 674, 678,
　　679, 680, 683
Portes, P., 112, 954
Portman, P. A., 492, 493, 494, 496, 501, 507
Portnoy, B., 485
Portuges, C., 32
Posch, P., 307, 313, 317, 318
Poschner, T., 324
Posner, J. K., 1015
Post, T. R., 444, 446, 447
Poster, N., 37
Postlethwaite, N., 63
Postman, N., 976
Potter, J., 864
Potthoff, S., 479
Pottorff, D. D., 726
Pound, L., 1186
Poundstone, C. C., 399
Pousada, A., 682
Powell, B. M., 394